Officers who died in the Service of British, Indian and East African Regiments and Corps 1914 – 1919

S.D. & D.B. Jarvis

The Naval & Military Press Ltd

Published by
The Naval & Military Press Ltd
Unit 10 Ridgewood Industrial Park,
Uckfield, East Sussex,
TN22 5QE England
Tel: +44 (0) 1825 749494
Fax: +44 (0) 1825 765701
www.naval-military-press.com
www.military-genealogy.com
www.militarymaproom.com

In reprinting in facsimile from the original, any imperfections are inevitably reproduced and the quality may fall short of modern type and cartographic standards.

INTRODUCTION

To compile a three volume set of the Officers who died in the Great War and who served in the British, Commonwealth and Colonial Regiments and Corps in alphabetical listing, is by any standard a monumental task. Every Commonwealth War Graves Register known to exist was carefully searched and the information extracted. With great patience the compilers checked the information given against other publications, many out of date, to enable readers to follow up further leads where appropriate. Discrepancies of a major nature are shown.

The conflict was so great, the number of deaths so enormous, that no reference book on the subject of the Great War can be perfect. The information given at the time was prone to mis-spelling and of course to mis-recording. The compilers could not judge what was right or wrong and have faithfully recorded what they read and what was written down. They have of course discovered many Officers not previously listed and great differences in units, rank and dates. The reader will need to do his own research into why these discrepancies occurred. An intriguing and hopefully rewarding task.

In their search to be as accurate as possible, the compilers checked names against town registers, national magazines and memorial books; the public school registers were particularly helpful. These are too numerous to list individually. For those who wish to research further, two main first opportunities exist - The Commonwealth War Graves Registers (the appropriate number is shown in the text), give in addition to what is listed some information on the next of kin and address. The British and Commonwealth War Graves Commission are based at 2 Marlow Road, Maidenhead, Berks SL6 7DX. In seeking further information from them it is strongly suggested a donation to their general fund would be welcomed. Secondly, the excellent information contained in the original HMSO Publication 'Officers Died' is now re-printed and available with additional sections from J.B. Hayward & Son, The Old Rectory, Polstead, Sussex C06 5AE. The information is given in regimental order and is therefore extremely helpful. The appropriate page number, if known, is shown in the text.

One further point concerns the Royal Flying Corps, as the Air Arm existed prior to the 1st April 1918 as a Corp, Volume 1 of this series contains the British Officers, Volume 3 the Commonwealth and Colonial. Volume 2 covers the Royal Naval Air Service and Royal Air Force.

Messrs S.D. and J.B. Jarvis are to be congratulated for what amounts to ten years diligent research. They will, in the process of their work, have laid low a number of "ghosts" and no doubt thrown up a great number of challenging questions.

Trevor J Davies March 1993

How to Interpret the Information Given

Examples

ABBATI, William Reginald, Lt ded 9.8.16, 3ESS p.264, CR Hamps 216, 2Lt. 7.8.16

SURNAME:	ABBATI
FIRST NAMES:	William Reginald
RANK:	Lieutenant
DECORATIONS:	None identified
CAUSE OF DEATH:	Died
DATE:	9.8.1916
UNIT:	3rd Battalion The Essex Regiment
OTHER REFERENCE:	Seen in Officers Died p.264
REGISTER:	CR Hampshire 216 (see Appendix 1)
INFORMATION FROM ALTERNATIVE SOURCES:	2nd Lieutenant Died 7.8.1916

ABRAHAM, Geoffrey William Pepperall, Capt dow 19.11.17, Glam Yeo p.203 CR Egypt 7, Pepperell, 24 Welch R.

SURNAME:	ABRAHAM
FIRST NAMES:	Geoffrey William Pepperall
RANK:	Captain
DECORATIONS:	None
CAUSE OF DEATH:	Died of Wounds
DATE:	19.11.1917
UNIT:	Glamorgan Yeomanry
OTHER REFERENCE:	Seen in Officers Died p.203
REGISTER:	CR Egypt 7 (see Appendix 1)
INFORMATION TAKEN FROM ALTERNATIVE SOURCES:	Possible spelling 'PEPPERELL' CR Unit '24 Welch R'

ACKROYD, Harold, V.C., M.C., TCapt Kia 11.8.17, RAMC att. 6Berks, p.145, CR Belgium 113

SURNAME:	ACKROYD
FIRST NAMES:	Harold
RANK:	Temporary Captain
DECORATIONS:	Victoria Cross, Military Cross
CAUSE OF DEATH:	Killed in action
DATE:	11.8.1917
UNIT:	Royal Army Medical Corp attached to 6th Battalion Royal Berks
OTHER REFERENCE:	Seen in Officers Died p.146
REGISTER:	CR Belgium 113 (see Appendix 1)

A

ABADIE,Eustace Henry Egremont,DSO.Maj kia 30-11-15 9Lancers p22 MR29,30-10-14

ABADIE,Richard Nevile.DSO.LtCol kia 10-7-17 KRRC p148 MR31

ABBATI,William Reginald Lt ded 9-8-16 3Ess p264 CR Hamps216,2Lt 7-8-16

ABBAY,Marmaduke John Norman Capt dow 10-5-15 IA 87Punjabis att47Sikhs p273 CR Suff106

ABBEY,G.Lt 7-9-20 RDC CR Shrop138

ABBEY,Noel Roland Lt kia 12-4-18 4GrenGds p49 MR32

ABBIS,Reginald Donaldson 2Lt dow 2-12-17 3att2YLI p142 CR Belgium18

ABBISS,John Lee Lt ded 25-7-18 1ESurr att7LightArmBtyMGC Motors p111&181 CR Iraq8

ABBOTT,Alfred 2Lt dow 26-4-18 EYorks att9YLI p83 MR30

ABBOTT,Clifford Hewson T2Lt dow 7-5-17 2Lincs p74 CR France1468

ABBOTT,Duncan William Sydney Elphinstone TCapt kia 26-9-15 10Y&L p158 MR19

ABBOTT,Edward John White Lt kia 17-5-15 2RIrFus p170 MR29

ABBOTT,Eric Goward 2Lt kia 14-3-17 1/5NStaffs p238 CR France281 dow

ABBOTT,Ernest Henry Fortescue.MC.Lt kia 9-7-18 4att2N&D p133 MR30 Capt

ABBOTT,Geoffrey Dyett Lt kia 2-11-14 1ConnRgrs p172 CR France706

ABBOTT,George Lt kia 23-8-18 Herts p252 CR France798

ABBOTT,George Shrubb 2Lt kia 19-7-16 2/4RBerks p234 CR France1887

ABBOTT,John Gurney 2Lt kia 21-9-17 6RB att57TMB p177 MR30

ABBOTT,Joseph Octavius 2Lt kia 28-7-17 RGA 179SB p37 CR Belgium29 J.D.

ABBOTT,Lionel Pilkington TLt kia 14-7-16 7Leic p87 CR France453

ABBOTT,Sidney Herbert 2Lt kia 4-11-18 2Beds p85 CR France521

ABBOTT,Thomas Aveling Capt&Adjt kia 24-5-15 2WRidRFA p24 CR France347

ABBOTT,Thomas Walker 2Lt kia 18-8-17 GL &11RFC p4 MR20

ABBOTT,Victor Stephen Henry 2Lt kld 15-9-16 SR &RFC p2 CR Wilts116

ABBOTT,W.F.Maj 28-2-21 RAMC CR Glouc9

ABBOTT,William David Rev ded 3-12-18 RAChDept p199 CR France 377

ABBOT-ANDERSON,Francis Wyatt LtCol ded 1-1-16 RLancs p58 CR Egypt9,2-1-16 Cmdg6Bn

ABBS,Bertie Edward T2Lt kia 26-3-18 7Suff p77 MR27

ABE,Frank E.T2Lt kia 23-7-18 8WYorks p80 CR France 1689

A'BEAR,Hedley John.MM.T2LtACapt kia 10-7-17 7RWSurr p55 CR Belgium15

ABECASIS,Arthur Philip T2Lt kia 9-4-17.3SomLI p79 CR France532 5Bn

ABEL,Frederick T2Lt drd 30-12-17 3Norf p73 CR Egypt6

ABEL,George Fowtrell.MM.2Lt ded 20-6-18 GL p189 Iraq6

ABEL,James Edgar.MC.T2Lt dow 22-12-17 PoW 6RWKent p140 CR France660

ABEL,John Duncan T2Lt kia 26-3-18 7SfthH p164 MR27

ABELL,Albert Reginald T2Lt ded 10-6-17 PoW 1Dev p76

ABELL,John Lloyd Williams Howard Capt kia 3-7-16 11Ches p95 MR21,William

ABELL,William Henry Maj kia 23-8-14 4Mddx p145 CR Belgium 242

ABERCROMBIE,Alexander Ralph,DSO.MC.Capt ded 31-12-18.1RWSurr p55 CR Surrey118

ABERCROMBIE,Alexander William LtCol ded PoW 5-11-15 2ConnRgrs p172 CR Germany4

ABERCROMBIE,Robert Henry Chester 2Lt kia 3-5-15 1/8Mddx p236 CR Belgium151

ABERCROMBY,John Stevenson T2Lt dow 29-4-17 17Mddx p145 CR France95

ABERDEEN,Louis Frederick 2Lt kia 10-9-16 3att12Lond p245 MR21,9-9-16

ABINGER,Bernard Russell.MC.2Lt 25-9-15 2RBerks MR32 served as RUSSELL

ABBISS,Frederick Thomas Lee Lt dow 27-10-17 76RFA p24 CR France64,ded

ABLETT,Arthur 2Lt dow 22-4-18 4MGC p181 CR France248

ABLETT,Frank Ellis 2Lt kia 20-9-17 Suff att1/8Lpool p77 MR30

ABLETT,Leslie Wallace T2Lt kia 15-10-17 NumbF att11Bn Res p59 MR30

ABRAHAM,Arthur Thomas,MC.2LtACapt kia 22-10-17 23Manch p153 MR30

ABRAHAM,Frederick Henry T2Lt kia 2-10-18 16LancF p91 CR France237 Henri

ABRAHAM,Geoffrey William Pepperall Capt dow 19-11-17 GlamYeo p203 CR Egypt7 Pepperell 24WelchR

ABRAHAMS,Arthur Charles Lionel Lt kia 13-4-18 3ColdGds p50 MR32

ABRAHAMS,Montague TMaj kia 3-9-16 16RB p177 MR21

ABRAHAMS,Robert Bernard 2Lt kia 14-9-16 4Yorks p220 MR21

ABRAM,Robert 2LtACapt kia 26-10-17 3 att2BordR p116 MR30

ABRAMS,Lawrence Golding TLt ded 3-11-18 RASC p192 CR France85

ABRAMS,Reginald Arthur Lt kia 4-3-17 8N&D p233 CR France281

ABREY,Charles Gordon 2Lt kia 21-7-16 O&BLI BucksBn p231 CR France832

ACHESON,Joseph T2Lt dow 7-6-18.2SLancs p125 CR France1778

ACHESON,Percival Havelock Maj kld 29-4-16 RASC p192 CREire70

ACHESON,Vincent Andrews TCapt kia 10-9-16 6 att7RInnisKF p104 CR Greece3

ACHURCH,William Henry T2Lt dow 6-12-17 2/5RWar p64 CR France398

ACKERLEY,Peter Roger TLt kia 7-8-18 8ESurr p111 CR France116

ACKERLEY,Ronald Hermann Lt kia 16-5-15 3att1RWelshF p97 CR France705

ACKLAND-ALLEN,Hugh Thomas Lt kia 23-10-14 1RWFus p97 MR29

ACKLOM,Spencer,DSO&Bar.MC.MajTLtCol kia 21-3-18 HLI att22NumbF p162 MR20

ACKROYD,Harold,VC.MC.TCapt kia 11-8-17 RAMC att6RBerks p194 CR Belgium113

ACKROYD,Thomas 2Lt kia 23-4-17 1 att9Beds p85 MR20

ACLAND,John Henry Dyke TCapt kia 12-7-16 RAMC att1SomLI p194 CR France643

ACLAND TROYTE,Heyl Leonard LtCol kia 17-4-18 5Lincs p269 CR France498,Hugh 4Dev att XI CpsHQ

ACOMB,Horace T2Lt kia 21-8-16.2Yorks att2Dev p89 CR France423,11Bn

ACTON,Armar Edward Rev Chap4Cl MID dow 4-11-17 RAChDept att2BordR p199 CR France64

ACTON,Charles Annesley TMaj kia 25-9-15 9RWelshF p97 MR19

ACTON,Norman Frederick T2Lt kia 23-4-17 4Worc p107 MR20

ACTON,Reginald 2Lt dow 9-5-15 5SLancs p230 CR France284

ACWORTH,Douglas Harry.MC.Maj ded 6-2-19 IA 55Rif p273 CR Egypt7

ACWORTH,Gordon William 2Lt dow 7-6-17 15Lond p249 CR Belgium11

ACWORTH,John Arden 2Lt dow 13-10-17 1/7Worc p225 CR Belgium16

ADAIR,Angus McPherson TLt kia 21-11-17 48MGC Inf p181 CR France1489

ADAIR,John Thomas TLt dow 22-8-15 10Beds att1BordR p85 MR4

ADAIR,William Finlay Capt kia 30-10-14 IA 129Baluchis p273 MR29

ADAM,Alan Gordon Acheson.MID Capt kia 21/22-1-16 5EKent p212 CR Iraq5

ADAM,Alexander Russell Lt kia 3-7-17 6SfthH attRFC p17&241 CR France481

ADAM,Allan Lt kia 1-10-18 7A&SH att2MGC Inf p186&243 CR France1483

ADAM,Arthur Innes Lt kia 16-9-16 1Camb p244 CR France518 Capt dow

ADAM,Arthur de Bels TCapt kia 1-7-16 18Lpool p71 MR21

ADAM,Douglas Walter TLt dow 4-4-18 LancF att18MGC p181 MR27

ADAM,Frank Dalziel Lt dow 16-7-18 6RB p177 CR France161 3Bn

ADAM,George 2Lt kia 22-10-17 att16RScots p53

ADAM,Gerald Wallace.MID 2Lt ded 10-8-19 Leic p263 MR70 &CR Europe180 att13Yorks

ADAM,James Robert T2Lt kia 18-8-16 13Mddx p145 MR21

ADAM,John Isabel TLt kia 10-5-18 A307RFA p24 CR France1106

ADAM,John Stewart 2Lt kia 11-8-18 D11RFA p208 CR Belgium11

ADAM,Matthew.MC.Lt kia 7-8-18 5RScotF attRAF p222&258

ADAM,Norman Macleod.MC.CaptAMaj kia 28-8-18 19RFA p24 CR Scot756

ADAM,Peter.MC.2Lt kia 31-7-17 3RB p177 MR29

ADAM,Ronald William.MC.2Lt ded 11-9-17 13/56RFA p24 CR Iraq8

ADAM,Walter Capt ded 3-11-18 EKentYeo attMGC Inf p186&204 CR Kent259 Lt

ADAM,Walter William TCapt kld 14-12-15 6RScotF p94 CR Belgum4 12-12-15

ADAM,William Frederick 2Lt kia 25-8-16 7 att5ScotRif p224 CR France453

ADAMS,Arthur Charles Henry 2Lt kia 21-3-18 1/2att2/8Worc p107 MR27

ADAMS,Arthur Joseph LtCapt kia 30-8-18 3RWar p64 CR France421 1Bn

ADAMS,Arthur Marston.MC.T2Lt dow 20-9-17 1/9Lpool p216 CR Belgium8

ADAMS,Aurnol Charles Andrew T2Lt kia 16/18-8-16 10RLancs p58 CR France294 Auriol

ADAMS,Bernard Pye TLt dow 27-2-17 11RWelshF p97

ADAMS,Briggs Kilburn T2Lt kia 14-3-18 18RFC p15 CR France134,Kilburn Lt

ADAMS,Caleb Henry T2Lt kia 20/22-9-17 10RWSurr p55 MR30

ADAMS,C.E.DCM.Lt 21-3-21 1RFus CR Notts112

ADAMS,Charles John Norman 2Lt dow 14-11-18 2GrenGds p49 CR France146

ADAMS,Dudley ACapt kia 21-3-18 RGA 130HB p37 MR27

ADAMS,Edward Carrington 2Lt kia 25-9-15 20Lond p251 CR France550 Carington

ADAMS,Ernest Frederick T2Lt kia 22-6-17 26RFus p66 CR Belgium154

ADAMS,Ernest Geoffrey T2Lt dow 26-6-18 8Norf p73 CR France84 7Bn

ADAMS,Frederick 2Lt kld 12-5-17 GL &53RFC p4 CR Belgium152

ADAMS,Frederick.MC.Lt selfInflictWound 29-11-20 IARO att45Sikhs p273 CR Iraq8

ADAMS,Frederick Leslie 2Lt kia 15-9-18 RGA 232SB p37 CR France841

ADAMS,Geoffrey Julian Balcombe 2Lt dow 27-9-18 1/5Lond p246 CR France113

ADAMS,Geoffrey Henry Cadwallader 2Lt kia 1-11-16 4Suff p217 MR21

ADAMS,George Allsop 2Lt kia 9-4-17 3 att7ESurr p111 CR France531

ADAMS,George Garnet Price Domel Lt 21-2-20 IARO CR EAfrica19

ADAMS,George Gordon Crymole Lt ded 9-3-18 RAMC p194 CR EAfrica11 &CR Tanzania 1,Crymoll

ADAMS,George Norman Capt ded 20-10-18 6SStaffs p255 CR Staffs78

ADAMS,George Stopford Maj kia 11-5-15 1LancF p91 CR Gallipoli1
ADAMS,Harold Towns Lt 28-3-18 GL &43RFC MR20
ADAMS,Henry Frederick Reginald Lt dow 20-10-17 A159RFA p24 CR Belgium13
ADAMS,Henry Gordon 2Lt kia 5-10-17 RFA SthMidBde p208 CR Belgium12
ADAMS,Hugh Irving TLt kia 1-7-16 1Hamps p120 CR France643
ADAMS,James Andrew T2Lt kia 17-4-18 11Mddx p145 CR France324
ADAMS,James Allison Wilson 2Lt kia 9-4-17 9RScots p212 CR France184 Alison
ADAMS,James Scovell T2Lt dow 8-8-18 7RWSurr p55 CR France69
ADAMS,John Bernard Pye TLt dow 27-2-17 1RWFus p97 CR France204
ADAMS,John Gould Capt kia 5-5-15 Leinst p174 MR29
ADAMS,John Hanna 2Lt kia 18-11-16 8NStaffs p156 CR France384
ADAMS,John Henry Capt ded 25-2-19 ArmyPayDept p268 CR Kent85
ADAMS,John Percy Fitzherbert Lt kia 14-10-17 4DLI att20RFC p4&160 CR Belgium11
ADAMS,John Wood Maj kia 3-9-17 6RScots p211 CR France8
ADAMS,Joseph 2Lt kia 23-7-16 3 att2RSuss p118 MR21
ADAMS,Lawrence Kingston Lt kia 16-5-15 7Lpool p215 CR France279 Laurence
ADAMS,Lestock Hanley TLt kia 22-4-18 1RB p177 CR France411 Handley
ADAMS,Ord T2Lt kia 20-3-16 RFA p24 CR Belgium73
ADAMS,Percy Ernest Capt kia 4-4-17 5N&D p232 CR France725
ADAMS,Percy Horace 2Lt kia 3-10-18 4 att1N&D p133 CR France184 Lt
ADAMS,Percy Lionel Lt dow 3-10-18 18Lond attMGC Inf p185&250 CR France194
ADAMS,Philip Rockley T2Lt kia 27-5-18 6SomLI att2Dev p79 MR18
ADAMS,Ralph.MC&Bar.Lt kia 1-7-16 1/8RWar p215 CR France742
ADAMS,Ralph Newton.MC.Capt kia 10-10-16 7RFus att23RFC p2&66 MR20
ADAMS,Reinhold Meitzen Maj dow 22-4-17 IA 51Sikhs p273 MR38
ADAMS,Robert 2Lt kia 12-8-15 5Norf p216 MR4
ADAMS,Robert Sefton LtACapt kia 5-10-17 12/35RFA p24 CR Belgium116
ADAMS,Robert Leonard Powys Lt kia 17-5-19 IA 1/35Sikhs p273 MR43
ADAMS,S.H.T.2Lt kia 28-3-18 GL & RFC p261&266
ADAMS,Stanley T2Lt dow 9-9-17 9NumbF p59 CR France1494
ADAMS,Theodore Dawson Capt kia 7-11-15 LancsRFA attRFC p17&207 CR France604,Dowson
ADAMS,Thompson 2Lt kia 7-10-16 4YLI att36MGC p186&235 MR21
ADAMS,Valentine Harold 2Lt dow 5-5-17 78RFC p4 CR France1032
ADAMS,Wilfred Evan 2Lt kia 14-5-17 212MGC p181 MR20
ADAMS,William John 2Lt drd 30-12-17 Norf p73 MR41
ADAMS-POSNER,Robert Cecil T2Lt kia 18-9-18 1KSLI p144 MR16
ADAMSON,Alexander Hutton 2Lt kia 9-4-17 5SfthH p241 CR France96,7Bn
ADAMSON,Alan John 2LtACapt kia 20-9-17 RGA 69SB p38 CR Belgium24
ADAMSON,Charles John Henry TCapt kia 22-9-17 NumbF att11Bn p59 MR30 20-9-17
ADAMSON,Charles Young TCapt&QM kia 17-9-18 8RScotF p94 CR Greece6
ADAMSON,Daniel Lt ded 7-6-19 RE att2S&M p43 MR43
ADAMSON,Duncan Francis Charles 2Lt kia 12-9-18 20att9Lond p251 MR16
ADAMSON,Francis Douglas Lt kia 16-11-15 2BordR p116 CR France279
ADAMSON,George T2Lt kia 15-9-15 12HLI p162 MR19,25-9-15
ADAMSON,George Addis T2Lt kia 12-10-17 6KOSB p101 MR30
ADAMSON,Gilbert Edgar Lt kia 25-8-18 7Mddx p235 CRFrance504,24-8-18
ADAMSON,Harry 2Lt kia 15-4-18 RGA 6SB p38 MR30
ADAMSON,Henry Bardell TCapt dow 30-10-16 21WYorks p80 CR France145
ADAMSON,James LtACapt kia 5-5-17 C242RFA p207 CR France68
ADAMSON,John Conway Lt kia 4-10-17 NumbF att1Lincs p59 MR30
ADAMSON,John Thomas Graves Maj ded 25-10-18 IA 119Inf p273 MR65
ADAMSON,Maurice Leslie 2Lt kia 1-7-16 RScotF att10IrRif p94 MR21
ADAMSON,Peter.MC.T2Lt kia 27-2-18 att1/4LNLancs p135 CR France765
ADAMSON,Robert Thorburn Adamson TLt kia 23-4-17 13RScots p53 MR20
ADAMSON,Robert William 2Lt kia 26-5-15 7DLI p239 MR29
ADAMSON,Travers Farrant T2Lt kia 1-7-16 9Dev p76 CR France330
ADAMSON,William TCapt kia 24-4-16 6LNLancs p135 MR38
ADAMSON,William Campbell TCapt kia 5-9-15 6RFC p1 CR Belgium140,kld
ADCOCK,Harold Meredyth TCapt kia 5-7-16 10LancF p91 MR21
ADCOCK,Harold Norman T2Lt kia 8-10-18 1EKent p57 CR France445
ADCOCK,Keith White Lt ded 30-10-18 RE p210 CR Herts81
ADCOCK,St.John Maj kia 9-5-15 3Leinst att1RLancs p174 MR29
ADDAMS-WILLIAMS,Donald Arthur T2Lt kia 13-8-15 4SWBord p99&257 CR Gallipoli17
ADDENBROOK,John Homfrey T2Lt kia 23-11-16 NStaffs att11Manch p156 CR France701,ADDENBROOKE Homfray

ADDENBROOKE,Arthur.MID TCapt dow 5-10-16 14War p64 CR Herefd &Worc144
ADDENBROOKE,Guy Besley 2Lt kia 7-5-15 YLI p142 MR27
ADDERLY,Douglas Herbert T2Lt kia 16-6-17 7Nhampt p137 MR29
ADDERLEY,William Harris 2Lt dow 27-10-18 9WRid & 59RAF p115 CR France398
ADDEY,George T2Lt kia 2-9-18 att7EYorks Res p83 MR16
ADDEY-JIBB,Arthur Harwood.MID Lt&QM dow 12-4-18 RAMC att94FA p194 CR France860
ADDIE,Robert Leatham 2Lt kia 20-11-17 2/5LancF p221 MR21
ADDINGTON,Cyril John Flinton T2Lt kia 2-7-16 16 att24Mddx p145 CR France35,Flintan dow
ADDINGTON,Geoffrey William 2Lt kia 1-12-17 2DLI p160 CR France711
ADDINGTON,William Leonard Maj ded 15-12-19 ExRWSurr p262 CR Devon72
ADDIS,David Malcolm 2Lt dow 9-6-17 26RFus p66 MR29
ADDIS,Henry Dansey T2Lt kld 24-1-17 GL & 43RFC p4&189 CR Oxford74
ADDIS,Ronald Forrester LtACapt kia 3-9-16 2KOSB att181MGC Inf p101&18 CR France402
ADDIS,Thomas Henry Liddon Lt kia 21-3-18 4RDubF p176 CR France212
ADDISON,Alfred Charles Capt kia 25-4-15 2Hamps p120 CR Gallipoli15
ADDISON,Arthur Joseph Berkeley TLtCol kia 1-7-16 9Y&L p158 CR France515
ADDISON,Frank T2Lt ded 22-3-16 8RSuss p118 CR France22
ADDISON,George Mellsome 2Lt dow 9-8-18 5SStaffs p229 CR Italy4
ADDISON,Noel Goodricke.MC.Lt kia 9-4-18 1KEdwsHorse p24 MR19
ADDY,James Carlton.MC.Capt kia 3-5-17 10EYorks p83 MR20
ADDY,Kenneth James Balguy T2Lt kia 13-10-15 1KRRC p148 CRFrance423 Balgay 3-10-15
ADDYMAN,Oscar James Lt kia 4-2-15 1EYorks p83 MR29
ADEANE,Henry Robert Augustus Capt kia 2-11-14 1CldGds p50 MR29
ADENEY,Robert Edward 2Lt ded 11-4-17 PoW 3RWSurr &48RFC p55&4 CR France1276,dow
ADEY,William Thomas Henworth 2Lt drd 10-10-18 W'mlnd&CumbYeo p206 CR Eire14
ADIE,Arthur A.DCM.2Lt kia 3-5-18 1/5RLancs p58 CR France106
ADIE,Harry Morton Ellis T2Lt kia 1-5-16 RFC p2 CR France62,Lt
ADIE,George Carl T2Lt kia 22-8-17 10DLI p160 CR Belgium116
ADIE,Robert Roland 2Lt kia 21-4-17 2DLI p160 CR France115
ADKIN,Arthur Wellesley 2Lt kia 3-6-17 20Lond p251 CR Belgium56
ADKIN,Frederick Edward.MM.T2Lt kia 24-9-18 RSuss att2Bn p118 CR France1700
ADLER,Henry George Vergettini 2LtAMaj kia 21-6-17 RGA 184SB p38 CR Belgium10,Vergottini
ADLERCRON,G.R.L.DSO.Capt 16-3-20 8Hrs MR65
ADLINGTON,Ernest Mason T2Lt kia 14-9-16 13 att9WYorks p80 CR France164
ADNEY,George Henry.MC.TLt kia 2-9-18 7TankCps p188 CR France1484
ADRIAN,William Kearns Lt kia 24-8-16 5RIrReg att1RIrRif p88 CR France423,ADRAIN
ADSETTS,William Henry 2Lt dow 1-10-15 3Y&L p158 CR France98 1Bn
ADSHEAD,Sydney Douglas T2Lt kia 23-4-17 18Manch p153 MR20
ADYE,Walter.CB.Col ded 3-9-15 GSO WarOfficeStaff p1 CR Lond4
AERTS,Francis Robert.MC.2Lt ded 26-12-19 13WelshR p264 CR Kent83
AGANOOR,Aganoor John 2Lt kia 15-9-16 17Lond p250 CR France432
AGAR,Richard Paterson 2Lt kia 14-10-16 2SfthH p164 CR France374
AGAR,Richard St.George Tracy Lt kia 29-9-18 RHA 16HQ p24 CR France725
AGAR-ROBARTES,Thomas Charles Reginald.Hon.MP.MID TLtACapt dow 30-9-15 1CldGds p50 CR France88
AGATE,Harold Capt kia 14-4-17 16Lond p249 MR20
AGATE,Norman Stanford 2Lt dow 23-3-18 18Lond p250 CR France177
AGATE,Sydney Herbert 2Lt kia 13-11-16 3 att4Beds p85 CR France220
AGELASTO,August.MC.MID Lt kia 8-11-16 1 att4Dors p123 CR France374 1 att6Bn
AGERUP,Harold Lt acckld 5-6-18 SL att222MGC &195RAF p201 CR Egypt8,GL
AGG,Arthur William TLt ded 2-4-16 SL p201 CR Glouc133
AGIUS,Richard Victor Joseph Roy Capt kia 26-10-17 2/3Lond p245 MR30
AGLIONBY,Arthur Hugh.MC.Maj dow 7-11-18 219RGA p209 CR France276
AGNEW,Andrew Eric Hamilton Capt ded 3-11-18 RDubF p176
AGNEW,Graham TCapt kia 26-9-15 13NumbF p59 MR19
AGNEW,James Watson 2Lt kia 21-5-15 1HLI p162 MR22
A'HERNE,David Joseph 2Lt 27-5-18 RGA 116SB MR18
AHERN,Patrick Joseph Lt&QM kia 9-9-16 7Leinst p174 MR21
AIKEN,James Douglas 2Lt ded 9-11-16 RFA attY14TMB p24 CR France1182 dow
AIKINS,Joseph Russell 2Lt mbk 26-3-18 59RFC p256 CR France1483

AIKMAN,William Hudson Lt dow 27-9-17 1/6HLI p240 CR France34,29-9-18
AIKMAN,William Saunders T2Lt kia 23-4-17 9NumbF p59 MR20,22-4-17
AIMER,George Edmond Vernon 2Lt kld 20-6-16 RFC p2 CR Mddx34
AINGER,Herbert Cecil Lt kia 4-10-17 3RScots &19RFC p4&53 MR20
AINGER,Thomas Edward 2Lt kia 21-8-15 BerksYeo p203 CR Galipoli5
AINLEY,Frederick William Rev Chap4Cl ded 5-12-18 RAChDept p199 CR France34
AINLEY,Hefford William Ernest Lt ded 4-2-17 D168RFA p24 CR France74
AINLEY,John Hirst 2Lt kia 21-6-18 1RB p177 CR France411
AINLEY,Kendrick Edward Denison 2Lt kia 9-6-15 RE p210 CR Gallipoli14
AINSCOUGH,Cyril LtACapt kia 7-8-15 5Manch p236 MR4
AINSCOUGH,Henry 2Lt kia 11-4-18 1BordR p116 MR32 13-4-18
AINSCOUGH,Thomas 2Lt kia 25-1-18 RGA 303SB p38 CR France711
AINSLEY,Archie Robson Lt kia 12-10-18 RGA 91SB p209 CR France1392
AINSLIE,Archibald 2Lt kia 19-4-17 4KOSB p224 MR34
AINSLIE,Denys Alfred Lafone Lt kia 24-10-14 1Dev p76 MR22,Lafore
AINSLIE,George.MC.TCapt dow 21-8-18 6KOSB p101
AINSLIE,Henry Percival LtCol ded 6-7-19 IA 1/63PalamcottahLI p273 CR Pakistan50A
AINSLIE,John 2Lt dow 11-4-17 9RScots p212 CR France95,9 att11Bn
AINSLIE,John Archibald Capt kia 19-5-17 KOSB p101 CR France184
AINSLIE,John Elliott T2Lt kia 28-9-15 12RScots p53 MR19,Elliot
AINSLIE,Montague Forwood TLt dow 17-5-16 12Lpool p71 CR Belgium11,17-4-16
AINSLIE,Walter Gordon 2Lt kia 10-11-16 RFA attX33TMB p24 MR21
AINSWORTH,Harry Lawrence Capt drd 30-12-15 IA 1/10GurkhaRif p273 MR41
AINSWORTH,Herbert Green 2Lt kia 9-10-17 9Manch p237 MR30
AINSWORTH,John Stirling Lt kia 14-10-14 11Huss p22 CR France324
AINSWORTH,William Maj kia 16-4-17 5LNLancs p234 CR France525
AIR,Charles Alexander Capt kia 25-9-15 4BlkW p230
AIRD,Allan Muir T2Lt kia 21-10-18 17 att18KRRC p148 CR Belgium140
AIRD,Archibald Thomas 2Lt kia 30-11-17 18Lond p250 MR17
AIRD,James Gilbert T2Lt kia 1-7-16 15LancF p91 MR21
AIREY,Henry William Sachs 2Lt kia 11-1-17 5WYorks p217 CR France505
AIREY,John Barker 2Lt ded 3-12-18 3DLI p265 CR Numb43,acckld
AIREY,Norman George 2Lt kia 22-11-17 2/W5Yorks p218 MR17
AIRTH,Rennie Alexander TLt kia 29-7-17 8Beds att7RFC p4&85 CR Belgium16
AIRY,Arthur Langton Lt kia 11-1-15 3 att1Nhampt p137 MR22
AIRY,James Oswald Capt 21-7-20 1Manch CR Eire77 &CR Eire14
AITCHESON,Thomas Charles 2Lt kia 19-10-16 2Hamps p120 MR21
AITCHISON,Andrew Leslie 2Lt dow 3-11-16 1KOSB p101 CR France833
AITCHISON,Douglas James Lt ded 17-4-18 RFA attRAF p269 CR Lond3 dow
AITCHISON,John T2Lt died 23-10-18 LabCps p266
AITCHISON,John Brebner 2Lt kld 10-5-15 5RScots p211 MR4
AITCHISON,Peter 2Lt kia 8-5-18 Yorks p254 MR30
AITCHISON,Ronald Andrew Colquhoun Lt dow 14-12-14 1RLancs p58 CR Belgium451
AITCHISON,Scott McDiarmid TLt kia 22-3-18 5 att1RInniskF p104 MR27
AITCHISON,Thomas Andrew Jamieson T2Lt dow 9-6-16 14 att12HLI p162 CR France423
AITCHISON,Thomas Donald 2Lt kia 28-6-15 4RScots p211 MR4
AITCHISON,Walter Maj kia 12-7-17 ScotHorse p205 CR Belgium6,attRGA HB
AITCHISON,William John.MID T2Lt kia 23-10-15 12HLI p162 CR France423
AITKEN,Alexander 2Lt dow 15-5-17 4GordH p241 CR France52
AITKEN,Andrew Danskine Lt kia 4-8-16 RE 2/2FC p210 CR Egypt2
AITKEN,Andrew Ramsey T2Lt acckld 2-3-18 RFC p15 CR Scot757,Ramsay
AITKEN,Archibald Bruce.MC.AMaj kld 4-8-19 RE att2S&M p254 CR Iraq8
AITKEN,Frank Thompson 2Lt kia 20-11-17 6SfthH p241 CR France1498
AITKEN,James 2Lt dow 3-5-17 5CamH p167 CR France1182
AITKEN,James Maj ded 29-7-17 RAMC p269 CR Scot761
AITKEN,James T2Lt kia 3-10-18 1GarBnWorc att11SomLI p107 CR France255
AITKEN,James Hunter 2Lt dedacc 2-6-16 7TrBnBlkW p231 CR Bucks60
AITKEN,John Christie.MC.Capt kia 25-9-15 2A&SH p172 CR France114
AITKEN,John Francis T2Lt kia 7-9-17 GL & 1/6LancF p189 CR Belgium8,6-9-17
AITKEN,John Malcolm T2Lt dow 12-10-18 D82RFA p24 CR France398
AITKEN,Robert Capt ded 17-1-19 RAMC SR p194 CR Iraq8
AITKENS,Albert Reginald Knight 2Lt dow 31-5-15 7Lond p247 CR France64
AITKENS,Cyril Arthur Charles Lt dow 10-7-16 RE p210 CR France397
AITON,Alexander Hamilton Capt kia 28-9-18 5HLI p240 CR Belgium84
AITON,William 2Lt kia 21-3-18 5 att3RB p177 MR27

AIZLEWOOD,Leslie Peach,MC.Maj kia 29-9-18 5Y&L &RAF p255
AKAM,James Rhodes Lt kia 1-7-16 18WYorks p80 MR21
AKED,George Lt kia 5-3-15 5Leic p220 CR Belgium33
AKED,Robert Basil Cautley.MC.Lt kia 21-3-18 2/5NStaffs p237 MR20
AKERMAN,Alexander Grant T2Lt kia 17-9-18 11Ess p131 CR France835
AKERMAN,Charles Savidge Annand Maj ded 26-9-15 RE HQ5SigCoy p43 CR France64
AKERMAN,Ralph Portland 2Lt dow 3-10-15 11Lond p248 CR Hamps64
AKHURST,Norman Walter TLt dow 8-6-18 35MGC p181 CR France63
AKRILL-JONES,Edward Trevor Lt kld 18-3-18 4N&D attRFC p15 CR Derby51
AKRILL-JONES,Robert Rowland 2Lt kia 9-4-17 2YLI CR France591
ALABASTER,Frederic Clifford 2Lt dow 25-8-16 5RWar p214 CR War3,Frederick
ALBAN,Clifton Frederick Lt dow 6-4-17 7Lond & 59RFC MR20 served as BAILEY.C.F.
ALBAN,Harry Chayton Lt kia 9-2-15 1Leinst p174 CR Belgium80
ALBERTSON,Armand Howard T2Lt kia 9-8-18 2TankCps p188 CR France649
ALBINSON,William Arthur 2Lt kia 26-4-18 3 att7RWSurr p55 CR France489
ALBRECHT,Charles Esmond Redlin Lt kia 24-8-14 2SLancs p125 MR15
ALBRECHT,John Ernest North 2Lt kia 1-8-17 33RFA p24 CR Belgium10 2-8-17 55RFA
ALBRIGHT,Martin Chicheley Maj dow 8-11-17 1/1WorcYeo p206 CR Palestine 8
ALBURY,Norman Howard T2Lt dow 15-9-17 GL &24RFC p4 CR France251
ALCOCK,Alfred 2Lt kia 21-8-16 18 att1Glouc p106 MR21
ALCOCK,Empson Lt kia 21-8-17 RFA 2NthMidBde p207 CR France1495
ALCOCK,Frank Lt ded 3-9-17 RhodR att3/2KAR p202 CR Tanzania1
ALCOCK,Randal Arthur Lt kia 1-9-18 7EYorks p83 CR France307
ALCOCK,Richard Evans Capt ded 1-3-17 RGA 99CoyMaltaGarr p38 CR Europe1
ALDANA,Juan Manuel TLt kia 21-4-17 12Worc p107 CR France531
ALDER,Thomas Gordon Edgecombe 2Lt kld 28-7-18 5ELancs &RAF p226&255 CR Glouc86
ALDERMAN,William.MC.Capt&QM kia 28-8-16 1Dors p123 CR France1472,31-8-18
ALDERMAN,William John.DSO.CaptALtCol kia 20-11-17 6RWKent p140 CR France379
ALDERSEY,Hugh Capt kia 10-3-18 ChesYeo p203 CR Palestine3,10ShropLI
ALDERSEY,Mark 2Lt kia 1-11-17 1Ches p95 MR30
ALDERSON,Albert Evelyn LtACapt drd 11-3-18 3RWSurr att1YLI p55 CR Greece3
ALDERSON,Alex George Jermyn 2Lt kia 19-10-16 5DCLI attMGC p186&227 CR Dors &C/146
ALDERSON,Arthur Roy TLt kia 22-3-16 RE 87FC p43 CR France423
ALDERSON,Bernard Henry Maj ded 2-9-17 IA 34PoonaHorse p273 CR France787
ALDERSON,Reginald.MC.ACapt dow 25-3-18 1/8LancF p221 CR France103
ALDERTON,Charles John Woodward 2Lt kia 20-11-17 7GordH p242 CR France662
ALDERTON,Colin Frederick T2Lt kia 7-7-16 12Manch p154 CR France667
ALDERWICK,Ernest Ewart Gladstone T2Lt kia 26-8-17 11Suff p77 CR France1462
ALDIN,Dudley Cecil 2Lt kia 15-5-16 RE 105FC p43 CR France68
ALDIS,Chas 2Lt ded 1-5-16 IARO att67Pujabis p273 CR Iraq1
ALDIS,Ralph Harry Lt kia 31-10-17 2/21Lond p251 CR Israel1
ALDOUS,Alan Edward T2Lt kia 3-7-16 8BordR p116 CR France393
ALDOUS,Stewart John Capt kia 26-3-16 5N&D p232 CR France68,Steuart 25-3-16
ALDRICH,Arnold 2Lt ded 1-5-18 1 att1/8Worc p107 CR Italy4,2-5-18
ALDRICH,Francis Pelham 2Lt kia 6-7-17 1/6NumbF p214 CR France421
ALDRICH,George Richard 2Lt kia 4-12-17 21Lond p251 MR17,1/23Lond
ALDRICK,Charles Pelham Gardner 2Lt kia 7-10-16 26RFus p66 CR France744
ALDRIDGE,Archie Horace.MC.2Lt dow 8-11-18 4RWSurr p212 CR France146
ALDRIDGE,Evelyn,OBE.MajALtCol ded 30-3-19 RGA p38 CR Hamps64
ALDRIDGE,Joseph George Rev 8-10-18 YMCA attSAfrBde CR France844
ALDRIDGE,Reginald John Petty Devenish Capt kia 7-10-14 2RSuss p118 CR France1329
ALDRIDGE,Reginald Percy T2Lt kld 26-3-18 39MGC p181 MR27
ALDWINKLE,Bernard Lt dow 3-11-18 RFA 421HB p24 MR70 &CR Europe179
ALDWINKLE,Ralph 2Lt kia 15-11-16 11RLancs att10LNLancs p58 CR France533
ALDWORTH,Douglas Gilbert Hayward 2Lt drd 10-10-18 att3RBerks p138 CR Eire14
ALDWORTH,Thomas Rupert Capt kia 11-3-15 2RBerks p138 CR France709
ALEXANDER,Alan Mansell 2Lt kia 8-12-17 2/16Lond p250 CR Palestine3
ALEXANDER,Alexander John 2Lt kia 27-11-17 5 att2/6WRid p227 MR17
ALEXANDER,Alfred Herbert 2Lt kia 3-12-17 6 att2Hamps p229 MR17
ALEXANDER,Alister Ralph Spiers Capt dow 9-2-16 IMS att2/7Gurkhas p273 CR Iraq1
ALEXANDER,Archibald Charles Edward Lt kia 11-3-15 3 att2RScotF p94 MR22

ALEXANDER,Charles.VD Maj 15-11-16 2HighBde RFA CR Scot386
ALEXANDER,Edward Mayne LtCol ded 11-8-16 SfthH p265
ALEXANDER,Frank Esmond T2Lt ded 25-7-16 98MGC Inf p181 CR France145,dow 27-7-16
ALEXANDER,Frank Wilson 2Lt kia 14-4-17 4 att16HLI p162 MR21
ALEXANDER,George Luard CaptTMaj kia 5-8-17 8Lond p247 CR France255
ALEXANDER,George Thomson Dickson T2Lt kia 11-4-17 2SfthH p164 CR France604
ALEXANDER,Gordon Reuben T2Lt kia 24-4-17 RSuss att2Bn p118 CR France379
ALEXANDER,Harold John 2Lt kia 25-7-18 7Lond p247 MR27
ALEXANDER,Harold Percy Maj kia 26-3-17 6Ess p232 MR34
ALEXANDER,Harry 2Lt kia 17-10-15 1GrenGds SR p49 CR France1059
ALEXANDER,Henry Talbot T2Lt kia 1-7-16 1Hamps p120 CR France1492
ALEXANDER,James.MID 2Lt kia 7-7-16 11NumbF p59 MR21
ALEXANDER,James Capt kia 2-12-17 16HLI p162 MR30
ALEXANDER,James Edward 2Lt kia 19-9-17 RFA 277ArmyBde p24 CR France285
ALEXANDER,James Kidd 2Lt kia 20-9-17 4 att9RScots p211 MR30
ALEXANDER,John T2Lt kia 15-7-16 8Leic p87 MR21
ALEXANDER,John Alexander Elliot TLt kia 16-8-15 12HLI p162 CR France149,15-8-15
ALEXANDER,John Petrie T2Lt ded 14-5-17 GL &4RFC p4 CR Scot244
ALEXANDER,John Rees 2Lt dow 4-9-18 6Lond p246 CR France833
ALEXANDER,John William Ewart 2Lt ded 14-4-16 BordR Ex10Norf p73&264 CR Norf301
ALEXANDER,Noel Legard T2Lt kia 1-7-16 9YLI p142 CR France267
ALEXANDER,Peter James.MC.Capt kia 12-10-17 7BlkW p231 CR Belgium125
ALEXANDER,Philip Mansell T2Lt dow 30-7-16 11 att5GordH p165 CR France833
ALEXANDER,Reginald LtCol dow 29-12-14 3RB p177 CR France284
ALEXANDER,Robert Lt dow 3-11-17 26RFA p24 CR Belgium3,117RFA
ALEXANDER,Samuel Aubrey Lt ded 15-11-18 5Mddx p269 CR Mddx40
ALEXANDER,Sydney Dawson Moray Maj 14-1-17 IOD MR66
ALEXANDER,Thomas Loudon 2Lt kia 8-5-17 10BlkW p128 MR37
ALEXANDER,Thomas Mitchell Lt kia 12-7-15 4KOSB p223 MR4
ALEXANDER,Thomas Wedderspoon.MID Maj kia 21-3-18 RGA att255RFA p209 MR20
ALEXANDER,Walter Lorenzo LtCol kia 14-5-15 2Yorks p89 CR France727
ALEXANDER,William LtCol ded 9-3-19 RAMC p269 CR Ches193
ALEXANDER,William Ewart 2Lt ded 14-4-16 10Norf p73 See ALEXANDER,John William Ewart
ALEXANDER,William Fairlie Lt kia 12-10-18 9HLI p240 CR France230
ALEXANDER,William Gemmell 2Lt kia 15-5-15 7Lpool p215 MR22
ALEXANDER,William Henderson Capt&QM ded 25-6-19 RE p262 CR Kent62
ALEXANDER,William Mercer T2Lt kia 1-7-16 17HLI p162 MR21
ALFORD,Allen Charles George 2Lt kia 3-9-16 10Glouc att3Worc p106 MR21,Allan
ALFORD,Edward Nicholas Capt ded 11-1-19 7Ess p232 MR43,2GarBnBeds
ALGAR,Arthur Patrick LtACapt kia 26-3-18 IARO att24Punjabis p273 CR Iraq8
ALGAR,Horace 2Lt ded 12-4-17 RE p269 CR Numb60
ALGEO,Norman Capt dow 30-11-17 3Leinst p174 CR France446
ALGEO,William Bensley Capt kia 17-5-16 1Dors p123 CR France1504
ALGER,George Crosbie T2Lt kld 7-6-17 GL &RFC p4 CR Scot398
ALINGTON,Geoffrey Hugh 2Lt kia 9-8-16 5RSuss p228 CR France296
ALINGTON,George Henry 2Lt kia 24-2-17 IARO att2/9GurkhaRif p273 MR38,23/24-2-17
ALISON,George Newdegate.MID Capt kia 1-7-16 SfthH &MGC Inf p181&164 CR France643
ALISON,Laughton Hassard 2Lt kia 15-5-15 1RBerks p138 MR22
ALLAM,Percy John 2Lt dow 22-5-18 PoW RLancs attTMB p58 CR Germany2
ALLAN,Alfred T2Lt kia 31-7-16 2HLI p162 see Allen,Alfred
ALLAN,Alwyn Munton.MC.Capt dow 21-4-18 1RWSurr p55 CR France40
ALLAN,Archibald.MC.Capt dow 17-6-18 4 O&BLI p231 CR Italy11
ALLAN,Arthur Gordon 2Lt dow 8-12-18 108RFA p24 CR France34,B106RFA
ALLAN,Charles Frederick Lt kia 28-6-15 4RScots p211 MR4
ALLAN,Frank Cecil T2Lt dow 29-9-16 4 att13DLI p160 CR France145
ALLAN,George 2Lt kld 14-3-16 19Lond p250 CR Scot531
ALLAN,George A.T2Lt kia 16-1-16 RGA p38 CR Belgium101
ALLAN,George McLachlan 2Lt dow 14-7-15 RE p210 MR4,Maclachan
ALLAN,Henry Somerset 2Lt dow 2-10-16 6Lond p246 CR France40
ALLAN,Hubert Gordon Rev 7-4-15 YMCA CR France1
ALLAN,Hugh Drummond Lt kia 24-4-17 3A&SH p172 CR France434,2Bn
ALLAN,James Grant TLt kia 25-9-15 9GordH p165 MR19
ALLAN,James Stanley 2Lt dow 22-10-16 3A&SH p172 CR France177

ALLAN,John 2Lt dow 4-11-16 GL &11RFC p2&189 CR France46
ALLAN,John.MC.T2LtACapt dow 9-6-17 6MGC HB p181 CR France285
ALLAN,John Love Strathearn T2Lt kia 25-9-15 7KOSB p101 MR19
ALLAN,John Steele T2Lt kia 12-10-15 9 att2RScotF p94 CR France744
ALLAN,JohnWilliam Anderson.MC. 2Lt dow 10-4-18 8BordR p116 see ALLEN,J.W.A.
ALLAN,Lawson Ellis Lt kia 26-4-17 W'morland&CumbYeo attRFC p17&206 MR20
ALLAN,Lewis Davidson TLt kia 27-9-18 8RScotF p94 CR France530
ALLAN,Marshall Thomson TLt kia 26/29-9-15 6RScotF p94 MR19
ALLAN,Noel James Capt ded 18-10-18 RAMC p253 CR Iraq6
ALLAN,Peter 2Lt dow 19-7-18 3 att5CamH p167 CR France134,kia
ALLAN,Ramsay 2Lt kld 22-4-18 GL &2RAF p189 CR France179
ALLAN,Robert 2Lt kia 23-4-17 8ScotRif att16KRRC p225 MR20
ALLAN,Robert Beausire Lt ded 5-4-18 4RScots p211 CR France64
ALLAN,Robert Gregor 2Lt kia 9-4-17 2KOSB p101 CR France550,Grigor
ALLAN,Wallace Capt ded 29-6-16 1GarrBnLincs p74 CR Egypt15,Ex7RScotF
ALLAN,William AssCommsyHonLt ded 28-11-16 IA S&TCps p273 CR Iraq6
ALLAN,William Alexander 2Lt kia 7-6-17 4 att11RScots p211 MR20 &CR France1896
ALLAN,William Halliday T2Lt kia 31-7-17 7/8KOSB p101 MR29
ALLAN,William Lewis Campbell HonMaj kia 12-10-14 3KOSB p101 CR France260,14-10-14 2Bn
ALLAN,William Stanley Lt kia 17-5-15 7Lpool p215 MR22
ALLAN-HAY,Edward James 2Lt ded 5-9-18 IA p273
ALLANSON,Henry Peter 2Lt kia 20-7-16 1 att2Suff p77 MR21
ALLARD,Philip Hayward LtACapt kia 23-6-17 3/45RFA p24 CR Belgium113,dow
ALLARDICE,Colin McDiarmid Lt kia 26-4-15 IA 14 att47Sikhs p273 CR Belgium101
ALLARDICE,Harry LtCol kia 1-7-16 IA 36JacobsHorse att13NumbF p273 CR France188
ALLASON,Lionel Theopilus Capt kia 7-10-14 1LNLancs p135 MR15
ALLATT,Henry Thomas Ward Col ded 8-5-16 SL &DCLI p201 CR Hamps1
ALLAWAY,Trevor Rhys.MC.Capt dow 29-6-16 3SWBord attWelshR p99 CR Egypt9,acckld
ALLBON,Bernard Charles Jeaves TCapt ded 3-2-19 3 att6Dors p123&257
ALLBERRY,Cecil Charles TCapt kia 25-9-16 10 att9Leic p87 MR21
ALLCHIN,Sidney Milton T2Lt kia 13-12-17 3RWKent p140 CR Belgium106,dow
ALLCHIN,Walter John T2Lt kia 26-10-17 14War p64 MR30
ALLCHORN,Edward Walter.MM T2Lt dow 5-11-17 1 att4EYorks p83 CR France64
ALLCOCK,Christian 2Lt dow 30-3-18 49MGC p181 CR Belgium3
ALLCOCK,Joseph 2Lt kia 16-10-18 54RGA attRE Sigs p38 CR France190
ALLCOCK,William Thomas Lloyd Capt kia 5-6-17 40RFC p4 MR20
ALLDAY,Stanley Owen Lt kia 13-10-15 1/5SStaffs p229 MR19
ALLDEN,Joseph Henry 2Lt kia 28-4-17 2/4 O&BLI p231 MR21
ALLEN,Albert Alexander 2Lt kia 11-10-17 GL &46RFC p4 CR France568
ALLEN,Alfred T2Lt kia 31-7-16 2HLI p162 MR21,ALLAN
ALLEN,Alfred James Benedict T2Lt kia 3-3-16 17RWelshF p97 CR France727
ALLEN,Archibald Stafford TLt kia 3-10-15 8RFus p66 CR France115
ALLEN,Arthur Haviland T2Lt kia 4-10-17 11 att1RDubF p176 MR30
ALLEN,Charles Arthur 2Lt kld 12-3-19 5NumbF &RAF p213
ALLEN,Charles Rayle.MC.Capt kia 27-9-18 6Manch p236 CR France712,Royle 7Bn
ALLEN,Charles St.Vincent 2Lt ded 16-2-17 3EKent attMGC Inf p57&181 CR Herts12
ALLEN,Cuthbert George Llewellin T2Lt dow 3-11-15 RE 175FC p43 CR Belgium11
ALLEN,Cyrus 2Lt kia 13-3-18 GL &RFC p15 CR France403
ALLEN,D.G.A. Capt kld 8-10-18 4DLI &RAF p160
ALLEN,Francis Edward Lt kia 11-4-18 1/5Y&L p238 MR30
ALLEN,Frederick John T2Lt kia 25-9-15 9Dev p76 CR France88,dow 27-9-15
ALLEN,Geoffrey Austin 2Lt kia 1-7-16 2Ess p131 MR21
ALLEN,Geoffrey Charles TLt dow 5-4-18 6EKent p57 CR France62
ALLEN,Geoffrey May 2Lt kia 2-9-16 GL &RFC p2&189 CR France233
ALLEN,Geoffrey Peake 2Lt kld 21-12-15 4RWSurr p212 CR Surrey6
ALLEN,George James T2Lt dow 12-10-17 att7RWKent p140 CR Belgium18
ALLEN,Harry TCapt dow 16-1-18 8Glouc p106 CR France398
ALLEN,Henry Edward TLt drd 24-4-17 GL attGambiaCoy WAFF p201 MR40
ALLEN,Herbert 2Lt kia 1-7-16 1/5SStaffs p229 MR21
ALLEN,Herbert Thomas TCapt kia 25-9-15 9SfthH p164 CR France114
ALLEN,Hugh Charles.DCM.2Lt kia 25-4-17 1/7BlkW p231 CR France604,23-4-17
ALLEN,Humphrey Decius TLt kia 1-7-16 10WYorks p80 CR France373

ALLEN,J.Capt&QM 15-9-20 10YLI CR Yorks547

ALLEN,James Lt&AssCommsy ded 22-10-18 IMS p273 MR65

ALLEN,John 2Lt ded 29-11-19 LabCps p266 CR Wales1

ALLEN,John Edric Russell.MIDx2 Lt dow 8-4-18 16Lancers p22 CR France145,Capt

ALLEN,John Francis Capt dow 4-11-14 LNLancs p135 CR Belgium57,5-11-14

ALLEN,John Hugh Lt kia 13-6-15 13Worc p107 CR Gallipoli6

ALLEN,John Stanley.MC.TMaj kia 11-4-18 9NumbF p59 MR32

ALLEN,John Thomas.MID Lt ded 18-2-16 RFA p24 CR Dorset &C/133,Capt

ALLEN,John William Anderson.MC.2Lt dow 10-4-18 8BordR p116 MR32,ALLAN

ALLEN,Kenneth Harris TLt dow 11-10-18 13 att9Manch p154 CR France446

ALLEN,Lawrence John Maynard T2Lt kia 2-7-16 6Wilts p152 MR21

ALLEN,Leslie John Spencer Capt dow 15-2-17 7Hamps p229 CR Iraq5

ALLEN,Lionel Raymund Whateley Lt kia 27-3-18 9SWBord attMGC12Div p99&181 MR27

ALLEN,Mary Ann SNurse ded 5-1-20 QAIMNS CR Lancs483

ALLEN,Maurice Reginald T2Lt kia 13-9-16 2N&D p133 MR21

ALLEN,Melville Richard Howell Agnew Lt ded 21-3-17 RFC p4 CR Beds&Hunts23

ALLEN,Merwyn Richard William T2Lt kia 2-8-17 7 att2/5Norf p73 CR France154,Mervyn

ALLEN,Norman TCapt kia 14-4-18 2 posted14RWar p64 CR France346

ALLEN,Owen Augustus Ellis TLt kld 3-11-17 GL &RFC p4 CR Camb1,O.E.A.

ALLEN,Percivall Knight TCapt kia 23-4-17 10WYorks p80 CR France531

ALLEN,Percy 2Lt kia 4-10-17 59RFA SR p24 MR30

ALLEN,Percy Hampson 2Lt kia 20-4-16 3Y&L p158 MR29

ALLEN,Percy Herman Charles Lt kia 9-5-15 3 att2ELancs p110 France566

ALLEN,Raymond Francis 2Lt kia 18-11-18 1/6RWar attRAF p258 CR Ches182,kld

ALLEN,Richard Gerrard Ross 2LtACapt kia 16-11-16 5WYorks attRFC p17&218 CR France742,2Lt

ALLEN,Richard Lancelot Baugh Lt ded 27-12-18 67RFA p261 CR Egypt9

ALLEN,Stephen Dexter T2Lt kia 27-8-18 Beds att4Bn p85 MR16,att7RFus

ALLEN,Stephen Henry Hammans Lt kia 27-3-18 3/5Dev att6NumbF p217 MR27

ALLEN,Sydney Raymond T2Lt kia 12-7-16 16Manch p154 MR21

ALLEN,Thomas 2Lt kia 25-2-15 1IrGds SR p52 CR France720,26-2-15

ALLEN,Thomas Gordon Lt kia 26-8-18 5EYorks p219 CR France432

ALLEN,Valentine Francis T2Lt kia 17-11-17 RB att16Bn p177 MR30

ALLEN,Walter Smith 2Lt kia 21-3-18 2/5N&D p232 MR20

ALLEN,Wellesley Roe Capt ded 11-3-19 RAMC att2Ech p194 CR Egypt9,GHQ 3Ech

ALLEN,William Lt ded 12-10-18 6Hamps p228 CR Asia82,1/4Bn

ALLEN,William Frederick 2Lt kia 9-10-17 3 att2/4ELancs p110 CR Belgium125

ALLEN,William Henry T2Lt kia 12-4-18 31MGC Inf p181 MR32

ALLEN,William Lynn.DSO.Maj kld 28-10-14 2BordR p116 MR29

ALLEN,William Maxey TLt kia 26-9-15 13NumbF p59 MR19

ALLEN,William Sproston Lt kia 14-3-18 1RFA attRGA252SB p207 CR Belgium19

ALLEN,W.J.Lt 20-1-17 EAUL attIntelDept CR EAfrica39

ALLENBY,Augustus Heathcote LtCol kia 7-8-15 IA att7RScotF p94&273 CR France222,H.A.

ALLENBY,Horace Michael Hynman.MC. Lt dow 29-7-17 14RHA p24 CR Belgium24

ALLENDER,George Frederick LtCol ded 29-9-16 5Lpool Res p269 CR Ches190,Col 2-10-16

ALLENDER,John Harold 2Lt kia 7-10-16 1Lond p245 MR21

ALLFREY,Frederick de Vere Bruce Lt kia 6-9-14 9Lancers p22 CR France1432,7-9-14

ALLFREY,Hugh Lionel Capt kia 19-9-18 10EKent p204 CR France212,18-9-18

ALLGOOD,Bertram Capt kia 6-12-14 1RIrRif p168 CR France768

ALLGOOD,George T2Lt kia 15-4-17 10RDubF p176 MR20

ALLIBAN,William Beaumont.MID Lt kia 5-5-17 2/5N&D p232 MR21

ALLIES,Alfric Evan Lt kia 16-8-15 8RWelshF p97 MR4,Ewan 15-8-15

ALLIN,Harold Arthur T2Lt kia 23-10-17 17LancF p91 MR30

ALLIN,Harold Wyse TLt dow 13-12-17 6KSLI p144 CR Egypt2

ALLINSON,Athelstan John William Ward.MID Lt kia 9-4-18 A121RFA p24 CR France1140

ALLINSON,Cyril Hugh 2Lt kia 13-11-16 3 att2Suff p77 MR21

ALLINSON,David.DCM.Lt kia 29-3-18 7ScotRif att12KRRC p224 MR27

ALLINSON,Fred.MC.T2Lt ded 27-3-17 GL 8RWSurr &70RFC p4 CR France1349

ALLISON,Charles Anderson TLt kia 12-3-15 2ELancs p110 CR France924

ALLISON,Gordon Lt kia 8-6-19 IA 3/1GurkhaRif p273 MR43

ALLISON,Harry Lt kia 27-8-18 3 att13RWelshF p97 CR France402

ALLISON,Henry James Noel Palmer Lt ded 4-2-19 3GordH CR Durham25

ALLISON,Hazlett Samuel.MID Maj kia 9-8-17 7RIrRif p168 MR29

ALLISON,James 2Lt kia 20-9-17 8RScots p211 MR30

ALLISON,James Stewart Lt ded 18-9-17 6BlkW att11GreekLabBn p231 CR Greece9

ALLISON,John Lt kia 24-11-17 9A&SH p244 CR France256

ALLISON,John T2Lt kia 21-3-18 14A&SH p172 MR20

ALLISON,Robert Stafford 2Lt kia 16-6-17 1DenbighYeo p203 CR Palestine8,dow

ALLISON,Thomas Capt kia 18-5-15 4CamH p242 MR22

ALLISON,Thomas McGregor TMaj kia 30-5-18 12Glouc p106 CR France1689

ALLISON,William Frederick 2Lt kia 23-4-17 7GordH p242 CR France604

ALLNUTT,Albert Edwin T2Lt kia 27-9-18 KSLI att7BnRes p144 CR France357

ALLOM,Charles Cedric Gordon Lt dow 20-10-17 C1NMidRFA p207 CR France145

ALLOTT,Thomas Richard T2Lt dow 4-11-18 1YLI p142 CRFrance206

ALLOWAY,Howard George 2Lt kia 30-11-17 4Leic p220 MR19

ALLPASS,Esmond Theodore T2Lt kia 21-8-15 9N&D p133 MR4

ALLPASS,Henry Blythe King 2Lt kia 16-9-16 4Ess att1Camb p232 MR21

ALLPASS,Samuel Rosslee TCapt dow 21-1-17 185MGC Inf p181 MR38

ALLPORT,Harrison Kingsley 2Lt kia 21-8-16 4A&SH p172 CR France453

ALLPORT,Ivor Merlin 2Lt kia 9-1-17 7Nhampt p137 CR France149

ALLPORT,Morton 2Lt ded 10-11-16 70RFC p2 MR20

ALLPORT,Thomas Coote Capt kia 1-8-15 5Y&L p238 CR Belgium85

ALLSOPP,Jerome Boileau.DSO.MIDx3 MajALtCol kia 27-5-18 SLancs p125 MR18

ALLTREE,Charles Derek TLt dow PoW 27-3-18 RWelshF att9Bn p97 CR France1277

ALLURED,Will T2Lt kia 14-9-16 6BordR p116 CR France251

ALMACK,Alfred Christopher Turnour 2Lt kia 27-9-16 MGC att3Nhampt p181

ALMACK,Edward Poulton Capt kia 25-1-16 RHA att85RFA p24 CR France430

ALMON,Harold Pryor 2Lt kia 31-7-17 3 att11LancF p91 CR Belgium34

ALMOND,Charles Percy Lt ded 5-4-17 RE BaseDepot p262 CR France145

ALMOND,George Hely-Hutchinson TCapt kia 9-8-18 RAMC 3CavFA p194 CR France652

ALMOND,Henry Tristram 2Lt kia 31-3-16 MGC att3GordH p181 CR France513 3GordH attMGC

ALMOND,Owen Edmund 2Lt kia 29-9-15 2LNLancs p135 CR EAfrica58

ALMOND,Rowland Latimer Lt kia 28-10-14 RE att21Coy3S&M p43 CR France98

ALNACK,A.C.T.3Nhampt attMGC p137 MR21,See ALMACK,A.C.T

ALSTON,Claude McCaul 2Lt kia 25-10-14 2RScotF p94 MR29,24-10-14

ALSTON,Ernest Alfred Brooke.MIDx3 MajTLtCol kia 10/11-8-17 2Nhampt att10DCLI p137 CR Belgium173,11-8-17

ALSTON,Garwood Kencingdale 2Lt kia 12-8-15 5Suff p217 MR4,Keningale

ALSTON,James 2Lt kia 28-9-18 5HLI p240 CR Belgium111

ALSTON,James William.MID MajTLtCol kia 15-4-15 2RIrRif p168 CR Belgium28

ALSTON,James William Hamilton TMaj ded 3-1-17 11A&SH p172 CR France430

ALSTON,John Capt kia 16-10-17 RAMC 103FA p194 CR Belgium12

ALSTON,John Douglas Lt kia 10-3-15 3 att2ScotRif p103 CR France260

ALSTON,Robert Charles Wallace Capt dow 18-8-15 1HLI p162 CR France924,kia

ALSTON,Rowland Evelyn 2Lt kia 17-8-16 B52RFA p24 CR France924

ALT,George Earl Capt kia 18-4-15 3YLI p142 CR Belgium152

ALTOFT,George Herbert 2Lt kia 17-7-17 4WYorks p80 CR Belgium132,G.A.

ALTY,Daniel 2Lt kia 9-9-18 9Lpool att2SStaffs p216 MR16,5-9-18

ALTY,Henry.DCM.2Lt dow 30-9-18 9Lpool p216 CR France256

ALVES,Alexander TLt kia 26-5-18 RASC att7RFus p192 CR France233

ALVES,John William Jerome Maj ded 29-10-18 IA 93BurmaInf p273 CR India48

AMBLER,Edward T2Lt kia 26-4-18 1/5Y&L p158 CR Belgium103

AMBLER,Edward Sharp Lt kia 8-5-18 2ScotsGds p51 CR France120

AMBLER,George Lt dow 3-8-17 6WYorks p218 CR Yorks410

AMBLER,Percy Capt dedacc 28-9-19 2/5Lpool CR Ches182

AMBLER,R.2Lt 24-11-18 13Lpool CR Lancs491

AMBRIDGE,William T2Lt kia 7-4-18 8 att6Beds p85 CR France798

AMBROSE,Donald 2Lt kia 21-3-18 23Lond p252 MR20

AMBROSE,Gerald Leslie 2Lt dow 28-5-19 IA 1/22Punjabis p273 MR43,27-5-19

AMERY,Harold Francis Saphir.MID Maj dow 24-11-15 1BlkW p128&263,ded CR Lond8

AMERY-PARKES,Douglas John.MC&Bar.LtAMaj dow 30-4-18 2Mddx att119MGC p145 181&258 CR France102

AMES,Ivan Wilson 2Lt ded 6-9-19.9RWKent p265 CR SAfrica42,Wilton

AMES,Peter Ashman Lt kld 21-11-20 GL &1GrenGds CR Lond9

AMES,Robert Henry TCapt kia 6-1-16 2Leic p87 MR38

AMES,William Kerr Lt dow 16-9-14 RWKent p140 CR France1227

AMESBURY,Frank Cholmondely Dering Maj ded 7-2-18 9WRid p115&268 CR Sussex111 ExIA WarwickRecs SL

AMESBURY,Hugh Frederick Raleigh 2Lt kia 20-11-17 5 att8Beds p219 CR France711

AMESS,Frederick Thomas 2Lt dow 22-7-17 3KOSB p101 CR Glouc11,3Beds
AMEY,Harold 2Lt kia 27-9-18 7KSLI p144 CR France437
AMIES,Arthur George T2Lt kia 9-10-17 1/5Y&L p158 CR Belgium125
AMIES,Kenneth Francis T2Lt kia 23-9-17 2/6NStaffs p156 CR Belgium10
AMOR,Ernest John T2Lt kia 15-5-16 14Mddx attRFC p2&145 CR France95,12-5-16
AMOROSO,Michele TLt kia 3-7-16 D96RFA p24 CR France189
AMOS,A.J.Lt 30-4-20 RE IWT CR Essex83
AMOS,Charles Edward 2Lt kia 22-3-18 40MGC p181 MR20
AMOS,Frank Edward T2Lt kia 20-9-18 A230RFA p24 CR France1495
AMOS,Gilbert Stratton 2Lt kia 14-9-14 2KOSB p101 CR France864
AMOS,John Vince Lt ded 13-2-17 RFA 37DAC p24 CR France345
AMOS,William Hope T2Lt kia 14-10-16 7EKent p57 CR France744
AMPHLETT,Richard Ferrand 2Lt kia 5-4-17 8Worc p226 CR France1495
AMPHLETT,Edward Maylie Capt kia 4-6-15 12Worc attRFus p107 CR Gallipoli6,Baylie
AMPHLETT MORTON,James Fairfax.MID 2Lt kia 10-1-15 KRRC p148 CR France260
AMPT,Norman Crosland T2Lt dow 22-8-15 1BordR p116 MR4
AMY,Adolphe Barbier 2Lt kia 19-9-16 9RIrRif p168 MR29,Barber
AMYATT-BURNEY,Horace A.Maj ded 8-3-19 RDC p253 CR Yorks38
ANCILL,S.J.Capt 4-7-20 GL DentalSurg CR Iraq9
ANCRUM,J.A.2LtACapt kia 16-7-18 8HLI p240 see below
ANCRUM,James Alexander,MC.Capt dow 17-7-18 9HLI p240 CR Belgium18
ANDERSEN,Peter Johansen See ANDERSON,P J
ANDERSON,A.John MajTCol ded 11-8-18 RASC p192 CR Greece9,10-8-18 DDST
ANDERSON,Abdy Fellowes Capt kia 23-4-15 3ScotRif attKOSB p103 MR29
ANDERSON,Alan James Ramsay 2Lt kia 20-10-14 3 att2RIrReg p88 MR22
ANDERSON,Albert Stewart T2Lt ded 1-2-17 9RInnisF p104 CR France285
ANDERSON,Alec David 2Lt kia 6-11-18 1GrenGds p49 CR France948
ANDERSON,Alexander Campbell Capt kia 20-4-15 RAVC p198 CR Belgium84
ANDERSON,Alexander Clairmonte Capt dow 23-11-14 IA 6Jats p273 CR France80,dedacc
ANDERSON,Alexander Douglas Lt kia 17-7-16 4Glouc p225
ANDERSON,Alexander John MajTCol ded 11-8-18 RASC p192
ANDERSON,Alexander Ronald 2Lt dow 8-10-15 3 att1HLI p162 CR France924
ANDERSON,Andrew 2Lt ded 29-10-19 RFA p261 CR Scot766,Lt
ANDERSON,Andrew Douglas McArthur Lt kia 8-5-15 9A&SH p244 MR29,MacArthur
ANDERSON,Andrew Stewart Maj kia 16-6-15 10Lpool p216 MR29
ANDERSON,Archibald John Scott 2Lt kia 27-8-16 3 att11Ches p95 CR France246
ANDERSON,Archibald Joseph TCapt kia 1-7-16 10WYorks p80 CR France373
ANDERSON,Arthur T2Lt kia 29-3-17 9RWar p64 MR38
ANDERSON,Arthur Ferneaux Dalgairno 2Lt kia 1-7-16 4 att1LancF p91 CR France221,Furneaux Dalgairns
ANDERSON,Basil Arthur.MC TCapt kia 21-3-18 5 O&BLI p129 CR France1061
ANDERSON,Bernard Gordon.MC TLt dow 8-8-16 10Lincs p74 CR Yorks323,Gordan
ANDERSON,Brian Hallam T2Lt kld 8-9-17 GL &RFC p4 see ANDERSON,F.B.H.
ANDERSON,Charles Alexander Kenneth 2Lt kia 10-11-14 1KRRC p148 MR29,12-11-14 att1RSFus
ANDERSON,Charles Alfred Walker TLtCol kia 18-9-16 1NStaffs att1/5RLancs p156 CR France374
ANDERSON,Charles Edward Capt kia 20-7-16 GordH att8Bn p165 CR France176,2Bn
ANDERSON,Charles Henry 2Lt ded 25-8-15.13HLI p265 CR Scot142
ANDERSON,Charles Hamilton Capt kia 19-12-14 HLI p162 MR22
ANDERSON,Charles Ogilvy Lt dow 2-10-15 2 att3RScots p53 CR France40,3 att2Bn
ANDERSON,Clifford William Lt kia 24-10-18 B190RFA p207 CR Belgium143
ANDERSON,Colin Knox Lt kia 23-8-14 3RWKent p140 CR Belgium201
ANDERSON,Duncan.MM.TLt ded 4-5-18 RASC p192 CR Surrey1
ANDERSON,David,MC.T2LtACapt kia 23-4-17 7CamH att44TMB p167 CR France1182
ANDERSON,David Lt kia 23-4-17 4GordH p241 CR France1194
ANDERSON,David TLt ded 13-9-17 RAMC 37MAC att4SH p194 CR France134
ANDERSON,David Alexander 2Lt kia 17-8-16 10/11HLI p162 MR21
ANDERSON,David Horace T2Lt kia 22-4-16 11 att2BlkW p128 MR38
ANDERSON,David William.MC&Bar Capt kia 8-8-18 6Lond p246 CR France1170,Wilson
ANDERSON,Denis Vipont Friend Capt kia 25-4-15 F Coy 1RDubF p176 CR Gallipoli15
ANDERSON,Donald Fraser Lt kia 27-4-18 4RWKent p234 CR Belgium188

ANDERSON,Donald Knox MC.TLtCol kia 3-12-17 MGC att61EKentDiv p57&181,TLt MR17
ANDERSON,Edward Darnley.DSO.TMaj ded 13-11-17 1NStaffs p156 CR France201
ANDERSON,Edward Kerr Capt kld 16-3-18 5HLI attRFC p17&240 CR Scot87
ANDERSON,Edwin Frederick Spurrier Lt dow 1-11-18 4NStaffs att35MGC Infp156 CR Belgium143,2-11-18
ANDERSON,Eric James Capt kia 13-11-16 6SfthH p241 CR France131
ANDERSON,Ernest Lionel Lane.MID 2Lt kia 10-11-14 1RSFus p94 MR29
ANDERSON,Francis TLt kia 18-11-16 7SLancs p125 MR21
ANDERSON,Francis Maj dow 28-1-17 2 att12RScots p53 CR France95
ANDERSON,Francis Brian Hallam T2Lt kld 8-9-17 GL &RFC p4 CR Norf151 see ANDERSON,B.H.
ANDERSON,Francis Sainthill.MC.CaptAMaj kia 25-8-18 A15RFA p24 CR France514
ANDERSON,Frank Gordon Donald TCapt kia 11-10-18 6Y&L p158 CR France405,9Bn
ANDERSON,Frederick Henry.MC.2Lt ded 15-5-18 50RFA p24 CR France1359
ANDERSON,Frederick Kinloch 2Lt kia 25-9-15 1/4BlkW p230 CR France705
ANDERSON,Fredk William Capt kia 29-3-18 RE 416FC p209 CR France184
ANDERSON,George Alexander Lt ded 27-2-19 4BlkW p269 CR Scot677,acckld 27-1-19
ANDERSON,George Grantham TCaptAMaj ded 3-11-18 RAMC att51GH p194 CR France40
ANDERSON,George John T2Lt kia 22-4-16 2BlkW p128 CR Iraq5
ANDERSON,George Ogilvie.DCM.2Lt kia 26-10-17 2GordH p165 MR30
ANDERSON,George Rutherford T2Lt kia 18-8-16 73MGC Inf p181 CR France400
ANDERSON,George Whitfield HonMaj&QM ded 31-8-15 SfthH attEgyptArmy p164 CR Egypt9,Whitefield
ANDERSON,Gerard Rupert Laurie 2Lt kia 9-11-14 3 att1Ches p95 MR29
ANDERSON,Goldie Fraser.MC.Lt kia 19-7-16 RE 90FC p43 CR France34,19-7-18
ANDERSON,Gordon Wright TCapt ded 20-11-18 RASC p192 CR Kent96
ANDERSON,Harry Frederick Cortlandt 2Lt dow 14-2-17 IA 102Grens p273
ANDERSON,Harry John 2Lt kia 10-4-18 3Wilts p152 CR Palestine9
ANDERSON,Henry Angus 2Lt kia 21-7-18 4GordH p241 CR France34
ANDERSON,Henry Lawrence LtCol dow 29-10-14 IA 9BhopalInf p273 CR France705
ANDERSON,Henry McDonald Lt kia 30-5-18 5NumbF att63MGC p186&213,McDonnell CR France84,dow
ANDERSON,Herbert Norman Scott T2Lt kld 24-12-17 GL &RFC p4 CR Scot151
ANDERSON,James TLt kia 20-8-16 SL &87TMB 26/10RFA p201 MR29
ANDERSON,James 2Lt kia 20-8-16 16ScotRif att87/2TMB p254 CR Belgium101
ANDERSON,James T2LtACapt kia 25-9-16 2KOSB p101 MR21
ANDERSON,James Capt dow 5-7-17 8HLI att5YLI p240 CR France8
ANDERSON,James Alexander T2Lt kia 19-10-16 11 att8BlkW p128 MR21
ANDERSON,James Kirkwood Capt dow 24-11-17 1/7ScotRif p224 CR Palestine3
ANDERSON,James Lennox 2Lt dow 25-5-17 1/7BlkW p231 CR France97
ANDERSON,James Morton 2Lt kia 1-5-17 C70RFA p24 CR France1182
ANDERSON,James Parker 2Lt ded 26-12-18 4SfthH p269 CR Scot199
ANDERSON,James Richard Haig Lt kia 11-5-15 2CamH p167 MR29
ANDERSON,James Skelton T2Lt dow 10-10-16 21KRRC p148 CR France833
ANDERSON,J.L.K. 2Lt kia about31-5-18 SL &RAF p201
ANDERSON,J.P Lt 9-6-20 IndDefForce 37Bn CR India97A
ANDERSON,John Capt ded 17-5-18 RAMC p253 MR43
ANDERSON,John Alexander 2Lt kia 21-3-18 2/4ELancs p226 MR27
ANDERSON,John Frederick Capt&Adjt kld 14-7-15 2 att10HLI p162 CR France727
ANDERSON,John Gavin Lt kia 3-5-17 212MGC Inf p181 CR France644
ANDERSON,John George.MC.MID Capt kia 21-3-18 RAMC att1/6BlkW p255 MR20
ANDERSON,John Macnabb Lt kia 17-6-15 3 att2RScots p53 MR29
ANDERSON,John Turnbull 2Lt kia 5-10-17 20MGC Inf p181 MR30
ANDERSON,John Victor Cortlandt Capt kia 8-6-18 IA CpsofGuides p273 CR Palestine9
ANDERSON,John William T2Lt kia 17-8-16 7CamH p167 MR21
ANDERSON,Jonas William.MC.Maj dow 26-3-18 RAMC 3FA p253 CR France103
ANDERSON,Joseph Henry 2Lt kia 9-12-17 21Lond p251 CR Palestine3,2/22Bn
ANDERSON,Lawrence 2Lt kia 11-10-15 4Lincs p217 MR19
ANDERSON,Leigh Maxwell Lt ded 3-2-15 9RInniskF p264 see below
ANDERSON,Leigh Maxwell TLt ded 1-9-15 9RIrFus p170&p264 CR Ireland71
ANDERSON,Macclesfield Heptinstall Maj kia 29-4-15 IA 33Cavalry p273 MR61

ANDERSON,Martin Alan.MC.Capt dow 9-5-17 RE 211FC p43 CR France113,Maj
ANDERSON,Mathew Capt kia 22-8-16 9HLI p240 CR France402
ANDERSON,Matthew T2Lt kia 11-6-17 6KOSB p101 CR France604
ANDERSON,Max Edward Alwyn TCapt dow 13-9-16 14Lpool p71 CR Greece6
ANDERSON,Mervyn Kebble T2Lt dow 11-5-15 2RIrReg p88 CR France102
ANDERSON,Norman Ruthven Maj kld By Sepoy 20-11-14 IA 130Baluchis p273 MR65
ANDERSON,Patrick Alexander T2Lt kld 19-10-17 GL &RFC p4 CR Scot235
ANDERSON,Percival Robert T2Lt kia 12-10-15 13WYorks p80 CR Gallipoli27
ANDERSON,Percy Hume Aufrey Capt kia 5-9-15 21Lancers p23 MR43,Allfrey
ANDERSON,Peter Johnson Lt kia 19-4-17 1/11Lond p248 CR Palestine8,ANDERSEN P Johansen
ANDERSON,P.G.Rodney LtCol 14-6-16 76Punjabis MR65
ANDERSON,Philip Maurice Ramsey.MID 2Lt dow 24-2-15 3RIrReg p88 CR France284
ANDERSON,Reginald D'Arcy Maj ded 14-8-17 RGA AOrdDept 384SB p38 MR38
ANDERSON,Reginald Dudley Bawawen 2Lt kia 1-7-16 15Y&L p158 CR France1492,Bawdwen
ANDERSON,Richard William Laurence T2Lt ded 12-6-17 GL &1RFC p4 Cr Belgium115,FltLt
ANDERSON,Robert 2Lt dow 23-3-18 2RScots p53 CR France103
ANDERSON,Robert Lt drd 29-5-18 SL &RE IWT p201 MR38
ANDERSON,Robert Ballantine Lt kia 19-4-17 1/4KOSB p223 CR Palestine8
ANDERSON,Robert Brown Lt ded 15-2-19 5RScotF p269 CR Kent129
ANDERSON,Robert Coventry 2Lt dow 4-11-17 282RFA p24 CR Belgium16
ANDERSON,Robert Cunningham Capt dow 27-9-15 1BlkW p128 CR France178,kia 26-9-15
ANDERSON,Robert Graham Lt kia 12-11-17 1/1GloucYeo p203 CR Palestine8
ANDERSON,Robert Lionel Lt drd 7-11-18 406RASC p192 CR France34
ANDERSON,Robertson Topping.MC.Lt kia 24-10-18 9HLI p240 CR France230
ANDERSON,Samuel Stephen 2Lt kia 30-12-15 5RScotF p222 CR Gallipoli6
ANDERSON,Thomas Binnie T2Lt dow 22-11-16 1BlkW p128 CR France397
ANDERSON,Vincent Tollemach T2Lt dow 13-4-18 1MGC p181 CR France88
ANDERSON,William.MC.2Lt kld 21-9-18 RGA114HB att7RAF p38 CR Belgium18
ANDERSON,Walter Kinloch LtACapt kia 22-7-18 5BlkW p230 CR France1695
ANDERSON,Wilfred Cruttenden Lt kia 30-10-14 2Beds p85 MR29
ANDERSON,William TLt kia 25-9-15 10ScotRif p103 MR19
ANDERSON,William T2Lt dow 23-4-17 1 att9BlkW p128 CR France113
ANDERSON,William 2Lt kia 4-6-17 1LovatScts p204 CR France1182
ANDERSON,William TLt dow 27-3-18 217RE p43 CR France185
ANDERSON,William TCapt ded 25-7-18 1LancF p91 CR Hamps57
ANDERSON,William TLt kia 20-10-18 15RIrRif p168 CR Belgium140,20Bn
ANDERSON,William Angus 2Lt ded 8-12-18 5A&SH p172 CR France1858 see below
ANDERSON,William Arthur 2Lt ded 8-12-18 6A&SH &RAF p255
ANDERSON,William Bruce.MC.2Lt kia 7-3-17 1/5GordH p242 CR France15,7-4-17
ANDERSON,William Christian Col ded 28-6-17 79RFA p261 CR Scot774
ANDERSON,William Francis Capt dow 10-12-15 3RFus p66 CR Belgium59,15-2-15
ANDERSON,William Francis Outram 2Lt kia 23-4-17 4GordH p242 CR France604
ANDERSON,William Harold 2Lt kia 13-6-17 5BordR p228 CR Belgium168
ANDERSON,William Henry Lt ded 4-12-18 RGA p38 CR Kent61
ANDERSON,William Herbert.VC.TMajALtCol kia 26-3-18 12HLI p162 CR France630,25-3-18
ANDERSON,William James Maj kia 19-10-15 WRidHQstaff 9ArmyCps p115 CR Gallipoli6
ANDERSON,William K.Lt ded 7-1-18 RFC CR Canada1430
ANDERSON,William Trevor Lt ded 8-4-17 6SfthH attRFC p269 CR Scot874,12-4-17
ANDERSON,William Wallace 2Lt kia 10-11-15 15RFA 526HB p24 CR France462
ANDERSON,W.J.Capt 26-8-17 EAMS CR EAfrica58
ANDERSON-MORSHEAD,Rupert Henry.DSO.MIDx3 CaptALtCol kia 27-5-18 Dev p76 MR18
ANDERTON,Albert.MC.&2Bars.LtAMaj dow 5-4-18 110RFA p24 CR France5,kia
ANDERTON,Edwards Lt ded 30-11-18 EAfrCensorDept CR EAfrica19
ANDERTON,Frank Westall 2Lt kia 1-7-16 3 att1LancF p91 CR France1492
ANDERTON,George Eric Asquith.MID Lt kia 22-3-18 LancF att119MGC p91&181 MR20
ANDERTON,James Devereux T2Lt kia 13-11-16 10Suff p77 CR France802
ANDERTON,William Frederick T2Lt kia 31-3-17 A15RFA p24 CR France68,Frederic
ANDERTON,William Lyon 2Lt kia 21-8-15 4WRid p227 MR29

ANDRE,Frederick William 2Lt kia 16-8-17 8Mddx p236 MR30
ANDREW,Arthur 2Lt kia 23-11-17 1Lond p245 MR17
ANDREW,Ellen ARRC Sister kia 21-3-18 TFNS att 58CCS CR France ?
ANDREW,Ernest John Lt kia 23-3-18 10 att1EYorks p83 MR27
ANDREW,Frank 2Lt kia 23-4-17 3BordR p116 MR20
ANDREW,Frank Douglas 2Lt dow 31-3-18 PoW 7Manch p237 CRFrance441,Lt
ANDREW,Frederick 2LtTLt kia 27-2-15 EYorks attWAfrR p83&200 CR WAfrica28,2Lt
ANDREW,Harold Lt kia 14-7-16 24Manch p154 MR21
ANDREW,Harry Townsend T2Lt kia 25-6-16 RE 96FC p43 CR Belgium6
ANDREW,Herbert Leslie 2Lt ded 14-10-18 6RWar att 137PoWCoyLabCps p214 CR France146
ANDREW,James Lionel 2Lt kld 13-12-17 RFC SR p4 CR Herts87
ANDREW,John 2Lt kia 1-7-16 3 att10YLI p142 CR France267
ANDREW,John James T2Lt dow 29-4-17 20NumbF p60 CR France40
ANDREW,Malcolm TLt kia 4-11-18 LancF att104TMB p91 CR France206
ANDREW,Robert Lt kia 8-5-17 12A&SH p172 MR37
ANDREW,William Dickie 2Lt kia 22-3-18 10 att15RScots p212 MR20
ANDREW-MARSHALL,Joseph Lt kia 20-11-17 6Lond att B'TankCps p246 MR17
ANDREWES,Charles Nesfield T2Lt ded 29-11-18 8LabCps p266 CR Kent154,ANDREWS
ANDREWES,George Lancelot LtCol ded 17-9-16 5Suff p269 CR Suff225,Col
ANDREWS,Alan Charles Findlay 2Lt kia 29-6-15 16RFus p66 MR4
ANDREWS,Alfred George T2Lt dow 14-10-18 4Mddx p145 CR France146
ANDREWS,Archibald TLtACapt dow 30-5-17 RFA 23DAC p24 CR Belgium11,29-5-17
ANDREWS,Arthur Alfred Capt ded 16-10-18 11Hamps p120 CR Hamps1
ANDREWS,Bertram John William T2Lt dow 31-7-17 13RSuss p118 CR Belgium16
ANDREWS,Charles Capt ded 21-7-18 RAOC p198 CR Essex118
ANDREWS,Charles Edward Maj kia 25-10-16 11HLI p162 CR France151
ANDREWS,Charles George Williams Capt kia 28-10-14 2BordR p116 MR29
ANDREWS,Charles Nesfield see ANDREWES,C.N.
ANDREWS,Charles Neville 2Lt kia 24-3-15 3LNLancs p135 CR France632
ANDREWS,Charles Raymond Capt kia 24-5-15 2Ches p95 MR29
ANDREWS,Charles William T2Lt kia 13-4-17 10WYorks p80 MR20
ANDREWS,E.C.H.MBE.Lt 17-5-20 RGA CR Lond29
ANDREWS,Eric Bernard 2Lt kia 16-9-18 RFA &RAF p208&258 CR France1252
ANDREWS,Edward Norman 2Lt dow 22-8-18 3EKent p57 CR France119,23-8-18
ANDREWS,Edwin Charles T2Lt ded 12-8-18 8RWKent p140 CR Hamps186
ANDREWS,Ellen Sister TFNS 21-3-18 p254 see ANDREW,E.
ANDREWS,Eric Cauty T2Lt kia 12-10-16 RE 9FC p43 MR21
ANDREWS,Francis Nicholas T2Lt dow 11-10-15 15RIrRif p168 CR France34,Lt
ANDREWS,Frank Henry.MC.2Lt kia 11-8-18 3 att1Glouc p106 MR19
ANDREWS,Frederick Charles 2Lt kia 16-3-15 3Leinst p174 CR France1141,2Bn
ANDREWS,Frederick Dudley.MC.Lt kia 14-8-17 1/4Glouc p225 CR Belgium27
ANDREWS,Frederick George Lt kia 21-10-14 4Lpool att2SLancs p71 MR22
ANDREWS,Frederick Seymour T2Lt kia 29-4-17 GL &13RFC p4 CR France40
ANDREWS,Geoffrey Fleetwood T2Lt dow 16-9-18 RGA 499SB p38 CR France526
ANDREWS,George Leonard TCapt kia 3-5-18 RGA 76SB p38 CR France41
ANDREWS,Glyndwr Levi TCapt kia 21-8-18 19 att16RWelshF p97 CR France432
ANDREWS,Hector George Robert Frank Lt kia 28-6-15 14WYorks p80 MR4
ANDREWS,Henry George 2Lt kia 25-3-18 1/7LancF p221 MR20
ANDREWS,Henry John.VC.MBE.TCapt kia 22-10-19 IMS p273 MR43
ANDREWS,Herbert George TLt kia 19-4-17 16Mddx p145 CR France418
ANDREWS,Horace Gibson TCapt kia 7-6-17 8Y&L p158 CR Belgium167
ANDREWS,James Alfrey Capt kia 1-7-16 2Dev p76 CR France1890,Allfrey
ANDREWS,John Alfred Raymond 2Lt kld 14-4-18 6Lincs attRAF p74 CR France31,kia
ANDREWS,John Leonard.MM.T2Lt dow 19-5-18 10RFus p66 CR France145,Lt
ANDREWS,Joseph Hamilton Millar 2Lt dow 16-8-17 11RIrRif p168 CR Belgium84
ANDREWS,Leigh Courtney T2Lt kia 3-7-16 9Lincs p74 MR21
ANDREWS,Leslie Ernest.MC.TCaptAMaj kia 20-9-17 10RWSurr p55 MR30
ANDREWS,Maynard Percy.MID Capt kia 15-8-15 4WRid p227 CR Belgium67
ANDREWS,Percy Heath Lt dow 28-3-18 RE 151 reposted73FC p43 CR France113,kia
ANDREWS,Reginald Lt kia 31-7-17 7LancF p221 MR29
ANDREWS,Reginald Hugo Catchpole 2Lt kia 8-5-17 12A&SH p172 MR37
ANDREWS,Robert Freeman T2Lt kia 15-11-16 10LNLancs p135 CR France533,Lt
ANDREWS,Robert Hutchinson T2Lt kia 25-9-15 1RIrRif p168 CR France684

ANDREWS,Sidney Mottram Capt 8-10-18 RAOC p198 CR France85
ANDREWS,Walter Capt kia 14-4-15 IA 95Inf att120Inf p273 CR Iraq6
ANDREWS,William 2Lt kia 25-4-15 1RDubF p176 CR Gallipoli15,26-4-15
ANDREWS,William Ernest LtTCapt kia 2-8-15 RIrRif p168 CR Belgium101
ANDREWS,William James Morrison T2Lt kld 4-6-17 GL &RFC p4 CR Ireland229
ANDREWS,William Thomas 2Lt kia 11-1-17 IARO 87Punjabis att2/124Baluchis p273 CR Iraq5
ANGAS,Lionel George T2Lt kia 3-5-17 3 att7Beds p85 MR20
ANGELL,Benjamin Eyre Lt kia 20-2-17 1KAR p202 CR EAfrica40
ANGELL,Geoffrey 2Lt kia 13-5-15 IA 1/8 att2/8GurkhaRif CR France631 p273
ANGLES,Robert.MC.T2Lt dow 13-11-17 Y&L p158 CR Durham182
ANGLISS,Henry James.DCM.Lt kld 21-11-20 RInniskF CR Lond1
ANGOOD,Percival George 2Lt kld 12-9-17 RFC p4 CR Camb84,11-9-17
ANGUS,H.C.2Lt 6-6-21 MGC Motors CR Scot235
ANGUS,James Robert ALtCol drd 17-9-17 16WelshR att11SWBord p126 CR France275
ANGUS,Leonard John Lt&QM drd 20-8-15 9Mddx p269 CR Herts30
ANGUS,Norman John 2Lt dow 18-9-17 4 att9GordH p242 CR France40
ANGUS,Raymond Brocklehurst 2Lt kia 22-9-15 RE p210 CR Gallipoli3
ANGUS,Robert Edward Lt kia 20-11-17 AyrYeo attRFC p17&203 MR20
ANGUS,Stewart 2Lt kia 2-7-16 RE 1FC p210 MR21,1-7-16
ANGUS,William John T2Lt kia 29-10-16 RScotF att1ScotRif p94 MR21,31-10-16
ANKER,Albert George Lt ded 8-8-19 8Lincs p263 CR Germany1
ANKETELL,Charles Edward.MM.2Lt kld 11-5-18 RFus att206RAF p66 CR France134
ANKETELL-JONES,John Hobart Capt ded 16-11-19 5Lancers attEgyptArmy RoO p261 CR EAfrica116
ANNAHEIM,George Herbert.MID TLt kia 4-10-18 1RMunstF p175 CR France256
ANNAND,Allan Young T2Lt kia 11-1-17 1HLI p162 MR38
ANNANDALE,F.W.Lt 29-3-20 3SStaffs CR Scot269
ANNE,Crathorn Edward Isham Charlton TMaj drd 15-4-17 GL &RFC p4 MR35
ANNELY,Ernest George 2Lt kia 4-5-17 5WYorks p218 MR20,3-5-17
ANNESLEY,Albemarle Cator.DSO.LtCol dow 8-7-16 8RFus p66 CR France44,7-7-16
ANNESLEY,Hon.Arthur Capt kia 15-11-14 10Huss p22 CR Belgium57,16-11-14
ANNESLEY,James Ferguson St.John TCapt ded 20-5-17 RAMC p267 CR Suff173,19-5-17
ANNESLEY,James Howard Adolphus.CMG.DSO.LtCol ded 22-4-19 1DragGds Ret p261 CR Surrey160
ANNESLEY,William Richard Norton.DSO.Maj 29-11-14 RWKent CR Scot142
ANNETT,Hugh Clarkson 2Lt kia 15-9-16 6DLI p239 CR France387
ANNS,Frederick 2Lt kia 6-11-15 4 att2Beds p85 CR France279
ANSCOMBE,Gilbert Allen Henry 2Lt kia 1-2-17 IARO att36Sikhs p273 CR Iraq5
ANSELL,Arthur George T2Lt dow 25-4-18 RE 1FdSurvCo p43 CR France102
ANSELL,George Kirkpatrick LtCol kia 1-9-14 5DragGds p21 CR France1230
ANSELL,Harry Clements 2Lt 9-5-20 RASC MT CR War134
ANSELL,Thomas ACapt kia 23-10-16 2ScotRif p103 MR21
ANSON,Arthur Lt kia 8-10-15 3GrenGds p49 CR France1726,11-10-15
ANSON,George Lechmere Capt kia 20-10-14 2N&D p133 MR32
ANSON,Harris Hartis 2Lt kia 30-8-18 5WRid p227 CR France421,Hortas
ANSON,Henry Percy Richmond Capt&Adjt kia 25-5-15 1 att8Mddx p145 CR Belgium46
ANSON,Nigel Frederick Edward.MC.2Lt kia 10-7-17 5 att2KRRC p148 MR31
ANSON,Stanley Edmund T2Lt kia 4-6-16 1EYorks p83 CR France189
ANSON,Walter Frank Vernon 2Lt kia 8-11-17 1/6RWelshF p223 CR Israel1
ANSTEE,Joseph 2Lt kia 1-7-16 2Lincs p74 MR21
ANSTEY,Alexander Burgess T2Lt kld 22-2-18 RFC p15 CR Oxford74
ANSTEY,George Alexander Capt kia 24-6-15 1Dev att2Ches p76 CR Belgium37
ANSTEY,Henry T2Lt kia 11-4-17 7RB p177 CR France532
ANSTICE,John Spencer Ruscombe.MID Lt kia 2-5-15 2RFus p66 CR Gallipoli2
ANSTIE,Edward Basil 2Lt kia 23-3-18 6 att2RB p177 MR27
ANSTRUTHER,John Arnold St.C.Lt kia 26-12-14 6DragGds att2LifeGds p21 MR29,30-10-14
ANSTRUTHER,R.E.MC.Capt 22-7-21 BlkW CR Scot92
ANTHONY,Albert Frederick T2Lt dow 10-4-18 18WelshR p126 CR France1094
ANTHONY,Clarence Case TCapt dow 15-12-15 13RFus p66 CR France1016
ANTHONY,Charles Stanley 2Lt kia 19-9-18 1/4Nhampt p234 CR Palestine9
ANTHONY,George Adam Moriarty Lt kia 24-1-16 9RWSurr attNigR p55&201 CR WAfrica56
ANTHONY,Henry Leonard Capt kia 2-5-17 RAVC 1/1LancsMobileSect p254 CR France1182
ANTHONY,John Richard Capt kia 25-5-17 6RWelshF att1RFC p17&223 CR Belgium18

ANTHONY,Percy TMaj kia 10-7-16 15WelshR p126 MR21
ANTHONY,Thomas Vaughan 2Lt kia 10-8-15 4Ches p222 MR4
ANTON,Edwin Vincent 2Lt kia 17-5-17 6 att5GordH p242 MR20,16-5-17
ANTROBUS,Cecil Hugh TCapt kia 26-9-15 6CamH p167 MR19
ANTROBUS,Charles Alexander Capt kia 25-4-15 KOSB p101 CR Gallipoli6
ANTROBUS,Edmund Lt kia 24-10-14 1GrenGds p49 MR29
ANTROBUS,Norman Briggs TCapt kia 1-10-15 4SLancs p229 CR Belgium28,2-10-15
APERGIS,Tassi Scott See ARERGIS,T.S
APLIN,Elphinstone D'Oyly Lt dow 13-5-15 2Glouc p106 CR France284
APLIN,Eric Scott LtACapt dow 11-3-18 2Worc p107 CR Belgium3
APLIN,Kenneth Sharland 2Lt kia 1-11-14 2RInniskF att2Bn p104 MR32,Shorland
APPELBEE,Thomas T2Lt kia 20-8-16 15WYorks p80 CR France727
APPERLEY,Basil Lang Marling T2Lt dow 19-4-17 8RWKent p140 CR France40,APPERLY 6Bn
APPERLEY,Charles Milton 2Lt kia 24-3-18 51MGC Inf p181 CR France924,28-3-18
APPERLY,B.L.M. see above
APPERLY,Arthur Lancelot 2Lt kia 27-8-16 5Glouc p225 MR21
APPLEBY,Eric Lt dow 28-10-16 48/2RFA p24 CR France105
APPLEBY,John Gill TLt kia 14-7-16 8SLancs p125 MR21
APPLEBY,Robert Charles Alfred Lt dow 28-6-16 1 att13RScots p53 CR France423
APPLEBY,Sidney Derrick 2Lt kia 18-7-17 11 att8LNLancs p135 MR29
APPLEGARTH,Thomas Forster 2Lt kia 5-11-16 6DLI p239 CR France385
APPLEGARTH,Thomas William T2Lt dow 20-3-18 PoW 11DLI p160 CR France652,ded 8-4-18
APPLETON,Aaron 2Lt kia 17-3-17 RFA &RFC p208 MR20
APPLETON,Francis Martin.VD.Maj ded 6-12-14 4SLancs p269 CR Kent267
APPLETON,Henry Metcalfe Capt ded 26-1-18 1DragGds &4RRofCav p261 CR Hamps1
APPLETON,Percy Robert Agnew 2Lt kia 3-5-17 4WRid p227 MR20
APPLETON,Richard Aidan Lt kia 21-3-18 2DLI p160 MR20
APPLEYARD,Benjamin Sydney T2Lt kia 29-9-18 6 att2Yorks p89 CR France273
APPLEYARD,Harry Elston T2Lt kia 14-7-16 12WYorks p80 CR France453
APPLEYARD,James Eric.MC.Capt kia 20-7-18 8WYorks p219 CR France622
APPLEYARD,John Ernest.MC.Lt kia 26-4-18 RE 222FC p43 CR France180
APPLEYARD,Richard TLt kia 4-8-16 14 att10N&D p133 CR France151,11Bn
APPLEYARD,William TLt kia 22-8-15 6Yorks p89 MR4
APPLIN,Geoffrey Walter Henry T2Lt kia 1-7-16 1Lincs p74 MR21
APPLIN,Richard 2Lt kia 29-4-17 GL &19RFC p4 MR20
APPS,Jack Harry Mason T2Lt kia 20-11-17 1NumbF p60 CR France1489,1/5Bn
APPS,Reginald Denman 2Lt kia 17-5-15 1RBerks p138 MR22
APSIMON,Arthur Injwerm TLt dow 4-8-17 14RWelshF p97 CR Belgium23,Tryweryn
APTED,Eardley Lt kia 1-8-17 9 att11RWSurr p55 MR29,Capt
ARBER,Archibald Guy T2Lt kia 21-10-15 BordR att1/7HLI p116 CR Gallipoli3
ARBERY,Ernest Edward T2Lt kia 6-6-17 GL &RFC p4 CR Belgium171
ARBERY,Frederick James TCapt dow 9-10-17 1DCLI p113 CR France139
ARBUCKLE,Hubert Hugh T2Lt kia 2-9-18 2RIrReg p88 CR France646
ARBUTHNOT,Aliser Dare Staveley Capt kia 8-3-16 RE att20S&M p43 MR38
ARBUTHNOT,Ashley Herbert Capt dow 15-5-15 12Lond p248 CR France1
ARBUTHNOT,Gavin Campbell 2Lt dow 6-8-15 7NStaffs p156 MR4
ARBUTHNOT,Gerald Archibald Lt kia 25-9-16 2GrenGds SR p49 CRFrance394
ARBUTHNOT,Hugh Hamilton 2Lt dow 28-12-15 IA 67Punjabis p273 CR Iraq1
ARBUTHNOT,John TLt dow 18-9-16 2GrenGds p49 CR France329,16-9-16
ARBUTHNOT,Kenneth Wyndham Maj kia 25-4-15 2SfthH p164 CR Belgium129,Windham
ARBUTHNOT,Lenox Stanley Capt kld 1-11-18 SL &RAF p201
ARBUTHNOT,Maurice Armitage.MC.LtTCapt ded 14-10-18 16Lancers p22 CR Surrey72
ARBUTHNOT,Ronald George Urquart Lt kld 3-12-18 16Lancers attRAF p22 CR Herts10
ARBUTHNOT,William John Capt 9-1-17 IARO att5Sikhs MR38
ARCH,Arthur James T2Lt dow 27-5-18 2RB p177 CR France1107
ARCHBOLD,John 2Lt kia 19-6-17 232RFA p208 CR Belgium34
ARCHBOLD,William Heslehurst T2Lt dow 21-10-18 RE 228FC p43 CR Belgium11
ARCHBUTT,William Henry Maj ded 8-2-15 9Manch p237 CR Egypt9
ARCHDALE,Charles William Capt kia 20-11-17 5 att7Norf p216 MR17
ARCHDALE,Dominick Mervyn TLt kia 13-11-16 1KAR attNyasaVolRes p202 CR EAfrica40
ARCHDALE,George Mervyn 2Lt dow 30-4-17 3 att1Berks p138 CR France95

ARCHDALE,Theodore Montgomery.DSO.LtCol drd 10-10-18 RHA p24 CR Eire3

ARCHDALE-PORTER,John Grey DSO.CaptAMaj dow 22-11-17 9Lancers p22 CR France439

ARCHDALL,Nicholas James Mervyn Maj kia 25-9-15 3 att5CamH p167 MR19

ARCHER,Albert Erskine Carson 2Lt kia 9-2-16 EKent att242RFC p2&57 CR France134

ARCHER,Eli Townend 2Lt kia 23-7-16 1/4YLI p235 MR21

ARCHER,Harry.DSO.MID LtAMaj kia 25-11-17 2Dev p76 MR30

ARCHER,Henry Charles 2Lt kia 8-10-18 1Mon p244 CR France1710

ARCHER,John William Butts Lt dow 16-2-15 EKent p57 MR29

ARCHER,Ronald Hedley T2Lt dow 27-12-17 1NumbF p60 CR France512

ARCHER,Thomas Lt kia 25-4-18 6KOSB p101 CR Belgium393

ARCHER,Walter Dunlop 2Lt kia 25-4-18 6WYorks p218 MR30

ARCHER-SHEE,George Lt kia 31-10-14 3 att2SStaffs p121 MR29

ARCHIBALD,James Duncan TLt dow 20-7-16 10Ess p131 CR France66

ARCHIBALD,John.MC&Bar.Capt dow 31-3-18 6GordH p242 CR France40

ARCHIBALD,Max Stanfield Eaton.MC.MID 2Lt dow 12-5-18 RE att18RAF p43 CR France95,kia

ARCHIBALD,William Maj dow 18-6-15 RE p209 CR Gallipoli6

ARDEN,Humphrey Warwick 2Lt dow 6-6-17 RGA 156HB p38 CR.France285

ARDEN,John Henry Morris.DSO.MID LtCol ded 22-7-18 25NumbF attRAF 2 att3CadetWing RoO p60 CR Egypt1

ARDEN,Reginald Douglas 2Lt kia 8-10-16 1/1Lond p245 MR21

ARDILL,Ivan Roy 2Lt kia 25-9-15 8KOSB p101 MR19

AREND,Ronald Sydney 2Lt kia 23-3-18 12RScots p53 MR27

ARERGIS,Tasso Scott 2Lt kia 10-9-18 10 att16Lond p248 MR21,APERGIS Tassi 10-9-16

ARGYLE,Percival Edgar T2Lt kia 9-4-17 1ELancs p110 CR France452

ARIS,Thomas Arthur TLt kia 16-4-17 23RFus p66 CR France1191

ARKCOLL,Frederick Thomas T2Lt kia 30-6-16 10 att7RSuss p118 MR19 12Bn

ARKLE,Norman Armitage T2Lt kia 1-7-16 20NumbF p60 MR21

ARKLESS,John William T2Lt kia 30-12-15 17 att15DLI p160 CR France1140

ARKWRIGHT,Frederick George Alleyne Capt kld 14-10-15 11Huss &RFC p22 CR Derby122,Frederic

ARMATAGE,Robert T2Lt dow 6-6-17 21NumbF p60 CR France95

ARMER,Arthur T2Lt kia 5-9-17 BordR att11Bn p116 CR Belgium24

ARMES,Raymond Linay TCapt kia 9-4-16 7NStaffs p156 MR38

ARMES,William Morriss.TD.LtCol kia 12-8-15 5Suff p217 MR4

ARMFIELD,Archie Seaward 2Lt kia 31-7-17 2IrGds p52 CR Belgium12

ARMISTEAD,Tom Elsworth.MC.2Lt kia 3-5-17 6WYorks p218 MR20

ARMIT,Napier.MC.Capt kia 4-8-16 16RScots p53 MR21

ARMITAGE,Alfred Cecil 2Lt kld 21-7-15 1RWSurr p55 CR France571

ARMITAGE,Arthur William Capt kia 1-10-16 8YLI p142 CR France239

ARMITAGE,Douglas William 2Lt kia 25-9-15 9RSuss p118 MR19

ARMITAGE,Eric 2Lt dow 4-10-17 46RFC p4 CR France49

ARMITAGE,Edward Stoney 2Lt kia 29-8-18 76RFA p24 CR France927

ARMITAGE,Ernest George T2Lt kia 14-7-18 RE 4SpecCo p43 CR France547

ARMITAGE,Francis Arthur William.DSO.MajALtCol kia 22-4-18 1WYorks att1Hamps p80 CR France250

ARMITAGE,Frank Rhodes.DSO Capt kia 30-7-17 RAMC att232RFA p253 CR Belgium7

ARMITAGE,Geoffrey Ambler TCapt kia 27-2-17 16WYorks p80 CR France580

ARMITAGE,George T2Lt kia 16-9-16 6DCLI p113 MR21

ARMITAGE,George Duncan T2Lt kia 6-8-15 11ESurr att2Hamps p111 MR4

ARMITAGE,George Jones 2Lt kia 17-6-17 GL &4RFC p4 CR Belgium10

ARMITAGE,J.A.R.Capt 19-7-19 15WYorks p52 CR Sussex178

ARMITAGE,John Basil Capt kia 17-5-17 5Ches p222 CR France581

ARMITAGE,Laurie Ritchie.MC.T2Lt dow 25-11-16 9WRid p115 CR Yorks447,Lt

ARMITAGE,Noel Lt kia 25-4-18 2/3ScotHorse att12Glouc p205 CR France18

ARMITAGE,Sidney Robert Lt kia 11-5-17 RASC NMidDivTrn p253 CR France223

ARMITAGE,William Harold TLt kia 22-5-16 9Yorks p89 CR France559

ARMOUR,Robert Stanley.MID TCapt ded 1-12-18 RAMC p194 CR EAfrica36,Maj

ARMSTRONG,Allan.DSO.LtCol dow 19-9-18 1/4Wilts p152 CR Palestine9

ARMSTRONG,Arthur Keith Capt dow 15-9-14 RAMC p194 MR15

ARMSTRONG,Arthur Sutcliffe Capt dow 31-5-17 1/1Camb p244 CR Belgium11

ARMSTRONG,Cecil 2Lt kia 21-9-16 12DLI p160 CR France703

ARMSTRONG,Charles Arthur MajTLtCol kia 1-10-15 2NumbF p60 CR France423

ARMSTRONG,Charles MacDonald 2Lt kia 25-9-16 10YLI p142 MR21,McDonald

ARMSTRONG,Charles Martin T2Lt kia 8-2-17 10RDubF p176 CR France339

ARMSTRONG,Christopher 2Lt kia 9-4-16 14RFus att6NLancs p66 CR Iraq5

ARMSTRONG,Denys Lt dow 3-10-16 5NumbF p213 CR France385,kia

ARMSTRONG,Edward Randolph Maj ded 25-2-21 IMS p273 MR43

ARMSTRONG,Edward William 2Lt dow 11-7-15 6 att3RB p177 CR Belgium11

ARMSTRONG,Ellen.MID Sister 20-3-19 QAIMNS CR France146

ARMSTRONG,Foster Moore Maj kia 25-9-17 251Numb RFA CR France592

ARMSTRONG,Frederick Edmund John Lt ded 27-10-19 IARO att1/69Punjabis p273 MR43

ARMSTRONG,George Canning Staples Lt kia 3-5-17 3RIrFus p170 CR France604

ARMSTRONG,George Pierce Lt kia 2-7-15 IA 34Sikhs p273 CR France768

ARMSTRONG,Gwin Henry TLt ded 28-10-18 Norf att4NigR p73&202 CR WAfrica40

ARMSTRONG,Guy Spearman 2Lt kia 28-9-15 ScotGds att1Bn p51 MR19,27-9-15

ARMSTRONG,George Carlyon 2Lt kia 25-1-15 CldGds att1Bn p50 MR22

ARMSTRONG,Harold 2Lt kia 14-11-16 21NumbF p60 MR21,28 att1/5Bn

ARMSTRONG,Harry William Thomas 2Lt dow 14-7-15 7ESurr p111 CR France922

ARMSTRONG,Helen Sister ded 20-3-19 QAIMNS p200

ARMSTRONG,Henry Leslie Lt kia 25-4-18 4 at6KOSB p223 MR30

ARMSTRONG,Henry Louis Winthrop T2Lt kia 29-11-15 7SomLI p79 CR France525

ARMSTRONG,Hilliard Mark T2Lt acckld 14-11-17 RFC p4 CR Scot235

ARMSTRONG,James Lt kia 28-3-17 RIM attRE IWT p273 MR64

ARMSTRONG,James Noble TLt kia 22-8-15 RAMC att2DLI p194 CR Belgium2

ARMSTRONG,John T2Lt kld 27-3-18 RFC p15 CR Ches28

ARMSTRONG,John Lewis Pasteur 2Lt kia 22-6-16 RASC att25RFC p17&253 CR France924,FltLt

ARMSTRONG,John Nicholas Fraser TMaj kia 5-7-16 RE 128FC p43 CR France372

ARMSTRONG,John Norman TLt dow 16-1-17 15 att8NumbF p60 CR France74,Capt

ARMSTRONG,John Owen 2Lt kia 15-7-16 10RFus p66 MR21

ARMSTRONG,John White T2Lt kia 21-10-18 20DLI p160 CR Belgium11

ARMSTRONG,Joseph Lt kia 5-5-17 2/4WelshRFA p207 CR France558

ARMSTRONG,Leonard William 2Lt kia 19-5-17 3 att1BordR p116 MR20

ARMSTRONG,Michael Richard Leader T2Lt kia 22-4-16 RE 150FC p43 CR France702

ARMSTRONG,R.V 2Lt 17-3-17 ImpCamCps Egypt CR Egypt2

ARMSTRONG,Sarah Jane Miss ded 12-12-18 VAD p200 CR Egypt9

ARMSTRONG,Sydney 2Lt kia 17-2-18 RFA attRFC p15&24 CR Essex211

ARMSTRONG,Sydney John 2Lt kia 26-9-15 12NumbF p60 MR19

ARMSTRONG,Thomas Herbert TLtACapt ded 15-5-17 13NumbF p60 CR France40,2Lt

ARMSTRONG,Walter Seymour TCapt ded 31-5-16 RAMC attMhowIndCavFA p194 CR France1,dow

ARMSTRONG,William Arthur 2Lt dow 26-10-18 3RInniskF p104 CR Ireland239

ARMSTRONG,William David 2Lt kia 12-10-18 1/4SfthH p241 CR France241

ARMSTRONG,William Kings Capt kia 11-4-18 4SLancs p229 MR19

ARMSTRONG,William Maurice(Pat) MC.MID Capt kia 23-5-17 10Huss att86BdeHQ p22 CR France1182

ARMSTRONG,William Wilberforce 2Lt kia 27-12-17 7BlkW p231 CR Palestine3

ARMSTRONG-DASH,Arthur Lt kia 22-4-18 12LancF p91 CR Europe58/57A,dow 1-5-18

ARMSTRONG-LUSHINGTON-TULLOCK,Graham de Montmorency Lt kia 5-10-14 1ConnRgrs p172 CR France1157,Montmorencey 5-11-14

ARNAUD,Frederick Cooper T2Lt kia 1-7-16 GL 16NumbF attTMB p189 CR France293,Lt

ARNELL,Douglas Carstairs Capt kia 13-7-16 2Hamps p120 MR21

ARNELL,Reginald Brandt T2Lt kia 30-7-15 7KRRC p148 MR29

ARNEY,Frank Stanley 2Lt kia 18-4-18 RFA 1MedTMB p208 CR Greece5

ARNHOLTZ,Ronald Henry Preuss Lt kia 23-8-18 1Herts att1Beds p252 CR France239

ARNISON,Edward Burra 2Lt dow 18-8-18 14RGA 11SB p38 CR France526

ARNOLD,Alban Charles Phidias T2Lt kia 7-7-16 18 att6RFus p66 MR21

ARNOLD,Alfred Huntriss Capt dow 30-12-16 2WYorks p80 CR Surrey2
ARNOLD,Alfred Lewis 2Lt kia 15-8-17 22Lond p251 CR Belgium115,24Bn
ARNOLD,Arthur Douglas T2Lt kia 9-4-16 10 att9RWar p64 CR Iraq5
ARNOLD,Arthur Edward.MC.2Lt kia 13-10-18 RE 416FC p210 CR France429,Ernest MM
ARNOLD,Barnard Marcus 2Lt dow 6-2-16 7KRRC p265&181 CR France102
ARNOLD,Bernard Marcus T2Lt dow 6-2-16 MGC p181
ARNOLD,Bernard William LtACapt kia 21-3-18 87/2RFA p24 MR20
ARNOLD,Edward Gladwin.MID Lt kia 21-3-18 RFA 232ArmyBde p24 MR27
ARNOLD,Frank William 2Lt kia 30-11-17 1RGLI p200 MR17
ARNOLD,Frederick Arthur T2Lt dow 13-10-18 RWKent att6Bn p140 CR France106
ARNOLD,Frederick Marshall Lt kia 27-3-18 1/5 att9RWelshF p223 MR20
ARNOLD,Geoffrey Francis Capt kia 8-3-16 5SomLI p218 MR38
ARNOLD,Hedley Graham 2Lt kia 11-4-18 2SWBord p99 CR France297
ARNOLD,Henry 2Lt dow 10-10-18 Dev att9Bn p76 CR France52
ARNOLD,Herbert Edward 2Lt ded 26-12-16 GL &5RFC p2&189 CRFrance1484
ARNOLD,Hugh TLt kia 11-8-15 8NumbF p60 MR4
ARNOLD,Hugo Cholmondeley 2Lt dow 12-6-17 4EKent p212 CR France40
ARNOLD,Joseph T2Lt kia 2-9-18 18 att1/5Manch p154 CR France308
ARNOLD,Joseph V Lt 3-9-18 4RWFus attRAF CR Yorks33
ARNOLD,Karl Ferdinand Franck William Capt kia 23-4-15 1Suff p77 CR Belgium167
ARNOLD,Leonard Frank Cecil.MC.Lt dow 21-12-19 3Lond att82Punjabis p269&273 MR43
ARNOLD,Margaret Trevener Miss ded 12-3-16 VAD p200 CR France1
ARNOLD,Oliver Vaughan 2Lt dow 11-8-16 6 att2Worc p107 CR War135,Vaughton
ARNOLD,Peter Forrester Capt ded 8-8-18 8LancF &RAF p221 CR Egypt1
ARNOLD,Thomas Sorrell 2Lt dow 11-10-17 3ESurr att2/7LancF p111 CR Belgium3
ARNOLD,Thomas Wilson TLt dow 15-9-16 8Beds attGoldCoastR p201 CR EAfrica39
ARNOLD,Victor Capt kia 15-1-17 1/4EKent p212 MR38
ARNOT,Arthur Alison McDonald 2Lt kia 12-4-18 GL &3RAF p189 CR France220,Lt
ARNOT,Colin T2Lt kia 22-3-18 1Glouc p106 MR30
ARNOT,L.A.D. see ARNOTT,L.A.D.
ARNOTT,David William Lt kia 3-9-16 2RWar p64 MR19 &CR France1890
ARNOTT,Evan Edward 2Lt dow 23-9-16 2WelshR p126 CR France385,Euan
ARNOTT,Frederick 2Lt kia 29-3-18 11DLI p160 MR27
ARNOTT,John(Punch).MC.Capt kia 30-3-18 15Huss p22 CR France1172
ARNOTT,Kenneth Hugh Lowden.DSO.MC.CaptTLtCol kia 30-5-18 2ELancs att7KSLI p110 CR France33
ARNOTT,Laurian Anthony Deane T2Lt kia 25-9-15 2GordH p165 MR19,ARNOT
ARNOTT,Robert Louis Irving 2Lt kia 19-9-18 IA 3CofGs 1CpsofGuidesInf p273 MR34
ARNOTT,Thomas Henry.MM.Lt 18-3-21 5BordR CR C'land&W'land6
ARNOTT,Thomas John 2Lt kia 26-10-17 2GordH p165 MR30
ARNOTT,W.Lt 15-8-20 2ScotRif CR Scot241
ARNOULD,Derek Clement Lt ded 7-5-18 4RFus attRTE p66 CR France40
ARNSTRONG,Forster Moore Maj kia 25-9-17 RH&FA p206 see ARMSTRONG,F.M.
ARON,Frederick Adolphus TLt kia 23-8-18 2SLancs p125 MR30
ARROW,George William Lt ded 25-1-19 GL p189
ARTAUD,Gerald Frank Deveniere TLt kia 26-9-17 7KSLI p144 MR30
ARTHUR,Alexander.MC.MM.T2Lt dow 1-10-18 25NumbF att1/7Lpool p60 CR France214
ARTHUR,David.MC.Capt ded PoW 31-7-17 IMS p273 CR Iraq8
ARTHUR,George Stuart 2Lt kia 1-7-16 5Ches p222 MR21
ARTHUR,Henry Bartle Compton Maj kia 10-8-16 5RFA p24 CR France267
ARTHUR,Hugh.MC.Capt kia 29-5-18 LabCps att48ChineseLabCps p189 CR France88
ARTHUR,John T2Lt kia 26-9-15 8GordH p165 MR19,25-9-15
ARTHUR,John Richard Capt 9-2-17 S&T Cps MR43
ARTHUR,William Herbert T2Lt kld 13-12-17 GL &RFC p4 CR Hamps4
ARTHURS,Thomas Andrew TLt ded 6-12-16 GL &134ChineseLabCps p189 CRFrance85 T.A.A.Capt

ARUNDEL-SMITH,Harold Edward 2Lt kia 23-7-16 13Lpool p71 MR21,Ex9Lancers
ARUNDELL,Reinfred Tatton Capt kia 3-2-15 1A 2Rajputs p273 CR Egypt8
ASCROFT,Robert Geoffrey Lees 2Lt kia 4-6-15 10Manch p237 MR4
ASH,Alfred William 2Lt kia 13-6-18 KRRC att12Bn p148 MR20
ASH,Basil Claudius Lt kia 20-9-14 2N&D p133 MR15 &CR France1893
ASH,Edwin Alexander Rays TLt dow 26-4-18 11 att10LancF p91 CR Belgium38
ASH,Gilbert Stanley 2Lt kia 3-9-16 14Hamps p120 MR21
ASH,John Rev Chap4Cl kia 7-9-17 RAChDept att48DAC RFA p199 CR Belgium10
ASH,John Cuxton TLt kia 2-7-18 8 att2Beds p85 CR France44,Luxton 3-7-18
ASH,Wilfred John Lt kia 16-2-15 3Mddx p145 MR29
ASH,William Behne TCapt kia 16-8-17 8NumbF p60 MR30
ASH,William Claudius Casson.DSO.TLtCol dow 29-9-16 23Mddx p145&258 CR France40
ASHBURNER,Daniel T2Lt kia 10-12-16 13Lpool p71 CR France5
ASHBURNHAM,Cromer Maj ded 11-9-19 KRRC p265 CR Sussex177
ASHBY,Donald Jesse 2Lt kia 17-7-16 4EYorks p219 CR Belgium60
ASHBY,George William Capt kia 25-9-15 6Lond p246 CR France149
ASHBY,Henry Herbert T2Lt kia 28-9-15 att3Mddx p145 MR19
ASHBY,Howard Dudley.MC.Maj ded 7-4-19 RGA A/A Bty p38 CR Germany1
ASHBY,Leslie T2Lt kia 20-10-18 LancF att2/5Bn p91 CR Belgium420
ASHBY,Samuel Lt&QM ded 13-2-16 10BordR p116 CR Sussex200
ASHBY,Thomas Philip T2Lt kia 5-9-18 7RSuss p118 CR France511
ASHBY-BROWN,Kenneth Capt kia 14-4-17 5ScotRif p224
ASHCROFT,Edward Davey Capt dow 30-11-17 RE 7FC p43 CR Palestine9
ASHCROFT,Edward Stanley TLt dow 12-5-18 PoW 17Lpool p71 CR Belgium140
ASHCROFT,Ernest TLt kia 25-9-15 8Dev p76 MR19
ASHCROFT,Frederick T2Lt kia 9-4-17 Lpool att18Bn p71 CR France595
ASHCROFT,George 2Lt kia 3-7-17 5LNLancs p234 MR29,Lt 31-7-17
ASHCROFT,John T2Lt kia 2-10-18 1/2 att16LancF p91 CR France237
ASHCROFT,John Robson.MC.LtTCapt kia 23-3-18 4 att9ScotRif p103 CR France1893
ASHCROFT,William TLt kia 22-3-18 19Lpool p71 CR France672
ASHCROFT,William Worsley.MID TLtAMaj kia 11-4-18 25MGC Inf p181 MR32
ASHE,Edward Neville.MC.Capt kia 21-3-18 8 att16Manch p237 MR27
ASHER,Albert T2Lt kia 24-9-18 1/2 att1/5Leic p87 CR France699
ASHER,Kenneth John Penrith T2Lt kia 1-7-16 10YLI p142 CR France189
ASHER,Ronald Stuart 2Lt kia 21-9-17 GL &46RFC p4 CR France924
ASHFORD,Isaac Dobson T2Lt dow 26-1-18 199MGC Inf 41Div p181 CR Italy74,kia
ASHFORTH,Dudley Sutton T2Lt kia 15-9-16 8RB p177 MR21
ASHFORTH,Isaac John 2Lt dow 27-4-16 IARO att15Lancers p273
ASHINGTON,Henry Sherard Osborn TLtACapt dow 31-1-17 7EYorks p83 CR France785
ASHLEY,Claude T2Lt kia 1-7-16.15 att2NumbF p60 MR21,att22Bn
ASHLEY,James 2Lt kia 2-5-18 RLancs p58 MR19
ASHLEY,Maurice 2Lt kia 23-11-17 1RIrFus p170 MR17
ASHMAN,Sidney John.MC.T2Lt kia 10-10-18 13Mddx p145 CR France916
ASHMAN,Stanley TLt kia 3-5-17 5 O&BLI p129 MR20
ASHMEAD-BARTLETT,Francis George Coningsby Capt kia 13-11-16 4Beds p85 CR France220
ASHMORE,Geoffrey William Paley Lt drd 4-5-17 RE WesternSigCoy p210 CR Italy13
ASHTON,Alexander Leslie T2Lt kia 1-7-18 6RWSurr p55 CR France61,Lt
ASHTON,Cyril James TLtACapt dow 12-3-18 6RWKent p140 CR France345
ASHTON,Edward Deakin T2Lt kia 1-7-16 9 att19LancF p91 CR France251
ASHTON,Edward Kitton Venning Lt ded 4-12-18 IA 29Lancers p273 CR Egypt1,Kittow 55Rif
ASHTON,Frederick James T2Lt kia 21-3-18 1/2 att11Leic p87 MR20
ASHTON,Frederick William Rev ded 18-11-18 RAChDept p254
ASHTON,George Francis TLt kia 20-10-18 42MGC p181 CR France270
ASHTON,G.G. 2Lt kia 23-7-18 5WRid attRAF p227
ASHTON,Hardnc Grey Lt dow 11-3-18 2/11Lond att25RFC p17&248 CR France88,Capt
ASHTON,Henry Oswald Lt kia 29-8-18 5Suff p217 CR France614
ASHTON,Herbert 2Lt kia 27-11-17 Y&L att2/5Bn p254 MR17

ASHTON,James Ormrod 2Lt 5-7-16 ACycCps att13Worc p181 MR21

ASHTON,John Richard Wilmot 2Lt dow 6-11-17 1/4ELancs p226 CR France1361

ASHTON,Robert Mark DCM.T2Lt kia 7-11-17 1/12LNLancs att2/19Lond p135 CR Israel1

ASHTON,Roger Hay 2Lt kia 30-7-16 2RScotF p94 MR21

ASHWELL,Alfred T2Lt kia 4-4-17 1 att10KRRC p148 CR France415

ASHWIN,Guy John Hamilton Lt kia 7-11-16 5DLI p238 CR France385

ASHWORTH,Brian Wilding T2Lt dow 4-8-17 11RWKent p140 CR France139

ASHWORTH,Edgar 2Lt kia 22-9-17 4 att6Ches p222 CR Belgium112

ASHWORTH,Edward Rose T2Lt kia 28-3-18 5MGC Inf p181 CR France777

ASHWORTH,Frank 2Lt dow 29-7-18 YLI att1/4Bn p142 MR30

ASHWORTH,Fred T2Lt dow 10-4-17 23NumbF p60 CRFrance53

ASHWORTH,Frederick Giles T2Lt kia 16-8-17 25MGC Inf p181 MR30

ASHWORTH,George T2Lt kia 2-10-16 19N&D att8LNLancs p135 MR21

ASHWORTH,George Bertram dow 10-8-16 3 att7Suff p77 CR France66

ASHWORTH,Hugh Stirling LtCol kia 26-3-17 4RSuss p228 MR34

ASHWORTH,James Francis Gordon 2Lt dow 25-6-16 9DLI p239 CR Belgium21

ASHWORTH,John Percival Curtis.MC.TLt kia 28-4-17 7Suff p78 MR20

ASHWORTH,Leonard 2Lt dow 12-4-18 13Y&L p158 MR32

ASHWORTH,L.T.LtCol ded 22-3-18 RFA p24 CR Nhampt161

ASHWORTH,Roger William Lt ded 26-4-18 8Hamps &15TrSqnRAF p229&258 CR Lond14,2Lt kld

ASKER,Arthur Howard 2Lt ded 30-1-17 6Ess p232 CR Staffs109

ASKEW,Cyril Horace 2Lt kia 9-4-17 1/8Mddx p236 CR France1185

ASKEW,Geoffrey.MC.2Lt dow 25-3-18 10TankCps p188 MR20

ASKEW,Henry Adam Capt kia 19-12-14 2BordR p116 MR32

ASKEY,Cecil Henry Leonard 2Lt dow 5-4-18 3 att8Lincs p74 CR France169,Lt

ASKHAM,Sydney Thomas T2Lt kia 21/22-8-16 9Suff p78 MR21

ASKHAM,William Capt kia 11-4-18 ACycCps p181 MR32

ASKWITH,Thomas Nowelle 2Lt kia 24-10-17 250RFA p24 CR Belgium13,Nowell

ASLACHSEN,Hector Shields T2Lt kia 23-4-17 4Lpool p71 CR France591

ASPDEN,Ernest Harold T2Lt kia 9-4-17 6RWSurr p55 CR France54

ASPDEN,Frank Hartley TLt dow 20-9-18 6RWSurr p55 CR France511

ASPDEN,Fred.MC.T2Lt kia 14-10-18 17LancF p91 CR Belgium157

ASPDEN,Ronald William.MM.2Lt dow 8-8-17 5RFus p66 CR Belgium16 2Bn

ASPINALL,Francis Clifford(Frank)2Lt kia 17-9-18 70RFA p24 CR France224

ASPINALL,Frank Toole T2Lt kia 1-8-16 16RWar p64 CR France397

ASPINALL,J.V.Capt 15-5-18 GL &11RAF CR France63

ASPINALL,Robert Lowndes.DSO TLtCol kia 3-7-16 11Ches p95 CR France296

ASPLAND,Stanley Richard 2Lt kia 3-10-18 61MGC p181 CR France1887

ASPREY,Bernard Noel Lt kia 24-2-15 1WYorks p80 CR France1140

ASPREY,Maurice Capt kia 12-8-16 3EKent attTMB p57 CR France164

ASQUITH,Arnold Senior 2Lt dow 2-10-18 9RScots p212 CR Belgium11,17Bn

ASQUITH,Ernest T2Lt kia 17-9-16 1EYorks att9YLI p142 MR21

ASQUITH,Gordon William 2Lt kia 2-12-17 3YLI p142 MR30

ASQUITH,Raymond Lt dow 15-9-16 3GrenGds SR p49 CR France294

ASSER,Harold Edward T2Lt kia 1-7-16 Mddx att16Bn p145 MR21

ASSER,Leslie Ernest T2Lt kia 10-8-18 5TankCps p188 CR France360

ASSHETON-SMITH,Thomas Capt ded 3-5-19 IARO attVetCps p273

ASSINDER,William Alfred 2Lt kia 16-6-18 6RWar p214 CR Italy3

ASTBURY,Thomas Leslie Capt kia 21-3-18 6SStaffs p229 MR20

ASTE,Norman Henry 2Lt dow 5-8-16 RGA 23HB p38 CR France430,4-8-16

ASTELL,Frances Ethel Sister ded 17-2-17 TFNS p254 CR Greece9

ASTELL,Somerset Charles Godfrey Fairfax.DSO.Capt ded 24-3-17 8NStaffs att37RFus p156 CR Numb4

ASTILL,Ernest William Dearle 2Lt kia 30-3-18 9Lond p248 MR27

ASTINGTON,Thomas Jeffery T2Lt kia 28-2-17 8ESurr p112 MR21

ASTLE,Albert George TLtACapt kia 3-5-17 8Leic p87 MR20

ASTLEY,Alexander Gifford Ludford Capt kia 5-3-17 14Huss p22 MR38

ASTLEY,Aston Giffard.MC TMaj kia 1-10-16 2RFus att61MGC p66&181 CR France397

ASTLEY,Christopher Basil Lt dow 27-7-18 10Lpool att1/6SfthH p216 CR France145

ASTLEY,Edward Dugdale D'Oyley.MID LtACapt kia 1-6-18 3 att1RBerks p138 CR France120

ASTON,Frederick Marriner TCapt kia 30-7-15 6DCLI p113 CR Belgium453,Frederic

ASTON,Henry Norman 2Lt ded 6-11-18 3Y&L p158 CR Yorks643,Capt

ASTON,Herbert Selwyn.MC.CaptTMaj dow 13-7-18 4HLI att9MGC p162&181 CR France27,kia

ASTON,Leonard Hugh T2Lt kld 6-9-17 GL &RFC CenFlySch p4 CR Surrey148

ASTON,Ronald Moseley Lt kia 14-3-15 2DCLI p113 MR29

ASTON,Walter Douglas Capt dow 2-11-17 1/1Camb p244 CR Belgium11

ASTWOOD,Edward Leicester Stuart T2Lt dow 20-9-16 26RFus p66 CR France145

ATACK,Percy T2Lt kia 4-7-18 6RROfCav attTankCps p23&188 CR France1170

ATCHISON,Charles Ernest.DSO.MajALtCol kia 24-8-17 KSLI p144 CR Belgium72,Cmdg6YLI

ATCHISON,George M HonCapt 15-4-18 GL CRCanada1245

ATCHISON,Harold Vivian 2Lt dow 26-8-18 RGA 19SB p38 CR France370

ATCHISON,John Osborne 2Lt kia 13-7-15 5YLI p235 CR Belgium85

ATHA,Leonard Edward T2Lt kia 5-3-18 GL &2RFC p15 CR France1203

ATHERLEY,Christopher Ernest Lt dow 17-6-15 11YLI att1RDubF p142 CR Gallipoli1

ATHERSTONE,George Henry Capt ded 21-2-18 RFA p24 MR65

ATHERTON,Edward.MC TLt ded 18-2-19 MGC &6Manch p266 CR Lancs176

ATHERTON,Francis Wright Lt kld 15-5-18 RFA att30RAF p24 MR38

ATHERTON,Walter Lt kia 30-12-17 4KSLI p235 CR France379

ATHOL,Charles Colbourne TLt kia 26-8-18 att21MGC p181 MR16

ATKEY,Freeman Archibald Haynes TCapt kia 5-7-16 9Yorks p89 CR France515

ATKIN,Charles Percy.MC LtAMaj kia 23-11-17 B70RFA 70ArmyBde p24 CR France415

ATKIN,George Dawson Hope 2Lt dow 16-7-16 4Lpool p71 CR France66

ATKIN,Jesse Marson Lt kia 7-11-14 N&D att3Worc p133 MR32

ATKIN,Keyser Capt dow 6-6-18 RAMC 1/1N.FA p253 CR France622

ATKIN,Richard Walter Lt kia 14-8-17 92RFA p24 CR Belgium86

ATKINS,Arthur Charles 2Lt kia 9-9-16 3 att1/12Lond p245 MR21

ATKINS,Basil Elmo.MID T2LtACapt kia 25-2-17 7NStaffs p156 MR38

ATKINS,Herbert de Carteret TLt dow 10-10-15 15DLI p160 CR France1

ATKINS,Herbert Lonsdale 2Lt kia 30-7-16 8RScotF p94 MR21

ATKINS,Kenneth Croydon 2Lt dow 30-5-18 6 att10Worc p107 MR18

ATKINS,Leslie Gordon 2Lt kia 25-5-18 1Lond p245 CR France177,24-5-18

ATKINSON,Ambrose TLt ded 7-7-17 RAMC att3Suff p194 CR Suff55

ATKINSON,Arnold Francis Crossley Lt ded 22-1-19 RE 75TC attS&M p262 MR43

ATKINSON,Arthur Wilfrid T2Lt kia 1-7-16 19Manch p154 MR21

ATKINSON,Bernard Stewart Capt kia 30-11-17 6SStaffs p229 CR France1498

ATKINSON,Charles Lt ded 4-7-19 171LabCps attChineseLabCps p266 CR France146

ATKINSON,Charles Mason TLt kia 9-8-17 RAMC 14FA TC att1Norf p194 CR France184

ATKINSON,Charles Richard 2Lt kia 16-10-15 2Y&L p158 MR29

ATKINSON,Edward William DSO.MBE Maj 22-7-20 1RInniskF MR67

ATKINSON,Elwyn Lt dow 18-5-17 D291RFA p207 CR France518

ATKINSON,Fred T2Lt kia 23-4-17 13KRRC p148 MR20

ATKINSON,Fred.MC TCapt kia 27/30-9-18 1 att9Lpool p71 CR France256

ATKINSON,Frederick Batty 2Lt kia 25-9-18 87RFA p24 CR France727

ATKINSON,Frederick St John Maj kia 30-11-17 IA 9HodsonsHorse CR France364

ATKINSON,Geoffrey Howard.MID Lt dow 1-2-17 IA 45Sikhs p273 MR38

ATKINSON,Geoffrey J Buddle Lt kia19-6-15 5Worc p107 CR Gallipoli6

ATKINSON,Geoffrey William Lt kia 19-7-16 O&BLI BucksBn p231 MR19

ATKINSON,George Louis TCapt drd 20/21-3-17 RAMC p194 CR Devon1

ATKINSON,Gilbert Lt dow 4-10-18 8DLI p239 CR Belgium38

ATKINSON,Guy Cheseldon Renell T2Lt dow 30-10-16 12 att2ELancs p110 CR France105,Reuell

ATKINSON,Harry 2Lt kia 28-9-17 RGA 155SB p38 CR Belgium79

ATKINSON,Harry John T2Lt kia 17-8-16 8YLI p142 CR France402

ATKINSON,Hon.Hector John Capt ded 26-5-17 RIrFus p170 CR Eire5

ATKINSON,Henry Noel DSO.MID 2Lt mbk 22-10-14 1/2Ches p256 CR France924,3 att1Bn

ATKINSON,Hugh MID T2Lt kia 22-11-17 10RIrRif p168 MR17

11

ATKINSON,James.MC.T2Lt kia 2-9-18 1RScotF p94 CR France646

ATKINSON,John T2Lt kia 24-3-18 2SStaffs p121 MR20

ATKINSON,John Broadwood TLt ded 24-12-15 5RIrFus p170 CR Egypt6,Capt

ATKINSON,John Cyril Lt kia 19-12-14 IA 59Rif p273 MR28

ATKINSON,John Ismay TLt kia 29-6-16 13NumbF p60 MR21

ATKINSON,Lawrence Evans TCapt kia 20-4-16 2Y&L p158 CR Belgium73,Laurence

ATKINSON,Lewis de Burgh.MID TLtACapt kia 16-8-16 2RSuss p118 MR21

ATKINSON,Lionel Edward Mapletoft Lt kia 9-5-15 3 att2RBerks p138 MR32

ATKINSON,Miles Linzee T2Lt kia 20-11-17 E'TankCps p188 CR France711

ATKINSON,Noel Mitford Henson T2Lt acckld 27-12-16 3ELancs &RFC p2&110 CR Glouc5,Milford

ATKINSON,Owen Dayott.MC.CaptAMaj dow 27-10-18 RE 200FC p43 CR France276,Dayot

ATKINSON,Richard Dermott 2Lt kia 16-7-16 16KRRC p148 MR21

ATKINSON,Rollo Edward Lt kia 20-2-16 9DLI p239 CR Belgium127

ATKINSON,Surtees.MC.CaptAMaj ded 7-2-18 RFA p24 CR Yorks38

ATKINSON,Thomas Joyce TMaj kia 1-7-16 9RIrFus p170 CR France339

ATKINSON,Victor Rupert 2Lt kia 23-11-17 1/6WRid p227 CR Belgium88

ATKINSON,William.MC.Lt dow 18-7-17 RFA 25DAC p24 CR Belgium11

ATKINSON,William Edward Capt kia 6-8-15 9DCLI p113 MR4

ATKINSON,William Ernest T2Lt kia 12-4-18 TankCps p188 MR32

ATKINSON,William Henry Jepson St.Leger Capt kia 12-5-15 1Drags p21 CR Belgium2,13-5-15

ATKINSON,William Noel Capt kia 29-6-15 IA 2/10GurkhaRif p273 CR Gallipoli6

ATKINSON-JOWETT,James TLt kia 16-9-16 11 att6YLI p142 MR21

ATLAY,Hugh Wordsworth.DSO.Maj kia 11-4-15 52RFA p24 CR Belgium58

ATOCK,Arthur George.MC.T2Lt kia 13-9-18 RE 155FC p43 CR France106,Lt

ATTENBOROUGH,John Haddon T2Lt kia 1-7-16 8Norf p73 MR21

ATTER,Christopher Francis Lt kia 21-3-18 1Leic p87 MR20

ATTERBURY,Lewis John Rowley 2Lt kia 7-10-16 4Lond p246 MR21

ATTFIELD,Sidney Hunrich Lt kia 19-4-17 9RWSurr attHamps p55 CR Palestine8

ATTREE,Francis William Wakeford Town Capt kia 10-5-15 1Suff p78 MR29,8-5-15

ATTRIDE,Raymond George.MID Capt kia 14-8-16 1/4RBerks p234 MR21

ATTWATER,Ernest T2Lt kia 22-3-18 58MGC Inf p181 CR France1473

ATTWATER,Humphrey St.John TCapt kia 26-6-16 1Nhampt p137 CR France149

ATTWATER,Reginald Henry 2Lt kia 9-4-17 1/8Mddx p236 CR France1185

ATTWELL,Ernest T2Lt kia 15-6-18 Worc att1/7Bn p107 CR Italy3

ATTWOOD,Algernon Foulkes Capt kia 8-10-14 4RFus p66 MR15,14-9-14

ATTWOOD,Langley Latton 2Lt kia 12-8-17 RGA 333SB p38 CR Belgium10

ATTWOOD,Stanley Albert Lt kia 3-10-18 15Lond p249 CR France82

ATWELL,Robert Erskine Lt kia 2-9-18 4ConnRgrs p172 CR Belgium89

AUBER,Charles St.Lo Lt kia 29-10-16 4RFA p207 CR France15,2Lt

AUBERTIN,William Aldworth Maj ded 20-2-19 13RWFus attOCB Egypt p97&257 CR Egypt9

AUBIN,Alfred Charles Capt kia 30-8-14 ELancs att2NigR p110 CR WAfrica57

AUBIN,John Fosbrooke Gerrard.DSO.MC&Bar.MID Capt kia 9-4-18 6DLI p239 MR32,Jehu

AUCHINLECH,Armar Leslie Capt kia 17-9-16 ScotRif 4SR att123MGC p181&254 MR21

AUCHINLECK,Daniel George Harold Capt kia 20-10-14 2RInniskF p104 CR Belgium451,21-10-14

AUCKLAND,Ernest T2Lt dow 30-10-16 24 att1Mddx p145 CR France105

AUCUTT,Donald.MID 2LtACapt kia 9-10-17 2RWar p64 MR30

AUDAER,Ernest Clifford 2Lt kia 1-7-16 13LancF p91 MR21,15 Ex13Bn

AUERBACH,Albert Arthur.MC.Lt kia 1-9-18 1 att3Lond p245 CR France216

AULTON-SMITH,Montague W. T2Lt kia 4-11-15 80RFA p24 CR Belgium35

AURET,Ben TCapt kia 21-9-16 112RFA p24 CR France430

AUSLIN,Percy Edward 2Lt dow 24-10-18 3SomLI p79 CR France612, AUSTIN 1Bn

AUST,Henry Ernest Lt kia 18-9-18 1/4Yorks p220 MR16

AUSTEN,Arthur Neville.MC CaptAMaj dow 28-3-18 A51RFA p24 CR France62

AUSTEN,Edward John Lt kia 21/23-3-18 3Lond p245 MR27,22-3-18

AUSTEN,Ernest.DCM.2Lt ded 25-8-16 14Huss p22 MR69

AUSTEN,George Alan 2Lt kia 26-10-17 9Dev p76 CR Belgium143

AUSTEN,William Henry Ambrose T2Lt kia 13-11-16 27 att17Mddx p145 CR France742

AUSTEN-CARTMELL,Arthur James Lt kia 1-6-16 1KRRC p148 CR France924

AUSTEN-CARTMELL,Geoffrie Hugh LtACapt kia 13-11-16 2HLI p162 MR21

AUSTEN-LEIGH,Arthur Alexander Capt kia 11-5-18 2/4RBerks p234 MR27

AUSTER,Norman Conway H. 2Lt kia 16-7-18 SWBord att27RAF p263 CR France1410,L.

AUSTIN,Arthur Hyndman Piercy Capt kia 4-8-16 13DLI p160 MR21

AUSTIN,Cyril Frederic 2Lt kia 10-3-15 2RWSurr p55 CR France706

AUSTIN,Cyril John T2Lt kia 16-5-18 1RLancs p58 CR France412

AUSTIN,Edgar William T2Lt kia 23-7-18 1Ches att4RSuss p95 CR France524

AUSTIN,Edward Gerrard T2Lt kia 18-9-18 Ches att2/24Lond p95 CR France369

AUSTIN,Frederick Hubert 2Lt ded 12-11-18 IA p273 CR France1848,1Ess

AUSTIN,Frederick William.OBE.Maj&QM ded 28-11-19 BordR p264 CR C'land&W'land17

AUSTIN,George Elliott Lt kia 27-8-17 6RWar p214 MR30

AUSTIN,George Frederick T2Lt kia 19-7-16 15Ches p95 MR21

AUSTIN,George Frederick T2Lt kia 11-10-17 RBerks att6Bn p138 CR Belgium23,Fredrick

AUSTIN,Harold Lunn Ferrier T2Lt kia 6-1-16 12 att9Worc p107 CR Gallipoli6

AUSTIN,Hubert Morell T2Lt kia 13-8-16 12HLI p162 CR France239,Morrell

AUSTIN,James T2Lt dow 21-6-17 13Manch p154 CR Greece7

AUSTIN,John Carson Lt kia 29-12-15 5RScotF p222 CR Gallipoli6,2Lt 30-12-15

AUSTIN,John Henry Edward Col ded 26-4-17 RAMC p194 CR Mddx16

AUSTIN,Oliver 2Lt kia 9-5-15 2RSuss p118 MR22

AUSTIN,P.E. see AUSLIN,P.E.

AUSTIN,Robert George T2Lt kia 26-10-18 257MGC Inf p181 MR38

AUSTIN,Stephen Phillip TLt dow 27-9-18 RASC att7LancF p192 CR France712,Philip kia

AUSTIN,Thomas Carnelly MacDonald TCapt kia 9-4-16 4SWBord p99 CR Iraq5

AUSTIN,Vernon James Lt kia 26-1-15 RFA p24 CR Kent177

AUSTIN,William Girvan Lt dow 23-8-17 5RScotF p222 CR Scot520

AUTERAC,Robert Sames T2Lt kia 18-10-16 28MGC p181 MR21

AVELING,Lancelot Neville Lt dow 29-4-15 ConnRgrs p172 CR France200

AVENT,E.Rev 25-8-20 Chap2Cl CR Yorks38

AVERDIECK,George Gerald TLt dow 14-9-16 10RB p177 CR Yorks292

AVERDIECK,Godfrey Harold T2Lt kia 11-3-16 16KRRC p148 CR France114

AVERILL,Thomas Hanson T2Lt kia 30-8-17 17Lpool p71 CR Belgium97

AVERY,Clare Havill LtACapt dow 11-4-17 2Ess att12TMB p131 CR France95

AVERY,Edward John 2Lt ded 1-2-15 4DCLI p227 MR43,Lt

AVERY,Frederick Graeme.MC.Capt kia 13-4-18 RE DivSigCoy att101InfBde p43 CR Belgium11

AVERY,Henry Norris T2Lt kia 5-6-18 6 att1RBerks p138 CR France120,Morris

AVERY,Joseph Francis T2Lt kia 31-7-17 10WelshR p126 CR Belgium65

AVERY,Thomas 2LtTCapt kia 16-6-15 5KSLI p144 CR Belgium58

AVERY,Sir William Eric Thomas Bart.MC.Maj ded 20-11-18 RASC attGdsDivMTCoy p192 CR France146

AVERY,William Ernest 2Lt kia 1-7-16 16NumbF p60 MR21

AWBERY,Charles Luker.MC.Capt kia 31-7-17 4Ess p232 MR29

AWDRY,Carol Edward Vere 2Lt kia 27-8-14 2RMunstF p175 CR France1751

AWDRY,Charles Selwyn.DSO.Maj kia 24-3-18 WiltsYeo p206 MR27

AWDRY,William Walter Lt dow 16-4-18 1 att6Wilts p152 MR30

AXTENS,Harold Surridge Lt kia 6-4-18 4 att7RWFus p223 CR France232

AYER,Leonard Stuart TCapt dow 15-7-16 13RWFus p97 CR France833

AYERS,George Mansfield Lt kia 31-7-17 38RFA p24 MR29

AYLES,Francis Powell Lt ded 1-6-18 GrenGds &RAF 5TrSqd p49 CR Dors&C/I111

AYLETT-BRANFILL,Capel Capt ded 11-5-16 GlamYeo p203 see BRANFILL,C.L.A.

AYLING,Arthur Henry T2Lt kia 28-4-17 25NumbF p60 MR20

AYLMER,Gerald Hans Hendrick Lt kia 16-4-17 2 att1RInniskF p104 MR20

AYLMORE,Alick Guyer Aylmer 2Lt kia 23-3-18 15Lond p249 MR20

AYMER,Alfred Ireland Lt dow 25-9-18 IARO att1/152Punjabis p273 CR Palestine9

AYNSLEY,Ronald Walker 2Lt dow 15-6-15 5NStaffs p238 CR France285

AYRE,Bernard Pitts TCapt kia 1-7-16 8Norf p73 CR France513

AYRE,Stanley Fawcett 2Lt kia 30-11-17 RFA 170ArmyBde p24 MR17

AYRES,Clement 2Lt kia 20-9-17 12RB p177 MR30
AYRES,Giles Frederick 2Lt kia 9-5-15 3Dors attLincs p123 MR32
AYRES,Stanley Frank TCapt kia 20-11-17 7ESurr p112 MR17
AYRES,Victor Albert 2Lt kia 1-9-17 4RFus p66 CR France568
AYRIS,Norman Lt kia 31-12-15 RE 98FC p43 CR France682
AYRTON,Frank Frederick Joseph Capt kia 28-6-15 16RFus p66 MR4
AYRTON,John 2Lt dow 29-4-17 1WYorks p80 CR France80
AYSCOUGH,Walter Guy.MC Capt kia 25-9-17 7Rajputs attBharatpurInf p273 CR EAfrica11 &CR Tanznia1,Maj
AYTOUN,Robert Merlin Graham Lt dow 27-8-14 2A&SH p172 CR France717

B

BABB,Royland Nettleton T2Lt ded 15-10-18 1/2WRid p115 CR France40,Roland Lt 9Bn
BABBAGE,John Colston 2Lt kia 18-11-16 2Manch p154 MR21
BABINGTON,Ralph Vivian 2Lt kia 9-10-17 3CldGds p50 CR Belgium87
BABINGTON,Thomas Zachary Dodson Lt died 16-10-18 IARO att49Bengalis p273 MR43
BACCHUS,William Hubert Ogden Capt dow 13-9-15 2Y&L p158 CR Belgium11
BACHE,Harold Godfrey T2Lt kia 15-2-16 10LancF p91 MR29,16-2-16
BACK,Courteny Douglas SubLt ded 16-6-16 RIM p273 CR Iraq6
BACK,Horace Aubrey 2Lt kia 22-9-16 3 att1Glouc p196 CR France453
BACK,Louis William Alexander T2Lt kia 23-4-17 4Lpool p71 CR France591
BACKHOUSE,Gerald Lovell 2Lt kld 2-8-16 Norf &RFC p2&73 CR Eire411
BACKHOUSE,Herbert Franklin T2Lt kia 25-8-18 4Mddx p145
BACKHOUSE,Henry.TD.LtCol drd 30-12-15 7Ches p222 MR41
BACKHOUSE,Horace Heptonstall.MC.TLt kia 23-8-18 8RLancs p58 CR France927
BACKHOUSE,Hubert Edmund ACapt kia 15-10-16 N&D att2Bn p133 MR21
BACKHOUSE,John William Capt kia 10-2-16 BucksBn O&BLI p231 CR France1327
BACKHOUSE,St.John Salmon 2Lt kia 3-4-18 10ELancs attRAF p110 CR Europe20,CamH
BACKHOUSE,William Henry T2Lt kia 13-3-18 1/6WYorks p80 CR Belgium72
BACKLAKE,Brian Ashber TLt kia 3-5-17 8RFus p66 MR20,Ashbee
BACKLAKE,Denis Ives T2Lt kia 19-10-16 1SomLI p79 MR21
BACKLER,Alfred Milne 2Lt ded 25-5-18 4Lond &RAF p246&258
BACKUS,Arthur Ronald.MC TCapt ded 23-9-17 1 att8RB p177 CR Belgium90
BACKUS,Charles Howard Capt ded 28-12-19 RAMC 7FA p267 CR Germany1
BACKWELL,Charles William T2Lt kia 22-6-17 20LancF attX35TMB p91 CR France212
BACON,Allan Harvey Lt kia 6/7-8-15 7Manch p237 MR4,6-7-15
BACON,Arthur Robert Dick Lt kia 25-4-17 1RBerks p138 CR France184
BACON,Basil Kenrick Wing Maj kia 13-12-14 1Worc p107 MR22
BACON,Charles Vallance TLt ded 4-11-18 RE p43 CR Kent61
BACON,Douglas Haviland Lt kia 16-11-16 60RFC p2 MR20
BACON,Dudley Francis Cecil 2Lt dow 1-11-15 4DLI attNumbF p168 CR Hamps182
BACON,Edward Sivewright Lt kia 31-8-17 RFA att66RFC p17&207 MR20
BACON,Frank William Capt ded 4-12-18 5Ess p232
BACON,John Lionel Rev ded 1-12-18 YMCA CRFrance85
BADCOCK,Arthur Lawrence T2Lt kia 13-10-15 6YLI p142 CR Belgium105,Lt
BADCOCK,Benjamin Morley 2Lt kia 9-7-18 5N&D p232 CR France109,1/6Bn
BADCOCK,Edmund Downes TLt kia 22-7-16 1Nhampt p137 MR21
BADCOCK,Harold John 2Lt kia 18-10-16 4Norf p216 CR France307
BADCOCK,Minden Francis.MC.Capt kia 26-3-18 2/5Glouc p225 MR27,27-3-18
BADCOCK,Stanley Edgar CaptTMaj kia 26-4-15 6DLI p239 MR29
BADDELEY,Alfred James Lt kia 23-10-18 RSuss att2TMB p118 MR16
BADDELEY,Edward Lawrence.TD Maj ded 6-6-15 1/8LancF p221 CR Gallipoli1
BADDELEY,John Frederick T2Lt kia 1-7-16 7EKent p57 CR France397
BADDELEY,Kenneth T2Lt kia 15-9-16 15Hamps p120 CR France277
BADDELEY,Percy Kynnersley T2Lt kia 29-6-16 RFA p24 CR France394
BADDOCK,Thomas Agnew TLt dow 3-12-17 8RB p177 MR30
BADDON,Wallace TCapt kia 3-9-16 147MGC p181 MR21

BADELOW,John George 2Lt dow 27-12-15 63RFA 6DAC p24 CR Iraq1
BADEN,Reginald T2Lt kia 26-6-17 6Beds p85 CR France513
BADENOCH,Ian Forbes Clark T2Lt ded 19-3-17 20RFus p66 CR France67
BADGLEY,James Chester T2Lt kia 7-6-17 1Wilts att58TMB p152 CR Belgium102,6Bn
BADHAM, Leslie Charles.MC.Capt 30-12-20 1ConnRgrs MR67
BADMAN,Raymond Clarence T2Lt kia 21-10-18 2SLancs p125 CR Belgium443
BADSWELL,Frank George 2Lt drd 4-5-17 Glouc p106
BAGGS,Harold Frank TLt dow 28-1-17 8WelshR p126 CR Iraq5
BAGGS,Henry Ernest 2Lt dow PoW 30-6-18 43MGC p181 CR Germany3, Lt 29-6-18
BAGGULEY,James Lionel TLt kldacc 6-12-17 13DLI p160 CR Belgium192
BAGLEY,Arthur Bracton MC.Capt dow 29-10-18 2 att8RDubF p176 CR France13
BAGLEY,Frank Adams MID Capt dow 2-10-15 2SLancs p125 CR Belgium11
BAGLEY,Thomas William Ashton.MID TMaj ded 14-11-15 RASC p192 CR Greece8
BAGNALL,George Barry Lt kia 23-4-17 6 att13RB p177 MR20
BAGNALL,John Angus 2Lt kia 15-9-16 4NumbF p213 CR France239
BAGNALL,Philip Walter Jowett 2Lt kia 10-8-15 6RWelshF p223 MR4
BAGNALL,Richard Gordon 2Lt kia 1-7-16 RGA 114HB p38 CR France296
BAGOT,Alan Desmond Sir Lt ded 11-1-20 RHGds CR C'land&W'land92
BAGOT,Edward Luke Henry 2Lt kia 10-9-16 WelshGds p53 CR France374
BAGOT-CHESTER,Greville John Massey Capt&BtMaj kia 28-11-17 2ScotsGds p51 CR France1498
BAGOT-CHESTER,Walter Greville.MC Capt dow 28-3-18 IA 2/3 att3/3GurkhaRif p273 CR Palestine9,Greville kia
BAGOT-De-La-BERE,Cyril John Lt 18-8-16 10Glouc MR21
BAGSHAW,Arthur Samuel T2Lt kia 22-8-16 7Wilts p152 CR Greece6
BAGSHAW,Frank Vivian Maj ded 29-11-18 RGA p269
BAGSHAW,Henry Kenyon TLt kia 13-4-18 197RASC att1/7WRid p192 MR30
BAGSHAWE,Edward George Clarkson Capt kia 20-7-16 5Yorks p220 CR Belgium60
BAGSHAWE,Geoffrey Hamilton 2Lt kia 13-5-15 5RRofCav att1DragGds p23 MR29,1Drags
BAGSHAWE,Leonard Vale Capt kia 16-6-15 3KOSB att1NumbF p101 MR29
BAILDON,Christopher Nevile T2Lt kia 3-5-17 21 att15DLI p160 MR20
BAILE,George Frederick Cecil TLt dow 9-11-17 RE p43 CR Lond8
BAILE,George William Rev Chap4Cl ded 27-1-18 RAChDept att64CCS p199 CR France40
BAILE,Robert Carlyle T2Lt kia 16-10-15 RE 76FC p43 CR France423
BAILES,John Thomas 2Lt dow 9-5-17 6DLI p239 CR Durham27,9Bn
BAILEY,Alfred John T2Lt kia 3-9-16 17KRRC p149 CR France701
BAILEY,Allan Richard 2Lt dow 15-6-17 A88RFA p24 CR Belgium102
BAILEY,Anthony Drummond 2Lt kia 16-12-16 8N&D att12RB p233 MR21
BAILEY,Anthony Yorke 2Lt kia 27-7-16 5 att1KRRC p149 MR21
BAILEY,Arnold T2Lt kia 24-3-18 8RLancs p58 CR France174
BAILEY,Arthur MacDougall Lt kia 22-8-18 7 att9Ess p232 CR France370
BAILEY,Arthur William Lt kia 4-6-15 9 OBLI p129 CR Gallipoli6
BAILEY,Cecil Arthur Lt kia 5-5-15 4WYorks att2WRid p80 MR29
BAILEY,Charles Lt ded 20-2-19 RGA p254 CR Ches44
BAILEY,Charles Frederick T2Lt kia 9-5-16 GL 8DubF attTMB p189 CR France223
BAILEY,Clifton Frederick Lt kia 6-4-17 7Lond att59RFC p17&247 MR20 See ALBAN C.F true name
BAILEY,Clive Maxwell T2Lt kia 3-8-17 GL &RFC p4 CR Surrey29
BAILEY,Dermot Harvey 2Lt kia 24-5-17 1/8RScots 211 France97,23-5-17
BAILEY,Donald William T2Lt kia 4-10-17 1 att12Glouc p106 CR Belgium125
BAILEY,Douglas Ingram Lt ded 16-11-18 12Lond att1GarBnRWar p248 CR Egypt15
BAILEY,Ernest T2Lt kia 28-10-16 21Lpool p71 CR France374
BAILEY,Felix Charles T2Lt dow 28-3-18 46RFC p15 CR France95,kld
BAILEY,Frank Lt kia 6-9-17 8LancF p221 MR30
BAILEY,George Haddon T2Lt dow 6-4-17 145MGC Inf p181 CR France363
BAILEY,Gerald Hinton T2Lt dow 20-10-15 13DLI p160 CR France285,Lt
BAILEY,Gerald Sergison Hon 2Lt kia 10-8-15 2GrenGds att1BnSpecRes p49 CR France279

BAILEY,Gilbert Maj kia 22-11-15 IA 104Rif p273 MR38
BAILEY,Guy Frederick.MC.Capt kia 7-7-17 2Y&L p158 CR France115
BAILEY,Guy Horsman.MC.LtAMaj kia 28-2-17 15RH&FA p24
BAILEY,Herbert Lt ded 24-5-15 RFA 2AC p24 MR43 &CR Pakistan50A
BAILEY,Herbert Packer.MC.2Lt kia 31-7-17 12ESurr p112 MR29
BAILEY,Hubert Percy Andrew T2Lt kia 24-11-17 17WelshR p126 MR17
BAILEY,Hugh Gardner Lt ded 31-1-19 8 att1/4SomLI p79 MR66
BAILEY,J.A.SenAssSurg 22-11-14 IMS MR66
BAILEY,James Connor Maxwell.OBE.MID Lt ded 13-4-19 RAMC p267 CR EAfrica35 &Tanzania1,Capt Conor
BAILEY,John Bodley 2Lt kia 20-9-17 1EYorks att7RFC p4&83 CR Belgium18
BAILEY,John Lancelot.Hon Capt ded 26-10-18 SWBord BrecknockBn p223 MR65
BAILEY,John William 2Lt drd 30-12-17 3Ches p95 MR41
BAILEY,John Winckworth 2Lt kld 31-3-16 RFC p2 CR Mddx34
BAILEY,Louis John T2Lt kia 17-6-17 GL &41RFC p4 CR Belgium11
BAILEY,Philip Gerald TCaptAMaj kia 26-4-17 36RFA p24 CR France265
BAILEY,Richard Percival Lt&QM ded 30-5-15 YorksHuss p206 CR Yorks34
BAILEY,Robert Humphrey David Lt kia 3-5-17 8SomLI p79 MR20
BAILEY,Robert Neale Menteith Lt dow 1-12-17 ERidYeo p206 CR Egypt9
BAILEY,Roland Henry Lt ded 4-1-19 C251RFA p24 CR France457
BAILEY,Tom Edmond Geoffrey.MC.Capt kia 2-4-19 6Beds att6Yorks p85&89 MR70 &CR Europe179
BAILEY,W.Nurse 23-9-18 VAD 38SH CR Italy12 see BAILY,W.
BAILEY,Walter Arthur Francis 2Lt kia 23-3-18 2 O&BLI p129 MR20,24-3-18
BAILEY,Walter George William TCapt kia 15-9-16 15Hamps p120 CR France1890
BAILEY,Wilson Rhodes T2Lt kld 19-1-18 RFC p15 CR Lancs157,Willie
BAILIE,Thomas Manbourg Douglas Maj kia 15-9-16 1IrGds p52 CR France394
BAILLIE,Alan La Touche TCapt kia 29-10-15 10ScotRif p103 CR France423
BAILLIE,Duncan Lt kia 2-11-14 IA 2/9GurkhaRif att1/9 p273 CR France924
BAILLIE,Evan Henry TCapt kia 25-9-15 10ScotRif p103 MR19
BAILLIE,Gawaine George Stuart.Bart 2Lt kia 7-9-14 2Drags p21 CR Scot728
BAILLIE,George Maj kia 18-11-14 RFA p24 MR29
BAILLIE,George T2Lt kia 5-6-17 21NumbF p60 MR20
BAILLIE,George Richard Lancelot Lt kia 3-10-18 6RInniskF p104 CR France234
BAILLIE,Hugh Montgomery Capt kia 21-3-18 16RIrRif p168 MR27
BAILLIE,Humphry John Lt kia 2-3-16 2Dors p123 CR Iraq1,Humphrey
BAILLIE,Ian Henry Capt dow 22-5-15 4CamH p242 CR France145
BAILLIE,John Henry 2Lt kia 3-5-17 15DLI p160 MR20
BAILLIE-HAMILTOM,Arthur Buchanan Capt kia 9-5-15 1SfthH p164 CR France721,BUCHANAN-BAILLIE-HAMILTON
BAILLON,Gerald Wolstan T2Lt kia 25-9-15 15Lpool p71 CR France163,1Bn
BAILWARD,Theodore Lt kia 29-4-15 IA 26Cav att7Lancers p273 MR38
BAILY,Arthur Alexander Russell 2Lt kia 4-11-18 RFA att17TMB p24 CR France737
BAILY,Denis Joseph.MC.TLt kia 21-2-17 9RMunstF p175 CR Belgium100
BAILY,Wilhelmina Miss ded 23-9-18 VAD StJAB 38SH p200 CR Italy12 see BAILEY,W.
BAIN,Alec Magnus Harold 2Lt kia 22-3-18 1/4Lincs p217 MR20
BAIN,Alexander Neill T2Lt kia 19-5-16 10GordH &7CamH p166&265 CR France423
BAIN,Andrew Lusk.MID Lt kia 4-11-18 1IrGds p52 CR France985
BAIN,Annie Watson Sister.MID kia 1-6-18 VAD StJAB p200 CR France40
BAIN,David McLaren Capt kia 3-6-15 3 att2GordH p166 CR France260
BAIN,John Meikle T2Lt kia 14-7-16 12 att9ScotRif p103 CR France513
BAIN,Nicol T2Lt kia 16-10-18 RWKent att8Bn p140 CR France206
BAINBRIDGE,Carlyle T2Lt kia 13-10-15 6EKent p57 France423
BAINBRIDGE,Eric Lt kia 5-9-16 GL &32RFC p2&189,ded MR20
BAINBRIDGE,James Scott Capt kia 22-3-18 4Yorks p220 MR27
BAINBRIDGE,John Stuart TLt kia 26-9-17 14Hamps p120 MR30
BAINBRIDGE,Thomas Emery T2Lt kia 9-4-17 29 att21NumbF p60 CR France265
BAINBRIDGE,Thomas Lindsay Lt kia 29-4-15 5NumbF p213 CR Belgium113
BAINBRIDGE,Wilfred Hudson Lt dow 15-3-16 6NumbF p213 CR France40
BAINBRIGGE,Philip Gillespie 2Lt kia 18-9-18 5LancF p221 CR France906
BAINES,Arthur Edward Carrow Lt kia 9-4-16 Lincs attRWelshF p74 MR38,Capt
BAINES,Athelstan Basil TCapt kia 3-4-17 6 O&BLI p129 CR France568

BAINES,Cecil Talbot Maj dow 26-4-17 RASC p253 CR Greece7
BAINES,Ellis Eylon TCapt ded 7-8-18 RAVC p198 CR France145,Eyton RAOC
BAINES,Frederick Athelstan Fanshawe 2Lt kia 25-5-15 4KRRC p149 MR29
BAINES,George T2Lt dow 3-6-17 GL 23Mddx att48RFC &48RFC p4 CR France40
BAINES,Henry Burgess 2Lt dow 4-6-17 C240(SM)RFA p208 CR France512
BAINES,Henry Parkyns Bridge T2Lt kia 3-2-17 15 att7Glouc p106 MR38
BAINES,Herbert 2Lt 14-1-17 RE CR Lancs255
BAINES,Hubert.MC.MID Capt dow 22-10-18 IA 75CarnaticInf p273 CR Asia62
BAINES,Jack Gordon Barrymore 2Lt kia 25-2-17 2RWar att2/3RFC p4&64 CR France167,kld
BAINES,John Hugh T2Lt kia 3-7-16 10Lincs p74 MR21
BAINES,Joseph TCapt kia 29-7-16 20Mddx p146 CR France115
BAINES,Kenneth James Mackenzie 2Lt kia 2-1-16 3Lpool p71 MR32
BAINES,Thomas Leo Rev Chap4Cl dow 31-5-18 RAChDept att152RFA p199 CR France31,kia
BAINTON,Herbert Sidney 2Lt dow 16-2-18 28Mddx p146 CR Kent175
BAIRD,Andrew Augustus Dering 2Lt kia 8-7-15 1Worc p107 CR France924,Arthur Lt
BAIRD,Barrington Hope Capt kia 21-12-14 1HLI p162 MR22
BAIRD,Charles Arthur Lt kia 12-10-18 9HLI p240 CR France230
BAIRD,Charles Edward Capt kia 1-7-16 SfthH p164 CR France1890
BAIRD,David Capt ded 22-12-17 WRid p264 CR France102
BAIRD,Joseph Franklin Montague Capt ded 10-9-17 9A&SH p269 CR Scot77
BAIRD,George Henderson Capt ded 9-11-19 RAMC p267 CR Ireland5
BAIRD,Gilbert Campbell T2Lt kia 28-7-17 Worc att229MGC p107&181 CR Palestine8
BAIRD,James Chap4Cl ded 13-2-19 RAChDept p199&258 CR France134
BAIRD,Leonard Barron.MC.Capt kia 20-4-17 RAMC att1/10Manch p253 CR France446
BAIRD,Louis Latham TLt dow 11-4-16 66RFA p24 CR Iraq5
BAIRD,Percy Thomas Charles Maj kia 15-2-15 CamH p167 CR Belgium80
BAIRD,William T2Lt kia 15-9-18 1Lpool p71 CR France530
BAIRD,William Frank Gardiner Capt dow 5-11-14 4Beds attLincs p85 CR France102
BAKE,Arthur Trevithick Tyack Lt kia 14-2-20 IA 126Baluchis p273 MR38
BAKE,Noel 2Lt kia 10-4-18 GL att1/6BlkW p189 MR19,ExMddx
BAKEL,Frank T2Lt kia 20-5-17 14Y&L p158 CR France644
BAKER,Albert Parkes 2Lt kia 22-8-17 3HLI att10DLI p162 CR Belgium125
BAKER,Alfred Parkes TLt dow 1-12-15 11RScots p53 CR France102
BAKER,Arnold Rennie 2Lt kia 16-8-17 GL att27RFC p4 CR France1032
BAKER,Arthur Brimfield 2Lt dow 26-9-16 3SStaffs att3MGC p181&254 CR France177
BAKER,Arthur Forbes LtTCapt kia 11-4-17 3DCLI att52RFC p4&113 CR France415,FltCmdr
BAKER,Arthur Leslie 2Lt kia 9-10-17 8WYorks p219 MR30
BAKER,Arthur William 2Lt kia 28-7-16 1/5YLI p235 MR21
BAKER,Aubrey Halliwell Capt kia 8-3-16 4SomLI p218 MR38
BAKER,Aveling John Wing 2Lt kia 23-3-18 4 att7A&SH p172 MR20
BAKER,Basil Howard Lt kia 22-5-18 2 att13RB p177 CR France81
BAKER,Bertram Reginald T2Lt kia 3-5-16 17RFus p66 CR France559
BAKER,Cecil Douglas Lt kia 29-7-17 1GrenGds SR p49 CR Belgium20,Capt
BAKER,Charles 2Lt kia 22-10-17 RGA 27SB p38 CR Belgium23
BAKER,Charles Hammond AssCommsy HonLt ded 14-7-17 IndMiscList attIMS p273 CR Iraq8
BAKER,Charles Tanqueray Capt kia 15-8-15 5Beds p219 CR Gallipoli4
BAKER,Colin Claude 2Lt dow 12-5-17 10N&D p133 CR France40,Claud
BAKER,Cyril Percival Lt dow 8-5-17 7O&BLI p129 MR37
BAKER,Douglas James T2Lt kia 28-4-17 24NumbF p60 CR France604
BAKER,Douglas Stanley Lt dow 23-7-16 RE 87FC p43 CR France74
BAKER,Edward Benjamin.MID Lt kia 26-10-14 3 att1Lpool p71 MR29
BAKER,Edward Carleton Capt dow 19-9-16 RE 228FC p43 CR France40
BAKER,Eric Trezier 2Lt kia 19-1-18 65RFC p15 MR20,Trezise
BAKER,Frank Alexander.MM.2Lt kia 1-10-18 14Lond p249 CR France647
BAKER,Frank Bernard T2Lt dow 17-9-16 EKent attRWSurr p57 CR France400

BAKER,Frank Vincent T2Lt kia 22-3-18 21 att7KRRC p149 MR27
BAKER,Frederick Gerald T2Lt kia 17-4-18 18WYorks p80 CR Belgium191
BAKER,Frederick Herbert 2Lt kia 24-3-18 58MGC p181 MR27,Harbert
BAKER,Frederick William Stewart Capt kia 20-9-17 4LNLancs p233 CR Belgium96,Stuart
BAKER,George Arthur 2Lt kia 29-11-17 RGA 342SB p38 CR Belgium176
BAKER,George Lionel John 2Lt kia 23-4-17 1Mddx p146 CR France434
BAKER,George Stanley Charles 2Lt kld 23-9-16 2DCLI p114 CR Glouc9,dedacc
BAKER,George William Capt dow 5-12-17 1/19Lond p250 CR France145
BAKER,Gordon Lennox ACapt kia 11-8-18 3Dors p123 CR France360
BAKER,Guy Talbot Lt kia 7-1-16 1/5EKent D'Coy p213 CR Iraq5
BAKER,Harold Carl 2Lt kld 8-10-16 49RFC p2 CR Kent7,dedacc
BAKER,Harold Glasspool.MC&Bar.TCapt dow 5-4-18 8SomLI p79 CR France62
BAKER,Harry Leslie MC.TLt kia 8-11-18 18Lpool p71 CR France930
BAKER,Herbert Norman Lt ded 30-8-17 Herts attigR p252 CR EAfrica39,Ex 28Lond
BAKER,Herbert Shorey.MIDx2 TCapt kia 4/5-4-16 9RWar p64 CR Iraq5
BAKER,Hubert George 2Lt kia 17-8-16 1/4Glouc p225 MR21
BAKER,James TLt&QM ded 4-6-17 SL p201 CR France145 Ex RFA
BAKER,James Henry T2Lt kia 1-7-16 8Y&L p158 CR France293
BAKER,John Bartrup Harwood T2Lt kia 1-9-17 8RFus p66 CR France1182
BAKER,John Francis Lt kia 28-8-18 13Lond p249 CR France568
BAKER,John Kildour TCapt kia 9-10-18 1ScotRif p103 CR France230,Kilgour
BAKER,Joseph T2Lt kia 29-6-17, NStaffs Res att6Bn p156 MR20
BAKER,Joseph Franklin 2Lt dow 16-11-18 79RGA 185SB p38 CR Nhampt76,Lt
BAKER,Joseph Leffler 2Lt dow 14-12-15 C76RFA p24 CR France345
BAKER,Kingsley.MC.Lt dow 30-3-18 A51RFA p24 CR France52
BAKER,Lawrence Edgar T2Lt kld 1-5-17 GL attRFC p4 CR Numb99
BAKER,Lionel Charles Edwin MC 2LtACapt kia 1-10-18 11RWSurr p55 CR Belgium112
BAKER,Micheal Granville Lloyd Capt kia 23-4-16 GloucYeo p203
BAKER,Neville Ernest TLt dow 31-7-17 RE attTankCps p43&188 CR Belgium124
BAKER,Osbert Clinton LtCol kia 9-5-15 1RIrRif p168 MR32
BAKER,Percy Gordon T2Lt dow 9-6-18 RE 81FC p43 MR34 moved fromCR France1693
BAKER,Reginald Cecil Capt ded 14-2-20 19TankCps CR Canada31
BAKER,Reginald Lawrence Capt kia 12-5-15 3Mon p244 CR Belgium126
BAKER,Richard Stanley Maj ded 13-11-18 IARO attS&TCps p273
BAKER,Robert Cunynhame Slade MC.Lt kia 9-8-17 1RBerks p138
BAKER,Robert Geoffrey DSO Maj kia 24-2-17 IA 82Punjabis p273 MR38,23-2-17
BAKER,Roger Dyke Maj dow 13-8-15 ELancs Staff 38InfBde p110 CR Greece10
BAKER,St John Vashon Capt ded 2-12-15 11Lancers CR India48
BAKER,Sidney TCapt dow 28-5-17 8SomLI p79 CR Mddx39
BAKER,Silvanus Wilfred T2Lt kia 26-9-15 8SomLI p79 MR19
BAKER,Sydney Harold TMaj kia 23-3-18 1Glouc att12Entrenching Bn p106 MR27
BAKER,Tom TCapt kia 1-7-16 10Lincs p74 CR France150
BAKER,Thomas LtACapt kia 28-7-17 RGA 203SB p38 CR Belgium24
BAKER,Thomas Sydney 2Lt kia 14-4-17 16Lond p250 MR20,Sidney
BAKER,Waldeman John 2Lt kia 25-10-17 83RFA p24 CR Belgium23
BAKER,Walter.MC.LtACapt dow 23-10-17 3 att14Glouc p106 CR Belgium16
BAKER,Walter George 2Lt kia 14-11-16 5RSuss p228 CR France392
BAKER,Walter Henry T2Lt dow 20-10-18 36MGC Inf p181 CR Belgium140
BAKER,Walter Percy 2Lt kia 14-7-16 3Dors att7RWar p123 MR21
BAKER,Ward T2Lt dow 21-9-17 11WYorks p80 CR Belgium11
BAKER,Wilfred Harry T2Lt kia 2-7-16 8SomLI p79 CR France74,3-7-16
BAKER,William Frank T2Lt kia 15-5-16 12 att11LancF p91 CR France68
BAKEWELL,George John T2Lt dow 16-11-17 GL 6BordR att21RFC p4 CR Belgium16
BALAAM,Augustus Orlando Lt kia 24-10-17 5Suff attRFC p17&217 CR France95,4Bn
BALBIRNIE,John Victor Elphinstone T2Lt kia 7-9-18 23RFus p66 MR19
BALBOUR,Frank Douglas MC Capt kia 23-3-18 NCycBn att15Lond p253 MR20,BALFOUR
BALCH,Percy Frederick Lt 26-2-19 RFC CR Lincs156
BALCHIN,John Richard Aubrey MC TLt dow 14-11-16 152MGC p181 CR France131,kia
BALCOMBE,Charles Percy Lionel MC&Bar TCaptAMaj dow 29-10-18 RE 11FC p43 CR France332
BALCOMBE-BROWN,William Edward 2Lt kia 29-6-15 68RFA p24 CR Belgium94
BALD,Alan Henry Capt kia 15-10-15 IA 2/3GurkhaRif p273
BALDERS,Arthur William Capt kia 27-11-15 Norf att1NigR p73&201 CR WAfrica58,26-11-15
BALDERSON,Eric Francis Richard 2Lt kia 28-3-16 C158RFA p24 CR France705
BALDERSON,Henry Leslie Paxton T2Lt kia 23-7-16 Dev attGlouc p76 CR France832
BALDERSTON,Chester Thomas 2Lt ded 26-6-17 C58RFA p24 CR France285,dow
BALDIE,John Boyd Lt kia 6-11-18 Fife&ForfarYeo &RAF p203&258
BALDING,Reginald Norman TLt dow 30-3-17 5Beds attMGC Inf p186&219 MR38
BALDOCK,Charley Blair LtCol ded 19-10-15 IA 108Inf p273 CR Asia63
BALDOCK,John William 2Lt dow 21-7-18 4YLI p235 CR France1415
BALDOCK,Thomas Agnew Lt dow 3-12-17 8RB CR Belgium84
BALDOCK,W.P Capt mbk 22-8-15 6Y&L p256 MR4
BALDRY,Arthur T2Lt kia 4-12-16 14Y&L p158 CR France342
BALDRY,Edgar George Lt 12-12-18 APD CR Norf162
BALDRY,Edwin James 2Lt kia 24-3-18 1NStaffs p156 MR27
BALDRY,William George Forsyth T2Lt dow 7-11-17 14 att11Ess p131 CR Iraq8
BALDWIN,Alan Aquilla Lt kia 26-4-18 5LNLancs p234 MR30
BALDWIN,Anthony Hugh ColTBrigGen kia 10-8-15 HQ Staff Cmdg38InfBde p1 MR4
BALDWIN,Austin Provost T2Lt kia 27-9-18 2Suff p78 CR France357
BALDWIN,David Aitken TLt ded 31-8-15 8Leic p87 CR France1017
BALDWIN,Herbert Donald TLt dow 18-7-16 156RFA p24 CR France833
BALDWIN,Frederick Charles 2Lt dow 11-5-18 2Beds p85 CR France142
BALDWIN,Harold John Taylor 2Lt kia 23-10-16 16Mddx p146 MR21
BALDWIN,Harry Sandford T2Lt kia 23-7-16 1DCLI p114 MR21
BALDWIN,Hugh Laurents Chenevix Capt kia 23-11-14 IA 58Rif p273 CR France80
BALDWIN,Hugh Reginald Lt kia 27-8-18 1IrGds p52 CR Frnce614
BALDWIN,J Engr 17-7-18 BRCS CR Iraq8
BALDWIN,Lancelot Hugh Maj 6-11-14 1/8GurkhaRif CR India97A
BALDWIN,Norman Edward 2Lt kia 8-10-16 5Lond p246 CR France432
BALDWIN,Osborne George de Courcy TCapt kia 26-1-16 8RMunstF p175 CR France222
BALDWIN,Terence Kennett James Lt kia 20-3-18 5RLancs p213 CR France1092,Kennet
BALDWIN,William Everton 2Lt dow 25-8-18 8Manch att18RAF p237 CR France41
BALDWIN,William Frederick MC TLtAMaj kia 27-5-18 RE 7FC p43
BALE,Thomas Henry Thriscutt Lt kia 24-4-18 3 att2Yorks p89 CR Belgium11,25-4-17
BALE,Thomas William 2Lt dow 10-8-18 13TankCps p188 MR16
BALES,Keith 2Lt kia 16-5-15 2BordR p116 MR22
BALES,Theodore Alfred Herbert T2Lt dow 13-10-18 6RR ofCav att7DragGds p23 CR France146
BALFOUR,Adrian Clive 2Lt kia 8-10-16 21Lond p251 CR France385
BALFOUR,Alan Scott 2Lt kia 13-1-18 RFA &RFC p15&24 CR France446
BALFOUR,Bernard Lt kia 16-4-18 1Lond &65RAF p245&255,21Bn MR20
BALFOUR,Evan Murray Macgregor.MC 2Lt kia 24-8-18 2ScotsGds p51 CR France502
BALFOUR,Frank Douglas.MC.Capt 23-3-18 NCycBn att15Lond MR20 see BALBOUR,F.D.
BALFOUR,George James 2Lt kia 15-9-16 6HLI p240 CR France402
BALFOUR,Guy Edward Capt ded 5-9-17 IA 98Inf MR67 p273
BALFOUR,Isaac Bayley Lt kia 28-6-15 14RScots p53 CR Gallipoli6
BALFOUR,James Alfred CaptAMaj kia 11-1-17 1HLI p162 CR Iraq5
BALFOUR,John.MC.Capt kia 21-3-18 2ScotsGds attDivSigCo p51 CR France1182
BALFOUR,John Melville.MC CaptAMaj kia 6-10-17 91RH&FA p24 CR Belgium12
BALFOUR,Percy DSO MajTLtCol kia 12-12-17 3Beds &HLI att2/7Worc p85 CR France439
BALFOUR,Robert 2Lt kia 20-5-18 4LNLancs p234 CR France204
BALFOUR,Robert Frederick Capt kia 28-10-14 1ScotsGds p51 MR29 &CR Belgium453

BALFOUR,Robert Wilson Maj ded 6-1-18 RGA 95SB p209 CR France512

BALFOUR,Thomas Henry.MC.Maj ded 16-3-20 RAMC MR43

BALFOUR-MELVILLE,James Elliot 2Lt kia 25-9-15 3 att2BlkW p128 MR19

BALKWILL,Albert Thomas James 2Lt kia 17-10-16 8BlkW p128 CR France385

BALKWILL,Charles Vince 2Lt kia 1-7-16 1/5Lond p246 MR21

BALKWILL,John 2Lt kia 1-7-16 6RWar p214 CR France605

BALKWILL,William Horniman 2Lt kia 9-4-17 2Wilts p152 CR France214

BALL,Albert.VC.DSO&2Bars.MC.Capt kia 7-5-18 7N&D att58RFC p17 CR France1279,7-5-17

BALL,Alec Radford 2Lt dow 17-8-17 3 att5Dors p123 CR Belgium18

BALL,Arnold Harding Lt kia 9-4-18 5RSuss p228 CR France163

BALL,Arthur 2Lt kld 19-2-17 3RLancs &57RFC p4&58 CR Egypt8

BALL,Arthur T2Lt kld 17-3-18 RFC p15 CR Scot252

BALL,Arthur Hugh.MC.2LtACapt dow 30-10-17 RGA 186SB p38 CR Belgium3,29-10-17

BALL,Arthur Sherley.MC.Lt kia 16-8-17 A186RH&FA p24 MR30,Shirley 2Lt C186

BALL,Benedict Hanly 2Lt kia 3-9-16 13 att14Hamps p120 MR21,Hanley

BALL,Catherine Sister drd 31-12-17 VAD p200 CR Egypt1

BALL,Charles Bent, Bart LtCol ded 17-3-16 RAMC p194 CR Ireland24

BALL,Charles Herbert Lt dow 3-4-18 WiltsYeo att5MGC Cav p186&206 CR France145

BALL,Frank Granville 2Lt kia 16-8-16 3 att9ESurr p112 MR21

BALL,George 2Lt kia 21-3-18 7N&D p233 MR20

BALL,George Frederick 2Lt ded 6-12-18 ACycCps 2/1HighCycBn p244 p269 CR Numb96,Lt

BALL,George William 2Lt kia 25-3-18 2Mddx p146 CR France1472

BALL,Gerald Harman.MC.T2Lt kia 12-4-18 31MGC Inf p181 MR32

BALL,Gerald Wheatley Lt kia 19-5-17 RE 445WRidFC p210 CR France1182

BALL,Henry Lt kia 13-1-16 3EYorks attRE 180TC p83 CR France279

BALL,Howell Thomas 2Lt kia 26-4-17 36RFA p24 CR France265

BALL,James.MC.Capt ded 23-1-18 1DCLI p114&257 CR Surrey1

BALL,John Joseph Barry Lt kia 27-6-16 2LondRFA p207 CR France1327

BALL,John Harry 2Lt dow 1-9-18 2/4LNLancs p234 CR France103,Lt

BALL,Joseph T2Lt kia 8-8-18 4TankCps p188 CR France487

BALL,Leslie Alfred Capt kia 4-10-17 10Mddx p236 MR30

BALL,Malcolm Edward Lt dow 10-4-16 RAMC att9Worc p194 MR38

BALL,Mark Christopher Lt dow 9-4-18 RE 231FC p43 CR France1094

BALL,Oliver Herbert T2Lt kia 28-9-16 10Yorks p89 CR France374

BALL,Oswald Frederic Grevatte T2Lt kia 5-4-17 GL RSuss att13RFC p4 CRFrance

BALL,Richard Anthony Lt kia 10-7-16 1/7Dev att1/8Worc p217 CR France1887

BALL,Robert Gordon TCapt ded 3-2-20 RAMC p267 CR Ireland24

BALL,Samuel George 2Lt kia 20-3-18 RWelshF p97 CR France646

BALL,Theodore Thomas Hollyman 2Lt kld 21-1-17 GL attVI Cps IntelDept p189 CR France46,dedacc

BALL,Thomas Henry Lt ded 22-1-18 RFA 25DAC p24&257 CR Lond28

BALL,Walter William T2Lt kia 24-11-15 10Yorks p89 CR France1140

BALL,William Charles 2Lt kia 27-9-18 2Manch p154 MR16

BALL,William Linnington 2Lt kia 5-11-18 NumbF att1RFus p60 CR France521

BALL,William Ormsby Wyndham Lt kia 25-9-14 RAMC p194 MR15,26-9-14

BALL-ACTON,Reginald Thomas Annesley Capt kia 22-5-16 7YLI p142 CR Belgium101,Maj

BALLAMY,Harold William Lt kia 15-8-17 B231RFA p207 CR France570

BALLANCE,Leslie Arthur Capt kia 28-9-16 4 att2KRRC p149 CR France277

BALLANTYNE,Allen James T2Lt dow 10-11-17 GL att46RFC p4 CR France49 see BALLANTYRE

BALLANLYNE,James Allan 2Lt kia 1-8-17 20DLI p160 MR29,Alan Lt

BALLANTYNE,Philip Hugh Lt kia 28-10-18 4SfthH p241 MR16

BALLANTYNE,William T2Lt kia 13-10-15 1BlkW p128 MR19

BALLANTYNE,W.C.AssSurg3rdCl 9-11-17 ISMD MR69

BALLANTYRE,Allen James T2Lt dow 10-11-17 GL att46RFC p4 CR France49,BALLANTYNE kld

BALLARD,Charles Naesmyth Bruere LtCol died 11-2-15 15RFA p24 CR France102

BALLARD,Charles Edward Penfold 2Lt kia 10-3-18 1WelshGds p53 CR France545

BALLARD,Charles William.MC.TCapt kia 25-11-17 7RSuss p118 MR17,Willard

BALLARD,Dennis Arthur.MID Capt kia 12-12-17 3RLancs p58 CR France155,1Bn

BALLARD,Ernest Fryer Capt ded 23-10-18 RAMC CR Sussex111

BALLARD,Frank Watson 2Lt kia 11-10-18 3 att1Nhampt p137 MR16

BALLARD,Godfrey Adolphus 2Lt kia 27-9-15 1/23Lond p252 MR19

BALLARD,Maurice Arnold 2Lt dow 29-5-15 23Lond p252 CR France473, Lt 30-5-15

BALLARD,Oliver Charles.MID 2Lt dow 17-10-18 21/2RFA p24 CR France1266,kia

BALLARD,Robert Francis Cooper T2Lt kia 30-7-16 2Beds p85 MR21

BALLEINE,Cuthbert Francis Capt kia 2-7-15 8RB p177 CR Belgium165

BALLINGER,Francis Allen 2Lt kia 22-5-15 4Lpool p71 MR22,Allan

BALLINGER,Henry John 2Lt kia 13-10-15 1Mon p244 MR19

BALLINTINE,Joseph Capt kia 1-7-16 11RInniskF p104 CR France383

BALLOCH,Humphrey Colquhoun 2Lt ded 2-6-15 3GordH p166 CR Scot280

BALLS,Frank William Lt ded 1-7-18 3Suff attRAF p78 CR Egypt1

BALMAIN,Roy Frederick.MC.TLtACapt dow 1-10-18 51RFA p24 CR Belgium157

BALMAIN,Walter.MM.2Lt kia 18-4-18 1BlkW p128 CR France279

BALME,Edward Nettleton.MC.Lt dow 22-4-18 3 att11Ess p131 CR Belgium18

BALMER,Pringle 2Lt kia 27-5-18 5DLI p239 MR18

BALMFORTH,Alfred Capt kia 31-7-17 8Manch p237 MR29

BALSHAW,Newton Kesteven Capt kia 13-4-18 16KRRC p149 MR32

BALSHAW,Walter 2Lt kia 20-10-14 2Manch p154 MR22

BALSOM,Ernest Henry TLt kia 30-8-18 14WelshR p126 CR France217

BALY,Cyril James Price Tyson Sugar Lt kia 15-9-16 1EKent p57 MR21

BAM,Cyril Turpin T2Lt kia 14-7-16 7Leic p87 MR21

BAMBER,Claude Charles Capt s/InflictedWound 26-1-19 IA RWar att3/9GurkhaRif p273 MR43

BAMBER,John Walton TLt kia 1-7-16 10YLI p142 CR France267

BAMBERGER,Cecil David Woodburn Capt kia 20-12-17 RE p43 CR France80,19-12-14

BAMBERGER,William Ewart Woodburn 2Lt kia 16-8-17 Glouc att1/5Bn p106 MR30

BAMBOROUGH,Thomas Clarence T2Lt dow 25-9-17 20DLI p160 CR France139

BAMBRIDGE,Bertram Stacpoole T2Lt kia 19-11-16 7EKent p57 CR France314,18-11-16

BAMBRIDGE,Harry Liddall.MC.2Lt kia 31-3-18 7EYorks p83 MR20

BAMBRIDGE,Rupert Charles.DSO.MC&Bar.MM.TCapt dow 23-5-18 10RFus p66 CR France145

BAMBRIDGE,William Herbert TLtACapt kia 19-8-17 24RFus p66

BAMFORD,Edwin Scott Capt dow 24-4-15 1Y&L p158 CR Belgium151,23-4-15

BAMFORD,Harold Walley 2Lt dow 26-11-15 1KSLI p144 CR France40

BAMFORD,Joseph Lamont.MIDx2 T2Lt kia 20-8-17 GL RScotsF &17RFC p4&94 CR Greece7

BAMFORD,Oswald Joseph Capt kia 13-10-15 6NStaffs p238 MR19

BAMKIN,Carl Jocelyn T2Lt kia 19-8-18 Dors att12Norf p123 CRFrance19

BAMKIN,Harold Picton 2Lt kia 19-7-15 7Suff p78 CR Belgium33

BAMPTON,James Henry TCapt dow 25-8-17 RAMC att70RFA p194 CR Belgium8

BANBURY,Charles William Capt kia 16-9-14 3CldGds p50 CR France1112,dow

BANBURY,Ralph Frontenac T2Lt died 8-1-16 9EYorks p83

BANBURY,William Michael Victor Capt kia 17-8-17 16RB p177 CRBelgium124

BANCE,Robert Arman T2Lt kia 9-8-16 9 att5RBerks p138 CR France150

BANCROFT,Stanley Fleming TLt kia 19-8-16 12 att10WelshF p97 MR21

BAND,George Laidman TCapt&Adjt kia 20-6-17 10NumbF p60 CR Belgium29

BAND,Lawrence T2Lt kia 28-4-17 17Lpool p71 CR France540

BANDEY,George Henry 2Lt ded 6-11-18 PoW 59MGC Inf p181 CR Europe149

BANES WALKER,Frederick Cecil 2Lt 9-5-15 2Dev CR France566 see WALKER,F.C.B.

BANES WALKER,Gerald Capt 22-11-17 1/5SomLI CR Palestine3

BANFIELD,Cyril Barnet 2Lt kia 21-3-18 RFC p15 MR20

BANHAM,Ernest T2Lt kia 29-9-18 13Y&L att10EYorks p158 CR Belgium49

BANHAM,Joseph John.MID TMaj kia 27-3-18 9RSuss p118 MR27

BANHAM,William Henry.MC.2Lt dow 8-9-18 A119RFA p24 France25

BANISTER,Charles Wilfred 2Lt kia 16-6-15 RFus p66 MR29

BANISTER,Maurice James TLt dow 17-2-16 7LNLancs p135 CR France727

BANKES,Edward Nugent Capt kia 26-4-15 3RDubF p176 MR29

BANKS,Arthur Byers.MID Lt ded 6-3-19 RGA p38&257 CR France85

BANKS,Arthur Chaplin 2Lt kia 22-6-16 2RWelshF p97

BANKS,Bertie Charlton 2Lt kia 5-11-16 8DLI p239 MR21,Charleton
BANKS,Charles Hunter Donaldson 2Lt dow 1-7-15 3Worc p107 CR Camb16
BANKS,Cyril D'Albini Sykes.MC.CaptAMaj ded 4-11-18 RGA 226SB p38
BANKS,Edward Francis 2Lt kia 28-2-17 2RFus p66 MR21
BANKS,Frederick 2Lt ded 2-6-18 1/2Ess &RAF p131 CR Lond12,3Bn
BANKS,Henry 2Lt kia 27-8-16 4Yorks p220 MR16
BANKS,Henry Crawford 2Lt kia 30-6-18 4RScots p211 CR France25,Harry
BANKS,John Cook.MC.TCapt kia 1-5-17 20KRRC p149 CR France581,2-5-17
BANKS,John Howard TLt dow 15-8-17 176MGC p181 CR Belgium12
BANKS,Leon Thomas Victor,MC.Maj dow 29-6-18 5RWar p214
BANKS,Percy Abbott,MC.T2Lt ded 22-2-19 RWKent &RAF p140
BANKS,Percy D'Aguilar,MID Capt kia 26-4-15 IA CpsofGuides att57Rif p273 MR29
BANKS,Randolph TCapt dow 5-7-17 161MGC p181 CR Palestine2
BANKS,Raymond D'Albini Sykes Capt kia 21-4-17 IA 9BhopalInf p273 MR38
BANKS,Thomas George Lt kia 26-4-18 RE p210 CR France880
BANKS,William T2Lt dow 6-4-18 PoW 11DLI p160 CR France987
BANKS,William John.MC.MID TCapt kia 30-7-16 15RFA p24 CR France397
BANKS,William Sykes Maj ded 19-2-16 Dors RoO p123
BANNATYNE,Douglas Alexander Lt kia 1-8-18 1/9RScots p212 CR France524
BANNATYNE,Edgar James.DSO.LtTMaj kld 11-9-17 19Huss &RFC p4&23 CR Glouc60
BANNATYNE,Ian McNiven 2Lt kia 18-11-16 9HLI p240 MR21
BANNATYNE,James Fitzgerald TMaj dow 14-5-16 11Huss att23Manch p22 CR France345
BANNATYNE,John Miller T2Lt dow 2-8-17 HLI att12Bn p162 CR Belgium7
BANNATYNE,Ninian John.MID Capt mbk 3-5-17 1Lpool p256 MR20
BANNATYNE,William Sterling LtCol kia 24-10-14 1Lpool p71 MR29
BANNEHR,Harold James Thomas Lt kia 5-11-15 7DLI p239 MR21,5-11-16
BANNELL,Leonard Henry 2Lt kia 3-12-17 2/6Glouc p225 see BANWELL,L.H.
BANNER,Frederick William T2Lt kia 12-5-17 7Yorks p89 MR20
BANNERMAN,Eric 2Lt kia 20-11-17 8A&SH p243 CR France712
BANNERMAN,G.G.Lt kld 8-6-19 RE attRAF p43
BANNERMAN,Oriel William Erskine Capt dow 3-2-15 IA 15Lancers p273 CR France102
BANNERMAN,Robert Gilroy TLt kia 25-7-16 157RFA p24 CR France399
BANNERMAN,Stanley Cyril Forster LtTCapt dow 7-11-17 RASC attRGA 375SB p192 CR Belgium23
BANNESTER,John 2Lt kia 4-10-18 16Lond p250 CR France567
BANNING,Percy Stuart Lt kia 4-11-14 2RMunstF p175 CR Belgium57
BANNISTER,Henry William T2Lt kia 14-6-17 10Lincs p74 CR France644
BANNISTER,Samuel Capt dow 15-4-17 4Worc p107 CR France113
BANNISTER,William George Lt kia 28-3-18 RGA 405SB p38 CR France1182
BANTICK,Reginald Arthur Jay Lt kia 19-5-15 19Lond p250 CR France279
BANTOCK,Arthur Thomas T2Lt dow 23-11-15 13RFus p66 CR Gallipoli27
BANTOFT,Edward Spencer 2LtTLt dow 10-9-16 5Lond p246 CR France23,11-9-16
BANWELL,L.H.MR17 See BANNELL,L.H.
BANYARD,James Hirst 2Lt kia 3-9-16 3 att1Beds p85 MR21
BARBE,Adrien Espinasson Lt ded 27-5-18 5HLI &RAF p240 MR41,drd
BARBER,Bradley King Bell 2LtTCapt kia 4-9-17 1NumbF att9RFC p4&60 MR20
BARBER,Frank William Lt kia 30-6-15 RGA 26HB p38 CR France571,2Lt
BARBER,Geoffrey Carew Capt kia 25-4-15 5Yorks p220 MR29
BARBER,George T2Lt kia 3-10-16 16 att18RFus p66 CR France374
BARBER,George Edward 2Lt kia 24-8-18 1GrenGds p49 CR France1489
BARBER,George Ernest 2Lt kia 7-7-16 10LancF p91 MR21
BARBER,Gordon TCapt kia 22-7-16 1CamH p167 CR France515
BARBER,Gordon Henderson.MC 2Lt ded 20-10-18 8Worc p226 CR France146
BARBER,Graham Brooke TLt kia 25-8-18 13KRRC p149 CR France578
BARBER,Harry Mason T2Lt kia 8-8-18 8ESurr p112 CR France247
BARBER,Henry Cecil T2Lt drd 9-11-17 14Glouc &WAFF p106 MR40,Lt
BARBER,Herbert Graham.MC.Capt kia 7-7-16 4Y&L p238 CR France702
BARBER,Herbert Sydney T2Lt dow 15-5-18 18 att10Mddx p146 CR France100
BARBER,John Lt kia 27-9-17 4Ess p232 CR France1361,Ex28Lond
BARBER,John Christian 2Lt kia 16-6-15 10Lpool p216 MR29
BARBER,Leonard Harry 2Lt kia 5-6-15 6Manch p236 MR4

BARBER,Maurice Capt MID kia 25-11-17 2/4Y&L p238 MR17,26-11-17
BARBER,Walter Edward 2Lt ded 9-11-16 RGA CR Kent83
BARBER,Wilfred 2Lt kia 27-11-17 Y&L p158 MR17
BARBER,Willard T2Lt kld 5-1-18 2Yorks p89 CR Belgium127
BARBER,William Geoffrey Wright 2Lt kia 1-7-16 1/5N&D p232 MR21
BARBER-STARKEY,William Henry Joseph Capt dow PoW 11-9-15 RFA p24 CR France717,11-9-14
BARBOR,Robert Christopher Lt ded 25-5-15 54RFA p24 CR Surrey 150
BARBOUR,Hastings Duncan 2Lt kia 21-10-17 GL &10RFC p4 CR Belgium383,Lt
BARCLAY,Allen 2Lt kia 24-4-15 RE p43 MR22
BARCLAY,David Frederick Lt kia 1-4-18 2DragGds A'Sqn p20 CR France1170,2-4-18
BARCLAY,David Stuart Lt dow 24-4-17 1ScotsGds p51 CR Norf137
BARCLAY,Edward Wilfred Howard 2Lt kia 27-1-18 2 O&BLI p129 CR France439
BARCLAY,Eric Callender.MID TLt kia 25-9-15 MGC Mtrs att3MGCS RFA p181 MR29,Ex12Ches
BARCLAY,F.Lt ded 1-11-18 RDC &RAF p253
BARCLAY,Geoffrey William.MC MID TMaj kia 28-7-16 1RB p177&258 CR Belgium73
BARCLAY,George Eric.MID Capt kia 24-1-17 RLancs att4Nig p58&201 CR EAfrica39
BARCLAY,George Reinhold TLt kia 30-10-18 GL Intelligence p189 CR Belgium393,Capt Ex7Suff
BARCLAY,Henry 2Lt kia 15-10-16 DLI att2Bn p160 CR France307,Harry
BARCLAY,James George Lt ded 23-7-17 6A&SH p243 CR Iraq8
BARCLAY,Marshall Stuart.MID TLt kia 28-3-18 17RScots p53 MR27
BARCLAY,Peter T2Lt kia 15-11-18 RE 180Co p43 CR France1495
BARCLAY,Rafe Hedworth Myddleton 2Lt kia 14-9-14 2KRRC p149 MR15
BARCLAY,Robert Stephen 2Lt kia 21-3-18 3 att16RScots p53 MR20
BARCLAY,Samuel Dugald 2Lt drd 10-10-18 5ScotRif p224 CR Ireland14
BARCLAY,Thomas Hubert Maj drd 4-5-17 1/1SurrYeo p205 CR Italy13
BARCLAY,William Kirk Lt dow 20-6-15 1/7BlkW p231 CR Scot105
BARCLAY-SMITH,J. AMatron ded 28-4-16 QAIMNS p200
BARDER,Sam Gerald T2Lt kia 30-9-16 8ESurr p112 MR21
BARDSWELL,Hamilton Ainsworth 2Lt kia 30-11-17 1/10Lpool p216 MR17
BARE,Arnold Edwin.MVO.Capt kia 30-10-17 28Lond p252 MR30
BARFIELD,John Claude Horsey 2Lt kld 29-6-15 3RFC p1 CR France200
BARFOOT,George Allan 2Lt kld 20-6-15 3Worc p107 CR Belgium112,20-6-18
BARFORD,Kenneth Purnell 2Lt mbk 27-3-18 2RFC p256 MR20
BARGH,George 2Lt kia 10-5-15 Lpool att1Suff p71 MR29
BARHAM,Wilfred Saxby TCapt dow 10-10-15 3 att1EKent p57 CR Belgium5,Wilfrid
BARING,Cecil Christopher T2Lt dow 21-3-18 8RWKent p140 CR France987,kia
BARING,Guy Victor Hon. MIDx2 TLtCol dow 15-9-16 1CldGds p50 CR France394
BARK,Norman Lt kia 1-10-18 6KOSB &RAF p101 CR Belgium157
BARK,Robert Charles T2Lt kld 28-3-18 RFC p15 CR Essex1,R.T.
BARKAS,John Charles Pearson Lt kia 15-9-16 DLI att10Bn p160 MR21
BARKBY,Hartley 2Lt kia 1-8-16 13/277WLancsRFA p208 CR France630,2-8-16
BARKER,Albion Mitchell 2LtTLt dow 19-7-17 20 att2/5LancF p91 CR Belgium11
BARKER,Arnold Septimus 2Lt died 29-5-17 7DLI CR Asia45
BARKER,Arthur 2Lt kia 9-10-17 6WYorks p218 MR30
BARKER,Arthur 2Lt ded 20-12-18 RGA 150HB p38 CR Germany1
BARKER,Arthur Edward James Col ded 8-4-16 RAMC p253 CR Greece7
BARKER,Cecil Massey Arbuthnot T2Lt kia 17-8-15 6RIrF p170 MR4
BARKER,Cecil Noel T2Lt kia 19-11-16 1Dors p123 MR21
BARKER,Charles Haydn 2Lt dow 8-10-18 1Lond p245 CR France146
BARKER,Charles Ivor T2Lt dow 17-3-16 6RWKent p140 CR France80,Ivo
BARKER,Charles William Tone.MC.Capt dow 24-3-18 15DLI p160 MR27
BARKER,Christopher James.MID TLtACapt dow 12-4-18 RE attHQ 30Div p43 CR Belgium20
BARKER,Clarence Moores Childe Capt kia 22-2-17 IA 126Baluchis att53Sikhs p273 MR38
BARKER,Edith Frances Miss ded 3-4-18 VAD 90Detachment p200 CR France134
BARKER,Edward CaptTMaj ded 2-1-16 Mddx attEss p146

BARKER,Edward Bannister Maj 2-1-16 Mddx attEss CR Gallipoli1
BARKER,Edward Walter Chap4Cl dow 18-3-18 RAChDept att176TMB p199 CR France518
BARKER,Frank Edward Lt ded 13-1-19 W'moreld&CumbldYeo &RAF p206&258
BARKER,Frederick Ernest T2Lt kia 13-10-17 10WYorks p80 MR30
BARKER,Geoffrey Capt kia 22-11-17 2/6WYorks p218 MR17
BARKER,George Frederick T2Lt kia 12-5-17 2Ess p131 CR France97
BARKER,Godfrey Maj 29-4-15 RM DrakeBn RNDiv CR Gallipoli6
BARKER,Gordon T2Lt dow 23-10-18 7EYorks p83 CR France332
BARKER,Harold Frederick.MID Maj kia 29-3-18 29RGA att126RFA p209 MR27,Frederic
BARKER,Harold William TLt dow 1-7-16 16Mddx p146 MR21
BARKER,Harry T2Lt kia 4-9-18 1LancF p91 CR France297
BARKER,Henry Arthur Eric T2Lt kia 20-11-17 YLI att2/4Bn p142 CR France530
BARKER,Henry Watson 2Lt kia 17-4-18 4Lincs p217 CR France285
BARKER,Herbert Leslie 2Lt kia 22-3-18 N&D att12Bn p133 MR27
BARKER,Holroyd Birkett Lt ded 15-8-17 RGA 134SB p38
BARKER,Hubert Joseph T2Lt dow 28-3-18 Mddx att1/8Bn p146 CR France266
BARKER,Hugh Edwin 2Lt ded 31-1-18 6RFus p66 CR Ireland33
BARKER,John Edward 2Lt kia 13-10-15 4Leic p220 MR19
BARKER,John Hawksworth Jackson Lt kia 7-8-15 5ELancs p226 CR Gallipoli2
BARKER,Nello Lt ded 14-3-17 6RScots p211 CR Lancs464
BARKER,Osmund Vincent T2Lt kia 28-11-17 97MGC Inf p181 MR30
BARKER,Paul Studholme.MC.TLtACapt kia 26-10-17 78RFA p24 CR Belgium25
BARKER,Percy T2Lt kia 13-4-18 33MGC Inf p181 CR France324
BARKER,Randle Barnett.DSO&Bar.TBrigGen kia 24-3-18 RWelshF Maj RoO p97 CR France430,99InfBde Ex RWFus
BARKER,Richard Raymond.MC.Maj kia 20-4-18 NumbF &3RAF p262 MR20
BARKER,Richard Vincent Capt kia 31-10-14 1RWelshF p97 MR29
BARKER,Robert Arnold.MC.TLtACapt dow 13-10-18 10N&D p133 CR France1393
BARKER,Sydney Clare Lt kia 21-3-18 4 att9Norf p216 MR20
BARKER,Theodore T2Lt kia 13-5-17 22Manch p154 MR20
BARKER,Thomas Chesman 2Lt kia 3-11-18 RE 218FC p43 CR France940,4-11-18
BARKER,William CaptTMaj dow 15-8-18 9Worc p107 MR4
BARKER,William Gordon Steiglitz Capt ded 1-12-16 ConnRgrs p172 CR Surrey128,2-12-16
BARKER,William Harold Capt dow 5-11-15 RGA HQ 24SB p38 CR Gallipoli29,Harald
BARKER,W.J.2Lt kld 27-4-18 GL &RAF p189
BARKER-MILL,William Claude Frederick Vaudrey TCapt kia 15-9-16 8RB p177
BARKLEY,Martin Bell 2Lt kia 2-9-18 4RScotF p222 CR France646
BARKWORTH,H.A.S.Maj 28-1-17 BordR CR Mddx26
BARKWORTH,Humphrey Robertson Capt dow 3-7-16 2NumbF p60 CR France44
BARLING,Harold T2Lt kia 15-6-16 8Leic p87 CR France283
BARLING,William Bingham 2Lt kia 12-3-15 6 att3Worc p107 MR29
BARLOW,Cecil George 2Lt dow 18-5-17 B156RFA p24 CR France113
BARLOW,Charles Alfred T2Lt dow 17-8-17 11RSuss att4RFC p4&118 CR Belgium11
BARLOW,Charles Leslie.DSO.BtLtCol kia 5-8-18 WYorks att1/5A&SH p80 CR France866
BARLOW,Cuthbert Charles Lambert Maj kia 1-11-14 1Lincs p74 MR29
BARLOW,Geoffrey Petrie.MC.2Lt kia 2-9-18 6N&D p233 CR France115
BARLOW,Harold Carver TLt kia 18-6-17 20LancF &9RFC p4&92 MR20
BARLOW,Harry Archibald T2Lt kia 10-7-17 16LancF p91 CR Belgium174
BARLOW,Harry Loftus TLt kld 18-3-18 RE &RFC p15&43 CR Hereford &Worc186
BARLOW,J.E.DSO.MC.Maj 3-6-20 2Yorks CR Iraq8
BARLOW,John Lancashire.MID T2Lt kia 23-9-17 GL &40RFC p4 CR France32
BARLOW,Leonard Monteagle.MC&2Bars LtTCapt kld 5-2-18 RFC SR p15 CR Surrey6
BARLOW,Lovel Hardwick T2Lt kia 16-8-16 13Lpool p71 MR21
BARLOW,Osborn.MC.TCapt dow 14-4-18 8SStaffs p122 CR Belgium183
BARLOW,Percy T2Lt kia 15-11-17 19Lpool p71 CR Belgium84
BARLOW,R.T.Capt kia 30-7-18 SL &RAF p201
BARLOW,Theodore Kenneth TLt dow 15-7-16 1SStaffs p122 CR France833,8Bn

BARLOW,William Howard 2Lt kia 2-5-17 GL &RAOC p266
BARLTROP,Eric Arthur Lt kia 23-4-17 RE(EAngla) att22RFC p17&210 CR France366
BARNABY,William Gordon.MID TCapt kia 23-8-16 7YLI p142 MR21
BARNARD,Albert T2Lt kia 1-10-18 2Suff p78 CR France359
BARNARD,Arthur Wilson T2Lt dow 29-3-18 12Suff p78 CR France40
BARNARD,Dudley Henry Lionel 2Lt ded 10-2-15 130RFA p24 CR France64
BARNARD,Edward Armstrong 2Lt kia 29-9-17 RFA att10RFC p4&24 CR France98
BARNARD,Ernest Yorke TCapt ded 5-3-18 GL &RFC p201&266 CR Lond8
BARNARD,Humphrey Denzil 2Lt kia 21-8-16 6 att3RB p177 MR21
BARNARD,Laurence Claude TMaj ded 12-1-18 RASC p192 CR France377
BARNARD,Lawrence Reginald 2Lt kia 1-10-16 17Lond p250 MR21
BARNARD,Lewis Harold TLt kia 25-8-16 GL attTMB p189 CR France294
BARNARD,Norman Arthur Southard T2Lt kia 8-7-16 18Lpool p71 CR France630
BARNARD,Robert Cyril TLt dow 5-9-17 RASC 58DivTrHQ p192 CR Belgium18
BARNARD-SMITH,William Woodthorpe Barnard T2Lt kia 21-10-16 38RFA p24 CR Frnce513
BARNARDISTON,Nathaniel Walter MajGen ded 18-8-19 Staff p261 CR Essex95
BARNE,M.DSO.TMaj ded 17-9-17 ScotsGds &1SuffYeo p205&51,17-8-17 CR Belgium18
BARNE,Seymour.MC.Capt kia 23-4-17 20Huss att35RFC p4&23 CR France95
BARNES,Arthur Randall 2Lt kia 4-10-17 3SomLI p79 MR30
BARNES,Arthur William TLt kia 11-4-18 9Ches p95 MR30,Capt
BARNES,Aubrey T2Lt kia 22-3-18 17Lpool p71 MR27
BARNES,Basil Goodall Lt dow 19-8-18 4 att10N&D p133 France13
BARNES,Benjamin King T2Lt ded 28-6-18 3NumbF att9RFus p60 CR France122
BARNES,Bertram Morris Lt kia 26-4-17 9 att12Manch p237 MR20
BARNES,David John T2Lt kld 25-4-17 GL &RFC p4 CR Kent7,24-4-17
BARNES,Edmund T2Lt kld 27-1-18 GL &RFC p15 CR Lincs61
BARNES,Edmund Lyndon.MID TCapt&Adjt kia 3-4-16 8RLancs p58 MR29
BARNES,Edward James 2Lt dow 4-5-18 5 att2RFus p66 CR France180,Lt
BARNES,Edward William 2Lt dow 10-7-17 5 att2KRRC p149 MR31
BARNES,Eric 2Lt kia 1-11-14 1Lincs p74 MR29
BARNES,Eric 2Lt kia 16-11-18 18Lond p250 CR Belgium195,6-11-18
BARNES,Eric Earle Capt kia 7-11-17 RE &102RFC p5&43 CR France1029
BARNES,Francis(Frank) T2Lt dow 1-7-16 22Lpool p71 CR France397,kia
BARNES,Frank 2Lt kia 28-10-17 20Lond p251 CR France646
BARNES,George Gaylor Lt kia 16-7-16 6 att3Worc p107 MR21
BARNES,George West LtCol 5-2-19 APD CR France40
BARNES,Harry Scott TLt kia 9-4-17 1NumbF p60 CR France581
BARNES,Henry T2Lt kia 25-9-15 11 att2GordH p166 CR France219
BARNES,Herbert Charles T2Lt kia 22-12-17 162MGC Inf p181 CR Palestine9
BARNES,Herbert George T2Lt kia 16-9-16 9 att7DCLI p114 MR21
BARNES,Herbert George T2Lt ded 31-8-17 KRRC att7Bn p149 CR Belgium8
BARNES,Hugh Cecil.MC.Lt kia 21-7-18 RSuss att2TMB p118 MR19,Cyril Capt
BARNES,James 2Lt dow 28-12-18 7N&D p233 CR France120,28-12-16
BARNES,John Backham 2Lt kia 9-5-17 87RFA p24 CR Belgium5,Buckham
BARNES,John Christopher Craven TCapt kia 29-5-16 8BordR p116 CR France68
BARNES,John Edward Templeman T2LtACapt kia 3-2-17 7Glouc p106 MR38
BARNES,John Robert Evans 2Lt dow 18-4-16 9 att6KSLI p144 CR France40
BARNES,Lawrence Fairbank T2Lt kia 24-7-17 YLI att10Bn p142 CR Frnce1186
BARNES,Leon Thomas Victor.MC.Maj 29-6-18 7KSLI CR France33
BARNES,Ralph George 2Lt kia 30-10-17 2/8Lond p247 MR30
BARNES,Vincent Kendall 2Lt kia 29-4-17 24RFus p66 MR20
BARNES,Walter Lt&QM ded 30-3-16 18Lond p269 CR Mddx53,30-6-16
BARNES,Wilfred Oliver T2Lt kia 18-11-16 10RFus p66 CR France701
BARNES,Will 2Lt kia 2-11-18 A26RFA p208 CR France1257
BARNES,William Sibson TLt kia 5-6-16 11BordR p116 CR France702
BARNET,D.G.Lt ded 31-10-18 RH&FA &11RAF p24 CR France512
BARNET,Henry Morton T2Lt dow 23-4-18 PoW 1KRRC p149 CR Germany3
BARNET,James Howieson 2Lt kia 1-8-18 4BlkW p230 CR France524
BARNET,James Knox TLt ded 2-11-18 RASC MT p192 CR Egypt9
BARNET,Walter 2Lt dow 22-11-18 6Dev p217 CR France146,BARNETT

BARNETT,Alan Gerrard Lt kia 22-8-17 7Lpool attTankCps p189&215 MR30
BARNETT,Bertram Leeds Thomas Capt ded 18-4-15 RASC p192 CR Hamps1
BARNETT,Bret Hercules 2Lt kia 10-8-17 11RFus p66 MR29
BARNETT,Carew Maj kia 12-8-15 6DCLI p114 CR Belgium84
BARNETT,Charles Edward TCapt dow 1-10-15 9ESurr p112 CR France1276
BARNETT,Charles Frederick Robert 2Lt kia 20-4-15 5Glouc p225 CR Belgium70,19-4-15
BARNETT,Denis Oliver TLt dow 16-8-15 2Leinst p174 CR Belgium5
BARNETT,Edwin Bertram Capt kia 30-10-17 8Lond attMGC Inf p186&247 MR30
BARNETT,Edwin James Lt kia 7-8-17 RE p210 CR Belgium29
BARNETT,Gerald 2Lt kia 3-11-15 3RScots p53 CR France423,13Bn
BARNETT,Gilbert Mortimer 2Lt kia 28-9-18 6WRid p227 CR France358
BARNETT,Guy 2Lt kia 11-3-15.5 att1Worc p107 MR22
BARNETT,Harold Thornton 2LtTLt dow 21-10-15 9ESurr p112 CR Belgium11,20-10-15
BARNETT,Harold Walter 2Lt kia 30-12-17 5SLancs p230 MR30
BARNETT,Harry Mortimer Stacey 2Lt kia 6-4-16 23RFA p24 CR Belgium28,107
BARNETT,Herbert William T2Lt kia 20-9-17 26RFus p66 CR Belgium112
BARNETT,Herbert William Capt kia 9-5-15 13Lond p249 MR32,Walter
BARNETT,James 2Lt kia 12-7-15 4RScotF p222&269 MR4
BARNETT,Lascelles De Barry TCapt kia 3-7-16 6RWKent p140 CR France1890
BARNETT,Lionel TLt ded 6-2-17 6Yorks p89 CR Glouc27
BARNETT,Phillip 2Lt kia 2-7-16 4Mddx p146 CR France267
BARNETT,Ralph Edward Fulton Lt kia 6-9-17 8LancF att125MGC Inf p221&186 CR Belgium125
BARNETT,Ralph Thurlby 2Lt kia 12-10-16 3 att2LancF p92 MR21
BARNETT,Reginald Walter.MC&Bar LtTMaj kia 12-8-18 KRRC attStaffDivHQ p149 CR Belgium40
BARNETT,R.T.F.Capt 12-2-20 RAMC CR Wales564
BARNETT,T.E.TD.Maj 5-12-18 6SStaffs CR Staffs57
BARNETT,Thomas William 2Lt ded 17-1-19 EYorks &RAF p83 CR Yorks244
BARNETT,Victor Baron TLt kia 25/27-9-15 12NumbF p60 MR19
BARNETT,Wilford Mainwaring Cornish 2Lt 13-9-15 IARO attS&T Cps MR43
BARNETT,William Augustus T2Lt dow 15-11-17 21RFC p5 CR Belgium20
BARNETT,William Raymond T2Lt kia 29-4-18 8 att1/5SStaffs p122 CR France572
BARNETT-BARKER,R.see BARKER,R.B
BARNEWALL,Reginald Nicholas Francis Mary.Hon Lt dow 24-3-18 5 att2Leinst p174 CR France329,Capt
BARNEY,Montagu Mydelton T2Lt kia 27-4-16 RE 253TC p43 CR France423,Middleton
BARNI,Noel Henry Louis TLt dow PoW 29-3-18 47MGC p181 CR France660
BARNICOT,Arthur William Capt 22-11-16 3/2MtdDivSigsRF CRSurrey57
BARNICOT,John Livingston 2Lt kia 22-12-16 3Lincs p74 CR France423,1Bn
BARNIDGE,John 2Lt dow 26-10-17 Manch att21Bn p154 MR30
BARNS,A Lt 20-4-17 RFC CRHamps4
BARNS,Charles Stanley Capt ded 22-7-18 17Lond attMGC p186&250,22-8-18 CR Essex40
BARNSLEY,Alan Capt kia 25/27-10-14 4LancF attNumbF p92 MR22
BARNSLEY,Thomas Kenneth Capt kia 31-7-17 1CldGds p50 CR Belgium12
BARNWELL,George Woodruffe T2Lt kia 13-4-18 RLancs att1/4YLI p58 MR30
BARON,Margaret Alice Nurse 22-10-18 VAD ELancs CR Lancs222
BARON,Stephen Timmis 2Lt kia 8-12-16 6Glouc p225 CR France251
BARON,Sydney Percival 2Lt kia 5-7-16 1N&D p133 MR21
BARON,William 2Lt dow 19-10-17 RGA 203SB p38 CR France1361
BARR,David Buik.MC.Capt dow 13-7-19 3ELancs p110 MR70 &CR Europe179
BARR,George Fleet TCapt ded 23-3-16 RAMC att42FA p194 CR France1182,Flett
BARR,Henry Keith Maj ?? 25-10-16 IA 38CenIndHorse p273
BARR,Herbert Carrick T2Lt kia 11-12-16 GL &RFC p2&189
BARR,Hugh TCapt ded 21-2-17 RAMC att42AmbTongaTrain p194 CR Greece7
BARR,Hugh T2Lt dow 30-9-18 35MGC Inf p181 MR30
BARR,James Lt dow 16-10-18 D121RFA p207 CR France398
BARR,James Hamilton TLt kia 1-9-18 11RIrRif att7/8RInniskF p168 CR Belgium89
BARR,John Lyle T2Lt dow 26-7-16 D159RFA p24 CR France51,Lt C157
BARR,John William T2Lt kld 14-11-17 GL &49RFC p5 CR Durham26
BARR,John William 2Lt kia 24-3-18 5 att8BlkW p231 MR27

BARR,John Young Lt kia 26-4-15 7A&SH p243 MR29,25-4-15
BARR,Ninian Horrell 2Lt kia 3-9-16 RFA p208 CR France233
BARR,Percival Fowler MC T2Lt kia 2-3-17 20Mddx p146
BARR,Samuel Tudor TLt kia 23-2-15 3Huss p21 CR Belgium112
BARR,William T2Lt kia 11/18-7-16 13NumbF p60 CR France188
BARR,William Arthur 2Lt kia 27-8-18 RGA 328SB p38 CR France1489,Ex 4SfthH
BARR,William Speirs TCapt dow 23-5-17 18HLI p162 CR France439
BARRACLOUGH,G W.MC 2Lt 29-9-18 6WRid CR France358 see BARRMCLOUGH,G W
BARRACLOUGH,William 2Lt kia 28-9-16 5WYorks p218 CR France383
BARRAN,Alfred Rawson T2Lt dow 31-3-18 9WRid p115 CR France62,kia
BARRAN,Roland Noel Lt ded 19-3-19 2LifeGds p20 CR Berks84,Capt
BARRAND,Sidney TLt kia 14-8-18 1KRRC p149 CR France1014,Sydney
BARRAS,William MM.2Lt dow 25-3-18 7A&SH p243 CR France300
BARRAT,William Topley T2Lt dow 25-4-17 26 att13Manch p154 CR Greece6
BARRATT,Ernest Bird Maj dow 7-5-16 IA 128Pioneers p273 CR Iraq8
BARRATT,Geoffrey Ravenscroft 2Lt dow 7-7-16 10LancF p92 MR21
BARRATT,George Herbert 2Lt kia 9-10-17 9Manch p237 MR30,Lt
BARRATT,Harold Charles Edward T2Lt dow 18-5-17 9Glouc p106 CR Greece7
BARRATT,John Leslie T2Lt kia 27-9-17 13Lpool p71 MR30
BARRATT,John Roland Lt ded 24-1-19 23GHQ Res MT 1144RASC p192 CR France40
BARRATT,Kenneth Franklin Lt kia 1-7-16 3Ess attMGC p131&181 MR21
BARRE,Gerald Benedict 2Lt kld 9-8-18 11RDubF &6RAF p176 MR20
BARRELL,Philip James 2Lt kia 1-5-15 Ess p131 MR29
BARRELL,Victor Henry T2Lt kia 22-8-18 11RFus p66 CR France177
BARRETT,Adrian Hamilton Silverton T2Lt kia 10-7-16 RWelshF att14Bn p97 MR21
BARRETT,Alec Roland TLt kia 4-10-17 10YLI p142 MR30
BARRETT,Arthur Edward T2Lt kia 22-8-17 KRRC att8Bn p149 MR30
BARRETT,Arthur Lennard 2Lt kia 1-10-17 1/2 att8Leic p87 MR30
BARRETT,Bernard Thomas T2Lt kia 12-4-18 15RWar p64 MR32
BARRETT,Cecil Roy.MC 2Lt dow 25-6-17 C113RH&FA p25 CR Belgium15
BARRETT,Charles John Chard Capt kia 13-11-14 RScotsF p94 MR29
BARRETT,Colin Frederick,MC.LtTCapt dow 23-9-18 8 att11YLI p142 CR Italy5
BARRETT,David Ernest SenAssSurg2Cl ded 8-10-18 IMS MR52
BARRETT,Edgar Bradley 2Lt ded 11-7-17 RE p269 CR Hamps4
BARRETT,Ernest William TCapt kia 29-5-16 29RFC p2 CR Belgium11,FltCmdr
BARRETT,Frederick Alan T2Lt kld 22-4-16 9Leinst att8Ches p174 MR38,8Ches att9Leic
BARRETT,George TLt kia 6-8-15 12RWar att2Hamps p64 MR4
BARRETT,Gerald Herbert Johnson Capt kia 24-4-16 IA 93BurmaInf p273 MR38
BARRETT,H.G.MM 2Lt 16-8-17 1Newfndland MR30
BARRETT,Hebron TLt dow 27-3-18 10RDubF p176 CR France185
BARRETT,Herbert Victor MC 2Lt dow 22-4-18 D110RFA p25 CR France100
BARRETT,Hugh Treherne Lt ded 6-11-17 SL NyassalandFldForce p201 CR EAfrica40
BARRETT,Jack Ainslake 2Lt kia 28-4-17 13Ess p131 MR20,John Aislabie
BARRETT,Jack Harper Phillip Lt ded 1-11-18 1Lincs &RAF p74 CR Lond12,Capt
BARRETT,John Ambrose T2Lt kia 31-7-17 16RB p177 CR Belgium96
BARRETT,Joseph Gordon.MC T2Lt kia 10-4-18 9LNLancs D'Coy p135 MR32
BARRETT,Keith Joy MID TLt dow 16-4-17 2RFus p66 CR France40,Capt
BARRETT,Knox Gordon 2LtALt kia 20-9-17 RFA attZ20TMB p25 CR Belgium12
BARRETT,Lindsay Alfred MC TMaj kia 17-3-16 1NumbF att1/4Yorks p60 CR Belgium5
BARRETT,L K W 2Lt kld 24-4-18 GL &RAF p189
BARRETT,Noel Bertram T2Lt kia 29-4-18 Ess att2Bn p131 CR France250
BARRETT,Norman Kenyon 2Lt kia 18-9-18 4Yorks att1EYorks p220 MR16
BARRETT,Philip Godfrey Capt kia 27-8-14 2RMunF p175 CR France1751
BARRETT,Reginald T2Lt kia 15-5-16 11LancF p92 CR France68
BARRETT,Reginald Albert Baber Lt kia 7-11-17 2/23Lond p252 CR Palestine1
BARRETT,Reginald James Lt kia 21-8-18 6Lpool p215 CR France619
BARRETT,Sophia Violet Nurse drd 10-10-18 VAD p200 MR40
BARRETT,Thomas Cyril T2Lt dow 4-7-16 Lincs p74 CR France207
BARRETT,Walter Ralph Lt kia 2-11-17 7Ess p232 MR34

BARRETT,Wilfred Varnish 2Lt dow 28-9-18 8RWar p215 CR France512
BARRETT,William T2Lt kia 11-8-16 11ELancs p110 CR France631
BARRICK,George Oliver James 2Lt kia 6-11-17 C168RFA p208 CR Belgium23
BARRIE,David Capt&QM ded 8-12-17 SL HLI p201 CR Surrey15
BARRIE,Walter 2Lt kia 7-6-17 3KOSB att6BordR p101 CR Belgium155
BARRIE,William Cowan Ogilvy Lt kia 14-10-16 5BlkW p231 MR21
BARRINGTON,Allan Leslie T2Lt kldacc 29-7-16 120MGC Inf p181 CR France550
BARRINGTON,Noel Scott Lt kia 10-3-15 1RIrRif p168 CR France706
BARRINGTON-KENNETT,Aubrey Hampden 2Lt dow 20-9-14 O&BLI p129 CR France1107
BARRINGTON KENNETT,Basil Herbert BtMaj kld 18-5-15 GrenGds attRFC p1&49 CR France727
BARRINGTON-KENNETT,Victor Annesley TMaj kia 13-3-16 RFC p2 CR France1504
BARRMCLOUGH,George William.MC.2Lt kia 29-9-18 6WRid p227 CR France358,BARRACLOUGH
BARRON,Francis Harry Lt ded 20-7-20 IARO attS&TCps p273 MR67
BARRON,James TMaj dow 27-9-15 7CamH p167 CR France924
BARRON,John George T2Lt kld 25-6-17 GL &RFC p5 CR Lond33
BARRON,Louis TLt kia 19-7-16 10BordR att2/6RWar p116 MR19
BARRON,Sydney William James Lt ded 25-7-18 IARO att53Sikhs p273 CR Egypt1
BARRON,Vincent 2Lt dow 4-11-18 4Nhampt p234 CR France146
BARROW,Alexander Egan Lt kia 4-10-17 3/4RWSurr B'Coy p212 MR30
BARROW,Alfred James.MC.Capt dow 24-6-18 PoW 10LancF p92 CR Germany3
BARROW,Edmund Sprotson Knapp 2Lt kia 8-5-17 4 att14RWar p64
BARROW,Ernest Isaac TLt kia 23-10-16 3SLancs att2ELancs p125 MR21
BARROW,Frederick William 2Lt kia 3-9-16 14 att13RSuss p118 CR France339
BARROW,Geoffrey Selwyn.OBE.LtTCapt ded 26-12-18 RFA att8DivCycCps p25 CR France1856
BARROW,Hector Henry 2Lt kia 20-10-15 8RFus p66 MR19
BARROW,Howard Cyril TLt kia 20-9-17 MGC p181 MR30
BARROW,James HonTLt&QM dow 1-6-16 8RBerks p138 CR France178
BARROW,Lawrence Alfred Howard T2Lt kia 1-9-16 10 att11RSuss p118 CR France1013,31-8-16
BARROW,Spencer Ellwood Lt dow 16-11-15 5RLanc p213 CR Lancs77
BARROW,Wynford Capt 1-3-20 20DeccanHorse CR France1571
BARROWCLIFF,Cyril Herbert Ford T2Lt kia 27-10-17 1/2Leic p87 MR30,6Bn
BARROWS,John Cecil Russell SubCdr ded 18-11-18 IA IOD p273
BARROWS,Maxwell Dalton 2Lt kia 3-10-18 1/5N&D p232 CR France375,Dalston
BARRS,Noel Coghlan 2Lt kia 15-9-16 11RWKent p140 MR21
BARRY,Cecil Lt kia 21-8-17 17RIrR &57RFC p5&88 CR Belgium125
BARRY,Francis Renton Capt kia 4-9-18 5ESurr p226 CR Belgium111
BARRY,Frederick Fitzgerald Lt 6-1-19 5WYorks CR Ches3
BARRY,James Lawrence.CMG.LtCol 12-6-20 1DragGds CR Lond12
BARRY,Nathaniel James Merriman Capt kia 20-10-17 SL EATrnptCps p268 CR Tanzania1,21-10-17
BARRY,R.2Lt 28-6-15 6Ess CR Essex5
BARRY,Robert Cooke Capt kia 18-7-16 17RScots p53 MR21
BARRY,Sheil Ronald 2Lt kia 7-10-16 11 att1/12Lond p248 MR21
BARRY,William Patrick T2Lt kia 25-8-18 9WRid p115 CR France239,28-8-18
BARRY-ROBERTS,Frederick Leslie Lt kia 22-12-17 IA 2 att7Rajputs p273 CR Asia62,2Lt
BARRY-WALSH,Stephen Michael Lt dow 8-9-15 RAMC 1CavFA CRFrance8
BARSTOW,Edmund Leonard James Lt kia 1-2-17 IA 35 att36Sikhs p273 CR Iraq5,2Lt
BARSTOW,John Eric Jackson Capt kld 27-1-19 NSomYeo &RAF p205&258
BARSTOW,John Baillie Maj kia 31-8-14 RE p43 CR France1063
BARSTOW,Michael William 2Lt kia 3-6-17 RGA 203SB p38 CR Belgium17
BARTELT,F.W.Capt ded 11-9-16 2/4SomLI p218 CR Somerset101
BARTEN,Donald.MM.2Lt kia 30-11-17 8RFus p66 MR17
BARTHOLOMEW,Benjamin James 2Lt kia 18-11-16 4CamH p243 CR France515
BARTHOLOMEW,Claude.MC.TCapt kia 15-9-16 1ScotsGds att&MGC Inf p52&181&258 CR France400
BARTHOLOMEW,George Hugh Freeland.MID TLtACapt dow 2-10-17 14A&SH p172 CR France398
BARTHOLOMEW,George Leo Walter 2Lt ded 6-4-19 RFus CR Essex1

BARTHOLOMEW,Guy Wollaston TCapt kia 25-8-16 7KRRC p149 CR France513
BARTHOLOMEW,William George 2LtTLt ded 26-4-15 BordR p116 CR Gallipoli3
BARTHORP,Arthur Herbert LtCol ded 18-6-18 Nhampt p265 CR Suff126
BARTHORP,Michael Arthur Raymond Lt kia 20-7-16 1Nhampt p137 MR21
BARTHORPE,Alec Scott Lt kia 25-4-18 14Lond p249 CR France54
BARTHROPP,Sidney Alfred Nathaniel Shafto 2Lt kia 29-1-15 RSuss att2Bn p118 CR France720
BARTLE,George T2Lt kia 2-11-16 18 att9RWelshF p97 MR21
BARTLEET,Henry Booth 2Lt kia 10-9-18 5Lond p246 CR France369
BARTLEMAN,Thomas Edward 2Lt kia 6-9-17 5SfthH p241 CR Belgium126
BARTLETT,Allan Owen T2Lt kld 16-10-18 RASC p192 CR Palestine3,kia 15-10-18
BARTLETT,Arthur 2Lt dow 12-4-18 PoW 4RWelshF p223 CR France706
BARTLETT,Cedric Drummond 2Lt ded 1-12-15 3KOSB p101 CR Scot237
BARTLETT,Cyril.MC.TMaj dow 14-11-17 13RSuss p118 CR France193
BARTLETT,Cyril Ward.MC.TCapt kia 9-10-18 11N&D p133 MR16
BARTLETT,Ernest Jack T2Lt kia 16-4-17 1WYorks p80 CR France115
BARTLETT,Herbert Claude.MC.MID TCapt kia 15-9-16 11Ess p131 MR21
BARTLETT,Howard John.MID TCapt ded 1-12-18 RASC p192 CR Italy6
BARTLETT,James 2Lt ded 6-5-18 GL RE IWT p189 CR Iraq6
BARTLETT,Leonard TLt kia 1-10-18 2 O&BLI p129 CR France256
BARTLETT,Leonard Percival T2Lt kia 9-4-17 5RBerks p138 CR France1182
BARTLETT,Lionel Arthur Capt dow 14-10-15 RE p43
BARTLETT,Lionel Arthur Lt kia 22-7-16 1RWKent p140
BARTLETT,Robert Nigel Oldfield TCapt dow 6-4-16 6ELancs p110 CR Iraq5
BARTLETT,Tom Brensley T2Lt kia 19-9-18 Dors att1/8Hamps p123 CR Palestine9
BARTLETT,William Bertram 2Lt kia 18-8-15 8Hamps p229 MR4
BARTLETT,William Herbert Lionel T2Lt kia 13-5-17 11Mddx p146 MR20
BARTLEY,Edward Hall LtACapt kia 31-7-17 2WYorks p80 MR29
BARTLEY,Frederick John Lt kia 26-3-17 1/5Ess p232 CR Palestine8,2Lt
BARTLEY,John.MC.T2Lt kia 31-10-18 14RWelshF p97 CR France1478
BARTLEY,Stanhope Cole Capt kia 12-3-16 RGA attD176RFA p38 CR France275
BARTOM,William Sidney 2Lt dow 26-4-18 Ess att10Bn p131 MR27,BARTON
BARTON,Albert Ernest.MID LtTCapt dow 24-5-17 6Dors p123 CR France1182,Maj
BARTON,Albert Thomas Lionel 2Lt kia 7-11-14 2RInnisF p104 MR32
BARTON,Arthur Everard Hale TLt kia 25-9-15 D20RFA p25 CR France114,2Lt
BARTON,Bernard TMaj kia 11-8-18 1/2Worc p107 CR France21,LtCol 1 att2/8Bn
BARTON,Charles Erskine Capt dow 23-8-18 4 att2RIrRif p168 CR France34
BARTON,Charles Geoffrey.MC.TCapt kia 17-10-18 6RInnisF p104 CR France660
BARTON,Charles John Lt kia 7-4-17 2/4 O&BLI p231 MR21
BARTON,Clarence Harry T2Lt kia 26-10-17 GL &6RFC p5 CR Belgium116
BARTON,Conwell Paris 2Lt kia 27-8-16 6ESurr att1/8RWar p226 MR21
BARTON,Edwin William 2Lt ded 27-4-17 2/5LancF p221 CR Lancs19
BARTON,Eric Percy Mervyn 2Lt kia 3-9-16 1Wilts p152 MR21
BARTON,Ernest Lt ded 1-4-19 RFA p269 CR Surrey148
BARTON,Francis Hewson Capt kia 2-11-14 IA 2/2GurkhaRif p273 CR Frnce706
BARTON,Frank Hubert T2Lt kia 5-11-18 1RFus att17LtTMB p66 CR France521
BARTON,Frederick Pembroke 2Lt dow 18-10-18 5Lincs p220 CR France725
BARTON,Frederick St.John Capt kia 24-7-15 1/4Hamps p120 CR Iraq6
BARTON,George Frank T2Lt kia 10-4-17 7Norf p73 CR France1182
BARTON,George Rawson Capt kia 9-4-18 11Ches p95 MR32,Rawdon 10-4-18
BARTON,Harold William Ferguson 2Lt kia 18-10-14 1RScotsF p94 MR22
BARTON,Harry 2Lt kia 22-3-18 3Lond p245 MR27
BARTON,Hugh Fabian T2Lt kia 12-2-16 9Norf p73 CR Belgium101
BARTON,James.MC.2Lt kia 17-8-18 RGA 11SB p38 CR France526,Capt
BARTON,Kenneth Cyril T2Lt kia 7-10-16 9RFus p66 MR21
BARTON,L.F.2Lt kld 17-5-18 GL &RAF p189
BARTON,Reginald Frederick Lt 17-6-17 2Suff p78 MR20
BARTON,Robert 2Lt kia 12-1-16 RFC p2 CR France1887
BARTON,Stanley Ernest 2Lt kia 31-7-17 1RFus p66 CRBelgium96
BARTON,Thomas Eyre 2Lt kia 16-7-16 14 att2RIrRif p168 CR France393
BARTON,Vivian Alfred 2Lt kia 22-9-17 C162RFA p25 CR Belgium15

BARTON,William Bernard T2Lt kia 28-4-17 103MGC Inf p181 MR20,Barton
BARTON,William Edgar 2Lt kia 22-3-18 9RInnisF p104 MR27
BARTON,William Ewart 2Lt dow 25-8-18 1Lond p245 CR France119
BARTON,William Sidney 2Lt 26-4-18 10Ess MR27 see BARTOM,W.S.
BARTRAM,Alan 2Lt kia 14-8-16 4RBerks p234 CR France293
BARTRAM,Arthur Allan T2Lt kia 30-9-16 8ESurr p112 MR21
BARTRAM,Harold Franc 2Lt kia 24-4-17 7Wilts p152 MR37
BARTRAM,Harry Brocklesby Capt ded 16-9-14 RHA p25 CR Kent8
BARTRAM,William Elliot Lt dow 1-5-17 1Lincs p74 CR France214
BARTRAM,Howard Laidlaw TCapt ded 8-7-18 7Yorks D'Coy p89 CR Yorks176,BARTRUM
BARTRUM,H.L. see BARTRAM,H.L.
BARTTELOT,Walter Balfour.Bart.DSO,MID MajBTLtCol kld 23-10-18 CldGds p50 CR Asia82
BARWELL,Edward Egerton Maj kia 29-10/2-11-14 IA 57Rif MR29,W.E.
BARWELL,Frederick Leycester Capt kia 29-4-17 16Lond p249 CR France1310
BARWELL,Humphrey Eames T2Lt kia 3-2-18 41RFC p15 CR France62
BARWELL,Hugh William Eames.MC.Capt kia 25-3-18 RFC p15 MR20
BASCOMB HARRISON,Arthur Montague Mattison 2LtTLt dow 27-10-15 RE 96FC p43 CR France345
BASCOMBE,Cecil Reginald T2Lt kld 10-10-17 RFC p5 CR Suff176
BASDELL,Frank George 2Lt drd 4-5-17 Glouc p106 CR Italy14
BASDEN,Maurice Duncan 2Lt kia 20-5-16 16Lond attRFC p17&250 CR France276
BASEDEN,Eric Lt kia 26-10-16 3 att2RBerks p138 CR France307
BASELEY,Albert Lawrence.MID Lt kia 11-8-17 2/6LancF p221 CR Belgium24
BASELOW,Henry Frank T2Lt kia 5-10-17 220MGC Inf p181 CR Belgium308
BASFORD,Bromley Alfred 2Lt kia 4-10-17 5N&D p232 CR Belgium165,6Leic
BASHFORD,Charles 2Lt kia 20-9-17 KRRC att21Bn p149 MR30
BASHFORD,Radcliffe James Lindsay.OBE.MIDx3 Maj ded 20-8-21 DADOS RAOC CR Wilts12
BASHFORTH,John Francis Cuthbert T2Lt kia 15-9-16 9Norf p73 MR21
BASING,George Limbery,CB Lord HonBrigGen ded 8-4-19 1RDrags p261 CR Hamps 122,Limbrey
BASKER,Reginald Hugh T2Lt kia 26-9-15 8SomLI p79 MR19
BASKERVILLE,Ralph Hopton Capt kia 9-4-18 GlamYeo att18WelchR p203 MR32,Ex 1Drags
BASKETT,Edmund Graham TCapt ded 27-10-18 GL 9 O&BLI attNigR p189&201 CR WAfrica45
BASKETT,Roger Mortimer T2Lt dow 14-11-16 14 att16Ches p95 CR France1182
BASKOTT,James Edward.MM.2Lt dow 11-12-17 RGA 193SB p38 CR Belgium18
BASON,Theodore Creceas T2Lt dow 29-4-18 Manch att1Worc p154 CR France29,Crescens Lt
BASS,Charles Brodie 2Lt kia 25-9-15 10Yorks p89 MR19
BASS,Charles Harold Capt kia 27-8-14 3 att2LancF p92 CR France611,26-8-14
BASS,Harold.MC TCapt kia 24-4-18 10Yorks att2WYorks p89 MR27
BASS,Phillip Burnett Lt kia 1-7-16 5Ches p222 MR21,Philip Burnet
BASSANO,Edward Arthur T2Lt kia 1-10-16 13 att11N&D p133 MR21
BASSETT,Geoffrey Edward Lt kia 21-3-19 RASC p192
BASSETT,George Sidney T2Lt dow 6-7-17 Res att10LancF p92 CR France113
BASSETT,Robert John TLt drd 10-12-18 RAMC p194 CR Eire78,10-10-18
BASSETT,William Frederick.MC.TLt kia 27-10-18 10BlkW att2RScots p128 MR70 &CR Europe180
BASSETT,William George Lt ded 17-12-15 5RScots p211 CR Ches3
BASSETT-SMITH,Thurstan Francis T2Lt ded 23-11-16 RFC p2 CR Cornwall123
BASSHAM,Reginald Owen 2Lt kia 31-5-17 5RB p177 CR France581
BASTARD,William Lt kia 27-10-14 Beds p85 MR29
BASTIAN,Stanley 2Lt kia 9-5-15 4SfthH p241 MR22
BASTIN,Eric Charles T2Lt kia 4-10-17 RWar att1/8Bn p64 MR30
BASTOW,Frank Capt kia 27-5-18 3WYorks p80 MR18
BASTOW,Norman Lt kia 23-10-16 3WYorks att23TMB p80 MR21
BASTOW,William Henry T2Lt ded 26-11-15 C66RFA attRNAS p25 CR Gallipoli1
BASWITZ,Albert.MC.MID Capt kia 16-9-16 1/22Lond p251 CR France453
BATCHELAR,Robert Thomas 2Lt kia 23-3-18 7RWSurr p55 MR27
BATCHELOR,Edward 2Lt kia 26-9-17 24Lond p252
BATCHELOR,Frederick Arthur MC.Capt 29-11-17 2/2KAR CR WAfrica30
BATCHELOR,Henry Washington TCapt kia 24-3-18 RAMC att43FA p104 CR France1063
BATCHELOR,Percival Horace T2Lt dow PoW 10-4-18 RWar att2/6NStaffs p64 CR Belgium241
BATCHELOR,T.A.Capt dow 29-11-17 2/2KAR p201
BATE,Alan Charles Lorraine Capt ded 25-10-18 RGA CR Herford &Worc154
BATE,Alfred Francis Lt kia 14-3-15 4RDubF att2Leinst p176 CR France1141
BATE,Eric Raoul Hender 2Lt kia 25-9-15.9ESurr p112 MR19,26-9-15
BATE,Frederick Over ALt kia 25-9-17 9MGC p181 CR Belgium8
BATE,George Beaumont T2Lt kia 29-4-17 18LNLancs &RFC p5&135 CR France646,9LNLancs att18RFC
BATE,Harold Lt kia 17-7-16 13 att12Manch p154 MR21,7-7-16
BATE,Maurice Charles Thornton 2Lt kia 13-8-17 2/9Lond p248 MR29
BATE,Thomas Lt kia 26-5-17 5RWelshF p223 MR34,26-3-17
BATEMAN,Arthur Cyril.MC.Capt kia 28-3-18 RAMC att7CamH p194 MR27
BATEMAN,Bernard Montague Basil.MC.Lt dow 24-7-15 113/21RFA p25 CR Mddx26
BATEMAN,Hubert Harry T2Lt kia 23-4-17 14 att4Worc p108 CR France155
BATES,Alfred Neville 2Lt kia 1-7-16 5N&D p232 CR France281
BATES,Allan Harold 2Lt kia 13-4-17 SR 25RFC p5 CR France1314
BATES,Archibald Claude.MC.Lt dow 20-10-17 6Nhampt p137 CR Belgium18
BATES,Arthur James Edmund T2Lt dow 30-7-17 RE 90FC p43 CR Herts29
BATES,Arthur William 2Lt kia 30-3-16 1Norf p73 CR France1182
BATES,Ernest Harold T2Lt kia 13-5-16 13Ches p95 CR France68,15-5-16
BATES,Eric George Henry Lt kia 23-8-16 BucksBn O&BLI p231 CR France393
BATES,Frances Mary SpProb ded 9-4-16 QAIMNS p200 CR Surrey41
BATES,Harold Christopher 2LtTLt kia 18-8-15 RE SR p43 CR France354
BATES,Harry Cecil TMaj kia 7-8-15 11Manch p154 MR4
BATES,John Hayes 2Lt kia 31-8-16 4YLI p235 CR France293
BATES,Leonard John.MC TLtACapt ded 9-11-17 TankCps p188 CR Ireland14,10-11-17
BATES,Lewis George T2Lt dow 24-5-17 RWar att6ELancs p64 CR Iraq8,24-5-16
BATES,Madeline Elsie dow 22-12-17 VAD BRCS CR Essex29
BATES,Percy Joseph T2Lt kia 28-3-17 RE 179Coy p43 CR France1182
BATES,Reginald Plumtre Lt kia 10-3-15 2Dev p76 CR France706,Raymond Plumtre
BATES,Stanes Geoffrey Capt kia 13-5-15 7Huss p22 MR29,Ex Adjt NSomYeo
BATES,Stanley Knight Lt kia 9-5-15 1/5RLancs p213 CR Belgium88
BATES,Thomas Oates Halliday 2Lt dow 12-4-16 IARO att89Punjabis p273 MR38,Holliday
BATES,Thomas William TLtACapt dow 12-10-18 49MGC Inf p181 CR France214
BATES,William T2Lt dow 13-5-18 101LabCps p189 CR Frnce145 Ex DLI
BATES,William George Henry Capt kia 26-4-15 1Leinst p174 MR29
BATESON,John.MC.Lt kia 14-10-18 A28RFA p25 CR Belgium157
BATH,Edgar Norman 2Lt kia 18-4-15 IARO att1/8Rajputs MR43
BATH,John Euel Witherden TCapt kia 22-12-15 5RBerks p138 CR France279
BATH,Reginald Fred 2Lt kia 7-10-16 10Lond p248 CR France374
BATHO,Arnold Capel 2Lt kia 15-9-16 8Mddx p236
BATHO,John.MID Lt dow 30-9-15 RE 54FC p43 CR France98
BATLEY,Arthur George 2Lt kia 27-9-18 4 att11Manch p154 CR France272
BATSON,Alfred William Lt kia 14-3-15 2DCLI p114 CR Belgium74
BATSON,Henry Thomas T2Lt kia 11-9-17 10RWSurr &48RFC p5&55 CR Belgium132
BATSON,Leonard Henry T2Lt kia 3-7-16 EKent p57 CR France393
BATSON,Robert Evelyn T2Lt kia 11-10-16 10LancF att7TMB p92 CR France293
BATT,Francis Joseph TLt kia 13-3-18 RFC p15 CR France699
BATTE,Sydney 2Lt dow 20-1-18 19Lond p250 CR France398
BATTEN,John Hardman T2Lt kld 18-2-18 RFC p15 CR Lancs179
BATTEN,John Henry Strode Capt kia 25-10-14 1Lpool p71 MR29
BATTEN,Joseph Keith Capt kia 27-9-18 5Beds p219 CR France1496,4Bn
BATTENBURG,Maurice Victor Donald KCVO.Prince.Lt kia 27-10-14 KRRC p149 CR Belgium57
BATTERSBY,Augustus Wolfe Lt ded 8-6-15 4ConnRgrs att2NigR p172 CR WAfrica61
BATTERSBY,Caryl Lionel Morse 2Lt kia 18-11-16 3YLI p142 CR France742

BATTERSBY,Charles Fremoult Preston Capt kia 4-11-14 113/25RFA p25 CR Belgium57
BATTERSBY,Eric May Capt kia 28-10-14 3 att1RWKent p140 MR22
BATTERSBY,Ernest Joseph 2Lt dow 13-6-17 18Lond att2/7Manch p250 CR France201
BATTERSBY,George Lefroy Maj ded 29-10-19 2/6RWFus p269 CR Ireland24
BATTERSBY,Henry Lewis Col ded 12-2-20 RAMC p267 CR Surrey159
BATTERSBY,J.C.LtCol 8-4-19 RAMC CR Ireland231
BATTERSBY,James Wilfred.MC.Capt kia 24-10-16 38RFA p25 CR France744,53/2RFA
BATTESBY,Philip Worsley Lt kia 7-7-17 WSomYeo attRFC p17&205 MR20
BATTISON,William.MC.Lt dow 13-10-18 7A&SH p243 CR Scot226
BATTLE,Arthur Newsum T2Lt kia 10-11-15 9Lincs att6Lancs p74 CR Gallipoli5
BATTLE,Edward Charles Vulliamy 2Lt kia 21-10-14 3Worc p108 MR22
BATTLEY,Frederick Walter T2Lt kia 21-4-16 11RSuss p118 CR France279
BATTOCK,Thomas William Lt kia 21-3-18 2/5ELancs p226 MR27
BATTY,Charles Frederick T2Lt kia 19-1-16 10DLI p160 CR Belgium73
BATTY,Geoffrey George Horn TCapt dow 27-9-16 6Nhampt p137 MR21
BATTY,William Liley Capt kia 25-10-16 4Yorks p220 MR21
BATTY-SMITH,Francis Clive TLt kia 4-6-16 13RFus p66 CR France505
BATTYE,Charles 2Lt kia 13-8-18 4WRid att1/8LancF p227 CR France5
BATTYE,Clinton Wynyard.DSO.MajALtCol kia 24-11-17KSLI att14HLI p144 CR France1496
BATTYE,Cyril Wynyard Lt kld 13-3-16 RBerks &RFC p138&2,Wynard CR Berks84
BATTYE,Harry 2Lt kia 21-3-18 8RWar p215 MR27,31-3-18
BATTYE,Hedley Morton Maj ded 4-6-15 IA 1/5GurkhaRif p273 MR4
BATTYE,Ivan Quinton Richmond 2Lt ded 19-5-21 IAUL att2RWar MR43
BATTYE,John 2Lt kia 25-3-18 5Yorks p221 MR27
BATTYE,Reginald T2Lt kia 23-10-18 LancF att1/7Manch p92 CR France287, 25-10-18
BATY,Bertie Cecil TCapt kia 16-9-16 23DLI p160 MR21
BAUGH,Bertram Percival 2Lt kia 16-6-18 RGA p38 CR France116
BAUGH,Charles T2Lt dow 5-4-18 9RFus p66 CR France62
BAUGH,James Thomas 2Lt dow 3-11-18 6Manch p236 CR France1266
BAUMANN,Maximillian Otto 2Lt kia 13-7-17 GL &70RFC p5 MR20
BAUMER,Derek Edward Lewis Venn Lt dow 21-10-17 32RFA p25 CR Belgium25
BAUSOR,Thomas Paul T2Lt kia 6-4-16 9KSLI &TMB p144 MR29
BAVA,Camille Bernard Colin 2Lt kia 26-9-15 14NumbF p60 CR France423
BAVIN,Geoffrey Wynne 2Lt kldacc 1-4-16 Lincs attRFC p2&74 CR Herts31
BAVIN,Nigel Benjamin Lt kia 23-5-15 3 att2Ess p131 CR Belgium96
BAVIN,William T2Lt kia 29-9-18 N&D att6Bn p133 MR16,1Bn
BAWDEN,Leslie John T2Lt dow 1-10-16 9 att6DCLI p114 CR France121
BAX,George Thomas T2Lt dow 8-9-16 15MGC Mtrs p181 CR France390,7-9-16
BAXENDALE,John Thompson 2Lt kia 18-7-17 RFA 30DAC att149Bde p25 CR Belgium15,17-7-17
BAXENDINE,John Young T2Lt kia 1-7-16 1BordR att5RScots p116 CR France1501
BAXTER,Alexander Carnegie.MC.Lt kia 17-4-17 6ScotRif att154MGC p186&224 CR France97
BAXTER,Andrew 2Lt kia 22-10-17 3 att16RScots p53 MR30,3 att17Bn
BAXTER,Angus Cameron 2Lt kia 31-7-17 4CamH p243 MR29
BAXTER,Arthur Sunderland T2Lt dow 2-1-16 18Mddx p146
BAXTER,Cecil Hubert 2Lt kia 1-2-17 A55RFA p25 MR38
BAXTER,Charles Arthur T2Lt dow 8-10-17 RWar att15Bn p64 CR Belgium112.kia
BAXTER,Edward Felix.VC.Lt kia 18-4-16 1/8Lpool p215 CR France1512,mbk
BAXTER,Frederick Cumber 2Lt kia 16-4-18 1/7WYorks p254 MR30
BAXTER,Fred Oscar.MC.Lt kia 17-3-17 IARO 33Punjabis att21RFC p273 CR France134,kld
BAXTER,Fredrick Bowden 2Lt ded 26-11-19 2WelchGds SR p262 CR W'land &C'Land85
BAXTER,Gavin Hector.MC.TLt dow 23-3-18 RE 157FC p43 CR France987
BAXTER,George William TLt kia 14-4-17 13 att2Hamps p120 MR20
BAXTER,Gerald William 2Lt kia 9-10-17 10Manch p237 MR30
BAXTER,Gordon Eyre T2Lt kia 8-10-18 2Dev p76 CR France97
BAXTER,Ian Alexander.MC.TCapt kia 30-5-18 9RWelshF p97 CR France1689
BAXTER,John Lt kia 10-11-17 1/5A&SH p243 CR Palestine8

BAXTER,John Denham 2Lt kia 7-11-18 18Lond p250 CR France1058
BAXTER,Leonard Arthur 2Lt kia 8-3-17 107RFA 23ArmyBde p25 CR France430
BAXTER,Leonard Josiah 2Lt dow 12-11-18 4EKent p212 CR France146
BAXTER,Leslie William Lt kia 28-5-18 95RFA p25 MR18
BAXTER,Paul Robert Elmhirst Lt kia 8-3-16 1Manch p154 MR38
BAXTER,Ralph Frederick 2Lt kia 25-9-15 2RSuss p118 CR France219
BAXTER,Rowland Percival 2Lt kia 16-9-16 5BordR p228 MR21
BAXTER,Walter Herbert LtCol ded 18-5-17 4Dors p229 MR66
BAXTER,William T2Lt kia 22-3-18 11Leic p87 MR20
BAXTER,William Hedley Bruce Capt kia 27-8-17 6RWar p214 CR Belgium125,5Bn
BAYARD,Reginald Aubrey Richard Lt kia 17-5-16 1EKent p57 CR Belgium73
BAYER,Henry Michael Capt ded 8-12-14 RAMC p269 CR Wales629
BAYETTO,Tone Hippolyte Capt 28-7-18 GL &RFC CR Mddx34
BAYFIELD,Herbert Lockington Lt dow 15-3-15 2Leic p87 CR France727
BAYFIELD,John Stanley Lucas 2Lt kia 29-8-18 14Lond p249 MR16
BAYLAY,George Frederick Lt kia 23-3-18 RE 1CavFdSqd p43 CR France605
BAYLEY,Albert Clarence 2Lt dow 13-12-17 14Lond p249 CR France145
BAYLEY,Charles Humphrey TCapt dow 7-8-17 9SLancs p125 CR France193
BAYLEY,Daniel James Capt kia 21-3-18 7GordH p242 MR20
BAYLEY,Edward Vincent 2Lt kld 24-2-17 6SStaffs attRFC p17&229 CR France1844
BAYLEY,George Baird.MID 2Lt kia 26-10-14 KOSB p101 MR29
BAYLEY,John Philip Lt dow 13-1-20 IA 1/34 att3/34SikhPnrs p273 MR43
BAYLEY,Norman David.MC.2Lt ded 20-10-18 3 att2RBerks p138 CR Hamps10
BAYLEY,Peter Ferguson 2Lt kia 23-3-18 9RB p177 MR27,Ex9HLI
BAYLEY,Reginald John 2Lt kia 29-4-17 13RFus p66 MR20
BAYLEY,Richard Joseph Capt ded 8-9-19 LabCps att40ChineseLabCps CR France375,acckld
BAYLEY,William Kercheval Maj kia 13-10-15 5RBerks p138 MR19
BAYLIS,Alfred Keppel T2Lt dow 24-4-18 2Suff p78 CR France40
BAYLIS,Charles John 2Lt ded 6-6-17 GL &42RFC p5 MR20
BAYLIS,Joseph Anno Jones TCapt kia 13-6-17 8SLancs p125 CR Belgium42
BAYLIS,Thomas Forbes 2Lt kia 14-7-17 20Lond p251 CR Belgium24
BAYLISS,John Edwin.MC.TLtAMaj dow 29-9-17 RFA A76ArmyBde p25 CR Belgium16
BAYLISS,Percival Baron.MID TLtACapt kia 3-10-18 TankCps p188 MR16
BAYLISS,Percy James 2Lt kia 27-9-18 RLancs p58
BAYLISS,Reginald Blencowe 2Lt dow 18-11-16 2Manch p154 MR21
BAYLY,Brian Brock.MC.TLtACapt dow 30-10-17 RE 254TC p43 CR Belgium3
BAYLY,Charles George Gordon Lt kia 20-8-14 RE 56FC att5RFC p1&43 CR Belgium406,22-8-14
BAYLY,Charles Ramsay TLt kia 29-3-18 29RH&FA p25 CR France266
BAYLY,Erskine Cochrane T2Lt kia 1-7-16 6RBerks p138 CR France513
BAYLY,Harry Ayrton T2Lt kia 14-6-17 12RFus p66 MR29
BAYLY,John.TD.Maj ded 26-2-18 RNDevYeo p203 CR Devon233
BAYLY,Launcelot Myles.MC.LtACapt dow 22-10-18 3RIrRif p168 CR Belgium20,5Bn
BAYLY,Noel Douglas Lt kia 27-11-17 2IrGds p52 CRFrance256
BAYLY,Vere Talbot T2Lt kia 8-5-16 7 att1Dors p123 CR France702
BAYNE,Edward Gordon TLt kia 4-10-17 2 att1ESurr p112 MR30
BAYNES,Denman Lambert Henry.MC.MID ACapt kia 14-10-18 RGA 115SB p38 CR Belgium112
BAYNES,Nigel William Francis Maj ded 19-3-15 3 att1Glouc p106 CR Bucks82, 20-3-15
BAYNES,Richard Henry Beindge Lt kia 14-7-16 1RWelshF p97 MR21
BAYNES,William Henry.MM.2Lt ded 12-10-18 1RWSurr p55&257 CR Kent175
BAYS,Albert William 2Lt kia 10-10-17 6 att4Mddx p146 CR Belgium56
BAYSPOOLE,Bernard Capt kia 9-4-16 6SLancs p125 MR38
BAYZAND,Alec T2Lt kia 10-10-16 19 att16N&D p133 MR21
BAZALGETTE,William Thomas Arnold 2Lt kia 9-5-17 1Dev p76 MR29
BAZELEY,Roland Arthur T2Lt kia 28-1-16 10 att9RSuss p118 MR29
BAZETT,Arthur Hugh Capt kia 10-8-15 4Ches p222 CR Gallipoli5
BAZIN,Geoffry Martyn Lt kia 19-9-15 1/2HAC p206 CR Belgium6
BAZLEY,Ernest Edward 2Lt kia 4-10-17 A298RH&FA p25 CR Belgium10
BAZLEY,Walter Neville Capt dow 23-5-15 1/6Manch p236 CR Gallipoli1

BEACALL,Arthur T2Lt kia 1-7-16 10 att11ELancs p110 CR France156

BEACALL,Hugh Lt&Adjt dow 14-5-15 2KSLI p144 CR France102

BEACH,John William Victor 2Lt ded 7-3-19 18TankCps CR Devon200

BEACH,Joseph Norman 2Lt kia 31-7-17 5SLancs p230 MR29

BEACH,Lionel H adwen Fletcher.DSO Capt ded 28-11-18 2/4RWSurr p212 CR Surrey6 F H

BEACHAM,Cecil James 2Lt kia 9-10-17 8Worc D'Coy p226 MR30

BEACHCROFT,Cyril Shakespear TLt kia 12-10-17 HouseholdBn p20 CR Belgium126

BEACHCROFT,Gerald William 2Lt kia 31-7-17 RLancs p58 MR29

BEACHCROFT,W.F.Lt ded 21-7-18 RH&FA &RAF p25 CR Berks39

BEADELL,Alfred George 2Lt kia 13-4-17 4Glouc p225 CR France212

BEADLE,George Whitmore.MC.Lt ded 8-3-19 501RASC p253 CR Germany1

BEADON,Basil Herbert Edwards Capt kia 10-8-15 7RWelshF p223 MR4,1-8-15

BEADON,William LtCol kia 13-1-16 IA 51Sikhs CR Iraq5

BEAFORD,Thomas Arthur 2Lt mbk 5-11-18 9WYorks p256

BEAGLEY,Frederick Parkman.MC 2Lt kia 26-8-18 4EKent p212 CR France177

BEAHAN,Arthur T2Lt kia 15-6-18 11NumbF Res p60 CR Italy4

BEAK,Basil Charles T2Lt ded 4-11-18 7MGC p181 CR Italy7

BEAK,Frank Leslie TLt kia 9-4-18 RH&FA att3CoSpecBde RE p25 MR32

BEAL,Arnold James 2Lt kia 1-7-16 12Y&L p158

BEAL,Edward Gerald TLt dow 6-11-18 1 att 8 N&D p133 CR France985,11Bn

BEAL,Ernest Frederick.VC.T2Lt kia 22-3-18 13Yorks p89 MR20

BEAL,Henry Benjamin Lt ded 23-6-19 RFA p25 CR Iraq1

BEALE,Alfred Percy Gordon Lt dow 28-3-17 D158RFA p207 CR France1182,Capt 28-3-18

BEALE,Cecil Charles T2Lt dow 29-1-17 16RB p177 CR Belgium6

BEALE,Clifford William TLt kia 3-3-16 7RSuss att36TMB p118 MR19

BEALE,Edmund Lansdowne LtACapt kia 22-3-18 1Camb p244 MR27

BEALE,Ernest Frederick T2Lt kia 28-4-17 17RFus p66 MR20

BEALE,Norman Stuart Charles Gascoigne T2Lt kia 18-8-16 7Nhampt p137 MR21

BEALE,Oscar Child T2Lt kia 4-10-16 12 att10RInniskF p104 CR Belgium100

BEALE,Robert Anthony 2Lt kia 15-3-17 1Glouc p106 CR France1472

BEALES,Frederick Charles Lt kia 4-11-18 4Lincs p217 CR France733

BEALES,George Ninian 2Lt kia 21-3-18 3 att22NumbF p60 MR20

BEALES,Henry T2Lt kia 9-5-17 1 att14Y&L p158 MR20

BEALEY,A C.Capt 22-11-17 2/4SomLI CR Palestine3

BEALEY,Frederick Arthur Harold Capt ded 17-11-18 PoW 2/6LancF p221 CR Germany3

BEALL,Albert Ernest Lt kia 29-9-17 1/5YLI p235 CR France1361

BEALL,Roy Dixon Lt kia 4-6-15 7RFA p25 CR France631

BEALL,Stephen Spencer ACapt kia 18-9-18 5EKent p213 CR France511,6Bn

BEAMAN,E R.H.Capt ded 17-12-18 RE &RAF p209

BEAMAN,William Archie.MC.Lt dow 10-4-18 7Worc p225 MR30

BEAMER,Archie Mainland T2Lt kia 4-2-18 22RFC p15 CR France31

BEAMISH,John Spread Hamilton Lt ded 2-11-15 KSLI p144 CR Surrey160

BEAN,Arthur Charles Stanley 2Lt dow PoW 14-10-18 24Lond p252 CRFrance567

BEAN,Bevis Heppel Lt kia 18-6-17 6RWelshF attRFC p17&223 MR20 &CR Belgium451

BEAN,Charles Reginald Chamberlayne 2Lt kia 26-10-15 1SStaffs p122 MR29,Chamberlin Lt 26-10-14

BEAN,Ernest Edward T2Lt ded 11-11-18 Norf p263 CR Norf209

BEAN,C.A Maj 30-5-18 7Lpool CR Ches192

BEAN,Humphrey LtACapt kia 19-9-18 1SfthH p164 CR Palestine9

BEAN,Kenneth Foster Lt dow 12-4-18 7RScots p211 CR France139

BEAN,Maurice Gordon Capt drd 30-12-15 IA 81Pnrs p273 MR41

BEAN,William Stuart Lt kia 21-1-18 RE att30RFC p17&210 CR Iraq8

BEANLAND,George Edward 2Lt kia 30-4-17 2N&D p133 CR France551

BEANLAND,John Everard 2Lt kia 26-5-18 161RFA attX32TMB p25 CR France924,initial E only

BEANLAND,Joseph Wilfred TCapt kia 14-8-15 7RWelshF p223 MR4

BEANLANDS,Bernard Paul Gascoyne.MC Capt ded 8-5-19 Hamps &RAF p120 CR Kent154,Gascoigne

BEAR,John Hon Lt&QM ded 18-12-17 NStaffs 258InfBn p156 CR Staffs109

BEAR,Sydney James 2Lt dow 31-7-17 4Mddx p146 MR29

BEARBLOCK,C H see BEARDLOCK,C.H.

BEARD,Edwin Cyril Lt kia 26-3-17 5Ess p232 MR34

BEARD,Frederick Gerald Vesey TLt kia 4-7-16 9 att4Worc p108 MR21

BEARD,Frederic Whiteley T2Lt kia 10-10-16 2WRid p115 MR21

BEARD,Harold Clifford 2LtTLt kia 8-10-16 1/5Lond p246 MR21

BEARD,Lewis Digby Mansergh T2Lt kld 19-10-16 MGC Inf p181 CR Ireland14

BEARD,Philip Lee TLt dow 9-9-16 15RWar p64 CR France51,Leo kia

BEARD,Valentine Edward 2Lt dow 24-11-17 RLancs p58 CR Greece6

BEARDLOCK,Charles Henry TLt dow 20-10-15 9Ess p131 CR France423,BEARBLOCK

BEARDMORE,Sydney Alfred 2Lt dow 1-9-18 1/14Lond p249 CR France103

BEARDSELL,Richard Ernest 2Lt kia 22-4-18 12LancF p92 MR37

BEARDSHAW,Reginald Dudley T2Lt dow 21-10-16 2SWBord p99 CR France277,Lt

BEARDSWORTH,James Lt ded 29-6-19 87RGA p262 CR Asia33

BEARMAN,Cecil Laurence T2Lt kia 23-8-18 7RWSurr p55 CR France515

BEARMAN,Frank TLt ded 5-8-17 7ELancs p110 CR Numb4,3Bn

BEARN,Octavius Leslie TLt kia 23-4-17 9BlkW p128 CR France924

BEARN,Percy Dare 2Lt kia 3-9-16 13 att14Hamps p120 MR21

BEART,Errol George Montague T2Lt kia 31-7-17 RASC attRGA 228SB p192 CR Belgium124

BEART,Vere Leopold Dunstan 2Lt kia 17-9-16 4 att13DLI p160 MR21

BEASLEY,Albert William.MM.2Lt kia 14-8-16 1/4RBerks p234 MR21

BEASLEY,James Joyce T2Lt kia 9-8-15 6RIrF p170 MR4

BEATER,Louis Nie Bohr 2Lt ded 13-3-15 3ConnRgrs p172 CR Ireland14 &CR Eire77,Niebuhr

BEATH,William Alexander 2Lt s/InflictWound 7-5-18 IARO att117Mahrattas p273 MR43

BEATON,Grover Cleveland MC.2Lt dow 30-9-18 RGA 143SB p38 CR France146

BEATON,William James T2Lt kia 24-9-17 174MGC Inf p181 MR30

BEATSON,Beaumont Crowther Oswald 2Lt kia 23-4-17 7BlkW p231 CR France604

BEATSON,Charles Ellis Stewart.MC CaptAMaj dow 3-10-17 105/22RFA p25 CR Belgium11,Elles Stuart

BEATSON,Roger Stewart Montresor TLt kia 1-7-16 6 att10YLI p142 CR France267,2-7-16

BEATSON,Walter William Gordon 2Lt kld 18-7-16 RFC p2 CR Beds23

BEATTIE,Charles TLt kia 20-7-18 GordH att1/7Bn p166 MR18,Capt

BEATTIE,G A.Capt 17-2-21 IraqRlys CR Iraq1

BEATTIE,George.MC T2Lt kia 23-4-17 11A&SH p172 MR20

BEATTIE,James Walker TCapt ded 23-7-18 RAMC p194 CR Durham28

BEATTIE,Malcolm Bartlett TLt dow 16-10-17 5RBerks p138 CR France113

BEATTIE,Maurice Alexander DSO.Maj 13-2-20 RGA Cmdg54SB CR Kent261

BEATTIE,Thomas Lt kia 27-10-18 11WRid p115 CR Italy8

BEATTIE,William 2Lt kia 15-4-17 7ScotRif p224 CR France672

BEATTIE,William Francis MC Lt dow 3-10-18 73/5RFA p25 CR France446,Frances Maj

BEATTIE,William Lindsey 2Lt kia 27-1-17 1BordR p116 CR France399,Lindsay

BEATTIE,William Marshall Lt kia 13-4-18 9HLI p240 MR32

BEATTIE-BROWN,William TCapt kia 9-4-17 25NumbF p60 MR20

BEATTIE-CROZIER,P Capt 19-5-15 IA 4Rajputs att15Sikhs CR France924

BEATTY,Arthur Harry Wolseley TLt kia 31-7-17 Manch att19Bn p154 MR29,2Lt

BEATTY,Benjamin George 2Lt kia 28-7-17 GL &45RFC p5 MR20

BEATTY,Carl John T2Lt kia 15-9-16 7RFC p2 CR France526

BEATTY,Charles Harold Longfield DSO TMaj dow 17-5-17 SL RWar ADC CanCpsHQ p201 CR War37

BEATTY,Charles St John Lt dow 16-9-16 4 att1RMunstF p175 CR France66

BEATTY,Desmond Henry 2Lt dow 21-2-15 4ESurr p112 CR France102,2Bn

BEATTY,Eric Edge TLt kia 29-4-16 6ConnRgrs p172 CR France178

BEATTY,Eric Leslie Finch T2Lt kia 23-6-16 GL 12N&D attTMB p189 CR Belgium17

BEATTY,Hugh Hogg TCapt kia 31-3-18 13RIrRif p168 MR27

BEATTY,Richard George Capt 9-6-15 IA 1Lancers MR67

BEATTY,William John.OBE.Maj ded 10-2-19 RASC p192 CR Belgium330

BEATY-POWNALL,George Ernest.DSO.MajALtCol dow 10-10-18 2BordR att1KOSB p116 CR Belgium11

BEATY-POWNALL,Thomas Trelawny 2LtACapt kia 24-3-17 3 att2BordR p116 CR France616

BEAUCHAMP,Edward Archibald 2Lt dow 22-12-14 1CldGds p50 CR France201

BEAUCHAMP,Eric Westgate 2Lt dow 23-11-17 2/4Dors att2/4Hamps CR Palestine3

BEAUCHAMP,Leslie Heron T2Lt kld 6-10-15 8SLancs p125 CR Belgium70

BEAUCHAMP,Penrith Sutton T2Lt kia 25-1-17 10Worc p108 CR Iraq5

BEAUCLERK,Aubrey Nelthorpe Maj died 22-4-16 2NStaffs p156 MR67

BEAUCLERK,Nevill Alfred de Vere Lt kia 20-6-15 12 att2Ess p131 MR4,17-6-15

BEAUFORT,Francis Hugh Capt kia 16-5-15 2 O&BLI p129 MR22

BEAUFORT,Ostcliffe Harold 2Lt kia 13-10-15 6NStaffs p238 MR19

BEAUFOY,Clive Marston T2Lt kia 25-9-18 10RWar p64 CR France1106

BEAUFOY,Katy A/Matron drd 26-2-18 QAIMNS p200 MR40

BEAUMONT,Charles Leslie T2Lt kld 20-5-17 GL &RFC p5 CR Suff173

BEAUMONT,D.J.Lt ded 24-11-18 11Glouc CR Surrey160

BEAUMONT,Eric Paton.MC.T Lt dow 2-4-18 17Lpool p71 CR France145,Capt

BEAUMONT,George.MC.Capt kia 9-4-18 6 att13ESurr p226 MR32

BEAUMONT,George Joseph TLt ded 18 -1-17 11ELancs p110 CR France41,24-1-17

BEAUMONT,James Hutchings Lt ded 24-6-17 2/7WRid p227 CR France102

BEAUMONT,John Barrie T2Lt kia 20-10-18 1Dev p76 CR France1388

BEAUMONT,Leslie T2Lt kia 17-8-16 12WYorks p80 MR21

BEAUMONT,Phillip Fairclough T2Lt kia 9-10-17 YLI att4Bn p142 MR30

BEAUMONT,Samuel George TCapt kia 25-9-15 5KSLI p144 MR29

BEAUMONT,Seymour James Gordon Maj ded 18-5-20 IA 101Grenadiers p273 CR Norf101,S.J.B.

BEAUMONT,Sydney.MC.T2Lt dow 28-3-18 ELancs att2/4Bn p110 CR France52

BEAUMONT,Thomas Somerville Capt kia 24-9-17 2/8Manch p237 CR Belgium173

BEAUMONT,Wilfrid Newton 2Lt kia 25-9-15 2BordR p116 MR19,Newlon

BEAUMONT-CHECKLAND,Montmorency Beaumont Lt kia 17-8-17 2/1WSomYeo MR30

BEAUMONT-EDMONDS,William George Beaumont 2Lt kia 17-9-16 22Lond p251 MR21

BEAUMONT-NESBITT,Wilfrid Henry.MC.LtACapt kia 27-11-17 2GrenGds p49 MR17

BEAUSIRE,Charles Edward 2Lt kia 14-2-15 12Lond p248 MR29

BEAUSIRE,Herbert Arthur William 2Lt kia 6-3-15 RFus p66 CR France683,15-3-15

BEAVEN,Charles Simeon 2Lt kia 14-4-18 7TankCps p188 MR32

BEAVER,John Denistoun Campbell 2Lt dow 15-5-18 KRRC att13Bn p149 CR Bucks12,17-5-18

BEAVER,Leslie Arnold T2Lt kia 21-9-18 7Lincs p74 CR France415,20-9-18

BEAVON,Donald James Lt 28-8-17 4Glouc p225 MR30

BEAVON,John Leonard 2Lt kia 1-7-16 26NumbF p60 MR21

BEAZER,Archibald Harold 2Lt dow 21-4-19 7Worc p225 CR Hereford & Worc189

BEBEE,Alexander Denman T2Lt kia 30-9-16 6RBerks p138 CR France246

BECHER,Edward Richard Fane 2Lt dow 19-7-16 8RMunstF p175 CR France223,Lt

BECHER,Harry Owen Dabridgecourt Capt kia 13-3-15 ScotRif p103 CR France83,Henry Da Bridgecourt

BECHER,Henry Sullivan Maj kia 2-11-14 IA 2/2GurkhaRif att34SikhPnrs p273 MR28

BECHER,John Pickard.DSO.Maj dow 1-1-16 8N&D p233 CR France51

BECHER,Maurice Andrew Noel Capt kia 26-4-15 1KOSB p101 MR4

BECK,Albert Edward Alexander.MC.Lt kia 12-8-15 5Norf p216 MR4

BECK,Arthur Evelyn.MC.Capt kia 19-4-17 1/5Norf p216 CR Palestine8

BECK,Aubrey Moore 2Lt kia 15-5-17 HAC p206 MR20

BECK,Bernard TCapt kia 18-8-16 3Lpool p71 CR France453

BECK,Charles Broughton Harrop 2Lt dow 15-8-15 7Ches p223 CR Greece10

BECK,Donald Coker Lt kld 21-9-16 RFA attRFC p17&207 CR Bucks120

BECK,Edmund Wallis TLt dow 9-1-16 8Beds p85 CR France102

BECK,Frank Reginald Capt kia 12-8-15 5Norf p216 MR4

BECK,Frederick Charles 2Lt kia 14-9-17 17Lond p250 MR29

BECK,Herbert Charles T2Lt dow 19-10-18 A152RFA p25 CR France34

BECK,Herbert Musgrove T2Lt kia 22-1-18 3 att6RFC p15 CR France300

BECK,J.A.Lt 26-1-20 RFA CR Iraq8

BECK,James Fenn T2Lt kia 28-4-17 5MGC Inf p181 MR20

BECK,John Stanley.MC.Capt kia 16-8-17 4Norf att17KRRC p216 CR Belgium124

BECK,Percy Latham 2Lt kia 6-3-15 RE &RMon SR p43 CR Belgium59

BECK,Philip Henry Harcourt Capt kia 2-4-17 2/6Glouc p225 CR France840

BECK,Theodore David Vodden 2Lt kia 16-9-16 6SomLI p79 MR21,Ex HAC

BECK,Thomas Mc.Lt kia 1-10-18 2HLI &48RAF MR20 p265

BECK,William Lt&QM ded 18-4-18 1KRRC p149 CR Yorks408

BECK,William.DCM.2Lt kia 26-4-18 6Y&L p158 MR19

BECK,William Crabbe.MID Maj kia 28-3-18 C301R&FA p206 CR Palestine3

BECKER,Charlie Hereward LtTCapt kld 8-8-18 3ESurr attRFus p112 CR USA187

BECKER,John Edward Lt ded 21-9-18 RE CR EAfrica36,20/21-9-18

BECKER,Jonathan Otto Gustavus Lt kia 12-3-15 2ESurr p112 CR Belgium168

BECKERLEG,Stephen Trevor Lt kia 15-10-15 3 att2DCLI p114 CR France526

BECKETT,Ernest Whitton 2Lt kia 22-3-18 1/4Leic p220 MR20

BECKETT,Frank Shaw T2Lt kia 31-5-18 RE 2SpCo p43 CR France25

BECKETT,Hubert Edge 2Lt kia 23-7-17 1/4Y&L p238 CR Belgium173

BECKETT,James Ranald T2Lt dow 4-7-16 17HLI p162 CR France74

BECKETT,John 2Lt kia 28-6-15 2BordR p116 CR France260

BECKETT,John Douglas Mortimer.DSO.MajTLtCol kld 9-2-18 10Hamps p120 CR Greece9,Douglass

BECKETT,Philip Arthur 2Lt kia 14-2-17 3 att7RWKent p140 MR21

BECKETT,Victor Louis Sydney TMaj dow 19-7-16 9Yorks p89 CR France833

BECKH,Robert Harold T2Lt dow 15-8-16 12EYorks p83 CR France924

BECKHAM,Arthur Thomas Grafton Capt kia 26-4-15 IA 32 att34SikhPnrs p273 CR Belgium58

BECKHUSON,Donald Frederic T2Lt kia 2-3-16 9WRid p115 CR Belgium167,Frederick

BECKINGSALE,Beauclerc Leigh TLt kia 21-3-18 RIrF att1Bn p170 MR27

BECKINGSALE,John Elgar T2Lt kia 23-8-17 6DCLI p114 MR30

BECKLEY,Eric White T2Lt dow 9-6-18 3DLI att36NumbF p160 CR France10

BECKTON,James Robson Lt kia 18-2-18 RE p210 CR France446

BECKTON,William Lt kld 23-3-18 5RWelshF &RFC p17&223 CR Egypt15

BECKWITH,William John.OBE HonCapt ded 21-12-18 RAOC p198 CR Belgium316

BECTON,H.Lt 23-9-19 RFA CR Essex176

BEDALE,Charles Lt ded 20-2-19 RGA p262

BEDALE,Charles Lees Rev Chap4Cl ded 8-3-19 RAChDept p254,H. CR Camb1

BEDBROOK,Ernest Arthur St.George T2LtAMaj ded 1-5-18 SWBord p99&263 CR USA169

BEDDOES,Henry Roscoe LtCol drd 15-1-19 4 att9RDubF p176 MR40

BEDDON,John Frederick Heber Capt kia 3-11-17 1/4Ess p232 CR Palestine8,BEDDOW

BEDDOW,Cecil Victor T2Lt kia 1-7-16 2Dev p76 CR France1890

BEDDOW,J.F.H. see BEDDON,J.F.H.

BEDDY,E.Col 8-5-19 29Punjabis CR Hamps64

BEDDY,Keith Charles Lt kia 6-2-18 RFC &5Hamps P261&269,kld CR Wilts1

BEDDY,Rafe Langdon Lt dow 4-6-15 IA 1/5GurkhaRif p273 CR Gallipoli3

BEDELL,E.A.Capt 5-2-17 ISMD MR69

BEDELL,F.SenAssSurg 22-10-18 ISMD MR66

BEDELL,H.J.AssSurg 18-10-18 IMS MR43

BEDELLS,Cecil Arthur 2Lt kia 26-9-15 11Ess p131

BEDFIELD,James Stewart EngrSubLt 24-4-19 RIM attRE IWT MR65

BEDFORD,Alan William T2Lt kia 20-11-17 WYorks att2/6Bn p80 CR France530

BEDFORD,Cecil Clarke T2Lt kia 8-3-16 1Manch p154 MR38

BEDFORD,Edward Terence Bertyn LtACapt kia 28-5-17 RGA 34SB 1AnzacCpsTroops p38 CR France518

BEDFORD,Kenneth Savile.MID Capt kia 12-10-16 Y&L att3Bn p158 MR37

BEDFORD,Robert Harold.MID Capt kia 25-3-18 6Manch p236 MR27

BEDFORD,Rowland.MC&Bar.TLt kia 13-9-18 9Dev p76 CR

France357,Roland

BEDFORD,Seaton Hall T2Lt kia 1-7-16 2RBerks p138 MR21
BEDFORD,Yhomas Arthur 2Lt kia 4-11-18 9WYorks CR France953
BEDFORD-PIM,Edward Woodley Lt ded 5-7-18 RH&FA p207 CR Kent91,RGA
BEDINGHAM,Albert T2Lt kia 25-2-17 Mddx att23Bn p146 CR Belgium28
BEDSON,Eric Hamilton Capt kia 7-8-17 8LancF att9RFC p221 CR Belgium20
BEDWELL,Charles Theodore Lt kia 12-4-18 1Y&L p158 MR30
BEDWELL,Victor Leopold Stevens 2Lt kia 18-8-16 4Suff p217 MR21
BEE,William Lt dow 24-9-17 RD94FA p207 CR Belgium11
BEEBY,Charles Stuart Lt kia 27-5-18 4Leic p219 MR18
BEEBY,William Sorley Marden Capt kia 3-5-17 4Y&L p238 MR20,Sorby Mardon
BEECH,John TLtACapt kia 12-5-18 RE 4FdSurCo p43 CR Belgium36,Ex 10SStaffs
BEECH,John Robert.CMG.DSO.LtCol ded 6-11-15 ScotHorse p205 CR Scot180
BEECH,Leonard 2Lt 11-12-20 2/5SStaffs CR Staffs60
BEECH,Norman William.DCM.2Lt kia 9-10-17 5WYorks p218 MR30
BEECH,Robert Clyde Capt kia 18-10-16 1RB p177 MR21
BEECH,Rowland Auriol James Lt kia 21-2-15 16Lancers p23 CR Belgium57
BEECH,Rowland John LtCol ded 30-8-19 WarYeo p269 CR Staff93
BEECHENO,James Herbert T2Lt dow 25-10-18 KRRC att13Bn p149 CR France332
BEECHER,Frank Alfred 2lt dow 16-9-16 6Lond p246 CR France188
BEECHEY,Frank Collett Reeves T2Lt dow 14-11-16 13EYorks p83 CR France120,Reeve
BEECHING,Geoffrey Charles Lt kia 12-9-18 12Lond p248 MR16
BEECROFT,William Henry 2Lt kia 22-7-18 6Glouc p225 CR France5
BEEDLE,Frank Symons Bussel.MC.2Lt kia 11-4-18 4 att7GordH p242 MR19
BEEMAN,Arthur Cecil Capt kia 26-10-14 1RWKent p140 MR22
BEEMAN,John Neville.MC.Lt kia 29-9-18 Mddx att1Bn p146 CR France407
BEER,Arthur Henry.MC.Lt dow 21-4-18 275RFA p207 CR France88
BEER,Edward Albert 2Lt kia 22-9-17 RGA 298SB p38 CR Belgium124
BEER,Harold Herbert T2Lt kia 23-4-17 14 att11Manch p154 MR20
BEER,Henry Oliver T2Lt kia 26-9-15 8RWKent p140 MR19
BEER,John Henry MajTLtCol kia 19-7-16 8RWar p214 MR32 &CRFrance1887,2/4Berks
BEER,Lewis Charles 2Lt kia 28-3-18 5DCLI p227 MR27
BEER,Robert Alexander T2Lt kia 5-10-17 12Glouc p106 MR30,4-10-17
BEER,Robert Gerald 2Lt kia 30-11-17 4 att6EKent p212 MR17
BEER,William John T2Lt kia 21-2-18 14RFC p15 CR Palestine3
BEERBOHM,Clarence Evelyn LtAMaj kia 26-9-17 12Lancers att162RFA p22 CR Belgium19
BEESLEY,Edwin.MC.T2LtACapt kia 27-9-18 1Lpool p71 CR France1483
BEESON,Ralph 2Lt drd 15-2-18 IARO 1S&M p273 MR66
BEESTON,Harold Lewis Lt ded 24-10-18 5RWKent p269 CR Kent95
BEETON,Arthur Charles Lt kia 23-8-15 1/6Ess p232 MR4
BEETON,Robert Henry T2Lt kld 1-2-18 RFC p15 CR Norf111
BEEVER,Jonathan Holt Lt kia 25-3-18 17RFA p25 MR27
BEEVER,William Henry Capt kia 1-7-16 1RB p177 MR21
BEEVOR,Felix Victor 2Lt kia 1-7-16 att51Mddx p146 MR19
BEEVOR,Vernon Saville.MC T2Lt kia 10-3-17 14 att10Ess p131 CR France239,Savile
BEGARD,Michael T2Lt kia 22-3-18 TankCps p188 MR27
BEGBIE,Alfred Vincent T2Lt dow 11-4-17 6CamH p167 MR20
BEGBIE,Sydney Claude Hamilton Lt ded 22-4-18 3ESurr attRAF p112 CR France1027,kia
BEGG,Arthur 2LtACapt ded 21-3-18 4Norf att2/5Lincs p216
BEGG,Alexander James.MC.TLt dow 10-7-16 17HLI p162 CR France51
BEGG,Alexander James Bartlett.MC.TLt kia 21-3-18 22NumbF p60 MR20,Bartlet
BEGG,Andrew Currie LtTCapt&Adjt kia 30-7-16 1/7BlkW p231 CR France1890
BEGG,Henry Capt kia 14-11-16 RAMC 2/1Highland FA p253 CR France3
BEGG,Henry Berners 2Lt kia 23-11-16 24RFC p2 MR20
BEGG,John Henderson Capt kia 23-7-16 8GordH p166
BEGG,Patrick Hunter Capt MurderedByHisBearer 24-8-21 IA 2/96Inf p273 CR Iraq8

BEGG,Robert Henderson Capt kia 24-12-15 RGA attStaff 6Div HQ p38 CR Iraq1,RA
BEGG,William 2Lt kia 13-11-16 5BlkW p231 CR France221
BEGG,William Pollock TCapt kia 9-4-18 RGA 157SB p38 MR32
BEGGS,Henry Parker Lt kia 1-7-16 8RIrRif p168 MR21,Capt
BEGGS,James T2Lt kia 9-4-18 21Mddx p146 MR32
BEHRENS,Robert Philip Lt dow 26-4-15 2SWBord p99 MR4,25-4-15
BEHRENS,Walter Louis 2Lt kia 9-7-17 C122RFA p208 CR Belgium23,10-7-17
BEILBY,Julius Henry Capt kia 23-4-16 RAMC p253 MR34
BEIT,Rupert Owen ACapt dow 29-7-17 RE p209 CR Belgium15,28-7-17 9ArmyTrpCoy
BEIT,Theodore Hamilton 2Lt ded 26-1-17 1Drags p21 CR Herts60
-BELAS,George Henry TCapt kia 3-6-17 RFA 4DAC p25 CR France96
BELAS,Reginald Charles William T2Lt kia 21-3-18 8RDubF p176 CR France212
BELCHAMBER,Ernest Henry T2Lt kia 23-4-17 7BordR p116 MR20
BELCHEM,Howard Matthew 2Lt dow 19-3-15 1/5NumbF p60 CR Belgium59,Lt kia
BELCHER,Austin Charles Sandham Capt&Adjt kia 10-8-15 5Wilts p152 MR4,Austen
BELCHER,Basil Henry 2Lt kia 1-7-16 2RBerks p138 CR France1890
BELCHER,Francis Terence Julian Lt kia 4-2-17 25Lond att1/6War p252 CR France1472
BELCHER,Frederick Percy TCaptAMaj dow 5-8-18 C92RFA p25 CR France34
BELCHER,Gordon.MC.Capt kia 15/17-5-15 3 att2RBerks p138&258 CR France632
BELCHER,Harold Thomas.DSO.LtCol ded 8-7-17 52RFA p25 CR Belgium29
BELCHER,Humphrey Gilbert TLt dow 7-8-15 5Wilts p152 MR4
BELCHER,Raymond Douglas.MC.DSO.TCaptAMaj dow 7-12-17 C63RFA p25 CR France13
BELCHER,Robert Henry Chap4Cl ded 25-10-16 25Lond CR Sussex185
BELCHER,Wilfrid Frank Lt dow 17-12-17 2/5NStaffs p237 CR France398
BELCHIER,Frank Elliot.MC.Capt kia 20-5-15 1ELancs p110 CR Belgium96
BELDING,Clare 2Lt kia 11-3-15 1Nhampt p137 MR22
BELEMORE,R.A.see BELLEMORE,R.A.
BELFIELD,Eric Capt mbk 31-7-17 4Mddx p256 MR29
BELFIELD,James Steward EngLt ded 21-4-19 RIM p273
BELFORD,Charles Roberts 2Lt kia 2-9-18 9BlkW p128 CR France1723
BELGRAVE,James Dacre.MC&Bar.Capt kia 13-6-18 1/2 2 O&BLI att60RAF p129 CR France105,Dacres
BELK,Charles Maj ded 16-12-17 RDC p253 CR Devon207
BELL,Adam Dickson Maj d 8-4-18 4Huss p21
BELL,Albert T2Lt kia 27-3-18 att118ELancs p110 MR20
BELL,Alexander 2Lt ded 27-2-19 1A&SH p266 CR Yorks2,27-1-19
BELL,Alexander Murray MacGregor Capt dow 28-4-15 RScotF p94 CR Lond8
BELL,Alfred Gordon.MC 2Lt dow 18-4-17 10DLI SR p160 CR France40
BELL,Alfred Herbert Capt kia 25-9-15 11RScots p53 MR19
BELL,Alfred Joseph TLt kia 13-5-17 2SStaffs p122 MR20
BELL,Alfred Roy Lancaster 2Lt dow 17-5-15 5RDubF p176
BELL,Arthur McLean TLt kia 20-5-18 BlkW att1GordH p128 CR France33
BELL,Arthur Walton 2Lt kia 28-3-18 1/9DLI p239 MR20
BELL,Aveling Francis T2Lt kia 12-8-15 4SWBord p99 MR4
BELL,Cecil Charles 2Lt kia 28-11-17 16LancF p92 CR Belgium63
BELL,Charles Henry.MC.Chap4Cl kia 23-8-18 RAChDept att1RBerks p199 CR France927
BELL,Charles Ockley 2Lt kia 12-10-14 Beds p85 MR29
BELL,Clifford Thiselton Capt ded 2-2-19 RAMC p253 CR Scot280
BELL,Colin T2Lt kia 29-10-17 N&D att15Bn p133 MR30,30-10-17
BELL,Cuthbert Patrick TLt dow 23-2-18 9Dev p76 CR Italy7
BELL,David 2Lt kia 6-10-18 13BlkW p205 MR16,7-10-18
BELL,Donald Simpson.VC.T2Lt kia 10-7-16 9Yorks p89 CR France267
BELL,Edward Augustine T/HonCapt drd 11-7-16 RAMC att5BRCHosp p194 CR France64
BELL,Edward Inkerman Jordan.MC&Bar.Capt kia 24-3-18 GL 17Mddx att Staff 99Inf Bde p189&258 CR France430
BELL,Edward Nevinson Lt ded 16-2-18 IARO att1/70BurmaRif p273 MR66

BELL,Edward William 2Lt TLt kia 8-12-17 209MGC p181 CR Palestine3
BELL,Elvis Albert T2Lt kia 22-9-17 GL &22RFC p5 CR Belgium17
BELL,Eric Norman Frankland.VC.TCapt kia 1-7-16 GL 9InniskF att109LightTMB p189 MR21
BELL,Eric Victor T2Lt dow 14-8-15 11Manch p154 MR4
BELL,Francis de Beauvoir Maj dow 24-4-15 2Norf p73 CR Iraq6
BELL,Francis Richard Lowry T2Lt kia 22-2-16 10 att2BordR p116 CR France189
BELL,Gawain Murdoch.DSO.Maj kia 31-7-17 11Hamps p120 CR Belgium6
BELL,George Henry LtCol ded 3-9-16 IA 9BhopalInf p273 MR67,27Punjabis
BELL,George Russell.MC.2Lt dow 4-12-18 C124RFA p25 CR France146
BELL,G.F Capt&QM 11-6-20 RASC CR Cornwall40
BELL,Guy Bayford Lt kia 28-4-17 5LancF att35MGC Inf p186&221 MR20
BELL,Harold 2Lt kia 13-11-16 13EYorks p83 CR France1890
BELL,Harold Stormont 2Lt mbk 2-12-17 att2/8Worc p256 MR17,dow
BELL,Henry 2Lt dow 17-10-17 8Yorks p89 see BELL,T.H.A.
BELL,Henry Capt dow 25-1-17 5BordR p228 CR France177
BELL,Henry Hogarth TCapt kia 5-9-16 4NumbF p213 CR France432,15-9-16
BELL,Henry Oswin.VD.TMaj ded 30-11-18 RASC p192 CR Yorks38
BELL,Hugh Randolph Ryan Lt dow 29-8-17 8Worc p226
BELL,Hugh Reginald.MID TCapt&Maj kia 3-9-18 11TankCps p188 CR France924
BELL,Jack Whateley TLt TCapt kia 26-3-17 1 att4Ess p131 CR Palestine8,Whately
BELL,James T2Lt kia 11-1-17 11RScots p53 CR France1182
BELL,James T2Lt kia 22-4-18 19DLI p160 CR France296
BELL,James Clifford Aveling Lt dow 30-5-18 175RFA p25 MR27,kld
BELL,James Donald Allen 2Lt kia 21/23-3-18 6LancF p221 CR France1494,21-3-18
BELL,James Ernest Kirkham TLt dow 5-8-16 8BordR p116 MR21
BELL,James Rogerson 2Lt dow 1-4-18 10RScots p212 CR France40
BELL,James William.MC.TCapt kia 7-11-18 21Manch p154 CR France951
BELL,John Capt dow 27-12-17 68RFC p5
BELL,John T2Lt kia 27-5-18 BordR att8Bn p116 MR18
BELL,John Cunningham TLt ded 22-11-15 RAMC att7RScots p194 CR Egypt3
BELL,John Dobree Lt ded 30-10-18 RFA 19CpsHQ attIntell p25 CR France34
BELL,John James Maj ded 2-3-15 AyrYeo p203 CR Scot547
BELL,John Mercer Grimshaw Lt dow 11-10-18 RFA att7RAF p25 CR France34
BELL,John Murray TCapt kia 27-9-15 9BlkW p128 CR France219,25-9-15
BELL,John Murray T2Lt kia 24-4-17 10HLI p162 MR20
BELL,John Scott 2Lt kia 1-8-17 RE 15FC p43 CR Belgium112
BELL,John Wilson 2Lt ded 18-2-17 RE p210 CRScot235
BELL,Joseph 2Lt kia 17-4-17 5WYorks p218 MR19
BELL,Kenneth Frederick Hamilton 2Lt kia 25-9-15 1Lond p245 MR32
BELL,Lee T2Lt kia 17-10-18 7RDubF p176 CR France716
BELL,Leonard TLt dow 22-5-18 3RB p177 CR France81
BELL,Leslie Harrison 2Lt ded 26-9-18 10Glouc att58RAF p106 CR France134,kld
BELL,Malcolm Arthur Russell Capt kia 20-12-14 IA 54Sikhs p273 CR France727
BELL,Norman 2Lt kia 18-8-17 10Ches att57RFC p5&95 CR Belgium140
BELL,Norman Henderson 2Lt kia 1-7-16 3 att1Hamps p120 MR21
BELL,Philip Lawrence Lt kia 10-8-15 10Hamps p120 MR4
BELL,Quentin David 2Lt kia 31-10-15 2GordH p166 MR29,31-10-14
BELL,Richard Logsdaile.MC.2Lt kia 9-4-18 1 att2/5Hamps p120 CR Palestine9
BELL,Robert de Houghan Mark.MID TLt kia 3-9-16 10KRRC p149 CR France39,Hougham
BELL,Robert James 2Lt kia 2-11-18 3 att1/4Nhampt p137 CR Palestine8,2-11-17
BELL,Robert Norman 2Lt kia 14-4-17 9DLI p239 CR France420
BELL,Robert Stephen T2Lt dow 17-4-18 10Ches p95 CR France40
BELL,Robert William Popham Capt kia 5-7-16 3 att2RIrReg p88 MR21
BELL,Samuel Edward.MC.TLt ACapt dow 19-11-16 7SLancs p125 CR France40
BELL,Sydney James 2Lt dow 13-10-16 7Lpool p215 CR Lancs381
BELL,Sydney Parker Capt kia 26-9-15D106 RFA p25 MR19
BELL,Thomas 2Lt kia 26-5-18 5RScotF p222 CR France268
BELL,Thomas Ernest 2Lt dow 1-4-18 5BordR p228 CR France145
BELL,Thomas Hector T2Lt kia 9-2-16 11 att9BlkW p128 CR France423
BELL,Tomas Henry Andrew 2Lt 17-10-17 8Yorks CR France145
BELL,Thomas Henry Stanley Capt kia 1-10-15 RAMC 36FA SR p194 CR France423,2-10-15
BELL,Walter Albert 2Lt kia 13-4-18 1DCLI p114 MR32
BELL,Walter Ernest 2Lt kia 25-4-18 8LancF p221 MR30 Ex19Bn
BELL,Walter Stanley 2Lt kia 16-4-18 12/13NumbF p60 MR30
BELL,William 2Lt dow 3-7-16 18DLI p160 CR France167
BELL,William Lt kia 10-4-17 7A&SH p243 MR20
BELL,William T2Lt dow 26-7-16 RE 252FC p43 CR France5
BELL,William 2Lt kia 3-5-17 5 att8BlkW p231 MR20
BELL,William Arundel T2Lt kia 14-6-17 BordR att8Bn p116 CR Belgium168
BELL,William Henry Dillon TCapt kia 31-7-17 1KEdwHorse p24 MR29
BELL,William James Knox.MC.2Lt kia 5-4-18 RGA 9SB p38 CR France5
BELL,William Robert T2Lt kia 12-10-17 11NumbF p60 MR30
BELL,Wilson Capt kia 5-3-17 2/4YLI p235 MR21,15-3-17
BELL-BATHURST,Basil Woodd Bambridge Capt AMaj dow 23-4-17 RHA p206 CR France512
BELL-HUGHES,John Otto T2Lt kia 28-9-17 Mddx att2/5LancF p146 MR30,20-9-17
BELL-IRVING,William 2Lt kld 28-10-15 10RScots attRFC p17&212 CR Scot617,Lt 27-10-15
BELL-IRVING,Kenneth Capt dow 22-10-17 8ESurr p112 CR Belgium16
BELL-IRVING,William Ogle.MC.Capt kia 29-11-17 11Huss p22 CR Palestine9
BELLAMY,Alfred Wraith 2Lt dow 22-10-17 Manch att23Bn p154 MR30
BELLAMY,Charles Henry TCapt dow 23-7-16 10Lincs p74 France145
BELLAMY,David Humphrey TLt ACapt kia 2-4-17 10 att9Dev p76 CRFrance568
BELLAMY,Frank William 2Lt dow 8-10-18 6 att4Beds p85 CR France914
BELLAMY,Geoffrey George Capt dow 1-9-18 7Dev att4MGC p156&217 CR France14,Maj
BELLAMY,Harold Edward Lt kld 28-7-18 19Mddx &RAF CR Ches158
BELLAMY,Howard Claxson.MID TLt kia 2-1-17 11RScots p53 CR France1182,3-1-17
BELLAMY,James Thomas Reynell 2Lt ded 14-11-18 RE 272RlyCoy p43 CR Syria2
BELLAMY,John Holland T2Lt dow 4-10-16 13 att11N&D p133 CR France177
BELLAMY,John James 2Lt kia 24-4-17 B116RFA p25 MR37
BELLAMY,Osmund Lt kia 21-3-18 315RFA p207 MR27
BELLAMY,Thomas Bilbous T2Lt dow 13-5-17 6RLancs p58 CR Iraq8,Billows
BELLASIS,Philip Joseph TCapt kia 24-8-16 5KSLI p144 MR21
BELLEMORE,Raymond Alfred Capt dow 8-6-17 4ConnRgrs p172 CR France285,BELEMORE
BELLEW,Alexander 2Lt kia 23-10-16 2ScotRif p103 MR21
BELLEW,Richard Courtenay 2Lt dow 21-8-17 2IrGds p52 CR Belgium16
BELLINGHAM,Alan 2Lt kia 26-10-17 4LNLancs p234 MR30
BELLINGHAM,Robert Charles Noel.MID Capt ded 4-3-15 RFA p25 CR Belgium80 &CR Belgium187
BELLIS,Cecil Magnus 2Lt dow 9-7-16 3 att13Ches p95 CR France23,3Bn
BELLOC,Louis 2Lt kia 26-8-18 RE &209RAF p254&257 MR20
BELLOT,Byson Lt ded 27-3-18 1/1NSomYeo p205 CRFrance52,Bryson
BELLWOOD,Frank TCapt kia 14-7-16 8Dev p76 CR France513
BELSCHNER,William Frederick T2Lt kia 8-10-18 25MGC Inf p181 CR France844
BEMAND,George Edward Kingsley T2Lt kia 26-12-16 RFA attY5TMB p25 CR France727
BEMROSE,Karl 2Lt kia 1-7-16 1/5N&D p232 MR21
BEMROSE,Roderick Henry.MC.Lt ded 7-11-18 C285RFA p207 CR France34
BENBOW,Edwin Louis.MC.Capt kld 3-5-18 RFA att85RAF p25 CR Belgium20,kia 30-5-18
BENBOW,Sidney T2Lt kia 29-9-18 10 att2Worc p108 CR France665
BENBOW,Walter Harold.MM.T2Lt kia 23-8-18 7KSLI p144
BENCE-TROWER,Alfred 2Lt kia 29-5-18 1ScotsGds CR France1014
BENCE-TROWER,Edward.MC.Maj dow 30-5-18 5SWBord p99 MR18
BENCH,James George 2Lt kia 24-4-17 10Hamps p120 MR37
BENCHER,Gilbert Alfred Lt dow 9-12-17 2/19Lond p250 CR Palestine3
BENDER,Alfred Courteney TLt kia 20-9-17 15Hamps p120 MR30
BENDING,Edward Owen 2Lt ded 24-1-19 KRRC CR Somerset40,Lt

BENEDICT,Albert Edward Julius Wilbraham Scott DSO Lt ded 16-12-15 RBucksYeo p269 CR Norf151
BENETT,Rita Mary Miss ded 3-11-18 VAD p268
BENETT-DAMPIER,J.T. see BENNETT-DAMPIER,J T
BENFORD,Charles George T2Lt kld 5-1-18 7DCLI p114 CR Belgium127
BENGER,Alfred Horace TMaj dow 17-4-17 11Leic p87 CR France223
BENGOUGH,Charles William 2Lt kia 21-3-18 RGA 277SB p38 CR France381
BENGOUGH,John Crosbie.MID TCapt kia 26-2-16 GloucYeo attDorsYeo p203 CR Egypt6
BENGOUGH,L.MC.Maj 7-2-21 Ches CR Germany1
BENHAM,Charles Henry TMaj ded 8-11-16 RAMC p253 CR Europe1
BENHAM,Frank Benham Capt dow 23-8-16 C81RFA p25 CR Staffs134
BENHAM,John Russell 2Lt dow 4-5-15 100RFA p25 CR France285
BENHAM,Malcolm Erick 2Lt kia 29-9-15 3Mddx p146 MR19,Erik
BENHAM,Ralph George T2Lt kia 11-9-18 6SomLI p79 CR France258
BENHAM,Walter Edward 2Lt ded 3-11-18 A245RFA p25 CR France146
BENINGFIELD,John Philip 2Lt dow 27-4-15 59RFA p25 CR Belgium35,Lt
BENINGFIELD,Maurice Victor 2Lt kia 10-3-15 1Worc p108 MR22
BENISON,Eric William 2Lt ded 13-8-15 RGA p209 CR Dorset/Cl135
BENISON,Robert Burton 2Lt kia 20-9-14 2ConnRgrs p172 CR France1329
BENJAMIN,Herbert Seymour Capt kia 9-10-17 1/8Worc p226 CR Belgium126
BENJAMIN,John Alfred TCapt kia 5-7-16 9WRid p115 CR France267
BENN,Alfred Maurice Lt kia 27-9-16 9WYorks p80 MR21
BENN,Bertie William T2Lt kia 19-7-16 8Norf p73 MR21
BENN,Joseph Reginald Tankard TCapt kia 2-9-15 RFA 11WRidHB p207 CR Belgium85,1-9-15
BENN,Oliver Williams Capt kia 6-6-15 9SomLI att1Ess p79 MR4
BENN,Walter Horace T2Lt kia 2-8-17 7Norf p73 CR France154
BENNALLACK,William Frederick 2Lt kia 17-10-18 RE 446FC p210 CR France1386
BENNELL,Donald Bruce Lt kia 16-4-17 315RFA p25 CR France265
BENNER,Walter TLt kia 2-9-18 16N&D att101TMB p133 MR30
BENNET,C.H. see BENNETT,C H.
BENNET,G.Lt 21-11-20 SL &RASC CR Lond9
BENNET,Helena Stewart SNurse ded 18-10-18 QAIMNS p200 CR Scot381
BENNET,James Hampton.MC.2Lt kia 22-9-16 4 att2RMunstF p175 MR21
BENNET,Trevor Moutray.MC.TLt kia 10-11-16 10RIrRif &RFC p169 see BENNETT,T M
BENNETT,Albert Henry 2Lt dow 6-11-16 6N&D p233 CR France134,6Leic
BENNETT,Alfred Charles DSO LtCol ded 16-1-15 WYorks p80 CR Essex268
BENNETT,Alfred John 2Lt kia 9-8-17 2Ess p131 MR20
BENNETT,Arnold John MC Chap4Cl ded 26-1-18 RAChDept attRAMC 230FA p199 CR Egypt2
BENNETT,Arthur Hugh T2Lt kia 18-8-16 6DCLI p114 MR21
BENNETT,Arthur Shirley TLt kia 14-7-16 9Leic p87 MR21
BENNETT,C.W.Lt ded 13-10-18 DCLI attRGA CR Italy19 see BENNETT,V C W
BENNETT,Charles Henry MC Lt drd 27-5-18 BucksYeo p203 MR41
BENNETT,Charles Hosken Lt died 25-2-19 RFA p261 BENNET
BENNETT,Charles Tudor MID Capt kia 22-7-16 3 att1RWKent p140 MR21
BENNETT,Claude Denman Capt dow 18-7-16 2/6WRid p227 CR France518
BENNETT,E.Lt 12-8-17 N&D CR Lond10
BENNETT,Edwin Herman T2Lt kia 5-5-18 29MGC p181 CR France24
BENNETT,Eric Fairfax MC TLt,ACapt kia 18-9-18 7RWSurr p55 CR France365
BENNETT,Ernest TLt ded 12-8-17 8LNLancs p135 MR29
BENNETT,Ernest Edward Sebastian Maj ded 26-3-19 IA 66Punjabis p273 CR India48
BENNETT,Francis Evans T2Lt kia 8-8-15 7RMunstF p175 MR4
BENNETT,Frank Dann Capt kia 21-3-18 5NStaffs p237 MR20,Dunn
BENNETT,Frederick Barberry Maj dow 22-10-18 C84RFA p206 CR France329
BENNETT,Frederick Martin 2Lt kia 10-9-18 20 att2/2Lond p251 MR16
BENNETT,Geoffrey Ernest Layton T2Lt kia 1-7-16 2Yorks p89
BENNETT,George Arthur T2Lt kia 3-12-17 RWar att2/6Bn p64 MR17
BENNETT,George Robert 2Lt kia 21-8-15 5ConnRgrs p172 MR4

BENNETT,George William 2Lt kia 3-12-17 W'land&C'landYeo p206 CR Palestine3
BENNETT,George William MC TLt,ACapt ded 29-11-18 Y&L att5Bn p158&258 CR Greece2,1Bn
BENNETT,Harold Capt mbk 14-11-14 IA 2/3GurkhaRif MR28
BENNETT,Harold Percy Lt kia 21-3-18 2Lond p245 CR france1893
BENNETT,Harold Presdee T2Lt kia 15-11-16 10LNLancs p135 MR21
BENNETT,Harold Stanley 2Lt kld 25-4-15 RGA p38 CR Glouc159
BENNETT,Henry Richard Lt ded 4-1-18 RHA 3CavDiv p25 CR France446
BENNETT,Henry Ryan TCapt kia 23-3-18 11Lpool p71 MR27
BENNETT,Herbert T2Lt kia 22-4-18 16RWelshF p97 MR27
BENNETT,Herbert Sydney TLt dow 18-10-18 1 att9SWBord p99 CR France1266
BENNETT,Ivan Provis Wentworth TCapt kia 14-7-16 7RWSurr p55 MR21 CR France1891,13-7-16
BENNETT,J.A 2Lt 5-2-20 RB CR War9
BENNETT,James T2Lt kia 28-11-16 RE 129FC p43 CR France149
BENNETT,John Alick T2Lt kia 22-8-18 9Ess p131 CR France370
BENNETT,John Benson T2Lt kia 28-3-18 3RB p177 MR27
BENNETT,John Blake T2Lt kia 21-3-18 GL &1Aircraft Supply Depot RFC p15 CR France102
BENNETT,John Edgar Capt kia 3-9-16 1 att2RIrReg p88 MR21
BENNETT,John Edwin Francis Theodore MM.2Lt kia 24-7-16 8RWar att143MGC p186&215 CR France150
BENNETT,John Francis 2Lt kia 26-8-18 9Hamps p229 CR France614
BENNETT,John Nicoll 2Lt kia 19-5-17 RGA 121SB p38 CR France729
BENNETT,John William Lt kia 13-10-15 3RMunstF p175 CR France219
BENNETT,Lawrence Ernest T2Lt kia 24-8-16 9 att1RWSurr p55 MR21
BENNETT,Leslie Punsfer 2Lt dow 16-2-17 4RWSurr p212 CR France164
BENNETT,Maurice Porter 2Lt dow 6-10-17 2RWSurr p55 CR France139
BENNETT,Philip Dennis Capt ded 24-2-19 5RWar p269 CR War102
BENNETT,Ralph T2Lt kia 4-9-18 10Worc att1Hereford p108 MR30
BENNETT,Reginald 2Lt kia 3-9-16 13Glouc p106 MR21
BENNETT,Reginald George 2Lt kia 26-10-17 5RLancs p213 MR30
BENNETT,Robert Davis T2Lt kia 7-12-17 GL 1ArmySupplyDepot RFC p5 CRFrance31
BENNETT,Robert Granville T2Lt kia 4-10-17 YLI att9Bn p142 MR30
BENNETT,Robertis Charles Rudolph Busby.MC.Lt kia 24-8-18 20Lond p251 MR16,Robertio
BENNETT,Sydney Garnet 2Lt kia 20-7-16 2Suff p78 MR21
BENNETT,Theodore John Lt kia 7-9-18 1/5Worc att17IndInf p273&108 MR52 CR Palestine3
BENNETT,Trevor Mountray.MC.TLt kia 10-11-16 RFC &10RIrRif p2 CR France530
BENNETT,Vere Raymond Lt kia 10-4-17 3N&D att64MGC Inf p133&181 CR France591
BENNETT,Victor Cyril Wentworth Lt ded 13-10-18 DCLI attRGAp114 CR Italy19,C.W.
BENNETT,Vivian Wilfred Lt kia 21-10-17 RE 209FC p43 CR Belgium23,208FC
BENNETT,Walter James T2Lt kia 4-7-16 14 att12RScots p53 CR France399
BENNETT,William Frank T2Lt kia 23-4-17 1Lpool p71 MR20
BENNETT,William Harns Capt ded 16-1-20 Mddx attHQ RAF MR53
BENNETT,William Henry 2Lt kia 11-4-17 8N&D p233 CR France616
BENNETT,William Henry Pope MC TLt,ACapt kia 3-3-18 13RSuss p118 MR21
BENNETT,William Munro Lt dow 18-6-16 8A&SH p243 CR France15
BENNETT,William Pyt Maj kia 15-7-16 RGA att162RFA p38 CR France188
BENNETT,Wilmer Annie Miss ded 21-11-18 VAD CR Surrey156
BENNETT-DAMPIER,John Tudor 2Lt kia 2-3-15 2Ches attN&D p95 CR Belgium89,BENETT
BENNETT-GOLDNEY,Francis TCapt,AMaj ded 26-7-18 SL & Staff p201 CR France477
BENNIE,Andrew T2Lt kia 30-9-18 17RScots p53 CR Belgium116
BENNIE,Hugh Osbourne Lt kia 31-7-17 5HLI attMGC p186&240 MR29
BENNIE,Robert Smith 2Lt kld 5-6-17 SR 45RFC p5 MR20
BENNIE,William Lt ded 10-10-17 RDC p269 CR Scot212
BENNIE,William Robertson 2Lt kia 2-12-17 7 att16HLI p240 MR30

BENNING,Murray Stuart Lt dow 1-11-14 3ESurr p112 CR France102

BENNISON,Miles 2Lt kia 1-10-17 9Yorks p89 MR30

BENNITT,Harry Pynson Capt dow 7-10-15 7SfthH p164 CR France40

BENNS,Arthur Lionel 2Lt kia 1-7-16 1/5Lond p246 MR21

BENSON,Alfred Hugh Maj ded 24-9-16 RAMC CR Yorks192

BENSON,Cyril Samuel T2Lt kia 24-4-17 6 O&BLI p129 CR France904

BENSON,Eric William TLtCol kia 15-9-16 9KRRC p149 MR21

BENSON,Frederick William.Sir.KCB.MajGen ded 19-8-16 RoO RemountSer p1 CR Canada1531,21Lancers

BENSON,George Agar Trevor.MC.2Lt kia 28-10-16 1Mddx p146 MR21

BENSON,Henry Lawrence.MID 2Lt kia 11-4-16 6NumbF p214 CR Belgium17,Laurence

BENSON,Hugh Cecil Lt kia 22-6-15 9RB p177 MR29

BENSON,Isaac TLtACapt kia 2-12-17 11BordR p116 MR30

BENSON,John Martin ACapt kia 27-5-18 4NumbF att149TMB p213 MR18

BENSON,John Peurice Capt kia 23-8-14 1ESurr p112 CR Belgium201

BENSON,Richard Erle LtCol dow 27-9-14 1EYorks p83 CR Wales54

BENSON,Thomas Brooke Lt kia 13-3-15 2RScotF p94 MR22

BENSON,Thomas Washington 2Lt kia 22-8-17 4RScots p211 CR Belgium92

BENSON,William Arthur 2Lt kia 21-3-18 6LancF p221 MR27

BENSON,William Roy Gwyn 2Lt kia 2-7-16 2SStaffs p122 CR France924

BENSTEAD,Harry Edwin 2Lt kia 14-4-17 7 att5Lond p247 CR France162

BENT,Percy Temple 2Lt kia 1-7-16 1KOSB p101 MR21,12Bn

BENT,Philip Eric.VC.DSO.TLtCol kia 1-10-17 9Leic p87 MR30

BENTALL,Ernest Hammond 2Lt kia 3-10-15 1KRRC p149 CR France423

BENTALL,William Douglas 2Lt kia 16-9-16 3 att6YLI p142 MR21

BENTHAM,George Andrew 2Lt kia 3-11-16 7ESurr &RFC p2&112,ded MR20

BENTHAM,Harley T2Lt dow 16-9-18 9WRid p115 CR France1184

BENTHAM,Richard Capt kld 8-11-16 7Manch attRFC p17&237 CR Lancs216

BENTHAM,Thomas TLt ded 12-3-19 SL RAMC p268 CR Surrey15

BENTINCK,Henry Duncan BtMaj dow 2-10-16 2CldGds p50 CR France145

BENTLEY,Arthur Fletcher 2Lt dow 11-3-16 13 att10N&D p133 CR France40

BENTLEY,Arthur Webb Butler 2Lt ded 2-12-18 3Yorks p89 CR Somerset157

BENTLEY,Basil T2Lt kia 11-9-17 2/5Y&L p158 CR France563

BENTLEY,Charles Arthur Campbell Capt kia 23-10-14 1RWar p64 CR France922

BENTLEY,Clarence Leslie 2Lt kia 28-10-14 2Manch p154 MR22

BENTLEY,Claud Louis 2Lt kld 23-12-16 15HLI p162

BENTLEY,Frank Mercer.MC.Capt kia 13-10-18 1/5LancF p221 CR France1266

BENTLEY,Frederick Donald.DCM.2Lt kia 30-11-17 GrenGds att1GdsMGC p49 CR FRance415

BENTLEY,Freeland Martell Lt kia 18-6-15 3 att2GordH p166 MR22

BENTLEY,Geoffrey Malcolm Capt dow 29-10-14 1Nhampt p137 CR Belgium57

BENTLEY,George Greenwood Lt dow 17-9-16 GL 13War att32RFC p2&189 CR France167,2Lt

BENTLEY,George Warwick T2Lt ded 13-1-17 GL RFus &3RFC p5 CR France927

BENTLEY,Gerald Wilson Capt kia 12-10-14 4Mddx p146 CR France1106

BENTLEY,Harry 2Lt drd 10-10-18 NumbF p60 MR40

BENTLEY,Howard Lidyard T2Lt kia 28-2-17 2RFus p66 MR21

BENTLEY,Joseph Elgey 2Lt kia 11-10-18 4WRid p227 CR France612

BENTLEY,Leonard Holt T2Lt ded 30-5-18 RASC p192 MR40

BENTLEY,Tom Capt dow 4-5-17 2/5WRid p227 CR France518

BENTLEY,Tom 2Lt dow 31-7-18 5YLI p235 CR France1358

BENTON,Frank T2Lt kia 15/17-9-16 15 att21KRRC p149 MR21,15-9-16

BENTON,John Walford 2Lt kia 28-9-16 19 att11N&D p133 MR21

BENTON,Ronald Mackenzie 2Lt kia 7-6-16 DLI att1AUL 53Sikhs p160&273 CR Iraq5

BENTON,Sydney T2Lt kia 27-10-17 1Norf p73 MR30

BENTON,William Manstead TCapt dow 17-8-16 12Manch p154 CR France833

BENZECRY,Solomon Lt kia 30-11-17 10Lond att17RFus p248 MR17

BENZIE,William Gardner 2Lt dow 10-4-17 8ScotRif p225 CR France113,9-4-17

BERESFORD,Charles Zaragoza de La Poer Lt kia 9-5-15 Nhampt p137 MR32

BERESFORD,Harold.MC.Lt dow 24-5-18 RFA p207 CR France180

BERESFORD,Percy William.DSO.MIDx2 LtCol dow 26-10-17 2/3Lond p245 CR Belgium36

BERESFORD,Rebecca Rose SNurse drd 26-2-18 QAIMNS p200 MR40

BERESFORD,Spencer Charles T2Lt kia 5-6-18 1RBerks p138 CR France120

BERESFORD,William TLt ded 30-3-17 RE IWT p43 CR Kent7

BERESFORD,William Maj ded 9-10-17 RDC p269 CR Somerset197

BERESFORD-POER,Hubert Piers.MID Maj kia 24-4-18 A91RFA CR France889

BEREY,Charles Eric Capt ded 10-12-19 IARO 9GurkhaRif attPoliticalDept p273 CR Iraq8

BERKELEY,Alfred Fitzhardinge Murray T2Lt kia 7-6-17 74MGC p181 CR Belgium43

BERKELEY,Christopher Lt kld 30-1-19 2CldGds &30TDS RAF p50 CR Mddx34,2Lt

BERKELEY,Maurice Henry Fitzhardinge Maj 1-1-18 RASC 27AmmPk CR Kent83

BERKELEY,Philip Charles Oswald TLtAMaj kia 29-9-18 123MGC Inf p181 CR France530

BERKELEY,Thomas Berkeley Hartman Lt ded 7-11-18 3Suff att7MGC p78&181 CR Italy9,Hardtman 9-11-18

BERKELEY,Thomas Mowbray Martin BtLtCol kia 20-5-16 BlkW CampCmdt 10Cps Staff DAQMG p1 CR France43

BERKLEY,John Humphrey Capt dow 8-4-16 10WYorks p80 CR France285

BERLAID,E.H.AssSurg 31-3-19 ISMD MR67

BERLEIN,Charles Maurice Lt kia 16-6-15 5 O&BLI p129 CR Belgium10

BERLEIN,Leslie Herman TLt kia 25-10-15 8RBerks p138 CR France219,Hermann

BERNARD,Arthur Basil LtACapt dow 4-5-17 PoW 5 att16KRRC p149 CR Germany1

BERNARD,Bernard Frederick Paul 2Lt kia 21-12-14 RWar p64 MR32

BERNARD,Frederick Joseph AssSurg2ndCl 22-10-14 ISMD CRFrance1841

BERNARD,George Robert.MC.T2Lt kia 8-4-17 RE 254Co p43 CR France80

BERNARD,Henry Claude T2Lt kia 3-9-16 7Glouc p106 MR21,att3Worc

BERNARD,Herbert Clifford Col kia 1-7-16 IARO att10RIrRif p265&273 CR France232

BERNARD,Lawrence Arthur Lt kia 20-9-14 2N&D p133 MR15 &CR France1893

BERNARD,Robert Lt kia 25-4-15 1RDubF p176 CR Gallipoli15,26-4-15

BERNERS,Hamilton Hughs Capt kia 14-9-14 1IrGds p52 CR France1112,Hugh

BERNEY,George Norman.MID Capt kia 6-11-17 1/1Hereford p252 CR Palestine1

BERNSTEIN,Maurice Leon.MC.T2Lt kia 10-4-18 11LancF p92 CR France1092

BERRIDGE,Jesse Dell.MC.TLt kia 24-5-18 RE JspecCo p43 CR France103

BERRIDGE,Victor Arnold T2Lt kia 6-3-17 Beds &34RFC p4&85 CR France424

BERRIDGE,William Alfred.MC.MM.2Lt ded 15-2-19 4Leic p269 CR Leic120,5Bn

BERIDGE,William Eric T2Lt dow 20-8-16 6SomLI p79 CR France833

BERRIE,Charlotte Sister ded 8-1-19 QAIMNS p200 CR Palestine3

BERRILL,Bernard Francis Gotch Lt kia 7-3-15 6RFus p66 MR29

BERRILL,Frank Gale Lt ded 28-9-18 57/43RFA p25 CR France113,dow

BERRIMAN,George WO ded 17-7-16 IA RIM p273

BERRINGTON,Caradoc Trevor Davies Capt kia 10-3-16 IA 15Lancers attC86RFA p273 CR France354

BERRY,Algernon Lawrence 2Lt kia 7-7-16 14 att8RFus p66 MR21

BERRY,Alexander James T2Lt kia 22-8-16 19 att20LancF p92 CR France630

BERRY,Andrew Reginald.CB.LtCol ded 24-3-17 2/9Lond p247 CR France120

BERRY,Bernard Lt kia 6-6-18 6Ches p222 CR France1689

BERRY,Claude Vincent Cameron 2Lt kia 27-7-17 112RFA p25 CR Belgium72

BERRY,David Douglas Anderson ACapt kia 26-9-17 2RScots p53 MR30

BERRY,Edward Fleetwood.MC.Capt kia 17-4-16 IA 2/9 att1/9GurkhaRif p273 MR38

BERRY,Edward James 2Lt kia 28-11-17 Manch att19Bn p154 CR Belgium112

BERRY,Eustace Carlton 2Lt kld 5-7-16 RFA attRFC p2&25 CR Numb4

BERRY,George Herbert 2Lt dow 9-10-17 D315RFA p25 CR Belgium11

BERRY,George Wilfred 2Lt kia 25-8-17 5DLI p239 CR France363,19Bn

BERRY,Harry T2Lt kia 1-11-18 WYorks p80 CR France1254

BERRY,James Frederick Williamson TLt ded 22-11-18 17 att1/5Lpool p71 CR France34,Wilkinson

BERRY,John Anthony T2Lt kia 25-9-15 2GordH p166 MR19

BERRY,John Granville.MC.2Lt mbk 16-8-17 2WYorks p256 MR30

BERRY,John Leslie TLt kia 4-7-18 13TankCps p188 CR France1170

BERRY,John Leslie 2Lt kia 12-10-18 7WRid p227 CR France718

BERRY,Oswald William 2Lt kia 8-4-17 9KOSB &48RFC p5&101 CR France924

BERRY,Percy Haycraft Lt drd 10-3-16 RAMC attBerksYeo p194 CR Egypt1

BERRY,Reginald 2Lt kia 30-5-16 4 att2SStaffs p122 CR France1896

BERRY,Reginald Douglas.MID TLt kia 12-5-17 12Y&L p158 CR France1191

BERRY,Samuel George TLt kia 22/23-3-18 7SomLI p79 CR France1061

BERRY,Tom Cecil Hayn Capt kia 30-8-18 5WelshR p230 CR France217,Haydn

BERRY,William T2Lt ded 4-7-17 56RASC DivTrain p192 CR Norf209

BERRY,William Herbert Stuart Lt kia 24-5-15 4RInniskF att2RIrReg p104 CR France285

BERRYMAN,John William T2Lt dow 27-11-17 15Yorks att2/4YLI p89 MR17

BERTHON,Leonard Tinne.MID TCapt kia 25-1-17 9RWar p64 CR Iraq5

BERTIE,Claude Peregrine Capt kia 19-3-17 6LondRFA att59RFC p17&207 CR France614

BERTIE,Ninian Mark Kerr 2Lt kia 8-5-15 KRRC p149 MR29,att4Bn

BERTIE,Richard Frederick Norreys Lt kia 20-11-17 BerksYeo p203 CR Palestine3

BERTINI,Umberto Michael Chap4Cl ded 30-9-18 RAChDept p268 CR Hamps144

BERTLIN,Hugh Anthony T2Lt kld 12-7-15 RE p43 CR Beds78

BERTRAM,Cyril Robertson 2Lt kld 18-6-16 1KEdwHorse &RFC p2&24 CR EAfrica7 &CR Tanzania1

BERTRAM,William Maj ded 18-2-15 11Manch p154 CR Scot789

BERTRAM WEARE,Albert James Capt ded 18-4-18 DLI 20Div CR War7

BERWICK,Robert George T2Lt kld 7-7-17 GL &RFC p5

BERWICK,William.TD.Lt&QM kia 11-9-18 5BordR p228 CR France511

BESCOBY,Edgar Laurence T2Lt dow 18-6-17 12RFus p66 CR Belgium11

BESLEY,Howard Napier 2Lt kia 29-6-17 1Lond p245 CR France581

BESLY,Barton Hope.MID Capt kia 25-10-14 1Dev p76 MR22

BESSELL,Mowbray TCapt kia 15/17-9-16 10RWSurr p55 MR21

BEST,Arthur Horris 2Lt dow 25-3-18 165RH&FA p25

BEST,Arthur Stephen Middleton TLt kia 23-2-17 RE 71FC p43 CR Iraq5

BEST,Douglas Kenneth Lt kia 16-8-17 6Ess att22RFC p17&232 CR France31

BEST,Edgar Harold T2Lt dow 18-9-18 2KRRC p149

BEST,Francis Behrens Lt kia 29-7-17 RASC attRFC p17&253 MR20

BEST,Frank Harrington Lt kia 13-2-17 SWBord BrecknockBn p223 MR38

BEST,Frank Robson Lt kia 2-1-16 4LNLancs p234 CR France702

BEST,Henry Reginald Lt ded 13-8-21 RASC CR Europe51

BEST,Jack TLt kia 15-5-18 34MGC p181 CR France59,Capt

BEST,James Henry T2Lt kia 25-6-16 RE 96FC p43 CR Belgium6,25-7-16

BEST,Norrys Aubrey 2Lt kia 19-7-17 3RFA p208 CR Belgium10

BEST,Stephen Wriothesley Lt kia 30-4-17 SWBord BrecknockBn p223 MR38

BEST,Thomas Andrew Dunlop.DSO&Bar.MajTLtCol kia 20-11-17 1/2RInniskF p104 CR France755

BEST,Thomas Edward Lt kia 9-8-15 8WRid p115 MR4

BEST,Wilfred Robert T2Lt dow 27-8-18 WRid p115

BEST-DUNKLEY,Bertram.VC CaptTLtCol dow 5-8-17 Cmdg2/5LancF p92 CR Belgium18

BESTALL,Edward Douglas Lt kia 3-7-16 9Ess p131 MR21

BESTER,R.A.Capt 16-3-21 GL &RlyTransOff attDADRT CR Germany1

BESWICK,John Charles 2Lt ded 22-4-17 PoW 11RLancs p58 CR France403

BETHELL,Charles Francis Ithel 2Lt kia 22-2-16 RE 70FC p43 CR France423,Ithell

BETHELL,Christopher.MID TCapt kia 20-2-16 10YLI p142 CR France922

BETHELL,Edward Walter Capt kia 21-9-18 1RWSurr p55 CR France369

BETHELL,Frank Harry 2Lt kia 25-9-15 3ConnRgrs p172 MR29,Lt

BETHELL,Richard Carrington T2Lt dow 22-5-16 11 att9Yorks p89 CR France570

BETHELL,Thomas Henry Capt kia 19-7-16 7RWar p214 MR32

BETHUNE,Henry Ewart MC LtTCapt kia 30-9-18 12HLI p162 CR Belgium116

BETHUNE,John Lt dow 29-10-17 A24RFA p207 CR Belgium3,28-10-17

BETLEY,Eric 2Lt kia 28-3-18 82RFC &RGA p261&262 MR20,Lt

BETTELEY,William Lawrence MC TCapt kia 25-6-17 7SomLI p79 CR France1488

BETTERIDGE,James Harper 2Lt kia 14-4-17 5BordR att16Lond p228 MR20

BETTESWORTH,Tom T2Lt dow 3-11-15 12RFus attRE 172FC p66 CR France40

BETTISON,Mark Hedley Capt kia 18-4-16 9DLI p239 CR Belgium37

BETTLES,Joseph T2Lt kia 7-11-18 5Leic p87 CR France1766

BETTRIDGE,R.F Lt 19-6-21 RFA CR Devon266

BETTS,Henry Lee T2Lt kia 20-9-17 26RFus p66 CR Belgium112,Lt

BETTS,John Hamilton TCapt kia 7-7-16 12Manch p154 CR France267

BETTS,John William 2Lt kia 9-5-15 2WelshR p126 MR22

BETTS,Thomas Walter T2Lt kia 31-7-17 17N&D p133 MR29

BETTY,Alfred William HonLt&QM ded 23-3-17 13RB p266 CR Somerset157

BEUTTLER,Charles Brereton Oakley 2Lt dow 24-12-16 A94RFA p25 CR France80

BEVAN,Alan Harry Reynolds Capt 30-12-20 9BhopalInf attPoliticDept CR Egypt7

BEVAN,Clement Beckford ACapt kia 20-7-16 3 att2Suff p78 MR21

BEVAN,Francis Harry Vaughan TCapt kia 19-4-17 GL &14RFC p5 MR34

BEVAN,Oliver Lewen 2Lt dow 25-10-18 RFA 25ArmyBde p25 CR France146

BEVAN,Percival Johnstone Lt kia 10-3-15 1KRRC p149 MR22

BEVAN,Thomas William TLtACapt ded 22-10-18 RE p43 CR France1359

BEVAN,Wilfrid 2Lt kia 3-12-17 GL &20RFC p5 MR20

BEVEN,Thomas T2Lt kia 3-7-16 9 att2SLancs p125 MR21

BEVERIDGE,Alan Primrose.MC&Bar.LtAMaj kia 16-9-18 RGA 35HB p38 CR France841

BEVERIDGE,Bernard Gordon.MC.Capt dow 21-3-18 RAMC 2/1HighlandFA p253 CR France307,kia

BEVERIDGE,David Alexander T2Lt ded 14-9-15 RFA HQ 54Bde p25 CR Europe1,13-9-15

BEVERIDGE,Douglas Lionel Lt ded 7-11-18 IA 1/94RussellsInf p273 MR65,2Lt

BEVERIDGE,Edmund Waller St.Clair Capt ded 24-11-19 IARO attLabCps p273 MR66

BEVERIDGE,James O'Shaughnessey Capt dow 22-11-17 RAMC att137FA p194 CR France245,Shaughnessy

BEVERIDGE,John Baxter TLt kia 22-10-16 14HLI p162 CR France115

BEVERIDGE,Walter Joseph Paterson TLtACapt kia 23-10-18 8GordH p166 CR France206,Patterson 1Bn

BEVERLAND,Charles Ferris T2Lt kia 4-12-16 2RInniskF p104 CR France568

BEVERS,Isaac Gwilym T2Lt dow 2-8-17 16RWelshF p97 CR Belgium16

BEVES,Trevor Howard.MC.Capt kia 1-7-16 1BordR p116 CR France35

BEVILLE,Alfred Geoffrey 2Lt kia 8-4-17 16Lond p250 CR France420

BEVINGTON,William Joseph ACapt kia 5-11-16 39RFA p25 MR21

BEVIR,Cyril Edward Francis Lt kia 29-10-15 76RFA p25 CR France1106

BEVIR,Raymond T2Lt kia 15-7-16 10RFus p66 MR21

BEVIS,Charles Thomas Capt ded 18-2-19 RE p255 CR Wales491

BEVON,William Victor Lt ded 29-11-17 RFC p261 CR Staffs78,17-11-17

BEWES,Reginald Charles Hope Lt kia 23-5-15 Lpool &RFC p1&71 CR France350

BEWICK,Norman 2Lt kia 22-1-18 157RFA p25 CR Belgium64

BEWICKE,Calverley George Lt kia 26-7-16 1WelshR p126 MR21

BEWICKE,Ralph Nathaniel 2Lt kia 29-9-16 8DLI p239 MR21,BEWICK

BEWICKE-COPLEY,Redvers Lionel Calverly Capt kia 21-12-16 CldGds p50

BEWLAY,Thomas Henry 2LtACapt dow 21-5-17 RGA 36SB p38 CR France1186

BEWLEY,Edward Capt ded 19-8-18 19RB p244 CR Egypt1

BEWLEY,Edward Neville 2Lt kia 26-6-17 2/6N&D p233 CR France662

BEWLEY,Frederick Norman T2Lt kia 20-9-17 N&D att16Bn p133 MR30

BEWLEY,Isaac Capt kia 10-10-18 7DLI p239 MR16,att13Bn

BEWSHER,Francis Alexander Lt dow 18-4-18 C255RFA p25 CR France134

BEYNON,Ernest John Wilson T2Lt kia 9-10-17 4Y&L p158 CR Belgium125

BEYNON,Ian William Arthur 2Lt dow 27-9-18 RGA 27SB p38 CR France433

BEYNON,William Charles 2Lt dow 3-5-17 4RWFus att2SWBord p223 CR France113,4-5-17

BEYTS,Julian Falvey DSO.TLtCol kia 5-10-17 15DLI p160

BEZUIDENHOUT,Pieter Hendrick Schalk MC 2Lt kia 24-12-16 A94RFA SR p25 CR France423

BHARGAVA,M.P Capt 6-10-19 IMS MR43

BHAT,K.H Lt drd 31-12-17 IMS MR41

BIANCHI,Edward Almachilde Lt kia 21-3-18 4 O&BLI att184TMB p231 MR27

BIBBS,Philip Henry Samuel Lt ded 25-10-19 RE p269

BIBBY,David Houghton TCapt kia 13-4-18 22NumbF p60 MR32
BIBBY,Francis Stephen 2Lt kia 20-7-16 3 att1ScotRif p103 MR21
BIBBY,Gerald Maurice Gosset T2Lt kia 6-3-17 GL 16RFC p5 CR France12
BIBBY,Henry Leigh Maj kia 4-5-17 LancsYeo p204 CR Italy14
BIBBY,John Patrick TLt kia 10-3-15 2ScotRif p103 CR France260
BIBBY,John Pengelly Lt 12-10-17 1GrenGds CR Belgium106 see BIDDY,J.P.
BIBBY,Joseph Morton 2Lt kia 3-5-17 8EYorks p83 MR20
BIBLE,Geoffrey Roskell T2Lt kia 1-7-16 101MGC Inf p181 MR21
BICE,William Francis T2Lt kia 4-9-16 10Norf p73 MR21,1Bn
BICK,Percy Arthur 2Lt kia 3-9-16 3 att2RIrReg p88 CR France402
BICKERDIKE,Robert.MC.Capt kia 20-11-17 6WYorks p218 CR France274
BICKERSTETH,Stanley Morris TLt kia 1-7-16 15WYorks p81
BICKERTON,William T2Lt kia 20-9-17 56MGC p181 CR Belgium22
BICKFORD,Arthur Louis Maj dow 9-3-16 IA CIE 56Rif p273 MR38
BICKHAM,Arthur Rushton.MID TLt ded 15-2-19 RGA 155HB p262 CR Ches183,Capt Ex RE
BICKLEY,George Howard TLtACapt kia 4-10-17 237MGC Inf p181 MR30
BICKMORE,Bertram George 2Lt kia 21-3-18 A232RFA p25 CR France672
BICKMORE,David Francis.DSO.LtALtCol kia 19-7-18 Norf att4GordH p73 MR18
BICKNELL,Herman Bysshe Bagshaw 2Lt kia 28-5-18 1Yorks p89 MR18
BICKNELL,Herman Kentigern TCapt ded 24-7-17 1 O&BLI p129 CR Iraq8
BIDDLE-COPE,Anthony Cyprian Prosper 2Lt kia 25-4-15 KSLI att2Bn p144 MR29
BIDDULPH,Leonard Shrapnell Capt dow 29-12-16 RFA attNigR p25&201 CR EAfrica38 &CR Tanzania1
BIDDULPH,Michael.OBE.LtCol 8-4-20 RAPayDept CR Asia51
BIDDULPH,Percival Vincent T2Lt kia 19-7-17 GL &1/3KAR p201 CR EAfrica38 &CR Tanzania1,Lt
BIDDULPH,Robert Assheton 2Lt ded 19-11-16 2DragGds p20 CR Eire487
BIDDULPH,Victor Roundell George 2Lt kia 15-9-16 5 att8RB p177 MR21
BIDDULPH,William 2Lt kia 3-9-18 4Ches p222 CR Belgium74
BIDDY,John Pengelly Lt kia 12-10-17 1GrenGds p49 CR Belgium106
BIDEN,Lawrance Trouse Gregory Vernon Lt dow 10-10-17 2RWar p64 CR Sussex112
BIDGOOD,Frank 2Lt kia 10-9-18 16Lond p250 CR France369
BIDGOOD,Thomas Aylmer Tattnall Lt dow 28-10-17 96RGA 91HB p38 CR Egypt2
BIDIE,George Maxwell Vereker Lt kld 8-7-16 RFC &RScots p2&53 CR Scot82,2Lt
BIDLAKE,Herbert Cooper Keith T2LtACapt kia 25-2-17 9Worc p108 MR38
BIDMEAD,Charles Hugh T2Lt kia 10-11-16 GL &25RFC p2&189 CR France88,Lt
BIDWELL,Claude Arthur Stephen T2Lt kia 21-9-15 10LNLancs p135
BIEDERMAN,Harry Charles Ernest 2Lt kia 10-8-17 OxfYeo att57RFC p17&205 MR20,BIEDERMANN
BIGELOW,Braxton.MID Capt kia 23-7-17 RE 170TC p43 CR France924
BIGG,Albert Charles T2Lt kia 31-7-17 18Lpool p71 MR29
BIGG,Walter Lt kia 27-5-18 8DLI p239 CR France1753
BIGGAME,Francis Joseph.MID TLt kia 16-8-17 8RMunstF att48TMB p175 MR30
BIGGAR,Kenneth T2Lt kia 26-9-15 6CamH p167 MR19,25-9-15
BIGGAR,William Francis Wilson 2Lt ded 20-10-18 10WYorks p81 p263 CR Scot621
BIGGE,John Neville.Hon Capt kia 15-5-15 1KRRC p149 MR22
BIGGER,John Alfred Whittard 2Lt kia 8-5-17 4 att1ESurr p112 MR20
BIGGERTON-EVANS,Arthur Basil George Lt ded 17-12-19 3SWBord p263 CR Europe17,Capt
BIGGS,Arthur Ridley T2Lt kia 2-7-16 6Wilts p152 CR France393
BIGGS,Bernard George Dawson Maj ded 1-12-16 5DLI p238 CR Durham88
BIGGS,George Henry WO ded 29-6-16 RIM p273 CR Iraq6
BIGGS,John Geoffrey.MC&Bar.Lt dow 1-9-17 NSomYeo att53MGC p186&205 CR France52
BIGGS,Seward T2Lt ded 26-11-18 332RASC attRWFus p192 CR France658
BIGHAM,William T2Lt ded 19-9-15 13NumbF p60 CR Staffs156,6-9-15
BIGLAND,George Braddyll 2Lt kia 15-6-15 5RLancs p213 MR22,1/4Bn
BIGNELL,Claude Arthur Capt ded PoW 21-11-16 IA 4Rajputs att24Punjabis p273 CR Iraq8
BIGNELL,Gurth Capt kia 15-7-16 6Beds p85

BIGSBY,Edgar Arthur 2Lt kia 25-9-15 8RWKent p140 MR19
BILBY,Eustace John 2Lt kia 16-8-17 Mddx att2Bn p146 MR30
BILL,J.H.LtCol 2-11-19 IndCivilServ CR Iraq8
BILL,John Alexander Patterson 2Lt kia 16-8-17 18 att12RIrRif p169 MR30
BILL,John Francis Capt dow 29-3-15 SWBord p99 CR France924,kia
BILL,Rodney Edward 2Lt kia 26-8-18 RGA 38HB p38 CR France924,27-8-18
BILLING,John T2Lt kia 2-9-18 EYorks att5YLI p83 CR France1484
BILLINGER,Hector Fussell T2Lt kia 23-11-16 8ELancs p110 MR21
BILLINGS,David Kitto 2Lt kld 15-9-17 RFC p5 CR War65,14-9-17
BILLINGS,Herbert T2Lt kia 6-4-16 9 att6Leic p87 MR38
BILLINGS,Hugh Bradish T2Lt ded 9-8-17 SR 29RFC p5 MR20,Braddish
BILLINGSLEY,Harold Hinton T2Lt kia 30-4-17 RWar att6ELancs p64 MR38
BILLINGTON,Frank Norman Lt kld 30-9-18 RAOC &RAF p198 CR France1483
BILLINGTON,Leslie Charles 2Lt kia 9-7-15 4 att2LancF p92 MR29,7-7-15
BILLINGTON,Whitworth Leonard T2Lt kia 17-5-17 RE Z'SpCo p43 CR France438
BILLMAN,Walter Melville Lt dow 5-11-16 6 att1Mddx p146 CR France105
BILSLAND,James.MC.T2Lt kia 9-6-16 11 att10ScotRif p103 CR France423
BILTON,E.B.MID ACapt kia 14-3-17 1/1HighCycBn att2/5YLI p253 CR France239,15-3-17
BILTON,Harold Charles Lt died 4-3-19 24Lond p269 CR Surrey152
BILTON,Lewis Edward Albert Samuel T2Lt kia 23-4-17 1EKent p57 CR France551,L.A.E.S.
BIMROSE,Charles 2Lt kia 3-10-18 1/6N&D p233 CR France375
BINDLOSS,Edward Alexander Morgan Maj kia 15-6-18 5RWar p214 CR Italy3
BINER,Benjamin Clive 2Lt ded PoW 21-7-18 18RIrRif att4EYorks p169 CR Germany1
BINER,Frank Amsden T2Lt kia 3-12-17 GL &22RFC p5 CR France31
BING,Eric Coppin Lt 15-8-18 2/3RFA CR Kent177
BINGEN,Carl Adolf Max Lt kia 11-2-16 5RSuss p228 CR France1327,Charles 10-2-16
BINGHAM,Arthur Doyle Lt ded 3-10-17 IARO RFC &RAVC p273 CR Lond2
BINGHAM,Bentinck Agliomby 2Lt kia 12-5-17 3 att10LancF p92 MR20
BINGHAM,David Cecil Lt kia 14-9-14 3CldGds p50 MR15
BINGHAM,Frank Miller Capt kia 22-5-15 5RLancs p213 MR29
BINGHAM,Frank Oldfield T2Lt dow 14-9-18 8 att9RFus p66 CR France145,Lt
BINGHAM,Harold 2Lt kia 15-9-18 C78RFA p25 CR France398
BINGHAM,John Warnock Capt ded 10-3-19 RAMC p194 CR Belgium241,10FA
BINGHAM,Montague Hearfield Lt kia 13-4-18 5YLI p235 MR32
BINGHAM,William Henry.OBE.LtCol S/InflictWound 18-3-20 IA 69Punjabis p273 CR Asia81
BINGHAM-DAY,Thomas Hulkes LtCol ded 11-4-17 4Dev p273 CR Wilts157,5Bn
BINGLEY,Arthur Noel T2Lt kia 14-6-16 110MGC p181 CR France283
BINKS,Basil Henry T2Lt kia 23-10-16 1RLancs p58 MR21
BINLEY,Percy Augustine.MC.T2Lt kia 23-8-18 10Ess p131 CR France430
BINNEY,Edward Hibbert 2LtALt&Adjt ded 11-10-17 N&D p133 CR Ches111,Capt
BINNEY,Leslie Wingfold 2Lt kia 15-4-18 126RFA p208 CR France149,Lt
BINNEY,Robert Humphrey.MC.ACapt dow 23-3-18 10Ess p131 CR France1893
BINNIE,David Willis 2LtTLt kia 27-5-17 5HLI p240 CR France1489,2Lt 9Bn
BINNIE,Philip 2Lt kia 26-9-17 5ScotRif p224 CR Belgium112
BINNIE,William Harold Lt kia 22-7-18 7RScots att206RAF p211,224&258 CR FRance134
BINNING,Albert Huteson T2Lt kia 13-11-16 13EYorks p83 MR21
BINNING,George Baillie Hamilton.Lord.CB.MVO.BrigGen ded 12-1-17 RHGds 1stMtdBde p20,204&261 CR Scot644
BINNING,Robert Inglis Capt ded 16-8-16 IA IMS p274 CR Iraq6
BINNING,William Barclay T2Lt dow 24-4-16 28MGC p181 CR France285
BINNS,Christopher 2Lt kia 26-9-17 RGA 154SB p38 CR Belgium19
BINNS,Clement Stanley T2Lt kia 1-7-16 20NumbF p60 MR21
BINNS,Eric Douglas 2Lt kia 7-10-16 7 att4Mddx p235 MR20
BINNS,George Alfred T2Lt kia 8-4-18 6Beds p85
BINNS,John Eric 2Lt kia 9-4-16 3 att5Wilts p152 MR38
BINNS,John Houghton T2Lt ded 4-9-17 GL &29RFC p5 CR Belgium125,Lt
BINNS,Raymond Louis T2Lt kia 10-7-16 8Yorks p89 CR France515,Raymund

BINNS,William Adam Ferrer 2Lt ded 18-5-20 6 att18KRRC CR Norf101
BINNY,Steuart Scott DSO TLtCol kia 3-3-16 10RWelshF p97 CR Belgium131,BINNY Ex 19Huss MR29,BINNEY
BINSTEAD,Gerald Charles MC CaptTMaj kia 8-4-15 2Ess p131 CR Belgium33,BINSTEED
BION,Kenneth Norman.MC.MIDx2 LtACapt kia 21-3-18 1 att2N&D p133 MR20
BION,Rupert Euston Lt kia 9-4-18 20Huss &40RAF p23 MR20
BIRBECK,Sidney Walker 2Lt kia 9-10-17 5WYorks p218 MR30
BIRCH,Arthur T2Lt dow 17-2-16 6RBerks p138 CR France246
BIRCH,Charles Richard Eli Lt&QM ded 12-8-17 9ESurr p112 CR France40
BIRCH,Edward Cecil Lt ded 26-1-19 3RWSurr &RAF p55 CR Surrey153
BIRCH,Eric Wykeham.MC Lt dow 17-1-17 4WRid attMGC p186&227 CR France62,Wykeham
BIRCH,Francis Wykeham Wallace 2Lt kia 23-1-20 IA 2/2 att2/9GurkhaRif p274 MR43
BIRCH,Frederick William Maj kia 17-4-16 4SWBord p99&274,IA Ret MR38,dow
BIRCH,George Owen Lt kia 14-9-14 WelshR p126 MR15,3 att2Bn CR France390
BIRCH,Gilbert Wilson Fitzroy TLtACapt kia 24-8-17 11YLI p142 MR30
BIRCH,Harold 2Lt dow 21-4-16 IARO att128Pnrs p274 CR Iraq6
BIRCH,Howard T2Lt kia 9-4-16 12 att8RWelshF p97 MR38
BIRCH,John 2Lt kia 5-7-15 13Worc p108 CR Gallipoli6
BIRCH,Leonard Capt kia 23-4-17 7BordR p116 MR20
BIRCH,Percy Hall 2Lt mbk 21-3-18 RGA 199SB p256 MR20
BIRCH,S C Capt ded 1-8-17 NumbF p60
BIRCH,W MBE.Capt 3-3-20 RHA CR Lond29
BIRCH,Walter Robert.MID TCapt kia 7-10-16 6 O&BLI p129 MR21
BIRCH,William Claud Kennedy.MC CaptAMaj kld 5-1-18 2Yorks p89 CR Belgium127
BIRCH,William Elric Hawthorn T2Lt kia 31-7-15 6DCLI p114 CR Belgium453,Lt
BIRCH-REYNARDSON,Edward Vere Lt kia 25-12-15 3 att1ESurr p112
BIRCHALL,Arthur Percival Dearman CaptTLtCol kia 24-4-15 RFus attCanInf p66 MR29
BIRCHALL,Edward Vivian Dearman.DSO Capt dow 10-8-16 O&BLI BucksBn p231 CR France40
BIRCHALL,Wilfred Arthur Lt kia 28-11-17 NottsYeo p205 CR Palestine3,SherRgrs
BIRCHAM,Humphrey Francis William.DSO TLtCol dow 23-7-16 2KRRC p149 CR France23
BIRD,E A Lt 29-8-20 CentIndRlyBn MR65
BIRD,Arthur Leonard 2Lt kia 6-9-17 2/5RWar p214 CR Belgium125
BIRD,Basil William MC&Bar MID TCapt dow 24-11-18 11N&D p133 CR France146
BIRD,Clement Eustace T2Lt dow 28-6-17 9RFus p66 CR France154,kia
BIRD,Charles Lt ded 6-8-18 RFA p261 CR Essex81
BIRD,Charles Edwin 2Lt kia 17-2-17 5Ess p232 CR France314
BIRD,Dudley Joseph de Anguld Lt kia 27-6-17 RFA attRFC p17&207 CR France421,Angulo
BIRD,Edward Kenelm Capt ded 27-9-19 IA 29 att20Punjabis p274 CR Egypt9
BIRD,Edwy Harold TCapt kia 24-2-17 10RWSurr p55 CR Belgium21
BIRD,Eric Hinckes Lt dow 27-6-16 1RFus att25RFC p266 CR France88 kia
BIRD,Eric James T2Lt dow 25-4-17 4Worc p108 CR France113
BIRD,Eric Stephen 2Lt kia 12-8-17 3 att8RIrF p170 CR Belgium125,6 att8Bn
BIRD,Ernest Walter Capt dow 27-7-16 1/6Glouc p225 CR France169
BIRD,Francis Clifford 2Lt kia 2-3-15 3KSLI p144 CR Belgium111
BIRD,George Brown.MC&Bar.TCapt kia 30-7-16 10RWar p64 MR21
BIRD,Henry Lt ded 12-4-19 1GrenGds att1/5KAR p49,201&257 CR EAfrica59
BIRD,Henry Tattersall 2Lt kia 27-3-18 160RFA p25 MR20
BIRD,John Greville Hobart Lt kiaAbout 25-10-14 RWSurr p55 MR29
BIRD,John Woodall T2Lt kia 21-12-17 RHGds HouseholdBn p20 CR France1182
BIRD,Laurie Edna SNurse ded 19-8-19 QAIMNS CR Surrey160
BIRD,Percy Charles Hilton T2Lt kia 5-4-16 10Norf att6LNLancs p73 MR38
BIRD,Raymond 2Lt kia 16-8-16 4Glouc p225
BIRD,Rex William T2Lt kia 24-8-16 1Wilts att7MGC Inf p181 MR21
BIRD,Robert MVO LtCol ded 30-3-18 IA CIE IMS p274 MR66
BIRD,Stanley Treadgold T2Lt dow 20-8-16 7KRRC p149 CR France177

BIRD,Walter Cyril TLt kia 4-3-17 8 att2Nhampt p137 MR21
BIRD,Wilfrid Stanley Lt kia 9-5-15 5 att2KRRC p149 MR22
BIRD,William Edmund T2Lt dow 28-4-17 RSuss p118 CR France102,2RFus
BIRD,William Gustave Capt ded 7-2-20 RASC CR Hamps1
BIRD,William Henry T2Lt kia 12-10-16 10 att2Beds p85 MR21
BIRD,William Ryder T2Lt kia 8-10-15 6 att8KRRC p149 MR29
BIRD,William Thornton Maj kia 12-7-15 7ScotRif p224 MR4
BIRDSEYE,Arthur Thomas T2Lt dow 25-4-18 2MGC p181 CR France62,Lt
BIRDSEYE,Douglas Martin T2Lt dow 10-2-17 8SStaffs p122
BIRDWOOD,C B.2Lt 18-7-18 CldGds CR Surrey4
BIRDWOOD,Christopher William Brodrick Capt dow 7-6-15 IA 1/6GurkhaRif p274 CR Gallipoli3
BIRDWOOD,Gordon Alic Brodrick 2Lt kia 19-9-14 SLancs p125 CR France1107,Alick 20-9-14
BIRDWOOD,Herbert Frederick Lt kia 2-3-16 20Lond attRFC p17&251 CR France1308
BIRDWOOD,Richard Lockington Capt kia 17-11-14 IA PoliticDept p274 CR Iraq6
BIRKBECK,Edward Lt kia 7-8-15 IA 128Pnrs att1/5GurkhaRif p274 MR4
BIRKBECK,George Lt ded 19-2-15 NorfYeo p204 CR Norf128
BIRKBECK,Gervase William Capt kia 19-4-17 5Norf p216 MR34,20-4-17
BIRKBECK,Morris Lt kia 14-7-15 IA 24Punjabis p274 CR Iraq6,14/15-7-15
BIRKBY,Henry Alexander T2Lt dow 20-4-16 9 att5RBerks p138 CR France80
BIRKETT-BARKER,Holroyd Lt ded 15-8-17 RGA 134SB CR Greece9
BIRKIN,Thomas Richard Chetwynd 2Lt kia 12-6-17 7DragGds att25RFC p5&21 CR France88,Lt
BIRKS,Alfred Owen T2Lt dow 13-3-18 1Dors p123 CR Belgium38
BIRLEY,Hugh Kennedy TCapt kia 23-7-16 19Manch p154 MR21
BIRLEY,Joseph Hornby TCapt kia 2-9-18 19Manch p154 CR France744
BIRMINGHAM,William Arthur T2Lt kia 9-8-15 6RIrF p170 MR4
BIRNEY,John Gordon Lt kia 11-1-17 1HLI p162 MR38
BIRNIE,Edward D'Arcy DSO MC TLtACapt dow 22-3-18 8BordR p116 CR France177
BIRNIE,Edward John Wilfrid 2Lt kia 14-2-15 2ESurr SR p112 MR29,Wilfred
BIRNIE,Gerald Lt dow 4-11-18 46/39RFA p25 CR France146
BIRNIE,William 2Lt kia 24-10-16 RE 2/2HighlandFC p210 CR France131
BIRNIE,William John Gordon Lt kia 23-11-18 8GordH att B'TankCps p166&188 MR17
BIRRELL,Andrew Smith T2Lt kia 9-4-17 6KOSB p101 CRFrance581
BIRRELL,George Henry Gordon 2Lt kia 12-5-15 9A&SH p244 MR29,10-5-15
BIRRELL,Stuart Erskin TCapt dow 11-7-16 6SomLI p79 MR20
BIRRELL,Thomas Yates TLt kia 17-2-16 8SStaffs p122 CR Belgium120,15-2-16
BIRRELL,William George MIDx2 MajGen ded 23-8-18 RAMC p194 CR Scot275
BIRRELL,William Henry 2Lt dow 20-9-18 8 att11ScotRif p225 CR Greece6
BIRRELL-ANTHONY,Henry Anthony 2Lt kia 8-5-15 1Mon p244 MR29
BIRT,Lascelles William TCapt dow 1-10-17 O&BLI att1/4Bn p129 CR Belgium18
BIRT,Lightly Harold DSO Capt kia 5-1-15 1RBerks p138 CR France727
BIRT,Wilfrid Beckett Capt ded 18-4-16 PoW 9ESurr p112 CR Germany1,Wilfred
BIRTLES,Leonard 2Lt kia 16-9-16 2DLI p160 MR21
BIRTLES,Roland Powell TLtACapt kia 4-3-17 1Worc p108 CR France439
BIRTWISTLE,Norman MC Lt dow 8-10-18 19Huss p23 CR France341
-BISCOE,Archibald Fairhead Lt ded 22-2-19 RASC p192 CR Germany1,attIICps
BISCOE,Arthur John Capt dow 12-3-15 1RIrRif p169 CR France102
BISCOE,Frederick Crozier Frazer Capt dow 19-5-15 2Worc p108 CR France80
BISHOP,Alfred Wedderburn T2Lt kia 12-5-17 1Hamps p120 MR20
BISHOP,Arthur Walter 2Lt kia 21-3-18 4 att9RSuss p228 CR France528,22-3-18
BISHOP,Basil Frederic MC MajALtCol kia 18-9-18 9SLancs p125 MR37
BISHOP,Bernard Bennett 2Lt kia 9-9-17 5DCLI attRFC p17&227 CR France1361
BISHOP,Charles Dudley 2LtACapt kia 17-4-18 2Worc p108 MR32
BISHOP,Charles Frederick T2Lt kia 4-4-18 13RFus p66 MR20
BISHOP,Charles Gamble DSO MC Maj kia 30-10-17 RE p209 CR Belgium23
BISHOP,Charles Harold MC T2Lt dow 23-10-18 13DLI p160 CR France441
BISHOP,Charles Trevor T2Lt kia 29-3-17 5Wilts p152 MR38

BISHOP,Colville Jones Lt ded 22-4-18 RASC attRGA p192 CR France134,James
BISHOP,Edwin Maurice Lt kia 18-10-14 3Dors attYLI p123 MR22
BISHOP,Ernest Eldred 2LtALt kia 14-3-17 RGA attY6TMB p38 CR Frnce149
BISHOP,Frank Ernest T2Lt kia 12-7-17 GL &57RFC p5 CR Belgium10
BISHOP,Frederick Capt ded 21-2-19 5Ches p269 CR Hamps202
BISHOP,George Bernard Hamilton Chap4Cl kia 27-5-18 RAChDept att6NumbF p199 MR18
BISHOP,Gerald Clement William T2Lt kia 11-8-17 Mddx att16Bn p146 MR29
BISHOP,John Edmund TCapt kia 18/19-4-16 10 att6ELancs p110 MR38
BISHOP,John Ellis 2Lt kia 21-9-17 7Lond p247 MR29
BISHOP,Keith Ford 2Lt kia 8-8-16 RGA 23HB p38 CR France430
BISHOP,Nigel Fyfe Watson 2Lt kia 13-10-15 1/5NStaffs p238 MR19
BISHOP,Parkyn Sydney 2Lt kia 30-11-17 8Lond p247 MR17
BISHOP,Ralph Murdock T2Lt dow 15-4-18 PoW 34MGC Inf p181 CR Belgium451
BISHOP,Rowland Bridgeman.MID LtACapt kia 19-4-17 1/4Nhampt p234 CR Palestine8,Bridgman
BISHOP,Samuel James Webb 2Lt kia 3-5-17 6Ess att7Mddx p232 MR20
BISHOP,Wilfrid T2Lt dow 6-7-17 BordR att11Bn p116 CR Belgium173
BISHOP,William Reason 2Lt kia 2-10-17 GL SStaffs att55RFC p5 CR Belgium140
BISPHAM,David Charles T2Lt kld 4-11-17 GL &RFC p5 CR Lond9
BISSEKER,Arthur Vanderkists Lt kia 4-10-17 6RWar p214 CR Belgium128,Vanderkiste
BISSEKER,John Wallis 2Lt kia 1-4-17 6RWar p214 CR France369
BISSET,J.L.Lt 26-3-21 RE CR Scot267
BISSETT,Edgar George William 2Lt dow 7-1-17 5GordH attRFC p17&242,BISSET CR Belgium18
BISSETT,Fenton Capt 16-4-18 4SomLI CR France88
BISSETT,George.DSO.MC&Bar.LtAMaj dow 18-10-18 1RScotF p94 CR France512,LtCol 10-10-18
BISSICKS,Francis Ronald T2Lt kld 2-1-17 GL &48RFC p5 &189 CR glouc9
BISSLEY,William Howe T2Lt kia 18-8-16 8RBerks p138 MR21
BITTLES,G.H.HonMaj ded 21-9-16 RAOC p267 CR Ireland181,IOD
BLACK,Allan Capt kia 27-5-18 RE 490FC p209 MR18
BLACK,Allan Maclean T2Lt kia 18-7-16 5CamH p167 CR France402
BLACK,Charles Morrison T2Lt ded 9-7-17 RIrRif attRInniskF p265 CR Ireland137,RIrFus
BLACK,Cyril Herbert Charles Pakenham T2Lt kia 18-8-16 13Mddx p146 MR21
BLACK,David T2Lt kld 3-10-17 GL &RFC p5 CR Scot591
BLACK,David Hammond 2Lt kia 8-5-18 20 att17Lpool p71 MR30,Hammond Dudley
BLACK,David Smith.MC.2LtTCapt kia 27-3-18 3 att7Suff p78 MR27
BLACK,Donald MacGregor Capt kia 6-8-15 1Ess p131 CR Gallipoli6
BLACK,Donald Walter Bryce T2Lt kld 3-1-18 RFC p15 CR Hamps57
BLACK,Eleanor Eileen Miss drd 4-6-18 VAD BRCS p200 MR40
BLACK,Eric Osborne Lt kia 9-5-15 2Lincs p74 MR32
BLACK,Ernest Charteris T2Lt kia 22-11-15 9 att7RScotF p94 CR France423
BLACK,Francis Henry LtTCapt kia 25-4-15 4 att1RWar p64 CR France705
BLACK,George Balfour.MC.LtTCapt dow 23-8-18 17Lancers att13TankCps p23&188 CR France1170
BLACK,George Bennett T2Lt kia 7-10-17 11A&SH p172 MR20
BLACK,George Dudley Austin TLt kia 21-6-16 22RFus p66 CR France924
BLACK,Hammond Dudley 2Lt 8-5-18 20 att17Lpool MR30 see BLACK,David Hammond
BLACK,J.LtCol 5-2-20 WarYeo CR Europe23
BLACK,James T2Lt dow 19-8-18 7/8KOSB p101 CR Belgium8
BLACK,James Ashton 2Lt kia 21-3-18 3DLI p160 CR France1484
BLACK,James Elliot,MC Capt kia 19-4-17 RAMC att8Beds p194 CR France115
BLACK,James Dykes.MC.Maj ded 5-7-18 5HLI p269 CR Scot756
BLACK,James George HonMaj ded 18-2-18 RLancs p262 CR Mddx29
BLACK,James Muir 2Lt kia 1-8-18 1/9RScots p212 CR France524
BLACK,James Somerville T2Lt kia 29-4-17 GL &16RFC p5 CR France134
BLACK,John Capt ded 26-9-17 RLancs p58 CR France145
BLACK,John TLt dow 23-8-18 6TankCps p188 CR France103
BLACK,John Montgomery T2Lt kld 5-2-18 RFC p15 CR Scot775

BLACK,John Neill.MID TCaptAMaj kia 9-4-17 6SomLI p79 CR France532
BLACK,Maurice Adam Maj kia 11-2-17 5DragGds &RFC p5&21 CR Europe58
BLACK,Maurice Charles Osborne Lt kia 24-8-16 GL 7BordR attTMB p189 CR France397,25-8-16
BLACK,Norman Annandale TCapt kia 23-5-16 A105RFA p25 CR France558
BLACK,Robert Robin 2Lt dow 22-10-18 1/5A&SH p243 CR Belgium11
BLACK,Robert Alaister McGregor TLtACapt kia 27-7-18 1/8GordH p166 CR France524
BLACK,Thomas Lloyd T2Lt kia 2-6-15 RE 171FC p43 CR Belgium4
BLACK,Thomas Porteous TCapt kia 9-8-15 9N&D p133 MR4
BLACK,Tom T2Lt kia 18-9-16 19 att17N&D p133 MR21
BLACK,W.N.2Lt 19-8-20 4KOSB CR Scot696
BLACK,William Rev Chap4Cl ded 10-7-18 RAChDept p199 CR France34
BLACK,William Duncan Thomson Rev kia 22-8-17 RAChDept att7CamH p199 CR Belgium8
BLACK,William McMillan Capt kia 31-10-14 IA 58Rif p274 CR France80
BLACK,William Thomas Lt kia 24-9-17 4Ess attRE p232 CR Belgium124
BLACK-HAWKINS,Claude Cranstoon Ridout Capt kia 10-8-15 2 att10Hamps p120 MR4,Cranstoun
BLACKABY,Arthur 2Lt kia 17-5-15 Ches p95 MR29
BLACKALL,Charles Walter.MIDx2 Capt kia 24-3-18 3EKent att4SStaffs p57 MR20,LtCol
BLACKALL-SIMONDS,George Prescott Lt kia 26-9-14 1SWBord p99 MR15
BLACKBOURN,Edgar Singleton T2Lt dow 29-9-16 7KRRC p149 CR France40
BLACKBURN,Charles James Critchley LtACapt kia 25-4-18 5WYorks D'Coy p218 MR30
BLACKBURN,Edward 2Lt kia 9-8-16 1/5LNLancs p234 MR21
BLACKBURN,Edward 2Lt kia 21-3-18 3 att2/7Manch p154 MR27
BLACKBURN,Ernest Lt kia 9-8-16 1/5LNLancs p234 MR21
BLACKBURN,Frank 2Lt kia 24-10-17 5ELancs attMGC p226&186 MR30
BLACKBURN,Geoffrey Gaskell TCapt kia 1-7-16 10WYorks p81 CR France373
BLACKBURN,George Stanley 2Lt dow 30-10-18 4BordR p228 CR Cumb'd&W'more'd40
BLACKBURN,Gideon 2Lt ded 18-2-19 1/7WYorks p269 CR Yorks344
BLACKBURN,Harry Clement T2Lt kld 23-3-18 1 att1/7WYorks p81 CR Belgium72
BLACKBURN,Harry Dudley Lt kia 5-4-17 1RBerks &43RFC p5&138 CR France924
BLACKBURN,John Herbert Lt ded 7-2-17 4YLI p235 CR Belgium11,8-2-17 9Bn
BLACKBURN,Norman Henry Gershorn.MC.T2Lt kia 23-10-18 RBerks att8Bn p138 CR France190
BLACKBURN,Reginald Herbert 2Lt ded 5-11-18 Beds p85&263,Lt
BLACKBURN,Stanley West T2Lt kia 9-10-17 Y&L p158 MR30
BLACKBURNE,Charles Harold.DSO.Capt&BtLtCol drd 10-10-18 5DragGds p21 CR Ireland27
BLACKBURNE,Harry Devereux Lt kia 27-9-17 9Lond p247 MR30
BLACKBURNE,John George.MID TMaj kia 22-8-15 9N&D Lt RoO p133 CR Gallipoli5
BLACKDEN,Arthur Worsley 2Lt kia 28-9-16 189RFA p25 MR21
BLACKDEN,Wilfred Worsley CaptTMaj ded 10-1-16 11NumbF p60 CR France40,Wilfrid
BLACKEBY,Joseph Edward T2Lt kia 21-2-18 RFC p15 CR Belgium13
BLACKER,Cecil Francis Lt dow 6-9-14 2ConnRgrs p172 CR Eire336
BLACKER,George Frederick Lt kia 9-5-15 3 att2Nhampt p137 MR32
BLACKER,John Robin 2Lt kia 28-9-15 1CldGds p51 MR19
BLACKER-DOUGLASS,Robert St.John.MC.Lt kia 1-2-15 1IrGds p52 CR France720
BLACKETT,Charles Robert 2Lt kia 25-4-15 KSLI p144 MR29
BLACKETT,William Stewart Burdett Lt dow 25-11-14 LeicYeo p204 CR Belgium150,Capt 24-11-14
BLACKIE,Albert Ferguson TCapt dow 17-4-17 16HLI p162 CR France583
BLACKIE,Frank Herndon Lt kia 11-4-18 8ScotRif att1KAR p225 MR52,Ex9HLI
BLACKIE,John.MC.Lt kia 22-10-18 8 att11RScots p211 CR France143
BLACKIE,John Stewart Lt kia 18-10-16 5 att1RB p177 MR21
BLACKLAWS,Alec Stuart.MC.2Lt kia 7-1-18 D161RFA p25 CR Belgium20
BLACKLEDGE,Ewan John 2Lt mbk 23-11-17 1Lpool &11RFC p256

MR20,Lt

BLACKLOCK,Algernon Haden 2Lt kia 21-10-14 2A&SH p172 CR France566

BLACKLOCK,Alice May Sister ded 13-8-16 TFNS p254 CR Iraq6

BLACKLOCK,William T2Lt ded 12-9-16 11BlkW p128 CR Europe1

BLACKMAN,George Hugh Willoughby TLt kia 30-7-16 2RScotF p94 MR21

BLACKMAN,Wilfred Ernest Arthur.MID T2Lt ded 14-10-18 MGC p181 CR Kent83,Capt

BLACKMAN,William.DCM.2LtACapt kia 8-5-17 1ESurr p112 MR20

BLACKMORE,Edwin 2Lt kia 16-8-16 1/5DCLI att9MGC Inf p186&227 MR21

BLACKSTOCK,John T2Lt kia 6-10-18 RASC att12NStaffs p192 CR France1140

BLACKWELL,Aubrey Francis.MC.Lt kia 2-6-17 6LondRFA p207 CR Belgium5

BLACKWELL,Basil Bernard 2Lt kia 3-9-16 3 att8EKent p57 CR France1890

BLACKWELL,Charles 2Lt kia 20-7-15 4RFus p66 CR Belgium37

BLACKWELL,Cyril T2Lt kia 1-7-16 16RFus p66 MR21

BLACKWELL,George John Rowland T2Lt kia 30-3-18 Manch att2/6Bn p154 MR27

BLACKWELL,Gerald Davis Lt kia 7-6-17 6NumbF att47MGC p186&213 CR Belgium60,Davies

BLACKWELL,Julian Victor T2Lt kia 11-4-18 11LancF p92 MR32

BLACKWELL,Samuel Frederick Baker.DSO.TCapt kia 20-11-17 TankCps p188 CR France711

BLACKWELL,Thomas T2Lt kia 27-3-18 7Suff p78 MR27

BLACKWELL,Walter TLt dow 28-9-18 11RDubF p176 CR Belgium38

BLACKWELL,William Gordon TLt kia 5-10-16 8RFus p66 MR21

BLACKWOOD,Henry Stear Lt dow 1-5-17 9Lond p248 CR War84

BLACKWOOD,John Angus 2Lt ded 10-9-16 3BlkW p128 p264 CR Scot760

BLACKWOOD,Miles Harry 2Lt kia 1-7-16 2SfthH p164 CR France643

BLACKWOOD,Walter Lennox TLt kia 31-7-17 RScotF attMGC Tanks p94 CR Belgium112

BLAD,Kenneth Sven T2Lt ded 26-11-18 RE &4TankCps p43&188 CR France1512,Lt

BLADEN,Eustace Clement T2Lt dow 4-11-15 11 att8WRid p115 CR Gallipoli27

BLADES,Laurence Turner 2Lt ?? 5-7-15 6 att1RB p177 CR Belgium85,Lawrence

BLADES,William Henry 2Lt kia 3-5-17 8RB p177 MR20

BLADON,Henry James 2Lt dow 1-9-18 4WelshR p230 CR France217,kia

BLADWELL,Leonard Joseph T2Lt kia 14-10-18 RE 237FC p43 CR Belgium157

BLAGBROUGH,George Stanley TMaj kia 11-12-16 EYorks att16WYorks p83 CRFrance203

BLAGDEN,Maurice Bernard 2Lt kia 21-9-18 1RWSurr p55 CR France369

BLAGDEN,Robert T2Lt dow15-5-16 10 att7Norf p73 CR France8,12-5-16

BLAGG,Sidney.MID T2Lt kia 29-7-18 N&D att1/4Suss p133 MR18

BLAGROVE,Richard Coore Lt&Adjt kia 12-8-15 DCLI att6Bn p114 CR Belgium84

BLAIN,Charles Victor 2Lt kia 3-9-16 1Ches p95 CR France453

BLAIN,Mary Maude Miss ded 15-3-19 WLA CR Ches131

BLAIR,Alexander McPherson TCapt kia 3-7-16 2SLancs p125 CR France293,Macpherson

BLAIR,Alexander Neville Lt ded 13-3-17 5BlkW p231 MR65

BLAIR,Claud Leslie.MC.TLt kia 16-6-17 RE 106FC p43 CR Belgium97

BLAIR,Duncan James Nugent Capt ded 10-1-17 5Lancers RoO attRFA p21

BLAIR,Edward James.MC.Capt kia 11-4-17 RAMC p253 CR France15

BLAIR,G.L.Maj 7-8-19 36Sikhs CR Lond14

BLAIR,George Young T2Lt dow 24-7-15 B63RFA p25 CR France263,kia

BLAIR,Herbert Samuel Penny 2Lt dow 31-10-16 3DCLI p114 CR Europe1

BLAIR,James Mcdonald T2Lt dow 9-4-18 35MGC p181 CR France116

BLAIR,John 2Lt dow 16-6-18 8 att10ScotRif p225 CR France14

BLAIR,John Lt dow 12-10-18 8DLI p239 CR Belgium38

BLAIR,Patrick Alexander.MC.Capt kia 23-4-17 9RScots p212 CR France545

BLAIR,Patrick Charles Bentley 2Lt dow 6-7-15 5RB p177 CR Belgium85

BLAIR,Patrick Edward Adam 2Lt kia 29-10-14 1BlkW p128 MR29

BLAIR,Richard Curwen Richmond.DSO.Capt kia 21-6-16 5BordR p228 CRBelgium97,Robert 21-7-16

BLAIR,Robert Hannay 2Lt kia 21-3-18 B79RFA p25 CR France568

BLAIR,Sidney Barclay 2Lt kia 16-5-15 3 att1RWar p64 CR France727,3 att2Bn

BLAIR,Thomas.MC&Bar.2Lt dow 21-11-18 6HLI p240 CR France34

BLAIR,William T2Lt kia 23-4-17 8SfthH p164 CR France536

BLAIR,William Alexander 2Lt dedacc 8-12-18 3 att2HLI p162 CR France289

BLAIR,William Kenneth Playfair Maj dow 14-5-15 96RFA p25 CR France102

BLAIR CUNYNGHAME,Ronald Ogilvy Capt dow 5-5-15 2GordH p166 CR France284

BLAIR-OLIPHANT,Philip Lawrence Kington.DSO.LtCol dow 8-4-1811/13RIrRif CRFrance145

BLAKE,A.R.2Lt 14-2-16 IARO MR65

-BLAKE,Alfred Joseph William.MID TLt kia 21-8-15 5ConnRgrs p172 MR4

BLAKE,Bernard Cecil Lt dow 9-4-18 A275RFA p207 CR France98

BLAKE,Cecil TLt ded 30-10-18 RAMC p194 p267 CR Staffs114

BLAKE,Cecil Francis John 2Lt kia 7-10-18 Mddx att2Bn p146 CR France545,Charles

BLAKE,Cecil Rodolph TCapt kia 4-4-17 10KRRC p149 MR21

BLAKE,Charles Edwin Norman.MC.LtAMaj kia 30-7-18 70RFA p25 CR France865

BLAKE,Charles Stanley TCapt kia 7-8-15 10SLancs p125 MR4

BLAKE,Christopher 2Lt kia 4-9-16 3 att1Beds p85 MR21

BLAKE,Edith S/Nurse drd 26-2-18 QAIMNS p200 MR40

BLAKE,Edward Algernon Cleader Maj kia 20-10-14 2DLI p160 MR32

BLAKE,Edward William Richmond 2Lt 31-7-17 4 att18SomLI MR29

BLAKE,Francis Seymour TCapt kia 1-7-16 15Lpool att2SWBord p71 MR21

BLAKE,Francis William.MC.T2Lt kia 31-10-18 19DLI p160 CR Belgium143

BLAKE,Geoffrey Stuart Lt kia 5-9-17 RE 203FC p43 CR France364

BLAKE,George Cyril TLt ded 5-11-17 GL 1/4WelchR attRecruitStaff p189 CR Yorks34

BLAKE,George Morley 2Lt kia 21-3-18 2/4ELancs p226 MR27

BLAKE,George Penderell TCapt kia 20-7-16 10RWelshF p97 CR France744

BLAKE,George Victor T2Lt kia 3-12-17 1KSLI p144 CR France911

BLAKE,Harold Frederick Capt kia 7-10-16 Wilts att13DLI p152 CR France385,Frederic

BLAKE,Harold Martin Joseph Lt dow 20-11-17 1RMunstF p175 CR France689

BLAKE,James Alexander Jeffrey Lt dow 18-8-16 RFA 47DAC p207 CR France1890,Jeffery

BLAKE,James Edward 2Lt kia 6-4-17 RE &45RFC p5&43 CR Belgium406

BLAKE,James Robert.MIDx2Capt kia 25-3-18 8 att14Worc p226 MR20

BLAKE,Jerrold Edward Capt kia 23-7-16 4 O&BLI p231

BLAKE,John Morgan 2Lt kia 4-10-17 1Dev p76 MR30

BLAKE,Maurice Frederic Lt kia 14-9-14 2KRRC p149 MR15

BLAKE,Norman Pilkington TCapt kia 14-7-16 8EYorks p83 CR France399

BLAKE,Reginald Joseph Albert TLt kia 13-4-18 1 att11ELancs p110 MR32

BLAKE,Reginald Howard 2Lt kia 1-6-18 2/8Lpool p71 CR France204

BLAKE,St.John Lucius O'Brien Acheson French.MC.TMaj kia 19-4-17 21Lancers attWorcYeo p23

BLAKE,Valentine Charles Joseph Capt kia 28-1-16 1IrGds SR p52 CR France1157

BLAKE,William Henry Maj ded 19-5-16 1RGA p209 CR Numb99

BLAKE,William Lovewell 2Lt dow 27-3-18 4Norf p216 CR France62

BLAKELEY,Frank Roland 2Lt kia 22-2-17 IA 53Sikhs p274 CR Iraq5

BLAKELEY,George Finney Maj ded 15-12-19 2/5RWar p269 CR Yorks588,dow

BLAKELY,John Douglas T2Lt kia 9-4-17 9GordH p166 CR France924

BLAKEMAN,Albert Victor T2Lt kia 7-10-18 SStaffs att1KSLI p122 CR France375

BLAKEMORE,John Edward.MC TCaptAMaj dow 5-10-17 42/24RFA p25 CR France98

BLAKENEY,Edward Charles William Lt ded 20-1-19 IARO 36JacobsHorse&44Cav p274 MR67

BLAKENEY,Leslie St.Leger Lt drd 28-3-15 2LancF &GoldCoastR p92&201 MR40

BLAKESTON,Bernard Moore 2Lt kia 25-3-17 IARO 1/1GurkhaRif p274 MR38

BLAKEWAY,James Maj ded 4-12-18 RAVC DADVS p254 CR France457

BLAKEWAY,Noel Carleton 2Lt kia 27-3-16 3 att1Dors p123 CR France392

BLAKEWAY,Philip John Thomas Chap1Cl ded 16-6-15 1MddxYe0 p204&268 CR Egypt8

BLAKEY,George 2Lt kia 16-9-16 9YLI p142 MR21

BLANCHARD,Frederick John.MID Capt kia 1-6-18 1/5DCLI p227 CR France31

BLANCHARD,Frederick Wilson Capt dow 26-1-18 PoW 1/2DCLI att2/5RWar p114 CR Germany3

BLANCHARD,John Balsillie 2Lt kia 13-10-15 6NStaffs p238 MR19,Baldsillie

BLANCHARD,Neville 2Lt ded 26-7-17 3 att2Dors p123 CR Iraq5

BLANCHARD,William Hutchison Capt ded 8-10-17 RAVC att155AFA p198

BLANCHETTE,Charles Matthew Lt ded 22-3-18 RAMC p267 CR War19

BLAND,Alfred Edward TCapt kia 1-7-16 22Manch p154 CR France397

BLAND,Braithwaite T2Lt dow 31-8-16 8RLancs p58 CR France201,Capt

BLAND,Bridgman Elsey Capt ded 26-10-17 5Lond p146 CR Essex208

BLAND,Cecil Francis Ramsden.MC.Lt kia 7-7-19 3RBerks att1SlavBritLegion p138&257 MR70 &CR Europe179

BLAND,Charles Edward TCapt kia 9-9-16 11Hamps p120 MR21

BLAND,Charles Ernest William.DSO.Capt kia 23-4-15 3 att2KOSB p101 MR29,3-4-15

BLAND,J.Capt ded 28-1-18 WYorks p263 CR Yorks408

BLAND,John George 2Lt dow 9-7-15 2RIrRif p169 CR France40,9-7-16

BLAND,Malcolm Gordon 2Lt kia 23-3-18 1KRRC p254 MR20

BLAND,Percy Richard Capt kia 3-5-17 3 att1Lpool p71 MR20

BLAND,Thomas Russell 2Lt kia 20-7-17 5NStaffs p238 MR19

BLAND-HUNT,Ernest Sydney de Vere Maj kia 4-9-15 RGA 6SB p38 CR Belgium84,Sidney De

BLANDE,Arthur Frederick William Lt kia 20-9-17 8Lond p247 MR29

BLANDY,Claude Milberne TCapt ded 8-4-16 110AC RFA p25 CR France145

BLANDY,Claude Reginald Bowe 2Lt ded 19-4-18 5SLancs p269

BLANDY,Francis Dawson.MC.LtCol kia 14-8-17 RAMC 24FA p253 CR Belgium15

BLANDY,Gerald Castleton 2LtACapt kia 9-10-17 4 att2RWar p64 MR30

BLANDY,Gurth Swinnerton.MC.TCapt dow 24-4-17 RAMC attRE 29Div p194 CR France40

BLANE,Hugh Seymour Capt dow 1-11-14 IA 19Lancers att5DragGds p274 CR Belgium170,31-10-14

BLANE,James Pitcairn TCapt dow 23-11-15 8KRRC p149 CR Belgium11

BLANE,Malcolm Gilbert Stewart Lt kia 25-9-15 3 att5CamH p167 MR19

BLANE,Sidney Taylor 2Lt kia 16-8-17 3 att11Manch p154 MR30

BLANFORD,Charles Edward Maj dow 11-7-15 RGA 30MountainBty p25 CR Iraq6

BLANFORD,Frank Burrell Capt ded 25-4-17 2RGLI p200 CR Dorset/Cl139,Lt

BLATCHLY,Walter John Atherton T2Lt kia 12-5-15 1Leinst p174 MR29

BLATHERWICK,Robert Hugh 2Lt kia 1-7-16 10WYorks p81 CR France373

BLATHWAYT,Gerald Wynter Capt kia 14-9-14 56/44RFA p25 CR France1329

BLATHWAYT,Henry Wynter Maj dow 30-11-17 A74RFA p25 CR France1498

BLAXALL,Harold Gurney 2Lt kia 8-10-17 7Mddx p235 MR20

BLAXLAND,John Bruce Capt kia 24-1-17 4SWBord p99 CR Iraq5

BLAXLEY,Stewart Lenton 2Lt kia 23-4-17 4RWelshF p223 CR France162

BLAZEY,John William Victor 2Lt kia 26-9-15 1RBerks p138 MR19,RegNo.2492

BLEADEN,Lionel TLt kia 6/9-7-16 13RFus p66

BLEASE,Harvey TCapt kia 7-8-15 15Lpool att7LancF p71 MR4

BLEASE,Richard Morris Stanley TCapt kia 3-5-17 15WYorks p81

BLEAZARD,Fred.DCM.2Lt kia 21-3-18 RFA 169ArmyBde p25 CR France1074

BLECH,Evelyn Lewis T2Lt kia 18-8-16 73MGC p181 CR France294, BLECK,17-8-16

BLECKLY,Henry Lt ded 25-5-21 2/1ChesYeo CR Ches11

BLEEZE,Frank James T2Lt kia 29-7-18 O&BLI att1/4RSuss p129 CR France524

BLENCH,Alfred Chapman T2Lt dow 6-7-16 20Manch p154 CR France300

BLENCOWE,Charles Edward T2Lt kia 3-5-18 RSuss att1Wilts p118 MR30

BLENCOWE,Ernest Cecil Blencowe TCapt kia 16-12-16 6Dors p123 MR29,16-2-16

BLENCOWE,Lawrence Cave 2Lt kia 29-6-17 2/10Lpool p216 MR32

BLENCOWE,Mabel Edith Sister ded 10-3-17 TFNS p254 CR France134

BLENCOWE,Oswald Charles T2Lt kia 7-10-16 6 O&BLI p129 MR21

BLENKINSOP,Edward Winnington 2Lt dow 26-9-15 3 att2War p64 CR France98

BLENKINSOP,Frank T2Lt kia 5-5-17 15DLI p160 MR20,6-5-17

BLENKINSOP,William Millford TLt dow 7-11-18 12DLI p160 CR Italy7

BLEST,Malcolm Alexander Capt ded 30-12-15 8Mddx p235 CR Surrey94

BLEW,Kynnersley 2Lt kia 12-4-18 3 att7RWKent p140 MR27

BLEWCHAMP,Ernest John T2Lt kia 14-7-16 7RWSurr p55 MR21

BLEWITT,Arthur TLtCol dow 4-9-17 5LabCps Ex KRRC p189 CR France134,Col KRRC att5LabCps

BLEWITT,Baker Arthur Rawson Capt kia 8-3-16 IA 1/9GurkhaRif p274 MR38

BLEWITT,John Henry.MID Lt dow 22-4-17 IA 54Sikhs att53 p274MR38,53 att54

BLIGH,Eric Lt kia 9-5-15 3 att2ELancs p110 CR France566

BLIGH,Frederick Arthur TMaj ded 15-11-15 8/154RH&FA p25 CR Hamps85

BLIGH,Jack Frederick.MC.AMaj kia 1-7-17 D121RFA p25 CR Belgium1

BLIGHT,Ernest James T2Lt kia 11-3-17 27NumbF p60 CR France1182

BLIGHT,Horace Vincent.MC.TLt kia 15-6-18 RASC att4RFus p192 CR France33

BLINCH,Wilfrid Joseph Hastings 2Lt kia 16-8-16 13Lpool p71 MR21

BLISS,Arthur Joseph 2Lt kia 9-9-16 4 att7Leinst p174 MR21,ExRAMC

BLISS,Charles.CIE.Maj dow 22-12-14 IA 1/1GurkhaRif p274 CR France201

BLISS,Francis Kennard T2Lt kia 28-9-16 59RFA 459HB p25 CR France251

BLISS,James.MC&Bar.Capt kia 31-7-17 1/6SfthH p241 CR Belgium36

BLISS,Thomas 2Lt dow 23-12-16 6SfthH p241 CR France251

BLISS,Wilfrid Marryat LtCol kia 10-3-15 2ScotRif p103 CR France260

BLISSETT,Percy Cecil 2Lt kia 9-10-17 HAC p206 MR30

BLOCK,F.J.Maj 22-9-18 3Glouc Ex RWar CR Sussex183

BLOCK,Maurice William Palmer Col ded 5-3-19 RH&FA p25 CR France1788

BLOFELD,Dudley.MC.2Lt kia 8-10-16 1/22Lond p251 MR20

BLOFELD,Robert Alban 2Lt dow PoW 20-4-17 8Hamps p229 MR34

BLOFIELD,Frank D'Arcy 2Lt kia 13-5-15 2LifeGds p20 MR29,BLOFIELD 12-5-15

BLOGG,Edward Basil.DSO.Maj dow 15-3-16 RE 4LondFC p209 CR France80,kia 16-3-16

BLOIS,Dudley George.DSO.LtCol dow 14-7-16 84RFA p25&258 CR France141

BLOIS-JOHNSON,Thomas Gordon.CMG.CIE.LtCol 5-11-18 IA 2/67Punjabis p274 MR67

BLOMFIELD,Arthur Eustace Lt ded 28-10-17 RFA 23DAC p207 CR Italy7,28-10-18

BLOMFIELD,Charles George Massie Maj kia 9-6-15 1RWar p64 CR Belgium85

BLONFIELD,William Henry T2Lt dow 26-10-17 RASC p192 see BONFIELD,W.H.

BLOOD,Bindon Capt kld 29-9-15 4Huss attRFC p1&21 CR Surrey162

BLOOM,Bertram T2Lt ded 30-6-18 3Lpool p71 CR Eire84

BLOOM,Henry TLt kia 14-2-17 12Yorks p89

BLOOMER,Arnold Grayson Lt dow 3-8-17 3 att2Lincs p74 CR Belgium7

BLOOMER,Guy Howard Walmesley T2Lt kia 5-9-18 2Lincs p74 CR France245

BLOOMFIELD,Arthur Herbert 2Lt kia 9-7-17 8Glouc p106 MR29

BLOOMFIELD,Gerald Arthur T2Lt kld 13-2-18 RFC p15 CR Berks37

BLOOR,Guy Hegan Lt ded 20-11-18 3RFA p207 CR Italy7

BLOOR,Ronald Terence 2Lt kia 23-1-18 5SStaffs p229 CR France115,1/6Bn

BLOOR,Vincent Uzielli 2Lt ded 25-8-14 2DLI p265 CR Staffs134

BLOOR,William Henry TLt/ACapt kia3-1-18 149RFA p25 CR Belgium15

BLOORE,Ronald Henry TLtACapt kia 28-4-18 14 att17Lpool p71 CR Belgium111

BLOSSE,Francis Lynch Capt ded 17-2-15 WIndReg p267

BLOTT,Thomas Watkin TLtACapt kia 9-4-17 24NumbF p60 CR France184

BLOUNT,Greville Hubert Robins Capt dow 23-9-14 RFA p25 CR France1839

BLOUNT,J.H.2Lt ded 6-7-18 1/2 O&BLI &RAF p129 CR Suff55

BLOWERS,Charles Paxton 2Lt dow 2-10-18 4Suff p217 CR France512,2Bn

BLOWS,Cyril Sydney George 2Lt kia 9-9-16 1/4Lond p246 MR21

BLOY,Laurence Henry Capt kia 29-6-16 5LancF p221 CR France1512

BLUE,Dougall Capt dow 11-5-15 ScotRif att2Bn p103 CR France345

BLUMER,John T2Lt dow 26-9-16 283RFA p25 CR France329

BLUMFELD,Hubert Winterbotham Lt kia 23-2-17 9Mddx attMGC p186&236 MR38

BLUMFIELD,William George 2Lt dow 21-3-18 RGA 186SB p38 CR Belgium85

BLUNDELL,William Kennedy TCapt ded 13-12-18 12Beds p254 CR Somerset25

BLUNDEN,Lewis 2Lt kia 22-7-16 5RSuss p228 CR France296

BLUNDEN,Oswald TCapt kia 4-7-16 16RB p177 CR France727

BLUNT,Charles George T2Lt kia 21-3-18 3RB p178 CR France725

BLUNT,Duncan Hamilton.DSO.MIDx2 MajTLtCol kia 3-10-17 1Dev p76 MR30

BLUNT,Ernest Lindsay LtACapt kia 2-11-18 RGA 24SB p38 CR France231

BLUNT,Francis Clifford 2Lt dow 14-10-15 1/4Leic p220 CR France98

BLUNT,Harold Ernest.MC.Capt ded 16-2-19 SussYeo p205 CR Belgium396

BLUNT,John 2Lt dow 15-10-15 5Lincs p220 CR France98

BLURTON,Cyril Evers 2Lt kia 22-10-17 1 att15N&D Z'Coy p133 MR30

BLY,Harold Alfred Edwin 2Lt ded 17-11-18 RGA p209 CR Essex274

BLYTH,Alick Frederick Lt kia 22-8-17 NCycBn att2/5Gloucp253 MR30,23-8-17

BLYTH,Benjamin Hall LtCol ded 13-5-17 RE

BLYTH,Dennis Carleton T2Lt kia 28-8-15 RE 93FC p43 CR Belgium28

BLYTH,Edward John 2Lt kia 26-3-18 RFC p15 MR20

BLYTH,Herbert Russel MajTLtCol ded 17-1-18 Ess 2GarrBn p131 MR65

BLYTH,James Charles 2Lt kia 13-4-17 5 att1KRRC p149 CR France728

BLYTH,James Reginald T2Lt kia 10-7-16 11RB p178 MR29

BLYTH,Reginald Crommelin Popham Capt kia 4-6-15 Glouc attRFus p106 MR4

BLYTH,Robert Paterson 2Lt kia 10-7-16 6CamH p167 CR Belgium58

BLYTH,Stuart Wynter Lt ded 13-11-15 5RWKent Res p269 CR Kent122

BLYTH,William TLt dow 7-11-18 46MGC Inf p181 CR France441

BLYTHE,Alan Lancelot Capt ded 27-11-18 1RFA CR Lancs196

BLYTHE,Harold T2Lt ded 10-2-17 GL &32RFC p5 CR France1489

BLYTHE,Norman Harry T2Lt kia 4-8-16 12Manch p154 MR21

BLYTHE,Percy Alfred.MID Capt kia 30-7-16 18Manch p154 CR France402

BLYTON,Arthur Allister 2Lt kia 5-9-18 A70RFA p208 CR France421

-BOADEN,William Freeman T2Lt kia 16-4-18 49MGC Inf p181 MR30

BOAG,Alfred 2Lt kld 29-4-16 7Lond attRFC p17&247 CR Mddx34,Lt

BOAG,Archibald Fullarton 2Lt kia 23-3-16 4A&SH p172 CR France114

BOAG,Herbert Edward T2Lt kia 31-7-17 MGC att B'BnTankCps p181 MR29

BOAL,James Spence 2Lt dow 29-1-17 RGA 109SB p38 CR France177

BOAL,John Kirk LtACapt kia 3-5-17 3 att1RIrF p170 MR20

BOAL,William Wainhouse T2Lt dow 10-10-18 7Nhampt p137 MR16,kia

BOARD,George William Lt kia 30-11-17 7ESurr p112 MR17,Ex RFC

BOARD,Richard Frank Lt dow 30-10-18 RE 479FC p210 CR France739,Capt kia

BOARD,William John 2Lt dow 22-9-18 130RFA att31Bde p25 CR Greece1

BOARDLEY,Harold TLt kia 26-9-17 8KSLI p144 MR30

BOARDMAN,Alfred 2Lt kia 21-9-18 RSuss att16Bn p118 MR16,Arthur

BOARDMAN,John Hopwood CaptTMaj dow 25-4-18 PoW 2 O&BLI att9RB p130 CR Germany3

BOARDMAN,Thomas Henry.DSO.TLtCol dow 5-8-17 8InniskF p104 CR Belgium7

BOARDMAN,William.DCM.2Lt kia 28-10-18 4SfthH p241 CR France1254

BOAS,Ernest George 2Lt kia 1-7-16 5 att13RIrRif p169 MR21

BOASE,Edgar Leslie Capt kia 30-7-16 1/4 att1/7BlkW p230 CR France1890

BOAST,Frederick 2Lt kld 28-12-19 23Lancs CR Ireland14

BOAST,John S.MC.Capt kia 22-3-18 2SLancs p125 CR France438

BOAST,Thomas Townshend MID 2Lt kld 29-9-18 3Norf p73 CR France905

BOBBY,Arthur Lawrence T2Lt kia 20-11-17 att16Mddx p146 MR17,Laurence

BOBBY,Sidney Fitzgerald T2Lt kia 1-7-16 GL 18DLI att93TMB p189 MR21

BOCKETT,Harold Arthur Palmer 2Lt kia 3-5-17 2HAC p206 MR20

BOCKING,Bernard.MC.T2Lt kia 21-8-18 12Yorks att11EYorks p89 CR France193

BOCKING,John Webb 2Lt kia 24-4-18 3YLI att2/4Lond p142 MR27

BODDAM-WHETHAM,Cecil Capt kia 14-12-14 3BlkW attGordH p128 MR29

BODDAM-WHETHAM,A C DSO.LtCol kld 22-6-19 4A&SH attRAF p172

BODDINGTON,Cecil Herbert TCapt kia 11-4-17 HouseholdBn p20 MR20,BODINGTON

BODDINGTON,Guy Livingstone Capt kia 19-12-16 6RWar p214 MR21,Livingston

BODDINGTON,Myles.MC.TCapt kia 1-7-16 6KSLI p144 CR Belgium4

BODDINGTON,Oswald William Lt kia 13-10-15 5NStaffs p238 CR France423

BODDINGTON,Ralph Thomas 2Lt kia 2-11-17 25Lond p252 CR Palestine8, 1/10Bn

BODDINGTON,Vincent Coke Chap4Cl ded 13-3-17 RAChDept att35GenHosp p199 CR Berks125

BODDY,G.G.D.T2Lt dow 27-3-16 9RFus p66 MR29,4Bn

BODEL,Frederick Ernest MC Capt kia 31-7-17 8Lpool p215 MR29,Frederic

BODEN,Anthony Drummond Maj kia 24-9-14 3RB p178 MR15

BODEN,Hugh Charles Wollaston TCapt kia 11-10-15 12N&D p133 CR Belgium111

BODEN,Samuel Standidge T2Lt kia 15-10-16 14DLI att14MGC Inf p160&181 MR21,15-10-16

BODENHAM,Charles James Lt kia 9-8-18 HampsYeo p203 MR30

BODENHAM,Henry Edward Charles Hyacinth Lt kia 7-9-16 49MGC Inf p181 CR France630

BODENHAM,S W 2Lt ded 25-10-18 RGA 117HB p38 CR Glouc9,Lt

BODEY,Alan Ralph Lt kia 28-6-16 7Lpool p215 MR20

BODGER,Robert Hendry Lt ded 15-7-18 IARO att1/32SikhPnrs p274 MR67,Capt

BODKER,John George TLt kia 20-11-17 Y&L att2/6WRid p158 CR France755,2/5Bn

BODKIN,Leo Francis.DSO.Maj ded 30-8-19 IA 113Inf p274 MR65,112Inf

BODLE,A Maj 3-3-15 RE CR Hamps179

BODMAN,Charles Walter T2Lt kia 24-8-18 15DLI p160 MR16

BODVEL-ROBERTS,Harold Owen.MC 2Lt dow 18-11-15 7Lond CR France1

BODY,Edward Upton.MC.TCaptAMaj kia 4-11-18 130/40RFA p25&258 CR France1081

BODY,Frank Lydford TCapt dow 18-6-17 8Beds p85 CR France80

BODY,Grant Trenavin Capt kia 14-9-14 1LNLancs p135 MR15

BODYCOMB,George Thomas T2Lt kld 18-2-18 RFC p15 CR Kent124

BOGLE,Albert T2Lt kia 10-8-17 12 att10RInniskF p104 MR29

BOGLE,Andrew Blyth McCulloch T2Lt kia 14-7-16 11RScots p53 CR France399

BOGLE,David Morrow 2Lt dow 1-9-16 2RInniskF p104 CR France100

BOGLE,George Stafford T2Lt dow 15-10-15 RE 68Coy p43 MR4

BOGLE,John.MC.Capt kia 20-9-17 5ScotRif p224 MR30

BOGUE,Patrick Yule T2Lt kia 23-7-17 9ESurr p112 CR Belgium29,24-7-17

BOGUE,Robert Alexander,MC.Lt dow 26-9-17 A Coy 16HLI CR Scot85

BOILEAU,Edmund Kenyvett LtACapt kia 18-10-17 RE p43 CR EAfrica11 &CR Tanzania1

BOILEAU,Edward Bulmer Whicher Lt kia 3-10-18 1Dors p123 CR France699

BOILEAU,Frank Ridley Farrer Col dow 26-8-14 RE Cmd &Staff 3Div p43 CR France34 &1202,28-8-14

BOIS,Dudley Gillespy Lt ded 4-10-15 RGA 6HB p38 MR4

BOLAND,Michael Thomas T2Lt kia 26-2-18 2RMunstF p175 CR France364

BOLAY,A R.2Lt kld 27-5-18 GL &65RAF p189 CR France71

BOLES,Hastings Fortescue 2Lt dow 24-5-15 17Lancers &RFC p1&23 CR France285,Lt

BOLES,Noel Henry Lt kia 11-1-16 2Dors attRNAS p123 CR Gallipoli1

BOLES,Robert Stephen T2Lt dow 6-5-18 1RDubF p176 CR France180,Lt kia

BOLGER,Katie SNurse ded 5-3-16 QAIMNS CR Wilts167

BOLITHO,Geoffrey Richard 2Lt ded 25-10-16 4RFC p2 CR France514 Ex DevR

BOLITHO,Victor Ayling T2Lt dow 9-4-17 HouseholdBn p20 CR France730

BOLITHO,William Edward Thomas DSO LtCol ded 21-2-19 1DevYeo CR Cornwall172

BOLITHO,William Torquill Macleod Lt kia 24-5-15 19Huss p23 MR29

BOLLAND,Frederick William Henry 2Lt kia 7-6-17 7RFus p66 MR29

BOLLAND,Theodore Julian Maj kia 9-5-15 9Lpool p216 MR22

BOLLOM,Johnson 2Lt kia 24-9-16 12DLI p160 CR France703

BOLLOND,John Wulstan Charles T2Lt kia 9-4-17 10Norf p73 CR France1182,BOLLAND

BOLSTER,C.Hawkes Capt 8-12-14 9KRRC CR Eire143

BOLSTER,Francis Julian LtACapt dow 4-4-17 RGA 31SB p38 CR France96

BOLSTER,George Emil Maj dow 23-10-14 RFA p25 CR Belgium57

BOLSTER,Richard MC.CaptAMaj kia 4-6-17 124/28RFA p25 CR France68,5-6-17

BOLT,Bertram Leslie T2Lt dow 13-5-16 7KSLI p144 CR France285

BOLTER,Charles Albert T2Lt kia 12-4-18 29MGC Inf p181 CR France298

BOLTON,Cecil Rawley TCapt kia 22-2-17 22Lpool p71 CR France420,19Bn

BOLTON,Edward Trevor.MID TLt kia 10-4-18 11Suff p78 CR France685

BOLTON,Geoffrey Charles 2Lt kia 1-8-16 17N&D p133

BOLTON,Gilbert Benson T2Lt kia 18-11-16 8NStaffs p156 CR France215

BOLTON,Gordon Wallace Capt kia 24-4-18 1EYorks p83 MR30

BOLTON,H S.Lt 22-3-21 RFA CR Scot533

BOLTON,Harry Hargreaves Capt dow 23-5-15 5ELancs p226 MR4,24-5-15

BOLTON,Henry Albert TCapt kia 1-7-16 23NumbF p60 MR21

BOLTON,Herbert Frederick TLt dow 3-5-17 10SLancs att103MGC p125&181 CR France95

BOLTON,John Lt dow 4-6-15 5ELancs p226,2Lt&Lt 2entries CR Gallipoli6

BOLTON,John Ritso Nelson.MID Lt dow 27-9-15 104/22RFA p25 CR France109,25-9-15

BOLTON,Maurice Baldwin.MC.Capt kia 21-3-18 5ELancs p226 CR France716,dow PoW 26-3-18

BOLTON,Percy James T2Lt dow 5-11-18 RWKent att7Bn p140 CR France341

BOLTON,Reginald Lightbown Capt drd 3-8-18 7Manch p237

BOLTON,Robert Frederick T2Lt dow 10-6-17 11NumbF p60 CR Belgium11

BOLTON,Stuart Lt kia 17-3-18 4RLancs p213

BOLTON,William Curtis.MC.TLt kia 1-7-16 8Y&L p158 MR21

BOLUS,Dorothy Kathleen Mary Miss drd 4-6-18 VAD p200 CR Devon2,Dorothea

BOMBER,Jeffrey Allan TLt kia 14-4-18 3Worc p108 MR32

BONATHAN,Frank Stanley.MC.2Lt kia 28-4-17 17Mddx p146 MR20

BONCKER,Barry Robert 2Lt kia 1-7-16 1EYorks p83 MR21

BOND,Alfred Dalton 2Lt ded 22-5-16 5Y&L p238 CR Yorks574,Lt

BOND,Bernard TLt dow 2-8-16 19 att11N&D p133 CR France44

BOND,Cecil William Capt kia 2-8-17 RAMC att97FA p194 MR29

BOND,Charles Edward TMaj kia 10-7-16 13WelshR p126 MR21,9-7-16

BOND,Charles Gordon Capt kia 25-11-15 2Wilts p152 CR France279

BOND,Charles Nesbit Lt dow 30-6-16 3SomLI att1/4Lincs p79 CR Frane281,Nesbitt kia

BOND,Charles Reginald 2Lt kia 26-9-17 2Suff p78 MR30

BOND,E.M.Sister 3-11-18 QAIMNS CR Lincs156

BOND,Edmund Lt kia 1-10-18 5WRid att32MGC p186&227 CR France237

BOND,Ernest Frederick T2Lt kia 26-9-18 RBerks att5Bn p138 CR France369

BOND,Frank Bertram T2Lt kia 24-10-18 31/35RFA p25 CR Italy7

BOND,Frederick Hamilton Bligh 2Lt dow 13-5-15 122RFA p25 CR Belgium101

BOND,Gustave Samuel 2Lt kia 9-4-18 B276RFA p25 CR France260

BOND,H.H.DSO.BrCol 10-11-19 RFA CR Eire71

BOND,Hubert Samuel Emery Lt kld 17-6-17 7WelshR attRFC p17&230 CR Wales17,2Lt

BOND,Reginald Edwin Maj kia 3-3-15 IA 4Rajputs p274 MR61

BOND,Robert Harold Lt kia 14-9-14 2KRRC p149 CR France1329,dow

BOND,Thomas Morgan T2Lt kia 3-5-15 11RIrRif p169 MR32

BOND,William Arthur.MC&Bar.TLtTCapt kia 22-7-17 YLI &40RFC p5&142 MR20

BOND,William Henry Hugh T2Lt kia 22-6-17 26RFus p66 CR Belgium154

BONE,Albert Edward Capt dow 3-11-18 B242RFA p25 CR France40,ded

BONE,Charles John T2Lt kia 9-8-18 14TankCps p188 CR France649,dow

BONE,George Drummond 2Lt kia 9-5-15 1/1BlkW p128 MR22

BONE,Harry Whittenburg 2Lt kia 25-9-15 1SStaffs p122 MR19,Whittenbury

BONE,John Craigie 2Lt kia 28-4-17 8RScots p212 CR France581

BONE,John Hugh 2Lt kia 22-7-16 6ESurr att1/5N&D p226 CR France504

BONE,Quintin TCapt kia 19-9-18 RLancs p58 CR Greece6

BONE,Ronald Walter 2Lt kia 12-10-17 5EKent p213 MR30

BONE,Thomas William TLtACapt ded 6-8-18 SomLI 1GarBn p79 MR43 &CR Pakistan50A

BONE,Victor Arnold TCapt kia 18-9-18 11RWelshF p97 CR Greece5

BONES,A.M.TLt kia 1916 KAR p202

BONEY,A.H.Lt 10-2-19 KRRC CR Lond14

BONFIELD,William Henry 2Lt kia 26-10-17 RASC CR Belgium172 seeBLONFIELD,W.H.

BONHAM,Denis Pierpont 2Lt dow 16-11-16 1HAC p206 CR France40

BONHAM,William Daniel T2Lt kia 14-10-17 7Norf p73 MR20

BONHAM-CARTER,Arthur Thomas Capt kia 1-7-16 3 att1Hamps p120 CR France1890

BONHAM-CARTER,Guy Capt dow 15-5-15 19Huss attOxfYeo p23 CR Belgium4

BONHAM-CARTER,Norman T2Lt kia 3-5-17 HouseholdBn p20 CR France546

BONNAR,James Crawford Lt kld 22-5-15 9A&SH p244 CR Scot82

BONNER,Augustine T2Lt kia 30-4-17 GL &13RFC p5 CR France1188

BONNER,Singleton.DSO.Maj dow 1-5-17 1SStaffs att10RFus p122 CR France40,LtCol

BONNER,William 2Lt kld 19-6-18 RLancs attRAF p58 CR France84

BONNEY,James Patterson T2Lt kia 6-10-17 RGA 351SB p38 CR Belgium20

BONNEY,Sydney Richard T2Lt kia 26-9-16 12 att10Ess p131 MR21

BONNIN,Ronald Homfray(Tom).MID Lt kia 24-8-18 1/2KOSB att47Inf p101 CR France210

BONNYMAN,Edward William.DSO.MC.TCapt dow 11-8-18 10A&SH p173 CR France29,BONNEYMAN

BONSER,Geoffrey Alwyn Gershom Capt kia 29-9-18 RAMC att12Norf p253 CR Belgium451

BONSER,Winfield Joice TCapt kia 25-9-15 12RB p178 MR32

BONSEY,Edwin Kenneth 2Lt dow 2-7-18 RGA 99SB p38 CR France31

BONSEY,Francis Henry William 2Lt ded 20-12-18 IARO p274 MR65

BONAHOR,John 2Lt dow PoW 26-7-18 2/6SStaffs p229 CR Germany4

BONSOR,Malcom Cosmo Capt kia 10-3-18 NorfYeo p204 CR Palestine3,Malcolm

BONVALOT,Edward St.Laurent 2Lt dow 9-10-15 RoO att2CldGds att2Bn p51 CR France80

BONYUN,Frank Vernon T2Lt kia 2-1-18 32RFC p15 CR Belgium18

BOOCOCK,Herbert Jennings 2Lt kia 6-11-17 7Worc att17Suff p226 CR Palestine1

BOOCOCK,William Narey 2Lt ded 3-3-19 RWar p263 CR War101

BOOKER,Stanley Charles.MC.Lt kia 10-10-16 2/7Worc p225 CR France631

BOOKLESS,James Donald 2Lt dow 24-5-15 4 CamH p243 CR France102

BOOMER,Walter Charter.MC.TCapt dow 1-10-18 12RIrRif p169 CR Belgium157

BOON,Arthur 2Lt kld 29-3-17 7Manch attRFC p17&237 CR War50

BOONE,Charles Frederick de Bohun Capt dow 23-9-14 2Ess p131 CR France462

BOONE,Henry Griffith.DSO.Maj dow 5-9-17 94RFA p25 CR Belgium18,6-9-17

BOONE,William Ernest 2Lt kia 20-4-15 YLI p142 MR29

BOONHAM,W.H.2Lt dow 10-8-20 3LancF CR Lancs102

BOOR,Alaric Pinder TLt dow 31-10-17 GL 7 O&BLI att13RFC p5 CR Palestine1

BOORNE,George Howard T2Lt kld 28-3-17 37RFC p5 CR Lancs103

BOOSEY,Frederick Cecil Lt kia 22-11-15 7Norf p73 MR38

BOOSEY,Noel Charles Lt dow 22-7-15 22Lond p251 CR France98,Capt

BOOSEY,Rupert George 2Lt kia 22-5-15 4DragGds p21 CR Belgium57,24-5-15

BOOTE,Charles Edward.TD.LtCol kia 1-7-16 5NStaffs p237 CR France576,Edmund

BOOTE,Charles William TCapt kia 4/5-4-16 8Ches p95 MR38

BOOTH,Ainslie TLt dow 30-4-16 RAMC att7KOSB p194 CR France423,kia

BOOTH,Arthur Wilfred T2Lt kia 22-3-18 19Lpool p71 MR27

BOOTH,Baron Brooke 2lt kia 15-9-16 7NumbF p214 MR21

BOOTH,Cecil Richard T2Lt dow 21-3-16 1GordH p166 CR France40

BOOTH,Cyril Talbot 2Lt kia 10-6-17 17Lond p250 MR29

BOOTH,Edward Arthur Lt mbk 23-9-19 GL NR p256 MR70 &CR Europe180

BOOTH,Francis Hardinge Follett ACapt kia 26-9-17 6 att1Worc p108 MR30,6 att2Bn

BOOTH,Fred T2Lt dow 24-4-18 56MGC p181 CR France95

BOOTH,Frederick Arthur.DCM.T2Lt kia 11-10-18 WYorks att1/7WRid p81 CR France612

BOOTH,Frederick Atkins T2Lt kia 27-9-15 2EKent p57 MR19

BOOTH,Harold Stanley T2Lt kia 1-7-16 11 att8Y&L p158 MR21

BOOTH,Herbert T2Lt dow 3-5-17 12WYorks p81 CR France1182

BOOTH,James,MC TLt kia 6-11-18 56MGC Inf p181 CR Belgium195

BOOTH,John 2Lt kia 7-10-16 6RFus p66 MR21,att8Bn

BOOTH,John Charles Lt ded 30-9-16 att281LondRFA p207 CR France145

BOOTH,John George 2Lt kia 22-11-17 2/6WYorks p218 MR17

BOOTH,John Lyon.MC.TLtACapt kia 18-4-18 2SfthH p164 CR France98

BOOTH,John Thomas T2Lt dow 19-11-17 GL &2AircraftSupplyDepot RFC p5 CR France40

BOOTH,Joseph William 2Lt dow 8-10-18 B93RFA p25 CR France256

BOOTH,Lawrence Elliot.MC&Bar.CaptAMaj kia 13-4-18 38RFA p25 CR Belgium89,Lawrence

BOOTH,Major William T2Lt kia 1-7-16 15WYorks p81 CR France74,Lt

BOOTH,Patrick Dick.DSO.MC.TCapt dow 2-12-17 26RFA DivTM Officer p25 MR17

BOOTH,Percival Edward Owen 2Lt kia 1-7-16 14Mddx &93MGC p181 CR France156

BOOTH,Philip Eustace 2Lt dow 4-12-17 11Mddx p146 CR France145

BOOTH,Philip John Lt ded 2-3-20 2RScotF p263 CR Asia51

BOOTH,Robert Hutchinson Capt ded 1-1-16 RASC 42ELancsFA p253 CR Europe1

BOOTH,William T2Lt dow 28-12-17 1RB &17RFC p5&178,28-2-17 &78RFC CR Belgium18,att7RFC

BOOTH,William Albert T2Lt kia 23-11-17 GL &8RFC p5 CR France403

BOOTH,William Leslie Capt dow 28-5-15 6Lond p246 CR France102

BOOTH,William Stanley 2Lt kia 8-7-16 4WRid p227 CR France252

BOOTHBY,Charles Geoffrey T2Lt kia 28-4-16 RE 177TC p43 CR Belgium114

BOOTHBY,Ernest Brooke T2Lt kia 10-7-16 13RB p178 MR29

BOOTHBY,John Henry Lt kia 23-7-16 U'RHA p25 CR France188

BOOTHROYD,Edwin 2Lt dow 21-3-18 PoW 4 att26N&D p133 CR Germany1,17-4-18

BOOTY,William George Stanbury T2Lt kia 30-10-16 GL &1KARif p201 CR EAfrica40

BOQUC,Robert Alexander.MC.TLt dow 26-9-17 16HLI p162

BORAIN,Harold Goldsmith 2Lt dow 5-11-17 22RH&FA p25 CR France40,27/32

BOREHAM,Harry Pendry T2Lt kia 16-4-18 18Mddx p146 MR32,Lt

BORLAND,George McPhearson 2Lt kia 14-4-18 3 att9NumbF p60 MR32,McPherson

BORLAND,Sydney Douglas 2Lt ded 6-11-18 IARO attS&TCps p274 MR43,Lt

BORMAN,George Wilson TLt dow 2-1-16 12N&D p133

BOROUGH,Alaric Charles Henry Lt kia 1-12-17 1WelshGds p53 CR France415

BOROUGH,George Herbert TCapt ded 7-11-16 RASC 578HT AuxCo att2Ind C Div p192 CR France40,8-11-16

BORRELL,Lancelot T2Lt dow 10-7-16 12NumbF p60 CR Numb19

BORRER,John Maximilian 2Lt ded 9-9-17 4RSuss p228 CR Egypt1,Lt

BORRETT,Alfred Frank Cyril LtACapt kia 24-11-17 11RGLI p200 MR17

BORRETT,Arthur Henry 2Lt kia 17-2-17 IA 2/8 att1/8GurkhaRif p274 CR Iraq5

BORRETT,M.A.Lt 24-6-21 IA 16Cav MR67

BORROUGH,Horace William ACapt dow 18-8-16 3 att1Dors p123 CR France114

BORROW,Cyril Ernest Lt ded PoW 24-3-19 Nhampt p265 CR Leic97

BORROW,Frederick Guy Lomer Lt dow 22-8-17 1/4Nhampt p234 CR Egypt1

BORST,Charles Louis 2Lt kia 24-11-17 4 att6RWSurr p212 MR17

BORTHISTLE,William John 2Lt kia 29-1-18 RMunstF &RFC p15&175 CR France1061

BORTHWICK,Arthur Pollock Sym 2Lt dow 15-4-18 58MGC p181 CR Frqnce145,Pollok

BORTHWICK,Donald Walker 2Lt kia 28-12-16 4RWSurr attMGC Inf p186&212 MR37

BORTHWICK,George Williamson T2Lt kia 28-6-16 6CamH p167 MR19

BORTON,Cyprian Edward Maj kia 2-8-17 IA 129Baluchis att&MalayStGdes p274 CR Asia62

BOSANQUET,Armytage Percy.MC.Capt kia 25-1-17 3DCLI att5Wilts p114 CR Iraq5

BOSANQUET,Graham Bromhead.MC Maj kia 1-7-16 1Glouc p106 CR France267

BOSANQUET,Lionel Arthur TLtCol kia 22-8-15 9N&D p133 MR4

BOSANQUET,Sidney Courthorpe 2Lt dow 17-12-14 SR att1Mddx p146 CR France1140,Courthope kia

BOSCAWEN,Vere Douglas Hon.2Lt kia 29-10-14 1CldGds p51 MR29

BOSCOWEN,George Edward.Hon.DSO.Maj dow 7-6-18 RFA 116SB p25 CR France1753

BOSHELL,Frederick Stephen T2Lt kia 23-7-18 5RBerks p138 CR France1014,1Bn

BOSHELL,Hugh Thomas Barron Capt kia 22-3-18 4 att10/11HLI p162 MR20

BOSHER,Alfred Henry Bruce 2Lt kia 16-8-17 45RFA p25 CR Belgium140

BOSTOCK,Alexander Gordon 2Lt ded 12-1-19 RGA p209 CR Suff83,Lt

BOSTOCK,Alfred Sidney 2Lt mbk 27-5-18 8DLI p257 MR18,D.S.

BOSTOCK,Archibald Thomas TCapt dow 30-9-15 14NumbF p60 CR France40

BOSTOCK,Clifford 2LtTLt kia 20-9-17 10RWar p64 MR30

BOSTOCK,Edward Lyon 2Lt dow 5-4-17 4RSuss p228 CR France164

BOSTOCK,Eric Norman MC 2Lt mbk 27-5-18 4Nhampt p257 MR18,2Bn

BOSTOCK,Guy Edwin TCapt kia 30-1-16 8RMunstF p175 CR France222

BOSTOCK,Hugh William 2Lt kia 12-6-15 6SStaffs p229 CR Belgium43

BOSTOCK,Joseph 2Lt kia 21-3-18 C'Coy10Ches p95 CR France1484,24-3-18

BOSTOCK,Neville Stanley 2Lt kia 22-4-17 B162RFA p25 CR France1182

BOSTOCK,Robert Ashton TCapt ded 17-8-17 RAMC p267

BOSTOCK-SMITH,Claude Lt kia 5-10-18 RE p210 CR Belgium44,attRFA

BOSTON,Lawrence TLt accded 6-5-16 9WYorks p81 CR Hamps1

BOSTON,Thomas TLt ded 25-12-18 10MGC Inf p181 CR Egypt9

BOSWALL,James Donaldson Capt kia 13-6-15 10SfthH att1Ess p164 MR4,6-6-15

BOSWELL,Claude Oliver Lt kia 9-10-17 5ELancs p226 MR30

BOSWELL,Denis St.George Knox.MIDx2 CaptTMaj ded 28-9-18 DCLI att82MGC p114&181 CR Greece2

BOSWELL,James Baxendale Maj&QM ded 23-3-16 RAMC 2/2FA p253 CR Yorks362

BOSWELL,Paul Victor 2Lt ded 29-6-19 D175RFA p261 CR Staffs52

BOSWELL,Percy George T2Lt kia 1-7-16 8YLI p142 MR21

BOSWELL,William Gerald Knox Capt dow 28-7-16 5 att2RB p178 CRFrance51

BOSWORTH,Arthur Wright 2Lt kia 26-9-15 8Lincs p74 MR19

BOSWORTH,Philip Charles Worthington Lt kia 26-9-15 8Lincs p74 MR19

BOSWORTHICK,William Howard 2Lt kia 7-11-18 1/5Dev p217 CR France924

BOTHAM,Arthur Frederick.MID 2Lt dow 18-6-17 D106RH&FA p25 CR Belgium11

BOTHAMLEY,Richard Arnold T2Lt kia 9-4-18 40MGC Inf p181 MR32 &CR France1896 ExWKentYeo

BOTHAMLEY,William Broughton 2Lt kia 25-9-16 4/10Mddx p236 CR France397

BOTHWELL,Alec.MC.TLtACapt kia 26-4-17 1GordH p166 CR France531,Alexander

BOTT,Charles Stuart 2Lt kia 17-4-17 Lincs p74 CR France1188,Lt

BOTT,Francis George Lt dow 20-8-20 1A 35ScindeHorse p274 CR Iraq6

BOTT,George 2Lt kia 9-2-17 6 att1RB p178 CR France115,3Bn

BOTT,George Gerald Randell.MC.Lt kia 13-4-18 3SLancs att8BordR p125&258 CR Belgium168

BOTT,John Arden TCapt ded 5-8-17 17RFus p263 CR Wales535

BOTT,John George 2Lt 18-9-18 1EYorks CR France666 See BUTT

BOTT,William Ernest TCapt kia 18-9-18 9RFus p66 CR France369

BOTTING,William Rolph 2Lt kia 25-9-17 3 att11RSuss p118 MR30

BOTTOMLEY,Edwin Rhodes 2Lt kia 2-6-17 RFA WRidDAC attRFC p17&208 CR France839,Lt

BOTTOMLEY,Eric William Capt kia 15-6-17 2/4Lond p246 MR20

BOTTOMLEY,Frederick T2Lt drd 4-5-17 3RWelshF p97 CR Italy14

BOTTOMLEY,Frederick T2Lt kia 2-9-18 YLI att5Bn p142 CR France617

BOTTOMLEY,Harry Roderick LtCol dow 18-5-15 2RWSurr p55 CR France80

BOTTOMLEY,John Cecil 2Lt kia 3-9-16 8WYorks p219 MR21

BOTTOMLEY,Thomas Reginald Lt kia 23-9-14 1EYorks p83 MR15

BOTWOOD,Edward Keightley Rev 28-7-16 RAChDept CR Devon11

BOUCH,John Lt ded 23-11-18 1/4ELancs att130RFA p207 CR Surrey1

BOUCHER,Alan Estcourt TCapt dow 25-7-16 9Leic p87 CR France145

BOUCHER,Albert Adolph T2Lt dow 16-10-16 7KSLI att8TMB p144 CR France203,Adolphe

BOUCHER,Alec Edward.MC TLt kia 18-11-16 11RWar p64 CR France339

BOUCHER,Arthur Guy 2Lt kia10-7-17 6 att2KRRC p149 MR31

BOUCHER,Basil Edward Cresswell MID Lt ded 10-5-19 1/2RWFus p263 CR Staffs91,Bazil

BOUCHER,Charles Bailey Lt kia 9-8-15 Y&L p158 MR29

BOUCHER,Henry Mason MC LtTCapt kia 23-4-18 3 att1SomLI p79 CR France98

BOUCHER,William Moore Lt kia 20-11-17 6RWKent p140 CR France379

BOUCHIER,Charles Arthur T2Lt kia 4-11-18 1/2 att9WRid p115 CR France206,Claude

BOUCK-STANDEN,Percy Edward Capt ded 31-10-18 3Hamps MinOfMuns p264 CR Glouc9

BOUGHEY,Anchitel Edward Fletcher TLt drd 10-10-18 8RB p178 CR Ireland14,Anchitel

BOUGHEY,Stanley Henry Parry VC.2Lt dow 4-12-17 1/4RScotF p222 CR Palestine8

BOUIE,Jean Auguste Andre T2Lt kld 24-3-17 GL &RFC p5 CR EAfrica66,BOUIC

BOULLY,Frederick Courtnay 2Lt kia 10-7-17 attRFA p208 MR31

BOULNOIS,Edmund TCapt kia 23-10-16 21WYorks p81 MR21

BOULT,Reginald Herbert Swinton 2Lt kia 8-8-16 6Lpool p215 MR21

BOULTBEE,Arthur Elsdale Lt kia 17-3-17 Nhants &25RFC p5&137 MR20 &CR France1896

BOULTER,George William Capt DC ded 4-7-18 IA MilWorksServ p274
BOULTER,Jack Edward Hewitt.MC. 2Lt dow 15-10-18 2RDubF p176 CR France528
BOULTER,Sidney Frederick 2Lt dow 18-2-17 25Lond p252 CR France177
BOULTIMG,Stanley Ernest 2Lt kld 14-4-17 4Suff attMGC p217 CR France1366,118TMB
BOULTON,Alec Gordon T2Lt ded 19-2-16 SL Intpr to 129Baluchis &APM HQ 3Army p201 CR France167
BOULTON,Arthur Vane 2Lt dow 25-2-17 1&2 att8Glouc p106 CR France40
BOULTON,Charles Valentine T2Lt kia 9-11-17 RE 314RdConstrCo p43 CR Belgium34
BOULTON,Christian Harold Ernest TLt kia 12-10-17 5CamH Staff p167 MR30
BOULTON,Clifford John.MC.TCapt kia 30-8-18 13WelshR p126 CR France217
BOULTON,Frederick Charles William T2Lt kia 30-7-17 8NStaffs p156 CR Belgium60,Lt
BOULTON,Harold Webster T2Lt kia 26-9-15 15DLI p160 MR19
BOULTON,James Babington 2Lt kia 17-2-17 3 att6Nhampt p137 CR France314
BOULTON,Wallace Dawson T2Lt kia 20-4-16 11 att7Glouc p106 MR38
BOUNDY,Frank Everard.MC.TLt dow 30-7-16 17Lpool p71&258 CR France294,kia
BOURCHIER,Arthur George 2Lt kia 9-5-15 2Berks p138 MR32
BOURDILLON,James Imbert Fulton Lt kia 15-7-16 RE 222FC p43 CR France432
BOURDILLON,Paul Aime 2Lt ded 20-3-19 RE
BOURDILLON,Tom Louis.MC.TMaj kia 24-8-17 KRRC att8Bn p149 CR Belgium125
BOURKE,Albert William 2Lt kia 9-5-15 3RIrF att2RIrRif p171 CR France566
BOURKE,Bertram Walter Capt kia 9-5-15 5 att2RDubF p176 MR29
BOURKE,Eustace George Walter Capt kia 16-6-15 KRRC att9Bn p149 CR Belgium165
BOURKE,James Gay Shute T2Lt kia 15-4-18 Lpool att1RWar p71 MR32
BOURKE,Patrick Miller 2Lt kia 25-7-16 28RFA 65HB p25 CR France397
BOURN,John 2LtTLt kia 31-7-17 8NStaffs p156 MR29,1Bn
BOURNE,Austin Spencer 2Lt dow 23-4-17 8SStaffs p122 MR20
BOURNE,Cecil Alfred.MC.CaptAMaj ded 11-12-18 RFA 411/126ArmyBde p25 CR France1142
BOURNE,Cyprian T2Lt dow 11-4-17 6RWSurr p55 CR France113
BOURNE,Gerald Hugh Temple T2Lt kia 18-3-17 KRRC &4RFC p5&149 CR France614
BOURNE,James Matthew 2Lt 17-6-18 2MadrasSMRRifs MR66
BOURNE,John Callander 2Lt kia 18-7-15 9Worc p108 MR4,Callender
BOURNE,Leonard Cecil.MC.T2Lt dow 14-8-17 2RFus p66 CR Belgium16
BOURNE,Ralph 2Lt kia 10-9-17 158RFA p25 CR Belgium24
BOURNE,Rowland Hurst 2Lt dow 24-10-18 RASC att7Suss p192 CR France1142
BOURNE,Stanley Mackenzie TLt kia 4/5-4-16 8RFus att8RWFus p66 MR38,4SWBord
BOURNER,Rowland Moody Nicholson T2Lt dow 28-3-18 3MGC p181 CR France64,Rowley Lt
BOURNS,Charles Lt kia 25-5-15 6 att4RB p178 MR29
BOUSFIELD,A.S.TLt ded 28-6-18 RASC p192 CR Wilts3
BOUSFIELD,Edmund Emerson LtCol dow 25-9-15 IA 123Rif att1/1GurkhaRif p274 CR France631
BOUSFIELD,Mary Cawston ARRC.MID Miss ded 24-2-19 VAD 8GH p200 CR France146
BOUSKILL,Edward T2Lt kia 4-10-17 21Manch p154 CR Belgium308,Lt
BOUSTEAD,Harry Atheling Russell Lt dow 5-4-17 8Mddx attRFC p17&236 CR France832
BOUSTEAD,Lawrence Clive.MID Lt kia 28-6-15 1RDubF W'Coy p176 CR Gallipoli6,29-6-15
BOVE-BLANDY,C.R.2Lt 18-4-16 5SLancs CR Lancs380
BOVE-BLANDY,S.R.Sister 13-1-19 QAIMNS CR Lancs380
BOVET,William MajTLtCol dow 5-7-18 RE CRE 12Div p43 CR France84
BOVEY,William Bernard 2Lt dow 15-11-16 19Lond p250 CR Belgium11
BOVILL,Charles Harry Lt dow 24-3-18 1CldGds p51 CR France113
BOVILL,Edward Henry 2Lt kia 1-7-16 1/16Lond p250 MR21
BOVILL,John Eric 2Lt kia 23-1-16 6DragGds p21 CR France423
BOW,George Clark 2Lt kia 25-3-17 7A&SH attMGC Inf p186&243 MR38
BOW,Herbert Christie 2Lt kia 23-3-18 7 att9ScotRif p224 MR27

BOWATER,George William 2Lt ded 20-2-17 RGA p38 CR War5
BOWDEN,Alfred John Hamilton.DSO.LtCol kia 2-3-17 2Mon p244
BOWDEN,Edward Ratcliffe Lt dow 29-4-15 6NumbF p213 CR France51,28-4-15
BOWDEN,Eric Gordon.MC.MID TMaj kia 22-7-18 11RWSurr p55 CR France924,LtCol
BOWDEN,Horace George Cecil T2Lt kia 11-3-17 45RFC 9Wing p5 CR Belgium11
BOWDEN,James T2Lt kia 30-3-18 66MGC Inf p181 MR27
BOWDEN,Norman 2Lt kia 25-4-18 8N&D attRAF p233&258 CR France1170
BOWDEN,Percival John 2Lt kia 15-4-18 1RWar p64 MR32
BOWDEN,Reginald Charles T2Lt dow 3-3-16 8RLancs p58 CR Belgium11
BOWDEN,Richard Thomas T2Lt kia 16-8-17 4Worc p108 MR30
BOWDEN,Walter Horace T2Lt kia 12-4-18 16Mddx p146 MR32,15-4-18
BOWDEN-SMITH,Ernest Baldwin Lt 26-6-16 RIM CR Iraq6
BOWDEN-SMITH,Walter Ardrian Carnagie Capt dow 28-8-14 RFus p66 CR Belgium244,Adrian Carnegie
BOWE,Eric Arthur T2Lt kia 27-5-18 DLI p160 MR18
BOWE,Stanley Gordon TLt dow 15-5-18 18 att2/5LancF p92 CR France10
BOWELL,Archibald Gordon Edward T2Lt kia 15-7-16 8Leic p87 MR21,14-7-16 Ex9Bn
BOWELL,Ernest Philip 2Lt kia 20-11-17 7 att2/5LancF p221 MR21
BOWELS,James Arthur Lt kia 26-8-14 RH&FA p25 see BOWLES,J.A.
BOWEN,Alan Lt kia 7-8-15 8Manch p237 MR4
BOWEN,Alfred John Hamilton.DSO&Bar.MID LtCol kia 2-3-17 22Mon CR France786
BOWEN,Cuthbert Edward Latimer Lt 1-12-14 EAfrPolice CR EAfrica44
BOWEN,Eynon George Arthur Lt ded PoW 8-9-16 RGA &RFC p2&38 MR20
BOWEN,Francis Moull Storer TLt kia 1-7-16 9RWKent att1InniskF p140 CR France339
BOWEN,Geoffrey Grenside.MC.LtTCapt kia 2-9-18 2LancF p92 CR France155
BOWEN,George Eustace Summers.MC.Capt dow 26-7-17 A83RFA p25 CR Belgium11
BOWEN,Henry Lt&QM kia 21-5-17 1/8ScotRif p225 CR Palestine8
BOWEN,Ivor Lt ded 25-2-17 RE 207FC p43 CR France95
BOWEN,Joseph Jones,MC Lt kia 9-4-18 18WelshR p126 CR France348,9-6-18
BOWEN,Leslie Harold Lt kia 22-12-15 3Lincs p74 CR France924,1Bn
BOWEN,Martin.MC.Capt dow 9-10-17 O&BLI 1/1BucksBn p231 CR France64
BOWEN,Roger Frederick Lt dow PoW 1-9-18 9RWar p64 MR61
BOWEN,Rowland George Breece Lt kia 9-5-15 1Lond p245 CR France348,11Bn
BOWEN,Thomas Henry T2Lt kia 2-8-16 6Leinst att11InniskF p174 CR Belgium339
BOWEN,William 2Lt dow 30-8-18 3 att15WelshR p126 CR France805
BOWEN,William Lloyd.MC.Lt dow 1-9-18 3 att6Mon p244 CR France924
BOWEN-COLTHURST,Robert MacGregor Capt kia 15-3-15 1Leinst p174 MR29
BOWER,A.E.Lt ded 4-7-19 RASC p267
BOWER,Alfred Percy T2Lt kia 1-11-18 1SomLI p79 CR France1079
BOWER,Charles Francis TLtACapt kia 13-9-17 16N&D p133 CR Belgium21
BOWER,Donald Robert T2Lt kia 20-9-18 CamH Res att1SfthH p167 CR Palestine9
BOWER,Edwin Harland Lt kia 21-3-18 2Y&L p158 MR20
BOWER,Frank.MID 2Lt dow 31-3-17 NumbF &60RFC p5&60 CR France164
BOWER,Frederic William TCapt kia 8-3-18 20RFus p66 CR Belgium112
BOWER,Gerard Rimington 2Lt kia 15-7-16 1RWSurr p55 MR21
BOWER,Henry Raymond Syndercombe Lt kld 18/19-12-14 5SStaffs p122 MR32,1Bn
BOWER,Maurice Syndercombe Lt ded 13-1-19 RASC MT p192&257 CR Europe20
BOWER,Thomas Geoffrey T2Lt kia 3-5-17 RHGds HouseholdBn p20 CR France1194
BOWER,William Carroll 2Lt ded 9-8-16 1RLancs p58 CR Belgium11
BOWER,William Charles Ernest TLt kia 19-10-16 RAMC att1NewfindlandR p194 CR France374
BOWER-SMITH,Cedric Gray Capt kia 4-11-15 Glouc &WAFF p201&106
BOWERMAN,Arthur James Lt kia 9-9-16 8SomLI &RFC p2 CR France882
BOWERS,Arthur Hugh Mansell Capt kia 9-8-15 2DLI p160 MR29
BOWERS,Frank Ewart 2Lt dow 31-3-18 5 att10RWSurr p212 CR France64
BOWERS,Frederick Henry Capt kld 29-5-17 RE p209 CR Lincs61

BOWERS,Thomas 2Lt ded 31-8-19 ACycCps p266 CR Norf179
BOWERS,Thomas James Lt kia 7-11-16 3N&D att7LNLancs p133 MR21
BOWERS,William Aubrey Lt dow 3-7-16 5NStaffs p238 CR France120,2-7-16
BOWERS-TAYLOR,Archibald Capt kia 7-6-17 1/6Manch p236 MR29
BOWES,Cyril Hulme T2Lt kia 1-7-16 2WRid p115 CR France1890
BOWES,Ellis Arthur 2Lt kia 12-3-18 4Leic p220 CR France369
BOWES,Roy.MC.TLtACapt dow 5-8-17 15RWelshF p97 CR Belgium16
BOWES,Stanley Ward 2Lt kia 29-9-15 3Dors attRFus p123 MR19
BOWES-LYON,Charles Lindsay Claude Lt kia 23-10-14 3 att1BlkW p128 CR Belgium96
BOWES-LYON,Fergus.Hon TCapt kia 27-9-15 8BlkW p128 MR19
BOWES-LYON,Gavin Patrick Lt kia 27-11-17 3GrenGds p49 MR17
BOWES-SCOTT,Harry George Rodney Lt kia 21-3-16 IARO att29Punjabis p274
BOWES-WILSON,George Hutton Capt kia 17-6-15 24Yorks p220
BOWES-WILSON,John Hutton LtCol 7-6-17 1WRid att9Y&L CR Belgium127
BOWHAY,Eustace Gilbert Capt kia 8-3-16 6Dev p217 MR38
BOWIE,Allan Stuart Hunter 2Lt dow 8-5-18 RGA 23SB p38 CR Belgium38
BOWIE,David Drummond.MM.MID TCapt dow 31-5-18 7KSLI p144 CR France33,MC
BOWIE,George T2Lt kia 12-10-17 RScots att11Bn p53MR30
BOWIE,Henry Lt kia 28-7-18 3 att6BlkW p128 CR France622
BOWIE,Ralph Archibald 2Lt kia 26-9-17 5Leic p220 MR30
BOWKER,Francis Jearrad LtCol kia 21-1-16 1/4Hamps p228 CR Iraq5
BOWKER,Robert Bucknall Maj 5-9-17 RE CR War14
BOWKER,Tom.MID T2Lt kia 9-4-18 244MGC Inf p181 CR France525
BOWLAND,Conrad Cloutman 2Lt dow 26-10-18 6Glouc p225 CR France332
BOWLBY,Geoffrey Vaux Salvin Capt kia 13-5-15 RHGds p20 MR29
BOWLBY,George Elliott Lowe TCapt kia 15-3-16 8Lincs p74 CR France922,Lowes
BOWLBY,Lionel Henry Salvin Lt dow 5-6-16 2Drags p21 CR Belgium167,kia 4-6-15
BOWLBY,Thomas Rupert Capt kia 17-9-14 1Norf p73 MR15
BOWLER,Alfred Arthur 2Lt kia 27-5-18 5NStaffs p238 CR France1755
BOWLER,Sydney 2Lt kia 21-10-17 RGA 237SB p38 CR Belgium36
BOWLER,Thomas Chester 2Lt dow 3-10-18 3 att1/4LNLancs p135 CR France88,Chesters
BOWLER,Thomas George 2Lt kia 30-6-17 RGA 6SB p38 CR Belgium339
BOWLER,William T2Lt kia 9-8-17 74MGC Inf p181 MR29
BOWLES,Alan John MID TCapt kia 10-4-16 1RBerks p138 CR France515,2Bn
BOWLES,Bernard Geoffrey T2Lt kia 3-9-16 EKent p57 CR France402
BOWLES,Edgar Branson 2Lt kia 31-3-18 108RFA 23ArmyBde p25 MR20,21-3-18
BOWLES,James Arthur Lt kia 26-8-14 28RFA p25 CR France716
BOWLES,John Campbell.MIDx2 Capt kia 19-2-15 RE 3FC p43 MR29
BOWLES,John George T2Lt kia 1-11-16 7SLancs p125 CR France384
BOWLES,Percy William MC 2Lt kia 10-9-18 C219 RFA p25 CR France308
BOWLES,Reginald Julian Albany Lt dow 20-7-16 3RWelshF p97 CR France66,2Bn
BOWLES,Wilfred Spencer 2Lt kia 10-7-16 5Ess attMGC Inf p186&232 CR France397
BOWLEY,Thomas Henry 2Lt kia 26-10-14 1Leic p87 MR32
BOWLING,Arthur Henry 2Lt ded 29-9-18 RGA 160SB p38 CR Mddx59
BOWLING,Edwyn Randolph 2Lt kia 4-6-16 9 att8RWKent p140 CR Belgium97
BOWLING,Victor Macdonald 2Lt kia 4-3-17 SR 29RFC p5 CR France158,acckld 12RFC
BOWLY,Reginald Walter TLt kia 29-5-18 22 att20Manch p154 CR France21,20Manch att1Ches
BOWMAN,Alexander White 2Lt kia 25-9-16 EYorks attMGC p83&181
BOWMAN,Anthony Harvey 2Lt dow 20-5-16 37RFA p25 CR France158
BOWMAN,Claude Herbert 2Lt kia 16-8-17 4 O&BLI p231 MR30
BOWMAN,Clive Septimus Lt 18-9-17 3 att11NumbF p60 MR30
BOWMAN,Edward Oliver 2Lt kia 31-10-18 NumbF att9Bn p60 CR France206
BOWMAN,Henry Arthur 2Lt kia 28-3-18 13Lpool p71 MR20
BOWMAN,Hugh James T2Lt kia 10-1-16 16Mddx p146 CR France163
BOWMAN,John T2Lt dow 23-11-15 5 O&BLI p130 CR Belgium140
BOWMAN,Leslie Spencer Lt kia 25-6-17 4Lancs att52RFC p17&213 MR20

BOWMAN,Robert Moore T2Lt kia 5-8-16 81RFA p25 CR France513
BOWMAN,William Powell Lt kia 17-10-16 19WYorks att11RFC p2&81 CR France568
BOWMER,Vernon.MC Lt ded 9-10-19 16N&D p264 CR Derby32
BOWN,Cecil Bertini Watkin TLt ded 20-3-17 4Aux(Petrol)RASC p192 CR France145
BOWN,Cyril Walter Lt dow 1-12-17 WSomYeo attH'TankCps p189&205 MR17
BOWN,Edward Elms T2Lt kia 2-11-17 GL att1/4Nhants p189 CR Palestine8
BOWN,William George 2Lt kia 31-7-17 44MGC Inf p181 MR29
BOWRAN,Robert Orton 2Lt kia 9-10-17 1/8WYorks p81 MR30
BOWRING,Arthur Hantague LtCol ded 14-9-19 RFA p261 CR Essex146
BOWRING,Francis Stephen Capt kia 22-11-15 IA 22Punjabis MR38
BOWRING,Frank Harvey TMaj kia 28-8-18 Lpool att9Bn p71 CR France592
BOWRON,Keith Stuart DCM.MID Capt kia 8-8-18 14 att2/10Lond p249 CR France116
BOWSER,Ida Thekla Sister 11-1-19 VAD StJ CR Sussex178
BOWSHER,William Henry.MC TLtACapt dow 25-10-18 20Manch p154 CR France231
BOWYER,Douglas Michael 2Lt kia 23-8-16 1BordR p116 CR Belgium101
BOWYER,Edgar George 2Lt kia 15-10-16 1Camb p245 MR21 Ex MonR
BOWYER,Edgar Raymond 2Lt kia 1-10-18 4Y&L p238 CR France406
BOWYER,Fritz 2Lt kia 25-7-16 GL &RFC p2&189,ded MR20
BOWYER,George Henry T2Lt kia 1-7-16 2SWBord p99 MR21
BOWYER,John Lt ded 10-7-21 RAOC CR Iraq6
BOWYER,John William TCapt kia 10-4-17 13RB p178 CR France154
BOWYER,Joseph.MC.HonLt&QM kia 9-6-17 11LancF p92
BOWYER-BOWER,Eldred Wolferstan Capt kia 19-3-17 3ESurr &59RFC p5&112 CR France614
BOWYER-SMITH,Cedric Gray Capt kia 4-11-15 Glouc att3NigR p201&106 CR WAfrica55
BOX,G.H.Lt kld 25-8-18 SL &RAF p201
BOX,Harold Francis Lt kia 29-10-18 5Ess attRE p232 CR France290
BOX,Philip John Murray TLt kia 7-8-15 Lincs p74 MR4
BOX,Raymond TLt dow 11-7-17 12Manch p154 CR France52
BOX,Reginald George 2Lt kia 30-11-17 7Ess p232 MR17
BOX,Roy Leslie 2Lt kia 9-10-16 RE 2/2WRidFC p210 CR France294,10-10-16
BOXALL,Alfred MC T2Lt dow 25-10-17 RE 262RlyCoy p43 CR Belgium165
BOXALL,Carze Lermithe Capt dow 4-5-15 2Hamps p120 MR4,Caryl Lermitte 27-4-15
BOXALL,William Gratbatch 2Lt dow 15-4-18 22Lond p251 CR France226,Greatbatch
BOXER,Hugh Edward Richardson DSO Maj kia 16-6-15 Cmdg 1Lincs p74 MR29,LtCol
BOYCE,Arthur Cecil Lt ded 10-8-17 RE p269
BOYCE,Charles Wallace 2Lt kia 24-10-18 4Glouc attMGC p186&255 CR France290
BOYCE,Perceval Capt kldRegMutiny 17-2-15 IA 5LightInf p274 CR Asia45,kia 15-2-15
BOYCOTT,Harold Charlton Lt dow 21-3-18 2CldGds p51 CR France1182
BOYD,Alexander Charles T2Lt kia 4-6-16 12RSuss p118 CR France114,5-6-16
BOYD,Brian.MM T2Lt dow 7-6-17 14RIrRif p169 CR France285
BOYD,Cecil Vincent 2Lt kia 23-11-17 8RIrRif p169 MR17
BOYD,Charles Gordon 2Lt kia 3-5-17 7N&D att9Leic p233 CR Frnce434
BOYD,David Thomas 2Lt kia 3-5-17 6ScotRif p224 CR France40
BOYD,Edward Fenwick.MID Lt kia 19-9-14 1NumbF p60 CR France1107,20-9-14
BOYD,Frederick Ennis 2Lt kia 20-5-17 5RDubF p176 CR France1191
BOYD,Gavin T2Lt kia 13-7-16 4SpBde RE p43 CR France503
BOYD,Gavin Haddow 2Lt kia 2-12-17 KRRC att16Bn p149 CR Belgium125
BOYD,George Francis Edward TLt ded 19-10-16 10SfthH attY51TMB p164 CR France64
BOYD,George Pratt 2Lt dow 3-9-17 1IrGds p52 CR Belgium13
BOYD,George Vallance McKinlay TCapt kia 1-7-16 17HLI p162 MR21
BOYD,Harold Alexander 2Lt kia 19-9-14 2RInniskF p104 CR France1435,7-9-14
BOYD,Henry Ormsby T2Lt kia 9-5-16 6SLancs p125 MR38

BOYD,Herbert Cust Lt ded 17-2-18 RASC p267 CR Canada1380,attYL1
BOYD,Hugh Lennox Fleming Capt kia 18-11-17 1BlkW p128 CR Belgium126
BOYD,James Duncan.MC.Lt kia 25-9-18 27RFA p25 CR France518,25-8-18,119RFA
BOYD,James Peter LtTCapt kia 25-9-15 2GordH p166 CR France115
BOYD,James Stanley Newtown LtCol 1-2-16 RAMC CR Mddx16
BOYD,James Wilson Brack TCapt dow 16-7-16 3 att2Y&L attTMB p158 CR Belgium6,kia
BOYD,John 2Lt kia 29-10-16 6 att1ScotRif p224 MR21
BOYD,John T2Lt kia 12-4-18 2RScotF p94 MR32
BOYD,John Lt ded 24-9-18 4CamH att2/1LovatScts p269 CR Scot455
BOYD,John Bain 2Lt kia 22-3-18 1/7GordH p242 MR20
BOYD,John Brodie Capt ded 8-7-19 RAMC p267 CR Scot204
BOYD,Nigel John Lawson 2Lt dow 12-10-14 1BlkW p128 CR Scot237
BOYD,Philip Bentinck 2Lt kia 13-4-17 GordH &59RFC p5&166 MR20
BOYD,Reginald Russell T2Lt dow 4-5-17 12ScotRif p103
BOYD,R.H. 2Lt kld 12-4-18 GL &5RAF p189 CR France95,Lt
BOYD,Robert Colin LtTCapt kia 14-7-16 8Dev p76 CR France453
BOYD,Robert Mitchell Stewart Lt kia 12-7-15 6HLI p240 MR4
BOYD,Stanley LtCol ded 1-2-16 RAMC p269
BOYD,Stuart Lt dow 7-10-16 N&D at1LNLancs p133 CR France177
BOYD,Thomas Cecil Lt dow 21-7-17 1 att7CamH p167 CR France64,Capt
BOYD,Thomas Moffatt TLt ded 25-10-18 RAMC p194 CR EAfrica90
BOYD,William Lt kia 5-11-16 8DLI p239 MR21
BOYD,William.MC.Lt kia 24-3-18 RFA att252RE p207 CR France512,25-3-18
BOYD,William Gaston(Tony)T2Lt dow 13-10-16 9RInniskF p104 CR France285
BOYD,William Graham TLt kia 16-8-17 9RIrF p171 MR30
BOYD,William Hatchell 2Lt kia 9-9-16 9RDubF p176 MR21
BOYD,William Noel Lawson 2Lt kia 23-4-15 2SfthH p164 MR29,25-4-15
BOYD CARPENTER,Victor Charles Douglas TLt kia 29-8-16 RE 89FC p43 CR France402
BOYD-MOSS,Ernest William.DSO.Maj kia 10-8-15 9Worc p108 CR Gallipoli13
BOYDELL,William Vernon 2Lt dow 8-6-15 8LancF p221 CR Gallipoli1
BOYDEN,Arnold Kingsley Maj ded 14-2-19 RASC GHQ p192&257 CR France40
BOYER,Charles Cyril Roslington Lt ded 23-11-19 RASC p267 CR Lincs25
BOYER,Ernest Alexander 2Lt kia 5-4-18 7 att1/22Lond p247 MR20
BOYER,Sydney James T2Lt kia 12-10-16 1RIrF p171 MR21,Lt
BOYERS,Edwin Capt ded 25-10-18 RAMC p194&267 CR Eire401
BOYES,James Ferguson 2Lt dow 25-8-18 15Lond p249 CR France100,Fergusson
BOYHAN,Thomas Francis 2Lt dow 12-9-16 3 att7RIrRif p169 CR France66
BOYLE,Charles Capes 2Lt kia 23-4-17 4EYorks p219 CR France162
BOYLE,David Erskine Lt kia 26-8-14 2LancF p92 MR15
BOYLE,Ernest Charles Patrick.DSO.LtCol kia 7-2-17 1HAC p206 CR France701
BOYLE,Godfrey Henry Patrick Maj ded 16-10-19 SfthH attRE Sigs p265 CR Surrey160,Col
BOYLE,James.Hon.Capt kia 18-10-14 1RScotF p94 MR22
BOYLE,John Antonio Saochey 2Lt kia 30-11-17 RGA 2/1LancsHB p38 MR17,Scochey
BOYLE,John Kennedy.MC.MIDx2 Lt ded PoW 21-10-18 7RDubF p176 CR Germany1,Kemmy 2RIrRif
BOYLE,Montgomerie Maj ded 27-3-19 RASC p253 CR Somerset172
BOYLE,Thomas Houston 2Lt kia 12-10-16 7 att2RScotF p94 MR21
BOYLE,William 2Lt kia 26-10-17 4LNLancs p234 MR30
BOYLE,William Scott TLt kia 4-1-17 11ScotRif p103 CR Greece6,4/5-1-17
BOYNE,Harry Horace 2Lt dow 21-7-16 4Suff attMGC Inf p186&217 CR France833,kia
BOYS,Edward Percival T2Lt kia 22-3-18 RE 5ArmySigCo p43 MR27,21-3-18
BOYS,Richard Harvey TLt kia 13-11-16 2 att4Beds p85 CR France220
BOYS,Sydney Charles TLt kia 23-6-18 RSuss att7Bn p118 CR FRance61,22-6-18
BOYS-STONES,George Lawden.MC.Capt dow 30-3-17 7Lancers att6CavBde CR Iraq8
BOYSON,Frank 2Lt kia 26-3-18 22DLI p160 MR27
BOYTON,Bertram Alfred Lt dow 9-11-17 A301RFA p207 CR Egypt2
BOYTON,Victor Henry Thompson 2Lt kia 31-5-17 RGA 289SB p38 CR Belgium4

BOYTON,Henry James Lt kia 14-12-16 4GrenGds p49 CR France785
BRABAZON,Alan.MIDx3 TCapt dow 8-3-18 6Leinst p174 CR Palestine3
BRABAZON,Hon.Ernest William Maitland Molyneux.DSO.Capt kia 17-6-15 CldGds p51 CR France114
BRABAZON,Terence Anthony Chaworth Lt dow 3-8-16 1Ess p131 CR Wilts179,Capt
BRABOURNE,W.W. see BRADBOURNE,W.W.
BRACE,F.E.SNurse ded 21-9-16 QAIMNS p200 CR Europe1
BRACELIN,Daniel Aloysius.MID T2Lt kia 20-7-18 BlkW att1/7Bn p128 CR France1695
BRACEWELL,Harry T2Lt dow 21-9-17 17N&D p133 CR Belgium15
BRACEY,Ernest Clifford 2Lt kia 28-9-18 SStaffs att5Bn p122 MR16
BRACEY,Frederick Sidney TLt kia 13-11-16 24RFus p66 CR France1491
BRACEY,Victor Charles Edelsten T2Lt kld 23-9-17 RFC p5 CR Somerset19
BRACHER,Frank Vivian TMaj kia 1-6-18 16 att9WelshR p126 MR19
BRACHER,Guy 2Lt kia 3-7-16 EKent p57 CR France251
BRADBEER,Alfred Harold 2Lt kia 21-10-16 3Manch att1LancF p154 MR21
BRADBEER,Francis Henry T2Lt kia 21-3-18 11Ess p131 MR20
BRADBEER,W.J.2Lt 8-8-20 RGA CR Somerset43
BRADBOURNE,Wyndham Wentworth.Lord.Capt kia 11-3-15 1GrenGds SR p49 MR22,BRABOURNE
BRABROOK,Edward John Lt kia 20-4-18 18Lond att8RAF p250&258 CR France40
BRADBURY,Austen.MC.TLtACapt kia 8-8-18 5TankCps p188 MR16
BRADBURY,Dennis John Freeland T2Lt dow 15-11-16 RLancs att10LNLancs p58 CR France131
BRADBURY,Edward Kinder.VC.Capt kia 1-9-14 RFA L'Btyp25 CR France1231
BRADBURY,Ernest Alfred 2Lt ded 2-5-17 3 att12Glouc p106 CR France12,dow 2-4-17
BRADBURY,George Hartley Lt 18-2-21 5Y&L CR Scot313
BRADBURY,Harry TLt ded 3-12-18 RE p43 CR Egypt1,DGO 53DivHQ
BRADBURY,Harry Claude T2Lt kia 16-4-18 18Mddx p146 MR32
BRADBURY,John Cregean Lt dow 6-10-18 2/7Lpool p215 CR France40,Cregeen
BRADBURY,Thomas Piers Lt kia 26-4-18 7WRid p227 MR30
BRADBURY,William Rowland T2Lt kia 7-9-18 WYorks att10EYorks p81 CR France297
BRADBY,Daniel Edward TCapt kia 9-4-17 9RB p178 CR France581
BRADDELL,Edward Terrence Lt dow 27-3-17 RE 484FC p210 CR Palestine8,Terence
BRADDYLL,Edward Clarence Lt kia 5-9-16 IA 10Lancers attRFC p274 CR Belgium140,5-9-15
BRADFIELD,James Thomas Capt kia 13-8-20 1/4SomLI CR Iraq8
BRADFORD,Alfred Royal Lt kia 14-10-16 1Camb p244 CR France293
BRADFORD,Cecil Aubrey Capt drd 24-4-17 Yorks attNigeria p89&201 MR40
BRADFORD,Evelyn Ridley,Bart LtCol kia 14-9-14 SforthH p164 CR France867
BRADFORD,Frederick Reith Campbell 2Lt kia 1-7-16 1/4Lond p246 MR21
BRADFORD,George William Bathhurst 2Lt kia 4-2-17 GL &15RFC p5
BRADFORD,James Barker.MC.T2Lt dow 14-5-17 18DLI p160 CR France113
BRADFORD,Roland Boys.VC.MC.BrigGen kia 30-11-17 2DLI &Staff 186InfBdeHQ p160 CR France529
BRADLEY,Arthur.MM.2Lt kia 24-8-17 YLI att6Bn p142 MR30
BRADLEY,Arthur Newsome Capt ded 6-11-18 RHA(WRid) p207 CR France403
BRADLEY,Augustus James Hector 2Lt kia 23-4-18 RGA 129HB p38 CR France62,dow
BRADLEY,Cyril Montague Lt kia 2-4-17 HQ 296RFA p207 CR France446
BRADLEY,Frank Gilbert Lt drd 3-1-21 1/8RWar CR Herefor&Worc208
BRADLEY,Frederick Hoysted.DSO.CaptALtCol kia 22-9-18 RAMC att15FA p194 CR France562
BRADLEY,Geoffrey Montagu.MID Lt kia 22-12-14 6RB attWelshR p178 MR22,2Bn
BRADLEY,George Joseph TCapt ded 17-2-19 LabCps 211EmpCoy p189 CR France40 Ex 2/2Lond
BRADLEY,George Page 2Lt kia 27-10-17 GL &43RFC p5 CR France924
BRADLEY,Gordon 2Lt kia 24-8-16 5 O&BLI p130 MR21
BRADLEY,Harry Thomas Lt&QM ded 2-4-17 MGC Inf p266 CR Notts68
BRADLEY,Horace Walter 2Lt kia 10-2-17 5RWFus p223 CR France631
BRADLEY,Hubert Mark 2Lt kld 27-5-18 21Lond p251 CR France44,kia 26-5-18

BRADLEY,James 2Lt kia 21-7-16 2Suff p78 MR21
BRADLEY,James T2Lt dow 26-10-18 RSuss att7Bn p118 CR France113
BRADLEY,John TCapt ded 17-2-19 RAVC att296RFA p198 CR France106
BRADLEY,John McDonald TLt dow 30-9-18 11RDubF p176 CR France512,17Bn
BRADLEY,Leslie 2Lt ded 11-7-16 IARO 56Rif MR65,Lt
BRADLEY,Philip Warden Lt kia 23-4-15 3 att1RWKent p140 MR29
BRADLEY,Reginald Ernest T2Lt dow 25-12-16 RE p43 CR France251
BRADLEY,Richard Lt kia 31-7-17 4RLancs p213 MR29
BRADLEY,R.J.LtCol 10-12-19 IMS CR Egypt2
BRADLEY,Robert Hubert Francis.MID T2Lt kia 25-1-17 9NStaffs p156 CR Iraq5
BRADLEY,Shephin Lt kia 25-5-15 Suff p78 MR29
BRADLEY,William Allan.OBE.MC.Capt ded 23-12-19 7DLI p269 CR Lond1
BRADLEY,Walter Robinson Lt ded 29-6-18 1N&D &RAF p133 CR Greece7
BRADLY,John Frank Lt dow 2-7-15 3 att1SWBord p99 CR Europe1
BRADNEY,Philip Edwin TCapt kia 31-7-16 6SomLI p79 CR Belgium58
BRADNEY,Walter 2Lt kia 24-3-18 1TankCps p188 MR27
BRADON,Harry 2Lt kia 16-11-16 1Suff p78 CR Greece3
BRADSHAW,Arthur Edwin Capt kia 13-10-14 IA 14Lancers att 15Huss p274 CR France1106
BRADSHAW,Arthur William Archibald 2Lt kia 25-9-15 1RWSurr p55 MR19
BRADSHAW,Bartle 2Lt kia 11-6-15 3BordR p116 CR Gallipoli6
BRADSHAW,Ernest Edwin TLt dow 30-9-17 D48RFA p25 CR Belgium17
BRADSHAW,Frank Seymour Capt kia 19-12-14 1SomLI p79 CR Belgium70
BRADSHAW,Harold James T2Lt dow PoW 18-5-17 1Norf p73 CR Palestine11,17-5-17,1/4Bn
BRADSHAW,Henry Herbert T2Lt kia 22-7-17 RE 74FC p43 CR Belgium6
BRADSHAW,Huyshe Arthur 2Lt BombAccident 19-8-16 IARO 112Inf p274 CR Iraq5
BRADSHAW,Percival Challon T2Lt kia 1-5-16 9 att6KOSB p101 CR Belgium137,Chalton
BRADSHAW,Peter Dennison T2Lt dow 14-7-16 15 att13NumbF p60 CR France176,kia
BRADSHAW,Richard Edward Kynaston Lt kia 1-7-16 1/12Lond p248 MR21
BRADSHAW,William Douglas 2Lt kia 31-10-16 88RFA p25 CR France251
BRADSHAW,William Robert T2Lt kia 19-2-17 5ConnRgrs p172 CR Belgium17,6Bn
BRADSTREET,Gerald Edmund.MIDx2 2LtTLt kia 7-12-15 RE 72FC SR p43 CR Gallipoli4
BRADSTREET,Lionel Arthur T2Lt kia 1-6-16 17Mddx p146 CR France924
BRADY,Charles TLt ded 15-8-15 RScots SL p53 p268 CR Scot279
BRADY,James TLt kia 26-8-18 15DLI p160 MR16
BRADY,Sydney Vincent.MC.2Lt ded 5-7-19 2Manch p265 CR Hamps119
BRAGG,Arthur Spencer T2Lt ded 28-3-19 10Ess p264 CR Essex43,Albert Lt
BRAGG,D.Lt 1-9-18 GL att1WAfrServBde CR WAfrica41
BRAGG,Frederick John T2Lt dow 25-9-17 Dev att1/9Lpool p76 CR Belgium3
BRAGG,Robert Charles T2Lt dow 2-9-15 58RFA p25 MR4
BRAGG,William Robyns Lt kia 3-12-17 1DevYeo p203 CR Palestine3
BRAGGINS,Albert Edwin 2Lt kia 29-4-18 7Worc p226 CR Belgium21
BRAIDE,G.F.W.LtCol 30-12-15 IMS MR67
BRAIDFORD,Percy.MC.2Lt kia 21-9-17 3DLI p160 MR30
BRAIDFORD,William T2Lt kia 24-7-16 19DLI p160 MR21
BRAIDWOOD,Robert Simpson.DCM.T2Lt kia 31-10-18 1/2 att1/8ScotRRif p103 CR Belgium140
BRAIN,Francis Sydney.MID TLt kia 3-10-18 RBerks att1Dors p138 CR France699,Capt
BRAIN,William Henry Oliver 2Lt kia 10-6-17 RGA 90HB p38 CR Belgium48,Lt
BRAINE,William Thomas Coker 2Lt kia 9-10-16 3 att2WRid p115 CR France374
BRAITHEWAITE,Michael Lloyd Lt kld 17-5-15 RFC p1 CR France473,BRAITHWAITE
BRAITHWAITE,Arthur 2Lt kld 11-3-18 5DLI p239 CR Durham164
BRAITHWAITE,Ernest 2Lt kia 22-7-16 14RWar p64 CR France432
BRAITHWAITE,Francis Joseph Maj kia 4-11-14 2LNLancs p135 MR47
BRAITHWAITE,Humphrey Layland T2Lt kia 10-7-16 RE p43 CR Belgium54
BRAITHWAITE,James Leslie 2Lt kia 22-7-16 Q'RFA attU'RHA p25 CR France188
BRAITHWAITE,Matthew Woodhouse Maj ded 9-11-18 7Ess p232 CR Essex10
BRAITHWAITE,M.D.Miss ded 3-3-19 VAD p200
BRAITHWAITE,M.L.see BRAITHEWAITE,M.L.
BRAITHWAITE,Philip Pipon.MID Capt kia 23-9-18 IARO att36Horse p274 CR Palestine11
BRAITHWAITE,Richard Wilfred TCapt kia 31-7-15 10DLI p160 MR29
BRAITHWAITE,Sydney Lt ded 4-12-16 SL p201
BRAITHWAITE,Valentine Ashworth.MC.2Lt kia 2-7-16 1SomLI p79 MR21
BRAITHWAITE,W.VD.Maj 18-2-17 7WYorks CR Yorks372

BRAKE,Frederick Carlton James T2Lt kia 21-3-18 10Worc p108 MR20
BRAKENBERRY,William Horace.MM.T2Lt dow 23-10-18 13KRRC p149 CR France1266
BRAKES,Bertram.DCM.Lt ded 5-1-18 2Leic att210MGC p87&181 CR Egypt2
BRAKSPEAR,Ronald William TMaj dow 2-10-15 8RBerks p138 CR France40
BRAKSPEAR,William Rae LtCol mbk 25-9-15 IA 2/3GurkhaRif p274 MR28
BRAMALD,John 2Lt kia 9-10-17 4YLI p235 MR30
BRAMBLE,George Henry Joseph 2Lt kia 1-7-16 3 att1Hamps p120 MR21,Gerald
BRAMELD,John Neville T2Lt dow 19-9-15 1KOSB p101 CR Gallipoli4
BRAMLEY,Arthur Henry 2Lt kia 8-6-18 1/2 att23Manch p154 CR France924
BRAMLEY,Cyril Richard Capt kia 20-2-17 2/5YLI p235 CR France339
BRAMLEY,Harold 2Lt kia 13-5-15 5YLI p269 MR29
BRAMLEY,Harry Brian T2Lt dow 15-7-18 13Lpool p71 CR France10
BRAMLEY,Samuel Leslie John 2Lt kia 23-9-17 SR 57RFC p5 CR Belgium140
BRAMPTON,Harry Lee T2Lt kia 7-6-17 3Worc p108 CR Belgium89
BRAMWELL,Charles Guy.MID Capt&Adjt kia 28-6-15 8ScotRif p103 MR4
BRAMWELL,Norman 2Lt kia 30-3-18 2/7LancF p221 MR27,Ex3/5Bn
BRAMWELL,William Dargue.Agent ded 1-12-18 EAIntelDept CR EAfrica36 Ex BowkersHorse
BRANCH,Albert 2Lt kia 1-7-16 4Mddx p146 CR France267
BRANCKER,James Donaldson Dulany.DSO.Maj kia 1-5-17 RGA 116SB p38 CR France581
BRAND,David Halyburton.MC.LtACapt kia 29-3-18 1ScotGds p52 CR France214
BRAND,Douglas William McLeod Capt dow 23-11-17 9Lond p247 CR France245,24-11-17
BRAND,Eric Jermyn T2Lt kia 23-8-18 1Ess p131 CR France578
BRAND,Ernest Stanley Capt kia 8-10-14 RFus attKAR p66&201 CR WAfrica28
BRAND,Geoffrey Jermyn T2Lt kia 1-7-16 GL att101TMB p189 MR21
BRAND,George Ellard Maj(Commsy) ded 6-8-18 IA MilWorksServ p274 CR India164
BRAND,Percy Alfred Easterling T2Lt kia 28-9-17 12RB A'Coy p178 MR30,20-9-17
BRAND,Robert.MC.T2Lt kia 8-5-18 RE 406RenfrewFC p43 CR France250
BRAND,Stanley Oliver TLtACapt kia 14-6-17 6Y&L p158 CR Belgium75
BRAND,W.J.H.Maj 20-1-20 LondScot CR Surrey47
BRANDER,Alfred Ernest 2Lt kia 13-11-16 8A&SH p243 CR France131
BRANDER,Bruce MacDonald Capt ded 30-11-18 RAMC attWaterTankCoy RASC p253 CR France1142,McDonald
BRANDER,J.Lt 19-7-19 RASC CR Scot287
BRANDER,Robert Brander 2Lt ded 27-9-17 RE p43 CR Cheshire31,Lt
BRANFILL,Capel Lisle Aylett Capt ded 11-5-16 GlamYeo p203 CR Egypt9 see AYLETT-BRANFILL,C.
BRANDON,Arthur Chester Capt&Adjt kia 21-1-16 4Hamps p228 MR38
BRANDON,Brian Lloyd T2Lt kia 4-9-18 KSLI att1/7Ches p144 CR Belgium100
BRANDON,Edgar Thomas Colin Lt kia 3-4-17 11RFC p5 MR20
BRANDON,William George T2Lt ded 13-7-18 7DCLI p114 CR Eire286
BRANDRAM,Christopher 2Lt dow 1-9-18 9 att2/4Lond p248 CR France833
BRANDRETH,Charles Reginald 2Lt kia 21-3-18 7 att2/8N&D p233 MR20
BRANDRETH,Lyall Maj Kia 4-6-15 2RFus p66 MR4,6-6-15
BRANDT,Douglas Robert Lt dow 6-7-15 RB p178 MR29,Druce
BRANFOOT,Clayton T2Lt kia 25-8-17 Lincs p74 CR France1462
BRANSURY,John Eric Cecil 2Lt ded 1-4-16 RGA 16HB p38 CR France15
BRANKER,Walter Robert.MC.T2Lt kia 5-10-18 KRRC att11N&D p149 CR France234
BRANNIGAN,Ernest Edward 2Lt kia 3-9-16 1/7WYorks p218 MR21
BRANSBURY,Vernon Dudley Bramsdon Lt kia 25-10-14 3Lincs p74 MR22
BRANTOM,William Harper.DCM.2Lt kia 3-7-16 15Lond p249 CR France558,4-7-16
BRASH,Edmund 2Lt dow 2-9-18 5 att13RWFus p223 CR France41
BRASH,James.DSO.MC.LtACapt dow 9-11-18 3 att7SfthH p164 CR France34
BRASH,John T2Lt kia 25-8-18 8 att1/5ELancs p110 CR France643
BRASH,Wilfred 2Lt kia 9-3-17 1/5RLancs p213 CR Belgium4
BRASIER,James Charles Capt&QM ded 26-12-16 1YLI p142 CR Greece7
BRASINGTON,Frederick Thomas T2Lt kia 9-10-17 GL &9RFC p5 MR20
BRASNETT,Thomas John Grose Jack T2Lt kia 13-10-15 7ESurr p112 MR19
BRASS,Ewart Stanley 2Lt kia 31-3-17 HAC p206 CR France568,1-4-17
BRASS,James Robson Lt dow 26/27-4-15 8DLI p239 CR Belgium44
BRASS,John.DCM.T2Lt accded 28-7-18 RASC 16ArmyAux HT Cps p102 CR France13
BRASSEY,Gerard Charles 2Lt kia 27-8-18 2CldGds p51 CR France615
BRASSEY,Harold Ernest TLtCol kia 15-7-16 RHGds att8SLancs p20 CR France296

BRASSINGTON,William Henry.MM.TLt kia 23-8-18 7TankCps p188 CR France518,25-8-18

BRASTED,Frederick Elliott Lt accded 18-8-17 7Ess p232 CR France113

BRATT,Alfred Charles LtACapt kia 4-10-17 1/5RWar p214 CR Belgium125

BRAUN,Charles Lema TCapt ded 19-6-17 Ess 2GarrBn p131 MR65

BRAWN,Mark.DCM.Lt&QM kia 1-9-18 4Beds p85 CR France592

BRAY,Aubrey Mellish.MC.TLt dow 8-8-18 8RBerks p138 CR France71,Capt

BRAY,Francis Patrick Maj kia 23-3-18 RE 518FC p209 MR20

BRAY,Frank Hugh 2Lt kld 28-5-18 3 att9RSuss p118 CR France149,kia

BRAY,George Thomas T2Lt dow 26-10-17 32RFus p66 CR France145

BRAY,George William Reginald TLt dow 16-8-16 7RBerks p138 CR Greece6

BRAY,Gerald Theodore 2Lt kia 9-8-15 2/5RWSurr p212 MR4

BRAY,Reginald Boydon T2Lt kia 23-10-18 9Norf p73 CR France190

BRAY,Sidney Herbert T2Lt kia 20-7-18 WYorks att8Bn p81 CR France622

BRAYBROOKS,Sidney T2Lt ded 3-2-19 LabCps att17RSuss p189 CR France134

BRAYDEN,Kevin 2Lt kia 23-12-17 18Lond p250 CR Palestine3

BRAYSHAW,Percy St.Quentin 2Lt ded 14-1-18 RFA p25 CR Belgium18

BRAYSHAY,William Stead Capt kia 6-4-17 RASC attRFC p18&253 CR Belgium406

BRAZIER,Albert Edward T2Lt kia 20-9-17 RWar att10Bn p64 MR30

BRAZIER,Anthony David Cecil T2Lt kia 10-3-17 3 att1RBerks p138 CR France393

BRAZIER,Charles Henry Lt ded 17-2-16 RGA p38 CR Essex81

BREARLEY,Arthur Joseph Capt kia 20-6-17 1/7Dev attRE N'Coy p217 CR Belgium15,20-6-17

BREARLEY,Norman Blackburn T2Lt kia 17/19-4-16 12 attRWar p64 MR38

BRECHIN,Robert Hood 2Lt kia 30-9-16 5SfthH att1A&SH p241 CR Greece3

BRECKELL,Edward Ryder Lt ded 8-2-18 3SLancs p215 CR Lancs2

BRECKELL,Ralph Leicester 2Lt kia 9-7-15 3SLancs att2LancF p125 MR29

BREE,Edward Russell Stapylton Lt kia 18-9-18 8DCLI p114 MR37

BREED,John Bennington 2Lt kia 31-7-17 RGA 236SB p38 CR Belgium102

BREEN,Thomas Francis Pennefather CaptAMaj kia 18-9-18 RAMC att142FA p194 CR France437

BREENE,Thomas Frederick TLt kia 1-7-16 1RWar attMGC p64&181 MR21

BREESE,William Laurence 2Lt kld 14-3-15 RHGds p20 CR France134

BREGAZZI,Edward 2Lt ded 9-11-18 1/5N&D p232 CR France65,8-11-18

BREINGAN,Samuel Karr 2Lt kia 26-5-17 3Y&L p158 CR Belgium127

BREMMER,George.DSO.MC.TCaptAMaj kia 23-3-18 RE 80FC p43 CR France1893

BREMNER,David T2Lt dow 9-7-16 10 att1BordR p116 CR France62

BREMNER,James TLt dow 24-6-17 1RScots p53 CR Belgium11,1/8Bn

BREMNER,John TCapt&QM ded 28-11-18 KAR p200 CR WAfrica30

BREN,Henry Alfred Hogarth Lt kia 9-9-16 4 att7Leinst p174 MR21

BRENAN,Byron Edward 2Lt kia 18-4-15 3Glouc p106 CR Belgium58,Lt 2Bn

BRENCHLEY,John,MC 2Lt kia 12-10-17 4CldGds p51 CR Belgium87

BRENDEL,John Daniel George T2Lt kld 27-1-18 RFC p15

BRENNAN,Jeremiah Lt kld 8-8-18 LancHussYeo att1IntelCps p204 CR France226

BRENNAN,John Henry Capt kia 19-10-14 3RWelshF p97 MR29

BRENNAN,Lester Luke T2Lt kld 25-2-18 99RFC p15 CR Wilts129

BRERETON,Charles MacLeod T2Lt kia 25-9-15 5CamH p167 MR19

BRERETON,Herbert TLt kia 21-12-16 GL att15RFC p2&189 CR France41

BRERETON,Leonard Leader 2Lt dow 29-4-17 1/5Beds p219 CR Egypt9

BRERETON-BARRY,William Roche 2Lt kia 16-8-17 10RDubF p176 MR30

BRESLAW,Geoffrey Reynell 2Lt kia 7-10-16 15Hamps p120 CR France385

BRESLIN,John 2Lt ded 11-7-17 1HLI p162 CR Iraq5

BRESSEY,Denys John 2Lt kia 14-10-17 12/35RFA p25 CR Belgium19

BRESSEY,Sydney Herbert.MM.T2Lt kia 21-9-18 RE 74DivSigCo p43 CR France1494

BRETHERTON,Walter Kington Lt ded 13-5-16 IARO attS&TCps p274 MR65

BRETON,Walter Guy Nicholas.DSO.MIDx2 Maj kia 14-9-17 RGA 2/1NMidHB p209 CR Belgium101

BRETT,Charles Arthur Hugh.DSO.MID LtCol kia 26-8-14 2Suff p78 MR15

BRETT,Ernest Edward 2Lt kia 23-4-17 BordR att7Bn p116 MR20

BRETT,Ernest Hugh William T2Lt dow 2-8-16 9 att1/5DCLI p114 CR France1887,kia

BRETT,Francis Joseph T2Lt kia 30-7-16 25Manch p154 CR France744

BRETT,Hugh Corthorn TCapt kia 29-7-16 7DCLI p114 CR France344

BRETT,Nora Veronica SNurse 20-5-15 TFNS CR War7

BRETT,W.G.A Capt 14-3-16 76Punjabis CR Devon72

BRETT,William Frank 2Lt dow 15-10-17 RGA 24SB p38 CR Belgium132,kia

BRETTELL,Sidney Walter TLt kia 10-7-16 10 att8SStaffs p122 MR21

BREUL,Oswald George Frank Justies T2Lt ded 16-10-17 RE 5CpsHQ p43 CR France134,Justus AR CableSect

BREW,Cyril Huleatt Lt dow 12-10-16 2IrGds SR p52 CR France145,Hulcatt

BREW,John George Maj dow 6-4-18 PoW 9RIrF p171 CR France987

BREWER,Cecil Harold 2Lt kia 4-10-17 4 att7LancF p92 CR Belgium83

BREWER,Edmund 2Lt dow 12-1-18 GlamYeo att12SWBordp203 CR France518

BREWER,John Angus.MID TCapt dow 18-9-18 9SLancs p125 CR Greece6,James

BREWER,John Giblett Lt ded 2-11-18 IARO attSap&Min p274 CR Lancs7,Giblette

BREWER,John Patrick Lt ded 20-7-19 1DragGds attMotor MGC p261 CR Hamps64

BREWER,Reginald England T2Lt kia 10-10-16 43/24RFA p25 CR France513

BREWER,Wilfred Aubrey TLt kia 21-11-17 1N&D p133 CR Belgium126

BREWERTON,Augustine T2Lt kia 26-9-16 12Mddx p146 MR21

BREWERTON,Robert Henry Lt kia 30-4-18 8 att19Lpool p215 MR30,Roland

BREWIN,Harold Rowland Nelson 2Lt kia 19-7-16 2Wilts p152 CR France1887,Roland 2/1 O&BLI

BREWIN,Harry Hedley T2Lt kia 12-8-18 15 att2Hamps p120 CR France28

BREWIS,Alfred Percy.MID LtTCapt dow 1-6-17 1NumbF att1/5ELancs p60 CR France905

BREWIS,H.W.MC.TCapt ded 4-6-18 10Glouc p264 CR Glouc27

BREWIS,John Arthur Gardner Lt kia 29-4-17 40RFC p5 MR20

BREWIS,Robert Henry Watkin MajTLtCol kia 18-12-14 2RWar p64 CR France253

BREWITT,James Leonard Lt dow 1-12-17 1/1StaffsYeo p205 CR Palestine9

BREWITT,William Sydney T2Lt kia 29-6-16 RFA p25 CR France394

BREWITT-TAYLOR,Raymond.MC.Capt kia 22-8-18 RAMC 7FA CR France504 see TAYLOR,R.B.

BREWSTER,Basil Stockbridge Lt kia 3-5-17 6Norf att2/5YLI p217 MR20

BREWSTER,Harold Staples Lt ded 6-12-16 RFC CR Canada1464

BREWSTER,Hugh Percival 2Lt kia 9-9-16 49MGC Inf p181 CR France785

BREWSTER,Richard Gardiner 2Lt kia 21-3-18 SlrHorse att7RIrReg p24 MR27

BRIAN,Arthur Gerald.MID TLt dow 16-10-17 10DCLI p114 CR Belgium3,Capt

BRIAN,Herbert Cecil 2Lt kia 9-5-15 RGA 59SB p38 CR France348

BRIANT,Thomas TSubCdr ded 10-11-17 IA CpsofMilStaffClerks p274

BRIARD,Ernest Felix Victor Capt kia 24-8-14 1Norf p73 CR Belgium198

BRIARD,John Fortescue 2Lt ded 15-10-19 IA 1/35Sikhs p274 MR43

BRICE,Ernest Maj ded 5-4-16 RAMC p269 CR Wales168

BRICE,Harry Copeland Lt dow 11-6-15 1/4Leic p219 MR29,Henry &CR France285

BRICE-SMITH,John Kenneth T2Lt dow 11-9-15 7Lincs p74 CR Belgium11

BRICKELL,Frederick William Lt kia 20-6-18 5DLI attMGC p186&238 MR30

BRICKLAND,Charles Hampton 2Lt kia 25-3-15 2RFus p66 MR4

BRICKMAN,Frederick William TLt kia 26-10-17 149MGC Inf p181 MR30

BRICKMANN,Hugh Morton Gairn TLt dow 1-10-16 GL 12ScotRif attTMB p189 CR France40,BRICKMAN

BRICKMANN,Noel.MID TCapt kia 29-10-16 3 att1ScotRif p103 MR21

BRICKNELL,Ernest Thomas Samuel T2Lt dow 20-10-16 9 att2SWBord p99 CR France401

BRICKWOOD,Arthur Cyril 2Lt ded 15-4-15 1Y&L p158 CR Hamps83

BRIDCUTT,John Henry.DSO.CaptALtCol kia 1-10-18 2RIrRif p169 CR Belgium157

BRIDDON,Charles Clark TCapt dow 30-9-17 177LabCps p189 CR Belgium16,Ex 17Y&L

BRIDGE,Donald Gerald Clive 2Lt dow 23-5-15 2RBerks p138 CR Lond2

BRIDGE,F.TLt ded 24-10-18 LabCps p266 CR Yorks575,2Lt

BRIDGE,George Francis Reginald 2Lt dow 15-4-18 7Worc p226 CR France31,2/8Bn

BRIDGE,John Kelly Capt ded 31-1-19 1/5LancF p221 CR Egypt9

BRIDGEMAN,Humphrey Herbert Orlando Lt kia 11-5-17 HouseholdBn p20 MR20

BRIDGER,Arthur Kynaston 2Lt kia 19-7-17 4Y&L p238 MR31

BRIDGER,Francis Albert Lt 77108 10-9-18 RFusPostal 2/2Lond

BRIDGER,Herbert John 2Lt kia 1-11-18 307RFA p25 CR France739

BRIDGES,Fitz-Stephen Henry Maj ded 24-9-16 IA 2/5GurkhaRif attKashmirLancers p274 MR67

BRIDGES,Fleming Hardy 2Lt kia 10-4-18 3 att8Glouc p106 MR30

BRIDGES,Roland Harley.DSO.MID MajALtCol ded 22-8-18 RAMC p194 CR Palestine9,drd

BRIDGES,Walter.MIDx2 Capt ded 25-1-19 RASC 1034MT Coy p192&257 CR Italy15,25-1-18

BRIDGES,William Robert 2Lt dow 23-4-17 3 att4Beds p85 CR France95,kia

BRIDGEWATER,Arthur Sidney.MC.T2Lt kia 8-10-18 9Dev p76 CR France234

BRIDGEWATER,Clement Joseph Bentley Capt kia 1-12-17 6Drags p22 CR France407

BRIDGEWATER,Samuel Ernest T2Lt kia 29-3-16 15N&D p133 CR France706,BRIDGWATER 30-3-16

BRIDGFORD,Stanley Lyon Capt dow 8-4-18 6Manch p236 CR Belgium353

BRIDGLAND,Neville Linton Lt kia 22-10-14 ESurr att1Bn p112 CR France705

BRIDGMAN,William Louis 2Lt dow 20-9-17 6RFus p66 MR30

BRIDGWATER,S.E. see BRIDGEWATER,S.E.
BRIDGWOOD,Dudley Edward 2Lt dow 10-10-17 1/5NStaffs p238 CR Staffs152
BRIDLE,C.Lt 11-3-19 Dors CR Dorset/Cl148
BRIDLE,Robert Reginald 2Lt kia 26-9-17 20Lond p251 MR30
BRIDSON,Charles Edward Ridgway.MID Capt dow 4-4-16 3 att8RLancs p58 CR Belgium15
BRIDSON,John Paul Ridgway 2Lt kia 25-9-15 8Dev p76 MR19
BRIEN,Charles 2Lt kia 27-8-16 5Glouc p225 CR France383
BRIEN,Desmond Cecil Bagge 2Lt kia 2-10-15 3 att2Ches p95 MR19
BRIEN,Frederick George TLt kia 30-4-18 RFA attY45TMB p25 CR France21,dow 20-4-18
BRIERCLIFFE,Louis Bernard Lt kia 31-3-17 3ELancsRFA p207 CR France53
BRIERLEY,Charles Leonard Maj dow 16-9-15 2LancF p92 CR Lancs413
BRIERLEY,George Raworth 2Lt dow 9-5-17 4YLI p235 CR France120,1-5-17
BRIERLEY,Harold Holland 2Lt kia 27-7-16 MGC Inf p181 MR21
BRIERLEY,Horace James TLt kia 7-8-15 9LancF p92 CR Gallipoli27
BRIERLEY,Hugh Colley Capt kia 23-6-17 6Manch p236 CR France755
BRIERLEY,Roger Christian Lt kia 14-7-17 5Ches p222 CR Belgium6,6Bn
BRIERLEY,Vincent.MC.T2Lt dow 28-5-18 8RLancs p58 CR France84,23-8-18
BRIERLEY,William Hunstone Capt kia 26-9-17 6N&D p233 CR Belgium96
BRIGGS,Arthur Desmond TCapt kia 25-9-15 9ScotRif p103 MR19
BRIGGS,Eric Mackie 2Lt kia 3-5-17 6LancF p221 CR France452
BRIGGS,Frederick Cecil Currer.DSO.Maj ded 22-11-19 2Lpool p263 MR43
BRIGGS,Frederick Clifton BtCol ded 30-12-16 3BordR p116 CR Lancs40
BRIGGS,Geoffrey Featherstone Lt kia 11-7-16 2/6Glouc p225 CR France1887
BRIGGS,George Clark.MID Capt kia 15/16-10-14 1RScotF p94 CR France1107,14-9-14
BRIGGS,Harley Knollys 2Lt kia 26-7-16 B166RFA p25 CR France188
BRIGGS,John Mackay TCapt&Adjt ded 2-10-16 18RIrRif p169 CR Ireland138,Mackey
BRIGGS,Orriell Lt/ACapt kia 4-11-18 8SomLI p79 CR France206,Orrie
BRIGGS,Oswald Kershaw Lt ded 22-4-20 2RFA p269 CR Yorks425,Capt
BRIGGS,Richard Stanley Lt kia 29-7-15 7WYorks p218 CR Belgium73
BRIGGS,Thomas.MC.2Lt kia 18-10-16 6LancF p221 CR France319
BRIGGS,William Lake Lt/TCapt kia 21-7-17 6LancF p221&269,Blake MR29,31-7-17 2/7 att2/5Bn
BRIGGS,William Lonsdale T2Lt dow 14-9-17 1RLancs att 1/5LancF p58 CR France40
BRIGGS-GOODERHAM,Ernest John Robinson 2Lt kia 13-12-16 36MGC Inf p181 CR France420
BRIGHT,Archibald Viccars Lt kia 7-6-17 3 att1N&D p133 CR Belgium127
BRIGHT,Cecil Desborough 2Lt kia 21-3-16 IARO 93BurmaInf p274 MR38
BRIGHT,Francis John 2Lt kia 20-9-17 32RFus p66 MR30
BRIGHT,Frank Arnold 2Lt kia 13-10-15 7N&D p233 CR France115
BRIGHT,Frederick George T2Lt kia 23-8-18 56MGC Inf p181 CR France927
BRIGHT,Harold Viccars Capt kia 21-9-18 4N&D p133 CR France835,2Bn
BRIGHT,John Leslie T2Lt kia 25-9-15 2RSuss p118 MR19
BRIGHT,Kenneth Coldwell Lt kia 18-8-16 2 att9RSuss p118 MR21
BRIGHTEN,Ralph Dalton Jarvis 2Lt kia 15-8-15 5Beds p219 CR Gallipoli4
BRIGHTMAN,Sidney Charles 2Lt kia 22-3-18 RE p210 MR34
BRIGINSHAW,Herbert William Oswald TLt ded 30-11-18 RASC p192 CR Ireland14,Henry
BRIGSTOCKE,Hugh Fraser TLt/ACapt kia 9-1-17 7/8KOSB p101 CR France151
BRIMFIELD,Ernest Gaskarth 2Lt kia 2-11-17 7Lond p247 CR Palestine8
BRIMS,James Sutherland.MID TLt kia 8-11-16 D79RFA p25 CR France430
BRINCKMAN,Denys Lt kia 10-6-15 1RIrF p171 CR Belgium4
BRIND,Ralph Montacute.MC.Capt kia 13-1-16 IA 37Dogras p274 CR Iraq5,2-2-16
BRINDAL,Gladstone 2Lt dow 24-3-16 6Glouc p225 CR France85
BRINDLE,John James 2Lt 6-3-20 5Lpool CR Lancs278
BRINDLE,John Laurence Capt ded 13-3-18 4LNLancs p233 CR Lancs346
BRINDLEY,Charles Stuart T2Lt kia 23-4-16 1/8 att1/4RScotF p94 CR Egypt2
BRINDLEY,Frank Ewart 2Lt dow 4-10-18 6NStaffs p238 CR France446
BRINE,Everard Lindesay Lt ded 24-9-18 1/4Hamps p228 CR Asia82
BRINK,Albert Drury 2Lt kia 20-9-17 6LancF p221 CR Belgium125
BRINK,Johannes Hieronymus Lt dow 11-4-17 RFA &14RFC p5&25 CR France564
BRINKWORTH,Arthur Robert 2Lt dow 7-9-16 14RWar p64 CR France630,kia
BRINKWORTH,Edwin John T2Lt dow 9-9-18 15DLI p160 CR France398
BRINKWORTH,Wilfred Henry Lt kld 4-8-18 RFus &215RAF p263 MR20,2Lt
BRINSLEY-RICHARDS,Roland Herbert Wyndham 2Lt kia 30-7-16 10WRid p115 MR21
BRINTON,M.G.SNurse 30-10-18 TFMS CR Durham1
BRISCO,Richard Brown.MC.TCapt kia 9-4-17 RE 172TC p43 CR France68

BRISCOE,Edward Villiers.MIDx2 Lt dow 27-8-16 1 att10RWar p64 MR29,Capt 26/27-8-16
BRISCOE,Frederick John Lt kia 11-5-15 3Y&L p158 CR Belgium58,10-5-15,1Bn
BRISCOE,Henry Whitby T2Lt ded 15-4-17 RIrF 3GarrBn p171 MR35,drd
BRISCOE,Mervyn Whitby TLt kia 23-7-17 RFA &6RFC p5&25 MR20
BRISTOL,Harold James TLt/ACapt dow 4-5-18 4SStaffs att10Ches p122 CR France100
BRISTOLL,Clarence T2Lt ded 9-11-18 ACycCps p181 CR France146
BRISTOW,Cuthbert George 2Lt kia 17-7-17 1 att3RWKent p140 MR20
BRISTOW,Percy Henry 2Lt kia 23-3-18 2/9Lond p248 MR27
BRISTOWE,Robert Owen.MID Lt kia 10-3-15 2Dev p76 CR France706
BRITT,Eric John Robert 2Lt kia 30-3-18 22Lond p251 CR Syria2
BRITTAIN,Edward Harold.MC.Lt/TCapt kia 15-6-18 2 att11N&D p133 CR Italy4
BRITTAIN,Frank Morris Engr ded 2-7-16 BRCS CR Iraq5
BRITTEN,Arthur Herbert.MC.TLt kia 14-4-18 8Glouc p106 MR30
BRITTEN,Charles Edward TLt dow 20-7-16 RFA 5DAC p25 CR France51,2Lt 29-7-16 2DAC
BRITTEN,Charles Wells.MID TLt/AMaj kia 26-4-17 RFA DTMO p25 CR Belgium167
BRITTEN,Edward William Capt kia 10-8-15 10Mddx p236 MR4
BRITTEN,Richard Spencer TMaj ded 18-8-18 RBucksHuss 5ArmyHQ p24 CR France31
BRITTEN,Thomas Xavier.MID LtCol dow 14-4-15 IA 110Mahrattas p274 CR Iraq6,15-4-15
BRITTIN,Edward Whicker T2Lt kia 31-7-17 20DLI p160 MR29,BRITTON 1-8-17
BRITTON,Arthur John Allan 2Lt kia 10-8-15 5WelshR p230 MR4
BRITTON,Herbert Edward 2Lt dow 15-10-16 62RFA p25 CR France188
BRITTON,William Kerr Magill 2Lt kld 23-5-17 1RMunstF &29RFC p5&175 CR Ireland248
BRITTS,Charles William Gordon 2Lt kld 6-11-15 4 att9ESurr p112 CR France1369,5-11-15
BROAD,Alfred Evans.MC.TLt dow 2-3-16 6Dors p123 CR France40
BROAD,Arthur Maurice TLt kia 12-7-16 15RFus attMGC Inf p66&181 CR France630
BROAD,Clifford Newman T2Lt dow 9-4-16 2RSuss p118 CR France178
BROAD,Francis Boase.MC.Lt/ACapt kia 24-10-18 1Mddx p146 CR France230
BROAD,Frank Cuthbert 2Lt kia 22-9-18 10Lond p248 CR France665
BROAD,Hubert Frederick Lt ded 25-10-18 3Leinst p174
BROAD,John Eric Lt kia 23-3-18 Herts p252 MR27
BROAD,Malcolm Percy Eyre 2Lt kia 9-10-17 5Y&L p238 MR30
BROAD,Reginald Leigh Maj ded 18-9-17 SL RE attIWT p268 CRGlouc5 Ex WelchR
BROAD,Richard Blunson.MID Lt/AMaj ded 6-11-18 U'RFA p25 CR France85,Blunsom
BROAD,Walter Victor Mantach Lt kia 22-3-18 15Lond p249 MR20,23-3-18
BROAD,William George.MM.T2Lt dow 28-3-18 19DLI p160 CR France44
BROADBENT,Cecil Hoyle 2Lt dedacc 1-3-16 4YLI p235 CR France43
BROADBENT,Edgar Richards.MC.Maj ded 31-10-18 8Huss p22 CR Mddx39
BROADBENT,George Carvel 2Lt kia 21-5-18 1/5SStaffs p229 CR France109
BROADBENT,Hermann TLt/ACapt&Adjt kia 15-2-17 Y&L att10Bn p158 CR France115
BROADBENT,Sidney TCapt kia 18-2-18 RFC p15 CR France765,Sydney
BROADBENT,Wilfred Stuart Stidston Lt kia 19-4-17 153MGC p181 CR Frnce451
BROADFOOT,William Allison 2Lt kia 13-7-15 6HLI p240 MR4
BROADHURST,Cecil Howard 2Lt dow 1-12-17 3Lpool p71 CR France518
BROADHURST,Gerald Henry Lt ded 8-5-17 52RFA p25 MR29
BROADHURST,Thomas Clifford 2Lt kld 28-9-17 GL &RFC p5 CR Lancs478
BROADLEY,Harry TCapt kia 6-8-17 2RInniskF p104 CR Belgium45
BROADRICK,Frederick Benjamin Dumaresq Maj ded 19-4-18 RFA p25 CR France25
BROADRICK,George Fletcher.MID LtCol kia 22-8-15 6BordR p116 MR4
BROADWAY,Hugh Alexander.MID 2Lt dow 30-3-15 RE 5FC p43 CR France102,Lt
BROADWAY,Neville Harris Lt kia 1-12-17 IA 2Lancers p274 MR28
BROADWOOD,Maximilian Francis 2Lt kia 24-8-14 1RWKent p140 CR Belgium20
BROADWOOD,Robert George.CB.LtGen dow 21-6-17 12Lancers Staff GOC 57Divn p1 CR France255
BROADWOOD,W.A.Capt 2-5-21 6LNLancs CR Lond1
BROCK,Alfred Herbert TCapt ded 3-11-19 RGA p269 CR Durham97,3-1-19 RE
BROCK,Alfred Lawrence Capt kia 14-4-17 6DLI p239 CR France162
BROCK,Algernon Bertram 2Lt dow 26-10-17 9Dev p76 MR30
BROCK,Cecil Howard TLt dow 4-11-18 8 att9Dev p76 CR France231,kia
BROCK,Edgar Nathaniel Loftus Capt kia 21-5-15 5 att3Worc p108 CR Belgium28,20-5-15
BROCK,Eric George.MC.Lt/ACapt kia 31-7-17 7Lpool p215 MR29

BROCK,George Selby Capt ded 7-10-18 IA IMS p274 CR Pakistan50A &MR43
BROCK,Herbert Leslie TLt kia 10-4-18 29MGC Inf p181 MR32
BROCK,Percy Douglas 2Lt kia 29-5-18 1Lincs D'Coy p74 CR France1332
BROCK,Sydney Edward.MC.Capt dow 11-11-18 10RScots p212 CR Scot725
BROCK-HOLLINSHEAD,Laurence Maj kia 26-9-15 8RWKent p140 MR19
BROCKBANK,Charles Norman TCapt kia 1-7-16 18Lpool p71 CR France397
BROCKBANK,Herbert T2Lt kia 28-4-17 27NumbF p60 MR20
BROCKIE,J.Capt 28-10-18 RFA CR Scot142
BROCKINGTON,Conrad Clive Lt kia 8-9-16 2WelshR p126 MR21
BROCKLEBANK,Bertram Vincent Lt kia 1-8-17 2CldGds p51 CR Belgium106
BROCKLEBANK,Lawrence Seymour 2Lt kia 26-8-14 3 ATT1RLancs p58 CR France611,BROCKELBANK
BROCKLEBANK,Ralph Royds 2Lt dow 16-5-17 1RWelshF p97 CR France518
BROCKLEBANK,Ralph Eric Royds Maj ded 13-2-21 5Lpool CR Ches193
BROCKLEBANK,Thomas Geoffrey Capt kia 5-8-16 277RFA p207 CR France141,dow
BROCKLEHURST,Archibald Henry Capt dow 29-7-16 1KRRC p149 CR France23
BROCKLEHURST,Edward Henry Capt kia 5-5-15 6Lpool p215 MR29
BROCKLEHURST,John Sidney T2Lt kld 1-11-15 14 att11Manch p154 CR Gallipoli27
BROCKLEHURST,Thomas Pownall TCapt kia 1-7-16 2RWSurr p55 CR France397
BROCKLEHURST,Wilfrid Stanley Maj 15-5-20 RWFus CR Wales537 Ex DerbyYeo
BROCKLESBY,Horace Markham 2Lt kia 1-7-17 113RFA p208 CR Belgium173
BROCKMAN,Albert John 2Lt kia 8-8-16 4RLancs p213 MR21
BROCKS,Archibald William T2Lt dow 10-3-18 PoW 3Ches att10Dev p95 CR Iraq8
BRODBECK,Edwin Charles 2Lt kia 26-7-18 7N&D p233 MR19
BRODBELT,Arthur Dell Lt dow 18-4-18 RGA 264SB p38 CR France98
BRODBELT,Guy Lt kia 14-4-16 9Lpool p216 CR France927
BRODHURST,Bernard Maynard Lucas Maj kia 27-4-15 IA 1/4GurkhaRif p274 CR Belgium92
BRODERICK,Herbert Thomas Lt dow 29-12-17 2/24Lond p252 CR Palestine3
BRODERICK,Thomas Joseph TLt kia 15-4-16 6RIrReg p88 CR France178
BRODIE,Allan TLt dow 27-7-16 13 att15HLI p162 CR France88
BRODIE,Charles Gordon Lt kia 23-5-17 5Lond att6RFC p18&246 CR Belgium11
BRODIE,Colin James 2Lt kia 9-9-16 1/4Lond p246 MR21
BRODIE,Douglas Edward TCapt kia 17-8-16 3 att1CamH p167 CR France432
BRODIE,Douglas Fontaine.MC.Lt kia 12-10-18 9HLI p240 CR France718
BRODIE,Duncan Smith T2Lt kia 15-6-18 8Y&L p158 CR Italy1
BRODIE,Ewen James Capt kia 12-11-14 1CamH p167 MR29
BRODIE,George T2Lt dow 2-8-17 8SfthH p164 CR Belgium8
BRODIE,Hugh Gordon Capt ded PoW 26-4-17 IA 103Mahrattas p274 CR Asia51
BRODIE,Hugh William TCapt kld 13-10-15 6EKent p57 MR19
BRODIE,John Capt dow 26-9-15 6RScotF p94 MR19
BRODIE,John 2Lt kia 13-11-16 4Beds p85 CR France220,Lt
BRODIE,John Miller T2Lt kia 15-5-18 Mddx att8Bn p146 CR France54
BRODIE,Mark Moyle T2Lt kia 7-1-16 10 att1SfthH p164 MR38
BRODIE,Mitchell Miller.MC.TLt dow 14-7-17 12NumbF p60 CR France145
BRODIE,Peter Bellinger Lt ded 12-8-16 4RWSurr att51ImpCamCps p212 CR Egypt9
BRODIE,Philip Wyndham Lt ded 18-11-18 1SfthH &RAF p164 CR Italy6,Capt
BRODIE,Sidney Edward T2Lt dow 17-4-17 17RFus p66 MR20
BRODIE,Walter Hamilton T2Lt kia 9-4-17 15RScots p53 CR France644
BRODIE,Walter Lorrain.VC.MC.ALtCol kia 23-8-18 2HLI p162 CR France745
BRODIE,William Alan 2Lt dow 13-5-18 3 att16RWelshF p97 CR France145
BRODIE,William Eastdale Lt kia 29-3-18 6ScotRif p224 CR Belgium8,1Bn
BRODIE-INNES,Ian Stuart.MID 2Lt mbk 25-9-15 8SomLI p256 MR19
BRODIGAN,Francis John Capt kld 9-5-15 1Glouc p106 MR22
BRODRIBB,William Carr Capt kld 26-8-14 3Manch p154 CR France716
BRODRICK,Edward TLt kia 31-7-17 13Manch p154 MR29,Capt
BRODRICK,Eric William 2Lt ded 22/23-7-16 PoW 5Yorks p221 CR Belgium132,dow
BROGDEN,Frederick Newman 2Lt kia 3-5-17 9EYorks att8TMB p83 MR20,8Bn
BROGDEN,Ingram Richard Rhodes TLt drd 15-4-17 RAMC p194 MR35
BROMBY,William Girdlestone Lt ded 29-5-21 10EYorks CR Yorks97
BROMET,John Neville Lt kia 30-11-17 63RFA p25 MR17,mbk
BROMFIELD,Harry Hickman.DSO.Maj dow 10-9-16 1WelshGds p53 MR21
BROMFIELD,William Henry 2Lt dow 31-10-18 RGA 278SB p38 CR France146
BROMHALL,John Coventry.MC&Bar.TLtAMaj kia 7-8-18 19MGC p181 CR France33
BROMHAM,Charles Adolphus Row Lt kia 17-10-18 5Dev attYLI p217 CR France190,2Lt
BROMILOW,John Nisbet Maj kia 1-7-16 Cmdg1RLancs p58 CR France742,2-7-16

BROMILY,James T2Lt kld 28-6-18 RASC MT RGA att391SB Amm Col p192 CR France770
BROMLEY,Cuthbert.VC.Tmaj drd 13-8-15 1LancF p92 MR4
BROMLEY,Hugh Frederic T2Lt kia 25-9-15 2RSuss p118 MR19
BROMLEY,John Edouard Marsden.DSO.TCaptAMaj kia 7-6-18 17/41RFA p25 CR France266
BROMLEY,John Ledger Lt ded 29-9-18 RASC MT &11RAF p192 MR20,kld Flying
BROMLEY-SMITH,H.R.2Lt ded 1-1-16 S p268
BROOK,Alexander.VD.LtCol dow 19-5-15 8RScots p211 CR France80,14-5-15
BROOK,Arthur Charles 2Lt kia 4-6-15 5Manch p236 CR Gallipoli2
BROOK,Cecil Frederick T2Lt ded 5-4-16 9 att8EYorks p83 CR Belgium11
BROOK,Charles William 2Lt kld 26-3-18 3WRid &RFC p15&115 CR Yorks644
BROOK,George William 2Lt ded 12-11-18 4WRid p269
BROOKE,Arthur Goulbourn T2Lt kld 10-12-16 RFC p2 CR Camb21
BROOKE,Cecil Berjew.DSO.2Lt kia 1-7-16 Yorks p90 CR France630,Charles Lt Ex Suff SR &1RWSurr
BROOKE,Cecil Rupert T2Lt kia 24-4-17 8GordH p166 MR20
BROOKE,Charles Pearson Joseph Lt kia 3-9-16 1Wilts p152 MR21
BROOKE,Clarence T2Lt kia 31-3-18 13EYorks p83 MR20
BROOKE,Cyril Thomthwaite 2LtACapt kia 22-8-17 3Dors att6SomLI p123 MR30
BROOKE,Frederick Arthur John Robertson TCapt kia 27-5-18 RAMC att1Wilts p194 MR18
BROOKE,George Lt dow 2-10-14 1IrGds SR p52 CR France1112,7-10-14
BROOKE,George Cecil.MID Maj kia 28-4-15 1BordR p116 CR Gallipoli3
BROOKE,George Miller Lt kia 25-4-18 1/7WYorks p218 CR Belgium104
BROOKE,George Townshend Capt kia 6-5-15 RE 1NMidFC p210 CR Belgium101,5-5-15
BROOKE,Gerald Douglas Capt kia 3-7-16 7Suff p78 MR21
BROOKE,Harold William TCapt kia 24-4-17 7EYorks p83 MR20
BROOKE,Henry Brian Capt dow 24-7-16 2GordH p166 CR Scot287
BROOKE,Henry Hastings Maj dow 19-2-20 4ConnRgrs CR Hamps220
BROOKE,Henry John 2Lt 27-2-20 Berks CR Ches51
BROOKE,Herbert Leonard 2Lt kia 12-4-18 7 att10Ess p232 MR27
BROOKE,James Anson Otho.VC.Capt kia 29-10-14 2GordH p166 CR Belgium116
BROOKE,John Josselyn 2Lt kia 4-10-17 2/6Suff att3/4RWSurr p218 MR30
BROOKE,Leonard.MC.2Lt kia 9-4-18 4LNLancs p234 CR France106
BROOKE,Percy TLtACapt kia 28-3-18 WYorks att9TMB p81 CR France1185
BROOKE,Richard Reginald Maude.MID Capt kia 31-5-15 1 O&BLI p130 MR38
BROOKE,Thomas Wickham.MC.Capt dow 30-11-17 6Lond p246 CR France530
BROOKE,Victor Reginald.CIE.DSO.Maj ded 29-8-14 IA 9Lancers p22 CR France1236
BROOKE,William Alfred Cotterill 2Lt kia 14-6-15 8Lond p247 CR France554
BROOKE,William John Capt dow 9-4-18 3KSLI att21Mddx p144 MR32,Maj
BROOKE-MURRAY,Kenneth Algernon TCapt dow 23-9-16 RASC att15RFC p2 CR France102
BROOKE-TAYLOR,Arthur Cuthbert Lt 4-6-15 6Manch MR4
BROOKER,James T2Lt kia 2-12-17 2RB p178 MR30
BROOKES,Ben 2Lt kia 21-3-18 att1NStaffs p156 MR27
BROOKES,Eric Guy.DFC.Capt kia 8-8-18 Worc &65RAF CR France526
BROOKES,Gordon Byron TCapt kia 16-9-16 9 att6DCLI p114 MR21
BROOKES,Harry T2Lt dow 12-4-18 17LancF p92 CR France64
BROOKES,Henry Richard Lt kia 4-11-14 IA 101Grenadiers MR47 p274
BROOKES,Percy 2Lt kia 22-11-17 6Ches p222 CR Belgium112
BROOKES,Ronald Baines 2Lt kia 13-3-18 RFC p15 CR France1643
BROOKFIELD,Sydney Freeman TCapt kia 3-9-16 17N&D p133 MR21
BROOKING,Hugh Cyril Arthur Capt ded 31-5-18 NSomYeo p155 CR Somerset96
BROOKING,Walter Arthur 2Lt kia 19-1-16 RHA attRFC p2&25 CR France1050,Lt
BROOKS,Archibald Buckley Capt kia 7-10-17 2/6Manch p236 CR Belgium84
BROOKS,Bazil Benjamin Burgoyne Capt kia 23-7-16 4 O&BLI p231 CR France832
BROOKS,Charles Alfred Capt kia 8-7-17 Wilts attRFC p5 MR34
BROOKS,Colin Robert Percy.MC.Lt dow 2-4-18 3Huss att4MGC Cav p2&182 CR France880
BROOKS,Ernest William TLtACapt kia 20-9-17 6 O&BLI p130 CR Belgium83
BROOKS,Francis Cyril 2Lt kld 17-8-17 RFA &47RFC p5&25 CR Surrey160
BROOKS,Frank Smith T2Lt kia 1-7-16 20Manch p154 CR France397
BROOKS,Frederick Jacob 2Lt kia 13/15-11-16 4 att2SStaffs p122 CR France156,Fredrick Lt 13-11-16
BROOKS,George Thomas 2Lt kia 30-11-17 1/13Lond p249 MR17
BROOKS,George William T2Lt kia 29-5-18 20KRRC p149 CR France98
BROOKS,Horace William.MC.T2Lt kia 4-11-18 8SomLI p79 CR France521
BROOKS,John Lt&Adjt ded 28-10-17 RDC p253 CR Lancs256
BROOKS,Leonard Samuel 1Lt kia 9-5-18 A50RFA p25 CR Belgium11

BROOKS,Leonard William 2Lt kia 6-7-17 8Hamps attRFC p18&229 CR France161,4Bn
BROOKS,Leslie Lt kia 25-9-15 4WYorks attLincs p81 MR32
BROOKS,Reginald St.George T2Lt kia 26-9-15 97RFA p25 CR France219
BROOKS,Rowland Causer 2Lt kia 4-6-15 6Manch p236 MR4
BROOKS,Thomas Edward Lt kia 13-5-17 LeicYeo p204 MR29 &CR Belgium152
BROOKSBANK,Hugh Freeth Gilbert T2Lt kia 8-7-16 1Worc p108 MR21,7-7-16
BROOKSBANK,Hugh Geoffrey.MID 2Lt dow 16-12-14 Yorks p90 CR Yorks308,Godfrey
BROOKSBANK,Stamp Lt kia 26-9-15 3Yorks p90 MR19,Capt
BROOKSMITH,John Douglas.MC.Capt mbk 21-3-18 47RFA p256 MR20
BROOM,Cyril Thomas 2Lt ded 15-7-15 10HLI p162 CR France525
BROOM,Frederick John Maurice 2Lt kia 7-6-17 8Mddx p236 CR Belgium29
BROOM,Frederick Jordan T2Lt kia 1-7-16 2SfthH p164 CR France643
BROOM,Lewis John.MBE.Capt 12-4-18 4WelchR att KAR CR EAfrica92
BROOMAN,Edward James.MC.T2LtALt kia 1-4-17 16LancF p92 CR France672
BROOMAN-WHITE,Ronald George 2Lt dow 15-5-15 4RInniskF attRIrF p104 CR Belgium4
BROOME,Louis George 2Lt dow 5-6-15 2RScots p53 CR France102
BROOME,R.C.CIE.MajGen 26-8-15 Army Remount Dept India CR Asia9
BROOMFIELD,James Taylor T2Lt kia 3-12-16 12 att 1Ess p131 CR France374
BROOMHALL,Harry 2Lt kia 22-3-18 8Worc att2RBerks p226 MR27
BROOMHALL,Oscar Arthur 2Lt dow 18-4-18 5Lpool att4RAF p255 CR France180,Lt
BROPHY,Ernest Gordon T2Lt kia 1-7-16 2WYorks p81 CR France296
BROPHY,John Bernard.MID 2Lt kld 24-12-16 2RFC p2 CR Lincs136,Lt
BROPHY,Thomas Joseph T2Lt kia 22-3-18 att2Leinst p174 MR27
BROSTER,Harold Broughton T2Lt kia 30-11-17 11KRRC p149 MR17
BROSTER,Robert Buck ACapt kia 11-10-18 4WRid p227 CR France612
BROTHERHOOD,Frank Ridgway T2Lt kia 15-9-17 GL &55RFC p5 CR France134
BROTHERS,Arthur Stanley TCapt kia 2-7-16 RE 178TC p43 CR France189
BROTHERS,Malam Capt kia 28-5-17 2/4ELancs p226 MR163
BROTHERTON,Vincent T2Lt dow 14-10-16 1WYorks p81 CR France105
BROUGH,Alexander T2Lt kia 18-11-15 12ScotRif att6Y&L p103 CR Gallipoli27
BROUGH,James Lindsay T2Lt kia 1-7-16 15RScots p53 MR21
BROUGH,John.CMG.MVO.LtCol ded 29-7-17 RH&FA GSO HQ61Div p26 CR France134,dow
BROUGH,John William.MIDx2 Lt&QM ded 20-10-18 1/1StaffsYeo p205 CR Lebanon1
BROUGHTON,Coote Edgar Capt kia 6-10-19 IA 34Horse attBhopalLancers p274 MR43
BROUGHTON,Ernest Chamier LtCol ded 17-12-14 3Y&L p158 CR Mddx16
BROUGHTON,Gerald Filose Capt kia 11-7-17 IA 17Inf p274 CR EAfrica40
BROUGHTON,Hugo Delves TCapt kia 4/5-4-16 8Ches p95 MR38 Ex 1Bn
BROUGHTON,Norman Walford.DSO.MID TCapt kia 9-9-16 RAMC att73RFA p194 CR France397,10-9-16
BROUGHTON,Thomas Dugdale T2Lt dow 10-4-18 7YLI p142 CR France164
BROUGHTON-ADDERLEY,Peter Handcock.MC.2LtACapt dow 16-10-18 1ScotsGds p52 CR France380
BROUN,Ernest Scott Capt kia 30-10-14 Yorks p90 MR29,Scot
BROUN,Richard Clive McBryde TLt kia 6-12-15 6RDubF p176 MR37
BROUNGER,William Henry Prescott T2Lt kia 9-4-17 22NumbF p60 CR France265
BROUNSWORTH,Edmund Arthur 2Lt dow 27-5-16 1Leic p87
BROWETT,Archibald T2Lt kia 20-11-17 37MGC Inf p182 MR17,Ex 9Lond
BROWETT,Arnold Leslie Thackall Capt kia 5-7-16 2/7RWar p214 CR France705
BROWETT,Reginald 2Lt kia 26-9-17 2/9Lond p248 MR30
BROWETT,Thomas Norman Lt ded 30-10-18 5Ess att1/7KAR p232&268 CR EAfrica36
BROWN,Aitken Capt dow 21-4-18 5BlkW p230 CR France40,1/6Bn
BROWN,Alan Francis Donald T2Lt kia 8-9-16 1Glouc p106 MR21
BROWN,Alan Moray Capt.MC.kia 13-3-15 IA 47Sikhs p274 CR France279,12-3-15
BROWN,Albert Edward T2Lt kia 9-10-18 1Leic p87 CR France235
BROWN,Alexander T2Lt kia 28-4-17 16RScots p53 MR20
BROWN,Alexander Henry T2Lt kia 9-8-18 6RWKent attRE 87FC p140 CR France636
BROWN,Alexander Johnstone TLt dow 11-4-18 1/5SfthH p164 CR France40,Capt
BROWN,Alexander Russell.MID TCapt kia 18-8-16 7KOSB p101 CR France432,17-8-16
BROWN,Algernon James T2Lt dow 1-12-16 2RB p178 CR France145
BROWN,Allan George TLt kia 27-10-18 10NumbF p60 CR Italy7,Alan
BROWN,Allison T2Lt kia 26-10-17 GordH att2Bn p166 CR Belgium112
BROWN,Andrew Cranstoun see BROWNE,A.N.

BROWN,Andrew Norman.MC.Lt kia 27-5-18 6DLI p239 MR18,Capt
BROWN,Angus Graham Capt kia 1-9-18 20Lond p251 CR France439
BROWN,Anthony William Scudamore Lt kia 18-8-16 6 att3RB p178 CR France402
BROWN,Archibald.MC.T2Lt kia 20-4-18 14A&SH p173 CR France113
BROWN,Archibald Campbell Lt kia 27-5-18 A95RFA p207 CR France1332
BROWN,Archibald Dimock Montagu TCapt kia 23-10-16 3 att1RLancs p58 MR21
BROWN,Archibald Gibson Capt kia 25-5-15 9A&SH p243 CR Belgium113
BROWN,Archie Maynard 2Lt kia 6-4-18 RGA 126HB p38 CR France343
BROWN,Arnold Nimmo ACapt ded 8-9-19 RGA 13SB p262 CR Germany1
BROWN,Arthur T2Lt dow 5-10-17 1Lincs p74 CR France139,kia
BROWN,Arthur Anthony.MC.LtACapt ded 4-3-18 271RFA p207 CR Palestine9
BROWN,Arthur George Maj 20-3-21 IMD CR India97A
BROWN,Arthur Horace Mortimer 2Lt kia 10-7-16 27Manch p154 CR France393
BROWN,Arthur Lyster T2Lt kia 25-9-15 2RWSurr p55 MR19
BROWN,Arthur Roberts 2Lt kia 6-4-17 RFA &2RFC p5&26 MR20
BROWN,Austin Hanbury.DSO.MC.Maj kia 27-3-18 RE 2FC p43 MR20
BROWN,Benjamin Albert TLt dow 4-10-17 RE 253FC p43 CR Belgium16,TC
BROWN,Benjamin Ewart ACapt kia 9-9-16 Lincs att1RMunstF p74 MR21
BROWN,Bernard Loftus.MC.Lt kld 1-11-20 RGA 26HB MR40
BROWN,Bertram TCapt kia 3-9-16 16RB p178 MR21
BROWN,Cecil Abraham Lt kia 23-4-17 6N&D p233 CR France58,Arthur
BROWN,C.F.Lt kia 25-7-18 1/2DLI attRAF p160
BROWN,Charles.MM.2LtACapt kia 25-4-18 RGA 242SB p38 CR Belgium11
BROWN,Charles Arthur 2Lt kia 5-7-17 4YLI p235 CR Belgium173
BROWN,Charles James Wilkins 2Lt dow 22-4-18 RGA 73SB p38 CR France88,Lt
BROWN,Charles King Valentine Maj ded 25-10-18 IA 102Grenadiers p274 MR65
BROWN,Charles Lawrie 2Lt dow 18-6-16 9RScots p212 CR France85
BROWN,Charles Roydon.MC.MID Capt kia 14-4-17 13Ess p131 CR France604,1Bn late9&13Bn
BROWN,Charles Tolme 2Lt kia 17-3-17 5A&SH p243 CR France728
BROWN,Charles William T2Lt dow 23-5-17 6KOSB D'Coy p101 CR Scot713
BROWN,Christopher 2Lt ded 24-10-18 8Worc p226 CR France146
BROWN,Christopher Wilkinson Capt kia 1-5-16 3 att1RScotF p94 CR Belgium28
BROWN,Claude Algernon Felix TLt kia 26-12-16 GL &RFC p2&190
BROWN,Claude Fitzgerad Sedley 2Lt kia 19-10-16 9LNLancs p135 CR France446,Fitzgerald
BROWN,Claude Joseph John Lt ded 18-11-18 3Nhampt att1/2KAR p137&201 CR EAfrica52
BROWN,Clive Andrews Capt ded 7-11-18 RE p210 CR Surrey6
BROWN,Colin Selwyn Capt kia 1-7-16 11BordR p116 CR France293
BROWN,Daniel T2Lt kia 25-9-15 12HLI p162 MR19,Ex 9Bn
BROWN,David Lt ded 23-9-15 8HLI att7RScots p240 MR4
BROWN,David Douglas T2Lt kld 27-9-15 13RScots p53 MR19
BROWN,David Hepburn TCapt kia 25-9-15 6KOSB p101 CR France219
BROWN,David Westcott Capt kia 17-7-16 6Leic p87 MR21,14-7-16
BROWN,Denis Sidney Lt SelfInflictWound 11-10-19 IA 1/39GarhwalRif p274
BROWN,Donald Andrew 2Lt ded 22/23-7-16 PoW 9DLI p239 CR France705
BROWN,Donald Morton TLt kia 17-10-18 CamH att1Bn p167 CR France1268
BROWN,Douglas Crow Lt dow 13-9-17 3RScots attMGC Inf p53&182 CR France1361,2Bn
BROWN,Douglas Knox.MC.Lt kia 30-11-17 9HLI att217MGC Inf p186&240 MR17
BROWN,Douglas Paton McRae 2Lt kia 24-11-16 22Lond p251 CR Belgium167
BROWN,E.C.Lt kia 18-10-18 RWKent &RAF p140 CR France341
BROWN,Edgar Archer 2Lt kia 23-8-18 2BucksBn O&BLI p231 CR France745
BROWN,Edward TLt kia 7-8-17 18 att2RIrRif p169 CR Belgium19
BROWN,Edward Dell T2Lt kia 16-8-17 KRRC A'Coy att12Bn p149 MR30
BROWN,Edward Frederick Montagu Lt dow 8-1-18 1/1Herts p252 CR Belgium20
BROWN,Edward James 2Lt ded 14-11-18 IARO attCentLaboratoryBaghdad p274 CR Iraq8
BROWN,Edward John 2Lt kia 17-8-17 45RFC p5 CR Belgium11
BROWN,Edwin Charles 2Lt dow 10-8-18 RWKent att7Bn p140 CR France69
BROWN,Edwin Percival Wildman Lt kia 4-9-16 1Norf p73 CR France402
BROWN,E.L Sister 19-2-19 QAIMNS CR Sussex111
BROWN,Eric Francis TLtACapt dow 1-4-17 5Wilts p152 MR38
BROWN,Eric Howard TLt kia 22-10-17 10Ess p131 CR Belgium126
BROWN,Eric Landon.MC.MID Capt kia 18-8-15 1SuffYeo p205&217,4SuffR CR France924,4SuffR
BROWN,Eric Metcalfe TLt kia 29-9-17 MGC A'HB p182 CR Belgium112 A'TankCps
BROWN,Eric Russell Wilkie 2Lt ded 19-11-18 IA 2/30Punjabis p274 CR Egypt9

BROWN,Eric William 2Lt kia 3-5-15 5SLancs p230 MR29
BROWN,Ernest LtACapt kia 20-11-17 2N&D p133 CR France379
BROWN,Ernest Albert Lt ded 23-11-18 RGA 188SB p38 CR France403
BROWN,Ernest Edward Lt kia 8-5-16 1Wilts p152 CR France68
BROWN,Ernest James 2Lt kia 31-7-17 4RWelshF p223 MR29
BROWN,Ewart Cudemore Lt dedacc 14-8-17 RFC CR Lincs181 Ex PPCLI
BROWN,Foss Hunter 2Lt kia 31-7-17 RE 76FC p43 CR Belgium20
BROWN,Francis.MC.T2Lt kia 5-4-18 Lincs att63TMB p74 MR27
BROWN,Francis Alfred Joseph T2Lt kia 9-9-16 6Leinst att8RMunstF p174 MR21
BROWN,Francis Arthur Noel 2Lt kia 21-7-16 1/7Worc p226 MR21
BROWN,Francis Clement.MID Lt kia 8-12-17 16Lond p249 CR Palestine3
BROWN,Francis Wrentmore TLt dow 16-9-16 23Mddx p146 CR France105
BROWN,Frank Frederick.MC.Lt ded 21-2-19 32RGA 35SB p38 France63
BROWN,Fred 2Lt kia 11-12-15 1 O&BLI p130 CR Iraq1
BROWN,Frederick Anderson Lt kia 26-10-17 7NumbF p214 CR Belgium126
BROWN,Frederick Arthur T2Lt kia 13-11-16 7RFus p66 CR France339
BROWN,Frederick Charles 2Lt mbk 7-8-15 9N&D p256 MR4
BROWN,Frederick David 2Lt kia 8-3-17 13EYorks p83 MR21
BROWN,Frederick Francis T2Lt ded 28-9-18 4MGC p182 CR France84
BROWN,Frederick George Capt kia 4-11-14 IA 101Grenadiers MR47 p274
BROWN,Frederick Henry 2Lt kia 29-5-18 6 att1RB p178 CR France250
BROWN,Frederick Peter T2Lt dow 24-5-18 3 att1ORWKent p140 CR France142
BROWN,Frederick Seddon Capt kia 26-5-15 5Manch p236 CR Gallipoli1
BROWN,Frederick Vincent Capt 35376 kia 1-9-18 NZFA p274 CR France745
BROWN,Frederick William Archer T2Lt kia 25-4-18 1Lincs p74 CR Belgium185
BROWN,G.B.DSO.LtCol 6-1-19 RFA CR Yorks501
BROWN,Geoffrey Hubert Lt kia 23-10-18 3 att2WelshR p126 CR France190
BROWN,George Capt kia 16/18-6-15 8Lpool p215 MR22
BROWN,George Alexander Capt ded 6-6-16 RE p43 CR Mddx77
BROWN,George Congdon T2Lt dow 8-5-17 11Worc p108 CR Greece7
BROWN,George Easter 2Lt drd 20-4-17 HAC p206 MR20
BROWN,George James Rankine T2Lt dow 21-5-17 2BlkW p128 CR Iraq5
BROWN,George Lothian TLt dow 15-11-17 LNLancs att1Bn p135 CR Belgium11
BROWN,George Miller.MC.Lt kia 28-11-17 12Lancers p22 MR17
BROWN,George Russell TLt kia 11-2-18 18NumbF p60 CRFrance592
BROWN,George Sydney Robert Johnston 2Lt dow 22-5-15 3 att 1RScotF p94 CR France102
BROWN,George Trevor Lt kld 12-2-17 6WelshR &RFC p18&230 CR Wales171
BROWN,George West Lt ded 23-2-18 Lincs 1GarrBn p74 CR Asia60,William 24-2-18
BROWN,Gerald Brindley Lt ded 21-4-18 5Manch p236 MR34
BROWN,Gerald Dick.MC.LtAMaj 14-4-18 3Wilts p152 MR32,1Bn
BROWN,Gerald Knapton Lt kia 3-5-17 2/6WYorks p218 CR France568
BROWN,Gilfrid Elliott T2Lt kia 18-11-16 11BordR p116 CR France803
BROWN,Gordon Hargreaves Capt kia 29-10-14 1CldGds p51 MR29
BROWN,Granville Albert Lt ded 18-2-19 RAOC 69XCD p198 CR Belgium11
BROWN,G.Selwyn 2Lt ded 25-7-19 RGA p262
BROWN,Guy Frank Courtney 2Lt dow 11-5-17 2/22HAC p206 CR France40
BROWN,H.W.S.Maj 19-1-17 Mddx CR Lond8
BROWN,Harold.DSO.MC.Maj kia 23-3-18 5Yorks p220 MR27
BROWN,Harold Atherton 2Lt kia 15-5-15 2Leic p87 MR22
BROWN,Harold Halstead 2Lt kia 18-7-16 3 att1GordH p166 MR21
BROWN,Harold James.MC.Capt dow 10-1-20 12SWBord CR Wales17
BROWN,Harold Masters.MC.T2Lt dow 9-7-16 5RBerks p138&258 CR France40
BROWN,Harold Montague 2Lt kia 9-4-16 3ELancs C'Coy p110 MR38
BROWN,Harold Vernon T2Lt kia 3-5-17 8 att11ESurr p112 MR20
BROWN,Herbert 2Lt ded 6-6-19 IARO att1/30Punjabis p274 MR65
BROWN,Herbert James Lt kia 6-11-17 1/7RWelshF p223 CR Palestine1
BROWN,Horace Leslie 2Lt dow 11-3-18 4EKent p212 CR France345
BROWN,Horace Manton.MC.Lt dow 14-4-18 4Suff p217 CR Belgium18
BROWN,Hubert William Lt dow 19-9-14 RIrReg att2NigR p88 CR WAfrica57
BROWN,Hugh T2Lt kia 31-7-16 6RIrRif p169 MR29
BROWN,Hugh Alexander T2Lt kia 14-7-16 9ScotRif p103 CR France399
BROWN,Ian Macdonald TCapt kia 15-11-16 RAMC att190RFA p194
BROWN,Ian Macgregor Knox 2Lt kia 25-9-15 11RScots p53 MR19
BROWN,James Capt kia 15-6-15 6ScotRif p224 CR France549
BROWN,James Alfred 2Lt kia 25-7-16 RFC SR p2 MR20
BROWN,James Cartmell Dennison 2Lt dow 28-4-15 5DLI p239 CR France200,27-4-15
BROWN,James Cavet 2Lt mbk 24-3-18 5A&SH p257

BROWN,James Ferguson T2Lt kia 24-4-17 14 att1/6Glouc p106 MR21
BROWN,James Hardie.MC Capt dow 7-6-18 1/6A&SH p243 CR France31
BROWN,James Herbert T2Lt dow 8-10-17 Yorks Res att2Bn p90 CR Belgium138,2WYorks
BROWN,James Leonard 2Lt kld 29-3-18 RFC p15 see BROWNE,James Lawrence
BROWN,James McDonald T2Lt kia 21-3-18 10RB p178 MR27
BROWN,James Macpherson Gordon Lt kia 6-5-15 3 att2KOSB p101 MR29
BROWN,James Stanley Lt kld 20-10-18 5ELancs &RAF p255&226
BROWN,James Sutherland TLt kia 30-9-17 SL att3NigR p201 MR52
BROWN,James Sydney T2Lt kia 20-10-18 12Manch att15Ches p154 CR Belgium402
BROWN,James Tod 2Lt dow 27-4-18 4BlkW p230 CR France100
BROWN,James Turner TLt drd 4-5-17 RAMC p194 CR Italy13
BROWN,James Westhall Lt kia 14-5-17 RFA 2/3HighlandHB attRFC p261&269 CR France418
BROWN,James William 2Lt dow 2-11-14 26RFA p26 MR29
BROWN,James William,MC Capt kia 21-3-17 11RScots p53 MR20
BROWN,John.MID T2Lt dow 11-8-16 RFA&RFC p2&26 CR Egypt2
BROWN,John T2Lt drd 4-5-17 3RWelshF GarrBn p97 CR Italy14
BROWN,John.MC&Bar.Capt dow 21-3-18 17RIrRif p169 MR27,8 att1Bn
BROWN,John.MC.Capt kia 21-3-18 2/7Manch p237 MR27
BROWN,John T2Lt dow 26-3-18 12HLI p162 CR France232,Lt
BROWN,John Lt kia 11-4-18 6SfthH p241 CR Belgium111
BROWN,John Capt kia 20-7-18 1/4GordH p241 CR Frnce622
BROWN,John Lt ded 27-6-19 4RScots p269 CR Scot262BROWN,John Albert Hunter ACapt kia 18-8-16 3 att1GordH p166 MR21
BROWN,John Alexander TLtACapt dow 22-10-18 9 att13RB p178 CR France287
BROWN,John Ambrose T2Lt kia 12-3-17 7YLI p142 CR France513
BROWN,John Arbuckle T2Lt dow 3-7-16 16HLI p162 CR France296
BROWN,John Carolan.MC.LtACapt kia 8-8-18 4ConnRgrs &1TankCps p172&188 CR France589
BROWN,John Cuthbert Backhouse TLt kia 29-9-18 Mddx att1Bn p146 CR France407
BROWN,John Dunlop 2Lt dow 3-12-17 6HLI p240 CR Belgium18
BROWN,John Edward LtACapt kia 14-9-18 D113RFA p26 CR Belgium188
BROWN,John Edward Guy Capt kia 22-2-15 2 att1RWKent attRBerks p140 CR Belgium133
BROWN,John Gordon Lt dow 5-2-17 SuffYeo p205 CR France624
BROWN,John Gordon.MC.Capt kia 5-10-18 RFus attRFA 47DivArtyHQ p66 CR France82
BROWN,John Rankine Capt dow 23-4-17 7HLI p240 CR Palestine2
BROWN,John Ritchie TLt dow 7-11-16 RAMC p194
BROWN,John Samuel 2Lt kia 18-5-17 RGA 61SB p38 CR France581
BROWN,John William.MC.T2Lt dow 1-8-17 Yorks Res att2Bn p90 CR Belgium18
BROWN,John William 2Lt kia 16-8-17 1/9 att1/5Lond p248 MR29
BROWN,John William 2Lt kia 16-10-17 7Yorks p90 MR30
BROWN,John William.MM.2Lt kia 11-4-18 10 att5Yorks p90 CR France1092
BROWN,Joseph Jackson TLt kia 5-8-18 2RScotF p94 CR France25
BROWN,J.W.Lt 10-11-14 RFA CR Belgium58
BROWN,Keith Andrews LtTCapt dow 22-9-18 1RWSurr A'Coy p55 CR France906
BROWN,Kenneth Ashby Capt 14-4-17 5ScotRif CR France434
BROWN,Kenneth Edward.MC&Bar.Capt dow 12-4-18 PoW 2/4 O&BLI p231 CR France934,13-4-18
BROWN,Kenneth Wallace 2Lt ded 24-8-17 6RWar p269 CR Numb39
BROWN,Laurence Clerke Lt kia 11-10-15 3 att1Glouc p106 MR19
BROWN,Lawrence Crawford T2Lt kia 16-8-17 8RInniskF p104 MR30,Laurence
BROWN,Lawrence Smith Blanche.MC.T2Lt kia 28-11-17 97MGC p182 CR Belgium63,Laurence 27-11-17
BROWN,Leonard James 2Lt kia 19-8-18 1ESurr att2RFus p112 MR32
BROWN,Lionel George Henry 2Lt ded 8-12-17 GL &52RFC p5 MR20
BROWN,Louis Foster TLt dow 15-5-18 115MGC p182 CR France13,14-5-18 38MGC
BROWN,Macdonald Warriner TCapt kia 12-10-16 17Manch p154 MR21
BROWN,Miles Wheelton Lt kia 25-9-15 2Leic p87 CR France1157
BROWN,Norman Algernon 2Lt ded 1-3-19 4Lond p246 CR Beds65,28-2-19
BROWN,Norman Watson 2LtTLt dow 1-5-17 3ELancs att103MGC p110&182 France113
BROWN,Osbert Harold.DSO.MC.TCapt kia 1-11-16 11Suff p78 CR France83
BROWN,Oscar Lt kia 24-4-15 IA 7Lancers att4DragGds p274 CR Belgium20
BROWN,Osmond Pickard 2Lt dow 31-7-17 3 att11RWKent p140 CR Belgium118,kia
BROWN,Oswald Stanley 2Lt kia 22-12-15 3 att1BlkW p128 MR19

BROWN,P.W.SubCdr 16-4-20 IndiaP&T Dept MR43
BROWN,Philip Anthony TLt kia 4-11-15 13DLI p160 CR France82
BROWN,Phillip Kentish 2Lt kia 13-10-15 9 att5Lincs p74 MR19
BROWN,Ralph Adair 2Lt kia 1-7-16 1/14Lond A'Coy p149 MR21
BROWN,Reginald Charles T2Lt kia 21-2-18 80RFC p15 CR France255
BROWN,Reginald Roy.MC.LtAMaj ded 31-10-18 RHA 14ArmyBde p26 CR France332
BROWN,Richard Clerke T2Lt kia 20-8-16 RE 103FC p43
BROWN,Richard Gavin Lt ded 14-2-16 RAMC p267 CR Hamps10
BROWN,Richard Stanley 2Lt ded 9-2-16 14Ches p95 CR Lancs7
BROWN,Richard Walker 2LtACapt kia 9-4-17 3 att2Wilts p152 CR France162,Walter
BROWN,Robert Lt ded 6-2-19 1/7HLI p254&265 CR Scot674
BROWN,Robert Lt ded 13-6-21 DCLI attS&T Cps MR43
BROWN,Robert Alexander 2Lt kia 16-9-18 14Lond p249 CR Belgium192,17-9-18
BROWN,Robert Cunningham 2Lt dow 11-4-17 9RScots p212 CR France95
BROWN,Robert Henry 2Lt dow 16-1-17 1/5WRid p227 CR France120
BROWN,Robert Laurie 2Lt kia 19-7-18 BlkW att8Bn p128 CR France324
BROWN,Robert Stanley 2Lt kia 1-7-16 16HLI p162 CR France293
BROWN,Robin Lowis Campbell T2LtALt dow 8-6-17 GL RFA attX8TMB p190 CR Belgium11
BROWN,Roland 2Lt kia 13-7-18 4Yorks p220 CR Belgium115
BROWN,Samuel T2Lt dow 27-9-18 CamH Res att11Bn p167 CR France25
BROWN,Sidney Frederick 2Lt ded 21-7-17 SR 21RFC p5 CR Belgium125,Capt
BROWN,Sidney Frederick 2Lt kia 15-5-18 RGA 239SB p209 CR France1182
BROWN,Sidney Wilfred 2Lt mbk 5-9-18 11ELancs p256 MR32BROWN,Stanley Newman T2Lt kia 27-8-18 RBerks att8Bn p138 CR France401
BROWN,Stewart Patrick T2Lt dow 31-12-17 RE 248FC p43 CR France398
BROWN,S.V.2Lt ded 9-11-18 3LancF p92 CR Staffs109
BROWN,Sylvester Samuel.MC.Lt kia 25-4-18 9Lond att&MGC p186&248 MR27
BROWN,Theodore Anthony.MC.2Lt kia 15-4-17 3 att1EKent p57 MR19,Capt
BROWN,Thomas 2Lt kia 4-9-16 1Norf p73 CR France402
BROWN,Thomas Campbell TLt ded 17-12-17 RASC p192 CR Surrey55
BROWN,Thomas Elliot Thorburn Lt dow 20-9-18 3KOSB p101
BROWN,Thomas Fletcher 2Lt kia 30-5-15 7Manch p237 CR Gallipoli2
BROWN,Thomas Muirhead TLt dow 16-4-18 RE 9 ObsGrp 1FdSurvCo p43 CR France102
BROWN,Tom T2Lt kia 13-11-16 10 att7ELancs p110 CR France384
BROWN,Valentine Oakley Lt kia 9-10-18 3DragGds p21
BROWN,Walter T2Lt kia 18-8-16 2A&SH p173 CR France432
BROWN,Walter Hugh SubCdr ded 23-2-19 IA S&TCps p274 CR Iraq6
BROWN,Walter Ravenhill.MC.Lt kia 21-11-17 7WYorks p218 CR France905
BROWN,Walter Sidney LtCol kia 6-7-16 Wilts p152 CR France246
BROWN,Wilfred Stephenson Capt ded 27-3-19 RAMC 19CCS p194 CR France85
BROWN,William 2Lt kia 5-10-17 1/4 att6BlkW p230 CR France592
BROWN,William T2Lt kia 1-3-18 3RMunstF att2RinniskF p175 CR Frnce1061
BROWN,William Lt kia 11-8-18 6RScots p211 CR France360
BROWN,William Chap4Cl ded 10-3-19 RAChDept p268 CR Hamps1
BROWN,William Archibald Ross T2Lt kia 22-11-17 H'TankCps p188 MR17
BROWN,William Charles Lt ded 7-11-18 RGA 387SB p38 CR Kent267
BROWN,William Clark 2Lt kia 21-5-17 4RScots p211 CR France522,21-5-18
BROWN,William Douglas Capt dow 29-12-17 LanarkYeo p204 MR34
BROWN,William Elmer TLt dow 18-5-18 RAMC att10FA p194 CR France10,att2WRid
BROWN,William George Chartens LtCol ded 26-5-19 RE p43 CR Sussex178
BROWN,William Gordon 2Lt kld 7-5-18 GL &19RAF p190 CR France95,kia
BROWN,William Herbert Lt dow 19-7-18 18DLI p160 MR32
BROWN,William Joseph Lt kld 21-2-18 1Cty of LondYeo &RAF p18&204 CR Egypt9
BROWN,William Leonard 2Lt kia 25-9-15 6N&D p233 CR Belgium82
BROWN,William Noel Sneade Lt ded 1-8-19 4SomLI p269 CR Berks71
BROWN,William Robertson T2Lt dow 30-9-17 1RScotF p94 CR Belgium16
BROWN,William Sandilands LtACapt kia 14-10-18 3NStaffs p156 CR Belgium112
BROWN,William Wallace Lt kia 28-6-15 7ScotRif B'Coy p224 CR Gallipoli6
BROWN,Winifred Maud Miss drd 31-12-17 VAD p200 CR Egypt1
BROWN,Wynyard Keith.MID Capt kia 4-6-15 IA 1/5GurkhaRif att9WYorks p274 MR4
BROWN,W.J.H.Capt kia 4-9-16 3 att15Norf p73 MR21
BROWN-CONSTABLE,John Cecil Lt kia 1-7-16 14Lond p249 CR France798
BROWNBRIDGE,Herbert Edward T2Lt ded 7-12-18 47MGC p182 CR France34
BROWNE,Alfred James Haslip 2Lt dow 23-4-17 8SStaffs p122 MR20

BROWNE,Andrew Cranstoun T2Lt kia 2-7-16 8SStaffs p122 CR France397,BROWN
BROWNE,Archibald Trevor TCapt kia 29-9-18 20DLI p160 CR Belgium111
BROWNE,Arthur Davies Lang 2Lt kia 11-9-17 3 att1ConnRgrs p172 MR38
BROWNE,Arthur George 2Lt kia 20-10-14 N&D p133 MR32
BROWNE,Arthur Richard Howe Lt kld 5-12-15 RFC p1 CR France518
BROWNE,Bernard Score.MC.TCapt kia 15-4-18 RAMC att2Ches p194 MR37
BROWNE,Charles Eric Wyndham 2Lt dow 24-10-16 2Ess p131 CR France105
BROWNE,Charles Nicholas Foster 2Lt kia 13-5-15 1Drags p21 CR Belgium2
BROWNE,Charles Pierson Capt dow 11-4-15 IA CpsofGuides att15Lancers p274 CR France924
BROWNE,Dominick Augustus Capt&Adjt kia 1-7-16 1RIrRif p169 MR21
BROWNE,Frank Douglas Maj dow 17-1-16 IA 56Rif p274 CR Iraq5
BROWNE,Frederick MacDonnell.DSO Maj dow 1-10-15 RE 38FC p43 CR France98,Macdonell
BROWNE,Geoffrey Dennis.MID Maj kia 19-9-16 C240RFA p206 CR France251
BROWNE,George Brownlie T2Lt kia 7-2-16 10 att9BlkW p128 CR France423
BROWNE,George Buckston.DSO.LtCol ded 6-1-19 RH&FA p261&269,Maj
BROWNE,George Edwin TLt dow 21-1-18 RFC p15 CR France446
BROWNE,Gordon Stewart Lt dow 27-11-14 1Wilts p152 CR Kent63
BROWNE,Harold Vernon Capt dow 7-9-15 DorsYeo p203 CR Gallipoli27
BROWNE,Henry Arthur T2Lt kia 26-10-18 Ess att2Bn p131 CR France1266
BROWNE,Herbert Maxwell T2LtALt kia 26-3-17 1/5Ess p131 CR Palestine8B
ROWNE,James Lawrence 2Lt kld 29-3-18 11ELancs attRFC p254&15,Leonard CR Lancs474
BROWNE,John Hazell T2Lt kia 20-4-16 12 att9RWar p64 MR38,18-4-16
BROWNE,Langford Kyffin T2Lt kia 9-4-17 32 att25NumbF p60 CR France265
BROWNE,Lionel Charles 2Lt kia 29-6-17 1/7N&D p233 CR France570,Lt 30-6-17
BROWNE,Lord Alfred Eden.DSO.ALtCol kia 27-8-18 HQ 186RFA p26 CR France54
BROWNE,Maurice.MID Capt kia 19-9-18 IARO att92Punjabis p274 CR Palestine9
BROWNE,Maurice Henry Dermot.Hon.MID Lt kia 29-9-15 1CldGds p51 CR France423
BROWNE,Maximilian Herbert.MC.TLtACapt kld 21-6-18 RIrRif att108TMB p169 CR France142,Maximillian
BROWNE,Montague Bernard 2Lt dow 30-4-16 8N&D p233 CR Ireland5
BROWNE,Percival Leathley Capt kia 9-8-15 6Lincs p74 CR Gallipoli5
BROWNE,Peter 2Lt kia 1-10-16 4 att6ConnRgrs p172 CR Belgium157,Lt
BROWNE,Robert Geoffrey.DSO.Maj ded 1-11-18 Manch p154 CR France1858
BROWNE,W.L.LtCol 6-2-20 RGA CR Lond28
BROWNE,William Angus TLt kia 21-9-17 8RInniskF &53RFC p5&104 CR France705
BROWNE,William Lindsay T2Lt dow 5-7-16 8YLI p142 CR France74
BROWNFIELD,Reginald John(Roy).MID Capt kia 18-12-14 2RWar p64 MR32
BROWNING,Charles Hunter Capt kia 26-8-14 124/28RFA p26 CR France716
BROWNING,Charles Stuart Capt kia 10-12-16 IA 129Baluchis p274 CR EAfrica38 &CR Tanzania1
BROWNING,Edwin Ormonde T2Lt kia 20-4-16 11 att7Glouc p106 MR38
BROWNING,Ernest George 2Lt dow 19-7-17 14Lond p249 CR France512
BROWNING,George Howard T2Lt kia 13-3-18 7 att1ELancs p110 CR France616
BROWNING,George Stamer TCapt ded 25-2-16 SL p201&257 CR Eire163,Stamer
BROWNING,James Alexander.MID Maj kia 31-10-14 2DragGds p20 CR Belgium89
BROWNING,Oakley Alsop 2Lt kld 11-8-17 GL &RFC p5 CR Yorks178
BROWNING,Reginald Arthur.MC.T2Lt dow 10-4-17 20NumbF p60 CR France53
BROWNING,Reginald Gordon Snell Capt kia 2-10-15 6WelshR p230 MR19
BROWNING,Stanley Forrester TCapt kia 3-5-17 GL &41RFC p5 CR Belgium125
BROWNING-PATERSON,Norman Alexander Capt kia 21-7-16 RFA &RFC p2&26 MR20
BROWNLEE,Wilfred Methven 2Lt ded 12-10-14 3Dors p123 CR Glouc5
BROWNLESS,John Wilson Lt dow 16-6-15 RAVC p198 CR Gallipoli3
BROWNLIE,John Reid T2Lt kia 29-6-16 11 att1ScotRif p103 CR France765
BROWNLIE,William.MC.TCapt kia 25-3-18 RAMC att13Yorks p194 CR France434
BROWNLOW,Charles Henry.GCB.Sir.FldMar ded 5-4-16 Commdg20Punjabis CR Berks47
BROWNLOW,Wilfred Herbert Cecil Capt kia 28-5-18 NumbF 2att12/13Bn p60 CR France1331
BROWNLOW,William Lionel 2Lt kia 9-5-15 NumbF att2BlkW p60 CR France631
BROWNRIGG,John Huleath Lt kia 14-4-15 2Norf p73 CR Iraq6
BROWNRIGG-JAY,George Harvey TLt kia 21-9-18 124MGC p182 CR France364
BROWNSON,Alfred Reginald TLt kia 18-9-18 11WelshR p126 CR Greece5
BROWNSON,Roger Dawson Duffield Capt ded 21-10-18 RASC p192 MR43,RAMC

BROWNSWORD,Douglas Anderson Capt dow 25-12-17 RASC p253 CR Greece22
BROWNSWORTH,E.A.2Lt dow 27-5-16 1Leic CR Belgium11
BROWSE,Reginald T2Lt kia 25-4-18 9ScotRif p103 MR30
BROXUP,John William T2Lt dow 24-4-17 10RWelshF p97 CR Lancs427
BRUCE,Alexander Angus 2Lt kia 24-6-18 B156RFA p26 CR Belgium36
BRUCE,Alexander Charles Arbuthnot.MID Capt kia 23-4-16 RASC p253 CR Egypt2
BRUCE,Andrew Moffat 2Lt kia 29-9-18 9HLI p240 CR France663
BRUCE,Bethune Duncan TCapt kia 27-9-15 13RScots p53 MR19
BRUCE,Charles James 2Lt dow 20-5-17 ACycCps 52Div p244 CR Egypt9
BRUCE,Charles William Capt kld 22-11-17 GordH &RFC p5&166 CR Essex86
BRUCE,Christopher Yule T2Lt kia 28-3-18 RE 176TC p43 CR France68
BRUCE,Colin TLt dow 5-9-18 14HLI p162 CR France52,6Bn
BRUCE,Douglas Fraser T2Lt kia 10-7-16 13RB p178 CR France832
BRUCE,Edward Tyrrell T2Lt dow 9-6-18 8MGC Inf p182 CR France622
BRUCE,Eric T2Lt ded 17-11-16 11 att2BlkW p128 CR Iraq5
BRUCE,Ernest John Webster.MC.Capt ded 17-4-19 94RFA p261 CR Lond8
BRUCE,George James.DSO.MC.TCapt kia 2-10-18 GL 109InfBde 36Div p190 CR Belgium157,BdeMaj Ex 13RIrRif
BRUCE,George McDonald Lt ded 18-2-19 4A&SH attCamH p173 CR Belgium316,MacDonald
BRUCE,Harry Kendal Walpole.MC.Maj kia 1-2-17 IA 1/2GurkhaRif p274 CR Iraq5
BRUCE,Henry Lyndhurst.Hon.Capt kia 14-12-14 3 att2RScots p53 MR29
BRUCE,Herbert William T2Lt kia 17-2-17 2BlkW p128 CR Iraq5
BRUCE,Jack Curtis 2Lt kia 25-3-18 2/4Leic p254 MR20
BRUCE,James 2LtACapt kia 25-7-17 256RFA p26 CR Belgium5
BRUCE,James Anderson Lt ded 6-1-19 AyrYeo &RAF p203&258
BRUCE,Jasper.MID Lt ded 17-2-19 2Remounts RASC attChes p95 CR France85
BRUCE,John Elliot Lidderdale Maj kia 29-5-15 26RGA p38 CR Gallipoli30
BRUCE,John Fryer 2Lt dow 28-2-18 2A&SH p173 CR Belgium3
BRUCE,John Gardiner Lt kia 14-4-18 ScotHorse att1ScotRif p205 MR32
BRUCE,John Russel TMaj kia 1-7-16 15RScots p53 Mr21
BRUCE,Jonathan Maxwell Maj kia 24-11-14 IA 107Pnrs p274 CR France80
BRUCE,Malcolm Ronald 2Lt kia 22-8-17 14Lond p249 CR Belgium125
BRUCE,Norman Martin TLt kia 7-8-15 6Yorks p90 MR4
BRUCE,Oliver T2Lt dow 9-6-18 PoW 2RB p178 CR France34
BRUCE,Philip Thomson Lt ded 30-5-18 10Lpool &43RAF p216,269&258,P.John MR20 Ex 87Sqn
BRUCE,Philip Thomerson 2Lt kia 31-5-18 10Lpool &RAF See Above
BRUCE,Robert.Hon.Capt kia 26-8-14 2A&SH p173 CR France716
BRUCE,Robert Lt dow 25-9-15 16LondRFA p207 CR France219
BRUCE,Robert 2Lt ded 7-7-16 IARO att14S&TCps p274 CR Iraq5,Lt
BRUCE,Robert James 2Lt kia 2-2-18 6SStaffs p229 CR France1483
BRUCE,Robert Lloyd TLt kia 19-11-16 11ScotRif p103 CR Greece6
BRUCE,Robert Stuart Malcolm T2Lt kld 17-8-17 GL att111RFC p5 CR Palestine2
BRUCE,Stanley Malcolm Maj kia 25-5-18 IA 37 att 15Lancers
BRUCE,Thomas Robert Capt ded 8-2-17 14Huss p22 CR Iraq5
BRUCE,Vincent Connell Lt kia 26-3-16 5GordH p242 MR20,Ex 13RScots
BRUCE,Wallace Edward Lt kia 31-7-17 1RFus p67 MR29
BRUCE,William.MC.2Lt kia 3-12-18 RE 206FC p210 CR Belgium337,dedacc
BRUCE,William Arthur McCrae.VC.Lt kia 19-12-14 IA 59Rif p274 MR28
BRUCE,William George Lt kia 25-4-18 RE att156RFA p210 MR30
BRUCE-CLARK,William Robert.MBE.Capt ded 1-12-18 14Lond &RAF p255 CR Camb16
BRUCE-LOCKHART,Norman Douglas Stewart Lt kia 25-9-15 7SfthH p164 MR19
BRUDENELL-BRUCE,James Ernest John Lt dow 11-4-17 1NhamptYeo p204 CR France113
BRUFTON,Howard Charles 2Lt kia 9-7-17 20RB &47RFC p18&244 CR Greece1,8-7-17
BRUFTON,Wilfred Eustace 2Lt dow 3-9-18 119/27RFA p26 CR France156,5-9-18
BRUMAN,Albert Victor T2Lt dow 31-5-18 19MGC Inf p182 CR France1693 &34
BRUMBLEY,Walter James Joshua.MC.2Lt kia 27-3-18 3 att7Norf p73 MR27
BRUNDLE,Henry Carlton Bulman LtTCapt kia 9-10-17 12LancF p92 MR37
BRUNDRETT,George Frederick 2Lt dow 24-8-18 5Ches att7KSLI p222 CR France145
BRUNGER,Robert.DSO.Capt kia 8-10-18 9Norf p73 CR France375
BRUNNER,Cecil Heywood Capt dow 25-10-17 RFA p207 CR Belgium16
BRUNNER,Francis Wilfred Maj kia 11-8-15 RE 67FC p43 CR Gallipoli5
BRUNO,Carlo TLt kia 29-4-16 RFC p2,261kld&268,CaptEAUL SL CR EAfrica13
BRUNSDEN,Edward James T2Lt dow 25-4-17 45MGC Inf p182 CR France113
BRUNSDON,Henry George 2Lt dow 24-4-17 1/9RScots p212 CR France53
BRUNSKILL,James Harold Capt kia 29-9-17 RASC NCycBatt p253 2entries CR France1361,ACycCps

BRUNSKILL,John Jesmond T2Lt kia 23-4-17 4Worc p108 MR20 &CR France1896,44Bn
BRUNSTROM,Waldemar.MC.2Lt kia 19-8-18 C223RFA p208 CR France1016,18-8-18
BRUNT,Henry John Francis Lt kia 25-9-15 3 att1RWelshF p97 MR19
BRUNT,John Jarvis 2Lt kia 24-3-18 12 att10RInniskF p104 CR France1170
BRUNT,William Edward T2Lt kia 1-7-16 22Manch p154 CR France397
BRUNT0N,Douglas Capt kia 9-10-17 HAC p206 MR30
BRUNTON,Edward Benjamin Durnford 2Lt kia 13-11-16 17Mddx p146 MR21
BRUNTON,Edward Henry Pollock TLt kia 8-10-15 RAMC att4GrenGds p194 CR France423
BRUNTON,George Lt dow 11-4-18 4 att8RScots p211 CR France88
BRUNTON,Hereward T2Lt kia 1-7-16 17HLI p162 MR21
BRUNTON,James McLeod 2Lt kia 1-8-17 6RScots p211 MR34
BRUNTON,Theodore Stuart Lt ded 3-6-19 IARO attS&M p274 MR65,13-6-19
BRUNWIN-HALES,Greville Oxley Capt kia 24-3-17 8Ess att13RFC p18&232 CR France95
BRUNWIN-HALES,Henry Tooke 2Lt kia 13-10-15 1/4Lincs p217 CR France423
BRUTON,Basil Vassar Capt kia 15-6-18 1/5Glouc p225 CR Italy2,dow
BRUTON,Thomas A.MM.2Lt kia 1-9-18 6 att4Worc p108 CR France285
BRUTTON,Eric West.MC.Lt kia 14-4-18 3Dev D'Coy attMGC p76&182 MR32
BRUTTON,Robert Hall.TD.Maj ded 15-1-16 1/5SomLI p218 MR65
BRUTY,Edward Douglas T2Lt kia 15-10-17 11NumbF p60 MR30,4Bn
BRYAN,Alfred.MC.Lt kia 23-8-18 3 att2HLI p162 CR France745
BRYAN,Cecil Clive.DSO.Maj kia 11-8-17 RE 490FC p209 CR Belgium15
BRYAN,Frederick Stawell.MC.TCapt kia 23-11-17 15 att21Mddx p146 MR17
BRYAN,Sterry James ACapt kia 8-2-17 1HAC p206 CR France339
BRYAN,Sydney Arthur T2Lt kia 1-7-16 9Y&L p158 MR21
BRYANS,John Lt dow 28-10-17 2/5LNLancs p234 CR Belgium16
BRYANT,Alan,DSO MajTLtCol kia 17-10-17 1Glouc p106 CR Belgium85
BRYANT,Alfred Francis Maj dow 26-11-17 RA attAyrshireRHA p26 CR Palestine9 ,kia
BRYANT,Frederick James Mansell 2Lt kia 26-3-17 4WelshR p230 MR34
BRYANT,Frederick Vivian James 2Lt ded 28-3-19 RGA p262 CR Herts12
BRYANT,George Herbert.OBE.MID HonMaj kia 1-8-18 RE p43 CR France34
BRYANT,Harvey.MC.2Lt kia 12-9-18 Hamps att2/4Bn p120 CR France530
BRYANT,Henry Grenville.DSO.Capt dow 1-5-15 2KSLI p144 CR Belgium383
BRYANT,John Evelyn TCapt kia 4-8-16 6 O&BLI p130 CR France643
BRYANT,Oliver Mackensie Beadon Lt kld 11-12-16 2/2KAR p201 CR EAfrica38 &CR Tanzania1
BRYANT,Reginald Eyre T2LtACapt kia 20-1-17 14DLI p160 CR France114
BRYANT,Richard Leslie Algernon 2Lt dow 23-5-17 7Suff attRGA 35TMB p78 CR France40,Lt ded
BRYANT,Thomas Capt kia 11-4-17 5Lincs p220 CR France366
BRYCE,David Grieg Maj ded 24-2-16 IA 76Punjabis p274
BRYCE,James TLt kia 27-5-18 17RIrRif p169 MR18
BRYCE,Samuel 2Lt kia 21-12-14 7DragGds p21 MR22
BRYCE,William Hulton T2Lt kia 2-3-16 14 att12RScots p53 CR Belgium53,Hutton
BRYCE-SMITH,Norgrave Ingram TLt kia 25-4-18 3 att6KOSB p101 MR30
BRYDEN,Richard Joseph.VD.Maj ded 16-1-15 RAMC p269 CR Kent129
BRYDON,Alec Whitworth Lt kia 31-8-15 4RWSurr p212 CR Gallipoli5 Ex 2/6Ches
BRYDON,John Earnsclinch Capt dow 27-6-17 RAMC p253 CR France592,Earnscleugh
BRYDON,Thomas Edward T2Lt dow 1-2-17 RE 88FC p43 CR Iraq5
BRYETT,Lewis Henry Frederick 2Lt dow 25-10-18 A307RFA p26 CR France380
BRYSON,Alexander 2Lt dow 25-6-17 5KOSB p224 CR Belgium11,7/8Bn
BRYSON,Andrew T2Lt dow 19-11-18 HLI att1/5Bn p162 CR France646,19-9-18
BRYSON,James Harvey T2Lt kia 20-10-18 RFA &X24TMB p26 CR France403,Y24
BRYSON,John T2Lt dow 14-10-17 NumbF att21Bn p60 CR Belgium25
BRYSON,Joseph 2Lt kia 6-10-18 1 att9RIrF p171 MR30
BRYSON,Lauder W.TCapt kia 30-7-16 14RWar p64 MR21,George Lander Unite
BRYSON,Thomas Harold 2Lt ded 27-2-19 GL 6/7RScotsF att207PoWCoy LabCps p190&266,TLt LabCps CR France134,Lt 28Bn
BRYSON,Thomas Lees Capt ded 16-4-19 LabCps attChineseLabCps p266 CR Asia45
BRYSON,William Miller 2Lt kia 1-9-18 1/1ERidYeo p206 CR France1484
BUBB,Harry Wilfred LtACapt dow 1-1-17 NStaffs attTMB p156 CR Staffs84
BUCH,Charles Justus T2Lt kia 14-9-16 9 att8Beds p85 MR21,13-9-16
BUCHAN,Alastair Ebenezar TLt dow 9-4-17 6RScotF p94 CR France113,Ebenezer
BUCHAN,Charles Rev T2Lt dow 2-12-17 1 att15LancF p92 CR Belgium84
BUCHAN,David,TLt kia 9-4-17 1GordH p166 MR20

BUCHAN,Ernest Norman.DSO.Capt kia 25-9-15 1Manch p154 MR19
BUCHAN,Francis Hall T2Lt dow 7-8-18 11RB p178 CR France547
BUCHAN,James 2Lt kia 22-3-18 LNLancs att15Bn p135 MR27
BUCHAN,James Wilson T2Lt kia 23-4-17 3ScotRif att5BordR p103 CR France1185
BUCHAN,John Crawford.VC.2Lt mbk 22-3-18 7 att8A&SH p257 CR France528
BUCHAN,Leslie Alexander T2Lt dow 30-7-16 6/40RFA p26 CR France51
BUCHAN,Roy Eric Victor T2Lt kia 27-3-16 40RFA p26 CR Belgium35
BUCHAN,William Erskine T2Lt kld 9-3-18 RFC p15 CR Hamps192
BUCHAN,William George T2Lt kia 12-10-16 7SfthH p164 MR21
BUCHANAN,Adam Heaton T2Lt kia 5-10-18 GordH att5Bn p166 CR France115
BUCHANAN,Andrew MacFarlane ALt dow 13-6-17 GL RFA &90TMB p190 CR Belgium11
BUCHANAN,Archibald Ure T2Lt dow 28-9-15 1GordH p166 CR Belgium11,27-9-15
BUCHANAN,Arthur Sanderson ACapt ded 15-2-19 RE p26CR Scot237
BUCHANAN,Claude Gray Capt kia 4-11-14 IA 53Sikhs att2/8GurkhaRif p274 MR28
BUCHANAN,David T2Lt kia 1-7-16 2SfthH p164 CR France643
BUCHANAN,David Neil Griffiths 2Lt kia 21-1-16 IARO att37Dogras p274 CR Iraq5
BUCHANAN,Edward Lawrie Capt kia 15-8-20 RFA &RAF CR Iraq8
BUCHANAN,Fraser Campbell 2Lt kia 9-4-17 13RScots p53 CR France924
BUCHANAN,Harold Cyril Dudley TLt dow 12-11-16 1Mddx p146 CR France40
BUCHANAN,James Herbert Lt kia 16-3-15 7RIrF attLeinst p171 CR Belgium28,4IrF 15-3-15
BUCHANAN,James MacKenzie TLt ded 18-2-18 RE 180FC p262 CR Scot674
BUCHANAN,James Robert TLt dow 1-4-18 13RIrRif p169 CR France145
BUCHANAN,Richard Brendan 2Lt dow 20-6-15 1/5RScotF p222 CR Gallipoli1
BUCHANAN,William Archibald Lt ded 2-6-16 1ConnRgrs &RFC p2 CR Wilts115,7-6-16
BUCHANAN,William Arthur Irvine Capt dow 24-7-17 RAVC 50MobileTrps p198 CR Belgium5,kia sect39Div
BUCHANAN,William Learmouth Capt dow 20-11-17 5HLI p240 CR Palestine9,Learmonth
BUCHANAN-BAILLIE-HAMILTON,Arthur.MID Capt 9-5-15 1SfthH CR France721 see BAILLIE-HAMILTON,A.B.
BUCHANAN-DUNLOP,Colin Napier.DSO.Maj kia 14-10-15 F'RHA p26 CR France423
BUCHANNAN,Alexander 2Lt kia 21-7-17 6 att16WYorks p218 CR France268
BUCK,Archibald Charles Watson 2Lt kia 9-8-16 10Lpool p216 MR21
BUCK,Arthur TLt kld 9-9-18 RE att67RGA p43 CR France570
BUCK,Bertram Forster TLt kia 3-9-16 17N&D p133 MR21
BUCK,Charles ACapt kia 15-5-18 1/4RBerks p234 CR Italy2,15-6-18
BUCK,Charles Melvill Lt mbk 24-1-17 IARO att53RFC p274 CR Belgium152
BUCK,Cyril Alfred Spencer.MM.2Lt kia 26-10-17 18 att2/3Lond p250 MR30
BUCK,Cyril Bernard Wilson.MC.Rev kia 29-9-18 RAChDept att5Leic p199&258
BUCK,Geoffrey Sebastian.MC.DFC.Capt kia 3-9-18 1Lond &RAF p245&258
BUCK,Robert Stanley Maj ded 11-3-19 GL LancF p263 CR Surrey6
BUCK,William Pallister T2Lt dow 24-10-18 NumbF att4RFus p60 CR France332
BUCKELL,Christopher James Allardyce 2Lt kia 19-4-17 3Norf p73 CR Palestine8
BUCKELL,Francis William Ashton Lt kia 21-3-18 4 att8RWSurr p212 MR27
BUCKELL,Harold Claude.MC.2LtTCapt kia 21-9-17 13DLI p160 MR30
BUCKERIDGE,Guy Dennis TLt kld 21-8-17 GL &RFC p5 CR Norf254,22-8-17
BUCKHAM,Norman Langley TLtACapt ded 30-10-18 RAOC GHQ p198 CR France65
BUCKINGHAM,Aubrey Webster Maj kia 17-11-14 3 att1GordH p166 CR Belgium84,1/5Bn
BUCKINGHAM,Henry Lt&QM ded 20-12-17 4Hamps p220 CR Iraq8
BUCKINGHAM,Maude Amy Matron 4-12-15 QAIMNS CR Lond8
BUCKINGHAM,P.E.MC.2Lt kld 8-11-18 1/2RWKent att7RAF p140 CR Belgium159,Lt
BUCKINGHAM,Thomas Nock Lt kia 26-10-17 6 att8Dev p217 MR30,Noel
BUCKINGHAM,William Albert T2Lt dow 3-10-18 Res att5Berks p138 CR France146
BUCKLAND,Cecil John 2Lt ded 19-8-18 1/4RFus &RAF p67 CR Wilts18,5Bn kld flying
BUCKLAND,Ernest Blas TLt kia 5-10-16 13ESurr p112 CR France115
BUCKLAND,John 2Lt kia 16-6-17 Y&L att12Bn p158 CR France644
BUCKLAND,John Arnold 2Lt kia 1-3-17 7SomLI p79 CR France744
BUCKLAND,Thomas Adrian TLt dow 18-10-15 7Norf p73 MR19,19-10-15
BUCKLE,Archie Stewart BrigGen ded 18-8-16 RA 17Div p26 CR France833
BUCKLE,Arthur Charles LtCol ded 21-12-18 Nhampt p137 CR Staffs125
BUCKLE,Christopher Galbraith.DSO.MC.ALtCol kia 27-5-18 2Nhampt p137 CR France1753

BUCKLE,Cuthbert Charles Corbett 2Lt kia 3-7-16 8RWKent p140 CR France1890,6Bn A'Coy
BUCKLE,Dudley Francis de Crespigny AMaj ded 24-4-19 3NumbF p254 CR Numb11A
BUCKLE,Harry Capt dow 4-10-14 PoW RFA p26 CR Germany1
BUCKLE,Matthew Perceval.DSO.Maj kia 27-10-14 1WKent p140 CR France924
BUCKLE,William T2Lt dow 7-6-17 8Yorks p90 CR Belgium11
BUCKLER,Annie Elinor SNurse ded 17-10-18 QAIMNS CR Hamps56
BUCKLER,Eric Wilson.MIDx2 Capt kia 16-6-15 6 att3Worc p108 MR29
BUCKLEY,Arthur Dashwood Bulkeley.CB.Col ded 3-4-15 Hamps p120 CR Wilts86
BUCKLEY,Edmund Cecil Gladstone Capt dow 5-8-16 6Lpool p215 CR France513
BUCKLEY,Edmund Maurice 2Lt dow 12-8-15 7RWFus p223 CR Gallipoli1
BUCKLEY,Edward Capt kia 30-9-17 3 att2Y&L p158 CR France550
BUCKLEY,Felix George.MC.TCapt dow 17-8-17 8NumbF p60 CR Belgium96
BUCKLEY,George William T2Lt kia 27-8-18 RBerks att8Bn p138 CR France515
BUCKLEY,Godfrey Lt kld 15-8-17 3 att9ELancs p110 CR Greece1
BUCKLEY,Hubert Hyde Lt kia 14-4-17 3 att1KSLI p144 CR France115
BUCKLEY,Humphry Paul Stenneth Capt dow 29-7-17 7EYorks p83 MR20
BUCKLEY,John F.Lt 23-2-19 3LancF p263 CR Ches72,Capt 3-3-19
BUCKLEY,John Herbert Wellington.MID Lt ded 5-3-19 RGA p262 CR Hamps240,Capt
BUCKLEY,Joseph Michael.MC.TCapt kia 23-12-17 9RB p178 CR Belgium101
BUCKLEY,Robert 2Lt dow 9-1-17 4Manch p154 CR France41
BUCKLEY,Sidney James 2Lt kia 24-3-18 5 att2SStaffs p229 MR20
BUCKMAN,James Leslie TCapt kia 15-9-16 12ESurr p112 MR21
BUCKMASTER,Charles Oliver Brook TLt ded 16-3-19 7DCLI p254 CR Hamps221
BUCKMASTER,Henry Augustine 2Lt kia 28-9-18 2/4LNLancs p234 CR France256
BUCKMASTER,Ralph Nevill Lendon.MID Capt kia 30-11-17 1/4LNLancs p233 MR17
BUCKNALL,Marc Antony 2Lt dow 6-3-17 3 att10DCLI p114 CR France177
BUCKNALL,Walter Harry Corfield Lt kia 3-5-17 2 att1NumbF p60 MR20,Capt
BUCKNELL,Harry Hill 2Lt kia 22-7-17 6WelshR p230 CR Belgium73
BUCKNELL,William Wentworth.MID Lt kia 10-8-17 103RH&FA p26 CR Belgium29
BUCKNILL,John Charles.MC.MIDx2 Lt kia 21-1-16 1/4Hamps p228 MR38
BUCKNILL,Llewllyn Morris.MID Maj dow 18-5-15 105RFA p26 CR France80
BUCKOKE,Oswald Lee T2Lt kia 8-7-17 11Suff p78 CR France366
BUCKTON,Arthur Scott TLtACapt dow 9-4-17 RGA 100SB p38 CR France1182
BUCKWORTH,Alan Benjamin 2Lt kia 16-8-17 3RInniskF p104 CR Belgium125
BUCKWORTH,Charles Raymond Lt kia 1-7-16 2SfthH attMGC Inf p164&182 CR France1890
BUCKWORTH,Wallace Alfred 2Lt kia 8-5-15 RInniskF p104 MR4
BUCKWORTH,William TLt kia 14-8-17 10RB p178 MR29 &CR Belgium152
BUDD,Edward.MC&2Bars.LtACapt kia 8-5-18 1IrGds p52 CR France925
BUDD,Eric Frank Corydon TLt dow 11-9-17 RE &52RFC p5&43 CR Belgium173
BUDD,Frederick George.MC.T2Lt dow 15-10-18 16KRRC p149 CR France398,MM
BUDD,Wrinch Joseph Charles Lt kia 28-6-15 9 att2SWBord p99 MR4
BUDDEN,Harold William T2Lt kia 14-9-16 12LancF p92 MR34
BUDDEN,Henry Richard 2LtTLt kia 25-9-15 3Dors att2Lincs p123 CR France349
BUDDEN,Ronald Anderson 2Lt kia 31-7-17 1Worc p108 MR29
BUDDICOM,Walter Digby Lt dedacc 6-6-18 4Huss p21 CR France40
BUDDS,Charles Walter 2Lt kia 8-9-18 5YLI p235 CR France415
BUDDS,Percy Harold Lt ded 29-10-18 6EKent att 12RAF p57 CR France40
BUDENBURG,Donald Harlow 2LtACapt kia 25-4-18 4 att17Manch p154 CR Belgium115,BUDENBERG
BUDGE,Hubert Lionel TLtCol dow 13-7-16 12RScots p53 CR France513
BUDGE,John Henry Capt dow 14-3-15 4SfthH p241 CR Scot968
BUDGE,Philip Prideaux.DSO.BtLtCol dow 11-9-18 323RFA p26 CR France103,232RFA
BUDGE,Preston Frederick TLt kia 8/9-5-17 12RWSurr attRBerks p55 MR37
BUDGEN,Sidney Norman Lt kia 4-10-17 A291RFA p207 CR Belgium20
BUDIBENT,Cecil T2Lt kia 25-9-15 2Lincs p74 MR32,Cedil
BUDIBENT,George Maj ded 2-10-18 RASC p254 CR Surrey3
BUDWORTH,Charles Edward Dutton.CB.CMG.MVO.MIDx10 MajGen 5-7-21 RA MR65
BUFTON,Edward Evan T2Lt ded 20-11-18 13Y&L p158 CR Wales429
BUGDEN,Robert Gordon TLt kia 24-8-15 5KSLI p144 CR Belgium165
BUGG,Herbert 2Lt kia 19-7-18 D106RFA p26 CR France570
BUGG,William Arthur Lt ded 9-6-20 IA TC att37Dogras p274 MR65,9-6-17
BUGLASS,Cyril T2Lt dow 23-3-18 12NumbF p60 CR France987
BUGLER,Leonard Herbert 2Lt 2-4-18 C'Coy 2/5Glouc CR Glouc15

BUIK,Henry Douglas 2Lt kia 9-4-17 5RScotF p222 CR France418,Lt 1Bn
BUIST,Charles Edward.MC.Capt dow 21-10-17 RGA 67SB p209 MR30
BUIST,George Bruce TLt kia 25-9-16 20Mddx p146 CR France115
BUIST,Kenneth Lt kia 25-1-15 1BlkW p128 CR France720
BILBECK,Henry Edmund TLt kia 6-11-16 16 att20RFus p67 MR21
BULKELEY,Charles Ivor Rivers Capt kia 16-5-15 2ScotsGds p52,C.S.R. MR22
BULKELEY,Edmund Burke Mabbot Capt ded 13-11-16 2Lpool p71 MR43
BULKELEY,Llewllyn Alfred Henry TCapt kia 10-4-18 RAMC att15Ches p194 CR France41
BULKELEY,Thomas Henry Rivers.CMG.MVO.Capt kia 22-10-14 2ScotsGds p52 MR29
BULKELEY-HUGHES,George Montagu Warren TLtACapt kia 27-2-17 6 att12KRRC p149 CR France374,Montague
BULKELEY-JOHNSON,Charles Bulkeley ADC BrigGen kia 11-4-17 2Drags Cmdg8CavBde p1 CR France104
BULKLEY,Howel Stephen Capt kia 19-7-17 IA 33Punjabis p274 CR EAfrica38 &CR Tanzania1
BULL,Alfred George 2Lt kia 6-8-18 5 att8KRRC p149 MR20
BULL,Arthur Henry 2Lt ded 14-12-18 2Dors p123 CR Egypt9
BULL,Benjamin Allen Capt kia 16-9-17 RAMC p253 CR Belgium23
BULL,Bernard George Sheen 2Lt kia 4-4-15 RE 1HomeCountiesFC p210 CR France924
BULL,Frederick John 2Lt kia 27-1-16 6Lond p246 CR France149
BULL,George.DSO.TBrigGen dow 11-12-16 RIrF Comdg8InfBde p171&258 CR France41
BULL,Geoffrey Spencer.MC.Capt S/InflictWound 25-3-16 IA 58Rif p274 CR Egypt3
BULL,Godfrey John Oswald Lt kia 8-7-15 RE 2ELancsFC p210 CR Gallipoli3
BULL,Henry Spencer.DSO.TMaj ded 30-7-18 6ELancs p110 CR Iraq6
BULL,John Edward 2Lt kia 29-9-15 3Dors attRFus p123 MR19
BULL,John Lionel Robin 2Lt kia 30-11-17 10KRRC p149 MR17 Ex 1Bn
BULL,Joseph William T2Lt dow 1-10-16 RE 98FC p43 CR France145
BULL,Lovelace Rowat TLt dow 3-5-17 MGC Inf p182 CR France1182
BULL,Percival John 2Lt kia 7-10-16 6 att9RFus p67 MR21
BULL,Robert Edward Bristow TLt kia 16-5-15 O&BLI p130 MR22
BULL,Ronald John Howard Capt kld 13-7-17 16Lond attRE p249 CR Belgium12
BULL,Ronald Page 2Lt kia 30-10-18 4Nhampt p234 CR France190
BULL,Wilfred Herbert TCapt kia 3-5-17 7Beds p85 CR France700
BULLARD,Ernest Gilbert Lt kia 1-8-15 IA IndPostalServs p274 CR France345
BULLEN,Henry Stanley Tempest Lt kia 14-4-17 D251RFA p207 CR France418
BULLEN,Roy Evans 2Lt dow 29-4-16 2KRRC p149 CR France149,Capt
BULLEN,William Francis 2Lt mbk 16-6-15 10Lpool p257 MR29
BULLER,Arthur Edward Adderley Capt ded 21-9-18 Inns of Court OTC att 1/5Norf p252 CR Palestine9
BULLER,Herbert Cecil.DSO.LtCol kia 3-6-16 RB &PPCLI p178 CR Belgium111,2-6-16
BULLER,Lesley Montagu Lt kia 24-8-14 1Lincs p74 CR Belgium202
BULLER,Richard Francis Montague Capt kia 24-8-18 7 att8Mddx p235 MR16,Maj
BULLIVANT,Alfred James T2Lt dow 21-7-16 17N&D p133 CR France80
BULLIVANT,Eric Claud 2Lt kia 24-3-18 18KRRC p149 MR20,Claude
BULLIVANT,Ritchie Pelham Capt kia 24-9-18 1Coy of LondYeo p204 MR34
BULLIVANT,Robert Walker 2Lt dow 1-5-17 SomLI att8Bn p79 CR France64,Roland Walter
BULLMAN,Haddon Robert Horsley 2Lt kia 30-11-17 3RWKent att71MGC Inf p140&182 CR France439
BULLOCK,Alan Marlowe 2Lt kia 4-11-18 15 att 1/4Lond p249 CR France1142
BULLOCK,Albert Edward T2Lt kia 26-10-18 2Worc p108 CR France1478
BULLOCK,Arthur Ernest TCapt kia 26-9-15 RAMC att4Mddx p194 CR Belgium6
BULLOCK,Charles Sidney 2Lt dow 6-9-18 1/4Ches p222 CR Belgium15
BULLOCK,Geoffrey Ernest Lt kia 16-7-18 5NStaffs att148RAF p238&255 CR France10
BULLOCK,Gervas Frederick 2Lt kia 31-7-17 11SWBord p99 MR29
BULLOCK,Henry Acton Linton 2Lt kia 14-7-16 7RWar p214 MR21
BULLOCK,Robert TLt kia 20-9-17 26RFus p67 MR30,BULLOCH 2nd entry as BULLOCK
BULLOCK,Robert Poe Story.OBE.Lt ded 17-2-20 IA 89Punjabis p274 CR Ireland165,Capt H.
BULLOCK,Robert Stanley Capt kia 17-4-16 IA 27Punjabis MR38 p274
BULLOCK,Thomas Eben Grainger 2Lt mbk 24-4-17 1EKent p256 MR19,22-4-17
BULLOCK,Thomas William MajALtCol kia 11-4-18 1Dors p123 CR France745
BULLOCK,William 2Lt dow 12-5-18 3Yorks p90 CR France65,6Bn
BULLOCK,William Acton 2Lt ded 25-10-18 RFus att2/17Lond p67 CR France34
BULLOUGH,Charles Berthold.DSO.Maj kia 25-4-18 RGA 117HB p38 CR France285

BULLOUGH,Frederick William 2Lt kia 8-11-17 RGA 152SB p38 CR Belgium106
BULLOUGH,John Leodius Lt kia 25-9-15 2A&SH p173 MR19
BULLOUGH,Thomas Horrolin Stanley T2Lt kia 7-7-16 11 att9LNLancs p135 MR21,Horrobin
BULMAN,Andrew Lt kia 12-7-15 4KOSB p223 MR4
BULMER,Charles Forsyth Lt kia 12-3-18 10Mddx p255 MR34,Ex WKentYeo
BULMER,Frank Stedman 2Lt kia 1-10-18 20Lond p251 MR21
BULMER,Geoffrey Percival.MC.Lt ded 15-2-18 GL &RFC p261&266 CR Hereford/Worc18
BULMER,John Legge 2Lt kia 3-5-17 4att5 O&BLI p231 MR20
BULTEAL,Sam Dominic CaptAMaj kia 5-4-17 45RFA p26 CR France511,BULTEEL
BULTEEL,Thomas Edward Lt kld 24-2-18 RFA &RFC p15&26 CR Wilts4
BUMPUS,Bernard Ebenezer.MID T2Lt kia 3-7-16 12NumbF p60 MR21
BUNBURY,Godfrey Hugh St.Pierre Capt kia 1-2-17 IA 15 att36Sikhs p274 CR Iraq5
BUNBURY,Hugh St.Pierre T2Lt dow 25-8-16 B70RH&FA p26 CR France40,90RFA
BUNBURY,Patrick Stanney St.Pierre 2Lt kia 19-12-16 2Suff p78 CR France133
BUNBURY,Thomas St.Pierre Capt kia 31-8-18 RFA &64RAF p26 CR France421
BUNBURY,Wilfred Joseph Capt kia 15-4-17 4NumbF p213 CR France162
BUNCE,George Owen 2Lt kia 12-5-15 2SWBord p99 MR4,9-5-15
BUNCE,Hugh Pollock T2Lt ded 5-10-16 8NStaffs p156 CR France200
BUNCH,Charles Walter 2Lt kia 13-11-16 RGA 128SB p38 CR France745,Lt
BUNCLE,Ronald 2Lt ded 16-10-15 RFA p208 CR Scot239
BUNDEY,Albert Arthur T2Lt kia 21-3-18 MGC p182 CR France307
BUNDLE,Harry Norman 2Lt kia 20-9-17 13Lond p249 CR Belgium125
BUNGARD,Eric George 2Lt mbk 30-11-17 3 att6EKent p256 MR17
BUNGEY,Gerald Edwards T2Lt kia 4-8-16 9RFus p67 MR21,Edward
BUNKER,Harold John T2Lt kia 28-9-17 9Yorks p90 MR30
BUNN,Ernest Walton 2Lt ded 11-6-18 5Suff p217 CR Suff176,kldacc
BUNN,Jack Coulson T2Lt kia 13-5-18 1/5SStaffs p122 CR France109
BUNT,Harry 2Lt kia 17-5-19 IARO att 1/15Sikhs p274 MR43
BUNTINE,Robert T2Lt dow 31-3-18 GordH att8/10Bn p166 CR France64
BUNTINE,Walter Horace Carlyle.MC.2Lt kld 19-6-17 4N&D &RFC p5&133,Carlisle CR Scot520
BUNTING,Henry.MC.TLtTCapt ded 5-2-18 1BordR p116 CR C'land&W'land68
BUNTING,Robert Russell TLt kia 6-8-15 12 att1Ess p131 CR Gallipoli6
BUNTING,Thomas Edward 2Lt kia 24-8-18 RIrF p171 CR France855
BUNTING,William.MC.TCapt kia 11-8-17 8Norf p73 CR Belgium19
BURBAGE,Edwin Joseph 2Lt dow 1-4-17 2/10Mddx p236 CR Egypt2
BURBIDGE,Howard Churchill T2Lt dow 13-9-16 13EYorks p83 CR France98
BURBRIDGE,Frederick T2Lt dow 28-8-18 15WYorks p81 CR France34,BURBIDGE
BURBURY,Francis William LtCol ded 11-9-1 3RWKent att24RB p265 MR67
BURBURY,John Francis 2Lt dow 23-2-15 RWKent p140 CR Belgium165,kia
BURCH,Charles Leonard 2Lt kia 18-8-16 6 att13Mddx p146 MR21
BURCH,Herbert Percival T2Lt ded 20-10-16 15MGC Motor p182 CR France188
BURCH,R.S.2Lt kia 28-6-18 Res &RAF p254
BURCH,Sydney Gasking Lt kia 13-11-16 SNottsHuss p205 CR France293
BURCHELL,Lawrence.MC 2Lt ded 31-12-18 RGA 153SB p38 CR Germany1
BURCHILL,Vivian TLt kia 2-6-16 22Manch p154 CR France329
BURD,Frederick Braham 2Lt kia 20-9-17 1/13Lond p249 MR20
BURDALL,Albert HonLt ded 3-1-16 RAOC p198 CR Kent7
BURDEKIN,Geoffrey Eric 2Lt kia 26-1-15 N&D attNLancs p133 CR France557
BURDEKIN,Sydney 2Lt kia 28-9-15 RFA p26 MR19,att10TMB
BURDESS,Matthew Forster Rev Chap4Cl kia 18-4-17 RAChDept att 1/6Glouc p199 CR France363
BURDETT,Charles Plantagenet Balfour T2Lt kia 7-7-16 15 att9RFus p67 CR France393
BURDETT,Edward Jerome Capt kia 25-6-15 IA 11Rajputs att89Punjabis p274 CR France708
BURDETT,Glanville 2Lt kia 4-10-17 1ESurr p112 MR30
BURDETT,H.SubCdr 17-10-18 S&T Cps CR Iraq8
BURDETT,Halford Gay Capt ded 3-3-16 2Coy of LondYeo p204 CR Kent267
BURDETT,Thomas George Deane.MC.Capt kia 6-11-17 1/7RWelshF p223 CR Palestine1
BURDETT,William Allen.MC.ACapt kia 31-7-17 1RFus p67 MR29
BURDETT,William Edward Capt kia 29-8-18 5RLancs p213 CR France646,Edwards
BURDGE,Reginald John 2Lt dow 9-10-17 C58RFA p26 MR21
BURDICK,Frederick William.MC.TCapt kia 29-8-18 20Lond att4RAF p251 CR France352,16-6-18
BURDIN,Frank Amesbury Lt kia 16-5-15 2RWar p64 CR France727
BURDITT,Stanley Wilbraham TLtACapt dow 1-10-17 RASC p192 CR France193,Sanley

BURDON,John Lt kia 8-3-16 1Manch p154 MR38
BURDON,Rowland TCapt kld 10-1-17 GL &RFC p5 CR Durham108
BURDON-SANDERSON,Guy Askew James 2Lt dow 21-2-17 3 att9NumbF p60 CR France145
BURFOOT,W.M.2Lt kld 22-5-18 3Dors &RAF p123
BURFORD,Francis Emery 2Lt kia 4-6-18 1Leic p87 CR Belgium3
BURFORD,Richard Ellis T2Lt dow 8-10-18 Ess att9Norf p131 CR France446
BURGE,Montague TMaj kia 1-7-16 23NumbF p60 MR21
BURGE,P.S.TCapt kia 12-7-18 SL attRAF p201
BURGES,Eric Laurence Arthur Hart 2Lt kia 23-10-14 3 att2Wilts p152 MR29,Lawrence
BURGES,George Herbert LtCol ded 6-8-19 3Glouc p264CR Berks47,Col
BURGES,James Alexander Stewart TLt dow 23-4-17 RAMC att49FA p194 CR France95
BURGES,Walter Travers 2Lt kia 8-5-17 3 att12Glouc p106 MR20
BURGES,William Armstrong Lt kia 10-3-18 1RIrRif p169 CR France706,10-3-15
BURGESS,Alexander James HonCapt ded 3-5-19 RAOC IA p267 CR Scot438
BURGESS,Charles Capt kia 11-10-18 RFA p207 CR France256
BURGESS,Eric Archibald 2Lt kia 17-2-17 6 att22RFus p67 MR21
BURGESS,Frank Harold Lt DCM kia 10-6-20 IA 2/102Grenadiers p274 MR43
BURGESS,Harold T2Lt kia 27-10-18 10NumbF p60 CR Italy9
BURGESS,Harold Torrence 2Lt kia 2-4-17 3Lond p245 CR France420,Torrance
BURGESS,Leonard George 2Lt kia 17-2-17 IARO att20Inf p274 CR Iraq5
BURGESS,Matthew Wylie TLt kia 23-7-18 2MGC Inf p182 CR France745
BURGESS,Philip Gulson T2Lt dow 14-10-15 8RWSurr p55 CR France1276,13-10-15
BURGESS,Reginald TLt ded 7-7-16 PoW ACycCps &22RFC p2&181,dow CR France927
BURGESS,Reginald Charles 2Lt kia 3-5-17 23RFus p67 MR20
BURGESS,Robert Balderston TCapt dow 10-12-15 RE p43 CR France285,9-12-15
BURGESS,Wallis Edward Lt&QM ded 30-9-16 ACycCps p266 CR Mddx44
BURGESS,Walter Capt kia 13-10-15 2RSuss p118 MR19
BURGESS,Wilfred Charles 2Lt kia 22-8-17 4SomLI p218 CR Belgium112,Wilfrid
BURGESS,William Frederick 2Lt kia 18-8-16 2Suff p78 MR21,Frederic
BURGESS,William Henry Langdon.MID Capt kia 20-7-16 3 att1ScotRif p103 CR France432
BURGESS,William Vernon T2Lt kia 19-7-16 RBerks att6Bn p138 MR21
BURGH,Edward Henry.MC.Lt dow 4-1-18 B223RFA p207 CR France755
BURGHOPE,Gerald Harry Vernon 2Lt kia 23-4-17 1RWSurr p55 MR20
BURGIS,Edward 2Lt kia 16-10-17 3 att18Manch p154 MR30
BURGOYNE,John Heywood 2Lt kia 31-10-16 88RFA p26 CR France251
BURGOYNE-JOHNSON,Luther Vincent Capt 26-4-15 8DLI MR29
BURGOYNE-WALLACE,Douglas Burgoyne Lt kia 3-3-15 IA 7Rajputs p274 MR61
BURKE,Charles James.DSO.MajA LtCol kia 9-4-17 1RIrReg attELancs p88 CR France452,2Bn
BURKE,Edward Terrence Lt&QM kia 25-4-18 Nhampt att9MGC p137&182 CR Belgium11,Terence
BURKE,Edward William 2Lt kia 14-9-16 6RFus att70RFC p2 CR France169
BURKE,Gordon William 2Lt ded 29-7-18 15RWFus p263 CR Lond7
BURKE,Henry Joseph Lt kia 25-9-15 1SStaffs p122 MR19
BURKE,J.Lt&QM 2-4-18 1/4LNLancs CR Lancs102
BURKE,John Capt ded 21-12-18 RAMC p194 CR Iraq8
BURKE,John Bernard Mary.MC.Capt dow 1-12-17 4GrenGds p49 CR France415
BURKE,John Errol T2Lt kia 21-8-15 5ConnRgrs p172 MR4
BURKE,John Laurence 2Lt kia 30-4-16 RGA Z25TMB p38 CR France68,29-4-16 2TMB
BURKE,Martin 2Lt kia 18-9-16 1WYorks p81 MR21
BURKE,Michael Arthur 2Lt kia 6-11-17 5BordR p228 CR Belgium13
BURKE Osborne Samuel T2LtACapt kia 25-9-16 C77RFA p26 CR France630
BURKE,Robert Alfred T2Lt kia 21-7-17 ConnRgrs att2Leinst p172 CR Belgium19,31-7-17
BURKE,Roland Edmund 2Lt kia 17-11-17 5Ess p232 CR France341
BURKE,Sydney Slaven 2Lt kia 22-12-17 2/18Lond p250 CR Palestine3
BURKE,Thomas Campbell Capt kia 19-12-14 IA 1/1GurkhaRif MR28
BURKE,Thomas Edward 2LtTCapt dow 14-4-17 1 att5KSLI p144 CR France120,11-4-17
BURKETT,Francis Edgar T2Lt kia 26-9-18 14DLI p160 MR19,26-9-15
BURKETT,Harold TCapt dow 5-6-17 10KSLI p144 CR France1186,10YLI
BURKETT,Harry William Bradly Lt kia 14-4-18 4Wilts p236 CR France285,Capt 1Bn
BURKETT,William Peter 2Lt kld 23-4-18 2Yorks p90 CR France180
BURKINSHAW,Francis William TCapt dow 30-3-16 9/19RFA p26 MR38

BURKINSHAW,Herbert Thornton 2Lt dow 20-9-18 LNLancs att5Y&L p135 MR16
BURLEIGH,Bennett Lt dow 15-7-15 7LancF p221 CR Gallipoli1
BURLEIGH,Finlay Swan 2Lt dow 2-10-18 1/4RScotF p222 CR France1184
BURLEIGH,James Emil.MC.T2Lt kia 12-10-17 12A&SH p173 MR30,Lt
BURLEIGH,Robert Lt kia 29-8-16 RE att15RFC p18&210 CR France220
BURLES,Thomas John 2Lt kia 24-6-17 RGA 21SB p38 CR Belgium1
BURLEY,Charles Frederick 2Lt kia 18-11-16 4 att10RWar p64 MR21
BURLEY,Cyril Percival T2Lt kia 9-8-18 7RSuss p118 CR France247,8-8-18
BURLEY,Ernest Sidney T2Lt ded 15-2-19 LabCps att112ChinLabCoy p189&257 CR France65
BURLEY,Robert James 2Lt dedacc 19-3-18 RFC 80CentTrStn CR Canada1688
BURLTON,,Arthur Vivian Capt kld 30-8-17 RASC attRFC p5 CR Yorks178
BURLTON,George Philip.MC.Lt kia 5-6-16 1Norf p73&258 MR20
BURLTON,Ralph Harry Lt kia 2-2-16 IA 34Horse att33Cav p274 MR38,1-2-16
BURLURAUX,John Rene Cornelius T2Lt kia 1-7-16 27NumbF p60 CR France393,Lt
BURMANN,Robert Moyle.DSO.MC.MIDx6 Capt kia 27-10-18 ELancs attHQ 7InfBde p110 CR France231
BURMESTER,Charles Mansel TCapt dow 8-10-18 3SWBord p99 CR France375
BURMESTER,Maurice George TLt dow 25-8-15 Ess att1Bn p131 MR4
BURN,Arthur George McCausland Capt kia 29-10-14 2ESurr p112 MR29
BURN,Arthur Herbert Rosdew 2Lt kia 29-10-14 1Drags p21 MR29,Posden
BURN,Arthur Morton Stanley 2Lt ded 7-6-17 IARO attS&M p274 MR65,BURNE Lt
BURN,Arthur Roland T2Lt kia 26-3-18 14 att6DLI p160 MR27
BURN,Arthur Sidney Pelham.MID 2Lt kia 2-5-15 6GordH p242 CR France768,Lt
BURN,Charles Scott Lt kia 3-11-17 1SfthH p164 MR38
BURN,Cuthbert John Lt kia 1-10-17 9Leic p87 MR30 Ex 3Bn
BURN,Hugh Henry.MC.TCapt dow 16-9-16 2CldGds p51 CR France105
BURN James T2Lt kia 17-10-17 NumbF att23Bn p60 CR Belgium83
BURN,Maurice Edward Pelham TLt kia 9-4-17 BlkW att8Bn p128 CR France924
BURN,William Gladstone Lt kia 9-5-15 13Lond p249 MR32
BURN-MURDOCH,Colin Thomas Capt kia 30-5-19 IA 20Inf attSWaziristanMil p274 MR43
BURNABY,Eustace Hotham Capt kia 5-8-15 7Glouc p106 MR4
BURNABY,Geoffrey Lt dow 23-10-16 1Lond p245 CR France40
BURNABY,Hugo Beaumont.DSO.LtCol dow 8-9-16 11RWSurr p55 CR France397
BURNAND,Cyril Francis 2Lt kia 11-3-15 1GrenGds SR p49 MR22
BURNAND,Geoffrey Chasmore Lt kia 7-4-17 SR 48RFC p5 CR France120,Chasemore 2Lt
BURNE,A.M.S.see BURN,A.M.S.
BURNE,Edward Robert.DSO.LtCol kia 1-10-18 15RFA p26 CR Belgium84
BURNE,Newdigate Owen Lt dow 27-10-17 IA 40Pathans p274 CR EAfrica38 &CR Tanzania1
BURNE,Thomas Oldbury 2Lt kia 25-3-18 2RBerks p138 MR27
BURNELL,Arthur Lt kia 20-7-18 5YLI p235 CR France1689
BURNELL,Arthur Coke Capt kia 18-3-16 2RB p178 CR France348
BURNELL,George Cuthbertson 2Lt dow 24-6-15 10Lpool p216 CR France102
BURNESS,Alfred Richard Lt dow 25-4-15 2SfthH p164 CR Belgium129
BURNET,Francis Alexander Lt kia 11-4-18 8RScots p211 MR32
BURNET,Robert LtCol dedacc 28-1-15 RAMC 2FA p253 CR Lancs346
BURNET,Stanley Lt 3-5-18 5Beds att17RAF CR Beds75
BURNETT,Charles Guy Arobiun Lt kia 30-6-16 7NumbF p214 CR Belgium60,Arbouin
BURNETT,Ian Alistair Kendale Capt kia 31-5-17 3 att8ELancs p110 MR20
BURNETT,John T2Lt dow 15-9-16 1Leic p87 MR21
BURNETT,John David Napier 2Lt kia 25-2-16 3 att6RWSurr p55 CR France423
BURNETT,Leslie Cecil James 2Lt kia 14-3-18 RFA p26 CR Belgium21
BURNETT,Maurice.MID Lt kia 14-4-15 RAMC p194 CR Iraq6,Capt
BURNETT,Noel Compton TLt kia 14-7-16 7Leic p87 MR21
BURNETT,Robert Capt ded 9-11-16 9Lpool p269 CR Lancs2
BURNETT,William.DSO.LtCol dow 3-7-16 5NStaffs p237CR France120
BURNEY,Geoffry Asteley Capt kia 7-7-16 ScotHorse att4RFC p18&205 CR France44
BURNEY,Gilbert Edward.MID TLt dow 28-9-15 GL 8GordH &Staff p190 CR France98,27-9-15
BURNHAM,Andrew William 2Lt kia 13-11-16 15RFus p67 MR21,att24Bn
BURNHAM,Albert Frederick James T2Lt kia 28-6-16 7Nhampt p137 CR Belgium17
BURNIE,Donald 2Lt kia 1-10-15 6WelshR p230 MR19,2-10-15
BURNIER,Richard Lt dow 21-2-18 att9RSuss p118 CR France446
BURNINGHAM,Ralph Horace T2Lt kia 22-3-18 10RWar p64 MR20
BURNLEY,Ernest Sidney T2Lt kia 5-11-18 9WYorks p81 CR France1142

BURNLEY-CAMPBELL,Colin William 2Lt kia 26-6-15 3A&SH p173 CR France681,27-6-15 1Bn
BURNS,David Chalmers 2Lt kia 30-9-18 BlkW att8Bn p128 CR Belgium163
BURNS,Digby TCapt drd 10-10-18 RAMC p194 CR Ireland14
BURNS,Francis.MC.T2Lt kia 31-7-17 SfthH att8Bn p164 MR29
BURNS,George William 2Lt dow 22-7-15 4NumbF CR France102
BURNS,Islay Ferrier T2Lt kia 10-7-17 97MGC Inf p182 MR31
BURNS,James Rattray.MC.Lt 10-6-18 ScotRif att193RAF CR Egypt1
BURNS,Joseph Dobson Rev Chap4Cldow 7-6-18 RAChDept attRGA p199 CR France180
BURNS,Percival Fossey-Thackaberry.MID T2Lt dow 21-3-17 13Lpool p71 CR France158,Fossy
BURNS,Robert Henry T2Lt kia 1-11-18 8RDubF p176 CR France1079
BURNS,Russell Johnstone T2Lt kia 16-9-16 10HLI p162 MR21
BURNS,Walter Bell Lt kia 9-10-17 3KSLI att 1/4Glouc p144 MR30
BURNS,Walter Scot Lt dow 1-7-15 RE p210 MR4
BURNS,William Lt kia 21-3-18 StaffsYeo att2N&D p205 MR20
BURNS,William Beaumont 2Lt kia 8-7-16 1Worc p108 MR21
BURNS-BEGG,Robert Col ded 9-1-18 SL Staff p201&268 CR Scot152
BURNSIDE,Edward Edmund T2Lt kia 21-3-18 16RIrRif p169 CR France1061
BURNSIDE,Eustace Bruce Caldecott TCapt&Adjt kia 12-10-17 7EKent p57 CR Belgium83
BURNYEAT,Hugh Ponsonby MajALtCol kia 30-10-18 RFA 65ArmyBde p26 CR France1482
BURNYEAT,Norman Quayle Maj dow 6-8-17 4RFA p206 CR Belgium24
BURR,Clifford John Frederick Lt 6-5-17 5RWKent MR66
BURR,Frederick Bonham 2Lt kia 12-3-15 3Worc ResOffList p108 CR Belgium17
BURR,Frederick Godfrey TCapt kia 26-9-15 7RScotF p94 CR France219
BURR,G HonLt&QM Acckld 6-6-17 Dev CR Hamps58
BURRELL,Arthur David Claypham TLt kia 15-8-17 MGC p182 MR29
BURRELL,Frederick George 2Lt kia 4-5-17 2RWar p64 MR20
BURRELL,John Stamp Garthorne 2Lt kia 10-8-15 4Ches p222 MR4,9-8-15
BURRELL,Percy Edmund 2Lt kia 21-8-15 3 att2SWBord p99 MR4
BURRELL,Raymond Francis Topham 2Lt kia 26-9-15 8RWKent p140 MR19
BURRELL,Stanley Walter TLt ded 22-7-16 RAMC p194 CR France833
BURRELL,Sydney 2Lt dow 20-7-16 1 att5Mddx p146 CR France833,Sidney
BURRETT,Mervyn Alan Lt ded 24-6-21 IA 16Cav p274
BURRIDGE,Guy Biddulph.MC.Lt kia 4-5-18 45/42RFA p26 CR France33
BURRIDGE,Henry Gardiner Lt kia 17-11-14 IA 107Pnrs p274 CR France80,dow 16-11-14
BURRIDGE,Richard Arthur Lt kia 29-12-21 IA 25Cav attIraqLevies p274
BURROUGH,Francis Thomas TCapt kia 1-7-16 6KSLI p144 CR Belgium4
BURROUGHES,Bernard Hollis Lt ded 11-12-19 RE p262 CR Suff83
BURROUGHES,Randall 2Lt kia 12-8-15 5Norf p216 MR4
BURROUGHES,Stephen 2Lt kia 4-11-18 KRRC att2Bn p149 CR France190
BURROUGHS,Bernard Prendergast 2Lt dow 16-3-17 1RDubF p176 CR France145
BURROW,Edward Lt dow 31-5-16 1ConnRgrs p172 CR France354
BURROW,Reginald Lt ded 15-2-19 1/8Lpool p269 CR Ches8
BURROWES,Guy Walter TLt kia 16-8-15 6RMunstF p175 MR4
BURROWS,Arnold Hayes TCapt kia 13-3-16 6Nhampt p137 CR France513
BURROWS,Arthur Cecil T2Lt dow 5-6-16 14 att8Ches p95 MR43
BURROWS,C.N.SubCdr kia 28-7-16 IndiaP&TDept CR Iraq5
BURROWS,Charles Selss.MC.TCapt kia 28-5-18 14NumbF p60 MR18
BURROWS,David T2Lt dow 3-7-16 MGC p182 CR France5
BURROWS,Donald TCaptAMaj ded 7-11-18 RAMC p194 CR Ches28
BURROWS,Edward William Montague Lt kia 26-8-16 42/2RFA p26 CR France630,Edmund Montagu
BURROWS,George William Cruttwell TLt kia 25-8-18 DCLI att7Leic p114 CR France385
BURROWS,James Cooke ACapt kia 14-4-18 4YLI p235 MR30
BURROWS,Leonard Righton T2Lt kia 2-10-15 9NumbF p60 CR Belgium132
BURROWS,Leonard Victor 2Lt kia 2-9-18 1/6N&D p233 CR France109,1-9-18
BURROWS,Percival Ernest.MC.Lt kia 19-9-18 3N&D att2/3GurkhaRif IA p133&274 CR Palestine9,Capt
BURROWS,Stanley Eric T2Lt kia 30-12-15 9 att5 O&BLI p130 CR Belgium20,dow 31-12-15
BURROWS,William Arthur 2Lt kia 15-9-16 3Lond p245 MR21
BURROWS,William George Ritson 2Lt kia 3-5-17 27MGC Inf p182 MR20
BURSTALL,Arthur 2Lt kia 24-9-18 4EYorks att 1WYorks p219 CR France1701
BURSTALL,John.MID Capt ded 12-4-19 RASC p192 CR France34,dow
BURT,Andrew Lt kia 18-12-14 8RScots p211 MR32
BURT,Arthur George LtCol kia 23-4-15 1Y&L p158 CR Belgium96

BURT,Charles Herbert 2Lt ded 27-10-18 3Coy of Lond Yeo p204 CR Surrey75
BURT,Frank Eliot Lt kia 3-10-18 1/6NStaffs p238 CR France341
BURT,Frank William 2Lt kia 5-7-16 1N&D p133 CR France390
BURT,Frederick Stanley TLt dow 21-2-17 16Lpool att6NLancs p71 CR Iraq5,Capt
BURT,James 2Lt kia 19-7-18 3 att8BlkW p128 CR France324
BURT,Lewis H.2Lt kld 31-10-17 RE Reinf att Works directorship Basra p43 MR38
BURT,Mary de Burgh Sister 7-4-16 ScotWomensHosp attSerbianArmy CR Greece7
BURT,Owen Lyndon TLt kia 23-7-17 GL &6RFC p5 MR21
BURT,Roger Frederick 2Lt kia 27-3-16 7NumbF p214 CR Belgium127
BURT,Theodore Charles Arthur TLt kia 15-7-16 12/35RFA p26 CR France399
BURT,William James Lt kia 18-8-16 6 att13Mddx p146 MR21
BURT-MARSHALL,William Marshall Capt dow 17-11-14 PoW 2A&SH p173 CR France1159
BURTON,Alexander Brown.MC.Capt kia 9-4-18 14HLI att13ESurr p162 MR32
BURTON,Alfred Lt kia 11-1-16 1RWSurr p55 CR France163
BURTON,Alfred Henry Wellesley Capt kia 23-10-16 7 att2Lincs p74 CR France1891
BURTON,Arthur Richard Capt kia 31-1-16 RFA p26 CR France745
BURTON,Arthur Robert LtCol ded 24-1-18 IA Cmdg94Inf att93 p274 CR Iraq6
BURTON,B.CB.CMG.MajGen 6-8-21 RA CR Cornwall40
BURTON,Charles Arthur T2Lt kia 23-3-18 14 att12Glouc p106 MR27
BURTON,Charles William Gordon 2Lt kia 22-11-17 6 att2RFus p67 MR17
BURTON,Cyril Henry 2Lt kia 1-7-16 1/7N&D p233 MR21
BURTON,Francis Charles Deane Maj ded 3-2-15 RFA p26&261,Capt CR Yorks396
BURTON,Francis Hugh T2Lt kia 14-10-18 15N&D p133 MR30
BURTON,Frank T2Lt dow 3-3-18 11RSuss p118 MR27,30-3-18
BURTON,Frederick Raymond Capt ded 16-4-19 LabCps 176PofW.Co p266 CR Kent38
BURTON,Geoffrey Bunnell Lt dow 3-8-17 1/6Lpool p215 CR Belgium11
BURTON,Geoffrey Walter Melvin Lt kia 3-7-16 EKent p57 CR France393
BURTON,George 2Lt kia 24-8-17 Mddx att13Bn p146 CR Belgium125
BURTON,George Ethelbert Earnshaw Lt dow 16-7-16 4Suff p217 CR France833,2Lt
BURTON,Gerard William.DSO.Maj kia 12-10-15 IA 2/39GarhwalRif p274 CR France765
BURTON,Henry Patrick Claude LtACapt kia 27-7-16 1Beds p85 MR21
BURTON,Henry Reginald 2Lt kia 11-9-18 3 att10DCLI p114 CR France1499
BURTON,Howard 2Lt dow 14-10-17 3SStaffs att 1/7RWar p122 CR Belgium16
BURTON,Hubert T2Lt kia 9-10-17 1/5Y&L p158 MR30,Herbert
BURTON,James Wilson.MID Capt ded 5-7-19 RAMC att18GH p267 MR43 &CR Pakistan50A
BURTON,John Lees T2Lt kia 24-4-17 9BlkW att 1GarrBnHLI p128 MR20,27-4-17 1BlkW att9HLI
BURTON,John Stanley 2Lt kia 16-5-16 GrenGds att2BnSR p49 CR Belgium84
BURTON,Kenrick Hammond Lt kia 16-6-18 6Lpool p215 MR30
BURTON,Louis LtAMaj dedacc 9-6-17 D70RFA p26 CR France225
BURTON,Percy Charles 2Lt kia 5-4-16 4EYorks p219 CR Belgium79
BURTON,Percy Herbert Capt kia 12-5-17 RAMC p253 MR20,att2/4Lond
BURTON,Reginald Cooksey 2Lt dow 9-4-16 IARO att 125Rif MR38 p274
BURTON,Reginald John 2Lt dow 15-4-18 PoW 8Worc p226 CR Belgium393
BURTON,Richard Lt dow 24-6-15 1N&D p133 CR France354,kia
BURTON,Richard TCapt ded 9-3-19 RASC p267 CR Kent268
BURTON,Robert Cecil Capt dow 16-3-15 2RB p178 CR Sussex176
BURTON,Sidney Rex T2Lt kld 11-9-17 GL &78RFC p5 CR Derby99
BURTON,Stephen John Maj kia 28-7-17 1CldGds p51 CR Belgium12,20-7-17
BURTON,Thomas John Lt dow 27-3-18 6DLI p239 CR France185
BURTONWOOD,Ernest T2Lt kia 1-9-18 13WelshR p126 CR France217
BURTT,Edward TLt drd 13-8-15 RASC att 18LabCoy p192 MR4
BURTT,William John 2Lt dow 23-3-18 RGA 286SB p38 CR France102
BURY,Edmond William TCapt kia 5-12-15 11KRRC p149 CR France525
BURY,Eric Lindsay.MC.T2LtTCapt ded 9-11-18 RE attRFA HQ2Cps p43 CR Glouc9
BURY,Harold Sterndale Entwisle 2Lt kia 25-1-15 1GrenGds SR p49 MR22
BURY,John Lt kia 5-7-15 ELancsRFA p207 MR4
BUSBY,Frederick William Merewether 2Lt dow 11-2-17 165RFA p26 CR France251
BUSBY,Harry Eldred T2Lt kld 11-9-17 GL &RFC p5 CR Mddx59
BUSBY,Reginald George Camden T2Lt kia 16-12-16 18DLI p160 CR France342
BUSBY,V.Capt ded 8-6-18 RE &RAF p43
BUSBY,William Baldwin T2Lt kia 15-2-17 12 att9Worc p108 CR Iraq5
BUSBY,William Walter.MC.Lt kia 13-11-16 D'Coy 13Ess p131 CR France1890,Capt

BUSE,Philip 2Lt kia 23-4-18 4 att1SomLI p218 CR France98
BUSH,Alfred John T2Lt kia 31-7-17 2Lincs p74 MR29
BUSH,Charles Gerald.DSO.TMaj ded 26-11-18 RASC 19DivTrn p192 CR France332,25-11-18 19
BUSH,Frederick Charles 2Lt dow 9-5-17 1Dev p76 MR20
BUSH,Hugh Godfrey de Lisle.MC.Lt dow 17-1-17 3Glouc p106 CR Glouc203
BUSH,James Cromwell.MC.Lt kia 7-10-17 Dors att22RFC p5&254 CR France1050
BUSH,John Stewart de Lisle Capt ded 25-8-17 PoW 3SomLI att41RFC p5&79 CR France660
BUSH,John Wheler T2Lt kia 25-9-15 RScotF p94 MR19,25/28-9-15
BUSH,Victor George Anderson TCapt kld 8-2-18 GL &RFC p15 CR Scot245
BUSH,Walter Donald Capt kia 4-6-15 4Worc p108 MR4
BUSHBY,Joseph Bryan 2Lt dow 9-10-18 6SStaffs p229 CR France446,1/5Bn
BUSHBY,Thomas Maj ded 1-1-16 RAMC p269 CR War84
BUSHE,Gervase Gray T2Lt dow 4-6-16 11Ches p95 CR France145
BUSHELL,Christopher.VC.DSO.CaptTLtCol kia 8-8-18 7RWSurr p55 CR France116
BUSHELL,Horace TLtACapt kia 6-9-18 57MGC Inf p182 CR France309
BUSHELL,R.H.C.2Lt kia 27-7-16 7RFus p67 MR20
BUSHELL,Roland 2Lt dow 26-9-17 A282RFA p208 CR Belgium36
BUSHER,Charles Joseph TLt dow 30-1-16 11WYorks p81 CR France285
BUSHER,Denis John Bryan T2Lt kia 24-4-17 8Lincs p74 MR20
BUSK,Edward Teshmaker 2Lt ded 5-11-14 RE attRFC p18&210 CR Hamps1,Lt
BUSK,George Laurence 2Lt ded 19-5-17 2RFA p208 CR Hamps13BUSS,Benjamin Capt dow 4-11-18 5EKent p213 CR Kent282
BUSS,Hilary Thomas T2Lt kld 21-1-18 RFC p15 CR Lincs100
BUSS,Percy Charles 2Lt kia 24-6-17 5 att1EKent p213 MR19
BUSS,Thomas Weston 2Lt kia 9-4-17 5 att6EKent p213 MR20
BUSSELL. Lt 11-6-15 NigR attS&TCps CR WAfrica58
BUSSELL,F.J.Lt 15-12-17 GL &NigR CR EAfrica35 &CRTanzania1
BUSSELL,Henry Richard 2Lt dow 17-8-17 5 att7SomLI p218 MR30
BUSSELL,John Garrett Capt kia 28-6-15 7RSuss p118 CR Belgium137
BUSSEY,Frank TCapt dow 15-8-17 1RE p43 CR Kent83
BUSSEY,Harry Martin 2Lt kia 3-5-17 3 att1RIrF p171 CR France604,Marslen
BUSSY,Cyril T2Lt kia 3-1-16 10 att8SStaffs p122 CR Belgium72
BUSSY,Julian T2Lt kia 29-9-16 7SStaffs p122 MR21
BUSWELL,Thomas Hubert 2Lt mbk 26-3-18 52RFC p256 MR20
BUSZARD,Stanley George Lt dow 8-12-17 NorfYeo p204 CR Palestine3
BUTCHARD,Robert Archibald TLt kia 5-11-16 31RFus p67 CR France374
BUTCHER,Arthur Algernon Lionel Hastings T2Lt kia 4-3-17 7RBerks p138 CR France1182
BUTCHER,Arthur James Basil 2Lt kia 3-9-16 17KRRC p149 CR France339
BUTCHER,Charles Geoffrey Lt kld 2-5-15 Dors p123 CR Belgium81
BUTCHER,Charles Leslie TCapt kia 24-7-16 2/7Worc p225 CR France1887
BUTCHER,Clarence Edward 2Lt kia 3-5-17 4Lond att8KRRC p246 MR20
BUTCHER,Cyril Arthur Mecrate T2LtACapt kia 6-7-17 GL 10Yorks att62TMB p190 CR France593
BUTCHER,Eugene Andrew Lt ded 23-11-19 IA TC att1/48Pnrs p274 MR66
BUTCHER,Francis Percival Herbert 2Lt kia 30-8-16 3 att1ELancs p110 CR Belgium127
BUTCHER,Frederick AMaj kia 22-5-18 A92RFA p26 CR France547
BUTCHER,Gilbert Thomas 2Lt kia 11-6-17 4NStaffs p156 CR Belgium127
BUTCHER,Harold Thomas T2Lt kia 17-2-16 11RB p178 CR Belgium73,18-2-16
BUTCHER,Henry Townsend BtCol kia 20-9-15 RFA p26 CR France219
BUTCHER,John Philip Henry 2Lt kia 22-5-16 18Lond p250 MR20
BUTCHER,Norris de Gruchy Lt&QM dow 23-5-18 13KRRC p149 CR France63
BUTCHER,Percival Drew Pitts Capt ded 3/4-11-18 RE 607Coy p255 CR Devon1,Lt 3-11-18
BUTCHER,Ralph Wycombe 2Lt kia 14-3-17 4 att22Manch p154 CR France576
BUTCHER,Richard Norman T2Lt dow 5-8-16 20Lpool p71 CR France66
BUTCHER,Vivian Haweis Lt dow 27-3-17 4Ess p232 CR Palestine8
BUTCHER,William Guy Deane Capt kia 16-8-17 1/5Lond p246 MR29
BUTLAND,George TLt kia 21-5-18 2Y&L p158 CR Belgium3
BUTLAND,William Henry T2Lt dow 31-1-16 10DLI p160 CR Belgium11
BUTLER,Archibald Stanley 2Lt kia 16-8-16 RFA 2/4SMid HB att25RFC p18&208 CRFrance88
BUTLER,Armar Somerset TLt kia 16-10-17 SLancs att7Wilts p125 CR Greece1,attRFC
BUTLER,Aubrey Edward Walter 2Lt kia 3-7-16 9 attRBerks p138 MR21
BUTLER,Bernard Arnold Barrington.DSO&Bar.LtCol dow 23-10-18 156RFA p26 CR France1478
BUTLER,Brian Danvers.Hon.TLt kia 18-8-16 13 att7KRRC p149 MR21

BUTLER,Charles Capt kld 27-8-17 RE attRFC p18&210,ded CR Yorks345
BUTLER,Charles Kingstone Capt&Adjt kia 1-7-16 10YLI p142 MR21
BUTLER,Charles Reginald Lt ded 28-11-18 19Lond p250 CR France1027
BUTLER,Clifford Hicks 2Lt kia 23-4-17 5BlkW p231 CR France604
BUTLER,Cyril Frank 2Lt dow 8-6-18 112RFA p26 CR France622
BUTLER,Desmond George Lt kld 17-3-18 Leinst &RFC p15&174 CR Mddx35,Capt 21-3-18
BUTLER,Edmund William.MC.TLtTMaj dow 18-4-18 2LifeGds att8Glouc p20 CR France40
BUTLER,Eric 2Lt kia 25-8-16 1Wilts p152 MR21
BUTLER,Eric Busvine 2Lt kia 30-9-17 D211RFA p208 MR30
BUTLER,Francis Mounilyan Lt ACapt kia 8-10-17 RFA 93ArmyBde p26 CR Belgium12
BUTLER,Frederick Harold 2Lt kia 1-1-16 1/6Lond p246 MR19
BUTLER,Geoffrey Lewis Lt kia 15-5-17 4 att11LancF p92 CR Belgium43
BUTLER,George Victor TLt kia 23-3-18 2/5Lincs p74 CR France927
BUTLER,Gordon Kerr Montague Lt ded 17-7-16 2ScotHorse attMGC p186&205 CR Egypt2,Montagu
BUTLER,Harold T2Lt kia 22-2-18 28RFC p15 CR Italy9
BUTLER,Harry 2Lt kia 25-3-17 70RFC p5 CR France245,Lt
BUTLER,James William 2Lt kia 3-5-17 3 att7EKent p57 MR20
BUTLER,John Fitzhardinge Paul.VC.DSO.Capt dow 5-9-16 2KRRC attGoldCoastR p149 CR EAfrica39
BUTLER,John Goodwin 2Lt dow 29-3-17 1/6WRid p227 CR France631
BUTLER,John Henry Rippon 2Lt dow 16-9-16 2CldGds p51 CR France105
BUTLER,John Leslie.MC.Capt dow 17-5-19 RFA Staff p26 MR43
BUTLER,John Ormond 2Lt ded PoW 11-4-18 GL 23RAF p15 CR Belgium241
BUTLER,Leonard Gray Capt kia 21-8-16 6 att3RB p178 MR21
BUTLER,Leonard William 2Lt kia 20-11-17 4 att7RIrF p171 CR France1489
BUTLER,Noel 2Lt kia 15-9-16 SR att1IrGds p52 CR France402
BUTLER,Owen James T2Lt kia 16-10-18 7Norf p73 CR France1284
BUTLER,R.A.Lt ded 20-7-18 RE &RAF p43
BUTLER,Richard Jefferson.MBE.Capt ded 1-7-19 YLI att8RWFus p265 MR43,kia att2SomLI
BUTLER,S.E.Sister ded 14-4-16 QAIMNS p200 CR Egypt3
BUTLER,Sidney Capt ded 22-1-19 16Lond p249 CR France65
BUTLER,Stanley Reginald.MM.2Lt kia 27-3-18 7SomLI p79 MR27
BUTLER,W.H.Capt&QM 21-8-21 RAMC CR Lond7
BUTLER,William T2Lt kia 22-3-18 7Leinst p174 MR27
BUTLER,William Andsley 2Lt kia 16-11-16 3SStaffs att1/8RWar p122 CR France239
BUTLER,William Martin CaptAMaj ded 5-3-19 RE 1MonSB p209 CR France1142
BUTLER-BOWDEN,Basil Joseph Bernard 2Lt kia 28-3-18 2LancF p92 MR20,BOWDON Lt
BUTLER-STONEY,Thomas Lt dow 1-10-17 1IrGds p52 CR Eire194,30-9-17
BUTLIN,Sir Henry Guy Trentham.MID Capt&Adjt kia 16-9-16 1/1Camb p244 MR21
BUTT,Alfred 2Lt kia 4-1-18 5Beds attRFC p15&85 CR Palestine3
BUTT,Charles Edward 2Lt kia 4-4-18 10Glouc p106 CR France1170
BUTT.F.W.2Lt kld 26-5-18 GL &RAF p190 see BUTT,W.F.R.
BUTT,George Lt&QM(Hon) ded 6-6-17 Dev p76
BUTT,Harry Alfred TCapt kia 8-6-16 14Glouc p106 CR France705
BUTT,AssSurg 26-10-18 ISMD MR65
BUTT,John George T2Lt dow 18-9-18 1EYorks p83 CR France666 SeeBOTT
BUTT,John Gillis Lt kia 29-10-14 RAMC att1GrenGds p194 MR29
BUTT,Lewis John Dalgleish T2Lt kia 4-7-16 16RB p178 CR France727
BUTT,Robert Acton T2Lt kia 9-1-16 9 att5KSLI p144 CR Belgium188
BUTT,William Frederick Reginald 2Lt dow 29-5-18 RGA 202SB p38 CR France29
BUTTANSHAW,Edward Henry Underwood Lt kia 27-4-15 EKent p57 CR Belgium84,dow 25-4-15
BUTTENSHAW,Leonard Horace Lt kia 27-6-18 4 att9WYorks p81 CR France223
BUTTER,Henry John TCapt kia 15-7-16 8BlkW p128 MR21,14-7-16
BUTTERFIELD,Charles Williams 2Lt kia 11-5-17 5NStaffs p238 MR19
BUTTERS,Henry Augustus T2Lt kia 31-8-16 B109RFA p26 CR France370,Harry
BUTTERWORTH,Benjamin 2Lt dow 25-3-17 3Manch p154 MR38
BUTTERWORTH,Edward Cyril T2Lt dow 21-11-17 9RFus p67 CR France446
BUTTERWORTH,F.2Lt kld 14-9-18 1/2WYorks attRAF p81 CR Belgium192
BUTTERWORTH,George Sainton Kaye.MC.Lt 5-8-16 13DLI MR21 See KAYE-BUTTERWORTH
BUTTERWORTH,Hugh Montagu TCapt kia 25-9-15 9RB p178 MR29
BUTTERWORTH,Harold.MC.Lt kia 20-9-18 RFA AA Bty p207 CR France327

BUTTERWORTH,Harold Winstone 2Lt kld 15-7-16 RFC p2 CR France924
BUTTERWORTH,Norman 2Lt kia 9-5-17 5Manch attRFC p18&236 CR France164,kld
BUTTERWORTH,Stanley Woodall Lt ded 16-1-18 7Ess p232 CR Suff55
BUTTERWORTH,Walter Cecil 2Lt kia 21-7-16 3 att1RWSurr p55 MR21
BUTTERY,Charles Henry 2Lt dow 1-10-16 6Lpool p215 CR France833
BUTTERY,Henry George 2Lt kia 27-9-18 5RWar p214 CR France415
BUTTERY,Robert Arthur T2Lt kia 15-6-18 1 att4 O&BLI p130 CR Italy2
BUTTERY,Walter 2Lt kia 20-8-18 5EYorks p219 CR France193
BUTTLE,Albert Edward TLt dow 2-10-18 17 att2RIrRif p169 CR Belgium38
BUTTLE,Bertram Haward T2Lt dow 1-10-17 RE att5Army HQ Z'SpCo p43 CR Belgium16,Howard
BUTTON,Charles Augustus 2Lt kia 27-5-18 45RFA p26 MR18
BUTTON,Norman Frederick TLt kia 4-11-17 1SomLI att11TMB p79 CR France154
BUXTON,Andrew Richard Lt kia 7-6-17 6RB p178 CR Belgium152,3Bn
BUXTON,Bertie Reginald 2Lt kia 1-7-16 1/2Lond p245 MR21
BUXTON,Hon.Denis Bertram Sydney 2Lt kia 9-10-17 2CldGds p51 MR30
BUXTON,George Barclay 2Lt kia 28-7-17 5Norf attRFC p18&216 MR20
BUXTON,Gurney White Capt ded 9-9-15 RAMC 2MtdBdeFA p253 MR4
BUXTON,Hugh Forster Lt dow 2-11-16 SR 5 att2RB p178 CR France105,3-11-16
BUXTON,Jocelyn Murray Victor 2Lt kia 1-7-16 6RB att25MGC Inf p178 MR21
BUXTON,Richard Percy ACapt kia 15-6-18 4 O&BLI p231 CR Italy2
BUY,Kenric Ellis Godson 2Lt dow 1-10-18 4BordR p228 CR France375,kia Ex NumbHuss
BYARD,Hubert 2Lt kia 6-11-17 1DCLI p114 MR30
BYATT,Harry Vivian Byatt Capt kia 14-3-15 RAMC att2RB p194 CR France768
BYERS,Henry Elliott 2Lt kld 12-11-16 3DCLI &RFC p2&114 CR Ireland14
BYERS,Henry Stagg TLt ded 3-2-16 RAMC p267 CR Europe1
BYERS,Richard Knight TCapt kia 20-7-16 8Glouc p106 MR21
BYFIELD,Arthur Thomas Stoneman Lt ded 24-3-15 3 att2DCLI p114 CR France64,2Lt
BYLES,Arthur Benzeville 2LtACapt dow 11-12-17 4 att2N&D p133 CR France446,Beuzeville
BYNG,Arthur Maitland Capt kia 14-9-14 RFus p67 MR15
BYNG,Francis Dacre TCapt kia 3-9-16 10RB p178 CR France294,Dacres
BYNG,Harry Gustave 2Lt dow 18-5-15 2BordR p116 CR France80,Gustav
BYNG,Leonard Gustave.MC.Lt dow 24-8-18 1GrenGds p49 CR France214,Gustav
BYNG,Percy Howard 2Lt ded 25-9-16 RFA 44Bty p26 CR Iraq5
BYRES,James Hope T2Lt kia 27-8-17 13RScots p53 MR30
BYRNE,Brennan Claude Sydney ObsOff 3-9-20 RE &47RAF CR Egypt9
BYRNE,Edward 2Lt kia 12-3-17 4GordH attRFC p18&242 CR France924
BYRNE,Edward T2Lt kia 23-8-17 6DCLI p114 MR30
BYRNE,Edward Aloysius T2Lt kia 24-4-17 11 att1RDubF p176 MR20
BYRNE,Edward James Widdrington Capt kia 29-4-16 3 att2SWBord p99 MR21,Edmund
BYRNE,Gerald William 2Lt ded 11-8-19 KSLI p265 CR Mddx53
BYRNE,Hubert Corbett 2Lt kia 2-9-18 5RSuss p228 CR Belgium111
BYRNE,Hugh Vyvian Edward.MC.TCapt kia 15-4-18 8 att9Norf p73 MR30
BYRNE,John Cahill Lt ded 11-10-18 IARO attOrdnanceDept p274 MR66
BYRNE,John Gilbert Lt kia 21-1-16 IA 37Dogras p274 CR Iraq5
BYRNE,Leo Francis T2Lt kia 21-8-16 6RIrReg p88 CR France178
BYRNE,Leslie Noel Lt ded 8-11-18 8Ess p232 CR Essex146
BYRNE,Louis Frederick T2Lt kia 1-7-16 24NumbF p60 CR France267
BYRNE,Patrick Anthony Laugan.DSO.MID 2Lt ded 17-10-16 129/30RFA &24RFC p2&26 MR20
BYRNE,Ralph Eugéne.MM&Bar.2Lt kia 4-4-18 C180RFA p26 CR France144
BYRNE,Samuel Hubert TCapt kia 13-9-16 9Suff p78 MR21
BYRNE,Thomas Edmond 2Lt kia 9-3-18 1WelshGds p53 CR France545
BYRNE,Vincent Cornel 2Lt kia 31-7-17 3 att1RIrRif p169 MR29,Connel
BYRNE,Walter T2Lt kia 30-9-18 LNLancs att1/4Bn p135 CR France572
BYRNE,William T2Lt dow 26-9-16 27NumbF p60 CR France285
BYRNE-JOHNSON,John Vivian.MID Capt kia 22-8-16 2RB p178 CR France423
BYRON,Clement John 2Lt kia 10-1-17 2HAC p206 CR France221
BYRON,Harry 2Lt kia 2-9-18 10Manch p237 CR France308
BYRON,Henry 2Lt dow 8-9-16 1/5SLancs p230 CR France188
BYTHEWAY,Gertrude Miss ded 31-12-17 VAD BRCS p200 CR Egypt1

C

CABLE,George Pickersgill 2Lt kia 9-5-15 5 att2RB p178 MR32
CABLE,Gordon Porter Capt ded 2-1-18 IARO attImpServTroops p274 CR Iraq8,attJaipurTransCps
CABLE,James Sydney Lt ded 5-9-18 RGA 46SB p38 CR France95,kldacc
CADDICK,Alfred Armstrong.MID TMaj kia 1-7-16 8RWar p214 MR21
CADDY,W.L.Capt 14-1-21 5Lancs CR Lancs71
CADE,Arthur Gordon.DSO.MC&Bar.MID CaptALtCol kia 26-4-18 2Mddx p146 MR30
CADE,Francis Thomas Darrel TCapt kia 6-9-16 11Hamps p120 MR21
CADE,Reginald Henry Maj kia 27-9-18 1/7LancF p221 CR France758,Harry
CADELL,Assheton Biddulph 2Lt dow 19-12-16 Dev att8RWKent p140 CR Belgium11,19-2-16
CADELL,Richard Lewis 2Lt dow PoW 28-5-18 RE 98FC p43 CR France1331
CADENHEAD,George 2Lt kia 10-5-15 3CamH p167 MR29
CADGE,Francis Edward Lt kia 30-4-15 1Ess p131 MR4
CADGE,William TLt kia 26-9-15 9Norf p73 MR19
CADIC,Bernard Francis Capt ded 20-8-16 RGA p209 CR Kent129
CADIC,Lawrence William Ludovic.MC.Capt dow 10-10-17 2Ess p131 CR Belgium83
CADMAN,Charles Joseph.MC.TLt kia 26-1-17 RE 150InfBdeSigs p43 CR France453
CADMAN,Edward Cadman LtCol kia 27-5-18 5RLancs p213 MR18
CADMAN,Philip Smelter Cadman Maj ded 31-3-19 ERidYeo p269 CR Yorks328
CADOGAN,Henry Osbert Samuel LtCol kia 30-10-14 1RWelshF p97 CR Belgium112
CADOGAN,William George Sidney.Hon.MVO.Maj kia 14-11-14 10Huss & Staff p22 CR Belgium57,12-11-14
CADZOW,Robert T2Lt kld 22-1-18 RFC p15 CR Scot783
CAESAR,Charles Patrick Lt 14-7-16 7KSLI MR21 see CEASAR,C.P.
CAESAR,George Theodore Lt dow 2-5-18 MGC &1ESurr attTankCps p112&182 CR France1170
CAFFRFEY,Charles James TCapt ded 1-7-16 RASC p192 CR Lond29
CAFFYN,Chalenor McCrae Humphrey Mannington 2LtTLt kia 28-3-17 ESurr att60RFC p5&112 CR France46,Chaloner
CAFFYN,Harold Hunt Capt kia 22-3-15 3 att1NStaffs p156 MR32
CAHILL,Alfred Gilbert 2Lt kia 8-10-16 3Lond p245 CR France374
CAHILL,John Archibald.MC.TCapt kia 16-8-17 RBerks p138 MR30
CAHILL,John Nugent Capt kia 16-8-17 13RIrRif p169 MR30
CAHILL,Patrick Leopold Lt kia 21-3-18 4RMunstF p175 CR France369
CAHILL,Thomas Laurence.MM.T2Lt kia 26-3-18 8 att1RDubF p176 MR27
CAIE,Robert George Hyndman TCapt ded 10-2-19 GL RFus p266 CR Surrey57,11-2-19
CAIGER,Frederick Howard Stewart 2Lt kia 11-11-16 92/17RFA p26 CR France432
CAIN,Alan Victor 2Lt kia 19-10-16 3 att2Hamps p120 MR21,18-10-16
CAIN,Edward 2Lt kia 2-12-17 2YLI p142 MR30
CAIN,Ernest William 2Lt kia 31-7-17 3Wilts p152 MR29
CAIN,Frank Backwell T2Lt dow 13-4-18 15HLI p162 CR France169
CAIN,Walter Frank Capt dow 3-5-17 17Lond p250 CR France113
CAIRD,Ernest Thomson T2Lt kia 24-3-18 11RScots p53 MR27
CAIRD,Frank Clagget 2Lt dow 22-11-16 3 att2InniskF p104 CR France74
CAIRD,John Roberts Capt kia 23-4-15 3att2KOSB p101 MR29,James Robert
CAIRN-DUFF,Norman 2Lt kia 25-4-18 RGA 242SB p38 CR Belgium11
CAIRNES,Alfred Bellingham TMaj kia 9-9-16 7RIrRif p169 CR France374
CAIRNES,Charles Beresford 2Lt kia 22-4-17 C146RFA p26 CR France616,148RFA
CAIRNES,William Jameson Capt kia 1-6-18 1Leinst &74RAF MR20
CAIRNIE,David Dandie.MC.2Lt kia 21-3-18 5SfthH p241 MR20
CAIRNS,George Morton 2Lt kia 13-11-16 6BlkW p231 CR France35
CAIRNS,George Ritchie 2Lt dow 4-1-16 RFA 52DAC p208 CR Gallipoli1
CAIRNS,George Thomas Lt kia 30-7-18 1/8ScotRif p225 CR France524,Thomson
CAIRNS,Herbert T2Lt kia 4-10-17 13KRRC p149 MR30
CAIRNS,James Lt kia 23-3-19 RASC p253 MR27,att2/4Lond
CAIRNS,John Anderson Gibson 2Lt kia 29-12-15 4KOSB p224 CR Gallipoli5
CAIRNS,Stanley Ewart.MC.Lt kia 30-9-18 7N&D p233 CR France1704
CAIRNS,William Anderson TLt kia 30-9-18 15 att17RScots p53 CRBelgium116
CAIRNS,William Jameson Capt kia 1-6-18 1Leinst &74RAF MR20
CALCOTT,Charles David TLt kia 23-4-17 15Lpool p71 CR France541
CALCUTT,Albert Birch 2Lt kia 30-3-18 13Glouc p106 MR27
CALDECOTT,John Leslie Lt kia 9-9-14 RGA p38 CR EAfrica80
CALDER,Alexander Lt kia 10-8-17 8 O&BLI &57RFC p5&130 MR20

CALDER,Alexander Frazer.MC.2Lt kia 19-7-16 3 att2A&SH p173 MR21
CALDER,Alexander Scott T2Lt kia 25-9-16 8 att10NumbF p60 MR21
CALDER,George MacBeth T2Lt kia 25-9-15 8SfthH p164 CR France219
CALDER,Harold Joseph.MID 2Lt kia 17-9-16 14Lond p249 CR France294,18-9-16
CALDER,John Kellick Lt kia 22-3-18 4SfthH p241 MR20
CALDER,John Stewart.MC&Bar.Capt kia 28-3-18 5Lond p246 MR20
CALDER,Kenneth William T2Lt dow 21-12-15 66RFA p26 CR Gallipoli1
CALDER,William Herbenton Lt dow 22-8-17 3/4KAR p202 CR EAfrica10 &CR Tanzania1
CALDER,William Menzies Grant T2Lt kia 15-9-16 13 att15Hamps p120 MR21
CALDER,William Paul T2Lt kia 14-6-17 18KRRC p149 MR29
CALDER-SMITH,Raymond Alexander 2Lt 1-7-16 3Lond MR21
CALDERON,George Lt kia 4-6-15 9 O&BLI att1KOSB p130 MR4
CALDERWOOD,Alex Taylor T2Lt kia 21-8-15 10Hamps p120 MR4
CALDERWOOD,William Sewell 2Lt kia 31-7-17 8ScotRif p225 MR29
CALDICOTT,Alan TCapt kia 7-12-16 GL 10LNLancs att1/2KAR p202 CR EAfrica38 &CR Tanzania1
CALDWELL,Anthony Steel T2Lt kldacc 4-5-17 GL &RFC p5 CR Yorks500
CALDWELL,Gavin Ralston Mure Lt kia 9-10-18 2CldGds p51 CR France1355
CALDWELL,James Robert McDonald T2Lt kia 26-10-18 RFA 403HB p26 MR38
CALDWELL,John Hay Lt kia 24-1-18 CamH attRFC p15&167,ded CR Iraq8
CALDWELL,Lindsay Roy Lt ded 6-1-20 IA 2/24BaluchistanInf p274 CR Palestine9,2/124Bn
CALDWELL,Robert Col 4-4-19 RAMC CR Devon258
CALDWELL,Robert Seddon T2Lt kia 11-6-18 8ACycCps p181 CR France1693
CALDWELL,Thomas.MM.T2Lt kia 3-10-18 1/2 att1/4KOSB p101 CR France242
CALE,Sidney 2Lt dow 29-8-17 5 att4Worc p108 CR Belgium16
CALEB,Clement Daryl Nicoll T2Lt kia 2-4-17 8Dev p76 CR France568
CALEY,Hugh William Capt ded 16-9-18 RASC p192 CR Berks84
CALEY,Pelham Russell 2Lt dow 14-8-17 9Lond p248 CR Belgium18,kia
CALEY,Vernon Christopher Russell.MC. ACapt kia 22-8-17 7RWar p214 MR30
CALIANDER,W.R.C.Lt 7-2-18 IARO MR66 see CALLANDER,W.R.C.
CALKIN,Brian Penry Bernard Lt kia 10-7-18 3 att8RWSurr p55 CR France161
CALKIN,John Ernest T2Lt kia 9-4-17 22NumbF p60 CR France265
CALLAGHAN,Arthur Nickson.MID TLt kia 30-8-17 14Lpool p71 CR Greece6
CALLAGHAN,Eugene Cruess 2Lt kia 27-8-16 19RFC p2 MR20
CALLAGHAN,J.C.MC.TMaj kld 2-7-18 1/2RMunstF att87RAF p175 CR France59,7Bn
CALLAGHAN,Joseph Patrick Aloysious 2Lt kia 1-7-16 64MGC p182 MR21
CALLAGHAN,Leslie Wilfred Capt kia 9-10-17 8WYorks p219 MR30
CALLAGHAN,Stanislaus Cruess LtTCapt kld 28-6-17 GL &RFC p5
CALLAN-MACARDLE,Kenneth 2Lt kia 10-7-16 17Manch p154 MR21,9-7-16
CALLANAN,Michael T2Lt kia 20-12-16 2RMunstF p175 CR France744
CALLANDER,William Ramsay Corson Lt ded 7-2-18 IARO p274 see CALIANDER,W.R.C.
CALLARD,Malcolm Ernest 2Lt dow 26-1-15 LNLancs p135 CR France80,25-1-15
CALLARD,Stanley Edwin 2Lt kia 23-4-15 2EYorks p83 CR Belgium96,Edwyn
CALLARD,William Kingsley 2Lt kia 1-7-16 5Leic p220 CR France281
CALLAWAY,Gilbert Charles 2Lt 28-4-17 2 O&BLI MR20 see CALLOWAY,G.C.
CALLAWAY,Robert Furley 2Lt kia 13-9-16 2N&D p133 CR France294
CALLEAR,Herbert TCapt kia 16-8-17 9RDubF B'Coy p176 MR30
CALLENDER,George Wilfred.MID TLtACapt kia 25-1-17 9Worc p108 CR Iraq
CALLENDER,Gerald Claude Lt kia 26-4-18 3RScots p53 MR30
CALLENDER,John Clement Lt kia 21-8-17 4 O&BLI p231 MR30
CALLENDER,Reginald Henry T2Lt kld 5-10-15 17DLI p160 CR France922
CALLEY,Oliver John Lt kia 12-3-15 1Wilts p152 CR Belgium60
CALLIER,E.F.M.Sister 22-6-19 QAIMNS CR Lond29
CALLINAN,Thomas William 2Lt kia 25-4-17 8DLI p239 MR29
CALLINGHAM,Frank Reginald T2Lt ded 26-2-19 N&D att10Bn p133 CR Lond12,25-2-19
CALLINGHAM,Stanley Breach Lt ded 18-1-19 6Norf p217 CR Essex137,5Bn
CALLISON,Robert William Lt kia 24-3-18 1/2 att8Leic p87 MR27
CALLOW,Donald 2Lt kia 2-7-16 1/5N&D p232 MR21,1-7-16
CALLOWAY,Gilbert Charles T2Lt kia 28-4-17 2 O&BLI p130 MR20,CALLAWAY
CALROW,William Robert Launcelot 2Lt kia 7-10-14 LNLancs p135 MR15
CALTHROP,Alfred Gordon.MID 2Lt kia 10-8-17 11RFus p67 MR29
CALTHROP,Calthrop Guy Spencer.Bart.LtCol ded 23-2-19 RE p269 CR Herts84
CALTHROP,Everard Ferguson MajTLtCol kia 19-12-15 38RFA p26 CR Belgium84
CALVERLEY,Geoffrey Walter.DSO.Lt kld 7-1-18 RIrRif attRFC p15&169 CR Wilts116
CALVERT,Cecilius Frederick Holcombe 2Lt kia 14-9-15 3SStaffs att2ELancs p122 CR France430,Cecil attRE 179Co

CALVERT,Eric Ruegg T2Lt kia 8-8-17 8RSuss p118 CR Belgium29
CALVERT,Francis 2Lt dow 19-9-17 2/4YLI p235 CR France512
CALVERT,Geoffrey Clifford TLt ded 15-1-19 16YLI p142 CR France1211
CALVERT,George Maj 25-8-20 RFA CR Devon50
CALVERT,James Howard T2Lt kld 24-4-16 6RIrRif p169 CR Ireland79
CALVERT,John Dutton Lt kia 14-2-15 RB p178 CR Belgium80,15-2-15
CALVERT,Lionel T2Lt kia 30-1-17 RE 175TC p44 CR France251
CALVERT,Reginald Cullen Capt dow 15-7-16 7WYorks p218 CR France74
CALVERT,Robert Mayson T2Lt kia 9-7-16 17Manch p154 CR France1890
CALWELL,Theophilus Legate.MC.TLt kia 7-10-16 9RFus p67 MR21
CALWELL,Walter Henry Lt dow 27-8-18 5 att2RIrRif p169 CR France100
CAM,Alan Noel T2Lt kia 16-8-17 RE 150FC p44 MR30
CAMBLE,Edward Maurice Baldwin TLt kia 1-7-16 8YLI p142 MR21,CAMBIE
CAMBLE,Graham Douglas Maj kia 25-9-15 40Pathans att10A&SH MR28
CAMBRIDGE,Thomas 2Lt kia 3-11-17 2/44RWKent p234 CR Palestine1,CAMBIDGE
CAMBRIDGE,William Kenneth 2Lt kia 26-3-18 331RFA p26 MR27
CAMBROOK,Horace.MC.T2Lt dow 17-10-16 8RWKent p140 CR France106
CAME,Harold Charles T2Lt kia 20-9-17 RWKent att11Bn p140 MR30
CAMERON,Alexander Leckie Capt kia 21-3-18 6 att8A&SH p243 MR27
CAMERON,Allan George Capt kia 25-9-14 1CamH p167 CR France1339
CAMERON,Archibald Capt kia 3-5-17 3 att5CamH p167 MR20
CAMERON,Archie.MM.2Lt kia 11-4-18 8BordR p116 MR32
CAMERON,Arthur Ian Douglas 2Lt dow 25-4-15 2SfthH p164 CR Belgium129
CAMERON,Charles Munnis T2Lt kia 12-6-16 RE 173TC p44 CR France178
CAMERON,Charles Peter Gwydyr.MC.Capt dow 30-4-18 RGA HvyArt attStaff 9CpsHQ p38 CR France100
CAMERON,Charles Tolmie 2Lt kia 21-3-18 4SfthH p241 MR20
CAMERON,Charles Wilson T2Lt kia 18-12-17 GL &21RFC p5 CR Belgium16
CAMERON,Colin Mackenzie Capt&Adjt kia 12-4-18 4SfthH p241 CR France194,11-4-18
CAMERON,Colin Neil Capt kia 10-8-15 7Ches p222 MR4
CAMERON,Cyril Henry 2Lt kia 12-3-15 N'RHA p26 CR France710
CAMERON,David.MIDx2 Capt&QM 1-1-20 1CamH CR Pakistan50A MR43
CAMERON,Donald T2Lt kia 25-3-18 3RFC p15 MR20
CAMERON,Donald Ronald Colin TLt kia 13-9-15 11HLI p162 CR France114
CAMERON,Douglas Robert Lt kia 31-7-17 3A&SH p173 CR Belgium46,dow
CAMERON,Duncan Lt ded 5-12-18 9A&SH attBaseDepotCarriers MGC p186&244 CR France40
CAMERON,Duncan Alexander.MC.Capt kia 1-12-17 IA CpsofGuides att38CentIndHorse p274 CR France446
CAMERON,Evan Stuart 2Lt kia 11-4-17 4 att6CamH p243 MR20
CAMERON,Ewen Arthur Lt kia 16-2-15 49RFA p26 MR29
CAMERON,Ewen Henry Lt ded 27-8-15 RDubF p266 CR Ireland24
CAMERON,Francis Blake TLt dow 19-8-16 7CamH p167 CR France74
CAMERON,Frederick Lt kia 23-4-17 7A&SH p243 CR France545
CAMERON,George Brown.MC.Lt dow 26-8-18 RASC p253 CR France832
CAMERON,George Grant 2Lt kld 16-10-17 4GordH attRFC p18&242 CR Scot280
CAMERON,Hector William Lovett Lt kia 14-9-14 1CamH p167 MR15
CAMERON,Henry Robley TLt ded 6-6-17 RFA 1stB ResBde p26 CR Sussex159
CAMERON,Hugh Alexander 2Lt dow 21-11-17 5Hamps p228 CR Palestine9,Lt
CAMERON,Hume Smith Capt kia 4-9-16 3Norf p73 CR France402
CAMERON,James Alistair Gordon 2Lt kia 18-11-16 3CamH p167 CR France515
CAMERON,James Callum 2Lt kia 23-4-17 4RScotF p222 CR France539
CAMERON,James Hunter Lt kia 25-9-15 9BlkW p128 MR19
CAMERON,James Macdonald 2Lt kia 10-5-15 368RFA p26 MR4
CAMERON,James Ritchie Capt kia 21-3-18 6LancF p221 MR27
CAMERON,John Capt ded 18-2-19 RAMC p267 CR Scot674
CAMERON,John Charles Schreiber Lt ded 28-5-18 SL(Censor) p268
CAMERON,John Gilmour 2Lt kia 9-11-16 CamH &RFC p2&167 CR France518,Ian
CAMERON,John Hunter.MID Lt ded 14-3-18 IARO att5MahrattaLI p274 MR66
CAMERON,John McAlister 2Lt ded 11-11-19 UL p269 CR Berks43
CAMERON,Kenneth.MC.CaptTMaj kia 26-9-18 2CamH p167 CR Belgium36,5Bn
CAMERON,Macdonald 2Lt kia 2-12-17 6HLI p240 MR30,Lt
CAMERON,Napier Charles Gordon Capt kia 26-9-14 1CamH p167 CR France1339
CAMERON,Nathaniel 2Lt dow 17-12-17 6SfthH p241 CR France52
CAMERON,Neil Kennedy Capt kia 25-9-15 5CamH p167 MR19
CAMERON,Percy Grant Lt kia 14-8-17 RGA &10RFC p5&38 MR20
CAMERON,Robert T2Lt dow 4-6-17 GL 7ScotRif att16RFC p5 CR France81

CAMERON,Robert Barton TLt kia 7-1-18 9RFC p15 CR Belgium18
CAMERON,Robert Campbell 2Lt dow 2-4-17 GL &8RFC p5 CR France120
CAMERON,Roy Douglas TLt kia 26-10-15 6CamH p167 MR19
CAMERON,Thomas Wright T2Lt kia 17-10-16 5CamH p167 MR21,18-10-16
CAMERON,Tom Finlayson Lt dow 30-4-18 2/14Lond p249 CR Palestine3
CAMERON,Waldo Hastie T2Lt kia 11-4-17 6CamH p167 CR France154
CAMERON,William Lt dow 27-10-15 1CamH p167 CR Scot447
CAMERON,William T2Lt kia 17-6-18 5CamH p167 CR France25
CAMERON,William George T2Lt kia 4-9-18 1/2WRid att 1/5LancF p115 CR France239
CAMERON,William Henry Veitch Capt kia 20-12-14 1HLI p162 MR22
CAMERON,William McAdam T2Lt kia 14-7-16 8BlkW p128 MR21
CAMIES,Ernest Arthur T2Lt kia 15-7-16 2RWFus p97 CR France701
CAMM,Bertram Cunliffe.MC.ACapt kld 7-1-18 2Yorks p90 CR Belgium127
CAMM,Percy 2Lt ded 10-11-18 4ELancs &RAF p226&258,kld 20-10-18
CAMMACK,Edith Mary SNurse ded 1-3-18 TFNS 4SthGH &GH Salonika p254 CR War100
CAMPBELL,Alexander Boswell Lt dow 13-9-17 SussYeo p205 CR Belgium20,Capt
CAMPBELL,Alexander Charles Penn TLt kia 26-9-15 9ESurr p112 MR19
CAMPBELL,Alexander Findlay T2Lt kld 22-9-17 GL &RFC p5 CR Scot395
CAMPBELL,Alexander John.MIDx2 Capt kia 29-7-18 1/5A&SH p243 CR France866
CAMPBELL,Alexander Mather T2Lt kia 22-3-18 8SfthH A'Coy p164 CR France1182
CAMPBELL,Allan William George Lt dow 20-9-14 CldGds p51 CR France1329
CAMPBELL,Angus Hamilton.MC.Lt ded 12-3-19 RE p262 CR Lond13,13-3-19
CAMPBELL,Archibald Augustus Ava.Bart.TLt kia 9-5-16 6CamH p167 CR France423
CAMPBELL,Archibald Douglas Lerago TCapt kia 18-11-15 15DLI p160 CR France1140
CAMPBELL,Archibald Thornsom TCapt ded 22-2-16 RAMC p194 CR Scot764
CAMPBELL,Archibald Wright TCapt dow 13-12-17 RAVC 6MtdBde p198 CR Egypt2
CAMPBELL,Aubone Charles.DSO.CaptTMaj dow 3-4-18 1KOSB att 11RScots p101 CR France62,2Bn
CAMPBELL,Brabazon 2Lt kia 18-12-14 4RWar p64 MR32
CAMPBELL,Bruce Hutchinson TLt kia 19-9-18 12A&SH p173 CR Greece5
CAMPBELL,C.C.K.Capt kia 28-9-15 3CamH attACycCps p167 MR19
CAMPBELL,Cecil Awdry Lt drd 4-10-18 RE 250FC p44 MR40,TC
CAMPBELL,Charles T2Lt dow 10-1-18 13KRRC p149 CR Belgium124
CAMPBELL,Charles T2Lt dow 20-4-18 11RFus p67 CR France300
CAMPBELL,Charles Arthur Lt kia 24-8-14 1Ches p95 CR Belgium197
CAMPBELL,Charles Bruce 2Lt ded 29-11-17 GL &49RFC p5 CR France403,48Sqn
CAMPBELL,Charles Duncan Mile.MBE.Maj ded 9-3-18 RFC p15 CR Kent83,Miles
CAMPBELL,Charles Frederick.MC.CaptAMaj kia 18-9-18 402/14RFA p26 CR France835
CAMPBELL,Charles Lionel Kirwan.CB.CMG.BtLtColTBrigGen ded 31-3-18 16Lancers5CavBde2CavDiv p23 CR Scot237
CAMPBELL,Charles Montage Gordon Capt ded 19-10-18 RAMC p194 CR France1858
CAMPBELL,Clarence Victor 2Lt kia 26-10-17 1/7N&D p233 CR France115
CAMPBELL,Claude Henry.DSO.TLtCol kia 14-3-16 1CamH att 12WYorks p167 CR France157,Cmdg1/4SfthH
CAMPBELL,Colin Archibald Heron Maj kia 29-9-17 C296RFA p26 CR Belgium84
CAMPBELL,Colin Boyd 2Lt kia 28-7-16 6MGC p182 MR21
CAMPBELL,Colin Frederick Fitzroy Capt kia 29-10-141ScotsGds p52 MR29
CAMPBELL,Colin Gernon Palmer.MC.2Lt dow 10-10-17 94RFA p26&258 CR France139
CAMPBELL,Colin Richmond 2Lt kia 11-1-17 3HLI p162 CR Iraq5
CAMPBELL,Colin St.George 2Lt kia 6-4-17 SR 45RFC p5 CR Belgium406
CAMPBELL,David Wylie T2Lt dow 28-9-18 2Suff p78 CR France278
CAMPBELL,Donald Lt kia 17-2-15 RAMC att2EYorks p194 MR29
CAMPBELL,Donald Lt kia 19-7-16 CldGds p51 CR Belgium73
CAMPBELL,Donald George TCapt kia 13-8-16 12HLI p162 CR France453
CAMPBELL,Donald William Auchinbolck Capt kia 23-11-14 4SStaffs attN&D p122 MR22
CAMPBELL,Duncan Capt kia 18-5-15 2BlkW p128 CR France924
CAMPBELL,Duncan 2Lt ded 27-11-18 RGA att4ArmyGunPark p38 CR France146
CAMPBELL,Duncan Donald Heron.MC.MID Capt kia 7-6-17 RGA att 112RFA p38 CR Belgium43
CAMPBELL,Duncan Frederick.DSO.MID LtCol ded 4-9-16 3BlkW Cmdg2/7WRid p227&264,Capt 9-9-16 CR Scot525,dow

CAMPBELL,Edward Lt kia 18-11-16 NStaffs att3rd p156 CR France384
CAMPBELL,Eric Octavius.Hon.DSO&Bar.TLtCol ded 4-6-18 8SfthH Staff p164 CR Wales416
CAMPBELL,Ernest Valentine Capt kia 26-9-15 4BlkW p230 MR19
CAMPBELL,Evan McDonald.MID T2Lt kia 5-10-17 RB att13Bn p178 CR Belgium112
CAMPBELL,Francis James Brook LtCol 1-7-18 IA MR65
CAMPBELL,Frederick Arthur 2Lt kia 22-3-18 2TankCps p188 MR27
CAMPBELL,Frederick Charles T2Lt kia 24-3-18 17RFus p67 MR20
CAMPBELL,Frederick William 2Lt ded 12-12-18 IARO att 105LabCps p274 MR43,11-12-18
CAMPBELL,Geoffrey Arthur.MID Lt kia 29-10-14 1CldGds p51 MR29
CAMPBELL,George Edward Forman Lt kia 7-8-15 IA 2/10GurkhaRif p274 MR4
CAMPBELL,George Wands T2Lt kia 18-11-16 16HLI p162 CR France533
CAMPBELL,Graham Douglas Capt kia 26-9-15 IA 40Pathans attA&SH p274
CAMPBELL,Guy.MC.MID TCapt ded 26-5-17 4MGC Motors p182 CR Lincs61
CAMPBELL,Harry La Trobe.DSO.TD.LtCol ded 19-2-19 RE p269 CR Glouc9
CAMPBELL,Henry Bethune 2Lt kia 23-2-15 A&SH p173
CAMPBELL,Henry Wallace 2Lt kia 22-6-16 6RWar p214 CR France1157
CAMPBELL,Hugh TLt kia 22-8-15 11Manch p154 CR Gallipoli5
CAMPBELL,Ian Dermid 2Lt kia 30-11-17 GL &24RFC p5 MR20
CAMPBELL,Ian Patrick 2Lt kia 9-5-15 1CamH p167 CR France279
CAMPBELL,Ian Stuart T2Lt kia 30-6-16 23NumbF p60 MR21
CAMPBELL,Islay McKinnon Lt dow 4-4-18 SussYeo att 11RScots p205 CR France145,Mackinnon
CAMPBELL,Ivan 2Lt dow 8-1-16 3A&SH attSfthH p173 MR38
CAMPBELL,Ivan.Hon.Capt ded 16-3-17 SL AssCensor p268
CAMPBELL,James 2Lt dow 23-7-18 8ScotRif p225 CR France865
CAMPBELL,James Archibald Lochnell Capt dow 19-3-15 1A&SH p173 CR Scot22 Ex 6GordH
CAMPBELL,James Henderson.MC.T2Lt kia 24-4-17 10/11HLI p162 MR20
CAMPBELL,John.MID.Capt kia 17-5-15 4CamH p242 MR22
CAMPBELL,John TCapt ded 19-2-19 RAMC p254 CR Lancs368
CAMPBELL,John Argentine TLt dow 2-12-17 6Drags p22 CR France660
CAMPBELL,John Beresford.Hon.DSO.Capt kia 25-1-15 CldGds p51 MR22
CAMPBELL,John Davies Lt kia 1-9-14 L'RFA p26 CR France1231
CAMPBELL,John Dundas T2Lt kia 24-8-16 9RWSurr p55 CR France432,1Bn
CAMPBELL,John Fyshe 2Lt dow 10-4-17 9A&SH p244 CR France95,8Bn
CAMPBELL,John Greenbank 2Lt kia 8-5-18 2Yorks p90 MR30
CAMPBELL,John Guy 2Lt dow 30-4-17 RGA 125SB p38 CR France1188,J.C.
CAMPBELL,John Kennedy T2Lt kia 28-7-17 GL &29RFC p5 MR20
CAMPBELL,John King T2Lt kia 21-4-16 RE 253Coy p44 CR France423
CAMPBELL,John Santiago Capt kia 28-9-17 9A&SH attRFC p18&243 CR France705
CAMPBELL,John W.DCM.2Lt dow 20-4-18 2SforthH p164 CR France10
CAMPBELL,John William Ronald.MC.Lt kia 14-4-18 3Worc p108 MR32
CAMPBELL,J.V.TLt ded 14-10-17 5CamH p167
CAMPBELL,Kenneth Gordon TLt kia 25-9-15 12HLI p162 CR France219
CAMPBELL,Kenneth James 2Lt kia 12-5-15 9A&SH p244 MR29
CAMPBELL,K.T.2Lt kia 17-6-18 GL &RAF p190
CAMPBELL,Lawford Bwine TLt kia 1-7-16 2RIrRif p169 MR21,Burne 12Bn
CAMPBELL,M.B.E.Maj ded 9-3-18 RFC p261
CAMPBELL,Montagu Irving Mitchell.MC.Maj dow 4-9-16 3ConnRgrs att2WelshR p172 CR France141
CAMPBELL,Neill Diarmid LtCol kia 12-4-18 8A&SH p243 MR32
CAMPBELL,Neil Leslie T2Lt kia 8-8-15 1/5RScots p53 CR Gallipoli6
CAMPBELL,Norman Phillips TLtACapt kia 3-5-17 RE 189Coy SpecBdeO SpCo p44 MR20
CAMPBELL,Oscar William 2Lt dow 24-6-17 RE 228FC p210 CR Belgium11
CAMPBELL,Quentin Hewes ACapt kia 19-7-17 5YLI p235 CR Belgium173
CAMPBELL,Robert Alexander Rankine 2Lt kia 1-7-16 2WYorks p81 MR21
CAMPBELL,Robert Gillies Capt ded 1-2-15 10SfthH p164 CR Scot926,Maj
CAMPBELL,Robert Burns Lt kia 3-5-17 5KOSB p224 MR20
CAMPBELL,Robert Charles Cowburn Capt dow 19-5-15 1KOSB p101 CR Lond4
CAMPBELL,Robert Colin 2Lt ded 28-11-18 1/1Lothian&BorderHorseYeo p204 CR Greece3
CAMPBELL,Robert William Procter Maj kia 15-11-15 RGA 2SB p38 CR France423
CAMPBELL,Ronald Walter Francis TCapt dow 11-8-16 10RFus p67 CR Scot22
CAMPBELL,Samuel MacDonnell TLt kia 1-7-16 GL 13LancF att86TMB p190 CR France221,2Lt
CAMPBELL,Stanley Frederick John 2Lt kia 27-8-18 1/6Lond p246 CR France214

CAMPBELL,Thomas Capt dow 3-8-16 RGA 19SB p38 CR France51
CAMPBELL,Thomas Callender TLt dow 8-10-15 RE 86Coy p44 MR4
CAMPBELL,Thomas Henderson Capt kia 4-5-16 6ScotRif p224 CR France114
CAMPBELL,Thomas Steel 2Lt kia 23-4-17 5RScotF p222 MR34
CAMPBELL,Tom Catto Pirie.MC Lt kia 28-3-18 4GordH p241 MR20,Catto
CAMPBELL,Torquil Lorne 2Lt kia 1-3-17 8 att1A&SH p243 CR France511
CAMPBELL,Victor Robert Wilkie T2Lt kia 7-9-18 RWelshF 3GarrBn att23Ches p97 CR France263,6-9-18
CAMPBELL,Walter Stanley.MC.Lt kia 7-10-16 1Lond p245 MR21
CAMPBELL,W.C.2Lt kia 23-4-17 7BordR p116 MR20
CAMPBELL,William.MC.TCapt kia 5-9-16 RAMC att7RFA p194 CR France188
CAMPBELL,William Lt kia 6-7-17 RFA &2RFC p5&26 CR France161
CAMPBELL,William.MC.2Lt kia 31-7-17 9RScots p212 CR Belgium73
CAMPBELL,William T2Lt kia 20-9-17 Mddx att23Bn p146 MR30
CAMPBELL,William Archibald Lt dow 21-9-17 1/7WYorks att10RFC p18&218 CR France98
CAMPBELL,William Barton Rev2Lt kia 19-4-17 5KOSB p224 MR34
CAMPBELL,William Kenneth Hamilton Maj ded 19-5-18 IA 12Pioneers p274 CR Devon237,9-5-18
CAMPBELL,William Mackenzie T2Lt kia 1-7-16 9RIrRif p169 MR21
CAMPBELL,William John 2Lt ded 25-5-15 RGA p38 CR Asia45
CAMPBELL,William Percy 2Lt kia 24-10-14 3 att2Wilts p152 MR29
CAMPBELL,William Robinson.DSO.Maj kia 13-5-15 14Huss p22 MR29
CAMPBELL,William Ulick Middleton Capt kia 14-3-15 1HLI p162 CR France279
CAMPBELL,William Watson 2Lt kia 9-1-17 7Manch p237 CR France701
CAMPBELL,Willie T2Lt kia 4-11-18 2/4Y&L p158 CR France1081
CAMPBELL,W.K.Lt 7-9-16 2DAC attRFC CR Canada 1203
CAMPBELL-IRONS,Arthur Capt kia 8-3-16 3HLI p162 MR38
CAMPBELL-JOHNSON,Patrick Seymour Campbell.MC.Lt dow 30-8-19 RFA p254 CR Essex29
CAMPBELL-MACGREGOR,John Rev dow 4-11-16 Chap4Cl attCamH CR France377
CAMPBELL-MURDOCH,Louis Forde 2Lt dow 19-9-16 2ScotsGds CR France300
CAMPBELL-ORDE,John Vernon TLt ded 14-10-17 5CamH p167&265,7Bn CR Scot44,kldacc
CAMPION,Edward MajTLtCol ded 25-2-16 2SfthH p164 CR Sussex136
CAMPION,Raoul Rene TLt kia 17-2-17 RGA att73 SR SBHvy p38 CR France314
CAMPION,William Ernest Maj kia 28-10-14 1EYorks p83 CR France82
CAMPKIN,Reginald Ernest 2Lt kia 28-3-18 4Lond p246 MR20
CAMPLIN,Ernest.MM.T2Lt kia 29-9-18 1 att6RWKent p140 CR France369
CANBY,Ronald Leslie Lt kia 8-5-17 6NStaffs p238 MR20
CANCELLOR,Desmond Bertram.MC.Lt kia 1-11-18 3 att1Hamps p120 CR France1252
CANDY,Douglas Bowhill 2Lt dow 25-9-16 4 att1Beds p85 CR France329
CANE,Leonard Dobbie TCapt&Adjt kia 24-1-16 20RFus p67 CR France114
CANE,Lionel Alfred Francis Capt kia 7-11-14 1ELancs p110 CR Belgium68
CANE,Maurice T2Lt kia 4-8-17 1/153RFA p26 CR Belgium96
CANE,Reginald Shapland T2Lt kia 1-7-16 1Hamps p120 MR21
CANEY,Charles.MC.2Lt dow 29-8-18 6EKent p57 CR France119
CANFOR,Arthur Reginald T2Lt kia 23-3-18 8ESurr p112
CANN,Leonard 2Lt kia 13-3-18 RFC p15 CR France34
CANN,P.R.2Lt dow 2-4-18 GL &RAF p190
CANNAN,Horatius James.DSO.TCapt dow 2-11-16 B78RFA p26 CR France145
CANNELL,Hugh Featherstone Cameron Lt dow 31-10-18 IA 1Lancers att72RAF p274 MR38
CANNING,Edward 2Lt kia 6-7-16 6KOSB p101 MR21
CANNING,Ernest Harold.DFC.2Lt kld 5-10-18 1Glouc &102RAF p106 CR France404
CANNON,Richard Lt kia 5-4-16 8Wilts p152 MR38
CANNON,Sidney Leslie 2Lt ded 14-9-18 KSLI attRAF p144 CR Egypt1,Lt
CANSDALE,Lionel.MIDx22Lt kia 29-3-18 1Dors p123 MR16,29-3-18
CANSFIELD,Victor Morton Lt kia 24-2-16 95RFA p26 CR France922
CANSINO,Joshua T2Lt kia 2-6-16 22Manch p154 MR21
CANTAN,Henry Thomas.CMG.LtCol kia 16-4-16 1DCLI p114 CR France1182
CANTLE,Leonard Heath Lt kia 8-4-17 SurrYeo attRFC p18&205 MR20
CANTON,Herbert Westrup LtTCapt kia 13-5-15 ELancs p110 MR29
CANTY,Frederick William T2Lt dow 29-6-18 3EYorks Res att2Y&L p83 CR France142
CAPE,George Augustus Stewart.CMG.TLtColTBrigGen kia 18-3-18 RFA 39DivArty p26
CAPEL CURE,B.A Capt dow 1-10-16 2Glouc CR Greece4 see CURE,B.A.C.
CAPELL,Arthur Edward T2Lt kia 13-11-16 10RWelshF p97 MR21

CAPELL,Arthur George Coningsby Capt kia 12-3-15 1Nhampt p137 MR21
CAPELL,Bruce Lorence.MC.2Lt kia 7-6-18 RGA 2/1NorthMidHvyBty p38 CR France504
CAPERN,Henry James T2Lt kia 22-3-18 10KRRC att59TMB p149 MR27,11Bn
CAPPELL,James Leitch Rev ded 23-1-8 RAChDept att1/9RScots p199 CR France85
CAPPER,Adam Clarke T2Lt kia 9-9-16 20 att7RIrRif p169 CR France402
CAPPER,Bass Durant TCapt kld 6-12-17 RFC p5 CR Ireland33
CAPPER,Charles Arthur TLt ded 11-3-19 ArmyPayDept p200 CR France134
CAPPER,Edward Walter Lt kia 14-4-17 MontgomeryYeo attRFC p18&204 MR20
CAPPER,Ernest Raphael.MC.TCapt dow 24-12-17 9Ess p131 CR Germany9
CAPPER,George William Maj ded 7-1-19 1EYorks GarrBn p83 MR66
CAPPER,John Beausire Copeland.MC.2Lt kia 26-9-16 A70RH&FA p26 CR France453
CAPPER,Thompson.Sir.KCMG.CB.DSO.MajGen dow 27-9-15 Staff ELancs GOC7Div p1 CR France201
CAPRON,Thomas Harvey Overbury TLt kia 26-3-17 1 att1/5Ess p131 CR Palestine8
CARBERY,Miles Bertie Cunningham Capt kia 18-10-14 1RIrF C'Coy p171 CR France1140,Cunninghame 17-10-14
CARBINES,Henry 2Lt mbk 27-3-18 8Lpool &RFC p257 MR20
CARBONELL,William Charles 2Lt dow 1-9-16 3 att1SStaffs p122 CR France66
CARD,Arthur Henry.MC.2Lt kia 26-9-16 12Mddx p146 MR21
CARD,John Victor.MC.Lt kia 25-3-19 3ESurr p112 MR70 &CR Europe179,Capt
CARD,Stormont Hays 2Lt kia 10-4-17 1SomLI p79 MR20
CARDELL,Edmund Powne.MC.Maj kia 21-3-18 46RFA p26 MR27
CARDEN,Derrick Alfred LtCol dow 25-5-15 SfthH att7A&SH p164 CR France200
CARDEN,Henry Charles.DSO.Maj kia 25-9-15 8Dev p76 MR19
CARDEN,John.CMG.LtCol dow 10-8-15 5Wilts p152 MR4 &MR22
CARDEN,John Rutter Maj dow 30-4-15 IA 15Sikhs p274 CR France102
CARDEN,Ronald Hugh 2Lt kia 14-3-15 SL attWilts p201 MR22
CARDEN,Ronald James Walter TLtCol kia 8-7-16 17Lancers att16RWelshF p23 CR France513,10-7-16
CARDEW,Edward Bellasis Capt kia 26-9-15 RE 7FC p44 MR19
CARDEW,George Eric.MC.Capt kia 9-4-18 4Dev att6DLI p220 MR32
CARDEW,John Haydon.MC.LtACapt dow 5-10-17 73RFA 5ArmyBde p26 CR Belgium16
CARDEW,Richard Cornelius Arthur 2Lt kia 24-4-18 3 att2Dev p76 CR France144
CARDWELL,Hugh Brodie Lt dow 9-8-18 B256RFA p207 CR France145
CARE,Graham Bristowe 2Lt kia 19-4-17 1/4RScots p211 CR Palestine8
CAREFULL,John Holt TCapt kia 21-3-18 12Lpool p71 MR27
CAREW,Coventry George Warrington TCapt dow 20-11-16 7 att1Dors p123 MR21
CAREW,Cyril Joseph Theodore 2Lt dow 29-4-15 2EYorks p83 CR France1
CAREW,Francis Ludovis 2Lt kia 30-10-14 20Huss p23 MR29,Ludovic
CAREW,Jasper 2Lt kia 14-10-14 WYorks p81 CR France276
CAREW,Robert Thomas Col ded 11-2-17 Leinst p266 CR Eire238
CAREW HUNT,Aubrey Noel Capt kia 5-6-16 3 att2 O&BLI p130 CR France68
CAREY,Allan Stewart T2Lt kld 27-5-17 GL &45RFC p5 CR Belgium140
CAREY,Arthur John Edward 2Lt kia 22-8-17 3 att8/10GordH p166 MR30,Lt
CAREY,Arthur Stanley Lt kia 15-9-16 1/8Mddx p236 CR France785
CAREY,Bertram Chepmell.MC.LtACapt dow 22-9-18 1Nhampt p137 CR France673
CAREY,Francis Ambrose 2Lt kia 15-9-16 32RFus p67 MR21
CAREY,Frederick Capt ded 22-1-16 RGA attAOD India p26 MR43 &CR Pakistan50A,Maj
CAREY,Henry Pattison TLt kia 7/11-8-15 9N&D p133 MR4
CAREY,Leicester William le Marchant Capt kia 17-10-14 RFus p67 MR22,19-10-14
CAREY,Leonard Arthur T2Lt kia 1-7-16 2Dev p76 MR21
CAREY,Loyd Carleton T2Lt kia 4-9-16 13 att1ESurr p112 MR21
CAREY,Mansell Ernest.MC.2Lt kia 30-11-17 1/4RWKent p234 MR17,Mansel
CAREY,M.J.MC.Lt&QM 16-11-20 GL &12RB CR Hamps202
CAREY,Richard Cyril T2Lt dow 8-7-16 12Suff p78 MR20,3-7-16
CAREY,Timothy S.J.Rev Chap4Cl ded 27-2-19 RAChDept p199 CR France1374
CAREY,Thomas Augustus 2Lt kia 5-12-17 1IrGds p52 MR17
CAREY,William Alexander Lt kia 29-12-17 2/19Lond p250 CR Palestine3
CARFRAE,Charles Francis Kirkpatrick Capt kia 25-9-15 O&BLI att5Bn p130 MR29
CARGILL,Duncan Campbell.MC.T2Lt kia 2-11-18 2SfthH p164 France1266,20-11-18
CARGILL,John Capt dow 24-4-17 7BlkW p231 CR France95
CARGIN,Norman J.A.T2Lt dow 1-5-16 7 att10NStaffs p156 CR Iraq6
CARLESS,Albert William Buchan Lt dow 27-9-15 5 att1Mddx p146 CR France98
CARLESS,Hugh Dobbie 2Lt dow 24-4-17 3GordH p166 CR France113

CARLESS,Wilfred Townsend Maj kia 12-8-15 1Hereford p252 MR4,Wilfrid Townshend
CARLESS,William Stanley Capt ded 18-12-18 RAVC p269 CR Hereford208
CARLEY,B.AssMatron 26-4-20 TFNS CR Suff68
CARLEY,Henry Victor T2Lt dow 14-10-15 7Norf p73 CR France 98,Harry Lt
CARLEY,Samuel Newman T2Lt kia 25-9-17 207MGC Inf p182 CR Belgium125
CARLEY,Thomas Morgan T2Lt kia 27-9-18 Manch att2/9Bn p154 CR France712
CARLILE,Edward Hildred Hanbury Capt kia 22-3-18 HertsYeo p204 MR20
CARLILE,Thomas T2Lt kia 16-8-17 11RInniskF p104 MR30
CARLINE,Norman John 2Lt kia 22-3-18 LNLancs att10Bn p135 CR France366
CARLINE,Thomas T2Lt kia 30-9-18 18Lpool att15LancF p71 CR France376
CARLISLE,Arthur Lewis Capt kia 29-8-18 4RASC 8DivTrain p192 CR France184,2Berks
CARLISLE,Francis Bruce Maj ded 31-12-14 4RWKent p234 MR65
CARLISLE,Frederick Albert 2Lt kia 15-9-16 2/4Lond p246 CR Belgium10
CARLISLE,John Edward Gordon Capt dow 11-5-15 IA 107Pnrs p274 CR France80
CARLISLE,Reginald TLtACapt kia 3-5-17 10EYorks p83 MR20
CARLISLE-CROWE,William Maynard Capt 11-11-14 RWar att1Nhampt MR29 see CROWE,W.M.C.
CARLOS,Ernest Stafford 2Lt kia 14-6-17 4EKent p212 CR Belgium56,Lt 8Bn
CARLTON,Claude Gray 2Lt kia 26-10-17 Dev att9Bn p76 MR30
CARLTON,Roy Septimus 2Lt ded 30-5-17 RFC p261 CR Kent83,Lt 8SLancs
CARLTON,William Fergus 2Lt kia 17-6-16 4EYorks p219 CR Belgium79
CARLYLE,George Pasley 2Lt kia 14-10-18 14Lond att9MGC Inf p249 CR Belgium157
CARLYLE,Robert 2Lt kia 12-7-17 1/5KOSB p224 CR Gallipoli2
CARLYLE,Thomas Johnstone Lt kia 5-10-17 5KOSB p224 CR Belgium84
CARLYLE,William Mackay 2Lt kia 26-10-16 60RFC p2 MR20
CARLYON,Lionel George T2Lt kia 3-5-17 9ScotRif p103 CR France604,W.G.
CARLYON,Thomas Tonkin 2Lt dow 28-6-18 RGA 99SB p209 CR France31
CARMAN,Leslie Guy.MID 2Lt kia 4-10-18 3EKent p57 CR France1890,7Bn
CARMICHAEL,Andrew T2Lt kia 12-10-17 6KOSB p101 MR30
CARMICHAEL,Andrew Gemmell T2Lt kia 11-4-17 6CamH p167 CR France311
CARMICHAEL,Archibald 2Lt dow 22-5-18 C108RFA p26 CR France71,D108
CARMICHAEL,Chalmers 2Lt kia 15-7-16 1/8N&D p233 MR21
CARMICHAEL,David Arthur Lt kia 17-4-18 3RFus att25MGC Inf p67&182 MR30,9Bn
CARMICHAEL,Douglas TCapt kia 25-9-15 9RB p178 MR29
CARMICHAEL,George Clement 2Lt kia 18-8-16 2A&SH p173 MR21 CR France393
CARMICHAEL,George Gordon Lt kia 1-8-18 4KOSB p223 CR France524,1/5Bn
CARMICHAEL,Gilbert 2Lt kia 21-3-18 10 att2/6Manch p237 MR27
CARMICHAEL,John T2Lt dow 25-3-18 20DLI p160 CR France62
CARMICHAEL,Robert Henry Morris Lt kia 12-7-15 5A&SH p243 MR4
CARMICHAEL,Thomas Sydney T2Lt dow 18-5-16 1LNLancs p135 CR France80
CARNAGHAN,James T2Lt kia 23-10-16 12ScotRif p103 MR21
CARNALL,Ronald Gundry TLt dow 29-11-16 143MGC p182 CR France177
CARNDUFF,Kenneth McLeod.MIDx2 Capt dow 11-1-16 RE 2FC p44 CR France423,12-1-16
CARNE,John Reeves T2Lt dow 25-7-17 12RSuss p118 CR Belgium11
CARNE,Maxwell Halford T2Lt dow 23-12-16 2DCLI p114 CR Europe1
CARNECY,James Maj kia 3-7-16 NStaffs att8Bn p156 MR21,CARNEGY
CARNEGIE,David Alexander 2Lt kia 2-4-17 B122RH&FA p26 CR Belgium1
CARNEGIE,Theodore Arthur Lt kia 16-8-17 12KRRC p149 MR30
CARNEGY,Frederick Alexander TLt kia 13-10-15 10Glouc p106 MR19
CARNEGY,Richard Lloyd Maj kia 10-8-15 RLancs IA 9GurkhaRif p58 CR Gallipoli17
CARNELL,Frederick Harry Wright.MC.TCapt kia 9-6-18 9WYorks p81&258 CR France223,9-5-18
CARNELLEY,Joseph Arthur TLt dow 16-6-16 RE 173TC p44 CR France285
CARNES,William Jameson Capt kia 1-6-18 Leinst &RAF p266
CARNLEY,Ronald Lt kia 27-5-18 5Leic p220 MR18
CARO,Jacob Pisa 2Lt kia 2-5-18 17Lond p250 MR27
CARPENDALE,Maxwell Montagu.MC.Maj ded 14-10-18 IA 36Horse p274 CR Syria2
CARPENTER,Bernard Melville 2Lt dow 3-4-18 6 att19Mddx p146 CR France40
CARPENTER,Cedric Theodore Arundel Lt dow 6-11-18 7Ches p223 CR France332
CARPENTER,Charles McElroy T2Lt kld 21-3-18 RFC p15 CR Shrop130
CARPENTER,Clarence 2Lt kia 17-2-17 23RFus p67 CR France314
CARPENTER,Ernest Lt kia 30-10-18 Worc &24RAF p264 MR20,3-10-18
CARPENTER,Henry Alfred Stanley T2Lt kia 2-9-16 130MGC p182 CR France151
CARPENTER,Herbert Montagu Soame TCapt kia 5-7-16 10WRid p115 CR France515

CARPENTER,Hubert Granville 2Lt dow 25-2-16 ACycCps 2LondDiv p244 CR France134,26-3-15
CARPENTER,John Neilson.MC.T2Lt kia 1-7-16 17HLI p162 MR21
CARPENTER,John Philip Morton TLt kia 15-9-16 RFA p26 CR France277,16-9-16
CARPENTER,Robert Leslie Lt kia 26-10-15 1/17Lond p250 CR France219
CARPENTER,Ronald Percy Victor TLt kia 6-9-18 57MGC Inf p182 CR France309
CARPENTER-GARNIER,John Trefusis Maj kia 14-9-14 1ScotsGds p52 CR France1328,15-9-14
CARPENTER-TURNER,Eric Walter Lt dow 9-8-16 2Hamps p120
CARR,Alexander Gunning Capt ded 14-2-19 RGA CR Lond2,dow
CARR,Alfred Rothwell 2Lt kia 9-4-17 9Lpool p216 CR France596
CARR,Arthur Clunes Hooper Lt dow 15-2-15 RE p44 MR29
CARR,A.W.2Lt ded 6-7-18 RIrF &22RAF p171 CR Egypt1,ConnRgrs
CARR,Basil Alderson 2Lt kia 25-7-17 RGA SR p38 CR Belgium24
CARR,Charles Frederick 2Lt dow 20-2-17 17 att4N&D p133 CR France64
CARR,Cyril(Dick).MC.TLt kia 11-4-18 RE 224FC p44 CR France193
CARR,Donald Neville.MC.LtTCapt ded 26-11-18 4BordR attSPersiaRif p116 MR61
CARR,Dudley Reed Lt kia 23-2-17 2Norf p73 MR38
CARR,Edgar Joseph Austin Lt dow 18-5-15 5RLancs p213 CR Lond9,Augustin
CARR,Eric Marcus T2Lt kia 1-7-16 12Y&L p158 MR21
CARR,Frank Clifford T2Lt dow 24-4-17 TurkPoW MGC p182 MR34,19-4-17
CARR,Frank Henry T2Lt dow 23-3-18 7Leic p87 CR France987
CARR,Frederick Wysses MajTLtCol ded 10-11-17 RAVC attEgyptianArmy p198 CR Yorks436,Ulysses
CARR,Hugh T2Lt dow 23-1-16 RE 172Coy p44 CR Belgium11
CARR,James 2Lt kia 21-3-18 296RFA p26 MR20
CARR,James Walter,MC.DCM.MID Lt ded 16-11-18 23RFus att99TMB p67 CR Surrey 1
CARR,John Cory Capt&QM kia 21-10-18 Lpool att2/5Bn p71 CR Belgium 406,20-10-18 2/6Bn
CARR,John Stanley Lt kia 31-7-17 5LNLancs p234 MR29
CARR,Leslie George.MC&Bar.Capt dow 27-4-18 1Lond att4SStaffs p245 CR France102
CARR,Martin Raymond Capt kia 18-9-14 2Worc p108 CR France1329
CARR,Robert Meredith TLt dow 29-5-18 10Lincs p74 CR France1332
CARR,Stanley Theodore TLt kia 27-9-16 11Manch p154 MR21
CARR,Victor Francis LtACapt kia 21-5-18 RGA 108HB p38 CR France106
CARR,William Parsons Lt kia 13-12-17 2/1Lond p251 CR Palestine3
CARR-ELLISON,Oswald Fenwicke-Clennall.MID Lt kia 5-10-18 2NumbF p60 CR France234,Clennell
CARR-HARRIS,Ernest Dale Capt kia 3-11-14 RE p44 MR47
CARR-WEST,Herbert St.John Maj dow 27-10-18 12DLI CR Italy7
CARRALL,John Edwin 2Lt kia 3-5-17 12EYorks p83 MR20
CARRE,Edward Mervyn TLt kia 16-10-16 8Lincs attRFC p74&2 CR France1327
CARRE,Gilbert Trenchard TLt kia 20-11-17 9 att6RWKent p140 CR France379
CARRETTE,Albert Ernest T2Lt kia 27-4-16 9RDubF p176 CR France423
CARRICK,James Douglas 2Lt kia 11-9-18 RFA attX42TMB p26 CR France568
CARRICK,John.MID TLt kia 31-7-17 6CamH p167 CR Belgium7
CARRICK,Richard Hamilton T2Lt kia 2-4-17 9Dev p76 CR France568
CARRIDEN,William Scott T2Lt ded 12-2-19 RASC p254&267 CR Scot754
CARRIE,Fred George Lt kia 26-10-17 5LNLancs p234 MR30
CARRIER,John Russell 2Lt kia 8-10-16 5Lond p246 MR21
CARRIGAN,Colin Herbert.MC&Bar.Capt kia 2-9-18 1RMunstF p175 CR France592
CARRINGTON,Charles Harold Lt kia 9-4-18 5DLI p238 MR32
CARRINGTON,Edmund Alfred 2Lt kia 18-10-15 2Wilts p152 MR19
CARRINGTON,Edward Worrell.MC.TCapt kia 27-9-15 RAMC att2Worc p194 CR France423
CARRINGTON,Harold Edward TCapt kia 15-9-16 15Hamps p120 MR21
CARRITT,Harry William TCapt kia 8-7-16 2Nhampt p137 MR21
CARROLL,Frederick Stanley T2Lt kia 21-11-16 7RInniskF p104 CR France432
CARROLL,Henry Arthur TLtCol ded 31-10-18 RMunstF p266 CR Hamps64
CARROLL,James Charles Lt dow 26-3-18 RGA att1TankCps p38 CR France300
CARROLL,James Francis Joseph R.Capt ded 24-3-19 RDubF p266 CR Ireland12
CARROLL,Patrick T2Lt kia 8-2-17 10RDubF p176 CR France339
CARROLL,William.MC.ACapt kia 3-5-17 12EYorks p83 CR France1191
CARROLL-LEAHY,Noel Edward Joseph kia 9-8-18 O/5RFA CR France1170
CARROTHERS,John Samuel 2Lt kia 16-8-17 8RInniskF p104 MR30
CARRS,Stuart TLt dow 28-7-16 RE 212FC p44 CR France51
CARRUTH,John TLt dow 10-10-18 6RDubF attRIrRif p176 CR France446
CARRUTH,Matthew 2Lt kia 9-9-16 6RIrReg att6ConnRgrs p88 MR21,4Bn
CARRUTHERS,Cameron Roy Capt kia 31-7-17 4CamH p242 MR29

CARRUTHERS,E.S.Maj ded 16-5-17 RE p44 CR Kent153
CARRUTHERS,George MacLellan T2Lt kia 10-8-17 11LancF p92 MR29
CARRUTHERS,Gordon T2Lt dow 27-11-18 1 att5WRid p115 CR France146
CARRUTHERS,James Mein Austin TCapt dow 26-4-17 16Mddx p146 CR France40
CARRUTHERS,William 2Lt kia 24-4-17 RE 154FC p44 Ex 3RIrRif CR France452,Lt
CARRUTHERS,William Alexander.MC.TLt dow 3-9-18 NumbF att1RScots p60 CR Greece6
CARRUTHERS,William Keith 2Lt kia 3-4-17 BucksBn O&BLI att2/4Lincs p231 MR21
CARRYER,Charles Ivan 2Lt kld 18-8-16 RFC p2,263&261,18-3-16 EYorks CR Leic63,13-8-16
CARSE,Robert Mercer 2Lt kia 12-4-18 174RFA p208 CR France881
CARSE,William Kenric T2Lt kia 13-2-17 GL &3RFC p5 CR France833
CARSLAW,John Howie Lt dow 26-11-17 A262RFA p207 CR Palestine3
CARSON,Charles Graham.MC.TCapt dow 28-11-16 13Ess C'Coy p131&258 CR France145,19-11-16
CARSON,Frederick Glover 2Lt kia 30-11-17 1KOSB p101 MR17
CARSON,Herbert William.DSO.CaptAMaj ded 12-10-18 RAMC p194 CR Syria2
CARSON,James Arthur Balfour Capt ded 9-8-18 GL RAMC attRAF p194&266 CR Egypt9
CARSON,Lindsay Hubert TCapt dow 31-10-18 10Ess p131 CR France1392
CARSON,Murray TCapt ded 20-4-17 RASC p192
CARSON,Richard Hartley 2Lt dow 4-9-17 1GrenGds p49 CR Belgium16
CARSON,Robert Maj dow 21-8-16 RGA 71HB p38 CR France232,24-8-16 139HB
CARSON,Samuel Murray Capt 20-4-17 RASC CR Kent175
CARSON,Sidney Thomas T2Lt kia 2-9-18 2RIrReg att1RMunstF p88 MR16
CARSON,Thomas Long 2Lt kia 31-7-17 GL 4RFC p5 MR20
CARSON,Thomas Wright 2Lt kia 27-12-15 6WRid p227 MR29 &CR Belgium453
CARSON,William John White 2Lt mbk 1-7-16 14RIrRif p256 MR21
CARSON-PACKER,Gaythorne Raymond Robertson T2Lt dow 5-10-15 C47RFA p26 CR Belgium11
CARSS,Herbert Crosley T2Lt dow 8-10-17 14NumbF p60 CR France134
CARSWELL,Henry Bradshaw Capt kia 6-10-18 7Ches p222 CR Belgium115
CARSWELL,John Dingwall TCapt kia 14-7-16 8BlkW p128 MR21
CARSWELL,John Jamieson T2Lt kia 25-9-15 10ScotRif p103 MR19
CARSWELL,Malcolm Shanks TLt kia 17-9-17 RBerks att2Bn p138 CR Belgium52
CARSWELL,Robert Nevin 2Lt kia 26-10-14 3 att2YLI p142 MR22
CARSWELL,William Alexander.MC.Capt dow 21-3-18 10 att1/7BlkW p128 MR20
CARSWELL-HUNT,William David.MC.Maj ded 5-4-17 7 att6DLI p239 CR France787
CART De LAFONTAINE,Alfred Edwin Cecil.MC.Capt kia 9-7-16 EYorks attHQ Staff 76InfBde3Div p83 CR France513,Edeward
CARTE,Alan Simpson 2Lt dow 9-6-17 12Lond p248 CR France512
CARTER,Albert 2Lt kia 12-4-17 RSuss att9Bn p118 MR20
CARTER,Alfred Cecil Capt ded 15-1-19 RASC p192 CR Europe42
CARTER,Alfred Henry LtCol ded 3-7-17 RAMC p267 CR Berks1,4-4-18
CARTER,Alfred John T2Lt kia 13-5-17 7Dev p76 CR France214
CARTER,Archibald Wren 2Lt kia 13-5-17 5Mddx p146 CR France427
CARTER,Arthur Donald Dundas Lt BombAcc 20-7-15 IA 2/4 att1/4GurkhaRif p274 CR France345
CARTER,Aubrey John.DSO.Maj kia 4-11-14 1LNLancs p135 MR29
CARTER,Audsley Ralph Maj dow 28-8-18 RGA attRAF 1Wing p38 CR France95
CARTER,Basil Ernest Arnold Lt ded 14-2-21 IARO 17Inf TC p274 MR66
CARTER,Bernard Robert Hadow T2Lt kld 7-11-17 GL &RFC p5 CR Glouc72
CARTER,Bertram 2Lt kia 18-9-18 1Camb p245 CR France369,Lt
CARTER,Cecil Edward.MID 2Lt kia 20-9-17 2/1Lond p245 CR Belgium10
CARTER,Charles Arthur.MC.T2Lt kia 14-10-18 29DLI p160 CR Belgium42
CARTER,Charles Oscar Percival 2Lt kia 26-4-18 Ess att10Bn p131 CR France425
CARTER,Cleary George Molyneux Capt kia 23-10-14 2Wilts p152 MR29
CARTER,Desmond Patrick Webb Lt ded 12-12-16 RE 1FldSigCo p44 CR France177
CARTER,Edward 2Lt kld 25-9-15 107RFA p26 MR29
CARTER,Edward Maurice Capt kia 11-8-20 IA 11Lancers p274 CR Iraq8
CARTER,Ernest 2Lt kia 15-6-18 C240RFA p26 CR Italy3
CARTER,Ernest Lionel.MM.2Lt kia 24-10-18 13RFus p67 CR France1480
CARTER,Frank Leslie Lt kia 22-4-17 ESurr &3RFC p5&112 CR France530,2Lt
CARTER,Geoffrey Herbert TLt dow 12-11-16 2RBerks p138 CR France513
CARTER,George Augustine T2Lt kia 5-12-17 GL &13RFC p5 CR France113
CARTER,George Herbert 2Lt ded 18-11-15 2/4RFA p269 CR Durham26
CARTER,George Sidney.MC.2Lt dow 28-11-17 9ESurr A'Coy p112 CR France145
CARTER,George Thomas T2Lt kia 10-3-16 10Norf p73 MR38
CARTER,Gerald Francis T2Lt dow 30-7-15 7KRRC p149 MR29

CARTER,Gerald Mark FlOff 17-1-20 RWar &RFC CR Hamps53
CARTER,Harold Major T2Lt dow 28-8-18 3Gar RWFus att13ELancs p110 CR France28,kia
CARTER,Harvey Gerald Carminow.MC.Capt kia 8-10-18 8Worc C'Coy p226 CR France1462
CARTER,Henry 2Lt kia 16-6-15 1NumbF p60 MR29
CARTER,Henry T2Lt kia 28-2-18 111LabCps p189 CR Belgium20
CARTER,Henry Gordon T2Lt kia 19-8-15 8NumbF p60 MR4
CARTER,Henry John 2Lt kia 22-10-18 1/7LancF p221 CR France287
CARTER,Henry William Whittard T2Lt kia 2-7-17 SL 59RFC p5 CR France446,Harry
CARTER,Herbert Augustine Maj.VC.ded 13-1-16 IA 101Grndrs att40Pathans p274 CR Cornwall177
CARTER,Herbert Francis George.MC.CaptBtMajTLtCol ded 28-2-19 YLI p142 MR70 &CR Europe193
CARTER,Hugh Harry Lt kia 8-10-18 1EKent p57 CR France445
CARTER,J.2Lt kld 30-10-18 RH&FA &RAF p26
CARTER,James Shuckburgh LtACapt kia 27-9-18 1GrenGds p49 CR France1497
CARTER,John 2Lt kia 29-5-18 15DLI p160 CR France1332
CARTER,John Allen TLt ded PoW 2-4-17 6DCLI p114 MR20,Alan
CARTER,John Lovelace.MC.2LtACapt ded 18-4-18 RASC 37DivTrain p192 CR Devon73
CARTER,John Robert Blackhall Graham LtCol ded 14-1-19 IA SuppList p274
CARTER,John Taylor 2Lt kia 9-10-17 7WYorks p218 MR30
CARTER,John Wilfred T2Lt kia 7-8-15 8WRid p115 MR4
CARTER,Malcolm Russell LtACapt kia 23-3-18 1 att8ESurr p112 MR27
CARTER,Norman Cecil T2Lt dow 23-7-16 13 att14RSuss p118 CR France80
CARTER,Percy Lt kia 9-4-18 4SLancs p230 CR France80
CARTER,Richard Ivens T2Lt dow 12-11-15 RE 68FC p44 CR Gallipoli27
CARTER,Richard Thellusson.MC.CaptAMaj dow 18-8-18 RGA 11SB 14Bde p38 CR France526
CARTER,Ronald John Frederick 2Lt kia 26-4-18 22Lond p251 MR27
CARTER,Seton Rodney T2Lt kia 14-4-17 17LancF att52RFC p5&92 CR France662
CARTER,Stephen Charles T2Lt kia 18-11-16 7RWKent p140 MR21
CARTER,Sydney Chatterton T2Lt dow 3-7-16 11N&D p133 CR France23
CARTER,Sydney Robert Eric 2Lt dow 8-7-16 4YLI p235 MR21
CARTER,Walter James T2Lt dow 29-8-18 1/7Worc p108 CR Italy5
CARTER,Walter James Coe T2Lt kia 14-7-16 8Dev p76 CR France453
CARTER,W.E.Lt 22-3-18 LdStrathconasHorse &RFC CR Wilts28
CARTER,Wilfred Arthur Douglas 2Lt kld 23-5-17 3Dors &RFC p5&123,Wilfrid CR Wilts28
CARTER,William Arthur Roise Capt kia 23-4-15 1/5RLancs p213 CR Belgium88
CARTER,William Henry Seaman TLt kia 14-7-16 13Lpool p71 MR21
CARTER,William James T2Lt kia 21-9-18 10Ess p131 CR France212
CARTER,William Leonard TLt ded 4-7-17 RE 40Coy p44 CR Asia33
CARTER,William Thomas Capt kia 12-10-16 7SfthH p164 MR21
CARTER-WOOD,Joseph Alan Lt kia 1-2-15 2CldGds p51 CR France720,Allan
CARTHEW,Sydney George 2Lt kia 26-3-18 2Dev p76 MR27
CARTLAND,Arthur Edward T2Lt kld 25-2-18 RFC p15 CR Sussex95
CARTLAND,Guy Trevor.MID Capt&Adjt kia 1-7-16 1RB p178 CR France1890,George
CARTLAND,James Bertram Falkner CaptAMaj kia 27-5-18 1Worc p108 MR18
CARTLEDGE,Charles Ashforth T2Lt kia 30-7-16 5Nhampt p137 CR France251
CARTMAN,James Victor 2Lt kia 19-6-18 5 att13Lpool p215 CR France33
CARTMELL,Thomas T2Lt dow 8-5-16 19LancF p92 CR France43
CARTTER,Arthur Edward Lt ded 4-4-19 3Lond CR Surrey152
CARTWRIGHT,Alfred Grahame Maj ded 5-8-17 7Yorks p263 CR Numb74,Col
CARTWRIGHT,Arthur 2Lt kia 30-9-18 7A&SH p243 CR France236
CARTWRIGHT,Charles T2Lt kia 19-4-16 8Beds p85 MR29
CARTWRIGHT,Donald Read TLtACapt dow 5-10-18 C153RFA p26 CR Belgium44
CARTWRIGHT,Eric Percival St.George 2Lt kia 12-8-16 4Leinst att45MGC p174&182 CR France515,13-8-16
CARTWRIGHT,Ernest 2Lt kia 1-11-18 5WRid p227 CR France1256
CARTWRIGHT,Ernest Mills T2Lt kia 14-4-18 11TankCps p188 CR France98
CARTWRIGHT,Frank 2Lt kia 22-3-18 19Manch p154 CR France1061
CARTWRIGHT,George Arthur T2Lt dow 28-11-17 WRid att2/7Bn p115 CR France398
CARTWRIGHT,George Crellin Capt kia 25-9-15 4 att2RWar p64 CR France423
CARTWRIGHT,John Digby 2Lt kia 9-8-15 DLI p160 MR29
CARTWRIGHT,Joseph Harry T2Lt dow 2-6-18 11 att20LancF p92 CR France84
CARTWRIGHT,Nigel Walter Henry 2Lt kia 21-9-17 20DLI p160 MR30

CARTWRIGHT,Pybus 2Lt kia 4-11-18 YLI &RAF p265
CARTWRIGHT,Ronald William St.George T2Lt kia 26-2-18 GL &16RFC p15 CR France95
CARTWRIGHT,Samuel Francis Lt dow 5-11-18 3 att6Y&L p158 CR France938,Capt
CARTWRIGHT,Stanley TLt kia 17-8-16 8Nhampt attMGC p137&182 CR EAfrica39
CARTY,Bertram Samuel T2Lt kia 21-8-16 12N&D p133 CR France400
CARTY,William George T2Lt kia 25-3-16 13 att10RWar p64 CR France1157
CARUS-WILSON,Trevor.DSO.TD.LtCol dow 27-3-18 1/5DCLI p227 CR France145
CARUTH,James Gordon 2Lt kia 25-9-15 5 att2RIrR p88 MR29
CARUTHERS-LITTLE,Arthur William Palling Capt kia 7/11-8-15 5Dors p123 MR4,7-8-15
CARVER,Basil Armitage 2Lt kia 21-8-16 6Drags p22 CR France68,kld
CARVER,Christian Creswell Lt dow 23-7-17 A83RH&FA p26 CR Belgium11
CARVER,Frank Maitland TLt kia 25-9-15 8Dev p76 MR19
CARVER,George Sholto Douglas 2Lt kia 1-7-16 2Dev p76 MR21
CARVER,Harold Quinan TLt kia 30-7-16 19Lpool p71 CR France294
CARVER,Lionel Henry Liptrah 2Lt kia 26-5-18 1IrGds p52 CR France925
CARVER,Oswald Armitage Capt dow 7-6-15 1/2RE p210 CR Gallipoli1
CARVER,Walter Lionel Capt kia 6-11-17 1/1Hereford p252 CR Palestine1
CARY,Launcelot Sulyarde Robert T2Lt kia 20-7-16 9Dev p76 MR21
CARY,Richard Harry 2Lt kia 1-7-16 9Lond p248 MR21
CARY-ELWES,Douglas George Lt kia 25-11-17 A262RFA p26 CR Belgium10,Dudley
CARY-ELWES,Wilfred Gervase Lt kia 27-11-17 2IrGds p52 MR17
CASE,Albert Robert.MC.TLtACapt kia 26-8-18 1EYorks p83 CR France385
CASE,Charles Henry 2Lt ded 29-9-18 12Manch &RAF p154 CR France376,11Bn
CASE,Elliott Dryden Lt kia 27-7-15 RE att2FC p44&210,kld CR France922
CASE,Frederick Marcus Beck T2Lt kia 10-8-16 7Norf p73 CR France150
CASE,Geoffrey Lt kia 22-3-18 2SLancs p125 MR27
CASE,George Robert Ashburner 2Lt kia 25-9-15 3 att2SLancs p125 MR29
CASE,Harry Ernest 2Lt kia 14-8-15 RE 1FC p210 CR France922
CASE,Harold John Turner.MID Lt ded 17-4-20 46RE CR Egypt9
CASE,John Wyatt T2Lt kia 21-10-16 8Norf p73 MR21
CASE,Joseph A.Lt dow 15-11-18 5 att1RFus p67 CR France146
CASE,Lionel Trevor Elliott TCapt kia 30-11-17 7ESurr p112 MR17
CASEBOURNE,Rowland Telford Lt kia 2-7-16 3Yorks att5WYorks p90 MR21
CASEBY,William Robert Brown.MC.T2Lt kia 25-4-17 RScots att1LancF p53 MR20
CASEMENT,Roger LtCol ded 21-12-17 58RFA p261 CR Eire539
CASEY.E.H.Capt 2-12-19 RIM WRid CR Asia20
CASEY,James Lt kia 30-10-14 1KRRC p149 MR29
CASEY,J.P.N.Capt ded 13-12-18 RAMC attRAF p253 CR Glouc9
CASEY,Michael Francis TCapt kia 19-7-16 9RMunstF p175 CR France223,18-7-16
CASH,Ernest Alfred T2Lt dow 17-6-17 14DLI p160 CR France178
CASH,Geoffrey Edwin Lt kia 27-8-16 6 att8LNLancs p135 CR France744
CASHIN,James 2Lt kia 13-10-17 102RFA p26 CR Belgium19
CASHMORE,Charles 2Lt 2-11-19 MGC Inf CR Lond14
CASHMORE,Edwin 2Lt dow 4-10-18 1/4Leic p220 CR France327
CASLEY,Hugh de Chastelai Lt kia 7-8-15 6Yorks p90 MR4
CASLON,Thomas White 2Lt kia 25-11-15 97RFA p26 CR France922
CASS,Hugh Launcelot 2Lt kia 19-6-15 3SWBord p99 CR Gallipoli6,2Bn
CASS,Leonard Francis TCapt ded 13-12-15 7RSuss p118 CR France260
CASS,William Edward T2Lt kld 4-6-17 GL &RFC p5 CR Kent269
CASSELL,Frank Lt 1-3-21 3RWar CR Surrey55
CASSELLS,Robert Wilson TCapt kia 1-7-16 17HLI p162 CR France293
CASSELS,Frank Lionel TLt kia 20-7-16 RE 222FC p44 CR France453
CASSELS,Hugh Kennedy TCapt kia 25-9-15 8RBerks p138 CR France552
CASSELS,Hugh Lindsay T2Lt kia 8-8-18 1TankCps p188 CR France360
CASSELS,Wilfrid Gardiner.MID TCapt kia 13-7-16 8BordR p116 CR France296
CASSERLY,William Alphonse 2Lt kia 1-3-17 5RMunstF att1RInniskF p175 MR21
CASSIDY,Bernard Matthew.VC.T2Lt kia 28-3-18 2LancF p92 MR20
CASSIDY,Cyril Martin 2Lt dow 17-5-15 1KRRC p149 CR France80
CASSIDY,Michael Bernard 2Lt kia 13-4-18 2IrGds p52 MR32
CASSIE,Leith 2Lt dow 11-12-17 3A&SH p173 CR Belgium11,2Bn
CASSON,Randal Alexander 2Lt kia 26-9-17 2RWelshF p97 CR Belgium126
CASSON,Thomas.MC.2Lt ded 17-5-17 6Ches p222 CR Ches160
CASSON,William.TD.TMaj kia 25-9-15 7Lond p247 CR France550
CASSWELL,Colin Garth Charles William Langlois TMaj kia 14-1-16 8Y&L p158 CR France525
CASSWELL,Eric Denison Seymour Capt kia 7-11-17 6RB att102RFC p5&178 CR France1029

CASSWELL,Frederick Charles T2Lt drd 13-8-15 10Beds att1Ess p85 MR4
CASTBERG,Francis Albert Harboe Capt dow 13-3-15 2Mddx p146 CR France345,Arthur
CASTELLI,Ernest Charles 2Lt kia 9-5-15 13Lond p249 MR32
CASTLE,Cecil Wells Lt kia 3-8-17 2SLancs p125 CR Belgium58,4-8-17
CASTLE,Cottam Harry Hunt Capt ded 30-10-18 6Glouc p225 CR Glouc19
CASTLE,Edward William 2Lt dow 25-8-18 RGA 126SB p38 CR France1170
CASTLE,Errington Edward TLt kld 12-8-17 GL &RFC p5 CR Yorks178
CASTLE,Sidney Batho Lt ded 4-1-16 6Mddx p146 CR France134
CASTLE,Tudor Ralph T2Lt kia 31-8-16 6RWSurr p55 CR France397
CASTLE,Vernon William Blyth Lt kld 15-2-18 RFC 43Wing p15 CR USA169
CASTOR,Richard Henderson.MID LtCol 30-12-20 1MS CR Lond14
CATCHPOLE,Charles Edward.MM.T2Lt kia 12-10-16 7Suff p78 MR21
CATCHPOLE,Thomas John Capt dow 3-11-17 1/5Suff p217 CR Palestine2
CATER,John White Capt kia 9-7-17 9Mddx p236 CR Germany3,dow
CATER,Walter Henry.MC.T2Lt ded 16-8-18 8RSuss p118 CR France145,dow
CATES,Geoffrey T2Lt kia 21-3-18 10 att2DLI p160 MR20
CATES,George Edward.VC.2Lt ded 9-3-17 2RB p178 CR France624
CATFORD,Cyril Herbert Barclay Lt dow 5-10-15 1DLI p160 CR France177
CATHCART,Augustus Ernest Capt kia 14-9-14 KRRC p149 CR France1342
CATHCART,David Andrew 2Lt kia 13-7-16 7RWKent p140 CR France630
CATHCART,Francis John T2Lt kia 3-6-18 A55RFA p26 MR38
CATHCART,Richard Robert 2Lt kia 16-8-17 1RInniskF p104 MR30
CATHER,Geoffrey St.George Shillington.VC.TLt&Adjt kia 2-7-16 9RIrF p171 MR21
CATHERALL,William Cecil 2Lt kia 2-11-17 Nhampt att1/5Norf p137 MR34
CATHIE,Archibald James T2Lt kld 11-7-16 GL &RFC p5 CR Glouc67
CATHIE,H.W.Lt 9-12-15 GL att3NigR CR WAfrica55
CATHRO,James Grant T2Lt kia 24-10-18 1ScotRif p103 CR France 230
CATLEY,James Thatcher Capt kia 12-9-17 HAC attRFA p206 CR Belgium102,Maj
CATLING,Bernard.MC.LtACapt dow 20-10-18 52/15RFA p26 CR France560
CATMUR,Graham Gunn Capt kia 30-6-18 RASC att6RWKent p192 CR France61
CATMUR,Harry Albert Frederick Valentine.MID Lt kia 1-7-16 3RSuss attMGC p118&182 MR21
CATNACH,Thomas Burnett T2Lt dow 19-4-17 26NumbF p60 CR France40,Burney
CATO,Geoffrey Maidens Walter Gaven T2Lt kia 6-11-17 GL &6RFC p5 CR Belgium11
CATON,Florence Missouri Sister 15-7-17 ScotWomensHosp attSerbianArmy CR Greece7
CATON,Frederic William T2Lt kia 28-6-16 RE p44 CR France559
CATON,Norman Newton.MC.Lt kia 21-4-18 C124RFA p26 CR France204
CATOR,Edward Philip Douglas LtACapt kia 11-4-18 RE 69FC p44 MR27
CATT,Archibald William.MC.2LtTLt ded 9-3-18 RWKent att3NigR p140&201 CR EAfrica35 &CR Tanzania1
CATTANACH,John TLt dow 27-7-15 RAMC att9RWar p194 MR4
CATTARNS,Glanvill Richards.MC.TCapt kia 12-2-17 6SLancs p125 MR38
CATTELL,Frank Douglas Bernard T2Lt kld 22-10-17 GL &RFC p5 CR Nhampt74
CATTERALL,Albert Lt kia 21-3-18 7N&D p233 CR France646
CATTERSON-SMITH,Thomas Mervyn Osborne.DSO.Capt dow 10-2-20 IA 1/12Pnrs att3/34Sikhs p274 MR43 &CR Pakistan50A
CATTLE,Eustace Shipstone.MC.2Lt kia 7-7-16 1/5Y&L p238 MR21
CATTLE,James Henry Nightingale Capt dow 1-5-17 D230RFA p207 CR France161
CATTLEY,Cyril Francis.MC.TMaj kia 30-11-17 1 att6EKent p57 MR17
CATTLEY,William.MC.2LtACapt kia 3-5-17 12EYorks p83
CATTO,Robert Kilgour Thom Capt kia 4-11-16 4GordH p241 CR France131
CATTO,Thomas Lt kia 22-8-18 4HLI C'Coy p162 CR France745,23-8-18
CATTO,William Basil T2Lt kia 11-9-16 23NumbF p60 CR France275
CAUDLE,Cedric 2Lt kia 3-5-17 HAC p206 MR20
CAUDWELL,Thord ACapt kia 30-11-17 16Lond p249 CR France1496
CAULFIELD,Algernon Montgomerie.DSO.Maj kia 7-8-15 6BordR p116 MR4,CAULFEILD DCM 9-8-15
CAULFIELD,Gordon 2Lt kia 30-11-17 3 att7SomLI p79 MR17
CAULFIELD,James Crosbie Lt kia 18-11-14 2Manch p154 CR Belgium42
CAULFIELD,St.George Robert Sanderson LtCol ded 29-4-16 RE p262 CR Suff55
CAULFIELD,Toby St.George 2Lt kia 16-6-17 45RFC p5 MR20
CAUNTER,John Charles Ashford Capt kia 28-10-17 1WelshR &60RFC p5&126 MR20
CAUNTER,Robert Lawrence Luscombe T2Lt dow 18-12-16 7Glouc p106 CR Iraq5
CAUSLEY,Frederick George.DCM.2LtACapt kia 31-7-17 7/8KOSB p101 MR29
CAUSTON,Jervoise Purefoy Capt kia 22-4-18 6Hamps p228 CR France250,1Bn

CAUTHERLY,Charles Stewart Lt kia 26-4-18 Herts p252 MR30
CAUTLEY,William Oxenham.DSO.Maj kia 9-5-15 3Suff p78 MR22
CAVANAGH,Bryan George.MIDx2 Capt&QM kld 24-5-19 GL attNigR p254 CR WAfrica54
CAVANAGH,Frank.MC.CaptAMaj dow 26-9-18 88/14RFA p26 CR France327
CAVANAGH,John 2Lt drd 26-2-18 GL RE IWT p190 MR38
CAVANAGH,Patrick Felix Lt kia 12-7-18 6RScots p211 CR France26
CAVAYE,George Ross LtCol 6-9-17 Staff CR Scot237 Ex CamH
CAVE,Arthur Douglas Lt ded 10-11-18 1/2DLI &RAF p160 CR Sussex111
CAVE,Edward Charles.MC.Lt dow 29-8-18 17Lond att56MGC p186&250 CR France84
CAVE,Eric Arthur 2Lt kia 13-2-16 24RFC p2 CR France34
CAVE,Frank 2Lt kia 17-2-17 4 att2SStaffs p122 MR21
CAVE,Joseph T2Lt dow 21-9-17 11WYorks p81&257 CR Belgium11
CAVE,Walter Henry Charles 2Lt kia 16-3-15 3 att1Dors p123 CR Belgium59,Lt 15-3-15
CAVE-PENNY,Evelyn Anthony Lt kia 8-6-18 IA CpsofGuides Inf p274 CR Palestine9
CAVELL,Hubert John TLt dow 22-4-17 11N&D p133 CR Somerset126
CAVENDISH,Hugh Crawford Maj kia 1-8-16 B87RFA p26 CR France453
CAVENDISH,Godfrey Lionel John Capt dow 22-12-14 IA 97Inf att1/9BhopalInf p274 CR France201
CAVENDISH,Lord John Spencer.DSO.Maj kia 20-10-14 1LifeGds p20 CR France924
CAWLEY,Harold Thomas Capt kia 23-9-15 6Manch p236 CR Gallipoli1 seeCR France1231
CAWLEY,John Stephen.MID Maj kia 1-9-14 20Huss 1CavBde p23 CR France1231
CAWLEY,Oswald Capt kia 22-8-18 10KSLI p205 CR France1231
CAWLEY,Robert Lt&QM ded 30-6-18 8RWFus p97 MR66
CAWOOD,William Benjamin Crane Capt ded 24-5-15 RFA p207 MR65
CAWS,Ronald Newton.MC.TCapt&Adjt dow 31-7-17 10Glouc p106 CR France1357
CAWS,Stanley Winther Lt kia 21-9-15 10RFC p1 MR20
CAWSON,George Adrian T2Lt kia 30-11-17 GL &56RFC p5 MR20
CAWSTON,George 2Lt ded 29-10-18 2RWSurr attRAF p55 CR Surrey83
CAY,Albert Jaffray Lt kia 23-4-16 WorcYeo p206 MR34
CAYFORD,George Everett T2Lt kld 16-7-17 GL &RFC p5 CR Essex1
CAYLEY,Francis Digby Edward T2Lt kia 29-9-15 8 att1KRRC p149 CR France423
CAYLEY,Sir George Everard Arthur Capt ded 15-11-17 RDC p253 CR Yorks186 Ex 3RWFus
CAZALET,Edward 2Lt kia 10-9-16 WelshGds p53 CR France394
CAZALET,Ronald de Bode.MC.TCapt ded 8-1-20 GL &TankCps p266 CR Asia81
CEASAR,Charles Patrick TLt kia 14-7-16 7KSLI p144 MR21,CAESAR
CECIL,Charles 2Lt kia 16-7-16 2/4RBerks p234 CR France1887
CECIL,George Edward 2Lt kia 13-9-14 4GrenGds 4Coy p49 CR France1108,1-9-14
CECIL,Rotherham Bagshawe 2lt kia 1-7-16 1/5N&D p232 MR21
CECIL,Rupert Edward Gascoyne 2LtTLt kia 11-7-15 4 att1Beds p85
CECIL,William Amherst.Hon.Capt kia 16-9-14 2GrenGds p49 CR France1112
CEMERY,Arthur Frank.MID Capt kia 19-7-17 1EYorks p83 CR France591
CENTENO,Leon 2Lt ded 6-7-16 4Suff p217 CR Suff55
CESARI,Sydney Fraser McAlpine Capt kia 3-10-15 RAMC att6FA p194 CR France80 3-9-15
CHADDOCK,John Glover 2Lt kia 30-3-18 RFA att86ArmyBdeSigSect RE p26 MR20
CHADS,Herbert Charles Lt dow 6-1-15 1NStaffs p156 CR France681
CHADWICK,Arthur Clarkson Capt&Adjt kia 29-10-15 1/4YLI p235 CR Belgium23
CHADWICK,Douglas Gordon Lt dow 20-7-16 O&BLI 2/1BucksBn p231 CR France345
CHADWICK,Edward Neale 2Lt kia 4-10-17 3SfthH p164 MR30
CHADWICK,Francis Joseph T2Lt kia 12-10-16 2Beds p85 MR21
CHADWICK,Frederick James.MID Capt dow 13-4-15 IA 104Rif p274 CR Iraq6
CHADWICK,James Henry.DSO.TLtCol kia 4-5-17 24Manch p154 CR France614
CHADWICK,John 2Lt kia 2-11-18 8LancF p221 CR France933
CHADWICK,John Collinge 2Lt kia 25-3-17 1/8WYorks p219 CR France1887
CHADWICK,Mabel Elizabeth Nurse ded 15-10-15 VAD 17GH CR Egypt3
CHADWICK,Norman Stuart T2Lt kia 6-11-17 5SLancs att12SomLI p125 CR Palestine1,dow
CHADWICK,Percival Miller Lt dow 22-9-18 RE 459FC p210 CR France835
CHADWICK,Richard Markham Lt dow 12-5-15 RGA 11SB p38 CR France80,2Lt kia 13-5-15
CHADWICK,R.M.Lt ded 17-3-16 2KAR attRhodesiaR p268
CHADWICK,W.E.A.VenArchdeacon 30-9-17 EAChapDept CR EAfrica38& CRTanzania1

CHAFFEY,Charles Russell T2Lt dow 10-3-17 23Manch p154 CR France692
CHAFFEY,Henry Percival 2Lt kia 10-8-17 HAC p206 MR29
CHAIZE,Jean Edward Gabriel T2Lt dow 18-8-17 RSuss att13Bn p118 CR France102
CHALAND,Maurice Leshe.MC.TLt dow 1-12-17 7Norf p73 CR France398
CHALCRAFT,George Arthur Lt dow 7-5-15 4WYorks att2WRid p81 CR Belgium35,5-5-15
CHALK,Theodore Wilson 2Lt kia 3-7-16 3 att7Suff p78 MR21
CHALKER,Eric.MID Lt kia 19-7-16 46/39RFA p26 MR21
CHALKLEY,Francis Henry.MBE.Maj ded 17-8-18 RAOC p267
CHALKLEY,Thomas Henry T2Lt kia 29-8-18 56MGC Inf p182 CR France593
CHALLEN,Christopher Frank.MID Capt dow 13-11-18 1/7Mddx p235 CR Lond14
CHALLENER,Arthur Cecil Lt kia 25-9-16 9Lpool p216 CR France277
CHALLENER,Percival Crawley T2Lt kia 12-12-17 13Lpool p71 CR France563
CHALLENOR,Norman Bowen Capt kia 31-7-15 3 att2RBerks p138 CR France349
CHALLINER,William Henry 2Lt dow 13-8-16 1/9Lpool p216 CR France141
CHALLINOR,Elizabeth Annie SNurse ded 26-10-18 QAIMNS CR Surrey118
CHALLINOR,Frederick William 2Lt kia 22-5-17 156RGA p38 CR France1186
CHALLIS,Alfred Edward HonLt ded 9-3-19 MGC Inf p266 CR Essex1
CHALLIS,Arthur Bracebridge.TD.Maj kia 21-9-18 RGA 133SB p209 CR France687
CHALLIS,Ivor James 2Lt kia 14-4-18 1/2 att11LancF p92 CR France298
CHALLIS,Thomas Archie.MC.2Lt ded 3-11-18 13TankCps p188
CHALLIS,Thomas Holt 2Lt dow 28-4-17 RGA 256SB p38 CR France113,27-4-17
CHALLIS,William Guy Fawcett TLt kia 13-7-16 3 att15Hamps p120 CR Belgium54,2Lt
CHALLONER,Alan Crawhall 2Lt kia 30-7-15 6DCLI p114 CR Belgium453
CHALLONER,Thomas Bennet Capt 3-11-15 RASC CR Lond29
CHALLONER,Thomas Rex.MC.Lt dow 25-7-16 RE 1FC p210 CR France102
CHALMERS,Archibald Douglas TLt ded 9-12-18 1A&SH p173 CR Greece9
CHALMERS,Arthur Lakes 2Lt kia 23-9-16 7Lpool p215 CR France401 Jakes
CHALMERS,David TLtACapt kia 18-9-18 GL 6Nhampt p137 CR France511
CHALMERS,Francis 2Lt kia 25-9-16 3 att1EYorks p83 MR21
CHALMERS,Henry Stewart LtACapt dow 29-9-17 C295RFA p207 CR Belgium11
CHALMERS,James.MC.DCM.TCaptAMaj kia 23-3-18 5RScots attMGC p187&211 MR27
CHALMERS,James Stewart T2Lt dow 7-10-16 12A&SH att1CamH p173 CR Scot387
CHALMERS,John Alexander T2Lt ded 21-10-18 LabCps 1032Coy p254 CR Syria2
CHALMERS,John Binny 2Lt ded 8-10-14 RFA p269 CR Wilts2 &CR Devon207
CHALMERS,John Cyril.MM.T2Lt kia 15-10-16 20NumbF p60 CR France275
CHALMERS,John Hunter.MID Capt&Adjt dow 25-3-18 5 att7A&SH p243 CR France300
CHALMERS,John James 2Lt ded 20-11-18 PoW 5GordH p242 CR Germany3,Lt
CHALMERS,John Leshe.MC.LtACapt kia 27-3-18 5RIrF p171 MR27
CHALMERS,John Robert Thornburn T2Lt kia 1-7-16 8SomLI p79 MR21
CHALMERS,John Stuart Maj kia 17-4-18 9HLI p240 MR32
CHALMERS,Ralph Capt kia 10-5-15 2Suff p78 MR29,8-5-15
CHALMERS,Robert Lt dow 25-5-15 15Lond p249 CR France98,26-5-15
CHALMERS,William Hamish 2Lt kia 13-4-16 IARO att19Punjabis p274 MR61
CHALONER,Richard Godolphin Hume Capt ded 3-4-17 3Wilts p152 CR France8
CHAMBERLAIN,Arthur 2Lt ded 11-2-19 5NStaffs p238
CHAMBERLAIN,Cyril John TLt kia 6-10-17 1RB p178 MR30,7-10-17
CHAMBERLAIN,Eric Dunstan 2Lt kia 30-11-17 att1/5LNLancs p135 MR17
CHAMBERLAIN,George Herbert T2Lt kia 4-10-16 14Ches p95 CR France1182,3-10-16
CHAMBERLAIN,James Russell Lt kld 2-6-16 RFC p2 CR Canada1688,Chamberlin
CHAMBERLAIN,John.MC.Capt kia 13-5-17 3SWBord att1WelshR p99 CR Belgium1,14-5-17 att14
CHAMBERLAIN,John Harold 2Lt dow 21-11-15 1Lond p245 CR France285
CHAMBERLAIN,John Robert William 2Lt kia 13-9-18 20 att2/10Lond p251 CR France511,CHAMBERLIN Capt
CHAMBERLAIN,Norman Gwynne Lt kia 1-12-17 1GrenGds p49 CR France439
CHAMBERLAIN,Rupert Maurice 2Lt dow 20-5-18 2ScotGds p52 CR France120
CHAMBERLAYNE,Arthur Lt dow 10-4-17 16LancF p92
CHAMBERLAYNE,Athelstone LtCol kia 14-1-20 IA 1Lancers Cmdg2/76Punjabis p274 MR43
CHAMBERLAYNE,Thomas Edmund Onslow TLt kia 18-8-16 73RFA p26 CR France397
CHAMBERLIN,Eric Valentine George 2Lt kia 31-12-17 RH&FA179ArmyBde p26 CR France905
CHAMBERLIN,Hugh Frederick Whitmore 2Lt kia 15-10-16 2DLI p160 MR21,CHAMBERLAIN

CHAMBERLIN,J.R.W. see CHAMBERLAIN,J.R.W.
CHAMBERS,Alfred Ernest.MC.TLt dow 29-10-18 26RFus p67 CR Belgium158
CHAMBERS,Anthony Gerald 2Lt kia 1-7-16 4Mddx p146 CR France267
CHAMBERS,Arthur Joseph Ferguson 2Lt dow 11-8-16 1/1WarYeo p205 CR Egypt2
CHAMBERS,B.K.ChEngr 19-6-17 RIM CR Iraq5
CHAMBERS,Charles Colhoun.MC.Capt kia 10-7-16 RGA 125B p38 CR France399
CHAMBERS,Cleveland Hugh 2Lt kia 3-9-16 8RBerks p138 MR21 &CR France390
CHAMBERS,C.P.E 2Lt 26-3-17 EgyptLabCps CR Egypt1
CHAMBERS,David Macdonald TCapt kia 20-2-17 12DLI p160 CR Belgium127
CHAMBERS,Edward Chandos Elliot T2Lt kia 1-7-16 19LancF A'Coy p92 CR France296
CHAMBERS,George Alfred 2Lt kia 22-8-17 1 att6SomLI p79 MR30
CHAMBERS,Henry 2Lt dow 11-8-18 1/1Camb p245 CR France69
CHAMBERS,James Edward 2Lt dow 1-10-16 4 att1WessexRFA p208 CR France177
CHAMBERS,John Paul 2Lt dow 4-4-17 4Ess p232 CR France80
CHAMBERS,L.E.AssSurg 26-8-21 IMD MR65
CHAMBERS,Norman Archibald 2Lt dow 17-8-16 3 att1Nhampt p137 CR France74
CHAMBERS,Percival Arthur T2Lt dow 10-4-16 10 att9RWar p64 CR Iraq5,6-4-16 11 att9
CHAMBERS,Percy Wilmot TCapt dow PoW 13-8-17 GL &22RFC p6 CR France1276
CHAMBERS,Philip Carlisle 2Lt kia 22-3-18 2TankCps p188 MR27
CHAMBERS,Robert SubCdr ded 23-7-22 IA IndOrdDept p274
CHAMBERS,Robert Avalon Montagu 2Lt dow 15-10-15 3Hamps att1Glouc p120 CR France88
CHAMBERS,Robert Seymour Bennet TLtACapt kia 24-12-17 8KRRC p149 CR Belgium126
CHAMBERS,Stanley Walter Graham Capt kia 24-11-17 11RWar p64 CR Belgium111
CHAMBERS,Stewart Capt kld 15-11-20 Lpool MR40
CHAMBERS,Wilfrid John TLt kia 18-8-16 11 att13ESurr p112 CR France550
CHAMBERS,William Trant.MID Maj dow 2-6-15 RFA 1DivHQ p26 CR France98
CHAMBERS,William Geoffrey Capt kia 15-5-18 1/2Lincs &49RAF p74 MR20
CHAMBERS-HUNTER,Charles Allardyce Jopp 2Lt kia 1-4-16 3 att1GordH p166 MR29
CHAMEN,Harold Ashcombe Lt dow 1-8-16 2Beds p85 CR France23
CHAMIER,Cyril Kinnaird Lt kia 23-4-15 Y&L p158 MR29
CHAMP,Leonard Lt ded 19-3-18 7Ess p232
CHAMPION,Eric Osbourne T2Lt kia 10-6-17 11SLancs C'Coy p125 CR Belgium165,11-6-17
CHAMPION,Leonard John Lt dow 4-10-18 NRhodPolice CR Tanzania1
CHAMPION,Reginald James Lt dow 18-7-17 1ScotGds attTMB p52 CR Belgium12,kia
CHAMPION,Rowland Laughton 2Lt kia 17-3-17 20Lond p251 CR Belgium167,Roland
CHAMPION,Sydney George TLt dow PoW 17-3-17 5RFus att2KAR p67&268 MR52
CHAMPION DE CRESPIGNY,Claude Norman Lt kia 1-9-14 2DragGds p20 CR Essex106
CHAMNEY,Harold D'Arcy 2Lt dow PoW 29-4-18 12Yorks p90 CR Germany3
CHAMPNEYS,John Dalrymple Lt dow 22-11-15 6Leic p87 CR France283
CHANCE,Albert Henry 2Lt kia 22-3-18 2/7RWar p214 MR27
CHANCE,Andrew Ferguson Capt kia 3-10-15 B85RFA p26 CR France727
CHANCE,Edward Seton CaptBtMaj kia 29-5-18 2DragGds att6Leic p20 MR18
CHANCE,Eric Godwin T2Lt kia 19-1-18 28RFC p15 CR Italy48
CHANCE,Eustace George St.Clair 2Lt kia 27-9-18 2CldGds p51 CR France1497
CHANCE,Frank Meryon 2Lt kia 25/26-5-15 24Lond p252 MR22
CHANCE,Guy Ogden de Peyster Lt kia 19-10-14 1RWelshF p97 MR29
CHANCELLOR,Geoffrey Ellis 2Lt kia 9-7-16 3RWSurr attRFC p2&55 CR France134,Lt
CHANCELLOR,Richard Albert Beresford TCapt dow 24-12-16 7RBerks p138 CR Greece1
CHANDLER,Cecil William.MC.TCapt kia 30-3-18 8RMunstF p175 CR France401
CHANDLER,Charles Robert T2Lt kia 29-9-15 2ESurr p112 CR France423
CHANDLER,Clive 2Lt kia 17-11-14 1Wilts p152 MR29
CHANDLER,Dorothy Maud Sister 15-11-17 QAIMNS CR Surrey91
CHANDLER,Edwin Spencer T2Lt kia 14-2-16 10N&D p133 MR29
CHANDLER,Eric Oatey 2Lt kia 11-4-18 RE 510FC p210 MR32
CHANDLER,Henry Leonard T2Lt kld 30-10-17 RFC p6 CR Lond14
CHANDLER,J.W.Lt 3-5-20 1Dev CR Devon1
CHANDLER,James Cook T2Lt kia 11-7-16 17 att11Ches p95 CR France296,12-7-16
CHANDLER,John.MC.2Lt kia 2-10-16 19Lond p250 MR21

CHANEY,Henry Edward.OBE.MIDx2 TMaj ded 27-2-19 LancF &RAF p263 CR Surrey150
CHANING-PEARCE,Wilfred Thomas.MC.TCapt kia 1-10-17 RAMC att18Lpool p194 CR Belgium75
CHANT,Thomas Roy Lt ded 7-11-18 13Lond p269 CR Herts110
CHANTRILL,Reginald Percy TLt kia 26-10-17 78RFA p26 CR Belgium25
CHAPLIN,Arthur Hugh Bates Maj dow 21-5-17 1/1Camb p244 CR Camb39,Capt
CHAPLIN,Aubrey Fletcher Lt kia 10-4-17 NhamtYeo p204 CR France418
CHAPLIN,Charles Montague 2Lt kia 26-9-17 1Camb p245 MR30
CHAPLIN,Charles Slingsby LtCol kia 30-7-15 9KRRC p149 MR29
CHAPLIN,Frederick Hardress Maj ded 27-5-16 RGA 154HB p38&209 CR Belgium6
CHAPLIN,Herbert 2Lt kia 19-10-17 4Suff &RFC p217 MR20
CHAPLIN,Humphrey Marmaduke Lt kia 11-5-15 3 att1Ches p95 MR29,Henry
CHAPLIN,Rowland Edward Ernest T2Lt kia 22-4-17 RE 7FC p44 CR France1185
CHAPLIN,Sydney Stranger Lt kia 21-3-18 2/5Manch p236 MR27
CHAPLYN,Cyril Edward T2Lt kia 26-4-18 10Ess p131 MR27
CHAPMAN,Albert Charles TCapt kia 20-8-16 RFA 29TrMortSchl p26 CR France701
CHAPMAN,Alfred John T2Lt ded 18-9-17 GL &41RFC p6 CR France660,kia
CHAPMAN,Alfred Reginald Lt kia 2-12-17 6MGC Inf p182 CR France529
CHAPMAN,Alfred Reginald Beeves Lt kia 6-6-16 1/5LNLancs p234 CR France504,Bewes
CHAPMAN,Alister Hillyar Darby Capt kia 27-9-15 1Drags p21 CR France178
CHAPMAN,Arthur Allsop Lt kia 25-4-17 7 att9WRid p227 CR France531
CHAPMAN,Arthur Donald 2Lt kia 1-7-16 1/5NStaffs p238 MR21
CHAPMAN,Arthur Frederick 2Lt kia 25-9-16 2ScotGds p52 CR France513
CHAPMAN,Arthur Gerald TLt ded 5-5-17 29Mddx p146 CR Essex81 Ex 5Lancs
CHAPMAN,Arthur Thomas Capt kia 26-4-15 3ESurr att1Hamps p112 CR Belgium152
CHAPMAN,Ben Fletcher T2Lt kia 19-4-17 RGA 1MtnBty Singapore p38 CR Palestine8
CHAPMAN,Bertie Robert Wyand 2Lt dow 13-6-18 1/4SLancs p230 CR France40
CHAPMAN,Charles Dudley T2Lt kld 19-1-18 RFC p15
CHAPMAN,Charles George.MID TLt dow 17-4-16 RE p44 MR38
CHAPMAN,Charles Lancelot.MC.Maj dow 22-8-17 D173RFA p206 CR Belgium11
CHAPMAN,Charles Meredith Bouverie.MC.LtTMaj dow 1-10-17 EKent att29RFC p6&57 CR Belgium18
CHAPMAN,Claude Bertram T2Lt kia 18-9-18 2Y&L p158 CR France1701
CHAPMAN,David Archibald James 2Lt kia 15-9-16 2ScotGds p52 MR21
CHAPMAN,David Markwell TLt kia 25-3-18 3RB p178 MR27
CHAPMAN,Donald John Stuart T2Lt dow 13-7-16 8RFus p67 CR France51
CHAPMAN,Douglas Collier Lt kia 20-10-18 RE 429FC p210 CR France1387
CHAPMAN,Edward Henry TLtCol kia 7-8-15 6Yorks p90 CR Gallipoli4
CHAPMAN,Edward Wynne Lt dow 17-11-14 3DragGds p21 CR Belgium57
CHAPMAN,Ernest Herbert Stuart Maj died 1-11-18 IA 31Lancers p275,Earnest CR Asia82
CHAPMAN,Frank Edward SubCdr ded 30-3-19 IA MilWorksServ CR Surrey1
CHAPMAN,Frank Reginald 2Lt dow 25-9-15 18Lond p250 CR France178,Lt
CHAPMAN,Fred 2Lt kia 22-8-18 1/23Lond p245 CR France396
CHAPMAN,Frederick Alan TLt dow 29-5-18 13Manch att1Worc p154 CR France1693 &CR France34
CHAPMAN,Fred Tarlington Lt dow 18-12-17 C173RFA p207 CR France518
CHAPMAN,Geoffrey Arthur T2Lt kia 28-3-16 11RScots p53 CR Belgium71
CHAPMAN,George Edwin Lt dow 27-9-16 5Yorks attMGC p187&221 CR France105
CHAPMAN,George Martin Lt kia 13-5-15 RAMC p194 CR Belgium45,Capt
CHAPMAN,Gordon Humphrey Capt kia 9-3-16 IA 53Sikhs p275 CR Iraq5,dow
CHAPMAN,H.F.2Lt 30-5-17 Leic CR Leics64
CHAPMAN,Henry Ernest.MC.Capt dow 22-3-18 G/17RHA p26 MR27
CHAPMAN,Henry James.MC.T2Lt kia 8-8-18 7RWKent p140 CR France247
CHAPMAN,Henry Randal 2Lt kia or dow 9-10-17 10Manch p237 MR30,Randall
CHAPMAN,Henry Reynolds Maj kia 27-6-15 10DLI p160 MR29,Harry
CHAPMAN,Herbert Foster.DCM.2LtTLt dow 29-5-15 1RWFus p97 CR France134
CHAPMAN,John Capt dow 30-5-17 5Leic p220
CHAPMAN,John TCapt kia 16-7-16 21Manch p154 CR France397,14-7-16
CHAPMAN,John Percy Lt kia 21-7-16 O&BLI 1/1BucksBn p231 MR21
CHAPMAN,Joseph Robert T2Lt kia 8-4-17 5KSLI p144 CR France581,9-4-17
CHAPMAN,Lawrence Vaughan TLt kia 25-9-15 2RB p178 MR32
CHAPMAN,Laurence Oxley 2Lt kia 31-7-17 5 att3RB p178 MR29
CHAPMAN,Leonard T2Lt dow 2-9-18 5RBerks p138 CR France145
CHAPMAN,Lewis Carlton T2Lt ded 16-4-17 GL &60RFC p6 MR20

CHAPMAN,Marion Dorothy Miss ded 10-8-18 VAD att17GH p200 CR Egypt1
CHAPMAN,Michael.MC.Lt kia 12-4-18 4GrenGds p49 MR32
CHAPMAN,Montague Gerald Herbert T2Lt kia 14-8-17 10RB p178 CR Belgium83,Lt
CHAPMAN,Perceval Christian Capt dow 1-5-15 IA RFA 26MtnBty p26 CR Egypt6
CHAPMAN,Raleigh George Aubrey Lt ded 1-3-19 RASC 7DivTrain p192 CR Italy59
CHAPMAN,Samuel Eric 2Lt kia 25-9-15 7CamH p167 MR19
CHAPMAN,Sidney George 2Lt dow 28-9-16 8 att7SStaffs p122 CR France74
CHAPMAN,Sydney Victor T2Lt kia 11-6-17 8NumbF p60 CR Belgium168
CHAPMAN,Theodore Victor.MC.LtACapt kia 12-5-17 2RWSurr p55 MR20
CHAPMAN,Wilfred Hubert TCapt kia 7-8-15 6Yorks p90 CR Gallipoli4
CHAPMAN,William Henry T2Lt kia 20-9-17 1/2 att11RB p178 MR30
CHAPMAN,William James 2Lt kia 26-3-18 1Camb p245 MR27
CHAPMAN,William Wetheral Lt kia 7-10-17 EKent attRFC p6&57 CR France1050
CHAPPEL,William Elden Lt kld 4-4-17 2/4DCLI attRFC p226 CR Egypt15
CHAPPELL,Edwin Francis T2Lt kia 3-2-16 RE 3FC p44 CR France423
CHAPPELL,Ernest Roland 2Lt dow 30-9-18 RGA C BtyAA p38 CR France106,Lt
CHAPPELL,Francis Harold T2Lt kia 3-9-16 16N&D p133 MR21
CHAPPELL,George Henry Lt ded 20-12-19 RASC p267 CR Mddx39
CHAPPELL,Stanley Lt kld 2-3-18 RFC p15
CHAPPLE,James Walter 2Lt dow 31-7-17 1GrenGds p49 CR Belgium12
CHAPPLE,Reginald Charles 2Lt kia 12-4-18 4DCLI p227 MR32
CHAPPY,Athol Isdale 2Lt kia 24-9-18 3 att11Ess p131 CR France835
CHARD,Robert Alexander Farmer TCapt kia 8-7-16 8RFus p67 MR21
CHARD,Thomas Norman T2Lt kia 23-4-17 1DCLI p114 MR20
CHARLES,Albert 2Lt kia 1-7-16 1/7N&D p233 MR21
CHARLES,Angus Alan Macgregor.MID Capt kia 20-12-14 73RFA p26 CR France571
CHARLES,B.S.2Lt ded 7-12-18 GL &RAF p190
CHARLES,Cecil Arthur 2Lt dow 22-9-18 12Lond p248 CR France194
CHARLES,George Harold 2Lt kia 31-10-18 14RWFus p97 CR France1478
CHARLES,James Arthur Mernman 2Lt dow 10-2-15 KSLI p144 CR Nhampt164
CHARLES,John James Percival.MC.TCapt ded 6-10-17 RAMC att1/1Herts p194 CR France 102
CHARLES,Leslie Stafford Capt ded 30-7-16 6Worc &60RFC p2&108 CR France528
CHARLESTON,Ebenezer T2Lt kia 20-9-17 KRRC att11Bn p149 MR30
CHARLESTON,Frederick 2LtTLt dow 7-7-15 2LancF p92 CR Belgium1
CHARLESWORTH,Alick Thomas Bentall 2Lt kld 30-5-17 GL &RFC p6 CR Lincs67,dedacc
CHARLESWORTH,Frederick T2Lt ded 1-2-19 2WRid p264 CR Yorks635,Lt
CHARLESWORTH,Frederick Raymond Capt dow 19-9-18 25RWFus p204 CR France194
CHARLESWORTH,George Lt kia 3-5-17 6WYorks p218 MR20
CHARLESWORTH,George Vernon 2Lt kia 28-9-18 6WRid p227 CR France358
CHARLESWORTH,Herbert T2Lt kia 26-10-17 91MGC Inf p182 CR Belgium112
CHARLESWORTH,John Stobart Maj 10-11-18 12YLI CR Yorks274
CHARLESWORTH,Reginald.MC.Capt dow 9-4-18 7Mddx p235 CR France185
CHARLESWORTH,Thomas Stephens T2Lt dow 10-7-16 25NumbF p60 CR France267
CHARLESWORTH,Walter Alexander T2Lt kia 7-2-17 3 att1Leic p87 CR France423
CHARLESWORTH,William Henry TMaj kia 15-9-16 6YLI p142 CR France402
CHARLEWOOD,William Henry TCapt dow 22-7-16 6NumbF p213 CR France285
CHARLTON,Arthur Nesbit.MC.LtTCapt kia 30-11-17 7Norf p73 MR17
CHARLTON,Bernard Hedley.MC.LtCol kia 22-3-18 4Yorks p220 CR France528
CHARLTON,Brian Lt kia 27-10-18 TankCps att82RAF p188 CR Belgium159
CHARLTON,Douglas Ferrier Lt kia 24-3-18 6DLI p239 CR France446,23-3-18
CHARLTON,Ernest Henry 2Lt kia 31-3-18 1/4EYorks p219 MR27
CHARLTON,Frank Tysor 2Lt dow 3-10-18 3SLancs attY55TMB p125 CR France98,Tysoe 1/5Bn
CHARLTON,George Fenwick Hedley.MID Capt kia 6-10-16 10SWBord p99 CR Belgium167
CHARLTON,Hugh Vaughan 2Lt kia 24-6-16 7NumbF p214 CR Belgium60
CHARLTON,John 2Lt kia 2-9-18 3 att1RScotF A'Coy p94 CR France433,Lt
CHARLTON,John Lawther 2Lt dow 15-9-18 18MGC p182 CR France145
CHARLTON,John Macfarlan TCapt kia 1-7-16 21NumbF p60 MR21
CHARLTON,Norman Ewart T2Lt kia 15-6-18 11NumbF p60 CR Italy3
CHARLTON,Ralph Turnbull 2Lt kia 20-9-17 20DLI p160 MR30,21-9-17 Ex 6NumbF
CHARLTON,Robert.MC.TCapt dow 5-10-17 11 att7SStaffs p122 CR Belgium16
CHARLTON,Robert Arthur Lt kia 21-3-18 3 att1WYorks p81 MR20
CHARLTON,St.John Alan Lt kia 26-10-14 4 att1Beds p85 CR France924

CHARLTON,William 2Lt kia 25-3-18 4 att2/5ELancs p226 MR27
CHARLTON,William Ferner 2Lt kia 18-9-16 6DLI p239 CR France239
CHARLTON,William Godfrey TLt kia 26-8-18 15DLI p160 CR France385
CHARLWOOD,William Roger T2Lt kia 18-7-17 1RWSurr p55 CR France421,6Bn
CHARMAN,Arthur Leonard Charles Lt 15-2-21 KentCycBn CR War7
CHARMAN,John Ewart 2Lt dow 25-9-17 1/4RSuss p228 CR Belgium140
CHARRIER,Paul Alfred Maj kia 27-8-14 2RMunstF p175 CR France1751
CHARRINGTON,Arthur Craven Capt dow 21-10-14 1Drags p21 CR Belgium57,20-10-14
CHARRINGTON,Edwin Milward Capt kia 13-11-16 3 att13Ess p131 MR21
CHARSLEY,Reginald Burton TMaj kia 30-11-17 12Lpool p71 MR17
CHART,Eric Nye Lt kia 25-9-16 1WYorks p81 MR21 CR France390
CHARTERIS,Ivo Alan.Hon.2Lt kia 17-10-15 GrenGds att1Bn SR p49 CR France257,Yeo
CHARTERIS,Thomas TCapt kia 27-9-15 10Yorks p90 MR19,26-9-15
CHASE,Archibald Alderman.DSO.Capt&BtMaj dow 11-3-17 RE attRSuss p44 CR France251
CHASE,Harold Charles 2Lt kia 8-6-17 4Lincs p217 MR20
CHASE,Philip Hugh.MID T2Lt dow 1-7-16 12Mddx p146 CR France66
CHATHAM,George Henry 2Lt kia 23-11-16 10RFus p67 MR21
CHATTAWAY,Philip Spencer 2Lt kia 14-10-16 6Ches p222 CR France293
CHATTERIS,Tom Brodie TCapt kia 9-8-15 N&D att2Bn p133 MR29
CHATTERLEY,D.R.Capt ded 7-9-14 RAVC p269
CHATTERTON,Alfred Henry Goodbarne Lt ded 21-7-17 215RFA p207 CR Iraq8
CHATTERTON,Arthur Measures T2Lt kld 30-7-17 GL &RFC p6 CR Wilts28
CHATTERTON,Harold Montagu Newnham T2Lt dow 18-6-16 9RWSurr p55 CR France285
CHATTERTON,Roden Latham Capt kia 28-3-18 Leinst attRFC p15&174 CR Kent205,kldacc 29-3-18
CHATTOCK,Reginald Harvey 2Lt kia 13-3-16 4Glouc p225 CR France643
CHAUDHURY,S.R.Capt 22-3-20 IMS MR43
CHAVASSE,Aidan Lt kia 4-7-17 17Lpool p71 MR29
CHAVASSE,Arthur Ryland TCapt ded 12-3-16 RAMC p194 CR France85
CHAVASSE,Noel Godfrey.VC&Bar.DSO.MC.Capt dow 4-8-17 RAMC att10Lpool p253 CR Belgium7
CHAVASSE,Percy Lt kia 8-10-18 IARO &59RAF p275 MR20
CHAVE,John Haydon TLt dow 15-4-18 19MGC p182 CR Belgium21
CHAVENTRE,Alfred 2Lt kia 1-9-18 126A HAC p26 CR France421,2A/126RFA
CHAWNER,Alain Percy Mark.MID 2Lt kia 20-10-16 13Ess p131 CR France400,Lt 21-10-16 3 att1Bn
CHAWNER,Meredith Andre Capt kia 21-5-17 2Ess p131 CR France311
CHAWORTH-MUSTERS,Patricius George Lt dow 12-1-15 1KRRC p149CR France80,11-1-15
CHAWORTH-MUSTERS,Philip Mundy.MC.LtTCapt kia 18-7-17 25RFA p26 CR Belgium5
CHAWORTH-MUSTERS,Robert.MC.Capt ded 10-10-18 12KRRC att3MuskCamp p149 CR Notts2
CHAWORTH-MUSTERS,Roger Michael 2Lt kia 7-5-17 Leic &56RFC p6&87 MR20
CHAYTOR,Alban Kingsford 2Lt dow 26-5-15 6 att3Worc p108 CR Belgium21
CHAYTOR,Hugh Cleivaux Capt kia 31-10-14 IA 26Cav att11Huss p275
CHEAPE,John de Caerick TLt kia 3-9-16 8 att1RSuss p118 CR France701,Carnch
CHEAPE,Leslie St.Clair Capt&adjt kia 23-4-16 1DragGds attWorcYeo p20 MR34
CHEATLE,Charles Chesterfield 2Lt kia 5-5-17 GL.&23RFC p6 MR20
CHEATLE,Walter John North Lt kia 25-4-15 1KOSB p101 CR Gallipoli6,26-4-15
CHECKLAND,Montmorency Beaumont Lt kia 16-8-17 WSomYeo p205
CHEERS,Donald Heriot Anson 2Lt kldacc 17-4-18 3ESurr attRAF p112 CR Scot235
CHEERS,Ronald Anson Vlascow 2Lt kia 27-9-15 3 att4SLancs p125 CR Belgium28,Vlassow 25-9-15
CHEESBROUGH,Harold T2Lt kia 4-9-18 WYorks att10EYorks p81 CR France262
CHEESE,Ernest Velmont TLt ded 30-7-16 ArmyPayDept p200 CR France145
CHEESE,William Gerard Chap4Cl ded 7-11-18 RAChDept att8Lincs p199 CR France146
CHEESEMAN,Anthony Alfred TLt kia 5-5-17 7EKent p57 MR20
CHEESMAN,Arthur Edwin Capt ded 26-9-16 1/5EKent p213 CR Iraq5
CHEESMAN,George Leonard TLt kia 10-8-15 10Hamps p170 MR4
CHEESMAN,John Frederick 2Lt kld 25-1-18 RFC p15 CR Suff83
CHEETHAM,Alan Humphrey Lt kia 16-12-16 2WRid p115 MR21
CHEETHAM,Charles Joseph LtCol ded 9-12-16 63RegDistRectgOff CR Lancs416
CHEETHAM,Frederick George Charles Beresford Lt ded 27-12-19 RH&FA p261
CHEETHAM,Herbert Lt kia 9-10-17 8WYorks att146TMB p219 CR Belgium125,1/6Bn
CHEETHAM,William Lt ded 6-2-20 RE p269 CR Lancs43

CHELL,Harold TLt dow 10-8-15 8RFus p67 CR France285
CHELLEW,John Maurice 2Lt dow 26-5-17 RGA 26SB p38 CR France512
CHENE,Charles Leslie 2Lt dow 21-4-18 5RScots p211 CR Germany4,11Bn
CHENE,Henry Maj kia 10-7-17 189RFA p206 CR Belgium29,Harry
CHENEVIX-TRENCH,Francis Maxwell Maj kia 31-10-14 RFA p26 CR Belgium58 2DivStaff
CHEPMELL,John Dobree Lt kia 10-4-18 2 att14RWar p64 MR32
CHEPMELL,William Dobree TLt kia 12-4-17 10RSuss attTMB p118 CR France480,9Bn
CHERRY,Alfred Douglas TLtACapt kia 4-4-17 Dors attSomLI p123 CR France162
CHESHIRE,Edgar Murray 2Lt kld 6-3-18 RFC p15 CR Surrey15
CHESHIRE,Eric Corveroy Lt kia 3-5-17 4RFus p67 MR20
CHESHIRE,Raymond Russell T2Lt kia 4-10-17 1/8RWar p64 MR30
CHESHIRE,William Robert T2Lt kia 1-7-16 1Ess p131 CR France220
CHESNEY,Charles Cornwallis Lt kia 24-11-15 IARO att117Mahrattas p275 MR38,22-11-15
CHESNEY,H.F.CMG.Col 21-3-20 RE CR Devon73
CHESTER,Greville Arthur Bagot 2Lt kia 13-10-14 3NStaffs p156 CR France193
CHESTER,Harry Keppel Capt dow 28-3-17 1/5Ess p232 CR Palestine2
CHESTER,James Leslie TLt kld 6-7-15 1/9Lpool p216 CR France114
CHESTER,Lewis Charles Bagot 2Lt kia 4-4-18 15LancF p92 MR20
CHESTER-MASTER,Richard Chester.DSO&Bar.BtMajTLtCol kia 30-8-17 13KRRC p149 CR Belgium183
CHESTERS,John Richards TLt kia 15-9-16 12ESurr p112 MR21
CHESTERTON,Frank Sidney 2Lt dow 11-11-16 C92RFA p26 CR France105
CHESTNUT,John Albon Lt dow 20-12-15 RFA 6DAC p26 CR France40,2t
CHETHAM-STRODE,Edward Randall Capt kia 1-10-17 3 att2BordR p116 MR30
CHETTLE,Ernest Frederick Lt dow 5-4-18 7Mddx att4RWFus p235 CR France102
CHETWOOD,Ernest Stanley.MID Capt kia 30-10-17 1/28Lond C'Coy p252 MR30
CHETWYND STAPYLTON,G.J.Maj kia 25-8-14 30/107RFA CR France206
CHETWYND-STAPYLTON,Henry Miles Capt kia 14-11-15 107RFA p26 CR Belgium15,dow
CHEVERS,Herbert Longmore Grant Maj ded 10-8-19 RAMC p267 CR Hamps218
CHEVERTON,Stanley Campbell Lt kia 27-1-17 1BordR p116 CR France399
CHEVERTON,Thomas Bird Maj kia 24-3-18 RFA p206 MR27
CHEVREAU,Louis Raymond de Montlehu T2Lt kia 22-3-18 16 att1/4NumbF p60 MR27
CHEW,George Douglas.MC.Capt kia 15-11-16 3NStaffs att11LNLancs p156 MR21
CHEYNE,Charles George 2Lt kia 14-4-18 6ScotRif p224 CR France324
CHIBNALL,George William Russell 2LtTLt kia 26-8-18 3DragGds att9WRid p21 MR16
CHIBNALL,Ronald Stanley TLt kia 31-7-17 8Suff p78 MR29
CHICHESTER,Edmund Basil Capt dow 7-11-14 3 att1EKent p57 CR France102
CHICHESTER,Henry Arthur Capt kia 20-10-14 3Dev p76 MR22
CHICHESTER,Robert Guy Incledon Capt kia 13-11-14 2HLI p162 MR29
CHICHESTER,William George Cubitt Lt kia 15-9-16 1Lond p245 CR France432,Capt
CHICK,Francis William Lt mbk 4-10-17 7 att1Dev p257 MR30
CHIDGEY,Percy Harold T2Lt dow 12-4-18 RE 200FC p44 CR Belgium38
CHIDSON,Laurence Drury.MC.TLtACapt kia 24-4-17 13KRRC p149 MR20,23-4-17
CHIGNELL,Hugh 2Lt kia 26-4-18 3Worc p108 MR30
CHILCOTT,Gilbert George Cardew 2Lt kia 18-4-17 1DCLI p114 MR20
CHILD,David Leslie Lt dow 11-9-16 2Lond p245 CR France329,2Lt
CHILD,Edward T2Lt kia 24-8-18 Mddx att1/8Bn p146 CR France927
CHILD,Gerald Julius Lt kia 18-4-15 YLI p142 MR29
CHILD,Gilbert Richard Gregory 2Lt kia 9-5-15 RSuss p118 MR22
CHILD,Henry Russell Capt kia 27-3-18 GL &11RFC p154&257 MR20
CHILD,James Martin.MC.Capt kld 23-8-18 1/2Manch &RAF p154 CR Essex40
CHILD,Joseph Alfred 2Lt kia 7-6-17 9Yorks att69TMB p90 CR Belgium167
CHILD,Philip Herbert T2Lt kia 23-8-18 16 att16RWar p64 MR16
CHILDE,Charles Murray TCapt dow 21-3-16 8Glouc p106 CR France345
CHILDE,Derrick Francis Lt kia 19-12-15 1/5Y&L p238 CR Belgium23
CHILDE-FREEMAN,John Arthur.MC.Capt kia 25-9-15 2RWFus p97 CR France114
CHILDE-PEMBERTON,Edward William Baldwin T2Lt dow 13-4-17 18 att11Huss p23 CR France12,Edmund Baldwyn
CHILDERHOUSE,Francis James Lt kia 23-9-16 9Lincs att2EYorks p74 MR37
CHILDS,George Willmot 2Lt dow 22-1-18 4Beds p85 CR France398
CHILDS,Robert Edward TLt dow 26-9-18 7RBerks p138 CR Greece6
CHILDS,Royden James 2Lt kia 27-7-16 3 att1RBerks p138 MR21
CHILES-EVANS,David Brynmor.DSO.LtCol kia 23-4-17 RAMC 3WelshFA p253 CR France80

CHILL,John Metcalfe 2Lt kia 8-11-16 att7EKent p57 MR21,18-11-16
CHILTON,F.Lt kia 20-6-15 13A&SH p173 MR4,4-6-15
CHILTON,Henry Lt ded 18-9-20 GL &RE IWT CR Iraq1
CHILTON,Hubert C.T2Lt kia 23-4-18 2LancF p92 France412,24-4-18
CHILVERS,Reginald Cuthbert T2Lt kia 19-4-17 10Norf p73 MR34
CHILVERS,Roland Clifford 2Lt kia 29-7-17 15Lond p249 CR France662
CHILWELL,Eric Robert T2Lt kia 16-9-16 7DCLI p114 MR21
CHINN,Lilian Ella Nurse 24-6-17 VAD attDevonportHosp CR Somerset49
CHINNERY,Esme Fairfax Capt kld 18-1-15 CldGds &RFC p1&51 CR Surrey86
CHINNERY,Harry Broderick TLt kia 28-5-16 13KRRC p149 CR France501
CHINNERY,Reginald Charles 2Lt kia 31-7-17 7Lpool p215 MR29
CHIPLIN,William Henry Capt kia 1-7-16 15RIrRif p169 MR21
CHIPMAN,John Douglas TLt kia 17-2-17 2SStaffs p122 MR21
CHIPPENDALE,Frank Dean 2Lt kia 10-4-18 4WRid p227 MR30
CHIPPERFIELD,Arnold Henry T2Lt kia 24-4-18 12Mddx att2/2Lond p146 MR27
CHIPPINDALL,Bertrand Thorold 2Lt kia 16-11-16 3SomLI p79 CR France339
CHIPPINGTON,Horace Leonard T2Lt dow 23-8-18 12Suff att16War p78 CR France84,24-8-18
CHIRSTIE,James Hugh CaptTMaj kia 24-5-15 4RIrReg p88 MR29,CHRISTIE,2Bn
CHISENHALE-MARSH,Harold Atherton Capt kia 28-9-18 9Lancers attSatff34DivHQ p22 CR Belgium11
CHISHOLM,Alasair Edward Lt kia 25-9-15 3RScots attRScotF p53 MR29
CHISHOLM,Alexander Lt kia 14-10-17 4 att7CamH p242 MR20
CHISHOLM,Edward Alexander.MC&2Bars.TMaj kia 7-11-18 C161RFA p26 CR France943,Ex 16CanadaFA
CHISHOLM,John Oliver TLt dow 23-7-18 RScots att1/8Bn p53 CR France1693 &CR France34
CHISHOLM,Kenneth James TLt dow 18-8-16 5Nhampt p137 CR France74
CHISHOLM,William Dempster T2Lt dow 23-3-18 5BordR p116 CR France987
CHISHOLM,William Malcolm Lt dow 27-8-14 1ELancs p110 CR France1349
CHISHOLM,William Turner 2Lt dow 1-9-16 2/23Lond p252 CR France95
CHISHOLM-BATTEN,James Forbes LtCol ded 17-3-15 ArmyPayDept p268
CHISHOLM-BATTEN,James Utermarck 2Lt kia 29-9-15 3Dors att3RFus p123 MR19
CHISHOLM BATTEN,John de Haviland CaptAMaj kia 7-8-17 RFA p26 CR Belgium89,Havilland
CHISLETT,Angus Robert Joseph Capt kia 24-4-17 8 att12HLI p240 MR20
CHISNALL,George Henry Lt dow 24-10-14 RAMC p194
CHISSELL,George Edwin.MC.TCapt dow 29-10-17 RAMC att1RWFus p194 CR Belgium11
CHISWELL,Henry Pettit.MC.Lt kia 25-3-18 RE 490FC p210 MR27
CHITTENDEN,Arthur George 2Lt kia 21-8-17 RFA p26 CR France255
CHITTENDEN,Arthur Grant Bourne 2Lt dow 9-9-14 Manch p154
CHITTY,Ernest Richard Inglis LtCol mbk 25-3-17 IA 105Mahrattas p275 MR38
CHITTY,James Malcolm 2Lt kia 1-12-17 4GrenGds p49 MR17
CHIVERS,Herbert T2Lt dedacc 18-6-18 RASC attRGA 153SB p192 CR France69
CHIVERS,Wreford 2Lt kia 17-8-17 GL &32RFC p6 MR20
CHOLMELEY,Eric Randolph Lt kia 1-7-16 2WYorks p81 MR21
CHOLMELEY,Harry Lenin Lt kia 1-7-16 3 att1BordR p116 MR21,Lewin
CHOLMELEY,Hugh Ralph 2Lt dow 14-6-15 45/42RFA p26 CR France285
CHOLMELEY,Hugh Valentine 2Lt kia 7-4-16 1GrenGds SR p49 CR Belgium84
CHOLMELEY,Montague Aubrey Rowley.Bart.Capt kia 24-12-14 2GrenGds RoO p49 MR22
CHOLMELEY,Roger James.MC.Capt drd 16-8-19 Ches p254 MR70 &CR Europe180
CHOLMONDELEY,Charles Almeric John Capt kia 28-10-14 2BordR p116 MR29
CHOLMONDELEY,Reginald Capt kld 12-3-15 RB att3RFC p1&178 CR France98
CHORLEY,Arthur Reginald Capt dow 28-4-18 1/4YLI p235 CR France102
CHORLEY,Charles Leonard.MC.T2Lt kia 26-4-18 1/2 att2/5LancF p92 MR19
CHORLTON,Herbert Bichonall 2Lt kia 26-3-18 2 att4ELancs p110 MR27
CHOVEAUX,Nigel Lt kia 14-3-17 1/5SStaffs p229 CR France281,Capt
CHOWN,Francis Jack T2Lt kia 20-9-17 GL att1RFC p6 CR Belgium112
CHOWN,William Leonard 2Lt kia 30-7-16 3Dors att2 O&BLI p123 MR21
CHOWNE,Gerard Henry Tilson TCapt dow 2-5-17 9ELancs p110 CR Greece6
CHOWNS,William Pharoah.MIDx2 Capt kld 5-1-21 IARO attS&TCps p275 CR Iraq8,Maj dow
CHREE,George William Johnstone.MC.TCapt&Adjt kia 14-7-16 1 att2RScots p53 CR France164,dow
CHRISTAIN,Albert T2Lt kia 27-9-18 TankCps p188 CR France662
CHRISTIAN,Aviet Thadeus Lt ded 6-11-18 IARO attWorksDirectorate p275 CR Iraq6
CHRISTIAN,Edward.MC.Capt dow 19-10-16 B235RFA p207 CR France40

CHRISTIAN,Edward Charles TCapt kia 11-9-16 7SStaffs p122 CR France251
CHRISTIE,Albert William Ernest 2Lt kld 27-9-15 2Worc p108 CR France281,27-9-16
CHRISTIE,Cedric Pasche T2Lt dow 16-12-15 11Lpool p71 CR France102
CHRISTIE,Denis Halstead T2Lt kia 21-9-18 11 att16RSuss p118 MR16
CHRISTIE,Dugald Roderick 2Lt kia 24-2-16 66RFA p26 MR38
CHRISTIE,Harold Reginald Morris 2Lt kia 16-7-16 4 att1ScotRif p103 MR21
CHRISTIE,Henry Robert Stark.DSO.OBE.LtCol ded 24-11-19 RE p262 CR Scot237
CHRISTIE,Herbert Bertram TLt ded 9-12-16 RemountService RASC p24 CR Lond14
CHRISTIE,James Allan T2Lt dow 6-11-17 6RWSurr p55
CHRISTIE,James Hugh Maj 24-5-15 2RIrReg MR29 see CHRISTIE,J.H.
CHRISTIE,John 2Lt kia 22-7-18 4SfthH p241 CR France1228
CHRISTIE,Lawrence William Lt ded 7-5-17 RIM attRE IWT p275 CR Iraq6
CHRISTIE,Lindsay Bruce Stark Maj ded 30-9-15 RA CR Scot237
CHRISTIE,Murray Inglis.DSO.T2LtACapt dow 24-3-18 32RFus A'Coy p67 CR France745
CHRISTIE,Paul Norman Jones 2Lt kia 9-10-17 1/2Beds C'Coy p85 MR30
CHRISTIE,Richard Colin Lt dow 15-12-15 RE 80FC p44 CR France22
CHRISTIE,Robert Francis Sanderson T2Lt kld 15-10-17 GL &RFC p6 CR War7
CHRISTIE,Robert Main Maj dow 15-5-18 10LabCps p189 CR France145
CHRISTIE,Ronald.MC.LtACapt dow 12-4-18 RASC attRGA p192 CR France1107
CHRISTIE,William Lt&QM ded 8-11-17 3GordH p166 CR Scot330
CHRISTIE,William Charles.MIDx2 Maj kia 13-10-14 1RWar D'Coy p64 CR France324
CHRISTIE,William Edward Tolfrey.CMG.OBE.DSO.MajTCol ded 22-10-18 RASC p192 CR SAfrica171
CHRISTIE-MURRAY,Maurice.MC.TLt dow 9-9-16 112RFA p26 CR France430
CHRISTISON,Frederick John TLt dow 4-12-15 10A&SH p173 CR Belgium4
CHRISTISON,Robert Colin Lt kia 25-9-17 10GordH p166 MR19
CHRISTMAS,Bernard Lovell Capt dow 11-5-16 1/3Lond p245 CR France,19-5-16
CHRISTMAS,Dudley Vivian LtStaffCapt kld 23-10-15 5Suff p217
CHRISTMAS,Edwin Cecil Russell T2Lt dow 7-10-16 18KRRC p149 MR21
CHRISTMAS,Leslie Frederick T2Lt kia 3-11-16 17 att14Mddx p146 CR France742,13-11-16
CHRISTOPHER,John Hosken 2Lt kia 22-2-17 IARO att92Punjabis p275 CR Iraq5
CHRISTOPHER,Leonard de Lona Capt kia 26-4-17 IA att40Pathans p275
CHRISTOPHER,Richard TLt kia 29-9-18 16TankCps p188 CR France212
CHRISTY,Basil Robert Francis 2Lt dow 3-10-16 1ColdGds p51 CR France105
CHRISTY,John George T2Lt kia 3-10-18 1/2 att1/5Leic p87
CHRISTY,Philip Archibald Lt kia 10-2-15 2Ess SR p131 CR Belgium33
CHRISTY,Stephen Henry.DSO.Capt kia 27-8-14 20Huss SR p23 CR France1445,3-9-14
CHRISTY,Stephen Edmund Fell Lt kia 12-7-16 1IrGds p52 CR Belgium84
CHRISTY,Thomas Hill 2Lt kia 12-4-18 EssYeo att10Ess p203 MR27,Hills
CHRONNELL,Hubert.MC.2LtACapt kia 31-7-17 1/5LNLancs p135 CR Belgium10
CHRYSTAL,George Gordon Lt kia 25-5-15 9A&SH p244 MR29
CHRYSTAL,Ian Campbell 2Lt kia 1-5-17 3 att9SfthH p164 CR France452
CHRYSTIE,James Alexander 2Lt kia 30-11-14 3 att2RScotF p94 MR29
CHRYSTIE,John Maj kia 17-11-14 RGA 1SB p38 CR Belgium57
CHUBB,Alan Travers 2Lt kia 9-9-16 11Hamps p120 MR21
CHUBB,Francis John MacLardie 2Lt kia 18-4-15 3 att2YLI p142 MR29
CHUBB,Geoffrey Capt kia 12-7-15 6RWSurr p55 CR Belgium137
CHUBB,Theodore 2Lt kia 17-2-17 10Lond attRFus p248 CR France314
CHURCH,Arthur.MC.Lt ded 14-2-18 EAfrIntelDept CR EAfrica1l& CR Tanzania1
CHURCH,Arthur Gilbert Walsh Capt kia 20-7-18 1/5Dev p217 CR France622
CHURCH,Frederick James.DCM.2Lt kia 10-5-15 2RDubF p176 MR29
CHURCH,Geoffrey William.MC.2Lt kia 3-5-17 7EKent p57 MR20
CHURCH,Harold Capt kia 19-7-16 O&BLI 2/1BucksBn p231 CR France1887
CHURCH,Horace Major Scrimshire 2Lt dow 10-2-18 7LancF p221 CR France98
CHURCH,John Victor Lt kia 10-12-17 3 att6KSLI p144 CR Egypt1,2Lt
CHURCH,John William Lt dow 30-3-18 Herts p252 MR27
CHURCH,W.A.Maj 17-6-20 DCLI CR Devon1
CHURCH,Walter Harry 2Lt kia 23-7-16 3 att1DCLI attTMB p114 MR21
CHURCH,William Campbell Capt kia 28-6-15 8ScotRif p224 MR4
CHURCHER,Bryan Thomas LtCol ded 31-12-18 RWSurr p55 CR Berks124
CHURCHER,Edgar TLt kia 14-7-17 3RB &32RFC p6&178 CR Belgium11
CHURCHFIELD,Sidney Percival T2Lt kia 1-7-16 4Mddx p146 CR France267
CHURCHILL,Arthur Lindsay Maury Capt ded 24-6-17 RAMC att18Lond p253 CR Egypt8
CHURCHILL,Charles Henry Matthew Capt kia 17-2-17 IA att20Inf p275 CR Iraq5
CHURCHILL,Clarence Harold 2Lt kia 15-12-17 RGA p38 CR Belgium101
CHURCHILL,George Ross Deas.DSO.LtCol kia 20-12-19 IA Cmdg2/19Punjabis p275 MR43
CHURCHILL,Herbert Payn T2Lt ded 20-10-15 RE p44 CR Europe1
CHURCHMAN,Charles Harvey Lt kia 3-5-17 6Suff att2/5WYorks p218 MR20
CHURCHWARD,Hubert Alan 2Lt kia 16-8-17 2Coy of LondYeo attRFC p18&204 MR20
CHURCHYARD,Arthur Stewart TCapt ded 28-1-17 6RB att1DubF p178 CR Mddx5
CHUTE,Challoner Francis Trevor Lt kia 27-8-14 2RMunstF p175 CR France1751
CHUTER,Harry Athelstan Lt kia 25-3-17 2RFus &70RFC p6&67 CR France234
CHUTTER,George Philip Lt kia 15-6-18 1/5Glouc p225 CR Italy2
CINNAMOND,Francis T2Lt ded PoW 13-11-18 10 att2RInniskF p104 CR Europe149
CITY,S.G.E.2Lt 30-5-17 IARO att1RGA MR67
CLACHAN,William James Capt kia 6-1-18 2Mddx att1KAR p146&202 CR EAfrica77
CLAGUE,George.MC.2Lt kia 14-3-15 1HLI p162 CR France279
CLAIRMONTE,George Egerton 2Lt kia 25/26-9-15 1Glouc p106 CR France550
CLAKE,see CLARKE,A.C.
CLANCEY,John Austin.MC.Maj ded 22-7-18 RIrF &MGC p171&182 CR Berks84
CLANCEY,Trevor John 2Lt kia 28-10-14 2BordR p116 MR29,24-10-14
CLANCY,George David Louis 2Lt drd 4-5-17 4RIrRif att1Leinst p169 CR Italy14
CLANCY,William John Lt ded 16-10-18 RASC p192 Lond29,Joseph
CLAPHAM,Alan Charles 2Lt kld 3-1-16 4EYorks p219 CR Belgium127
CLAPHAM,Barnard Aubrey Lt dow 27-3-17 4Ess p232 CR Palestine8
CLAPHAM,Christopher Albon T2Lt kia 10-2-16 8Y&L p158 CR France347,Christofer
CLAPHAM,Edgar Lt dow 5-11-18 6WRid p227 CR France332
CLAPHAM,Graham Windyer 2Lt dow 10-5-17 71RFA p26 CR France113
CLAPHAM,Robert Sydney T2Lt dow 28-9-17 12WYorks p81 CR Belgium16
CLAPP,Alfred Henry Lt ded 15-5-17 RAVC p198 CR France207
CLAPP,Leonard Bishop T2Lt dow 2-10-17 BordR att1Bn p116 CR Belgium16
CLAPP,William Gilbert Elphinstone 2Lt dow 29-4-17 NorfYeo att7Norf p204 CR France113
CLAPPEN,Wilfred Joseph 2Lt dow 22-9-16 10DLI p160 CR France833
CLAPPERTON,James Hugh Maj dow 7-5-17 B317RFA p206 CR France40
CLAPTON,Arthur 2Lt kia 5-9-16 32RFus p67 MR21,15-9-16
CLARE,Arthur Vernon 2Lt kia 15-9-16 21Lond p251 CR France385
CLARE,Horace Townshend.MID LtAMaj kia 29-4-18 A245RFA p26 CR Belgium8
CLAREMONT,Frederick Victor Leszynski 2Lt kia 14-8-17 RGA 184SB p38 CR Belgium23
CLARK,Algernon Basil.MC.MIDx2 Capt kia 3-10-18 3BlkW att2RAF p128 CR France223
CLARK,Alan Glover 2Lt kia 21-9-18 3 att1ScotRif p103 CR France666
CLARK,Albert Victor.MC.2Lt dow 2-1-18 5Beds p219 CR France398
CLARK,Alexander.MC.Lt&QM dow 13-4-18 9SforthH p164 CR Belgium38
CLARK,Alfred Matthews Lt kia 20-11-17 1/4RLancs p213 MR21,Mathew
CLARK,Alick Morton 2Lt kia 27-1-17 1BordR p116 CR France374
CLARK,Allan La Barte Capt kia 18-9-18 RAMC att12Ches p194 MR37
CLARK,Andrew Scott Duncan T2Lt dow 22-4-17 9RScotF att1/4Bn p94 CR Egypt2
CLARK,Anthony Dalzell TCapt dow 4-12-17 N&D p133 CR Egypt2
CLARK,Archibald Strachan T2Lt kia 8-10-18 13Lpool p71 CR France338
CLARK,Arthur Lt 26-1-20 RASC CR Egypt6
CLARK,Arthur Henry T2Lt dow 3-5-18 PoW 49MGC Inf D'Coy p182 CR France1029
CLARK,Arthur James Richard Lt dow 9-10-16 8RFus p67 CR France833,kia
CLARK,Arthur Vivian T2Lt kia 20-4-16 GL att7Glouc p190
CLARK,Basil Vyse Lt kia 24-7-18 121RFA p26 CR France4
CLARK,Bruce Lt kia 9-11-16 1/4Glouc p225 MR21
CLARK,C.B.Capt kia 3-11-16 SL att1KAR p202 MR50
CLARK,Charles 2Lt kia 24-3-18 19Lond p250 CR France216
CLARK,Charles.MC.MID LtAMaj kia 25-4-18 295RFA p26 CR France745
CLARK,Charles Augustus 2Lt kia 1-7-16 5 att1RB p178 MR21
CLARK,Charles Douglas.TD.LtCol ded 22-1-20 5RWKent p269 CR Kent95
CLARK,Charles Inglis Capt ded 6-3-18 RASC 976MT p192 CR Iraq8
CLARK,Charles William T2Lt kia 20-11-17 RWKent att6Bn p140 CR France379
CLARK,Charlie T2Lt kia 9-4-18 2 att5LancF p92 CR France1106
CLARK,Claude Frederick 2Lt dow 10-4-18 4Nhampt p234 CR France34,6Bn
CLARK,Clifford Stanley Lt ded 30-5-19 465/65RFA p26 CR Germany1
CLARK,Colbert Walter 2Lt kia 26-4-18 13RB p178 MR27
CLARK,David Ian Graham 2Lt kia 20-9-17 4SfthH p241 CR Belgium83

CLARK,Donald Gordon.DSO.MC.Capt dow 13-4-18 1/6GordH p292 CR France40
CLARK,Douglas Maj dow 29-6-15 8HLI p240 MR4
CLARK,Douglas Scott Dalrymple Capt kia 15-9-16 18KRRC attTMB p149 MR21 &CR France1890
CLARK,Egbert Douglas Lt dow 15-2-17 2Ches p95 CR Iraq5
CLARK,Ellis 2Lt kia 1-5-15 1LancF p92 CR Gallipoli1,25-4-15
CLARK,Eric Alan 2Lt kld 20-3-18 5RFC p15 CR Lancs386
CLARK,Eric Foster TLt kia 1-1-17 EKent &RFC p6&57 CR France833
CLARK,Eric Groby 2Lt kia 23-4-17 6 att1Mddx p146 MR20
CLARK,Eric Henry Lloyd 2Lt kia 1-7-16 5/3RFA p208 MR21
CLARK,Ernest Vaughan 2Lt kia 29-11-17 RFus &20RFC p6 MR20
CLARK,Frank Adams Maj dow 20-11-17 1/5Dev p217 CR Palestine9
CLARK,Frank Nelham 2Lt kld 29-4-17 GL &RFC p6
CLARK,Fred Sumner 2Lt kia 14-10-18 10Lpool att1/4SfthH p216 CR France611
CLARK,Frederick Percy Capt&QM 8-10-18 3Huss CR Kent180
CLARK,George 2Lt kia 3-11-17 RGA 189HB p38 CR Palestine8
CLARK,George Ernest Cecil TCapt kia 9-1-16 8LNLancs p135 CR Belgium70
CLARK,George Mackay Lt dow 12-11-17 4RScots p211 MR34
CLARK,George Milburn T2Lt kia 14-7-18 12Yorks att1WYorks p90 CR Belgium3
CLARK,George Reginald Heylin.MID Lt kia 26-8-18 7NStaffs p156 MR38
CLARK,Gerald Maitland TMaj kia 14-7-16 9Nhampt p137 MR21,6Bn
CLARK,Harold Conquest.MC.Lt dow 7-2-18 3 att2Wilts p152 CR France1063,Capt
CLARK,Henry Featherstone T2LtTLt kia 3-5-17 11Dev att2/6Glouc p76 CR France1701
CLARK,Henry Robert Ernest see CLARKE,H.R.E.
CLARK,Herbert George Lt ded 16-4-18 IARO attStaffBombay p275 MR65
CLARK,Horace Arthur Capt kia 14-9-16 24Lond p252 CR France387
CLARK,Hugh Reginald Stanley T2Lt kia 18-8-16 11GordH p166 MR21
CLARK,James.CB.LtCol kia 10-5-15 9A&SH p243 CR Belgium6
CLARK,James Smith 2Lt kia 3-5-17 6GordH att5CamH p242 MR20
CLARK,James Tony 2Lt kia 9-9-16 2Suss p118 MR21
CLARK,Jasper Lt kia 2-10-18 6A&SH p243 CR France236
CLARK,John T2Lt kld 6-8-17 GL &RFC p6 CR Scot122
CLARK,John Dormet 2Lt kia 27-5-17 6 att1ScotRif p224 MR20,Dormer
CLARK,John Frederick 2Lt ded 10-9-18 6Mddx &RAF p265
CLARK,John Harold.MID 2Lt kia 25-9-15 3 att2Wilts p152 MR19
CLARK,John Ladyman TCapt ded 16-12-18 RAVC attIndVetHosp p198 CR Egypt9
CLARK,John MacTaggart Capt ded 18-11-18 8RWSurr attDLI p55 CR Essex146
CLARK,John Ryder 2Lt kia 20-10-17 RGA 196SB p38 CR Belgium87,dow
CLARK,Laurence Fraser T2Lt dow 7-12-17 1EKent p57 CR France446
CLARK,Lyonel Latimer 2Lt kia 2-8-16 LeicRFA attRFC p208 CR France837
CLARK,Marcus Broadfoot TLt kia 25-9-17 2A&SH p173 CR Belgium112
CLARK,Neville Arthur Lt dow 28-11-17 1CldGds p51 CR France398
CLARK,Noel T2LtACapt dow 1-4-18 2Nhampt p137 CR France145
CLARK,Norman Lt kia 18-3-18 RFA att54RFC p18&207 CR France333,FlLt
CLARK,Norman Henry 2Lt dow 25-11-17 BedsYeo p203 CR France298,Harry
CLARK,Norman Pickslay T2Lt kia 24-8-16 7 att2RMunstR p175 MR21
CLARK,Oscar William T2Lt kia 22-7-16 1ESurr p112 MR21,23-7-16
CLARK,R.A.Ronaldson Lt ded 19-10-18 RH&FA &RAF p26
CLARK,Reginald Burton 2Lt dow 1-5-17 60RFC p6 CR France13,CLARKE
CLARK,Reginald William T2Lt kia 19-8-17 3 att17N&D p133 CR Belgium120
CLARK,Richard T2Lt kia 15-5-15 8 att7KOSB p101 CR France423,14-5-16
CLARK,Robert TCapt dow 7-11-18 RAMC att20Huss p194 CR France943
CLARK,Roland Hope T2Lt dow 24-3-18 16RB p178 CR France300
CLARK,Samuel Clarkson Lt dow 17-9-18 1GordH p166 CR Scot798
CLARK,Sidney George 2Lt kia 4-4-18 15Lond p249 CR France296
CLARK,Stanley Lowndes TLt kia 13-4-18 ACycCps att13Lpool p181 CR France88
CLARK,Stewart T2Lt kia 21-3-18 7RB p178 MR27
CLARK,Sydney Capt kia 2-10-16 RAMC 5LondFA p253 CR France397
CLARK,Thomas James Maj&QM ded 10-9-16 RE p269 CR Kent46
CLARK,W.R.LtCol 4-2-19 IMS CR Lancs401
CLARK,Walter Llewellyn T2Lt;TCapt kia 23-5-17 GL &6RFC p6 CR Belgium11
CLARK,William T2Lt kia 27-3-17 16Manch p154 CR France214
CLARK,William 2Lt kia 23-4-17 5A&SH p243 CR France434
CLARK,William Brown TCapt kia 12-3-17 RAMC att2ScotsGds p194 CR France329
CLARK,William Campbell 2Lt dow 27-10-18 7A&SH p243 CR France13
CLARK,William Frederick Hunter 2Lt dow 23-2-18 3RScotF p94 CR Greece7,CLARKE
CLARK,William Henry 2lt kia 6-7-17 8Mddx attRFC p18&236 MR20
CLARK,William Muir T2Lt kia 20-11-17 BlkW att1/7Bn p128 CR France398

CLARK,William Sowerby.MC.TCapt kld 10-7-17 10EYorks p83 CR France68,dedacc
CLARK,William Spenceley TCapt kia 1-7-16 12Y&L A'Coy p158 CR France1890,dow
CLARK-KENNEDY,Alexander Kenelm Capt kia 19-4-17 1/5KOSB p224 CR Palestine8
CLARK-KENNEDY,Archibald Douglas Hewitt.MID Capt dow 18-9-18 5RScotF p222 CR France646,kia
CLARKE,Albert Edward T2Lt kia 20-4-16 2Y&L p158 CR Belgium73
CLARKE,Albert Edward 2Lt dow 9-7-16 6RWar p214 CR Germany1
CLARKE,Alexander Maj ded 2-8-18 SL 7Hrs RecruitOff p268 CR Essex80
CLARKE,Alexander Norwall 2Lt kia 24-8-18 7A/317RFA p26 CR France577
CLARKE,Alfred Lord 2Lt kia 27-3-18 3 att2/6LancF p92 MR27
CLARKE,Algernon Percy 2Lt dow 24-7-15 23Lond p252 CR France98
CLARKE,Ambrose Childs 2Lt kia 10-5-15 1/4Leic p220 CR Belgium99
CLARKE,Arthur 2Lt ded 17-11-18 1Worc p264 CR Staffs61
CLARKE,Arthur Aubrey.MC.Lt kia 1-10-17 7Leic p87 CR Belgium112,Capt
CLARKE,Arthur Cecil Grafton T2Lt kia 28-5-18 2/6RWar p64 CR France1161
CLARKE,Arthur Cyril T2Lt kia 9-4-17 2Wilts p152 CR France214,CLAKE
CLARKE,Arthur Henry Gilbert 2Lt kia 9-9-16 Nhampt p137 CR France432
CLARKE,Arundel Geoffrey 2Lt kia 1-7-16 5RB p178 CR France744
CLARKE,Austin Basil.MC.Capt kia 23-11-17 RAMC att1/9Lond p194 CR France245
CLARKE,Booth Frederick 2Lt kia 26-1-17 2ESurr p112 MR37
CLARKE,Brian Lloyd Lt dow 19-4-15 1A 23Cav &RFC p275 CR France200
CLARKE,Cecil Andrews.MM.MIDx2 2Lt kia 23-4-17 1/7Mddx p235 CR France15,24-4-17
CLARKE,Charles Basil 2Lt kia 21-4-16 66RFA p26 MR38
CLARKE,Charles Edward 2Lt 27-9-18 WYorks att20RAF CR France1061
CLARKE,Charles Henry Geoffrey Mansfield Maj ded 27-7-19 RB p266 CR Bucks91
CLARKE,Charles Louis TLt kia 8-10-16 7Nhampt p137 CR France81
CLARKE,Charles St.Aubyn 2Lt ded 30-7-18 IA 74Punjabis p275 MR66
CLARKE,Claud Fitzroy Maj ded 30-6-18 20DeccanHorse CR Surrey37
CLARKE,Claude Hamilton Law 2Lt ded 22-3-18 RFC p15 CR Mddx39
CLARKE,Cyril T2Lt dow 16-6-16 11 att8ESurr p112 CR France23,kia
CLARKE,Cyril George TLt dow 26-9-15 8EYorks p83 CR France178
CLARKE,Cyril John Digby Lt dow 15-9-17 RASC p253 CR Belgium10
CLARKE,David T2Lt kia 22-3-18 11Ches p95 MR20
CLARKE,Donald T2Lt kia 26-8-16 GL &7RFC p2&190 CR France44
CLARKE,Edward George.MID LtTCapt kia 13-11-16 7RFus p67 CR France220
CLARKE,Edward Rupert 2Lt kia 9-4-17 4Lond p246 MR20 CR France581,9KRRC
CLARKE,Edwin Alfred 2Lt dow 1-10-16 2/20Lond p251 CR France95
CLARKE,Edwin Charles Kaye.MC.Capt kia 31-8-18 Inns of Court OTC p252 MR16
CLARKE,Eric Fitzgerald Capt kia 9-4-17 3Lond p245&204,3Co of LondYeo CR France419
CLARKE,Eric Groby T2Lt kia 23-4-17 7BordR p116
CLARKE,Ernest George 2Lt 23-4-17 7BordR MR20
CLARKE,Francis Arthur T2Lt kia 31-7-16 1Norf p73 CR France402
CLARKE,Francis Charles Erlin Lt dow 11-10-17 3Worc &5RFC p6&108 CR France113
CLARKE,Francis Herbert.MC.2Lt kia 1-11-18 RFA 28ArmyBde p26 CR Belgium140,124RFA
CLARKE,Frederick John Noel 2Lt kia 29-6-15 6 att3Worc p108 MR29 &CR Belgium453
CLARKE,Frederick Thomas Phillip 2Lt kia 19-4-17 11Lond p248 MR34
CLARKE,Geoffrey d'Almaine Campbell TLt kia 11-1-16 RFA att92TMB p26 CR France515
CLARKE,George Alexander T2Lt kia 21-3-18 8RDubF p176 CR France660,Lt
CLARKE,George Edward 2Lt kia 23-7-16 10RWar p64 MR21
CLARKE,George Henry 2Lt kia 22-4-18 3 att1Norf p73 CR France21,21-4-18
CLARKE,George Thomas TLt dow 18-9-18 C/114RFA p26 CR Greece1
CLARKE,Gerald Foulkes T2Lt dow 6-10-17 8 att1DCLI p114 CR Belgium11
CLARKE,Gilbert Roderick Bernard 2Lt dow 13-6-18 7ScotRif p224 CR France102
CLARKE,Gordon Elstone.MC.T2Lt kia 28-8-16 6DCLI p114 MR21
CLARKE,Hamlet John 2Lt kia 21-5-18 1Dors p123 CR France502
CLARKE,Harold Frank TLt kia 25-9-15 5 O&BLI p130 MR29
CLARKE,Harold Joyce Lt kia 17-5-15 3 att1RBerks p138 MR22,16-5-15
CLARKE,Harold Martin Lt kia 26-9-15 1/17Lond p250 CR France550
CLARKE,Harold Percival Lt dow 9-5-15 6 att2RB p178 MR32,kia
CLARKE,Harry Charles TLt kia 6-7-17 48RFC p6 CR France403
CLARKE,Harry Herbert TLt ded 14-7-18 4RRofCav p261

50

CLARKE,Henry Colin TCapt ded 25-5-16 170RASC p192 CR France80,Harry
CLARKE,Henry Hugh Franklin T2Lt kia 24-9-17 87RFA p26 CR France179
CLARKE,Henry Robert Ernest 2Lt dow 3-6-16 15Lond p249 CR France98,CLARK 3-6-15
CLARKE,Hilary Calvert TLt dow 31-8-18 31MGC Inf p182 CR France324
CLARKE,Horace Yelverton Chatfield 2Lt kia 23-4-17 2SWBord p99 MR20
CLARKE,Hugh Robert 2Lt ?-8-21 RMunstF CR Eire408
CLARKE,H.W.2Lt dow 2-9-18 28Lond &RAF p255
CLARKE,Ian Alexander TCapt kia 16-11-16 RAMC att1Dors p194 CR France131
CLARKE,Ian Hay Steuart Lt mbk 2-11-14 IA 57Rif p275
CLARKE,James Burford 2Lt kia 2-9-18 4SLancs p230 CR France511
CLARKE,James Henry Fisher T2Lt kia 1-7-16 7Yorks p90 CR France397
CLARKE,James Leonard Courtney Lt kia 5-1-17 IARO att47Sikhs p275 MR38,5-11-17
CLARKE,John Edward Langton.MC.Lt kia 14-9-14 50RFA p26 CR France1329
CLARKE,J.Gay TCapt kia 27-9-15 9RSuss p118 MR19
CLARKE,Job Lt 16-10-15 S&TCps MR65
CLARKE,John Capt kia 9-9-15 RAMC 1FA p253 CR Gallipoli27
CLARKE,John 2Lt kia 18-9-18 5SLancs &35RAF p230 MR20
CLARKE,John Lt ded 24-10-18 16Manch p154 CR Germany1
CLARKE,John Granshields Lt 26-3-16 RIndMarine CR India97A
CLARKE,John James Gordon ACapt kia 28-4-17 6Ess p232 MR21,13Ess att 1O&BLI
CLARKE,John Kingham 2Lt kld 22-7-18 3ConnRgrs &RAF p172
CLARKE,John Michell LtCol ded 21-4-18 RAMC p253 CR Glouc9
CLARKE,John Percy Dalzell 2Lt ded 21-2-15 Worc p264 CR Surrey160
CLARKE,John Seymour Denison TLt kia 10-11-17 13A&SH p173 CR Palestine18
CLARKE,Joseph.MC.Lt kld 1-10-19 Worc &99RAF p264 MR65
CLARKE,Kenneth Herbert 2Lt kia 30-9-17 1/6A&SH p243 CR Belgium127,Lt
CLARKE,Leonard Lt dow 4-10-17 4 att7KSLI p235 CR Belgium16
CLARKE,Leonard William T2Lt dow 14-11-16.11ELancs p110 CR France2
CLARKE,Montagu Christian Cuthbert Lt kia 10-5-15 1A&SH p173 MR29,8-5-15
CLARKE,Mordaunt Edward Leonard Hannam Lt kia 26/27-8-14 3Worc p108 CR France657,26-8-14
CLARKE,Nathaniel Fuhrmann T2lt kld 1-6-17 GL &RFC p6 CR War135
CLARKE,Neville Dutton 2Lt ded 18-4-16 5RIrRif p171&265 CR Ireland33,10-4-16
CLARKE,Nicholas Vincent T2Lt kldacc 19-6-17 GL &57RFC p6 CR Egypt8
CLARKE,Percy Thomas T2Lt kia 19-8-18 3 att1/5Suff p78 CR Palestine9
CLARKE,Peter TLt dow 30-7-16 GL Wilts Cmdg13LgtTMB p190 CR France51,Capt
CLARKE,Reginald Burton see CLARK,R.B.
CLARKE,Richard John Capt kia 10-3-15 IA 8Rajputs att1/39GarhwalRif p275 CR France355 &CR France1887
CLARKE,Richard Stanley.MC.T2Lt kia 4-10-18 47MGC Inf p182 CR France1106
CLARKE,Robert George 2Lt kia 9-9-18 72RFA p26 CR France439
CLARKE,Robert Shuttleworth TCapt kia 25-9-15 5KSLI p144 MR29
CLARKE,Robert William Capt ded 10-8-16 RAVC p254 CR Egypt9,19-8-16
CLARKE,Roland Harry 2Lt ded 23-5-18 3 att1RWKent p140 CR France65,Lt
CLARKE,Roland Harwood TLt drd 21-2-17 20RFA p26 MR35
CLARKE,Russell Frank 2Lt kia 21-5-17 15Lond p249 MR20
CLARKE,S.S.S.Maj 11-5-18 CamH CR Scot45
CLARKE,Samuel Frank 2Lt kia 7-8-17 6Hamps p229 CR Belgium10
CLARKE,St.A.2Lt 30-7-18 74Punjabis MR66 see CLARKE,C.St.A.
CLARKE,Sidney Herbert.MC&Bar.LtTCapt kia 2-9-17 3Wilts att1AircraftDepotRFC p6&152 CR France134
CLARKE,Stanley Vingoe Lt kia 6-5-17 5Dev p217 CR France407,2Bn
CLARKE,Stephen Rev Chap4Cl 4-10-17 RAChDept att7LancF p199 MR30
CLARKE,Thomas Henry 2Lt kia 28-9-18 4ELancs p226 CR Belgium50
CLARKE,Thomas Purcell Lt kia 30-9-16 6Y&L p158 MR21
CLARKE,Thomas Veitch Lt accdrd 30-9-20 IA 9Horse att41Dogras p275 CR Palestine9
CLARKE,Vincent Charles T2Lt dow 12-10-16 10DLI p160 CR France158,Capt dedacc
CLARKE,W.A.Col 18-4-15 9Y&L CR Hamps1
CLARKE,Walter Stanley Arnold 2Lt kia 10-7-16 6Dors p123 MR21
CLARKE,Walter Sidney 2Lt kia 25-6-16 5 att2RMunstF p175 MR20,Sydney
CLARKE,Wilfred John 2Lt dow 9-9-16 5 att8RDubF p176 MR21
CLARKE,Wilfrid Randall TLt kld 4-2-18 RFA &RFC p15&26 CR Lincs61
CLARKE,William Frederick Hunter see CLARK,W.F.H.
CLARKE,William Hamilton 2Lt kia 12-3-15 5Worc p108 CR Belgium17,3Bn
CLARKE,William Mitchell 2Lt kia 12-11-16 RE 1/1FC p210 CR France392
CLARKEN,George Capt ded 3-1-19 RFA p254 CR Yorks294,Maj

CLARKSON,Amos.MC.TLt dow 24-10-18 WYorks att8Bn p81 CR France380
CLARKSON,Charles Capt ded 12-2-17 2/4WRid p227 CR France169
CLARKSON,Donald James 2Lt kia 9-8-18 1/6N&D att6Bn p133 CR France109
CLARKSON,Harold 2Lt kia 11-4-17 MGC D'HB att D'TankCps p182 MR20
CLARKSON,John James TLt kia 30-12-17 10A&SH p173 CR France439
CLARKSON,John Osborne Price 2Lt kia 10-3-17 13Huss p22 MR38
CLARKSON,Leslie Cecil Bentinck Capt ded 31-3-17 RASC p192 CR France102
CLARKSON,Thomas T2Lt kia 22-3-18 23Manch p154 MR20
CLARKSON,Wilfred Bamforth T2Lt ded 20-6-18 2Y&L p158 CR France142,Wilford
CLATWORTHY,Thomas Eland 2Lt kia 7-1-16 IARO att37Dogras p275 MR38,6-1-16
CLAUGHTON,Ian Drummond TLt kia 2-3-16 11Suff p78 CR France83
CLAUGHTON,John Harold 2Lt kia 30-11-17 35MGC p182 MR17
CLAUGHTON,Wilfred Maj ded 24-3-18 25LabCps p189 CR France102,Wilfrid
CLAXTON,Eric Abley 2Lt dow 31-7-17 KRRC att18Bn p149 MR29
CLAY,Arthur Joseph CaptTMaj ded 18-2-15 2/6NStaffs p238&255 CR Staffs180
CLAY,Henry George Walter 2Lt kia 29-7-16 1ESurr p112 MR21
CLAY,Lionel Pillean Capt kia 18-2-18 YorksDrag p206 CR France446,Pilleau
CLAY,Louis John 2Lt kia 5-4-18 6LancF p221 CR France745
CLAY,Vernon Harcourt.MC.T2Lt dow 26-10-16 10LancF p92 CR Yorks738
CLAY,Vivian Hastings Capt kia 18-10-16 2Wilts p152 MR21
CLAYDON,Archer William Ridge Lt ded 31-5-18 3KAR p202 CR EAfrica47,SL att1/6KAR
CLAYE,Charles Geoffrey Lt kia 5-7-18 5N&D &RAF p232&258,6-5-18
CLAYE,Geoffrey Woolley Lt dow 29-3-17 1/7Ches p223 CR Egypt2
CLAYHILLS,George.DSO.Capt kia 2-11-14 1ELancs p110 CR Belgium68
CLAYPHAN,George Alfred T2Lt kia 4-12-17 GL &12RFC p6 CR France214
CLAYTON,Albert James.MC.2Lt dow 24-8-18 2Lond p245 CR France100
CLAYTON,Arthur Oliver.MID Capt kia 21-3-18 3 att2Wilts p152 MR27
CLAYTON,Benjamin Chipchase.MC.T2LtACapt kia 16-8-17 2WYorks p81 MR30
CLAYTON,Charles Cam Thackwell 2Lt dow 19-7-17 1Glouc p106 CR Belgium24
CLAYTON,George 2Lt kia 17-10-16 1WYorks att11RFC p2 CR France568,Lt
CLAYTON,George 2Lt dow 24-10-16 1WYorks &11RFC p81
CLAYTON,Harold Robert Capt kia 4-6-15 1LancF C'Coy p92 CR Gallipoli6
CLAYTON,J.A.Capt 20-3-20 CentIndRlyBn MR65
CLAYTON,James Edward.MC.LtAMaj kia 24-6-18 B155RFA p26 CR France924
CLAYTON,James Gardner TCapt kia 20-8-16 Dors att1Nhampt p123 CR France387
CLAYTON,John Alfred 2Lt ded 5-3-19 8N&D p269 CR Notts85
CLAYTON,John Arnold.MID 2Lt kia 26-3-17 7Ches p223 MR34
CLAYTON,Keith Herbert Lt kia 22-8-18 1/1Camb p244 CR France196
CLAYTON,Norman 2Lt kia 23-8-16 1/4RBerks p234 MR21,23-7-16
CLAYTON,Norman Lt dow 13-4-18 RFA attPortugueseCps p26 CR France134
CLAYTON,Norman 2Lt kia 14-10-18 1/4YLI p235 CR France1196
CLAYTON,Richard Stopford Lt ded 26-1-16 4HLI CR Scot241
CLAYTON,William Ernest Albert T2Lt dow 22-4-16 9Ches p95 CR France345
CLAYTON-SMITH,Albert Butler Henkersfeldt Lt kia 19-12-15 1/5YLI p235 CR Belgium23,Heukensfeldt
CLAYTON-SMITH,Horace Edward Henkersfeldt.MC.Lt kia 23-7-17 1/5YLI p235 CR Belgium173,Capt
CLEAL,Harry.MC.T2Lt kia 10-12-17 11Ess B'Coy p131 CR France711
CLEALL,Ernest Harry TCapt drd 4-5-17 92RGA p38 CR Italy13
CLEALL,Percy Cawdell Lt dow 26-8-18 6 att10Ess p232 CR France481
CLEARY,Michael Hugh 2Lt kia 28-3-18 GL &62RFC p261&266 MR20
CLEARY,Robert Ernest T2Lt kld 18-12-17 GL &RFC p6 CR Shrop52
CLEASBY-TAYLOR,Ian 2Lt kia 4-12-17 8RScots CR France307
CLEAVE,Norman 2Lt kia 8-11-18 6RWar p214 CR France965,10Bn
CLEAVER,Claude Rex Capt dow 19-7-15 IA 29Punjabis p275 CR EAfrica13
CLEAVER,Digby Crunden 2Lt kia 29-12-15 RFC p1 CR France200
CLEAVER,Eric Arnold TLt dow 3-7-17 GL &RFC p6 CR France219 ExEYorks
CLEAVER,Frank T2Lt dow 3-10-18 RE ROD SurveyCoy p44 CR France113
CLEAVER,Frederick Canning Rev Chap4Cl 17-6-17 CR Iraq6
CLEAVER,Herbert Leonard HonLt&QM ded 11-11-14 2/5SLancs p269 CR Lancs164
CLEAVER,Horace Gregory T2Lt kld 17-3-18 RFC p15 CR Oxford74
CLEE,Thomas Howard 2Lt ded 7-11-18 10Worc att23LancF p108 CR France1028
CLEEF,Henry Victor T2Lt kia 6-12-17 8RWSurr p55 CR France366
CLEEVE,Frederick John Stewart BtCol ded 13-10-16 RFA 10DAC p26 CR Greece7
CLEEVE-EDWARDS,Cecil T2Lt kia 16-10-18 RE 2FC p44 CR France777

CLEGG,Albert SubCdr ded 13-7-19 IA S&TCps p275
CLEGG,Alexander 2Lt kia 1-7-16 13LancF p92 MR21
CLEGG,Alfred Victor Capt kia 7-8-15 6LancF p221 CR Gallipoli1
CLEGG,Frank Cecil TCapt kia 22-8-15 6BordR p116 MR4
CLEGG,James Lt dow 25-5-15 10Manch p237 MR4
CLEGG,John Hamer Capt dow 4-6-15 10Manch p237 MR4
CLEGG,Joseph TCapt kia 16-9-16 6YLI p142 MR21
CLEGG,Lionel TLt kia 22-8-18 7TankCps p188 CR France798
CLEGG,Percy T2Lt kia 1-7-16 1Lancs p58 CR France643
CLEGG,Richard Bagnall Lt kia 18-7-16 RE 15FC p44 CR France144
CLEGG,Robert Burton 2Lt kia 17-2-17 C250RFA p208 CR France1472
CLEGG,Robert Leslie Lt kia 3-9-17 4LancF att45RFC p6&92 CR France285
CLEGG-HILL,Arthur Reginald.Hon.DSO.TLtCol kia 18-9-18 12Ches p95 MR37
CLEGHORN,Allan James T2Lt ded 7-9-16 11 att1GordH p166 CR France201
CLEGHORN,Herbert Stuart Capt kia 2-9-17 RE att1AircraftDepotRFC p18&210 CR France134
CLELAND,Frank Lee TCapt dow 5-7-16 RAMC att2Ess p194 CR France145,4-7-16
CLELAND-HOLLAMBY,Douglas MacDonald T2Lt kld 22-8-17 RWKent &RFC p6&140
CLELLAND,Robert Marshall 2Lt ded 22-12-18 IARO attSap&Min p275 MR66
CLEMENT,Carleton Main.MC.Capt kia 19-8-17 GL &22RFC p6 MR20
CLEMENT,Herbert TLtACapt kia 10-10-17 3 att14RWar p64 MR30
CLEMENT,Hubert Arnold 2Lt kia 3-5-17 att83BlkW p128 MR20
CLEMENT,Walter Albert 2Lt kia 21-3-18 59MGC p182 MR20
CLEMENT,William Honeycott Lt ded 27-6-19 18Lond p255 CR Palestine11,CLEMENTS
CLEMENTS,Claude Casburn 2Lt kia 9-10-18 4RBerks p234 CR France916
CLEMENTS,F.C.Lt kia 6-9-15 3SStaffs A'Coy p122 CR France163,dow
CLEMENTS,Francis Carey 2Lt dow 11-1-17 RE BO CableSect attF'CpsSigCo p44 CR France158
CLEMENTS,F.W.R.Col 2-3-15 RE CR Hamps34
CLEMENTS,George William Valentine Capt&QM 3-3-16 Drags CR Norf209
CLEMENTS,Louis Walter ACapt kia 9-10-17 3Norf p73 MR30
CLEMENTS,Reginald Francis.MC.TLt kia 14-8-18 7RSuss p118 CR France633
CLEMENTS,Robert Cooper 2Lt kia 7-8-18 4NumbF p213 CR France193,8-8-18
CLEMENTS,Thomas Lipton T2Lt kia 23-3-18 11 att9RInniskF p104 MR27
CLEMENTS,W.G.LtCol 16-1-20 RAMC CR Hamps13
CLEMENTS,William Hunter.MSM.2Lt kia 16-8-17 11RInniskF p104 CR Belgium96
CLEMENTS,William Vincent Lt ded 28-2-19 RASC MT att58SBAmmCol p192 CR Belgium267,2Lt 20-2-19
CLEMENTZ,Denis Murray T2Lt kia 6-3-18 24RFC p15 CR France1203
CLEMES,Percival Henry 2Lt kia 2-12-17 IA 6Cav p275 CR France415
CLEMETSON,David Louis Lt kia 21-9-18 PembrokeYeo p205 CR France212
CLEMINSON,Robert 2Lt kia 25-9-16 3 att1EYorks p83 MR21
CLEMSON,John Oliver LtCapt dow 9-12-15 RNDevYeo p203 CR Gallipoli26
CLENCH,Gordon McDakin.TD.Maj ded 26-7-18 3RFA CR Scot381
CLENDINNING,T.H. See GLENDINNING
CLENT,James Tom HonCapt ded 20-4-17 ArmyPayDept p200 CR Mddx66
CLEPHAN,William Richmond.MC.2Lt kia 7-7-17 6NumbF p214 MR20
CLERK,Beauchamp Capt kia 11-3-15 IA 82Punjabis att59Rif p275 CR France727
CLERK,Robert Vere Capt&Adjt kia 28-6-15 ScotRif p103 MR4
CLERK,Ronald Malcolm Capt kia 9-4-17 RLancs att6RWSurr p58 CR France1182
CLERKE,Francis William Talbot Lt kia 21/26-9-16 2CldGds p51 CR France218,26-9-16 &CR France374
CLERKE-BROWN,Richard 2Lt 20-8-16 RE 103FC CR France402
CLERY,Carleton Lumley St.Clair 2Lt kia 12-3-15 ULIA att4Lpool p71&275 CR France1106
CLERY,Daniel Richard Lt kia 10-8-15 6RDubF p176 MR4
CLERY,James Albert.CB.SurgGen 10-2-20 AMS CR Lond29
CLERY,John Cosney Lewis 2Lt kia 1-5-17 78RH&FA p26 CR France418
CLERY,John Francis Capt kia 16-8-17 RMunstF att1RIrRif p175 MR30
CLERY,Noel Cairns.MC.TCapt kia 24-7-16 RFA DivHQ p26 CR France399
CLESHAM,Thomas Henry T2Lt kia 1-7-16 17Manch p154 MR21
CLEVELAND,Alfred Sherwood 2Lt kia 16-10-16 2N&D p133 MR21
CLEVELAND,Ernest Herbert 2Lt kia 31-7-16 13N&D att8Y&L p133 CR France515
CLEVELAND,Frederick Walter.MC.MID Chap4Cl dow 11-10-18 RAChDept att1/6NStaffs p199 CR France146
CLEWS,Robert.MC.TLt dow 28-4-18 RE 235ArmyTroopCoy p44 CR France102
CLIBBORN,Cecil Hamilton Capt dow 7-4-16 IA 92Punjabis p275 MR38
CLIBBORN,Cuthbert John Hamilton.MID Capt kia 14-12-15 D'RFA p26 CR France275

CLIDERO,Herbert T2Lt kia 1-9-18 1Yorks att8WYorks p90 CR France1484,2Bn
CLIEVE,James Francis Maj&QM ded 7-2-19 RWFus p263 CR Wales,6-2-19
CLIFF,Cecil Robson Lt ded 3-10-18 161RFA p27 CR Yorks323
CLIFF,Frank Pearce TLt kia 4-10-17 10Yorks p90 MR30
CLIFF,Grosvenor Talbot Maj dedacc 10-2-18 3DragGds p21 CR France446
CLIFF,Harold Martin.MID LtCol ded 1-2-17 RDubF p176 CR Lond8
CLIFF,Herbert Theodore Maj kia 13-10-14 3WYorks p81 CR France193
CLIFF,Percy Jack 2Lt dow 16-6-17 4 att5NStaffs p156 CR France178,John
CLIFF,Reginald Bertram Talbot Capt dow 23-9-15 1RFA p207 CR Belgium11
CLIFF-McCULOCH,Walter Alexander TLt kia 27-2-18 7RIrRif p169 CR France423,McCULLOCHN 27-2-16
CLIFFORD,Anthony Clifford 2Lt kia 2-6-15 3DragGds RoO p21 CR Belgium4
CLIFFORD,G.K Lt 1-7-18 13Lond CR Devon107
CLIFFORD,Henry Francis Maj kia 9-1-17 1/1GloucYeo p203 CR Egypt2
CLIFFORD,Henry Frederick Hugh.DSO.TBrigGen kia 11-9-16 2Suff attStaff Cmdg149InfBde p78&258 CR France430
CLIFFORD,Herbert Edward Capt dow 19-7-16 2SAfrInf CR France145
CLIFFORD,Herbert James TLtACapt kia 20-9-17 11KRRC p149 MR30
CLIFFORD,Hugh Gilbert Francis Lt kia 1-7-16 Lincs p74 CR France393
CLIFFORD,Leonard Price 2Lt kia 7-6-17 23Lond p252
CLIFFORD,Norman Charles T2Lt ded 13-2-19 ExMGC p266 CR Hamps 138
CLIFFORD,Ralph Montague Lewis TCapt kia 15-10-16 GL 11Ess attTMB p190 MR21
CLIFFORD,Walter Francis Joseph 2Lt kia 27-9-15 IrGds SR att2Bn p52 MR19
CLIFFORD,Watling Wallis T2Lt dow 12-10-17 8RFus p67
CLIFFORD,Wigan.DSO.MajTLtCol kia 20-6-17 1 att10NumbF p60 CR Belgium29,Wigram
CLIFFORD,William James 2Lt kia 25-4-17 GL &48RFC p6 MR20
CLIFT,Marcus Henry T2Lt kia 8-11-17 11EYorks p83 MR20
CLIFT,Maurice Richard 2Lt dow 4-8-16 3Dors att9Dev p123 CR France40
CLIFTON,George Leake Cecil Lt ded 22-7-17 RFC 2AircraftDepot p6 CR France62
CLIFTON,Harold Norton 2Lt dow PoW 1-2-15 1CldGds p51 CR France924
CLIFTON,Hubert Arthur T2Lt dow 6-4-16 10ELancs p110 CR Iraq6,8-4-16
CLIFTON,Hubert Everard.MC.2Lt dow 4-10-16 1Dev p76 CR Devon258
CLIFTON,Percy James.DSO.MID Maj dow 26-8-18 A232RFA p206 CR France119,kia
CLIFTON,Ralph 2Lt dow 22-5-17 RFA att14DivHQ p27 CR France 102
CLIFTON,William Gerard Talbot 2Lt kia 31-3-17 3 O&BLI att11RFC p6&130 CR France1311
CLIMIE,Agnes Murdoch SNurse kia 1-10-17 TFNS 58GH p254 CR France134,30-9-17
CLIMO,Verschoyle Crawford Maj ded 19-2-19 Manch MinOfPensions p265 CR Hamps159
CLINTON,Walter Lawrence Capt ded 22-11-18 KRRC p149 CR Europe56
CLISSOLD,Harry.DSO.Maj kia 28-9-17 RE 474FC p209 CR Belgium20,Henry
CLIVE,Percy Archer.DSO.TLtCol kia 5-4-18 1GrenGds Cmdg1/5LancF p49 MR20
CLIVE,Percy Robert H.Viscount Capt dow 31-10-16 1WelshGds p53 CR Wales358
CLIVE-SMITH,Colin Metcalfe T2Lt kia 24-3-18 12RB p178 CR France987
CLIVELY,John Harold 2Lt kia or dow 3-5-17 4Y&L p238 MR20
CLIXBY,Edward Denis 2Lt kia 13-10-15 4Lincs p217 MR19
CLODE-BAKER,George Edmund Lt kia 1-7-16 5Lond p246 CR France798
CLOETE,Harry Durie.MC.Maj gunwound 29-2-20 IA 92Punjabis att2AssamRif p275 MR66
CLOETE,Lawrence Balfour.MC.LtCol 25-1-20 41Dogras MR65
CLOSE,Barry Samuel Lt kia 27-9-18 1IrGds p52 CR France1497
CLOSE,Charles Paul T2Lt dow 14-11-16 10RDubF p176 CR France74
CLOSE,Frederick Mackdonald.MIDx2 Col dow 30-3-19 RA CR Suff98
CLOSE,Henry Burke Lt ded 1-11-18 RDubF att1/2Bn p176&257 CR Ireland12
CLOSE,Max Arthur 2Lt kia 14-3-15 1HLI p162 CR France279
CLOSE,Robert William Mills Lt kia 27-5-18 4Yorks p220 MR18
CLOSE,William Collins 2Lt kia 20-3-17 3 att6Nhampt p137 MR20
CLOSE-BROOKS,Arthur Brooks.MC.Capt dow 10-1-17 3Manch p154 CR Iraq5
CLOSEBROOKS,John Charles Lt kia 30-10-14 1LifeGds p20 MR29
CLOTHIER,John Keith Capt kia 7-12-14 1WYorks p81 CR France82
CLOTHIER,Robert Frank Capt kia 3-11-14 IA 13Rajputs p275 MR47
CLOUDESLEY,Hugh TLt kia 1-7-16 7RWSurr p55 CR France397
CLOUGH,Alan TCapt kia 1-7-16 16WYorks p81 MR21
CLOUGH,Charles Eric Maj ded 12-3-15 RASC 28DivTrn p253 CR France134
CLOUGH,Edgar T2Lt ded 14-10-18 RE 97FC p44 CR France123
CLOUGH,Ernest Rowan Butler 2Lt dow 27-6-16 Dev att11DLI p76 CR Belgium6

CLOUGH,Gilbert Seymour T2Lt dow 27-3-18 65MGC p182 CR France40,Lt 55Bn
CLOUGH,Harry Collier T2Lt kia 30-7-16 14 att18Manch p154 MR21
CLOUGH,Hugh Francis Lt kia 14-3-17 4RWKent p234 MR38
CLOUGH,Mary SNurse ded 12-10-16 QAIMNS p200 CR Europe1
CLOUGH,Morris Capt kia 25-4-18 18WYorks p81 MR30
CLOUGH,Thomas Capt mbk 2-2-19 IARO att1/72Pujabis p275 MR34
CLOUGH,Walter George 2Lt kia 18-9-18 1Lincs p74 CR France415
CLOUTMAN,Thomas Henry T2Lt dow 7-3-17 16Mddx p146 CR France145
CLOUTMAN,Wolfred Reeve.MIDx2 TLt kia 22-8-15 RE 178Coy p44 CR France189,21-8-15
CLOVER,Harwood Linay TLt ded 25-12-16 7RDubF C'Coy attRFC p2&176 CR Suff225,23-12-16
CLOW,David James.DCM.2Lt kia 24-8-18 4BordR att15DLI p228 MR16
CLOW,George Robert T2Lt kia 17-3-16 9BlkW p128 MR19
CLOW,Oswald William 2Lt kia 25-4-18 156RFA p27 MR30
CLOWES,Charles George Edric Lt dow 18-2-15 1 att3KRRC p149 CR France284
CLOWES,Henry Arthur LtCol ded 8-3-16 1StaffsYeo p205 CR Egypt9
CLOWES,Warren Peter Lt kia 30-3-18 8Huss p22 CR France1172
CLUBB,Howard William Lt kia 27-3-17 6Ess p232 MR34
CLUE,Henry May T2Lt kia 30-7-16 10 att7RLancs p58 MR21
CLULOW,Frederick Reginald 2Lt dow 24-4-18 3 att1N&D p133 CR France29,25-4-18
CLUNIE,William Halkerston 2Lt kia 26-4-18 9RScots p212 CR Belgium185,6-4-18
CLUNIES ROSS,H.E.Capt 27-9-18 KAR CR Sussex 30 See ROSS,H.E.Clunies
CLUTTERBUCK,Arthur Stanley 2Lt kia 14-7-16 8Worc p226 CR France643
CLUTTERBUCK,Arthur Vincent Maj ded 31-10-16 1 att3Ess p131 CR Suff54,LtCol
CLUTTERBUCK,Bernard Valentine 2Lt kia 13-7-17 RFA attZ29TMB p27 CR Belgium12,14-7-17
CLUTTERBUCK,David TLt dow 6-5-17 126/28RFA p27 CR France95
CLUTTERBUCK,Henry Capt kia 31-8/2-9-14 RLancs p58 CR France1350,26-8-14
CLUTTERBUCK,Hugh Guy Daniel 2Lt mbk 19-4-16 IARO att1/7GurkhaRif p275 MR38,17-4-16
CLUTTERBUCK,Norman Eckstein Lt kia 24-4-17 8Worc p226 CR France1495
CLUTTERBUCK,Peter Lt kia 20-10-14 1EYorks p83 MR32
CLYDESDALE,Robert Alexander Crawford 2Lt ded 27-2-19 Fife&ForfarYeo p255 CR Scot97
CLYNE,Daniel Miller Lt kia 23-7-18 1/5SfthH p241 CR France1697
COADE,William Henry Lt dow 5-11-18 3Leinst p174 CR Surrey1
COADY John 2Lt 21-8-18 ConnRgrs att2RIrReg MR16
COAKLEY,Charles Stewart T2Lt kia 30-10-17 KSLI att1/4Bn p144 MR30
COAKLEY,G.H.Cdr 28/29-9-19 IndMiscList attMilWks MR43
COAKLEY,Joseph Lynch Capt ded 19-10-17 LabCps p189&266,RoO RB CR Eire86 Ex RB
COALES,Stephen James T2Lt dow 18-9-16 6RWKent p140 CR France158
COAPE-ARNOLD,R.de N.Lt ded 28-6-18 6SStaffs &RAF p229
COAR,Edward Roland T2Lt dow 8-1-18 2ELancs p110 CR Belgium11
COATE,Alfred Melbourne 2Lt kia 28-8-18 36RFA p27 CR France927
COATE,William Henry TLtACapt kia 25-10-17 16ACycCps p181 MR37
COATES,Alan David Lt kia 27/28-4-15 4Lond p246 CR Belgium101,28-4-15
COATES,Arthur 2Lt kia 27-10-16 4Yorks p220 MR21
COATES,Basil Montgomery T2Lt kia 7-9-15 10RB p178 MR32
COATES,Cecil Evelyn Maj kia 23-7-16 6Glouc p225 CR France832
COATES,Clifford Marsh 2Lt kia 3-5-17 RGA 174SB p38 MR20,Marsden 146SB
COATES,Donald Newton 2Lt kia 21-3-18 25NumbF p60 MR20
COATES,Frederick Noel T2Lt dow 4-4-17 22NumbF p60 CR France1182
COATES,George Henry Capt ded 25-12-15 2/9DLI p239 CR Durham88
COATES,George Washington Tate.MID 2Lt kia 10-3-15 33RFA p27 MR22
COATES,Harold Capt kia 25-9-15 1Lincs p74 MR19
COATES,Harold Brearley T2Lt kia 1-7-16 7Yorks p90 CR France397
COATES,Harold Edward TMaj kia 3-5-17 13Lpool p71 MR20
COATES,James Ernest 2Lt dow 22-8-18 RGA 336SB p38 CR France103
COATES,John 2Lt kia 15-8-18 ERid of YorksYeo att1EYorks p206 CR France19
COATES,Percy T2Lt kia 15-4-16 RE 180Co p44 CR France423
COATES,Stanley Harvey 2Lt kia 7-6-17 4EKent p212 CR Belgium131
COATES,Sydney T2Lt kia 27-5-17 GL att52RFC p6 CR France1468
COATES,W.F.Capt dow 30-4-15 6 att1RFus p67 CR France683
COATH,Leonard Charles 2Lt kia 4-9-16 10 att1Norf p73 MR21
COATS,Eric Robert Lt kia 17-5-17 1ScotsGds p52 CR France927
COATS,J.LtCol 11-5-19 RAMC CR Scot503
COATS,John Alexander Hamilton 2Lt dow 8-8-16 10RScots att164TMB p255 MR21
COATS,Lawrence Armstrong T2Lt kia 28-10-15 15 att8NumbF p60 CR Gallipoli4

COATS,Thomas T2Lt kia 30-9-18 5CamH p167 CR Belgium157
COATS,William Evans T2Lt dow 4-11-17 17RScots p53 CR France145
COATSWORTH,Alfred Henry T2Lt dow 8-9-16 1RWar att10MGC p64 CR France1,9-9-16
COBB,Francis Walker 2Lt ded 28-3-18 42RFC p15 CR Mddx48,Walter
COBB,Frederick Charles TCapt kia 25-9-15 6KOSB p101 CR France114
COBB,James Cassels Lt kia 23-8-18 5RWKent p235 CR France177
COBB,John Elbridge 2LtTLt dow 14-8-17 RASC att21RFC p6&192 CR Belgium16
COBB,Kenneth Rhodes Capt kia 1-7-15 15KRRC p149 CR Gallipoli6
COBB,Reginald T2Lt kia 13-10-16 5RBerks A'Coy p138 CR France277
COBB,Reginald John Preston 2Lt kia 11-10-17 WRid &56RFC p6&115 MR20
COBB,Sydney James T2Lt dow 20-7-16 8RMunstF p175 CR France64,Sidney
COBB,T.W.2Lt 15-12-20 EgyptLabCps CR Hamps18
COBB,William Ralph.MC.LtACapt dow 5-10-17 RWKent p140 MR30
COBBETT,Arthur Irvin Brooke 2Lt dow 23-8-18 1DCLI p114 MR16
COBBETT,Charles Newberry Capt ded 7-10-19 RAMC p267 CR Dorset52
COBBOLD,Charles Augustus TCapt kia 13-10-15 7Suff p78 MR19
COBBOLD,Charles Townsend 2Lt kia 3-10-16 32RFA p27 MR21
COBBOLD,Edgar Francis Wanklyn Lt kia 12-1-16 7Ches attRFC p18&223 CR France924
COBBOLD,Robert Henry Wanklyn Lt kia 9-9-15 6 att2RB p178 CR France276
COBBOLD,Robert Towshend T2Lt kia 25-9-15 6RFA p27 CR Belgium6,Rowland
COBDEN,Frank Pargeter Lt kia 7-7-18 MGC att 104RAF p182 CR Germany3
COBHAM,Elijah Rev Chap4Cl dow 19-9-17 RAChDept attKAR p199 CR EAfrica8 CR Tanzania1,kia
COBHAM,Frederick George Brian Lt kia 8-8-18 1Camb p244 CR France196
COBON,Harold Gardiner.MC.2Lt dow 24-1-18 NorfYeo p204 Egypt9
COBURN,Charles 2Lt kia 31-7-17 KRRC att18Bn p149 MR29
COBURN,Frederick Isaac.MID TLt ded 4-10-17 1RASC SupplyCoy p192 CR France85
COCHRAN,Frances Alexander 2Lt kia 25-9-15 1GordH p166 CR Belgium112,Francis
COCHRAN,Herbert Philip Gordon.DSO.LtCol kia 24-3-18 Mddx att15Ches p146 CR France402
COCHRAN,Lionel Francis Abingdon Capt kia 4-2-15 IA 72Pujabis att92 p275
COCHRANE,Cyril Lt kia 25-9-15 1GordH p166 MR29
COCHRANE,Donald James Capt kia 8-5-15 65RFA p27 MR29
COCHRANE,Edwin Arthur Lt dow 4-8-18 4 att2/6NStaffs p156 CR France10,1/6Bn
COCHRANE,George T2Lt kia 19-9-17 att7RB p178 CR Belgium42,18-9-17
COCHRANE,George King Hicks T2Lt kia 25-3-17 1HLI att 1/1Gurkhas IA p162&275 MR38
COCHRANE,Hugh Paterson Maj kia 20-9-17 8 att2/5LancF p221 MR30
COCHRANE,Reginald.MID 2Lt kia 18-8-17 B282RFA p27 CR Belgium36
COCHRANE,Walter Francis Capt kia 19-4-17 1/4KOSB p223 CR Palestine8
COCHRANE,William T2Lt kia 26-9-17 1RScotF p94 CR Belgium125
COCK,Hubert Charles Langslow Maj kia 22/24-11-15 17RGA attStaff p38 MR38
COCK,John Herbert 2Lt kia 14-4-17 GL &60RFC p6 CR France1310
COCKADAY,Aubrey George.MID Lt dow 31-10-18 10/147RFA p27 CR France241
COCKAYNE,Arthur Edward 2Lt kia 1-7-17 5NStaffs p238 MR19
COCKBURN,Charles James Lt.MC.kia 7-1-16 IA 6Jats p275 MR38
COCKBURN,George Percival Lt kia 23-3-18 6Suff att7RWSurr p218 MR27
COCKBURN,Henry Howard 2Lt kia 1-4-17 4RIrReg att2RInniskF p88 CR France675
COCKBURN,James 2Lt kia 12-10-16 4A&SH att90MGC p173&182 MR21
COCKBURN,John 2Lt kia 25-4-15 RWar p64 MR29
COCKBURN,Robert Bowes TCapt ded 27-9-18 RAVC att130RFA p198 CR Greece18
COCKBURN,Robert Claude Radcliffe Lt ded 25-11-18 IA 36Sikhs p275
COCKCROFT,Arthur Clarence T2Lt kia 1-7-16 11 att10YLI p142 CR France267
COCKE,Robert Sturgeon Capt ded 16-11-18 RAMC p267 CR Lond14,20-11-18
COCKER,Arthur Wilfred Kingsley 2Lt kia 30-11-17 17RFus p67 MR17
COCKER,Thomas Edge LtACapt kia 21-3-18 A/153RFA attY36TMB p27
COCKERELL,Andrew Pepys 2Lt kia 15-8-16 2KRRC p149 CR France397
COCKERELL,Donald Chessum 2Lt kia 6-11-18 5Lond p246 CR Belgium195
COCKERELL,Samuel Pepys 2Lt ded 20-3-15 RFC p1 CR Egypt8,Lt
COCKERILL,George Edward LtTCapt dow 3-7-16 PoW 16Lond B'Coy p249 CR France1484
COCKETT,Edward Allan T2Lt dow 9-9-16 1Glouc p106 CR France833
COCKETT,William Arthur 2Lt mbk 26-10-17 3 att2GordH p256 CR Belgium112
COCKEY,John Edmund Percival 2Lt kia 30-7-16 20Lpool p71 MR21

COCKFIELD,Charles Francis 2Lt kia 27-8-16 RGA 142SB p38 CR France630
COCKING,Charles Oscar John 2Lt kia 11-4-17 5SLancs p230 CR France705
COCKING,Frank Kenneth Lt kia 23-7-16 3DCLI p114 MR21,Stennett
COCKLE,Clarence Tapscott Lt kia 10-9-18 5Suff p217 MR30
COCKRELL,William Archer Lt ded 11-11-17 RemountService RASC p24 CR Berks113
COCKRILL,Alick Charles 2Lt kia 23-4-17 4Norf p216 MR20
COCKRILL,Charles Whalley Lt kia 2-2-18 C180RFA p207 CR France364
COCKS,Edward James Trist.MID 2Lt kia 5-8-18 5Worc p108 CR France28,4Bn
COCKS,Edward Louis 2Lt kia 8-8-16 17Mddx p146 MR21
COCKS,John Stanley Capt ded 29-1-19 RAMC att 1EgyptDetHosp p194 CR Lebanon1,Maj
COCKS,Percy Frank Anderson Lt ded 25-5-16 5RWSurr p212 MR38
COCKS,Willard Fleetwood TLt dow 9-4-17 3Lincs p74 MR20
COCKSEDGE,Robert James 2Lt kia 25-9-18 1Norf p73 CR France905
CODD,Herbert Charles Capt ded 6-11-18 IARO attLabCps p275 MR69,19-3-20
CODD,Stephen Arthur Herbert T2Lt kia 9-9-16 11 att 10Glouc p106 MR21
CODDINGTON,Charles Ernest 2Lt kia 4-12-17 10Lpool attRFC p17&216 CR France120
CODDINGTON,Hubert John Capt kia 7-7-15 DLI p160 CR Belgium92
CODE,Harold T2Lt kia 25-8-18 Manch p154 CR France239
CODNER,Christopher Cardew 2LtACapt kia 3-5-17 1SomLI p79 CR France1194
CODRINGTON,Ernest LtCol ded 20-4-16 IA 120Inf p275 CR Iraq1
CODY,John 2Lt kia 21-8-18 ConnRgrs att 2RIrReg p172
CODY,Samuel Franklyn T2Lt kia 23-1-17 GL &41RFC p6 CR Belgium115
COE,Frederick Hermann Lt ded 28-4-17 6LancF p269 CR Lancs475
COE,George T2Lt kia 1-7-16 1 att 11BordR p116 MR21
COE,Herbert James T2Lt kia 8-8-18 2TankCps p188 CR France526
COE,James George Lt dow 1-10-18 4SfthH p241 CR Belgium157
COE,Joseph William Maj ded 21-10-17 RAVC att59Div p254 CR France145
COE,Sydney Urie Charles T2Lt kia 30-11-17 16KRRC p149 CR Belgium125
COFFEE,Francis Warren 2Lt kia 16-8-17 5 att 14RIrRif p169 MR30
COFFEY,Charles Reay Lt kld 27-5-18 GL &RAF p190 MR20
COFFIN,Sebright Edward 2Lt dow 20-12-15 3 att2RScots p53 CR Belgium11
COGAN,Lionel Gatrell Lt ded 7-10-18 IA 1/153Inf p275 MR65, 1/153Punjabis
COGGIN,Algernon Oswald TLt kia 27-10-16 20RFus p67 CR France374
COGGINS,Wilfred George 2Lt dow 15-12-16 4RWKent att 16RB p234 CR France145
COGHILL,Hugh Bernard Mackay Capt kia 25-9-15 4HLI p162 MR19,2Bn
COGHILL,Norman Harry Lt dow 28-3-18 ScotsGds attMGC p52 CR France62,attGds MGR
COGHILL,Sinclair Baxter T2Lt kia 9-9-16 5 att 8RInniskF p104 MR21
COGHLAN,Clifford Edward Leslie Lt kia 27-8-17 SStaffs att9Bn p122 MR30
COGHLAN,Joseph Patrick.MC.Lt kia 20-9-17 RE 228FC p44 CR Belgium124
COGHLAN,Thomas Reginald 2Lt dow 24-10-18 3RIrF p171 CR Belgium358
COGHLAN,William Humphrey Lt kia 26-8-14 11/15RFA p27 CR France716
COHAN,E.M.2Lt 5-8-14 RFA CR Lancs181
COHEN,Aaron Simeon Lt kia 25-9-15 RAMC att8SomLI p194 MR19
COHEN,Adolph Broadfield TLt dow 22-7-17 17WYorks p81 CR France145
COHEN,Benjamin TLt dow 3-7-17 RAMC att 122RFA p195 CR Belgium18,kia
COHEN,Cecil Hope Lt ded 18-11-18 RGA Sig p38 CR Mddx40
COHEN,Dudley Trevor 2Lt dow 20-11-17 4 att 7RSuss p228 MR17
COHEN,Edward.MC.T2Lt kia 31-7-17 12RFus p67 MR29
COHEN,George Herbert Lt kia 16-5-15 5Lpool p215 CR France279
COHEN,Harold T2Lt ded 18-7-15 9RBerks p138 CR Mddx27,8Bn
COHEN,John Icely TCapt dow 11-8-17 Dev p76 CR Belgium16,3ELancs
COHEN,Moss.MM.LtACapt dow 24-9-18 2DLI p160 CR France835
COHEN,Moss 2Lt kia 15-9-16 21Lond p251 CR France385
COHEN,Simon Capt ded 23-11-19 LabCps p266 CR Egypt9,dow 22-11-19 EgyptLabCps
COHEN,Solomon Maurice Lt kia 9-9-16 12Lond p248 MR21
COILL,Caesar Alfred Capt ded 11-11-18 RGA p269
COKE,Arthur George.Hon.2Lt kia 21-5-15 2Coy of LondYeo p204
COKE,Langton Sacheverell Lt kia 31-10-14 1IrGds RoO p52 MR29
COKE,Leigh Rigby Capt kia 2-11-17 8Hamps p229 CR Palestine8
COKER,Cadwallader John Lt kia 22-6-15 1WelshR p126 CR Belgium37
COKER,John Cadwallader.MID Lt dow 26-9-14 1SWBord p99 CR France1329
COLBECK,Leonard George 2Lt ded 3-1-18 C59RFA p27&261 MR40
COLBORN,Albert George Lt ded 10-10-18 RH&FA p27 CR Oxford73
COLBORNE,Reginald Elgar 2Lt ded 6-11-18 IARO p275 MR65

COLBORNE,Richard Arthur Pell Rev Chap4Cl kia 28-5-18 RAChDept att 1/1Lond p199 CR France54
COLBOURNE,Eric Krabbe.MC.2Lt dow 27-6-15 3 att 1RBerks p139&258 CR France98
COLBOURNE,Frederick William Lt ded 25-2-19 RAOC 3rdArmy p198 CR France
COLBY,Laurence Robert Vaughan.MID Maj kia 24-10-14 1GrenGds p4 MR29
COLCHESTER,Bernard Valentine T2Lt kia 25-4-17 6Beds p85 MR20
COLCOTT,Ernest Harry 2Lt kia 11-9-16 1/8Mddx p236 CR France164,COLLCOTT
COLCUTT,Thomas Mills.MID T2Lt kia 9-9-18 8Glouc p106 CR France1106
COLDHAM,George Herbert TLt dow 17-9-16 64MGC p182 CR France188
COLDICOTT,Arden Cotterell.MC.Capt kia 16-8-18 15RWar p64 CR Germany1,dow 14-8-18
COLDICOTT,Hubert Eric 2Lt kia 21-5-17 15 att 2/6Lond p249 MR20
COLDRICK,Thomas 2Lt kia 21-3-18 7 att 10Worc p226 MR20
COLDWELL,Edward Smith 2Lt 15-2-19 RE CR Lond12
COLDWELL,Herbert David T2Lt kld 11-3-18 RFC p15 CR Wilts116
COLDWELL,Norman Goodman.MC.T2Lt dow 16-5-18 2WRid p115 CR France40
COLDWELL,Vincent Capt ded 18-4-16 IA 4Cav p275 CR Iraq6
COLDWELLS,Charles Albert T2Lt kia 28-9-15 108RFA p27 CR France219
COLDWELLS,Francis Baker 2Lt kia 1-7-16 2Dev p76 MR21
COLE,Arthur Willoughby George Lowry.CB.DSO.ColTBrigGen dow 9-5-15 Staff 25InfBde p1
COLE,Cecil Clark 2Lt dow 13-10-17 RGA 149Bde p38 CR Belgium16
COLE,Charles Henry 2Lt kia 4-10-16 11Lond p248 MR21
COLE,Clarence Claridge T2Lt kia 8-5-18 2Y&L p158 CR Belgium3
COLE,Clifford Spearing Lt kia 19-6-16 2/5Glouc p225 CR France706
COLE,Cyril Charles 2Lt ded 14-11-18 13Ess &RAF p131
COLE,Cyril Lawson Capt ded 14-3-19 2/5Glouc p225 CR France40
COLE,David T2Lt kia 3-7-16 16RIrRif p169 CR France252
COLE,Dorothy Helen Sister ded 24-10-18 TFNS CR Surrey180
COLE,Emily Helena Sister 21-2-15 QAIMNS CR France64
COLE,Ernest T2Lt dow 8-8-16 14 att 8Yorks p90 CR France44
COLE,Ernest Lockett T2Lt kia 27-9-16 8Nhampt p137 MR21
COLE,Frederick John Lt kia 19-4-17 4Norf p216 MR34
COLE,Henry Munroe Capt ded 4-12-18 4Dev att 1/4Wilts p220 CR Egypt2,Maj
COLE,Herbert William 2Lt kia 14-4-18 3 att 1ScotRif p103 MR32
COLE,Humfrey Theodore Shuldham 2Lt dow 12-2-17 19Lond p250 CR France41
COLE,Humphrey Porteus T2Lt dow 3-4-16 9Dev p76 CR France22
COLE,Kenneth Leonard Lt kia 29-9-15 3Y&L p158 MR19
COLE,Leonard Baker TCapt ded 9-5-18 RAVC p268 CR France119
COLE,Leslie Stewart 2Lt kia 3-10-15 3 att 2Ches p95 MR19
COLE,Maxwell Gerard T2Lt kia 18-5-17 GL &1RFC p6 CR Belgium152,Lt
COLE,Mowbray Lyster Stanley Owen Capt ded 14-9-14 4RFus p67 MR15
COLE,Nigel Edwin Fitz Roy 2LtTLt kia 5-10-17 6EKent C'Coy p57 CR France154
COLE,Percival James Lt dow 22-9-16 WessexRFA p207 CR France105
COLE,Reginald Price 2Lt kia 20-5-17 7HLI p240 MR20
COLE,Richard Harry 2Lt kia 25-7-16 1SWBord p99 MR21
COLE,William Maurice.MC.2Lt dow 29-6-18 1/5Leic p220 CR France10
COLE,William Norman 2Lt kia 5-2-17 7SLancs p125 MR21
COLE,Wilfred Samuel TLt ded 11-5-16 25RFus p67 CR EAfrica52,Wilfrid
COLE,William Thomas 2Lt kia 29-7-18 4Yorks p220 CR France1689
COLE-HAMILTON,Arthur Richards TLtCol dow 10-8-15 6ELancs p110 CR Gallipoli12
COLE-HAMILTON,Con William Eric Capt kld 2-7-17 2RScots att 20RFC p6&53 CR Herts87
COLEBROOK,Geoffrey Bathurst 2Lt kia 27-7-15 1RWSurr p55 CR France721,26-7-15
COLEBROOK,Leslie Charles T2Lt kia 1-2-17 14Hamps p120 CR Belgium4
COLEMAN,Arthur T2Lt kia 1-7-16 20NumbF p60 MR21
COLEMAN,Edward Charles Lt kia 2-4-17 114RFA attA'TMB p207 CR Greece5
COLEMAN,Eric 2Lt kia 31-7-17 3Norf attMGC p73&182 MR29
COLEMAN,Ernest Harold 2Lt kia 15-2-15 2RIrF p171 MR29
COLEMAN,Frederick Charles T2Lt kia 25-9-15 6Wilts p152 MR19
COLEMAN,Fred Creighton 2Lt kia 23-4-17 3 att 1Norf p73 CR France58,Lt
COLEMAN,Gerald Arthur Capt ded 6-2-19 RDC &RFus p253 CR Lond1
COLEMAN,Herbert Edward Evatt 2Lt kia 9-9-16 2RSuss p118 MR21
COLEMAN,John Albert David 2Lt kia 3-5-17 9Mddx p236 MR20,10 att 12Bn
COLEMAN,John Roberts T2Lt ded 26-11-18 RE SpecBde p44 CR France1029
COLEMAN,Sydney Capt dow 14-10-18 1Lond p245 CR France214

COLEMAN,Walter William 2Lt ded 12-3-19 6MGC Inf p266 CR Kent301,Lt
COLERIDGE,Luke Frederick Rennell 2Lt kia 22-12-14 1CldGds p51 MR22
COLES,Albert Edward 2Lt mbk 4-10-17 1SomLI att11TMB p256 MR30
COLES,Arthur Norman TLt kia 24-8-16 8RB p178 CR France400
COLES,Crewe 2Lt kia 4-6-15 4ELancs p226 MR4
COLES,Daisy Kathleen Mary Miss kia 30-9-17 VAD BRCS 58GH p200 CR France134
COLES,Donald Mackintosh Lt kia 25/27-10-14 3 att 1NumbF p60 CR France567,27-10-14
COLES,Edgar Ralph Capt kia 12-5-15 3DragGds p21 MR29
COLES,Frederick George.MC.2Lt kia 25-9-17 RFA attY16TMB p27 CR France616
COLES,Henry James Capt kia 30-6-17 5N&D p232 MR20
COLES,Herbert 2Lt kia 18-11-17 2RB A'Coy p178 MR30
COLES,Herbert Stonehouse Capt kia 16-5-15 RWFus p97 MR22
COLES,James Hugh.DSO.CaptALtCol kia 24-4-18 1EYorks p83 MR30
COLES,Lionel George TCapt kia 1-7-16 16RScots p53 CR France267
COLES,Reginald Walter T2Lt kia 12-10-17 RWKent att7Bn p140 MR30
COLES,Rowland Humphrey Lt kia 9-5-17 WSomYeo attRFC p18&205 CR France415
COLES,Sidney Harcourt Lt kia 12-10-14 4Mddx p146 CR France1106
COLES,Thomas Wallace Lt dow 1-5-16 A184RFA p27 CR France80
COLES,William Henry Lt kia 27-12-17 5Yorks p220 CR Belgium125
COLES,William Price Vivian.MM.2Lt kia 7-10-16 7Lond C'Coy p247 CR France385
COLEY,Allen Cowen TLt kld 6-3-18 RFC p15 CR Hamps4
COLEY,Joseph Alfred 2LtACapt kia 22-3-18 5 att4RFus p67 MR20
COLEY,William John 2Lt kia 15-7-16 1Dors p124 CR France296,Lt
COLFER,James Richard TLt ded 26-2-17 9RMunstF p175 CR France64
COLFOX,Thomas David 2Lt kia 14-6-18 42RFA p27 CR France33,41RFA
COLGATE,Roger Edward.MM.2Lt kia 18-11-16 3 att8Glouc p106 MR21
COLGATE,Roy TCapt dow 12-7-16 114MGC p182 CR France66,Robert 13-7-16
COLIN,Felix Augustus 2Lt kia 3-5-17 1 att7ESurr p112 MR20
COLLCOTT,Ernest Harry see COLCOTT,E.H.
COLLCUTT,Philip Martin Blake TLt kia 12-5-17 7EYorks p83 MR20
COLLEDGE,Arthur Vincent Lt kia 10-8-19 4Worc att45RFus p254 MR70 &CR Europe180
COLLEN,John 2Lt mbk 25-10-16 7RInniskF &7RFC p256 MR20
COLLEN,Norman Owen T2Lt kia 25-9-16 EYorks p83 CR France385
COLLEN,William Stewart T2Lt kia 7/10-8-15 6RInniskF p104 CR Gallipoli5,Lt 7-8-15
COLLENS,Edwin Theobald Lt dow 3-9-18 1Lond p245 CR France103,2Lt
COLLER,Bernard Tarrant Lt kia 26-9-16 GL &RFC p2&190,ded MR20
COLLER,Charles Mervyn Capt kia 21-3-18 4 att9Norf p216 MR20
COLLES,Arthur Grove Capt kia 12-3-15 RDubF att1RIrRif p176 MR22
COLLETT,Arthur Leigh T2Lt dow 18-11-16 8Glouc p106 CR France384,Lt
COLLETT,Clive Franklyn.MC.LtTCapt kld 23-12-17 70RFC p6&258 CR Scot235
COLLETT,Thomas Theodore 2Lt dow 15-2-17 7Yorks p90 CR France105
COLLEY,Archibald 2Lt kia 14-3-15 2DCLI p114 MR29
COLLEY,Douglas James 2Lt kia 29-11-16 6Lpool p215 MR29
COLLEY,Ernest Vincent 2Lt dow 23-8-17 B'TankCps p88 MR30
COLLEY,Harold 2Lt kia 1-7-16 18WYorks p81 MR21
COLLEY,Harry Leonard.MC.2Lt kia 4-11-18 WYorks att2YLI p81 CR France933
COLLEY,Philip Wellesley 2Lt ded 31-10-18 A156RFA p27 CR Hamps1,21-10-18
COLLEY,Robert Archibald Lt kia 22-3-18 8DLI att25MGC p187&239 MR20
COLLEY,William Arthur TCapt kia 1-7-16 12Y&L p158 MR21
COLLIE,M.A.T.LtCol 3-12-18 IMS CR Lancs40
COLLIER,Bertram T.T2Lt dow 5-11-16 31 att25NumbF p60 CR France297
COLLIER,Ernest Stebbing 2Lt kia 2-4-18 9RGA p38 CR France1071
COLLIER,Frederick 2Lt dow 11-5-17 2/8Manch p237 CR France134
COLLIER,Frederick Herbert Mark TLt kia 23-4-17 15N&D p133 MR20
COLLIER,George T2Lt dow 9-8-18 8MGC p182 CR France95
COLLIER,Guy Cecil Lt kia 23-7-18 3 att10ScotRif p103 CR France865
COLLIER,Harry Ronald.MC.LtACapt kia 17-4-18 1KOSB p101 CR France324
COLLIER,Hubert Charles de Zoete 2Lt dow 4-4-17 21Manch att91TMB p154 CR France156
COLLIER,John Thomas T2Lt kia 2-11-17 3RWar att 1/4Norf p64 CR Palestine8
COLLIER,Reginald Charles 2Lt ded 17-11-18 RGA 196SB p38 CR France85
COLLIER,Reginald John T2Lt kld 12-2-18 RFC p15 CR Ireland107
COLLIER,Samuel Francis Capt kia 22-3-18 6Manch p236 MR27
COLLIER,Samuel Robert T2Lt kia 20-7-16 6RBerks p139 MR21
COLLIER,Sidney.MC.Lt kia 28-3-18 6Manch attRFC p18&236 CR France58
COLLIER,Simon.MC.Lt kia 14-9-18 2Wilts p206 CR France80 Ex WiltsYeo
COLLIN,Joseph Henry.VC.2Lt kia 9-4-18 4RLancs p213 CR France1106
COLLIN,Kenneth Glenfield T2Lt kia 12-10-16 12Lpool p71 CR France385
COLLINGE,John Chisholm 2Lt dow 25-10-17 PoW 8LancF p221 CR Germany2
COLLINGE,Wharton Rye Lt dow 7-8-17 2/6Lpool p215 CR France345
COLLINGS,Eric D'Auvergne 2Lt kia 23-8-16 1RWSurr p55 CR France399
COLLINGS,Frank Reginald 2Lt kia 3-12-17 16NumbF p60 MR30
COLLINGS,Harry Colston 2Lt kia 19-9-18 RGA 284SB p38 CR France673
COLLINGS,L.L.2Lt ded 3-10-18 2DLI &RAF p160
COLLINGS,Sydney Walter T2Lt kia 20-4-18 11RFus p67 CR France300,Sidney
COLLINGS,Walter.MC.Lt kia 10-4-18 1/3Mon p244 CR France19,11-4-18
COLLINGS,William Norman TLt kia 6-10-18 2NumbF p60 CR France234
COLLINGS-WELLS,John Stanhope.VC.DSO CaptALtCol kia 27-3-18 4Beds p85 CR France516
COLLINGWOOD,Carlton Capt dow 8-8-16 4SLancs p229 CR France141
COLLINGWOOD,George Albert T2Lt kia 10-8-15 6BordR p116 CR Gallipoli5,COLLINWOOD
COLLINGWOOD,Gordon Francis TLt dow 28-3-18 RGA 405SB p38 CR France113
COLLINGWOOD-THOMPSON,Edward James Vibart 2Lt dow 10-9-14 2RWFus CR France1445
COLLINS,Albert Shepherd 2Lt dow 25-9-17 5ScotRif p224 MR30,10Bn
COLLINS,Alexander Kilpatrick T2Lt kia 29-5-18 12/13NumbF p60 MR18
COLLINS,Alfred John 2Lt kia 29-9-18 1DCLI p114 CR France245
COLLINS,Arthur Duppa T2Lt dow 1-4-17 GL &52RFC p6 CR France105
COLLINS,Arthur Edward Jeune.MID Capt kia 11-11-14 RE 5FC p44 MR29
COLLINS,Arthur Michael Austen Lt ded 28-10-18 IA 38Dogras att 1/1Brahmans p275 MR66
COLLINS,Charles.MID Lt dow 28-7-16 1KRRC p149 MR21
COLLINS,Charles Bury.CMG.DSO.LtColTCol ded 1-3-17 RE p44 CR EAfrica39
COLLINS,Charles Edwin Lt kia 21-3-18 24RFA p27 MR20
COLLINS,Claude Henry James T2Lt dow 16-4-18 18NumbF p60 MR30
COLLINS,Ernest Stanley 2Lt kia 31-7-17 1Worc p108 MR29
COLLINS,Francis John Lt accdrd 25-3-17 RIM attRE IWT p275 CR Iraq6
COLLINS,Frank Basil 2Lt kia 22-8-17 1RFA p208 CR Belgium10
COLLINS,Frederick William T2Lt ded 29-4-16 1LifeGds p20 CR France134
COLLINS,George Edwin T2Lt kia 11-1-18 2RB p178 CR Belgium22
COLLINS,Harold George TLt kia 9-4-17 RASC &48RFC p6&192 CR France120
COLLINS,Harold Stafford T2LtACapt ded 17-11-17 GL EgyptLabCps p190 CR Egypt1
COLLINS,H.B.Maj ded 12-9-18 RAMC p269 CR Hamps246
COLLINS,Henry Herbert John Chap4Cl kia 9-4-17 RAChDept att9BlkW p199 CR France924
COLLINS,Herbert Charles TLt died 11-2-17 24Manch p154 CR France40
COLLINS,Horace Alexander TLt kia 18-9-17 SStaffs att246RFA attRE49SigCo p122 CR Belgium17
COLLINS,James Henry William.MC.T2Lt dow 6-5-17 6LNLancs p135 CR Iraq8
COLLINS,John Ferdinando T2Lt kia 28-3-18 56MGC Inf 182 CR France184
COLLINS,John Gerrard TMaj kia 27-9-15 8BlkW p128 MR19
COLLINS,John Stratford Lt kia 5-4-18 RSuss att12Bn p118 CR France516
COLLINS,L.E.2Lt kld 5-4-18 GL &100RAF p190 CR France1404
COLLINS,Lionel Drummond Kyrle 2Lt kia 11-5-16 3 att13RScots p53 CR France423
COLLINS,Maurice Lt kia 11-9-18 RGA 305SB p38 CR France1484
COLLINS,Neville Lancelot 2Lt kia 15-8-16 3 att2RSuss p118 CR France432
COLLINS,Newton Henry T2Lt kia 27-4-16 5RInniskF p104 CR France115,7Bn
COLLINS,Norman Cecil 2Lt kia 9-8-16 3 att7Suff p78 MR21
COLLINS,Percival George TLt kia 18-8-16 6DCLI p114 MR21
COLLINS,Percy Hugh Campbell.MC.Capt 11-8-20 1Y&L CR Wilts115
COLLINS,Percy Robert Murdoch.DSO.CaptAMaj dow 25-6-17 RGA 13SB p38 CR Belgium29,kia
COLLINS,Philip Capt kia 30-7-15 7RB p178 CR Belgium116
COLLINS,Reginald Thomas.DSO.MajTLtCol kia 18-9-18 RAMC att17FA p195 CR France835
COLLINS,Robert Hayes Maj kia 20-5-17 6Lond p246 CR France614
COLLINS,Robert Simpson T2Lt kia 9-3-18 2RFC p15 CR France98
COLLINS,Samuel William 2Lt kia 21-3-18 2/7N&D p233 MR20
COLLINS,Stanley Thomas Lt dow 29-4-17 5LancF p221 CR France80,2Lt
COLLINS,Thomas TLtACapt ded 23-2-19 RAOC p198 CR France403
COLLINS,Vincent Henry 2Lt kia 12-2-17 IARO att102Grenadiers p275 CR Iraq5
COLLINS,Vivian Donald Berry Lt kia 9-5-15 13N&D attGurkhaRif p133 MR22

COLLINS,Valentine St.Barbe Lt kia 2-9-18 SL &RAF p268 MR20
COLLINS,William 2Lt kia 30-7-16 3 att8Glouc p106 MR21
COLLINS,William Geoffrey Lt dow PoW 21-1-18 7Norf p73 CR Germany2
COLLINS,William Henry Lt kld 7-3-18 YorksHussYeo attRFC p206&18 CR Wilts3
COLLINSON,Arthur Amery Capt kia 25-9-15 9ESurr p112 MR19
COLLINSON,Frank Graham.VD.HonCol ded 3-3-19 6Lond p269 CR Italy15,LtCol
COLLINSON,George Edward Cleather Lt kld 13-4-17 CamH &RFC p6&167 CR Devon230
COLLINSON,Jeffreys Lewis William 2Lt kia 15-7-16 3 att2SLancs p125 CR France393
COLLINSON,John Harold 2Lt kia 21-3-18 18MGC p182 MR27
COLLINSON,William Holmes 2Lt kia 5-1-16 6NumbF p214 CR Belgium127
COLLIS,Bert Humphrey Lt dow 20-12-15 3 att9Suff p78 CR Belgium11
COLLIS,Frank Reginald Maj kia 27-9-16 2NthMidRFA p206 CR France630
COLLIS,Hugh Humphrey 2Lt dow 12-4-17 5Suff p217 CR France113
COLLIS,Percy Harold 2Lt dow 31-7-17 4Hamps p228 CR Belgium36,12Bn
COLLIS,William Henry TCapt kia 9-5-17 7RInniskF p104 CR Belgium60
COLLIS-BROWNE,Alfred Ulick.MID Lt kia 13-4-15 1YL1 p142 MR29
COLLIS-SANDES,Maurice James.MID Capt kia 17-2-17 11RFus B'Coy p67 CR France314
COLLISON,Edgar Henry 2Lt ded 26-6-16 4Norf p216 CR Norf184
COLLISON-MORLEY,Harold Duke.MID MajTLtCol kia 25-9-15 EKent Cmdg19Lond p57 CR France219
COLLISSON,Edwin Read CaptAMaj kia 13-10-15 1/6SStaffs p229 MR19
COLLISSON,Evelyn Ernest Arnold T2Lt kia 23-2-16 2Beds A'Coyp85 CR France699
COLLOT,Thomas Alexander 2Lt kia 1-7-16 6RBerks p139 CR France513
COLLYER,Arthur Alan.OBE.LtCol ded 11-12-19 RAPC p268 CR Scot204 Ex Beds
COLLYER,Arthur Hamilton 2Lt dow 23-4-17 5GordH p242 CR France451
COLLYER,William James T2Lt kia 31-7-17 RSuss att13Bn p118 MR29
COLLYMORE,Hubert Aubrey Lt kia 17-4-18 9Beds att25MGC p85&182 MR30
COLLYNS,Robert Henry.MC.TLt dow 1-6-18RE97FC p44 CR France1693 &CR France34,Maj
COLMER,Arthur Cecil 2Lt kia 1-7-16 A96RFA p27 CR France188
COLNETT,Richard Dauntesbey Capt mbk 13-8-18 8Ess p257&275,IA 3/151Punjabis MR34,2entries
COLOMB,George Lushington.DCM.Lt kia 22-11-16 4Lond &RFC p246 CR France169
COLOMB,Mervyn William 2Lt dow 11-5-15 4Lond attRFC p18&246 CR Hamps1
COLQUHOUN,A.S.2Lt kld 20-4-18 GL &RAF p190
COLQUHOUN,Ernest Forbes Campbell 2Lt kia 26-9-17 3 att2RWFus p97 CR Belgium126
COLQUHOUN,Ivor Kenneth T2Lt ded 9-9-15 14WelchR p126 CR Wales165
COLQUHOUN,Phillip Hugh Leslie Campbell.MC.Capt kia 19-9-18 3 att1BlkW p128 CR France835,Lumsden
COLQUHOUN,Robert Clark T2Lt dow 3-7-16 9RScotF att2ScotRif p94 CR France40
COLQUHOUN,Robert Fletcher TLtACapt kia 16-11-16 13 att15HLI p162 MR21
COLQUHOUN,William Wallace TCapt kia 25-9-15 11HLI p162 MR19
COLSON,Anthony Francis Douglas.MC.Lt kia 10-11-17 RFA p207 CR Belgium10
COLSON,Cecil.MC.CaptAMaj kia 14-12-16 RGA 21SB p38 CR Belgium4
COLSON,Douglas Fairley.DSO.Maj ded 3-2-19 RE 521FC p209 CR Syria2
COLSON,Edward.MID Maj dow 20-1-16 IA 41Dogras p275 CR Iraq5
COLSTON,Harold Kelway Maj kia 23-4-15 1Y&L p158 MR29
COLTHART,Robert Herd Capt dow 2-11-18 14BlkW p203 CR France1033
COLTHURST,Arthur Beadon TCapt kia 25-10-16 14Glouc p106 CR France1182
COLTMAN,Richard Lester 2Lt kia 27-11-17 CldGds att2GdsMGCps p254 MR17
COLTMAN,Walter Joseph 2Lt dow 2-6-17 2/6Lond p246 CR France518
COLTON,Stanley Edmonds.MC.2Lt kia 28-3-18 1NumbF p60 MR20
COLVER,Edward Watkin.MID Lt kia 28-6-15 RE 455FC p210 MR4
COLVER,Henry Capt kia 19-12-15 1/5Y&L p238 CR Belgium23,dow
COLVILL,George Chaignian Capt kia 30-11-17 SIrHorse att7RIrReg p24 CR France1489,Chaigneau
COLVILL-JONES,Robert.MC.Capt 4-11-18 13RB &RAF CR France733
COLVILLE,Harold Linklater T2Lt dow 6-7-16 9SomLI p79 CR France145
COLVILLE,Henry George Coulson Capt kia 22-9-15 1KSLI attHQ16InfBde p144 CR Belgium92
COLVIN,Kenneth Colquhoun 2Lt ded 6-9-15 RASC att348Co p192 CR Wilts2
COLVIN,Robert Alexander Capt&Adjt kia 10-3-15 2WYorks p81 CR France279
COLVIN,Russell Alexander TCapt kia 1-5-17 10A&SH p173 CR France451
COLWELL,Albert Edward 2Lt kld 23-2-18 RFC p15 CR Mddx66
COLYER,Wilfred Victor 2Lt kia 22-10-18 Hamps att15Bn p120 CR Belgium408

COLYER-FERGUSSON,Thomas Riversdale.VC.2LtACapt dow 31-7-17 Nhampt p137 CR Belgium72
COMBE,Boyce Anthony Lt kia 11-11-14 6RFus att4Bn p67 MR29
COMBE,George Henry Richard TLt kia 15-9-16 7RB p178 MR21
COMBE,Samuel Barbour Lt 1-10-14 NIrHorse MR22
COMBE,Stanley Greatrex Lt ded 11-10-18 3Co of LondYeo p204 CR Egypt8,attImpCamCps
COMBE-CEATON Frank T2Lt kia 14-10-18 ESurr att 12Bn p112 CR Belgium157
COMBER,Andrew Pater Capt ded 29-6-15 7Dev p269 CR Lond8
COMBER,Turner.MC&Bar.T2LtACapt kia 19-9-18 9Ess p131 CR France369
COMBER-TAYLOR,Eric Horace Capt kld 16-6-18 GL &10RAF p190 CR France142
COMBRIDGE,Leslie Ernest T2Lt kia 22-8-18 6EKent p57 CR France370
COMLEY,Edgar Cyril.MC.Lt kld 27-9-18 4RMunsF p175 CR France686
COMMINS,Arthur Edward 2Lt kia 23-4-17 150MGC p182 MR20
COMMON,Henry Alder 2Lt dow 4-10-18 1/2 att1/4KOSB p101 MR16
COMPSTON,John Milton T2Lt kia 8-10-18 WYorks p81 CR France375
COMPTON,Cyril Henry 2Lt kia 23-7-16 3RWKent att 19Manch p140 MR21
COMPTON,Florence D'Oyly Sister ded 15-1-18 QAIMNS att65GH p200 CR Iraq6,drd
COMPTON,Guy T2Lt kia 27-7-17 RSuss att9Bn p118 MR29
COMPTON,Harold William TLtCol dow 7-7-17 12RFus p67 CR France40
COMPTON,Neville George T2Lt kia 20-4-17 9Worc p108 MR38
COMPTON,Rex Lt kia 12-8-17 5Ess p232 MR29
COMPTON,Lord Spencer Douglas Lt kia 13-5-15 RHGds p20 MR29
COMPTON,William Henry Capt ded 6-12-18 RAMC p195 CR Sussex183
COMPTON,William Horace Gordon 2Lt dow 17-6-17 B186RFA p27 CR Belgium5,kia
COMPTON,William Walter 2Lt kia 25-4-18 RH&FA p27 CR France139
COMPTON-SMITH,Geoffrey Lee.DSO.Maj kld 30-4-21 2RWFus CR Eire95
COMPTON-SMITH,Roger Noel 2Lt dow 27-5-15 6Manch p236 CR Gallipoli2
COMPTON-THORNHILL,Richard Anthony Lt kia 16-9-14 1ScotsGds p52 MR15,14-9-14
COMRIE,Alexander T2Lt ded 15-8-16 RE 257Coy p44 CR France98,kldacc
COMRIE,William Ritchie 2Lt dow 27-11-17 HLI att16Bn p162 CR Belgium18
COMYN,David Charles Edward Ffrench Maj kia 12-5-17 10LancF p92 MR20
CONAN-DAVIES,Brynmor Ivan HonLt ded 23-11-18 7Y&L p158 CR Lond14
CONCANNON,James Aloysius 2Lt kia 3-5-17 2LancF p92 MR20
CONDER,Philip Capt ded 15-7-17 IA 24 att19Punjabis p275 CR Iraq8
CONDI,Allen George 2Lt kia 1-10-16 4BordR p228 CR France239,5Bn
CONDIE,George Rev Chap4Cl ded 30-6-18 RAChDept p199 CR Scot674
CONDON,David Lt ded PoW 23-7-17 1NumbF p60 CR Germany2
CONDON,Thomas 2Lt kld 28-5-16 A108RFA p27 CR Belgium97
CONDUITT,Robert Bruce 2Lt kia 16-4-15 1SfthH p164 CR France924 Ex 14Lond
CONEN,James Henry T2Lt kia 25-7-18 12Manch p154 MR27
CONEYBEARE,Herbert William T2Lt dow 24-10-16 2Lincs p74 MR21
CONGLETON,Henry Bligh Fortescue Parnell.Lord.MID Lt kia 10-11-14 GrenGds p49 CR Belgium134
CONGREVE,William La Touche.VC.DSO.MC.Capt&BtMaj kia 20-7-16 RB p178 CR France23
CONHEENY,Gerald,MC T2Lt kld 5-12-18 1/5RLancs p58 CR Germany4,Lt
CONIBEAR,Arthur Edward 2Lt dow 14-10-17 1/6Lpool p215 CR France40,Lt
CONLAN,Arthur Underhill 2Lt kia 22-5-16 18Lond p250 MR20
CONLEY,William Cockayne.MC.TLt kia 26-10-17 1SStaffs att91TMB p122 MR30
CONLIN,Bernard Francis 2Lt dow 9-10-16 28RFA p27 CR France833
CONMEE,John Alphonsus Lt kia 3-5-17 4Y&L p238 MR20
CONN,James Fullerton Caldwell Capt dow 1-5-17 7A&SH p243 CR France64,Fullarton
CONNAL,Alexander Campbell 2Lt kia 9-4-18 RGA 99SB p39 CR France572
CONNAL,Arthur William Campbell Lt kia 24-10-16 53/38RFA p27 MR21
CONNELL,Alfred Hamilton CaptTMaj kia 28-9-15 2RScotF p94 CR France257
CONNELL,Harry Bertram LtCol dow 16-11-16 RAMC p195 CR France74
CONNELL,John Capt ded 18-5-20 RAMC p267 CR Berks112
CONNELL,Sydney Dennis Lt kia 28-11-14 Manch p154 MR22
CONNELL,Victor John Alexander BtMaj ded 7-7-20 IA 13Lancers attGuidesCav p275 MR43
CONNELL,William Patrick.MID LtACapt kld 24-11-18 55RFA p27 CR Iraq8
CONNELLAN,Peter Martin Maj kia 20-10-14 Hamps p120
CONNELLY,Montagu Edward Lt ded 14-1-18 RFC p15 CR USA228,2Lt
CONNER,Frederick Attenborrow T2Lt kia 1-7-16 2SfthH p164 MR21,Frederic
CONNER,Richard Maj dow 7-9-15 Glouc p106 CR Surrey160

CONNERY,Michael Henry.MC.LtCol ded 25-4-21 1/9Manch CR Lancs416
CONNING,Thomas Rothsay.MC.Lt kia 27-5-17 2RWFus p97 CR France1489
CONNOCHIE,Robert Hope see CONOCHIE,R.H.
CONNOLLY,Hugh Aloysius 2Lt kia 27-8-18 IrGds att4GdsMGReg p52 CR France568
CONNOLLY,James Harris TCapt ded 23-10-18 RAMC p195
CONNOLLY,John Henry T2Lt dow 1-9-16 6RMunstF att11RIrRif p175 CR France285
CONNOLLY,Matthew G Capt 4-9-19 RAVC CR Canada1087
CONNOR,Albermarle Dare Maj ded 9-7-20 IA 1/42Deolali p275 MR65
CONNOR,Amos Lloyd 2Lt dow 30-6-17 2N&D p133 CR France178
CONNOR,Cleveland Alexander TLt kia 23-10-18 ChinLabCps att1/8Worc p189 CR France231
CONNOR,Isaac Joscelyn Maj kia 25-7-16 RE 101FC p44 CR France372
CONNOR,James Patrick.MC.2Lt kia 7-6-17 B119ArmyBde RH&FA p27 CR Belgium165
CONNOR,Samuel Maurice 2Lt kia 10-8-17 5Beds p219 MR29
CONOCHIE,Robert Hope 2Lt kia 31-7-17 4KOSB p224 MR29,CONNOCHIE
CONOCHIE,Robert Pollock 2Lt kia 19-5-18 8ScotRif p225 CR France547,18-5-18
CONOLLY,B.D.Capt&QM 6-2-21 RAMC CR Kent7
CONRAN,Owen Mostyn Maj kia 29-7-17 RLancs att10RFC p6&58 CR France98,28-7-17
CONRAN,Percy Wogan Drysdale Capt dow 12-4-18 1LancF p92 CR France352
CONRATH,Percy Thorpe T2Lt kia 4-9-18 20DLI p160 MR32
CONROY,Bernard 2Lt kia 5-7-15 2RDubF p176 CR Belgium23,6-7-15
CONROY,Hugh Tracey T2Lt ded 28-10-18 LabCps att85IndLabCoy p189 CR France52
CONSIDINE,Christopher Daniel 2Lt kia 24-5-15 2RDubF p176 MR29
CONSIDINE,Heffernan James.MC.Capt kia 27-10-16 4 att2RIrReg p88 CR Belgium17
CONSIDINE,John William Capt kia 25-9-15 2RMunstF p175 CR France219,Maj
CONSIDINE,Patrick Francis Lt dow 12-7-15 4RScots p211 CR Europe4
CONSTABLE,Archibald Thomas Wynne CaptTMaj dow 16-10-15 9Ess p131 CR France98
CONSTABLE,Arthur Leslie 2Lt kia 17-3-17 43RFC p6 CR France924
CONSTABLE,Basil John Leslie Clymping Capt kia 9-8-15 1/4RSuss p228 CR Gallipoli5
CONSTABLE,Douglas Oliaphant Lt kia 25-9-15 4GrenGds SR p49 CR France374
CONSTABLE,Ralph TCapt kia 25-9-16 10NumbF p60
CONSTANCE,William Ernest 2Lt kia 9-8-18 7 att8Lond p247 CR France247
CONSTANTINE,Frank Iveson T2Lt dow 20-8-18 22NumbF att2Lincs p60 CR France84,Francis Ivison kia
CONSTANTINE,Hebden Stringer 2Lt dow 13-5-17 2/7Worc C'Coy p226 CR France610
CONSTANTINE,Herbert Norman.MC.Capt kia 27-5-18 4Yorks p220 CR France1753
CONSTANTINE,Robert Baxandall Capt ded 4-3-19 2/6WYorks p218 CR Yorks408
CONSTANTINE,William.MC.TLt kia 18-9-18 7BordR p116 MR16
CONSTERDINE,Arthur Edward TCapt kia 26-12-16 WYorks att9Bn p81 CR France701
CONSTERDINE,Henry Stanley Lt ded 11-6-18 RE IWT p262 CR Scot241
CONSTERDINE,V.C.SNurse 6-11-18 QAIMNS CR Notts84
CONSTERDINE-CHADWICK,Robert Thompson Consterdine TLtACapt kia 4-10-18 17 att3RFus p67 CR France234
CONVERY,J.A.Lt 11-3-18 RFA CR France1277
CONWAY,Arthur Septimus.DSO.Maj kia 17-6-17 1NStaffs p156 CR Belgium127
CONWAY,Brian Wiseman TLtACapt kia 4-10-17 22Manch p154 MR30
CONWAY,Edgar Philip Maj kia 10-8-15 6RMunstF p175 CR Gallipoli27
CONWAY,Guy T2Lt kia 29-9-18 11RWSurr p55 MR30
CONWAY,Joseph Michael T2Lt kia 7-7-16 7RLancs p58 MR21,8-7-16
CONYERS,Charles MajTLtCol dow 12-5-15 RIrF p171
CONYERS,Harold Cater T2Lt kia 22-9-18 2 att8Glouc p106 CR France1106
CONYERS,Walter Neville T2Lt kia 13-8-16 8RBerks p139 MR21,19-8-16
CONYBEARE,Edward Bruce.MC.MIDx2 Capt kia 5-4-16 1 att9Worc p108 MR38
CONYBEARE,Maynard Henry Crawford Lt ded 14-1-15 114Mahrattas&7Yorks CR Devon238
CONYNGHAM,Cecil Allan Taylor Capt kia 4-11-14 RAMC p195 MR47
CONYNGHAM,Victor George Henry Francis Lt ded 9-11-18 7RIrReg p24 CR Eire459
COOBAN,Adrian Deighton TMaj kia 16-7-16 16KRRC p149 CR France432
COOCH,Charles Rollo Lt kia 17-12-14 BordR B'Coy p116 CR France525
COOCH,T.A.Capt 17-9-19 Worc &2RAF CR France457
COOIL,Caesar Alfred Capt 11-11-18 RGA CR Wales491
COOIL,Henry Stuart T2Lt kia 9-9-18 YLI att9Bn p142 CR France415

COOK,Albert Edward T2Lt kia 20-2-18 ESurr att2/22Lond p112 MR34
COOK,Alexander James Lt kia 28-4-17 4Lincs p217 CR France1495
COOK,Alfred Burton TCapt kia 20-11-17 GL att57RFC p6 CR France134
COOK,Alfred John Lt ded 8-6-19 RE att1S&M p44 MR43
COOK,Arthur Basil Kemball T2Lt kia 7-7-16 9RFus p67 MR21
COOK,Arthur Clifford T2Lt kia 16-8-16 16 att4Lpool p71 CR France453
COOK,Arthur Thomas 2Lt dow 9-8-16 3 att8Glouc p106 CR France833
COOK,B.E.2Lt ded 7-11-18 RE p44 CR Wilts56
COOK,Bernard 2Lt kia 6-9-16 7Lpool p215 MR21
COOK,Cecil Haddon T2Lt kia 22-10-17 23Manch p154 MR30
COOK,Charles Adam T2Lt kia 11-3-16 1Beds p85 CR France924,Adams
COOK,Charles Reynolds T2Lt kia 29-5-18 2Hamps p120 CR France24
COOK,Charles Stanley Blannin 2Lt kia 15-9-16 3/5SomLI att1/8Lond p218 CR France252
COOK,Cyril Annesley TCapt kia 25/26-9-15 8RWSurr p55 MR19
COOK,Cyril Edward Lt dow 8-7-17 2RSuss p118 CR France98
COOK,Cyril Frank T2Lt kia 5-8-17 32RFus p67 CR Belgium116
COOK,Cyril Mountfort 2Lt kia 27-8-17 7Worc p226 CR Belgium125
COOK,Cyril Ramsay 2Lt kia 9-6-17 4N&D att9Bn p133 MR29
COOK,E.J.SubCdr 9-10-14 S&T Cps MR43
COOK,E.K.SNurse 8-9-17 QAIMNS CR Egypt1
COOK,Earl Allen T2Lt kld 22-3-18 RFC p15 CR Bucks96
COOK,Edwin Archibald Douglas Lt ded 11-1-20 2CamH p265 CR Canada423
COOK,Edwin Berkeley.MVO.LtCol dow 4-11-14 1LifeGds p20 CR Kent252
COOK,Ernest Arnold Lovell.MC.Maj mbk 1-11-18 122RFA p256 MR16
COOK,F.W.Lt&QM 1-1-18 EYorks CR Yorks2
COOK,Francis Richardson TLt kld 22-2-18 EYorks &RFC p15 CR Egypt15
COOK,Frank Ecaden.MC.Lt kia 20-10-18 1/10Manch p237 CR France287,Eaden
COOK,Frederick Charles Lt dow 9-10-19 Beds attRAF CR Beds75
COOK,Frederick James T2LtTCapt dow 30-11-15 10BordR att1/4RScots p116 CR Gallipoli3
COOK,Geoffrey Bruce TLt kia 1-10-18 RE IWT att1/5LNLancs p44 CR France256
COOK,George Albert 2Lt kia 10-3-15 2Mddx p146 CR France706
COOK,George Trevor-Roper.CMG.DSO.MIDx2 LtCol kia26-3-18 20Huss p23 MR27
COOK,Gerald Haslam Capt dow 25-7-15 IA 101Grenadiers p275 CR EAfrica6 &CR Tanzania1
COOK,Godfrey Burton Lt dow 29-3-18 PoW 19Huss p23 CR France1266,23-3-18 20Bn
COOK,Harold Joseph Bede Lt dow 28-5-18 B46RFA p27 CR France33,Capt kia
COOK,Henry 2Lt kia 23-4-17 4RScots p211 CR France545
COOK,Henry James T2Lt dow 6-10-15 8YLI p142 CR France40
COOK,Henry Rodham T2Lt kia 7-9-17 12Manch p154 CR France1190
COOK,Henry Vincent 2Lt kia 21-3-18 7 att11Ess p232 MR20
COOK,Horace Herbert T2Lt kia 25-3-18 RE 438FC p44 MR27
COOK,Horace Montague 2Lt kia 21-3-18 7Lond p247 CR France1893
COOK,Howard Mortimer TLt kia 9-8-18 12MGC p182 CR France59
COOK,Humphrey Noel Felix T2Lt kia 26-6-17 11RWSurr p55 CR Belgium29
COOK,James Robert Capt kia 26-4-15 IA 21Punjabis att47Sikhs p275 CR Belgium96
COOK,John T2Lt kia 23-10-16 22DLI p160 CR France400
COOK,John Blair.DSO.MC.LtCol kia 24-11-17 1/5RScotF p222 CR Palestine3
COOK,John Duncan Howe Capt kia 28-9-17 IA 1/5GurkhaRif p275 CR Iraq8,Home
COOK,Kenneth Richmond T2Lt dow 30-7-16 8BlkW attTMB p128 CR Surrey152
COOK,Leonard Nield.MC.2Lt kia 7-7-17 3RLancs p58 CR France379
COOK,Norman George 2Lt kia 29-6-17 4 att6NStaffs p156 CR France550,28-6-17
COOK,Percy Mellows T2Lt kia 4-10-16 18KRRC p149 MR21
COOK,Philip Harry 2Lt kia 19-7-17 8Lond p147 CR Belgium118
COOK,Philip John Cecil 2Lt kia 14-10-18 7WelshR p230 CR France258
COOK,Randolph 2Lt kia 9-4-17 7ScotRif att9KRRC p224 CR France581
COOK,Reginald Cyril T2Lt dow 11-7-18 RB att8Bn p178 CR France84,13Bn
COOK,Reginald William.MC.2Lt kia 1-9-18 3Dev p76
COOK,Richard Edward T2Lt dow 13-4-18 11Suff p78 CR Belgium18
COOK,Robert Alexander T2Lt kia 30-6-16 2KOSB p101 MR20
COOK,Robert Guy T2Lt kia 9-2-17 3Worc p108 CR Belgium138,Lt
COOK,Robert Leslie 2Lt kia 7-8-15 6Lincs p74 MR4
COOK,Taylor 2Lt ded 21-3-17 7A&SH p243 CR France15
COOK,Thomas 2Lt kia 2-10-15 12Ess att6Lincs p131 MR4
COOK,John Valentina see COOKE,J.V.
COOK,Walter 2Lt kia 16-4-18 5N&D p232 CR Belgium183

COOK,William Edward 2Lt kia 12-3-17 2YLI p142 CR France649
COOK,William Edwin T2Lt dow 27-4-18 1/2 att4Yorks p90 CR France1142
COOKE,Alan Welldon Hands Capt kia 24-3-18 22DLI p160
COOKE,Archibald Ernest 2Lt dow 1-5-18 1Leic p87 CR France142
COOKE,Arthur 2Lt ded 22-8-17 2/6N&D p233 CR France699
COOKE,Arthur Francis.MID 2Lt kia 4-3-17 29RFA p27 CR France626
COOKE,Cecil Pybus T2Lt kia 22-8-17 KSLI att5Bn p144 MR30
COOKE,Charles Earsham.MC.Lt dow 24-5-17 1/9Manch p237 CR France145
COOKE,Charles Ernest.MID 2Lt kia 25-5-15 3 att1RIrF p171 MR29
COOKE,Charles Herbert T2Lt kia 21-9-17 2RB p178 CR Belgium52
COOKE,Charles Taylor Capt kia 10-8-15 7Ches p222 MR4
COOKE,Charles Reginald 2Lt ded 12-2-19 7LNLancs p274 CR Lancs481
COOKE,Denys Capt kia 18-4-18 3 att1BlkW p128 CR France279
COOKE,E.K.SNurse ded 8-9-17 QAIMNS p200
COOKE,Ernest Richard TCapt kia 25-4-16 8RIrF p171 CR France423,26-4-16
COOKE,George Frederick Lt ded 22-10-19 5Mddx p265 CR Ches197
COOKE,George Josiah 2Lt kia 23-11-17 2/2Lond attRFC p18&245 CR France1361,kldacc
COOKE,Hans Hendrick Anthony Capt kia 24-1-17 ConnRgrs att3NigR p172&201 MR50
COOKE,Harold Esmond.MC.Capt kia 30-11-17 12Lpool p71&258 MR17
COOKE,Henry Frederick.MID 2Lt kia 4-8-16 7RSuss p118 MR21
COOKE,Hugh William Fothergill Maj kia 14-5-15 IA 24Punjabis CR Iraq6
COOKE,I.A.E.Lt kia 19-7-17 SL attTMB p201
COOKE,J.K.Maj 29-7-15 Ches CR Ches186
COOKE,James Gore Capt kia 8-10-16 16N&D p133 MR21
COOKE,John T2Lt ded 20-6-16 DLI &RFC p2&160 CR France518
COOKE,John Howard TLt ded 9-10-18 RASC MT attRGA p192 CR France123
COOKE,John Irwin Lt dow 3-9-17 RE 4LROD p44 CR Belgium15,33LROC
COOKE,John Valentina.MC.TLtACapt kia 1-10-18 11RWSurr attTMB p55 CR Belgium116,COOK Valentine
COOKE,Leslie Frederick T2Lt kia 26-9-16 12 att10Ess p131 CR France396
COOKE,Reginald Charles.MC.T2Lt kia 7-7-16 9WelshR p126 MR21
COOKE,Samuel Arthur LtCol ded 26-3-18 IA 38CentIndHorse p275 CR Hamps7
COOKE,Sydney Philip 2Lt ded 4-11-18 8Norf p73&263 CR Norf209,Sidney
COOKE,Thomas Lt ded 30-5-17 RGA att18HAC p39 CR France113
COOKE,Vincent Joseph.MC.Lt dow 1-3-21 7Mddx CR Scot359
COOKE,William Harry Coleman TCapt kia 1-9-18 1YLI GarrBn att2/6DLI p142 CR France496
COOKE,William Henry 2Lt kia 9-8-15 2N&D p133 MR29
COOKE,William Wesley 2Lt kia 25-4-18 9MGC Inf p182 MR30
COOKSEY,Joseph Arnold 2Lt kia 1-5-17 RGA 116SB p39 CR France581
COOKSEY,Kenneth Bassano 2Lt kia 8-4-17 3RWKent &RFC p6&140 CR France924
COOKSEY,Maurice Wilfrid T2Lt dow 13-4-17 RE B SpCo p44 CR France12,Wilfred M.
COOKSON,Alan Capt kia 27-6-17 10Lpool p216 CR France275
COOKSON,Bernard T2Lt kia 10-4-17 EYorks Res att1Bn p83 CR France162
COOKSON,Mostyn Eden Maj kia 14-9-14 2RSuss p118 MR15
COOLE,Arthur Evans 2Lt ded 14-5-19 IA 1/32SikhPnrs p275 CR Sussex24
COOMBE,Leslie Clarence T2Lt kia 25-3-18 1 att1/5DCLI p114 MR27
COOMBE,Samuel Barbour Lt ded 1-10-14 NIrHorse p24
COOMBE,William John TLt kia 1-10-16 7DCLI p114 MR21
COOMBE,William Robert Lt kia 27-5-18 NottsYeo p205 MR41,drd
COOMBER,Harry Alan.MC.Lt dow 29-4-18 RGA 138HB p209 CR France145
COOMBER,Horace Bertram Capt kia 12-10-17 8Manch attRFC p18&237 CR Belgium157
COOMBES George 2Lt kia 16-8-17 RIrF att7/8Bn p171 CR Belgium128
COOMBES,George Wilson T2Lt kia 3-5-17 1RLancs p58 CR France604
COOMBES,Herbert Victor 2Lt kia 28-3-18 21Lond p251 MR20
COOMBES,John Edwin Henshaw Lt dow 1-4-18 5BordR p228 CR France145
COOMBS,Claude Stuart T2Lt dow 6-7-16 6RWKent p140 CR France102
COOMBS,Debenham Stuard Lt ded 31-10-18 7Ess Res p269 CR Hereford208
COOMBS,Henry Whitaker TLt dow 2-7-16 18NumbF p60 CR France23
COOMBS James Roy 2Lt kia 24-3-18 RFA 93ArmyBde p27 MR20
COOMBS,Percy Douglas 2Lt kia 14-4-17 7 att1Ess p232 MR20
COONEY,Albert George Lt kia 12-5-17 291RFA p27 MR20
COONEY,Charles Robert T2Lt kia 9-10-16 7RDubF att2RIrRif p176 MR21,Richard
COONEY,Edmund Luke T2Lt kia 4-6-17 9RDubF p176 CR Belgium182
COONEY,Patrick Augustine T2Lt kld 22-8-17 LabCps attEgyptLabCps p189 CR Egypt2

COOPER,Anne.MID Sister ded 17-11-19 QAIMNS p268 CR Lancs30
COOPER,Albert Frederick T2Lt dow 9-5-18 11Mddx p146 CR France142,1Bn
COOPER,Alexander Stewart Capt dow 25-4-15 1KOSB p101 MR4,26-4-15
COOPER,Alfred Lynn 2Lt kia 15-9-16 19Lond p250 CR France390
COOPER,Arthur T2Lt dow 10-7-16 14Manch p154 CR France119
COOPER,Arthur Charles Capt kia 16-5-15 1/4Leic p219 CR Belgium99
COOPER,Arthur Herbert Augustus Lt kia 4-10-17 4RWSurr p212 MR30
COOPER,Arthur Miles Gilpin 2Lt ded 23-10-16 12RBerks p265
COOPER,Astley de Borde T2Lt dow 7-7-15 RE 1SigCo p44 CR France80
COOPER,Cecil Bernard 2Lt kia 9-8-17 A38RH&FA p27 CR Belgium7
COOPER,Cecil Davey T2Lt dow 29-1-18 3ResReg of Cav att6Wilts p23 CR France905
COOPER,Cecil Fletcher Maj ded 5-9-16 D121RFA p27 CR France64
COOPER,Charles Morris Lt kia 20-10-18 7Manch p237 CR France287
COOPER,Clarence Edwards Nooth Lt kia 16-9-16 3Lincs attRFC p2&74 CR France105 dedacc 2Bn
COOPER,Clarence Percy TLt dow 2-4-17 Ess att1/4 p131 CR Egypt2
COOPER,Claude Huntley.MM.T2Lt drd 17-1-18 9Yorks p90 CR Italy7
COOPER,Clifford T2Lt kia 22-4-18 18Mddx p146 CR France490
COOPER,Clifford Edward Gordon T2Lt kldacc 26-11-17 GL &62RFC p6 CR Kent7
COOPER,Corin Henry Benedict TLt dow 20-11-16 RE 178FC p44 CR France40,TC
COOPER,Cyril Ashley T2Lt kld 29-6-17 GL &RFC p6 CR Scot520
COOPER,Cyril Henry 2Lt kia 6-4-16 RGA 132HB p39 CR Belgium4
COOPER,David Cameron Lt kia 23-7-18 6GordH p242 CR France622,Donald
COOPER,Donald Keith T2Lt kia 9-9-16 1Nhampt p137 CR France432
COOPER,E.S.Maj 27-11-20 11RWFus CR Norf231
COOPER,Edward George Capt kia 4-8-16 3Lpool att1KAR p71&268 CR EAfrica40
COOPER,Ernest Walter T2Lt dow 13-10-18 9Ess p131 CR France106
COOPER,Francis Nicholas Nooth Lt kia 21-11-17 RASC &SWBord p192 CR France911
COOPER,Frank Douglas Towers 2Lt kia 22-7-16 2RScots p53 MR21,23-7-16
COOPER,Frank Penley T2Lt kia 26-9-16 17 att16RWar p64 MR21
COOPER,Frederick Edmund TLt dow 18-12-18 26RFus p67 CR Dorset20
COOPER,Frederick John T2Lt kia 27-5-18 SLancs p125 MR18
COOPER,Frederick William.MC.TLt kia 17-4-18 RE 105FC p44&258 MR30
COOPER,Frederick William Harvey.MM.T2Lt kia 9-3-18 10EKent p57 CR Palestine3
COOPER,G.C.M.ACapt ded 23-11-18 RE attRAnglesey p44 CR Surrey2
COOPER,Geoffrey Rowsell 2Lt ded 8-11-16 3RBerks p139
COOPER,George Frederick T2Lt kia 24-2-17 RASC p192 CR France749
COOPER,George Spencer T2Lt kia 17-2-17 6Nhampt p137 MR21
COOPER,George Stanley Capt ded 28-6-15 5RWKent p235 MR66
COOPER,Harold Leslie T2Lt kia 31-3-18 7EYorks p84 MR20
COOPER,Henry Mark Hugh Lt dow 29-7-15 1KEdwardsHorse p24 CR Lond2
COOPER,Henry Weatherley Frank T2Lt dow 28-4-17 7RFus p67 CR France113,29-4-17
COOPER,Herbert Ambrose TCapt kia 21-6-16 11RFC p2 CR France95
COOPER,Herbert Leonard 2Lt kia 16-9-16 7Mddx p235 CR France785
COOPER,Horace Burnaby 2Lt kia 23-10-18 4 att1Wilts p236 CR France1477
COOPER,Horace Charles Henry T2Lt kld 15-4-17 GL &RFC p6 CR Wilts116
COOPER,Howard Frank Byrne 2Lt kia 1-7-16 1KOSB A'Coy p101 CR France339
COOPER,Hubert T2Lt dow 30-3-18 16RB p178 CR France52
COOPER,Jack Oliver TCapt kia 23-7-16 att21RFC p2 MR20
COOPER,James 2Lt ded 5-11-18 TankCps p266 CR Lancs14
COOPER,James Alfred 2Lt kldacc 17-5-16 7N&D p233 CR France747,2Bn
COOPER,John Bruce Capt ded 21-11-15 RASC p192&253
COOPER,John Stephen TLt kia 25-3-17 GL &70RFC p6 CR France568
COOPER,Joseph T2Lt kia 26-9-16 14 att11Manch p154 MR21
COOPER,Leonard Gosse T2Lt kia 9-8-15 4SWBord p99 MR4
COOPER,Leonard Russell T2Lt drd 23-10-15 RFA 29DAC p27 MR35
COOPER,Maurice Stanley Charles T2Lt dow 10-8-16 9 att6Beds p85 CR France197,9-8-16
COOPER,Nowell Edwin Lt dow 16-10-18 1HuntsCycBn att2Suff p253 CR France560
COOPER,Oliver Henry Donald Lt kia 8-5-17 6HLI p240 MR37
COOPER,Percy TLt kia 22-3-18 18MGC p182 MR27,23-3-18
COOPER,Percy Newbery TLt dow 6-7-16 1N&D p133 CR France23
COOPER,Percy Valentine T2LtACapt kia 8-8-18 7RWSurr p55 CR France247
COOPER,R 2Lt 8-11-16 RBerks CR Surrey148
COOPER,Richard 2Lt kia 8-6-17 1 att10RWar p64 MR29

COOPER,Robert Charles TLt dow 12-4-18 18WelshR att119TMB p126 CR France25
COOPER,Ronald 2Lt dow 16-6-17 119RFA p27 CR Belgium127
COOPER,Spencer Bruce T2Lt dow 24-4-18 Wilts p152 CR France119,Lt
COOPER,Sydney Gordon 2Lt dow 17-9-15 4 att1RWar p64 CR France344
COOPER,Thomas Gill T2Lt ded 25-3-18 49MGC p182 CR France145
COOPER,Victor Travers T2Lt kia 22-6-17 1/8RWar p64 CR France381
COOPER,William 2Lt kia 25-9-15 1SStaffs p122 MR19
COOPER,William Campion Lt mbk 13-12-15 IA 53Sikhs att59Rif p275 MR41,drd 30-12-15
COOPER,William Dermot.MID Capt kia 30-8-17 AyrYeo p203 CR Palestine8
COOPER,William F.T2Lt kia 31-7-17 12RFus p67 CR Belgium112
COOPER,William Ferguson 2Lt dow 28-6-17 2KOSB p101 CR France21
COOPER,William Marsden 2Lt kia 17-2-17 2Worc p108 CR France511
COOPER,William Randolph 2Lt kia 13-5-18 4LNLancs p234 CR France261
COOPER,Willie.OBE.VD.LtCol 18-12-20 5WRid CR Yorks643
COOPER-BROWN,Arthur Neville 2LtACapt dow 27-10-18 3 att2Ess C'Coy p131 CR France613
COOPER-KING,Reginald Garret Maj dow 20-12-14 2WYorks p81 CR France768,21-12-14
COOPER-MARSDIN,Arthur Cooper Rev ded 16-8-18 RAChDept Ret p268
COOPER-SMITH,Reginald Burston 2Lt kia 10-3-17 5Ess p232 CR France624
COOTE,Arthur Eyre 2Lt kia 1-7-16 8RIrRif p169 MR21,1/2-7-16
COOTE,Charles Gartside Eyre Lt kia 22-3-18 11Huss p22 MR27
COOTE,George Bertrand Lt kia 27-5-18 RWKent att50MGC p182&140,Bernard MR18
COOTE,Philip Edward 2Lt kia 15-9-16 8Lond p247 CR France390
COOTE,Richard Markham TCapt kia 13-10-15 8RBerks p139 MR19
COPE,Edward Moseley Lt ded 3-6-19 NStaffs att52Leic p254 CR Germany1
COPE,George Eric TLt kia 1-7-16 20NumbF p60 MR21
COPE,Gerald Quin 2Lt dow 24-5-17 2/9Manch p237 CR France134
COPE,W.G.Capt 6-9-18 Yorks CR Mddx16
COPELAND,Douglas Chatterton Bruce.MC.Capt dow 21-6-18 12Lond p248 CR Essex75
COPELAND,Eric Neville Van de Ben TLt kia 26-3-18 63MGC p182
COPELAND,Frederick.MID Maj kia 6-6-15 IA 69Punjabis p275 CR France924
COPELAND,John Stuart T2Lt dow 20-2-17 2YLI p142 CR France62,Lt
COPELAND,Rupert Ramsay.DSO.MC.MIDx2 LtCol kld 24-7-20 39RFA MR38
COPELAND,William Alan 2Lt kia 25-4-15 1RScots p53 CR Belgium4
COPEMAN,Ernest Hugh 2Lt kia 18-3-16 6RWKent att37MGC p140&182 MR19
COPEMAN,Herbert Guy Hele 2Lt kia 3-9-16 6 O&BLI p130 CR France294
COPEMAN,Robert George Henry T2Lt dow 12-1-16 9Ess p131 CR France80
COPINGER,John Patrick 2Lt kia 10-9-17 4 O&BLI p231 CR Belgium96
COPLAND,Dudley Charles James 2Lt kia 9-5-15 1N&D p133 CR France566
COPLAND,George Harold T2Lt kia 31-7-17 18Lpool p71 MR29
COPLAND,Reginald Wallace ACapt kia 16-7-19 IA 3/1GurkhaRif p275
COPLEY,Alan T2Lt kia 2-4-17 19Manch p154 CR France596,Allan
COPLEY,Alfred Beresford T2Lt kia 26-8-17 101MGC Inf p182 CR France1461
COPNER,Arthur Bruce Lt kia 25-9-15 Dev p76 MR19
COPPACK,Charles Richard Stewart 2Lt dow 24-3-18 22 att24RFus p67 MR20,25-3-18 24 att22Bn
COPPARD,Stuart Benjamin Hayes T2Lt kia 20-11-17 GL att57RFC p6 CR France134
COPPARD,William John T2Lt dow 23-3-18 24RFus p67 MR20
COPPEN,William Joseph Lt kia 2-11-17 2Lond p245 MR34
COPPIN,Richard Alfred TCapt kia 11-4-17 6RWSurr B'Coy p55 CR France531,12-4-17
COPPING,Arthur Milton.MM.2Lt kia 18-9-16 6Lond p247 MR21
COPPOCK,Hugh Searle.MID TLt kia 10-4-18 3 att25Lancs p125 MR32
CORAH,Leslie Capt kia 13-10-15 4Leic p219 MR19
CORAH,Sydney Lt kia 3-10-18 5Leic p220
CORBALLY,Lewis Capt dow 6-5-15 RFA p27 CR France284
CORBAN,Joseph 2LtTLt kia 17-7-17 10Y&L p158 CR Belgium100
CORBAN-LUCAS,Percival Laurence TCapt dow 15-12-16 1RSuss att9Worc p118 MR38
CORBEN,Victor Leslie 2Lt ded 22-7-18 26RFus p67
CORBET,George Frederick Francis 2Lt dow 25-1-16 WelshR p126 CR Surrey160
CORBET,John Hugh T2Lt kia 13-1-18 KSLI &RFC p15&144 CR France1276
CORBET,Reginald Vincent Campbell Lt kia 25-4-15 1RDubF p176 MR4
CORBET,Roland James.Bart.Lt kia 15-4-15 3CldGds p51 CR France279
CORBETT,Alfred Edward TCapt kia 1-7-16 11BordR p116 MR21
CORBETT,Charles Craustron TCapt ded 31-1/3-2-18 RAVC p268 CR Belgium18,Cranston 3-2-18

CORBETT,Charles Harold Maj kia 13-5-15 18Huss p23 CR Belgium126
CORBETT,Cyril Dudley Hely LtCol 4-12-18 RAMC &RAF CR Mddx26
CORBETT,David Bertram T2Lt kia 3-7-16 17RIrRif p169 CR France232
CORBETT,Frank Harvey.MC.TCaptAMaj kia 5-5-18 B75RFA p27 CR France745
CORBETT,Frederick St.John Chap3Cl ded 14-3-19 3Lond p269 CR Mddx34
CORBETT,Harry 2Lt kia 23-7-16 1Dev att1/6Glouc p76 MR21
CORBETT,Herbert Vincent Capt kia 17-10-18 1Camb att11Ess p244 CR France441
CORBETT,John Whitworth 2Lt kia 14-7-17 8N&D p233 CR France1489
CORBETT,Reginald David de la Cour Maj ded 25-12-17 IA 48Pnrs attRFC p275 CR Iraq8
CORBETT-WILSON,Denys Lt kia 10-5-15 RFC p1 CR France924
CORBIN,Charles Robert Peel TLt dow 21-10-16 11Worc p108 CR Greece7
CORBIN,Christopher Lt kia 5-6-17 RGA 141HB p39 CR Belgium2
CORBISHLEY,Ronald Heathcote 2Lt kia 28-7-17 8Dev &57RFC p6&76 CR Belgium149
CORBITT,John Frederick Lt ded 1-1-17 RDC p253 CR Numb3
CORBOLD,Henry Maurice Lt ded 26-8-16 19RFC p2 CR France528
CORBRIDGE,Arthur.MC.T2Lt kia 20-5-17 4Lpool p71 CR France434
CORBYN,Edwin Christian LtCol kia 1-12-17 IA 18Lancers p275 CR France417
CORCORAN,Alban Thomas 2Lt dow 2-12-17 3 att2YLI p142 CR Belgium20
CORCORAN,William James Maj dow 25-10-14 5Mddx p146 CR France80
CORDER,Hugh Gerald Annerley Lt kia 9-5-15 WelshR p126 MR22
CORDER,Terence Spence Lt 13-4-21 RFA CR Iraq6
CORDES,Hugh de Bary.MC.2Lt kia 27-9-18 1ScotsGds p52 CR France1497
CORDEUX,Edward Henry Noble Lt kia 1-10-15 7N&D p233 CR Belgium122
CORDINER,Roy Grote.MC.TCapt kia 4-10-17 8Lincs p74 MR30
CORDNER,James,MC TLt kia 16-4-18 17RIrRif p169 CR Belgium64
CORDNER,James Henry TLt dow 8-8-18 15TankCps p188 CR France699
CORDON,Henry James 2Lt dow 17-10-16 2Wilts att21TMB p152 CR Hamps1
CORE,Charles Gooch 2Lt kia 10-8-17 11RFus p67 MR29
COREN,Edward Walker 2Lt dow 15-6-15 RFA p27 CR Belgiumn165
CORFIELD,A.B Sister 2-2-16 QAIMNS CR Egypt3
CORFIELD,Egerton Anson Frederick T2Lt dow 17-6-17 153RFA p27 CR France200
CORFIELD,Frederick.J.A.Lt 19-10-20 1/1 O&BLI CR Ches56
CORFIELD,Herbert Roy Lt dow 5-11-17 266RFA p207 CR Palestine1,Hubert Ray 2Lt
CORFIELD,Hubert Vernon Auchitel T2Lt kia 6-7-16 7ELancs p110 MR21,Anchitel,7-7-16
CORISH,Thomas Power T2Lt kia 16-9-16 12Lpool p71 MR21
CORKE,Frederick William 2Lt kia 10-4-18 10Lincs p74 MR32
CORKE,Guy Harold T2Lt kia 17-9-16 15 att22NumbF p60 CR France402,15 att12Bn
CORKE,Hubert William T2Lt kia 19-4-16 10Glouc C'Coy p106 CR France149
CORKER,Francis Llewelyn Lt kia 4-6-17 14WelshR p126 MR19,5/6-6-16
CORKILL,Ernest 2Lt kia 28-2-17 4LancF p92 CR France390
CORKRAN,Reginald Seymour 2Lt dow 15-6-15 2GrenGds SR p49 CR Surrey45,11-6-15
CORLESS,John Stanley T2Lt kia 17/19-9-18 2N&D p133 MR16
CORLETT,Douglas Lt ded 9-10-16 RIM p275 CR Iraq6
CORLETT,Douglas Stephen TLtACapt dow 12-11-18 3RFus p67 CR France146
CORLEY,Edward Cecil T2Lt kia 23-2-17 7RWKent p140 MR21
CORLEY,Frederick Charles 2Lt kia 12-4-18 BordR att8Bn p116 MR32
CORLEY,William Raymond.MID T2Lt kia 27-3-18 9ESurr p112 MR27
CORMAC-WALSHE,Edward Joseph Capt dow 5-11-14 2Leinst p174 CR France102
CORMAC-WALSHE,Henry Capt dow 7-11-17 125/29RH&FA p27 CR Belgium16,Harry
CORMACK,Reginald Ormiston T2Lt kia 1-7-16 15DLI p160 MR21
CORMACK,Sidney.MC.2Lt dow 19-11-17 D15RFA p27 CR France146,19-11-18
CORN,Frederick T2Lt kia 29-4-18 2Ess p131 CR France250
CORNABY,George Ernest.MCABar.TCapt dow 23-9-18 11RFus p67 CR France34
CORNABY,Hubert Arthur T2Lt kia 15-7-16 10Yorks p90 MR21
CORNELIUS,Cecil Victor Powell Lt kia 10-11-14 3WelshR p126 MR29
CORNELIUS,Frank Stuart.MC.T2Lt kia 3-10-17 8Dev p76 CR Belgium112
CORNELIUS,Herbert Walter T2Lt kia 20-7-18 1Beds p85 MR32
CORNELL,Arthur George T2Lt kia 7-7-16 9NumbF p60 MR21
CORNER,Cecil Gerald Sedgeley Lt,ded 29-12-20 IA IMS p275 CR Egypt6,Sedgerley
CORNER,Edward Franklin T2Lt kia 25-9-15 8RKent p57 MR19
CORNER,Herbert Edward TLt ded 30-10-17 GL attGoldCoastR p201 CR Hamps13
CORNES,Henry Percy Griffiths T2Lt kia 27-9-17 23RFus att99TMB p67 CR France163

CORNFOOT,David Henry Harman Capt ded 2-5-16 9Lond p247 CR Lond8
CORNFORD,Ross Lt kia 17-8-17 GL 7RSuss att22RFC p6 CR Belgium132
CORNFORD,William Day 2Lt kia 22-7-16 1RWKent p140 MR21
CORNFORTH,Norman Leslie T2Lt kia 18-1-18 2RFC p15 CR France98
CORNISH,Charles Lawson Lt kia 13-11-14 2HLI p162 MR29
CORNISH,William Oliver T2Lt kia 20-9-17 GL &32RFC p6 MR20
CORNOCK-TAYLOR,Gerald Oldroyd.OBE ALtCol ded 14-2-19 SL p201 CR France1512,CBE GL
CORNWALLIS,Fiennes Wykeham Mann Capt kld 15-5-21 17Lancers CR Kent239
CORNWELL,Joseph T2Lt dow 29-5-16 13RSuss p118 CR France80
CORP,Benjamin.MC.Capt kia 18-9-16 1WYorks p81&258 MR21
CORRALL,Arthur 2Lt dow 24-12-15 2Dors p124 CR Iraq1
CORRIDON,Vesey Richard T2Lt dow 8-10-16 55MGC p182 CR France74,3-10-16
CORRIDON,W.J.Capt 19-11-17 IMS MR43
CORRIE,William Ronald 2Lt dow 23-4-17 1 att8EYorks p84 CR France40
CORRIGALL,John.MID LtACapt dow 8-5-18 5SfthH p241 CR Scot871
CORRIGAN,Francis Stanislaus TLt kia 31-8-18 13Lpool p71 CR France433 Ex Lancs
CORRIS,William Henry 2LtACapt dow 31-8-18 1RB p178 CR France14
CORRY,Armar Valentine Lowry.MC.Lt kia 12-9-16 1GrenGds p49
CORRY,E.J.Lt 18-3-20 WYorks CR Yorks447
CORRY,Frank Moring 2Lt dow 13-12-17 8N&D att65RFC p18&233,7Bn CR Belgium11,12-12-17
CORRY,John Beaumont.DSO.Maj kia 5-11-14 RE p44 CR France706
CORRY-SMITH,A.C.Lt 30-12-20 Mon CR War7
CORSCADDEN,Francis Theodore George T2Lt dow 18-6-16 14RIrRif p169 CR France44
CORSCADEN,James Noel 2Lt kia 17-10-18 4 att6InniskF p104 CR France190
CORSE-SCOTT,Alexander Capt ded 13-3-19 RScots p254 CR Scot711
CORTIS,John Halsted 2Lt kia 15-6-15 3 att2Wilts p152 MR22
CORTLANDT-ANDERSON,Harry Frederick Lt dow 14-2-17 102Grndrs CR Iraq5
CORY,Charles Willoughby 2Lt kia 12-8-15 5Suff p217 MR4,Woolnough
CORY,Cyril Noel Capt kia 31-10-16 RFA attTMB p27 CR France394
CORY,E.Q.2Lt ded 9-8-18 3RRofCav CR Beds8
COSENS,Harold Stanley Frederick Lt kia 27-10-14 1EYorks p84 CR France82
COSGROVE,Albert Bruce T2Lt dow 31-5-16 22NumbF p60 CR France208,acckld
COSGROVE,Gordon Sallnow 2Lt kld 4-11-17 GL &RFC p6 CR Lond14
COSSAR,James 2Lt dow 16-8-16 3 att12HLI p162 CR France145
COSSAR,Norman Thomson T2Lt kia 15-5-17 7RB p178 CR France594
COSSER,George Alfred Lt ded 15-5-16 6Hamps p229 MR38
COSTA,Luigi Gausche T2Lt kld 19-3-18 RFC p15
COSTEKER,John Henry Diver,DSO BtMaj kia 25-4-15 RWar 88InfBde 29Div p64 CR Gallipoli15 Dives
COSTELLO,Archibald Gordon 2Lt kia 15-9-16 17Lond p250 CR France432
COSTELLO,Edward William Lt kia 1-7-16 3RInniskF att87MGC Inf p104&182 MR21
COSTELLO,Gabriel Patrick T2Lt kia 16-8-15 5RIrReg p88 MR4
COSTER,Cecil Vincent.MC.TLt kia 24-9-18 17MGC Cav p182&258 CR Palestine11 Ex WKentYeo
COSTER,Ernest.MC.T2LtACapt kia 26-9-17 1/2RWFus p97 MR30
COSTER-EDWARDS,John Francis Capt dow 11-11-18 3 att24RWFus CR France34
COSTIN,Bruce Duffus LtTCapt dow 24-10-14 1WYorks p81 CR France102
COSTIN,Henry William 2Lt kia 1-8-17 10RWKent p140 MR29
COSTLEY,Horace George Thompson Maj kia 7-2-16 IA 44Inf p275 MR38,Thomson
COTCHIN,Joseph 2Lt kia 9-10-17 1Beds p85 MR30
COTES,Digby Charles Bathe TCapt dow 15-10-18 7NStaffs p157 CR Belgium20
COTGRAVE,Christopher Russell Farmar Capt ded 29-12-17 Worc att100TMB p108
COTHILL,William Henry Thomas T2Lt kia 23-10-18 1Beds p85 CR France1476
COTMAN,R.A.TLt kia 26-3-18 4RFC p15 CR France98,2Lt
COTSWORTH,John Henry 2Lt kia 28-9-18 4Ches p222 CR France364
COTTAM,Clement John T2Lt kia 18-12-15 4Mddx p146 CR France682,19-12-15
COTTAM,Horace Charles Bowman.MC.Capt kia 30-9-18 7Hamps p229 CR France357
COTTAM,Hubert Frank 2Lt kia 23-3-18 3 att7Y&L p158 MR20,28-3-18
COTTEN,Leonard John Lionel.MC.Lt ded 13-6-20 Hamps CR Hamps10
COTTER,George Edmund Sackville Capt ded 19-4-17 RGA p262 CR Norf101,RA
COTTER,George Herbert 2Lt kia 12-4-15 5Lond p246 CR Belgium71
COTTER,Harold Cecil 2Lt kia 10-4-18 1/2 att11LancF p92 MR32
COTTER,Harry John.CIE.DSO.BrigGen ded 28-6-21 Late RA MR40
COTTERELL,Basil William 2Lt kia 30-10-18 3N&D attRAF p133 CR Belgium241
COTTERELL,Frederick Hampson Lt dow 16-12-16 5SStaffs p229 CR France300,acckld

COTTERELL,Robert Victor 2Lt kia 23-4-17 5 att8SStaffs p229 MR20
COTTERILL,Arthur Capt kia 21-3-18 5NStaffs p237 MR20
COTTERILL,Denis TCapt ded 2-12-18 RAMC att20CCS p195 CR France441,50CCS
COTTERILL,Frank T2Lt dow 11-11-18 Y&L p158 CR France289
COTTERILL,Harold Gordon Knight Lt ded 6-6-17 RFA att35RFC p6&27,dow CR France234
COTTERILL,John Henry 2Lt dow 15-3-17 3 att2BlkW p128 MR38
COTTIER,Walter Kaneen 2Lt dedacc 23-8-18 1/8 att1/6Lpool p215 CR France34
COTTLE,Frank Lt ded 9-2-19 RASC p267 CR Ches182 Ex RE
COTTLE,Sidney Joseph TLt kia 31-7-17 Dev attMGC p76 CR Belgium113
COTTLE,Walter Edward Worsdale Lt kia 31-7-17 GrenGds att1GdsBde MGR p49&53 MR29
COTTON,Arthur Edward 2Lt kia 7-7-16 13Ches p95 MR21
COTTON,Aubrey Nightingale TCapt kia 30-6-16 12RSuss p118 CR France631
COTTON,Brian Gordon Hamilton Capt dow 8-11-17 2/17Lond p250 CR Palestine1
COTTON,Harold Temple.DSO.LtCol kia 3-9-16 2SLancs p125 MR21
COTTON,Herbert Joseph Maj ded 23-5-16 IA 99Inf att76Punjabis p275 CR Iraq8
COTTON,John T2Lt dow 1-7-16 150RFA p27 CR France141
COTTON,Montague Arthur Finch Capt kia 18-5-15 6Lond p246 CR France260
COTTON,Ralph Charles Fairbairn.MID Lt dow 28-3-18 1/1HampsYeo attMGC p187&203 CR France1799
COTTON,Robert Douglas.MC.2Lt ded 5-4-19 14Lond p249 CR Hereford110
COTTON,Robert Hugh Alban T2Lt ded 12-10-18 RASC p192 CR Italy6
COTTON,William John Stanley T2Lt dow 23-8-17 Suff p78 CR Belgium172,Norf att1/4Bn
COTTON,William Martin Vernon 2Lt kia 21-12-16 GL &RFC p2&190 MR20
COTTON,Willoughby Lynch Capt ded 6-1-18 SL KSLI p201 CR Shrop19
COTTRELL,George Frederick 2Lt kia 11-5-15 RGA 108HB p39 CR Belgium135
COTTRELL,Harold William 2Lt kia 30-9-16 2SLancs p125 CR France832
COTTRELL,John Prince T2Lt dow 24-8-18 1RWKent att7RFus p140 CR France84
COTTRELL,Leonard Samuel Joscelyn TLt kia 13-4-18 9ACycCps p181 MR32
COTTRELL,Percy Bagliatto.MC.MID TLt dow 27-9-18 GL p190 CR Greece1,Baglietto
COTTRELL-DORMER,Charles Melville.DSO.Lt dow 8-2-15 3CldGds p51 CR France80
COTTRELL-DORMER,Clement Lt kia 27-10-14 2ScotsGds p52 MR29,26-10-14
COUCHE,Henry John.MC.Lt kia 9-1-20 MGC p266 CR Asia81
COUCHER,George Walter 2Lt kia 15-4-18 4 O&BLI p231 CR France248,16-4-18
COUCHMAN,Cyril Seymour 2Lt kia 8-5-17 2/6NStaffs p238 MR21
COUGHLAN,Julius Edward.MC.DCM.ACapt kia 25-10-16 1Mddx p146 MR21
COULDREY,Douglas John 2Lt dow 31-10-17 24 att2/22Lond p252 CR Palestine1
COULDRIDGE,Jack Oswald Lt kia 6-11-16 12 att2Worc p108 MR21
COULES,Eric Allan Gifford 2Lt kia 28-10-17 RE 129FC p44 CR France527
COULL,Andrew Mearns T2Lt kia 3-7-17 RE 178TC p44 CR France439
COULL,John Frederick TLt kia 30-9-18 RFus att23Bn p67 CR France914
COULL,James Christie Lt ded 13-2-19 RFA p269 CR Numb96
COULSON,Arthur.MM.2Lt kia 27-3-18 NumbF att1/5Bn p60 CR France526
COULSON,Coulson Tregarthen.MC.Capt dow 8-9-18 RGA 546SB p209 CR France100
COULSON,Jack Baxter 2Lt dow 20-6-16 5Lincs p220 CR France1
COULSON-MAYNE,Eric William Lt dow 25-4-17 5DLI D'Coy p238 CR France120
COULTAS,Thomas Bestwick TLt kia 26-9-16 6EYorks p84 CR France251
COULTER,Sidney 2Lt kia 25-8-18 12Manch p154 CR France402
COULTER,Thomas 2Lt ded 25-11-19 RASC p267 CR Egypt9,Lt
COULTER,Walter McFarlane.MC.Capt kia 20-5-17 6 att9HLI p240 MR20
COULTER,William Hugh Lt kia 22-2-15 5Lancers p21 CR Belgium57
COULTARD,Ernest TLt ded 12-11-18 RASC attCanadaForestryCps p192 CR France1798
COULTARD,Eustace Frank T2Lt kia 6-4-16 9 att1 O&BLI p130 MR38
COULTHWAITE,James 2Lt kia 5-8-17 5BordR p228 CR France614
COULTHURST,Temple Capt kia 11-10-18 6WRid p227 CR France612
COULTON,Aubrey Ewan Capt kia 20-7-16 6Norf att6RWar p217 MR32,19-7-16
COUNSELL,Christopher Herbert 2Lt dow 6-7-16 3 att2Hamps p120 CR France169
COUNSELL,Henry Cecil 2Lt kia 27-5-18 45RFA p27 MR18
COUNSELLOR,Thomas Bell Small.MM.2Lt ded 8-12-18 7NumbF p214 CR Belgium330
COUNT,William Charles LtACapt kia 5-7-17 63/14RFA p27 CR France570
COUPAR,Sydney Bell Nicoll.MID Capt ded 30-12-18 7A&SH p243 CR France512
COUPE,Albert Capt kia 9-4-17 9Lpool p216 MR20

COUPE,Thomas Harold Lt ded 26-7-17 4Lancs attRFC p18&226 CR Lancs199,kid
COUPER,Charles Miller Capt dow PoW 28-9-15 4BlkW D'Coy p230 CR France347
COUPER,James Mudie Lt dow PoW 4-4-18 B256RFA p207 CR France1252
COUPER,John Ralph TLtACapt kia 15-11-16 10LNLancs p135 MR21
COUPLAND,Henry Lt dow 24-4-15 5RLancs p213 CR France284
COUPLAND,John Charles Gerald Lt kia 6-5-17 RFA &2RFC p6 MR20
COUPLAND-SMITH,Frederick Vyvyan TLt kia 2-7-17 173RFA p27 CR Belgium62
COURAGE,Godfrey Michell.MID T2Lt kia 1-7-16 6RBerks p139 CR France513
COURT,Eric McClintock Wathen TCapt kia 6-8-16 13 att4Worc p108 MR4
COURT,Gordon Frederick 2Lt kia 16-9-16 MGC HvyBrch p182 MR21
COURT,Reginald Walter Southwood 2Lt kia 26-3-17 1Hereford p252 MR34
COURT,Richard T2Lt kia 9-4-18 RLancs p58 MR19
COURT,Robert Ambrey TCapt kia 26-4-17 9WYorks att8WRid p81 CR France529
COURT,William Hubert Roylance Capt kia 24-5-15 9Lancers p22
COURTENAY,Arthur Patrick 2Lt dow 28-6-15 IARO att8Cav p275 MR66,Lt
COURTENAY,Hugh.DSO.MC.BtMajLtCol dow 23-8-18 1Beds p85 CR France84
COURTENAY,K.S. see COURTNAY,K.S.
COURTENAY,Michael Hudson LtCol dow 4-1-16 RGA Cmdg1HB p39 CR Iraq1
COURTHOPE,William George Lt ded 21-10-18 4Beds &RAF p85 CR France1858
COURTHOPE-MUNROE,John Wilfrid T2Lt ded 24-1-16 RASC 597MTCoy p192 CR Egypt3,Wilfred
COURTICE,G.R.A.Rev 3-6-17 IndEcclesDept MR65
COURTICE,Reginald Leyster T2Lt kia 2-7-16 8Lincs p74 MR21
COURTIS,John Harold.MIDx2 Capt kia 22-11-15 1 O&BLI p130 MR38
COURTNAY,Kilcoursie Sigismond Lt kia 11-8-18 3Dors p124 CR France360,COURTENAY Sigismund
COURTNEY,Edward Derek Lt ded 9-8-18 55RASC MT'Coy GHQ TrpSplyCol 192 CR France40
COURTNEY,F.Capt 17-7-20 LabCps CR Wales613 Ex RWFus
COUSANS,Guy Newson 2Lt kia 9-9-16 3InnisF att70RFC p2&264,Newsome CR France23
COUSENS,George Edward T2Lt kia 24-8-18 Mddx att1/8Bn p146 CR France214
COUSIN,Arthur Norman TCapt kia 7-12-17 12Y&L p158 CR France184
COUSIN,John Denholm Lt kia 9-4-18 4HLI p162 MR32
COUSINS,Charles Hope 2Lt dow 27-4-15 1Ess p131 MR4
COUSINS,Donald Threlkeld Lt kia 10-4-17 4EKent p212 CR France420
COUSINS,Eric Cyril 2Lt kia 21-3-18 13 att2N&D p133 MR20
COUSINS,Leonard T2Lt kia 14-4-17 1Ess p131 MR20
COUTTS,Norman Vawdrey 2Lt dow 26-9-15 9ESurr p112 MR19
COUTTS,Paul Campbell T2Lt kia 23-8-18 MGC p182 CR France239
COUTTS,Robert Disher Lt kia 25/27-9-15 4GordH p241 MR29
COUTTS,Walter Gordon T2Lt kld 2-12-17 GL &RFC p6
COUTTS,William Ernest Capt kia 22-3-18 6BlkW p231 CR France245,dow
COVELL,Howard Charles T2Lt ded 26-6-16 C69RFA p27 CR Iraq6
COVENEY,William Robert 2Lt ded 23-7-19 RE 303RdConst p262 CR Kent179
COVENTRY,Edgar Ernest Capt kia 1-11-14 1ELancs p110 CR Belgium68
COVENTRY,Eric T2Lt kia 20-7-16 20RFus p67 MR21 See ZEEDERBERG real name
COVENTRY,Leslie Corbett Capt kia 27-5-18 NottsYeo p205 MR41,drd
COVENTRY,William St.John.MID Lt kia 22-10-14 Beds p85 MR22
COVENTRY,Wyndham John Capt dow 1-1-16 IA 7Lancers p275 CR Iraq5
COVENTRY-DAVIES,Charles Capt ded 7-8-19 GL &11RWFus p266 CR France1775
COVINGTON,Edwin Thornton 2Lt kia 9-3-17 4ESurr att6NLancs p112 MR38
COWAN,Albert Arthur 2Lt ded 16-7-18 RFA &RAF p27 CR Egypt9
COWAN,Adam TLt kia 18-11-16 RE 82FC p44 CR France215
COWAN,Andrew Galbraith Maj murdered 1-6-15 IA 74Punjabis att53Sikhs p275 CR Egypt15
COWAN,Basil Terence Reilly Lt kia 6-8-15 Lincs attManch p75 MR4
COWAN,Charles John Alexander Capt dow 25-3-18 3RScots p53 CR France699
COWAN,Dennis Walker Lt ded 2-11-18 RFA p269 CR Lancs14
COWAN,Douglas Henderson 2Lt kia 26-8-14 1Hamps p120 MR15
COWAN,Eric Hamilton Lt ded 28-2-16 RGA p209 CR Lancs14
COWAN,George Deas.MID Maj kia 23-4-18 9RScots p212 CR France248
COWAN,Henry Vivian.CB.CVO.Col ded 24-1-18 RA p27 CR Devon37
COWAN,James.MM.2Lt ded 25-10-18 ScotHorse p205 CR Scot212
COWAN,John Grave Capt kia 16-8-15 4Ess p232 MR4
COWAN,John Orr Craig Capt kia 14-7-16 3RScots p53 CR France399
COWAN,Philip Chalmers Capt kia 8-11-17 8Manch attRFC p18&237 MR20
COWAN,Reginald Percival T2Lt ded 16-8-15 6BordR p116 MR4
COWAN,Robert Craig 2Lt kia 24-10-14 3RScots p53 MR22

COWAN,Ronald 2LtTLt kia 13-7-15 6HLI p240 CR Gallipoli1,dow
COWAN,Sidney Edward.MC&2Bars.TCapt kia 17-11-16 29RFC p2 CR France647
COWAN,William Wilson Lt kia 14-4-17 8RScots attRFC p211 CR Scot239,6-6-19 &CR France583,14-4-17
COWARD,Henry TLt dow 20-4-17 1BordR p116 CR France120
COWARD,John Bayman 2Lt kld 26-3-18 RFC p15 CR France300
COWARD,Leslie Graham Capt kia 25-9-15 5 att1Mddx p146 CR France114
COWD,Arthur Martin Chap4Cl ded 22-12-18 RAChDept att81FA p199 CR France1571
COWDELL,Charles Joseph Morton T2Lt kia 12-9-17 RE 212FC p44 CR Belgium37
COWDEROY,Horace 2Lt kia 15-9-16 20Lond p251 CR France432
COWDY,Harold Evans T2Lt kia 16-8-17 9RIrF p171 MR30
COWE,Archibald TCapt kia 2-12-17 RAMC att2Lincs p195 MR30
COWELL,Albert Victor John Capt ded 29-1-15 6RB p178 CR Yorks106
COWELL,Charles Stanley TLt ded 13-4-17 GL &RFC p190 CR Durham28
COWELL,George Edmund Maurice Maj kia 30-12-17 RFA p206 CR France398
COWELL,Henry Pulleine John Maj dow 9-8-15 RFA p27 MR4
COWELL,Jocelyn Gore 2Lt kld 28-1-18 RFus attRFC p15&67 CR Dorset70
COWELL,John Edward 2Lt kia 29-11-17 NStaffs att2/6Bn p157 MR17
COWEN,Henry Walter 2Lt kia 29-9-18 RGA 6SB p39 CR France528
COWHERD,John.MC.T2Lt kia 29-9-18 5 att4Worc p108 CR Belgium112
COWIE,Alexander Gordon Capt dow 6-4-16 SfthH p164 CR Iraq5
COWIE,Arthur William Spring T2Lt kia 8-7-16 7Lincs p75 CR France397
COWIE,Daniel MacDougall TCapt dow 17-9-16 10/11HLI p162 CR France197
COWIE,George 2Lt kia 22-10-17 GL &54RFC p6 CR Belgium125
COWIE,Gerald James Hardwicke.MC.T2Lt kia 23-4-17 10RFus p67&258 MR20
COWIE,Henry Benedict T2Lt kia 10-7-16 10WelshR p126 CR France297
COWIE,Hugh Norman Ramsay.CMG.DSO.Maj dow 20-5-15 1Dors p124 WestWoodhayChurchyard Berks
COWIE,John George Capt ded 26-2-19 6GordH p269 CR Scot838
COWIE,Lionel Jack Hardwicke T2Lt kia 24-4-17 2RFus p67 MR20
COWIE,William T2Lt dow 28-9-16 13RScots p53 CR France40
COWIE,William Anderson.MC.LtACapt dow 30-5-18 9RWFus p97 MR18
COWIN,Henry Hampton T2Lt kia 1-7-16 21Manch p154 CR France397
COWING,Ralph Henry 2Lt dow 15-7-15 3Y&L p158 CR France285
COWL,John Douglas 2Lt kia 23-4-17 4EYorks p219 MR20
COWLAND,Herbert Samuel 2Lt kia 15-4-17 291RFA p27&208 CR France568
COWLEY,Alexander 2Lt kia 1-7-16 8N&D p233 MR19
COWLEY,Charles Selwyn Lt kia 9-5-15 1Nhampt p137 MR22
COWLEY,Francis Llewellyn ACapt ded 18-3-19 RE p262 CR Kent46
COWLEY,Frank Wheatley.MC.TLt dow 9-8-18 11EYorks att92LightTMB p84 CR France134
COWLEY,Frederick John Bodenham T2Lt kia 11-8-18 Glouc att1Dors p106 CR France360,Bodnum
COWLEY,George Evelyn.MID TMaj dow PoW 18-6-18 8RDubF p176 CR France716
COWLEY,Victor Travers TLt kia 23-7-18 7/8KOSB C'Coy p101 CR France865
COWLING,Alexander 2Lt kia 26-4-18 1Camb p245 MR30
COWLING,Frederick Watkin 2Lt dow 20-10-18 5DLI p239 CR France337
COWMAN,Frederick Gregory.DCM.2Lt kia 28-9-18 6Lpool p215 CR France914
COWPE,George Bleazard Lt kia 31-7-17 6Ches p222 MR29
COWPER,Frank Neville 2Lt kia 12-10-16 7Suff p78 MR21
COWPER,Geoffrey Moore.MID TCapt dow 3-10-18 RAMC attDors p195 CR France113
COWPER,Gordon Capt ded 2-2-19 9GordH p166 CR Belgium321
COWPER,Leonard Harris T2Lt dow 7-11-16 32 att20NumbF p60 CR France297
COWPER,Ronald Macphail T2Lt kia 27-4-16 14HLI p162 CR France423
COWPER-COLES,S.W.Capt kld 14-10-18 RASC &RAF p192 CR Belgium18
COWTAN,Francis Scott Capt kia 24/25-4-17 WiltsYeo att7Wilts p206 CR Greece5
COX,Albert Henry 2Lt kia 24-7-16 RGA 109SB p39 CR France397
COX,Arthur George T2Lt kia 15-12-17 GL &42RFC p6 CR Italy7
COX,Arthur Johnson T2Lt kia 3-5-17 8EYorks p84 CR France924
COX,Cecil Arthur TCapt dow 16-10-16 26RFus p67 CR France121
COX,Cecil John 2Lt dow 24-4-18 RGA 331SB p39 CR France37,Lt
COX,Charles Frederick Lt kia 31-3-18 3N&D p133 CR France988
COX,Clarence Frederick Stuart.MC.TLt kia 29-10-17 10N&D p133 CR Belgium87
COX,Clarence Rupert TCapt dow 13-4-17 12RSuss &RFC att5Wing p6&118 CR Egypt2
COX,Derek Percy 2Lt kia 21-8-17 GL &27RFC p6 CR France924
COX,Douglas Weld 2Lt dow 17-5-15 3Suff p78 CR Belgium383,Lt

COX,Edgar William.DSO.MajABrigGen drd 26-8-18 RE StaffGHQ 1stEch p44 CR France40
COX,Ernest 2Lt dow 8-12-17 3 att7SomLI A'Coy p79 CR France319
COX,Eustace Richard Alan Calthrop.MC.Capt ded 18-3-17 3Dev p76 CR Berks19
COX,Francis Henry 2Lt kia 23-10-16 1RWar p64 MR21
COX,Frederick Percy 2LtTCapt kia 3-5-17 3 att9Leic p87 MR20
COX,George Beckett 2Lt kia 16-8-17 7Lond p247 MR29
COX,George Cyril Addison.MC.Capt 2-6-21 1BordR MR43
COX,George Henry Lt kia 30-10-14 3 att2KOSB p101 MR22
COX,George Pottinger Capt kia 24-12-15 1Ess p131 CR Gallipoli1
COX,George Walker Capt kia 3-5-17 1RWar att1Ess p64 MR20,Maj
COX,Harleigh Capt kia 3-7-16 8Glouc Res p106 MR21
COX,Harold 2Lt dow 16-4-18 12Lond attMGC Inf p187&248 CR Belgium168
COX,Harold Edward Leys Capt kia 1-7-16 9Lond p247 MR21
COX,Henry Bowerie TCapt kia 8-8-16 1/5Lpool p215 MR21,Harry
COX,Henry George 2Lt kia 3-7-16 EKent p57 CR France251
COX,Henry Hayr 2Lt kld 16-5-17 A64RFA attRFC p208 CR France98
COX,Henry Jack TCapt kia 31-7-17 12RFus p67 CR Belgium112
COX,Hugh Bertram Hamilton 2Lt kld 29-1-17 RFA &RFC p6&27 CR Lancs403,Lt
COX,John Alonzo.DSO.Maj kia 29-9-18 1HighCycBn att12HLI p253 CR Belgium88
COX,John James 2Lt dow 29-5-15 2Leic p87 CR France345,Lt
COX,John Lennox Lt kia 19-9-18 4 att11ScotRif p103 CR Greece5
COX,John Ramsay Capt kia 11-3-15 6Worc p108 MR22
COX,Joseph Henry Silvanus 2LtTLt kia 30-9-17 93LabCps p189 MR30
COX,Leonard Albert T2Lt kia 10-6-18 KSLI p144 CR France547
COX,Lupton James T2Lt kia 18-4-18 1Glouc p106 CR France765
COX,Margaret Annie SNurse 7-2-19 TFNS CR Eire492
COX,Norman John TLt kia 23-8-15 7RSuss p118 CR France1140
COX,Percival Elliot Capt dow 23-5-17 4NumbF p213 CR France1184
COX,Percy Cyril 2Lt kia 28-4-17 25NumbF p60 MR20
COX,Reginald John Ponsonby Maj kia 27-9-15 A&SH att8GordH p173 MR19
COX,Richard 2Lt kld 24-8-18 2/7Mddx p235 CR France504,kia
COX,Robert Ernest 2Lt kia 11-3-15 HLI p162 MR22
COX,Robert William Talbot.MID T2Lt kia 15-2-16 6Dors p124 CR Belgium131
COX,Theodore Russell 2Lt kia 27-9-15 14DLI p160 MR19
COX,Thomas Henry 2Lt kia 21-6-17 4ScotRif p103 CR Belgium115
COX,Walter Ewart 2Lt kia 18-5-17 4Glouc Z'Coy p225 CR France1701
COX,William Charles LtCol ded 21-4-19 1/4SomLI p218 CR Egypt15
COX,William George T2Lt ded 22-9-18 RE p44 CR Iraq8
COX,William Joseph LtTCapt kia 16-5-15 1RBerks p139 CR France632
COXE,Arthur Nelson 2Lt dow 3-11-14 105RFA p27 CR Belgium135
COXE,Cecil Henry 2Lt kia 1-7-16 6RFC p2 CR France452
COXE,Eric Noel T2Lt dow 9-6-17 SStaffs att7Bn B'Coy p122 CR France285
COXHEAD,Maurice Edward CaptTMaj kia 3-5-17 9RFus p67 CR France1182
COXON,Herbert Archibald 2Lt kia 1-7-16 14Lond p249 MR21
COXON,Percy Hunter.MC.TCapt kia 13-4-18 8BordR p116 CR Belgium168
COXON,William Basil 2Lt kia 11-4-18 NumbF p60 CR France297
COXON,William Hugh 2Lt kia 11-3-15 3N&D p133 MR22
COXSON,Lawrence Frederick 2Lt kia 17-10-16 12RSuss p118 CR France383
COXWELL,W.S.G.Lt dow 18-10-17 RhodR att2KAR p202 CR Tanzania1,att1Bn
COY,Alfred Reginald 2Lt kia 2-7-16 7WYorks p218 MR21
COY,John Christopher Capt kia 27-9-18 12/13NumbF GarrBn p60 CR France415
COYLE,Clement William Lt ded 19-2-19 GL Cmd &Staff p190 CR France1028
COYLE,Leonard Joseph T2Lt kia 23-11-16 10KRRC p149 MR21
COYNE,Cecil Thomas TCapt kia 27-8-17 9WYorks p81 CR Belgium83
COYNE,John Joseph Aloysius T2Lt kia 10-8-17 9RDubF p176 MR29
COZENS,Leslie Capt dow 14-10-15 5SStaffs p229 CR France98
COZENS-BROOKE,John Gilbert Somerset Lt kia 18-10-14 3 att1RScots p94 MR29
COZENS-HARDY,Raven 2Lt kia 9-10-17 4Norf p216 MR30
CRABB,Leonard George Bruce 2Lt kia 12-3-15 2ESurr p112 CR Belgium168
CRABB,Thomas Henry,MC 2Lt dow 18-3-16 4RFus p67 CR Belgium11
CRABBE,Campbell Tempest Eyre Lt kia 27-9-15 3GrenGds p49 MR19
CRABBE,Hubert Lyon Bingham 2Lt kia 15-5-18 3Huss &RAF p21 CR France513
CRABBE,John T2Lt dow 6-5-16 13RScots p53 CR France257
CRABTREE,Fred Walmseley TLt kia 15-8-15 7Yorks p90 CR Belgium111
CRABTREE,John Hebron 2Lt kia 26-9-17 4KSLI p235 MR30
CRABTREE,Lawrence C.T2Lt kia 24-4-18 WYorks p81 CR France424
CRABTREE,Stephen Mark Lt kia 28-6-16 18EYorks p84 CR France744
CRABTREE,Walker.MM T2Lt kia 21-8-18 1SomLI p79 CR France250,Walter
CRABTREE,William Henry 2Lt ded 10-2-15 8Lincs p75 CR Yorks500

CRACKNELL,Charles George Raphael Lt dow 29-12-17 1 att2/24Lond p252 CR Palestine3
CRACROFT,Robert Brian Lt kia 10-7-16 3EYorks p84 CR France453,7Bn
CRACROFT-WILSON,Clive Winthorpe TLt ded 12-11-18 4SWBord p99 MR65
CRADDOCK,Percy Frederick Capt kia 25-2-17 6RWFus p223 CR Belgium23
CRADDOCK,Reginald 2Lt kia 21-3-18 5NStaffs p238 MR20
CRADDOCK,Victor 2Lt dow 11-10-18 5SStaffs p229 CR France375
CRADOCK WATSON,Arthur Vivian See WATSON,A.V.C.
CRAFTER,James.MC.Lt ded 7-7-17 PoW 20Lond attRFC p18&251 MR20
CRAGG,John Francis T2Lt kia 1/3-7-16 8Lincs p75 MR21,1-7-16
CRAGG,Sydney Bolton T2Lt kia 9-11-17 GL &25RFC p6 CR France1553
CRAGGS,John James 2Lt kia 17-2-17 6 att1KRRC p149 CR France251
CRAGGS,Mabel Olive Nurse 20-1-15 BRCS CR France461
CRAGGS,Percival 2Lt kia 30-9-18 13Y&L p158 CR Belgium451
CRAIG,Archibald.MC.LtACapt kia 23-3-18 3GordH att267TMB p166 MR27
CRAIG,Arthur Francis Capt dow 4-10-18 1/4RWKent att30MGC p187&234 CR France25
CRAIG,Charles Frederick T2Lt kia 3-7-16 17RIrRif p169 CR France232,10Bn
CRAIG,Donald Leslie Langford.MC.Lt kia 31-7-17 RFA p207 MR29
CRAIG,Edmund Robert T2Lt dow 1-6-16 17RScots p53 CR France80
CRAIG,Eric Ericksen T2Lt kia 30-8-16 20 att10RIrRif p169 CR Belgium43,Erichsen
CRAIG,George Barton 2Lt kia 21-2-18 60RFC p15 CR Belgium158,Lt
CRAIG,George Robert.MC.Lt kld 19-8-17 ELancs &RFC p6&110,19-7-17 CR Lancs277
CRAIG,Gordon Robert T2Lt dow 3-4-18 7Beds p85 CR France185
CRAIG,Hedley William T2Lt kia 15-4-17 RE &RFC p6&44 CR Iraq8
CRAIG,Henry David Cook.MC.MID Maj ded 13-2-20 2HLI p265 MR70
CRAIG,Isaac Murray ACapt kia 22-8-18 RE 66FC p44 CR Palestine9
CRAIG,J.2Lt kld 11-4-18 GL &RAF p190
CRAIG,James Glen.MC.2Lt kia 23-4-18 3 att2RScots p53 CR France88
CRAIG,James Young TLt dow 24-10-17 3A&SH att1/2KAR p173&202 CR EAfrica35 &CR Tanzania1
CRAIG,John Arnott Taylor T2Lt kia 1-7-16 11RInniskF D'Coy p104 CR France215
CRAIG,John Beverley 2Lt kia 3-6-17 RH&FA p208
CRAIG,John MacAdam Lt dow 1-11-14 1A 57Rif att58 p275 CR France80,McAdam
CRAIG,John William Archibald Capt dow 26-8-16 1BerksRHA attB300RFA p207 CR France53 J.W.J.26-7-16
CRAIG,Robert Clark Capt kia 22-7-17 RGA p209 CR Belgium10,215SB
CRAIG,Robert Hunter T2Lt kia 21-3-18 9NumbF p60 CR France1489
CRAIG,Robert William.MC.T2Lt kia 17-4-18 34MGC Inf p182 MR32
CRAIG,R.Stewart 2Lt kld 22-4-18 GL &RAF p190 CR France103
CRAIG,Thomas Forrest TCapt ded 2-2-18 RAMC p195 MR41,dow
CRAIG,Thomas Patrick TLt kia 22-3-18 7Leinst p174 MR27
CRAIG,Walter George 2Lt ded PoW 5-11-18 11DLI p160 CR Europe149
CRAIG,William 2Lt kia 8-5-18 5ScotRif p224 CR Belgium111
CRAIG,William Colston T2Lt dow 20-1-17 10 att6SLancs p125 CR Iraq5,Willie
CRAIG,William Tait TLtACapt kia 21-9-18 1ScotRif p103 CR France666
CRAIG,William Younger Lt kia 20-9-17 5Lpool p215 MR30
CRAIGE,George 2Lt ded 28-10-18 10Lpool p216 CR Lancs149
CRAIGHEAD,John Marr T2Lt kld 25-9-17 EKent p57 CR Belgium21
CRAIGMILE,Alexander Murray.MC.Capt kia 29-3-18 6RB p178 CR France544
CRAIK,John Beverley 2Lt 3-6-17 2(Lond)RFA CR France96
CRAIKE-PICKERING,M.S.C.MC.TLt ded 14-4-18 MGC p182 CR Sussex 110
CRAM,Hubert Arthur T2Lt dow 16-4-18 16KRRC p149 CR Belgium102
CRAM,John Edwin.MC.2Lt kia 30-9-18 4Yorks att2/4WRid p220 CR France358
CRAMB,Wilfrid Brown 2Lt kia 14-4-17 4A&SH &9RFC p6&173 CR France913,Lt
CRAMER,George L'Estrange Lt dow 16-7-15 4RMunstF p175 CR France80,kia 2Bn
CRAMER-ROBERTS,Edward Herbert 2Lt kia 10-8-15 3EKent p57 CR Belgium97,2Bn
CRAMER-ROBERTS,Walter Evelyn BtLtCol ded 12-3-19 2Norf p263 CR Lond4
CRAMP,George Herbert 2Lt dow 18-11-18 RGA 301SB p39 CR France34,233SB
CRAMPTON,Edgar Walter 2Lt kia 9-10-17 5 att2RFus p67 MR30
CRAMPTON,William.MC.Lt ded 17-2-19 A94RFA p27,2Entries CR France40
CRAMSIE,Arthur Butler Lt kia 8-5-15 2 att5NumbF p60 MR29
CRANE,Charles Edward 2Lt dow 18-9-14 1DCLI p114 CR France1107
CRANE,Herbert Donovon T2Lt kia 22-3-18 10LNLancs B'Coy p135 CR France366
CRANE,John Robert Capt ded 8-5-18 RAVC p269 CR Notts84
CRANE,Lancelot 2Lt ded 15-3-18 RGA 159HB p39 CR France40
CRANE,Lucius Francis T2Lt kia 8-10-18 14Worc p108 CR France530
CRANE,Reginald Hooper T2Lt kia 4-10-17 1EYorks p84 MR30
CRANE,William Henry Lt ded 13-3-18 GL p266 CR Norf77

CRANK,Harry T2Lt kia 22-10-17 1/2 att 17LancF p92 MR30
CRANMER,Guy Paterson 2Lt kia 9-10-17 5YLI p235 MR30
CRANMORE,George William Lt kia 19-7-18 10Lond p248 CR France886
CRANSTON,Archibald Lindsay 2Lt dow 16-8-18 5KOSB p224 CR France28,1Bn
CRANSTON,John Tennent 2Lt kia 15-7-16 9HLI p240 CR France402
CRANSTON,William Weir TLt kia 18-12-17 RE 173TC p44 CR Belgium12
CRANSWICK,George Alec 2Lt kia 18-11-17 Y&L &23RFC p6&158 MR20
CRANSWICK,Gilbert 2Lt kia 26-10-16 4EYorks p219 CR France387
CRANWILL,Valentine Arthur Butler.MC.LtACapt kia 24-4-18 2ELancs p110 CR France304
CRAPP,Cyril Frederick T2Lt ?? 22-5-17 GL &78RFC p6 CR Sussex182
CRAPPER,Charles.MM.2Lt dow 26-4-18 3 att5Yorks p90 CR Yorks740
CRASTON,Frank Marshall Lt kia 28-8-17 5ELancs att 13Manch p226 CR Greece5
CRASTON,John 2Lt dow 19-4-15 3 att 1RWKent p140 CR Belgium165
CRATHORNE,Frederick TLt kia 14-1-16 GL attRE 252TC p190 CR France76
CRAUFURD,John Gordon Capt kia 22-11-15 IA 37Dogras att12DivSigCo p275 MR38
CRAVEN,Asa T2Lt kia 19-10-16 8 att 1BlkW p128 CR France385
CRAVEN,Austen James Arthur TLt ded 27-8-18 SL &RA p201 CR Lond9,Austin
CRAVEN,Brian Thornthwaite T2Lt kia 1-7-16 RFA p27 CR France513
CRAVEN,Frank 2Lt kia 28-3-18 2WYorks p81 MR27
CRAVEN,George Alfred Senior Lt dow 15-9-17 RFA p207 CR France592
CRAVEN,George Edward Rev ded 7-12-18 RAChDept p199 CR Greece9
CRAVEN,Leo Lt ded 31-10-20 IA TC attRGA 6MtnBty p275 MR66
CRAVOS,Cyril Stephen T2Lt kia 2-3-17 GL &5RFC p6 CR Greece927
CRAWFORD,Alexander Basil TCapt kia 10-5-16 17WYorks p81 CR France631
CRAWFORD,Cecil James 2Lt kia 23-10-17 7 att12Mddx D'Coy p235 MR30
CRAWFORD,Charles Noel 2Lt kia 8-4-16 1Nhampt p137 CR France551
CRAWFORD,Daniel David Dunlop Lt ded 10-12-17 RE att25RlwyCps S&M p44 CR EAfrica10 &CR Tanzania1
CRAWFORD,David Lt ded 10-12-17 IARO attS&M p275
CRAWFORD,Donald T2Lt kia 27-7-16 9MGC 99Coy p182 MR21
CRAWFORD,Edward Lt dow 27-5-15 3 att2RInniskF p104 CR France64
CRAWFORD,George Rainier.CB.Col ded 22-8-15 10WRid IA Retd p115 CR Glouc31
CRAWFORD,Gerald Shakespear Maj dow 10-8-17 6SWBord p99 CR Belgium11
CRAWFORD,James T2Lt dow 19-7-16 7CamH p167 CR France80
CRAWFORD,James Carpenter 2Lt kia 1-10-16 20Lond p251 CR France385
CRAWFORD,John Cane 2Lt kia 31-8-16 F14RHA p27 CR France397
CRAWFORD,John Russell 2Lt dow 27-9-16 13 att9N&D p133 CR France246,kia
CRAWFORD,John Stirrit 2Lt ded 5-3-19 5RScotF p269 CR Scot514
CRAWFORD,Kelvin Capt kia 11-4-18 MGC &60RAF p266 MR20
CRAWFORD,Kenneth Clark 2Lt kia 2-9-18 4RScotF p222 MR16,1 att 14Bn
CRAWFORD,Reginald Waring Lindsay 2Lt dow 13-7-16 C63RFA p27 CR France51
CRAWFORD,Robert T2Lt died 15-11-18 12HLI p162 CR Scot679
CRAWFORD,Robert McLarg T2Lt kia 14-8-16 8RFus att10HLI p162 MR21,McLay
CRAWFORD,Robert Stobo 2Lt kia 17-5-17 2RScotF RoO p94 CR France279
CRAWFORD,Sydney George 2Lt drd 10-10-18 1RDubF p176 CR Scot660,Lt 3Bn
CRAWFORD,William Charlton T2Lt kia 17-11-16 GL &RFC p2&190 MR20
CRAWFORD,William Montgomery T2Lt dow 5-9-18 12HLI p162 CR Scot685
CRAWFORD,William Scott 2Lt kia 15-4-17 14Lond p249 CR France162
CRAWFORD-KEHRMANN,Jessel Lt kia 24-1-15 3RB attSStaffs p178 CR France681
CRAWFORD-LESLIE,Reginald William Henry Maj ded 3-4-16 ScotHorse Res p269 CR Scot310
CRAWFORD-WOOD,Guy Lt kia 1-7-16 1WelshGds p53 CR Belgium6,2Lt
CRAWHALL,Fritz Portmore 2Lt kia 10-3-15 KRRC p149 MR22
CRAWHALL,Neil Grant Lt kia 7-7-16 Manch att2ELancs p154 MR21
CRAWLEY,Albert T2Lt dow 9-5-17 7Lincs p75 CR France40,Lt
CRAWLEY,Eric TLt ded 26-2-17 10RInniskF p104 CR France285
CRAWLEY,Eustace Maj kia 2-11-14 12Lancers p22 MR29
CRAWLEY,Henry Thomas 2Lt dow 6-5-18 4Worc p108 CR France24
CRAWLEY,Thomas Henry Ouseley Capt kia 6-5-15 Worc p108 MR4
CRAWLEY-BOWEY,Thomas Russell TCapt dow 30-8-16 14Glouc p106 CR France66,BOEVEY
CRAWLEY-BOEVEY,Edward Martin Capt kia 24-12-14 1RSuss attRFus p118 CR Belgium17
CRAWSHAW,Charles Neville.MC.Capt&Adjt kia 19-9-18 8RScotF p94 MR37
CRAWSHAW,T.H.Lt 5-9-20 1/5Y&L CR Yorks575
CRAWSHAY,Mervyn Capt kia 31-10-14 5DragGds p21 MR29
CRAYMER,Douglas Charles 2Lt kia 15-9-18 RGA 232SB p39 CR France841
CREAGH,Aubrey Osborne Capt kia 14-4-15 IA 120Inf p275 CR Iraq6

CREAGH,Henry James Perceval.MC.MID TLtACapt dow 23-11-18 11Suff p78 CR France13
CREAGH,Leo Capt kia 20-12-14 1Manch p154 MR22
CREAGH,O'Moor Charles Lt kia 23-4-18 RFA 108ArmyBde p27 MR20,O'Moore 23-3-18
CREAGH,Reginald Simon Macnamara TLt ded 5-12-17 14RB p178 CR Lond9
CREAGH,William Nagle 2Lt dow 7-3-17 3Leinst p174 CR Belgium100
CREAN,John Fitzgerald Capt ded 17-10-18 LancHuss p269 CR Lancs10
CREAN,Theodore Capt kld 26-10-14 Nhampt &RFC p1&137 MR20
CREAR,Malcolm Charlton 2Lt ded 3-8-17 RH&FA &RFC p27 see CRERAR,M.C.
CREASEY,Arthur Andrew 2Lt kia 14-7-17 1Beds att22RFC p6&85 CR France95
CREASY,Francis Symons T2Lt kia 23-4-17 8SStaffs p122 MR20
CREASY,Harry William Hay TCapt kia 13-6-16 11Ess p131 CR Belgium73
CREASY,Robert Leonard.MC.LtAMaj dow 22-10-18 D190RFA p27 CR Belgium392
CREBBIN,William Arthur.MC.TCapt kia 4-4-18 8RB p178 MR27
CREE,Adrian Victor T2Lt kia 17-2-16 10RWFus p97 MR29
CREE,Arthur Thomas Crawford Lt kia 12-5-15 7DLI p239 CR Belgium165
CREE,Charles Edward Victor Lt kia 20-7-16 6N&D p233 CR France504
CREE,James Fleming 2Lt kia 3-9-18 3 att22NumbF p60 CR France258
CREE,Robert Scott Capt dow 14-11-17 1/8ScotRif p225 CR palestine2
CREE,William Cecil Holt Capt ded 24-10-14 RFA p27 CR Cornwall40
CREED,Charles Odell 2Lt dow 2-6-15 2GrenGds SR p49 CR France145
CREERY,Ronald Hulbert.MC.2Lt dow 23-4-17 RGA 121SB p39 CR France113
CREES,William 2Lt kia 1-7-16 2RWSurr p55 CR France630
CREEY,Cuthbert John 2Lt kia 20-10-16 21RFC p2 CR France833,CREERY
CREIGHTON,Oswin Chap4Cl kia 15-4-18 RAChDept att42RFA p199 CR France98
CRELLIN,Douglas Mark T2Lt ded 25-12-18 RE p262 CR Lancs156,Lt Worc
CRELLIN,William Anderson Watson.DSO&Bar.CaptTLtCol dow 8-10-18 15N&D p133 CR Belgium11
CREMEN,Leonard Francis Lt ded 4-6-15 IA 14Sikhs p275 CR Gallipoli3
CREMETTI,Max Arthur Eugene T2Lt kld 14-8-17 GL &RFC p6 CR Mddx17
CREMIN,Bernard Felix Ambrose 2Lt kia 11-10-16 10A&SH att26TMB p173 MR21
CREMONINI,James Henry T2Lt kia 18-10-17 66RFC p6 CR France31
CRERAR,Donald Campbell Lt kia 24-4-18 4RFA attRE 254TC p207 CR France144
CRERAR,John Lt kia 31-7-17 5A&SH p243 CR Belgium96
CRERAR,Malcolm Charlton 2Lt kld 3-8-17 RFA &RFC 5Wing p6&27 seeCREAR,M.C.CR Palestine2
CRESSEY,George Ernest Lister Lt kia 26-9-15 2Yorks p90 MR19
CRESSWELL,Alfred Sackville Capt kia 13-3-15 2EKent p57 CR Belgium17
CRESSWELL,Clarendon Hyde Capt ded 29-10-18 LancsYeo p269 CR Scot239,CRESWELL
CRESSWELL,Edward Arthur Capt kia 13-10-15 6SStaffs p229 MR19
CRESSWELL,Francis Joseph Capt kia 24-8-14 1Norf p73 CR France1196
CRESSWELL,Frank T2Lt kia 18-5-16 9Leic p87 CR France283
CRESSWELL,H.O.TCapt ded 7-6-18 SL p268 CR Surrey80,H.C.
CRESWELL,Leonard Curtis Lt dow 13-10-16 3Y&L p158 CR Greece4
CRESWELL,Ronald Arthur 2Lt kia 13-1-16 2 O&BLI p130 CR France152,13-11-16
CRESWICK,Wilfred Bertram Capt kia 10-4-16 4YLI attRE 179FC p235 MR21
CRESSY,Charles Howard T2Lt kia 25-9-15 8RWSurr p55 MR19
CREW,Denis Meirville Lt dow 5-7-17 7Ches p223 MR29 &CR Belgium310,Dennis
CREWDSON,Dorothy Mary Lynerette.MM.Sister ded 13-3-19 VAD p200 CR France40,Dorothea Lynette 12-3-19
CREWDSON,Theodore Wright TCapt dow 6-11-16 20Manch p154 CR France102
CREWE,Clifford Whatley T2Lt kld 13-8-17 GL &RFC p6 CR Mddx66
CREYKE,Edmund Ralph Capt kia 5-7-16 5YLI p235 CR France702
CRICHTON,Alexander Godfrey T2Lt kia 16-8-15 7RDubF p176 MR4
CRICHTON,Arthur James.MC.T2Lt kia 15-7-16 1RWSurr p55 MR21
CRICHTON,Cyril William Alfred 2Lt kia 10-3-15 3Lond p245 CR France727,C.A.W.
CRICHTON,Henry Richmond Lt dow 22-2-17 IA 54Sikhs att51 p275 CR Iraq5
CRICHTON,Henry William.MVO.DSO.Viscount.MajBtLtCol kia 31-10-14 RHGds p20 CR Belgium116
CRICHTON,Herbert Clowe T2Lt dow 7-10-16 18Manch p154 CR France188
CRICHTON,Hubert Francis Maj kia 1-9-14 1IrGds p52 CR France1113
CRICHTON,John Arthur Maj 6-2-17 6Hamps attRE 1WT CR Iraq6
CRICHTON,John Drummond TCapt kia 22-3-18 9LNLancs p135 MR20
CRICHTON,McVeag Maj kia 19-12-20 IA 1/103Mahrattas p275 MR43,McVeagh
CRICHTON,Norman 2Lt kia 16-11-16 4SforthH p241 MR21
CRICHTON,Robert Renfrew 2Lt kia 20-11-17 6GordH p166 CR France1498
CRICHTON,Ronald 2Lt kia 22-8-17 5RWar p214 CR Belgium126

CRICHTON-BROWNE,Cecil Harold Verdin.MC.CaptAMaj ded 13-12-18 3KOSB p101 CR Belgium241

CRICHTON-STUART,Lord Ninian Edward LtCol kia 2-10-15 6WelshR p230 CR France80

CRICK,Cyril George Lt kia 27-8-17 HuntsCycBn att2/8Worc p253 MR30

CRICK,Walter Haliburton Routledge ACapt kia 9-4-18 4Dors p229 CR Palestine9

CRICK,William Edward T2Lt dow 9-4-17 9YLI p142 CR France214

CRIGHTON,Harold Reginald 2Lt kia 10-4-18 10Lpool p216 MR19

CRIGHTON,John TLt kia 27-9-15 8BlkW p128 CR France219,25-9-15 9Bn

CRIGHTON,John Arthur Maj ded 6-2-17 5Hamps p228

CRIGHTON,John Fairweather TLt kia 18-7-16 8BlkW p128 MR21,CRICHTON

CRIMMIN,Florence Lt kia 24-4-17 RNDevYeo p203 MR37

CRIPPEN,George Oliver Lt kia 14-5-15 5SLancs p230 MR29

CRIPPIN,Harry William.MC.Capt kia 8-9-16 RFA 56DivHQ p27 CR France

CRIPPS,Henry Reginald HonCapt ded 6-1-15 lateRE p262

CRIPPS,Reginald Edward T2Lt kia 5-11-17 RBerks att6Bn p139 MR30

CRISP,Cyril Bright Lt kia 16-8-17 5SomLI p218 CR Belgium106

CRISP,Ernest Geoffrey T2Lt dow 16-12-15 15RWar p64 CR France625,kia

CRISP,Francis Edward Fitzjohn 2Lt kia 5-1-15 1GrenGds p49 CR France566

CRISP,Frederick George T2Lt kia 9-10-17 16RWar Res p64 MR30

CRISP,Harold Dudley 2Lt kia 6-11-17 RFC p6 MR40

CRISP,Reginald 2Lt kia 29-3-18 att74EKent p212 MR27

CRISP,Stanley Searle AMaj dow 8-12-17 RFA 63A/ASec Bty p27 CR Italy7

CRISPIN,Hugh Trevor LtCol kia 30-10-14 2RSuss p118 MR29

CRITCHLEY,Frank T2Lt dow 10-4-18 SLancs att1/4Bn p125 CR France98

CRITCHLEY,John T2Lt kia 11-7-16 11RWar p64 MR21

CRITCHLOW,Charles T2Lt kia 26-10-17 21Manch p154 MR30

CRITTENDEN,Frederick 2Lt ded 7-9-17 RGA 170SB p39 CR Surrey15

CROAGER,Norman Eustace Sassoon T2Lt kld 8-11-17 GL &RFC p6 CR War98

CROAGER,Lawrence William 2Lt kia 3-5-17 2Ess p131 MR20

CROAL,Kenneth McFarlane T2Lt kia 19-10-18 6RFus att2/10RScots p67 MR70 &CR Europe179

CROALL,John James Capt kia 4-10-17 5RScotF p222 MR30

CROCKER,Edward TCapt kia 24-4-17 13ESurr p112 CR France379

CROCKER,Francis George T2Lt kia 14-7-16 8EYorks p84 MR21

CROCKER,Joseph Lt kia 19-9-17 5WRid p227 MR30

CROCKER,Percival James Wilberforce TLt ded 16-11-18 2 att1/5RWKent p140 CR Iraq8

CROCKET,John Lt kia 25-9-14 RAMC att1CamH p195 CR France1339

CROCKETT,Charles Love T2Lt kia 28-4-16 12RInniskF p104 CR Ireland196

CROCKETT,Clifden James Lt kia 18-8-16 4Nhampt att6War p234 CR France832

CROCKETT,Laurence Charles Capt ded 17-10-18 RAMC attSL DentalSurg p195 CR Nhampt78,Lawrence

CROCKETT,R.B.Lt&QM 8-4-21 GL CR Glouc168

CROFT,Benjamin Capt kia 10-11-18 28 att10Lond p252 CR Belgium256

CROFT,Cyril Talbot Burnley 2Lt kld 8-12-15 SomLI &RFC p1&79,Burney CR Somerset222

CROFT,Eric.MC.MID LtACapt ded 17-1-18 106/22RFA p27&261 CR Lond29,kldacc

CROFT,George Wheeler TLt kia 16-2-18 Lincs &48RFC p15&75 CR France1203,kld

CROFT,Herbert Archer.Bart.Capt kia 11-8-15 1Hereford p252 MR4

CROFT,Herbert Arthur 2Lt kia 14-2-17 GL &2RFC p6 CR France924

CROFT,John Arthur Christopher 2Lt kia 18-4-15 4RWar att2WRid p64 MR29

CROFT,Leslie Robert 2Lt kia 30-10-14 RSuss p118 MR29

CROFT,Randal William Shuckburgh TCapt kia 12-5-17 7Yorks p90 MR20

CROFT,Robert John 2Lt kia 21-3-15 2Glouc p106 CR Belgium28

CROFT-SMITH,Edwin Spencer 2Lt kia 8-5-15 1KRRC p149 MR29,10-5-15

CROFTON,Charles Woodward Maj kia 10-8-15 9Worc RoO NStaffs p108 CR Gallipoli13

CROFTON,Edward Vivian Morgan Lt kia 14-7-17 RE 61FC p44 CR Belgium102

CROFTON,Hugh Lefroy Capt kia 22-5-15 RInniskF p104 CR Gallipoli6

CROFTON,Thomas Horsfall.MC.Capt kia 21-3-18 3 att6ConnRgrs p172 MR27

CROFTS,Charles Howard.MC.T2Lt kia 20-7-18 RLancs attYLI p58 MR18

CROFTS,Edmund Cyril Iveson 2Lt dow PoW 28-4-18 1KOSB p101 CR Germany3

CROFTS,Frederick Wilkinson.MC.Capt dow 15-9-16 17Lond p250 CR France188

CROFTS,George Robert Murray Lt kia 9-5-15 3 att2WelshR p126 MR22

CROFTS,R.DSO.Maj 16-2-16 RAMC CR Eire138

CROFTS,William Lt kia 5-12-17 6LancF att2/7RWar p221 MR17

CROGER,Nathaniel William 2Lt dow 25-9-18 RGA 434SB p39 CR France13

CROGGAN,Josiah Fenwick Sibree TCapt ded 18-11-18 14 att10N&D p133 CR France52,CROGGON

CROKER,Frederick Reginald 2Lt kia 27-4-17 6LancF &RFC p221 MR20

CROLE,David Clement TCapt kia 23-3-18 RAMC att19Huss p195 MR27 &CR France1890

CROLEY,Frank William Capt dow 14-8-16 1ARO RE 178TC attS&M p275 CR France197

CROLL-JONES,Eustace Alvanley 2Lt kia 15-4-18 RFA 9/38ArmyBde p27 MR30

CROMARTY,Donald Everard Capt 7-3-20 RGA CR Mddx25

CROMB,David Rankin T2Lt kia 23-4-17 3 att13RScots p53 CR France421

CROMBIE,Ian Osborne TCapt kia 28-7-16 11Mddx p146 CR France296

CROMBIE,James 2Lt dow 24-6-18 7HLI p240 CR France169

CROMBIE,James McHattie 2Lt dow 2-7-17 3 att10RWKent p140 CR Belgium11

CROMBIE,John Eugene Capt dow 23-4-17 4GordH p241 CR France113

CROMBIE,Stewart Phyn Lt kia 4-12-18 1/5KOSB p224 CR Palestine8

CROMBIE,William Edgar.MC.Lt kia 31-8-18 7RWar attRAF p214&258

CROMBIE,William Lauder 2Lt kia 1-7-16 3RScots p53 MR21

CROMBIE,William Maurice Lt ded 17-2-19 IA IMS p275 CR Kent157,Capt

CROMIE,Henry Julian TCapt kia 23-10-16 3 att1Hamps p120 MR21

CROMIE,Maurice Francis Lt 4-6-15 3 att2Hamps MR4

CROMIE,Samuel Osborne Lt dow 17-11-16 2CldGds p51 CR France105,2Lt

CROMPTON,Arthur Harold T2Lt kia 3-7-16 7BordR p116 CR France397

CROMPTON,Cyril T2Lt ded 17-9-15 11YLI p142 CR Lancs267

CROMPTON,Henry Dent 2Lt kia 4-12-16 WLancsRFA att4RFC p18&208 CR France59,Harry

CROMPTON,Nigel George.MID TLt kia 5-11-15 RE 1-1FCp44 CR France275

CROMPTON,Thomas Lt kia 13-4-18 1RWSurr p55 MR32

CRONE,Bertram John Fenwick T2Lt dow 13-9-16 7Lancs p58 CR France922

CRONE,Percy Alexander 2Lt kia 8-9-16 4 att7RMunstF p175 MR37

CRONEEN,Laurence 2Lt kia 28-4-17 6RScots p211 MR20

CRONEY,Reginald Harry Talbot 2Lt kia 9-8-18 1 att8NStaffs p157 CR France33

CRONHELM,Arthur Geoffrey Lt kld 6-9-17 2/22Lond att23RFC p18&251 CR Egypt1

CRONIN,Harold William Lt dow 2-12-17 5Beds p219 CR Palestine8

CRONIN,John Francis 2Lt ded 10-3-17 14DLI p160 CR Europe51

CRONK,William Guy 2Lt kia 26-10-14 3EKent attKRRC p57 MR29

CRONSHAW,Thomas Edgar T2Lt dow 8-3-17 11ELancs p110 CR France339

CRONUN,William Benn TCapt ded 1-2-18 RAVC p198 CR France85,CRONYN

CROOK,Ernest Richard T2Lt dow 13-10-16 D59RFA p27 CR France59

CROOK,Harry 2Lt dow 20-4-18 17Lpool p71 MR30

CROOK,Leslie Arthur,MC TLtACaptAAdjt kia 25-9-17 1RWSurr p55 MR30

CROOK,Philip Joseph Lt kia 9-11-17 D of LancsYeo p204 CR Palestine8

CROOK,William George T2Lt kia 9-3-18 10RFus p67 CR Belgium113

CROOKE,Charles Croydon TLt ded 22-11-18 LabCps p266 CR War66

CROOKE,Elliot Hampden TCapt kia 3-7-16 8Glouc p106 MR21

CROOKE,Hugh Neville 2Lt kia 10-12-16 RE 67FC p44 CR France701

CROOKE,Walter T2Lt kld 12-11-17 GL &40RFC p6 CR Surrey6

CROOKES,Ronald Orme T2Lt kia 4-6-16 24RFus p67 CR France549

CROOCKEWIT,Alexander Edward 2Lt dow 26-10-17 3 att1Beds p85 CR Belgium11

CROOKHAM,Hugh Antony Rupert TLt dow 3-8-15 1Camb p244 CR France1

CROOKS,Edward Neilson 2Lt kia 22-3-18 12KRRC p149 CR France1204

CROOKSHANK,Wilfred Plassy Capt kia 8-3-16 IA 1/1GurkhaRif att123Rifs p275 MR38

CROOKSTON,William John 2Lt kia 12-4-18 4ScotRif att8BordR p103 MR32

CROOM,William Charles 2Lt kia 7-6-17 10Lond p248 MR29

CROOM-JOHNSON,Brian Lt kia 9-5-15 4RWFus p223 MR22

CROOME,William Hardman Capt kia 30-11-17 8Ess p232 MR17

CROPLEY,Reginald John T2Lt dow 22-9-18 1Beds p85 CR France512

CROPLEY,William 2Lt kia 21-9-18 4Suff p217 CR France212

CROPPER,Alexander 2Lt dow 22-10-16 Wilts att22RFC p2&152 CR France59

CROPPER,Edward Percival.MC.Lt kia 25-3-18 2WYorks p81 MR27

CROPPER,John TLt drd 21-11-16 RAMC p195 MR35

CROPPER,Thomas Andrew Lt dow 19-4-18 D75RFA p27 CR France84,2Lt

CROPPER,William 2Lt kia 22-8-16 6 att19Lond p247 MR16

CROSBIE,John Colin Lt dow 7-9-17 RGA att70RFC p6&39 CR France31

CROSBIE,Thomas Edward Chapman.MC&Bar.T2LtACapt dow 15-4-18 9RIrF p171 MR30

CROSBIE,Walter Robert Lt kia 12-4-18 4 att1/7BlkW p230 MR19

CROSBY,Arthur Barnard Lifford 2Lt dow 24-4-17 5DLI p239 CR France120

CROSBY,Frederick Howard 2Lt kia 7-3-18 2/17Lond p250 CR Palestine3

CROSBY,John Claude Parry T2Lt dow 21-1-18 1Lpool p71 CR France769,kia

CROSBY,Timothy Hugh Stowell Lt kia 3-2-18 5DLI att 1AircraftDepot RFC p238 CR France134,kld
CROSFIELD,Guy Henry Goad Lt kia 26-1-18 5 att1RB p178 CR France154
CROSHAW,Oswald Moseley.DSO.LtCol dow 26-9-18 QOGlasgowYeo att53AustInf p203 CR Belgium165,26-9-17
CROSHER,William John 2Lt dow 20-5-17 RGA 239SB p39 CR France40
CROSIER,Vernon Swann 2Lt dow 6-4-18 7Lond p247 CR France62
CROSLAND,G.W.K.DSO.Maj 31-12-19 WRid CR Yorks643
CROSLAND,John Herbert Lt ded 13-4-19 3RWFus att6KAR p97,202&266,GL MR46
CROSLAND,Trevor Allington 2Lt kia 22-6-16 2RWFus p97 CR France924
CROSLAND,William Philip T2Lt kia 16-8-17 2WYorks p81 MR21
CROSLEY,Cecil.MID 2Lt kia 16-8-15 RIrFus att5Bn p171 MR4
CROSS,Alfred 2Lt kia 13-11-16 1Lpool p71 CR France131
CROSS,C.E.P.Lt 4-10-18 3RFus CR France234 see CROST,C.E.P.
CROSS,David Ronald.MC.MID Lt kia 21-2-15 16Lancers p23 MR29
CROSS,Dennis Patrick.MC.LtACapt kia 24-8-18 2Beds p85 CR France177
CROSS,Ernest 2Lt kia 24-4-18 5 att2Mddx p146 CR France144
CROSS,Frank Alan T2Lt kia 25-2-17 7Glouc p106 MR38 Ex 1RFus
CROSS,Fred Capt ded 5-5-18 IARO att15CarnaticInf p275 CR India164
CROSS,George Herbert TCapt kia 30-9-18 RASC att9RIrFus p192 CR Belgium157
CROSS,Henry Hazelock Graham T2Lt kia 13-11-16 10RDubF p176 CR France220,Havelock
CROSS,Howard 2Lt dow 27-9-18 5Lond p246 CR France113
CROSS,James Lt dow 3-9-17 RFA 41DAC 10Cps p27 CR France139
CROSS,James Capt ded 9-11-19 RAMC p267 CR Lancs171
CROSS,John TCapt ded 21-7-18 RAMC p195 MR66
CROSS,Leslie Lt dow 30-9-15 44RFA p27 CR France345
CROSS,Maurice Assheton Capt kia 18-8-16 1LNLancs D'Coy p135 CR France402
CROSS,Philip Frank 2Lt kia 22-7-16 1RWKent p140 MR21
CROSS,Philip Frederick Lt kia 9-9-16 4 att6RIrReg p88 MR21
CROSS,Reginald Carlton Lt kia 7-6-18 DorsYeo attSLancs p203 CR France204
CROSS,Robert Singlehurst Lt ded 2-1-20 10Lpool p269 CR Lancs1
CROSS,Ronald Sydney TCapt kia 27-7-16 18WYorks p81 CR France631
CROSS,Russell W.Lt kld 24-7-19 RFC CR Canada116
CROSS,Samuel Allison 2Lt kia 14-1-18 KRRC att2Bn p149 MR30
CROSS,Sidney William T2Lt dow 23-10-18 RWKent att10Bn p140 CR Belgium143
CROSS,Solomon TCapt kia 22-3-18 RAMC att11Suff p195 MR20
CROSS,Thomas Edward Kynaston Capt kia 13-7-17 B70RFA p27 CR Belgium6
CROSS,Wilfrid 2Lt kia 22-7-16 4Leic p220 CR France745
CROSSE,Edward Arthur Willson 2Lt kia 27-9-18 1CldGds p51 CR France1497
CROSSE,Ewins Charles Marlborough Lt dow 16-5-15 Leic p87 MR22
CROSSE,M.E.B.2Lt kia 13-3-15 2Yorks p90 CR France279
CROSSE,Robert Grant TLt dow 14-7-16 7RWKent p140 CR France630
CROSSE,Thomas Latymer TCapt kia 3-7-16 7BordR p116 CR France397
CROSSLAND,Albert Lt ded 7-8-19 5YLI p269 CR Yorks323
CROSSLE,Howard Maj ded 26-11-19 IMS p275 MR43
CROSSLEY,Allen Hastings Lt dow 10-5-17 1/1Hereford p252 CR Egypt9,Alan
CROSSLEY,Arthur Reginald Gordon TLt ded 10-3-19 WYorks p263 CR Yorks468,Capt
CROSSLEY,Brian.MID Lt kia 17-5-15 3 att2HLI p162 MR22
CROSSLEY,Cyril 2Lt kia 1-7-16 15LancF p92 MR21
CROSSMAN,Guy Danvers Mainwaring T2Lt kia 10-7-16 13WelshR p126 CR France453
CROSSMAN,Lionel Gordon Capt ded 11-12-17 RAMC p253 CR Iraq6
CROSSMAN,Richard Douglas.MC.LtACapt kia 27-9-18 3RScots p53 CR France437
CROSSMAN,William Ronald Morley 2Lt kia 2-11-14 2KRRC p149 MR29
CROST,Christopher Edric Percy Lt kia 4-10-18 3RFus p67 CR France234,CROSS
CROUCH,Alan T2Lt kia 25-8-16 RB att42TMB p178 CR France402
CROUCH,Augustus Barton T2Lt kia 27-4-17 10Lincs p75 MR20
CROUCH,Clarence Cecil.MC.2Lt dow 22-10-17 A50RFA p27 CR France40
CROUCH,Frederick Charles.MID LtAMaj dow 2-11-17 RGA 113HB p39 CR Belgium165
CROUCH,Foster Brooke TLt kia 23-3-18 10DCLI p114 MR20
CROUCH,George Percy T2Lt dow 4-10-17 1DCLI p114 CR Belgium72
CROUCH,Lionel William Capt kia 21-7-16 O&BLI BucksBn p231 CR France832
CROUCH,William Ballard 2Lt kia 13-4-17 RGA 270SB p39 CR France924
CROUCHER,Cecil 2Lt ded 26-2-17 6N&D p233 CR France120
CROUCHER,Frederick William 2Lt kia 27-4-15 1RWKent p140 CR Belgium96
CROUGH,Francis Harris.MC.Capt kia 21-3-18 5 att2LancF p221 MR27,CROUCH Harrie

CROUSAZ,Cecil Francis Lt kia 31-11-14 1SStaffs p122 MR29,31-10-14
CROW,Arthur Arnold Pte kia 10-10-17 Ess Ex LNLancs CR Belgium83 Resigned Capt re-enlisted as Pte
CROW,Charles Maurice 2Lt kia 23-4-17 16RFC p6 CR France32
CROW,Henry Paterson Capt ded 9-11-18 RAMC p195 MR66
CROW,Norman Howard 2Lt kia 14-9-17 GL &56RFC p6 CR Belgium140
CROWDER,Harry 2Lt kia 14-3-17 1Lpool p71 MR21
CROWDY,James Dunscomb.DSO.Maj kia 14-1-20 IA 2/5GurkhaRif p275 MR43
CROWE,Cecil Alexander T2Lt kia 9-9-16 7RInniskF D'Coy p104 CR France402
CROWE,Harold Archer 2Lt dow 1-6-15 1Lond p245 CR France345
CROWE,Hugh Barby Lt drd 28-10-15 RFus p67 MR4
CROWE,William Herbert SubCdr 2561/33233 ded 24-6-20 IA IndOrdDept p275 CR Iraq8
CROWE,William Maynard Carlisle Capt kia 11-11-14 RWar attNhampt p64 MR29,CARLISLE-CROWE
CROWLEY,Cedric Hugh Lt kia 25-4-15 4 att2RWar p64 MR29,att 1Bn
CROWLEY,Cyril Raymond 2Lt kia 4-10-17 1Dev p254 CR Belgium125
CROWLEY,Daniel Joseph Lt ded 27-9-19 RAMC p267 MR65
CROWLEY,Frederick Augustus T2Lt kld 26-2-18 SL &RFC p15 CR Essex211
CROWLEY,John Cyril Capt kia 11-9-16 4RWSurr p212 CR Iraq6
CROWLEY,Philip TLt kia 7-7-17 RLancs p58 CR France379
CROWTHER,Eric Stuart 2Lt dow 21-11-16 7GordH p242 CR France40,Lt
CROWTHER,Ernest T2Lt kia 25-10-18 RE 92FC p44 CR France716
CROWTHER,George 2Lt kia 28-6-17 1/4WRid p227 CR France258
CROWTHER,Leslie Oakes TCapt kia 6-12-16 GL &12RFC p2&190 CR France46
CROWTHER,Leslie Taylor 2Lt kia 15-6-15 5WRid p227 CR France347,16-6-15
CROWTHER,Norman 2Lt kia 14-10-18 3Ches att15Suff p95 CR France567
CROWTHER,Percy TCapt ded 14-9-16 RASC p192 CR Hamps205
CROWTHER,Philip Townsend TLt kia 5-5-17 RE 211FC p44 CR France1191
CROWTHER,Stanley Lorne 2Lt kia 20-9-17 29RFC p6 CR Belgium123
CROWTHER,William Osborne T2Lt kia 24-11-16 3 att9N&D p133 CR France701
CROXSON,Sidney T2Lt ded 16-9-16 8Dev p76 CR France145
CROYDON-FOWLER,Hilgrove TLt kia 12-10-18 2Worc 1stGarrBn p108 MR16,Hillgrove
CROYSDALE,Marjorie Sister ded 2-3-19 QAIMNS p200 CR France40
CROZIER,Gerald Irvine Lt ded 28-6-20 6Leinst CR Asia53
CROZIER,James Cyril Baptist 2Lt kia 27-8-14 2RMunstF B'Coy p175 CR France1751
CROZIER,Percy Beattie Capt kia 19-5-15 IA 4Rajputs att15Sikhs p275
CROZIER,Thomas Alexander.MC.TLt kia 23-3-18 11RWSurr p55 CR France307
CROZIER,William Magee Lt kia 1-7-16 9RInniskF p104 MR21
CRUDDAS,Hugh Wilson.DSO.LtCol dow 20-1-16 IA 41Dogras att 1/4Suff p275 CR France178,kia
CRUDDAS,Sandwith George Peter T2Lt kia 20-9-15 6DCLI p114 CR Belgium84,21-9-15
CRUESS-CALLAGHAN,Stanislaus Capt ded 27-6-17 44RFC CR Canada1601
CRUICKSHANK,Alexander Douglas.MC.T2Lt kia 23-10-18 50MGC Inf p182 CR France1386
CRUICKSHANK,Andrew John Tuke 2Lt kia 7-7-16 RGA att70RFC p2&39 CR France134
CRUIKSHANK,Arthur Henry Prinsep Capt dow 28-4-15 IA 32SikhPnrs att34 p275 CR France200
CRUICKSHANK,Donald Edward 2Lt kia 9-4-16 10BordR att5Wilts p116 MR38
CRUICKSHANK,Eric TCaptAMaj dow 26-9-18 D87RFA p27 CR France88
CRUICKSHANK,Ernest Alec Watson Lt kia 21-8-18 48/36RFA p27 CR France1014
CRUICKSHANK,Guy Lindsay.DSO.MC.Capt kia 15-9-16 RFC p2 CR France1465
CRUICKSHANK,Harold Arthur Lt dow 28-9-15 3 att2RScotF p94 CR France80
CRUICKSHANK,Harold Thomas Capt kia 25-9-15 1 att8KOSB p101 MR19
CRUICKSHANK,Isabella Sister drd 10-4-17 QAIMNS p200 CR France85
CRUICKSHANK,James 2Lt dow 3-8-16 7ScotRif p224 CR France145
CRUICKSHANK,Kenneth George 2Lt ded 12-7-17 GL &32RFC p6 MR20
CRUICKSHANK,Philip TCapt kia 1-7-16 RInniskF p104 MR21
CRUICKSHANK,Raymond Alfred 2Lt kia 23-4-17 3Mon p244 CR France427,2Bn
CRUICKSHANKS,Ernest TCapt kia 17-10-15 14 att9KRRC p149 See WESTON,J.true name
CRUIKSHANK,Eric Onslow Lt kia 19-9-14 3Wilts p152 CR France864
CRUISE,Henry B.Capt ded 23-4-17 SL NyasalandFF p268 CR EAfrica78,Richard 22-4-17
CRUM,Stewart Alexander 2Lt kia 1-7-16 2SfthH p164 CR France1890
CRUM-EWING,Alexander.MID 2Lt kia 22-12-14 3SfthH att1CamH p164 MR22
CRUMPTON,Thomas 2Lt kia 17-4-18 RGA 6SB p39 MR32

CRUNDWELL,Alan Lt kia 23-3-18 11Lpool p71 MR27
CRUTTWELL,Hugh Lockwood 2Lt kia 12-10-17 RGA 118SB p39 CR Belgium19
CRYER,Bernard Noel 2Lt kia 15-9-17 7Lond p247 MR29
CRYER,Harold James T2Lt kld 13-10-17 GL &RFC p6
CRYMBLE,Cecil Reginald Lt kia 20-11-14 3 att1RIrF p171 MR32
CRYMBLE,John Gordon T2Lt dow 28-12-16 9RIrF p171 CR France285
CRYMBLE,William Capt ded 12-10-16 RAMC p195 CR Egypt15
CUBBON,Francis Richard.MC.Capt mbk 9-6-17 IA 72Punjabis attRFC p275 MR20
CUBEY,Joseph Berkeley TCapt kia 1-7-16 23NumbF p60 CR France393
CUBIE,Adam 2Lt kia 30-7-18 119/27RFA p208 CR France21
CUBITT,Alick George.Hon.Lt kia 24-11-17 15Huss p22 MR17
CUBITT,Bryan Barton TLt kia 26-9-15 8EYorks p84 MR19
CUBITT,Edward Randall Capt kia 12-8-15 5Norf p216 MR4
CUBITT,Eustace Henry Capt kia 19-4-17 1/5Norf p216 CR Palestine8
CUBITT,Henry Archibald Capt kia 15-9-16 3CldGds p51 CR France513
CUBITT,Terence Algernon Kilbee.MC.Capt kia 22-8-18 4Norf p216 CR France281,1Bn
CUBITT,Victor Murray TLt kia 12-8-15 5Norf p216 MR4
CUBITT,William Hugh.Hon.Lt dow 24-3-18 1Drags p21 CR France1063
CUBITT-IRELAND,Leslie Woodhouse 2Lt kia 12-2-17 12Manch CR France786
CUDMORE,Milo Massey.MC.TLt kia 27-3-16 RFA 31THBty p27 MR29
CUFFEY,Maurice O'Connor Lt kia 20-5-15 att2RDubF p176 MR29
CUFFLEY,Joseph Ison.MC.T2Lt dow PoW 31-3-18 61MGC Inf p182 CR France1061,Lt
CULL,Arthur Tulloch Capt kia 11-5-17 1SfthH &48RFC p6&164 MR20
CULL,Leslie TLt kia 8-11-17 21MGC Cav p182 CR Palestine1
CULL,Percival Stuart.MIDx2 2Lt kia 14-4-18 3 att1NumbF p60 CR France1896
CULLEN,C.F Lt 1-4-20 1/4Y&L CR Germany1
CULLEN,Gerald Somerville Yeats 2Lt kia 11-4-17 1RIrF p171 CR France604
CULLEN,Harry William 2Lt 21-8-20 7LancF CR Staffs6
CULLEN,James.MC.2Lt dow 3-10-18 1RIrF p171 CR Belgium38
CULLEN,John T2Lt kia 15-9-16 13A&SH p173 CR France239
CULLEN,Ralph Neville 2Lt kia 6-12-15 6RIrF p171 MR37
CULLEN,Thomas T2Lt dow 22-9-18 33MGC Inf p182 CR France906
CULLEN,William Barbour Alexander Kennedy Maj ded 29-3-21 IA p275 MR69
CULLEN,William Geoffrey Langley 2Lt ded 30-3-15 8RScots p212 CR Scot237,9Bn
CULLEN,William Harold T2Lt kia 11-7-16 113MGC p182 MR21
CULLERNE,Alan Baird.MC.T2Lt kia 23-10-18 7RWKent p140 CR France717
CULLEY,Geoffrey Matthew George TCapt kia 15-9-16 11RWKent p140 CR France277
CULLEY,Walter Duncan T2Lt dow 12-7-17 Hamps att1Bn p120 CR France10,12-7-18
CULLIMORE,H Capt 15-2-15 JohoreForces CR Asia45
CULLIMORE,John.MIDx2 TLt dow 16-4-18 8Ches p95 CR Iraq5
CULLIMORE,Joseph Albert T2Lt kia 23-5-16 8RIrF p171 CR France423
CULLIMORE,Smart TCapt kia 20-2-16 11SWBord p99 CR France727
CULLINAN,Robert Hornidge TCapt kia 8-5-15 7RMunstF p175 MR4
CULLING,Harold William T2Lt kia 7-7-16 9WRid p115 MR21
CULLIS,Edmund Herbert 2Lt ded 19-8-17 RE p269 CR Glouc102
CULLIS,Henry Thoreau TLt kia 10-12-15 15 att12RB p178 CR France276
CULLY,Leslie T2Lt dow 27-10-17 91MGC p182 CR Belgium11
CULME-SEYMOUR,George.MID Capt kia 7-5-15 KRRC p149 MR29
CULPEPER,A.G.Lt 9-5-20 IMD MR65
CULPIN,Charles Henry T2Lt dow 15-5-17 1 att10Glouc p106 CR France88,Lt
CULSHAW,Ronald Henry 2Lt kia 14-7-18 3WYorks p81 CR Belgium3,1Bn
CUMBERLAND,Andrew John T2Lt kld 3-1-18 RFC p15 CR Shrop52
CUMBERLAND,Brian Clark Capt kia 15-8-15 5Beds A'Coy p219 CR Gallipoli4
CUMBLEY,Reginald T2Lt kia 19-9-18 RBerks att8Bn p139 CR France212
CUMING,Arthur Eric MacMorrough.MC.LtACapt dow 26-10-18 1RIrF p171 CR France34
CUMING,William Edward T2Lt kia 31-7-17 5ConnRgrs attRInniskF p172 CR Belgium106
CUMMING,Adam Smith 2Lt dow 20-4-17 5A&SH p243 CR Palestine8
CUMMING,Alex Bryant Lt kia 22-4-16 3BlkW p128 CR Iraq5
CUMMING,Alfred Lionel T2Lt kia 7-6-17 GL att15RFC p6 CR France41
CUMMING,Andrew Alexander 2Lt ded 6-2-18 4RScots p211 CR Scot742
CUMMING,Anthony Dyson Lt kia 6-3-17 4LNLancs attMGC p187&234 CR France624
CUMMING,Colin Edward Lt dow 25-2-15 103RFA p27 CR Belgium151
CUMMING,Edward John Capt ded 15-11-18 IA 102Inf p275
CUMMING,Frederick Kenneth 2Lt kia 23-10-18 3 att14BlkW p128 CR Belgium428
CUMMING,George T2Lt kia 9-7-16 8SLancs p125 MR21
CUMMING,Gilmour 2Lt kia 21-3-18 5 att1/7BlkW p231 MR20
CUMMING,H.R.DSO.BrigGen 5-3-21 Staff CR Mddx26 Ex DLI
CUMMING,James Leslie T2Lt kldacc 24-3-18 64RFC p15 CR Scot380
CUMMING,Lewis Robertson 2Lt kia 28-9-14 1BlkW p128 MR15
CUMMING,Lionel George T2Lt kia 9-5-17 8Dev p76 MR20
CUMMING,Robert John Alfred 2Lt kia 27-8-17 7 att1/6HLI p240 CR France162,Lt
CUMMING,Robert Scott.MC.Capt 14-3-21 RAMC CR Iraq6
CUMMINGS,Eric.MID Capt ded 26-4-16 IA 93Inf p275 CR Iraq5
CUMMINGS,Ralph Michael 2Lt kld 15-1-18 RFC p15 CR USA77,16-1-18
CUMMINGS,Thomas Horsfield 2Lt ded 15-7-18 5DLI p239 CR Durham39
CUMMINGS,William Capt kia 18-5-17 RAMC p253 CR France614
CUMMINGS,William Allen Wesley 2Lt kia 13-4-18 MGC p182 CR France193,Lt
CUMMINS,Archibald Wilfred.MID SubAssSurgCl3 17-7-15 IMS CR France354
CUMMINS,Fenton King.MC.LtACapt kia 21-3-18 6ConnRgrs p172 CR France365,Lt
CUMMINS,Harry Jackson.MID Lt kia 21-8-15 IA 1/5GurkhaRif p275 MR4
CUMMINS,Herbert Charles Bruce TCapt dow 7-5-16 9SfthH p164 CR France264
CUMMINS,Herbert Waller Lt kia 24/25-5-15 4Yorks p220 MR29,24-5-15
CUMMINS,Ian Ashley Marsham Maj ded 20-7-18 RGA p39 MR21 &CR Ireland14
CUMMINS,Leslie T2Lt kia 1-7-16 10Lincs p75 MR21
CUMMINS,Thomas Coote 2Lt kia 25-3-18 3Y&L p158 CR France385,7Bn
CUMMINS,Thomas Morris 2Lt ded 7-11-18 3Lond p269 CR Mddx40,Lt 8-11-18
CUMNER,Cyril William 2Lt kia 24-4-18 1Lond p269 CR France144
CUMPSTON,Basil Lancelot T2Lt dow 10-5-17 2BordR p116 CR France518
CUNDALL,Cecil.MC.LtACapt kia 30-11-17 2RInniskF p104 MR30
CUNDALL,Hubert Walter 2Lt kia 1-7-16 1Lond p245 MR21
CUNDALL,John Ernest 2Lt kia 3-5-17 5YLI p235 CR France1186
CUNDALL,Stanley T2Lt kia 21-4-18 9YLI p142 CR Belgium102,20-4-18
CUNDLE,Thomas William 2LtTLt kia 27-9-17 GL att2KAR p202 CR EAfrica38 &CR Tanzania1
CUNNINGHAM,Charles Arthur Capt kia 10-8-15 6BordR p116 MR4
CUNNINGHAM,George Edmund Maj ded 6-12-18 IARO attASC p275 CR Asia82,CUNNINGHAM
CUNNINGHAM,James Campbell see CUNNINGHAM,J.C.
CUNINGHAME,Alfred Keith Smith.MID TCapt kia 25-9-16 2GrenGds D'Coy p49 CR France394
CUNINGHAME,Boyd Alexander Maj ded 16-3-17 5A&SH attNRhodRif CR WAfrica8
CUNINGHAME,William John see CUNNINGHAME,W.J.
CUNLIFFE,Clement Wallwork 2Lt kia 24-9-17 6Manch p236 CR Belgium173
CUNLIFFE,Edward Gilbert TLt kia 25-3-18 37MGC p182 CR Belgium19
CUNLIFFE,Ernest Nicholson Maj ded 31-3-19 RAMC p255 CR C'land&W'land108
CUNLIFFE,Foster Hugh Egerton.Bart.TMaj kia 10-7-16 13RB p178 CR France150,dow
CUNLIFFE,G.Capt 23-2-20 HertYeo CR Kent281
CUNLIFFE,James Grimshaw.MC.TCapt dow 1-8-17 18Manch p154 CR Belgium11
CUNLIFFE,John Brooke Maj ded 20-4-17 NhamptYeo p204 CR Shrop63
CUNLIFFE,John Leonard TCapt kia 4-9-16 21Manch p154 MR21
CUNLIFFE,Robert Ellis T2Lt kia 9-5-15 SL att2RBerks p201&254 MR22 &MR32
CUNLIFFE,Thomas Hathorn LtCol ded 25-5-15 9Manch p237 CR Lancs472,Hethorn
CUNLIFFE,Thomas Henry Withers Capt kia 4-6-15 1LancF p92 CR Gallipoli1
CUNNACK,George James.MC.TLtACapt dow 17-10-18 RE 180TC p44 CR France846
CUNNELL,Donald Charles Capt kia 12-7-17 5Hamps &RFC p228 CR France285
CUNNINGHAM,Alexander Campbell T2Lt kia 21-8-15 RMunstF p175 MR4
CUNNINGHAM,Alexander Pinman.MM.T2Lt dow 19-9-18 2KRRC p149 CR France327
CUNNINGHAM,Archibald John Lt kia 24-3-18 A110RFA p27 MR20
CUNNINGHAM,Arthur Joseph.DCM.2Lt kia 15-9-16 18Lond p250 CR France432
CUNNINGHAM,Bernard Camelis Josh TCapt kia 21-3-18 7RDubF p176 CR France212
CUNNINGHAM Charles Albert Glentworth Capt kia 6-6-15 12ScotRif att1KOSB p103 MR4
CUNNINGHAM,Charles Clement Francis Capt dow 19-8-16 2A&SH p173 CR France176
CUNNINGHAM,Charles Stewart 2Lt kia 1-2-17 IARO att36Sikhs p275 CR Iraq5
CUNNINGHAM,David T2Lt ded 27-10-17 2Yorks p90&263 CR France285
CUNNINGHAM,Douglas Murray 2Lt dow 11-6-18 3 att4/5BlkW p128 CR France113
CUNNINGHAM,Edward 2Lt kia 28-1-18 11RFC p15 MR20
CUNNINGHAM,Edward Hamilton T2Lt kia 11-8-18 Hamps att1Dors p120 CR France360

CUNNINGHAM,Edward Malcolm.MC.LtTCapt kia 4-8-17 2 att9WRid p115&258 CR France97,5-8-17
CUNNINGHAM,George Edmund see CUNINGHAM,G.E.
CUNNINGHAM,Harold John.MC.TCapt dow 4-10-17 6Beds p85 CR Belgium132
CUNNINGHAM,Hugh Rose 2Lt kia 26-4-18 12RScots p53 MR30
CUNNINGHAM,James T2Lt kia 1-7-16 9 att7Beds p85 MR21
CUNNINGHAM,James Campbell 2Lt kia 14-3-16 15RFC p2 CR France518,CUNINGHAM
CUNNINGHAM,James Michael TLtACapt dow 28-3-18 7Suff p78 CR France169
CUNNINGHAM,James Nelson TLt dow 19-10-17 GL &56RFC p6 CR France297
CUNNINGHAM,Joseph Francis Crowley T2Lt kld 28-11-17 GL &RFC p6 CR Mddx68
CUNNINGHAM,Kenneth Edward Capt dow PoW 3-5-17 2WRid p115 MR20
CUNNINGHAM,Lyman Holden 2Lt kld 14-1-18 RFC p15 CR Wilts121
CUNNINGHAM,Peter Nesbit 2Lt kia 2-12-17 HLI att17Bn p162 MR30
CUNNINGHAM,Robert William Capt kia 1-7-16 9Lond p247 MR21
CUNNINGHAM,Samuel Andrew Capt kia 12-7-15 5RScotF p222 MR4
CUNNINGHAM,Stuart Gordon 2Lt kia 22-10-17 12/35RFA p27 CR Belgium19
CUNNINGHAM,William 2Lt kia 1-10-18 4 att1RIrF p171 MR30
CUNNINGHAM,William John Lt&QM ded 18-5-15 ShropYeo p205
CUNNINGHAM REID,Duncan Flower 2Lt kia 19-12-15 IARO 17Lancers attRFC p275 CR Belgium379
CUNNINGHAME,William John Maj ded 19-3-19 NottsYeo (SNottsHuss) p205 CR Germany1,CUNINGHAME
CUNNINGTON,Cecil Henry Lt ded 24-10-17 215MGC Inf p266 CR Lond12,26-10-17
CUNNINGTON,Edward Charles TCapt kia 23-3-18 RAMC att95FA p195 CR France924
CUNNINGTON,Joseph Herbert 2Lt ded 19-10-18 Ex RE p262 CR Devon107
CUNNISON,Alan Watson 2Lt kia 29-10-16 3 att1ScotRif p103 MR21 &CR France34
CUPPLES,William Capt kia 25-9-15 3RInniskF p104 MR29
CURE,Basil Alfred Capel Capt dow 1-10-16 2Glouc p106 CR Greece4,CAPEL CURE
CURETON,Edward Robert Maj ded 18-5-16 KOSB attHamps p120 CR Hamps202
CURGENVEN,William Charles Capt kia 21-10-14 SWBord p99 CR Belgium115
CURLE,William Sydney Noel.MC.Maj dow PoW 23-3-18 B107RFA p27 CR France441
CURLETT,Patrick Alexander Lt kia 3-7-15 3Lpool p71 CR France163
CURLEY,Alfred T2Lt kld 5-3-18 11RFC p15 CR Lancs18
CURLEY,Francis Lt kia 25-9-15 AngleseyRE p44 MR19
CURLING,Edward Charles James Lt&QM ded 2-5-17 RAMC att133FA p195 CR France102
CURLING,Edward Thomas Lt kld 15-2-18 22Lond att93RFC p18&251 CR Hamps192
CURLING,Frank Trevor ACapt kia 31-8-18 18Lond p250 CR France218
CURNOCK,George Ashwin Lt kia 14-8-17 6 att10RB p178 MR29
CURPHEY,William George Sellar.MC.TCapt ded 15-5-17 GL &32RFC p6 CR France924
CURR,Thomas 2Lt kia 4-10-16 4 att18HLI p162 CR France1182
CURRALL,Norman Frank 2Lt kia 18-10-16 1ELancs p110 MR21
CURRAN,Henry 2Lt kia 25-4-17 10RWelshF p97 CR France531
CURRAN,Nevil William.MC.MID Lt kia 4-10-16 2 att3RIrReg p89 MR32
CURRER,Thomas Russell 2Lt kia 26-9-17 1RScotF p94 MR30
CURREY,Donald Saunders Capt kia 24-4-17 1Mon att7RBerks p244 MR37
CURREY,George Capt ded 15-11-19 RAVC p268 CR C'land&W'land17
CURREY,George Grafton TCapt kia 22-8-15 6Yorks p90 MR4
CURREY,Vere Fortrey Maj kia 13-10-15 7Suff p78 MR19
CURRIE,Adam TCapt kia 28-3-18 17RScots p54 MR27
CURRIE,Clarence Algernon TLt dow 19-12-15 RE p44 CR France285
CURRIE,Claud George Ironside Maj ded 3-12-16 Dors p264 CR Lond8
CURRIE,Frederic Rivers Lt kia 8-8-15 3 att1KSLI p144 MR29 &CR Belgium453,Frederick
CURRIE,Gilbert Heron.DCM.2Lt kia 12-10-16 3 att10A&SH p173 CR France924
CURRIE,Harold Maxwell T2Lt kia 1-8-17 1/2 att10ScotRif p103
CURRIE,Horatio Charles Lt ded 24-4-18 KAR &SL p268 CR EAfrica92
CURRIE,James Alexander Vance Lt kia 13-3-17 10Lond p248 CR France175
CURRIE,James Hamilton Lt kia 25-8-18 3Hamps p120 CR France28,2Bn
CURRIE,John Eugene Havelock T2Lt kia 11-9-15 8 att1RScotF p94 MR22
CURRIE,R.A.M.CMG.DSO.MIDx4 BrigGen 30-3-20 SomLI &GenStaff CR Europe150A
CURRIE,William George.MC.2Lt kia 22-3-18 1Lincs p75 CR France364,28-3-18
CURRIE,William Thomson Capt dow 31-7-18 3 att1/5GordH p166 CR France1225

CURROR,William Edwin Forrest 2Lt kia 1-7-16 14Lond p249 CR France798
CURRY,Ralph.MID Capt dow 9-4-18 8DLI p239 CR France193
CURRY,Vernon Edward T2Lt kia 23-4-17 1Beds p85 MR20
CURRY,William Gordon T2Lt kia 7-6-17 12 att13Ches p95 CR Belgium89
CURRY,William Horace.DSO.2LtACapt kia 25-10-17 3 att1SStaffs p122 MR30
CURRY,William Leonard TCapt dow 9-11-16 RGA 87SB p39 CR France74
CURSHAM,Francis George Maj ded 31-8-18 8N&D p269
CURSHAM,Geoffrey Lt kia 12-10-17 1RLancs p58 MR30
CURTEIS,Lancelot 2Lt kia 4-7-16 8BordR p116 MR21,3-7-16
CURTEIS,R.Nurse 14-11-18 VAD CR Hamps1
CURTICE,Frederick Russell Lt dow 17-11-16 C79RFA p27 CR France74
CURTIES,Dudley Thomas Lees Lt ded 24-10-18 2HAC p206 CR Italy12,25-10-18
CURTIES,Lionel Charles Alfred TCapt kia 25-10-15 GL attMGC p190 MR29
CURTIS,Arthur.MC.Capt kia 27-8-18 3Lond p245 MR16
CURTIS,Eric Calvin 2Lt kia 28-7-18 5SfthH p241 CR France865
CURTIS,Ernest John 2Lt dow 22-1-18 5 att7RWKent p235 CR Belgium106,kia
CURTIS,Evelyn St.George 2Lt kia 3-5-17 7 att12Mddx p235 MR20
CURTIS,Frank Warren 2Lt kia 14-8-17 9RFC p6 CR Belgium18
CURTIS,Frank William TLt kia 4-11-17 6Leic A'Coy attKSLI p87 MR30
CURTIS,Harry Reginald TMaj kia 18-9-18 11RWFus p97 CR Greece5
CURTIS,Henry Edward 2Lt drd 21-2-17 RE 117ConstnCoyRlwy p44 MR35
CURTIS,Henry Neville T2Lt kia 25-7-17 GL &45RFC p6 CR France1049
CURTIS,Henry Thomas 2Lt dow 12-2-17 24Lond p252 CR France41
CURTIS,Hubert James Lt kia 4-11-18 SL att87RAF p201 MR20
CURTIS,Horace Lt kia 7-8-15 9WYorks p81 MR4
CURTIS,Jocelyn Stewart 2Lt kia 21-3-18 3RB p178 MR27
CURTIS,John Handel 2Lt kia 24-11-17 4 att18WelshR p230 MR17
CURTIS,Keith Saxby T2Lt kia 26-10-17 14RWar Res p64 MR30
CURTIS,Ralph Luxmore T2Lt ded PoW 21-9-17 GL &48RFC p6 CR Belgium140
CURTIS,Robert Henry T2Lt kia 20-9-17 10RWSurr p55 MR30
CURTIS,Thomas Britt T2Lt dow 25-10-17 11Ches p95 CR France80,kia
CURTIS,William 2Lt kia 14-3-15 1Manch p154 CR France706,Lt 12-3-15
CURTIS,William Charles T2Lt kia 3-10-18 5TankCps p188 MR16
CURTIS,William Edward 2Lt kia 18-8-16 5RWar p214 MR21
CURTIS,William Michael.Bart.Capt ded 19-1-16 RDC p253 CR Shrop74
CURTIS-BEALS,Harold T2Lt kld 15-3-18 GL &38RFC p15 CR Egypt9,Harry
CURTIS-RALEIGH,H.T.R.Capt 27-9-14 2Berks MR65
CURTLER,Frederick Gwatkin Oldham Lt kia 21-10-14 5 att2Worc p108 MR29
CURWEN,Cecil Neil TLt kia 15-9-16 18KRRC p149 MR21,Niel
CURWEN,Gilbert Christopher 2Lt kia 3-6-18 16Lond p250 CR France887
CURWEN,Henry Stanley T2Lt kia 13-10-15 7Norf p73 MR19
CURWEN,Wilfred John Hutton Capt kia 9-5-15 6 att3RFus p67 MR29
CURWEN,William Lynedoch.MC&Bar.TLt dow 30-10-17 RGA att27MtBty SR p39 CR EAfrica10 &CR Tanzania1
CURZON,Fitzroy Edmund Penn LtCol kia 9-9-16 6RIrReg p89 CR France513
CUSACK,Reginald Ernest 2Lt ded 15-4-15 4RDubF p176 CR Kent71,Lt
CUSACK,Thomas William Stanley 2Lt ded 25-6-19 18Lond p269 CR Staffs114
CUSHEN,Aylett Cameron 2Lt kia 30-6-16 11RSuss p118 MR19
CUSHING,Geoffry Edgar 2Lt kld 29-12-17 RFC p6 CR Suff83,Lt
CUSHING,Robertson Macaulay 2Lt dow 30-4-18 RGA 190SB p39 CR Belgium3
CUSHNY,Donald Lt kia 14-4-15 Dors p124 CR Iraq6
CUSSELL,Stanley James T2Lt kia 29-5-18 RASC p192 MR18
CUST,Bertram Mitford T2Lt kia 9-11-15 10Yorks p90 CR France1140
CUTBILL,Bernard TCapt ded PoW 24-3-18 8Norf p73 CR France481
CUTBUSH,Douglas.MC.2LtACapt kia 10-4-17 5 att4Mddx p146 CR France545
CUTCLIFFE,John TLt kia 26-8-16 1EYorks att9WRid p84 CR France385,2Bn
CUTHBERT,Charles Louttit T2Lt dow 18-8-16 9ESurr p112 CR France141
CUTHBERT,David TCapt kia 7-10-16 29 att8RFus p67 MR21
CUTHBERT,David Wilson Harper T2Lt dow 9-4-17 9BlkW p128 CR France113
CUTHBERT,Gordon Capt kia 27-4-15 8Mddx p235 MR29
CUTHBERT,James Harold.DSO.Capt dow 27-9-15 1ScotsGds p52 MR19
CUTHBERT,John George Gunn TLt dow 19-10-16 28MGC p182 CR France177
CUTHBERT,J.Stewart Ross Lt dedacc 28-12-17 RFC CR USA228
CUTHBERT,Leonard Arthur.MC.Capt kia 20-12-19 IA 2/19Punjabis p275 MR43
CUTHBERT,Olaf Ranson TCapt kia 1-7-16 8Y&L p158 CR France246
CUTHBERT,Reginald Vaux T2Lt dow 28-4-17 8SfthH p164 CR France113
CUTHBERTSON,Edward Hadley Lt ded 24-7-17 RWar p64 CR Iraq5,Hedley
CUTHBERTSON,Eric Ian 2Lt kia 23-10-17 RGA 327SB p39 CR Belgium85
CUTHBERTSON,George Chapman.MC.Capt dow 8-4-18 GL &54RAF 22Wing CR France145

CUTHBERTSON,Hugh 2Lt kia 14-4-18 B275RFA p27 CR France109
CUTHBERTSON,Norman William Maj ded 12-2-15 1BlkW CR Mddx16
CUTHELL,Algernon Hubert.MID TMaj kia 22-8-15 9WYorks p81 MR4
CUTLER,Edward Trevor 2Lt kia 9-8-17 7 att2Ess p232 MR20
CUTLER,Frank 2Lt kia 18-9-16 14DLI p160 CR France744
CUTLER,Harold Arthur Lt kia 23-3-18 39MGC p182 MR27
CUTLER,Herbert Cecil Lt kia 10-5-17 2/1WorcYeo attRFC p18&p206 CR France1495
CUTLER,Leslie Durban 2Lt ded 8-10-18 13Lond p269 CR Kent99,2-10-18
CUTLER,Stuart le Geyt LtTCapt kia 9-8-17 RASC &21RFC p6&p192,Staurt Le Guyt CR Belgium16
CUTLER,William Reynolds T2Lt kia 18-11-17 GL &70RFC p6 CR France40
CUTTLE,Geoffrey 2Lt kia 14-3-15 2Yorks p90 MR22
CUTTLE,George Robin 2Lt ded 9-5-18 RFA &RAF p27 MR20
CUTTLE,George William 2Lt kia 4-6-17 8EYorks p84 CR France154,5-6-17
CUTTING,Edward James 2Lt kia 9-10-18 4RBerks att7Nhampt p234 CR France270
CUTTS,Leonard Edwin TLt ded 11-10-18 RE 256TC p44 CR France1063
CUTTS,Thomas Bernard TCapt kia 20-7-16 15N&D p133 CR France294
CUXSON,Basil Pryce 2Lt kia 14-7-15 2RScots p54 CR Belgium167
CUZEN,Richard 2Lt kia 5-4-18 6Nhampt p137 CR France587

D

Da COSTA,Oscar Michael John LtCol ded 11-10-18 IA 35ScindeHorse p275 MR65
DACRE,Brian TCapt kia 12-10-18 9WRid p115 CR France230
DACRE,John Kenneth.MC.Lt dow 30-9-16 71RFA p27 CR France197
DACRES,Leonard Seymour Lambert Capt ded 20-4-19 IARO attPoliticalDept p275 CR Iraq8,att21Cav
DADD,Edmund Halton.MC.TCapt kia 3-9-16 1RWFus p97p258 MR21,Hilton
DADD,Ivor Llewellyn T2Lt ded 17-7-17 RE IWT p44 CR Iraq6,DADDS
DADD,Reginald John T2Lt kia 5-4-18 7RFus p67 MR20
DADSWELL,Clifford Irwin 2Lt kia 7-7-16 3 att7RSuss p118 CR France1890
DAFFEN,Harold Charles Lt kld 26-4-16 2/8N&D p233 CR Ireland14,kia
DAFFURN,Oswald.MC.2Lt kia 1-4-18 1BordR p116 MR32
DAFT,Harry 2Lt kia 13-4-17 17Lond p250 CR France184
DAGGE,Albert Lima 2Lt kia 1-7-16 B168RFA p27 CR France215
DAGGETT,Cedric Hunton.MC.Capt kia 11-2-17 23NumbF p60 MR32
DAGLISH,John William 2Lt 10-12-19 DLI CR Durham23
DAIN,Sidney Edward T2Lt ded 7-12-18 RE PostalSect p44 CR France52
DAINES,Allan Edward 2Lt kia 30-12-17 7RFus p67 MR21
DAINES,Roland Lewis T2Lt kia 3-8-17 32RFus p67 MR29
DAINES,Sidney T2Lt kia 16-5-18 1Hamps p120 MR19
DAINTITH,James T2Lt kia 13-8-17 RE 150FC p44 CR Belgium101
DAINTON,Howard Hillier T2Lt dow 5-4-18 14Glouc att7RWKent p106 CR France37,1Bn
DAKERS,John 2Lt kia 12-5-17 14Lond p249 MR20
DAKIN,Albert Edward T2Lt dow 16-9-18 Wilts att2Bn p152 CR France88
D'ALBERTANSON,Ronald.MC.2Lt dow 8-8-16 3ESurr att6Dors p112 CR France176
DALBIAC,Charles James Shelley 2Lt kia 16-6-15 1NumbF p60 MR29
DALBY,Herbert Charles T2Lt kia 1-7-16 11Y&L p158 MR21
DALBY,Herbert Ernest Maj ded 14-10-17 RAMC p195 CR Iraq6
DALE,Alfred Parks T2Lt kld 15-3-18 57RFC p15 CR Egypt8
DALE,Alwyn Percy.OBE.Maj kia 1-3-17 5WYorks p218 CR France514,Alwyne
DALE,Andrew Murray Capt ded 1-5-19 Ex YLI p265
DALE,Arthur 2Lt dow 12-3-15 1NStaffs p157 CR France681
DALE,Arthur 2Lt kia 25-9-16 Dev p76 MR21
DALE,Arthur William 2Lt kia 1-7-16 7NumbF p214 CR Belgium60
DALE,Charles Lt ded 16-10-18 337RFA p207 CR Iraq8
DALE,Frank Cottrell 2Lt dow 26-5-18 4Ches p222 CR Ches84
DALE,Harry T2Lt kia 24-4-18 TankCps p188 CR France424
DALE,James Ritchie TLt ded 14-1-19 RE 96FC p262 CR Surrey1
DALE,John Ernest 2Lt dow 14-9-17 Ess att9Bn p131 CR France113
DALE,Rayner William Maj ded 25-8-16 RFA p27 CR Scot253,RGA
DALE,Robert Clunie 2Lt kia 18-8-16 B109RFA p27 CR France370
DALE,Robert Jacomb Norris Lt kia 31-1-18 9Manch BallSect &RFC p237 CR Italy7
DALE,Robert Percy.MC.LtTCapt kia 25-10-18 4 att9ScotRif p103 CR Belgium140
DALEY,Alexis T2Lt dow 14-4-17 1/2NStaffs att2Y&L p157 CR France8
DALEY,Richard T2Lt kia 25-10-18 LancF att2/5Bn p92 CR Belgium406,dow
DALGLEISH,George Walter.MID LtCol ded 17-2-19 RFA 2DAC p27 CR Germany1

DALGLEISH,William.MC.Lt kia 12-11-17 4RScots p211 MR34,DALGLIESH
DALGLISH,Charles Antoine de Guerry Capt dow 9-9-14 BlkW p128 CR France1451,8-9-14
DALGLISH,James Wilson 2Lt kia 14-2-16 3 att4Yorks p90 CR Belgium5
DALGOUTTE,George Cork T2Lt kia 3-5-17 8RB p178 MR20
DALL,John T2LtTCapt ded 12-10-18 1HLI p162 MR66
DALLAS,A.S.MC.Lt 30-1-21 RA MR66
DALLAS,George Barnes Lt kia 1-9-19 SomLI att8MGC Inf p254 MR70 &CR Europe179
DALLAS,John Sweetland Capt dow 12-9-15 IA 1/6GurkhaRif p275 CR Egypt3
DALLAS,Raymond Vivian Leslie.MC.TCapt kia 13-4-18 9NumbF p60 MR19
DALLAS,William Frederick Lt kia 9-4-16 WelchR att6ELancs p126 MR38
DALLAS,William Loraine Seymour Chap4Cl kia 20-9-17 RAChDept att5Lpool p199 MR30
DALLAS,William Reid 2Lt kld 24-12-18 RASC MT att215RAF CR France134
DALLEY,John Pomeroy Lt mbk 15-10-17 IARO att20RFC p275 MR20,14-10-17
DALLOW,William Ewart 2Lt kia 9-4-17 7KSLI p144 CR France581,Ewart W.
DALMAHOY,John Francis Cecil Capt kia 26-4-15 IA 40Pathans p275 CR Belgium96
DALRYMPLE,Hew T2Lt kia 1-7-16 8SomLI p79 MR21
DALRYMPLE,Ian Douglas Capt kia 5-5-15 2HLI att2KOSB p162 MR29
DALRYMPLE-CLARK,Douglas Scott.MC.Capt 15-9-16 18KRRC attTMB CR France1890
DALRYMPLE-WILLES,Patrick Lt ded 29-9-18 RLancs &RAF p58
DALTON,Charles LtCol dow 18-9-14 RAMC p195 CR France1139
DALTON,George Henry 2Lt dow 14-8-16 3RIrReg att4 O&BLI p89 CR France354
DALTON,Horace Montague T2Lt kia 3-5-17 8EYorks p84 MR20
DALTON,J.G.2D/147Sister 20-3-16 QAIMNS CR Scot26
D'ALTON,James George 2Lt kia 27-10-17 162RFA p27 MR30
DALTON,Richard Gregory T2Lt kia 31-8-17 18WYorks p81 CR France268
D'ALTON,Thomas Joseph 2Lt dow 9-6-17 4RIrReg att7InnisKF p89 CR France40,DALTON
DALY,Alexis 2Lt dow 14-4-17 1/2NStaffs attY&L CR France8 see DALEY,A.
DALY,Arthur Charles de Burgh 2Lt kia 9-9-16 5RDubF p176 CR France402
DALY,Cyril Francis St.Felix T2Lt kia 14-10-17 7RWSurr p55 MR20 6Bn
DALY,Darby T2Lt kia 4-10-18 ConnRgrs p172 CR France1495,2MunstF
DALY,Donald Lynott Lt ded 12-4-15 SL &3NigR CR WAfrica46
DALY,Thomas.CMG.Col ded 15-4-17 RAMC p195 MR35,drd
DALY,Valentine Maurice 2Lt dow 20-4-18 30MGC p182 CR France64
DALY,William Cecil Thomas 2Lt kia 18-8-16 3RB p178 CR France400
DALZELL,Thomas Frost 2Lt kia 21-3-18 18MGC p182 MR27
DALZELL-WALTON,Hubert Pulteney.MID TLtCol kia 9-9-16 8RInniskF p104 CR France329
DALZIEL,Charles Sutherland 2Lt kia 8-1-17 7DLI p239 CR France453
DALZIEL,John Morrison T2Lt kia 14-11-18 RScots att2/10Bn p54 MR70 &CR Europe179
DAMAN,Geoffrey Windeath 2Lt kia 24-5-15 4SfthH p241 CR France924,Windeatt Lt
DAME,John William Malvern 2Lt kia 27-11-17 2IrGds p52 MR17
DAMER,Wilfred Percy T2Lt kia 18-11-16 7RWSurr p55 CR France535
DAMES,William Stanley 2Lt ded 17-7-19 RE p262 CR Lincs179
DAMIAND,Walter Henry Alexander 2Lt dow 2-7-16 2RDubF p176 CR France167,DAMIANO
DAMPIER,Glenny William 2Lt kia 11-12-16 10RFC p2 CR France765
DANAHER,Mary SNurse ded 12-10-18 QAIMNS p200 CR Palestine8
DANBRIDGE,William Leslie Lt dow 5-10-18 RAMC att103FA p195 DANDRIDGE
DANBY,Charles David.MC.Capt kia 18-7-18 RE &RAF p210 CR Durham182,kld
DANBY,Francis Geoffrey Lt kia 27-12-17 5Yorks p220 CR Belgium125,28-12-17
DANCE,Charles Edward LtCol ded 23-7-18 RE p44 CR Lond4
DANCER,Alfred Christopher.MC.TLtACapt kia 4-10-17 5Dors p124 MR30
DANCKWERTS,Richard William Lt kia 21-12-14 1Glouc p106 CR France260,2Lt 22-12-14
DANCY,George.MC.Lt&QM ded 2-6-19 1 O&BLI p130 MR70 &CR Europe179
DANDRIDGE,George Sidney T2Lt kia 1-7-16 7RWSurr p55 CR France397
DANE,Victor Lewis Yate Capt kia 22-11-15 IA 22Punjabis p275 MR38
DANE,Wilfred Spencer T2Lt kia 18-11-16 12 att10Worc p108 MR21
DANES,Thomas T2Lt ded 13-11-18 RASC p192 CR Glouc9
DANGAR,Clive Colingwood.MC.MID TMaj ded 4-7-18 GL HQ AIF p190 CR Australia112,Collingwood
DANGERFIELD,William Cecil Hay.MID TLt&Adjt kld 26-12-16 11ScotRif p103 CR Greece6
DANIEL,Archibald Morris T2Lt kia 4-10-17 1RWKent p140 CR Belgium125

DANIEL,Ernest Lt kia 21-10-18 4 att1RIrRif p169 CR Belgium140
DANIEL,Fleetwood Earnscliffe T2Lt kld 20-12-17 GL&RFC p6 CR Wilts115
DANIEL,Ralph Picton TCapt kia 31-7-17 17RWelshF p97 CR Belgium106
DANIEL,Thomas George TLt kia 23-11-17 22 att19RWelshF p97 MR17
DANIELL,Archibald Steuart Lindsey.MID 2Lt kia 19-12-14 1RB p178 CR Belgium71
DANIELL,Edward Henry Edwin.DSO.TMajLtCol kia 20-10-14 RIrReg p89 MR22
DANIELL,Francis Edward Lloyd.DSO.TLtCol dow 4-3-16 SfthH GenStaff 21Div p164 CR France922,kia
DANIELL,George Francis Blackburne 2Lt kia 24-4-17 6 att2RFus p67 MR20
DANIELL,Hubert John Capt ded PoW 19-8-16 IA 20Punjabis p275 CR Iraq8
DANIELL,Neville Reay.DSO.CaptTLtCol kia 4-10-17 DCLI Cmdg9YLI p114 MR30
DANIELL,William Raymond Maj dow 1-12-17 IA 1/123Rif p275 CR Egypt2
DANIELS,Cecil William T2Lt ded 4-11-18 1N&D p133&257
DANIELS,Edwin Ambrose TLtACapt kia 21-10-16 8SLancs p125 MR21
DANIELS,Fred.MC.2Lt kia 3-12-17 2/5RWar p214 MR17
DANIELS,George 2Lt kia 20-11-17 1/8Lpool p215 MR21
DANIELS,James T2Lt kia 28-9-18 1Ches p95 CR France415
DANIELS,James Alfred TLtACapt dow 21-9-17 Hamps att15Bn p120 CR Belgium11
DANIELS,Russell John Lt ded 29-8-18 2ScotsGds p52 CR Lond10
DANIELS,Thomas Harold Rayner 2Lt kia 9-4-16 RLancs p58 MR38
DANN,Ernest T2Lt dow 22-11-15 6Beds p85 CR France1016
DANN,Henry Norman Groves T2Lt kia 15-9-17 GL &55RFC p6 CR France134
DANN,Tom Vincent 2Lt kia 13-10-15 6SStaffs p229 MR19
DANN,Wilfred 2Lt dow 30-10-17 3 att12Glouc p106 CR Belgium11
DANN,Wilfred Stephen 2Lt kld 16-5-18 3EKent att70RAF p57 CR France63,dow
DANNAHY,William T2Lt kia 25-10-16 92RFA p27 CR France513
DANNE,Arthur William Brian Lt kia 30-3-18 3 att13Glouc p106 MR27
DANSEY,Felix Ramon Arthur 2Lt kia 25-7-18 7Lond p247 CR France62
DANSON,Francis Rudolf Lt 10-8-15 4Ches MR4
DANVERS,Charles 2Lt kia 9-4-17 15RWar p64 MR20
DANVERS,Robert William Ford 2Lt kia 26-8-17 3Suff p78 CR France1462
DANZIG,Morris William TLt drd 15-4-17 RAMC p195 MR35
DANZIGER,Charles William Jack 2Lt dow 15-5-17 9Manch p237 CR France518
DARBISHIRE,Arthur Dunkinfield 2Lt ded 26-12-15 RGA p39
DARBY,Ernest 2Lt ded 4-6-15 10SWBord p99 CR Wales571,Lt 3-6-15
DARBY,Frederick.MID 2Lt kia 29-11-14 1Worc p108 MR22
DARBY,John Sprake Capt kia 28-3-18 4RBerks p234 CR France1170
DARBY,Joseph Capt 27-6-16 IndMilWksServ CR War6
DARBY,Maurice Alfred Alexander.MID Lt kia 11-3-15 1GrenGds p49 CR Shrop60
DARBY,Norman Leslie 2Lt kia 16-8-17 5Manch p236 CR Belgium96,Lt
DARBY,William Edward Cleve Augustus Lt kia 11/13-10-15 1Mon p244 MR19,Clere
DARBY-GRIFFITH,Octavius Sidney.MC.TCaptAMaj kia 27-5-18 11 att9LNLancs p135 MR18
DARBYSHIRE,Graham Hirtzell Capt kia 7-10-17 RFA p207 CR Belgium10,8-10-17
DARBYSHIRE,Percy Capt ded 30-5-18 Res p269 CR Lancs256
DARCH,Stanley Percival 2Lt kia 22-4-16 10Glouc p106 CR France149
D'ARCY,Lionel George 2Lt kia 20-12-16 ConnRgrs &RFC p2 MR20
D'ARCY-IRVINE,Charles William Capt kia 6/12-8-15 6Leinst p174 MR4
DARDIER,Leonard Henry T2Lt dow 4-10-15 RHA 30Bty p27 CR France423
DARGIE,Arnold Maj kia 18-9-17 RGA 137HB p209 CR France161
DARKE,Hugh Cubt Maj ded 12-7-16 220RFA p269 MR67,Cuff
DARKER,Ernest Naismith 2Lt dow 10-9-17 RGA 262SB p39 CR Belgium16
DARKER,Neil Campbell 2Lt kia 3-5-17 2RScots p54 MR20
DARKER,Richard Owen 2Lt kia 12-4-18 2RFus p67 MR32
DARLEY,Desmond John 2Lt kia 1-7-16 11Suff p78 MR21
DARLEY,John Evelyn Carmichael.MID LtCol kia 31-3-18 4Huss p21 CR France988
DARLEY,William Hastings La Touche.OBE.Maj ded 11-10-18 IA 12Pnrs attStaff DAAG GHQ 3Ech p275 CR France146
DARLING,Alan Heppell T2Lt kia 10-7-16 8Yorks p90 CR France515
DARLING,Claude Henry Whish T2Lt kia 12-12-15 3 att2RIrRif p169 CR Belgium137
DARLING,Jack.MC.2Lt dow 26-10-18 4RIrF p171 CR Belgium159,John
DARLING,Robert.MC.Lt kia 16-9-18 9Lpool p216 CR France433
DARLING,James William Kingsley Capt kia 11-8-18 5RScots p211 CR France360
DARLING,William Oliver Fortesque Lt kia 16-10-15 3 att1RIrRif p169 CR France276
DARLINGTON,Tom.MC.MM.Lt kia 1-10-18 11RWSurr p55 MR30
DARLINGTON,William Charles 2Lt kia 4-11-17 2/4RWKent p234 CR Palestine1
DARLOW,John William Edward.MC.TLt kia 29-8-18 1RWKent att16RWar p140 CR France1484

DARNELL,Charles Verdon 2Lt kia 25-4-17 ConnRgrs &25RFC p6&rp172 MR20
DARNEY,Clarence Edwin 2Lt kia 2-9-18 7BlkW p231 CR France511
DARNEY,Henry Whiting Lt ded 8-9-19 IARO attMilPolice p275
DARRAGH,James Robinson Lt dow 5-7-17 1/6WRid p227 CR France98
DARRAGH,Matthew Sloan 2Lt kia 20-3-17 6WRid p227 MR19
DARREL,Richard Frederick William T2Lt ded 26-2-19 TankCps p188 CR Essex5
DARRELL,Albert 2Lt kia 25-12-15 1ESurr p112 MR21
DARRICOTTE,Gilbert Haley 2Lt kia 6-9-18 1HuntsCycBatt p253 CR France511
DARRINGTON,Clarence Philip Lt dow 27-11-18 1/5Lond p246 CR France40
DARRINGTON,Harold Edgar Lt dow 20-11-17 9Mddx att27RFC p18&rp236 CR France88 Ex 5Lond
DARSIE,George Lt dow 31-7-18 Fife&ForfarYeo p203 CR France1225
DART,Hugh TCapt dow 2-7-16 13Y&L p158 CR France5,1-7-16
DARTNALL,Albert John T2Lt kia 20-11-17 RLancs att1/4Bn p58 MR21
DARTNELL,Wilbur.VC.TLt kia 3-9-15 25RFus p67 CR EAfrica58,William Thomas
DARTON,Edward John 2Lt ded 30-4-15 RE 80FC p44 CR Essex146
DARTS,William 2Lt kia 8-3-17 RFA 66Bde p27 CR Iraq8
DARVELL,Frederick William.MC.2Lt kia 27-5-18 BordR att8Bn p117 MR18
DARVELL,George William 2Lt kia 8-5-18 6RWar p214 MR19
DARWALL,Gordon Cecil Capt ded 31-3-17 3SomLI attACycCps p79&263 CR Lond8
DARWELL,Claude Randall T2Lt kia 10-8-15 6BordR p117 CR Gallipoli5
DARWELL,Thomas Walter 2Lt kia 18-9-18 RWelshF att14Bn p97 CR France415
DARWIN,Erasmus 2Lt kia 25-4-15 4Yorks p220 MR29
DARWIN,John Henry Bradshaw Lt dow 5-12-17 8Manch p237 CR France660
DASHWOOD,Claude Burrand Lewes TMaj dow 26-4-16 9NumbF p60 CR France285
DASHWOOD,Ernest George Capt kia 12-5-15 1/4 O&BLI p231 CR Belgium71
DASHWOOD,Lionel Albert T2Lt kia 16-5-15 O&BLI p130 MR22
DASHWOOD,Robin Henry Lyndsay LtACapt kia 27-5-18 2WYorks p81 MR18,Robert Lindsay
DASHWOOD,Ronald Phillimore T2Lt kia 7-10-16 15 att12RB p178 CR France307
DASHWOOD,Wilfred James Lt dow 2-8-17 1GrenGds p49 CR Belgium16
DAUBENEY,George Henry James Lt kia 26-9-15 6 att2Worc p108 CR France423
DAUBENEY,Giles Robert 2Lt kia 23-4-15 3 att1RWKent p140 MR29
DAUBENY,Charles John Odinel LtACapt dow 16-6-17 3 att1SomLI p79 CR France95
DAUBER,John Henry LtCol drd 13-8-15 RAMC p253 MR4
DAUKES,Archibald Henry MajTLtCol kia 7/11-8-15 7SStaffs p122 MR4
DAUN,Edward Charles Lt kia 14-9-14 RSuss p118 MR15
DAUNT,Barry 2Lt kia 22-9-18 RSuss att7Bn p118 CR France369
DAUNT,Conrad O'Neill 2Lt kld 29-9-18 8SLancs &RAF p125 CR France329,Lt
DAUNT,Giles Wellacott 2Lt kia 9-4-16 10 att6SLancs p125 MR38,Vellacott
D'AUVERGNE,Francis Arthur Payne Lt kia 12-4-18 1RGLI p200 CR France297
DAVALL,Cecil George T2Lt kia 23-8-18 2Suff p78 CR France927
DAVENPORT,Allen Arthur Orme.MC.Lt dow 24-3-18 1/2 att4ELancs p110&258 CR France650
DAVENPORT,Arthur Lt kia 23-8-18 6RB p178&266,11MGC CR France927
DAVENPORT,Barnabas Tom Wilcox 2Lt kia 15-12-17 RWar att1/4Norf p64 CR Palestine9
DAVENPORT,Cyril Francis T2Lt dow 2-8-16 14Hamps A'Coy p120 CR France80
DAVENPORT,Edmund Sharrington T2Lt ded PoW 3-1-18 RFC p15 MR20
DAVENPORT,Francis Edward Alexander 2Lt kia 21-3-18 1KSLI p144 MR20
DAVENPORT,Frank Maturin Capt kia 22-11-15 O&BLI p130 MR38
DAVENPORT,Fred.DSO.MC.Maj kia 25-9-17 A296RFA p206 CR Belgium84
DAVENPORT,Harold 2Lt kia 21-3-18 RGA 122SB p39 MR27
DAVENPORT,Hughes Nares.MC.Maj kia 26-3-18 2/4 O&BLI p231 CR France1203,24-3-18
DAVENPORT,Leonard Merriott 2Lt dow 6-9-16 3 att7RIrFus p171 CR France66
DAVENPORT,Robert 2Lt kia 3-5-17 2LancF p92 MR20
DAVENPORT,Robert 2Lt dow 20-10-18 1/5ELancs p226 CR France270
DAVENPORT,Thomas Lowe 2Lt kia 27-4-17 4RFA A'Coy p208 CR France581
DAVENPORT,Vyvyan Hope Lancelot 2Lt kia 14-7-16 8Leic p87 MR21
DAVEY,Archibald Henry Pingston TMaj kia 14-10-17 1RGLI p200 CR Belgium83
DAVEY,Albert Victor Patrick 2Lt kld 2-6-18 RFA &2RAF p27 CR France1564,Lt
DAVEY,Charles Leonard TLt kia 17-10-18 18MGC Inf p182 CR France660
DAVEY,Charles Richard.MC.MM.T2LtACapt dow 30-10-18 7Lincs B'Coy p75 CR France40
DAVEY,Ernest Charles 2Lt ded 1-11-18 RGA 210SB 98Bde p39 CR France146
DAVEY,Herbert 2Lt kia 18-4-17 3 att6ELancs p110 MR38
DAVEY,Hubert Burgoyne Lt 5-12-18 SWBord CR Hereford208

DAVEY,John Burneford Lt ded 2-3-19 EX RFA p261 CR Somerset201
DAVEY,John Stanley Lt kia 17-11-14 NSomYeo p205 CR Belgium57
DAVEY,Reginald Lt kia 5-5-18 6RSuss att1KAR p228&268 MR52
DAVEY,Reginald Hubert Lt ded 28-11-19 1RGLI p268 CR France34
DAVEY,Roland Alfred T2Lt kld 8-8-17 GL att14RFC p6 CR Palestine2
DAVEY,Sydney Guy LtAMaj kia 25-3-18 4Norf att40MGC p187&216,ded MR20
DAVEY,Thomas Kerrison 2Lt dow 31-3-18 6 att1RB p178 CR France40
DAVEY,Wilfrid Charles TLt dow 21-11-17 RASC att15RFC p6&192,Wilfred CR France398
DAVEY,William Aubrey Carthew T2Lt kia 21-8-18 9Ches p96 CR France33
DAVEY,William Hamilton.OBE.Maj ded 29-8-20 27NumbF B'Coy CR Ireland40
DAVEY,William Henry.MC.2Lt kia 9-9-16 4Lond p246 MR21
DAVEY,William Roy 2Lt kia 1-7-16 12Lond p248 CR France798
DAVID,Arthur Walter 2Lt kia 14-9-18 1SWBord p99 CR France725
DAVID,Edward Harold 2Lt kia 5-11-18 1Ches p96 CR France521
DAVID,Frederick John Louis T2Lt dow 18-9-18 SWBord att15WelshR p99 CR France415
DAVID,Lionel Adolf David T2Lt kia 1-7-16 7Yorks A'Coy p90 CR France397
DAVID,Thomas William Capt kia 27-7-17 5WelshR p230 CR Belgium23,4Bn
DAVID,William Jenkin 2Lt kia 27-5-18 NumbF Res att6Bn p60 MR18
DAVIDSON,Alexander Bonn 2Lt kld 26-9-16 RFC SR p2 CR Kent160
DAVIDSON,Alexander James 2Lt kia 8-4-17 4SfthH p241 CR France728
DAVIDSON,Alexander Ritchie Lt kia 21-4-16 3SfthH p164 MR38
DAVIDSON,Andrew Pearson T2Lt kia 5-9-16 11 att2GordH p166 MR21
DAVIDSON,Archibald Randall Capt kia 15-6-17 1GordH p166 MR20,14-6-17
DAVIDSON,Arthur Gerrard 2Lt kia 9-9-18 4GordH attRFC p18&241,Lt CR France1361
DAVIDSON,Charles 2Lt kia 26-10-17 GordH p166 MR30
DAVIDSON,Charles Lingard 2Lt kia 6-8-15 13N&D p133 MR4
DAVIDSON,Christopher Edmund Grant Capt kia 13-10-15 1 att6EKent p57&257 CR France423
DAVIDSON,David Adams 2Lt kld 28-7-17 RGA 179SB p39 CR Belgium29
DAVIDSON,Donald Alastair Leslie.MC.MID Capt kia 30-4-17 9RFC p6 MR20
DAVIDSON,Donald Frederick Cluney Cdr ded 30-4-18 IA att9Div S&TCps p275 CR Iraq8
DAVIDSON,Douglas Byers Capt mbk 30-10-14 IA 2/8GurkhaRif p275 MR28
DAVIDSON,Duncan Hemelin Capt kia 9-5-15 SforthH p164 MR22
DAVIDSON,Edward Gordon.MC.Capt dow 2-4-18 19Huss p23 CR France145
DAVIDSON,Farquhar Biggam 2Lt dow 10-9-15 1/6HLI p240 CR Gallipoli3
DAVIDSON,Francis Charteris Capt kia 10-5-17 IARO attSWaziristanMil p275 MR43
DAVIDSON,George Leslie Capt kia 2-12-17 4 att16HLI p162 MR30
DAVIDSON,George William Smyttan 2Lt kia 25-9-16 1CamH p167 CR France453
DAVIDSON,George Wilson T2Lt dow 27-12-17 15WYorks p81 CR France184
DAVIDSON,Gerald Louis.MC.TLt dow 11-7-16 6Dors p124 CR France833
DAVIDSON,Gordon Parsons Lt kia 3-5-17 1RScotF p94 MR20
DAVIDSON,Henry Hutcheon ACapt ded 27-1-21 IARO att15LabCps p275 MR43
DAVIDSON,Henry Steele Lt kia 17-5-15 3 att1HLI p162 MR22
DAVIDSON,Hugh Douglas T2Lt kia 28-8-16 6YLI p142 CR France402
DAVIDSON,Ian Sprot 2Lt kia 11-11-14 A&SH p173 CR Belgium96
DAVIDSON,James.MID Capt kia 30-11-17 RAMC attKRRC p195 MR17
DAVIDSON,James T2Lt dow 27-5-18 NumbF att15DLI p60 MR18
DAVIDSON,James Eadie.DSO.TCaptAMaj dow 16-10-18 RGA 19SB p39 CR France528
DAVIDSON,James Samuel TCapt kia 1-7-16 13RIrRif att108MGC Inf p169&182 CR France1890
DAVIDSON,John HonLt&QM ded 19-12-15 13HLI p162 CR Scot671
DAVIDSON,John T2Lt dow 15-10-17 BordR att8Bn p117 CR France1180
DAVIDSON,John Philip 2Lt kia 9-8-16 1/10Lpool p216 MR21
DAVIDSON,John Whitworth Lt dow 5-3-17 4 att10N&D p133 CR France164
DAVIDSON,Norman Randell.DSO&Bar.MajBTLtCol dow 5-10-17 RHA HQ4Div p27 CR Belgium16
DAVIDSON,Ralph Ivan Meynell Lt dow 24-11-14 Manch p154 CR France705
DAVIDSON,Robert Henry Walter T2Lt kia 1-7-16 8Dev p76 CR France330
DAVIDSON,Robert William TLt kia 12-10-17 10A&SH p173 MR30
DAVIDSON,Roland Cooper TLt kia 1-7-16 20NumbF p60 MR21
DAVIDSON,Ronald Riach TCapt kia 27-3-16 12RScots p54 CR Belgium15
DAVIDSON,Sydney 2Lt kia 21-5-18 GL &RAF p190 CR Belgium24
DAVIDSON,Thomas Andrew 2Lt dow 9-4-18 RGA 12SB p39 CR France31
DAVIDSON,W.H.2Lt 6-9-17 32SikhPnrs MR67 see DAVISON,W.H.
DAVIDSON,William 2Lt kia 31-10-17 GL &10RFC p6 MR20
DAVIDSON,William 2Lt kia 23-3-18 7 att9ScotRif p224 MR27

DAVIDSON,William Adrian 2Lt dow 2-7-16 2GordH p166 CR France633
DAVIDSON,William Leslie.CB.Col ded 3-8-15 RFA 4GenBaseDepot p27 CR France145
DAVIDSON,William Mason Lt dow 29-3-18 5GordH p242 CR France103,26-3-18
DAVIDSON,William Thomas Chorley Capt kia 13-10-14 Dors p124 MR22
DAVIDSON-HOUSTON,Charles Elrington LtCol mbk 25-9-15 IA 58Rif p275 MR28
DAVIDSON-SMITH,Adam 2Lt 2-10-18 4RScots CR France699
DAVIE,Archibald Charles T2Lt kia19-9-18 1Wilts p152 CR France1106
DAVIE,Frank.MM.2Lt dow 2-6-17 4EYorks p219 CR Yorks2,11Bn
DAVIE,Fred TLt kia 1-4-17 1 att1/7HLI p162 CR Palestine8
DAVIE,Henry William Wilson VetSurgeon drd 23-11-15 RAVC p198 CR USA234A
DAVIE,John.MC.T2LtACapt kia 11-5-18 GL &13RScots p190 CR France113
DAVIE,Robert Chapman Capt ded 4-2-19 RAMC p253 CR Scot530
DAVIE,Sidney John 2Lt kia 10-10-17 1/8Manch p237 CR Belgium24
DAVIES,A.C.R.2Lt ded 27-10-15 5NStaffs p238 CR Mon19
DAVIES,Alun Edwards 2Lt kia 28-5-18 12/13NumbF p60 MR18
DAVIES,Alan Wilmot Lt kld 23-4-16 45RFA attRFC p2&rp27 CR Lond28
DAVIES,Albert 2Lt kld 19-6-17 GL &55RFC p6 CR Essex1
DAVIES,Albert Gordon 2Lt dow 1-8-17 7RWelshF p223 CR France285
DAVIES,Aldborough Henry 2Lt dow 18-4-16 RFA p27 MR38
DAVIES,Arthur 2Lt ded 19-10-18 IA(TC) attMtnArt RGA p275 CR Pakistan50A
DAVIES,Arthur Charles Capt kia 10-8-15 6RWelshF p223 MR4
DAVIES,Arthur Cyril Richard 2Lt ded 27-10-15 5NStaffs &RFC p261&269
DAVIES,Arthur Peter T2Lt kld 22-3-18 RFC p15 CR Ches182
DAVIES,Arthur Trevor Capt kia 7-6-17 5WelshR p230 MR29
DAVIES,Bengiman Evan Stedman TCapt kia 31-7-17 11SWBord p99 MR29
DAVIES,Benjamen Jones Capt kia 19-5-17 3SWBord p99 MR20
DAVIES,Benjamin Daniel Rowland T2Lt kld 11-3-18 RFC p15 CR Wales163,D.D.R.
DAVIES,Brinley Owen Lt kia 22-4-18 WelshR att16RWFus p126 MR27
DAVIES,Cecil James Lt died 25-11-18 RFA p207 CR Egypt9
DAVIES,Cecil Lloyd T2Lt dow 25-11-16 28Mddx att2RBerks p146 CR France105
DAVIES,Charles Albert 2Lt kia 22-9-18 7SWBord p99 MR37
DAVIES,Charles Bernard Lt kia 9-6-16 3RDubF p176 CR France514
DAVIES,Charles Hugh T2Lt kia 17-1-16 9WelshR p126 CR France727
DAVIES,Clifford Thomas 2Lt kia 7-6-17 10RWKent p140 MR29
DAVIES,Cyril Nutcombe Lt ded 1-3-19 RE p254&262,ACapt CR Surrey29
DAVIES,Cyril Thomas Morris Capt kia 1-7-16 6RWar p214 MR21
DAVIES,D.O.Capt 22-5-17 7RWFus CR Wales693
DAVIES Dan TCapt dow 10-9-17 10WelshR p126 CR Belgium23
DAVIES,David T2Lt kia 13-11-16 10RWFus p97 MR21
DAVIES,David Benyon Lt kia 11-8-17 GL &52RFC p6 CR Belgium173
DAVIES,David Claude Graham Lt dow 15-5-15 RGA 1SB p39 CR France80,Claud Lt
DAVIES,David Daniel 2Lt dow 26-8-18 235RFA p208 CR France209,kia
DAVIES,David Ethelstone TLt kia 18-6-17 10WelshF p97 CR France531
DAVIES,David Evan 2Lt kia 29-4-17 GL att12RFC p6 MR20
DAVIES,David Guy.MC.TCapt kia 4-4-17 10KRRC p149 CR France415
DAVIES,David Harold T2Lt dow 18-11-18 PoW Wilts att1Bn p152 CR Germany3
DAVIES,David James 2Lt kia 31-7-17 MGC HB C'Bn p182 MR29
DAVIES,Donald Frederick.MID T2Lt kia 15-4-18 22 att23RFus B'Coy p67 CR France103
DAVIES,Edward Stanley TCapt kia 10-9-18 NStaffs att8Bn p157 CR France80
DAVIES,Edward Thomas 2Lt kia 13-10-18 RGA 140SB p39 CR France147
DAVIES,Edwin Alfred Capt ded 25-1-15 8Lpool p215 2entries CR Lancs2
DAVIES,Ellerton Osborne 2Lt kld 2-4-15 1/2Mon p244 CR Belgium33
DAVIES,Emlyn H.Rev 18-3-18 YMCA attIndLabCps CR France699
DAVIES,Ernest Frank T2Lt kia 24-8-16 7DCLI p114 CR France400,25-8-16
DAVIES,Ernest Glyn TCapt kia 5-7-16 19WelshF p97 CR France550
DAVIES,Ernest Owen 2Lt kia 9-9-18 5NStaffs p238 CR France80
DAVIES,Evan TMaj kia 27-7-17 15WelshF p97 CR Belgium86,28-7-17
DAVIES,Evan James 2Lt kia 28-3-18 1WelshGds p53 MR20
DAVIES,Evan Walter T2Lt kia 26-3-17 GL 1/7RWFus p190 CR Palestine8
DAVIES,Fairfax Llewelyn Lt kia 8-7-17 6Norf p217 CR France646
DAVIES,Francis Hugh Lt kia 10-12-17 3 att1Dors p124 CR Belgium22,9-12-17
DAVIES,Frank Arnold 2Lt kia 1-7-16 5Ches p222 CR France798
DAVIES,Frederick 2Lt kia 12-9-18 5NStaffs p238 CR France662,9Bn
DAVIES,Frederick Anscombe T2Lt kia 14-5-17 12Y&L p158 MR20,13-5-17
DAVIES,Frederick Charles TCapt kia 17-10-17 RAMC att9NumbF p195 CR Belgium85
DAVIES,Frederick George T2Lt kia 6-2-16 9RB p178 CR Belgium85

DAVIES,Geoffrey Boisselier T.Capt kia 26-9-15 11Ess p131 MR19
DAVIES,Geoffrey David T.Lt dow 28-11-17 18WelshR att119TMB p126 CR France398
DAVIES,George Herbert Lt kia 9-8-15 3 att 1KSLI p144 MR29
DAVIES,George Llewelyn 2Lt kia 15-3-15 6KRRC att4RB p149 CR Belgium111
DAVIES,George Price T2Lt kia 29-9-18 2SWBord p99 CR Belgium116
DAVIES,George Stewart Berrington Lt ded 26-10-19 RB p266 CR Wales214
DAVIES,Geraint.MC.Capt dow 14-4-18 4NumbF p213 CR Belgium183,9Bn
DAVIES,Gilbert Vere Faithfull T.Lt kia 23-4-17 13RScots p54 MR20
DAVIES,Glyn Lloyd T2Lt kia 15-2-17 4SWBord p99 MR38
DAVIES,Graham T.Lt dow 27-7-17 A121RFA p27 CR Belgium12
DAVIES,Griffith 2Lt dow 1-5-15 24Lond p252 CR France80,Lt
DAVIES,Griffith 2Lt kia 2-10-15 1WelshR 126 MR19
DAVIES,Gwynonfryn Albert Hayden 2Lt kia 7-6-17 3Mon attRFC p18&244 MR20,Haydn
DAVIES,Harold Bellamy T2Lt kia 3-11-17 7RWar attEss p64 CR Palestine8
DAVIES,Harold Blakeney 2Lt kia 23-4-16 1WYorks p81 CR Belgium73
DAVIES,Harold Casamajor Capt kia 26-9-14 2WelchR p126 CR France1328
DAVIES,Harold Percival 2Lt kia 11-4-17 MGC D'Bn p182 MR20
DAVIES,Harry T2Lt dow 10-4-16 2RBerks p139 CR France515,kia
DAVIES,Harry Harding 2Lt kia 10-11-17 3 att 1SWBord p99 MR30
DAVIES,Harry Llanover.MID Lt dow 25-10-14 RHA p27 MR29
DAVIES,Harry Noel T2Lt kia 1-7-16 10 att 11ELancs p110 MR21
DAVIES,Henry T2Lt kia 13-11-16 6 att2 O&BLI p130 CR France1491
DAVIES,Henry Robert Griffith Lt kia 13-10-15 5NStaffs p238 MR19
DAVIES,Herbert Howard Capt kia 24-8-17 10DLI D'Coy p160 MR30
DAVIES,Hugh Frederick.MID 2Lt kia 3-7-15 1/5Ches p222 CR Belgium28,Frederic
DAVIES,Hugh Mercer.DCM.2Lt kia 12-10-18 RE 430FC p210 CR France1392
DAVIES,Idris Powell 2Lt dow 21-8-18 7Ches att7KSLI p223 CR France745
DAVIES,Ivor Garfield T2Lt kia 8-8-18 Wilts att2Bn p152 CR France411,Ifor
DAVIES,Ivor Theophilus 2Lt kia 22-6-15 5 O&BLI p130 MR29
DAVIES,James Gordon T.Capt dow 9-2-16 10WelshR D'Coy p126 CR France727
DAVIES,James Gordon 2Lt kia 1-6-17 1KSLI p144 MR19
DAVIES,James Parton T2Lt kia 26-10-18 KSLI att7Ches p144 CR Belgium406,25-10-18
DAVIES,James Thomas T.Lt dow 14-4-18 1SomLI p79 CR France88
DAVIES,John 2Lt kia 30-3-18 RWar att 1Bn p64 MR20
DAVIES,John Charles T2Lt dow 12-4-17 18RWelshF p97
DAVIES,John Hickman T2Lt kia 9-10-17 2RWar p64 CR Belgium308
DAVIES,John Howard 2Lt kia 4-7-17 4 att2RWelshF p223 CR Belgium23
DAVIES,John James 2Lt dow 29-9-17 3 att9WelshR p126 CR France193
DAVIES,John Llewelyn T.Maj kia 25-9-15 11Ess p131 MR19
DAVIES,John Morris T2Lt kia 8-10-18 16RWelshF p97 MR16
DAVIES,John Rhys 2Lt dow 28-11-17 23Lond p252 CR Palestine3
DAVIES,John Wesley T.Lt kia 26-3-16 16RWelshF p97 CR France727
DAVIES,Joseph Charles Gladstone Lt drd 6-1-18 RFA p207 MR34
DAVIES,Joseph Ithel Jehu T2Lt dow 3-9-16 8 Cmdg1RWFus p97 CR France402,Lt kia
DAVIES,Kenneth Lt ded 5-11-18 6SStaffs p255 CR Staffs78
DAVIES,Kenneth George T.Lt kia 19-5-17 RE H CableSect p44 CR France68
DAVIES,L.C.MC.Lt ded 16-3-18 5ScotRif &54TrgDepotStn RFC p224 CR Hamps98
DAVIES,Leonard T.Lt.ACapt kia 3-6-17 5 att9RB p178 CR France1185
DAVIES,Leslie Capt kia 15-9-16 15Lond p249 CR France432
DAVIES,Leslie Frederick St.John.MC.MID T.Capt.AMaj ded 10-11-18 20MGC p182 CR Lebanon1
DAVIES,Lindsay Ramsay T2Lt dow 5-7-16 18Lpool p71 CR France66
DAVIES,Llewelyn Crighton.MC.2Lt kld 16-3-18 3ScotRif att RFC p18&224,Llewellyn ded 5Bn
DAVIES,Maurice Albert Mervyn T2Lt kia 25-9-15 Dev p76 MR19
DAVIES,Noel John T2Lt kia 27-4-16 8RDubF p176 CR France178
DAVIES,Norman Stollard Lt kia 2-9-18 7Ess p232 CR France427
DAVIES,Owen Griffith 2Lt kia 15-11-16 6A&SH p243 CR France533
DAVIES,Percy Hier Lt.TCapt kia 16-8-17 17 att15WelchR p126 MR30
DAVIES,Ralph Howell T.Lt kia 9-4-16 9RWar p64 MR38
DAVIES,Reginald Charles T2Lt kia 1-6-16 19NumbF p60 CR France1106
DAVIES,Reginald Charles Spurgeon 2Lt kia 21-3-18 17Lond p250 MR20
DAVIES,Rhys Beynon 2Lt kia 1-5-17 4NumbF attRFC p18&213 CR France1744
DAVIES,Richard Cecil.VD.Maj ded 17-5-17 RE p44 CR Ches28
DAVIES,Richard Harry Seymour T.Lt dow 29-7-16 C88RFA p27 CR France145
DAVIES,Richard Hutton.CB.MajGen ded 9-5-18 Staff p1 CR Lond4
DAVIES,Robert Finden Capt kia 9-9-16 9Lond p247 MR21

DAVIES,Robert Glynne T.Capt kia 14-8-16 4Lpool p71 CR France432
DAVIES,Robert Humphrey T2Lt kia 23-8-18 13RWelshF p97 CR France516
DAVIES,Robert Lloyd T.Lt kia 12-4-17 RE 129FC p44 CR France480
DAVIES,Robert Thomas T2Lt dow 2-4-17 21Manch p154 CR France620
DAVIES,Robert William Marengwyn T2Lt kia 6-4-17 22NumbF &52RFC p6&60,59Sqn CR France1321,Maengwyn
DAVIES,Roland Arthur Llewelyn T.Lt kia 4-10-18 3RFus p67 CR France1495
DAVIES,Rudolph Ellis Lt dow 11-8-17 1/7WRid p227 CR Belgium172
DAVIES,Sydney Bruce 2Lt kia 26-3-18 5ESurr p226 MR27,ESurr att9Bn
DAVIES,Sydney Francis T2Lt dow 15-11-17 11RSuss p118 CR Belgium112
DAVIES,Sydney George T2Lt kia 31-7-17 9RWelshF p97 MR29,Sidney
DAVIES,T.H.T.Lt ded 26-10-18 RE p44 CR Shrop97
DAVIES,Thomas Lt ded 20-9-18 RE p262 CR Wales1
DAVIES,Thomas Howell Capt 6-10-19 11SWBord CR Wales199
DAVIES,Thomas John Carlyle 2Lt kia 2-10-15 1WelshR p126 MR19
DAVIES,Thomas Llewelyn.MC.Maj kldacc 16-9-18 RFA attRAF p27 CR Wales167
DAVIES,Tom Llewelyn 2Lt kia 26-5-17 RE IWT p44 MR38
DAVIES,Trevor Arthur Manning Lt kia 1-7-16 RFA NMidDAC p207 CR France798
DAVIES,T.W.E.Lt.ACapt ded 20-5-18 RFA No1depot RFA p27 CR Kent100
DAVIES,Valentine Clements.MC.T.Capt dow 10-7-16 6/40RFA p27 CR France141
DAVIES,Wallis Rowland Henry Rochfort 2Lt ded 8-3-16 3SomLI p79
DAVIES,Walter T2Lt kia 18-9-18 9RLancs p58 CR Greece5,19-9-18
DAVIES,Walter Ambler 2Lt 15-6-15 4LNLancs MR22 See DAVIS
DAVIES,Walter Bomford 2Lt ded 3-11-18 SomLI p263 MR65
DAVIES,Walter Llewelyn T2Lt dow 15-7-16 7KSLI p144 CR France66
DAVIES,Walter Owen 2Lt kia 27-11-17 2/5WRid p227 MR17
DAVIES,Wilfred John Lt kia 5-11-16 70RFA p27 CR France385
DAVIES,William T2Lt kia 10-4-17 13RFus p67 CR France154
DAVIES,William Capt kia 11-4-18 2SWBord p99 MR32
DAVIES,William Bryan 2Lt ded 18-9-16 6N&D p269 CR France46
DAVIES,William Edward 2Lt dow 29-1-16 1/5Ches p222 CR France639
DAVIES,William John Lt dow 14-10-18 RGA 140SB p39 CR France214,1/4SB
DAVIES,William Lloyd T2Lt kia 31-7-17 13RWFus C'Coy p97 CR Belgium86
DAVIES,William Robert T.Lt kia 1-11-18 19NumbF p60 CR France143
DAVIES,William Thomas Lt dow 13-4-18 6SWBord p99 CR Belgium183
DAVIS,Alistair Ingram 2Lt kia 11-4-18 4A&SH p173 MR32
DAVIS,Anthony Hugh 2Lt kia 6-4-16 10 O&BLI p130 MR38,1Bn
DAVIS,Arthur George 2Lt kia 16-8-17 11Lond p245 MR29
DAVIS,Basil Raymond Lt kia 20-9-17 RFus &45RFC p6 CR Belgium157
DAVIS,Bernard Samuel 2Lt kia 9-4-17 5BordR p228 CR France214,Capt
DAVIS,Brian Charles 2Lt dow 22-8-18 7 att1/22Lond p247 CR France119
DAVIS,C.H.G.Lt 23-3-21 IAUL att2RWSurr MR43
DAVIS,Cecil Capt dow 27-3-17 5WelshR p230 MR34
DAVIS,Charles 2Lt kia 4-10-17 RGA 210SB p39 CR Belgium23
DAVIS,Charles Edwin T2Lt drd 15-9-18 14RWar Res p64 CR France13
DAVIS,Charles Henry 2Lt kia 24-5-15 2 att5BordR p117 CR Belgium101
DAVIS,Charles Stewart 2Lt kia 1-7-16 5 att2Mddx p146 CR France393
DAVIS,Clement John Burton Capt dow 29-9-17 RE 470Coy p210 CR Belgium3
DAVIS,Cyril Arthur Ernest T2Lt kia 31-7-17 A108RFA p27 CR Belgium7
DAVIS,Cyril York T.Capt kia 15-9-16 12ESurr p112 MR21
DAVIS,Douglas Stalman Lt ded 27-1-19 HAC p206 CR Italy15
DAVIS,Edward Bernard T2Lt kia 31-7-17 225MGC Inf p182 CR Belgium112
DAVIS,Edward Thomas Lt kia 27-12-17 24Lond attMGC p187&252,Edwin CR Palestine3
DAVIS,Eugene T2Lt kia 28-3-18 2Dev p76 MR27
DAVIS,Francis Edward T2Lt kia 9-10-17 9 att 1/5YLI p142 MR30
DAVIS,Fredk John Stockham Maj ded 4-11-18 5Dev p217 CR Devon69
DAVIS,George Edward Lt kia 11/13-10-15 RE p210 MR19
DAVIS,George Frederick.MID Maj mbk 15-8-15 11Lond p257 MR4
DAVIS,George Leith Blakeman 2Lt kia 27-9-18 23RFus p67 CR France714
DAVIS,Gronow John.DSO.LtCol ded 20-6-19 IA 22Punjabis att9KRR p275 CR Mddx26
DAVIS,Guy Clifton Lt ded 11-5-18 1/7NumbF p214 CR France1525
DAVIS,H.R.2Lt 22-12-17 RFC CR Norf261
DAVIS,Harold Charles 2Lt kia 4-4-17 4Lond p246 CR France662,att11KRRC
DAVIS,Harold Charles 2Lt kia 26-6-18 9Ess att104RAF p131 CR France1632
DAVIS,Harry.MM.2Lt 20-5-19 3RWar att59RAF CR Germany1
DAVIS,Henry Carlisle Monsell Lt kia 7-4-20 IA 2/3GurkhaRif att2/5 p275 MR43
DAVIS,Henry Christopher 2Lt kia 2-7-16 16KRRC p149 MR19

DAVIS,Henry Ouseley Capt kia 27-10-14 5 att2RIrRif p169 MR22
DAVIS,Henry William Warren Lt kia 18-4-15 1WelshR p126 CR Belgium167
DAVIS,Herbert Gough Lt kia 14-2-15 3Norf p73 CR Belgium98
DAVIS,Herbert Nathaniel Lt dow 22-2-15 RE 3FC p210 CR Belgium58
DAVIS,Herbert Pinder T2Lt dow 29-7-16 13Ess p131 CR France141
DAVIS,Horace John 2Lt kia 6-2-17 3Lincs att15RFC p6&p75 CR France41
DAVIS,Hugh Courtenay 2Lt kia 5-8-16 3RBerks attRFC p2&p139 CR France31
DAVIS,Hugh Courtney T2Lt kia 25-7-16 20LancF p92 MR21
DAVIS,James Walden Fortune McNaught Lt kia 17-1-15 SWBord p99
DAVIS,John Charles Reginald Lt kia 13-5-15 3 att2Ess p131 MR29
DAVIS,John Henry TCapt ded 21-6-16 RAMC p267 CR Ireland33
DAVIS,Joseph T2Lt kld 20-1-18 RFC p15
DAVIS,Joseph Frederick.MC.Lt ded 19-3-19 RE p269 CR Hamps1
DAVIS,Lawrence Alan T2Lt kia 23-6-17 GL &4RFC p6 CR Belgium11
DAVIS,Leigh Jacob Capt kia 15-9-16 19Lond p250 CR France390
DAVIS,Leo Edwin 2Lt kia 7-8-15 5Manch p236 MR4
DAVIS,Leslie James George 2Lt kia 5-4-18 4EKent p212 CR France196
DAVIS,Leslie Sansome Lt kia 30-9-18 RH&FA &RAF p261
DAVIS,Maurice Oliver Arthur 2Lt dow 1-3-18 13 att18Lond p249 CR France398
DAVIS,Mellville Allen Duff.MC.T2Lt ded 29-5-18 KRRC att9Bn p149 CR Lancs43
DAVIS,Norman K.2Lt kia 4-10-17 YLI att9Bn p142 MR30
DAVIS,Oswyn St.Leger LtCol dow 5-4-18 6Manch Cmdg8LancF p236 CR France745,DAVIES
DAVIS,Owen Mazzinghi T2Lt kia 27-6-16 9EYorks p84 CR France643
DAVIS,Philip Henry Halton 2Lt dow 9-11-18 3Manch p154 CR France341
DAVIS,Percy Hill T2Lt dow 26-10-17 14RWar Res p64 CR Belgium165,kia
DAVIS,Percy Warren Theodore 2Lt kia 30-3-17 1EKent p57 MR19
DAVIS,Ralph Salway T2Lt kia 16-9-16 7Dors att6SomLI p124 MR21
DAVIS,Reginald 2Lt kia 20-10-16 GL &RFC p2&p190 CR France833
DAVIS,Reginald Noël.MID TCapt kia 12-10-16 3 att2WRid p115 CR France374
DAVIS,Reginald Percy 2Lt dow 5-10-15 4RWelshF p223 CR France259,DAVIES
DAVIS,Richard Christopher 2Lt kia 8-3-16 3 att1Manch p154 MR38
DAVIS,Richard Samuel Lt dow 22-3-18 2/5Leic p220 MR20
DAVIS,Robert 2Lt dow 11-1-17 IA 59Rif p275 CR Iraq5,10-1-17
DAVIS,Sidney Alfred 2Lt kia 22-8-17 5Glouc p225 MR30 Ex 1/4Bn
DAVIS,Sidney John 2Lt dow 28-3-18 5SStaffs p229 CR France40,4Bn
DAVIS,Thomas Edward George T2Lt kia 27-5-17 2RWelshF p97 CR France644
DAVIS,Thomas William 2Lt ded 14-11-18 5Beds att43TMB p269 CR Norf209
DAVIS,Uriah Philip 2Lt kia 16-4-17 10Lond att20RFus p248 MR20
DAVIS,Vivian Alfred 2Lt kia 4-9-18 9RIrFus p171 CR Belgium89
DAVIS,Wallace Howard 2Lt kia 1-7-17 4 att2N&D p133 MR19
DAVIS,Walter Ambler 2Lt kia 15-6-15 4LNLancs p234 MR22,DAVIES
DAVIS,Walter Arthur T2Lt kia 1-7-16 11N&D p133 CR France246
DAVIS,Wilfred Allen 2Lt kia 21-4-15 4 att1ESurr p112 MR29,Wilfrid
DAVIS,Wilfred Jervis Lt kia 30-6-16 7NumbF p214 CR Belgium60,Wilfrid
DAVIS,William T2Lt kia 18-10-16 12 att9Ess p131 MR21
DAVIS,William.MID Lt 28-5-21 2NumbF CR India97A
DAVIS,William Jeffery Capt&Adjt kia 30-7-15 8KRRC p149 MR29,T.
DAVIS,William Rhys Lancelot TLt&ACapt kia 23-4-17 10N&D p133 MR20
DAVIS,William Richard TCapt kia 28-9-15 2EKent p57 MR19
DAVIS,William Stanley Lt kia 22-3-18 5 att4Beds p219 MR20
DAVIS,William Thomas Hadley 2Lt kia 21-3-18 2DLI p160 MR20
DAVISON,Charles Montague 2Lt dow 10-4-18 4NumbF p213 CR France1094
DAVISON,Charles William Joseph T2Lt kia 14-9-16 9WYorks p81 MR21
DAVISON,Edmund 2Lt kia 24-9-17 3 att11RSuss p118 MR30
DAVISON,Frederick William 2Lt kia 17-4-18 Y&L p158 MR30
DAVISON,Guy Middleton TCapt ded 30-11-18 RE IW&DconstructSect p44 CR Kent25
DAVISON,Henry James Goddard 2Lt kia 4-6-15 13WYorks att3LancF p81 MR4
DAVISON,Joseph Jonathan 2Lt dow 23-6-17 2DLI p160 CR France178
DAVISON,Ralph Lt kia 9-5-15 3 att1Nhampt p137 MR22
DAVISON,Robert.MC.Lt dow 8-10-16 12Lpool p71 CR France105
DAVISON,Robert Charles 2Lt dow 19-5-17 5 att4RFus p67 CR France40
DAVISON,Rosnell Montague Rasnell TCapt dow 27-1-19 3NStaffs att8Leic p157 CR Surrey148,Rashell Rashell
DAVISON,Rutherford Willoughby 2Lt dow 10-10-16 3Lond p245 CR France105
DAVISON,Stuart 2Lt kia 14-9-14 2KRRC p149 CR France1329
DAVISON,William Hope 2Lt ded 6-9-17 IARO att2/32Pnrs p275 MR67,DAVIDSON
DAVISSON,Bertram 2Lt ded 22-2-19 RE p262 CR Lancs34,Lt RGA

DAVITT,Felix William T2Lt kia 12-4-18 12GordH p166 MR32
DAVOREN,Ambrose Joseph Stanislaus Lt kia 18-7-17 RFA Z25TMB p207 CR Belgium5
D'AVREY,William Septimus 2Lt kia 22-11-15 IARO att48Pnrs p275 MR38
DAVSON,Thomas Gordon Lt kia 13-5-15 RHGds p20 MR29
DAVY,Howard Samuel 2Lt kia 15-2-15 2RIrRif p169 CR Belgium17
DAVY,John Alfred Lt kld 8-11-16 GL &RFC 19ResSqd p2&p190 CR Surrey160
DAVY,John Evelyn.DSO.Maj ded 9-12-18 266RFA p206 CR Italy6
DAVY,Philip Francis.MC.T2Lt.ACapt kia 4-11-18 13RB p178 CR France733
DAVY,Reginald 2Lt kia 21-10-18 3ESurr p112 CR France1388,20-10-18 1Bn
DAVY,William Edward TCapt&Adjt kia 7-7-16 18Ches p96 MR21,13Bn
DAVY,William James 2Lt kia 7-7-16 6SomLI p79 MR21,18-8-16
DAVY,William Reginald Capt kia 21-8-18 7Ess att10TankCps p189&232 MR16
DAW,Frederick Pole Lt.ACapt kia 18-10-16 4Worc p108 CR France307
DAW,Reginald Samuel TCapt dow 25-9-16 9KRRC B'Coy p149 CR France177,25-8-16
DAW,T.Maj&QM 10-1-20 1Mddx CR Mddx46
DAW,Thomas Herbert TCapt kia 9-5-15 2ELancs p110 CR France706
DAW,William Westaway T2Lt ded 12-11-18 RE 171TC p44 CR France34
DAWE,Alfred Henry T2Lt kia 11-4-17 13KRRC p149 MR20
DAWE,James Jeffery Lt on or since7-6-18 GL &24RFC CR France649
DAWE,Richard Henry O'Neill 2Lt kia 13-9-16 1Dev p76 CR France785
DAWE,Sydney Charles.MC.Capt kld 13-2-18 5Lincs p220 CR France439
DAWES,A.E.Sister 23-10-18 QAIMNS CR Beds23
DAWES,Arthur Irwin TCapt ded 22-6-17 9SomLI att10Gurkhas p79 CR Asia51
DAWES,Charles Edmund 2Lt dow 28-1-15 1LNLancs p135 CR France721
DAWES,George Hugh TLt&A/Adjt kia 16-9-16 5BordR p228 CR France432
DAWES,Hubert.MM.James 2Lt kia 8-5-18 3Suff att2Yorks p78 CR Belgium102
DAWES,Morris 2Lt kia 26-4-18 Ess att10Bn p131 MR27
DAWES,Oswald Stephen Bernard 2Lt kia 8-5-17 5NStaffs att14Y&L p238 MR20
DAWES,Roy Samuel 2Lt kia 9-9-16 13Lond p249 MR21
DAWES,Sidney Francis 2Lt kia 9-10-18 RGA 236SB p39 CR France341
DAWES,Walter Richard Aston Capt kia 23-8-14 1Wilts p152 CR Belgium261
DAWES,William Henry George T2Lt kia 29-9-18 8TankCps p188 CR France1495
DAWKINS,Charles John Randle 2Lt kia 25-9-15 9WelshR p126 CR France260
DAWKINS,Charles Tyrwhitt.KCMG.CB.MajGen ded 4-10-19 Commd &Staff p261
DAWKINS,Frank Lt ded 11-10-18 RE &RAF p44
DAWKINS,Frederick Clifton.MC.2Lt dow 2-9-17 A86RFA p27 CR Belgium11
DAWKINS,Guy Stacey T2Lt dow 25-9-16 ScotsGds att2Bn p52 CR France66
DAWKINS,Norman Leslie T2Lt kia 14-4-18 Y&L att1/5Bn p158 MR30,13-4-18
DAWN,Arthur Lt&QM drd 8-2-19 IARO att1/70BurmaRif p275 MR66
DAWN,Harold Frederick 2Lt mbk 22-1-17 IARO att6Jats p275 MR38,22-1-16
DAWNEY,Hugh.Hon.DSO.Maj kia 6-11-14 2LifeGds p20 CR Belgium140,DAWNAY
DAWS,Edwin 2LtTLt kia 2-11-17 16 att1/4RScots p54 CR Palestine8
DAWS,Harold T2Lt kld 26-12-16 10DLI p160 CR France1182
DAWSON,Albert George CaptALtCol kia 22-4-17 4Mddx p146 CR France604,23-4-17
DAWSON,Alfred.MC.Maj kia 20-5-17 88/14RFA p27 CR France570
DAWSON,Allan T2Lt kia 3-9-16 22MGC p182 CR France402
DAWSON,Anthony Lt kia 13-7-16 5 att2RB p178 CR France423
DAWSON,Arthur T2Lt kld 21-1-18 RFC p15 CR Scot396
DAWSON,C.C.Lt ded 23-9-16 3KAR p202 MR46, see DAWSON Mc.
DAWSON,Cecil Hubert Thrower Lt&QM mbk 24-3-18 10RIrRif p256 CR France1216,23-4-18
DAWSON,Dan Magill TLt dow 8-9-16 24NumbF A'Coy p60 CR France145
DAWSON,David Stewart 2Lt ded 20-10-17 3GordH p265 CR Scot280,Lt
DAWSON,Douglas James Septimus 2Lt ded 26-1-15 4Ess p269 CR Essex16
DAWSON,Eveline Maud Matron drd 10-4-17 QAIMNS p200 CR France40
DAWSON,Francis Rudolf Lt kia 10-8-15 4Ches p222
DAWSON,Frank Maitland Fraser 2Lt kia 20-9-17 4GordH p242 MR30
DAWSON,Frederick Albert.MC.T2Lt kia 7-8-18 8ESurr p112 MR27
DAWSON,Frederick Charles Blakeman T2Lt kia 3-5-17 11RFus attHAC p67 MR20
DAWSON,Frederick William 2Lt kia 8-9-16 5SLancs p230 CR France400
DAWSON,Gerald Moore TLt kia 1-7-16 18Lpool p71 MR21
DAWSON,Harold 2Lt kldacc 14-7-17 7Lond p247 CR France662
DAWSON,Harold Percy T2Lt kld 9-3-18 RFC p15 CR Mddx1
DAWSON,Harold William T2Lt kia 4-10-17 GL &19RFC p6 CR France285
DAWSON,Herbert Edward Capt kia 14-9-14 1Lincs p75 MR15
DAWSON,Herbert George T2Lt ded 29-5-18 12Manch attRE 86FC p154 CR France106,11Bn

DAWSON,Herbert Henry Mawson T2Lt kia 19-7-16 148RFA p27 CR France400
DAWSON,James 2Lt ded 2-4-17 3 att2BlkW p128 CR Scot625
DAWSON,James 2Lt kia 29-5-18 BordR att15DLI p254 MR18,28-5-18
DAWSON,John T2Lt kia 25-9-15 11 att4GordH p166 MR19
DAWSON,John T2Lt dow 22-7-16 9DLI p160 CR France1415
DAWSON,John Douglas Maj kia 28-6-15 7RScots p211 MR4
DAWSON,John Leonard T2Lt ded 6-5-16 10 att1/5Beds p85 CR Egypt15
DAWSON,John Stewart Lt ded 14-8-18 IARO att2S&M p275 MR65
DAWSON,Leonard T2Lt kia 4-6-15 13 att1WYorks attLancF p81 MR4
DAWSON,Leonard Leslie TLt kia 27-5-18 1N&D p133 CR France1332
DAWSON,M.C.Lt 23-9-16 3KAR MR46 see DAWSON,C.C.
DAWSON,Norman Currey TLt kia 28-3-18 13Lpool p71 MR20
DAWSON,Niel Creaton T2Lt dow 12-7-16 16N&D attTMB p133 CR France80,kia
DAWSON,Phillip Lt kia 26-3-18 RE 283ArmyTroopCoy p210 CR France526
DAWSON,Reginald Todd 2Lt kia 13-11-16 3 att2RScots p54 CR France742
DAWSON,Richard Long Capt kia 20-11-14 CldGds p51 CR Belgium134
DAWSON,Roger Graham 2Lt kia 18-9-15 3 att6Nhampt p137 CR France511,18-9-18
DAWSON,Sydney TLt&Adjt kia 1-7-16 8Y&L p158
DAWSON,Thomas Reginald 2Lt dow 4-2-16 19Lond p250 MR20
DAWSON,Walter Henry Mountiford Westropp 2Lt kia 24-5-15 2Ches p96
DAWSON,Wilfred Leedham 2Lt kia 3-12-17 2/6RWar p214 MR17
DAWSON,William T2Lt kia 11-4-17 SfthH p164 CR France604
DAWSON,William Arthur TLt kia 23-7-16 7 att11LNLancs p135 CR France432
DAWSON,William Ernest Capt ded 16-9-18 RFA &RAF p207&258 CR Mon81
DAWSON,William Healey 2Lt kia 20-7-18 7WYorks p218 CR France622,2/8Bn
DAWSON,William Ordford Charles Maj drd 22-1-17 IA IndCivVetDept p275,MR41,30-12-15 O'C.
DAWSON,William Robert Augrue.DSO&3Bars.CaptTLtCol dow 3-12-15 6RWKent p140 CR France40,Aufrere,3-12-18
DAWSON-DAMER,George Seymour.Hon.2Lt dow 12-4-17 10Huss p22 CR France104,13-4-17
DAWSON-GREENE,Charles John 2Lt dow 23-4-18 4GrenGds p49 CR France40
DAWSON-SCOTT,John Kearsley Capt kia 29-11-14 RE 5FC p44 MR29,29-10-14
DAWSON-SMITH,Charles Frank Lt ded 11-1-20 4 O&BLI att5KAR p269 CR EAfrica59
DAWSWELL,George Alec 2Lt kia 20-3-16 19Lond p250 CR France924
DAY,Charles Norris 2Lt kia 1-5-18 RGA 298SB p39 CR France139
DAY,Charles Spencer 2Lt dow 25-4-18 D59RFA p27 CR France106
DAY,Dennis Ivor T2Lt dow 7-10-15 106RFA p27 CR Hunts104
DAY,Douglas Knowles T2Lt dow 19-11-15 10 att6ELancs p110 CR Gallipoli27
DAY,Francis Innes Maj 21-12-14 2RMunstF p174 MR22,22-12-14
DAY,Francis Thomas Pressland TCapt dow 25-3-18 15WYorks p81 CR France103
DAY,Frederick Charles Capt kia 31-7-17 RFus att12Bn p67 MR29
DAY,Geoffrey Reynolds Lt kia 27-8-16 5Beds att 1/8RWar p219 MR21
DAY,George Francis Hermitage 2Lt kia 11-9-16 125RFA attRGA 42SBp27 MR21,10-9-16
DAY,George Samuel Lt kia 1-10-18 12Lond &RAF p250&258&248
DAY,Gerald Harlow 2lt kia 24-4-17 12Worc att7RBerks p108 MR37
DAY,Gerald Philip Lt dow 26-9-16 2Lincs p75 CR France105
DAY,Harry Montague TLt kia 15-4-18 59MGC Inf p182 MR32
DAY,Henry Brodie 2Lt kia 4-2-18 1Camb C'Coy p245 CR France439,3-2-18
DAY,Henry James 2Lt kia 7-7-17 71RFA p27 CR Belgium72
DAY,Henry Julian Dunlop TLt ded 3-12-18 MGC Inf p182 CR Norf132
DAY,Herbert T2Lt kia 10-7-16 8LNLancs p135 CR France832
DAY,Herbert James 2Lt dow 8-8-17 Glouc &11RFC p6&106 CR France214
DAY,Horace Frederick T2Lt kia 5-9-16 8NStaffs p157 CR Belgium89
DAY,Hubert Francis T2Lt kia 10-8-17 11RFus p67 MR29
DAY,Hubert Victor T2Lt kia 9-4-17 13RFus p67 MR20
DAY,James Arthur Percival SubCdr ded PoW 29-4-16/11-2-17 IA S&TCps p275 MR38
DAY,John Charles 2Lt kia 9-5-17 3RSuss &52RFC p7&p118 CR France415
DAY,John Edward TCapt dow 6-4-17 6RIrReg A'Coy p89 CR France285
DAY,Leslie Terrett TLt kia 1-7-16 RFA attTMB p27 MR21
DAY,Maurice 2Lt kia 9-5-15 RBerks p139 MR32
DAY,Maurice Charles 2Lt kia 3-11-14 IA 13Rajputs p275 MR47
DAY,Norman Leslie T2Lt kia 14-9-16 14Lpool p71 MR37
DAY,Oliver 2Lt dow 3-9-17 17WYorks p81 CR France658
DAY,Owen Heathcote Lacy Capt kia 6-8-15 2Hamps p120 CR Gallipoli6
DAY,Percy Oliver James T2Lt kia 19-7-16 17KRRC p149 CR France727
DAY,Reginald Harry TLt kia 4/5-4-16 12 att9RWar p64 CR Iraq5

DAY,Richard.MC.Maj dow 23-2-18 RFA p206 CR Belgium10
DAY,Samuel Albert 2Lt kia 10-11-16 3 att15WYorks p81 CR France342
DAY,Shirley Cuthbert.MC.TLtACapt kia 12-10-17 10N&D p133 MR30
DAY,Sidney 2Lt kia 11-8-16 5Y&L p238 CR France293
DAY,Walter Evan Capt kia 5-6-16 RE p44 CR Belgium137
DAY,William Leonard Lt kia 6-4-17 BordR &59RFC p7&117 MR20
DAYSH,Maurice T2Lt kia 23-4-18 12WYorks p81 CR France2,10Bn
D'CRUZ,Peter Clement AssSurg 2-2-16 ISMD MR59 &CR EAfrica61,2-2-17
DEACON,Charles.MC.MID LtAMaj dow 14-5-18 113RFA p27 CR France102
DEACON,Ernest Cecil Watson 2Lt kld 22-4-18 YLI att27RAF p143 CR France140,kia
DEACON,Edmund LtCol kia 13-5-15 EssYeo p203 MR29
DEACON,Raymond Eric 2Lt kia 7-8-15 10NStaffs att8LancF p157 MR4
DEACON,Stanley Alfred T2Lt kia 28-2-17 10Glouc p106 CR France1472
DEACON,William Warren.MC.Lt kia 22-8-18 1/5RLancs p213 CR France106,23-8-18
DEAKIN,Cedric Guy 2Lt kia 20-5-16 14Huss p22 MR38
DEAKIN,Cedric Kenworthy Lt kia 21-3-18 2/8Manch p237 MR27
DEAKIN,Charles Joseph John King T2Lt dow 2-7-16 16Mddx p146 CR France62
DEAKIN,George Welsley TCapt ded ?-2-16 RE IWT p262 CR Ches8,Welsby,21-3-16
DEAKIN,Robert Hartley 2Lt kia 22-7-17 IA 10Jats att45RFC p275 MR20
DEAKIN,William Ewart T2Lt kia 4-3-17 1Worc p108 MR21,Wilfrid
DEALTRY,Herbert Arthur Berkeley Capt kia 26-9-15 9ESurr p112 MR19
DEAN,Albert.MC.T2Lt dow 15-10-18 29DLI p160 CR France25
DEAN,Arthur T2Lt kia 8-11-16 21 att10LancF p92 CR France307
DEAN,Arthur Lt selfInflictGunshot 22-3-21 IA 80CarnaticInf att2/154Inf p275
DEAN,Arthur LeRoy 2Lt kld 9-8-17 RFC p7 CR Norf58
DEAN,Arthur Reginald.DCM.2Lt kia 4-7-17 4EYorks p219 CR France1489,3-7-17
DEAN,Cyril Edward Brietycke.MID 2Lt kia 15-9-16 RGA 121HB p39 MR21,Brietzcke
DEAN,Frank.MID 2Lt kia 31-10-14 KRRC p149 MR29
DEAN,George Frederick 2Lt kia 16-10-17 162RFA p27 MR30
DEAN,George Murray Lt kia 13-9-18 5GordH p27 p242 CR France115
DEAN,Harold.MC.T2LtACapt kld 5-1-18 2Yorks p90 CR Belgium127
DEAN,Harry T2Lt kia 11-4-18 EYorks p84 CR Belgium19,2Y&L
DEAN,Hedley T2Lt kia 21-3-18 10WYorks p81 MR20
DEAN,Henry James Lt ded 27-8-18 RE p262 CR Norf101,Capt
DEAN,John Henry Ellis.MC&Bar. TCapt kia 27-5-15 13 att10Ches p96 MR18
DEAN,Josiah Stanley Capt dow 27-5-17 7Lpool p215 CR France102
DEAN,Langley 2Lt ded 19-6-19 IARO 10EKent att2/28Punjabis p275 CR India48
DEAN,Leonard Lawson 2Lt kia 3-10-18 1LNLancs p135 CR France1710
DEAN,Reginald Evan 2Lt kia 7-6-17 10 att21Lond p248 CR Belgium60
DEAN,Rosser Fellowes Marriott 2Lt kia 1-7-16 4RWar att93MGC p64&p182 CR France156
DEAN,Thomas Albert Wray 2lt dow 8-5-18 20Lpool p71 MR30
DEAN,Thomas Walton T2Lt kia 7-6-17 9Yorks p90 MR29
DEAN,William 2Lt kia 1-7-16 3 att10RIrRif p169 MR21
DEAN,William Homer 2Lt kia 11-10-15 7N&D p233 MR19
DEAN-PITT,D.C.Maj 5-2-17 AssSec BRCS CR France461
DEANE,A.Lt 23-3-21 IA 2/154Inf MR65
DEANE,Arthur Denman T2Lt kia 14-7-17 1 att2RIrReg p89 MR21
DEANE,Arthur Francis T2Lt kia 16-8-17 167MGC Inf p182 CR Belgium167
DEANE,Arthur Reginald Lt dow 14-11-17 5RSuss p228
DEANE,Denis 2Lt kia 23-10-14 2RWar p64 MR29
DEANE,Ernest Cotton.MC.Capt kia 25-9-18 RAMC att2Leic p195 CR France1157
DEANE,George Frederic T2Lt kia 22-4-17 11Ess att18TMB p131 CR France115
DEANE,George Frederick 2Lt ded 29-11-17 RE p269 CR Berks85
DEANE,Gordon Alexander Capt dow 11-4-18 PoW 1RIrFus p171 CR France928
DEANE,John Henry Maj kia 30-4-15 Hamps p120 MR4
DEANE,Lancelot Colin William.DSO.MC.MIDx2 TMajALtCol kia 29-5-18 6SWBord p99 CR France 1689
DEANE,Richard John 2Lt kld 18-7-17 117/26RFA p27 CR Belgium29
DEANE,Wellesley Venables.MID 2Lt kia 24-9-17 D95RFA p208 CR Belgium19
DEANE,William.MC.Lt kia 20-3-20 4Norf &20RAF p269 MR43
DEANE-OLIVER,Richard Edward TLt kia 8-9-16 RE 75FC p44 CR France515,7-9-16 74FC
DEANE-SPREAD,Frederick Bradshaw Lt kia 25-9-15 IARO att58Rif p275 MR28
DEANS,Albert Victor 2Lt mbk 11-4-18 7 att12Yorks p256 CR France1092
DEANS,Geoffrey Chase Capt kia 6-5-15 4Worc p108 CR Gallipoli6

DEANS,Harold Mackenzie Capt kia 17-9-18 3 att7/8KOSB p101 CR France115
DEANS,William Wilkie TCapt dow 4-1-16 RAMC att54RFA p195 CR Gallipoli1
DEAR,Roy Evers T2Lt kia 30-4-17 RWar att6ELancs p64 MR38
DEARE,F.A.LtCol ded 24-1-15 RBerks p139 CR Berks121
DEARDEN,James Ferrand.DSO.MC&2Bars.Capt ded 6-10-19 RFus p263 CR Glouc31
DEARDEN,Walter Lt kia 19-12-16 NStaffs p157 MR38
DEARNALEY,Irvine 2LtTCapt kia 23-11-15 9Manch p237 CR Gallipoli6
DEAS,John Cairns Lt ded 31-12-19 3BlkW p264 CR Mddx26,30-12-19
DEAS,William Darling TLt dow 30-9-15 11A&SH p173 CR France1142
DEASE,Maurice James.VC.Lt kia 23-8-14 4RFus p67 CR Belgium242
DEASE,Trevor Herbert Llewellyn 2Lt kia 12-10-16 4 att1RIrFus p171 CR France1890
De BECK,George Clifford T2Lt kia 18-2-17 23RFus p67 MR21
DeBEER,Bendix Hallenstein 2Lt kia 10-7-17 RGA 94SB p39 CR Belgium173
DEBELL,Francis 2Lt kia 9-10-17 4Y&L C'Coy p238 CR Belgium125
DEBENHAM,Herbert.MID TLt dow 9-8-15 6ELancs p110 MR4
DEBENHAM,Herbert Austin 2Lt kia 1-11-18 4RWKent p234 MR16
DEBENHAM,Keith Lt dow 4-12-16 3HLI p162 CR Lond4
DEBERIGNY,Charles Etienne 2Lt dow 29-4-17 43RFC p7 CR France32,kia 45Sqn
De BLABY,Reginald Swithun Capt dow 9-8-16 3 att4LNLancs p135 CR France23
DeBLAQUIERE,John.Hon.Lt kia 10-3-15 2ScotRif p103 CR France260
DeBRUYN,Douglas Bayly 2Lt kld 27-5-16 RLancs &RFC p2&58,ded CR Camb16
DeBURGH,Francis Vavasour Cdr 7-12-18 RIM MR65
DeBURGH,Thomas.MID Lt mbk 17-9-14 IA 13Lancers att5 p275 MR28
DeBURIATTE,John Philip 2Lt kia 12-3-15 2ESurr p112 CR Belgium168
DeBURIATTE,Warwick Huxley Lt ded 19-10-18 RGA 92SB p262 CR Bucks69
De BUSSY,Walter 2Lt kia 14-10-16 6Y&L att82RFC p265 CR Belgium157,DeBUSSEY 14-10-18 RAF
DeCANDOLE,Alec Corry Vully Lt kia 3-9-18 4Wilts attMGC p187&236,4-9-18 CR France95
De CANN,Harold John T2Lt kia 29-7-16 9 att2Lincs p75 CR France423
De CASTRO,James Vivian Reynell Capt kia 1-10-15 3Suff p78 CR Belgium167
DeCAUX,Harry T2Lt kia 15-10-18 29DLI p160 CR Belgium42
De CAUX,William TCapt kia 15-9-16 9Norf p73 MR21
De CHAZAL,Robert Lt kia 9-4-16 11LNLancs p135 MR38
DECK,Richard Frank T2Lt kia 30-9-15 2Suff p78 CR Belgium115,Richmond
DeCONWAY,John Lt mbk 15-6-17 LovatScouts &RFC p257 MR20
DeCOUNDOUROFF,George 2Lt mbk 25-7-19 SL p256 CR Asia81
DeCOURCY,Henry Joseph.MID 2Lt kia 18-1-17 3Leinst att6RIrReg p174 CR France149
DeDENNIE,Thomas Geoffrey 2Lt kia 4-10-17 4Dev p220 MR30
DEDMAN,William Albert Lt ded 4-2-18 1/8WYorks p219 CR France200
DEEDES,Arthur Gordon Rev ded 29-11-16 RAChDept p199 CR Surrey160
DEEDES,Herbert Philip TCapt kia 16-7-16 16KRRC p149 MR21
DEEKS,Edward Charles Lt ded 4-8-19 RFA 31DAC p261 MR65,3DAC
DEEKS,Frederick William 2Lt dow 13-9-15 RH&FA 69Bty28Div 31Bde p27 CR France40
DEEMING,Frank Tetlow TLtACapt kia 21-3-18 12NumbF p60 MR27
De FALLOT,Carl Clare Capt kia 15-6-15 6LNLancs p135 CR Gallipoli3,15-7-15
DeFERRANTI,Basil Ziani.MC.Maj dow 12-7-17 RGA 21SB CR France64
DeFONTAINE,Edward Harold Lt dow 17-11-15 19Lond p250 CR France1
DeFRECE,Cyril T2Lt kld 10-8-16 RFC p2 CR Mddx41
De FREYNE,Arthur Reginald French.Lord.Capt kia 9-5-15 3 att1SWBord p99 CR France924
DEFIES,Frederick.MID Lt kia 6-4-18 5 attMddx p146 MR37
DeGEX,Francis John.CB.CMG BrigGen ded 2-4-17 Staff BaseCommdt Rouen p1 CR France145
DeGUNZBERG,Baron Alexis George 2Lt kia 6-11-14 11Huss attRHGds p22 CR Belgium134,RHG att11Huss
DEHN,Thomas George Rudolph 2Lt dow 19-4-17 3Wilts attBerks p152 CR Lancs30
De HOUGHTON,Vere Capt kia 11/13-10-15 Lincs p75 MR19
DEIGHTON,Bartholomew James LtTCapt kia 25-9-15 1Mddx p146 MR19
DEIGHTON,Frederick Hamilton Lt dow 18-6-15 1KOSB p101 CR Europe1
DEIGHTON,Gerald William.MC.MID Capt kia 3-7-16 7Suff p78 MR21
DEIGHTON,John Capt dow 20-9-16 RAMC att1/5RLancs p195 CR France833,19-9-16
DeJASTRZEBSKI,Hubert Stephen Slepowron 2Lt dow 5-4-17 24Lond p252 CR France164
DeKNOOP,John Julius Jersey Capt kia 7-8-16 1/1ChesYeo att61ImpCamelCps p203 CR Egypt2

DeLaBERE,Charles Edward 2LtACapt&Adjt kia 10-9-18 66RGA p39 CR France433
DeLaBERE,Cyril John Baghot TLt kia 18-8-16 10Glouc p106
De LACEY,John Matthew 2Lt kia 23-9-17 18WYorks &57RFC p7&p81 CR Belgium140
DeLACOUR,Herbert Hedges Hyde Lt dow 3-12-19 RNDevYeo p269 CR Surrey37
De LACY-WHITE,Cyril T2Lt ded 27-6-18 13WelshR p126 CR France145,Capt
De La FONTAINE,Henry Victor Mottet.DSO.MajTLtCol kia 5-8-17 9ESurr p112 CR Belgium15,dow
DeLaHAYE,Cyril T2Lt dow 23-5-18 RE N SpecCo p44 CR France41
DELAHUNT,Peter Godfrey 2Lt dow 28-8-18 4 att1/7BlkW p230 CR France14
DELAINE,Frederick John TCapt ded 21-3-18 RAVC att119RFA p198 CR Canada1691
DeLALOUBERE,John Louis Claude Alfred Lt ded 24-9-17 RDC p253 CR Camb16
DELAMAIN,Frank Gun 2Lt kia 21-9-16 104RFA p27 CR France453
DELAMAIN,Henry Cresswell 2Lt ded 17-4-15 3Dors p124 CR Hamps28
DELAMERE,Percy Herbert TCapt ded 23-2-18 RAMC p195 CR Hamps7
DELAMOTTE,Hubert Thomas.MC.MID Capt dow 30-10-18 IA 29Punjabis CR Surrey160
DeLANDRE-GROGAN,Leon Victor St.Patrick.MC.TLt kia 13-10-18 Y&L p158 MR32
DELANEY,James Alfred Leo T2Lt kia 10-6-17 7RLancs attTMB p58 CR Belgium102
DELANEY,Michael Capt 29-3-19 16GpHQ RAF &Yorks CR Yorks557
DELAP,John Follansbee Bredin 2Lt kia 18-10-16 1Yorks p90 CR France744
DeLaPASTURE,Charles Edward Capt kia 29-10-14 1ScotsGds p52 MR29
DELARUE,Francis T2Lt dow 23-7-18 10ScotRif p103 MR18
DeLaRUE,Thomas Capt ded 28-7-17 RLancs p58 CR Lancs77
DELAVOYE,F.B.Capt 11-8-16 RASC CR Surrey158
DELEPINE,Helenus George Sheridan 2Lt kia 17-4-15 1DCLI p114 CR Belgium165
DeLISLE,Alexander Charles Nicholas March Phillipps TLt kia 20-11-17 GL 9Leic &21RFC p7 CR Belgium16
DeLISLE,Richard de Beauvoir 2Lt mbk 21-1-16 IA 97Inf p275 MR38
DeLISLE-SMITH,Frank Lt ded 31-10-18 RH&FA p27
DeLUSIGNAN,Raymond Lt kia 25-4-15 RDubF p176 CR Gallipoli15,26-4-15
DELL,Louis Michael T2Lt kia 14-7-16 7KSLI p144 MR21
DELL,Reginald TLt dow PoW 8-5-18 20MGC Inf p182 CR France928
DELL,Stephen Arthur Hayton 2Lt dow 5-10-17 RGA 15SB p39 CR France446
DELLER,Harold James 2Lt kia 30-7-17 104RFA p27 CR Belgium29
DELLOW,Richard 2Lt ded 8-7-19 19NumbF p262 CR Durham8
DELMAR-WILLIAMSON,George Frederick Lt kld 12-7-18 1/2BlkW &RAF p128 CR Glouc31
DELMEGE,Eyre Bolton Massy.MC.MID Capt kia 23-10-16 2ELancs p110 CR France307,dow
DELMEGE,James O'Grady 2LtTLt ded 27-5-15 4DragGds p21 CR France285,dow
DeMATTOS,Gerald Comber Capt dow 11-8-19 9ELancs p254 MR70 &CR Europe179,Maj
DE MAYO,J. ? RE PMR attROD CR Egypt2
DEMETRIADI,L.P.LtCol 26-10-18 RAMC CR Yorks645
DeMEZA,Jacob.MC.MID Capt kia 22-8-18 19Lond p250 CR France210,Jack 23-8-18
DeMOUBRAY,Leslie St.John Capt ded 6-9-19 5RBerks p254&265 CR Kent230,Leslye
DEMPSTER,David Burns.MC.LtACapt kia 26-10-17 3KOSB att2BordR p101 MR30
DEMPSTER,Francis Erskine 2Lt kia 23-7-16 3 att1CamH p167 MR21
DEMPSTER,George Henry Capt kia 20-12-14 IA 35Sikhs att1/9Inf p276 MR28
DEMPSTER,Ian MacKay 2Lt kia 24-2-18 52RFC p15 CR France1266,25-2-18
DEMPSTER,James Lionel Cathcart.MID Lt dow 24-11-15 IA 66Punjabis p76 MR38
DENBY,Isaac Cecil 2Lt kia 27-6-17 6 att1/4WRid p227 CR France258
DENDRINO,Stephen 2Lt ded 27-9-16 RFC p2 CR France1185
DENDY,Ralph.MC.TCapt kia 15-10-18 RASC HT att2SWBord p192 CR Belgium157
DeNEUFVILLE,Eustace Charles.DSO.Maj mbk 21-3-18 RGA 262SB p256 MR20
DENHAM,Aubrey Crawshaw Lt ded 1-4-15 6Beds att10Bn p85 CR Yorks643
DENHAM,Francis Bardon Lt kia 7-7-16 5 att1Worc p108 MR21
DENHAM,George Parsons TCapt dow 14-4-17 10A&SH A'Coy p173 CR France40
DENHAM,Reginald Grainger Lt kia 30-5-18 Wilts att11TMB p152 CR France1689
DENHAM,W.A.Lt 27-5-18 RFA att50DAC MR19
DENHAM,Wm.Malcolm 2Lt kld 3-1-18 RFC p15 CR Beds23
DENHAM-COOKES,Arthur Brownlow Capt ded 5-11-18 24Lond CR Essex176
DENHOLM,Thomas Stobie T2Lt dow 5-4-18 PoW 7CamH p167 CR France1276
DENIS-MARKLEW,Leslie Ernest 2Lt dow 12-10-17 7Lincs p75 MR30
DENISON,Archibald Campbell.MID Capt kia 25-9-15 2BlkW p128 MR19
DENISON,Bertram Noel Capt dow 15-9-14 2YLI p143 CR France717

DENISON,Gerald Evelyn Henry T2Lt kia 25-9-15 12RB p178 CR France768
DENISON,Harry.DSO.Maj dow 28-8-17 RHA p27 CR Belgium16
DENISON,John William.MC.Lt kia 18-9-18 6WRid p227 CR France415
DENISON,Robert Charles TCapt kia 27-8-16 8RWar p214 CR France383
DENISON,William Frank Evelyn T2Lt dow 22/28-3-18 15N&D p133 CR France300,26-3-18
DENLEY,Herbert Owen T2Lt kia 30-3-18 1Worc attCamelCps p27 MR34
DENMAN,Frank Christopher 2Lt kia 17-8-17 84/11RFA p27 CR Belgium13
DENMAN,Percy Darrell 2Lt kia 1-7-16 2Yorks p90 CR France630
DENMAN,Richard Charles Lt kia 1-12-17 4GrenGds p49 CR France662,2-12-17
DENMAN-JUBB,Cyril Oswald Capt kia 24-8-14 2WRid p115 CR Belgium201
DENNE,Vincent Alured T2Lt ded 5-1-17 10 att7RLancs p58 CR France169
DENNE,William Henry.DSO.Maj dow 21-2-17 Beds p85 CR Glouc51
DENNEHY,W.C.Capt ded 22-7-17 IA IndPostalDept p276 CR Iraq6
DENNES,Wilfred.MC.TCaptAMaj kia 21-3-18 82RFA p27 MR27
DENNETT,Stephen Hepworth T2Lt kld 11-5-17 8KSLI &23RFC p7&p144 CR Egypt1
DENNETT,Thomas,Frank Preston Thwaites 2Lt dow 5-8-17 4RWSurr att52RFC p18&p212 CR Belgium24,4-8-17
DENNETT,William Charles 2Lt kia 27-3-18 3RFC p15 MR20
DENNING,John Edward Newdigate Poyntry 2LtACapt dow 26-10-16 1Lincs p75 CR France833,Poyntz
DENNIS,Albert Claude.MID TCapt dow 27-7-16 7RWKent att12Mddx p146 CR France145
DENNIS,Charles Cowley 2Lt kia 25-9-18 1/19Lond attRFC p18&p250 CR France120
DENNIS,Edward 2Lt kia 22-3-18 7N&D attRFC p18&p233 MR20
DENNIS,Frederick Claude T2Lt kia 1-8-16 17N&D p133 CR France765
DENNIS,George Stanley Lt ded 1-7-19 11DLI p265 CR Germany1
DENNIS,James Owen Cuninghame Lt kia 24-10-14 12/35RFA p27 MR29
DENNIS,John Edmund William Lt kia 23-8-14 DCLI p114 MR15,Edward
DENNIS,John Neville.MC.TLt dow 15-10-17 11NStaffs att41MGC p157&p182 CR France139
DENNIS,L.V.TLt kia 31-7-18 SL attRAF p201
DENNIS,Michael Frederick Beauchamp.DSO.MajTLtCol kia 19-5-18 7/8KOSB p101 CR France68
DENNIS,Richard Thomas T2Lt ded 19-12-18 17RIrRif p169 CR France34
DENNIS,W.Lt 7-2-16 EAfrIntelDept CR EAfrica56
DENNISON,Harry Glanville 2Lt ded 24-2-19 RGA p254&p262 CR Mddx77
DENNISON,James 2Lt kia 9-9-18 RGA 101SB p39 CR France298
DENNISON,Ralph Edward McKie 2Lt kia 9-5-15 5RSuss p228 MR22
DENNISS,Charles Sherwood LtCol 8-12-17 RE CR War6
DENNISS,Kenneth George T2Lt kia 15-7-16 16KRRC p149 MR21
DENNISS,Thomas Vivian Bartley.MID Capt dow 28-8-18 RBerks p139 CR Mddx83,LtCol
DENNISTON,Jack Evelyn T2Lt dow 20-9-16 10 att1BlkW p128 CR France453,21-9-16
DENNISTOUN,James Robert Lt dow PoW 9-8-16 NIrHorse &RFC p2&p24 CR Germany3
DENNY,Barry Maynard Rynd 2Lt dow 26-10-14 Lpool p71
DENNY,Ernest 2Lt dow 4-8-17 15Lond att17KRRC p249 CR Belgium16
DENNY,James T2Lt kia 23-10-18 1RIrFus p171 CR Belgium140
DENNY,Leonard George 2Lt ded 21-4-17 133RFA p27 CR Mddx26,dow
DENNY,Leon Serena Capt kia 13-5-15 1DragGds RoO att5DragGds p21 MR29
DENNY,Thomas David William.MM.2Lt ded 6-3-19 3Glouc p264 CR Kent234,Lt
DENNYS,Cecil Hector Massy Capt kia 9-2-17 IA 4GurkhaRif p276 MR65,25-4-20
DENNYS,Edward Massy Capt kia 9-2-17 IA 2/4GurkhaRif p276 CR Iraq5
DENNYS,Kenneth Rose 2Lt kia 9-5-15 RMunstF p174 CR France924
DENNYS,Richard Molesworth TCapt dow 24-7-16 10LNLancs A'Coy p135 CR France145,Molesworth
DENOVAN,Allan McNab 2Lt kia 26-3-18 1RFC p15 MR20,Macnab
DENROCHE-SMITH,Archibald John Lt kia 13-9-14 18Huss p23 MR15
DENSHAM,Walter Henry.MC.Lt dow 5-4-18 ELancsRFA p207 CR France62
DENT,Arthur Evelyn.MID LtACapt kia 9-4-17 1 att9KRRC p149 CR France581
DENT,Cornelius Costall 2Lt kia 20-5-16 10HLI p162 CR France423,21-5-16
DENT,Edgar Dent Capt kia 12-4-18 2IrGds p52 CR France346
DENT,Joseph Leslie.DSO.MC.Capt&BtMaj kia 11-4-17 2SStaffs p122 CR France182
DENT,Reginald Teesdale 2Lt kia 24-3-18 6 att2RB p178 MR27
DENT,Wilfred Harry TMaj kia 27-9-15 10Yorks p90 CR France924,26-9-15
DENTON,Arthur Capt kia 16-8-15 5Ess p232 MR4
DENTON,Arthur 2Lt kia 16-6-17 20 att2Lond p251 MR20
DENTON,Brian Maurice TLt kia 19-8-16 6SomLI p79 CR France402

DENTON,George Clarke.MIDx3 Maj kia 9-10-16 IA 12Pnrs attJindInf p276 CR EAfrica36
DENTON,Philip Sydney 2Lt kia 13-8-17 A&SH att10CamH p173 MR21
DENTON,Reginald 2Lt 30-1-19 9Lpool CR Ches175
DENTON-CARDEW,Warnell de Montigny T2Lt kia 30-11-17 KRRC att12Bn p150 MR17
DENWOOD,Thomas William 2Lt ded 22-10-18 3RLancs att2/6Suss p58 MR67,2/6Lancs
DENYER,Augustus Andrew.MC.T2Lt kia 7-6-17 9Y&L p158 MR21
DENYER,Horace Frederick.MID TLt kia 13-7-17 12Ches p96 CR Greece6
De PARAVICINI,John Marcus Maj kia 30-11-17 KRRC att11Bn p150 MR17
De PASS,Crispin Asabel 2Lt kia 22-3-18 2TankCps p188 MR27,Asahel
De PASS,Frank Alexander.VC.Lt kia 25-11-14 IA 34 PoonaHorse p276 CR France80
DePASS,William Hugh David Lt kia 25-3-18 6 att13Mddx p146 CR France692
DePENNINGTON,Alan Lt kia 4-9-17 4ELancs p226 CR Belgium113
DEPENTHENEY-O'KELLY,Henry Arundel Capt dow 19-5-15 18Huss RoO p23
DePENTHENY-O'KELLY,Edmund Capt ded 14-2-19 LancF p263 CR Lond9
De PIERRES,Eric Noel 2Lt dow 16-9-17 C190RFA p27 CR Belgium15
De PLEDGE,Edward Karl TCapt kia 3-6-16 15WYorks p81 CR France5
De POMEROY,Norman 2Lt kia 20-10-16 GL &RFC CR France647
DEPREZ,Austin Edward Capt kia 12-11-15 C62RFA p27 CR France423
DEPUIS,Alfred 2Lt dow 8-8-16 1Lincs p75
DERBYSHIRE,Albert 2Lt kia 30-4-17 9Ess p131 MR20
D'ERF Wheeler,Geoffrey Noel Popham 2Lt kia 26-9-16 7 att5Dors p124 MR21
D'ERF Wheeler,Percival Francis Crommelin Capt kld 24-7-17 3Dors &RFC p7&p124
DERING,Rupert Cholmeley Yea Capt dow 19-4-15 2KOSB p101 CR Belgium151
De RITTER,Victor Frank T2Lt dow 9-8-16 1SomLI p79 CR Belgium11,kia
DeROCHIE,Curtis Matthew 2Lt kia 14-7-17 27RFC p7 CR Belgium175
DeROSS,Adam Gower Sutherland T2Lt kia 14-2-17 GL &3RFC p7 MR20
DeROSSE,Joseph Albert.MC.Lt ded 2-12-18 IARO att2S&M p276 CR Egypt9,Capt
DeROTHSCHILD,Evelyn Achille.MID Maj dow 17-11-17 BucksYeo p203 CR Palestine14
DeROUGEMONT,Maurice Henry 2Lt kia 16-5-15 2RWSurr p55 CR France279,dow
DERRICK,Alan James 2Lt kia 15-11-16 7NumbF p214 MR21
DERRICK,John Leslie TCapt kia 27-8-17 6Yorks p90 MR30
DERRICK,Leslie James 2Lt kld 3-5-18 3EKent att15RAF p57 CR France116
DERRIMAN,Gerard Lysley Capt dow 7-8-15 4GrenGds RoO p49 CR France1
DERRY,Daniel 2Lt ded 18-4-18 5NStaffs p238 CR Belgium18
DERRY,Douglas Alfred Laurie TLt dow 9-10-16 2Y&L p158 CR France374
DERRY,Richard Courtnay Powell T2Lt kia 6-8-15 2Hamps p120 CR Gallipoli6,Lt
DeRUTZEN,Alan Frederick James Lt kia 7-8-16 1/1Pembroke Yeo att61ImpCamelCps p205 CR Egypt2
DERWENT,Robert Ivor T2Lt kia 1-7-16 18WYorks p81 CR France156
DESAGES,Owen Loftus 2Lt kia 27-5-18 Wilts p152 MR18
DESAGES,Wilfrid Roland Capt kia 21-3-18 24Lond p252 MR20,Wilfred
DESAI,F.C.Capt 7-11-17 IMS MR43
DeSALIS,George Roldolph 2Lt kia 21-6-17 8Mddx p236 CR France594
DeSALIS,Jerome Joseph Fane 2Lt dow 3-10-15 8Mddx p236 CR Mddx62,Lt 3Bn
DeSALIS,Peter Fabin Fane 2Lt kia 22-1-17 3 att2SfthH p164 CR France511
DeSATGE,Frederick Gordon Capt kia 15-9-16 1 att7KRRC p150 MR21
DeSAUMAREZ-BROCK,Ranulf Steinthal TLt kia 24-5-17 RFA Y23TMB p27 CR Belgium6
DESBOROUGH,Laurence Vernon Lt kia 30-11-17 RFA att15RFC p18&207 MR20
De SEGUNDO,Robert Charles Edward Stewart 2Lt kia 17-2-17 1Lpool p71 CR France239
DESLANDES,Denis George T2Lt kia 27-11-16 7ESurr p112 CR France175
DESPARD,Charles Beauclerk.DSO.MC.TCapt kia 18-4-18 InniskDrags att9RIrFus p171 MR30
DESPARD,Ernest Richard T2Lt dow 26-9-17 ETankCps p188 CR Belgium16
DESPARD,Marcus Carden 2Lt kia 19-7-17 3InniskF p104 CR Belgium85,1Bn
DESPICHT,Leonard Terry.MC.MID Lt&Adjt kia 11-2-17 4Beds p85 CR France220
DESPREZ,Warwick Haynes T2Lt kia 24-8-18 3Glouc att7RWKent p141 CR France177
DeSTACPOOLE,Robert Andrew 2Lt kia 20-9-14 2ConnRgrs p172 MR15
DeSTACPOOLE,Roderick Algernon Antony.MID 2Lt kia 11-3-15 RFA 1Bty p27 CR France705,Anthony
De St CROIX,Aubrey.MIDx2 Capt kia 3-2-17 IA 2/119Inf p276 MR38
De Ste CROIX,Wilfred Hungerford T2Lt ded 24-7-17 RASC p192 CR Iraq8
DeSt.PAER,Louis Emile.MC.Maj dow 8-5-18 B246RFA p206 CR Belgium8

DES-VOEUX,Frederick William Lt kia 14-9-14 2GrenGds p49 CR France1112
DES VOEUX,Harold Charles 2Lt dow 11-6-15 IAUL attRMunstF p276 CR Gallipoli1,Lt
DES VOEUX,Seymour Capt dow 1-2-17 IA 36Sikhs p276 CR Iraq5
DeTEISSIER,Aubrey T2Lt kld 12-10-17 GL &RFC p7 CR Essex45,2-10-17
DeTRAFFORD,Henry Joseph Capt kia 25-9-15 3 att 1SStaffs p122 MR19
De TRAFFORD,Ralph Edric Galfrid Antony Lt kia 25-4-15 2RFus p67 MR4,Eric Galrid
DeTRAFFORD,Reginald Francis Lt dow 9-5-15 3RLancs attGlouc p58 CR France727
De TRAFFORD,Thomas Cecil Capt kia 10-11-14 RFus p67 MR29
De TUYLL,Maurice Arthur Capt kia 13-5-15 10Huss p22 CR Belgium45
DEUCHAR,Alic Guthrie Capt kld 22-11-17 NCycBn attRFC p269 CR Numb4
DEUCHAR,Robert 2Lt ded 27-5-16 3/2ScotHorse p269 CR Numb75
DEVAS,Arthur Edward Lt ded 15-2-15 Ess p131 CR Somerest139,1-2-15
DEVAS,Bertrand Ward TLt kia 13-11-16 2Suff p78 CR France801
DEVENISH,Arthur Henry Noel Maj ded 5-10-16 RFA p27 CR Surrey160
DEVENISH,Donald Henry TLt ded 17-1-16 14WelshR p126 CR France80,17-1-15
DEVENISH,George Weston Lt kia 6-6-17 RFA &35RFC p7&p27 MR20
DEVERELL,Richard Seddon T2Lt ded 4-11-16 14 att15WYorks p81 CR Lond2
DEVEREUX,Frederick Herbert T2Lt kia 31-7-17 23Mddx p146 MR29
DEVEREUX,Humphrey William Lt kia 26-6-16 5SStaffs p229 CR France747
DeVILLE,Charles Arthur 2Lt kia 20-7-18 2/5WYorks p218 CR France622
DeVINE,Hatton Bertram St.John Rev kia 27-4-18 RAChDept att 10GordH p199 CR France423
DeVINE,Henry 2Lt ded 17-2-19 10RIrF p265 CR Ireland14,RIrRif
DEVINE,John Ross.MC.Lt kia 26-8-17 15RScots p54 MR21
DEVIS,Francis 2Lt kia 11-4-17 4 att2RWar p64 CR France604
DEVITT,Guy Francis Ormond T2Lt kia 30-7-15 7RB p178 MR29,Ormand
DEVITT,Herbert John 2Lt kia 12-9-18 16 att13KRRC p150 CR France245
DEVLIN,Henry Little Lt kia 19-9-17 5A&SH att9RFC p18&243,Harry CR Belgium18
DEVONSHIRE,Feray Vullramy Lt 20-7-19 7Huss &RAF MR43
DeVRIES,Harry Kumbring 2Lt kia 20-11-17 3 att5RBerks p139 MR17
DEW,Albert William John 2Lt kia 10-4-17 7 att26NumbF p214 MR20
DEW,Frederick Thomas T2Lt kia 24-8-17 10DLI A'Coy p160 MR30
DeWAEL,Cecil Hubert Lt dow 6-4-18 LondRFA p207 CR France64
DEWAR,Alan Douglas 2Lt ded 22-6-19 RE p262 CR Lond14
DEWAR,Alexander.MID Lt dow 21-12-14 RE 15FC p44 CR France768
DEWAR,David(Sonnie).MID TLt kia 22-3-18 14MGC Inf p182 CR France1061
DEWAR,George TLt kia 3-2-16 RAMC att48FA p195 CR France747
DEWAR,Harold Ernest.MC.T2Lt dow 12-7-16 11Ches p96&258 CR France833,11-7-16
DEWAR,Ian Dalrymple TCapt kia 16-3-16 5CamH p167 CR Belgium53,17-3-16
DEWAR,James Evan 2Lt kia 8-10-16 5Lond p246 MR21
DEWAR,James Melville TLt kia 16-10-18 1/7BlkW p128 CR France760
DEWAR,James Tyrie T2Lt kia 14-2-17 13RIrRif p169 CR Belgium43
DEWAR,Margaret Smith SNurse kia 12-3-17 QAIMNS p200 CR Greece9
DEWAR,Robert Lt kia 18-11-16 17HLI p162 CR France534
DEWAR,Robert Johnman.DCM.2Lt dow 3-10-18 153RFA p27 CR Belgium44,5-10-18
DEWAR,William Capt kia 22-3-18 9ScotRif p103 MR27
DEWARBURG,Hermann Vivian T2Lt kia 7-10-16 122MGC p182 CR France744
DEWDNEY,Clifford Mostyn French Capt kia 4-4-18 14Glouc att7RWKent p106 MR27
DEWE,William Horsley LtCol ded 31-3-18 RDC p253 CR Sussex 128
DeWEND,Douglas Fenton Lt kia 11-11-14 2WRid p115 MR29
DEWES,Bryan Osmond T2Lt kia 30-7-15 1Mddx p146 CR France707
DEWHIRST,Alfred Guy T2Lt kld 10-8-18 RASC MechTransport p192 CR France145
DEWHURST,George Charnley Littleton TLt kia 1-7-16 1RB p178 CR France1890
DEWHURST,Joseph Mullineaux Lt dow 7-11-17 1/4ELancs p226 CR France1361
DEWHURST,Robert William Millington.MID TLt dow 26-4-16 5Wilts p153 CR Iraq5
DeWIND,Edmund.VC.2Lt kia 21-3-18 15RIrRif p169 MR27
DEWING,Robert Edward.DSO.CaptALtCol kia 4-4-18 RE att8RBerks p44 MR27
DeWINTON,Walter Frederick 2Lt kia 6-9-14 3CldGds p51 CR France1402 &CR France1895
DeWOLF,George Le Blanch TLt kia 14-2-16 3 att9RSuss p118 CR Belgium72
DEXTER,E.I.Lt ded 4-5-18 9NumbF attRAF p60
DEY,Herman Francis 2Lt kia 31-7-17 5Lpool p215 MR29

DIACK,William 2Lt kia 20-9-17 4GordH C'Coy p213&242 MR30
DIAMOND,Julius.MC.Lt kia 8-10-17 KOSB &7RFC p7&p101 MR20
DIBB,William Reginald.MC.Lt dow 27-5-18 RFA X37TMB p27 CR France745
DIBBEN,Harold William 2Lt kia 30-9-17 4KSLI p235 CR France1182
DIBBS,Thomas Graythwaite Burton T2Lt kia 27-8-15 7Y&L p158 CR Belgium111
DICK,Alexander Young T2Lt dow 1-10-16 13 att15HLI p162 CR France134
DICK,Andrew Campbell T2Lt dow 23-10-18 2KRRC p150 CR France146,24-10-18
DICK,Andrew Robertson T2Lt kia 18-7-18 1BordR p117 MR32
DICK,Arthur James Seaber Lt kia 22-3-18 1RInnskF p104 MR27
DICK,Charles William Lt ded 9-11-18 RAF CR Scot237
DICK,George Frederick Graeme 2Lt kia 9-5-15 N&D p133 CR France566
DICK,James.MM.2Lt dow 28-10-17 9DLI p239 CR Belgium18
DICK,John Campbell Capt kia 9-5-15 RMunstF p175 MR22
DICK,John Young Farquhar T2Lt dow 14-11-16 HLI p162 CR France1492
DICK,Norman Brabazon 2Lt kia 28-4-17 6 att17Mddx p146 MR20
DICK,Robert Henry.MIDx3 Lt 15-3-21 4RFus CR Iraq6
DICK,Thomas Aitken Maj ded 27-1-19 RFA p254 CR Surrey1
DICK,Watson Tullock.MC.Capt&Adjt kia 18-9-18 7SWBord p99 CR Greece5
DICK,William LtCol 12-11-17 RAMC CR Mddx53
DICKASON,Reginald Percy 2Lt kia 14-2-17 6 att1Mddx p146 CR France511
DICKENS,Cedric Charles Maj kia 10-9-16 13Lond p249 MR21 &CR France218,9-9-16
DICKENS,Guy TCapt dow 17-7-16 13KRRC p150 CR France300,DICKINS
DICKENS,Maurice Wilfred Lt kia 27-2-18 25RFC p15 CR France40
DICKENS,William Castle.MID T2Lt kia 13-10-18 1 att10LancF p92 CR France315
DICKENSON,Aubrey Greville Newton TLt dow 1-7-16 2KRRC p150 CR France80,2Lt
DICKENSON,Lawrence Aubrey Fiennes Wingfield Lt dow 10-5-15 4Beds attRIrRif p85 CR France345
DICKERSON,Charles Henry T2Lt kia 14-7-16 11A&SH p173 MR19
DICKERSON,Jersey Horrex T2Lt kia 22-4-18 15N&D p133 MR27
DICKETTS,George Humphrey Lt dow 21-7-18 3/24RFA p27 CR France11,111/24RFA
DICKEY,Robert George Alexander Capt ded 14-11-18 5Manch C'Coy p236 CR Lancs210
DICKIE,Cecil Barron Lt kia 18-7-18 BlkW &107RAF p264 MR20
DICKIE,Edward Gordon TLt kia 30-11-17 GL &84 att54RFC p7 CR France1472,2Lt
DICKIE,Herbert 2Lt kia 2-10-16 8SLancs p125 CR France535,21-10-16 3Bn
DICKIE,Robert Bruce 2Lt kia 1-6-18 7 att1GordH p242 CR France33
DICKIE,William 2Lt kia 1-7-16 6BordR att9KOSB p117 MR21
DICKIN,Albert Edward T2Lt kia 21-10-16 13Ches p96 CR France314
DICKINS,Albert Light Moody.MC.Capt kia 21-3-18 7N&D p233 MR20
DICKINS,G. see DICKENS,G.
DICKINS,Wyndham Harold TCapt dow 28-9-15 12N&D p133 CR France51,Maj
DICKINSON,Alan Piele.MC.Capt dow 1-6-18 10Lpool p216 CR France106,Peile kia
DICKINSON,Arthur Frowde TLt kia 22-3-18 14NumbF p60 MR27
DICKINSON,Arthur Thomas Searle.MIDx3 Maj kia 24-11-15 IA 51Sikhs attHQ Staff30Bde p276 MR38,22-11-15
DICKINSON,Bruce Norman T2Lt kia 29-6-16 10RWKent p141 CR Belgium30
DICKINSON,Colin James Henry T2Lt kia 28-7-16 15Ches p96 CR France453
DICKINSON,Digby Cecil Cales 2Lt kia 18-8-18 2SWBord p99 CR France28
DICKINSON,Edward Capt kia 28-6-15 11Yorks p90 MR4
DICKINSON,Francis Arthur Maj dow 11-4-15 DCLI p114 CR Somerset118
DICKINSON,Francis John Twysden LtTCapt kia 17-9-18 2att7SWBord p99 CR Greece5
DICKINSON,Frederick William 2Lt kia 17-3-18 7Leic p87 MR21
DICKINSON,Geoffrey Garbutt 2Lt kia 2-10-17 B255RFA p208 CR Belgium10
DICKINSON,George Bairnsfather Lt kia 3-5-15 3ELancs p110 MR29
DICKINSON,George Sidney TCapt kia 2-7-16 7Lincs p75 CR France630
DICKINSON,Harry Chap4Cl kia 30-10-17 RAChDept att1/28Lond p199 CR Belgium123
DICKINSON,Henry Waite Lt dow 9-8-18 PoW 12/13NumbF p60 CR Germany3
DICKINSON,Herbert.MC.LtACapt kia 27-5-18 10Glouc att2Mddx p106 MR18
DICKINSON,Hubert John 2Lt kia 20-9-16 2Lincs p75 CR France452
DICKINSON,Hugh Carey CaptTLtCol ded 18-12-18 1SomLI att2/3KAR p202&79 CR EAfrica36,att3/3KAR
DICKINSON,Humphrey Neville 2Lt dow 13-10-16 3 att6RWKent p141 CR France145
DICKINSON,John.MC.Lt kia 9-4-17 72RFA p207 CR France68,8-4-17
DICKINSON,John 2Lt kia 28-8-17 3RScots p54 CR Belgium88

DICKINSON,John Archibald Lt kia 13-4-18 4 att1RWSurr p212 MR32
DICKINSON,John Malcolm Lt dow 12-6-18 2RSuss CR France10 see DICKISON,J.M.
DICKINSON,Leonard T2Lt kia 11-4-18 12Y&L p158 MR32
DICKINSON,Leslie Alfred T2Lt dow 17-11-17 1Norf p73 CR Herts30
DICKINSON,Lewis George 2Lt kia 1-10-15 6N&D C'Coy p233 CR Belgium131,30-9-15
DICKINSON,Lionel St.Clair 2Lt kia 16-9-16 1Lond p245 CR France785
DICKINSON,Raymond Scott 2LtTCapt kia 2-10-15 16Lond p249 CR Belgium44
DICKINSON,Ronald Francis Bickersteth.MID Capt kia 16-6-15 10Lpool p216 MR29
DICKINSON,Talbot.MC.Lt kia 31-7-17 8LancF p221 MR29,2/5Bn
DICKINSON,Thomas Arthur 2Lt kia 1-7-16 1/6SStaffs p229 MR21
DICKINSON,Thomas Malcolm.DFC.Capt ded 4-1-21 IA 16Cav attRFC p276 CR Egypt15
DICKINSON,Walter Stanley T2Lt kia 23-4-17 8Lincs p75 MR20
DICKINSON,William 2Lt kia 29-3-17 5LancF p221
DICKINSON,William Henry Egerton de Brissac Maj dow 19-10-18 113/25RFA p206 CR France725,29-10-18
DICKINSON,William Vicris.CMG.Col ded 28-10-17 Staff AAG GHQ3Ech p1 CR France145 lateWelchR
DICKISON,John Malcolm Lt dow 12-6-18 2RSuss p118 CR France10,DICKINSON,J.M.
DICKS,Francis James Neville 2Lt dow 27-5-18 2/8Worc p226 CR France31
DICKSEE,Lawrence Rowland Arthur 2Lt kldacc 2-5-16 3N&D D'Coy p133 CR Durham27,9-5-16
DICKSEE,Maurice John Lt kia 14-9-18 9Mddx att10RFus p236 CR France245
DICKSEE,Reginald Frank 2Lt kia 8-10-18 6N&D p233 CR France849
DICKSON,Alan James Lt kia 14-11-14 HLI p162 MR29
DICKSON,Angus Lt kld 15-10-16 1/5RLancs p213 CR Belgium4,14-10-16
DICKSON,Arthur TLtCol kia 1-7-16 1SLancs att10WYorks p125 CR France373
DICKSON,Arthur Francis Lt kia 14-7-18 IARO att34PoonaHorse p276 CR Palestine3
DICKSON,Arthur Herbert 2Lt ded 13-10-15 LNLancs p135 CR Lancs52,7-10-15
DICKSON,Ashley Gordon.MID Maj dow 18-6-17 RHA attC123RFA p206 CR France
DICKSON,Barrington Blomfield Capt kia 9-5-15 1Nhampt p137 MR22
DICKSON,Cyril Garlies Lt kia 4-11-14 2LNLancs p135 MR47
DICKSON,Edward John Quayle.MC.TCapt kia 26-10-17 RE 255TC 1stCps p44 CR Belgium11
DICKSON,Edwyn David Lt kia 28-4-17 10Lincs p75 MR20
DICKSON,George Lt kia 12-7-15 7HLI p240 MR4
DICKSON,George Arthur Hamilton.MVO.Maj ded 16-2-18 5Worc attLabCps p108 CR Mddx26
DICKSON,George Hubert Murray 2Lt kia 26-10-18 6BlkW p231 CR France1256
DICKSON,Henry Goudie 2Lt dow 5-2-17 IARO att82Punjabis p276 CR Iraq5
DICKSON,Hugh Barclay Lt kia 12-10-17 3 att8BlkW p128 MR30
DICKSON,J.A.Capt 4-4-17 IA CR Cornwall123
DICKSON,James 2Lt kia 16-9-16 21Lond p251 CR France385
DICKSON,John Gavin 2Lt kia 8-3-16 4 att1HLI p162 MR38
DICKSON,John Hamilton 2Lt kia 14-9-14 att1CamH p167 MR15
DICKSON,Mary C.Nurse ded 16-2-17 VAD p200 CR France145
DICKSON,Robert.DCM.ACapt kia 27-5-18 7DLI p239 CR France1753
DICKSON,Robert Adair 2Lt kia 2-8-17 4 att6RIrReg p89 MR29
DICKSON,Robert Cecil Capt ded 16-6-19 RAMC p267&254 MR65
DICKSON,Robert Maxwell T2Lt kia 22-3-18 11Lpool att8RB p71 CR France1061
DICKSON,Sam.MC.ACapt kia 20-10-18 1/5Manch p236 CR France287
DICKSON,Sigurd Ayton 2Lt kia 1-2-17 102RFA p27 CR Belgium72
DICKSON,Thomas Graeme Capt 27-4-20 RAMC CR Derby58
DICKSON,Walter Felix T2Lt kia 1-8-18 11Ess p131 CR Belgium3,dow 31-7-18
DICKSON,Walter Michael T2Lt kia 26-9-15 11A&SH p173 MR19
DICKSON,William Herbert 2Lt kia 7-6-17 2/4LNLancs p234 CR Belgium31
DICKSON,William Tillie Lt dow 9-7-16 6RInniskF p104 CR France167,Capt &CR France1490,Lt
DIETRICHSEN,Frederick Christian Capt kia 26-4-16 2/7N&D p233 CR Ireland5,25-4-16
DIGBY,Charles 2Lt dow 10-7-18 RGA 123SB p39 CR France924
DIGBY,G.H Maj 20-11-14 DorsYeo CR Dorset28
DIGBY,John Kenelm Lt kia 4-8-15 1/7Norf p73 CR Belgium71
DIGBY-JONES,Charles Kenelm TCapt ded 25-9-18 RE p44 MR70 &CR Europe195
DIGGENS,Martin Charles TCapt kia 30-6/1-7-16 13RSuss p118 CR France924
DIGGES La TOUCHE,Averell Lt 25-9-15 5 att2RIrRif MR29
DIGGES La TOUCHE,Denis Capt kia 8-8-15 8WelshR p126 MR4

DIGGLE,Joseph T2Lt kia 23-8-18 2RWelshF p97 CR France41,24-8-18
DIGNAN,Albert Guy Lt kia 21-3-18 SIrHorse att7RIrReg p24 MR27
DIGNAN,Joseph Patrick 2Lt kia 16-10-16 4ConnRgrs att8RinniskF p172 CR Belgium17
DIGNEN,George William 2Lt kia 24-10-18 3 att1NumbF p60 CR France206
DILBEROGLUE,Augustus Lt kia 1-4-18 3Huss p21 CR France485,Lt
DILBEROGLUE,Richard Nicholas Lt kia 15-9-16 1CldGds p51 CR France374
DILL,John Rowe Lt&Adjt kia 6-5-15 IA 69Punjabis p276 CR France924
DILL,Robert Foster.DSO.Capt kia 11-4-15 IA 129Baluchis p276 CR France924
DILLING,John Francis TLt kia 10-8-18 15LancF p92 MR16
DILLIWAY,George Goldin TLtACapt ded 10-10-18 RASC attH'Coy CamelTransCps p192 CR Palestine3,Golden
DILLON,Charles Edward Maxwell 2Lt kia 31-7-17 10RWKent p141 CR Belgium88
DILLON,Edeveain Charles Barclay 2Lt kia 13-10-16 3RDubF p176 CR France374,2Bn
DILLON,George Charles Tracy 2Lt kia 23-7-16 6Glouc p225 MR21,Tracey
DILLON,Harry Chester Wentworth Lt kia 24-11-15 IA 26Punjabis att24 p276 MR38,22-11-15
DILLON,Henry Mountiforort.DSO.Maj ded 13-1-18 2 O&BLI p130 CR Oxford32
DILLWYN-VENABLES-LLEWELYN,John Lister Capt kia 10-7-17 3CldGds p51
DILNUTT,Eric William LtTCapt kia 2-3-16 8RFus p67 MR19
DILWORTH,Maclean Proctor Lt kia 20-10-14 1N&D p133 CR France924,20-11-14
DILWORTH,Robert Kildahl 2Lt kia 28-12-16 2RMunstF p175 MR21
DILWORTH-HARRISON,Douglas Roy 2Lt 27-3-18 10 att1/8DLI MR27
DIMENT,Harry Stanley T2Lt kia 23-5-17 GL &6RFC p7 CR Belgium11
DIMENT,William James Gregory T2Lt kia 26-9-17 8EYorks p84 CR Belgium125
DIMERY,George Wentworth T2Lt ded 4-4-17 15WYorks p81 CR Yorks373
DIMMER,John Henry Stephen.VC.MC.CaptTLtCol kia 21-3-18 KRRC att2/4RBerks p150 CR France725
DIMMOCK,James Bolton 2Lt dow 16-5-17 3RWSurr p55 CR France40,2Bn
DIMOND,Francis Robert 2Lt kia 31-7-17 17Lpool p71 MR29
DIMSDALE,Edward Charles Capt kia 8-5-15 RB p178 MR29
DINAN,Francis Arthur 2Lt kia 31-7-17 113RFA p27 MR29
DINAN,Frederick Charles Capt dow 29-9-17 1Ess p131 CR Belgium18
DINAN,George Albert T2Lt kia 9-9-16 6 att8RDubF p176 MR21
DINEEN,C.H.see DINNEN,C.H.
DINES,Joseph T2Lt kia 27-9-18 13Lpool p71 CR France358
DINES,Percy John Francis T2Lt dow 1-7-16 Dev p76 CR France513
DINGLE,Arthur James TLt kia 22-8-15 6EYorks p84 MR4,Capt
DINGLE,John Lt kia 10-9-16 2NumbF p60 CR Greece3
DINGLEY,Alfred Claude.MIDx3 TCapt kia 19-4-16 7NStaffs p157 MR38
DINGLEY,Norman Oliver TLt dow 5-5-17 6Worc att93MGC p108&182 CR France113,kia
DINGLEY,William T2Lt dow 29-4-17 7Suff p78 CR France113
DINGWALL,J.D.2Lt kld 21-4-18 GL &RAF p190
DINGWALL-FORDYCE,James Lt dow 27-9-15 2A&SH CR France98
DINNEN,Campbell Hackwood Capt kia 4-3-18 Lpool attKAR p71&p200 CR WAfrica28,DINEEN 4-3-15
DINNIS,George Hugh 2Lt kia 28-4-18 16Manch p154 CR Belgium115
DINSDALE,Frank 2Lt kia 1-7-16 12Y&L p158 CR France802
DINSLEY,Francis Hugill 2Lt ded 8-3-19 2CldGds p262 CR Beds29
DINSMORE,M.Edmund TCapt ded 12-11-18 SL RAMC DentalCps p201 CR Ireland196
DINSMORE,John Hastings 2Lt kia 3-5-17 3 att6EKent p57 MR20
DINWIDDIE,James Travers Blount LtTCapt dow 13-9-15 BordR p117 CR Glouc143
DINWIDDY,Conrad Hugh 2LtACapt dow 26-9-17 RGA 13SB p39 CR Belgium11,27-9-17
DINWOODIE,David Wallace 2Lt kia 19-4-17 8ScotRif p225 CR France1495
DIPLOCK,Douglas Gerard 2Lt dow 5-4-18 PoW 30MGC Inf p182 CR France1266
DIPPIE,Harry Peckham 2Lt kia 18-7-16 11GordH p166 CR France402
DIPPLE,Thomas Denis Lt ded 30-11-18 O&BLI BucksBn p231 CR Sussex144
DISNEY,Arthur William T2Lt kia 30-11-17 9RFus p67 MR17
DISNEY,Brabazon Thomas CaptAMaj kia 17-10-17 RGA 166SB p39 CR Belgium19
DITCHFIELD,Samuel Eric 2Lt kia 31-7-17 4 att7/8KOSB p224 MR29
DITMAS,Thomas Owen Bulteel Lt kia 14-1-15 1Dev p76 CR Belgium169
DIX,Cyril Bernard T2Lt kia 9-8-17 8ESurr p112 MR29,10-8-17
DIX,Geoffrey Stewart 2Lt dow 6-5-15 5NStaffs p238 CR France284
DIX,Herbert Golden,MC T2Lt kia 14-2-17 7RWKent p141 CR France314
DIX,Stephen Hamilton.MC.MajTLtCol kia 4-10-17 Leinst Cmdg12/13NumbF p174 CR Belgium125
DIXEY,Edmund Harry T2Lt dow 3-7-16 10Suff p78 CR France66,8Bn

DIXON,Albert Ernest Lucas T2Lt kia 8-5-18 3RSuss att23RFus p118 CR France214
DIXON,Alfred Charles 2Lt kia 4-2-16 19LancF p92 CR France1504
DIXON,Arthur Edward Basil Lt dow 6-6-15 5LNLancs p234 CR Belgium2
DIXON,C.Lt kia 19-9-18 NCycBn &RAF p253
DIXON,Cecil Hargreave TLt kia 28-11-17 GL &9RFC p7 CR Belgium18
DIXON,Charles George Lt kia 9-5-15 RIrReg attRIrRif p89 MR32
DIXON,Charles Howard Lt dow 12-9-17 RFA p27 CR Herts108
DIXON,Charles John(Ian) 2Lt kia 22-6-17 9DLI p239 CR France162
DIXON,Charles Penrose 2Lt dow 25-10-17 GL att9RFC p7 CR Belgium18
DIXON,Charles Ralph Capt dow 5-5-15 Ess p131 MR4
DIXON,Claude Dudley T2Lt dow 28-7-16 10 att6Leic p87 CR France145
DIXON,Clive MacDonnell Maj kia 6-11-14 16Lancers p23 CR Belgium170,5-11-14
DIXON,Cuthbert Stuart T2Lt kia 3-5-17 7ESurr p112 MR20
DIXON,Cyril Burton.MC.TLt dow 12-11-18 2/4Y&L p158 CR France332,14-11-18
DIXON,Cyril Masxfield Lt kia 30-8-15 4Y&L p238 CR Belgium85
DIXON,Ernest 2Lt kia 19-8-16 10RWelshF p97 MR21
DIXON,Ernest Edward 2Lt kia 9-6-17 RGA 168SB p39 CR Belgium4
DIXON,Frederick T2Lt kia 18-9-18 3Worc p108 CR France632
DIXON,Frederick John Cruse T2Lt dow 6-9-16 1BlkW p128 CR France66
DIXON,Frederick William T2Lt kia 9-10-17 5Y&L p158 MR30
DIXON,Geoffrey Francis Lt ded 1-8-18 IARO att72CamelCps p276 MR61
DIXON,George.MID 2Lt kia 20-10-14 2Manch p154 MR22
DIXON,George T2Lt kia 6-8-15 RE 170TC p44 CR France163 Ex CldGds
DIXON,George LtCol ded 24-4-17 RASC p267 CR Lond14
DIXON,H.O.Lt 8-11-18 4EKent CR Kent28
DIXON,Harold George 2Lt kia 4-11-18 3Dors &RAF p124 CR France521,Lt
DIXON,Harry TLt kia 6-10-18 9Yorks p90 CR France234
DIXON,Harry Yorston 2Lt kia 13-7-15 11Y&L att9Manch p158 CR Gallipoli2
DIXON,Henry Edward Otto Murray 2Lt dow 10-4-17 4SfthH p241
DIXON,Henry Eric TCapt kld 19-8-17 GL &62RFC p7 CR Yorks543
DIXON,Henry Oliver 2Lt kia 6-9-17 RGA 32HAG p39 CR Belgium24
DIXON,Henry Philip Norman T2Lt kia 4-9-17 26NumbF p60 MR21
DIXON,Hubert Bradshaw Capt kia 12-3-15 N&D p133 MR22
DIXON,James Capt&Adjt kia 10-3-15 2Mddx p146 CR France706
DIXON,James Alfred TLt kia 10-8-15 6BordR A'Coy p117 CR Gallipoli5,9-8-15
DIXON,James Evelyn Bevan TCapt kia 1-7-16 6RWar p214 CR France1890
DIXON,James Galloway T2Lt kia 12-10-16 17Lpool p71 MR21
DIXON,James W.2Lt kia 5-8-17 RE 152FC p44 CR Belgium17
DIXON,John Francis 2Lt kia 12-4-16 4Y&L p238 MR30
DIXON,John George T2Lt kia 16-6-17 13NumbF p60 MR20
DIXON,John Henry 2Lt ded 1-5-19 RE 85FC p262 CR Egypt2
DIXON,John Vibart 2Lt kia 6-3-17 3NMidRFA p208 CR France745
DIXON,John William T2Lt kia 22-10-17 Manch att23Bn p154 MR30
DIXON,Kenneth 2Lt dow 25-11-16 6WRid p227 CR France203
DIXON,Leonard Frederick T2Lt kia 21-5-18 11 att2SWBord p99 CR France24,Lt 22-5-18
DIXON,Norman Ferguson.MID ACapt dow 5-10-17 6BlkW attMGC p187&231 CR Belgium72
DIXON,O.D.TLt ded 4-11-18 2YLI p143 CR Yorks323
DIXON,Peter Sydenham TLt kia 7-8-18 7RSuss p118 CR France196
DIXON,Robert Archibald 2Lt kia 12-4-16 2Dors p124 MR38
DIXON,Robert Harrison Maj ded 16-11-15 RASC 54Div p253 CR Europe1
DIXON,Robert William.MM.T2Lt kia 5-9-18 26RFus p67 CR Belgium37
DIXON,Sidney Thomas 2LtTLt dow 20-11-17 3 att4Worc p108 CR France439
DIXON,Thomas Herbert.MC.TCapt kia 25-8-18 12Manch p154 CR France402
DIXON,William H.2Lt dow 23-6-18 3SfthH att25RAF p164 CR France40
DIXON,William Alexander 2Lt kia 16-8-17 3 att8RIrFus p171 MR30
DIXON,William Francis Trevor T2Lt kia 20-7-16 15N&D p133 MR21
DIXON,William Hutton 2Lt kia 22-4-18 3 att8SfthH p164 CR France54,21-4-18
DIXON,William Stanton 2Lt kia 30-4-18 2/4Lincs attLeic p217 CR Belgium11,Swanston
DIXON-NUTTAL,Frederick John Lt kia 21-5-15 RE 1FC p210 CR Belgium96,J.F.
DIXSON,Thomas Storie Lt kld 8-12-16 1CldGds p51 CR France1568
DOAKE,Samuel Henry.DSO.CaptAMaj kia 30-3-18 RFA 52ArmyBde p27 CR France268
DOBB,Robert Alan Capt ded 22-12-17 30RFA p27 CR Iraq8
DOBBIE,Alexander Middleton 2Lt dow 13-4-18 6BlkW p231 CR France10
DOBBIE,Herbert William 2Lt kia 14-11-16 3 att1RBerks p139 MR21
DOBBIE,John Shedden Lt kia 5-10-17 3GordH C'Coy p166 MR30,Capt 2Bn
DOBBIE,Robert Shedden Lt dow 12-4-17 11A&SH CR France40

DOBBIE,Robert William ACapt kld 23-12-18 18HLI &RAF p162
DOBBIE,William James 2Lt kia 7-6-17 2RIrRif p169 CR Belgium43
DOBBIN,Fergus Le Fanu 2Lt kia 16-7-19 IAUL 2/6GurkhaRif att3/1 p276 MR43
DOBBIN,George Frederick T2Lt kia 16-8-15 6RIrFus p171 MR4
DOBBIN,Robert Alexander Sheridan Lt kia 25-9-15 RGA p39 MR19
DOBBIN,William Leonard Price.MC.Lt kia 21-3-18 3RIrRif p169 MR27,2Bn
DOBBS,Arthur Hugh Capt mbk 22-4-16 IA 76Punjabis att92 p276 MR38
DOBBS,George Eric Burroughs CaptBtMajALtCol dow 17-6-17 RE AD Sigs p44 CR Belgium11
DOBBS,Hugh Cathcart Capt kia 25-5-18 IA 3/124Baluchis p276 CR Asia82
DOBBS,William Carey Capt kia 31-7-17 2Mddx p146 MR29
DOBBYN,Robert Newport T2Lt kld 23-11-16 GL &RFC p2&190 CR Eire215
DOBBYN,William Augustus Nelson T2Lt kld 4-1-17 18LancF p92 France813,4-2-17 15Bn
DOBELL,Caleb Clifford Lt ded 17-11-18 RE 256TC p44 CR Sussex178
DOBELL,Colin Macpherson Lt dow 30-5-18 1 att9RWelshF p97 CR France622
DOBIE,James Jardine.DSO.MC.Capt kia 30-9-18 3Huss p21 CR France911
DOBIE,Kirkpatrick Smith.MC.MM.2Lt kia 26-10-17.3 att2GordH p166&258 MR30
DOBIE,William Findlay Robertson Lt kia 14-12-14 1GordH p166 CR Belgium155
DOBIE,William Murray Lt kia 9-4-16 3 att1RWKent D'Coy p141 CR France1182
DOBINSON,Stanley Raine TLt kia 31-3-18 10 att1/4Yorks p90 MR27
DOBINSON,Thomas William.MID TCapt ded 1-12-18 RE 183TC p44 CR France717,183FC
DOBINSON,William.MC.T2Lt kia 22-10-17 18LancF p92 MR30
DOBSON,Alfred Frederic Otterbine Lt kia 15-6-15 8N&D p233 CR Belgium17,Ottobine
DOBSON,Arthur Edward John T2Lt kia 7-6-17 GL &45RFC p7 MR20
DOBSON,Edward TCapt kia 10-7-17 17HLI p162 CR Belgium24
DOBSON,Eric Trist Lt ded 8-6-20 IA 74Punjabis att2/124Baluchis p276
DOBSON,Frank Rayner T2Lt kia 28-9-18 3Y&L att10EYorks p158 CR France262
DOBSON,G.M.Maj 17-9-19 RAMC CR Wales564
DOBSON,George Lt kia 11-4-18 4 att6BlkW p230 MR19
DOBSON,Harold Percy TLtACapt kia 16-10-17 20NumbF p60 CR Belgium83
DOBSON,Harold Pierce.MID Capt kia 5-4-16 9Worc p108 MR38
DOBSON,James Robinson T2Lt kia 19-2-17 9RIrFus p171 CR France285
DOBSON,John 2Lt dow 4-5-17 RIrFus p171 CR France95
DOBSON,Montague Charles BdeMaj kld 26-9-15 RFA 21Div p27 CR France423
DOBSON,Nathaniel George TLt dow 17-11-18 BordR att1Camb p117 CR France146
DOBSON,Reginald Graham.MIDx2 Maj ded 4-1-19 6WYorks att75MGC p218&187,4-1-18 CR Egypt2
DOBSON,Thomas Ernest T2Lt dow 11-4-15 3MGC p182 CR France40,11-4-18
DOCKER,George Arthur Murray Capt kia 17-11-14 RFus p67 CR Belgium32
DOCKING,Robert James TLt dow 10-2-17 9EKent &43RFC p7&p57 CR France31
DOCKREE,Gilbert Arthur 2Lt kia 15-9-16 6Lond p247 MR21
DODD,Ernest John 2LtTLt kia 17-7-17 C177RFA p27 CR Belgium6
DODD,F.Capt 14-2-20 RGA CR Lancs2
DODD,Francis Joseph T2Lt ded 31-10-18 63MGC Inf p182 CR Lincs61
DODD,Herbert 2Lt kia 23-10-18 5Ches p222 CR Belgium408
DODD,Herbert Robert T2Lt kia 21-3-18 10Ess p131 MR27
DODD,James Forrest 2Lt kia 28-2-17 1LancF p92 CR France216,7Bn
DODD,John O'Connell TLt kia 7-11-18 6RMunstF p175 CR France968,2Bn
DODD,Neville 2Lt kia 1-7-16 1/6WYorks p218 CR France1890
DODD,Percy Reed Capt kia 10-3-15 2ScotRif p103 CR France260
DODD,Stanley Preston 2Lt dow 25-11-17 1/7Ches p223 CR Egypt2
DODD,Walter De Courcy Lt ded PoW 31-10-17 5RMunstF &11RFC p7&p175 CR France568,Courcey kia
DODD,Westgarth John 2Lt dow 19-9-18 RFA X38MidTMB p27 CR France415
DODDRELL,Kenneth Curling 2Lt kia 19-9-18 2 att1/4Wilts p153 CR Palestine9
DODDS,Benjamin William Pedley.MC.Lt kia 8-8-19 IARO att34ResMtnBty p276 MR38,7-8-19
DODDS,Cave Bradburne 2Lt kia 25-9-15 12NumbF p60 MR19
DODDS,Cecil T2Lt kia 5-10-18 13DLI p160 CR France844
DODDS,Cecil James Capt kia 22-9-16 6 att1RMunstF p175 MR21
DODDS,Herbert Alexandra Christopher 2Lt ded 13-6-16 3/5Y&L p238 CR Surrey15
DODDS,Robert William Lee Lt kia 25-9-15 13NumbF p60 MR19,26-9-15
DODDS,Walter Milbourne TCapt dow PoW 14-10-18 8NumbF p60 CR Europe149,Meibourne 23Bn
DODDS,William Henry T2Lt kia 6-11-16 20NumbF p60 CR France82
DODGE,Walter Robert.MM.T2Lt kia 2-10-17 20Manch p154 CR Belgium308

DODGSHON,Angus John Charles Lt kia 10-11-17 5Glouc p225 CR France1190
DODGSHON,John Hampson 2Lt kld 2-10-16 SurrYeo &RFCp205 CR Wilts116,1-10-16
DODGSON,David Scott Lt kia 13-11-14 2RGA 1SB p39 MR22
DODGSON,Francis TCapt kia 10-7-16 8Yorks p90 MR21 CR France1890
DODGSON,Guy Capt dow 14-11-18 Herts p252 CR France658
DODGSON,John Henley 2Lt kia 7-6-17 5RWKent p235 MR29
DODGSON,Kenneth Vernon TLt kia 25-9-15 8Dev p76 MR19
DODGSON,Reginald Henry Lutwidge Lt ded 14-3-18 RDC p269 CR Shrop67
DODGSON,Vernon Colville TLt dow 5-3-16 14 att11Mddx p146 CR France423
DODINGTON,Thomas Marriott Lt kia 2-7-16 1SomLI p79 MR21
DODKINS,Lionel Claud FlOff ded 13-6-21 25Lond repostedBordR &31RAF CR Surrey6
DODS,John Ballantyne Lt dow 11-4-18 1/8RScots p211 CR France201
DODS,William Henry Gordon Lt kia 21-10-14 Leic p87 MR32
DODSON,Henry Howard 2Lt kia 27-6-17 8Hamps p229 CR France245
DODSON,Herbert Edwin 2Lt kia 28-4-17 5 att9Norf p217 CR France551
DODSON,Herbert Leigh Midelton Lt ded 25-8-18 RASC att73&46RFC p15&192,kia CR France421
DODSON,Joseph Edward T2Lt kia 10-10-18 RWKent att10EKent p141 CR France82
DODWELL,Oscar Wilfred 2Lt kia 10-5-15 1Y&L p158 MR29
DOE,Alfred Bramhill 2Lt kia 23-4-17 6BlkW A'Coy p231 CR France604
DOGGART,Norman Alexander Capt 10-10-18 RAF &ScotRif CR Oxford69
DOGGETT,George Patrick 2Lt dow 4-7-17 7WRid p227 CR Camb16
DOHERTY,John T2Lt kia 16-8-17 8RDubF p176 MR30
DOHERTY,Joseph 2Lt kia 3-7-16 RGA 113HB p39 CR France203
DOHERTY,Mary Agnes Sister ded 5-9-16 QAIMNS p200 CR Greece7
DOHERTY,Patrick T2Lt dow 1-8-17 1RIrRif p169 CR Belgium11
DOHERTY-HOLWELL,Raymond Vernon.DSO.MID Maj kia 9-1-17 RE AD Sigs 8CpsHQ p44 CR Belgium5,LtCol
DOIDGE,Reginald Chamberlain TCapt kld 2-3-16 17LancF p92 CR France356
DOIG,David Lt 3-4-19 RGA CR Scot14
DOLAMORE,Arthur William.MID Capt kia 14-4-17 10Mddx att5EKent p236 MR38
DOLAN,Stephen Christopher 2Lt kia 16-8-17 RInniskF att49TMB p104 MR30
DOLBY,Horace Adams Lt kia 7-5-17 3 att1Leic p87 CR France115,1 att3Bn
DOLD,Cedric Lewis.MC. TCapt kia 5-10-18 RAMC att1SWBord p195 CR France725
DOLL,Philip Walter Rudolph Lt kia 31-10-14 1/8Lpool p71
DOLLEY,Reginald Charles Francis 2Lt kia 30-6-17 6N&D p233 MR20,1-7-17
DOLLING,Caledon Robert John Radcliffe T2LtACapt kia 20-8-16 2RWelshF p97 CR France453
DOLMAN,Leonard 2LtTLt dow 31-12-17 8Beds p85 CR France518
DOLPHIN,Eric John Weston Lt kia 7-11-14 1Hamps p120 CR Belgium69,Capt
DOLPHIN,Harold Maximilian Burton 2Lt ded 31-8-20 2/56PunjabRif attSeistanLevyCps p276 MR43,Lt
DOLPHIN,Samuel 2Lt kia 24-3-18 4SStaffs p122 CR France307 Ex 1/6ScotRif
DOLPHIN,Vernon Ommanney Maj kia 7-6-17 17RFA p27 CR France1182,8-6-17
DOMAN,George Herbert Ryder 2Lt dow PoW 11-6-18 12/13NumbF p60 CR Europe149
D'OMBRAIN,Roland Maund 2Lt kia 8-3-16 IARO att53Sikhs p276 MR38,DOMBRAIN
DOMEGAN,Christopher Patrick Lt drd 10-10-18 RIrFus &RAF p171 CR Eire437
DOMELEO,Robert Frearson TLt ded 10-12-18 RE ROD p44 CR France34,DOMLEO
DON,Alexander Duff Brownlee Lt kia 21-10-16 RE 2FC p44 CR France374
DON,Archibald William Robertson TLt ded 11-9-16 10BlkW p128 CR Greece7
DON,Daird Fairweather T2Lt kia 1-7-16 14 att2N&D attSWBord p133 MR21
DON,Frederick Alexander LtCol ded 24-5-18 IA S&TCps p276 CR Asia60
DON,Reginald Gilbert 2Lt kia 15/16-9-14 1BlkW p128 MR15,15-9-14
DON,Robert Macpherson Lt kia 8-4-17 10BlkW p128 MR37,8/9-4-17
DON,Thomas Douglas 2Lt kia 21-7-18 5BlkW p231 CR France324
DON,Valentine Grantham Lt kia 26-8-15 8RWKent p141 MR19,26-9-15
DONAGHY,Robert Andrews 2Lt kia 28-5-18 RGA NRidHB p39 MR18,Andrew
DONAHOO,Malcolmson Gardiner.MC.TLt dow 31-1-17 8YLI p143 CR Belgium11
DONAHUE,P.Capt&QM 26-5-21 RGA CR Essex9
DONALD,Alan James Ingram 2Lt kia 4-6-15 6Manch p236 MR4
DONALD,Andrew Patrick 2Lt ded 1-2-18 RE 7PontConstCo p262 CR Lond1,Lt
DONALD,Colin George Hamilton 2Lt kia 8-8-18 2SfthH p164 CR France250
DONALD,George Lt 12-9-20 RE IWT MR65
DONALD,Ian Strathy 2Lt dow 7-8-16 5ScotRif p224 CR France85
DONALD,James 2Lt ded 15-10-16 IARO att2S&M p276 MR43

DONALD,Robert Capt ded 3-5-16 RAMC p269
DONALD,Robert.MC.TLt kia 28-4-17 24NumbF p60 MR20
DONALD,William Clark 2Lt kia 31-7-17 4CamH p243 MR29
DONALD,William Francis Maxwell.MC.Capt kia 19-9-18 9HLI p240 CR France1496
DONALDSON,Alexander Cleveland TCapt kia 6-8-15 8CamH att1Ess p167 CR Gallipoli6
DONALDSON,Alexander Howard Lt kia 12-10-18 9HLI p240 CR France230
DONALDSON,Cleweth Thomas Lee 2Lt kia 14-4-17 GlasgowYeo att52RFC p18&p203 CR France662
DONALDSON,Denis Harrison 2Lt kia 25-9-15 7Lond p247 CR France550
DONALDSON,Geoffrey Boley Capt ded PoW 19-7-16 7RWar p214 MR32
DONALDSON,George Lt kia 16-5-17 6GordH p242 CR France546
DONALDSON,Herbert Graham 2Lt kld 16-2-18 20Lond attRFC p18&251,ded
DONALDSON,James Capt kia 23-8-17 7 at9BlkW p231 CR Belgium8
DONALDSON,James TCapt ded 5-12-18 RAMC att2/22Lond p195 CR Egypt1
DONALDSON,John.MC.Lt kia 25-3-18 8Manch att5RWar p237 MR27
DONALDSON,John James T2Lt kia 1-7-16 20NumbF p60 MR21
DONALDSON,Norman.MID Lt kia 10-3-15 45RFA p282 MR22
DONALDSON,Stuart T2Lt kia 28-9-18 15HLI p162 CR Belgium101
DONALDSON,Wilfred Wallace Douglas 2Lt dow 19-4-17 1/4RScotF p222 CR Palestine2
DONALDSON,William T2Lt kia 5-6-17 12RScots A'Coy p54 CR France604
DONALDSON-SELBY,Victor Montague 2Lt ded 31-8-17 3Lincs p263 CR Lond8,dow
DONCASTER,Guy Capt kia 8-6-18 IARO att CpsofGuides Inf p276 CR Palestine9
DONCASTER,Robert Ivan T2Lt kia 1-7-16 15LancF p92 CR France293
DONE,Neville Savage 2Lt kia 10-3-17 6 att22RFus p67 MR21
DONE,Robert Lt dow 13-10-18 15Ches p96 MR30
DONELAN,William Lawrence T2Lt kia 5-4-17 8EKent p57 CR France161
DONGREY,Hayden Harry T2Lt kia 23-3-18 41MGC p182 CR France1896,DONGRAY
DONKERSLEY,Reynold.MC.2Lt kia 20-7-18 2/5WYorks p218 CR France622
DONKIN,Samuel Thornton 2Lt kia 25-12-15 7NumbF p214 CR Belgium127
DONLEY,David C.B.2Lt dow 3-9-17 2ELancs p110 CR France285
DONNALLY,Robert Charles TLt kia 21-10-16 RH&FA 147Bde97Bty p28
DONNAN,William LtCol ded 13-8-19 IA attStaff p276 CR Iraq6,Col Ex Lincs
DONNELL,Arthur Patrick 2Lt kld 5-12-16 NumbF &RFC p2&60 CR Norf247,Lt
DONNELLY,Gilbert TLt kia 21-3-18 1RMunstF p175 MR27
DONNELLY,James Alexander 2Lt dow 31-3-18 GL &59RFC p15 CR France62
DONNELLY,John Verney.MID ACapt kia 9-10-17 9Manch C'Coy p237 MR30
DONNER,Eric Robert TCapt kia 3-9-16 11RB p178 MR21,Robin
DONNOLLY,Robert Charles Lt 21-10-16 97/147RFA p28 MR21
DONOHUE,Thomas 2LtTLt dow 8-2-17 8BordR p117 CR France285,2Lt
DONOVAN,Bridget SNurse ded 3-4-16 QAIMNS p200 CR Hamps11
DONOVAN,Cyril Bernard.MC.TLt kia 25-3-18 2RDubF p176 MR27
DONOVAN,John 2Lt kia 26-4-18 5YLI p235 MR30
DONWORTH,Thomas Francis TCapt drd 28-7-16 RAVC att109RFA p198 CR France34 &CR France30
DOONER,Alfred Edwin Claud Toke.MID Lt&Adjt kia 30-11-14 1RWelshF p97 CR Belgium112,30-10-14
DOONER,John Graham.DSO.LtCol kia 31-7-18 RFA Staff 34DivHQ p28 CR France524
DOOGAN,George William TLt kia 21-10-16 11RSuss p118 MR21
DOOLEY,Thomas 2Lt kia 1-5-15 2Leic p87 CR France727
DOOTSON,Herbert 2Lt dow 5-11-17 RFA 66Bty p28 MR38
DORAN,Edward Sheridan 2Lt kia 1-11-16 RFA p28 CR France374
DORAN,Frank Beecher Lt kia 13-8-17 20CanadaInf CR Belgium18
DORAN,Louis Godfrey T2Lt kia 23-10-16 7 att2RDubF p176 MR21
DORE,Alfred Clarence T2Lt kia 1-7-16 101MGC p182 CR France267 Ex Y&L
DORE,Sidney Arthur.MID T2Lt kia 24-4-18 11 att1/7Mddx p146 CR France54
DORE,William Hayward Lt kia 25-9-16 1WYorks p81 MR21
DORINGTON,Thomas Philip Maj kia 12-11-14 1Dragoons p214 CR Belgium57
DORMAN,Anthony Godfrey.MC.TLt kia 13-11-16 13EYorks p84 MR21
DORMAN,Edward Crump Capt kia 1-5-15 1RMunstF p175 MR4
DORMAN,Thomas Robert Hobart 2Lt dow 21-2-16 2RMunstF p175 CR France779
DORNTON,Harold Shafto 2Lt kia 1-7-16 1/5N&D p232 MR21
DORRELL,Evelyn Percy 2Lt dow 14-10-18 4RWSurr p212 CR France380,kia
DORRELL,Harold George Harcourt T2Lt kia 3-4-16 10DLI p160&257,H.G.Hugh CR France420,2-4-16
DORRINGTON,Percy 2Lt kia 12-10-17 10N&D p133 MR30,Lt
DOSWELL,Frank.MM.2Lt ded 29-2-19 6RWSurr p262 CR Surrey6

DOTHIE,Elvery Ashton 2Lt kld 9-5-15 ELancs p110 MR32
DOTHIE,John Howard T2Lt kia 27-6-16 2BordR p117 CR France394
DOUCET,Gerald Danby 2Lt kia 26-10-17 7NumbF p214 MR30
DOUDNEY,Charles Edmund Rev dow 16-10-15 RAChDept att18Bde6Div p199 CR Belgium11
DOUDNEY,Hugh Denham ACapt kia 31-7-17 12RFus p67 MR29,Densham
DOUGAL,John Braes T2Lt kia 1-7-16 15RScots p54 MR21
DOUGAL,Robert Joseph TLt kia 1-7-16 21NumbF p60 MR21
DOUGALL,Eric Stuart.VC.MC.LtAMaj kia 14-4-18 A88RFA p28 CR Belgium192
DOUGHTY,E.A.MM.2Lt kld 14-4-18 GL att4RAF p190 CR France31,Albert Edward
DOUGHTY,George T2Lt kia 20-11-16 13RScots &RFC p2&54 CR France518
DOUGHTY,George Harry 2Lt kia 25-4-17 18Manch p154 MR20
DOUGHTY,George Marbrook.MC.Lt kia 21-8-17 22Mddx att17MGC Inf p146&182 CR Belgium167
DOUGHTY,Gordon Gray T2Lt kia 11-4-18 1KOSB p101 MR32
DOUGHTY,John Henry Lt ded 25-8-19 RFA Ex RAOC p261
DOUGHTY,Robert Cecil T2Lt kld 26-2-18 101RFC p15 CR France1063
DOUGHTY-WYLIE,Charles Hotham Montagu.VC.CB.CMG.LtCol kia 28-4-15 RWelshF p97 CR Gallipoli15A,26-4-15
DOUGLAS,Alexander Gawain TLt kia 15-8-16 10 att 1Leic p87 CR France220
DOUGLAS,Alexander Stark 2Lt dow 28-10-18 3 att1/6BlkW p128 CR France52
DOUGLAS,Alfred William.MM.2Lt dow 3-9-16 14RWar p64 CR France23
DOUGLAS,Allen Grant.MC.Capt kia 30-11-17 14Lond p249 CR France1496
DOUGLAS,Archibald 2Lt kld 16-10-16 RFA attRFC p2&28 CR France82
DOUGLAS,Archibald Halliday Lt kia 16-9-16 9RScots A'Coy p212 CR France922
DOUGLAS,Andrew T2Lt dow 19-2-16 3 att2BlkW p128 CR Iraq5
DOUGLAS,Brian Charles O'Driscoll Capt kld 21-10-18 ConnRgrs attRAF p172 CR Mddx66
DOUGLAS,Bruce Francis Sholto 2Lt kia 14-4-15 4 att2SStaffs p122 CR France80,Lt
DOUGLAS,Bryce Lt kia 13-11-17 IA 1/101Grens att58Rif p276 CR Palestine9
DOUGLAS,Charles Camelon Lt dow 25-5-16 1/4CamH p242 CR France157,Cameron
DOUGLAS,Charles Whittingham Horsley.GCB.ADC.Col ded 25-10-14 Ch of Staff CR Lond8
DOUGLAS,David Tocher T2Lt dow 1-11-17 3ELancs p110 CR Lancs472
DOUGLAS,G.S.Maj 10-2-16 ScotRif CR Scot263
DOUGLAS,George Archibald Percy Capt dow 30-11-15 10Lond p248 CR Egypt3,Adjt 1/6Ess
DOUGLAS,Henry Guy Stuart Capt ded 8-9-19 GL &3ScotRif p266 CR Mddx39
DOUGLAS,Ian Victor.MC.2Lt kia 25-10-17 RGA 180SB p39 CR Belgium124
DOUGLAS,James Capt&QM ded 11-2-19 RAMC 1/1FA p253 CR Scot235,11-12-19
DOUGLAS,John Charles Edward TMaj dow 18-12-15 10Yorks p90 CR France285
DOUGLAS,John Gordon Lt kia 12-4-18 7SfthH p164 CR Belgium124
DOUGLAS,John Norman Turnbull Capt mbk 12-4-18 23NumbF p256 MR32
DOUGLAS,Kenneth Mackenzie TLt ded 9-12-18 GL 7SfthH attKAR p164,202&266 CR EAfrica86,Capt
DOUGLAS,Leslie Hall Lt kia 9-7-15 RE 2FC p210 CR Belgium98
DOUGLAS,Malcolm TMaj ded 17-11-18 MGC p182 CR Shrop19
DOUGLAS,Norman Dighton 2Lt kia 12-12-19 IARO att3CpsofGuides p276 MR43
DOUGLAS,Percy T2Lt ded 25-5-17 7EYorks p84 CR Yorks81
DOUGLAS,Robert.MID Lt dow 15-7-15 1/5KOSB p224 MR4
DOUGLAS,Robert Greenshields 2Lt ded 14-8-16 1SuffYeo attSuffR p205 CR Egypt1
DOUGLAS,Robert Jeffray.CMG.TD.LtCol kia 3-7-16 5ScotRif p224 CR France80
DOUGLAS,Robert Morrison Wilson 2Lt kia 29-3-18 5GordH p242 MR27
DOUGLAS,Ronald Ross T2Lt dow 30-8-17 7/8KOSB p101 CR Belgium11
DOUGLAS,Sholto TCapt kia 28-1-16 16Mddx p146 CR France114
DOUGLAS,Stafford E.Maj ded 15-2-20 A&SH CR Somerset197
DOUGLAS,William Anderson Capt kia 24-8-16 5RScots p211 2entries 6Bn MR21
DOUGLAS,William Gurwood.MC.2Lt ded 26-2-19 111RFA p261 CR Scot674
DOUGLAS,William Sholto Maj dow 14-11-14 RE p44 CR France102
DOUGLAS,William Campbell 2Lt dow 17-8-17 3 att1KOSB p101
DOUGLAS,William Millar 2Lt kia 19-8-17 5KOSB p224 MR30
DOUGLAS,William Robert 2Lt kia 5-10-18 1/10Lpool p216 CR France1725,Robertson
DOUGLAS,W.R.B.CIE.Cdr drd 28-6-19 RIM MR64
DOUGLAS-CROMPTON,Sidney Harold Lionel 2Lt kia 7-6-17 5RFus p67 MR29
DOUGLAS-DICK,Archibald William John Joseph Lt kia 11-11-14 1ScotsGds p52 MR29
DOUGLAS-HAMILTON,Angus Falconer.VC.TLtCol kia 26-9-15 6CamH p167 MR19
DOUGLAS-HAMILTON,Leslie Reginald Coventry TCapt kia 25-7-16 7CamH attLancF p167 CR France630,Lesley 24-7-16
DOUGLAS-JONES,William Eric Vyvyan 2Lt ded 15-1-15 33RFA p28 CR France768

DOUGLAS-PENNANT,Alan George Sholto.Hon.Lt kia 29-10-14 1GrenGds p49 MR29
DOUGLAS-PENNANT,Charles.Hon.Lt kia 29-10-14 CldGds p51 CR Belgium115
DOUGLAS-PENNANT,George Henry.Hon.MID Capt kia 11-3-15 1GrenGds RoO p49 MR22
DOUGLAS-WILLAN,Stanhope William Howard Sholto LtACapt kia 17-2-17 2SStaffs p122 MR21
DOUGLAS-WILLAN,Walter Gordon Maj kia 24-3-18 4DLI att22NFusGarrBn p160 MR27
DOUGLASS,Archibald Henry TLt dow 8-4-18 9ESurr p112 CR Mddx53,Capt
DOUGLASS,George Percival.MC.Lt dow 25-8-18 157RFA p28 CR France100 Ex AustInf
DOUGLASS-JAMES,William Lt dow 25-9-15 RGA p39
DOULL,Gilbert Laurie T2Lt dow 11-3-17 11ScotRif D'Coy p103 CR France164
DOUST,Charles Bowden 2Lt kia 1-7-16 5Lond p246 MR21
DOUTHWAITE,Robert Christopher Morris Lt ded 19-6-19 8Y&L p158 CR Europe58A
DOVE,Charles Bertram Capt kia 21-3-18 3 att8BordR p117 CR France563
DOVE,Edward Maddison.MC.TLt dow 23-3-18 8ESurr p112 MR27
DOVE,Etienne Howard T2Lt kia 30-3-17 1RWelshF p97 CR France616
DOVE,Lewis Lt dow 1-4-18 BedsYeo attOxfYeo p203 CR France185
DOVE,Patrick Edward Lt kia 14-6-17 1GordH p166 MR20
DOVE,Percy Matthew Maj kia 15-5-15 2N&D p133 CR Belgium451
DOVE,Sydney Ernest T2Lt kia 16-8-16 8RWKent p141 CR France294
DOVE,Tom.MC.TCapt kia 16-8-17 12KRRC p150 MR30
DOVER,William Lt kia 28-4-17 5 att7Norf p216 MR20
DOVETON,J.H.Maj 19-4-15 16Cav MR66
DOVEY,Wiliam Edward 2Lt kia 23-10-16 1RLancs p58 MR21
DOW,A.Lt 23-2-17 CamH CR Scot966
DOW,Allan Gladstone T2Lt kldacc 17-8-17 GL &RFC p7 CR Kent125
DOW,David Edward.MID 2Lt dow 17-5-17 1/6SfthH p241 CR France95
DOW,James Robertson T2Lt kia 11-4-18 2SLancs p125 MR32
DOW,John T2Lt kia 25-3-18 12Lpool p71 MR27,12KRRC
DOW,John Capt ded 5-11-18 IA IMS p276 CR Asia82
DOW,Samuel Hugh T2Lt kia 30-12-16 9ScotRif p103
DOW,Walter 2Lt kia 19-12-15 1/8ScotRif p225 CR Gallipoli3
DOW,William T2Lt dow 2-2-17 9BlkW p128 CR France177,kia
DOW,William John Lt kia 22-8-17 5A&SH p243 MR30
DOWDELL,Ernest George.MC.2Lt kia 22-3-18 3 att8BordR p117 MR20
DOWDEN,Reginald Stanley 2Lt kia 16-8-17 1Lond p245 MR29
DOWDESWELL,Horace Scott 2Lt kia 3-11-17 1/5WelshR p230 CR Palestine1
DOWDING,Charles Gordon.MC.Capt dow 17-11-17 IA 87Punjabis att2SigCo p276 CR EAfrica11 &CR Tanzania1
DOWDING,Lionel 2Lt kia 7-1-16 Leic p87 MR38
DOWEND,John Middleton 2LtACapt kia 24-11-17 26NumbF p60 CR France592
DOWENS,James Alexander 2Lt kia 17-10-18 4KOSB p224 CR Belgium157
DOWLING,Frederick Payne Lt kia 7-8-17 1RDubF p176 MR29
DOWLING,Geoffrey Charles Walter TCapt kia 30-7-15 7KRRC p150 MR29
DOWN,Charles Boileau.MID Maj ded 10-5-19 40RGA p39 p262 CR Beds23
DOWN,John Aubrey Maj ded 28-11-18 8Mddx p235 CR Mddx26
DOWN,John Eric Lt kia 29-9-18 6Mddx C'Coy att63Div MG'Bn p146 CR France602
DOWN,Robert Hayward Lt dow 17-8-16 4Glouc p225 CR France74
DOWN,William Oliphant.MC.Capt dow 23-5-17 4RBerks p234 CR France530
DOWNER,Frederick 2Lt kia 2-4-17 5Manch att2/7N&D p236 MR21
DOWNES,Arthur Chernocke 2Lt dow 20-11-14 2Ches p96 CR Belgium150
DOWNES,Benjamin 2Lt kia 2-6-18 18Lond p250 CR France887
DOWNES,Donald Ltt 2Lt dow 5-10-18 4Worc p108 CR Belgium38
DOWNES,Gilbert George TCapt dow 11-8-15 Lincs p75 CR Greece10
DOWNES,Herbert Laidlow.MID Lt kia 15-6-15 8Lpool p215 MR22
DOWNES,Howard Gray 2Lt kia 12-3-17 RE 517FCp210 CR Belgium5,13-3-17
DOWNES,Oswald 2Lt 1-7-16 2DLI CR Hereford9
DOWNES,Villiers Chernocke Lt dow 18-10-14 3Beds p85 CR France134
DOWNES,W.D.MC.Capt 5-8-20 RSuss attNigR HQ CR WAfrica42
DOWNEY,George Jamieson T2Lt ded 24-4-18 11RLancs p262 CR Wilts115,25-4-18 3Bn
DOWNEY,Sydney James Livingstone T2Lt kia 7-6-17 14RIrRif p169 CR Belgium61,Livingston
DOWNEY,William Edmund Capt drd 19-7-17 RAOC p198 MR37,ded
DOWNHAM,Harold 2Lt dow 29-9-18 1/7LancF p221 CR France512
DOWNIE,Andrew Marshall Maj dow 20-7-15 1/5HLI p240 CR Egypt3
DOWNIE,James Maitland Capt ded 28-10-18 RAMC p195 CR Iraq6

DOWNIE,James Wallace 2Lt kia 22-10-17 6ScotRif p224.MR30
DOWNIE,Leslie E.V 2Lt 9-4-17 4SfthH CR France15
DOWNIE,Nelson 2Lt dow 17-5-17 IARO att1/4GurkhaRif p276 MR43
DOWNIE,Reginald Alexander Forbes 2Lt dow 24-3-18 1 att3CamH p167 MR27,att5Bn
DOWNIE,Robert.MC.DCM.Capt kia 6-11-18 5ScotRif p224 CR France937
DOWNIE,Robert Theodore Manners Lt ded 24-1-16 3/5HLI p240 CR Ches69
DOWNIE,William Kimmond Capt ded 3-2-20 RGA CR Hamps11
DOWNING,Alfred Edward 2Lt dow 27-5-18 9LNLancs p135 MR18
DOWNING,Ernest Gillespie TLt kia 3-5-17 4RFus p67 MR20
DOWNING,Francis Geoffrey Lt ded 27-10-16 5Mddx attRE p146 CR Eire160
DOWNING,George Guy Barry Lt kld 4-9-17 GL &RFC p7 CR Wales20
DOWNING,Henry Francis TCapt kia 3-9-16 7Leinst p174 MR21
DOWNING,Herbert George.MC.2Lt kia 6-11-17 GL &29RFC p7 MR20
DOWNING,James 2Lt kia 3-9-16 3 att6RIrReg p89 MR21
DOWNMAN,Bernard Vincent Ridout T2Lt kia 21-9-16 9 att13N&D p133 CR France296
DOWSE,Benjamin Thomas John Lt gunshotWounds 25-1-21 IA 2/30Punjabis p276 MR43
DOWSE,Henry Harvey 2Lt ded 10-11-18 RASC &139RAF p192 CR Italy12
DOWSE,Robert Joseph Gordon.MID Lt TCapt ded 19-12-18 RASC VIIICps TrpsMTCoy p192 CR France1277
DOWSE,Thomas William T2Lt dow 7-9-16 RE 34DivSigs p44
DOWSE,William Arthur Clarence Lt kia 3-7-16 11Ches p96 MR21
DOWSON,Humphrey.MC.TCapt kia 15-9-16 9KRRC p150 CR France402
DOWSON,Oswald John Capt kia 3-5-17 1/4RBerks p234 MR21
DOWSWELL,Charles Victor 2Lt kia8-10-16 9Lond p248 MR21
DOYLE,A.A.K.C.Capt 1-11-18 1Hamps CR Hamps83
DOYLE,Christopher.J.G.2Lt kia 15-8-17 2RDubF p176&257 MR29,15-7-17 8Bn
DOYLE,Denis Rev kia 18-8-16 RAChDept att2Leinst p199
DOYLE,Edward Percival T2Lt dow 5-7-16 11WYorks p81 CR France833
DOYLE,Eric Douglas.MC.Lt kia 29-7-17 190RFA p28 CR Belgium154
DOYLE,Francis Hubert Lt dow 12-10-16 RAVC p198 CR Egypt9
DOYLE,Henry T2Lt kia 17-1-17 ACycCps attNFus p181 CR France82
DOYLE,Henry James 2Lt dow 11-10-17 2/9Manch p237 CR Belgium3
DOYLE,James Charles.MC.Capt kia 27-5-18 RGA p39 MR18
DOYLE,John Francis Innes Hay.CMG.DSO.BrigGen ded 19-2-19 RFA attStaff p28 CR Belgium316
DOYLE,John Joseph TLt kia 10-8-15 6RDubF p176 MR4
DOYLE,Michael William 2Lt kld 22-3-18 RFC p15 CR Hamps13
DOYLE,Thomas Walter T2Lt dow 9-8-16 17 att16RB p178 CR Belgium11
DOYLE,William Joseph.MC.Chap4Cl kia 17-8-17 RAChDept att8RDubF p199 MR30 &CR France141
DOYNE,Philip Denys Lt kia 29-12-15 4 O&BLI p231 CR France1327,28-12-15
DRABBLE,Charles Frederick Lt kia 13-8-18 19DLI att18RAF p160 CR France1483
DRAG,A.M.HonLt&Comm 3-10-18 IndPostalServ CR Iraq8
DRAGE,Arthur William.MM.T2Lt kia 26-9-18 18Mddx p146 CR France439
DRAGE,George T.Maj drd 19-10-18 RIrRif p169 CR Ireland137
DRAISEY,Edwin Rowland Watts TLt kia 15-9-16 8Beds p85 MR21
DRAKE,Ernest Francis TLt ded 10-12-18 Ches p263
DRAKE,Francis T2Lt kia 27-3-18 WYorks att2/4YLI p81 MR20
DRAKE,Frederic Augustus Capt drd 27-5-18 WarYeo p205 MR41
DRAKE,Gerald Edward T2Lt dow 26-1-18 att10Worc p108 CR France905
DRAKE,Godfrey Ward T2Lt dow 1-8-17 2Yorks p90 CR Belgium11,2WYorks
DRAKE,Henry Mackay 2Lt dow 16/18-6-15 8Lpool p215 CR France410,17-6-15
DRAKE,Leonard T2Lt dow 5-10-16 11N&D p133 CR France177
DRAKE,Percy Albert T2Lt kia 13-10-16 11Glouc p106 CR France293
DRAKE,Robert Edward Capt dow 8-9-14 1Lincs p75 CR France1117
DRAKE,Robert Flint Lt kia 17-11-14 10Huss p22 CR Belgium57
DRAKE,Walker 2Lt kia 26-6-16 RHA p28 CR France131
DRAKE,Wilfred Wallace T2Lt dow 16-8-17 2Dev att23TMB p76 CR Belgium8
DRAKE-BROCKMAN,Paris Villiers 2Lt kia 18-7-18 1EKent p57 CR Belgium40
DRAKE-BROCKMAN,Ralph Zouch.MC.2Lt dow 29-9-17 46RFA p28 CR Belgium42
DRAKE-CUTLIFFE,Bernard Henry Hamilton 2Lt 11-4-21 Dev CR Devon91
DRAKEFORD,Harold Arthur T2Lt kia 5-4-18 8SomLI p79 MR20
DRAKELEY,Reginald Kenneth T2Lt dow 19-4-16 9RWar p64 CR Iraq5
DRANFIELD,W.B.AssSurg 19-2-17 ISMD CR EAfrica38 &CR Tanzania1
DRAPE,Norman 2Lt dow 15-7-17 RGA 28SB p39 CR France95
DRAPER,Arnold Inman TMaj kia 21-10-17 17Lpool p71 CR Belgium17
DRAPER,Arthur Reginald Olley Lt&QM dow 16-4-18 18NumbF p60 MR32
DRAPER,Cecil Frederick Napier Lt dow 17-6-16 1Mddx p146 CR France80

DRAPER,Dudley Lt ded 21-2-18 RFA p28 CR Mddx26
DRAPER,James 2Lt dow 10-11-18 4 att2LNLancs p234 CR France34
DRAPER,Mark Denman T2Lt kld 7-2-17 GL &RFC p7 CR Derby3
DRAPER,Roger Francis TCapt kia 22-8-15 6Y&L att8WRid p158 MR4
DRAYCOTT-WOOD,William 2Lt kia 29-6-15 2SStaffs p122 CR France163
DRAYSON,John Douglas.MC.TLt ACapt kia 10-4-17 93RFA p28 CR France548,9-4-17
DREDGE,Stanley TLt kia 15-6-18 23MGC p182 CR Italy4
DRENNAN,James Wilson TLt dow 12-8-17 10RInniskF p104 CR Belgium7
DRENNAN,Robert Hugh Capt 26-7-17 RAMC CR Kent129
DRESCHFELD,Henry Theodore Capt ded 19-2-15 13Manch p154 CR Lancs489
DRESSER,Bruce William.MC.Lt dow 20-9-18 27RFA p28 CR France13,120Bty
DRESSER,Harry Jex CaptAMaj kia 2-6-18 1 att15Ches p96 CR France60
DREW,Alan Appleby Lt kia 10-3-15 4ScotRif p103 CR France706,2Bn
DREW,Charles George TLt ACapt kia 12-4-18 1RIrFus p171 CR Belgium168
DREW,Frederick James 2Lt kia 29-3-18 RGA 230SB p209 CR France184
DREW,Frederick William T2Lt kia 5-11-16 9 att7EYorks p84 MR21
DREW,J.T Lt 3-9-19 ConnRgrs CR Devon92
DREW,Richard William 2Lt kia 25-6-18 3 att12Glouc p106 CR France352
DREWE,Abrian.MID T2Lt ACapt kia 12-7-17 RGA 262SB p39 CR Belgium10
DREWERY,Arthur Bancroft 2Lt kia 20-10-16 19RFC p2 CR France169
DREWERY,George William 2Lt kia 22-3-18 1/4EYorks p219 MR27
DREWETT,Charles T2Lt dow 29-6-16 12EYorks p84 MR21
DREWETT,Herbert Benn 2Lt kia 30-10-17 4EYorks p219 CR Belgium126,Ben
DREY,Adolphe.MC.TLt kld 9-5-17 RASC &58RFC p7&192,Adolph ded CR Egypt15
DRIFFIELD,Herbert George T2Lt dow 1-8-17 2Lond att10RWKent p141 CR Belgium5
DRINKILL,Frederick Maurice Lt dow 1-7-16 2RFus p67 CR France35
DRINKWATER,Leonard Wilfred 2Lt kia 3-10-17 RFA p208 MR30
DRISCOLL,D.O'Neill Lt ded 13-8-18 1/4Mddx &RAF p146 CR Surrey152
DRIVER,Bernard Henry.MC.2Lt AMaj kia 4-10-17 2RWSurr p55 CR Belgium115
DRIVER,Graham Dudley TLt ded 5-5-15 RASC p192 CR Mddx26,George
DRIVER,Harry.DSO.MC.Capt kia 10-8-19 Beds att45RFus p254 MR70 &CR Europe179
DRIVER,Harry Farrant.MC.Lt dow 28-8-18 1/1Camb p244 CR France370
DRIVER,Percy Scott Lt kia 26-3-18 RASC attRFC p18&253 MR20
DRIVER,Thomas Stanley Lt ded 2-12-18 4RRofCav p261 CR Essex120
DRON,John Kent Lt kia 13-10-18 6HLI att1KOSB p240 CR Belgium157
DROUGHT,Charles Frederick TCapt dow 31-12-15 7Lincs p75 CR France40
DROUGHT,George Thomas Acton Maj dow 14-6-15 RFA p28 CR Eire533,15-6-15
DROUGHT,Robert Victor.MC.2Lt dow 9-6-17 3 att14RirRif p169 CR France285,3 att7Bn
DROVER,Charles Peacock TLt kia 23-3-18 8 att1GordH p166 CR France174
DRUERY,Dudley Victor 2Lt dow 18-10-18 13Lond p249 CR France146
DRUITT,Charles Lambert.MID TLt kia 13-10-16 9SfthH p164 CR France177
DRUITT,Joseph 2Lt kia 9-5-15 RBerks p139 MR32
DRUMMOND,Alexander Gilmour.MC.2Lt dow PoW 5-4-18 3 att6BlkW p128 CR Germany1
DRUMMOND,David Robert Lt kia 3-11-14 2ScotsGds p52 MR29
DRUMMOND,Douglas Torne 2Lt dow 3-5-17 3 att5CamH p167 MR20,Torrel
DRUMMOND,Eric Grey Maj kia 14-11-14 IA 2/4 att2/3GurkhaRif p276 CR France80
DRUMMOND,Francis T2Lt kia 5-7-16 9NumbF p60 CR France
DRUMMOND,Harry T2Lt kia 31-10-18 17LancF p92 CR Belgium143
DRUMMOND,Harvey Gerald Binns.MC.Lt kia 3-9-18 1ScotsGds p52 CR France646
DRUMMOND,Henry Claude Capt kia 24-7-16 7A&SH p243 CR France453
DRUMMOND,Henry Murray T2Lt dow 26-5-16 8 att9BlkW p128 CR Hereford96
DRUMMOND,John Davidson 2Lt kia 9-10-17 YLI att5Bn p143 MR30
DRUMMOND,John Grey T2Lt kia 13-10-15 RE 176TC p44 CR France765
DRUMMOND,Keaisley Mathwin.MC.Capt dow 24-3-18 6NumbF p213 CR France650,Kearsley
DRUMMOND,Nigel Felton Lt kld 20-12-16 6 att1KRRC p150 CR France817,Capt
DRUMMOND,Patrick Campbell T2Lt kia 25-9-15 8KOSB p101 MR19
DRUMMOND,Robert Charles Crosbie 2Lt kia 28-11-17 2CldGds p51 CR France256
DRUMMOND,Robert Kenneth.MC&Bar.TCapt dow 24-7-18 6CamH p167 CR France1228
DRUMMOND,Samuel Frederick 2Lt kia 29-7-17 17RFus p67 CR France572
DRUMMOND,Spencer Hensage Capt kia 30-7-15 7RB p178 MR29,Heneage
DRUMMOND,William Young T2Lt kia 11-7-16 13A&SH p173 CR France630

DRUMMOND-FRASER,Haddo Reginald.MC.Capt 1-8-18 5Ches att1Hereford CR France524

DRUMMOND-FRASER,Murray 2Lt kia 3-6-15 1/5Ches CR Belgium28

DRURY,Alfred Aloysius T2Lt kia 16-11-16 161RFA p28 CR France1013

DRURY,Follett McNeil.MID Lt kia 7-1-18 1/1Herts p252 CR Belgium20

DRURY,Gordon Vallancy TMaj ded 19-11-17 O&BLI 35TrgRes p130&266,GL George CR Wilts3

DRURY,Harold Strickland Lt kia 1-7-16 3 att8YLI p143 MR21

DRURY,Leonard George.MC.T2Lt dow 11-9-18 YLI att9Bn p143 CR France13

DRURY,Philip Blackett TCapt ded 15-7-16 18NumbF p60 CR Numb4

DRURY,William Symes TLt kld 29-1-16 8RDubF p176 CR France178,6Bn

DRURY-LOWE,William Drury.DSO.TLtCol kia 25-9-16 1GrenGds p49 CR France374

DRYBURGH,Joseph T2Lt dow 26-6-18 1 att7/8KOSB p101 CR France95

DRYDEN,John Thomas Lt ded 28-7-17 RAOC p198 CR Iraq5

DRYDEN,Norman McLeod Capt ded 24-11-15 1/6NumbF p270 CR Yorks303,23-11-15

DRYDEN-SMITH,Henry Dalby TCapt kld 14-12-15 RFC p1

DRYERRE,Robert Henry T2Lt kia 1-10-16 11 att7DCLI p114 MR21

DRYNAN,James Hugh St.Clair 2Lt kia 8-5-18 5ScotRif p224 MR30

DRYSDALE,Alexander T2Lt kld 25-3-18 RFC p15 CR Lancs114

DRYSDALE,Alexander Icely Maj kia 28-7-16 A87RFA p28 MR21

DRYSDALE,Alexander Nicholson.MC.TCapt dow 15-4-17 17HLI p162 CR France583

DRYSDALE,Donald Roy Lt dow 25-9-16 5Dors p124 CR France145

DRYSDALE,Hamilton Dunbar Capt kia 1-9-15 IA 26Punjabis att11RScots p276 CR France114

DRYSDALE,Ian Staveley 2Lt kia 18-9-15 11RB p178 CR France924

DRYSDALE,John.MC.2LtACapt kia 11-4-18 4GordH p241 MR19

DRYSDALE,Joseph Dudley TLt kia 23-10-16 2Lincs p75 CR France307

DRYSDALE,Roger Gillespie 2Lt ded 15-4-15 RWar p263 CR Hamps28

DRYSDALE,William.DSO.BtLtCol kia 29-9-16 2RScots Cmdg7Leic p54 CR France432

DUBERLY,Grey William Maj kia 13-3-15 1GrenGds RoO p49 MR22

DUBERLY,Vernon Conrad Capt kia 6-2-16 IA 17Cav p276 MR50

DUBOIS,Latimer Ridley 2Lt kia 7-4-17 18Lond p250 MR20

DuBOULAY,Arthur Housse Mayne.DSO.MajBtLtCol ded 25-10-18 RE AQMG3rdArmy p44

DuBOULAY,Hubert Lionel Houssemayne 2Lt kia 3-9-16 3 att1Wilts p153 MR21

DUBS,Charles Edward Douglas Capt ded 6-11-18 17Lancers p23 CR Scot546

DuBUISSON,John Edmund 2Lt ded 11-10-16 99RFA p28 CR Greece7

DuCANE,Hubert John.CB.MVO.TBrigGen ded 15-6-16 RH&FA GenStaffSthArmy p28 CR Essex212

DUCAT,Richard Maj dow 11-11-14 IA 20Inf p276 CR Iraq6

DUCHESNE,Richard Ernest T2Lt kia 8-10-16 7Nhampt B'Coy p137 CR France81

DUCKERS,Margaret Ellison SNurse ded 16-5-18 QAIMNS p200 CR Greece9

DUCKETT,Harold Ager 2Lt dow 7-6-17 9HLI p240

DUCKETT,Kenneth Lees 2Lt dow 22-8-16 9HLI p240 CR France176

DUCKETT,Vincent George T2Lt kia 23-3-18 14 att11DLI p160 MR27

DUCKETT,William Garnard.MC.2Lt kia 27-3-18 300RFA p28 MR27,Barnard

DUCKITT,Charles Stanley TCapt kia 3-5-17 18WYorks p81 MR20

DUCKSWORTH,Walter Clarence T2Lt kia 8-10-18 WelshR att1KSLI p126 CR France235

DUCKWORTH,Bernard 2Lt kia 28-7-16 1Ches p96 MR21

DUCKWORTH,Eric 2Lt kia 7-8-15 6LancF p221 MR4

DUCKWORTH,Herbert Hartley Lt kia 24-3-18 3/6LancF att2/7War p221 MR27

DUCKWORTH,Percy Blezard 2Lt kia 9-4-17 WarwickRFA p208 CR France418

DUCKWORTH,William T2Lt kia 25-3-18 20 att18LancF p92 MR27

DUCKWORTH,William Henry T2Lt dow 21-4-16 20LancF p92 CR France1,14-4-16

DUDDELL,Arnold Leslie Lt dow 27-9-17 3SStaffs att6Yorks p122 CR Belgium23

DUDDLE,William Kearsley 2Lt kia 20-8-17 8LancF p221 MR30,19-8-17

DUDDY,George Lionel Alfred T2Lt kia 10-4-18 11Suff p78 CR France685

DUDER,Harvey Stevens Capt kia 31-7-17 8Lpool p215 MR29

DUDGEON,Arthur TLt ded 19-11-18 RGA attRE 4FldSurvCo p39 CR France134

DUDGEON,Frederick Charles 2Lt kia 28-10-18 8Huss p22 MR38

DUDGEON,Ralph de Seton Maj 29-4-18 MilAccDept MR67

DUDLEY,Arthur Walter T2Lt kia 30-3-18 2 att8Worc p108 MR27

DUDLEY,Bernard John Cherleton Capt kia 24-1-17 Dors att3NigR p124&201 MR50

DUDLEY,Charles Leonard 2Lt kia 14-6-15 1/7Manch p237 CR Gallipoli6,4-6-15

DUDLEY,David Capt kia 9-5-15 IA 91Punjabis att6Jats p276 CR France924

DUDLEY,Eric Whittington 2Lt kia 30-6-16 13RSuss p118 MR19

DUDLEY,Henry Pemberton 2Lt kia 3-9-16 3Leinst att2IrReg p174 CR France402

DUDLEY,Herbert Edward.MID T2Lt kia 23-8-17 6SomLI p79 CR Belgium165

DUDLEY,Leonard Gray Capt dow 24-11-14 IA 6Jats p276 CR France80,Grey

DUDLEY,Leonard Thomas.MC.Lt dow 8-10-18 10RFus p67 CR France398,Capt

DUDLEY,Noel Montague Charles 2Lt dow 11-10-16 1/5Lpool p215 CR France40

DUDLEY,Samuel Robert TLt ded 21-12-15 RAMC p267 CR Essex1

DUDLEY,Walter Joseph TLt kia 16-6-15 4RFus p67 MR29

DUDLEY-HILL,William Capt 13-5-15 1LNLancs CR France80

DUDMAN,David.MID Lt&QM ded 26-4-19 11Leic p87 CR Germany1

DUERDEN,Charles 2Lt dow 24-3-18 87RFA p208 CR France13

DUERDEN,Edgar Lt dow 17-8-17 A150RFA p28 CR Belgium8

DUERDEN,Henry T2Lt kld 27-7-17 GL &RFC p7 CR Lancs235

DUERDEN,John Lt dow 10-6-17 2/4 att2/5ELancs p226 CR France769,2Lt

DUERDON,George 2Lt kia 10-4-18 4LNLancs attRFC p234&258,5Bn CR France37

DUFF,Alexander 2Lt kia 28-6-15 7ScotRif p224 MR4

DUFF,Beauchamp Oswald Capt kia 7-11-14 IA 1/1GurkhaRif att2/2 p276 MR28

DUFF,Beauchamp Patrick T2Lt kia 25-9-15 5CamH p167 MR19

DUFF,Edward Algernon ACapt ded 22-9-19 8TankCps p266 CR Asia81

DUFF,Guy Leith Assheton Capt dow 2-9-16 RFA p28 CR Scot141

DUFF,Hugh John.DSO.MC.Maj kia 6-9-18 2LovatScouts p204 CR France518,10CamH

DUFF,James 2Lt dow 9-4-17 RGA 167SB p39 CR France120,69SB

DUFF,James Mitchell Lt ded 24-8-19 7ScotRif p255 CR Burma129A,John

DUFF,John 2Lt dow 25-8-18 3 att1RInniskF p104 CR France855

DUFF,John Creran Lt kia 10-6-15 2GordH p166 MR22,Crera 18-6-15

DUFF,Peter Tyrie T2Lt kia 20-9-18 1/5SLancs p125 CR France106

DUFF,Robert George Vivian.Bart.Lt kia 16-10-14 2LifeGds RoO p20 CR Belgium380,Robin

DUFF,Sidney Hamilton 2Lt kia 13-4-18 18WelshR p126 MR32,9-4-18

DUFF,William Lt kia 28-6-15 1/7ScotRif D'Coy p224 CR Gallipoli6

DUFF,William 2Lt kia 18-11-16 13HLI p162 CR France534

DUFF,William Peter.MC.2Lt kia 23-4-17 8N&D p233 MR20

DUFF-GORDON,Cosmo Lewis Lt kia 3-9-16 Hereford att13MGC Inf p187&252 CR France402

DUFFELL,James Henry 2Lt kia 22-3-18 5TankCps p188 MR27

DUFFIELD,Arthur Edward 2Lt kia 16-8-17 8Mddx p236 MR30

DUFFIELD,William Ernest Capt ded 7-2-19 Ex RASC p267 CR Lond1

DUFFIN,Charles Francis TLtACapt kld 13-3-18 GL 9RIrRif attLabCps 127PoWCoy p190 CR France134

DUFFUS,Gordon Charles 2Lt kia 16-1-17 A235RFA p208 CR Belgium28

DUFFUS,William Lt dow 1-12-17 1/6GordH p242 CR France398

DUFFY,Alexander Noel T2Lt kia 18-11-16 8NStaffs A'Coy p157 CR France284

DUFFY,D.J.P.Lt 20-2-20 RMunsF att3NigR CR WAfrica39

DUFFY,Joseph Vincent TCapt ded 7-12-18 RAMC p195 CR EAfrica36

DUFFY,Thomas Bryan TCapt dow 16-8-18 1/2 att15DLI p160 France4,17-8-18

DUFTY,Thomas Ernest Lt kia 19-5-15 5Yorks p220 CR Belgium4

DUGDALE,Charles Cyril Lt dow PoW 27-5-18 4DLI attYLI p160 MR18

DUGDALE,Daniel TCapt kia 28-9-18 10EYorks p84 CR France262

DUGDALE,James.DCM.T2Lt dow 7-7-18 ELancs att1Bn p110 CR France31

DUGDALE,John Ainscow Capt ded 22-10-19 Norf p263 CR Lancs86

DUGDALE,Joseph Warrior 2Lt ded 3-1-18 27LabCps p189 CR France145

DUGDALE,Richard William.MC.Rev kia 24-10-18 RAChDept att1Norf p199 CR France658

DUGGAN,Charles William Maj drd 10-10-18 RAMC p195 MR40

DUGGAN,Frederick Capt kia 21-3-16 RH&FA p28 CR France275

DUGGAN,George Grant TCapt dow 16-8-15 5RIrFus p171 MR4

DUGGAN,Herrick Stevenson TLt dow 21-10-15 RE 70Coy p44 CR France80,18-9-15

DUGGAN,J.HonMaj&Commy 27-2-21 IOD CR Yorks548

DUGGAN,John Rowswell Lt kia 16-8-15 5RIrReg p89 CR Gallipoli4

DUGGAN,Joseph Henry William 2Lt kia 6-11-17 14Glouc &20RFC p7&106 MR20

DUGGAN,Thomas Alphonsus T2Lt kia 13-11-16 7ELancs p110 CR France384

DUGMORE,William Francis Brougham Radcliffe.DSO.MajALtCol kia 12-6-17 1NStaffs RoO p157 CR Belgium127

DUGNOLLE,John Henry 2Lt kia 25-9-15 2RSuss C'Coy p118 CR France219

DUGUID,Alexander Ritchie 2Lt kia 3-5-17 4EYorks p219 CR France777

DUGUID,Charles Frederick.DSO.MC.Capt kia 13-5-17 22Manch p154 MR20

DUGUID,Clarence Donald.MM.T2Lt kia 18-9-18 13WelshR p126 CR France415

DUGUID,James T2Lt kia 9-4-16 7NStaffs p157 MR38

DUHAN,Francis Taylor Maj kia 26-4-15 IA 19Punjabis att57Rif p276

DUHEAUME,Herbert Thomas TCapt ded 5-8-16 RAMC p195 CR Dorset162
DUIRS,Mearns William T2Lt kia 25-9-15 7KOSB p101 MR19
DUKE,Alexander Leonard LtCol ded 27-2-18 IMS p276 MR43
DUKE,Barry Pevensey Lt kia 3-11-14 3 att2RSuss p118 MR29
DUKE,John.MC.TCapt dow 22-4-18 11Ess p131 CR Belgium18
DUKE,Valentine Gordon Capt kia 10-7-16 RGA 26SB p39 CR France188
DUKES,Samuel SubCdr ded 21-10-16 IA S&TCps p276 CR France300
DULEY,Edwin Joseph T2Lt kia 2-11-16 7BordR p117 CR France744
DULSON,Matthew Harvey 2Lt kia 11-4-17 3DragGds p21 MR20
DUMARESQ,Herbert William Maj ded 14-1-16 RB p178 CR Surrey27
Du MAURIER,Guy Louis Busson.DSO.LtCol kia 10-3-15 3RFus p67 CR Belgium17,9-3-15
Du MOULIN,Francis Louis.MC.CaptALtCol kia 7-11-18 RSuss Cmdg1EYorks p118 CR France935
DUMSDAY,Cyril Robert Capt kia 27-4-15 8Mddx p236 CR Belgium152
DUMVILLE,E.2Lt kia 26-6-18 6WRid &RAF p227
DUN,Leslie Finlay Capt kia 28-9-15 10Lpool p216 CR Belgium6
DUNBAR,Arbuthnot John Capt kia 17-3-15 RFA 114Bty p28 CR France705
DUNBAR,John Campbell 2Lt kld 18-9-18 1/5HLI &RAF CR Egypt9
DUNBAR,William John Lt ded 20-11-17 RE p262
DUNBAVANO,Hubert 2Lt kia 25-8-16 RE p210 CR France400
DUNCAN,Alexander Lt kia 25-3-18 4Manch att40MGC p154&182 CR France927
DUNCAN,Alexander Bell 2Lt dow 5-8-16 IARO att28Cav p276 CR Asia82
DUNCAN,Alexander John Farquharson 2Lt dow 31-3-18 4 att8/10GordH p242 CR France40
DUNCAN,Alick Thomas 2Lt kia 2-3-17 12ESurr p112 CR Belgium28
DUNCAN,Arthur Paul 2Lt ded 26-5-18 1Mon p270 CR Mon52
DUNCAN,Arthur Seymour 2Lt kia 9-4-18 17Mddx p146 CR France298
DUNCAN,Charles Eric T2Lt kia 24-11-16 3RB p178 CR France115
DUNCAN,Charles Walter T2Lt kia 22-11-17 att6Nhampt p137 CR Belgium106
DUNCAN,Christopher William.MC.2LtTLt kia 20-11-17 4NStaffs attA'TankCps p157,188&258 MR17
DUNCAN,Daniel McFie T2Lt kia 2-10-18 1/2KOSB p101 CR France699
DUNCAN,David Cyril 2Lt kia 21-8-18 14Lond p249 MR30
DUNCAN,Edward Francis.MC.Chap4Cl kia 11-3-17 RAChDept att103InfBde p199 CR France1182
DUNCAN,Edward Henry 2Lt dow 24-3-18 93RFA p28 CR France62,25-3-18
DUNCAN,Emile Horace George TCapt ded 28-10-16 RAMC p195 CR Surrey2
DUNCAN,Garnet George Lt kia 15-12-16 SL attGoldCoastR p254 CR EAfrica38 &CR Tanzania1
DUNCAN,George Balfour 2Lt kia 30-7-16 3 att2RScotsFus p94 MR21
DUNCAN,George Stewart Lt kia 23-9-17 6GordH p242 MR30
DUNCAN,H.Capt 20-6-21 RAMC CR Scot935
DUNCAN,Harold Forrester.MC.Lt dow 29-3-17 3/5HLI attRFC p18&240 CR France169
DUNCAN,Harry T2Lt kia 23-4-17 18Manch p154 MR20
DUNCAN,Henry John Maj kia 8-8-16 5Lpool p215 CR France630
DUNCAN,Herbert Richard Lt ded 26-4-19 RASC p192 CR Scot359
DUNCAN,Isabella Lucy May Sister ded 1-3-17 QAIMNS 13StatHosp p200 CR France64
DUNCAN,J.M.T2Lt ded 6-6-18 RE 1WT p44 CR Scot495,20-11-17
DUNCAN,James 2Lt ded 19-4-19 TankCps p266 CR Scot840
DUNCAN,James Athol Gordon T2Lt kld 15-2-18 RFC p15 CR Hunts83
DUNCAN,John TLt kia 31-7-17 10HLI p162 MR29
DUNCAN,John Donald Parland 2Lt kia 16-6-17 13NumbF p60 MR20
DUNCAN,John Francis TCapt&radjt kia 25-9-15 10ScotRif p103 MR19
DUNCAN,Leonard George Capt ded 15-6-21 RE 136RlyConstCoy MR43
DUNCAN,Kenneth 2Lt kia 9-5-17 6Dev p217 MR20
DUNCAN,Kenneth William Allen 2Lt kia 8-5-18 10Lpool att6SfthR p216 MR20
DUNCAN,Malcolm 2Lt dow 21-9-17 1/7Lpool p215 CR Belgium3,Capt
DUNCAN,Philip Courtnay 2Lt kia 30-10-17 8Lond p247 CR Belgium126
DUNCAN,Robert Gordon Campbell 2Lt kia 3-5-17 10A&SH p173 CR France924
DUNCAN,Ronald Wingrave Capt kia 9-3-16 RAMC attLeic p195 MR38
DUNCAN,Stuart Capt kia 13-11-14 Glouc RoO att2SLancs p106 MR29
DUNCAN,W.A.TD.LtCol 18-12-17 MddxHuss CR Mddx26
DUNCAN,Walter.MIDx2 Lt ded 19-12-18 8Lpool p215 CR Lancs2
DUNCAN,William Balfour Bethune Lt ded 3-9-16 4BlkW p230 CR France701
DUNCAN,William Williamson Kerr Lt ded 29-2-16 RAMC p270 CR Scot877
DUNCANSON,Ian Ferguson 2Lt kia 12-10-17 8A&SH p243 CR Belgium126
DUNCANSON,Roy 2Lt kia 7-7-16 3 att9WRid p115 MR21
DUNCANSON,Stuart Ray 2Lt kia 11-8-17 1Mon att11Ches p244 CR Belgium125

DUNCANSON,Una Marguerite Nurse drd 31-12-17 VAD p200 CR Egypt1
DUNCOMBE-SHAFTO,Arthur.DSO.Capt kia 12-9-14 RScots p54
DUNCUM,Eric Cundy Lt 7-12-20 B84RFA CR Africa81
DUNDAS,Cecil Henry Lt dow 2-3-15 1WelshR p126 CR Belgium58 20-2-15
DUNDAS,David George Minden.MID 2Lt ded 10-2-18 IA 17Inf p276 MR66,Maj
DUNDAS,George.MC&Bar.Lt dow 2-9-18 161RFA p28 CR France119,kia A61RFA
DUNDAS,Henry Lancaster Neville.MC&Bar.LtACapt kia 27-9-18 1ScotsGds p52 CR France530,Nevill
DUNDAS,Richard Charles LtCol kia 25-9-15 11RScots p254 CR France924
DUNDERDALE,William Henry T2Lt kia 11-1-17 21Manch p154 MR21
DUNDON,James St.John TLt ded 17-6-16 RAMC p195 CR Iraq6
DUNDON,Sydney Jack 2Lt kia 16-8-16 13Lpool p71 MR21
DUNFORD,Ernest Thubron T2Lt dow 23-4-17 PoW GL &12RFC p7 CR France1276
DUNFORD,Roy Craig.DSO.Capt dow 10-11-16 1/6NumbF p213 CR Numb3
DUNGEY,Francis Herbert T2Lt kia 3-5-17 1EKent p57 MR19
DUNGLISON,William T2Lt dow 21-8-18 1NumbF p60 CR France745
DUNHILL,Carlos Miguel Guillermo Capt kia 1-12-15 RE att17S&M p44 MR38
DUNKERLEY,Harold TCaptAMaj dow 23-3-18 RAMC att95FA p195 CR France924
DUNKIN,Alfred Davy Hosking T2Lt kia 3-10-18 N&D att1/8Bn p133 CR France375,Davey
DUNKLEY,Alexander 2Lt kia 9-4-16 12 att9Worc p108 MR38
DUNKLEY,Henry Newman T2Lt kia 21-9-17 1/2 att12ESurr B'Coy p112 MR30
DUNLOP,Alesander Hamilton 2Lt kia 6-11-17 AyrYeo p203 CR Palestine1,12RScotsF
DUNLOP,Archibald Ballantine Henderson.MC.Capt dow 20-9-18 1Camb p244 CR France194
DUNLOP,Brian John 2Lt kia 31-7-17 3GrenGds p49 CR Belgium13
DUNLOP,Charles 2Lt dow 22-10-14 RInniskF p104 CR France473,Lt
DUNLOP,Christian Dolymythe Hamilton 2Lt kia 16-6-15 10Lpool p216 MR29,Dalrymple
DUNLOP,Colin Edward 2Lt kia 3-2-17 IARO att1/2GurkhaRif p276 CR Iraq5
DUNLOP,Frederick Cleave Strickland Capt kia 8-11-14 1Manch p154 CR France706
DUNLOP,George Harry Melville TMaj ded 3-7-16 RAMC 4GH p195 CR France40
DUNLOP,George Malcolm Capt kia 25-4-15 RDubF p176 CR Gallipoli15
DUNLOP,Harry Holmes Kerr Lt ded 12-2-19 RASC 1034 MT Coy p192 CR Italy15
DUNLOP,James Lt dow 1-11-18 4RScots p222 CR Belgium159,2-11-18
DUNLOP,James Wilkie TLt ded 5-3-17 5RIrReg p89 CR Surrey18
DUNLOP,John Francis Logan Lt dow 7-5-18 RGA 139HB p39 CR France71
DUNLOP,John Gunning Moore 2Lt kia 27-8-14 2RDubF p176 CR France660
DUNLOP,Julian Silver Strickland.MID Capt kia 24-10-14 1SStaffs p122 MR29
DUNLOP,Kenneth Strickland 2Lt kia 26-9-15 4 att1SStaffs p122 CR France423
DUNLOP,Launcelot Lindsay Brook T2Lt kia 3-7-16 11Ches p96 MR21
DUNLOP,William.MC.MM.2Lt dow 30-10-18 39RFA p28 CR France1270,51RFA
DUNLOP,William Eric Brook 2Lt kia 19-5-17 5BordR p228 MR20
DUNLOP,William James T2Lt kia 21-9-16 RFA p28 CR France430
DUNLOP-SMITH,R.Capt 12-6-17 33Punjabis CR EAfrica38 &CR Tanzania1
DUNMAN,Charles Norman Innes 2LtTLt kia 31-7-17 15Mddx attMGC Inf p146&182 CR Belgium112
DUNMAN,Victor William TLt dow 19-9-17 SL att2/2KAR p202 CR EAfrica52
DUNN,Arthur Gibson TLt kia 5-9-17 RAMC 129FA p195 CR Belgium83
DUNN,Clifford Martyn.MIDx2TCapt kia 25-11-17 17WelshR p126 CR France256,24-11-17
DUNN,Ernest George 2Lt kia 10-6-17 10Lpool attMGC Inf p187&216 CR France777
DUNN,Francis William Morgan 2Lt kia 10-8-15 5WelshR p230 MR4
DUNN,Frank Mewborne T2Lt kia 23-9-17 10DLI p160 CR Belgium78
DUNN,Frederick Charles Robert TLt kia 9-7-16 11LancF p92 MR21,10-7-16
DUNN,Frederick Oswald TLt kld 19-3-16 23NumbF p60 CR France275
DUNN,Gerald Morton 2Lt kia 13-10-18 RGA 140SB p209 CR France147
DUNN,Godfrey Lawrence Capt 21-9-20 1/1KentCycBn CR Kent268
DUNN,Gwynne Morgan T2Lt dow 23-2-17 9WRid p115 CR France105
DUNN,Harold Black T2Lt kia 30-8-18 1/5Dev p76 CR France1484
DUNN,Henry Joseph 2Lt kia 26-11-17 4RWKent p234 CR France1461
DUNN,Herbert 2Lt ded 25-10-15 8ScotRif p225 CR Egypt3
DUNN,Herbert Harman TLt kia 26-9-16 12Lpool B'Coy p71 MR21 &CR France1890
DUNN,Hugh Aubrey Fairfield 2Lt drd 21-5-16 RE p44 CR Wales37
DUNN,James 2Lt ded 14-11-18 IARO att2S&M p276 MR40,Lt
DUNN,James Shannon T2Lt kia 4-10-17 2KOSB p101 MR30
DUNN,John 2Lt kia 21-6-17 7ScotRif p224 CR Belgium115

DUNN,John 2Lt.MM.dow 1-2-18 3Suff p78 CR Frnce518,kia
DUNN,John.MM.2Lt kia 20-9-18 56RFA p28 CR France484
DUNN,John Cragg Lt dow 25-3-16 3Dors att59TMB p124 CR Belgium11
DUNN,John Hubert Malcolmson 2Lt kia 25-9-16 18RFA p28 CR France832
DUNN,John Robert Collard 2Lt kia 20-8-15 5WelshR p230 MR4
DUNN,John Valentine TCapt kia 15-8-15 7RMunstF p175 MR4,7RDubF
DUNN,Malcolm T2Lt kia 9-4-18 22NumbF p60 CR Belgium451
DUNN,Martin 2Lt kia 16-5-17 5BlkW p231 CR France97
DUNN,Philip Morgan TCapt kia 3-2-17 8RWelshF p97 CR Iraq5
DUNN,Ralph Ellis T2Lt dow 1-7-16 1SomLI p79 MR21
DUNN,Ralph John 2Lt kia 25-9-15 RE p44 MR19
DUNN,Robert James Armstrong Capt kia 23-4-17 4GordH p241 CR France1194
DUNN,Robert William Henry Brighen Col ded 8-1-17 Staff RFus 13ResInfBdeCdr p1 CR Wales613
DUNN,Robin Gaspar Lt kldacc 19-3-19 1/5Lincs p255 CR Kent268,Capt 18-3-18
DUNN,Spottiswoode Robert.TD.LtCol dow 29-6-15 1/4RScots p211 MR4
DUNN,Thomas Capt kia 19-4-17 1/5KOSB p224 CR Palestine8
DUNN,Thomas Edward Doncaster Lt dow 21-12-14 2ScotRif p103 CR France768,22-12-14
DUNN,William T2Lt kia 24-3-18 7Lincs p75 CR France216
DUNN,William John T2Lt kia 17-7-16 6KOSB p101 CR France744
DUNN-PATTISON,Richard Phillipson Capt kia 8-3-16 6Dev p217 MR38
DUNNACHIE,William James Nimmo Lt kia 15-4-16 RE 250TC p44 CR Belgium37,2Lt
DUNNAGE,Arthur 2Lt kia 1-9-16 5 att3RB p178 CR France402
DUNNE,Arthur Sydney Lt kia 2-7-17 6Drags p22 CR France1495
DUNNE,John Geoffrey David Baird Lt ded 12-11-18 3RDubF p176 CR France1028,1 Ex3Bn
DUNNE,Walter Edwin 2LtTLt ded 18-10-15 2LancF p92 CR France167
DUNNET,Donald 2Lt kia 15-6-15 5SfthH p241 MR22
DUNNETT,Raymond Frederick.MC.Lt kld 17-11-17 5Worc &RFC p7&108 CR Hamps153
DUNNING,Reginald Percy 2Lt kia 21-3-18 2/6N&D p233 MR20
DUNNINGTON-JEFFERSON,Wilfred Mervyn 2Lt kia 22/29-4-15 7 att3RFus p67 MR29,27-4-15
DUNPHY,K.P,MC Lt 19-5-20 2Leinst CR Eire381
DUNSCOMBE Charles William TLtACapt dow 14-3-17 13Ess p131 CR France177
DUNSCOMBE George 2Lt ded 6-11-18 PoW 17Manch p154 CR Europe149
DUNSFORD,Reginald Martin Capt ded 18-10-18 RGA 397SB p270 CR Hamps57
DUNSHEE,Ernest Rowland T2Lt dow 11-8-18 1/2 att5WRid p115 CR France40
DUNSMURE,Colin Hamilton Terrot 2Lt kia 25-9-15 5CamH p167 MR19
DUNSMURE,Henry Alexander Henderson Lt kia 20-2-15 2CamH p167 CR Belgium28,Alistair
DUNSTAN,Guy Pierce T2Lt kia 1-7-16 11BordR p117 CR France293,Peirce
DUNSTAN,Hedley T2Lt kia 18-8-17 Y&L &55RFC p7&158 CR France285
DUNSTAN,John Leonard Lt ded 28-10-18 GL &RAF LR Lond14
DUNSTAN,Sidney Chap4Cl ded 16-7-18 RAChDept p199 CR Notts68
DUNSTERVILLE,Graham Eardley Lt 30-10-14 1Dev p76 MR22
DUNVILLE,John Spencer.VC.2Lt dow 25-6-17 1Drags p21 CR France363,26-6-17
DUNWELL,Frederick Leslie 2Lt kia 4-1-16 5RFus p67 CR Belgium28,Fredrick
DUNWOODY,Hugh Henderson T2Lt kld 31-7-16 10 att9RIrRFus p171 CR Belgium48
DUNWOODY,John Myles 2Lt kia 4-5-17 4RDubF p176 CR Italy14
DUNWOODY,Samuel T2Lt kia 5-10-18 17RIrRif p169 CR Belgium157
DUPE,Cyril Harry 2Lt dow 21-3-18 C149RFA att30DAC CR France1203
Du PLERGNEY,Victor Wilder 2Lt dow 18-4-18 1 att2/5Lincs p75 CR Belgium38,DuPLERGNY
DUPLOCK,Marten Cave TLt kia 2-4-18 7Beds p85 MR27
DUPRES,Ernest Cruzick TLtACapt kia 29-8-18 9RFus p67 CR France630
DUPUIS,Alfred 2Lt dow 8-8-16 1Lincs CR France46
DURAND,Francis William Capt kia 21-12-14 3 att2RMunstF p175 MR22,22-12-14
DURAND,Reginald Heber Marion Lt dow 29-6-17 IA 38CentIndHorse p276 CR France446
DURANT,Christopher Gilbert T2Lt kia 18-10-16 13 att4Worc p108 MR21
DURANT,Hugh.DCM.MID 2Lt kia 20-1-16 9Lancers p22 CR France423
DURANT,Noel Henry Colin Fairfax Lt kia 30-11-17 1IrGds p52 MR17
DURANT,Norman Lt kia 12-3-16 1Glouc p106 CR France149
DURBAN,Percy 2Lt kia 25-3-18 3GrenGds p49 CR France214,DURBIN
DURDLE,Reginald William Lt kia 18-9-18 4EKent p212 CR France369
DURHAM,Edward Lt kia 26-11-14 RB p178 MR22
DURHAM,William Elyrin Wakeman Maj kia 19-9-19 IA 27LightCav p276 MR43,Glynn

DURINGTON,Thomas Philip Maj kia 12-11-14 1Drags p21
DURLACHER,Eric Alexander Ogilvie.MC.2LtACapt kia 20-5-17 5 att2Worc p108&258 MR20
DURLACHER,Philip Alfred.MC.Lt ded 12-5-18 148MGC p266 CR Surrey160
DURNAN,Edward T2Lt kia 16-10-17 14Y&L p158 CR France184
DURNFORD,Richard Selby TCapt kia 31-7-15 9KRRC p150 MR29
DURNFORD,Robert Chichester.DSO.Capt kia 21-6-18 1/4Hamps p228 CR Asia82
DURNO,Ronald Walpole 2Lt kia 24-2-17 RFA attY41TMB p28 CR Belgium21
DURNO-STEELE,Frederick Arthur Lt kia 9-5-17 7 O&BLI p130 MR37
DUROSE,Sydney Truman Capt kia 2-4-17 7N&D p233 CR France366
DURRAD,Francis Albert Capt kia 8-11-17 RASC &22RFC p7&192 MR20
DURRANT,Alec William TLt kia 13-11-16 184RFA p28 CR France1013
DURRANT,Arthur Michael.MC.TLtACapt kia 5-12-16 RE 257TC p44 CR France705,257FC
DURRANT,Christopher Martin TLt kld 31-7-18 SL p201
DURRANT,Dudley Garton 2Lt kia 16-8-16 1/5Glouc p225 MR21
DURRANT,John TLt ded 17-10-18 3N&D p133 CR France1858
DURRANT,Lombe Atthill 2Lt kld 6-6-18 GL &65RAF p190 CR France71,kia
DURRANT,T.Capt ded 16-5-18 SL &RAF p201
DURRANT,William Blencowe 2Lt kia 9-5-17 6 att2RB p178 MR32,8-5-15
DURRANT,William Henry Gilbert T2Lt kia 26-9-15 6Dors att2Wilts p124 CR France423,Heinz
DURSTON,Charles Giles 2Lt kia 7-10-16 12Lond p248 MR21
DURTNELL,Richard Neville.MID T2Lt kia 28-4-17 11Suff p78 MR20
DURWARD,Andrew.MC.LtACapt kia 16-10-18 6KOSB p101 CR Belgium157
DURWARD,Ronald Gibson Stewart Lt kia 11-8-18 1RScots p54 CR France360
DUSGATE,Richard Edmund T2Lt ded PoW 19-12-17 RE &46RFC p7&p44 CR France1142,dow
DUSSEE,Arthur Norman 2Lt kia 1-7-16 4 att19LancF p92 CR France296
DUST,Frank William.MC.Maj kia 23-4-17 RFA p206 MR20
DUTCH,Ernest James T2Lt dow 6-1-17 14 att25/7RFus p67 CR EAfrica39,25Bn
DUTHIE,Bertie T2Lt kia 23-10-18 GordH p166 CR France206,Bert 24-10-18 3 att1NumbF
DUTHIE,D.O.2Lt kia 23-8-18 GL &2RAF p190 MR20
DUTTON,Alfred Laurence T2Lt kia 11-4-17 RE 95FC p44 CR France568
DUTTON,Charles T2Lt kia 7-7-16 10LancF p92 MR21
DUTTON,Charles TCapt dow 28-7-16 2SStaffs p122 CR France141,29-7-16
DUTTON,Geoffrey 2Lt dow 8-9-17 4 att8RSuss p228 CR Belgium16
DUTTON,Gerald Alexander 2Lt ded 5-5-16 4SStaffs p122 CR Dorset160
DUTTON,John Gordon.MC&Bar.TCaptAMaj dow 5-4-18 D107RFA p28 CR France1233
DUTTON,Joseph Issacher 2Lt kia 21-3-18 82RFA p28 MR27
DUTTON,Richard T2Lt ded 19-8-17 GL &48RFC p7 CR Belgium132
DUTTON,Thomas Dutton Capt kia 3-11-17 5 att2/4RWKent p235 CR Palestine1,Daniel 4-11-17
DUVALL,John Richard Rev dow 6-10-17 RAChDept att13Manch p199 CR Greece1,att7Wilts
DUVOISIN,John Hurll 2Lt kia 15-7-16 9HLI p240 MR21
DUXBURY,Andrew Marshall Lt dow 30-3-18 1 att6 O&BLI p231 MR27
DUXBURY,Arthur T2Lt kia 9-4-18 5RLancs p58 CR France98
DUXBURY,Herbert Cecil T2Lt ded 11-5-17 GL &54RFC p7 MR20
DWYER,Charles Henry.MID TCapt kia 17-11-16 10Worc p108 MR21
DWYER,Harold Beecher 2Lt kia 16-4-16 IARO att103Mahrattas p276 CR Iraq1
DWYER,J.O.2Lt 10-9-16 7RIrF &TMB CR France66
DWYER,James Jameson.DSO.Capt ded 19-2-19 RAMC p195 CR France65
DYCHE,John TLt dow 28-1-17 8RWelshF p97 CR Iraq5
DYE,George Harry Gordon TLt dow 21-11-17 9Norf p73 CR France398
DYE,Norman Sawford 2Lt kia 25-3-18 N&D att16Bn p133 MR27
DYER,Arthur Francis Rayner TCapt&Adjt kia 30-9-17 GL att1KAR p202 CR EAfrica11 &CR Tanzania1
DYER,Cecil MacMillan 2Lt kia 9-4-15 6 att4RB p178 MR29
DYER,Charles James 2Lt kia 7-3-17 RGA 150SB p39 CR France550
DYER,Charles Nettleton Capt ded 14-7-16 HAC A'Bty p206 CR Egypt15,Chester
DYER,Edward Arnold Lt kia 28-6-15 9KSLI p144 CR Gallipoli6
DYER,Francis Lloyd Capt kldByArabs 15-4-15 IA 83BurmaInf p276 CR Asia82,Frank 93Bn
DYER,Frederick Vivian Alma LtTCapt kia 25-9-15 1Mddx p146 CR France114
DYER,Harry Frank 2Lt dow 28-8-17 1/6WRid p227 CR France102
DYER,Herbert Arthur 2Lt kia 7-12-17 GL &65RFC p7 MR20
DYER,James Edward Stanley 2Lt kia 9-10-17 6LancF p221 MR30
DYER,John Swinnerton.Bart.MC.Capt kia 31-7-17 1ScotsGds attDAQ MG GdsDiv p52 CR Belgium12

DYER,Laurence Charles Lt kia 19-4-17 4EKent att2/10Mddx p212 CR Palestine8
DYER,Percy Maitland Lt kia 1-9-17 RE 208FC p44 CR France366
DYER,R.MM.Lt ded 30-12-18 SL p201
DYER,Ralph Gibb T2Lt kia 23-2-17 RE 92FC p44 CR France832
DYER,Stewart B.B.DSO.Maj ded 26-1-17 3Wilts CR Europe42 Ex2LifeGds
DYER,Sydney Beresford Hope 2Lt dow 10-7-18 104LabCps p189 CR Staffs61
DYER,William Oscar 2Lt dow 28-10-17 RGA 276SB p39 CR France193
DYKE,Cyril John 2Lt kia 7-11-17 24 att2/22Lond p252 CR Palestine1
DYKE,E.P.W.2Lt kld 30-10-18 8Y&L &RAF p158 CR Belgium205
DYKE,Francis Hart 2Lt kia 27-9-17 RWKent att7LNLancs p141 CR Belgium20
DYKE,George Bewsey TLt kia 26-4-16 RGA 18SB p39 CR Belgium15
DYKE,Walter Ball TCapt kia 10-4-18 RGA 155SB p39 CR Belgium90
DYKES,Alfred McNair LtCol kia 26-8-14 RLancs p58 MR15
DYKES,James Johnstone Capt kia 12-7-15 5KOSB p224 CR Gallipoli2
DYMOCK,Robert Townsend Vaughan Lt dow 27-10-15 1KSLI p144 CR Belgium2
DYMOKE,Walter George T2Lt dow 3-10-16 6RBerks p139 CR France62
DYMOND,John Jordan 2Lt kia 12-4-18 1/5SLancs p230 CR France260
DYMORE-BROWN,Hugh Patterson 2Lt ded 21-2-19 9RBerks Ex att5Bn p265 CR Berks117
DYSON,Charles Capt kia 6-4-17 2/8WYorks C'Coy p219 CR France568
DYSON,Charles Bertram Lt kia 25-3-18 1/5ELancs p226 CR France560
DYSON,Harold Edward 2Lt kia 31-7-16 4Y&L p238 CR France246
DYSON,Hubert Archibald.MID LtACapt kia 18-11-16 7EKent A'Coy p57 CR France314
DYSON,S.G.2Lt ded 1-6-18 GL &RAF p190
DYSON,Stanley William TLtACapt dow 5-10-17 11Manch p154 CR Belgium16
DYSON,William Hubert 2Lt dow 14-7-16 16Lond p250 CR France1512
DYSON,William Webster 2Lt kia 26-8-16 1RIrFus p171 CR Belgium127

E

EADE,Aylmer 2Lt kia 9-10-17 3 att2Yorks p90 CR Belgium83
EADDY,Charles Thomas 2Lt kia 9-7-16 4 att8NStaffs p157 MR21
EADIE,David 2Lt kia 10-5-18 5ScotRif p224 MR30
EADIE,James 2Lt kia 15-5-17 5SfthH p241 MR20
EADIE,James Albert Lt kia 27-5-18 9A&SH attMGC p187&244 MR18
EADIE,Robert Allan T2Lt kia 6-8-16 7Lincs p75 CR France399
EADIE,William TCapt kia 18-10-16 5CamH p167 CR France385
EADON,Alfred Mitchell 2Lt dow 21-8-15 6Yorks p90 MR4
EAGAR,Denis Geoffray 2Lt kia 28-9-18 160RFA p28 MR30
EAGAR,Francis Russell 2Lt kia 9-5-15 RFA 36Bty p28 CR France525
EAGAR,Rowland Tallis.MID 2Lt kia 8-8-18 RFus att9Bn p67 CR France141
EAGAR,William George Massy Capt kia 21-8-15 3 att1RMunstF p175 MR4
EAGLE,Frank Walter Lt kia 6-6-16 RE 2/1FC p210 CR France281
EAGLE,Gerald Charles T2Lt kia 12-10-16 7Suff p78 MR21
EAGLESFIELD,William James.MM.MSM.2Lt ded 15-11-18 8LancF p221 CR France146
EAGLETON,John Ronaldson Lt dow 3-9-18 C291RFA p207 CR France177
EAITCH,Ernest 2Lt dow 2-11-18 1/17Lond p250 CR France1887
EAKIN,Robert Andrew Capt dow 24-9-17 1KSLI p144 CR Mddx49
EALAND,Frederick John Arthur T2Lt kia 26-9-15 8SomLI p79 MR19
EALES,Charles Wilfred Lt kia 27-9-18 2Dev p76 MR16
EALES,Francis Daw Sherbrooke 2Lt kia 3-5-17 9Leic p87 MR20
EALES,Frank 2Lt ded 2-3-19 12RB p266 CR Durhan64,Lt
EALES-WHITE,Henry Hewlett Capt mbk 25-7-15 6RScotF p256 MR19,27-9-15
EAMES,Arthur Horwood 2Lt kia 1-7-16 1EYorks p84 MR21
EAMES,Fred 2Lt kia 19-9-18 1/3Yorks att1/5Ess p90 CR Palestine9
EAMES,William Stanley Lt dow 16-2-16 7 att12RFus p67 CR Belgium11
EARDLEY,George Arthur T2Lt kia 27-11-17 RLancs att2/5YLI p58 MR17
EARDLEY-WILMOT,F.L.Lt 19-3-15 EOntarioR CR Belgium111
EARDLEY-WILMOT,Gerald Howard T2Lt dow 10-3-16 20MGC p182 MR21 CR France22,9Dev MGSect
EARDLEY-WILMOT,Theodore.DSO.MajTLtCol kia 22-3-18 Y&L att12Suff p158 MR20
EARL,Agnes Kerr Sister 19-3-19 ScotWomensHosp CR Europe57
EARL,Harry Walter T2Lt kia 18-9-18 2RSuss Res p118 MR16
EARLAND,Reginald John T2Lt dow 30-1-17 2SWBord p99 CR France105
EARLE,Cedric 2Lt kia 4-9-18 4EYorks p219 CR France298,Lt
EARLE,Charles Edward LtCol ded 11-8-17 16Ches p96 CR Lond14
EARLE,Ernest Clifford Lt kia 27-5-18 D250RFA p207 MR18

EARLE,John Vincent Lt kia 20-6-15 1N&D att WAFF p201&133 CR WAfrica6
EARLE,Noel Vansittart Lt ded 9-3-16 EKent attN&D p57 CR Surrey160,Capt
EARLE,Walter Colby Capt ded 7-4-15 Ches p96 CR Ches28
EARLE,Wallace Sinclair T2Lt kia 16-4-16 GL &9RFC p2&190 MR20
EARLE,Wilfrid Antony 2Lt kia 23-4-17 4EYorks p219 MR20
EARLEY,William T2Lt kia 11-10-18 Mddx att13Bn p146 CR France270
EARLY,Egbert Edward 2Lt kia 13-10-15 5Lincs p220 MR19
EARLY,Frank D.Capt ded 15-5-18 LdStrathconasHorse CR Canada1595
EARNSHAW,Oscar T2Lt kia 2-6-16 RE p44 MR29
EARY,Frederick Charles.MC.TCapt kia 24-3-18 7DCI p114 MR27
EASDON,A.R.SubAssSurg 10-9-18 IMS CR Iraq8
EASON,Alan 2Lt ded 20-1-16 9RBerks p139 CR Berks93
EASON,Raymond Praed TLt dow 1-7-16 10Lincs A'Coy p75 CR France267
EASON,Sampson TLt kia 7-8-15 5Dors p124 MR4
EASSON,David Lt kia 21-3-18 19Lond p250 MR20
EASSON,David,Ernest Craik Maj kia 13-7-15 6HLI p240 MR4
EAST,Alfred Tomlin 2Lt dow 25-12-15 IARO 1 att3S&M p276 CR Iraq1,25-9-15
EAST,Gordon Doulton LtTCapt kia 30-7-17 RAMC att3GrenGds p195 CR Belgium12,31-7-17
EAST,Herbert Hinton Rev kia 5-8-17 RAChDept att3Ches p199 MR29
EAST,Hubert James Capt kia 10-5-15 1Y&L p158 MR29
EAST,John TCapt kia 1-7-16 15DLI p160 MR21
EAST,Kingsley Dunmore TLt kia 27-5-16 18LancF p92 CR France632
EAST,Lionel William Fellow.CMG.DSO.ColTBrigGen kia 6-9-18 RFA Staff Cmdg X111C HvyArt p28 CR France88,Pellow
EAST,Sydney Clark 2Lt kia 9-10-17 HAC Inf p206 MR30
EAST,William Frederick Ernest T2Lt kia 16-11-16 12 att8ELancs p110 CR France153
EASTERBROOK,Henry George Lt dow 25-4-18 9Lond p248 CR France13
EASTERBROOK,William Reginald.MC.Lt dow 17-7-18 3Ches p96 CR France31,1Bn
EASTGATE-SMITH,Charles William TLtACapt kia 27-8-18 2Manch p154 CR France526
EASTHAM,Clement Vincent T2Lt kia 3-5-17 KSLI att7Bn p144 MR20
EASTMAN,William Viviash T2Lt kia 4-10-17 KRRC att13Bn p150 MR30,Vivaish
EASTON,Arthur Aitken.MID T2Lt kia 2-3-16 10HLI p162 CR Belgium30
EASTON,Cyril.MC.Capt kia 23-4-17 4EYorks p219 CR France162
EASTON,Jack Leslie 2Lt kia 21-3-18 RGA 277SB p39 MR27
EASTON,Percy Thomas Capt&QM ded 26-11-18 Mddx att8NigR p146,26-11-16&201&265 CR Lond5
EASTOP,David Lt dow 14-2-20 RFA CR Kent127
EASTWOOD,Benjamin.MC.TCapt kia 30-5-18 8Glouc p106 CR France1410
EASTWOOD,Donald Capt kia 20-9-17 6Lpool p215 MR30
EASTWOOD,Edmond Patrick 2Lt kia 22-3-18 2Leinst p174 CR France1494
EASTWOOD,Frank Molyneux Lt dow 30-10-14 1RWSurr p55 MR29
EASTWOOD,Frederick Arthur Jervis TLtACapt dow 6-6-17 D103RFA p28 CR Belgium1
EASTWOOD,John William T2Lt kld 28-1-18 10N&D p133 CR France530
EASTWOOD,Leslie T2Lt ded 19-9-15 6RLancs p58 CR Egypt3
EASTWOOD,Ronald.MID Lt dow 5-12-17 RE 42ELancsFC p210 CR France765
EASTWOOD,Sam Lt dow 10-5-18 2/5LNLancs p234 CR France84
EASTWOOD,Thomas Capt 10-1-17 RAVC CR Ches127
EASTWOOD,William.MID TMaj kia 11-8-15 RIrRif att6Bn p169 MR4
EATHORNE,Francis John T2Lt kia 31-7-16 24RFus p67 MR21
EATON,Alexander Robert Charles TLt kia 23-8-18 1Beds p85 CR France239,Alexandra
EATON,Charles William TCapt dow 9-8-17 11Leic p87 CR Belgium19
EATON,Clifford Gwatkin 2Lt kia 24-4-17 1/8Worc p226 MR21
EATON,George Hubert TLt kia 25-3-18 6MGC Inf p182 CR France1893
EATON,Guy Wellesley TCapt kia 6-9-16 8RIrF p171 MR21
EATON,Harold T2Lt kia 31-7-17 13Glouc p106 CR Belgium20
EATON,James Willcox T2Lt kia 1-7-16 20Manch p154 CR France397
EATON,John Rodman Lt dow 8-9-17 RASC p192 CR Belgium16
EATON,William T2Lt kia 6-9-18 18RIrRif p169 CR Belgium42,2Bn
EATON-JONES,Stafford Thomas T2Lt kia 28-10-16 22 att4Lpool p71 MR21
EATON-RICHARDS,Julian David 2Lt kia 25-9-15 2RSuss p118 MR19
EAVES,Alfred Thomas TLt kia 3-10-16 10RWSurr p55 MR21
EAVES,Frederick William D.2Lt kia 21-3-18 1 att7RIrReg p89 MR27
EAVES,Wilberforce Vaughan.MBE.Capt 10-2-20RAMC CR Lond29
EBBUTT,John Horace Lt ded 21-2-19 HuntsCycBn p253 CR France40,1Camb

EBDEN,Francis Thomas Powney Maj ded 9-10-19 IA 73CarnaticInf p276 CR Iraq8

EBERHARDIE,Donel Clemons ACapt ded 7-4-18 IARO RecruitgOff p276 MR66,EBARHARDIE

EBERLI,John Frederick 2Lt dow 16-8-17 3 att2RIrReg attTMB p89 CR Belgium8

EBERLIN,Frederick Harold Maden 2Lt kld 25-7-17 3YLI &RFC p7&143,ded CR Notts84

EBERY,Wilfred T2Lt kia 14-2-16 10N&D p133 MR29

EBORALL,John Arthur T2Lt dow 25-2-17 32RFus p67 CR Belgium21

EBSWORTH,Alexander E.MC.CaptALtCol kia 21-9-18 SLancs att9NumbF p125 CR France255

ECCLES,Arthur John Tolcher.MC.Lt ded 26-11-18 4ESurr attRE p112 CR France289

ECCLES,Charley Gordon TCapt kia 25-5-17 GL &41RFC p7 CR Belgium168

ECCLES,David Roderick T2Lt kld 5-12-17 GL &RFC p7 CR Glouc60

ECCLES,Henry T2Lt kia 28-2-17 3 att7 O&BLI p130 CR Greece6

ECCLES,Horace Dorset Capt kia 16-8-17 RAMC att13RIrRif p195 CR Belgium96

ECCLES,John Dennison.MC.Capt dow 27-9-16 9Lond p247 CR Mddx16

ECCLES,John Vivian William T2Lt drd 4-5-17 RLancs p58 CR Italy14

ECCLES,Robert Col ded 30-10-15 9Lpool p270 CR Lond8

ECCLES,Walter 2Lt kia 30-5-16 4LNLancs p234 CR France175

ECCLESTONE,James T2Lt dedacc 14-5-17 1LifeGds p23 CR Staffs135

ECHIN,C.P.SubCdr 27-10-17 S&T Cps MR43

ECHLIN,Frederick St.John Ford North Lt dow 27-9-16 5RFus &RFC p2&67 CR France518

ECKERSLEY,Herbert T2Lt kia 15-11-17 731LabCps p189 CR Belgium92

ECKLEY,Frederick George 2Lt kia 27-11-17 F'TankCps p188 CR France357

ECKSTEIN,L.A.Lt dow 23-11-16 1/2KARif p268 CR EAfrica38 &CR Tanzania1,L.W.

EDDEN,Henry Stewart Capt kia 21-8-15 RInniskF p104 CR Gallipoli5

EDDIE,George Richard Lt ded 3-11-18 1/4Y&L p238 CR France34

EDDISON,John Radley 2Lt kia 22-4-15 1/8N&D p233 CR Belgium17,21-4-15

EDDISON,Richard de Paiva Lt kia 10-8-17 2/4LNLancs p234 CR France922

EDDISON,Tom Denton Lt kia 30-7-16 14 att19Lpool p71 MR21

EDDY,Charles T2Lt kia 9-10-17 Mddx att16Bn p146 MR30

EDE,Edward Dickens 2Lt dow 13-6-18 5NStaffs p238 CR France145,9Bn Ex 9Lond

EDE,Edwin William.MC.T2LtACapt kia 30-8-18 11RFus p67 CR France786

EDEN,Arthur George 2Lt kia 21-5-18 7Ess p232 MR34

EDEN,Bernard Lt kia 9-5-15 att2Nhampt p137 MR32

EDEN,John Lt kia 17-10-14 12Lancers p22 CR Belgium132

EDEN,William Alfred Morton.Hon.Lt kia 3-3-15 4KRRC p150 MR29

EDENS,Lionel George T2Lt kia 3-9-16 8RBerks p139 CR France389

EDEY,Sydney T2Lt kia 28-4-18 8Leic p87 MR30

EDEY,William John T2Lt kia 1-2-18 1Ess p131 CR Belgium22

EDGAR,Bernard Roy T2Lt kia 31-7-17 23MGC Inf p182 CR Belgium167

EDGAR,Elizabeth SNurse drd 26-2-18 QAIMNS p200 MR40

EDGAR,George Geoffrey TLt dow 28-8-16 9KRRC p150 CR France145

EDGAR,John Hammond Lt dow 24-2-16 9DLI p239 CR Belgium127

EDGAR,John Maxwell LtACapt kia 22-3-18 4SStaffs p122 MR20

EDGAR,Robert Gerald Capt kia 4-6-15 1/6Manch p236 CR Gallipoli2

EDGAR,Surrey 2Lt kia 7-10-16 7Lond p247 MR21

EDGE,Edward Holden 2Lt kia 22/23-3-18 8Lond p247 CR France1893,22-3-18

EDGE,Frank Goodair 2Lt dow 10-8-17 4LNLancs p234 CR Belgium11,9Bn

EDGELER,Percival Lt 17-8-18 MilLabCps(EA) CR Surrey102

EDGELL,Richard Fayrer Arnold Lt kia 5-5-15 3 att2KOSB p101 MR29

EDGHILL,Arthur Richard Lt kia 9-10-17 ChesYeo p203 MR30

EDGHILL,Ashley Gay.MC.LtACapt dow 15-4-18 15LancF att96TMB p92 CR France62,kia

EDGINGTON,William 2Lt kia 8-5-15 RFA p28 MR29

EDGINTON Robert Walter Lawrence Lt kia 3-6-15 1/5RWar p214 CR Belgium339

EDINGBOROUGH,Noel Duncan T2Lt kia 1-7-16 15Mddx att109MGC p146&182 MR21

EDINGER,Frank Harrison Chap4Cl kia 26-2-18 RAChDept p199 MR40,drd

EDINGER,Walter Mark Valentine T2Lt kia 23-8-18 1 att4RWar p64 CR France239

EDIS,Robert Wilkie Henderson Capt ded 5-5-16 9Mddx 5SupplyCo p270 CR Mddx25

EDIS,Walter Owen Lt kia 29-3-18 BedsYeo p203 MR27

EDKINS,Charles 2Lt kia 29-10-18 4Lond p246 CR Belgium406,30-10-18 7Bn

EDKINS,Harrison 2Lt kia 16-9 16 1/2Lond p251 France239,15-9-16

EDKINS,Philip Eric 2Lt dow 16-7-16 7RWar p214 CR France833

EDLMANN,Ernest Elliot.DSO.Maj dow 17-4-15 RGA 23MtdBty p39 CR Iraq6

EDMANDS,Francis Douglas T2Lt dow 1-12-17 RASC 952MT attRGA p192 CR Palestine9

EDMANSON,Joe Lt kia 2-7-16 7 att13YLI p143 CR Belgium101,2Lt

EDMETT,Arthur William TLt dow 16-3-18 10RWKent p141 CR Kent232

EDMISTON,Allan John 2Lt dow 16-8-18 4ScotRif CR Scot812

EDMOND,James 2Lt kia 20-8-17 HLI p162 MR34

EDMOND,John Adamson Capt kia 30-11-17 RAMC att60FA p195 MR17

EDMOND-JENKINS,William Hart TMaj dow 1-7-16 25NumbF p60 CR France430

EDMONDS,Albert Henry Lt dow 30-5-18 4Glouc p225 CR France145,2-6-18

EDMONDS,Edward Peregrine Pell 2Lt ded PoW 18-3-18 3RFC p15 CR France1252

EDMONDS,Harold Sylvester.MC.T2Lt dow 20-4-18 2Wilts p153 CR France40

EDMONDS,Leonard 2LtTLt kia 3-11-17 2/4RWKent p141 CR Palestine1

EDMONDS,Walter T2Lt kia 14-7-16 9ScotRif p103 MR21

EDMONDS,Walter John LtACapt ded 19-5-19 1/6Dev p217 CR Devon91

EDMONDSON,Frank Capt kia 11-4-17 1 att8ELancs p110 MR20

EDMONDSON,Percival Henry.MC.Lt dow 28-6-18 RHA attRGA 309SB p207 CR France116

EDMONSON,Kenneth James TCapt kia 4-6-16 3 att1Lincs p75 CR France188

EDMONSTONE,Norman Stuart Lt dow 7-11-17 2/16Lond p249 CR Palestine1

EDMONSTONE,William George TLt kia 14/16-9-16 2CldGds p51 CR France374,15-9-16

EDMUNDS,Cecil Harry Lt kia 23-3-18 21Lond p251 CR France439

EDMUNDS,Charles Vincent 2Lt kia 26-3-17 1/5Ess p232 CR Palestine8

EDMUNDS,David Gwynne TLtLtACapt kia 25-11-17 18WelshR p126&257 MR17

EDMUNDS,Guy Victor 2Lt kia 23-5-16 21Lond p251 MR20

EDMUNDS,Gwynne Rhys Lt kia 20-7-16 18 att2RWFus p97 MR21

EDMUNDS,Vivian Spence T2Lt kld 6-9-17 GL &37RFC p7 CR Sussex55

EDMUNDS-DAVIES,John Charles 2Lt dow 12-4-17 18 att10RWFus CR France52

EDMUNDSON,Charles Robert Eubank.MC.TCapt kia 1-7-16 8Y&L p158 CR France239

EDRIDGE-GREEN,Henry Allen 2Lt ded5-11-18 23RWFus &RAF p97

EDSELL,George Alfred Lt ded 15-8-15 RAMC p270 CR Surrey148,LtCol

EDWARD,Bernard Joseph.MC.2Lt dow 18-4-18 3 att9LNLancs p135 CR France65,Lt

EDWARD,Borlase Maj kia 18-3-17 RGA 247SB p39 CR France1182,EDWARDS

EDWARD,James Daniel 2Lt dow PoW 26-4-18 6HLI p240 CR Germany3

EDWARDES,Cecil.Hon.Capt kia 20-11-17 ScotHorseYeo attTankCps p189&205 MR17

EDWARDES,George D'Arcy TMaj kia 10-7-16 1Drags att13WelshR p21 CR France397

EDWARDES,Henry Arthur T2Lt kld 16-2-18 RFC p15

EDWARDES,Henry Frederick Edgcumbe 2Lt kia 6-3-17 3 att1DCLI p114 CR France80,6-2-17

EDWARDES,Owen 2Lt kia 1-7-16 2KRRC p150 MR20

EDWARDES,Thomas Lt kia 11-4-18 5Y&L p238 MR30

EDWARDES-CRATE,Ian Ronald.MC.T2Lt dow 10-10-18 9Yorks p90 CR France528,EDWARDS

EDWARDS,Alfred Ford Collins AssSurg2Cl 12-3-15 IMS MR28 CR France31

EDWARDS,Albert Campbell T2Lt kia 24-3-18 6 att7DCLI p114 MR27

EDWARDS,Albert John 2LtTLt kia 2-8-17 26RFus p67 MR29

EDWARDS,Alfred Cecil.MC.TCapt dow 25-7-17 RAMC att1/4YLI p195 CR France13

EDWARDS,Alfred Joseph 2Lt dow 10-4-16 3RScots att6LNLancs p54 MR38

EDWARDS,Algernon Stuart TLt kia 31-7-17 17RWFus p97 MR29

EDWARDS,Anthony Hepburn Lt kia 1-4-18 5 O&BLI p130 MR27

EDWARDS,Arthur 2Lt kia 16-6-17 4EKent p212 MR29

EDWARDS,Arthur T2Lt kia 17-9-17 3Y&L p158 MR30

EDWARDS,Arthur Corbett Capt kia 25-9-15 8RWKent p141 MR19

EDWARDS,Arthur Ernest T2Lt kia 1-9-18 7EYorks Ex8Bn p84 CR France307

EDWARDS,Arthur Joseph T2Lt kia 27-9-18 RWar att16Bn p64 CR France415

EDWARDS,Arthur Noel Capt dow 24-5-15 9Lancers p22 CR France285,25-5-15

EDWARDS,Arthur Strother Capt ded 2-5-18 MGC &RAF p182

EDWARDS,Arthur Webb 2Lt kia 10-10-17 GL &41RFC p7 CR France421

EDWARDS,Bernard Wallace TCapt kia 14-8-17 10RB p178 MR29

EDWARDS,Bert.MID Lt kia 2-9-18 D281RFA p28 CR France214

EDWARDS,Brian Wallie 2Lt ded 10-11-18 4RDubF &59RAF p176 CR Mddx46,Lt Ex RE

EDWARDS,C.H.Capt 27-8-20 RAMC CR Scot359

EDWARDS,Charles 2Lt kia 29-1-17 6EYorks p84 CR France150

EDWARDS Charles O'Reilly.MC.Capt kia 13-12-15 RE 57FCp44 CR Belgium1

EDWARDS,Clement Edward Alexander 2Lt ded 5-12-18 5 att11Worc p108 CR Devon247

EDWARDS,Colin Hyde 2Lt dow 22-5-17 1ESurr p112 CR France1276

EDWARDS,Cuthbert LtTCapt dow 17-4-18 RASC att7RWKent p192 CR France185,Glouc
EDWARDS,Donald William.MC.Capt kia 6-4-17 RASC att45RFC p7&192 CR Belgium406
EDWARDS,Edward Capt kia 17-8-16 1/2Mon p244 CR Belgium4
EDWARDS,Edward T2Lt kia 30-5-17 4Worc p108 MR20
EDWARDS,Edward.MC.ACapt kia 21-3-18 1Lincs p75 MR27
EDWARDS,Edward Ernest T2Lt kia 17-12-17 3Ches att1/4RSuss p96 CR Palestine3
EDWARDS,Edward Walter TCapt kia 23-11-17 18WelshR p126 MR17
EDWARDS,Edwin Allen James Lt dow 31-12-14 3 att1Beds p85 CR Surrey95
EDWARDS,Eric 2LtTLt kia 22-11-17 12SWBord p99 MR17
EDWARDS,Eric Lea Priestley Capt kia 20-9-14 1EYorks p84 MR15
EDWARDS,Eric Wilson.MC.TLtACapt kia 30-11-17 6RWSurr p55 MR17
EDWARDS,Ernest Victor 2Lt kld 16-2-18 GL attRFC p15 CR Egypt8
EDWARDS,Evan Chap4Cl ded 27-11-18 RAChDept p199 CR Lancs2
EDWARDS,Francis Andrew Lloyd T2Lt dow 10-8-16 5RBerks p139 CR France74
EDWARDS,Francis William Lloyd.OBE.MID LtCol 19-12-20 KRRC CR Wales677
EDWARDS,Frank Glencairn de Burgh Lt kia 12-10-14 I/12RHA p28 CR France350
EDWARDS,Frederick Thomas.MC.T2Lt kia 20-10-18 8Lpool p71 CR Belgium406
EDWARDS,Geoffrey Otto Charles 2Lt kia 7-7-16 9WRid p115 MR21
EDWARDS,George T2Lt ded 24-9-16 GL &RFC p2&190 MR20
EDWARDS,George Eric.DSO.ACapt kia 20-11-17 6SforthH p241 CR France1498
EDWARDS,George Percy.MC.Lt dow 2-10-18 D155RFA p28 CR France214
EDWARDS,George Richard Owen.DSO&Bar.TMaj dow 17-6-17 C173RFA p28 CR Belgium97
EDWARDS,Gerald John Capt dow 9-6-17 20Lond attKRRC p251 CR France518
EDWARDS,Gordon Stafford TCapt kia 28-9-16 8WRid p115 MR21
EDWARDS,Griffith Oliver.MC.T2Lt kia 20-9-17 11NumbF p60 CR Belgium84
EDWARDS,Guy Thulkeld TCapt kia 31-7-16 24RFus p67 MR21,Threlkeld
EDWARDS,Harold Ethelstan Lt kia 25-9-15 3 att2RWar p64 MR19
EDWARDS,Harold Thomas Capt kia 8-5-15 1Mon p244 CR Belgium96,Thorne
EDWARDS,Harold Welleson Hurst 2LtACapt kia 18-11-16 8Glouc p106 CR France215,Wellstone
EDWARDS,Harri Willis 2Lt kia 28-4-17 1/5ELancs p226 MR21
EDWARDS,Harry 2Lt kia 7-10-16 12Lpool p71 MR21
EDWARDS,Harry T2Lt ded 17-2-18 SStaffs p264 CR Staffs4
EDWARDS,Henry Arthur 2Lt 16-2-18 RFC CR Essex9
EDWARDS,Henry Laidley Garland Lt dow 16-5-15 3 att1RWFus p97 CR France260
EDWARDS,Howard Joseph 2Lt dow 9-10-17 7Worc p226 MR30
EDWARDS,Hywell 2Lt dow 22-11-17 2SWBord p100 CR France398
EDWARDS,J.Maj 23-5-16 RGA CR Ireland12
EDWARDS,James Harry TLt kia 7-1-17 14DLI p160 CR France114
EDWARDS,James Tudor 2Lt kia 13-9-15 3Lpool p71 CR France924
EDWARDS,John T2Lt kia 22-3-18 3RB p178 MR27
EDWARDS,John Francis Coster LtACapt dow 10-11-18 3 att24RWFus p97
EDWARDS,John Henry 2Lt kia 21-9-18 6 att25RWFus p223 CR France924
EDWARDS,John Hugh Evan Lloyd 2Lt kia 20-9-17 34/139RFA p28 CR Belgium102
EDWARDS,John Ivor Jones T2Lt kia 31-10-18 2 att24RWFus p97 CR Belgium140,Ivon
EDWARDS,John Kelvin Lt ded 28-11-18 7Ches p222 CR France1142,5Bn
EDWARDS,John Llewelyn 2Lt kia 7-9-17 C75RFA p28 CR Belgium12
EDWARDS,John Rathbone 2Lt kia 6-7-16 7DCLI p114 CR France4
EDWARDS,John Robert T2Lt ded 15-11-18 704LabCps p189 CR France40
EDWARDS,John Stanley.MC.ACapt dow 24-4-18 LancHussYeo p204 CR Belgium38
EDWARDS,John Wesley.MC.2Lt kia 8-11-17 1/1WorcYeo p206 CR Palestine8
EDWARDS,Kenneth Grenville TLt kia 8-5-18 13RWFus p97 CR France60
EDWARDS,Lancelot Maj dow 15-4-15 1Lincs p75 CR France102
EDWARDS,Leo 2Lt ded 8-6-16 1Norf p73 MR20
EDWARDS,Leslie Edward.MC.TCapt dow 6-12-17 6 att8RFus C'Coy p67 CR France145
EDWARDS,Lewis George T2Lt kia 20-9-17 KRRC att11Bn p150 MR30
EDWARDS,Llewllyn Albert Lt ded PoW 21-3-18 7RWar p214 CR France672,Capt
EDWARDS,Llewllyn Foster.MC.TLt dow 12-4-18 8SLancs p125 CR France139
EDWARDS,Norman Roy 2Lt kia 19-4-17 8ScotRif p225 MR34
EDWARDS,Osborne Montague TLt kia 23-8-18 37MGC Inf p182 CR France577,25-8-18
EDWARDS,Oswald James T2Lt ded 10-12-18 RE 456FC p44 CR France146
EDWARDS,Percival Charles.DCM.TMaj kia 27-9-18 15RWar p64 CR France245
EDWARDS,Percy Howarth Lt kia 24-5-15 5NumbF p214 MR29
EDWARDS,Philip Arthur CaptTMaj kia 18-3-16 1LNLancs p135 CR France149

EDWARDS,Philip Percival 2Lt kia 25-4-17 7Worc p226 MR21,Perceval
EDWARDS,R.2Lt ded 15-6-15 6RB p266 CR Surrey95
EDWARDS,Reginald Howard 2Lt kia 22-9-16 19RFC p254 MR20
EDWARDS,Robert Maj ded 26-5-20 RAMC CR C'land&W'land17
EDWARDS,Robert Amor Lt dow 14-7-18 1WYorks p81 CR Belgium11
EDWARDS,Roland Frederick.MC.TLt dow 8-10-18 11RWSurr p55 CR Belgium11
EDWARDS,Roy 2Lt dow 30-11-17 10RB p178 MR17
EDWARDS,Spenser Ernest 2Lt ded 9-3-17 4EKent p212&270 CR Surrey160
EDWARDS,Stanley Robert TLt kia 24-9-15 8SStaffs p122 CR Belgium111,25-9-15
EDWARDS,W.E.CMG.Col 25-7-21 RA CR Lond28
EDWARDS,Walter 2Lt kia 26-4-16 6Lond p247 CR France924
EDWARDS,Wilfred William.MC.T2Lt dow 22-1-17 17RFus p67 CR France41
EDWARDS,William TCapt dow 28-3-18 RASC p192 CR France62
EDWARDS,William Armino Lt dow 1-11-17 GlamYeo p203 CR Palestine1,2Lt 24WelchR
EDWARDS,William Augustus Spencer Maj dow 30-4-16 NStaffs att7Bn p157 CR Iraq5
EDWARDS,William Francis Boucher Capt kia 14-4-15 IA 24Punjabis p276 CR Iraq6
EDWARDS,William Hardinge Colvin.MC.MID TCapt kia 9-5-15 1BlkW p128 CR France632
EDWARDS,William Ian.MC.TCapt&Adjt kia 5-8-17 11LancF p92 MR29
EDWARDS,William Victor Capt kia 29-12-17 7RDubF p176 CR Palestine3
EDWARDS-TROLLIP,John 2Lt kia 27-8-18 7Lond p247
EDYE,Charles Vivian de Grete Lt kia 30-10-14 2DCLI p114 MR29
EGAN,Pierce John Chap4Cl ded 6-4-16 RAChDept p199 CR Egypt3,att1BWIndR
EGERTON,Arthur George Edward MajTLtCol kia 29-9-15 1ClдGds p51 CR France423
EGERTON,Arthur Oswald 2Lt kia 25/26-9-15 att5KSLI p144 MR19
EGERTON,Bertram Gustavus T2Lt dow 8-9-16 9N&D p133 CR France296
EGERTON,Brian Raleigh Lt kia 23-10-18 RE 87FC p44 CR France1296 &CR France1080
EGERTON,Charles Caledon Lt kia 18-4-15 2WRid p115 CR Belgium59
EGERTON,Edward Brassey TCapt dow 1-9-16 17Lancers D'Sqn p23 CR France158
EGERTON,George Algernon Maj dow 13-5-15 19Huss p23 CR France284,LtCol
EGERTON,James Boswell.MIDx2 Maj kia 27-10-18 IA 23Cav p276 MR38
EGERTON,John Frederick T2Lt dow 3-4-16 8KRRC ADC p150 CR France62
EGERTON,Louis Edward William Capt kia 1-8-17 BucksYeo p203 CR Belgium12,Edwin
EGERTON,Philip de Malpas Wayne LtACapt kia 8-10-18 19Huss p23 CR France341
EGERTON,Philip Graham Capt dow 18-10-18 3BlkW att2/19Lond p128 CR Egypt1
EGERTON,Phillip John Lt dow 17-10-14 BordR p117 CR Belgium57,Philip
EGERTON,Robert.MC.CaptTMaj kia 23-12-17 2RIrF &59RFC p7&171 CR France518
EGERTON,Robert Randle Lt kia 15-11-14 RE 1FC p44 CR Belgium96,16-11-14
EGERTON,Rowland Le Belward 2Lt kia 30-11-14 RWFus p97 MR32
EGERTON-GREEN,Charles Scroop Lt kia 1-7-16 2KRRC p150 MR20
EGERTON-GREEN,John William Capt dow 9-10-17 1RB p178 CR France102
EGERTON-WARBURTON,John Capt dow 30-8-15 ScotsGds p52 CR Ches136
EGGLESTONE,Ernest 2Lt ded 2-6-19 20DLI p160 CR Germany1
EGGLETON,Frank.MID Lt kia 21-10-17 17RFA p28 CR Belgium12
EGGLETON,Robert 2LtTLt dow 15-11-17 33RFA p28 CR Belgium16
EGLINGTON,Ferdinand Capt kia 1-7-16 1/5SStaffs p229 MR21
EGLON,H.E.Lt 19-7-17 SL attNigR CR EAfrica38 &CR Tanzania1
EGNER,Frederick Albert 2Lt kia 6-1-18 GL &6RFC p15 CR France62
EGREMONT,Godfrey Leonard Hobart Lt ded 2-5-18 8Manch p237 CR France1439
EHRHARDT,John Albert T2Lt kia 26-3-18 1TankCps p188 MR27
EICKE,E.C.LtCol 29-3-18 APD CR Mddx26
EICKE,Owen Macaulay.MC.TLt kia 5-11-16 62RFA p28 CR France374
EILLS,William.MC.Maj kia 9-4-18 C275RFA p206 CR France98,dow
EILOART,Cyril Howard T2Lt kia 26-9-18 IrGds att4GdsMGReg p52 CR France756
EILOART,Frank Oswald ACapt kia 3-5-17 1/1Lond p245 MR20
EINEM-HICKSON,Samuel Vernon Lt kia 4-11-14 2LNLancs p135 MR47
EISTOB,Wilfrith.VC.DSO.MC.TLtCol kia 21-3-18 16Manch p154
EKIN,James 2Lt kia 1-7-16 8Y&L p158 CR France293
EKIN,Leslie Montrose.MC.kia 1-7-16 8Y&L CR France246
EKINS,Franklin George.MC&Bar.Lt ded 27-1-19 1RIrReg p89 CR France1849
EKINS,Willingham Richard 2Lt kia 3-5-17 3 att11EYorks p84 MR20
ELAM,Charles Lt kia 1-7-16 12Y&L p158 CR France744

ELBOROUGH,Alfred Charles Ernest TCapt dow 30-7-15 6YLI p143 CR Belgium11
ELCHO,Hugo Francis Charteris, Lord LtTCapt kia 23-4-16 GloucYeo p203 MR34
ELD,Arthur William TLt kia 19-4-17 2Lincs p75 CR France407
ELDER,Alexander T2Lt kia 1-7-16 15RScots p54 CR France267
ELDER,James Capt kia 29-12-17 13RScots p54 CR Belgium94
ELDER,James 2Lt kia 21-3-18 6BlkW p231 MR20
ELDER,William Gardner Lt ded 10-2-18 2/20Lond p251 CR Lond32
ELDERFIELD,Henry T2Lt ded 11-11-18 NumbF att163ChineseLabCps p61 CR France52
ELDERKIN,John Victor 2LtALt dow 23-9-17 59RFA p28 CR Belgium23
ELDERS,John Francis 2Lt kia 28-10-17 16Lond p250 CR France646
ELDERTON,Fothergill Rex.MID Lt kia 25-9-15 3 att2RWar p64 MR19
ELDRED,John Sturgess 2Lt dow 27-11-14 2Leinst att2RIrRif p174 CR France102
ELDRIDGE,John Thomas T2Lt kia 18-9-18 2KRRC p150 CR France1700
ELEY,Ralph Corben 2Lt kia 24-3-18 19Lond p250 CR France216,Corban,dow
ELEY,William Arthur Derrick 2Lt kia 17-2-17 5 att1KRRC p150 CR France314
ELFORD,Arthur Douglas TLt kia 13-11-16 12EYorks p84 MR21
ELGEE,Hugh Francis Capt kia 6-7-15 SWBord attEgyptArmy p100 CR Gallipoli6
ELGEY,Eric 2Lt kia 19-3-17 RFA attRFC p18&208 CR France614
ELIAS,Hywel James T2Lt kia 5-6-17 21NumbF p61 MR20 &CR France1059
ELIFFE,M.Sister ded 25-5-16 QAIMNS p200
ELIOT,Geoffrey Lionel T2Lt kld 2-7-17 GL &RFC p7 CR Mddx17
ELIOT,Peter Douglas Colin Capt kia 25-2-17 IA 14Lancers p276 MR38
ELIOT,William Lawrence Lt kia 20-9-14 1WYorks p81 MR15
ELIOTT,Hugh Russell Capt kia 12-10-14 3Worc p108 CR France260
ELIOTT-LOCKHART,Percy Clare.DSO.LtCol dow 12-3-15 IA 59Rif p276 CR France632,kia
ELKINGTON,Thomas Garrett T2Lt dow 4-3-16 2Suff p78 CR Belgium11
ELKINGTON,Walter Henry T2Lt kia 22-3-18 11Hamps p120 MR27
ELLA,Alfred Newsam 2Lt ded 18-11-18 RGA 180HB p39 CR Greece9
ELLEN,Arthur Charles 2Lt dow 6-6-17 RGA 156HB p39 CR France297
ELLEN,Eric Adrian TLtACapt kia 30-1-17 2ELancs p110 CR France624
ELLEN,Harry John.MC.2Lt kia 14-9-18 2/20Lond p251 CR France755
ELLER,Cyrus Radcliffe Lt dow 30-5-17 8Manch p237 CR France1266
ELLERAY,Robert Lincoln T2Lt kia 18-4-18 2/6N&D p133 MR32
ELLERBY,Harry T2Lt kia 11-9-18 A122RFA p28 France398
ELLERINGTON,Robert.MC.TLtAMaj dow 29-3-18 39MGC p182 CR France185
ELLERKER,W.T Capt 14-12-21 RGA attIntel GHQ CR Germany1
ELLERSHAW,Wilfrid TBrigGen drd 6-6-16 RA p28 MR40,5-6-16
ELLERTON,Charles Fleetwood TCapt kia 21-5-16 10Ches p96 CR France68,19-5-16
ELLICE,Alexander TCapt dow 18-10-16 5CamH p167 CR France177
ELLICE,Andrew Robert Lt dow 29-9-16 4GrenGds SR p49 CR France105,2Lt
ELLICOTT,Frederick Arthur John 2Lt kia 8-7-16 6KOSB p101 CR France400,dow 9-7-16
ELLIFFE,Margaret Sister 24-5-16 QAIMNS CR Surrey160
ELLIKER,William Harold ACapt ded 19-2-19 RE p254 CR Staffs183
ELLINGHAM,Victor Edward 2LtTLt kia 1-10-17 Leic p87 MR30,2-10-17
ELLIOT,Alexander Shiels Lt kia 28-6-15 8HLI p240 MR4
ELLIOT,Edward John Capt kia 23-5-18 RAMC att10StyHosp p195 CR France134
ELLIOT,Gavin William Esmond.Hon.Lt dow 6-8-17 2ScotsGds p52 CR Belgium18
ELLIOT,Henry Gratten Capt kia 20-9-14 Dev p76
ELLIOT,Hugh Maj kld 26-7-15 11Lpool p71 CR Belgium84
ELLIOT,Hugh Lt ded 21-6-16 1 att14Lpool p71 CR Greece7
ELLIOT,James Brown T2Lt kia 22-11-17 RScots p54 CR Palestine3
ELLIOT,John Lt kia 3-8-17 108RFA p28 MR29
ELLIOT,Nichol T2Lt dow 9-7-17 1Nhampt att2TMB p137 MR31,10-7-17 Ex28Lond
ELLIOT,Thomas Archibald Scott T2Lt dow 6-8-17 CamH att7Bn p167 CR Belgium18
ELLIOT,Thomas Victor Guppy Lt dow 16-10-15 1RFA p207 CR France200
ELLIOTT,Charles Allen.CMG.DSO.LtCol 15-8-19 RE MR43 &CR Pakistan50A
ELLIOTT,Charles Arthur Boileau 2Lt dow 12-4-17 1SomLI p79 CR France113
ELLIOTT,Charles Howard Capt kia 27-4-15 IA 58Rif p276 CR France924,ELLIOT
ELLIOTT,Clarence William T2Lt kia 14-4-18 1RWSurr p55 MR32
ELLIOTT,Clifford Wilfrid 2Lt kia 12-8-17 23RFC p7 MR20
ELLIOTT,Duncan Lt kia 15-4-18 3BordR &4RAF p264 MR20
ELLIOTT,Edward Lt dow 25-10-18 B181RFA p28 CR Dorset53
ELLIOTT,Elizabeth Nurse 27-10-18 TFNS CR Durham109
ELLIOTT,Eric Cuthbert John TLt kia 22-11-17 GL &27RFC p7 CR France95
ELLIOTT,Eustace Trehane T2Lt kia 9-4-17 9 att8EYorks p84 MR20,10-4-17
ELLIOTT,F.Lt 2-2-16 3Lincs CR EAfrica61

ELLIOTT,Frank Phelps T2Lt kia 23-8-18 1Manch p154 CR France643
ELLIOTT,Frederick 2Lt dow 2-8-16 1/6SfthH attMGC p187&241 CR France176
ELLIOTT,Frederick Guy TLt kia 22-3-18 3Worc p108 MR20
ELLIOTT,Frederick William 2Lt kia 19-7-16 B166RFA p28 MR21
ELLIOTT,Geoffrey Edmund 2Lt kia 12-10-16 3 att2WRid p115
ELLIOTT,Geoffrey Faber 2Lt kia 31-8-16 4 att8SStaffs p122 MR21,ELLIOT
ELLIOTT,George Edward T2Lt dow 20-5-16 13RSuss p118 CR France80
ELLIOTT,George Keith Lt kia 8-9-18 3 att25RWFus p97 CR France365
ELLIOTT,Gerald Even Capt kia 21-7-16 6Glouc p225 MR21,Ewen
ELLIOTT,H.G.Capt 20-9-14 1Dev CR France1107
ELLIOTT,Harold Seymour Lt RegMutiny 17-2-15 IA 5LightInf p276 CR Asia45,kia 15-2-15
ELLIOTT,Henry Christopher T2Lt dow 20-12-17 RE 150FC p44 CR France52
ELLIOTT,Henry Ernest.MC.ACapt ded 2-3-19 RGA 152HB p39 CR Germany1
ELLIOTT,Herbert John 2LtTLt kia 2-11-17 1RWarGarrBn att1/4Nhampt p64 CR Palestine8
ELLIOTT,Horace William 2Lt kia 13-11-17 3SomLI p79 CR Palestine9
ELLIOTT,J.C.Rev 5-10-20 Chap4Cl CR Derby30
ELLIOTT,James Dunsmore T2Lt kia 22-10-17 16Ches p96 MR30,John Dunsmoor
ELLIOTT,James Harold 2Lt kia 29-11-16 2RWar p64 CR France221
ELLIOTT,John Benjamin George 2Lt kia 16-8-17 4Lond p246 MR29
ELLIOTT,John Forster TCapt ded 30-9-17 RAMC p267 CR Ireland146,Lt
ELLIOTT,John MacCreary Lt 16-4-17 LdStrathconasHorse &60RFC MR20
ELLIOTT,John William 2Lt kia 21-3-18 12/13NumbF p61 MR27
ELLIOTT,Leila Mabel Nurse 2-3-20 TFNS CR Scot241
ELLIOTT,Oswald Carr Finnes T2Lt kia 14-10-16 10GordH p166 CR France515,Fiennes
ELLIOTT,Phillip Lloyd 2Lt kia 21-10-14 1DCLI p114 CR France279
ELLIOTT,Philip Maurice 2Lt kia 1-7-16 3Mddx p146 CR France239
ELLIOTT,Reginald William Sidney kia 24-11-14 IA 1/7att2/8 GurkhaRif p276 CR France80
ELLIOTT,Robert Chambers Macdonald T2Lt kia 24-8-16 5KSLI p144 MR21
ELLIOTT,Thomas Brignall T2Lt kia 1-7-16 10RIrRif p169 MR21
ELLIOTT,Thomas Nichol 2Lt kia 11-4-18 7Lpool p215 MR32
ELLIOTT,Vere Arthur Edmonstone LtACapt kia 25-3-18 B165RFA p28 CR France745
ELLIOTT,Walter 2Lt kia 13-11-16 7RFus p67 CR France220
ELLIOTT,Walter Leonard Lt ded 21-11-16 9RB p178 CR France46
ELLIOTT,Wilfrid Edmund 2Lt kia 26-9-16 5Dors p124 MR21,ELLIOT
ELLIOTT,William LtACapt dow 3-9-18 RGA 374 att309SB p39 CR France833
ELLIOTT,William Herron,MBE Capt ded 28-1-20 RAMC 36CCS CR Germany1
ELLIOTT,William James.MC.2Lt dow 30-6-18 6RWKent p141 MR27
ELLIOTT-COOPER,Neville Bowes.VC.DSO.MC.TLtCol dow PoW 11-2-18 8RFus p67 CR Germany2
ELLIS,Basil Herbert Lt kia 16-6-15 5KSLI p144 CR Belgium115
ELLIS,Bryan Grogan Langley 2LtTCapt kia 13-10-17 RGLI att50BallSect 5WingRFC p7&200 CR Egypt9
ELLIS,Ceredig T2Lt dow 19-7-16 15RWFus p97 CR France51
ELLIS,Clifford Walker 2Lt kia 1-7-16 9 att2YLI p143 CR France267,3 att9Bn
ELLIS,Cyril Brooks 2Lt kia 13-11-16 HAC p206 CR France339
ELLIS,David Ithel.MC.Maj dow 9-4-18 285RFA p28 MR32
ELLIS,Douglas Quirk Lt ded 8-2-18 RFC CR Canada1667
ELLIS,Douglas Wilmshurst TLt kia 24-5-17 13Ches p96 CR Belgium43
ELLIS,Edward Charles TLt kia 7-8-15 11Glouc att15MunstF p106 CR Gallipoli6
ELLIS,Edward Miller.MC.Capt kia 7-8-18 HAC att5Lond p206 CR France44
ELLIS,Ernest Dennis TLt kia 27-9-18 4Beds p85 CR France1496 Ex10Bn
ELLIS,Evelyn Charles 2Lt kia 3-5-17 HAC p206 MR20
ELLIS,Francis Bevis TCapt kia 25-9-16 10NumbF p61 CR France239,26-9-16
ELLIS,Frederick Alfred T2Lt kia 22-3-18 11Ess p131 MR20
ELLIS,Frederick William 2Lt kia 3-3-18 1/13Lond p249 CR France184
ELLIS,G.R.Capt 28-6-18 RAMC CR Glouc126
ELLIS,George Adams Maj kia 10-3-15 ScotRif p103 CR France260
ELLIS,George Barker TLt kia 21-7-16 D51RFA p28 CR France399
ELLIS,George Frederick 2Lt kia 30-3-15 RE 173MinCoy p44 CR France706
ELLIS,Guy Stuart T2Lt kia 12-7-17 GL &57RFC p7 CR Belgium10
ELLIS,Harry T2Lt kia 9/12-4-17 8RLancs p58 MR20
ELLIS,Herbert Dudley 2Lt kia 25-9-15 RGA p39 MR19
ELLIS,Herbert Pearce.MC.Lt dow 1-12-17 GloucYeo p203 MR34
ELLIS,Horace Nickson.MC.T2Lt kia 9-10-18 6MGC Cav p182 CR France190

ELLIS,Hughie Lodwick Maldwyn T2Lt dow 5-5-17 1/2RWFus p97 CR France518
ELLIS,James Capt dow 24-4-17 7GordH p242 CR France113
ELLIS,James Clive T2Lt ded PoW 21-4-18 4TankCps p188 CR France364,dow
ELLIS,James Graves St.John T2Lt dow 11-10-15 RE p44 CR Gallipoli27
ELLIS,James Norman 2Lt kia 2-12-17 3 att2YLI p143 CR Belgium125,1-12-17
ELLIS,John Chute 2Lt dow 6-6-17 106RFA p28 CR Belgium11,Lt
ELLIS,John William 2Lt kia 27-5-18 4RWFus p223 CR France215,24-5-18 10Bn attRNDiv
ELLIS,Philip Challinor Lt kia 17-10-16 14HLI &1RFC p2&162,ded CR France705
ELLIS,Rae Adam Capt dow 22-9-18 25RWFus p204 CR France194
ELLIS,Reginald Denni Capt kia 8-6-17 1/4Lincs p217 CR France550,Dennie
ELLIS,Reginald Walter TLt kia 18-6-17 GL &9RFC p7 MR20
ELLIS,Robert Bruce.MC.Capt&Adjt dow 21-11-16 6BlkW p231 CR France40
ELLIS,Robert Charles T2Lt ded 31-5-18 PoW 2RB p178 CR France1755
ELLIS,Robert Percy 2Lt dow PoW 6-4-18 3RDubF p176 CR France934,2Bn
ELLIS,Robert Thomas Hugh 2Lt kia 13-10-17 19RWFus p97 CR Belgium168,12-10-17
ELLIS,Shirley Duncan.MC.T2Lt ded 19-3-16 RE 173Coy p44 CR France80
ELLIS,Thomas Arthur Capt 20-11-18 Min of Muns &RAF CR Ches28
ELLIS,Thomas Martin Capt kia 18-4-15 WRid attWYorks p115 CR Belgium115
ELLIS,Trevor Edgar.MID T2Lt kia 10-4-18 40MGC Inf C'Coy p182 MR32
ELLIS,Victor Richard Helps.MC.T2Lt kia 28-4-18 11RSuss p118 MR30,Help
ELLIS,William 2Lt kia 29-7-18 7Lpool p215 CR France745
ELLIS,William Ewart Simpson 2Lt kia 13-1-17 4SomLI p218 CR France785
ELLIS,William Forrest 2Lt kia 9-9-16 1/8Lpool p215 MR21
ELLIS,William John 2Lt kia 23-3-18 4 att9RWFus p223 MR20
ELLIS,Yvo Lempnere TLt kia 29-5-16 13Hamps p120 CR France114
ELLISON,Cuthbert Joseph ACapt ded 18-2-19 RGA p270 CR Berks2
ELLISON,Douglas Heins Capt dow 14-1-20 IA 95Inf att1/109 p276 MR43,Hems
ELLISON,Frederick John Gwynn 2Lt kia 16-8-17 1 att13RIrRif p169 MR30
ELLISON,Samuel T2Lt dow 25-3-18 2ELancs p110 CR France987
ELLISON,Samuel Charles TLt ded 17-7-17 RAMC p195 CR Egypt1
ELLISON,Stanley John 2Lt kia 1-7-16 5SStaffs p229 CR France644
ELLISON,Theodore Tarleton T2Lt kia 14-3-16 12 att1/6WelshR p126 CR France149
ELLISON,William Ronald 2Lt dow 20-6-15 RFA p28 CR Lancs164
ELLWOOD,Albert.MC.Capt kia 14-4-18 4RLancs p213 CR France1106
ELLWOOD,Charles Hugh Lt kia 2-6-15 4Lincs p217 CR Belgium98,1-6-15
ELLWOOD,Francis James Lt kia 4-10-17 1EYorks p84 CR Belgium167
ELLWOOD,Goeffrey Thomas Lovick TLt kia 17-7-16 6Leic p87 MR21,14-7-16
ELLY,Cyril John T2Lt dow 6-9-18 N&D att 1/8Bn p133 CR France10
ELMES,King TCapt kia 28-9-18 RAMC att2/16Lond p295 CR Belgium42
ELMHIRST,Ernest Christopher 2Lt kia 7-8-15 8WRid p115 MR4
ELMHIRST,William TCapt kia 13-11-16 9EYorks p84 CR France742,8Bn
ELMITT,Austin Joyce,MC ACapt kia 24-11-17 17WelshR p126 MR17
ELMITT,George Carleton Brooksley 2Lt kia 16-8-17 7RIrRif p254 MR30,Brooksby
ELMITT-BROWNE,Austin T2Lt dow 15-6-18 2WRid p115 CR France10,15-6-18
ELMSLIE,Ernest George T2Lt kia 26-9-17 2RScots p54 MR30
ELMSLIE,Kenward Wallace Lt kia 4-11-14 4DragGds p21 MR29
ELPHICK,Kevin 2Lt dow 28-9-16 4 att2RIrRif p169 CR France44
ELPHICK,William Roy 2Lt ded 7-6-16 IA 108Inf p276 MR65,Lt
ELPHINSTONE,Arthur Percy Archibald.MID TLtCol kia 1-7-16 22NumbF p61 MR21
ELPHINSTONE,Montague TMaj kia 22-3-17 RASC attRFC p7&192 CR France833
ELRINGTON,Gerard Gordon Clement 2Lt kia 2-11-14 EYorks p84 MR29,31-10-14
ELRINGTON-BISSET,Walter Faviere T2Lt kia 25-9-15 9GordH p166 MR19
ELSE,William Edwin TLt&Capt kia 3-1-18 17N&D p133 CR Belgium10
ELSMIE,George Edward Douglas LtCol murdered 18-6-17 IA 25Cav p276 MR43
ELSOM,Harold 2Lt kia 28-4-17 10Lincs p75 MR20
ELSON,Edwin Arthur 2Lt kia 9-9-16 9Mddx p236 MR21
ELSON,George Henry.MM.T2Lt ded 8-12-18 1/2 att14Leic p87 CR France1027
ELSTOB,Wilfrith.VC.DSO.MC.LtCol 21-3-18 16Manch MR27
ELSTON,Charles Douglas Capt dow 22-11-17 Nhampt p137 CR Lond4
ELSWORTH,George Herbert 2Lt ded 27-6-16 IARO att62Punjabis p276 CR Iraq6
ELSWORTH,Harold Lt kia 21-8-18 4RScotF p222 CR France214
ELTHAM,Charles William Lt kia 3-11-16 1RWSurr p55 MR21
ELTON,Alfred George Goodenough Col ded 17-11-19 ConnRgrs p266 CR Hereford191
ELTON,Arthur Bayard Maj ded 12-1-16 Ex Yorks p263
ELTON,Arthur Charles Lt kia 24-7-15 2RWKent p141 CR Iraq6
ELTON,Frederick John T2Lt dow 11-9-15 C48RFA 14Div p28 CR Belgium11

ELTON,George Kenward 2Lt kia 18-10-16 5Hamps p228 MR21
ELTON,Gordon Daubeney Gresley,DSO.MC Capt kia 5-11-17 RIrF p171 CR Belgium20
ELVERSON,Ronald Whidborne Lt kia 25-9-18 9ESurr p112 MR16
ELVEY,Charles Leslie 2Lt kia 9-4-17 5Suff p217 CR France581
ELVIDGE,Jabez Gordon 2Lt kia 17-11-17 3 att1/7WYorks p81 MR30
ELVIDGE,Laurence T2Lt dow 9-8-16 5ConnRgrs attRInniskF p172 CR Belgium165
ELVIN,Arthur George 2Lt ded 13-10-17 1/4Suff p217 CR Egypt2
ELVIN,Sydney James.MID 2Lt dow 13-4-18 1/4EYorks C'Coy p219 CR France31
ELWELL,Ernest Edward 2LtTLt kia 6-10-17 17 att21Manch p154 MR30
ELWIN,Frank Harold 2Lt kia 14-3-15 3 att2Wilts p153 MR22,12-3-15
ELWOOD,Robert Vernon T2Lt kld 17-11-17 GL &RFC p7 CR Yorks38
ELWORTHY,Edward Pearce 2Lt kia 11-8-15 RE 67FC p44 CR Gallipoli5,Lt 9-8-15
ELWORTHY,Thomas.MID T2Lt kia 3-5-17 1RLancs p58 CR France604 Ex RE
ELY,Denis Herbert James TCapt kia 1-7-16 15DLI p160 MR21
ELY,Percy Alfred Lt ded 17-11-18 1KEdwsHorse attNZEF CR Lond8
EMANUEL,Oliver Lt 25-9-15 1Wilts MR29
EMBERTON,Percival Harvey T2Lt kia 1-7-16 1SStaffs p122 CR France397
EMBLEM,Harold.MC.2Lt 23-4-18 8 att1N&D MR27
EMBREY,Cyril Stewart.MC.MIDx2 2Lt kia 12-10-18 1/6SStaffs p229 CR France847
EMERSON,Frank 2Lt kia 26-8-18 5Lond p246 CR France630
EMERSON,Harold Theodore T2Lt kia 10-7-16 8LNLancs p135 MR21
EMERSON,James Samuel.VC.T2Lt kia 6-12-17 9RInniskF p104 MR17
EMERSON,John Miller T2Lt dow PoW 8-4-18 8MGC Inf p182 CR France526 Ex 1NumbF
EMERSON,Max William Pailthorpe 2Lt kia 5-7-16 5YLI p235 CR France702
EMERTON,Harry Burton.MC.TLtAMaj kia 27-9-18 B178RFA p28 CR France686
EMERY,Burkett John Lt kia 11/13-10-15 RE p210 MR19
EMERY,George William T2Lt kia 20-11-17 F'TankCps p188 MR17
EMERY,Ewart Arthur Edwin T2Lt kia 23-3-18 RE 16SigCoy p44 MR27
EMERY,Walter Herbert Vernon T2Lt ded 26-10-18 7ELancs p264 CR Lond4
EMINSON,George 2Lt kia 1-9-18 21Lond p251 MR16
EMINSON,Robert Astley Franklin 2Lt kia 20-7-16 6KRRC attMGC Inf p150&182 CR France515
EMINTON,Frederick Arthur 2Lt kia 23-4-17 18Manch p154 MR20
EMLEM,Harold,MC 2Lt kia 23-4-18 8N&D p233
EMMANUEL,Oliver Lt kia 25-9-15 Wilts p153
EMMENS,Richard Reeve 2Lt kia 4-9-16 GL attTMB p190 CR France432,Lt
EMMERSON,Alfred 2Lt dow 4-4-17 5Leic attRFC p18&220 CR France120
EMMERSON,Henry Hetherington TMaj kia 25-9-16 10Leic p87 MR21
EMMERSON,Jabez.MID 2Lt kia 13-10-15 4Leic p220 MR19,Joseph Son of Jabez
EMMET,Frederick Herbert TCapt kia 14-7-16 9Leic p87 MR21
EMMET,Robert 2Lt ded 30-10-15 1LifeGds p20 CR Lond9,29-10-15
EMMETT,Alexis Renwick Lt kia 12-2-16 ISMD att2LNLancs MR50
EMMETT,Charles Percival LtACapt dow 28-6-18 1 att8ESurr p112 CR France31
EMMOTT,John Barlow Lt kia 4-6-15 10Manch p237 CR Gallipoli6
EMMOTT,Rennie.MM.2Lt kia 31-7-17 7ELancs p110 MR29
EMMS,Harry T2Lt kia 6-8-16 8SomLI p79 CR France549
EMPEY,Simeon Robert Franks 2Lt ded 17-8-16 3RIrRif att9LNLancs p169 CR France4
EMSLEY,John Alfred Capt ded 1-12-18 6WYorks p270 CR Yorks408
EMSLIE,Alexander 2Lt kia 16/17-5-17 6GordH p242 MR20
EMSLIE,Herbert Robertson 2Lt kia 24-10-17 6 att11A&SH p243 CR France545
ENDEAN,Frank Edgar T2Lt kia 24-3-18 15RIrRif p169 MR27
ENDERBURY,Frederick Albert 2Lt kia 9-2-16 10HLI p162 CR Belgium30
ENDERBY,Arthur Aaron TLt dow 2-8-17 4RFus p67 CR France512
ENGALL,John Sherwin 2Lt kia 1-7-16 16Lond attMGC p187&250 MR21
ENGINEER,G.S Lt 30-5-16 IMS CR Egypt13
ENGLAND,Edward Parker.DCM.LtCol ded 10-1-21 RFA CR Devon29
ENGLAND,Ernest William Lt kia 26-9-16 3 att7YLI p143 MR21
ENGLAND,John Humphrey.MID T2Lt kia 31-7-17 14WelshR p126 MR29
ENGLAND,John Kenneth T2Lt dow 5-9-18 4ESurr p112 CR France145,8Bn
ENGLAND,Raymond Maj kia 26-8-14 88RFA p28 CR France1354
ENGLISH,Alfred Cecil 2Lt kia 30-12-17 28Lond p252 MR21
ENGLISH,Charles Arthur 2Lt kia 6-5-17 4BordR p228 MR20
ENGLISH,Eric T2Lt kia 7-8-15 13WYorks att1/8Manch p81 CR Gallipoli2
ENGLISH,Frederick Garnet 2Lt kia 13-11-16 3 att13Ess p131 CR France1890
ENGLISH,Richard Cornforth TLt ded 25-7-16 RASC p192 CR Lincs100
ENGLISH,Robert Ernest Capt kia 13-5-15 NSomYeo p205 MR29
ENNIS,Charles Francis 2Lt kia 20-11-17 1RMunstF p175 CR France689

ENNIS,Edward Armstrong 2Lt dow 30-10-18 3Leinst p174 CR Ireland12
ENNIS,Reginald Joseph 2Lt kia 16-8-17 1RIrRif p169 MR30
ENRIGHT,Anthony Basil 2Lt dow 11-5-17 D17RFA p28 CR France40
ENRIGHT,Thomas 2Lt dow 20-4-18 RIrRif p169 CR Lond9
ENRIGHT,Thomas Louis TCapt ded 19-3-18 RAMC p195 CR Greece7
ENSOR,Charles Edward James Lt ded 18-10-19 RGA p270 CR Hamps57
ENSOR,John Collen Lt dow 26-11-17 17WelshR p126&257 CR France512
ENSOR,William James Alfred 2Lt kia 3-10-18 1/6NStaffs p157 CR France1706
ENTWISTLE,Charles Egerton Lt dow 22-3-18 8Manch p237 CR France987
ENTWISTLE,Charles Herbert TLt kia 9-4-18 231MGC Inf p182 CR Palestine9
ENTWISTLE,Frederick 2Lt kia 9-10-17 1Norf p73 CR Belgium112
ENTWISTLE,John Edward T2Lt kia 24-10-18 24Manch A'Coy p154 CR Italy9
ENTWISTLE,John Maurice Binley Capt ded 2-12-18 Worc p108 CR Egypt1,1-12-18
EPPSTEIN,William Reginald TCapt dow 4-9-18 20DLI p160 CR Belgium11
EREAUT,Harold John Capt 8-6-16 EAMS CR EAfrica58
ERICSON,Eric Charles.MM.T2Lt kia 18-9-18 RSuss att7Bn p119 CR France369
ERLE,Christopher TCapt ded 10-2-17 1Nhampt GarrBn p137 CR Egypt1
ERLEBACH,Arthur Woodland T2Lt kia 5-7-17 GL &57RFC p7 CR France134
ERLEBACH,Edward Eustace 2Lt kia 7-2-17 45RFC p7 CR France1032
ERMEN,Godfrey Henry Capt ded 4-5-15 6WRid p227 CR Yorks481
ERRINGTON,A.H.P.2Lt kia 30/31-11-14 YLI p143 MR32
ERRINGTON,James Capt kia 30-8-15 7DLI p239 CR France681
ERSKINE,Neil 2Lt dow 23-8-18 1Lpool p71 CR France103
ERSKINE,Ralph TCapt ded PoW 1-1-18 GL &66RFC p15 CR Italy9,kia
ERSKINE,Thomas Barrie.MC.2LtTCapt dow 20-7-15 4A&SH att1GordH p173 CR Belgium6,kia
ERSKINE,Walter Augustus Capt kia 24-5-15 108RGA p39 CR Belgium135
ERVINE,Charles James T2Lt dow 6-4-16 27NumbF p61 CR France285
ERWOOD,Cecil Victor T2Lt kia 17-2-17 19 att1KRRC p150 CR France314
ESDAILE,Arthur James Lt kia 7-11-18 1Dev p76 CR France937
ESDAILE,George Augustus Churchill 2Lt kia 10-8-17 281RFA p208 CR Belgium19
ESDALE,Robert Blair T2Lt kld 13-11-17 GL &RFC p7 CR Canada256
ESMONDE,Geoffrey 2Lt kia 7-10-16 26NumbF p61 CR France922
ESMONDE,John Joseph TCapt ded 17-4-15 RAMC p195 CR Eire205
ESPIE,Thomas Fletcher Lt ded 6-2-19 5RIrF p171 CR Ireland79
ESSEX,Percy Clifford 2Lt kia 9-9-16 2/5LancF p221 MR21
ESSEX,Robert Charles Lt dow 14-5-18 B162RFA p207 CR France142
ESSON,Alfred Charles T2Lt dow 23-10-17 17LancF p92 CR Belgium16
ESTALL,Arthur Cecil TCapt dow 8-8-17 RASC p192 CR France102
ESTEN,Gerald Philip TLt kia 6-8-15 9RWSurr attEss p55 MR4
ESTRIDGE,Edward Wilfred 2Lt kia 13-11-16 3 att12EYorks p84 MR21
ETCHES,Alfred Joseph Edward TLt kia 11-4-17 GL &52RFC p7 CR France415
ETHELSTON,Herbert Wicksted Lt kia 14-3-15 1GrenGds p50 MR22
ETHERIDGE,Cecil Norbert Lt kia 29-3-18 2RB p178 CR France544
ETHERIDGE,Eckley Oxtoby 2Lt kia 12-7-17 149RFA p28 CR Belgium15,ETHEREDGE
ETHERIDGE,Hugh Dimsdale,MC.MM T2Lt dow 2-10-18 17RFus p67 CR France512
ETHERINGTON,Herbert Field 2Lt dow 8-1-16 2DragGds p21 CR France80,8-1-15
ETLINGER,Henry Capt dow 27-4-15 IA 9BhopalInf p276
EUSTACE,Thomas George Lt kia 28-6-15 4 att1RMunstF p175 MR4
EVAN-JONES,Hilary Gresford.MID Lt kia 16-2-15 1WelshR p126 MR29
EVANS,Albert Ashley 2Lt kia 24-9-18 1KSLI att2Y&L p144 CR France835
EVANS,Albert Aylward TCapt kia 16-6-17 13NumbF p61 MR20
EVANS,Albert Illtyd 2Lt kia 17-8-17 RFA 85Bty att92Bde p28 CR Belgium5
EVANS,Albert John 2Lt kia 15-6-17 19Lond p250 MR20,att2/2Bn
EVANS,Alfred Henry Courtenay T2Lt kld 22-3-18 11ELancs att107RFC p15 CR Wilts3
EVANS,Arthur 2Lt ded 31-3-15 18WelchR p126 CR Wales203
EVANS,Arthur 2Lt kia 18-10-16 3 att9Ess p131 MR21
EVANS,Arthur Ernest TCapt kia 24-6-17 19WelshR p126 CR Belgium23
EVANS,Arthur Frederick Lt kia 30/31-10-18 4RWFus &RAF p255,Frederic p223,5Bn
EVANS,Arthur John TLtACapt kia 2-7-18 10SWBord p100 CR France41
EVANS,Arthur Leslie 2Lt kia 20-7-16 2Suff p78 MR21
EVANS,Arthur Stuart LtCol ded 2-1-20 RE MR43
EVANS,Bernard T2Lt ded 8-4-17 GL &55RFC p7 CR France481,Lt
EVANS,Bertram Trevor T2Lt kia 22-4-18 13RWFus p97 MR27
EVANS,Charles Edward Maj kia 6-8-18 RE 82FC p44 CR France33
EVANS,Charles Heyland 2Lt kia 26-10-14 2BordR p117 MR29
EVANS,Charles Wilmot.MC.Capt kia 1-7-16 1 att4SStaffs p122 MR21

EVANS,Christmas Richard.MC.Capt ded 11-4-19 WelshR p264
EVANS,D.M.W.Lt 10-4-19 Mon CR Wales195
EVANS,David.MC.Capt kia 20-7-16 1ScotRif p103 MR21
EVANS,David 2Lt kld 14-9-16 1RE S'Coy p44 CR France1106
EVANS,David T2Lt dow 24-9-17 NumbF att1Bn p61 CR Belgium18
EVANS,David Edgar Lt kia 18-9-18 14WelshR p126 MR37
EVANS,David Edward 2Lt kia 26-8-18 3RWFus p97 CR France432
EVANS,David Owen TLt kia 12-2-16 17RWFus p97 CR France631
EVANS,David William T2Lt kia 8-10-18 1/2 att14RWFus p97 CR France1345,Williams
EVANS,Dennis Leslie 2Lt dow 15-12-17 21Lond F'Coy p251 CR Palestine9
EVANS,Douglas Houghton 2Lt kia 13-8-16 7ESurr p112 MR21
EVANS,Douglas Lane TCapt dow 26-9-16 6Nhampt p137 CR France41
EVANS,Douglas Osmond 2Lt kia 8-8-16 1Lpool p71 MR21
EVANS,Edward TLt kia 9-4-17 RAMC att10RWFus p195 CRFrance418
EVANS,Edward TCapt ded 21-5-18 RAVC p268 CR Wales713
EVANS,Edward Herbert Sandford LtTCapt kia 22-7-16 18LancF p92 CR France63
EVANS,Edward Juson T2Lt kia 3-7-16 9 att8Glouc p106 CR France393
EVANS,Edward Meredyd Lloyd Capt kia 14-3-16 5RLancs p213
EVANS,Edward Tilney T2Lt kld 19-2-18 GL &RFC p15 CR Essex1
EVANS,Edward Williams.MID Rev ded 10-2-19 RAChDept p268 CR Cornwall135
EVANS,Edwin T2Lt dow 22-11-16 2Mddx p146 CR France40
EVANS,Emrys T2Lt kia 29-4-16 RE 253TC p44 CR France423
EVANS,Eric Ben T2Lt kia 11-11-17 1/2 att2/8LancF p92 CR Belgium45
EVANS,Eric Charles Lt kia 23-3-18 5RWSurr p212 CR France1893
EVANS,Ernest 2Lt dow 21-9-18 RGA 91SB p39 CR France194
EVANS,Fisher Arthur Haslett Freke TLtACapt kia 11-1-17 RLancs p58 MR38
EVANS,Forrest Dinnett 2Lt kld 27-3-18 RFC p15 CR Wilts1
EVANS,Francis Bernard T2Lt kldacc 17-2-18 RFC p15 CR Norf61
EVANS,Francis Graham Lt ded 26-9-16 4RWFus p223 CR Wales609,25-9-16
EVANS,Frank Dudley 2Lt kld 9-6-16 4RWar &RFC p2&64 CR War65
EVANS,Frank Montague 2Lt kia 4/5-4-16 3RWSurr att9RWar p55 CR Iraq5,5-4-1
EVANS,Frederick Henry TLt kia 9-10-17 9 att15WYorks p81 MR30
EVANS,Frederick William T2Lt dow 28-10-16 13WelshR p126 CR Belgium11
EVANS,Frederick Woodham T2Lt dow 26-5-17 21Mddx &20RFC p7&146 CR France705 Ex 16Lond
EVANS,Frew Ferguson T2Lt kia 13-2-17 8 att4SWBord p100 MR38
EVANS,Geoffrey Maynard.MC.Chap4Cl kia 11-8-17 RAChDept p199 CR Belgium310
EVANS,George.MID 2Lt kia 3-10-18 1/6SStaffs p229 CR France443
EVANS,George Edwin T2Lt kia 26-3-18 1 att8ESurr p112 MR27,25-3-18
EVANS,George Ernest Knightly 2Lt kia 3-9-16 3Leinst att2RIrRif p174 CR France402
EVANS,Godfrey Stanton Lt ded 30-6-17 RDC p253 CR Essex255,Thomas
EVANS,Griffith William 2Lt kia 22-4-18 6RWFus &RAF p223&258 CR Lincs181,21-4-18
EVANS,Harry TLt kia 26-3-18 11WYorks p81 CR France745,Capt
EVANS,Harry Charles T2Lt kia 23-8-18 32MGC Inf p182 CR France526
EVANS,Henry Cope,DSO.2Lt kia 4-9-16 GL &RFC p2&190,ded 3-9-16 MR20
EVANS,Henry Robert Noel 2LtTCapt kia 16-8-17 8 att7DCLI p114 MR30
EVANS,Herbert Theodore Penrhys Lt kia 4-10-16 98RFA p28 CR Greece3
EVANS,Hew Reginald Lt ded 15-12-16 RDC p253 CR Kent61
EVANS,Horace Thomas Royston 2Lt kia 8/9-5-17 4 att15RWar p64 CR France777
EVANS,Hubert William T2Lt dow 24-5-17 6EKent p57 CR France40
EVANS,Hugh Arthur TLt ded 3-6-15 RAMC p195
EVANS,Hugh Elwyn.MC.Lt kia 26-3-18 5Yorks p220 MR27
EVANS,Hugh George 2Lt kia 4-9-18 5Lpool att16Dev p215 CR France511
EVANS,Hugh Robert 2Lt kia 19-9-18 18 att9WelshR p126 MR19
EVANS,Hugh William T2Lt kld 30-8-17 GL &35RFC p7 CR Essex48
EVANS,Humphrey Pennefather TLt kia 1-7-16 2SWBord p100 MR21
EVANS,Hywel Llewellyn 2Lt kia 26-9-17 7 att2RWFus p223 MR30,Llywelyn
EVANS,James Bansall TLt kia 20-8-16 20RFus p67 MR21
EVANS,James Reginald T2Lt ded 19-10-18 RE 3ResBn p44 CR Staffs52
EVANS,Jane Sister drd 26-2-18 QAIMNS p200 MR40
EVANS,John 2Lt ded 29-10-18 EYorks &13RAF p84 CR France332
EVANS,John.MC.MID 2Lt kia 19-9-18 1RWFus p97 CR France660
EVANS,John Arthur 2Lt kia 27-1-17 4RWFus att1/2Lond p223 CR France924
EVANS,John Baynes Lt kia 23-3-18 4Lond p246 MR20
EVANS,John Edward Martin Lt dow 9-2-18 8Manch &48RFC p237 CR France987
EVANS,John Eric Capt dow 9-5-15 4RWFus p223 CR France80,kia 10-5-15

EVANS,John Ewart 2Lt kia 27-9-18 Dev p76 CR France245
EVANS,John Harold Lt ded 12-12-19 WelshR p264 CR France1142,7RWFus
EVANS,John Henry Grant.DCM.2Lt dow 7-2-17 1DCLI p114 CR France80
EVANS,John Owen 2Lt kia 23-11-17 TankCps p188 MR17
EVANS,John Rayner Lt kia 8-10-18 1Mon p244 CR France1710
EVANS,John Trevor Stuart TCapt dow PoW 7-5-18 GL &19RWFus p190 CR France742
EVANS,John William T2Lt dow 10-4-17 11N&D p133 CR Belgium11
EVANS,Kenneth George Ogle 2Lt kia 31-3-18 6KSLI p144 CR France988
EVANS,Lawrence Picton Lt kia 21-8-18 6 att4RFus p67 CR France618
EVANS,Leonard Austin T2Lt ded 27-3-18 1TankCps p188 CR France52,dow
EVANS,Leslie Morier T2Lt kia 12-11-17 RASC p192 CR Belgium10
EVANS,Lewis Lt&QM ded 28-10-18 8Glouc p106 CR France34
EVANS,Margaret Ellen Miss ded 22-7-17 VAD att83GH p200 CR France64
EVANS,Neville Vernon 2Lt kia 16-8-17 3SWBord p100 CR Belgium106
EVANS,Noel Everard 2Lt dow 11-11-18 RFA 121Bty27Bde p28 CR France146
EVANS,Norman 2Lt kia 25-7-16 1SWBord p100 CR France832
EVANS,Norman Edward T2Lt kia 4-11-18 17RWFus p97 CR France735 Ex RFC
EVANS,Norman Emryn T2Lt dow 3-10-16 2SLancs p125 CR France74,Emrys
EVANS,Norman Harden Lt dow 19-4-17 2/4RWKent p234 CR Palestine8
EVANS,Oscar James T2Lt kia 5-1-16 8RWFus p97 MR4
EVANS,Percival Richard TLt,AMaj dow 6-9-17 D74RFA p28 CR Belgium16
EVANS,Percy Charles David TCapt dow 22-12-15 13WelshR MGOffr att114Bde p126&182
EVANS,Philip T2Lt kld 24-1-17 GL&RFC p7&190,12-1-17 CR Hamps1
EVANS,Philip Henry 2Lt kia 3-5-17 2Ess p131 MR20
EVANS,Raymond T2Lt kia 12-1-17 9 att4SWBord p100 CR Iraq5
EVANS,Rees Tudor Capt kia 10-8-15 5WelshR p230 MR4
EVANS,Rhys Trevor 2Lt kia 1-9-17 4 att14RWFus p223 MR30
EVANS,Richard Lt dow 10-8-17 1/6N&D p233 CR France80
EVANS,Richard Hellier Agard Lt kia 5-11-17 IA 127BaluchiLI att2/124Baluch MR38
EVANS,Richard Parry T2Lt kia 14-5-17 1RWFus p97 CR France644
EVANS,Richard Stanley Lt kia 10-8-15 5WelshR p230 MR4
EVANS,Richard William Picton.MID Maj ded 13-9-18 4WelshR p229 CR Palestine8
EVANS,Robert Cecil Lt kia 6-4-18 4RWFus A'Coy p223 CR France232
EVANS,Robert Charles T2Lt kia 24-8-18 15WelshR p126 CR France832
EVANS,Robert Pritchard T2Lt dow 11-4-17 14WelshR p126 CR Belgium18,Pritchard
EVANS,Roy Galloway TLt kia 26-8-18 9 att2SWBord p100 CR France28
EVANS,Rupert Ancrum 2Lt ded 25-1-16 3WYorks p81 CR Hereford162
EVANS,Samuel Houching Maj&QM ded 7-7-17 RASC p192 CR Scot764
EVANS,Stewart Nicholson Lt kld 9-7-17 2/6Suff attRFC p18&218 CR Suff83
EVANS,Thomas George T2Lt kia 20-9-17 SLancs att1/4Bn p125 CR Belgium10
EVANS,Thomas Richard.DSO.TMaj&Lt Col kia 3-10-18 RWFus att1/6NStaffs p97 CR France375
EVANS,Tudor Eglwysbach 2Lt kia 1-7-16 8ESurr B'Coy p112 CR France513
EVANS,Walter George 2Lt ded 14-12-17 1Norf p263 CR Herts37
EVANS,Walter Richard Capt ded 15-12-16 Leic p263 CR Wales30,Maj
EVANS,William HonLt&QM ded 27-5-16 5Leinst p174
EVANS,William Ashton T2Lt dow 16-11-16 9Ches p96 CR France62
EVANS,William David Russell Lt kia 10-8-15 5WelshR C'Coy p230 CR Gallipoli5
EVANS,William Edwards 2Lt kia 1-5-17 3 att13RWFus p97 CR Belgium73
EVANS,William Henry Lt kia 2-11-17 1/5Ess p232 CR Palestine8
EVANS,William James,DCM Lt 27-5-16 5Leinst CR Eire322
EVANS,William Jones TCapt dow 13-9-17 RAMC att2/1SMidFA p195 CR Belgium10
EVANS,William Laurence TLt kia 11-8-16 RAMC att1/6Lpool p195 CR France630
EVANS,William Pearce.MM.Lt 31-7-20 B307RFC CR France113
EVANS,Willie Herbert TMaj kia 14-8-15 11RScots p54 CR France727,William
EVANS-FREKE,Percy Charles.Hon.LtCol kia 13-5-15 LeicYeo p204 CR Belgium35,Cecil
EVANS-JONES,William Rev kia 8-10-18 RAChDept att2RWFus p199
EVANSON-JONES,Tom Alec Edward 2Lt 7-8-15 11Manch MR4
EVATT,George Raleigh Kerr Capt kia 14-11-14 1Mddx A'Coy p146 CR France347
EVATT,James Millar Capt kia 21-3-18 RAMC att330RFA p195 MR27
EVE,Frederick Samuel.Sir.LtCol ded 15-12-16 RAMC CR Essex56
EVE,William Henry Capt kia 5-3-17 13Huss p22 CR Iraq8
EVELEGH,Rosslyn Curzon Capt kia 19-9-14 2 O&BLI p130 CR France1111
EVERARD,Christopher Philip Capt kia 11-1-17 3HLI p162 MR38
EVERARD,Clement Charlie TLt kia 7-9-16 9N&D p133 CR France296

EVERARD,Ernest Victor T2Lt dow 23-6-17 8LNLancs A'Coy p135 CR France40
EVERARD,John Guy Lt kia 12-3-15 3HLI p162 CR France279
EVERED,Henry Robert Hastings T2Lt kia 1-7-16 27NumbF p61 MR21
EVERETT,Charles Alfred Stanley 2Lt dow 17-6-17 2/4Lincs p217 CR France1468
EVERETT,George Gordon Capt kia 1-5-17 IA 2/67Punjabis p276 MR43
EVERETT,Walter Reginald T2Lt dow 4-9-17 Ess att1Bn p131 CR France179,Lt kia
EVERETT,William Thomas 2Lt kia 6-11-18 4RWSurr p212 CR France979
EVERETT,William Wallis TCapt kia 9-10-18 9 att2Norf p73 CR France443,8-10-18
EVERINGHAM,Guy T2Lt kia 8-4-17 GL 16RFC p7 CR France1321
EVERITT,John Paxman T2Lt kia 1-7-16 15WYorks p81 MR21
EVERITT,John Wilson 2Lt ded PoW 12-4-18 5KRRC C'Coy p150 CR France652,dow 12Bn
EVERITT,Rupert Edward 2Lt kia 24-6-17 RGA 299SB p39 CR Belgium1
EVERITT,William Needham,MC Lt kia 3-9-17 16 4WRid p227 MR21
EVERS,Bertram Saxelbye TCapt kia 14-9-16 9WYorks p81 MR21
EVERS,Ernest William.MC.TCapt kia 23-11-17 15 att21Mddx p146 MR17
EVERS,Hugh Lancelot.MC&Bar.Capt kia 1-11-18 2/8Worc p226 CR France290
EVERS,Leslie Montague 2Lt kia 30-3-18 6Yorks p90 Mk19
EVERSDEN,Robert Ernest Capt kld 5-8-19 3SuffYeo att47RAF p270 CR Asia81,15-8-19
EVERSFIELD,Charles John T2Lt kia 25-9-16 10YLI p143 MR21
EVERSHED,Albury Lt kia 1-7-16 1/6NStaffs p238 MR21
EVERSHED,Ernest Bernard 2LtTLt kia 27-9-17 GL RFus att1/2KAR p202 CR EAfrica11 &CR Tanzania1,28-9-17
EVERSHED,Philip Douglas Lt kia 22-8-18 7 att19Lond p247 CR France210
EVERSON,Charles Percy 2Lt kia 7-10-16 5DCLI p227 MR21
EVERSON,Harry Thomas T2Lt kia 7-11-18 8RWKent p141 MR16
EVERTON,Bird.MID Lt kldacc 19-4-20 2Dors B'Coy CR Ireland196
EVERTON,Maryon Jeffrey T2Lt kia 9-7-16 13 att10SWBord p100 CR France453,Jeffreys
EVERTON,Robert Frederick Lt ded 8-4-19 RGA 61Coy p39 MR65
EVERTON,Walter Hassell T2Lt ded 30-5-18 RASC attCamelTransport p192 CR Palestine9
EVEZARD,George Lt ACapt dow 9-5-17 1RWar p64 CR France95
EVILL,Chetwode Percy.MC.TCapt ded 17-7-18 IARO attS&M p276 MR69
EWEN,George Thomas.MC.Capt kia 8-3-16 3Manch p258&154 MR38
EWART,Archibald John T2Lt kia 28-9-16 11 att8WRid p115 CR France1170
EWART,Cecil Frederick Kelso TCapt kia 1-7-16 11RIrRif p169 MR21
EWART,James Henry HonBrigGen ded 1-1-16 4SfthH p270 CR Scot199,Col
EWART,Keith Penicuik 2Lt kia 4-1-18 27RFC p15 CR France920
EWART,Richard Henry Charles TLt dow 16-10-18 10 att14BlkW p128 CR France769
EWART,William Grieve Lt kia 30-3-18 Fife&ForfarYeo att13RScots p203 MR20
EWBANK,John Walter,MC &Bar LtTCapt kia 30-11-17 1BordR p117 MR17
EWBANK,Leonard 2Lt kia 23-2-16 5BordR p228 CR Belgium127
EWEN,Edgar Hunter Lt kld 1-5-17 5RScotF p222 CR Scot517
EWEN,Guy Cuthbert Lt kia 24-1-17 SL att3NigR MR50
EWEN,Henry Spencer.MC.Lt kia 5-4-18 1/23Lond p252 MR20
EWEN,Philip Keith Somerville TLt kia 3-9-16 17KRRC p150 CR France701
EWEN,William James Lt ACapt kia 25-3-18 3 att8RWKent p141 MR27
EWENS,G.W.F.Col 9-9-14 IMS MR67
EWENS,Thomas William T2Lt kia 30-3-17 13NumbF p61 CR France927
EWIN,Arthur.DCM.HonLt&QM kia 7/11-8-15 9N&D p133 MR4
EWING,Arthur Harold.MC.LtACapt&Adjt dow 8-9-18 1EYorks p84 CR France84
EWING,Douglas James.MM.2Lt ded 24-6-18 4 att2/6RWar p263 CR France1161
EWING,Douglas Ramsay Maj ded 31-5-17 ScotRif att66Bde HQ p103 MR37
EWING,Gordon Craig.MC.2Lt kia 20-9-18 4Lond p246 CR France369
EWING,Harold Gordon T2Lt kia 9-4-17 18Lpool p71 MR20
EWING,James.MID Capt dow 12-4-17 RAMC att8RWFus p195 MR38
EWING,James Adie T2Lt kia 31-7-17 11A&SH p173 MR29
EWING,James Robert Capt ded 19-5-15 RSuss p119 CR Sussex201
EWINGS,John George Vivian Lt kia 3-10-18 1YLI p143 CR France234
EXELL,Noel Jardine TCapt dow 31-7-15 9KRRC p150 MR29
EXLEY,A.T.2Lt kld 22-4-18 11NumbF &RAF p61
EXLEY,Charles Lt ded 11-10-15 RIM p276 CR Iraq6
EXLEY,George Allan 2Lt kia 14-1-17 5YLI attRFC p18&235 CR France158, Lt
EXLEY,John Henry TCapt ded 11-3-19 RAOC p267 CR Yorks361
EYDEN,Herbert.MC.Lt kld 7-4-18 RGA &21RAF p39 CR Belgium18,Capt
EYKYN,Gilbert Davidson Pitt Capt kia 25-4-15 RScots p54 MR29
EYLES,Harold Morley Lt kia 6-11-16 6Worc p108 CR France432
EYNAUD,P.A.M.Lt kia 21-3-18 MaltaR attRMunstF p201 CR France369

EYRE,Arthur Noel 2Lt kia 26-9-18 6N&D &57RAF p233&258,Lt MR20
EYRE,Charles Howard Lt kia 25-9-15 6 att2KRRC p150 CR France219
EYRE,Harry 2Lt kia 17-9-18 2N&D p133 MR16
EYRE,Henry Joseph Bagshawe Lt dow 14-7-17 1IrGds p52 CR Belgium115,Harry
EYRE,Henry Wright Capt dow 29-7-16 2/6Glouc p225 CR France134
EYRE,Sebert Henry Robert 2Lt kia 14-4-17 1Ess p131 MR20
EYRE,Thomas Herbert T2Lt kia 17-7-17 1/2 att7Yorks p90 CR France97,16-7-17
EYRE,William TCapt dow 19-8-15 12WelshR attLancF p126 CR Egypt6
EYRE-POWELL,John William Alcock Rev kia 16-4-18 RAChDept attHQ 27LabCps p199 MR30
EYRES,H.T.2Lt ded 9-11-18 RWSurr &101RAF p55 CR France1754
EYTON,Robert William.MID TLt kia 22-3-18 7RB att41TMB p178 MR27
EYTON-Lloyd,John Wathen T2Lt kia 24-6-17 GL 10RFC p7 CR France98
EZARD,Herbert Henry T2Lt kld 30-5-17 24RFC p7 CR Wilts4
EZRA,David Lt kia 6-8-18 RGA 192SB p39 CR France247

F

FABER,Cecil Valdemar T2Lt kia 30-7-15 9KRRC p150
FABER,John Benbow.MC.Capt kia 18-9-16 RE 1/3FC p210 MR20
FABER,Stanley Colt Maj kia 30-3-17 47RFA p28 CR France182
FABER,Walter Louis TLt kia 24-8-16 5KSLI p144 MR21
FABIAN,Arthur Stanley LtTCapt kia 3-9-16 8 att13RSuss p119 CR France701
FAGAN,James Edward T2Lt dow 5-10-16 6 att8RInniskF p104 CR Belgium17,6-10-16
FAGAN,Jasper Gilbert Lt dow 22-11-15 IA 119Inf p276 MR38
FAGAN,Niel 2Lt dow 20-7-16 6 att1RB p178 CR Sussex4
FAILES,Gerald Watson.DSO.MC TCapt kia 15-4-18 9Norf p73 MR30
FAIR,Arthur Edward Balfour Maj kia 16-8-17 122RFA p28 CR Belgium12
FAIR,George Lt kia 1-10-18 1/4KOSB p223 CR France403,dow
FAIR,George Patrick Conroy 2Lt kia 1-7-16 1SomLI p79 CR France643
FAIR,James Conroy 2Lt kia 25-9-15 1CldGds p51 MR19,27-9-15
FAIR,James Gerald 2Lt kia 19-3-17 D of LancsYeo attRFC p18&204
FAIR,V.A.MC.Lt kld 29-9-18 KRRC att212RAF p265 CR Belgium140
FAIRALL,Harry Gustavus.MC.2Lt ded 5-11-18 4Leic p270 CR Leic63
FAIRBAIRN,Andrew Hubert 2Lt ded 5-6-15 3 att2RIrReg p89 CR Belgium125
FAIRBAIRN,George Eric 2Lt dow 20-6-15 10DLI p160 CR France285
FAIRBAIRN,Harry Lawson 2Lt kia 2-8-17 4CamH p243 MR29,att10Lpool
FAIRBAIRN,Maurice T2Lt kia 7-7-17 11RLancs p58 CR France379
FAIRBAIRN,W.R.Lt 12-1-17 11ESurr CR Surrey38
FAIRBAIRNS,Arnold.MID TLtACapt kia 14-10-18 10Yorks att13WRid p90 CR France347
FAIRBAIRNS,Joseph Maurice 2Lt kia 20-8-17 RFA 8DAC p28 CR Belgium5
FAIRBANK,Stanley Reginald T2Lt kia 4-4-18 8ESurr p112 MR27
FAIRBURN,Herbert Francis Lt dow 15-9-20 RFA CR Sussex110
FAIRBURN,William Ross Lt ded 12-1-17 ESurr p264
FAIRCLOUGH,Egerton.MID LtCol kia 10-4-18 Cmdg1/4SLancs p229 CR France80
FAIRCLOUGH,Eric Montague T2Lt dow 25-2-17 10RWSurr p55 CR Belgium11
FAIRCLOUGH,Robert Justice Capt dow 31-5-15 5Lpool p215 CR France102,30-5-15
FAIRCLOUGH,Robert Leslie 2Lt ded 5-5-17 RE 218Coy p262 CR France609
FAIRE,Reginald Alfred Capt kia 14-10-15 4Leic p219 MR19
FAIRER-SMITH,Aubrey TLt kia 25-4-18 RASC att182SBAC p192
FAIRGRIEVE,Alexander Oman Lt ded 25-12-18 IA 41Dogras p276 MR43,25-10-18 37Bn
FAIRGRIEVE,Robert 2Lt dow 24-11-17 RGA 86SB p39 CR Essex13
FAIRHURST,Lambert Supt 9-12-18 CombLabCps MR65
FAIRLEY,Duncan Lt kia 1-7-16 14Y&L p158 CR France156
FAIRLEY,Gilbert 2Lt kia 9-4-17 1RScotF p94 CR France418
FAIRLEY,James Fairburn TCapt ded 9-11-15 RAMC att11GH p195 CR France102
FAIRLEY,Philip Ernest.DCM.Capt ded 2-4-19 18Lond p250 CR Ireland68,dow
FAIRLEY,William Kerr T2Lt kia 12-8-18 1/2 att12RScotF p94 CR France19
FAIRLEY,Frank Capt kia 23-10-14 RScotF p94 MR29
FAIRLIE,Edward TCaptAMaj kia 30-3-18 7 att17KRRC p150 MR27
FAIRLIE,James Gordon TLtCol kia 22-4-16 Cmdg6LNLancs p135 MR38
FAIRLIE,Jno Ogilvy TCapt kia 27-9-15 10HLI p162 CR France98
FAIRLIE,Norman Edwin 2Lt kia 21-10-14 3 att2A&SH p173 MR32
FAIRTLOUGH,Frederick Howard.CMG.TLtCol kia 25/27-9-15 8RWSurr p55 MR19,26-9-15

FAIRTLOUGH,Gerald Harold.MC.Capt dow 13-6-18 RE 423FC p210 CR France40,Gerard Howard
FAIRWEATHER,Cyril John 2Lt kia 22-3-18 4 att14Hamps p228 MR27
FAIRWEATHER,Joseph CaptTMaj kia 15-1-17 4SWBord p100 CR Iraq5
FAIRWEATHER,Leslie John Edgar Cuthbert TLt dow 19-3-16 3Lincs p75 CR France922
FAIRWEATHER,William Lyall T2Lt kia 22-3-18 8RB p178 CR France1061
FAITHFUL,Eric Basil Francis Capt kia 10-3-18 3ConnRgrs att1RIrReg p172 CR Palestine3
FAITHFULL,Florence Mary Nurse drd 15-1-18 VAD BRCS p200 CR Iraq6
FAITHFULL,Francis William Alexander 2Lt kia 3-7-15 3 att2SfthH p164 CR Belgium23
FAITHFULL,Sidney Leigh T2Lt ded 15-8-16 RE 256TC p44 CR France15
FAKER,Frank Leonard T2Lt kia 13-11-16 12EYorks p84 MR21
FALBY,Edward Frederick 2Lt kia 9-9-16 1/4LNLancs p234 MR21
FALCK,Jack Randell 2Lt kld 7-12-17 GL &RFC p7 CR Hamps57
FALCOMER,William Meek 2Lt kia 13-5-16 3 att11RScots p54 CR Belgium71,FALCONER
FALCON,Francis Capt kia 6-8-15 12Worc p108 MR4
FALCON,Geoffrey William Lockhart TLt kia 6-8-15 11ESurr p112 MR4
FALCONAR-STEWART,Ian Stewart 2Lt dow 24-7-16 10A&SH p173 CR France1
FALCONAR-STEWART,Ronald Dundas.DSO.CaptTLtCol kia 19-9-18 12A&SH p173 CR Greece5
FALCONER,James Page Lt kia 5-8-18 4RScots p210 CR France26
FALCONER,James Rankin T2Lt kia 25-9-15 10HLI p162 CR France114
FALCONER,John Keith Lt kia 31-7-17 HampsYeo att14Hamps p203 MR29
FALCONER,Robert Whitfield TLt kia 1-7-16 16NumbF p61 MR21
FALCONER,William Keay Lt kia 26-4-15 7A&SH p243 CR Belgium129,25-4-15
FALCY,Humphrey Ned.MC.T2Lt kia 21-11-16 23NumbF p61 CR France275
FALKINER,Frederick Ewen Baldwin.MC.2Lt kia 21-8-17 15RIrRif &57RFC p7&169 CR Belgium125,17Bn
FALKINER,George Stride 2Lt kia 16-8-17 2RDubF p176 MR30
FALKNER,Arthur Newstead TCapt dow 20-7-16 8LNLancs p135 CR France145
FALKNER,Clarence Beach Capt kia 25-10-17 2/2Lond p245 MR30
FALKNER,Leonard Lt kia 25-9-15 8Lincs p75 MR19
FALKNER,William Harold 2Lt kia 20-10-17 RFC p7 CR France62,Lt kld
FALKONS,Robert TCapt kia 1-7-16 30 att27NumbF p61 MR21
FALL,Patrick Joseph Lt dow 15-11-16 15 att17Mddx p146 CR France203
FALLE,Bertram Vernon TCapt kia 16-8-15 6RIrF p171 MR4
FALLOON,T.SubAssSurg 3-1-20 IMS CR Iraq8
FALLOWES,John Tyrrell Champion TLt kia 15-9-16 9Suff p78 MR21
FALLOWFIELD,William Gordon T2Lt kia 25-9-15 2A&SH p173 CR France114
FALLOWS,Ernest Hamilton 2Lt kia 25-3-18 IrGds attGdsDivMGR p52&53 MR20
FALLOWS,James Albert.TD.LtCol kia 7-6-15 8LancF p221 CR Gallipoli1,6-6-15
FALSIDE,William James Chap4Cl ded 7-10-18 RAChDept p199 CR Italy19
FALVEY-BETTS,J.DSO.LtCol kia 5-10-17 15DLI CR Belgium96
FANE,Horatio Alfred.MC.Capt dow 11-8-18 OxfYeo p205 CR France587
FANE,Octavius Edward.DSO.MC.CaptAMaj dow 18-9-18 RGA 128HB p39 CR France836,SB
FANGHANEL,Frederick Charles 2Lt kia 1-7-16 1/4Lond p246 MR21
FANNING,Vivian Edward LtACapt kia 14-11-16 2 O&BLI p130 CR France152
FANSHAWE,Harvey Vernon 2Lt dow 11-10-17 1IrGds p52 CR Belgium16
FANSHAWE,Leighton Dalrymple TLt kia 3-8-17 7MGC p182 MR29
FARADAY,Roy Lt kia 7-6-17 2/6Lond att74MGC p187&246,Ray CR Belgium43
FARAGHER,Edward Sayle 2Lt kia 9-10-17 2LancF p92 MR30
FARDELL,Gervase.MC.Capt kia 29-9-18 5 att1KRRC p150 CR France1483
FARDELL,Hubert George Henry Lt kia 23-4-15 3 att2ESurr p112 CR Belgium167
FAREBROTHER,Harcourt Sutcliffe TCapt dow 24-7-16 Norf p73 CR Lincs162,Lt
FAREIRA,John E.AssSurg 21-5-18 ISMD MR68
FAREY,Cecil Victor.MC.2Lt dow 11-8-17 4 att7ESurr p112 CR France113
FARGUS,Frederick Brian Arthur Lt kia 1-1-15 9Lond p248 MR29
FARIE,Claude Allan Gilbert Lindsay Hamilton Capt dow 15-3-16 1HLI &RFC p2&162 CR Iraq5
FARIS,Sturton Johnston T2Lt kia 30-7-16 17Lpool p71 CR France294
FARISH,Samuel TLt kia 24-4-17 1KOSB p101 MR20
FARLEY,Ernest Harold T2Lt kia 3-7-16 9Ess p131 MR21
FARLEY,Frederick Albert 2Lt kia 1-7-16 1/2Lond p245 MR21
FARLEY,George Herbert 2Lt kia 16-8-17 3RInniskF p104 MR30
FARLEY,Harry William Lt kia 24-4-18 RWKent att8Bn p141 MR20
FARLEY,Joseph Thomas T2Lt ded 1-9-18 16Manch p154 CR France40
FARLEY,M.Matron ded 1-6-18 QAIMNS p200 CR Ireland24

FARLEY,William T2Lt kia 15-6-16 15RWar p64 CR France1182
FARMAR,Cyril Herbert Berkeley Capt kia 19-4-17 1/10Lond p248 CR Palestine8
FARMAR-COTGRAVE,Christopher Russell Capt 29-12-17 2Worc att100TMB CR France1371
FARMER,Arthur William 2Lt kia 7-6-17 5BordR p228 MR29
FARMER,Charles George Edgar TLt kia 18-8-16 7KRRC p150 MR21
FARMER,Cyril.DSO.MC.Maj dow 3-8-17 RGA 183Bty83Bde attRFA p39 CR Belgium18
FARMER,Frederick George 2Lt ded 1-5-15 1ARO MR43
FARMER,Frederick Stanley T2Lt dow 20-7-17 1/2 att14Worc p108 CR France184,kia
FARMER,George Barten 2Lt kia 14-6-18 5ELancs p226 CR France5,15-6-18
FARMER,Henry Charles Maclean 2Lt kia 10-5-15 6 att4KRRC p150 MR29
FARMER,Henry Gamul TCapt dow 12-11-15 7SfthH p164 CR Germany1
FARMER,James Douglas Herbert 2Lt kia 4-11-14 9/41RFA p28 MR29
FARMER,James Inglesby 2Lt kia 9-5-15 2KRRC p150 MR22,Inglesby
FARMER,Roland Devonport Capt kia 22-3-16 5Leic p220 CR France68
FARMER,William McDowall Lt kia 9-4-16 14RScots att8RWFus p54 MR38
FARMILOE,George Frederick 2Lt kia 26-6-17 2HAC p206 CR France614
FARNES,Henry Charles T2Lt kia 6-7-17 GL &48RFC p7 CR France421
FARNHAM,Frank Jefferson 2Lt kld 15-4-17 RGA 239SB p39 CR France593
FARNHAM,Ralph Capt dow 31-10-18 6LancF p221 CR Belgium11
FARNWORTH,James 2Lt kia 9-8-16 1/5LNLancs p234 MR21
FARQUARSON,James T2Lt kia 23-4-17 11A&SH p173 CR France531,FARQUHARSON
FARQUARSON,John Charles Lancelot Lt kia 31-10/1-11-14 14Lond p249
FARQUHAR,Dean Maj ded 11-10-20 1A att7MGC Motors p276 MR43,12-10-20
FARQUHAR,Francis Douglas.DSO.LtCol kia 20-3-15 CldGds attPrcessPatCanLI p51
FARQUHAR,Hobart Brooks Capt kia 21-5-16 15Lond p249 MR20,22-5-16
FARQUHAR,James Edward Mainwaring TMaj kia 15-9-16 6CamH p167 CR France432
FARQUHAR,John Oswald Lt kia 23-3-18 RGlasgowYeo att 10Ess p203 MR27
FARQUHAR,Ronald George T2Lt kia 29-3-17 9RWar p64 MR38
FARQUHAR,Rupert,MC Lt dow 17-9-17 4GrenGds p50 CR Belgium12
FARQUHAR,Walter Randolph Fitzroy.Bart Capt kia 15-10-18 RFA 59Div p207 CR France570
FARQUHAR,W.R.Lt ded 23-3-18 RFA p28 CR Surrey1
FARQUHAR-THOMPSON,Douglas T2Lt kia 13-10-15 10GordH p166 MR19
FARQUHARSON,Francis David Capt dow 11-4-18 5RScots att4Yorks p210 CR France1094
FARQUHARSON,Frank Lumsden Lt kia 4-6-15 6GordH p242 MR22,3-6-15
FARQUHARSON,Hugh Joseph T2Lt ded 27-8-16 2Norf p73 CR Iraq6
FARQUHARSON,John(Ian) 2Lt dow 23-8-18 4 att 1GordH p242 CR France226
FARQUHARSON,John Charles Lancelot Lt 31-10/1-11-14 LondScot MR29
FARQUHARSON,Lewis Shaw Capt kia 12-5-18 1RScots p54 CR Belgium4
FARQUHARSON,Norman Kenneth T2Lt kia 29-8-18 2/5RLancs D'Coy p58 CR France568
FARQUHARSON,Peere William Nesham 2Lt kia 7-10-16 26RFus p67 CR France744
FARQUHARSON-ROBERTS,Donald.MC.TCapt kia 20-11-17 7 att4ESurr p112 MR17
FARR,Charles Gordon.MID 2Lt dow 25-3-18 4 att6KOSB p224 CR France40
FARR,Percival Ward Lt kia 31-7-17 4Mddx p146 MR29
FARRAN,Charles T2Lt kia 24-8-16 9KRRC p150 MR21
FARRAN,Edmond Baker 2Lt drd 8-8-15 5BlkW p255 CR Scot118,18-8-15
FARRAN,Edmond Chomley Lambert Capt kia 16-6-15 3 att2RIrRif p169 MR29
FARRAN,George Francis Maj kia 18-7-16 98RFA p28 CR France515,A88RFA
FARRANT,Archibald William TLt ded 6-11-18 87MGC p182 CR Berks23
FARRANT,George T2Lt kia 9-2-17 6RLancs p58 MR38
FARRANT,Robert George Capt ded 18-12-17 MilLabCps CR EAfrica58
FARRAR,Ernest Bristow 2Lt kia 18-9-18 3 att16Dev p76 CR France1463
FARRAR,Fred T2Lt dow 4-10-17 8Lincs p75 CR Belgium132
FARRAR,Herbert Ronald 2Lt kia 24-12-14 3Leic att2Manch p87 CR Belgium97
FARRAR,John Frederick T2LtACapt ded 2-11-18 2WYorks p81 CR France1277
FARRAR,John Harold.MIDx2 Capt kia 9-5-15 3 att 1Nhampt p137 MR22
FARRAR,Julian Gordon Knowles TCapt kia 14-9-16 12LancF p92 MR37
FARRAR,Valentine Anstruther TLt dow 15-3-16 17LancF p92 CR France495,17-3-16
FARRAR,William Watt TLt ded 10-8-16 RAMC p195 MR65
FARRELL,Adrian Lt dow 23-8-16 4EYorks p219 CR Yorks5
FARRELL,Bede Capt kia 24-4-15 4EYorks p219 MR29
FARRELL,Bryan Usher Lt 27-6-21 RASC 11MT MR43

FARRELL,Francis 2Lt ded 23-2-19 15RIrRif p265 CR Ireland33,Lt
FARRELL,J.E.J.Capt 19-11-17 5Ches CR Yorks256
FARRELL,John Leo T2Lt kia 16-3-18 17RIrRif p169 CR France1061
FARRELL,Joseph.DCM.MID TCapt ded 28-7-18 1Dev p263 CR Devon1
FARRELL,Reginald T2Lt kia 14-7-16 6Nhampt p137 MR21
FARRELL,Stanley Knox 2Lt kia 20-7-18 1/6BlkW p231 CR France1695
FARREN,John 2Lt kia 13-11-16 7RWSurr attSuff p55&263, Suff att7RWKent CR France802,Lt 3 att2Suff
FARREN,William Ignatius George Lt ded 29-3-18 3RWFus p97 CR Wales497
FARRER,Fred 2Lt kld 28-11-17 RFC p7 CR Kent231,Lt
FARRER,Henry Wyndham Francis Blackburn.MC&2Bars.CaptAMaj kia 30-10-18 30RFA p28 CR France1270
FARRER,Lyonel Henry St.George T2Lt ded 28-10-15 5 O&BLI p130 CR France102,9Bn
FARRER,Richard Bracken Lt kia 8-6-17 1/5Leic p220 CR France161
FARRIER,Archibald Manaton 2Lt dow 29-12-14 SWBord p100 CR France765
FARRIER,Douglas Towry 2Lt kia 1-10-17 RGA 219SB p39 CR Belgium124
FARRIMOND,Harry Carrington TLt ded 14-3-19 ELancs p264 CR Lancs368
FARRIMOND,Joseph T2Lt kia 21-7-16 8Nhampt att 1/5Glouc p137 MR21
FARRIN,Stuart Thomas 2Lt dow 7-12-17 RE 263RlyCo p44 CR Belgium84
FARRINGTON,Alfred Jack Lt ded 27-8-17 5RWar p214 CR Belgium126,John
FARRINGTON,F.L.Lt 16-12-20 S&M MR67
FARRINGTON,George William 2Lt kia 28-6-18 3 att12Glouc p106 CR France352
FARRINGTON,William Bowker 2Lt kia 25-3-18 6Manch p236 MR20
FARROW,Brian 2Lt kia 1-7-16 4 att2LancF p92 CR France742
FARROW,Charles Oswald 2Lt ded 2-12-18 RFA p261 CR Durham59
FARROW,Clifford Willis 2Lt dow 9-4-18 3 att4Dors p124 CR Palestine9
FARROW,Eric Tom 2LtTCapt kld 7-2-17 GL &RFC p7 CR Mddx34
FARROW,Jack TCapt kia 9-4-16 4SWBord p100 CR Iraq5
FARTHING,Leonard.MC.LtACapt kia 16-11-16 2ELancs p110 CR France744
FARTHING,William Edgar 2Lt dedacc 8-2-17 RGA 159HB p209 CR Devon1
FARWELL,John Edmund T2Lt kia 30-5-18 NumbF att4Bn p61 MR18
FASKALLY,Percy Blake Capt ded 18-12-19 RFus p263 CR Lond14,17-12-19
FAST,William Jack 2LtACapt kia 24-3-18 3 att12RSuss p119 MR27
FAULDER,Eric Amyas Wareing 2Lt kia 18-9-18 10WYorks p81 MR16
FAULDER,Harold.MIDx2 LtTCapt kia 26-4-18 3 att1/4Y&L p158 MR30
FAULKE,William James TLt kia 21-3-18 9Norf p73 MR20
FAULKNER,Charles Edward Arthur 2Lt dow 19-9-18 5Lpool p215 CR France530
FAULKNOR,Robert Sylvester John Capt kia 25-9-15 1LNLancs p135 CR France1723
FAULKS,Edgar TLt dow 26-9-15 RAMC att95RFA p195 MR19
FAULKS,Levi T2Lt kia 14-4-18 1Leic p87 MR30
FAUNCH,Ernest Alfred 2Lt kia 4-5-17 RGA 212SB p39 CR France557
FAUSSET,Charles Reginald 2Lt kia 3-5-15 3 att 1/2RIrReg p89 MR29,2-5-15 1Bn
FAUSSET,Stewart Simon Lt kia 31-7-17 9Lpool p216 MR29
FAUSSET,Robert Clifford TLt dow 16-11-16 C74RFA p28 CR Lond4
FAUSSET,William Willoughby Bernard Capt ded 6-12-18 GL p190&257 CR Lond4
FAVELL,William Reginald Lt kia 2-7-16 4Y&L p238 CR France702
FAWCETT,Bertram James Acton.MID Capt dow 24-4-17 8ELancs p110 CR France95
FAWCETT,Edward Bertram.MID Capt kia 22-4-16 1A 92Punjabis p276 MR38,21-4-16
FAWCETT,Frank Aldridge 2Lt kia 1-7-16 1/5SStaffs p229 MR21
FAWCETT,Fred 2Lt ded 12-11-18 D of LancsYeo &RAF p255
FAWCETT,Geoffrey Lt kia 14-6-18 RASC p253 CR France62,8Lond
FAWCETT,John 2Lt kia 8-5-18 3 att2Yorks p90 CR Belgium111
FAWCETT,John Bellars 2Lt kia 21-3-18 RGA 233SB p39 MR27
FAWCETT,Joseph John 2Lt kia 23-3-18 9RInniskF p104 CR France1203
FAWCETT,Leopald George Frederick Elliot Capt kia 6-11-17 LanarkYeo p204 CR Palestine1,12RScotsF
FAWCETT,Richard Wilfrid 2Lt dow 26-9-15 4 att2SStaffs att15TMB p122 CR France80
FAWCETT,Robert Heath 2Lt kia 26-4-15 4 att1Beds p85 CR Belgium133
FAWCETT,Woodford T2Lt kia 21-3-18 5 O&BLI p130 CR France1061
FAWCUS,Walter.MC.TCapt kia 25-3-18 19NumbF p61 MR27
FAWDRY,Alfred George 2Lt kia 4-5-17 2RWar p64 MR20
FAWKNER,Leslie Charles 2Lt kia 26-10-16 15RFC p2 CR France156 See FOCKEN,L.C.true name
FAWSITT,Thomas Ruby 2Lt kia 16-9-16 3 att9Y&L p158 MR21
FAYLE,Barcroft Joseph Leech Capt kia 24-10-16 RAMC att2WYorks p195 CR France390
FAYLE,Gerald Leigh Bleeck Lt kia 22-7-16 RE 59FC p44 MR21

FAYRER,J.O.S.LtCol 19-10-18 5GurkhaRif CR Lond4
FAYRER,Joseph Steward 2Lt kia 21-1-16 IA 37Dogras p276 CR Iraq5
FAZACKERLEY,Harold.MC.T2Lt kia 25-8-18 LNLancs att1/4Bn p135 CR France106
FAZACKERLEY,Joseph 2Lt dow 24-10-18 13Manch p154 CR France13
FAZACKERLY-WESTBY,Gilbert Basil Joscelyn Capt kia 21-4-15 9Lond p247 MR29,J.B.
FAZAN,Roy 2Lt kia 9-5-15 5RSuss p228 MR22
FEAR,Edgar Leslie Brinsdon T2Lt dow 11-4-18 SomLI 3Coy p79 MR34
FEAR,Robert Stanley T2Lt dow 5-3-18 5Worc att15RFC p15&108 CR France398
FEARN,Charles Frederick 2Lt kia 4-7-15 4RInniskF att2MunstF p104 CR France80
FEARN,Herbert T2Lt kia 12-10-17 8ESurr p112 CR Belgium126
FEARNHEAD,John Hayes 2Lt dow 13-8-16 1/7Lpool p215 MR21
FEARNLEY,Ethel SNurse 23-11-14 QAIMNS CR France102
FEARNLEY,William 2Lt kia 1-7-16 2GordH p166 CR France331
FEARNLEY-WHITTINGSTALL,George Herbert TLt kia 3-8-16 11NumbF p61 CR France430
FEARNSIDE-SPEED,Ronald Nelson de Dieskan Lt kia 25-9-15 7Lond p247 MR19
FEASBY,Harold T2Lt kia 11-4-18 Y&L att1/5Bn p158 MR30
FEATHER,Reginald Albert 2Lt kia 16-8-17 9Hamps p229 MR30
FEATHERSTONE,Cecil Frederick Lt kia 25-4-15 3 att2ESurr p112 MR29
FEATHERSTONE,George Herbert T2Lt kia 1-7-16 9YLI p143 MR21
FEATHERSTONE,Marshall Breckon T2Lt kia 2-9-17 RE 2SpecCoy p44 CR Belgium88
FEATHERSTONE,Reginald Benjamin Capt kia 18-12-14 2Dev p76 MR22
FEATHERSTONE,Thomas.MC.T2Lt kia 25-4-17 12 att11Worc p108 MR37
FEATHERSTONE,Walter 2Lt ded 3-10-17 GL &RFC p7 CR Bucks36
FEATHERSTONE,William Lt kia 13-9-16 5Yorks p220 CR France453
FEATHERSTONE,William Davies.MC.Lt kia 23-3-18 D77RFA p207 CR France307
FEATHERSTONHAUGH,Edwyn Maj dow 27-4-15 1RDubF p176 MR4 See FETHERSTONHAUGH,E.
FEATHERSTONHAUGH,Harry TCapt kia 8-7-16 8RFus p67 MR21
FEATHERSTONHAUGH,Richard Collingwood Lt dow 14-5-15 KRRC p150
FEAVERYEAR,Albert George 2Lt kia 5-9-18 7 att19Lond p247 CR France511
FEDDEN,Cecil Olchar Lt acckld 7-1-18 IARO attRFC p276 CR Numb34 lost at sea
FEDDEN,Raymond Henshaw 2Lt kia 3-5-17 2HAC p206 MR20
FEETHAM,Alan 2Lt kia 18-9-16 5BordR p228 CR France453
FEETHAM,Edward.CB.CMG.TMajGen kia 29-3-18 Staff Commdg39Divn p1
FEGGETTER,John Halifax,MC TLt kia 4-10-17 12/13NumbF p61 MR30
FEHILY,Thomas TCapt kia 13-4-18 RAMC att2RFus p195 MR32
FEILD,John Forbes 2Lt kia 16-9-16 7DCLI p114 MR21
FEILDEN,Oswald Henry Capt dow 29-9-17 2/5Leic p220 CR Belgium18
FEILDEN,Granville John Henry 2Lt kia 25-4-15 2SfthH p164 CR Belgium129
FEILING,Hubert St.Lawrence.MID 2Lt kia 20-11-16 1BlkW p128 CR France397
FELIX-BROWN,Claud A kia 26-12-16 GL attRFC CR Belgium4
FELL,David Malcolm 2Lt kia 17-7-16 166RFA p28 CR France188
FELL,George Charles Huntley 2Lt dow 24-7-17 C82RFA p208 CR Belgium29
FELL,Harold 2Lt kia 5-11-16 6DLI p239 MR21
FELL,Matthew Henry 2Lt kia 17-9-16 5Yorks p221 CR France239
FELL,Sidney Fitzroy T2Lt kia 10-7-16 12 att3Worc p108 MR21
FELLOWES,A.H.G.Capt ded 2-4-18 att54RFC p261 CR France446,11-3-18
FELLOWES,Coulson Churchill.Hon.Capt ded 22-10-15 1LifeGds p20 CR Hunts102
FELLOWES,Cyril Walter 2Lt kia 21-3-18 att2/6NStaffs p157 MR20
FELLOWES,Hedworth George Ailwyn.MC.Capt kia 12-5-17 IA 11Lancers p276 CR France730
FELLOWES,Robert 2Lt kia 10-3-15 1KRRC p150 MR22
FELLOWES,Rupert Caldwell Butler LtACapt kia 21-8-18 1ColdGds 4Coy p51 CR France103
FELLOWS,Arthur Simpson 2Lt kia 1-4-17 7Worc p226 CR France369
FELLOWS,Basil Hamilton Abdy 2Lt dow 22-3-17.3 att5RBerks p139 CR France46,FELLOWES
FELLOWS Mervyn 2Lt dow 25-8-17 C173RFA p28 CR Belgium11
FELLOWS Richard Woodhouse TLt kia 15-9-16 14 att2N&D p133 CR France374
FELTON,Hubert Ratcliffe 2Lt kia 9-10-17 7Worc p226 MR30,17Bn
FELTS,Percival Claude T2Lt kia 23-7-17 GL &6RFC p7 CR Belgium11
FEMNER,Cyril Frederick Hamilton 2Lt kia 24-9-16 2ScotGds p52
FENCHELLE,George John T2Lt dow PoW 30-6-16 12RSuss p119 CR France924
FENDALL,Charles Magrath TLt kia 14-12-15 RFA p28 MR29
FENDALL,Denis John 2Lt dow 8-8-17 RFA att4RFC p28&7,kia 7-8-17 CR Belgium19
FENDER,Edward Henry LtACapt kia 9-10-17 7WYorks p218 MR30

FENERAN,Frank Edward Capt kia 10-3-15 Lpool p71 MR22
FENN,Edward Gerald Palmer T2Lt kia 19-9-18 3RWFus GarrBn att1/5Ess p97 CR Palestine9,6Bn
FENN,John Edmund.MC.Lt kia 9-4-18 1/8Lpool p215 CR France260
FENN,Roland Pitt 2Lt kia 25-3-18 GL &18RFC p7 MR20
FENN-SMITH,Warren Kemp T2Lt kia 18-1-18 20RFC p15 CR France98
FENNELL,Frederick Vibond Lt kld 30-6-18 GL &8RAF CR France1564
FENNELLY,James Philps T2Lt kld 24-12-17 GL &RFC p7 CR Mddx17
FENNEMORE,George Charles T2Lt ded 3-11-18 RE p44 CR Iraq6
FENNER,Alan Thomas T2Lt dow 8-12-17 NStaffs att2/6Bn p157 CR France52
FENNER,Arthur.MC.LtTCapt ded 20-11-18 RASC HT25DivTrn p192 CR France146
FENNER,C.F.H.2Lt 24-9-16 2ScotsGds MR21
FENNER,Claude Cambridge LtCol kia 23-11-14 IA 59Rif p276 CR France727
FENNER,John Prebble T2Lt dow 8-8-17 7EYorks p84 CR France113
FENNER,Thomas 2LtACapt kia 22-3-18 3RB p178 MR27
FENNER,Walter Noel Lt dow 2-7-17 RFA p207 CR France13
FENNING,Algernon Esme Hal Maj kia 6-8-15 6Y&L p158 MR4
FENTIMAN,Frederick William 2Lt dow 24-3-18 BordR att8Bn p117 MR20
FENTON,Alan Hughes 2Lt mbk 4-3-17 43RFC p256 MR20
FENTON,Arthur Edward T2Lt kia 14-6-17 RWKent att11Bn p141 MR29
FENTON,Bede Liddell CaptTMaj kia 15-7-16 1Dors p124 MR21
FENTON,Charles Edwin T2Lt ded 19-8-17 12RIrRif p169 CR France40
FENTON,David Houston 2Lt kia 8-9-15 4WRid p227 CR Belgium167
FENTON,Douglas Annand Lt kia 9-9-16 3 att2ScotRif p103 CR France423,10-9-16
FENTON,Geoffrey Russell Lt kia 20-9-14 2ConnRgrs p172 MR15
FENTON,Gilbert Francis Rowland TLt kia 4-7-16 16RB p178 MR19
FENTON,William Vernon T2Lt dow 16-9-15 8Yorks p90 CR France684
FENWICK,Anthony Lionel.MID TLtACapt kia 16-2-18 6Lincs p75 CR France115
FENWICK,Maurice Edward Edmonds T2Lt kia 2-4-17 8Dev p76 CR France568
FENWICK,Percival Fenwick 2Lt kia 1-7-16 RFA p28 CR France700
FENWICK,William 2Lt dow 22-5-18 PoW 5 att10RWSurr p212 CR Germany1
FENWICK,William Cecil 2Lt ded 7-10-16 21RFC p2 MR20
FENWICKE-CLENNELL,Thomas Percival Edward Capt ded 20-2-19 Loth&BordHorseYeo p270 CR Greece9
FERARD,George Deas Lt kia 21-2-18 2Dev p76 MR30
FERGIE,Alexander Bancroft T2Lt kia 20-9-17 LNLancs att1/4Bn p135 MR30
FERGUSON,A.2Lt 22-9-18 EAfrMilLabCps APD CR EAfrica90
FERGUSON,Adam Lt dow 1-9-18 AustMGC 2Coy CR France119
FERGUSON,Alan TLt dow 4-7-16 9WRid p115 CR France207
FERGUSON,Alexander Crichton Capt ded 12-2-19 2RScots att8TMB p54&257,2Lt CR Germany1,Crighton
FERGUSON,Alexander Lundie Hunter TLt kia 23-7-16 8 att1/4GordH p166 MR21,22-7-16
FERGUSON,Alexander Robertson 2Lt kld 14-6-16 1/3ScotHorse p205 CR Egypt2
FERGUSON,Alva John T2Lt kld 4-8-17 127MGC p182
FERGUSON,Arthur Douglas Lt kia 12-10-17 6SforthH p241 MR30
FERGUSON,Arthur Alexander Lt dow 26-9-15 7Lond p247 CR France178,25-9-15
FERGUSON,Charles Edgar 2Lt kia 18-10-17 GL &22RFC p7 CR Belgium453
FERGUSON,David Raeside TLt kia 17-11-17 RE 135ArmyTrpsCoy p45 CR Belgium12
FERGUSON,Donald Francis 2Lt kia 7-5-17 ScotHorse att2GordH p205 MR20
FERGUSON,Douglas Chalmers T2Lt dow 26-1-17 10HLI p162 CR France145
FERGUSON,Duncan MacIntyre Grant Lt dow 14-5-15 3 att2KOSB p101 CR France102
FERGUSON,Fritz Eberhard.MC.Capt kia 7-10-19 IA 3CpsofGuides p276 MR43
FERGUSON,George Douglas.DSO.TCapt dow 23-4-17 RAMC att27RFA p195 CR France1325
FERGUSON,Harold Gowan.MC.Maj ded 30-11-18 RE p209 CR Lond14,Gowans
FERGUSON,Henry Horatio Edward TCapt dow 23-9-17 14HLI D'Coy p162 CR France398
FERGUSON,Henry Innes TCapt kia 14-7-16 17HLI p162 MR21
FERGUSON,Hugh Mortimer TCapt kia 11-6-17 9SStaffs p122 CR Belgium127
FERGUSON,Ian Alexander Grant TCapt kia 11-5-16 13RScots p54 CR France423
FERGUSON,J.Engr ded 12-7-17 IndLabCps attRE IWT Iraq6
FERGUSON,James Maj kia 22-7-16 9RScots p255 MR21
FERGUSON,James T2Lt kld 12-3-17 GL &RFC p7 CR Bucks51
FERGUSON,James Capt ded 9-10-18 SL IAUL RAMC p268 MR43
FERGUSON,James Arthur Ross Lt kia 9-5-15 3RSuss att1YLI p119 MR29
FERGUSON,James Ernest 2Lt kia 20-4-17 4 att10RDubF p176 MR20
FERGUSON,James Duncan.MID TLt dow 27-10-16 11Ess p131 CR France105

FERGUSON,James McKee TCapt kia 22-12-17 RAMC att6ConnRgrs p195 CR France1463
FERGUSON,John 2Lt kia 23-10-16 4 att2ScotRif p103 MR21
FERGUSON,John Capt kia 30-11-17 RAMC att1/12Lpool p195 MR17
FERGUSON,John 2LtTLt ded 8-7-18 14HLI p162 CR Scot167,3Bn
FERGUSON,John James Moore TCapt ded 19-11-18 7 att2Beds p85 CR France146,Charles
FERGUSON,Leonard R.C.T2Lt dow 20-7-16 13RScots p54 CR France134,Lt
FERGUSON,Norman Douglas 2Lt ded 1-7-19 LabCps 8Coy p266 CR France446
FERGUSON,Percy Grant 2Lt kia 10-3-15 Wilts p153 MR22
FERGUSON,Peter 2Lt kia 28-10-18 3A&SH p173 CR France1196
FERGUSON,Philip TCapt ded 27-1-19 RAMC p267 CR Surrey91
FERGUSON,Philip Hew.MC.CaptAMaj kia 22-10-17 152RFA p28 CR Belgium12
FERGUSON,Rachel SNurse ded 26-6-18 QAIMNS p200 CR Italy16
FERGUSON,Robert George.MC.T2LtACapt ded PoW 11-6-18 1RScotF p94 CR France924
FERGUSON,Robert William 2Lt kia 13-11-16 5GordH p242 CR France1501
FERGUSON,Roderick Mackenzie 2Lt kia 13-11-16 4GordH p242 CR France1490
FERGUSON,Samuel Cranswick 2Lt kia 8-9-18 8Lond p247 CR France511
FERGUSON,Stanley McEwan Lt ded 15-9-18 1A 17Cav p276 MR67 Ex 2Lt SfthH
FERGUSON,Thomas Capt kia 13-11-16 6BlkW p231 CR France35
FERGUSON,Thomas Jenkins T2Lt kia 30-8-18 15TankCps p188 CR France214
FERGUSON,Victor John Lt kia 21-8-18 2LifeGds att2GdsMGReg p20&53,21/22-8-19 CR France16
FERGUSON,William.MC.TCapt kia 1-11-16 12 att2Worc p108&258 MR21
FERGUSON,William Percival 2Lt kia 9-4-17 9RScots p212 CR France184
FERGUSON-DAVIE,Arthur Francis.CIE.DSO.LtCol dow 12-4-16 1A 51Sikhs p276 MR38
FERGUSON-POLLOCK,Robert Cuthbert Maj kia 11-4-17 IA 32Lancers p276 MR38
FERGUSSON,Douglas Hubert Lewin Lt dow 2-2-16 1CamH p167 CR Lond14
FERGUSSON,Edward Keith Ogilvy.MID TCapt kia 26-1-16 8SfthH p164 CR France178
FERGUSSON,Fitz-James Shillington T2Lt kia 22-3-18 12RB p178 CR France672
FERGUSSON,James Adam Hamilton 2Lt kia 20-9-14 HLI p162 MR15
FERGUSSON,James Grant T2Lt kia 14-7-16 8BlkW p128 MR21
FERGUSSON,James Scott Elliott Gillon Lt kia 27-4-15 5 att3Mddx p146
FERGUSSON,Kenneth Mountney James Lt kia 31-7-17 2Lincs p75 MR29
FERGUSSON,John Wright TLt ded 9-5-17 2SfthH p164 CR France40 Ex 9RScots
FERGUSSON,Robert Allan Arklay LtACapt kia 14-9-16 CldGds p51 CR France374,15-9-16
FERGUSSON,Robert Arthur 2Lt kia 15-4-17 6 att17RFus p67 CR France1321
FERGUSSON,Robert Frank Lt kia 12-7-15 1/5RScotF D'Coy p222 CR Gallipoli2
FERGUSSON,William Albert 2Lt dow 15-5-17 4Leic p220 CR France178
FERNALD,Van Dyke Lt ded 23-7-18 3RWSurr att139RAF p15&55 CR Italy9,kia
FERNANDES,Dudley Luis De Tavora.MID 2Lt kia 23-10-14 Beds p85 MR29
FERNIE,Andrew John T2Lt kia 12-10-17 11RScots p54 MR30
FERNIE,Roy Mackenzie Lt kia 16-8-15 RE 6SigCoy p210 CR Belgium59
FERNYHOUGH,Samuel Lt ded 7-5-18 4 att18Manch p154 CR Ches184
FERRABY,Robinson Lt ded 7-4-16 4EYorks p219 CR France64,dow
FERRAR,Walter Hughes Capt kia 2-11-14 2WelshR p126 CR Belgium57,31-10-14
FERRIE,Robert Leighton Moore.MC.2Lt kia 3-1-18 46RFC p15 CR France49
FERRIER,Gilbert Colin Cunninghame 2Lt kia 11-11-14 7 att4RFus p67 MR29
FERRIER,John Kinmont T2Lt dow 23-8-18 13RB D'Coy p178 CR France518
FERRIER,Robert Ernest 2Lt kia 15-10-16 4BlkW p230 CR France293
FERRILL,Tom Archibald 2Lt kia 16-8-17 3 att2WYorks p81 MR30
FERRIMAN,Frederick Samuel T2Lt kia 7-6-17 GL 6 O&BLI att25RFC p7 CR Belgium140
FERRIS,Alfred William 2Lt dow 5-3-17 2/3Lond p245 CR France120
FERRIS,Henry Norman 2Lt kia 9-10-17 4Glouc p225 CR Belgium126
FERRIS,James T2Lt kia 2-12-17 16HLI att97TMB p162 MR30
FERRIS,Samuel Bernard Clutton 2Lt ded 6-4-15 10Huss att11ResCavR p22 CR Wilts176
FERRIS,William Small T2Lt kia 7-6-17 12RIrRif p169 CR Belgium62
FERRYMAN,William Edward LtACapt dow 12-10-18 2ScotsGds p52 CR France337
FESTING,Arthur Hoskyns.CMG.DSO.Maj kia 9-5-15 RIrRif p169 MR32
FESTING,Hubert Wogan.DSO.MajLtCol kia 21-3-18 15DLI att10YLI p160 MR27
FETHERSTONHAUGH,Ashly Elliot Herbert Maj kld 20-3-19 14KHuss p261 CR Eire510
FETHERSTONHAUGH,Edwyn Maj 27-4-15 1RDubF MR4 See FEATHERSTONHAUGH,E.
FETHERSTONHAUGH,George Rupert Alexander 2Lt kia 25/27-10-14 RFus p67 MR22

FETHERSTONHAUGH,John Lennox 2Lt kia 10-11-14 2A&SH p173 MR32
FETHERSTONHAUGH-FRAMPTON,Philip Tregonwell Lt kia 3-5-15 RWar att2EKent p64 MR29,Tregenwell
FEURER,Sydney Moss 2Lt kia 22-7-18 RBerks att27RAF p254 CR France1107
FEVERSHAM,Charles William Reginald.Earl LtCol kia 15-9-16 21KRRC attYorkHussYeo p150&206 CR France744
FEW,Robert James Donald Lt dow 27-10-18 1Dors p124 CR Oxford69
FEWELL,Charles William T2Lt ded 6-11-18 O&BLI p130 CR Essex50
FFOLKES,William Rupert Compton 2Lt kia 30-12-17 5 att1KRRC p150 CR France530
FFRENCH,Edward Fulke.Hon.2Lt ded PoW 13-11-18 296RH&FA p28
FFRENCH,Ernest Dudley 2Lt kia 16-7-19 IA CpsofGuides att3/1GurkhaRif p276 MR43,ffRENCH
FFRENCH,Evelyn Wilson Capt kld 23-12-18 RFA &RFC p28 CR Mddx26
FIDLER,Canel Watt 2Lt dow 19-5-17 7A&SH attRFC p18&243,Carrell CR France297
FIDLER,Frederick Capt kia 26-4-15 1Hamps p120 MR29
FIDOE,Norman Godfrey T2Lt kia 21-3-18 1Leic p87 MR20
FIELD,Alfred John Lt ka 11-4-18 1/5NumbF p213 MR32
FIELD,Arthur Clarence Henley T2Lt dow 4-4-16 14RFus att4SWBord p67 MR38,5-4-16
FIELD,Arthur Dudley Lt kia 4-7-16 RGA 61SB p209 CR France430
FIELD,Arthur Montague 2Lt mbk 22-3-18 4Leic D'Coy p257&270,dow 13-4-18 CR France716
FIELD,Arthur Roland.MC.2Lt kia 17-9-18 C70RFA p28 CR France179
FIELD,A.W.Capt kia 9-1-18 48RFC p15 CR France238
FIELD,Charles Abel T2Lt dow 12-11-18 RWSurr att8Bn p55 CR France40
FIELD,Charles Cecil T2Lt kia 30-3-16 RWKent att2Suff p141 CR Belgium124
FIELD,Cyril Decimus 2Lt kia 4-6-15 5Worc p108 MR4
FIELD,Dave Hamilton Lt 22-4-15 RGA 2HB MR29
FIELD,Edwin Arthur T2Lt kia 14-9-16 14 att9WYorks p81 CR France293
FIELD,Francis Morgan TLtACapt kia 31-3-18 7EYorks p84 MR20
FIELD,George Walton T2Lt kia 25-9-15 10Glouc p106 CR France1723
FIELD,Gordon Stewart T2Lt kia 16-6-17 12NumbF p61 MR20
FIELD,Harold William T2Lt kia 27-5-18 9ACycCps p181 CR France1894
FIELD,Hassel Dyer.MID TCapt dow 28-9-17 RAMC att134FA p195 CR France139,Hassell
FIELD,Henry Lionel 2Lt kia 1-7-16 6RWar p214 CR France1890
FIELD,Howard LtTCapt kia 6-8-15 4Worc p108 MR4
FIELD,John Alan Francis TLtCol ded 23-4-18 13SWBord p100 CRKent179 Ex 13Ches
FIELD,John Archibald Capt kia 13-7-16 RE 92FC p45 CR France164
FIELD,John Morton T2Lt kia 11-4-18 7RSuss p119 CR France423
FIELD,John William 2LtTCapt kia 20-9-15 1RIrRif p169 CR France924
FIELD,Kenneth Douglas.DSO.LtCol kia 30-11-17 RGA 38SB p39 MR17
FIELD,Leslie Jack T2Lt kia 4-11-18 RBerks att8Bn p139 CR France230
FIELD,Linwood.DSO.MC.CaptAMaj kia 26-10-17 RFA p28 CR Belgium25
FIELD,Norman Lt kia 14-8-17 5Manch att25RFC p18&236 CR France924
FIELD,Oliver 2Lt kia 18-7-15 9DLI p239 CR France683
FIELD,Reginald George 2Lt dow 6-4-18 10Huss p22 CR France145
FIELD,Robert Alister.MC.LtACapt kia 2-4-17 2Yorks p90 CR France1186
FIELD,Samuel Hatten 2Lt kia 31-7-17 4SLancs p230 MR29
FIELD,Stephen Capt ded 10-4-15 PoW RAMC p195 CR Germany4
FIELD,Sydney Hubert 2Lt dow 9-8-16 4 att1RInnıskF p104 CR Belgium165
FIELD,Vincent Alfred 2Lt kia 20-9-17 10RWSurr p55 MR30
FIELD,William Christian T2Lt kia 31-7-17 2RB p178 MR29
FIELD,William James.MC.2Lt kia 31-7-17 1RFus p67 MR29
FIELDEN,Gilbert Sutcliffe T2Lt ded 18-7-17 9RLancs p58 CR Greece1
FIELDEN,Norman Leyland Lt ded 22-2-19 RGA p254 CR Herts110
FIELDER,Charles Lt mbk 22-9-18 11WelshR p256 CR Greece5
FIELDER,Edgar John T2Lt kia 9/12-4-17 RLancs p58 CR France182,Lt 8-4-17
FIELDHOUSE,Walter Benjamin T2Lt ded 1-11-18 2Lpool p71 MR43
FIELDING,Alexander.MC.T2Lt dow 26-10-18 26RFus att124TMB p67 CR Belgium158
FIELDING,Arthur William T2Lt kia 16-4-18 Y&L att6Bn p158 CR France163,15-4-18
FIELDING,Edward Fleming TLt kia 24-10-15 SomLI attKAR p200 CR WAfrica28
FIELDING,Francis Willoughby 2Lt kia 1-7-16 9Lond p248 CR France798
FIELDING,Frank T2Lt kia 4-10-17 1 att7LancF p92 MR30
FIELDING,George Rudolf TMaj kia 24-7-15 9N&D p134 CR Gallipoli14
FIELDING,Gerald Trueman 2Lt ded 27-5-18 B88RFA 19DAC p261 CR Belgium11,17-4-18

FIELDING,Henry Crossley Capt kia 12-9-15 IA 3A8Dogras att59Rif p276 CR France355 &CR France1887

FIELDING,Henry Simon.Hon.LtACapt dow 9-10-17 2CldGds p51 CR FEILDING 11-10-17

FIELDING,Herbert Hilton 2Lt kia 28-3-17 6Manch p236 CR France616

FIELDING,Joseph.MID 2Lt ded 16-12-17 GL RE attIWT p190 CR Iraq6

FIELDING,Joshua Maj ded 20-1-17 BRCS Ex 4DragGds CR Egypt8

FIELDING,S.Lt&QM ded 12-11-14 N&D p134 CR Derby97

FIELDING,F.Thomas.MID Capt&QM ded 31-10-18 4WRid p270 CR Yorks619

FIELDS,Edward Cotman T2Lt dow 22-6-16 27NumbF p61 CR France23,Cotnam

FIENNES,John Eustace Capt dow 18-6-17 2GordH p166 CR France113

FIFE,Alexander John LtCol ded 7-2-17 4Yorks attMGC p90,182,187&220 CR France40

FIFE,Gilbert 2Lt dow 16-7-16 9HLI p240

FIFIELD,Percival T2Lt kia 22-3-18 17KRRC p150 MR27

FIGG,Donald Whiteley.DSO.LtCol dow 5-3-17 24Lond &RFus p252 CR France624

FIGGINS,Henry Francis 2Lt kia 16-9-16 6Lond p247 MR21

FIGGIS,Lenox Paton.MC.TLtACapt kia 27-8-18 6EKent p57 CR France370

FIGGIS,Neville Johnstone TLt kia 10-8-15 6Leinst p174 CR Gallipoli18

FIGGURES,Douglas Lionel.MM.2Lt dow 15-10-18 C46RFA p28 CR France25

FILE,Harold William T2Lt kia 13-7-16 7RWKent p141 MR21

FILGATE,Thomas William Capt dow 29-9-15 8RMunsF p175 CR France178

FILLEUL,Leonard Amaurie 2Lt kia 21-10-14 SomLI attO&BLI p79 MR29,Amauri

FILLINGHAM,Reginald John.MC&Bar.LtAMaj dow 29-9-18 RGA 41SB p39&258 CR France194

FILMER,Robert Marcus.Bart.MC.TCapt dow 27-1-16 4GrenGds p50 CR France345

FILMER,Vivian Reginald Royal 2Lt kia 25-11-17 2Drags p21 CR France379

FILMER-STRANGEWAYS-ROGERS,Arthur Edmund 2Lt dow 4-11-18 3GrenGds p50

FILTNESS,John.MIDx2 Lt dow 22-5-18 D161RFA p28 CR France103,Capt

FINCH,Aubrey Malcolm Cecil Capt kia 7-7-19 4SfthH p241 MR70 &CR Europe179

FINCH,Ernest Wilfred Rupert Lt dow 7-8-16 4SfthH A'Coy p241 CR France74,kia

FINCH,Frank Marshall 2Lt kia 22-9-18 2RBerks p139 CR France604

FINCH,Frederick George Capt 3-7-21 IndOrdDept MR67

FINCH,George Capt ded 8-10-18 RAMC p253 CR Iraq6

FINCH,Herbert Marshall.DSO.LtCol kia 9-5-15 1RBerks p139 MR22

FINCH,Hugh Adair 2Lt kia 27-8-18 2GrenGds p50 CR France614

FINCH,Philip Gerard.MC.Lt kia 28-3-18 1NumbF p61 MR20

FINCH,Russell Claude 2Lt ded 5-11-18 22Lond p270 CR Essex209

FINCH,Tom 2Lt dow 20-10-17 6N&D p233 CR Derby98

FINCH,William Capt ded 22-2-19 RE CR C'land&W'land17

FINCH-NOYES,Charles William Fabin 2Lt kia 3-9-16 9LNLancs p135 MR21

FINCHAM,George Edmund Heygate 2LtTCapt kia 9-3-16 6RFC p2 CRBelgium11,Lt

FINDLATER,Percival St.George TCapt kia 28-3-18 RASC 21DivTrn p192 CR France79

FINDLAY,Arthur Bertram Lt dow 30-7-15 15 att7KRRC p150 MR29

FINDLAY,Cyril Olney 2Lt dow 17-10-17 4SomLI p218 CR France193

FINDLAY,Edward John 2Lt kia 9-5-15 14Lond p249 CR France80,Lt

FINDLAY,Ernest Robert 2Lt dow 5-10-17 255RFA p208 CR Belgium36

FINDLAY,Ian Caulcutt 2Lt dow 10-8-15 3Y&L p158 CR Belgium5,Calcutt 2Bn

FINDLAY,James T2Lt kia 16-6-17 12NumbF p61 MR20

FINDLAY,John 2LtACapt kia 25-4-18 6KOSB p101 MR30

FINDLAY,John Alexander.DSO.MIDx3 Maj kia 8-11-17 1/5HLI p240 CR Palestine8

FINDLAY,John Tulloch Lt kia 28-6-15 8ScotRif p225 MR4

FINDLAY,Lorimer TCapt kld 14-6-17 HLI GL &RFC p7 CR Scot398

FINDLAY,Neil Douglas.CB.BrigGen kia 10-9-14 Cmdg1Div RA p28 CR France1107

FINDLAY,Robert de Cardonnel Capt kia 11-3-15 4SfthH p241 MR22

FINDLAY,Robert Scott Capt kldacc 22-5-15 9A&SH p243 CR Scot76

FINDLAY,Ronald James T2Lt kld 24-12-17 RFC p7 CR Wilts3,FINLAY

FINDLAY,Scott T2Lt kia 8-5-18 19Manch p154 MR30

FINDLAY,Struthers 2Lt kia 4-8-16 ACycCps 52LowlandDiv p244 CR Egypt2

FINDLAY-HAMILTON,John Eric Lt kia 16-6-15 3 att2RScotF p94 MR22

FINDON,Robert TLt kia 18-4-18 RE 9FC p45 CR France250

FINE,S.2Lt kld 18-5-18 GL &RAF p190

FINEGAN,Herbert Marion Capt kia 16/18-6-15 8Lpool p215 MR22

FINIGAN,Wilfred James T2Lt kia 28-3-18 15MGC p182 MR20

FINK,Lawrence Alexander Lewis,MC 2LtACapt kia 5-10-17 2Beds p85 CR Belgium17

FINK,Sydney Lt dow 20-4-17 2/5SLancs p230 CR France769

FINKE,Richard Fenwick Capt kia 9-5-15 RSuss p119 MR22

FINLAY,A.TCapt ded 7-6-18 RAMC p267 CR Surrey41,5-6-18

FINLAY,Edward Norman Alison 2Lt kia 4-7-16 16RB p178 MR19

FINLAY,Eric Lionel 2Lt dow 20-3-16 6Dev p217 CR Iraq6

FINLAY,George Guy Lt kia 14-7-18 3 att2RIrReg p89 MR27

FINLAY,George Malcolm TCapt kia 5-11-17 14Hamps p120 CR Belgium105,Malcolme Ex 1Leinst

FINLAY,James Nelson 2Lt kia 28-3-18 14Lond att7CamH p249 MR20

FINLAY,John Cuthbert Capt kia 23-11-16 26NumbF B'Coy p61 CR France922

FINLAY,Robert Alexander Lt kia 9-5-15 5RDubF att1RIrRif p176 MR32

FINLAY,Thomas Pretsell Lt kia 25-9-15 3 att2GordH p166 MR19

FINLAYSON,Alexander.MID ACapt kia 22-3-18 6HLI att4NumbF p240 CR France34 &CR France834

FINLAYSON,Alexander Cunningham 2Lt dow 9-4-17 4RFC p7 CR France832

FINLAYSON,Alexander Moncrieff T2Lt dow 23-7-17 10 att7SLancs p125 CR France183

FINLAYSON,Bernard Stuart 2Lt dow 13-4-18 1 att1/4SfthH p164 CR France88

FINLAYSON,John T2Lt kia 23-3-18 5 O&BLI p130 CR France1061

FINN,Bernard William 2Lt kia 13-11-16 12 att13Ess p131 MR21

FINN,Francis William Lt kia 5-10-17 C74RFA p28 CR Belgium12,4-10-17

FINN,Michael AssCommsyHonLt ded 15-4-18 IA IOD p276 CR Iraq6

FINN,Thomas Joseph 2Lt ded 20-11-18 5RInniskF p104 CR France85,4Bn

FINN,William Joseph Rev kia 25-4-15 RAChDept p199 CR Gallipoli15

FINNEMORE,Henry James T2Lt dow 27-3-18 RSuss &RFC p16&119

FINNEMORE,Percival Edward Lt kia 26-10-17 Dev p76 MR30

FINNERTY,Wilfrid Edward 2Lt kia 22-3-18 10Lincs p75 MR20

FINNEY,Edwin Newland 2Lt kia 19-5-17 Leinst att6CycBn p174 CR France452

FINNEY,John.MC.2Lt ded 8-2-19 11RInniskF p257&104 CR France1028

FINNEY,Thomas 2Lt kia 21-3-18 3Y&L p158 MR20,2Bn

FINNIE,Bertram Knott Capt kia 1-10-15 5Lincs p220 MR29

FINNIMORE,David Keith Lt ded 10-5-17 RE 2PontoonPk p45 CR Hamps1

FINNIMORE,Henry James 2Lt 27-3-18 7Suss attRFC CR France300

FINNIS,John Fortescue LtCol dow 14-1-16 IA 53Sikhs p276 MR38

FINNIS,William Frank 2Lt dow 2-5-17 RGA 250SB p39 CR France924

FIPPARD,Richard Clift TCapt kia 4-6-15 14WYorks attLancF p81 MR4

FIRBANK,Godfrey Benjamin Joseph 2Lt kia 11-9-16 23RFC p2 MR20

FIRMIN,John Eric Robert T2Lt kia 10-8-15 5Wilts p153 MR4

FIRMIN,Maurice Harold Cuffe TLt kia 26-2-16 11LNLancs p135 MR20

FIRMINGER,Thomas T2Lt kia 3-9-16 9 att8EKent p57 CR France372

FIRTH,Arnold 2Lt kia 15-4-17 RFA p208 CR France568

FIRTH,Charles Ronald 2Lt ded 9-11-18 1/5WYorks p218 CR Germany3

FIRTH,Edwin Norris Lt ded 16-3-18 8WYorks p219 CR Yorks469,dow

FIRTH,Ernest Hartley TCapt kia 1-7-16 13Y&L p158 CR France156

FIRTH,Fred TLt kia 24-8-18 12 att10WYorks p81 MR16

FIRTH,Harold Lt kia 9-10-17 6Yorks p90 CR Belgium 126

FIRTH,James William Lt 1-10-18 Norf &108RAF MR20

FIRTH,John Stanley 2Lt kia 9-10-17 2 att3RWar p64 MR30,3 att2Bn

FIRTH,Joseph Oliver 2Lt kia 18-11-17 4LNLancs p234 CR France364

FIRTH,Percy 2Lt dow 28-7-18 2Yorks att2/8WYorks p90 MR18

FIRTH,Richard Charles Dundas Lt ded 21-12-14 9SLancs p125 CR Scot921

FISCHEL,Claude Henry Capt kia 14-9-18 RAMC att7Leic p195 CR France398

FISCHER,Alexander William.MID TLt dow 12-5-16 8Dev p76 CR France67,2Lt

FISCHER,John Bosman Capt kia 7-8-15 10NStaffs att8LancF p157 MR4

FISH,Barrow Edmondson T2Lt kia 3-9-16 11RSuss p119 CR France339

FISH,Benjamin Leslie TLt dow 30-10-18 12 att18Mddx p146 CR France332

FISH,Frank Edward Capt kia 17-5-17 3 att2Yorks p90 CR France279,Francis

FISH,Jack T2Lt kia 22-7-16 10Worc p108 CR France744

FISH,John Leslie 2Lt kia 3-7-16 7Suff p78 CR France393

FISH,Robert John 2Lt kia 30-9-17 4Lincs p217 CR France1723,Lt

FISH,W.R.MC.Capt kld 2-6-18 GL &RAF p190

FISHBOURNE,Charles Edward TLtCol dow 6-10-16 1 Cmdg8NumbF p61 CR France145

FISHBOURNE,Charles Eustace Lt ded 10-6-15 RE p45 CR Wales619,Capt 6-10-?

FISHBOURNE,Derrick Haughton Gardiner 2Lt kia 6-5-17 RGA 99SB p39 CR France1182

FISHBOURNE,Morgan 2Lt drd 1-1-17 2Co LondYeo p204 CR Greece16,FISHBURNE

FISHER,Alexander McEwan T2Lt kia 24-4-17 10ScotRif p103 MR20

FISHER,Arthur James 2Lt kia 25-10-16 GL &21RFC 14Wing p2&190 CR France306

FISHER,Arthur Maxwell TCapt kia 12-10-17 RAMC p195 CR Belgium23,58FC

FISHER,Cecil Eric Haig 2Lt dow 24-7-15 RE 15FC p45 CR France254
FISHER,Charles Heath.MC.2Lt kia 14-10-18 4 att12ESurr p112 CR Belgium157
FISHER,Charles John.DCM.2Lt dow 28-7-17 2Nhampt p137 CR Lond14
FISHER,E.J.SubAssSurg3Cl 27-1-16 IMS CR Iraq6
FISHER,Edmund 2Lt kia 16-11-16 3 att8ELancs p110 CR France153,Eddie
FISHER,Edmund Montague Prinsep 2Lt ded 31-3-18 RFA 36DAC p28 CR Hamps30
FISHER,Edward Henry 2Lt kia 9-4-18 KEdwHorse p24 MR19
FISHER,Edward Humbert 2Lt kia 19-5-15 Yorks p90 MR22
FISHER,Eric Whitmore Capt ded 14-10-18 IARO att1 19Inf p276 MR65
FISHER,Frank Capt kia 13-9-14 RWKent p141 MR15
FISHER,Frank Maj kia 26-9-17 RE 470FC p209 CR Belgium10
FISHER,Geoffrey Herbert 2Lt dow 25-10-15 8N&D p233 CR France40
FISHER,George Kenneth Thompson Capt kia 3-9-17 1/4Norf p216 CR Palestine8
FISHER,George William 2Lt kia 18-11-17 1/4Suff C'Coy p217 CR Belgium125,17-11-17
FISHER,Harold.DSO.Capt kia 15-12-14 1Manch p154 CR France571
FISHER,Harold TLt dow 14-4-18 RE 184TC p45 CR France180
FISHER,Harry Laireate 2Lt kia 27-10-18 10DLI p160 CR Italy9,Laureate 12Bn
FISHER,Henry Bruges ALtCol kia 3-10-16 Wilts att12Y&L p153 CR France727
FISHER,Henry Mornington.MC.2Lt kia 31-10-18 RFA attY31TMB p28 CR Belgium143
FISHER,Herbert 2Lt kia 11-4-18 NumbF att1/5DLI p61 MR32
FISHER,Henry Brean Lt dow 24-7-16 9MGC Inf p182 CR France833
FISHER,Herbert Learoyd Hammond Lt kia 8-8-16 1/8Lpool attMGC p187&215 MR21
FISHER,Herbert George.DSO.ALtCol ded 29-7-19 RFA p261 CR Wales26
FISHER,Hubert Patrick T2Lt kia 9-7-16 9KSLI p144 CR France643
FISHER,Hugh Bell TLt dow PoW 23-11-17 2RMunstF p175 CR Belgium140
FISHER,James Capt ded 23-2-19 4Lancs CR Lancs40
FISHER,John 2Lt dow 17-4-18 1 att2/5Lincs p75 CR France285
FISHER,John ACapt ded 17-4-19 5BordR p270 CR Surrey2
FISHER,John Campbell.MID ACapt dow 6-5-17 6RScotF p94 CR France1182,Maj 1Bn
FISHER,John Hammond.MC.2Lt dow 7-9-18 6WYorks att2/4YLI p218 CR France85
FISHER,John Hylton 2Lt kia 29-11-16 1/5WRid p227 CR France281
FISHER,John Joseph T2Lt dow 2-5-16 1NStaffs p157 CR France285
FISHER,John Wilfred.DSO.TCapt dow 8-7-16 10N&D p134 CR France833
FISHER,Leslie Benito TLt kia 14-8-15 12KRRC p150
FISHER,Mortimer Capt kia 20-9-14 1WYorks p81 MR15
FISHER,Norman Hill Lt dow 16-4-17 2/4LNLancs p234 CR France769
FISHER,O.G.Chap4Cl 4-11-20 CR Iraq8
FISHER,Percy Harold T2Lt dow 4-7-16 10RSuss attMGC p182&119 CR France203
FISHER,Percy Watkins.DCM.2Lt kia 12-9-16 22RFus p67 CR France1326,Watkiss
FISHER,Raymond Wadhams TCapt kia 13-9-16 NumbF p61 CR Greece6
FISHER,Robert 2Lt kia 14-11-16 3SStaffs att10Y&L p122 MR21
FISHER,Thomas Edward Coney Lt kia 1-7-16 1ELancs p110 MR21
FISHER,Wilfred T2Lt kia 9-5-15 1LNLancs p135 CR France80
FISHER,Wilfrid Frederick 2Lt kia 24-7-17 3 att12RSuss p119 MR29
FISHER,William Horace Arthur 2Lt kia 4-10-18 1/6RWar p64 MR30
FISHER,William Sefton Capt kia 23-3-18 4 att6Nhampt p234 MR27
FISHER-BROWN,Charles George Cranleigh.MID2Lt kia 10-8-15 5Wilts p153 MR4
FISHER-BROWN,Douglas Gordon 2Lt dow 28-6-18 RGA 2ArmyA/ASect p39
FISHER-BROWN,Kenneth Cuthbert 2Lt kia 13-11-16 1/7WRid p227 CR France281
FISHER-ROWE,Laurence Rowe LtCol dow 12-3-15 1GrenGds p50 CR France768,13-3-15
FISHER-SMITH,Alan Archibald Lt kia 1-8-17 CldGds att1GdsBdeMGC p53 CR Belgium106
FISHLOCK,Albert Ernest T2Lt dow 7-9-18 10Hamps p120 CR Greece6
FISKE,Dudley Lt dow 22-8-18 C86RFA p28 CR France119
FISKE,Harold Lt kia 20-12-16 GL &18RFC p2&190,ded CR France518
FISON,Frank Henry Lt kia 19-7-16 6Norf p217 CR France567,2/6Glouc
FISON,James Frederick Lorimer.MC.MIDx2 LtTCapt dow 2-11-17 6Suff p218 CR Suff133,4Bn
FITCH,Alfred Cyril T2Lt kia 2-4-17 2RWSurr p55 CR France1489
FITCH,Aubrey Sugden 2Lt kia 26-3-17 4RSuss p228 MR34
FITCH,Cecil Alexander Gordon 2Lt dow 18-9-18 RGA 260SB p39 CR France327
FITCH,Christopher John TLt kia 16-2-16 6Dors p124 CR Belgium131,Jack
FITCH,Conrad William TLt kia 3-7-16 6RWSurr p55 CR France251
FITCH,Douglas 2Lt kia 16-10-17 162RFA p28 CR Belgium21

FITCH,Louis Cifford.MM.T2Lt kia 28-7-18 1RFus p67 CR France161
FITCH,Matthew Craig.MC.Lt ded 9-12-18 RScots att2/10Bn p54 MR70 &CR Europe179,Capt
FITCH,Philip Henry Burt.MC.Lt kia 23-7-17 D177RFA p207 CR Belgium6
FITCH,W.S.Cdr 13-1-18 IA MiscList MR65
FITCH,Walter Frederick.MC.TCapt ded 1-11-18 GL 7Suff attBrMilMission p190 CR USA234
FITCH-JONES,Owen Edward TLt kia 13-5-17 13/275RFA p28 CR Belgium4
FITNESS,William John TLt ded 22-11-16 RAOC p198 CR Greece9
FITT,Charles William TLt kia 19-5-17 207MGC Inf p182 CR Belgium136
FITT,Norman Eric Lloyd 2Lt ded PoW 26-6-17 RIrF p171 MR20
FITTON,Hugh Gregory.CB.DSO.ADC.TBrigGen dow 20-1-16 Staff Cmdg101InfBde p1 CR Belgium11
FITTON,Norman 2Lt kia 14-11-16 7 att22RFus p67 MR21
FITTON,W.2Lt.MM.kldacc 19-8-18 1/2LancF &6RAF p92 CR France1525
FITTON,Walter Verdi 2Lt dow 29-9-16 2RFA p208 CR France74
FITZ-GIBBON,John Augustus TMaj ded 25-1-16 RGA p39
FITZBROWN,Eric 2Lt 1-7-16 18Lpool MR21
FITZBROWN,Geoffrey T2Lt dow 24-10-16 23DLI p160 CR France105
FITZCLARENCE,Augustus Arthur Cornwallis.MID Capt kia 28-6-15 2RFus p67 MR4
FITZCLARENCE,Charles.VC.BrigGen kia 12-11-14 Staff p1 MR29,IrGds
FITZE,Gerald Gadsden Lt kia 25-11-14 RHA p28 MR29,28/31-10-14
FITZGERALD,Alfred Edward TLtCol dow 13-7-16 ESurr att15DLI p112 CR Bucks50
FITZGERALD,Gerald 2Lt kia 1-7-16 26NumbF C'Coy p61 CR France150,Lt
FITZGERALD,Gerald Hugh Capt kia 13-9-14 4DragGds p21 CR France1339
FITZGERALD,Gerald Thomas TCapt kia 3-12-15 15DLI p160 CR France1140,30-12-15
FITZGERALD,Herbert 2Lt kia 9-4-18 6Lpool p215 CR France98,Lt
FITZGERALD,John Desmond Lt drd 10-10-18 4SLancs p230 MR40
FITZGERALD,Loftus de Vallentin MajALtCol kia 16-9-18 RIrF att2RInniskF p171 CR France285
FITZGERALD,Lord Desmond Maj&Adjt ded 3-3-16 1IrGds p52 CR France8
FITZGERALD,Maurice Robert Lt ded PoW 19-4-18 2IrGds p52 CR Belgium409
FITZGERALD,Oswald Arthur Gerald.CMG.LtCol drd 5-6-16 IA 18Lancers &Staff CR Sussex144
FITZGERALD,Robert William T2Lt dow 4-10-18 10RDubF p176 CR France1184
FITZGERALD,Roy James.MC.MID Lt kia 1-7-18 12Glouc att35RAF p106 CR France71
FITZGERALD,Thomas David T2Lt kia 30-7-16 8Glouc p106 MR21
FITZGERALD,William Wilks T2Lt kia 27-7-17 GL &25RFC p7
FITZGIBBON,Brian Normanby.MID TLt kia 21-8-16 6RIrReg p89 CR France178
FITZGIBBON,G.J.LtTCapt kia 20-11-17 10RDubF p176 CR France616
FITZGIBBON,John Augustus Maj 26-1-16 RGA CR Lond9
FITZGIBBON,Harold T2Lt kia 27-3-18 12RFC p16 CR France62
FITZGIBBON,John.MC.Chap3Cl kia 18-9-18 RAChDept att17FA p199 CR France835
FITZGIBBON,Michael Joseph TLt kia 15-8-15 7RDubF p176 MR4
FITZ GIBBON,Richard Apjohn.MID Lt dow 4-2-15 IA 128Pnrs p276 CR Egypt8
FITZHERBERT,Gilbert Clare.MC.Lt kia 18-9-18 2Y&L p158 MR16
FITZHERBERT,Harold Lancelot TLt kia 30-6-16 13RSuss p119 CR France924
FITZHERBERT,Wyndham Waterhouse Capt kia 7-7-17 13RSuss att55RFC p7&119 MR20
FITZHERBERT-BROCKHOLES,Thomas Joseph Capt&Adjt dow 14-3-15 2RB p178 CR France768
FITZHUGH,Godfrey Capt kia 31-10-17 MontgomeryYeo p204 CR Palestine1,25RWFus
FITZHUGH,Harold T2Lt kia 31-7-17 8ELancs p110 MR29
FITZMAURICE,Archibald Hamilton Lt kia 12-3-18 RFC p16 MR20
FITZMAURICE,John Herbert 2Lt kia 25-3-18 6KSLI p144 MR27
FITZMAURICE,Lindsay TLtACapt kia 18-11-16 8SomLI p79 CR France339
FITZMAURICE,Maurice Alexander Ross Geraldine Lt kia 5-8-15 RE 21FC S&M p45 CR France924,6-8-15
FITZPATRICK,Dudley Thomas Francis Lt kia 27-10-14 3 att2SStaffs p122 MR29
FITZPATRICK,Gabriel Roy Capt kia 14-9-14 3WelshR p126 MR15
FITZPATRICK,John Joseph 2Lt kia 30-7-16 2 att8RMunstF p175 CR France223,29-7-16
FITZPATRICK,Thomas Gordon.MID TCapt kia 6-9-16 8RIrF p171 CR France1890
FITZROY,Michael Algernon 2Lt kia 15-4-15 4SfthH D'Coy p241 CR France924,Capt 17-4-15
FITZSIMONS,Terence 2Lt kia 4-4-16 3 att7RSuss p119 MR19
FITZWILLIAMS,John Kenrick Lloyd.MC.Maj kia 30-8-18 Z5A'RFA p28 CR France421,25ArmyBde

FLACK,Wilfred George.MC&Bar.Lt dow 7-9-17 1RFus p67 CR France40
FLACK,William Arthur.DCM.2Lt dow 19-12-15 RGA 27TMB p39 CR France102
FLAGG,Allston TCapt kia 26/27-9-15 10Norf att1/58Rifs p73&276,Alston 25-9-15 CR France705
FLAHERTY,John Ernest T2Lt ded 12-7-18 6Mddx p146
FLANAGAN,George Anton T2Lt kia 30-6-18 6RWSurr p55 MR27
FLANAGAN,Joseph Samuel Lt kia 23-8-18 20Lond p251 CR France1170,22-8-18
FLANEGAN,Lionel Christopher TLt kia 20-11-17 Ess &TankCps p188&264,Flanagan MR17
FLANIGAN,Edmund Hughes Lt ded 17-6-16 RAMC 102FA p195 CR Ireland105
FLATAU,A.Theodore TCapt kia 1-7-16 8ESurr p112 CR France513
FLATT,Harry T2Lt kia 28-11-17 6Y&L C'Coy p158 CR France551
FLAVELL,Alfred Victor 2Lt ded 4-5-18 Worc &RAF p264
FLAXMAN,Alfred Edward 2Lt kia 1-7-16 1/6SStaffs p229 MR21
FLAXMAN,Walter James 2Lt ded 27-5-17 RASC attS&TCps p192 MR38
FLECKNOE,Percy James Deane Lt dow 25-11-17 64RFA p28 CR Belgium3
FLEET,Aylmer Louis Elliot.MC.CaptAMaj kia 10-9-18 B56RFA p28 CR France433
FLEET,Leonard T2Lt kld 27-10-17 GL &RFC p7 CR Lancs33,Leanord
FLEET,Vernon Jesse Lt dow 10-9-18 RFA att3SpCoy RE CR Berks125
FLEET,William Alexander 2Lt kia 18-5-18 1GrenGds 3'Coy p50 CR France120
FLEET,William Henry.MC.2Lt dow 19-4-16 6BlkW p231
FLEETWOOD,Cyril Percy 2Lt dow PoW 12-7-16 9Lond p248 CR France716,Lt
FLEMING,A.2Lt dow 29-4-18 GL &RAF p190
FLEMING,Alfred.MC.T2Lt dow 1-7-18 27MGC Inf p182 CR France134
FLEMING,Charles Christie.DSO.Col dow 24-12-17 RAMC ADMS51DivStaff p195 CR France512
FLEMING,Charles Elphinstone Maj ded 2-3-15 RAMC p195 CR Scot812
FLEMING,Ernest Cole.MC.MID Maj kia 18-7-17 C121RFA p28 CR Belgium23
FLEMING,Ernest William T2Lt ded 4-11-18 13KRRC p150 CR France1480
FLEMING,Frank 2Lt kia 11-4-18 4SfthH p241 MR30
FLEMING,Frederick Nelson 2Lt ded 22-6-18 RGA 321SB p39 CR Germany3
FLEMING,Frederick William Oswald 2Lt dow 20-12-15 4WRid p227 CR Belgium11
FLEMING,Geoffrey Montagu Mason Lt kia 16-6-15 RAMC att2Beds p195 CR France279
FLEMING,George TLt dow 18-7-16 7 att1RScotF p94 CR France51
FLEMING,George 2Lt kia 29-5-18 3 att2ScotRif p103 CR France924
FLEMING,George Eric Pearce Lt 1-6-18 IARO att3/39GarwhalRif CR Pakistan50A
FLEMING,Harold Winning 2Lt kia 6-10-17 1/2Beds p85 MR30,5-10-17 1Bn
FLEMING,Henry Roland 2Lt kld 24-11-14 RFC p1 CR Wilts1
FLEMING,Hugh Lt kia 30-9-18 5HLI p240 CR Belgium116
FLEMING,Hugh Joseph T2Lt kia 24-8-16 7 att6Dors p124 CR France342
FLEMING,Ian Grant.MC.MID Capt kia 31-7-17 6GordH p242 CR Belgium27
FLEMING,James.MC.Lt kia 21-3-17 11RScots p54 CR France1182
FLEMING,James Hamilton Capt kia 13-10-15 1/5NStaffs p237 CR France258
FLEMING,James Sword T2Lt dow 29-9-18 1GordH p166 CR France40
FLEMING,James Wellington 2Lt kia 12-7-17 29RFC p7 MR20
FLEMING,John Allister 2Lt dow 22-7-16 1RWKent p141 MR21
FLEMING,John Joseph.MID TCapt kia 13-10-17 26NumbF p61 MR30
FLEMING,Joseph 2Lt kia 15-9-16 6HLI p240 CR France387
FLEMING,Malcolm James Henderson Lt dow 14-7-15 5A&SH p243 MR4
FLEMING,Reginald Henry T2Lt kia 11-7-16 15RWFus p97 MR21
FLEMING,Robert Alexander 2Lt dow 31-7-16 1/7BlkW p231 CR France833
FLEMING,Robert John T2Lt kld 29-1-18 RFC p16 CR Scot237
FLEMING,Richard Thomas Cyril Willis 2Lt dow 4-8-16 RH&FA p208
FLEMING,Thomas.MID T2Lt dow 20-10-18 RGA 71Bty21Bde p39 CR France725
FLEMING,Valentine.DSO.Maj kia 20-5-17 OxfYeo p205 CR France1495
FLEMING,Wilfrid Allan.MC.Capt dow 10-8-17 1Dev &56RFC p7&76 CR Belgium140
FLEMING,William James Calbard Capt ded 2-12-18 6GordH p270 CR Scot835
FLEMMING,Douglas Sidney T2Lt dow 1-6-17 9RLancs p58 CR Greece7
FLEMMING,Herbert Otto Capt dow 7-5-15 9Lond p247 CR Lond12
FLENLEY,Edmund Bernard 2Lt kia 9-4-17 5 att13Lpool p215 CR France581
FLESHER,Frederick Arthur Lt dow 27-9-16 6RWar p214 CR Yorks361
FLETCHER,Amiraux Silver.MID 2Lt kia 7-8-15 IARO att1/5GurkhaRif CR Gallipoli17
FLETCHER,Arnold Lockhart TLt dow 30-4-17 4Leinst att193MGC p174&182 CR France145
FLETCHER,Arthur TCapt ded 14-2-18 2GarBnRIrF attGarBnLpool p171 CR Greece3
FLETCHER,Arthur Frederick T2Lt kia 12-5-18 Nhampt att6Bn p137 CR France177

FLETCHER,Arthur Henry Felix 2Lt kld 22-5-17 13Huss &RFC p7&22,11Bn CR Surrey2
FLETCHER,Arthur Joseph T2Lt kia 23-4-17 13RFus p67 MR20
FLETCHER,Arthur Philip T2Lt kia 1-10-15 RE p45 CR Belgium132
FLETCHER,Arthur Stanley T2Lt kia 11-7-16 11SWBord p100 MR21
FLETCHER,Charles Alexander 2Lt kld 20-10-18 Worc &RAF p264
FLETCHER,C.W.Maj&QM 19-4-17 Ex ESuss CR Hamps7
FLETCHER,Donald Lockhart 2Lt ded 28-4-17 4 att6Leinst p174 CR Greece3,dow
FLETCHER,Edward Stewart 2Lt kia 3-5-17 6WYorks p218 MR20
FLETCHER,Eric Graham Lt kia 3-7-16 SLancs att2Bn p125 CR France402
FLETCHER,Ernest 2Lt kia 15-9-16 15Lond p249 CR France402
FLETCHER,Franklyn Haward Capt ded 5-6-18 RDC CR Sussex4
FLETCHER,Gareth Hamilton 2Lt kia 25-1-15 GrenGds SR p50
FLETCHER,George Herbert 2Lt kia 2-6-17 WYorks &4RFC p7&81 MR20
FLETCHER,George William 2Lt dow 9-8-16 3 att1RInniskF p104 CR Belgium11
FLETCHER,Gilbert Harding Capt kia 1-7-16 5NStaffs p237 CR France281
FLETCHER,Guy Verney Lt ded 24-4-16 RAMC att19DAC p195 CR France31
FLETCHER,Henry Mungles 2Lt kia 7-6-17 RFA attY30TMB p28 CR Belgium127
FLETCHER,Herbert Philips.DSO.Maj ded 3-8-16 1Co of LondYeo attRFC p18&20 CR Lond12,kld
FLETCHER,Herman T2Lt kia 13-11-16 7LNLancs p135 MR21
FLETCHER,Horace William 2LtTLt dow 26-3-17 9 att7RWFus p97 MR34
FLETCHER,Jack Haslip 2Lt kia 20-10-18 2ScotsGds p52 CR France320
FLETCHER,John T2Lt kia 28-9-18 LNLancs att2/4Bn p135 CR France256
FLETCHER,John Harwood Cash 2Lt kia 1-7-16 1/7N&D p233 MR21
FLETCHER,John Holland Ballett Lt dow 13-5-15 7Lond p247 CR France80
FLETCHER,Joseph Harold TCapt kia 25-11-17 RWFus att19Bn p97 MR17
FLETCHER,Leslie Morley T2Lt kld 5-7-17 GL &RFC p7 CR War67
FLETCHER,Malcolm 2Lt dow 8-9-17 9 att17HLI p240 CR France1361
FLETCHER,Maurice.MC.TCapt dow 9-9-16 6RMunstF C'Coy p175 CR France197
FLETCHER,Noel William Scott 2Lt dow 7-3-17 11DLI p160 CR France374
FLETCHER,Reginald William 2Lt kia 31-10-14 118/26RFA p28 MR29
FLETCHER,Robert Henry TLt kia 27-7-16 14 att17RFus p67 MR21
FLETCHER,Robert Ronald Radcliffe Lt ded 29-10-19 3 att6SLancs p264 MR65
FLETCHER,Roland Sackville Capt kia 1-11-14 1NumbF p61 MR29
FLETCHER,Thomas May.MC.Lt kia 1-8-17 20DLI p254&258 MR29
FLETCHER,Thomas Murray Kilpin T2Lt kia 23-4-17 1Beds p85 MR20,Kelpin
FLETCHER,Tom Walter 2Lt kia 26-9-17 N&D att2/5Bn p134 MR30
FLETCHER,Walter George.MIDx2 2Lt kia 20-3-15 2RWFus B'Coy p97 CR France684
FLETCHER,William Alfred Littledale.DSO.MIDx2 LtCol ded 14-2-19 Res 2/6Lpoc p270 CR Lancs181,dow
FLETCHER,William George T2Lt kia 3-7-16 11NStaffs att2SLancs p157 MR21
FLETCHER,William Guy T2Lt dow 14-10-16 11SLancs p125 CR Kent129
FLETCHER,William Henry Anthony 2Lt ded 2-7-16 11 att7NStaffs p157 CR Iraq6
FLETT,Arthur David Lt kia 9-4-17 7RScots p211 CR France644,16Bn
FLETT,Frederick T2Lt kld 9-3-18 1SfthH p164 CR Egypt8,accded
FLETT,John Edmund Lt ded 15-11-15 7RScots p211 CR Gallipoli3
FLETT,William Henry.MC.Lt 19-4-16 6BlkW CR France95
FLEWITT,Edward Luke 2Lt kia 7-1-18 1/7N&D p233 CR France115,Lake
FLEXEN,Harold Augustus T2Lt dow 29-7-16 1Mddx p146 CR Mddx48
FLIN,Richard Valentine 2Lt kia 8-8-18 Ess att10Bn p131 CR France141
FLINDT,Leighton Harold Richard Edward 2Lt dow 4-10-16 3NStaffs att8Leic p157 CR France145
FLINN,Cyril Herbert 2Lt kia 14-4-17 1Ess p131 MR20
FLINN,Edgar Wormald 2Lt kia 13-11-16 34RFA &RFC p2&28 MR21
FLINN,Philip Woolven Lt kia 20-9-17 5SLancs p230
FLINT,Charles William T2Lt kia 1-7-16 26NumbF p61 MR21
FLINT,Harvey Priestman.MC.2Lt kia 27-5-18 9 att8Leic p87 MR18
FLINT,Ralph Stacey.MSM.MIDx3 2Lt kia 27-3-18 6RWSurr p55 MR27
FLINT,Robert Bradford.DSO.Lt dow 23-1-15 RE p45 CR Belgium98
FLINT,Wilfred Ernest 2Lt kia 1-7-16 1/7N&D p233 CR France281
FLINT,William Henry Maj ded 2-11-17 RAMC Res p270 CR Hereford110
FLINTOFF,A.Sister 9-11-18 TFNS att3GH CR Lond1
FLINTOFF,Randolph Alex TLt kia 25-6-16 10EYorks p84 CR France5,24-6-16
FLITCROFT,Joseph 2Lt ded 2-11-18 RGA p39&257 CR Lancs438
FLITCROFT,S.2Lt ded 17-2-19 SLancsF CR Lancs256
FLOOD,Dundas Charles TLt ded 27-10-18 8Leinst p174 &263,8Leic CR Lond14,8Leic
FLOOD,Robert Samuel.MC.TCapt kia 5-12-17 9RIrF p171 CR France711
FLORY,Percival James T2Lt kia 22-8-18 4Beds p85 CR France745

FLORY,Robert James.MC.2Lt kia 28-6-17 2HAC p206 CR France614
FLORY,William Henry 2Lt kia 21-3-18 2/4 O&BLI p231 MR27
FLOWER,Alfred Chegwin Lt kia 25-9-16 4GrenGds SR p50 CR France374
FLOWER,Frederick Godfrey T2Lt kia 18-12-17 GL &21RFC p7 CR Belgium16
FLOWER,H.J.DSO.Maj ded 31-1-19 Ex KRRC p265
FLOWER,Leopold Arthur Lacon Capt kia 7-10-16 7Lond p247 CR France385
FLOWER,Oswald Swift TLtCol dow 12-7-16 13RWFus p97 CR France633
FLOWER,Victor Augustine.DSO.Maj kia 15-8-17 13Lond p249 CR Belgium115,LtCol
FLOWER,Wilfred Joseph 2Lt dow 18-8-17 1/7Worc p226 CR Belgium18
FLOWERS,Herbert T2Lt kia 1-9-16 8RWKent p141 CR France402
FLOWERS,Humphrey French Lt kia 14-10-18 RFA att82RAF p207 CR Belgium157
FLOWERS,John Arthur T2Lt kia 1-9-16 10 att7RSuss p119 MR20
FLOWERS,William Henry Field T2Lt dow 15-4-18 1/5Y&L p158 CR France324
FLOYD,Hayden T2Lt dow 11-7-16 PoW GL &11RFC p2&190 CR France927
FLOYD,Henry Murrell Capt kia 28-6-15 2RDubF p176 CR Gallipoli6
FLOYD,Howard Grimley T2Lt kia 9-4-18 1/5Dev p76 CR Palestine9
FLUCK,Harold Graham T2Lt dow 3-11-17 6Mddx att 1/4Nhampt p146 CR palestine1,2/10Bn
FLUKE,Arthur Charles.MID 2Lt kia 10-1-15 116/26RFA p28 MR22
FLUKE,Samuel TLtACapt kia 16-8-17 11RInniskF p104 MR30
FLUX,George Belben Capt ded 18-3-18 RAMC p267
FLUX,Leonard Taylor T2Lt kia 1-11-16 12 att2Worc p108 MR21
FLUX,L.G.T2Lt ded 18-6-18 13TankCps p188 CR Hamps41,16-6-18
FLYNN,George Axen Wallace T2Lt kia 25-9-15 10ScotRif p103 MR19
FLYNN,Horace Justice Dillon Capt bombAcc 23-10-17 IARO att 1/101Gren p276 CR Egypt8
FLYNN,John Hoskins T2Lt kia 30-9-17 GL &60RFC p7 CR France134
FLYNN,Joseph Michael T2Lt dow 11-5-18 25NumbF p61
FLYNN,Percy 2Lt kia 10-11-17 5 att2RMunstF p175 MR30
FLYNN,Thomas Lt&QM ded 23-7-18 LabCps p266 CR Yorks294
FOALE,William Ernest Lt ded 1-5-19 RGA A/ABty CR Lond8
FOCKEN,Leslie Charles 2Lt kia 26-10-16 15RFC p2 CR France156 see FAWKNER,L.C.
FODEN,Frank Joseph 2Lt kia 9-9-16 1/4Lond p246 MR21
FOGARTY,Gerald Joseph Lt kia 26-8-17 3RIrReg &9RFC p7&89 CR Belgium18
FOGARTY,William Joseph Capt kia 21-3-18 SIrHorse att7RIrReg p24 MR27
FOGERTY,John Frederick Cullinan Lt kia 25-9-17 RE 227FC p45 CR Belgium124
FOGERTY,William Perrott Lt ded 19-10-19 IA 58att57Rif p276 CR Egypt1,57att58Rif
FOGG,Thomas Holt TLt kia 26-3-18 RE 288ArmyTrpsCo p45 CR France526
FOGGIN,G.W.2Lt 14-7-18 NthCycBn att48RAF CR France71
FOGGO,Watson Henry TLt ded 20-5-18 5LancF p92 CR Ches3
FOISTER,Percy Reuben.DCM.2Lt kia 13-1-16 2Leic B'Coy p87 MR38
FOIZEY,Harold Egbert TLt kia 1-7-16 18WYorks p81 CR France156
FOLEY,Alfred Montague 2Lt kia 9-9-16 11 att2RSuss p119 CR France345,dow 3-8-16
FOLEY,F.Y.Capt&QM 12-5-18 RASC attRAF CR Hamps64
FOLEY,Geoffrey Robert T2Lt dow 17-5-17 7SomLI p79 CR France95,Lt
FOLEY,John TCapt kia 1-7-16 25NumbF p61 MR21
FOLEY,Michael Alphonsus Lt ded 25-4-19 6Leinst p174 CR Egypt9
FOLEY,Michael James Aloysius Capt kia 10-8-15 10Mddx p236 MR4
FOLEY,Thomas Algernon Fitzgerald Lt kia 25-10-14 Norf p73 MR22
FOLEY,Thomas William Winspear Lt kia 9-9-16 3 att7Leinst p174 MR21
FOLEY,William Alfred LtACapt dow 1-11-17 RIrF p171 CR France398
FOLINGSBY,Thomas Grueber 2Lt dow 23-6-16 7RFA p208 CR France480,22-6-16
FOLJAMBE,Hubert Francis Fitzwilliam Brabazon Maj kia 14-9-14 2KRRC p150 MR15
FOLJAMBE,Josceline Charles William Saville.Hon.MIDx3 CaptBtMaj kia 6-4-16 1 O&BLI p130 MR38
FOLKER,Edgar Reginald 2Lt kia 20-2-15 3Y&L p158 MR29
FOLLETT,George 2Lt kia 19-9-18 6RB att 1/10Lond p178 CR Palestine9
FOLLETT,Gilbert Burrell Spencer,DSO.MVO BtLtColTBrigGen kia 27-9-18 CldGds 3GdsBdeHQ p51 CR France756
FOLLIOTT,Charles Russell Hastings Lt kia 10-3-18 RFC p15 CR France525,FFOLLIOTT
FOLLIOTT,John 2Lt kia 19-9-18 2DLI p160 CR France835
FOLLIS,Thomas 2Lt dow 24-2-17 7DCLI p114 CR France105
FOLLIT,Charles Albert Roy.DSO.MC.TCapt dow 20-8-16 10RWFus p97 CR France23
FOLLIT,John Fraser Lt ded 21-10-18 IARO att29Lancers p276 CR Syria2
FOLLIT,Reginald William 2Lt dow 28-4-17 GL &13RFC p7 MR20

FOOKS,Edward Luckham 2Lt kia 31-10-16 129RFA p28 MR37
FOORD,Charlton Willoughby Hougham T2Lt dow 19-12-16 60MGC p182 CR France67
FOORD,George Howard T2Lt dow 13-10-15 RASC 176Depot p192 CR Gallipoli1,Lt
FOORD-KELCEY,John Mordaunt 2Lt kia 1-7-16 2RWSurr p55 CR France397
FOORD-KELCEY,William Beverly.MC.Lt kia 24-9-18 C104RFA p207 CR France446
FOOT,David Victor T2Lt kldacc 4-5-17 GL &RFC p7 CR Scot721
FOOT,Douglas Eric 2Lt kia 13-10-15 8RBerks p139 MR19
FOOT,James Stanley Capt kia 30-7-16 1/7WelchR att2/4Glouc p230 CR France1887
FOOT,Victor Edward 2Lt ded 25-11-18 1WelshGds p53 CR France289
FOOT,William John Hawken Lt ded 28-10-19 IARO att 109Inf p276 MR69
FOOTE,Trevor Maudsley AMaj kia 10-7-17 8LNLancs p135 CR Belgium10
FOOTNER,Arthur Henry T2Lt kia 6-8-15 1Ess p131 MR4
FOOTNER,Harry Erlegh TCapt kia 1-8-16 RGA 35HB p39 CR France515
FOOTT,Alexander Boyd Capt ded 21-7-18 RAMC att49FA p195 CR Palestine3
FORAN,Edward Cornelius 2Lt kia 28-12-17 5RMunstF p175 CR Palestine3
FORBES,A.J.Lt kia 21-10-17 3KAR attLovatScouts
FORBES,Albert.MID Capt kia 30-8-18 8Manch p236 CR France308
FORBES,Alec.MID Capt kia 3-9-16 2RWar p64 CR France402
FORBES,Alexander 2LtACapt dow 22-3-18 HLI att 17Bn p162 CR France512
FORBES,Alexander Bruce 2Lt dow 29-10-18 1/88A&SH p243 CR France241
FORBES,Alexander Stewart TLt dow 17-8-16 10SfthH att 181MGC p182 CR France95
FORBES,Arthur Maj kia 17-4-16 IA 128Pnrs p276 MR38
FORBES,Arthur T2Lt kia 27-9-17 RE 11FC p45 CR Belgium19
FORBES,Arthur John Lt kia 21-10-17 1LovatScouts att 1/3KAR p204&268 CR EAfrica11 &CR Tanzania1
FORBES,Beatrice Georgina Frederica SNurse 12-5-18 TFNS CR War7
FORBES,Douglas Tulloch 2Lt dow 17-1-16 17Lond p250 CR France201
FORBES,Donald Keith Lt kia 15-2-15 Suff p78 MR29
FORBES,Duncan T2Lt kia 28-3-18 3RScots p54 MR20
FORBES,Fergus George Arthur.Hon.Capt dow PoW 23-8-14 RIrReg p89 CR Belgium242
FORBES,Fergus Robert TLt kia 25-9-15 RE p45 MR19
FORBES,George Francis Reginald.MID LtCol dow 17-3-15 RIrReg p89 MR29 &CR France284
FORBES,Gordon Stewart Drummond.CMG.DSO.Maj dow 21-7-15 7KOSB p101 CR France109
FORBES,Gordon William 2Lt ded PoW 18-10-17 24RFC p7 CR Belgium132,kia
FORBES,Harry Seymour Capt ded 3-11-18 2/1StaffsYeo p205 CR France40
FORBES,Henry James 2Lt kia 18-8-18 3 att 1KOSB p101
FORBES,Hunter Capt kia 6-4-16 IA 51Sikhs p276 MR38
FORBES,James T2Lt kia 12-12-15 RE 67FC p45 CR Gallipoli27
FORBES,Joel Scott Lt kia 1-4-17 RGA 78SB p209 CR France518
FORBES,John Donald T2Lt dow 29-9-15 10LancF p92 CR Belgium11
FORBES,Kenneth 2Lt kia 10-2-15 5Lond p246 CR Belgium136
FORBES,Lawrence Lt dow 9-7-17 5Lond p246 CR Lond12
FORBES,Leonard Noel Lt kia 19-9-18 6Ess p232 CR France369
FORBES,Leslie Alexander 2Lt kia 27-5-17 4 att 1ScotRif p103 CR France568
FORBES,Muirton Warrand Lt kia 24-5-18 2AustInf CR France28
FORBES,Noel Edmund 2Lt dow 12-5-15 20RFA p28 CR France80,Lt
FORBES,Robert Struthers 2Lt kia 24-4-17 8A&SH p243 CR France415
FORBES,William Alexander Stanhope 2Lt kia 3-9-17 3DCLI p114 CR France294
FORBES,William Guthrie.MC.Maj dow 26-9-18 RGA 135HB p209 CR France278
FORBES-MENZIES,Alastair.DSO.Capt 4-5-18 17RFus CR France924
FORBES-ROBERTSON,Kenneth Capt kia 8-11-14 1 att2SfthH p164 MR32,7-11-14
FORBES-ROSS,Ralph Morison 2Lt 20-2-15 2Lancs MR29
FORBES-SEMPHILL,Robert Abercromby.Hon.Lt dow 2-6-15 5GordH p242 CR France727,kia
FORD,A.2Lt kia 9-5-17 RFus p67 MR29
FORD,Alfred Murnie Lt dow 28-7-18 8SfthH p164 MR18,Marnie
FORD,Alfred Winn.MC.2Lt kia 18-9-18 45/42RFA p28 CR France530
FORD,Arthur Llewelyn T2Lt kia 27-9-15 12Lpool p71 CR France525
FORD,A.V Maj 13-12-18 RAMC CR Hamps 217
FORD,Cecil George 2Lt drd 10-10-18 NorfYeo p204 MR40
FORD,Charles Bell Capt kia 30-9-19 IA 103MahrattaLI att 1/7GurkhaRif p276 MR38
FORD,Clement Charles LtTCapt kia 2-7-16 1SomLI p79 CR France643
FORD,Clement William 2Lt kia 31-7-17 5RLancs p213 CR Belgium125

FORD,David Milne 2Lt dow 3-11-18 7ScotRif p224 CR France332
FORD,E.G.Capt 7-10-15 RAMC CR War96
FORD,Francis William.MC.2LtACapt kia 26-9-17 1Camb p244 MR30
FORD,Frank Stephen.MID Capt&QM ded 24-3-18 1Ess p131 CR France64
FORD,Frederick Austin 2Lt kia 27-8-18 RE DivSigCo p45 CR France927
FORD,Herbert Alfred.MC.2Lt kia 11-8-18 1Dors p124 MR16
FORD,Herbert Walter 2Lt kia 10-8-17 5RWSurr p212 MR29
FORD,James Ernest T2LtACapt kia 4-10-17 1KOSB p101 MR30
FORD,John T2Lt ded 16-6-16 25RFus p67 CR EAfrica13
FORD,John Ballard Berkley Capt dow 16-2-17 2 att7RWKent p141 CR France177
FORD,Kenneth George Haslam TLt dow 1-12-15 11Ches p96 CR France285
FORD,Lawton Stephen 2Lt kia 1-7-16 2RWSurr p55 MR21
FORD,N.2Lt kld 5-4-18 RE &RAF p45
FORD,Norman Stanley.MC.2Lt kld 19-7-18 11RWSurr &RAF p55 CR Wilts116
FORD,Reginald James TCapt kia 2-7-16 17Manch p154 CR France397,1-7-16
FORD,Richard 2Lt kia 3-2-17 C177RFA p28 CR Belgium10,3-8-17
FORD,Richard Jellard.MC.Capt kia 9-5-15 1Worc p108 CR France566
FORD,Richard Nagle.MC.CaptTMaj kia 6-1-18 11RFus p67 CR France62
FORD,Robert Englefield ACapt dow 3-4-17 5LNLancs att55TMB p234 CR Belgium11,1Bn
FORD,Robert Willoughby Lt ded 10-5-19 1/11Lond p270 CR Essex275,Capt
FORD,Royston Dearmer 2Lt kia 15-3-17 1RIrReg p89 MR29,Royster
FORDE,Henry Rawson.MC.LtACapt kia 2-12-17 2YLI D'Coy p143 CR Belgium125
FORDE,John Patrick 2Lt dow 16-8-17 9RDubF p176 MR30
FORDE,Kenneth Rowley Lt kia 23-7-15 3EKent p57 CR Belgium98
FORDE,Lionel Winnington 2Lt kia 8-6-18 Dors att6Bn p124 MR27
FORDER,Charles Frederick 2Lt kia 9-9-16 3 att2RSuss p119 CR France389
FORDHAM,Charles George Harry Lt&QM ded 29-10-17 GL p190 p266 CR Numb4,Henry George
FORDHAM,Reginald Frederick 2LtACapt kia 5-11-17 5Ess p232 CR France522
FORDYCE,Ernie Lawrence Dingwall Capt ded 5-12-16 IA 84Punjabis attAssamMilPolice p276 MR66
FORDYCE,James Dingwell T2Lt dow 27-9-15 A&SH p173
FOREMAN,Granado Walter 2Lt kia 14-7-17 SR 22RFC p7 CR France95
FOREMAN,Harry Clennell TLt kia 24-10-18 3 att9NumbF p61 CR France739
FOREMAN,John Eugene TLt ded 9-7-17 RAMC p195 CR Egypt1
FORESHEW,Henry John Hulbert 2Lt kia 15-4-17 6 att3RB p178 MR20
FORESTIER,Walter Waldorf.MC.TCapt kia 12-3-18 1 att1/4DCLI p114 CR Palestine9
FORGE,Arthur Fyfe T2Lt kia 4-10-17 8Lincs p75 MR30
FORGE,Henry Noel Francis 2Lt kia 20-11-17 5Beds p219 CR France667
FORGE,William Frederick 2Lt kia 1-7-16 2Mddx p146 MR21
FORMAN,Francis 2Lt kia 14-7-16 3Dors att7RWar p124 MR21
FORMAN,Moses TLt dow 11-4-17 8ELancs p110 CR France581
FORMBY,Myles Lonsdall Capt kia 26-10-14 Wilts p153 MR22
FORMBY,Richard William Lt kia 16-2-17 RE p45 CR France294
FORMBY,Thomas Hope Capt kia 13-10-16 1Camb p244 MR21
FORREST,Austin Lancelot T2Lt kia 3-9-16 11KRRC p150 MR21
FORREST,Bertram Thomas Alexander 2Lt kia 27-12-17 LanarkYeo att14BlkW p204 CR Palestine3
FORREST,Charles Evelyn.DSO.Maj kia 22-11-15 O&BLI p130 MR38
FORREST,Evelyn Arthur Atherley TLt ded 9-12-15 11 att7Glouc p106 CR Europe1
FORREST,Frank Capt dow 13-9-14 RAMC p195 CR France1107
FORREST,Henry Dacre T2Lt kia 7-4-18 WYorks att5WRid p81 CR France745
FORREST,James Capt ded 6-10-15 RWKent attASC p265 CR Lond7
FORREST,John William T2Lt kia 27-10-15 7SfthH p164 MR19,27-9-15
FORREST,Laurence Bernard 2Lt kia 20-5-17 16KRRC p150 MR20
FORREST,Percy Huskinson 2Lt dow 21-3-18 7Leinst att16MGC Inf p174&182 CR France1495,16Bn
FORREST,R.F.Lt 17-1-19 GL &1/1WAfrServBde CR WAfrica53
FORREST,Reginald Lt kia 27-9-16 5LNLancs p234 CR France744
FORREST,Thomas Lt ded 28-5-18 RAMC attPatialiaLancers p195 CR Iraq8
FORREST,Walter Torrie Maj kia 19-4-17 1/4KOSB p223 CR Palestine8
FORREST,William Robinson 2Lt kia 12-9-18 7DLI p239 CR France530
FORRESTER,Cecil James K.TLt ded 13-1-19 RASC attRAMC 28DivFA p254 CR Greece9
FORRESTER,Hugh Fielding 2Lt dow 22-4-16 2BlkW p128 MR38
FORRESTER,James.MC.2Lt kia 8-5-18 13RB p178 MR27
FORRESTER,James David TCapt kia 15-11-16 RAMC attRNavyDiv p195 CR France701,14-11-16
FORRESTER,Patrick Hamilton T2Lt dow 11-10-15 8BlkW p128 CR Scot231

FORRESTER,Robert Edgar Capt kia 16-6-15 1BlkW p128 CR France720
FORRET,David James T2Lt dow 28-12-15 9 att1KOSB p101 CR Gallipoli1
FORRET,Robert Smith Leiper.MC.2Lt dow 15-5-18 7ScotRif p224 CR France10 6Bn
FORRETT,Percival Donald Capt kia 5-2-16 5NumbF p213 CR Belgium309
FORRYAN,Donald T2Lt kia 16-9-16 9YLI p143 MR21
FORSAITH,Hugh John 2Lt kia 18-8-17 55RFC p7 CR France285
FORSDIKE,Charles William 2Lt dow 13-6-18 129/42RFA p28 CR France10
FORSDIKE,Harold Brooke TLt kia 1-7-16 14Y&L p158 MR21
FORSELL,Alan Richard Lt kia 14-10-15 4Leic p219 MR19
FORSHALL,John Lt kia 12-4-18 C123RFA p28 CR France204
FORSHAW,George Leslie Fresson T2Lt kia 19-11-17 LancF att3/5Bn p92 CR Belgium115
FORSHAW,Joseph 2Lt dow PoW 4-10-18 1/5LNLancs p234 CR France612
FORSTER,Alfred Henry Lt dow 10-3-19 2Drags p21 CR Hamps43
FORSTER,Arthur Paul TCaptAMaj ded 24-9-18 47MGC p182 CR France88,25-9-18
FORSTER,Christopher Jack ALt kia 21-7-17 RFA att3RE 3CoSpecBde p28 CR Belgium11
FORSTER,Eric Murray 2Lt kia 3-5-17 3 att2Ess p131 CR France451
FORSTER,Francis Arthur 2Lt ded 6-4-19 RGA 443SB p39 CR Germany1,Lt
FORSTER,Frederick Albert Capt dow 23-8-15 RFus p67 CR Belgium242
FORSTER,Frederick Richard.MC.2Lt dow 3-10-17 159RFA p28 CR France145
FORSTER,George Norman Bowes.CMG.DSO.BrigGen kia 4-4-18 RWar attStaff42InfBde p64 MR27
FORSTER,George Richardson.MID TCapt kia 25-8-17 19DLI p257&160 CR France363
FORSTER,Harold Ker 2Lt dow PoW 8-12-17 6Lond p247 CR France924
FORSTER,Harold Thomas.DSO.MC.LtAMaj dow 29-5-18 RBerks att2Nhampt p CR France1693 &CR France34
FORSTER,Henry William Broderick Lt ded 22-1-19 7Mddx p270 CR Mddx68,d
FORSTER,Herbert Cyril Capt kia 25-5-15 3RFus p67 MR29
FORSTER,Hugh Murray TCapt dow 28-9-15 8KOSB p101 CR France178,Maj 15
FORSTER,James Ernest HonMaj kia 29-9-15 3 att1Y&L p158 CR France550
FORSTER,James Henry Lt kia 29-9-15 RE 2/1FC p210 CR France423,dow
FORSTER,John 2Lt kia 14-9-14 KRRC p150 MR15
FORSTER,John.MC.CaptAMaj dow 2-10-18 7RFus p67 CR France1184
FORSTER,John Percival TCapt kia 1-7-16 22NumbF p61 MR21
FORSTER,John Stanley Capt dow 23-8-18 B285RFA p207 CR France504,22-8-1
FORSTER,Lionel Archibald Capt ded PoW 4-11-14 Ches p96 CR France1276,d
FORSTER,Ralph T2Lt ded 22-11-18 MGC p182 CR War81,Lt
FORSTER,Ralph Louis Francis 2Lt kia 3-5-17 1EKent p57 MR19
FORSTER,Thomas T2Lt ded 26-2-19 6Y&L p265 CR Ches128
FORSTER,Thomas Burton 2Lt kia 10-6-16 3 att2RIrReg p89 CR France394,dow
FORSTER,Thomas Foreman.MID ACapt kia 31-10-17 7DLI p239 CR Belgium1
FORSTER,Walter Johnson Capt kia 31-5-17 3 att8ELancs p110 MR20
FORSTER,William Edward Blake 2Lt ded 12-6-15 RFA p28 CR Eire49
FORSTER,William Oxley Lt dow 22-9-16 8DLI C'Coy p239 CR France177
FORSTER-BROWN,James Cameron TLt dow 27-8-16 12RB p178 CR France14
FORSTER-MORRIS,Herbert Gloyne Forster 2Lt dow 10-10-15 1SWBord p100 France1
FORSYTH,Andrew Alexander T2Lt kia 12-10-18 12 att9RScots p54 CR France
FORSYTH,Cusack Grant.DSO.TLtCol kia 14-9-16 NumbF 2 att6Yorks p90 CR France246
FORSYTH,David 2Lt ded 17-5-15 7HLI p270 CR Scot812,17-6-15
FORSYTH,Gordon Amhurst 2Lt kia 27-8-16 8RFus p67 CR France420
FORSYTH,Gordon Oliver TLt kia 11-10-18 37MGC Inf p182 CR France1396
FORSYTH,James T2Lt kia 13-7-16 7RWKent p141 MR21
FORSYTH,James Corson T2Lt kia 31-8-17 1Worc p108 CR Belgium54,30-8-17
FORSYTH,John 2Lt dow 28-3-18 3 att17HLI p162 CR France225
FORSYTH,John Alexander Stewart Lt ded 5-11-19 RB att517LabCps p266 CR France113
FORSYTH,John Charles 2Lt kia 11-10-18 ScotHorse p205 CR France660,13Blk
FORSYTH,John Cusack.MID Lt&Adjt kia 22-9-14 23RFA p28 CR France1110
FORSYTH,Maxwell Hanton.DSO.MC.TMaj dow 11-3-18 9ScotRif p103 CR France1066 Ex 8GordH
FORSYTH,Roy Anderson 2Lt kia 28-11-17 RFA att7RFC p7&28 CR Belgium16
FORSYTH,Samuel Sanford.MID Lt kia 25-9-15 RFA 43TrHowBty p28 MR29
FORSYTH,W Lt 28-10-18 IA MiscList CR Pakistan50A MR43
FORSYTH,Walter William T2Lt ded 7-12-18 HLI att2Bn p162 CR France289

FORSYTH,William Capt dow 20-10-15 1/7GordH p242 CR France300
FORSYTH,William 2Lt dow 1-4-16 6A&SH p243 CR France95
FORSYTH,William Allan Capt kia 27-6-18 56RFA &79RAF p28 CR Belgium31
FORSYTH,William Forbes 2Lt kia 15-9-18 10RScots p212 CR France179
FORSYTH,William James Samuel 2Lt kia 13-5-17 3KOSB p101 CR France777
FORSYTH,William Laing 2Lt kia 22-3-18 5 att4SforthH p241 MR20
FORSYTH,William Matthew T2Lt dow 20-4-17 16Mddx A'Coy p146 CR France40
FORSYTH,William Walker 2Lt ded 1-3-19 3A&SH p266 CR Scot684
FORSYTH-GRANT,Ivor.MID Lt dow 19-10-15 2LovatScouts p204 CR Gallipoli26
FORT,Lawrence Capt kia 16-2-15 2EKent p57 MR29
FORTH,Charles 2Lt kia 30-7-17 2/10Manch p237 CR Belgium24
FORTESCUE,Grenville TCapt kia 4-9-15 11RB p178 CR France707 Ex 4Bn
FORTESCUE,William Aubrey Lt kia 12-10-16 3 att2LancF p92 CR France390
FORTUNE,Henry George 2Lt kia 17-1-17 3/6WelshR att132MGC Inf p187&230 CR Iraq5
FORTUNE,John TCapt ded 27-12-18 RAMC att27CCS p195 MR61
FORTUNE,Rutherford Lamond T2Lt dow 15-1-17 16RScots p54 CR France275
FORTUNE,Stanley Welsh 2Lt kia 13-3-16 10RB p178 MR29
FORWARD,Charles Arthur 2Lt kia 25-9-15 2Beds p85 MR19
FORWOOD,Thomas Brittain Capt kia 8-5-15 RLancs p59 MR29
FOSBERY,Frank Sidney Thomas T2Lt kia 21-3-18 21MGC p182 MR27
FOSBROOKE,Cuthbert 2Lt kia 19-7-17 6DLI p239 CR Belgium29,22Bn
FOSDICK,John Hyland TLt dow 31-7-15 7RB p178 CR Belgium11
FOSKETT,Herbert Edward 2Lt kia 28-4-17 5 att6Beds p219 MR20
FOSS,Frederick George Lt kia 6-11-17 1/6RWFus p223 CR Palestine1
FOSS,Gilbert Harry T2Lt kia 3-7-16 8BordR p117 MR21
FOSSETT,Reginald Graham T2Lt kia 3-10-18 5TankCps p188 CR France375
FOSTER,Alfred 2Lt kia 14-4-17 27/32RFA p28 CR France451
FOSTER,Alfred David.MC.2LtTCapt kia 5-5-17 8RSuss p119 CR France592
FOSTER,Archibald Courtenay Hays Lt kia 20-9-14 Hamps attKAR p120&202 MR50,18-9-14
FOSTER,Arthur Cedric 2Lt dow 12-3-15 1GrenGds SR p50 CR France500
FOSTER,Arthur Edward 2Lt kia 10-4-17 3 att7YLI p143 CR France905,9-4-17
FOSTER,Bernard La Trobe Lt kia 24-7-16 19Manch p154 CR France744,23-7-16
FOSTER,Charles Clifford Lt kia 29-7-18 5Ches p222 CR France524
FOSTER,Charles Finch Lt kia 27-3-18 9Lancers p22 CR France424
FOSTER,Douglas Cameron Capt kia 14-4-17 ScotRif p103 CR France434
FOSTER,Edward T2Lt kia 23-4-17 10RFus p67 MR20
FOSTER,Ethelbert Harold(Bert) Lt kia 8-10-18 4WelchR p230 CR France1345
FOSTER,Frank 2Lt ded 23-9-19 RGA 155SB SR p262 CR Lancs34
FOSTER,Frank Hawley T2Lt kia 3-6-17 GL &45RFC p7 MR20
FOSTER,Franklin James T2Lt kia 23-8-17 GL &11RFC p7 CR France120,Frank
FOSTER,George T2Lt kia 16-5-17 102RFA p28 CR Belgium127
FOSTER,George Haslewood T2Lt kia 21-3-18 RE 179TC p45 CR France1182
FOSTER,George Major Solloway T2Lt kia 3-7-16 10Worc p108 CR France393
FOSTER,H.Capt 29-6-17 IOD MR66
FOSTER,Harry Langton 2Lt kia 7-6-17 4WKent p234 CR Belgium154
FOSTER,Harold John Brittain Capt kia 14-4-17 Beds att1Ess p85 MR20
FOSTER,Heaton 2Lt kia 16-4-18 1EYorks p84 MR30
FOSTER,Hedley Roy Capt kia 22-8-17 BucksBn O&BLI p231 MR30
FOSTER,Herbert Knollys 2Lt kia 30-10-14 1Glouc p106 MR29
FOSTER,James Sloman T2Lt drd 13/14-8-15 9SomLI p79 MR4,13-8-15
FOSTER,John Capt kia 23-4-17 5SStaffs p229 MR20,8Bn
FOSTER,John 2Lt kia 25-4-18 4RScots p211 MR30
FOSTER,John Bowden T2Lt kia 11-10-18 7WYorks p81 CR France612
FOSTER,John Cecil.MC.MID TCapt kia 20-8-17 6Lincs p75 CR Belgium10
FOSTER,John Maurice 2Lt kia 23-7-16 4GordH p242 CR France432
FOSTER,John Rowland Maj 22-2-20 RAMC CR Lancs233
FOSTER,Joseph T2Lt dow 14-10-18 20DLI p160 CR Belgium11
FOSTER,Laurence Talbot Lisle TLt kia 5-8-15 16DLI att5Manch p160 CR Gallipoli6,7-8-15
FOSTER,Leonard T2Lt dow 13-8-16 15WYorks p81 CR Yorks388
FOSTER,Leslie Arthur Clifford T2Lt kia 12-4-18 13Lpool p71 CR France88,13-4-18 Lt
FOSTER,Norman Kessen TCapt ded 2-12-18 RAMC p195 MR41
FOSTER,Norman Rae Lt kia 26-3-17 1/7Ches p223 CR Palestine8,Roe
FOSTER,Percy George T2Lt dow 2-4-16 7RSuss p119 CR Sussex178
FOSTER,R.D.Lt mbk 7-8-15 6Lincs p256 MR4
FOSTER,Reginald T2Lt kldacc 3-1-18 RFC p16 CR Yorks368
FOSTER,Robert Clow 2Lt kia 10-4-18 11Suff p78 MR32

FOSTER,William Arthur Lt ded 20-2-19 5Manch &RAF p270 CR Dorset50
FOSTER,William Augustus Portman Lt dow PoW 11-11-14 1SStaffs p122 CR Germany3,Capt
FOSTER,William Leo Gorrill TCapt kia 2-7-18 RASC p192 CR France
FOTHERGILL,Reginald Alfred Lt ded 20-7-20 2/5Glouc CR Glouc11
FOTTRELL,Brendan Joseph 2Lt kia 15-3-15 3 att1RIrReg p89 MR29
FOUBISTER,John Leask 2Lt kld 8-10-17 GL &31RFC p7 CR Surrey6
FOUCAR,James Lewis Maj kia 8-5-15 12Lond p248 MR29
FOULDES,Thomas John.MID Capt kia 25-6-18 A114RFA p28 CR Greece6
FOULDS,Maurice Frank 2Lt kia 30-10-17 19 att2/6Lond p250 MR30
FOULGER,Maurice T2Lt kia 9-8-15 KSLI p144 MR29
FOULIS,James Bell TCapt kia 18-10-16 5CamH p167 MR21
FOULKES,Charles Henry Lt 11-9-20 6WRid CR Eire166
FOULKES,George Boyd TCapt kia 12-8-16 6RScotF p94 MR21
FOULKES,Thomas Howard.CIE.LtCol kldByTribesmen 14/15-11-20 IMS p276 MR43,15-11-20
FOULKES-WINKS,Oswald Woodward T2Lt kia 20-7-16 13Mddx att75TMB p146 CR France285
FOULSHAM,Arthur Percy 2Lt kia 20-7-17 RGA 245SB p39 CR Belgium29
FOUNTAIN,John Alfred Arnott T2Lt kia 1-7-16 10YLI p143 CR France267
FOURMY,William Reginald 2Lt dow 28-1-18 28MGC Inf p182 CR France439
FOWELL,John 2Lt kia 12-10-17 4 att8SStaffs p122 MR30
FOWKE,Mansergh Cuthbert Capt kia 30-8-14 2Manch p154 MR15
FOWLE,Michael Randolph 2Lt kia 24-11-14 2Wilts p153 MR29,24-10-14
FOWLE,Louis Richard.MID Lt kia 4-6-15 IA 14Sikhs p276 MR4
FOWLE,William Ernest Lt ded 1-5-19 RGA p262
FOWLE,William Meade Capt dow 16-3-16 RE p45 CR Sussex112
FOWLER,Alan Arthur Capt kia 28-4-15 2CamH p167 MR29
FOWLER,Alexander George.MID TCapt kia 1-1-18 GL &1KAR p202 CR EAfrica77
FOWLER,Bernard Edwin Lt kia 22-3-18 19MGC p182 MR20
FOWLER,Cecil Dashwood Melman Lt kia 25-9-15 1RWSurr p55 MR19,Milman
FOWLER,Charles Jefford T2Lt dow 1-6-16 22RFus p67 CR France95
FOWLER,Christopher George Capt kia 6-4-17 1/6Norf p217 CR France568
FOWLER,Claude Oliver 2Lt kia 23-10-18 5Beds p219 CR France1476
FOWLER,David Dennys 2Lt kia 16-3-17 RFC p7 CR Sussex114,17-3-17
FOWLER,Edward Wareham Lt kia 15-7-16 1/7RWar p214 MR21
FOWLER,Evelyn Philip Lt ded 5-10-17 BlkW p264
FOWLER,F.W.Capt 8-6-19 RE CR Mddx70
FOWLER,Francis Reginald 2Lt kia 18-10-16 3Leinst att2RIrRif p174 MR21
FOWLER,Frank Archibald 2LtACapt kia 28-7-17 RGA 295SB p39 CR France922
FOWLER,George Edward T2Lt kia 28-10-17 1 att12Glouc p106 MR30
FOWLER,George Glyn Lt dow 26-9-15 2KRRC p150 CR France88
FOWLER,George Herbert LtCol kia 15-10-15 Cmdg1/8N&D p233 CR France109
FOWLER,Horace Vernon Lt 15-7-17 RIM MR65
FOWLER,John Dudley 2Lt kia 30-11-14 5Lancers p21 MR29
FOWLER,John Edward.Sir.Capt kia 22-6-15 4SfthH p164 CR Scot936
FOWLER,John Orr 2Lt kia 19-8-17 GL &45RFC p7 MR20
FOWLER,Kenneth Ryeland T2Lt kia 3-6-15 RFA p28 CR Belgium28
FOWLER,Norman John T2Lt kia 23-4-17 1RWSurr p55 MR20
FOWLER,Ralph 2Lt kia 16-9-16 6DCLI p114 MR21
FOWLER,S.H.SubCondr 5-2-15 S&T Cps MR66
FOWLER,Valentine TMaj kia 2-6-17 10Yorks p90 CR France1489
FOWLER,William 2Lt kld 16-11-16 RFC p2 CR Scot398
FOWLER,William Maurice T2Lt dow 26-9-18 2RSuss p119 CR France673
FOWLIE,Charles Wilson Lawson Maj kia 30-5-15 5GordH p242 CR France705
FOWLIE,James Lawrence Lt kia 23-4-17 1 att10HLI p162 CR France1182,24-4-17
FOWNES,Henry Harley Maj dow 17-3-17 210 att174RGA p209 CR France120
FOX,Alan Geoffrey Capt kia 9-5-15 RE attRFC p1&45 CR France163
FOX,Albert Victor 2Lt kia 3-9-16 10RB p178 MR21
FOX,Andrew J.TLt kia 1-9-18 6 att4RBerks p139 CR France346
FOX,Andrew Stewart 2Lt kia 13-10-15 6NStaffs p238 MR19
FOX,Arthur.MC.ACapt kia 8-5-15 3 att1KSLI A'Coy p144 CR France115
FOX,Arthur Clause.DSO.LtCol drd 15-4-17 RAMC p195 MR35
FOX,Cecil Croker TLt kia 15-9-16 12ESurr p112 MR21
FOX,Charles Alexander Newcombe.MC.Lt kia 26-9-17 4NStaffs att2Worc p157&258 CR Belgium19,Capt 25-9-17
FOX,Charles James T2Lt kia 22-7-16 1RWKent p141 MR21
FOX,Charles Joseph 2Lt kia 29-6-16 16 att2RFus p67 CR France35
FOX,David T2Lt kia 15-10-17 11WYorks p81 MR30
FOX,Douglas Charles 2Lt kia 23-7-16 1NumbF p61 CR France432

FOX,Francis Nevil Wilson T2Lt kia 31-7-17 14WelshR p126 CR Belgium96
FOX,Francis Parker T2Lt kia 1-7-16 9RInniskF p104 MR21
FOX,Frank Herbert T2Lt kia 23-8-16 1Beds p85 CR France518
FOX,Frederick Donald T2Lt kia 5-11-16 19 att17N&D p134 MR21
FOX,G.H.Lt 6-5-21 RASC CR Lancs34
FOX,Geoffrey Noel Storrs 2Lt kia 28-3-18 5 att2WYorks p218 MR27
FOX,George 2Lt dow 24-5-15 RFA p28 CR Belgium4,Lt kia
FOX,George Herbert 2Lt kia 23-4-16 RFA att G'HQ Intelligence p28 MR34
FOX,Gerald Vincent TLt kia 10-7-18 4MGC Inf p182 CR France411
FOX,H.A.AssSurg 19-10-18 IMD MR65
FOX,Harold Sidney George 2Lt kia 8-4-17 4SfthH p241 CR France15,9-4-17
FOX,Harry Norton T2Lt kia 23-4-17 1Norf p73 MR20
FOX,James John T2Lt kia 11-9-18 Norf att12Bn p73 CR Belgium451
FOX,James Joseph.MID T2Lt kia 1-9-18 11RInniskF p105 CR France297
FOX,John T2Lt ded 18-11-17 5ConnRgrs p172 CR Egypt7
FOX,John Robert 2Lt ded 16-8-18 10Manch &RAF p270
FOX,Lawrence Anselm Storrs TLt dow 27-4-18 21WYorks p81 CR France102
FOX,Leslie Herbert 2Lt kia 11-7-16 4 att2Beds p85 MR21
FOX,Leslie William Capt kia 31-7-17 10Lpool p216 MR29
FOX,Maurier James 2Lt ded 10-1-19 4 att17Hamps p270 CR Kent27,Maurice John
FOX,Michael Stanley T2Lt kia 20-11-17 RWSurr att6Bn p55 MR17
FOX,Owen Gurney 2Lt kia 6-2-17 3 att1Dors p124 CR France221
FOX,Ralph Talbot 2Lt kia 25-8-18 4YLI p235 CR France614
FOX,Reginald Wilson LtCol kia 8-3-16 6Dev p217 MR38
FOX,Sidney Thomas 2Lt kia 21-9-17 RGA 230SB p39 CR Belgium113
FOX,Thomas Herbert LtACapt kia 31-3-18 17/41RH&FA p28 CR France41
FOX,Thomas Noel 2LtTLt ded 12-12-18 SomLI att79MGC Inf p79&182 CR Europe20
FOX,Vincent Lt kia 26-8-14 RAVC p198 CR France658
FOX,Victor William Darwin Lt kia 18-5-15 1IrGds SR p52 CR France727
FOX,Walter Henry Lt kia 16-6-15 4SStaffs att2Beds p122 MR22
FOX,Wilfred Armstrong 2Lt kia 29-7-15 4Lincs p217 CR Belgium98
FOX,William Archibald.MC.Lt 6-11-17 4RSuss p228
FOXALL,Thomas William T2Lt kia 2-10-18 RWFus 3GarrBn att25GarrBnLpool p97 CR France1887
FOXELL Edward William Lanchester TCapt ded 11-6-17 7EKent att3ArmyGasSchl p57 CR France225
FOXON,Harold Richard Lt kia 28-8-18 7 att9Ess p232 CR France397
FOY,Ernest Reginald 2Lt kia 11-4-17 1SomLI p79 MR20
FOY,Martin Victor Capt kia 13-10-14 1RWSurr p55 CR France1329
FOY,William Archibald.MC.Lt 6-11-17 1/4RSuss CR Palestine1
FOYSTER,Ellen Lucy Sister drd 10-4-17 QAIMNS p200 CR France85
FOYSTER,Philip Tillard LtTCapt dow 11-12-16 RE 86FC p45 CR France40
FRADD,Kingsley Meredith Chatterton 2Lt kia 1-7-16 2Lond attMGC p187&245
FRAME,Robert T2Lt kia 28-3-18 RLancs p59 CR France452
FRAMPTON,John Guy Lt dow 11-10-18 1Mon p244 CR France725,4-10-18
FRAMPTON,John Reginald T2Lt kia 3-7-17 13Glouc p106 CR Belgium10
FRAMPTON,William John Goulbourn Shipdern Capt kia 24-4-18 2ELancs p110 MR27
FRANCE,Arthur Alderson T2Lt dow 7-10-16 RE p45 CR France513
FRANCE,Errol Martin T2Lt kia 30-7-16 10Worc p108 CR France432,Lt
FRANCE,John Galbraith 2Lt kia 12-4-17 8 att9ScotRif p225 MR20
FRANCE,William T2Lt kia 8-10-18 12/13NumbF p61 CR France1345
FRANCE-HAYHURST,Frederick Charles LtCol kia 9-5-15 4RWFus p223 CR France924
FRANCIS,Ainslie Norman.MC.MM.2Lt dow 30-4-18 1LancF p92 CR Lancs475
FRANCIS,Alan Buller T2Lt kia 24-8-16 9 att7DCLI p114 CR France390 &CR France399
FRANCIS,Basil Hugh 2Lt kia 4-2-15 3RScots att2HLI p54 CR France765
FRANCIS,Christopher Thomas TCapt dow 26-5-16 13RScots p54 CR France8
FRANCIS,Dudley Collins 2Lt kia 13-11-16 5Y&L A'Coy p238 CR France1327
FRANCIS,Edward Griffith 2Lt kia 21-5-16 8Lond p247 MR20
FRANCIS,Francis Gustave 2Lt kia 6-8-15 3 att1Ess p131 CR Gallipoli6
FRANCIS,Hugh Gordon.MC.MID TLtACapt kia 22-3-18 RE 104Coy p45 MR27
FRANCIS,John Capt kia 2-6-15 1/5RWar D'Coy p214 CR Belgium339
FRANCIS,Philip Arthur 2Lt kld 1-6-18 4Manch p154 CR France1416,kia att10Ches
FRANCIS,Richard John Lt dow 31-3-15 2Y&L p158 CR France922
FRANCIS,Vere T2Lt dow 20-4-17 3 att2Suff p78 CR France40
FRANCIS,William George 2Lt kia 10-3-18 66RFC p16 CR Italy75
FRANCIS,William Joseph 2Lt kia 22-3-18 11RFus p67 MR27
FRANCIS,William Pollock 2LtTLt kia 22-10-17 12RScots p54 MR30

FRANCKE,William Henry Lt ded 10-12-19 GL &LabCps 399PoW Coy 270 CR Scot235
FRANK,Edward T2Lt kia 7-8-15 6Yorks p90 MR4
FRANK,Robert James Brownlaw Lt dow 6-6-16 1/4RSuss p228 CR Egypt8,Brownlow
FRANKAU,Paul Ewart Lt kia 2-11-17 20RB p244 CR Palestine8
FRANKENSTEIN,Cyril Joseph T2Lt kia 23-8-18 13TankCps p188 CR France117
FRANKENSTEIN,Oscar Reginald 2Lt kia 26-3-17 5WelshR p230 MR34
FRANKHAM,A.A.Lt ded 17-2-19 RGA 218SB p262 CR Hamps 4
FRANKLAND,Edgar 2Lt kia 24-10-18 9 att15DLI p239 MR16
FRANKLAND,John Cecil 2Lt kia 10-1-17 5LNLancs p234 MR29
FRANKLAND,Robert Cecil Colville Capt kia 7-8-15 3NStaffs att8LancF p157 MR
FRANKLAND,Thomas Hugh Colville BtMaj kia 25-4-15 RDubF p176 MR4
FRANKLAND,Thomas Pemberton T2Lt kia 29-7-16 RGA 51 att109SB p39 CR France397
FRANKLEN-EVANS,George Philip 2Lt dow 18-9-18 4DLI p160 CR France327
FRANKLIN,Arthur John 2Lt kia 9-4-18 18WelshR p126 MR32
FRANKLIN,Benjamin Lester TLt kia 4-5-17 12Mddx &70RFC p7&146,dow CR France285
FRANKLIN,Cyril Edward Lt dow 20-2-17 RE p210 CR France251,kia
FRANKLIN,Edgar John LtTCapt drd 17-4-17 C58RFA p28 MR40
FRANKLIN,Francis 2Lt kia 3-5-15 3RFus p67 MR29
FRANKLIN,Frederick Robert 2Lt kia 9-12-17 10RIrRif p169 MR21
FRANKLIN,George T2Lt kia 20-10-18 3 att2NStaffs p157 CR France658
FRANKLIN,L.C.Lt 20-4-19 RASC CR Hunts65
FRANKLIN,Leslie Willoughby Lt dow 16-10-18 10/147RFA p28 CR France686
FRANKLIN,Percival George Capt kia 18-7-17 8Manch att1/8Lpool p236 MR29 C Belgium10
FRANKLIN,Rodney Vernon TLt kld 24-6-17 GL &16RFC p7 CR Egypt15
FRANKLIN,Thomas Alderman.MC.Capt dow 27-11-17 1/5Beds p219 CR Palestir
FRANKLIN,William Ernest T2Lt kia 1-4-18 10Worc p108 CR Belgium48
FRANKLIN,William Hyslop TLt kia 25-9-15 6KOSB p101 MR19,26-9-15
FRANKLIN,William Joseph T2Lt kia 5-10-16 11ESurr att7Suss p112 MR21
FRANKLYN,George William 2Lt kia 7-6-17 23Lond C'Coy p252 CR Belgium112
FRANKLYN,Henry TCapt kia 8-7-16 8RFus p67 MR21
FRANKLYN,William Edmund.KCB.Sir LtGen 27-10-14 Yorks CR Mddx39
FRANKS,Braham Alfred T2Lt kia 24-10-15 11 att8WRid p115 CR Gallipoli27,23-10-15
FRANKS,George Despard.CMG.DSO.LtCol kia 8-10-18 19Huss p22 CR France8
FRANKS,Harold Cooper T2Lt kia 15-6-18 2Suff p78 CR France33
FRANKS,John Ferguson.MC.Capt&Adjt dow 22-9-15 3KRRC p150 CR France692,kia
FRANKS,Lionel 2Lt dow 5-5-17 4 att8EYorks C'Coy p219 CR France145
FRANKS,Rolland Sutton 2Lt kia 12-10-17 8 att1ESurr p112 MR30
FRANKS,Spencer Capt kia 22-3-18 2SLancs p125 CR France481,28-3-18
FRASER,Alan Cumming.MC.2Lt kia 31-8-18 7Lond p247 CR France630
FRASER,Alan Simon 2Lt kia 24-3-18 RE HighlandFC p210 CR France1063,Lt
FRASER,Alexander.VD.LtCol kia 17-5-15 4CamH p242 MR22,18-5-15
FRASER,Alexander 2Lt kia 13-10-15 1BlkW p128 MR19
FRASER,Alexander 2Lt kia 30-11-17 att1/5LNLancs p135 MR17
FRASER,Alexander Evan Lt kia 2-5-15 2Mon p244 CR Belgium92
FRASER,Alexander Roderick 2Lt dow 26-4-17 3 att6SLancs p125 CR Iraq8
FRASER,Andrew.MC&Bar.Capt dow 20-4-18 2CamH p167 CR France95
FRASER,Andrew Knowles.MC.Capt kia 20-11-17 4SfthH p241 MR17
FRASER,Angus McIntyre Lt dow 19-6-18 1/6A&SH p243 CR France65
FRASER,Arthur Cecil T2Lt kld 22-1-18 RFC p16 CR Lincs61
FRASER,Arthur Ian.DSO.MID Maj kia 30-11-17 IA 9HodsonsHorse p276 CR France364,Ion
FRASER,Arthur Leslie 2Lt dow 1-7-17 RGA 27SB p39 CR France88
FRASER,Arthur William.DSO.T2Lt kia 1-7-16 1BordR p117 CR France1501
FRASER,C.Lovat Capt 18-6-21 14DLI CR Herts24
FRASER,Campbell Robertson 2Lt kia 17-4-18 1Lpool D'Coy p71 MR32,Lt 4Bn
FRASER,Charles Douglas 2Lt kia 22-3-18 3Lond p245 MR27
FRASER,D'Arcy Mackenzie TMaj kia 7-8-15 IA 75Carnatic att6Lincs p75&276 C Gallipoli5
FRASER,Donald TCapt kia 1-7-16 RE p45 CR France68
FRASER,Donald.DSO.Chap2Cl kld 2-6-18 RAChDept p199 CR France204
FRASER,Donald Charles 2Lt kia 3-5-17 5 att9RFus p67 MR20
FRASER,Duncan McNeill 2Lt ded 16-10-19 9HLI p270 CR Scot752
FRASER,Eldred Leslie T2Lt kia 20-11-17 HTankCps p188 MR17
FRASER,Frederick Gordon.MC.MID TCapt kia 14-6-17 12 att11RWKent p111 MR20

FRASER,Geoffrey Norris 2Lt kia 12-3-15 3 att2BordR p117 MR22
FRASER,George Allan 2Lt kia 15-5-17 2HAC p206 MR20
FRASER,George Dick T2Lt dow 3-6-18 13RB p178 CR France145
FRASER,Harold Reginald Drummond.MC.LtACapt kia 1-8-18 5Ches p222
FRASER,Henry Hubert Lt kia 27-5-18 3 att5Yorks p90 MR18
FRASER,Herbert Heron T2Lt dow 18-10-17 SfthH att8Bn p164 CR France40
FRASER,Herbert Ross T2Lt kia 24-8-16 17RScots p54 CR France630
FRASER,Hugh 2Lt kia 13-11-16 9A&SH p244 CR France131
FRASER,Hugh Crawford TCapt kia 5-8-15 2 att6RScotF p94 CR France727
FRASER,Hon Hugh Joseph.MVO.Maj kia 28-10-14 2ScotsGds p52 MR29
FRASER,Ian Catto T2Lt kia 25-9-15 2A&SH p173 CR France114
FRASER,J.R.CMG.LtCol 11-6-20 1LNLancs CR Mddx26
FRASER,James 2Lt dow 28-3-18 4BlkW p230 CR France145
FRASER,James 2Lt dow 20-5-18 330RFA p28 CR France142
FRASER,James Carstairs Lt kia 21-3-18 5SfthH p241 MR20
FRASER,James Herbert Lt dow 9-7-16 2Mon att107MGC p187&244 CR France74
FRASER,James Howie Lt kia 29-10-14 2GordH p166 MR29
FRASER,James Leslie Lt ded 1-4-19 3SfthH p265 CR Ches181,31-3-19
FRASER,James Lovat Hasack TLt dow 18-2-17 75MGC p182 CR France263
FRASER,James Scholfield.MID Maj kia 13/14-1-16 1/5EKent p212 CR Iraq5
FRASER,John T2Lt dow 6-4-18 47MGC p182 CR France169,5-4-18
FRASER,John Alexander Capt dow 28-8-14 2A&SH p173 CR France1394
FRASER,John Courtenay.MC.Lt drd 9-9-18 GrenGds attGdsMGR p50&53 MR40
FRASER,John Irwin see FRAZER,J.I.
FRASER,Kenneth John.MC.T2Lt kia 27-5-18 10DLI p160 MR18
FRASER,Lachlan Henry Veitch.MID Lt kia 24-2-15 4Mddx p146 CR Belgium104
FRASER,Lachlan Ronald 2Lt kia 25-9-15 1ARO att69Punjabis p276 MR28
FRASER,Laureston Ross 2Lt kia 21-3-18 14Lond p249 CR France184,Lauriston
FRASER,Mackenzie Hamilton Capt ded 28-6-19 SfthH p254&266,A&SH CR EAfrica49
FRASER,Madge Neill Nurse 8-3-15 ScotWomensHosp CR Europe57
FRASER,Malcolm Goulding 2Lt kia 1-7-16 2ScotRif p103 MR21
FRASER,Oswald Campbell T2Lt kia 9-4-17 9BlkW p128 CR France924
FRASER,Owen Alan Denholm 2Lt ded 1-11-19 ULIA att3CpsofGuides p276 MR43
FRASER,Patrick Grant 2Lt kia 3-5-17 3GordH att8BlkW p166 MR20
FRASER,Patrick Neill TLt kia 1-7-16 11NStaffs att2BordR p157 MR29
FRASER,Percy William Norman.DSO.Capt kia 22-2-15 2CamH p167 CR Belgium28
FRASER,Peter Campbell 2Lt dow 23-7-16 1NumbF p61 MR21
FRASER,R.A.2Lt kld 18-5-18 GL &RAF p190
FRASER,Rowland TCapt kia 1-7-16 6 att1RB p178 MR21
FRASER,Hon Simon 2Lt kld 29-10-14 3 att2GordH p166 MR29
FRASER,T.P.27-8-14 WAfrMedServ CR WAfrica58
FRASER,Thomas Lt kia 1-7-16 2Ess p131 MR21
FRASER,Thomas Francis TCapt kia 7/11-8-15 9WYorks p81 MR4,8-8-15
FRASER,Victor Murray Drummond 2Lt dow 3-6-15 5Ches p222
FRASER,Wallace TCapt kia 30-7-16 19Lpool p71 CR France294
FRASER,William T2Lt dow 29-9-15 1BlkW p128 CR France88
FRASER,William 2Lt kia 25-10-16 RFC p2 MR20
FRASER,William 2LtACapt kia 9-4-17 1GordH A'Coy p166 CR France581
FRASER,William Alan TCapt ded 7-7-17 RE 26DivHQ p45 CR Greece7
FRASER,William Augustus Cumming Maj ded 14-6-15 1Dors p124 CR Iraq6
FRASER-CAMPBELL,William Baillie 2Lt kia 23-3-18 8A&SH p243 MR27
FRASER-TYTLER,Patrick Seton TCapt kia 3-8-16 D36RFA p28 CR France630
FRATER,David George.MC.2Lt kia 17-4-18 A255RFA p208 CR France202,16-4-18
FRAYLING,Herbert Joseph T2Lt kia 30-8-18 1DCLI p114 CR France518
FRAYLING,Michael Stapleton 2Lt kia 16-9-18 C183RFA p28 MR21
FRAYNE,Ernest TLt dow PoW 17-5-18 16 att2Mddx p146 CR Germany3
FRAZER,Alexander.MC.2Lt kia 13-8-16 10HLI p162 CR France151,10/11Bn
FRAZER,Douglas Villers Capt kia 16-8-17 RFA p207 MR30
FRAZER,John Irwin Lt kia 14-9-14 2ConnRgrs p172 CR France1107,FRASER
FRAZER,John Gordon LtCol ded 1-8-16 1Dev GarrBn p76
FREAKES,Alexander John 2Lt dow 3-9-18 RFA p208 CR Surrey1
FREAM,William Lt kia 21-7-16 1/5Glouc p225 MR21
FRECHVILLE,William Ralph.MID Capt kia 9-1-20 RE p262 CR Asia81,FRECHEVILLE
FREDERICK,Thomas.MC.TCapt dow 14-12-17 9Norf p73 CR France13
FREE,Ernest Robert 2Lt ded 16-7-18 RGA X'SB p209 CR Camb2
FREEAR,Eric Charles 2Lt kia 13-4-17 4Beds p85 CR France644,15-4-17
FREEDMAN,Bertie T2Lt kia 3-7-17 15Lpool att1/9Manch p71 CR France755

FREEDMAN,Phineas T2Lt kia 3-10-17 6EKent p57 CR France154
FREELAND,Hugo Wharncliffe Lt kia 14-8-16 RGA p39 CR Belgium113
FREELAND,John Buchan 2Lt kia 26-7-17 2Yorks p90 MR29
FREEMAN,Arthur Cyril Bruce Lt kia 27-9-18 3Huss &2RScotF p94 CR France530
FREEMAN,Douglas Lt kia 26-9-17 16AustInf CR Belgium88
FREEMAN,Edward TMaj kia 3-3-16 10RWFus p97 CR Belgium131
FREEMAN,Eric Allen TLt kia 18-8-16 9 att6DCLI p114 MR21
FREEMAN,Eric Payne TCapt ded PoW 23-3-18 14Hamps p120 CR France511
FREEMAN,Francis Basil 2Lt kia 1-7-16 1/8RWar p215 CR France700
FREEMAN,Francis Hubert T2Lt kia 1-7-16 19LancF p92 CR France393
FREEMAN,Frank Albert 2Lt kia 1-7-16 2KRRC p150 MR20
FREEMAN,Frank Ernest Allien 2Lt kia 21-3-18 RFA 18DAC att83Bde p28 MR27
FREEMAN,Frederick John 2Lt dow 3-7-16 4 att2WYorks p81 CR France74
FREEMAN,George Cyril TLtACapt kia 1-10-16 6RBerks p139 CR France246
FREEMAN,H.P.Lt 21-1-18 RFC CR Mddx26
FREEMAN,Herbert Joseph TCapt dow 29-10-18 142RASC 16DivTrain att13InniskF p192 CR France1034
FREEMAN,James 2Lt kia 20-8-17 RGA 225SB p39 CR Belgium124
FREEMAN,James Edward Hutton 2Lt kia 24-4-16 7RWSurr att29RFC p2&55 CR Belgium11
FREEMAN,John Bentley 2Lt kia 20-9-17 3 att11RWKent p141 MR30
FREEMAN,John Roland.MID T2Lt dow 12-2-17 23NumbF p61 CR France285
FREEMAN,John William 2LtTLt kia 24-9-17 RE X CpsSigCo p45 CR Belgium102
FREEMAN,Joseph.MC.T2Lt dow 9-4-18 21Mddx p146 MR32
FREEMAN,Noel 2Lt kia 5-4-18 3RWSurr p55 CR France1170
FREEMAN,Noel William.MC.TCaptAMaj kia 21-3-18 68/14RFA p28 MR20
FREEMAN,Peter 2Lt dow 19-9-18 RGA 284SB p39 CR France835,Lt
FREEMAN,Robert Stuart Lt ded 29-8-19 RASC MT p267 CR Mddx15
FREEMAN,Russel Herbert.MC.Maj kia 21-7-18 Worc &73RAF p264 CR France524
FREEMAN,Tom T2Lt kia 17-2-17 6Nhampt att54TMB p137 CR France314
FREEMAN,Tristram Lt kia 12-3-15 6Worc p108 CR Belgium17,3Bn
FREEMAN,William Thomas LtCol ded 23-12-18 RAMC CR Berks86
FREEMAN,William Winter T2Lt kia 30-11-17 11DLI p160 CR France415,Winters
FREEMAN-COWEN,Cecil 2Lt kia 23-6-16 175RFA p28 CR France430
FREEMAN-THOMAS,Gerald Frederick.Hon.2Lt kia 14-9-14 1CldGds p51 MR15,Gerard
FREEMANTLE,Ronald Percy Cowen 2Lt kia 30-4-17 9RFC p7 CR France1483
FREEMANTLE,William George Lt kia 4-6-15 7Manch p237 MR4
FREENEY,Patrick Joseph T2Lt kia 8-10-18 6RDubF att198L TMB p176 CR France845
FREER,Arthur Martin 2Lt dow 12-4-18 3DLI p160 CR France298
FREER,John William Lt dow 29-6-15 10Leic p87 CR Greece10
FREESTON,Cecil James T2Lt kia 18-9-17 7Yorks p90 CR France1190
FREESTONE,William Herbert Rev kia 14-12-16 RAChDept p199 CR Greece9
FREETH,Richard Victor Canston Lt kia 13-7-16 4RBerks p234 CR France631
FREMANTLE,Thomas Francis Halford T2Lt dow 17-10-15 5 O&BLI C'Coy p130 CR France40
FRENCH,Albert Anthony T2Lt kia 3-9-16 11RSuss p119 MR21
FRENCH,Allan George 2Lt kia 23-5-16 15RWar p64 MR20
FRENCH,Bertram St.George TCapt kia 1-7-16 15Lpool attRInniskF p71 CR France339
FRENCH,Cecil John.MC.Lt 28-9-18 4CanadaMGC CR France256
FRENCH,Charles John TMaj dow 2-7-16 5KSLI attRE 255TC p144 CR France178
FRENCH,Charles Stockley Lt kia 25-4-15 2RDubF p176 MR29
FRENCH,Claude Alexander Capt dow 1-6-15 2RIrReg p89 CR France64
FRENCH,Digby Manifred Capt kia 11-9-18 4Suff p217 CR France511,FFRENCH
FRENCH,Edward Fulke.Hon.2Lt ded 13-11-18 PoW 296RFA p28 CR Egytp3
FRENCH,Ernest Aloysius.Hon.Lt dow 16-8-17 2SWBord p100 CR Belgium16
FRENCH,Ernest Shaw Lt kia 12-9-18 5YLI p235 CR France755
FRENCH,G.H.2Lt 26-6-19 RFA CR Ches97
FRENCH,George Philip.Hon.Lt kia 9-5-15 3 att1SWBord p100 CR France924
FRENCH,John Lawson TLt ded 26-9-17 RASC 1ColGHQ p192 CR France95,2Lt
FRENCH,Percival Vincent T2Lt dow 19-7-16 16DLI p160 CR France630
FRENCH,P.H.Capt ded 12-11-14 RE p45 CR Eire57
FRENCH,Robert Douglas 2Lt kia 15-9-16 6Lond p247 MR21
FRENCH,Robert Mason Jackson Capt dow 19-2-16 3RWFus p97 CR Hamps13
FRENCH,Sidney Arthur TLt kia 20-3-18 7RWKent p141 MR21
FRENCH,Thomas Hugo T2Lt kld 13-1-17 GL &RFC p7 CR Essex231
FRENCH,Valentine Douglas 2Lt dow 17-6-15 5KSLI p144 CR Belgium80 &CR Belgium187
FRENCH,Victor James Somerset 2Lt kia 10-10-18 1IrGds p52 CR

France337
FRENCH,William Alexander Smith 2Lt kia 12/16-5-17 6SfthH p241 MR20
FRENCH,William Cotton Maj kia 12-3-15 IA 2/3GurkhaRif p276 CR France727
FRENCH-BLAKE,St J.L.O'B.A,MC Maj 19-4-17 21Lancers attWorcHuss CR Palestine18
FRENCH-BREWSTER,Robert Abraham Maj ded 17-2-17 IrGds SR p52 CR Lond8
FREND,Hugh Palliser T2Lt kia 20-3-17 6Nhampt p137 CR France420
FREND,John Arthur Edward 2Lt kia 17-1-17 281RFA p28 CR France705
FREND,William Reginald Capt&Adjt kia 21-9-14 2N&D p134 MR15 &CR France1893
FRERE,Bartle Laurie Stuart.MID Lt kia 13-11-16 4Beds p85 CR France220
FRERE,Edgar 2Lt dow 22-5-16 8Lond p247 MR20
FRERE,Frederick John Henry Tobias.MC.Capt kia 10-6-17 RAMC att6Lincs p195 CR Belgium17,9-6-17
FRERE,Gilbert Raper TLt&Adjt dow 26-10-15 10RB p178 CR France345,Capt
FRERE,Lionel Basil 2LtTLt dow 29-9-15 DLI att2EYorks p160 MR19
FRESTON,Charles Albert Edward 2Lt dow 25-3-18 5 att23RFus p67 MR20
FRESTON,Hugh Reginald 2Lt kia 24-1-16 3 att6RBerks p139 CR France515
FRETTINGHAM,Arthur Cyril 2Lt ded 27-2-17 19WelshR p264 CR Notts84
FRETWELL,Arthur Richard Lt dow 1-4-18 5SomLI p218 CR France62,5WYorks
FREW,David Thomas Crichton TCapt ded 29-9-16 RAMC att2RIrR p195 CR Scot764
FREW,James Robertson TLtACapt dow 23-11-16 RFA 63Bde12Div p28 CR France177
FREW,John William.MC.TCapt dow 8-10-18 RAMC att2/3WRidFA p195 CR France146,Williamson
FREW,Robert Dunlop Black Capt kia 3-8-17 RAMC 1/3FA p253 CR Belgium11
FREY,Emile 2Lt kia 26-8-18 5Lond p246 CR France214
FRICKER,Albert Charles T2Lt kia 27-2-17 10EYorks p84 CR France156
FRICKER,Arthur Warwick TLt kia 29-5-16 1Nhampt p137 CR France149
FRICKER,Edwin T2Lt kia 29-9-16 7RWKent p141 MR21
FRIEAKE,Gordon Minter 2Lt ded 1-8-16 1/4 O&BLI p231 CR France145
FRIEDBERGER,William Sigismund Capt kia 24-5-15 3 att5RFus p67 MR29
FRIEND,Charles Philip Lt ded 15-10-18 RFA p28 CR Europe41
FRIEND,Frank Howard TLt dow 29-9-15 2Wilts p153 CR France201,Haward
FRIEND,George Burton Taddy TCapt kia 25-7-15 6EKent p57 CR Belgium33,26-7-15
FRIEND,Henry John T2Lt kia 4-10-17 8SomLI p79 CR Belgium116
FRIEND,James Bertie T2Lt kia 21-8-18 17 att13Lpool p71 MR16,Joseph
FRIEND,Joshua J.T2Lt kia 9-9-17 NumbF att20Bn p61 CR France1461
FRIEND,Philip Emlyn 2Lt kia 7-7-16 MGC p182 CR France267
FRIEND,Stanley John 2Lt dow 22-4-18 7RWSurr p55 CR France145
FRIPP,George 2Lt dow 4-6-18 1Dors p124 CR France924
FRIPP,John Trude 2Lt kia 13-10-15 3Lincs p75 MR19
FRIPP,Joseph Harry T2Lt ded 12-3-18 12RFus p67 CR Lancs164
FRIPP,Tom Olphert 2Lt kia 30-6-18 RGA 177SB p39 CR Belgium2
FRISCH,Charles 2Lt kia 17-4-16 IARO att1/9GurkhaRif p276 MR38
FRISCH,Maurice 2Lt kia 25-8-16 5 att2RB p178 MR19
FRISCHLING,Geoffrey Hepworth T2Lt kia 14-8-18 9 att12ESurr p112 CR Belgium11,Lt
FRITCHLEY,Joseph Bertram 2Lt kia 27-8-18 6Lond p247 MR16
FRITH,Henry George T2Lt kia 31-7-17 17Manch p154 MR29
FRITH,Reginald William Lt ded 7-2-18 Herts p270 CR Essex83
FRITH,William Wesson LtACapt kia 3-11-17 RGA 169SB p39 CR Belgium176
FRITZBROWN,Eric T2Lt kia 1-7-16 18Lpool p71
FRIZELL,Richard Alexander TCapt kia 10-11-17 2RMunstF p175 MR30
FRIZELLE,Archibald 2Lt kia 1-5-16 75RH&FA B'Bty p28 CR Belgium4
FRIZELLE,Edwin Samuel 2Lt kia 3-8-15 5LancF p221 CR Gallipoli1
FRIZONI,Oscar Lorenzo Lt kia 13-11-16 12EYorks p84 MR21
FRODSHAM,William Thomas Lt kia 9-9-16 5SLancs p230 CR France402
FROLICH,John Charles Cecil 2Lt kia 15-9-16 21Lond p251 CR France385
FROMANT,Herbert Dudley Sands T2Lt kia 29-4-17 26NumbF p61 CR France451
FROST,Alan Capt kia 17-10-17 28Lond att259MGC Inf p187&252 CR EAfrica11 &CR Tanzania1
FROST,Alfred Iago 2Lt kia 1-7-16 2Mddx p146 MR21,Ingo
FROST,Arthur 2Lt dow 23-3-18 2 att8Worc p108 MR27
FROST,Arthur Byfield.MC.Lt kia 23-3-18 4RWSurr p212 MR27
FROST,Arthur Colin T2Lt kia 25-9-15 11A&SH p173 MR19
FROST,Charles Dale Capt kia 22-11-15 IA 110MahrattaLI p276 MR38
FROST,Colin Blomfield TLt kia 24-7-18 44RFA p28 CR France248
FROST,Cyril Haddon TLt kia 26-10-18 RFA 403HB p29 MR38
FROST,E.H.Capt 8-9-20 MGC Inf CR War129

FROST,Edmund Lionel Lt kia 16-6-15 4SLancs p230 MR29
FROST,Eric George Capt kia 26-1-16 1/7Mddx p235 CR France768
FROST,Evelyn Fairfax Meadows Capt dow 20-12-15 5HLI p240 CR Gallipoli1
FROST,Francis Conrade Shenstone 2Lt kia 21-3-18 4 att8EKent p212 MR27
FROST,George SubCdr drd 1-1-17 IA S&TCps p276 MR35
FROST,George Jesse T2Lt dow 9-9-15 7Suff p78 CR France285
FROST,James John TLt kia 7-7-16 11NumbF p61 MR21
FROST,John Wiliam.MC.Lt ded 23-3-19 2Nhampt p137 CR Oxford69
FROST,Joshua 2Lt dow 29-9-16 8DLI p239 CR France453
FROST,Kenneth 2Lt kia 22-2-15 1RWKent p141 MR29
FROST,Kingdon Tregosse Lt kia 4-9-14 3Ches p96 MR15
FROST,Percy Causton T2Lt kia 8-9-18 KSLIatt10Bn p144 CR France364
FROST,Robert Wall 2Lt kia 3-7-16 10 att7Suff p78 MR21
FROST,Ronald William.MC.Lt kia 10-10-17 94RFA p29&258 CR Belgium19
FROST,Thomas Lawrence Capt&Adjt kia 28-3-15 1Ches p96 CR Belgium165,Laurence
FROST,William Edward.MM.2Lt ded 9-10-19 1Lincs p263 CR Ireland14,Lt 8-10-19
FROST,William Frank 2Lt kia 17-10-18 21RFA p208 CR France341
FROUD,Harold William Lt dow 27-7-17 5DLI p238 CR France518
FROWD-WALKER,R.S.CMG.LtCol 16-5-17 10Glouc CR Kent97
FRY,Alfred Andrew Capt ded 27-6-19 3Mon &RAF p244
FRY,Alfred Harold 2Lt dow 30-10-16 1/22Lond C'Coy p251 CR France40
FRY,Arthur Charles 2Lt dow 28-2-17 2/4 O&BLI D'Coy p231 CR France164
FRY,Charles Augustus Capt kia 1-4-18 6Ess att2GarBnSuff p232 CR France65,2-18
FRY,Charles Edward Lt kia 17-11-17 D23RFA p29 CR France266,17-4-17
FRY,Edward Meaburn.MC.Lt kia 23-8-18 D211RFA p207 CR France643
FRY,Edwin Harries Sargood Maj dow 25-5-18 RGA 126SB p209 CR France84
FRY,Horace Charles 2Lt ded 24-2-17 10RWKent attRFC p7,kld p18&235,5Bn p141,p212 CR Kent127,23-2-17
FRY,John Desford Lt kia 15-9-16 1Lond p244 CR France785
FRY,John Libby 2Lt kld 20-2-17 RFC p7 CR Wilts116
FRY,John Thomas Lt&QM ded 3-10-15 RAMC p195 CR France8
FRY,Leonard 2Lt kia 19-7-16 6Glouc p225 CR France525
FRY,Leslie.MC.2Lt dow 9-11-18 3RScotF attMGC p94&182
FRY,Leslie Harrington.MID Lt kia 9-8-18 19Huss p23 CR France652
FRY,Stephen Gabriel 2Lt kia 22-5-15 IARO att1/1GurkhaRif p276 MR28
FRY,Walter Burgess Maj ded PoW 17-3-15 RAMC p195 CR Germany4
FRY,Wilfred 2Lt dow 3-11-18 10Lond p248 CR France146
FRY,William Henry TLt dow 26-5-17 88MGC p182 CR France113
FRYE,Lionel Henry 2Lt kia 16-6-18 1/2 att1/5Glouc p106
FRYER,Charles William 2Lt dow 1-8-18 1/12LNLancs p135 CR France248
FRYER,Christopher John Gwynne.MC&Bar.Lt kia 4-11-18 1Herts p252 CR France206
FRYER,Eric Hamilton Lt kia 3-8-16 4 att2/5LancF p92 MR21
FRYER,James Whaley 2Lt kia 1-7-16 22NumbF p61 MR21
FRYER,John Maj ded 2-3-20 7Huss p261 CR Dorset53
FRYER,John Percival T2Lt kia 22-3-18 8BordR p117 MR20
FRYER,Stanley Phillipps 2Lt kia 27-10-18 30RFA attY1TMB p29 CR France127C
FRYER,William Arthur TLt kia 3-10-18 KRRC att4Bn p150 CR France234
FRYER,William Basil 2Lt kld 26-12-16 3/5SStaffs attRFC p18&229 CR Egypt1
FUDGE,Alfred TLt dow 22-2-18 9Suff att101RFC p16&78 CR France1063
FUGE,Frederick Henry TLt kia 13-8-16 6SomLI p79 MR21
FUGEMAN,William Alfred TCapt kia 1-12-17 23RFus C'Coy p67 CR France149
FULLALOVE,George Young 2Lt 13-8-17 55RFC CR France134
FULLARD,Norman 2Lt dow 22-5-18 5 att2YLI p235 CR France226
FULCHER,Bernard Vincent.MC.MIDx2Lt kia 17-11-14 2SLancs p125 MR29
FULCHER,Oliver Arthur 2Lt ded 29-6-16 RGA p39 CR Iraq6
FULFORD,Reginald Hardwick Chap4Cl kia 15-12-16 RAChDept p199 MR38
FULKES,John Greville 2Lt kia 13-11-16 3 att13Ess p131 MR21
FULLER,Bernard T2Lt kia 4-11-18 7RWKent p141 CR France660
FULLER,Charles Stephen.MC.T2Lt kia 11-11-17 GL &1RFC p7 CR France285
FULLER,Cyril John T2Lt dow 22-7-16 6RBerks p139 CR France141
FULLER,Dunstan Milley.MC.TCapt kia 10-8-17 11RFus p67 MR29
FULLER,Edward James.MC&Bar.MM.Lt ded 28-7-19 RGA 3Bty p262 CR Surrey
FULLER,Ernest Paget 2Lt kia 20-9-17 4 att10RWSurr p212 MR30
FULLER,Gardner Henry 2Lt ded 26-2-15 RASC p192&257
FULLER,Gordon Howard 2LtACapt kia 7-7-18 3 att2 O&BLI p130 CR France745
FULLER,H.2Lt 24-2-15 RASC CR Staffs108

...R,Henry Arthur.MID dow 26-4-18 RE 490LCp10 CR France29
FULLER,Herbert Foster Maj ded 8-11-19 IA S&TCps p276 MR43
FULLER,Herbert Walter 2Lt kia 21-8-18 14Lond p249 CR France285
FULLER,Hugh William 2Lt kia 18-9-18 5Suff p217 CR France369
FULLER,John Henry Middleton Capt kia 4-11-14 IA 83Inf att63PalamcottahLI p276 MR47,WallajahbadLI
FULLER,John Severn.MID LtTCapt ded 15-3-19 177RFA p29 CR Asia33
FULLER,Leonard Arthur Lt kia 17-5-17 8DLI att1RFC p18&239 CR France604
FULLER,Leslie Thomas Easterbrook 2Lt kia 18-9-16 24Lond p252 MR21
FULLER,Morris Richard T2Lt kia 11-4-17 10RFus p68 MR20
FULLER,Oliver Lionel 2Lt ded 18-10-18 PoW 20Lond p251 CR Germany1
FULLER,Percy D.2Lt kia 18-8-16 6DCLI p114 CR France402
FULLER,William Lt&QM 3-1-20 GL att1GarBnSomLI CR Europe5
FULLER,William Blyth Capt kia 16-5-15 2RWSurr p55 CR France279
FULLER-MAITLAND,William Alan Capt dow 19-9-14 1CldGds p57 MR15
FULLERTON,Frank T2Lt kia 31-7-17 LNLancs att 1/4Bn p135 MR29
FULLERTON,James Basil Lt kia 9-8-17 A240RFA p207 CR Belgium10
FULLERTON,John Kenneth Capt dow 15-8-17 1/6Glouc p225 CR Belgium20
FULLERTON,William Francis Hannan 2Lt kia 22-10-16 GL &RFC p2&190,ded CR France598
FULLIN,John Francis.MC.2Lt kia 22-3-18 5RMunstF p175 MR27
FULTON,Alexander T2Lt kia 19-8-16 13RScots p54 CR France515
FULTON,Andrew 2Lt kia 23-4-17 6A&SH p243 CR France434
FULTON,Andrew Wilfred TMaj kia 12-8-16 1/9Lpool p216 MR21
FULTON,Cecil John TLt dow 29-4-17 7RIrF p171 CR France80
FULTON,Charles Mathew Capt ded 23-7-20 IA 33Cav p276 MR67,24-7-20 23Cav
FULTON,D.T.MC MID Capt 11-8-20 RE IWT CR Egypt2
FULTON,Ernest Alan T2Lt kia 3-10-16 25 att 19Mddx p146 MR21
FULTON,George Koberwein.DSO.TCaptALtCol kia 14-4-18 9Ches p96 MR30 Ex6Wilts
FULTON,Harry Townsend.CMG.DSO.BrigGen dow 29-3-18 IA Cmdg3NZRifBde p276
FULTON,Hugh 2Lt kia 9-10-18 9HLI p240 CR France550
FULTON,James Fleming T2Lt kia 12-10-16 5CamH att26TMB p167 CR France385
FULTON,John Duncan Bertie.CB.MajTLtCol ded 11-11-15 RFA &RFC p1&29 CR Lond4
FULTON,Samuel Duff 2Lt ded 21-10-19 RGA p262 CR Scot288
FUNNELL,Cecil Herbert Michael Capt dow 30-4-16 RGA 128HB p39
FUNNELL,Harry Edward.DSO.TMaj ded 10-12-18 MGC attGHQ Italy p182 CR Italy65
FURBER,Gilbert George 2Lt dow 22-7-17 12Y&L p158 CR France113,Lt kia
FURLEY,Bernard Edward.MID TMaj kia 13-10-15 6EKent p57 MR19
FURLEY,Francis Edward Lt kia 22-3-18 1/4EYorks p219 CR France836
FURLEY,Percival Henry Biddulph 2Lt kia 1-6-19 IA 1/41Dogras p276 MR43
FURLEY,Robert Basil 2Lt kia 25-1-16 O&BLI BucksBn p231 CR France1327
FURLEY,Wolseley Haig.MID Lt kia 26-4-18 3RScots p54 MR30
FURLONG,Philip James T2Lt kia 30-7-16 19Lpool p71 MR21
FURMSTON,Clement Barrington T2Lt kia 9-4-17 154MGC Inf p182 CR France184
FURNEAUX,Phillip Templer Lt kia 26-10-14 1Lpool p71 MR29
FURNEAUX,William Edington.MC.TMaj kia 24-3-18 9SfthH p164 CR France511
FURNELL,Cecil Herbert Michael Capt 30-4-16 RGA 128HB CR Belgium11
FURNELL,Thomas Capt dow 31-7-18 1/7Ches p222 CR France145
FURNESS,Godfrey Gordon Lt kia 9-2-17 3 att2N&D p134 CR France423
FURNESS,James Collins LtCol kia 26-2-18 RAMC p195 MR40,drd
FURNESS,Montague Smith 2Lt kia 29-6-17 3/45RFA p29 CR Belgium115
FURNISS,Charles Frederick T2Lt dow 16-4-18 14Y&L p158 CR Belgium38
FURNISS,James 2Lt kia 31-7-17 4RIrRif p169 MR29
FURNISS,Kevin Robert Lt dow 29-4-17 PoW StaffsYeo att23RFC p18&205 CR France403
FURSE,Edmund William LtCol kld 19-5-18 88RFA p29 CR France1410
FURSE,George Armond Capt dow 16-9-14 44RFA p29 CR France1329,Armand
FURSE,William Henry T2Lt kia 1-7-16 21NumbF p61 CR France150,dow
FURZE,Alfred TCapt&Adjt kia 16-9-16 7YLI p143 MR21
FURZE,Claude Capt dow 6-4-18 5Lond p246 CR France2
FURZE,Frederick Capt kia 20-9-17 5Lond p246 MR29
FURZE,Nevil Ford 2Lt kia 14-3-17 2RWSurr p55 CR France514
FUSSELL,James Gerald Lt kia 1-7-16 1/8RWar p215 MR21
FUSSELL,John William Hugo 2Lt kia 19-7-16 3 att6 O&BLI p130 CR France525
FUTERS,Norman Ratcliffe LtACapt kia 27-9-18 1NumbF p61 CR France357
FYFE,Austyn James Claude 2Lt kia 23-3-17 RFA &55TMB p208 CR Belgium4
FYFE,Charles Clarke 2Lt kia 21-3-18 6BlkW p231 MR28

FYFE,Gilbert 2Lt 16-7-16 9HLI CR France833
FYFE,Thomas Alexander.MC.Capt dow 29-8-18 1/5HLI p240 CR France145
FYFE,William Quentin Lt kia 21-3-18 5GordH p242 MR27
FYFFE,John James T2Lt kia 14-9-16 13WYorks p81 CR France293
FYLDES,Aubrey William 2Lt kia 9-8-15 1/4ELancs p226 CR Gallipoli2
FYNN,Robert Charles T2Lt kia 25-3-18 4Beds p85 MR20 &CR France390
FYNNEY,Frederick Adolphus TLt ded 27-11-18 TankCps p266 CR Kent175,Capt ExLpool
FYSH,Charles Edward.DSO.MC&Bar.Maj kia 28-7-18 6SfthH p241 CR France1697
FYSON,Geoffrey Lt kia 4-9-18 3 att1RScots p54 MR37
FYSON,George Dumill T2Lt kia 20-4-16 11Glouc p106 MR38,Dumillo 7Bn
FYSON,Harold George 2Lt kia 12-10-16 2Beds p85 MR21
FYVIE,William 2Lt kia 26-8-17 3RScots p54 CR France1461

G

GABAIN,William George.MC.Capt kia 24-3-18 Inns of CourtOTC SL att 2RB p201&252 CR France605
GABB,Richard George T2Lt dow 6-8-15 12 att1Ess p131 CR Gallipoli6
GABB,Stanley Frederick T2Lt dow 8-12-16 76MGC p182 CR France169
GABBETT,Pulteney Charles LtCol ded 11-7-16 IMS p276 CR Iraq5
GABBETT,Richard Edward Phillip LtCol kia 16-5-15 1RWFus p97 CR France279,Phillips
GABBETT-FAIRFAX,Thomas Oliver 2Lt kia 14-8-17 11RB p178 MR29
GABELL,Douglas Ridley Clunes 2Lt kld 12-7-18 Glouc &RAF p264
GABRIEL,Allan TLt dow 23-8-16 15N&D att105TMB p134 CR France23
GADDUM,Russell Charles Sydney T2Lt kia 10-9-16 17RFus p68 CR France344
GADNEY,Gilbert Sims T2Lt kia 3-7-16 8Glouc p106 MR21
GADSDEN,Crawford Cunningham Lt dow 16-10-17 4RWSurr att101RFC p18&212 CR France134
GADSDON,Frank Bannatyne T2Lt kia 7-6-17 9Ches p96 CR Belgium153
GAFFIKIN,George Horner TMaj kia 1-7-16 9RIrRif B'Coy p169 CR France396
GAFFNEY,James.MC.TCapt kia 8-10-18 RDubF p176 CR France844
GAFFNEY,Leon Arthur T2Lt dow 12-8-15 6RMunstF p175 CR Gallipoli27
GAGE,Brenton Albert Hamilton.MC.MIDx2 LtTCapt dow 29-5-15 7/4RFA p29 CR France631
GAGE,John Capt ded 7-11-16 11RDubF p176
GAGE,John Munro TCapt ded 29-11-18 RAMC p195 CR Greece2,att57RFA
GAGE,John Stewart Moore 2Lt kia 1-7-16 9RInniskF p105 MR21
GAGLIARDI,Louis Patrick.MID Capt accdrd 5-9-17 IARO att37Lancers p276 CR Iraq5
GAGNE,John 2Lt kia 24-5-17 GL &43RFC p7 MR20
GAILLIE,O.E.DSO.MC.Capt kia 7-12-17 RH&FA p29
GAINEY,Henry Charles T2Lt kia 14-7-16 8Dev p76 CR France453
GAIR,Henry Burgh 2Lt dow 15-5-18 4Dors att14PnrCoy p229 CR France84,13-5-18,1Bn
GAIR,Thomas Lt kia 10-9-17 A276RFA p207 MR30,9-9-17
GAISFORD,Lionel Lt kia 23-11-14 IA 58Rif WAFF p276 CR France80
GAISFORD,Robert Sandeman Lt kia 30-1-18 RFA att34RFC p16&29 CR Italy9,Capt
GAISFORD,Walter Thomas MajTLtCol kia 25-9-15 7SfthH p164 MR19
GAITSKELL,Cyril Egremont Lt dow 19-10-14 2Leinst p174 CR France922
GALBRAITH,Alexander Norman Capt 16-2-15 CeylonPlantersRifCps CR Eire541
GALBRAITH,Alfred Hugh T2Lt kld 24-2-18 57TrSqnRFC p16 Egypt8
GALBRAITH,Arthur Hugh Courtney Lt dow 9-9-18 RGA 285SB 83Bde p39 CR France145,Courtrey 284SB
GALBRAITH,David Boyd 2Lt kia 20-8-15 7HLI p240 CR Gallipoli1
GALBRAITH,Donald James Findlay Lt kia 25-1-15 9HLI p240 CR France765
GALBRAITH,James Robert 2Lt ded 20-9-17 A64RFA p29 CR Belgium8
GALBRAITH,Norman Dunlop Lt kia 22-8-18 7HLI p240 CR France113
GALBRAITH,William Brodie Lt dow 14-7-15 7HLI p240 CR Gallipoli1
GALBRAITH,William Thomas T2Lt kld 26-2-18 RFC p16 CR Scot214
GALE,Arthur Witherby.DSO.TCapt kia 10-4-16 2LifeGds attRFA RoO p20 CR Belgium11
GALE,Charles William Lt ded 20-2-19 Ex16GarrBn YLI p265 CR Surrey57
GALE,Harold William T2Lt kia 8-8-18 7RSuss att5RBerks p119 France141
GALE,Henry James 2Lt kia 21-3-18 1Lincs p75 MR27
GALE,Henry John Elliott.MC.MM.T2Lt kia 7-6-18 RE 1SpCoy p45 CR France31,8-6-18
GALE,Herbert Anthony.MC&Bar.ACapt dow 12-8-18 6 att2Wilts A'Coy p153 CR France31
GALE,John Hugh 2Lt kia 14-9-16 70RFC p2 CR France374

GALE,Marmaduke Henry Littledale Maj kia 28-6-15 IA 8Cav p276 MR66
GALE,Ralph George 2LtTLt kia 12-10-17 8SStaffs p122 MR30
GALE,Ralph Goulstone TLt kia 26-3-18 RE B SpecCo p45 CR France570
GALE,Robert Grafton TLt kia 24-4-18 RASC 24DSC att2/5Glouc p192 CR France248
GALE,William Newlyn Capt kia 3-5-17 4Y&L p238 MR20
GALL,Campbell McKenzie Lt kia 18-8-18 6KOSB p101 MR32
GALL,Grant Lt kia 21-3-18 3RScots attRE 3FdSurvCo p54 CR France245
GALL,William John Reid 2Lt dow 18-4-18 RGA 346SB p39 CR France31
GALLAGHER,Roland Henry Capt ded 25-6-15 MGC p182 CR France102
GALLAGHER,William Augustine.MID Capt kia 12-3-15 2ELancs p110 CR France1106,10-3-15
GALLAUGHER,Henry.DSO.Capt kia 7-6-17 11RInniskF p105 CR Belgium62
GALLAUGHER,Robert Rankin T2Lt ded 23-2-17 4Worc p108 CR France300
GALLETLEY,Ian Lt kia 3-8-16 C258RFA p207 CR France188
GALLEY,Ralph Rowlands 2Lt kia 22-3-18 11DLI A'Coy p160 CR France1206
GALLICHAN,Francis Ernest 2Lt kia 28-7-16 10NStaffs att99MGC p157 CALLICHAN &182 MR21,27-7-16
GALLIE,Arthur Lockhart Maj ded 23-9-15 Dors p124 CR Devon237
GALLIE,Charles 2Lt kia 22-8-15 RScotF attRFC p1&94 CR France924
GALLIE,Edward Archibald TLt kia 1-7-16 17HLI D'Coy p162 CR France293
GALLIE,Oscar Eugene.DSO.MC.Capt kia 7-12-17 A156RFA CR Belgium10
GALLIERS,Richard Sidney 2LtACapt kia 31-5-18 2Wilts p153 CR France1689
GALLIMORE,Henry Burrows Capt kia 26-5-17 D312RFA p207 CR France568
GALLIMORE,Hubert Thomas Keith Lt kia 29-3-18 4KSLI att6Ches p235 MR27
GALLINGER,George Harry T2Lt kia 31-10-17 GL &18RFC p7 CR France88
GALLO,Antonio Marie.MC.2Lt kia 31-7-17 5Beds p219 MR29
GALLOWAY,Bernard Thomas 2Lt kia 6-10-16 8Mddx p236 MR21
GALLOWAY,Frederick Philip TLt dow 12-11-17 27RFC p7 CR France40
GALLOWAY,Graeme Stuart Montgomerie T2Lt kia 4-7-16 4Lpool p71 CR France114
GALLOWAY,Harold Bessemer CaptTMaj kia 25-9-15 7SforthH p164 MR19
GALLOWAY,James Blyth 2Lt ded 17-11-18 RFA p208 MR65
GALLOWAY,Reginald Edgar Charles TCapt ded 11-2-19 RAOC 121Coy p198 CR France40
GALLOWAY,Robert Herbert 2Lt kia 24-3-18 8TanksCps p188 CR France245
GALLOWAY,Ronald Moncrief Lt kia 28-6-15 7RScots p211 MR4
GALLOWAY,William Ernest 2Lt kia 6-11-17 1/4WelshR p230 CR Palestine1
GALSWORTHY,Edgar T2Lt kia 27-9-18 11TankCps p188 CR France379
GALSWORTHY,Lionel Richmond Lt 8-3-21 RFA CR Norf101
GALTON,Francis William Joseph.MID Lt kia 23-4-17 1Dev p76 MR20
GALTON,Theodore Hugh 2Lt kia 21-10-14 Worc att3Bn p108 MR22
GALTRY,Raymond T2Lt kia 9-10-17 1/2 att6Yorks p90 MR30
GALWAY,Edgar Seaman SubCdr kia 7-5-15 IA S&TCps p276 CR Gallipoli30
GALWAY,Reginald Hugh Maj dow 15/17-2-15 RGA 80Coy p39 CR Asia45,15-2-15
GAMBELL,Dennis Clayton Lt kia 30-4-18 2/19Lond p250 MR34
GAMBLE,Frank Burfield 2Lt kia 1-7-16 1/7N&D p233 CR France281
GAMBLE,George T2Lt dow 24-9-17 2RB p178 CR France262
GAMBLE,Hugh Valentine Lt kia 3-5-17 2SfthH p164 CR France546
GAMBLE,James Frederick 2Lt kia 24-6-16 1RWar p64 CR France35,Lt 25-6-16
GAMBLE,John Walcote TLt dow 22-5-16 2DLI B'Coy p160 CR Belgium11,14Bn
GAMBLE,Ralph Dominic.MC.Lt kia 22-8-18 1CldGds p51 CR France103
GAMBLE,Richard Maurice Brooks 2Lt kia 16-5-15 7Lpool p215 CR France279
GAMBLE,Richard Sumner 2Lt kia 22-5-15 7ELancs att1/1GurkhaRif p264&276 MR22
GAMBLE,Walter Rayes.MC.TCapt dow 12-6-17 9Yorks p90 CR Belgium11,Raynes
GAMBLIN,John Louis 2Lt kia 8-5-15 RFA p29 MR29
GAME,Hubert John TLt kld 8-6-17 RFA &RFC p7&29 CR Norf247
GAME,Reginald Francis 2Lt ded 10-10-18 3BlkW att60MGC Inf p128 CR Palestine9
GAME,Walter Harold 2Lt kia 23-4-17 5Yorks p221 MR20
GAMESON,George Henry Molyneux 2Lt dow 14-3-17 3 att8NumbF p61 CR France514
GAMLEN,Robert Arthur Winnington LtACapt kia 30-11-17 4Worc p108 CR France1483
GAMMAN,Edward 2Lt kia 26-10-17 RGA 306SB p39 MR30
GAMMAN,Gilbert T2Lt kia 10-8-15 5Wilts p153 MR4
GAMMELL,Henry Stobart.MC.LtACapt kia 31-8-18 1GordH p166 CR France927
GAMMIE,Herbert Forsyth TLt kia 14-9-18 1CamH att7NStaffs p167 CR Asia81
GAMON,John Lionel Percival Lt kldacc 4-6-18 1BordR att51NumbF p117 CR Ches30
GAMON,Maurice Partridge TCapt kia 1-7-16 2LancF p92 CR France1890

GAMON,Sidney Percival Capt kld 23-3-18 5Ches attRFC p18&222 CR Ches117,Sydney
GANDAMALL,James Rev ded 10-10-18 IA CR Iraq6
GANDAR-DOWER,Leonard Francis 2Lt ded PoW 3-5-17 2HAC p206 MR20
GANDER,Leslie Stephen T2Lt dow 5-6-18 SfthH att1/4Bn p164 CR France40
GANDON,Ralph T2Lt kia 26-9-16 Dors att7Bn p124 MR21
GANDY,Clement Joseph.MC.2Lt kia 31-7-17 RE 234FC p45 CR Belgium96
GANDY,George Joseph 2Lt kia 15-5-17 2Leic p87 CR France727
GANDY,William Hendry.MID Capt kia 12-7-15 7HLI p240 MR4,Henry
GANE,Wilfred Errol.MC.Lt dow 8-12-17 D301RFA p207 CR Palestine3
GANLY,Roger.MC.Capt kia 29-9-16 LancF att11Bn p92 MR21
GANNON,John Howard T2Lt kld 9-10-17 3 att11RWFus p97 CR Greece6,8-10-
GANSON,Andrew T2Lt kia 14-12-16 10HLI p162 CR France392
GANT,Alfred Claude T2Lt kia 17-10-16 2KRRC p150 CR France341
GANT,Harold Holden 2Lt kia 1-9-18 2Lond p245 CR France216
GANT,Leslie John Lt ded 15-7-19 RH&FA 19BdeAmmCol p261 CR Egypt1
GANTSMAN,Ernest T2Lt kia 10-11-17 KRRC att9Bn p150 CR Belgium10
GARBETT,Ronald Vivian T2Lt kia 5-1-18 10RFC p16 CR Belgium11
GARBUTT,James Reston Gardiner TLt kia 1-12-15 RAMC att8KOSB p195 CR France423
GARBUTT,Lawrence Mark T2Lt dow 10-8-18 3Ess att9Norf p131 CR France142
GARD,Frederick TLt kia 28-6-18 1DCLI p114 CR France20
GARDEN,Charles Robert John 2Lt ded 5-5-16 B69RFA p29 CR Iraq5
GARDEN,John James 2Lt kia 3-5-17 5RWSurr p212 CR France357
GARDINER,Alec Maj kia 20-12-14 RE p45 MR22
GARDINER,Alexander Anson 2Lt kia 26-1-17 IARO att13/2S&M p276 CR Iraq5
GARDINER,Archibald Macalister T2Lt dow 24-5-16 12A&SH p173 CR France80,11Bn
GARDINER,Arthur Lt dow 26-3-18 19Lond p250 CR Palestine9
GARDINER,Ashley James T2Lt dow 24-10-18 1SomLI A'Coy p79 CR France241
GARDINER,Charles Lt kia 25-4-18 4 att6KOSB p223 MR30
GARDINER,Charles Thomas 2Lt dow 1-6-15 3RFus p68 CR France102
GARDINER,Ellis Hubert Lt dow 7-10-18 1/7Ches A'Coy p223 CR Belgium11
GARDINER,Eric John Lt kia 19-4-17 5Norf p216 MR34
GARDINER,Ernest.MID Maj kia 2-3-15 RE 1FC p209 MR29
GARDINER,Evelyn Francis.MC.Lt kia 30-7-16 3SfthH att90MGC p182 MR21
GARDINER,Francis John 2Lt ded 28-3-17 IARO att40Pathans p276 CR EAfrica38 &CR Tanzania1
GARDINER,Frederick Thomas LtACapt kia 31-7-17 HLI att12Bn p162 MR29
GARDINER,Godfrey Deman T2Lt kia 13-9-16 9Suff p78 MR21,GARDNER Derm
GARDINER,Ivan Jephson Lt drd 27-5-18 5Norf &RAF p216 MR41
GARDINER,James Totton 2Lt dow PoW 1-11-18 RIrRif p169 CR Belgium342
GARDINER,Kenneth Edward MacAlpine T2Lt ?? 17-10-15 14RFus att8Lond p68 CR France219
GARDINER,Kenneth John Rattray LtTCapt ded 1-2-17 SL RE att2/3KAR SL p202 MR46
GARDINER,Paul Wrey Lt kia 27-5-18 4Manch att1Worc p154 MR18
GARDINER,Robert Edward 2Lt kia 26-7-17 RGA 285SB p39 CR Belgium17
GARDINER,Stanley Tysol T2Lt kia 27-6-16 RE 55FC p45 CR Belgium6,Tysoe
GARDINER,William Edward Mansfield 2Lt kia 20-7-16 5Lond p246 CR France2
GARDINER,William MacPherson T2Lt kia 16-1-18 RB p178 MR30
GARDNER,Albert Abercrombie T2Lt kia 23-4-17 8SfthH p164 CR France536
GARDNER,Alex Young Fraser Lt ded 15-11-18 RASC p253 CR Scot237
GARDNER,Alfred Ernest 2Lt kia 13-1-17 1/4YLI p235 CR France504
GARDNER,Alfred Linton TCapt kia 9-4-18 RAMC 107FA att4NStaffs p195 CR France41,10-4-18
GARDNER,Andrew Abercrombie Lt kia 6-9-18 6A&SH att57MGC Inf p187&243 CR France309
GARDNER,Arnold 2Lt ded 13-7-19 10RSuss p264
GARDNER,Burnett Gilroy Craufurd 2Lt ded 7-5-15 RE 171TC p45 CR France1,Crawford
GARDNER,Caldwell Lt kia 11-9-16 6A&SH p243 CR France394
GARDNER,Cyril Gower Lt kia 14-9-16 2 att3GrenGds p50 MR21
GARDNER,Eric Mawdsley 2Lt kia 10-4-17 3SomLI p79 MR20
GARDNER,Eric Melford 2Lt kia 27-9-18 8 att28Lond p247 CR France1496
GARDNER,Francis Henry T2Lt dow 17-10-18 1/2Leic p87 CR France847
GARDNER,Frederick George Benjamin T2Lt kia 25-7-16 D166RFA p29 CR France188
GARDNER,George Capt kia 21-8-15 21Lancers attBucksYeo p23 CR Gallipoli5
GARDNER,George Ryding Sankey Maj ded 26-6-16 B265RFA p206 CR Egypt8,Sanky

GARDNER,Henry Montfort LtCol 28-10-18 4Lincs CR Glouc27
GARDNER,James 2Lt kldacc 27-11-16 RFC p2 CR Scot810
GARDNER,John.MC.TCapt dow 27-9-17 6/7RScotF p94 CR Scot674
GARDNER,Leonard Clement Lt dow 2-6-18 RGA 139HB p39 CR France69
GARDNER,Maurice Leigh 2Lt kld 19-1-15 RFC p1 CR Mddx26
GARDNER,Maurice Reginald George 2Lt kia 27-5-18 1Worc p108 MR18
GARDNER,Norman T2Lt kia 2-10-18 3WRid att16LancF p115 CR France237,Capt
GARDNER,Richard Pringle McKay 2Lt kia 18-8-16 2A&SH p173 CR France393,GARDENER
GARDNER,Robert 2Lt kia 5-5-15 5RLancs p213 MR29
GARDNER,Robert Bell 2Lt kia 7-1-18 5HLI p240 CR Palestine9
GARDNER,Robert MacGregor Stewart Maj kld 31-10-14 1Glouc p106 MR29
GARDNER,Robert Oswald Capt kia 8-5-15 3Mon B'Coy p244 CR Belgium152
GARDNER,Sidney T2Lt kia 27-3-18 11ELancs p110 MR20
GARDNER,Thomas Lt kia 22-7-16 2/20Lond p251 CR France68,28-7-16
GARDNER,Wedderburn Mackenzie T2Lt dow 23-8-17 8SfthH p164 CR Belgium11
GARDNER,William T2Lt kia 24-3-18 10 att15DLI p160 MR27
GARDNER,William Bristow.MC.T2LtACapt kia 28-3-18 2Wilts p153 MR27
GARDNER,William James 2Lt dow 26-9-16 1Leic attWYorks p87 CR France329
GARDNER,William Sutton 2Lt kia 6-3-17 RFA att57RFC p29&7 CR France46
GARDNER,Wilie T2Lt dow 17-10-17 WYorks att1/8Bn p81 CR France64
GARDOM,John Charles TLt kia 6-8-15 12 att1Ess p131 CR Gallipoli6
GARFIT,Thomas Noel Cheney Lt kia 30-4-15 2DLI p160 CR France1140
GARFORTH,William Godfrey Willoughby Lt kia 16-5-15 2ScotsGds p52 CR France705
GARLAND,Cecil William Robert 2Lt kia 20-2-18 Lpool att1/7Bn p71 CR France765
GARLAND,Francis Henry 2Lt kia 23-10-18 4 att8Glouc p225 CR France270
GARLAND,George Arthur T2Lt kia 16-9-16 21DLI p160 MR21
GARLAND,George Harry Charles 2Lt ded 4-3-17 RFA 113Bty 25Bde p29 CR France833
GARLAND,James Harvey Lt dow 12-11-15 5GordH p242 CR France43
GARLAND,James Richard TCapt kia 1-7-16 2Lond p245 CR France798
GARLAND,John Jeffrey T2Lt dow 9-7-18 1/2Glouc p106 CR France21,James
GARLAND,Wilfred.MID T2Lt kia 8-5-17 7 O&BLI p130 MR37,Wilfrid
GARLICK,Charles Sidney T2Lt dow 16-7-16 8Wilts p153 CR France141,20KRRC
GARLICK,Frank Arthur 2Lt kia 20-2-16 13RFC p2 CR France448
GARLICK,Hilda Mary SNurse ded 12-8-17 TFNS CR War7
GARLICK,John Munro Lt dow 2-12-17 4A&SH p173 CR France398
GARLICK,Vivian Lt kia 15-6-18 O&BLI 1/4BucksBn p231 CR Italy2
GARMENT,Leonard Charles T2Lt kia 21-3-18 10LancF p92 MR20
GARNER,A.E.C. Sister ded 12-3-17 QAIMNS p200 CR Mddx13
GARNER,Edward Harold 2Lt kia 27-8-18 4Lond p246 MR16
GARNER,Frank Leslie T2Lt kld 20-12-16 GL &RFC p2&190
GARNER,Reginald William T2Lt kia 13-11-16 MGC p182 CR France156
GARNER,Robert Leonard 2Lt kia 24-8-18 11Lond p248 MR16
GARNER,Walter Percy 2Lt kia 13-4-18 18WelchR p264 CR France1059
GARNER-SMITH,Eric John Lt kia 25/26-5-15 1/24Lond MR22
GARNET,Grosvenor 2Lt kia 9-10-17 3LancF p92 CR Belgium83
GARNETT,Alfred Edward 2Lt kia 29-9-17 3Y&L p158 CR France550,30-9-17 2Bn
GARNETT,Claude Lionel Capt dow 31-12-15 RGA 86HB p39 CR Iraq1,30-12-15
GARNETT,Errol Russell Maj kia 18-10-16 2Wilts p153 CR France385
GARNETT,Ewanda Berckeley T2Lt kld 27-1-18 RFC p16
GARNETT,Harold Gwyer CaptAMaj kia 3-12-17 SWBord p100 MR17
GARNETT,Henry Knowles Lt ded 6-11-15 RFA p207
GARNETT,Ivan William T2Lt kia 12-2-16 6KSLI p144 CR Belgium101
GARNETT,Jerry Knowles Lt ded 6-11-15 3ELancsRFA p207 CR Europe1
GARNETT,Kenneth Gordon.MC.TLt dow 22-8-17 RH&FA p29
GARNETT,Laurence Henry TLt kia 7-6-17 A110RFA p29 CR Belgium6
GARNETT,Phillip Nigel Lt dow 11-10-14 RBerks att1KAR p139&268 CR EAfrica80
GARNETT,William Herbert Stuart TLt kld 21-9-16 GL &RFC p2&190 CR Wilts116
GARNETT,William Patrick Lt dow 30-3-17 3RBerks attRFC p7&139 CR France81
GARNETT-BOTFIELD,Alfred Clulow Fitzgerald Lt kia 9-5-15 SWBord p100 MR22
GARNETT-BOTFIELD,Charles Sidney.MID Capt dow 14-12-14 2Beds p85 CR Shrop100
GARNHAM,Percival 2Lt ded 25-10-18 6Glouc p225 CR Italy11
GARNIER,Denys Keppel Capt dow 7-12-16 2Glouc p106 CR Greece3,6-12-16
GARNIER,John Warren Capt dow 29-5-15 3RWSurr p55 CR Sussex178,28-5-15
GARNONS-WILLIAMS,A.Aylmer Curtis.MC.Capt ded 14-5-18 SWBord &RAF p100 CR Sussex27
GARNONS-WILLIAMS,Richard Davie LtCol kia 25-9-15 12RFus p68 MR19,Davies

GARRAD,Edward Victor T2Lt kia 22-4-16 14RFus att6LNLancs p68 MR38
GARRARD,Frederick George.MC.2Lt dow 22-5-18 2GordH p166 CR Italy10
GARRARD,Harry Vernon Lt kia 2-11-14 BordR p117
GARRARD,Percy.DCM.Maj ded PoW 18-9-18 4KAR att24Lond p252,202&268 CR EAfrica77,24Lond att2/4KAR
GARRARD,Reginald Herbert T2Lt kia 23-4-17 16KRRC p150 CR France568
GARRARD,Stanley Charles T2Lt kia 28-8-15 14 att8RB p178 CR Belgium84
GARRARD,William Garth Blackall Lt kld 19-10-17 2NumbF p61 CR Greece1
GARRATT,Leslie Thomas T2Lt dow 3-7-16 32RFus p68 CR France285
GARRATT,Reginald Horatio 2Lt kia 29-9-17 GL &1RFC p7 MR20,GARRATT-REED 20-9-17
GARRAWAY,Wilfrid Fletcher 2Lt accdrd 5-11-16 IA 82Punjabis p276 CR Iraq5
GARRETT,Arthur Dale 2Lt kia 17-4-18 RE 456FC p45 MR30
GARRETT,Arthur ffolliott.OBE.Maj 28-3-20 RE CR France1571
GARRETT,Charles Harold Rev kia 26-9-17 RAChDept att2/6SStaffs p199 CR Belgium8
GARRETT,Dalton Gilbert Knox Lt kia 30-9-18 RAMC att133FA p195 CR France511
GARRETT,Henry Fawcett TCapt kia 22-8-15 6EYorks p84 CR Gallipoli5
GARRETT,Henry William 2Lt kia 24-3-18 20Lond p251 MR20
GARRETT,Hubert Frederick Lt kia 4-6-15 6EYorks p84 MR4,9Bn att1RDubF
GARRETT,Hyde Tregillas 2Lt kia 20-5-17 GL &23RFC p7 MR20,Tregellas
GARRETT,Maurice Humphris 2Lt kia 2-9-18 15Lond p249 MR16
GARRETT,Stephen Capt kia 12-3-15 4Suff p217 CR France768
GARRETT,William Oakley 2Lt kia 24-11-15 IARO att3S&M p277MR38,22/24-11-15
GARRETT,William Robert 2Lt ded 6-5-19 11N&D p134 CR Nhampt1
GARRETT-SMITH,Louis Lt dow 31-7-15 RE 61FC SR p45 CR Belgium5
GARRETY,J.F.T2Lt kia 21-9-18 ScotRif att1Bn p103 CR France666
GARRIOCH,John Thomas LtAMaj dow 3-4-18 RGA 173SB p39 CR France169,GARRIOCK
GARRITT,John Crossland 2Lt kia 30-5-17 7WYorks att1/6DLI p218 CR France622,1-6-18
GARROD,Alfred Noel TLt kia 25-1-16 RAMC att100FA p195 CR France80
GARROD,Basil Rahere Lt ded 4-2-19 1LNLancs &149RAF p135 CR Germany1
GARROD,Ronald Percival 2Lt kia 22-5-15 6Lond p247 CR France260
GARROD,Thomas Martin 2Lt dow 10-5-15 3LNLancs p136 CR France80,Lt
GARRUD,Owen Henry Lt kia 24-8-18 8Lond p247 CR France1187
GARRY,John Lt kia 12-2-17 IARO att102Gren p277 CR Iraq5,2Lt
GARRY,Kenneth T2Lt dow 18-6-17 13NumbF p61 CR France512
GARSIA,Oliver Dunham Melville Lt dow 18-9-14 2 att1DCLI p114 MR15
GARSIDE,Frank Gerald Lt kia 27-8-18 9Lond p248 CR France560
GARSIDE,Thomas Oughtibridge 2Lt kia 5-4-17 4RBerks p234 CR France1495
GARSTIN,Charles William North 2Lt dow 24-8-14 9Lancers p22 CR Belgium197
GARSTIN,Denys Norman.DSO.MC.TLtACapt kia 15-8-18 MGC p182 MR70 &CR Europe179,Denis 10Huss
GARSTIN,William Fortescue Colborne TMaj kia 7-8-15 5RIrF p171 CR Gallipoli ,9-8-15
GARTON,Arthur T2Lt kia 24-9-18 2RSuss p119 CR France375
GARTON,Arthur Richmond,MID Lt kia 26-4-15 6NumbF p213 MR29
GARTON,Edward Clive 2Lt dow 2-9-18 5RB p178 CR France1182
GARTON,Herbert Westlake TCapt kia 15-9-16 9RB p178 MR21
GARTON,Reginald William TLt kia 1-7-16 11SLancs p125 MR21
GARTON-SPRENGER,H.A Lt 25-7-21 4Beds CR SAfrica72
GARTSIDE-TIPPINGE,Francis 2Lt kia 6-11-17 GL &19RFC p7 MR20
GARVAN,Edmund William Lt kia 23-4-17 RFA 80Bty p29 CR France557
GARVEY,Ivan Harold.MC.Capt dow 20-2-17 3 att6ConnRgrs p172 CR Belgium17
GARVIE,Alexander Cockburn 2Lt kia 23-4-17 1/6BlkW p231 CR France604,Coburn
GARVIE,Ernest Leonard,MC 2Lt ded 15-6-18 9HLI attTMB p240 CR France142
GARVIE,James Alexander.MC.Lt kia 21-8-18 2KOSB p101 CR France798
GARVIE,Peter Thomas TLtACapt kia 25-6-17 RGA 13SB p39 CR Belgium29
GARVIN,Gerard Capt 22-7-16 7SLancs MR21
GARVIN,Roland Gerard TCapt kia 22-7-16 7SLancs p125 MR21
GARVIN,Samuel 2Lt kia 27-3-17 9 att1/7RWFus p97 CR Palestine8
GARVIN,William Myles Frederick T2Lt kia 23-9-17 1Ess p131 MR30
GARWOOD,Gerald Dennis 2Lt kia 13-11-16 4 att15RWar p64
GASCOIGNE,Ivo Clifton Lt dow 12-4-18 1GrenGds p50 CR France225
GASCOYNE,Charles Capt dow PoW 8-5-17 2/7N&D p233 CR France716
GASCOYNE,Francis Paul 2Lt kia 22-3-18 8 att11RWar p215 MR27
GASCOYNE,William Elhanan 2Lt kia 22-8-17 2/4 O&BLI p231 CR Belgium125

GASCOYNE-CECIL,John Arthur.MC.Capt kia 27-8-18 75RFA p207 CR France214
GASCOYNE-CECIL,Randle William Lt kia 1-12-17 RH&FA p207 MR17
GASCOYNE-CECIL,Rupert Edward Lt kia 11-7-15 1Beds CR Belgium127
GASELEE,Alec Mansel 2Lt kia 24-5-15 15Huss p22 MR29
GASHION,Stanley Michael 2Lt kia 8-5-17 1ESurr p112 MR20
GASKAIN,Cecil Stavley Lt kia 7-5-17 RA attRFC p18&207 MR20
GASKELL,Arnold Joseph 2Lt kia 2-11-18 12NorfYeo D'Coy p204 CR Belgium140
GASKELL,David Lyndsay Stranack T2Lt dow 12-1-16 16WelshR p126 CR France495,Lt dedacc
GASKELL,Frank Hill TLtCol dow 17-5-16 16WelshR p126 CR France345
GASKELL,John Charles Temple Capt kia 5-8-17 IA 69Punjabis att129Baluchis p277 CR EAfrica38 &CR Tanzania1,Maj
GASKELL,Joseph Lt&QM ded 5-4-17 NSomYeo p205 CR Essex146
GASKELL,Reginald Robinson Lt kld 15-12-16 RE attRFC p18&210 CR Yorks3
GASKELL,Lawrence Norris T2Lt dow 1-3-18 RFC p16 CR France15
GASKELL,Wallis William Penn 2Lt kia 25/26-5-15 24Lond p252 MR22,25/26-6-15
GASKIN,Robert Bertram T2Lt kia 9-9-17 23NumbF p61 CR France1461
GASPER,Horace Le Geyt Lt kia 20-12-19 IA 2/119Inf att1/103MahrattaLI p277 MR43,19-12-19
GASSON,R.S.Lt 25-12-17 6Mddx CR Lond10
GASTON,James.MC.TCapt dow 5-11-18 RAMC att4Suff p195 CR France1059
GATACRE,Edward George Capt dow 20-2-16 2WRid p115 CR France3
GATACRE,John Kirwan.MID Capt kia 12-10-14 IA 11Lancers att4Huss p277 CR France324,13-10-14
GATCHELL,James Harcourt Cecil.MC.TCapt kia 27-9-17 RAMC att11Suss p195 CR Belgium167
GATE,Leslie Charles Thomas 2Lt kia 30-10-17 10Beds p86 MR30
GATEHOUSE,John 2Lt ded 25-3-16 IARO att6Jats p277 CR Iraq6
GATEHOUSE,Richard Francis Capt kia 13-9-14 NumbF p61 CR France864
GATELY,John Edward Lt ded 13-6-16 IARO att2Lancers &MGC p277 CR Lancs169,3-6-17
GATENSBY,Samuel TLt ded 24-11-18 10RIrRif p169 CR Ireland33,5-11-19 15Bn
GATES,Alan Ferrier 2Lt dow 20-8-17 B307RFA p29 CR Belgium8,21-8-17
GATES,Alfred William.MC.MID 2Lt kia 3-7-16 3 at2SLancs p125 MR21
GATES,Arthur Noel T2Lt kia 1-3-17 RE 176TC p45 MR20
GATES,Douglas Leslie 2Lt kia 1-10-15 1Suff p78 MR19
GATES,Eric Chasemore Lt kia 14-3-15 13Lond p249 CR France710,Capt 12-3-15
GATES,Henry T2Lt kia 18-10-18 RE 23FC p45 CR France1268
GATES,Horace John T2Lt kia 19-11-17 EKent &RFC 16Wing p57 CR Greece 3
GATFIELD,Reginald Alfred Lt dow 7-6-17 16Lond attMGC Inf p187&249 CR France297
GATH,Charles Henry 2Lt kia 30-10-14 3Huss p21 MR29
GATHORNE-HARDY,Alfred Cecil TCapt kia 25-9-15 9ScotRif p103 MR19
GATRELL,Reginald James Hurst.MC.Lt kia 1-7-16 3 att1EYorks p84 MR21
GATTENS,Charles Lt kld 15-6-19 RE &RAF p45
GATWARD,Frederick James.MM.T2Lt dow 25-4-18 13TankCps p188 CR Belgium11
GAUKROGER,Hubert T2Lt kia 2-4-17 1Manch p154 CR France672
GAUL,Ernest T2Lt kia 23-10-18 Lincs att6Leic p75 CR France1477,Capt
GAUL,Lawrence John Littlewood TLt ded 12-4-17 ArmyPayDept CR France88
GAULD,Alexander George Capt kia 15-9-16 19Lond p250 CR France390
GAULD,George ALt ded 24-6-19 RB APM attKRRCp178&254 CR France65
GAULD,Gordon Smith Mellis.MC.Lt kld 25-3-18 RFA &RFC p16&29 CR Lincs61
GAULT,Arthur Alexander T2Lt dow 10-10-18 11DubF D'Coy p176 CR France380
GAULT,John Victor 2Lt kia 23-10-16 5 att 1RIrRif p169 CR France307
GAULT,Robert Anderson Lt kia 16-9-16 4GrenGds SR p50 MR21
GAULTER,Charles Pendrick 2Lt kia 18-8-16 3 att4Lpool p71 MR21
GAULTER,Cuthbert Vivian Lt kia 7-5-17 5RLancs att7RFC p18&213 MR20
GAUNT,Benjamin William Lt kia 7-9-18 3Y&L att63TMB p158 CR France745
GAUNT,Edward 2Lt dow 28-9-16 5WYorks p218 MR21
GAUNT,Eric Thomas Capt kia 9-10-17 RAMC p195 MR30
GAUNT,Kenneth MacFarlane 2Lt kia 25-9-15 2 att4RWar p64
GAUSSEN,Arratoon William David Capt kia 17-5-15 HLI p162 MR22
GAUSSEN,David Newbold T2Lt kia 31-7-16 9 att1Beds p86 CR France176
GAUSSEN,John Samuel.CBE.Col ded 13-10-19 ArmyPayDept p268 CR Hamps7
GAVAGHAN,Colin 2Lt kia 13-3-18 55RFC p16 CR Germany3
GAVIN,Neil Murphy TLt dedacc 12-3-16 RAMC 6FA p195 CR France88
GAVIN,Noel John Hay.MC.TCapt ded 2-11-17 RAMC p195
GAVIN,Robert Fitzaustın Lt kia 25-9-15 2RIrRif p169 MR29
GAWAN-TAYLOR,Francis 2Lt kia 9-8-15 3Y&L p158 MR29
GAWAN-TAYLOR,Norman 2Lt kia 24-4-17 3 att1&L CR Belgium116
GAWN,Thomas 2Lt kia 6-8-15 2Hamps p120 MR4

GAWNE,William Zacharias T2Lt kia 9-4-17 8BlkW p128 CR France729
GAY,Edgar Percy T2Lt dow 6-1-17 6DCLI p114 CR France158
GAY,Edmund 2LtACapt kia 12-8-15 1/5Norf p216 MR4
GAY,Frederick Hollington 2Lt dow 25-3-17 16RFC p7 CR France32
GAY,John(Jock).2Lt kia 10-10-15 RFC p1 CR France924
GAY,John TCapt ded 29-5-16 30NumbF p61
GAYER,Alexander Edward Capt&Adjt ded 23-11-18 6ELancs p110 CR Surrey1
GAYER,Edward John 2Lt kia 4-10-17 1Lincs p75 MR30
GAYES,Thomas Samuel 2LtACapt kia 10-4-18 11BordR p117 CR France214
GAYFORD,Thomas Frederick Marter 2Lt kia 23-11-17 RE 203FC p45 CR Belgium20,204FC
GAYFORD,William George T2Lt dow 26-9-15 69RFA p29 CR Egypt6
GAYNER,William John 2Lt ded 9-5-17 2/4SomLI attRFC p218 p261 CR France270,kld
GAYNOR,Brian Seymour Capt ded 1-11-20 IA 23Cav p277 MR65
GAZE,Geoffrey Atkinson Capt kia 15-9-16 Cmdg15Lond B'Coy p249 CR France432
GEAKE,Boyd Burnet T2Lt kia 1-7-16 9Y&L p158 CR France246,Lt
GEARD,Reginald Cheniston Capt murdedByTribesmen 27-7-20 IA 15Lancers attPoliticalDept p277 CR Asia82
GEARD,Walter Leslie Maj kld 26-6-16 C282RFA p206 MR21
GEARE,William Duncan Rev kia 31-7-17 RAChDept att165InfBde p199 CR Belgium10
GEAREY,Albert Edward.MC.Capt dow 17-10-18 8N&D p233 CR France847
GEAREY,Edward 2Lt kia 1-1-15 CamH attHLI p167 MR22,20-12-14
GEARY,Ronald Fitzmaurice 2Lt kia 15-1-16 21Lond p251 CR France149
GEARY-SMITH,Alexander Capt kia 7-8-15 9WYorks p81 MR4
GEBBIE,James Francis Roy Lt dow 4-10-14 SLancs p125 CR France1839
GEDDES,Alastair Cosmo Burton.MC.TMaj kia 19-4-17 GL &RFC 17KiteBallCo CR France1485
GEDDES,Alistair Alexander Francis 2Lt kia 16-6-15 3 att2RScotF p94 MR22
GEDDES,Arthur Alexander TCapt ded 5-7-16 28RASC MotorAmbConvoy p192 Pakistan50A MR43
GEDDES,Augustus David LtCol kia 28-4-15 2EKent p57 CR Belgium84,Col
GEDDES,David Scott T2Lt kia 26-10-17 3Manch p154 CR Belgium116
GEDDES,Donald 2Lt kia 5-4-16 1SfthH att7Bn p164 MR38
GEDDES,John Gordon.CB.CMG.Col ded 26-8-19 RFA p261 CR Sussex55
GEDDES,John Rowland Lt 3-11-17 1CenOntario att23RFC CR Belgium16
GEDDES,Robert Stirling T2Lt kia 9-10-16 12MGC Inf p183 CR France294
GEDDES,William Murray Capt kia 27-9-15 2Wilts p153 CR France423
GEDDIE,George Alexander 2Lt kia 19-9-16 4CamH p243 CR France374,20-9-16
GEDDIS,Samuel McKee TLt kia 19-9-18 1Leic p87 CR France835
GEDGE,Basil Johnson Rev dow 25-4-17 RAChDept attRAMC 78FA p199 CR Greece5
GEDGE,Cecil Bertie 2Lt kia 25-9-15 3Lond p245 MR19
GEDGE,Edward Leonard.MID Lt kia 23/24-8-16 RH&FA p207 CR France251,GEDYE
GEDGE,Peter TLt kia 13-10-15 7Suff p78 MR19
GEE,Albert Edwin 2Lt ded 14-12-17 RGA p262 CR Lond33,dow
GEE,Donald T2Lt kld 31-1-18 RFC p16 CR Hamps192
GEE,Edward Topping Lt ded 12-2-19 12Lpool CR Lancs2
GEE,Ernest Desmond Farrell Maj kia 25-4-18 RGA 263SB p39 CR Belgium21
GEE,Frank Lionel T2Lt kia 5-9-17 RE 203FC p45 CR France364
GEE,Geoffrey Richard Dudley 2Lt kia 4-6-17 3RSuss &21RFC p7&119 MR30
GEE,George Edward TCapt dow 27-7-16 15RScots p54
GEE,Herbert Lt kia 10-7-15 16Lpool p71 CR Gallipoli6
GEE,Reginald Claud Moline.MC.TLtACapt kia 7-11-18 15DLI p160 CR France9
GEE,Robert Francis McLean 2Lt dow 27-10-14 3 att5Wilts p153 CR Sussex144
GEE,Thomas.MID Lt dedacc 13-11-17 B122RH&FA p29 CR Wales165
GEEN,William Purdon 2Lt kia 31-7-15 9KRRC p150 MR29
GEERE,Douglas Joseph 2Lt kia 23-2-16 D71RFA p29 CR France554
GEERING,S.Capt 20-10-19 RFus CR Surrey15
GEERING,Sydney Cecil 2Lt dow PoW 3-5-18 4Lond p246 CR France425
GEESON,Leslie Frederic T2Lt kld 15-6-17 GL &RFC p7 CR Surrey2
GEFEALL,George 2Lt kia 23-3-18 2/4 O&BLI p231 MR27
GEGGIE,William Millar McG.T2Lt kia 4-10-17 227MGC p182
GEIDT,Charles Uppleby Lt kld 10-4-18 GL CamH &RAF p190,C.W. CR Egypt
GELDER,George Douglas TCapt kia 4-11-18 9WRid p115 CR France206
GELDERD-SOMERVELL,Roger Frederick Churchill 2Lt dow 13-3-15 1GrenGds SR p50 MR22,11-3-15
GELIOT,William Henry 2Lt kia 1-7-16 4Lincs p217 CR France281
GELL,Christopher Gawall 2Lt kia 18-9-16 1WYorks p81 MR21

GELL,James Bainton Stowell T2Lt kia 9-10-18 56RFA p29 CR France332
GELL,Philip 2Lt ded 5-9-17 3Ches att217InfBn p96 CR Eire94
GELLATLY,John Stewart 2Lt kia 31-7-17 9RScots p212 CR Belgium36
GELLATLY,Robert 2Lt kia 23-4-17 13RScots p54 MR20
GELME,Reginald William T2Lt ded 27-7-16 RE p45 CR Iraq6
GEMMELL,Alexander Capt ded 4-1-19 SL antiGas School p268 CR Scot239
GEMMELL,Andrew Steveson Lt ded 5-3-19 5HLI p240 CR Scot674
GEMMELL,Cecil Woodburn 2Lt kia 24-4-17 8 att10ScotRif p225 MR20
GEMMELL,George Manners 2Lt kia 13-11-16 13Ess p131 CR France1890
GEMMELL,James Brown Richardson 2Lt kia 16-7-17 2HLI p162 CR France721
GEMMELL,John TCapt kia 25-9-15 12HLI p162 CR France219
GEMMELL,Kenneth Alexander Lt kia 16-6-15 10Lpool p216 MR29
GEMMELL,Stewart Armour Capt dow 22-7-15 6HLI p240 CR Egypt3
GEMMELL,Stuart Sterling 2Lt kia 21-3-18 3 att7CamH p167 CR France1182
GEMMELL,Thomas 2Lt dow PoW 7-5-18 7A&SH D'Coy p243 CR France1142
GEMMELL,Wallace Alexander Capt ded 29-3-16 RASC p253 CR Egypt2
GEMMILL,John Adshead T2Lt kia 1-7-16 16HLI p162 CR France293
GEMMILL,William.DSO.LtCol kia 25-3-18 8RScots p211 MR20
GENGE,John T2Lt dow PoW 24-3-18 2Y&L p158 CR France568
GENNINGS,Cecil Samuel 2Lt kia 13-8-16 7ESurr p112 MR21 &CR France390
GENT,Alfred Harry Thomas.MC.2Lt dow 3-10-18 1/5N&D p232 CR France446
GENT,Frank Ernest Lt kia 7-8-15 9WYorks p81 MR4,9-8-15
GENT,George Edward 2Lt kia 14-9-17 379RFA p29 CR France275
GENT,Thomas Samuel T2Lt kia 24-7-15 7RB p178 MR29 CR Belgium453
GEOGHEGAN,James Randolph Capt kia 7-11-14 RInniskF p105 CR Belgium451
GEOGHEGAN,Stannus 2Lt dow 18-3-18 2A&SH p173 CR Belgium3,Lt kia 17-3-18
GEOGHEGAN,William George Richard 2Lt dow 13-4-17 2RInniskF p105 CR France583
GEORGE,Alan Lee T2Lt dow 14-4-18 15RWar p64 CR France21
GEORGE,Athelstan Key Durrance Lt dow 14-9-14 1Dors p124 CR France1429
GEORGE,Edward Barcroft 2Lt kia 16-9-16 4 att15DLI p160 CR France744
GEORGE,Edward Royston TLtACapt ded 12-8-17 RE 264Co p45 CR Belgium18
GEORGE,Elmor Wright T2Lt kia 10-5-18 15WelshR p126 CR France232
GEORGE,Eric Coe T2Lt ded 15-9-15 10Glouc p106 CR France98
GEORGE,Frank Alfred 2Lt kia 17-10-18 6WelchR p230 CR France1269
GEORGE,Frank William.MID T2Lt kia 22-8-15 5Dors p124 MR4
GEORGE,Frederick Ralph Lt kia 5-11-14 1ConnRgrs p172 CR France1157
GEORGE,Henry William Hotton 2Lt dow 19-3-19 10RWKent p265
GEORGE,Herbert Duncan King Lt ded PoW 6-4-17 2RDubF &48RFC p7&176 CR France1276
GEORGE,Ion Barry Maj ded 5-5-18 RIrReg p89 CR Surrey1
GEORGE,L.Lt ded 12-5-18 RASC &RAF p192
GEORGE,Laurence Edgar Capt kia 28-6-15 9SomLI p79 MR4
GEORGE,Thomas T2Lt kia 27-8-18 16RWFus p97 CR France432
GEORGE,Thomas William T2Lt kld 18-10-17 GL &RFC p7 CR Scot963
GEORGE,William 2Lt kia 12-3-15 BlkW p128 CR France924
GEORGE,William King Capt kia 25-1-15 3Glouc p106 CR France279
GEORGESON,Dan Horace.MIDx2 TLtACapt kia 9-3-18 8SfthH p164 CR France1182
GEORGESON,William 2Lt kia 3-4-18 5HLI p240 CR France745
GEPP,Nicholas Melvill TCapt kia 6-8-15 11YLI att1Ess p143 CR Gallipoli6
GERAGHTY,Thomas 2Lt kia 26-9-17 8EYorks p84 MR30
GERALD,Harold T2Lt kia 2-12-17 Worc att2/8Bn p108 MR17
GERARD,Gilbert Meade Capt ded 3-5-16 HLI p162 MR38
GERARD,Tom Overton T2Lt kia 10-7-16 MGC 112Coy p183 MR21
GERDS,Frederick Niven T2Lt kia 1-6-15 RE 176TC p45 CR France631
GERMAIN,Harry Gordon 2Lt 12-7-16 17NumbF p61 MR21
GERMAN,Frederick Francis TCapt ded 27-3-16 RAMC p195 CR Lancs149
GERMAN,Hugh Bernard.MC.TCaptAMaj kia 18-9-18 RAMC att17FA p195 CR France835
GERMAN,Ivon Hector.MC.TLtACapt ded 1-12-18 1Hamps p120 CR France40
GERMAN,William Henry Capt dow 16-3-16 1/6Dev p217 CR Iraq5
GERMANY,Ernest Albert Capt&QM ded 13-5-19 RAVC p268 CR Lond28
GEROW,Albert Augustus T2Lt kld 28-2-18 RFC p16 CR Hamps98
GERRARD,Harry Vernon Lt kia 2-11-14 2BordR p117 MR29
GERRARD,James Spinks Lt ded 13-2-19 RASC p267 CR Scot247
GERRARD,John Maurice Harold 2Lt dow 28-8-18 74RFA p29 CR France927
GERRARD,Robert Finlay Capt kia 18-4-17 4RScots att1/6Glouc p211 CR France363,Maj
GERTSON,Frederick.DCM.2Lt kia 16-4-18 12/13NumbF p61 MR30

GETHIN,Percy Francis 2Lt kia 28-6-16 3 att8Dev p76 CR France330
GETHIN,Richard Patrick Wilmot Lt kia 25-9-15 2RMunstF D'Coy p175 CR France219
GETHING,Hugh Bagnall 2Lt kia 21-8-15 1/1GloucYeo D'Sqn p203 CR Gallipoli5
GETHING,William Gordon 2Lt kia 22-9-17 2/6SStaffs p122 MR30,23-9-17
GETTING,Eric Noel Capt kia 28/29-9-15 1RBerks p139 MR19
GETTY,James Houghton Capt kia 3-5-17 12WYorks p81 MR20
GHOSH,N.Capt 22-12-19 IMS MR43
GIBAUD,Ernest John 2Lt kia 24-4-17 12Hamps p120 MR37,25-4-17
GIBB,Alexander Lt kia 5-6-17 RFA V63H TMB p207 CR France184
GIBB,Alexander Reid Capt kia 12-10-16 105RFA p207 CR Belgium137
GIBB,C.L.G.Capt 23-1-20 RE CR Ches31
GIBB,George Blaikie Capt kia 1-9-18 17Lond p250 CR France785
GIBB,George Calder 2Lt kia 17-4-17 3 att4Lpool p71 MR32
GIBB,George Eben TLt kia 25/26-10-18 HLI p162 MR38
GIBB,James Robertson 2Lt kia 4-11-18 6A&SH p243 CR France521
GIBB,James Shirra Capt kia 29-7-18 1/5A&SH p243 CR France524
GIBB,John Hardie T2Lt kia 31-7-17 KRRC att18Bn p150 MR29
GIBB,Richard 2Lt kia 11-5-15 1A&SH p173 MR29
GIBB,Robert Andrew 2Lt kia 19-4-17 1/5KOSB p224 CR Palestine8
GIBB,William Lt 19-2-17 APD CR Scot277
GIBB,William Alexander LtCol ded 10-3-15 RAMC att6Suff CR Suff83
GIBB,William Ian 2Lt kia 14-4-17 11Lond p248 MR20
GIBBENS,George T2Lt dow 2-4-18 2Mddx p146 CR France185
GIBBES,Frederick William T2Lt ded 13-10-17 GL &54RFC p8 CR Belgium132
GIBBINGS,Frank 2Lt kia 2-12-17 RBerks att2Bn p139
GIBBINS,Gwynn Gilbert TLt kia 26-7-17 RE 107FC p45 CR Greece6
GIBBINS,Roland Bevington Capt kia 3-12-17 2/8RWar p214 MR17
GIBBON,Frederic T2Lt kia 8-10-18 12/13NumbF p61 MR16
GIBBON,Frederick William T2Lt kia 25-8-18 1NumbF p61 CR France239
GIBBON,John Taylor T2Lt kld 6-2-17 GL &20RFC p8 CR Belgium115
GIBBON,Oliver Vernon 2Lt kia 3-4-16 12WYorks p81 CR Belgium124
GIBBON,Wilfrid St.Martin Lt ded 24-4-18 IA 2/89Punjabis p277 MR43
GIBBONS,Alfred St.Hill.MID TLtCol dow 15-7-16 13Lpool p71 CR France119
GIBBONS,Charles Barry 2Lt kia 24-8/1-9-14 2RIrReg p254 CR Belgium242,24-8-14
GIBBONS,Edward Ingram Lt kia 29-4-17 20LancF p92 MR21
GIBBONS,Edward Stephen.DSO.MajALtCol kia 19-9-18 Mddx Cmdg7HLI p146 CR France686
GIBBONS,James Bryan Lt kia 10-3-20 RGA p262 MR43
GIBBONS,John T2Lt dow 6-6-17 Dors att6Bn p124 CR France40
GIBBONS,Percy James T2Lt kia 7-10-16 3 att1ESurr att1RWKent p112 MR21
GIBBONS,Thomas Pilling.MC.Capt kia 22-3-18 1Herts p252 CR France528
GIBBONS,Wilfred Ernest Capt ded 20-12-17 RAMC p270 CR Leic63
GIBBS,Archibald Edward T2Lt kia 25-4-17 11Worc p108 MR37
GIBBS,Bernard.MC.MID 2Lt kia 6-7-15 6 att1RB p178 CR Belgium85
GIBBS,Cecil Charles T2Lt kia 27-3-17 GL &14RFC p8 CR Egypt2
GIBBS,Cecil Thomas T2Lt kia 9-4-17 9Ess p131 CR France531
GIBBS,David Angus 2Lt 24-3-18 6 att2RB p178 MR27
GIBBS,Edward Reginald Chap4Cl kia 29-3-18 RAChDept att1GrenGds p199 CR France1183
GIBBS,Eustace Lyle Capt dow 11-2-15 NSomYeo p205 CR Belgium57,kia
GIBBS,Gilbert Fincher T2Lt kia 28-4-17 8SomLI p79 MR20
GIBBS,Harold Walter Lt dow 25-3-18 158RFA p207 CR France113
GIBBS,Henry Sampson Capt&Adjt ded 9-2-18 DLI p265 MR66
GIBBS,Horace Austen 2Lt kia 29-4-17 1RBerks p139 CR France777
GIBBS,Ivan Richard TCapt kia 25-9-15 10Glouc p106 CR France1723
GIBBS,John Angel.DSO.TMaj kia 20-9-17 9WelshR p126 CR Belgium17
GIBBS,Lawrence Henry.MC.TLtACapt kia 18-9-18 10LancF p92 CR France415
GIBBS,Leslie Lt kia 26-9-15 8RWKent p141 MR19
GIBBS,Percy Roland T2Lt ded 17-3-16 14Worc p108 CR Devon69
GIBBS,Philip Henry Samuel Lt ded 25-10-19 RE CR Sussex111
GIBBS,Ronald Charles Melbourne 2Lt dow 29-10-14 2ScotsGds p52 MR29,28-10-14
GIBBS,Stanley Gordon Maj kia 20-9-17 RASC DAQMG 1AnzacCpsHQ p192
GIBBS,Thomas Charles.MC.Lt kia 31-8-18 7 at9Ches p223 MR18,31-5-18
GIBBS,Walter Septimus T2Lt kia 17-10-18 2KRRC p150 CR France341
GIBBS,Walter William T2Lt kia 22-4-18 RE 1FldSurCo p45 CR France268
GIBBS,William Alexander Lt ded 10-3-15 RAMC p270
GIBBS,William Beresford.MID TLtCol kia 3-9-16 3Worc p108 CR France246,dow

GIBBS,William Henry Herbert.MC.T2Lt kia 21-8-18 RASC 329SBAmmCol p192 CR France31
GIBLIN,Eric Lewis Capt kia 28-9-15 RAMC att24Lond p253 CR France107,Louis
GIBSON,A2Lt 13-12-15 IARO att110MahrattaLI CR Iraq5
GIBSON,Albert Fisher 2Lt kia 24-3-17 4Leinst att4RFC p8&174 CR France561
GIBSON,Albert Henry T2Lt kia 1-7-16 12 att9RInniskF p105 MR21
GIBSON,Alexander Douglas Lt kia 11-9-18 9Lpool p216 CR France482
GIBSON,Alwyn Morland 2Lt dow 27-9-16 6WYorks att1/6TMB p218 MR21,Alcwyn
GIBSON,Arthur 2Lt dow 6-7-17 RH&FA attY29TMB p29 CR Belgium16
GIBSON,Arthur Douglas T2Lt kia 9-4-17 22NumbF p61 CR France644
GIBSON,Arthur Ferrall Lt ded 29-10-18 RASC 14DivnTrain p193 CR Lond29
GIBSON,Arthur Lionel 2Lt kia 8-8-15 1/7WRid p227 CR Belgium67
GIBSON,Athol Thomas Capt kia 21-10-14 3 att2SLancs p125 MR22
GIBSON,Bertrand Dees.DSO.MID LtCol kia 27-5-18 4NumbF p213 CR France1753
GIBSON,Cecil Mervyn 2Lt kia 5-5-17 1/5Y&L p238 CR France705
GIBSON,Charles Leslie.MC.Lt dow 3-9-18 17Lond p250 CR France177
GIBSON,Charles Methven 2Lt kia 14-10-16 4BlkW p230 CR France215
GIBSON,Charles Sydney 2Lt kia 1-7-16 4RWar attMGC p183 CR France638,2War att22MGC. Inf
GIBSON,Edgar Daniell T2Lt kia 9-10-17 GL &2RFC p8 CR France98
GIBSON,Franklin Reginald TLt ded 20-9-18 RGA 80Bde 176SB p39 CR Berks116
GIBSON,Frederick James Lt 28-12-20 6LNLancs CR Iraq8
GIBSON,George Henry 2Lt kia 27-8-17 2 att9WYorks p81 CR Belgium96
GIBSON,Gerald Dudley 2Lt dow 16-8-18 5Lancers p22 CR France145
GIBSON,Griffiths Ifor 2Lt 12-8-17 11WYorks att6RFC CR Belgium11
GIBSON,Harold.DSO.Capt dow 17-10-17 RAMC att71FA p195 CR France40
GIBSON,Harold Wolfe Lt kia 24-3-18 1Wilts p153 MR20
GIBSON,Harry Olivier Sumner Lt kia 19-4-17 11Lond p248 CR Palestine8
GIBSON,Henry T2Lt kia 30-9-18 Y&L att13Bn p158 CR Belgium451
GIBSON,Henry William T2Lt dow 27-11-16 2RDubF p176 CR France8
GIBSON,Herbert Edwin 2Lt kia 7-8-17 4 O&BLI p231 MR29
GIBSON,Horsburgh 2Lt dow 22-12-16 7A&SH p243 CR France62
GIBSON,Howard Graeme Maj ded 12-2-19 RAMC p195 CR France52
GIBSON,Hugh Stuart LtTCapt ded 19-2-19 5SStaffs p270 CR Lond12
GIBSON,Ivor Griffith T2Lt dow 11-8-17 11WYorks &6RFC p8&81
GIBSON,James TLt kia 5-10-17 13MGC Inf p183 MR30
GIBSON,James 2Lt kia 12-10-17 9A&SH p244 MR30
GIBSON,James Douglas Lt kia 25-3-18 RE 401FC p210 CR France385
GIBSON,James Guthrie 2Lt dow 12-9-17 PoW 3 att6CamH p167 CR Germany3
GIBSON,James William T2Lt kia 9-8-18 8TankCps p188 CR France526
GIBSON,Jesse Lt ded 7-3-19 RDC p270 CR Leic24
GIBSON,John 2Lt kia 19-6-16 2/7Dev attRFC p18&217 CR France120
GIBSON,John TLt kia 5-7-16 9Yorks p90 MR21
GIBSON,John Anthony 2Lt dow PoW 27-8-17 9RInniskF p105 CR Germany1,27-9-18
GIBSON,John Auchenlosh 2Lt kia 27-5-17 RGA 116SB p39 MR18
GIBSON,John Lancelot Lt kia 27-5-18 D251RFA p207 MR18
GIBSON,John Seear T2Lt dow 15-10-16 8Beds att16TMB p86 MR21
GIBSON,John Thomas T2lt kld 10-2-18 RFC p16 CR Wilts 28
GIBSON,Leonard TCapt ded 1-8-18 GL p190 CR Devon 69
GIBSON,Malcolm Reginald TLt kia 8-10-15 7ESurr p112 CR France423,8-10-16
GIBSON,Margaret Annabella Campbell.MM.UnitAdmintr ded 17-9-18 QMAAC p200 CR France13
GIBSON,Matthew Henry.MC&Bar.TLtACapt dow 28-10-18 RIrRif att12Bn p169 CR Belgium20,kia 29-10-18
GIBSON,Norman James Lt kia 21-11-17 4GordH p241 CR France256
GIBSON,Ollyett Archibald M.2Lt dow 27-8-16 RH&FA p29
GIBSON,Pendarves Christopher Foll TLt kia 10-4-17 13RFus p68 MR20
GIBSON,Percy Montague.MC.MM.2Lt dow 6-9-18 5Mddx att17Lond p146 CR France833
GIBSON,Reginald James 2Lt kia 28-6-15 4RScotF p211 MR4
GIBSON,Robert Lt kia 5-5-15 2KOSB p101 MR29
GIBSON,Robert 2Lt 23-7-16 1/9RScots CR France402
GIBSON,Robert Bowness Lt kia 11-7-16 3 att2Beds p86 CR France630
GIBSON,Robert Gray Nicol Lt kia 21-3-18 6 att2RScots p211 MR20
GIBSON,Ronald 2Lt dow 12-12-15 IARO att110Mahrattas p277
GIBSON,Samuel Archibald Gibson.MC.2Lt dow 26-8-17 3Wilts att2/1 O&BLI p153 CR Belgium11,Currie 3/1Bn
GIBSON,Thomas Ernest 2Lt kia 28-11-17 2/5WYorks p218 MR17
GIBSON,Walter Reginald 2Lt kia 4-10-17 8Lincs p75 MR30

GIBSON,William 2Lt kia 1-7-16 14 att15RScots p54 MR21
GIBSON,William Ramshaw 2Lt ded 16-6-18 8LNLancs p264 CR Lancs111,17-6-1
GIBSON-CRAIG,Archibald Charles.Bart.Lt kia 13/17-9-14 2HLI p162 MR15 14-9-14
GIDDINGS,Frank.MM.2Lt kia 2-12-17 att2Berks p139 MR30
GIDDY,Napier Llewellyn 2Lt kia 15-8-16 1Nhampt p137 CR France387
GIDLEY,Frederick William Lt kia 27-3-17 1 att4Ess p131 MR34
GIELGUD,Henry Lex Francis Adam.MC.MajALtCol kia 30-11-17 7Norf p73 MR17
GIERRIER,Elias George T2Lt drd 30-11-18 GL &IWT p190
GIFFARD,Colin Hay Capt kia 8-3-16 IA 1/1GurkhaRif p277 MR38
GIFFARD,Edmund Hamilton LtAMaj dow 10-11-18 2RFA p29 CR France332
GIFFARD,Robert Capt dow 1-11-14 RFA p29 CR Belgium57
GIFFARD,Sydney Lt kia 3-5-15 RFA p29 CR Gallipoli1
GIFFARD,William Carter.DSO.BrCol 25-4-21 WelchR CR C'land&W'land45
GIFFEN,James.MC.LtACapt dow 22-12-16 2CamH p167 CR France177
GIFFORD,Gordon Arthur Lt kia 10-7-17 LNLancs att2TMB p136 MR31
GIFFORD,Harry William.MID TCapt kia 15-7-16 1LNLancs p136 MR21
GIFFORD,Norga Ernest TCapt kia 14-7-16 7Leic p87 MR21
GIFFORD,William Roy 2Lt kia 7-10-16 4Lond p246 CR France744
GIFFORD-WOOD,Leslie Keith 2Lt mbk 22-8-15 6Yorks p256 MR4
GILBANKS,Richard Parker TLt kia 10-8-15 6BordR p117 MR4
GILBART,William Stuart T2Lt dow 26-9-16 9Leic p87 CR France833
GILBERT,Archibald Holmes T2Lt kia 21-9-17 GL &22RFC p8 CR Belgium46
GILBERT,Bernard Ryland Joseph 2Lt kia 1-12-17 1/5SStaffs p229 CR France115,30-11-17
GILBERT,Bertram Thomas Chesterton Lt kia 22-4-17 4Leic p219 MR29
GILBERT,Christopher Choaler TLt kia 28-9-16 11 att8WRid p115 MR21,Chowler 29-9-16
GILBERT,Edward Burton T2Lt kia 21-3-18 25RFus p68 CR France245
GILBERT,Frank Charles Henry TLt dow 23-4-16 14Hamps p120 CR France279,21
GILBERT,Frank William 2Lt kia 11-10-17 2Ess p131 MR30
GILBERT,Gilbert Garnet T2Lt kia 18-3-18 9RLancs p59 CR Greece5
GILBERT,Herbert James.MID T2Lt kia 22-3-18 16RB p178 MR27
GILBERT,George Hewitt 2Lt kia 15-6-18 7Worc p226 CR Italy3
GILBERT,James Ponsonby Capt drd 30-12-15 IA 6Jats p277 MR41
GILBERT,John Driffield Lt kia 18-10-17 SussYeo attRFC p18&205 MR20
GILBERT,John Ewart TCapt ded 6-11-18 24RFus p68 CR Cornwall40
GILBERT,Joseph Plumptre 2Lt kia 11-4-17 4Hamps p228 CR France1193,dow
GILBERT,Kenneth Nigel Wilson.MC.ACapt ded 15-10-18 32RFA &RAF p29 CR Norf138
GILBERT,L.S.T2Lt kia 4-4-16 13RFus att8RWFus p68 MR38
GILBERT,Reginald Herbert 2Lt dow 8-8-18 6SfthH p241 CR Oxford69
GILBERT,Reginald William,MC T2Lt dow 21-7-16 53MGC p183 MR21
GILBERTSON,Graham Sydney 2Lt kia 28-11-17 4 att7Beds p86 MR30
GILBEY,Eric Lt kia 10-3-15 5RB p178 CR France709
GILCHRIST,Alexander Arthur T2Lt kia 3-9-16 A&SH att1CamH p173 CR France453
GILCHRIST,Archibald 2Lt kld 3-10-18 1/4RB &RAF p178 CR France234,Lt kia
GILCHRIST,Ivan Hamilton Learmouth 2Lt kia 2-10-15 2NumbF p61 CR France423,Lt 2/5Bn
GILCHRIST,John TCapt dow 29-8-15 9BlkW p128 CR France98
GILCHRIST,Robert Crooks Capt kia 19-12-14 IA 46Punjabis att59Rif p277 CR France571
GILDEA,John Arthur Knox 2Lt kia 11-7-16 2RWar p64 MR21
GILDER,Tom Norman 2Lt ded 4-11-18 IA 47Sikhs p277 MR66
GILDERTHORP,Ellwood TLt dow 11-4-18 29MGC p183 CR France25
GILDERTHORP,Guy 2Lt kia 12-4-18 8RWar p215 CR France248
GILES,Edward Victor T2Lt kia 3-7-16 9 att5RBerks p139 MR21
GILES,Eric Capt dow 16-7-16 4Lond p246 CR France1
GILES,Geoffrey T2Lt kia 1-7-16 2GordH p166 CR France331
GILES,George Edward TLt kld 11-11-16 RFC p2 CR Glouc9,2Lt
GILES,Thomas William T2Lt dow 14-12-17 7EYorks p84 CR France134,Wilfred
GILES,Victor Marshall T2Lt kia 28-6-16 7RIrRif p169 CR France423
GILES,Walter Lt kia 13-7-16 RGA 32SB p39 CR France630
GILES,William Charles 2Lt kia 12-10-17 11 att8SStaffs p122 MR30,Lt
GILES,William James.DCM.T2Lt kia 6-4-18 6RWSurr p55 CR France296
GILES,William Stanley T2Lt kia 2-11-17 3RWar att1/4Norf p64 CR Palestine8
GILFILLAN,Arthur Wayland Lt ded 7-11-18 RFus &RAF p263
GILFILLAN,Donald Roy T2Lt kia 26-2-17 11Mddx p146 CR France1182
GILHESPIE,Charles Salkeld T2Lt dow 12-12-17 3LNLancs att1/5SLancs p136 CR France145

GILHESPY,Henry White Capt ded 3-11-19 RASC MT CR Asia53,Harry
GILHESPY,John William T2Lt kia 20-7-16 12 att 1ScotRif p103&167 MR21
GILKINSON,Donald Stewart Capt kia 20-9-14 5ScotRif p103 CR France1329,Dugald
GILKINSON,James David Lt kia 26-8-14 2A&SH p173 CR France716
GILL,Basil Every Capt kia 18-10-16 2Yorks p90 MR21
GILL,Charles Treverlyn 2Lt kia 1-7-16 4 att 22Manch p154 CR France630,Treverbyn
GILL,Colin 2Lt kia 31-7-17 12RFus p68 MR29
GILL,Daniel Aloysius T2Lt kia 24-10-16 18WYorks p81 CR France342
GILL,Eric Longden 2Lt kia 30-11-17 4Y&L p238 CR France245
GILL,Erold Waring TLt dow 25-7-16 86RH&FA p29
GILL,Francis Edwin Capt ded 28-2-15 RE p45 CR Lancs380
GILL,Frank Brooks 2Lt kia 3-9-16 6WRid p227 CR France293
GILL,Frank Hubert T2Lt kia 16-8-17 2WYorks p81 MR30
GILL,Frank Malcolm Capt kia 25/26-5-15 24Lond p252 MR22
GILL,George AssSurg 22-9-17 IMS MR66
GILL,Gordon Evans Maj ded 12-3-19 RE p254
GILL,Hugh Goddard Lt kia 12-3-18 13WYorks attRFC p16&81 CR France660,10Bn
GILL,Jack Woodward T2Lt kia 19-11-15 6YLI p143 CR Belgium101
GILL,John Brown Lt ded 20-1-21 6A&SH CR Scot874
GILL,John Ignatius T2Lt kia 7-6-17 11WYorks p81 MR29,7-6-16
GILL,Kenneth Carlyle.MC.MID Capt dow 22-10-18 1Camb &22RAF p244&258 CR France1512,23-10-18
GILL,Leonard Edward 2Lt kia 17-9-17 7N&D attMGC p233&187 CR France545
GILL,Noel Brendan 2Lt kia 23-4-17 18Manch p154 MR20
GILL,R.Capt 6-3-20 RAMC CR Hamps64
GILL,Rowland.MC.MM.2Lt kia 19-4-18 17Lpool p71 MR30
GILL,William Gerald Oliver 2Lt kia 27-3-17 1/7Ess p232 CR Palestine18
GILL,William Hutton Pridmore TCapt ded 26-1-17 RASC p193 CR France300
GILL,William Rey 2Lt kia 21-8-17 O&BLI 2/1BucksBn p231 CR Belgium96
GILLARD,Frederick T2Lt kia 24-8-18 9YLI p143 MR16
GILLENDER,Alfred Williamson 2Lt dow 10-4-17 3SStaffs att7Lincs p122 CR France97
GILLESPIE,Alexander Douglas 2Lt kia 26-9-15 4 att 2A&SH p173 MR19
GILLESPIE,Charles Lt dow 20-9-15 4 att 2HLI p163 CR France98
GILLESPIE,David Andrew 2Lt dow 24-1-17 3 att 2BordR p117 CR France41
GILLESPIE,D.V.2Lt kia 5-4-18 GL &RAF p190
GILLESPIE,Francis Sydney TCapt dow 18-6-16 13RSuss p119 CR France345
GILLESPIE,Franklin Macaulay.MID TLtCol kia 9-8-15 4SWBord p100 MR4
GILLESPIE,Gordon Wood 2Lt kia 13-4-17 9Mddx attRFC p18&236 MR20
GILLESPIE,James Capt kia 30-7-16 1/7BlkW p231 CR France1890
GILLESPIE,John Lt ded 9-7-19 IndianMGC p266 CR Iraq8,9-8-19
GILLESPIE,Rollo 2Lt kia 25-9-15 3 att 2SLancs p125 MR29
GILLESPIE,Thomas T2Lt kia 14-3-17 2BlkW p128 MR38
GILLESPIE,Thomas Cunningham 2Lt kia 18-10-14 2KOSB p101 MR22
GILLESPIE,William TCaptAMaj dow 9-4-18 RE 218FC p45 CR France169,206FC
GILLESPIE,William Edward T2Lt kia 11-9-18 7RB att 12Lond p178 CR France415
GILLESPIE,William Robert Beauchamp.MID TMaj kia 8-9-17 7RBerks p139 MR37
GILLETT,Edward Francis T2Lt dow 29-9-15 53RGA p39 CR France80,Lt
GILLETT,Frederick Tremlow T2Lt kia 22-7-16 1RWKent p141 MR21
GILLETT,George Maurice Gerald TCapt kia 26-9-16 6Leic p87 MR21
GILLETT,Herbert Edward Lt ded 23-11-18 1/1DerbyYeo p203 CR Greece9
GILLETT,Richmond Edward T2Lt dow 29-4-16 5RInniskF p105 CR France423
GILLHAM,Reginald George William 2Lt kia 26-9-17 RSuss att 13Bn p119 MR30
GILLIAT,Cecil Glendower Percival Capt dow 14-10-14 RWar p64 CR France200
GILLIAT,Reginald Horace Crosbie Capt kia 6-4-15 5Leinst att 1ConnRgrs p174 CR France1157
GILLIAT,Robert Vincent Lt dow PoW 25-5-18 10Manch p237 CR France1615
GILLIAT-SMITH,Arthur Lt 1-11-14 RE 26FC MR29
GILLIATT,Francis Ralph 2Lt kia 26-7-17 1/5Lincs p220 CR France223
GILLIATT,Otho Claude Skipwith Capt kia 30-10-14 1RB p178 CR Belgium32
GILLIES,Charles Percival.MC.TLt dow 5-5-16 MGC p254 CR France40,Percivale Capt
GILLIES,Forbes T2Lt kia 27-8-16 89MGC Inf p183 CR France765
GILLIES,Halliday Gordon 2Lt kia 13-11-16 3 att 1RScotF p94 MR21
GILLIES,James T2Lt kia 1-7-16 2RWSurr p56 CR France630
GILLIES,James Brown Capt dow 14-11-16 4GordH p241 CR France131,kia 13-11-16
GILLIGAN,John Joseph 2Lt kia 25-4-18 B123RFA p29 CR France204

GILLILAND,Valentine Knox Capt kia 8-5-15 RIrRif att 2Bn p169 MR29
GILLILAND,William Miller LtAMaj kia 28-4-15 RInniskF p105 CR Gallipoli3,W.M.M.Lt
GILLISON,Andrew.MID Rev 22-8-15 RAChDept att 14AustInf CR Gallipoli18
GILLMAN,Angus George.MC.Maj kia 29-4-17 52/15RH&FA p29 CR France68
GILLON-FERGUSSON,James Scott Elliot Lt 27-4-15 5Mddx MR29
GILLOT,Oswald Cronek T2Lt kia 7-6-17 RE 68FC p45 CR Belgium168
GILMAN,Ronald John Lt ded 15-7-18 WarYeo p205 CR France40
GILMAN,William Harold 2Lt kia 14-6-18 8Lond p247 CR France62
GILMER,Ernest Richard T2Lt kia 12-10-16 1RIrF p171 MR21
GILMON,John Charles AssSurg 1-7-15 IMS CR India97A
GILMORE,Alexander William Francis.MC.2Lt kia 23-11-17 15RIrRif p169 MR17
GILMORE,Andrew 2Lt kia 11-3-15 1RIrRif p169 MR22
GILMORE,John Kenneth TCapt kia 22-8-16 6Glouc p225 MR21
GILMORE,Thomas Francis.MC.Lt kia 8-11-18 4 att 5ConnRgrs p172 MR16
GILMOUR,Alastair Stuart T2Lt kia 15-9-16 11A&SH p173 CR France453
GILMOUR,Allan Capt ded 16-12-17 1LovatScts p204 CR Greece4,10CamH
GILMOUR,Archibald Keltie TCapt kia 16-8-16 7KOSB p101 CR France188
GILMOUR,D.Capt ded 19-8-16 RAMC CR Scot237
GILMOUR,Douglas TLt dow 16-2-16 7SfthH attTMB p164 CR France285
GILMOUR,Elphinstone Forrest 2Lt kia 28-3-18 1/4RScotF att8TMBp222 MR20
GILMOUR,G.L.T2Lt ded 12-8-17 RE IWT p45 CR Scot228
GILMOUR,Herbert James Graham Lt kia 19-9-14 3Worc p108 MR15
GILMOUR,James Lt kia 30-3-18 8 att 9ScotRif p225 MR27
GILMOUR,Robert Wallace T2Lt kia 21-3-18 9RInniskF p105 MR27
GILMOUR,William T2Lt kia 4-12-16 13ScotRif att 6Lancs p103 MR38,9-4-16
GILMOUR,Willis John Oberlin 2Lt kia 15-5-15 ScotHorse p205 MR37,Williejohn 15-5-17 13BlkW attSNottsYeo
GILPIN,Albert John T2Lt kia 17-9-16 11KRRC A'Coy p150 CR France374
GILPIN,Ernest Henry Capt kia 21-3-18 2DLI p160 MR20,Harry
GILPIN,George Lt dow 7-10-18 1/8Manch p114 CR France40
GILPIN,Norcliffe William Bernard 2Lt ded 1-6-17 RDC p253 CR Wilts115
GILPIN,Robert Lt dow 3-7-15 63RFA p29 CR Iraq6
GILROY,George Bruce.MC.TCapt dow 15-7-16 8BlkW p128 CR France23
GILROY,Kenneth Reid Lt dow 12-3-15 2BlkW p128 CR France727
GILSON,Alexander Ivan 2Lt kia 17-3-17 GL &RFC p8 MR20
GILSON,Edward Norman 2Lt dow PoW 5-11-18 2Y&L p158 CR Germany3
GILSON,Francis Gerald Maj dow 17-9-20 6Worc CR Hereford201
GILSON,George 2Lt kia 1-9-18 5Lond p246 MR16
GILSON,Leo Herbert TLt dow 29-7-16 7Suff p78 CR France51
GILSON,Robert Quilter TLt kia 1-7-16 11Suff p78 CR France515
GIMBLETT,Raymond John 2Lt ded 20-2-19 RFA 15DAC p29 CR Belgium316
GIMINGHAM,Charles Henry.MID Capt kia 9-11-17 1Herts attRFC p18&252 CR Greece3
GIMSON,Rupert Maj 10-3-21 6Ches CR Ches98
GIMSON,Walter Stanley.MC.T2LtACapt kia 16-8-17 GL YLI att 61TMB p190 CR Belgium23
GINDER,Thomas Wilfred T2Lt kia 21-3-18 13Ess p131 MR20
GINN,Harold Etridge T2Lt kia 8-7-17 3Worc p108 CR France1890
GINN,S.W.Capt&Adjt 21-8-21 2EYorks CR Iraq8
GIOVANETTI,Albert Harcourt T2Lt kld 3-2-18 57ResSqnRFC p16 CR Egypt8
GIPPS,Reginald Nigel Lt kia 7-11-14 ScotsGds p52 MR29
GIRARD,Geoffrey Marcus Erskine T2Lt kld 16-11-17 7Leinst p174 CR France689
GIRARDOT,Markham Henry Capt kia 30-4-15 Ess p131 CR Gallipoli2,28-4-15
GIRARDOT,Paul Charcowt 2Lt kia 17-9-14 2 O&BLI p130 CR France1111,Chancourt
GIRDLESTON,Morrell Andrew Capt kia 25-3-15 1A 41Dogras p277 CR France924,GIRDLESTONE
GIRDLESTONE,H.W.Lt kld 30-4-18 RH&FA &4RAF p29 CR France134,RGA
GIRLING,Charles John 2Lt kia 23-10-16 1Hamps p120 MR21
GIRLING,Stephen Eastough TLt kia 29-9-18 9 att 7DCLI p114 CR France379
GIROD,Milton 2Lt kld 19-3-16 3Ches &RFC p2&96,ded
GIRVAN,Frederick William LtACapt kia 26-10-17 8Dev p76 MR30
GIRVIN,Colin Bertram TCapt ded 5-11-18 3RDubF p176 CR Yorks181,dow
GISSING,Alexander 2Lt ded 9-10-18 3 att 2SStaffs p122 CR France146
GITTINGS,Charles T2Lt kia 21-3-18 2 att 2/5ELancs p110 CR France528
GITTINS,Albert.MC.TLt kia 25-5-17 5KSLI p144 CR France162
GITTINS,Henry Neville Capt ded 20-3-17 RGA 170SB p209 CR France169,Harry
GITTINS,Herbert 2Lt dow 2-6-17 5LNLancs p234 CR France255
GIUSANI,see GUISANI,S.J.J.V.A. CR France220

GIVEN,Robert 2Lt kia 27-5-18 19RIrRif att4EYorks p169 MR18
GJEMS,Albert Ole Müller 2Lt kia 8-8-17 5 att2RFus p68 MR29
GJERS,Lawrence ACapt kia 4-10-17 3 att2SfthH p164 MR30
GLACKEN,Hugh Frank Capt 16-1-18 MilWksServ MR65
GLADDEN,Leslie Charles Lt kia 20-4-18 3 att2Ess p131 CR France250
GLADSTONE,Elsie Mabel.ARRC.Sister ded 24-1-19 QAIMNS p200 CR Belgium265
GLADSTONE,John Ravenhill TCapt kia 23-8-18 6Leic p87 CR France742
GLADSTONE,Ralph Oscar T2Lt kia 2-11-17 RE 421WLancsFC p45 CR Belgium23
GLADSTONE,William Glynne Charles Lt kia 13-4-15 3RWFus p97 CR Wales637,1Bn
GLADSTONE,William Herbert.MC.LtACapt kia 27-9-18 1CldGds p51 CR France1497
GLADWELL,John Henry T2Lt kia 12-10-17 1 att7RWKent p141 CR Belgium20,dow 14-10-17
GLADWIN,Ralph Hamilton Fane Lt kia 26-10-14 2ScotsGds p52 MR29
GLAISBY,Kenneth Lt kia 1-11-17 2Bde att134Bty RFA p207 CR Belgium83
GLAISTER,George Lt kia 31-7-17 1/5LNLancs p234 CR Belgium10
GLAISTER,George Frederick TLt kia 1-8-18 2TankCps C'Coy p188 CR France300
GLANCY,Hugh G.2Lt kia 30-9-18 3RMunsF attMGC p183&175 CR France348
GLANFIELD,Barnard St.John Capt dow 31-8-16 4Suff p217 CR France397,Bernard
GLANFIELD,Gordon T2Lt kia 12-11-15 9Norf p73 CR Belgium92,11-11-15
GLANVILL,Ernest Mure Capt kia 2-11-14 RAMC attRScotsGreys p195 MR29
GLANVILLE WEST,Herbert T2Lt kia 19-8-18 Norf att12Bn p73 CR France193
GLASFURD,Duncan John TBrigGen dow 12-11-16 A&SH HQ 12AustInfBde p173
GLASGOW,William James Nesbitt.MC.MID TCapt dow 7-10-16 RE 93FC p45 CR France203,Nesbit
GLASIER,Philip Mannoch.DSO.LtCol kia 2-6-18 16Lond p249 CR France54,Mannock
GLASS,A.Lt 24-11-19 RGA CR Durham113
GLASS,David William Capt kia 18-9-16 5BordR p228 CR France239
GLASS,James Fraser 2Lt dow 26-4-15 2SfthH p164 CR Belgium151
GLASS,John Meldrum T2Lt kia 25-10-18 SfthH p164 CR France1256
GLASS,Leonard George 2Lt kia 9-10-17 1/2LancF p92 MR30
GLASS,William 2Lt kia 23-4-17 6BlkW p231 CR France924
GLASSCOCK,Sydney Frederick TLt kia 20-11-17 TankCps p188 MR17
GLASSON,Donald Havelock 2Lt dow 12-3-17 47RFC p8 CR Europe58
GLASTONBURY,Harold Mynett 2Lt dow 1-7-16 5 att1RIrRif p169 MR21
GLAZE,Donald Stuart T2Lt kia 26-10-17 SStaffs att1Bn p122 MR30
GLAZEBROOK,Philip Kirkland.DSO.Maj kia 7-3-18 1/1ChesYeo p203 CR Palestine
GLEAVE,Fergus 2Lt kia 22/23-7-16 10Glouc p106 MR21
GLEAVE,Harold Mason.MID Capt kia 6-3-17 3 att1N&D A'Coy p134 MR21 CR France624
GLEAVE,Thomas Reginald Lt kia 11-10-16 1/5SLancs p230 CR Belgium4
GLEDHILL,Annie Sister ded 17-10-18 QAIMNS p200 CR Palestine8
GLEDHILL,George Richard 2Lt kia 3-9-16 2/5WRid p227 MR21
GLEDSDALE,Arthur 2Lt kia 31-7-17 10Lpool p216 MR29,Arnold
GLEDSDALE,Irving Lt kia 13-7-17 3 att15Ches p96 CR France363
GLEDSTANES,Sheldon Arthur Capt dow 9-5-15 Beds p86 CR France284
GLEDSTONE,Herbert Reginald ACapt kia 25-5-18 NumbF att4Beds p61 MR27
GLEED,George Alfred.MID Lt dow 6-9-16 1Ches p96 CR France66,Capt
GLEED,John Victor Ariel 2Lt ded 7-7-17 45RFC p8 CR Belgium74
GLEESON,John Francis.MC.HonLt dow 2-2-18 8RMunsF p175 CR Eire167,Capt
GLEESON,Timothy TCapt&QM ded 22-12-18 SL Sch of Musk p201 CR Surrey148,28-12-18 ESurr
GLEGG,Arthur Livingstone 2Lt kia 10-8-15 6 att2KRRC p150 CR France114
GLEGG,Cuthbert Kemp TCapt kia 19-5-16 10ScotRif p103 CR France219,Charles
GLEGG,Robert.MID Lt kia 19-7-15 RE 1/2HighlandFC p210 CR France924
GLEGG,Walter Scott 2Lt kia 15-9-16 6 att9KRRC p150 MR21
GLEN,Alec 2Lt kia 29-12-15 Manch att8RFC CR France274
GLEN,Alexander Lt ded 21-9-16 RAMC p267 CR Yorks294,GLENN
GLEN,David 2Lt dow 24-4-17 4Suff p78 CR France120
GLEN,David Alexander 2Lt kia 28-12-15 Manch &RFC p1&154
GLEN,David Corse TLt kia 25-9-15 8RBerks p139 CR France219
GLEN,David Robert 2Lt kia 28-3-18 1/4 att1RScotF p222 MR20
GLEN,Donald Roy T2Lt kld 12-2-18 RFC p16 CR Kent25,GLENN
GLEN,James Capt 16-9-18 5ScotRif &70RAF MR20
GLEN,John Todd 2Lt kia 27-11-15 4ScotRif att1RMunstF p103 MR4
GLENCROSS,Andrew 2Lt kia 18-4-18 BlkW att1TMB p128 CR France279
GLENDAY,Alexander Goncalves Capt kia 8-8-15 RE 21S&M p45 CR France924
GLENDAY,Ferdinand Goncalves Capt kia 15-9-16 12NumbF attRFC p2&61 CR France167,dow

GLENDINNING,Arthur William Frederick T2Lt kia 14-7-16 12RScots p54 MR21
GLENDINNING,Duncan Retallick Lt kia 16-11-17 1/7Mddx p235 CR France307
GLENDINNING,James Graham 2Lt dow PoW 16-12-17 3Mon att57RFC p18&2 CR Belgium140,2-12-17
GLENDINNING,Thomas Henry TCapt kia 19-4-17 ACycCpsLowlandDiv p244 MR34,Clendinning
GLENIE,George Richard 2Lt kia 11-9-16 1/4RLancs p213 MR21
GLENIE,Julian William Lt accShotByServant 26-9-20 IA 3/70BurmaRif p277 CR Iraq6 Ex1KEdwHorse
GLENN,Archibald Patrick T2Lt kia 14-9-16 15WYorks p81 CR France631
GLENN,Cecil William TLt kia 28-1-17 RASC att1RInniskF p193 MR21
GLENNIE,John Herbert 2Lt kia 1-7-16 1KOSB p101 CR France220
GLENNON,Francis Henry T2Lt kia 16-11-16 10 att8ELancs p110 MR21
GLENNY,Ernest Howard Lt ded 9-10-18 RAMC p195 CR Iraq6
GLENNY,H.Q.Lt 18-11-14 SL attNigR CR WAfrica33
GLENNY,Thomas Alexander Maj kia 25-9-15 7KOSB p101 MR19
GLENTWORTH,E.W.C.G.de V.Viscount.Capt ded 18-5-18 WarYeo &RAF p205
GLEW,Aubrey Edward 2Lt kia 8-9-16 24RFC p3 CR France300
GLIDDON,Ernest Frank Leslie Nevill 2Lt dow 5-6-18 4 att1Dors p229 CR France
GLIDDON,G.C.Capt 11-5-15 MO 10CanadaInf CR France284
GLIDDON,Maurice.MC.TLtACapt dow 16-8-17 B108RFA p29 CR Belgium8
GLIDDON,Reginald Arthur 2Lt kld 9-5-18 13Mddx &RAF p146 CR Lond33,Lt
GLORNEY,Ernest Edward 2Lt kld 25-10-16 RFC p3 CR Ireland5,Lt
GLOSSOP,Bertram TLt kia 4-9-16 9Dev p76 MR21,6-9-16
GLOSSOP,Ernest Edward 2Lt dow 4-5-15 SomLI p79 CR France284
GLOSSOP,Walter George Cave Lt kld 20-6-21 RFA CR Surrey11
GLOSTER,Francis Beresford Lt kia 3-12-17 RASC &20RFC p8&193 MR20
GLOSTER,Gerald Charles Edward Lt kia 6-11-17 1Dev p76 MR30
GLOSTER,Henry Colpays Lt kia 13-3-15 6GordH p242 MR22
GLOVER,A.C.SubCdr 22-7-20 S&T Cps MR43
GLOVER,Alexander Milligan Thomson Lt kia 17-8-17 KOSB &70RFC p8&101 MR20
GLOVER,Ben Hilton 2LtACapt kia 1-7-16 7RWKent att50TMB p141 CR France3
GLOVER,Brian Edward.DCM.T2Lt ded 13-3-16 GL &8RFC p3&190 CR France421,kia
GLOVER,Clifford Lee Lt kia 18-5-18 Ches &48RAF p263 MR20
GLOVER,Cyril John 2Lt dow 8-10-16 10Lond p248 CR France105
GLOVER,G.M.MC.Capt 24-7-20 2Manch MR38
GLOVER,George Wright.DSO.Lt dow 31-8-18 6 att1RB p178 CR France95,1-9-1
GLOVER,John Bertram 2Lt kia 16-6-18 RGA 309SB p39 CR France116,HAC
GLOVER,John Grenside 2Lt kia 8-11-15 4YLI p235 MR30
GLOVER,Leonard James 2Lt dow 1-11-17 B82RH&FA p29 CR Belgium16
GLOVER,Richard Bowie Gaskell.MID Capt kia 5-11-15 1Lond p245 CR France2
GLOVER,Ronald Howard 2Lt kia 25-9-17 RFA X19TMB p208 CR France285,dow
GLOVER,Samuel Lawrence T2Lt ded 12-1-16 10WRid p115 CR France924,kld
GLUCKMAN,Philip Lt kia 8-10-16 25Lond p252 MR21
GLYKA,Anthony Isidore 2Lt kia 12-10-16 1RWar p64 MR21
GLYN,Charles Reginald 2Lt kia 9-1-17 IA 110MahrattaLI att105 p277 MR38
GLYN,Guy Godfrey TLt ded 16-8-15 RE 109Co RlyConSect p45 CR France51
GLYN,Richard Spencer Lt kia 20-10-14 1EKent p57 MR32
GLYNN,Alfred Henley 2Lt dow 12-2-17 15Lond p249 CR France41
GLYNN,Bernard James 2Lt kia 29-5-17 34RFC p8 CR France1170
GLYNN,Martin T2Lt kia 29-9-18 10 att2Worc p108 CR France665
GOADBY,John Clifton 2Lt kia 28-8-18 13Lond p249 CR France568
GOATCHER,Fred TLt dow 31-10-17 9Suff p78 CR France179
GOATER,Horace Benjamin Capt kia 10-8-18 8RDC att2/4Berks p253 CR France3
GOBEY,Alfred John Lt 19-11-20 2DLI CR Durham1
GOBY,James Henry ACapt ded 29-10-20 IARO attS&M att122RlyConstCoy p277 MR43
GODBER,Hugh Gerald TCapt kia 11/18-7-16 13NumbF p61 CR France188,12-7-16
GODBY,Thomas Stanley T2Lt kia 20-11-17 6Mddx att8Lpool p146 MR17
GODDALL,Cecil Clarence 2Lt kia 7-7-16 3 att6Dors p124
GODDALL,Clarence William 2Lt kia 15-11-16 2SStaffs p122
GODDARD,Alec Spencer 2Lt kia 30-11-17 7Norf p73&257 MR17
GODDARD,Eric 2Lt kia 4-7-16 1/7WRid p227 MR21
GODDARD,Frederick Sidney 2Lt kia 15-12-17 4RFus p68 CR France614
GODDARD,Gordon Cecil T2Lt kia 16-10-18 9ESurr p112 CR France206
GODDARD,Harold 2Lt kia 9-10-17 5WYorks p218 MR30
GODDARD,John Lister TLt kia 15-9-16 9Norf p73 MR21

GODDARD,Kenneth Aquinas McKenzie 2Lt kia 11-7-16 5Worc p108 CR France430,Acquinas lt
GODDARD,Norman Molyneux T2Lt dow 2-7-17 SStaffs att9Bn p122 CR France285
GODDARD,Philip Henry Thomas T2Lt kia 26-9-16 11RFus p68 MR21
GODDARD,Ralph Garnett 2Lt kia 9-10-17 1HAC p206 MR30
GODDARD,Sydney George 2Lt kia 30-6-16 2RSuss p119 MR20
GODDARD,Sydney Vernon Lt dow 23-3-18 2/17Lond p250 CR Palestine3
GODDARD,William Neale TLt kia 13-6-17 1/2LancF p92 CR France765
GODDARD,William Thomas 2Lt dow 13-10-17 2/35RFA p29 CR France40
GODET,L.De G.2Lt kia 1-6-18 GL &RAF p190
GODFREY,Arthur Pole TLt kia 11-4-17 HouseHoldBn RHGds p20 MR20
GODFREY,Edward T2Lt kia 31-7-17 RWKent att10Bn p141 MR29,GODFERY
GODFREY,Frederick 2LtTCapt kia 16-8-16 4RFus p68 MR21 CR France1890
GODFREY,Harry Frederick 2Lt kia 1-7-16 1/5N&D p232 MR21
GODFREY,Henry 2Lt kia 9-9-16 5LancF p221 CR France402,8/9-9-16
GODFREY,Herbert Arthur T2Lt kia 12-5-17 11Mddx p146 MR20
GODFREY,Hugh 2Lt kia 1-7-16 2RBerks p139 MR21
GODFREY,John Leslie 2Lt dow 7-5-18 C113RFA p29 CR France180
GODFREY,Leonard George 2Lt kia 20-7-16 10RWFus p97 MR21
GODFREY,Leonard Powell TCapt dow 23-8-17 14WelshR p126 CR Belgium18
GODFREY,Norman Carter T2Lt kia 16-4-18 5TankCps p188 MR32
GODFREY,Oliver Cyril 2Lt ded 23-9-16 27RFC p3 CR France452,kia
GODFREY,Stephen Mervyn Lt dow 30-12-17 28Lond p252 MR21
GODFREY,Victor 2Lt kia 1-7-16 2RScotF p94 MR21
GODFREY,William Frank 2Lt kia 3-9-16 4NStaffs att72TMB p157 CR France402
GODFREY,William John 2Lt kia 3-9-16 1BlkW p128 MR21
GODFREY-FAUSSETT,Owen Godfrey.DSO.LtCol kia 2-5-15 Ess p131
GODFREY-PAYTON,Arthur Capt dow 29-8-16 7RWar p214 CR France74
GODLEE,John T2Lt kia 19-7-16 RFC p3
GODLEY,Gerald Annesley George Lt kia 26-3-18 RASC 15DivTrain p193 CR France113
GODLEY,John Lindley 2Lt ded 31-8-19 RB att286MGC Inf p266 MR43
GODMAN,Frederick Tyrell TCapt ded PoW 12-10-17 9RSuss p119 CR Germany3
GODMAN,Lawrence.DSO.MajALtCol dow 30-9-17 46RFA p29 CR France285
GODMAN,Walter Williams Wynn 2Lt kia 24-1-15 KRRC p150 CR France727
GODOLPHIN-OSBORNE,Maurice Capt dow 25-2-15 RB p178 CR France284
GODSAL,Alan T2Lt kia 30-7-15 7RB p178 MR29
GODSAL,Walter Hugh.DSO.MC.Maj dow 26-3-18 2DLI p160 CR France300
GODSILL,Stanley Lt kia 23-12-17 18Lond p250 CR Palestine3
GODSON,Albert Bernard Lawrence 2Lt kia 3-8-17 NStaffs att9Bn p157 CR Belgium17
GODSON,William Curry TLt kia 3-5-17 46RFA p29 CR France1185,1-5-17
GODWARD,Eric James 2Lt kia 25-8-15 7Mddx p235 CR France525
GODWIN,Charles Cayley 2Lt mbk 17-10-16 1RFC p256 CR France705
GODWIN,Colin Harold 2Lt kia 1-7-16 15Y&L p158 MR21
GODWIN,George 2Lt kia 28-9-16 17RFA p29 CR Belgium84
GODWIN,Harold North T2Lt dow 31-7-17 Lpool att209LabCps 209EmplCoy p189 CR France200
GODWIN,John Charles Raymond T2Lt kia 7-7-16 10 att7RSuss p119 MR21
GODWIN,Leslie Wentworth 2Lt kia 10-10-16 3 att16N&D p134 CR France215
GODWIN,Louis Vionnet T2Lt kia 23-10-16 2RB p178 MR21
GODWIN,Philip Edgar 2Lt kia 7-1-16 IARO att6Jats p277 MR38,6-1-16
GODWIN,Sidney William 2Lt kia 2-10-16 19Lond p250 MR21
GODWIN,Thomas Ernest Lt kia 21-8-17 GL &RFC CR Belgium140
GODWIN,William Bernard 2Lt kia 17-2-17 9 att12Mddx p236 MR21
GODWIN-WILLIAMS,Frederick James HonCapt ded 23-11-18 RWSurr p56&262 CR Nhampt151
GOEPEL,Robert Mackie Lt kia 17-9-16 5SfthH att123MGC p187&241 MR21
GOFF,Alfred Laurence T2Lt kia 16-1-17 14RFus att6LNLancs p68 MR38,Lawrence
GOFF,Charles Edward.MC.LtCol kia 8-8-16 1Lpool p71 MR21
GOFF,R.W.Lt 13-12-16 Leinst CR Kent217
GOFF,William Setten.MC.Lt kia 22-4-17 7RWFus p223 CR France296
GOFFE,William Reginald T2Lt kia 30-7-16 2 O&BLI p130 MR21
GOFFEY,John Graham 2Lt kia 3-9-16 12KRRC p150 CR France339,23 att17Bn
GOING,Charles Henry Bernard Lt kia 18-8-17 2RhodR C'Coy attKAR p202 CR Tanzania1
GOLBY,Arthur Hugh 2Lt dow 13-8-17 4RSuss p228 CR Belgium18
GOLD,Cecil Argo TLt&Adjt kia 3-7-16 5RBerks p139 CR France251
GOLD,Charles Read.DSO.Capt kia 21-11-17 DerbyYeo attDLI p203 CR France1266
GOLD,George Rome 2Lt kia 27-5-18 Hamps att2Berks p120 MR18
GOLD,Percy 2Lt kia 19-7-16 2ScotsGds p52 CR Belgium6,2-7-16

GOLDBERG,Frederick William 2Lt kia 3-10-16 3RWSurr att7RDubF p56 CR Greece3
GOLDBERG,Herbert Walter 2Lt dow 31-7-15 3RWSurr p56 CR France145
GOLDBY,William Charles T2Lt kia 22-8-18 18KRRC p150 CR Belgium11,21-8-18
GOLDEN,Alfred William T2Lt kia 25-3-18 9RSuss p119 MR27
GOLDEN,Frank Charles Allen TLt kia 26-12-15 12DLI p160 France83
GOLDER,William TLt kia 5-10-18 13DLI p160 CR France844
GOLDIE,Amyas Leigh TLt kia 6-8-15 11Glouc att4Worc p106 MR4
GOLDIE,Barre Herbert 2Lt dow 29-4-15 IARO att32Lancers attPatialaLancers p277 CR Egypt8
GOLDIE,George Henry Lt kia 14-9-14 1LNLancs p136 MR15
GOLDIE,Mark Leigh.DSO.MVO Maj ded 5-3-15 V'RHA p29 CR France31
GOLDIE,Paul Francis T2Lt kia 25-9-15 1LNLancs p136 MR19
GOLDIE-TAUBMAN,Gerald TCapt ded 15-9-15 RGA ComdtDetnBks p39 CR Lancs410
GOLDING,Edgar Lt kia 19-9-17 RASC attRFC p18&253 CR France658
GOLDING,Eric.DCM.2Lt kia 15-7-16 1Mddx p146 MR21
GOLDING,Frank 2Lt kia 21-5-17 17 att2/1Lond p250 MR20
GOLDING,Frank Alfred T2Lt kia 1-7-16 9YLI p143 CR France267
GOLDING,Harold T2Lt dow 25-8-17 7RWSurr p56
GOLDING,Harold Gordon Lancelot Lt ded 3-12-20 IA 1/35Sikhs p277 CR Palestine9 Ex 8SLancs
GOLDING,Harold William.MID TCapt kia 31-10-18 RASC att8SomLI p193 CR France206
GOLDING,Thomas James LtTCapt kia 26-9-17 RAMC p195 CR Belgium34
GOLDRICK,A.C.Lt kia 30-8-18 1KAR &SL p268 CR EAfrica90
GOLDRING,Frank Carter TLt kia 13-11-16 8RLancs p59 MR21
GOLDS,Frank T2Lt kia 5-10-16 11ESurr att7RSuss p112 CR France374
GOLDS,Gordon Brewer T2Lt kia 1-7-16 18Lpool p72 CR France397
GOLDS,Ingram Thomas ACapt kia 30-11-17 7ESurr p112 MR17
GOLDSELLER,Leon David Lt dow 14-4-17 5WRid p227 CR France614
GOLDSMID,Sidney Alexander 2Lt ded 7-11-14 3Worc p108 CR France924
GOLDSMITH,Amy Alice Victoria SNurse ded 5-3-19 TFNS att57GH p254 CR France1571
GOLDSMITH,Bertie Lt dow 13-10-18 30/39RFA p29 CR France146
GOLDSMITH,Frank.MC.TMaj dow 27-9-17 14Hamps p120 MR30
GOLDSMITH,Herbert Francis Lt kia 27-9-18 6LancF att63MGC p187&221 MR16
GOLDSMITH,Henry Mills Lt kia 9-5-15 Dev att2Lincs p76 MR32
GOLDSMITH,Lewis Wilberforce TCapt kia 5-11-16 7Yorks p90 MR21
GOLDSPINK,Edward Newell T2Lt kia 31-7-17 Lpool p72 MR29
GOLDSTEIN,Selwyn TLt ded 8-6-17 RE 173Coy p262 CR Belgium5
GOLDSWORTH,Duncan William Lt kia 25-9-15 3 att2SLancs p125 MR29
GOLDSWORTHY,Thomas.MID Lt kia 12/14-4-18 5DCLI attMGC p227 MR32,12-4-18
GOLDTHORP,Guy TCapt kia 23-4-17 10RFus p68 MR20
GOLDTHORPE,Arthur Francis T2Lt kia 12-5-17 7EYorks p84 MR20
GOLIGHTLY,George Frederick T2Lt dow 7-5-17 19DLI p160 CR France610
GOLLIN,Edgar Bearman T2Lt dow 14-5-17 13Lpool p72 CR France113,Capt
GOLLOP,R.J.Capt 28-5-20 3Dors CR Devon206
GOMERSALL,William Ellis TLt kia 1-7-16 22Manch p154 MR21
GOMME,Edward Elfred Coote TLtACapt kia 18-6-17 2Suff p78 CR France421
GONNE,Michael Edward.MC.Capt kia 7-8-18 RFus &54RAF p68&257 CR France526,8-8-13
GONNER,Edward Dermot Leslie 2Lt ded 2-7-18 5RWar p214 CR Ches198
GONNER,Edward Maurice.MC.TCapt kia 23-4-17 16KRRC p150&258 MR20
GONSALVES,D.R.Maj 15-3-21 IMD MR66
GOOCH,Edward Sinclair.MID Maj dow 21-9-15 BerksYeo p203 CR Scot430 Ex7Huss
GOOCH,Geoffrey Fulthorpe TLtACapt kia 19-9-18 RGA 25SB p39 MR16
GOOD,Thomas Henry TCapt dow 8-9-16 9RDubF p176 CR France23
GOOD,William Henry T2Lt kia 16-8-15 7RMunstF p175 MR4
GOOD,William Knight Lt kia 27-2-18 5RScots p211 MR30
GOODACRE,Harry 2Lt ded 29-5-19 3Lincs p263 CR Lincs61
GOODALE,Arthur William 2Lt kia 9-8-15 1KSLI p144 MR29
GOODALL,Albert James Gill TLt kia 1-7-16 2RBerks p139 CR France251
GOODALL,Arthur 2Lt dow 20-2-18 12Lond p248 CR Lond1
GOODALL,Arthur Charles T2Lt kia 6-11-16 7Yorks p90 MR21
GOODALL,Cecil Clarence 2Lt 7-7-16 3 att6Dors CR France1890
GOODALL,Clarence William 2Lt kia 15-11-16 2SStaffs p122 CR France1890,13-11-16
GOODALL,Edward Orme Clement TLt dow 9-11-17 23RFA p29 CR Belgium18

GOODALL,Frank Basil Lt kia 21-8-15 3BordR p117 MR4
GOODALL,Garnett Arthur Cumberland 2Lt kia 20-7-16 4Suff p217 MR21
GOODALL,George Mortimer Langdon 2Lt kia 9-5-15 3 att2ELancs p110 CR France566
GOODALL,George Percy TCapt kia 14-2-16 N&D p134 MR29
GOODALL,Harold Armitage 2Lt kia 22-3-18 RFA attZ16TMB p29 MR27
GOODALL,Marcus Herbert Capt dow 14-7-16 1/5Y&L p238 CR France74
GOODALL,Robert Leslie T2Lt kia 18-9-18 12Manch p154 CR France415 Ex 7HLI
GOODALL,William David Lt ded 11-5-21 6RScots CR Canada155
GOODBAN,Montague Sidney T2Lt kia 19-5-17 ESurr &22RFC p8&112 CR France439
GOODBODY,Henry Edgar Capt kia 12-5-15 4Leinst p174 MR29
GOODBODY,Owen Frederick T2Lt ded 20-10-15 RE 72FC 13Div p45 CR Egypt3,Lt
GOODCHILD,Stanley Cecil 2Lt kia 1-7-16 2Ess p131 MR21
GOODCHILD,Stewart John 2Lt kia 28-3-18 3 att7KSLI p144 MR20
GOODCHILD,Victor George Lt ded 31-10-18 GL &RAF p190
GOODDEN,Frank Widenham LtTmaj kld 28-1-17 RFC p8 CR Hamps1
GOODDEN,Henry William Lt kia 9-5-15 RAMC att2RIrReg p195 MR29
GOODE,Alfred T2Lt kia 29-3-17 NStaffs p157 MR38
GOODE,George Mortlock Lt kia 24-5-17 GL &43RFC p8 MR20
GOODE,Thomas Lord 2Lt kia 15-6-18 5RWar p214 CR Italy3
GOODES,George Leonard.MC&Bar.Capt kia 6-10-16 4Lond &140TMB p246 CR France453
GOODEVE,Lionel TMaj kia 26-8-15 6RScotF p94 CR France423,1Bn
GOODEVE,S.M.Lt 20-11-17 21RFC CR Belgium 16
GOODEVE,Thomas Edward.OBE.TCaptAMaj kld 26-1-19 RE p45&257 CR Syria2
GOODFELLOW,Arthur James Capt dow 7-8-15 8LancF p221 CR Gallipoli3
GOODFELLOW,Edward Arthur Fitzherbert 2Lt kia 21-2-16 3ConnRgrs att60TMB p172 CR Belgium23
GOODFELLOW,Eric Hector.MID TLt kia 9-3-16 28/9RFA p29 MR38
GOODFELLOW,Hugh Douglas TCapt dow 17-12-15 D49RFA p29 CR Belgium11
GOODFELLOW,James Gordon.MC.Lt.AMaj kia 23-3-18 RE 416FC p209 CR France184
GOODFORD,Charles James Henry.MC.Lt kia 1-7-16 1Hamps p120 CR France643
GOODHAND,Reginald Frederick SubCdr ded 16-7-17 IA IndOrdDept p277
GOODING,Herbert Robert Withom Lt kia 13-5-15 5Lond p246 MR22
GOODING,Samuel Jewell 2Lt dow 11-12-17 15ImpCamCps CR Egypt9
GOODING,William Thomas 2Lt kia 22-3-18 1/2 att6/7RScotF p94 MR20
GOODISON,Frank Bowler Lt dow 26-5-17 PoW 5SStaffs attRFC p18&229 CR Germany3
GOODLER, Cdr 19-2-15 S&T Cps CR Iraq6
GOODMAN,Basil Harris 2Lt kia 25/27-9-15 9Norf p73 MR19
GOODMAN,Claude Pendarvis 2Lt kia 18-8-16 4Lpool p72 CR France432
GOODMAN,Douglas Lt dow 24-11-17 RASC att12SWBord p253 MR17
GOODMAN,Eric George T2Lt kia 12-4-18 6Dors p124 MR20
GOODMAN,Gilbert Anthony 2Lt kia 28-10-18 10LNLancs att66RAF p136 CR Italy9,Lt 1Bn
GOODMAN,Geoffrey Thomas Lt kia 1-6-17 RFA p207 CR Belgium21
GOODMAN,Harold Harry 2LtACapt kia 16-8-17 3 att2Dev p76 MR30,Henry
GOODMAN,James 2Lt kia 11-4-17 NhamptYeo p204 MR20
GOODMAN,John Everatt T2Lt kia 14-8-17 GL &53RFC p8 CR France285
GOODMAN,Joseph 2Lt kia 11-4-17 5RLancs att10LNLancs p213 MR20
GOODMAN,Percy Nathaniel TCapt kia 3-3-16 13RFus 1Coy p68 CR France501
GOODMAN,Reginald Moon.MID 2Lt kia 16-5-15 SL att2BordR p201 CR France279
GOODRICH,Frank Edward.MC.TCapt kia 12-9-16 60RFC p3 CR France95,kldacc
GOODRICH,Walter Michael 2Lt kia 25-3-18 8 att6Manch p237 CR France1472
GOODRICK,John William 2Lt drd 26-2-18 GL RE HR17 &IWT p190 MR38
GOODRICK,Walter Robert.MC.Capt kia 1-1-17 7DLI p239 CR France453
GOODSON,Harold Walter.MC.2LtTCapt kia 11-10-18 3 att6Dors A'Coy p124 CR France
GOODWAY,James T2Lt kia 27-12-17 7Yorks p90 CR France1498
GOODWILL,Goodwill,Cyril 2Lt kia 3-9-16 5WYorks p218 CR France383
GOODWIN,Cecil Herbert 2Lt dow 13-10-18 D189RFA p29 CR France686
GOODWIN,Cecil Stanley TCapt kia 31-8-16 A109RFA p29 CR France370
GOODWIN,Dudley Fletcher 2LtACapt dow 7-3-17 157RFA p29 CR France699
GOODWIN,Eric Lindsey TLt kia 12-10-16 13 att17Manch p154 MR21
GOODWIN,George 2Lt ded 19-10-17 1/7Ches p223 CR Egypt1
GOODWIN,Harold Desborough Lt kia 1-7-16 16Mddx p146 CR France1500
GOODWIN,Harold James 2Lt kia 24-4-17 RGA 135SB p39 CR France1182
GOODWIN,John T2Lt kia 29-11-17 1KRRC p150 MR17

GOODWIN,John TCapt&QM ded 22-2-19 RAMC p254 CR Lancs98
GOODWIN,John Stanley 2LtTLt kia 28-3-17 1SStaffs att22Manch p122 MR20
GOODWIN,Norman William 2Lt kia 16-9-17 1Mddx attRFC p8&146 CR Belgium383
GOODWIN,Stuart Wycliffe.MC.T2Lt kia 31-3-18 11BordR p117 CR France745
GOODWIN,William Alexander Delap TLt kia 1-7-16 11Y&L p158 CR France246
GOODY,Geoffrey Riddel TLt kld 14-7-18 9KRRC att 10TrResBn p150 CR France3
GOODY,Gilbert Alexander T2Lt dow 6-11-16 22 att16KRRC p150 CR France105
GOODYEAR,Duncan Matheson TLt kia 29-6-17 GL &57RFC p8 CR Belgium6
GOODYEAR,Frank Percy.MSM.2Lt ded 8-2-19 RASC p193 p267 CR Wilts194
GOODYEAR,Frederick T2Lt dow 23-5-17 Ess att2Bn p131 CR France95
GOODYEAR,Frederick George.MC.Lt dow 18-12-17 24Lond p252 CR Egypt7
GOODYEAR,Raymond Norman 2Lt kia 24-4-17 6ESurr p226 CR France415
GOODYEAR,Roland 2Lt kia 12-4-18 9MGC Inf p183 MR30
GOOLD,Louis 2Lt dow 11-5-18 122/52RFA p29
GOOLDEN,Alexander Wood Capt kia 15-7-19 IA 3/124BaluchistanInf p277 MR4
GOOLDEN,Donald Charles 2Lt kia 15-8-16 6 att4RFus p68 CR France630,14-8-1
GOOSENS,Adolphe Anthony Lt dow 17-8-16 7Norf p73 CR France74
GOOSEY,H.2Lt kld 8-8-18 3NumbF &RAF p61
GOPSILL,Kenneth Lloyd TLt kia 15-2-18 ESurr att43RFC p16&112 CR France345,Capt
GORBUTT,Isaac Lt ded 19-3-19 11WYorks p263 CR Lincs156
GORBUTT,Martha Sister 28-7-20QAIMNS CR Lond29
GORDON,Adam Fraser 2Lt dow 11-8-16 10LNLancs p136 MR21
GORDON,Adrian Charles.DSO.LtCol kia 12-12-17 RFA 235Bde p206 CR France755
GORDON,A.E.Maj ded 19-12-16 RGA p39 CR Wales372
GORDON,Albert William 2Lt dow 12-8-17 32RFC p8 CR France40
GORDON,Alec McDougall.MC.MID Capt dow 7-11-17 246RFA p207 CR Belgium10
GORDON,Alec William.MC.CaptAMaj kia 6-8-18 RE 56FC p45 CR France33
GORDON,Alexander John Maxwell Capt kia 27-11-17 1/16Lond p249 CR France530
GORDON,Alexander Maurice Lt kia 23-1-16 1RFus p68 MR29,20-1-16
GORDON,Alexander Weston LtCol ded 20-12-18 3RIrF p171 CR Glouc27
GORDON,Alistair Campbell Miller T2Lt dow 1-3-17 6RScotF p94 CR Lond14
GORDON,Alister Fraser.CMG.DSO.TBrigGen dow 31-7-17 GordH Cmdg153Bde Staff p166 CR Belgium11
GORDON,Arthur Forbes T2Lt dow 18-4-18 1CamH p167 CR France10
GORDON,Bernard Vernon 2Lt kld 14-12-16 RFC p3 CR Numb86
GORDON,Bertram Gorges Reginald.DSO.TLtCol kia 20-7-16 2GordH p166 CR France176
GORDON,Cecil Philip George Capt kld 21-3-18 4SStaffs attRFC p16&122 CR Glouc67
GORDON,Charles Campbell Boswell 2Lt kia 28-4-17 3SomLI p79 MR20
GORDON,Charles Cecil CaptAMaj kia 4-6-17 110RH&FA p29 CR Belgium42
GORDON,Charles Ewan Lt kia 27-8-18 5RScots att1/5RScotsF p211 MR16 CR France162
GORDON,Charles William Eric BrigGen kia 23-7-17 BlkW 123InfBde p128 CR Belgium15
GORDON,Colin.MID Capt kia 16-8-17 2Lond p245 MR29
GORDON,Colin Graham 2Lt kia 1-7-16 3GordH p166 CR France331
GORDON,Cosmo George 2Lt dow 17-9-14 1Nhampt p137 CR France1107
GORDON,David Elder 2Lt kia 15-7-16 12RScots p54 CR France399
GORDON,Donald 2Lt kia 17-7-17 256RFA p208 CR Belgium5
GORDON,Donald Jervis Gordon T2Lt kia 3-7-16 8BordR p117 CR France233
GORDON,Douglas Lt kia 14-8-17 7A&SH att10RFC p18&243 CR France924
GORDON,Douglas Neave 2Lt kia 21-2-17 1/6SStaffs p229 CR France502
GORDON,Douglas Stanley 2Lt kia 21-2-18 RFA &2RFC SR p16&29 CR France9
GORDON,Elizabeth Marjorie Miss died 11-9-17 VAD StJAB p200 CR Greece9
GORDON,Eldred Pottinger 2Lt kia 22-11-15 IARO att104Rif p277 MR38
GORDON,Eric Alexander T2Lt kia 21-3-18 HLI att10/11Bn p162 MR20
GORDON,Ernest Arthur Woodhall 2Lt dow 29-7-17 4YLI p235 CR France13
GORDON,Geoffrey Lt kia 30-4-15 12Lancers p22 MR29
GORDON,George Duff TLt kia 12-3-15 2Nhampt p137 CR France768
GORDON,George Strachan 2Lt kia 19-8-17 7ScotRif attRFC p18&224 CR France1495
GORDON,Gerald Montague TCapt&Adjt kia 9-6-17 5 att12RFus p68 CR Belgium
GORDON,Gilbert Thomas T2Lt dow 28-9-15 8GordH p166 CR France98
GORDON,Harold Eastly 2Lt dow 23-2-17 5Lond p246 CR Belgium11
GORDON,Henry Lt dow 19-12-15 3 att2KOSB p101 CR Gallipoli1,Harry 3 att1Bn

GORDON,Henry Bernard TLt kia 7-7-16 7RSuss p119 MR21

GORDON,Ivan Hugh Maj accShot 2-9-17 IA 56Rif attKapurtalaInf p277 CR EAfrica13

GORDON,J.C.H.2Lt 23-1-21 3GordH CR Scot341

GORDON,James Gaspar 2Lt kia 5-3-17 5 att6GordH p242 MR20

GORDON,James Willison Nugent Lt kia 22-2-15 5BlkW p231 CR France706,William

GORDON,John Cameron 2Lt kia 21-3-18 8RBerks p139 MR27

GORDON,John Frederick Strathearn Capt dow 19-11-14 ScotRif att1RScotF p103 CR Belgium150

GORDON,Lewis.DSO.Capt dow 18-10-15 GordH p166 CR Gallipoli3,BdeMaj 129Bde

GORDON,Maitland Lockhart Capt kia 7-5-17 3 att2GordH p166 MR20

GORDON,Michael Patrick Rev dow 27-8-17 RAChDept p199 CR Belgium24

GORDON,Peter,T2Lt kia 24-8-18 12 att18KRRC &4CamH p150 CR Belgium11,9Bn

GORDON,Reginald Clegg.DSO.Maj kld 26-3-18 RGA Lowland HB p209 CR France156,R.G.

GORDON,Robert T2Lt dow 4-12-16 99MGC p183 CR France40

GORDON,Robert Charles Lowther T2Lt dow 30-9-15 8GordH p166 CR France64

GORDON,Robert Eddington Capt kia 15-9-14 Nhampt p137 MR15

GORDON,Robert Hope Lt kia 8-8-16 1/8Lpool p215 MR21

GORDON,Robert Norman Capt kia 28-10-14 2BordR p117 MR29

GORDON,Roland Elphinstone.MC.CaptAMaj dow 30-8-18 C251RFA p29 CR France119

GORDON,Ronald Granville 2Lt kia 19-9-18 3 att2RSuss p119 CR France699

GORDON,Ronald Henry Capt kia 18-7-16 3 att1GordH p166 MR21

GORDON,Ronald Steuart Capt kia 2-11-14 IA 57Rif p277

GORDON,Sidney Eustace Laing Lt kia 13-3-15 6 att4RFus p68 MR29

GORDON,Sidney George T2Lt kia 20-9-17 16RB p178 MR30

GORDON,Thomas Seton T2Lt dow 22-1-16 11BordR p117 CR France43

GORDON,W.D.Lt 7-2-20 S&T Cps MR66

GORDON,W.H.Lt 30-10-16 CanadaFldArt 2DAC CR France133

GORDON,William Lt kia 9-5-15 CamH p167 MR22

GORDON,William Bonnalie.MID Capt ded 2-11-19 RAMC p267 CR Yorks474

GORDON,William Hyde Eagleson TLt dow 30-9-15 8GordH p166 CR France40

GORDON,Victor Frederick.MC.Lt dow 1-7-18 GL YLI attTMB p190 CR Mddx9

GORDON,Vivian TCapt kia 25-9-15 8GordH p166 MR19

GORDON-DUFF,Lachlan Capt kia 24-10-14 3 att1GordH p166 CR France348

GORDON-IVES,Victor Maynard Gordon Lt dow 16-9-14 3CldGds p51 CR France1107

GORDON-JONES,Eric 2Lt dow 1-8-17 2Mddx p146 CR Belgium11

GORDON-KIDD,Arthur Lionel.DSO.LtTCapt dow 27-8-17 4DragGds attRFC p8&21 CR Belgium18

GORDON-LENNOX,Lord Bernard Charles Maj kia 10-11-14 2GrenGds p50 CR Belgium134

GORDON PATCHETT,Reginald Lt 7-3-18 MilLabCps CR EAfrica53

GORDON-RALPH,Philip James Gordon Capt kia 6-8-17 2RIrReg p89 CR Belgium7

GORDON-SALE,H.Lt 9-3-15 3KAR p268

GORDON-SMITH,Gordon TLtACapt kia 24-10-18 RWKent att10Bn p141 CR Belgium408

GORDON-SMITH,Norman 2Lt kia 19-12-15 HLI attRFC CR Belgium379

GORDON-STEWARD,Charleton William TMaj kia 12-4-17 NumbF Staff198InfBde p61 CR France765

GORE,Annesley Charles Edward St.George Capt kia 26-6-15 IA 2/9 att1/9GurkhaRif p277 CR France631

GORE,Arthur Holmes Capt kia 12-8-15 8Hamps p229 MR4

GORE,Francis T2Lt dow 26-3-17 23Mddx p146 CR Belgium11

GORE,Gerard Ribton 2Lt dow 20-12-14 3 att2RWFus p97 CR France345,kia 1Bn

GORE,Leonard Joseph Capt kia 3-5-17 7 att12Mddx p235 MR20

GORE,Robert Clements.CB.CMG.BrigGen kia 14-4-18 A&SH Cmdg101InfBde p173 CR Belgium11,13-4-18

GORE,Sidney Kingston Lt kia 28-10-14 1RWKent p141 MR22

GORE,William Frederick.MM.T2Lt kia 27-9-18 2RIrReg att1RMunstF p89 CR France256

GORE-BROWN,Harold Thomas Thirlwall 2Lt dow 23-8-16 6 att7KRRC p150 CR France833

GORE-BROWNE,Eric Antony Rollo Maj drd 3-7-18 Dors att2/3KAR p124&268 MR46

GORE-JONES,Stanley Fox Lt kia 7-6-17 1Wilts CR Belgium43

GORE-LANGTON,Montague Vernon.MC.Capt kia 9-10-15 1IrGds p52 CR France423

GORELL,Henry Gorell.Lord.DSO.Maj dow 16-1-17 RFA 19Bty47Div p206 CR Belgium11

GORELL-BARNES,Charles Roper.DSO.MC.TCapt dow 21-4-18 GL att8RB p190 CR France52

GORFUNKLE,Isaac TLt kia 12-8-18 13 att1LancF p92 CR France193

GORING-Jones,Michael Derwas.CMG.DSO.TBrigGen ded 19-5-19 Staff 57InfBde p261 MR65

GORMAN,D.T.MC.LtACapt dow 22-6-19 2Hamps p120 MR70 &CR Europe179

GORMAN,Gerald Francis 2Lt kia 30-7-16 12RWar p64 MR21,14Bn

GORMLEY,Thomas 2Lt mbk 12-6-18 1 att7/8KOSB p156 MR20

GORNALL,George 2Lt kia 27-3-18 16RFC p16 MR20

GORNELL,Noel Christopher T2Lt kia 21-3-18 RE 157FC p45 CR France364,dow

GORRIE,Alexander Keith T2Lt kia 26-4-16 11HLI p163 CR Belgium137

GORRIE,John William 2Lt kia 19-7-16 7Worc p226 CR France832

GORRINGE,Arthur Arnold Capt ded 3-5-20 Ex RASC CR SAfrica63

GORRINGE,Edward Clifton.MC.TCapt kia 5-9-18 7RSuss p119 CR France511

GORRINGE,Noel Rupert Lt kia 10-4-18 4Nhampt attMGC p234&187 MR32

GORRINGE,Wilfred Stuart Capt dow 10-6-18 RE 82FC p210 CR France622

GORST,E.W.2Lt kia 25-10-14 1RFus p68 MR32

GORST,James 2Lt ded 29-5-17 42RFA p29 CR France113

GORT,Albert Henry 2Lt ded 6-11-18 RDC p253 CR Suff55

GORTON,Arthur Llewellyn Lt kia 20-10-18 IARO att1/10GurkhaRif p277 MR38,29-10-18

GORTON,George Herbert T2Lt kia 10-7-16 11 att9Yorks p90 MR21

GORTON,Lionel John 2Lt kia 16-4-18 1Lincs p254 MR30

GOSCHEN,Christopher Gerard TCapt kia 25-9-16 4GrenGds SR p50 CR France374

GOSCHEN,Hon George Joachim.MID 2Lt dow 19-1-16 1/5EKent p213 CR Iraq5

GOSDEN,Dudley Walter TLt kia 6-7-16 1Wilts p153 MR21,8-7-16

GOSLETT,John Southcote 2Lt ded 11-11-15 1/1NorfYeo p204 CR Egypt3,Lt

GOSLEY,George Andrew Hay 2Lt dow 16-10-16 1/9A&SH att1/14Lond p244 CR France145

GOSLING,Charles.CMG.ColTBrigGen kia 12-4-17 Staff &KRRC p1 CR France729

GOSLING,Douglas Edward Lt kia 20-5-15 RE p210 CR Belgium98

GOSLING,Frank T2Lt kia 26-4-18 5Y&L p158 CR Belgium102

GOSLING,Frederick Horace 2Lt kia 7-6-17 32RFus p68 CR Belgium111

GOSLING,Frederick William TCapt kia 20-7-16 23Manch p154 MR21

GOSLING,Gerald Noel.MC.Lt kia 7-7-19 1Glouc p106 MR70 &CR Europe179

GOSLING,Leonard Buchanan T2Lt ded 27-10-18 10TankCps p188 CR Dorset94

GOSLING,William Robert.MM.2Lt kia 21-3-18 2Wilts p153 MR27

GOSNELL,Harold Clifford 2Lt kia 1-7-16 1/2Lond p245 MR21

GOSNEY,Reginald Wilkie 2Lt kia 23-11-15 IARO att76Punjabis p277 MR38,22-11-15

GOSS,Edward Herbert Allan.MID TLt kia 1-7-16 7EKent p57 CR France397

GOSS,Edward Oliver 2Lt dow 14-10-18 4 att10RWSurr p212 CR Belgium112

GOSS,Hubert John.MC.2Lt kia 15-7-16 10Ches p96 MR21

GOSS,Raymond George Frederic 2Lt kia 13-8-15 1/5NStaffs p238 CR Belgium127,Frederick

GOSSAGE,Guy Winwood Maj ded 24-12-17 RFA p206 CR Shrop145

GOSSCHALK,Edward Meyer Lt kia 28-8-16 3 att6YLI p143 CR France402

GOSSE,Robert Buchanan Wilkes 2Lt dow 1-4-17 7Ches att1/6War p223 CR France511

GOSSE,William Hay.MC.TCaptAMaj kia 5-4-18 A79RFA p29 CR France41

GOSSELIN,Alwyn Bertram Robert Raphael.DSO.Capt kia 7-2-15 GrenGds p50 CR France720

GOSSET,Claude Butler Gosset Maj ded 16-2-16 Ches attRE 19SigCoy p96 CR France134

GOSSET,René Frankland ACapt kia 25-9-16 1EYorks p84 CR France1890

GOSSETT,William Beresford 2Lt kia 1-11-14 RFA p29 CR Belgium57

GOSSLING,Donald Foley 2Lt dow 10-6-17 2/9Manch p237 CR France80

GOSTLING,Thomas Harold 2Lt ded 2-8-19 Leic p263 CR War32

GOSWELL,Oliver Owen 2Lt kia 30-4-18 15Lond p249 MR34

GOTCH,Duncan Hepburn 2Lt kia 11-3-15 1Worc p108 MR22

GOTCH,Geoffrey William Lt ded 22-10-18 RGA &RAF p39

GOTCH,Roby Middleton Capt kia 1-7-16 7N&D p233 MR21,Myddleton

GOTELEE,Geoffrey Harris TLtACapt kia 18-9-18 7SWBord p100 MR37

GOTHE,Cecil Rudolph Lt ded 10-2-19 RGA p270

GOTT,Albert Ernest T2Lt kia 18-11-16 10RWar p64 MR21

GOUDIE,Alexander Currie T2Lt kia 20-9-17 9ScotRif p103 MR30

GOUDIE,Alexander Malcolm Lt dow 18-8-16 3Leinst att17MGC Inf p174&183 CR France329,2Bn

GOUDIE,Humphrey Blaikie T2Lt kia 17-8-16 7CamH p167 MR21

GOUGH,Bernard Bradley TLt kia 17-2-16 RAMC att8SStaffs p195 CR Belgium120

GOUGH,Bert Harold 2Lt kia 9-4-18 4RLancs p213 CR France1106

GOUGH,Cyril Lt ded PoW 8-9/9-11-18 4EYorks p219 CR Belgium353,11-10-18
GOUGH,Dermot Humphrey.MC.Lt ded 7-10-19 10Huss p261 CR Glouc40
GOUGH,Eric John Fletcher Capt kia 30-12-14 IrGds p52 CR France727
GOUGH,George Henry Waldron.MID Lt kia 15-12-17 1/7Ches p223 CR Palestine3
GOUGH,George William Blanthorne TLt kia 10-8-15 6Leinst p174 CR Gallipoli18
GOUGH,Harold Stuart TLt kia 17-6-16 11KRRC p150 CR Belgium4,16-6-16
GOUGH,Harry Stanley Lt ded 13-3-18 8Manch &RFC p237 CR Wilts115
GOUGH,Henry Percy Bright.MC&Bar.TMaj dow 22-4-18 17WelshR p126 CR France100,Harry
GOUGH,Horace Frederick.DSO.2Lt kia 21-9-17 NStaffs att8Bn p157 CR Belgium22
GOUGH,John Bloomfield.MID Lt kia 9-9-14 RHA p29 CR France1445,8-9-14
GOUGH,John Bolle Tyndale Maj kia 22-3-18 1Herts p252 CR France365
GOUGH,John Edmond.VC.ADC.KCB.CMG.BrigGen dow 21-2-15 Staff p1 CR France768,22-2-15
GOUGH,John Noel 2Lt kia 8-3-18 RFA attY29TMB p29 CR Belgium22
GOUGH,Leo Walter THon2Lt ded 23-4-18 GL IntelCps p190&257 CR France1571
GOUGH,Norman Lt kia 19-7-16 7Worc p225 CR France832
GOUGH,Owen Lt drd 30-12-15 IA 12Cav p277 MR41
GOUGH,Roland Ivor.DSO.TCapt dow 14-10-16 15RWar p64 CR France145
GOUGH,Rupert.MC.2Lt dow 28-10-17 RH&FA 71Bty p29 CR Belgium16
GOULD,Arthur Edmund T2Lt kia 13-5-16 13Ches p96 CR France68,14-5-16
GOULD,Cecil Arbuthnot Capt kia 26-3-17 5Ess p232 MR34
GOULD,Chalkley Vivian TLtAMaj kia 9-6-17 115/25RFA p29 CR Belgium102
GOULD,Clifford.MC.Lt kia 24-8-18 14RFA p29 CR France1014
GOULD,Eric Melville 2Lt kia 1-7-16 3 att2Dev p76 MR21
GOULD,Ernest William 2Lt kia 10-4-18 4SLancs att1/5SomLI p230 CR Palestine9
GOULD,Francis Hunt Capt kld 6-6-15 1Mddx p146 CR France922
GOULD,Francis William 2Lt kia 9-10-17 7Worc p226 MR30
GOULD,Frank Allan Capt ded 17-4-19 Res p270 CR Surrey160
GOULD,Frederick James 2Lt ded 12-12-18 RGA 143HB p39 CR Greece2
GOULD,Gerald Oscar Alan 2Lt dow 25-6-16 13KRRC p150 CR France120,George
GOULD,Henry Charles Hamerton 2Lt dow 15-4-17 32RFA p29 CR France95,27RFA
GOULD,James Robertson Sabiston.MID T2Lt dow 15-4-18 268MGC p183 CR France64
GOULD,Jay.CBE.LtCol ded 1-6-19 ADMS IMS p277 CR Asia60,2-6-19
GOULD,Joseph William T2Lt kia 13-10-18 1Y&L p158 CR France316
GOULD,Patrick Wallace T2Lt kia 24-8-16 9KRRC p150 MR21
GOULD,Ralph Bohn T2Lt dow 20-12-16 4SWBord p100 CR Iraq5
GOULD,Roy Ernest 2Lt kia 27-3-17 7Ess p232 MR34
GOULD,Walter Harvey Russell Lt kia 26-9-17 GL &70RFC p8 MR20
GOULD,William Justin TLt kia 23-8-15 5Nhampt p137 CR Belgium137
GOULDBY,James Henry 2Lt kia 25-8-16 5 att7Lincs p220 MR21
GOULDEN,E.C.Capt drd 28-3-15 NigR MR40
GOULDEN,Frederick Charles Capt drd 28-3-15 NigForces CR Eire58
GOULDEN,William Charles T2Lt kia 12-2-18 Mddx att2Bn p146 CR Belgium125,Wilfred
GOULDING,Frederick Ernest T2Lt ded 5-8-18 9RIrRif p169 CR France100
GOULDING,George Percival Kimber 2LtTLt dow 31-7-17 7ELancs p110 CR Belgium152
GOULDING,Reginald T2Lt kia 27-9-17 YLI att2Bn p143 CR Belgium24
GOULDSBURY,Henry Cullen TCapt ded 27-8-16 9RBerks EAUL att1KAR p139 CR EAfrica19,2Bn
GOUNDRY,John Firth 2Lt kia 16-8-17 9 att1/19Lond p248 MR29
GOURD,Percy TCapt kia 18-4-16 3SLancs p125 MR38
GOURLAY,Alexander Smith Forrest 2Lt kia 24-3-18 3 att2ScotRif p103 MR27
GOURLAY,George T2Lt kia 14-11-17 73MGC Inf p183 CR France528
GOURLAY,John Norman 2Lt kia 1-7-16 3SfthH p164 CR France605,2Bn
GOURLAY,William Norris TCapt kia 6-6-17 5CamH p167 CR France64
GOVAN,Douglas Moncrieff.MID Maj kia 28-6-15 IA 1/5GurkhaRif p277 MR4
GOVER,William Arthur Capt kia 3-3-15 IA 7Rajputs p277
GOW,James Lightfoot T2Lt kia 1-7-16 9 att1KOSB p101 CR France220
GOW,John Halley T2Lt kia 15-7-16 1Mddx p146 MR21
GOWAN,Arthur Blackmore Lt kia 14-7-16 RE 1/3DurhamFC p210 MR21,Blackwood
GOWAN,J.C.Capt 16-8-15 1/4Ess CR Gallipoli4
GOWANS,Alexander Douglas Stuart 2Lt dow 27-4-17 6BlkW p231 CR France95,Lt
GOWANS,William Maj dow 2-5-15 2YLI p143 CR France200
GOWANS,William Ireland T2Lt kia 13-10-17 25NumbF p61 MR30
GOWAR,Lancelot John T2Lt kld 1-5-17 GL &RFC p8 CR Mddx53
GOWER,Francis John Harman 2Lt ded 23-11-17 E TankCps p100 MR17

GOWER,John Richard.MBE.MIDx2 Capt&QM 24-4-20 23WelchR att7SWBord CR Wales76
GOWING,William Lee 2Lt dow 12-12-17 1/4Norf p216 CR Palestine9
GOWSELL,Leonard Lt dow 20-4-18 GL &4RAF CR France134
GOZNEY,Charles Marsh.MC.Capt 15-8-20 RAMC MR38
GRACE,Alfred Alexander Gordon T2Lt kld 26-6-17 GL &22ResRFC p8 CR Egypt
GRACE,Frank LtACapt dow 5-11-17 RFA 19Bty p29 MR38
GRACE,Handley Carleton TCapt dow PoW 2-9-17 6Nhampt A'Coy p137 CR Belgium393
GRACE,Joseph 2Lt kia 19-8-17 15Ches p96 CR France363
GRACE,Mervyn Bruce Lt kia 8-5-17 6NStaffs p238 CR France1495
GRACEY,Horace Charles Capt kia 18-10-16 1RB p178 CR France1891
GRACIE,Hugh Colin Stuart T2Lt dow 26-11-17 18WelshR p126 CR France398
GRACIE,John James.MC.Lt kia 17-9-18 1 att7/8KOSB p101 MR19
GRACIE,William James T2Lt kia 26-4-17 9NStaffs p157 CR France924
GRADON,F.M.Capt ded 18-9-20 RE IWT HQ Staff CR Iraq6
GRADWELL,Charles Edward Lt 21-3-18 RB att59MGC p178&183 MR27
GRADWELL,George Francis 2Lt kia 28-2-17 1RDubF p176 MR21
GRADY,Walter Henry 2Lt kld 22-4-15 RFus att3Bn p68 MR29,25-4-15 6Bn
GRAEME,Laurence Oliphant.CMG.MIDx3 TLtCol kia 10-3-16 1CamH p167 CR France178,GRÆME Lawrence
GRAFTON,William Salter T2Lt kia 15-8-18 9YLI p143 CR France233
GRAFTON-GRATTON,Thomas Walter 2Lt ded 24-2-19 RGA p254 CR Surrey148,24-1-19
GRAFTON-WIGNALL,John Dighton Capt kia 26-1-17 IA 82Punjabis p277 MR3
GRAHAM,Alan Moir Capt kia 20-12-14 IA 2/5GurkhaRif att2/2 p277 MR38
GRAHAM,Alec George Malcolm Capt kia 22-12-14 6Worc attNLancs p108 MR2
GRAHAM,Alexander.MID Capt dow 19-10-15 RAMC att1/7Ess p253 MR4
GRAHAM,Alexander Cecil Capt kia 10-9-16 1GrenGds SR p50 CR France394,12-16
GRAHAM,Andrew TLt kia 30-12-17 9BlkW att44TMB p128 CR France1182
GRAHAM,Andrew James Lt kia 26-9-17 6ScotRif p224 CR Belgium45
GRAHAM,Archibald Foster.MID 2Lt kia 11-11-15 RGA 6SB p39 CR Belgium84,Forster
GRAHAM,Archibald Stuart Bullock Lt kia 31-10-14 2GordH p166 MR29
GRAHAM,Arthur Thomas T2Lt kia 27-3-18 42MGC p183 MR20
GRAHAM,Austin Graham MajTLtCol dow 11-4-18 14 att5Yorks p220 CR France1094,5 att4Bn
GRAHAM,Bertram Robert LtCol kia 11-3-16 3KAR CpsofGuides p277&268 CR EAfrica56
GRAHAM,Cecil Erskine Capt kia 1-7-17 2BordR att 1/5NStaffs p117 MR29
GRAHAM,Cecil Hollingsworth 2Lt kia 19-9-16 3RDubF attTMB p176 CR Belgium4,20-9-16
GRAHAM,Cedric Kenny Onslow T2Lt kia 16-9-16 15DLI p160 MR21
GRAHAM,Charles Hamilton Malise Lt kia 12-4-18 1RLancs p59 CR France604,1-4-17
GRAHAM,Cyril TLt kia 27-5-15 5BordR p228 MR29 CR Belgium45
GRAHAM,Donald Hatt Noble TCapt kia 27-9-15 9BlkW A'Coy p128 CR France219,25-9-15
GRAHAM,Duncan.DCM.2Lt kia 30-9-18 7A&SH p243 CR France236
GRAHAM,Duncan Charles Capt kia 28-4-17 7Norf p73 MR20
GRAHAM,Edwin Michael T2Lt kia 4-10-17 1DCLI p114 MR30
GRAHAM,Eric Clive 2Lt kia 9-1-17 3 att1Manch p154 CR Iraq5
GRAHAM,Eric Montrose Lt dow 2-4-15 SWBord p100 CR Lond8
GRAHAM,Ernest William 2Lt kia 18-10-16 12BordR att1ELancs p117 MR21
GRAHAM,Fenton Weiss Lt kia 4-10-15 4DLI att1YLI p160 CR France924,14-10
GRAHAM,Francis.DSO.MC.CaptAMaj kia 28-3-18 71RFA p29 CR France1182
GRAHAM,Francis Noel TCapt dow 16-11-16 11RWar p64 CR France62
GRAHAM,George Humphrey Irving Maj kia 7-2-16 IA 44MerwaraInf MR38 p27
GRAHAM,George Lionel Capt ded PoW 11-4-18 7RWar D'Coy p214 CR France1061
GRAHAM,George Lyons T2Lt kia 18-7-17 6RDubF p176 MR30
GRAHAM,George Stanley TLt ded 19-6-16 RAMC p195 CR Iraq5
GRAHAM,George William T2Lt kia 20-9-17 Mddx att5LancF p146 MR30
GRAHAM,Hamilton Carruthers 2Lt kia 26-8-18 8Lond p247 CR France626
GRAHAM,Harry Capt&QM ded 10-1-16 HLI p265 CR Lond35
GRAHAM,Henry 2Lt kia 28-6-17 IA 74Punjabis att67 p277 MR38
GRAHAM,Henry Balfour 2Lt kia 9-5-17 3 att10BlkW p128 MR37
GRAHAM,Hugh Christison 2LtTLt kia 9-6-17 9RScotF att33MGC p183&94 CR Belgium60,8-6-17
GRAHAM,Hugh Colborne T2Lt kia 1-10-17 1/2 att9Yorks p90 MR30
GRAHAM,James Lawson TLt dow 30-9-18 9RInniskF p105 MR30

GRAHAM,John Capt kia 16-6-15 10Lpool p216 MR29
GRAHAM,John 2Lt kia 16-9-16 10DLI p160 MR21
GRAHAM,John Arthur.MC.MID TMaj kia 20-3-16 7Lincs p75 CR France922
GRAHAM,John Frederick TMaj kia 1-7-16 A150RFA p29 CR France630
GRAHAM,John Hamilton Thom TLt kia 6-7-16 6KOSB p101 MR21,4-7-16
GRAHAM,John Robertson.MC.2Lt dow 22-9-16 C96RH&FA p29 CR France145,Roberson
GRAHAM,John Stanley 2Lt kia 30-8-18 4WelshR p230 CR France217
GRAHAM,John Wilfrid Lt kia 21-12-14 1CamH att3HLI p167 MR22,22-12-14 HLI attCamH
GRAHAM,Kenneth Stuart 2Lt kia 24-3-18 9SfthH p164 CR France785
GRAHAM,Lachlan Seymour 2Lt dow 29-8-17 7HLI p240 CR Belgium11,Lt 12Bn
GRAHAM,Lionel Lovell Capt kia 26-9-17 1Camb p244 MR30
GRAHAM,Malcolm G.MC.2LtACapt kia 26-10-17 2GordH p166 MR30
GRAHAM,Malcolm Hewley Lt kia 15-6-15 3 att2Yorks p90 MR22
GRAHAM,Marmaduke Whitaker Capt kia 24-7-15 2RWKent p141 CR Iraq6
GRAHAM,Percy Gordon TCapt kia 1-7-16 16NumbF p61 MR21
GRAHAM,Peter Capt kia 30-8-18 GL CamH att1KAR p167,202&266 CR EAfrica90
GRAHAM,P.N.Capt 28-11-20 NumbF CR Berks1
GRAHAM,Richard 2Lt kia 10-1-15 2ScotRif p103 CR France567
GRAHAM,Robert Lynedoch.MID Lt kia 16-9-17 GL &19RFC p8 CR Belgium125
GRAHAM,Robert Main T2Lt kia 4-10-16 10WRid p115 MR21
GRAHAM,Ronald McLeod 2Lt kia 12-3-15 Ess attRScotF p131 MR22
GRAHAM,Thomas Eric.MC.2Lt kia 24-3-18 2ScotRif p103 CR France1890
GRAHAM,Thomas Harold T2Lt dow 25-10-16 17RB p178 CR France105,2Bn
GRAHAM,Thomas Leslie.MC.Lt ded 23-5-19 3SfthH p265 CR Kent268
GRAHAM,Walter Ap.S.J. Maj ded 23-2-18 RAMC p267
GRAHAM,W.L.C.Capt 14-7-15 IARO CR Scot208
GRAHAM,William Capt kia 3-5-17 6DLI p239 MR20
GRAHAM,William LtCol ded 5-11-17 RAMC p267 CR Ireland57
GRAHAM,William George.MID Capt kia 24-6-15 5NumbF p213 CR Belgium43
GRAHAM,William James T2Lt kia 31-7-17 18Lpool p72 MR29
GRAHAM,William John T2Lt kia 22-11-17 18RIrRif p169 MR17
GRAHAM,William Rennie TLt kia 1-10-18 9RIrF p171 CR Belgium157
GRAHAM-CLARKE,John Altham Stobart 2Lt kia 1-7-16 9KOSB att6BordR p101 CR France339
GRAHAM-KING,Reginald 2Lt kia 23-3-18 4 att6Dors p229 CR France385,25-3-18
GRAHAM-MENZIES,Alastair Lt 1-1-15 1ScotGds MR22
GRAHAM-MONTGOMERY,Graham John Early Capt kia 24-4-17 12Hamps p120 MR37
GRAHAM-ROE,Archibald Chaceley T2Lt kia 29-4-17 KRRC att1Bn p150 MR20,28-4-17
GRAIL,Clifford George TCapt dow 23-7-15 7NStaffs p157 MR4
GRAINGER,James Francis Stuart TCapt dow 12-8-15 11BlkW att1KOSB p128 CR Gallipoli6
GRAINGER,John Henry 2Lt kia 15-9-16 4EYorks p219 CR France239
GRAINGER,John Scott 2Lt kia 1-7-16 1/2Lond p245 MR21
GRAMSHAW,Hugh 2Lt ded 28-2-16 3SStaffs p122 CR Numb49,Lt
GRAMSHAW,Robert Wilfred Raleigh 2Lt dow 27-1-15 3 att2RSuss p119 CR France80
GRAND,Hugh Stevenson.MID T2Lt kia 28-4-17 11Suff p78 CR France604
GRANDAGE,William Briggs LtCol dow 14-5-17 235RFA p206 CR Belgium11
GRANDIN,Richard John 2Lt kia 18-5-17 RASC &60RFC p8&193 MR20
GRANET,Edward John.CB.TBrigGen ded 22-10-18 RA p29 CR Europe51
GRANGE,James Burness T2Lt kia 20-4-18 21WYorks X'Coy p81 CR France250
GRANGER,Ernest Every Wyatt.MID TCapt kia 16-8-17 att9LancF p92 MR30
GRANGER,Frank T2Lt dow 15-12-16 20Manch p154 CR France74,14Bn
GRANGER,Frederick Collins.MC.MID T2Lt dow 30-3-17 1Glouc p106 CR France145
GRANGER,Harold Mossman 2Lt 29-5-15 1/7Manch CR Gallipoli2
GRANGER,William Thomas Lt dow 21-9-17 4Wilts p236 CR Belgium154
GRANSDEN,Victor Eric T2Lt kia 26-4-18 10RIrRif p169 CR Belgium64
GRANSMORE,Rodney Capt kia 28-9-15 Mddx p147 MR19
GRANT,Alan.MID 2Lt dow 3-9-18 1RScotF p94 CR France103,Allen
GRANT,Alan Francis Montague T2Lt dow 18-6-16 9RWSurr p56 CR France285
GRANT,Albyn Evan Powell 2Lt kia 14-8-15 7RWFus p223 MR4
GRANT,Alexander Capt kia 13-11-16 6GordH p242 CR France131
GRANT,Alexander 2Lt dow 24-4-17 7HLI p240 CR Palestine2
GRANT,Alexander 2Lt kia 27-9-18 1GrenGds p50 CR France1497
GRANT,Alexander George William LtCol kia 25-9-15 8Dev attWAfrR p76&200 MR19

GRANT,Arch TLtACapt kia 30-11-17 1Ess p131 MR17
GRANT,Charles Bruce 2Lt dow 8-12-17 9HLI p240 CR France64,Lt
GRANT,Charles William TLtCapt dow 12-10-17 11RScots p54 CR Belgium20
GRANT,Clifton Brown.MID TCapt kia 27-7-16 99MGC Inf p183 CR France1890
GRANT,D.2Lt kia 28-4-15 7CamH p168 MR29
GRANT,Daniel Menzies T2Lt dow 4-8-18 1/5A&SH p173 CR France1225
GRANT,Donald 2Lt kia 20-11-17 6SfthH p241 CR France1498
GRANT,Douglas Lt kia 30-11-17 1KOSB p101 MR17
GRANT,Edmund Henry T2Lt dow 2-8-16 16KRRC p150 CR France145
GRANT,Edward Macpherson Capt kia 14/15-4-16 HLI p163 MR38
GRANT,Ferns Nelson Capt kia 9-5-15 5RSuss p228 MR22
GRANT,George Campbell TLt dow 14-10-15 RE 96FC p45 CR France345
GRANT,George Leonard TCapt kia 11-10-15 RAMC attLondonScottish p195 CR France222
GRANT,Harold Allan 2Lt ded 27-9-18 4SStaffs att7NStaffs p122 CR Asia82
GRANT,Harold Duncan 2Lt ded 27-3-19 1Dev p76 CR France34
GRANT,Harold Edward T2Lt kia 3-9-16 17 at16RB p178 MR21
GRANT,Henry Norman 2Lt kia 1-7-16 1LancF A'Coy p92 CR France1492
GRANT,Hubert Anthony Capt kia 24-11-14 2Leic p87 CR France727
GRANT,Humphrey de Butts Capt kia 3-10-15 A63RFA p29 CR France219
GRANT,Ian Alan William Lt kia 24-4-17 70RFA p29 CR France1188
GRANT,Ivan Thorold T2Lt kia 9-10-16 10RWKent p141 CR France432
GRANT,James.MC.T2Lt kia 23-10-18 16N&D att8RBerks p134 CR France716
GRANT,James Gibson 2Lt ded 19-2-19 10Lpool p270 CR Lancs14
GRANT,John T2Lt kia 1-7-16 15RScots p54 MR21
GRANT,John 2Lt ded 24-11-18 5DLI attMGC p187&239 CR Greece2
GRANT,John Anderton 2Lt kia 14-5-18 3 att8RSuss p119 CR France196
GRANT,John Cardross.MC.TCapt kia 27-1-16 10ScotRif p103 CR France178
GRANT,John Mann.DCM.T2Lt kia 9-4-17 11RScots p54 CR France645
GRANT,John Russell 2Lt kia 8-5-18 6ScotRif p224 CR Belgium111
GRANT,John Spence.MC.2Lt kia 9-4-17 6GordH p242 CR France728,Capt Rev
GRANT,Joseph Brabazon Theobald Capt kia 16-8-15 6RMunstF p175 MR4
GRANT,Kenneth Henry T2Lt kia 26-8-16 10 att8SfthH p164 CR France453
GRANT,Nigel Alexander James 2Lt dow 24-4-17 1/4GordH p242 CR France40
GRANT,Noël 2Lt kia 25-5-17 B156RFA p29 CR France311
GRANT,Percy Kenmure.MID TLt ded 6-11-18 RASC attGHQ p193 CR France1027
GRANT,Percy Victor 2Lt kia 3-4-18 10Glouc att9RB p106 MR27
GRANT,Philip Thomas Wilson T2Lt kia 15-10-15 8 att5Wilts p153 CR Gallipoli5
GRANT,Reginald Walter Capt ded 26-11-18 8RWKent p265 CR Mddx39
GRANT,Richard Craven Capt kia 2-9-18 3ScotRif &209RAF p264 MR20
GRANT,Robert T2Lt kia 13-6-17 GL &29RFC p8 CR Belgium375
GRANT,Robert William Gordon Capt kia 24-5-17 7Manch p237 CR France905
GRANT,Ronald Cameron TLt ded 16-10-16 RE p45 CR France62
GRANT,Sidney Robert T2Lt kia 18-4-18 1MGC Inf p183 CR France765,Sydney
GRANT,Stanley Chadwick T2Lt kia 3-9-16 2RIrReg p89 MR21
GRANT,Stanley Kenneth TLt kia 26-3-18 9ESurr p112 MR27
GRANT,Stuart.MC.LtACapt kia 3-12-17 2/5RWar p214 MR17
GRANT,Theodore.MC&Bar.Capt kia 28-5-18 3Worc attSAfrDefForce p108 MR18
GRANT,Thomas Francis.MC&Bar.Lt kia 11-4-18 1/5SfthH p241 CR France201,10-4-18
GRANT,William Gordon 2Lt kia 17-4-17 1/7HLI p240 CR Palestine8
GRANT,William Hugh 2Lt kia 29-9-15 7SfthH p164 MR19,30-9-15
GRANT,William St.Clair.MC.TCapt&Adjt kia 26-9-18 5CamH p168 CR Belgium36
GRANT-DUFF,Adrian.CB.LtCol kia 21-9-14 BlkW p128 CR France1341,14-9-14
GRANT-PETERKIN,Cosmo Gordon Capt dow 12-9-17 ScotHorse att1/5GordH p205 CR Belgium16
GRANT-SUTTIE,Archibald Ronald Lt dow 23-7-17 L15RHA p29 CR Belgium16
GRANTHAM,Charles Alpe Lt kia 3-3-17 IA 33Cav p277 CR Iraq6
GRANTHAM,Edward Rodney Hasluck 2Lt dow 31-3-17 1NumbF p61 CR France1182
GRANTHAM,Edward Mason Capt kia 27-2-15 3Lincs p75 CR Belgium166,1Bn
GRANTHAM,Ernest Joel LtACapt ded 6-12-18 RAOC attRGA p198 CR France65
GRANTHAM,Ernest Russell T2Lt kia 27-11-17 9ESurr p112 CR France1461
GRANTHAM,Frederick William Capt kia 9-5-15 2RMunstF p175 MR22
GRANTHAM,Hugo Frederick 2Lt kia 28-6-15 3Ess p131 CR Gallipoli6
GRANTHAM,Percy William 2Lt kia 26-9-17 5Lincs p220 CR Belgium123,W.P.Lt
GRANTHAM,Richard Aubrey Fuge T2Lt kia 4-3-17 2Lincs p75 CR France439
GRANTHAM,William Capt dow 30-11-18 PoW 4WRid p227 CR Germany3
GRANVILLE,Basil Rayond 2LtACapt kia 23-4-17 7RFus p68 MR20

GRANVILLE,Clifford Paul McGarry Capt kia 5-5-18 1Mddx att3/1KAR p147&268 MR52

GRAPES,John Wellington 2Lt dedacc 24-7-17 8AustInf CR France251

GRASETT,Elliot Blair Lt kia 25-9-15 IA 28Punjabis att33 p277 MR28

GRASSICK,Peter TLt kia 25-10-18 A&SH p173 CR France1258

GRASSICK,William Henderson 2Lt ded 9-2-19 A86RFA p29 CR France34

GRASSIE,John Ainslie Aymer 2Lt kia 21-3-18 5BlkW p231 MR27

GRATTAN,John LtCol dow 26-4-17 IA 55Rif att53Sikhs p277 CR Iraq8

GRATTAN-BELLEW,William Arthur.MC.2LtTMaj dow 24-3-17 ConnRgrs &29RFC p8&172 GRATTON CR France46

GRATTON,Albert.MM.2Lt kia 20-11-17 RGA 211SB p39 CR Belgium84

GRATTON,George Harry T2Lt kld 4-3-18 RFC p16 CR Mon67

GRATTON,Reginald Ernest 2Lt kia 31-7-17 5LancF p221 MR29

GRATWICK,Harold Duncan Lt ded 18-2-19 4Dev p270

GRATWICK,Philip Charles Lt 30-3-19 9ACycCps p243 MR27

GRAVES,Adrian Hubert.MC&Bar.TLtACapt kia 22-3-18 40MGC p183 MR20

GRAVES,Algernon Frederick Charles TCapt dow 26-8-17 PoW 7RInniskF p105 CR Belgium140

GRAVES,Evelyn Paget CaptTmaj kia 6-3-17 RFA Cmdg60RFC p8&29 CR France46

GRAVES,Francis George 2Lt kia 20-9-17 4 att16N&D p134 MR30

GRAVES,George Henry T2Lt ded 22-2-19 5 att7RFus p263 CR Kent7,Lt

GRAVES,Harry Steele Lt dow 24-11-17 1/6BlkW p231 CR France145

GRAVES,Horace Jocelyn.MC.TLt dow 14-10-18 13Yorks att8WYorks p90 CR France146

GRAVES,James Singleton Lt kia 15-6-18 6 att2Worc p254 MR32,6 att4Bn

GRAVES,John TCapt dow 16-4-17 MGC IA 36JacobsHorse p183&277 CR France512

GRAVES,Lionel Percival 2Lt ded 24-12-18 9KOSB p264 CR Wales536,Lt 21-12-18

GRAVES,Robert James TLt ded 28-1-17 2RIrReg HS 2GarrBn p89 CR Ireland14 &CR Eire77

GRAVES,Thomas Molyneaux Lt dow 22-4-16 IA 76Punjabis att56Rif p277 MR38

GRAVES,Walter Francis Lt kia 9-11-14 3 att1Beds p86 MR29 &CR Belgium167

GRAVES-KNYFTON,Reginald Barrett Maj ded 29-10-18 4SomLI p218 MR66,Benett

GRAVES-SAWLE,Richard Charles Lt kia 2-11-14 2CldGds p51 MR29

GRAY,Alexander Allen.MC.T2Lt kld 3-2-17 GL &RFC p8&190 CR Mddx66

GRAY,Alexander Jackson Maj kia 7-11-17 10RScots att2/19Lond p212 CR Palestine1

GRAY,Alexander Tudhope 2Lt kia 21-4-17 6 att 10ScotRif p224 MR20

GRAY,Andrew 2Lt kia 9-5-15 1BlkW p128 MR22

GRAY,Anthony Frederick Lt kia 26-8-18 1/1Camb p244 CR France196

GRAY,Arthur Frederick 2Lt drd 10-10-18 SuffYeo p205 MR40

GRAY,Arthur John Capt kia 31-7-17 1/1Camb p244 CR Belgium94

GRAY,Cecil Edward Patrick 2Lt dow 11-10-17 RFA attL'RHA p29 CR Belgium106,10-10-17

GRAY,Charles Dixon Lt kia 9-9-18 1ELancs p110 CR France1887

GRAY,Charles Rutherford T2Lt dow 23-11-17 11A&SH p173 CR France545

GRAY,Charles Shortland Capt kia 13-10-15 4Lincs p217 MR19

GRAY,Charles William T2Lt dow 4-12-17 23Manch p154 CR Belgium63

GRAY,Cyril Seaton 2Lt dow 21-4-17 1Ches p96 CR France40,2Wilts

GRAY,Cyrus Keswick 2Lt kia 14-4-17 18Lond p250 MR20

GRAY,David 2LtACapt kia 6-6-17 RGA 234SB p39 CR Belgium4

GRAY,David Gordon 2Lt kia 31-7-17 4RWKent p234 CR Belgium88

GRAY,David William T2Lt kia 18-7-16 5CamH p168 MR21

GRAY,Douglas Huon Lt kia 3-7-16 GL &RFC p3&190 MR20

GRAY,Douglas William 2Lt kia 18-11-16 111MGC Inf p183 MR21

GRAY,E.B.Lt 20-12-17 RGA CR Lond28

GRAY,Edis John William 2Lt kia 27-9-15 14DLI p254 MR19

GRAY,Edmund Trevennin T2Lt kia 22-10-15 15DLI p160 CR Belgium70

GRAY,Edward Cecil TCapt dow 2-5-17 11Manch p154 CR France512

GRAY,Edward Jasper 2Lt kia 31-3-18 6RB p178 CR France544

GRAY,Edward Leadbetter 2Lt kldacc 22-3-18 13RFC p16 CR Scot569

GRAY,Francis Henry Tower TLt drd 21-7-18 GL RASC attWAFF p190&201 CR Devon96

GRAY,Frederick Hodskinson 2Lt kia 1-4-17 HAC Inf p206 CR France568

GRAY,Frederick William.MC.2Lt kia 21-8-15 DorsYeo p203 CR Gallipoli5

GRAY,Geoffrey Thomas 2Lt kia 24-3-17 RE &8RFC p8&45 CR France120

GRAY,George 2Lt kld 28-4-16 4RDubF p176 CR Ireland14,kia

GRAY,George T2Lt ded 8-2-19 labCps p189 CR France65,Lt

GRAY,George Donald TLt ded 5-5-17 2/4Y&L p158 CR France518

GRAY,George Ernest Marshall T2Lt kia 14-7-16 14NumbF p61 MR21

GRAY,George Godfrey T2Lt dow 10-1-17 5 Q&RBI 1 p130 CR France120

GRAY,George Robert TLt dow PoW 31-10-17 GL &84RFC p8 CR France1029

GRAY,Gerald Montague 2Lt kia 7-10-16 3 att6RWKent p141 MR21

GRAY,Harry Albert.MC.TLt dow 15-7-18 1RWKent p141 CR France31

GRAY,Hubert James Stirling Capt kia 27-3-17 4RSuss p228 MR34

GRAY,Hubert McKenzie ACapt kia 10-8-17 11RFus p68 MR29

GRAY,James Maj kia 28-6-15 1/4RScots p211 CR Gallipoli6

GRAY,James Blackhall 2Lt kia 27-10-18 4GordH p242 CR Italy9

GRAY,James Cook.MC.ACapt kia 22-12-17 11BordR p117 CR Belgium9

GRAY,James Roy ACapt ded 18-2-19 10TankCps p266 CR Surrey1

GRAY,John Capt kia 12-4-16 IA 36Sikhs p277 MR38

GRAY,John T2Lt kia 24-3-18 8TankCps p188 CR France307

GRAY,John Lt kia 21-9-18 5 att2A&SH p243 CR France666

GRAY,John 2Lt ded 26-11-18 18WYorks p81 CR Numb3,3Bn

GRAY,John Arthur.DCM.2Lt kia 4-3-17 2RBerks p139 CR France216

GRAY,John Hunter Wood TCapt&QM ded 17-11-18 17RFus p68 CR France289

GRAY,John James Enslie 2Lt kld 18-3-17 1DCLI p114 CR Hamps234,17-3-17

GRAY,John Parnwell 2Lt ded 13-9-18 D47RFA 14DAC p29 CR Lincs100,Lt

GRAY,John Purves T2Lt dow 1-10-18 12 att1RInniskF p105 CR France262

GRAY,Julian Frederick.MC.Capt dow 10-7-17 RE att1S&M p45 CR Palestine9,10 7-18

GRAY,Leonard Capt ded 31-7-17 1/5Ess p232 CR Egypt1

GRAY,Leslie Austin T2Lt kia 12-10-16 13 att4Worc p108 CR France390

GRAY,M.2Lt 16-8-16 3DubF att10RIrRif CR Belgium48

GRAY,Magnus Nigel.MID Lt dow 21-6-15 3 att1ScotRif p103 CR France83

GRAY,M.Nurse 23-1-16 ScotWomensHosp CR France1866

GRAY,Martin Kenion T2Lt kia 28-8-16 6YLI p143 CR France402

GRAY,Maurice LtACapt kia 8-8-18 7MGC Cav att2DragGds p21&183 CR France652

GRAY,Meredith 2Lt kia 16-8-16 3RDubF att10RIrRif p176

GRAY,Norman McNeil Maj dow 9-2-16 45/42RFA p29 CR Lond8,Macneill

GRAY,Patrick Walworth 2Lt dow 9-5-17 153RFA p29 CR France113

GRAY,Peter 2Lt kia 18-6-18 10Lpool p216 CR France266

GRAY,R.M.McC.MC.Lt 30-9-18 46CanadaInf CR France113

GRAY,Roderick Hubert.MC.2Lt dow 2-12-17 1'7RFA p29 CR France518

GRAY,Thomas Robert 2Lt dow 24-11-17 4Yorks att7YLI p220 MR17

GRAY,Victor Samuel Lt kia 8-8-18 4Suff &48RAF p270 MR20

GRAY,Vivian 2Lt kia 18-8-16 3 att9Lpool p72 MR21

GRAY,William Harrington TCapt ded 23-11-19 RAMC p267

GRAY,William Leslie 2Lt dow 28-9-18 4Suff p217 CR France512

GRAY-BUCHANAN,Walter Bruce Capt&Adjt kia 10-3-15 2ScotRif p103 CR France260

GRAY-CHEAPE,Hugh Annesley.DSO&Bar.LtCol drd 27-5-18 WorcYeo p206 MR

GRAYFOOT,Blenman Buhot.CB.ded 30-9-16 IA IMS p277 CR Egypt1

GRAYSON,Ambrose Dixon Holdrege Capt kia 13-10-14 1RFA p29 MR22

GRAYSON,George 2Lt dow 24-12-18 155RFA p29 CR Durham102

GRAYSON,John Henry TLt kia 20-11-17 6RIrReg p89 CR France689

GRAZEBROOK,Charles Alvery Capt kia 10-3-15 6 att1KRRC p150 MR22,Alverey

GREANY,John Wingate.DSO.Capt&Adjt kia 9-4-16 5Wilts p153 MR38 mbk

GREATHEAD,Alan TCapt kia 20-11-17 9RFus p68 MR17

GREATHEAD,John Harding T2Lt kld 11-1-18 GL &RFC p16 CR Herts87

GREATHEAD,John Rivers T2Lt kia 23-10-16 2RB p178 CR France307

GREATHED,Robert Napier LtCol 26-3-20 RFA CR Devon207

GREATOREX,Janet Mary Sister ded 2-4-16 TFNS CR War151

GREATOREX,Thomas Anthony Capt 17-1-19 4EKent CR Devon230

GREATWOOD,F.S.2Lt ded 12-4-18 1/2RSuss &RAF p119 CR Kent7,drd

GREATWOOD,Harold 2Lt dow 20-10-17 36RFA p29 CR Belgium63

GREATWOOD,Walter Capt kia 8-3-16 IA 123Rif att1/1GurkhaRif p277 CR Iraq1

GREAVES,Eric.MC.TLt dow 21-11-18 7RDubF p176 CR France146

GREAVES,Frederic T2Lt kia 1-6-18 7RLancs att1/4LNLancs p59 CR France106

GREAVES,George Harold T2Lt kia 5-3-17 2WYorks p81 CR France439

GREAVES,John 2Lt dow 31-3-18 2/7RWar p214 CR France185

GREAVES,Reginald Lt ded 22-2-19 RGA 125B p39 CR France1029

GREAVES,Thomas Capt dow 1-7-18 1/6N&D p233 CR France10

GREAVES,Victor T2Lt dow 28-11-17 WRid att2/5Bn p115 CR France398

GREEN,Alan Edward 2Lt kia 2-10-15 5SStaffs p229 MR19,13-10-15

GREEN,Alan Herbert T2Lt dow 26-2-18 RE &32RFC p45&16,25-2-18 CR Italy

GREEN,Alfred TLt kia 19-9-17 5RFus att2/2KAR p202 CR EAfrica8 &CR Tanzania1,1/4Bn

GREEN,Allan T2Lt kia 19-8-17 21WYorks p81 CR France97,Lt

GREEN,Arthur Lt kia 26-3-18 9Manch p237 MR27

GREEN,Arthur Lt ded 3-12-19 SL RE &1WT p268 CR Iraq6
GREEN,Arthur Dowson.DSO.Maj kia 28-9-14 Worc 17 InfBde p108 CR France1112
GREEN,Arthur Fairbrother 2Lt kia 21-3-18 2/6NStaffs p238 MR20
GREEN,Arthur Knowles 2Lt kia 30-9-17 148RFA p29 CR Belgium17,Knolles
GREEN,Arthur Percival TLt kia 6-7-16 7Norf D'Coy p73 CR France430,Perceval
GREEN,Arthur Vivian 2Lt kia 17-8-17 5RDubF p176 MR30
GREEN,Basil.MC.2Lt kia 1-7-17 5NStaffs p238 MR19
GREEN,Benjamin Cecil 2Lt kia 24-4-17 5ELancs att126MGC Inf p187&226 MR21
GREEN,Cecil Ernest 2Lt kia 26-8-18 5Lond p246 CR France329
GREEN,Cecil Henry T2Lt dow 9-10-16 6 O&BLI p130 CR France105
GREEN,Charles Arthur.MC.2Lt kia 13-7-17 RGA 2/3LowlandHB p39 CR France592,2/1Bn
GREEN,Charles Ernest T2Lt kia 14-7-16 9 att7KSLI p144 MR21
GREEN,Charles Henry.MID CaptAMaj dow 8-11-17 1SStaffs att3NigR p122&201 CR EAfrica13 &CR Tanzania1
GREEN,Charles James LtACapt kia 16-4-18 13RSuss p119 CR Belgium21
GREEN,Charles Layton T2Lt kia 9-6-17 GL 11Ess att53RFC p8 CR France285
GREEN,Charles Taylor 2Lt kia 26-10-17 2RWSurr p56 MR30
GREEN,Clifford Whittington LtTCapt dow 27-6-15 RBerks p139
GREEN,Cuthbert 2Lt kia 15-10-16 2DLI p160 MR21
GREEN,Cyril Mortimer Lt kia 6-11-17 16RSuss p119 CR Palestine1,Capt
GREEN,Daniel Abbott 2Lt kia 13-11-16 3 att1Lpool p72 MR21
GREEN,Daniel Cottle 2Lt kia 25-2-17 22Lond attMGC Inf p187&251 MR38
GREEN,David T2Lt kia 1-8-17 23MGC p183 MR29
GREEN,Demetrius Frederick Edward Joseph.MID Lt ded 15-10-18 GL 9NumbF p190 CR France457
GREEN,Edward Scott Waring 2Lt kia 28-8-16 1Mddx p147 CR France399,27-8-16
GREEN,Edward Unsworth.MC.TCapt kia 10-8-17 9LNLancs p136 MR29
GREEN,Edwin Charles 2Lt kia 26-3-18 4NStaffs p157 CR France300
GREEN,Eric De Wilde T2Lt dow 15-4-18 1RWSurr p56 CR France102
GREEN,Ernest Arthur James Capt kia 21/22-10-20 2/67Punjabis MR43
GREEN,Ernest Michael TLt kia 3-9-16 14Hamps p120 CR France742,Capt
GREEN,Ernest Newham Chap4Cl ded 26-3-16 RAChDept p199 CR Mddx42
GREEN,Frank T2Lt kia 17-9-16 5RIrF p171 CR Greece3
GREEN,Frank 2Lt kia 3-11-16 4YLI p235 CR France1327
GREEN,Frank Lt dow 28-12-17 5Yorks p220 CR Belgium11
GREEN,Frank Clifford 2Lt kia 16-6-15 1Lincs p75 MR29
GREEN,Frederick George.MC.T2Lt kia 3-10-18 LNLancs att1/4Bn p136 CR France242
GREEN,Geoffrey George Miers T2Lt kia 28-3-18 WYorks att5YLI p81 CR France798
GREEN,George Birch T2Lt kia 11-6-18 1RWFus att7KSLI p97 CR France33
GREEN,George Owen TCapt kia 23-8-15 9WelchR p126 CR France1157
GREEN,Gilbert Pitcher T2Lt dow 25-10-16 13Ches p96 CR France44
GREEN,Geoffrey Walter Ashdown 2Lt kia 8-3-18 RFA &59RFC p16&29 CR France518
GREEN,Harold T2Lt kia 28-2-17 1RDubF p176 MR21
GREEN,Harold Stewart.DCM.2Lt kia 4-4-18 4DragGds p21 CR France196
GREEN,F.Harold Syddal 2Lt dow 1-5-17 12SWBord p100 CR France85
GREEN,Henry Arthur 2Lt kia 9-10-18 4RWKent p234 CR France332
GREEN,Henry Edwin Capt dow 13-10-16 22Lond p251 CR France177
GREEN,Henry Morris TCapt kia 4-8-16 9RFus p68 CR France446
GREEN,Herbert.MC.Rev kia 24-8-17 RAChDept att41MGC p199 CR Belgium19
GREEN,Herbert John T2Lt kia 4-3-17 GL &43RFC p8 CR France924
GREEN,Herbert Walter.DSO.MajBtLtCol dow 31-12-18 EKent attRWSurr p57 CR France146
GREEN,Herbert William 2Lt kia 16-8-17 5RSuss p228 CR Belgium10
GREEN,Herbert William T2Lt kia 12-10-17 2ScotsGds p52 MR30
GREEN,Horace Salkeld.MID Maj kia 20-9-17 7Lond p247 CR Belgium125
GREEN,Hubert Bishop 2Lt kia 13-4-18 7 att2Worc p226 MR32
GREEN,Hugh James Bernard Chap4Cl ded 8-12-18 RAChDept att20DivDetls p199 CR France134
GREEN,Hugh Mortimer Capt kia 10-8-15 4WelshR p230 MR4
GREEN,James T2Lt dow 21-7-16 7SLancs p125 CR France188
GREEN,James 2Lt dow 27-9-18 2Mddx p147 CR France268
GREEN,James Archer Capt kia 23-3-17 16Lond p249 CR France419
GREEN,James 2Lt kia 23-3-17 16Lond p249 CR France419
GREEN,John Alexander TLt ded 18-8-18 8SStaffs attAnsonBnRNDev p122 CR France69
GREEN,John Berks 2Lt kia 11-1-17 8Manch p237 MR21
GREEN,John Feetham 2Lt kia 5-11-16 7DLI p239 CR France385,Frettiam
GREEN,John James HonCapt&QM ded 9-12-17 10WYorks p81 CR Essex1

GREEN,John Leslie.VC.Capt kia 1-7-16 RAMC att5N&D p253 CR France281
GREEN,Joseph George Airey 2Lt kia 23-11-17 TankCps p188 MR17
GREEN,Leslie Alan 2Lt kia 13-11-16 6 att23RFus p68 CR France131,Lt
GREEN,Malcolm Charles Andrew LtCol kia 17-11-14 SLancs p125 MR29
GREEN,Norman T2Lt kia 25-1-17 7NStaffs p157 CR Iraq5
GREEN,Norman Wilson 2Lt kia 23-4-17 4EYorks p219 MR20
GREEN,Oswald Robert John TLt dow 5-7-16 9WelchR p126 CR France833
GREEN,Percy T2Lt kia 9-9-18 9YLI p143 CR France415
GREEN,Percy Harold T2Lt kia 26-3-18 9RInnisF p105 MR27
GREEN,Philip Louis Samuel 2Lt kia 18-9-16 4 att1WYorks p81 MR21
GREEN,Philip Sydney TCapt ded 13-11-18 RAMC 32SH p195 CR France34
GREEN,Phillip 2Lt kia 28-3-18 1/4EYorks p219 MR27,Philip
GREEN,Reginald Cumberland Lt dow 18-5-16 1Beds p86 CR France1182
GREEN,Richard Scott Lt kia 14-10-15 4Leic p219 MR19
GREEN,Richmond Edward Ormond Lyttleton T2Lt kia 19-2-16 6KSLI p144 CR Belgium73
GREEN,Robert Edward 2Lt kia 21-3-17 20Lpool p72 MR20
GREEN,Rupert Anthony Lt kia 25-3-18 Mddx att23Bn p147 MR20
GREEN,St.John T2Lt kia 6-12-17 12 att9RInniskF p105 MR17
GREEN,Thomas.DCM.22489 2Lt dow 28-10-16 RGA 10SB p39 CR France515
GREEN,Thomas Claud Erskine T2Lt kia 31-7-17 8RWSurr p56 MR29
GREEN,Thomas Seaman TLt kia 13-2-17 GL &3RFC p8 CR France833
GREEN,Thomas William T2Lt dow 14-8-18 2TankCps p188 CR France34,Lt
GREEN,Vivian Unsworth 2LtTLt kia 26-3-17 15 att10Mddx p147 MR34
GREEN,William Bruce T2Lt kia 29-3-18 11Mddx p147 CR France266,Willie
GREEN,William Eddowes Lt dow 6-7-16 1Dors p124 CR France74,3Bn
GREEN,William Osmond T2Lt kia 1-7-16 10RIrRif p169 MR21
GREEN,William Wesley 2Lt kia 9-4-17 1EYorks p84 CR France162
GREENALL,Jack Eckersley D.Capt kia 31-3-18 LanarkYeo attRAF p255&204 CR France300
GREENALL,James Mackintosh Capt died /-11-19 RASC p267
GREENE,Aldrich Wells 2Lt kia 17-2-18 27RFC p16 CR France1887
GREENE,Charles Kendall Capt 25-3-16 EKent CR Ireland14 &CR Eire77
GREENE,Ernest Alfred Jeffries Capt kia 22-10-20 IARO att2/67Punjabis p277
GREENE,Godfrey Robert 2Lt kia 3-9-16 116MGC Inf p183 MR21
GREENE,Henry.MIDx2 Lt kia 21-8-15 IA 92Punjabis att1/6GurkhaRif p277 MR4
GREENE,Henry Caldwell 2Lt kia 29-4-18 5RMunstF att 1RIrRif p175 CR Belgium96,Harry
GREENE,Henry Roundell Capt ded 27-6-18 Hamps attGCR WAAF p120 CR Hamps10
GREENE,John 2Lt kia 3-11-16 Wilts att6Bn p154 MR21
GREENE,Quincey Shaw LtACapt kia 28-3-18 3CldGds p51 MR20
GREENE,Richard Ernest 2Lt dow 3-2-19 9RInniskF p105 CR France34,Lt
GREENE,Robin TCapt ded 21-9-18 RE PostalServ p45 MR65
GREENER,Arthur Stephen.MC.LtACapt dow 18-4-18 1NumbF p61 CR France10
GREENER,Francis Pemberton 2Lt kia 15-2-15 2ESurr p112 MR29
GREENER,Henry 2Lt kia 14-4-17 6DLI p239 CR France162
GREENER,Leysters Llewellyn.MC.Capt kia 5-12-17 2/6RWar p214 MR17
GREENER,Noel Hindmarsh TLt kia 25-9-15 6KOSB p101 MR19
GREENFIELD,Benjamin Lt ded 28-11-18 RFA p254 CR Scot862
GREENFIELD,Eric Frank T2Lt kld 13-2-17 2KRRC p150 CR France145
GREENFIELD,Fredk 2Lt kia 2-5-17 GL attRAOC p266
GREENFIELD,Gerald Henry 2Lt dow 17-8-17 B242RFA Bde p29 CR Belgium11
GREENFIELD,Richard Mentieth.CB.BrigGen ded 25-4-16 RInniskF GenStaff InshCommand p1 CR Herts84
GREENFIELD,Ronald William Lt kia 23-10-16 1RB p178 MR21
GREENFIELD,Thomas Bevil T2Lt kia 19-9-15 RE 1/2FC p45 CR Gallipoli17
GREENHALGH,Harold Fifield T2Lt kia 9-4-18 RAOC p198 CR Belgium3
GREENHALGH,Hugh Charles T2Lt kia 5-5-17 20Mddx p147 CR France439
GREENHALGH,James Arthur 2Lt kia 22-10-14 Ches p96 MR22
GREENHALGH,Maurice Lomax T2Lt kia 25-9-15 15Lpool p72 CR France625
GREENHILL,Campbell.MC.TLt kia 10-8-17 3Worc p108 MR29
GREENHILL,Frederick William Ridge Lt kia 10-10-17 3GrenGds p50 MR30
GREENHILL,Reginald Fowler Capt dow 1-1-18 15LancF p92 CR France64
GREENHILL,Thomas Watson Lt kia 11-2-16 4DragGds p21 CR France423
GREENHOUS,Ernest Brereton TLt kia 26-8-17 1RScotF &9RFC p8&94,T2Lt CR Belgium18
GREENHOW,Denys Edward T2Lt kia 6-3-17 45RFC p8 CR Belgium11
GREENLAND,Charles Stirling Walter Lt kia 9-5-15 2Glouc p106 CR Belgium167
GREENLAND,Richard 2Lt kia 13-4-17 9DLI p239 CR France420

GREENLEES,Charles Fouracres T2Lt kia 1-7-16 9RWSurr p56 CR France35
GREENLESS,George Dickson 2Lt kia 1-12-17 4BlkW p230 CR Palestine3
GREENOP,Garnet Arthur Claude 2Lt kia 9-7-16 RFA 172Bty p29 CR France701,8-7-16
GREENOUGH,William Gladstone 2Lt kia 21-10-18 4 att1/6Manch p154 CR France287
GREENSHIELDS,John Arthur.MC.2Lt kia 27-5-18 5 att9YLI p235 CR France622,Capt
GREENSHIELDS-LEADBETTER,Alan Edmonstoune.MID Maj kia 4-8-17 L15RHA CR Belgium12
GREENSLADE,Francis Harold 2Lt kia 31-5-18 A52RFA p29 CR France268
GREENSMITH,J.Cdr 29-5-20 IA MiscList CR Asia60
GREENSTED,Walter 2Lt dow 22-10-18 A50RFA p29 CR Belgium147
GREENSTREET,Ernest Henry T2Lt ded 15-2-19 19Mddx p147&257 CR Germany1
GREENSTREET,Frederick George Maj kia 9-1-17 IA 103MahrattaLI att105 p277 MR38
GREENUP,John Bertram 2Lt kia 12-10-17 5 att1RB p178 MR30,13-10-17
GREENWAY,Douglas Howard Wilson T2Lt kia 17-10-15 13 att4Worc p108 CR Gallipoli4
GREENWAY,Frederick Charles Garton 2Lt kia 14-7-16 8Leic p87 MR21
GREENWAY,Kenneth T2Lt kia 27-11-15 13 att4Worc p108 CR Gallipoli4,18-11-15
GREENWELL,John T2Lt kia 24-10-18 12/13NumbF p61 MR16
GREENWELL,Thomas William Maddison Lt kia 19-7-18 6NumbF att17LancF p213 CR France139
GREENWELL-LAX,Anthony William Capt kia 11-10-16 RGA 43SB p39
GREENWOOD,A Maj 10-6-19 IMD MR65
GREENWOOD,Arthur Donald T2Lt kia 30-8-18 2Beds p86 CR France397
GREENWOOD,Cecil James Lt kia 9-8-18 10Lond p248 CR France1170
GREENWOOD,Charles 2Lt kia 22-3-18 RLancs att6Wilts p59 MR20
GREENWOOD,Charles Norman.MC.2Lt dow 5-9-18 A70RFA p29 CR France95
GREENWOOD,Charles Stuart 2Lt ded 21-7-16 11RFus p68
GREENWOOD,Cyril Stewart T2Lt kia 20-8-16 1Nhampt p137 CR France387
GREENWOOD,Ernest 2Lt ded 31-10-18 4LNLancs p270 CR Yorks730
GREENWOOD,Gerald Wyatt Capt ded 17-11-18 B210RFA p207 CR Lancs381
GREENWOOD,Harold Sutcliffe T2Lt kia 22-7-16 14RWar p64 CR France432
GREENWOOD,Henry Smith.VD.LtCol 4-5-16 RE CR Surrey160
GREENWOOD,Herbert T2Lt dow 8-6-17 122MGC p183 MR29
GREENWOOD,Isidore Herbert Lt dow 6-7-18 10 att8Mddx p236 CR France54
GREENWOOD,James Barton Lt kia 13-10-18 19LancF att1/4Y&L p92 MR16
GREENWOOD,James Hurst.MC.TLt dow 24-7-18 11RWKent p141 CR Hamps13
GREENWOOD,John Exley T2Lt ded 11-9-17 GL &RFC p8 CR Yorks583
GREENWOOD,John Francis Bernal Lt kia 2-5-15 1RLancs p59 MR29
GREENWOOD,Joseph LtCol 27-12-15 RE CR Lond9
GREENWOOD,L.A.2Lt dow 13-4-18 GL &RAF p190
GREENWOOD,Leonard Montague.DSO.MC&Bar.TMaj ded 17-10-18 13DLI p160 CR France146
GREENWOOD,Tom 2Lt kia 31-8-18 5Lpool p215 CR France433
GREENWOOD,Tom Stanley T2Lt kia 7-7-16 14 att12Manch p154 MR21
GREENWOOD,Victor John Maj kia 18-4-18 D275RFA p206 CR France109
GREER,Donald Allister Lt ded 12-7-16 1ConnRgrs p172 CR Iraq5,Alister
GREER,Eric Beresford.MC.MajALtCol kia 31-7-17 2IrGds p52 CR Belgium12
GREER,Francis St.Ledger.MC.Lt ded 1-2-17 2IrGds p52 CR France833
GREER,James Kenneth Macgregor.MC.Lt dow 3-10-16 11rGds p52 CR France145
GREER,Morrice Capt kia 16-6-17 RAMC attRWFus p253 CR Palestine8
GREEVES,Arthur Frederick Wellesley T2Lt dow 20-9-17 8NStaffs p157 CR Belgium21,Frederic
GREEVES,John 2Lt kia 1-7-17 5NStaffs p238 MR19
GREG,Arthur Tylston Capt kia 23-4-17 3Ches &55RFC p8&96 CR France1074
GREG,Robert Phillips 2Lt dow 3-5-18 4Ches p222 CR Belgium11,11Bn
GREGERY,James Langdale T2Lt kia 13-5-17 8Yorks attRE 101FC p90
GREGG,Charles Edward 2Lt kia 15-6-17 1/5RLancs p213 CR Belgium10
GREGG,George Philip 2Lt kia 26-3-17 7Ches p223 MR34
GREGG,Reginald Lt kia 1-10-18 6Manch p236 CR France376
GREGG,Robert Lt kia 9-8-15 2DLI p160 MR29
GREGG,William Henry 2Lt kia 1-7-16 5 att1RIrRif p169 MR21
GREGGE-HOPWOOD,Edward Byng George.DSO.MajALtCol kia 20-7-17 1CldGds p51 CR Belgium12
GREGOR,George Trevor.VD.LtCol kia 1-7-17 RFA 1WelshHB p206 CR Belgium1
GREGORY,Alfred John Reginald.DSO.Maj ded 4-12-18 RGA 120HB XIXCps p39 CR France717
GREGORY,Arthur Skelton T2Lt kia 22-9-19 2LNLancs att2FLancs p136 CR France184

GREGORY,Fleming Clement.MC.Capt dow 29-11-17 3County of LondYeo p20 CR Palestine9
GREGORY,Frank TLt kia 16-4-18 19LancF p92 MR30
GREGORY,Geoffrey Francis Gregory Lt kia 25-9-15 RBerks p139 MR32
GREGORY,George T2Lt kia 26-9-17 7Y&L p158 CR Belgium13
GREGORY,Godfrey Levinge Capt ded 5-1-18 6DLI CR Berks125
GREGORY,Henry Vincent Lt kia 15-3-17 3 att12Lpool p72 CR France513
GREGORY,Herbert Capt&QM ded 23-10-19 MGC Inf CR Lancs179
GREGORY,Herbert Thomas T2LtACapt dow 13-10-17 7RWKent p141 CR Belgium64
GREGORY,James Alfred TLt dow 13-4-17 RAMC 52FA att12Manch p195 CR France113
GREGORY,James Langdale 2Lt 13-5-17 8Yorks attRE 101FC CR Belgium127
GREGORY,John George 2Lt dow 8-1-16 6Lond p247 CR France178
GREGORY,John Sheridan TCapt kia 19-2-18 RASC attRFC p16&193 CR France369
GREGORY,Kenneth Stuart Lt kia 10-11-17 2/7RWFus att3MGC Inf p187&223 MR30
GREGORY,Percy John T2Lt kia 4-10-17 12/13NumbF p61 MR30
GREGORY,Reuben Henry.MC.TCapt kia 9-6-17 10N&D p134 MR29
GREGORY,Robert.MC.LtTMaj kia 23-1-18 4ConnRgrs att66RFC p16&172 CR Italy48
GREGORY,Stanley T2Lt kia 8-6-18 1/10Manch p154 France5
GREGORY,Stanley Harris T2Lt kia 13-11-16 15 att24RFus p68 CR France152
GREGORY,Stephen Barnes Lt ded PoW 3-6-16 4Dev p220 MR38
GREGORY,Sydney Maurice 2Lt kia 18-5-15 6Lond p247 CR France260
GREGORY,Thomas William Capt dow 22-3-18 4 att16NumbF p213 MR20
GREGORY,Walter Stanley T2Lt kia 30-4-17 5Wilts p153 MR38
GREGSON,Alan Herbert T2Lt kia 19-4-17 RWKent att2/4Bn p141 CR Palestine
GREGSON,Edward Maurice Capt kia 28-6-16 4LNLancs p233 MR20
GREGSON,Francis Robert Capt dow 15-5-17 SL att4AustDiv p201 CR France13,Maj
GREGSON,Herbert 2Lt kia 30-11-17 35MGC p183 MR17
GREGSON,William Pilkington T2Lt dow 18-10-18 16TankCps p188 CR France
GREGSON-ELLIS,Reginald George TCapt dow 17-4-17 O&BLI BucksBn p231 CR France511
GREIFFENHAGEN,Norman T2Lt dow 24-12-18 1EKent p57 CR Belgium11,24-15
GREIG,Hugh Irwin Maj kia 2-11-17 RGA p39 CR Belgium176
GREIG,James Gordon Hamilton 2LtTLt dow 13-8-15 6EKent D'Coy p57 CR France285
GREIG,John William Henry 2Lt kia 26-3-15 IARO att25Cav p277 MR43
GREIG,Morland John Maj kia 17-10-15 1RNDevYeo p203 CR Gallipoli27
GREIG,Ronald Henry.DSO.Maj kia 28-8-16 RE 54FC p45 CR France372
GREIG,Roy Scott Capt kia 28-3-18 14Lond att6CamH p249 CR France924,dow
GREIG,William Ewing Capt dow 27-5-15 5Lpool p215 CR France102
GRELL,Louis George Neville Lt ded 5-6-18 10WYorks att27Punjabis p81&p277 MR66
GRELLIER,Arthur Bertean 2Lt kia 26-3-18 LancF att2/7Bn p92 MR27,Berteau
GRELLIER,Gordon Harley T2Lt kia 31-10-18 RGA 51SB p39 CR France737
GRENFELL,Francis Octavius,VC Capt kia 24-5-15 9Lancers p22 CR Belgium4,
GRENFELL,Gerald William.Hon.T2Lt kia 30-7-15 8RB p179 MR29
GRENFELL,Julian Henry Francis.DSO.Hon.Capt dow 26-5-15 1Drags p21 CR France102
GRENFELL,Riversdale Nonn Capt kia 14-9-14 BucksYeo att9Lancers p203 CR France1328,Nonus
GRENNAN,Gerald Lismore T2Lt kia 12-10-16 20Lpool p72 MR21
GRENVILLE-GREY,Wilfred Hanbury Lt dow 16-5-15 1KRRC p150 CR France632,Wilfrid
GRENVILLE WELLS,Nigel Lt 9-10-19 WeldhGds CR Palestine3
GRESHAM,Gordon 2Lt dow 18-6-16 4EYorks p219 CR France285
GRESHAM,John Francis Lt ded 16-2-19 4EYorks p219 CR France377
GRESHAM,Leonard Stanley 2Lt dow 7-5-17 1/1Yorks ERidYeo p206 CR Egypt2
GRESLEY,Roger.MC.LtAMaj dow 6-9-18 A119RFA p29 CR France298
GRESLEY-COX,Edward Louis T2Lt kld 22-2-18 17/16RFC p16 CR Greece3
GRESSON,John Edward 2Lt kia 24-5-15 3 att2Ches p96 MR29
GRESWELL,Eric Walter Lt kld 9-6-18 8Ches att111RAF p96 CR Palestine9,kia
GRESWELL,H.G.Capt dow 18-8-16 RE 154FC p45 CR France88
GRESWOLDE-WILLIAMS,Francis Humphrey John Lt kia 3-8-17 SL att3/4KAR p202 CR EAfrica10 &CR Tanzania1,F.H.T.3/2Bn
GRETTON,Horace Edward Capt kia 16-8-17 2Lond p245 MR29
GRETTON,Rupert Harold TCapt kia 17-12-15 8Beds p86 MR29

GREVELINK,Edward James Yzenhoed Lt ded 6-6-17 2WRid &RFC p8&115 CR France403

GREVES,Thomas Samuel 2Lt ded 28-6-19 3 att11Hamps p264CR Sussex72

GREVILLE,David Onslow 2Lt kia 3-5-17 16WYorks p81 MR20

GREVILLE,George Gordon Francis Lt dow 31-3-18 4Huss p21 CR France988

GREVILLE,Sydney T2Lt kia 19-4-17 NStaffs p157 CR France366

GREW,Hubert 2Lt kia 2-7-15 7KRRC p150 CR Belgium165

GREW,Walter Ernest T2Lt kia 7-10-17 16RWar p64 MR30

GREY,Alice Annie Sister 21-8-16 ScotWomensHosp attSerbianArmy CR Greece7

GREY,Charles Joscelyn Eden(Robin).DSO.Maj 15-5-21 2GrenGds CR Lond4

GREY,Gordon Louis 2Lt ded 3-6-17 SNottsHuss p270 Lond8

GREY,John Ivor 2Lt kia 15-9-16 7NumbF p214 CR France387

GREY,Norman Lt kia 26-10-17 5LNLancs p234 CR Belgium126

GREY,Patrick Riddle T2Lt kia 26-9-16 15 att8NumbF p61 MR21

GREY,Sidney James 2Lt kia 1-8-18 14Lond att6Ca p249 CR France878

GREY-SMITH,Melville Capt kia 19-11-17 IARO att2/3GurkhaRif p277 CR Palestine9

GRIBBELL,Arthur Frank TCapt ded 13-3-16 RFA p29 CR Sussex128

GRIBBELL,Leslie Terrell T2Lt ded 31-3-16 3Dev p76 CR Dorset52

GRIBBEN,James Grenfell 2Lt kia 12-6-17 1/6SStaffs p229 CR France149,11-6-17

GRIBBLE,Charles Ethelburt.MC.LtACapt dow 15-10-18 3 att7Leic p87 CR France560

GRIBBLE,Charles Herbert Lt kia 30-11-17 4EKent p212 att1RGLI

GRIBBLE,Horace Dewey TLt ded 13-7-18 SL att1NigR p201&268 CR WAfrica41

GRIBBLE,Julian Royds.VC.Capt ded PoW 25-11-18 1 att10RWar p64 CR Germany3,kia

GRIBBON,John Stewart 2Lt kia 27-5-18 7YLI att2RB p143 MR18

GRIBBON,Montagu Claude Capt kia 9-12-15 IA 67Punjabis p277 MR38

GRICE,Harold George Lt dow 27-3-18 4RScots p211 CR France145

GRICE,Howard Thomas 2Lt kia 25-3-18 2ScotRif p103 CR France1203

GRICE,Lawrence Victor TLt kia 13-4-18 21NumbF p61 MR32

GRICE,Leslie Clark 2Lt dow 20-4-17 23/40RFA p208 CR France1185

GRICE,Maurice Chuma Lt accdrd 4-7-18 14ACycCps p244 CR Italy8

GRICE,Percival Samuel Henry Lt kia 2-9-18 2/17Lond p250 CR Belgium89

GRICE,Thomas Gerald CaptTMaj dow 15-6-16 3 att2ScotRif p103 CR France203

GRIDLEY,F.SubCdr 30-6-15 S&T Cps MR66

GRIER,Francis Nemo Lt&QM ded 30-4-18 SL p201 CR Egypt1

GRIER,William TLt drd 15-4-17 RAMC p195 MR35

GRIERSON,James Moncrieff.KCB.CVO.CMG.ADC.Sir.LtGen ded 17-8-14 Staff RA p1 CR Scot756

GRIERSON,John T2Lt kia 21-3-18 13Lpool p72 MR20

GRIERSON,John Henry Clifford 2Lt kia 31-7-17 3GordH p166 MR29

GRIERSON,John Livingstone Hailes T2Lt kia 1-7-16 3 att2RScotF p94 MR21

GRIERSON,Robert Lt&QM ded 14-2-16 2/5KOSB p270 CR Scot621

GRIERSON,Stanley Virtue 2Lt kia 31-8-18 3 att2SfthH p164 CR France421

GRIESBACH,Claude Walter 2Lt kia 23-10-16 2RBerks p139 MR21

GRIEVE,Alan Edward 2Lt kia 3-7-16 2SLancs p125 MR21

GRIEVE,C.C.Maj 22-9-20 2CamH CR Ireland14 &CR Eire77

GRIEVE,David Harley T2Lt ded 31-10-18 12LabCps p189 CR France34

GRIEVE,James TLt kld 21-2-17 3SLancs &RFC p8&125 CR Lancs149

GRIEVE,James Ross.MC.TCaptAMaj kia 4-4-18 C107RFA p29 CR France988

GRIEVE,Nicholas Harrington 2Lt kia 13-11-16 3 att1RScotF p94 CR France742

GRIEVE,William Percival 2Lt kia 16-2-15 Mddx att3Bn p147 MR29

GRIEVE,William Robertson Capt kia 28-4-17 7HLI p240 MR20

GRIEVES,James 2Lt kia 20-9-18 5NumbF p213 CR France530

GRIFFEN,Harold Samuel T2Lt dow 9-4-17 KSLI att5Bn p144 CR France418,GRIFFIN

GRIFFIN,Basil Walker T2Lt dow 2-12-17 2Lincs p75 MR30

GRIFFIN,Cecil Scott James Capt kld 11-10-17 1GordH attRFC p8&166 CR Devon76

GRIFFIN,Charles John T2LtACapt kia 1-9-16 2RWSurr p56 MR21

GRIFFIN,Clive.MC.Lt dow 11-11-16 3RFA p207 CR Greece7

GRIFFIN,Douglas Morley T2Lt dow 16-7-16 18Lpool p72 CR France51

GRIFFIN,Edward Stanley 2Lt kia 31-7-17 6Lpool p215 MR29

GRIFFIN,Edward William Lt kia 16-9-18 6Glouc attRAF p225&258 CR France792

GRIFFIN,George Edward TCapt kia 1-7-16 9YLI p143 MR21

GRIFFIN,Hedley Saunders 2Lt dow PoW 31-8-17 4RBerks p234 CR Belgium140 Ex HAC

GRIFFIN,Innes Edward Capt dow 19-2-16 1/4 O&BLI p231 CR France167,18-2-16

GRIFFIN,John James Wahal T2Lt kia 15-11-16 6Beds p86 CR France533,James John W.

GRIFFIN,Leslie Stuart Herbert.MID TLt kia 18-8-16 10Glouc p106 CR France386

GRIFFIN,Lilian Sister ded 5-9-16 TFNS p254 MR37

GRIFFIN,P.G.DSO.Maj 26-3-21 16RFA CR Palestine9

GRIFFIN,Reginald Herbert 2LtACapt dow 7-7-17 RFA attRGA 21SB p29 CR Belgium18,kld

GRIFFIN,Sidney James Capt dow 26-3-18 1 att3 O&BLI p130 CR Iraq8

GRIFFITH,Allex James William 2Lt kia 25-3-17 2Dors G'Coy p124 MR38,Allix Lt

GRIFFITH,Arthur Charles Fleming Lt kia 8-10-18 2 att17RWFus p97 CR France234

GRIFFITH,Edward William Collisson Capt dow 1-2-19 10RIrRif p254&257 CR Sussex185

GRIFFITH,Frank.VD.Col ded 4-1-17 R6FA p206 CR Kent91

GRIFFITH,Geoffrey Foster.MID Capt kia 26-9-17 9Lond p247 MR30

GRIFFITH,George Herbert Col ded 20-9-17 RE DepDir ofWorks p45 MR65

GRIFFITH,Gerald Lt kia 26-8-14 1Hamps p120 MR15

GRIFFITH,Henry Hall TCapt kld 2-11-17 45RFC p8 CR Sussex139,63Sqn

GRIFFITH,Henry Rathbone TLt ded 21-5-16 RAMC p267 CR Shrop93

GRIFFITH,John Gwynne Maj kia 24-5-15 IA 32Lancers attHQ9CavBde p277 CR Belgium57

GRIFFITH,John Herbert 2Lt kia 27-3-18 15WYorks p81 CR France927

GRIFFITH,Oswald 2Lt kia 27-2-15 80RFA p29 CR Belgium170,Lt

GRIFFITH,Rupert Varden De Burgh Lt kia 12-3-15 3RFus p68 CR Belgium17

GRIFFITH,Thomas Comber Lt dow 8-7-19 LNLancs p257&136 See GRIFFITHS.T.C. MR70 &CR Europe179

GRIFFITH,Trevor Llewelyn ALt kia 30-10-17 D82RFA p29 CR Belgium10

GRIFFITH,Walter Stanley Currie T2Lt kia 10-8-15 6Leinst p174 CR Gallipoli18

GRIFFITH,William Henry.MC.T2Lt dow 5-7-17 15RWFus p97 CR Belgium18

GRIFFITH,William Henry Lt 14-12-17 MilWksServ MR65

GRIFFITH,William Key 2Lt kia 26-9-17 12Lond p248 MR30

GRIFFITH,William Llewelyn T2Lt dow 22-9-17 WelshR att9Bn p126 CR Belgium183

GRIFFITH,William Starbuck Maj ded 23-7-15 RAMC p270 CR Wales389

GRIFFITH,William Walter Gilbert LtCol kia 22-4-17 IA 32Lancers p277 MR38

GRIFFITH-JONES,William Lionel Phillips.MC.Lt kld 12-7-16 3 att2DLI p160 CR Belgium5,dedacc

GRIFFITHS,Allen Rhys T2Lt kia 9-8-15 53/2RFA p29 CR Belgium59

GRIFFITHS,Arthur Ivor T2Lt kia 3-8-17 12Suff p78 CR France439

GRIFFITHS,Charles Jewell Thomas Lt ded 7-11-18 RDC p270 CR Hamps7

GRIFFITHS,Charles Ridley T2Lt dow 1-5-17 7RFus p68 CR France95

GRIFFITHS,Christopher William TLt dow 7-11-18 RE 123FC p45 CR France146

GRIFFITHS,D.H.Chap4Cl 15-12-15 CR Mon89

GRIFFITHS,David George.MC.Lt dow 15-12-18 84RFA p29 CR Wales231,17-12-18

GRIFFITHS,Edwin Arthur TLt kia 27-2-18 11SWBord att115TMB p100 CR France275

GRIFFITHS,Edwin Harold 2Lt dow 23-10-18 6RWFus attTMB p223 CR Italy9,kia 22-10-18

GRIFFITHS,Edwin John T2Lt kia 28-2-18 111LabCps p189 CR Belgium20

GRIFFITHS,Egbert Clarence T2Lt ded 27-2-19 5KRRC p265 CR Surrey2

GRIFFITHS,Francis Noot Gifford Lt dow 2-6-15 10Manch p237 CR Gallipoli1

GRIFFITHS,Frank Calvert 2Lt dow 14-2-17 3 att7Yorks p90 CR France105

GRIFFITHS,Frederick James Capt kia 1-9-18 20 att4Lond p251 CR France216

GRIFFITHS,George Clement TCapt kia 28-6-15 13 att1LancF p92 CR Gallipoli6

GRIFFITHS,George Richards TLt dow 15-9-16 1KRRC p150 CR France203

RIFFITHS,Gwyn Arthur TLt kia 2-6-17 15WelchR &35RFC p8&126 CR France839

GRIFFITHS,Harry James T2Lt dow 9-8-16 9 att1SomLI p79 CR Belgium11

GRIFFITHS,Henry Hingley TLt ded 26-10-18 SStaffs p264 CR Hereford186

GRIFFITHS,Hugh T2Lt ded 1-12-18 RE 310RdConstCo p45 CR France13

GRIFFITHS,Iorworth T2Lt kia 5-7-16 7ELancs p110 MR21 Iorwerth

GRIFFITHS,J.L Sister 30-10-15 QAIMNS CR Egypt3

GRIFFITHS,John.MID TCapt kia 1-7-16 12RIrRif p169 CR France339

GRIFFITHS,John Enos 2Lt kia 23-4-18 5Glouc p225 CR France248

GRIFFITHS,John Herbert 2Lt dow 29-5-18 B175RFA p29 CR France504,A174RFA

GRIFFITHS,John Joseph 2Lt dow 23-3-18 11Lpool p72 MR27

GRIFFITHS,John Llewelyn T2Lt kia 26-6-16 15 att12NumbF p61 CR France188

GRIFFITHS,John Neville TCapt kia 30-11-17 RAMC att58HAG p195 CR France245

GRIFFITHS,Leon David T2Lt dow 29-4-17 24RFus att5TMB p68 CR France95,Lt

GRIFFITHS,Lewis Herbert T2Lt kia 11-9-18 Norf att12Bn p73 CR Belgium451

GRIFFITHS,Nicholas T2Lt kia 10/11-7-16 7 att6SWBord p100 CR France150,11-7-16

GRIFFITHS,P.R.LtCol 13-7-20 RAMC CR Mddx26

GRIFFITHS,Reginald Hopkins Hill.MC.2Lt kld 17-10-18 9WelshR &RAF p126 CR Belgium140,Hopkin

GRIFFITHS,Royston Swire TLtAMaj ded 17-3-17 RGA 123SB p39 CR France1182

GRIFFITHS,Thomas Comber Lt dow 8-7-19 LNLancs att1SlavoBritLegion p136 SeeGRIFFITH.T.C.

GRIFFITHS,Walter 2Lt kia 21-11-17 1LancF p92 MR17

GRIFFITHS,Walter Edward Lambourn TCapt kia 26-4-17 9Glouc p106 CR Greece6

GRIFFITHS,Walter Harold T2Lt kia 4-10-16 7RWKent p14 CR France383,30-9-16

GRIFFITHS,William Charles TLt kia 21-10-18 10RInniskF p105 CR Belgium140

GRIFFITHS,William Dillwyn 2Lt kia 18-9-18 4WelshR p230 CR France1463,dow

GRIFFITHS,William George T2Lt kia 9-3-18 1 att1/5RWFus p97 CR Palestine3

GRIFFITHS,William Henry Capt&QM kia 7-8-15 6LancF p221 MR4

GRIFFITHS,William John.MC.Capt kia 24-11-17 17WelshR p126 MR17

GRIFFITHS,William Percival TCapt kia 30-3-16 10RWFus p97 MR29

GRIGG,George Irving 2Lt dow 21-7-17 RGA 234SB p39CR Belgium16

GRIGG,Harry Hasting Capt kia 16-5-15 IA 1/3GurkhaRifatt2/3 p277CR France631,Hastings

GRIGG,John Capt ded 14-10-18 EAfrSupplyCps CR EAfrica47

GRIGG,Lionel Francis T2Lt kia 29-7-16 1ESurr p112 MR21,28-7-16

GRIGG,Malcolm Howard 2Lt kia 9-7-16 26Manch p154 MR21,17Bn

GRIGGS,Horace Edward TCapt kia 5-10-15 9Ess p131 MR19

GRIGSON,Francis Henry T2Lt kia 9-8-15 9RWar p64 MR4

GRIGSON,Kenneth Walton.MC.Capt kia 20-7-18 7Dev att2/5WYorks p217 CR France622

GRIGSON,Lionel Henry Shockforth 2Lt kia 9-5-17 3Dev p76 MR20,Shuckforth

GRIMBLE,Henry T2Lt kia 28-9-16 8Suff p78 MR21

GRIME,Joseph Crookes 2Lt kia 26-3-18 17LancF p92 MR27

GRIMES,John Arthur.MC.T2Lt kia 7-3-18 1RBerks p139 CR France662

GRIMMOND,Alfred 2Lt kia 14-7-16 2RScots p54 CR France164

GRIMSDELL,Gerald Lucien.MC.TCapt ded 6-7-18 8SLancs p125 CR Mddx15,28-7-18

GRIMSDELL,Reginald Edward 2Lt kia 25-9-16 4Lond p246 MR21

GRIMSELL,Gerald Lucien.MC.Capt ded 6-7-18 SLancs p264

GRIMSEY,Walter James Lt drd 3-10-18 RFus attNigR CR Lond2 Served as SINCLAIR,F.

GRIMSHAW,Cecil Thomas Wrigley.DSO.Maj kia 26-4-15 1RDubF p176 CR Gallipoli15

GRIMSHAW,Ewing Wrigley LtCol kia 21-6-16 IA 62Punjabis p277 CR Iraq5,21-1-16

GRIMSHAW,Geoffrey Harrison T2Lt kia 10-7-16 6 att8LNLancs p136 MR21

GRIMSHAW,Harold Shrieves T2Lt dow 24-5-17 Manch att21Bn p154 CR France518

GRIMSHAWE,Charles Ronald Vaughan Lt mbk 28-5-18 22DLI p256 CR France1331

GRIMSLEY,William Henry TLt kia 6-10-18 14 att9Yorks p90 CR France844

GRIMSTON,Horace Sylvester Lt kia 23-10-14 2Wilts p153 CR Belgium308,21-10-14

GRIMWADE,Arthur Macrae Capt 6-9-20 RASC CR Hamps11

GRIMWADE,Edward Ernest 2Lt kia 17-9-16 3 att9LancF p92 MR21,Lt

GRIMWOOD,Bertie Constantine Ruffell.MC.Lt kia 7-11-17 RHA attRFC p8&29 MR20

GRIMWOOD,John Chisnell Lt kia 3-12-17 5Suff p217 MR17,att2/5RWar

GRINDELL,John Flint Lotherington Capt kia 20-6-17 7DLI p239 CR Belgium29,22Bn

GRINDLAY,Alexander Brown T2Lt ded 24-3-17 11RScots p54 CR France787

GRINDLAY,William T2Lt kia 30-5-18 DLI p160 MR18

GRINDLEY,Herbert Taylor Lt kia 19-10-15 RE p45 CR Belgium6

GRINHAM,Philip Richard John Lt kia 3-5-17 10Mddx p236 MR20

GRIPPER,Edward Cutbush Capt dow 5-12-17 7YLI p143 CR France40

GRIPPER,Walter Vincent Thomas Capt kia 24-7-16 3 att1ESurr p112 CR France397

GRISEWOOD,Francis 2Lt kia 30-6-16 11RSuss p119 MR19

GRISEWOOD,George Maria Joseph Alphonsus Capt ded 27-3-16 11RSuss p119 CR France345

GRISOT,Reginald T2Lt kia 6-8-18 11RFus p68 CR France209

GRISSELL,Bernard Salwey.DSO.MajTLtCol kia 19-4-17 Cmdg1/5Norf p73 CR Palestine8

GRISSELL,Francis Lt kia 15-9-16 1CldGds p51 MR21

GRIST,Cecil Howard Lt kia 3-5-17 7RWKent p141 MR20

GRIST,Henry Noel T2Lt kia 27-5-17 RE 173TC p45 CR Belgium23

GRIST,Percival Charles Hugh Lt kia 18-9-18 25Lond p252 CR France369

GRIST,Ronald Lt ded 15-5-18 18RB p244 CR Burma122A

GRISTWOOD,George Henry 2Lt dow 16-9-16 3 att1Leic p87 CR France105

GRITTON,S.Lt 5-10-18 IndPostalServ CR Iraq8

GROBEL,Peter,Rev ded 1-1-17 RAChDept p199 CR France102

GROCOTT,Frederick William 2Lt kia 17-7-17 3 att6RWKent p141 MR20

GROGAN,Gerald Forman TLt kia 8-1-18 RE 183Co p45 CR Belgium23

GROGAN,Hubert Lawrence.MC.LtACapt kia 6-5-18 4Worc p108 CR France24,5-18

GROGAN,James Colin Lt kia 4-6-15 KOSB p101 CR Gallipoli6

GROGAN,Richard Lawrence Renny 2Lt kia 30-1-17 RE 183Coy p210 CR France374

GRONOW,Charles David T2Lt dow 18-4-18 55MGC p183 CR France88

GROOM,Cyril Lt kia 30-12-17 28Lond p252 MR21

GROOM,Noel TLt kia 20-9-17 9Yorks p90 MR30

GROOMBRIDGE,Clement Thomas 2Lt ded 23-11-15 4Leic p270 CR Essex86

GROOME,Robert Edward Charles 2Lt dow 4-3-15 65RFA p29 CR Belgium151

GROOME,Thomas Mason Capt ded 1-6-16 6Manch Res p270 CR Ches182

GROSART,William David 2Lt dow 15-4-17 5LNLancs p234

GROSE,Albert George 2Lt ded PoW 9-11-17 GL &4RFC p8 MR20

GROSE,Guy Charles George 2Lt kia 9-10-17 9WYorks A'Coy p81 CR Belgium12

GROSE-HODGE,Dorrien Edward 2Lt kia 24-4-15 3Suff p78 CR Belgium152,27-15

GROSER,Arthur Geoffrey Lt kia 7-10-16 7Mddx p235 CR France374

GROSER,Arthur Hugh 2Lt kia 22-9-16 3 att1RWFus p97 CR Belgium54

GROSS,Geoffrey Yates Capt kia 9-4-16 1RWKent p141 CR France1182

GROSS,Herbert George 2Lt kia 16-9-16 9YLI p143 MR21

GROSS,Robert John T2Lt kld 26-2-18 GL &RFC p16 CR Essex185,25-2-18

GROSS,William Henry Bright 2Lt kia 3-11-16 1RWSurr p56 MR21

GROSSART,Archibald Campbell 2Lt kia 23-7-18 10Lpool att1/5SfthH p216 CR France1697

GROSSART,Robert Dykes T2Lt kld 9-2-17 18WelchR &RFC p8&126 CR Scot60

GROSSART,William David 2Lt kia 15-4-17 4/5LNLancs CR France255

GROSSMAN,Victor David T2Lt kia 17-9-16 24NumbF p61 CR France515,15-9-1

GROSVENOR,Hugh Williams.Lord.Capt kia 25-10-14 1LifeGds p20 MR29,30-10-14

GROSVENOR,Richard Eustace.Hon.Capt kia 13-10-15 RFA p29 CR France423

GROSVENOR,Thomas TLt kia 17-9-17 7Lincs att57RFC p8&75 CR Belgium175

GROSVENOR,Thomas Robert 2Lt kia 14-8-17 13Lond p249 MR29

GROTE,Arthur Lloyd TCapt ded 9-7-18 RE IWT p45 CR Iraq6

GROUND,Edward George Lt kia 15-8-15 11Lond p248 MR4

GROUND,Francis William T2Lt kia 25-4-17 44MGC p183 MR20

GROUND,John Kingston T2Lt kia 19-6-16 10RWKent p141 CR Belgium137

GROUNDS,Keble 2Lt dow 15-9-16 4 att2N&D p134 MR21

GROUTAGE,Joseph Harry 2Lt kia 29-3-18 8RWar att61DivHQ p215 MR27,2/5B

GROVE,Charles Frederick Smith.MC.TLtACapt kia 8-8-18 1TankCps p188 CR France589

GROVE,Ernest Richard 2Lt kia 10-2-17 7Lpool p215 CR Belgium112

GROVE,James Percival 2LtTCapt kia 31-7-17 9Manch p237 MR29

GROVE,John Archibald.MID TMaj kia 10-8-18 RASC HT 32DivTrn p193 CR France692

GROVE,Percival Allen 2Lt dow 7-7-16 1/5RWar p214 CR France145,5-7-16

GROVE,Philip Cranston 2Lt kia 11-4-17 2SfthH p164 CR France604,Cranstoun

GROVER,Alice Jane Sister ded 6-2-19 QAIMNS 21GH p200 CR Egypt1

GROVES,Ernest 2Lt kia 31-3-18 7EYorks p84 MR20

GROVES,Francis Neville Lt kia 8-5-15 3Mon p244 MR29

GROVES,Harold Rienzi Milton T2Lt dow 14-10-17 28MGC p183 CR Belgium23,Rienzie

GROVES,Joseph Capt ded 19-10-18 6WRid p227 CR France377

GROVES,Leonard Alloway Lt kia 3-9-15 11RSuss p119 CR France1890

GROVES,Reginald Edward T2Lt kia 9-4-18 20Mddx p147 MR32

GROVES,Richard Lt dow 24-10-17 6 att1N&D p233 CR France64

GROVES,Robert Harry.MC.2Lt dow 12-4-17 3Lond C'Coy p245 CR France120

GROWSE,John Hartley LtTCapt dow 1-4-18 2Nhampt p137 CR France145

GROWSE,Robert Henry Maj ded 12-2-19 RASC F'Cps MT Coy p193 CR Germar

GRUBB,Donald James T2Lt kia 15-8-15 5RInniskF p105 MR4

GRUBB,Lawrence Ernest Pelham 2Lt kia 18-11-14 YLI p143 MR29

GRUBY,Thomas William T2Lt dow 19-7-16 8BordR p117 CR France40

GRUCHY,Francis Le Maistre Capt kia 22-10-14 Leic p87

GRUMMITT,Hugh Cecil 2Lt ded 25-3-19 4EYorks p270 CR Yorks46

GRUMMITT,Joseph Roland Lt ded 14-11-18 4EYorks p219 CR Yorks46

GRUNDTVIG,Humphrey Halgrim.MC.TLt dow 22-3-18 11Leic p87 CR France5

GRUNDY,Cecil Boyce 2Lt dow 16-11-15 6 att1Mddx p147 CR France80

GRUNDY,Edwin Dan Worth TLt dow 19-8-18 3LNLancs att11ELancs p136 CR France134

GRUNDY,Frederick William David T2Lt dow 26-2-17 9RIrF p171 CR France145
GRUNDY,George Edward Lt kia 22-7-15 9RWar p64 MR4
GRUNDY,Ronald Edwin 2Lt kia 1-7-16 2Mddx p147 CR France393
GRUNE,Gilbert Dennis James Lt kia 13-3-16 RFA attRFC p207 CR France421
GRUSELLE,Henri Ernest John 2Lt kia 30-11-17 1/13 att 1/2Lond p249 MR17
GUBBIN,John Richard Francis 2Lt dow 20-11-17 PoW 47RFC p8 Europe58
GUBBINS,Richard Rolls.DSO.BtLtCol drd 25-1-18 KSLI p144 CR France85,SomLI
GUDGEON,Frederick Gustavus TCapt kia 28-6-15 16 att2RFus p68 MR4
GUDGEON,Robert Eustace.MC.Capt dow PoW 2-4-18 RFA p207 CR France1266
GUDGEON,Sidney 2Lt kia 14-5-15 3 att2Manch p154 CR Belgium56,Lt
GUDGEON,Thomas Wallace Lt kia 25-8-18 5RScotF attTankCps p189&222 CR France614
GUERNSEY,Heneage Greville Finch.Lord.Capt kia 14-9-14 1IrGds p52 CR France1112
GUERRIER,Elias George TLt drd 30-11-18 GL attRE IWT p190 CR Iraq5
GUEST,Cyril Stuart T2Lt dow 5-8-16 10SStaffs att9ELancs p110 CR Greece6
GUEST,Ernest William 2Lt dow 26-2-18 RLancs att25RFC p16&59 CR France88
GUEST,Frederick Charles Herbert Lt dow 3-6-17 RASC p253 CR France1182
GUEST,Ivor Arthur Melville Lt kia 6-11-17 1CapeCps CR EAfrica11
GUEST,John Aloysius T2Lt dow 27-7-16 24 att17Mddx p147 MR21
GUEST,John Eric Cox 2Lt dow 20-9-18 7RWar CR Italy10
GUEST,Reginald Victor 2Lt dow 28-8-16 2/8RWar p215 CR France134
GUEST,Sidney 2Lt kia 11-4-18 4SLancs p230 MR19
GUEST,Thomas Heald TMaj kia 1-7-16 13Y&L p158 MR21
GUEST-WILLIAMS,Wynne Austin Capt kia 25-9-15 RBerks p139 MR32
GUILDING,John 2Lt kia 18-8-17 8Worc p226 MR30
GUILDING,Sidney Cecil Lansdowne 2Lt ded 4-11-18 106RH&FA p29 CR Italy12
GUILLEBAUD,E.C.2Lt 3-6-15 11Worc CR Somerset33
GUILLIBAND,Geoffrey Peter Lt kia 10-8-15 6LNLancs p136 MR4,GUILLEBAUD
GUINEY,Edward Castray Capt drd 14-2-18 SL attNyassalandFieldForce p201&202,KAR
GUISANI,St.John Joseph Vincent Anthony T2Lt kia 13-11-16 10RDubF p176 CR France220,GIUSANI
GUISE,Henry George Christopher Lt kia 6-5-15 5Glouc p225 CR Belgium70
GUISE,James William T2Lt dow 19-8-17 5 O&BLI p130 CR Belgium8
GUISE,Reginald Edward.MC.Lt kia 29-6-18 12GloucYeo p203 CR France352
GULBENKIAN,Krikor T2Lt kia 20-9-17 Mddx att23Bn p147 MR30
GULL,Francis William Lindley CaptAMaj kia 25-8-18 1 att 13RB p179 CR France518
GULL,Leonard Joseph T2Lt kia 24-7-17 90MGC p183 MR29
GULLAND,Alexander Falkland Lt dow 16-6-17 3EKent p57 CR Belgium11,Capt 8Bn
GULLICK Arthur Louis TLt kia 3-10-15 EKent p57 CR France552
GULLILAND,John Hutchison TCapt dow 18-7-16 11Ess p131 CR Belgium11
GUMBLEY,Donald Charles Beric 2Lt kia 3-9-16 3 att1Wilts p153 MR21
GUMMER,Basil Austin 2Lt kia 12-8-16 1/9Lpool p216 MR21
GUMMER,Fred T2Lt kia 9-8-18 15TankCps p188 CR France526
GUMMER,Stanley Capt kia 9-10-17 5Y&L p238 MR30
GUNDILL,Robert Percy 2Lt kia 2-10-18 YLI &108RAF p265 MR20
GUNDLE,G.W.Lt kia 27-9-17 KAR p202
GUNDRY,William Lt&QM ded 19-1-18 GL p190 CR Lancs179
GUNINGHAM,William John Lt&QM 18-5-15 ShropYeo CR Lond4 Ex RHG
GUNN,Arthur T2Lt kia 5-5-17 2WRid p115 MR29
GUNN,Charles Mortimer Austin Capt kia 20-5-17 5ScotRif p224 MR20
GUNN,David TLt kia 13-10-17 SfthH att7Bn p164 Belgium123
GUNN,Edmond Alan 2Lt ded 13-2-19 RGA 77SB p39 CR Belgium265
GUNN,James Campbell T2Lt kia 27-5-18 Hamps att2RBerks p120 MR18
GUNN,Kenneth Lt kia 14-4-16 3 att 1BlkW p128 CR France178,4-4-16 2 att1Bn
GUNN,Marcus Sinclair..C Lt dow 6-9-16 1BlkW p128 CR France833
GUNN,Murray Grant 2Lt kia 7-12-17 23RFC p8 MR20
GUNN,Ronald William Craig 2Lt kia 6-1-17 3 att 12N&D p134 CR France115
GUNN,Walter Roderick Hamilton 2Lt kia 1-9-18 3Lond p245 CR France216
GUNN,Wilfred Herbert 2Lt kia 26-3-18 331RFA p29 MR27
GUNNELL,J.F.R Lt 8-4-20 Dors att51War CR Germany1
GUNNER,Arthur Henry Edmund T2Lt kia 26-3-18 11RSuss p119 CR France402
GUNNER,Benjamin George,MC LtTCapt kia 7-10-15 1NumbF p61 CR Belgium6
GUNNER,Frank Lt kia 14-4-18 4 att 12ScotRif p103 MR32
GUNNER,John Hugh Capt dow 9-8-18 HampsYeo att15HampsR p203 CR Belgium21
GUNNER,William Henry.MC.2Lt kia 29-7-17 GL &60RFC p8 CR France924
GUNNERY,Cedric Leopold T2Lt kia 22-5-17 GL &46RFC p8 CR France354

GUNNING,Edward George Francis TCapt ded 10-6-19 RFA attRAOC p254 CR France65,acckld
GUNNING,Frank Douglas 2Lt kia 1-7-16 6 att11RInniskF p105 MR21
GUNNING,John Walter 2Lt kia 24-3-18 1Wilts p153 MR20
GUNNING,Orlando George.CMG.DSO.MID BrigGen ded 14-11-17 IA 36Sikhs p277 CR SAfrica172
GUNNING,William Herbert 2Lt dow 31-10-16 3 att 10Hamps p120 CR Europe1
GUNNIS,Geoffrey George.MC.TCapt dow 13-10-16 3GrenGds p50 CR France145
GUNNIS,Ian Fitzgerald Stuart 2Lt kia 4-7-17 2GrenGds p50 CR Belgium84
GUNSON,Henry Edward Rev ded 23-8-18 RAChDept p199 CR Hamps10
GUNSON,Leslie Robert Schrader TLt kia 18-7-16 RGA 31HB p39 CR France399
GUNSTON,Frederic John Dover.MC.LtACapt dow PoW 14-7-18 6Worc p108 CR France1027,2Bn
GUNTER,Francis James Lt kia 24-5-15 11Huss p22 MR29
GUNTER,Robert Benson Nevill.Bart.LtCol ded 16-8-17 SL 3Yorks p201 CR Belgium5,Benyon
GUNTHER,Charles Emil TLt kia 24-9-18 2LifeGds att2GdsMGReg p20&53 CR France1701
GUNTHER,Geoffrey Robert.MC.2Lt kia 4-11-18 3GrenGds p50 CR France1080
GUNTHER,Norman Otto Frederick.MC.2Lt kia 11-7-17 att6REKentYeo p204 MR20,12-7-17
GUNTON,John Welby 2Lt kia 9-8-16 9SomLI &70RFC p3&79 MR20
GUNTON,Reginald Oliver 2Lt kia 21-3-18 3Lond p245 CR France1893
GURDON,Philip Norman Lt kia 9-10-16 IA 14Sikhs attJindInf p277 CR EAfrica36,Capt
GURNELL,Robert Matthew T2Lt kia 21-5-17 18RIrRif p169 CR Belgium100
GURNEY,Elizabeth Shepherd SNurse drd 10-4-17 QAIMNS p200 CR France85
GURNEY,Frederick Arthur T2Lt ded 23-3-16 5Nhampt p137 CR France40
GURNEY,Kenneth Gerard 2Lt ded PoW 17-12-17 5Glouc p225 CR France660,dow
GURRIN,Reginald Wells 2Lt dow 5-8-17 3 att12ESurr p112 CR Belgium167
GUSH,William George T2LtACapt kia 23-4-17 RFus p68 CR France777
GUTHE,Cecil Rudolph Lt 10-2-19 RGA CR Durham180
GUTHE,Thomas Percival Maj dow 13-1-16 1DurhamRFA p206 CR France40
GUTHRIE,Albert John Lt kia 30-7-16 5GordH p242 MR21
GUTHRIE,Alexander Capt ded 29-12-16 RDC 35ProtCoy p253 CR Scot386
GUTHRIE,Alexander Lt kia 12-7-17 1HighlandRFA Y32TMB p207 CR Belgium173
GUTHRIE,Arthur Calderwood 2Lt kld 9-8-18 RE att42RAF p45 CR France31
GUTHRIE,Charles Wilford Lt kia 1-8-17 13RScots p54 CR Belgium125
GUTHRIE,David Michall Chap4Cl dow 21-11-16 RAChDept att8ELancs p199 CR France41
GUTHRIE,George Watson TLt kia 13-11-16 RAMC RNDiv p195 CR France220
GUTHRIE,Hector MacLennan Lt kia 4-6-15 3 att 1LancF p92 MR4
GUTHRIE,Hugh Smith 2Lt ded PoW 31-3-18 7BlkW p231 CR France924,dow
GUTHRIE,John Mack.MC.Capt kia 28-7-18 6BlkW p231 CR France1689
GUTHRIE,John Noel Capt kia 18-5-15 IrGds p52 CR France727
GUTHRIE,Robert Forman Capt kia 9-8-16 10Lpool p216 MR21
GUTHRIE,Robert Gilbert Lt ded 7-11-18 3RFA p207 CR Yorks3
GUTHRIE,Stuart 2Lt kia 4-4-18 5 att2/6Lond p246 MR20
GUTHRIE,Thomas T2Lt dow 27-6-18 6CamH p168 CR Scot752
GUTHRIE,Thomas Errol Capt kia 3-7-16 RAMC attNZ MedCps p195
GUTHRIE,William Colville 2Lt ded 7-11-18 C52RFA p208 CR France403
GUTHRIE,Willie Forrester Lt kia 26-4-18 4 att9ScotRif p103 CR Belgium74
GUTHRIE-SMITH,Ronald Cameron 2Lt kia 19/22-12-14 1HLI p163 CR France644,Lt 20-12-14
GUTMANN,Walter 2Lt dow 7-5-17 D71RFA p29 CR France40
GUTTERIDGE,Eric Lancelot T2Lt kia 14-7-16 10Leic p87 MR21
GUTTERIDGE,Richard Charley Lt kia 28-5-18 2/6 att 15DLI p239 CR France1331
GUTTERIDGE,Richard Howard 2Lt kia 2-10-16 9Lond p248 MR21
GUY,Christopher Godfrey Capt dow PoW 12-8-17 1/4Nhampt C'Coy attRFC p18&234 CR Belgium5
GUY,Norman Glass 2Lt kia 27-5-18 3 att7Leic p87 MR18
GUY,Reginald Churchill T2Lt kia 24-8-18 8RBerks p139 CR France177
GUY,Ronald Litterdale Lt kia 26-10-17 6 att1/7NumbF p213 MR30,Lidderdale
GUYON,George Sutherland LtCol kia 1-7-16 2RFus p68 MR21
GWYER,Alexander Grant Capt kia 22-10-14 6DragGds RoO p21 CR Belgium74,Alastair
GWYER,Charles Percy Capt kia 8-8-15 1 att8WelshR p126 MR4
GWYER,Cyril Lt kia 27-8-18 2GrenGds p50 CR France614
GWYN,Reginald Augustine Jerome 2Lt dow 3-3-16 2Lincs p75 MR29,Jermy
GWYNN,John Chap4Cl dow 12-10-15 RAChDept att 1IrGds p199 CR France80
GWYNNE,Henry Stanley 2Lt kia 24-11-17 6RWar p214 CR Belgium111

GWYNNE,Hubert Llewellyn 2Lt kia 18-11-16 8NStaffs p157 MR21
GWYNNE,John Fitzgerald.MC.MID Capt kia 9-7-15 RAMC p195 CR Belgium85
GWYNNE,L.H.Lt 10-3-18 EAUL CR EAfrica10 &CR Tanzania1
GWYNNE,Owen Perrott 2Lt kia 7-1-16 IARO att92Punjabis MR38 p277
GWYNNE,Roderick Thynne Sackville 2Lt dow 23-5-15 4YLI p235
GWYNNE-GRIFFITH,Gilbert Digby Mansel TLtACapt dow 2-7-18 RE attSPersiaRif p45 CR Asia82
GWYNNE-VAUGHAN,Kenneth Duncan T2Lt kia 6-9-16 15RFus att33MGC Inf p68&183 CR France296
GWYTHER,Edwin Thomas T2Lt dow 28-5-18 SStaffs att1/6Bn p122 CR France40
GWYTHER,Guy Llewelyn T2Lt kia 6-1-16 2Leic p87 MR38
GYE,Denison Allen TLtACapt kia 28-2-17 15RHA p29 CR France786
GYLE,Ernest Woods 2Lt kia 18-10-18 7BlkW p231 CR France1271
GYLLENCREUTZ,James Randolph TMaj drd 10-4-17 RAMC p195 CR France85
GYVES,John James T2Lt kia 3-6-18 11RDubF p176 CR France24,1Bn

H

HAARER,Philip McLellan 2Lt kia 28-11-16 15RFC p3 CR France41,22-11-16
HAASE,Edward George Louis T2Lt kia 3-7-16 9 att5RBerks p139 MR21
HABERSHON,Kenneth Rees TCapt kia 12-2-16 12RB p179 CR Belgium5
HABERSHON,Leonard Osborne TCapt kia 13-11-16 12EYorks p84 MR21
HABERSHON,Philip Henry T2Lt kia 25-9-15 9KRRC p150 MR29
HABERSHON,Sidney Heathcote 2Lt kia 8/13-4-18 12Suff p78 MR32
HABLUTZEL,George Rudolph 2Lt kia 1-7-16 1RLancs p59 MR21
HACK,Adrian Henry TLt kia 1-7-16 8YLI p143 CR France246
HACK,Charles Edward Capt kia 5-11-14 ConnRgrs p172 MR22
HACK,John Frederick Charles Lt kia 26-9-16 RGA 117HB p39 CR France401
HACKER,Norman Capt kld 26-10-17 2Dors p124 CR Iraq8
HACKETT,David Frederick Mackness.MM.Lt kia 22-8-18 1Leic p87 CR France383
HACKETT,Eric Adrian Nethercote T2Lt kia 9-9-16 6RIrReg p89 MR21
HACKETT,Harry Osborne 2LtTLt dow 28-8-17 11WelchR p126 CR Belgium16,Osbourn 16Bn
HACKETT,Henry Robert Theodore 2Lt kia 2-11-15 1RDubF p176 CR Gallipoli4
HACKETT,Learo Aylmer Henry.MC.TCapt kia 24-4-18 10RIrRif p169 CR Belgium64
HACKETT,Venice Clementine Henrietta Miss ded 13-10-18 VAD BRCS p200 CR Eire476
HACKETT,Walter Ralph TLt kia 3-10-16 7RWKent p141 MR21
HACKETT,William TLt ded 15-11-18 RE Ex 8SStaffs p45 CR Staffs67
HACKFORTH-JONES,Arthur Lt kia 8-8-18 3Glouc att7RWKent p106 MR16
HACKING,Walter William 2Lt kia 21-3-18 N&D att2/8Bn p134 MR20
HADDEN,Archibald Robert Capt kia 25-4-18 9Lond p247 CR France425
HADDEN,Arthur.MC.2Lt kia 8-3-16 IARO att53Sikhs MR38 p277
HADDEN,Cyril Martin ACapt kia 28-3-18 3 att1RScotF p94 MR20
HADDEN,Eustace Waller Russell Maj ded 11-6-16 1/4 O&BLI p231 CR France51
HADDEN,Francis Albert Lt 22-6-19 RAMC CR Mddx42
HADDEN,Frank John TLt ded 5-5-16 RemountServ 42RASC p24 CR Egypt9
HADDEN,John Hazlett Millar T2Lt kia 31-10-16 20RIrRif p169 CR Greece3
HADDEN,Nigel Clement Charles TCapt dow 9-4-16 RFA 14Bty p29 MR38
HADDER,Robert 2Lt kia 19-7-16 5Glouc attMGC p225
HADDOCK,Joseph Henry T2Lt kia 24-3-18 14RIrRif p169 CR France1203
HADDOCK,Wilfrid Spencer T2Lt dow 16-7-17 9SLancs p125 CR Greece7,Spence
HADDOCK,William.MC.TLt kia 24-9-18 1WYorks p81 CR France835
HADDOCK,William Theodore TLt ded 30-1-16 1/5Suff p217 CR Egypt3
HADDON,Harold Esmond.MIDx3 Lt kia 24-12-15 IA 119Inf p277 CR Iraq1
HADDON,Harwood Albert T2Lt kia 26-9-17 att2/8N&D p134 CR Belgium125
HADDON,Hugh Reid Capt ded 12-7-15 5RScotF p222
HADDON,Thomas Capt dow 20-4-18 PoW 2/7Ches p222 CR France934
HADDON,Vernon 2Lt kia 10-8-17 11RFus p68 MR29
HADDON,Walter T2Lt dow 27-9-15 7KOSB p101 MR19,25-9-15
HADDON-SMITH,Walter Basil Capt kia 16-5-15 RWSurr p56 MR22
HADDOW,H.R Capt 12-7-15 5RScotF CR Egypt
HADDY,Stephen Edgar T2Lt dow 16-8-17 4Hamps p228 CR Belgium16
HADEN,Frederick Haughton 2Lt kia 4-11-17 1RB att11TMB p179 CR France154
HADENHAM,Lawrence George T2Lt dow 18-7-16 9ESurr p112 CR France285,Lt
HADFIELD,Edgar T2Lt kia 22-3-17 10WelshR p126 CR Belgium23
HADFIELD,James Robert TLt ded 9-3-16 13Manch p154 CR Greece7
HADFIELD,Wilfred John Mackenzie Lt ded 10-9-14 SLancs p125 CR France1845 &CR France34,dow

HADINGHAM,Roy Matthew Lt kia 22-6-16 4Glouc p225 MR19,26-6-16
HADLAND,Spencer Austin Capt kia 24-3-18 2RB p179 MR27
HADLEY,Cyril Vernon 2Lt kia 3-7-16 10Worc p108 MR21
HADLEY,Ernest Sidney 2Lt kia 27-8-17 4Glouc p225 MR30
HADLEY,Peyton Sheldon.MC.TLtACapt ded 24-10-18 7Nhampt p137 CR Norf60,25-10-18
HADLEY,Reginald Bracebridge Lt mbk 31-10-14 1/2SWBord p256 MR29
HADOW,Arthur de Salis BtCol kia 27-9-15 10Yorks p80 CR France551,15Bn
HADOW,Erlan Godfrey.MC.TCapt kia 29-5-17 17WYorks p81 CR France415
HADOW,Gerald Francis Lt kia 15-6-15 2Yorks p90 MR22
HADRILL,Arthur William TLt kia 12-8-15 9Lincs attRMunstF p75 MR4
HADWEN,Charles Eugene.MM.T2Lt kia 12-9-18 RB att13Bn p179 MR16
HADWEN,Noel Waugh Capt kia 1-7-16 2WRid p115 MR21
HAEFFNER,Frederick Wilfred 2Lt kia 9-7-16 149RFA p29 CR France699,151RF
HAGGAR,Harry Douglas Fox Lt kia 17-8-16 3LNLancs p136 CR France630
HAGGARD,Mark Capt dow 15-9-14 2WelchR p126 CR France1329
HAGGART,David Lt kia 14-6-18 1SfthH p164 CR Palestine9,3Bn
HAGGART,James 2Lt dow 3-1-18 4 att14BlkW p230 CR Palestine9
HAGGART,William Jackson Lt kia 31-8-18 4Glouc p225 CR France518,12Bn
HAGGARTY,John Joseph T2Lt dow 11-9-16 29 att22NumbF p61 CR France275,
HAGGER,William Alexander Capt ded 12-7-15 126Baluchis MR43
HAGGO,Aubrey Paxton 2Lt kia 18-8-16 4RScotF p222&221 CR France832
HAGON,Charles Douglas 2Lt dow 3-8-17 4SomLI p218 CR France52,8Bn
HAGUE,Albert Edward 2Lt kia 5-8-16 1/4LNLancs p234 MR21
HAGUE,Harold William 2Lt kia 16-6-18 D47RFA p29 CR France98
HAGUE,James Herbert 2Lt kia 23-4-17 7Manch p237 MR20
HAGUE,Leonard 2Lt kia 26-4-18 13Glouc p106 MR30
HAGUE,Sydney George.MC.TLt dow 21-9-18 1/2Beds p86 CR France194
HAGUE,Walter 2Lt dow 31-3-18 PoW 2/5N&D p232 CR Belgium241
HAHN,Benno Oscar Linsengen T2Lt kld 13-10-17 GL &RFC p8 CR Wilts116,Linsingen
HAIG,Alexander Weir.MM.2Lt dow 17-10-18 1 att1/5GordH p166 CR France163,Lt
HAIG,David T2Lt kld 5-7-18 4/5BlkW p128 CR France145
HAIG,Ernest Herman LtCol ded 28-12-14 RE p45 CR Essex81
HAIG-BROWN,Alan Roderick.DSO.LtCol kia 25-3-18 23Mddx p147 CR France5
HAIG-SMELLIE,Herbert Hamilton T2Lt dow 26-4-17 7Norf p73 CR France113,k
HAIGH,Allen Mortimer T2Lt kia 13-4-18 RLancs att1/4YLI p59 MR30
HAIGH,Arthur Gordon T2Lt kia 15-2-16 RE 172Coy p45 MR29
HAIGH,Charles Roderick Lt kia 7-11-14 RWSurr p56 MR29
HAIGH,Edward 2Lt kia 19-12-15 5YLI p235 CR Belgium23
HAIGH,James Aspinall Lt dow 22-11-17 2/5WRid p227 CR France398
HAIGH,John Caleb 2Lt kia 2-10-18 3RDubF attRIrRif p176 CR Belgium157
HAILE,Robert.MC.TLt dow 29-10-18 10Ess p131 CR France1392
HAILES,Joseph HonCapt kia 1-9-15 RAOC p198 CR Gallipoli18,DADOS 54EAngliaDiv
HAILSTONE,Dudley William T2Lt kia 7-7-18 1DCLI p114 CR France20
HAILSTONE,George Rupert Capt kia 6-11-17 1/7RWFus p223 CR Palestine1
HAILSTONE,Ralph Puroglove T2Lt kia 18-10-16 13 att2Hamps p120 MR21,Pursglove
HAILWOOD,John 2Lt kia 15-10-18 1/4LNLancs p234 CR France1725,16-10-18
HAIN,Edward Capt kia 11-11-15 1DevYeo p203 CR Gallipoli27
HAIN,Edward Sydney T2Lt kia 21-11-17 KRRC att11Bn p150 MR17
HAINES,Alec C.Lt dow 8-5-15 RDubF p176
HAINES,Alexander Crichton Cooper 2Lt dow 8-5-15 2RDubF CR France102
HAINES,Alfred Godfrey Victor TLt dow 22-4-17 15N&D p134 CR France674,G.A.V.
HAINES,Ernest Andrade T2Lt kia 3-9-16 11 att9ESurr p112 MR21
HAINES,Ernest Edward.MC.T2Lt ded 11-2-17 14Lpool p72 CR Berks125
HAINES,Frank Percy Lt kia 15-6-17 8Leic p87 MR20,16-6-17
HAINES,Herbert Henry 2Lt kia 15-5-17 3Lond p245 CR France536
HAINES,Stephen Gilbert 2Lt dow 4-5-17 C70RFA p29 CR France40
HAINING,William John 2Lt kia 28-1-17 3 att1KOSB p101 MR21
HAINING,William Stobo T2Lt kia 20-11-17 TankCps p188 CR France712
HAINSBY,Fernley Winter 2Lt kia 26-3-18 RFC p16 MR20
HAIR,Donald Campbell 2Lt kia 3-10-16 6KSLI p145 MR21
HAIR,Eric Francis Wilson T2Lt dow 27-8-17 2Mddx p147 CR Lond28,Edwin
HAIRE,George TLt dow 7-1-17 6ConnRgrs p172 CR Belgium17
HAIRSINE,Owen.MC.LtTCapt kia 7-6-17 RAMC p195 CR Belgium2
HAIST,Orville Dwight T2Lt kld 5-7-17 GL &37TrSqnRFC p8 CR Lincs181
HAIZELDEN,Benjamin 2Lt dow 30-8-18 2/10Lond p248 CR France119

HAKE,Osmond George 2Lt kld 14-5-16 GL &RFC p3 CR Hamps15,Ormond
HAKEWILL,Thomas George T2Lt kldacc 11-2-16 11NStaffs att17RFC p3&157 CR Egypt3
HALCOMB,Leslie Broughton Maj kia 25-10-18 B295RFA p206 CR France1044
HALCOMBE,Norman Marshall TMaj ded 13-2-19 RE attRAF p255 CR Egypt7
HALCROW,Arthur Palmer Lt kia 23-4-17 3 att2Hamps p120 MR20
HALCROW,John William 2LtTLt kia 7-7-16 3Dors &4RFC p3&124 CR France44
HALCROW,Thomas Tulloch 2Lt kia 3-5-17 1 att2RScots p54 MR20
HALDANE,Arthur Cuthbert T2Lt kia 14-8-16 10SforthH p164 CR Belgium23
HALDANE,Colin Kennedy T2Lt dow 18-10-16 26Manch attMGC p154&183 CR France513
HALDANE,Douglas William 2Lt dow 9-4-17 9HLI p240 CR France1182
HALDANE,James Oswald 2Lt dow 9-8-16 6RB p179 CR Belgium73
HALDANE,Laurence Aylmer.DSO.TMaj kia 2-4-16 2Nhampt &Staffs p137 CR France480
HALDANE,Robert Patrick Lt dow 13-6-15 6BlkW p231 CR France1106
HALDEN,Alexander 2Lt drd 26-2-18 GL RE &1WT p190 MR38
HALDINSTEIN,Frank Worlfe Capt dow 7-3-17 RE p210
HALE,Alfred LLewellyn TCapt kia 8-7-18 10RWSurr p56 CR Belgium11
HALE,Frank Ernest T2Lt kia 25-8-18 13KRRC p150 CR France578
HALE,George Edwin T2Lt kia 22-3-18 39MGC p183 MR27
HALE,Harold John 2Lt kia 24-3-18 15DLI p160 MR27
HALE,Herbert Charles Lt dow 2-11-17 4Yorks p220 CR Belgium16
HALE,S.F.Lt ded 31-5-19 12Hamps p120
HALE,William T2Lt dow 9-8-18 2Worc p108 CR France34,1Bn
HALE,William John Douglas TCapt kia 28-4-17 10RWFus p97 CR France531
HALE,William Webb Lt ded 12-4-17 2/6ESurr attRDC p253 CR Surrey 83
HALES,Arthur Hoare.MC.TCapt kia 6-7-16 1Wilts p153 MR21
HALES,Charles Edward Hoare 2Lt ded 22-11-17 1Wilts p265 CR Somerset30
HALES,Eli George LtCol ded 23-11-18 RE Res p270 CR Sussex112
HALES,Walter Percy Capt ded 1-11-18 IARO att3/124BaluchistanInf p277 CR Asia82
HALES,William Clifford T2Lt kia 23-10-16 8 att2RBerks p139 CR France307
HALEY,Arthur 2Lt kia 1-6-18 3Ess &55RAF p131 CR France1667
HALFACRE,Cecil William T2Lt ded 19-10-16 7RBerks attTMB p139 CR Greece1
HALFHIDE,Charles Edward Nelson TLtAMaj kia 24-5-18 7ELancs attMGC p110&183 CR France41
HALFORD,Arthur Henry.DCM.2Lt dow PoW 30-5-18 RB att7Bn p179 CR France1615
HALFORD,Edward Frederick TLt ded 10-10-18 RE p45&257 CR Surrey104,Frederic
HALFORD,William Stanley 2Lt kia 15-9-16 20Lond p251 CR France432
HALFPENNY,William Henry 2Lt dedacc 24-11-18 11LancF att49RAF p92 CR Lancs2,Lt
HALL,Alan Ryder Lt kia 30-5-18 6NumbF p213 MR18
HALL,Albert Loader TCapt kia 4-4-18 8ESurr D'Coy p112 CR France424
HALL,Alexander Kilburn Capt kia 7-10-16 6RWKent p141 MR21
HALL,Allan Bernard Lt kia 3-5-17 ACycCps att11EYorks p181 MR20
HALL,Allan Gordon Maj kia 24-4-18 C210RFA p206 CR France745
HALL,Arthur Ernest Lt mbk 22-8-15 6Yorks p256 MR4
HALL,Arthur Gordon.MID Capt kia 26-10-14 2Beds D'Coy p86 CR Belgium115
HALL,Arthur Henry.MC.TLtACapt kia 19-11-16 2 att8SomLI p79 CR France339
HALL,Arthur James Melville 2Lt kia 15-9-16 20Lond p251 MR21
HALL,Aubrey Frederick TLt kia 8-8-18 RE 92FC p45 CR France209
HALL,Basil Claude Capt kia 25-8-18 8Manch p237 CR France643
HALL,Bruce Lt kia 25-9-15 SStaffs p122 MR19
HALL,Burton Howard Capt kia 4-11-14 IA 98Inf p277 MR47
HALL,Cecil Charles Hatfield.DSO.MIDx2 Maj kia 27-5-18 22DLI p160 MR18
HALL,Charles 2Lt dow 13-8-16 O&BLI BucksBn p231 MR21
HALL,Charles 2Lt kia 28-3-17 8EKent attM'LTMB p57 CR France161
HALL,Charles Sidney T2Lt kia 7-4-17 GL &60RFC p8 CR France581
HALL,Charles Stuart 2Lt kia 12-1-17 1Mon p244 CR France1014
HALL,Charles William Lt dow 10-8-17 465/65RFA p29 CR France139
HALL,Clarence Espent Lyon TLt kia 7-7-16 5SWBord p100
HALL,Clifford Sheppard T2Lt kia 3-7-16 6RWSurr p56 CR France251
HALL,David Henry TCapt dow 14-5-18 RAMC att2SfthH p195 CR France10
HALL,David Sidney.MC.Capt kia 20-11-17 9A&SH attRFC p18&243 CR France134
HALL,Douglas Alexander TLt kia 25-4-17 10Y&L p158 CR France1193,Capt 23-4-17
HALL,Durham Donald George.MC.2LtTCapt dow 27-3-18 Yorks att80RFC p16&90 CR France62,kia

HALL,Edward Charles 2Lt kia 30-11-17 13Ess p131 MR17
HALL,Edward Henry TLt kld 27-11-16 DCLI attRFC p3 CR Yorks38
HALL,Edward Lawrence 2Lt kia 30-11-17 att1/5LNLancs p136 MR17
HALL,Edward Lionel T2Lt kia 27-3-18 9RSuss p119 MR27
HALL,Edwin Lincoln.MC.2Lt kia 22-4-17 3 att2Leic p87 MR38
HALL,Eric Watson.MBE.Capt kia 26-9-17 2/4Lincs p220&270 CR Belgium101
HALL,Ernest Leslie 2Lt kia 21-3-18 att2Wilts p153 MR27
HALL,Ernest Louis T2Lt dow 6-11-17 11Leic p87 CR Belgium11,5-11-17
HALL,Frances Mary.RRC.MID Matron ded 7-7-19 QAIMNS p268 MR43
HALL,Francis Edward Charles 2Lt kia 16-8-16 2Suff p78 MR21
HALL,Francis Henry T2Lt kia 30-9-18 1 att9RIrF p171 CR Belgium157 ExRIrRif
HALL,Frank Leslie Lt kia 27-8-17 4Glouc p225 MR30
HALL,Fred 2Lt kia 22-9-16 Dors attRFC p3&124 CR France294
HALL,Frederick Grainger TCapt kia 7-7-16 13Ches p96 CR France1890,Frederic
HALL,G.L.D.2Lt kld 2-5-18 GL &RAF p190
HALL,Geoffrey T2Lt kia 23-10-16 2Mddx p147 MR21
HALL,Geoffrey.MC.TLt kia 20-11-17 9RFus p68 MR17
HALL,Geoffrey Evans T2Lt kia 25-4-17 1 att9Norf p73 CR France149
HALL,George.MID Capt dow 23-4-18 14Lond p249 CR France39
HALL,George Dorrington Lt dow 17-9-18 1/5Dev p217 CR France1184
HALL,George Elliott 2Lt dow 29-5-18 RGA 196SB p39 CR France95,kia
HALL,George Ferner Mansfield Lt kia 28-9-15 RBerks p139 MR19
HALL,George Foden Rooking T2Lt kia 28-6-17 RE 103FC p45 CR Belgium29
HALL,George Hanney Lt ded 6-12-19 IARO att4/39GarhwalRif p277 MR40,Capt
HALL,George Henry.MSM.T2Lt kld 24-12-17 RFC p8 CR Nhampt
HALL,George Wilfred 2Lt kia 20-11-17 GL &3RFC p8 CR France336
HALL,Gerald Percy 2Lt kia 13-11-14 4 att2HLI p163 CR Belgium126
HALL,Gilbert Sudbury 2Lt dow PoW 30-11-16 RFC p3 CR France598
HALL,Gordon William 2Lt kld 21-8-16 GL &3RFC p3&190 CR Norf209,Lt
HALL,H.W.Lt 24-12-20 Manch CR Sussex110
HALL,Harford Greville 2LtTLt kia 4-3-17 1N&D p134 MR21
HALL,Harold T2Lt kia 15-2-16 7Lincs p75 MR29
HALL,Harold Platt.MC.2Lt dow 9-11-18 C83RFA p29 CR France146
HALL,Harry Herbert 2Lt kia 2-12-17 6N&D p233 CR France668
HALL,Harry Spencer Lt ded 14-3-15 RAMC p195 CR Staffs125
HALL,Harry Sydney Hopton Hadley Capt ded 24-10-18 3RWKent p141 CR India97A
HALL,Henry Capt kld 25-9-18 RFA 18AC p207 CR Palestine3,kia
HALL,Henry Armstrong.CBE.Rev 12-5-21 CR Yorks381
HALL,Henry Cecil T2Lt kia 4-10-17 Hamps att1Bn p120 MR30
HALL,Henry Charles T2Lt kia 4-9-18 Wilts att15Hamps p153 MR30
HALL,Henry Guy Fitzwilliam TLt kia 13-11-16 10DCLI p114 CR France1491
HALL,Henry John 2Lt kia 19/20-7-16 54AustInf CR France82
HALL,Henry Lewes.MM.2Lt kia 30-11-17 KRRC att10Bn p150 MR17,Lewis
HALL,Henry Leonard Lt kia 27-10-18 RGA 14SB p39 CR France1271
HALL,Herbert Cecil Victor TLt kia 13-6-17 12DLI p160 CR Belgium127
HALL,Herbert John 2Lt kia 7-4-17 5GordH p242 CR France15
HALL,Herbert John Elliott Lt ded 7-2-19 RFA p254 CR Lond3
HALL,Hugh.MC.Lt kia 15-9-17 9DLI p239 CR France538
HALL,Hugh Wilfred 2Lt kia 15-5-17 2/3Lond p245 MR20
HALL,Humphrey Evans LtTCapt kia 27-11-15 2Norf p73 MR38,23-11-15
HALL,J.W.H.Capt ded 19-10-18 TankCps 776RFA CR Essex75
HALL,James Henry 2Lt kld 26-7-18 6LancF &RAF p255
HALL,James Herbert William TLtACapt ded 19-10-18 TankCps p188&261,RH&FA
HALL,James Hervey Lt 25-8-18 LancF &RAF CR Lancs263
HALL,James Muir 2Lt dow 23-4-17 51RFA p29 CR France1182
HALL,James Thomson T2Lt dow 9-6-17 9YLI p143 CR France40,8Bn
HALL,John Edward Kenyon 2Lt dow 22-9-15 3 att2SWBord p100 MR4
HALL,John Francis Ashley 2Lt kia 14-8-18 1EYorks &21RAF p84 CR France88
HALL,John Gilbert 2Lt kia 3-5-17 6WYorks p218 MR20
HALL,John Martindale 2Lt kia 28-8-16 3 att8BordR p117 CR France246
HALL,John McRobb T2Lt kia 1-7-16 21NumbF p61 MR21
HALL,John Pearson Herbert T2Lt kia 1-11-18 19NumbF p61 CR Belgium143
HALL,John Ramsay Fitz-Gibbon 2Lt kia 24-5-15 2RDubF p176 MR29
HALL,John Reginald T2Lt kia 10-7-16 15WelshR p126 MR21
HALL,John Smith Lt kia 21-3-18 7RB p179 MR27
HALL,Joseph T2Lt kia 31-7-17 72MGC p183 MR29
HALL,Joseph Stanley 2Lt kia 5-5-17 12EYorks p84 MR20

125

HALL,Kenneth Stuart TLt kia 25-1-16 15NumbF att21DivACycCps p61 CR France922
HALL,Louis Sylvester Lt kia 27-5-18 RE 490FC p210 MR18
HALL,Luther T2Lt kia 22-9-16 22RFA p29 CR France397,21-9-16
HALL,M.E.A.2Lt ded 27-3-15 14WYorks p81
HALL,Malcolm Wilfrid Forrester Lt kia 20-5-17 5 att1RInniskF p105&257 MR20,Wilfred
HALL,Mark Walter 2Lt kia 5-12-17 2/7N&D p233 CR France1498
HALL,Miles Arthur 2Lt kia 23-4-17 150MGC p183 MR20
HALL,Norman Bodger.MC.TLt dow 2-11-18 12DLI att68TMB p160 CR Italy9
HALL,Norman de Haviland T2Lt dow 7-10-16 1Suff p78 CR Greece7
HALL,Percy George T2Lt kia 30-6-16 23 att26NumbF p61 CR France430
HALL,Percy Mark Capt ded 4-1-19 13Beds p86
HALL,Percy Shene Bernard Capt kia 9-8-16 1EKent p57 CR Belgium47,Sheen
HALL,Peveril Austin 2Lt ded 5-11-18 RE p45 CR Nhampt31
HALL,Ralph Gordon T2Lt kld 23-1-18 GL &RFC p16 CR Canada256
HALL,Ralph Prescott TLt ded 22-3-19 RAOC p267 CR Yorks98
HALL,Reginald 2Lt kia 8-10-18 4Wilts p236 CR France234
HALL,Reginald Clifford.MC.LtACapt kia 20-11-17 5Y&L p238 CR France530
HALL,Robert Lane 2Lt kia 27-5-18 2Nhampt p137 MR18
HALL,Robert Macpherson Maj ded 8-7-15 IA 25Cav att6 p277 MR43
HALL,Roger Holinsworth TLtACapt dow 11-7-17 RFA AntiAircraftGrp p29 CR Belgium24,12-7-17
HALL,Samuel Lt kia 4-6-15 8Manch p237 MR4
HALL,Sidney LtACapt dow 21-3-18 RGA146Bty p39 MR20
HALL,Stanley Alexander Lt dow 10-4-18 RE 156Coy p210 CR France145
HALL,Sydney Lt kia 18-10-18 Manch &RAF p154
HALL,Theodore Newman Lt dow 15-8-16 4 O&BLI p231
HALL,Thomas Lt&QM ded 21-10-17 HLI p265 CR Scot525
HALL,Thomas 2Lt kia 27-3-18 4NumbF p213 MR27,1/6Bn
HALL,Thomas 2Lt dow 19-6-18 4 att11Ess attTMB p232 CR France142
HALL,Thomas Kershaw 2Lt kia 9-10-17 RFA 6/241Bde p29 MR30
HALL,Thomas Storey Inglis 2Lt kia 9-4-16 5 att6RLancs p59&p270,9-4-15 MR38,11-4-16
HALL,Thomas Peter Moubray T2Lt ded 12-12-18 5RRofCav p23 CR Egypt15
HALL,Walter 2Lt dow 15-11-18 5 att2Yorks p221 CR France34
HALL,Warwick Lt dow 1-7-16 SStaffs p122 CR France397
HALL,Wilfred Rodenhurst.MC.TLt kia 21/22-3-18 11Suff p78 MR20
HALL,William.MC.2Lt kia 21-3-18 6 att2/8Worc p108 MR27
HALL,William Brown Lt dow 25-8-18 ACycCps att24Lond p181 CR France119
HALL,William Charles TMaj ded 17-12-17 19RIrRif p169 CR Ireland146,17-12-18
HALL,William Ernest Lt kia 23-5-15 5RFus p68 CR Gallipoli6
HALL,William Francis TLt kia 7-10-17 20Manch p154 MR30
HALL,William Hingston 2Lt kia 5-4-18 6Nhampt p137 MR27
HALL,William Holden 2Lt kia 26-9-17 D51RFA p208 CR Belgium20
HALL,William Hubert TLt kia 19-2-17 53MGC p183 MR21
HALL,William Stephen Lt drd 10-10-18 5SLancs p255 CR Ireland14
HALL,William Teesdale 2Lt kia 19-5-17 24RFC p8 CR France1061,Teasdale Capt
HALL-BROWN,John TMaj kia 7-7-16 10N&D p134 CR France397
HALL-WATT,Richard 2Lt kia 13-10-17 1GrenGds p50 CR Belgium106,13-11-17
HALLAM,Alice Violet Sister541 ded 18-12-16 VAD StJAB p200 CR France40
HALLAM,Horace George Searle Lt kia 1-12-17 RASC attImpCamelCps p253 CR Palestine9
HALLAM,Howard T2Lt kia 4-10-17 RWar att1/6Bn p64 MR30
HALLAM,Robert Samuel 2Lt kia 20-7-16 15N&D p134 MR21
HALLAM-BOTHAM,G.TMaj kia 3-8-16 10NumbF p61 CR France430
HALLARAN,William Col ded 23-1-17 RAMC p195 MR65
HALLER,Edward Denison T2Lt kia 3-6-17 GL &45RFC p8 MR20
HALLER,John Henry Lyle.MID Capt kia 12-3-15 3ESurr p112 CR Belgium17
HALLETT,Arthur Mapleton Capt kia 2-6-16 D125RFA p29 CR France745
HALLETT,Henry William Percy TCapt dow 12-10-18 Mddx att2Bn p147
HALLETT,Samuel William Lt dow 15-7-16 1Mddx p147 MR21
HALLEWELL,George Noble T2Lt dow 10-10-16 167MGC p183 CR France513
HALLEY,Clifford Richard Brice T2Lt kia 2-10-17 GL &57RFC p8 CR Belgium140
HALLEY,Edward Harland TLt kia 26-11-17 RFA att12TMB p29 CR France407
HALLEY,Jack Jacob TLt kia 26-7-16 13Worc att25MGC Inf p108&183 CR France423,HALLE
HALLEY,James Mitchell White.MC TCaptAMaj kia 24-10-18 RE 62FC p45 CR Belgium442
HALLEY,William Carr 2Lt ded 28-5-17 RGA 327SB p209 CR France113,Curr
HALLEY-JONES,Percival.MC.Capt kia 9-8-18 7Lond p247 CR France1170

HALLIDAY,Balfour 2Lt dow 4-7-17 1/7WYorks p218 CR France769
HALLIDAY,Charles Graham Rivers 2Lt kia 13-6-17 RE 225FC p45 CR Belgium10
HALLIDAY,Charles Walter Alexander 2Lt dow 17-11-16 53/2RFA p29 CR France105
HALLIDAY,Hugh Maclean LtCol ded 10-12-20 IA SuppList p277 CR India97A ExYLI
HALLIDAY,John 2Lt kia 8-5-18 2Yorks p90 MR19
HALLIDAY,John Alexander Capt ded 13-11-14 11Huss p22 CR Wilts145,dow
HALLIDAY,Leigh Hales 2Lt kia 31-7-17 8 att7Nhampt p137 MR29
HALLIDAY,Morrice Frederick John 2Lt kia 7-6-17 Glouc &RFC p8&106 CR Belgium126
HALLIDAY,Thomas Owens T2Lt kia 21-3-18 9RIrRif p169 CR France1061
HALLIFAX,John Dampier Lt kia 17-5-15 2Yorks D'Coy p90 CR France279
HALLIGAN,Matthew Lt kia 18-11-17 RDubF &RFC p8&176 CR France62
HALLIWELL,Eric John Lt kia 11-9-17 RFA SR &57RFC p8&29 CR Belgium158
HALLIWELL,Fred T2Lt kia 22-4-18 11Manch p154 CR France115
HALLIWELL,Frederick T2Lt kia 12-10-18 17Manch p154 CR France192,12Bn
HALLIWELL,Wilfrid Newbold T2Lt dow 21-9-16 9Yorks p90 CR France177
HALLMARK,Percy Harold T2Lt kia 2-9-18 24Y&L p159 CR France646
HALLORAN,J SubCdr 17-1-21 IA S&TCps CR Pakistan50A MR43
HALLOWES,Alexander Boyle T2Lt ded 31-5-17 RASC p193 CR Lond8
HALLOWES,Geoffrey Blackwood 2Lt kia 4-9-16 1RWKent p141 CR France294
HALLOWES,John Chaworth LtACapt kia 28-10-18 7Huss p22 MR38
HALLOWES,Rupert Price.VC.MC.T2Lt kia 30-9-15 4Mddx p147 CR Belgium167
HALLPIKE,Christopher George 2Lt kia 6-4-18 RGA 68SB p39 CR France196
HALLUM,Howard George.MC.2Lt dow 12-1-18 2/5Hamps p228 CR Egypt7
HALLUMS,E.C.SubAssSurg 12-3-16 IMS CR Iraq1
HALLWARD,Basil Murray TLt kia 9-4-17 B79RFA p29 CR France704
HALLWARD,Kenneth Leslie TLt kia 28-5-18 3Worc p108 CR France
HALLY,John Capt kia 30-7-16 6BlkW p231 MR21
HALPIN,William Oswald TCapt dow 10-8-18 RAMC att4Huss p195 CR France1170
HALSALL,Donald Court T2Lt kia 9-10-17 1/2 att3/5LancF p92 MR30
HALSE,Clive Harold 2Lt kia 24-4-17 GL &70RFC p8 CR France660
HALSE,Lionel William T2Lt ded 17-10-18 12Glouc p106 CR Yorks22,dow
HALSEY,Eric Charles 2Lt kia 19-6-17 7Lond p247 CR France689
HALSEY,Francis William T2Lt kia 14-11-15 RGA att3TMB p39 CR France423
HALSEY,Frederick 2Lt kia 10-8-17 7Beds p86 CR Belgium112
HALSTEAD,Arthur.MC.TLt ded 1-8-17 10WRid p115CR France134,dow
HALSTEAD,Arthur Frederick Lt kia 28-6-15 15RB p179 MR4
HALSTEAD,James Thornton T2Lt kia 7-12-16 LNLancs attTMB p136 CR Belgium136
HALSTEAD,John James T2Lt kia 21-3-18 7BordR p117 CR France245
HALSWELLE,Wyndham.MID Capt kia 1-4-15 1HLI p163 CR France706,HALSWELL 31-3-15
HALY,Andrew Stuart 2Lt dow 8-7-15 3RLancs attELancs p59 CR Belgium85
HALY,William Hele 2Lt kia 14-10-16 2Hamps p120 MR21,Heli
HAM,Frank Livingstone 2Lt ded 13-2-16 KEdwHorse p24 CR Eire322
HAM,Frederick William T2Lt ded 6-5-17 GL &158ResRFC p8 CR Egypt15
HAMAR,Alfred John Lt dow 8-4-17 RFC 55Sqd 9Wing p8 CR France300
HAMBLETON,H.R.Cdr 24-8-15 IndMilWksServ MR66
HAMBLETON,Walter Edwin 2Lt kia 21-3-18 4 att10Ess p232 MR27
HAMBLEY,Francis William T2Lt kia 31-7-17 2ELancs p110 MR29
HAMBLIN,John Edward TLt kia 24-3-18 12Suff p78 MR20
HAMBLIN,William Ebb Lt kia 24-5-16 RE 5FC p45 CR France573
HAMBLY,Alan Gordon 2Lt dow 22-5-17 1Dev p76 CR Devon2
HAMBLY,Dudley Charles T2Lt kia 14-5-17 6Dors p124 MR20
HAMBRO,Percival 2Lt dow 23-3-18 1KRRC p150 CR France177
HAME,Arthur William LtACapt kia 21-5-18 RFA attX21TMB p29 MR18
HAMEL,H.P.J.G.T2Lt kia 10-1-18 RFC p16 CR France113
HAMEL,Robert Sydney 2Lt kia 12-4-18 1RGLI p200 MR32
HAMER,Arthur Derrick Capt kia 6-11-18 NCycBn p253 CR France957
HAMER,Frank Capt kia 7-6-17 9Manch p237 MR4
HAMER,Harold TLt ded 6-6-17 GL 3LNLancs &56RFC p8 CR France383
HAMER,Hubert James Tudor Lt kia 4-11-14 IA 108Inf att101Grens p277 MR47
HAMER,John T2Lt kia 22-3-18 6KSLI p145 MR27
HAMER,Maurice T2Lt kia 27-3-18 WYorks att5YLI p81 MR20
HAMER,Samuel T2LtACapt kia 14-4-17 26NumbF p61 CR France644
HAMER,Thomas Pryce TLt kia 7-7-16 11SWBord p100 MR21
HAMILL,William Lt kia 16-8-17 7Manch p237 MR30
HAMILTON,Albert Edward T2Lt kia 18-8-17 26RFus p68 CR France855

HAMILTON,Alexander Beamish.CB.BrigGen ded 30-12-18 Staff p261 CR Dorset95

HAMILTON,Alexander Turnbull Rossell TLt kia 9-5-17 5BordR p228 MR20

HAMILTON,Andrew Douglas Lt ded 26-4-19 310RFA p29 CR Germany1

HAMILTON,Archibald Charteris Capt kia 28-6-15 7KOSB p101 CR Gallipoli6

HAMILTON,Archibald Gilbert Capt ded 15-2-19 RE p45&257 CR France40

HAMILTON,Archibald Hamilton Capt ded 4-11-16 13RIrRif p265 CR Ireland33

HAMILTON,Archibald James Rowan Lt dow 21-10-15 2IrGds SR p52 CR France423

HAMILTON,Archibald Lindsay T2Lt kia 10-6-17 13DLI p160 CR Belgium127

HAMILTON,Archibald Samuel LtCol dow 13-10-15 14DLI IA Retd p160 CR Mddx29

HAMILTON,Arthur Anson Shirley 2Lt dow 24-11-16 3 att1Berks CR France40

HAMILTON,Arthur Donald T2Lt kia 20-10-17 RE 101FC p45 CR Belgium21,19-10-17

HAMILTON,Arthur John Lord Capt kia 6-11-14 IrGds SR p52 MR29,L.A.J.

HAMILTON,Arthur Leslie Lt kia 25/26-10-18 3HLI p163 MR38

HAMILTON,Arthur Percival.MC.TLtCol kia 15-9-16 RWSurr att19Lond p56 CR France453

HAMILTON,Bernard St.George TLt kia 28-6-17 15MGC p183 MR20

HAMILTON,Cecil Claude 2Lt kia 16-8-17 3ConnRgrs att2RIrF p172 MR37

HAMILTON,Cecil Fife Pryce Capt dow 27-10-14 1ScotsGds p52 CR Belgium57

HAMILTON,Charles Gough 2Lt ded 12-10-19 Norf p263 CR Hereford51,11-10-19

HAMILTON,Chatham Anson Shirley 2Lt dow 24-11-16 3 att1RBerks p139

HAMILTON,Claud William T2LtACapt dow 6-11-17 RGA 287SB p39 CR Belgium72

HAMILTON,David Love 2Lt kia 21-3-18 BlkW att6Bn p128 MR20

HAMILTON,Douglas 2Lt kia 9-5-15 RIrRif att1Bn p169 MR32

HAMILTON,D.R.T2Lt kld 23-1-18 RFC p16 CR War5

HAMILTON,Edward TLt kia 14-4-18 GL att9RIrRif p190 MR30

HAMILTON,Eric T2Lt kia 15-2-17 GL &54RFC p8 CR France927

HAMILTON,Francis Walker Douglas Capt ded 24-2-19 RFA Res p254 CR France457,WRid attDirShipReprs

HAMILTON,Francis William T2Lt dow 3-3-16 8RWKent p141 CR Belgium11

HAMILTON,Geoffrey Cecil Monck T2Lt kia 7-9-16 8RDubF p176 CR France294

HAMILTON,George Lt dow 26-11-17 2ScotsGds p52 CR France398

HAMILTON,George Cyril Rae Lt kld 18-6-16 RFC CR Canada 256

HAMILTON,George Edward Archibald Fitzgeorge 2Lt kia 18-5-18 1GrenGds p50 CR France120

HAMILTON,George John T2Lt kia 9-6-17 16RScotsF p54 MR21

HAMILTON,Guy Stanley Gerald TLt&Adjt kia 1-8-17 3RWSurr p56 MR29

HAMILTON,Harold Gerard Hans TCapt dow 27-7-17 7BordR C'Coy p117 CR France1182

HAMILTON,Harry Austin Maj kia 25-1-16 23RFA p29 CR Belgium11

HAMILTON,Hector Macdonald 2Lt kia 22-3-18 3 att1RInniskF p105 MR27

HAMILTON,Henry McCartney T2Lt kia 14-5-16 7KOSB p101 CR France423

HAMILTON,Herbert Otho Lt kia 25-9-15 12NumbF p61 MR19

HAMILTON,H.J.Capt ded 13-6-18 DCLI &RAF p114

HAMILTON,Hubert Ian Wetherall.CB.CVO.DSO.MajGen kia 14-10-14 Staff p1 CR Kent179

HAMILTON,Hugh Wallace LtCapt dow 20-3-18 4A&SH p173 CR France145

HAMILTON,James 2Lt kia 5-11-16 4BordR p228 CR France385

HAMILTON,James Capt kia 3-1-17 6ScotRif p224 CR France392,1-1-17

HAMILTON,James Montgomery.MC.T2LtACapt dow 19-9-18 10LancF p92 CR France278

HAMILTON,James Russell T2Lt kia 22-10-17 17LancF p92 MR30

HAMILTON,John 2Lt kia 1-7-16 11RInniskF p105 MR21

HAMILTON,John 2Lt kia 23-3-18 4 att6NumbF p213 MR27

HAMILTON,John Alfred.DSO.Maj 19-7-21 RASC MR43

HAMILTON,John Dundas Lawrie Maj acckld 22-5-15 7RScots p211 CR Scot249,James

HAMILTON,John Guthrie 2Lt kia 21-3-18 2/7LancF p221 MR27

HAMILTON,John Percy T2Lt acckld 8-3-18 GL &RFC p16 CR Egypt1

HAMILTON,John Stewart 2Lt kia 21-3-18 10 att3RB p179 MR27

HAMILTON,Leslie d'Henin.Hon.MVO.Maj kia 29-10-14 1CldGds p51 MR29

HAMILTON,Mervyn James Capt dow 28-11-14 1GordH C'Coy p166 CR Belgium150

HAMILTON,Noel Crawford T2Lt kia 14-7-16 6Nhampt p137 MR21

HAMILTON,Norman Butler Lt kia 24-7-18 5Lancs p213 CR France261

HAMILTON,Ralph Gerard Alexander.Hon.LtCol kia 31-3-18 Cmdg106RFA p206 CR France1008

HAMILTON,Richard Marchbank 2Lt ded 7-12-18 IARO attMGC Inf p277 MR65

HAMILTON,Robert Ainslie TLt kia 28-3-18 RASC att5YLI p193 MR27

HAMILTON,Robert Gordon 2Lt kia 27-9-16 D77RFA p29 CR France630

HAMILTON,Robert Peyton 2Lt dow 25-9-15 20Lond p251 CR France178,Lt

HAMILTON,Robert Victor T2Lt kia 1-7-16 9RIrRif p169 MR21

HAMILTON,Ronald Eric 2Lt kia 23-4-17 1Dev p76 MR20

HAMILTON,Ronald Millie 2Lt kld 3-6-17 5Ches p222 CR France417

HAMILTON,Thomas Lt kia 12-5-17 7WYorks p218 CR France646

HAMILTON,Thomas T2Lt kia 8-12-17 10RInniskF p105 CR France379

HAMILTON,Tom Knox Lt kia 1-6-15 3 att1RWar p64 CR Belgium96,Ion

HAMILTON,Vyvyan Lodwick 2Lt kia 14-6-17 6 att18KRRC p150 MR29

HAMILTON,Wallace Bernard T2Lt kia 9-8-16 10 att6Beds p86 MR21

HAMILTON,William LtACapt ded 13-8-17 RE 183TC p45 CR Belgium16,14-8-17

HAMILTON,William Lt kia 30-9-18 3ConnRgrs att1InniskF p172 CR Belgium157

HAMILTON,William Arnold T2Lt kia 4-6-17 6ConnRgrs p172 CR Belgium60

HAMILTON,William Lees T2Lt kia 20-9-17 RE 237FC p45 CR Belgium102

HAMILTON,William Robert 2Lt kia 12-10-17 CldGds att4GdsMGReg p51&53 MR30

HAMILTON-AGNEW,A.E.Capt 3-11-18 RDubF CR Bucks32

HAMILTON-COX,A.F.OBE.Col 5-3-21 SthnCommdArmyPayDept CR Wilts129

HAMILTON-COX,Cecil Francis T2Lt kia 27-8-17 8WRid p115 MR30

HAMILTON-DALRYMPLE,John Raphael.MID Lt dow 23-4-15 2KOSB p111 MR29

HAMILTON-FLETCHER,Gareth 2Lt 25-1-15 3GrenGds att1ScotsGds MR22

HAMILTON-GRACE,Raymond Sheffield CaptBtMaj ded 4-8-15 13Huss p22 CR France353

HAMILTON-GRIERSON,James Gilbert 2Lt kia 12-7-15 5RScotF p222 CR Gallipoli2

HAMILTON-JOHNSTON,Douglas Charles Capt kia 21-1-16 2BlkW p128 MR38

HAMILTON-JOHNSTON,Ewen Colquhoun Richardson Lt kia 1-9-18 2 att1/4KOSB p101 CR France646

HAMILTON-JONES,Charles Nugent T2Lt kia 20-9-17 Mddx att9Lpool p147 MR30

HAMILTON-TEMPLE-BLACKWOOD,Lord Ion Basil Gawen Temple ded PoW 4-7-17 2GrenGds p50 MR29

HAMLETT,George Froude 2Lt kia 13-8-17 3 att1BordR p117 MR29

HAMLEY,W.S.Capt 28-10-19 IARO CR Lond4

HAMLEY,William Walter T2Lt dow 26-3-18 6Dors p124 CR France62

HAMLYN,Alfred Ernest T2Lt kia 16-7-16 9DCLI p114 CR Belgium11,7Bn

HAMLYN,Wilfrid Stephen T2Lt kia 24-8-17 6DCLI p114 MR30

HAMM,William George.MC.T2Lt kia 2-5-17 13EYorks p84 CR France777

HAMMANS,A.W.Maj 13-6-16 DCLI CR Oxford44

HAMMANS,Arthur John Spencer.MC.CaptAMaj kia 3-7-17 1DCLI p114 CR France184

HAMMERSLEY,Alan George 2Lt kia 14-3-17 5NStaffs p238 CR France579

HAMMERTON,Gilbert TLt kia 4-9-16 MGC p183 MR21

HAMMETT,Noel Henry Franklin Lt ded 7-9-17 IARO attASC 258MT p277 CR Europe51

HAMMICK,Ernest Lumley 2Lt ded 16-5-16 IARO 1/73CarnaticInf p277 MR66

HAMMICK,Eustace.MC.Capt dow 8-10-18 IA 17Inf p277 CR Egypt9

HAMMICK,Stephen Frederick.MID Capt dow 18-4-16 O&BLI p130 CR Iraq6

HAMMOND,Anthony Edgar 2Lt kia 28-11-17 12Lancers p22 MR17

HAMMOND,Douglas William 2Lt kia 24-5-15 2EKent p57 MR29

HAMMOND,Edward William 2Lt ded 2-10-18 1Worc p108 CR Glouc86

HAMMOND,Ernest William Frost.MC.2Lt kia 3-5-17 HAC p206 MR20

HAMMOND,Frederick Robert Cyprian 2Lt kia 6-7-15 2Lond p245 CR Belgium11,5-7-15

HAMMOND,Gilbert Philip 2Lt kia 10-9-14 2KOSB p101 MR15,26-8-14

HAMMOND,Guy Neville Lt 19-7-16 SL &2NigR CR WAfrica52

HAMMOND,Hugh Jerrold TLtACapt ded 23-3-18 2Glouc p106 CR Greece9

HAMMOND,Jack Cecil T2Lt kia 11-4-17 7Nhampt A'Coy p137 CR France570

HAMMOND,John Martin Richard Lt kia 25-9-15 11Ess p131 MR19,26-9-15

HAMMOND,John Maximilian.DSO.TLt dow 15-3-17 RAMC att10Dev p195 CR Greece1

HAMMOND,Kenneth Lowton Charles T2Lt kia 22-3-18 23NumbF p61 MR20

HAMMOND,Leonard TLt kia 5-7-16 10WRid p115 CR France515

HAMMOND,Paul TCapt dow 25-2-16 8ELancs p110 CR France121

HAMMOND,R.W.LtCol 26-8-18 RE CR Ireland24

HAMMOND,Richard Martin Lt dow PoW 20-5-18 RFA attX66TMB p29 CR Germany3

HAMMOND,Robert Whitehead.MC.TCapt dow 30-9-17 26RFus p68 CR France1361,LtCol

HAMMOND,Thomas Hill T2Lt kia 31-10-18 35MGC Inf p183 CR Belgium143

HAMMOND,Thomas Percival 2Lt dow 15-6-18 RGA 137SB p39 CR Italy5

HAMMOND,William Cecil Capt kia 24-4-17 8DCLI p114 CR Greece5

HAMMOND,William Walter Maj kia 5-5-18 RGA 139HB p39 CR France44,Walker

HAMMOND-CHAMBERS,Henry Borgnis Baret TCapt kia 21-7-16 7RLancs p59 MR21

HAMMONDS,Denys Huntingford.DSO.MC.CaptAMaj kia 30-3-18 RE 225FC p45 MR27,125FC

HAMNETT,Frederick George T2Lt ded 15-11-18 GL KRRC &XV CpsHQ IntelCps p190 CR France1027

HAMPE-VINCENT,Percival Campbell Capt dow 26-10-14 IA 129Baluchis p277

HAMPSALL,E.SubCdr 23-2-21 S&T Cps MR65

HAMPSHIRE,Stanley Lt kia 9-10-17 2/4ELancs p226 CR Belgium125

HAMPSON,Alfred Eric T2Lt kia 8-7-16 10Ches att7TMB p96 MR21

HAMPSON,Edgar TLt kia 1-7-16 15 att16LancF p92 MR21

HAMPSON,Frank 2Lt kia 30-11-17 3 att1Lpool p72 MR17

HAMPSON,Harold Norman 2Lt dow 8-4-17 4SLancs att&RFC p18&230 CR France285

HAMPSON,James Stanley 2Lt kia 21-5-18 4SLancs att1/4LNLancs p230 CR France106

HAMPSON,Norman T2Lt kia 15-2-17 11LNLancs p136 MR38

HAMPTON,F.A.F.2Lt ded 23-8-18 15NumbF &RAF p61 CR Mddx17,Lt

HAMPTON,George Kenneth Lt kia 16-8-15 1/4Norf p216 CR Gallipoli4

HAMPTON,George William Betts 2Lt kia 11-3-17 4Suff att2RFC 1Wing p18&217 CR France423,Lt

HAMPTON,William Orr 2Lt kia 1-7-16 3Norf &70MGC Inf p73&183 CR France293

HANAFY,Sydney Reginald T2Lt dow 24-11-17 GL &46RFC p8 CR France512

HANBURY,Claude Everard Robert Capt kia 9-10-17 1IrGds p52 CR Belgium12,2Bn

HANBURY,Evan Robert Maj kia 24-3-18 LeicYeo att14MGC p187&204 MR27

HANBURY,Herbert Wood Capt kia 15-11-16 1/7Mddx p235 CR France785

HANBURY-SPARROW,Brian.MC.Capt kia 26-8-18 3KSLI att7NStaffs CR Asia 81

HANBURY-TRACY,Algernon Henry Charles.Hon.CMG.TMaj ded 3-12-15 RHGds p20 CR Surrey151

HANBURY-TRACY,Hon Felix Charles Herbert Lt kia 19-12-14 att2ScotsGds RoO p52 MR32,Hubert

HANBURY-WILLIAMS,Charles Ferdinand Reiss Lt ded 16-12-16 2 O&BLI p130 CR Mon9,19-12-16

HANBY,Edward Wrey 2Lt ded 30-4-17 6 att23Mddx p147 CR Sussex178

HANBY,Francis James 2Lt kia 30-6-16 12RSuss p119 MR19

HANCOCK,Albert Leslie 2Lt kia21-5-16 1/7Lond p247 MR20

HANCOCK,Arthur T2Lt kia 17-10-18 50MGC Inf p183 CR France1386

HANCOCK,Francis De Berckem Maj ded 6-5-16 IARO attPolitcalDept p277 CR Asia60

HANCOCK,Frank Pine 2Lt kia 16-8-18 KRRC att2Bn p150 MR19

HANCOCK,Harold T2Lt kia 19-9-18 16RWFus p97 CR France415

HANCOCK,John Eliot.DSO.TCapt kia 21-3-18 9Norf p73 MR20

HANCOCK,John Henry TLt kia 9-6-17 RE 129FC p45 CR Belgium28

HANCOCK,John Maurice T2Lt kia 7-3-18 65RFC p16 CR Belgium18

HANCOCK,Ralph Escott.DSO.Lt kia 26-10-14 Dev p76 MR22,29-10-14

HANCOCK,Ralph Longhurst Lt kia 27-8-17 8Worc p226 MR30

HANCOCK,Robert David 2Lt kia 21-3-18 24MGC p183 MR27

HANCOCK,William T2Lt kia 28-9-17 14NumbF p61 CR Belgium19

HANCOCK,William Reginald Lt kia 24-4-17 RNDevYeo p203 MR37

HANCOCKS,William Capt kia 9-10-17 7Worc p225 MR30

HAND,Maurice William Lt kia 25-6-15 1Ches p96 CR Belgium107,25-1-15

HAND,Moreton Capt kia 31-7-17 20DLI p160 MR29

HANDCOCK,Henry R.2Lt kia 18-8-16 3Leinst p174 CR France630

HANDCOCK,Reginald Henry Birbeck HonLt drd 17-2-17 RAOC p198 CR France300

HANDFIELD-JONES,Neville Montague 2Lt kia 25-9-15 108RFA p29 CR Belgium112

HANDFORD,Everard Francis Sale 2Lt kia 15-10-15 8N&D p233 MR19

HANDFORD,Frederick Stanley 2Lt kia 27-1-16 4 att9ESurr p112 MR29

HANDFORD,Henry Basil Strutt Capt kia 15-10-15 8N&D p233 MR19

HANDFORD,John Willis T2Lt dow 24-3-18 20N&D p134 CR France177

HANDFORD,Reginald Stuart 2Lt dow 9-8-16 6RB p179 CR Belgium11,1Bn

HANDLEY,Guy Frederick Beckham.MC&Bar.Lt kia 27-8-18 2CldGds 3Coy p51 CR France615

HANDLEY,Herbert Eustace 2Lt kia 25/26-5-15 23Lond p252 MR22,25-5-15

HANDLEY,Walter T2Lt kia 25-3-18 9RWFus p97 MR20

HANDS,Cecil T2Lt kia 12-10-17 13DLI p160 MR30

HANDS,Frederick ACapt kia 27-5-17 RE 1SigConstCoy p45 CR France201

HANDS,Reginald Harry Myburgh TCaptAMaj dow 20-4-18 RGA attSAfrHvyArt73SB p39

HANDYSIDE,Arthur Cruikshanks 2Lt dow 17-4-18 1/4SLancs p230 CR France88

HANDYSIDE,Arthur John T2Lt kia 24-10-18 1NumbF att4RFus p61 CR France1082

HANDYSIDE,John T2Lt dow 18-10-16 16 att18Lpool p72 CR France389

HANDYSIDE,Percy James Alexander Capt kia 1-7-16 2Lond p245 CR France798 7-16

HANDYSIDE,Thomas Fosbery Lt kia 29-12-17 4RDubF p176 CR Palestine3

HANEWINKEL,Ernest Eberhard Capt kia 31-8-15 19Lond p250 CR France80,30 8-15

HANFORD,Albert William TLt kia 23-4-18 15Ches p96 CR France41,22-4-18 18Bn

HANHAM,P.B.Col 20-2-17 RFA CR Surrey106

HANKEY,Donald William Alers 2Lt kia 12-10-16 1RWar p64 MR21

HANKIN,E.M.Lt&QM 17-5-20 GL &CentIndRlyBn MR65

HANKINSON,Richard Hooton Lt kia 21-6-17 14 att1/6Manch p154 CR France7.

HANKINSON,Robert Prothero 2Lt dow 23-2-17 IARO att56Rif p277 CR Iraq5

HANLAN,Edward Gordon Lt dedacc 9-8-17 RFC CR Canada1689

HANLEY,Alfred T2Lt dow 24-5-18 DLI p160 CR Lancs33

HANLEY,Bartholomew 2Lt kia 23-8-17 4RScots p211 CR Belgium115

HANMER,Alexander John.MC.2Lt dow 7-10-16 3 att6EKent p57 CR France145

HANMER,Lambert Alfred Graham.DSO.MIDx2 LtCol dow 29-4-18 IA 21Cav p2 MR38

HANN,Cecil Collins 2Lt kia 22-10-16 GL &3RFC p190&3 CR France833

HANNA,David Wishart.MC.T2Lt dow 24-6-18 8RFus p68 CR Surrey150

HANNA,Douglas Murray TCapt kia 25-9-15 8RBerks p139 CR France219

HANNA,Frank Leslie Lt ded 26-7-18 RASC p267 CR Ireland137,3A&SH ExRASC(HorseTransport)

HANNA,John Henry 2Lt kia 20-9-17 19Lond p250 MR29

HANNA,William Neil 2Lt ded 20-11-18 RH&FA &RAF p261

HANNAFORD,Ida Durant SNurse 14-3-18 QAIMNS CR Surrey160

HANNAFORD,Stanley John Lt kia 5-10-17 1ELancs p110 CR Belgium83,2Lt

HANNAFORD,William Allan T2Lt kia 23-11-17 5SomLI p79 CR Palestine3

HANNAH,Charles William Cooper 2Lt kia 28-9-16 3 att2Dev p76 CR France115

HANNAH,Edward Meale.MC.T2Lt dow 16-8-17 1 att6KSLI p145 MR30

HANNAH,Henry William 2Lt kia 10-2-17 5RScots p211 CR France131

HANNAH,James 2Lt drd 21/22-4-16 2/4RGA p209 CR Scot677,21-4-16

HANNAH,John George 2Lt dow 30-11-17 1Lpool p72 CR France364

HANNAH,R.L.MC.TCapt kia 25-3-18 12HLI p163 CR France630

HANNAH,Robert 2Lt kia 16-8-17 7RIrRif p169 MR30 Ex Tpr W'land &C'landYe

HANNAM,Francis John Capt kia 5-7-16 2/4Glouc C'Coy p225 CR France1887

HANNAM,Sydney Philip.MC.Lt kia 11-7-16 161RFA p29 CR France702

HANNAN,George Giles T2Lt dow 17-8-17 8Suff p78 CR Belgium8

HANNAN,George Madder TMaj ded 13-10-15 9ScotRif p103 CR Kent234

HANNAN,Henry Monteith LtCol kia 21-6-15 8ScotRif p224 CR Gallipoli6

HANNAN,James Maxwell Adair T2Lt kia 23-7-18 9TankCps p188 CR France987

HANNAN,Stanley Livingstone LtACapt kia 30-11-17 D275RFA p207 MR17

HANNAN,William David.MC.Capt kia 14-10-18 1/8ScotRif p225 CR Belgium15

HANNAY,David TCapt ded 17-1-18 RAVC att7RHA p198 CR France145

HANNAY,Herbert Thomas 2Lt kia 28-3-18 1/4Lond p246 MR20

HANNING,James Henry Rowland 2Lt kia 26-9-15 8Lincs p75 MR19

HANNING,James Talmage 2Lt kia 27-11-16 9RFC p3 MR20

HANNON,John Coulson 2Lt kia 18-8-16 3Lpool p72 CR France432

HANNON,Norman Leslie 2Lt kia 16-5-15 7Lpool p215 CR France279

HANNON,Thomas James 2Lt dow 1-12-17 4KSLI p235 CR France398

HANNYNGTON,John Arthur BrigGen.CB.CMG.DSO.ded 21-8-18 IA 129Baluch p277 CR Egypt8

HANSARD,Arthur John St.Leger Capt S/InflictGunshot 7-10-20 IARO 2/89Punja att98Inf p277 MR66

HANSELL,Kenneth Joyce Nelson Lt kia 21-3-18 4Leinst &26MGC att1RIrRif p169&183 MR27

HANSELL,William Booth Capt kia 27-5-18 6DLI p239 MR18

HANSEN,Carl Frederick Vilhelm Lt dow 31-7-17 9Lpool att165MGC p187&21 CR Belgium46

HANSEN,William George 2Lt kia 25-9-16 1/9Lpool p216 MR21

HANSFORD,John Scriven Lt ded 21-12-18 2/8Lpool p270 CR France788

HANSON,Harold Capt dow 1-12-17 5WRid p227 CR Belgium3,1/4Bn

HANSON,James Arthur 2Lt kia 14-4-18 att1/5WYorks p81 CR France193

HANSON,Norman.MM.2Lt dow 12-10-18 9WYorks p81 CR France214

HANSON,Sydney Capt drd 27-5-18 NottsYeo p205 MR41

HANSON,Wilfred Clements Lt dow 15-9-17 A232RFA p207 CR Belgium18

HANSON,William Edward T2Lt kia 28-4-17 NumbF att26Bn p61 MR20

HANSTOCK,John Walter 2Lt dow 30-10-18 RE 12FC p210 CR France1266

HANWRIGHT,Thomas.DCM.2Lt kia 3-10-16 2DCLI p114 CR Greece3

HARBEN,Kenneth Tucker 2Lt kia 13-8-18 5Lond p246 CR France23,dow 9-8-18

HARBISON,Robert 2Lt kia 28-9-18 5HLI p240 CR Belgium124
HARBORD,Cecil Gordon TLt kia 1-9-16 14Y&L p159 CR France631
HARBORD,Frank Robert Rev dow 8-8-17 RAChDept p199 CR Belgium7
HARBORD,George Alfred Lionel Lt kia 1-7-16 3 att1RInniskF p105 MR21
HARBORD,John.MC.Capt dow 10-7-18 NorfYeo p204 CR France65
HARBORD,Philip Anthony Assheton.MC.Lt dow 1-12-17 2GrenGds p50&257 CR France439,Assheton
HARBORD,Stephen Gordon.MC.LtACapt kia 14-8-17 D153RFA p29 CR Belgium10
HARBOTTLE,John LtACapt kia 21-3-18 1Leic p87 MR20
HARBOTTLE,Stanley James Lt kia 26-10-17 91MGC Inf p183 MR30
HARCOURT,Howard Leslie 2Lt dow 18-3-17 5RWar A'Coy p214 CR France164
HARCOURT,Joseph 2Lt dow 5-10-18 Leic att12NStaffs p87 MR32
HARD,William Thomas 2Lt kia 23-3-18 3Lond p245 MR27
HARDAKER,Harold 2Lt kia 19-12-15 1/5Y&L p238 CR Belgium23
HARDCASTLE,John Balfour Capt 30-7-16 2 O&BLI MR21
HARDCASTLE,Sydney Philip TCapt kia 30-7-16 3 att2 O&BLI p130
HARDEN,Allen Humphrey Capt kia 21-10-14 2 O&BLI p130 MR29
HARDEN,Arthur James Victor 2Lt kia 25-9-15 RSuss p119 CR France219
HARDER,John Charles Victor.MID 2Lt dow 26-4-18 D50RFA p29 CR Belgium185
HARDEY-MASON,Harold Victor 2Lt kia 3-5-17 4EKent p212 CR France427
HARDICKER,James Ogden CaptHonLtCol ded 7-4-19 7Manch Res p270 CR Lancs30
HARDIE,David Whyte T2Lt kia 18-11-17 48RFC SR p8 CR Belgium176
HARDIE,Frederick Capt dow 20-9-17 RAMC p253 CR France297
HARDIE,John T2Lt kld 7-2-18 RFC p16 CR Kent127,5-2-18
HARDIE,Norman T2Lt kia 27-3-17 RE 2FC p45 CR France511
HARDIE,William 2Lt dow 18-4-17 4 att13LancF p92 CR France610,4 att15Bn
HARDIMAN,Wilfred James 2Lt ded 4-12-18 4ELancs p270 CR Lancs381,J.W.
HARDING,Arthur Dennis Lt dow 30-10-14 4 att1Glouc p106 CR Belgium57
HARDING,Arthur Keith.MC.TCapt kia 24-10-18 10RWKent p141 CR Belgium408
HARDING,Charles Egerton Hugh CaptBtMaj ded 10-12-17 RFus p68 CR France40
HARDING,Claude Stephen TLt ded 22-1-18 GL Norf att4/4KAR p190&202 CR EAfrica8 & CR Tanzania1
HARDING,Clive Scotland Lt kia 6-8-15 11ESurr att2Hamps p112 MR4
HARDING,Donald Stanley.MC.T2LtACapt kia 10-4-17 13RFus 3Coy p68 CR France311
HARDING,Eric Stanley Milthrop Lt kia 6-7-17 2/5Lpool p215 CR France922
HARDING,Francis Edward Basil Capt dow 1-12-15 RFA 21Bty p29 CR France145
HARDING,Frederick John T2Lt dow 22-9-17 12ESurr p112 CR Belgium116
HARDING,Geoffrey Harold 2Lt ded 3-9-17 13RWar attRFC p261&263 CR Berks71
HARDING,George Clifford Capt 14-4-19 RAVC 14MobileSect att3Huss CR Shrop37
HARDING,George Helliwell Lt kia 27-3-18 79RFC p16 CR France141
HARDING,George Herbert Capt ded 23-5-18 GL RAMC p266 CR Lancs2
HARDING,Henry George.MC.Lt kia 4-10-17 1Hamps p120 MR30
HARDING,Homer 2Lt ded 3-10-18 IARO TC p277 MR66
HARDING,Isabel Lois ded 15-2-19 VAD CR War7
HARDING,Jack Maynard 2Lt kia 26-10-14 1RWKent p141 MR22
HARDING,James Golding Lt kia 30-10-17 RFA att21TMB p29 CR Belgium112
HARDING,James Philip Capt dow 10-11-17 2RMunstF p175 MR30
HARDING,John (Jack) Samuel TLt kia 8-11-15 11NumbF p61 CR France83
HARDING,Joseph 2Lt kia 6-10-17 3 att2BordR p117 MR30
HARDING,Lionel Cox Lt dow 18-6-15 RGA 5MtnBty p39 CR France285
HARDING,Lionel Henry Powys.MC.2Lt kia 23-10-18 1/2 att6Leic p87 CR France1477
HARDING,Norman Ernest Jasper MajTLtCol ded 10-8-16 RAMC att12SH p195 MR65
HARDING,Reginald.MC.2Lt kia 28-3-18 3 att6RWSurr p56 CR France233
HARDING,Reginald William Fowler Capt kia 7-11-17 18Lond p250 MR34
HARDING,Robert Denis Stewart Lt kia 9-11-14 4 att1Beds p86 MR29,7-11-14
HARDING,Samuel Collis.MM.T2Lt kia 22-8-17 F'TankCps 18Coy p188 MR30
HARDING,Sydney Allen.MID T2Lt dow 3-9-17 1AircraftDepotRFC SR p8 CR France134,Lt
HARDING,Wilfred John.MC.Chap4Cl kia 31-10-17 RAChDept attDrakeBn p199 MR30,Wilfrid
HARDING,William Arthur Capt kia 8-8-15 8WelshR p126 MR4
HARDING,William Kesterton 2Lt died 26-6-19 5Beds p219 CR France146
HARDINGE,Edward Charles.Hon.DSO.MID Lt dow 18-12-14 15Huss p22 CR Kent141
HARDINGE,Henry Ralph.Hon.2Lt kia 9-5-15 2RB p179 MR32
HARDINGE,Patrick Robert.MC.TMaj dow 17-6-16 1 att10ScotRif p103 CR France80

HARDINGHAM,Robert Cecil.MC.CaptTMaj dow 18-9-17 1Mddx att3/2KAR p147&268 CR EAfrica10 &CR Tanzania1,2Bn
HARDMAN,Adrian Thomas Lt dow 30-3-16 4RFus p68 CR Belgium11
HARDMAN,Archibald TLtACapt kia 4-10-17 9YLI p143 MR30
HARDMAN,Basil Brocas Lt kia 29-10-18 IARO att1/10GurkhaR p277 MR38
HARDMAN,Cecil William TLt kia 21-9-16 23Manch att70RFC p3&154 CR France169
HARDMAN,Frederick McMahon 2Lt kia 29-10-14 4RFus p68 MR22
HARDMAN,Hudson Beauford Lt kia 17-8-16 3 att7CamH p168 MR21
HARDMAN,Kenrie Capt kia 25/26-10-18 3HLI p163 MR38,Kenric
HARDMAN,Robert Taylor T2Lt kia 1-7-16 RE p45 MR21
HARDMAN,Tom Walker T2Lt kia 18-7-17 11Lpool p72 CR Belgium102
HARDMAN,Wallace George.MID T2Lt kia 9-1-17 13Manch p154 CR Iraq5
HARDMAN,William Frederick Kerr.MC.T2Lt dow 28-10-17 RE 171Co p45 CR Belgium3
HARDS,E.2Lt ded 10-6-18 RGA p262 CR Kent191,Lt
HARDWICK,Nathaniel Charles 2Lt dow 15-9-17 10DCLI p114 CR Belgium173
HARDWICK,Oswald William T2Lt kia 9-5-17 1Dev p76 MR20
HARDWICK,Philip Edward,DSO LtCol dow 9-6-19 10Huss p22
HARDWICK,William West 2Lt dow 11-6-15 5 att2Mddx p147 CR France345
HARDWICK-TERRY,Leonard Alfred TLtACapt kia 31-8-17 RE att24RFC p8&45 CR France251
HARDY,Alan Herbert 2Lt kld 14-10-15 REKentYeo attRFC p18&204 CR Kent191
HARDY,Charles Edwin TCapt kia 13-4-18 22NumbF p61 MR32
HARDY,Charles Eric T2Lt kia 23-10-18 19MGC Divl p183 CR France270
HARDY,Edgar Leslie TLt dow 7-10-18 WYorks attRE p45&81 CR France272
HARDY,Ferdinand H.TLt kia 4-9-16 2RFus att22MGC p68&183 MR21
HARDY,Frederick 2Lt kia 9-9-17 3 att21NumbF p61 CR France1461
HARDY,Gathorne T2Lt dow PoW 30-4-18 10RIrFus p171 CR France393
HARDY,Geoffrey 2Lt dow 27-5-17 D312RFA p208 CR France518
HARDY,Guy John Meredith Lt dow 1-8-17 3CldGds p51 CR Belgium16
HARDY,Harold TCapt kia 15-4-18 13RIrRif p169 MR30
HARDY,James Henry Chap4Cl kia 5-5-18 RAChDept RGA att1/1WelchR p199 CR Belgium3
HARDY,Leonard Basil Lt kia 11-2-15 2Worc p108 CR France765
HARDY,Ralph Miller Lt kia 4-11-15 5 att16HLI p240 CR France940
HARDY,Reginald Herbert William Lt ded 4-11-17 3WelchR p126 CR Mon34
HARDY,Richard Luard TCapt&Adjt kia 24-8-17 KRRC att8Bn p150 CR Belgium112,Luord
HARDY,Ronald Montagu Capt kia 23-7-17 7RB p179 MR29
HARDY,Theodore Bayley.VC.DSO.MC.Rev dow 18-10-18 RAChDept att8Lincs p199 CR France146
HARDY,Victor Harnott Lt kia 25-10-14 Y&L att1Lincs p159 MR22,26-10-14
HARDY,Walter John 2Lt ded 21-8-17 15RFA L'Bty p29 CR Staffs84
HARDYMAN,John May Maitland.DSO.MC.MIDx2 TMaj kia 24-8-18 8SomLI p79 CR France745,LtCol
HARDY-SMITH,Arnold Capt ded 16-5-19 16RWar p64 CR Greece9,1Bn
HARE,Alexander Balfour 2Lt kia 31-10-16 2RH&FA p29 CR France396
HARE,Bernard Urmston.MID T2Lt kia 25-9-15 14 att1Mddx p147 MR19
HARE,Edward Henry 2Lt kia 23-7-19 6RDubF att1Yorks p176 MR43,Lt
HARE,Edward John T2Lt kia 24-3-17 GL &15RFC p8 CR France518
HARE,Evan Alfred Amyas 2Lt kia 10-3-15 2Mddx p147 CR France706,E.Amyas Alfred
HARE,George TLt kia 27-12-17 7RDubF D'Coy p176 CR Palestine3
HARE,Harry Vivian Capt kia 20-9-14 2DLI p160 MR15
HARE,John Alfred T2Lt kld 1-3-17 10Suff &RFC p8&78 CR Camb103
HARE,John Maxwell 2Lt kia 24-5-17 6DLI p239 MR29
HARE,Robert Stuart MacLaine Capt kia 6-8-15 1Ess p131 CR Gallipoli6
HARE,Stanley Grant T2Lt kia 19-4-17 15Mddx p147 CR Palestine8
HAREL,Louis Octave 2Lt kia 18-8-17 GL &11RFC p8 CR France1295
HARES,Vincent Colin TLt kia 30-11-17 6KSLI p145 CR Palestine3
HARFORD,Edward Bridges.MID Capt ded 15-7-18 4SomLI p255 CR Sussex144
HARFORD,George Lawrence Lt kia 17-2-15 2RLancs p59 CR Belgium133,16-2-15
HARFORD,John Henry Lt kia 25-10-16 3 att7SWBord p100 MR21,26-10-16
HARGER,Edwyn Oscar T2Lt dow 23-9-18 RE 171TC p45 CR Belgium192
HARGER,Frank Eric T2Lt kia 16-12-15 C49RFA p29 CR Belgium58
HARGRAVE,Ernest Lawton T2Lt kld 22-9-17 GL &79RFC p8 CR Hamps31
HARGRAVE,W.G.2Lt kia 17-4-18 GL &RAF p190
HARGREAVE,Frederick Parker TLtACapt kia 20-11-17 7YLI p143 MR17
HARGREAVES,Alan Knyveton.DSO.Capt kia 9-5-15 2RB p179 CR France566
HARGREAVES,Clifford.MIDx2 2Lt kia 22-8-18 22Lond p251 CR

France247
HARGREAVES,Cyril Augustus T2Lt dow 15-8-17 43RFC p8 CR France178
HARGREAVES,Frank.MID TLt kia 12-7-16 19RWFus p97 CR France550
HARGREAVES,Harold 2Lt kia 23-8-18 4YLI p235 CR France526,2Bn
HARGREAVES,James Pater 2Lt kia 9-10-17 126RFA p29 MR30
HARGREAVES,Leopold Reginald.MC.Capt dow 25-9-16 IrGds p52 CR France294
HARGREAVES,Norman Lt kia 23-11-16 4ELancs att29RFC p18&226 CR France158
HARGREAVES,Ralph Walter TLt kia 1-12-17 1WelshGds p53 MR17
HARGREAVES,Reginald Anthony Lt kia 28-6-17 4DLI p160 MR19
HARGREAVES,Sydney Jasper 2Lt dow 19-5-18 1GrenGds p50 CR France84
HARGREAVES,Thomas Charles.DSO.Maj kia 23-3-18 23Lond p252 MR20
HARGREAVES,William Henry Lt 8-5-18 15Mddx attRAF CR Palestine3
HARGREAVES,Willoughby Frankland T2Lt kia 21-2-18 66RFC p16 CR Italy7
HARIES-JONES,Llewelyn Albert 2Lt kia 30-7-16 27Manch p154
HARINGTON,Herbert Hastings LtCol kia 8-3-16 IA 84Punjabis att62 p277 MR38,HARRINGTON
HARINGTON,William Guy.DSO.Maj kia 28-9-17 IA 2/5GurkhaRif p277 CR Iraq8
HARKER,E.K.2Lt dow 18-4-18 RGA &RAF p39 CR Belgium38
HARKER,George Cuthbert Warburton Capt dow 1-12-17 12Lond p248 CR France513
HARKER,George Ernest 2LtTLt kia 19-5-17 23/40RFA p29 CR France1182
HARKER,Herbert Charles 2Lt dow 25-3-18 393RFA p30 CR France103
HARKER,John Gordon 2Lt dow 28-9-18 SussYeo p205 CR France278
HARKER,Lewis T2Lt kia 1-10-18 2YLI p143 CR France375
HARKER,Robert Percy 2Lt kia 20-3-15 1NStaffs p157 CR France681
HARKNESS,Percy Yarborough Capt kia 1-7-16 2WYorks p81 MR21
HARKNESS,Raymond TLt kia 23-11-17 119MGC Inf p183 CR France1498
HARLAND,Hugh Baxter T2Lt ded 28-10-17 RE BaseDept p45 CR France285
HARLAND,Reginald Wickham Capt kia 30-10-14 1Hamps p120 CR Belgium69
HARLAND,Richard 2Lt kia 16-6-18 RGA 254SB p40 CR France18
HARLAND,Sidney 2Lt kia 25-5-18 RGA 214SB p40 CR France247
HARLE,Richard John Patterson.MC.2LtTLt ded 26-4-17 KOSB att2A&SH p101 CR France40,Paterson Capt dow
HARLEY,Albert Edward T2Lt kia 15-4-18 NStaffs p157 CR France298
HARLEY,Arthur Darent Lt kia 1-7-16 6SStaffs p229 MR21
HARLEY,Benjamin Chapman 2Lt kia 1-7-16 14RIrRif p169 MR21
HARLEY,Frederick William 2Lt kia 3-6-17 7BlkW att70RFC p18&231 CR Belgium410
HARLEY,George Melven TCapt kia 25-9-15 12HLI p163 MR19
HARLEY,John Lt kia 4-6-15 13Worc p108 MR4
HARLEY,Katherine Mary 7-3-17 IntDept attSerbianMinister CR Greece7
HARLEY,Robert Alexander TMaj ded 20-10-17 24RWFus p270 CR Lancs1,19-10-17
HARLING,Tom Lough T2Lt kia 26-10-17 Manch att21Bn p154 MR30
HARMAN,Arthur.DCM.Capt&QM ded 26-6-15 1KRRC p150 CR France80
HARMAN,Arthur George 2Lt kia 20-10-18 1/6Manch p237 CR France287
HARMAN,Brian Relton Lt ded 4-11-19 IA 110MahrattaLI att125Rif p277 CR Egypt9,3-11-19
HARMAN,Cecil Rochfort 2Lt kia 10-11-17 1Glouc p106 CR Belgium26
HARMAN,Charles Edward Col ded 5-1-15 9RDubF p266 CR Ireland5
HARMAN,George Malcolm Nixon.DSO.Maj kia 27-11-14 RB p179 CR France1095,28-11-14
HARMAN,John Augustus TLt kld 18-11-17 RFC p8 CR Lincs136,17-11-17
HARMAN,John Bower 2Lt kia 26-8-14 29/22RFA p30 CR France657
HARMAN,L.W. Lt ded 27-10-18 RH&FA &RAF p207
HARMAN,William 2Lt kia 27-3-18 A106RFA p30 CR France588
HARMER,Gerald T2Lt kia 11-8-16 9NStaffs p157 MR21
HARMON,Wilfred Baldwin T2Lt kia 1-8-17 21KRRC p150 MR29
HARMOOD-BANNER,Walcot TCapt kia 30-8-15 3 att1SWBord p100 CR France114,29-8-15
HARMS,William T2Lt kia 4-3-17 21NumbF &59RFC p8&61 CR France502
HARMSWORTH,Cecil John 2Lt dow 9-1-17 2Suff att3Mddx p78 CR Greece3
HARMSWORTH,Harold Alfred Vyvyan St.George.Hon.MC.Capt dow 12-2-18 2IrGds p52 CR Lond12
HARNETT,Donald Alfred 2Lt kia 7-10-16 3 att6EKent p57 MR21
HAROLD,John Peter Bevan Lt dow 16-2-18 RFA attRFC p16&30 CR France40
HAROLD-BARRY,J.Capt kia 24-5-15 3RDubF p176 MR29
HAROLD-BARRY,John Gerard 2Lt kia 7-7-16 5RMunstF p175 CR France115,1Bn
HARPER,Alan Gordon T2Lt kia 1-6-17 187RFA p30 CR Belgium29
HARPER,Alexander Simpson TLt kia 12-10-17 8BlkW p128 MR30

HARPER,Alfred George Montague Norton Capt kia 16-10-17 SL att41L NigR p201,2entries
HARPER,Arthur 2Lt dow 1-4-17 2BordR p117
HARPER,Charles 2Lt ded 27-11-18 2KSLI p145 CR Greece2
HARPER,Charles Croke 2Lt kia 3-5-17 3 att5 O&BLI p130 MR20
HARPER,Clarence Rucil 2Lt kia 15-7-16 6WYorks p218 CR France246
HARPER,Edgar Henry TLt kia 10-7-16 8SStaffs p122 MR21
HARPER,Ernest Macowan TLt kia 9-8-15 7RMunstF p175 MR4
HARPER,Frederick Henry TLt dow 20-4-18 RE 11FC p45 CR Belgium38
HARPER,Gordon Philip 2Lt kia 29-9-18 4Lpool p72 CR France407
HARPER,Hal 2Lt kia 19-7-16 6RWar p214 MR32
HARPER,Harold Raymond T2Lt kia 4-11-18 1/2 att2/4WRid p115 CR France1081
HARPER,Hugo Alfred 2Lt kia 15-4-17 3 att2SforthH p164 CR France407
HARPER,James 2Lt kia 28-6-18 3 att1Ches D'Coy p96 CR France21
HARPER,John Alexander.MC.TCapt kia 14-2-17 RAMC att7Yorks p195 CR France786
HARPER,John Boughton T2Lt kia 12-10-17 7Lincs p75 MR30
HARPER,Owen Tannett 2Lt kia 22-3-18 1Leic p87 MR20
HARPER,Reginald Alexander 2Lt dow 16-9-17 2/1Lond p245 CR Belgium16
HARPER,Rennie T2Lt kia 14-10-18 1LancF p92 CR Belgium157
HARPER,Robert Charles Middleton 2Lt kia 19-4-17 GL att1/5Norf p190 MR34
HARPER,Tom T2Lt kia 4-6-17 1/2 att7LancF p92 MR29
HARPER,Walter Lacon Lt kia 1-7-18 3 att6Nhampt p137 CR France44,30-6-18
HARPER-SMITH,Septimus William 2Lt ded 19-10-19 RFus attLabCps p266 CR Yorks294,Lt
HARPLEY,Robert Ableson 2Lt kia 5-7-16 5YLI att148MGC Inf p235 MR21
HARPUR,Edward Percival H.TLt dow 11-9-16 7RIrRif p169 CR France66,RIrF
HARRAGIN,William Piercy Lt ded 1-11-18 A&SH attKAR CR EAfrica36
HARRIES,Eric Guy Capt dow 17-8-15 1/7RWFus p223 CR Greece10
HARRIES,Frederick Ebenezer Melville T2Lt kia 26-2-17 12KRRC p150 CR France744
HARRIES,Gilbert James St.Clair T2Lt kia 24-8-17 10DLI p160 MR30
HARRIES,Howard Lock T2Lt kia 13-11-16 18 att10RWFus p97 CR France156,Locke
HARRIES,James Francis Lt ded 30-6-18 6ESurr p226 CR Ches182
HARRIES,John Elvet 2Lt kia 23-4-17 3 att2SWBord p100 MR20
HARRIES,William Frank Reginald T2Lt kia 26-9-18 MGC Cav p183 MR34
HARRIES,Wyndham Trevor T2Lt kld 21-8-17 GL &3RFC p8 CR Sussex55
HARRIES-JONES,Llewelyn Albert 2Lt 30-7-16 27Manch MR21
HARRIGAN,William Piercy TLt ded 1-11-18 GL 11A&SH attKAR p173,202&266
HARRIMAN,Charles Henry T2Lt kia 29-10-17 GL &43RFC p8 CR France88
HARRIMAN,Horace William.MC.TCapt kia 1-9-18 8 att9WRid p115 CR France74
HARRINGTON,Charles Stanley Lawrence Lt ded 27-5-17 3ConnRgrs p172 MR38.drd
HARRINGTON,E.HonLt&QM ded 28-7-15 RASC p193 CR Lond9
HARRINGTON,George Christmas 2Lt ded 30-10-17 6DragGds p21 CR Kent232,L
HARRINGTON,Herbert Andrzey Biernaski Lt dow 9-12-14 3 att1Hamps p120 CR Hamps11,HARINGTON MR32,Andrzer
HARRINGTON,Philip William 2Lt kia 13-1-17 5Worc p108 CR Iraq5
HARRINGTON,Walter 2Lt kia 22-6-17 5WelshR p230 CR Belgium43 13Ches 21-17
HARRINGTON,Walter John 2Lt ded 18-5-19 LabCps att20RB p266 MR40
HARRIS,Albert James 2Lt kia 17-10-16 1RLancs p59 MR21
HARRIS,Albert Hansen 2Lt kia 26-9-15 8RWKent p254 MR19
HARRIS,Alfred Abraham 2Lt kia 9-9-16 10Mddx C'Coy p236 CR France294
HARRIS,Alfred Edward T2Lt kia 2-7-18 12MGC Inf p183 CR France704
HARRIS,Alfred George 2Lt kia 11-4-17 7WelshR p230 MR20,att2/6WYorks
HARRIS,Antrobus Taft 2Lt kia 19-3-16 4Beds att1Lincs p86 CR France922,Lt
HARRIS,Arthur Edward Crawford 2Lt dow 11-9-17 2/7RWar p214 CR Belgium18
HARRIS,Arthur Harold 2Lt dow 4-7-18 1 att16RWFus p97 CR France169,Lt
HARRIS,Arthur Lea Capt kia 31-7-17 4LNLancs p234 MR29
HARRIS,Arthur Stanley 2Lt kia 31-7-17 6Lpool p215 MR29
HARRIS,Aubrey TLt kia 4-9-16 21Manch A'Coy p154 MR21
HARRIS,C.B.Lt 3-3-19 6WelchR attMGC Inf CR Wales168
HARRIS,Cecil Alfred 2Lt dow 3-11-16 4RWSurr att4Suff p212 CR France105
HARRIS,Cecil St.John 2Lt ded 10-9-15 5SomLI p218 CR Somerset173
HARRIS,Charles Cecil 2Lt kia 13-6-17 4NStaffs p157 CR Belgium127
HARRIS,Charles Henry 2Lt dow 19-9-18 RWFus att11Bn p97 CR Greece6
HARRIS,Charles Montagu TLt dow 28-8-15 RAMC att7RScotF p195 CR France51
HARRIS,Charles Noel 2Lt kia 21-4-17 IA 123Rif att125 p277 MR38

HARRIS,Christopher Samuel 2Lt kia 27-5-17 6WYorks p218 MR19
HARRIS,Claude Leslie(Jim) Capt dow 2-5-18 HAC A'Bty p206 CR Palestine3
HARRIS,Edward.MC.Capt dow 25-4-18 RGA p209 CR Belgium38
HARRIS,Edmund George 2Lt dow 26-6-17 2/7WRid p227 CR France518
HARRIS,Eric Wallace Lt dow 4-11-17 RGA 213SB p40 CR Belgium11
HARRIS,Ernest Charles TCapt kia 23-10-16 12WRid p115 CR France400
HARRIS,Ernest Edward 2Lt ded 21-4-17 6 att1RIrF p171 CR Germany1 dow
HARRIS,Frank 2Lt kia 15-7-16 3 att10Ches p96 MR21
HARRIS,Frederick James Lt kia 13-4-18 6HLI C'Coy p240 CR Belgium89,9Bn
HARRIS,Frederick T.2Lt dow 19-9-15 B49RFA p30 CR Belgium5
HARRIS,F.W.Davie LtCol ded 20-6-17 RAMC p195 CR Surrey64
HARRIS,Hamilton Snow TCapt kia 1-7-16 13 att11N&D p134 CR France246
HARRIS,Harold Cecil Dunstan Lt 4-11-19 1Mon CR Ireland33
HARRIS,Harold Maltby 2Lt kia 16-6-17 3Co of LondYeo p204 MR29,Malthy
HARRIS,Harry Thomas Hopkinson Capt kia 20-1-16 IA 92Punjabis p277 MR38
HARRIS,Henry TLt kia 4-10-16 10WRid attNhampt p115 CR France239,Harry,5-10-16 attNumbF
HARRIS,Henry James Fraser drd 27-2-16 IARO p277 CR Kent8
HARRIS,Henry James Lawrence TLt dow 6-11-16 16 att14Hamps p120 CR France293,Capt
HARRIS,Henry Lionel T2Lt dow 1-12-15 RE 105FC p45 CR France285
HARRIS,Herbert Brutus Aubrey Lt mbk 10-8-17 7RWSurr p256 MR29
HARRIS,Herbert Cecil TCapt kia 3-7-16 6RWKent p141 MR21
HARRIS,Howard Kilbourne.MC.Capt kia 22-2-18 3 att11Ess p131 CR France568
HARRIS,Hubert Alfred TCapt kia 31-7-17 RAMC att61RFA p195 CR Belgium13 74RFA
HARRIS,Hugh Ripley Lt ded 20-11-18 RH&FA att1TMB p30 CR France1858
HARRIS,Jack St.Clair Gainez 2Lt kia 22-2-15 SStaffs p122 CR France924,Gainey
HARRIS,John Anthony.MC.Capt kia 26-11-17 12Yorks p90 MR17
HARRIS,John Lionel 2Lt kia 7-4-16 IARO att125Rif p277 MR38,6-4-16
HARRIS,Johnny Stringer Lt kia 23-3-18 4SforthH p241 MR20
HARRIS,Joseph Cecil Capt kia 16-8-17 RAMC 3FA att A'CCS p253 CR Belgium8
HARRIS,Joseph Walter Lt kia 2-6-15 1Lincs p75 MR29
HARRIS,Leslie George Hamlyn 2Lt kia 2-11-14 N&D p134 MR29
HARRIS,Lyn Arthur Philip TCapt&Adjt kia 10-7-16 16WelshR p126 CR France397,11-7-16
HARRIS,Nathan Leonard.MC.TCapt kia 28-8-18 9RWFus p98&258 CR France98
HARRIS,Percy Cuthbert Capt kia 17-2-15 Suff p78 MR29,16-2-15
HARRIS,Percy George T2Lt kia 11-8-17 17RWFus &21RFC p8&98 MR20
HARRIS,Philip Dawson Capt kia 21-3-18 1NStaffs p157 MR27
HARRIS,R.D.AssSurg 16-7-21 IMS MR43
HARRIS,Reginald Arthur 2Lt kia 9-10-17 4 att9WYorks p81 CR Belgium83
HARRIS,Reginald Samuel 2Lt dow 24-6-17 5Mddx p147 CR Belgium11,13Bn
HARRIS,Reginald William TLt kia 3-9-16 4WYorks attZ1TMB p81 MR21
HARRIS,Robert Arthur TCapt drd 21-11-17 GL p190 MR40
HARRIS,Robert Edward TLt kia 4-11-18 8NStaffs p157 CR France984,2Lt
HARRIS,Robert Hugh 2Lt kia 28-9-16 11 att8WRid p115 MR21
HARRIS,Roland James Lt kia 16-9-16 6DLI p239 MR21,17-9-16
HARRIS,Roland Milton 2Lt kia 7-6-17 2Yorks &60RFC p8&90 CR France46
HARRIS,Rowland Hanwell.MC.2Lt kia 27-12-17 2/15Lond p249 CR Palestine3,Roland
HARRIS,Sydney Ernest T2Lt dow 15-5-18 2/4LNLancs p136 CR France145
HARRIS,Theodore Trevor 2Lt dow 4-10-16 2/7Mddx p235 CR France105
HARRIS,Thomas William.MID 2Lt kia 27-3-18 19DLI p160 MR27
HARRIS,Vernon T2Lt kia 9-4-16 12 att9RWar p64 MR38
HARRIS,Walter Lewis 2Lt kia 10-2-17 10Dev p76 MR37
HARRIS,Walter Read 2Lt ded 10-10-18 1/5Suff att1/1Camb p217 CR France123
HARRIS,Wilfred Ernest Lt kia 15-9-17 RFA 62TMB p207 CR France538
HARRIS,William Edward 2Lt dow 19-12-15 2DLI p160 CR Belgium11
HARRIS,William Gregory 2Lt kia 3-2-17 7Glouc p106 MR38
HARRIS,William Handel 2Lt kia 26-8-18 16RWFus p98 CR France432
HARRIS,William Lawson.MC.Lt kia 30-7-16 2RScotF C'Coy p94 MR21
HARRIS,William Robert Capt ded 15-2-19 RASC p193 CR France52
HARRIS,William Trengwreath Lt drd 15-4-17 RAMC p195 MR35
HARRISON,Alfred Herbert Maj ded 3-11-18 RFA p30&257 CR Essex81
HARRISON,Bernard Percy Bartlan T2Lt kld 6-1-18 RFC p16
HARRISON,Brian T2Lt kia 10-7-16 14RWFus p98 CR France397
HARRISON,Brian Charles TCapt dow 12-8-18 11 att5BordR p117 CR France649
HARRISON,Cecil Eustace Maj kia 14-3-15 2RB p179 CR France709,12-3-15
HARRISON,Cecil George Bradford T2Lt kia 13-8-16 8RBerks p139 MR21
HARRISON,Charles Augustus LtCol ded 28-10-16 RE p270

HARRISON,Charles Geoffrey Lt kia 27-11-17 2/4Y&L p238 MR17
HARRISON,Charles Gordon.MC.T2Lt dow 26-9-18 3 att2SLancs p125 CR Belgium192
HARRISON,Charles Hibbert Lt kia 31-7-17 RFA D91HB p30 CR Belgium85
HARRISON,Christopher Rene Lt dow 23-5-15 3 att2Leic p87 CR France102
HARRISON,Cyril Cazalet Lt kia 19-9-14 3Worc p108 MR15,20-9-14
HARRISON,Cyril Henry T2Lt kia 6-9-17 10SLancs att1/5LancF p125 MR30
HARRISON,Dennis Riley T2Lt kia 3-5-17 BlkW att8Bn p128 MR20
HARRISON,Donald Howard Lt kia 16-9-18 C306RFA p207 CR France768
HARRISON,Douglas Roy Dilworth T2Lt kia 27-3-18 10DLI p160
HARRISON,Edgar Brooks 2Lt dow 28-9-16 7WYorks p218 CR France74,29-9-16
HARRISON,Edward 2Lt kia 28-4-17 RGA 158SB p40 CR France729
HARRISON,Edward Lt 17-5-18 RE &24RAF MR20
HARRISON,Edward Donald 2Lt kia 25-7-16 3RWKent att19Manch p141 MR21
HARRISON,Edward Frank.CMG.DSO.TLtCol ded 4-11-18 RE p45 CR Lond4
HARRISON,Edward Rainsford.MID Capt ded 25-12-18 RASC 524Coy 61DivTrn p253 CR France52
HARRISON,Eric Lt kia 30-6-15 3 att1Leic p87 CR Belgium44
HARRISON,Ernest Hesketh ACapt kia 18-9-18 5ESurr p226 CR France511,8Bn
HARRISON,Everard Capt kia 18-4-17 RAMC att1/6Gloucp253 CR France363
HARRISON,Francis Harold Lt kia 2-9-16 3Yorks att85RE SpBde p90 CR France150,att5RE
HARRISON,Francis Ingleby LtACapt dow 8-5-18 3 att1RWKent p141 CR France31,kia
HARRISON,Frank T2Lt drd 25-4-17 NStaffs p157 MR38
HARRISON,Frank Cecil Capt dow 13-10-18 RAMC p195 CR France612
HARRISON,Frank Cyril T2Lt dow 4-5-18 Lpool att 1/5Bn p72 CR France88
HARRISON,Frank Talbot T2Lt kia 3-5-17 8ESurr p112 MR20
HARRISON,Frederick Alfred 2Lt kia 9-9-163Leinst att6RIrReg p174 CR France402
HARRISON,Frederick William,MC 2Lt kia 27-5-18 8DLI p239 MR18
HARRISON,Geoffrey T2Lt kia 1-7-16 MGC Inf p183 CR France393
HARRISON,George Carmichael TLtACapt dow 10-1-17 RGA 6A/ABty 24HAG p40 CR Belgium11
HARRISON,George Frederick Whitby T2Lt dow 30-9-17 3RRofCav attWiltYeo att6Wilts p23CR Belgium17
HARRISON,George Herbert.MC.2Lt dow 21-8-16 3 att1LNLancs p136 CR France833
HARRISON,George Launcelot Godwin 2Lt kia 7-11-17 4 att11RSuss p228 MR30
HARRISON,George Victor.MC.Lt dow 26-8-18 3 att1Lpool p72 CR France84
HARRISON,H.G.Capt &Adjt 24-7-20 2Manch MR38
HARRISON,Halford Claude Vaughan MajTLtCol ded 1-4-16 RFA 16HAG p30 CR France201
HARRISON,Henry Malcolm Lt dow 19-3-15 3 att2Glouc p106 CR Belgium28 28-3-15
HARRISON,Henry Neville Baskcombe.MVO.Capt dow 16-3-15 2DCLI p114 CR Belgium151,kia
HARRISON,Herbert Le Grew TLt ded 12-3-18 GL RE p266 CR Mddx16,Greu
HARRISON,Herbert William 2Lt dow 9-6-17 3 att1Lincs p75 CR France145
HARRISON,Henry Leslie Lt ded 28-10-18 4Yorks attRAF p220 CR Lond14
HARRISON,James Spink T2Lt dow 28-5-18 2DLI p160 CR France142
HARRISON,James Molyneux LtCol ded 10-3-19 RASC p254 CR Yorks361,13-3-19
HARRISON,John,MC 2Lt kia 16-4-17 6RWar p214 CR France669
HARRISON,John.VC.MC.2Lt kia 3-5-17 11EYorks p84 MR20,mbk
HARRISON,John 2Lt kia 31-7-17 4 att1LancF p92 CR Belgium34
HARRISON,John Adshead T2Lt kia 12-4-18 31MGC p183 CR France352
HARRISON,John German Capt ded 11-4-18 RFA X32TMB p207 CR France145,dow
HARRISON,John Henry T2Lt kldacc 31-8-16 11 att7Lincs p75 CR France1014
HARRISON,John William 2Lt kia 7-6-17 18Lond attRFus p250 CR Belgium154
HARRISON,Leonard Arthur T2Lt kia 17-7-16 12DLI p160 MR21
HARRISON,Leonard John Harrison 2Lt kia 24-5-15 IAUL att2LancF p277 MR29
HARRISON,Leonard John T2Lt dow 17-4-18 18 att1RIrF p171 CR Germany3
HARRISON,Lionel Joseph Briggs TCapt kia 27-3-18 5 att16N&D p134 CR France526,3 att16Bn
HARRISON,Maurice Cazalet TCapt kia 12-10-16 1RWar p64 MR21
HARRISON,Noel Stuart TLt kia 30-7-16 9 att2 O&BLI p130 MR21
HARRISON,Osmond 2Lt ded 5-2-19 RGA p270 CR Durham26,Lt
HARRISON,P.W.CBE.LtCol 5-3-20 3LNLancs CR C'land&W'land107
HARRISON,Percy Day 2Lt ded 12-3-17 4RSuss p228 CR Hamps15,HARRISSON
HARRISON,Percy Pool Capt dow 20-10-17 5N&D p232 CR France145
HARRISON,R.Lt ded 17-5-18 RE &RAF p210
HARRISON,R.A.2Lt 9-2-19 RMunstF CR Eire78

HARRISON,Richard Scorer Molyneux Maj kia 16-8-15 IA 51Sikhs att7RDubF p277 MR4

HARRISON,Ronald 2Lt kia 18-9-16 11 att16Lond p248 CR France402

HARRISON,Ronald TLt kia 10-11-17 11BlkW att1/5A&SH p128 CR Palestine8

HARRISON,Roland Damer.DSO.Maj kia 16-9-17 RFA p30 CR France369,HARRISSON

HARRISON,Roland Edgar TLt kia 27-2-16 1DLI p160 CR Belgium127,2Lt 8Bn

HARRISON,Samuel Dunlop Henderson TLt dow 29-10-18 1 att11RInniskF p105 CR France1034,kia 11 att13Bn

HARRISON,Stanley T2Lt kia 23-10-16 1Hamps p120 MR21

HARRISON,Stanley Sextus Barrymore.MC.AMaj dow 10-10-18 RAMC att1/3NMidFA p195 CR France34

HARRISON,Thomas Charles 2Lt kia 21-3-18 43MGC p183 MR27

HARRISON,Thomas Percy 2Lt kia 9-4-18 RFA p208 MR19

HARRISON,Thomas Walter Lt drd 10-10-18 1/4Lincs p217 MR40

HARRISON,Tom Marriott TCapt dedacc 3-4-17 3 att13NumbF p61 CR France40

HARRISON,W.M.Sister 3-4-20 QAIMNS MR66

HARRISON,Wilfred Ernest.MC.TCapt dow 10-4-18 11Suff p78 MR32

HARRISON,William 2Lt dow 5-7-16 3GordH att2SfthH p166 CR France62

HARRISON,William Lt dow 17-9-16 7Lpool p215 CR France23

HARRISON,William Lt kia 29-9-18 7ScotRif p224 MR30

HARRISON,William Henry TLt kia 24-1-17 4Ess p232 MR50

HARRISON,William Sandilands LtCol ded 12-4-15 RAMC p195 CR Lancs284

HARRISON,William Stanford Bennett T2Lt kia 7-7-17 9LNLancs p136 MR29

HARRISS,Reginald Edmund TCapt kia 12-5-17 10LancF p92

HARROP,James Allinson T2Lt kia 8-10-18 KSLI att1Bn p145 MR16

HARROP,James Lawton 2Lt dow 13-9-18 LNLancs att4Bn p136 CR France686

HARROP,Tom T2Lt kia 28-4-18 17Lpool p72 MR30

HARROP,Tom Lt ded 31-3-20 LabCps CR Lancs42

HARROP,William Henry Lt kia 9-10-17 4ELancs p226 MR30

HARROW,Leonard Phillip.DCM.Lt kia 28-8-18 16Lond p249 CR France214

HARROWER,Alan Pat TLt dow PoW 26-3-18 12NumbF p61 CR France528

HARROWER,James.VD.TCapt dow 15-9-16 14HLI p163 CR France188,kia 10/11Bn Ex 14Lond

HARROWER,Peter.MC.T2Lt kia 17-10-18 16 att12RScots p54 CR Belgium140

HARROWING,John Stanley.MC.TLt kia 4-5-17 2RWar ExRASC p64 MR20,Capt

HARRUP,Frederick Charles Leonard.MC.T2Lt kia 21-9-18 9RFus p68 MR16

HARRY,Alfred Edward Capt kia 3-1-16 3 att1Ches p96 CR France394

HARRY,Reginald Charles 2Lt kia 29-8-16 ACycCps SthMidDiv p244 CR France220

HARRYMAN,Geoffrey Charles T2Lt dow 8-8-16 25Manch p154 CR France145,16Bn

HARRYMAN,Sydney T2Lt dow PoW 24-3-17 13Glouc att88RFC p8&106 CR France924

HARSTON,Frank Northey.MC.MIDx2 LtTCapt kia 22-4-18 ELancs attStaff 11InfBde p110 CR France250,Maj

HARSTON,William Harvey 2Lt kia 23-11-17 8Nhampt &52RFC p8&137 CR France1361,7Bn

HART,A.F SubAssSurg2Cl 31-8-15 IA IMD CR Asia60

HART,Albert TLt kia 30-6-18 RASC att6RWKent p193 CR France61

HART,Andrew Chichester 2Lt kia 1-7-16 109MGC p183 CR France215,Lt Ex 11RInniskF

HART,Arthur Charles Capt kia 7-5-15 2NumbF p61 MR29

HART,Cecil Lyon Capt kia 1-7-16 3WRid p115 CR France643

HART,Charles Crowther 2LtTLt kia 14-11-17 3WRid att3/3KAR p115&202 CR EAfrica11 &CR Tanzania1

HART,Clarence Herbert Lt kia 23-10-18 5 att2Beds p219 CR France190

HART,Clifford John TCapt kia 9-8-16 Worc &RFC p3&108 CR France525,RFC attWorc

HART,Conway John TLt kia 10-10-16 16N&D p134 CR France383

HART,Cornelius Henry 2Lt kia 17-10-18 RGA 130SB p40 CR France340

HART,David Provan.MC.Lt 27-12-18 LNLancs CR Scot807 Served as PROVAN,D.H.

HART,Edgar Oswald T2Lt kia 10-7-16 13 att9Yorks p90 MR21

HART,Edward Alexander TCapt kia 9-4-16 7NStaffs p157 MR38

HART,Ernest 2Lt kia 26-10-18 2Ess p131 CR France1266

HART,Ernest George Lt kia 30-8-18 13Lond p249 CR France308

HART,Francis Henry Lt ded 4-7-18 10Manch att42MGC Inf p187&255CR Lancs34

HART,Frank Arthur Squire T2Lt kia 16-9-16 9SomLI p79 MR21

HART,Frederick Reginald.MC.Lt dow 28-1-17 1Herts p252 CR Mddx39

HART,George Washington TLtAMaj kia 15-3-17 189RFA p30 CR Belgium28

HART,H.J.Capt 1-5-17 EAfrRlys CR EAfrica47

HART,Howard Victor.MC.Lt kld 23-3-19 6Lond p246 MR70 &CR Europe180,6Yorks Ex6Lond

HART,Hyla Padgham TLt kia 5-10-18 13DLI p160 MR16

HART,James.MC.LtACapt kia 1-11-18 1/6WRid p115 CR France1256

HART,James Arthur 2Lt ded 18-12-19 5Nhampt p265 CR Europe51,Lt

HART,James Wilson.MC&Bar.Capt kia 24-3-18 10RWSurr p56 MR20

HART,John Gordon Lt kia 28-8-17 7HLI p240 MR34,Capt

HART,John Harcourt Welby.MIDx2 TLt kia 20-9-18 Dev att1Manch p76 MR34

HART,John Sidney Lt dow 18-4-18 1 att1/5ELancs p110 CR France84

HART,Neil Lancefield T2Lt kia 31-7-17 218MGC p183 MR29

HART,Laurence George Capt kia 3-11-14 IA 61Pnrs p277 MR47

HART,Percival Frank Lt dow 3-5-17 3 att1Beds p86 CR France64

HART,Reginald Munro Lt dow 25-7-16 1Glouc p106 CR France703

HART,Richard George 2Lt kia 30-7-16 3 att10RWar p64 CR France390

HART,Robert Arthur 2Lt dow 1-8-17 6 att1Worc p108 CR Belgium7

HART,Samuel Edward 2Lt dow 30-4-17 7GordH p242 CR France40

HART,Thomas T2Lt kia 5-4-18 63MGC p183 CR France41

HART,Walter 2Lt kia 7-6-17 4Y&L p238 MR29

HART,William Cecil Frederick Nicol Lt kia 1-4-18 11RLancs &57RAF p59 MR20

HART-DAVIES,Ivan Beauclerk Lt kld 27-7-17 RFC SR p8 CR War

HARTE,George William 2Lt kia 5-3-18 2RMunstF p175 CR France364

HARTE,Irvine William Bagot Maj kia 21-6-17 IA 2/6GurkhaRif p277 MR43

HARTE,Joseph 2Lt kia 6-6-17 5RScots p211 CR France546

HARTE,Michael Joseph Capt kia 21-3-18 RASC att2/6N&D p193 MR20

HARTE-MAXWELL,Percival Maxwell Lt kia 11-4-16 4ConnRgrs att1RIrRif p172 France515,2Lt

HARTER,Clements Jesse Lt kia 16-6-15 3 att4RFus p68 MR29

HARTER,Herbert Hatfield Lt kia 9-10-17 GrenGds att2GdsMGReg p50&53 CR Belgium106,Hatfeild

HARTER,John Collier Foster T2Lt kia 28-11-17 3RRofCav attNottsYeo p23 CR Palestine9,James

HARTER,John George Capt dow 3-4-16 1DLI 151Bde p160 CR Belgium11

HARTERT,Joachim Charles TLt kia 28-10-16 8EYorks p84 CR France133

HARTFORD,Hugh Irving St.John Capt kia 22-10-14 Ches p96 MR22

HARTIGAN,Edward Patrick T2Lt kia 20-11-17 RMunstF att57RFC p8&175 CR France134,kld

HARTIGAN,Jeremiah Austin Chap4Cl ded 16-7-16 RAChDept p199 CR Iraq5

HARTIGAN,Kenneth Leslie Stewart Lt ded 2-11-19 IA 35ScindeHorse att36JacobsHorse p277 CR Egypt1

HARTIGAN,Thomas Jerome T2Lt kia 18-8-16 8Nhampt p137 CR France402

HARTILL,John Harry TCapt ded 25-1-16 GL 3Ches p96 CR War100

HARTINGTON,John Ernest Lt dow 13-7-17 5LancF att164MGC p187&221 CR Belgium11

HARTLE,Julian Walter Leslie 2Lt ded 10-3-20 IARO attMilWorksServ p277 MR4

HARTLEY,Alfred Lt dow 9-10-18 RGA 263SB p40 CR France725

HARTLEY,Arthur Rowland 2Lt dow 9-11-17 5SStaffs p229 CR Yorks719

HARTLEY,Bernard Harold TLt kia 4-11-16 20LancF p92 CR France924

HARTLEY,Charles Fletcher.MID 2Lt kia 27-11-17 CldGds att2GdsBde MGC p53 MR17

HARTLEY,Christopher Lt kia 1-9-17 C210RFA p207 CR Belgium84

HARTLEY,D'Arcy John Joseph Lt kia 14-7-16 7DragGds attMGC p21&183 MR2

HARTLEY,Edmund Lt kia 18-5-18 2LancF p92 CR France412

HARTLEY,Frederick Lynn 2Lt kia 23-8-18 3 att1ESurr p112 CR France239

HARTLEY,Herbert Henry T2Lt kia 14-3-18 48RFC p16 CR France446

HARTLEY,Horace Neville 2Lt kia 13-10-15 1/6NStaffs p238 MR19

HARTLEY,James Ernest 2Lt kia 26-10-17 5LNLancs p234 MR30

HARTLEY,James Harold 2Lt kia 22-7-17 RMunstF &45RFC p8&175 CR France

HARTLEY,John Armitage 2Lt kia 19-12-15 4WRid p227 CR Belgium11

HARTLEY,John Bernard Capt kia 4-6-15 1KOSB p101 MR4

HARTLEY,Noel Thomas.MC.TCapt kia 5-11-18 9WYorks p81&258 CR France1142

HARTLEY,Norman Curtis 2Lt dow 20-1-18 RFA 19DAC p30 CR France905

HARTLEY,Reginald TLt kld 26-10-15 10Worc p108 CR France260

HARTLEY,Reginald Humphrey 2Lt kia 3-5-17 7 att1Mddx p235 MR20

HARTLEY,Richard T2Lt kld 11-11-16 8EYorks p84

HARTLEY,Walter John TCapt kia 16-8-15 5RIrF p171 MR4

HARTLEY,Walter Lockwood Lt kia 13-10-15 5Lincs p220 MR19

HARTLEY,William Edwin T2Lt kia 2-10-15 2Ches p96 MR19,1-10-15

HARTLEY,William Garfield Capt dow 9-8-16 48AustInf CR France74

HARTLEY,William Guest.MM.T2Lt dow 8-8-18 9Ess p131 CR France888

HARTLEY,William Holliday.MC.Lt dow 22-3-18 8Huss p22 MR27

HARTLEY,William Ismay Spooner TLt kia 1-7-16 8YLI p143 CR France246

HARTLEY,William John Capt kia 21-5-17 2/6Lond p246 MR20

HARTLEY,William Reginald 2Lt dow 20-12-15 7LancF p221 CR Gallipoli6

HARTLEY,William Stuart.MC.TCapt dow 8-10-18 9Manch att1LNLancs p237 CR France380

HARTMANN,Carl Herbert Lt kia 2-7-18 5RWKent p235 CR France516

HARTNALL,Archibald John Maj ded 6-3-17 2RFA p206 MR65

HARTNELL,Cuthbert LtACapt kia 16-7-15 8WYorks p219 CR Belgium96

HARTNELL,Edward Bush Capt ded 25-4-16 RAMC 1/4LondMtdBdeFA p253 CR Egypt9

HARTNELL-SINCLAIR,St.John Leslie 2Lt kia 25-9-15.3ESurr att2WelshR p112 MR19

HARTNETT,Joseph Mary Patrick SubCdr ded 18-2-15 IA S&TCps p277

HARTNETT,Michael Charles Lt kia 19-9-17 RMunstF attRFC p8&175 CR Belgium

HARTNOLL,Herbert Nicholas Lt&QM ded 28-5-16 RE p45

HARTNOLL,Hugh Peter Lt kia 12-12-14 1Worc p108 MR22

HARTNOLL,James Capt ded 20-5-17 RFA 1/1BerksBty p207 CR Egypt2

HARTNOTT, SubCdr 19-2-15 S&T Cps CR Iraq6

HARTOPP,Charles William Liddell 2Lt kia 13-10-15 7Suff p78 MR19

HARTREE,Cyril 2Lt kia 29-5-18 RGA 201SB p40 CR France25

HARTREE,Eric Mursell TLt kia 8-8-18 RASC att8RBerks p193 CR France247

HARTSHORN,Arthur William TLt dow 9-1-18 98MGC p183 CR Belgium11

HARTSHORN,Laurence Alec Lt dow 26-3-18 2DLI att18LTMB p160 CR France1483,4Bn

HARTT,Harold 2Lt kia 5-5-17 9Lpool p216 CR Belgium4 7Bn

HARTWELL,Barry Capt kia 30-10-14 IA 2/8GurkhaRif p277 MR28

HARTY,James Johnson TLt ded 6-3-17 RAMC p195 CR Eire88

HARTY,John Joseph 2Lt dow 27-9-16 1RMunstF att10RIrRif p175 CR France285

HARTY,Wilfrid A.2Lt kia 8-8-17 11RDubF p176 CR Belgium115

HARTY,William David T2Lt kia 30-9-18 KSLI att1/4Bn p145 CR France80

HARVARD,Kenneth O'Gorman Lt kia 1-8-17 2GrenGds p50 CR Belgium106

HARVARD,Lionel de Jersey LtACapt kia 30-3-18 1GrenGds p50 CR France1183

HARVEST,G.Maj 14-10-18 5Lond CR Lond13

HARVEST,Gordon Lindsay.MC.Lt dow 20-6-17 5Lond p246 CR France518,21-6-17

HARVEY,Albert Henry T2Lt kia 7-10-16 9RFus p68 MR21

HARVEY,Alec Wright Capt dow PoW 27-3-18 8ScotRif p225 CR France660

HARVEY,Alexander Scott TLt dow 29-3-18 2GordH A'Coy p166 CR France95

HARVEY,Alfred Wallace TCapt dow 7-9-16 RAMC att55RFA AmmCol p195 CR Iraq5

HARVEY,Austin Mozart.MBE.Lt mbk 27-10-18 5Dev p257

HARVEY,Bernard Sydney Capt kia 1-7-16 1/5Lond p246 MR21

HARVEY,Charles Claud Lt dow 3-4-16 7A&SH p243 CR France95,Cleland

HARVEY,Charles Lewis Capt dow 10-5-17 2/4Lincs p220&270 CR Lincs29

HARVEY,Charles Milne Lt kia 25-11-14 2Mddx p147 CR France1157,23-11-14

HARVEY,Claude Lindsay 2Lt kia 23-3-18 4 att7RWSurr p212 MR27

HARVEY,Douglas.DSO.Capt kia 10-2-17 IA 31Punjabis attStaff 35InfBde p277 CR Iraq5

HARVEY,D.S.Capt 29-10-21 RAMC CR War7

HARVEY,Douglas TLt kia 27-3-18 2GrenGds p50 CR France214

HARVEY,Douglas Lennox 2Lt kia 2-11-14 9Lancers p22 CR Belgium98

HARVEY,Douglas Preston.MC.T2Lt kia 20-11-17 164MGC p183 MR17

HARVEY,Edward Byron Atkins T2Lt kia 15-4-17 8RWKent B'Coy p141 CR France149

HARVEY,Edward George Capt kia 16-6-15 1Wilts p153 MR29

HARVEY,E.H.Capt 31-7-16 RE CR Hamps7

HARVEY,Eric Howard.MC&Bar.Capt kia 30-9-18 2/5Glouc A'Coy p225 CR France769

HARVEY,Ernest Anthony 2Lt ded 14-11-17 IARO att29Lancers p277 MR65,15-11-17

HARVEY,Frank Lennox Lt kia 30-10-14 9Lancers p22 MR29

HARVEY,Frederick William TLt kia 9-8-15 10SLancs att6LancF p125 CR Gallipoli1

HARVEY,George LtTCapt kia 21-6-17 RGA 336SB p40 CR France163

HARVEY,George Denis 2Lt kia 9-10-17 3CldGds p51 MR30

HARVEY,George Winfred.MC.LtACapt kia 12-4-18 A169RFA p207 CR France881,13-4-18

HARVEY,Gerald Franklyn Lt kia 8-11-15 RFA attRFC p1&30 CR Belgium11

HARVEY,Gilbert Aberdein Capt dow 25-11-17 RAMC att1RLancs p195 CR France113

HARVEY,Harry Thomas Lt kia 31-7-17 5Suff att23MGC p187&217 MR29

HARVEY,Henry Burnett T2Lt kia 30-3-18 13Glouc p106 MR27

HARVEY,Herbert Lt 23-5-20 IARO MR66

HARVEY,Herbert Alexander TLt kia 12-10-16 Beds att1Ess p86 MR21

HARVEY,James Capt kia 16-5-15 7Lpool p215 MR22,17-5-15

HARVEY,James.MID 2Lt kia 1-7-16 2SfthH p164 MR21

HARVEY,James T2Lt dow 26-2-17 2SfthH p164 CR Iraq5

HARVEY,James Walter TLt ded 25-8-17 RASC p267 CR Norf30,2Lt

HARVEY,John 2Lt dow 10-9-18 1RB p179 CR France13

HARVEY,John Alan T2Lt kia 20-11-17 11RDubF p176 CR France1489

HARVEY,John Albert T2Lt kia 4-4-18 7RWSurr attTMB p56 MR27

HARVEY,John Alexander 2Lt kia 25-9-15 6GordH p242 MR19

HARVEY,John Forsyth TCapt kia 23-3-18 9RInniskF p105 MR27

HARVEY,John Lawrence T2Lt kia 24-4-17 4SfthH p164 CR France545

HARVEY,John William Lt ded 26-12-18 IARO att2/56Regt p277 CR India97A

HARVEY,Kenneth Watson Lt dow 27-9-15 RFA 19A/Asect p30 CR Belgium11

HARVEY,Leslie 2Lt kia 25-4-15 8Mddx p236 MR29

HARVEY,Oliver Colin 2Lt kia 4-7-16 3 att7SLancs p125 MR21

HARVEY,Phillip Parmenter 2LtACapt kia 8-8-18 10Ess p131 MR16

HARVEY,Ralph de Warenne 2Lt dow 7-6-16 3Dors att1KRRC p124 CR France145,Warrenne

HARVEY,Richard Ernle TCapt&Adjt dow 27-10-15 9BlkW p128 CR France554,25-9-15

HARVEY,Richard Prentice Maj kia 9-5-15 3 att2RBerks p139 MR32

HARVEY,Robert Clive Lt kia 14-10-15 1/4Leic p219 MR19,13-10-15

HARVEY,Robert George Bosworth 2Lt kia 25-12-17 1/5Lincs p220 CR France163,kldacc

HARVEY,Rollo d'Aubigne ACapt kia 9-9-16 2RSuss p119 CR France432

HARVEY,Ronald Marmaduke Dawnay 2Lt kia 20-4-15 4NStaffs att1Beds p157 MR29 CR France453

HARVEY,R.W.2Lt ded 22-10-18 17RFus &RAF p68

HARVEY,Sidney Lancelot,DSO.MC Maj ded 8-1-19 RE 500FC p209 CR Asia81

HARVEY,Stanley 2Lt kia 9-4-17 4NStaffs att9YLI p157 CR France162

HARVEY,Stanley Alfred George TLt kia 21-3-18 8RBerks p139 MR27

HARVEY,Thomas 2Lt ded 29-4-17 3RLancs p59 CR Iraq8

HARVEY,Thomas Daniel.MC.TLt ded 17-10-18 MGC att2/1NigR p183&201 CR WAfrica54

HARVEY,Thomas Francis Lt kia 7-6-18 6SfthH &49RAF p270 MR20

HARVEY,Wickham Leathes Lt kia 3-3-15 IA 7Rajputs p277 MR61

HARVEY,William 2Lt kia 25-9-15 3Lpool p72 CR France163,1Bn

HARVEY,William 2Lt dow 14-10-16 NumbF att27Bn p61 CR France297

HARVEY,William Anthony Lt ded 7-11-17 4Norf attRFC p18&216 CR Europe51

HARVEY,William Clayton TLt kia 14-7-16 20KRRC p150 CR France513

HARVEY,William Henry T2Lt kia 23-10-18 A88RFA p30 CR France323,22-10-18

HARVEY,William James St.John TBrigGen dow 1-2-16 BlkW p128 CR Iraq5

HARVEY,William Mitchell 2Lt kia 10-7-16 13WelshR p126 MR21

HARVEY,William Reginald TLt dow 23-9-17 B95RH&FA p30

HARVEY JAMES,A.K.MID Capt 15-4-17 1EKent CR France551

HARVEY-JONES,F.M.MC.2Lt 18-6-17 3Worc att8BordR CR France285

HARVEY-KELLY,Hubert Dunsterville,DSO CaptTMaj kia 29-4-17 RIrReg &19RFC p89&8 CR France604

HARVIE,Eric Fulton.MC.Lt kia 15-6-18 2GordH p166 CR France33,Capt 1Bn

HARVIE,James 2Lt dow 8-6-16 D92RFA p30 CR France40

HARVIE,Patrick Joseph TLt kia 16-4-17 9NumbF p61 CR France1188

HARVIE,Stuart McLaren 2Lt dow 1-6-18 2 att6KRRC p150 CR France10

HARVISON,Robert Albert Lt ded 9-2-19 3RMunstF p266

HARWOOD,Colin Crisp T2Lt ded 6-11-17 2MGC Inf p183 CR Notts68

HARWOOD,Gerald.AFC.Lt kldacc 1-5-19 3Suff attRAF p78 CR Kent103

HARWOOD,Percy Gregory Shelley Lt dow 31-12-17 1/4RSuss p228 CR Palestine3

HASELDEN,Cyril Gerrard TLt ded 27-11-18 RE attAustCpsHQ p45 CR France931,Capt

HASELDEN,Edgar Adolphus TCapt dow 9-7-16 11WYorks p81 CR France833

HASELDINE,Frederick HonLt&QM ded 2-12-14 8WRid p115 CR Leic13

HASELER,Maurice Noble TLt dow 4-7-16 2RWar p64 MR21

HASELER,William Hereward TLtACapt kia 20-11-17 'B'TankCps p188 MR17

HASELGROVE,Bertram Thorpe 2Lt dow 3-9-18 9Lond p248 CR France833

HASKINS,Victor Bradshaw 2Lt kia 20-11-15 3ESurr att5KSLI p112 CR Belgium84

HASLAM,Arthur Dixon TLt dow 2-11-18 9NumbF p61 CR France398

HASLAM,Bernard John.DSO.Maj kia 26-8-18 RE p45 MR61,LtCol

HASLAM,Charles Stanley Lt kia 10-11-17 YorkHussYeo p206 MR20,9WYorks

HASLAM,Herbert 2Lt kia 16-9-17 14Manch &6RFC p8&155 MR20

HASLAM,James Lt kia 30-10-17 28Lond p252 MR30

HASLAM,Robert T2Lt ded 29-3-18 12LancF p92 CR Greece1

HASLAM,Wilfred Henry Wescott Lt kia 7-2-16 4RWKent p234 CR Iraq6

HASLAM,William T2Lt kia 21-3-18 Manch att2/7Bn p155 MR27,24-3-18

HASLAM,William Kenneth Seale Capt kia 27-4-17 4RFA p207 CR France581

133

HASLER,Algernon 2Lt dow 18-9-16 2GrenGds SR p50 CR France833
HASLER,Arthur Thomas.MC.Lt&QM drd 4-5-17 RAMC att40CCS p195 CR Italy14
HASLER,Gordon Beverley T2Lt kia 26-7-16 9 att7Beds p86 CR France513
HASLER,Julian BrigGen kia 26-4-15 EKent p57 CR Belgium101
HASLER,Leonard Melsome TLt dow 21-9-17 2Ess att17MGC p131&183
HASLETT,Thomas Sinclair.MC.TLt kia 22-11-17 10RIrRif p169 MR17
HASLOCK,John Charles Simeon T2Lt dow 2-11-15 att7Glouc p106 MR4
HASLUCK,Sidney Vandyke.MID 2Lt kia 4-6-15 IARO att89Punjabis p277 MR4
HASSARD,Edward John,MC Lt ded 7-11-18 B110RH&FA p30
HASSELL,Robert De Bray.CMG.LtCol 22-2-20 RA CR Sussex225
HASSLACHER,James Alfred Charles Capt kia 29-12-17 2/20Lond p251 CR Palestine3
HASTINGS,Aubrey Joseph T2Lt kia 5-10-15 7ESurr p112 CR France108
HASTINGS,George Herbert Capt kia 5-2-15 1Mddx p147 CR France922
HASTINGS,George William 2Lt kia 1-8-17 3Mon att10Ches p244 CR Belgium3,Williams
HASTINGS,H.M.Sister 23-7-18 TFNS CR Scot613
HASTINGS,James Smith 2Lt ded 25-6-16 4GordH p270 CR Scot281
HASTINGS,Joseph Edward T2Lt kia 18-7-16 11 att8BlkW p128 MR21
HASTINGS,Joseph Lorton T2Lt kia 12-5-17 10LancF p92 MR20
HASTINGS,Leslie Lt kia 21-1-16 IA 102Grens p277 CR Iraq5,Capt
HASTINGS,Noël Henry Bruce TCapt kia 7-6-17 8Glouc p106 CR Belgium102
HASTINGS,Percy Maj dow 2-9-14 RWKent p141
HASTINGS-MEDHURST,Francis Leslie 2Lt kia 17-10-14 2Worc p108 MR22
HASTWELL,Hugh Norman 2Lt kia 30-6-18 10AustInf CR France193
HASTWELL,Wilfrid Maurice T2Lt kia 7-4-17 MGC p183 CR France266
HASWELL,Frederick 2Lt dow 23-4-15 3EYorks p84 MR29
HASWELL,Gordon TCapt kia 1-7-16 9YLI p143 CR France189
HATCH,Andrew Basil 2Lt ded 10-10-14 9Mddx p255 CR Mddx58,Lt
HATCH,George John Lt kia 6-4-17 17Lond attRFC p18&250 MR20 &CR France924
HATCH,Henry Bertram William T2Lt kia 18-11-16 57MGC Inf p183 MR21
HATCH,Jesse.MC.DCM.MM.Lt dow 23-10-18 RGA 95SB p40 CR France270
HATCH,Laurence Collier Lt kia 27-9-15 11DLI p160 MR19,14Bn
HATCH,Nicholas Stephen 2Lt kia 1-7-16 13RIrRif p169 CR France744
HATCH,Norman Claud 2Lt kia 21-10-16 2SLancs p125 CR France832
HATCH,Philip Randall TLt kia 7-10-16 6EKent p57 MR21
HATCH,Reginald William Lt kia 3-9-16 17 att10RB p179 MR21
HATCH,William Leonard Ringrose Lt kia 25-1-15 2RIrF p171 MR29
HATCHER,Reginald Gordon Lt dow 20-9-17 1/4RLancs p213 CR Belgium18
HATFIELD,Alfred Charles.MC.2LtACapt dow 21-9-17 8Y&L p159 CR Belgium11
HATFIELD,Arthur Percival Chap4Cl ded 9-7-18 RAChDept 1stBGH p199 CR Iraq5
HATFIELD,Charles Eric.MC.Capt kia 21-9-18 10EKent p204 CR France1462
HATFIELD,Roy Berriman Lt dow 24-5-15 8Lond p247 CR France80,kia
HATHAWAY,Sidney T2Lt kia 12-1-16 11RFC p3 CR France518
HATHAWAY,Thomas Hervey 2Lt kia 17-2-15 3RLancs p59 MR29
HATHERELL,Eric James 2Lt mbk 25-4-17 9WRid p256 MR20
HATHORN,Charles Nicholls 2Lt kia 10-8-15 6LNLancs p136 MR4
HATHORN,Noel McDonall.MID 2Lt kia 14-7-15 IARO att76Punjabis p277 CR Iraq6,McDouall
HATT,Arthur Beach TCapt kia 1-7-16 8SomLI A'Coy p79 CR France267
HATT,Edward Beach TCapt kia 26-8-16 7SomLI C'Coy p80 CR France400
HATT,Harold Ernest Lt drd 23-3-19 RASC p270 CR Oxford36,29-1-19
HATTAM,Harold Colin Lt kia 26-9-17 5 att 1/4Suff p217 MR30
HATTE,Edward Stokes T2Lt kia 16-8-17 7RIrRif p169 MR30
HATTER,Bernard 2Lt kia 25-9-15 2 att3Leic p87 MR19
HATTON,Bryan 2Lt kia 23-4-16 1/1WorcYeo p206 CR Egypt2,Brian
HATTON,Christopher 2Lt 9-12-15 SStaffs CR Lincs69
HATTON,Ernest Robert.MID 2Lt kia 8-5-18 2Wilts p153 MR30
HATTON,Frederick Charles 2Lt kia 30-10-14 2Yorks p90 MR29
HATTON,Horace Walter Smeathman LtACapt kia 23-8-18 3 att2SStaffs p122 CR France927
HATTON,John Alfred 2Lt kia 3-5-17 7 att12Mddx p235 MR20
HATTON,Robert Andrew Maj dow 23-10-18 RFA 123SB p206 CR France332
HAUGHTON,Alfred John 2LtTLt kia 23-6-15 9DLI p239 CR Belgium17 24-6-15
HAUGHTON,Charles Stanley Lt ded 4-2-19 23RB p244 CR Ches8,5-2-19
HAUGHTON,Thomas Greenwood TLt kia 1-7-16 12RIrRif p169 CR France701
HAVELOCK,Beresford Arthur Jardine TMaj kia 14-9-18 1 att7NStaffs p157&265,14-9-15 Y&L CR Asia81
HAVELOCK,Ernest Wilfrid TLt dow 18-9-16 26RFus p68 CR France833,Wilfred
HAVERFIELD,John Campbell Lt dow 14-7-15 IARO att24Punjabis p277 CR Iraq6

HAVERS,Frederick Charles 2Lt kia 27-5-18 5Lincs p220 MR18
HAVERSON,James Blain Lt dow 25-6-16 RAMC 104FA p195 CR France430
HAVILAND,John Doria TLt dow 16-7-16 10RFus p68 CR France833
HAWARD,Godfrey TLt kia 15-11-16 99MGC Inf p183 MR21
HAWARD,Hereward Warren T2Lt dow 1-7-18 7 att2Beds p86 CR France69,Lt
HAWARDEN,Robert Cornwallis.Viscount.Lt dow 26-8-14 3CldGds p51 CR France932
HAWDON,Cecil 2Lt kia 27-6-16 4Yorks p220 CR Belgium182
HAWDON,Noel Elliot Chap4Cl ded 16-11-18 RAChDept CofE att45TMB p199 C France34
HAWDON,Rupert Ayrton.MIDx2 TLtACapt kia 4-11-18 RGA 35SB p40 CR France1081
HAWES,Adrian Lancelot TLt kia 8-10-18 52MGC Inf p183 CR France602
HAWES,Ernest Harington T2Lt kia 5-6-17 20NumbF p61 MR20
HAWES,Frederick Maxwell 2Lt kld 14-9-17 RGA &RFC p8 CR Camb37
HAWES,Godfrey Charles Browne TCapt drd 10-4-17 RAMC p195 CR France85
HAWES,Herbert TLt kia 20-10-18 11 att1ESurr p112 CR France1388
HAWES,Robert Frank Capt dow 23-9-14 1Leic p87 CR France1107
HAWKE,Albert Edward Mountain Aysh T2Lt dow 11-9-16 19 att2KRRC p150 CR France833
HAWKE,Edward Anthony Francis Lt ded 27-12-18 20/7RFA p261 CR Cornwall10 9Bde
HAWKE,Ernest William 2Lt kia 11-5-17 7 att1Hamps p229 MR20
HAWKE,William Baldwin 2Lt kia 7-10-16 7Mddx p235 MR21
HAWKEN,Alfred George WO explosion 8-11-20 RIM p277
HAWKEN,G.W.2Lt 18-5-18 GL &RAF CR Hamps192
HAWKEN,William Victor Lt kia 26-4-16 2/7N&D p233 CR Mddx53
HAWKER,Albert Victor TLt ded 23-12-18 8 att9Glouc p106 CR France1571
HAWKER,Charles William Seymour Lt ded 13-3-18 13Hamps p264 CR Europe5
HAWKER,Frederick James T2Lt dow 16-7-16 8Glouc p106 CR France40
HAWKER,Gilbert Victor Lt ded 1-7-20 IARO attS&TCps p277 MR65
HAWKER,Lance George.VC.DSO.TMaj ded 23-11-16 RE &24RFC p3&45 MR20
HAWKER,Reginald Sudlow Capt dow 9-11-17 1DevYeo attMGC p203 CR Egypt2
HAWKES,Gerald Arthur 2Lt dow 3-7-18 RGA att521SB p40 CR France31
HAWKES,John Aubrey T2Lt dow 11-9-18 7Leic p87 CR France439,kia
HAWKES,John Cornock TLt kia 30-7-15 RAMC att8KRRC p195 CR Belgium35 Cornick
HAWKES,Percival Warburton Capt kia 9-4-18 5Lpool p215 MR19
HAWKES,Septimus James LtACapt ded 10-7-18 3RBerks p139 CR Berks86
HAWKESWORTH,Francis Henry Stanley 2Lt kia 25-1-15 3BordR attWelshR p11 MR22
HAWKINS,Alexander Edward CaptAMaj dow 12-12-17 B181RFA p30 CR France398
HAWKINS,Charles Francis Maj kia 25-4-15 RFA 46Bty p30 CR France1106
HAWKINS,Clarence Vincent Tom Capt kia 26-9-17 5SStaffs p229 MR19
HAWKINS,F.C.Lt dow 15-11-17 2KAR p268
HAWKINS,George Arthur LtCol ded 2-6-19 IA attS&TCps p277 CR Surrey1
HAWKINS,Gilbert William TLt dow 15-11-16 15 att13KRRC p150 CR France70
HAWKINS,Harold George T2Lt dow 24-7-15 11Mddx p147 CR France922
HAWKINS,Harold Ingleby Capt mbk 16-6-17 2Lond p257 MR20
HAWKINS,Herbert Edward 2Lt kia 11-5-17 1/14Lond p249 CR France537
HAWKINS,Herbert Edwin TCapt kia 1-7-16 10Ess p131 CR France513
HAWKINS,Humphrey Caesar.MC.2Lt kia 23-4-18 B121RFA p30 CR Belgium11
HAWKINS,John Bawtree TCapt&Adjt ded 30-8-16 SL 18InfBaseDepot p201 CR France40
HAWKINS,John Henry T2Lt dow 8-2-18 WYorks att8Bn p81 CR France266
HAWKINS,John Noel Capt dow 30-7-16 27Manch p155 CR France742
HAWKINS,John Stephen 2Lt kia 23-7-17 22Lond p251 CR Belgium122,24-7-17
HAWKINS,Kenneth Edwards.MC.LtACapt kia 22-3-18 7RFus p68 MR20
HAWKINS,Kenneth James T2Lt kia 8-8-18 1TankCps A'Coy p188 CR France587
HAWKINS,L.H.Lt 8-10-19 2Suff CR Surrey148
HAWKINS,Lionel Hope Lt kia 31-10-14 1DragGds p20 MR29
HAWKINS,Oliver Luther 2Lt dow 26-4-15 3EYorks p84 CR France200
HAWKINS,Stanley.MC.Capt kia 29-5-18 HAC p206 MR18
HAWKINS,Walter Elmslie 2LtTLt dow 8-6-17 8Glouc p106 CR Belgium11
HAWKINS,Wilfred Francis Capt 21-4-21 RAMC CR Ireland33
HAWKINS,William Percy TLt dow 12-10-15 6KSLI p145 CR France40
HAWKRIDGE,Joseph Arnold T2Lt dow 6-11-16 15RFus att9RSuss p68 CR France12
HAWKS,Albert John Everdale 2Lt dow 15-6-17 79RFA p30 CR France113
HAWKS,Aubrey Meldrum Wood Lt kia 27-9-18 4RScots p211 CR France484

HAWKSEY,Bernard Richard Lt kia 28-9-18 5LancF p221 CR France658
HAWKSLEY,George Lt kia 22-3-18 4 att7/8RInniskF p105 CR France329
HAWKSLEY,John Plunkett Verney.DSO.MIDx3 TLtCol kia 8-8-16 110RFA p30 CR France515
HAWKSLEY,Walter Linney Maj kld 3-4-16 RAMC 98FA p253 CR France300
HAWKSWELL,Lewis Bertram Lt dow 18-9-18 6WYorks &RAF p255
HAWKSWORTH,Henry Charles Harold.MC.Lt kia 21-3-18 10Ess p131 MR27
HAWKSWORTH,Stanley Harcourt T2Lt kia 20-9-17 7Lpool p72 MR30
HAWLEY,Cyril T2Lt kld 23-7-17 GL &RFC p8 CR Yorks547
HAWLEY,Cyril Francis Capt kia 2-11-14 2KRRC p150 MR29
HAWLEY,F.SNurse 20-6-18 QAIMNS CR Staffs153
HAWLEY,Nellie MilProb Nurse drd 31-12-17 QAIMNS p200 CR Egypt1
HAWLING,Thomas Albert T2Lt kia 4-11-17 RLancs att9YLI p59 MR30
HAWORTH,Arthur T2Lt kia 19-7-16 16Lpool attMGC p72&183 CR France1157
HAWORTH,Harold Stanley Lt kia 13-8-16 4YLI p235 CR France293
HAWORTH,Herbert TLt kia 7-6-17 11 att8LNLancs p136 CR Belgium102
HAWORTH,Montague Burgess Lt kia 23-3-18 5ESurr p226 CR France1893
HAWORTH,Percy Geoffrey du Val Lt kia 30-7-16 18Manch p155 CR France402
HAWORTH,Philip Theodore 2Lt dow 3-5-17 D86RFA p30 CR France40,Capt
HAWORTH,Thomas Eldred Curwen T2Lt dow 2-12-17 9Ess p131 CR France398
HAWORTH-BOOTH,Benjamin Booth Maj 8-11-19 ERidYeo CR Mddx26
HAWTHORN,William T2Lt dow 31-12-15 RE 172TC p45 CR France40,Lt
HAWTREY,John James Alexander 2Lt ded PoW 17-9-17 GL 60RFC p8 CR Belgium140
HAWTREY,Ralph TLt kia 3-9-16 RE 179TC p45 CR France430
HAY,Alfred Chalmers 2Lt kia 9-4-17 3 att8/10GordH p166 MR20
HAY,Andrew Peter T2Lt kia 29-4-16 1KOSB D'Coy p101 CR France35
HAY,Archibald MajTLtCol kia 3-2-17 8RWFus p98 CR Iraq5
HAY,Arthur Leslie 2Lt dow 26-4-17 4 att10/11HLI p163 CR France113
HAY,Arthur Vincent.Lord Capt kia 14-9-14 1IrGds p52 CR France1112
HAY,Charles Edward Erroll Lt dow 9-8-18 17Lancers p23 CR France29
HAY,Donald Yalden Lt kia 11-8-17 2/5RWKent att20RFC p18,235&212,Malden RWSurr CR France134
HAY,Douglas Woulfe.MC.Lt kia 29-9-18 6 att1Mddx p147 CR France407
HAY,E.J.A.Lt 5-9-18 IA 2/41Dogras MR65
HAY,Edward Hutton 2Lt dow 11-6-17 1/7GordH p242 CR France113
HAY,Frank Tochetti TLt kia 26-9-15 7RScotF p94 MR19
HAY,Geoffrey William.MID Capt kia 9-5-15 3 att1LNLancs p136 MR22
HAY,James Barromew.DSO.TLtCol ded 2-8-19 SL GHQ p268 CR Egypt8
HAY,James Blackwood 2Lt ded 29-10-18 4Y&L p238 CR Italy12
HAY,James Duncan T2Lt dow 15-12-17 1/5RLancs p59 CR France145
HAY,James Henry Webster TCapt&Adjt kia 30-11-15 9SfthH p164 CR Belgium5
HAY,James Lyle T2Lt kia 3-7-16 12NumbF p61 CR France267
HAY,J.M.Lt mbk 24-3-18.MID Ches &62RFC p256 MR20
HAY,John 2Lt kia 23-1-17 40RFC SR p8 CR France31
HAY,Robert T2Lt kia 28-7-18 5Dev p76 MR18
HAY,Robert TLt ded 9-10-18 RASC MT p193 CR France34
HAY,Robert TLt ded 7-1-19 9 att2NLancs p254 CR Belgium302
HAY,Roger Bolton.MC.Lt dow PoW 17-7-17 3WYorks att48RFC p8&81 CR Belgium175,2Bn
HAY,William T2Lt dow 1-4-16 12ScotRif att1RScotF p103 CR Belgium11
HAY,William George TCapt ded 7-8-16 11 att8BlkW p128 CR France12
HAY,William Stevenson Brown TCapt kia 5-10-18 RAMC att53RFA p195 CR Belgium44
HAY-JAN,Henry Gordon 2Lt 15-2-17 8Wilts CR Iraq5
HAY-WEBB,A.B.Capt 23-8-15 1/5GurkhaRif MR4
HAY-WEBB,Charles Robert Forbes TCapt kia 28-12-16 235RFA p30 CR Belgium28
HAY-SMITH,Alan Douglas 2Lt 26-3-17 4Ess MR34
HAYBITTLE,Richard William Lt dow 8-1-18 185MGC p183 CR Iraq5
HAYCRAFT,Alan Montague Lt kia 1-7-16 6 att2RFus p68 CR France1501
HAYCRAFT,Leonard Courtenay 2Lt kia 7-10-16 4Lond p246 MR21
HAYCROFT,Frank Alexander T2Lt kia 10-8-17 KRRC att10Bn p150 MR29
HAYDEN,Leon Anthony 2Lt dow 14-1-17 2RIrReg p89 CR France200
HAYDEN,William Clarence Capt kia 19-9-15 1HAC p206 CR Belgium6
HAYDOCK,Tom Lt dow 2-9-18 1/7ScotRif p224 CR France103
HAYDON,Alan TLt ded 28-12-18 RE 71FC p45 CR Surrey1
HAYDON,Edgar Frederick Bewes 2Lt kia 19-7-16 51/39RFA p30 MR21
HAYDON,Geoffrey Miles TLtACapt kia 16-8-17 8SWBord p100 CR Belgium106,dow
HAYDON,George Francis 2Lt kia 19-8-16 C175RFA p30 CR France1890,18-8-16
HAYE,Basil Lt drd 10-10-18 2RBerks p139 CR Ireland14

HAYE,Philip Lt ded 2-4-19 3RBerks att82MGC p183&139 CR Asia81
HAYES,Arthur 2Lt kia 25-3-18 3 att4Beds p86 MR20
HAYES,Cedric George Lt kia 9-4-18 RE 422FC p210 CR France260
HAYES,Charles Bianconi Capt kia 10-8-15 10Hamps p120 MR4
HAYES,Charles Robert 2Lt ded 25-3-19 IARO p277 CR India97A
HAYES,Claude Julian Patrick ACapt kia 9-8-16 1RFus p68 CR France164
HAYES,Ernest de Launoy Maj kia 10-3-15 ScotRif p103 CR France260,Lannoy
HAYES,Gordon Stanley T2Lt kia 15-6-18 1/2RWKent att5Glouc p141 CR Italy2
HAYES,Harry Urmston 2Lt kia 13-10-15 1BlkW p128 MR19,Urmson
HAYES,Herbert Henry TCaptAMaj kia 1-10-18 RGA 409SB p40 CR France439
HAYES,John Carolin.MC.Lt ded 19-11-18 2CldGds p57 CR France85
HAYES,John Henry 2Lt kia 31-7-17 5 att17RWFus p223 MR29
HAYES,Leo John 2Lt kia 10-10-18 3 att18Lpool p72 CR France190
HAYES,Leonard Frank 2Lt kia 29-4-18 1/5SStaffs p229 CR France572,Capt
HAYES,Marshall HonLt ded 23-3-19 15Ches p263 CR Sussex19
HAYES,Mortimer Frederick TLt kia 10-7-16 8EYorks p84 CR France531,Capt 29-4-17
HAYES,Reginald 2Lt kia 22-7-17 GL &45RFC p8 MR20
HAYES,Reginald Pole 2Lt kld 12-3-16 3SomLI p80 CR France55,Lt 6Bn
HAYES,Richard Johnson(Dick) T2Lt kia 4-11-18 7Wilts p153 CR France929
HAYES,Robert Harnett 2Lt dow 1-8-17 4ConnRgrs att2Leinst p172 MR29,Lt
HAYES,W.Rice Maj 19-2-19 RFA CR Yorks417
HAYES,William.DSO.Capt ded 20-10-18 RWSurr p56 CR Italy12
HAYES,Willie 2Lt dow 25-9-18 RGA 143SB p40 CR France146
HAYES-NEWINGTON,Charles Wetherell.MID TCapt kia 11-5-15 2Ches p96 MR29,8-5-15
HAYES-NEWINGTON,Harold May 2Lt kia 10-3-15 1Lpool p72 CR France1106
HAYES-SADLER,Edwin John Berkley Lt kia 28-10-14 RE p45 MR22

HAYES-SADLER,Ernest Reginald Capt kia 30-10-14 IA 2/8GurkhaRif p277 CR France1887
HAYES-SADLER,Gerard Ralph Lt kia 3-9-16 2RWar p64 CR France402
HAYES-SHEEN,George Edward Capt ded 19-2-15 6RIrRif CR Ches8
HAYFIELD,Allan Sydney T2Lt dow 6-10-16 7EKent p57 CR France74
HAYHOE,Alfred Charles 2Lt kia 27-7-16 1Beds p86 MR21
HAYHURST,John 2Lt kia 19-4-18 2Ess p131 CR France250,18-4-18
HAYHURST,Thomas Lt drd 13-8-15 RAMC 2/1FA p254 MR4
HAYLETT,Newman T2Lt dow 19-8-16 166RFA p30 CR France197
HAYLEY,Cyril William Seafort Burrell TCapt dow 18-9-15 10HLI p163 CR France98
HAYLOCK,Henry Capt kia 11-5-15 1/4Leic p219 CR Belgium99
HAYLOR,Charles Alexander Lt kia 17-2-17 10Mddx p236 CR France314
HAYMAN,Alfred George.MC.Capt kia 8-9-16 2WelshR A'Coy p126 CR France432
HAYMAN,J.H Lt dow 18-7-17 ASC 29MT att29SB CR Belgium16
HAYMAN,William Deacon T2Lt kia 13-8-17 1/11Hamps p120 CR Belgium10
HAYMAN,William Muir.DSO.TMaj dow 13-7-17 RE 92FC p45 CR France145
HAYMES,George Noel 2Lt mbk 19-8-18 IA 1/89Punjabis att125Rif p277 MR34
HAYNE,Moreton 2Lt ded PoW 10-10-16 LancF &25RFC p3&92 CR France604
HAYNES,Albert TCapt ded 20-7-17 7NStaffs p157 CR Iraq8
HAYNES,Charles Graham.MC&Bar.Lt kia 23-10-18 4KRRC &RAF p265 CR France349,Capt
HAYNES,Charles Henry 2Lt kia 26-3-18 3 att8NStaffs p157 CR France798,Lt
HAYNES,Bernard Hamer 2Lt ded 20-12-17 RFA p261 CR Lancs40
HAYNES,Clifford Skemp T2Lt kia 1-7-16 15DLI p161 MR21
HAYNES,Francis Edmund Lt kld 20-4-18 1/5Suff p217 CR Palestine9
HAYNES,George James T2Lt kia 16-6-18 17 att13Mddx p147 MR20
HAYNES,George John TCapt ded 30-9-17 RASC p193 CR Scot357,LtCol
HAYNES,G.W.N.R.Capt kld 30-5-19 6RMunstF attRAF p254 CR Germany1
HAYNES,James 2Lt kia 29-3-16 11NumbF p61 CR France160
HAYNES,John Eustace Tarleton 2Lt kia 23-3-18 1 att2/8Worc p108 MR27
HAYNES,John Lorenzo Patrick Lt mbk 11-3-18 4LNLancs attRFC p257 CR France1277
HAYNES,Samuel 2Lt dow 4-10-18 4SomLI att58MGC p187&218 CR France146
HAYNES,William Charles 2Lt kia 3-5-17 3 att5 O&BLI p130 MR20
HAYNES,William George 2Lt kia 27-6-17 1/4Suff p217 CR France593
HAYNES,William Gray TLt kia 25-9-15 8RBerks p139 CR France552
HAYNES,William Harold Capt kld 26-9-18 6Yorks &RAF p90
HAYS,Samuel Copping Athanasius Capt ded 19-7-19 RASC p267 CR Lond2
HAYTER,Arthur Cecil Thomas Lt dow 1-11-14 Norf p73 MR29

HAYTER,Eric Francis Seafourth 2Lt kia 21-3-18 RFA 87Bty27Bde p30 CR France435
HAYTHORNTHWAITE,Rycharde Mead 2Lt kia 24-5-15 2EKent p57 MR29
HAYTON,Walter James 2Lt kia 16-9-16 4Yorks p220 MR21
HAYWARD,Bertram Richard 2Lt kia 6-6-15 RFA p30 MR4
HAYWARD,Cecil Bernard TCapt kia 27-7-16 23RFus p68 MR21
HAYWARD,Charles Oswald TLt kia 17-1-16 7Lincs &RFC p3&75 CR Belgium140
HAYWARD,Edward John 2Lt kia 12-11-15 5 att2RFus p68 CR Gallipoli4,Lt
HAYWARD,Edward Ronald 2Lt kia 20-12-16 RFA 99Bty p30 CR Greece9
HAYWARD,Ernest Frank Walton T2Lt kia 5-10-16 11Hamps p120 CR Belgium5,2Bn
HAYWARD,Ernest Harold Lt kia 24-4-17 7Wilts p153 MR37
HAYWARD,Herbert William.MID 2Lt kia 23-7-16 6YLI p143 MR20
HAYWARD,Herbert William T2Lt kia 26-9-16 8 att6Nhampt p137 MR21
HAYWARD,John Stratton T2Lt kia 7-7-16 11Wilts p153 MR21,1Bn
HAYWARD,Kenneth Alfred Capt ded 22-11-18 RH&FA p30
HAYWARD,Marcus Henry Hugh 2Lt dow 26-3-18 3 att7SomLI p80 CR France587
HAYWARD,Milward Cecil Lt ded 23-8-16 RAMC p255 CR Berks1
HAYWARD,Robert Edward T2Lt kia 27-3-18 att1NStaffs p157 MR27
HAYWARD,Walter 2Lt kia 21-3-18 1 att5NStaffs p157 MR27
HAYWARD,William Hugh T2Lt kia 31-8-18 12Manch att52TMB p155 CR France374
HAYWOOD,Charles Oswald TLt kia 18-1-16 7Lincs &RFC p75
HAYWOOD,Ernest.DCM.2Lt kia 27-5-18 5SLancs p230 MR18
HAYWOOD,Philip 2Lt kia 22-11-17 2/6WYorks p218 MR17
HAYWOOD,Sydney TLt kld 26-10-16 ELancs&RFC p3 CR Iraq5
HAYWORTH,Frederick 2Lt kia 12-5-17 7A&SH p243 MR20
HAYWORTH,Harry Asher 2Lt kia 15-4-17 7A&SH p243 CR France1182
HAZARD,Charles Piper 2Lt kia 21-4-16 1KSLI p145 CR Belgium73
HAZARD,Douglas TLt dow 17-10-18 RASC attMddx p193 CR France113
HAZARD,Douglas George Lt kia 23-5-15 3 att2KSLI p145 MR29 CR France453
HAZARD,William Noel T2Lt kia 26-8-18 14WelshR p127 CR France402,27-8-18
HAZEL,Dudley David Fraser Lt dow 25-4-17 6WRid p227 CR Mddx16
HAZELDENE,John Turner Clough 2Lt kld 9-5-15 4RWFus p223 CR France632,HAZLEDENE
HAZELL,Dudley Howard Lt kld 27-9-18 2RLancs attRFC p59&16 CR France924
HAZELL,Frederick Pung T2Lt dow 19-5-18 101LabCps p189 CR France145 Ex 12Nhampt
HAZELTON,Edwin Hills TBrigGen ded 25-7-16 RAVC IndVetCps p198 MR65,24-7-16
HAZZARD,William.MC.T2Lt dow 28-3-18 15WYorks p81 CR France62
HEAD,Albert Everest TLt kia 1-7-16 20NumbF p61 CR France267
HEAD,Arthur.MM.2Lt dow 6-9-18 44RFA p30 CR Fance177
HEAD,Arthur William George T2Lt kia 1-8-17 117MGC Inf p183 CR Belgium126
HEAD,Basil William Lt kia 31-7-17 Herts p252 MR29
HEAD,Bernard Maj kia 12-8-15 5RWFus p223 MR4
HEAD,Edward Keith Lt dow 11-12-16 4Y&L p238 CR Nhampt144
HEAD,Frank William.MID Lt dow 17-10-18 RE p210 CR France375
HEAD,Herbert George 2Lt kia 18-12-15 IARO att117Mahrattas p277 CR Iraq1
HEAD,Henry d'Esterre Lt dow 1-6-15 RDubF p176 CR France285
HEAD,Leslie Dymoke TCapt kia 1-7-16 9YLI p143 CR France267
HEAD,Mark T2Lt kia 28-12-15 8RFC p1 CR France1205
HEAD,Raymond Evelyn.MC.LtACapt ded 24-11-18 3Lpool p72 CR Esex13
HEAD,Reginald Capt kia 28-4-15 BordR p117 CR Gallipoli3
HEADEN,Herbert Harry Lt 6-5-20 3RMunstF CR Egypt9
HEADING,William Henry Chap4Cl ded 21-11-18 RAChDept p199 CR Camb84
HEADINGTON,Arthur Hutton Lt kia 27-11-17 BerksYeo p203 MR34,Capt
HEADLAM,J.2Lt kld 30-5-18 GL &RAF p190
HEADLEY,Herbert Marshall T2Lt kia 11-3-17 RFA att18RFC p8&30 CR France614
HEAGERTY,Richard Browne 2Lt kia 3-5-17 1/2Lond p245 MR20
HEAGERTY,William Thomas TMaj dow 31-1-17 13RSuss p119 CR Belgium11
HEAL,Cecil Ambrose 2Lt dow 3-7-15 3 att1Wilts p153 CR Belgium11
HEAL,Charles Henry 2Lt dow 9-5-15 SWBord p100 CR Gallipoli6
HEAL,Walter George 2Lt ded 23-10-18 RFA p261 CR Hamps7
HEALD,Douglas 2Lt dow 6-10-17 6RB p179 CR Belgium16
HEALD,Geoffrey Yates TCapt kia 1-7-16 15LancF p92 CR France293
HEALD,Thomas Penrose T2Lt kia 13-10-17 GL &6RFC p8 CR Belgium84
HEALD,William Margeson Lt ded 9-9-18 RAMC att16LancF p195 CR France145
HEALE,Arthur George.MC.Lt dow 23-4-18 41/42RFA p30 CR France40
HEALE,Ernest Newton LtCol ded 12-6-16 IA 121Pnrs att14NumbF p277 CR France1

HEALE,George Reginald Charles Capt dow 3-5-17 10WRid p115 MR29
HEALEY,Arthur Wilfred T2Lt kia 1-9-18 att1Wilts p153 CR France560
HEALEY,Philip 2Lt kia 25-9-15 3Manch att1LNLancs p155 MR19
HEALEY,Richard Elkanah Hownam Lt&Adjt kia 22-7-16 1RWKent p141 MR21
HEALING,George William 2Lt kia 4-10-18 22Lond p251 CR France161,3-10-18
HEALING,Kenneth 2Lt kia 27-4-17 6N&D p233 CR France1495
HEALY,Dermott Joseph 2Lt kia 5-8-17 5RMunstF att74TMB p175 MR29
HEALY,Edward Lt kia 7-6-17 6 att8BordR p117 MR29
HEALY,George Ernest HonLt ded 3-3-19 RASC Retd p267 CR Eire63
HEALY,Guy Rambant Lt kia 11-3-16 4RMunstF att3KAR p175&202 CR EAfrica56,3Bn
HEALY,John Frederick Lt kia 1-7-16 3 att9RIrRif p169 CR France383,2-7-16
HEANEY,Paul.DCM.MID 2Lt kia 21-10-14 RLancs p59 MR32
HEAP,Frederick William 2Lt kia 23-4-17 5DLI p239 CR France1487
HEAP,Wilfred Herbert T2Lt kia 25-2-17 RB att12Bn p179 CR France744,Wilfrid
HEAPE,Brian Ruston LtACapt kia 16-5-17 RH&FA 162BdeA/Bty p30 CR France1182
HEAPS,Norman Costine.MID 2Lt ded 10-2-19 5Lpool p270 CR Belgium316,Normand
HEARD,Charles Miller 2Lt kia 10-4-17 1 att8ELancs p110 MR20
HEARD,Francis George Lt ded 15-3-17 RAMC p267
HEARD,Geoffrey Richard TCapt kia 3-7-16 RAMC att10RWar p195 CR France150,2-7-16
HEARD,Robert James Bannatyne Capt dow 5-5-15 1LancF p92 CR Egypt6 4-5-1
HEARD,Robert Rankin 2Lt kia 23-4-17 7BlkW p231 CR France604
HEARD,Robert H.Warren.MC&Bar.Lt ded 3-3-19 IrGds p254 CR Eire114
HEARN,Albert Henry 2Lt kia 1-10-17 1/2 att1/8Leic p87 MR30
HEARN,Edward Thomas Hills 2Lt kia 11-9-17 RFA &57RFC p8&30 CR Belgium140,kld
HEARN,George Harold 2Lt dow PoW 12-5-17 1ESurr p112 CR France924
HEARN,John Stanley T2Lt kia 12-10-16 7Suff p78 MR21
HEARN,Leonard Webb T2Lt kia 18-10-17 6DCLI p114 CR Belgium84
HEARN,Robert Cecil.MC.Capt kia 30-4-18 2/20Lond p251 CR palestine3
HEARNDEN,Harry Crespin Stephens TLt kia 6-8-15 9RWKent att2Hamps p141 MR4
HEARSCH,Edward 2Lt ded 28-6-15 RFA p30 CR Mddx40
HEARSON,Richard Philip TLt kia 23-3-18 1RR ofCav att5Lancers p23 MR27
HEASMAN,George Harry TLt kld 20-1-18 RFC p16 CR Sussex165
HEASTEY,George Rodney 2Lt kia 20-7-16 3RWFus p98 CR France397
HEATH,Alfred Chap4Cl kia 30-6-18 RAChDept att9WRid p199 CR France76
HEATH,Arthur George TLt kia 8-10-15 6RWKent p141 MR19
HEATH,Arthur Morris 2Lt kia 12-4-18 33MGC p183 MR32
HEATH,Edmund Griffith Capt kia 25-9-15 97RFA p30 CR France219
HEATH,Geoffrey Capt kia 10-8-15 1/7Ches p222 MR4
HEATH,Gerard Bower 2Lt dow 22-5-18 2CldGds p51 CR France84
HEATH,Henry Newport Charles.CB.MajGen ded 22-7-15 Staff CmdgSMidDiv p CR Surrey160,29-7-15
HEATH,Henry James Lt kia 17-7-16 16Mddx p147 CR France1500,1-7-16
HEATH,John Lionel 2LtTLt kia 2-10-15 1YLI p143 MR19,1-10-15
HEATH,John Oswald TLt kia 7-10-16 11RWKent p141 MR21
HEATH,Leonard George Capt dow 14-3-16 NottsYeo p205 CR France1,Nhampt att1Lancers IA
HEATH,Maurice Gordon.MID LtCol kia 25-9-15 2RWSurr p56 MR19
HEATH,Percy Macclesfield LtCol ded 14-7-17 IA 110MahrattaLI att105 p277 C Iraq8
HEATH,Percy Voltelin Lt dow 1-9-15 RHGds p20 CR France1419,4-9-14
HEATH,Raymond Leopold Greig Capt kia 25-9-15 2RWSurr p56 MR19
HEATH,Roger Meyrick T2Lt kia 15-9-16 6SomLI p80 MR21
HEATH,Sidney Stuart 2Lt kia 23-4-17 7BordR p117 MR20
HEATH,Walter Rowland TLt kia 23-8-16 O&BLI 1/1BucksBn p231 MR21
HEATH,William Charles T2Lt kia 22-5-18 1/2 att10DCLI p114 CR France502
HEATH,William Hutsby 2Lt kia 1-7-16 1/6NStaffs p238 MR21
HEATH,William Rufus Kennard 2Lt kia 25-2-16 1Glouc p106 CR France551
HEATH-CALDWELL,Martin Frederick 2Lt kia 16-5-15 RHA p30 CR France80
HEATHCOAT-AMORY,Ludovic.MID Capt dow 25-8-18 1DevYeo att32DivHQ p203 CR France119
HEATHCOCK,Ethelbert Agnew Lt dow 29-9-17 1/4DCLI p226 CR Palestine2
HEATHCOCK,Thomas TCapt kia 10-7-16 7EYorks p84 CR France453
HEATHCOTE,James Shirley 2Lt dow 28-8-17 1CldGds p51 CR Lond8
HEATHCOTE,Martin Arthur.MC.TLt dow 10-7-16 10RFus B'Coy p68 CR France833

136

HEATHCOTE,Ralph Noel T2Lt dow 17-11-16 12EYorks p84 CR France203
HEATHCOTE,William Godfrey T2Lt kia 23-11-17 GL &29RFC p8 CR Belgium3
HEATHER,Percy Arthur Lt kia 12-7-17 1Nhampt p137 MR31
HEATHERINGTON,Eric 2Lt kia 4-5-17 2RWar p64 MR20
HEATLEY,Leonard TCapt dow 17-8-17 12Lpool p72 CR Belgium16
HEATLY,Charles Frederick T2Lt dow 17-4-18 16RWFus att38DivSnipingCoy p98 CR France134
HEATLY,Henry Francis Lt kia 22-2-15 2Yorks p90 CR France924
HEATLY,John Firth 2Lt kia 21-3-18 RWKent att7Bn p141 MR27
HEATON,Charles Darrell T2Lt kia 26-8-17 143MGC Inf p183 CR Belgium125
HEATON,Eric Rupert T2Lt kia 1-7-16 14 att16Mddx p147 CR France1500
HEATON,Harold Sinclair T2Lt kia 22-4-18 13 att17RWFus p98 CR France516
HEATON,Herbert Walker Lt kia 5-9-17 7LancF p221 CR Belgium84,Walter
HEATON,Ivon.MID TLtACapt dow 14-10-17 7RWKent p141 CR France13
HEATON,Lionel James 2Lt kia 29-8-18 3 att1RWFus p98 CR France374
HEATON,Norman Child 2Lt kia 3-5-17 1/1Lond p245 MR20
HEATON,Philip Ralph.DCM.TLt ded 4-1-17 1/2KAR p202 CR EAfrica38 &CR Tanzania1
HEATON,Robert Capt kia 25-9-17 5SLancs p230 CR Belgium22
HEATON,Stanley Tomlinson 2Lt kia 27-9-16 6WYorks p218 MR21
HEATON,William 2Lt kia 3-5-17 2/5WRid p227 MR20
HEATON-ELLIS,Charles Edward Robert TLt kia 19-3-16 6YLI p143 CR France420
HEATON-ELLIS,David.MC.Capt kia 27-5-18 2RB p179 MR18
HEAUMANN,Richard Capt kia 8/10-9-16 2Lond p245
HEAVEN,George Frederick Victor TCapt kia 25-1-16 16RWar p64 CR France394
HEAVEN,Norman Edwin 2Lt kia 21-3-18 66MGC p183 MR27
HEAVER,Douglas Cams T2Lt kia 4-8-16 8RFus p68 MR21
HEBBERT,Robert Francis Capt ded 19-3-16 IA 1MS p277 CR Iraq6
HEBBES,Arthur Ernest Lt kia 28-11-17 4Suff attNigR p217 MR40,drd
HEBBLETHWAITE,Abraham Rhodes T2Lt kia 3-10-15 RFA 88Bty p30 CR France727
HEBBLETHWAITE,C.J.Lt 7-4-15 GL &NigR CR WAfrica47
HEBBLETHWAITE,George T2Lt kia 7-7-16 10LancF p92 MR21
HEBBLETHWAITE,John Christopher TLt kia 26-6-16 RFA p30 CR Belgium4 22-6-16
HEBDEN,Alan 2Lt kia 8-5-17 6BlkW p231 MR20
HEBDEN,George Spencer T2Lt kia 22-4-17 2Leic p87 MR38
HEBDEN,Robert Coke TCapt ded 25-2-16 RE 201Coy p45 CR France22
HEBELER,Roland Stuart TCapt dow 16-9-15 7RWSurr C'Coy p56 CR France22
HEBERDEN,Arthur Clements 2Lt kia 10-7-17 5 att2KRRC p150 MR31,6 att2Bn
HEBRON,William T2Lt kia 25-10-18 20DLI p161 MR30
HECKFORD,Percy James 2Lt kia 31-10-16 RGA 114HB p209 CR France393
HECKROODT,Benjamin TMaj ded 6-10-18 6RSuss p228 CR Iraq8
HECHT,Marcus Francis TMaj kia 3-9-16 17KRRC p150 CR France220
HEDDERWICK,Charles Stuart 2Lt kia 28-2-15 2RScots B'Coy p54 CR Belgium104
HEDDERWICK,Guy 2Lt kia 22-9-16 1RRofCav &RFC p3&23 CR France306,Lt
HEDDERWICK,James Alexander Lt ded 6-11-18 RGA 56A/ACoy p40 CR Mddx26
HEDDING,James Lawrence 2Lt dow 28-3-16 3Dors att1Mddx p124 CR France80,Lt
HEDGCOCK,Frederick Leslie T2Lt kia 30-9-18 D57MGC Inf p183 CR France256,29-9-18
HEDGES,Charles Cuthbert.MC.Lt kia 8-10-18 4Berks p234 CR France338
HEDGES,William Herbert.MC.Capt ded 21-8-16 RE 1FC p210 CR France120,dow 22-8-16
HEDGES,William Robert.MC.2Lt kia 18-9-18 2TankCps p188 MR16
HEDGLAND,Charles Samuel.MID TLt kia 17-4-18 33MGC Inf p183 CR Belgium167
HEDLEY,Gerald Montague.MID TCapt ded 4-10-18 RE 29Coy p45 CR France146
HEDLEY,James Frederic TLt ded 13-1-16 RASC p193 CR Wilts142
HEDLEY,John Hunt 2Lt kia 8-3-18 5 att4Mddx p147 CR Belgium112,4 att8Bn
HEDLEY,John Ralph.DSO.LtCol ded 15-7-17 6 Cmdg5NumbF p213 CR France214
HEDLEY,Joseph Walton Capt dow 13-9-16 2/5LancF p221 CR France833,12-9-16
HEDLEY,William Alexander Cosgrave.MID TLt dow 19-7-18 8 att1EKent p57 CR Belgium40
HEDLEY,William James TLtACapt kia 7-6-17 11RWSurr p56 CR Belgium29
HEDWORTH,Thomas Hedworth 2Lt drd 10-10-18 1Worc p108 MR40
HEENAN,Michael Cornelius Capt kia 12-1-16 Leinst att2Wilts p174 CR France513
HEENAN,Thomas George Graudon 2Lt kia 21-3-18 4RDubF p176 MR27
HEFFERMAN,William T2Lt kld 25-10-17 GL &RFC p8 CR France790
HEFFERNAN,Francis Joseph Christopher LtCol ded 16-7-17 RAMC p196 CR Iraq5
HEFFERNAN,William Patrick 2Lt kia 9-5-15 3RIrRegatt1Glouc p89 MR22
HEGARTY,Andrew TLt kia 16-12-15 RAMC &RFA p196 CR Belgium58

HEGARTY,Edward 5432.MC.ACapt kia 3-9-16 3 att2RIrReg p89 CR France402
HEGGIE,David Rev ded 23-10-17 RAChDept att2/7RScots p199 CR Eire322
HEGGIE,David Alexander 2Lt kia 3-8-15 9 att1RScotF p94 CR Belgium82
HEGGS,Frederick William 2Lt kia 21-8-16 2Y&L p159 CR France156
HEIGHAM-PLUMPTRE,L.G.2Lt dow 4-6-18 1Beds &RAF p16&86 CR France1564
HEINEMANN,John Walter TCapt dow 6-3-16 20RFus p68 CR France114
HEINING,Wilfred Hardinge Capt kia 6-4-16 IA 54Sikhs att51 p277 MR38,HEINIG
HELBY,John Alfred Hasler 2Lt dow 3-8-16 2RDubF p176 CR Belgium11
HELDMAN,Harry Randolph TLt kia 27-9-15 9RSuss p119 MR19
HELE-SHAW,Henry Rathbone Lt kia 19-7-16 GL &RFC p3&190 CR France366
HELLARD,John Alexander 2Lt kia 2-7-16 3 att1SomLI p80 CR France1890
HELLIAR,Leonard Jeffrey 2Lt kia 14-5-17 236RFA p208 CR Belgium11
HELLICAR,Geoffrey Theodore 2Lt kia 27-7-16 2/20Lond p251 CR France68,26-7-16
HELLIER,Fred ACapt kia 12-10-16 3 att14DLI p161 MR21
HELLIER,Leonard Gordon T2Lt dow 16-12-17 3 att11BordR p117 CR Belgium18
HELLMERS,Alfred 2Lt dow 11-5-15 1RIrRif p169 CR France345
HELLYER,George Edgcombe TCapt dow 22-8-15 10Hamps p120 MR4
HELLYER,Sidney Hannaford 2Lt dow 8-5-15 4EYorks p219 CR Devon47
HELM,Frank Lt kia 4-6-15 8Manch p237 MR4
HELM,Henry Paul Dundas.MID Capt ded 6-11-18 2BordR &RAF p117 CR C'land&W'land17
HELME,Guy Masterman Lt dow 30-10-17 1CldGds p51 CR France40
HELME,Harold Lutwyche Capt kia 18-9-14 1LNLancs p136 MR15,14-9-14
HELME,Richard 2Lt kia 25-9-15 1LNLancs p136 MR19
HELME,Robert Barnard Lt kia 25-6-17 1Drags p21 CR France363
HELME,Thomas Herbert Capt dow 3-11-18 16Lond p249 CR Surrey88
HELMORE,Ernest Creswell 2Lt dow 1-1-17 1 att15N&D p134 CR France1182
HELMORE,Stanley Thomas John 2Lt kld 14-5-18 23RFus &18RAF p68 CR France21,kia
HELMS,Percy T2Lt dow 5-10-18 9Yorks p90 CR France194
HELSDON,Harold Leofric 2Lt kia 26-11-16 3Dors att1/7RWar p124 MR21
HELYAR,Maurice Howard Capt kia 24-1-15 RB p179 CR France285
HEMANS,George Willoughby Maj kia 4-3-17 IA 29Lancers p277 CR France430
HEMELRYK,Eugene John Vincent 2Lt kia 23-4-17 2LancF p92 CR France412
HEMING,Charles Leonard Parlett Lt dow 12-2-17 2Leinst p174 CR Kent177,ded
HEMING,Maurice Ivory T2Lt kia 1-7-16 2RBerks p139 MR21
HEMINGWAY,Horace Vincent T2Lt dow 2-10-18 36MGC p183 CR Belgium38
HEMINGWAY,James 2Lt kia 9-5-15 3 att1SforthH p164 CR France721
HEMINGWAY,Kenneth Stanley LtACapt kia 21-3-18 Worc att10Bn p108 MR20
HEMINGWAY,Maurice William,MC Lt mbk 27-5-18 33RFA p256 MR18
HEMINGWAY,Ralph Eustace 2Lt kia 15-10-15 8N&D p233 MR19
HEMINGWAY,Stewart TLt dow 6-4-16 4SWBord p100 MR38 ExSthIrHorse
HEMMANT,Maurice TLt kia 14-8-17 5 att11RB p179 MR29
HEMMERDE,Charles Eric.MC.Lt kia 27-9-18 6RWKent p141 CR France415
HEMMING,Francis William Capt kia 24-4-17 1/8Worc p226 CR France1495
HEMMING,Frank James.MC.Lt kia 13-4-18 5 att2Worc p108 MR32
HEMMING,Jesse Clifford 2Lt kia 27-8-17 8Worc p226 MR30
HEMMING,William Norman T2Lt ded 15-11-17 GL &65RFC p8 CR France285,dow
HEMPHILL,Richard Patrick T2Lt ded 24-3-17 6Leinst attaRFC p8&174 CR Egypt9,Capt acckld
HEMPSON,Claude Dawson.DSO.TCapt kia 8-3-17 10Suff att6RLancs p78 CR Iraq8
HEMSLEY,Ernest James.MC.T2Lt kia 4/5-9-18 12RSuss att10RWSurr p119 CR Belgium185,4-9-18
HEMSLEY,Godfrey Hamilton 2Lt kia 12-10-17 C255RFA p30 CR Belgium10
HEMSLEY,James Mortimer 2Lt ded 28-7-17 RFA attDerajatMtnBty p30 CR Africa38 &CR Tanzania1
HEMSTEAD,John 2Lt kia 16-4-17 106RFA p30 MR20,HEMSTED
HEMSWORTH,Augustus Hethersett 2Lt ded 6-6-15 YLI p265 CR Norf288
HEMUS,Cyril Harcourt.MC.2Lt dow 27-3-18 B87RFA p30 CR France62,28-3-18
HEMUS,Donald George TLt kia 22-3-18 3Worc p108 MR20
HENDERSHOT,Charles Cecil T2Lt kld 6-2-18 RFC p16 CR Canada1114
HENDERSON,Albert N.Maj kia 23-7-16 10RWar p64 MR21
HENDERSON,Alec Stewart Capt dow 25-4-15 1Lond A'Coy p245 CR France254
HENDERSON,Alexander Rennie Lt kia 25-9-15 4GordH p241 MR29
HENDERSON,Alfred Roche T2Lt kia 28-4-17 Mddx att17Bn p147 MR20
HENDERSON,Andrew Hubert Millin 2Lt kia 12-7-15 4KOSB p224 MR4
HENDERSON,Andrew William TCapt kia 1-7-16 1RB p179 MR21
HENDERSON,Angus 2Lt kia 3-5-17 1RScotF p94 MR20
HENDERSON,Archibald Wright T2Lt kia 30-12-17 223MGC p183 MR21

HENDERSON,Arthur Lt kia 4-8-16 9HLI p240 CR Egypt2 ACycCps 52Div
HENDERSON,Arthur.VC.MC.2LtACapt kia 24-4-17 4A&SH p173 CR France591
HENDERSON,Arthur Francis Maj kia 12-9-14 IA 27LCav Staff p277 MR28
HENDERSON,Arthur Gordon Lt kia 18-5-19 IA 1/9GurkhaRif p277 MR43
HENDERSON,Arthur Percy 2Lt dow 19-6-17 RGA 49SB p40 CR France40,18-6-17
HENDERSON,Benjamin Hall Blyth 2Lt dow 18-6-18 5CamH p168 CR France134
HENDERSON,Bertram Mackay.MC.MID LtACapt dow 7-4-18 PoW GordH att7Bn p166 CR Germany3
HENDERSON,Cecil Ivanhoe T2Lt kia 26-11-17 1 att13ESurr p112 CR France481
HENDERSON,Charles Edward Piercy.MC.Capt kia 17-11-16 B71RFA p30 CR France453
HENDERSON,David Capt kia 15-9-16 8Mddx att19Lond p236 CR France390
HENDERSON,David.KCB.KCVO.DSO.Sir LtGen 17-8-21 A&SH CR Scot520
HENDERSON,Donald 2Lt kia 11-1-15 6 att1KRRC p150 CR France727
HENDERSON,Duncan Frank Capt kia 8/9-8-16 1InniskF p105 CR Belgium47,9-8-16
HENDERSON,Edward Elers Delaval.VC.Lt kia 25-1-17 NStaffs att7Bn p157 CR Iraq5,Delavel Cmdg9War
HENDERSON,Edward Francis Lt kia 27-3-18 4 att6EKent p212 CR France233
HENDERSON,Elmes Pollock Capt&Adjt kia 25-6-16 IA 106Pnrs p277 MR43,29-6-16
HENDERSON,Eric 2Lt kia 7-6-17 8Lond p247 MR29
HENDERSON,Eric Joseph.MC.2LtTCapt kia 25-3-17 70RFC SR p8 CR France518
HENDERSON,Eric Lockhart Hume Capt dow 21-5-15 RMunstF p175 CR Egypt3,20-5-15
HENDERSON,Everard Francis Scott Maj kia 6-7-16 2Leic p87 MR38
HENDERSON,G.A.F.Lt ded 4-7-18 GordH attRAF p166
HENDERSON,Geo.Ballingham 2Lt ded 31-10-18 63MGC p266 CR Scot127
HENDERSON,George Gartly T2Lt kia 6-8-16 17HLI p163 CR France114
HENDERSON,George Stuart.VC.DSO&Bar.MC.MIDx5 Capt 24-7-20 2Manch MR38
HENDERSON,George York.MC.Lt kia 22-11-17 RIrRif att10Bn p169 MR17
HENDERSON,Graeme Von Hope Lt kia 16-6-17 2/2Lond p245 MR20,Bonhote
HENDERSON,Harold Winfred Lt ded 13-11-18 3 att24Manch p155 CR Italy7
HENDERSON,Henry May MajALtCol kia 10-3-17 RE 18Div p45 CR France251
HENDERSON,Ian Henry David.MC.Capt ded 21-6-18 A&SH attRAF p173 CR Scot520
HENDERSON,J.SurgGen 12-4-19 IMS CR Kent83
HENDERSON,J.Capt 22-11-20 IOD MR65
HENDERSON,Jacob Johnson Lt dow 17-10-18 15SuffYeo p205 CR France769,16-10-18
HENDERSON,James LtTCapt ded 16-7-17 RAMC p196 CR Canada1691
HENDERSON,James.MC.AMaj kia 11-4-18 4GordH p241
HENDERSON,James Angus Smith Lt kia 25-3-18 7 att1/8A&SH p243 MR27
HENDERSON,James Francis Lt kia 27-3-18 4EKent p212
HENDERSON,James Fuller TLtACapt kia 26-4-18 7RWSurr p56 CR France489
HENDERSON,James Graeme T2Lt kia 3-12-17 1 att1/5RLancs p59 CR France658
HENDERSON,James Greig Mitchell.MC.MID 2Lt kia 18-8-16 4RB p179 CR France402,3Bn
HENDERSON,James Hugh T2Lt kia 7-11-15 11 att8WRid p115 CR Gallipoli27,2-11-15
HENDERSON,James Macdonald.MC&Bar.Maj kia 11-4-18 4GordH att7A&SH MR19
HENDERSON,James Norman Maj kia 28-6-15 1/4RScots p211 CR Gallipoli6
HENDERSON,James Percy T2Lt kia 11-9-17 21NumbF p61 MR21
HENDERSON,James Richard 2Lt ded 29-11-14 2/4BlkW p128&270 CR Scot386,28-11-14
HENDERSON,James Sowers 2Lt kia 22-3-18 RGA 33SB p40 CR France439
HENDERSON,John Easton TLt ded PoW 26-4-18 14NumbF p61 CR France716
HENDERSON,John Thomas Capt kia 15-9-16 4NumbF p213 CR France239
HENDERSON,Kenneth Selby Capt kia 2-6-18 SL &1RAF p268 MR20
HENDERSON,Michael William MajTLtCol kia 27-9-15 9BlkW p128 CR France219
HENDERSON,Neil Emslie Nelson 2Lt kia 11-4-18 1KOSB p101 MR32
HENDERSON,Noel Charles 2Lt kia 25-9-15 2BlkW D'Coy p128 CR France347,9-10-15
HENDERSON,Norman William Arthur Lt kia 10-11-14 RScotF p94 MR29
HENDERSON,Patric Gordon T2Lt dow 2-5-18 2WRid p115 MR19
HENDERSON,Raymond Montgomerie Hume Lt kia 20-9-14 2ConnRgrs p172 MR15
HENDERSON,Robert 2Lt dow 16-4-17 4GordH p242 CR France95
HENDERSON,Robert Francis Watt Lt dow 15-10-18 1/6RScots p211 CR France40,Capt
HENDERSON,Robert Morley Chap4Cl ded 3-2-19 RAChDept p199 CR Belgium265

HENDERSON,Robert Stanley Lt kia 13-10-18 1/6GordH p242 CR France271,Stanislaus Robert
HENDERSON,Thomas T2Lt kia 6-8-17 8RIrRif p169 MR29
HENDERSON,Thomas 2Lt kia 23-11-17 'B'TankCps p188 MR17
HENDERSON,Thomas Adam.MID 2Lt kia 25/27-9-15 6GordH p242 MR19
HENDERSON,Thomas Eric 2Lt kia 3-8-16 1SStaffs p122 CR France402,31-8-16
HENDERSON,Thomas Harvey.MC.TCapt kia 30-11-17 6 att10RB p179 MR17
HENDERSON,Walter 2Lt kia 8-3-19 9HLI att13RFus p240 CR Belgium112
HENDERSON,Walter TLt ded 29-10-18 RE attGHQ p45 CR France457 Ex 9RScot
HENDERSON,William 2Lt kia 21-3-18 1 att2DLI p161 MR20
HENDERSON,William 2Lt kia 9-4-18 14HLI p163 MR32
HENDERSON,William Alexander Capt kia 10-11-14 D/2A&SH p173 MR32
HENDERSON,William Douglas 2Lt kia 18-11-16 8NStaffs p157 CR France384
HENDERSON,William Fraser 2Lt kia 8-8-16 17Mddx p147 MR21
HENDERSON,William George 2Lt kia 23-4-17 4GordH p242 MR20
HENDERSON,William James.MC.MID TCapt kia 6-7-16 9LNLancs p136 MR21
HENDERSON,William James 2Lt kia 3-5-17 4 att12RScots p211 MR20
HENDERSON,William Lewis.MID TCapt dow 3-5-16 10WYorks C'Coy p81 CR France40
HENDERSON-BEGG,John Henderson Capt kia 23-7-16 4GordH p241 MR21
HENDERSON-HAMILTON,Charles Campbell TCapt kia 21-8-15 12ScotRif att1KOSB p103 MR4
HENDERSON-HAMILTON,James Campbell TLt kia 27-9-15 9BlkW p128 CR France219
HENDIN,Harold Percival Lt kia 28-4-17 10Lincs p75 MR20
HENDRIKS,Augustus Mark Capt kia 25-5-15 RFus att1WYorks p68 MR32
HENDRY,Alistair 2857.MID Lt kia 27-9-17 189RFA p207 MR30
HENDRY,Archibald Thomas 2Lt ded 23-10-16 3CamH p168 CR Scot501,Thomson
HENDRY,Charles Arthur 2Lt kia 27-3-18 9RFus p68 MR27
HENDRY,Hector Victor Baird 2Lt ded 6-10-16 7BlkW p270 CR Scot136
HENDRY,James.MC.TCapt dow 6-9-16 16RScots p54 CR France145
HENDRY,John B.Maj ded 28-8-19 RASC p267 CR Scot754
HENDRY,John Taylor ACapt ded 16-6-19 4RLancs p213 CR France65,2/5Bn
HENDRY,William T2Lt kia 27-7-16 17Mddx p147 MR21
HENDRY,William 2Lt kia 5-3-17 19Lond p250 CR Belgium56
HENEKER,Frederick Christian Maj kia 1-7-16 Leinst att20NumbF p174 CR France393,Cmdg21NumbF
HENERY,Hewett Walter Lewis Lt kia 19-4-17 5KOSB p24 CR Palestine8
HENLEY,Anthony Warton 2Lt dow 21-1-17 C156RFA p30 CR France40
HENLEY,Frederick T2Lt kia 27-10-16 20RFus p68 MR21
HENLEY,Frederick Louis T2Lt kia 1-10-16 13 att11N&D p134 MR21
HENLEY,Henry Thomas T2Lt kia 8-3-17 7RIrRif p169 CR Belgium17
HENMAN,Herbert Cecil 2Lt dow 25-9-17 RGA att18CpsHQ 3SB p40 CR Belgium16
HENMAN,Richard Mox.MC.LtAMaj ded 3-11-18 RFA p30 CR Berks85
HENMAN,Sydney TLt kia 10-8-17 RE 86FC p45 CR Belgium23
HENN,Edward Henry Lovett T2Lt kia 25-9-15 9RB p179 MR29
HENNA,John Ramsey 2Lt kia 9-9-16 3 att6RIrReg p89 MR21
HENNELL,Arthur T2Lt kia 3-1-18 14Worc p108 CR France668
HENNELL,Robert Alexander 2Lt kia 28-8-18 4 att1/7A&SH p173 MR16
HENNEY,Herbert Norman 2Lt kia 25-4-17 17RFA p30 CR France1182
HENNINGSEN,Cecil Eric 2Lt kia 30-11-17 ShropYeo p205 CR Palestine3,Lt
HENRI,Frank TCapt kia 15-6-18 11NumbF p61 CR Italy3
HENRIQUES,Philip Brydges GutterIz T2Lt dow 24-7-15 8KRRC p150 CR Belgium11
HENRIQUES,Ronald Lucas Quiand Lt kia 14-9-14 2 att1RWSurr p56 CR France1329,Quixano
HENRY,Arthur Richard T2Lt kia 23-4-17 5 att1Mddx p147 CR France434
HENRY,Charles Lennox 2Lt kia 16-8-17 3 att7RIrF p171 MR30
HENRY,Charlotte E.SNurse drd 26-2-18 QAIMNS p200 MR40
HENRY,Claude Lt kia 19-9-14 3Worc p108 CR France1107
HENRY,Cyril Charles Lt kia 26-9-15 Worc att2nd p108 MR19
HENRY,Dermot Jepson T2Lt kia 9-7-17 5 att1RIrF p171 CR France546
HENRY,Douglas John Luther Martin 2Lt dow 25-9-17 4GordH p242 CR Belgium1
HENRY,George Cecil 2Lt dow 9-12-17 3Suff p78 CR Palestine3
HENRY,John Lt kia 13-4-18 9ACycCps p244 CR France324
HENRY,John Allan.MC.TCapt kia 14-7-17 11RScots p54 MR21
HENRY,Norman.MC.TCapt kia 8-5-18 17Lpool p72 MR30
HENRY,Walter T2LtACapt kia 8-10-16 RFA attW40TMB p30 MR20
HENRY,William Ernest Lt kia 1-5-16 1RIrF p171 CR France283
HENSHALL,Charles TCapt kia 8-7-16 18Manch p155 CR France630

HENSHALL,Donald Edward 2Lt dow 14-9-16 D238RFA p208 CR France177
HENSHILL-WOOD,Alexander Russell Lt dow 27-9-16 9Lpool p216
HENSHAW,A.H.SubCdr 11-4-21 S&T Cps MR43
HENSHAW,Isabel Sister ded 11-8-19 RAMC CR Canada116
HENSLEY,Wilfrid Henry Capt kia 21-3-18 6SomLI p80 MR27
HENSMAN,Henry John.MC.2Lt kia 18-9-18 1Herts p252 MR16
HENSON,Albert Cecil Maj kia 22-8-15 4Nhampt p234 MR4
HENSON,Stanley Benskin 2Lt kia 19-12-14 1SomLI p80 CR Belgium70
HENSTOCK,Arthur Frank Newman.MC.Capt kia 22-3-18 15N&D p134 MR27
HENSTOCK,Kenneth Parnell Lt kia 23-8-14 4Mddx p147 CR Belgium242
HENTY,Arthur Frank TCapt kia 4-3-16 11Mddx p147 MR19
HENTY,George Herbert Maj kia 30-11-17 7Suff p78 MR17
HENWOOD,John Edwin T2Lt dow 1-7-16 9RWSurr p56 CR Egypt9,acckld
HEPBURN,Andrew Munro 2Lt kia 3-9-16 6 att11RB p179 MR21
HEPBURN,Archibald James Capt kia 29-5-15 8Manch p237 CR Gallipoli2
HEPBURN,Arthur Jacobs 2Lt kia 30-3-18 RGA 173SB p40 France156
HEPBURN,David Laughton Inkster 2Lt kia 25-4-18 6WYorks p218 MR30
HEPBURN,George TLt kia 22-3-18 RE 98FC p45 CR France511
HEPBURN,Malcolm Arnold 2Lt kia 30-11-14 2SfthH p164 CR France339
HEPBURN,Reginald Lt ded 14-6-19 38RFA p30 MR43
HEPBURN,Reginald Victor 2Lt kia 16-9-18 GL &RAF CR France365
HEPBURN,Roger Paul.MC.T2Lt dow 3-8-17 RE 30DivSigCo att21InfBde p45 CR Belgium11
HEPBURN,William Duncan Capt kia 28-4-15 SfthH att5RScots p164 MR4
HEPBURN-STUART-FORBES-TREFUSIS,John Frederick.DSO.Hon.BrigGen dow 24-10-15 IrGds20InfBde p52 CR France279
HEPBURNE-SCOTT,Alexander Noel 2Lt kia 16-5-15 2ScotsGds p52 MR22
HEPNER,Herman 2Lt kia 8-5-17 4 att11ScotRif p103 MR37
HEPPELL,Harry Denby 2Lt kia 5-4-17 4Berks p234 CR France1495
HEPPELL,Thomas Reginald Capt kia 15-9-16 21Lond p251 CR France385
HEPPENSTALL,George Percival 2Lt kia 24-4-18 1Glouc att2Mddx p106 MR27 &CR France390
HEPPLE,Francis James TLt kia 28-4-17 11NStaffs att5MGC p157&183 MR20
HEPPLE,John TMaj drd 30-12-16 RAMC YorksFA p255 CR Yorks591
HEPTON,Arthur Lt dow PoW 13-4-18 5Yorks p220 CR France328
HEPTON,William TLt ded 9-11-18 4RRofCav att5DragGds p23 CR France1278
HEPWORTH,Arthur Montagu.MC.Lt dow 4-5-18 4RWSurr &RAF p212&258 CR Palestine9
HEPWORTH,Frederick Joseph 2Lt kia 20-5-17 3RMunstF attRInniskF p175 CR France155,19-5-17
HEPWORTH,George Percy Capt dow 27-10-18 RFA 4TrnDepot p207 MR65
HEPWORTH,Henry James Jephson 2Lt kia 16-8-17 12Lpool p72 MR30
HEPWORTH,Laurence Frederic Capt ded PoW 9-3-17 2Suff p78 CR Germany3
HEPWORTH,W.J.H.Capt 11-6-18 RAMC CR Durham62
HERALD,James Herbert Crossland Lt dow 24-1-15 8DLI p239 CR Belgium4,24-1-16
HERALD,Thomas T2Lt kld 20-10-17 GL &RFC p8 CR Wilts28
HERAPATH,Alfred Maltravers 2Lt kia 1-7-16 8Y&L attMGC p159 CR France156
HERAPATH,Norman Finnis 2Lt kia 11-4-17 1SomLI p80 MR20
HERAPATH,Randolph Fitz Roy Boehm LtACapt kia 3-7-16 1Lincs p75 CR France267
HERBERT,Alfred James Anthony 2Lt dow 17-9-17 ACycCps 2LdnDiv p244 CR Belgium16
HERBERT,Allan Douglas 2Lt dow 29-9-15 4Mddx p147 CR Belgium11
HERBERT,Charles Stanley.MC.Capt kia 27-5-18 15DLI p161 CR France1331
HERBERT,Cyril Joseph T2Lt kia 13-3-18 7Leinst p174 CR France365,23-3-18
HERBERT,Edmund Widdington T2Lt kia 16-10-18 1 KSLI att1/4Ches p145 CR Belgium112
HERBERT,Edward Grafton.MC.2LtACapt kia 9-4-18 10War attMGC p65&183 CR France1092,10-4-18
HERBERT,Elidye John Bernard.Hon.Capt kia 12-11-17 GloucYeo att 19MGC p187&203, Elidyr CR Palestine8
HERBERT,Harry Bentley 2Lt kia 22-5-15 IARO att1/1GurkhaRif p277 MR28
HERBERT,Hubert Leslie TLt kia 7-8-15 8GordH p166 CR France727,Hugh
HERBERT,John William Lt ded 2-7-18 5RSuss p228
HERBERT,Johnstone Erskine Galway Lt kia 23-4-17 5Yorks p220 MR20
HERBERT,Malcolm Cavagnari Norton Lt dow 2-1-15 1Glouc p106 CR France202
HERBERT,Owen William Eugene 2Lt kiaAbout 27-10-14 23RFA p30 MR22
HERBERT,Reginald Strickson Lt kia 21-5-17 2/11Lond p248 MR20
HERBERT,Robert Bingley Capt kia 30-9-15 RE p210 CR France149
HERBERT,Ronald Crouch T2Lt kia 1-7-16 7RWSurr p56 CR France397
HERBERT,Ronald Young.MID Lt kia 23-9-17 RFA p207 CR Belgium21
HERBERT,Thomas William Percy TLtACapt kia 1-8-17 9WelshR p127 CR Belgium111
HERBERT,William Alfred 2Lt kia 1-10-16 9DCLI att8YLI p114 MR21
HERBERT-SMITH,Vere 2Lt kia 22-3-15 5RB p179 CR France681,3Bn
HERBERT-STEPNEY,Herbert Arthur Maj kia 7-11-14 1IrGds p52 MR29
HERBERTSON,Andrew Hunter Lt kia 16-5-17 KRRC att7Bn Res p150 MR20
HERBERTSON,John.TD.Maj kia 12-7-15 4KOSB p223 MR4
HERBERTSON,William Gray T2Lt kia 25-9-15 8KOSB p101 MR19
HERBISON,Charles William TCapt dow 17-9-16 1Leic p87 CR France23
HERD,Horace Falkland Capt kia 27-12-14 WelchR p127 CR France260
HERD,James Semple T2Lt kia 16-10-17 52MGC p183 CR Belgium83
HERD,John 2Lt dow 23-9-17 1/4GordH p242 CR Belgium18
HERD,Oswald Alexander TCapt kia 24-9-16 14DLI p161 CR France374
HERDMAN,Arthur Widdrington Lt kia 25-10-14 1KSLI p145 MR32
HERDMAN,George Andrew T2Lt kia 1-7-16 18Lpool p72 MR21
HERDMAN,James Lt dow 9-5-17 5RScots att4NumbF p211 CR France40
HERDMAN,Thomas Anderson Lt kia 21-9-18 7RScots p211 CR France1496
HERINGTON,Percy Godfrey T2Lt kia 15-2-17 8RWFus p98 CR Iraq5
HERIOT,George Edward 2Lt ded 11-12-15 3Co ofLondYeo p204 CR Egypt9,13-12-15
HERISTON,Frank TLt kia 5-7-16 9Yorks p90 MR21
HERITAGE,Audrey Nurse ded 31-10-18 VAD CR Sussex178
HERITAGE,H.A.2Lt ded 28-6-18 14Lond &RAF p249
HERIZ-SMITH,Ambrose Joseph Cocks Lt kia 8-3-16 6Dev p217 MR38
HERIZ-SMITH,Denzil Mitford Heriz T2Lt dow 17-2-17 6Nhampt A'Coy p137 CR France314
HERMAN,George Alfred Lt kia 20-7-16 1Camb p244 MR21
HERMAN,Robert Douglas 2Lt ded PoW 22-9-16 2/5SLancs attRFC p18&230 CR France368,dow
HERMGES,Arthur Cyril Gustave T2Lt dow 19-5-17 5RInniskF p105 MR20
HERMON,Edward William.DSO.TLtCol kia 9-4-17 KEdwHorse &24NhamptF p24 CR France184,Cmdg24NumbF
HERMON-HODGE,George Guy Capt dow 7-7-16 RHA att165RFA p30 CR France169
HERMON-HODGE,John Percivald 2Lt kia 28-5-15 1/4 O&BLI p231 CR Belgium71
HERN,William Stanley TMaj kia 10-8-15 3Wilts p153 MR4
HERNE,David Joseph 2Lt kia 27-5-18 RGA 116SB p40
HERON,Ernest Stewart Lt kia 28-3-18 1/5Ches p222 CR France184
HERON,James T2Lt kia 28-3-18 2LancF p92 MR20
HERON,Jon Maxwell Maj kia 26-3-17 1/5Ess p232 CR Palestine
HERRICK,Harry Eustace Capt kia 11-5-17 RIrR p171 CR France546
HERRICK,John Riversdale Warren Capt dow 4-10-20 IA 3/2GurkhaRif att1/11 p277 CR Iraq6,24-10-20
HERRIES,Fred T2Lt dow 19-12-17 3BordR att10DLI p161 CR Belgium3
HERRING,Horner Reginald Capt kia 23-4-17 5DLI p238 MR20,Homer
HERRINGHAM,Geoffrey Wilmot Capt kia 31-10-14 6Drags att5DragGds p22 MR29
HERRIOTT,John.MC.T2Lt ded 17-2-19 41MGC p183&257 CR France40,Lt
HERRISON,Roger Orme LtCol ded 18-9-17 6RRofCav att4AustFABde p23
HERRON,Alec Rowan 2Lt kia 10-3-17 6 att1KRRC p150 MR22
HERRON,Cyril Douglas 2Lt kia 13-5-15 2DragGds p21 CR Belgium45
HERRON,Kenneth Chester Lt kia 24-4-18 EssYeo &RAF p203&258
HERRON,Reginald Maurice T2Lt dow 12-6-17 13RSuss p119 CR Belgium11
HERRON,Walter Fitzroy.MID TLt ded 3-4-16 4DragGds p21 CR France40,kldacc
HERSCHELL,Ernest Capt dow 26-9-16 6Lpool p215 CR France833
HERSEE,Charles Patrick Allen T2Lt kia 3-3-16 9RFus p68 MR19,2-3-16
HERTSLET,Harold Cecil 2Lt kia 1-7-16 6 att16Mddx p147 CR France35
HERTSLET,Warren Eccles Lt kia 15-8-15 10Lond p248 CR Gallipoli5
HERVEY,Douglas Frederick Lt dow 17-5-17 1/5Norf p216 CR Egypt9
HERVEY,Gerald Arthur Lt kia 8-8-17 1/1RGA p209 CR Belgium19
HERVEY,Thomas Percy Arthur T2Lt kia 15/17-9-16 21KRRC p150 CR France374,15-9-16
HESELTINE,William Wasney Lt dow 20-10-18 RGA 284SB p40 CR France146
HESELTON,George Robert TLt kia 2-6-17 13DLI p161 CR Belgium127
HESELWOOD,George Robert Fettes Lt ded 15-4-15 ArmyPayDept p200 CR Kent61
HESKETH,James Ernest Bytheway T2Lt kia 22-4-17 GL &11RFC p8 MR20
HESKETH,John.MIDx2 T2Lt kia 14-10-18 WYorks att1/6Bn p81 CR France761,dow
HESKETH,Thomas Humphrey Lt ded 28-1-19 1RRofCav p261 CR Scot674,21Lancers
HESKETH,William T2Lt dow 9-6-17 10Ches p96 CR France285
HESKETH,William Cecil TLt kia 9-10-16 149RFA p30 CR France744
HESKETT,John 2Lt kia 15-4-18 3 att2WRid p115 CR France98

HESLOP,Fred T2Lt kia 26-4-18 1WYorks p81 CR Belgium101
HESLOP,George Henry TCapt kia 1-7-16 16Mddx p147 CR France1500
HESLOP,Harold Linton Capt ded 30-10-17 RAMC att7DLI p270 CR Belgium38
HESLOP,William T2Lt kia 5-11-16 16DLI att64TMB p161 CR France114
HESLOP,Walter Lt ded 5-4-18 8SWBord p100 CR Durham88
HESS,Arthur Frank Maj dow 14-7-16 8WYorks p219 CR Yorks361
HESS,Augustus George 2Lt dow 25-2-15 RFA N'Bty p30 CR Belgium165
HESS,Henry.MID 2Lt&Adjt dow 28-10-16 5 att2Mddx p147 CR France105
HESS,Ivan Henry 2Lt kia 15-11-16 3EKent p57 CR France314,16-11-16
HESSELTINE,William T2Lt kia 21-8-16 9RB p179 CR France402
HESSLER,Jacob Andrew Norman Capt kia 27-5-18 5DLI p238 MR18
HESSLER,Jacob Kruse Müller.MID Capt kia 23-3-18 5DLI p238 MR27
HESTER,Edgar Hazel Capt&Adjt kia 16-8-17 2 att7RInniskF p105 CR Belgium167
HETHERINGTON,Arthur TLt kia 22-3-18 9YLI p143 MR27
HETHERINGTON,Guy Capt kia 27-3-17 7Ess p232 MR34
HETHERINGTON,John TLt ded 24-11-18 MGC Inf p183 CR Lincs69
HETHERINGTON,Stephen Owen T2Lt kia 29-9-16 11LancF p92 CR France383
HETHERINGTON,Thomas Alexander 2Lt kia 1-11-18 8RWar p215 CR France1079
HETHERINGTON,Thomas William TLt kia 17-7-16 12DLI p161 MR21
HETT,Roland Thorsten TLt dow 26-10-16 RASC att2Lincsp193 MR21
HETTERLEY,H.C.SNurse 30-5-17 QAIMNSCR Nhampt164
HEUMANN,Richard Capt kia 10-9-16 2Lond CR France218
HEUSTON,Fred Gibson 2Lt kia 15-8-15 6RIrFus p171 MR4
HEVENINGHAM,Lionel Joseph.MID 2Lt kia 7-10-18 C158RFA p30 CR France115
HEWART,Gordon Morley T2Lt kia 9-5-15 6Lincs p75 CR Gallipoli5,9-8-15
HEWAT,Anthony Morris Coates Capt kia 8-9-14 RScots p54 CR France1443,Coats
HEWAT,Bertie Barron.MC.2Lt kia 1-12-17 246RFA p30 MR30
HEWAT,George Michael Fitz Gerald 2Lt kia 10-3-15 1AUL att2SStaffs p122&277,mbk MR28
HEWAT,James Govan Argyll Capt dow 16-4-18 6BlkW p231 CR France88
HEWER,Charles 2Lt kia 23-8-18 1/1Camb p245 CR France196
HEWER,Charles William Lt kia 22-8-17 9A&SH p244 MR30
HEWER,Richard Tuckey 2Lt kia 21-11-17 1BerksYeo p203 CR Palestine3
HEWETSON,Arthur T2Lt kia 24-3-18 8Lancs p59 CR France174
HEWETSON,Charles Herbert Maj kia 23-7-16 11Glouc p106 MR21
HEWETSON,John Dixon.MID TCapt dow 30-5-18 10 att1SStaffs p122 CR France1693 &CR France34,8Bn
HEWETSON,John Jervis Lt murderedByLanceNaik 2-4-21 IA 1/8GurkhaRif p277 MR43
HEWETSON,Richard John Philip Capt dow PoW 3-7-18 3 att9LNLancs p136 CR France1329
HEWETT,Edmond Geoffrey Capt kia 2-12-15 2/4RWSurr p212 CR Gallipoli26
HEWETT,Ernest Arthur Frederick 2Lt kia 28-3-18 18Lpool att2Ess p72 MR27
HEWETT,George Edward Capt kia 12-3-15 Worc RoO att6Bn p108 CR Belgium17 WIndR att3Worc
HEWETT,Harold Capt kia 4-1-18 RBerks &113RFC p16&139 CR Palestine3,Harald
HEWETT,Henry Walter O'Connell Capt kia 25-9-15 IA 41Dogras attStaffBareillyBde p278 MR28
HEWETT,Herbert Arthur TCapt dow 20-10-18 10RWar p65 CR France403
HEWETT,Stephen Henry Philip 2Lt kia 22-7-16 19 att14RWar p65 MR21
HEWETT,William John.MID Capt kia 9-5-15 3RMunstF p175 CR France924
HEWISON,Charles Runciman TLt drd 4-5-17 RE p45 CR Italy14
HEWISON,Geoffrey Joseph 2Lt kia 15-7-16 3RMunstF p175 CR France267
HEWISON,John Edward 2Lt dow 19-4-17 4RScots p211 CR France97,9Bn
HEWITSON,John T2Lt kia 11-11-17 23NumbF p61 CR France536
HEWITT,Hon Archibald Rodney.DSO.Capt kia 25-4-15 2ESurr p112 MR29
HEWITT,Arthur Kidman T2Lt kia 20-9-17 3Norf att 1/8Lpool p73 MR30
HEWITT,C.J.Maj 21-7-21 S&T Cps MR65
HEWITT,Cedric Atkinson Lt kia 27-10-18 11NumbF p61 CR Italy9
HEWITT,Denis George Wyldborn.VC.2Lt kia 31-7-17 2 att14Hamps p121 MR29,Wyldbore
HEWITT,Ernest Henry.MID Lt kia 15/16-6-15 4RLancs p213 MR22
HEWITT,Frederick Whitmore Chap4Cl kia 28-9-15 RAChDept att20InfBde p199 CR France423,27-9-15
HEWITT,George Alfred Guest Capt kia 27-11-17 2/5Y&L p238 MR17
HEWITT,Gordon Hughes Lt dow 24-9-14 2SLancs p125 CR France473
HEWITT,H.D.Lt dow 27-10-18 3EKent &RAF p57
HEWITT,Holt Montgomery TLt kia 1-7-16 109MGC p183 CR France383
HEWITT,Humphrey St.John 2Lt kia 9-7-18 5Lond p246 CR France177
HEWITT,James Francis Lt kia 26-10-14 1ScotRif p103 MR32

HEWITT,James Gordon T2Lt ded 14-11-18 WYorks att2/7Bn p81 CR Yorks410
HEWITT,James Percy 2Lt kia 5-4-18 4 att8SomLI p218 MR20
HEWITT,Robert Edward Talbot 2Lt kia 7-6-17 3 att6RIrReg p89 CR Belgium17
HEWITT,Robert Westbrooke.DSO.MajTLtCol dow 30-9-17 14Huss p22 CR Iraq
HEWITT,Sydney Rangeley.OBE.MIDx2 Chap4Cl ded 16-2-19 RAChDept attRAM 6FA p199&257 CR Germany1
HEWITT,Thomas 2Lt kia 27-3-18 7Norf p74 MR27
HEWITT,William Arthur T2Lt kia 1-7-16 9RInniskF p105 MR21
HEWITT,William George 2Lt kia 14-10-14 3RScots p54 CR France1106
HEWITT,William Taylor T2Lt dow PoW 16-4-18 36MGC Inf p183 CR France34
HEWLETT,Harold Alcester Tom Capt kia 23-8-18 4Lond p246 MR16
HEWLETT,Harry Campbell T2Lt kia 28-4-17 7Suff p78 MR20
HEWSON,Charles Victor 2Lt kia 9-7-16 21RFC p3 CR France598
HEWSON,Falkiner Melton Capt ded 22-10-18 RAMC p196 MR65
HEWSON,Henry Holland Capt died 7-11-19 RASC p267 CR Surrey1,Hilliard
HEWSON,Joseph Edward T2Lt kia 10-7-16 8ELancs p110 CR France515
HEWSON,Stanley Barton 2Lt kia 27-8-18 6Lond p247 MR16
HEWSON,Wilfrid John.MID TLt dow 25-10-18 9NumbF p61 CR France332,Wilfred
HEXT,Charles Wilfred Maj ded 21-7-19 IA S&TCps p278 CR Egypt1
HEXT,Francis John.DSO.MC.CaptAMaj dow 9-5-18 41/42RFA p30 CR Cornwall
HEXT,Thomas Madewood 2Lt kia 29-4-17 5 att12KRRC p150 MR20,Marwood 2 4-17 att1Bn
HEYCOCK,Edwin T2Lt kia 27-8-18 2 att14RWFus p98 CR France432
HEYES,A.E.2Lt dow 14-4-18 GL &21RAF p190 CR Belgium38
HEYES,John Peter Capt ded 6-7-16 RAVC att42Div p253 CR Europe1
HEYES,William 2Lt kia 27-2-17 2Worc p108 CR France511
HEYGATE,Claud Raymond Capt kia 1-7-16 2 att10YLI p143 CR France267
HEYGATE,Reginald 2Lt kia 11-6-18 2KOSB p101 MR32
HEYLAND,Arthur Alexander Lt kia 22-5-15 IA 2/5GurkhaRif att1/1 p278 MR28
HEYLAND,J.R.L.MC.Capt 11-3-15 9GurkhaRif CR France727
HEYMAN,John Archibald TCapt ded 2-2-19 RASC p267 CR Lond12
HEYMAN,John Henry TLt dow 18-7-17 RASC p193
HEYNES,Dudley Hugo 2Lt kia 16-5-18 402/14RFA 14ArmyBde p30 CR France8
HEYS,William George.TD.LtCol dje 4-6-15 8Manch p237 CR Gallipoli1
HEYWARD,Harvey Heale T2Lt kia 10-10-16 15DLI p161 CR France400,Harry Neale Ex 2Bn
HEYWARD,Maurice 2Lt kia 20-7-16 3 att8Dors p124 MR21
HEYWOOD,Albert Bertine T2Lt kia 4-10-17 10YLI p143 MR30
HEYWOOD,Arthur George Percival Maj dow 12-9-18 1/6Manch p236 CR France145
HEYWOOD,Aubrey Talley Lt kia 3-9-17 GL &45RFC p8 MR20
HEYWOOD,Bertram Charles Percival.TD.Col ded 28-10-14 Manch CR Staffs177
HEYWOOD,Charles Clement Lt kia 25-4-18 RFA p207 MR30
HEYWOOD,F.K.Lt kld 1-10-18 RASC &RAF p193
HEYWOOD,Herbert 2Lt kia 25-9-15 1Manch p155 CR France924
HEYWOOD,Herbert Capt dow 22-8-17 8Mddx attMGC p147&183 CR Belgium
HEYWOOD,James George Cross Lt kia 30-8-15 B1/4Nhampt p234 CR Gallipoli17,dow
HEYWOOD,Robert Myles Lt dow 15-2-15 3EKent p57 CR Belgium151
HEYWOOD,Stanley Lt kia 4-6-15 8Manch p237 MR4
HEYWOOD,Thomas Aston 2Lt dow 6-6-15 4ELancs p226 CR Gallipoli6
HEYWOOD,W.H.V.Capt 7-9-20 IndDefForce CR Derby98
HEWORTH,Frederick James.CB.DSO.TBrigGen kia 9-5-16 Comdg3ScotGds p1 Belgium6
HEYWORTH,Heyworth Potter Lawrence Capt kia 6-8-15 7NStaffs p157 CR Gallipoli31
HEYWORTH,J.P.Lt 27-2-20 RFA CR Ches74
HEYWORTH,Peter George 2Lt dow 12-5-17 10Worc att57TMB p108 CR Belgium11,Capt 50TMB
HEYWORTH,Wilfred Alexander 2Lt kia 23-5-16 5Lpool p215 CR France927
HIBBARD,Edmund John 2Lt kia 9-4-17 12Lond p248 CR France1185
HIBBARD,Nelson Stuart 2Lt kia 14-7-17 1LNLnacs p136 CR Belgium173
HIBBARD,Richard 2Lt kia 6-11-18 KSLI att4Bn p145 CR France521
HIBBERT,Arthur James 2Lt ded 14-8-17 B79RFA p30 CR France102
HIBBERT,Cyril Gordon Reuss Capt kia 16-6-15 1/4LNLancs p234 MR22
HIBBERT,Howard Morley 2Lt kia 1-7-16 1/5N&D p232 MR21
HIBBS,Laurence Bosdet T2Lt ded 21-3-16 RJerseyMil att7RIrRif p201 CR France
HIBBS,Richard John Walmsley Lt kia 8-10-18 3 att22Manch p155 CR France846
HICHENS,James Bryan TLt kia 16-7-16 16KRRC p150 MR21,Byrn 15-7-16

140

HICHENS,William Thomas 2Lt kia 3-9-16 9 att1DCLI p114 CR France294
HICK,Harold Crispen T2Lt kia 12-7-16 19Lpool p72 CR France630
HICK,Joseph Marsden 2Lt kia 17-4-18 7WRid p228 CR France139
HICK,Pantland Capt ded 17-4-15 RAMC p270
HICKEY,Arthur Aidan 2Lt kia 25-10-18 2/5LancF p221 CR Belgium420
HICKEY,Denis.MC.T2Lt ded 7-11-18 2Leinst p174 CR France1028
HICKEY,Eugene Francis Lt ded 10-3-21 RDubF CR Europe51
HICKEY,Robert Francis 2Lt dow 16-8-17 9RDubF p176 MR30
HICKFORD,Albert T2LtACapt dow 10-5-17 14DLI p161 CR France8
HICKIE,Charles Sinclair Lt dow 1-10-17 6RFC SR p8 CR Belgium11
HICKING,Francis Joseph T2Lt kia 1-7-16 13 att1WYorks p81 CR France373
HICKING,George Graham TLt kia 1-7-16 6Y&L p159 MR21
HICKLENTON,Donald Stuart 2Lt kia 24-8-18 86RFA p30 CR France1170
HICKLEY,Henry Dennis Capt mbk 18-4-16 IA 2/7GurkhaRif att1/9 p278 MR38
HICKLEY,Richard Trollope North Lt kia 24-3-18 Herts p252 MR27
HICKLING,Edward Robert Eyre 2Lt dow 27-10-14 3Glouc attNLancs p106 CR Belgium150,Lt 26-10-14
HICKLING,John Christopher 2Lt kia 11-4-16 9Mddx p236 MR38
HICKMAN,Arthur Kendrick Lt kia 5-4-16 3 att8WelchR p127 MR38,RWFus
HICKMAN,Ernest John 2Lt kia 16-8-15 1/4Ess p232 CR Gallipoli4
HICKMAN,Harry Claude 2Lt kia 23-3-18 13RSuss p119 CR France365,Lt
HICKMAN,John George 2Lt kia 4-10-17 C50RFA p30 CR Belgium10
HICKMAN,Philip Gregory 2Lt dow 31-10-17 6SStaffs p229 CR France102
HICKMAN,Poole Henry TCapt kia 15-8-15 7RDubF p176 MR4
HICKMAN,Terence 2Lt kia 26/27-6-16 2Leinst p174 MR29,26-6-16
HICKMAN,William Christie 2Lt kia 1-7-16 175RFA p30 CR France393
HICKMOTT,Sydney Richard 2Lt dow 1-10-18 4RWKent p234 MR30
HICKOX,Edwin Baskerville.MC.TMaj dow 15-8-17 9Ess p131 CR France113
HICKS,Arthur Supt ded 16-6-19 NWFProvPolice MR43
HICKS,Arthur Leslie TLt ded 4-4-18 11Leic p87 CR France924,dow
HICKS,Basil Perrin TLt kia 25-9-15 8RBerks p139 CR France219
HICKS,Charles Albert T2Lt kia 3-10-18 6RInniskF p105 CR France375
HICKS,Charles Hubert Lt kia 21-7-18 8N&D p233 CR France28
HICKS,Edwin Theodore Capt ded 12-5-17 2/4Lincs p220&270 CR France833
HICKS,Eric Raymond.MC.Lt ded 25-12-18 RFA 60DivHQ p207 CR Egypt1
HICKS,Ernest 2Lt kia 9-10-16 2/18Lond p250 CR France68
HICKS,Frank Alan.MC.Lt kia 21-8-18 4RFus p68 CR France214
HICKS,Frederick Richard LtCol dow 12-6-15 Hamps p121 CR Cornwall128
HICKS,Harleigh Lionel Adrian Oswald 2Lt kia 12-4-18 5 att1/8Mddx p147
HICKS,Harry Ronald 2Lt kia 12-10-17 GL &19RFC p8 CR Belgium157
HICKS,Lawrence Frederick Lt dow 5-11-18 2Wilts p153 CR France321
HICKS,Robert 2Lt kia 26-5-18 23Lond p252 CR France177,25-5-18
HICKS,Walter Gerald T2Lt dow 12-8-15 8RFus p68 CR France12
HICKS,William Goss 2Lt dow 3-7-17 RGA 260SB p40
HICKSON,Horace Grant T2Lt kia 6/12-8-15 6Leinst p174 MR4
HICKSON,James Ferguson 2Lt dow 31-7-17 1/9Lpool p216 CR Belgium7
HICKSON,Reginald Davies.MC.TCapt dow 30-4-17 9Ess p131 MR20
HIDDINGH,Stephen Van Der Poel LtACapt kia 3-5-17 4RFus p68 MR20
HIDER,Arthur Leslie George 2LtTLt kia 27-5-17 8SStaffs A'Coy p122 CR France544
HIELD,John Hamer Capt kia 3-9-16 16RB p179 MR21
HIGGERTY,Frederick Charles 2Lt mbk 30-11-17 8Lond p257 MR17
HIGGIN,Harold Sinclair Capt ded 11-1-19 IARO att75CarnaticInf p278 MR65
HIGGIN,James Laurence.MID Capt kia 30-6-15 IA 1/10 att1/9GurkhaRif p278 MR4,29/30-6-15
HIGGIN-BIRKET,William Capt mbk 2-12-14 1/2LancF p256 MR32,28-10-14
HIGGIN-BOTHAM,Charles Egerton 2Lt kia 5-11-16 9DLI p239 MR21
HIGGINBOTHAM,Charles Ernest Maj kia 11-3-15 2Nhampt p137 MR22
HIGGINBOTHAM,Robert Edward 2Lt kia 29-9-18 B115RFA p30 CR Greece5
HIGGONBOTTOM,Frederick T2Lt ded 6-4-17 9Ches &23RFC p8 MR20
HIGGINS,Arthur Aken TCapt ded 25-10-18 RAVC att115RFA p198 CR Greece5
HIGGINS,Arthur Henry 2Lt ded 29-10-19 RGA 258SB p262 CR Staffs61
HIGGINS,Claud Wilfred 2Lt drd 25-4-17 NStaffs p157 MR38
HIGGINS,Claude D.2Lt kia 22-9-16 21RFC p3 CR France446
HIGGINS,Cuthbert George 2Lt dow 1-7-16 6WYorks p218 MR21
HIGGINS,Douglas Stanley TLt kia 9-4-17 9 att5 O&BLI p130 CR France581,Capt dow
HIGGINS,Frederick 2Lt kia 27-7-18 1/7GordH p242 CR France622
HIGGINS,George Frederick TMaj kia 10/12-7-16 17Lpool p72 MR21,10-7-16
HIGGINS,Harry Vincent 2Lt kia 3-9-16 116MGC Inf p183 CR France1890
HIGGINS,Herbert Edward Powell Capt kia 10-8-15 6RLancs p59 MR4

HIGGINS,Hugh Stevenson 2Lt kia 28-3-18 13RScots p54 MR20
HIGGINS,John WO ded 2-8-16 RIM p278
HIGGINS,Michael Aloysius Lt kia 31-3-17 3Leinst p174 CR France480,2Bn
HIGGINS,P.J.Lt 18-2-20 RGA CR Ches18
HIGGINS,Percy Clynton Capt kia 22-9-17 1KSLI attNigR p145&201 CR EAfrica8 &CR Tanzania1
HIGGINS,Stanley T2Lt kia 28-9-18 2/7Lpool p72 CR France686,27-9-18
HIGGINS,Thomas.MC TLt dow 15-11-16 RE 130FC p45 CR France40
HIGGINSON,Ernest George T2Lt kld 4-10-17 GL &73RFC p8 CR Scot235
HIGGINSON,George Neale TLt kia 23-11-16 16LancF p92 CR France153
HIGGINSON,John Herbert 2Lt kia 30-11-17 5RHA p30 CR France1483
HIGGINSON,John Thomas Gordon T2Lt kld 1-11-17 GL &RFC p8 CR Ches51
HIGGINSON,John Victor.MC.Capt ded 23-9-19 2RWFus p263 CR Shrop97
HIGGINSON,Robert 2Lt kia 15-8-16 5RLancs p213 MR21
HIGGINSON,Thomas Cecil Lt kia 15-9-16 GrenGds attMGC SR p50 MR21
HIGGINSON,Tom Arthur TCapt kldacc 19-9-15 6KSLI p145 CR France706
HIGGINSON,William Clifton Vernon T2Lt kia 20-11-17 GL &3RFC p8 MR20
HIGGINSON,William Frederick Capt kia 25-4-15 1RDubF p176 CR Gallipoli15
HIGGITT,Leonard Henry Lt dow 30-10-17 4NStaffs att9YLI p157 CR France40
HIGGON,Archibald Bellairs Maj kia 10-9-15 RFA p30 CR Gallipoli20,9-9-15
HIGGON,John Arthur Maj kia 20-7-16 PembYeo p205 CR France82
HIGGS,Harry Leonard 2Lt kia 25-3-18 5Lond p246 MR20
HIGGS,John Phillip Lt dow 14-4-18 OxfYeo attMGC p205 CR France185
HIGGS,Lucien Herbert T2Lt kld 8-6-17 RFC SR p8 CR War65
HIGGS,Marcus Webb T2Lt kia 23-10-18 att9Dev p76 MR16 CR France231
HIGGS,Reginald Frank T2Lt kia 22-9-18 1RWSurr p56 CR France407
HIGH,Gilbert Cecil 2Lt kia 14-3-17 2/6Norf att2/5YLI p217 CR France239
HIGH,Robert Donald 2Lt kia 22-3-18 4GordH p242 MR20
HIGHAM,Percy Harrowell.MC.2Lt kia 17-2-17 6Nhampt p137 MR21
HIGHAM,Wilfred T2Lt kia 27-9-18 2/5RLancs p59 CR France530,Capt
HIGHFIELD,George Harold 2Lt dow 4-7-15 3Y&L p159 CR Belgium17
HIGHMORE,Charles Bowyer 2Lt ded 26-2-19 MGC p254 CR Surrey154
HIGHT,Norman Dudley John.MC.2Lt kia 24-3-18 3 att10Ess p131 CR France1893
HIGHTON,Harold Victor 2Lt kia 25-3-18 RFC p16 MR20
HIGMAN,Frederick James 2Lt dow 17-10-18 3 att1YLI p143 CR Scot764
HIGMAN,Michael T2Lt kia 18-8-16 6DCLI p114 MR21
HIGNETT,William Rowland 2Lt kia 3-5-17 4 att12EYorks p219 MR20
HIGSON,Frederic Stewart.MC.TLtACapt kia 31-8-17 17WelshR p127 CR France415
HIGSON,John Turnbull T2Lt dow 4-8-18 Nhampt att2Bn p137 CR Germany3
HIGSON,Richard Henry 2Lt kia 23-10-16 16 att2LancF p92 MR21
HIGSON,William Marsh T2Lt dow 9-4-17 8RLancs p59 CR France113,kia
HILARY,Henry Jephson 2Lt dow 3-6-17 17RH&FA p30 CR France113,2-6-17
HILDAGE,Harry 2Lt kia 15-4-17 27RFA p30 CR France1325
HILDER,Harold Sutton Lt kia 3-5-17 att7EKent p57 MR20
HILDER,Maurice Lake.MC.LtTCapt kia 3-5-17 5 att23RFus p68 MR20
HILDERSLEY,Stanley Kentfield Edwards T2Lt kia 12-9-16 6Yorks p90 CR France246
HILDITCH,Charles Henry 2Lt kia 23-10-18 27RFA p30 CR France206
HILDITCH,Richard.MID TLt kia 14-9-16 14Lpool p72 MR37
HILDITCH,Victor Cadifer.DSO.MC.ALtCol ded 11-2-19 RFA p261 CR Wales166,Cadifor
HILDRETH,Ernest T2Lt kld 18-10-16 14Yorks attRFC p3&90 CR Norf247
HILDYARD,Robert Aubrey 2Lt kia 20-12-16 1RLancs p59 CR France630
HILEY,Frank TCapt kld 13-2-18 8Yorks p90 CR Italy7
HILL,Adam Cyril Darley 2Lt kia 16-8-17 RIrRif CR Belgium125
HILL,Albert Charles Leonard 2Lt kia 27-5-18 4Berks p234 CR France248
HILL,Alec Leslie 2Lt kia 26-12-17 4 att1Dev p220 CR Italy48,kld
HILL,Alexander Lt kia 12-10-18 9HLI p240 MR16
HILL,Alexander Sidney 2Lt kia 9-10-17 6Glouc p225 MR30
HILL,Alan Purdie Dunlop Capt ded 8-2-19 RGA att59RAF p30&40 CR Belgium330,Maj
HILL,Alfred 2Lt kia 13-9-17 1/5NStaffs p238 CR France115
HILL,Alfred Saunders 2Lt kia 20-11-17 RGA 109SB p40 CR Belgium92
HILL,Andrew Bruce 2Lt kia 27-9-18 7RWar p214 CR France415
HILL,Arthur James 2Lt kia 8-7-16 2Wilts p153 MR21
HILL,Arthur Lionel T2Lt kia 25-9-15 1Mddx p147 MR19
HILL,Arthur Moberly 2Lt kia 9-4-17 NSomYeo att1SomLI p205 MR20
HILL,Arthur Rowland Maj kia 3-10-15 2Ches p96 MR19
HILL,Austen Shelbourne 2Lt dow 3-6-17 6Lond p247 CR France614

HILL,Barry Lt kia 1-7-16 10RIrRif p169 MR21
HILL,Benjamin Godlonton.MC.2Lt dow 5-6-17 RFA p208 CR Belgium102
HILL,Beresford Winnington TLt kia 4-3-17 GL 10RB &r59RFC p8 CR France502
HILL,Bertram Gilbert 2Lt kia 25-9-15 3 att2RWar p65 CR France260
HILL,Brian Edward TCapt dow 2-10-18 RASC att1TankCps p188&193 CR France446
HILL,Cedric Lloyd Graham 2Lt kia 5-11-16 5 att8DLI p239 MR21
HILL,Charles Douglas Lucas T2Lt kia 14-2-16 9RSuss p119 CR Belgium72
HILL,Charles Edward HonLt ded 16-3-18 LabCps p266 CR Mddx46
HILL,Charles Edward TCapt kia 28-9-15 13Mddx p147 MR19
HILL,Charles Edward Cecil Lt kia 17-4-16 HLI p163 MR38
HILL,Charles Glencairn,CMG.DSO TLtCol kia 26-6-15 1RBerks p139 CR France1106
HILL,Charles Herbert TCapt kia 21-8-15 11Y&L att1RinniskF p159 MR4
HILL,Charles Percy Capt kia 19-8-16 4NStaffs p157 CR France513
HILL,Douglas Agar Worsley TLt dow 14-8-18 6EKent p57 CR France13
HILL,Edwin Arundel TMaj dow 26-10-18 8RSuss p119 CR France1170
HILL,Eric Alfred TLt kld 12-1-17 SL p201 CR Asia81,ded
HILL,Eric Battley 2Lt ded 19-11-16 5Ess attTMB p232 CR France121,1/6Bn
HILL,Ernest Hatton Capt ded 11-4-18 7WRid p227 CR Yorks619
HILL,Frederick.DCM.Capt kia 8-8-18 15Lond p249 CR France141
HILL,Frederick Thomas Cecil TMaj kia 7-8-15 6Y&L p159 CR Gallipoli26
HILL,Gerald Leader Capt kia 26-9-17 5Lincs p220
HILL,Gerald Stanley 2Lt kia 15-9-16 1Lond p245 MR21
HILL,George SubCdr ded 26-11-18 IA MilWksServ p278 CR EAfrica36 Ex 9Lancers
HILL,Guy Charles Dunlop Lt drd 4-5-17 2KSLI p145 CR Italy14
HILL,Harold Belfit Lt kld 6-9-18 3RWKent attRAF p141
HILL,Henry Hamp TCapt dow 8-3-16 11WYorks p81 CR France924
HILL,Henry Oswald William.MC.TCapt ded 21-10-17 GL &52RFC p8 MR20
HILL,Henry Tavener 2Lt kia 18-10-14 2RWar p65 MR29
HILL,Henry William T2Lt kia 10-8-15 6BordR p117 MR4
HILL,Horace Frederick.MC.TCapt dow 5-9-17 18Mddx p147 CR Belgium37
HILL,Hugh.MVO.DSO.BtLtCol kia 10-9-16 RWFus Staff p98 CR France80
HILL,James 2Lt ded 21-10-16 RGA 16HB p40 CR France64
HILL,James Alfred Lt TCapt kia 17-4-18 1Leic p87 MR30
HILL,James Macgregor T2Lt dow 10-11-16 2NumbF p61 CR Greece9
HILL,Jeremiah Charles Holmes T2Lt dow 2-5-17 9Ess p131 CR France113
HILL,Jesse Adolphus Henry Capt ded 1-3-19 RFA p254 CR Essex14
HILL,John Edward TCapt dow 24-3-18 PoW 9Norf p74 CR France274
HILL,John Newton T2Lt ded 11-8-16 SL CamelTransportCoy 1CamCps p201 CR Egypt2
HILL,John Robertson Lt kia 2-6-15 3DLI p161 CR Belgium44
HILL,John Robertshaw T2Lt kia 6-5-17 RE P'SpCoy p45 CR France560
HILL,John Rowland T2Lt kia 5-8-16 13YLI p143 CR France643
HILL,Joseph T2Lt ded 23-11-18 MGC Inf p183 CR Wales78,Lt
HILL,Leonard Coulthard.MC.LtACapt ded 10-10-18 RFA att4ArmyArtySchool p30 CR France52,Maj
HILL,Leonard Grenville 2Lt kia 9-11-16 48RFA p30 CR France174
HILL,Lionel George Capt kia 17-2-15 2EYorks p84 MR29
HILL,Mark Carr TLt kia 17-7-16 6Leic p87 MR21,14-7-16
HILL,Maurice Cridland Lt kia 24-5-15 5NumbF p213 CR Belgium96
HILL,Michael.DCM.T2Lt kia 19-7-16 RE 3SigCo p45&259 CR France513
HILL,Nicholas Weatherby.MC.LtACapt kia 16-1-17 2 O&BLI p130 CR France280
HILL,Norman Ernest Albert 2Lt ded 27-3-15 14WYorks p254 CR Dorset141
HILL,Oldham Cyril Darley 2Lt kia 16-8-17 4 att7RIrRif p169
HILL,Percy Joseph TLt kia 3-10-18 1YLI p143 CR France234
HILL,Phillip Aubrey Capt kia 23-4-17 att2SWBord BrecknockBn p223 MR20
HILL,R.Lt 24-11-20 Glouc CR Devon68
HILL,Ralph Grenfell Lt kia 20-2-17 1KAR p202 CR EAfrica40,19-2-17
HILL,Reginald Byng Tower LtTCapt kia 3-6-17 8Ess p232 CR France115
HILL,Reginald Gordon.MC.TLt kia 11-10-17 RAMC att1CldGds p196 CR Belgium12
HILL,Reginald Percy 2Lt dow 25-8-18 A72RFA p30 CR France924
HILL,Richard Maj ded 17-2-15 3Yorks p90 CR Yorks171
HILL,Richard Alexander TLt kia 10-4-17 RGA 138HB p40 CR France480
HILL,Richard Alexander Gathorne Lt kia 12-8-18 SomLI &204RAF p263 MR20
HILL,Robert William Capt dow 31-7-17 1Camb p244 CR Belgium101
HILL,Stanley Frederick.MC&Bar.Capt kia 4-11-18 4Glouc p225 CR France977
HILL,Sydney Moir-Byres 2Lt kia 25-9-15 3GordH attCamH p166 MR19
HILL,Thomas Edward 2Lt dow 21-4-18 RGA 156B47HABde p40 CR France145
HILL,Thomas Hooton 2Lt kia 13-11-16 4Beds p86 CR France220

HILL,Thomas Wilson T2Lt kia 10-7-17 HLI att16Bn p163 CR Belgium24
HILL,Tom Warner T2Lt ded 14-10-17 4MGC Inf p183 CR Yorks543
HILL,Victor Baillie.MC.Capt dow 15-1-18 6KRRC p150 CR France64
HILL,Walter Edward Lt kia 23-9-14 3NStaffs p157 CR France1111,25-9-14
HILL,Walter Henry T2Lt kia 20-11-17 RB att10Bn p179 MR17
HILL,Wilfred Stuart T2Lt kia 31-7-17 RB p179 CR Belgium167
HILL,Wilfrid Dudley Capt dow 13-5-15 3 att1LNLancs p136
HILL,Wilfrid James T2Lt dow 17-9-16 6DCLI p114 CR France833
HILL,William.MID HonLt&QM ded 11-10-15 8RWFus p98 CR Gallipoli26
HILL,William TLt kia 30-10-17 RFA 86ArmyBde p30 CR Belgium19
HILL,William Alfred TLtACapt kia 23-3-18 7DCLI att61TMB p114 CR France106
HILL,William Carlisle.MC.TLt kia 7-6-17 2RIrRif att74TMB p169 MR29
HILL,William Ernest TLt kia 8-8-18 9RFus B'Coy p68 CR France247
HILL,William Henry Ostler 2Lt dow 25-9-15 2Yorks p90 MR19
HILL,William Reginald.MC&Bar.Lt ded PoW 6-11-18 4 att12DLI p161 CR Germany4
HILL,William Robb 2Lt dow 24-8-18 4BlkW p230 CR France266,kia
HILL,William White Lt dow 20-4-17 ImpCamelCps CR Palestine2
HILL-TREVOR,Hillyer George Edwin Lt kia 21-12-14 1ScotsGds p52 MR22
HILL-WILLIAMS,J.Lt 3-3-17 PoliticDept CR EAfrica46
HILLAS,Arthur Benedict Edward Capt kia 23-4-17 7GordH p242 CR France644
HILLBROOK,Wallace Capt 22-7-16 UgandaMS CR EAfrica52
HILLEBRANDT,Frederick Edmund T2Lt kld 22-3-17 GL &RFC 5Wing p8 CR Essex48,HILLEBRANT
HILLER,Alan Menzies.MID 2Lt kia 16-5-15 3RWSurr p56 CR France279,2Bn
HILLERNS,Hero Wilhelm Oswald.MID Maj kia 14-4-17 B251RFA p206&207 CR France418
HILLIAR,Gordon Edward 2Lt kia 26-9-15 3SLancs attELancs p125 CR France276,dow
HILLIER,Cyril Anthony Hudson 2Lt dow 27-2-15 2Mon p244 CR Suff138,26-2-15
HILLIER,Frederick William 2Lt ded 2-12-19 IA 8Cav p278 MR43,3Lancers att27LtCav
HILLIER,Geoffrey Stuart Drummond TCapt kia 30-3-18 13Glouc p106 MR27
HILLIER,Maurice 2Lt kia 9-4-17 6KOSB p101 CR France645
HILLIER,Sidney Napier T2Lt kia 25-3-18 6SWBord p100 MR20
HILLIER,W.D.Capt 15-11-18 20DLI CR Ches147
HILLING,Sophie.ARRC.Sister ded 12-10-18 QAIMNS p200 CR France123
HILLMAN,Harold Alexander Moore TLt kia 1-7-16 11 att7Yorks p90 CR France39
HILLMAN,Horace James T2Lt ded 25-3-19 RE SpBde p262 CR Mddx68,Lt
HILLMAN,Leslie Harris Lt kia 31-7-17 2RB p179 MR29
HILLMAN-MILLER,James TLt dow 10-8-15 4SWBord p100 MR4
HILLS,Arthur Edward TCapt kia 28-5-18 14NumbF p61 MR18
HILLS,Arthur Hyde 2Lt kia 19-4-17 8Hamps p229 MR34
HILLS,Charles Herbert 2Lt dow 5-9-16 3Manch p155 CR France188
HILLS,Cyril.MC.T2Lt kia 30-8-18 2Suff p78 CR France433
HILLS,Ernest Leslie TLt dow 26-11-15 12RWFus att1NigR p98&201 CR WAfrica58
HILLS,Frederick Mervyn 2Lt kia 27-7-17 3 att7Nhampt p137 CR Belgium115,3 att2Bn
HILLS,Geoffrey Wilfrid 2Lt kia 14-6-17 10Lond p248 CR France568
HILLS,Laurence Clifford T2Lt kia 3-7-16 1Lincs p75 MR21
HILLS,Malcolm Arthur T2Lt kia 15-9-16 1EKent p57 MR21
HILLS,Maud Ellen Sister ded 22-7-18 TFNS p254 CR Surrey160
HILLS,Walter Edward.MID T2Lt kia 26-6-17 KRRC att16Bn p150 CR France1489
HILLS,William Frederick Waller TLt kia 6-3-17 GL RFA att57RFC p8 CR France4
HILLYARD,Noël Hardcastle Lt dow 23-4-17 223RFA p207 CR France95
HILLYER,James Excelsior 2Lt kia 27-10-17 RGA 186SB p40 MR30
HILLYER,Philip Charles T2Lt kia 31-8-18 13Lpool p72 CR France433
HILLYER,William Harold,MC Capt kia 22-5-16 RE 1/4FC p210 CR France80
HILTON,A Maj 4-3-15 RAMC CR Egypt9
HILTON,Arthur T2Lt kia 9-10-17 5Y&L p159 MR20
HILTON,Clarence Stuart Capt kia 1-7-16 2Mddx p147 MR21
HILTON,Fawcett T2Lt kia 3-7-16 1Lincs p75 MR21
HILTON,George 2Lt kia 8-8-16 4RLancs p213 MR21
HILTON,Harold 2Lt kia 26-11-17 14HLI p163 MR17
HILTON,Henry Denne 2Lt kia 19-12-14 5 att4Mddx p147 CR Belgium17,20-12-
HILTON,Herbert Philip Capt kia 16-2-15 3Mddx p147 MR29
HILTON,Murray Venables BtColTCol kia 20-10-15 Cmdg7ELancs p110 CR France737 Ex Worc
HILTON,Oscar.MC.ACapt dow 14-11-18 RFA p254
HILTON,Reginald Musgrave 2Lt kia 23-4-17 6 att4Mddx p147 MR20

HILTON,Robert 2Lt ded 29-4-18 16Manch &13RAF p155 MR20,6-4-18 5Bn
HINCHCLIFFE,Frank Beatson 2Lt kia 4-11-18 5WRid p227 CR France206
HINCHLIFF,Cyril Stanley T2Lt kld 4-9-17 GL &RFC p8 CR Sussex9
HINCHLIFFE,Charles Ernest.MM.2Lt kia 20-7-18 YLI att4Bn p143 MR18
HINCHLIFFE,George William 2Lt kia 26-6-18 15WYorks att93TMB p81
HINCKLEY,Douglas Roy 2Lt kia 13-1-17 12Y&L att5RFC p9&159 CR France927
HINCKLEY,John 2Lt kia 27-3-18 RGA 24SB p40 CR France1170
HINCKS,Bertram 2Lt kia 18-12-16 5 att10KRRC p150 CR France402
HIND,Arthur Charles Sinclair Capt kia 14-4-15 IA 110MahrattaLI p278 CR Iraq6
HIND,Charles Raymond.MID Lt kia 30-5-16 2SStaffs p122 CR France924,29-5-16
HIND,Ernest William Gayles 2Lt kia 1-7-16 15RIrRif p169 MR21
HIND,Frank Capt dow PoW 29-10-14 EYorks p84 CR France1887
HIND,Frank Farmer T2Lt kia 16-7-16 6Leic att110TMB p87 CR France453
HIND,Henry Basil Lindsay Lt kia 22-11-15 3SomLI attO&BLI p80 MR38
HIND,I.F.Capt ded 12-8-18 SL &RAF p201
HIND,Jesse Francis Montague TLt kia 27-9-16 9N&D p134 MR21
HIND,Lawrence Arthur.MC.LtCol kia 1-7-16 1/7N&D p232 MR21
HIND,Reginald Charles 2Lt kia 6-2-18 A160RFA p30 CR France592
HINDE,Cyril de Villiers.MC.Lt ded 11-1-17 2RBerks p139 MR29,11-7-17
HINDE,Kenneth 2Lt kia 3-2-17 5RLancs p213 CR France624
HINDE,William Henry Rousseau LtTCapt ded 22-10-18 RASC p193 CR Yorks361
HINDLE,Alfred Herbert 2Lt kia 12-5-18 26/17RH&FA p30 CR Belgium36
HINDLE,Harold Burn TLt kia 27-3-18 G'RHA p30 MR27
HINDLE,Ralph.DSO.LtCol kia 30-11-17 4LNLancs p233 CR France212
HINDLE,Stephen T2Lt kia 26-3-18 4TankCps p188 CR France395
HINDLEY-SMITH,Evelyn Hay Capt 16-5-18 5Manch CR Hamps214
HINDMARSH,George Edwin 2Lt ded 16-6-17 23RB p244 MR67,G.E.S.
HINDS,Ralph William Gore.MID Lt kia 16-5-15 2RInniskF p105 CR France279
HINDS,William Pugh TLt dow 2-2-16 15RWFus p98 CR France345
HINDSLEY,Eric TLt dow 11-4-17 1SStaffs p122 CR France64
HINDSON,Leslie Reginald Probyn Lt kia 10-6-17 A187RFA p30 CR Belgium15 Lesley
HINDSON,Reginald Gordon 2Lt ded 13-9-14 RFA p30 CR C'land&W'land17
HINE,Claude Annesley T2Lt dow 16-10-16 2 att10RWSurr p56 CR France833
HINE,Godfrey Valentine Brooke Lt kia 6-10-15 2IrGds SR p52 CR France423,2Lt
HINE,Harold Bowman Egerton Lt ded 31-8-18 7Hamps p229 CR Iraq5
HINE,Herbert Josiah.MM.T2Lt kia 25-8-18 6EKent p57 CR France430
HINE,T.C.2Lt kia 20-7-16 20RFus p68 MR21
HINE-HAYCOCK,Ralph Hugh Capt kia 3-5-17 1 att10YLI p143 CR France1186
HINES,Austin T2Lt dow 15-12-15 10DLI p161 CR Belgium11
HINES,Charles William Maj kia 24/25-6-15 7DLI p239 MR29,26-5-15
HINES,Harold William.MC.DCM.2Lt kia 7-10-17 RFA 113ArmyBde p30 MR30
HINGSTON,Edward Maj kia 28-3-15 RE 54FC p45 CR France768
HINGSTON,Frank Leonard Capt kia 26-4-15 1DCLI p114 CR Belgium151,Frederick
HINGSTON,George Bennett LtCol dow 16-6-15 RE p45 CR Egypt3
HININGS,Frederick William Crowther Capt kia 25-9-16 3 att1EYorks p84 MR21
HINKLEY,Arthur 2Lt kia 7-8-15 1/5LancF p221 MR4
HINKLEY,Siegfried Thomas T2Lt kia 3-7-16 6EKent C'Coy p57 CR France393
HINNELL,Thomas Squier 2Lt kia 12-8-15 5Suff p217 MR4
HINTON,Charles Allan.MC&Bar.Capt&Adjt kia 22-5-18 RE 46Div p210 CR France109
HINTON,Godfrey Bingham.CMG.LtCol kia 21-3-18 RFA 26ArmyBde p30 CR France518
HINTON,Norman Charles 2Lt dow 4-4-18 6RFus p68 CR France62,Lt 13Bn
HINTON,Walter Reginald T2Lt kia 14-7-16 2BordR p117 CR France453
HINXMAN,Alfred James TLt kia 10-8-15 5Wilts p153 MR4
HIPKIN,Henry James T2Lt kia 17-7-18 att7SfthH p165 MR32
HIPKINS,Fredk Wystan.MC.Capt kia 3-10-18 6N&D D'Coy p233 CR France375
HIPKINS,Norman.MID Capt kia 28-9-18 6NStaffs p238 CR France375
HIPPISLEY,Harold Edwin 2Lt kia 23-10-14 att1Glouc SR p106 MR29
HIPWELL,Charles Stanley.MC.Lt kia 14-10-16 16Lond p249 CR France15,15-10-16
HIPWELL,H.Reginald 2Lt kia 23-4-17 4SfthH attMGC p187&241 CR France604
HIRD,Christopher T2Lt kia 19-4-17 8WRid att1/4Nhants p115 CR Palestine8
HIRD,Frederick TLt kia 29-7-16 GL WRid att10TMB p190 MR21,dow
HIRD,Joseph William Smith T2Lt dow 26-1-17 7NStaffs p157 CR Iraq5
HIRE,Frederick TLt ded 12-10-18 RE p262 CR Belgium38
HIRONS,William John T2Lt kia 21-3-18 7Lincs p75 MR20
HIRSCH,David Philip.VC.MID Capt kia 23-4-17 4Yorks p220 MR20
HIRSCHBEIN,served as HURSTBOURNE,Walter Hirsch

HIRSCHORN,Cecil T2Lt ded 21-2-18 1Wilts att9Dev p153 CR Italy12,HIRSCHHORN
HIRST,Alfred Edison 2Lt kia 3-9-16 4WRid p227 MR21
HIRST,Cecil Pollock T2Lt kia 1-7-16 8Dev p76 CR France397
HIRST,Charles Capt kia 3-9-16 1/4WRid p227 MR21
HIRST,Fred Philip Lt ded 19-2-19 RGA p209 CR Europe1
HIRST,Gerald William 2Lt kia 26-2-17 3Lpool p72 CR France744
HIRST,Harold Capt kia 24-6-15 1/4YLI p235 CR France684
HIRST,Harold Hugh Lt ded 24-2-19 GL 21Manch attRE p266 CR Berks117
HIRST,Henry Denne LtCol ded 16-5-18 3EKent p57&251 CR Kent164
HIRST,James.MM.2Lt kia 14-9-18 20Lond p251 MR16
HIRST,Leonard George.MC.TLt ded 18-10-18 RE p254 CR France52
HIRST,Stanley Ewart 2Lt kia 24-10-17 RGA 200SB p40 CR Belgium19
HIRST,Wilfred Bertram 2Lt dow 22-4-15 4Lincs p217 CR Belgium98
HIRST,William T2Lt kia 1-7-16 14Y&L p159 CR France5
HIRST,William Henry T2Lt kia 1-8-18 WYorks att10Bn p81 CR France61
HISCOCK,Ernest Henry TCapt kia 25-1-17 9Worc p109 CR Iraq5
HISCOCK,Leonard Ernest T2Lt kia 10-8-15 9Worc p109 CR Gallipoli13
HISLOP,Alec Herbert 2Lt ded 24-12-17 14Lond p249 CR France95
HISLOP,Arthur Fowler Maj ded 19-3-19 IA S&TCps p278 MR43
HISLOP,Frederick Laurence 2Lt kia 23-4-17 6A&SH p243 CR France546
HISLOP,George Capt dow 28-11-17 RAMC N&D FA p253 CR Egypt9
HISLOP,James.MC.TLtACapt kia 31-7-17 CamH att6Bn p168 CR Belgium125
HISLOP,James Ambrose Lt kld 9-9-15 RAMC p254 CR Scot776,8HLI
HISLOP,John.MC.TLtACapt kia 22-9-17 8Beds p86 MR30
HISLOP,John Arthur TCapt ded 8-7-16 19Manch p155 CR Lancs464
HISLOP,John Hogben T2Lt dow 11-4-17 15RScots p54 CR France95
HISLOP,Percy Robert T2Lt dow 7-12-17 17Mddx p147 CR France145
HISLOP,Robert Wallace TLtACapt kia 22-7-17 RE 251TC p45 CR France163
HISLOP,Robert Wilson Lt 4-7-17 1/4 att1/6SfthH CR Belgium11
HISLOP,Walter Balmer 2Lt kia 28-4-15 5RScots D'Coy p211 CR Gallipoli2
HISSEY,Maurice Henry ACapt kia 26-10-16 2RBerks p139 MR21
HITCH,George Stuart Lt ded 9-11-18 5Lpool attRAF p215&258 CR Ches182,Stewart
HITCH,Gerald Henry Sibbald TCapt ded 10-2-19 RASC p254
HITCHCOCK,Cyril Augustus T2Lt kia 21-4-16 1KSLI p145 CR Belgium73
HITCHCOCK,Edward Arthur Lt dow 29-9-18 1/6HLI p240 CR France1184
HITCHCOCK,Herbert William TLt kia 13-11-16 MGC Inf att11TankCps p183 CR France383
HITCHCOCK,Reginald Francis 2Lt kia 14-4-18 25MGC p183 MR32
HITCHEN,Stanley Lucas T2Lt kia 6-6-16 17WYorks p81 CR France727
HITCHIN,George Robert Capt kia 14-8-16 RAMC 2/1FA p253 CR France141
HITCHINGS,Francis Noel Wells Lt kld 3-12-18 5RWSurr att6EKent p212 CR France1196,ded
HITCHINGS,Henry Mayne 2Lt kia 18-8-16 GL 7RIrRif att48TMB p190 CR France423,HITCHINS
HITCHINGS,Richard Gordon LtACapt kia 10-7-17 RFA 38DAC p30 CR Belgium16
HITCHINS,Henry William Ernest LtCol kia 28-4-15 1Manch p155 CR Belgium101,26-4-15
HITCHON,James Foldys Lt kia 1-7-16 10 att11ELancs Y'Coy p110 CR France802
HITNER,Victor Jacob TLt ded 20-7-18 RASC attLabCps p193 CR France145
HOADE,Reginald William 2Lt kia 15-7-16 2/7 att1Mddx p235 MR21
HOARD,Henry Herbert Hoare 2Lt kia 9-9-17 3 att21NumbF p61 CR France366
HOARE,Allen Brodie Capt kia 26-10-17 5LNLancs A'Coy p234 MR30,Alan
HOARE,Archibald Capt dow 27-11-17 12KRRC p150 CR France446
HOARE,Charles Morgan Lt kia 24-8-15 15Huss p22 MR15,24-8-14
HOARE,Edward 2Lt kia 9-5-16 1GrenGds SR p50 CR Belgium84
HOARE,Eric Sutherland 2Lt dow 11-11-16 53/2RFA p30 CR France105
HOARE,Evelyn Melville Shovell T2Lt kia 28-3-18 6EKent p57 MR27
HOARE,Frank William Capt kia 23-4-17 1Norf p74 MR20
HOARE,Frederick William Ernest Capt kia 10-8-17 HAC att11RFus p206 MR29 &CR France453
HOARE,George Henry 2Lt dow 1-6-17 RGA 93SB p40 CR Belgium11
HOARE,Gerard Croft 2Lt ded 1-8-17 6RB p179 CR Essex167
HOARE,Henry Colt Arthur Capt dow 20-12-17 DorsYeo p203 CR Egypt1,B Sqn
HOARE,Henry James Rev ded 5-8-17 RAChDept p268
HOARE,Henry Joseph 2Lt kia 15-8-15 10Lond p248 MR4
HOARE,Percival Hugh Trench Lt dow 8-1-15 3 att1ELancs p110 CR Belgium68,kia 2-1-15
HOARE,Percy James T2Lt kia 18-9-18 A117RFA p30 CR France528

HOARE,Reginald Arthur Capt kia 19-9-18 PembYeo attKSLI p205 CR France1701
HOARE,Richard Lennard Capt kia 1-7-16 12Lond p248 CR France798
HOARE,Robert Victor 2Lt ded 10-5-17 IA 22Cav p278 CR Iraq8
HOARE,Robert William Capt kia 9-10-17 7Worc C'Coy p225 CR Belgium126
HOARE,Vincent Robertson Maj kia 15-2-15 12Lond p248 CR Belgium58
HOARE,Walter John Gerald.DSO.TCapt kia 25-10-16 11RFus p68 CR France280
HOARE,Wilfred Gurney Capt kia 10-3-15 3DLI att2Wilts p161 MR22
HOARE,William George 2Lt kia 16-6-15 HAC p206 MR29
HOATHER,Harold Lt ded 4-5-19 WYorks p263 CR Sussex190
HOBART,Hobart Douglas Capt dow 21-4-16 IA 24Punjabis att53Sikhs p278 MR38,Lt 20-4-16
HOBART,Joseph Claud Antonie 2Lt ded 3-2-16 1/5RSuss p228 CR Lond9
HOBART-HAMPDEN,George Miles Awdry 2Lt kld 17-9-17 O&BLI &RFC p130&9 CR Bucks116,Lt
HOBBES,Narelli Sister ded 10-5-18 QAIMNS p200 MR38,Narrelle
HOBBS,A.S.Capt 16-10-18 IARO MR66
HOBBS,Alan Victor T2Lt kia 15-12-15 GL &RFC p17&190 CR France1144
HOBBS,Arnold William.MM.2Lt kia 9-4-17 3 att10YLI p143 CR France1186
HOBBS,Arthur Edward Singleton TCapt ded 16-10-18 IARO attArmyRemount Dept p278
HOBBS,Arthur Harold Capt kia 2-10-15 1WelshR p127 MR19
HOBBS,Cecil William St.John 2Lt ded 31-5-16 RASC p267 CR Mddx29
HOBBS,Charles James Willoughby.DSO.Maj dow 16-10-16 2N&D p134 CR France105,LtCol
HOBBS,Eric 2Lt kia 1-7-16 2RWSurr p56 CR France397
HOBBS,Frank Matthew 2Lt kia 16-9-14 4RFus p68 MR15,14-9-14
HOBBS,Geoffrey Brian TLt kld 7-9-15 10NumbF att9RFC p61&1,Bryan CR Kent15,2Lt
HOBBS,Geoffrey Harold Chapman 2Lt kia 16-9-16 7Dors att6SomLI p124 MR21
HOBBS,Gerald Parker 2Lt dow 15-10-17 2Ess p131 CR Belgium16
HOBBS,H.E.2Lt kia 25-5-15 2NumbF p61 MR29
HOBBS,Henry Bede Lt kia 15-3-17 10Lpool p216 CR France513,Bedo
HOBBS,Herbert Victor T2Lt kia 7-4-17 17Manch p155 CR France214
HOBBS,John.MC.2Lt dow 28-6-15 1RScots p54 CR France285
HOBBS,Joseph Spencer Lt ded 8-6-18 1RFA p270 CR Herts87
HOBBS,Reginald George T2Lt kia 20-9-17 11KRRC p150 CR Belgium8
HOBBS,Victor William John Lt kia 9-8-18 4EKent p212 CR France209
HOBBS,William George TLt kia 25-9-15 8RBerks p139 MR19
HOBBY,Grenville Howard.MM.T2Lt kia 20-10-18 17 att14WelshR p127 CR France230
HOBDAY,Charles Frederick ACapt dow 1-12-17 3 att1Ess p131 CR France398
HOBDAY,Victor Maitland 2LtTCapt kia 7-6-17 11WYorks p81 CR Belgium127
HOBDAY,William Edward.DCM&Bar.T2Lt kia 11-4-17 13RB p179 CR France154
HOBDELL,Arthur Bert Falvey 2LtACapt dow 16-4-18 3 att6Wilts p153 CR Belgium18,Birt Falwey
HOBDEN,Charles Frank T2Lt ded 16-9-15 RGA p40 CR Europe23
HOBDEN,Ernest 2Lt kia 20-10-18 RGA 328SB p40 CR France319
HOBHOUSE,Paul Edward.MID Capt kia 21-3-18 6SomLI p80 MR27
HOBKINSON,Charles Wilfred T2Lt dow 23-8-15 6Y&L p159 MR4
HOBLYN,Walter Frederick 2Lt dow 1-10-15 att4CldGds p51 CR France88,Lt 2-10-15
HOBSON,Allen Faber.DSO.MIDx2 Maj kia 28-8-16 RE 2/1FC p209 CR France296,Alan
HOBSON,Alwyne Chadwick Lt kia 13-5-15 2LifeGds p20 MR29
HOBSON,Andrew John Hay Lt kia 9-10-17 8WYorks p219 MR30
HOBSON,Archibald Campbell LtCol ded 19-12-17 IA 99Inf att2/10Jats p278 MR66
HOBSON,Charles Cuthbert Lt ded 20-2-19 2Co ofLondYeo p204 CR Lond28
HOBSON,Edgar Charles T2Lt dow 20-5-17 PoW 15RWar p65 CR Germany1
HOBSON,Geoffrey Hamilton 2Lt dow 14-4-17 1Hamps p121 CR France40
HOBSON,John Alfred.MC.T2Lt kia 2-12-17 175MGC p183 CR France177 &CR France711
HOBSON,John Collinson TLt kia 31-7-17 1/6MGC p183 MR29
HOBSON,Leslie Faber 2Lt ded 12-7-15 4Y&L p238 CR Belgium1 dow
HOBSON,Nathaniel James Fennel Lt drd 10-10-18 5Lpool p215 MR20
HOBSON,Owen Ellis.MID TCapt kia 27-9-18 6 att4Beds p86 CR France1496
HOBSON,Robert Carl.MC&Bar.MID TCapt ded 10-11-18 GL NumbF 50Div p190 CR Devon2
HOCKADAY,Harold Francis Henry Legg 2Lt kia 10-10-17 4Dev 2Coy p220 MR30,Lugg
HOCKADAY,Sidney Reginald Capt dow 2-9-16 2Mon p244 CR Belgium11
HOCKEN,Stephen Lotan T2Lt kia 3-9-16 10KRRC p150 MR21
HOCKEY,Jessie Olive Sister 14-8-17 QAIMNS Res CR France64

HOCKIN,George Chamberlain Lt kia 24-11-15 IA 1/7 att2/7GurkhaRif p278 MR38,22-11-15
HOCKING,Edward Cuthbert 2Lt kld 28-10-18 RFA &151RAF p30 CR France646,Lt
HOCKING,Herbert Victor LtACapt kia 13-4-18 1DCLI p114 CR France18
HODDER,Charles William Rev ded 21-10-18 RAChDept p268 CR Surrey152
HODDING,Cuthbert Francis Capt ded 8-12-18 4Wilts CR Wilts129
HODDING,Frederick Capt ded 21-10-19 IARO att118LabCps p278 CR Pakistan50A MR43
HODDING,Henry Ellis.MC.TLt dow 8-11-18 10N&D p134 CR France332
HODDING,James Douglas T2Lt dow 10-7-16 10RFus A'Coy p68 CR France833
HODES,Francis Percy T2Lt dow 24-7-16 14RWar p65 CR France44,Lt
HODGART,Matthew.MC.Maj kia 9-10-17 RE 406FC p209 CR Belgium23
HODGE,Andrew Buckland Lt dow 31-7-17 3Leinst p174 MR29
HODGE,Arthur Egerton Lt kia 13-6-17 1NStaffs p157 CR Belgium127
HODGE,Frederick George 2Lt kia 31-10-17 2/21Lond p251 CR Palestine1
HODGE,George William 2Lt kia 27-4-18 2/4Lincs p217 MR30
HODGE,Jack Wheaton Lt kia 12-10-16 2WRid p115 CR France374
HODGE,Leslie Richard 2Lt kia 17-7-17 4Ess p232 MR20
HODGE,Lionel Bryant Capt dow 10-11-17 2/22Lond p251 CR Egypt2
HODGE,Lionel Clifford 2Lt kia 30-11-17 6RWKent p141 MR17
HODGE,William Bardo TLt ded 4-11-18 6 att11RScotF p94 CR France40
HODGES,Albert Rowland Cortis 2Lt kld 20-3-18 Mddx &RFC p16&147 CR Norf73
HODGES,Alfred John Carter 2Lt kia 23-8-18 20Lond p251 CR France119,Lt dow
HODGES,Archibald Gordon TLt kia 15-9-16 8Beds p86 MR21
HODGES,Arthur Thomas 2Lt ded 2-3-19 Ches p263 CR Glouc86
HODGES,Bernard T2Lt dow 16-4-18 KRRC att16Bn p150 MR32
HODGES,Charles Edward 2Lt kia 16-6-15 4RFus p68 CR Belgium116
HODGES,Daniel Alfred 2Lt kia 5-5-17 3 att10RWKent p141 CR Belgium152
HODGES,Edward Norman.MC.TCapt ded 22-6-18 RASC p193 CR France788
HODGES,Eric Colpoys 2Lt dow 15-7-16 2RIrReg p89 CR France833
HODGES,Harold Augustus.MID Capt kia 22-3-18 3Mon att11SLancs p244 CR France987,24-3-18
HODGES,Harold Henry T2Lt dow 13-7-16 7Leinst p174 CR France423,Henry Harold
HODGES,Harold Wardale 2Lt kia 9-5-15 6 att2KRRC p150 MR22
HODGES,Henry Burden 2Lt kia 18-4-15 2YLI p143 MR29
HODGES,James William T2Lt kia 21-3-18 ELancs att5Bn p111 MR27
HODGES,John Cyril Lt kld 17-9-16 RGA attRFC p3&40 CR War67
HODGES,John Percy 2Lt kia 25-4-18 6KOSB p101 CR Belgium21
HODGES,Sydney Howard 2Lt kia 17-10-14 4RFus p68 CR France567
HODGINS,Charles Francis Burgoyne 2Lt kia 25-9-15 2Wilts p153 CR France924
HODGKINS,James Percy 2Lt dow 26-9-17 2/4Leic p220 CR Belgium16
HODGKINSON,Alan.MID Lt kia 1-7-16 2RWar p65 CR France397
HODGKINSON,G.Lt dow 18-10-17 3/2KAR p202
HODGKINSON,Geoffrey Still Lt kia 24-7-17 A277RH&FA p30 CR Belgium7
HODGKINSON,George Cedric TLt dow 4-7-16 Yorks att8Y&L B'Coy p90 CR France833
HODGKINSON,Harry 2Lt kia 9-9-18 Manch att12Bn p155 CR France415
HODGKINSON,Hans Gerald 2Lt dow 18-10-17 5WRid att3/2KAR p255 CR EAfrica11 &CR Tanzania1,Lt
HODGKINSON,James Percival TCapt kia 2-11-16 15N&D p134 CR France1182
HODGKINSON,John T2Lt kia 17-4-18 18NumbF p61 MR32
HODGKINSON,John Francis Capt dow 10-11-14 3DragGds p21 CR France102
HODGKINSON,William Lt kia 9-10-18 6Lpool &RAF p270
HODGKISS,Frederick.MC.2Lt dow 8-10-17 3 att2/4LNLancs p136 CR France11
HODGSON,Albert Hodgson T2Lt kia 22-1-17 GL &52RFC p9 CR France134
HODGSON,Alec Edmund Smart 2Lt kia 12-10-16 3Y&L p159 MR21
HODGSON,Arthur Dawson TLt kia 20-7-16 15N&D p134 MR21
HODGSON,Charles T2Lt dow 9-8-16 18 att15RScots p54 CR France74
HODGSON,Charles Basil Mortimer Capt dow 1-4-18 3RWSurr att2/24Lond p56 CR Egypt9
HODGSON,Charles Edward.DCM.T2Lt kia 2-10-18 KRRC att18Bn p150 CR Belgium112
HODGSON,Christopher Anthony Rowlandson Capt kia 18-12-14 3RWar p65 MR32
HODGSON,Christopher Michael Lt dow 17-6-17 B276RFA p207 CR Belgium10
HODGSON,Clarence Mortimer TCapt kia 18-9-16 14DLI C'Coy p161 CR France374
HODGSON,Cyril Arthur Godwin Capt ded 20-3-18 RNDevYeo p203 CR Egypt9

HODGSON,Cyril Francis 2Lt kia 11-1-17 IA 2/124BaluchistanInf p278 CR Iraq5

HODGSON,Evelyn Mary Sister ded 21-12-18 QAIMNS att28GenHosp p200 CR Greece9

HODGSON,Eric Godfrey 2Lt dow 22-5-15 IARO att40Pathans p278 CR France102

HODGSON,Francis Faith.MID Capt dow 17-5-15 IA 84Punjabis att58Rif p278 CR France924

HODGSON,Frederick James TLt ded 5-5-18 GL &1KAR p202 CR SAfrica144

HODGSON,George Bailey TCapt kia 13-4-17 GL &59RFC p9 MR20

HODGSON,George Graham Lt kia 9-5-15 2RBerks p139 MR32

HODGSON,George William Houghton Lt dow 6-11-14 2BordR p117 CR France102

HODGSON,Hamilton Capt kia 6-5-15 Lincs attHamps p75 MR4

HODGSON,Isaac Harvey TLt dow 20-4-16 1BordR p117 CR France67,2Bn

HODGSON,John T2Lt kia 27-10-18 12DLI p161 CR Italy9

HODGSON,John TLt ded 16-11-18 RE TransStores p45 CR France134

HODGSON,John Charles Capt kia 28-6-15 10BordR p117 MR4

HODGSON,John Edward.OBE.LtCol ded 5-11-18 RAMC att12ArmyCps attStaff p196 CR Greece19

HODGSON,John Henry.MM.TLt kia 30-4-18 4Mddx p147 CR France204

HODGSON,John Joseph 2Lt kia 13-8-17 RE 184TC p45

HODGSON,John Solomon Riddell Lt kia 25-3-17 2Dors p124 MR38

HODGSON,Maurice Kirkham Capt dow 12-3-15 1N&D p134 CR France768,kia 13-3-15

HODGSON,Michael Reginald Kirkman Capt kia 17-3-15 RFus attYLI p68 MR29

HODGSON,Oswald Arthur 2Lt kia 16-4-17 28 att9NumbF p61 MR20

HODGSON,Philip Ormiston 2Lt dow 13-3-15 2ELancs p111 CR France768,kia

HODGSON,Reginald 2Lt kia 27-6-16 7Leinst p174 CR France423

HODGSON,Reginald Drury TCapt kia 21-3-18 82RFA p30 MR27

HODGSON,Richard Everleigh Lt kia 16-9-18 4Lpool &204RAF p72 CR Belgium24,Eveleigh 15-9-18

HODGSON,Richard Victor 2Lt kia 20-6-17 22DLI att5DCLI p161 CR Belgium29

HODGSON,Rupert Ernest Lt kia 31-8-16 1NStaffs p157 CR France397

HODGSON,William Hope TLt kia 17-4-18 RFA 11ArmyBde p30 MR30

HODGSON,William Noel TLt kia 1-7-16 9Dev p76 CR France330

HODGSON-JONES,Douglas Sacre.MID TCapt ded 13-2-19 RE p262 CR Lancs34

HODKIN,Wilfred Capt kia 14-1-20 IA 1/109Inf p278

HODKINSON,Harold Hale 2Lt kia 8-8-16 10 att1/4RLancs p59 MR21

HODKINSON,Leonard 2Lt kia 14-9-17 15RWFus &53RFC p9&98 CR France285

HODKINSON,Peter 2Lt kia 23-10-18 7 att20DLI p239 MR16

HODSON,Bertie John TLt kia 21-3-18 5RIrReg att1RIrRif p89 MR27

HODSON,Edward Hutchinson TLt kia 24-3-18 15Ches p96 MR27

HODSON,George Benjamin.CB.DSO.BrigGen dow 29-1-16 IA Cmdg33Inf p278 CR Europe1,25-1-16

HODSON,Robert Charles T2Lt kia 8-5-17 RE 279RlyCo p45 CR France523

HODSON,Sydney 2Lt kia 21-3-18 5 att9KRRC p150 MR27

HODSON,Thomas George Smith Capt drd 10-4-17 RAMC p196 CR France85

HODY,Edmund Hody Maj ded 15-3-19 RASC VI Cps MT Coy p254 CR Germany1,15-6-19

HOEY,Fredk Cyril T2Lt kld 7-6-17 GL &RFC p9 CR Wilts28

HOFFA,James Michael Crosby Lt ded 28-7-17 1/3KAR p202 CR EAfrica38 &CR Tanzania1

HOFMEYER,Robert Ernest Murray 2Lt kia 24-4-17 5Yorks attMGC p221

HOFMEYR,Jan Hendrik T2Lt kia 27-10-17 N&D att1/8Bn p134 CR France115

HOFMEYR,Richard TLt ded 11-9-17 YLI &RFC p9&143 MR37

HOFMEYR,Robert Ernest Murray 2Lt kia 24-4-17 5Yorks att63MGC p187 MR20

HOG,Archibald Swinton Capt dow 20-8-15 5ConnRgrs p172 CR Europe1

HOGAN,Arthur Alan TLt kia 24-1-18 N&D att15Bn p134 CR Belgium83,2Lt

HOGAN,Edmund James Patrick Lt ded 11-2-20 IARO attS&TCps p278 MR67,13-2-20

HOGAN,Jack Graham 2Lt kia 28-3-18 1Hamps p121 MR20

HOGAN,Robert Garret Roche 2Lt kia 12-3-15 2RBerks p139 MR22

HOGAN,Robert James Lt ded 10-6-20 IARO attFollowersCentDept p278 MR69

HOGARTH,Archibald McDonald Lt dow 9-7-16 A104RFA p30 CR France188,Archie

HOGARTH,John Scott 2Lt kia 25-3-17 4KOSB p224 CR France68

HOGBEN,Frank T2Lt kia 12-10-16 7Norf p74 MR21

HOGBEN,Frederick 2Lt kia 23-10-16 3SStaffs att8Lincs p122 MR21

HOGBEN,Henry Francis Thomas Lt kia 22-11-15 10Mddx p236 MR38

HOGBEN,Leslie Thomas T2Lt kld 23-10-17 RFC p9 CR Kent177

HOGBEN,William Iggulden 2Lt kia 18-8-16 12WYorks p81 MR21

HOGBIN,Raymond T2Lt kia 20-9-17 32RFus p68 MR30

HOGG,Archibald TLt ded 14-10-18 RAMC p267 CR Scot685

HOGG,Clement Stuart T2Lt dow 6-4-17 RE Z SpCo p45 CR France95

HOGG,David Adams T2Lt kia 9-2-17 15HLI p163 CR France131

HOGG,Frank Alexander T2Lt dow 17-6-16 10 att1NStaffs p157 CR France285

HOGG,Hardinge Monteith Maj kia 22-4-17 IA 32Lancers p278 MR38

HOGG,Ian Graham.DSO.LtCol dow 2-9-14 4Huss p21 CR France1129

HOGG,Ivan Dayrell Meredith Capt kia 4-11-14 IA 101Grens p278 MR47

HOGG,J.S.Capt 12-8-17 RE 2FC CR Scot674

HOGG,James TCapt kia 24-9-16 14A&SH p173 CR France115

HOGG,James T2Lt kia 2-12-17 5RB p179 MR30

HOGG,Lewis Stephen Capt&Adjt kia 25-9-15 9RWFus p98 MR19

HOGG,Robert Morrison T2Lt dow 1-4-18 2DLI p161 CR Germany1

HOGG,Theodore Alan TCapt kia 21-3-18 2NStaffs p157 MR20

HOGG,Walter Gordon TLt kia 24-5-17 15RIrRif p169 CR Belgium100

HOGGE,Thomas Henry.MC.Lt kia 5-10-17 24RFA p30&258 CR France179

HOGGAN,Claude Ashley Rien Lt kia 30-5-18 46MGC p183 CR France109,Rieu

HOGGARD,Ernest John 2Lt kia 5-11-16 3RWSurr attMGC Inf p56&183 CR France385

HOGGARTH,Norman Scott T2Lt dow 30-5-18 PoW 6Leic p87 CR Germany3

HOGGETT,Frank Reginald T2Lt dow 18-7-16 10RWSurr p56 CR Lancs34

HOGHTON,Frederick Aubrey BrigGen ded 12-4-16 IA Cmdg17Inf p278 CR Iraq1

HOHLER,Arthur Preston LtCol ded 7-3-19 10Mddx p270 CR Bucks76

HOILE,George Vincent.MBE.Capt&QM 29-5-20 GL Ex RFA CR Surrey15

HOJEL,J.G.LtCol 21-3-19 IMS MR65

HOLAWAY,Charles Edmund 2Lt kia 11-8-17 ChesYeo attRFC p18&203 MR20

HOLBECH,David T2Lt kia 8-4-17 18KRRC p150 CR Belgium28

HOLBECH,William Hugh Lt dow 1-11-14 2ScotsGds RoO p52 CR War57

HOLBERTON,Philip Vaughan.MIDx5 ALtCol kia 26-3-18 6Manch p155 CR France518,2Bn

HOLBOROW,Frederick Bernard T2Lt kia 16-4-18 16KRRC p150 MR32

HOLBROW,Thomas Leonard Stanley.MC.Capt kia 28-3-18 RE 156FC p45 CR France899,Maj

HOLCROFT,Gilbert Culcheth 2Lt kia 9-8-15 2DLI p161 MR29

HOLCROFT,Raymond Boycott T2Lt kia 1-7-16 9Dev p76 CR France330

HOLDCROFT,Eric Crane T2Lt kia 4-10-17 RFus Res att13Bn p68 CR Belgium125

HOLDCROFT,Walter Leigh.MC&Bar.2Lt kia 5-8-18 1 att6NStaffs p157 MR19

HOLDCROFT,William Lawrence T2Lt kia 29-7-16 2SStaffs p122 MR21,28-7-16

HOLDEN,Cecil Alexander Nalorett 2Lt kia 28-5-19 22Punjabis p278 MR43,Lt 27-5-19 &CR Ireland24,Capt 22-11-18 2Leins

HOLDEN,Edward Charles Shuttleworth.DSO.LtCol 18-5-16 DerbyYeo CR Surrey160

HOLDEN,Ernest Airlie T2Lt dow 17-10-16 8LNLancs C'Coy p136 CR France59

HOLDEN,H Maj 3-3-20 IndOrdDept CR Burma129A

HOLDEN,Harold 2Lt kia 20-9-17 5LNLancs p234 CR Belgium96,1/4Bn

HOLDEN,Hyla Napier.DSO&Bar.LtCol kia 26-10-18 IA 5Cav attLancers p278 CR Lebanon1

HOLDEN,John 2Lt kia 28-9-18 4ELancs p226 CR Belgium50

HOLDEN,Joseph Rogers 2Lt kia 5-8-16 RE p210 CR France513,Roger

HOLDEN,Leigh 2Lt kia 9-6-15 4SLancs p230 MR29 &CR France453

HOLDEN,Leonard Neil TLt kia 9-7-16 11LancF p92 MR21

HOLDEN,Norman T2Lt dow 29-10-18 5SWBord p100 CR France380

HOLDEN,Norman Victor Lt&QM dow 4-6-15 6LancF p221 CR Gallipoli1

HOLDEN,Oswald Addenbrooke Chap4Cl kia 1-12-17 RAChDept att60InfBde p199 CR France379

HOLDEN,Vernon.DSO.MC.TMaj dow 2-10-18 10RWKent attWSurr p141 CR Belgium188

HOLDEN,William Leak 2Lt kia 4-1-17 19Manch p155 CR France927

HOLDER,Charles Vincent T2Lt kia 24-8-16 5KSLI p145 MR21

HOLDER,Tom S.TCapt ded 26-11-18 DCLI p114&257 CR Cornwall40

HOLDERNESS,William Harold 2Lt kia 17-4-16 6N&D p233 CR France68

HOLDICH,Godfrey William.VC.DSO.LtCol 13-4-21 RGA MR69

HOLDING,Alfred William TLt&QM ded 27-7-16 RAMC p196 CR Sussex144

HOLDING,James Capt&Adjt kia 1-8-18 1/4Ches p222 CR France524

HOLDROYD,Percy T2Lt kia 5-5-17 YLI att2/5Bn p143 MR20

HOLDSWORTH,Arthur Mervyn.MID LtCol dow 7-7-16 2RBerks p139 CR France40

HOLDSWORTH,Charles John T2Lt kia 8-5-17 Dev p76 CR France568

HOLDSWORTH,Ernest T2Lt kia 23-9-17 GL &29RFC p9 CR Belgium18

HOLDSWORTH,Godfrey Edward LtACapt kia 24-3-18 1 att4SStaffs p122 MR20

HOLDSWORTH,Henry Bernard Capt kia 10-4-18 8DLI p239 MR32

HOLDSWORTH,Joseph Arthur.MC.LtACapt ded PoW 17-6-18 5LancF p221 CR Germany4,2/8Bn

HOLDSWORTH,Vavasour Mervyn 2Lt kia 20-12-15 22Lond p251 CR

France423
HOLE,Ernest George T2Lt ded 10-12-18 RASC p193 CR France1830
HOLE,Michael T2Lt kia 19-9-17 10KRRC p150 MR30
HOLE,William Arthur TLt kia 1-7-16 15RScots p54 MR21
HOLFORD,Leonard Brocklesby 2Lt dow 20-2-19 10Lpool p216 CR Ches181,1/16Bn
HOLGATE,Harold Arthur T2Lt kia 25-9-16 14 att 1ESurr p112 MR21
HOLLAND,Albert Capt kia 21-9-18 6RSuss &RAF p158&228
HOLLAND,Archibald Clare 2Lt kia 27-7-16 1Beds p86 MR21
HOLLAND,Arthur Leslie 2Lt kia 21-4-17 6 att2RB p179 CR France407
HOLLAND,Basil Thomas 2Lt kia 10-3-15 2BlkW p128 MR22
HOLLAND,Charles.MC.Capt kld 25-1-18 8RFC p16 CR Sussex27
HOLLAND,Charles Stewart Maj kia 24-8-14 RFA p30 CR Belgium201,23-8-14
HOLLAND,Charles Trevenent T.Lt kia 9-5-15 33RFA p30 CR France348
HOLLAND,Clarence Jennings T2Lt kia 14-8-18 RLancs att1/4Bn p59 MR19
HOLLAND,Cyril Capt kia 9-5-15 RFA p30 CR France631
HOLLAND,Edward.MC.2Lt kia 13-9-16 1ScotsGds p52 MR21
HOLLAND,Edward Hugo T2Lt kia 23-4-17 4Worc p109 MR20
HOLLAND,Edward Matthew Lt kia 6-11-16 2Worc p109 MR21
HOLLAND,Ernest T2Lt kia 19-7-17 9SStaffs p122 CR Belgium29
HOLLAND,Frank Sidney Lt kia 27-11-17 2/6WRid p227 MR17
HOLLAND,Frederick 2Lt dow 22-8-17 3 att 1N&D p134&257 CR France40
HOLLAND,George Percival T2Lt kia 18-3-18 RWar att7Norf p65 CR France255
HOLLAND,Gerald Edward.CB.CMG.CIE.DSO.MIDx2 TBrigGen ded 26-6-17 RE IWT Staff p1 CR Wales460
HOLLAND,Harold Richard 2Lt kia 12-4-18 Mddx att1/8Bn p147 MR20
HOLLAND,Jack Harold 2Lt ded 16-6-18 22RFus attRAF p68 CR France1233
HOLLAND,John Dixon Cuyler T2Lt kia 13-11-16 2 O&BLI p130 CR France152
HOLLAND,Ralph TLt&QM ded 21-8-16 RAMC p196 CR Eire322
HOLLAND,Ralph Bertram TCapt kia 2-10-16 7RWKent B'Coy p141 CR France383
HOLLAND,Ralph Lingard 2Lt kia 8-2-17 RGA 255SB p40 CR France285
HOLLAND,Reginald Capt kia 4-4-18 2/4 att8Berks p234 MR27
HOLLAND,Richard Edward T2Lt kia 24-10-18 1Mddx p147 CR France230
HOLLAND,Samuel Clifford.DSO.Maj ded 13-9-19 1KDragGds RoO p261
HOLLAND,Thomas Welsby Lt kia 18-9-18 4 att16RWFus p223 CR France415,2Lt
HOLLAND,Tyrrel Evelyn.MC.Capt ded 11-1-19 GL att12RB p254 CR Lond4
HOLLAND,Vivian Ernest Capt dow 8-11-18 7Huss p22 CR Iraq8
HOLLAND,Wallace Derry Ayre Capt ded 13-8-17 IA 11Lancers p278 MR43
HOLLAND,William Francis Claude TCapt ded 8-11-17 GL &4DLI p190&265 CR Essex261
HOLLAND,William Rawlinson Garside.MC.T2Lt dow 18-9-17 10WYorks att50TMB p81 CR France1190
HOLLAND-MARTIN,Geoffrey Robert 2Lt kia 26-3-18 16Lancers p23 MR27
HOLLANDS,Wilfrid George 2Lt kia 12-10-16 7 att4RFus p68 CR France156
HOLLES,Frederick Tetherley Noel 2Lt ded 11-9-16 3ELancs p111 CR Iraq5
HOLLICK,Percy Hood.MID 2Lt&ACapt kia 8/9-5-17 3 att15RWar p65 MR20
HOLLIDAY,Alfred Rowland 2Lt kia 20-11-17 5Lond p246 CR France379
HOLLIDAY,Henry Lowther 2Lt kia 15-12-17 3 att9BordR p117 CR Greece5
HOLLINGBERY,Raymond Archibald Robert Lt kia 6-7-16 2 att3RWFus p98 CR France765
HOLLINGS,John Herbert Butler Lt kia 30-10-14 21Lancers p23 MR29
HOLLINGSHEAD,Amos Lt&QM ded 26-7-17 Yorks p90 CR Yorks176
HOLLINGSWORTH,F.Lt 26-4-15 1RhodR MG Sect CR SAfrica18
HOLLINGSWORTH,Frank Edwin 2Lt kia 15-9-16 A&SH &RFC p3 CR France1896 &CR France382
HOLLINGSWORTH,John Frederick T2Lt dow 2-10-16 14RSuss att7ESurr p119 CR France105
HOLLINGSWORTH,John Gordon Lt kia 12-8-15 10Mddx p236 MR4
HOLLINGWORTH,Leonard T2Lt kia 28-9-16 11 att1Dev p76 MR21
HOLLINGWORTH-BROWN,Robert Lt ded 27-12-19 RFA p261 MR65,28-12-19
HOLLINS,Edward Ralph Lambert TCapt dow 3-3-16 9RLancs p59 CR Belgium11,8Bn
HOLLINS,Herbert Francis TMaj ded 19-8-17 RGA 157HB p40 CR Iraq6
HOLLINS,James Piggott TLt&QM ded 3-2-16 13Lpool p72 CR Belgium15
HOLLINS,William Humphrey 2Lt kia 15-6-15 8N&D p233 CR Belgium17
HOLLINS-FISHER,Sydney Capt ded 28-9-18 9Mddx p236 MR65
HOLLINSHEAD,Shadrach 2Lt kia 27-3-18 3 att11ELancs p111 MR20
HOLLIS,Arthur Reginald TLt kia 12-9-18 10DCLI p114 CR France530
HOLLIS,Basil Lt kia 31-7-17 5BlkW p231 MR29
HOLLIS,Charles Frederick Griffith.MC.Lt 2-8-18 1EKent p57 CR Belgium40
HOLLIS,Frederick Alwin 2Lt ded 17-12-16 2/6BlkW p270 CR Norf209,16-12-16

HOLLIS,John Gordon.MID TLt kia 14-7-16 7Leic p87 MR21
HOLLIS,Percival Claude 2Lt kia 21-3-18 RGA 146SB p40 MR20
HOLLIS,Victor William.MC.2Lt kia 22-8-17 281RFA p30 CR Belgium19
HOLLIS,Walter Henry Lt kld 22-7-16 RDC p253 CR Sussex 189
HOLLIST,Anthony May Capron Capt kia 25/27-9-15 8EKent p57 MR19
HOLLMAN,George Leslie T2Lt dow 5-3-18 DLI p161
HOLLMAN,William Harold 2Lt kia 16-10-18 4RWKent p234 MR16
HOLLOM,Ernest Albert Bruce TLt kia 24-7-16 53RFA p30 CR France399
HOLLOMAN,Arthur TLt&QM kia 12-12-16 RAMC p196
HOLLOWAY,Arthur Grayston 2Lt kia 24-3-18 6 att16N&D p233 MR27
HOLLOWAY,Bernard Henry TCapt kia 27-9-15 9RSuss p119 MR19
HOLLOWAY,Claude Abrey Marseille Capt 19-12-19 RWKent &RAF CR Kent289
HOLLOWAY,Henry Francis.MC.2Lt&ACapt kia 11-4-18 7ELancs att9WelshR p111&258 MR30
HOLLOWAY,James T2Lt kia 27-9-18 MGC Inf p183 CR France905
HOLLOWAY,James Clinton.MID LtCol ded 11-1-17 RDC Staff p1&253,Hollway CR Nhampt60 Ex Lincs&1A
HOLLOWAY,Leonard T2Lt kia 9-4-17 20NumbF p61 MR20
HOLLOWAY,Robert James.MID Lt&QM ded 14-8-16 5NumbF p213 CR Numb5,dow
HOLLOWAY,William Robert T2Lt kia 20-9-17 69MGC Inf p183 MR30
HOLLOWELL,Francis John 2Lt kia 7-7-16 3Worc p109 CR France1890
HOLLYWOOD,Arthur Carson TLt kia 1-7-16 9RIrF p171 MR21
HOLLYWOOD,James T2Lt kia 1-7-16 18 att12RIrRif p169 MR21
HOLM,Frank Diederick T2Lt/TLt kia 14-5-17 RE &27RFC p9&45 CR France62,2Lt
HOLMAN,Arthur Vincent Capt ded 9-1-17 Hereford p252 CR Glouc32
HOLMAN,Cecil Graham 2Lt dow 5-9-17 KOSB &8RFC p9&101 CR France214
HOLMAN,Donald TLt kia 8-8-18 11Mddx att7RWSurr p147 CR France247
HOLMAN,Geoffrey Lt kia 9-4-15 2KSLI p145 MR29
HOLMAN,Gerald Chaplin Lt kia 17-9-17 GL &41RFC p9 CR France1277
HOLMAN,Guy Henry Wallis Lt dow 6-7-16 1Wilts p153 CR France296
HOLMAN,John Lt dow 29-10-14 4DragGds p21 CR France102
HOLME,Alexander Charles Lt kia 6-9-14 Glouc att3NigR p106&268 CR WAfrica1
HOLME,Bertram Lester TLt dow 25-4-16 12RWFus p98 CR Iraq5
HOLME,George Weston 2Lt kia 22-12-16 RFA 50DAC p208 CR France388,23-12-16
HOLME,James Edward Capt kia 9-10-17 16RWar p65 MR30
HOLME,Ronald Henry Paull Lt dow 9-11-14 KOSB p102 CR Scot567
HOLMES,Akehurst Wilson 2Lt dow 28-7-17 RGA 295SB p40 CR France297
HOLMES,Albert Arundel Capt ded 19-5-15 2/5RSuss p228 CR Essex45
HOLMES,Albert Edward 2Lt kia 18-9-18 2Y&L p159 MR16
HOLMES,Alfred Raymond Cdr ded 26-6-16 IA MilWksServ p278 CR Iraq6
HOLMES,Andrew T2Lt dow 24-10-18 13DLI p161 CR France231
HOLMES,Archibald 2Lt kia 4-2-18 RFC p16 MR20
HOLMES,Aubrey T2Lt kia 1-7-16 2Ess p131 CR France1491
HOLMES,Basil Ralph Gardiner 2Lt kia 2-10-17 A38RFA p208 CR Belgium8
HOLMES,Bryan Hanby 2Lt ded 9-11-18 5RFA p30 CR Scot235
HOLMES,Cecil Crampton.MID LtTCapt dow 26-8-14 1Lincs p75 CR Belgium202,Crompton
HOLMES,Charles James Maj ded 5-4-16 RAMC p196 CR Lancs76,LtCol
HOLMES,Cuthbert Blace 2Lt dow 28-9-17 1/4LNLancs p234 CR Belgium18,Black kia
HOLMES,Cyril TLt ded 21-12-15 WelshR att8Bn p127 CR Greece11,Capt
HOLMES,Cyril Ernest Jackson 2Lt kia 24-6-17 3/5ELancs att2/5Lpool p226 CR France922
HOLMES,Duncan McPherson Studdert T2Lt kia 4-3-16 9Ches p96 MR19
HOLMES,Eric Cecil Lt dow 3-4-18 5DLI p238 CR France145
HOLMES,Ernest Cameron T2Lt kia 14-11-16 13KRRC p150 CR France701
HOLMES,Francis Lennox Lt kia 23-10-14 1SStaffs p122 MR29
HOLMES,Frederick 2Lt dow 10-5-15 RInniskF att4LNLancs p105 CR France80
HOLMES,George 2Lt kia 9-4-17 1EYorks p84 CR France162
HOLMES,George Francis Edwin T2Lt kia 25-10-16 15N&D p134 CR France118
HOLMES,Henry Ball Maj dow 27-11-15 RIrF p171 CR Eire286
HOLMES,Hubert Lee Maj ded 22-4-18 IA 122Inf p278 CR Surrey11
HOLMES,James Fyfe.MC.2Lt mbk 23-3-18 9ScotRif p256 MR27
HOLMES,John Alexander 2Lt ded 26-4-16 4Leinst p174 CR France285
HOLMES,Leslie Stuart 2Lt ded 14-12-18 3SomLI p80 CR Lond12
HOLMES,Oswald Matthews T2Lt dow 25-8-17 6YLI p143 CR Belgium11
HOLMES,O.W.2Lt kia 16-8-17 7RInniskF p105 MR30

HOLMES,Reginald Eden LtACapt kia 4-6-18 1ScotsGds p52 CR France1014
HOLMES,Robert T2Lt ded 16-2-18 6RLancs p59 MR66
HOLMES,Robert Bryan 2Lt dow 1-7-16 5 att2KRRC p150 CR France178,Brian
HOLMES,Robert Reginald John Capt ded 26-3-16 RAMC 81FA p253 CR Europe1
HOLMES,Thomas George Lt kia 6-5-17 100RFC SR p9 CR France1277
HOLMES,Thomas Gerald 2Lt kia 27-3-18 A16RFA p30 CR France588
HOLMES,Thomas Symonds 2Lt kia 12-11-14 RWSurr attEKent p56 CR France276,11-11-14
HOLMES,Vernon Raines.MC.Lt kia 14-10-16 6Ches p222 CR France293
HOLMES,Wilfred Bertram 2Lt kia 20-8-17 4Ches p222 MR30,Wilfrid 20-9-17
HOLMES,William.CMG.DSO.VD.MajGen kia 2-7-17 SL Staff AustDivHQ Ex AIF p1
HOLMES,William Henry T2Lt kia 15-12-17 7SfthH p165 CR France415
HOLMES,William James Maj 5-2-21 RAOC attIACC CR Germany1
HOLMS,Andrew Stuart TLt kia 1-7-16 RE 177TC p45 CR Belgium4,Lt
HOLMS,John Cyril Capt dow 10-9-15 9Lond p247 CR France513
HOLMS,William T2Lt kia 16-9-16 10/11HLI p163 CR France239
HOLNESS,Frederick Reginald T2Lt ded 2-2-19 6Lincs p263 CR Essex7,4Bn
HOLOHAN,P.Capt dow 19-8-15 1RMunstF CR Egypt6
HOLROYD,Benjamin 2Lt kia 13-11-16 1/5SfthH p241 CR France131
HOLROYD,Clifford 2Lt kia 3-5-17 2/6WRid p227 MR20
HOLROYD,Lister TCapt dow 12-9-16 7EYorks p84 CR France121
HOLROYD-SMYTH,Charles Edward Ridley.DSO.MC.CaptTLtCol dow 23-9-18 3DragGds att 15DLI p21 CR Somerset37
HOLROYDE,John Sheffield 2Lt kia 10-5-17 EYorks &55RFC p9&84 CR France288
HOLT,Arthur Edward 2Lt dow 25-10-17 RGA 233SB p40 CR Belgium72
HOLT,Denis Ralph William Capt ded 31-12-19 IA 3/34SikhPnrs p278 MR43,31-1-20
HOLT,Follett Hallett Lt kia 22-8-18 3 O&BLI attTankCps p130&188 CR France370
HOLT,Fredk George Bradley 2Lt kia 5-4-18 24Lond p252 MR20
HOLT,Geoffrey Vesey 2Lt kia 2-9-15 91RFA p30 CR Belgium23
HOLT,Herbert Wilfred 2Lt kia 23-8-14 RE p45 CR Belgium242
HOLT,Hubert Granville,MC TLt kia 6-10-17 GL &9RFC p9 CR Belgium18
HOLT,John Leonard 2Lt kia 16-3-18 88RFC p16 CR France1266
HOLT,John William Capt kia 27-8-17 4WRid p227 CR Belgium126,8Bn Ex 4Bn
HOLT,Joseph Capt kia 4-6-15 6Manch p236 MR4
HOLT,Laurence Guy.MC.TCapt kia 27-9-16 1LNLancs p136 CR France385,3Bn
HOLT,Leslie Capt kia 11-3-18 2/10Lond p248 CR France1893
HOLT,Percy James T2Lt dow 6-9-18 6Beds att1/1Herts p86 CR France145
HOLT,Wilfred T2Lt kia 16-8-17 12Manch p155 CR Belgium96
HOLT,Wilfrid 2Lt kia 3-5-17 18WYorks p81 MR20
HOLT,William Frederick Sloane T2Lt ded 1-7-18 19Manch p155 CR Lancs474
HOLT,William Leslie T2Lt kia 23-12-17 10Y&L p159 CR Belgium131,22-12-17
HOLT,William Parkinson Capt kia 24-6-17 RASC attRFC p18&253 CR France1310
HOLTOM,Charles Cecil TLt kia 31-10-17 181MGC p183 CR Palestine1
HOLTOM,Charles Fifield 2Lt dow 4-8-16 1/5NStaffs p238 CR France120
HOLTOM,John Nicholson 2Lt ded 22-10-16 RFC p3 MR20
HOLTON,Francis Keatley Lt kld 27-10-17 1Mddx att98TMB p147 CR Belgium48,2Lt
HOLTON,George James Paul 2Lt dow 16-9-18 1Co ofLondYeo p204 CR France1184
HOLTON,John Arthur 2Lt kia 4-10-17 103RFA p30 CR Belgium21 Ex EssYeo
HOLWILL,William Bertram 2Lt dow PoW 16-5-18 66MGC Inf p183 CR France928
HOLYMAN,Leslie Edward 2Lt kia 9-3-17 1/5EKent p213 MR38
HOLYOAKE,Ralph LtCol ded 18-5-19 RAMC p267 CR Mddx48
HOMAN,Arthur Douglas CaptAMaj dow 9-5-17 RIrReg att70HLI p89 CR Greece1
HOMAN,Claude Knox TLt kia 18-9-15 6Dors p124 CR Belgium111
HOMAN,H.B.2Ld kld 4-4-18 GL &RAF p190
HOMAN,Henry Leslie Capt kia 10-3-15 2Mddx p147 CR France706
HOMAN,Ralph William LtTCapt dow 11-8-15 1EKent p57 CR Belgium11
HOMAN,Russell Charles TLt kia 22-3-18 15N&D p134 MR27
HOME,Robert TCapt kia 23-4-17 RAMC p196 17FA CR France80,22-4-17
HOME,Walter Gabriel.MID Maj dow 13-11-14 6DragGds p21 MR29,31-10-14
HOMER,Charles William T2Lt kld 27-10-17 GL &RFC p9 CR Suff173
HOMER,William Howard Claude.MC.Lt kia 26-4-18 6Glouc p225 MR30
HOMERSHAM,Arthur Jones Lt kia 18-2-18 25Lond attRFC p18&252 CR France765,Alfred
HOMERSHAM,Ronald 2Lt kia 30-4-18 4EYorks att4RAF p219 CR France134
HOMFRAY,John Richards Lt kia 11-11-14 1SWBord p100 MR29 CR France453,1Worc
HOMFRAY,Richard Pophin Capt ded 3-3-18 7Worc p225
HONAN,Matthew TCapt kia 14-11-16 10SLancs p125 CR France384

HONE,Gilbert Bentott 2Lt kia 18-8-17 121RFA p30 CR Belgium23,17-8-17
HONE,Nathaniel Frederick Lt kia 1-7-16 3 att9RIrRif p254 CR France446
HONER,Douglas James Lt ded 4-6-17 RFA attRFC p18&207 MR20
HONESS,Albert Edward T2Lt kia 9-4-18 Mddx att21Bn p147 MR32
HONEY,Alexis Cowper 2Lt dow 10-2-18 5 att4Worc p109 CR France40
HONEY,Geoffrey Henry Le Sueur T2Lt kia 21-10-16 5 att17KRRC p150 MR21
HONEY,George Ronald.MC.TLt dow 25-9-18 9 att8RLancs p59 CR Greece5
HONEYBALL,Wilfred Chennell 2Lt kia 21-3-18 14MGC p183 MR27
HONEYMAN,Herbert Tom Allan 2Lt kia 10-12-17 RScotF &15RFC p9&94 MR20
HONEYMAN,Norman Stark 2Lt kia 22-10-17 8RScots p212 MR30
HONEYWILL,Stanley Ross 2Lt kia 8-10-18 4RFus p68 CR France912
HONYCHURCH,Terence William 2Lt dow 22-9-16 1/7Mddx att167TMB p235 CR France105
HOOD,Andrew Smith Lt ded 24-7-18 RE p210 CR Scot395
HOOD,Charles Ivo Sinclair Chap4Cl dow 15-4-18 RAChDept att41RGA p199 CR Belgium11
HOOD,Douglas Edward 2Lt kia 14-4-17 1Beds p86 CR France549
HOOD,Edward Thesiger Franklin.DSO.LtCol dow 15-5-18 LincsYeo Cmdg38RFA p204 CR France180,Frankland
HOOD,Ernest William 2Lt kia 25/27-9-15 5Yorks p221 MR19
HOOD,Gilbert Brackenbridge 2Lt kia 19-2-18 2/19Lond p250 CR Palestine3
HOOD,James Minto Lt 23-2-20 GL RE attIWT CR Europe5
HOOD,John Lt kia 18-8-17 8A&SH att57RFC p18&243 CR Belgium140
HOOD,John William.MID Lt ded 15-11-18 RGA 39SB p40 CR France1142
HOOD,Oswald T2Lt kia 1-9-16 10 att11RSuss p119 CR France1013
HOOD,Percy Charles 2Lt dow 20-9-18 3 att1/5Norf p74 CR Palestine9
HOOD,Richard Edward.MIDx2 Lt ded 7-8-19 1/2RFA p270 CR Lancs149,Maj
HOOD,Ronald Paton 2Lt kia 28-9-17 GL &43RFC p9 MR20
HOOD,Thomas 2Lt kia 12-10-16 3 att7Suff p78 MR21
HOOD DANIEL,Arnold Frost Capt 28-1-17 2/5EKent C'Coy CR Ches62
HOOD-ROWAN,Maxwell 2Lt kia 12-8-16 1/9Lpool p216 MR21
HOOK,Cyril Walter Keenan TLtACapt kia 23-4-17 16Manch p155&257 CR France162
HOOK,Duncan TLt kia 7-8-15 9LancF p92 CR Gallipoli27
HOOK,F.M.L.AssNurse 10-11-18 QAIMNS CR Dorset111
HOOK,Gerald Francis 2Lt kia 13-4-18 8BordR p117 MR32
HOOK,Robin T2Lt kia 9-8-15 9LancF p92 CR Gallipoli27,7-8-15
HOOK,Valentine.MID TCapt kia 3-5-17 7RWSurr p56 CR France538
HOOKE,Alfred Douglas Lt kia 28-4-17 4Mddx p147 MR20
HOOKE,Utten Lamont LtCol dow 21-6-17 3/4RWSurr p212 CR France545
HOOLE,Geoffrey 2Lt kia 15-9-16 1/15Lond C'Coy p249 CR France432,Geoffry
HOOLE,Ronald Herbert 2Lt kia 21-8-16 8RWSurr p56 MR21
HOOLEY,Arthur Wellesley.MC.MID Lt ded 9-2-19 RASC att11RWSurr p193 CR Belgium267
HOOLEY,Basil Terah.MC.Maj ded 28-10-18 7N&D p233 CR Derby146
HOOLEY,Tom Williamson T2Lt dow 3-9-17 45LabCps p189 CR France139
HOOPER,Alfred Henry Capt kia 10-3-15 2Mddx p147 CR France706
HOOPER,Arthur James 2Lt kia 26-8-17 8Lond att7KRRC p247 MR30
HOOPER,Bernard Keith 2Lt kia 26-9-17 12Lond p248 MR30
HOOPER,Charles Frederick Aubrey Albert Anderson.MID TCapt ded 11-11-18 Wilts p254 CR Durham124,Frederic
HOOPER,Charles Winsmore.MID Capt kia 25-9-15 2HLI p163 MR19
HOOPER,Colin Holt Lt dow 28-9-15 20Lond p251 CR France1
HOOPER,David Ernest 2Lt kia 30-4-17 3 att2ELancs p111 CR France566
HOOPER,Ernest Jesse Joseph TLt dow 24-11-17 12SWBord p100 MR17
HOOPER,Eustace Woodrow Noel T2Lt kia 7-1-18 15DLI p161 CR France369
HOOPER,Henry H.Hoskin T2Lt kia 28-8-18 Lincs p75 CR France385
HOOPER,John Hamilton Morris 2Lt kia 30-11-17 1/16Lond p250 CR France1496,Morriss
HOOPER,Leonard John T2Lt kia 26-9-16 5Dors p124 CR France832
HOOPER,Ronald Morley Lt kia 21-3-18 RGA 3FldSurCo p40 CR France245
HOOPER,Sidney Frederick Lt kia 12-3-15 3Wilts attDCLI p153 CR Belgium17
HOOPER,Stuart Huntly HonLtCol ded 31-5-15 RHA DAAG p30 CR Hamps19
HOOPER,William T2Lt kia 3-10-18 1 att1/5SStaffs p122 CR France341
HOOPS,Guy Staveley T2Lt ded 27-2-17 RFA p30 CR Hamps15
HOOPS,Harry Albert Mostyn 2Lt kia 16-8-17 4RIrF attRIrRif p171 MR30
HOOTON,Edward Cedric Lt kia 26-6-16 2/8RWar p215 MR19,27-6-16
HOOTON,Henry Hurst TLt dow 5-5-16 14RIrRif p169 CR France40,5-8-16
HOOTON,Nelson Mackrow 2Lt kia 16-8-17 17Lond p250 MR29
HOPE,Charles Edward T2Lt kia 22-3-18 17Manch p155 MR27
HOPE,Charles Bateman 2Lt kia 26-2-16 1/1DorsYeo p203 CR Egypt6

HOPE,George Everard.MC.LtCol kia 10-10-17 GrenGds att l/8LancF p50 CR Belgium173

HOPE,Herbert Alfred T2Lt dow 28-7-17 25RFC p9 CR France88

HOPE,Humphrey Brian Thompson Lt kia 26-4-17 4Nhampt attRFC p18&234 MR20 Thomasson

HOPE,James Horatio Maj kia 18-4-16 HLI p163 CR Iraq5

HOPE,John Angus 2Lt kia 22-10-17 16RScots p54 MR30

HOPE,Percy Beckett TLt ded 25-12-17 RASC p193 CR France40

HOPE,Reginald Addison TLt kia 31-7-17 1NStaffs p157 CR Belgium20

HOPE,William Edward Lt kia 6-11-14 1IrGds SR p52 MR29

HOPE,William Henry Webley.CMG.LtCol ded 13-5-19 RGA p40 CR Mddx6,kldacc

HOPE-EVANS,Timothy Idwal TCapt kia 23-11-17 19RWFus p98 MR17

HOPE-JOHNSTONE,Henry Murray.MC.CaptAMaj dow 31-7-17 att12RFus p68 CR Belgium15

HOPE-JOHNSTONE,William Gordon Tollemache Lt kia 25-10-14 RFus p68 MR22

HOPE-LUMLEY,Reginald Lewis TLt kia 11-10-17 2RBerks att37TrainingRes p139 CR France297

HOPE-WALLACE,James Lt kia 15-9-17 4NumbF p213 CR France594

HOPES-HEELIS,E.Capt 29-3-20 EAfrMilLabCps CR EAfrica47

HOPEWELL,Charles 2Lt kia 24-3-18 YLI att64TMB p143 MR27

HOPEWELL,James Handley Lt kia 14-7-16 6Leic p87 MR21

HOPEWELL,Robert George TCapt kia 3-9-16 17N&D p134 MR21

HOPGOOD,John Lambert T2Lt dow 17-8-16 8RWSurr p56 CR France66

HOPKIN,Robert Thomas T2Lt kia 20-9-17 16RB p179 MR30

HOPKINS,Arthur Emlyn.MC.LtACapt kia 21-3-18 2/5ELancs p226 MR27

HOPKINS,Arthur Maskern TLt dow 18-11-16 7SLancs p125 CR France215

HOPKINS,Arthur Martyn T2Lt kia 28-3-18 11KRRC p150 MR27

HOPKINS,Charles Randolph Limes Lt kia 18-12-14 2ScotRif p256 CR France706,Innes

HOPKINS,Daniel Idwal 2Lt kia 23-4-17 2SWBord p100 MR20

HOPKINS,Edward Favill George 2Lt kia 30-3-17 181RFA p30 CR France448

HOPKINS,Eric Arthur 2Lt kia 5-5-15 3 att 1Beds p86

HOPKINS,Francis Gethin TLt ded 2-2-16 RAMC p196 CR Devon2

HOPKINS,Frederick Lt ded 17-6-19 GL attIA p254&266 MR65

HOPKINS,George Henry Stanton T2Lt kia 31-7-17 45MGC p183 MR29

HOPKINS,Gerald Broughton TLt kia 17-9-18 7/8KOSB p102 MR19

HOPKINS,Henry Greenfield Berkeley TLt dow 29-7-17 MGC HB p183 CR Belgium18

HOPKINS,Herbert Leslie.MID Lt kia 19-9-14 RAMC p196 CR France1107

HOPKINS,Lawrence Hilton Capt kia 7-10-18 HuntsCycBn p253 CR France547

HOPKINS,Lewis T2Lt kia 26-9-15 8SomLI p80 MR19

HOPKINS,R.W.Chap4Cl 24-4-18 RAChDept CR Belgium11

HOPKINS,Trevor 2Lt ded 13-9-19 WelshR p264 CR Wales76

HOPKINS,William Jones T2Lt dow 8-10-16 11EYorks p84 CR France495

HOPKINSON,Charles Reginald Thompson Capt kia 6-9-14 ESurr att3NigR p112 CR WAfrica48

HOPKINSON,Edward.MC.Lt mbk 23-4-17 8N&D p257 MR20

HOPKINSON,Eric Humphrey.MC.MID Lt ded 2-6-15 1Camb p244 MR32

HOPKINSON,George Silkston 2Lt kia 18-1-18 5N&D p232 CR Belgium20,Silkstone

HOPKINSON,Hugh James Pearson TLt dow 6-11-15 RE 67FC p45 CR Gallipoli27

HOPKINSON,James Garland Capt kia 25-9-15 4GordH p241 MR29

HOPKINSON,Rudolph Cecil.MIDx2 Lt dow 9-2-17 RE 12DivCycCo p45 CR Camb3

HOPLEY,Geoffrey William Vanderbyl 2Lt dow 18-5-15 GrenGds SR p50 CR Mddx19,12-5-15

HOPLEY,Thomas Henry 2Lt kia 10-10-18 RGA 132HB p40 CR France1392,Lt 11-10-18

HOPPER,James Arthur.MC.T2Lt kia 10-4-17 26NumbF p61 CR France644

HOPPER,Raymond T2Lt kia 11-1-17 GL &60RFC p9 CR France95

HOPPER,Robert Edward 2Lt kia 28-4-17 5WYorks p218 MR19

HOPPER,William Joseph Lt kia 6-9-18 6DLI attMGC p239&187,15DLI CR Belgium89

HOPPS,William Leonard T2Lt dow 22-5-16 25NumbF p61 CR France67

HOPSON,Albert Edward Lt kia 11-4-18 7DLI p239 MR32

HOPTON,Edward Michael Lt ded 17-3-16 1/1ShropYeo p205 CR Egypt6

HOPTON,Guy William Capt kia 27-7-15 RBerks att5Bn p139 CR Belgium71

HOPWOOD,Alan Clement T2Lt dow 18-9-18 RE 152FC p45 CR France755

HOPWOOD,Edwin John TLt kia 9-4-16 10 att6ELancs p111 CR Iraq5

HOPWOOD,Frederick Ernest TLt ded 26-10-18 RE ROD p45 CR France770

HOPWOOD,Frederick William.MM.2Lt kia 27-8-18 RBerks att8Bn p139&259 CR France399

HOPWOOD,Marcus 2Lt kia 3-9-16 10 att13RSuss p119 MR21

HOPWOOD,Norman T2Lt kia 23-10-18 19MGC Inf p183 CR France270,15Bn

HOPWOOD,Robert Gerald Capt kia 24-8-16 RB &70RFC p3&179 MR20

HOPWOOD,Robert Hervey TLt kia 5-2-16 16Mddx p147 CR France114,4-2-16

HORAN,Charles Robert.MC.TLt kia 10-11-17 8 att2RMunstF p175 MR30

HORBRUGH,Robert Patrick LtCol ded 5-9-14 IA Bera&CentProvComm Ex MadrasLancers

HORBURY,George Squire T2Lt kia 21-5-16 4Lpool p72 CR France163

HORE,Cecil William 2Lt kia 26-4-17 A47RH&FA p30 CR Belgium15,26-8-17

HORE,Charles Owen.CMG.Col ded 14-2-16 SL p201

HORE,Kennett Scarborough Lt kia 25-9-15 1/19Lond p250 CR France219

HORE,Percy Standish Capt kia 12-3-15 IA 52Sikhs att59Rif p278 CR France727

HORE,Ruthven Pomfret 2Lt dow 2-10-15 3Dors att1WelchR p124 CR France80

HORE,William Barras Capt kia 7-8-15 IA 120Inf att9WYorks p263&278 MR4

HORGAN,Matthew SubCdr 13-7-18 IOD MR66

HORKINS,Richard Earl TCapt kia 27-9-16 RAMC attRFA 77HB p196 CR France630

HORLER,Edwin T2Lt kia 31-7-17 122MGC Inf p183 CR Belgium124

HORLEY,Engelbert Lutyens Rothwell T2Lt kia 4-9-17 Manch att16Bn p155 CR Belgium24

HORLICK,Gerald Nolekin.MID Maj ded 5-7-18 GloucYeo attMGC p187&203 CR Egypt1

HORN,Arthur Henry Harvey 2Lt kia 2-9-18.24Lond p252 MR16

HORN,Edmund Eric T2Lt kia 4-3-17 2Mddx &8RFC p9&147 CR France120

HORN,Francis Cuthbert Lt dow 28-5-18 4 att2Manch p155 CR France622

HORN,John Bernard T2Lt kia 26-10-17 LNLancs att2/4Bn p136 MR30

HORN,John Cyril T2Lt kia 29-4-17 13EYorks p84 CR France777

HORN,John Hetherington T2Lt kia 13-10-18 1LNLancs att4Y&L p136 CR France316,6Bn

HORN,Robert.DSO&Bar.MC.TLtCol kia 18-4-18 7SfthH p165 CR Belgium11

HORNABROOK,Leonard Charles 2Lt dow 21-5-18 3 att1/4Leic p87 CR France4

HORNBEAK,George Henry 2Lt kia 2-10-17 22RFA p30 CR Belgium112

HORNBY,Cecil Geoffrey.OBE.MC.MajTLtCol ded 30-12-18 ELancs attWAFF p111&201 CR WAfrica4

HORNBY,Cyril Blurton S.2Lt ded 15-4-15 KSLI p145 CR Nhampt79

HORNBY,Geoffrey Phipps 2Lt kia 10-5-15 3Suff p78 MR29,8-5-15

HORNBY,Gerald Barford T2Lt kia 12-7-16 10Yorks p90 CR France397

HORNBY,Hugh Langton HonCapt dow 5-6-18 RInniskF Ex 8Bn p105 CR Sussex112

HORNBY,Joseph Henry.MID Lt kia 7-11-18 RE 94FC p45 CR France521

HORNBY,Richard Arthur Capt kia 9-4-18 Mddx att21Bn p147 MR32

HORNBY,William T2Lt kia 12-10-16 17Lpool 1Coy p72 CR France385

HORNBY,William Raymond 2Lt kia 4-6-15 4ELancs p226 MR4

HORNCASTLE,Cyril Charles Schubert Lt ded 8-1-19 RH&FA p30&257 CR Egy 10Div Staff

HORNCASTLE,Edward Henry Lt kia 27-5-18 10Manch p237 MR18

HORNCASTLE,Leonard Harry.MC.Capt kia 20-5-17 1Wilts &11RFC p9&153

HORNE,Alexander Capt kia 14-9-14 1CamH p168 MR15

HORNE,Charles Walter Capt ded 27-12-19 IARO att38CentIndHorse p278 CR Devon258

HORNE,Cyril Henry Morton TCapt kia 27-1-16 7KOSB p102 CR France222

HORNE,David Douglas TCapt kia 1-7-16 29 att21NumbF p61 MR21

HORNE,Herbet George McMillan 2Lt kia 13-4-17 19Lond attRFC p18&250 MR

HORNE,James Anthony 2Lt kia 1-7-16 16Lond p250 CR France798

HORNE,John Austen T2Lt ded 2-11-18 6RRofCav p23 CR Kent298,6DragGds

HORNE,Leonard John Lt kia 15-6-18 2/4YLI p235 CR France745

HORNE,Robert Stevenson 13051 Lt ded 29-7-18 7A&SH &5/4KAR p243&268 EAfrica12 &CR Tanzania1,9Bn

HORNE,Thomas Wardlaw 2Lt kia 22-8-17 3 att8SfthH p165 MR30

HORNER,Bernard Lt ded 5-3-17 8LancF p221 CR France164

HORNER,Edward William Lt dow 21-11-17 18Huss p23 CR France398,kia

HORNER,Frederick Julian.MC.TLtACapt dow 15-4-18 RWar att2Ches p65 CR Greece3

HORNER,Karl Christian 2Lt dow 4-4-17 8WYorks attRFC p18&219 CR France46,7Bn

HORNER,Walter Aitken 2Lt ded 24-3-15 15Lpool p72 CR Lancs11

HORNER,William Arthur TLt dow 13-12-17 10KRRC p150 CR France40

HORNER,William Jackson 2Lt dow 15-7-17 RGA attV39TMB p40 CR Belgium11,RFA

HORNSBY,George Westome 2Lt kia 4-6-15 1ARO att14Sikhs p278 MR4

HORNSBY,Harold Gibson T2Lt kia 1-7-16 7Yorks p90 CR France372

HORNSBY,John Philip Skipworth TCapt kia 2-9-18 10SWBord ACoy p100 CR France216

HORNSBY,Richard Lionel T2Lt kia 7/11-10-15 Lincs p75 MR4,7-10-15

HORNSBY,William T2Lt kia 21-8-17 6SomLI p80 MR30
HORNSEY,John Frederick Lt kia 24-3-18 RAMC att6KSLI p196 MR27
HORNUNG,Arthur Oscar 2Lt kia 6-7-15 3 att2Ess p131 MR29
HORNUNG,John Peter.MC.T2Lt dow 20-2-16 95RFA p30 CR France922
HORRABIN,Maurice Pinney 2Lt mbk 30-11-17 4 att6EKent p257 MR27
HORRELL,? 9-1-20 VAD CR Egypt10
HORRIDGE,Robert Lt kia 17-11-14 3 att2Manch p155 CR Belgium98,4 att2Bn
HORROCKS,John Hon Lt&QM ded 23-10-15 1EYorks p84 CR Belgium5
HORROX,Henry M.T2Lt kia 1-7-16 24NumbF p61 MR21
HORSBRUGH,Boyd Robert TLtCol ded 11-7-16 RASC p193 CR Surrey32
HORSER,Stanley Cottrell Seymour TCapt kia 12-10-16 17Lpool p72 MR21
HORSEY,Cyril James T2Lt dow 22-11-16 7SLancs p125 CR France145
HORSEY,Thomas Frederick Charles SudCdr 7-3-16 IA MiscList CR India48
HORSFALL,Alfred Garnett.DSO.MajALtCol kia 9-10-17 2WRid p115 CR Belgium23
HORSFALL,Arthur Mendelssohn 2Lt kia 9-5-15 2RMunstF p175 MR22
HORSFALL,Basil Arthur.VC.2Lt kia 27-3-18 1 att11ELancs p111 MR20
HORSFALL,Cuthbert 2Lt dow 17-2-18 Worc att2/8Bn p109 CR France1204
HORSFALL,Cedric Fawcett Capt kia 18-9-16 6WRid p227 CR France246
HORSFALL,George Rowland T2Lt kia 20-11-17 14Y&L att48RFC p9 CR France1361
HORSFALL,Henry Francis Coghlan TCapt dow 22-4-16 6LNLancs p136 CR Iraq6,kia
HORSFALL,John Brown T2Lt kia 25-7-17 124MGC p183 MR29
HORSFALL,John Joseph TCapt dow 19-1-17 8WRid p115 CR France41
HORSFALL,Robert Elcum TCapt kia 20-11-17 12Lpool p72 MR17
HORSFALL,Vernon Adams 2Lt kia 3-9-16 4WRid p227 CR France1890
HORSFIELD,John Francis Lt kia 26-7-17 6Manch p236 CR Belgium24
HORSFORD,Harry Curwin Capt dow 8-4-17 5RBerks p139 CR France1182
HORSFORD,Thomas Gavin Moor Lt kia 16-6-15 2Beds p86 MR22
HORSFORD,Thomas Herbert O'Bryen Lt dow 14-3-15 2WYorks p81&257 CR France768
HORSLEY,Claude Cressy Lt dow 29-11-17 4NStaffs p157 CR France64,28-11-17
HORSLEY,Ernest T2Lt kia 14-8-17 10KRRC att59TMB p150 CR Belgium23
HORSLEY,John TCapt kia 16-5-15 3 att2BordR p117 CR France279
HORSLEY,Oswald.MC.Capt kld 19-8-18 GordH &RAF p166 CR Hamps179
HORSLEY,Ralph Neville 2Lt kia 27-8-17 7Worc p226 MR30
HORSLEY,Sir Victor Alexander Haden.Bart.CB.Col ded 16-7-16 RAMC p196 CR Iraq5
HORSLEY,Wilfred Palmer.MC.TCapt kia 2-7-17 GL &53RFC p9 CR France285
HORSNELL,Alick George T2Lt kia 1-7-16 7Suff p78 MR21
HORST,George Phillip 2Lt kldByTribesmen 18-4-16 IARO att24Punjabis p278 MR43
HORT,Courtenay Randell Lt ded 10-5-16 RGA 49SB p209 CR France145,Randall
HORTON,Frank.MC.2Lt drd 10-10-18 3Lpool p72 MR40
HORTON,H.F.MC.Lt 27-2-21 1WYorks CR Yorks38
HORTON,James Henry.DSO.MIDx2 LtCol ded 23-7-17 IMS DADMS III Cps p278 CR Iraq8
HORTON,Stanley Tom T2Lt kia 9-4-17 2Wilts p153 CR France595
HORTON,Victor John 2Lt kia 3-12-17 D161RFA p30 CR Belgium20,2-12-17
HORWITZ,Samuel Salmen Lt kld 21-10-16 3N&D attLNLancs p134 CR France390,Sydney
HORWOOD,Archibald Alfred 2Lt kia 28-3-18 1/6DLI p239 MR27
HORWOOD,Richard George 2Lt dow 8-5-18 20Lond A'Coy p251 CR France88
HORWOOD,Ronald Bentall 2Lt kia 1-7-16 3 att1Ess p131 CR France339
HOSE,Cyril Arthur Sparling 2Lt kia 10-9-16 1/5Lpool p215 CR France198
HOSE,Robert Henry 2Lt kia 18-3-17 5Beds p219 CR France420,2Bn
HOSEGOOD,Archibald Harding T2Lt kia 26-11-17 86MGC p183 CR France667
HOSEGOOD,Gilbert 2Lt kia 10-9-16 2Dev p76 CR France423
HOSEGOOD,Henry Arnold 2Lt kia 24-2-15 5RFus p68 CR Belgium17 3Bn
HOSEGOOD,Ralph T2Lt kia 23-7-16 12Glouc attTMB p106 CR France397
HOSEGOOD,William Leman Lt ded 15-8-18 4SomLI att4KAR p218&268 CR EAfrica36
HOSKEN,Ernest Dryden 2Lt kia 14-10-17 7CamH p168 MR20
HOSKEN,Henry Richard 2Lt kia 11-8-17 54MGC p183 MR29
HOSKEN,Victor Frederick 2Lt kia 7-10-16 7Lond p247 MR21
HOSKEN,Wilfrid 2Lt kia 21-8-15 6EYorks p84 MR4
HOSKIN,Alfred TCapt dow 4-7-17 RAVC att10Cps p198 CR France285
HOSKING,Cyril Gordon Lt kld 26-10-14 102RFA &4RFC p1&30 MR20
HOSKING,Herbert Edward Capt kia 3-2-17 IA 66 att62Punjabis p278 CR Iraq5,62 att66
HOSKING,Herbert John Roy 2Lt kia 23-7-16 7 att3LNLancs p136 MR21,3 att7Bn

HOSKINS,Cyril Lt kia 1-7-16 1/8RWar p215 MR21
HOSKINS,Francis Desmond 2Lt dow 2-10-15 1NStaffs p157 CR Belgium5,30-9-15
HOSKINS,George 2Lt kia 5-11-16 3 att10LancF p92 CR France401
HOSKINS,George Chandos.MC.T2Lt kia 11-3-17 GL 2RFC 1Wing p9 CR France423
HOSKINS,Joseph Capt died 7-10-18 4Dors p270 CR Dorset33,6-10-18
HOSKINS-ABRAHALL,Christopher Henry 2Lt kld 22-12-17 RFA attRFC p9&30,Hoskyns CR Devon237
HOSKYN,Frank Hebden 2Lt ded 19-11-19 IA TC att1/109Inf p278 MR43 2/102Grdrs Ex 1/109Inf
HOSKYN,John Henry 2Lt kia 20-9-17 9Lpool p216 MR30
HOSKYNS,Edwin Cecil Leigh Lt kia 20/21-10-14 1RWFus p98 MR29,20-10-14
HOSKYNS,Henry Charles Walter,DSO Maj kia 25-9-15 1Lincs p75 MR32
HOSKYNS-ABRAHALL,Bennet Edmund 2Lt dow 25-4-18 RGA 242SB p40 CR Belgium11
HOSLER,Albert Edward T2Lt kia 26-8-17 att7RB p179 MR30
HOSLEY,William James Seymour.MID Maj kia 25-9-15 6KOSB p102 CR France114
HOSSACK,Allan John.MM.T2Lt dow 27-4-18 14DLI p161 CR France144
HOSSELL,Leslie Cartmell Capt kia 8-8-16 1/8WYorks p219 MR21
HOSTE,George Michael Lt kld 7-10-16 16Lond p249 2entries1 kia MR21
HOSTE,William Graham.Bart 2Lt kia 9-5-15 RB p179 MR32
HOTBLACK,G.T.2Lt 22-3-21 Ess CR Sussex187
HOTCHKIN,Lambert Annesley 2Lt kia 8-10-16 21Lond p251 MR21
HOTCHKIS,Gilbert T2Lt kia 23-4-17 GordH p166 CR France162
HOTCHKISS,Felix James Bishop Lt kia 3-5-17 10 att13Mddx p236 MR20
HOTCHKISS,Henry TLt ded 19-6-18 RASC 17MT SP p193 CR France95,kia
HOTSON,Herbert Charles 2Lt kia 18-11-16 3 att2YLI p143 MR21
HOTSON,William Hugh McIntosh T2Lt kia 10-9-18 11N&D p134 CR Italy5,9-9-18
HOUFTON,Charles Morley Lt dow 12-11-15 8N&D p233 CR France924
HOUGH,Eric Bernard Capt kia 29-4-18 19Lpool p72 MR30
HOUGH,Geoffrey Goadsby TLtACapt ded 8-9-18 KRRC OC 214PoW Coy p150 CR France833
HOUGH,Topham Becher Dabridgecourt T2Lt kia 17-1-16 8EYorks p84 CR Belgium28
HOUGHAM,Bertram William.MC.LtACapt kia 6-9-18 3RWKent att5RBerks p141 CR France
HOUGHTON,Albert William 2Lt dow 31-3-18 10EYorks p84 CR France40
HOUGHTON,Arthur T2Lt kia 22-3-18 3Worc p109 MR20
HOUGHTON,George T2Lt kia 27-8-18 12WYorks att6Dors p81 CR France385
HOUGHTON,John.MM.T2Lt kia 14-12-17 18Manch p155 MR30 Ex 21Bn
HOUGHTON,John Reginald.MC.ACapt kia 21-3-18 1Lond p245 MR20
HOUGHTON,John Reginald Capt dow 22-3-18 6Manch attMGC Inf p187&236 CR France528,Maj
HOUGHTON,Noel.MID TMajALtCol kia 13-9-17 16N&D p134 CR Belgium21
HOUGHTON,Philip Squarey Capt kia 1-7-16 9Lond p247 MR21
HOUGHTON,Ralph 2Lt kia 20-3-18 6RWar p214 CR France1701,21-3-18
HOUGHTON,Tom Whitfield 2Lt ded 21-4-19 MGC Motors p183 CR Syria2
HOUGHTON,William T2Lt kia 9-4-16 11 att15RFus att8RWFus p68 MR38
HOULDSWORTH,William Gillbert Lt dow 23-9-14 ScotsGds p52 CR France462,Gilbert
HOULSTON,Edgar Charles Chap4Cl drd 4-5-17 RAChDept p199 CR France1571
HOULT,Alfred John LtAMaj ded 2-11-18 RGA 181HB p40 CR palestine11
HOULT,Arthur T2Lt ded 17-11-16 12EYorks p84 CR France74
HOULT,Robert Percy T2Lt kia 16-8-17 2WYorks p81 MR30
HOUNAM,George Leslie 2Lt kia 5-3-18 19DLI CR Belgium83
HOUNSON,George James T2Lt ded 20-9-17 Dev attLabCps p76 CR Devon2,19-9-17
HOURIHANE,Thomas Cormac Lt kia 1-2-20 IA 1/26Punjabis att4/39GarhwalRif p278 MR43,2-2-20
HOURSTON,David William Lt kia 11-8-18 7ScotRif p224 CR France25,9Bn
HOUSE,Horace George T2Lt kia 28-3-18 1Hamps p121 MR20
HOUSE,Joseph Francis T2Lt kia 24-3-18 Wilts att2RBerks p153 MR27
HOUSE,Malcolm Hutchinson T2Lt kia 3-5-17 8RB p179 MR20
HOUSECROFT,Harold 2Lt kia 19-11-14 4 att1ESurr p112 CR Belgium89
HOUSEHOLD,Ernest Scott 2Lt ded 22-7-17 5Ess p232 CR France113,dow 21-7-17
HOUSSEMAYNE DUBOULAY,Arthur.DSO.MajBrLtCol 23-10-18 RE 3Army GHQ CR France1512
HOUSTON,Arthur Oswald T2Lt kia 26-3-18 9RInniskF p105 MR27
HOUSTON,Cyril Thomas Lt ded 22-7-18 GL &RAF p190
HOUSTON,Frederick Neville.MC.Capt kia 1-7-16 Y&L p159 MR21
HOUSTON,Hugh TLt kia 24-10-17 17RScots Z'Coy p54 CR Belgium126

HOUSTON,John Cunningham T2Lt kia 14-10-18 1/2NumbF att9MGC Inf p61&183 CR Belgium157
HOUSTON,Kenneth D'Aguilar Capt kia 24-3-18 18Lond p250 MR20
HOUSTON,Thomas Cameron Capt dow 25-8-16 RAMC p253 CR France176
HOUSTON,William Houston TCapt dow 28-3-16 12RScots att1RScotF p54 CR Belgium11,Robertson
HOUSTON,William Wylie T2Lt kia 17-8-17 RE 226FC p45 CR France163,18-8-17
HOUSTON-BOSWALL,George Reginald.Bart.Capt kia 27-9-15 4GrenGds RoO p50 MR19
HOVELL,Mark T2Lt kia 12-8-16 1N&D p134 CR France423
HOVENDEN,Arthur Lester 2Lt kia 3-5-17 3 att7ESurr p112 MR20
HOW,Henry James 2Lt kia 14-4-17 9Lond p248 MR20
HOW,John Christian 2Lt kia 2-4-17 2RWSurr p56 CR France1489
HOW,William Alexander 2Lt kia 12-4-18 1RScotF p94 MR19
HOWARD,Addison James Lt kia 4-9-16 3 att1Beds p86 CR France294
HOWARD,Albert Leonard TLt kia 18-9-18 1LNLancs p136 CR France375
HOWARD,Alfred Heywood Capt kia 10-8-15 4WelshR p230 MR4
HOWARD,Alfred Lewis 2Lt kia 21-11-17 City of LondYeo p204 MR34
HOWARD,Arthur James 2Lt kia 30-4-17 2Hamps p121 MR4
HOWARD,Bernard Henry Maj kia 8-3-16 IA 47Sikhs p278 MR38
HOWARD,Cecil Cunningham T2Lt dow 23-5-16 8LNLancs A'Coy p136 CR France95
HOWARD,Cedric Stewart T2Lt kia 28-9-16 7Beds F'Coy p86 CR France383
HOWARD,Charles Reginald.OBE.TCapt kia 6-9-18 RAMC attKAR p196 CR EAfrica90
HOWARD,Dennis Brook.MC.T2LtACapt kia 22-10-17 35RFA p30 CR Belgium19,12RFA
HOWARD,Edgar Stacey T2Lt kia 9-8-18 6TankCps p188 MR16
HOWARD,Edward Douglas 2Lt kia 20-9-17 4RLancs p213 MR30
HOWARD,Eric Stanley T2Lt kia 18-5-17 RE att60RFC p9&45 CR France46
HOWARD,F.G.SNurse 18-11-14TFNS CR Wales135
HOWARD,F.J.C.Maj 6-6-20 8Huss CR Yorks335
HOWARD,Francis Stanley Capt kia 28-11-15 3Lond p245 MR19
HOWARD,Frederic George.MVO.DSO.MajTLtCol kia 19-10-15 RE p46 CR Belgium1,9-10-15
HOWARD,George Blake Lt ded 10-6-20 1ARO attFollowersCentDept p278 MR66
HOWARD,George Oscroft 2Lt ded 14-11-18 5SStaffs p229 CR Yorks561
HOWARD,Gilbert Gordon Lt dow 29-10-18 6Glouc p225 CR France528
HOWARD,Guy Robert.DSO.Maj ded 23-10-18 1/2Ess &18RAF p131 CR France113
HOWARD,Harry Elsmore T2Lt dow 8-4-17 25NumbF p61 CR France265
HOWARD,Henry Charles Mowbray.MID Lt kia 29-9-15 Y&L p159 MR19
HOWARD,Herbert Arthur T2Lt dow 29-9-18 GordH att1Bn p166 CR France512,kia
HOWARD,Herbert Quey.DCM.2Lt dow 8-8-18 2Lond p245 MR16
HOWARD,James Kelvey Lt kia 11-2-17 5N&D attRFC p18&232 CR France924
HOWARD,John Allan Lt dow 9-5-18 3 att1Ess p132 CR France745
HOWARD,John Brereton Capt dow 6-4-18 4RWFus A'Coy p223 CR France232
HOWARD,John Turner TLt ded 18-6-18 RE 5FldSurCoy p46 CR France13
HOWARD,Kenneth Salwey LtTCapt kia 6-10-18 N&D att1Bn p134 CR France184
HOWARD,Leslie Rayner TLt kia 27-3-16 4RFus p68 MR29
HOWARD,Lewis Charles.DSO.TLtCol dow 23-12-15 8SomLI p80 CR France922
HOWARD,Lionel George T2Lt dow 12-4-17 5RBerks p139 CR France40 see HOWARD-GREEN true name
HOWARD,Louis Meredith TLtCol dow 2-7-16 24NumbF p61 CR France393
HOWARD,Lyulph Walter Mowbray TLt kia 15-9-15 7RWSurr p56 CR France189
HOWARD,Michael Francis Stafford Pte 10246 2HAC MR30 Ex Lt 18Huss attScotsGds
HOWARD,Norman TLt dow 1-8-15 5Nhampt p137 CR France922
HOWARD,Percy Edward TCapt ded 21-10-18 GL RAMC p266 CR Bucks51
HOWARD,Percy Edward Napier 2Lt kia 27-10-14 RIrReg p89 MR22
HOWARD,Philip Granville James Fitzalan.Hon.Lt dow 24-5-18 1WelshGds p53 CR France103
HOWARD,Richard Jackson T2Lt kia 17-3-16 9BlkW p128 CR France1723
HOWARD,Robert Henry Palmer.Hon.2Lt kia 9-5-15 4 att2ESurr p112 CR Belgium46,8-5-15
HOWARD,Victor Charles 2Lt drd 15-4-17 4ESurr p112 MR35
HOWARD,Walter Leslie TLt dow 16-8-17 48MGC p183 CR Belgium16,176MGC
HOWARD,William TCapt dow 8-10-15 8EKent p57 CR France1
HOWARD,William T2Lt kia 24-4-18 18Mddx att2Nhampt p147 MR27
HOWARD,William Aloysius 2Lt kia 24-4-17 7/8KOSB p102 MR20
HOWARD,William George 2Lt dow 20-12-17 RGA 119SB p40 CR Belgium3
HOWARD,William Hyson 2Lt kia 11-9-18 2Manch attX32TMB p155 CR France1061
HOWARD-GREEN,L.G.2Lt served as HOWARD,L.G.
HOWARD-VYSE,Richard Capt kia 14-9-14 1LNLancs p136 MR15
HOWARTH,Alfred Doran Capt ded 26-3-18 6LancF p270 CR Lancs30,2/4Bn
HOWARTH,Charles Thomas.DCM.2Lt dow 28-5-18 149MGC Inf p183 CR Derby97 Ex N&D
HOWARTH,Frederick Ewart 2Lt kia 31-5-18 74RFA X'GdsTMB p30 CR France74
HOWARTH,Gilbert Lt dow 29-3-18 RGA 60SB p209 CR France644,2Lt 28-3-18
HOWARTH,Harold Victor Lt dow 2-5-18 1/5Dev p217 CR Palestine9
HOWARTH,J.Lt 6-5-20 LabCps CR Lancs112
HOWARTH,John 2Lt dow 10-9-16 RE 1FC p210 CR Derby26
HOWARTH,John Dearden T2Lt dow 1-8-17 9LNLancs p136 CR Belgium11,Lt 8B
HOWARTH,Norman 2Lt kia 13-7-16 3SLancs p125 CR France150,2Bn
HOWARTH,Norman 2Lt kia 22-3-18 2Yorks p90 MR27
HOWARTH,Norman Capt died 6-9-18 3RLancs &RAF p59 MR20
HOWARTH,Tom Hartley 2Lt dow 6-12-17 59MGC Inf p183 CR France716
HOWARTH,Wallace 2Lt kia 16-8-17 49MGC Inf p183 CR Belgium167
HOWAT,George T2Lt kia 26-8-18 ScotRif att2KOSB p103 CR France239,25-8-18
HOWATT,James Capt kia 28-6-15 7ScotRif p224 CR Gallipoli6
HOWATT,William Howatt 2Lt kia 3-5-17 7ScotRif att9RB p224 MR20,Henry
HOWCROFT,Laurence Walter TLt kia 20-11-17 1/2Hamps p121 CR France1483
HOWDEN,Francis William T2Lt dow 30-3-18 11 att1RDubF p176 CR France64,Frank
HOWDEN,George Bruce 2Lt ded 8-5-18 2DCLI p114 CR Devon152
HOWE,Arnold Ewart 2Lt kia 30-10-17 28Lond A'Coy p252 CR Belgium126
HOWE,Charles Kingsley T2Lt kia 1-7-16 6RBerks p139 CR France513
HOWE,Claude Arthur Capt kia 20-11-17 4RWFus att1/5LNLancs p223 MR17,30-11-17
HOWE,Edward Lt ded 4-1-17 22WYorks p81 CR Numb36
HOWE,Ernest TLt dow 14-12-16 RAMC att83FA p196 CR Greece9
HOWE,Frederick Norman.MID 2Lt kia 25-4-18 84/11RFA p30 MR30
HOWE,George Herbert 2Lt kia 28-3-18 RGA 151SB p40 CR France1182
HOWE,James Ashwell T2Lt kld 13-2-18 14RFC p16 CR Derby57
HOWE,James Roche Lt kia 18-10-18 3RMunstF B'Coy p175 CR France190
HOWE,Robert Ernest 2Lt kia 4-10-17 1EYorks p84 CR Belgium84
HOWE,Thomas Sydney Curzon.MC.2Lt kld 17-4-18 ConnRgrs &54RAF p266 MR20
HOWE,William Thomas.MM.2Lt kia 4-11-18 5 att9WYorks p218 CR France1142
HOWELL,Arthur Anthony.CMG.BrigGen ded 15-1-18 3Lond p270 CR Surrey160
HOWELL,Aubrey Hamilton Lt kia 6-1-16 2Leic p87 MR38
HOWELL,Augustus William 2Lt kia 15-4-17 6 att3RB p179 MR20
HOWELL,Charles Joseph Lt kia 25-1-17 Y&L attMGC Inf p159 CR Iraq5
HOWELL,Douglas Bert T2Lt kia 24-3-18 2HLI p163 MR20
HOWELL,Edmund Lally.MID TCapt kia 27-7-16 5 att1KRRC p150 MR21
HOWELL,Evan Idres Lt ded 21-4-18 4Nhampt att72RAF p234 CR Wales135
HOWELL,Ernest Alfred Russell LtCol drd 30-12-15 IA S&TCps p278 MR41
HOWELL,Francis Slinger 2Lt kia 2-8-17 GordH att8/10Bn p166 CR Belgium58,dow 31-7-17
HOWELL,George Woodbourne.MSM.2Lt kia 22-6-18 17 att1/2RWFus p98 CR France4,1/2att17
HOWELL,Herbert Edgar 2Lt kia 9-5-15 2ELancs p111 MR32
HOWELL,John T2Lt kia 25-9-15 9KRRC p150 MR29
HOWELL,John Edwin 2Lt 7-7-16 3 att16WelshR MR21
HOWELL,Maurice Ives Berthon 2Lt kia 25-9-15 1RWSurr p56 MR19
HOWELL,Norman Asquith T2Lt kia 23-12-16 6KSLI p145 CR France744
HOWELL,Norman Bulmer.MID Lt kia 24-7-15 2RWKent p141 CR Iraq6
HOWELL,Norman Eliott.MID Capt kia 7-1-16 IA 82Punjabis attStaff 35Bde p278 MR38
HOWELL,Philip.CMG.TBrigGen kia 7-10-16 4Huss Staff p21 CR France41
HOWELL,Reuben Harrison T2Lt dow 29-3-18 11 att2RDubF p177 CR France145
HOWELL,Richard David.MC.2Lt kia 15-9-18 3 att2WelshR p127 CR France673
HOWELL,Roland Basil 2Lt kia 2-10-15 4NStaffs p157 MR19
HOWELL,Thomas Chap4Cl kia 1-12-17 RAChDept att6KSLI p199 CR France379
HOWELL,Wilfred Symonds T2Lt kia 25-4-16 9ESurr p112 CR Belgium97
HOWELLS,Courtney Philip T2Lt kia 30-9-18 3Yorks att5YLI p90 France912
HOWELLS,David Geoffrey T2Lt ded 1-12-18 52RFus p68 CR Ches3
HOWELLS,Denzil 2Lt dow 13-4-18 5ELancs attY&L p226 CR Belgium183
HOWELLS,Edmund Sydney TLt kld 27-3-18 RFC p16 CR Wales389
HOWELLS,F.A.C.Lt 24-3-20 5Worc CR Glouc109
HOWELLS,George Davey 2Lt kia 28-2-18 1Mon att15Ches p244 CR Belgium83

HOWELLS,George James 2Lt kia 23-11-17 GL &8RFC p9 CR France403,kld
HOWELLS,Graham T.Capt dow 2-5-16 14WelshR A'Coy p127 CR France345,kia
HOWELLS,Hugh T.2Lt kld 10-4-17 GL &RFC p9 CR Mon76
HOWELLS,James T.2Lt kia 21-3-18 RWSurr att8Bn p56 MR27
HOWELLS,John Edwin T.2Lt kia 20-11-17 E15TankCps p188 CR France711
HOWELLS,John Hubert 2Lt kia 9-10-17 RFA att15RHA p30 CR Belgium12
HOWELLS,John Wesley 2Lt kia 23-7-17 7LancF p221 MR34
HOWELLS,Phillip George Herbert T.2Lt kia 18-11-16 10NStaffs p157 CR France384
HOWELLS,Reginald Lt dow PoW 30-5-18 1Hereford p252 CR Germany3,HOWELL 1/3Bn
HOWELLS,William John T.Capt dow 10-8-15 8WelshR p127 MR4
HOWES,Charles William T.CaptAMaj kia 22-4-18 19DLI p161 CR France296
HOWES,Edward 2Lt kia 2-8-16 9NumbF p61 CR France397
HOWES,Harold Edward Lt kia 1-8-18 1/6Ches p222 CR France524
HOWES,Henry Edward.MM.Lt 18-1-21 ESurr CR Surrey107
HOWES,Hugh Gilbert 2Lt kia 8-3-16 1ARO att2Rajputs p278 MR38
HOWETT,William T.2Lt kia 18-9-18 RSuss att7Bn p119 CR France369
HOWFIELD,John Arthur.MC.2Lt kia 1-9-18 75RFA p30 CR France214
HOWIE,David Dickie 2Lt ded 19-1-16 2RFA p270 CR Egypt9,Lt
HOWIE,George Francis 2Lt kia 21-3-18 3 att16RScots p54 MR20
HOWILL,John Edwin 2Lt kia 7-7-16 16WelshR p127
HOWIS,Francis Thackeray T.2Lt dow 8-12-15 12Ess att6Lincs p132 CR Gallipoli27
HOWITT,Adam Gordon.MC.T.Capt kia 5-8-17 12ESurr p112 MR29
HOWKINS,Ernest Lt kia 4-8-16 1/5RHA p207 CR Egypt2,M.
HOWKINS,George Addington T.2Lt kia 25/27-9-15 12NumbF p61 MR19
HOWLETT,Charles Wilfred T.2Lt kia 1-7-16 9YLI p143 CR France189
HOWLETT,John Harold T.2Lt kia 26-9-17 215MGC Inf p183 MR30
HOWLEY,Jasper Joseph.DSO.Maj kia 11-3-15 1Lincs p75 CR France525,2Bn
HOWMAN,Henry Roger T.Maj kia 25/26-4-18 13Glouc p106 CR Belgium115
HOWSE,Basil Thomas 2Lt ded 18-9-18 C99RFA p30 CR Greece7
HOWSE,Harold Edward.MID ACapt kia 16-8-17 3 att2RBerks p139 MR30
HOWSON,C.J.Lt ded 5-7-18 Lpool &RAF p72
HOWSON,Frederick John Lt 18-10-18 126/29RFA MR65
HOWSON,George Rowland Paget T.2Lt kia 9-4-17 1RLancs p59 CR France729
HOWSON,John Frederick Lt ded 18-10-18 RH&FA p30
HOY,Andrew Burn Lt dow 2-6-18 4RScots p211 CR France95
HOY,Arthur 2Lt kia 3-11-16 RE p210 CR France1327
HOY,John Leonard 2Lt kia 21-3-18 2/7N&D p233 MR20
HOY,William Capt ded 17-9-16 RAPC p200 CR Yorks98
HOYLAND,Godfrey Algernon.MC.LtACapt dow 3-10-18 36RFA p30 CR France
HOYLAND,John Fraser Capt kia 26-9-16 4 att9LancF p92 MR21
HOYLE,Basil William Edmond T.Capt kia 25-9-15 9RWFus p98 MR19
HOYLE,Frederick Harold T.2Lt dow 20-4-18 2WYorks p82 CR France145
HOYLE,Geoffrey Morgan Lt kia 9-8-15 3 att2N&D p134 MR29
HOYLE,Harold 2Lt kia 23-7-16 7LNLancs p136 CR France432
HOYLE,Humphrey King 2Lt kia 1-5-15 5LancF p221 MR4,7-5-15
HOYLE,John Baldwin.MC.T.Lt kia 1-7-16 7SLancs p125&258 CR France393
HOYLE,Walter Maynard 2Lt ded 11-5-17 Norf p263 CR Mddx26
HOYLE,William T.2Lt kia 9-4-17 8EYorks p84 CR France581
HOYLES,Arthur Harry Child 2Lt ded 2-12-17 5HLI attRFC p18&240,Henry MR20
HOYNE-FOX,Leslie Vincent Capt ded 14-10-18 1A 120Inf p278 CR Iraq8,13-10-18
HOYS,Cecil Thomas Gray T.2Lt kia 15-9-16 150MGC Inf p183 CR France239
HOYTE,Raymond Wilson Lt kia 21-3-18 2/7N&D p233 MR20
HUBBACK,Francis William 2Lt dow 12-2-17 2/6Lond p247 CR France120
HUBBARD,Adrian George T.2Lt dow 30-8-16 9 att8EKent p57 CR France23
HUBBARD,Alfred T.2Lt kia 17-2-17 8Suff p78 CR France314
HUBBARD,Alfred William.MID T.2Lt kia 25-1-17 8RWFus p98 MR38
HUBBARD,Archibald Charles 2Lt kia 8-11-17 5 att2KRRC p150 MR30
HUBBARD,Bertram John.MC.Capt kia 1-12-17 4GrenGds p50 CR France415,Lt
HUBBARD,Leslie Victor T.2Lt kia 31-8-16 13Mddx p147 CR France432
HUBBARD,Percy William(Peter).MM.T.2Lt kia 6-6-18 16LancF p92 CR France924
HUBBARD,William Dickenson Lt kia 8-7-16 3 att2Yorks p90 MR21,Dickinson
HUBBERT,Francis Stanley William 2Lt kia 23-5-15 2EYorks p84 MR29,23-4-15
HUBBLE,Frederick Richard T.2Lt ded 2-8-18 RASC MT 36Div p193 CR France134
HUBBLE,Harry Leonard 2Lt kia 15-4-18 4Lincs p217 MR30
HUBBLE,Harry Ronald 2Lt kia 20-5-17 3 att4Lpool p72 MR20
HUBER,Edgar William 2Lt kld 2-11-16 1MaltaReg p201 CR Greece7
HUBER,H.W.Lt kia 7-1-16 MaltaReg attRInniskF p201 MR4
HUBERT,Donald Franklyn Lt kia 14-3-17 1A 9BhopalInf p278 MR38,Capt

HUBY,O.M.2Lt ded 11-9-18 5RWar &RAF p214
HUBY,Owen Meredith Lt kld 23-10-18 5RWar attRAF p255 CR Yorks1
HUCKER,Wilfred Thomas 2Lt dow 23-12-17 3 att8SomLI p80 CR France285
HUCKETT,Arnold Walter Lt kia 10-8-15 5Wilts p153 MR4
HUCKLE,Henry William 2Lt kia 5-9-18 1Camb p245 CR France511
HUCKLEBRIDGE,Sidney Eames Lt ded 7-3-19 21WYorks p82 CR Belgium243
HUCKS,B.C.Capt ded 7-11-18 GL &RAF p190
HUDDART,Cuthbert Edmund Arnold T.Capt ded 29-1-17 RAMC p267 CR Lond8
HUDDART,Lindow Hereward Leofric T.Lt ded 5-2-17 GL RE att1NigR p201 CR EAfrica39
HUDDART,Robert Edward Thorne 2Lt kia 30-6-16 5 att2RB p179 CR France251
HUDDLESTON,Maurice Louis T.2Lt kia 1-7-16 15DLI p161 CR France267
HUDDLESTON,Purefoy Gauntlett Capt kia 25-3-16 RE 84FC p46 CR Belgium1
HUDDLESTONE,Sydney Chantler 2Lt kia 25-1-15 3 att2BlkW p128 MR22
HUDDY,Edward T.2Lt kia 30-7-16 11Glouc p106 MR21
HUDLESTONE,Harold Robert T.2Lt dow 2-7-16 14Mddx p147 CR France513
HUDSON,Alban John Benedict.MC.Lt kia 7-6-17 3Worc p109 CR Belgium62
HUDSON,Allan Harrison 2Lt dow 13-6-15 1/9Manch p237 CR Gallipoli1
HUDSON,Arthur Cyril T.Maj dow 2-10-16 3 att11RFus p68 CR France102
HUDSON,Arthur Henry William 2Lt kia 1-7-16 1RLancs p59 MR21
HUDSON,Arthur Hensley T.Capt kia 31-7-17 6RBerks D'Coy p139 CR Belgium112
HUDSON,Arthur Thomas Rawlings Lt kia 12-4-18 2/7DLI p239 MR32,11-4-18
HUDSON,Aubrey Wells Lt dow 20-9-14 5 att2Worc p109 MR15
HUDSON,Austin Patrick Capt kia 1-9-17 5LancF p221 MR30,31-8-17
HUDSON,Charles Edward 2Lt dow 18-12-16 3/7Mddx p235 CR France59
HUDSON,Charles Herbert 2Lt kia 16-5-15 Lpool p72 CR France279
HUDSON,Cuthbert Newton Lt kia 29-3-17 2/5Lpool p215 CR France82
HUDSON,Edward Stanley T.2Lt dow 13-2-17 10Dev p76 CR Greece1
HUDSON,Elijah Rennison 2Lt ded 18-1-19 RGA 46A/ACoy p262 CR Lond14
HUDSON,Ernest LtCol ded 14-10-16 1A IMS p278
HUDSON,Francis Reginald LtT.Capt kld 21-3-18 RFC p16 CR Devon248
HUDSON,Frank T.Lt kia 12-10-18 12Manch p155 CR France192
HUDSON,Frank Hobbs T.2Lt dow 26-4-18 1Worc p109 CR France39
HUDSON,George Trevor T.2Lt kia 2-10-16 7RWKent p141 CR France383,29-9-16
HUDSON,Godfrey.MC.Maj kia 12-4-18 MGC p183 MR32
HUDSON,Godfrey Burnside 2Lt kia 18-4-18 3 att1Glouc p106 CR France765
HUDSON,Harold Baldwin T.2Lt kia 13-11-16 10 att4Beds p86 CR France220,14-11-16
HUDSON,Harold Edwin T.2Lt kia 27-9-15 10Ess p132 CR France430
HUDSON,Harry 2Lt dow 25-4-18 RGA 177SB p40 CR Belgium38 26-4-18
HUDSON,Harry T.Lt kia 21-9-18 RScots att1/4Bn p54 CR France646
HUDSON,Henry Erns.MC.2Lt kia 18-6-18 N&D att9Bn p134 MR19
HUDSON,Horace Sayer 2Lt ded 17-11-18 9Manch att2MGC Inf p187&237 CR France289
HUDSON,Jocelyn Hope T.Lt dow 12-1-16 C49RFA p30 CR Belgium11
HUDSON,John Burgoyne 2Lt kia 25-10-16 4Yorks p220 MR21
HUDSON,John William Willoughby Lt kld 30-11-15 1/5RWar A'Coy p214 CR France281,kia
HUDSON,Leslie Sidney 2Lt kld 28-10-17 3Glouc att49RFC p106&9 CR Kent7 1Bn
HUDSON,Robert Arthur.DSO.MajALtCol kia 9-10-17 8WYorks p219 MR30
HUDSON,Robert Dennis T.2Lt kia 25-1-16 109RFA p30 CR Belgium28,Denis
HUDSON,Roland Burton 2Lt kia 19-7-16 O&BLI BucksBn p231 MR19
HUDSON,Thomas Heylyn Capt&Adjt kia 13-10-15 5RBerks p139 CR France149
HUDSON,Thomas James 2Lt kia 20-5-17 GL &11RFC p9 CR France481
HUDSON,Wilfred 2Lt dow 8-2-16 RE ERidCoy p210 CR Belgium11,Wilfrid
HUDSON-KINAHAN,Cecil Barton T.Lt ded 30-12-15 SL att4KAR p202 CR EAfrica52
HUDSON-KINAHAN,Daniel Dickinson Lt kia 9-4-16 2IrGds SR p52 CR Belgium72
HUDSPETH,Arthur 2Lt kia 19-9-16 10SStaffs att13DLI p122 MR21
HUDSPITH,Walter Leonard.MC.T.Lt kia 7-11-18 1Mddx p147 CR France941
HUFFINGTON,Thomas ACapt dow 8-2-17 7Yorks p90 CR France329
HUGGAN,James Laidlaw Lt kia 16-9-14 RAMC att3CldGds p196 MR15
HUGGAN,Robert Elliott Lt ded 29-5-18 9HLI att3/1KAR p240&268 CR EAfrica77
HUGGAN,Thomas T.2Lt kld 24-7-17 RFC p9 CR Yorks383
HUGGARD,Hewitt Lt kia 7-8-15 6EYorks p84 MR4,9-8-15
HUGGARD,Lewis Dudley Richard T.LtACapt kia 26-6-17 13Y&L p159 CR France1191
HUGGETT,Sidney George T.2Lt kia 18-9-18 RSuss att7Bn p119 CR France369
HUGGETT,William Wyndham T.2Lt dow 24-4-16 4SWBord att10Bn p100 CR France354

HUGGINS,Douglas Frank Capt kia 29-8-18 1Lond p245 CR France924
HUGGINS,R.H.Capt ded 27-6-19 3KAR p268
HUGH-JONES,Kenneth Herbert 2LtACapt kia 20-9-17 5 att12RB p179 CR Belgium83
HUGHES,Alan Stuart T2Lt kia 18-11-16 8NStaffs p157 CR France384
HUGHES,Albert Edward 2Lt kia 4-8-18 Lpool att1/9Bn p72 CR France261
HUGHES,Alexander Arbuthnot Capt kia 1-7-16 2SWBord p100 CR France1490
HUGHES,Alfred 2Lt kia 1-7-18 RE 526FC p210 CR France250
HUGHES,Arthur Maj kia 16-5-15 7Lpool p215 CR France279
HUGHES,Arthur.DCM.TCapt&QM ded 11-2-19 GL 18LancF att2Sch of Cookery p190 CR Germany1
HUGHES,Arthur Price Capt 31-3-21 17RWFus CR Wales535
HUGHES,Aubrey Noel T2Lt kia 26-9-16 5Dors p124 MR21
HUGHES,Benjamin Thomas T2Lt kia 17-3-18 13RWelshR att13RWFus p127 CR France275
HUGHES,Bryan Desmond.MC.TCapt kia 6-8-18 8RDubF p177 CR France28,1Bn
HUGHES,Burroughs Maurice Maj kia 15-9-15 4Norf p216 CR Gallipoli17
HUGHES,Charles Henry T2Lt kia 30-8-18 14WelshR p127 CR France217
HUGHES,Charles Walter TCapt dow 1-10-18 14RWar p65 CR France512
HUGHES,Christopher James Capt ded 13-5-16 4ConnRgrs p172 CR Iraq6
HUGHES,Cyril Rodyk TLt kia 4-7-16 7LNLancs p136 MR21
HUGHES,Daniel 2Lt kia 23-7-16 8GordH p166 MR21
HUGHES,Douglas Duncan 2Lt kia 10-7-16 11 att8SStaffs p122 MR21
HUGHES,Edward TCapt dow 16-9-16 2DLI p161 CR France329
HUGHES,Edward John.MC.Lt kia 20-10-18 3Lpool att13RWFus p72 CR France223,2Lt
HUGHES,Edward Malcolm LtCol ded 11-9-16 IA 14JatLancers p278 CR Iraq6
HUGHES,Edward Phillip T2Lt kld 27-7-17 RFC p9 CR Shrop145
HUGHES,Edward Reginald Graham 2Lt kia 25-9-15 2 O&BLI p130 CR France279
HUGHES,Edward William TLt ded 30-1-18 RAVC att23VetHosp p198
HUGHES,Eric 2Lt kld 14-11-17 RFC SR p9 CR Scot235
HUGHES,Eric James Walrond 2LtACapt kia 20-9-17 MGC Inf att4N&D p183 MR30
HUGHES,Ferdinand T2Lt kia 29-5-18 25MGC p183 MR18
HUGHES,Frederick TLt kia 12-10-16 1SLancs attY&L p125 CR Greece3,3Bn
HUGHES,Frederick Deeton Lt kia 21-10-14 1ELancs p111 CR Belgium451
HUGHES,Frederick Gordon 2Lt kia 26-6-16 3 att12NumbF p61 CR France188
HUGHES,Frederick Lee Maj kia 2-3-17 IA 20Inf attSWaziristanMil p278 MR43
HUGHES,Frederick Peter.MC.Lt dow 6-8-18 RE 511FC CR France71
HUGHES,Fred Micklewright 2Lt kia 23-3-18 1/1 att5 O&BLI BucksBn p231 MR27
HUGHES,Geoffrey Lt dow 5-8-18 1GrenGds p50 CR France502
HUGHES,George 2Lt kld 12-8-17 7KSLI p145 CR France256,kia
HUGHES,George Augustus.MC&Bar. 2Lt dow 4-11-17 6WRid p227 CR France658
HUGHES,George William Victor 2Lt kia 27-11-17 YLI att2/5Bn p143 MR17
HUGHES,Gladys Corfield SNurse 6-11-18 QAIMNS CR Shrop101
HUGHES,Gordon McGregor 2Lt kia 8-8-16 9 att5RBerks p139 MR21
HUGHES,Guy Ferguson Lt ded 21-12-15 HP IA EmpCycCo GdsDiv RHGds p20 CR France1106
HUGHES,Guy Wiley 2Lt dow 31-12-14 Mddx p147 CR France284
HUGHES,Harold 2Lt kia 11-4-18 GL &7RAF p190 CR Belgium18
HUGHES,Harold 2Lt dow 23-4-17 27RFA p30 CR France1325
HUGHES,Harold Bickley Drewe Capt kia 16-5-15 3RWar attHLI p65 MR22
HUGHES,Harold George.MC.TLt kia 4-5-17 197MGC p183 CR France1193
HUGHES,Henry Kent Capt kia 9-5-15 1YLI p143 MR29
HUGHES,Horatio Clement T2Lt kia 18-9-18 1 att11RWFus p98
HUGHES,Hugh Darrell 2Lt kia 14-1-17 3 att8RWFus p98 MR38,High
HUGHES,Irvin John Lt kia 13-1-16 IA 1/9GurkhaRif p278 CR Iraq5
HUGHES,John.MC.Lt kia 9-10-17 4 att16RWar p65 CR Belgium125
HUGHES,John Arthur.MID Lt dow 26-1-15 4RWFus p223 CR France80
HUGHES,John Edwyn T2Lt dow 19-8-16 10RWFus p98 CR France141
HUGHES,John Gwilym TLt kldacc 3-11-16 20 att9RWFus p98 CR France52
HUGHES,John Henry T2Lt kia 3-7-16 8WKent p141 CR France393
HUGHES,John Hugh Edward 2Lt kia 10-7-17 RGA 156SB p40 CR France591
HUGHES,John Lawrence TLt kia 1-10-17 17WelshR &25RFC p9&127 CR France88
HUGHES,John Meirion Lt 16-6-18 4SLancs &103RAF MR20
HUGHES,John Norman.MC&Bar.2Lt dow 2-8-18 4Ches p222 CR France1225
HUGHES,John Richard Hammond 2Lt ded 29-6-18 5RFA p208 CR France145
HUGHES,John Walter 2Lt kia 8-10-18 3 att1Ess p132 CR France1345
HUGHES,John William.MC.TLt kia 15-4-18 2WRid p115 CR France98
HUGHES,Lestocq 2Lt kia 26-9-16 5 att12Mddx p147 MR21

HUGHES,Lewis Reginald 2Lt dow 19-5-15 4NStaffs attRScotF p157 CR France8
HUGHES,Lionel Holford 2Lt kia 29-10-14 3 att1NStaffs p157 CR France82
HUGHES,Maurice Thomas T2Lt kia 30-5-16 20 att13RWFus p98 CR France115
HUGHES,Myrddin McKelvie.MC.Lt kia 16-5-18 402/14RFA 14ArmyBde p30 CR France889
HUGHES,Norman Alfred TCapt kia 18-9-18 11WelshR p127 CR Greece5
HUGHES,Norman Labrey 2Lt kia 26-9-19 Dev att1 O&BLI p76&257 MR70 &C Europe180,27-6-19
HUGHES,Oscar Cecil Lawrence Lt kia 18-8-17 RAMC att2KAR p196 CR EAfrica &CR Tanzania1
HUGHES,Owen T2Lt kia 30-11-15 RE 54FC p46 MR19
HUGHES,Percy Canynton T2Lt dow 3-10-18 11WelshR attSWBord p127 CR Greece6,3RWFus att7SWBord
HUGHES,Peter Capt kia 25-3-18 KRRC att11Bn p150 MR27
HUGHES,Peter Fredk.MC.Lt dow 7-8-18 RE 511FC p210 MR27
HUGHES,Rhys T2Lt dow 1-8-16 20LancF p92 CR France51
HUGHES,Robert Baskerville T2Lt kld 31-5-17 GL &RFC p9 CR Staffs153
HUGHES,Robert Charles 2Lt kia 17-8-18 15Lond p249
HUGHES,Robert Maurice Lt 1-8-19 EYorks CR WIndies36
HUGHES,Robert Peyton Lt kia 4-11-14 IA 101Grens p278 MR47
HUGHES,Sam T2Lt kia 6-11-17 WelshR att10Bn p127 MR32
HUGHES,Sidney Russell T2Lt kia 30-9-18 23 att11RFus p68 CR France212
HUGHES,T.O.AssPoliticAgent 16-4-16 MakranLevy Cps MR43
HUGHES,Tegerin TCapt dow 1-4-16 10RWFus p98 MR29
HUGHES,Thomas 2Lt kia 8-10-18 4WelshR p230 CR France1346
HUGHES,Thomas T2Lt ded 14-12-18 6ELancs p111 MR65,Lt
HUGHES,Thomas Derfel 2Lt kia 3-5-16 4 O&BLI p231 CR France1327
HUGHES,Thomas Hector Capt kia 15-10-14 Worc p109 CR France279
HUGHES,Thomas McKenny.MIDx2 TLt kia 5-2-18 KRRC att53RFC p16&150 C Belgium11,6-2-18
HUGHES,W.2Lt kld 19-11-18 RH&FA &RAF p30
HUGHES,Walter 2Lt kia 8-3-18 3 att2YLI p143 CR Belgium12
HUGHES,William T2Lt kia 3-3-16 10RWFus p98 MR29
HUGHES,William 2Lt kia 26-3-18 10 att1/9Manch p237 MR27
HUGHES,William.MC.T2Lt dow 14-9-18 8 att2Beds p86 CR Surrey18
HUGHES,William Francis.MC.MM.T2Lt dow 7-9-18 17RFus p98&254 CR France103
HUGHES,William Frederick TLt kia 20-11-17 10RIrF p171 CR France1489
HUGHES,William George T2Lt kia 23-7-18 12Lpool p72 MR20
HUGHES,William Price T2Lt kia 24-8-18 10SWBord p100 CR France246
HUGHES,William Sladen Lt kia 14-9-14 RSuss p119 MR15
HUGHES,William Thomas ded 8-4-17 IARO CR India48
HUGHES-DAVIES,Arthur Gwynne.MC.Lt kia 20-9-18 7RWFus att53MGC Inf p187&223 CR Palestine3
HUGHES-DUDLEY,Robert Charles 2Lt PoW 17-8-18 CivServRif MR16
HUGHES-GAMES,Joshua Brewer.MC.Capt ded 17-10-18 18DLI p265 CR Shrop
HUGHES-GIBB,Charles Pomery Capt dow 25-7-16 158RFA p30 CR France23
HUGHES-GIBB,Harold Francis TLt kia 18-4-17 B62RFA p30 CR France731,19-4-17
HUGHES-HALLETT,Harold Hereward Maj ded 16-6-19 NStaffs p265 CR Sussex184
HUGHES-HUGHES,William Montagu TCapt kia 25-9-15 9WelshR p127 CR France260
HUGHES-JONES,Harry Llewelyn TLt kia 3-3-16 11Mddx p147 MR19
HUGHES-ONSLOW,Arthur Maj ded 17-8-14 10Huss RoO p22 CR France87
HUGHES-ONSLOW,Denzil TMaj kia 10-7-16 6Dors p124 CR France370
HUGHESDON,Arthur Hamilton Lt kia 27-9-18 59RFA p30 CR France274
HUGHMAN,Cecil Mackenzie Capt dow 18-9-16 1/8Mddx C'Coy p236 CR France66
HUGHMAN,Leopold Alexander Capt kia 5-3-16 11Mddx p147 MR19
HUGHSTON,Johnston.MID TCaptAMaj dow 14-9-18 RAMC att68FA p196 CR Greece1,John
HUGILL,Edwin Abbot TCapt ded 25-9-17 17RFus p68
HUGILL,Valentine Francis Herbert 2Lt kia 16-10-16 16RFus &42RFC p3&68 C France82
HUGO,Reginald Graeff TLt dow 28-3-18 10/11HLI p163 CR France40
HUGO,Stephen Hofmeyr Capt kia 21-8-16 2RBerks p139 CR France423
HUIE,Henry William Richard Lt kia 11-8-18 9RScots p212 CR France360
HUISH,Francis T2Lt kia 28-7-18 Dev p76 CR France1689
HUITT,Richard Henry William 2Lt ded 13-12-17 RGA 77HAG p40 CR Belgium84
HULEATT,Francis Hugh.MC.CaptAMaj dow 28-2-17 C83RFA p30 CR France177

HULBERT,George Dodson 2Lt kia 9-8-18 18Huss p23 CR France652,Dodgson
HULE-KELLY,George Harvey Capt kia 20-10-14 NStaffs p157
HULKS,Henry John TCapt kia 3-9-16 17KRRC p150 CR France701,Harry
HULL,Edward Cecil Gordon Lt dow 26-8-17 30/39RFA p30 CR Belgium24
HULL,Edwin Charles T2Lt kld 17-3-18 RFC p16 CR Beds23
HULL,Joseph Laurence T2Lt dow 19-10-16 13Worc p109 CR France188
HULL,Lyonel Hyde Rochfort Lt kia 25/26-5-15 21Lond B'Coy p251 CR France279,25-5-15
HULLEY,Arthur Henry Booth TLt ded 4-12-18 RFA p30 p261 CR Hamps64
HULLETT,William Ernest T2Lt dow 7-12-17 Norf att7Bn p74 CR France446
HULM,Glynn TLtACapt ded 28-11-18 7 O&BLI p130 CR Greece9,WO
HULM,Wynne Odyerne TLt dow 25-9-15 8Dev p76 CR France88
HULME,Arthur T2Lt kia 23-10-18 20Manch p155 CR France231
HULME,Clarence Waller.MC.2Lt kia 16-9-18 317RH&FA p30 CR France245
HULME,Wilfred Lt ded 14-11-18 3Lpool att6TMB p72 CR Lancs463,Wilfrid 5Bn
HULSE,Edward Hamilton Westrow.Bart Capt kia 13-3-15 2ScotsGds p52 CR France347,12-3-15
HULTON,Alan Edward Grey TLt dow 6-5-15 RASC 173HTCoy p193 CR Glouc9
HULTON,Benjamin William T2Lt dow 5-7-18 13TankCps p188 CR France29,Wright Lt kia
HULTON,Cecil Harry Joy.MC.T2LtACapt kia 4-11-18 16LancF p92 CR France1479
HULTON-HARROP,Hugh de Lacey Lt kia 12-5-15 1LifeGds RoO p20 MR29,Lacy CR France453 Ex5Lancers
HULTON-SAMS,Frederick Edward Barwick TLt kia 30-7-15 6DCLI p114 CR France453
HUMBERSTON,Herbert Lt ded 20-10-18 Leic p263 CR Bucks80,2Lt
HUMBERT,Ernest Graham Johnston Lt dow 8-6-15 9RBerks att2Hamps p139 CR Gallipoli1
HUMBLE,Robert 2Lt kia 7-9-15 9A&SH p244 CR Belgium6
HUMBLE-CROFTS,Cyril Mitford TCapt kia 30-6-16 13RSuss p119 MR19
HUMBLY,William Leeuwin Lt kia 23-8-18 RBerks att1Bn p139 CR France927 HUMBLEY
HUMBY,Frederick Harry Lt dow 9-11-18 6 att2/7RWar p214 CR France13
HUME,Arthur James T2Lt dow PoW 21-5-18 1TankCps p188 CR France1076
HUME,Arthur Sinclair Vernon Maj ded 21-9-15 3ScotHorse p205 MR4
HUME,Charles Geoffrey Lt kia 20-10-14 1SStaffs p122 MR29,26-10-14
HUME,Edward Archibald TCapt dow 27-8-15 7SStaffs p122 MR4
HUME,George Minchin 2Lt kia 12-6-15 RE 2FC p210 MR29 &CR France453
HUME,Robert Anseley Cuthbert LtCol dow 1-5-15 1BordR p117 MR4,Ouseley
HUME,Ronald TLt kia 6-4-17 20RFus &20RFC p9&68 p68 MR20
HUME-GORE,Gustavas Lt kia 17-10-17 7A&SH att4KAR p243&268 CR EAfrica30 &CR Tanzania1
HUME-KELLY,George Harry Capt 20-10-14 1NStaffs CR France681
HUME-WRIGHT,Maurice Gabriel TLt kia 10-7-16 8Yorks p90 CR France515
HUMFREY,B.J.H.LtCol 1-9-15 IA ArmyRemountDept CR Hamps245
HUMFREY,Douglas Herbert Washington Lt kia 16-5-15 3 att2 O&BLI p130 MR22
HUMFREY,John Edward Hampinstall T2Lt ded 28-7-18 3SLancs att18Y&L p125 CR France134
HUMFREY,Wiliam Knox Lt kia 26-8-14 2LancF p92 MR15
HUMMEL,Raymond T2Lt kia 19-5-16 18WYorks p82 CR France643
HUMMERSTONE,Lawrence George Lt kia 21-8-18 5Lond &12RAF p255&246,2Lt CR France103
HUMPHREYS,David Virgil T2Lt kia 24-4-17 14A&SH p173 MR21
HUMPHREY,Elsie M.Sister 19-4-20 TFNS CR Cornwall168
HUMPHREY,Eric Sutherland Capt kia 5-6-15 8LancF p221 CR Gallipoli1
HUMPHREY,Ernest Graham 2Lt dow 29-3-18 48RFC p16 CR France62
HUMPHREY,Idwal Ben T2Lt dow 14-9-16 14Lpool p72 CR Greece6
HUMPHREY,Joseph Herbert T2Lt kia 20-9-17 1/2 att8Glouc p107 CR Belgium22
HUMPHREY,Richard Ronald 2Lt kia 31-8-19 5Yorks p221 CR France777
HUMPHREY,Thomas Albert 2Lt kia 3-5-18 8RWSurr att205RAF p56 CR France425
HUMPHREY,Vincent Ernest TLt ded 26-10-18 RASC 3ArmyEFC p193 CR France1512
HUMPHREY,William.MC.2Lt dow 24-10-18 4 att3RDubF p177 CR France40
HUMPHREY,William Pryn 2Lt kia 27-5-18 1/4Lond p246 CR France54,Pryor
HUMPHREY-DAVY,Darrel Norman O'Neale T2Lt kia 12-2-17 att14 Hamps p121 CR Belgium4,1-2-17
HUMPHREY-JONES,Cecil TCapt kia 24-11-17 19RWFus p98 MR17
HUMPHREYS,Arthur Cecil Capt kia 10-5-15 7LancF p221 MR4
HUMPHREYS,Dashwood William Harrington.DSO.Maj kia 17-2-17 IA 1/8GurkhaRif p278 MR38
HUMPHREYS,Dudley Francis 2Lt dow 16-5-15 2RWSurr p56 CR France80
HUMPHREYS,Frederick Charles.MC.TCapt kia 4-10-17 8SomLI p80 MR30

HUMPHREYS,George Geoffrey Prendergast Maj dow 30-10-14 IA 127BaluchistanLI att129Baluchis p278 CR Belgium186
HUMPHREYS,John Alan 2Lt kia 31-8-17 C64RFA p30 CR Belgium8
HUMPHREYS,John Theodore Gordon 2Lt kia 19-7-17 IA 40Pathans p278 CR EAfrica38 &CR Tanzania1
HUMPHREYS,Laurence Olsen T2Lt dow 13-11-15 7RLancs p59 CR France98
HUMPHREYS,Noel Forbes.MC.MID TCapt dow 27-3-18 10TankCps p188 CR France40
HUMPHREYS,Percy Lloyd TCapt kia 31-7-17 15WelshR p127 CR Belgium66
HUMPHREYS,Richard Grain 2Lt kia 28-9-17 13KRRC p150 MR30
HUMPHREYS,Roy Lt kia 4-9-18 RASC p193 MR30
HUMPHREYS,Spencer Noel.MC.2Lt kia 10-2-17 116RFA p30 MR37
HUMPHREYS,Stanley Howard 2Lt kia 20-11-17 4 att7ESurr p112 MR17
HUMPHREYS,Victor Richard 2Lt kia 24-9-16 2RBerks p139 CR France423
HUMPHREYS,William George 2Lt kia 9-9-16 2RSuss p119 MR21
HUMPHREYS,William Thomas LtTCapt&QM kia 4-10-18 3RFus p68 CR France234
HUMPHREYS-JONES,Shon Theodore Lt kia 14-11-17 RFA 86ArmyBde p30 MR30
HUMPHRIES,Cecil Frederick George.DSO.MC&Bar.DCM.TCaptALtCol dow 22-8-18 1DCLI att1Norf p114 CR France281,kia
HUMPHRIES,Leslie Glendower T2Lt kia 16-9-17 GL &4RFC p9 CR Belgium112
HUMPHRIES,Thomas 2Lt kia 1-7-16 15WYorks p82 MR21
HUMPHRIES,Walter Rawleigh Lt kia 27-7-16 18WYorks p82 CR France631
HUMPHRISS,Edward Victor 2Lt kia 11-4-17 NhamptYeo p204 MR20
HUMPHRY,Laurence Maj ded 5-2-20 RAMC p270 CR Camb9,LtCol
HUMPHRYS,Edward Thomas TCapt ded 3-5-16 2ScotRif GarrBn p103 MR65,BtMaj
HUMPHRYS,Leslie Palmer 2Lt dow 13-12-16 1HAC p206 CR France40
HUMPHRYS,Stewart Francis.MID T2Lt kia 26-8-16 20 att14RFus p68 CR France389
HUNKIN,William Burrows Clement.MC.TLt kia 3-11-18 14RWFus p98 CR France1478,4-11-18
HUNNYBUN,Gerald Norman.MC.MID TMaj kia 23-10-18 9Yorks p90&258 CR France231
HUNSTON,John Norman T2Lt dow 15-7-16 6Beds p86 CR France515,Lt
HUNSTON,Robert Donald T2Lt kia 28-9-16 10 att7Beds p86 CR France383
HUNSTONE,George Neil T2Lt kia 28-6-17 11RFC p9 CR France120
HUNSTONE,William Henry TMaj ded 18-2-19 GL p266 CR Yorks185
HUNT,Alfred John 2Lt dow 28-11-14 30RFA p30 CR France102
HUNT,Alfred Stanley 2Lt kld 20-8-17 GL &RFC p9 CR Wilts28,FltLt
HUNT,Alfred Thomas Lt ded 31-10-18 RFA p30&261 CR Lond29
HUNT,Arthur George 2Lt kia 4-11-18 IrGds att4GdsMGR p52&53 CR France1080
HUNT,Arthur Warner T2Lt dow 28-4-18 Ess att11Bn p132 CR France142
HUNT,Benjamin Owen T2Lt dow 23-5-17 10WRid p115 CR Belgium11
HUNT,Cecil Edwin Capt mbk 19-12-14 IA 34SikhPnrs p278 CR France705,dow
HUNT,Charles Francis 2LtACapt kia 25-9-15 2RB p179 CR France276
HUNT,Claude Holdsworth TCapt dow 2-4-17 RFA att18CpsHQ p30 CR France120
HUNT,D.A.DSO TCapt dow 30-11-17 SL att1/4KAR p202 MR52
HUNT,Edward Wallace Alleyne.MC.2Lt kia 1-5-17 GL &18RFC p9 CR France243
HUNT,Francis Henry Walter TCapt dow 27-9-15 5KSLI p145 CR Belgium140
HUNT,Frederick Arthur Lt ded 21-11-18 RHA p30 CR Wilts115
HUNT,Frederick Frank 2LtTLt kia 27-6-15 4Lond p246 CR France631
HUNT,Frederick William Capt kia 31-10-14 IA 19Lancers att4Huss p278
HUNT,George Ede 2Lt kld 21-7-18 5YLI &RAF p255 CR Yorks172
HUNT,Geoffrey Albert T2Lt kld 6-9-17 GL &RFC p9 CR Mddx28
HUNT,George Ward Capt kia 9-5-15 2Nhampt p137 MR32
HUNT,Gerald Ponsonby Sneyd.CMG.DSO.MajALtCol kia 23-3-18 1RBerks p139 CR France41
HUNT,Harold Montague 2Lt dow 27-8-15 3 att6EKent p57 CR France119
HUNT,Henry Hope 2Lt kia 26-10-18 10Lond &8LancP p248&258
HUNT,James T2Lt kia 16-11-16 10 att8ELancs p111 CR France153
HUNT,James Charles Marjoribanks Lt kia 10-8-16 B47RFA p30 CR France453
HUNT,John Goldsworth TLt dow 11-3-19 RASC p255
HUNT,John Henry Sneyd 2Lt kia 16-9-16 23Lond p252 MR21
HUNT,John Reginald Lilly 2Lt kia 1-7-16 5N&D p232 CR France576
HUNT,John William Reynolds 2Lt kia 28-4-17 11Suff p78 MR20
HUNT,Lawrence Herbert Lt kia 4-12-17 21Lond p251 MR17
HUNT,Louis Gordon 2Lt kia 22-9-18 9Lond p248 CR France369
HUNT,Noel Guy Lt dow 5-4-17 4Berks p234 CR France511
HUNT,Percival George Havelock Lt kia 8-11-17 GL RFA att92TMB p190 CR France184
HUNT,Ralph Leslie T2Lt kia 15-10-16 11Ess p132 MR21

HUNT,Reginald Frank Lt ded 29-5-18 RFA Y8TMB p207 CR France1755,dow
HUNT,Reginald Thomas Headley 2Lt dow 12-4-18 10DLI p161 MR32
HUNT,Robert Lancelot Gibbs TCapt kia 7-10-16 6 O&BLI p130 CR France432
HUNT,Roger Victor Cecil T2Lt dow 1-10-18 B155RFA p31 CR France40
HUNT,Ronald Francis 2Lt kia 25-4-15 3RWar p65 MR29
HUNT,Sidney Herman 2Lt kia 22-8-17 19Lond p250 MR29
HUNT,Sidney William T2Lt kia 26-10-16 12 att13Ess p132 CR France643
HUNT,T.H.Maj 29-4-18 RAMC CR Yorks619
HUNT,William George Philip.MC.TCapt dow 15-8-17 10Ess p132 CR France40
HUNT,William Julian T2Lt kia 11-7-16 112MGC p183 MR21
HUNT,William Victor Lt dow 17-10-18 MGC att82RAF p183 CR Belgium20
HUNTER,A.H.Lt&QM 16-2-17 1Dors CR Hamps219
HUNTER,Albert Richmond.MC.Lt ded 11-2-19 23NumbF p61 CR France34
HUNTER,Alexander 2Lt kia 20-11-17 2/5LancF p221 MR21
HUNTER,Alexander Forbes 2Lt kia 23-5-16 21Lond p251 MR20
HUNTER,Alfred James 2Lt kld 6-8-18 1/4Mddx att101RAF p147 CR France29,Lt kia 7-8-18 17Bn
HUNTER,Archibald T2Lt kia 2-7-16 14 att9Ches p96 MR21
HUNTER,Archibald.MC.TMaj ded 10-10-18 5CamH p168 CR Ireland24
HUNTER,Archibald T2Lt kia 7-11-18 9YLI p143 CR France930
HUNTER,Archibald 2Lt ded 15-9-19 KOSB p264 CR Scot746
HUNTER,Archibald Douglas 2Lt kia 23-4-17 9Lond p248 CR France1193
HUNTER,Archibald Smith.MC.Capt dow 29-8-18 1/7A&SH p243 CR France145
HUNTER,Arthur David Capt kia 7-8-15 6Manch p236 CR Gallipoli2,Douglas
HUNTER,Arthur Lawrence T2Lt kia 8-8-18 9RFus p68 MR16
HUNTER,Atholl Gunning Capt kia 22-4-17 IA 32Lancers p278 MR38
HUNTER,Bentley Moore TCapt kia 31-7-17 RAMC att1/1Camb p196 MR29
HUNTER,Charles Gawain Raleigh Lt kia 24-4-15 2YLI p143 MR29
HUNTER,Charles James TLt ACapt ded 4-11-18 LabCps p189 CR Lond14,4-11-19 Ex Beds
HUNTER,D.F.Capt 29-3-20 RAMC CR Ches182
HUNTER,David Maj ded SRussia 18-10-19 SL p268 CR Asia81
HUNTER,Douglas William.DSO.TCapt kia 25-3-18 RAMC att10WYorks p196 MR20
HUNTER,Eric Hamilton.MID 2Lt kia 7-8-15 IARO att1/5GurkhaRif p278 CR Gallipoli17
HUNTER,Frederick Lt ded 9-12-19 SL RE attIWT p268 CR Wales564
HUNTER,George Arnold Lt ded 3-8-17 ScotHorse att265MGC Inf p187&205 CR Egypt7
HUNTER,George Edward Capt kia 26-4-15 6NumbF p213 MR29
HUNTER,George Frederick Gordon Lt 9-2-19 EAfrMilLabCps CR Scot308
HUNTER,George Stuart.MC.TLt dow 10-11-18 RASC att13RB p193&258 CR France658
HUNTER,Godfrey Jackson 2Lt kld 26-4-16 5Lancers p22 CR Ireland14
HUNTER,Harry T2Lt dow 5-11-17 GL &RFC p9 CR France64
HUNTER,Herbert 2Lt kia 26-4-18 1/4RLancs p213 CR France106
HUNTER,Herbert.MC.Lt dow 23-10-18 1EKent p57 CR France924,Capt 6Bn
HUNTER,Hope Capt ded 3-12-17 14Lond p249 CR Egypt2 2LondScot
HUNTER,Howard Tomlin Capt kia 27-4-15 6NumbF p213 MR29,26-4-15
HUNTER,Hugh Michael Lt dow 6-4-15 3 att2Wilts p153
HUNTER,Hugh Swinterton Forsyth T2Lt kia 29-4-16 1KOSB p102 CR France35
HUNTER,Jack Lt&QM drd 27-5-17 NottsYeo p205 MR41,27-5-18
HUNTER,James Cecil 2Lt dow 2-9-18 5Lond p246 CR France833
HUNTER,James Gladstone 2Lt kia 14-3-17 4RScots att1/5SStaffs p211 CR France281
HUNTER,James Kenneth Lt kia 6-9-17 RE 427FC p210 CR Belgium125
HUNTER,James MacMillan T2Lt kia 17-10-18 KRRC att2Bn p150 CR France341
HUNTER,James Whitaker T2Lt dow 9-7-16 5Nhampt p137 CR France23,8-7-16
HUNTER,James Williamson 2Lt dow 14-11-16 2RScots p54 CR France74
HUNTER,John Maurice T2Lt kia 2-7-16 6Wilts p153 CR France267
HUNTER,Johnston Shaw Kirker 2Lt kia 30-6-16 D/157RFA p31 CR France631
HUNTER,Leslie Aubrey William Lt ded 3-11-18 4SfthH p255 CR Norf209
HUNTER,Leslie Whitaker Lt kia 14-8-16 4 O&BLI p231 CR France832,13-8-16
HUNTER,Martin Lt dow 11-4-18 9Lancers p22 CR France64
HUNTER,Melville Adrian Cecil 2Lt dow 15-11-15 4HLI att7SStaffs p163 CR Gallipoli27
HUNTER,Nigel Duncan Ratcliffe.MC&Bar.Capt kia 26-3-18 RE 228FC p46 CR France560
HUNTER,Norman Archbold T2Lt kia 3-9-17 26NumbF p61 CR France1461
HUNTER,Norman Frederick Lt dow 16-6-15 4RWar att4RFus p65 MR29
HUNTER,Patrick Colin T2Lt dow 16-10-17 2NStaffs attRFC p9 CR Greece1
HUNTER,Percy Talbot Langley Lt ded 19-7-16 1/14Lond p249 CR France40,Lungley 2Lt
HUNTER,Peter T2Lt kia 17-4-16 RE 251TC p46 CR France163
HUNTER,Philip Needham Chap4Cl ded 14-3-19 RAChDept p268 CR Kent180
HUNTER,Richard Jocelyn Capt dow 25-8-18 5 att21Lond p246 CR France141
HUNTER,Robert Lt kia 5-6-17 RFA p207 CR Belgium127
HUNTER,Robert Gibson Lt kia 23-4-17 7A&SH A'Coy p243 CR France545
HUNTER,Ronald Gordon 2Lt dow PoW 25-4-18 1RDubF p177 CR Germany4
HUNTER,Thomas Lt kia 16-7-17 RE 474FC p210 CR Belgium36
HUNTER,Thomas Murray Capt ded 22-5-16 5SfthH p270 CR Scot975
HUNTER,Thomas Vicars Capt kia 5-12-17 RB &66RFC p179&9 CR Italy45
HUNTER,Thomas William.MC.Lt dow 24-10-18 113/25RH&FA p31 CR France1266
HUNTER,Wilfred Cleaver 2Lt kia 29-12-15 RGA 121HB p40 CR Belgium35
HUNTER,William 2Lt dow 10-10-16 10Ches p96 CR France44,Lt kia
HUNTER,William Alexander Dobson Lt kia 1-10-18 3 att8BlkW p128 CR Belgium157
HUNTER,William John Kenny T2Lt ded 26-10-17 3HLI p163 CR Scot235
HUNTER,William Mortimer 2Lt kia 29-6-17 4RInniskF p105 CR Belgium23
HUNTER,William Samuel T2Lt ded 1-2-16 9RWKent p141 CR Wilts142,Wallace
HUNTER,William Scott T2Lt kia 1-8-17 10ScotRif p103 MR29
HUNTER,William Stuart T2Lt kia 31-7-17 8Lincs p75 MR29
HUNTER-BLAIR,Alister 2Lt kia 9-5-15 CamH p255 MR22
HUNTINGTON,George Waldeof 2Lt kia 24-7-16 8 att6KRRC p150 MR21,24-8-1 6 att8Bn
HUNTINGTON,John.MC.Lt dow 12-8-18 5BordR p228 CR France29
HUNTINGTON,Nigel Jocelin Searanche Lt kia 17-11-14 Lincs p75 MR22
HUNTLEY,Edward Kenneth 2Lt kia 20-9-17 3 att6 O&BLI attRB p130 CR Belgium126,HUNTLY
HUNTLEY,John Fenwirk TLt kia 9-4-17 25NumbF B'Coy p61 CR France265,Cap
HUNTLY,Louis Francis 2Lt kia 26-4-17 1GordH p166 MR20
HUNTON,Frederick Capt kia 4-5-17 RAMC p253 CR Palestine2
HUNTRISS,Cyril John.MC.MID TCapt kia 1-7-16 1EYorks p84 MR21
HUNTRISS,Harold Edward Capt kia 17-5-15 2Beds p86 CR France279
HUNTRISS,William TLt ded 23-10-18 9WRid attWAFF p201&115 CR WAfrica3
HUNTSMAN,Benjamin Canning Capt kia 7-4-17 2/8N&D p233 MR21
HUNWICK,Edward Noel T2Lt dow 30-8-18 1/2ELancs p111 CR France307
HURD,Angier Percy Lt kia 30-3-18 1Herts p252 CR France425
HURD,Douglas William Capt dow 17-9-16 7Mddx p235 CR France329
HURD-WOOD,John Grahame TCapt kia 4-8-16 GL 68InfBdeHQ p190 CR France430
HURDMAN,Cyril 2Lt kia 19-7-16 3SStaffs att2/6RWar p122 MR32
HURLBATT,Edgar Simon.MC.Maj kia 27-3-18 7 att2/8Manch p237 MR27,Simm LtCol
HURLBUTT,Percivald.MC.HonCapt ded 8-6-18 7RWFus p223 CR Wales637
HURRELL,Colin John Richard Capt kia 2-11-17 10Lond p248 CR Palestine8
HURST,Aubrey Clive 2Lt dow 22-1-18 39RFC p16 CR Belgium18
HURST,Charles Ernest T2Lt kia 14-9-16 11 att6Yorks p90 CR France293
HURST,Henry Cubbin T2Lt kia 28-9-16 6Yorks p90 MR21
HURST,Herbert William 2Lt dow 10-10-17 C295RFA p31 CR France40
HURST,John Julius Lt kia 31-10-17 2/22Lond p251 CR Palestine1,Jules
HURST,Richard Henry 2Lt kia 29-9-18 9Lpool att12Norf p216 CR Belgium451
HURST,Sydney Bailey 2Lt kia 26-8-18 5RScotF p222 CR France1185
HURSTBOURNE,Walter Hirsch 2Lt kia 23-6-17 4WessexRFA p208 CR Belgium1
HURST-BROWN,Cecil 2Lt dow 26-9-15 2 O&BLI p130 CR France80,25-9-15
HURST-BROWN,Dudley 2Lt dow 15-6-15 129/30RFA p31 CR Belgium28
HURT,Seymour Frederick Aukland Albert Capt kia 18-10-14 RScotF p94 MR22
HURWORTH,Charles Reginald Lt kia 26-3-18 5Yorks p220 MR27
HUSBAND,Donald Irons 2Lt kia 16-8-16 4A&SH p173 CR France515
HUSBAND,George Staunton.DSO.Capt ded 21-2-17 IA IMS p278 MR61
HUSBAND,Joseph Sim.MIDx2 TLtAMaj dow 11-4-18 C59MGC p183 CR France262
HUSBAND,Kenneth D'Ombrian 2Lt kia 28-3-18 2Wilts p153 MR27,D'Ombrain
HUSBAND,Peter,Ross T2Lt kia 25-9-16 1BlkW p128 MR21
HUSBAND,William T2Lt dow 25-6-18 NumbF att15DLI p61 CR Derby76
HUSEY,Ralph Hamer.DSO&Bar.MC.MIDx4 BrigGen dow PoW 30-5-18 5Lond Cmdg25InfBde p246 CR France1329
HUSK,Frederick John.MID 2Lt dow 21-3-18 RGA 301SB p40 MR27
HUSKINSON,Frederick John Capt kia 1-7-16 RInniskF p105 MR21
HUSKISSON,Claude Alexander 2Lt kia 15-6-17 6 att1Hamps &TMB p229 CR France546
HUSKISSON,Herbert George 2Lt dow 27-1-17 6Hamps p229 CR Iraq5

HUSSEY,Charles Francis T2Lt kia 5-10-18 Glouc att1/5th p107 CR France375
HUSSEY,Edmund Dobson 2Lt kia 9-4-18 Mddx att21Bn p147 MR32
HUSSEY,Edmund Thornber 2Lt kia 7-6-17 1RMunstF p175 CR Belgium155
HUSSEY,Frank.MM.2Lt kia 4-10-17 8RWar A'Coy p215 MR30
HUSSEY,Frank William Lt kia 24-9-18 4Leic p219 CR France375
HUSSEY,Harold Edward T2Lt kia 25-3-17 3Dev att1Manch p76 MR38
HUSSEY,Hubert Murray.MC.2Lt kia 6-8-12 2 att1/6SStaffs p122 CR France98
HUSSEY,Michael Edward 2Lt 4-9-15 att81Pars MR67
HUSTON,William TCapt kld 6-12-17 RAVC attRASC 37DivTrn p198 CR France285
HUTCHEON,Samuel Wyness T2Lt dow 4-9-16 11 att12HLI p163 CR France40
HUTCHEON,Thomas T2Lt dow 12-8-16 7RScotF p94 CR France23,13-8-16
HUTCHESON,Andrew Guy.MC.TCapt&Adjt kia 14-7-16 9ScotRif p103&258 CR France399
HUTCHESON,Gordon James Lt ded 27-5-18 GL &RAF p190 CR France102
HUTCHESON,James McLeod T2Lt kia 21-9-17 12ESurr p112 MR30
HUTCHESON,John T2Lt kia 8-9-15 10N&D p233 CR Belgium112
HUTCHESON,Norman Heber Lt kia 12-3-15 RIrRif p169 MR22
HUTCHINGS,Edgar John 2Lt ded 9-11-15 10Lond p248 CR Europe1,dow
HUTCHINGS,Kenneth Lotherington Lt kia 3-9-16 4 att12Lpool p72 MR21
HUTCHINGS,Thomas Clifton TCapt dow 19-7-17 1LancF p92 CR Belgium16
HUTCHINS,Alfred John Avalon T2Lt dow PoW 22-3-18 2RSuss p119 CR Belgium140
HUTCHINS,C.F.MM.2Lt 15-1-19 RGA CR Glouc176
HUTCHINS,Cedric Page TLt kia 14-11-17 SL att1/3KAR p202 CR EAfrica11 &CR Tanzania1
HUTCHINS,Douglas Markham 2Lt dow 2-8-16 5Mddx att1/4 O&BLI p147 CR France167
HUTCHINS,Frederick Charles T2Lt kia 22-4-18 13RWFus p98 MR27
HUTCHINS,Ralph 2Lt ded 3-6-16 8Mddx p236 CR Surrey78
HUTCHINS,Richard Capt ded 13-5-15 4RMunstF p175 CR Eire48
HUTCHINSON,Albert T2Lt kia 8-10-18 att2Y&L p159 MR16
HUTCHINSON,Ambrose Lt kia 19-1-18 6Lpool attRFC p18&215 CR Belgium132
HUTCHINSON,Andrew Levy Lt kia 21-3-18 7RSots att31MGC p211&187,Hutchison MR20
HUTCHINSON,Anthony Christopher Campbell TMaj ded 18-11-18 30MGC p183 CR Surrey1,Clark
HUTCHINSON,Arthur George T2Lt dow 10-3-18 1/2SStaffs att1/4Ches p122 CRPalestine3
HUTCHINSON,Arthur Norman 2Lt kia 21-3-18 7Worc p226 MR37
HUTCHINSON,Basil Stewart Cayley Lt kia 20-9-14 EYorks p84 MR15
HUTCHINSON,Benjamin.MC.2Lt kia 3-5-17 11EYorks p84 MR20
HUTCHINSON,Bert 2Lt dow 12-8-18 3 att15LancF p92 CR France145,3 att5Bn
HUTCHINSON,Cecil Dunbar TLt dow PoW 12-8-17 7SStaffs &57RFC p9&122 CR Belgium140
HUTCHINSON,Cecil Leigh 2Lt kia 31-7-17 3 att2ELancs p111 MR29
HUTCHINSON,Edgar Francis 2Lt dow 24-5-15 4Yorks p220 CR Belgium165
HUTCHINSON,Edwin Octavius.MID TLt dow 21-9-18 RE 78FC p46 CR France906
HUTCHINSON,George Hanley Lt kia 2-3-16 4Yorks Y'Coy p220 CR Belgium5
HUTCHINSON,George Russell 2Lt kia 26-11-17 2/8WYorks p219 MR17
HUTCHINSON,Hanley Lt dow 1-9-17 2/5WYorks p218 CR France512
HUTCHINSON,Harry T2Lt kia 30-9-18 9 att3YLI p143 CR France375,att2Bn
HUTCHINSON,Henry William Lt kia 13-3-17 2/4Leic p87 CR France1472
HUTCHINSON,Herbert 2Lt kia 27-9-18 1 att3Beds p86 MR16
HUTCHINSON,Hugh Maxwell Lt dow 29-11-17 26NumbF p61 CR France214,HUTCHISON
HUTCHINSON,Ivan 2Lt kia 22-8-18 5EYorks p219 CR France514,Lt
HUTCHINSON,Jack Clifforde Lt kia 22-3-18 6ESurr p226 MR20,att4Leic
HUTCHINSON,James Gwynne Lt kia 10-11-17 246RFA p207 CR Belgium10
HUTCHINSON,James Walter LtTCapt dow 25-9-15 2Beds p86 MR19
HUTCHINSON,John Cayley Lt kia 5-8-15 IA 3 att1/3GurkhaRif p278 CR France1157
HUTCHINSON,John Summerscales Capt kia 3-9-14 2SLancs p125 CR France206,26-8-14
HUTCHINSON,Leslie Gwynne TLt dow 10-9-18 10EYorks p84 France297
HUTCHINSON,Peter 2Lt kia 11-9-18 4LNLancs p234 CR France1496
HUTCHINSON,Tom 2Lt kia 18-9-18 YLI att9Bn p143 CR France407
HUTCHINSON,Tom Macintosh T2Lt kia 13-11-16 13EYorks p84 CR France802
HUTCHINSON,William T2Lt kia 22-11-17 5 att2/8WYorks p218 MR17
HUTCHINSON,William John T2Lt kia 25-5-17 88MGC Inf p183 CR France311
HUTCHINSON,William Stanhope.MC&Bar.T2LtACapt dow 8-9-18 12/13NumbF B'Coy p61 CR France41

HUTCHINSON,W.J 2Lt 24-1-17 WRid attWIndR CR SAfrica171
HUTCHISON,Andrew Levy Lt kia 21-3-18 7RScots attMGC p187&211,HUTCHINSON
HUTCHISON,David Fancourt.MID 2LtACapt kia 29-8-18 3 att2YLI p143 CR France327
HUTCHISON,Donald Herbert 2Lt kia 9/10-8-15 16Lond p250 CR Belgium112,10-8-15
HUTCHISON,Edward TMaj kia 1-7-16 17HLI p163 CR France296
HUTCHISON,Innes Owen.MID T2Lt kia 7-1-16 2BlkW p128 MR38,Capt
HUTCHISON,James T2Lt kia 26-7-16 27Manch p155 CR France513
HUTCHISON,John McMaster TLt kia 22-10-16 9GordH p166 CR France239
HUTCHISON,John William 2Lt dow 26-11-17 1/8RScots p212 CR Palestine3
HUTCHISON,Robert Hamilton TLt kia 13-10-15 8 att1BlkW p128 MR19
HUTCHISON,Seton Marshall TLtACapt ded 8-1-18 Hamps att2WIndR p121
HUTCHISON,Thomas T2Lt kia 20-5-16 10/11HLI p163 CR France423,21-5-16
HUTCHISON,Thomas Walter Capt dedacc 22-11-15 10RScots p212 CR Scot725
HUTCHISON,William Murray.MC.MID Capt dow 27-4-16 1Lpool p72 CR France32
HUTCHISON,William Ramsay TCapt kia 22-3-18 6/7RScotF p94 MR20
HUTH,Austin Henry Capt kia 20-4-15 4ESurr p112 MR29,1Bn
HUTLEY,Horace Abrey 2Lt kia 2-4-18 7WRid p228 CR France298,12-4-18
HUTSON,Douglas Bertram Lt ded 23-7-18 RASC p193 CR Lond28
HUTSON,Harold T2Lt dow 26-3-18 10 att9YLI p143 CR France364
HUTSON,Harry Austen Capt kia 28-5-18 GL attLancF p190 MR18
HUTSON,William Cecil 2Lt kia 21-3-18 C51RFA p31 MR27
HUTT,Ernest Reginald 2Lt kia 25-9-15 6RScotF p94 MR19
HUTT,Francis Rodes TCapt kia 25-9-15 7KOSB C'Coy p102 CR France219
HUTT,Harold Vernon 2Lt kia 26-1-15 2RSuss p119 CR France720
HUTT,Walter Beresford 2Lt dow 29-9-18 RGA 527SB p40 CR France113
HUTTON,Alexander TCapt kia 8-7-16 2HLI A'Coy p163 CR France924
HUTTON,Andrew Donald TCapt kia 3-7-16 15HLI p163 CR France296
HUTTON,Frederick Robert Hughes Lt kia 12-5-15 9A&SH p244 MR29,10-5-15
HUTTON,George Adolph Lt drd 19-9-14 RE 3SigCoy p46 CR France1110
HUTTON,John Barnabas Lt kia 13-10-15 5SStaffs p229 MR19
HUTTON,Lorne de Hutton T2Lt kia 24-3-18 41MGC Inf p183 CR France518
HUTTON,Richard 2Lt kia 7-11-14 3Leic att2RWar p87 MR29
HUTTON,Robert Capt kia 22-8-17 ScotHorse p205 MR30
HUTTON,Stanley Fell T2Lt kia 9-11-18 12Yorks p90 MR32,11-4-18
HUTTON,Walter Forbes T2Lt kia 14-7-16 8 att11BlkW p128 MR21,11 att8Bn
HUTTON,William Wallace 2Lt kia 28-10-17 7Lond attRFC p18&247 MR20
HUTTON-BALFOUR,Archibald Gibson T2Lt dow 22-3-18 3 att6KOSB p102 CR France511
HUTTON-SQUIRE,Robert Henry Edmund.DSO.MID Maj dow 8-4-17 RGA att85RFA p40 CR France12
HUXLEY,John Scott T2Lt kia 16-7-16 100MGC p183 MR21,15-7-16
HUXLEY,Joseph 2Lt kia 22-4-18 10 att14RWFus p98 CR France296
HUXLEY,Robert Charles 2Lt kia 7-5-18 8RWar p215 MR19
HUXTABLE,Geoffrey.MBE.2Lt 10-12-18 MilLabCps CR EAfrica36
HUYTON,John 2Lt kia 28-5-17 4N&D att51TMB p134 CR France544
HYAMS,Alec Hallenstein Lt kia 3-5-17 9 att3RFus p68 MR29
HYATT,Valentine 2Lt kia 24-3-18 RFC p16 MR20
HYATT,William Joseph Lt mbk 24-10-18 4LabCps att9Dev p256&189,kia MR16
HYDE,Arthur Clarendon Maj kia 22-11-15 O&BLI p130 MR38
HYDE,Charles Stuart T2Lt kia 1-7-16 16WYorks p82 MR21
HYDE,Cyril 2Lt kia 1-12-17 RGA &35RFC p9&40 MR20
HYDE,Eustace Emil Lt kia 12-10-16 4 att1RIrF p171 CR France744
HYDE,Francis Cecil Lt kia 9-4-17 1RWKent p141 CR France523
HYDE,Gilbert Arthur T2Lt kia 4-10-17 YLI att9Bn p143 MR30
HYDE,Herbert Walter T2Lt dow 20-5-16 16RWar p65 CR France1182,kia
HYDE,Herbert William 2Lt kia 17-5-15 RSuss att2RInniskF p119 MR22
HYDE,James Charles 2Lt kia 1-7-16 1/5N&D p232 MR21
HYDE,Leslie Arthur 2Lt ded 26-10-15 RHA p31 CR Eire356
HYDE,Patrick George Maj ded 2-3-15 RAMC p267 CR Hamps1
HYDE,Percival G.Lt ded 15-11-18 GL attWT Ret p266
HYDE,William Frederick T2Lt kia 8-11-18 10RWar att2Lincs p65 CR France965
HYDE,William Nelson Capt&QM dow 16-10-16 2RWar p65 CR France264
HYDE,William Sisson Lt dow 7-11-18 5Lincs p220 CR France658
HYDER,Alfred William T2Lt kia 2-9-18 15ACycCps p181 CR France285
HYETT,Frank 2Lt kia 30-11-17 RGA 52HAG p40 CR France245
HYLAND,Albert Clive LtTCapt dow 10-8-18 RASC att6EKent p193 CR France69

HYLAND,Frederick Hunter 2Lt kia 23-5-15 Yorks &RFC p1&90 CR France350
HYLAND,Herbert Bright T2Lt kia 19-7-16 100MGC p183 MR21
HYMAN,Ezra Herbert 2Lt dow 1-11-18 3Glouc att11SLancs p107 CR France528
HYMAN,Robert Leslie T2Lt kia 23-8-17 6DCLI p114 MR30
HYMAN,Walter William 2Lt kia 1-7-16 26NumbF p61 MR21
HYNE,Charles Godfrey Haggas Cutcliffe Lt dow 21-11-16 2IrGds attTMB p52 CR Yorks482
HYNES,Ernest Stanley Patrick 2Lt kia 10-11-16 EKent &25RFC p3&57 CR France88,Lt
HYNDMAN,James Valentine TCapt dow 7-7-16 14RIrRif p169 CR France64
HYRONS,Francis Austin T2Lt kia 13-9-16 13 att2N&D p134 MR21
HYSLOP,James.MM.Lt kia 5-11-18 14Lond p249 CR France1142
HYSLOP,James T2Lt ded 15-2-19 RE p255 CR Scot510
HYSLOP,John Wallet 2Lt kia 26-10-17 3 att2GordH p166&257 MR30
HYSLOP,Ninian Steele T2Lt kld 30-10-17 RFC p9 CR Iraq6
HYSLOP,Thomas Anderson.MC.T2Lt kia 22-3-18 10 att4Yorks p90 MR27
HYSLOP,William Douglas T2Lt dow 25-3-18 8BlkW p128 CR France62
HYTTEN,Edwin Christopher 2Lt kia 12-11-15 8Hamps p229 CR Belgium182,12-11-16 11Bn

---

I

I'ANSON,John Francis Capt kia 20-9-14 3WYorks p82 MR15
I'ANSON,Leonard Percy Lt kia 25-4-15 4Yorks p220 MR29
IBBERSON,Henry Joseph 2Lt kia 5-10-17 220MGC Inf p183 CR Belgium308
IBBITSON,William Beveridge T2Lt kia 1-7-16 10WYorks p82 CR France373,Lt
IBBOTSON,Arnold Lt kia 13-10-18 1/4Y&L p238 CR France316
IBBOTSON,Edwin.MC.2Lt kia 11-4-17 10LNLancs p136 MR20
IBBOTSON,George Sharples 2Lt kia 14-5-18 5LNLancs p23 MR19
IBBOTSON,Roskell Lt kia 2-5-17 4 att2RIrF p171 CR Greece3 Ross
IBBOTSON,Robert 2Lt kia 28-4-17 5 att13Ess p232 MR20
IBBOTSON,Tom T2Lt kia 25-9-16 7Leic p87 CR France402
IBBS,John Thomas 2Lt dow 20-3-17 7Worc p226 CR France164
IDDON,Harold 2Lt dow 23-8-18 D173RFA p31 CR Lancs114
IDE,Thomas Norman 2Lt kia 2-7-16 2Ess p132 CR France643
IDESON,Joseph Henry T2Lt kld 13-3-17 N&D &RFC 12TrainingBn p134&9 CR Yorks438
IDLE,Wilfrid Ernest 2Lt kia 25-2-17 26RFus att17Lond p250 CR Belgium102,Wilfred 24-2-17
IEVERS,Oliver Goldsmith LtCol ded 12-2-16 SL IA Censor p268 CR Eire406
IKIN,Alfred Edward T2Lt kia 11-3-18 GL att93RFC p16 CR France88
ILBERY,Oscar Reginald 2Lt kia 1-7-16 2YLI p143 CR France1890
ILES,Charles Cochrane Lt dow 19-12-14 RAMC att2ELancs p196 CR France768
ILES,John Francis TLt kia 2-6-17 B165RFA p31 CR France644
ILES,John Owen Lt kia 25-9-15 1SStaffs att1RWFus p122 MR19
ILES,Percy Henry 2Lt kia 11-4-17 16 att1RWar p65 MR20
ILIEVE,William Arthur 2Lt kia 9-10-17 Ess att2Bn p132 CR Belgium126
ILIFF,Frederick John 2Lt kia 13-10-15 1/6SStaffs p229 MR19
ILIFFE,Thomas Dealtrey T2Lt kia 10-9-18 1 att2YLI p143 CR France672,Dealtry
ILLING,Francis 2Lt dow 8-5-18 5 att13RFus p68 CR France84
ILLINGWORTH,Frank 2Lt kia 15-12-16 2EYorks p84 CR Greece3
ILLINGWORTH,Fred Donald Roberts TLt kia 23-4-17 1Beds p86 MR20
ILLINGWORTH,Frederick William Lt ded 6-2-19 4ScotRif &RAF p264
ILLINGWORTH,Guy Russell ACapt ded 21-1-21 IA 1/91Punjabis p278 MR65
ILLINGWORTH,Harold Locke 2Lt kia 23-3-18 17Lond p250 MR20
ILLINGWORTH,John.MC.Lt dow 3-6-18 8WYorks p219 CR Belgium188,1/6Bn
ILSLEY,Alfred Lewis T2Lt ded 23-11-17 ELancs p111 CR Berks27
IMBER,William Arthur 2Lt kia 27-8-17 7RWar p214 MR30
IMPEY,John Eugene Lt kia 27-3-16 1Lincs attMGC p75&183 MR29
IMRIE,Arthur Leslie 2Lt kia 30-11-17 D275RFA p208 MR17
IMRIE,Daniel McLachlan 2Lt dow 16-11-17 GlasgowYeo p203 CR Belgium18
INCE,Hugh Ethelred McCarthy.MID LtAMaj kia 4-11-16 52/2RFA p31 CR France374
INCE,William Campbell Lt kia 2-6-16 8CanadaMGC CR Belgium106
INCH,George Edward 2Lt kia 22-9-17 1/2 att6Beds p86 MR30
INCH,John 2Lt kia 20-6-16 1/9 att1/8A&SH p244 CR France15
INCH,Robert Stuart Mark.MC.TLt kia 22-10-18 8Norf p74 MR30
INCHBALD,John Chantry Elliot.MID TLtACapt kia 2-4-17 9Dev p76 CR France568,Chantrey
INCHBOLD,Gerald Lt kia 31-5-17 4N&D &55RFC p9&134 CR France134
INCHES,Robert Kirk.DFC.2Lt kia 26-8-18 RE &RAF p46

INCHLEY,William Lt kia 19-12-15 3 att9WRid p115 CR Belgium84
IND,William Ernest.MC.Capt&Adjt dow 7-6-17 15Lond p249 CR Belgium11
INESON,James Walker T2Lt kia 18-5-17 18DLI p161 CR France644,19-5-17
INGERSOLL,James Hamilton 2Lt kia 29-9-16 2Lincs p8&75 CR France251
INGESTRE,Charles John Alton Chetwynd.Viscount.MVO.Capt ded 8-1-15 RHGd p20 CR Staffs143
INGHAM,Alan T2Lt kia 14-3-17 32Manch p155 CR France576,22Bn
INGHAM,Clarence 2Lt kia 21-8-18 RGA 65SB p40 CR France1182
INGHAM,Claud Mary Leo 2Lt kia 19-11-16 4ConnRgrs att9InniskF p172 CR Belgium100
INGHAM,Horace.MC.TLtAMaj kia 24-4-18 2WYorks p82 MR27
INGHAM,Major T2Lt kia 13-4-18 WYorks att1/7Bn p82 MR30
INGHAM,Robert John Fitzgerald.DSO.MajALtCol dow 1-7-17 RGA 58HAG HQ p40 CR Belgium11
INGLE,Aubrey Charles Bertram CaptHonMaj ded 8-1-17 4HLI attScotRif p163 MR65
INGLE,Roland George T2Lt kia 1-7-16 Lincs p75 CR France515
INGLEBY,Norman Ward.MID Capt kia 27-5-18 4EYorks p219 CR France1329
INGLES,Alexander Wighton Maj kia 20-9-14 1WYorks p82 MR15
INGLES,Robert Adam 2Lt kia 21-3-18 16RScots p54 MR20
INGLESANT,Thomas George 2Lt kia 20-8-16 7N&D p233 CR France504
INGLETON,Hubert John Lt dow 2-11-18 4 att1/8LancF p92 CR France146
INGLIS,Alexander TLt kia 11-4-17 8GordH p166 CR France531
INGLIS,Alexander Alves 2Lt kia 26-9-16 RE att126FC p46 MR21
INGLIS,Arthur McCulloch.DSO.TMaj ded 12-5-19 Glouc p255 CR Glouc32
INGLIS,Charles North Dalrymple Lt kia 25-9-15 IARO att2/8GurkhaRif p278 MR
INGLIS,David Capt kia 19-2-14 IA 1/4GurkhaRif p278 MR28
INGLIS,Douglas Ian 2Lt kia 7-2-17 3RDubF p177 CR Belgium17
INGLIS,Henry Montgomery 2Lt kia 13-3-15 6GordH p242 MR22
INGLIS,Herbert McClelland LtCol 17-9-17 MedCps CR NZ194
INGLIS,James HonLt&QM ded 28-11-15 GL p190 CR Scot799
INGLIS,James Arthur Chetwynd Lt kia 9-5-15 4HLI attSfthH p163 MR22
INGLIS,James Malcolm T2Lt dow 26-10-18 9RIrF p171 CR France34
INGLIS,James Normand.MC.Capt kia 22-4-16 BlkW p128 CR Iraq5
INGLIS,John Alfred Pigon Lt kia 26-9-15 RE p46 CR France554
INGLIS,Maurice Paterson TCapt kia 17-9-16 RAMC att1/5BordR p195 CR France453
INGLIS,Robert.MC.Lt dow 5-10-18 13BlkW p205 CR France194
INGLIS,Robert Anderson T2Lt kia 21-9-15 GL &19RFC p9 CR France705,ANDERSSON Lt
INGLIS,Rupert Charles Lt dow 29-6-15 3SWBord p100 MR4
INGLIS,Rupert Edward Rev kia 18-9-16 RAChDept p199 MR21
INGLIS,Sidney Herbert T2Lt dow 5-6-17 GL &16RFC p9 CR France12
INGLIS,William Logan 2Lt kia 2-10-17 4RScotF attRFC p18&222 CR Belgium383,Lt
INGLIS,William Wiley TLt kia 20-11-17 11DLI p161 CR France379
INGLIS,William Raymond Col ded 30-3-16 33RFus p68 CR Essex258
INGOLDBY,Roger Hugh.MID T2Lt kia 1-7-16 2RDubF p177 CR France744
INGOUVILLE-WILLIAMS,Edward Charles.CB.DSO.MajGen kia 22-7-16 Commdg34Div p1 CR France44
INGPEN,Norman Cecil TCaptAMaj dow 4-12-17 175MGC Inf p183 CR France4
INGRAM,Arthur Charles LtACapt kia 26-3-18 4Beds att4ELancs p86 MR20
INGRAM,Arthur Herbert Lt kia 6-9-18 Glouc att8Bn p107 MR19
INGRAM,Edgar Charles 2Lt kia 27-3-18 RWar att7Norf p65 MR27
INGRAM,Edith A.Nurse kia 13/14-8-18 VAD 55GH p200 CR France34,14-8-18
INGRAM,Eric Talbot Allan.MC.Lt kia 4-11-18 2RInniskF attX32TMB p105 CR France190
INGRAM,Gerald Sclater Lt kia 21-10-14 RWSurr p56 MR29
INGRAM,Henry John T2Lt dow 22-9-17 RB att16Bn p179 CR Belgium15
INGRAM,John Aldred 2Lt kia 23-4-17 6 att16Manch p237 MR20
INGRAM,Thomas Lewis.DSO.MC.TCapt kia 16-9-16 RAMC att1KSLI p196 CR France374
INGRAM,William Harold Lt kia 4-6-15 8Manch p237 MR4
INGRAM-JOHNSON,Reginald James Theodore 2Lt dow 10-7-15 DLI attELancs p161 CR France297
INGRAMS,Frank Ridley.MC.T2Lt kia 3-9-16 9ESurr p112&258 MR21
INGS,John Walter Lt kia 18-9-18 RE 56FC p46 CR France756
INIGO-JONES,Henry Richmond Lt kia 4-9-14 1ScotsGds p52 MR15,14-9-14
INKPEN,Wilfred T2Lt kia 26-10-17 2BordR p117 MR30
INKSTER,Walter 2Lt kia 25-9-15 4GordH p242 MR29
INMAN,Arthur Walter Patrick Col 17-6-20 RAMC CR Ireland5
INMAN,Desmond Hague TLt kia 17-2-17 RE 80FC p46 CR France314

INMAN,Edwin Lt kia 1-7-16 10Lincs p75 CR France150
INMAN,Leslie Yardley 2Lt dow 5-4-16 3RScots attWilts p54 MR38,6-4-16
INMAN,Richard Hugh TLt kia 28-6-18 11ELancs p111 CR France352
INNES,Albert James Langlands Lt ded 11-3-20 RAMC CR Scot241
INNES,Alexander Berowald Lt kia 16-6-15 1/7GordH p242 CR France727,18-6-15
INNES,Alfred James 2Lt kia 3-5-17 13Lpool p72 MR20
INNES,Donald McLeod 2Lt dow 7-10-18 BlkW att14Bn p128 CR France52,6-10-18
INNES,Edgar Arthur.CMG.LtCol kia 1-7-16 1/8RWar p214 MR21
INNES,Edward Arthur Robert(Jack) Lt d ed 15-7-19 IARO att4Cav p278 MR43
INNES,Frederick Arthur.MC.2Lt kia 3-9-16 4WRid p227 CR France293
INNES,Ian Charles Lt kia 2-11-14 IA 2/2GurkhaRif p278 MR28
INNES,James Brydon Lt kia 20-7-15 4KOSB p223 MR4
INNES,James David T2Lt dow 5-8-17 24NumbF p61 CR France446
INNES,James Stuart d'Anvergne.MC&Bar.Lt kia 5-8-17 189RFA p31 CR Belgium29 34RFA
INNES,John Alfred 9-9-18 BRCS CR France34
INNES,Patrick McLeod 2Lt kia 30-4-17 RGA 111SB p40 CR France268
INNES,Robert Prentice T2Lt kia 21-9-18 1/7RScots p54 CR France1496
INNES,Ronald Stewart T2Lt kia 7-8-15 11Manch p155 MR4
INNES,William Robert Capt kia 13-11-16 6Ches p222 CR France293
INNES-BROWN,Ambrose Robin.CMG.DSO.TMajALtCol kia 10-4-18 6KOSB p102 CR Belgium21
INNES-CROSS,Sydney Maxwell 2Lt kia 27-10-14 RIrRif p169CR France525
INNES-HOPKINS,J.R.Capt 25-5-15 5CanadaInf CR France727
INNOCENT,Edward John TLt kia 3-7-16 9RWKent p141 CR France397
INSKIPP,Douglas T2Lt kia 16-4-17 143MGC p183 CR France669
INSOLE,George Claude Latham.MC.MID LtACapt kia 12-4-18 1WelshGds p53 CR France745
INSTONE,Edwin Lloyd T2Lt dow PoW 4-8-17 SStaffs att7Bn p122 CR Belgium383
INWARDS,Horatio 2Lt kia 15-6-17 2Lond p245 CR France1489
INWOOD,Charles Hawkins T2Lt kia 16-8-17 145MGC Inf p183 MR30
IONIDES,Ambrose Constantine TLt kia 16-10-15 15 att9KRRC p150 MR29
IONIDES,Theodore Alexander 2Lt dow 16-11-16 3 att2 O&BLI p130 CR France203
IPSWICH,William Henry Alfred Fitzroy.Viscount.Lt kldacc 23-4-18 5CldGds attRAF p51 CR Suff173
IRA-SMITH,Herbert William Edwin Capt ded 7-12-20 1/5Beds &RAF CR Asia82
IRELAND,Albert 2Lt dow 9-7-16 D50RFA p31 CR France66
IRELAND,Arthur George T2Lt dow 19-10-17 5ResRofCav att1/1NumbHuss p23 CR Belgium16
IRELAND,Arthur William 2Lt kia 23-11-17 D256RFA p31 CR France711
IRELAND,Cubitt Austen.MC.Lt kia 14-10-17 6 att7Norf p217 MR20
IRELAND,de Courcy Maj ded 28-1-15 IA 36Sikhs p278 CR Asia20
IRELAND,Herbert Victor Lt&QM ded 13-11-18 1BordR attMGC p117&183 CR Yorks1
IRELAND,Herbert Richard Hall.MC.Maj dow 28-3-18 3Leinst att2MunstF p174 CR France145,LtCol
IRELAND,H.F.Lt dow 22-7-17 1/3KAR p202 CR EAfrica38 &CR Tanzania1
IRELAND,James 2Lt ded 24-7-18 RFA p31 CR Ireland33
IRELAND,James Balleny TLt kia 5-5-17 1 att7Glouc p107 MR20,11 att12Bn
IRELAND,James Reginald 2Lt kia 28-10-16 3 att2A&SH p173 MR21
IRELAND,John Balfour 2Lt kia 8-9-16 9BlkW p128 CR France402
IRELAND,John Thomas Craig Chap4Cl drd 4-5-17 RAChDept p199 CR Italy14
IRELAND,Joseph Knowles Capt kia 7-10-16 26RFus p68 MR21
IRELAND,Leslie Woodhouse Cubitt T2Lt kia 12-2-17 Manch p155
IRELAND,Robert Clifford 2Lt dow 7-11-16 133RFA p31 CR France832
IRELAND,Robert Megans.Sir.KBE.CB.CMG.Col ded 3-9-19 APD p268 CR Hamps8,Megaw
IRELAND,Samuel James T2Lt kia 12-10-16 17Lpool p72 MR21
IRELAND,Walter Ernest Lt kia 26-3-17 1/6RWFus p223 CR Palestine8
IRELAND,William 2Lt kia 25-9-15 2RSuss p119 CR France219
IRELAND,William Farquhar T2Lt kia 9-4-17 8GordH p166 CR France265
IRISH,Edward 2Lt kia 20-6-15 1/5WYorks p218 CR France566
IRISH,Edwin Charles 2Lt kia 26-12-17 2ELancs p111 MR30
IRLAM,George Arthur 2Lt kia 21-6-17 Manch att2/8Bn p155 CR France258
IRONS,William Morley T2Lt dow 13-4-18 5Y&L p159 CR Belgium11
IRONSIDE,Arthur Douglas 2Lt kia 22-9-17 D295RFA p208 CR Belgium84
IRONSIDE,Harold Allan TMaj ded 15-10-16 96MGC p183 CR France80
IRONSIDE,James Paul T2Lt dow 29-10-17 GL &28RFC p9 CR Belgium18
IRONSIDE,John Gladstone 2Lt ded 17-12-17 5GordH attMGC Inf p242 CR EAfrica11 &CR Tanzania1
IRONSIDE,Oliver Dalton Lt ded 1-4-19 RFA p207 MR65

IRONSIDE,William Stewart.DSO.MC.Lt.AMaj kia 2-11-18 24RFA p31 CR France717
IRVIN,Thomas William Lt dow 20-5-16 5GordH p242 CR France225
IRVINE,Charles 2Lt kia 24-8-18 4 att2RScots p211 MR16
IRVINE,Charles Knowles TCapt kia 14-8-17 10RB p179 MR29
IRVINE,Charles Wallace T2Lt kia 14-10-18 1RInniskF p105 CR Belgium157
IRVINE,Christopher Theodore Corne.MID Lt dow 28-6-15 IA 25Punjabis att29InfBde p278 CR Gallipoli3 att69Punjabis
IRVINE,Edward White 2Lt kia 27-3-18 186RFA p31 MR20
IRVINE,Francis Duncan Maj kia 1-5-15 RE p46 MR4
IRVINE,Fred Catterson 2Lt kia 19-5-18 RGA 297SB p40 CR France113
IRVINE,Gerard Byrom Corrie Maj dow 15-5-17 IA 9BhopalInf p278 CR Iraq5
IRVINE,Gerard Foster TCapt dow 24-10-16 1RWar p65 MR21
IRVINE,Harold TLt dow 29-6-15 13Worc attRMunstF p109 MR4
IRVINE,John Laird Gallwey Capt kia 8-7-15 A&SH p173 CR France82
IRVINE,Paget George Capt dow 26-11-15 6Glouc p225 CR France1327
IRVINE,Robert 2Lt kia 1-9-18 12 att7/8RInniskF p105 CR Belgium89
IRVINE,Robert Charles.MID TCaptAMaj ded 10-11-18 RAMC 63FA p196 CR France13
IRVINE,Thomas Walter LtCol drd 26-1-19 IMS MR43
IRVINE,William Henry T2Lt kld 25-10-16 RFC p3 CR Wales119
IRVINE,William Magnus 2Lt kia 22-3-18 NumbF att12RFC p16&61 MR20
IRVINE-WATSON,John 2Lt kia 14-8-17 B110RH&FA p31
IRVING,Alexander AMaj ded 15-2-19 A&SH attCamH p266 CR Surrey160,1SfthH
IRVING,Alfred 2Lt kia 26-10-18 IA 15Sikhs att14 p278 MR38
IRVING,Archibald Denys 2Lt dow 16-9-18 82RFA p31 CR France511
IRVING,Aubrey Gordon Lt dow 10-3-15 RE attRFC 2Wing p1&46 CR France706
IRVING,David Piercy 2Lt kia 30-7-16 3 att2RScotF p94 MR21
IRVING,Ernest T2Lt kia 5-10-17 BordR att2Bn p117 CR Belgium125
IRVING,Herbert Rufus Evelyn.MC.T2Lt kia 31-10-18 1/2 att17LancF p92 CR Belgium143
IRVING,Robert 2Lt kia 2-8-16 2/5RLancs D'Coy p213 CR France630,Richard
IRVING,Thomas Henry 2Lt kia 19-8-16 3Lpool p72 CR France432
IRWIN,Andrew Herbert 2Lt kia 18-4-15 IAUL att8Rajputs p278 MR43
IRWIN,Aubrey Joseph T2Lt kia 3-9-18 2Hamps p121 MR32
IRWIN,Charles Patrick Michael Lt kia 9-9-16 3 att7RIrF p171 CR France402,10-9-16
IRWIN,Eric Conway.MC.Maj dow 19-7-17 IA 20Inf att40Pathans p278 CR EAfrica38 &CR Tanzania1
IRWIN,Frederick T2Lt kia 16-8-17 9RInniskF p105 CR Belgium96
IRWIN,Herbert Quintus Capt kia 26-4-15 1ConnRgrs p172 CR Belgium92
IRWIN,Horace Charles.MM.T2Lt kia 20-7-18 10A&SH att1/4SfthH p173 CR France622
IRWIN,James Ross T2Lt kia 2-9-18 2 att7RIrReg p89 CR Belgium89
IRWIN,Lancelot Bolton Lt ded 11-8-14 IA 52Sikhs p278 MR43
IRWIN,Richard Nynian TLt kia 6-3-17 9Glouc p107 CR Greece6,Nyniau
IRWIN,Thomas Whitmore Crommelin Lt dow 31-10-18 2N&D p134 CR Surrey1
IRWIN,W.H.SNurse 18-11-18 TFNS CR Surrey160
IRWIN,William Hetherton 2Lt dow 12-2-17 7HLI p240 CR France164
IRWIN,William James 2Lt kia 16-8-17 RIrRif att7Bn p169 MR30
ISAAC,Arthur Whitmore 2Lt kia 7-7-16 5Worc p109 MR21
ISAAC,Dudley Charles.MIDx2 TCapt kia 10-4-17 NStaffs att41MGC Inf p183 CR France1185
ISAAC,Frank Philip T2Lt kia 9-8-15 1KSLI p145 MR29
ISAAC,George Duncan ACapt ded 13-12-17 RGA 77HAG HQ p40 CR Belgium84,dow
ISAAC,George Gower Maj ded 31-7-16 RASC p253 CR Lond12
ISAAC,John Edmund Valentine.DSO.Capt kia 9-5-15 2RB p179 CR Belgium96
ISAAC,William Jones 2Lt kia 26-4-16 1/19Lond p250 MR20
ISAACS,Bernard Clifford T2Lt dow 1-8-17 89MGC p183 CR France64
ISAACS,Francis Harold T2Lt kia 30-9-18 1Suff att11RScotF p78 CR France1106
ISAACS,Henry Rowland 2Lt kia 9-4-17 4 att7Suff p217 MR20
ISAACS,Vincent Harcourt 2Lt kia 21-9-18 9RFus p68 CR France369
ISAACSON,Colin de Slutevalle.MC.Capt dow 11-6-17 SL &Staff EAfrUL p190&268 CR EAfrica10 &CR Tanzania1,Stuteville
ISARD,Cyril Bickford Capt kia 15-8-15 10Lond p248 MR4
ISBISTER,Leonard Stanley 2Lt kia 9-9-16 1/12Lond p248 MR21
ISHAM,John Vere 2Lt ded 3-6-16 5DragGds p21 CR France40
ISHERWOOD,Arthur 2Lt kld 8-12-16 6NumbF att149TMB p214 CR France1568
ISHERWOOD,Francis Edmund Bradshaw.MIDx2 LtCol kia 8-5-15 2Y&L Cmdg1Bn p159 MR29 &MR32
ISHERWOOD,H.2Lt 23-10-18 RAF &LNLancs CR Lancs257
ISHERWOOD,Norman Lt kia 6-9-17 1/6LancF p221 CR Belgium125

ISHERWOOD,Norman George T2Lt kia 8-10-15 RE 174TC p46 CR France637
ISHERWOOD,Samuel Guy Lt dow 20-9-18 7WYorks p218 CR France278
ISHMAEL,Henry Plummer 2Lt kia 4-11-14 IA SpServOff p278 MR47
ISLE,William Collinson Lt dow 13-8-15 7SStaffs p122 CR Greece10
IUNG,Henry Adolph 2Lt dow 9-5-15 3 att1NumbF CR France102
IVATT,Harold Alfred.MC.Capt kia 21-5-18 1/5SStaffs p229 CR France109
IVATTS,Selwyn.MC.2Lt kia 8-10-17 B93RFA p31 CR Belgium12
IVE,David 2Lt kia 23-10-14 RWSurr p56 MR29
IVE,Frank T2Lt kia 7-10-16 6 O&BLI p130 MR21
IVENS,Frank Harold Howe 2LtACapt kia 21-10-16 11RSuss p119 MR21
IVES,Henry James Mansfield 2Lt dow 28-4-17 C255RFA p31 CR France95
IVES,Kenneth Hill 2Lt ded 9-12-14 8WYorks p219 CR Yorks361
IVESON,Frank Taylor Lt kia 30-6-15 16DLI p161 CR Gallipoli2
IVESON,James Henry TLtACapt kia 23-3-18 20DLI p161 MR20
IVESS,Thomas Francis Capt ded 5-11-18 4RBerks p270 CR Surrey157
IVEY,Thomas.OBE.Capt&QM ded 23-10-19 O&BLI p264 CR Surrey1
IVORY,John Arthur TLt kia 27-9-18 MGC Inf p183 CR France1496
IZARD,Francis Vallance Capt kia 17-2-15 RGA p40 CR Asia45,16-2-15
IZARD,George Henry T2Lt kia 10-8-18 7Norf att35L TMB p74 CR France196 Ex RWar
IZAT,Alan.MC.Capt kia 2-1-17 RE 103FC p46 CR France177
IZON,Edgar Godfrey ACapt kia 27-9-18 RWar att14Bn p65 CR France518

J

JACK,Christina Sister ded 22-10-18 QAIMNS p200 CR Scot862
JACK,Douglas Peacock 2Lt kia 18-9-18 4EKent p212 CR France365
JACK,Gavine 2Lt kia 25-9-15 2RScots p54 MR29,Gavin
JACK,Henry Claude 2Lt kld 1-9-16 HLI &RFC p3&163 CR Hamps4
JACK,James Charles.DSO.MC&Bar.MID Maj dow 31-5-18 D150RFA SR p31 CR France71
JACK,Robert Lawrence Munro 2Lt dow 27-2-17 5GordH att16RFC p18&242 CR France95,26-2-17
JACK,Thomas 2Lt kia 9-4-17 6RScots p211 CR France184
JACK,Thomas Barclay TCapt dow 24-8-18 RASC att10Lond p193 CR France119
JACK,William Boyd.MC.TCapt dow 11-10-18 RAMC att1/5Leic p196 CR France847
JACKMAN,Gerald Radcliffe T2Lt kia 21-4-17 17WelshR p127 CR France439
JACKMAN,Harold.MC.T2LtACapt kia 21-3-18 7KRRC p150 MR27
JACKMAN,Henry Croome 2Lt ded 28-11-15 9EKent p57 p262 CR Glouc182
JACKMAN,John Robinson Lt kia 22-7-18 6WRid &RAF p227 CR France518,17-6-18
JACKMAN,Osbert William,MM 2Lt dow 7-11-18 1RWSurr p56 CR France952
JACKS,Edmund Cecil 2Lt kia 25-10-16 3Dev p76 MR21
JACKS,Harold Capt ded 27-1-19 7DLI att4NigR p239 CR WAfrica41,26-1-19
JACKSON,Alan James 2Lt kia 27-4-15 att3Mddx p147 MR29
JACKSON,Albert Leslie 2Lt dow 18-3-17 4Mddx p147 CR Lond10,Lt
JACKSON,Alexander Maclean.MC.Lt dow 27-4-17 RE 12FC p46 CR France80,Maj
JACKSON,Arthur T2Lt kia 2-11-16 7BordR p117 CR France307
JACKSON,Arthur T2Lt kld 7-2-17 GL &24RFC p9 CR Mddx1
JACKSON,Arthur Frederick 2Lt kia 27-8-18 10Lond p248 MR16
JACKSON,Arthur Gordon 2Lt kia 25-2-17 3 att6SLancs p125 MR38
JACKSON,Arthur Graham 2Lt kia 6-10-18 13Lond p249 CR France149
JACKSON,Arthur Lloyd TLtACapt kia 24-4-18 409/96RA p31 MR27
JACKSON,Arthur Rushton T2Lt kia 25-4-18 23RFus C'Coy p68 CR France214
JACKSON,Arthur Selby T2Lt kia 16-9-16 9YLI p143 MR21
JACKSON,Arthur Thomas T2Lt dow 8-11-18 8 att 1/5Glouc p107 CR France341
JACKSON,Bertram Rolfe TCapt kia 15-9-16 1CldGds p51 CR France372
JACKSON,Bertram Washington Lt kia 14-9-14 2KRRC p150 MR15
JACKSON,Cecil Thomas Lt kia 31-8-18 1/12LNLancs attRAF p255 CR Egypt1
JACKSON,Cedric Arthur TLt kld 5-11-17 12Y&L &RFC p159&9 CR Derby127
JACKSON,Charles 2Lt kia 10-10-18 1/2LancF p92 CR France190
JACKSON,Claude Stewart Capt kia 9-10-17 3CldGds p51 MR30
JACKSON,Crosby 2Lt kia 1-8-18 4RScots p211
JACKSON,Cyril Compton LtCol kia 22-11-15 IA 103MahrattaLI p278 MR38
JACKSON,Daniel Talbot T2Lt kia 30-9-18 1 att2/5Glouc p107 CR France1887
JACKSON,David Capt ded 3-9-15 6RScots p211 CR Lancs34
JACKSON,David T2Lt kia 16-12-17 8BlkW p128 CR France415
JACKSON,Donald Lt ded 20-9-19 RASC p267 CR Scot52
JACKSON,Donald Fisher.MIDx2 Lt kia 11-10-18 20Huss p23 CR France341

JACKSON,Donald Richard Field Lt kia 27-8-17 5WRid p227 MR30
JACKSON,Douglas William TLt dow 18-5-17 att1KSLI p145 CR France178
JACKSON,Dudley William Gerald Capt dow 13-4-16 1 att10RWFus p98 CR France40
JACKSON,Edward Cecil TLt kia 30-5-16 15N&D p134 MR19
JACKSON,Edward Fergusson.MC.LtTCapt dow 22-9-18 7SfthH p165 CR Palestine9,Lt
JACKSON,Edward Philip 2LtACapt kia 30-11-17 1RBerks p139 CR France924
JACKSON,Edward Phillips 2Lt kia 9-5-15 3RWar attSWBord p65 MR22,Lt
JACKSON,Ernest 2Lt kia 1-7-16 3LancF p92 MR21
JACKSON,Ernest.DSO.MC&Bar.LtAMaj dow 15-4-18 RE 458FC p209 CR France64
JACKSON,Ernest Alexander 2Lt kia 27-5-18 6 att8BordR p117 MR18
JACKSON,Francis 2Lt kia 27-9-18 25 att2/20Lond p252 CR France755
JACKSON,Frank Wigmore.MC.Capt kia 9-6-17 RE 421FC p210 CR France922
JACKSON,Frederick Charles.DCM.Lt&QM dow 11-8-17 21Lond p251
JACKSON,Frederick Howard Capt kia 28-10-14 4 att2ConnRgrs p172 MR29
JACKSON,Frederick John 2Lt kia 14-10-18 1/3Lond &RAF p270 CR Belgium157
JACKSON,Frederick Vyvyan Milbourne Maj kia 13-4-18 A245RFA p206 CR Belgium10 14-4-18
JACKSON,George TLt kia 26-9-15 11A&SH p173 MR19
JACKSON,Geoffrey Laird.MID LtACapt kia 9-4-17 1RB p179 CR France728
JACKSON,George TCapt kia 25-8-17 18HLI p163 CR France363
JACKSON,George Conway TLt kia 25-9-15 6KOSB p102 MR19
JACKSON,George Dewar 2Lt kia 14-9-16 3GrenGds p50 MR21,15-9-16
JACKSON,George Henry.MC.2Lt kia 31-7-17 att2RB p179 MR29
JACKSON,George William TLt kia 7-5-17 7NumbF attRFC p18&214 MR20
JACKSON,Godfrey Lt dow 15-9-17 1/4ELancs p226 CR Belgium8
JACKSON,Hamilton Ray T2Lt dow 26-7-17 RASC attRGA 245SB p193 CR Belgium11,kia
JACKSON,Harold TCapt kia 7-6-17 GL 41RFC p9 CR Belgium56
JACKSON,Harold Edward 2Lt kia 12-6-17 6WYorks p218 MR19
JACKSON,Harold James T2Lt kia 4-6-18 10LancF p92 CR France220
JACKSON,Harold Willows Lt dow 14-5-17 4EYorks p219 CR France113
JACKSON,Harry T2Lt kia 9-10-17 WRid att1/7Bn p115 MR30
JACKSON,Harry 2Lt ded 25-10-18 RGA 4SAR Bde p40 CR Hamps1
JACKSON,Henry Douglas.MC.2Lt kia 26-10-16 4EYorks p219 CR France387
JACKSON,Henry Hall.MC.Capt ded 28-11-18 15Huss p22 CR Yorks256
JACKSON,Henry Medland T2Lt kia 19-9-18 RASC att1/10Lond p193 CR Palestine
JACKSON,Henry Stewart TLt kia 1-7-16 8YLI p143 MR21
JACKSON,Henry Teasdale T2Lt kia 8-10-17 13NumbF att8Leic p61 MR30
JACKSON,Herbert T2Lt kia 21-3-18 11 att2RDubF p177 MR27
JACKSON,Herbert Meynell T2Lt kia 18-6-17 GL 53RFC p9 MR20
JACKSON,Herbert Percival Lt kia 25-9-15 A296RFA p207 CR Belgium84
JACKSON,Herbert William Lt kia 20-1-18 12/13NumbF p61 CR France439
JACKSON,Horace T2Lt kia 21-3-18 16MGC p183 CR Belgium45
JACKSON,James Battle T2Lt kia 23-4-17 2RWFus p98 CR France162
JACKSON,James Crosby 2Lt kia 1-8-18 4 att9RScots p211 CR France524
JACKSON,John Lt kld 22-5-15 9A&SH p244 CR Scot80
JACKSON,John 2Lt kia 19-8-16 3Dors att2/5Glouc p124 CR France1887
JACKSON,John T2Lt kia 20-9-17 26RFus p68 MR30
JACKSON,John Alfred 2Lt kia 4-5-18 6ScotRif p224 CR France114
JACKSON,John Bell Lt kia 7-6-17 RScots &43RFC p9&54 MR20
JACKSON,John Cooper 2Lt kia 31-7-17 3 att16Manch p155 MR29
JACKSON,John Edward.DSO.Capt ded 25-10-17 1/8Lpool p270 CR Lancs7
JACKSON,John Henry 2Lt kia 9-9-16 5LancF p221 MR21
JACKSON,John Male 2Lt ded /-9-17 DLI p265
JACKSON,John Montague Hammick TLt dow 18-8-15 5 O&BLI p130 CR Devon7
JACKSON,John William TLt kia 17-10-17 11N&D p134 CR Belgium72
JACKSON,Lancelot 2Lt kia 1-7-16 1BordR p117 MR21
JACKSON,Leonard 2Lt kia 22/23-7-16 15RWar p65 MR21
JACKSON,M.MIDx2 Lt&QM ded 23-5-18 RE 3Army Spec Coy p46 CR Sussex30
JACKSON,Malcolm Race T2Lt kia 25-3-18 Manch att1/6Bn p155 MR20
JACKSON,Martin de Carle 2Lt kia 5-11-16 RFA p31 MR21
JACKSON,Nicholas William Goddard 2Lt kia 9-9-16 1Nhampt p137 CR France4
JACKSON,Noel Bower 2Lt kia 6-12-17 2/5N&D p233 CR France711
JACKSON,Patrick Arthur Dudley 2Lt kia 4-1-17 2RIrRif p169 CR Belgium53
JACKSON,Raymond Wilfred 2Lt kia 9-10-17 4Y&L p238 MR30,Raymund
JACKSON,Robert T2Lt kia 13-4-18 9SfthH p165 CR Belgium21
JACKSON,Robert Cameron T2Lt kia 24-9-17 233MGC Inf p183 MR30

JACKSON,Robert Raimes.MC.Capt dow 1-11-17 105/29RFA p31 CR Belgium16
JACKSON,Robert William.MC.DCM.T2Lt kia 23-10-18 1 att16WYorks p82 CR France1266
JACKSON,S.S.Lt 29-9-15 EAfrTransCps CR EAfrica52
JACKSON,Samuel Lt kia 20-3-18 3 att2RIrReg p89 MR21
JACKSON,Sidney Douglas 2Lt kia 3-5-17 31/35RFA p31 CR France616
JACKSON,Sidney Foster Lt kia 17-11-17 7WYorks p218 CR Belgium308
JACKSON,Stanley T2Lt kia 10-11-17 12Manch p155 MR30
JACKSON,Stanley Foster Capt kia 4-6-15 1/6Manch D'Coy p236 Gallipoli6,dow
JACKSON,Stanley Richardson TMaj dow 31-12-15 19Lond p250 CR France88
JACKSON,Stewart Spiers.MC.2Lt kia 21-3-18 1 att2/8Worc p109 MR27
JACKSON,Theodore Walter TCapt ded 4-10-18 RASC HT p193 CR France25,Walton
JACKSON,Theophilus Rudolph.MC.TCapt dow 25-3-18 7DCLI p114&258 CR France987
JACKSON,Thomas Lt kia 12-7-15 5RScotF p222 MR4
JACKSON,Thomas Leslie.MC.TCapt kia 2-7-16 9Ches p96 CR France267
JACKSON,Walter 2Lt kia 9-10-17 7WYorks p218 MR30
JACKSON,Walter Lt dow 8-11-17 LanarkYeo p204 CR Palestine1,9-11-17 12RScotF
JACKSON,Wilfred Flower Lt kia 28-10-18 IARO attCpsofGuidesCav p278 MR38
JACKSON,Wilfred George Lt kia 27-4-15 1EKent p57 MR32
JACKSON,William.MC.T2Lt dow 26-8-18 3NumbF att15DLI p161 CR France84
JACKSON,William T2Lt kia 30-9-18 11RDubF att23RFus p177 CR France914
JACKSON,William Brabazon Mather Capt kia 27-4-17 2/6N&D p233 CR France1495,dow 28-4-17
JACKSON,William Ewart Capt kia 9-1-17 3 att1Manch p155 CR Iraq5
JACKSON,William Hickin T2Lt kia 3-5-17 15WYorks p82 MR20
JACKSON,William John Humphrey 2Lt dow 26-3-18 12 att6RInniskF p105 MR34
JACKSON-BARSTOW,John Eric Capt 27-1-19 NSomYeo &RAF CR Somerset197
JACKSON-TAYLOR,John Curzon 2Lt kia 21-3-18 1KSLI p145 MR20
JACOB,Anstey Ross 2Lt dow 18-9-16 4DLI p161 CR France833
JACOB,Arthur Henry Augustus Lt dow 16-7-16 4RFus p68 CR France40
JACOB,Arthur Leslie Hamilton TLt kia 25-9-15 18Lond p250 MR19
JACOB,Cecil Otway Reed Capt kia 29-11-17 2Dev att2/5Lincs p77 MR21 &CR France1498,3Dev
JACOB,Donald Allen 2Lt dow 13-11-17 1/4Lincs p217 CR France90,Lt 12-11-17
JACOB,Gwynne.DCM.MM&Bar.Lt kia 1-8-19 EYorks att45RFus p255 MR70 &CR Europe179
JACOB,Henry William James 2Lt kia 26-10-17 16Lond p250 MR20
JACOB,John Victor Reed Lt ded 16-3-19 RGA &RAF p255
JACOB,Victor Vivian Lt kia 25-9-15 2 O&BLI p130 MR19
JACOBI,Walter Thomas T2Lt dow 21-10-16 14RWar p65
JACOBS,Alan Edward Aflalo.MC.2Lt kia 7-8-16 8ESurr p112 MR32
JACOBS,Daryl.MID 2Lt kia 10-4-17 4SLancs p230 MR32
JACOBS,Henry 2Lt kia 6-7-18 5 att8RLancs p213 CR France98,Harry
JACOBS,Henry Houston 2Lt kia 25-9-15 8Lincs p75 MR19
JACOBS,Joel 2Lt kia 20-7-16 5Yorks p221 CR Belgium60
JACOBS,John Harry.MC.ACapt kia 11-10-18 1RFus A'Coy p68 CR France270
JACOBS,Robert Capt dow 20-7-18 RAMC p253 CR France46,kia
JACOBSON,Lyonel Hugh.MC.TLt kia 29-4-17 D50RFA p31 CR France96
JACOT,Conrade William T2Lt kld 23-6-17 GL RFC p9 CR War67
JACOT,Edward Lt kia 6-6-17 42RFC p255 MR20
JACQUES,David Wright 2Lt dow 1-12-16 1 att 10RWSurr p56 CR France200,kia
JACQUES,Edward William Rigbye Lt kia 17-8-16 1Nhampt p137 CR France387,16-8-17
JACQUES,Francis Augustus LtCol kia 4-6-15 1A 14Sikhs p278 MR4
JACQUES,Geoffrey Plateras Lawson 2Lt kld 5-10-16 RFC p3 CR Essex50
JACQUES,George Sheriff Harkus 2Lt kia 27-6-16 6NumbF p214
JACQUES,William Gladstone 2Lt kia 17-10-18 5N&D p233 CR France847
JACSON,Mainwaring George ColTBrigGen ded 2-6-15 RoO Staff p1 CR Shrop95
JAFFE,Joseph TCapt kia 1-8-18 RAMC att2/4SomLI p196 CR France524
JAFFRAY,John Henry.Bart.2Lt kia 23-4-16 WorcYeo p206 MR34
JAFFREY,William.MC.Lt kia 23-3-18 6 att8A&SH p243 MR27
JAGGER,Arthur Stannus T2Lt dow 1-10-18 9RWFus p98 CR France98,Lt 30-9-18
JAGGER,Harry 2Lt kia 10-6-18 1LancF p92 CR France24
JAGGERS,William John 2Lt kia 20-9-17 RFA B277ArmyBde p31 CR Belgium112
JAGO,Edward Arthur 2Lt kia 1-7-16 3 att2Dev p77 MR21
JAGO,Henry Harris.MC.LtACapt kia 24-4-18 2Dev p77 MR27
JAGOE,Charles Bateman T2Lt kia 26-7-17 16RIrRif p169 CR Belgium5
JAKINS,Walter Vosper T2Lt kld 10-7-17 GL &54RFC p9 CR Essex40

JALLAND,Boswell Victor 2Lt kia 9-4-17 3EYorks p84 CR France162
JALLAND,Henry Herbert Lt kia 18-10-18 3 att1BlkW p128 CR France1271
JALLAND,Robert Miles T2Lt kia 26-8-18 6Leic p87 CR France385
JALLAND,Stephen Lt kia 9-8-15 6EYorks p84 MR4
JAMES,Albert TLt dow 28-3-18 10MGC p183 CR France169
JAMES,Albert Hazlewood H.2Lt ded 20-12-18 RH&FA p208 CR Wilts142
JAMES,Albert John Stanley.DSO.MC.TMajA.LtCol kia 28-3-18 10RWFus Comdg8RLancs p98 MR20
JAMES,Alfred 2Lt dow 8-3-18 1/4SLancs p230 CR France88
JAMES,Archibald Hugh.DSO.ALtCol kia 26-3-18 8NumbF att8WYorks p61 CR France745
JAMES,Alyn Reginald Capt kia 24-3-18 24RWFus &RFC p203 MR20
JAMES,Arthur Lt kia 3-1-17 7Yorks p90 CR France374
JAMES,Arthur Keedwell Harvey TCapt kia 15-4-17 GL p190
JAMES,Arthur Ling Capt kia 8-8-16 7Suff p78 MR21
JAMES,Baron Trevinnen.MIDx2 LtTCapt kia 13-7-15 RE &RFC p1&46 MR20,Trevenen
JAMES,Basil Lister 2Lt dow 25-11-16 4EKent p212 CR France177
JAMES,Bernard Ashworth TCapt kia 18-8-16 13Mddx p147 MR21
JAMES,Bernard William Austin 2Lt kia 14-10-17 18 att6Lond p250 CR France644
JAMES,Burnet George Lt kia 26-9-15 RFA att7RFC p18&207 CR Belgium83
JAMES,Charles Kenneth.DSO&Bar.ALtCol kia 19-5-18 6BordR p117 CR France745
JAMES,Charles Llewellyn T2Lt kia 10-5-18 WelchR att15Bn p127 CR France232
JAMES,Clement Wilbraham 2Lt kia 1-7-16 15WYorks p82 MR21
JAMES,Donald Croft 2Lt kia 19-7-16 2/4Glouc p225 MR21
JAMES,Douglas Attwood Lt kia 25-4-15 BordR p117 CR Gallipoli3,Capt
JAMES,Douglas Charles 2Lt dow 1-10-15 1SStaffs p122 CR France473,Douglass Lt 30-9-15
JAMES,Edward Scott TCapt ded 19-8-17 B102RH&FA p31
JAMES,Enoch Lewis T2Lt kia 18-2-17 14RWFus p98 MR29
JAMES,Eric Gwynne.DSO.MID TCapt&Adjt dow 15-10-16 1KSLI p145 CR France145
JAMES,Eric Samuel Pennant Kingsbury Capt kia 17-3-15 6KRRC p150 CR Belgium28 4Bn
JAMES,Evan T2Lt kia 27-7-17 3 att15WelshR p127 CR Belgium23
JAMES,Francis Arthur TCapt dow 18-9-15 5Manch p236 CR Gallipoli3
JAMES,Frank Lt kia 1-11-18 3 att1SWBord p100 CR France1268
JAMES,Frank Clifford 2Lt dow PoW 4-5-17 1RBerks p139 CR France1276,Lt
JAMES,Frederick T2Lt kia 20-5-17 4Lpool p72 CR France434
JAMES,George Henry 2Lt dow 8-5-17 3 att2Hamps p121 CR France40
JAMES,George Millais Capt kia 3-11-14 EKent 1 att2InfBde p57 MR29
JAMES,George Sidney Lt kia 4-6-15 5Manch p236 CR Gallipoli2
JAMES,Gwilym T2Lt dow 8-10-18 13RWFus p98 CR France398
JAMES,Gwilym Christopher Bowring Lt dow 23-11-17 3 att2SWBord p100 CR France398
JAMES,Gwilym Gregory Maj ded 19-12-19 IMS p278 CR Iraq8
JAMES,Gwynne Lewis Brodhurst Lt kia 18-7-17 IrGds attTHB p52 CR Belgium12
JAMES,Henry John T2Lt kia 9-4-17 24NumbF p61 CR France184
JAMES,Henry Stoddart 2Lt kia 23-4-17 5BordR p228 CR France1185
JAMES,Henry Vernon Lt dow 12-4-18 41/42RFA p207 CR France201
JAMES,Herbert Walter 2Lt kia 4-10-17 13NumbF att9YLI p61 MR30
JAMES,James Wright TCapt kia 7-10-16 15Hamps p121 MR21
JAMES,Joe Conquest TCapt dow 14-7-16 5RBerks p139 CR France64
JAMES,John Capt dow 8-10-18 RAMC att18HLI p196 CR Belgium157,kia
JAMES,John Stephen Harvey 2Lt kia 16-5-15 1KRRC p150 MR22
JAMES,Kenneth Lister 2Lt kia 3-5-17 4 att6EKent p212 MR20
JAMES,Merridith Charles Clifton T2Lt dow 27-10-16 1Worc p109 MR21,Meredith
JAMES,R.A.Capt kia 16-7-18 5Mddx &RAF p255
JAMES,Ralph Lionel 2Lt died 3-8-17 7RWFus attRFC p223 CR Surrey157
JAMES,Reginald Arthur Capt 16-6-18 5Mddx & 54RAF MR20
JAMES,Reginald Valpy ded 15-7-19 IARO attRailways p278 MR67
JAMES,Richard Arthur Brodie TCapt kia 13-9-16 9ELancs p111 MR37
JAMES,Richard Walter T2Lt kia 8-5-17 11ELancs p111 CR France1191
JAMES,Robert Kenneth Lt kia 27-5-18 4YLI p235 MR18
JAMES,Roy Francis T2Lt kia 2-9-18 18Manch p155 CR France308
JAMES,Rupert Frederick Lt kia 27-3-18 11EYorks p84 CR France927
JAMES,Samuel Forest T2Lt kia 18-11-16 8Glouc p107 MR21
JAMES,Vivian Gwynne Lt kia 26-3-17 12att1/7RWFus p98 MR34
JAMES,W.Douglass Lt 24-9-15 RGA TMB CR France98
JAMES,Walter Capt kia 25-6-15 10DLI p161 CR Belgium165
JAMES,Walter Ibbe Lt kia 25/27-9-15 3RWFus p98 MR19

JAMES,Wilfred Sydney T2Lt kia 24-11-17 19RWFus p98 MR17
JAMES,Wilfred Rowland TLt kia 16-9-16 23DLI p161 MR21
JAMES,William David T2Lt kia 23-5-18 9LNLancs p136 MR20
JAMES,William David.MM.2Lt kia 8-10-18 13RWFus p98 CR France1346
JAMES,William Maynard Capt&Adjt kia 8-10-18 1Mon p244 CR France1710
JAMESON,Alan Battersby 2Lt kia 21-7-16 1Camb p245 CR France765
JAMESON,Anthony Mildmay 2Lt kia 1-9-16 2Leinst p174 CR France399,Antony
JAMESON,Edmund James.DSO.TLtCol dow 27-3-17 5Leinst Cmdg1/4Ess p174 CR Palestine2 John
JAMESON,Francis John TLt kia 25-9-15 12 att9ScotRif p103 CR France114
JAMESON,Harold.MC.DCM.2Lt kia 5-1-17 6RFC SR p9 CR Belgium11,42Sqdn
JAMESON,Harold Gordon 2Lt kia 16-8-15 RE 65FC p46 MR4
JAMESON,Harry Roderick Victor 2Lt kia 11-4-17 2SfthH p165 MR20
JAMESON,Horace Armytage.MC&Bar.Maj kia 24-3-18 311RFA p206 MR27
JAMESON,Ian Herbert Sydney TCapt kia 23-4-17 8SfthH p165 CR France536
JAMESON,James Leslie.MC.Lt kia 2-7-16 1/5WYorks p218 MR21
JAMESON,John 2Lt kia 30-8-18 1Dev p77 CR France1484
JAMESON,John Louis SubCdr 10-2-16 MilWksServ MR65
JAMESON,Robert Alexander 2Lt kia 21-7-18 1/8RScots p212 CR France622
JAMIESON,Colin Miller 2Lt kia 21-5-17 15Lond p249 MR20
JAMIESON,Crawford Lt kia 23-4-17 9RScots p212 CR France604
JAMIESON,Douglas Lt kia 9-7-17 RE 401FC p210 CR Belgium10
JAMIESON,Eric Liew Ellen 2Lt kia 22-8-17 A&SH p173 CR Belgium128,Lieuellen
JAMIESON,George William Lt kia 28-3-18 5 att10ScotRif p224 CR France57
JAMIESON,Gerald Alister.MID Maj dow 28-2-16 IA 9BhopalInf p278 MR65
JAMIESON,Jessie Smith SNurse ded 30-12-18 TFNS CR Scot236
JAMIESON,John T2Lt kia 3-4-18 9 att16LancF p92 CR France804
JAMIESON,John.DCM.2Lt kia 29-4-18 23NumbF p61 MR20
JAMIESON,John Melvill 2Lt kia 28-4-17 7N&D p233 France1495
JAMIESON,John Prior Capt dow 13-10-17 3 att1RLancs p50 CR Belgium16
JAMIESON,Leonard Foster TLt ded 27-6-18 RAMC att302RFA p196 CR Egypt1
JAMIESON,Nicol Capt kia 13-8-15 4RScotF p222 MR4
JAMIESON,Robert Lindsay T2Lt kia 3-9-16 12A&SH att1CamH p173 MR21
JAMIESON,Thomas 2Lt ded 5-9-19 4 att6WYorks p263 CR Germany1,drd
JAMIESON,William Patterson TLt kia 6-4-17 MGC HB p183 CR France581
JAMISON,James Clawson Capt kia 22-11-17 10RIrRif p169 MR17
JAN,Henry Gordon Hay T2Lt kia 15-2-17 8Wilts p153
JANASZ,James George Gee 2Lt kia 15-6-15 3Dors att2Wilts p124 MR22
JANE,William Maj dow 24-4-18 RE p209
JANES,Edmund 2Lt kia 13-5-18 RGA 70HAG 161SB p40 CR Fraance523,13-5-17
JANES,George Frederick HonMajT/QM ded 13-8-18 RASC p193&257
JANES,Willis T2Lt dow 22-1-17 6KOSB p102 CR France1
JAPP,William Neville 2Lt kia 25/26-9-15 1/20Lond p251 MR19,25-9-15
JAQUES,Arthur TCapt kia 27-9-15 12WYorks p82 MR19
JAQUES,George 2Lt kia 25-9-17 B236RFA p31 CR Belgium21
JAQUES,George Sheriff Harkus 2Lt kia 27-6-16 6NumbF CR Belgium17
JAQUES,John Barclay.MC.AFC.FlOff 1-4-20 DLI att216RAF CR EAfrica116
JAQUES,Joseph 2Lt kia 26-9-17 1NumbF p61 MR30
JAQUES,Joseph Hodgson Maj kia 27-9-15 12WYorks p82 MR19
JAQUES,William 2Lt dow 30-12-17 1RMLI CR France398
JARAH,Charles T2Lt dow 20-6-17 22DLI p161 CR Belgium29
JARDINE,Charles Hunt TLt kia 3-5-18 13RScots att2/2KAR p54&202 CR EAfrica92
JARDINE,Douglas Graeme Burness.MC.Capt ded 5-8-18 1/2HLI &RAF p163 CR Europe74,kia
JARDINE,Graham Brymmer Thomas 2Lt kia 18-10-16 13A&SH p173 CR France385,Brymner
JARDINE,Henry Marshall Lt kia 23-7-16 6 att2RScots p211 MR21
JARDINE,J.A Capt 19-3-20 RAMC CR Egypt2
JARDINE,Richard Webster 2Lt kia 23-7-16 7LNLancs p136 MR21
JARDINE,Robert Gordon 2Lt kia 20-7-16 56RFC SR p9 MR20
JARDINE,Ronald James 2Lt kldacc 13-9-17 2Drags attRFC p9&21 CR Scot582
JARDINE,William.Bart.TMaj ded 13-12-15 3KOSB p102 CR Scot582
JARINZOFF,Dmitri.MC.MID TLtACapt kia 8-10-17 10 att6ELancs p111 MR30
JARMAN,Andrew Hatch T2Lt kia 1-7-16 20NumbF p61 CR France393
JARMAN,Harry Love TCapt kia 15-1-17 RAMC att7SWBord p196 CR Greece6
JARRED,Geoffrey William 2Lt ded 30-12-17 3RBerks p139 CR Egypt1,drd
JARRETT,Aylmer Vivian.DSO.Capt dow 22-6-15 2Y&L p159 CR Belgium2
JARRETT,Charles Harry Brownlow Maj kia 25-4-15 1RMunstF p175 CR Gallipoli1
JARRETT,Herbert Horace 2Lt dow 6-12-17 5NStaffs p238 CR France145
JARRETT,Hubert Cecil Delacour LtCol ded 21-12-19 IA 1/19Punjabis p278 CR India48

JARROTT,Samuel Fox Armitage TLt dow 12-10-16 2DLI p161 CR France105,2Lt
JARVIE,John T2Lt dow 17-4-17 7/8KOSB p102 CR France787
JARVIE,Thomas Russell T2Lt kld 10-9-17 RFC p9 CR Scot780
JARVIS,Alan Bishop Capt kia 10-8-17 10Mddx att1RFC p18&236 CR Belgium14
JARVIS,Archibald Thomas TLt ded 24-9-16 12Ess att1YLI p132 CR Greece7
JARVIS,Arthur Bernard T2Lt kia 3-8-17 C177RFA p31 CR Belgium10
JARVIS,Arthur Septimus Guy 2Lt kia 31-10-14 1Nhampt p137 CR Belgium132
JARVIS,Cecil.DSO.MC.Maj kldByNativeMob 18-3-19 IA 20DeccanHorse p278 C Egypt9
JARVIS,Charles Edward TLt kia 18-7-17 10WYorks p82 CR France97
JARVIS,Charles Wemyss Barron 2LtACapt kia 30-7-16 3RWKent att7RDubF p14 MR21 att1Bn
JARVIS,E.MacD.2Lt kld 6-6-18 GL &RAF p190
JARVIS,Edwin Leonard T2Lt kia 4-9-18 Hamps att2Bn p121 CR Belgium451
JARVIS,Ernest Cory TCapt kia 28-8-16 6 att8SLancs p125 MR21
JARVIS,Frederick Charles T2Lt kia 7-7-16 2Nhampt p137 MR21
JARVIS,George Frederick Jervaulx.MC.TLt dow 28-9-18 5RRofCav att9WYorks p2 CR France113
JARVIS,James Warden TLt dow 26-9-15 7KOSB p102 CR France88
JARVIS,John 2Lt kia 21-3-18 5NStaffs p238 MR20
JARVIS,John Baxter Capt ??? 10-4-19 RAOC p267
JARVIS,Louis Archibald Lt kia 16-5-15 2ScotsGds p52 CR France279
JARVIS,Ralph Himsworth.MC.LtTCapt kld 27-2-18 RFC p16 CR Surrey157
JARVIS,William Simpson T2Lt kia 8-11-18 7Lincs p75 CR France930,Simpkin
JAVES,John Walter Capt 3-11-20 ImpWarGravesComm CR Greece9
JAVES,Robert Charles T2Lt kia 15/17-9-16 10RWSurr p56 MR21,16-9-16
JAY,Arthur Palmer T2Lt kia 21-3-18 2RRegofCav att7BordR p23 MR20
JAY,Frank Goldsmith T2Lt kia 29-9-18 KRRC att18Bn p150 CR Belgium116
JAY,H.B.maj 20-8-17 DCLI CR Mddx26
JAY,William Oak Lt kia 25-4-17 8RLancs p59 MR20
JAYE,Harold Conway T2Lt dow 9-7-16 11WYorks p82 CR France833,13Bn
JEAKES,John William TLt dow 12-10-17 RBerks att6Bn p139 CR Belgium126
JEAL,Walter T2Lt kia 1-7-16 GL att15RScots p190 MR21
JEAVONS,Rechab Vivian 2Lt kia 30-8-17 RFA p208 MR30
JEBB,Arthur Beresford T2Lt kia 17-6-16 RFA attX16TMB p31 CR France223,
JEBB,Hope Emile 2Lt dow 21-3-18 2DLI p161 MR20
JEBSON,George James 2Lt kia 23-1-17 RGA 113HB p40 CR France133
JECKS,Albert Edward Lt 15-5-21 RASC MR65
JEEVES,Charles Anthony Victor.MM.T2Lt kia 20-9-17 Dev att9Lpool p77 MR30
JEFF,Andrew Russell T2Lt kia 13-8-16 12HLI p163 CR France1170
JEFFARES,Richard Thorpe.MID Capt dow 6-10-17 4 att2RIrRif p169 CR France8
JEFFCOAT,Stanley Ferns T2Lt dow 29-4-17 22RFus p68 CR France184
JEFFCOCK,Harold Charles Firth Lt dow 30-5-17 8N&D p233 CR France446,Ca
JEFFCOCK,Robert Salisbury 2Lt kia 1-7-16 1/6SStaffs p229 MR21
JEFFERIES,James Leslie TLt kia 9-9-16 11Hamps p121 CR France1890
JEFFERIES,Maurice Arnold T2Lt kia 19-7-16 10SLancs p125 MR19
JEFFERIES,Richard Oliver Geary.MC.TLtACapt kia 29-9-18 8TankCps p188 CR France375
JEFFERIES,Stanley Saunders 2Lt kia 10-8-18 8TankCps p188 CR France526
JEFFERSON,Elgie Blyth Barwise Capt kld 15-5-19 1Lpool attRAF p72 CR France1359,15-5-16
JEFFERSON,Hamilton Lt kia 16-8-17 4 O&BLI p231 MR30
JEFFERSON,Ralph James 2Lt kia 25-2-17 3 att6SLancs p125 MR38
JEFFERY,Charles Launcelot 2LtACapt dow 23-9-17 1 att10RB p179 MR30
JEFFERY,Claud Gifford Capt dow 23-10-14 2Yorks p90 CR Belgium57,Giffard 2 10-14
JEFFERY,George Reginald T2Lt kia 13-2-16 20Huss p23 CR France423,Lt
JEFFERY,Harold Greensmith 2Lt kia 4-7-18 GL &58RAF CR France223
JEFFERY,John T2Lt kia 20-9-18 18 att9WelshR p127 CR France631
JEFFERY,Ronald Edward 2Lt kia 25-5-17 GL 55RFC p9 CR France421,Roland
JEFFERY,Tom Forbes 2Lt dow 17-4-18 156RFA p31 CR Belgium18,16-4-18
JEFFERY,William T2Lt dow 7-10-17 att10RB p179
JEFFERYS,Charles Thomas Claude Rev ded 20-11-18 RAChDept p199 CR Somerset26
JEFFERYS,Montagne Gane Lt kia 18-1-17 10Mddx p236 MR38
JEFFORD,William Arthur 2Lt kia 8-5-15 12Lond p248 MR29
JEFFREE,Johnson Vivian 2Lt kia 10-8-18 3Lond p245 CR France1170 Ex HAC
JEFFREY,Ernest Lt kia 24-3-TA 4RScots p211 MR20
JEFFREY,Joseph Hunter 2Lt kia 23-10-18 2DLI p161 CR France1266
JEFFREY,Reginald Harry 2Lt kia 11-4-17 4 at1RWar p65 CR France544

JEFFREYS,Alexander Harry ACapt kia 6-11-16 20NumbF Ex 19Bn p61 CR France82,19Bn
JEFFREYS,Charles Thomas Claude Rev ded 20-11-18 RAChDept p268
JEFFREYS,Charles Wilfred 2Lt kia 17-10-17 KSLI att5Bn p145 MR30
JEFFREYS,Darell Richard Capt kia 11-7-15 1Dev p77 CR Belgium56
JEFFREYS,Hubert Leslie 2Lt kia 29-4-17 13RFus p68 MR20 JEFFERYS
JEFFREYS,William Stanley TLt kia 10-7-16 13WelshR p127 MR21
JEFFRIES,Harold John Fotheringham Capt kia 26-9-15 1/5Leic p220 CR Belgium11,Maj
JEFFRIES,Herbert TLt dow 20-9-18 Yorks att12MGC attYorks p90&183 CR France194
JEFFRIES,Philip TLt ded 3-12-18 15MGC Motors p183 MR43
JEFFRIES,Thomas 2Lt kia 14-8-17 3Lond p245 MR29
JEFFRYS,James Herbert 2Lt mbk 27-5-18 7 att2ELancs p256 CR France1894
JEHU,John Howard Lt kia 28-11-17 1Co of LondYeo p204 CR Palestine3,MddxHuss
JEKYLL,Arthur Cyril Albert TCapt kia 11-5-16 RAMC att13RScots p196 CR France423
JELF,Charles Gordon T2Lt kia 13-10-15 6EKent p57 CR France423
JELLEY,William Frederick.MC.2Lt dow 2-11-17 6Yorks p90 CR France145
JELLICOE,Eric Maitland Lt kia 1-7-16 6N&D p233 CR France281
JEMMETT,Charles William Lt kia 15-3-18 5EKent p213 CR France1712
JEMMETT,George Elwick 2Lt dow 17-12-17 13Lond p249 CR France13
JEMMETT-BROWNE,Antoney Edward Capt kia 11-9-14 2RSuss p119 CR France1113,Antony 10-9-14
JENINGS,George Pierce Creagh Lt kia 6-11-14 1KSLI p145 MR32
JENKIN,Louis Fleeming.MC&Bar.Capt kia 11-9-17 GL 9LNLancs &1RFC p9 MR20
JENKINS,Aneurin 2Lt kia 13-4-18 6SWBord p100 MR32
JENKINS,Arthur Emlyn TLt dow 4-12-16 20MGC p183 CR France131
JENKINS,Arthur Lewis Lt kld 31-12-17 4DCLI attRFC p18&226 CR Surrey152
JENKINS,Charles T2Lt kld 21-3-18 RFC p16 CR Wales367
JENKINS,Christopher Hutchinson LtTCapt dow 22-5-17 3RSuss &45RFC p9&119 CR France285
JENKINS,Cyril Donald Thomas Lt kld 2-10-16 3RWFus &RFC p3&98 CR Wales171
JENKINS,Cyril Frank Bingham TCapt dow 13-10-17 11SWBord p100 CR France64
JENKINS,David Chap4Cl ded 6-3-19 RAChDept p255 CR Wales118
JENKINS,David Lewis Lt kia 26-9-17 5RWFus p270&230,WelchR MR30,5 att10Bn
JENKINS,David Roy Capt kld 21-1-17 RFA attRFC p18&207 CR Wales7
JENKINS,Donald Fraser.MC.2Lt kia 13-11-16 6SfthH p241 CR France131
JENKINS,Edgar Ernest.MC.TLtACapt kia 25-3-18 RWar att1/5LancF p65 MR20
JENKINS,Edgar Kynnersley TCapt dow 23-9-16 2DCLI p114 CR Greece3
JENKINS,Edward Geoffrey T2Lt dow 26-10-18 1NumbF p61 CR France40
JENKINS,Edward Tuberville Llewellin Lt dow 25-7-16 RE 59FC p46 CR France23,2Lt
JENKINS,Edwin Walter Capt ded 9-11-16 Hamps CR Hamps13
JENKINS,Ernest 2Lt kia 2-9-18 40RFA p31 CR France214
JENKINS,Ernest Stanley 2Lt kia 24-11-17 5WelchR p230 CR France256
JENKINS,Francis Howard T2Lt kia 2-9-18 12SomLI p80 CR France439
JENKINS,Frederick John TMaj ded 22-1-19 RASC p267 CR Mddx13,23-1-19 dow
JENKINS,Garrett Primrose 2Lt kia 7-9-17 C75RFA p31 CR Belgium12
JENKINS,George Cliffe 2Lt kia 3-5-17 att2/5Y&L p159 MR20
JENKINS,James Temple Lt kia 20-9-17 4SfthH p241 MR30
JENKINS,John.MC.TMajALtCol dow 9-10-18 20KRRC att1Mon p150 CR France446
JENKINS,John Ernest TCapt dow 25-11-17 12SWBord p100 CR France398
JENKINS,Kenneth Gordon Lt dow 31-3-18 NSomYeo p205 CR France62
JENKINS,L.DSO.MC.LtCol ded 20-11-18 RGA &RAF p209
JENKINS,Llewellyn Maynard T2Lt dow 2-12-16 10WelshR p127 CR Belgium1
JENKINS,Patrick Graham 2Lt kia 9-4-17 4CamH p243 CR France924,7Bn
JENKINS,Ralph Conway T2Lt kld 2-12-17 GL RFC p9 CR Hamps4
JENKINS,Ralph George Lt ded 21-5-16 RGA p270 CR Wales35
JENKINS,Richard 2Lt kia 11-11-16 7Manch p237 MR21
JENKINS,Richard Borlase 2Lt dow 17-1-16 25WBord att9RFC p3&100 CR France34,18-1-16
JENKINS,Richard Owen.MC.2Lt dow 21-9-17 1/5Lpool p215 CR Belgium3,Lt
JENKINS,Robert Alfred Capt kia 21-1-16 1A 97Inf p278 MR38
JENKINS,Robert Henry Charles 2Lt dow 19-10-16 8Lond p247 CR France145
JENKINS,Samuel Clifford T2Lt dow 21-8-18 2Wilts p153 CR France10
JENKINS,Sidney Emlyn T2Lt kia 22-4-18 NStaffs att16RWFus p157 CR France296,Sydney 15 att16RWFus
JENKINS,Sidney Oswald 2Lt kia 22-8-18 3RWFus att10KSLI p98 MR19

JENKINS,Sydney Randell Lt dow 26-9-15 3 att2WelshR p127 MR19
JENKINS,Thomas Frederick TMaj ded 26-2-19 GL 16WelchR att1ArmyMSch p190 CR France788
JENKINS,W.W.L.2Lt dow 25-6-18 1/2DCLI &RAF p114
JENKINS,William T2Lt kia 11-10-18 Dors att6Bn p124 CR France230
JENKINS,William Alexander 2Lt dow 14-4-17 7A&SH p243 CR France95
JENKINS,William Charles 2Lt kia 4-10-17 RGA 66SB p40 CR Belgium101
JENKINS,William Edwin Capt kia 1-10-15 2NumbF p61 MR19
JENKINS,William Edwin 2Lt kia 23-11-17 ESurr &60RFC p9&112 CR Belgium125
JENKINS,William Marenday TLt kia 3-10-16 23WelshR p127 CR Greece3,Marendaz
JENKINSON,John Capt kia 13-10-15 6NStaffs p238 MR19
JENKINSON,John Banks.MID Capt kia 14-9-14 RB p179 CR France1329
JENKINSON,John Wilfred Capt kia 4-6-15 12Worc attRFus p109 MR4
JENKS,Alan Robert Constantine.MC.TLtAMaj kia 31-7-17 RE 61FC p46 CR Belgium17
JENKS,Arthur Leslie Lt dow 7-10-18 3 att2Dors p124 CR Egypt2
JENKS,John Edward TCapt dow 4-7-16 12RIrRif p169 CR France74
JENNER,George Reginald 2Lt dow 2-8-16 1/3 att1EYorks p84 CR France46
JENNER,John Thomas Russell 2Lt kld 21-12-17 GL 43RFC p9,R.J.CR Canada1143
JENNER-CLARKE,John William TLt kia 16-9-16 GL 6DCLI att43TMB p190 MR21
JENNINGS,Alexander LtTCapt ded 7-4-17 PoW RFA att29RFC p9&31 MR20
JENNINGS,Arnold John Capt kia 2-2-17 1 att6Leinst p174 CR France149
JENNINGS,Basil Spencer T2Lt dow 7-11-15 14 att6WYorks p82 CR Gallipoli27
JENNINGS,Charles Francis T2Lt kia 8-4-17 13Yorks p90 CR France439,Lt
JENNINGS,Francis Henry Cuthbert TLt ded 7-2-18 201MGC p183 CR Hamps11
JENNINGS,Francis Montgomery Capt ded 11-11-18 8Huss &2RRofCav p22&261 CR Eire148
JENNINGS,Francis William TLt kld 26-3-16 3Leics p87 CR Yorks63
JENNINGS,Gouldbourne Hayward 2Lt kia 10-8-16 20 att10RWFus p98 MR21,18-8-16
JENNINGS,H.A.K BrigGen 15-1-21 RA Staff CR India48
JENNINGS,Harold Victor Edgar 2Lt kia 29-5-18 14NumbF p61 MR18
JENNINGS,Henry Arthur 2Lt kia 29-4-17 6 att3Worc p109 CR France68,30-4-16
JENNINGS,Herbert Blake Lt dow 25-7-17 RGA 240SB p209 CR France398
JENNINGS,Hugh Cotton 2Lt dow PoW 3-5-17 RASC att12EYorks p193 CR France1277,Cotter
JENNINGS,H.W.McIvor T2Lt ded 29-2-16 RFA p31 CR Eire506
JENNINGS,Isaac Gaitskell 2Lt kia 21-3-18 5BordR p228 MR27
JENNINGS,John Gilderdale Maj mbk 10-8-15 1A 66Punjabis att6RDubF p278 MR4,Jack
JENNINGS,Richard William.MID TLt dow 3-7-16 10Worc C'Coy p109 CR France370
JENNINGS,Sidney James 2Lt kia 30-3-18 3ESurr attRE FldSur p112 CR France425,Sydney
JENNINGS,Thomas Edward ACapt kia 11-12-17 4Norf p216 CR palestine9
JENNINGS,William 2Lt dow 31-7-18 5Yorks p221 CR France1333
JENNINS,Harry T2Lt kia 12-11-16 8SStaffs p122 CR France307
JENNISON,Alfred Denzil 2Lt ded 17-9-16 14Lpool p72 CR Europe1
JENNISON,James Leonard 2Lt kia 3-5-17 15WYorks p82 MR20
JENNISON,Norman Lees.MC.TLtACapt ded 30-10-18 20Manch attTMB p155 CR Italy12
JENNS,Frank Arthur T2Lt dow 6-4-18 13Ess p132 CR France41
JENSON,Cyril Thornton T2Lt kia 10-5-16 25Manch attTMB p155 CR France625
JEPHSON,Charles Mitchell Warren Lt kia 27-12-17 5RWSurr p212 CR Palestine3
JEPHSON,Edward Jermy TCapt kia 15-9-16 10 att9Norf p74 MR21
JEPHSON,Howard 2Lt kia 23-4-17 6SStaffs p229 MR20
JEPHSON,John Noble.MID Maj dow 29-8-15 6RMunstF p175 CR Greece10
JEPHSON,William Jermy T2Lt kia 26-9-18 C175RFA p31 CR France451
JEPSON,Albert Clarence Leonard 2Lt kia 12-10-16 3Y&L p159 CR France432
JEPSON,Arthur George Leslie.MID Capt kia 16-9-16 2Lond p245 MR21,15-9-16
JEPSON,Joseph Jordan 2Lt kia 2-10-18 6LancF p221 CR France237
JEPSON,Norman Richard T2Lt kia 15-10-15 14 att2RFus p68 CR Gallipoli4,14 att2Bn
JEPSON,Stanley Capt ded 24-2-19 4NStaffs p157 CR France1028
JERGENSON,E.T.Lt kia 4-5-18 GL attKAR p266
JERRARD,Charles Frederick.MC.Capt ded 15-5-19 1Dors RoO p124&257 CR Germany1
JERRETT,Sidney(Jim) 2Lt dow 8-5-17 28RH&FA p31 CR France95,123RFA Ex H'RHA
JERVIS,Arthur Cyril LtTCapt kia 3-7-18 3Lpool att2/3KAR p72&202 CR EAfrica90
JERVIS,John Cedric TLt kia 26-10-16 5RFC p3 CR France133

161

JERVIS,Percy William 2Lt kia 3-4-17 5RWFus p223 CR France616
JERVIS,Robert Norrie TLt kia 5-1-16 RE 83FC p46 CR France525
JERVOIS,Philip Harding Lt dow 28-10-17 RGA 177SB p40 CR Belgium84,2Lt
JERWOOD,John Hugh.MC.Maj kia 21-3-18 10DLI att6SomLI p161 MR27
JESSON,Arthur 2Lt kia 16-11-16 6Beds p86 MR21
JESSON,Robert Witford Fairey.MID TCaptAMaj kia 22-2-17 5Wilts p153 MR38
JESSOP,Frederick Devereux.MC.TCapt kia 16-9-16 12ESurr p112 CR France277,15-9-16
JESSOP,George Edward Lt kia 10-4-18 8WYorks att6NumbF p219 MR32
JESSOP,John William LtCol kia 4-6-15 4Lincs p217 CR Belgium98
JESSOPP,Augustus John TLt kia 12-5-17 GL RFC p9 CR France777
JESSOPP,Walter Leverton TLt kia 31-7-17 MGC p183 MR29
JESSUP,Francis Reginald TCapt kia 1-7-16 1BordR p117 MR21
JESSUP,William Henry Gray.DSO.HonCapt dow 24-12-18 6DCLI p114
JESTIN,Martin T2Lt kia 7-6-17 7RIrF p171 MR29
JEUDWINE,Spencer Henry Capt kia 1-7-16 att2Lincs p75 MR21
JEUNE,Hugo St.Helier TCapt dow 12-5-17 9Glouc p107 CR France32,12Bn
JEWELL,Dudley Mark Hayward T2Lt kia 20-1-16 RE att18RFus p46 CR France279,RFus attRE
JEWELL,Edward Herbert T2Lt kia 15-5-16 11LancF B'Coy p92 CR France68,16-5-16
JEWELL,Frank Ernest T2Lt kia 15-12-17 RLancs att1/4YLI p59 CR Belgium101
JEWELL,J.B.Lt 6-4-18 GL &RFC CR Mddx34
JEWELL,William John T2Lt kia 1-9-18 12 att10SWBord p100 MR16
JEWHURST,George Stanley 2Lt dow 19-2-18 20Lond p251 CR France755
JEWITT,Dermod Patrick 2Lt kia 23-4-16 WorYeo p206 MR34
JEWITT,Joseph T2Lt kia 1-11-18 WYorks att1/7Bn p82 CR France1254
JEWSON,William Henry TMaj kia 19-4-17 4Norf p216 MR34
JEYNES,Harry.MC.MM.T2Lt kia 22-3-18 1Lincs p75 MR27
JICKLING,Frank T2Lt kld 23-10-17 GL RFC p9 CR Shrop52
JINKS,Mary Nurse 29-9-19 TFNS CR Scot358
JOACHIM,B.I.H.Lt 20-10-18 IMS MR67
JOB,Bernard Craig Keble 2Lt kia 18-4-15 3RWKent p141 MR29
JOB,Ernest Dalzel Capt kia 11-7-16 28Lond attMGC p187&252 CR France453
JOBLING,Ernest.MID ACapt kia 23-10-18 6ACycCps p181&257 CR France206
JOBLING,Harold Edward 2Lt dow 9-9-17 7Leinst p174 CR France593
JOBLING,Henry Douglas 2Lt dow 22-1-18 RFA p208 CR Yorks428
JOBLING,John Beresford TCapt ded 4-11-18 17LabCps p189 CR France332
JOBLING,Joseph Higgin TLt kia 1-12-17 10LancF p92 MR30
JOBSON,McGregor Maj dow 3-5-18 PoW 4KOSB p223 CR France1029
JODE,Gordon Robert Lovelace 2Lt kia 19-8-18 12Norf p204 CR France193
JOEL,Harold Walter ACapt kia 7-6-17 21Lond p251 CR Belgium122
JOFFE,William.DSO.2Lt kia 1-10-18 5YLI &RAF p270
JOHN Hugh Graham 2Lt mbk 16-6-15 3Y&L att1NumbF p256 MR29
JOHN,Iorwerth Glyndwr 2Lt kia 24-2-16 3 att1SWBord p100 CR France1723,25-2-16
JOHN Lennox William McClure 2Lt dow 24-9-16 1Lincs p75 CR France833,ded
JOHN,Wilbur Arnold Lt kia 1-8-18 SussYeo &RAF p205&258 CR Belgium112
JOHNS,Arthur T2Lt kia 25-9-17 RE 183TC p46 CR Belgium16
JOHNS,Arthur Hugh TLt kia 1-9-16 10 att11RSuss p119 CR France344
JOHNS,Bernard Digby TCapt kia 17-2-16 10RWFus p98 MR29
JOHNS,Bradley Cooper 2Lt ded 23-10-18 RGA 43A/ACoy p40 CR Essex122,22-10-18
JOHNS,Edward Tregonwell 2Lt dow 3-4-18 3 att6Dors p124 CR France103
JOHNS,Graham Lt kia 27-9-18 1ScotsGds att2TMB p52 MR16
JOHNS,Harold Thomas T2Lt kia 11-1-17 9 att8WelshR p127 MR38
JOHNS,Herbert 2LtACapt kia 11-4-18 1RGLI p200 MR32
JOHNS,Hubert Hilditch 2Lt ded 29-5-17 3BordR p117 MR65
JOHNS,Owen Llewellyn.MC.T2Lt kia 28-6-16 RFA attY33TMB p31&258 CR France296
JOHNS,Stephen T2Lt kia 14-3-16 RE 255Co p46 CR France705
JOHNSON,Alan Barrie.MC.Lt kld 27-1-18 45RFC CR Lincs181
JOHNSON,Alec.MC.Capt kia 18-9-18 1Camb p244 CR France369
JOHNSON,Alexander Downing 2LtTCapt kia 25-9-15 3 att2SStaffs p122 CR France163
JOHNSON,Alfred William.MC.TLtACapt dow 17-4-18 RE 1FldSur p46 CR France40
JOHNSON,Anthony.MC&Bar.2Lt kia 13-4-18 6 att2Worc p109 CR Belgium42,14-4-18
JOHNSON,Arnold Leslie Capt kia 14-10-18 5NStaffs p237 MR30
JOHNSON,Arthur Dennis 2Lt ded 16-10-17 RFA p270 CR Wales171
JOHNSON,Arthur Ellis T2Lt kia 20-7-17 Y&L att2Bn p159 MR19
JOHNSON,Arthur Graham MajTLtCol kia 17-9-17 RFA 33DAC p31 CR Belgium15

JOHNSON,Bernard Copestake 2Lt kia 14-5-17 2/7WRid p228 CR France690
JOHNSON,Charles Maj ded 15-1-17 RAMC p267
JOHNSON,Charles Cuthbert 2Lt kld 9-6-15 RE 1FC p210 MR4,6-6-15
JOHNSON,Clive Armstrong 2Lt kia 22-1-16 IARO att6Jats p278 MR38,Capt 21-1-
JOHNSON,Cecil Marland 2Lt kld 6-6-18 GL &2RAF p190 CR France12
JOHNSON,Cyril Benton LtCol kia 21-9-17 1/6N&D p233 CR France258
JOHNSON,Cyril Goode 2Lt kia 7-6-17 149RFA p31 CR Belgium6
JOHNSON,Derrick Sivewright 2Lt kia 4-12-16 ACycCps HomeCountDiv attRFC p18&244 CR France924
JOHNSON,Donald Frederick Goold TLt dow 15-7-16 2Manch p155 CR France29
JOHNSON,Edmund George 2Lt kia 24-8-18 1 att12Lond p245 MR16
JOHNSON,Edward Fielder TCapt kia 7-12-17 B310RFA p31 CR France530,6-12-
JOHNSON,Edward Francis 2Lt dow 7-11-18 5 att1Mddx p147 CR France930
JOHNSON,Eric Guildford 2Lt kia 25/26-9-15 8RWSurr p56 MR19
JOHNSON,Eric Hope Lt kia 22-12-17 8LancF p221 MR30
JOHNSON,Ernest Edward Chap4Cl ded 1-12-18 RAChDept att15LancF p199 CR France717
JOHNSON,Evelyn Walter James T2Lt dow 20-7-16 7Beds p86 CR France145
JOHNSON,Francis Hugh 2Lt kia 15-9-16 1/19Lond p250 CR France1890
JOHNSON,Frank L.Lt 6-9-17 BrWIndR attRFC CR Egypt1
JOHNSON,Fred Blacktin T2Lt kia 31-5-17 13RB p179 MR20
JOHNSON,Frederick Henry.VC.TCaptAMaj dow 26-11-17 RE 231FC p46 MR17 73FC
JOHNSON,Frederick Stansfield T2Lt kia 4-11-18 C92RFA p31 CR France
JOHNSON,G.J.J.Lt 17-5-15 IA 32Lancers CR EAfrica60
JOHNSON,Geoffrey Barham TCapt kia 23-11-15 7Norf p74 CR France423
JOHNSON,Geoffrey Robert T2Lt dow 7-8-15 7Glouc p107 MR4
JOHNSON,George Arthur Moxey Tuker 2Lt kia 21-5-17 19Lond p250 MR29
JOHNSON,George Bernard.DSO.Maj kia 18-4-18 A275RFA p206 CR France109
JOHNSON,George William TLt kia 24-4-18 8MGC p183 MR27
JOHNSON,Gilbert Ernest TLtACapt ded 4-7-18 14ACycCps p181 CR Italy8,drds
JOHNSON,Harold T2Lt dow 14-7-16 75MGC p183 CR France44
JOHNSON,Harold George Lt kia 7-8-17 1GrenGds p50 CR Belgium106
JOHNSON,Harold Richard Lt kld 19-1-16 3RFC p3 CR France88
JOHNSON,Harry Lt&QM 27-5-18 GL att9CpsCycBn MR19
JOHNSON,Harry Cecil.DSO.BtMaj dow PoW 1-1-15 KRRC p150 CR France598
JOHNSON,Henry Lt&QM kia 27-5-18 GL p254
JOHNSON,Henry Earlam 2Lt kia 4-6-16 5KRRC p150 CR France149
JOHNSON,Henry Norman Lt kia 2-11-17 5Manch p236 CR Belgium175
JOHNSON,Horace 2Lt kia 28-4-17 5SStaffs p270 MR20
JOHNSON,Horace James.DSO.LtCol kia 7-8-15 8WRid p115 CR Gallipoli27,JOHNSTON
JOHNSON,Horace Samuel T2Lt kld 9-3-18 RFC p16 CR Lincs181
JOHNSON,Howard Fife 2Lt kia 9-3-17 1/5EKent p213 MR38
JOHNSON,Hubert Alfred T2Lt kia 27-2-17 GL &8RFC p9 CR France120
JOHNSON,James Alexander Campbell Capt kia 21-8-18 8Lpool p215 CR France618
JOHNSON,James William Lt kia 30-11-17 8Mddx p236 MR17
JOHNSON,John T2Lt kia 9-1-17 133MGC Inf p183 MR38
JOHNSON,John Burgoyne LtCol ded 9-1-20 8DLI Res p270 CR Durham140
JOHNSON,John Chapman 2Lt kia 8-7-15 3 att1RWar p65 CR Belgium23
JOHNSON,John Frederic 2Lt kia 9-4-16 9RLancs p59 MR38
JOHNSON,John Frederick Lt dow 30-10-15 4Leic p219 CR France201
JOHNSON,Joseph John Claud 2Lt dow 5-4-18 SR att48RFA p31 CR France62
JOHNSON,Laurence Bertrand 2Lt dow 15-4-18 3 att1SomLI p80 CR France10
JOHNSON,Laurence Frederick T2Lt kia 16-6-17 8Dev p77 MR20
JOHNSON,Leslie Nethercote.MC.2Lt kia 3-6-17 6N&D p233 CR France570
JOHNSON,Luther Vincent Burgoyne Capt kia 26-4-15 8DLI p239 MR29,See BURGOYNE-JOHNSON
JOHNSON,Malcolm Johnson Williams Lt ded 18-2-19 RFA p207 CR War47
JOHNSON,Malcolm Thomas 2Lt kld 16-11-17 4 att12ESurr p112 CR Italy56
JOHNSON,Maurice Richard Wheatley Lt kia 28-6-18 IARO att21KohatMtnBty p278 CR Asia82
JOHNSON,Mervyn-Taylor Lt dow 17-10-14 2SWBord p100 CR France1329,14-9
JOHNSON,M.H.SNurse 5-9-15 QAIMNS CR Egypt9
JOHNSON,Newton Farring T2Lt kia 16-8-16 15 att26RFus p68 CR Belgium54, 8-16
JOHNSON,Norman Alfred Power.MID 2LtTCapt kia 27-11-15.1LancF p92 MR4,Nelson
JOHNSON,Norman Teasdale 2Lt kia 16-4-17 3 att8RWKent p141 MR20,Leasdale
JOHNSON,Owen Bennett Goold T2Lt kia 9-4-17 11Suff p78 CR France265

JOHNSON,Percy Clarkson 2Lt kia 16-5-15 8Manch p237 MR4
JOHNSON,Phillip Norman.MC.Capt dow 16-10-18 1/4Y&L p238 CR France214
JOHNSON,Philip Walter 2Lt dow 18-5-15 3RWSurr p56 CR France632
JOHNSON,Pieter Cedric Earlam 2Lt kia 28-1-17 GL &RFC p9 MR20
JOHNSON,Raymond Albert.MC.TLt kia 24-4-18 1N&D p134 CR France144
JOHNSON,Rayner Harvey.MC.LtAMaj kia 26-9-18 RGA 122HB p40 CR France759,27-9-18
JOHNSON,Reginald Travernor Capt kia 13-10-15 5NStaffs p237 MR19
JOHNSON,Richard Colling TLt kia 31-7-17 RE SpCo p46 CR Belgium96
JOHNSON,Richard Digby.MID Maj kia 24-5-15 3RDubF p177 MR29
JOHNSON,Richard Ethelbert MajHonCol ded 29-10-15 GL p270 CR Yorks5 Ex EYorkRGA
JOHNSON,Robert 2Lt kia 24-4-17 4NumbF p213 MR20
JOHNSON,Robert Blissett Powell.MC.TLt kld 19-9-18 RGA 109HB p40
JOHNSON,Robert Deane TCapt kia 6-7-16 23RFus p68 CR France924
JOHNSON,Robert Harold Jervis 2Lt kia 13-3-15 2Ess p132 CR Belgium33
JOHNSON,Ronald Gordon Mayson Maj 30-9-20 RGA CR Berks73
JOHNSON,Ronald Lindsay TLtACapt kia 29-5-17 RFA HQDiv 23TMB p31 CR Belgium6
JOHNSON,Russell Lowell T2Lt kld 12-11-17 GL &RFC p9
JOHNSON,Samuel.MC.Lt kia 24-9-18 RFA attRGA 303SB p207 CR France421
JOHNSON,Samuel Clement Lt ded 8-2-19 RFA p270 CR Hamps15
JOHNSON,Sidney Frederick LtTCapt kia 10-1-17 3 att2BordR p117 CR France534
JOHNSON,Stanley T2Lt kia 20-7-16 2Suff p78 MR21
JOHNSON,Stanley Morrell T2Lt kld 25-5-17 GL &RFC p9 CR Yorks22
JOHNSON,Stephen Henry ACapt kia 20-5-17 GL att 19TMB p190 MR20
JOHNSON,Sydney 2Lt dow 30-8-18 5WRid p227 MR16
JOHNSON,Thomas TLt kia 1-7-16 16HLI p163 MR21
JOHNSON,Thomas.MC.Lt kia 4-9-16 1BlkW p129 CR France432,3-9-16
JOHNSON,Thomas T2Lt dow 4-8-17 217MGC p183 CR Belgium18
JOHNSON,Thomas Henry Fielder.DSO.Maj ded 9-3-19 6Dors p264 CR Norf101
JOHNSON,Thomas Pelham.DSO.LtCol ded 12-6-18 RASC 15DivTrn p193 CR France113
JOHNSON,Victor Reginald William Lt dow 28-3-15 3 att2Wilts A'Coy p153 CR France706
JOHNSON,Walter Charles Littley 2Lt 30-7-17 6 att16Mddx MR20
JOHNSON,Wilfrid Lloyd T2Lt kia 19-4-16 2BordR p117 CR France394
JOHNSON,William 2Lt dow 16-5-15 2Leic p87 CR France727
JOHNSON,William T2Lt dow 12-11-16 8SStaffs p122 MR21
JOHNSON,William Charles Littley T2Lt kia 30-5-17 6 att16Mddx p147
JOHNSON,William Godfrey Easlam Capt dow 13-10-17 1/5Manch p236 CR France1361
JOHNSON,William Herbert 2Lt dow 28-6-17 4LNLancs p234 CR Lancs381
JOHNSON,William Inglis Capt dow 15-10-15 4Lincs p217 CR France80
JOHNSON,William Morton TCapt kia 2-7-16 16Manch p155 MR21
JOHNSON,William Roland 2Lt kia 1-7-16 1/6SStaffs p229 MR21
JOHNSON,William Stanley T2Lt dow 17-3-17 7ESurr p112 CR France158
JOHNSON-SMYTH,Edward Chap4Cl ded 10-2-17 RAChDept p199 CR France145
JOHNSTON,Adrian Alexander Hope Lt kia 2-7-16 5 att4Mddx p147 CR France267
JOHNSTON,Alec Leith TLt kia 22-4-16 1KSLI p145 CR Belgium73
JOHNSTON,Alexander 2Lt kia 25-3-18 10EYorks p84 MR20
JOHNSTON,Alexander Maj ded 22-9-18 RAMC p267 CR Scot80
JOHNSTON,Alexander Francis 2Lt kia 10-9-16 11 att1/6Lond p248 MR21
JOHNSTON,Alexander Vyvyan TLt kia 18-8-17 12Lpool p72 MR30,17-8-17
JOHNSTON,Alfred Roy T2Lt kia 24-4-17 GL &RFC p9 MR20
JOHNSTON,Andrew 2Lt kia 30-10-17 RFA &RFC p9
JOHNSTON,Andrew Robert 2Lt kia 29-7-18 5HLI attD'Coy 5KOSB p240 CR France866
JOHNSTON,Andrew Yaill Pollok 2Lt kia 5-10-17 5KOSB p224 CR Belgium112,Yuill
JOHNSTON,Arthur Annan 2Lt dow 16-4-17 B291RFA p208 CR France145
JOHNSTON,Basil 2Lt kia 3-9-16 6 att11RB p179 CR France294
JOHNSTON,Benjamin 2Lt ded PoW 3-11-18 11KRRC p150 CR Europe149
JOHNSTON.C.E.L.Maj 18-3-21 RGA CR Beds70
JOHNSTON,Charles Ernest.DSO.TD.Maj kia 23-3-18 6SfthH p241 MR20
JOHNSTON,Charles Moore TCapt kia 1-7-16 9RIrRiF C'Coy p171 CR France233
JOHNSTON,Charles Wright T2Lt kia 12-10-17 11RScots p54 MR30
JOHNSTON,David Ernest T2Lt ded 12-11-17 RASC 954MT p193 CR Iraq8
JOHNSTON,Donald Clark Capt dow 13-9-18 1 att1/8ScotRif p103 CR France145
JOHNSTON,Edward John Farquharson Capt kia 12-4-15 1RScots p54 CR Belgium151
JOHNSTON,Elliott Capt kia 1-7-16 13RIrRif p169 MR21

JOHNSTON,Evelyn Sandiland Capt 14/15-5-20 RGA 27MtnBty MR43
JOHNSTON,Foster Crampton 2Lt dow 23-4-17 13ESurr p112 CR France164,Forster
JOHNSTON,Francis Earl.CB.MIDx4 TBrigGen kia 7-8-17 NStaffs att3NZealandBaseHQ p157 CR France285,att1NZ
JOHNSTON,Francis WO ded 16-2-18 RIM p278
JOHNSTON,Frank.MID CaptTMaj dow 31-5-18 7KSLI p145 CR France33
JOHNSTON,Geoffrey Stewart Lt kia 14-5-15 EssYeo p203 MR29
JOHNSTON,George Mitchell Capt kia 3-4-16 RJLI att7RIrRif p201 CR France423,1-4-16
JOHNSTON,Gilbert Henderson T2Lt kld 15-12-17 GL &RFC p9 CR Scot228
JOHNSTON,Godfrey Julius Jeppe Lt ded 17-5-15 IA 32Lancers p278
JOHNSTON,Gordon Black Lt ded PoW 22-10-18 1/4RSuss p228 CR Iraq8
JOHNSTON,Henry Edward.DCM.2Lt dow 16-3-18 SussYeo p205 CR Palestine3
JOHNSTON,Herbert Augustus 2Lt kia 4-3-16 1RFC p3 CR France922
JOHNSTON,Hugh Bertie Henriques.DSO.Maj dow 27-10-16 RH&FA p31 CR France453,RGA 21HB
JOHNSTON,Hugh McColl Capt dow 4-4-18 RAVC att1RDrags p198 CR France37,kia
JOHNSTON,James Annandale 2Lt kia 2-7-16 3 att1SomLI p80 MR21
JOHNSTON,James Cecil TCapt kia 9-8-15 6RIrF p171 MR4
JOHNSTON,James MacCormac Caldwell TLt kia 27-5-16 RAMC att3Worc p196 CR France68
JOHNSTON,James Tait TLt kia 28-9-16 6BordR p117 CR France293,JOHNSTONE
JOHNSTON,James Valentine 2Lt kia 3-4-17 7HLI p240 CR France672
JOHNSTON,John 2Lt kia 10-4-18 RE 81FC p210 MR30
JOHNSTON,John Edwin T2Lt kia 10-7-16 4 att10SStaffs p122 MR21
JOHNSTON,John Henry Capt ded 18-5-18 6LancF p270
JOHNSTON,John Leslie 2Lt kia 12-5-15 O&BLI p130 MR22
JOHNSTON,John Lionel Lukin TCapt dow 21-6-16 2Leinst p174 CR France285,Lyonel
JOHNSTON,John Thomas Capt kia 27-5-17 10 att1/9RScots p212 MR20
JOHNSTON,Joseph Allen TCapt kia 18-2-17 9RIrF p171 CR Belgium43
JOHNSTON,Leslie.MC.2Lt dow 25-7-16 7Worc p226 CR France345
JOHNSTON,Octavius Ralph Featherston Capt kia 1-7-16 4Mddx p147 CR France267
JOHNSTON,Paul Headley 2Lt dow 11-6-18 C74RH&FA p31 CR France103,Lt
JOHNSTON,Percy Ellwood LtACapt dow 12-9-16 3DLI att2NumbF p161 CR Greece4
JOHNSTON,Richard George Mann Maj kia 25-8-16 C162RFA p31 CR France188
JOHNSTON,Robert Graham Lt kia 18-7-16 7SfthH p165 MR21
JOHNSTON,Robert London T2Lt kia 13-12-15 17Manch p155 CR France281,Loudon
JOHNSTON,Robert Neilson 2Lt kia 22-7-16 8ScotRif p225 MR34
JOHNSTON,Rowland Ivan 2Lt dow 28-8-18 2 att3RIrRif p169 CR France34
JOHNSTON,Sinclair Beatty 2Lt died 27-5-17 3 att7EKent p57 MR20
JOHNSTON,Stuart TLt kia 12-8-16 B70RFA p31 CR France703,dpw
JOHNSTON,Thomas James T2Lt kia 21-3-18 12 att7/8RInniskF p105 MR27
JOHNSTON,Thomas McKinnon 2Lt kia 13-11-16 3 att1RScotF p94 CR France742
JOHNSTON,Thomas Peacock Lt kia 20-5-17 ShropYeo attRFC p205&18 CR France120,2Lt
JOHNSTON,Walter Robertson Lt kia 6-9-18 A112RFA p207 CR France511
JOHNSTON,William Henry.VC.Maj kia 8-6-15 RE p46 CR Belgium115
JOHNSTON,William Holden 2Lt kia 30-7-16 17Lpool p72 CR France294
JOHNSTON,William Saville Lt dow PoW 23-3-18 7A&SH p243 CR France256
JOHNSTON,William Tardiff T2Lt kia 13-4-17 12Manch p155 CR France581,Tordiff
JOHNSTON,William Vincent TCapt ded 12-12-17 RAMC p196 CR Eire322
JOHNSTON-STEWART,Herbert Eustace Hathorn Capt kia 17-5-15 2HLI p163 MR22
JOHNSTON-STUART,Cyril George Lt kia 16-4-18 13EYorks p84 MR30
JOHNSTONE,Arthur James 2Lt kia 5-4-17 5RScotF p222 CR France1182
JOHNSTONE,Frederick John Lawrie.MC.Lt dow 29-8-16 2KRRC p150 CR France51,Capt
JOHNSTONE,George Dreyer 2Lt kia 19-12-16 7Lond p247 CR France1157
JOHNSTONE,George Smith Lt kia 26-8-18 3 att2KOSB p102 MR16
JOHNSTONE,Gilbert Lumley TCaptAMaj kia 4-10-16 96RFA p31 CR France389
JOHNSTONE,Godfrey Gleeson T2Lt dow 30-1-18 2RFC p16 CR France345
JOHNSTONE,Henry Archer TCaptAMaj kia 21-3-18 152RFA p31 CR France162
JOHNSTONE,Hugh Bertie Henriques Maj dow 27-10-16 RGA p262
JOHNSTONE,Hugh Noel 2Lt 1-6-2 2/8WYorks CR C'land &W'land54
JOHNSTONE,J.H.MC.Capt 18-5-18 Lpool&LancF CR Ches182
JOHNSTONE,James 2Lt dow 17-4-18 9HLI p240

JOHNSTONE,James Lt ded 20-10-19 LabCps p266 CR Scot238,CamelTransCps
JOHNSTONE,James Henry Walter Maj kia 15-9-14 115/25RFA p31 CR France1328,Waller
JOHNSTONE,John TCapt kia 9-9-16 7Leinst p174 MR21
JOHNSTONE,John Andrew Lt kia 20-5-18 RFA attRFC p31 CR France200
JOHNSTONE,John Douglas Lt kia 31-7-17 4RLancs p213 MR29
JOHNSTONE,John Pultney Hope Lt accDrd 15-2-18 IA 66Pujabis p278 MR66
JOHNSTONE,Melville 2Lt kia 16-7-17 27RFC SR p9 CR France134,Capt
JOHNSTONE,Nelson Lt ded 9-12-15 RAMC p270 CR Camb16
JOHNSTONE,Nelson Gordon.MC.2Lt kia 30-12-17 9BlkW att44TMB p129 CR France1182,Capt att22
JOHNSTONE,Reginald Fitzroy Lews Lt kia 8-9-14 1CamH p168 CR France1425
JOHNSTONE,Richard TCapt ded 8-4-19 NumbF p262 CR Durham26
JOHNSTONE,Richard Michael TCapt kia 25-3-18 12HLI p163 CR France630
JOHNSTONE,Robert Maj 6-10-17 7ScotRif CR Scot237
JOHNSTONE,Robert Brown Whylock 2Lt kia 19-7-18 51RFA p31 MR32
JOHNSTONE,Robert James Halliday Lt kia 26-9-17 5BlkW p231 MR30
JOHNSTONE,William 2Lt kia 30-3-16 8BlkW p129 CR Belgium71
JOHNSTONE,William James 2Lt kia 28-6-15 4RScots p211 MR4
JOHNSTONE,William Jeffray.MC.Lt kia 28-12-17 Fife&ForfarYeo p203 CR Palestine3
JOHNSTONE,William Joseph Capt dow 18-12-17 7Lond p247 CR France398
JOHNSTONE,William McCall T2Lt kia 13-2-16 152RFA p31 CR France275
JOHNSTONE,William Rutherford Mushet 2Lt kld 20-8-21 IAUL att1Leinst p278 MR66
JOICE,Philip Sidney T2Lt dow 1-12-17 16Ches p96 CR Belgium16 1Bn
JOICE,Reginald John TLt kia 30-4-17 60RFA p31 CR France96,1-5-17 C50RFA
JOICEY,Clive Montague LtTCapt kia 5-6-17 4NumbF p213 CR France604
JOICEY,Sidney James Drever.Hon.TCapt&Adjt kia 20-3-16 10NumbF p61 CR France557,Sydney
JOICEY-CECIL,John Francis James Lt kia 25-9-16 4GrenGds p50 CR France374
JOLLEY,John Andrew Benjamin T2Lt kia 11-10-15 2 att5Lincs p75 MR19
JOLLEY,Robert James 2Lt dow 22-8-18 1Ches p96 CR France84
JOLLIE,Francis Ormonde Holden Capt kia 25-4-15 2ESurr p112 MR29
JOLLY,Benton Ord T2Lt dow 9-2-17 7Yorks p90 CR France105
JOLLY,Frederick Capt ded 20-8-18 HertsYeo p204 CR Herts91
JOLLY,Percy 2Lt kia 13-7-17 4RLancs p213 France759JOLLEY
JOLLY,R.2Lt 26-11-19 4GordH CR Scot500
JOLLY,Trevor Blake 2Lt kia 20-9-17 3 att12ESurr p122 MR30
JONAS,Frank Charlton Capt kia 31-7-17 1Camb p244 MR29
JONES,A.Capt 17-4-17 RE CR Surrey97
JONES,A.A.Col 23-9-15 MysoreImpServTrps MR66
JONES,A.E.Capt 9-4-18 1/6Lpool CR France88
JONES,Albert Capt kia 9-4-18 6Lpool p215
JONES,Alfred Cotton.MC.TCapt kia 2-7-16 8Lincs p75 MR21
JONES,Alfred Ivan Noel Lt ded 22-11-19 Norf att19Lond p263 MR34
JONES,Alfred Gwilym Capt ded 27-1-16 RAMC p196 MR43 &CR Pakistan50A
JONES,Alfred Roy 2Lt kia 23-3-18 RWar att2/7Bn p65 MR27
JONES,Archibald Wilson LtCol ded 22-2-17 4HLI attRemounts p163 CR Wales658
JONES,Arnold Seymour Lt dow 27-3-15 4SLancs p230
JONES,Arthur 2Lt kia 27-5-18 11LancF p92 MR18
JONES,Arthur T2Lt kia 23-8-18 8DCLI att3MGC p114&183,22-8-18 CR France927,5MGC
JONES,Arthur Ewart T2Lt kia 8-8-15 8WelshR p127 MR4
JONES,Arthur Godman T2Lt dow 1-7-17 10EYorks B'Coy p84 CR France113
JONES,Arthur Henry 2Lt ded 15-3-16 RFA p208 CR Shrop111
JONES,Arthur Leslie Gwynne 2Lt kia 4-5-18 RGA 252SB p40 CR Belgium8
JONES,Arthur Lloyd.MC.TCapt dow 3-9-18 14RWFus p98 CR France703
JONES,Arthur Mervyn Lt dow 21-11-16 1ScotsGds p52
JONES,Arthur Meredydd.MC&Bar.Lt dow 10-4-18 50MGC p183 MR32
JONES,Arthur Trevor TLt dow 19-6-17 17WelshR C'Coy p127 CR France439,Capt
JONES,Arthur Vernon.MID TCapt ded 16-2-19 GL &RWFus p255 CR France40
JONES,Arthur William 2Lt kia 31-3-17 HAC p206 CR France568
JONES,B.M.Lt kld 28-9-18 RE &RAF p256
JONES,Barham Ivor Lewis 2Lt kia 22-6-15 3SWBord p100 CR Gallipoli6,B.J.L.
JONES,Basil Rev ded 25-10-18 RAChDept p199 CR France85
JONES,Basil Gordon Dawes.MC.Lt kia 23-9-16 1 att2WelshR p127 MR21,23-10-16
JONES,Beatrice Isabel Matron I/C 14-1-21 QAIMNS CR Iraq8
JONES,Bryan John.DSO&Bar.Maj kia 20-10-18 1Leinst att15RIrRif p174 CR Belgium140,LtCol
JONES,Brynley Lewis Capt ded 26-12-18 3Mon p270 CR Mon4

JONES,Cecil Hughes TCapt kia 18-9-18 11RWFus p98 CR Greece5,Hugh
JONES,Cecil Norman 2Lt ded 9-11-17 3 att15WelshR p127 CR France255
JONES,Charles Arnold T2Lt dow 1-5-18 RASC att2Berks p193 CR France29
JONES,Charles David T2LtALt ded 7-3-18 8WRid attBritPortugueseMission p1 CR France345
JONES,Charles Douglas TLt kia 28-10-16 9YLI p143 CR France114
JONES,Charles Edward Coursolles TCapt kia 4-7-16 10RWar p65 MR21
JONES,Charles Henry Lt kia 10-4-16 RE 1/2FC p210 CR France68
JONES,Charles Lambert TLt kld 15-6-16 10Glouc p107 CR France149
JONES,Charles Taylor.MID T2Lt kia 25-9-15 2RWSurr p56 MR19
JONES,Cledwyn Lloyd 2Lt kia 21-3-18 2/7N&D p233 MR20
JONES,Clifford T2Lt kia 2-8-17 15RWFus p98 MR29
JONES,Cyril Gordon TLt kia 20-11-17 9Norf C'Coy p74 CR France379
JONES,Cyril Hammond Montague LtACapt ded 14-11-18 RGA p40 CR Wilts142,14-11-17
JONES,Dan Llewellyn T2Lt dow 14-3-16 9WelchR p127 CR France345
JONES,Daniel Thomas 2Lt kia 4-5-17 3 att1RWFus p98 MR20
JONES,David TCapt kia 12-7-16 10WelshR p127 MR21
JONES,David T2Lt kia 24-7-18 3SWBord att1KSLI p100 CR Belgium40
JONES,David 2Lt kia 18-9-18 3WelchR att11RWFus p127 CR Greece5 att11RF
JONES,David 2Lt kia 8-10-18 10SWBord p100 CR France845
JONES,David John.MC.T2Lt ded 4-12-16 RE 178TC p46 CR France102
JONES,David Raymond Lt kia 17-4-18 RE p210 CR Belgium102
JONES,David William Llewellyn Lt dow 2-7-16 3Lond p245 CR France120,1-7-
JONES,Douglas Grainger 2Lt kia 4-6-15 6 att4Worc p109 MR4
JONES,Douglas Llewellyn TLt kia 22-8-17 6Lincs B'Coy p75 MR30,Capt
JONES,Edward Earle 2Lt dow 1-8-16 4Yorks Y'Coy p220 CR France285
JONES,Edward Pitcairn 2Lt dow 13-5-16 5 att9RB p179 CR France46
JONES,Edward Stanley Lt ded 28-11-18 RAOC p198 CR Wales107
JONES,Edwin 2Lt dow 14-4-18 RGA 1/1NMidlandHB p40 CR Belgium183
JONES,Edwin 2Lt kia 23-8-18 5Mddx att2/16Lond p147 CR France139
JONES,Edwin Evan 2Lt ded 25-9-19 LabCps p266 CR Wales725,Lt
JONES,Edwin Jones TCapt kia 13-6-17 2/6LancF p221 CR France765,James
JONES,Edwin Tudor Capt kia 3-9-16 3 att1RWFus p98 MR21
JONES,Emyr Griffiths.MM.2Lt dow 18-9-18 3 att7SWBord p100 MR37
JONES,Eran Brindle HonCapt ded 10-11-18 19RWFus p263
JONES,Eric 2Lt kia 2-7-16 1/9Lpool p216 CR France174
JONES,Eric Arthur Owen 2Lt kia 18-9-16 16Lond p250 MR21
JONES,Eric Irvine 2Lt kia 22-3-18 2/19Lond p250 CR Palestine3
JONES,Ernest Hugh T2Lt kia 26-10-17 188MGC Inf p183 CR Belgium126
JONES,Ernest Kerrison TCapt kia 3-7-16 8 att9RWFus p98 MR21,2-7-16
JONES,Ernest Rae Capt kia 2-9-14 1Ches p96 CR Belgium216,24-8-14
JONES,Ernest William T2Lt ded 9-11-15 8WelchR p127 CR Europe1
JONES,Evan 2Lt kia 6-11-17 1/6RWFus C'Coy p223 CR Palestine1,Capt
JONES,Evan Brindle Capt ded 10-11-18 B'Coy 19RWFus CR Wales462
JONES,Evan Gwilym T2Lt dow 31-8-18 13WelchR p127 CR France84
JONES,Evan Harries.MC&Bar.2Lt kia 25-4-18 87RFA p31 MR30
JONES,Evan Lawrence TCapt kia 30-9-18 RAMC att2HLI p195 CR France1483
JONES,Evan Lewis T2Lt kia 13-11-16 10NStaffs att76MGC p157&183 CR Frar
JONES,Evelyn Llewellyn Hustler 2Lt kia 26-3-17 12 att1/5RWFus p98 MR34
JONES,F.D. Lt kia 7-7-16 10LancF p92 MR21
JONES,Felix Ernest.MC.Lt kia 16-8-17 4 O&BLI p231 MR30
JONES,Francis George.MID LtCol dow 9-5-15 Cmdg 1RInniskF p105 MR4,5-5
JONES,Francis Leonard Clarence.MC.MM.2Lt kia 1-9-18 2RWFus p98 CR France216
JONES,Francis Maynard Harvey.MC.2Lt dow 18-6-17 6Worc p109
JONES,Frank Riddell T2Lt kia 18-11-16 17HLI p163 CR France534
JONES,Fred 2Lt kia 24-5-15 9Manch p237 CR Gallipoli2
JONES,Frederick James.MM.2Lt kia 26-10-17 21Lond p251 MR20
JONES,Frederick S.C.2Lt kia 30-11-16 1LancF attMGC p92&183 CR France63
JONES,Frederick Thomas Averay 2Lt dow 5-12-17 3/1Hereford p252 CR France145
JONES,Frederick Wigan Lt dow 21-12-16 8RWar p215 CR War10
JONES,Frederick William James.MC.2Lt ded 24-10-18 RFA p261 CR Glouc5
JONES,G.M.Lt 13-12-18 W'land &C'landYeo CR Wales684
JONES,Geoffrey Anthony St.John Lt kia 14-6-16 4Mddx p147 CR France397
JONES,Geoffrey Brian T2Lt kia 18-9-18 SWBord att13WelshR p100 CR France415
JONES,George 2Lt kia 21-5-18 1/5SStaffs p229 CR France109
JONES,George Alfred Prime Capt kldacc 28-5-16 8EKent attRFC p3&57 CR Kent269

JONES,George Frederick.MC.T2LtACapt kia 28-3-18 7KSLI p145 MR20
JONES,George Harold Price Lt kia 30-5-18 7KSLI p145 CR France33
JONES,George James LtTCapt kia 7-4-17 GL RFC p9
JONES,George Morris 2Lt dow 14-7-16 4LNLancs p234 CR Lancs342
JONES,George William T2Lt kia 15/16-5-16 11Ches att6SWBord p96 CR France68
JONES,George William 2Lt dow 12-4-18 12Y&L p159 MR32
JONES,George Worthington.MC.Maj dow 10-11-17 RH&FA p206
JONES,Gerald.MC.Capt kia 2-11-17 7Ess p232 CR Palestine8
JONES,Gertrude Ellen Sister drd 10-4-17 QAIMNS p200 CR France85,Eileen
JONES,Gladys Maud Miss ded 21-8-17 VAD BRCS p200 CR Greece9
JONES,Griffiths Vaughan 2Lt dow PoW 24-4-18 4KSLI p235 CR Germany1,Griffith
JONES,Gwilym T2Lt kia 10-9-18 8Lincs p75 CR France530
JONES,Gwilym Rhys 2Lt kia 10-8-15 6RWFus p223 MR4
JONES,Gwilyn Arthur Tegid 2Lt kia 25-10-17 RGA 41SB p209 CR Belgium13
JONES,Harold 2Lt ded 26-12-17 RDC p253 CR Lancs463
JONES,Harold Edward T2Lt kia 22-11-17 GL &41RFC p9 CR France62
JONES,Harold Garfield 2Lt kia 8-10-18 A286RFA p31 CR France482,A288RFA
JONES,Harold Madoc.MIDx2 TLt kia 31-7-17 17RWFus p98 MR29
JONES,Harold Vivian TLt kia 10-7-16 13RWFus p98 CR France453
JONES,Harry.MID Lt kld 15-5-18 4Lond p246&270,ded CR Hamps1
JONES,Harry Edward 2Lt ded 12-10-17 22RFC p9 CR Surrey1
JONES,Harry Reynolds T2Lt kia 17-3-18 80RFC p16 CR France987
JONES,Henry John Rutherford TCapt ded 26-2-16 RAMC p196 CR Mddx51
JONES,Henry Myrddin.MID T2Lt kia 13-11-16 10RWFus p98 CR France156
JONES,Henry Paul Mainwaring TLt kia 31-7-17 MGC p183 MR29
JONES,Herbert 2Lt dow 4-11-18 5SLancs p230 CR France716
JONES,Herbert Francis T2Lt kia 10-7-16 10WelshR p127 MR21
JONES,Herbert Japson.MC.Capt dow 12-11-18 RH&FA p207
JONES,Herbet Joaquin 2Lt dow PoW 29-3-18 4 att7RIrReg p89 CR France658
JONES,Herbert Thomas 2Lt kia 4-11-18 3 att10SWBord p100 CR France34 &CR Frnce734
JONES,Herbert Wynn Lt dow 24-3-18 WelshHorseYeo attMGC p187&205,Wyman CR France650,25RWFus
JONES,Hilda Lilian Sister ded 28-10-18 QAIMNS p200 CR Devon1,L.H.
JONES,Horace Birchall 2Lt kia 1-7-16 1/6NStaffs p238 MR21
JONES,Horace Edwin 2Lt kia 21-3-18 SStaffs att2/6Bn p122 MR20
JONES,Hubert Victor Edward T2Lt kia 25-10-18 12RIrRif p169 CR Belgium140
JONES,Hugh T2Lt kia 3-9-16 10RWFus p98 MR21
JONES,Hugh T2Lt kia 27-9-16 11SStaffs att7Leic p122 MR20
JONES,Hugh.MC.TCapt ded 10-11-18 13Glouc p107 CR Glouc109
JONES,Hugh Ivor 2Lt ded 22-6-18 B51RFA attRE p31 CR France134
JONES,Hugh Laurie T2Lt ded 29-4-18 RASC attS&TCps p267 MR66,Lt
JONES,Hugh M.TLt kia 30-7-16 19Lpool p72 MR21
JONES,Hywel Herbert Saunders 2Lt kia 4-3-17 3RWSurr p56 CR France511
JONES,Ivor Cynric Salusbury Lt dow 21-9-16 5YLI p235
JONES,Ivor Dryhurst TLt kia 10-4-18 5SWBord D'Coy p100 MR30
JONES,Ivor Wyn 2Lt dow 9-6-17 7RWFus att1/24Lond p223 CR Belgium11,Wynne Lt
JONES,Jaffrey Fryer Selous 2Lt dow 26-8-16 2SpBde RE F'Coy CR France145
JONES,James Andrew.DSO.MC.MajALtCol dow 14-10-18 2DLI att17LancF p161 CR Belgium112
JONES,James Arthur.MID TCapt dow 8-10-18 10SWBord D'Coy p100 CR France845
JONES,James Brinley TLt kia 31-5-17 10WelshR att25LabBn p127 CR Belgium73
JONES,James Forbes.MID Maj dow 29-3-17 7A&SH p243 CR France40
JONES,James Melville Lt kia 27-8-17 RFA p207 MR30
JONES,James Richard Tudor 2Lt kia 23-7-18 3LNLancs p136 CR France524,2Bn
JONES,James Thomas 2Lt dow 24-8-17 20Lond p251 CR Belgium11
JONES,Jesse 2Lt kia 11-11-14 2O&BLI p130 MR29
JONES,John Arllwyd 2Lt kia 20-9-17 WelchR att9Bn p127 MR30
JONES,John Daniel Lt ded 21-2-16 RFA p31 CR France85
JONES,John Harold T2Lt kia 1-10-17 1RWFus p98 MR30
JONES,John Harold Ryle T2Lt kia 4-7-16 7SLancs p125 MR21
JONES,John Humphrey 2Lt kia 8-10-18 SWBord att5RWFus p223 CR France1346,15WelchR
JONES,John Langdale Maj ded 14-5-17 RAMC p196 MR43
JONES,John Lewis T2Lt ded 13-8-17 3WelchR p127 CR Wales278
JONES,John Llewelyn Thomas Capt kia 16-8-17 3Lond D'Coy p245 CR Belgium112
JONES,John Myddleton T2Lt kia 1-7-16 17DLI p161 MR21
JONES,John Owen T2Lt kia 6-6-17 WelshR att 16Bn p127 MR29

JONES,John Sydney 2Lt died 27-8-17 189RFA p208 CR France139
JONES,John Thomas.MC.TCapt ded 28-3-18 RASC HQ DivTrn p193 CR France65
JONES,John Victor 2Lt kia 14-7-16 3Dors att7RWar p124 MR21
JONES,John Wilfred T2Lt kia 16-11-16 20 att9WelshR p127 CR France246,Wilfrid
JONES,John William T2Lt kia 8-8-18 10KSLI attImpCamelCps p145 MR34
JONES,John Ynys Palfrey T2Lt kia 30-8-18 14WelchR p127 CR France217
JONES,Joseph Maurice 2Lt kia 15-2-17 6 att9Worc p109 CR Iraq5
JONES,Joseph Stephen Lt 27-8-20 GL &RE IWT MR38
JONES,Kenneth Champion T2Lt kia 1-7-16 1ELancs p111 MR21
JONES,Kenneth James Devison TLtACapt kia 3-5-17 SStaffs att6Leic p122 MR20
JONES,Kingsmill William.DSO.Capt kia 2-8-18 RAMC attEKent p253 CR Belgium40
JONES,Lilian Kate Nurse ded 6-6-16 VAD p200 CR Mon67
JONES,Lawrence Henry Capt kia 4-10-17 2 att1ESurr p112 CR Belgium12
JONES,Lawrence Bertram 2Lt kia 23-10-16 2Lincs p75 MR21,Laurence
JONES,Leonard 2Lt kia 16-5-15 3 att1RWFus p98 MR22
JONES,Leslie Philips Lt dow 6-6-15 9RBerks att2Hamps p139 CR Gallipoli2,kia
JONES,Leslie Seymour Ross 2Lt kia 7-10-18 3Dev &65RAF p263 CR Belgium371,6-10-18
JONES,Lewis Farewell.MID Maj kia 1-7-16 1/12Lond p248 MR21 &CR France390
JONES,Lewis Jeremy Capt mbk 29-10-14 IA 9BhopalInf p278
JONES,Llewellyn James Capt dow 16-3-16 WIndR att7ESurr p112 CR France80
JONES,Llewellyn Price T2Lt kia 20-9-17 3 att9WelchR p127 MR30
JONES,Loftus Edward Percival TCapt kia 3-8-15 7Yorks p90 CR Belgium166,Perceval
JONES,Louis Gueret Walter Southwell 2Lt dow 20-6-17 1Mon B'Coy p244 CR France178
JONES,Lumley Owen Williames.DSO.TBrigGen ded 14-9-18 Cmdg13Ess Staff p132 CR France84
JONES,Max Greville.MC.Lt kld 12-6-18 1/2NumbF &55RAF p61 CR France1678
JONES,Maurice TLt dow 27-9-18 ELancs att14RWar p111 CR France568
JONES,Merfin Harman Salisbury T2Lt kia 11-8-18 YLI att8Bn p143 MR16,Merfyn Salusbury
JONES,Mervyn Lt 21-11-16 1ScotsGds SR CR France105
JONES,Oliver Saint Michael TLt kia 4-10-17 N&D att9Bn p134 MR30
JONES,Otto Hamilton T2Lt dow 23-11-15 15RIrRif p169 MR17
JONES,Owen Cecil Maj dow 30-12-17 1/7RWFus p223 CR Palestine3
JONES,Owen Gwilym 2Lt kia 26-3-17 7RWFus p223 MR34
JONES,Owen Morris Lt kia 31-10-18 6RWFus p223
JONES,P.H.MC.Capt&QM 23-1-21 Lincs CR Lincs181
JONES,Penry T2Lt kia 20-9-17 1/2 att10Worc p109 MR30
JONES,Percy.DCM.VD.Capt dow 3-11-17 1ARO att13Lancers p278 CR Iraq8
JONES,Percy Barrett Capt kia 28-9-15 3Mddx p147 MR19
JONES,Percy Griffith 2Lt kld 2-7-18 RE &RAF p46
JONES,Philip Allsworth T2Lt dow 27-9-16 21KRRC p150 CR France833
JONES,Raymond John TLt kia 10-7-16 RAMC att129FA p196 CR France513
JONES,R.Colville 2Lt kld 4-11-18 13RB &RAF p179
JONES,Reginald George Capt kia 30-8-18 2/20Lond C'Coy p251 CR France617
JONES,Reginald George T2Lt kia 20-10-18 10WYorks p82 CR France658
JONES,Reginald Rees.DSO 2Lt dow 25-8-17 1WelshGds p53 CR Belgium18
JONES,Rhys Harris TLt kia 8-10-18 1/2 att6SWBord p100 CR France845
JONES,Richard T2Lt kia 21-10-16 2SLancs p125 MR21
JONES,Richard Alum T2Lt kia 20-11-17 D'TankCps p188 CR France1483
JONES,Richard Archibald TMaj kia 21-5-16 15RWar p65 CR France1182
JONES,Richard Basil Brandram.VC.TLt kia 21-5-16 8LNLancs p136 MR20
JONES,Richard Harold 2Lt kia 14-1-17 6LancF att1Lond p221 CR France1887
JONES,Robert Arthur Capt kia 10-9-14 122/28RFA p31 MR15,26-8-14
JONES,Robert Carl Molsch 2Lt dow 13-11-16 3 att5SWBord p100 CR France74,Moesch
JONES,Robert Henry T2Lt kia 29-9-16 13 att18WYorks p82 CR France134
JONES,Robert Nelson Lt kia 31-7-17 4Nhampt attMGC p187&234 MR29
JONES,Robert Roland Aknll 2Lt kia 9-4-17 4YLI p235
JONES,Rowland T2Lt dow 13-10-18 1/2 att9WRid p115 CR France398
JONES,Russell Shedden 2Lt kia 3-9-16 6 att3Worc p109 CR France246
JONES,Russell Hafrenydd 2Lt kia 10-8-15 7RWFus p223 MR4
JONES,Samuel Victor Charles Lt dow 23-9-16 3 att6RDubF p177 CR Greece3
JONES,Sidney Herbert 2Lt kia 28-7-18 4GordH p242 CR France1689
JONES,Simon James TLt dow 5-6-18 8SLancs p125 CR France622,2Bn
JONES,Stanley Capt kia 16-5-15 1RWFus p98 CR France279
JONES,Stanley T2Lt dow 25-2-17 14RWFus p98 CR Belgium23
JONES,Stanley Cottmore 2Lt kia 3-9-16 RE 2/1FC p210 MR21,Cotmore

JONES,Stanley Fox Gore T2Lt kia 7-6-17 Wilts p153
JONES,Stuart Kirby Lt dow 17-9-14 RAVC att25RFAp198 CR France473,18-9-14
JONES,Sydney Douglas Selborne 2Lt kia 2-9-16 26RFA p31 CR France397
JONES,Sydney Everard T2Lt kia 8-8-15 8WelshR p127 MR4
JONES,Sydney James TLt kia 15-9-16 11RWKent p141 MR21
JONES,T.H.Maj 18-3-16 QueensBays CR Kent27
JONES,Tom Bright Capt kld 11-4-18 GL &RAF p190 CR France95
JONES,Thomas 2Lt kia 31-7-17 161RH&FA p31 CR Belgium24
JONES,Thomas Alex Evansen T2Lt kia 7-8-15 11Manch p155
JONES,Thomas Capel Lt kia 26-10-17 3Lond p245 MR30
JONES,Thomas Edward Painton Capt kia 15-9-16 1/6Lond p246 MR21
JONES,Thomas Esmor Lt kia 6-4-18 4RWFus p223 MR27
JONES,Thomas Glasfryn Chap4Cl dow 12-4-17 RAChDept att11SWBord p199 CR Wales238
JONES,Thomas Idwal.MM.Lt kia 31-8-18 18Lond p250 CR France785
JONES,Thomas John.MC.TLtACapt dow 22-4-18 A122RFA p31 CR Belgium11
JONES,Thomas Lewis.MC.Lt dow 10-10-18 1/8Worc p226 CR France446,9-10-18
JONES,Thomas Lloyd Rees Lt 29-9-19 SWBord CR Wales306
JONES,Thomas Luke.MC.T2Lt dow 9-10-18 RASC attRGA 27SB p193 CR France214
JONES,Thomas Mozart 2Lt ded 6-7-18 RGA 262SB p40 CR Wales177,26SB
JONES,Thomas Stephen 2Lt kia 26-9-17 1/2 att10RWFus p98 MR30
JONES,Thomas William TLt kia 11-3-17 RAMC att27NumbF p196 CR France1182
JONES,Thomas William Allen 2Lt kia 31-7-17 4Ches p222 CR Belgium96
JONES,Thomas William Hathway.OBE.Maj 7-4-19 IARO CR EAfrica54 Ex 94Inf
JONES,Titho Glynne Lt kia 20-4-17 1/7RWFus p223 CR Palestine8
JONES,T.L.R.Lt ded 29-9-19 SWBord p263
JONES,Tom Wason T2Lt kia 8-10-18 SWBord att15WelshR p100 CR France1346
JONES,Trevor Benjamin TLt kia 18-9-18 16WelshR p127 CR Greece5,6Bn
JONES,Vavasor 2Lt kia 19-5-15 7RWFus p223 CR France427
JONES,Victor Trevor T2Lt kia 18-9-18 WelshR att17Bn p127 MR16 17 att14Bn
JONES,Wallace.MC&Bar.LtAMaj dow 15-10-18 C174RFA p31 CR France760
JONES,Walter George Cotterell T2Lt kld 17-3-18 RFC p16 CR Hunts104
JONES,Walter Joseph TLt dow 15-10-17 7Norf p74 CR France113
JONES,Walter Truran T2Lt kia 12-10-16 17Manch p155 MR21
JONES,Watkin Morgan Lt kia 29-3-18 RE 258TC p46 MR27
JONES,W.H.A.Capt 17-11-17 RWFus CR Surrey152
JONES,Wilfrid Griffith Lt kia 6-4-18 7RWFus p223 CR France232
JONES,William Bartholomew 2Lt kia 27-5-18 134MGC p183 MR18
JONES,William Edgar Lt kia 10-4-18 10RWar p65 MR30
JONES,William Edgar Chap4Cl dow 24-10-18 RAChDept att9Yorks p199 CR France234,kia 8-10-18 att2RWFus :-
JONES,William Henry 2Lt kia 27-5-18 1 att4Yorks p90 MR18 [&CR France528,24-10-18 att9Yorks
JONES,William Hugh 2Lt kia 21-6-17 7RWFus p223 CR Belgium23,16Bn
JONES,William James Lt kia 28-6-16 6Lpool p215 CR France506
JONES,William Orlando Maj kia 26-8-17 10SWBord p100 CR Belgium23,Capt
JONES,William Saville Lt kia 27-5-18 4NumbF p213 MR18
JONES-BATEMAN,Francis Capt kia 4-11-18 13RWFus p98 CR France521
JONES-BATEMAN,Llewelyn Capt dow 19-3-17 A103RFA p31 CR France88
JONES-BATEMAN,Lloyd Newton.CMG.LtCol ded 25-7-17 1Norf p74 MR65
JONES-MANLEY,David Henry George Capt kia 6-11-17 6RWFus p223
JONES-NOWLAN,Thomas Chamney 2Lt dow 27-5-17 3 att1RDubF p177 CR France113
JONES-PARRY,Ivor Norman Lt dow 12-5-17 RGA 171SB p209 CR France614
JONES-PARRY,John Jeffreys Bulkeley TMaj kia 30-7-15 6DCLI p114 CR Belgium35
JONES-ROBERTS,Peter Chap4Cl 23-6-21 CR Wales491
JONES-SAVIN,John Savin T2Lt kia 27-3-17 ACycCps att11RWFus p98 CR Greece6
JONES-VAUGHAN,Evan Nanney Capt kia 26-10-14 2RWFus C'Coy p98 CR France82
JONES-VAUGHAN,Hugh Thomas Charles Maj ded 20-11-18 RB p179 CR Asia60
JORDAN,Edward 2Lt kia 9-4-18 7ESurr p112 MR32
JORDAN,Francis Hugh Dormer 2Lt ded 23-7-18 RGA p262 CR Scot241
JORDAN,Hugh Stewart Latimer 2Lt kld 20-8-17 RFA attRFC p9&31 CRMddx37
JORDAN,James.MC.Lt kia 8-8-15 5DragGds p21 CR France526
JORDAN,John Edward 2Lt ded 9-2-16 1/7Worc p226 CR France3,10-2-16
JORDAN,Leslie Tiel.MID Lt kia 6-6-16 RE 2/1FC p210 CR France281
JORDAN,Louisa Sister ded 6-3-15 ScotWomensHosp CR Europe57
JORDAN,R.A.A.Y.Maj 14-6-20 KSLI CR Somerset31
JORDAN,William T2Lt kia 8-11-16 GL &45RFC p3&190 CR France134,Willie
JORDON,John Lt dow 19-6-15 9 att2SWBord p100 CR Gallipoli1,JORDAN

JORDON,Leonard Owen.MC.Capt kia 4-11-18 Hereford p252 CR France1087,JORDAN
JORDON,Percy Thomas Lt kia 21-8-15 3 att15RInniskF p105 MR4,att1Bn
JORDON,Victor Harry Capt kia 7-10-16 7Lond p247 MR21
JOSCELYNE,Arthur Kennett T2Lt dow 26-6-17 RBerks att5Bn p139 CR France1182
JOSCELYNE,Clement Percy 2Lt dow 10-10-17 3 att11Suff p78 CR Belgium16
JOSCELYNE,Frank Henry Tremlett TLtACapt kia 19-11-16 8SomLI p80 CR France339
JOSCELYNE,Lawrence Arthur.MC.T2Lt dow 1-10-17 7SomLI p80 CR Belgium11
JOSELAND,Arthur Noel Lt kia 22-9-17 4ESurr attNigR p112&201 CR EAfrica22 &CR Tanzania1
JOSELAND,Frederick Osborn 2Lt kia 10-9-16 12Lond p248 MR21
JOSEPH,Alan Edward TLt dow 10-5-17 14RWar p65 CR France8
JOSEPH,Cyril John Gadalja 2Lt ded 13-10-14 21Lond p251&270 CR Mddx40,Gedaliah
JOSEPH,Horace 2Lt kia 20-7-16 Dev p77
JOSEPH,Jack Benjamin T2Lt kia 8-1-17 RE 185TC p46 CR France53
JOSEPH,John Herbert TCapt kia 1-8-17 17Lpool p72 CR Belgium116
JOSEPH,John Rhys 2Lt ded 23-4-17 GL RFC p9 CR Scot235,Lt
JOSEPH,Stewart Hugh LtAMaj dow 18-8-17 RE 227FC p46 CR Belgium124
JOSEPH,Wilfred Gordon Aron T2Lt kia 19-4-17 1Nhampt att 1/5Norf p137 CR Palestine8
JOSEPH,William Franklin George T2Lt kia 27-5-18 6 att2RBerks p139 MR18,att7Bn
JOSEPHI,Ernest Henry TLt ded 23-1-17 8RASC p193 MR21 CRMddx40
JOSEPHS,Joseph 2Lt kia 1-7-16 12Lond p248 CR France798
JOSLIN,Francis John Maj kia 18-4-15 RWKent p141 MR29
JOTCHAM,Fred T2Lt dow 27-9-18 RE 4SpCo p46 CR France298
JOTCHAM,Walter Morse 2Lt kia 19-8-17 1/8Worc p109 CR Belgium96
JOTHAM,Eustace.VC.Capt kia 7-1-15 IA 51Sikhs attNWaziristanMil p278 MR43
JOURDAIN,Charles Edward Arthur.DSO.LtCol kia 29-7-18 2LNLancs p136&25? CR France524
JOURDAIN,Ernest Nevill Capt kia 16-2-15 1Suff p78 MR29
JOWERS,Joseph Frank Lt kia 24-3-18 5 att6SomLI p218 MR27
JOWETT,Alan 2Lt kia 29-6-17 2/10Lpool p216 CR France705
JOWETT,Eric Craven Lt dow 9-7-16 GL &RFC p3&190 CR France514 Ex 12NumbF
JOWETT,Harold Crossley 2Lt kia 1-9-18 7LancF p221 CR France307
JOWETT,John Sutcliffe ACapt dow 22-9-18 4 att1/5Manch p155 CR France13
JOWETT,Sydney Ferguson 2Lt kia 27-5-18 12 att5Yorks p90 MR18
JOWETT,William Hall T2Lt dow 28-6-16 20Lpool p72 CR France67
JOWITT,Arthur Lt kia 25-4-15 1RWar p65 MR29
JOWITT,Thomas Lawrence Maj dow 17-7-15 5HLI p240 CR Greece10
JOY,Edward Sydney T2Lt kia 19-8-16 8RBerks A'Coy p139 CR France432
JOY,Frederick Charles Patrick 2Lt kia 16-6-15 3 att2RIrRif p169 MR29
JOY,George Bruce Lt dow 21-5-15 3WelchR att1HLI p127 MR22
JOY,Gwyn.MC.2Lt dow 16-7-17 2/10Lond p248 CR France145,
JOY,Thomas Cyril Bruce LtTCapt kia 11-2-15 2Dev att2Dors p77 CR Iraq1,1Bn
JOYCE,Alexander Hugh Sinclair.MM.T2Lt dow 20-8-18 12Norf p74 CR France1
JOYCE,Eric Gordon 2Lt kia 31-10-16 4Suff A'Coy p217 CR France294,30-10-16
JOYCE,Frank Bernard.MC.TCapt kia 21-4-18 10N&D p134 CR France252
JOYCE,Frank Postlethwaite TLt kia 29-5-17 7BordR p117 CR France604
JOYCE,Frederick George Lt kia 29-9-17 3 att2SWBord p100 CR Belgium106
JOYCE,George Edgar TLt kia 20-9-16 10 att7Leic p87 MR21
JOYCE,James T2Lt kia 22-8-15 9LancF p92 MR4
JOYCE,Norman Roy Lt kld 1-4-18 GL &23RAF p190 MR20
JOYCE,Philip Solomon Lt mbk 6-3-17 60RFC p256 MR20
JOYCE,Walter Herbert 2Lt kia 22-3-18 8Lond p247 MR27
JOYCE,William Alfred T2Lt kia 28-3-18 4MGC p183 MR20
JOYNSON,Leonard Charles Billingsley Lt kld 6-5-15 1/6SStaffs p229 CR Belgium170
JUBB,James Critchley 2Lt kia 23-7-16 1/4YLI p235 MR21
JUCKES,George Francis 2Lt kia 6-7-15 6 att1RB p179 CR Belgium85
JUCKES,Thomas Roland Lt kia 9-5-15 3 att2RSuss p119 MR22
JUDD,Alan Cecil.MC.Rev kia 21-3-18 RAChDept att2/5N&D p199 MR20
JUDD,Frank King T2Lt kia 30-11-17 5RBerks p139 MR17
JUDD,Frederick George Kerridge T2Lt kia 24-5-15 2RDubF p177 MR29
JUDD,Morris Stanley T2Lt acckld 18-8-17 RWKent att7Bn p141 CR France134
JUDD,William Bush TMaj ded 2-2-18 RASC 15DivTrain p193&257 CR Hamps221

JUDE,Leo Gerald Simon TLt.ACapt kia 15-11-16 10LNLancs p136 CR France534
JUDGE,Charles Harland Lt dow 17-5-15 4EYorks p219 CR France1
JUDGE,Leopold James T2Lt kia 3-5-17 GL 7Leic att110TMB p190 MR20
JUDGE,Wilfred Justice 2Lt dow 21-8-16 5 att1RFus p68 CR France66
JUDGE,William Spencer 2Lt dow 26-7-16 A105RFA p31 CR France145
JUKES,Andrew Monro Capt ded 18-10-18 IMS p278 CR Egypt15
JUKES,Arthur Starr 2Lt ded 6-3-17 10Lond p248 CR Egypt15
JUKES,Frederick T2Lt kia 20-9-17 9WelchR p127 MR30
JUKES,Michael Egerton Ewart TLt kld 4-9-15 14Manch p155 CR Staffs125
JULER,George Critchett Lt kia 31-8-14 5Lancers p22 MR15
JULIAN,Ernest Lawrence TLt dow 8-8-15 7RDubF p177 MR4
JULIUS,Cecil Herbert 2Lt kia 9-4-16 3 att6ELancs p111 MR38
JULL,Leslie Hubert Lt kld 3-1-18 NStaffs &RFC p16&157 CR Kent243
JUMP,John Herbert.MC.Lt kia 15-9-17 4LNLancs p234 CR France275
JUNG,Henry Adolph 2Lt ded 9-5-15 3 att1NumbF p61
JUNIPER,John Harvey 2Lt kia 30-4-17 7RFus p68 MR20
JUPE,Charles Eric ACapt kia 26-10-17 8Dev p77 MR30
JURGENS,Sydney George TLt dow 17-8-15 6RLancs p59 CR Egypt3
JURGENSON,Emil Theodore Lt kia 4-5-18 GL att1KAR p268 MR52
JURY,George Risehieth 2Lt kia 14-9-16 7Lond p247 MR21
JURY,Reginald 2Lt dow 6-10-17 4WRid p227 CR France1360
JUSTICE,George Hercules ACapt dow 31-7-17 7RInniskF att7NLancs p105 CR Belgium111,kia

K

KAHN,Edgar 2Lt kia 5-5-15 1Leinst p174 MR29
KANE,Augustine George 2Lt mbk 24-6-18 8SWBord attRAF p99&100,kia CR Greece6 3Bn
KANE,Frederick Paul 2Lt kia 1-11-16 GL &29RFC p3&190 CR France95
KANE,James Gabriel T2Lt kia 22-10-18 8 att10SWBord p100 CR France190
KANE,John Francis Aloysius Capt kld 22-3-15 Dev &RFC p1&77 CR Lond9
KANE,Robert Romney Godred.DSO.CaptALtCol dow 1-10-18 1RMunstF p175 CR France1184
KANE-SMITH,James.MC.Lt kia 27-5-18 110RFA p31 MR18
KANN,Edward Henry TLt kia 21-10-17 102RFC p9 CR Belgium383
KANN,Raymond Victor Lt RScotsF &RAF CR Lond12
KARNEY,David Noel T2Lt.ACapt kia 21-3-18 11 att2RDubF p177 MR27
KARRAN,John Bowler T2Lt kia 1-7-16 9 att2SWBord p100 CR France1490
KARSLAKE,Harry Howard T2Lt kia 23-4-17 Dev att1DCLI p77 MR20
KARSLAKE,William Reginald Lt ded 29-12-17 PembrokeYeo p270 CR Devon53
KATINAKIS,Francis Beresford.MC.Lt dow 27-3-18 3DragGds p21 CR France1422
KATON,Arthur Robert.DCM.Capt 6-9-15 8SStaffs CR Staffs109
KATZ,Sampson Goldston TLt ded 19-7-18 8RLancs p262 CR Mddx40,Goldstone
KAUFFMAN,Albert Edward T2Lt ded 17-10-18 RASC p193 CR Palestine11
KAUNTZE,Cedric Ernest Wheldon Lt kia 1-10-15 3Worc p109 CR Belgium112
KAVANAGH,Bernard Chap4Cl dow 21-12-17 RAChDept p199 CR Palestine3
KAVANAGH,Edward 2Lt kia 30-7-16 18Manch p155 MR21
KAVANAGH,John William 2Lt ded 11-3-18 RFC p16 CR Kent28,FltLt 10-3-18
KAVANAGH,Thomas Osborne Joseph Lt kia 24-8-18 3 att1RIrFus p171 CR France855
KAY,Albert T2Lt kia 1-8-17 26RFus p68 CR Belgium88
KAY,Charles William Lt ded 3-11-18 4 att2LNLancs p234 CR France34
KAY,Collin Lowther 2Lt dow 12-10-16 12MGC Inf p183 MR21
KAY,Geoffrey Clarkson AMaj kia 29-3-18 5LancF attMGC p187&221 CR France644
KAY,George Alexander T2Lt kia 9-8-15 N&D p134 MR29
KAY,George Frederick 2Lt ded 16-9-19 LabCps p264 CR Scot241 Ex BordR
KAY,George Philip.MC.2Lt ded 21-10-18 172RFA p31 CR Egypt7
KAY,George Pollard 2Lt dow 29-6-17 46RFC p9 CR France354
KAY,Henry Norman Lt kia 21-8-18 7Manch p237 CR France514
KAY,John T2Lt kia 30-9-18 10 att1LNLancs p136 CR France516
KAY,John Alexander ACapt kia 9-10-17 6LancF p221 MR30
KAY,John Calvert 2Lt kia 15-7-16 11LancF p92 MR21
KAY,Lawrence Herbert T2Lt kia 18-11-15 12 att9RWar p65 CR Gallipoli4
KAY,Maurice Alfred 2Lt kia 30-4-17 GL &56RFC p9 MR20
KAY,Melville Herbert 2Lt kia 5-11-16 8DLI p239 CR France385
KAY,Noel Rawstone Wilkinson Lt dow 5-7-18 15RHA L'Bty p31 CR France102,Rawstorre
KAY,Robert Roland 2Lt kia 23-3-18 5DLI p239 MR20
KAY,Stanley Burnett Capt ded 28-1-18 7Yorks &RFC p16&90 CR Yorks361
KAY,Walter Haddow T2Lt kia 23-3-18 att6GordH p166 CR France757
KAY,William Lt dow 21-3-18 8LancF attMGC p187&221 MR27
KAY,William Algernon Ireland.Bart.CMG.DSO.MIDx6 BrigGen kia 4-10-18 KRRC Cmdg3InfBde p150 CR France725
KAY,William Henry.MC.Chap4Cl kia 5-4-18 RAChDept att5Dors p199 CR France223
KAY,William Joseph O'Neill Beaumont T2Lt ded 19-11-18 2BlkW p129 CR Lebanon1
KAY-ROBINSON,Hugh Thomas.DSO&2Bars.LtCol 26-4-18 12 att13RSuss MR30
KAY-SHUTTLEWORTH,Edward James.Hon.TCapt kld 10-7-17 GL 7RB 218InfBde p190 CR C'land &W'land86
KAY-SHUTTLEWORTH,Lawrence Ughtred.Hon.ACapt kia 30-3-17 D11RFA p31 CR France81
KAYE,Eric Priestley 2Lt kia 3-5-17 7WRid p228 MR20
KAYE,Frank Leon T2Lt dow 11-4-17 5 att9RFus p68 CR France113
KAYE,Frederick William Capt 8-1-19 IndOrdDept CR India97A
KAYE-BUTTERWORTH,George Saintow TLt kia 4-8-16 13DLI p161
KEABLE,Harold Charles Linford T2Lt kia 25-9-15 8RBerks p139 CR France552
KEAN,Francis John TLt dow 25-11-18 RASC p193 CR Lond9,ded
KEAN,James Rankin 2Lt dow 1-10-18 1/4RScotF p222 CR France34
KEAN,John Herdman Capt kia 1-12-17 1/5RLancs p213 MR17
KEANE,Albert Graham 2Lt dow 8-5-17 7 att2ScotRif p224 CR France1468
KEANE,Edward Dawson TCapt ded 31-10-18 RAMC att689MT Coy ASC p196 CR Europe58
KEANE,William May Augustine 2Lt kia 4-11-16 3 att8RIrF p171 CR Belgium17,Mary
KEARLEY,Harold 2Lt kia 3-2-18 15Lond attRFC p18&249 CR Belgium18
KEARNEY,Arthur Joseph Lt kia 9-9-16 att1RMunstF p175 MR21
KEARNEY,I.M.Sister ded 25-12-16 QAIMNS forIndia p278 CR Iraq6,26-9-16
KEARNS,Arthur Clark Rose Lt ded 7-6-16 1Glouc attWorc p107 CR France85,Clarkson
KEARNS,Reginald Arthur Ernest Holmes.CMG.LtCol ded 24-11-18 RASC p253 CR Surrey93
KEARNS,Thomas Joseph.CB.CMG.MIDx3 Col 30-6-20 RASC CR Kent24
KEARSLEY,John Stewart Lt kia 22-11-15 O&BLI p130 MR38,Steuart
KEARTON,Frank T2Lt kia 21-11-17 11KRRC p150 MR17
KEARTON,James Linton Graham Lt dow 3-12-17 1WelshGds p53 CR France398
KEAST,William Reginald 2Lt kia 21-8-17 66RFC SR p9 MR20
KEATES,Richard John.MC.2Lt.ACapt kia 20-8-18 RGA 23BdeHQ p40 CR France177
KEATING,David Timothy TLt dow 21-4-18 1/4Y&L p159 CR Belgium38
KEATING,George 2Lt kia 17-2-15 2Ches p96 CR Belgium131
KEATING,George Henry Lt kia 18-9-18 2/1Camb p244 CR France369
KEATING,Harold Francis Amboor kia 28-6-18 RE 210FC p46 CR France19
KEATING,Henry Sheehy Lt kld 20-1-15 IrGds p52 CR France727
KEATING,John Lt kld 17-2-15 2Ches p96 CR Belgium131
KEATING,John Baker T2Lt kia 20-7-16 15 att7N&D p134 MR20
KEATING,Robert Pears Capt kia 18-7-17 1/8Lpool p215 CR Belgium10 Richard
KEATING,Thomas Joseph TLt.ACapt kia 14-6-18 RFA att63RAF p31 CR Iraq8
KEATING,William Britten.MC.TCapt ded 11-10-18 9SfthH p165 CR Belgium11
KEATINGE,Eustace Gabriel Lawrence Lt kia 13-4-18 NumbF p61 CR Belgium307
KEATS,Frederick Thorold TLt kia 25-5-16 8Suff p78 CR France513
KEAY,C.H.Capt 9-5-21 RAMC CR Cornwall1
KEAY,James Gordon Lt dow 2-7-16 2/5RWar p214 CR France345
KEAY,Robert Naismith 2Lt dow 30-11-16 6BlkW p231 CR France102
KEAY,Wilfrid Farrar TLt&Adjt kia 16-9-16 9YLI p143 MR21
KEBBLEWHITE,Fred Edgar 2Lt kia 14-8-17 8N&D attRFC p18&233 CR France285
KEBLE,Eustace Charles 2Lt kia 21-3-18 att1NStaffs p157 MR27
KEDGLEY,Alfred Edmund.MM.2Lt kia 17-10-18 C83RFA p31 CR France1392
KEDIE,William Thomas Capt kia 21-8-15 1BlkW p129 MR22
KEE,William.MC.ACapt dow PoW 24-3-18 7 att1RDubF p177 MR27
KEE,William John TCapt ded 20-12-18 RAVC attRHA14ArmyBdeHQ p198 CR Canada1028
KEEBLE,Alfred Ernest TCapt dow 5-8-18 6MGC Inf p183 CR Belgium11
KEEBLE,Arthur Theodore T2Lt dow 28-6-17 RE 8SigCo p46 CR Belgium11
KEEBLE,John Harold T2Lt kld 27-10-17 GL &RFC p9 CR Suff121
KEEFE,Cecil Henderson TCapt kld 5-2-18 RFC p16 CR Norf207,FltCmdr
KEEFE,Ronald Conray Murray.MC.TCapt kia 27-3-18 19Manch p155&258 MR27 Raymond Conrad
KEELE,Charles Acland TCapt kia 12-7-16 14RB p179 CR Belgium5,12Bn

KEELER,Oscar Alan.MC.2Lt kia 20-9-17 7Lond att 17KRRC p247 MR29
KEELEY-AYRES,H.Maj&QM 26-6-20 GL CR Iraq8
KEELIHER,William John 2Lt kia 25-7-18 1BordR p117 CR France40
KEELING,Bertram Francis Eardley.OBE.MC.Lt 20-9-19 RE CR Egypt9
KEELING,Charles Henry 2Lt ded 28-10-18 A15RFA H'Bty15Bde p31 CR France40
KEELING,G.B Lt ded 19-3-16 RIM MR64
KEELL,Herbert Alfred 2Lt kia 9-10-17 3 att2Ess p132 MR30
KEEN,Arthur Clive Capt kia 10-5-17 1/7Mddx p235 CR France531
KEEN,Aubrey Owen TLt dow 4-8-18 11RScots p54 CR France134
KEEN,Edward William 2Lt ded 5-7-18 IARO att1/6GurkhaRif p278 CR Iraq1
KEEN,James Raglan Lt dow 19-10-17 5RSuss p228 CR Belgium20,8Bn
KEEN,Stephen Whitworth.MC.Lt dow 21-8-18 2Lond &RAF p245&258
KEEN,William Allan Capt dow 6-9-18 7Mddx p235 CR France833
KEENAN,John TCapt ded 26-3-17 11RDubF p177 CR Ireland12
KEENE,Alfred.CMG.DSO.BtCol ded 21-4-18 RGA p255
KEENE,Hector Conway Lt 11-7-18 2/112Inf MR43
KEENE,John Pearce 2Lt kia 24-11-15 IARO att2/7GurkhaRif p278 MR38,22/24-11-15
KEENLYSIDE,Cecil Alexander Headlam Capt kia 20-7-15 1Camb p244 CR France922
KEENLYSIDE,Guy Francis Headlam Capt dow 29-10-14 1RWKent p141 CR France102
KEENLYSIDE,Thomas Edward Lt dow 21-4-18 18NumbF p61 CR Belgium38
KEEP,Douglas Scrivener Howard.MC.TCapt kia 14-7-17 7Beds p86 CR Belgium15
KEEP,Douglas William T2Lt kia 16-10-18 9ESurr p113 CR France206
KEEP,John Drummond 2Lt kia 13-10-18 5Lond p246 CR France273
KEEP,Walter Fischer T2Lt kia 7-6-17 15Hamps p121 CR Belgium154
KEEPFER,William Robert Cyril 2Lt kia 4-11-16 3 att2RWFus p98 CR France230 Ex 3DragGds
KEEPING,Claude Jeffery Capt kia 24-8-18 8Mddx p236 CR France927
KEESEY,George Ernest Howard TCapt kia 24-8-16 8RB p179 CR France1890
KEEVIL,Cecil Horace Case TCapt kld 13-6-17 18WYorks &RFC p9&82 CR Lond12
KEHOE,William Charles 2Lt dow 24-4-17 70RFA p31 CR France1182
KEIGHLEY,Linden Raynes 2Lt dow 3-12-17 4RLancs p213 CR France446,Rayner
KEIGHLEY,Richard Ernest Clayton Capt kia 1-8-17 RGA 1SB p209 CR Belgium34
KEIGHLEY,William Munkley TLt kia 1-7-16 10WYorks p82 CR France373
KEIGHTLEY,Philip Charles Russell Lt ded 2-3-19 RGA 262SB p255 CR Ireland56,Capt
KEIGWIN,Henry David 2Lt kia 20-9-16 3 att19LancF p92 CR France296
KEIL,Alexander Peter McLennan EngLt ded 11-10-16 RIM p278 CR Iraq5
KEILLER,George William Capt ded 9-3-19 RE RlySubComm p46 CR Germany1,Weston
KEIR,Edward Hugh T2Lt kia 28-10-17 GL 3Lancs att16RFC p9 CR France95,Lt
KEITH,Alexander Gill TCapt kia 26-11-15 11 att1GordH p166 CR Belgium21,27-11-15
KEITH,Alexander Graham T2Lt ded 18-12-18 HLI p265 CR Scot245,Lt
KEITH,Alexander James T2Lt kia 14-7-16 12Mddx p147 MR21
KEITH,Douglas Hay T2Lt kia 31-8-17 18HLI att18DLI p163 CR France268,17Bn
KEITH,George Elphinstone TCapt ded 6-12-18 RAMC p196 CR Italy16
KEITH,Malcolm T2Lt kia 26-9-17 8EYorks p84 CR Belgium16
KEITH,Noel Lt kia 22-5-17 8Lpool p215 CR France922
KEITH,Patrick Hay Lt kia 15-6-15 6ScotRif p224&225,8Bn MR22
KEITH-BRUMBY,Harry Catherall 2Lt ded 31-10-16 13DLI IARO att98Inf p161&278 CR EAfrica12 &CR Tanzania1,Lt
KEITH-MURRAY,Alastair William 2Lt kia 8/9-5-17 3BlkW p129 MR37,8-5-17
KEKEWICH,Arthur St.John Mackintosh.MID Capt kia 25-9-15 8Dev p77 MR19
KEKEWICH,George Capt dow 28-10-17 1Lond p204&245 CR Palestine1
KEKEWICH,Hanbury Lewis Maj kia 6-11-17 SussYeo p205 CR Palestine1,Capt
KEKEWICH,John Capt kia 25-9-15 8EKent p57 MR19
KEKEWICH,Robert George.CB.MajGen 5-11-14 EKent CR Devon185
KELK,Arthur Frederick Hastings,MC T2Lt kia 9-3-17 14WelshR p127 CR Belgium23
KELL,Douglas Fearn 2Lt dow 24-4-17 1/7GordH p242 CR France95
KELL,Waldegrave Frank Sydney 2Lt dow 23-7-17 10 att1/5Suff p78 CR Palestine2
KELLACHER,Sydney Arthur.MC.Lt dow 4-8-17 34RFA p31 CR France13
KELLAS,Arthur Capt kia 6-8-15 RAMC 89FA p253 CR Gallipoli1,Maj
KELLEHER,Bartholomew TLt kia 27-9-18 RASC att8Lancs p193 CR France357
KELLER,Francis Frederick Lt dow 22-5-17 2/6Lond p246 MR20
KELLER,Roderick Leopold.MC.2Lt kld 15-8-18 RWar attRAF p65 CR Herts10,Capt
KELLETT,Richard Henry Villiers 2Lt kld 21-8-16 B74RH&FA p31 CR France203,Lt dow

KELLETT,William T2Lt kia 22-1-17 8SomLI att10RFC p9&80 CR France98
KELLIE,Esmond Lawrence 2Lt kia 19-4-15 Beds p86 MR29
KELLIE,John.MID Rev kia 1-8-17 RAChDept att6CamH p199 MR29
KELLIE,Kenneth Harrison Alloa TCapt kia 25-6-16 RAMC 104FA p196 CR France430
KELLIE,Leslie Lawrence 2Lt kia 1-2-17 102RFA p31 CR Belgium72
KELLIE,William Reid 2Lt kia 18-6-18 10Lpool p216 CR France279
KELLOCK,Harold Plumer Lt dow 6-10-18 NIrHorse att13/17RFA p24 CR Franc
KELLY,Alfred George Lt ded 18-3-20 RASC CR Lond3
KELLY,Brian Edmund T2Lt kia 2-12-17 2Y&L p159 MR17
KELLY,Charles Leonard 2Lt kia 20-9-18 LNLancs &204RAF p264 MR20 &CR Belgium452
KELLY,Charles Patrick TLt kia 2-7-16 RAMC 96FA p196 CR France141
KELLY,Edward Denis Festus Capt kia 30-10-14 1LifeGds p20 MR29
KELLY,Edward Rowley 2Lt kia 7-7-15 3BordR attLancF p117 MR29
KELLY,George Henry Fitzmaurice LtCol kia 23-11-14 IA Cmdg34SikhPnrs p278 CR France571
KELLY,Harry Holdsworth Capt kia 24-10-14 RE 38FC p46 CR France82
KELLY,Henry John T2Lt kia 20-9-17 KRRC att21Bn p150 MR30
KELLY,Henry Newton Maj kia 25-9-15 IA 33Punjabis p278 CR France705
KELLY,James Sheil 2Lt dow 29-3-18 2/8LancF p221 CR France145
KELLY,John James T2Lt dow 12-4-17 7Leinst p174 CR France557,Capt kia 2Br
KELLY,John Lawson.MC.Lt kia 4-11-18 RE 407FC p210 CR France1272
KELLY,Joseph Cresswell Lt ded 28-9-17 IARO att4/3GurkhaRif p278 MR43
KELLY,Joseph Francis Mary LtCol ded 22-8-16 RAMC p196 CR Wilts129
KELLY,Kenneth George Lt kia 27-5-18 MGC Inf p183 CR France1753
KELLY,Oscar Raphael T2Lt kld 2-5-17 GL NumbF &53RFC p9 CR Belgium152
KELLY,Percy Ewart 2Lt kia 27-4-15 8Mddx p236 MR29
KELLY,Percy Patrick T2Lt kia 1-7-16 10ESurr A'Coy p113 CR France513,8Bn
KELLY,Philip Edward TLtCol kia 10-10-18 1 att9RIrFus p89&265 CR Belgium
KELLY,Robert Houston Lt kia 1-1-18 6A&SH att1KAR p243&268 CR EAfrica7
KELLY,Robert Maitland Lt kia 11-1-17 RNDevYeo att5Dors p203 MR21
KELLY,Terence O'Neil William 2Lt dow 2-5-15 4GordH p242 CR France40
KELLY,Thomas.MC.TMaj kia 26-6-17 11RWSurr p56 CR Belgium111
KELLY,Thomas Aloysius.MC.Capt kia 2-10-16 24Lond p252 CR France453
KELLY,Thomas Cameron T2Lt kia 27-3-16 19HLI p163 CR France515,16Bn
KELLY,Thomas Joseph Lt kia 7-11-17 IARO attMysore&HyderabadImpSerCav p278 CR Palestine8
KELLY,William John 2Lt kia 25-9-15 6GordH p242 MR19
KELLY,William Peter TCapt dow 12-11-16 26NumbF p61 CR France285
KELLY-LAWSON,George McFarquhar 2Lt 9-8-17 RGA CR Belgium23
KELSALL,John Lindsay TLt kia 28-8-17 86RFA p31 CR Belgium19
KELSEY,Arthur Edward Capt drd 26-2-18 RAMC p196 MR40
KELSEY,Herbert Burleigh T2Lt kia 17-2-17 12Mddx p147 MR21
KELSEY,Leon de Barr 2Lt kia 16-9-16 23Lond p252 MR21
KELSEY,Pryce Atwood Clive TCapt dow 26-7-15 EKent p57 CR France285
KELSEY,William TLt dow 23-9-16 RH&FA p31 CR Yorks575
KELSON,Gerald Miles.MC.Capt ded 27-12-19 KEdwsHorse p261 CR SAfrica14
KELWAY-BAMBER,Claude Herschel 2Lt kia 11-11-15 GL RFC p1&190 CR Belgium140
KELYNACK,Richard Henry 2Lt kia 4-10-17 1DCLI p114 MR30
KEMBER,Walter 2Lt kia 1-9-17 7LancF attRFC p18&221 Belgium140
KEMBER,Walter Herbert TCapt kia 7-6-17 8SLancs p125 MR29
KEMBER,Cyril Stewart 2Lt kia 27-5-18 3Suff att2/4RBerks p78 CR France248
KEMBLE,Harold William Capt 2-1-20 GloucHuss CR Glouc61
KEMBLE,Henry Herbert.DSO.MC.LtCol dow 7-6-17 15Lond p249 CR Belgium11,23Bn
KEMBLE,Henry Noel Lt kia 20-7-16 2Suff p78 CR France513,Capt
KEMISH,Charles Lt&QM 14-7-15 RASC AdvHorseTrans p193 CR Gallipoli
KEMP,Albert 2Lt kia 1-7-16 10RInniskF A'Coy p105 MR21
KEMP,Alexander.MC.Lt dow 26-7-18 RE 34DivSigs 101BdeHQ p210 CR France145
KEMP,Alexander Gordon 2Lt dow 7-5-17 4GordH C'Coy p242 CR France40
KEMP,Alfred Greatrex T2Lt kia 10-8-15 9RWar p65 MR4
KEMP,Ambrose Ernest William 2Lt dow 10-12-17 1/19Lond p250 CR France1
KEMP,Basil Aubrey 2Lt kia 3-5-17 9 att7Mddx p236 MR20
KEMP,Bernard Herbert 2Lt ded 23-10-19 Ex MGC Inf p266 CR SAfrica52
KEMP,C.M.F.SNurse ded 4-7-18 QAIMNS 40GH p200 CR Iraq6
KEMP,Charles George T2Lt kia 24-9-17 1RWSurr p56 MR30
KEMP,Charles John 2Lt kia 25-5-15 5RScots p211 MR4

KEMP,Charles Matthew.DSO.TMaj dow 9-10-17 21Manch p155 CR Belgium308
KEMP,Douglas Gordon.MC.2Lt kia 21-3-18 RE p210 CR France568,dow
KEMP,Elsie Margaret Sister kia 20-10-17 TFNS 58CCS p254 CR France139
KEMP,Eric Arthur T2Lt kia 30-11-17 7ESurr p113 MR17
KEMP,Ernest Charles 2Lt kia 6-9-16 9Yorks &RFC p3&90,ded MR20
KEMP,Frank 2Lt kia 22-7-16 11YLI att56MGC Inf p143&183 MR21
KEMP,Frederick Owen T2Lt kia 23-10-16 2Mddx p147 CR France390
KEMP,George Arnold.MID 2LtTLt ded 12-1-18 3YLI att3/3KAR p202&143,9YLI CR EAfrica10 &CR Tanzania1
KEMP,George Hubert 2Lt kld 1-6-18 15DLI att20RAF p161 CR France134,kia
KEMP,Godwin Francis Lt kia 23-4-17 3 att1BordR p117 MR20
KEMP,Harold George 2Lt kia 21-10-15 2RB p179 CR France276
KEMP,Horace Douglas Meadows T2Lt dow 31-8-16 8RSuss p119 CR Oxford69
KEMP,James Ogilvie Capt ded 12-12-17 5RScots p211 CR C'land &W'land45
KEMP,John Thomson 2Lt kia 11-4-18 25MGC p183 MR32
KEMP,Kenneth Reginald Flint T2Lt ded 18-10-18 RASC p193 CR Devon68
KEMP,Louis Augustus T2Lt dow 22-3-18 9LNLancs p136 CR France512
KEMP,Norman 2Lt kia 9-9-16 5LancF p221 MR21
KEMP,Percy Vickerman LtACapt dow 31-5-18 4 att1DLI p161 CR France40
KEMP,Reginald 2Lt kia 26-8-18 8Manch p237 CR France832
KEMP,Sydney Frank.MC.2Lt kia 16-4-18 O&BLI BucksBn p231 CR France248
KEMP,Thomas T2Lt kia 1-7-16 20Manch p155 CR France397
KEMP,Thomas Norman Cameron.MC.Capt kia 17-5-19 IA 1/9GurkhaRif p278 MR43
KEMP,William Meadows 2Lt kia 28-2-17 5 att16Mddx p147 CR France216,3 att16
KEMP-WELCH,Maurice T2Lt kia 11-4-17 10Yorks p90 MR20
KEMPE-ROBERTS,John Archer Clinton 2Lt kia 10-3-18 RFC p16 MR40
KEMPSEY-BOURNE,Frank Leonard T2Lt kia 11-7-16 11RWar p65 MR21
KEMPSTER,Alec Albert Dresden Lt kia 25-9-15 66/4RFA p31 CR France705
KEMPSTER,Stephen Alec T2Lt kia 8-6-17 17Mddx p147 CR France184
KEMPSTON,Noel Chester 2Lt kia 12-10-16 4ConnRgrs att9InniskF p172 CR Belgium100
KEMPSTON,Robert James Lt kia 24-5-15 2RDubF p177 MR29
KEMPTHORNE,Harold Sampson Lt kia 24-8-17 RFA p207 CR Belgium72
KENCH,Leonard Sheldon Capt dow 29-6-16 2/7RWar p214 CR France134
KENDALL,George 2Lt ded 15-10-18 3WYorks &RAF p263 CR Ches56
KENDALL,John Haywood 2Lt kia 14-4-15 Dors p124 CR Iraq6
KENDALL,Locke Francis William Angerstein TLt dow 22-11-17 9Norf att21MGC Cav p74&183 CR Palestine9
KENDALL,Percy Dale 2Lt kia 25-1-15 10Lpool p216 CR Belgium186,Lt
KENDALL,Rose Elizabeth Sister drd 26-2-18 QAIMNS p200 MR40
KENDALL,Thomas Linaker 2Lt kia 1-8-16 3BordR &MGC p183 CR France513
KENDEL,Benjamin 2Lt kia 14-6-18 21Lond p251 CR France59
KENDERDINE,Tom Herbert Gordon TLt kia 9-9-16 LancF att2/5Bn p92 CR France402
KENDLE,Robert Hastings Maj ded 12-8-15 5Suff p217 CR Gallipoli4
KENDRICK,Arthur Percy Lt dow 9-10-17 1KAR p202 CR EAfrica40
KENDRICK,Frederick Howard 2Lt dow 16-10-15 5SStaffs p229 CR France201
KENDRICK,Haden Mostyn 2Lt kldacc 18-9-16 5SStaffs &RFC p229 CR Staffs47,Lt
KENEALLY,W.Cdr 9-6-20 IndMiscList MR65
KENEALY,John William Kieman 2Lt ded 21-8-15 4IrRReg p89 CR Eire350
KENION,Hugh Cyril T2Lt kia 1-7-16 2LancF p92 CR France742
KENNA,Paul Aloysius.VC.DSO.ADC.BrigGen dow 30-8-15 3MountedBde Staff p1 CR Gallipoli26,21Lancers
KENNARD,Arthur Molloy.DSO.TLtCol ded 2-1-17 179RFA p31 CR Scot214
KENNARD,Lionel Edward Maj ded 10-12-19 15KHuss RoO p261 CR Hamps19
KENNARD,Maurice Nicholl.MC.MIDx3 TLtCol kia 1-7-16 18WYorks p82 MR21 Ex 6DragGds
KENNARD,Patrick Noel Capt kia 14-7-16 1EYorks p84 MR21
KENNARD,Robert 2Lt kia 7-7-16 2RSuss p119
KENNARD,Terence Evelyn Lt kia 26-2-18 RFA &5RFC p16&31 CR France95
KENNARD,Willoughby Arthur.DSO.Capt ded 30-10-18 13Huss p22 CR France40,Maj
KENNARD,Winwood Read 2Lt kia 30-6-16 54MGC p183 CR France513,Reade
KENNAWAY,Arthur Lewis Lt kia 21-8-15 1DorsYeo p203 CR Gallipoli5
KENNEDY,Alastair McKinnon Lt ded 18-10-18 2/2RE p256 CR Scot442
KENNEDY,Alexander.MC.T2LtACapt kia 26-3-18 11RScots p54 MR27
KENNEDY,Andrew Macpherson T2Lt kia 26-3-18 20 att18LancF p92 MR27
KENNEDY,Archibald Edward Capt kia 26-8-14 2A&SH p173 CR France716
KENNEDY,Arthur St.Clair 2Lt ded 6-3-15 3RDubF p177 CR Ireland14 &CR Eire77
KENNEDY,Charles TLt dow 16-11-16 D102RFA p31 CR France145,D113RFA

KENNEDY,Charles Noel Jardine Capt kia 30-7-16 RScotF p94 MR21
KENNEDY,Charles Seccombe Craufurd.MC.Capt kldacc 22-8-16 1N&D attRE p134 CR France200
KENNEDY,David Hew.MC.T2Lt kia 31-7-16 2RScotF p94 MR29
KENNEDY,D.C.2Lt kia 16-10-14 HLI p163
KENNEDY,Donald 2Lt kia 30-8-18 1GordH p166 CR France927
KENNEDY,Douglas Stewart.MC.Capt kia 12-3-18 62RFC p16 CR France660
KENNEDY,Duncan Cameron Lt kia 9-9-16 9HLI att47MGC Inf p240 MR21
KENNEDY,Edwin Alfred 2Lt kia 12/16-5-17 6SfthH p241 MR20
KENNEDY,Gilbert Capt ded 11-12-18 1RMunstF p175 CR France65
KENNEDY,Gilbert McClelland 2Lt kia 16/18-6-15 6ScotRif p224 MR22,15-6-15
KENNEDY,Gilbert Stuart.MID Capt kia 12-3-15 IA 1/9GurkhaRif p278 MR28
KENNEDY,H.A.Lt 22-8-17 GL &RFC CR France924
KENNEDY,Herbert Alexander Capt dow 28-10-14 2RIrRif p169 CR France80
KENNEDY,Horas Tristram TLt kia 6-6-17 2RScotF attRE p94 CR France263
KENNEDY,Hugh Victor Strain T2Lt kia 16-8-17 14RIrRif p169 MR30
KENNEDY,Humfrey Hays MajALtCol kia 29-7-18 2 att8SfthH p165 CR FRancr524
KENNEDY,James T2Lt dow 26-9-15 1CamH p168 CR France178,Lt
KENNEDY,James T2Lt kia 21-3-18 8 att1RIrRif p169 CR France1061
KENNEDY,James Joseph TLt dow 17-10-18 6 att11RInniskF p105 CR France846
KENNEDY,James Patrick 2Lt kia 19-6-18 18Lond attMGC p187&250 MR32
KENNEDY,James Robert LtCol ded 3-8-17 IA 96Inf att90Punjabis p278
KENNEDY,James Wallace.MID ACapt kia 27-5-17 4 att1ScotRif p103 MR20
KENNEDY,John 2Lt kia 23-4-17 ScotRif att7BordR p103 MR20
KENNEDY,John T2Lt kia 20-4-18 BordR att15DLI p117 CR Belgium15
KENNEDY,John Alexander Capt dow 6-8-16 6SfthH p241 CR France74
KENNEDY,John Edwin TLt kia 25-9-15 8SfthH p165 MR19
KENNEDY,John Gilbert T2Lt kia 14-9-16 1Leic p87 MR21
KENNEDY,John Horace 2Lt kia 10-1-15 2SomLI attScotRif p80 CR France567
KENNEDY,John Murray Stewart TLt kia 10-8-15 9SfthH p165 CR France765
KENNEDY,John Patrick Francis Capt kia 24-4-18 5 att2RB p179 CR France424
KENNEDY,John Pitt Capt kia 10-3-15 2ScotRif p103 CR France260
KENNEDY,J.N.C.Maj 20-4-15 RE CR Hamps1
KENNEDY,Miles Arthur Claude.DSO.Capt ded 2-11-18 IA 1/8GurkhaRif p278 CR Pakistan50A
KENNEDY,Nigel.MID Lt kia 22-10-14 RScotF p94 MR29,25-10-14
KENNEDY,Norman 2Lt dow 31-10-17 1/2RScotF p94 CR France134
KENNEDY,Paul Adrian Capt kia 9-5-15 4 at2RB p179 MR32
KENNEDY,R.B.C.2LtTLt ded 10-8-17 Ches p96 CR Eire234,RDubF
KENNEDY,Robert 2Lt dow 10-7-16 2 att3RScotF p94 CR France66
KENNEDY,Rolf Darab T2Lt kia 27-3-18 23RFC p16 MR20
KENNEDY,Ronald Sinclair.MC.TCapt kia 17-4-18 RAMC att76FA p196 CR France856,Sinclair
KENNEDY,Samuel Lancelot Richard Alexander Edgar 2Lt kia 15-9-16 8Lond p247 CR France432
KENNEDY,Thomas Christian 2Lt kia 25-11-15 C97RFA p31 CR France922
KENNEDY,Thomas James TLt kia 9-9-16 8RInniskF p105 MR21
KENNEDY,Tristram Gervias Lt dow 28-3-18 A301RFA p31 CR Palestine3
KENNEDY,Walter Douglas Lt kia 19-4-17 5RScotF p222 MR34
KENNEDY,Walter Louis 2Lt kia 3-9-16 12RSuss p119 CR France339
KENNEDY,William HonMaj&QM ded 29-5-15 KEdwHorse p24
KENNEDY,William.MC.MajALtCol kia 23-11-17 18HLI att18WelshR p163 MR17
KENNEDY,William Robert T2Lt kia 25-9-15 2A&SH p173 CR France114
KENNEFICK,Edward Hamerton Capt kia 8-7-16 Ess p132 MR21
KENNEFICK,John George Hamerton Capt kia 20-4-18 3 att2Ess p132&257 CR France250
KENNELLY,Leslie William TLt dow 9-10-15 9RSuss p119 CR France134
KENNETH,Archibald Capt kia 12-7-15 4RScotF p222 MR4
KENNINGTON,Harry Lt kia 27-10-17 52RFA p207 MR30
KENNY,Cecil John Lt kia 24-3-18 3RIrReg attMGC Inf p89&183 CR France1203
KENNY,Cecil Stacpoole 2Lt ded 11-11-15 KSLI p265 MR40,drd
KENNY,Francis Joseph Leo T2Lt kia 9-8-16 5ConnRgrs attRInniskF p172 CR Belgium47
KENNY,John Mary Joseph TLt kia 23-9-16 RASC &RFC p3&193 MR20
KENNY,Laurence Henry T2Lt kia 26-6-16 10 att8Suff p78 MR21
KENNY,William David.VC.Lt kia 2-1-20 IA 4/39GarhwalRif p278 MR43
KENNY,William George Stanhope Capt kia 10-3-15 IA 1/39GarhwalRif p278 CR France355 &CR France1887
KENRICK,Herbert William Mascall Capt ded 24-3-19 RoO att11Huss p22 CR Germany1
KENT,Alan Williamson 2Lt dow 27-4-15 7NumbF p214 CR Belgium4

KENT,Charles Ronald.MC.T2Lt kia 20-10-18 6 att5Dors p124 CR France192
KENT,Charles Stuart 2Lt kia 24-10-18 4BlkW p230 CR France1258
KENT,Edward Montague Wayne Lt kia 26-8-14 1Hamps p121 MR15,Swayne
KENT,Ernest TLt dow 8-4-17 2Ess &24RFC p9&132 CR France699
KENT,Frederick Charles 2Lt kia 5-7-17 7Worc p226 CR Belgium34
KENT,George Edward Lt kia 24-3-18 3 att8RLancs p59 MR20
KENT,George Herbert Stanton Capt kia 24-3-18 RE 490FC p46 MR27
KENT,Harold 2Lt kia 4-8-17 3 att8SWBord p100 CR Belgium101
KENT,Harold 2Lt dow 16-11-17 A50RH&FA p31 CR France1361
KENT,James Maddison Lt dow 5-8-15 3DLI p161 CR Belgium11,2Bn
KENT,Lionel Victor 2LtTLt dow 31-7-17 3SWBord p100 CR Belgium84 Ex 28Lond
KENT,Percival Naylor MajALtCol ded 8-4-18 3DragGds p21 CR France40,18-4-18
KENT,Peter Francis 2Lt kia 6-2-18 3RFC p16 CR France568
KENT,P.J.2Lt ded 2-9-16 N&D p264 CRWales17,P.G.
KENT,Ralph E Dawson LtCol kia 27-5-18 4Yorks att81TrainResBn p90 MR18
KENT,Sidney T2Lt kia 13-12-17 43MGC Inf p183 MR30
KENT,W.J.SubCdr 17-3-18 MilWksServ MR43
KENT,Walter John 2Lt kia 24-8-18 17Lond p250 MR16
KENT,William James Capt kia 7-8-15 13WYorks attManch p82 MR4
KENT,William John 2Lt kia 12-3-15 RFA 53Bty p31 CR France1106
KENT,William Morley 2Lt kia 21-2-18 RFC p16 CR Belgium158,Lt
KENTFIELD,Edwin Nelson T2Lt kia 17-2-17 23RFus p68 MR21
KENTISH,Ernest George 2Lt ded 27-2-18 B'RHA p31 CR Iraq8
KENTISH,Harold Edward Capt kia 30-3-18 RE 281ArmyTroopsCo p46 MR27
KENWARD,Robert 2Lt 7-7-16 2RSuss MR21
KENWORTHY,Donald LtTCapt kia 17-5-17 1SomLI p80 CR Belgium96,17-5-15
KENWORTHY,Stanley TCapt kia 1-7-16 17Manch p155 CR France397
KENYON,Charles Wilton T2Lt kia 16-3-16 10RSuss attT47TMB p119 CR France924
KENYON,James T2Lt kia 21-3-18 Manch att2/6Bn p155 MR27
KENYON,James Maj ded 22-12-18 Res 5LancF p270 CR Lancs321,22-11-18
KENYON,James Henry Turner Capt ded 28-9-18 RAVC p268 CR Derby98
KENYON,John De Winton 2Lt kia 16-5-15 4 att1Lpool p72 MR22
KENYON,William Douglas Capt dow 16-9-18 1/7Ches p222 CR France25
KEOGH,Alfred Alexander T2Lt kia 12-5-17 Mddx att11Bn p147 CR France1188
KEOGH,Frederick Bertram.MC.Capt kia 8-8-18 4ConnRgrs att1TankCps p172&188 CR France360
KEOGH,Henry Claude 2Lt kia 4-4-17 3 att13RSuss p119 CR Belgium127
KEOGH,James Lynch.MID Capt&QM ded 18-1-19 RAMC 83FA p253 CR Asia81
KEOGH,John 2Lt kia 22-3-18 3 att2Leinst p174 CR France365,Lt
KEOGH,Thomas T2Lt ded 16-12-18 RE IWT p46 CR India97A
KEOGH,William Gerald TLt ded 12-10-18 6Leinst att2/4NumbF p174 CR EAfrica116
KEPPELL,Albert Edward George Arnold.Hon.MID Lt kia 31-7-17 2RB p179 CR Belgium88
KEPPELL-PALMER,Stuart Leslie.MC.TLtACapt kia 3-10-18 3TankCps LtBn p188 CR France234
KEPPIE,Charles Browning T2Lt dow 27-3-18 2RB p179 CR France145
KER,Arthur Milford Capt kia 14-10-14 GordH p166 CR France1106
KER,Bruce Ralph Capt ded 28-11-19 SL p268
KER,Cecil Howard Capt kia 15-9-14 1Beds p86 MR15
KER,Frederick Roxburghe 2Lt kia 20-9-17 6Lond p247 MR29
KER,Laurence Arthur 2Lt ded 4-4-15 9RScotF p94 CR Scot677,kldacc
KER,Thomas Darling 2Lt kld 1-6-16 RE p46 CR Egypt2
KER-GULLAND,Reginald Glover 2Lt dow 12-11-14 14Lond p249 CR Belgium135
KERFOOT,Edwin Capt ded 8-3-20 5Manch p270 CR Lancs443
KERKHAM,Francis Leslie 2Lt kia 14-10-17 3 att7Norf p74 MR20
KERLEY,Bertram Frederick 2Lt kia 10-9-17 6SWBord p100 CR Belgium23 Fredrick
KERMODE,Edgar Marsden.DSO.MC&Bar.DCM.2Lt dow 27-7-18 2/5WYorks p218 CR France1697,26-7-18
KERNAGHAN,Graham Hemery TLt kia 1-7-16 8YLI p143 CR France246 &CR France1890
KERNAGHAN,John T2Lt dow 1-10-18 9RIrF p171 CR Belgium84
KERNICK,Charles Sylvester TLt dow 1-12-17 14MGC Inf p183 CR France446
KERR,Adam TCapt dow 3-11-18 10N&D p134 CR France1478
KERR,Alan Graham Lt kia 26-10-18 5ScotRif p224 CR France206
KERR,Alexander Lt dow 30-4-15 5RScots p211 MR4
KERR,Alexander Crerar 2Lt kia 1-1-17 RE 91FC p46 CR France515
KERR,Andrew Alan 2Lt kia 26-3-18 16KRRC p150 MR30
KERR,Arthur Douglas Garnett Odell 2Lt kia 3-8-16 10Mddx att1/5LancF p236 MR21

KERR,Daniel Lt kia 6-7-15 14Ches attSWBord p96 MR4
KERR,Daniel Eugene.MID Lt kia 10-6-18 RFA 87Btyp31 CR Belgium18
KERR,David.MC.T2Lt kia 12-8-16 6/7RScotF p94 CR France151
KERR,David Anselm 2Lt kia 13-10-14 3RScots p54 CR France708 &CR France1158,13-10-14 2Bn
KERR,David,Bryce TCapt kia 1-7-16 16HLI p163 MR21
KERR,David Chesne 2Lt kia 12-10-17 4RScots p211 MR30,Chesney
KERR,Donald 2Lt kia 1-7-16 14Lond p249 MR21
KERR,Edward Bournes TLt dow 26-5-16 12RB p179 CR Belgium11
KERR,Finlay 2Lt kia 4-7-16 2RIrReg p89 MR21,Lt 5-7-16
KERR,Frederick Walter.DSO.Col kia 31-10-14 1Div HQ Staff p1 CR Belgium58 1GordH
KERR,George Augustus L'Estrange 2Lt kia 30-6-18 2Beds p86 CR France516
KERR,Harry Smellie 2Lt dow 25-4-18 4RScots p211 MR30
KERR,Henry Thomas Frederick.MC.2Lt kia 25-9-15 2A&SH p173 CR France114
KERR,Henry Grace 2Lt dow 1-7-17 9Lancers p22 CR France178
KERR,Henry Thomas Ross 2Lt ded 3-7-16 PoW 8att6CamH p168 MR19
KERR,Hubert Rainsford Gordon Lt kia 21-12-14 1HLI p163 MR22,19-12-14
KERR,James 2Lt kia 1-7-16 4 att16HLI p163 MR21
KERR,James 2Lt kia 13-11-17 1/5KOSB p224 CR Palestine9
KERR,James Lt kia 21-3-18 3 att1RIrRif p169 MR27
KERR,James Campbell 2Lt ded 30-3-19 9HLI p240 CR Iraq6
KERR,James Elkin TLt dow 10-9-17 202MGC Inf p183 CR Belgium173
KERR,James Melrose 2Lt drd 4-9-16 1/5RScotF p222 CR Egypt7,3-9-16
KERR,John Murdoch 2Lt kia 13-11-16 8 att1RScotF p94 CR France742,1 att8Bn
KERR,John Robert Capt ded 7-11-17 12RDC p253 CR Lancs98
KERR,John William T2Lt kia 28-3-18 10ScotRif p103 CR France57
KERR,Leslie Henry Fox TLt dedacc 24-11-16 RASC 9DivTrain 106Coy p193 CR France169
KERR,M.T.SNurse 17-1-15 TFNS 2ScotGH CR Scot501
KERR,Norman James T2Lt dow 20-12-16 97MGC p183 CR France40
KERR,Peter Campbell T2Lt kia 18-8-18 1 att1/7LancF p93 CR France5
KERR,Robert 2Lt dow 7-6-17 19Lond p250 CR Belgium165
KERR,Robert Goodman.MC.TMajALtCol kia 11-7-18 7RInniskF att9RIrF p105 CR France855
KERR,Robert Thomas 2Lt kia 23-10-16 4Y&L p238 CR France927
KERR,William Walton.DSO.MC.CaptALtCol kia 3-5-18 2BordR p117 CR Italy2
KERR,William TLt kia 2-9-18 6RScotF att4MGC Inf p94&183 CR France1182,4MGC att6RScotF
KERR,William John Lt dow 10-3-15 2ScotRif p103 CR Glouc124
KERR,William Niven 2Lt ded 26-11-18 19Lond p250 CR France1030
KERR-CLARK,St.Ruan Robertson TCapt kia 25-9-15 7SfthH p165 MR19
KERRICH,Henry Latham Lt dow 27-9-17 3N&D p134 CR Belgium93
KERRICH,John Herbert Capt kia 14-9-14 2WelshR C'Coy p127 CR France1329,Maj
KERRIDGE,Oswald Alfred T2Lt dow 23-7-16 16DLI p161 CR France145
KERRISON,Roger Orme LtCol ded 18-9-17 Suffyeo CR France64
KERRY,Albert 2Lt kia 22-3-18 1RFus p68 MR27
KERRY,Arnold John St.Ledgier.MID Lt ded 14-2-18 16Manch p155 CR Camb16,Legier dow
KERSEY,William Henry Myddleton Capt kia 17-10-17 RGA 166SB p209 CR Belgium19
KERSHAW,Ellis T2Lt kia 1-7-16 13 att1LancF p93 MR21
KERSHAW,Henry Valder Capt kia 15-9-16 19Lond p250 MR21
KERSHAW,Joseph Harrison Lt ded 16-9-19 10Manch p256 CR Egypt2
KERSHAW,Kenneth Robert Beresford T2Lt kia 25-9-15 9GordH p166 CR France554
KERSHAW,Milton 2Lt kia 7-11-14 att2Glouc SR p107 MR29
KERSHAW,Ryder Samuel 2Lt kia 11-5-17 7LancF SR att1/1Lond p221 CR France581
KERSHAW,Thomas James T2Lt dow 23-1-17 11LancF p93 CR France264
KERTLAND,Edwin Blow 2Lt kia 16-6-15 3RIrF att2RIrRif p171 MR29
KERWOOD,Lionel Maj kia 21-10-16 1/8Worc p226 MR21
KERWOOD,Philip Malcolm Lt kia 25-6-15 8Worc p226 CR France285
KESBY,Thomas Herbert TCapt kia 15-9-16 EKent att70MGC Inf p57&184 CR France390
KESSACK,James O'Connor TCapt kia 13-11-16 25 att17Mddx p147 MR21
KESSLER,Edgar Capt kia 4-6-15 1/6Manch A'Coy p236 CR Gallipoli2
KESTELL-CORNISH,Robert Vaughan.MC&Bar.MIDx3 LtTCapt dow 17-6-18 Dors attStaffDivHQ p124 CR France102
KESTEVEN,Thomas Carew.Lord.Capt dow 4-11-15 LincsYeo p204 CR Somerset199,5-11-15

KETTLE,Rupert Arthur Lt kia 26-3-18 3Huss p21 CR France1063
KETTLE,Thomas Michael TLt kia 9-9-16 9RDubF p177 MR21
KEVILL-DAVIES,William Albert Somerset Herbert Lt dow 15-5-15 9Lancers p22 CR France285
KEW,George Richard ACapt dow 8-11-17 8SLancs p125 CR France98
KEWLEY,George Raymond T2Lt kia 20-5-15 8LNLancs p136 MR20
KEWLEY,John Tasker TLt dow 16-1-17 6LNLancs p136 CR Iraq5,Capt
KEY,Douglas Polson Lt dow 25-8-15 RE 78FC p46 CR Belgium82
KEY,Frederick Bertram 2Lt kia 1-7-16 8RWar p215 MR21
KEY,Hart Reginald 2Lt kia 13-4-18 6WRid p227 MR30
KEY,William Partridge Lt kia 11-9-15 1 att 11YLI p143 CR France1059
KEYES,Cleveland.MC.TCaptAMaj dow PoW 24-3-18 C83RFA p31 CR France1703
KEYMS,Thomas Booth 2Lt kia 19-7-16 B84RFA p31 CR France402
KEYS,Joseph Nicholas Douglas.MC.LtACapt kia 21-9-17 11Ess p132 CR France149
KEYS,Malcolm T2Lt dow 31-8-16 8BordR p117 CR France44
KEYSER,Richard Norman Lt kld 22-8-17 3ELancs attRFC p9&111
KEYZOR,Herbert Louis Abraham T2Lt kia 9-3-18 1SWBord att25RWFus p100 CR Mddx66,kldacc CR Palestine3,2Bn
KHALAF,E.Capt ded 1-10/31-12-19 MO 3EgyptStatHosp CR Egypt2
KIBBY,H.C.2Lt ded 27-10-18 10Mddx &RAF p236
KIDD,Alastair Wilson TLt ded 26-10-18 RE 1BaseParkCo p46 CR France65,MiningCoy
KIDD,Balmer T2Lt dow 19-3-18 137MGC Inf p184 CR France98
KIDD,Cecil Christian.MID TCapt drd 28-2-18 RE 8FldTrpCo p46 CR Palestine2
KIDD,Charles Roland Capt 8-7-20 RAMC CR Hamps64
KIDD,Claude Bernard.MC.TCapt kia 24-3-18 15Ches p96 MR27
KIDD,Edward John Cecil 2Lt kld 10-4-18 5WYorks &RAF p270 CR Yorks474
KIDD,Guy Egerton.DSO.Maj kia 26-9-16 A70RFA p31 CR France453
KIDD,Herbert Dickie 2Lt kia 17-5-15 4CamH p243 MR22
KIDD,James Forrest 2Lt ded 1-11-18 12KRRC &20RAF p150 CR France937,Lt kld
KIDD,J.G.Capt 24-9-14 Cps of Army Schlmstrs MR67
KIDD,John Newman Capt kia 19-1-16 6DragGds p21 CR France423
KIDD,Leonard Cameron.MC.Lt kia 12-10-16 3RFC p3 MR20
KIDD,Philip Chabert 2Lt kia 30-10-14 Yorks p90 MR29
KIDD,Robert John Lt dow 24-4-21 IA 1/1 att1/11GurkhaRif p278 MR43,2/1Bn
KIDD,Vivian Norval.MC.TMaj ded 21-3-17 8WRid.Staff p115&258 CR France169
KIDD,William Sidney Lt kia 21-3-18 att2RMunstF p175 MR21
KIDDELL,George Bartam Pearce 2Lt ded 27-2-17 1RIrF p171 CR France67
KIDDER,Milton Ellory T2Lt kld 19-5-17GL RFC p9 CR Norf209,Elroy
KIDDIER,Ernest 2Lt kia 17-9-18 RGA 244SB p40 CR France686
KIDDLE,Cyril Frank 2Lt kia 25-4-18 4 att1/5WYorks p82 MR30
KIDDLE,Geoffrey Capt ded 29-7-16 7RFA p31 CR Iraq6
KIDDS,George Frederick T2Lt kia 25-7-17 11Mddx p147 CR France581
KIDNER,Thomas Clatworthy Capt kia 26-10-16 RAMC att2Mddx p196 MR21
KIDSON,Charles Wilfrid Lt kia 17-10-18 5 att2RDubF p177 CR France190
KIDSTON,William Hamilton Campbell Capt ded 8-8-17 9A&SH p243 CR France40,1/8Bn
KIELY,Florence Patrick 2Lt kia 24-6-17 4 att9RIrF p171 MR29
KILBORN,Leslie Bertram 2Lt dow 10-4-17 6GordH p242 CR France95,1/8Bn
KILBY,Arthur Forbes Gordon.VC.MC.Capt kia 25-9-15 2SStaffs C'Coy p122 MR19 CR France1059
KILBY,John T2Lt dow 21-8-16 10Glouc att7TMB p107 CR France2
KILBY,William Watson Capt ded 19-2-19 SL p268
KILGOUR,Alexander Lt kia 18-4-18 7BlkW p231 CR France279
KILGOUR,Arthur Wilson TLt/Capt kld 27-7-17 RFC SR p9
KILGOUR,Charles David Winton T2Lt dow 4-11-18 RFA 25ArmyBde p31 CR France1266
KILGOUR,Henry LtCol ded 24-11-15 2/5Dev p217 CR Egypt9
KILKELLY,John George Joseph Capt kia 24-3-18 RMunstF &RFC p16&175 MR20
KILKENNY,Edward Charles Randolph.MC.LtAMaj kia 26-6-17 A186RFA p31 CR Belgium5
KILLBY,Chester Winterbon Lt kia 21-3-18 C307RFA p207 MR27
KILLEN,Edward Osborne Brice TLt kia 15-1-17 RE 71FC p46 CR Iraq5
KILLICK,R.N.Lt 8-12-19 RWKent CR Kent289
KILLICK,Richard 2Lt kia 18-5-15 1/6Manch p237 MR4,15-5-15
KILLICK,Sidney Herbert Capt dow 18-11-16 1SLancs attHQ Staff p125 CR Iraq5
KILLICK,Sydney Howard 2Lt ded 16-5-18 8ESurr attMGC p113&184 CR France145
KILLINGBACK,Stanley Gordon Lt kia 10-8-16 RE p210 CR France15,11-8-16
KILLINGLEY,Hastings Grewatt Lt kia 23-10-16 2RDubF p177 MR21,Grevatt
KILMISTER,Harold Howard Linsdell.MC.Lt kia 22-8-18 5 att9RFus p68 CR France370

KILNER,Charles Ussher T2Lt dow 8-10-16 1Suff p78 CR Greece3
KILNER,Thomas Richard Burgess.MM.T2Lt kia 18-6-18 9N&D p134 CR France115
KILPIN,Franklin James 2Lt kia 16-4-18 RGA 250SB p40 CR Belgium21
KILPIN,Thomas Bennett T2Lt dow 15-6-17 RFA attY25TMB p31 CR France262
KILROE,Francis Joseph T2Lt dow 28-8-18 1HLI attRInniskF p163 CR France134
KILSBY,George Alfred 2Lt kia 18-9-18 4Nhampt p234 CR France212
KILVERT,Harry T2Lt dow 1-8-17 9RWFus p98 CR France285
KIMBELL,Harry John Sullings TLt ded 28-5-16 RAMC p196 CR Lond10
KIMBELL,Richard Evison 2Lt kia 16-4-17 14Huss &60RFC p9&22 CR France604
KIMBER,Basil Liddon T2Lt kia 10-7-16 7Lincs p75 MR21 Ex 5Lond
KIMBER,Henry Cyril Dixon Lt dow 22-6-16 19/7RFA p207 CR France12
KIMBER,John William Lt dow 11-5-18 4BlkW p230 CR France40,1Bn
KIMBER,Reginald Ernest T2Lt kia 20-9-17 8Glouc p107 MR30
KIMBERLEY,W.R Lt 26-9-20 GL &RASC CR Egypt6
KIMPTON,Frank Capt ded 14-3-19 RE p46&257 CR Iraq6
KIMPTON,Norman Herbert 2Lt dow 14-7-17 1RFA p208 CR Belgium12
KINAHAN,James T2Lt dow 8-10-18 23RFus p68 CR France407
KINCAID,Andrew Duncan 2Lt dow 23-3-18 BlkW att8Bn p129 MR27
KINCAID,James Brown TLt kia 23-4-17 13RScots p54 MR20
KINCAID,John Brown 2Lt kia 3-5-17 1RScotF p94 MR20
KINDER,Geoffrey George.MC.Capt kia 20-7-18 8WYorks p219 MR18
KINDER,Richard Clement TCapt kia 20-9-17 GL att26RFus p190 MR30
KINDER,Thomas Harry Capt kia 3-7-16 7Suff p78 MR21
KINDERSLEY,Douglas Cumming Paget.DSO.Capt kia 22-6-17 3HLI att2KOSB p163 CR France184
KINDERSLEY,Lionel Nassau 2Lt kia 25-11-17 15Huss p22 MR17
KINDLEYSIDES,Charles Frederick T2Lt dow 4-10-18 ACycCps att22NumbF p181 CR France106,5-10-18
KING,Alan Howard T2Lt kia 22-8-19 9RFus p68 CR France370
KING,Albert TLt kia 23-8-16 RFA p31 CR France833
KING,Albert 2Lt kia 31-5-17 3Mon p244 MR20,2Bn
KING,Alexander Duncan Campbell 2Lt kia 24-5-15 18Huss SR p23 CR Belgium2
KING,Alexander Lindsay T2Lt kia 9-4-18 HL1 att10/11Bn p163 CR France705
KING,Alfred John 2Lt dow 17-6-18 6 att4NStaffs A'Coy p238 CR France122
KING,Alfred Nelson TLt kia 10-5-16 C53RFA p31 CR Belgium71
KING,Andrew Buchanan Maj dow 28-5-15 7A&SH p243 CR France200
KING,A.P.Lt ded 12-10-16 12Suff p263 CR Suff224
KING,Arthur Bernard T2Lt kia 7-7-16 12Manch p155 MR21
KING,Arthur Montague Maj kia 15-3-15 RB p179 MR29
KING,Arthur Philip 2Lt kia 24-11-17 2Mddx p147 CR Belgium126 Ex 1Lancs
KING,Arthur Towers Lt kia 17-11-17 1/1LincsYeo p204 CR Palestine9
KING,Arthur William 2Lt kia 17-9-16 17Lond p250 CR France432,15-9-16
KING,Berry 2LtTLt kia 3-5-17 3YLI &25RFC p9&143 CR France88,6Bn
KING,Bertie Allen T2Lt dow 29-4-17 7EYorks p84 CR France113
KING,Charles Lt dow 10-5-17 1/1GlamorganRHA p207 CR France1182
KING,Charles Arthur Cecil.MIDx2 Col kia 30-10-14 2Yorks p90 MR29
KING,Charles Eustace Dickson.MC.Capt&Adjt kia 11-10-16 2YLI p143 CR France114
KING,Charles Frederick 2Lt kia 20-9-17 Dev att 1/6Lpool p77 MR30
KING,Charles Leonard 2Lt kia 22-3-18 Herts p252 CR France528
KING,Charles Sealy Lt kia 9-5-15 RMunstF p175
KING,Charles William 2Lt kia 25-9-15 2SStaffs p122 MR19
KING,Cuthbert TMaj kia 11-4-17 44MGC attRWSurr p184 CR France924
KING,Cyril Henry Marshall 2Lt kia 30-9-16 GL &60RFC p3&190 CR France95
KING,Cyril William T2Lt kia 9-11-17 52MGC Inf p184 CR Belgium126
KING,Daniel Arthur TLt ded 22-7-17 RE IWT p46 CR Iraq5
KING,David 2Lt kia 31-7-17 15RWFus p98 MR29
KING,David Taylor T2Lt kia 1-7-16 2GordH p166 CR France331
KING,Douglas Reid.MC.MID Capt kia 7-6-17 RAMC att74FA p196 CR Belgium152
KING,Ebenezer.MC.2Lt kld 17-3-17 3KOSB attRFC p9&102 CR Lincs181
KING,Edmund Harold T2Lt dow 3-7-16 6Wilts p153 CR France833
KING,Edward Gordon Macgregor 2Lt kia 17-7-16 KSLI attGlouc p145 CR France246
KING,Edward Roly Capt dow 23-4-18 3Norf A'Coy p74 MR38,Roby
KING,Edward Westcott 2Lt dow 20-10-18 B79RFA p31 CR France332
KING,Eric George T2Lt kia 21-3-18 8RBerks p139 MR27
KING,Eric George Lauder Lt kia 22-7-17 1GrenGds p50 CR Belgium12 Lander
KING,Frank Maxfield TMaj kia 22-3-18 KRRC att9LNLancs p150 MR20
KING,Frank Radcliffe T2Lt kia 14-9-16 14Lpool p72 MR37

KING,Frederick Cross T2Lt kia 23-10-16 17RIrRif att25MGC Inf p184 CR France307

KING,Frederick Harvey Lt kia 12-10-16 1WIndiaR att2WRid p192 MR21

KING,George 2Lt kia 12/13-2-17 3 att9Suff p78 MR19

KING,George Charles.MID Capt ded 4-7-21 RAMC 2FA CR Ches62

KING,Gilbert Stewart TCapt kia 3-4-17 15WYorks p82 MR20,3-5-17

KING,Gordon Wick 2Lt kia 9-4-16 8Ches p96 MR38

KING,Hamilton Boyd 2Lt kia 7-6-17 22Lond p251 CR Belgium120

KING,Harry T2LtACapt kia 3-9-16 11 att3Worc p109 CR France246

KING,Harry Garfield T2Lt kia 26-4-18 Ess att10Bn p132 MR27

KING,Harold Dudley 2Lt kia 6-10-18 Worc att1/8Bn p109 CR France1462

KING,Henry Alfred 2Lt ded 4-11-18 IA TC attS&TCps p278 MR61

KING,Henry Arthur.MC.2Lt kia 1-7-17 RFA D'Bty121Bde p31 CR Belgium1

KING,Henry Frederick T2Lt dow 7-5-17 9Leic p87 CR France120

KING,Henry Frederick Irwin Lt ded 5-11-18 D165RFA p31 CR Belgium159

KING,Herbert TLt dow 6-10-17 RAOC p198 CR Belgium8

KING,Herbert Garner T2Lt kia 10-9-16 2NumbF p61 CR Greece3

KING,Herbert Grenfell.MC.Capt kia 22-3-18 16NumbF p61 CR France34 &CR France834

KING,Horace Reginald Edward Lt kia 28-3-18 4Ess p232 MR20

KING,Hubert Weston 2Lt kia 10-11-18 10 att1Lond p248 CR Belgium256

KING,Hugh Denham 2Lt kia 13-3-17 2/10Lond p248 CR France175

KING,Humphrey Stuart.MC.TLtACapt kia 4-10-18 2NumbF p61 CR France375,3-10-18

KING,James Lt&QM drd 14-6-16 RAVC 20VetHosp p198 CR Egypt9,13-6-16

KING,James Norman 2Lt kia 18-4-18 4LNLancs p234 CR France1106

KING,John Alexander 2Lt kia 12-9-16 4GordH p242 CR France922

KING,John David.DCM.2Lt ded 30-6-18 242RFA attSigSubSect p31 CR France95

KING,John Francis BtMaj ded 26-9-19 Suff att3Ech GHQ p263 CR Egypt1

KING,John Rose.MC.TLt kia 22-4-18 18 att10WYorks p82 CR France2

KING,John Skelton Clarke.DCM.2Lt kia 3-5-17 1/4 O&BLI p231 CR France1327

KING,Joseph 2Lt kia 4-10-18 3ConnRgrs att2RMunstF p172 CR France1495

KING,Kerry.DCM.2Lt dow 25-9-18 RGA 7Bty 3BdeMtnArty p40 CR Greece5

KING,Leonard.MC.Lt kia 18-4-17 1/6Glouc p225 CR France363

KING,Lucas Henry St.Aubyn Lt kia 8-5-15 4KRRC p151 MR29

KING,Maurice T2Lt ded 24-6-17 GL attEgyptLabCps p190 CR Egypt2

KING,Maurice Edmund Lt kia 15-3-16 13Mddx p147 MR29

KING,Nathaniel Walter Ryder Lt kia 21-2-15 16Lancers p23 CR Belgium57

KING,Nita Madeline Miss ded 25-5-17 VAD p200 CR France64

KING,Noel Gilbet Bryan Lt kia 7-6-17 1Wilts p153 MR29

KING,Norman 2Lt dow 26-5-18 IrGds att4GdsMGR p53 CR France63 see OLIVER,H.A.B.true name

KING,Norman Toynbee Lt kia 22-3-18 3DragGds p21 MR27

KING,Percy T2Lt dow 5-8-17 7ESurr p113 CR France113,kia

KING,Percy James Church.MM.2Lt kia 24-10-17 RFA p208 CR Belgium21

KING,Percy Reginald 2Lt kia 30-7-16 18Manch p155 MR21

KING,Philip Douglas Atwood 2Lt kia 18-12-16 2RSuss p119 CR France744

KING,Reginald 2Lt dow 15-9-18 1Mon att1SWBordp244 CR France526

KING,Reginald Duncan 2Lt kia 19-4-17 8Hamps p229 MR34

KING,R.F.C.Maj 19-3-18 RFC 6Mddx CR Sussex125

KING,Richard T2Lt dow 18-4-16 6SLancs p125 CR Iraq5

KING,Richard Henry T2Lt kia 27-6-17 N&D att12Bn p134 CR Belgium115

KING,Robert T2Lt kia 29-9-18 1SWBord p100 CR France672

KING,Robert Anderson Ferguson Smyly 2Lt dow 23-5-15 2RDubF p177 CR France102,Andrew

KING,Robert Neal Capt kia 1-11-14 Lincs p75 MR29

KING,Robert Thomas 2Lt kia 31-7-18 6SfthH p241 CR France27

KING,Robert William 2Lt kia 27-3-18 1Camb p245 MR27

KING,Samuel Perston Lt kld 13-10-17 LincsYeo p270 CR Oxford1

KING,Solomon T2Lt kia 13-10-16 23NumbF p61 CR France275,Solomon

KING,Stewart William LtCol ded 25-12-15 IA 17Inf p278

KING,Sydney Lt kia 31-7-17 Herts p252 MR29,Simmonds

KING,Sydney Robert HonCapt ded 19-11-16 RAOC p198 CR Lond14

KING,Sydney William Thacker 2Lt kia 10-8-15 4Ches p222 MR4

KING,Thomas Shirley Capt kia 3-5-17 4 att7ESurr p113 MR20

KING,Victor Algernon Robert T2Lt kia 29-9-17 233MGC Inf p184 MR30

KING,Victor Reginald TLt dow 13-5-18 GL Nhampt attRE Sigs p46&190 CR France180

KING,Wilfred Frank T2Lt kld 4-11-17 GL RFC p9 CR Kent90

KING,William 2Lt mbk 11-4-18 1LancF p256 MR32

KING,William T2Lt dow PoW 26-6-18 6 att7DCLI p114 CR Germany4

KING,William BRCS 19-10-18 CR Dorset50

KING,William Albert de Courcy.DSO.MajALtCol kia 27-5-17 RE 36DivHQ p46 Belgium97

KING,William Galbraith T2Lt kia 7-7-16 9RScotF att1MunstF p94 CR France115,6-7-16 8Bn

KING,William Hugh Lt kia 11-4-18 8Ess att7RAF p258&232 CR Belgium18,kld

KING,William Oliver Redman Lt ded 28-2-19 SL p268

KING,William Thomas 2Lt kia 29-8-18 5RWKent p235 CR France1484

KING,W.J.Lt ded 16-5-18 1/2NStaffs &RAF p157

KING-CHURCH,Cyril Edward Capt dow 25-9-15 7Lond D'Coy p247 CR France107

KING-HARMAN,Lawrence Hope Capt kld 26-10-16 RHA att30RFC p3&31 CR Iraq5

KING-MASON,S.D.Capt 10-06-20 RFA attNigR CR WAfrica3

KING-SALTER,Nigel Henry.MIDx2 Capt kia 3-6-19 IA 1/6GurkhaRif attStaff 55InfBde p278 CR Iraq8

KING-STEPHENS,Lionel Eustace 2Lt dow 20-12-16 8N&D p233 CR France120

KINGCOMBE,Alexis Randolph Lt dow 28-6-15 11Yorks p90 CR Gallipoli6

KINGDON,Arthur Francis TCapt kia 9-10-17 6Y&L p159 MR30

KINGDON,Leonard 2Lt kia 12-1-16 Worc &RFC p3&109 CR Belgium406

KINGDON,Oliver.MC.MID TCapt kia 24-4-18 7Beds p86 MR27

KINGDON,Robert Claude Hawker 2Lt kia 9-4-17 123RFA p31 CR France68,19-4

KINGHAM,Albert Edward.MID TLt kia 6-9-16 8RIrF p171 CR France1890,KINGHAN

KINGHAM,George William Ambrose 2Lt drd 9-11-17 3EKent attWAFF p57&20 CR Mddx39,Lt 1Bn

KINGHAM,Leonard Arthur Lt kia 11-8-17 1 att6RBerks p139 CR Belgium113,10-8

KINGHAM,Rolland Hill T2Lt kia 23-3-18 7MGC p184 MR20,17MGC

KINGSBURY,Edward Harrison TLt ded 17-8-17 GL RE IWT p190 CR Egypt8

KINGSFORD,Reginald John T2Lt kia 1-7-16 10Y&L p159 MR21

KINGSLEY,Albert Thomas 2Lt kia 26-4-18 4SStaffs p122 CR Belgium21

KINGSLEY,Eric T2Lt dow 7-7-16 12Manch p155 MR21

KINGSLEY,Gerald Cecil Lt kia 23-10-14 LNLancs p136 CR Belgium126

KINGSMAN,Roland Walter 2Lt kia 12-10-17 10MGC Inf p184 CR Belgium167

KINGSTON,Harold William Fellemans Lt kia 21-8-15 9RWSurr attRInniskF p56 M

KINGSTON,Nugent Arthur T2Lt kia 1-4-18 1RWar p65 CR France924

KINGSTON,William Lt 16-8-17 7RIrRif MR30

KINGSTON,William.MC.MID 2Lt kia 16-8-17 3RMunstF att1RIrRif p169&175 M

KINGSTON-BLAIR,Oliphant Philip Laurence.DSO.TLtCol dow 8-4-18 11RIrRif p

KINGSWELL,Frank Alford TLt kia 22-3-18 RB att8Bn p179 MR27

KINGSWELL,Leonard William TLtACapt kia 26-3-18 14 att1Hamps att7CpsRei p121 MR20

KINGTON,Edwin Lt dow 17-9-16 11RFA p31 CR France74

KINGTON,William Miles.DSO.Capt kia 20-10-14 1RWFus p98&127,WelshR M

KINGWELL,Francis Robert T2Lt dow 14-10-16 11Mddx p147 CR France833

KINGWELL,Hugh Robert TLt dow 24-8-18 11TankCps p188 CR France927

KINKAID,David Brown Lt 23-4-17 13RScots MR20

KINKAID,John Brown 2Lt 3-5-17 1RScotsF MR20

KINKEAD,Richard Crofton George Moore Capt kia 31-10-14 RAMC att10Huss p196 CR Belgium57,30-10-14

KINKEAD,Thompson Calder T2Lt kld 4-9-17 GL 3RFC p9 CR Sussex55,3-9-17

KINLOCH,James Moncrieff Thompson 2Lt kia 11-7-15 RE p46 MR29

KINMONT,John Collie Capt ded 18-11-17 3CamH attl'TankCps p168&188 CR France398

KINNA,James Eckersley.MC.TLt ded 12-9-17 16LancF p93 CR France40,Charle

KINNACH,Samuel James T2Lt kia 15-7-16 10Yorks p90 MR21

KINNAIRD,Hon Arthur Middleton.MC.Lt kia 27-11-17 1ScotsGds p52 CR France755

KINNAIRD,David T2Lt kia 5-12-17 26NumbF p61 CR France592

KINNAIRD,Douglas Arthuron.Hon.Capt kia 24-10-14 1ScotsGds p52 CR Belgium104

KINNAIRD,Francis Joseph Capt dow 6-6-15 4 att2SStaffs p122 MR22

KINNAIRD,John Kay T2Lt ded 6-11-18 LabCps p189 CR Scot252

KINNEAR,Alexander Hope T2Lt dow 19-7-17 6CamH p168 CR Belgium16

KINNEAR,Charles Annesley 2Lt kia 16-10-16 50RFA p31 CR France397

KINNEAR,J.L.DSO.MC.Maj kld 28-4-18 1/2Lpool &RAF p72

KINNEAR,Katherine Ferrars Nurse ded 3-9-17 VAD CR France1360

KINNELL,Guy Reeve BtMaj ded 9-12-19 4WYorks p263 CR Dorset110

KINNIBURGH,John Donaldson T2Lt kia 6-11-17 GL att14BlkW p190 CR Palestine1 Ex A&SH

KINRADE,Edward T2Lt kia 23-10-18 22NumbF att2Lincs p61 CR France1475

KINROSS,George Irvine Lt kia 12-9-16 2/22Lond p251 CR France157

KINSEY,Albert Thornley T2Lt kia 16-8-17 7SomLI p80 CR Belgium453
KINSLEY,Lawrence Millais 2Lt kia 15-10-16 11Ess p132 CR France307
KINSMAN,Cecil Henry 2Lt dow 28-3-16 RE p210
KIPLING,John Lt kia 27-9-15 2IrGds p53 MR19
KIPPAX,Arthur Hadden T2Lt kia 1-7-16 7EYorks A'Coy p84 CR 372
KIPPAX,James Elliott 2Lt kia 22-9-16 4ELancs p226 CR France758
KIPPS,George Stewart TLt kia 22-8-18 RASC att4Worc p193 CR France28
KIRBY,Alexander Claude 2Lt kia 24-7-18 3 att 1/5N&D p134 CR France109
KIRBY,Alister Graham Capt ded 29-3-17 5Lond p246 CR France1571
KIRBY,Arthur Maurice Lt kia 25-9-17 5DLI attMGC Inf p187&238 MR30
KIRBY,Francis Emile Capt ded 6-12-15 RAOC CR Lond35
KIRBY,Frederick William T2Lt kia 21-9-17 GL 19RFC p9 CR France705
KIRBY,George TLt dow 8-5-18 1LancF p93 CR France65,2Lt
KIRBY,George Ernest T2Lt kia 23-7-16 10Glouc p107 MR21
KIRBY,James Sabey 2Lt kia 10-2-17 10Dev p77 MR37
KIRBY,Kenneth Cameron Lt kia 18-9-18 4Norf p216 CR France369
KIRBY,Richard Elston LtTCapt kldacc 1-6-18 RGA 22CpsHvyArty attStaff p40 CR France1367
KIRBY,Robert Arthur T2Lt kia 11-5-17 11MGC p184 MR20
KIRBY,Sidney Henry T2Lt kia 19-12-15 10BordR att5HLI p117 CR Gallipoli3
KIRBY,Walter Ernest 2Lt mbk 10-7-15 IARO att15Sikhs p278 MR28
KIRBY,William Howard Lee TLt ded 11-12-16 2Suff GarrBn p78
KIRK,Alfred Charles 2Lt kia 31-3-18 13Lond p249 CR France44
KIRK,Arthur T2Lt dow 12-8-16 9SWBord att1/4RScotF p100 CR Egypt7
KIRK,Arthur 2Lt kia 28-6-18 4EYorks p219 CR France352
KIRK,Charles Edmund 2Lt kia 6-8-17 6Beds p86 CR Belgium17,5-8-17
KIRK,Charles Gordon TCapt kia 20-7-18 14Y&L p159 CR France1693 &CR France34
KIRK,Gerald 2Lt dow 24-4-15 1/5RLancs p213 CR Belgium151
KIRK,Gerard Arthur Lt dow 20-7-16 3 att1Lincs p75 CR Lincs98,Garard
KIRK,Harold Raymond 2Lt kia 31-7-17 4SomLI p218 MR29
KIRK,Henry Buchanan TBrigGen ded 12-5-16 A&SH 93InfBde p173 CR France1
KIRK,James.MC.Chap4Cl dow 1-4-18 RAChDept att2SfthH p199 CR France64
KIRK,James.VC.2Lt kia 4-11-18 10 att2Manch p237 CR France1479
KIRK,John Alexander 2Lt kia 13-10-18 5KOSB p224 CR Belgium112
KIRK,John Thomas.MC.2Lt kia 28-3-18 15MGC p184 MR20
KIRK,Joseph Lingard 2Lt ded 10-2-16 1/10Manch p237&270 CR Ches160
KIRK,Leslie Christiern TCapt kia 9-10-17 9WYorks p82 MR30
KIRK,Percival Gordon Capt kia 13-8-17 1Camb attRFC p18&244 CR France134
KIRK,Richard.MC.Capt kia 13-11-16 6Ches p222 CR France293
KIRK,Ronald Leslie 2Lt kia 2-9-18 7 att1Lond p247 MR16
KIRK,Thomas James 2Lt dow 2-7-16 2Ess p132 MR21
KIRK,Tom 2Lt kia 4-6-15 1/10Manch p237 MR4
KIRKALDY,John Givens Capt drd 13-8-18 GL attRE p46 MR41,Maj
KIRKBY,John Nevil 2Lt kia 25-9-16 3 att2Y&L p159 MR21
KIRKBY,William TLtACapt ded 1-11-18 5MGC p184 CR France332
KIRKCALDY,Charles Henry 2Lt kia 10-3-15 1SfthH p165 CR France706,KIRKALDY
KIRKCALDY,Ray H.2Lt mbk 25-3-18 24RFC p256 MR20
KIRKHAM,William Laben T2Lt dow 21-10-16 9RWKent p141 CR France59
KIRKHOUSE,George Capt kia 9-4-18 6DLI p239 CR France346
KIRKLAND,Frederick William 2Lt kia 1-7-16 att1RB p179 MR21
KIRKLAND,James Towers.MC.TCapt kia 18-9-18 RAMC 141FA att1Glouc p196 CR France836
KIRKLAND,William Harrison Capt kia 25-9-15 7CamH p168 MR19
KIRKLEY,Frank Robson.MC.Lt ded 13-11-18 B102RFA p31 CR Italy11
KIRKNESS,Thomas Robert 2Lt kia 18-8-17 GL &32RFC p9 MR20
KIRKPATRICK,Athol 2Lt kia 3-5-17 3 att6EKent p57 MR20
KIRKPATRICK,Edward Hartley Maj kia 15-5-15 2 O&BLI p130 MR22
KIRKPATRICK,Harry Fearnley.DSO.ALtCol dow 27-3-18 EKent attRN Div"Anson" p57 CR France62
KIRKPATRICK,Hugh Cunningham Bruce.DSO.MC.CaptTMaj kia 1-10-18 KOSB StaffGHQ p102
KIRKPATRICK,John Crighton TLt kia 10-12-17 GL &20RFC p9 CR Belgium11
KIRKPATRICK,Robert Buist 2Lt kia 23-6-18 3 att1DCLI p114 CR France20,dow
KIRKPATRICK,Samuel T2Lt ded 30-9-18 PoW LancF att2/5Bn p93 CR Germany3
KIRKUP,Philip Austin.MC.TMaj kld 11-4-17 7DLI attRFC p18&239 CR Durham28
KIRKUS,Cuthbert Hayward 2LtACapt kia 31-7-17 RGA 283SB p40 CR Belgium17
KIRKWOOD,Robert Patrick Lt kia 5-10-17 2 att1KOSB NStaffs p102 MR30
KIRKWOOD,William John T2Lt kia 11-11-15 Yorks att6Bn p90 CR Gallipoli27
KIRKWOOD,William Lithgow 2Lt kia 4-10-18 4KOSB p224 MR16

KIRSH,Charles Sidney 2Lt kia 19-4-15 Beds p86 CR Belgium165
KIRSOP,Conrad Robert John Capt ded 13-10-17 262RFA p207 CR Palestine2
KIRTLAND,John 2Lt kia 12-3-15 2ESurr p113 CR Belgium168
KIRTON,Ralph Imray.AFC.2Lt ded 22-11-18 KOSB &RAF p102 CR Lond3
KIRTON,William Henry 2Lt 1-11-20 2/24Lond CR Herts30
KIRWAN,Laird 2Lt ded 20-8-18 6SLancs &30RAF p125 CR Iraq8,Lt
KIRWAN,R.M.Chap4Cl 23-5-16 CR Mddx51
KIRWAN,Theodore James 2LtACapt ded 11-6-19 RASC p193 CR Asia82
KITCHEN,Fred Tudor 2Lt kia 28-5-18 6SWBord p100 MR18
KITCHEN,George Rowland 2Lt kia 9-4-18 3 att4SomLI p80 CR Palestine9
KITCHEN,Harold Rosslyn Lt kia 27-9-16 3 att8WRid p115 MR21,KITCHIN
KITCHENER,Cecil Lt ded 30-10-18 RGA 94Coy p40 MR43 &CR Pakistan50A
KITCHENER,Horatio Herbert.Earl.KG.KP.GCB.OM.GCSI.GCMG.GCIE.FldMar drd 6-6-16 Staff p1 MR40,5-6-16
KITCHER,Henry Ernesy TCapt kia 7-8-16 5Dors p124 CR France174
KITCHIN,Anthony Walter Brook T2Lt kia 24-9-15 7RWSurr p56 CR France189
KITCHIN,Ernest Harold TCapt kia 21-10-16 17 att15KRRC p151 MR21,21/22-10-16 15 att17Bn
KITCHIN,Francis Leslie TLt kld 11-4-17 11Glouc &4RFC p9&107,kia MR20
KITCHIN,John Buchanan LtACapt dow 5-5-17 6EKent p57 CR France113
KITCHING,Edward Allen 2Lt ded 8-9-15 2/2RFA p208 CR Yorks159,Lt
KITCHING,Fred 2Lt kia 10-7-18 4Yorks p220 CR Belgium188,5Bn
KITCHING,George Allenby 2Lt kia 22-4-18 4 att10N&D p134 CR France41
KITE,Ralph Bertram.MC.Capt dow 10-12-16 3 att2 O&BLI p130 CR France1
KITHER,James Frederick TLt kld 12-12-17 GL RFC 62Aerodrome p9 CR Kent7
KITSON,Edward Gerard Templeman 2Lt dow 3-9-16 3DCLI p114 CR France329
KITSON,Frederick Neill Edmonstone Lt dow 15-8-17 5BlkW p231 CR France922,14-9-16
KITSON,Harold 2Lt dow 21-10-18 5Yorks p221 CR France1287
KITSON,John Henry 2Lt kia 14-4-18 5WRid p227 MR30
KITSON,Richard Buller.MID Capt kia 13-11-17 IA 58Rif p278 CR Palestine9
KITTERMASTER,Arthur Noel Colley TCapt kia 4/5-4-16 9 att12Worc p109 MR38
KITTLE,Ernest Arthur Lewis TLt dow 10-10-18 6RRofCav att3DragGds p23 CR France528
KIVER,Herbert William 2Lt kia 17-4-17 6ESurr p226 CR France161,9Bn
KLEAN,Michael Graham T2Lt kia 1-7-16 16NumbF p61 CR France293
KLEE,Arthur Milton T2Lt kia 8-8-18 10TankCps p188 MR16
KLEIN,Albert John 2Lt kia 14-10-18 5Ess p232 CR France550
KLEMANTASKI,Louis Arthur.MID T2Lt kia 27-5-16 8RBerks p139 CR France161
KNAGGS,Francis Henry TCapt ded 24-6-17 RAMC p196 CR Yorks643
KNAGGS,Kenneth John 2Lt kia 16-3-18 4RWar attRFC p16&65 CR France1281
KNAGGS,Victor St.George Lt dow 12-8-18 G5RFA p31 CR France69
KNAPP,Arthur Douglas TLt ded 27-5-17 NyasaFldForce p201 CR EAfrica15 &CR Tanzania1
KNAPP,Oswald Reed 2Lt dow 13-9-16 2Welch p127 CR France833
KNAPP,Percival Ernest Maj kia 7-1-16 IA 51Sikhs p278 CR Iraq5
KNAPP,Simon Stock.DSO.MC.Rev dow 1-8-17 RAChDept att2IrGds p199 CR Belgium16
KNAPP,Valentine Powell T2Lt kld 18-7-16 7ESurr p113 CR France3
KNAPP-FISHER,Cyril Edward Holme T2Lt dow 31-7-15 6YLI p143 CR Belgium11
KNAPPS-FISHER,S.B.2Lt ded 6-10-14 3NStaffs p265 CR Lond14
KNAPTON,Odber Augustus Lt kia 18-9-14 RWar p65 CR France864
KNATCHBULL,Reginald Norton.DSO.LtCol ded 24-7-17 2Leic p87 CR Iraq8
KNATCHBULL-HUGESSEN,Maurice Astley.MC.Lt kia 25-9-16 2GrenGds SR p50 CR France394
KNEALE,John Francis T2Lt kld 21-12-17 GL RFC p9 CR Shrop145
KNEATH,David John 2Lt dow 3-8-18 5Ches p222 CR France145
KNEE,George Creasy Lt kia 3-5-17 4 att8EYorks p219 CR France421,Capt
KNELL,Edward Charles.MC.2Lt kia 9-8-18 8Lond p247 MR16
KNELL,William HonMaj&QM ded 22-7-17 Lincs attRFC p75 CR Mddx66
KNELLER,Frederick Kneller 2Lt kia 21-3-18 8RFC p16 MR20
KNIFTON,Charles William McKinley 2Lt kia 23-11-17 2RSuss p119 MR30,22-11-17 McKinlay
KNIFTON,James McKinley 2Lt kia 21-7-18 3 att2RSuss p199 MR19
KNIGHT,Arthur Gerald.DSO.MC.TCapt kia 20-12-16 RFC p3 CR France927
KNIGHT,Alan Collingwood Lt dow 29-6-15 14RB attRDubF p179 CR Gallipoli3,28-6-15
KNIGHT,Albert James.MC.2Lt dow 2-6-17 3 att11N&D p134 CR Belgium11
KNIGHT,Alexander William T2Lt dow 14-10-15 12 att9RWar p65 CR Gallipoli27
KNIGHT,Alfred Howard Capt ded 10-12-15 1/5RSuss p228 CR Kent86
KNIGHT,Allan 2Lt kia 23-3-18 5 att11SLancs p230 MR27,24-3-18

KNIGHT,Arthur George Lt kia 29-6-15 9RFus p68 CR Belgium33
KNIGHT,C.R.Wentworth Lt ded PoW 21-6-19 SL p201
KNIGHT,Edgar Frederick 2Lt kia 28-5-16 3Lond p245 CR France1014
KNIGHT,Edward 2Lt kia 20-9-18 4RScotF p222 CR France646
KNIGHT,Edward James 2Lt kia 12-5-17 7 att10LancF p221 MR20
KNIGHTM,E.F.Maj 5-7-17 8Lpool CR Sussex125
KNIGHT,Ernest Alexander T2Lt kia 24-9-17 233MGC Inf p184 MR30
KNIGHT,Francis Ernest T2LtACapt kia 4-3-17 2Nhampt p137 MR21
KNIGHT,Frederick Thornton 2Lt kia 13-5-15 3 att1ELanc p111 MR29
KNIGHT,Geoffrey St.John Lt dow 10-9-18 4RInniskF att14TankCps p105&188 CR France34
KNIGHT,George Gordon Lt dow 17-6-18 1/1DorsYeo p203 CR Palestine3
KNIGHT,George Harold T2Lt kia 6-10-17 RFC GL 11BallCo p9 CR Belgium20
KNIGHT,Gerald Fetherston Lt ded 30-10-19 Dev &RAF p263
KNIGHT,Gerald Robert Frank Capt dow 17-8-17 6Ess att1/1 O&BLI p232 CR Belgium16
KNIGHT,Guy Cunninghame LtCol dow 11-9-14 1LNLancs p136 CR France1134
KNIGHT,Harold Harrison Lt kia 27-3-18 1/9Manch p237 CR France927
KNIGHT,Henry James Capt kia 21-3-18 6BlkW C'Coy p231 CR France646,dow
KNIGHT,Herbert William 2Lt ded 6-6-16 6N&D p270 CR Essex1
KNIGHT,Hugh Eric Coleraine Capt kia 11-4-18 3 att1ELancs p111 MR32
KNIGHT,James Matthew 2Lt kia 20-5-18 C165RFA p31 CR France504
KNIGHT,James William T2Lt dow 12-12-17 10Y&L p159 CR Wilts115
KNIGHT,James Burghleigh Caxton 2Lt kld 15-4-18 GL &RAF p190 CR Egypt9
KNIGHT,John Hall.VD.LtCol kia 13-10-15 5NStaffs p237 MR19
KNIGHT,John Oswald 2Lt kia 2-11-16 3 att11RWKent p141 CR Belgium152,31-10-16
KNIGHT,John Owen Coldhan T2Lt kia 30-11-17 6RWSurr p56 CR France415
KNIGHT,John Peake.DSO.MIDx2 TCapt kia 31-8-16 35RFA p31 CR France397 Ex RHA
KNIGHT,John Percival Lt kia 26-3-18 1/7DLI p239 MR27
KNIGHT,Maynard Mansfield Lt ded 28-1-19 IARO att1MadrasLabCps p278 CR Iraq8
KNIGHT,N.T.CIE.Capt 18-10-18 RIM MR66
KNIGHT,Osbert Richmond.MC.Lt kia 6-4-17 4RWSurr attRFC p18&212 CR France522
KNIGHT,Philip T2Lt kia 28-5-17 6 att7Nhampt p137 CR Belgium28
KNIGHT,Phillip T2Lt kia 29-9-18 16KRRC p151 CR France212
KNIGHT,Philip Clifford 2Lt kia 1-7-16 SomLI p80 MR21
KNIGHT,Raymond Edward.DCM.2Lt kia 21-7-16 1/5Glouc p225 CR France150,22-7-16
KNIGHT,Richard Brodnax Capt dow 5-9-18 3 att4Beds p86 CR France145
KNIGHT,Robert Halley Capt kia 19-9-18 4Wilts p236 CR Palestine9
KNIGHT,Robert Valentine Harold 2Lt kia 19-7-16 1Nhampt p137 CR France703
KNIGHT,Walter Foster TLt kia 27-2-17 14 att16WYorks p82 CR France580,Forster
KNIGHT,William Bernard 2Lt kia 21-4-15 4NStaffs p157 MR29
KNIGHT,William Leonard TLt ded 26-2-19 2Ess p132 CR France34
KNIGHT-BRUCE,Algernon James Lewis 2Lt kia 10-3-15 33RFA p31 CR France706
KNIGHTON,Gerald Godfrey.MID TMaj dow 30-4-17 5 O&BLI p130 CR France214
KNIGHTS,Henry Thorne TCapt kia 19-10-16 2Yorks att21TMB p90 CR France385
KNIGHTS-SMITH,Bernard Arthur 2Lt kia 5-9-15 12RB C'Coy p179 CR France1157
KNIPE,Edward Arthur 2Lt dow 26-9-16 2KOSB p102 CR France630,kia
KNOCKER,Arthur Paget LtCapt kia 7-2-15 1Hamps p121 CR Belgium69,8-2-15
KNOLLYS,Frederick Roger Alexander Nicholas Maj dow 24-9-15 CityofLondYeo p204 CR Lond14
KNOTT,Archibald Sherbrooke.MC&Bar.T2Lt dow 25-4-18 2RBerks p139 CR France71
KNOTT,Charles Singleton 2Lt kia 23-3-18 11RFus p68 MR27
KNOTT,Donald James Vivian T2Lt kia 7-10-16 12 att11RWKent p141 CR France744
KNOTT,Ernest Capt kia 22-3-18 6Manch p236 MR27
KNOTT,Frederick Vernon TLt kia 21-3-16 19ACycCps p181 CR France705
KNOTT,Frederick William T2Lt kia 7-6-17 9Yorks p90 MR29
KNOTT,Henry Basil TCapt dow 7-9-15 9NumbF p61 CR Blegium84
KNOTT,James Leadbitter.DSO.TMaj kia 1-7-16 10WYorks p82 CR Belgium84
KNOTT,Ralph Leonard Lt 25-9-15 12NumbF p61 MR19
KNOTT,Robert Cecil TCapt dow 14-8-16 28 att20NumbF p61 CR France924
KNOTT,Stanley T2Lt ded 1-2-18 RASC p267 CR Suff45
KNOTT,Stuart Wallace 2Lt kia 24-4-18 3Lond p245 MR27
KNOTT,Sydney James 2Lt dow 8-7-16 5 att3Worc p109 CR France44
KNOTT,Thomas Albert 2Lt dow 25-11-14 1RBerks p139 CR France102

KNOWLES,Andrew Brooks 2Lt kia 11-6-16 IARO att17Cav p278 CR EAfrica29,Lt
KNOWLES,Arthur Yalden Lt dow 26-8-17 RFA 2ReinfCo 5thArmy p31 CR France40
KNOWLES,Eustace Oliver.OBE.Capt 11-3-20 GL attRE IWT CR Iraq6 Ex RIM
KNOWLES,F.2Lt 26-5-20 5RRofCav CR Ches114
KNOWLES,Frank Henry Capt kia 3-5-17 5WYorks p218 MR20
KNOWLES,Gavin Tenison Royle Lt kia 1-7-16 1/5SStaffs p229 MR21
KNOWLES,George Clarence 2Lt dow 10-6-17 3 att9Yorks p90 CR Belgium11
KNOWLES,Harold Leslie 2Lt kia 30-1-17 10GordH p166 MR21
KNOWLES,Harry Wilfred.MC.2LtTLt kia 8-6-17 1 att11WYorks p82 CR Belgium127
KNOWLES,Hedley Lt kia 30-5-15 1/6WRid p227 CR France82
KNOWLES,Henry Rylands.MC.TCapt kia 30-7-15 RAMC att7RLancs p196 MR21
KNOWLES,J.C.B.Lt 3-4-20 5ELancs CR Lancs193
KNOWLES,John Lyndon 2Lt kia 18-8-16 5 att7RB p179 MR21
KNOWLES,Jonathan Edward Capt kia 23-8-14 Mddx p147 CR Belgium244
KNOWLES,Richard Arthur Lees.MC.Lt kia 25-2-17 KRRC att4Bn p151 CR Greece1
KNOWLES,Richard Cameron TLt kia 10-7-16 114MGC Inf p184 MR21
KNOWLES,Stephen 2Lt dow 24-10-16 5 att2RB p179CR France105
KNOWLES,Vincent Lt&QM ded 14-10-15 RE p46 CR Yorks5
KNOWLES,Walford Vernon 2Lt kia 31-12-17 3 att2RBerks p139 CR Belgium126
KNOWLES,William Scott.MC.Capt kldByRobbers 26-11-20 IA 1GurkhaRif attSPersiaRif p278 CR Asia82
KNOWLING,Francis John Dobree.MC.TCapt kia 8-3-18 10A&SH p173 CR Belgium12
KNOWLSON-WILLIAMS,Henry William T2Lt kld 11-7-17 GL RFC p9
KNOX,Alexander William Coningham Capt kia 19-10-14 2RIrReg p89 MR22
KNOX,Andrew Ronald T2Lt kia 12-12-15 RE 185TC p46 CR France430
KNOX,Arthur Rice.DSO.Maj ded 22-4-17 RFA p261 CR Lond29,23-4-17
KNOX,Arthur Victor Lt kia 6-6-17 5 att1NumbF p213 MR20
KNOX,Charles Duncan 2Lt kia 17-3-17 Suff &43RFC p9&78 MR20
KNOX,George 2Lt kia 9-4-16 8RLancs p59 MR29
KNOX,Hubert LtCol kia 13-10-16 Manch att16Bn p155 CR France432
KNOX,James Meldrum.DSO&Bar.LtCol dow 23-9-18 1/7RWar p214 CR Italy
KNOX,John.MC&Bar.T2Lt dow 23-10-18 13RIrRif p169 CR France34
KNOX,John Laurence T2Lt kia 20-11-17 7RSuss p119 MR17,Lawrence
KNOX,John Stanley T2Lt dow 11-7-16 7RInniskF p105 CR France115
KNOX,John Vesey Lt kld 4-1-18 18Lond attRFC p18&250 CR Ireland145
KNOX,Robert TCapt kia 17-4-16 1HLI p163 MR38
KNOX,Thomas Cowe 2Lt kia 19-8-18 7Lpool att12Norf p215 CR France19,Cowl
KNOX,William Capt ded 20-2-16 3CamH &13RFC p3&168 CR France448
KNOX,William 2Lt kia 24-3-18 54RFC p16 MR20
KNUBLEY,Robert Leavitt.MC.MID LtACapt dow 9-7-16 3Wilts p153 CR France44,7-7-16
KOCH,Marcus Addison T2Lt kia 22-9-15 2KSLI p145 CR France1472
KOE,Archibald Stephen LtCol dow 25-4-15 1KOSB p102 MR4,26-4-15
KOE,Philip Stephen 2Lt kia 31-7-16 1/4Y&L C'Coy p238 CR France246
KOEBEL,Charles Edward Capt dow 24-8-15 RWSurr attLancF p56 MR4
KOHN,Wilfred Arthur T2Lt kia 1-7-16 11ELancs p111 CR France156
KOHNSTAM,Oscar Jacob Charles 2Lt kia 29-6-16 4NStaffs attMGC Inf p157&18 CR France513
KOHNSTAMM,Norman Mortimer Joseph Capt kia 22-3-18 18Manch &RFC p16&155 CR France511,23-3-18
KORTRIGHT,Mountney Coesvelt William Lt kia 21-5-17 1Ess p132 CR France311,Mounteney
KRAMER,Gerald.MM.Lt kia 31-8-18 5ESurr p226 CR France563
KRAUSS,Dennis Hillel 2Lt dow 7-4-17 5NStaffs p238 CR France1
KRIEKENBECK,Ronald Edward Elliott Maj mbk 18-4-16 IA 128Pnrs p278 MR38,KOIEKENBEEK
KROENIG-RYAN,Alexander Charles Thomas Lt kia 24-10-18 8Mddx p236 CR France190,23-10-18
KROG,Eustace John.MC.TLt kia 7-9-18 1EYorks p84 CR France262
KROHN,Edmund Otto 2Lt kia 1-3-18 84RFC p16 CR France1893,Lt
KROHN,Nicholas Adolf 2Lt kia 16-5-15 2BordR p117 MR22
KROLIK,Elliot.MC.TCapt kia 23-10-17 16RB p179 CR Belgium124
KRUGER,Dirk Jacobus T2Lt kia 1-4-18 23Manch p155 CR France44,Lt 2-4-18
KUHN,Alfred Edgar Lt dow 18-5-15 2Beds p86 CR France80
KURTEN,Gaston Pierre Peter TLtAMaj kia 24-4-18 RGA 291SB p40 CR France30
KYD,Frank Proctor T2Lt kia 18-8-16 11ESurr attRWar p113 CR France293
KYDD,Chester Bishop T2Lt kia 3-5-17 3 att7Beds p86 MR20
KYDD,Henry John Naysmith Lt ded 13-5-18 LabCps p266 CR Numb96 Ex 2WYorks

KYDD,John William Albert T2Lt dow 26-3-18 19LancF p93 CR Belgium72
KYLE,David Logan 2Lt kia 19-5-15 RE p46 CR Belgium115
KYLE,Hugh Gavin 2Lt kia 12-7-15 4RScotF p222 MR4
KYLE,John Stott.MC&Bar.Lt dow 22-5-18 D123RFA p31 CR France63
KYNASTON,John Oswald Maurice TLt kia 21-9-18 74MGC Infp184 CR France1462
KYNCH,Harold Egerton Vivian Maj ded 31-5-19 Ches att183LabCps p189 CR France268
KYNOCH,Alexander Bruce TCapt kld 8-3-18 RFC p16 CR Mddx15
KYNOCH,Alfred Stewart T2Lt kia 13-3-18 52RFC &GL p16 CR France1203
KYNOCH,Colin Smith 2Lt kia 26-4-15 6DLI p239 MR29
KYRKE-SMITH,Arthur Kyrke Capt dow 23-9-14 1Lpool p72 CR France1110,kia
KYSH,Claude James Anthony Lt ded 27-11-18 1RWKent p141 CR Norf26
KYTE,Henry Edward T2Lt dow 22-11-17 14RIrRif p169 CR France512

L

LABERTOUCHE,Guy Neal Landale Maj dow 14-4-15 IA 122Inf att119 p278 CR Iraq6
LABETT,John William Hooper T2Lt kia 25-1-17 9Lincs p75 MR38
LABDON,Percy Miller T2Lt kia 26-9-17 RE 469FC p46 CR Belgium130
LABOUCHERE,Arthur Maxwell.DSO.TMaj dow 30-4-18 5 O&BLI p130 CR France1142
LACAITA,Francis Charles.MC.LtTCapt kia 3-4-18 17Lancers att1MGC p23&184 MR20
LACE,Walter Henry.MC.Maj kia 8-11-18 RE 439FC p209 CR Belgium406
LACER,see LACEY,E.A.
LACEY,Edred Severs 2Lt kia 21-10-16 17 att11Ches p96 MR21
LACEY,Everitt Arthur 2Lt ded 16-5-19 4Lpool p270 CR Wales671,LACER 7Bn
LACEY,Frank Philip Sleigh T2Lt ded 29-3-18 RASC MT &RFC p193 CR Egypt15
LACEY,Gordon Herbert.MC.2Lt dow 29-9-18 9Lond p248 CR France146
LACEY,Thomas Henry T2Lt dow 4-9-16 17KRRC p151 CR France169
LACEY,Wilfred Lt kia 31-3-18 RFA 59DAC attY59TMB p207 MR20
LACEY,William George.MC.Lt dow 4-11-18 RASC &27RAF p267 CR France154
LACEY,William Stocks TLt dow 11-10-16 RAMC att11RWKent p196 CR France833
LACHLAN,Cecil George.MIDx2 T2Lt kia 31-8-17 17WYorks p82 MR21
LACK,Frederick George 2Lt kia 30-3-18 21Lond p251 CR Syria2
LACK,John Westlake TCapt dow 26-7-16 8Suff p78 CR France51
LACK,Reginald Walter.MM.MID 2Lt kia 29-9-16 13 att1RWFus p98 MR32
LACK,Reg Lambert T2Lt dow 18-7-16 14RIrRif p169 CR Surrey96
LACON,Sidney John Boileau Maj kia 12-4-18 RWar attVIIICps MT RASC CR Belgium3 see LOCON,S.J.B.
LA COSTE,Charles John Constable.MC.TCapt kia 9-10-17 GL att1/8WYorks p190 MR30
LACY,Francis Prior.MC.2LtTCapt kia 13-8-15 W'land&C'landYeo attRE 170TC p206 CR France163
LACY,Thomas Joseph 2Lt kia 7-4-18 48A'RFA p31 CR France2,8-4-18 B48
LACY,Wilfrid Henry TCapt kia 7-10-16 15Hamps p121 CR France744
LACY,William Braithwaite 2Lt dow 14-12-17 15Lond p249 CR France398
LADD,Alfred Caldier Maj kia 25-3-18 14Worc p109 MR20
LADE,John Harvey 2Lt dow 5-10-17 WarYeo att1/5WarR p205 CR Belgium16
LADELL,John Francis TLt kia 20-7-16 20Mddx p147 CR France149
LADLER,Ernest George T2Lt ded 3-12-18 700LabCps p189
LAFERLA,H.G.Capt 4-7-19 2MaltaR CR Europe4
LAFERRIERE,L.S.Capt.MC.29-5-20 RGA CR Lond9 served as MARTIN,L.S.
LAFONE,Alexander Malins.VC.Maj kia 27-10-17 1MddxHuss p204 CR Palestine1
LAFONE,Claude Alexander.DSO.Capt kia 14-3-15 2Dev D'Coy p77 CR France706,12-3-15
LAFONE,Eric William.MC.TCapt kia 15-6-18 12DLI p161 CR Italy4
LAGDEN,Ronald Owen Capt kia 3-3-15 6KRRC p151 MR29
LAIDLAW,Andrew T2Lt kia 9-9-16 2Manch p155 MR16
LAIDLAW,James Clelland T2LtACapt kia 6-11-17 3ScotRif p103 CR Belgium13
LAIDLAW,John Leslie T2Lt dow 20-7-16 10A&SH p173 CR France23
LAIDLAW,Walter Sibbald TLt kia 23-11-17 RE 203FC p46 CR Belgium20
LAIDLAW,William Simpson 2Lt kia 30-8-18 250RFA p31 MR16
LAILEY,Eric Lillywhite T2Lt kia 29-2-16 7DCLI p114 CR Belgium23
LAINE,Charles Janion T2Lt kia 30-7-16 89MGC Inf p184 MR21
LAINE,Thomas de Jersey T2Lt kia 21-11-17 1RGLI p201 MR17
LAING,Alexander Arthur Lt kia 28-11-17 RE p210 CR France364
LAING,Alexander Torrance TCapt dow 24-7-16 13NumbF p61 CR France145

LAING,Charles William 2Lt kia 24-4-15 2EKent p57 MR29
LAING,David Patrick Lt kia 20-10-15 2RIrReg p89 MR22
LAING,Dudley Ogilvie TCapt kia 1-7-16 22NumbF p61 MR21
LAING,Ernest Edward T2Lt kia 29-7-17 7EYorks p84 CR France604
LAING,George T2Lt dow 10-4-17 9ScotRif p103 CR France95
LAING,Gerald Ogilvie TCapt kiaa a 5-6-17 20NumbF p61 MR20
LAING,Gilbert James 2Lt kia 12-3-15 ULIA att1RIrRif p169 p278 MR28
LAING,Henry Davidson Capt kia 13-3-15 6GordH p242 MR22,Harry
LAING,Harry Needham 2Lt kia 17-9-16 4Yorks p220 MR21
LAING,Ivan.MC.Lt kia 30-11-17 2CldGds p51 CR France662
LAING,James Alexander T2Lt kia 14-10-18 10RWSurr p56 CR Belgium157
LAING,James Gordon Maj kia 3-10-18 28Lond attMGC p187&252 CR France1887
LAING,James MacDougall Lt kia 23-3-18 25MGC p184 MR20
LAING,John Darg T2Lt kia 24-10-17 GL 19RFC p9 CR France1032
LAING,John Spence 2Lt ded 12-6-19 RASC p267
LAING,N.P.Capt 31-10-19 RAMC CR Lancs387
LAING,Robert MacLeod 2Lt kia 20-7-16 4 att1ScotRif p103 MR21
LAING,St.Clair King Nixon T2Lt ded 2-4-17 7RMunstF p175 CR France285
LAING,William McClymont Black 2Lt dow 21-6-16 1RScotF p94 CR Belgium11
LAIRD,Andrew Clark 2Lt kia 22-11-16 5BlkW att15RFC p18&231 CR France41,22-12-16
LAIRD,Arthur Donald T2Lt kia 1-7-16 17HLI p163 CR France246
LAIRD,Colin TLtACapt kia 20-9-17 19Lpool p72 MR30
LAIRD,Frank 2Lt mbk 25-3-18 8NStaffs att56TMB p256 MR20
LAIRD,Homer Warring T2Lt kia 8-10-17 GL RFC p9 CR France285
LAIRD,Hugh Blackhall 2Lt kia 8-7-16 3 att2Yorks p90 MR21
LAIRD,James Duncan T2Lt kia 25-3-18 12KRRC p151 MR27
LAIRD,James Ritchie 2Lt dow 22-7-16 5ScotRif p224 CR France44
LAIRD,Louis Wilfred T2Lt kia 2-9-18 NumbF att23LancF p61 CR France298
LAIRD,Matthew James Donald Capt kia 23-4-16 RE 2/2FC p210 CR Egypt2
LAIRD,Ninian Parker T2Lt kia 26-3-18 1 att7/8KOSB p102 MR20,28-3-18 3 att7/8Bn
LAIRD,William 2Lt kia 1-12-17 3CldGds p51 CR France662
LAIRD,William Allan Lt dow 18-9-15 3 att1RScotF p94 CR France64
LAIRD,William Weir 2Lt kia 4-11-16 5GordH p242 CR France131
LAIT,Wilfrid Francis James T2Lt kia 3-8-17 3 att8BordR p117 MR29
LAITHWAITE,John TLt kia 22-2-16 20Manch p155 CR France370
LAKE,Frank Gilbert Lt kia 31-7-17 Herts p252 MR29
LAKE,James Louis Engelburt Rey 2Lt dow 24-8-15 3 att1BordR p117 CR Greece10
LAKE,John Stephen Raymond Capt kia 16-6-16 1 att3SWBord p100 CR France550,3 att1Bn
LAKE,Noel Graham Lt kia 25-3-18 2/5Glouc p225 MR27,24-3-18
LAKE,Reginald St.George Lt kia 17-11-16 4 O&BLI p231 CR France392
LAKE,Thomas Ashton 2Lt kia 13-8-18 6N&D p233 MR19
LAKE,William TCapt kia 28-7-16 3 att2SStaffs p122 CR France390
LAKE,William Martin 2Lt dow 28-6-16 RGA attP34MedTMB TMB p40 CR France515
LAKEMAN,Arthur Frederick 2Lt kia 5-8-18 4BlkW att15TankCps p189&230,kld CR France300
LAKEMAN,Harold Leslie T2Lt kia 22-8-18 RASC att7LancF p193 CR France514
LAKEMAN,John Pearce T2Lt dow 20-4-17 NumbF att20Bn p61 CR France40,Pearse
LAKEMAN,Reginald Noel 2Lt kia 3-10-18 5N&D p233 CR France375
LAKIN,Charles Lt dow 21-8-16 4 O&BLI p231 CR France74
LAKIN,H.W. Mech 27-9-16 RIM CR Iraq5
LALONDE,Lionel Victor Pollock 2Lt ded 31-3-16 9SomLI p80 CR France1,45MGC
LAMAISON,Leonard William Henry Lt kia 2-7-16 2/5RWar p214 CR France1157
LAMAISON,Wilfrid Lawrence.MID Lt dow 23-8-18 16Lond att1/6NStaffs p249 CR France10,Laurence
LAMB,Cameron.DSO.Capt dow 29-12-14 2BordR p117 CR France64
LAMB,Cecil Walter TCapt ded 15-11-15 RFA p31 CR Hamps17
LAMB,Dudley William Lt kia 22-3-18 14Lond p249 MR20
LAMB,Eric Robert Lt ded 2-11-18 5Manch p236 CR France341
LAMB,Ernest Edwin 2Lt kia 26-9-16 3RWKent att9LancF p141 MR21
LAMB,Everard Joseph Capt kia 1-11-14 3NumbF attYLI p61 MR29
LAMB,Edward Woolard Peniston 2Lt kld 24-4-18 GL &11RAF p190 CR France62,kia
LAMB,Francis Cardno 2Lt kld 7-9-16 RFC p3 CR Mddx17
LAMB,Francis James Ongley 2Lt ded 24-7-18 RGA attArmyAmmoPark p40 CR Iraq8
LAMB,Frank Muller Lt kia 21-3-18 7N&D p256 MR20
LAMB,George Ross 2Lt kia 20-4-17 7HLI p240 MR34

LAMB,Harold Alfred 2Lt kld 9-7-18 12Lancers att98RAF p22 CR France31,Lt kia 1Bn
LAMB,Harold George Wellesley 2Lt kia 8-10-18 6 att10RFus p68 CR France1345
LAMB,James Scott T2Lt kia 10-9-18 RB att2Bn p179 CR France369
LAMB,John 2Lt ded 28-7-17 5RScots p211 CR Scot 235
LAMB,John T2Lt dow 17-10-17 RE 179TC p46 CR Belgium16
LAMB,John Albert 2Lt kia 14-10-18 4WYorks att13WRid p82 CR France82,Lt
LAMB,John McNair T2Lt kia 4-11-18 A82RFA p31 CR France1478
LAMB,Joseph 2Lt dow 16-8-17 153RFA 36DAC p31 CR Belgium10
LAMB,Launcelot Rupert TLt kia 25-5-17 2RLancs p59 CR Greece5
LAMB,Patrick James TLt dow 31-7-18 RGA 14DAC p40 CR France33
LAMB,Raymond Wildman.MC.TLt ded 14-11-18 60MGC Inf p184 CR Egypt9
LAMB,Thomas 2Lt ded 30-6-16 4YLI p235 CR Numb20
LAMB,Walter TLt kia 1-7-16 22NumbF p62 MR21
LAMBARDE,B.A.Nurse 5-3-19 VAD RNHosp CR Kent147
LAMBART,Gerald Edgar Oliver Fortescue CaptAMaj dow 28-3-16 1RScotF p94 CR Belgium11
LAMBDIN,John Reginald.MC.Lt dow 24-9-18 7WYorks p218 CR France327
LAMBE,Frederick William TLt dow 10-11-16 5Norf p216 CR France515
LAMBE,Percy TLt kia 7-11-15 9 att6EKent p57 MR19
LAMBERT,Arnold Stuart.MC&Bar.MID LtAMaj ded 25-12-18 RE 459FC p46 CR Belgium330
LAMBERT,Arthur Frere MajALtCol kia 2-11-17 3RWSurr att10Lond p56 CR Palestine8
LAMBERT,Charles Henry TLt ded 17-8-15 RAVC attRFA p198 CR Egypt3
LAMBERT,Cyril John Noël.MC.Lt kia 2-9-18 103/40RFA p31 CR France214
LAMBERT,Douglas T2Lt kia 13-10-15 6EKent p57 MR19
LAMBERT,Eric Noel.MC.TCapt dow 7-6-17 3 att8Yorks p90 CR Belgium127
LAMBERT,Ernest Charles TLt dow 30-6-16 RAMC att12ESurrp196 CR France102
LAMBERT,Francis Courtenay Maj ded 29-3-16 RAMC p196 CR Iraq1
LAMBERT,Francis Henry Lt dow 14-6-15 3 att1Hamps p121 MR29
LAMBERT,Frederick Charles 2Lt kia 28-3-18 5YLI p235 MR20
LAMBERT,Frederick William Manley T2Lt ded 25-2-19 2SStaffs p264 CR Surrey15
LAMBERT,Geoffrey Fontaine 2Lt dow 15-4-16 1Herts p252 CR France145
LAMBERT,George 2Lt kia 22-4-15 3RFus p68 MR29
LAMBERT,George T2Lt kia 23-4-17 7CamH D'Coy p168 CR France1182
LAMBERT,George T2Lt kia 29-9-18 1 att2Worc p109 CR France665
LAMBERT,Harry Redcliffe 2Lt kia 21-3-17 RE 476SthMidFC p210 CR France1472
LAMBERT,Henry McLaren Capt kia 13-5-15 1Drags p21 CR Belgium2
LAMBERT,Henry Stuart 2Lt kia 11-1-16 5Yorks A'Coy p221 CR Belgium5
LAMBERT,Jack Fellowes 2Lt kia 30-7-15 9KRRC p151 MR29
LAMBERT,James Edward Downes TLt kia 2-11-15 6Nhampt p137 CR France637,1-11-15
LAMBERT,John Henry TCapt dow 9-8-16 25NumbF p62 CR France12
LAMBERT,John Lewis TMaj ded 20-10-16 4RASC ArmyAuxHorseCo p193 CR France300
LAMBERT,John Mounsey Capt kia 28-10-14 3 att1NumbF p62 CR France924
LAMBERT,Kenneth Capt kia 9-5-15 1YLI p143 CR Belgium152
LAMBERT,Leonard Walter T2Lt kia 28-3-18 RFus att4Bn p68
LAMBERT,Marie Louise Benjamin Hector Maj ded 24-8-19 RASC p267 MR70 &CR Europe180,Louis
LAMBERT,Maurice Borington TLt kia 7-8-15 6Yorks p90 MR4,Bovingdon
LAMBERT,Maurice Gustave Louis 2Lt kia 5-1-17 10Worc att7Berks p109 MR37
LAMBERT,Montague Arthur T2Lt kia 2-10-18 KRRC att18Bn p151 CR Belgium112
LAMBERT,Percy Gerald T2Lt kia 21-3-18 25NumbF p62 MR20
LAMBERT,Philip Felix 2Lt kia 3-5-17 2WRid p115 MR20
LAMBERT,T.S.CB.CMG.BrigGen kld 20-6-21 Staff CR Surrey1
LAMBERT,Walter Col ded 20-12-14 RAOC p267 CR Lond28,24-12-14
LAMBERT,William T2Lt dow 2-6-16 18HLI p163 CR France80,kia
LAMBERT,William Fairlie 2Lt kia 23-3-16 3 att9ScotRif p103 CR France390 &CR France1160
LAMBERT-SHEA,Joseph Patrick.MC&Bar.DCM.Capt&QM dow 1-12-17 2DCLI CR France398
LAMBOURNE,Reginald Bertram 2Lt dow 5-1-16 3 att2Hamps p121 CR Gallipoli1
LAMBOURNE,William 2Lt kia 9-8-18 23Lond p252 MR16
LAMBROUGHTON,Hugh T2Lt dow 12-4-18 1RScotF p94 CR France202
LAMBROUGHTON,Matthew T2Lt ded 16-11-18 3SfthH p165 CR France1027
LAMBTON,Edward Capt ded 28-3-16 PembrokeYeo p205
LAMBTON,Francis.Hon.2Lt kia 25-10-15 RHGds p20 MR29,30-10-14
LAMBTON,Geoffrey Lt kia 1-9-14 CldGds p51 CR France1108
LAMBTON,L Capt 28-3-16 PembrokeYeo CR Egypt9
L'AMIE,H.St Clair Lt 5-10-20 WRid att2Ches CR Ireland14

LAMMERT,Rennie Dean T2Lt kia PoW 23-3-18 10 att8Glouc p107&257,dow 29-3-18 CR France403
LAMOND,George Alexander Walker TLtCol ded 25-2-18 RE IWT p46 CR Asia9
LAMONT,Alexander 2Lt drd 10-10-18 9Lpool p216 CR Ireland14
LAMONT,Geoffrey Simpson.DSO.2Lt kia 5-11-18 1GrenGds p50 CR France1080
LAMONT,James Kenneth Lt kia 27-10-17 RFA 4HB p207 CR Belgium101
LAMONT,John 2Lt kia 11-5-16 7KOSB p102 CR France423,12-5-16
LA NAUZE,George Mansfield Lt kia 9-5-15 4RIrRif p169 MR32
LA NAUZE,William Lt kia 16-5-15 4RIrRif p169 MR29
LANAWAY,Francis Charlton T2Lt kia 21-8-18 RSuss att7RFus p119 CR France51
LANCASTER,Alice Hilda SpMilProbat drd 3-6-18 TFNS p254 CR France64
LANCASTER,Arnold Busk.MM.T2Lt dow 11-4-18 29MGC p184 CR France1094
LANCASTER,Charles Edward TLt kia 21-3-18 3 att1Leic p87 MR20
LANCASTER,Dudley Wood 2Lt ded 23-1-18 SStaffs p264
LANCASTER,Ernest Randolph T2Lt kia 12-10-16 16MGC Inf p184 MR21 Ex 7D
LANCASTER,Gerald William.MC.Capt dow 14-9-18 3Mon att15WelchR p244 C France34
LANCASTER,Henry Robert 2Lt kia 2-11-17 1/4Ess p232 CR Palestine8
LANCASTER,Howard Vincent T2Lt dow 21-11-17 3 att1Leic p87 CR France398
LANCASTER,James Capt kia 8-5-15 3Mon p244 MR29
LANCASTER,James Norman T2Lt kia 10-8-15 9Worc p109 MR4
LANCASTER,John Cecil Maj kia 8-5-15 1RWar p65 MR29 &CR Belgium152
LANCASTER,Joseph Clement 2Lt kia 29-4-18 3 att9LNLancs p136 MR30
LANCASTER,Joseph William Lt&QM ded 1-1-16 7LancF p270 CR Kent268
LANCASTER,Percy T2Lt kia 15-9-16 122MGC Inf p184 MR21
LANCASTER,Robert T2Lt kia 28-4-17 7Norf p74 CR France531
LANCASTER,Thomas Erwin 2Lt kia 1-7-16 2SfthH p165 MR21
LANCASTER,William Oliver T2Lt kia 26-10-17 21Manch p155 MR30
LANCASTER-BELL,A.Ray Lt kia 17-5-15 2DubF CR Belgium4
LAND,Ronald John Lt kia 20-3-18 3Y&L attMGC p159&184 MR20,21-3-18
LANDALE,Cyril TCapt kia 21-8-18 13KRRC p151 CR France1014
LANDALE,Douglas Blackwood Lt kia 23-10-14 3RB p179 CR France681
LANDALE,James Russell Capt kia 8-3-16 IA 2Rajputs p278 MR38
LANDELL,William TLt dow 22-7-17.14A&SH p173 CR France398
LANDERS,George Maxwell 2Lt kia 28-3-18 8RLancs p59 MR20
LANDON,John Robert LtACapt kia 3-9-16 15RWar p65 MR21
LANDON,William Henry Fitz Roy Capt kia 15-2-15 3Suff attBeds p78 CR Belgium98,Fitzroy
LANDREY,Cecil Thorpe TLt kia 21-4-18 RE 251TC p46 CR France88
LANE,Arthur Bloomfield TCapt kia 20-11-17 10RB p179 MR17
LANE,Charles Henry 2Lt dow 21-8-18 2 att10RIrRif p169 CR France100,kia
LANE,Charles Willington Tremayne.MC.CaptAMaj dow 4-4-18 7DragGds p21 C France185
LANE,Edward Alfred Joseph Ardan Lt kia 1-7-16 1/9Lond p248 MR21
LANE,Edward Dion.MC.T2Lt dow PoW 8-12-17 59MGC Inf p184 CR France658
LANE,Edward F.Capt ded 13-4-19 3Hamps p121 CR Staffs140
LANE,Edward George Arthur Campbell 2Lt kia 30-9-18 Leinst att12RIrRif p174 Belgium157
LANE,Eric Arthur Milner 2Lt kia 8-3-16 3Manch p155 MR38
LANE,Ernest Albert 2Lt kia 1-9-18 3 att2Ess p132 CR France531
LANE,Frank 2Lt kia 16-5-17 17Lond p250 MR20
LANE,Frank Ashton T2Lt kia 31-7-17 18Lpool p72 MR29
LANE,Frank Nowell.MID Capt ded 11-8-18 IA 2/7GurkhaRif p278 CR Palestine
LANE,Frederick William 2Lt dow 19-5-17 8Lond p247 CR France40,Frederic
LANE,Geoffrey Horsburgh Capt kia 19-12-19 IA 1/103MahrattaLI p279 MR43
LANE,George James.MID 2Lt dow 29-6-16 1RBerks p139 CR FRance40
LANE,George Ronald Capt&Adjt kia 16-9-16 2CldGds p51 CR France374,15-9-
LANE,Harold Frank 2Lt kia 14-10-15 11RScots p54 CR Belgium122
LANE,Hector Allan Lt kia 13-5-15 ELancs p111 MR29
LANE,Henry Clarence Horsburgh T2Lt kia 10-7-17 1BordR p117 MR29
LANE,Jocylyn Henry Cambridge 2Lt ded 16-10-18 4CldGds p51 CR France40,Jocelyn
LANE,John Austen T2Lt ded 27-10-17 542LabCps p189 CR Sussex144,RGA
LANE,John Boyd Armstrong T2Lt dow 13-9-16 6RIrF p171 CR France145
LANE,John Elston 2Lt kia 3-5-17 4 att7EKent p212 MR20
LANE,Maurice.MC.MM.LtACapt kia 29-12-17 2/20Lond p251 CR Palestine3
LANE,Reginald William 2Lt kia 9-11-18 1/2Hamps &RAF p121 CR France276
LANE,Shales Frederick TCapt kia 18-9-18 9Norf p74 CR France1701
LANE,Sydney Henry TLtACapt kia 5-4-18 RGA 38HB p40 CR France924
LANE,Thomas Edward Moore TMaj ded 17-4-19 5KSLI p265 CR Lancs410
LANE,William George 2Lt dow 7-11-17 1/1WorcYeo p206 CR Egypt2

LANE-FOX,George Henry Capt 29-10-20 GL CR Surrey1
LANE-JOYNT,Albert William Lt kia 26-2-16 Dors attMGC p184 CR France279
LANE-MULLINS,James Brendan 2Lt kia 14-6-17 RFA att29DAC p31 CR France1182
LANE-NICHOLS,Douglas William TCapt kia 20-8-16 8RWSurr p56 MR21
LANES,Ewart Reginald.MC.Capt kia 22-3-18 8Lond p247 MR27
LANG,Arthur Lt kia 29-8-16 6A&SH p243 CR France394
LANG,Arthur Horace 2Lt kia 25-1-15 2GrenGds attScotGds p50 MR22 &CR France1896
LANG,Frederick Murray Capt dow 18-12-15 6A&SH p243 CR France43,17-12-15
LANG,Graeme Gordon T2Lt kia 11-4-17 7KOSB p102 MR20
LANG,Henry Astell Maj kia 9-6-15 4Worc p109 CR Gallipoli6,6-6-15
LANG,James Corbet Capt kia 12-7-15 1KOSB p102 MR4
LANG,John Capt ded 15-4-17 GL Res CR Scot717
LANG,Norman TLt kia 24-8-18 MGC DivBn p184 CR France393
LANG,Sidney Drummond 2Lt dow 26-2-17 5YLI p235 CR France177,kia 23-2-17
LANG,William Brymner LtTCapt kia 12-7-15 6A&SH p243 2entries Bryner 5Bn MR4
LANG-BROWNE,John Agnew Capt kia 16-5-15 2RWSurr p56 CR France279
LANGDALE,Edward George.MC.MID Lt kia 13-10-15 5Leic p220 MR19
LANGDALE,Harold Carthew Lt kia 26-9-17 13RSuss p119 MR30
LANGDALE,Mary Agnes Nurse 9-2-17 VAD CR Wilts115
LANGDON,Arthur Charles 2Lt dow 27-10-18 7 att15Hamps p229 CR Belgium158
LANGDON,Cecil Rev kia 31-10-17 RAChDept att11BordR p199 CR Belgium36
LANGDON,Douglas Eckley 2LtACapt kia 23-4-17 1DCLI p114 CR France547
LANGDON,John Henry.MC.Lt kld 5-6-18 2Glouc att195RAF p107 CR Egypt8
LANGDON,John Stafford T2Lt ded 24-10-18 RE IWT p46 CR France65
LANGDON,Lawrence TLt dow 14-3-16 14Hamps p121 CR France254,Laurence
LANGDON,Wilfrid Max TCapt kia 21-5-16 10Ches p96 CR France68
LANGDON,William Chappell Croeder.MID TLt dow 10-3-17 RGA attRE 3FldSurCoy p40 CR France120,Crocker
LANGFORD,Albert Frederick 2Lt kia 10-7-16 3Worc p109 MR21
LANGFORD,Arthur Hector Allan T2Lt dow 1-8-16 17N&D p134 CR France80
LANGFORD,Claude Charles 2Lt ded 23-2-18 6DragGds p21 CR War7
LANGFORD,Colin Cecil CaptAMaj dow 9-4-18 295RFA D'Coy p31 CR France169
LANGFORD,John Joseph T2Lt kia 15-9-16 18KRRC p151 CR France277
LANGFORD,Wallace George T2Lt dow 27-6-16 18KRRC p151 CR France285
LANGFORD,William John Lt kia 19-7-16 6Glouc p225 MR19
LANGHAM,Cecil Richard Capt kia 16-8-17 5RSuss p228 CR Belgium10
LANGHAM,John 2Lt kia 18-9-18 TA 7 att10N&D p233 MR16
LANGLANDS,Alan 2Lt kia 9-5-15 3 att1SWBord p100 CR France631
LANGLER,John Bickford.MC.Lt ded 31-10-18 RFA p31 CR Lond29
LANGLEY,Alfred 2LtACapt kia 20-9-17 6Wilts D'Coy p153 MR30
LANGLEY,Arthur Cecil Lt kia 23-9-17 34RFA p207 CR Belgium102
LANGLEY,Eric Erskine Lt ded 22-1-20 IARO att114LabCps p279 MR43
LANGLEY,Francis Jasper 2Lt kia 27-8-18 2GrenGds p50 CR France614
LANGLEY,Harry Gustave Lt ded 28-1-19 RDC p256 CR Ches74
LANGLEY,S.TD.Maj 20-1-21 GlasgowYeo CR Scot764
LANGRISHE,Hercules Ralph Lt kld 16-2-17 MontgomeryYeo attRFC p204&18 CR Eire362 &CR Ireland14
LANGSDALE,William Anthony.MM.MID T2Lt kia 22-3-18 12N&D p134 MR27 CR France390,22-3-16
LANGSTONE,Arthur 2Lt dow 19-5-17 20Lond p251 CR Belgium11,19Bn
LANGSTONE,Frederick Herbert Lt kia 17-4-18 88RFA 19DAC p31 MR30
LANGTON,Arthur Henry Brodie Lt dow 12-9-16 2KRRC p151 CR France23
LANGTON,David Elland T2Lt dow 10-4-17 36MGC p184 CR France113
LANGTON,Hugh Gordon 2Lt kia 26-10-17 4Lond p246 CR Belgium126
LANGTREE,Charles Henry Lt dow 3-8-16 159RFA p31 CR France23
LANGWILL,Trevor 2Lt ded 17-4-17 GL 60RFC p9 CR France1276,dow
LANGWORTH,Harold Samuel T2Lt dow 9-9-17 BordR att8Bn p117 CR Belgium34
LANGWORTHY,William Southmead Lt kia 4-10-17 7Dev p217 MR30
LANHAM,Walter James 2Lt kia 21-8-18 1/6SStaffs p229 CR France109
LANSDALE,Ernest Conway Lt ded PoW 30-9-16 RASC attRFC p18&253 CR France306,kia
LANSDALE,William Morris Capt kia 26-8-18 RAMC att5RBerks p196 CR France370
LANSDOWN,Francis Arthur Stanley T2Lt ded 14-8-17 SL att1BrWIndR p201 CR Palestine2,Lt
LANSTRY,Reginald Redfern Lt dow 27-9-15 11A&SH p173 CR France51
LANT,Edwin 2Lt kia 8-9-17 88RFA p208 CR France179
LANT,Thomas 2Lt kia 1-11-16 6NumbF p214 CR France388
LANYON,William Mortimer Capt kia 5-4-15 1RIrRif p169 CR France707

LAPP,Austin Ross T2Lt kld 9-3-18 RFC p16
LAPTHORN,Owen Heckford 2Lt kia 29-5-17 D102RFA p31 CR Belgium127,28-5-17
LARCOMBE,Archibald Herbert T2Lt ded PoW 26-10-18 2WRid p115 CR Germany3
LARCOMBE,Henry Reginald Reader 2Lt kia 2-9-17 6RFus p68 CR Kent7
LARCOMBE,Reginald Fred 2Lt kia 10-9-18 CityofLondYeo att2/2Lond p256 MR16
LARDNER,Dion Albert T2Lt kia 4-9-16 9 att1Beds p86 MR21
LARDNER,Roland 2Lt kia 26-5-18 Y&L &RAF p265
LARGE,Charles Edward Lt kia 27-5-18 45RFA p31 MR18
LARGE,Ernest T2Lt ded 8-3-19 RASC 13FldBakerySD p255 CR France40
LARGE,Ernest L.Capt dow 21-5-15 5Lond p246 CR France102
LARGE,Harold Bowater T2Lt kia 10-3-17 9RWar p65 MR38
LARGE,Harold Emmott TCapt dow 9-10-15 10RB p179 CR France706,8-10-15
LARGE,Herbert Edward Capt kia 16-2-15 3Mddx p147 MR29
LARGE,John Gerald Lt ded 4-6-18 RE p210 CR Lincs115
LARGE,Percy Francis T2Lt dow 28-6-17 3DLI p161 CR France285
LARGE,Philip Martin Maj. kia 27-4-15 Mddx p147 MR29
LARGE,Ronald Murray LtACapt kia 4-11-18 7RFus p68 CR France521,3Bn
LARGEN,Edward Charles 2Lt kia 23-7-16 3 att1DCLI p114 MR21
LARKEN,Frederick James 2Lt kia 15-11-16 7NumbF p214 CR France430,14-11-16 1/4Bn
LARKEN,John Savage 2Lt kia 21-9-18 10EKent p204 CR France364
LARKIN,Frederick Joseph.MC.2Lt kia 7-11-17 2/22Lond p251 CR Palestine1
LARKIN,J.P.D.DSO.DCM.Maj 4-11-19 7KOSB &RAF CR Durham28
LARKIN,William James 2Lt kia 25-12-16 1Lincs p75 CR France423
LARKING,Ronald Guy.MC.Capt kld 1-4-18 RE 38DivSigCoy p46 CR France297,dedacc
LARKINS,Charles Horace T2Lt dow 21-11-17 16Mddx p147 MR17
LARKINS,Edward Arthur Malcolm Lt kia 18-7-15 2ELancs p111 CR France924,18-1-15
LARKINS,John Colin TLt kia 4-6-16 15RWar p65 CR France1182
LARKINS,L.H.TCapt kia 4-7-18 13TankCps p188 CR France1170
LARSEN,Hubert Victor 2Lt dow 23-8-18 3 att2SLancs p125 CR Belgium184,Herbert
LASCELLES,Arthur Moore.VC.MC.TCapt kia 7-11-18 3DLI p161 CR France930
LASCELLES,Edward Rowley Lt kia 2-9-18 25Lond p252 CR France624
LASCELLES,Francis Hope TLt kia 22-8-17 42MGC Inf p184 MR30
LASCELLES,Guy Ernest 2Lt kia 24-3-18 5RB p179 CR France605
LASCELLES,Harold Leslie TLt kld 11-3-17 GL RFC p9 CR Lond8
LASCELLES,John Frederick.MC.MID Lt kia 31-7-15 RB &RFC p1&179 CR France167
LASCELLES,Ronald Hastings.DSO.MajALtCol ded 16-2-19 RHA p261 CR Lond28
LASENBY,Searlin 2Lt kia 20-9-17 3 att1Surr att127BdeHQ p113 MR20,Scarlin MR30,Scarlin,12Bn
LASH,Augustus Oliver Maj dow 11-9-18 7RIrRif p169 CR France40
LASKEY,George.MM.T2Lt kia 16-10-18 RWKent att8Bn p141 CR France206
LASLETT,Henry Clinton.MC.T2Lt dow 2-8-16 D149RH&FA p31 CR France23
LASSEN,Reginald Capt ded 18-10-19 RASC MT p267 CR Yorks408
LASSETTER,John James Wilder T2Lt kia 8-3-17 11 att6LNLancs p136 MR38
LAST,Arthur James 2Lt dow 9-12-18 RH&FA p31
LAST,Basil Herbert T2Lt kia 23-4-17 17Mddx p147 CR France728
LAST,Ernest Reginald.MC.Capt kia 24-3-18 att1Lpool p72 MR20
LAST,Leonard Walter 2Lt kia 22-8-18 1Norf p74 CR France281 Ex HAC
LAST,Leslie Sydney 2Lt kld 21-2-18 RFA &RFC p16&31
LATER,Joseph Oswald TLt dow 13-7-16 MGC Inf p184 CR Lancs37
LATHAM,Arthur James T2Lt ded 4-2-16 RE 185TC p46 CR France430
LATHAM,Edgar Retief T2Lt kld 20-10-17 GL 72RFC p9 CR Wilts4
LATHAM,Francis Pulsford Maj ded 26-2-16 3WelshR att1GarrBnWelshFus p127 CR Europe23
LATHAM,Percy 2Lt kia 20-8-15 8Hamps p229 MR4
LATHAM,Stephen Grey.DSO.MC&Bar.CaptALtCol kia 24-4-18 3 att2Nhampt p137 CR France144
LATHAM,Thomas Jones TLt kia 3-10-15 RAMC attRE p196 CR France423
LATHAM,Thomas Selby Lt dow 29-11-17 A18RFA p207 CR Belgium11
LATHAN,William T2Lt kia 24-9-18 RSuss att17Bn p119 CR France276
LATHBRIDGE,Staughton Charles Archelas 2Lt dow 31-10-15 RE 1/4FC p210 CR France80,Lt
LATHBURY,George Lionel Lt ded 24-2-19 6NStaffs p270 CR Staffs85
LATHEY,Arthur Richard T2Lt ded 25-10-18 GL RE p266 CR Surrey1
LATIMER,Alfred.MM.kia 4-10-18 RFA &RAF p261 CR Italy2
LATIMER,Francis T2Lt kia 7-7-16 12Manch p155 MR21

LATIMER,Hugh 2Lt kia 3-7-16 8RWKent p141 MR21,3 att6Bn
LATIMER,Kenneth T2Lt kia 27-2-18 9NStaffs p157 CR Belgium17
LA TOUCHE,Averell Digges Lt kia 25-9-15 5 att2RIrRif p169
LATTA,Alexander James Jobb 2Lt kia 5-8-16 62RFA p31 CR France296,Jopp
LATTA,Charles Keith Lt kia 29-11-15 2GordH p166 MR29,29-10-14
LATTA,Robert William Campbell T2Lt dow 22-10-17 2SfthH p165 CR France64,Lt
LATTER,Francis Robinson Capt dow 3-5-17 7RWKent p141 MR20
LATTER,George Walter William T2Lt kia 11-7-16 3RB p179 CR Belgium100
LATTEY,James Cumming Maj kia 5-5-18 RFA attRGA 1/1WelshHB p31 CR Belgium3,RFA att1/1WelchR
LATTO,William Duncan 2Lt ded 21-2-18 4GordH p242 CR France512
LAUDER,George Gordon 2Lt kia 30-7-16 1Lpool p72 MR21
LAUDER,John Currie Capt kia 28-12-16 1/8A&SH p243 CR France393
LAUDERDALE,John Maitland 2Lt kia 18-9-16 1/8DLI p239 MR21,17-9-16
LAUGHLAND,George Thomson T2Lt dow 21-6-17 15HLI p163 CR Belgium24
LAUGHLIN,James Courtney T2Lt kia 1-7-16 20Lpool p72 CR France699
LAUGHLIN,Philip Herbert TLt dow 21-12-17 1RWSurr p56 CR Palestine3
LAUGHTON,Geoffrey T2Lt kia 5-12-17 26NumbF p62 CR France592
LAUGHTON,H.P.W.Lt kia 28-5-18 10Mddx &RAF p236
LAUGHTON,Hubert Henry Schomberg TLt ded 25-11-18 2Worc attMGC p109&184 CR Surrey91
LAUGHTON,Joseph Thornton T2Lt dow 29-9-18 1Beds p86 CR France146
LAUNCETON,Roy.MC.TCapt kia 24-3-18 16 att2Mddx p147 CR France1472,24/25-3-18
LAURENCE,Bertie Standish 2Lt kia 9-9-15 1/2Co ofLondYeo p204 CR Gallipoli5
LAURENCE,Dudley Sydney 2Lt kia 23-10-16 6 att1RB p179 CR France432
LAURENCE,Stuart 2Lt kia 17-9-16 10RWKent p141 CR France400
LAURENSON,Laurence Capt ded 14-7-16 7GordH p270 CR Scot1014
LAURIA,Jack Victor T2Lt dow 18-6-16 14N&D attRE p134 CR France285
LAURIE,Alfred William 2Lt dow 22-11-16 RGA 42SB p40 CR France388
LAURIE,Donald Saunders.OBE.Capt ded 11-2-19 RE p46 CR Belgium406
LAURIE,Eric Unwin.MC.Lt kia 24-3-18 58MGC Inf p184 CR France1893
LAURIE,George Brenton.MID LtCol kia 12-3-15 RIrRif p169 CR France705
LAURIE,James Alexander Lt kia 3-5-17 6KOSB p102
LAURIE,John William TLtACapt kia 12-8-18 6EKent p57 CR France209,9-8-18
LAURIE,Wilfrid Walter LtACapt kia 19-5-17 3 att2KOSB p102 CR France184
LAURIE,William Joseph Cornwall 2Lt kia 6-1-17 IARO att2/124Baluchis p279 CR Iraq5
LAVARACK,Adolph Keith TLt kia 5-7-16 10WRid p115 CR France515
LAVELLE,James Delargey T2Lt kia 20-8-15 12HLI p163 CR France550
LAVELLE,Patrick Joseph Aloysius.MIDx2 Capt kia 4-10-18 5RScots p211 CR France602,RScotF
LAVELLE,William James 2Lt kia 21-3-18 4 att1/8RInniskF p105 MR27
LAVENDER,Frank Ashley 2Lt kia 14-3-17 1/5SStaffs p229 CR France281
LAVENDER,Harry Richard 2Lt kia 28-8-18 5RSuss p228 CR France630
LAVENDER,John Elliott 2Lt kia 28-4-17 10Lincs p75 MR20
LAVER,Francis Reynell Lt kia 9-4-18 4SStaffs p122 CR Belgium451
LAVERICK,Frederick Gordon T2Lt kia 23-7-17 7ELancs p111 CR Belgium102
LAVERS,Victor Alfred.MC.T2Lt dow 22-4-17 1RBerks p139 CR France145
LAVERTON,Frederick King 2LtTLt kld 19-12-17 3Glouc &RFC p9&107 CR Glouc88,3/9Bn
LAVERTY,Joseph T2Lt kia 16-8-17 13RIrRif p169 MR30
LAVILLE,Samuel Eustace Blythe TCapt kia 18-8-16 3Leinst p174 CR France630,2Bn
LAW,Alan Drummond TLt dow 3-5-17 4 att10A&SH p173 MR20
LAW,Alan Hugh T2Lt kia 4-11-18 16LancF p92 CR France231
LAW,Cecil Edward T2Lt kia 30-9-18 1LancF p92 CR Belgium20
LAW,Charles Arkley 2Lt kld 19-2-18 RFC p16 CR Norf247,13-2-18
LAW,Charles John Lt kia 19-4-17 3KOSB p102 CR Palestine8
LAW,Charles Lindsay Qwyder T2Lt kia 30-9-15 2Suff p78 CR Belgium167,Lindsey Gwydr
LAW,Charles Orlando TCapt ded 29-12-18 RE p262 CR Lond4,2-1-19
LAW,Edgar Felix Lt kia 5-4-18 6Nhampt p137 MR27
LAW,Edward Michael Fitzgerald 2Lt kia 11-8-18 Dors att1Bn p124 CR France360,Lt
LAW,Harry.MIDx2 Lt dow 7-7-15 1RWFus p98 CR Lincs14,21-7-15
LAW,Henry Merrick Burrell 2Lt kia 8-8-16 18RFC p3 CR France32
LAW,Henry Milner 2Lt kia 9-4-17 6SfthH p241 CR France15
LAW,James Kidston Capt kia 21-9-17 RFus &60RFC p9&68 MR20
LAW,John Gordon T2Lt kia 20-10-18 1ESurr p113 CR France1388
LAW,Malcolm Colin McGregor Lt dow 29-12-15 6WRid p227 CR Belgium1

LAW,Robert Archibald Fitzgerald.MC&Bar.2LtACapt dow 31-10-18 1 att7Wilts p153 CR France146
LAW,Thomas Pakenham 2Lt dow 27-8-15 IrGds SR att2Bn p53 MR22
LAW,William John.MID TLtCol kia 19-12-15 7LancF p221 CR Gallipoli6
LAWDER,Arthur William Charles 2Lt dow 15-4-17 155RH&FA p31 CR France120,A.G.
LAWDER,Noel Wilfred TMaj kia 4-9-16 1Beds p86 MR21
LAWES,Charles Gilbert TLt kia 27-10-16 9RWFus p98 MR21
LAWES,Thomas Eric 2Lt kia 18-6-17 3Suff p78 CR France421
LAWFORD,Edward Enfield Lt mbk 13-6-17 IARO att20DeccanHorse p279 MR28
LAWFORD,Herbert Martin Benson TCapt kia 7-10-16 9RFus p68 MR21
LAWLEDGE,Francis Mott 2Lt kia 10-10-16 RE attRFC p3&46 CR France644,Matt
LAWLER,Guy Feinagle Lt kiaWithArabs 22-4-20 IA 2Lancers C'Sqdn p279 CR Palestine11,Feinaigle
LAWLER,Lionel Alfred Ballantyne Lt ded 8-3-19 RASC p193&257 MR40
LAWLESS,Barry Joseph Anthony 2Lt kia 17-7-17 12Lond att56TMB p248 CR Belgium12
LAWLOR,Edward Fredk 2Lt kia 27-11-16 2Mon p244 CR France744
LAWRANCE,John Henry 2Lt kia 20-8-17 3 att2DCLI p114 CR France184
LAWRENCE,Alexander TCapt&Adjt dow 19-9-16 1GordH att10RWSurr p166 CR France833
LAWRENCE,Bertram Capt kia 27-10-14 1EYorks p84 CR France82,28-10-14
LAWRENCE,Brian Lightly 2Lt kia 1-6-15 att2Mddx p147 MR32
LAWRENCE,Charles Alfred.MC.TLtACapt kia 24-4-18 7Beds p86 MR27
LAWRENCE,Charles Philip 2Lt dow 29-4-16 IARO att27Punjabis p279 MR38
LAWRENCE,Christopher Hal 2Lt kia 13-10-14 6 att2KRRC p151 MR15,4 att2Bn
LAWRENCE,Edward.MC.DCM.LtACapt kia 28-3-18 10 att1NumbF p62 MR20
LAWRENCE,Edward William TCapt kia 10-7-16 RAMC att13RWFus p196 MR21
LAWRENCE,Francis Alfred John 2Lt kia 12-4-18 10Ess p132 MR27
LAWRENCE,Frank Helier 2Lt kia 9-5-15 3Glouc p107 MR22
LAWRENCE,Frederic Wilson Capt ded 9-12-15 Res GL 3/5Lpool p270 CR Lancs381
LAWRENCE,George Aubrey Kennedy.DSO.CaptTLtCol kld 28-1-17 RFA attRFC p10&31 CR Surrey160
LAWRENCE,Guy Francis Lt kia 27-8-17 2GrenGds p50 CR France924
LAWRENCE,Harold Raymond Lt ded 28-10-18 12NStaffs attTMB p157 CR Lancs381
LAWRENCE,Harold Roy 2Lt dow 12-7-17 2/6Lond p247 CR France398
LAWRENCE,Harry Joseph 2Lt kia 26-4-18 4Ess p232 CR France425
LAWRENCE,Henry 2Lt kia 17-1-17 5 att6Yorks p221 MR21
LAWRENCE,Humphrey Richard Locke Lt drd 30-12-15 IA 34SikhPnrs p279 MR41,Capt
LAWRENCE,James Linton TCapt dow 3-7-16 15RScots p54 France119
LAWRENCE,John George.MC.2Lt ded 15-2-18 Norf att2WIndiaR p74&192 CR EAfrica35 &CR Tanzania1
LAWRENCE,John James T2Lt kia 23-10-18 11RFus p68 CR France190
LAWRENCE,Joseph Reginald Mark 2Lt kia 16-8-16 3 att9ESurr p113 CR France294
LAWRENCE,Lawrence Arthur 2Lt kia 16-8-17 83/122RFA p31 CR Belgium23
LAWRENCE,Malcolm Eyton Lt kia 10-1-15 6 att2KRRC p151 MR22 &CR France1059
LAWRENCE,Michael Charles TCapt dow 16-9-16 1CldGds p51 CR France105
LAWRENCE,Norman Alan 2Lt kia 30-4-17 RFus &16RFC p10&68 CR France55
LAWRENCE,Oliver John 2Lt kia 26-5-15 8Lond p247 CR France261
LAWRENCE,Percy 2Lt kld 9-8-18 7Leinst &RAF p174
LAWRENCE,Rudolph Russell 2Lt kia 24-8-16 5KSLI p145 MR20
LAWRENCE,Thomas Edward 2Lt dow 22-9-18 7RSuss p119 CR France194
LAWRENCE,Walter Capt kld 2-1-15 7Ess attRFC p18&232 CR France284
LAWRENCE,William George 2Lt kia 23-10-15 O&BLI &RFC p1&130 CR France1266
LAWRENCE,Lawrence,William Lyttleton.DSO.Maj kia 31-10-14 1SWBord p100 MR29
LAWRENCE-TOWNSEND,Robert Edward Capt 2-3-18 5Mddx CR Kent61
LAWRENSON,Harold 2Lt kia 25-5-18 RGA 214SB p40 CR France247
LAWRENSON,Raymond Fitmaurice Lt dow 5-9-17 16Ches p96 CR France446
LAWRENSON,Reginald Robert.DSO&Bar.MajTLtCol dow 27-4-18 WIndia att18HLI p192 CR France40
LAWRIE,Allan James Capt kia 16-5-15 6ScotRif p224 CR France348
LAWRIE,Andrew Ralph TLt kia 22-8-17 D'TankCps p188 MR30
LAWRIE,Edward LtCol 22-8-15 IMS CR Sussex183
LAWRIE,Francis Allan TCapt ded 25-9-18 1ScotRif GarrBn attManch p103 MR66,26-9-18
LAWRIE,James Alexander Lt 3-5-17 6KOSB MR20

LAWRIE,James Hunter 2Lt kia 9-8-16 3 att7KOSB p102 CR France188
LAWRIE,John Charles CaptHonMaj ded 7-5-15 3Ess p132 CR Essex185
LAWRIE,Norman Ernest 2Lt kia 9-5-15 13Lond p249 MR32
LAWRIE,Robert Rossiter 2Lt dow 8-4-18 22Lond E'Coy p251 CR Palestine9
LAWRIE,Thomas Helm 2Lt kia 25-7-18 9RScots p212 CR France865
LAWS,Alfred Victor 2Lt kia 25/27-10-14 1NumbF Z'Coy p62 MR22
LAWS,Bernard Courtney Lt dow 25-5-15 3 att1Y&L p159 CR Belgium165
LAWS,Cecil William TLt kia 27-5-18 N&D p134 MR18,Willie
LAWS,Philip Umfreville.MC.TCapt kia 20-9-17 16N&D p134 CR Belgium124
LAWS,Selwyn Vernon T2Lt kia 25-5-18 9Ches p96 CR France31
LAWSON,Alexander Sutherland 2Lt kia 11-11-14 1BlkW p129 MR29
LAWSON,Alfred 2Lt kia 16-9-16 9DLI p239 MR21
LAWSON,Arthur Ashley T2Lt ded 19-3-18 TankCps p266 CR Hamps13
LAWSON,Arthur Bertram.DSO.BtMajA/LtCol kia 24-6-18 11Huss att2/5Glouc p22 CR France248
LAWSON,Arthur Cresswell T2Lt kia 19-11-16 11GordH attScotRif p166 CR Greece6
LAWSON,Arthur Cyril T2Lt dow 6-7-17 7RB p179 CR Lond4
LAWSON,Arthur James.MIDx3 TLtACapt kia 22-3-18 8Leic att110TMB p87 CR France669
LAWSON,Arthur James 2Lt ded 17-12-18 SL att1RdCps p201 CR EAfrica52
LAWSON,Cecil David Norton T2Lt kia 26-9-15 8RWKent p141 MR19
LAWSON,David T2Lt kia 9-10-17 5Y&L p159 MR30
LAWSON,Edward Grey 2Lt kia 14-11-16 7NumbF p214 CR France385
LAWSON,Frank Harry Reginald Lt ded 19-11-19 BucksHuss p270 CR Lond8
LAWSON,Frederick Henry Capt kia 24-5-15 5NumbF p213 MR29
LAWSON,Gavin T2Lt kia 4-8-16 12 att 1/8ScotRif p103 CR Egypt2
LAWSON,George McFarquhar Kelly 2Lt kia 9-8-17 RGA 5SB p40
LAWSON,George William 2Lt kia 11-4-18 10 att5Yorks B'Coy p90 MR32
LAWSON,Harry Sackville Lt kia 5-2-18 RFA p207 CR France1066
LAWSON,Henry Heaton Chap4Cl kia 24-3-18 RAChDept att2NhamptR p199 CR France692
LAWSON,James Burnett TLt kia 27-3-18 2ScotRif p103 MR27
LAWSON,James McKercher T2Lt kia 1-7-17 1/2KOSB p102 CR France184
LAWSON,John Lawson T2Lt kia 14-10-16 10SfthH p165 MR21
LAWSON,John Low Maj ded 15-6-16 RASC p267 CR Hamps15
LAWSON,John Wilson.MC.TLtACapt kia 24-3-18 41MGC p184 CR France927
LAWSON,Joseph TLtACapt kia 22-3-18 18Lpool p72 MR27 21-3-18
LAWSON,Joseph Percy 2Lt kia 8-8-15 6RLancs p213 MR21
LAWSON,Norman Wilfrid Lt kia 14-11-16 5NumbF B'Coy p213 CR France385
LAWSON,Oswald Head Maj dow 17-3-16 IA 26Punjabis p279 CR Iraq5
LAWSON,Reginald Hugh.MC.MID TLt kia 24-8-16 7RB p179 CR France397
LAWSON,Robert Lt kia 27-5-18 7DLI p256 MR18
LAWSON,Robert Wybergh Gordon T2Lt kia 18-7-16 1GordH p166 MR21
LAWSON,William TLt kia 27-3-16 1DLI p161 CR Belgium56,2Lt 17 att8Bn
LAWSON,William TLt kia 24-4-17 14A&SH p173 CR France415
LAWSON,William T2Lt kia 19-9-18 1 att8RScotF p94 CR Greece5
LAWSON,William Bernard Webster Lt kia 22-10-14 1ScotsGds p52 MR29
LAWSON-JOHNSTON,Arthur McWilliam.MC.Lt dow 22-2-17 2GrenGds p50 CR France105
LAWSON-SMITH,John Lt kia 20-10-14 1WYorks p82 MR22
LAWSON-SMITH,Thomas Edward Lt kia 1-11-14 13Huss p22 MR29
LAWSON-WALTON,J.E.Capt 31-12-19 GL att4KAR CR EAfrica51
LAWTHER,Arthur Leonard 2Lt dow 23-5-16 RFA 22Bty 8HB p208 CR France12
LAWTON,Arthur 2Lt ded 4-9-19 RGA p262 CR Staffs105
LAWTON,Edward Gerald Capt dow 12-4-18 2ESurr p113 CR EAfrica116
LAWTON,Eric Reginald T2Lt kia 10-8-17 12Manch p155 CR France604
LAWTON,Robert Charles Lt dow 16-10-15 5Leic p220 CR France98,17-10-15
LAWTON,William T2Lt kia 3/6-7-16 8NStaffs p157 MR21
LAWTON,William Victor TLt dedacc 8-7-18 RE 7PontoonPk p46 CR France142
LAX,Anthony William Greenwell.MID Capt kia 11-10-16 RGA 43SB p262 CR Greece6
LAX,Donald T2Lt kia 25-10-18 4 att20DLI p161 MR30
LAXTON,Archer Benjamin 2Lt dow 21-7-17 C110RFA p31 CR Belgium11
LAXTON,Reginald Earl T2Lt kia 10-6-17 16WYorks att93/1TMB p82 CR France5
LAY,Harold Frank Douglas 2Lt kld 7-3-18 RFC p16 CR France64,dedacc
LAY,John Frederick Lt 28-10-18 IARO att2/67Punjabis MR43 &CR Pakistan50A
LAYARD,Arthur Austen McGregor Maj ded 5-6-17 RE p46 CR Essex146
LAYARD,Frank Stanley.MC.2Lt kia 19-5-17 1BordR p117 CR France427,Stanlie dow
LAYARD,Peter Clement Lt kia 23-8-18 4Suff p217 CR France927
LAYBOURNE,John Oscar 2Lt kia 26-3-17 1/7Ches p223 CR Palestine8
LAYCOCK,Donald Stanley 2Lt dow 24-3-18 70/34RFA p208 CR France560

LAYCOCK,Joseph Harold 2Lt kia 7-10-16 2 att18KRRC p151 MR21
LAYCOCK,Lewis James Penard TLt kia 31-7-17 7Nhampt p137 MR29,Louis
LAYMAN,Douglas Arthur Campbell T2Lt dow 22-2-16 17LancF p92 CR France80
LAYMAN,F.H.Maj 2-10-17 RDC CR Surrey162
LAYNG,George Reginald Stuart T2LtALt dow 18-8-16 GL 10Glouc att1TMB p190 CR France44
LAYTHORPE,Roger Marmaduke 2Lt dow 8-7-16 3 att7SLancs p125 CRKent7,10-7-16
LAYTON,Roland Churchill Capt kia 30-4-18 NottsYeo p205 MR34
LAYTON-BENNETT,Geoffrey Ernest 2Lt 1-7-16 2Yorks CR France630
LAZARUS,Cyril Henry Lt kia 27-5-18 7Leic p87 CR France1755
LAZONBY,Julian Cecil 2Lt kia 23-11-17 B'TankCps p188 MR17
LEA,Gerald Ernest Capt kia 16-9-14 2Worc p109 CR France1329
LEA,Hilda Louisa SNurse 10-5-16 QAIMNS CR Surrey160
LEA,John T2Lt dow 15-7-16 8Leic p87 CR France207
LEA,Maurice Bertram T2Lt kia 18-8-16 7Nhampt p137 MR21
LEA-SMITH,Leslie Arthur TLt kia 7-7-16 6EKent p57 CR France251
LEACH,Edward Savory Wykeham Capt kia 3-5-17 1 att7ESurr p113 MR20
LEACH,Eric Thomas 2Lt dow 14-10-18 1Worc p109 CR Belgium406
LEACH,Ernest Walter Vindin ACapt kia 2-1-17 3 att2RIrRif p169 CR Belgium53
LEACH,Errol William Carlisle ALt kia 15-5-17 11ELancs p111 CR France777
LEACH,Francis James Capt dow 26-4-15 KSLI p145 CR Devon10
LEACH,Fred Lt kld 16-6-18 1/8Manch &RAF p256 MR65
LEACH,George.MM.2Lt kia 28-4-18 3 att19Manch p155 MR30,17Bn
LEACH,Gerald Kimball TLt kia 10-8-15 6BordR p117 MR4,Kemball
LEACH,Gordon Pemberton Capt kia 20-8-15 B66RFA p31 CR Gallipoli3,19-8-15
LEACH,Grey de Leche 2Lt ded 3-9-16 1ScotsGds p52 CR France23
LEACH,Herbert Lt kia 22-4-17 2Y&L p159 CR France551
LEACH,J.Capt 28-2-20 RFA CR Hamps4
LEACH,Robert Edward TCapt dow 29-11-17 RAVC att64RFA p198 CR Belgium10
LEACH,Sidney 2Lt kia 10-8-18 4TankCps p188 MR16
LEACH,Walter John T2Lt kia 11-10-18 RE 4FldSurBn p46 CR Belgium84
LEACH,William Alfred 2Lt ded 5-3-19 RFA 96BdeAC p31 CR France1029
LEACHMAN,Gerald Evelyn.CIE.DSO.LtCol 12-8-20 RSuss CR Iraq8
LEACROFT,Richard Frederick T2Lt kia 10-11-15 12Worc p109 CR France114,2Bn
LEACROFT,Ronald John Ranulph.MC.Capt kia 1-7-16 1SomLI p80 CR France1491
LEADBETTER,Alan Edmonstoun Greenshields LtAMaj kia 4-8-17 RH&FA L'Bty15Bde p31
LEADBETTER,Duncan 2Lt dow 6-8-18 82RH&FA p31 CR France71,7-8-18
LEADBITTER,Francis John Graham T2Lt kia 5-3-17 11KRRC p151 CR France374
LEADBITTER,Geoffrey George 2Lt mbk 19-4-17 4Nhampt p257 MR34
LEADER,Benjamin Eastlake Capt kia 12-10-16 3RWSurr att2WRid p56 MR21
LEADER,Francis William Mowbray Capt kia 26-8-14 2ConnRgrs p172 CR France943
LEADER,Reginald John Carey T2Lt kia 28-4-16 14DLI p161 CR Belgium23
LEAH,Wilfred Reginald 2Lt kia 10-9-16 1/4RLancs p213 CR France393
LEAHY,Eugene Patrick TCapt dow 18-9-16 RAMC att61FA p196 CR France105
LEAHY,Noel Edward Joseph Lt kia 10-8-18 5RH&FA p31
LEAHY,Percy Edward.MID TMajA/LtCol kia 17-7-18 6Y&L p159 CR France223
LEAK,Charles Henry Capt&QM ded 24-9-17 RE p46 CR Surrey15
LEAK,Reginald 2Lt dow 26-8-15 6LancF p221 MR4
LEAK,Reginald T2Lt dow 14-7-16 13Lpool p72 CR France141
LEAKE,Eric Gilbert.MC.Capt dow 31-7-18 7Manch att59RAF p258&237,Lt CR France84
LEAKE,Eric Larkin Wheadon Lt kia 4-6-15 LancF p92 MR4
LEAKE,George Dalton Capt kia 13-5-15 1ELancs p111 CR Belgium96
LEAKE,George Ernest Arthur.DSO.Capt dow 2-6-17 2/4Lond p246 CR France145
LEAKE,Russell Madley.MC&Bar.LtACapt kia 18-9-18 3 att1LNLancs p136 CR France375,Medley
LEAKEY,Herbert Nettleton Chap4Cl ded 24-7-17 RAChDept p199 CR EAfrica35 &CR Tanzania1
LEAL,George Lt kia 7-8-17 RFA att9RFC p10&31 CR Belgium20
LEAMAN,Mark Reginald 2Lt kia 5-4-18 42MGC p184 MR27,6-4-18
LEAMAN,Douglas Arthur 2LtTLt dow 14-8-17 4Norf p216 CR Belgium11,8Bn
LEAN,Hugh Henry.MC.Capt kia 29-7-17 153HLI p163 CR Belgium5
LEANING,Reginald William 2Lt kld 31-5-18 9Lpool p216 CR France40
LEAPINGWELL,Henry Byng Capt mbk 21-1-16 IA 97Inf p279 MR38
LEARED,Paul Lupus Maj ded 7-3-18 IA 1/7GurkhaRif attStaff 53Div p279 CR Iraq8
LEARMOUTH,Eric Charles Allan Lt kia 9-10-17 7WYorks p218 MR30
LEAROYD,Digby Guy TLt ded 13-12-17 GL RE IWT p46 CR Iraq6
LEAROYD,Ernest Smith T2Lt kia 23-11-17 20Mddx p147 MR17 CR France1059

LEAROYD,Geoffrey Ernest Douglas Capt ded 29-10-18 21Lancers p23 MR43

LEARY,Eric Lt dow 21-6-15 RIrReg p89 CR France1140

LEARY,Ernest Richard 2Lt dow 23-7-16 3Y&L attMGC p159&184 CR France300

LEARY,George Godfrey Whitney TLt kia 25-9-18 10Glouc p107 CR France1723

LEASK,James Cunliffe.MC.Capt kia 30-3-18 5NumbF p213 MR27

LEASK,John T2Lt kld 26-3-17 GL RFC p10 CR Scot876

LEASON,Thomas Herbert T2Lt dow 16-9-16 9YLI p143 CR France188

LEAT,Edwin John 2Lt dow 8-6-18 Dors att6Bn p124 MR27

LEAT,Frederick Charles 2Lt kia 27-5-18 2Dev p77 CR France1332

LEATER,Henry.MID Lt kia 21-3-18 2/9Manch p237 CR France1464,Capt

LEATHAM,Bertram Henry.DSO.MajA.LtCol kia 26-9-15 2Yorks att2Wilts p90 CR France423

LEATHAM,Edward Hubert Lt kia 31-10-14 12Lancers p22 MR29

LEATHER,Christopher Lt kia 25/27-10-14 3 att1NumbF p62 MR22

LEATHER,Ernest Arthur TMaj kia 10-2-16 15 att27NumbF p62 CR France347

LEATHER,Edward Wilberforce Capt kia 18-4-15 3Yorks att2YLI p90 MR29

LEATHER,J.Capt 18-9-14 IOD MR66

LEATHER,John Francis.MID Capt ded 16-10-18 RASC att1/4KSLI p253 CR France123

LEATHERDALE,Donald Ryan 2Lt kia 22-7-16 1RWKent p141 MR21

LEATHERLAND,Frederick Arthur T2Lt kia 7-8-18 11RFus p68 MR27

LEATHERLAND,Percy John T2Lt drd 10-10-18 3Lpool p72 CR Ireland14,Lt

LEATHES,Robert Herbert de Mussenden 2Lt kia 18-4-17 B62RFA p31 CR France731

LEATHLEY,William George T2Lt kia 1-7-16 8SomLI p80 MR21

LEAVER,Stanley Horace T2Lt kia 9-4-18 17Mddx p147 MR32

LE BAS,Owen Vincent Lt kia 7-11-15 RWSurr &RFC p1&56 CR France604

LEBISH,Frank Roland 2Lt dow 25-7-17 D173RFA p31 CR Belgium11

LE BLANC-SMITH,Charles Ralph TLt kia 27-11-15 8RB p179 CR Belgium73

LE BLOND,Robert Cecil Gamage du Plessis Capt ded 17-5-15 12RB p179

LE BRASSEUR,Robert Henry Hubert Lt ded 24-5-16 RFC p261 CR Norf209,Robin

LE BRETON,Vivian Bertram Lt kia 9-8-18 10Lond p248 CR France1170

LE BRUN,Lewis Appleby T2Lt kia 31-10-18 3Hamps att11SomLI p121 CR Belgium406

LEBY,Maitland Benn.MC.ACapt kia 12-4-18 2IrGds p53

LE CHAVETOIS,Grantley Adolphe ACapt dow 21-1-18 22Lond p251 CR Lond3,22-1-18

LECHE,Arthur Victor Carlton 2Lt kia 1-7-16 3SomLI p80 CR France1890

LE CHEMINANT,Cyril T2Lt kia 9-8-17 7Suff p78 MR20

LECHERTIER,Jacques Alfred 2Lt kia 4-11-18 D211RFA p31 CR France1082

LECHLER,Frederick Gordon 2Lt ded 24-9-16 IARO att62Punjabis p279 CR Iraq6

LECHLER,Henry Nicholson T2Lt kia 4-4-16 10 att6SLancs p125 MR38

LECHMERE,Nicholas George Berwick Lt kia 17-10-15 2ScotsGds p52 MR19

LECKENBY,Harold T2Lt kia 9-4-17 26NumbF C'Coy p62 CR France184

LECKIE,Graham 2LtTLt kia 7-7-17 RGA &21RFC p10&40 CR Belgium115

LECKIE,John.MC.TLtAMaj dow 29-8-18 56MGC Inf C'Coy p184 CR France103

LECKIE,John Harvey Lt kia 13-5-15 1Drags p21 MR29,13-6-15

LECKIE,Malcolm.DSO.Capt dow 29-8-14 RAMC p196 CR Belgium202,28-8-14

LECKIE,Otway Trevor MacRitchie Capt dow 13-4-15 IA 104Rif p279 CR Iraq6

LECKIE,Walter Alan TLt dow 21-2-16 RE 90FC p46 CR Belgium137

LECKY,Averell Lt dow 19-10-14 2Leinst p174 CR France681,20-10-14

LECKY,John T2Lt kia 16-7-16 18RIrRif p169 MR21

LECKY,John Rupert Frederick Capt kia 28-9-15 7RFus att2Norf p68 MR38

LECOMBER,Philip Hebdon Lt kia 27-3-18 2/7Manch p237 MR30

LEDBITTER,Herbert Peter Rev ded 28-2-17 RAChDept attAMTD Base p199 CR France1

LEDGARD,Frank Cooper Lt kia 23-10-14 2Yorks p90 CR Belgium140

LEDGER,Harold Partington T2Lt kia 20-11-17 GL 3RFC p10 CR France911

LEDGER,Horace Martin Capon 2Lt kia 22-12-15 IARO attFrenchSeaplaneFlight p279 MR34

LEDGER,Raymond Kerwood Lt kia 13-4-15 6RB attRWFus p179 CR France348,dow

LEDGER,Robert John 2Lt dow 11-3-17 7RSuss p119 CR France46,dedacc

LEDINGHAM,Andrew 2Lt kia 22-3-18 4GordH p242 MR20

LE DOUX,Vietch,Dallas Gerard Lt kia 4-8-16 3 att7RSuss p119 MR21

LEDUC,John Charles Romuald T2Lt kld 7-11-17 GL RFC p10 CR Kent125,Jean-Charles Lt

LEDWARD,George William Capt ded 12-8-15 5Suff p217 MR4

LEE,A.M.Capt 2-11-20 LNLancs CR Lond14

LEE,Arnold Thomas 2Lt kia 1-9-18 RGA 87SB p40 CR France419

LEE,Arthur Basil 2Lt kia 2-7-16 5WYorks p218 MR21

LEE,Audley Andrew Dowell.MC.TCapt kia 1-10-17 9Leic A'Coy p88 MR30

LEE,Bernard George TLt dow 22-3-18 D180RFA p31 CR France987,Capt

LEE,Charles Alexander Cmdr ded 6-2-18 RIM CR Italy6

LEE,Charles Frederick 2Lt dow 27-4-17 9Lpool p216 CR France95

LEE,Charles Harold 2Lt kia 20-9-17 RGA 249SB p40 CR Belgium112

LEE,Charles Henry.MC.Maj ded 26-2-20 24Manch CR Lancs95

LEE,Charles Percy 2Lt kia 22-10-18 3Lond &RAF p246&258

LEE,Charles Stuart 2Lt kia 30-12-15 RE 126FC p46 CR France1140

LEE,Edgar Charles T2Lt kia 1-6-16 17Mddx p147 CR France924

LEE,Edward Capt kia 14-10-16 Herts p252 CR France293

LEE,Eric Hanson T2Lt dow 19-9-16 9 att1KSLI p145 CR France105

LEE,Ernest Lt kia 11-7-15 4WRid p227 CR Belgium106

LEE,Ernest William 2Lt kia 28-9-16 1/5WYorks p218 CR France383

LEE,Frank Stanley TLt kia 22-3-18 13RB p179 MR30

LEE,Frederick Gurdon Driffield TLt ded 1-3-16 2/6Norf p217 CR Norf172

LEE,Frederick Henry Norris Lt dow 4-7-16 IrGds SR att1Bn p53 CR France102

LEE,George Jonston Capt ded 29-8-20 IARO attMechTrans p279 CR Dorset85,attRB

LEE,George Thomas Hutteman Lt ded 26-10-18 IARO attS&TCps p279 MR66

LEE,Harry Norman Capt kia 19-12-14 IA 59Rif p279 MR28

LEE,Hector McLean T2Lt kia 18-10-16 5CamH p168 MR21

LEE,Henry Lt dow 22-11-17 1RInniskF p105 CR France300

LEE,Henry Duncan 2Lt kia 5-8-17 42/5RFA 5ArmyBde p31 CR Belgium12

LEE,Herbert Malachi T2Lt kld 26-9-17 GL 62RFC p10 CR Kent7

LEE,Herbert Victor 2Lt dow 17-11-16 3 att1Suff p78 CR Greece3

LEE,Holdsworth T2Lt kia 31-5-17 8Lincs p75 CR Belgium97,31-7-17

LEE,J.S/AssSurg 6-8-20 IMS MR67

LEE,Jack.MC.Capt kia 31-7-17 6Ches p222 MR29

LEE,James Clifford 2Lt dow 1-8-17 2RBerks p139 CR Belgium11

LEE,James Denton 2Lt dow 22-1-18 10Manch p237 CR Yorks606

LEE,James Francis 2Lt kia 11-9-18 8Lpool p216 MR16

LEE,John Arthur 2Lt kia 16-9-16 3 att5KSLI p145 MR21

LEE,John Mitchell 2Lt kia 27-9-15 7BordR p117 MR29,25-9-15

LEE,John William 2Lt kld 31-3-18 2SWBord attRFC p16&100 CR Egypt1,Lt 8B

LEE,Joseph Bagnall TLt kia 8-8-15 6RMunstF p175 MR4

LEE,Kenneth Willoughby.MC.Capt dow 27-9-16 A95RFA p32 CR France40

LEE,Lennox Cleland Lee 2Lt kia 1-2-15 1IrGds SR p53 CR France720

LEE,Leonard Bernard 2Lt kia 30-11-17 RE 83FC p46 CR France1483

LEE,Leonard Harry Capt bombAcc 23-10-17 IA 110Mahrattas att2/101Grens p2 CR Egypt8

LEE,Lionel Shaw 2Lt kia 25-9-15 5 O&BLI p130 MR29

LEE,Michael Philip Edward.MC.Lt kia 26-3-18 6DragGds p21 MR28

LEE,Noel.VD.BrigGen dow 22-6-15 6Manch Cmdg42Div p236 CR Europe1

LEE,Noel Esmond TCapt kia 24-8-17 8KRRC p151 MR30

LEE,Percy William T2Lt kia 9-4-17 KSLI att5Bn p145 MR20

LEE,Philip Warburton LtAMaj kia 11-10-17 29RFA 3ImpDivArty p32 CR Belgium10

LEE,Richard T2Lt kia 13/16-10-15 10 att7Suff p78 MR19

LEE,Richard Henry Driffield Capt kld 23-6-17 1/6Norf attRFC p217&19 CR Norf172,FltCmdr

LEE,Robert Carswell T2Lt kia 4-11-18 18Lpool att10LancF p72 CR France206

LEE,Robert Ernest TCapt drd 10-10-18 RAMC p196 CR Ireland5

LEE,Sidney Edward 2Lt kia 11-4-17 3 att1GordH p166 MR20

LEE,Thomas 2Lt kia 9-4-18 50MGC Inf p184 MR32

LEE,William Lt kld 19-8-18 5RIrF &RAF p171 CR Egypt15

LEE,Walter Noel Oliff T2Lt kia 25-9-15 1SStaffs p122 MR19

LEE,William Melbourne 2Lt kia 21-3-18 RFA 298ArmyBde p32 MR27

LEE,William Robert Charles Paul 2Lt kia 10-7-15 7RFus attRWFus p68 CR France684

LEE-KIRBY,W.H Lt 11-12-16 1GarBnEss CR Egypt1

LEE-STEERS,John Henry Gordon Lt kia 17-11-14 GrenGds p50 CR Belgium134,STEERE

LEE-WOOD,Alfred Capt 1-7-16 15LancF MR21

LEEB,Mercer Eric Capt ded 10-7-19 LNLancs &RAF p264 CR Sussex144

LEECE,Edwin Stanley TLt dow 24-11-17 18WelshR p127 MR17

LEECE,Francis Ballantyne 2Lt kia 12-10-16 2WRid p115 MR21

LEECH,Arthur Charles Capt kia 4/5-6-15 5Manch p236 CR Gallipoli2

LEECH,Arthur William.MC.Lt dow 12-4-18 6NumbF p213 CR France134

LEECH,Bernard Jack T2Lt kia 9-10-17 148MGC Inf p184 MR30

LEECH,Cecil Darley Farran LtTCapt ded 2-3-18 2NStaffs p157 MR67

LEECH,Geoffrey Charles Martyn TLt dow 9-4-17 5KRRC p151 CR France120,9Bn

LEECH,Harry Maj kia 31-7-17 8Lpool p215 CR Belgium125,Henry
LEECH,James Alexander T2Lt kia 10-10-18 12 att5RInniskF p105 CR France1394
LEECH,Norman Black 2LtTCapt dow 10-5-17 10EYorks p84 CR France40,Bleeck
LEECH,Percy Leonard T2Lt kia 27-8-18 13WelshR p127 CR France432
LEECH,Robert Edward Holt T2Lt kia 30-9-18 KSLI att1/4Bn p145 CR France80
LEECH,William Frederick.DSO.T2Lt dow 18-8-17 GL &9RFC p10 CR Belgium18
LEECHMAN,Colin Barclay Lt kia 26-9-14 3Huss p21 MR15,24-9-14
LEED,David 2Lt kia 12-8-18 1/2Hamps &209RAF p121 MR20
LEEDHAM,Richard Walter 2Lt kia 24-10-18 6RWar p214 CR France321
LEEDHAM,William T2Lt kia 4-9-18 Hamps att15Bn p121 MR30
LEEDS,John Stanley 2Lt kia 19-9-15 HAC p206 CR Belgium6
LEEK,Major Frederick William T2Lt kia 20-11-17 TankCps p188 MR17
LEEKE,Charles Lt dow 11-4-16 1GrenGds MGC SR p50 CR France40
LEEKE,Henry Alan Lt ded 29-5-15 9RWar CR Hamps1 see LEERE,H.A.
LEEKE,Ralph Henry CaptTMaj ded 5-11-15 RB att4KAR p178&202 CR EAfrica56
LEEMING,Alfred Johnson,MID 2LtACapt kia 31-7-17 6RFus p68 CR Belgium167
LEEMING,James Arthur.OBE.TLt ded 4-10-18 RE 170TC p46 CR France146
LEERE,Henry Alan Lt ded 29-5-15 9RWar p65 CR Hamps1,LEEKE
LEES,A.G.H.Capt 6-8-14 RDubF CR Ireland2
LEES,Algernon Henry.MIDx2 Maj ded 8-11-19 RASC p267 CR Wilts190
LEES,Clifford.MC.Lt dow 5-11-18 3WRid att15LancF p115 CR FRance441
LEES,Edmund Hastings Harcourt Capt kia 28-10-14 2BordR p117 MR29
LEES,Eric Brown Maj kia 31-7-18 W'land&C'landYeo p206 CR France61
LEES,Frank Priestman 2Lt kia 17-6-16 4NumbF p213 CR Belgium60
LEES,James Lowry.MC.TLtACapt kia 23-8-18 6TankCps p188 CR France745
LEES,James Malcolm Lt kia 22-8-16 1NStaffs p157 CR France513
LEES,Jasper 2Lt drd 28-3-15 4HLI attNigR p163&201 MR40
LEES,John Capt kia 19-4-17 5RScotF p222 MR34
LEES,Paul Beveridge Lt ded 18-6-19 SL 12GravesReg p255&268 CR Germany1
LEES,Percival Booth T2Lt kia 19-7-16 16Hamps att14Glouc p121 MR21
LEES,Percy Beresford 2Lt kia 11-3-15 3Nhampt p137 MR22
LEES,Robert Milne T2Lt kia 21-3-18 80RFC p16 CR France987
LEES,Robert Wallace T2Lt kia 3-9-16 7 att2KOSB p102 MR21
LEES,Thomas Evans Keith.Bart.Lt dow 24-8-15 DorsYeo p203 MR4
LEES,Thomas Prior Maj kia 21-4-15 9Lond p247 MR29
LEES,William Henry 2Lt ded 25-6-19 9Ches p96 CR Lancs475
LEESE,Cecil Francis Winton Lt kia 30-5-19 IA 27Punjabis attSWaziristanMil p279 MR43,31-5-19 29Bn
LEESON,Alexander Neve.DSO.Lt kia 22-10-17 RHA &30RFC p10&32 CR Iraq8
LEESON,Ian Alister Capt kia 10-7-17 97MGC p184 CR Belgium24 11-7-17
LEESON,James Thomas Chap4Cl kia 23-4-17 RAChDept att 13RFus p199 CR France452
LEETCH,Ernest Ashley.MM.Lt ded 19-3-19 RH&FA p261 CR Yorks528
LEETE,Frank Evelyn 2Lt dow 10-12-17 9Lond p248 CR Herts81
LEETE,Sydney John 2Lt kia 28-7-17 8Worc att57RFC p19&226 CR Belgium140
LEETE,William John Hurthwaite TCapt kia 21-1-16 11LancF p93 CR Belgium30,Hurstwaite
LEETHAM,Reginald LtACapt kia 12-10-17 5 att1RB p179 MR21
LEFAUX,John Faulkner 2Lt dow 15-10-18 15RHA p32 CR Belgium20
LEFEBORE,R.H.2Lt kld 13-4-18 GL &RAF p190
LEFEBVRE,Henri Homer TLt ded 15-12-17 RAVC p198 CR Surrey1
LE FEUVRE,Walter Tom TLt ded 8-1-17 RE p46 CR Wales498
LE FLEMING,Lawrence Julius.MID BtLtCol kia 21-3-18 ESurr att9Bn p113 MR27
LE FRANC,Guy Antoine Lt kia 16-7-21 IA 99LabCps p279 MR43
LEFROY,Bertram Percival.DSO.TLtCol dow 27-9-15 2RWar p65 CR France109,25-9-15
LEFROY,Francis Percival 2Lt kia 28-4-16 RE 73FC p46 CR France223
LEFROY,Frazer Kent 2Lt dow 8-4-17 11RFA p32 CR France12,Keith 7-4-17 85RFA
LEFROY,Gerald 2Lt kia 24-8-16 5 att2RMunstF p175 MR21
LEFROY,Tracy Edward.MIDx2 Maj ded 5-12-17 8RWar p214 CR France379
LEFTWICH,Nigel George Lt kia 15-4-18 Ches att2Bn p96 MR37
LEGALLAIS,Reginald Walter TLt kld 15-9-17 RFC p10 CR Dorset162
LEGARD,Geoffrey Philip Lt kia 8-5-15 2NumbF p62 MR29
LEGARD,George Bruce.MIDx2 Capt&Adjt kia 27-10-14 1RWKent p141 CR France924
LEGARD,Ralph Hawksworth Capt kia 9-8-15 4 att2DLI p161 MR29,Hawkesworth
LEGARD,Reginald John Lt dow 9-5-15 2WYorks p82 CR France345
LEGAT,Andrew Ronald.MC.Lt kia 28-3-17 A317RFA p207 CR France924
LEGATE,Francis Lt kia 27-8-18 5HLI p240 MR16
LEGG,Charles T2Lt ded 15-9-18 RE 203FC p46 CR France100

LEGG,Frederick William T2Lt kia 9-10-17 1Ess p132 MR30
LEGG,Horace Gordon Lt kia 24-3-18 22DLI p161 MR27,25-3-18
LEGG,William Norman TLt dow 24-3-16 7KSLI p145 CR France40,2Lt
LEGGAT,William 2Lt dow 2-7-15 7ScotRif p224 CR Europe1
LEGGAT,William 2Lt kia 13-10-18 3CamH p168 CR France271
LEGGATT,Ashley Gordon Scott T2Lt kia 16-9-16 C47RFA p32 CR France389
LEGGATT,Eric Gerard 2Lt kia 15-7-16 4 att10A&SH p173 MR21
LEGGATT,Jack T2Lt kia 5-4-16 6LNLancs p136 MR38,LEGGAT
LEGGATT,Logie Colin 2Lt kia 31-7-17 2CldGds p51 CR Belgium106
LEGGATT,Matthew 2Lt kia 26-3-18 5LancF attRFC p19&221 MR20,LEGGAT
LEGGE,David St.Clan 2Lt kia 14-7-16 7RWSurr p56 MR21
LEGGE,Gerald.Hon.TCapt kia 9-8-15 7SStaffs p122 MR4
LEGGE,Hugo Molesworth Lt kia 5-5-15 RFus p68 MR29
LEGGE,Reginald Charles Lt kia 16-9-16 MGC D'Coy HB p184 MR21
LEGGE,Ronald George Capt kia 18-12-14 2Dev p77 MR22
LEGGE,W.H.Lt 11-2-17 RFC CR Essex40
LEGGE-BOURKE,Nigel Walter Henry Lt kia 30-10-14 2CldGds p51 MR29
LEGGE-WILKINSON,Benjamin Claude T2Lt ded 4-1-16 RWar 1GarrBn p65 CR EAfrica116
LEGGETT,Alan Randall Aufrère.MID Lt kia 30-10-14 1NStaffs p157 CR Kent179,31-10-14
LEGGETT,Eric Henry Goodwin.DSO.Maj ded 30-7-16 188RFA p32 CR France134
LEGGETT,Wilfred Noël Maj kia 14-7-16 RGA 77SB p40 CR France232
LEGGOTT,Joseph Parkinson TLt dow 16-8-17 14RFA p32 CR France178
LEGGOTT,William Evers T2Lt kia 29-7-16 21Mddx p147 CR France115,30-7-16
LEGROVE,Walter 2Lt kia 25-4-18 12Lond p248 MR28
LEHFELDT,William Robert Alexander TLt dow 11-10-16 16N&D p134 CR France40
LEHMANN,Frederick Hope Maj ded 3-10-17 RDC p253
LEICESTER,Donovan Nicolas T2Lt kia 8-5-17 12Glouc p107 MR20
LEICESTER,James 2Lt ded 27-5-19 1Ches p263 CR Ches127,Lt 26-5-19
LEIGH,Benjamin Hilton TCapt ded 9-10-18 RAMC p267 CR Surrey91
LEIGH,Bernard Henry TLt kia 18-8-17 9RBerks att159LabCps p189 CR Belgium23
LEIGH,Chandos.DSO.Maj ded 29-8-14 KOSB p102&258 CR Belgium201
LEIGH,Edward Maj kia 1-5-15 2Hamps p121 CR Gallipoli2
LEIGH,Edward Henry Lt kia 9-5-15 2RB p179 MR32
LEIGH,Harvey Tunstill 2Lt kia 14-10-18 17LancF p93 CR Belgium157,Harry
LEIGH,Henry Clifford Capt kld 24-10-16 RFC p3 CR Lancs24,25-10-16
LEIGH,Henry Godfrey Thomas T2Lt ded 11-11-18 LabCps p189 CR France34
LEIGH,Herbert ACapt kia 14-10-18 1/7Ches p223 CR Belgium112
LEIGH,John Charles Thomas TCapt kia 3-7-16 EKent p57 CR France393
LEIGH,John Egerton TCapt kia 4-4-17 10KRRC p151 CR France662
LEIGH,Percy Lemprière Capt dow 29-8-16 RGA 29SB p40 CR France203
LEIGH,Robert Graham Lt ded 6-2-18 SL RecDuty p268 CR Berks125,6Nhampt
LEIGH,Rupert.Hon.Maj ded 14-8-19 Ex 4RIrDragGds p261
LEIGH,William Booth 2Lt kia 30-11-17 LNLancs att1/5Bn p136 MR17
LEIGH-BENNETT,Arthur.DSO.MC.Capt kia 3-10-15 2CldGds p51 CR France423
LEIGH-BENNETT,Olliph Spencer Lt dow 17-11-18 1CldGds p51 CR Sussex112
LEIGH-PEMBERTON,Percy Lt dow 27-7-16 4Mddx CR France145
LEIGH-PEMBERTON,Thomas Edward Geoffrey Lt kia 11-1-15 13Lond p249 CR France706
LEIGHTON,Archibald TCapt kia 2-9-18 RASC att1/5Lond p193 CR France511
LEIGHTON,Arthur 2Lt kia 14-11-16 3 att7SLancs p125 MR21
LEIGHTON,Bryan Baldwin Mawddy.Bart.TD.Maj ded 19-1-19 W'land&C'landYeo Res p270
LEIGHTON,George Roger Lt kia 7-8-18 6HLI &RAF p270
LEIGHTON,Harold.MC.TLt ded 26-5-17 88MGC Inf p184 CR France1182
LEIGHTON,John Burgh Talbot.MC.CaptTMaj dow 7-5-17 ScotsGds &23RFC p10&52 CR France41
LEIGHTON,Roland Aubrey Lt dow 23-12-15 1/7Worc p225 CR France3
LEISHMAN,Thomas Hugh 2Lt kia 23-4-17 5RScotF p222 MR20
LEISHMAN,Walter Algernon Lt ded 19-2-19 Dors p255 CR Hamps7
LEITCH,Alexander Harold Percival T2Lt dow 22-5-18 10RB p179 CR France81
LEITCH,Andrew J.Capt 11-2-19 RAMC CR Berks125
LEITCH,Eoin,Capt kia 31-7-17 5A&SH p243 MR29
LEITCH,George Fraser T2Lt kia 26-4-16 12 att9ScotRif p103 CR Belgium30
LEITCH,Neil TCapt kia 20-5-16 11HLI p163 CR France257
LEITCH,Vivian Bissett 2Lt kia 16-4-15 10Lpool p216 CR Belgium111
LEITH,Douglas Meldrum Watson.MC.Lt kia 21-3-18 4GordH p241 CR France245
LEITH,John T2Lt kia 23-8-18 16 att14RWar p65 CR France239

LEITHAM,Herbert Wilson 2Lt dow 17-10-18 5 att8BlkW p231 CR Belgium370
LELAND,John Henry Frederick 2Lt kia 10-8-15 5RWFus p223 MR4
LELAND,Walter Alfred 2Lt kia 4-6-15 10Beds att1RDubF p86 MR4
LELEU,Sydney Francis T2Lt dow 11-4-17 7KSLI p145 CR France46
LELIEVRE,Albert Frederick Henry T2Lt dow 4-8-16 17RFus p68 CRFrance23,14Bn
LEMAN,Douglas Walter Capt kia 28-3-18 21Lond p251 CR Syria2
LEMAN,Thomas Henry Capt kia 1-7-16 1/7N&D p233 CR France281
LE MARCHAND,John Wharton Jones Lt kia 9-8-15 IA 56Rif att1/6GurkhaRif p279 MR4
LE MARCHANT,Edward Herbert Charlie Lt dow 29-10-16 1Hamps p121 CR France145,Capt
LE MARCHANT,Henry Neville Capt kia 7/11-8-15 5Dors p124 MR4
LE MARCHANT,Louis St.Gratien.DSO.LtCol kia 14-9-14 1ELancs p111 CR France1445
LE MARCHANT,S.H.2Lt dow 25-5-15 6 att3RFus p68 CR Surrey62
LEMASS,Herbert Justin 2Lt kia 23-10-16 2RDubF p177 CR France432
LE MAY,Algernon Edward Lt dow 24-7-17 A235RFA p207 CR Belgium11
LE MAY,Lionel Henry LtACapt ded 24-2-19 SL att6KAR p202&257 MR46
LE MESSURIER,Cecil Cooper T2Lt kia 15-11-16 6Beds p86 CR France534
LEMESSURIER,Thomas T2Lt kld 30-1-18 RFC p16 CR Hamps90
LE MESURIER,Algernon Paul 2Lt mbk 9-3-17 IA 6GurkhaRif att27Punjabis p279 MR38,Arthur Edward
LE MESURIER,Clive 2Lt kia 29-4-15 IARO att33Cav p279 MR61,Lt
LE MESURIER,Frederick Neil Capt kia 25-4-15 att2RDubF p177 MR29
LE MESURIER,Havilland T2Lt kia 29-8-16 9KRRC p151&257 MR21,24-8-16
LEMMY,Frederick George TLt kia 14-7-16 11RScots p54 CR France399
LEMON,Adrian Leigh Lt kia 29-11-16 6DragGds att4MGC p21&184 CR France256
LEMON,Archie Dunlop TLt kia 1-7-16 12RIrRif p169 MR21,Dunlap
LEMON,David Wardlow.MC.T2Lt kia 22/23-3-18 7Leinst p174 CR France528,22-3-18
LEMON,Lionel Theodore T2Lt kia 12-4-17 6Dors p124 CR France531
LE MOTTEE,Edward D'Albert Maj kia 25-9-15 Glouc DivStaff p107 MR19
LEMPRIERE,Henry Anderson.DSO.LtCol kia 23-12-14 7DragGds p21 MR22
LENDON,Penry Bruce.MVO.Capt kia 21-10-14 3RLancs p59 CR Belgium32
LENDRUM,A.C.MC&Bar.Capt kld 27-10-20 RInniskF CR Ireland239
LENDRUM,Charles James William Kane.MID AMaj dow 13-11-16 3 att1RInniskF p105 CR France145
LENDRUM,Harold Bruce Lt dow 1-8-17 1/6SfthH p241 CR Belgium16
LENDRUM,James Herbert Reginald Chap4Cl kia 22-8-18 RAChDept att8Lancs p199 CR France745
LENKE,Ernest Capt ded 2-6-15 RFA p207 CR France102
LENNARD,Edward Stuart Russell T2Lt kia 14-9-17 GL 9RFC p10 CR Belgium18
LENNARD,Edward Wood 2Lt kia 30-11-17 4 att1RIrRif p169 MR30
LENNARD,Richard Granger T2Lt ded PoW 6-5-17 24NumbF p62 CR Belgium266
LENNARD,Samuel Frederic 2Lt kia 30-3-16 1/4Leic p220 CR France68,Lt
LENNOX,Alexander Dick 2Lt kia 18-10-17 5RScotF attRFC p222&19 CR Belgium453
LENNOX,Alfred James T2Lt kia 20-1-17 2RIrRif p169 MR32
LENNOX,Frederick William Lt ded 1-11-18 9DLI p239 CR Durham15
LENNY,Lancelot Arthur TLt kia 20-12-17 5RIrF att9ELancs p171 CR Greece6
LENOX-CONYNGHAM,Hubert Maxwell.DSO.MID BtLtCol ded 15-3-18 RAVC p198 CR Ireland17
LENOX-CONYNGHAM,John Staples Molesworth LtCol kia 3-9-16 Cmdg6ConnRgrs p172 CR France513
LENTAIGNE,Victor Aloysius 2Lt kia 14-9-14 2ConnRgrs p172 MR15
LENTON,Gerald T2Lt dow 27-7-17 2Beds p86 CR Belgium11
LENTON,Harold Bertram 2Lt kia 30-10-17 7RFus p68 MR30
LENZ,William Adolph Philip 2Lt kia 6-11-17 RGA 148SB p40 CR Belgium19,Ardolph
LEON,Edward Joseph 2Lt kia 7-10-16 8Lond p247 CR France385
LEON,John Temple Capt ded 30-3-16 RAMC p270 CR Surrey162
LEONARD,Denis.MM.T2Lt kia 6-11-18 2Yorks p90 CR France949
LEONARD,Francis 2Lt ded 4-7-15 RGA p40 MR43
LEONARD,Francis Patrick Mapletoft TLt dow 29-4-16 8RInniskF p105 MR19
LEONARD,George.DCM.TLt&QM ded 1-9-16 8SStaffs p122 CR France1
LE PAGE,George William TMaj kia 26-1-16 6RIrReg D'Coy p89 CR France178
LE PETON,Clive Alfred Lt kia 15-8-17 8 att7RInniskF p105 MR29
LE PETON,Desmond Alexander 2Lt dow 9-8-16 1SomLI p80 CR Belgium11
LE POER TRENCH,Nugent Charles 2Lt kia 16-1-17 9ESurr CR France115 see TRENCH,N.C.Le P.
LEPPER,Harper Mervyn.MC.2Lt kia 9-4-16 Mddx att8RWFus p147 MR38
LERESCHE,Alfred Sunderland 2Lt kia 3-9-16 1/7WYorks p218 CR France1890

LERMITTE,Henry James LtCol ded 20-6-18 EssYeo &RScotF p261 CR Essex196
LE SAUVAGE,Ernest Davies.MID 2Lt kld 30-5-16 1Dors att&RFC p3&124 CR Dorset149
LESLIE,A.F.Capt 25-8-21 RE CR Wales17
LESLIE,A.M.Maj 21-4-19 Suff CR Sussex95
LESLIE,Alexander William 2Lt dow 23-4-17 4Leic p220 CR France12
LESLIE,Cecil George.MC.Maj ded 11-8-19 3DragGds p261 CR Eire260
LESLIE,Charles Joseph 2Lt dow 24-4-18 5 att2WYorks p218 MR27
LESLIE,Donald Wilfred Russell Lt ded 20-2-21 IARO att41MuleCps p279 CR India48,D.R.W.
LESLIE,Edwin Victor Downie 2Lt kia 8-4-17 4SfthH p241
LESLIE,Frank King Capt kia 25-4-15 2RFus p68 MR4
LESLIE,George Constable Lt dow 15-8-17 5BlkW p231 CR France40,9Bn
LESLIE,George Muir T2Lt kia 3-10-15 2HLI p163 CR France423,2-10-15
LESLIE,Leslie Francis Ellington 2Lt kia 20-8-17 1KAR p202 CR EAfrica40,Lt
LESLIE,Norman Jerome Beauchamp Capt kia 19-10-14 3RB p179 CR France681
LESLIE,Richard Fitzgerald William Ferris Maj kia 22-8-15 5Dors p124 MR4
LESLIE,William Capt kia 12-1-16 70RGA p40 CR Asia62,dow
LESLIE,William Robert Norman 2Lt kia 25-1-15 3Glouc p107 CR France260,Lt 1Bn
LESLIE-SMITH,Gilbert Capt kia 14-7-15 IA 24Punjabis p279 CR Iraq6
LESSELS,Robert Murray 2Lt kia 29-7-18 RWSurr p56 CR France524
LESTER,Albert Edward.MC.2Lt kia 8-5-18 13Lond p249 MR27
LESTER,Ernest Charles Lt kia 3-7-15 10 att1BordR p117 CR Gallipoli6
LESTER,Eric Peter T2Lt kia 13-10-15 13 att2Worc p109 MR19
LESTER,Frank Capt dow PoW 25-3-18 6ESurr p226 CR France375
LESTER,Gerald James Rev ded 16-12-18 RAChDept attCMELocoWorks p199 CR France146
LESTER,John Beaumont TCapt kia 15-9-16 18KRRC p151 CR France277
LESTER,William Owen Ernest 2Lt kia 4-4-18 4 att8ESurr p113 MR27
LESTER-SMITH,Henry 2Lt kia 15-7-17 4Ches p222 CR Belgium152,14-7-17
LE STRANGE,Roland Capt ded 20-2-19 Staff CmdgChinLabCps CR Norf61
LE SUEUR,Ernest Geoffrey Carrington LtTCapt kia 26-7-17 1Yorks p90 MR29
LE TALL,Cyril Herbert Capt kia 30-8-18 1Lond p245 CR France646
LETHBRIDGE,Brian Hugh Bridgeman TLt dow 19-7-17 8Beds p86 CR France115,kia
LETHBRIDGE,Cecil Augustus Lt kia 3-5-17 8RFus p68 MR20
LETHBRIDGE,Fred.DCM.2Lt kia 24-4-18 2Dev p77 CR France144
LETHBRIDGE,Patrick Lionel TCapt&Adjt kia 25-9-15 7KOSB p102 MR19
LETHBRIDGE,William Bernard Lt ded 14-5-20 61Pnrs CR Devon12
LETHBRIDGE,William Henry T2Lt kia 4-10-17 12/13NumbF p62 MR30
LETHEBE,Herbert Thomas TLt kia 2-9-18 11TankCps p188 CR France924
LETHEM,John 2Lt kia 1-12-17 246RFA p208 MR30,Lt
LE THICKE,Gerald Mann 2Lt ded 23-7-15 5SWBord p100 CR Berks28
LETT,John Millard T2LtACapt kia 22-3-18 3Worc p109 MR20
LETTERS,Thomas Arthur Lt kia 13-3-15 3GordH p166 MR22
LETTS,Arthur Kingdon Maj ded 5-6-20 RWFus attMGC Inf
LETTS,Bertram Chiene TLt ded 21-10-15 RAMC 13CCS p196 CR Egypt3
LETTS,John Herbert Towne.MC.Capt kldacc 11-10-18 1/2Lincs &64RAF p75 CR France103
LEVACK,George MacLeod Capt kia 7-10-16 RAMC att6 O&BLI p253 MR21
LEVASON,Desmond George Granville Capt dow 27-3-17 1/1Hereford p252 CR Palestine8
LEVENE,Nathan Neville 2Lt kia 8-8-16 1/8Lpool p216 MR21
LEVENTHORPE,John Algernon.MID Lt kia 22-1-15 RE p46 CR Belgium74,23-1-
LEVENTON,Raymond Sylvester T2Lt drd 5-11-17 GL 49RFC p10 CR Kent7
LEVER,Harold Brasington 2Lt ded PoW 23-10-18 5Beds p219 CR Belgium406
LEVER,Harrie,Reginald.OBE.LtCol ded 16-11-20 RASC MT MR43
LEVER,Harry Marshall.DCM.Lt 23-5-20 1RScots Ex Capt KAR CR Burma129
LEVER,Joseph.MC.T2Lt dow 1-10-18 1KRRC p151 CR France512
LEVERETT,John Ivison 2Lt ded 27-3-19 LovatScts p270 CR Mddx26,Lt
LEVESON,Rudolph Marcus TLt kia 18-12-17 10DLI p161 MR30
LEVESON-GOWER,Ronald Charles Granville Gresham Lt dow 1-8-17 2CldGds p51 CR Belgium16
LEVESON-GOWER,William George Gresham Lt kia 9-10-18 1CldGds p51 CR France332
LEVETT,Richard Henry 2Lt ded 20-8-16 3RWKent p141 CR Kent279
LEVETT,Richard William Byrd 2Lt kia 10-3-17 6 att1KRRC p151 CR France430
LEVI,Albert 2Lt dow 12-6-19 4Beds p86 CR Mddx40,LEVY
LEVI,Frederick Joseph 2Lt kia 21-3-18 1 att2/5Lincs p75 MR20
LEVI,Harry T2Lt kia 30-11-17 9RFus p68 MR17

LEVICK,Arthur Lascelles 2Lt kia 15-9-16 3 att6YLI p143 CR France402
LEVICK,Percy T.Capt kld 15-3-18 RAMC attGdsDAC p196 CR France266
LEVIE,Peter MacLeod.MC.Capt kia 24-10-18 1/4BlkW p230 CR France1258
LEVIN,Charles Norton.MC.Capt kia 21-3-18 21NumbF att102TMB p62 MR27
LEVINGE,Henry George.MIDx2 LtCol kia 10-8-15 6LNLancs p136 MR4
LEVINGE,Richard William.Bart.Lt kia 24-10-14 1LifeGds RoO p20 CR Belgium101
LEVINSTEIN,Gerald Edward TLt kia 12-10-16 26 att17Manch p155 MR21
LEVIS,James Henry Bruce T2Lt kia 12-8-15 6RIrRif p169 MR4
LEVITA,Francis Ellison Lt kia 12-10-14 4Huss p21 CR France324
LEVITT,Robert TLtACapt dow 7-7-17 6LNLancs p136 CR Iraq8
LEVITT,Sydney Neville T2Lt kia 29-9-18 16KRRC p151 CR France212
LEVY,A.2Lt 12-6-19 4Beds CR Mddx40
LEVY,Arthur Herbert Lt kia 31-7-17 232RFA p208 CR Belgium7
LEVY,Josiah 2Lt kia 19-4-17 1/4Norf p216 CR Palestine8
LEVY,M.B.MC.Capt 12-4-18 2IrGds MR32
LEVY-TEBBIT,Isaac 2Lt ded 4-12-15 19Lond p270
LEWER,Richard Roy TLt dow 21-7-16 16KRRC p151 CR France833
LEWES,Frederick Henry Meredith Capt dow 2-7-16 5N&D p232 MR21,1-7-16
LEWIN,Cecil Charles Humphreys.MC.Capt kia 2-11-18 4SomLI p218 CR France1257
LEWIN,Edward Chaloner TLt kia 27-9-18 RWKent att1Bn p141 CR France415
LEWIN,Edward Hale Capt kia 8-3-16 IA 46Punjabis att82 p279 MR38
LEWIN,Francis Harold.MC.MIDx2 TCapt kia 12-10-17 7RWKent p141 CR Belgium23
LEWIN,Frederick Henry Capt ded 8-12-15 3ConnRgrs p172 CR Eire432 &CR Ireland14
LEWIN,John Wesley 2Lt kia 24-9-18 LabCps att5Leic p88 CR France699
LEWIN,Kenneth Robert TLt kia 9-3-16 7DCLI p114 CR Belgium23
LEWIN,Rex Richard Lt kia 25-9-15 3 att2RSuss p119 MR19
LEWINGTON,Frank Samuel T2Lt kia 21-3-18 9Norf p74 MR20
LEWINGTON,George Longley T2Lt kld 23-12-17 GL RFC p10 CR Mddx6
LEWINSTEIN,Harry 2Lt kia 22-7-16 1RWKent p141 CR France432
LEWIS,Alfred Drysdale TLt kia 24-3-18 RE 62FC p46 MR27
LEWIS,Alfred Ernest George TLt kia 6-9-17 195MGC Inf p184 CR Belgium112
LEWIS,Alfred John T2Lt kia 1-8-18 1 att7/8KOSB p102 CR France864
LEWIS,Archibald Ernest T2Lt kia 28-9-17 1KSLI p145 CR France550
LEWIS,Arthur Glanmor 2Lt kia 11/13-10-15 3SWBord att1Mon p100 CR France550,12-10-15
LEWIS,Arthur Glynne Lt ded 10-7-17 IARO att13Lancers p279 CR Iraq8
LEWIS,Arthur Milton.MID Capt kia 8-8-19 IA 1/52Sikhs p279 MR38
LEWIS,Arthur Ralph Pollard 2Lt kia 23-3-18 93RFA SigSubSec p32 CR France518
LEWIS,Arthur Starkey TLt kia 4-5-17 1RWFus GarrBn p98 MR20
LEWIS,Benjamin Alfred T2Lt kia 8-11-18 YLI att2Bn p143 CR France928
LEWIS,Brinley Richard TLtAMaj kia 2-4-17 B122RH&FA p32 CR Belgium1
LEWIS,Cecil Hallowes Maj ded 28-5-15 RASC 1DivTrn p193 CR France145
LEWIS,Charles HonLt&QM ded 14-6-17 RASC p193 CR Egypt1
LEWIS,Charles 2Lt kia 21-3-18 6 att16Manch p237 MR27
LEWIS,Charles Edward 2Lt kia 9-9-16 1/4Lond p246 MR21
LEWIS,Charles Vernon TLt ded 18-8-15 11SWBord att3Dors p100 CR Wales491
LEWIS,Clifford Stanley Lt dow 19-9-16 2/6Glouc p225 CR France345
LEWIS,Cuthbert Preston T2Lt kia 8-6-17 RE 2SpCoy p46 CR France297
LEWIS,Cyril William Victor Lt kld 3-10-17 6 att1Mddx p147 CR Wales289
LEWIS,David Elwyn 2Lt dow 18-9-18 16RWFus p98 CR France415
LEWIS,David Jacob T2Lt kia 28-2-17 2RFus p68 MR21
LEWIS,Denys Mervyn 2Lt kia 25-4-17 1/7Worc p226 MR21
LEWIS,Donald Swain.DSO.TLtCol kia 10-4-16 RE attRFC p3&46 CR Belgium11
LEWIS,Douglas David Raymond 2Lt dow 22-4-17 8DLI p239 CR France418
LEWIS,Edgar Capt kia 8-3-16 1/4SomLI p218 MR38
LEWIS,Edmund Llewellyn 2Lt kia 26-12-16 1/7Ess att24RFC p19&232 MR20
LEWIS,Edward Pugh 2Lt kia 6-10-17 GL 9RFC p10 CR Belgium18
LEWIS,Edward Richard Hampton 2Lt dow 25-4-17 4Worc Z'Coy p109 CR France113,Edwin
LEWIS,Edwin Maj dow 30-9-18 1/6SStaffs p229 CR France327
LEWIS,Ernest Hastings Maj kia 12-8-15 8Hamps p229 MR4
LEWIS,Francis Alexander 2Lt kia 5-2-18 53RFC p16 CR Belgium11,Frank Arthur
LEWIS,Frank T2Lt dow 31-7-17 7MGC p184 CR Belgiu19
LEWIS,Frank Arthur T2Lt kld 28-3-18 RFC p16 CR Scot398
LEWIS,Frederic Homer T2Lt kia 29-4-18 10 att1RIrRif p169 MR30
LEWIS,George Arthur Dunally 2Lt kia 8-7-15 4SStaffs attRWFus p122 MR29
LEWIS,George Hardy LtTCapt dow 29-9-15 4 att2ESurr p113 CR France98,27-9-15

LEWIS,George Herbert Lt 9-12-16 APDept CR Lond29
LEWIS,Gerald Sidney TCapt kia 7-7-16 11Mddx A'Coy p147 CR France296
LEWIS,Gordon T2Lt dow 18-4-18 10WelshR p127 CR France765
LEWIS,Graham Knight TLt dow 1-11-18 1HLI p163 CR Iraq8
LEWIS,Graham Lawson Lt dow 9-7-16 4 att2LancF p92 CR France1
LEWIS,Granville Vernon Loch T2Lt kldacc 5-10-17 RFC p10 CR Mddx17
LEWIS,Harold LtCol kia 1-7-16 IA 37Lancers Cmdg20Manch p279 CR France397
LEWIS,Harold 2Lt dow 29-4-17 151MGC p184 CR France145
LEWIS,Harold Lockwood T2Lt kia 23-10-17 24NumbF p62 MR30
LEWIS,Harold Nicholson.MM.T2Lt kia 18-10-17 1/2 att17LancF p92 MR30
LEWIS,Harris 2Lt kia 25-9-16 1/7Lpool p215 MR21,Harry
LEWIS,Harry Arthur.DCM.MID Maj kia 1-7-16 9Y&L p159 MR21
LEWIS,Harry Blundell 2Lt kia 2-12-17 1/7Lond p247 MR17
LEWIS,Henry Clifford Capt kia 4-10-17 10Mddx p236 MR30
LEWIS,Henry William T2Lt kia 12-10-18 RE 154FC p46 CR France287
LEWIS,Herbert 2Lt drd 5-5-17 RASC 917&MT Co p193 MR37
LEWIS,Herbert Monce 2Lt kia 4-11-15 10Mddx p236 MR4
LEWIS,Herbert Owen Roland.MC.T2Lt kia 1-10-17 1/2 att9Yorks p90 MR30
LEWIS,Hugh Berwyn T2Lt ded 12-2-19 LabCps 775AreaEmployCoy p189 CR France1142
LEWIS,Hugh Frederick.MID Capt kia 19-10-14 2RWSurr p56 CR Belgium160
LEWIS,James Windsor Lt kia 6-6-16 1WelshGds CR Belgium6
LEWIS,John Charles Capt kia 20-11-17 1Mon att6KSLI p244 MR17
LEWIS,John Clifford 2Lt dow 27-3-18 RGA 24SB p209 CR France185
LEWIS,John Dunning Gaunt Lt kia 24-9-18 3KSLI p145 CR France725
LEWIS,John Emrys T2Lt kia 1-7-16 8SomLI p80 CR France267
LEWIS,John Nicholas Lt kia 8-8-15 8WelshR p127 MR4
LEWIS,John Thorpe TCapt kia 9-8-15 Lincs p75 MR4
LEWIS,John Walter Lt kia 6-6-16 1WelshGds p53
LEWIS,John Walter 2Lt dow 15-7-16 3 att8Dev A'Coy p77 CR France119
LEWIS,Joseph Henry T2LtACapt kia 8-10-18 17RWFus att1/7Ches p98 CR France234
LEWIS,Lance Will T2Lt kia 9-8-16 7KRRC attMGC Inf p151&184 CR France294
LEWIS,Lawrence Reddrop TCapt kia 11-7-16 11SWBord p100 MR21
LEWIS,Leonard Geoffrey 2Lt mbk 31-8-18 1 att2Wilts p256 MR29,31-7-17
LEWIS,Leonard Glynne.MC.T2Lt kia 24-11-17 18WelshR p127 MR17
LEWIS,Llewelyn T2Lt kia 1/12-7-16 17RWFus p98 MR21
LEWIS,Lloyd Edward Lt kia 24-9-18 5N&D p232 CR France375
LEWIS,Ludwig T2Lt kia 6-7-17 2MGC Inf p184 CR Belgium173
LEWIS,Morgan Henry Lt dow 20-6-15 4RScotF p222 CR Gallipoli1
LEWIS,Nevill Graham Nuscomb Hart Capt kia 17-9-17 3Mon p244 CR Belgium20,Newcome
LEWIS,Norman George Lt ded 12-2-19 18KRRC A'Coy p265 CR Glouc5
LEWIS,Norman Victor TLt kia 13-11-16 15 att13EYorks p84 MR21
LEWIS,Reginald Cameron.MC.TCapt kia 1-7-16 2RBerks p139 CR France393
LEWIS,Reginald Walter Morton TLt ded 3-10-18 1 att9Worc p109 CR Asia82
LEWIS,Richard Percy MajALtCol kia 8-9-17 Dev attManch p77 CR Belgium84,7-9-17
LEWIS,Robert Frederick T2Lt kia 20-9-17 17KRRC att117TMB p151 MR30
LEWIS,Robert George TLt kia 23-9-18 74MGC Inf p184 CR France1494
LEWIS,Stephen Henry Lt kia 28-8-15 5ConnRgrs p172 MR4
LEWIS,Thomas William T2Lt dow 27-10-17 1RWFus p98 CR Belgium112
LEWIS,Trefor 2Lt dow 27-5-18 RFA att37TMB p32 CR France63
LEWIS,Trevor Edward TCapt kldacc 28-8-15 5SWBord p100 CR France345
LEWIS,Wallenstein Ryan.MC.TCapt dow 25-3-18 RE 284AT Co p46
LEWIS,Walter Henry.MID Lt dow 4-8-17 D107RFA p32 CR France40,2Lt
LEWIS,William Owen 2Lt mbk 27-5-17 4 att2WelshR p257 MR20
LEWIS,William Thomas 2Lt kia 27-3-17 1/7Ess p232 CR Palestine8
LEWTAS,Oscar Capt kia 9-7-16 3 att2Manch p155 MR21
LEWTHWAITE,Charles Gilfred.MC.Lt kia 29-7-17 231R FA p208 CR France570,Gilfrid
LEWTON-BRAIN,James Andrew T2Lt dow 14-8-17 8Norf p74 CR Belgium11
LEWTY,Thomas Edmund.MID 2Lt kia 14-3-17 5NStaffs p238 CR France579
LEY,Christopher Francis Aden Capt kld 16-3-18 NottsYeo attRFC p19&205
LEY,Geoffrey Arthur Henry 2Lt kia 30-7-17 3Dev attTankCps p77 CR Belgium126
LEY,James Wickham.DSO.Maj ded 22-10-18 2NStaffs p157 CR Asia82,7Bn
LEY,John Howard 2Lt kia 9-9-16 1RMunstF p175 MR21
LEY,Maurice Aden Lt kia 1-11-14 EKent att1Lincs p75&262 CR Belgium101
LEY,Maurice Carew 2Lt kia 1-7-16 2Dev p77 CR France393
LEYBOURN,Frederick Percy.MM.MID T2Lt ded 1-11-18 17Manch att6Ches p155 CR France276,19Bn

LEYBOURNE,Philip Edwin.MC&Bar.Capt kia 4-9-18 8Hamps p229 CR Belgium111

LEYLAND,Herbert Edward T2Lt dow 17-10-17 RE 179TC p46

LEYLAND,Reginald Hamilton ALtCol kia 24-9-18 2RB p179 CR France184,Rex

LEYS,Colin McLaren T2Lt kia 15-9-16 8Beds p86 MR21

LEZARD,Arthur Gower Capt kia 31-1-16 13RB p179 CR France745

LIARDET,Frederick Charles Evelyn Lt ded 13-12-17 5Dev attRFC p217&19,dow CR Devon128

LIAS,Ronald John Mortlock TLt kia 23-2-16 9RSuss p119 CR Belgium72

LIBERTY,John Ince Lt kia 28-11-17 RFA 38ArmyBde p32 CR Belgium19

LIBBY,Alfred Thomas TLt kia 20-9-17 12ESurr p113 MR30

LIDDELL,Arthur John T2Lt dow 5-10-17 YLI att8Bn p143 CR France8

LIDDELL,John TLt kia 30-3-18 RE 144ArmyTroopCo p46 MR27

LIDDELL,John Aidan.VC.Capt dow 31-8-15 A&SH &RFC p173&1,Adrian CR Hamps106

LIDDELL,John Henry Tandy Lt dow 17-11-16 6 att1KRRC p151 CR France120

LIDDELL,John Robert Hugh T2Lt kld 10-11-17 GL RFC p10 CR Lancs421

LIDDELL,Lily Nurse ded 29-9-18 VAD BRCS p200 CR Egypt9

LIDDELL,Mathew Henry Goldie 2Lt ded 17-4-16 7ScotRif &54RAF p224&256,17-4-18 MR20,no date

LIDDELL,Robert 2Lt ded 24-1-19 Ess att1/7Bn p132 CR Italy6

LIDDLE,Horace Septimus HonCapt ded 1-6-18 Ex LabCps p266 CR SAfrica53 RFus

LIDDLE,William Capt ded 27-9-18 9RScots attRE 11DivSigs p212 CR France95

LIDGETT,John Cuthbert TLt kia 23-3-18 11SLancs p125 CR France1203,24-3-18

LIDIARD,Richard John Abraham 2Lt kia 1-7-16 3Lond p246 CR France1327

LIDINGTON,Norman Herbert T2Lt kia 15-9-16 1Nhampt att11Ess p137 MR21

LIDSEY,William John 2Lt dow 22-3-17 4 O&BLI &16RFC p19&231 CR France95

LIEBENTHAL,Louis George Lt kia 4-6-15 8CamH att1Ess p168 MR4

LIEBERT,Bernard Robert Maj kia 13-5-15 LeicYeo p204 MR29

LIEBERT,Frederick Alexander Charles Capt kia 17-11-14 NSomYeo p205 CR Belgium57 Ex 3DragGds

LIFETREE,Ernest Henry T2Lt kia 20-5-16 16N&D p134 CR France279

LIGHT,Eric 2Lt mbk 26-3-18 40MGC p256 MR20

LIGHT,George Joseph 2Lt kia 8-11-17 RGA 142SB p40 CR France777

LIGHTBODY,James Gordon Lt ded 27-4-19 1A 36Horse p279 MR65

LIGHTBODY,Wilfred Petre TLt kia 26-9-15 9Norf p74 MR19

LIGHTBOURN,Robert T2Lt kia 26-7-17 8Glouc p107 CR Belgium60 Lt

LIGHTFOOT,Francis Bertram 2Lt kia 30-12-17 28Lond p252 MR21

LIGHTLEY,Albert 2Lt kia 31-3-18 7EYorks p84 MR20

LILICO,Percy T2Lt kld 16-2-18 RFC p16 CR Numb58,Lt

LILLEY,Edmund Arthur Howe TLt kia 31-7-18 6Beds att112TMB p86 CR France1014,Capt

LILLEY,William David Hetherington 2Lt dow PoW 11-8-16 8Lpool p216 CR France1266

LILLEY,William Fred.MM.2Lt kia 24-4-18 6RWar p214 MR19

LILLIE,Frank William T2Lt kld 18-12-16 9YLI p143 CR France423,Capt

LILLIE,Frederick Sutherland Maj kia 15-3-15 1RIrReg p89 CR Belgium28

LILLINGTON,Conrad Ivan 2Lt kia 8-3-16 1/4SomLI p218 MR38

LILLIS,Martin Michael Arthur TLt kia 11-4-17 RIrReg &3RFC p10&89 CR France833

LILLY,Arthur John 2Lt kia 4-4-17 6RWar p214 CR France669

LILLY,Thomas Maj 24-9-19 RAOC CR Yorks361

LILLYWHITE,Frederick Thomas Sherwood T2Lt dow 26-5-17 2Mddx p147 CR France145

LILLYWHITE,Robert John TCapt kld 26-11-16 GL &RFC p190&3,LILLYWHILTE CR Sussex88

LIMB,Harry TLtACapt ded 23-10-18 RE IWT p46 CR France1359

LIMBERY,Charles Roy.MC.Capt kia 1-7-16 1SStaffs p122 CR France397

LIMBERY,Kenneth Thomas.MC.TCapt kia 26-9-17 RAMC att133FA p196 CR France139

LIMBRICK,Arthur William Wentworth 2Lt kia 14-3-17 3 att2RWSurr p56 CR France514

LIMERICK,Victor 2Lt ded 20-8-19 RFA &5RAF p256&258 CR Germany1,Lt

LIMONT,William Eric T2Lt kia 14-7-16 15 att12NumbF p62 MR21

LIMRICK,Paul Osborne Lt kia 12-9-16 8Lpool p215 CR France402

LINAKER,Archibald Frederick Richard TLt kia 9-9-18 SLancs att2LNLancs p125 CR Belgium15,Fredrick 2LNL attSL

LINCEY,Charles Edgar 2Lt kia 31-7-16 1/4RLancs p213 CR France453

LINCOLN,C.Joseph AssSurg 23-7-21 IMD MR66

LINDBERG,Thomas Henry TMaj ded 24-4-15 SL p201 CR Yorks245

LINDE,Henry Eyre T2Lt dow 24-6-17 7RInniskF p105 Cr Belgium60

LINDEN,Norman Eric T2Lt dow 4-9-18 10TankCps p188 CR France34

LINDEN,Samuel McCullagh.MID 2Lt kia 31-7-17 RGA 90HAG p40 MR29

LINDLEY,Ernest William 2Lt ded PoW 18-2-17 9Manch attRFC p19&237 CR France604

LINDLEY,Foster 2Lt dow 5-9-18 7EYorks p84 CR France41,Lt

LINDLEY,Harry Lt&QM ded 27-1-16 6Leic p88 CR Leic63

LINDLEY,John Bennett 2Lt dow 19-5-17 RFA V2HvyTMB p208 CR France265

LINDLEY,Thomas Grenville 2Lt dow 24-9-17 1/20 att2/10Lond p251 CR Belgium18

LINDOP,Eugene Lancelot Erskine.MC.Capt dow 30-1-16 1A 41Dogras p279 CR Iraq6

LINDOP,Herbert Cyril Lt kia 20-9-17 5NStaffs att10KRRCp238 MR30

LINDOW,Edwin 2Lt dow 11-8-16 3 att6Dors p124 CR France397

LINDREA,George Patrick Maj kia 18-7-16 B305RFA p206 CR France1887

LINDREA,Wilfred George 2Lt kia 30-3-18 4Glouc p225 CR France1170

LINDSAY,Adam 2Lt dow 1-8-18 10RScots p212 CR France1225

LINDSAY,Alexander Cuthbert TLt ded 10-2-18 GL RE IWT p46 CR Iraq6

LINDSAY,Archibald Thurston Thomas Lt kia 26-3-18 RE 7ATCoy attMon p46 C France281

LINDSAY,Bernard Wilfred Capt dow 22-11-16 B187RFA p207 CR France34

LINDSAY,Charles Stephen Capt dow 11-4-16 1A 55Rif att53Sikhs p279 MR38

LINDSAY,Claud Frederic Thomas.MID Capt kia 31-3-18 RFA 33Bty p32 CR France1003,Maj

LINDSAY,Courtenay Traice TLt ded 28-4-16 RASC p193 CR Bucks57

LINDSAY,David Lt kia 15-4-17 7HLI p240 MR41

LINDSAY,David Paton TCapt ded 2-12-18 RAMC p196 CR EAfrica36

LINDSAY,Douglas Alexander Capt kia 15-5-15 5RScots p211 CR Gallipoli2

LINDSAY,Douglas Alexander T2Lt kia 25-9-15 10ScotRif p103 MR19

LINDSAY,Francis Howard Maj kia 1-7-16 14Lond p249 MR21

LINDSAY,George Lt kia 7-5-17 5 att11RScots p211 CR France97

LINDSAY,George Walter Thomas Capt kld 26-6-17 RFA attRFC p10&32 CR Wales16

LINDSAY,Henry.MC.Capt kia 8-8-16 1/4LNLancs p234 MR21

LINDSAY,James T2Lt kia 12-4-18 23NumbF p62 MR32

LINDSAY,James Arthur Capt ded 24-6-15 RGA p270

LINDSAY,James Basden T2Lt ded 8-8-18 RASC BaseSupplyDepot p193 CR Iraq6

LINDSAY,T.H.Capt 24-6-15 RGA CR Scot237

LINDSAY,William 2Lt kia 31-7-17 3 att2RScotF p94 MR29

LINDSAY,William Alexander Hewes 2Lt kia 31-7-16 4 att2HLI p163 MR21

LINDSAY,William Henry.MC.TCapt kia 3-9-18 9ESurr p113 CR France480

LINDSAY,William Horn 2Lt dow 30-5-19 6BlkW p129&257 CR Scot385

LINDSAY-SMITH,Campbell Lt 10-11-15 11 att8GordH CR Belgium125

LINDSAY-YOUNG,Laurence Hingston Capt dow 25-12-18 1RScotF &RAF p95 Hamps7

LINDSEY,Douglas Lt kia 17-12-17 3 att5Dors p124 CR France550,Capt

LINDSEY,Paul 2Lt kia 2-6-17 4 O&BLI p231 CR France162

LINDSLEY,George Vincent 2Lt dow 16-3-17 3 att2RWFus p98 CR France145

LINE,Eric Alfred Thiselton T2Lt ded 16-12-16 RASC 26DivTrain p193 CR Greec

LINE,John Young Alexander T2Lt dow 13-3-16 8NStaffs D'Coy p157 CR France

LINES,Francis Leonard Lt kia 19-4-17 1/4Nhampt p234 CR Palestine8

LINES,Herbert T2Lt kia 20-9-17 KRRC att10Bn p151 MR30

LINES,Sidney Martin 2Lt kia 13-5-15 1/5Lond p246 MR29 CR Belgium453

LINES,Thomas.MC.DCM.T2Lt dow 5-4-18 16LancF p92 CR France804

LINFORD,Ivor Hutchison.MC.TCapt kia 21-3-18 12Ess p132 MR27 10Bn

LING,Arthur Leonard 2Lt dow 3-11-18 5Lancs p213 CR France52,Lt

LING,Fergus Graham Capt ded 16-12-18 KEdwsHorse p24 CR W'land&C'land2

LING,Frederick William TCapt&Adjt kia 27-6-17 8RFus p68 CR France154

LING,Godfrey Frank Mackwood.MC&2Bars.Capt kia 23-5-18 2/7WYorks att185TMB p218 CR France798

LING,Leonard Simpson 2Lt kia 23-4-17 3 att1Norf p74 MR20

LINGARD,John Reginald Lt kia 21-8-15 6Manch p236 MR4

LINGEMAN,John Florris 2Lt dow 28-4-17 1EssYeo p203 CR France102

LINGWOOD,Edward St.Hilary T2Lt kia 3-5-17 7Beds p86 MR20

LINK,F.L.C.2Lt kld 7-6-18 GL &RAF p190

LINK,Horace Arthur 2Lt kia 9-9-16 1HAC p206 CR France161

LINKLATER,William Irvine 2Lt kia 5-4-18 B77RFA p32 CR France232

LINN,Peter 2Lt kia 22-10-17 16RScots p54 CR Belgium126

LINNELL,Robert McCheyne Capt ded 17-3-15 RAMC p196 CR Beds34

LINNING,John HonMaj&QM ded 16-9-14 1BlkW p129 MR15

LINSELL,Johnson Hugh T2Lt kia 25-9-15 Mddx p147 MR19

LINSTEAD,Douglas Walter T2Lt kia 6-5-16 12RFus 3Coy p68 CR Belgium339

LINTON,Charles Strangways.DSO.MC.MajALtCol kia 20-11-17 4Worc p109 CR France439

LINTON.F.P.Surg 18-10-18 IMS MR61
LINTON,Frederick Tom.MC.T2Lt kia 22-4-18 16RWFus p98 CR France296
LINTON,Henry McEwan TLt dow 28-9-15 12HLI p163 CR France178,kia 26-9-15
LINTOTT,Evelyn Henry TLt kia 1-7-16 15WYorks p82 MR21
LINTOTT,Harry Chamen Lt dow 22-3-18 5Lond p246 CR France398
LINTOTT,Richard 2Lt kia 3-5-15 5Lond p246 MR29
LINZELL,Harold Harding.MC.T2Lt kia 3-7-16 7BordR p177 CR France397
LINZELL,Stanley James.MC.Capt kia 3-4-17 RAMC p196 CR France1204
LIPP,Charles Napier 2Lt kia 31-7-17 6SfthH p241 MR29
LIPP,Frank 2Lt dow 30-5-16 2ScotRif att8RWFus p103 MR43
LIPP,Vernon Robertson 2Lt kia 17-6-16 5 att12RFus p68 CRBelgium339
LIPPIATT,William George T2Lt kia 10-8-18 6RWSurr p56 CR France636
LIPSCOMBE,Eric Lancelot Lt kia 9-5-15 3 att2RBerks p139 MR32
LIPSETT,Louis James.CB.CMG.TMajGen kia 14-10-18 RIrReg Staff DivHQ 18/1 p89 CR France686
LIPTROTT,Eric Carr.MID Lt dow 26-11-14 IA 6Jats p279 CR France102
LISBY,Leslie Norman Lt dow 5-11-17 4RSuss p228 CR Palestine1,2Lt
LISH,John Robertson 2Lt kia 4-10-17 3Lincs p75 MR30
LISLE,John Wynne 2Lt kia 3-5-17 15WYorks p82 MR20
LISLE,Robert Ernest Bentham Capt kia 30-3-18 8 att9DLI p239 MR20
LISMER,Alfred Bass TLt ded 26-10-18 RE CR Nhampt32
LISSAMAN,Arthur John TLt kia 13-4-17 23RFus p68 MR20
LISTER,Arthur Hugh.CMG.LtCol ded 17-7-16 RAMC p253 MR41
LISTER,Charles Alfred.Hon.MID 2LtTLt ded 26-8-15 1Co ofLondYeo p204 CR Greece 10,28-8-15
LISTER,Frederick William.MC.Maj ded 24-2-19 WorcYeo attTankCps p189&206 CR War22
LISTER,Herbert Dixon 2Lt kia 4-9-18 4WelchR p230 MR30
LISTER,Herbert Henry Holden 2Lt kia 4-5-17 2RWar p65 MR20
LISTER,John Curtis T2Lt kia 20-5-17 17RFA p32 MR20
LISTER,John Raymond T2Lt kia 15-12-15 11 att8WRid p115 CR Gallipoli27
LISTER,Matthew William Capt kia 19-7-17 5 att9SStaffs p229 CR Belgium29
LISTER,Philip Thomas T2Lt dow 10-4-17 10YLI p143 CR France214,9-4-17
LISTER,Thomas Frederick T2Lt kia 28-4-17 27NumbF p62 MR20
LISTER,William Howard.DSO.MC&2Bars.TCapt kia 9-8-18 RAMC att21FA p196 CR Italy3
LISTON,William Prosper Lt kia 12-4-17 5Leinst p174 CR France557 see PROSPER LISTON
LITCHFIELD,Frederick George TLt kld 24-9-17 GL &RFC p10 CR Kent109
LITCHFIELD,Thomas 2Lt kia 31-7-17 3 att7Nhampt p137 MR29
LITHFIELD,John 2Lt kia 22-10-14 Beds p86 MR29
LITSTER,Hugh Sinclaire 2Lt dow 20-4-16 3Dors p124 CR Iraq5
LITTEN,Raymond TCapt kia 1-7-16 6RBerks p139 CR France513
LITTLE,Adam T2Lt kia 21-7-18 1/6SfthH p165 CR France1697
LITTLE,Andrew 2Lt kia 25-4-15 9DLI p239 MR29
LITTLE,Charles Hope LtCol ded 18-6-18 Cmdg4Wilts p236 CR France1571
LITTLE,Donald Alexander Duncan 2Lt ded 22-8-17 LanarkYeo att14BlkWp270 CR Egypt7
LITTLE,Harry Ewart T2Lt kia 18-9-18 2RSuss p119 CR France725
LITTLE,Henry James T2Lt kia 20-9-17 EKent att5SLancs p57 CR Belgium125
LITTLE,Herbert James Lt kia 26-3-18 1/7DLI p239 MR27
LITTLE,Henry Walter 2Lt kia 30-8-18 5WRid p227 CR France421
LITTLE,John.DCM.T2Lt kia 24-4-17 8GordH p166 MR20
LITTLE,John.MC.Capt dow 17-10-18 RE 90FC p46 CR Belgium405
LITTLE,John Russell 2Lt kia 3-5-17 KOSB att6Bn p102 MR20
LITTLE,John Wishart Maj ded 7-5-18 IA IMS p279 MR43
LITTLE,Norman James Richard T2Lt kia 13-3-17 11RFus p68 MR21
LITTLE,William 2Lt kia 1-10-16 6DLI p239 MR21
LITTLE,William 2Lt kia 24-4-18 RFA p208 CR France196
LITTLEBOY,Frederick Graham TLt dow 7-12-15 RWKent att9Worc p141 CR Gallipoli4
LITTLEBOY,Wilfrid Evelyn TLt kia 9-10-17 16RWar p65 CR Belgium112
LITTLEDALE,Arthur Charles.MID Maj dow 9-5-15 RFA 19Bty p32 CR France924,kia
LITTLEDALE,Robert TCapt kia 30-11-17 5Nhampt p137 CR France662
LITTLEDALE,Willoughby John Lt kia 23-3-18 2 O&BLI A'Coy p130 CR France307,Capt
LITTLEJOHN,John T2Lt kia 26-10-16 2WYorks p82 CR France1891
LITTLEJOHN,Stanley William 2Lt kia 23-9-17 RGA 142SB p40 CR Belgium94
LITTLER,Frank T2Lt kia 23-7-17 2 att8SLancs p125 CR Belgium11
LITTLER,James Tattock Lt kia 7-8-15 8LancF p221 MR4

LITTLER,John Edward T2Lt dow 4-5-18 11LancF p92 CR France100
LITTLER,Tom T2Lt kia 3-7-17 GL 1RFC p10 CR France285
LITTLETON,Cecil Francis Henry TLt dow 6-5-17 1 att5CamH p168 CR France95,Capt
LITTLEWOOD,Charles William Stephen.MC.2Lt kia 10-7-17 RE 7FC p46 CR France1185
LITTLEWOOD,Frederick William TLt kia 5-3-16 8Y&L p159 CR France347
LITTLEWOOD,George Patrick TCapt kia 3-9-16 17N&D p134 CR France339
LITTON,Reginald T2Lt kia 8-9-16 10 att2ELancs p111 CR France423
LIVERMORE,Ernest Bernard 2Lt kia 15-9-16 24Lond p252 MR21
LIVERSEDGE,Alexander Frederick 2Lt kia 25-3-18 Mddx att2Bn p147 MR27
LIVERSIDGE,Albert T2Lt dow 2-7-16 15WYorks p82 CR France62
LIVERSIDGE,Harold 2Lt kia 23-7-16 1DCLI p114 CR France402
LIVESAY,George Augustus Bligh Lt kia 28/29-5-16 5SWBord p100
LIVESEY,Alan George Hilton Lt kia 25-9-15 3 att1LNLancs p136 CR France1723,2Lt
LIVESEY,Cyril Joseph Glanville T2Lt kia 4-1-18 2Mddx p147 MR30
LIVESEY,Harry TCapt kia 1-7-16 11ELancs p111 MR21
LIVESEY,Joseph Harold 2Lt kld 30-11-17 1/4LNLancs p234 MR17
LIVINGSTON,William Montgomery T2Lt dow 15-4-17 6RIrF p171 CR France95,Lt
LIVINGSTONE,Frank Darley TCapt dow 22-3-18 RASC 15DivTrn p193 CR France113,kia
LIVINGSTONE,Frederick James H.T2Lt kld 12-1-18 RFC p16 CR Lincs136
LIVINGSTONE,Frederick Maurice T2Lt dow 4-11-18 16LancF p92 CR France341
LIVINGSTONE,Harold Gordon 2Lt kia 1-5-15 64RFA p32 CR Belgium20,5-5-15
LIVINGSTONE,Robert TLt ded 10-11-16 RE p46 CR Essex10
LIVINGSTONE-LEARMOUTH,Nigel James Christian Capt kia 22-8-15 15Huss attDorsYeo p22 CR Gallipoli5,21-8-15
LIVOCK,Eric Stuart Lt dow 8-11-17 4RWSurr attRFC p19&212 CR Belgium18
LIVSEY,Ernest Claude T2Lt kia 13-11-16 12EYorks p84 MR21,13-9-16
LIVSEY,William Mylrea 2Lt drd 2-6-17 RFA 5ResBde p32 CR Eire506
LLANGATTOCK,John McLean.Lord Maj dow 31-10-16 RFA p206 CR France102
LLARENA,Eustace Fernando 2Lt kia 18-6-15 2Suff p78 MR29
LLEWELLIN,C.H.OBE.MC.DCM.Capt 26-11-20 RE CR War16
LLEWELLIN,William Mervyn Johnes 2Lt kia 17-8-18 2SWBord p100 CR France1723,1Bn
LLEWELLYN,Arthur.OBE.LtCol 27-4-20 Comdg 3SomLI CR Somerset10
LLEWELLYN,Edward Thomas TLt dow 18-5-18 RWFus 4GarrBn att9Bn p98 CR France40
LLEWELLYN,Gwenyth Miss ded 4-11-18 VAD BRCS p200 CR France146,Gwynedd 3-11-18
LLEWELLYN,Harold Alfred TLt kld 14-6-16 8SWBord p100 CR Greece1
LLEWELLYN,John Herbert TCapt kia 24-8-16 5KSLI p145 CR France402
LLEWELLYN,John Horace TLt dow 9-10-17 RFA A/ABty p32 CR Belgium165,kia
LLEWELLYN,Thomas Edward.MM.2Lt kia 27-10-18 30RFA p32 CR France1270
LLEWELLYN,Vivian T2Lt kia 3-11-18 14RWFus p98 CR France1478,4-11-18
LLEWELLYN-JONES,Vivian Bruford Lt kia 4-5-15 2Suff att1WelshR p78 CR Belgium96
LLOYD,Alan Scrivener TLt kia 4-8-16 C78RFA p32 CR France188
LLOYD,Arthur Lt ded 4-2-18 2Ches p96&257 CR Ches8
LLOYD,C.M.C.Capt 25-4-16 2Hamps CR Lond12
LLOYD,Charles Edward MajHonLtCol ded 8-10-15 6RIrReg p89 CR Hamps1
LLOYD,Charles Gordon Lt ded 9-6-15 10RWFus p98 CR Hamps1,7-6-15
LLOYD,David Rhys Cadogen TLt kia 16-6-17 GL RFC p10 CR France568,Cadwgan
LLOYD,Dennis Montford Anthony 2Lt kia 22-3-18 6RWar p214 MR27
LLOYD,Duncan Ian Dowes Lt kia 14-8-15 IA 1/5Gurkhas att1/6 p279 MR4
LLOYD,Edward Raymond.MID Capt&Adjt kia 3-12-14 2RInniskF p105 CR France598,dow
LLOYD,Edward Stanley.MC.Lt ded 23-11-18 RH&FA HQ312Bde p32 CR France717
LLOYD,Ernest Alfred Collyer Lt kia 31-7-17 1ScotsGds p52 CR Belgium106
LLOYD,Ernest Henry TCapt dow 2-4-18 5RBerks p139 CR France145,2-4-18
LLOYD,Ewan Christian 2Lt dow 5-10-18 1SWBord p100 CR France725
LLOYD,Francis Burrows T2Lt kia 3-10-16 2Dev p77 CR France115
LLOYD,Francis Charles Aylmer TLt dow 8-10-15 12 att2HLI p163 CR France40
LLOYD,Francis Oswald T2Lt kia 12-2-16 9 att6KSLI p145 MR29
LLOYD,Frank 2Lt kld 1-2-19 5Worc &RAF p264
LLOYD,Frank Lewis Capt kia 1/4-10-15 Ches p96 MR19
LLOYD,Frank Stuart TMaj dow 5-9-17 13RWFus p98 CR Belgium16
LLOYD,Gerald Aylmer LtTCapt kia 16-2-15 1WelshR p127 CR Belbium166
LLOYD,Gilbert Kingsley 2Lt ded 21-2-16 3KSLI p145 CR Greece9,2Bn
LLOYD,Gilbert Lewis 2Lt kia 30-11-17 21Lond p251 MR17

185

LLOYD,Gwion Llewelyn Bowen Capt kia 7/11-8-15 5Dors p124 MR4,11-8-15
LLOYD,H.TLt kia 19-7-17 1/3KAR p202 CR EAfrica38 &CR Tanzania1
LLOYD,Harvey Richard.MID TCapt dow 6-9-16 6RIrReg p89 CR France66,Rickard
LLOYD,Henry John Graeme TCaptHonMaj ded 13-4-19 DCLI p264
LLOYD,Herbert T2Lt kia 12-8-16 7Nhampt p137 MR21 18-8-16
LLOYD,Hesperus David Watkins Maj kia 12-3-15 2ScotRif p103 CR France708,Watkiss 10-3-15
LLOYD,Hugh Clifford Chetwode LtTCapt ded 25-2-16 1DCLI p114 CR France64
LLOYD,Ira Cyril T2Lt ded 24-11-18 1/2Worc p109 CR France146
LLOYD,James.MC.LtTCapt dow 21-4-18 Glouc att8Bn p107 CR France40
LLOYD,James Percival T2Lt kia 25-7-17 1/2 att16RWFus p98 CR Belgium66,att15Bn
LLOYD,John Francis Selby Maj kia 18-6-15 6NStaffs p238 CR Belgium89
LLOYD,Lewis John Bevenall Lt kia 25-4-15 9KSLI p145 MR29
LLOYD,Llewellyn T2Lt dow 1-8-17 11SWBord p100 CR Belgium16
LLOYD,Lyndsey 2Lt kia 9-10-17 3 att2Hamps p121 MR30
LLOYD,Marteine Kemes Arundel Capt kia 15-9-16 2GrenGds SR p50 CR France402
LLOYD,Meyricke Entwisle Capt kia 23-10-14 RWFus p98 MR29,24-10-14
LLOYD,Mervyn Capt dow 15-3-15 3NumbF p62 CR Surrey106
LLOYD,Owen Robert.MC.2LtACapt dow 20-9-17 3 att7KSLI p145 CR Belgium83
LLOYD,Reginald Conway T2Lt kia 3-11-16 1RWSurr p56 MR21
LLOYD,Richard Glyn Lt kia 13-9-16 19Lpool p72 MR19
LLOYD,Richard Serjeantson 2Lt kia 18-6-17 GL 1RFC p10 MR20
LLOYD,Robert Arthur 2Lt kia 27-4-15 Lpool p72 CR Belgium101
LLOYD,Robert Courtois 2Lt kia 22-8-18 4 att7RIrReg p89 CR France139,dow
LLOYD,Robert Love.MID Maj dow 9-12-15 RWFus 158BdeHQ p98 CR Gallipoli26
LLOYD,Samuel Ernest Lt kia 16-3-16 1/7Worc p225 CR France3
LLOYD,Thomas Glyn TCapt kia 10-5-18 15WelshR p127 CR France232
LLOYD,Thomas Lancelot T2Lt ded 8-4-19 3RRofCav p261 CR Lincs44
LLOYD,Thomas Newburn Chetwoode Capt ded 25-4-16 Hamps p121
LLOYD,Thomas Richard Beamish T2Lt ded 20-2-16 RASC p193 CR Ireland14 &CR Eire161
LLOYD,Thomas Yale T2Lt kia 12-7-16 10WelshR p127 CR France453
LLOYD,Valentine.MC.Lt kia 23-10-18 3 att11Leic p88 CR France1475
LLOYD,Walter.MID Capt kia 7-8-15 8RWFus p98 CR Gallipoli31
LLOYD,Walter Henry Capt kia 4-8-18 RAMC att1/20Lond p253 CR France59
LLOYD,Walter Reginald LtCol kia 14-9-14 1LNLancs p136 MR15
LLOYD,William Benjamin 2Lt kia 10-8-17 3 att7Nhampt p137 MR29
LLOYD,William Henry Aloysius Capt kldBySepoy 16-7-16 IA 122Infatt101Grens p279 CR EAfrica2 &CR Tanzania1
LLOYD,William Merrick Ellis 2Lt kia 19-5-17 40RFA p32 CR France1182
LLOYD,William Robert T2Lt kia 12-7-16 15 att2RWFus p98 MR27
LLOYD,Wymond Howard Capt ded 9-3-16 Hereford p252
LLOYD,Wynell Hastings T2Lt kld 17-4-18 RE 123FC p46 CR France44
LLOYD-BAKER,Michael Granville Lloyd.MID Capt 23-4-16 GloucYeo MR34
LLOYD-EVANS,Edward Meredydd Capt 14-3-16 5Lancs CR France504
LLOYD-JONES,Edward Wynne.MID Capt kia 10-8-15 1/7RWFus p223 CR Gallipoli5
LLOYD-JONES,Harold 2Lt ded 1-7-18 RWFus p263 CR Wales227
LLOYD-JONES,Ivor Thomas.MID Capt kia 26-3-17 1/7RWFus p223 CR Palestine8
LLOYD-JONES,John TCapt ded 11-3-16 2Yorks p90 CR Wales531
LLOYD-JONES,Percy Arnold.DSO.MID Maj dow 22-12-16 RAMC p196 CR France120,LtCol
LLOYD-WILLIAMS,David Gray 2Lt kia 10-8-15 6RLancs p59 MR4
LLOYD-WILLIAMS,Kelyth Pierce T2Lt kia 17-10-16 17WelshR p127 CR France149
LLOYDS,Cyril Edwin Fowler 2Lt ded 9-1-19 RGA p262 CR Oxford51
LLUELLYN,Raymond Chester TCapt kia 13-8-18 7Lincs p75 CR France526
LOADER,Ernest Stanley 2Lt kia 4-11-18 2RSuss p119 CR France1272
LOADER,Graham Chard Capt kia 12-8-15 8Hamps p229 MR4
LOAM,Ernest Harold T2Lt kia 7-5-18 RE 56FC p46 CR France33
LOCH,Alex Arthur Francis.DSO.MID Capt kia 22-7-16 1SWBord p100 MR21
LOCH,Arthur Cuthbert 2Lt ded PoW 1-8-16 1ARO att104Rif p279 CR Iraq8,LOCK
LOCHEED,R.W.2Lt kld 28-5-18 GL &RAF p190
LOCHRIN,Michael James Capt kia 23-10-14 RAMC att1Nhampt p196 MR29,Joseph
LOCK,A.S. see LOCH,A.S.
LOCK,George Maj 11-9-20 3LNLanc CR Hereford113
LOCK,James Alexander 2Lt kia 25-9-16 10NumbF p62 CR France239
LOCK,James Palmer 2Lt dow 2-2-18 63RFA p32 CR France769
LOCK,Thomas Henry Lt&QM ded 9-11-18 RNDevYeo p256 CR Eire398,19-11-18
LOCK,William Absalom TLt kia 25-9-16 6Wilts p153 CR France260

LOCKE,Frank William 2Lt 13-10-15 RE 1ArmyHQSigCoy CR France80
LOCKE,Harold Capt drd 10-10-18 RIrReg p89 MR40
LOCKE,Robert Douglas T2Lt kia 2-3-16 2Suff p78 CR Belgium131,Lt
LOCKERBIE,Herbert T2Lt kia 21-8-18 3MGC Inf p184 CR France924
LOCKET,George Eimer 2Lt kia 28-6-18 3 att1Suff p78 CR Belgium37,28-6-15
LOCKETT,Clifford Vincent Lt ded 12-2-19 5Ess p270 CR Mddx80
LOCKETT,Garstang Bradstock.MC.LtACapt dow 4-11-18 ChesYeo att1Ches p203 CR France380
LOCKETT,William Henry T2Lt kia 7-10-16 16 att12DLI p161 MR21
LOCKEY,Ernest William 2Lt kia 8/10-9-16 2Lond p245 CR France402
LOCKHART,Alan Ross T2Lt ded 7-12-17 13Manch p155 CR Greece9
LOCKHART,George Barclay Capt kia 14-4-17 HighCycBn attRFC p19&253 CR France58
LOCKHART,Gerald Bevis TLt kia 10-8-15 6LNLancs p136 MR4
LOCKHART,James Herbert 2Lt kia 30-7-16 7BlkW p231 CR France785
LOCKHART,John Sutherland Lt kia 10-5-15 3RScots p54 CR Belgium21,Jack 2Br
LOCKHART,Reginald Frank 2Lt dow 10-7-17 13Lond attMGC p187&249 CR Belgium24
LOCKHART,Robert Hamilton T2Lt kia 11-11-15 9 att7RScotF p95 CR France423
LOCKIE,James.MC.Capt kia 22-3-18 12/13NumbF att2Lincs p62 MR27
LOCKING,Thomas Edgar Lt dow 20-1-18 RGA p209 CR France64
LOCKLEY,Henry James T2Lt kia 22-3-18 11LancF p92 MR20
LOCKLEY,Rupert Edward Holder Maj ded 21-10-15 GordH attWAFF p201&265 CR Berks43,20-10-15
LOCKTON,George Woodhams TCapt dow 21-10-17 RGA 153SB p40 CR France193
LOCKWOOD,Albert 2Lt kia 7-10-18 RGA 93SB p40 CR France375
LOCKWOOD,Frank T2Lt kld 4-11-17 GL RFC p10 CR Yorks652
LOCKWOOD,George 2Lt dow 3-11-17 10YLI E'Coy p143 CR France145
LOCKWOOD,Joshua Capt&QM ded 16-12-18 GL att4Dev p270 CRYorks677,YL
LOCKWOOD,Reginald Ughtred Lt ded 10-1-19 IARO att14LabCps p279 MR66
LOCKWOOD,Richard William Mark 2Lt kia 14/15-9-14 2CldGds p51 CR France1112,14-9-14
LOCKYEAR,Horace 2Lt kia 20-5-18 6Lincs p75 CR France115
LOCKYER,Felix Courtenay 2Lt kia 12-2-17 8Dev p77 MR21
LOCON,Sidney John Boileau CaptTMaj kia 12-4-18 4RWar attRASC MT VIIICps p65 CR Belgium3,LACON
LODER,Robert Egerton Capt dow 2903017 1/4Suss CR Palestine2
LODER,William Victor 2Lt kia 10-5-18 4Wilts p236 CR Palestine9
LODER-SYMONDS,John Frederick Maj kia 31-11-14 1SStaffs p122 MR29,1-11-
LODER-SYMONDS,Robert Francis Capt ded 3-3-15 1Ches p96 CR France145
LODER-SYMONDS,Thomas Lenthall Lt kia 9-5-15 2ScotRif p103 CR France525
LODER-SYMONDS,William Crawshay Capt ded 30-5-18 Wilts &RAF p153 CR Berks56
LODGE,Bernard Grime.MID 2Lt kia 24-8-17 4 att10DLI p161 MR30
LODGE,Gerald Aylmer Bleackley Lt kia 5-6-15 8LancF p222 CR Gallipoli2,6-6-
LODGE,John 2Lt dow 18-3-18 RGA 190SB p40 CR Belgium11
LODGE,John William HonCol ded 23-8-17 3Yorks Cmdg2HSGarrBn p90 CR Yorks100
LODGE,K.A.2Lt ded 5-11-18 1LancF p92 CR Ches31,4Bn
LODGE,Ralph Nesbit 2Lt kia 1-7-16 3 att15LancF p92 MR21
LODGE,Raymond 2Lt dow 14-9-15 2 att3SLancs p125 CR Belgium113
LODGE,Richard Cuthbert TLt kia 27-8-17 16RScots p54 MR21
LODGE,Ronald Edward Somerville Lt kia 25-9-15 2Leic p88 MR19
LODGE,Tom.MC.T2Lt dow 21-5-18 2/4 O&BLI p130 CR France248
LODGE,William Wass 2Lt dow 17-4-18 6 att1Mddx p147 CR Belgium18
LODGER,Robert Egerton Capt dow 29-3-17 4RSuss p228
LODWICK,John Thornton.DSO.Capt drd 30-12-15 IA 2/3GurkhaRif p279 MR41
LOE,Harold Charles.MC.T2LtACapt kia 27-9-18 1Beds p86 MR16
LOEWE,Leopold TCapt kia 6-4-16 23RFA p32 CR Belgium28,107Bty
LOFT,A.A.Capt 15-6-16 RFA CR Yorks705
LOFT,Percy Trotter 2Lt kia 24-3-18 6 att18KRRC p151 MR20
LOFTHOUSE,George Hood 2Lt kia 23-4-17 4EYorks p219 MR20
LOFTING,Charles Edgar T2Lt dow 10-1-17 8NumbF p62 CR France701
LOFTUS,Henry Gordon TCapt kia 26-9-15 10Y&L p159 MR19
LOFTUS,Kenneth 2Lt ded 9-11-18 RFA p208 CR Surrey1
LOFTUS,William.MC.MID LtTCapt&Adjt dow 25-4-17 11RScotF p95&262 CR France40
LOGAN,Alexnder Taylor 2Lt kia 23-3-18 5CamH p168 MR27
LOGAN,Alfred Thomas.MID Capt kia 16-9-16 RAMC att3GrenGds p196 MR21
LOGAN,Arthur Capt kia 11-6-15 4RScotF p222 MR4

LOGAN,Crawford Randolph Capt kia 3-7-16 7Suff p78 CR France393
LOGAN,David Herbert Hosken 2Lt kia 1-7-16 2BordR p117 CR France394
LOGAN,Edward Townshaw.DSO.LtCol kia 25-9-15 15DLI att3Ches p161 MR19,Townshend 26-9-15
LOGAN,George Baillie Lt dow 6-5-17 2/8N&D p233 CR France122
LOGAN,Gordon Christie Lt kia 31-7-17 4BlkW p230 MR29
LOGAN,Hubert Henderson TCapt kia 15-9-16 10RWKent p141 CR France432
LOGAN,Hugh Lt ded 24-2-19 LeicYeo p204 CR Belgium406
LOGAN,John 2Lt kia 19-4-17 4RScotF p222 MR34
LOGAN,John Francis T2Lt kia 12-4-18 1RScotF p95 CR France410
LOGAN,John Hastie.MC.2LtACapt kia 1-8-17 13RScots p54 MR29
LOGAN,Joseph LtTCapt ded 21-4-18 2HLI p265 CR Scot798
LOGAN,Lionel Stuart Maj accShot 2-11-14 IA S&TCps p279 CR France354
LOGAN,Richard T2Lt kia 10-7-16 15HLI p163 CR France296
LOGAN,Robert 2Lt kia 12-10-17 3 att7SfthH p165 MR30
LOGAN,Robert 2Lt kia 20-10-18 4KOSB p224 CR France658
LOGAN,Rowland Octavius Capt kia 17-10-15 O&BLI att5Bn p130 CR Belgium113,Roland 16-10-15
LOGAN,Walter 2Lt kia 13-12-16 5ScotRif att1/6SStaffs p224 CR France745
LOGAN,William Alexander Ross 2Lt ded 19-2-19 MGC Inf p255 CR Scot503,Lt
LOGIE,Alexander Graham Spiers Capt ded 1-2-19 RAMC p270 CR Scot627
LOGIE,James Paton T2Lt kia 1-10-18 BordR att1GordH p117 CR France359
LOGSDAIL,Hugh 2Lt kia 19-9-18 RGA 99SB p40 CR France276
LOGSDON,Frank Lionel de Marche 2Lt kia 4-10-17 YLI att9Bn p143 MR30,Manché
LOMAS,Frank 2Lt kia 4-6-15 7Manch p237 MR4
LOMAS,George Archibald Colin.DCM.2Lt kia 22-5-16 20Lond p251 CR France924
LOMAS,George Guest TLt kia 22-3-18 Manch att2/6Bn p155 MR27
LOMAS,Harold TLt kia 1-7-16 20Manch p155 CR France397
LOMAS,John Henry T2Lt kia 30-8-16 4Lpool att98TMB p72 CR France402
LOMAX,Edward Harold TLtACapt kia 13-8-17 8SLancs p125 CR Belgium34
LOMAX,Gerald David 2Lt dow 11-5-15 3WelshR att2RBerks p127 CR France768
LOMAX,John 2Lt kia 18-8-16 3DCLI attRWar p114 CR France832
LOMAX,John Herbert TCapt dow 22-11-15 9RWar att9EKent p65 MR4
LOMAX,Samuel Holt.CB.LtGen dow 10-4-15 Staff p1 CR Hamps1
LOMAX,William Sinnott Lt kia 30-7-16 3 att7RScotF p95 MR21
LOMER,Henry Charles TCapt kia 5-5-17 GL 10RFC p10 CR France98
LONDON,Stanhope Francis.DCM.T2Lt kia 18-11-16 8NStaffs p157 CR France384
LONES,Percy East Capt kia 28-4-17 RAMC att5FA p196 CR France184
LONEY,Robert 2Lt kia 1-7-17 5N&D p233 MR19
LONG,Alfred Pocock Lt kld 23-3-17 7Mddx attRFC p19&235 CR Wilts25
LONG,Arthur Glanville Holland 2Lt dow 13-8-17 9Lond p248 CR Belgium7
LONG,Arthur Trevor D'Arcy Lt kia 21-8-15 1RInniskF p105 MR4
LONG,Arthur William Emanuel 2Lt kia 24-8-16 8 att1RWSurr p56 CR France390
LONG,Austin Theodore Lt kia 22-8-17 10RScots p212 MR30
LONG,Basil Andrew TCapt ded 10-2-17 11RLancs p59 CR France833
LONG,Bernard Wilfrid T2Lt kia 16-8-17 16WYorks p82 CR Belgium308
LONG,Charles Bernard 2Lt ded /-/-19 CldGds SR p262
LONG,Charles Henry T2Lt ded 19-2-18 HLI 1GarrBn p163 CR Scot235
LONG,Charles Percy T2Lt kia 13-4-17 RE att46RFC p10&46 CR Belgium11
LONG,Cyril Edwin Arnold Capt kia 27-3-18 15WYorks p82 CR France927
LONG,Daniel Edward 2Lt kia 28-5-18 1Lond p245 CR France54,Dennis
LONG,Francis Stuart Lt 8-9-16 1/5SLancs MR21
LONG,Francis William 2Lt dow PoW 28-6-16 94RFA p32 CR Belgium140
LONG,Frank Stevenson TLt kia 26-9-15 11Ess p132 MR19
LONG,Frederick Edward.MC.TCapt kia 24-8-17 1Lpool p72 CR Belgium19,11Bn
LONG,Frederick Joseph John Lt kia 31-7-17 RFA 37Bty p208 CR Belgium34
LONG,Guy Steer T2Lt kia 28-9-16 8Suff p78 CR France1170
LONG,Harold Dudley 2Lt kia 21-5-16 7Lond p247 MR20
LONG,Henry Archibald 2Lt kia 15-9-16 4NumbF p213 MR21
LONG,Horace Victor T2Lt dow 28-6-17 13NumbF C'Coy p62 CR France145
LONG,James William Capt kia 8/10-9-16 1/2Lond p245 MR21
LONG,John.MM.T2Lt kia 12-4-18 18DLI p161 CR France298
LONG,John T2Lt kia 4-11-18 RBerks att8Bn p139 CR France738
LONG,John Thomas 2Lt kld 10-10-17 53RFC &17Mddx p10 CR France285,dow
LONG,Leslie Paul Lt kia 25-9-15 1/20Lond p251 MR19 &CR France924
LONG,Reginald Stuart Lt kia 9-9-16 5SLancs p230
LONG,Violet Alice Lambton.OBE.DepChContr drd 2-8-18 QMAAC p200 MR40,3-8-18
LONG,Walter.CMG.DSO.MIDx2 TBrigGen kia 28-1-17 2Drags Cmdg56InfBde p21 CR France203

LONG,William Charles.MC.T2Lt dow 31-8-18 9RFus p68 CR France145
LONG,William Herbert Berkeley 2Lt dow 31-5-18 RGA 261SB p40 CR France84
LONG-INNES,Selwyn Lt kia 4-8-15 3RLancs p59 CR Belgium97,2Bn
LONG-PRICE,Cecil Evelyn Capt kia 7-8-15 9WYorks p82 MR4
LONGBOTHAM,Cyril Murgatroyd Capt ded 12-1-20 IA 1/72Punjabis p279 CR Europe51,dow
LONGBOTTOM,Donald Hough 2Lt kia 8-8-16 5Lpool p215 CR France630,Haigh
LONGBOTTOM,Edward Brooke Lt kia 9-10-17 7WYorks p218 CR Belgium123
LONGBOTTOM,Henry 2Lt kia 9-8-15 6SLancs p125 MR4
LONGBOTTOM,Robert T2Lt kia 31-7-15 7KRRC p151 MR29,30-7-15
LONGBOURNE,Hugh Richard.DSO.Capt kia 3-5-17 3RWSurr p56 CR France538,7Bn
LONGBOURNE,William Louis Jennings Lt kia 9-8-15 5 att2/4RWSurr p212 MR4
LONGCROFT,Thomas Roy 2Lt kia 25-9-15 3 att2Leic p88 MR19
LONGDEN,Alfred Henry Capt ded 2-3-19 5N&D p232 CR Notts32
LONGDEN,Ernest William Maj ded 21-8-18 4Y&L p238 CR Yorks543
LONGDEN,Frederick Cecil Capt kia 24-8-18 4 att15DLI p161 MR16
LONGFIELD,Charles Edmund.MID TCapt kia 10-3-18 6RMunstF p175 CR Palestine3
LONGFIELD,John Percival.MVO.Capt kia 30-9-15 3Norf p74 CR France166
LONGFORD,Thomas.KP.MVO.Earl BrigGen kia 21-8-15 HQ Cmdg2Mtd Bde Staff p1 CR Gallipoli5
LONGHURST,C.R. TMaj ded 8-3-18 NumbF p62 CR Numb74
LONGHURST,Harold George Fairfax TMajALtCol kia 12-10-17 6RBerks p139 MR30
LONGHURST,Seaward T2Lt kia 1-7-16 11N&D p134 CR France232
LONGLEY,Frank Arthur John 2Lt kia 18-6-17 7Lond att17KRRC p247 CR Belgium10,19-6-17
LONGLEY,Leslie Gordon T2Lt kia 12-7-16 15Lpool att19LancF p72 CR France296,Lt
LONGMAN,Frederick Lt kia 18-10-14 4RFus p68 MR22
LONGMAN,Valentine Sandford TLtAMaj kia 1-9-18 19RFA p32 CR France568
LONGMORE,Charles Gerard LtACapt ded 24-11-18 270RFA p207 CR Lebanon1
LONGRIDGE,Archibald Owen Carwithen Rev ded 12-10-18 RAChDept att11GH Boulogne p199 CR Devon200
LONGRIDGE,James Atkinson.CMG.LtCol kia 18-8-16 IA 43Erinpura attStaffHQ p279 CR France430
LONGSHAW,Charles Henry 2Lt dow 21-7-15 5SLancs p230 CR France345,2/4Bn
LONGSTAFF,Jack Campbell 2Lt kia 7-7-16 1/5Y&L p238 MR21
LONGSTER,William Ernest T2Lt kia 28-7-16 10Ches p96 CR France220
LONGTHORPE,Frederick T2Lt dow 20-9-18 TankCps p188 CR France278
LONGTON,Edward John 2Lt kia 6-6-15 3 att1Ess p132 MR4
LONGTON,John Lt kia 31-7-17 RASC &4RFC p10&193 MR20
LONGUEHAYE,James Stanley T2Lt kia 7-10-16 12 att6RWKent p141 MR21
LONGWORTH,Eustace Counsellor TCapt kia 26-9-16 9LancF p92 MR21
LONGWORTH-DAMES,Thomas Dudley Lt ded 28-11-19 6CarabDragGds p261 CR Eire475 &CR Ireland14
LONNEN,Leslie Edgar John Lt kld 16-8-16 RFC p3
LONSDALE,Arthur Carr Glyn Lt kia 10-3-15 6KRRC att2RScotF p151 CR France525
LONSDALE,James Raymond McLintock Lt ded 29-10-14 4Huss p21 CR Ches198
LONSDALE,Thomas Wilkes.MC.TCapt dow 5-6-16 7DCLI p114 CR France134,kia
LOOBY,Patrick Chap4Cl kia 26-10-17 RAChDept p199 CR Belgium1216
LOOK,John Leopold TLt dow 1-9-18 1Glouc att1/5Dev p107 CR France84,2Lt
LOOKER,Arthur Donald T2Lt kia 8-10-18 Suff 1GarrBn att15Ess p78 CR France1092
LOOKER,Leonard Davies 2Lt kia 1-8-17 5RWSurr p212 MR29
LOOMES,Herbert Rueben Lt kia 14-9-14 1LNLancs p136 MR15
LOOS,Cecil George Bertram Lt kia 13-3-15 3Worc p109 CR Belgium17,12-3-15
LORD,Arthur John Harry.DCM.2Lt kia 18-9-18 1/2 att7Leic p88 CR France415
LORD,Albert Edward.MM.T2Lt dow 29-4-18 12Yorks p90 CR Yorks467
LORD,Arthur Capt dow 12-2-17 3WelshR p127 CR Belgium18
LORD,Arthur George 2Lt kia 20-7-16 3 att2RWFus p98 MR21
LORD,Charles Henry TMaj ded 30-12-14 10RWFus p98 CR Hamps13
LORD,Cuthbert Edward HonMaj dow 23-6-15 3 att1SStaffs p122 CR France102
LORD,Douglas Frears Lt kia 26-5-17 RFA X27TMB p208 CR Belgium167,27-5-17
LORD,Ernest Joseph T2Lt kia 21-3-18 4TankCps p188
LORD,Eustace Charles Gabriel 2Lt kia 8-5-18 1IrGds p53 CR France925
LORD,Evelyn Geoffrey TLt ded 25-6-18 37MGC Inf p184 CR Lancs491
LORD,Frank Samuel 2Lt dow 12-3-15 2Dev p77 CR France768
LORD,George Hammond Lt kld 30-11-17 256RFA p208 CR Belgium18
LORD,Henry Otto TLt kia 1-7-16 26Manch p155 CR France397

LORD,Hugh Cecil 2Lt kia 26-10-17 Dev p77 MR30
LORD,John Frederick Wilson 2Lt kia 9-4-17 5YLI p235 CR France1185
LORD,Reginald Hollins.MC.Capt dow 25-11-18 B245RFA p207 CR France146
LORD,Roland Capt kia 8-10-18 3 att2NumbF p62 CR France338
LORENZEN,Otto Hans Hermann 2Lt dow 2-7-16 7Mddx p235 CR France120
LORIMER,Hugh Cowan Lt ded 27-11-18 5DCLI p270 CR Devon153
LORIMER,James Bannerman Capt kia 3-5-17 5CamH att8RB p168 MR20
LORIMER,John Scott.MC.2LtTCapt kia 5-11-17 1Norf att95TMB p74 MR30
LORIMER,Robert 2Lt kia 14-3-17 4RScots att1/5SStaffs p211 CR France281
LORING,Charles Buxton Maj kia 21-12-14 IA 37Lancers att34PoonaHorse p279 MR28
LORING,Charles Michael 2Lt kia 3-9-16 2RWar p65 MR21
LORING,Robert Nele 2Lt kia 16-6-15 5 att3Worc p109 MR29
LORING,Walter Latham LtCol kia 23-10-14 1RWar p65 MR29
LORING,William Capt dow 24-10-15 ScotHorse p205 MR4
LORY,J.J.Capt 12-12-18 MilLabCps CR EAfrica36
LOSH,James Norman Merryweather 2Lt kia 4-10-17 3Lincs p75 MR30
LOTAN,William Desmond Guthrie T2Lt kld 10-12-16 RFC p3 CR Eire319
LOTT,John Cyprian.MC.2Lt kia 13-4-18 3 att11ELancs p111 CR France193
LOTT,John English.MC.T2Lt dow 21-8-17 RE 4FldSurCo p46 CR France1468,21-5-17
LOTT,William T2Lt kia 7-10-16 14RSuss p119 MR21
LOUDON,James Brugh Livingstone Lt kia 13-4-18 6ScotRif p224 MR32
LOUDON,Robert TLt kia 13-9-18 13RScots p54 CR France179
LOUDON,Robert Gavin Morton Lt kia 12-5-16 6ScotRif p224 CR France114,11-5-16
LOUDON-SHAND,Stewart Walter.VC.TMaj kia 1-3-17 10Yorks p90 CR France189,1-7-17
LOUDOUN,Thomas 2Lt kia 8-6-18 2BlkW p129 CR Palestine9,LOUDON
LOUGH,Frederick George 2Lt kia 21-3-18 B88RFA p32 CR France905
LOUGHER,Gwylym Robert Lt&QM ded 21-9-17 RAMC WelshCCS p254 CR Egypt9
LOUIS,Gerald John TCapt dow 23-5-16 RASC 19MT AuxCoy p193 CR France924,22-5-16
LOUSADA,Bertie Charles Capt kia 9-5-15 1Y&L p159 MR29
LOUSADA,Edward Arthur Lt kia 2-11-14 2RSuss p119 MR29
LOVATT,Charles.MC.T2Lt kia 12-4-18 26NumbF att4Beds p62 CR France252
LOVE,Henry John.MM.T2Lt dow 2-11-18 RBerks Resatt2/4Bn p139 CR France332
LOVE,James Ellis T2Lt kia 2-9-18 18Manch p155 CR France308
LOVE,James Robert T2Lt kia 17-8-17 3RMunstF p175 MR30,18-8-17
LOVE,Reysom 2Lt kia 3-12-17 8 att2/5RWar p215 MR17
LOVE,Ronald Andrew 2Lt dow 1-11-18 9RInniskF p105
LOVE,Ronald Barclay T2Lt kia 15-3-16 8Lincs p75 CR France922,Lt
LOVEBAND,Arthur.CMG.LtCol kia 25-5-15 2RDubF p177 MR29
LOVEBAND,Arthur Reginald TCapt kia 6-12-14 1WYorks p82 CR France82
LOVEDAY,Charles Norton T2Lt kia 12-10-17 54MGC Infp184 MR30
LOVEDAY,Claude Godfrey 2Lt kia 10-10-16 2N&D p134 CR France374
LOVEDAY,Francis William.DSO.BtLtCol ded 15-9-19 RA p261 CR Devon207,16RGA
LOVEGROVE,Sidney Joseph Capt dow 14-3-16 NStaffs att3KAR p157&202 CR EAfrica52
LOVEITT,Alan Percy Charles 2Lt kia 25-7-16 7RWar p214 MR21
LOVELACE,Ronald Desmond Weston(Dick) 2Lt kia 26-10-17 1RWKent p141 MR30
LOVELACE-TAYLOR,Arthur George T2Lt kia 9-10-16 1RWar p65 MR21
LOVELL,Charles Ernest TLt dow 21-3-17 RE 62FC p46 CR France46
LOVELL,Clarence John 2Lt kia 19-10-17 RGA 274SB p40 CR Belgium84
LOVELL,Cyril Thomas T2Lt kia 14-6-18 9MGC &RFC p184 CR France27,15-6-18
LOVELL,Edward Caton 2Lt kia 12-11-17 5LancF p221 CR Belgium128
LOVELL,John Anthony 2Lt kia 22-1-16 2LifeGds B'Sqdn p20 CR France423
LOVELL,John Cuthbert TLt kia 1-8-17 10ScotRif p103 CR Belgium7
LOVELL,Leslie Graham T2Lt kia 11-4-17 GL 48RFC p10 MR20
LOVELL,Robert Clifford T2Lt kia 26-1-18 101RFC p16 CR France200,kld
LOVELL,William Leslie 2Lt kia 27-7-17 8RWKent &25RFC p10&141 CR France88
LOVELOCK,Clifford Andrew Lt ded 20-11-18 5 att26RWFus p223 CR France34,LOVELUCK
LOVER,Charles TLt ded 1-9-18 NStaffs attY&L p157 CR Ches19
LOVEROCK,Harold George 2Lt dow 5-8-16 1/1WarYeo p205 CR Egypt2
LOVETT,Alfred Crowdy.CB.CBE.TBrigGen ded 27-5-19 1Glouc p107&257 CR Yorks185
LOVETT,Owen.MID Capt kia 24-4-17 10Dev p77 MR37,25-4-17
LOVETT-THOMAS,Richard Sackville.MC.2Lt dow 12-3-17 165RFA p32 CR France1327

LOW,Alexander Petrie Capt kia 14-7-16 RAMC att7SfthH p253 MR21
LOW,Alexander Sturrock T2Lt kia 23-6-17 10ScotRif p103 CR Belgium6
LOW,David Carmichael 2Lt kia 18-7-16 1GordH p166 MR21
LOW,David Finlay 2Lt kia 26-10-17 16RScots p54 MR30
LOW,Eustace Bertram T2Lt kia 24-3-17 GL 4RFC p10 CR France561
LOW,George 2Lt kia 25-9-15 4GordH p242 MR29
LOW,George Alexander 2Lt kia 28-9-18 2RScotF p95 CRBelgium112
LOW,James Morrison Lt kia 1-7-16 2SfthH attMGC p165&184 MR21
LOW,John 2Lt kia 10-1-18 13KRRC p151 MR30
LOW,John Jackson.MC.MM.T2Lt kia 3-12-17 RE F'SpCo p46 CR Belgium307
LOW,John James 2Lt kia 3-8-17 1 att13NumbF p62 MR20
LOW,Joseph Davidson McKenzie 2Lt kia 13-7-16 6RScots p211 MR21
LOW,Thomas Cartrae Capt ded 30-10-19 MGC Inf p266 MR43,Carfrae
LOWCOCK,R.J.DSO.MC.Maj ded 22-7-18 N&D &RAF p134 CR Wilts4
LOWDEN,Norman.MID 2Lt kia 21-3-18 9RInniskF att109TMB p105 CR France672,Lt
LOWDER,Noel Reginald 2Lt kia 3-5-17 1RWar p65 MR20
LOWE,Albert Frank TLt ded 23-2-19 TankCps p266
LOWE,Alexander Lt kia 24-11-17 10SWBord Brecknock p223 CR France922
LOWE,Arthur Cecil.CMG.DSO.TLtColBrigGen kia 24-11-17 RFA p206 CR Belgium84
LOWE,Arthur Denis Worsley.MC.2Lt kia 4-10-17 3SWBord p100 MR30
LOWE,Ernest Archer 2Lt kia 26-9-17 5Lincs p220 MR19
LOWE,George Alexander T2Lt kia 4-12-16 15RScots p54 CR France83,Lt
LOWE,George Ernest.MC.2Lt kia 28-10-18 15WelshR p127 CR France230
LOWE,George Stanley 2Lt kia 18-9-18 RFus att9Bn p68 CR France212
LOWE,Henry Griffith Pagan.DCM.T2Lt kia 8-11-16 GL &45RFC p3&190 CR France134,kld
LOWE,Henry Shanten Lt dow 21-10-14 2Worc p109 CR France477,Stanley
LOWE,James William TLt ded 3-8-19 RE p262 CR Lebanon1
LOWE,John Edmund.MC.2Lt kia 1-7-17 5NStaffs p238 MR19
LOWE,Joseph T2Lt kia 26-3-18 8 att1RDubF p177 MR27
LOWE,Maurice Lt kia 27-6-17 GL 19RFC p10 CR Belgium115
LOWE,Norman McGregor.DCM.2Lt kia 10-1-16 14Lond p249 CR France423
LOWE,Richard Conway.MC.MID TCapt kia 18-8-16 6RWar p214 CR France83
LOWE,Richard Heath Capt kia 9-10-17 6Ess p232 MR30
LOWE,Ronald Charles Lt dow PoW 18-8-18 8Lpool p215 CR France525
LOWE,Thomas Henry T2Lt kia 23-4-17 7BordR p117 MR20
LOWE,William TLt kia 5-7-16 7ELancs p111 CR France267
LOWE,William Erl Bridson.MC&Bar.ACapt kia 28-5-18 2ELancs p255 MR18
LOWE,William James T2Lt kia 27-4-16 8CamH attTMB p168 CR France480
LOWE,William Norman ACapt kia 24-11-17 14HLI att13ESurr p163 MR17
LOWENSTEIN Jack Charles 2Lt kld 9-5-18 GL &RAF p190 CR France102
LOWER,Neil Eustace T2Lt kia 30-6-17 9MGC Inf p184 CR France550,Lt
LOWERY,Allan Maxwell TCapt dow 24-3-17 GL 70RFC p10 MR20
LOWERY,Thomas.DCM.T2Lt kia 3-8-17 15DLI p161 CR France1489
LOWES,Ernest Ion 2Lt dow PoW 2-6-18 5DLI p239 CR France1753
LOWIS,John Rollo Capt kia 4-9-18 HampsYeo p203 CR Belgium111
LOWNDES,Charles Arthur 2Lt kia 13-10-15 5NStaffs p238 MR19
LOWNDES,Richard Forbes 2Lt kia 14-11-16 5 att1KRRC p151 CR France533
LOWNDS,Reginald Herbert T2Lt ded 17-3-17 GL 43RFC p10 MR20
LOWRIE,James Harold T2Lt dow 25-1-17 9 att7EYorks p84 CR Europe1
LOWRIE,John Edward T2Lt kia 18-6-17 HouseholdBn p20 CR France546,17-6
LOWRY,Auriol Ernest Eric.DSO.MC.CaptALtCol kia 23-9-18 2WYorks p82 CR France268
LOWRY,Cyril John Patrick Lt kia 25-3-18 2WYorks p82 MR27
LOWRY,Henry Cooke Capt ded 11-7-16 RAVC p198 CR Iraq6
LOWRY,John T2Lt ded 4-5-17 9 att2KSLI p145 CR Greece7
LOWRY,Joseph Ewart TLt kia 25-8-18 2RIrReg p89 CR France239,2Lt
LOWRY,Sidney Henry.MC.Capt kia 31-7-17 Herts p252 MR29
LOWRY,Vyvyan Charles Lt kia 9-4-18 5ESurr attMGC p187&226 CR France10
LOWRY,William Augustine Harper 2Lt mbk 4-6-15 IARO att14Sikhs p279 MR
LOWRY COLE,Arthur Willoughby George.CB.DSO.BrigGen dow 9-5-15 Staff 25InfBde CR France566
LOWRY-CORRY,A Maj 12-2-21 RAOC CR Egypt3
LOWRY-CORRY,A.V.MC.Lt 12-9-16 1GrenGds CR France394
LOWRY-CORRY,Frederick Richard Henry TLt dow 30-9-15 C47RFA p32 CR France40
LOWSON,Courtenay Patrick Flowerdew Lt kld 3-11-17 1RB attRFC p10&179 CR Scot187
LOWSON,Matthew Stewart 2Lt kia 14-7-16 2BordR p117 CR France432

LOWSON,Norman Couttie.MC.TCapt dow 6-3-17 RE 7DivSigs p46 CR France41
LOWSON,Wilfred Robert 2Lt kia 16-9-16 5Yorks p221 CR France239,15-9-16
LOWSON,William 2Lt dow 17-11-16 8RScots p212 CR France74
LOWTH,Francis Robert Leslie.MID Capt mbk 22-8-18 2 att9LancF p256 MR4
LOWTH,John Leslie T2Lt kia 4-10-17 12/13NumbF p62 MR30
LOWTHER,Carl T2Lt kia 16-8-17 11Manch p155 MR30
LOWTHER,Ernest Frederick T2Lt kia 14-6-18 2Manch att96TMB p155 CR France924,4-6-18
LOWTHER,Rowland TCaptAMaj ded 10-11-18 RASC MT p193 CR France1028
LOWTHER,Thomas Beresford Lt kia 4-6-15 2LancF att1NumbFp92 MR29
LOWTHER,William 2Lt kia 27-5-18 Yorks p90 MR18
LOWY,Walter Albert TCapt dow 3-9-18 13 att10Hamps p121 CR Greece6
LOXLEY,Arthur Harry 2Lt kia 9-4-17 4NStaffs att6YLI p157 CR France581
LOXLEY,Charles Eric Smart.MID TCapt ded 18-12-18 Ess attMGC Inf p132&184 CR Egypt9
LOXTON,Charles Edward Holden 2Lt dow 23-5-15 1/5NStaffs p238 CR Belgium170
LOXTON,Lionel D'Estelle T2Lt kia 29-8-18 10SWBord p100 CR France217
LOY,Martin William TLt kia 28-8-16 RAMC p196 CR France246
LOYD,Alfred William Kirkman Maj ded 13-2-19 1RSuss p264 CR Kent280,2Bn
LOYD,Alwyne Travers Capt kia 28-9-17 5EKent att32RFC p19&213 CR Belgium11
LOYD,Geoffrey Archibald.MID Lt dow 13-11-14 2ScotsGds p52 CR Belgium150,kia
LOYD,Godfrey Beaumont.MC.Capt dow 1-12-17 12KRRC D'Coy p151 CR France446
LOYD,Lewis Frederick Innes AMaj ded 21-9-18 2/1LovatScouts attWorcHuss p204 CR Essex242
LOYD,Reginald Percy.MC.LtACapt kia 1-12-17 3CldGds p51 France662
LUARD,Charles Elmhurst.DSO.Maj kia 15-9-14 1Norf p74 MR15
LUARD,Edward Bourryan.DSO.TLtCol dow 24-4-16 KSLI p145 CR Belgium11,Bourryua
LUARD,Peter Dalbiac Lt mbk 19-9-18 3 att11ScotRif p256 MR37
LUBBOCK,Eric Fox Pitt.Hon.MC.TCapt kia 11-3-17 GL &45RFC p10 190&258 CR Belgium11
LUBBOCK,Harold Fox Pitt.Hon.Lt kia 4-4-18 2GrenGds p50 CR France1183
LUBY,Thomas William 2Lt kia 5-10-16 6 att3Worc p109 CR France246
LUCAS,Aberon Thomas.Lord Capt kia 3-11-16 HampsYeo &RFC p203 CR France568,Auberon
LUCAS,Albert James T2Lt dow 16-5-17 GL 66RFC p10 CR France120
LUCAS,Algernon 2Lt kld 28-4-16 KEdwsHorse p24 CR Ireland14,29-4-16
LUCAS,Arthur Geoffrey.MC.Lt dow 25-11-17 IA 127Baluchis att2/124 p279 CR Iraq8
LUCAS,Charles Lucas Clement 2Lt dow 30-6-17 Nhampt att7Bn p137 CR Belgium11,Leslie
LUCAS,Christopher Hollins T2Lt kia 11-4-18 8NStaffs p157 MR30,10-4-18
LUCAS,Clifton Malet T2Lt kia 10-7-16 4SWBord att15WelshR p100 MR21
LUCAS,Ernest Lt kia 18-9-18 2 att7SWBord p100 MR37
LUCAS,Ernest Henry Austin Lt kia 7-6-17 5Y&L p238 MR29
LUCAS,Frederick Gerald Bazalgette.MC.TCapt dow 10-8-17 6Beds p86 CR France285,Frederic
LUCAS,Frederick Richard 2Lt kld 21-10-16 RFC p3 CR Essex1,20-10-16
LUCAS,Gerald Blunt Capt dow 16-5-16 IA 38CentIndHorse att13RFC p279 CR France15
LUCAS,Harold Clement Montagu Lt mbk 2-11-14 IA 2/2GurkhaRif p279 MR28
LUCAS,James Edward T2LtACapt kia 5-5-17 10DLI p161 CR France581
LUCAS,John T2Lt dow 28-12-17 17RFus p68 CR France512
LUCAS,Keith Capt kld 5-10-16 attRFC p19 CR Hamps1
LUCAS,Lord Alberon Thomas Capt kia 3-11-16 HampsYeo attRFC p19
LUCAS,Malcolm Hugh.DSO.LtCol ded 2-8-20 IA 37Lancers InspGenSPersiaRif p279
LUCAS,Norman Carey T2Lt dow 2-10-16 6RIrRif p169 CR Greece4
LUCAS,Perceval Drewett T2Lt dow 6-7-16 10 att2BordR p117&257 CR France51,Percival
LUCAS,Reginald Blockley Capt kia 3-7-16 RAMC att7Norf p196 MR21
LUCAS,Robert Capt ded 1-11-18 52/15RFA p32 CR France40
LUCAS,Roy Herbert Charles TLt kld 25-12-15 RAVC att20RFA p198 CR France816
LUCAS,Sidney Richard 2Lt ded 6-11-18 RASC p193 CR Nhampt55
LUCAS,Thomas Charles Harvey Lt kia 6-2-17 Suff &20RFC p78&10 CR Belgium115
LUCAS,Thomas Farquhar Lt kia 16-6-17 3RWar att20BallCoRFC p10&65 CR Belgium6
LUCAS,Thomas Henry Lt kld 15-5-18 Hamps &RAF p121 CR Egypt9
LUCAS,Victor Carrington.MC.Lt kia 7-6-17 A236RFA p208 CR Belgium167
LUCAS,Wilfrid 2Lt kia 23-12-16 100RFA p32 CR Greece6 23/24-12-16
LUCAS,William Herbert TLt dow 21-1-16 8NStaffs p157 CR France345

LUCAS-TOOTH,Archibald Leonard Lucas.Bart Maj ded 12-7-18 2/1B'HAC p206 CR France95
LUCAS-TOOTH,Douglas Keith Lucas.DSO.Capt kia 13-9-14 9Lancers p22 CR France1340,dow 14-9-14
LUCAS-TOOTH,Selwyn Lucas Capt kia 20-10-14 LancF p263 CR Belgium32
LUCHFORD,Harry George Ernest.MC.Capt kia 2-12-17 20RFC p10 MR20
LUCIE-SMITH,Evan Lt kia 25-4-15 RWar p65 CR 32,Euan
LUCK,John Lewis T2Lt dow 6-9-18 WYorks att1/7Bn p82 CR Kent285
LUCK,Nelson Amos T2Lt kia 15-6-18 1RWKent att1/10 O&BLI p141 CR Italy2
LUCK,Percy 2Lt 4-11-19 Lincs CR Beds75
LUCKETT,John Spokes Lt dow 24-5-15 RIrReg p89 CR France285
LUCKHURST,William 2Lt kia 24-4-17 4Yorks p220 MR20
LUCKING,Frank Horatio 2Lt kia 28-4-17 3 att10Lincs p75 MR20
LUCKMANN,Harold John.MC.T2Lt kia 10-4-18 11 att10Worc p109 MR30,LUCKMAN
LUCY,Reginald Eric Lt dow 20-3-15 2Nhampt p137 CR Devon1,19-3-15
LUDLAM,Eric Wollaston 2Lt kia 28-3-18 7Manch p237 MR20,8Bn
LUDLOW,Ernest.MC.Lt kld 16-2-18 4GrenGds p50 CR Surrey160
LUDLOW,Frank Hubert Charles 2Lt kia 23-11-17 1/20 att1/2Lond p251 MR17
LUDLOW,John Coape ACapt dow 15-12-16 1RInnsikF D'Coy p105 CR France145
LUDLOW,Leonard Gordon Sutton Lt kia 11-8-18 4YLI p256 MR30
LUDLOW,Lionel 2Lt kia 8-10-17 9Lond p248 MR21
LUDLOW,Stratford Walter Capt kia 1-7-16 1/8RWar C'Coy p214 CR France1890
LUFF,Edgar William Guy Lt kia 25-3-18 63MGC p184 MR20
LUGARD,Edward March 2Lt kld 30-7-18 1RLancs &RAF p59 CR Lond8
LUGER,Arthur LtACapt dow 13-8-18 1Leinst p174 CR Palestine3
LUGTON,George Deane 2Lt kia 30-11-17 8ScotRif p225 CR France647,Deans 30-11-18
LUIS,Eric George Vincent T2Lt kia 6-10-16 6 O&BLI p130 MR21
LUKE,John Norman 2Lt kia 9-9-18 5DLI p239 CR France908
LUKER,Frank Percy 2Lt ded 1-11-18 1GarrBn Worc &RAF p264 CR Bucks39
LUKEY,Charles Ximius Lt kia 24-6-16 1RWar p65 CR France35,Charley Ximines
LUKIS,Charles Pardy.Hon.Sir.KCSI.VD.SurgGen ded 21-10-17 IA IMS p279 MR65
LUKIS,Leofwin Collings Fellowes 2Lt kia 6-1-17 Ess &27RFC p10&132 CR France808
LUKIS,Theodore Stewart Capt dow 15-3-15 13Lond p249 CR France102
LUKYN,Stanley Edward.MC.2Lt kld 10-4-17 3RWSurr attRFC p56&10,ded CR Mddx76,1Bn
LUKYN-WILLIAMS,Herbert Temple TCapt dow 26-3-18 RAMC att15N&D p196 CR France
LUMB,Herbert T2Lt ded 8-10-17 A66RFA p32 MR4
LUMB,Joseph William.MC.2Lt dow 30-10-18 1/4WRid p227 CR France40
LUMGAIR,Robert Robertson Morrison Capt kia 19-4-17 1/4KOSB p223 CR Palestine8
LUMLEY,Corale Nurse 25-11-18 VAD CR NZ243
LUMLEY,Frederick William 2Lt kia 10-4-17 27NumbF p62 MR20
LUMLEY,Henry Ralph 2Lt kia 11-3-18 RFC p16 CR Lond12
LUMLEY,Richard John 2Lt kia 17-10-14 11Huss p22 CR Belgium69
LUMMIS,Ralph 2Lt kia 4-10-17 Lincs att12/13NumbF p75 MR30
LUMSDEN,Alfred Forbes.DSO.BrigGen kia 24-6-18 RScots Staff 46InfBdeHQ p54 CR France113
LUMSDEN,Bertie Noel Capt kia 23-4-15 SfthH p165 CR Belgium128
LUMSDEN,Carlos Barron TMaj ded 8-3-16 18HLI p163 CR France354
LUMSDEN,Charles Ramsey Capt kia 26-8-14 1GordH p166 MR15
LUMSDEN,David Aitken Capt kia 1-5-15 4Lpool p72 MR29
LUMSDEN,Henry Tailyour Capt ded 21-6-15 CamH &RFC p168&1,kld CR Scot294
LUMSDEN,Joseph Charles T2Lt kia 11-10-18 2NumbF p62 CR France1392
LUNAN,George Harold Lt kia 13-5-15 RAMC p196 CR Belgium126
LUNAN,James 2Lt kia 20-9-17 4GordH p242 CR Belgium126,Lt
LUND,Charles Lt kia 19-2-20 IA 1/8GurkhaRif att3/11 p279 MR43
LUND,Clifford Bullen Lt ded 31-12-19 RASC p267 CR Surrey1
LUND,Gilbert William T2Lt kia 9-10-17 WYorks att1/7Bn p82 MR30
LUND,Tom Clough Lt kia 23-3-18 1/4NumbF p213 MR27
LUND,William Bullen TLt drd 13-8-15 RASC p193 MR4
LUNDIE,Eric Balfour 2Lt kia 12-9-17 3CldGds p51 MR30
LUNDIE,James Edward 2Lt dow 29-3-18 4/5BlkW p230 CR France145
LUNDIE,Robert Charles.DSO.MIDx2 CaptAMaj dow 15-10-18 RE 93FC p46 CR France658,14-10-18
LUNDIUS,James Philip kia 28-5-16 1/5GordH p242 CR France15
LUNN,Frank Victor 2Lt kia 31-5-18 8Lpool p216 CR France204
LUNN,Gilbert Alfred Lt ded 15-10-18 2/6RSuss p228 MR67

LUNN,Henry Anderson Capt ded 5-3-17 RAMC attColabaSHospBombay p196 MR65
LUNN,Herbert Charles Lt kia 22-3-17 3 att1RScots p54 MR20
LUNN,Ralph William 2Lt dow 17-6-17 B15RFA p32 CR France1182
LUNNON,George John 2Lt kia 27-4-15 2DCLI p114 MR29
LUNO,Evanston Holt Lt kia 20-7-18 4GordH p241 CR France622
LUNT,Arthur Towers T2Lt dow 17-8-16 15Lpool p72 CR France66,13Bn
LUNT,Christopher 2Lt kia 10-8-17 3 att9LNLancs p136 MR29
LUNT,Douglas Gordon Capt kia 16-7-16 5RWar p214 CR France832
LUPTON,Francis Ashford Maj kia 19-2-17 8WYorks p219 CR France514
LUPTON,Frank T2Lt kia 25-4-17 10Y&L p159 MR20
LUPTON,Frank William T2Lt kia 4-8-16 att9RFus p68 MR21
LUPTON,Joseph Brookes 2Lt kia 20-11-17 2/5LancF p221 CR France924
LUPTON,Lionel Martineux Lt kia 16-7-16 RFA p208 CR France296
LUPTON,Maurice Capt kia 19-6-15 7WYorks p218 CR France525
LUPTON,Reginald TCapt dow 22-8-15 9WYorks p82 MR4,8-8-15
LUPTON,Reginald Banister T2LtACapt kia 1-8-17 12RSuss p119 CR Belgium20
LUSCOMBE,Gridland John T2Lt kia 3-5-19 9 att7Beds p86 MR20
LUSCOMBE,Henry Lt kia 11-4-17 3Lond p245 CR France1185
LUSH,Charles William T2Lt kia 14-11-16 11RWar p65 CR France156
LUSH-WILSON,Herbert Geoffrey Maj kia 21-7-16 Y15RFA p32 CR France131
LUSHINGTON,Cecil Henry Gossett Lt kia 3-7-16 10Worc p109 MR21
LUSHINGTON,Sydney Edward James Chippendale TLt dow 25-9-16 GL 11Hamps att41Div ADC HQ p190 CR France40
LUSK,James Capt dow 28-12-15 1/6ScotRif p224 CR France300
LUTENER,George Arthur T2Lt kia 31-1-17 RE 15FC p46 CR France624
LUTENER,Richard Arthur Maurice T2Lt kia 6-4-16 6KSLI p145 CR Belgium73
LUTYENS,Charles Grae Capt dow 8-8-15 6ELancs p111 CR Gallipoli20,9-8-15
LUTYENS,Charles John Lionel Lt dow 3-10-17 A156RFA p32 CR Belgium131
LUTYENS,Cyril Arthur George Lt kia 9-10-17 3CldGds p51 MR30
LUTYENS,Lionel Gallwey.MC.CaptAMaj dow 6-1-18 123/28RFA p32 CR Belgium12
LYALL,Archibald Lt kia 2-7-16 15HLI B'Coy p163 CR France296,3-7-16
LYALL,Charles Genie Capt kld 18-10-14 1Lincs p75 MR22,George
LYALL,David Ivor 2Lt kia 18-10-16 3 att2Wilts p153 MR21
LYALL,Francis Gerald 2Lt kia 9-12-16 1BordR p117 CR France374
LYALL,George William 2Lt ded 7-12-17 6ResRegofCav p24 CR Wilts115 6-12-17
LYALL,James T2Lt dow 14-11-16 1GordH p166 CR France203
LYALL,James Thomson TLt kia 2-7-16 15HLI D'Coy p163 CR France296,3-7-16
LYBURN,John Jardine 2Lt ded 13-10-16 116RFA p32 CR Greece7
LYCETT,Lawrence Henley 2Lt dow 31-5-18 3 att1SStaffs p122 MR18,att4Bn
LYCETT,Timothy.DSO.LtCapt dow 5-10-18 12KRRC p151 CR France106
LYCETT,William Bernard T2Lt dow 24-7-16 8Nhampt att1/5Glouc p137 CR France169,kia 3Bn
LYDDIARD,Francis Alfred 2Lt ded 22-4-19 RGA p262 CR Surrey15
LYDDON,Ernest Hugh Capt kia 31-10-14 Beds p86 MR29
LYDDON,Frederick Cyril 2Lt dow 26-4-15 ULIA att4Lpool p279 CR Belgium4
LYDEKKER,Cyril Richard Lt kia 15-8-15 5Beds p219 CR Gallipoli4
LYDEKKER,Gerard Owen Lt&QM ded 14-6-17 1/5Beds p219 CR Egypt1
LYDE-MALCOLM,Sackville Malcolm Berkeley Capt ded 17-10-18 NumbF p262 CR Mddx66
LYE,Gilbert 2Lt dow 27-7-16 4 att23Manch p155 CR France23,Lt kia 21-7-16
LYE,Robert Cobb.DSO.LtCol ded 28-6-17 IA 2/34SikhPnrs p279 MR67,27-6-17
LYELL,Charles Henry.Hon.Maj ded 18-10-18 RGA p209 CR USA234
LYELL,David 2Lt kia 12-7-15 7RScots p211 MR4
LYELL,James Francis Ronaldson Lt kld 25-11-17 3 att2RScots p54 CR France563
LYLE,Geoffrey Samuel La Warre 2Lt dow 29-4-17 2 O&BLI p130 CR France95
LYLE,Hedley Robert T2Lt kia 24-5-16 9GordH p166 CR France423,23-5-16
LYLE,James Vernon T2Lt kia 23-1-17 GL 45RFC p10 CR France140
LYLE,John Clevendon Capt ded 6-12-16 RASC p253 CR Cornwall148
LYLE,Thomas Basil 2Lt kia 9-5-15 1BlkW p129 MR22
LYLE,William TLtCol kia 1-7-16 23NumbF p62 CR France150
LYNAM,James Michael.MC.Lt ded 29-12-16 RAOC p198 CR Ireland12
LYNCH,Bartholomew Patrick TLt kia 15-9-16 RB att9Bn p179 MR21
LYNCH,Colmer William Donald.DSO.TLtCol kia 2-7-16 9YLI p143 CR France189,1-7-17
LYNCH,Denis T2Lt kia 23-3-18 10 att15WYorks p82 MR20
LYNCH,Francis William 2Lt kia 27-4-15 4 att1ConnRgrs p172 CR Belgium92,26-4-15
LYNCH,Gilbert Edwin Lt kia 21-3-18 7DLI att7RIrRif p239 MR27
LYNCH,Harold Francis 2Lt kia 16-5-15 1RWFus p98 CR France279

LYNCH,James Meacher 2Lt kia 1-10-18 4RScots p211 CR Belgium160
LYNCH,James Stewart Lt kia 30-11-17 1RGLI p201 MR17
LYNCH,James Walker T2Lt kia 31-7-17 MGC HB p184 CR Blegium63,TankCps
LYNCH,Jasper Beverley Capt kia 5-3-17 IA 12Cav attStaff 6CavBde p279 MR38
LYNCH,John 2Lt kia 3-5-15 RFA p32 MR29
LYNCH,Joseph Edward TCapt kia 26-9-15 10Yorks p90 MR19
LYNCH,Michael John Lt ded 15-10-18 IARO att100LabCps p279 MR43,2Lt
LYNCH,Palric Stephen.MC.ACapt kia 27-12-16 7 att2Leinst p174 CR France149
LYNCH,Reginald Francis.MID Capt kia 8-3-16 2Manch p155 MR38 Ex 1Bn
LYNCH,Thomas 2Lt dow 29-4-17 20LancF p92 CR France610
LYNCH-STAUNTON,Eric Margrave 2Lt kia 9-5-17 3Lond p246 MR20
LYNCH-STAUNTON,Geoffrey 2Lt kia 5-3-17 13Huss p22 MR38
LYNCH-STAUNTON,Reginald Kirkpatrick.DSO&Bar.MIDx5 BtLtCol dow 7-11-18 220RFA p32 CR Iraq8
LYNDALL,Joseph Gwynne T2Lt kia 3-5-17 8KRRC p151 MR20
LYNDEN-BELL,Donald Percival Lt kia 25-4-15 1RIrF p171 CR Belgium96
LYNDEN-BELL,Colin Sutherland Lt ded 21-2-18 IA 99Inf att13Rajputs p279 CR Iraq
LYNE,Charles Vyvyan TCapt kia 18-10-16 17WelshR p127 CR France149,19-10-1
LYNE,Cyril Lionel Bishop 2Lt kia 13-11-16 11Ess p132 MR21,13Bn
LYNES,Arthur Cecil D'Arcy 2Lt kia 10-7-15 1RBerks p139 CR Belgium121
LYNES,Wynne Parr Capt ded 8-10-16 5KRRC p151
LYNESS,Harold T2Lt dow 2-9-16 9RIrF p171 CR France285
LYNN SHAW,Henry Capt kia 3-7-16 10War CR France150
LYON,A.Maj 21-1-20 BordR CR Ches143
LYON,Alexander Patrick Francis.MID Lt kia 9-9-14 1GordH p166 CR France1391,27-8-14
LYON,Charles James Lt kia 13-1-14 1RScotF p95 MR29,13-11-14
LYON,Claude Edward T2Lt kia 27-5-16 B165RFA p32 CR France5
LYON,Claude Stuart.MC&Bar.LtAMaj kia 21-3-18 53/2RFA p32 CR France563
LYON,Donald Halliday 2Lt kia 20-9-17 10WRid p115 MR30
LYON,Edward Lycett TMaj dow 17-9-16 18Huss att7SomLI p23 CR France23
LYON,Eric T2Lt kia 4-11-18 1/2WRid att15LancF p115 CR France940,1/3Bn
LYON,Francis Charles Lt kia 13-4-18 4GrenGds p50 MR32
LYON,George William.MC.Lt kia 16-4-18 RE 511LondFC p210 CR France880
LYON,Reginald Anthony Lt kia 13-8-17 ACycCps att6Norf att1/7WRid p217 CR Belgium24
LYON,Robert Capt kia 30-7-16 5GordH p242 MR21
LYON,Robert 2Lt kia 17-3-17 5A&SH att1/8MGC p187&243 MR20
LYON,Walter Scott Stewart Lt kia 8-5-15 9RScots p212 MR29,Stuart
LYON-HALL,Clarence Espeut Capt dow 29-3-17 1/4Suss CR Palestine2
LYONCLARK,Basil L.TCapt dow 9-7-17 3/3KAR p202 CR EAfrica38 &CR Tanzania1
LYONE,Alexander Martin.MC.T2Lt dow 26-9-17 11NumbF p62 CR France8
LYONS,Basil 2Lt kia 19-7-17 5RBerks p139 MR20
LYONS,Denis James 2Lt kld 15-11-16 4 att6ConnRgrs p172 CR Belgium17
LYONS,Edward Thomas T2Lt kia 4-10-17 1/2Lancs p111 MR30
LYONS,Henry James T2Lt kia 23-9-17 7RLancs p59 CR Belgium20
LYONS,Robert Victor T2Lt kia 24-3-18 14 att23RIrRif p169 MR27
LYONS,Vincent Aloysius T2Lt dow 23-8-17 18HLI p163 CR France446
LYONS,W,Maj 26-10-16 RASC CR Hamps1
LYONS,William Barry CaptBtMaj dow 4-9-16 2RIrReg p89 MR21 France51,LtCol 2RMunstF
LYONS,William Holmes St.John Lt ded 1-11-18 6Mddx att2/4 O&BLI p147&257 CR Ireland137
LYONS,William Thomas.MID TCapt&Adjt kia 3-3-16 10RWFus p98 CR Belgium131
LYONS,William Thomas.MC.TCapt kia 19-7-16 8RLancs p59 MR21 18-7-16
LYS,Francis George Bryan T2Lt kia 14-7-16 6Nhampt p137 MR21
LYSONS,Nigel Lucius Samuel Maj kia 21-10-14 RLancs p59 CR Belgium32
LYTE,Owen Nevill TLt ded 31-10-18 RASC 6DivMTCoy p193 CR France441
LYTHGOE,Jeffrey Wentworth T2Lt kia 22-7-16 14RWar p65 CR France432
LYTTLE,E.Cdr 6-2-17 S&T Cps MR65
LYTTON,Percy Arthur Bertram 2Lt kia 4-2-18 RIrReg att58RFC p16&89 MR20
LYWOOD,Kenneth Primrose Gifford Lt kia 24-3-18 RFA O'Bty p32 MR27

M

MAASDORP,C.R.T2Lt ded 28-3-18 PoW RFC p16 MR20
MAASDORP,Norman TCapt dow 28-8-16 RFA p32 CR Lond8
MABEN,James Armstrong TLt kia 23-8-18 DorsR att6Bn p124 CR France215

MABEY,John Hume Capt dow 18-11-17 2/23LondR p252 CR Egypt9
MABON,John Craig Ferrie T2Lt kia 14-10-18 ScotRif att1/8Bn p103 CR Belgium112,11-10-18
MABY,Lionel Bruce 2Lt kia 12-9-18 2ScotGds p52 CR France1484
MACADAM,James Ferrier Lt ded 19-11-18 1/4EssR p232 CR Egypt9
MACADAM,John Lt dow 18-8-15 4EssR p232 MR4
MACALEVEY,William Francis TCapt kia 27-9-16 RAMC att54FA p196 CR France293
MACALISTER,George Howden 2Lt 24-8-16 5RScotF att78MGC MR37
MACALISTER,William Grierson Maj kia 20-7-16 5ScotRif p224 MR21
MACALLEN,James Capt dow 9-2-17 RAMC att6ELancR p196 CR Iraq5
MacALPINE-DOWNIE,James Robert LtCol dow 21-3-18 1/8A&SH p243 CR France1203
MACAN,Hugh O'Donoghue LtACapt dow 1-9-18 4ESurrR p113 CR France833
MACAN,Hugh Turner TLt kia 23-3-18 21MiddxR p147 MR20
MACAN,Robert Basil Capt kia 13-6-15 IA 28Cav att30Lancers p279 CR Belgium4
MACANDREW,Colin Geen Orr 2Lt kia 2-10-17 AyrYeo att29RFC p19&p203 CR Belgium140
MACANDREW,Henry John Milnes.Sir.KCB.DSO.MajGen ded 16-7-19 IA Comdg5CavDiv p279 CR Lebanon1
MACANDREW,Ian Maclean.MID Lt kia 25-12-14 1SfthH p165 MR22
MacANDREW,John McLean Capt ded 11-10-17 GL 3SfthH p190 CR Scot886,Maj
MacANDREW,Ronald TLt kia 16-8-15 5RIrReg p89 MR4
MacARTHUR,Alaster Capt kia 13-11-16 8A&SH p243 CR France131
MacARTHUR,Daniel Reid 2Lt kia 21-9-18 7ScotRif p224 CR France666
MACARTHUR-ONSLOW,Arthur William Capt kia 5-11-14 16Lancers p23 CR Belgium89
MACARTNEY,Hussey Burgh George Capt kia 24-6-15 1RFus p68 CR Belgium92
MACARTNEY,Thomas Hendry 2Lt kia 7-6-17 19LondR attMGC p187&p250 CR Belgium48 attTankCps
MACASKILL,George Hasken 2Lt ded 4-7-18 EssR &RAF p132
MACAULAY,Bruce Wallace 2Lt kia 3-5-17 att2SfthH p165 MR20
MACAULAY,Colin Alexander T2Lt kia 9-4-16 12ScotRif p103 MR38
MACAULAY,George Cecil Gordon 2Lt kld 2-5-17 3EYorks p84 CR France777
MACAULAY,Horace Lt kia 25-4-18 3 att7SfthH p165 MR30
MACAULAY,James 2Lt kia 4-11-18 13RB p179 CR France733
MACAULAY,John B.Lt 8-2-19 Leinst CR Ireland14
MACAULAY,John Shaw 2Lt dow 4-1-18 25RFC p16 CR France134
MACAULAY,Maxwell Stanley 2Lt kia 7-5-18 Loth&BordHorse p204 CR Palestine3
MACAULEY,William Ingham.MIDx2 CaptTMaj RAVC kld 14-5-17 p198 CR France564
MACAUSLAND,Oliver Babington 2Lt kia 9-5-15 ULIA att1RIrF p279 MR28
MACBEAN,Duncan Gillies Forbes TCapt kia 18-6-15 2GordH p166 CR France765
MACBETH,Harold John 2Lt kia 15-9-16 17LondR p250 CR France432
MACBETH,John Duncan Gilmour 2Lt kia 19-4-17 5HLI p240 MR34
MACBETH,Margaret Ann 2ResM1009 SNurse 30-10-18 QAIMNS CR Scot200
MacBETH,Stanley Lt kia 15-9-16 1/18Lond p250 CR France432
MacBETH,Thomas Mcbeth Mathieson Lt 5-9-17 2Lond CR Belgium27
MacBETH,William David 2Lt kia 23-4-17 1/5BlkW p231 CR Lond1,18-2-19 Worc &CR France604,23-4-17
MacBEY,George Munro.MC.Lt kia 22-3-18 6SfthH p241 MR20
MacBRAYNE,D.C.H.2Lt 21-6-17 GL &11RFC CR France1277
MacBRAYNE,John Burns TLt kia 1-7-16 17HLI p163 CR France1890
MacBRYAN,Edward Crozier Lt kia 2-7-16 3 att1SomLI p80 MR21,1-7-16
MACCABE,Robert Maxwell 2Lt kia 23-4-15 8LondR p247 CR France80,Lt dow
MacCALL,Henry Dobree Capt kia 25-9-15 IA 33Pujabis p279 CR France1157
MacCALLUM,William Hay 2Lt kia 27-8-18 7HLI p240
MacCARTHY,Cornelius Aloysius 2Lt drd 19-7-17 9RDubFus p177 MR38
MacCARTHY-O'LEARY,William Felix Lt kia 6-9-16 1RMunstFus p175 MR21,7-9-16
MacCOLL,George Edwardes TMaj kia 5-8-17 8RIrRif p170 MR29
MacCOMBIE,William John TCapt kia 17-7-16 6KOSB p102 MR21
MacCORMAC,Menotte Campbell Capt kia 16-5-17 7GordH p242 CR France604,Menotti
MacCORMICK,Alexander Campbell 2Lt kia 11-10-16 4A&SH C'Coy p173 CR France115,14Bn
MacCULLOCH,William Bruce TCapt kia 11-4-17 10HLI p163 MR20
MacCULLOCK,Sigurd Harold 2Lt dow 20-12-15 2SfthH p165 CR France344,Lt
MacCUNN,John Francis TCapt dow 25-9-15 6CamH p168 MR19,F.J.
MacDANIEL,Francis George Vernon Lt kia 20-11-17 2RMunstFus p175 CR France275
MacDANIEL,James Robertson 2Lt kia 18-8-17 3RDubFus att57RFC p10 &177 CR Belgium140

MacDERMID,Donald Russell T2Lt kia 28-6-16 16HLI p163 CR France296
MACDERMOT,Hugh Maurice T2Lt kia 7-8-15 6RIrFus p171 MR4,9-8-15
MacDERMOTT,Robert Wilson T2Lt kia 9-1-16 8RIrRif p170 CR France35,8-1-16
MACDONALD,Alexander 2Lt 14-7-16 13Lpool MR21
MACDONALD,Alexander Lindsay.MC.LtTCapt kia 26-8-17 BlkW &9RFC p10&p129 CR Belgium18
MacDONALD,Alexander Robert,MC 2Lt kia 28-3-18 7CamH p168 MR20
MACDONALD,Alan Leslie 2Lt kia 19-5-17 2/8ManchR p237 CR France258
MACDONALD,Andrew Moffat TCapt kia 11-5-16 13RScot p54 CR France423
MACDONALD,Angus MacGillivray.DSO.ACapt kia 21-11-17 4SfthH p241 CR France1498
MACDONALD,Archibald Alexander 2Lt dow 17-4-16 4CamH p243 CR France285
MACDONALD,Archibald Hillcoat.DCM.T2Lt dow 5-3-16 ScotRif att1Bn p103 CR France163
MacDONALD,Charles Gordon 2Lt kia 15-6-15 6ScotRif p224&p225,8Bn MR22
MACDONALD,Charles Hodgson Barrington 2Lt kia 23-3-15 RFA 44Bty p32 CR France706,25-3-15
MACDONALD,Charles Philpot Lt kia 7-1-16 IARO att102Grens p279 MR38
MacDONALD,Claude Keith 2Lt kia 27-9-15 10A&SH p173 MR19
MACDONALD,Colin Capt kia 24-11-15 IA 1/7 att2/7GurkhaRif p279 MR38,22-11-15
MacDONALD,David Johnston Lt kia 29-10-17 RGA p209 CR Belgium12
MACDONALD,Donald Theodore.MC.Capt dow 15-3-20 IA 125Rif p279 CR Iraq8,14-3-20
MACDONALD,Edgar.MC.Capt dow 3-1-20 RFA CR Scot675
MacDONALD,Evan Ronald Horatio Keith 2Lt kia 20-9-14 2HLI p163 MR15
MacDONALD,George Anderson 2Lt kia 18-8-17 10A&SH p173 MR21,McDONALD
MacDONALD,George Cockburn 2Lt ded 17-11-18 5HLI p240 CR Scot530
MACDONALD,George Harper T2LtACapt kia 5-9-16 2GordH p166 MR21
MACDONALD,George Mortimer 2Lt ded 8-8-17 IARO att5Cav p279 MR43
MacDONALD,Godfrey Evan Hugh.Hon.Lt dow 2-11-14 1ScotGds p52 MR29
MacDONALD,Guyon Kenneth Capt ded 21-11-19 3N&D &RAF p264
MacDONALD,Hamish.MC.Lt kia 14-7-19 13Huss p22&p257 MR38
MACDONALD,Hector Robert 2Lt kia 22-2-17 1SfthH p165 CR Iraq5
MACDONALD,Hugh T2Lt kia 5-6-17 22NumbFus p62 MR20
MACDONALD,Hugh Ferguson T2Lt ded 20-5-18 11RScot p54 CR Scot752,kldacc
MACDONALD,James Cecil T2Lt ded 27-4-16 1CamH p168 CR France88
MacDONALD,John Capt 13-7-15 5HLI MR4
MacDONALD,John TCapt dow 23-7-16 5CamH p168 CR France51
MacDONALD,John 2Lt kia 29-10-16 5ScotRif p224 MR21
MACDONALD,John TCapt dow 11-4-17 16RScot p54 CR France95
MACDONALD,John 2Lt kia 27-5-18 RGA 286SB p40 MR18
MACDONALD,John Alexander TLt kia 30-11-17 1WYorks p82 MR17
MacDONALD,John Doran TCapt dow 18-3-16 SL GravesRegn p201 CR France285
MacDONALD,John McPhail.MC.2Lt kia 23-9-17 6ScotRif p224
MacDONALD,John P.Capt ded 20-11-20 RAMC CR Canada547
MACDONALD,John Row Mackenzie 2Lt kia 3-3-17 9RScot p212 CR France15
MACDONALD,John Stewart 2Lt kld 5-7-18 15LondR att2/5LancF p249 CR France106,kia
MacDONALD,Kenneth Lt kia 16-8-15 5NumbF &21RAF p270 MR20
MACDONALD,Malcolm TLt kia 10-10-16 10BlkW p129 MR37
MacDONALD,Murdock Donald T2Lt kia 18-7-16 7CamH p168 CR France423,Murds
MacDONALD,Neil.MC.2Lt kia 25-4-18 RGA 263SB p40 CR Belgium21 McDONALD
MACDONALD,Neville Douglas Maj ded 19-1-18 2Wilts CR Dorset51
MacDONALD,Percy 2Lt kia 21-4-17 7DLI p239 CR France594
MacDONALD,Percy Brooming Capt ded 19-5-17 8Yorks p263 CR Mddx26,McDONALD
MACDONALD,Robert Brown Aitchison T2Lt kia 17-8-16 9BlkW p129 CR France703
MacDONALD,Roderick T2Lt kia 1-7-16 23NumbFus p62 MR21
MacDONALD,Roderick John Macpherson 2Lt dow 20-4-17 4SfthH p241 CR France40
MacDONALD,Ronald.TD.Maj dow 10-6-16 4CamH D'Coy p242 CR France1571
MACDONALD,Ronald.DCM.Lt 29-2-20 2Yorks CR Lancs43
MACDONALD,Ronald Duncan 2Lt kia 31-10-17 82RFA p32 CR Belgium23
MACDONALD,Ronald Hugh Charles T2Lt kia 10-12-16 14DLI p161 MR19
MacDONALD,Ronald Ian.Hon.Capt ded 17-10-18 3CamH attGenStaff CR France1848
MACDONALD,Ronald Mosse Lt kia 3-11-14 1CamH p168 MR29

MACDONALD,Simon TLt kia 1-7-16 23NumbFus p62 CR France700

MACDONALD,Somerled Lt ded 30-11-19 IA 1/54Sikhs p279 CR Scot359

MACDONALD,Sydney Lt kia 2-9-18 8RScot p211 CR France646,1/4Bn

MACDONALD,Sylvester Patrick Joseph.MC.2LtACapt kia 7-6-17 3WorcR p109 CR Belgium89

MacDONALD,Thomas HonLt&QM ded23-11-14 5RIrReg p89 CR Eire186,McDONALD

MACDONALD,Walter Halli-Burton TLt ded 22-1-16 RAMC attNo2Sec ForthDefs p196 CR Scot237

MACDONALD,Wilfred Ferguson T2Lt kia 23-5-17 GL &18RFC p10 CR France381

MACDONALD,William Alexander Capt kia 23-7-18 1/5SfthH p241 CR France1697

MacDONALD,William Alexander LtACapt ded 18-2-19 RAOC p267 CR Essex88 Ex 14Lond

MacDONALD,William Forbes 2Lt kia 23-11-17 RFA p208 CR France415

MacDONALD,William Francis.MC.2Lt kia 1-9-18 3 att2SfthH p165 CR France421,31-8-18

MacDONALD,W.S.2Lt ded 28-1-18 RFC CR Canada1667

MACDONALD-BROWN,Ian Capt kia 15-11-16 RAMC att109RFA CR Belgium28

MACDONALD-MORETON,Norman Charles Henry.MC.TCapt kia 13-10-15 5KRRC p151 CR France692,3Bn

MacDONELL,Alastair Somerled 2Lt kia 13-10-15 3CamH p168 MR19,Alasdair 1Bn

MacDONNAGH,William John 2Lt kia 11-9-18 8MddxR p236 MR21

MacDONNELL,Colla Ion 2Lt kia 9-10-17 4Glouc p225 MR30

MACDONNELL,Francis William Joseph TMaj ded 4-10-15 14 att9WYorks p82 CR Europe4,4-12-15

MACDONNELL,Herbert Creagh Capt dow 24-5-15 RIrReg attRFC p1&p89 CR France200,23-5-15

MacDONNELL,Hugh Edward EdmundCapt ded 22-1-17 4ESurr p264 CR Devon2

MACDONNELL,John Henry O'Connell de Courcy Lt dow 14-10-18 6ConnRgrs attLeinst p172 CR Belgium157,kia

MACDOUGALD,Llewellyn George Duncan T2Lt kia 16-8-17 8RInnisFus p105 MR30

MACDOUGALL,Alastair Lt 30-4-18 CamH att2/14Lond CR Palestine3

MacDOUGALL,Alexander Lt kia 30-4-18 CamH p242

MacDOUGALL,Alexander 2Lt ded 26-10-18 LancF p263

MacDOUGALL,Allen TCapt kia 4-8-16 22RFus p69&p257 CR France394,Allan

MacDOUGALL,Archibald LtACapt kia 31-10-18 8ScotRif p225 CR Belgium140

MacDOUGALL,David Graham Mather Lt kia 27-7-17 5KOSB att1/3KAR p224 CR EAfrica38 &CR Tanzania1

MacDOUGALL,D.C.Lt kia 27-7-17 1/3KAfrR p202

MacDOUGALL,Dugald 2Lt ded 8-2-18 6A&SH p270 CR Scot677

MacDOUGALL,Edward Greaves TCapt kia 26-10-15 6CamH p168 MR19

MACDOUGALL,Finlay Neil Lt kia 18-8-16 3BlkW p129 CR France432

MacDOUGALL,Iain Capt&Adjt 1-9-14 2GrenGds CR Scot41

MACDOUGALL,Ian Capt kia 13-9-14 GrenGds p50

MACDOUGALL,Stewart of LUNGA TLtCol kia 21-7-15 10GordH p166 CR France107

MacDOWEL,Benjamin George Lt kia 22-9-15 3ConnRgrs p172 CR France924,1Bn

MACDOWELL,Charles Michael Vere Capt dow 28-4-17 1/6BlkW p231 CR France102

MacDOWELL,M.Miss 3-7-18 ScotWomensHosp CR Greece9

MACDOWELL,Robert T2Lt kia 25-2-17 NStaffR p157 MR38

MacDUFF,Alexander Capt kia 24-4-15 2CamH p168 MR29

MacDUFF,William Brown 2Lt kia 2-12-17 5BordR p228 MR30

MACE,Alban Bodley Rev 3-10-16 RAChDept 3 att2DCLI p199 CR Greece3

MACE,Alfred Reginald Lt ded 18-10-19 RASC MT p267 CR Essex1

MACE,Ernest 2Lt kia 10-8-17 4Nhants p234 CR Belgium125

MacEWAN,Maxwell 2Lt kia 5-7-17 5ESurrR p226 CR France439

MACEY,Clifford James T2Lt kia 25-5-15 Dors p124 CR France285

MACFADYEN,John Dennis Goulty.MC.TLt kia 8-8-18 1MGC p187 CR France485,1TankCps

MacFADYEN,Neil Douglas 2Lt kia 6-5-15 3 att2CamH p168 MR29,5-5-15

MACFADYEN,R.Lt 8-10-19 1CamH CR Scot808

MACFADYEN,Walter.MID Lt kia 7-5-17 RScot p54 CR France1182,Capt

MACFARLAND,George Adams TCapt dow 17-10-17 RAMC att23StnHos p196 CR Mddx16

MACFARLANE,Alastair Hunter Lt kia 12-5-15 8RScot p211 MR29 2Lt 9Bn

MACFARLANE,Alexander 2Lt kia 2-12-17 91RFA p32 CR France662

MACFARLANE,Donald McIntyre T2Lt kld 18-4-18 9ScotRif &RAF p103 CR Egypt9,McFARLANE Lt

MacFARLANE,Harold Embleton T2Lt kia 14-7-17 GL att55RFC p10 CR France134

MacFARLANE,Ian TCapt ded 18-7-17 RAMC attEgyptHospl p196 CR Egypt2

MacFARLANE,Ian Cameron 2Lt kia 14-9-16 11 att6YorkR p91 MR21

MacFARLANE,John Tennant Lt 26-9-15 MGC p184 MR19

MACFARLANE,Keith Dix Lewis TLt kia 14-4-17 9ScotRif p103 MR20

MACFARLANE,Kenneth Capt ded 7-12-16 5HLI p240 CR Scot764

MACFARLANE,Leslie Kerr 2Lt kia 23-8-18 8RScot p212 CR France927 2Bn

MACFARLANE,Robert.MC.Capt kia 21-4-17 3 att2BlkW p129 MR38

MACFARLANE,Robert George 2Lt 6-3-16 177RE CR Belgium11

MACFARLANE,Ronald Wallace 2Lt kia 3-9-16 RGA 152HB p40 CR France232

MacFARLANE,Wallace Bird 2Lt kia 10-3-15 5 att2Middx p147 MR22

MacFARLANE,William Barr 2Lt dow 20-7-15 5KOSB p224 MR4

MacFARLANE,William Cargill Stuart 2Lt kia 27-8-16 4A&SH p173 CR France23

MacFARLANE,William MacCallum.DSO.TMaj kia 19-2-17 15HLI att1/5SfthH CR France15

MacFARLANE,William Smith.MC.Lt kld 20-6-18 5RScots CR Scot237

MacFARLANE,William Walter 2Lt kia 12-4-18 D256RFA p208 CR France1106,McFARLANE

MacFARLANG-GRIEVE,Alwyn Ronald 2Lt kia 17-3-17 1/8A&SH p243 CR France728,Lt

MacFARQUHAR,Murdo Mackenzie T2Lt kia 15-9-16 9 att7/8KOSB p102

MacFARREN,Ernest T2Lt dow 8-11-16 7RIrRif p170 2entries CR France285

MacFAYDEN,Robert Lt ded 8-10-19 CamH p265

MacFIE,Claud William 2Lt kia 16-6-15 3SStaffs att2Beds p122 MR22

MacFIE,Robert Alexander 2Lt kia 20-11-17 2/5LancFus p221 MR21

MacGEORGE,Henry Warwick LtTCapt kia 25-9-15 1SStaffs p122 MR19

MacGEORGE,William Henry LtCol ded 16-12-16 RDC p253

MACGEOUGH-BOND,Ralph Shelton 2Lt dow 22-8-17 D46RFA p32 CR Belgium124

MACGILL,Mary Mitchell Matron 11-3-15 QAIMNS CR Hamps1

MACGILVARY,Alexander Renfrew 2Lt kia 29-11-17 1/7ScotRif p103&p224,MACGILVRAY CR Palestine9,McGILVRAY

MacGILVRAY,John Duncan 2Lt kia 18-2-17 4CamH att2/10Lpool p270 MR32

MacGILVRAY,Martin Lt drd 10-11-17 RE attWAFF CR Scot50

MacGLASHAN,Alexander 2Lt kia 27-9-18 7ScotRif p224 CR France686,McGLASHAN

MacGRATH,Roger.MC.TCapt dow 5-5-18 RAMC att28FA p196 CR France102,McGRATH

MACGREGOR,Alexander Henry Campbell Maj kia 15-3-15 RIrFus p171 CR Belgium111,14-3-15

MacGREGOR,Alexander John Lindsay Capt dow 8-10-18 3/13BlkW D'Coy p205 CR France446

MacGREGOR,Alfred Horace.MID Capt kia 11-9-16 14LondR p249 MR21 10-9-1

MACGREGOR,Amyas.MC.Lt dow 13-10-16 RE 1LondFC p210 CR France513,C

MACGREGOR,Andrew Hamilton.MID Capt kia 13-11-16 6SfthH p241 CR France131

MacGREGOR,Andrew Steven 2Lt kia 23-4-17 RFA p208 CR France1188

MacGREGOR,Colin Alexander T2Lt kia 26-9-15 9GordH p166 MR19

MacGREGOR,Cortland Richard Lt kia 5-5-15 2SWBord p100 MR4,Cortlandt

MacGREGOR,Donald Alastair Capt dow 15-8-15 2RBerkR p139 CR Germany2

MacGREGOR,Donald Argyle Douglas Ian TLt kia 30-11-17 GL &41RFC p10 MF

MacGREGOR,Douglas 2Lt kia 13-11-16 8A&SH D'Coy p243 CR France131,McGREGOR

MacGREGOR,George 2Lt kia 25-9-15 8SfthH p165 MR19

MACGREGOR,James.MC.T2Lt kia 10-4-18 11RScot p54 MR30

MACGREGOR,James Lt 12-7-18RFA CR Scot752

MACGREGOR,James Hamilton 2LtTLt kia 10-1-17 3BedR att132MGC Inf p138&184 CR Iraq5

MacGREGOR,John Atholl 2Lt kia 21/26-9-16 2CldGds p51 CR France218 &CR France374,Lt 26-9-16

MacGREGOR,John Campbell Rev ded 4-11-16 RAChDept p268

MACGREGOR,Kenneth Cortlandt 2Lt kia 26-2-15 2KOSB p102 MR29

MacGREGOR,Peter Maj 15-11-17 RAMC CR Yorks644

MacGREGOR,Ralph Alexander Montgomery Lt dow 26-9-18 RGA 136SB p40 C France1484,Montgomerie

MacGREGOR,Reginald Kinloch TCapt kld 23-4-16 RAMC p196 CR France1372

MacGREGOR,Rhoderic 2Lt dow 23-7-17 RASC SR MT attT'CpsSiegePk 76SB D/ p193 CR France40

MacGREGOR,Robert Murray Lt dow PoW 9-5-15 1/13LondR p249 MR32

MacGREGOR,Ronald Lt ded 1-5-17 1LovatScts att2/2KAR p204 CR EAfrica47,17

MacGREGOR,Thomas Charles Stuart T2Lt kia 8-6-17 GL &53RFC p10 MR20

MACGREGOR-WHITTON,Percy William Thomas TCapt kia 9-7-16 2RScotFus MR21

MacHAFFIE,John T2Lt kia 21-9-17 GL &29RFC p10 CR Belgium84

MacHARDY,David Scott T2Lt kia 1-7-16 16HLI p163 MR21

MACHARG,Ebenezer Maitland Capt kia 23-10-16 3 att1ScotRif p103 MR21

MACHARG,James Anthony Boyd 2Lt kia 29-10-16 6ScotRif p224 MR21
MACHELL,Humphrey Gilbert 2Lt ded 12-6-18 3BordR p117 CR France145,8Bn
MACHELL,Maurice Irving 2Lt kia 16-9-16 3 att5KSLI p145 MR21,15-9-16
MACHELL,Percy Wilfrid.CMG.DSO.LtCol kia 1-7-16 11BordR p117 CR France43
MACHEN,Frederick James 2Lt kia 3-6-17 1/20LondR p251 CR Belgium56
MACHON,C.F.E.Lt 16-9-20 3Glouc CR Glouc9
MacHUTCHEON,John Chisholm T2Lt dow 2-8-16 15N&D p134 CR France23
MACHUTCHISON,William Frederick Lt kia 26-3-18 7RDubFus p254 MR27
MacILDOWIE,Edward John Howard 2Lt kld 1-11-16 9HLI p240 MR21
MacILWAINE,Julian Mackay Capt kia 22-3-18 5RIrRif att12RFC p16&170 MR20
MACINDOE,Cecil Alexander Dunn Capt kia 28-6-15 8ScotRif p225 CR Gallipoli2
MACINDOE,J.G.Maj 5-10-16 RAMC CR Devon74
MACINDOE,Ronald Christian Black Capt kia 28-6-15 8ScotRif p225 MR4
MacINNES,Duncan Sayre.CMG.DSO.BrigGen dedacc 23-5-18 RE p46 CR France40
MACINTOSH,Eric Lt kld 31-7-17 Herts p252 MR29
MacINTOSH,Henry Maitland TCapt dow 26-7-18 A&SH p173 CR France1225
MACINTOSH,John T2Lt kia 23-7-16 14RWarR p65 MR21
MACINTOSH,John Douglas Capt kia 6-5-15 5RScot p211 MR4
MacINTOSH,John Hill 2Lt kia 14-4-17 6HLI p240 MR21
MACINTOSH,Kenneth Alexander 2Lt kia 24-8-18 6HLI p240 CR France162
MACINTOSH,Kenneth John.MC.Lt dow 16-1-20 1/5 att2/5GurkhaRif p279 MR43
MACINTOSH,Thomas Gordon Gall T2Lt kia 18-8-18 11RScot p54 CR France26
MACINTOSH,William Henry Lt ded 9-11-18 4GordH p270 CR Scot244
MacINTYRE,Charles Frederick Davis T2Lt kia 6-11-18 27RFA 37HB p32 CR France937
MacINTYRE,D.Capt 30-5-19 2GurkhaRif CR Europe51
MacINTYRE,George Duncan TLt kia 10-7-16 15 att7YorkR p90 CR France267
MacINTYRE,Ian Campbell Lt kia 22-11-17 CamH att108MGC Inf p168&p184 CR France529
MacINTYRE,John Taylor 2Lt kia 25-8-17 9 att18HLI p240 MR21
MACINTYRE,Peter Brown Capt dow 3-8-17 4SfthH p241 CR Belgium23
MacINTYRE,Robert Cochran.MC.Lt kld 30-9-18 6A&SH p243 CR France236,6/10Bn
MacINTYRE,Thomas Lt kia 1-7-16 16N'umbFus p62 MR21
MacIVER,Andrew Tucker Squarey Capt kia 24-4-15 RE p210 CR Belgium21
MacIVER,Donald Lt 24-3-18 3SLancs att2/7RWar MR27
MacIVER,Donald John 2Lt dow 14-10-15 TA 4CamH p243 CR France1,McIVER
MACIVER,Duncan T2Lt kia 11-10-16 5CamH att26TMB MR21
MacIVER,Ian Lt kia 11-8-16 5RFA p32 CR France267,10-8-16
MacIVER,Kenneth TCapt kia 27-3-18 CamH Res att5Bn p168 MR27
MacIVER,Kenneth Ogg Mackenzie TLt kldacc 30-10-18 KRRC att1KAR p151&266 CR EAfrica77
MacIVER,Reginald Squarey Lt kia 1-7-16 4LancF p93 CR France643,2Bn
MacIVER,Robert Troutbeck 2Lt kia 11-9-15 1RScot p54 CR France82
MACK,Arthur Stanley Lt kia 9-4-17 3RLancs p59 CR France729,1Bn
MACK,Arthur Paston TLtCol kia 15-9-16 9Suff p78 CR France294
MACK,Edward Geoffrey 2Lt kia 27-9-15 3 att2Wilts p153 CR France423,Edgar
MACK,Isaac Alexander TLt kia 1-7-16 Suff attTMB p78 CR France267,Capt
MACK,Thomas T2Lt kia 26-1-16 DLI att9Bn p161 CR Belgium115
MACK,Thomas Arthur 2Lt kia 9-4-17 6GordH p242 CR France184
MACKADAM,Harold James T2Lt kia 30-12-17 7RFus p69 MR21
MacKAIN,Henry Fergus T2Lt kia 27-2-17 GL &13RFC p10 CR France95,Lt
MacKAIN,James Fergus Capt kia 23-11-14 IA 34SikhPnrs p279 CR France279
MacKAY,Alexander Rinnison T2Lt kia 13-3-16 13 att15HLI p163 CR France430,Kinnison
MACKAY,Alexander William.MC.TCapt dow 28-9-17 26RFus p69 CR France1361
MACKAY,Angus 2Lt dow 16-11-16 5SfthH p241 CR France102
MACKAY,Angus T2Lt dow 10-5-18 24RFus p69 CR France84
MACKAY,Arnold Langley 2Lt dow 31-10-16 3 att2RScotF p95 CR France40
MACKAY,Charles SubCdr ded 15-6-16 PoW IA S&TCps p279
MacKAY,Charles Alexander.MID Capt kia 21-3-18 5SfthH p241 MR20
MacKAY,Charles William Donaldson 2Lt kia 17-8-16 8CamH p168 CR France239
MacKAY,Claude Lysaght 2Lt dow 7-6-15 2WorcR att2ManchR p109 CR France102
MACKAY,Donald 2Lt dow 17-11-18 5SfthH p241 CR France40
MACKAY,Donald Paley Maj kia 9-10-17 5WYorks p218 MR30
MacKAY,Douglas Duncan Anderson Lt kia 14-10-18 RE &RAF p270
MacKAY,Eric Reay Capt kia 13-6-15 13A&SH p173 MR4
MACKAY,Frederick William.MC.Capt dow 24-10-18 1/4YLI p235 CR France146
MacKAY,George Douglas Lt dow 23-4-17 1ARO att56Rif p279 MR38,2Lt
MacKAY,George Lawrence Forbes Lt kia 11-4-17 Leinst p174 CR France570,12-4-17
MacKAY,George Newton.MC.Lt 24-7-18 GordH att6MGC CR Belgium11
MACKAY,Gordon T2Lt kia 16-8-17 24Middx att16MGC Inf p147&184 MR30,44MGC
MACKAY,Hamish Strathy Lt kia 9-9-16 RGA 1HampsHB att22RFC p19&p209 CR France882
MACKAY,Harry William Mackintosh Lt kia 6-3-18 6GordH att18RFC p19&242 CR France31
MacKAY,Henry Neil T2Lt kia 28-11-16 12A&SH p173 CR Greece6
MACKAY,Ian.MID CaptTMaj 28-3-18 4CamH p242 MR20
MacKAY,Ian Darrock T2Lt kia 21-3-18 14A&SH p173 MR20
MacKAY,Ian Forbes TCapt kia 25-9-15 8GordH p166 MR19
MacKAY,James Lt kia 25-9-15 3 att1GordH p166 CR Belgium453
MACKAY,James Alasair Culbard.MC.Capt dow 22-7-16 6SfthH p241 CR France66
MacKAY,James Bruce TCapt dow 3-5-17 21WYorks p82 CR France97
MacKAY,James Ivan 2LtTCapt kia 5-10-17 3WRid att70RFC p115 CR Belgium11
MacKAY,John 2Lt kia 23-4-17 5BordR p228 CR France1185
MacKAY,John Alexander 2Lt kia 11-9-17 57RFC p10 CR Belgium158
MACKAY,John Mitchell.MID T2Lt kia 10-8-17 RE 130FC p46 CR Belgium112
MACKAY,John William TLt dow 20-8-17 7CamH p168 CR France64
MACKAY,Kenneth.MC.Capt dow 7-11-18 6GordH p242 CR France40,6/7Bn
MACKAY,Malcolm 2Lt dow 7-4-18 7A&SH p243 CR France113
MACKAY,Mark Sprot T2Lt kia 23-4-17 7CamH p168 CR France1182
MACKAY,Philip Storrs 2Lt kia 14-4-17 3 att1KOSB p102 CR France162
MACKAY,Samuel Francis Henderson Capt kia 13-6-17 5ELancs p226 MR19
MACKAY,Terence Faulkner T2Lt kia 3-10-18 KRRC att4Bn p151 CR France234
MacKAY,William Gidden 2Lt kia 25-9-15 3GordH p166 MR29
MacKENNA,Peter Fraser Maj ded 26-11-18 3/5RScotF Res p270 CR Scot520
MACKENSON,Christopher 2Lt dow 16-8-17 RB p179
MacKENZIE,Adrian Somerset T2Lt kia 1-4-17 GL 10HLI att15RFC p10 CR France41,Lt
MACKENZIE,Alan Keith Capt dow 16-9-16 3GrenGds p50 CR France23,Allan
MACKENZIE,Albert James.MC.2Lt dow 13-12-17 4 att2ScotRif p103 CR France64
MACKENZIE,Alexander Alan LtACapt kia 23-3-18 4SfthH p241 MR20
MACKENZIE,Alexander Kenneth 2Lt kia 1-9-18 2SfthH p165 CR France427
MacKENZIE,Alexander Ritchie Doughty 2Lt kia 22-3-18 4GordH p242 MR20,McKENZIE
MACKENZIE,Alistair 2Lt kia 24-3-18 3 att9SfthH p165 MR27,Alastair
MACKENZIE,Archibald TCapt dow 4-6-18 1NumbFus p62 CR France10
MACKENZIE,Bernard Francis Lt kia 28-6-18 4SLancs p230 CR France352
MACKENZIE,Boyce Mackey Scobie TLtACapt kia 22-3-18 8RWSurr p56 MR27
MACKENZIE,Charles Alexander Chandos Capt mbk 21-12-14 IA 20DeccanHorse p279 MR28
MACKENZIE,Colin Landseer 2Lt kia 20-9-14 2HLI p163 CR France1329
MACKENZIE,Cortlandt Graham Gordon Lt kia 25-10-14 RScotFus p95 MR29,29-10-14
MACKENZIE,Cyril Atkinson Capt kia 24-12-17 2/7Lpool p215 CR Belgium12
MACKENZIE,David Ferguson Capt kia 17-5-15 4CamH p242 MR22
MACKENZIE,Donald Lt&QM kia 30-9-18 5N&D p232 CR France375
MACKENZIE,Donald Charles Lt dow 20-1-15 1SfthH p165 CR Surrey112
MACKENZIE,Donald Lawson 2Lt kia 1-10-18 5SfthH p241 CR Belgium157,McKENZIE
MACKENZIE,Donald Stamford Forth Lt dow 31-7-17 177RFA p32 CR Belgium7
MACKENZIE,Duncan T2Lt ded 7-1-17 BlkW p264 CR Wales664,4-1-17
MACKENZIE,Edward Forbes 2Lt kia 14-12-14 RScot p54 MR29
MacKENZIE,Eric James Bethune Capt kia 8-7-16 29/42RFA p32&257 CR France513,Maj
MACKENZIE,Francis Edgar 2Lt kia 23-4-17 8ScotRif att13KRRC p225 MR20
MACKENZIE,Francis Ramsay 2Lt kia 1-7-16 2SfthH p165 MR21
MACKENZIE,Frederick Boyce ACapt ded 4-7-18 RGA 71HB p262 CR Hamps23
MACKENZIE,Frederick Obrè Capt kia 3-3-15 IA 7Rajputs p279 CR Iraq6
MACKENZIE,Frederick Thomas Lt 23-3-18 169RFA MR20
MacKENZIE,Frederick Wallace Capt ded 30-7-17 RAMC CR Scot591
MacKENZIE,George Arthur T2Lt kia 25-9-15 8GordH p166 MR19
MACKENZIE,George Laing.MC.T2Lt dow 13-4-18 SfthH att1/4Bn p165 CR France10
MACKENZIE,Gilbert Marshall Capt kia 21-4-16 SfthH p165 MR38
MACKENZIE,Henry Deedes Nutt TCapt kia 4-10-17 RAMC att95RFA p196 CR Belgium19
MacKENZIE,Henry Pierce.MID TCapt kia 25-9-15 9ScotRif p103 CR France114
MacKENZIE,I Nurse 2-11-18 QAIMNS CR Scot990
MACKENZIE,Ian.MC.Capt 21-3-18 5SfthH MR20
MACKENZIE,Ivan Emilio Mario TCapt kld 12-10-17 RFC p10 CR Hamps4
MACKENZIE,Jack Ronald Lewes Lt kia 21-4-17 SfthH p165 MR38

MACKENZIE,James Lt kia 16-5-15 ScotGds att2Bn p52 CR France279
MACKENZIE,James Alexander 2Lt kia 20-9-17 4SfthH p241 MR30
MACKENZIE,James Graham Lt kia 4-8-16 16RScot p54 MR21
MacKENZIE,John.VC.Maj kia 17-5-15 1Beds p86 CR France279
MACKENZIE,John TLt kia 26-9-16 8NumbF p62 MR21
MACKENZIE,John 2Lt kia 28-10-17 RGA 11SB p40 CR Belgium23
MacKENZIE,John 2Lt kia 1-12-17 GL &RFC p10 MR20
MACKENZIE,John Gladstone Capt kia 21-5-16 AustAMC 6FA CR France275
MACKENZIE,John Kincaid T2Lt kia 27-5-18 BordR att8Bn p117 MR18
MACKENZIE,Keith Bethune Capt kia 12-11-14 2SforthH p165 MR29
MacKENZIE,Keith Ingleby 2Lt kia 8-4-17 A&SH &RFC p10&p173 CR France1321
MACKENZIE,Kenneth TCapt kia 1-7-16 24NumbF p62 MR21
MacKENZIE,Kenneth Capt kld 9-9-18 9RScot p212 CR France541,27-8-18
MACKENZIE,Kenneth Fitzgerald 2Lt 14-7-16 SfthH att26MGC MR21
MACKENZIE,Kenneth Lee Warner Maj ded 27-11-14 IA 62Punjabis p279 CR Egypt15
MACKENZIE,Lynedoch Archibald LtACapt dow 19-10-15 RE p210 MR4
MACKENZIE,Mark Kinkaid Lt kia 1-2-16 4KRRC att3RB p151 CR France1894,Kincaid 25-9-14
MACKENZIE,Maurice.MID TLt kia 28-11-15 RAMC att2RIrRif p196 CR France921
MacKENZIE,Murdo John 2Lt kia 28-6-15 RFA p208 CR Gallipoli6
MACKENZIE,Murdock T2Lt kia 5-11-15 9BlkW p129 MR19
MACKENZIE,Murray Mitchell.MID T2Lt dow 21-11-16 10 att1/4SfthH p165 CR France59
MacKENZIE,Noel Olliffe Compton 2Lt kia 1-7-16 1/13LondR p249 MR21
MacKENZIE,Percy Melville Capt kia 6-10-18 2GordH p166 CR France686
MACKENZIE,R.H.Col 19-1-16 4ScotRif CR Scot237
MACKENZIE,Richard Devon Samuels T2Lt dow 1-7-17 8SfthH p165 CR Belgium2,Devern
MACKENZIE,Roderick Ian 2Lt dow 11-4-15 1BlkW p129 CR France80
MACKENZIE,Ronald Angus Hugh Lt kia 7-2-15 1Leinst p174 CR Belgium80,McKENZIE
MACKENZIE,Ronald Patrick 2Lt kia 19-4-17 1/5RScotFus p222 CR Palestine8
MACKENZIE,Simon 2Lt kia 7-12-16 4SfthH p241 CR France1182
MACKENZIE,Thomas Graham T2Lt dow 31-8-17 13 att5/6RScot p54 CR Belgium24
MACKENZIE,William Alexander Lt kia 17-5-17 9KOSB att167MGC Inf p102&184 CR France537
MACKENZIE,William Archibald 2Lt dow 29-9-18 2/5Lancs p213 CR France1184
MACKENZIE,William Sinclair 2Lt 28-4-17 4 att16RScots p211 MR20
MACKENZIE,William Stuart Capt ded 22-8-21 IA 1/124Baluchis p279 MR43
MACKEOWN,John Harold T2Lt kld 5-10-17 5 att1ConnRgrs p172 CR Iraq8
MACKESON,Christopher.MID 2Lt&Adjt dow 16-8-17 2RB CR Belgium7
MACKEY,Edward Reeves.DCM.Lt kld 15-3-17 GL &RFC p10 CR Herts87
MACKIE,Alexander Mackay 2Lt kia 21-10-18 4DLI C'Coy att9MGC Inf p161&p184 CR Belgium140
MACKIE,Frank James T2Lt kia 29-5-17 19Lpool p72 CR Belgium4
MACKIE,George 2Lt dow 12-4-17 9RScot p212 CR France266
MACKIE,George Neville Capt kia 26-4-15 IA 54Sikhs att57Rif p279
MACKIE,Harold Lt dow 18-11-17 9RB p179 CR Belgium16
MACKIE,James D.TCapt kia 10-4-16 12LpoolR p72 CR Belgium23
MACKIE,James Logan LtACapt kia 27-12-17 1/1AyrYeo p203 CR Palestine3
MACKIE,Norman Lindsay LtACapt dow 28-9-15 14LondR attMGC p187,Lindsey&p249,25-9-15 MR19
MACKIE,Reginald Ernest Capt kia 28-6-15 4RScot p211 MR4
MACKIE,Thomas Sinclair Lt kia 18-11-16 3 att8NStaffs p157 MR21,Thomson
MACKIE,William 2Lt ded 29-4-16 6RScot p211 CR Scot722,Lt
MACKILLOP,Donald TLt kia 20-7-16 3 att1ScotRif p103 MR21
MACKINDER,H.J.H.WO accdrd 14-6-16 RIM p279
MACKINLAY,James Lt ded 17-1-19 RDC p256 CR Lancs170
MACKINLAY,Robert Wallace.MC.Capt ded 6-2-19 RE 3SiegeCoy p210 CR Belgium316
MACKINNON,Alastair Lt ded 14-10-16 8A&SH attMGC p187&243,kld CR France397
MACKINNON,Alexander Hood 2Lt kia 14-9-14 1CamH p168 MR15
MACKINNON,Archibald Donald T2Lt kia 13-10-18 51MGC Inf p184 CR France271
MACKINNON,Brice Bunny.MC.Lt ded 5-8-18 3 att10BlkW p129 CR France145
MACKINNON,Bruce Lt dow 2-10-18 4HLI att97TMB p163 CR France528
MacKINNON,Charles Frank Capt ded 14-6-19 1/6KAR CR SAfrica30
MACKINNON,Colin Alexander John 2Lt kia 25-9-15 1Middx p147 MR19
MACKINNON,Duncan Lt kia 9-10-17 1ScotGds p52 MR30

MACKINNON,Duncan T.Capt dow 12-4-18 RAMC att9HLI p196 CR France324
MACKINNON,Farquhar Donald Lt dow 4-10-17 IARO att129Baluchis p279 CR EAfrica38 &CR Tanzania1
MacKINNON,Francis James Ogilvie Capt kia 16/17-5-15 3 att2GordH p166 CR France279
MACKINNON,Frank Irvine TCapt ded 30-12-18 RAMC p196 CR Syria2
MACKINNON,Gordon.MC.Lt kia 8-11-17 KOSB att1/5Bn p102 CR Palestine8
MacKINNON,John T2Lt kia 21-4-18 8SfthH p165 CR France57
MacKINNON,John Angus 2Lt kia 22-8-17 4Berks p234 MR30
MacKINNON,Kenneth Lt kia 7-4-17 8N&D p233 CR France725
MacKINNON,Lachlan T2Lt kia 30-6-16 8CamH p168 CR France423,6Bn
MacKINNON,Lionel Neil Alexander Capt kia 6-11-15 CldGds att5NigR p51&201 CR WAfrica58
MACKINNON,Louis Charles Bowden Fuller 2Lt kia 21-3-18 RE 518FC p210 MR20,Fullarton
MACKINNON,Mary SNurse drd 26-2-18 TFNS p254 MR40
MacKINNON,Neil Alexander Lt kia 19-9-18 3SuffR p78 CR Palestine9
MacKINNON,Ronald Fullerton.MC.TLt kia 21-10-16 11LancF att9LNLancs p93 MR21
MacKINNON,Roy Livingston.MID Capt dow 15-4-21 4GordH CR Scot280
MACKINNON,Vincent Walter Kenneth.MID Lt kia 21-7-15 IA 53Sikhs p279 CR Asia60
MacKINNON,William Capt kia 11-5-17 1/14LondR p249 CR France537
MACKINTOSH,Alastair Hugh Capt kia 14-9-14 CamH p168 MR15
MACKINTOSH,Angus Alexander Capt ded 14-10-18 RHGds p20
MACKINTOSH,Charles Gustave Rochefort T2Lt kia 5-4-17 GL &RFC p10 CR France1484
MACKINTOSH,Donald.VC.Lt kia 11-4-17 3SfthH p165 CR France604
MACKINTOSH,Douglas Bruce Capt kia 24-7-16 BlkW att1KAR p129&268 CR EAfrica40
MACKINTOSH,Douglas Fraser Lt 2-10-17 50RFA att55RFC served as MATHEWS,G.
MACKINTOSH,Edwin Hampson TLt kia 25-9-15 8BlkW p129 MR19
MACKINTOSH,Ewart Alan.MC.Lt kia 21-11-17 5SfthH p241 CR France1498
MACKINTOSH,Gerard 2Lt ded 26-3-17 IARO attS&TCps p279 CR Iraq6
MACKINTOSH,Henry Leith 2Lt dow 5-3-15 1SStaffs p122 CR France254,Harry
MACKINTOSH,James Lawton 2Lt kia 1-5-15 ULIA att 1HLI p163&279 CR Belgium101,Lt
MACKINTOSH,John Capt kia 23-7-18 6SfthH p241 CR France1697
MACKINTOSH,John James TLt ded 1-4-16 RAMC att1GarrBn Ess p196 CR Egypt8
MACKINTOSH,John Lachlan Lt 9-1-16 ArabRifs CR EAfrica50
MACKIRDY,Charles David Scott Lt dow PoW 22-3-18 11Huss p22
MACKNIGHT,Thomas William Finglan TLt ded 4-9-16 RAMC p196 MR65,Fingland
MACKLE,Augustine Mary 2Lt dow 16-8-17 5BordR att1/6Lond p228 CR Belgium19,Austin
MACKLIN,David Harold 2Lt kia 27-3-18 5BedR p219 CR France393,4Bn
MACKLIN,John James Malcolm TLt kia 12-3-18 RLancs att12LancF p59 CR Greece5
MACKPHERSON,Donald 2Lt dow 11-11-17 RH&FA p208
MACKRETH,John TLt kia 15-9-16 RE 41DivSigCo p46 MR21
MACKRIDGE,Ralf Leslie 2Lt kia 26-4-18 4 att1WYorks p82 MR30
MacKRORY,Ernest William T2Lt kia 14-7-16 1SStaffs p122 MR21
MACKWORTH,Arthur Christopher Paul TLt ded 25-11-17 RB p266 CR Oxford71
MACKWORTH,Francis Julian Audley Maj kia 1-11-14 RA p32 CR France1106
MacLACHLAN,Alexander Fraser Campbell.CMG.DSO.MajTLtCol kia 22-3-18 KRRC p151 CR France672
MACLACHLAN,David Corson T2Lt ded 18-5-17 MGC HB p184 CR France40
MacLACHLAN,James Menzies.MC.T2LtACapt kia 2-12-17 GL att97/LTMB p191 MR30
MacLACHLAN,Kenneth Douglas Mackenzie Capt dow 27-4-15 SfthH p165 CR France134
MacLACHLAN,Kenneth Gilbert 2Lt kia 23-4-17 8 att13RScot p212 MR20
MACLACHLAN,Peter Malcolm.MC.TCapt dow 26-3-18 RAMC att15Hamps p196 CR France62,McLACHLAN
MACLACHLAN,Robert Hugh Muir dow 2Lt kia 23-3-18 4 att12RScots p211 MR27,McLACHLAN
MACLACHLAN,Ronald Campbell.DSO.TBrigGen kia 11-8-17 RB Staff Cmdg112InfBde p179 CR Belgium183
MACLACHLAN,Walter Miller 2Lt ded 11-7-16 13HLI att6SLancs p163 CR Iraq5,1 att6Bn
MacLACHLAN,William Smith 2Lt kia 29-8-18 1/14LondR p249 CR France646,McLACHLAN
MacLAGAN,Gilchrist Stanley Lt kia 25-4-15 3 att1RWar p65 MR29
MACLAGAN,James Graham Lt kia 1-8-18 1/5LNLancs p234 CR France113

MacLAGAN,Philip Whiteside.MID Lt kia 16-4-16 5Bord p228 CR Belgium37

MacLAGAN,Thomas Duncan Ogilvie.MC&Bar.Capt kia 30-4-18 2/14Lond p249 CR Palestine3

MACLAREN,Frank Nairne Capt kia 15-4-16 IA 1/9GurkhaRif p279 MR38,14-4-16

MacLAREN,Donald Graeme 2Lt kia 29-6-17 10Lpool p216 MR32

MacLAREN,Ernest Cecil Capt kia 1-7-16 15LancFus p93 CR France215,McLAREN

MacLAREN,Robert T2Lt dow 24-7-16 16Ches p96

MacLAUGHLIN,Alexander Wilson Lt mbk 29-10-17 1RFC p256 MR20

MACLAVERTY,Colin Johnston Capt kia 18-9-16 1KSLI p145 MR21

MACLAY,Ebenezer Lt dow 11-4-18 1ScotGds p52 CR France62

MACLAY,James Webster 2Lt kia 28-6-15 7ScotRif p224 CR Gallipoli6

MACLAY,William Strang 2Lt dow 25-6-15 8ScotRif p225 MR4

MacLEAN,Alec Clarkson TLt kia 9-4-18 RE 296RlyCo p46 CR France1094

MacLEAN,Alexander Harvie Maj kia 26-8-14 2A&SH p173 CR France716

MacLEAN,Alexander Murchison TCapt kia 12-4-18 ScotHorse &10RAF MR20

MACLEAN,Alfred Knowles T2Lt kia 27-9-18 8NumbF p62 MR16,McCLEAN

MacLEAN,Alfred Peter Lt kld 17-9-18 4RScot &RAF p211&p258 CR Egypt15

MacLEAN,Alistair Fitzhugh Capt kia 8-8-15 IA 33Punjabis att14Sikhs p279 MR4

MacLEAN,Andrew De Vere Capt kia 19-9-14 ESurr p113 CR France864,17-9-14

MACLEAN,Archibald T2Lt kia 18-8-18 1KOSB p102 CR France28

MacLEAN,Arthur Kirkpatrick Lt kia 26-8-14 2A&SH p173 CR France716

MacLEAN,David 2Lt kia 14-7-18 1GordH p166

MACLEAN,Donald T2Lt dow 12-10-16 6CamH p168 CR France385

MACLEAN,Donald 2Lt kia 21-9-16 6ScotRif p224 CR France666

MACLEAN,Donald Frederick Durant TMaj ded 10-12-17 10RFus p69 CR Berks83

MACLEAN,Donald Lewis Lt 21-11-20 RB CR Ireland14

MACLEAN,Dugald Black.MC.TCapt kia 29-8-16 RAMC att8ELanc p196 CR France115

MACLEAN,Dugald Fitzroy 2Lt dow 23-7-16 KSLI att1/4Glouc p145 MR21

MACLEAN,Frederick William T2Lt dow 14-6-17 GL &29RFC p10 CR France46,McLEAN

MACLEAN,G.H.MC.Capt 30-8-20 Ches CR EAfrica116

MACLEAN,Ivan Clarkson.DSO.MC&Bar.TCapt dow PoW 4-4-18 RAMC att2RB p196 CR France441

MACLEAN,Henry Chevers TCapt kia 1-7-16 9RInnisF p105 MR21

MacLEAN,James Acheson.MC.Lt kia 30-9-17 D148RFA p32 CR Belgium17,2Lt

MacLEAN,Kemp T2Lt kia 28-3-18 13RScot p54 MR20

MACLEAN,Malcolm Alexander 2Lt kia 13-10-15 3CamH p168 MR19

MACLEAN,Moira Francis Allan Capt kia 17-2-15 RGA p40 CR Asia45,15-2-15

MacLEAN,Raymond Alastair T2Lt kia 13-11-16 3 att6SfthH p165 CR France131,McLEAN

MACLEAN,William Archibald Lt kia 12-3-15 3HLI p163 CR France279,1Bn

MACLEAN,William Macfarlane.MC.2Lt 24-3-18 5 att1/8A&SH MR27

MACLEAR,Basil Capt kia 24-5-15 2RDubFus p177 MR29

MACLEAR,Basil George Hope.MC.2Lt kia 26-7-16 4GrenGds p50 CR Belgium73

MacLEAR,Harry.DSO.LtCol kia 15-3-16 ELanc att3RScots p111 CR France222

MacLEAR,Percy Maj kia 30-8-14 RDubF Cmdg2NigR p177 CR WAfrica57,LtCol

MacLEAY,George Cameron T2Lt kia 17-8-16 8CamH p168 MR21,McLEAY

MacLEHOSE,James Colin T2Lt kia 14-2-17 16RB p179 CR Belgium6

MACLEHOSE,Norman Crawford Lt kia 26-5-15 8LondR p247 CR France261

MACLELLAN,George Douglas 2Lt kia 28-4-17 5HLI p240 MR20

MACLELLAN,Lewis.MC.Lt kia 30-11-17 1/5HLI p240 CR Palestine9

MACLELLAN,Malcolm TCapt kia 25-9-15 11A&SH p173 MR19,26-9-15

MacLENNAN,Iain Donald Forrest 2Lt kia 12-5-17 3 att1GordH p166 CR France1182

MacLENNAN,John Maj ded 9-8-16 1GordH p265 CR Scot287

MacLENNAN,Roderick Ward T2Lt kia 23-12-17 GL &60RFC p10 CR France200

MACLEOD,Alastair Roderick Lt kia 25-4-15 15RHA p32 MR4

MACLEOD,David.DSO.TLtCol ded 19-12-17 8GordH p166 CR France113

MACLEOD,Daniel Mackay 2Lt ded 9-7-18 7NumbF p214 CR Scot674

MACLEOD,Donald Capt kia 28-9-15 1/10Lpool p216 CR Belgium6

MACLEOD,Donald Lt drd 10-5-17 RE GL attIWT p191 MR38

MACLEOD,Donald.MC.T2Lt kia 1-7-17 BordR att1Bn p117 CR Belgium23

MACLEOD,Donald Angus 2Lt dow 5-10-17 3KOSB p102 CR France139

MACLEOD,Donald Kerr 2Lt kia 18-10-17 86RFA p32 CR Belgium19

MACLEOD,George Calder T2Lt kia 19-4-17 9 att1/5KOSB p102 CR Palestine8

MACLEOD,George Charles Sholto Capt dow 13-5-15 2BlkW p129 CR France80

MacLEOD,Ian Breac Lt kia 17-4-15 2BlkW p129 CR France924

MacLEOD,Ion Keith Falconer Capt kia 27-4-18 RAMC 75FA CR Belgium11

MACLEOD,John TLt kia 6-1-16 1SfthH p165 MR38

MACLEOD,James Herbert Negroe TLt kia 29-6-16 8KOSB p102 CR France423,Neynoe 2Lt

MACLEOD,John Capt ded 12-7-19 RAMC att11Lancers p267 CR Iraq8

MACLEOD,Victor Charles Augustus T2Lt kia 18-7-17 10 att1/8ScotRif p103 CR Palestine8

MACLEOD,William Bannatyne Capt kia 12-1-17 IA 121 att34SikhPnrs p279 CR Iraq5,McLEOD 11/12-1-17

MacLUCKIE,Reginald William TCapt kia 11-8-16 3A&SH att9WYorks p173 CR France158

MACLURE,Gordon Stanley 2Lt dow 16-6-16 RFA attZ32TMB p32 CR France145

MACMAHON,Charles Edward Valentine 2Lt ded 9-3-16 1LNLancR p136 CR Lancs102,McMAHON 13-3-16

MacMAHON,John Aquila Lt dow 12-5-15 RAMC att3SomLI p196 CR Mddx80

MacMASTER,Donald Cameron Deford TLt kia 26-9-15 6CamH p168 CR France219,25-9-15

MacMEEKEN,Guy Steel Peebles.MC.TLtACapt dow PoW 5-5-18 12RScot p54 CR France1142

MacMEEKEN,James T2Lt kia 27-5-18 NumbF Res att5Bn p62 CR France1753

MACMICHAEL,Michael William Annesley Capt dow 16-9-16 11Ess A'Coy p132 CR France66,Lt

MACMILLAN,Cameron TLtACapt kia 22-8-17 8SfthH p165 MR30

MACMILLAN,Edwin James 2Lt kia 12-1-17 4 att8RIrF p171 MR29

MacMILLAN,James Alexander(Sandy) 2Lt kia 20-7-18 1/4SfthH p241 CR France622

MacMILLAN,James Bonthron.DSO.TMaj kia 30-11-17 7DCLI p114 MR17

MacMILLAN,John 2Lt 24-3-18 LanarkYeo att9RScots MR27

MACMILLAN,John 2Lt dow 24-9-18 8ScotRif p225 CR France278,McMILLAN 1Bn

MACMILLAN,Robert Alexander Cameron T2Lt kia 11-4-17 2SfthH p165 CR France604

MacMILLAN,Stephen Alexander Lt dow 9-5-15 IARO att58Rif p279 CR France80

MACMILLAN,Thomas 2Lt kld 12-2-17 GL &RFC p10 CR Scot675

MACMILLAN,Thomas Muir 2Lt 19-8-17 4SAInf CR France662

MacMULLEN,E.R.Lt 30-6-16 EAUL CR EAfrica2 &Tanzania1

MACMULLEN,Frederick Charles Kendall LtCol ded 19-6-16 IA 27Cav attStaff GenHQ p279 CR Iraq5,12Bn

MacMULLEN,George Reade Maj ded 28-1-16 SL IA Retd p201 CR War75

MacMURCHY,Ian Ure T2Lt kia 9-10-17 GL &9RFC p10 MR20,McMURCHY

MacNAB,Alexander 2Lt dow 24-10-18 D186RFA p32 CR France241

MACNAB,Angus Capt kia 1-11-14 RAMC att14Lond p254 MR29

MACNAB,Colin Lawrence.CMG.BrigGen ded 13-10-18 Staff p254 CR Essex254 Ex Suss

MACNAB,James T2Lt kia 19-8-15 8NumbF p62 MR4

MacNAE,Robert.MC.2Lt kia 10-10-16 10Lpool p216 CR Belgium4

MacNAGHTEN,A.C.R.S.Lt 29-11-14 1BlkW MR29

MACNAGHTEN,Arthur Douglas.Bart T2Lt kia 15-9-16 8RB p179 CR France432

MACNAGHTEN,Edward Harry.Bart.2Lt mbk 1-7-16 1BlkW att12RIrRif p256 MR21

MACNAGHTEN,Stewart Cecil Capt ded 9-11-18 RASC p253 CR Norf210,Steuart

MACNAGHTON,Arthur Edward Harry T2Lt kia 31-7-16 13RSussR p119 CR France727,MACNAGHTEN Hay

MACNAMARA,Charles Carroll Maj dow 15-7-16 1RIrRif p170 CR Herts29,Carroll Charles LtCol 16-7-16

MACNAMARA,Colin George Herbert Rawdon 2Lt kia 17-8-15 IARO Inf attCpsofGuides p279 MR43

MACNAMARA,George CaptAMaj dow 25-5-17 2Wilts p153 CR France178,kia 27-5-17

MACNAMARA,George Frederick 2Lt kia 17-8-16 4 att8RDubF p177 CR France115

MacNAMARA,Joseph Bernard 2Lt kia 19-10-16 3 att2WRid p116 CR France374,McNAMARA

MacNAMARA,Kevin Parnell 2Lt kia 29-6-16 RFC p3 MR20

MACNAMARA,Maccon John 2Lt kia 26-3-18 2RDubF p177 MR27

MACNAUGHT,Frederick Clement TLt kia 25-9-15 RE 91FC p46 MR19

MACNAUGHTON,Angus Charles Rowley Stuart Lt kia 29-10-14 BlkW p129

MacNEECE,James Douglas Gaussen Capt kia 16-8-16 39RFA p32 MR21

MACNEILL,Andrew Duncan TCapt kia 29-7-17 RGA 21HB p40 CR Belgium9

MacNEILL,Archibald 2Lt kia 25-3-16 6A&SH p243 CR France15,26-3-16

MACNEILL,William Mackinnon 2Lt kia 12-10-14 16Lancers p23 CR France324

MACNICOL,Angus John Bayne TLt dow 18-4-17 D50RFA p32 CR France95

MacNICOL,Douglas Oswald Lt kia 5-1-18 1/4RWSurr att57RFC p19&212CR Egypt8 2Lt RWKent

MacNICOL,Harry Mansfield TLt kia 19-7-16 8Norf p74 MR21

MACNICOL,Horatius Bonar 2Lt drd 30-7-15 10RScot p212 CR Scot239

MACNIE,George Francis T2Lt kia 5-9-16 5ConnRgrs att6RDubF p172 CR Greece3

MacNIVEN,Alister Orr Lt kia 5-9-17 7HLI attRFC p19&240,6Bn

MACONACHIE,Arthur Delano 2Lt kia 1-7-16 9YLI p143 CR France267

MACONCHY,George Alexander.MID Capt kia 14-1-20 IA 2/5GurkhaRif p279 MR43

MACOUAT,John T2Lt kia 12-4-17 12RScots p54 CR France604

MacPHERSON,Arthur Vincent Claresholm TLt kia 25-8-15 14HLI att5RScots p163 CR Gallipoli4,McPHERSON Capt 4Bn

MacPHERSON,Donald William.MID Maj kia 16-11-16 IA 62Punjabis attStaffIndInfBde p279 CR Egypt15 McPHERSON

MACPHERSON,Duncan Stuart Ross Lt kia 24-11-14 IA 1/7 att2/8GurkhaRif p279 CR France80,23-11-14

MACPHERSON,Ewen Fergus Lord 2Lt kia 10-8-16 5RFA p32 CR France267

MACPHERSON,George TLt dow 15-9-16 MGC 4Sect p184 CR France105

MACPHERSON,George Denis Maj kia 27-9-15 13RScot p54 MR19 kld 26-9-15

MACPHERSON,Henry Douglas T2Lt kia 14-10-17 29RFC p10 CR Belgium18

MACPHERSON,Hugh Bannerman.MC.Lt kia 27-9-18 95RFA p32 CR France530

MACPHERSON,James Capt kia 10-3-15 4CamH p242 CR France1157

MacPHERSON,John Lt kia 1-7-16 1/7N&D p233 MR21

MacPHERSON,John Cook T2Lt kia 25-9-15 11 att1GordH p166 MR29

MACPHERSON,John Symon Lt dow 15-3-18 6GordH p242 CR France8

MACPHERSON,Maximillian.MIDx2 Capt kia 4-10-17 3 att1SfthH p165 MR30,3 att2Bn

MACPHERSON,Neil Maj kia 31-10-14 IA 2/2GurkhaRif p279 MR28

MACPHERSON,Robert Duncan Mearns 2Lt kia 25-10-15 7SfthH p165 MR19,25-9-15

MacPHERSON,Robert David T2Lt drd 6-6-16 8GordH p166 CR Scot900,5-6-16

MACPHERSON,Robert Nasmyth Maj kia 18-4-17 IA 40Pathans p279 CR EAfrica38 &CR Tanzania1

MacPHERSON,Ronald Charters Capt dow 18-4-18 B256RFA p207 CR France202

MacPHERSON,T.D.2Lt 11-11-18 RFA CR Scot253

MACPHERSON,William Meikle T2Lt kia 18-9-18 6MGC Inf p184 CR France1701

MacQUEEN,Alexander Norman 2Lt kia 25-3-17 6GordH attRFC p19&242 CR France568

MacQUEEN,John Ellison LtCol kia 25-9-15 6GordH p242 MR19

MACQUEEN,Roderick Reid TCapt kia 15-5-16 7RScotF p95 CR France423,Lt

MACQUEEN,Thomas Malcolm TLt kia 15-7-16 8ELancR p111 MR21

MACRAE,Alexander William Urquhart Capt kld 11-8-18 5RScot p211 CR France360,kia

MacRAE,Alfred Reginald AssComm ded 1-7-16 CR Iraq6

MacRAE,Archibald John Lt dow 5-10-18 4CamH att8SfthH p242 CR France106

MACRAE,Charles Alexander TLt ded 22-4-16 RASC p193 CR France1564,McRAE

MacRAE,Charles Eric 2Lt kia 10-11-16 1/4SfthH &RFC p19&241 CR France169

MACRAE,Charles Mackenzie Lt kia 5-7-15 1/4Hamp p228 CR Iraq6

MACRAE,Donald Alastair Lt ded 16-11-18 5SfthH att15MGC p187&241 CR Belgium406

MACRAE,Duncan Mackenzie 2Lt kia 4-10-17 3 att2SfthH p165 MR30

MACRAE,Frank Laing 2Lt kia 25-9-15 8SfthH p165 MR19

MACRAE,George Duncan T2Lt kia 27-3-18 31MGC Inf B'Coy p184 CR France745

MacRAE,George Pitt Taylor 2Lt kia 9-4-17 4SfthH p241

MACRAE,Ivor Alexander 2Lt dow 15-10-14 3 att2KOSB D'Coy p102 CR France80,14-10-14

MACRAE,John Nigel Capt kld 11-4-18 GL &83RAF p191 CR France88

MACRAE,John Alexander T2Lt kia 18-7-16 11 att8BlkW p129 MR21

MACRAE,John Harold 2Lt kia 25-8-16 4 att18ScotRif p103 CR France453,att1Bn

MACRAE,Joseph Nixon T2Lt kia 18-2-18 11BordR p117 CR Belgium126

MACRAE,Kenneth Matheson.MC.TMaj kia 1-11-18 124/28RFA p32 CR Belgiu140

MacRAE,Patrick Cameron Capt ded 5-3-17 RAMC 80FA p196 CR Scot458

MACRAE,William Charles Macintyre LtACapt kia 27-9-18 3RASC att14DivTrain p193 CR France429,29-9-18

MACREADY,Oscar Henry TCapt dow 3-12-17 16RIrRif p170 CR France512

MacREADY,William Capt kia 14-4-15 IA 120Inf p279 CR Iraq6

MACREIGHT,Arthur William James Lt ded 23-11-15 18Lond p250 CR Hamps15

MACREIGHT,Lionel Albert Lt kld 22-3-18 3 att2SLancs p125 MR27

MACRORIE,Roderick Douglas Capt kia 2-11-17 1/4RScot p211 CR Palestine8

MACROSTIE,Ernest James 2Lt kia 21-5-19 25Lond p252 MR43

MACROSTY,Henry Hugh TLt kia 19-12-15 C53RFA p32 CR Belgium84

MACRURY,Norman Lt kia 4-6-15 11BlkW attKOSB p129 MR4,McRURY

MacSHERRY,Dermot Joseph 2Lt kia 4-6-17 3 att6ConnRgrs p172 CR Belgium60

MacSWINEY,Joseph Ray.MC.Lt ded 2-11-18 10Lpool p216 CR Ches8,Capt

MacTAGGART,Murdoch Archibald.MID Capt kia 16-5-17 8A&SH p243 MR20

MACTAVISH,Hugh 2Lt kia 22-3-18 4ScotRif att8BordR p103 MR20

MACTAVISH,Roswell Murray.MC.TCapt ded 6-2-19 GL attStaff 45InfBde p191 CR France134

MACTIER,Henry MacKinnon Maj kia 12-3-15 IA 2/39GarhwalRif p279 CR France355 &CR France1887

MACVICAR,Neil T2Lt dow 4-5-17 2 att1/6SfthH p165 CR France40

MacVICKER,John Everard Churchill Lt ded 22-7-18 GL attRAF p191 CR France429

MacWALTER,Charles Christopher 2Lt kia 1-7-16 RLancs p59 MR21

MACWATT,Norman Ian Lt kia 1-7-16 2SfthH p165 MR21

MacWHIRTER,Thomas.MC.Maj kia 27-4-17 9GordH p166 MR20

MacWILLIAM,Frank T2Lt kia 2-6-18 7BordR p117 CR France4 McWILLIAM

MacWILLIAM,James Julian Gordon TLt kia 14-12-14 GordH p166

MADAN,Nigel Cornwallis TLt kia 3-3-16 8RLancs p59 MR29,2-3-16

MADDEN,Gerald Hugh Charles MajTLtCol dow 12-11-15 1IrGds p53 CR Eire46

MADDEN,Thomas Hylton 2Lt kia 10-3-15 1Lpool p72 CR France1106

MADDEN,William Henry TCapt dow 24-3-18 16RIrRif p170 CR France1063,kia

MADDEN,William Thomas TLt kia 14-4-18 1DCLI p114 CR France18

MADDER,Robert 2Lt kia 20-7-16 3/5GloucR att145MGC p187 CR France150

MADDERS,Hubert Franklin 2Lt kia 1-7-16 168RFA p32 CR France296

MADDEVER,Robert William Digory 2Lt dow 22-10-17 4SomLI p218 MR30

MADDICK,Herbert Capt dow 28-10-15 5Lancers p22 CR Surrey160

MADDICK,Sidney Alfred TLt ded 2-12-18 20Lpool att 1/6KAR p72&202 CR EAfrica52

MADDISON,Bertram Lionel TLtCol kia 1-7-16 2Yorks att8Y&L p91 CR France24

MADDISON,Geoffrey T2Lt kia 28-8-18 7Norf p74 CR France370

MADDISON,George Lionel Temple Lt kia 17-7-17 RFA p208 MR29

MADDISON,Walter 2Lt ded 24-11-17 RFC p10 CR Lond10

MADDOCK,Owen Loftus 2Lt kia 7-10-16 9Lond p248 CR France374

MADDOCKS,John Onslow TLt kia 4-6-16 17 att15RWar p65 CR France1182,Anslow

MADDOX,Cecil Edwards Capt 16-4-17 63PalamcottaLI MR61

MADDOX,Cecil Richard Capt kld 6-4-17 IA 63LI p279

MADDOX,Cyril Percy T2Lt kia 20-11-17 Yorks att2/4YLI p91 CR France530

MADDOX,Edward Harry.MID TLt kia 27-8-18 RE 18DivSigCo p46 CR France51

MADDOX,John Mortimer 2Lt kia 12-8-16 3 att10LancF p93 MR21

MADDOX,Leonard George.MC&Bar.2Lt kld 30-8-18 1/22Lond p251 CR France785

MADDRELL,James Keggan TLt kia 23-4-17 90MGC p184 MR20

MADDRELL,John Denis Hugh Lt dow 13-12-16 1/5DCLI p227 CR France40

MADELEY,Claude Neville 2Lt kia 19-1-18 43RFC p16 CR France1316

MADELEY,Sydney 2Lt dow 11-3-15 KRRC p151 CR Belgium28

MADEN,Harold T2Lt kia 29-7-17 18Manch p155 MR29

MADEN,William Henry T2Lt dow 4-10-17 GL DCLI att95TMB p191 CR Belgium165

MADGE,Charles Albert.MID TLtCol kia 10-5-16 SL RWar p201 CR France80

MADLEY,Lewis George T2Lt kia 14-5-17 1RWFus p98 MR20

MADOCKS,Henry John TLtCol kia 25-9-15 9RWFus p98 CR France260

MADORE,William Douglas LtACapt dow 10-2-17 RE 254TC p46 CR France80

MAFFETT,Henry Telford Capt kia 20-10-14 2Leinst p174 CR France1140

MAFFEY,Henry TLt&QM dow 1-5-16 RAMC att139FA p196 CR France858,18-5-

MAGAWLY CERATI DECLRY,Valerio Awby.DSO.CaptTLtCol kia 10-5-17 6Drag Cmdg7RB p22,10-8-17 CR France1185,de CALRY

MAGENIS,R.H.C.2Lt kia 15-9-14 3RIrRif p170 MR15

MAGER,William George 2Lt kia 1-7-16 13Lond p249 CR France1327

MAGGS,Eric William Bristow T2Lt kia 20-8-18 11KRRC p151 CR France547,Bristowe

MAGGS,George Ernest T2Lt dow 14-7-16 8RBerks p139 CR France176

MAGILL,Thomas Edmund 2Lt kia 3-9-16 6RIrReg p89 MR21

MAGINN,Philip Albert Charles.MC.Capt kia 15-9-16 18Lond p250 CR France45

MAGINNESS,Oscar Gladstone.MID TLt dow 15-12-15 RAMC attC51RFA p196 C Belgium11

MAGNAY,John Christopher Frederick Lt kia 23-4-17 1Norf p74 MR20

MAGNAY,Philip Magnay.MIDx3 CaptTLtCol kia 13-4-17 RFus Cmdg12Manch p CR France924,Mathew

MAGNESS,Thomas Charles 2Lt kia 22-8-17 1/5RWar p214 MR30

MAGNIAC,Erskine.MID LtCol kia 28-4-17 IA 27Punjabis p279 MR38

MAGNIAC,Meredith.DSO.MajTLtCol kia 25-4-17 1/2LancF p93 CR France418

MAGOOKIN,William Douglas.DCM.2Lt kia 21-3-18 12RIrRif p170 MR27

MAGOR,Arthur Curgenven Capt kia 17-10-14 3 att2Wilts p153 MR29

MAGOVERNY,John Henry Capt ded 19-4-19 RAMC attCamH p267 CR Asia81

MAGRANE,George Fairfield 2Lt kia 7-6-17 RGA 161SB p40 CR Belgium451,261

MAGRATH,Beauchamp Henry Butler TMaj kis 2-6-16 8ELancs p111 CR France745,5Bn

MAGRATH,Meyrick Magrath.DSO.CaptAMaj kia 2-8-18 291RFA p32 CR France887

MAGUIRE,Cecil Augustine 2Lt kia 31-7-17 4 att2ScotRif p103 MR29

MAGUIRE,Edward Alphonsus T2Lt kia 8-10-18 RFus att4Bn p69 CR France338

MAGUIRE,Francis Patrick 2Lt kia 27-4-18 5Leinst p174 CR France24

MAGUIRE,Henry T2Lt dow 15-7-16 RE 124FC p46 CR France66
MAGUIRE,Hugh 2Lt kia 9-9-16 3ConnRgrs att7InnisF p172 MR21
MAGUIRE,John Reginald T2Lt kia 18-8-16 3 att12WYorks p82 MR21
MAGUIRE,M.2Lt 21-8-18 3Ches CR France239
MAGUIRE,Matthew Laurence.MC.2LtTLt kia PoW 28-4-17 1ConRgrs &30RFC p10&172 MR38,dow
MAHAFFY,Henry Irwin T2Lt kld 22-10-17 RFC p10 CR Ireland107
MAHER,Cyril Benjamin Lt ded 25-7-17 IARO att7IndLabCps p279 CR Iraq8,25-7-19
MAHER,John Charles Lt kia 14-4-18 2IrGds p53 CR France352
MAHOMED,Claude Atkinson Etty Lt kia 31-7-17 1ScotGds p52 CR Belgium106
MAHON,James Harold Capt dow 13-9-16 1/8Lpool p215 CR France66
MAHON,Oswald Sydney Wilson 2Lt dow 14-4-17 5 att7Lpool p214 CR France13
MAHONEY,Frank.MC.2Lt kia 6-10-17 2BordR p117 CR Belgium165
MAHONEY,Herbert James.MM.MID LtACapt dow 24-10-18 RGA 184SB p40 CR France1196
MAHONEY,Thomas.MC.MID Capt&QM ded 10-1-18 2RIrReg p89 CR France145,MAHONY
MAHONY,Brian Gerald 2Lt kld 3-9-18 1/2RMunstFus att189RAF p175 CR Lond4,MAHONEY
MAHONY,Edmund Joseph TLt kia.27-9-18 1RMunstF p175 CR France530
MAHONY,Edward Archibald Lt kia 16-8-17 3RIrRif p170 MR30
MAHONY,Frederick Henry.MID Capt dow 22-10-14 ChesR p96 CR France80
MAHONY,James TLt dow 4-3-17 11RWSurr p56 CR Belgium11
MAHONY,Norman T2Lt dow 23-6-18 LancF att1/2Bn p93 CR France10,2/5Bn
MAHONY,Thomas George T2Lt kia 13-7-16 19LancF p93 MR21
MAHONY-JONES,G.J.Capt 7-4-17 GL &RFC CR France285
MAHOOD,Charles Cleland T2Lt dow 16-9-16 9KOSB p102 CR France177
MAIBEN,W.SubCdr 2-3-15 IA S&TCps CR Asia60
MAIDEN,Albert Augustus T2Lt kia 16-9-16 6YLI p143 CR France329,dow
MAIDLOW,John Southern Maj dow 23-8-14 RFA p32 CR Belgium241
MAIL,Frank Oswald 2Lt kia 9-10-18 78RFA p32 CR France660
MAIN,Alfred Leonard Lt ded 3-10-19 2Worc p264 CR Staffs60,2Lt 5Bn
MAIN,Donald Alexander Mill.MC.Capt drd 6-9-18 6HLI p240 MR70 &CR Europe180,5-9-18 Ex9 att2/10RScots
MAIN,Eric Arthur 2Lt ded 26-2-18 6RRofCav attNSomYeo p24 CR France987
MAIN,George Ernest Lt kia 12-10-17 KOSB att6Bn p102 MR30
MAIN,John Capt dow 18-8-16 6ScotRif p224 CR France300
MAIN,John Alexander.MC.TLt kia 27-3-18 RE 278RlyCo p46 CR France174
MAIN,Percy Rowland 2Lt kld 28-9-16 15HantR attRFC p3&p121 CR Hamps9,23-9-16
MAINE,William John Samuel AssSurg drd 27-2-16 IMS RAMC p279 CR Kent8,W.J.C.
MAINPRISE,Bertie Wilmot.MIDx4 Maj kia 12-3-16 RE attHQBde p46 CR EAfrica56
MAINSTONE,James Francis 2LtACapt kia 4-10-17 1 att12Glouc p107 MR30
MAINWARING,Cyril Lyttleton Lt ded 16-2-19 RGA 422Bty p262 CR Surrey15,17-2-19
MAINWARING,Frank Harry George Carver Capt ded 6-1-19 3Co ofLondYeo att104MGC p187&204 CR France40
MAIR,Edward Millett 2Lt kia 3-9-16 3 att1CamH p168 MR21
MAIR,George Hay Lt ded 14-12-18 3RWFus attRSuss p98 CR Camb16
MAIR,John Gordon T2Lt dow 5-8-18 RE 150FC p47 CR France100
MAIR,William Craig.MC.Capt kia 22-3-18 4 att2RScotF p222 MR27
MAIS,Herbert Roxburgh.MID TLt dow 30-11-17 RE 70FC p47 CR France439
MAISEY,Albert Henry 2Lt dow 16-2-17 6Mddx p147 CR France164
MAISEY,Alfred George 2Lt kia 12-5-17 6RWSurr Inf p56 CR Belgium125 &CR France421
MAISH,William Edward.MC.T2Lt kia 12-10-17 27MGC p184
MAITLAND,Alexander 2Lt kia 20-5-17 9HLI p240 MR20
MAITLAND,Alexander McLean 2Lt kia 1-8-16 RE 1/2FC p210 CR France189
MAITLAND,Alfred Henry.Hon.Maj kia 19-9-14 1CamH p168 MR15,14-9-14
MAITLAND,Arthur Dudley TLt kia 1-7-16 13WYorks p82 CR France743,14 att16Bn
MAITLAND,Arthur James T2Lt kld 22-9-17 GL &RFC p10 CR Mddx5
MAITLAND,Edgar Francis Lt kia 24-9-17 6Manch p236 CR Belgium173
MAITLAND,Graham Macdonell 2Lt kia 26-1-16 1IrGds p53 MR29,Macdowall 1-11-14
MAITLAND,Henry Maitland.MC.TCapt ded 10-11-18 GL p191 CR France1848
MAITLAND,James Moule Hamilton T2Lt dow 23-4-17 2A&SH p173 CR France434
MAITLAND,John Dalrymple T2Lt kia 22-2-16 9WRid p116 MR29
MAITLAND,John Pelham Blanchard Capt ded 2-8-15 11YLI p143 CR Yorks321
MAITLAND,Keith Andrew Ramsay.MC&Bar.LtAMaj kia 4-10-17 A76RFA p32 CR Belgium12

MAITLAND,William Ebenezer 2Lt dow 24-12-14 3SfthH att2BlkW p165 CR France202
MAITLAND,William Renmure 2Lt kia 18-11-16 5Mddx attTMB p147 MR19
MAITLAND-ADDISON,Alec Arthur Creighton 2Lt dow 27-10-14 1ChesR p96 CR France102
MAITLAND-MAKGILL-CRICHTON,Charles Julian TMaj kia 25/27-9-15 10GordH p166 MR19
MAJOR,Arthur Oswald Capt kia 23-11-17 1/5SomLI p218 CR Palestine3
MAJOR,Charles William Wykeham Chap4Cl ded 19-3-19 RAChDept p199 CR Germany1
MAJOR,Cyril Birdee 2Lt kia 5-11-16 7EYorks p84 MR21 Bisdee
MAJOR,Harold TLt kld 19-10-15 14Mddx p147 CR Belgium82
MAJOR,Stanley T2Lt kia 3-3-17 3 att1EKent p57 CR France149
MAKANT,Angus Virtue Capt dow 14-3-15 5LNLancs p234 CR France922
MAKEHAM,Eric Noel T2Lt ded PoW 28-8-17 13Mddx p147 MR29,10-6-17
MAKIN,Stanley T2Lt kia 22-3-18 9YLI p143 MR27
MAKINNON,Charles Frank Capt mbk 14-6-19 SL att1/6KAR p257&p201,McKINNON ded
MAKINS,Geoffrey.MVO.Capt dow 23-8-15 3KRRC p151 CR France345
MAKINS,Hugh Capt dow 4-11-15 16LondR p249 CR Belgium2
MAKINSON,Frederick Valentine 2Lt kia 14-4-18 3Lpool p72 MR32
MALCOLM,Alan Alexander Lt kia 17-5-18 17Lancers &98RAF p23 MR20
MALCOLM,Albert Victor Sadler T2Lt kia 17-2-17 16 att11RFus p69 CR France314
MALCOLM,Archibald Houlder Lt kld 24-8-18 9HLI p240 CR France1186,kia
MALCOLM,Archibald Hugh T2Lt kia 16-5-17 1KOSB p102 MR20
MALCOLM,Geoffrey Cooper T2Lt kld 27-9-17 3YLI attRFC p10&p143,kia CR Essex73
MALCOLM,George John.MID TMaj kia 9-7-16 RFA attRFC p3&p32 CR France134
MALCOLM,Henry Alexander Drummond 2Lt dow 17-2-17 RFA Z33TMB p32 CRFrance624 Ex 2KEdwHorse
MALCOLM,James Waddell.MID 2Lt kia 12-7-15 5HLI p240 MR4
MALCOLM,John Evelyn LtACapt ded 19-2-19 RE 271RailCo p47 CR Belgium406
MALCOLM,Kenneth James Lt kia 19-2-18 2/20Lond p251 CR Palestine3
MALCOLM,Pulteney LtACapt kia 25-8-18 1GrenGds p50 CR France1487
MALCOLM,Robert James TCapt dow 15-7-16 2RScot p54 CR France23 true name STEWART,Malcolm Hector
MALCOLM,Sidney John TCapt kia 20-9-17 1/8A&SH p173 CR Belgium96,Sydney
MALCOLM,Stuart Renton Lt ded 22-11-18 RGA 38SB p40 CR France1725,39SB
MALCOLM,Thomas 2Lt dow 23-10-17 3 att18HLI p163 CR Belgium16
MALCOLM,William Aberdein Maj ded 3-10-15 RAMC att1/11Lond p253 CR Europe1
MALCOLM,William Noel 2Lt dow 12-6-15 RE 271RlyCoy p47 CR Europe7
MALCOLMSON,Hubert TLt&Adjt dow 16-9-16 6RIrReg p89 CR Eire185
MALCOLMSON,James Grant Capt ded 22-12-14 27/18Lond p250 CR Lond8
MALCOLMSON,John Joseph Maj ded 4-6-15 RFA p206 CR Hamps221
MALCOLMSON,Keith Grant Capt ded 30-8-21 RGA CR Lond8
MALCOLMSON,Thomas Stuart Capt kia 10-12-17 17RFA att15RFC p19&206 MR20
MALE,Arthur Ernest TLt ded 3-7-17 RMunstF att6ConnRgrs p175 CR France134,kldacc
MALE,Arthur Philip TLt kia 23-11-17 121MGC p184 MR17
MALEHAM,Edgar Hubert T2Lt dow 29-3-18 2 att9Y&L p159 CR France62,23-3-18
MALEHAM,Stewart TCapt kia 1-7-16 13Y&L p159 CR France802
MALET,Frank Louis TLt kia 4-6-15 12RWar att2Hants p65 MR4
MALET,Hugh Arthur Grenville Lt kia 18-4-15 2KOSB p102 MR29
MALEY,Frederick 2Lt kia 14-10-18 4WRid p227 CR France612
MALEY,J.Cdr 30-12-19 IOD MR43
MALIGNY,H.A.Lt kia 5-3-21 RASC CR Surrey16
MALINS,Edward Francis T2Lt dow 12-4-18 2SWBord p100 CR France25
MALKIN,James Andrew 2LtACapt kia 4-9-16 2BordR p117 MR21
MALKIN,Norman Harry T2Lt dow 14-5-17 12Y&L p159 CR France113
MALLALIEU,Joseph 2Lt dow 7-11-17 1/7WRid p228 CR France8,6-11-17
MALLALUE,Maxwell.MC.MID Capt kia 24-8-16 9KRRC p151 MR21
MALLAM,Clifford Angus.MC&Bar.LtTCapt dow 29-10-18 3 att5RBerks p139 CR France1277
MALLANDAINE,Herbert Ernest 2Lt kia 9-3-16 IARO att97Inf p279 MR38,8-3-16
MALLEN,William James T2Lt kia 16-8-17 11 att8RDubF p177 MR30
MALLETT,Eric Sydney 2Lt kia 1-7-16 1ELancs p111 MR21
MALLETT,Hubert.MIDx2 Lt ded 3-2-19 5ESurr p271 CR Lond4,Capt Ex RWSurr
MALLETT,Phillip Henry John.MC&Bar.LtACapt dow 12-11-18 1Glouc p107 CR France146,P.F.H.
MALLETT,William James 2Lt kia 21-3-18 2/4 O&BLI p231 MR27
MALLETT,William Victor Lancelot Lt kia 22-3-18 5ESurr p226 MR20

MALLEY,F.L.Lt 19-7-21 RDubF att2/1KAR CR EAfrica36
MALLEY-MARTIN,J.MC.2Lt kld 30-10-18 1/2BordR &RAF p117 CR France332
MALLINS,Claude Joseph O'Conor Lt kia 2-11-14 2ConnRgrs p172 MR29
MALLINSON,Charles Heathcote Capt dow PoW 26/27-6-18 11ELancsR p111 CR Germany3,26-6-18
MALLINSON,Eric Lt kia 7-7-16 3 att9WRid p116 CR France267
MALLINSON,John Whiteley.MID 2Lt kia 14-2-16 6RB attMGC p179&184 MR29
MALLINSON,Richard Capt kia 1-8-17 ChesR p96 MR29,Maj
MALLOCH,David TLt kld 14-9-16 RE SpecBde p47 CR France74,2Lt dedacc
MALLOCH,Lyon Robert MacGregor.MC.Capt kia 18-11-17 5ScotRif p224 CR Belgium72
MALLOCK,Charles Herbert.DSO.Maj dow 5-11-17 23RFA p32 CR Belgium18
MALLONEY,John Charles T2Lt kia 9-4-17 1 att26NumbF p62
MALLORY,John Charles 2Lt kia 9-4-17 1 att26NumbF p62 CR France265
MALONE,Brian Wilmot L'Estrange Lt kia 23-4-17 1Dev p77 MR20
MALONE,Briston Miniss 2Lt kia 16-8-17 9RIrF p171 MR30,Bristow
MALONE,Joseph James T2Lt kia 16-8-17 9RDubF p177 MR30
MALONE,M.P.SubCdr 4-3-19 IOD MR43 Ex ConnRgrs 6657
MALONE,Patrick Arthur 2Lt ded 13-2-19 RMunstF p266 CR Ireland12
MALONE,William Adolph 2Lt kia 16-5-17 13Ches p96 MR29,Adolphe
MALONEY,Francis Joseph ACapt dow 20-7-16 12RScot p54 CR France145
MALPAS,John Louis Lt kia 29-7-16 2SStaffs p122 MR21
MALPAS,Reginald Arthur 2LtTLt dow 18-11-17 3DorsR att7SomLI p124 CR Surrey160
MALPASS,Charles Edward.MC.ACapt kia 8-10-18 11RWKent att28Lond p141 CR France915
MALTBY,Alfred Henry 2Lt kld 4-6-18 GL &4RAF p191 MR20
MALTBY,Charles Robert Crighton TLt dow 27-8-16 12RB p179 CR France141
MALTBY,Charles Thomas T2Lt dow 27-3-18 Norf att7Suff p74 CR France62
MALTBY,E.W.Capt&QM 18-1-20 2/1LancHuss CR Lancs343
MALTBY,Gerald Capt ded 9-7-19 IARO attS&TCps p279 MR65,9-6-19
MALTBY,Phyllis May Nurse ded 6-12-18 VAD CR Surrey160
MALTON,Michael Innes T2Lt kia 22-8-18 7EKent p57 CR France430
MALTON,Paul Locock 2Lt dow PoW 3-9-18 1DCLI p114 CR France1027
MAN,Frederic Cecil Lt ded 21-2-19 3Hamps att3GurkhaRif p121 CR Egypt15 2/5Hamps att2/3GRifs
MANBY-COLGRAVE,Gerald Thomas TLt dow 21-4-17 RASC attRGA 221SB p193 CR France53
MANCE,Henry Eric 2Lt kia 15-9-16 10RWSurr p56 MR21
MANDALL,Harry 2Lt ded 18-5-19 RE p262
MANDER,Alfred Ernest Capt kia 9-10-17 4WRid A'Coy p227 MR30
MANDER,D'Arcy Wentworth Maj kia 20-9-14 2DLI p161 CR France1329
MANDER,Thomas James 2Lt ded 9-11-18 IARO attDir of Lab p279 CR Asia82
MANDERS,George Benjamin TLt dow 24-4-16 66/4RFA 66Bty p32 CR Iraq5
MANDERS,Neville Col kia 7-8-15 RAMC p196 CR Gallipoli20,9-8-15 DDMS AnzacAMedServ
MANDERS,S.G.Capt ded 9-12-18 9RWFus &RAF p98
MANDERSON,Horace Leslie 2Lt kia 9-4-16 11 att6LNLancs p136 MR38
MANDEVILLE,Pierce Capt kia 28-9-16 5WYork p218 CR France383
MANDLESTAM,Joseph 2Lt ded 6-3-16 RE p262
MANFIELD,Neville Phillip Lt kia 9-9-16 4Nhants attRFC p19&234 MR20
MANFORD,Reginald Valentine Lt kia 8-8-18 59/18RFA p208 CR France196
MANGER,Eric 2Lt kia 10-7-17 2MGC Inf p184 MR31 &CR Belgium173
MANGER,Gerald T2Lt kia 21-3-18 2RGLI p201 MR30
MANGER,John Kenneth 2Lt kia 8-5-15 2NumbFus p62 MR29
MANGIN,Frederick Meredyth LtCol ded 31-12-18 RAMC p196 MR69
MANGIN,Reuben Addison.MM.T2Lt dow 7-5-18 2WYorks p82 CR France145,7-4-18
MANIFOLD,William Herbert 2Lt kia 26-4-17 15/36RFA p32 CR France265
MANISTY,Henry Scott.MC.Lt kia 16-10-17 RE 18CpsHQ p47 CR Belgium11/5,14-10-17
MANKELOW,Archibald Henry.MC.Lt kia 14-5-15 1A 1/39GarhwalRif p280 CR France631
MANKTELOW,Walter Stanley T2Lt kia 21-3-18 2 att2/5ELancs p111 MR27
MANLEY,Charles Percival Henry.MC.T2Lt dow 4-10-18 8RWKent p141 CR France34
MANLEY,D.H.George Capt kia 6-11-17 1/6RWFus CR Palestine1
MANLEY,George Sydney 2Lt ded 30-11-18 3EYorks p84
MANLEY,Hamilton Douglas T2Lt kia 27-3-18 7RSuss p119 MR27
MANLEY,John 2LtTCapt kia 18-9-17 19RFC p10 CR France285
MANLEY,John Dundas 2Lt kia 26-9-14 RE SR p47 CR France1328
MANLEY,John Hunter Capt kia 9-1-17 IARO att59Rif p280 CR Iraq5

MANLEY,Terence Wood T2Lt kld 6-3-18 RFC p16 CR Kent180,2-3-18
MANLOVE,Leonard Cecil Tong 2Lt kia 3-8-16 3 att2Hamps p121 CR Belgium47
MANLY,Eric Cecil John Lt kia 18-7-17 B82RFA p32 CR Belgium29
MANN,Agnes Greig SNurse drd 10-4-17 QAIMNS p200 CR France85
MANN,Alexander David 2Lt kia 20-11-17 1/6SfthH p241 CR France1498
MANN,Alexander James T2Lt dow 10-4-17 8BlkW p129 CR France95
MANN,Arthur Longbottom TCapt kia 30-3-18 RE 328Co p47 MR27
MANN,Basil Stainforth Capt kia 27-11-17 2/6WRid p227 MR17
MANN,Charles Frederick Lt ded 4-12-18 22Lond CR Essex73
MANN,Charles Humphrey Dalla T2Lt kia 30-9-16 21 att13DLI p161 MR21
MANN,Charles Julian Lt kia 3-10-18 20Huss p23 CR France375
MANN,Frederick Christmas 2Lt kia 12-3-15 1NStaffs p157 CR France681
MANN,George Bertram 2Lt dow 29-9-19 9RFus CR Ches97
MANN,George William TCapt kia 24-7-18 MGC F'HB p184 CR Belgium16
MANN,Henry William.MID Lt kia 30-3-18 178RFA p32 CR France504,Harry
MANN,Horace Lt ded 25-12-18 3DorsR att1KAR p124&202 CR EAfrica86
MANN,Horace Walpole T2Lt kia 10-8-15 6LNLancs p136
MANN,Horatio Geoffrey Cornwallis.MC.2Lt kia 17-7-17 6RWKent p141 MR20
MANN,Horatio Gordon Capt kia 10-8-15 6LNLancs p136 CR Gallipoli19
MANN,Hugh Wallace TCapt dow 12-11-17 5CamH p168 CR France13
MANN,James Saumarez.MID Capt kia 22-7-20 6RWKent attPoliticDept CR Iraq8
MANN,John Anderson.MC.Lt kia 9-8-16 5ScotRif &RFCp224 CR France525
MANN,John Charles.MC.MID ACapt kia 26-9-17 2RWFus p98 MR30
MANN,John William 2Lt dow 22-8-18 4EKent p212 CR France209,7Bn
MANN,Lawrence John T2Lt kia 12-7-17 16NumbF p62 MR31
MANN,Nevill Swire Maj dow 12-4-16 LNLancs att6Bn p136 CR Iraq5
MANN,Osric Alwyn T2Lt kia 5-4-16 10RLancs p59 MR38,Lt
MANN,Percy Charles T2Lt kia 31-7-17 KRRC att17Bn p151 MR29
MANN,Robert Lamplough Lt kia 23-12-14 7DragGds p255 MR22,21-12-14
MANN,Robert Leonard 2Lt kia 9-10-16 3 att16RWFus p98&257 CR Belgium73
MANN,Robert Mathers.VD.TMaj ded 20-11-17 GL &ScotRif p191 CR Scot795
MANN,Stanley Walter 2Lt kia 1-11-16 9RFC p3 MR20
MANN,Stephen William.MM.T2Lt kia 27-3-19 GL att2Lond p191,255&257 MR7 &CR Europe179,kldacc
MANN,Theodore John Lewis 2Lt dow 28-4-18 173RFA p32 CR France142,Lt
MANN,Thomas Edward 2Lt kia 30-7-18 B10RFA p208 CR France865,31-7-18
MANN,William George 2Lt kia 28-11-17 GL &7RFC p10 CR Belgium162
MANNERS,Cecil Frederick T2Lt ded 17-6-17 692RASC MTC p193 MR43
MANNERS,Henry Fairholm T2Lt kia 28-4-17 7Norf p74 MR20
MANNERS,Hugh T2Lt kia 24-4-17 52MGC p184 MR20
MANNERS,James Herbert T2Lt ded 28-6-17 RE p47 CR France8
MANNERS,John Neville.Hon.Lt kia 1-9-14 2GrenGds p50 MR15
MANNERS,Lord Robert William Orlando.CMG.DSO.LtCol kia 11-9-17 Cmdg10NumbF p62 CR Belgium19
MANNERS,Richard Henry Hedges Maj ded 27-11-19 1A 106Pnrs att107 p280 MR
MANNERS-SMITH,Frederick Maj dow 3-11-14 1A 2/3GurkhaRif p280 CR France80
MANNING,George 2Lt kia 28-1-16 ESurr p113 MR29,19-10-14
MANNING,George Alfred Lt kia 26-9-17 RE 438FC p210 MR30
MANNING,John Carlton T2Lt dow 17-2-17 3 att10Ches p96 CR France285
MANNING,Nicol Page 2Lt kia 6-10-18 4RScot p211 CR France1723
MANNING,Robert Charles.DSO.MC.TMaj dow 6-9-18 RE 170TC p47 CR France
MANNING,Victor Lionel T2Lt kia 23-3-18 25MGC Inf p184 CR France307,dow
MANNOCK,Edward.VC.DSO.MC.Maj kia 26-7-18 RE &85RAF p47 MR20
MANOUKIAN,Zavern T2Lt kia 3-9-18 LancF att2/5Bn p93 CR France106
MANSBRIDGE,William Kenneth Elliott 2Lt kia 4-10-17 4Lond p246 MR30
MANSEL,Jestyn Llewelyn Capt kia 20-12-14 7DGds p255 MR22
MANSEL,John Delalynde Col ded 15-12-15 RemountService RB p24 CR Dorset102,11-12-15
MANSEL-CAREY,Spencer Lort Maunsel T2Lt dow 24-2-16 8 att9Dev p77 CR France22,Mansel kia
MANSEL-HOWE,Charles Iorworth Lt kia 9-8-18 23Lond p252 MR16
MANSEL-PLEYDELL,Edmund Morton Lt kia 12-3-15 3Dors attWorc p124 MR29
MANSEL-PLEYDELL,Henry Grove Morton.MC.Lt kia 17-5-16 1Dors p124 CR France1504
MANSEL-PLEYDELL,John Morton T2Lt dow 22-9-16 A107RFA p32 CR France3
MANSELL,Charles Paul T2Lt kia 3-9-16 16RWar p65 MR21
MANSELL,Harry Champion T2Lt kia 30-6-17 15MGC p184 MR29
MANSELL,Leslie Wyndham 2Lt kia 20-4-17 DerbyYeo p203 MR19,22-4-17
MANSELL,Walter Reynolds Capt dow 16-4-18 5SStaffs p229 CR France40,2Bn

MANSELL,William Du Pre TCapt kia 12-10-16 2LancF p93 MR21,MANSEL

MANSELL,William Stanley 2Lt kia 11-9-17 3ESurrR &22RFC p10&113 CR France705,1RFC

MANSER,William Edward Maj ded 8-4-17 RE p47 MR40

MANSERGH,Harry Read TLt dow 12-11-16 1 att1/9Lpool p72 CR France40

MANSERGH,John Loftus Otway Lt kia 25-9-15 RWar att2Bn p65 MR19

MANSERGH,Wilmsdorff George Lt kia 26-8-15 Manch p155 MR15,26-8-14

MANSFIELD,Eric Oswald T2Lt kia 24-8-18 8KRRC p151 CR Belgium11

MANSFIELD,George 2Lt kia 22-3-18 1Leic p88 CR France438

MANSFIELD,George Stanley 2Lt kia 22-3-18 1/4 att1EYork p219 MR27

MANSFIELD,Gerald Turner T2Lt kia 15-9-16 11RWKent p141

MANSFIELD,Harold T2Lt dow 12-4-16 1Ches p96 CR France40

MANSFIELD,Harold Barton T2Lt kia 13-11-16 10RDubF p177 CR France220

MANSFIELD,Harold Lawrie 2Lt dow 3-5-17 18WYorks p82 MR20

MANSFIELD,Harry John T2Lt kia 27-9-18 15TankCps p188 CR France357

MANSFIELD,John Roy 2Lt kia 18-6-17 RGA 121HB p40 CR Belgium29

MANSFIELD,Maurice Charles Lt ded 11-2-19 SL Intel Petrograd p268 MR70 &CR Europe180,11-2-16

MANSFIELD,Oscar Marshall T2Lt kia 14-3-17 2Leic p88 MR38

MANSFIELD,Reginald Horace T2Lt dow 1-10-18 121/27RFA p32 CR France512

MANSHIP,Charles Edward 2Lt kia 24-7-18 15N&D p255 MR30

MANSON,Bruce Edward Alexander Maj kia 3-11-14 IA 61Pnrs p280 MR47 Capt

MANSON,Charles Claude Edmonstoune.MC.2Lt kia 4-12-15 IARO att1/4GurkhaRif p280 MR4

MANSON,Gerald Patrick.MC.TCapt kia 24-8-18 6SomLI p80 MR30

MANSON,John Cochrane T2Lt kia 7-7-16 9RFus p69 CR France393

MANSON,Richard 2Lt kia 1-10-18 4GordH p242 CR France359,dow

MANTERFIELD,John Thomas 2Lt kia 21-9-18 Lincs attMGC p75&p184 CR France212

MANTLE,Alexander Lt kia 23-5-17 7Lond p247 CR France568

MANTON,Thomas T2Lt dow 22-10-17 7Y&L p159 CR Belgium25

MANTZ,Victor Frank T2Lt kia 25-10-18 1EssR p132 CR France1480

MANUEL,Vane Carrington T2Lt kld 18-12-17 GL &56RFC p10 CR Essex48

MANWARING,Jack Lancaster.MC.2Lt ded 15-11-16 3 att9RWFus p98 CR Kent279

MAPLES,Kenneth James Capt kia 16-5-15 3 att2SStaffs p122 MR22

MAPLES,William Evelyn MajALtCol kia 14-12-16 WRid att6NLancs p116 MR38,15-12-16

MAPLESON,Gerald Horsley T2Lt kia 26-4-17 2 att2/4RWSurr p56 CR Palestine8

MAPPLEBECK,Gilbert William.DSO.LtTCapt kld 24-8-15 Lpool &RFC p1&72

MAPPLEBECK,Gordon Whitfield ACapt dow 30-7-17 NStaffs att4Bn p157 CR Belgium15,4 att1Bn

MAQUIRE,Maurice 2Lt kia 21-8-18 3Ches p96

MARCH,Arthur John Jethro T2Lt ded 24-10-18 RE 50DivSig p47 CR France146

MARCH,Joseph Cyril Capt kia 14-1-20 IARO att2/5GurkhaRif p280 MR43

MARCH,William Francis George 2Lt dow PoW 24-10-17 GL &23RFC p10 CR Belgium140,Lt

MARCH-PHILLIPS,Spencer Leslie T2Lt kia 20-11-17 1TankCps p188 MR17

MARCHANT,Arthur Charles AssSurg kia 11-3-16 IA IndSubMedDept p280 CR EAfrica56

MARCHANT,Charles G.Capt kld 3-5-15 20Lond p251 CR France765,Silverlock

MARCHANT,Charles Stewart 2Lt kia 4-6-17 5 att9RDubF p177 CR Belgium182

MARCHANT,Charles Victor 2Lt kia 30-11-17 15Lond p249 MR17

MARCHANT,Francis George Wake 2Lt dow 25-10-16 RWKent &3RFC p3&141 CR France833,22-10-16

MARCHANT,Francis Scott Lt kia 22-3-18 5BordR att2TankCps p189&228 MR27 CR France307

MARCHANT,Frederick Louis 2Lt kld 20-11-17 7EssR p232 MR17

MARCHANT,Godfrey Maj ded 17-6-19 IA 29Lancers p280 MR43

MARCHANT,Harold Edgar 2Lt kia 5-6-16 Dev p77 CR France251

MARCHANT,Hugh Stephen Lt kia 7-1-16 1/5EKent p213 CR Iraq5

MARCHANT,Richard Henry 2Lt kia 26-1-16 9ESurr p113 CR Belgium125

MARCHANT,Sydney T2Lt dow 6-7-16 12NumbF p62 CR France119

MARCHETTI,Alexander Lt kia 15-3-16 5 att2RB p179 CR France348

MARCHETTI,Eustie 2Lt kia 8-11-16 149RFA p32 CR France374

MARCHMENT,William James LtACapt kia 4-11-18 RFA X32TMB p32 CR France190

MARDEN,Arthur Cecil 2Lt ded 11-12-17 RGA 117HB p40 CR Belgium101

MARE,Arthur Llewellyn TLtAMaj kia 27-5-18 33RFA p32 MR18

MARGERISON,Caleb Walden.MID TLt dow 6-7-16 11BordR p117 CR France44

MARGERISON,Thomas 2Lt kia 13-4-17 HuntsCycBn attRFC p19&253 CR France604

MARGERRISON,James T2Lt kia 14-8-18 10Yorks att150TMB p91 CR France40

MARGESSON,Edward Cuninghame Maj kia 25-4-15 2SWBord p100 MR4

MARGETSON,Emil Alexander 2Lt kld 16-6-17 GL &RFC p10 CR Mddx13

MARGETTS,Percy Alexander T2Lt kia 5-12-15 9 att6Lincs p75 CR Gallipoli4

MARGOLIOUTH,Alfred Henry 2Lt kia 2-4-17 5YLI &RFC p19&235 CR France924

MARILLIER,Frederick Charles Jennens 2Lt kia 30-10-14 2RSuss p119 MR29

MARILLIER-MILLER,Ralph T2Lt kia 30-7-16 25Manch p155

MARINDIN,Henry Eden Allan,MC T2Lt dow 8-10-18 KSLI att1/4Bn p145 CR France80

MARION,Donald 2Lt kia 9-5-15 SfthH p165

MARION-CRAWFORD,Harold Francis 2Lt kld 16-4-15 IrGds p53 CR France279

MARJORIBANKS,Alexander Capt&Adjt ded 28-9-14 52Sikhs attNWaziristanMil MR43

MARJORIBANKS,Marmaduke Edward 2Lt kia 21-11-17 1NumbF p62 CR France563

MARK,Hannah Dunlop Nurse 10-10-18 TFNS CR Wales4

MARK,James Wilson 2Lt dow 7-8-17 2RIrReg p89 CR Belgium7

MARKER,Raymond John.DSO.LtCol ded 13-11-14 GrenGds Staff p51 CR Devon87

MARKES,Thomas Maxwell 2Lt kia 1-10-17 1RLancs p59 CR Belgium23

MARKES,John Carlon.MIDx2 Maj kia 19-7-16 Leinst p174 CR France513 Ex LancF

MARKHAM,John Addis Capt kia 7-5-15 1EYorks p84 CR Belgium451

MARKHAM,Montagu Wilfred 2Lt kia 29-8-17 2ScotGds p52 MR30

MARKHAM,Ronald Anthony.MIDx2 Maj dow 26-10-14 2CldGds p51 CR Leic117,25-10-14

MARKHAM,Walter Henry James T2Lt dow PoW 27-3-18 NumbF att1/5Bn p62 MR27

MARKHAM-ROSE,Kenneth Lt kia 3-5-15 Ess attWAFF p132&201,3-5-16 CR WAfrica23

MARKS,Arthur Sampson Lt ded 25-10-18 Ex GL p267

MARKS,C.H. LtTCapt kia 23-10-15 Middx &RFC p1&147 CR France1266

MARKS,Charles Bernard.MC.T2Lt kia 23-10-18 ESurr att8Bn p113 CR France229

MARKS,Craig Royston T2Lt kld 3-5-17 GL &RFC p10 CR Lincs53

MARKS,George Frederick Handel LtCol ded 3-5-15 RAMC p196 MR65

MARKS,Horace Owen TLt kia 29-10-16 111RFA p32 CR France150,C110RFA

MARKS,Isidor David T2Lt kia 10-7-16 11WRid p116 CR France267

MARKS,James Albert 2Lt kia 25-2-17 NStaffs p157 MR38

MARKS,James Ganly Lt kia 23-3-18 5SfthH p241 CR France245

MARKS,John Hyman TLt kia 24-10-18 15DLI p161 CR France1477

MARKS,Nathaniel Capt ded 27-7-18 3/24Lond p252 CR Mddx40,Maj

MARKS,Philip Moses 2Lt kia 29-9-15 4 att5Middx p147 MR29

MARKS,S.A.Lt 16-2-20 RE CR Lancs9

MARKUS,Eugene Bernays.MC.2Lt dow 5-4-17 1RScotF p95 CR France40

MARKWICK,Frederick Thomas T2Lt kia 6-8-15 12 att1Ess p132 MR4

MARKWICK,William Percival Lt kia 5-9-18 5Norf p216 CR France511

MARLER,Wilfred Earlstone 2Lt dow 4-5-17 1SomLI p80 CR France95

MARLEY,Grace Margaret Prob 12-10-16 TFNS 2S GenHosp CR Wilts100

MARLEY,William Capt kia 23-4-17 5DLI B'Coy p238&239,6Bn CR France162

MARLIN,Harold James 2Lt kia 12-4-17 3SStaffs att1Lincs p122

MARLOR,Eric 2Lt kia 3-5-17 6WRid p227 CR France1489

MARLOW,Albert Leopold Craddock T2Lt dow 4-4-17 KRRC att10Bn p151 CR France364

MARLOW,Charles Dwyer T2Lt kia 17-8-17 8RDubF p177 MR30

MARLOW,George 2Lt dedacc 26-8-16 6LancF p221 CR Ches123

MARLOW,John Maj ded 29-2-16 3RIrReg p89

MARLOW,Kenneth Conway Lt ded 3-2-18 8RFus p263 CR Camb16,MARLOWE 3-12-18

MARLOW,Percy 2LtTCapt dow 7-6-17 Wilts att6Bn p153 CR Belgium102

MARLOW,Stanley John Lt kia 19-4-17 1/4Nhampt p234 CR Palestine8

MARLOWE,Cecil Arthur T2Lt dow 18-10-18 1/2Yorks att1/7WYorks p91 CR France34

MARMION,M.Sister ded 25-1-19 QAIMNS p200 CR Lond9

MARNER,George Lionel Stuart Lt kia 8-4-17 10Leic att2Bn B'Coy p88 MR38,Capt

MARNER,T.Cdr 24-5-19 IA OrdDept CR India164

MARNHAM,Hugh Cecil 2Lt kia 22-8-16 SussYeo attRFC p19&205 CR France727

MARNOCH,Margaret Bella SNurse 13-11-18 TFNS CR Scot333

MARONA,Charles Antonio RevChap ded 28-2-15 Suss RGA p271 CR Sussex134

MARQUARD,John TLtACapt kia 23-8-18 13RFus p69 CR France518

MARR,Frederick Sidney.MC.TLtACapt kia 30-8-17 B47RFA p32 CR Belgium15

MARR,Hugh Boyd 2Lt kia 16-12-16 19Lond p250 CR Belgium127

MARR,James Scott TCapt kia 18-11-16 17HLI p163 MR21

MARRABLE,Edmund Douglas Lt ded 25-4-18 1105RFA &RAF p208 CR Kent193,kld

MARRIOTT,Arthur Pelham.MC.LtACapt kia 7-4-17 11RFA 85Bty p32 CR France12

MARRIOTT,Frederick Ernest T2Lt kia 30-7-15 7RB p179 MR29
MARRIOTT,Geoffrey Vaughan 2Lt kia 22-4-18 N&D att1Bn p134 MR27
MARRIOTT,George Edward Joseph Capt ded 6-7-17 1/6LancF p271 CR France755
MARRIOTT,Herbert Norman TCapt kia 13-11-16 12EYorks p84 CR France1890
MARRIOTT,Hugh Digby T2Lt kia 9-10-15 15RB p179 CR Belgium84
MARRIOTT,John Douglas 2Lt kia 26-9-17 1ScotRif p103 CR Belgium112
MARRIOTT,John Francis Laycock 2Lt ded 26-1-15 7DCLI p114 CR Hamps1
MARRIOTT,Joseph Percy SubCdr ded 17-7-17 IA Cps of MilStaffClerks p280
MARRIOTT,K.M.H.Lt kia 28-9-18 1/2WRid &RAF p116
MARRIOTT,Norman Clarke Capt kia 17-8-17 5Leic p220 MR19
MARRIOTT,Osborne Delano TLtACapt kia 27-8-17 8WRid p116 MR30
MARRIOTT,Richard Henry.MC.Lt kia 18-9-16 KSLI p145 CR France374
MARRIOTT,Stanley George T2Lt kia 21-10-16 RE 2FC p47 CR France374
MARRIOTT,W.T.Maj ded 26-12-15 16DLI p265
MARRIOTT-WATSON,Richard Brereton.MC.Lt kia 24-3-18 2RIrRif p170 MR27
MARRIS,Horace Frost.MC.TLt dow 12-12-17 RE 76FC p47 CR France446
MARROW,Edward Armfield Capt kia 25-4-15 1KOSB p102 CR Gallipoli6
MARRS,Frederick Mallinson 2Lt kia 4-3-17 1Worc p109 MR21
MARSDEN,G.DSO.Capt 24-9-16 12Ches CR Mddx26
MARSDEN,Harold 2Lt dow 14-8-17 6 att1/8Lpool p215 CR France134
MARSDEN,Harold 2Lt ded 5-6-18 8WRid p116,257&264,3Bn CR Yorks375
MARSDEN,Herbert William 2Lt dow 11-9-18 1/4LNLanc p234 CR France106
MARSDEN,Humphrey Miller 2Lt kia 11-10-18 7WRid A'Coy p228 CR France612
MARSDEN,James Alfred Capt kia 21-4-18 RE p210 CR France300
MARSDEN,John Horace.MC.Capt kia 27-4-17 6N&D p233 CR France1495
MARSDEN,John William 2Lt kia 20-11-17 2/5LancF p221 MR21
MARSDEN,Morris James T2Lt kia 20-9-17 214MGC Inf p184 MR30
MARSDEN,Philip Sidney Lt kia 30-5-17 9Manch p237 CR France905
MARSDEN,Reginald Lt kia 4-6-15 8Manch p237 MR4
MARSDEN,Wallis Austin Jonathan Lt dow 20-7-17 RFA p208 CR Wales251
MARSDEN,W.C.Capt 19-12-20 RAMC CR Hereford/Worc110
MARSDEN-SMEDLEY,George Futvoye 2Lt kia 18-8-16 5RB p179 MR21 3Bn
MARSH,Alford Stanley TCapt kia 6-1-16 8SomLI p80 CR France922,Alfred 5-1-16
MARSH,Bertie Cecil Capt gunshotWound 15-12-19 IA 1/69Punjabis p280 MR43 Ex 8Ches
MARSH,Charles Frederick William ACapt kia 22-9-18 12Ches p96 MR37
MARSH,Charles Walter Brockwell TLt kia 13-10-15 6EKent p57 MR19
MARSH,Clarence Eric Lt ded 31-10-18 RE p271 CR Staffs52
MARSH,Cuthbert Alban 2Lt dow 24-6-18 SLancs att42RAF p125 CR France31,dedacc
MARSH,Douglas Charles Earle 2Lt dow 8-4-18 6DragGds p21 CR France145,11-4-18
MARSH,Edward Waters Harbin Capt&Adjt drd 30-12-15 IA 13Rajputs att6SLancs p280 MR41
MARSH,Francis Bedford 2Lt dow 5-10-16 4RWSurr attMGC p187&212 CR France177
MARSH,Frederick Courtney Maj kia 7-8-15 BordR att6Bn p117 MR4 Francis Courteney
MARSH,Gilbert Howe Maxwell Capt kia 1-11-14 IA 41Dogras p280 CR France80
MARSH,Harold 2Lt kia 4-10-18 5 att3RFus p69 CR France234
MARSH,Harry Victor T2Lt dow 22-10-16 8Norf p74 CR France59
MARSH,Henry Francis Freke.MC.Capt&Adjt dow 2-2-17 IA 1/2GurkhaRif p280 CR Iraq5
MARSH,Henry Herbert TLt kia 12-2-16 10WelshR p127 CR France727,2Lt
MARSH,Henry Herbert Stanley Maj dow 2-4-15 RE 4FC p209 CR France80
MARSH,Henry Sidney 2Lt kia 13-11-16 78RFA p32 CR France430
MARSH,John Lt ded PoW 23-10-18 1WorcYeo p206 CR Iraq8
MARSH,John Edward Joseph 2Lt kia 24-9-17 1Camb p245 MR30
MARSH,John Lockwood.MID Capt kia 16-10-15 1/4Y&L p238 CR Belgium23
MARSH,John Theodore Templeman 2Lt dow 28-6-18 D15RFA p32 CR France31
MARSH,Joseph T2Lt kia 23-11-17 15RIrRif p170 MR17
MARSH,Nicholas Clayton T2Lt kia 25-9-15 16Lpool p72 CR France163,1Bn
MARSH,Philip Everard Graham.MC.Capt kld 20-12-18 RASC &RAF p193 CR Essex10
MARSH,Ralph Hedley T2Lt kia 12-4-18 7RWKent p141 MR27
MARSH,Robert Cecil T2Lt dow 19-9-18 2MGC p184 CR France40,17-9-18
MARSH,Robert Neville Caldicot 2Lt kia 3-7-16 3KOSB attMGC Inf p102 CR France1012,1Bn
MARSH,Victor Braine T2Lt kia 3-9-16 6 O&BLI p130 CR France513
MARSH,William Bernard T2Lt kia 21-3-18 12NumbF att1Lincs p62 MR27
MARSH,William John Grimstead Lt dow 7-11-17 IA 127Baluchis att2/124 p280 CR Iraq8

MARSH,Zacheus Stanley T2Lt kia 10-10-17 GL &52RFC p10 CR France1361
MARSHALL,Albert 2Lt ded 12-6-19 RFA p32 MR65
MARSHALL,Albert Herbert Bathurst T2Lt kia 22-5-18 GL att3RB p191 CR France81,Alfred Lt
MARSHALL,Alexander Balfour 2Lt kia 14-4-16 3ScotRif att5ConnRgrs p103 MR
MARSHALL,Allan Gow TCapt kia 12-2-17 17HLI p163 CR France803
MARSHALL,Ambrose 2Lt kia 15-4-17 4Beds att1Hereford p252 CR Franmce644
MARSHALL,Andrew Fairlie Wilson 2Lt ded PoW 26-9-18 10EYorks p84 CR Germany3
MARSHALL,Archibald James 2Lt kia 26-10-17 LNLancs att2/5Bn p136 MR30
MARSHALL,Arthur Norris 2Lt kia 31-7-16 1Beds p86 MR21
MARSHALL,Arthur Raymond 2LtACapt&Adjt dow 2-2-18 RGA 34HAG p40 CR France145
MARSHALL,Augustus de la Pere 2Lt kia 9-5-15 8ELancs p111 MR32,22-5-15
MARSHALL,Bernard Gouldsmith 2Lt kia 5-4-16 1Nhants p137 CR France551
MARSHALL,Bernard Sanderson.MC.Lt kia 7-6-17 GL &20RFC p10 MR20
MARSHALL,Cecil Clyde 2Lt kia 24-6-17 RGA 21SB p40 CR Belgium1
MARSHALL,Charles Bertram Capt drd 13-8-15 RAMC p254 MR4
MARSHALL,Charles Samuel T2Lt dow 2-4-18 1Suff GarBn p78 CR France65
MARSHALL,Claud T2Lt kia 27-7-17 7SStaffs p122&p257,Claude CR Belgium73
MARSHALL,David.MC.2Lt kia 13-5-17 2/5LancF p221 CR France106
MARSHALL,Donald Ewan 2Lt kia 8-8-17 4WYorks &18RFC p10&p82 CR France201,7-8-17
MARSHALL,Douglas Cargill Lt kia 28-6-15 LancF p93 MR4
MARSHALL,Dudley 2Lt kia 26-9-17 6 att4RFus p69 MR30
MARSHALL,Duke 2Lt dow 22-2-19 A159RFA p32 CR Surrey1
MARSHALL,Edward Leslie.MC&Bar.TCapt dow 1-9-18 9RInnisF p105 CR France324
MARSHALL,Ernest William.MC.LtACapt kia 22-4-18 3SomLI p80 CR France98,1Bn
MARSHALL,Evelyn Saffery.MIDx2 TCapt dow 6-4-16 9RWar D'Coy p65 MR38
MARSHALL,Francis Capt dow 30-9-14 1Lpool p72 CR France473
MARSHALL,Frank TCapt kia 17-3-16 24Manch p155 CR France370
MARSHALL,Frederick Guy Lt kia 22-3-15 GrenGds p50 CR France279
MARSHALL,George Garth Lt kia 4-11-14 11Huss p22 CR Belgium57
MARSHALL,George Leonard Lt dow 26-9-15 3Lincs p75 CR France254,2Bn
MARSHALL,Harry T2Lt dow 5-11-18 1/5Lpool p72 CR France769
MARSHALL,Harold.MC.LtCol ded 10-9-18 7Hamp Cmdg1/4RFus p229 CR Hamps22
MARSHALL,Harold Sanders 2Lt kld 31-1-18 6NStaffs attRFC p19&238 CR Staff
MARSHALL,Harry TLt kia 30-9-18 15LancF p93 CR France376
MARSHALL,Harry Cecil T2Lt kld 23-12-17 GL &RFC p10 CR Surrey91
MARSHALL,Henry T2Lt kia 1-8-18 7RWSurr p56 CR France116
MARSHALL,Henry Turnbull Maj ded 21-9-15 IA 1Brahmans p280 MR43
MARSHALL,Herbert T2Lt kia 13-4-17 10WYorks p82 MR20
MARSHALL,Herbert William Hare TLt kld 26-8-17 GL &RFC p10 CR Somerset
MARSHALL,Hubert Graham Hamilton T2Lt kia 2-9-18 TankCps p188 CR France427
MARSHALL,James Neville.VC.MC&Bar.LtCol 4-11-18 IrGds att16LancF CR France1479
MARSHALL,Jenner Stephen Chance 2Lt dow 21-10-14 2 O&BLI p130 CR Belgium57,23-10-14
MARSHALL,John Lt drd 15-4-17 RAMC p196 MR35
MARSHALL,John TLt kia 18-9-18 15WYorks p82 CR France285,Capt
MARSHALL,John Lt kia 24-10-18 4BlkW p230 CR France1258
MARSHALL,John Arthur Lt kia 6-4-17 HuntsCycBn att45RFC p19&253 CR Belgium406
MARSHALL,John Edward Capt kia 30-3-15 1DCLI p114 CR Belgium17
MARSHALL,John Hamilton T2Lt kia 23-10-16 8ELancs p111 MR21
MARSHALL,John Morice Maitland Lt dow 23-10-15 4Ess p232 CR Gallipoli18
MARSHALL,John Neville.VC.MC.LtALtCol kia 4-11-18 IrGds att16LancF p53
MARSHALL,John Percival Lt dow 4-11-17 B282RFA p32 CR Belgium20,D'Bty
MARSHALL,John Willoughby Hadfield 2Lt kia 21-3-18 3Y&L p159 MR20
MARSHALL,John Woodall.MC.TLt kia 1-7-16 27NumbF p62 CR France267
MARSHALL,Laurance Herbert T2Lt dow 22-4-18 RE 9FC p47 CR France145
MARSHALL,Louis 2Lt kia 23-11-17 GL &65RFC p10 MR20
MARSHALL,Mary P.MID SNurse kia 12-3-17 QAIMNS p200 CR Greece9,Bethia
MARSHALL,Matthew 2Lt kld 11-8-18 6RScot p211 CR France360,kia
MARSHALL,Philip Spencer Lt kia 15-8-17 B3/307RFA p208 CR Belgium10
MARSHALL,Robert Burnaby.MID Lt dow 14-9-19 1ESurr p255 MR70
MARSHALL,Robert Wilson 2Lt kia 27-5-18 7 att1A&SH p243 CR Palestine9,29-5-18

MARSHALL,Roger 2Lt kia 20-9-14 2DLI p161 MR15
MARSHALL,Roger Charles Lt ded 7-1-18 RFA p208 CR Camb97
MARSHALL,Stanley 2Lt dow 18-4-18 7LancF p256 CR France716
MARSHALL,Sydney James T2Lt kia 8-8-18 3RRofCav att15Huss p23 CR France649,Lt
MARSHALL,Theodore Samuel Simon 2Lt ded 31-7-17 RE p271 CR Cornwall140
MARSHALL,Thomas Frederick T2Lt kia 30-10-17 1ESurr p113 MR30
MARSHALL,W.E.Lt ded 27-6-18 RASC &RAF p253
MARSHALL,Wilfred Lt kia 4-6-15 10Leics p88 MR4 Wilfrid
MARSHALL,William Lt kld 27-4-15 8DLI p239 MR29
MARSHALL,William Cornelius T2Lt kia 29-9-18 11Lpool p72 CR France666,4Bn
MARSHALL,William Gainer Lt dow 19-8-15 RFA p208 MR29
MARSHALL,William Macandrew Capt kia 19-3-18 IA 37Dogras att PoliticalDept p280 CR Iraq8
MARSHALL,William Robert 2Lt kia 12-10-16 3 att7Suff p78 CR France560,Rowland
MARSHALL,William Thomas.VC.LtCol 11-9-20 19Huss CR Scot127
MARSHALL-LEWIS,Frank TLt kia 13-9-17 GL &43RFC p10 CR France88,2Lt
MARSHAM,John Ralph Theodore 2Lt ded 27-2-19 LabCps Ex 11Worc p266 CR Hamps202
MARSHAM-TOWNSEND,Ferdinand 2Lt kia 16-5-15 ScotGds att2Bn p52 CR France279
MARSHFIELD,Harold William T2Lt kia 14-8-18 9ESurr att10RWSurr p113 CR Belgium11
MARSLAND,Eric Forbes 2Lt kia 7-10-16 6 att8RFus p69 MR21
MARSLAND,James Francis.MC.Lt dow 18-8-15 2Leinst p174 CR Belgium11,15-8-15
MARSLAND,John.MC.TLt kia 23-7-17 8RSuss p119 CR Belgium29
MARSLAND,Sydney Hammond TLt kia 7-8-15 11Manch p155 MR4
MARSON,Eric Newton T2Lt kia 10-8-15 9RWar p65 MR4
MARSON,John Charles 2Lt kia 8-8-15 8WelshR p127 MR4
MARSON,William Henry 2Lt kia 1-7-16 1/6NStaff p238 MR21
MARSTERS,John Victor Harold TLt kia 25-9-15 6KOSB p102 MR19
MARSTON,Arthur Bright T2Lt dow 14-7-16 7RWSurr p56 CR France402,kia
MARSTON,Felix William T2Lt dow 24-7-16 10RWar p65 CR France300
MARSTON,Guy Eric Millett TLt dow 9-2-18 1War attRE 130FC p47 CR France512
MARSTON,Percy Ingram T2Lt dow 20-9-17 22DLI p161 CR France297
MARTEN,Charles Peter TLtCol kia 15-9-16 1WYorks Cmdg18KRRC p82 CR France1890
MARTEN,Harold Charles Capt kia 7-8-15 7SStaffs p122 MR4
MARTEN,Henry Humphrey.MID 2Lt kia 13-8-15 6KRRC att2Manch p155 CR France699,Lt
MARTEN-SMITH,Cecil Eugene T2Lt kia 13-11-17 2RSuss p119 MR30
MARTHEWS,Leonard Gordon 2Lt dow PoW 20-4-18 2SLancs p125 CR Germany1 Lt 22-4-18
MARTIN,Albert Emanuel 2Lt kia 2-9-18 3 att2/4YLI p143 CR france617
MARTIN,Albert Trever de Monteval Maj dow 10-12-17 2WIndR att5WelshR p192 CR Palestine3,Trevor Morteval RWFus
MARTIN,Alfred T2Lt kia 3-9-16 1RWKent p141 CR France294
MARTIN,Alfred John T2Lt dow 2-8-16 7 att10ESurr p113 CR France44
MARTIN,Alfred Stanley 2Lt dow 26-10-18 6RWSurr p56 CR France146,24-10-18
MARTIN,Algernon 2Lt kia 30-7-18 70RFA p32 CR France865
MARTIN,Arthur 2Lt kia 28-6-16 10Mddx att 1/4Lancs p236 MR20
MARTIN,Arthur Derisley Capt kia 18-4-16 IA 36Sikhs att47 p280 MR38,17-4-16
MARTIN,Arthur Henry Col ded 27-8-18 RASC p253 CR Sussex111,24-8-18
MARTIN,Arthur Herbert T2Lt ded 5-3-19 RE 19RlyOpCo p262 CR Greece9
MARTIN,Arthur James Capt kld 15-5-15 8HLI p240 CR France727,kia
MARTIN,Arthur William 2Lt dedacc 14-3-17 61WelshR p127 CR Wales673
MARTIN,Aylmer Richard Sancton LtCol kia 9-5-15 RLancs p59 MR29
MARTIN,Basil Cuthbert Danvers 2Lt kia 4-6-15 13Worc p109 MR4
MARTIN,Bertram Charles.MM.T2Lt kia 13-4-17 4RFus p69 MR20
MARTIN,Cecil Hampson Capt kia 2-10-16 2ELancs p111 CR France423
MARTIN,Charles Andrew.MID Capt kia 6-12-15 6RDubF p177 MR37,8-12-15
MARTIN,Charles Herbert George Lt kld 2-5-15 1/3Mon p244 MR29 &CR Belgium453
MARTIN,Charles Stanley T2Lt kia 4-10-17 6Leic p88 CR Belgium165
MARTIN,Claude 2Lt kia 1-12-17 3CldGds p51 CR France662
MARTIN,Clive Victor LtCol kia 27-3-17 IA 29Lancers attStaff 10CpsHQ p280 CR Belgium11
MARTIN,Cuthbert Thomas.DSO&Bar.MIDx3 TBrigGen kia 27-5-18 HLI staff151InfBde p163 MR18
MARTIN,Cyril Basnett Lt kia 30-3-18 21Lond p251 CR Syria2
MARTIN,Cyril Stephen Bignold Capt dow 2-3-16 IA 90Punjabis p280 MR65,Cecil

MARTIN,David Archibald 2Lt kia 25-3-18 1 O&BLI p130 MR38
MARTIN,Douglas Bain 2Lt dow 9-10-18 C52RFA p32 CR France113
MARTIN,Douglas Francis de Renzy 2Lt kia 13-4-17 1NumbF p62 MR20
MARTIN,Duncan Lenox TCapt kia 1-7-16 9Dev p77 CR France330
MARTIN,Edward James T2Lt dow 21-12-17 att1/4SfthH p165CR France512
MARTIN,Edward Nugent Meredyth 2Lt kia 30-9-16 5Lancers RoO attMGC Cav p22 CR France630
MARTIN,Edward William Sidney.MID TCapt dow 16-2-17 RAMC att9Worc p196 CR Iraq5
MARTIN,Edwin John 2Lt kia 4-9-18 1Lond p245 CR Belgium89
MARTIN,Eldred Joseph Lt kia 1-7-16 3 att2RWar C'Coy p65 CR France189
MARTIN,Eric Tomlinson T2Lt kia 1-10-16 9DCLI att8YLI p114 MR21
MARTIN,Ernest 2Lt kia 18-7-16 D306RFA p32 CR France1887
MARTIN,Ernest 2Lt ded 16-12-17 RGA 15HB p40 CR Staffs84
MARTIN,Ernest Ivor T2Lt kia 18-8-18 6KOSB p102 CR France324
MARTIN,Ernest William T2Lt kia 27-7-16 1Norf p74 MR21
MARTIN,Fairlie Russell 2Lt kia 29-6-17 1RScotF att57RFC p10&p95 CR Belgium96
MARTIN,Felix William 2Lt dow 24-7-16 10RWar p65
MARTIN,Francis Henry 2Lt kia 24-11-17 RE 84FC p47 MR17
MARTIN,Frank Henry.MC.2Lt kia 28-3-18 2CldGds p51 CR France214,Lt
MARTIN,Frederick Arthur T2Lt dow 7-9-15 2N&D p134 CR Belgium2
MARTIN,Frederick Nathaniel 2Lt kia 24-10-18 3 att1RWar p65 CR France1260
MARTIN,G.J.Capt 1-3-20 6RIrReg attStaff APM CR Europe23
MARTIN,Geoffrey Clogstoun 2Lt kia 2-8-16 3RDubF p177 CR France423,Lt 9Bn
MARTIN,George Charles Russel Lt ded 12-9-18 Y&rL attN&D p159 CR Kent203,kldacc
MARTIN,George Elvyn 2Lt kia 4-4-18 5 att7RWSurr p212 MR27
MARTIN,George Ernest Capt kia 2-8-17 11Ches p96 CR Belgium112
MARTIN,George Ernest T2Lt kld 29-11-17 GL &RFC p10 CR Wilts115
MARTIN,George Henry 2Lt kia 26-12-17 3 att2Nhants p137 CR Belgium125,27-12-17
MARTIN,George Johnston 2Lt kia 26-9-17 13RSuss p119 MR30
MARTIN,George Patrick Winfield TLt kia 2-10-18 8NumbF Y'Coy p62 CR France273
MARTIN,George Russell Courtney Lt kia 1-7-16 6RWar p214 CR France1504
MARTIN,George Styles Lt kia 23-4-17 5 att18Manch p236 MR20
MARTIN,Gordon Eric T2Lt kia 14-8-17 10RB p179 MR29
MARTIN,George William TMaj kia 17-9-18 17NumbF p62 CR France686
MARTIN,Harold TLt kia 31-7-17 12RFus p69 MR29
MARTIN,Harold James.MID Lt 12-4-17 3SStaffs att1Lincs CR France1186
MARTIN,Harold Young Capt kldacc 14-4-17 5Manch p236 CR Scot387,13-4-17
MARTIN,Harry Edward 2Lt kia 16-11-16 60RFC p3 CR France95
MARTIN,Harry Forster 2Lt kia 29-9-18 1SWBord p100 CR France672
MARTIN,Henry.DCM.2Lt ded 22-10-18 RGA p40 CR Derby2
MARTIN,Henry Lloyd TCapt kia 28-9-16 7RWSurr p56 MR21
MARTIN,Henry Yarde T2Lt dow 14-9-16 9Leic att9ELancs p88 CR Greece6
MARTIN,Herbert 2Lt dow 26-5-15 80RFA p32 CR France285,27-5-15
MARTIN,Herbert Ernest T2Lt kia 14-10-18 16 att1/8ScotRif p103 MR30
MARTIN,Horace Edmund Capt dow 19-6-16 8Mddx p236 CR France1
MARTIN,Hugh Waldyve Maj ded 2-6-18 IA 59Rif p280 MR65
MARTIN,James Adam 2Lt kia 12-7-15 6HLI p240 MR4
MARTIN,James Martin 2Lt kia 24-4-18 409/96RFA p32 CR France303
MARTIN,James Nelson 2Lt kia 21-3-18 RFA 61TMB p32 MR27
MARTIN,John.MC.Capt kia 9-4-17 8/10GordH A'Coy p166 CR France924
MARTIN,John 2Lt kia 19-12-17 RGA 229SB p40 CR Italy7
MARTIN,John Kingsley TCapt kia 1-8-15 10DLI p161 MR29
MARTIN,John Muir Lt kia 6-11-18 7ScotRif p224 CR France936
MARTIN,John Sinclair Lt kia 9-5-15 1RIrRif D'Coy p170 MR32
MARTIN,Joseph Skinner Capt&QM ded 13-2-19 GL 2/8Manch p254 CR Lancs34,Jonathan
MARTIN,Jules Stainmetz ACapt ded 15-12-18 RAMC att19SH p196 CR EAfrica92,Steinmentz
MARTIN,L.S.Capt see LAFERRIERE,L.S. true name
MARTIN,Lawrence Henry T2Lt kia 23-11-17 9RIrF p171 CR France1496,Laurence
MARTIN,Marcel James Capt&Adjt kia 9-5-17 16RWar p65 CR France184
MARTIN,Margery 0/1144 Trail AssAdmintr ded 17-5-18 QMAAC p200 CR Scot253,Marjorie
MARTIN,Marshal TLt ded 18-2-19 Dev 1GarBn p77&257 CR Palestine11
MARTIN,Norman.DSO.Lt kia 22-7-16 5 att1CamH p168 CR France515,23-7-16 3 att1Bn
MARTIN,Peter McEwan ACapt kia 2-12-17 11BordR p117 MR30

MARTIN,Rankin.MM.T2Lt ded 12-7-18 RE 176Co p47 CR France95
MARTIN,Reginald Frank 2Lt kia 30-6-17 1/5N&D p233 MR20
MARTIN,Reginald Poole TLt ded 2-12-18 RE p47 CR Devon36
MARTIN,Richard Archer Walcott 2Lt kia 16-8-17 3RDubF p177 MR30
MARTIN,Robert Lt kia 4-9-17 2/1ScotHorse attRFC p19&205 CR France134
MARTIN,Robert Douglas T2Lt kia 26-8-16 1Wilts p153 MR21
MARTIN,Ronald Hutton Capt kia 24-3-18 MunstFus attRFC p16&175 MR20
MARTIN,Ross T2Lt dow 25-10-18 12TankCps p188 CR France380
MARTIN,Rowland Hill.CB.CMG.CIE.BtCol ded 31-1-19 1Norf GarrBn p74 MR65
MARTIN,Sidney Grant 2Lt dow 18-4-17 13/17RFA p32 CR France581,Lt
MARTIN,Sidney Todd Lt kia 1-7-16 6 att 1RInnisF p105 MR21
MARTIN,Stanley.MM.2Lt kia 18-9-18 2Lond p245 CR France369
MARTIN,Stanley Charley James T2Lt dow 25-7-16 15Hamp attTMB p121 CR France285,Curley,26-7-16
MARTIN,Thomas.MC.Lt kia 31-10-18 5ScotRif p224 CR Belgium140
MARTIN,Thomas Dick 2Lt dow 18-6-18 119/27RH&FA p32 CR France20
MARTIN,Thomas Whittle.MC.Capt kia 9-4-17 RAMC att11RScot p196 CR France645
MARTIN,Trice T2Lt kia 7-6-17 11RWSurr p56 CR Belgium29
MARTIN,Walter Percival T2Lt kia 24-8-16 7DCLI p114 CR France400
MARTIN,Wilfred Arthur T2LtACapt kia 3-8-17 3RB p179 MR29,Wilfrid
MARTIN,William Francis Maj kia 13-5-15 LeicYeo p204 MR29 CR Belgium152
MARTIN,William Gerald TLtACapt kia 14-1-17 12KRRC p151 CR France785
MARTIN,William Harold 2Lt kia 14-9-16 24Lond p252 CR France453,Harrod
MARTIN,William Henry 2Lt ded 27-11-18 9 att6KSLI p145 CR Ireland136,27-10-18
MARTIN,William Howard T2Lt kia 31-7-17 3 att2RWFus p98 MR29
MARTIN,William Murdoch 2Lt kia 22-8-17 13RScot p54 MR30
MARTINDALE,Alfred Horace T2Lt kia 1-10-15 1YLI p143 MR19,4/5-10-15
MARTINDALE,John Ball TLt dow 1-8-16 LancF att2LNLancs p93 CR France1225,Bell
MARTINDALE,Laurence 2Lt kia 31-3-18 2/4WRid p227 CR France924,21-3-18
MARTINDALE,Stanley 2Lt kia 4-9-16 2BordR p117 MR21
MARTINDALE,Warine Frederic Lt kia 15-9-16 1ScotGds p52 MR21
MARTINEAU,Alfred John Maj kia 17-4-17 RGA 19SB p209 CR France161
MARTINEAU,Clement Capt dow 5-5-18 PoW 10RWar p65 CR Belgium393
MARTINNANT,Archibald A.Maj 11-12-18 MadrasBarrackDept MR65
MARTINSON,Karl Ludwig TLt dow 1-6-17 RFA attRFC p10&32 CR France285
MARTLE.W,Raymond Douglas Lt 4-6-21 TankCps CR Europe51
MARTYN,Cecil Radcliffe.MIDx2 Rev ded 3-3-19 RAChDept p199 CR France146
MARTYN,Edgar Spear Capt kia 30-11-17 6RWKent p141 MR17
MARTYN,Harold Henry Capt kia 21-3-18 3 att2Wilts p153 MR27
MARTYR,John Francis Capt dow 11-8-15 1 att6RIrRif p170 MR4
MARVIN,Donald 2Lt kia 9-5-15 1SfthH p165 CR France721
MARVIN,Henry Leslie 2Lt kia 27-10-17 GL &6RFC p10 CR Belgium116,26-10-17
MARWOOD,Charles Phillip Lysaght Capt dow 24-11-15 RWar att1NigR p65&201 CR WAfrica58
MASCALL-THOMPSON,Cecil TCapt ded 21-1-16 RASC p193 CR Dorset139
MASCORD,Alfred Edgar 2Lt kia 6-5-18 6RWar p214 CR France1161
MASEFIELD,Charles John Beech.MC.2Lt dow PoW 21-8-17 1/5NStaffs C'Coy p238 CR France924,Capt 2-7-17
MASEFIELD,Robert Maj kia 24-10-14 KSLI p145 MR32
MASH,Oswald Nelson.MC.TLt kia 1-6-17 D174RFA p32 CR France504
MASHITER,Thomas Alexander Greenwood TLt kia 31-8-17 10Y&L att 1/5LancF p159
MASKELL,George Lt&QM kia 21-3-18 10ScotRif p103 CR France1182
MASKELL,Wilfred Fred 2Lt kia 22-11-17 1/4Lincs p217 CR France115
MASKELL,William Charles.DSO.MC.LtAMaj dow 15-12-17 C189RFA p32 CR France446
MASLIN,Leonard Frank,MC TLt ded 20-5-18 21MGC p184 CR France40
MASON,Albert Thomas T2Lt ded 1-3-18 LabCps att66IndLabCo p189 CR France770
MASON,Allan Edward Glendinning T2Lt dow 30-6-16 7Leic p88 CR France62,Alan Glendenning
MASON,Arthur Edmund 2Lt kia 8-8-18 8Lond C'Coy p247 CR France141
MASON,Arthur Edward Wright Capt kia 2-3-16 7 att8RFus p69 MR19,Knight
MASON,Arthur Humphrey Capt kia 21-8-15 NorfYeo p204 MR4,Humfrey 1/5NorfR
MASON,Arthur Pelham T2Lt kia 22-8-17 8 att1SomLI p80 CR France250
MASON,Arthur Walton T2Lt kia 11-5-17 GL &7RFC p10 CR France528
MASON,Cecil Wyatt T2Lt kia 8-4-17 11RScot p54 CR France97
MASON,Charles 2Lt kia 27-9-18 3RWKent att5MGC p141 MR16
MASON,Charles Douglas Forrest 2Lt 20-4-20 1/3Lpool CR Wales646

MASON,Charles Harold T2Lt kia 6-7-17 7RWSurr p56 CR Belgium29,7-7-17
MASON,Charles Henry.MC.2Lt dow 10-9-18 3Lond p246 CR France446
MASON,Derick Cecil 2Lt kia 10-11-17 1SWBord p255 MR30
MASON,Douglas Howard 2Lt kia 28-4-17 13Ess p132 MR20
MASON,Edward 2Lt kia 9-5-15 3 att2Nhampt p137 MR32
MASON,Ernest TLtACapt dow 5-10-17 9YLI p143 CR France139
MASON,Fanny SNurse drd 10-4-17 QAIMNS p200 CR France85
MASON,George T2Lt kld 4-5-17 GL&RFC p11 CR Scot235 Ex 28Lond
MASON,George 2Lt kia 20-5-17 8 att2Worc p226 MR20
MASON,George 2Lt kia 15-4-18 1 att2/6NStaffs p157 MR32
MASON,George 2Lt kia 16-9-18 RGA Ex BSM 444SB p40 CR France161,15-9-18
MASON,George Sowersby T2Lt kia 8-10-18 2Y&L p159 CR France443
MASON,George William TLt kia 9-4-17 19Lpool p72 CR France592
MASON,Gerald Francis Lt kld 1-9-17 3Hamp att12MGC p121&184,ded CR Hamps87
MASON,Godfrey Jackson 2Lt kia 30-1-18 1/6 att1/8LancF p221 CR France765
MASON,Gordon T2Lt kia 7-6-17 15 att21KRRC p151 CR Belgium29
MASON,Herbert John.MC.Lt ded 16-12-18 Manch att23Bn p155 CR Norf85
MASON,Hubert Harry Leslie 2Lt dow 12-10-17 1RWar p65 CR Belgium16
MASON,James Philip 2Lt kia 9-4-17 3 att7ESurr p113 CR France96
MASON,John Norman.MC.TLt dow 13-10-18 2RRofCav att 1/1DorsYeo p23 CR Egypt1
MASON,Kenneth Ralph 2Lt kia 21-6-15 4Suff p217 CR France631
MASON,Lancelot William Hart 2Lt kia 14-4-17 5WYork p218 CR France115,1Bn
MASON,Norman George Minta.MC.Maj kld 13-9-18 RFA RNDivAmmCol p206 CR France560
MASON,Overton Trollope 2Lt kia 1-7-16 1/9Lond p248 MR21
MASON,Peter 2Lt kia 17-2-17 6 att 1KRRC p151 CR France314
MASON,Philip Granville.DSO.Maj kia 26-9-15 3DragGds p21 CR France423
MASON,Randall Stewart 2Lt kia 14-3-15 6RB p179 CR France709
MASON,Richard TLtACapt kia 23-11-17 13Yorks p91 MR17
MASON,Robert Brereton T2Lt kia 10-10-18 15MGC Inf p184 CR France705
MASON,Rowland Charles Lt dow 30-9-14 3LNLanc p136 CR War12
MASON,Royston Alfred Robson 2Lt dow 20-11-17 5 att2RFus p69 CR France439
MASON,Stanley Hopkins T2Lt kia 26-9-16 8Suff p78 CR France314
MASON,Thomas Henry 2Lt dow 24-7-15 3Middx p147 CR France1
MASON,Vere Karsdale T2Lt kia 3-8-16 11Suff p78 MR21
MASON,Vernon T2Lt kia 1-4-18 1 att9NumbF p62 CR France275
MASON,Wilfrid Howard T2Lt kia 9-3-17 RE 72FC p47 CR Iraq8
MASON,William James T2Lt kia 20-9-17 11RB p179 MR30
MASON,William John TCapt kia 3-7-16 8Glouc p107 MR21
MASON-MACFARLANE,Carlyon Will Capt kia 5-9-16 7Huss att18ImpCamelCps p22
MASSEY,Albert Francis T2Lt kia 28-3-18 8MGC att3Hamp p184 MR27
MASSEY,George Hocken 2Lt kia 27-6-16 A53RFA p32 CR France699
MASSEY,John Hamon.MC.MID Capt kia 27-5-18 5/45RFA p32 CR France1332
MASSEY,Louis Oger 2Lt kia 21-8-16 1RFus p69 CR France390
MASSEY,William Clayton 2Lt kia 5-11-18 4Lincs p217 CR Belgium204,6-11-18
MASSEY-LYNCH,Wilfrid John T2Lt kia 4-4-18 6RRofCav att3DGds p24 MR27,Wilfred
MASSIAH-PALMER,Werner William Thomas.OBE.TMaj ded 17-2-19 GL &13NumbF p262 CR Mddx21,LtCol
MASSIE,A.H AssSurg 9-8-16 IMS CR Pakistan50A MR43
MASSIE,John Hamon.DSO.Maj dow 15-11-14 RGA 26HB p40 CR Belgium58
MASSIE,Sidney Edward 2Lt kia 8-5-17 att1SomLI p80 MR20
MASSON,Alexander 2Lt dow 1-10-14 4SfthH p241 CR Belgium157
MASSON,Alex James 2Lt kia 23-3-18 9Manch p237 MR27
MASSON,J.HonMaj&QM ded 1-5-15 RScotF p95 CR Hamps7
MASSON,James 2Lt kia 28-7-18 7GordH p242 CR France1689
MASSON,James Alexander 2Lt dow 8-5-17 RGA 38HB p40 CR France1185
MASSY,Haworth Peel Capt ded 10-12-14 Leinst att4NigR p174&201 CR WAfrica50
MASSY-BERESFORD,John Clarina Lt kia 28-8-18 310RFA p32 CR France5,23-8-
MASSY-MILES,Henry Godfrey.MC.TCapt dow 26-4-18 RAMC att1/8Lond p196 France145,Harry
MASSY-WHEELER,George Godfrey.VC. 13-4-15 IA 7Lancers CR Iraq6
MASTER,Charles Lionel.MID Capt kia 12-10-14 2RIrRif p170 CR France260
MASTER,George Gilbert Onslow Lt kia 25-7-16 1/4Glouc p225 CR France296
MASTERMAN,Frederick Michel 2Lt kia 1-7-16 3 att10RIrRif p170 MR21
MASTERMAN,Robert Chauncey TLt kia 1-7-16 9LancF p93 MR21
MASTERS,Alexander Capt kia 23-11-14 IA 34SikhPnrs p280 CR France279

MASTERS,Charles William 2Lt kia 30-8-17 5 att8RFus p69 CR France154,5 att9Br.
MASTERS,Geoffrey T2Lt kia 9-4-17 9RFus p69 CR France531
MASTERS,George Edward Lt mbk 4-6-15 IA 89Punjabis att14Sikhs p280 MR4
MASTERSON,Christopher John 2Lt kia 2-9-17 10 att1Worc p109 CR Belgium50,Lt
MASTERSON,Frank 2Lt kia 5-4-18 9RFus p69 CR France516,MASTERTON
MASTERSON,George Cuthbert Dillon Capt ded 25-2-17 RLancs p262 CR Hamps8
MASTERTON,William Murray 2Lt dow 10-6-17 6RScot p211 CR France113
MASTIN,Frank T2Lt kia 2-11-17 1N&D 1stGarrBn att 1/4Nampt p134 CR Palestine8
MATEAR,Norman Hirst Lawrence.MID TCapt kia 25-9-15 2RWar p65 MR19
MATHER,Alan William Lt ded 29-10-18 3BlkW &RAF p129 CR Lincs61
MATHER,Alfred Lushington 2Lt kia 7-1-17 3Y&L p159 CR Belgium4
MATHER,C.H.T2Lt dow 18-3-16 12NumbF p62 CR France285
MATHER,Donald 2Lt kia 2-11-17 5Manch p236 CR Belgium24
MATHER,Edward Noel 2Lt kia 26-4-15 6NumbFus p214 MR29
MATHER,Edward William 2Lt dow 13-10-16 RE 1FC p210 CR France300
MATHER,George 2Lt kia 8-10-16 25Lond p252 MR21,4-10-16
MATHER,John Wilfred TCapt kia 10-8-15 6LNLanc p136 MR4
MATHER,John Kearsley Lt kia 18-2-15 Y&L p159 MR29
MATHER,Norman 2Lt kia 9-8-16 1/10Lpool p216 MR21
MATHER,Robert T2Lt kia 27-3-18 20Lpool p72 MR27
MATHER,Volney 2Lt kia 31-7-17 12LNLanc p234 CR Belgium125
MATHERS,George Eric TLt kia 8-10-18 6MGC p184 CR France235
MATHESON,Alexander Percival Lt kia 13-7-17 GL &55RFC p11 CR Belgium344,Perceval
MATHESON,Andrew Scott T2Lt dow 10-4-17 7SfthH p165 CR France95,Lt
MATHESON,Archibald Angus T2Lt ded 20-12-17 RASC HQ BaseSupplyDepot p193 CR France145
MATHESON,Claude Bruce 2Lt kia 23-9-17 5 att2RB p179 CR Belgium52
MATHESON,George Hugh T2Lt kia 3-12-17 14DLI p161 MR17
MATHESON,Harry Mackay 2Lt ded 24/26-12-17 RFC attAust FC p11 CR Palestine8
MATHESON,Herbert 2Lt kia 23-3-18 13 att15Lond CR France716
MATHESON,Homer Lindsay T2Lt kia 16-8-16 9ESurr p113 MR21
MATHESON,Ian Kenneth LtACapt dow 13-5-17 3 att2SfthH p165 CR France40,Lt
MATHESON,James 2Lt kia 26-3-16 4A&SH p173 MR32
MATHESON,James Frederick.MC.TCapt dow 19-4-18 RAMC att7Norf p196 CR France145
MATHESON,James McDonald TCapt kia 30-11-17 RAMC att17Mddx p196 CR France530
MATHESON,John T2Lt kia 9-4-17 10HLI p163 MR20
MATHESON,John Hugh Capt dow 24-4-17 6GordH p242 CR France113
MATHESON,John James 2Lt dow 13-8-18 7CamH att 1/5A&SH p168 CR France145,Lt
MATHESON,John MacLean 2Lt kia 26-6-18 4RScot p211 MR32
MATHESON,Malcolm Angus.MC.Capt dow 27-9-16 6GordH att 15TankCps p242 CR France433
MATHESON,Roderick Kyrle 2Lt dow 8-9-16 3RWKent att20Manch p141 CR France245
MATHEW,C.V.D.Waynflete T2Lt kia 21-8-17 RE 48DivSigCo p47 MR30
MATHEW,George Dudley Capt dow 10-5-15 IA 2/2GurkhaRif p280 CR Belgium140 &CR France924
MATHEW,J.D.Cdr 29-7-21 MilWksServ MR66
MATHEW,Murray Chamberlain Gervase.MID Lt dow 4-7-15 IA 28Punjabis att14Sikhs p280 CR Egypt3
MATHEWS,Anthony Edward T2Lt kia 19-7-16 11Dev att2/6Glouc p77 CR France1887
MATHEWS,Arnold.MID TLt dow 14-4-16 14Ches p96 MR38
MATHEWS,Avard Yuill 2Lt dow PoW 26-10-18 1York att1WYork p91 MR16
MATHEWS,Edward Stanley TLt kia 2-10-18 1 att2Mddx p147 CR France407,26-9-18
MATHEWS,George 2Lt kia 2-10-17 RFA att55RFC p11&32
MATHEWS,Hubert Victor 2Lt kia 26-8-16 135/32RFA p32 CR Belgium127
MATHEWS,Hugh Spencer Capt kia 22-7-16 14RWar p65 CR France432
MATHEWS,John Laurence Lt ded 28-12-17 3RSuss attRE DivSigs p264 CR France31,29-12-17 7Bn
MATHEWS,Joseph Henry T2Lt kia 27-3-18 5RBerks p139 MR27
MATHEWS,Robert Arthur Cecil Lt kia 18-10-16 3 att1ELancs p111 MR21
MATHEWS,Thomas Hugh Lt kia 2-11-14 1ELancs p111 CR Belgium68
MATHEWS,Walter Vivanti Dewar Maj dow 9-12-17 RGA 102SB p40 CR France398
MATHEWS,William Scott TLt kia 15-9-16 18KRRC p151 CR France1890
MATHEWSON,George Gillespie.MID TLt kia 27-3-18 RE 5FC p47 MR27
MATHEWSON,Hamilton TCapt dow 27-10-16 RAMC att2Nhampt p196 CR France105
MATHEWSON,James Kenneth 2Lt kia 14-9-18 D113RFA p32 CR Belgium188
MATHEWSON,Kenneth Lt kia 3-8-16 RFC p3 CR France161
MATHIAS,Charles Arthur Stirling.MC T2Lt kia 3-5-17 7EKent p57 MR20
MATHIAS,John Edmund 2Lt drd 11-10-16 5WelshR p230 CR Wales12
MATHIAS,John Harold Tudor 2Lt kia 25-11-17 5 att17WelshR p230 MR17
MATHIESON,Herbert Gerard Lt kia 10-3-15 3Lond p245 CR France706
MATHIESON,John T2Lt kia 5-8-18 3A&SH att7SfthH p173 CR France27
MATHIESON,Kenneth Ronald Lt kia 1-11-14 1IrGds p53 MR29
MATHIESON,Stanley 2Lt dow 16-8-18 7ScotRif p224 CR France85
MATHIESON,William 2Lt kia 25-5-18 4Beds p86 MR27
MATHIESON-MACBETH,Thomas McBeth Lt kia 5-9-17 8Lond p247
MATHVIN,Douglas Gatecliffe 2Lt kia 9-5-15 1/9Lpool p216 MR22,MATHWIN
MATON,Leonard Evelyn Leigh.MC.MIDx2Capt kia 9-5-17 1Dev p77 MR20
MATTESON,Leonard Maj ded 11-4-16 RASC SR p193 CR Lond8
MATTEY,Charles Percival T2Lt ded PoW 22-1-17 1Beds p86 CR France924
MATTHAMS,Lawrence T2Lt kia 13-10-18 49MGC Inf p184 CR France270
MATTHEW,Frank Henry 2Lt kia 9-10-15 RGA p40
MATTHEW,Wilfrid John 2Lt kia 19-5-18 5Lond p246 CR France196
MATTHEWS,Alfred Apsley T2Lt dow 12-9-16 9ESurr p113 CR France145
MATTHEWS,Arthur James TCapt ded 21-11-18 15SLanc p125
MATTHEWS,Bertram Cash TLt kia 24-3-17 2RScot p54 CR France645
MATTHEWS,Charles Henry 2Lt dow 22-3-18 1RFus p69 CR France987 Ex 2CldGds
MATTHEWS,David T2Lt kia 29-5-18 6ConnRgrs p171 CR France178
MATTHEWS,Ernest Alan 2Lt kia 2-4-18 8SomLI &RAF p255 CR France630,Lt 11Bn
MATTHEWS,Edward Alexander 2Lt kia 14-3-15 3Nhants p137 MR22,10-3-15
MATTHEWS,Edward Philip TLt dow 16-9-16 8RB p179 CR France66
MATTHEWS,Edwin Harold 2Lt kia 8-8-16 1/7Lpool p215 MR21
MATTHEWS,Edwin Martin Lt kia 8-11-16 1/4Glouc p225 MR21
MATTHEWS,Francis Harold T2Lt kia 24-7-17 266MGC p184 MR29
MATTHEWS,Frank Arthur TLt kia 24-4-17 10RSuss &9RFC p11&119 MR20
MATTHEWS,Frank Reginald Lt dow 23-3-18 12ESurr p113 MR20
MATTHEWS,George T2Lt dow 2-7-18 PoW WYorks att1/6Bn p82 CR Germany1
MATTHEWS,Godfrey Estcourt.CB.CMG.TBrigGen dow 13-4-17 198InfBde RMLI Staff p1
MATTHEWS,Harold Carey Maj ded 25-4-15 4York p220 MR29 CR Belgium453
MATTHEWS,Henry 2Lt kia 15-1-17 24RFus att47RFC p11 CR Greece7
MATTHEWS,Henry Arthur 2Lt dow 25-10-17 465/65RFA p32 CR Belgium16
MATTHEWS,Henry Aylmer Vallance.MC.TCaptAMaj ded 8-11-18 Cmdg14Div RASC MT p193 CR France1028
MATTHEWS,Herbert Lewis Lash 2Lt kia 9-9-16 11 att1/5Lond p248 CR France1890
MATTHEWS,John Brice TCapt kia 14-2-17 7RWKent p141 CR France314
MATTHEWS,John Bredel.MC.LtTCapt kia 1-10-17 3NStaffs att8Leic p157 MR30,Budel
MATTHEWS,John Edward Norman 2Lt died 4-8-19 1Suff att8N&D p263 CR Greece9
MATTHEWS,John Herbert Capt kia 13/14-9-14 1NumbF p62 MR15,Hubert 15-9-14
MATTHEWS,L.G.MID Chap1Cl 26-5-16 CR Lond9
MATTHEWS,Leonard Mansfield TLt ded 25-6-18 RASC MT p193 CR France1358
MATTHEWS,Leslie Herbert 2Lt kia 28-3-18 RWar att2/6 p65 MR27
MATTHEWS,Lewis Joseph Rev ded 26-5-16 RAChDept p199
MATTHEWS,Mervyn Lt dow 28-1-15 RE p47 CR Glouc24
MATTHEWS,Myles Lewis Wyan TCapt kia 3-7-16 6RWKent p141 MR21
MATTHEWS,Noel Anwyl 2Lt kia 15-9-16 11Lond p248 CR France277,3 att8Bn
MATTHEWS,Richard Malcolm T2Lt kia 20-9-17 9York p91 MR30
MATTHEWS,Robert John Lt ded 2-11-18 4Norf p187&216 CR Lincs61
MATTHEWS,S.W.Capt 15-11-18 RAMC CR EAfrica8 &Tanzania1
MATTHEWS,Samuel Wauchope TLt ded 15-9-18 RAMC attMLB p196
MATTHEWS,St.John Bell T2Lt dow 25-11-15 6RBerks p139 CR France22
MATTHEWS,Thomas.MBE.LtACapt dow 27-6-18 RGA 521Household SB p40 CR France31,251SB
MATTHEWS,Walter Franey Capt kia 28-9-17 4Dors p229 CR Iraq8
MATTHEWS,Wilfrid Vernon.MC.T2Lt kia 1-10-18 11 att1/5BordR p117 CR France375
MATTHEWS,William Frederick Capt kia 18-8-18 1SWBord att 1ELanc p100 CR France21
MATTHEWS,William Henry 2Lt kia 28-9-18 RGA 2/1Lowland HB p41 CR France446
MATTHEY,Edward Granville Capt kia 1-7-16 1LancF p93 CR France1492
MATTHYSSENS,Francis Alexander TCapt ded 23-6-16 1/4WelshR p230 CR Egypt1

MATTMAN,A.M.Lt 22-7-21 RFA SR CR Lond14
MATTOX,Charles Douglas Lt 15-6-20 RFA attIntCps CR Asia51
MATTS,Frank 2Lt kia 24-7-16 5War p214 CR France832
MATURIN,W.K.(Kay)Lt 29-1-15 UgandaPoliceBn CR EAfrica128
MAUBSELL,George Wyndham 2Lt kia 23-2-17 IARO att2S&M p280
MAUCHLINE,Allan Bryce T2Lt kia 14-10-18 SfthH att9Bn p165 CR Belgium157
MAUD,Charles Carns,DSO Capt kia 19-12-14 1SomLI p80 CR Belgium70
MAUD,Frederick T2Lt kia 20-9-17 124MGC Inf p184 MR30
MAUD,Frederick Stanley.MC.T2Lt kia 3-10-18 att2YLI p143 CR France375,Sidney
MAUDE,Frederick Stanley.Sir.KCB.CMG.DSO LtGen ded 18-11-17 Staff GOCinChief MEF p1 CR Iraq8
MAUDE,Gerald William Edward Capt ded 5-11-19 1Yorks p263 MR43
MAUDE,Gervase Henry Francis 2Lt dow 9-4-17 att8RFus p69 CR France113
MAUDE,John William Ashley T2Lt kia 24-8-15 10KRRC p151 CR France707,Achley 23-8-15
MAUDE,Louis Edward Joseph 2Lt kia 1-7-16 11YLI p143 CR France267
MAUDE,M.B.MC.Lt 24-1-21 4RFus CR Iraq8
MAUDE,Michael Day Wade Capt dow 14-10-17 3 att9Yorks p91 CR Yorks485
MAUDE,Robert Henry Ernest 2Lt ded 12-9-16 2WYorks GarBn att3NStaffs p82 CR Cornwall1
MAUFE,Statham Broadbent.MID TMaj dow 5-7-16 11WYorks p82 CR France833
MAUGHAN,Alfred William 2Lt kia 24-6-17 RGA 285SB p41 CR Belgium17
MAUGHAN,John.MID Capt kia 17-2-16 4Yorks p220 CR Belgium5
MAUGHAN,William Douglas T2Lt kia 19-11-17 17NumbF p62 CR Belgium23
MAUL,Richard Selby Lowndes 2Lt kia 30-7-16 2 O&BLI p130 MR21
MAULE,Edward Barry TLt kia 6-2-17 18HLI &20RFC p11&p163 CR Belgium112
MAULE,Geoffrey Lamb Capt ded 15-11-18 RAMC att27CCS p196 CR Iraq8
MAULE,Robert Lt kia 27-5-15 5RScot p211 CR Gallipoli3
MAULE-FRENCH,Eric Herbert Justus 2Lt kia 27-8-18 7Lond p247 CR France164,FFRENCH
MAULEVERER,Richard De Burgh 2Lt dow 13-11-17 3 att2ELancs CR Scot252
MAULKINSON,Harry Young T2Lt dow 4-6-17 7Lincs p75 CR Lincs202
MAULTSAIS,Wesley 2Lt 22-5-15 9RScots D'Coy CR Belgium453
MAUNSELL,Douglas Slade Lt kia 6-9-16 2RMunstF p175 MR21,5/6-9-16
MAUNSELL,Edwin Richard Lloyd Capt kia 1-7-16 1RDubF p177 CR France35
MAUNSELL,George Wyndham 2Lt 23-2-17 IARO attS&M MR38
MAUNSELL,Herbert Stofford Lt dow 1-9-15 3RWar p65 CR France98,2Bn
MAUNSELL,Marian Jane Nurse ded 7-1-19 VAD BRCS p200 CR Egypt9
MAUNSELL,Reginald Harcourt Proctor 2Lt kia 27-4-18 RGA 128SB p41 CR Belgium188
MAUNSELL,Robert George Frederick Capt drd 4-5-17 RE p210 CR Italy14
MAUNSELL,Thomas Bowyer-Lane Capt kia 1-5-15 1LancF p93 CR Gallipoli,25-4-15
MAUNSELL,Wilfrid Innocent Capt kia 8-2-15 2ScotRif p103 CR France567
MAURICE,Charles Henry Pryse 2Lt dedacc 24-1-17 3RBerks p139 CR France120
MAURICE,Francis Thomas 2Lt ded 29-10-18 1GrenGds p262
MAURICE,John Capel 2Lt kia 7-10-18 RBerks att2Bn p139 CR France184
MAURICE,Sterling 2Lt dow 11-5-15 RE 2FC p210 CR Belgium11
MAVETY,John Le Roy TLt ded 13-12-15 RAMC 46Div p196 CR France495
MAVOR,Robert George Innes.MC.2Lt kia 23-4-17 7A&SH p234 CR France545
MAW,Arthur Rogers Capt kia 21-3-18 10Manch p237 MR27
MAW,George Oliver TCapt dow 10-7-16 RAMC att13StatHospl p196 CR France430,attRB
MAW,Harry H.T2Lt kia 22-8-18 Beds p86 CR France239
MAWBY,Edwin George Lt kia 27-9-15 WelshGds p53 MR19
MAWBY,Thomas Henry 2Lt kia 24-6-18 4Lond p246 CR France1182
MAWDSLEY,Burton James Platt Lt kia 6-2-16 IA 17Cav p280 CR EAfrica42,Barton
MAWDSLEY,John Edmund Lt kia 24-4-17 10 att6RLancs p59 MR38
MAWDSLEY,Norman Hargreaves Lt ded 17-6-18 6RFus p69 CR Hamps15
MAWHOOD,Claude George T2Lt kia 14-9-16 8WRid p116 MR21
MAWSON,Alan John Lt ded 4-12-18 5NumbF p256 CR Numb5
MAXFIELD,Hugh Lt 8-12-18 MilLabCps CR EAfrica36
MAXTED,Spencer Edward Chap4Cl 19/20-7-16 AustInf CR France525
MAXWELL,Alexander Edward Lt dow 7-5-17 GL 20Mddx att121TMB p191 CR France1468
MAXWELL,Arthur Lt&QM ded 19-3-19 GL att4RWSurr p271
MAXWELL,Arthur Edwin Lt ded 18-3-20 RE attDORE Constantinople p271 CR Asia51
MAXWELL,Aylmer Edward Capt kia 9-10-14 1LovatSc CmdgCollingwoodBn RND p271 CR Belgium342,Aymer LtCol
MAXWELL,Charles William Lt kia 24-11-14 IA 2/8GurkhaRif p280 CR France279,23-11-14
MAXWELL,Clyde Fairbanks 2Lt kia 3-7-16 9Ess p132 MR21

MAXWELL,David.MC&Bar.Capt dow 3-8-18 5BlkW p231 CR France1225
MAXWELL,Eustace Lockhart LtCol mbk 20-7-16 IA 11Lancers att23Manch p280 MR28
MAXWELL,Francis Aylmer.VC.CSI.DSO.BrigGen kia 21-9-17 IA Cmdg27InfBde 9Div p280 CR Belgium84
MAXWELL,Harley Hyslop 2Lt dow 24-10-18 1CamH p168 CR France725
MAXWELL,Henry T2Lt kia 10-10-16 13Ches p96 CR France280,Capt 11-10-16
MAXWELL,Hon.Henry Edward.DSO.Col ded 2-3-19 SL BlkW p268 CR Eire251
MAXWELL,Ian Bouverie Capt kia 31-1-14 3 att1SWBord p100 MR29,31-10-14
MAXWELL,James Lt kia 21-8-15 11Lond p248 CR Gallipoli27
MAXWELL,James McCall Lt kia 1-6-16 459/118RFA p32 CR Belgium5
MAXWELL,John 2Lt kia 12-7-15 5RScotFus p222 MR4
MAXWELL,John.DSO.MC.CaptALtCol dow 4-12-17 7RB att8KRRC p179 CR Belgium84
MAXWELL,John Duncan T2Lt dow 18-7-17 11Suff p78 CR France446
MAXWELL,Joseph.MM.2Lt ded 26-3-18 3RScotF p263 CR Scot683
MAXWELL,Peter Benson Capt dow 24-9-14 EYorks late35Sikhs p84 CR France1110
MAXWELL,Power MacMurrough.MC.CaptAMaj dow 1-10-17 B95RH&FA p32 C Belgium11
MAXWELL,Richard D'Arcy TLtACapt kia 23-10-18 2RScot p54 CR France292
MAXWELL,Richard Drummond Capt ded 3-6-16 RAMC p271 CR Scot239,6-3-1
MAXWELL,Richard Henry Perceval Lt kia 23-7-18 3 att10ScotRif p103
MAXWELL,Robert Greenwood TCapt kia 7-1-16 3SfthH p165 MR38
MAXWELL,Ronald Erskine Wilford TMaj kia 25-9-16 6KOSB p102 CR France55
MAXWELL,Stanley Woods T2Lt dow PoW 27-7-16 8RIrRif B'Coy p170 CR France1266
MAXWELL,Thomas T2Lt kia 9-9-16 8RDubF p177 CR France294
MAXWELL,Walter T2Lt ded 11-2-18 1SWBord p100 MR66
MAXWELL,Wellwood 2Lt dow 16-9-16 20Lond p251 CR France197,15-9-16
MAXWELL,William Francis John Lt kia 13-8-15 5KOSB p224 CR Gallipoli2
MAXWELL,William Gardner.MC.BtMaj ded 11-12-18 8GordH GSO att3CpsSch p166 CR France13
MAXWELL,William Jardine Capt ded 26-8-16 2CamH att10SoudanInf EgyptAm p168 CR EAfrica116
MAXWELL,William Leigh LtCol kia 12-5-15 IA 127Baluchis attRMLI p280
MAXWELL,William Nisbet 2Lt kia 12-10-16 3 att7SfthH p165 CR France489
MAXWELL,William Stewart 2Lt kia 21-3-18 56RFC p16 MR20,27-3-18
MAXWELL-HERON,Basil Charles Montague TCapt SL ded 22-9-16 p201 CR Lond4
MAXWELL-MOFFAT,Alexander Logan Nathan Lt ded 21-11-14 2Dors p124 CR Iraq6,dow
MAXWELL-STUART,Alfred Joseph 2Lt dow 24-8-18 1CldGds p51 CR France84
MAXWELL-STUART,Edmund Joseph TLt kia 26-4-16 RE 175Coy p47 CR Belgiu
MAXWELL-STUART,Henry Joseph Ignatius 2Lt kia 9-10-17 3GrenGds p51 CR Belgium106,CldGds
MAXWELL-STUART,J.J.Lt 2-3-16 9WRid CR Belgium15
MAY,Adrian Robson 2Lt kia 8-9-16 5Lpool p215 CR France188
MAY,Charles Campbell.MID TCapt kia 1-7-16 22Manch B'Coy p155 CR France
MAY,Charles Richard Allen Lt ded 18-8-20 IA 56Rif p280 CR Egypt10
MAY,Claude Boyle.MC.TCapt kia 19-11-17 6BordR p117 CR France550
MAY,Ernest Bernard.DCM.T2Lt kia 4-10-16 30MGC p184 CR Greece3
MAY,Ernest Edward.DCM.2Lt kia 28-8-16 20Manch p155 CR France402
MAY,Francis Henry T2Lt kia 29-9-18 1TankCps p188 MR16
MAY,Frederick Wilson Laughton TCapt dow 8-6-17 11RIrRif p170 CR Belgium
MAY,George Neville TCapt dow 29-5-18 RGA 243SB att87SB p41 CR France145,343SB
MAY,Harold Costwick 2Lt dow 27-3-15 3DorsR p124 CR France102,Gostwyck
MAY,Herbert Cecil 2Lt dow 29-9-18 6 att18KRRC p151 CR Belgium116
MAY,Herbert Edwin Lt drd 6-12-17 SurrYeo p205 MR37
MAY,James Percy Maj kia 12-2-17 IA 102Grens p280 CR Iraq5
MAY,John Hayes 2Lt kia 20-11-17 9Lond p248 CR France530
MAY,Leo Cuthbert 2Lt kia 27-6-18 3 att12Glouc p107 CR France352
MAY,Paul Archer 2Lt kia 15-4-17 1Dev p77 MR20
MAY,Percy William T2Lt kia 13-11-16 10 att7ELancs p111 MR21
MAY,Peter Langton 2Lt kia 13-2-16 2Drags SR p21 MR19
MAY,Ralph Edward 2Lt kia 12-7-15 5HLI p240 MR4
MAY,Richard Trelawney.MID TCapt kia 7-7-16 7RSuss A'Coy p119 MR21
MAY,Richard Wallis 2Lt kia 9-8-15 2DLI p161 MR29
MAY,Stanley Harris Lt kia 27-8-16 11LNLancs att2RWar p136 MR21
MAY,Thomas George T2Lt kia 6-8-17 143MGC p184 CR Belgium9
MAY,Walter Gould 2Lt kia 3-9-16 Hamps 1GarrBn p121 CR France339

MAY,Wilfred John.MC.T2L dow 1-8-17 2WYorks p82 CR Belgium11
MAY,William Clarence 2Lt kia 26-10-17 NumbF att1/5Bn p255 MR30
MAY,William Ernest Edward Frederick 2Lt kia 24-11-16 1/22Lond p251 CR Belgium167
MAY,William John T2Lt dow 23-3-18 Y&L p159 CR France177
MAYALL,James 2Lt dow 13-11-18 4KOSB p271 CR Lancs441
MAYBANK,John Gunter TLt kia 15-9-16 2YLI p143 CR France114,2Lt
MAYBERRY,Richard Lt kia 15-11-17 3RScotFus &70RFC p11&95 MR20 &CR Belgium167
MAYBERY,Richard Aveline.MC&Bar.Lt kia 19-12-17 21Lancers att56RFC p11&23 CR France1483,Capt
MAYBIN,James Johnstone TCapt kia 14-7-16 11RScot p54 CR France399
MAYBREY,Arthur James 2Lt kia 22-7-16 10Glouc p107 MR21
MAYBROOK,Walter Richard T2Lt kia 24-4-16 1Wilts p153 CR France68
MAYBURY,Arthur.DCM.2Lt kia 19-7-17 1 att5RBerks p139&257 MR20
MAYBURY,Francis Joseph 2Lt dow 5-10-18 5 att1RMunstF p175 CR France40,Lt
MAYBURY,Reginald 2Lt kld 23-4-17 6 att18Manch p237 MR20
MAYCOCK,Frederick William Orby.DSO.Maj kia 25-5-15 1Suff p78 CR Belgium125
MAYER,Frank TLt kia 3-10-18 RFus att4Bn p69 CR France338,8-10-18
MAYER,Frank Bertram Lt kia 13-10-15 5NStaff p238 MR19
MAYER,Frederick Percy Fry Lt ded 30-4-17 NigR CR WAfrica3
MAYER,Gerald Max.MID Lt dow 16-2-17 1Lond p245 CR France40,Capt
MAYER,John Stuart Lt kia 29-1-18 8Manch p237 CR Belgium72
MAYERSBACH,Jack Frederick T2Lt kia 4-5-18 13RB p179 CR France1014
MAYES,Robert Campbell.MC.2Lt dow 19-10-18 22Lond p251 CR France496,Capt
MAYES,Walter Herbert 2Lt kia 9-1-17 IARO att1S&M p280 MR38
MAYFIELD,Leonard Augustus T2Lt kia 27-9-18 NumbF att1Bn p62 MR16
MAYLIN,Bertram Henry 2Lt kia 11-4-18 8 att2/7Lond p247 MR32
MAYNARD,Frederick Creber Lt dow 20-9-18 RGA 119HB p41 CR France1184
MAYNARD,Frederick Owen Capt ded 12-1-20 RAVC CR Egypt2
MAYNARD,Hugh Charles Lt kia 15-9-16 1CldGds p51 MR21
MAYNARD,John Edwin.MC.Maj dow 17-10-18 6Lond p246 CR Hamps64
MAYNARD,John Wilmot 2Lt kia 24-4-15 3KRRC p151 MR29
MAYNARD,Michael James Lt kia 8-10-16 1/5Lond p246 MR21
MAYNE,Augustus Blair Maj ded 4-12-17 RH&FA 3DAC Ex CenIndHorse p32 CR Surrey113
MAYNE,Cecil Robert 2Lt kia 30-11-17 2/5 att7YLI p235 MR17
MAYNE,Denis John Heriot 2Lt kld 12-10-17 RIrRif &57RFC p11&170 CR Mddx16
MAYNE,George Rufane Talbot.MC.TLt dow 10-11-18 RASC p193 CR Eire394
MAYNE,Jasper Moone 2Lt kia 9-5-15 RFA p32 CR France525,Moore
MAYNE,Victor Charles Moore Lt kia 19-2-16 1SWBord p100 CR France1896 &CR France1723
MAYO,Percy Austin 2Lt kld 9-5-16 3Dors p124
MAYO,William Charles TLt kia 7/11-8-15 9N&D p134 MR4,7-8-15
MAYS,Alexander Walter 2Lt ded 14-11-16 IARO att14JatLancers p280
MAYS,Cecil Clarence 2Lt kia 30-3-18 1GrenGds p50 France1183
MAYS,Charles Cecil Wildman Lt drd 25-1-18 RAMC p196 CR France85,RASC
MAYS,Frederick William 2Lt ded 20-7-17 A69RFA p32 CR Iraq8
MAYS,W.H.2Lt 14-11-16 14Lancers MR65
MAYSON,Frank Eric Halton T2Lt kia 28-8-16 6YLI p143 CR France402,Hutton
MAYWOOD,James Henry LtTCapt kia 23-8-18 1DCLI p114 CR France239
MAZENGART,George Richard Bostock 2Lt kia 29-7-16 3 att1ESurr p113 MR21,MAZENGARB
McADIE,David Alister Alexander.MC.2Lt kia 22-8-17 5SfthH p241 MR30,MACADIE
McADIE,George 2Lt 22-3-18 14A&SH p173 MR20
McADOREY,John 2Lt dow 5-5-18 2/10Manch p155 CR France84
McAFEE,Lewis Alexander Capt kia 30-7-15 8RB p179 MR27
McALINDON,Thomas.MC.2LtACapt ded 17-9-18 2RIrRif p169 CR Ireland74
McALISTER,Clara SNurse drd 10-4-17 QAIMNS p200 CR France85
McALISTER,George Howden 2Lt kia 24-8-16 5RScotF &78MGC p187&222 MR37
McALISTER,Gordon Duncan 2Lt kia 10-4-18 4KSLI A'Coy p235 MR30
McALISTER,Hugh 2Lt ded 17-9-17 Y&L p159 CR Surrey1
McALLISTER,Angus TCapt ded 29-8-17 RE p46 CR Italy6,Andrew
McALLISTER,Charles ACapt kia 27-5-18 9DubF att2WYorks p177 CR France1753
McALLISTER,Robert 2Lt kia 30-10-17 8Lond p247 CR Belgium83
McALPIN,James Montgomerie T2Lt kia 11-4-17 8KOSB p102 MR20
McANDREW,Alister 2Lt kia 24-12-14 1BlkW p129 MR22
McANDREW,Charles Arthur Worthington 2Lt kia 26-4-17 24RFA p32 CR France257

McANDREW,Charles Roy 2Lt kia 21-9-18 WarYeo attMGC p187&205 CR France369
McANDREW,George Burbury LtCol kia 14-3-15 2Lincs p75 CR France525,10-3-15
McARA,Duncan 2Lt dow 29-4-17 3HLI p163 CR France95
McARDLE,Hugh Francis Lt kia 18-9-17 KEdwHorse &41RFC p10&24 MR20
McARDLE,Peter Paul T2Lt kia 26-4-18 1/2Ches att1/4Y&L p96 MR30
McARDLE,W.R.Capt 28-8-21 IMD MR65
McARTHUR,Dugald T2Lt dow 21-4-17 2BlkW p129 MR38
McARTHUR,John TCapt kia 27-2-17 GL &12RFC p10
McARTHUR,Lawrence William.MC.Capt kia 27-5-17 HAC att12RFC p19 CR Belgium140 &CR France46
McARTHUR,William Bell.MC.T2Lt kia 9-4-17 1RScotF p95 CR France418
McAULEY,Bernard Capt kia 7-8-15 6BordR p117 MR4
McAULEY,Francis Willmer TCapt kia 21-5-16 B230RFA p207 CR France281,McAULAY
McAULIFFE,Cornelius Rev ded 6-10-16 RAChDept p199 CR Eire167
McAULIFFE,George Henry 2Lt kia 29-10-14 CamH att2GordH p168 MR29
McBAIN,Frederick Thomas T2Lt kia 9-4-18 13Yorks p90 CR France82
McBAIN,John Mortimer 2Lt dow PoW 9-7-16 231RFA p32 CR France1484
McBEAN,Donald Lt kia 15-3-16 RWFus att10Bn p98 MR29
McBEAN,William T2Lt kia 12-5-16 11A&SH p173 CR France423
McBLANE,David McMurtrie 2Lt kia 12-10-17 4RScots MR30
McBRAYNE,David Cecil Hope T2Lt dow PoW 21-6-17 GL &11RFC p10
McBRIDE,Alfred Henry 2Lt dow 1-11-14 2HLI p163 CR Belgium58
McBRIDE,Andrew Best.MC.Capt kia 24-4-18 2/5Beds p219 CR France303
McBRIDE,Arthur King TCapt kia 7-6-17 12RIrRif p169 CR Belgium100
McBRIDE,John Gordon 2Lt kld 8-10-18 3Glouc &20RAF p107 MR20
McBRIDE,Joseph LtAMaj kia 23-4-17 27RFA p32 CR France1325
McBRIDE,William Wilson 2Lt dow 5-12-17 RGA 229SB p40 CR Italy7,kia
McBRIEN,Hubert John T2Lt kia 4-11-18 2DubF p177 CR France521
McBRINN,John Charles 2Lt kia 3-9-16 4RIrReg p89 CR France402,5Bn
McBURNEY,James Wilson T2Lt kia 16-8-17 14RIrRif p169 MR30
McCABE,Albert Peter Patrick.MID 2Lt kia 16/17-5-15 2RWSurr p56 CR France279
McCABE,Daniel.Sir Col 29-9-19 1Manch CR Lancs35
McCABE,Daniel James Bernard 2Lt kia 31-7-17 8Lpool p216 MR29
McCABE,John Bertram 2Lt kia 28-3-18 6LancF p221 MR27
McCAHON,Robert Lt dow 30-3-18 RE 69FC SR p46 CR France62
McCAIG,George Mann 2Lt dow 18-10-18 306RFA 61DAC p32 CR France403,kia
McCAIG,Peter Lt 27-9-18 ScotHorse att54RAF CR France147
McCAIG,William George 2Lt 1-10-18 13RAF CR France256
McCALL,Alfred Ward 2Lt dow 30-9-18 3 att11RScotF p95 CR France525
McCALL,Archibald.MC.2Lt dow 23-8-17 4KOSB p224 CR France40,7/8Bn
McCALL,Eric Hutchinson 2Lt ded 7-9-16 V'Bty RHA p32 CR Iraq6,Hutchison
McCALL,Gavin.MC.DCM.MM.ACapt kia 28-3-18 10ScotRif p103 CR France57
McCALL,Gilbert Stewart Lt dow 20-5-18 5SfthH p241 CR Scot112
McCALL,Mathew Brown Wright 2Lt kia 12-7-15 4RScotF p222 MR4
McCALL,Robert Alfred T2Lt kia 25-9-15 9Ches p96 CR France260
McCALL,William.DSO.LtCol ded 27-6-18 RAMC p253 CR Scot522
McCALLION,Frank Mungo.MC.TLt dow 20-7-18 4SfthH p165 CR France622
McCALLUM,Alexander Meikle TCapt dow 3-4-17 16HLI p163 CR France1204
McCALLUM,Charles 2Lt ded 6-11-18 1/10Lpool p216 CR Lancs4
McCALLUM,Donald T2Lt kia 25-9-15 10ScotRif p103 MR19
McCALLUM,Daniel Capt kia 3-9-16 51AustInf CR France516
McCALLUM,Duncan TCapt kia 22-9-17 12ESurr p113 MR30,21-9-17
McCALLUM,Edward 2Lt drd 30-12-17 13Lond p249 MR41
McCALLUM,George Lt 31-7-15 RAMC att5DCLI p196 MR29
McCALLUM,John 2Lt kia 15-9-16 3CamH p168 CR France239
McCALLUM,Malcolm Campbell 2Lt kia 18-11-16 7ScotRif att15HLI p224 CR France1890
McCALLUM,Norman 2Lt kia 31-7-17 11A&SH p173 MR29
McCALLUM,Rae Bruce T2Lt kia 2-9-17 4 att9RFus p69 CR France154,Ray
McCALLUM,William Hay 2Lt 27-8-18 7HLI MR16
McCAMMON,Charles Duncan 2Lt kia 3-7-16 9RWFus p98 CR France393
McCAMMON,Thomas Valentine Plaisted LtCol dow 28-4-17 5 att20RIrRif p169 CR France40,5RIrRif att2Hamps
McCANCE,Finlay 2Lt dow 22-5-15 2BordR CR France102
McCANCE,Robert 2Lt kia 21-11-17 5ScotRif p224 CR Belgium22
McCANDLISH,William Ewart 2Lt kia 24-3-18 20Lond p251 MR20
McCANN,Bertie Joseph 2Lt 12-11-16 18RIrRif p169 CR Belgium48,14-11-16
McCANN,Francis Lt&QM dow 27-1-16 RASC p193 CR Egypt6,24-1-16

McCANN,William Robert 2Lt dow 11-10-16 7DLI p239 CR France387

McCARTER,John Wylie T2Lt kia 6-12-17 12 att9RInnisF p105 2 entries MR17

McCARTHY,Alexander T2Lt kia 23-8-18 13RFus p69 CR France518

McCARTHY,David.MC.Lt kia 7-10-18 Lpool p72

McCARTHY,J.C.T.Lt 2-1-16 3ConnRgrs attTMB CR France721

McCARTHY,John Maj&QM ded 30-9-19 RASC RetPay p267 CR War135

McCARTHY,John Charles Thomas Lt kia 2-1-16 3ConnRgrs attTMB p172

McCARTHY,Noel Fisher 2Lt kia 18-10-16 2Yorks p90 MR21

McCARTHY,Terence Cormac.MC.Lt kia 7-7-20 IA 1/6Jats att I/99Inf p279 MR38

McCARTHY,Thaddeus Francis.MC.2Lt kia 14-4-18 4LNLancs p234 MR32,Lt

McCARTHY,William Offley Capt dow 26-8-16 2RhodR CR Tanzania1

McCARTHY,William Ronald Ware 2Lt kia 2-11-17 3BordR attPoW Camp p117 CR Palestine3 att3Norf

McCARTNEY,Hugh Lt ded 4-11-15 RAVC p270 CR Scot682

McCARTNEY,Robert Stuart 2Lt dow 9-1-18 WelshR att17Bn p127 CR France518

McCASH,John Watson Lt kia 22-11-16 6BlkW attRFC p19,231&208,23-11-17 MR20

McCASKIE,John T2Lt kia 23-3-18 6Dors p124

McCASKIE,Roy Whyte.MC&Bar.Lt dow 5-8-18 6SfthH p241 CR France85,White

McCASKILL,Kenneth TLt kia 27-9-18 1GordH p166 CR France1483

McCAUCE,Finlay 2Lt dow 22-5-15 3 att2BordR p117

McCAUL,Alexander Theodore Wigram Capt ded 8-8-15 RFA p261 CR Mddx43,21-8-15

McCAUSLAND,Arthur John Kennedy T2Lt kia 10-8-15 6BordR p117 MR4

McCAUSLAND,David Capt kia 22-11-17 12RIrRif p169 MR17

McCAY,James Frederick Daniel Lt kia 27-3-18 15RIrRif p169 MR27

McCAY,Thomas Fulton 2Lt kia 22-11-17 10RIrRif p169 MR17

McCLARENCE,Stanley T2Lt kia 10-4-17 27NumbF p62 CR France644

McCLATCHEY,Samuel Edward.MID Capt 25-3-18 RAMC att18WelshR p196 MR20

McCLATCHIE,Edward Alexander T2Lt dow 10-8-17 12RInnisF p105 CR Belgium18

McCLAY,J.Maj 17-1-17 RAMC CR Yorks38

McCLAY,Samuel Whitfield 2Lt dow 4-10-17 12 att1Lincs p75 CR Belgium112

McCLEAN,Angus Neil 2Lt 22-6-15 8 att1Wilts MR29

McCLEAN,J Lt 16-7-18 SL RE attIWT CR Asia82

McCLELLAN,Alfred 2Lt dow 13-10-17 5RIrRif p170 CR France297,McCLELLAND 1Bn

McCLELLAN,Allan John 2Lt kia 1-7-16 18 att15RIrRif p170 MR21

McCLELLAN,Greville Edward Gordon Capt kia 20-10-15 5 att2Worc p109 CR France114

McCLELLAND,Albert 2Lt 2-4-17 5HLI CR France164

McCLELLAND,Herbert 2Lt dow 2-4-17 5HLI p240

McCLELLAND,Samuel George 2Lt kia 25-9-15 8KOSB p102 MR19

McCLELLAND,Thomas 2Lt kia 16-5-15 7Lpool p215 CR France279

McCLELLAND,William Alan TMaj dow 18-1-18 N&D att15Bn p134 CR Belgium20

McCLENAGHAN,Arthur Bryant Phelps 2Lt kia 16-6-15 1Wilts p153 MR29

McCLENAGHAN,George Mayo Capt dow 8-11-18 1RWKent p141 CR France937

McCLEVERTY,Robert Jim Capt kia 29-10-14 IA 47Sikhs p279 MR28,28-10-14

McCLINTON,John Stuart TCapt kia 5-7-16 7SLancs p125 MR21

McCLOUGHIN,Robert James Capt kia 18-9-14 Beds p86

McCLOUGHLIN,Kenelm Rees.MID Capt kia 25-9-15 IA 14Sikhs att11RScots p279 MR28

McCLUGGAGE,William TLt kia 1-7-16 12RIrRif A'Coy p170 CR France1890

McCLUMPHA,Cyril Dudley Capt ded 9-7-21 IARO att1/112Inf p279 MR43

McCLURE,Charles Russell.MID Maj kia 21-10-14 19Huss p23 CR Belgium451

McCLURE,E.R.Lt 27-6-19 MilLabCps CR EAfrica51

McCLURE,Ernest.MID Lt kia 1-7-16 10RInnisF p105 MR21

McCLURE,Hugh Cecil 2Lt kia 23-10-18 RGA 146SB p40 CR France717,Lt

McCLURE,John 2Lt dow 24-11-17 4 att1RIrF p171 CR France398

McCLURE,John Richard Smyth.MID TLtACapt ded 29-10-18 RE 250TC p46 CR Lond13

McCLURE,T.A.2Lt ded 28-5-18 1/2ConnRgrs &RAF p172 CR Eire512

McCOLL,Duncan Colvin 2Lt kia 18-10-16 3 att5CamH p168 MR21

McCOLL,Ednor Ernest 2LtALt dow 24-10-17 3RScot p54 CR Belgium16,16Bn

McCOLL,William Laurence T2Lt dow 18-7-16 7EKent p57 CR France145,Lawrence Lt

McCOLLOCK,James T2LtACapt kia 22-8-17 7CamH p168

McCOMBE,William Joseph Pogue T2Lt kia 23-4-17 10N&D p134 MR20

McCOMBIE,Christian Nurse 15-1-19 TFNS CR Scot353

McCOMBIE,L.H.D.Lt 3-7-15 IntelDept CR EAfrica125

McCONAGHEY,Charles Jack Lt kia 22-4-16 2BlkW p129 MR38

McCONAGHEY,Maurice Edwin.DSO.MajALtCol kia 23-4-17 1RScotF p95 CR France1185

McCONAGHY,William.DSO.Maj ded 4-7-18 RAMC p196 CR Egypt15

McCONNAN,George Capt kia 9-8-16 10Lpool p216 MR21

McCONNAN,James T2Lt kia 20-9-16 14 att11Manch p155 CR France150,19-9-16 Lt

McCONNEL,Harold Jeffrey 2Lt ded 31-5-18 1RIrRif att98RAFp170 CR Belgium132,Lt 5Bn

McCONNEL,Merrick Hugh.MID Maj dow 14-9-17 B295RFA p32 CR Belgium11

McCONNELL,Frederick James T2Lt ded 10-3-18 RFC p16 CR France285

McCONNELL,Horace Lincoln Cyril.MC.Lt mbk 24-11-17 IARO attRFC p279 CR Syria2,dow PoW 22-11-17

McCONNELL,Primrose.MC.TCapt kia 18-9-18 101RFA DBty p32 MR37

McCONNELL,Reginald Bryan T2Lt kia 22-1-17 6KOSB p102 CR France182,Brian

McCONNELL,Robert Wallace TLt kia 9-4-16 10RLancs p59 MR38

McCONNELL,William Clark Lt kia 9-7-16 3 att2RIrRif p170 MR21

McCONNELL,William Gardiner TCapt dow 13-10-17 RAMC att10Y&L p196 CR France285

McCONNOCHIE,Norman.MC.MID Capt kia 29-3-18 11HampR p121 MR27

McCONNOCHIE,William Jamieson 2Lt kia 8-11-15 5RFC p1 CR Belgium11,8-10-15

McCORMAC,Herbert Hood TLt kia 15-8-15 5RInnisF p105 MR4

McCORMACK,Campbell McNeill.MC&2Bars.CaptAMaj kia 22-9-18 RAMC att15F p196 CR France562

McCORMACK,Edward 2Lt kia 1-11-18 4GordH p242 CR Belgium435

McCORMACK,George 2Lt ded 28-10-18 TankCps p188 CR Dorset109

McCORMACK,John Joseph TCapt kia 28-4-17 27NumbF p62 CR France604

McCORMACK,Joseph Francis TCapt kia 4-10-17 9N&D p134 MR30

McCORMACK,Thomas Lt kia 15-9-16 42MGC p184 MR21

McCORMICK,Edward John TLt kia 14-5-17 7RInnisF &12/8RFC p10&p105 CR France214

McCORMICK,Frank Pockell T2Lt dow 9-8-18 18 att9NumbF p62 CR France20,Pockett

McCORMICK,Gregory Day LtCol kia 21-12-19 IA 72Punjabis att2/122Inf p279 MR43

McCORMICK,Harry Lt dow PoW 8-5-17 5ELancs attMGC Inf p187&226 CR France1276

McCORMICK,James Gardiner 2Lt kia 16-5-15 2Worc p109 MR22,Lt

McCORMICK,John Lt dow 28-7-18 2/4YLI p235 CR France1693

McCORMICK,John Hugh Gardiner Capt kia 19-10-14 4 att2RWar p65 MR29

McCORMICK,Mark Huston 2Lt kia 23-4-17 RMunstF att1RInniskF p175 MR20

McCORMICK,William John T2Lt kia 8-11-17 RB att1lBn p179 CR France439

McCORQUODALE,Archibald Lt dow 25-7-16 RFA attA/ABty p32 CR France513

McCOSH,Edward.MC.Maj dow 26-9-18 9HLI p240 CR France906

McCOSH,Thomas.MC.Capt 16-4-17 RAMC att11WelshR p196 CR Greece6

McCOULL,William Sinclair Lt kia 3-5-17 MGC HB D'Bn attTankCps p184 MR20

McCOURT,Cyril Douglas 2Lt kia 8-10-16 21Lond p251 MR21

McCOWAN,Hew Lt kia 28-6-15 8ScotRif p225 MR4

McCOWAN,James T2Lt kia 16-6-18 SWBord att7KSLI p100 CR France33

McCOWAN,Robert McCaig.MC.2Lt dow 1-11-18 5 att2ScotF p222 CR France34

McCRACKEN,Benjamin Brayshan Victor T2Lt dow 23-8-17 10RInnisF p105 CR Belgium11,Lt 9Bn

McCRACKEN,Henry Joy 2Lt ded 17-10-17 GL &111RFC p10 CR Egypt2,Lt

McCRACKEN,James Henderson T2Lt kia 26-9-17 1RScotF p95 MR30

McCRACKEN,Peter Alexander Earle Lt kia 16-9-18 9HLI p240 CR France686

McCRAE,Alexander Bissett.MC.Lt kia 18-9-18 5ScotRif p224 CR France415

McCRAE,George Capt kia 28-6-15 4RScots p211 MR4

McCRAITH,Bernard Maj ded 29-1-19 RE 1BasePkCoy p209 CR France65,26-1-19

McCREA,Alexander 2Lt 27-6-17 RGA 58SB p40 CR Belgium1

McCREADIE,John 2Lt kia 21-3-18 255RFA p208 MR20

McCREATH,Andrew Berghans Lt dow 11-12-17 2/7NumbF att5KOSB p214 CR Egypt9

McCREDIE,John Forrest 2Lt kia 30-11-17 235MGC p184 MR17

McCREERY,Mona J.M.Capt ded 21-10-18 3RDubF p177 CR Eire355

McCREERY,Robert Bruce Lt kld 15-5-21 17Lancers CR Dorset87

McCRONE,John Milloy.MC.MID T2Lt kia 28-8-16 11A&SH p173 CR France515

McCROSTIE,Charles Hutchison T2Lt kia 1-7-16 GL 19HLI att14TMB p190 CR France1170

McCUBBIN,Percy Griffith 2Lt kia 23-4-18 7RB p179 MR27

McCUDDEN,John Anthony.MC.2Lt kia 18-3-18 84RFC p16 CR France1266

McCULLAGH,Alexander Henry T2Lt kia 16-8-17 11RInnisF att109TMB p105 CR Belgium96

McCULLAGH,Edwin Samuel T2Lt kia 7-6-17 14 att13Ches p96 CR Belgium168

McCULLOCH,Alexander Fenton T2Lt kld 16-8-17 GL &62RFC p10 CR Glouc67,McCULLOUGH

McCULLOCH,David French Capt ded 19-3-19 RASC p267 CR Lond32,Trench

McCULLOCH,Frederick James 2Lt kia 8-11-17 RGA &53RFC p10 &p40 CR Belgium111,McCULLOGH

McCULLOCH,James Arthur TCapt kia 27-9-18 1/8LancF p93 CR France712

McCULLOCH,John Capt 9-4-17 5GordH p242 MR20

McCULLOCH,John Allan 2Lt kia 21-12-17 RFA Z52DivMedTMB p32 CR Palestine9

McCULLOCH,John Wyndham Hamilton TCapt dow 21-10-15 8BordR p117 CR France285

McCULLOCH,Kenneth Lt kia 12-10-17 RFA p208 CR Belgium12

McCULLOCH,Kenneth Lionel Nevill 2Lt kia 1-6-17 6 att16Middx p147 MR20

McCULLOCH,R.C.S.Capt 1-3-19 RASC CR Scot228

McCULLOCH,Robert Arthur Douglas 2Lt kia 3-5-15 RLancs p262&93,LancF MR29

McCULLOCH,Robert Maxwell TLt kia 19-4-17 D106RFA p32 CR France149,20-4-17

McCULLOCH,Thomas LtCol 25-6-15 RAMC p196 CR Hamps64

McCULLOCK,James T2LtACapt kia 22-8-17 7CamH p168 MR30,McCULLOCH

McCULLOUGH,Robert James T2Lt kia 22-10-17 16Ches p96 MR30

McCULLOUGH,William John 2Lt kia 3-2-17 6DLI p239 CR France1182

McCURDY,John 2Lt dow 9-8-16 2Hamps p121 CR Belgium5

McCURRACH,Alexander 2Lt kia 18-10-16 CamH p255 CR France385

McCURRACH,George 2Lt 1-7-16 13HLI p163 MR21

McCURRICH,Laurence Oliphant Capt ded 25-10-18 IARO attRlyTrgCps p279 MR66

McCURRY,Alexander 2Lt mbk 25-4-18 9MGC Inf B'Coy p256 MR30

McCURRY,Walter Tennyson Lt kia 14-3-15 RAMC p196 CR Belgium59

McCUSKER,Patrick Joseph TLt kia 13-11-16 10DubF p177 CR France220

McCUTCHAN,Frank Marsh T2Lt dow 14-5-17 RE 212FC p46 CR France1186

McCUTCHEON,Hugh Edward 2Lt kia 3-9-16 7WorcR att4RFC p19&226 CR France44

McCUTCHEON,John Cecil Lt dow 2-10-16 6RIrF CR Greece4,ded RIrRif

McDERMOTT,Edward.MC.T2Lt kia 12-4-18 10EYorks p84 CR France193

McDERMOTT,J.W.Capt 8-5-19 IARO CIE CR Sussex111

McDERMOTT,Lawrence Alphonsus T2Lt kia 11-10-18 8RWSurr p56 CR France270

McDERMOTT,Robert Keith Capt 20-9-18 3 att1SfthH p165 MR34

McDIARMID,David Lt kia 10-8-16 164MGC p184 MR21

McDIARMID,Kenneth.MID Capt kia 18-4-15 3 att2KOSB p102 MR29

McDONACH,Patrick 2Lt kia 18-11-14 RWKent attSuff p141 CR Belgium89,McDONAGH

McDONALD,A.Lt 19-7-17 1/3KAR CR Tanzania1

McDONALD,Archibald Joseph Lt ded 3-11-18 1LovatScts p204 CR France34

McDONALD,Alexander T2Lt kia 14-7-16 13Lpool p72

McDONALD,Alexander T2Lt kia 30-7-16 9 att2KOSB p102 MR21

McDONALD,Angus George T2Lt ded 29-12-15 20KRRC p151 CR Lancs2

McDONALD,Archibald Lt kia 19-7-17 1/3KAR p202 CR EAfrica38

McDONALD,Charles 2Lt ded 28-11-18 14Lond attMGC Inf p270 CR Lond14,MACDONALD

McDONALD,Donald Alexander T2Lt kia 25-8-15 12ScotRif att5RScots p103 CR Gallipoli4

McDONALD,Edward Lawson Lt 22-11-17 12 RIrRif p170 MR17

McDONALD,Harold Stewart 2Lt kia 21-9-18 6ScotRif p224 CR France663

McDONALD,Harry Alexander Capt ded 5-2-18 ACycCps p243 CR Kent175,6-2-18

McDONALD,Henry Rhodes T2Lt kld 22-12-17 GL &RFC p10

McDONALD,James Vallence 2Lt dow 17-4-18 3 att6/7RScotF p95 MR30

McDONALD,John Capt kia 13-7-15 5HLI p240

McDONALD,John 2Lt ded 21-11-16 29 att22NumbF p62 CR Scot935,MACDONALD kldacc

McDONALD,John Mellis Capt mbk 20-7-16 1ScotRif p256 MR21

McDONALD,John Patrick CaptQM ded 25-3-15 RFA p32 CR Scot764

McDONALD,J.McP.MC.Lt 23-9-17 6ScotRif CR Belgium83

McDONALD,Kenneth William Lt dow PoW 4-9-17 RE LowlandFC attRFC p19&210 CR Belgium140

McDONALD,Lachlan John TLt kld 19-1-18 91RFC p16 CR Hamps192 MACDONALD

McDONALD,Mark William 2Lt drd 2-8-15 4RInnisF p105 CR Ireland45

McDONALD,Norman 2Lt dow 25-12-16 3LNLancs p136 CR EAfrica38 &CR Tanzania1,MACDONALD 2Bn

McDONALD,Ronald Graham.MC.TLtACapt dow 16-8-17 8NumbF p62 CR Belgium8

McDONALD,Samuel 2Lt 25-9-15 7CamH p168 MR19

McDONNELL,Archibald Clark Maj ded 4-10-16 Res RWSurr p270

McDONNELL,Charles Edward TLt kia 26-9-16 12Middx p147 MR21

McDONNELL,Frank Joseph TLt ded 26-5-18 24 att9NumbF p62&257 CR Lancs169

McDONELL,George Oscar Lt dow 18-3-18 RGA att12RFC p16&40 CR France214

McDONNELL,Herbert James Winter T2Lt kia 31-7-17 Middx att4Bn p147 MR29

McDONNELL,John de Courcy 2Lt ded 14-12-15 4GordH p270 CR Yorks294,MacDONNELL

McDONNELL,John LtCol kia 29-9-18 5Leinst att1InniskF p174 CR Belgium84

McDONNELL,John Joseph Chap4Cl kia 9-4-18 RAChDept att55MGC p199 CR France572

McDONNELL,Martin Joseph 2Lt dow 24-1-17 2RIrRif p170 CR France285

McDONNELL,Schomberg Kerr.Hon.GCVO.KCB.Maj dow 23-11-15 5CamH p168 CR Belgium11

McDONNELL,Thomas John T2Lt kia 1-11-17 1/2 att26NumbF p62 MR20

McDOUGAL,A.Lt 26-10-18 LancF CR Scot686

McDOUGAL,Ronald Lt kia 20-10-14 1EKent p57 MR32,McDOUGALL

McDOUGALL,Alexander Ernest 2Lt dow 20-2-18 10/11HLI p163 CR France145,Lt

McDOUGALL,Duncan Albert Herbert 2Lt 9-5-15 1SfthH p165 CR France721

McDOUGALL,George.MC.Capt kia 30-3-18 2/8Manch attMGC p187&237 MR27

McDOUGALL,John MacColl 2Lt kia 26-3-18 9SfthH p165 CR France343,MacDOUGALL

McDOUGALL,Lionel Robert 2LtACapt kia 8-4-17 2YLI Cmdg97TMB p143 CR France1701,8-8-17

McDOUGALL,Sydney Lt 7-8-15 6Manch p236 MR4 Sidney

McDOWALL,Archibald 2Lt kld 12-1-18 3ELancs attRFC p16&111 CR Essex50

McEACHRAN,Charles 2Lt kia 3-2-17 5Dev p217 CR Iraq5,Lt

McEACHRAN,Neil Lt kld 20-5-19 3HLI att59RAF p163 CR Germany1

McELNEY,Robert Gerald.MC.Capt kia 21-3-18 RAMC att77FA p196 CR France512

McELROY,Frederick William.DSO.Lt ded 16-11-18 7TankCps p188 CR France788,Capt

McELROY,George Edward Henry Capt kia 31-7-18 RGA &RAF p40

McELROY,John Oliver Capt ded 5-3-19 Relsd PoW 14Manch p255 CR Eire499 &CR Ireland14,4-3-19

McENERY,John Aloysius Capt kld 26-10-14 RE p46 MR29

McENTIRE,James Thomas LtCol 29-10-18 RAMC O/C 20StatHosp p196 CR Greece9

McENTIRE,James Virtue 2Lt ded 3-8-15 14Lond p270 CR Lond4

McERVEL,John Harold TMaj kia 8-8-16 1Manch attLpool p155 CR France400

McEUEN,James Stewart Capt kia 21-12-14 IA 20DeccanHorse p279 MR28

McEVOY,Frank Osmond T2Lt kia 9-4-17 3 att7ESurr p113 CR France96

McEWAN,David Grant T2Lt kld 23-1-16 10WelshR attTMB p127 CR France631

McEWAN,Donald Fraser 2Lt kia 30-7-16 6BlkW p231 MR21

McEWAN,Fraser 2Lt 24-3-18 GordH att44TMB p166 MR20

McEWAN,George Cameron T2Lt kia 9-4-17 1SfthH A'Coy p165 CR France924,2 att7Bn

McEWAN,George Edward 2Lt kia 15-11-16 9 att6Beds p86 MR21

McEWAN,George Lammie Lt 21-7-15 6HLI p240 MR4

McEWAN,James Robert Dundas Lt kia 12-10-16 2RScotF p95 MR21 McEWEN

McEWAN,Robert William Capt kia 14-4-17 5ScotRif p224 CR France162

McEWAN,William Gray TLt kia 27-10-18 22Manch p155 CR Italy9,2Lt

McEWEN,Charles James 2Lt kia 18-11-16 5HLI p240 CR France534

McEWEN,David Campbell 2Lt dow 10-4-17 1/9RScots A'Coy p212 CR France95,MacEWEN

McFADDEN,Robert Edgar 2Lt kld 12-10-18 10Mddx p236 CR France206

McFADYEN,John Craig 2Lt kia 6-6-17 RFA 11DAC p32 CR Belgium89

McFADYN,John Dennis Goulty.MC.TLt kia 8-8-18 1TankCps p188

McFALL,Thomas Lamont T2Lt kia 7-8-17 9RInnisF p105 CR Belgium45

McFARLAN,Arthur Keith 2Lt kia 15-5-16 11LancF p93 CR France68

McFARLAND,Foster Murray Lt kld 3-9-18 SL &RAF p268 MR20

McFARLAND,Francis John Elliott 2Lt kia 22-7-18 4RIrF p255 MR30

McFARLANE,Alexander Laidlaw T2Lt dow 2-9-18 1MunstF p175 CR France95

McFARLANE,George Capt&QM ded 23-9-17 RASC p193 CR Lond28

McFARLANE,James Arthur T2Lt kia 16-9-16 9HLI p163 CR France453,12Bn

McFARLANE,John.MC.2Lt kia 23-4-17 RFA p208 CR France266

McFARLANE,John Tennant TLt kia 26-9-15 MGC p184 see MacFARLANE,J.T.

McFARLANE,Robert George T2Lt dow 6-3-16 RE 177Co p46

McFARLANE,Robert Speedon 2Lt kia 3-7-16 15HLI p163 CR France1890,MACFARLANE

McFARLANE,Ronald Aitchison Lt kia 25-9-15 13RScot p54 MR19

McFARLANE,Walter T2Lt dow 15-1-17 RLancs att38MGC Inf p59&184 CR Iraq5

207

McFARLANE,William Capt&QM ded 1-1-19 7WRid p227 CR Egypt9
McFARLANE,William Arthur 2Lt ded 8-2-19 3CamH p168 CR Belgium329,7-2-19
McFARLANE,William Hannah Lt kia 27-5-18 1/8A&SH p243 CR France498
McFERRAN,Maurice Anderdon.MC.2Lt 21-3-18 5 att2RIrRif p170 MR27
McFERRAN,Thomas Malcolm T2Lt kia 21-6-17 GL &1RFC p10 MR20
McGAFFIN,Robert Clanrye 2Lt dow 5-7-16 RGA 10HSB p40 CR France251
McGAIN,Ashley Waterson T2Lt kia 1-7-16 11Suff p78 MR21
McGARRY,William Frederick Cecil 2Lt kia 10-8-15 6RDubF p177 MR4
McGARVIE,Hector Archer 2Lt kia 8-7-17 52RFA p32 CR Belgium29
McGAVIN,Charles Abercrombie 2Lt ded 24-11-17 7KRRC p265
McGAVIN,Peter Liddell 2Lt kia 14-8-17 GL &25RFC p3 CR France924
McGEACH,William Morice Lt ded 10-2-19 3SLancs p255 CR Lancs405
McGECHAN,George Ross 2Lt 28-3-18 GordH att8/10Bn p166 MR20
McGEE,Thomas 2Lt kia 24-4-18 9 att2RB p179 MR27
McGEOCH,William T2Lt kia 13-10-16 KOSB att8TMB p102 CR France344
McGEORGE,Thomas Leslie 2Lt kia 7-8-15 5Manch p236 MR4
McGERGOW,Robert Dudley Wilson 2LtTLt kia 21-9-17 5DragGds &RFC p21
McGHEE,Harry TCapt kia 8-5-17 11ScotRif p103 MR37
McGHEE,Thomas Aloysius T2Lt kia 28-9-18 3CamH p168 CR Belgium46
McGHEE,William 2Lt kia 9-4-17 4 att7RScotsF p222 MR20
McGHIE,John Allen Lt 18-10-16 RIM MR65
McGIBBON,R.A.Sister 6-3-19 QAIMNS CR Ireland80
McGIBBON,Richard Forsyth T2Lt kia 23-4-17 10SfthH p165 CR France536
McGIBBON,Richard Forsyth T2Lt dow 16-11-16 15HLI p163 CR France74
McGIBBON,William Patrick 2Lt kia 23-9-17 4 att20DLI p161 MR30
McGIBNEY,Francis George 2Lt kia 3-5-17 4 att1RIrF p171 CR France604
McGILDOWNY,William.DSO.TMaj dow 27-5-17 RGA 124SB p40 CR France729,26-5-17
McGILL,Douglas T2Lt kld 27-10-17 GL &RFC p10 CR Scot523
McGILL,George Thomas.MC.LtACapt kia 3-5-17 2RScot p54 MR20
McGILLEWIE,Malcolm TLtACapt ded 24-5-18 RGA 390SB p40 CR Italy11
McGILLEWIE,Nigel 2Lt kia 12-10-17 6KOSB p102 CR Belgium126
McGILLICUDDY,John TLt kia 1-7-16 26NumbF p62 CR France150
McGILLICUDDY,Richard Hugh.MC.TCaptAMaj ded 20-10-18 RAMC p196 CR Hamps64,21-10-18
McGILLIVRAY,Charles Allister 2Lt kld 14-2-18 RFC p16 CR Wilts3
McGILLIVRAY,David T2Lt kia 29-9-18 15HLI p163 CR France375,dow
McGILLIVRAY,John 2Lt 14-7-16 7SfthH att2LovatScts p165 MR21
McGILLYCUDDY,Richard Hugh.MC.Maj 21-10-18 RAMC CR Hamps64
McGILTON,James 2Lt 23-3-18 8RIrRif p170 MR27
McGINITY,Henry Cuthbert ChapCapt ded 8-11-18 RAChDept att23FA p199 CR Italy7
McGINN,James Joseph AssCommsy&Lt ded 17-9-19 IA S&TCps p279 MR65
McGINN,Wilfrid Joseph T2Lt kld 18-2-18 34RFC p16 CR Shrop52
McGIVENEY,Philip.DSO.T2Lt dow 2-6-18 17LancF p93 CR France84
McGLASHAN,John Ewing Lt 12-7-15 5A&SH p243 MR4
McGONAGIL,Charles John.MC.TLt&QM ded 5-11-18 8Y&L p159 CR Italy9
McGOWAN,John Spence 2Lt 1-7-16 2Dev p77 MR21
McGOWAN,Joseph TLt ded 19-9-15 RAMC p196 CR Europe1,MacGOWAN,18-9-15
McGOWAN,Sidney.MC.Capt kia 25-5-17 5KOSB att 1/6NStaffs p224 MR20
McGOWAN,William 2Lt kia 9-9-16 7Leinst p174 MR21
McGRANE,Peter Leo 2Lt kia 20-5-17 3RIrReg att1InnisF p89 MR20
McGRATH,Noel George Scott Lt dow 5-11-14 2DragGds p21 CR France102
McGRATH,P.N.AssSurg 22-2-17 IMD MR66
McGREGOR,Alexander 2Lt kia 11-4-18 4 att1/7BlkW p230 MR19
McGREGOR,Andrew William 2Lt kia 27-2-16 10 att9BlkW p129 CR France178
McGREGOR,Charles T2Lt kia 24-3-18 7DCLI p114 MR27
McGREGOR,David Capt kia 24-9-18 2A&SH p173 CR France666
McGREGOR,David Stuart.VC.Lt kia 22-10-18 6RScots att29MGC p187 CR Belgium141
McGREGOR,Donald Hamilton T2Lt kia 23-8-18 1GordH D'Coy p166 CR France618,MacGREGOR
McGREGOR,Ian Alexander 2Lt kia 10-9-16 2RFus att2NumbF p69 CR Greece3 15 att2NumbF
McGREGOR,Ian Lacy Lt 18-7-16 5CamH p168 MR21
McGREGOR,James 2Lt 20-5-17 9HLI p240 MR20
McGREGOR,Marcus 2Lt kia 3-10-15 att3Ches p96 MR19
McGREGOR,R.Lt ded 3-5-17 2/2KAR p202
McGREGOR,Robert Roy 2Lt ded 6-10-18 6SLancs p125 MR66
McGREGOR,Roderick Dear Capt mbk 9-4-18 RAMC att18WelshR p256 MR32,MacGREGOR

McGREGOR,Ronald Alexander Lt 9-4-18 6SfthH p241 MR19
McGREGOR,Ronald Malcolm 2Lt kia 24-5-15 2Ches p96 MR29
McGREGOR,W.2Lt 4-10-20 Worc CR Scot674
McGRIGOR,James Neil Grant 2Lt dow 7-11-14 GordH p166 CR Bucks55
McGRORY,John Joseph 2Lt kia 28-9-18 7A&SH p243 MR30
McGUFFIE,Arthur John Capt kia 29-11-17 1/7ScotRif p224 CR Palestine9
McGUINESS,John Norman 2Lt kia 21-3-18 11RDubF att2RMunstF p177 MR27
McGUIRE,Brian 2Lt kia 14-9-14 2DubF p177 CR France864
McGUIRE,Edward Lt 25-9-15 11HLI p163 MR19
McGUIRE,Robert Blayrey T2Lt kld 30-4-17 23Middx p147 CR Belgium15,Blayne
McGUSTY,Barry Edge 2Lt ded 15-5-18 3Leinst p266 CR Ireland24
McGUSTY,George Ross TLt dow 14-6-16 8RIrRif p170 CR France51
McHAFFIE,Arthur David 2Lt ded 4-10-17 IARO attS&TCps p279 MR43 &CR Pakistan50A
McHALE,George Nolan 2Lt kia 20-9-17 5Lpool p215 MR30
McHALE,John Richard Jarlath TLt kia 24-3-18 19Lpool p72 CR France1203,MacHALE
McHARDY,John Lt kia 24-7-18 1/5GordH p256 CR France865
McHARDY,Stewart John 2Lt kia 30-4-18 7Lond p247 CR Palestine3
McHARDY-YOUNG,James William T2Lt kia 19-8-15 RGA 6TMB p40 CR France721
McHARRIE,Robert Capt kia 9-6-18 5 att1RScotF p222 CR France33
McHATTIE,James William Lt kia 25-4-18 5Y&L att20RAFp238 CR France134
McHOUL,James Stewart T2Lt dow 26-8-17 16RScot p54 MR21,MacHOUL
McHUGH,Edward James Lt ded 31-10-18 4 att1RInnisF p105 CR France40,6Bn
McHUGH,Terence HonLt&QM dow 20-5-18 RAVC p198 CR France40
McILLVAINE,John Joseph Chap4Cl drd 26-2-18 RAChDept att2/7N&D p199 MR40
McILWAINE,Arthur Arnold 2Lt kia 5-3-16 1LNLanc p136 CR France551
McINDEOR,Malcolm Neil Lt dow 26-10-18 14Lond att7CamHp270 CR Wales168,26-10-19
McINDOE,William Reid 2Lt kia 6-8-18 5 att1GordH p242 CR France33,5-8-18
McINNES,John Edward 2Lt kia 1-7-16 1/5N&D p233 MR21
McINNES,Percy Norman Leopold 2Lt dow 20-7-16 3/5Yorks p221 CR France28
McINNES,Robert Donald T2Lt dow 30-3-18 17LancF p93 CR France44
McINNES,William Miller T2Lt kia 25-1-17 5Wilts p153 CR Iraq5
McINTOSH,Angus Alexander Capt 15-10-18 RHGds CR USA234
McINTOSH,Charles George Gordon T2Lt dow 28-9-15 8BlkW p129 CR France98,kia
McINTOSH,Daniel 2Lt dow 20-5-18 RGA 297SB p40 CR France95
McINTOSH,James 2Lt kia 13-11-16 1GordH p166 MR21
McINTOSH,James Marshall 2Lt kia 16-6-15 2RIrRif p170 MR29
McINTOSH,James Robert Hay.DCM.2Lt kia 22-3-18 7BlkW p231 MR20
McINTOSH,John 2Lt kia 22-3-18 16 att1/5NumbF p62 CR France834 Ex 19Hu
McINTOSH,John 2Lt kia 9-4-18 RGA 217SB p209 MR19
McINTOSH,Joseph Francis TLt drd 10-10-18 3 att2RWFus p98 CR Ireland14
McINTOSH,Robert Rae Lt kia 20-4-15 7CamH p168 MR29,24-4-15
McINTOSH,William TLt dow 6-7-16 23NumbF p62 CR France145,22Bn
McINTOSH,William Alexander 2Lt kia 26-9-17 2RScot p54 MR30,Lt
McINTOSH,William Matthew dow Lt 1-7-16 17HLI att97TMB p163 MR21
McINTYRE,Aaron 2Lt 29-7-16 25AustInf CR France1890
McINTYRE,Alexander Cameron.MC.Maj dow 24-3-18 8A&SH p243 CR France40,MACINTYRE
McINTYRE,Donald William 2Lt kia 28-6-17 Y&L att1/4Bn p159 MR20
McINTYRE,Francis T2Lt kia 3-5-17 8EYorks p84 MR20
McINTYRE,Frederick Malcolm T2Lt dow 2-5-16 RE 176TC p46 CR France224
McINTYRE,James Lennie T2Lt dow 14-5-18 10RFus p69 CR France145
McINTYRE,John Caldwell T2Lt dow 5-10-15 11 att2Yorks p91 CR France924,L
McINTYRE,John Watson 2Lt ded 30-3-17 4KOSB p224 CR France1182
McINTYRE,Malcolm T2Lt dow 21-9-16 6CamH p168 CR France40,Lt
McINTYRE,Reginald John TLt kia 25/26-10-18 HLI att1Bn p163 MR38
McINTYRE,Robert William.MBE.T2Lt kia 25-7-18 11EYorks p84 CR France19
McINTYRE,Sidney Colin 2Lt dow 25-3-18 6 att10DCLI p114 MR20
McINTYRE,Walter Graham T2Lt dow 21-8-18 att1BordR p117 CR France134
McIVER,Donald Lt kia 24-3-18 3 att2/7SLancs p125
McIVER,Hector Capt 30-4-21 RASC CR Palestine5
McIVER,James Noble 2Lt kia 25-8-17 8RScots p212 CR Belgium88
McIVER,Kenneth MacKenzie TLt kld 30-10-18 KAR &KRRC p202
McIVER,Kenneth Patrick John TLt dow 26-1-16 SL &NigR p201 CR WAfrica56
McJANET,Arthur William T2Lt kia 31-10-17 GL &18RFC p10 CR France88,McJANNET

McJANET,Walter Guy 2Lt dow 24-8-18 2Beds p86 CR Oxford69

McJANET,William Robert Benjamin Capt 14-7-16 10 att7SfthH p165 MR21,McJANNET Benny

McJANNET,Hector William.MID Capt ded 28-10-18 C261RFA p207 CR Egypt9,dow

McKAY,Alexander Matheson.MC.TLt dow 18-5-18 RE 179TC p46 CR France145

McKAY,Alfred Edwin Capt kia 28-12-17 RFC SR p10 MR20

McKAY,Alexander Steele 2Lt kia 10-4-18 3RScot p54 MR32

McKAY,Edward Horatio Lt dow 21-9-18 1SfthH p165 CR Palestine3

McKAY,Ernest Lt kia 19-9-15 1/7Ches p223 CR Gallipoli4

McKAY,Frederick.DCM. Lt dow 28-2-17 1RWFus p98 CR France204,MACKAY

McKAY,George Newton TLt kia 24-7-18 6MGC p184

McKAY,Harry.MC.Capt kia 10-4-18 4CamH p242 CR France260

McKAY,Henry Marshall Capt kia 13-11-14 RE p46 CR France706

McKAY,James Ivan 2LtTCapt kia 5-10-17 WRidR &RFC p10

McKAY,John Thomas Ralph Lt kia 30-3-18 IARO att58Rif p279 CR Palestine9

McKAY,William James 2Lt ded 29-9-19 LabCps CR Ireland183

McKEAN,Hugh Capt kia 7-7-16 12Manch p155 MR21

McKEAN,Kenneth Victor Lt ded 27-9-19 1MddxHuss att 1/1DorsYeo p270 CR Lebanon1

McKEAND,David Gray TCapt ded 23-3-19 11WYorks p263 CR Yorks597

McKECHNIE,Alexander 2Lt kia 21-3-18 9KRRC p151 MR27

McKEE,Alexander Lt kia 22-11-17 10RlrRif p170 MR17

McKEE,John Albert T2Lt kia 1-12-17 2SStaffs p122 CR France530

McKEE,Patrick Joseph 2Lt kia 10-8-17 3 att2RlrRif p170 MR29

McKEE,William Dickson Lt kia 11-8-17 12RlrRif p170 MR29

McKEEVER,James Holden Lt dow 20-9-17 4Ches p222 CR France193

McKEEVER,Louis Lawrence.MC.Capt 8-11-17 RAMC att1/4RScotsF p196 CR Palestine8

McKELLAR,Archibald Peter 2Lt dow 22-7-18 7A&SH p243 CR France1415

McKELLAR,Frederick Charles Marshall.MC.T2Lt kia 21-8-18 1Lincs p75 CR France514

McKELLAR,John Thomson 2Lt kia 13-11-16 8A&SH A'Coy p243 CR France131,Lt

McKENDRICK,David 2Lt kia 30-11-17 59MGC p184 MR17

McKENNA,John Charles Xavier TMaj ded 20-4-17 9NStaffs p157 CR France46

McKENNA,Justin Morell TLt kia 2-10-17 GL KRRC attRFC p10 CR France924

McKENNA,Reginald Talkington 2Lt kia 10-10-18 1 att8NumbF p62 CR France611

McKENNEY,William James 2Lt ded 9-5-16 6HLI p240 CR Scot237,16Bn

McKENNY,Edward Richard T2Lt kia 18-10-18 12 att6RInnisF p105 CR France660

McKENZIE,Alan A.Capt ded 3-11-19 RE IWT p262 CR Wales568,MACKENZIE Ex RNR

McKENZIE,Alexander TLt kia 7-6-17 11RWSurr p56 CR Belgium29

McKENZIE,Alexander Capt ded 25-5-19 RAMC p267 CR Scot286,Lt

McKENZIE,Angus.MC&Bar.Capt kia 4-11-18 2Manch p155 CR France1479

McKENZIE,Arthur Murdo.MC.TLtACapt ded 8-9-18 RE 6DivSigCo p46 CR France34

McKENZIE,Frederick Thomas Lt kia 23-3-18 RHFA p208

McKENZIE,Gordon William T2Lt kia 20-9-17 GL &RFC p10 CR Belgium18

McKENZIE,Ian.MC.Capt kia 21-3-18 5SfthH p241

McKENZIE,Ian Hume Townsend 2Lt ded 12-11-18 3HLI p265 CR Camb16,MacKENZIE

McKENZIE,James Kinnell T2Lt kia 30-10-15 10 att8SfthH p165 CR France423

McKENZIE,John Alexander.MC.Capt dow 10-4-18 RAMC att6DLI p196 CR France1094,MACKENZIE 9-4-18

McKENZIE,Kenneth Buchanan Capt kia 25-9-15 IA 123Rif att58 p279 MR28

McKENZIE,Kenneth Fitzgerald 2Lt kia 14-7-16 MGC p184

McKENZIE,Kenneth Fitzpatrick TLt kia 25-9-15 5CamH p168 CR France219,MACKENZIE

McKENZIE,Kenneth Nowell 2Lt kia 4-6-15 9EYorks p84 MR4

McKENZIE,Leslie TLt dow 2-4-18 9BlkW p129 CR France40

McKENZIE,Robert Andrew T2Lt kia 10-11-17 KRRC att9Bn p151 CR Belgium101

McKENZIE,William 2Lt dow 12-6-18 2/14Lond p249 CR Palestine3

McKENZIE,William Sinclair.DSO.2Lt kia 21-4-17 1SfthH p165 MR38

McKERGOW,Robert Dudley Wilson 2LtTLt kia 21-9-17 5DragGds &RFC p10 CR Belgium84

McKERRELL,Augustus De Segar.CB.TBrigGen ded 24-4-16 CommdgTayDefences Staff p1 CR Scot237 Ex CamH

McKERRELL,William Archibald Struthers Lt dow 10-4-18 8RScots att4RAF p211&258 CR France98

McKERROW,Charles Kenneth TCapt dow 20-12-16 RAMC att10NumbF p196 CR Belgium11

McKERSIE,Archibald James Lt dow 16-7-15 p240 CR Egypt6,Capt

McKEY,Hugh Aloysius 2Lt kia 25-3-18 5 att18HLI p240 MR27

McKIE,Douglas Hamlin 2Lt dow 11-4-17 3 att27NumbF p62 CR France184,kia

McKIE,Eric 2Lt kia 24-3-18 KRRC att11Bn p151 MR27

McKIE,William Purdon Lt kia 20-9-18 1/7HLI p240 CR France1496,MACKIE

McKIERNAN,Evelyn James SubCdr ded 14-6-16 IA S&TCps p279 CR Iraq6

McKIERNAN,Michael Vincent.MM&Bar.2Lt dow 11-5-18 6ConnRgrs p172 CR France145

McKIEVER,Victor Comley 2Lt dow 18-5-15 3 att2Manch p155 CR Belgium56,28-5-15

McKILLOP,James Bunting 2Lt kia 27-9-18 5RScotRif p224 CR France484

McKIMMIE,Alexander T2Lt kia 23-5-17 GL &6RFC p10 CR Belgium11

McKIN,John Nelson Burdette 2Lt kia 10-3-18 RFC p16 CR France525

McKINLAY,David Oliver 2Lt kia 21-10-17 28MGC p184 Belgium63

McKINLAY,Robert Galloway 2Lt kia 25-9-15 10HLI p163 MR19

McKINLEY,James Gordon 2Lt dow 3-6-15 RGA attRE p40 CR France200

McKINLEY,Samuel Brown.MC.Capt dow 7-2-19 12RScots p54 CR Scot757

McKINNEL,Bryden Capt kia 16-6-15 10Lpool p216 MR29,McKINNELL

McKINNEY,George TLt kia 16-8-17 13RlrRif p170 MR30

McKINNEY,Joseph James Moore 2Lt kia 27-3-18 12RlrRif p170 MR27

McKINNIE,Peter T2Lt kia 4-10-17 10MGC Inf p184 MR30

McKINNON,C.F.Capt ded 14-6-19 SL att1/6KAR p201&255

McKINNON,James Beaton T2Lt kia 7-6-17 23Middx p147 CR Belgium111

McKINNON,J.F.Lt mbk 28-11-17 65RFC p256 MR20

McKINSTRY,James McNeil T2Lt dow 2-12-16 2RInnisF p105 CR France44

McKINSTRY,Ronald William T2Lt kia 23-9-16 A48RFA p32 CR France399

McKINTY,Alexander Joseph(Allister) 2Lt drd 27-2-16 IARO p279 CR Scot280

McKIRDY,Gillies T2LtACapt kia 11-2-17 4Beds p86 CR France220,MACKIRDY

McKIRDY,Robert Fingland Capt kia 12-7-15 5A&SH p243 MR4

McKISACK,Lawrence Hill Wilson Lt kld 13-11-16 5Lancers attRFC p3&p22 CR Ireland33 Ex RGA &RE

McKNIGHT,Samuel TCapt kia 29-9-18 17RScots p54 CR Belgium72

McKNIGHT,Thomas T2Lt kia 21-2-17 10RInnisF p105 CR Belgium54

McLACHLAN,Berry.MC.Lt dow 11-10-18 C4RHA p32 CR France660

McLAGAN,James 2Lt kld 8-6-16 RE 61FC p270 CR Scot761

McLAGEN,Frederick Charles Albertus T2Lt ded 26-5-17 3LancF p263 CR Lond11

McLAGGAN,James Murray.MC.TCapt kia 4-10-18 RAMC att2RFus p196 CR France234,3Bn

McLAINE,Donald Lt dow 2-4-18 1/8LancF p221 CR France145

McLARDIE,Archibald 2Lt kia 25-12-15 5A&SH p243 CR Gallipoli3

McLARE,Alexander Vernon.MC.Lt kia 12-4-18 8DLI p239 MR32,Vernor Capt

McLAREN,Athole Stewart 2Lt kia 18-9-18 7Lond p247 CR France369

McLAREN,Donald Lt kia 3-5-17 1 att6KOSB p102 MR20

McLAREN,Eustace 2Lt kia 22-11-17 2/5Y&L p238 MR17

McLAREN,Hon Francis Walter Stafford T2Lt kld 30-8-17 GL &RFC p10 CR Surrey114

McLAREN,Frederic Monteath 2Lt kia 12-8-17 GL &RFC p10 MR20

McLAREN,James T2Lt dow 12-1-17 6KOSB p102 CR France1182

McLAREN,James Capt kia 21-11-17 7A&SH p243 MR17

McLAREN,John Francis Capt kia 28-9-15 4CamH p242 MR19

McLAREN,Malcolm Colquhoun.MC.TLt kia 22-10-18 7Leic p88 CR France192,MacLAREN Capt 23-10-18

McLAREN,Quentin 2Lt kia 26-10-16 6BlkW p231 CR France35

McLAREN,Richard Juson Maj dow 2-8-17 2WYorks p82 CR Belgium11

McLAREN,Robert T2Lt dow 24-7-16 16Ches p96 CR France141

McLAREN,Robert John Capt kia 1-7-16 14Ches att2SWBord p96 CR France1501

McLAREN,Samuel Bruce TLt dow 13-8-16 RE 35DivSigCo p46 CR France51

McLAREN,Thomas James 2Lt kia 25-1-16 RFA p32 CR Belgium101

McLAREN,William Somerville 2Lt dow 19-11-17 GL &48RFC p10 CR France1361

McLAUCHLAN,Alan Stewart Lt kia 28-3-18 RGA 405SB p209 CR France1182,MACLAUCHLAN

McLAUCHLAN,Andrew Youngson Greig 2Lt kia 28-9-18 8Manch p237 CR France379

McLAUGHLIN,Arthur Lt kia 9-5-15 3 att1RlrRif p170 MR32

McLAUGHLIN,Edmund Coldicoate Lt kia 18-5-15 6Lond D'Coy p246 CR France260

McLAUGHLIN,Edward Archibald Crofton T2Lt kia 9-11-15 7SfthH p165 CR Belgium127

McLAUGHLIN,Hubert Guy Bromilow 2Lt dow 12-10-16 3 att7SfthH p165 CR France385,Lt

McLAUGHLIN,Hubert James.DSO.LtCol ded 25-3-15 Remount Service p24 CR Hamps1,28-3-15

McLAUGHLIN,L.T.Lt 19-4-17 4WYorks attRFC CR Hamps4

McLAUGHLIN,William Pulteney Michael Dalzell Maj ded 6-12-19 IA 107Pnrs p279
McLAURIN,Robert 2Lt kia 7-6-17 10RIrRif p170 CR Belgium97,Lt
McLAY,Archibald.MC.2LtACapt kia 21-3-18 1/2 att6Leic p88 MR27
McLAY,Joseph T2LtACapt ded 9-10-18 16RB p179 CR France770
McLEAN,Angus Neil 2Lt kia 22-6-15 p153
McLEAN,Atholl Archibald T2Lt kia 1-7-16 11Suff p78 CR France515
McLEAN,Charles John Lt kia 20-9-17 9RScots p212 MR30
McLEAN,Colin LtCol kia 13-3-15 6GordH p242 CR France705
McLEAN,Donald 2Lt kia 14-7-18 1GordH CR France33
McLEAN,Donald Gordon TLt kia 4-2-18 GL &45RFC p16 CR Italy7
McLEAN,Gordon Davis TLt kia 21-8-18 7TankCps B'Coy p188 CR France514
McLEAN,Hugh Archibald Capt ded 7-11-18 RAMC p271 CR Scot756
McLEAN,James Monteith 2Lt kia 28-4-17 HLI p163 MR20
McLEAN,John Lt kld 16-7-18 GL RE attIWT p191 MR38
McLEAN,John Victor T2Lt dow 17-7-16 6RBerks p139 CR Mddx26,9Bn
McLEAN,Joseph Richard Garratt Lt kia 9-5-18 2A&SH p173 MR30
McLEAN,Robert TLt kia 11-7-16 RE 76FC p46 CR Belgium73
McLEAN,Robert Drysdale 2Lt kia 26-10-17 C64RFA p32 CR Belgium8
McLEAN,Thomas William 2Lt kia 21-9-17 GL &RFC p10 MR20
McLEAN,Walter Lt dow 17-11-17 6WYorks p218 CR Belgium72,Capt
McLEAN,William James 2Lt dow 12-8-16 1Ess p132 CR Belgium11
McLEAN,William Mcfarlane 2Lt kia 24-3-18 5A&SH p243
McLEAN,William Wood.MC.Lt kia 23-9-18 2A&SH p173 CR France666
McLEAN-RICHARDSON,Pelman Archibald Capt ded 19-11-18 IARO attS&TCps p279
McLEAR,Geoffrey D'Olier.MC.Lt died 29-1-19 IARO att2/39GarhwalRif p279 CR Kent177,MACLEAR
McLEAVY,C.E.SubCdr 17-11-15 IA CR Lond2
McLEAY,Duncan Matheson 2Lt kia 23-3-17 6A&SH attRFC p243 p19 CR France511
McLEISH,Gordon 2Lt 31-7-18 RAF CR Scot387
McLELLAN,Allan John 2Lt 1-7-16 18 att15RIrRif MR21
McLELLAN,Harold Noble 2Lt kia 9-7-16 2Manch p155 MR21
McLELLAN,James 2LtTLt kia 4-10-17 3HLI attMGC Inf p163&184 MR30
McLELLAN,Joseph Taylor TLt kia 21-3-18 55MGC Inf p184 CR France765,MacLELLAN
McLELLAN,Samuel TLt drd 16-10-17 GL RE &IWT p191 CR France1359
McLELLAN,Thomas Ancott Capt kia 25-9-16 9A&SH p243 CR France402
McLELLAND,Robert Carrick Lt dow 17-8-16 9HLI p240 CR Scot764
McLENNAN,Farquhar John 2Lt kia 18-8-16 1GordH p166 MR21
McLENNAN,John Lawrence.MC.Capt kia 28-8-19 RASC attRAF p267 CR Asia81
McLENNAN,William Ross 2Lt kia 21-3-18 5BordR p228 MR27
McLEOD,Alexander Lt drd 3-3-18 RE IWT CR France134
McLEOD,Angus 2Lt kia 20-11-17 4SfthH p241 CR France1498,dow
McLEOD,Archibald Alastair Capt kia 2-11-14 1Glouc p107 MR29
McLEOD,Daniel Edward 2Lt kia 1-12-16 B86RFA p32 CR France251
McLEOD,Douglas Keith 2Lt dow 21-10-18 24RFA 43Bty p32 CR France146
McLEOD,Elmer George T2Lt dow 23-11-17 GL &46RFC p10 CR France214
McLEOD,George MacFarquhar 2Lt kia 7-4-17 7GordH p242 CR France15
McLEOD,George Munro Lt ded 22-5-18 RAMC p271 CR Scot757,MacLEOD
McLEOD,G.M.2Lt 7-4-17 7GordH CR France15
McLEOD,John 2Lt dow 25-4-17 5ScotF p222 CR France1185
McLEOD,Ian Keith Falconer TCapt kia 27-4-18 RAMC att75FA p196
McLEOD,Matthew Paul 2Lt kia 14-11-16 6BlkW p231 CR France35
McLEOD,Roderick Patterson 2Lt ded 14-12-18 RE p46 CR Sussex112,MacLEOD Paterson
McLEOD,W.A.Rev ded 18-11-16 YMCA CR Greece7
McLEOD,William.MC.Capt dow 18-5-19 RAMC p196 MR43
McLERNON,Robert William 2Lt kia 8-5-15 RFA p32 CR Belgium132
McLINTOCK,Arnold.MIDx2 Capt kia 3-9-16 5WRid p227 CR France383
McLINTOCK,John Lawrie Lt kia 26-2-18 RFC p16 MR20
McLOUGHLIN,James Patrick Lt dow 24-5-15 4DubF attRIrRif p177 CR France285
McLURE,David T2Lt ded 8-3-18 2KRRC att4ArmyMuskSchool p151 CR France134
McMAHON,Bruce Metcalfe Capt ded 3-5-19 RAVC p198 CR Germany1
McMAHON,Norman Reginald.DSO.BrigGen kia 11-11-14 RFus attHQ10InfBde p69 MR32
McMAHON,Patrick 2Lt dow 11-6-17 4RIrRif p170 CR France285
McMAHON,Patrick Stan T2Lt dow 29-12-15 8MunstF p175 CR France80,Senon
McMAHON,T.SubCdr 19-12-20 MilWksServ MR65
McMAKING,Oscar Lennox 2Lt kia 11-9-17 LincYeo attRFC p19&204 MR20
McMANUS,Terence Joseph Lt ded 23-12-19 2Mddx p265 CR Sussex144,dow

McMASTER,Charles.MC.TLtACapt kia 16-8-17 7RIrRif attTMB p170 MR30
McMASTER,Hugh.DSO.MC.Maj dow 2-12-17 A46RH&FA p32 CR France64
McMASTER,John Wallace Lt dow 11-9-18 RGA att35SB p40 CR France103
McMASTER,Philip George TLt kia 20-6-18 18MGC p184 CR France196
McMICHAEL,Douglas William T2Lt dow 17-4-16 8Beds p86 CR Belgium73,20-4-16
McMICHAEL,John Edward Lt ded 12-5-17 EAUL 4/3KAR p202 CR EAfrica35 &C Tanzania1
McMICHAEL,John Douglas Wield 2Lt kia 23-5-16 5Worc p109 CR France68,Wyl 3Bn
McMICHAEL,Walter Buchanan Lt kia 26-7-16 1/7GordH p242 CR France453
McMICKING,Gilbert Thomas Gore 2Lt ded 11-11-18 Camb p245 CR Europe97
McMILLAN,Donald Cameron 2Lt dow 11-3-16 12KRRC p151 CR France8,2Bn
McMILLAN,George T2Lt kia 31-7-17 2ELancs p111 MR29
McMILLAN,Hugh Dobie TLt kia 19-7-18 8BlkW p129 CR France324,dow
McMILLAN,John Lt dow 15-3-15 4SfthH p241 CR France102
McMILLAN,John 2Lt kia 24-3-18 LanarkYeo p204
McMILLAN,John Casely 2LtTCapt dow 6-2-17 RScotFus &4RFC p10&95 CR France59
McMILLAN,John Mackie Lt kia 1-8-18 7/8KOSB p102 CR France864,MACMILLAN
McMILLAN,J.S.TLt ded 12-3-18 GL RScots att3/3KAR p191&202 CR EAfrica35 &CR Tanzania1
McMILLAN,Neil T2Lt dow 29-11-16 1BlkW p129 CR France59,kia
McMILLAN,Kenneth Gregor 2Lt kia 16-8-17 33/33RFA p32 CR Belgium113
McMILLAN,William Calderwood SenAssSurg &Lt ded 24-10-17 IA ISMDept p279 CR Iraq8
McMILLAN,William McLeod Capt kia 25-9-15 11A&SH p173 MR19
McMINN,Hugh Bell TMaj ded 27-6-18 GL DAD RlyTrans p266 CR France40,27-7-18
McMINN,John Capt kia 27-5-18 14RIrRif p170 MR18
McMONNIES,Stuart Menzies 2Lt kia 20-11-17 4SfthH p241 MR17,21-11-17
McMORDIE,James Wilson 2Lt kia 18-11-16 9KSLI att2YLI p145 MR21
McMURDO,G.D.Capt 4-11-19 HLI CR Scot808
McMURDO,John Coke Capt kia 25-4-15 1Ess p132 MR4
McMURDO,John Hamilton T2Lt kia 27-5-18 NumbF Res att5Bn p62 MR18
McMURRAY,John Capt kia 12-10-17 12RScots p54 MR30
McMURRAY,Bertie Stedman Joseph Maj ded 12-6-18 IA 108Inf attSPersiaRif p279 CR Asia82
McMURRAY,Stuart 2Lt kia 7-8-17 2/2Lond attRFC p19&245 CR France201,8-8-
McMURTRIE,John.MC.TCaptAMaj kia 26-7-17 RE 151FC p46 CR Belgium23
McMURTEIE,S.G.Chap4Cl 14-6-19 CR Ches178
McMUTRIE,Robert Lindsay TLtACapt kia 21-8-18 1RScotF p95 CR France618
McNAB,Alexander 2Lt dow 27-4-18 147RFA p32 CR France102
McNAB,J.B.McC.Lt 14-2-19 RE CR Belgium241
McNAB,James Fortune 2Lt dow 6-4-16 4A&SH att1KOSB p173 CR France35,MACNAB
McNAB,John Borrie McCulloch Lt kia 14-2-19 RE p210 CR Belgium241
McNAIR,Eric Archibald.VC.TCapt ded 12-8-18 9RSuss p119 CR Italy12
McNAIR,Robert Schemehorn T2Lt kld 17-3-18 RFC p16 CR Scot520,Schermerhorn
McNALLY,James Maj&QM ded 28-4-17 ConnRgrs p172 CR Eire301
McNALLY,Thomas Patrick 2Lt kia 30-9-17 10Y&L p159 CR Belgium17
McNALLY,William Wright.MC.2Lt kia 8-10-17 4Worc p109 MR30
McNAMARA,Joseph Charles 2Lt kia 2-6-17 GL &4RFC p10 MR20
McNAMARA,Vincent T2Lt ded 29-11-15 RE 136FortressCoy p46 CR Gallipoli1,dow
McNAMEE,John Joseph TLt dow 1-9-18 9RInnisF p105 CR France100,MacNAME 3-9-18
McNAUGHT,Douglas Ramson T2Lt kld 27-3-17 8GordH p166 CR Mddx15
McNAUGHT,Ernest Henry 2Lt kia 18-7-16 12RFus p69 CR Belgium116
McNAUGHT,James T2Lt kia 7-1-17 2RScots p54 CR France1890
McNAUGHT,James McGeogh Capt ded 13-11-19 4RWSurr p271
McNAUGHT-DAVIS,James Walden Fortune Lt 17-1-15 1SWBord CR France721
McNAUGHTON,Algernon 2Lt kia 30-9-18 10Lond p248 MR16
McNAUGHTON,Hamish Ian 2Lt kia 24-4-17 100RFA E'Bty p32 CR Greece6
McNAUGHTON,Norman George.MC.Capt kia 24-6-17 57RFC p10 MR20
McNAUGHTON,William James 2LtTLt dow 31-12-15 5ScotF p222 CR Gallipoli1
McNEIL,Francis George 2Lt kia 8-3-18 GL &70RFC p16 CR Belgium140
McNEIL,John Fraser 2Lt dow 9-9-15 D256RFA p32 CR France14
McNEIL,Robert T2Lt kia 6-2-16 6KOSB C'Coy p102 CR Belgium137
McNEILE,Henry Donald LtCol kld 20-12-15 1Drags p21 CR France1586
McNEILE,John LtCol kia 12-7-15 4KOSB p223 MR4

McNEILL,Alan Gordon.MC.CaptBtMaj dow 10-1-17 RE 2/2WLancFC p46 CR Belgium11

McNEILL,Donald Augustus 2Lt kia 16-11-16 7RFC p3 CR France742,MACNEILL

McNEILL,John 2Lt drd 26-2-18 GL RE &IWT p191 MR38

McNEILL,John Charles 2Lt kia 3-5-17 2Ess p132 MR20

McNEILL,Leslie Ernest TLt ded 25-3-19 4RIrDragGds p261 CR Surrey13

McNEILL,Malcolm.CMG.DSO.LtCol ded 3-6-17 11A&SH p173 CR France13

McNEILL,Neil 2Lt kia 11-11-14 1BlkW p129 MR29

McNEILL,Nigel Lorne 2Lt kia 1-7-16 3 att2GordH D'Coy p166 CR France331

McNEILL,Robert Archibald 2Lt kia 9-4-17 21NumbF p62 CR France265,MACNEILL

McNICHOL,James Percival 2Lt dow 20-6-18 4 att10A&SH p173 CR France84,Lt

McNICOL,John Hart.MC.TCaptAMaj ded 8-10-18 RAMC att86FA p196 CR Greece1,McNICHOL

McNICOLL,David Graham.DSO.MID LtCol dow 20-9-17 20DLI p161 CR Belgium15

McNICOLL,Godfrey Robert 2Lt kia 20-11-17 5BlkW p231 CR France712,Lt

McNICOLL,Malcolm David.MC.Capt dow 21-11-17 2/4YLI p235 CR France398,20-11-17

McNIFF,Francis Joseph 2Lt kia 13-3-18 24NumbF attRFC p16&62 CR France699

McNIVEN,Alastair T2Lt dow 1-5-17 7CamH p168 CR France113,MacNIVEN Lt

McNIVEN,Alister Orr Lt kia 5-9-17 7HLI &RFC p271 MR20

McNULTY,Michael John Lt kia 4-9-15 5 att9DubF p177 MR32

McPHAIL,Alexander Banks.MC.LtACapt dow 31-10-18 RGA 2SB p40 CR France146

McPHAIL,Peter John Stewart Lt ded 26-11-18 RGA p256 CR Scot239

McPHEE,Arthur David.MC.Capt 8-10-18 GL &CamH CR Scot246

McPHEE,Douglas 2Lt ded 21-2-19 RGA 1SB p40 CR Germany1

McPHERSON,Allen Ross T2Lt kld 26-1-18 RFC p16 CR Canada1688

McPHERSON,Archibald Austin Oliver Lt dow 26-5-18 RE 416FC p210 CR France95,MACPHERSON

McPHERSON,Ian Charles 2Lt kia 25-9-15 3 att2GordH p166 MR19

McPHERSON,Leonard Alfred T2Lt kia 28-7-17 GL &43RFC p10 CR France258

McPHERSON,Robert David 2Lt drd 6-6-16 8CamH p265 CR Scot900,5-6-16 see MacPHERSON.R.D.

McPHERSON,William Lt kia 8-5-17 A101RFA p208 CR Greece6

McQUAKER,George Wilson 2Lt kia 13-11-17 1/4ScotF p222 CR Palestine9

McQUEEN,John T2Lt kia 24-4-17 13HLI p163 CRFrance421,MACQUEEN

McQUESTIN,Matthew Lt kia 28-3-18 1/4RScotsF att87TMB p222 MR20

McQUIBAN,William TCapt ded 2-5-18 RAMC p196 CR Egypt2

McQUINN,Wallace.MC.T2Lt de 6-8-18 PoW 16Manch p155 CR Germany4

McRAE,Archibald Douglas Lt ded 11-7-16 IA 80CarnaticInf p279 CR India164

McRAE,Archibald Ludovic 2Lt kia 12-10-17 5CamH p168 MR30

McRAE,Archibald William Capt kia 4-6-17 20RIrRif p170

McRAE,Peter McKay T2Lt kia 24-12-17 7Nhants attRE 129FC p137 CR France528,MACRAE

McRAE,Ronald Gwynnyd Montague T2Lt kia 28-1-18 24RFC p16 CR France1203

McRAE,William 2Lt kia 27-3-18 42MGC p184 MR20

McRAE,William Gordon 2Lt kia 26-10-17 GL &19RFC p10 MR20,21-9-17

McREADY-D'IARMID,Alistair Malcolm Cluny.VC.TLtACapt kia 1-12-17 4 att17Mddx p147 MR17

McREYNOLDS,John Bernard HonLt&QM kia 12-11-16 11EYorks p84 CR France203

McROBERTS,Thomas T2Lt kia 13-8-17 20RIrRif p170 CR Belgium125

McSHANE,John Chesterton T2Lt dow 28-7-16 RE 229FC p46 CR France80

McSHANE,Vincent TLt kia 21-8-15 15NumbF att2SWBord p62 MR4

McSHERRY,Bernard 2Lt kia 13-4-19 2Manch p155 CR France804,14-4-18

McSORLEY,Frederick William.MID 2Lt kia 5-4-17 20NumbF p62 CR France1182

McSWEENEY,Felix Joseph T2Lt kia 30-7-17 Middx att 19Bn A'Coy p147 CR Belgium102

McSWEENY,Randal Roderick Lt ded 15-3-17 4HLI p163 CR France40,2Lt 10-3-17

McSWINEY,Eugene John Capt ded 26-12-16 RAMC p196 CR Eire122

McSWINY,Claude O'C T2Lt kia 14-7-16 9 att7KSLI p145 MR21

McTAVISH,I.A.B 2Lt kld 15-5-18 GL&RAF p191

McTAVISH,James Duncan 2Lt kia 23-4-17 GordH att7Bn p166 MR20

McVEIGH,Joseph 2Lt kia 28-3-18 3 att9BlkW p129 MR20

McVEIGH,William John TLt kia 28-12-17 7MunstF p175 CR Palestine3,6Bn

McVICAR,Thomas Graham 2Lt kia 28-3-18 4 att5BlkW p230 MR27

McVICAR,William Lt&QM ded 17-7-19 GL MGC Inf 116TrainingBn p266 CR Lincs61

McVICKER,Edgar Harold TLt kia 10-9-16 RAMC att2/5LancF p196 CR France397,9-9-16

McVICKER,John William T2Lt kia 14-7-16 13Lpool p72 MR21

McVITTIE,George Henry 2Lt ded 12-3-15 2/4BordR p228 MR40,8-3-15

McWHA,Archibald John 2Lt kld 2-1-17 RFC CR Kent180,Lt 5-1-17

McWHA,George Henry 2Lt kia 20-9-17 LNLancs att1/5Bn p136 MR30 see MEWHA

McWHAE,John Wilson Lt kia 21-6-17 189RFA p32 CR Belgium127

McWHANNELL,John.MC.2Lt dow 3-7-16 2Wilts p153 CR France23

McWHINNIE,Charles Routledge Lt dow 1-7-18 3 att6RWSurr p56 CR France41

McWILLIAM,Charles Thomas Lt kia 18-3-16 5GordH att51DivCycCoy p242 CR France157

McWILLIAM,Hamish Lt kia 29-5-16 2 att9BlkW p129 CR France423

MEACOCK,Robert Hugh T2Lt dow 19-10-16 21DLI p161 CR France46,19Bn

MEAD,Anthony George Lt ded 26-5-19 SL attRE p268CR Hamps186

MEAD,Bernard Wallace 2Lt dow 2-6-15 4RFus p69 CR France285

MEAD,Christopher.MID Lt kia 28-9-15 4 att2ESurr p113 MR19

MEAD,Edward 2Lt dow 22-4-18 6LancF p221 CR France145

MEAD,Evelyn Augustus Kew Capt 13-3-19 161/20RASC CR Surrey15

MEAD,George John 2Lt kia 22-2-17 IARO att92Punjabis p280 CR Iraq5

MEAD,Horace Warren TCapt kia 13-7-16 8RSuss p119 CR France630,MEADE

MEAD,John Robert Capt ded 15-12-17 RE 335RoadConsCo p47 CR Derby135

MEAD,Joseph Frederick 2Lt kia 23-8-14 4RFus p69 CR Belgium242

MEAD,Ralph Edward Culverhouse T2Lt kia 29-9-17 7EKent p57 CR Belgium3

MEAD,Robert John T2Lt dow 2-8-15 8RFus p69 CR France922

MEAD,Thomas Hallard T2Lt kia 24-7-16 72RFA p32 CR France423

MEADE,Alfred de Courcy.MC.Maj dedacc 15-12-18 RE p262 CR Ches18,14-12-18

MEADE,Cyril 2Lt kia 5-4-17 2/5Glouc p225 CR France674

MEADE,Evelyn Augustus Kew Capt ded 13-3-19 161/20RASC p255 CR Surrey15

MEADE,Michael.MC.Capt kia 9-4-18 5Lpool p215 CR France279

MEADE,Richard Gilbert Trevor T2Lt dow 10-10-17 MGC Cav p184 MR38 &CR Iraq8 Ex 14Huss

MEADE,Richard John Frederick Philip.MIDx2 Lt kia 4-6-15 IA 14Sikhs p280 CR Gallipoli3

MEADE,Robert Percy T2Lt kia 11-7-16 13RB p179 MR21

MEADE,Wakefield Waldo Lt kia 20-6-15 6 att3Worc p109 MR29 CR Belgium453

MEADOWCROFT,James T2Lt ded 7-11-18 RE 476FC p47 CR France332

MEADOWS,Albert Henry Capt kia 8-8-16 8Lpool p215 CR France402

MEADOWS,Christopher Bentley.MC.T2Lt kia 19-5-18 1RLancs p59 CR France412

MEADOWS,Daunt Capt 13-10-19 IndVetCps CR Pakistan50A

MEADOWS,Reginald Melville TLt kia 4-9-18 12ESurr p113 CR Belgium111

MEADS,John Arthur.MC.TCaptAMaj kia 10-10-17 10N&D p134 CR Belgium83

MEADWAY,Brian Wilton 2Lt ded 4-6-18 7Nhants att56RAF p137 CR Herts87,Lt

MEAKIN,Herbert Percy TCapt kia 25-9-16 3CldGds attGdsTMB p51 MR21

MEAKIN,Kenneth William Glenny 2Lt dow 16-5-15 5NStaffs p238 CR France285

MEAKIN,Sidney Arthur Lt kia 17-10-15 4 att1NStaffs p157 CR France681,17-12-14

MEAKIN,Thomas T2Lt kia 21-10-18 Leic att11Bn p88 CR France1266

MEAKIN,Walter Kendrick Capt kia 15-8-15 5Beds p219 MR4

MEAKINS,Robert William Spencam 2Lt kia 27-8-16 1RWKent p141 MR21

MEAL,William Capt ded 27-5-19 1Worc GarBn p264&255

MEALING,Maurice Edmund 2Lt kia 24-3-18 KSLI att56RFC p16&p145,ded MR20

MEARES,Cecil Stanley TCapt kia 30-7-16 19 att24RFus p69 CR France402

MEARES,Ellen Caroline Miss ded 24-2-19 VAD BRCS CR Surrey1

MEARNES,Henry Gould T2Lt dow 20-8-16 1GordH p166 CR France66,Gauld

MEARNS,Angus Hughes Lt ded 24-6-17 9BlkW &57RFC p129&11,Hughs kia MR20

MEARS,Edward de Quincey 2Lt kia 13-7-16 10Ess p132 MR21,14-7-16

MEARS,Francis Peel TCapt ded 22-2-19 RASC p255 CR Kent83,Perl

MEARS,James William 2Lt kia 12-11-14 HLI p163 MR29

MEARS-DEVENISH,John Augustus T2Lt dow 22-3-18 12 att1RFus p69 CR France987

MEASDY,Thomas Percy 2Lt kia 30-9-16 2Glouc p107 CR Greece3

MEASURES,John Charles T2Lt kia 30-9-16 6Y&L p159 MR21

MEASURES,Percy Lt kia 31-12-17 1/5Leic p220 CR France163,30-12-17

MEASURES,William Henry.MC.T2Lt kia 22-8-18 5 att11RFus p69 MR16

MEAUTYS,Denzil Hatfield Lt dow 7-5-17 3 att12WYorks p82 CR France40,1 att12Bn

MEAUTYS,Paul Raymond.MC.Capt kia 16-6-17 2NStaffs p157 CR France1185

MEAUTYS,Thomas Gilliat Lt kia 26-9-14 1WYorks p82 CR France1329,22-9-14

MEDCALF,Edwin Francis T2Lt dow 11-6-17 3 att8Leic p88 CR France518,kia

MEDCALF,William Archer T2Lt dow 15-10-17 15N&D p134 CR France139

MEDCRAFT,Alexander Raymond T2Lt kia 18-9-18 Hamps att12Bn p121 MR37 &end ofCR Greece1

MEDHURST,William Richard 2Lt ded 4-1-17 5RWKent p271

MEDLAND,James Edward Percy 2Lt kia 23-3-18 RE 64FC p210 MR20
MEDLEN,Leslie Lashbrook T2Lt kia 22-12-17 GL &16RFC p11 CR France95
MEDLEY,Bertram Anthony 2Lt kia 25-9-15 HLI p163 MR19
MEDLICOTT,Edward Morley TLt kia 11-4-16 2RBerks p139 CR France515
MEDLICOTT,Harold William 2Lt kld 21-5-18 RFC p16 MR20
MEDLICOTT,Sidney Neville T2Lt dow 6-10-15 A61RFA HB p32 CR France98
MEDWORTH,Frank Oswald.MC.TCapt kia 13-5-18 2Manch p155 CR France924
MEE,Ernest Campbell 2Lt kia 3-9-16 4WRid p227 MR21
MEE,George Hamilton TLt kia 22-8-15 6EYorks p84 MR4
MEECHAM,David Jeffreys T2Lt kia 27-3-17 11RWFus p98 CR Greece6,28-3-17
MEEK,Hubert Kingsley TCapt kia 15-9-16 14KRRC p151 CR France402
MEEK,John Lt kia 24/26-5-15 7DLI p239 MR29,24-5-15
MEEK,William T2Lt kia 17/19-9-18 2N&D p134 CR France835,18-9-18
MEEKE,William Stanley Capt kia 1-7-16 2Middx p147 CR France393
MEEKING,Norman Arthur 2Lt kia 1-7-16 9Lond p248 MR21
MEENAGHAN,John 2Lt kia 21-3-18 4ConnRgrs p172 CR France1495
MEERS,John Henry TCapt dow 9-10-15 RAMC attLNLancs p197 CR France178,10-10-15
MEERS,Philip James Lt ded 6-12-19 IA 2/69Punjabis p280 MR43,Capt
MEES,Rudolf Lt kld 14-11-18 GL&RAF p191
MEESON,Fitzalan Ridware Lt dow 4-11-18 13/17RH&FA p32
MEFF,William Blann Lt dow 14-11-16 1/7GordH p242 CR France41,kia
MEGAW,William Cecil Kennedy.MC.Capt&Ajt kia 31-3-15 1Norf p74 CR Belgium59
MEGENEY,Horace William LtACapt kia 21-9-18 72RFA p32 CR France439
MEGGS,Stewart Gordon 2Lt ded 3-3-17 RGA 213SB p209 CR France300
MEGGY,Frederick Arthur LtACapt kia 31-8-18 4Ess p232 CR France496
MEGSON,Robert Hargraves.MIDx2 Capt kia 23-4-17 16Manch p155 MR20
MEHARG,Robert John Lt ded 4-3-17 RIM attRE IWT p280 CR Iraq5
MEHEGAN,Daniel Joseph 2Lt kia 21-3-18 10 RDubF att 2RMunstF p177 MR27
MEIKLE,James Drysdale T2Lt kia 4-11-18 13KRRC att111TMB p151 CR France1430
MEIKLE,Robert Jardine 2Lt kia 15-9-16 4DLI p161 CR France374
MEIKLE,William Reginald Dempster 2Lt kia 30-11-17 1KOSB p102 MR17
MEIKLEJOHN,Kenneth Forbes Lt&Adjt kia 26-9-14 1CamH p168 CR France1329,25-9-14
MEIKLEJOHN,Robert 2LtTCapt dow 15-11-15 7ScotRif p224 CR Gallipoli3
MEIN,Dudley Gerald.MC.Lt kia 26-10-18 IA 31Lancers attMysoreLancers p280 CR Lebanon1
MEIR,Wilfrid Ault.MID TLtACapt kia 11-4-18 8NStaffs p157 CR Belgium89,dow 10-4-18
MEIRE,Walter Herbert Geoffrey T2Lt kia 26-9-15 9Norf p74 MR19
MEISTER,Charles Gustave Clark.MC.Chap4Cl kia 18-4-18 RAChDept att10A&SH p199 CR Belgium21
MELDRUM,Ernest Alexander 2Lt kia 25-9-15 IARO att2/8GurkhaRif p280 MR28
MELDRUM,George Dundas 2Lt kia 16-12-16 5GordH p242 CR France832
MELDRUM,I.Sister 2-2-18 TFNS CR Scot677
MELDRUM,Ronald 2Lt kia 9-10-17 HAC Inf p206 MR30
MELHADO,Owen Stirling.MID T2Lt dow 7-12-15 6 att11Yorks p91 CR Europe9
MELHUISH,Alan George James 2Lt kia 21-3-18 7N&D p233 MR20
MELHUISH,Jan Vaughan Brenbridge T2Lt kia 27-10-15 7SomLI p80 CR France707,Ian Bremridge
MELHUISH,Leslie T2Lt kia 27-11-17 1/2Yorks att2/5YLI p91 MR17
MELLAND,Edward Guy Lt kia 30-6-15 8Ches attWYorks p96 CR Belgium96,1-7-15
MELLARD,Richard Bartlett Lt kia 1-7-16 5NStaffs p238 CR France576
MELLENFIELD,Cecil Beven T2Lt kia 23-10-16 7SLancs p125 CR France383
MELLER,Arthur William 2Lt kia 29-1-16 1EYorks p84 MR15,20-9-14
MELLERS,George Henry Reginald Capt kia 14-10-15 7N&D p233 MR19,13-10-15
MELLES,Gordon Frank Lt ded 6-11-15 2RFA HQ Staff p208 CR Egypt3
MELLING,Charles Flower.MC.ACapt mbk 13-5-18 1LancF p227 MR32
MELLING,Harold Lt kld 7-11-18 5Ches attRAF p256
MELLIS,Andrew Douglas John T2Lt kia 17-10-15 5 O&BLI p130 CR Belgium113,Lt
MELLIS,George Duncan Capt kia 30-11-17 C255RFA p207 CR France662
MELLIS,James 2Lt kia 15-6-18 5 att1GordH p242 CR France33
MELLIS-SMITH,Samuel Grant 2Lt kia 11-2-17 IARO 1/4 att2/4GurkhaRif p280 CR Iraq5
MELLISH,John George T2Lt kia 10-3-17 5Wilts p153 MR38
MELLISH,Henry Tupper Capt ded 4-10-17 RASC p267 CR Scot241
MELLISH,Richard Coppin T2Lt kia 25-9-15 1Middx p147 CR France114
MELLISH,Roy Thompson T2Lt kia 7-3-18 79RFC p16 CR France987
MELLISS,Montague Stanley CaptHonMaj ded 4-3-19 Res p271

MELLO,Arnold 2Lt dow 17-11-15 14Lond p249 CR France201
MELLOR,Francis Rigby TLt dow 15-1-17 10 att6ELancs p111 CR Iraq5,16-1-17
MELLOR,Frank Johnson Lt dow 19-9-16 2N&D p134 CR France105
MELLOR,Harold Welton TCapt ded 28-5-18 15RFus att2KAR p69 CR EAfrica90
MELLOR,John Lewis 2Lt kia 26-6-16 C163RFA att231TMB p32 CR France643
MELLOR,N.Lt drd 10-10-18 4WRid &RAF p256
MELLOR,Percy 2Lt kia 13-10-15 5NStaffs p230 MR19
MELLOR,Richard 2Lt kia 16-6-17 2/5Manch A'Coy p236 CR France163
MELLOR,Roy TLt kia 1-7-16 22Manch p155 MR21
MELLOR,Vincent Charles Serecold Lt ded 21-3-19 KRRC p255 CR Somerset161
MELLOR,Walton Capt kia 23-8-14 2RIrReg p89 CR Belgium242
MELLY,Hugh Peter Egeston Mesnard 2Lt kia 2-7-16 1Lancs p59 CR France643,Egerton 1-7-16
MELLY,Reginald Ernest Lt kia 30-7-16 20Lpool p72 MR21
MELROSE,James Douglas Leitch AMaj dow 25-4-18 RGA 29SB p271&206,RHFA CR Belgium40
MELROSE,Thomas Nelson 2Lt kia 14-11-16 5NumbF p213 MR21
MELTON,Arthur Francis Capt kia 27-11-17 2/6WRid p227 MR17
MELVILL,Melvill Leopold 2Lt kia 31-10-17 108/23RFA p33 CR Belgium11
MELVILLE,Alan Maj dedacc 8-8-16 IA 122Inf p280 MR43
MELVILLE,David.MC.ACapt kia 26-10-18 4 att5CamHp242 CR Belgium140
MELVILLE,David Charles T2Lt kld 21-1-18 RFC p16 CR Essex1
MELVILLE,David William 2Lt kia 21-3-18 14A&SH p173 MR20
MELVILLE,Harry George.DSO.CIE.Col ded 7-12-18 IMS p280 CR Iraq8
MELVILLE,Harry Taylor TLt kia 31-7-18 GL &RAF p191
MELVILLE,Hugh Colquhoun 2Lt kia 14-2-16 13 att10N&D p134 MR29
MELVILLE,John 2Lt kia 27-11-17 2/5WRid p256 MR17
MELVILLE,Joseph Thomson 2Lt kia 16-9-16 6HLI p240 CR France402
MELVILLE,Stuart Powis T2Lt kia 23-1-16 11N&D p134 CR France348,Bowie
MELVILLE,Sydney John Craig 2Lt kia 8-10-16 109RFA p208 CR France401
MELVILLE,William Woodfall Lt kia 9-5-15 6 att2KRRC MR22
MELVIN,Will Simpson 2Lt kld 23-8-18 1/4RB &RAF p179 CR France223
MENCE,William Charles Capt ded 25-7-19 RAMC CR Devon15
MENDEL,Reginald William Wynn 2Lt ded 19-9-17 RFA p33 CR Lond8
MENDS-GIBSON,Ollyett Archibald 2Lt dow 27-8-16 106/22RFA CR France23
MENNIE,James T2Lt kia 18-9-18 7RSuss p119 CR France369
MENNIE,John Henderson 2Lt kia 10-4-17 4CamH att2/10Lpool p243 CR France705,11-4-17
MENZIES,Alastair Forbes.DSO.TLtACapt kia 4-5-18 17RFus p69
MENZIES,Alastair Graham TLt kia 1-1-15 ScotGds p52
MENZIES,Alexander Lawrence 2Lt dow 21-9-16 C48RFA p33 CR France145,Lt
MENZIES,Archibald Rudge Wilson Lt kia 25-11-17 2ScotGds p52 MR17
MENZIES,Arthur John Alexander.DSO.CaptAtCol kia 9-8-18 RAMC Cmdg3Cav p197 CR France652
MENZIES,Harry 2Lt kia 29-4-17 23NumbF p62 MR20
MENZIES,Robert John.MID Capt kia 31-7-17 6BlkW p231 CR Belgium96
MENZIES,Vere Gordon Maj mbk 21-1-16 IA 97Inf p280 MR38
MENZIES,William Alan 2Lt dow 14-6-17 RGA 163SB p41 CR Belgium29
MEO,Giovanni Batista Lt kia 10-6-16 12Lond p248 CR France1327,Battista
MEPHAM,Horace Leslie 2Lt kia 11-4-18 6 att2RFus p69 MR32
MERCER,Alfred Stephen T2Lt kia 13-3-17 A155RFA p33 CR France133
MERCER,Andrew 2Lt dow 22-10-15 1BlkW p129 CR France40
MERCER,Archibald Ariel Maj kia 17-11-15 2Dors p124 CR Iraq6,17-11-14
MERCER,Eric Cameron 2Lt kia 13-10-14 ULIA att2LancF p93&280 CR France1
MERCER,Eric Dawson T2Lt dow 2-5-17 10LancFus p93 CR France40
MERCER,George Enos T2Lt kia 3-10-18 8 att1/4Leic p88 CR France375
MERCER,Hugh William Welch LtCol ded 14-6-18 IA p280
MERCER,John Edgar ACapt ded 3-12-19 RFA attHQ HejazOps p271 CR Egypt15,acckld
MERCER,S.Minchin Maj ded 27-6-19 RASC RetIA p267 CR Yorks438
MERCER,Thomas Milbourn 2Lt mbk 23-11-17 TankCps p256 MR17
MERCER,W.H.W.LtCol 14-6-18 86CarnaticInf MR65
MERCER,William.MBE.TLt&QM ded 13-11-18 MontgomYeo p271 CR Greece9 12-18 RASC attExpForce
MERCER,William Malcolm Lt kia 28-11-17 4KOSB p223 CR Palestine9
MERCHANT,Alfred Douglas Lt kia 10-4-18 6 att1LancF p221 MR32
MERCHANT,Arthur Douglas Mount-Stephen T2Lt kld 13-5-17 GL &68RFC p1 CR Yorks38
MERCHANT,Herbert George T2Lt kia 28-9-16 9 att7Beds p86 MR21
MERCHANT,Reginald Frank 2Lt kia 21-3-18 36MGC Inf p184 CR France1061

MERCHANT,W.MC.Capt&QM 6-2-20 RAMC CR Hamps1
MERCHANT,William John 2Lt kia 7-10-16 7Lond p247 MR21
MERCIER,H.B.2Lt ded 3-11-18 RlrRif &RAF p170
MERCIER,Y.W.2Lt kia 25/27-9-15 3 att1RScotF p95 MR29
MERE,Colin Leigh TLt kia 10-8-15 6RLancs p59 MR4
MEREDITH,Arthur Llewellyn 2Lt dow 4-6-18 1Mon p243 CR France10
MEREDITH,E.M.2Lt kld 13-4-18 GL&RAF p191 CR Belgium38
MEREDITH,Eric Dunfee T2Lt kia 4/10-10-16 32RFus p69 MR21,7-10-16
MEREDITH,Gerald.MC.TCapt ded 27-3-18 11KRRC p151 CRFrance145
MEREDITH,John Collins 2Lt kia 23-9-18 43/24RFA p33 CR France835
MEREDITH,Malcolm Hereward 2Lt kia 10-11-15 4Worc p109 CR Gallipoli4
MEREDITH,Maurice Neville.MC.2Lt kia 26-10-18 IARO 1Lancers attMysoreLancers p280 CR Lebanon1,Lt
MEREDITH,Owen Watkin Wynn Hardinge T2Lt dow PoW 20-11-17 GL &64RFC p11 CR France421
MEREDITH,William John Lt dow 20-2-15 3MunstF attSLancs p175 CR Belgium182
MEREDITH,William Morris TCapt ded 7-12-18 Lpool p263 CR Norf128
MEREWETHER,Christopher Kerr Capt dow 19-12-17 1/4Wilts p236 CR Egypt7,Ken 20-12-17
MEREWETHER,John Alwarth TCapt kia 15-9-16 9RB p179 MR21
MERIVALE,Francis Lt ded 17-10-18 1/7NumbF p214 CR France146,17-11-18
MERIVALE,John William Capt kia 15-9-16 1/7NumbF A'Coy p214 CR France387
MERK,John William Albert 2Lt ded 15-4-17 IA 1/6GurkhaRif p280 CR Iraq8
MERRELL,Arthur Walter 2Lt kia 8-5-17 1/2 att12Glouc p107 MR20
MERRETT,Arthur Edwin T2Lt kia 18-12-16 15Hamps p121 CR Belgium28
MERRETT,Harold Edmund T2Lt dow 17-8-18 10N&D p134 CR France145
MERRICK,Herbert Frederick Rivers Lt kia 3-5-17 2RBerks p139 MR21
MERRICK,Thomas Barker.MC.TLtACapt kia 2-9-18 4MGC Inf p184 CR France421
MERRICK,Thomas James.DSO.MC.LtAMaj ded 8-11-18 87RFA p33 CR France13
MERRIFIELD,Percy 2Lt kia 21-3-18 Worc att2/8Bn p109 MR27,MERIFIELD
MERRIKIN,George Houlden 2Lt kia 27-8-18 2Lond p245 CR France1186
MERRILES,John Sutherland 2Lt kia 19-6-15 5RScots p211 CR Gallipoli6
MERRIMAN,Charles Henry T2Lt kia 9-4-17 2Wilts p153 CR France162
MERRIMAN,Gordon Holland Capt kia 12-5-15 95RFA p33 CR Belgium115
MERRIMAN,Sydney Thomas Lt ded 3-6-21 IA 1/97DeccanInf p280 MR65
MERRITT,Frederick Charles LtAMaj kia 17-6-17 B15RFA p33 CR France1182
MERRY,George William Henry 2Lt kia 21-3-18 16MGC Inf p184 CR France1495
MERRY,Norman Cuthbert TCapt kia 15-7-16 10Ches p96 MR21,14-7-16
MERRY,Ralph Valentine T2Lt kia 1-7-16 18Lpool p72 CR France397
MERRYFIELD,Leopold Reginald TCapt dow 28-8-16 13ESurr p113 CR France102
MERRYMAN,William Robert Hill.MID T2Lt kia 15-8-16 8RB p179 CR France399,MERRIMAN
MERRYWEATHER,Charles Walter TMaj kia 23-11-16 16LancF p93 MR21
MERSON,Marshall Lt kia 3-5-17 5RScotsF p222 MR34
MERSON,William Murison Smith Capt kia 13-11-16 7GordH p242 CR France131
MERTS,Walter Scott T2Lt ded 28-7-16 RE p47 CR Wales137,MERTZ
MESHAM,Robert Seymour TLt kia 19-4-18 SL MilLabCps WAAF p201&268 CR EAfrica92
MESSENGER,Henry Frederick Roy 2Lt kia 22-8-15 6Yorks p91 MR4
MESSENGER,L.W.2Lt ded 4-7-18 RH&FA &RAF p33
MESSENGER,Wilfred Chaundler TCapt dow 16-9-17 12RB p179 CR France145
MESSER,Allan Ernest Capt dow 17-2-16 1KRRC p151 CR France8
MESSERVY,Ernest Dyce Capt kia 20-7-17 21Lond attRFC p19&251 MR20
MESSERVY,Gerald.MC.CaptAMaj kia 9-10-18 16/41RFA p33 CR France914,8-10-18
MESSOM,Harold 2Lt kia 16-5-15 2RWSurr p56 CR France279
MESTON-REID,James Capt ded 6-11-18 RE p210 MR70 &CR Europe179
METCALF,Cecil David Lt kia 20-4-18 7Lond p247 CR France880
METCALF,George 2Lt dow 12-4-18 15RScots CR Belgium11
METCALF,Lister 2Lt kia 8-8-16 4Lancs p213 MR21
METCALFE,Francis.MID Capt ded 10-7-18 RAMC 1FA p256 CR Numb7
METCALFE,George 2Lt dow 12-4-18 10RScots p212
METCALFE,George Christopher TCapt ded 16-3-19 RAMC p267 MR66
METCALFE,Harry 2Lt kia 4-4-17 7N&D att11RB p233 CR France905
METCALFE,Ian Morehouse Lt dow PoW 1-11-17 3Worc p109 MR19
METCALFE,John Chaytor TMaj kia 7-7-16 13Ches p96 CR France393
METCALFE,Johnn Clifford.MC.Capt dow 20-3-16 RAMC 1/1FA p254 CR Belgium11,20-3-18
METCALFE,Joseph Stephen 2Lt kia 17-1-17 3Mon p244 MR19
METCALFE,Lawrence T2Lt ded 25-12-17 16WYorks p263 CR France184,Laurence Lt
METCALFE,Wilfred Charles TLt dow 19-8-16 11ESurr p113 CR France51,9Bn

METCALFE-SMITH,Bertram Cecil Lt dow 22-4-18 4 att21WYorks p82 CR France10
METGE,Randolph Cole Capt ded 4-10-19 Ex 5Leinst p266 CR Eire440
METHUEN,Cameron O'Bryen Harford Capt kia 20/21-10-14 RWar p65 MR29,20-10-14
METHVEN,David George Capt kia 20-10-14 SfthH p165 CR France1140
METHVIN,Donald Capt kia 12-9-18 2CamH p168 CR Greece6
METSON,Herbert Frank 2Lt dow 9-8-16 D70RFA p33 CR France23
METTAM,Athol Roy 2Lt kia 16-8-17 WYorks att217MGC Inf p82&184 MR30
METTHAM,John Arthur TLtACapt ded 12-11-18 RE p47 MR70 &CR Europe179
MEUGENS,Geoffrey Ellsworth Maj ded 30-10-18 TankCps p188 CR Kent268
MEVDELL,Colin Grant 2Lt kia 10-8-17 43RFC p11 CR France88,MEUDELL Ex AustImpF
MEWBURN,Simon William Richard Capt kia 20-5-16 14Huss p22 MR38,21-5-16
MEWHA,George Henry 2Lt kia 20-9-17 LNLancs att1/5Bn p136 MR30
MEWS,John Keith Capt dow 24-8-18 1Lond p245 CR France103
MEYER,Alan Wallace 2Lt ded 11-3-18 RGA 289SB p41 CR Italy7
MEYER,Constant Clifford William Lt dow 3-7-16 2Lincs p75 CR France119
MEYER,Herbert Frederick 2Lt kld 15-10-17 GL &RFC p11 CR Shrop52
MEYER,James Leopold Maj died 22-6-17 RE p47 MR65
MEYER,Llewellen 2Lt kia 11-6-16 6DLI p239 CR Belgium21
MEYER-GRIFFITH,Harold Walter Gooch Maj kia 28-5-15 LNLancs p136 CR WAfrica28
MEYERS,H.Deverell TCapt ded 30-10-18 RASC p193 CR Ireland24
MEYERS,Stanley Arthur 2Lt kia 26-10-17 1Lond p245 MR30
MEYNELL,Edward James Hugh.MC.Capt dow 4-10-18 1/5SStaffs p229 CR France446
MEYNELL,Hugo Charles T2Lt dow 27-9-15 12Ess p132 CR France80
MEYRICK,John Charles 2Lt kld 26-7-16 4LNLancs p234 CR Lancs92
MEYRICKE,Robert James Francis TMajALtCol kia 17-2-17 11RFus att6Nhampt p69 CR France251
MEYRICKE,Rupert John Chabert Maj ded 25-1-16 58RFA p261 CR Europe1,26-1-16
MEYSEY-THOMPSON,Claude Henry Meysey.Hon.Capt dow 17-6-15 3RB p179 CR Yorks249
MIALL-SMITH,George Eric.MC.Lt kia 25-9-17 8Norf &11RFC p258,11&74,25-3-17 CR France120
MIALL-SMITH,Ralph Arnold TLt kia 26-9-16 11RFus p69 MR21
MICALLEF,Paolo Capt ded 11-12-16 2MaltaR p201 CR Europe4
MICHAELIS,Grant Moritz Lt kia 23-9-15 RE 1/2FC p210 CR Gallipoli17
MICHELL,Arthur T2Lt kia 12-10-17 7RWKent p141 MR30
MICHELL,James Douglas T2Lt ded 9-10-18 2/4KAR &MGC p202 CR SAfrica144
MICHELL,John Colloryan Capt kia 28-8-14 12Lancers p22 CR France1715
MICHELL,Noel Burgess TCapt kia 22-3-18 11RFus p69 MR27
MICHELL,Robert Williams.MID TCapt dow 20-7-16 RAMC p197 CR Camb3
MICHELMORE,Jeffery Edwards Morton Lt kia 9-4-18 6 att13ESurr p226 MR32
MICHELMORE,Robert Frank 2Lt dow 7-7-16 16Middx p147 CR France245
MICHELSON,Arthur Conrad 2Lt kia 18-10-17 B64RFA p33 CR Belgium125
MICHELSON,Walter 2Lt dow 27-7-16 14DLI p161 CR Belgium11
MICHIE,Christopher Young Lt kia 21-11-17 7ScotRif p224 CR Belgium22
MICHIE,Henry George Lt kia 26-9-16 15 att8NumbF p62 MR21
MICHIE,John 2Lt kia 15-7-17 D15HLI p163 CR Belgium24
MICHIE,John Boyd TLt ded 31-12-18 RAMC p197 MR70 &CR Europe179
MICKLE,Kenneth Aubrey.DSO.Capt ded 30-7-19 4/22RGA p262 CR Australia307
MICKLETHWAITE,Harold Chandos T2Lt dow 25-3-18 1EYorks p84 CR France699
MICKLEWRIGHT,James T2Lt kia 3-11-18 RE 178TC p47 CR France1259
MIDDLECOTE,Edwin William Alfred George Lt kia 3-10-18 16KRRC attRAF p151 CR France915
MIDDLEDITCH,Archibald Milne Lt kia 1-7-16 12Ess p132 CR France1890
MIDDLEDITCH,Arnold Warden T2Lt ded 19-6-16 O&BLI p130 CR Herts30
MIDDLEHURST,John T2Lt kia 26-10-17 LNLancs att2/5Bn p136 MR30
MIDDLEMASS,Robert McGregor 2Lt dow 29-9-16 3 att7/8KOSB p102 CR France40
MIDDLEMIS,Herbert 2Lt kia 23-10-17 24/27NumbF p62 MR30
MIDDLEMISS,Thomas Elmslie Lt kia 17-10-17 RHFA p208 CR Belgium9
MIDDLETON,Alexander Samuel 2Lt dow 30-9-18 3 att1CamH p168 CR France145,30-9-15
MIDDLETON,Arthur Claud 2Lt dow 7-6-15 8LancF p221 CR Gallipoli1
MIDDLETON,Edward Geoffrey 2Lt kia 3-9-14 Suff p78
MIDDLETON,Edwin Relfe Barrett 2Lt kia 9-4-17 6SfthH p241 CR France15,9-4-18
MIDDLETON,Ernest Lt kia 26-2-16 DorsYeo p203

MIDDLETON,Frank Capt kia 17-11-14 Dors p124 CR Iraq6

MIDDLETON,George Hilton Lt kia 10-8-19 RAMC p255 MR70 &CR Europe180 Ex 2RFA

MIDDLETON,George North T2Lt kld 22-2-18 RFC p16 CR Scot398

MIDDLETON,Henry Capt kia 23-4-18 RE 456FC p210 CR Belgium15

MIDDLETON,James.MC.T2Lt kia 2-9-18 7KSLI p145 CR France1484

MIDDLETON,James Russell TLt dow PoW 21-6-17 GL &11RFC p11 CR Germany1 Ex CamH

MIDDLETON,John TCapt dow 2-10-17 8WRid p116 CR Belgium23

MIDDLETON,Leonard William T2Lt kia 8-11-17 GL &53RFC p11 CR Belgium111

MIDDLETON,R.MC.Capt 4-4-18 15Lond CR France1142

MIDDLETON,Reginald 2Lt kia 3-9-16 8WYorks p219 CR France383

MIDDLETON,Thomas Lt kia 1-7-16 16HLI att97TMB p163 MR21,Capt

MIDDLETON,Thomas Stanley 2Lt kia 19-5-17 3 att1BordR p117 MR20

MIDDLETON,William Archie Arbuthnot Capt kia 25-4-15 2SfthH p165 MR29

MIDDLEWOOD,Albert 2Lt kia 3-5-17 2WRid p116 MR20

MIDGLEY,Albert T2Lt dow 18-6-18 1/2Worc p109 CR Italy10,2 att 1/7Bn

MIDGLEY,Arthur T2Lt dow 15-7-16 9MGC p184 CR France66

MIDGLEY,Ellis Reginald 2Lt kia 15-11-15 1/5YLI p235 CR Belgium23,17-11-15

MIDWOOD,Harry 2Lt dow 25-12-16 13Y&L p159 CR France74,Lt

MIDWOOD,Lilian Nurse drd 31-12-17 VAD p200 CR Egypt1

MIERS,Douglas Nathaniel Carleton Capel Capt kia 25-9-14 1CamH p168 CR France1339

MIERS,Maurice Colin Capel MajALtCol dow 9-8-17 5Middx att8SomLI p147 CR Kent61

MIERS,Richard Henry Probyn Capt kld 12-12-17 GlamYeo att31RFC p19&203 CR Hunts113,FlOff

MIGHELL,Philip T2Lt dow 12-10-17 GL &5RFC p11 CR France113,Lt

MIGNON,Jephson George TLtCol kia 15-7-16 8Leic p88 MR21,Jepson

MILBANK,Robert Charles Alfred Palso Edmund Capt dow 10-5-15 3 att2WRid p116 CR France102

MILBANKE,John Peniston.Bart.VC.LtCol kia 21-8-15 SherwoodRgrs p205 MR4

MILBOURNE,Leslie TLt dow 10-7-16 7LNLancs p136 CR France102

MILBURN,Richard Gerald 2Lt dow 10-2-15 4ESurr p113 CR Belgium115

MILBURN,Robert Norman T2Lt kia 20-7-18 YLI att2/9Bn p143 MR18

MILBURN,William Hudson 2Lt kia 15-7-16 4Suff p217 MR21

MILDMAY,B.W.StJ 2Lt kld 16-4-18 GL &RAF p191

MILEMAN,Vernon Wallace.MC.Capt kia 16-9-17 7Lond p247 MR29

MILES,Alfred Crosfield Vernor T2Lt kia 24-8-15 2WelshR p127 CR France114

MILES,Allan Oswald T2Lt kia 30-6-16 11 att13Glouc p107 MR19

MILES,Cyril Vernor Capt kia 25-9-15 2WelshR p127 MR19

MILES,Francis James Lt dow 6-11-17 366/268RFA p208 CR Palestine1,kia

MILES,George Henry 2Lt kia 13-9-17 1RWKent att6RFC p11&141 CR Belgium11,12-9-17

MILES,Gordon TLt kia 7-10-16 14 att9Yorks p91 MR21

MILES,Guy Ralph.MC.TLt dow 10-3-18 4RRofCav att5DGds p23 CR France446,George

MILES,Harold Gordon T2Lt kia 4or5-8-16 10DCLI p114 MR21,4-8-16

MILES,Henry Robert T2Lt kia 18-7-16 6ConnRgrs p172 CR France178,16-7-16

MILES,Herbert Francis T2LtACapt kia 3-9-16 2KOSB p102 CR France402

MILES,Herbert Talbot Lt kia 16-4-17 D291RFA p208 CR France518

MILES,Jesse Samuel 2Lt kia 19-6-18 1/2 att1/6Glouc p107 CR Italy11

MILES,John Guildford Capt kia 27-6-18 6Norf p217 CR France61

MILES,John Harris 2Lt kia 27-9-15 7 att4RFus p69 CR Belgium6

MILES,Leonard Percy 2Lt kia 7-10-16 6 att8RFus p69 CR France560

MILES,Maurice W.Holt Capt ded 25-11-18 Ex RAMC p267

MILES,Richard Douglas.MC.2Lt dow 17-8-17 4 att9RIrF p171 CR Belgium8

MILES,Robert Patrick Capt kia 30-12-14 KSLI p145 CR France768,Patric

MILES,Robert William TCapt dow 1-6-17 13 att11N&D p134 CR Belgium127

MILES,Roger Thomas William T2Lt kia 1-10-17 1/2 att7Leic p88 CR Belgium125,2-10-17

MILES,W.N.2Lt ded 24-7-18 14Worc &RAF p109

MILEY,Miles Lt dow 30-12-15 1RFA p208 CR France102

MILHOLLAND,Frederick Raymond TCapt dow 26-2-18 7 att6Yorks p91 CR France98

MILHOLM,David Archibald T2Lt kia 18-11-16 16HLI p163 MR21

MILL,James Drysdale 2Lt kia 15-10-15 3 att1KOSB p102 CR Gallipoli3

MILL,Leonard Binning Lt kia 9-8-16 10Lpool p216 MR21

MILL,Robert Cowper King Lt kia 3-9-16 5BlkW p231 CR France701

MILL,William Henry 2Lt kia 12-7-15 5RScotF C'Coy p222 CR Gallipoli2

MILLAIS,Geoffrey de Carteret TLtACapt dow 21-8-18 1Beds p86 CR France342

MILLAR,Arthur James Lt kia 25-4-15 3 att1RIrRif p171 MR29,Capt

MILLAR,Arthur Liberty Capt kia 15-4-18 6 att4RB p179 CR Greece3

MILLAR,Audley Charles Hyde.MC.TCapt dow 16-10-17 3 att9Yorks CR Belgium72,15-10-17

MILLAR,David Hopkin Lt dow 30-5-18 4 att5RScots p211 CR France84,kld

MILLAR,Douglas Archibald T2Lt kia 18-7-16 11 att1GordH p166 MR21

MILLAR,Duncan Crerar Reeve Lt dow 10-4-18 12Yorks att21TMB p91 CR France1094,13Bn

MILLAR,George Rev ded 26-8-17 RAChDept att13GenHosp CR France 102

MILLAR,George Inglis 2Lt kia 8-4-17 RFA p208 CR France266

MILLAR,G.R.SubCdr ded 1-1-18 IA RlyCps p280

MILLAR,Ian Arthur 2Lt dow 30-9-16 6RIrRif p170 CR Greece3

MILLAR,Ion Keith T2Lt kia 27-7-16 1ESurr p113 MR21

MILLAR,James T2Lt kia 25/27-9-15 9BlkW p129 CR France219

MILLAR,James 2Lt dow 25-4-18 Res att1/6WYorks p82 MR30

MILLAR,James 2Lt kia 24-9-18 13TankCps p188 CR France1701

MILLAR,James 2Lt ded 12-6-19 5RIrReg p263

MILLAR,James Ainslie 2Lt kia 25-9-15 RScotF p95 MR29,Anslie

MILLAR,James Joseph Francis 2Lt kia 12-6-19 5RIrRif CR Germany1

MILLAR,James Lytton 2Lt kia 29-7-16 5 att15RIrRif p170 CR France423,28-7-16 1Bn

MILLAR,James Roland TCapt kia 16-8-17 11DubF p177 CR Belgium45,16-8-18

MILLAR,James Steele Hair T2Lt ded 13-1-19 Mddx p265 CR Scot199

MILLAR,John Lt kia 29-7-18 6ScotRif p224 CR France524

MILLAR,John Pitcairn Lt kia 21-9-18 6ScotRif p224 CR France407 Ex14Lond

MILLAR,John Wilson Lt ded 14-10-18 6A&SH p271 CR Scot685,Willson

MILLAR,Leonard 2Lt dow 19-7-16 17DLI p161 CR France630

MILLAR,Robert Bain TLtACapt kia 24-7-18 17RScots attMGC p184 CR Belgium1

MILLAR,Robert Curle Lt kia 25-9-15 8SfthH p165 MR19

MILLAR,Robert Given T2Lt dow 16-8-16 9KOSB p102 CR France134,7/8Bn

MILLAR,Robert Gordon 2Lt dow 11-5-17 4 att11A&SH p173 CR France40

MILLAR,Robert Spiers Lt kia 18-9-18 6A&SH p243 CR France375

MILLAR,Stanley Gemmell TCapt kia 1-7-16 103MGC Inf p184 MR21

MILLAR,Walter Gordon Capt kia 8-7-16 3 att7EYorks p84 CR France453,7-7-16

MILLAR,William 2Lt kia 23-8-18 6TankCps p188 CR France927

MILLAR,William Linton TCapt ded 23-10-18 RAMC p197 CR France770

MILLAR,William McKay T2Lt kia 18-9-18 KSLI att10Bn p145 MR16

MILLARD,Albert Wardle Lt dow 25-2-18 A641RFA p33 CR France345

MILLARD,Alfred George T2Lt dow 7-8-17 9ESurr p113 CR Belgium88 See WILLARD

MILLARD,David Edward Hall 2Lt kia 23-4-17 3RWSurr p56 MR20

MILLARD,Edgar John T2Lt dow 31-7-17 8RWSurr p56 CR Belgium7,kia

MILLARD,Harold TCaptAMaj dow 11-4-17 7Nhants p137 CR France570

MILLARD,Henry Albert.MM.Lt dow 16-9-16 58/35RFA p33 CR France23,Harry

MILLARD,John Barnard T2Lt kia 25-6-17 8EKent p57 CR Belgium29 Ex HAC

MILLEN,W.D. See MILLER,William Donnell

MILLER,Alan 2Lt dow 14-10-16 3 att2Yorks p91 CR France188

MILLER,Albert Guy TCapt kia 29-12-15 RAMC att12Mddx p197 CR France370

MILLER,Andrew Lindsay 2Lt kia 12-10-17 9A&SH p243 MR30

MILLER,Andrew Richard Stuart 2Lt dow 21-4-18 3 att2KOSB p102 CR France31

MILLER,Archibald Craig Capt ded 3-10-15 RGA p271&209,kld CR Scot241

MILLER,Archibald Ingram TLt kia 11-3-17 RAMC att47RFA p197 CR France1182

MILLER,Archibald William Buchanan Lt ded PoW 13-7-17 1KOSB &RFC p11&102 CR Belgium140

MILLER,B.MC.2Lt kld 29-5-18 RGA SR &RAF p41 CR Belgium36

MILLER,Bertram Charles St.Clair 2Lt kld 29-11-17 RE attRFC p11&47 CR Kent231,Lt

MILLER,Charles Wilde 2Lt kia 7-6-17 11WYorks p82 CR Belgium127

MILLER,Clement Francis Patrick 2Lt ded 4-10-18 IARO att46DivSigs p280 MR65

MILLER,Cyril Rowland Eyre Lt dow 25-11-14 4ScotRif attKOSB p103 CR France102,23-11-14

MILLER,David Joseph 2Lt kia 12-4-18 3 att9RIrF p171 MR30

MILLER,Dudley Melville TLt kia 28-4-17 11Suff p78 CR France604

MILLER,Edwin George 2Lt kia 23-4-17 3 att7GordH p166 CR France604

MILLER,Ernest Cyril Capt kia 23-10-14 3 att1LNLancs p136 CR Belgium126,Ex 1

MILLER,Francis John 2Lt kia 1-7-16 7RWSurr p56 CR France397

MILLER,Francis Samuel Lt dow 7-6-17 RE p210 CR Mddx25,2Lt

MILLER,Frank Edwin Commsy&Maj gunshotWound 11-10-20 IA IndOrdDept p280 MR65

MILLER,Frank Henry 2Lt kia 27-5-18 2RBerks p139 MR18

MILLER,Frederic Charles Lt kia 24-4-18 6Glouc CR France248

MILLER,Frederick David T2Lt dow 4-2-18 20RFC p16 CR Belgium11

MILLER,Frederick Richard Maj ded 4-2-16 RAMC p271 CR Hamps15
MILLER,Frederick William Joseph MacDonald Lt kia 24-10-14 2GrenGds p50 MR29,23-10-14
MILLER,George 2Lt dow PoW 31-3-18 RFC p16 CR Belgium241
MILLER,George Bell 2Lt kia 1-5-17 2HLI att18RFC p163&257 CR France244
MILLER,George Blair T2Lt kia 24-4-17 2HLI att18RFC p11 MR20,28-4-17
MILLER,George Clark Capt kia 26-8-18 5RScotF p222 CR France419
MILLER,George Frederick 2Lt kia 23-3-18 4 att11Ches p96 MR20
MILLER,George Gibbs.MID TLt ded 17-11-18 RE 8FldSurCo GHQ p47 CR Greece9
MILLER,George Gordon Darley 2Lt kia 15-9-19 RFA p255 MR70,1-9-19
MILLER,George James Capt dow 29-8-18 A56RFA p207 CR France103
MILLER,George James 2Lt kia 29-9-18 4Lincs p217 CR France407
MILLER,George Sefton TCapt kia 8-9-16 RAMC att1FA p197 CR France397
MILLER,George William 2Lt kia 15-12-17 2Ess p132 MR20
MILLER,Godfrey Lyall 2Lt kia 14-9-14 RE 11FC p47 CR France1107
MILLER,Gordon Stanley Reed 2Lt dow 24-12-16 6RSuss att11KRRC p228 CR France145
MILLER,Harold Patterson 2Lt dow 27-4-18 8ScotRif p225 CR France142
MILLER,Henry Thornton Lt kia 6-5-15 3EYorks att2WRid p84 MR29
MILLER,Henry William Waltson 2Lt kia 30-7-16 6BlkW p231 MR21
MILLER,Howard Todd Lt kia 21/26-3-18 LondIrRif p250 MR20
MILLER,Ian MacLeilain Lt kia 25-9-15 3A&SH p173 CR France114,Iain MacLellan 2Bn
MILLER,Inglis Francis Rowley Lt dow 13-9-14 RInnisF p105 CR France598
MILLER,Jack Humphrey Capt ded 25-8-17 3LNLancs attEgyptArmy p136 CR Egypt1
MILLER,James.MC.2Lt kia 11-3-18 6CamH p168 MR20
MILLER,James.DCM.2Lt kia 25-3-18 2SStaffs p122 MR20
MILLER,James Lt 31-7-18 5SfthH CR Scot862
MILLER,James Lt kia 14-10-18 3 att11Ches p96 CR Belgium157,3 att16Bn
MILLER,James Archibald Montgomerie 2Lt kia 16-4-17 7NumbF p214 MR20
MILLER,James Arthur T2Lt kia 28-3-18 GL &24RFC p16 CR France891,dedacc
MILLER,James Brand Scott 2Lt kia 14-3-18 RGA 252SB p41 CR Belgium19
MILLER,James Cooper Capt dow 24-11-17 14Lond p249 CR France512
MILLER,John Capt kia 19-8-15 6RWFus p223 MR4
MILLER,John.MC.T2Lt kia 1-8-17 10HLI p163 CR Belgium125
MILLER,John T2Lt kia 2-12-17 HLI att17Bn p163 MR30
MILLER,John.MC.Lt dow 12-11-18 7A&SH p243 CR France13
MILLER,John Austin Lt ded 3-4-20 4Ess p271 CR Essex50
MILLER,John Charles 2Lt kia 27-7-15 6DLI p239 CR France922
MILLER,John Donald Gardiner TLt dow 15-11-15 9BlkW p129 CR France423,Capt
MILLER,John Eric Hale 2Lt kia 11-1-16 3 att1NumbF p62 CR Belgium28 Hall
MILLER,John Kingsley Lt kia 19-9-18 24RWFus p203 CR France212
MILLER,John Lockhart Lt kia 21-5-16 8Lond p247 MR20
MILLER,John McGregor 2Lt kia 8-10-16 167MGC p184 MR21,7-10-16
MILLER,Joseph Ewing Bruce Lt dow 24-5-15 5 att1RIrRif p170 CR France134
MILLER,Kenneth Steven 2Lt kia 1-8-17 3ScotRif p103 MR29,4 att10Bn
MILLER,Maurice 2Lt ded 5-8-17 4RScots CR Scot242
MILLER,Neville 2Lt 28-6-17 5SStaffs 3RWar MR20
MILLER,Peter,Spence 2Lt drd 26-2-18 GL RE &1WT p191 MR38
MILLER,Ralph Marillier 2Lt 30-7-16 25 att17Manch MR21
MILLER,Reginald de Hochepied Marillier T2Lt dow 27-10-18 RWFus 3GarrBn p98
MILLER,Rex de Hochepied Marillier.MM.2Lt dow 27-10-18 3RWFus CR France1392
MILLER,Robert.MC.Lt dow 25-4-17 3 att10ScotRif p103 CR France113
MILLER,Robert Fordyce 2Lt kia 4-9-16 9Dev p77&235 CR France402
MILLER,Robert Goldie 2Lt kia 17-3-17 4A&SH att5RFC p11 CR France3
MILLER,Stanley 2Lt kia 1-7-16 11RInnisF p105 CR France526
MILLER,Thomas Alexander Grant Lt kia 27-4-15 1KOSB p102 MR4,26-4-15
MILLER,Thomas Murray T2Lt kia 27-1-16 7KOSB p102 CR France222
MILLER,Thomas Peacock T2Lt kia 26-3-18 LancF att6Bn p93 MR27
MILLER,Tom Drysdale.MC.TCapt kia 21-10-16 8BordR p117 MR21
MILLER,Walter T2Lt dow 30-4-17 11A&SH p173 CR France40
MILLER,Walter Douglas 2Lt kia 2-10-16 RGA attRFC p19&209 MR20
MILLER,Walter Roy 2Lt kia 15-9-18 1GrenGds att4GdsMGR p50 CR France1484
MILLER,William Donnell 2Lt kia 23-6-18 7GordH att4ResBn p242 CR France266,MILLEN
MILLER,William Edward 2Lt dow 17-7-16 7Lond p247 CR France224
MILLER,Wilfred Heard 2Lt kia 4-7-16 7SLancs p125 MR21,Wilfrid
MILLER,William Henry Capt kia 18-4-16 IA 74Punjabis att59Rif p280 CR Iraq5
MILLER,William Reginald Francis TLt kia 24/25-4-17 10Dev p77 MR37

MILLER-HALLET,Stewart Alexander T2Lt kia 11-7-16 11SWBord p100 MR21
MILLER-STIRLING,Edward George Bradshaw Lt dow 14-3-17 2BlkW p129 MR38
MILLER-STIRLING,H.J.G.S.Lt 16-10-17 GL attNigeriaR MR52
MILLETT,James Noble Layton 2Lt ded 13-3-18 73RFC p16 MR20
MILLICAN,John Stamper T2Lt dow 3-7-16 2WRid p116 CR France167,Lt
MILLICAN,Reginald Isaac 2Lt dow 23-3-18 4Middx p147 CR Belgium165
MILLICHAP,Frank Henry Lt dow 24-4-16 6SLancs attWRid p125 MR38 &CR Iraq5,WRid att6SLancs
MILLIGAN,Alastair T2Lt dow 30-4-17 5CamH att1/7A&SH p168 CR France40,3Bn
MILLIGAN,Donald Samuel Eccles Lt kia 9-10-17 RAMC 1/3FA att1/7Worc p197 CR Belgium20,12-10-17
MILLIGAN,Frank Joynt T2Lt dow 13-3-18 80RFC p16 CR France987
MILLIGAN,Frederick Albert T2Lt ded 29-4-16 7RInnisF p105 CR France115
MILLIGAN,George Berry Lt kia 24-3-18 152RFA p33 MR20
MILLIGAN,Herbert Ward TLt kia 21-11-17 16 att1LancF p93 MR17
MILLIGAN,James Henry.MID Lt mbk 25-9-15 IA 58Rif p280 MR28
MILLIGAN,John Richard 2Lt mbk 8-3-16 IARO att59Rif p280 MR38,att55Rif
MILLIGAN,Percy Bass TCapt kia 30-9-18 12HLI p163 CR Belgium116
MILLIKEN,Frank Stevens T2Lt dow 4-5-17 19Lpool p72 CR France13
MILLIKEN,James 2Lt kld 31-12-18 11RIrRif &RAF p170 CR Ireland42,MILLIKIN 12Bn
MILLIKEN,Joseph Dalton Lt 30-6-16 EAUL CR EAfrica123
MILLIN,Edward Job.MID TCapt kia 1-7-16 2YLI p143 MR21
MILLISHIP,William Griffin T2Lt kia 7-6-17 GL &1RFC p11 MR20
MILLNER,William Capt kia 13-10-15 5SStaffs p229 MR19
MILLS,Albert Edward 2Lt kia 16-8-17 3 att2RBerks p139 MR30
MILLS,B.A.J.Capt 23-2-21 6Dev CR Iraq8
MILLS,Ben Holt 2Lt dow 29-4-17 6Manch p237 CR France120,5Bn
MILLS,Charles Gordon 2Lt kia 26-1-15 1CldGds p51 CR France720,25-1-15
MILLS,Charles Thomas.Hon.2Lt kia 6-10-15 2ScotGds p52 MR19
MILLS,Edgar Edward.MC.Capt mbk 22-9-18 7SWBord p256 MR37,18-9-18
MILLS,Frank Symons Capt&Adjt kia 5-8-17 att7SomLI p80 CR Belgium23
MILLS,George Carlton Lt kld 4-11-17 RFC p11 CR Hamps4
MILLS,George Charles 2Lt kia 10-7-16 11WYorks p82 CR France832
MILLS,Gerald Desmond CaptTMaj kia 19-5-17 N&D &19RFC p11&134 CR France62
MILLS,Harry Forster Capt kia 21-3-18 46RFA p33 MR27
MILLS,Henry Jackson Lt kia 30-5-18 2Middx att19MGC p147&184 MR18
MILLS,Henry Valentine 2Lt kia 25-6-17 RGA 321SB p41 CR Belgium10
MILLS,John R.Lt&QM ded 11-8-14 RASC p193 CR Lond4
MILLS,John Birchell 2Lt dow 16-4-17 4RWFus p223 CR France64,Lt
MILLS,John Coleridge Lt kia 25-9-15 10HLI p163 MR19
MILLS,John Richard LtQM dow 7-5-18 11Huss p22 CR Kent179
MILLS,John Thomas HonCapt ded 22-12-14 RAOC p198 CR Lancs48
MILLS,Kenneth Le Gai 2Lt dow 11-11-17 GL &10RFC p11 CR France98
MILLS,Mansfeldt Charles Nightingale T2Lt kia 29-12-15 RE p47 CR France922
MILLS,Norman Hope Vandeleur T2Lt kia 17-9-17 146MGC p184 CR Belgium24
MILLS,Percy Trevenson Capt kia 8-2-15 3 att1RWKent p141 CR Belgium98
MILLS,Robert Cecil Lloyd TLt ded 28-2-19 6Nhampt att54TMB p265 CR Norf195,3Bn
MILLS,Robert Henry TMaj kia 10-7-16 14RWFus p98 CR France397
MILLS,Robert Nicholas Fenwick Capt kia 21-9-17 RASC attRFC p19&253 CR France705,23-9-17
MILLS,Samuel T2Lt kia 18-11-16 2YLI p143 MR21
MILLS,Tenlon Lewis TCapt dow 5-8-15 2 att11Middx p147 CR France922,Teulon kia
MILLS,Thomas Arthur Reginald Lt kia 26-9-17 5N&D p232 MR30
MILLS,Thomas Henry Lewis TCapt kia 14-7-16 8EYorks p84 CR France399
MILLS,Tom Rethanan Lt kia 4-6-15 6Manch p236 MR4
MILLS,Trevor Blake T2Lt ded 24-5-17 PoW 13ESurr p113 MR21
MILLS,William Checkley 2Lt kia 23-7-16 3 att2Yorks p91 MR21
MILLS,William Edward 2Lt kia 8-8-16 1/4SLancs p230 MR21
MILLS,William Henry 2Lt kia 5-10-17 1 att12Glouc p107 MR30,4-10-17
MILLS,William John 2Lt dow 4-9-18 20NumbF att20RAF p62 CR France142
MILLS,William Longley Lt kia 9-5-17 RFA &45RFC p11&33 CR France1039
MILLS,William Robert Granville 2Lt kia 16-2-17 103RFA p33 CR Belgium127
MILLS,William Thomas Capt 25-10-15 RAMC p197 CR Eire475 &CR Ireland14
MILLWARD,Charles T2Lt kia 22-3-18 11Leic p88 MR20
MILLWOOD,Frederick James T2Lt kia 23-10-18 186RFA p33 CR France1196
MILLSON,Avlan Ewen ACapt kia 9-4-17 6RFus p69 CR France418,4Bn

MILLSON,Edgar George Butlin 2Lt kia 18-6-16 4Beds p86 CR France1182
MILM,George Gordon.MC.TCapt kia 22-4-18 16 att15Ches p96 CR France41
MILN,William Wallace TLt kia 24-5-18 26NumbF att4Beds p62 MR18
MILNE,Alexander Lt kia 18-9-16 14DLI p161 CR France374
MILNE,Alexander James Bolton Lt kia 22-8-17 4 att9GordH p241 CR Belgium101
MILNE,Alexander Nichol Capt kia 7-8-15 6Manch p236 MR4,Nicol
MILNE,Alexander Richard Capt kia 31-7-17 Herts p252 MR29
MILNE,Allan Smith 2Lt kia 26-6-17 5GordH p242 CR Belgium5
MILNE,Clifford T2Lt kia 14-5-18 LNLancs att4Bn p136 MR19,13-5-18
MILNE,David 2Lt kia 21-9-18 HuntsCycBn att10Ess p253 CR France212
MILNE,Donald Farrow TLt kia 5-11-17 20 att1Manch p155 MR38
MILNE,Douglas Thwaite Capt dow PoW 28-3-18 4 att7CamH p242 MR20
MILNE,Eric Sutcliffe 2Lt kia 28-10-17 att12/13NumbF p62 CR Belgium127,12Bn
MILNE,Esmond William Capt dow 12-8-17 RGA 5SB p207 CR Belgium18
MILNE,George Smith Mitchell TLt kia 14-10-17 8/10GordH p166 CR France545
MILNE,George William T2Lt dow 22-10-17 22RFA p33 CR Belgium19 23RFA
MILNE,Helen Sister ded 23-11-17 QAIMNS p200 MR65
MILNE,Herbert Wardlaw Capt kia 27-9-15 IA 74Punjabis att6CamH p280 MR28
MILNE,Irvine McKenzie T2Lt kia 31-8-17 1RScotF p95 CR France245
MILNE,J.Lt 29-9-18 4A&SH CR France666
MILNE,James Gordon Capt kia 8-8-17 5HLI p240 MR34,10-8-17
MILNE,James Robertson.MID Capt ded 30-10-18 GL p191 CR France146
MILNE,James William.MIDx2 LtCol ded 21-6-19 IA Cmdg82Punjabis p280 MR43
MILNE,John Archibald Dickie 2Lt kia 12-10-17 2/1ScotGds p52 CR Belgium12,11-10-17
MILNE,John Theobald.MC.MID Capt mbk 24-10-17 48RFC p256 MR20
MILNE,John Vincent Percy 2Lt kia 25-9-16 NumbF att10Bn p62 MR21
MILNE,Joseph Lt kia 29-9-18 4A&SH p173 CR France666
MILNE,Joseph Ellis.DSO.MID Capt kia 22-2-17 RAMC p254 CR Belgium11
MILNE,N.L.Mabel Sister dow 2-10-17 TFNS 58GH p254 CR France134
MILNE,Patrick George TCapt kia 22-4-18 RAMC att93FA p197 CR France24
MILNE,Sydney Septimus Brown.DCM.Lt ded 29-10-18 5BlkW attMGC Inf p187&271 CR Scot396,dow
MILNE,William 2Lt kia 27-9-15 1GordH p166 MR29
MILNE,William TCapt dow PoW 25-7-18 49MGC Inf p184 CR Germany2 Maj
MILNE,William.MC.CaptTMaj kld 13-4-17 NLancs &25RFC p11&136 MR20 CR Scot239
MILNE,William Charles Lt ded 29-10-17 IARO att121Pnrs p280 CR Iraq8
MILNE-HENDERSON James Young.MID Lt kia 31-7-17 11HLI p163 MR29
MILNE-HENDERSON John Milne 2Lt kia 28-1-18 11RFC p16 MR20
MILNE-HOME,David William LtCol ded 27-7-18 RGA p41&257 CR Scot563
MILNER,Archibald Berry T2Lt kia 4-11-18 24MGC Inf p184 CR France521
MILNER,Archibald Donald LtACapt kia 23-3-18 1 att9Ches p96 MR20
MILNER,G.F.CMG.DSO.BrigGen 20-6-21 1ResCav CR Yorks305 Ex1LifeGds 5&17Lancers
MILNER,John Lt kia 26-4-16 1Wing 10RFC p3 CR France345
MILNER,John Lewis 2Lt kia 9-5-15 62/8RFA p33 MR29 CR Belgium453
MILNER,Lawrence Frank Lt kia 25-9-15 9Lpool p216 MR19
MILNER,Roy Denzil Pashley 2Lt kia 20-9-14 2N&D p134 CR France1893
MILNER-MOORE,Douglas Owen Capt ded 23-4-18 IA RE attEAMilRlys p280 CR EAfrica47
MILNES,Sydney Herbert Capt kia 7-8-15 5LancF p221 MR4
MILROY,Alexander Anderson 2Lt dow 4-7-18 6 att3Lpool p215 CR France10
MILROY,Eric 2Lt kia 18-7-16 8BlkW p129 MR21
MILROY,Peter 2Lt kia 30-11-17 1KOSB p102 MR17
MILSOM Sidney Lt kia 30-7-15 8RB p179 MR29
MILTON,Edward Thomas TCapt kia 26-9-15 13NumbF p62 MR19
MILTON,Ernest Edward Lt kia 23-1-17 RGA 113HB p41 CR France133,2Lt
MILTON,George Herbert 2Lt kia 25-10-16 21/2RFA p33 CR France515
MILTON,John Munro 2Lt kia 25-9-15 13NumbF p62 MR19
MILWARD,Etienne Geoffrey TCapt dow 2-9-16 7DCLI p114 CR France66
MILWARD,Philip Henry TCapt dow 7-12-15 7RB p179 CR Belgium11
MILWARD,Stanley Reginald 2Lt kia 11-8-16 35MGC p184 MR21
MILWAY,Edwin Horace T2Lt kia 8-10-18 10RFus p69 CR France1185,Capt
MIMS,Harold Dickman Lt kia 27-9-18 4Dors p229 CR France274
MINCER,Frank T2Lt kia 23-10-18 1 32MGC p184
MINCHIN,Hubert Charles Loder Lt mbk 20-12-14 IA 125Rif p280 MR28
MINCHIN,William Smith.MC.CaptQM kia 20-4-18 11RFus p69 CR France300
MINNAAR,C.W.R.2Lt kia 16-11-16 3 att8ELancs CR France153
MINOGUE,John O'Brien.CMG.LtCol ded 26-10-16 3 att9WYorks p82
MINOR,Philip.MID Lt kld 29-5-18 5DLI p239 MR18,kia

MINOR,Ronald 2Lt kia 1-7-16 2RLancs p59 CR France156,Roland 3Bn
MINORS,Ronald Towers Capt kld 27-3-19 7Worc attRAF p256 CR Belgium265
MINOT,Laurence.MC.Capt kia 28-7-17 57RFC p11 CR Belgium140
MINNAAR,Charles William Rorich 2Lt kia 16-11-16 3 att8ELancs p111
MINSHALL,Thomas Charles Wynn Capt dow 25-3-18 4RWFus p223 CR France267,Wynne
MINSHUALL,A.M.Sister ScotWomensHosp 21-4-15 CR Europe57
MINSHULL,George Henry.MC.T2Lt kia 20-10-18 15WelshR p127 CR France230
MINSHULL,John Lewis.MID Capt kia 2-4-17 3Lond p245 CR France420
MINTER,Charles Biron Capt ded 27-6-15 4/7Mddx p271 CR Mddx26
MINTER,F.2Lt kia 23-10-18 32MGC Inf CR France1266
MINTO,William Blair Griffiths.TD.dedacc 2-7-19 RGA p271 CR Scot280,Bain Ex 151SB
MINTOFT,Henry Stephen 2Lt kia 4-10-17 3EYorks p84 CR Belgium152
MINTY,George Capt kia 23-11-17 5GordH p242 CR France1498,6Bn
MINTY,Reginald T2Lt kia 22-5-18 RB att3Bn C'Coy p179 CR France81
MIRFIN,Joseph Colin T2Lt dow 17-8-17 6Y&L p159 CR Yorks543
MISELL,William T2Lt kia 20-10-18 ScotRif att10Bn p103 CR Belgium423
MISKIN,Maurice James.MC.TLtACapt kia 17-10-18 1TankCps p188 CR France660,Maj
MISSEN,Edward Roland Cecil 2Lt kia 4-10-18 2Lond B'Coy p245 CR France647
MISQUITH,Joan Charles 2Lt dow 4-2-17 A/102RFA p33 CR Belgium11 Juan Car
MITCHEL,Frederick David Capt dow 24-11-17 10RIrFus CR France512
MITCHELL,Alexander Charles Oswald.MID Lt kia 30-4-17 att4SWBord B'Coy BrecknockBn p223 MR38
MITCHELL,Alexander Goble Lt kld 30-5-18 6 att4Middx p147 CR France84,4 att6Bn
MITCHELL,Andrew 2Lt dow 2-8-17 2Leinst p174 CR Belgium11
MITCHELL,Andrew Neill Lt kia 30-12-15 5RScotF p222 CR Gallipoli6
MITCHELL,Archibald 2Lt kia 25-4-18 4RScots p211 MR30
MITCHELL,Archibald McKerrow.MC.2Lt kia 6-7-17 1/23Lond p252 CR Belgium118
MITCHELL,Arthur Gorman 2Lt kia 13-5-16 5 att2RIrRif p170 CR France68
MITCHELL,Bertram Earnshaw T2Lt ded 4-2-17 12 att7ELancs p111 CR France40
MITCHELL,Charles Douglas 2Lt dow 26-3-18 4 att2HLI p163 CR France62
MITCHELL,Charles Henry 2Lt kia 3/4-9-16 1/6WYorks A'Coy p218 CR France383,3-9-16
MITCHELL,Charles Johnstone.DSO.Maj ded 16-10-18 O&BLI p130 CR Sussex183,16-11-18
MITCHELL,Charles Richard Gerald Lt kia 1-4-18 6DragGds p21 MR27
MITCHELL,Charles Wand Chap4Cl dow 3-5-17 RAChDept att8EYorks p199 CR France1182
MITCHELL,Clement Alexander TCapt kia 13-10-16 13Lpool p72 CR France156,14-10-16
MITCHELL,Edward Noel TLt kia 15-2-16 8Beds p86 CR Belgium92
MITCHELL,E.P.H.2Lt kld 7-5-18 BordR &RAF p117 CR Egypt9
MITCHELL,Eric Arthur 2Lt kia 27-10-14 2SLancs p125 MR22
MITCHELL,Eric Harrison TCapt kia 29-4-16 RA attRFC p3&33,Erik
MITCHELL,Francis James 2Lt kia 27-9-18 4RScots p211 CR France437
MITCHELL,Francis Sidney TLt kia 15-2-16 RAMC att9RSuss p197 CR Belgium7
MITCHELL,Frank 2Lt kia 12-5-17 50MGC p184 MR20
MITCHELL,Frank Warley 2Lt kia 7-6-18 2Manch p155 MR20
MITCHELL,Frank Kinniburgh 2Lt kia 8-5-18 8ScotRif p225 MR30
MITCHELL,Frederick McLellan.MC.LtACapt kia 2-5-18 18Huss attWorcYeo p23 CR Palestine3
MITCHELL,George 2Lt kld 22-7-15 3 att1BlkW p129 CR France109,dedacc
MITCHELL,George 2Lt kia 1-2-17 IA 45Sikhs p280 CR Iraq5
MITCHELL,George Alan Capt ded 29-11-19 RAMC p267 CR Asia51
MITCHELL,George Clarkstone 2Lt kia 21-3-18 3 att2N&D p134 MR20
MITCHELL,George Henry 23784 Lt kia 22-8-17 11A&SH p173 MR30,Capt
MITCHELL,George James T2Lt kia 19-7-16 11Dev att2/6Glouc p77 MR19
MITCHELL,Gordon T2Lt dow 17-8-17 RE 96FC p47 CR Belgium23
MITCHELL,Guy Spencer Tmaj kia 15-5-17 3 att11Lpool p72 CR France581
MITCHELL,Harry 2Lt dow 28-9-18 7Manch p237 CR France214
MITCHELL,Henry 2Lt dow 3-4-18 11EYorks p84 CR France102
MITCHELL,Henry Harrison TLt dow 23-2-16 11ELancs p111 CR Egypt7
MITCHELL,Henry Theophilus Kelly Lt kld 12-11-15 1RSuss p119 MR43,11-11-
MITCHELL,Henry William 2Lt kia 22-1-17 5 att4DCLI p227 CR Palestine3,Lt
MITCHELL,Herbert Stanley Lt kia 21-3-18 4RWKent p234 MR27
MITCHELL,James T2Lt kia 26-4-16 GL &RFC p3&191
MITCHELL,James 2Lt 19-10-18 7 att13BlkW CR France982
MITCHELL,James 2Lt ded PoW 23-10-18 7BlkW p231

MITCHELL,James Alexander 2Lt kia 15-3-17 5BordR p228 CR France513
MITCHELL,James Arthur 2Lt kia 27-9-18 6NumbF p214 CR France439
MITCHELL,James Campbell Lt kia 13-1-16 IARO att56Rif p280 MR38
MITCHELL,James Douglas TLt ded 9-10-18 GL &KAR p191
MITCHELL,James Lawson Maj kia 16-3-16 24RFA p33 CR Belgium4
MITCHELL,James Marshall Lt kia 22-3-18 HLI att2Bn p163 MR20
MITCHELL,James Porter T2Lt dow 29-9-18 16HLI p163 CR France528
MITCHELL,James Thornburn ACapt dedacc 16-3-17 10 att7Leic p88 CR France80
MITCHELL,James Thomas Rankin.DSO.TMajALtCol dow 1-4-18 13RScots attA&SH p54 CR Scot808
MITCHELL,J.H Capt 26-10-17 7RScots CR Belgium18
MITCHELL,John 2Lt dow 3-4-18 7ScotRif att25RAF p224&258 CR France52,Lt
MITCHELL,John Brine.MC.Capt kia 15-9-15 8Lond p247 CR France432
MITCHELL,John Halliburton Capt dow 26-10-17 7RScots p211
MITCHELL,John Harris 2Lt mbk 1-2-17 IARO 36Sikhs p280 CR Iraq5
MITCHELL,John Horsley 2Lt kia 19-5-17 RGA 305SB p41 CR Belgium138,Lt
MITCHELL,John Innes Lt ded 9-7-18 RGA p271 CR Scot60
MITCHELL,John Leischman 2Lt dow 4-6-17 18Lond p250 CR France52
MITCHELL,John Marshall TLt kia 9-5-17 11ScotRif p103 MR37
MITCHELL,John McGeorge 2Lt kia 25-9-15 5 O&BLI p130 MR29
MITCHELL,John Monfries Capt kld 22-5-15 7RScots p211 CR Scot249
MITCHELL,John Patrick Cameron 2Lt kia 21-4-17 4HLI &16RFC p11&163
MITCHELL,Joseph Spencer 2Lt dow 5-10-16 70RFC p3 CR France169,dedacc
MITCHELL,Julian Alan Spencer Capt dow 28-9-14 3KSLI p145 CR France1110
MITCHELL,Lawrence Adams.MC.LtTCapt kia 22-10-18 D123RFA p33 CR France287
MITCHELL,Leslie James T2Lt kld 22-12-17 GL &RFC p11
MITCHELL,Lewis Medcalfe 2Lt kia 11-8-18 1/5WYorks p218 CR Belgium188
MITCHELL,Norman R.Lt ded 6-6-18 RScot &RAF p54
MITCHELL,Norman Reid T2Lt kia 5-12-17 KRRC att20Bn p151 CR France1488
MITCHELL,Patrick James T2Lt dow 17-8-17 RE 83FC p47 CR Belgium16
MITCHELL,Percy Maschwitz Lt kia 6-11-17 1/1Herts p252 CR Palestine1
MITCHELL,Peter,Harper.MC.dow 14-9-17 1/4GordH p242 CR Belgium18
MITCHELL,Robert Clapperton T2Lt dow 26-7-18 7CamH p168 CR France1225,27-7-18
MITCHELL,Robert Thomas Lamont.MC.Lt ded PoW 29-11-18 4GordH p241 CR Belgium320
MITCHELL,Robert William Page T2Lt dow 10-10-17 16Middx p147 CR Belgium16
MITCHELL,Robert William Hamilton Capt ded 9-5-17 RoO 3 att2RInnisF p105 MR21 CR Ireland196
MITCHELL,Ronald Walter Lt dow 19-11-17 EKentYeo p204 CR Egypt7 10EKent
MITCHELL,Terence Hargreaves 2Lt dow 6-11-16 2/5DCLI att145MGC 48Div p187&227 CR France703,kia 5-11-16
MITCHELL,Thomas Maj dow 12-4-17 1Suss att8Ches p119 CR Iraq8
MITCHELL,Thomas T2Lt ded 4-11-18 14NumbF attGHQ LewisGSch p62 CR France40
MITCHELL,Thomas Frederick.MC.2Lt dow 4-10-18 5 att8N&D p233 CR France446
MITCHELL,Thomas Hume T2Lt dow 16-4-18 66MGC p184 CR France145
MITCHELL,Thomas James T2Lt kia 10-7-16 11Yorks p91 MR21
MITCHELL,Tom Illingworth CaptAMaj dow 12-4-18 16Middx p147 CR France40,13Yorks
MITCHELL,Walter Victor 2Lt kia 27-11-15 3Beds attTMB p86 MR19
MITCHELL,William 2Lt kia 28-4-17 25NumbF p62 MR20
MITCHELL,William TLt kia 24-3-18 RE 41DivSigCo p47 MR20
MITCHELL,William George 2Lt kld 23-3-18 RFC p16 CR Surrey6
MITCHELL,William Henry T2Lt kia 1-11-18 61MGC Inf p184 CR France290
MITCHELL,William Henry Lister 2Lt kia 20-9-17 5Lond p246 MR29
MITCHELL,William Holford Lt drd 15-4-17 4ESurr p113 MR35
MITCHELL-INNES,Gilbert Robert Lt dow 13-5-15 19Huss p23 CR Belgium4
MITCHELSON,George Stanley Lt 25-1-20 SLancs CR Ches3
MITCHISON,Malcolm Lt ded 4-11-18 13Lond p249
MITCHISON,William Anthony Lt kia 20-9-17 RE 19DivSigCo p47 CR Belgium124
MITCHLEY,Sydney Robert T2Lt kia 12-10-16 10 att7Norf p74 MR21
MITFORD,Hon Clement Bertram Ogilvy,DSO Maj kia 13-5-15 10Huss p22 CR Belgium4
MITTON,Harold Lt kia 29-7-17 RFA &10RFC p11 CR France98
MITTON,Thomas Ewart TLt kld 24-12-17 RE GHQ Sig p47 CR Belgium20
MOAKES,John Curtis TLt kia 5-9-16 RE 155FC p47 MR21
MOBBERLEY,Lionel Westwood.MC.Lt kia 11-9-16 24Lond p252 CR France453
MOBBS,Edgar Roberts.DSO.TLtCol kia 31-7-17 7Nhants p137 MR29
MOBBS,Edward Thomas 2Lt kia 7-5-17 1ESurr p113 MR20

MOBERLY,Henry Stuart Lt kia 25-9-15 IA 74Punjabis att69 p280 MR28
MOCATTA,F.E.Capt 26-8-19 RFA &RFC CR Mddx27
MOCATTA,Robert Menzies 2Lt kia 10-8-15 1/5RWFus p223 MR4
MOCKFORD,Joseph 2Lt dow 8-4-17 1Lond p245 CR France120
MOCKLER,Francis George Ross.MC.MID Capt kia 1-7-16 2RIrReg attMGC p89&184 MR21
MOCKLER-FERRYMAN,Hugh Lt kia 16-9-14 2 O&BLI p130 France1111
MOCKRIDGE,George Ewart Lt kia 1-7-16 64MGC p184 MR21
MOFFAT,Hugh Francis Baillie.MC.T2LtACapt dow 27-9-18 8RLancs p59 CR France756
MOFFAT,John Alexander T2Lt dow 11-8-18 RE 69FC p47 CR France69
MOFFAT,John Everard 2Lt kia 9-4-18 10Lpool p216 MR19
MOFFATT,Archibald Shirving Woolery LtCol kia 16-5-15 2BordR p117 MR22
MOFFATT,Cecil Henry T2Lt dow 1-8-16 2/5LancF p93 CR France66
MOFFATT,Durward Forbes 2Lt kia 30-11-17 7ESurr p113 MR17
MOFFATT,Edmund Craig Forbes Capt dow 30-5-17 8N&D p233 CR France446
MOFFATT,James Robert Capt kia 15-2-15 1Leinst p174 MR29
MOFFATT,Stanley L.T2Lt dow 13-8-16 2LancF p93 CR France630
MOFFETT,John Leeson 2Lt kia 11-3-15 RScotF p95 CR France279,10-3-15
MOFFITT,James Prior.MC.Capt kia 3-12-17 1 att14DLI p161 MR17
MOGGRIDGE,Charles Francis Blayney Lt kia 10-4-18 IARO att2/3GurkhaRif p280 MR34
MOGRIDGE,Basil Fullelove West 2Lt kia 13-10-15 4Leic p220 MR19
MOGRIDGE,Lewis 2Lt kia 12-4-18 8Lpool att5RAF p216&258 CR France95,Lt
MOHAN,Harry Deacon Capt kia 11-4-16 10RLancs p59 MR38
MOHAN,Thomas TCapt kia 23-3-18 RAMC att10SHosp p197 CR France134
MOIR,Archibald Gifford.MID Lt kia 26-4-15 7A&SH p243 CR Belgium167,25-4-15
MOIR,Douglas.MC.Lt dow 22-7-18 7CamH att 1/2KAR p168&202 CR EAfrica90,das
MOIR,Douglas Dana Drew Kinnaird 2Lt kia 23-7-16 2Yorks p91 MR21
MOIR,G.Capt 10-6-19 IARO att94Inf MR65
MOIR,George Andrew Christie Capt kia 7-4-17 5GordH p242 CR France15
MOIR,James McMurchy T2Lt kia 25-9-15 1BlkW p129 CR France115
MOIR,John Andrew Alexander 2Lt kia 16-6-15 2A&SH p173 CR France82
MOIR,John Elliot Maj ded 26-1-17 IA 10Lancers attStaff6CavBde p280 CR Iraq6
MOIR,Reginald Lt ded 9-11-15 RE SR p47 CR Surrey160
MOIR,Robert Bruce Oliphant 2Lt kia 9-4-17 3HLI att2DLI p163 MR19
MOIR-BYERS,James Sandilands Lt ded 28-9-15 1/3ScotHorse p271 CR Numb4
MOKE-NORRIE,Geo Stuart 2Lt kia 7-10-16 3 att6EKent p57 CR France307
MOLAY,W.F.MSM.MID Lt 9-4-21 RASC CR Wilts115
MOLE,Harold Pearce 2Lt kia 3-9-16 11RSuss p119 MR21
MOLE,William.MID 2Lt dow 28-8-17 10DLI p161 CR Belgium18
MOLESWORTH,Charles Willoughby Murray.Hon.2Lt dow 15-4-17 1DCLI p114 CR France81,Lt
MOLESWORTH,Ernest Kerr Maj kld 31-1-15 RE att2S&M p47 CR France1169,31-12-14
MOLINEUX,Albert Ward Spencer 2Lt kld 28-7-16 RFC p3 CR Staffs78,MOLINEAUX
MOLINEUX,George King LtTCapt kia 5-5-15 2NumbF p62 MR29
MOLL,Albert Donald Campbell TLt kia 25-9-15 10ScotRif p103 MR19
MOLL,John Arnold Lt dow 21-9-19 RFA p255 CR Mddx26
MOLL,Tobias Mortimer T2Lt kia 15-7-16 9Leic p88 CR France207
MOLLARD,Alfred Edward.DCM.2Lt ded 7-11-18 10TankCps p188 CR Lancs34
MOLLETT,Frederick Norman Lt dow 18-7-18 9Hamps &107RAF p271 CR France1107
MOLLISON,William Allan Lt dow 1-10-18 2/6WRid att52MGC p227&187 CR France34
MOLLMAN,Herbert Bernard ACapt kia 1-2-17 4 att2Leinst p174 CR France149
MOLLOY,Brian Charles Baskerville Capt kia 1-11-14 OxfHuss p205 MR29
MOLLOY,Henry Edward 2Lt kia 22-8-17 O&BLI 1/1BucksBn p231 MR30
MOLLOY,Joseph Geale.MC.T2Lt kia 2-9-18 1Norf p74 CR FRance512
MOLLOY,Michael Vallanery 2Lt kia 9-8-15 2N&D p134 MR29,Vallancey
MOLLOY,Wilfred Cyril 2Lt dow 10-5-18 PoW 16RScots p54 CR Germany3
MOLONEY,Bertram Weldon Capt kia 28-2-15 1ELancs p111 CR Belgium68
MOLONEY,Frank T2Lt kia 9-4-18 RB att6SomLI p179 CR Palestine9,att 1/5Bn
MOLONY,Charles Albert TCapt kia 14-7-16 13Lpool p72 MR21
MOLSON,Eric Elsdale Lt kia 2-4-15 3RScots p54 CR Belgium104,1-4-15
MOLYNEUX,Benjamin,MC Lt dow 8-11-18 3 att11Ches p96 CR France332 att9Bn
MOLYNEUX,Eric Seymour.MID ACapt kia 30-11-17 Worc attIIICpsCycBn p109 CR France439
MOLYNEUX,Ian Moore Lt dow 10-7-18 1/7RScots p211 CR France95
MOLYNEUX,James Herbert 2Lt kia 16-8-17 12KRRC p151 MR30

217

MOLYNEUX-MONTGOMERIE,George Frederick Maj 22-10-15 3GrenGds CR France423

MOLYNEUX-SEEL,Edmund Harrington Maj ded 6-8-15 SL Lpool p201&268 CR Lancs152,5-8-15

MOLYNEUX-SEEL,Louis Edmund Harington Capt dow 6-1-15 BordR p117 CR Belgium140

MOMBER,Edward Marie Felin.DSO.MC.Capt dow 20-6-17 RE 177TC p47 CR Belgium11,Maj

MONAGHAN,Denis Laurence Capt kia 24-11-17 1TankCps p188 MR17

MONAT-BIGGS,Eric 2Lt kia 3-5-16 2Lincs p75

MONCK,Charles Henry Stanley.Hon.Capt kia 21-10-14 3CldGds p51 CR Belgium115

MONCKTON,Christopher 2Lt kia 1-7-16 RIrF &RFC p3&171 CR France839

MONCKTON,Francis Algernon Lt kia 8-11-14 1ScotGds p52 MR29

MONCKTON,Geoffrey Valentine Francis Lt kia 25-1-15 1ScotGds p52 MR22

MONCKTON,Marmaduke Henry Lt kia 9-7-15 RGA att8RFC p1&41 CR France285

MONCRIEFF,Charles George Conradi T2Lt dow 24-11-16 9 att12EYorks p84 CR France52

MONCUR,James Melville 2Lt kia 17-4-17 8RScots p212 CR France1182

MONCUR,William George T2Lt dow PoW 25-12-17 11RScots p54 CR France660

MOND,Francis Leopold Capt kia 15-5-18 RFA attRAF p207&258

MONDAY,Joseph Cyril 2Lt kia 3-5-17 3 att8BlkW p129 CR France1190

MONEY,Charles Arthur Gilbert Maj kia 13-12-16 IA 130Baluchis att129 p280 CR EAfrica38 &CR Tanzania1

MONEY,Duncan Goff 2Lt kia 16-2-18 4RFC p16 CR France525

MONEY,Eric William Lt kia 11-4-17 ACycCps attMGC HB D'Bn p181&183 MR20 1-4-17 TankCps

MONEY,George Russell 2Lt kia 1-7-16 4Middx p147 CR France267

MONEY,Gerald Hugh Kyrle 2Lt kia 27-7-16 18DLI p161 CR France631

MONEY,Henry Ironside.MID Capt kia 20-12-14 IA 1/1GurkhaRif p280 MR28

MONEY,Noel Campbell Kyrle Capt dow 6-9-15 IA 22Punjabis att5ConnRgrs p280 CR Europe1,Maj

MONEY,Roy Granville Kyrle 2Lt kia 9-4-17 3EKent p58 CRFrance531,Capt

MONIE,Roy Douglas John TLt dow 18-4-17 282RFA p33 CR France558

MONILAWS,Selwyn Macgeorge Lt kia 12-8-18 8RScots att12RScotFp211 CR France19

MONK,Alan Lt kia 26-10-17 att8Dev p77 MR30

MONK,Charles LtCol ded 11-7-16 RAMC p271

MONK,Ernest William Capt kia 29-3-18 1/4Lond attRFC p19&246 CR France167

MONK,George Bertram 2Lt kia 18-12-14 2RWar p65 MR32

MONK,Gerald Patrick Baillow Capt kia 3-10-15 1WelshR p127 CR France423,de Baillou

MONK,J.M.DSO.MC.Maj 24-10-20 Worc attEgyptArmy CR EAfrica116

MONKHOUSE,Alfred Ernest T2Lt kia 1-7-16 11BordR p117 MR21

MONKHOUSE,John Arthur Lt&QM ded 23-1-17 RAMC p254 CR Lond1

MONKHOUSE,Joseph Thompson Capt kia 27-4-15 6DLI p239 MR29

MONKHOUSE,Robert Alexander 2Lt kia 9/11-4-17 6GordH p242 CR France265

MONKMAN,Fred Kerbey T2Lt dow 28-9-17 26RFus p69 CR Belgium11

MONKS,Charles Phatean Lt kia 17-6-15 RH&FA p33 CR Belgium4,Phetean

MONKS,D.E.Maj 11-12-18 RlySurSiestanBengal NWRly MR61

MONREAL,George TMajALtCol dow 11-4-18 Res att6Wilts p153 CR Belgium183

MONRO,Harold Oswald 2Lt dow 21-5-17 9HLI p240 CR France214

MONRO,Kenneth Edward Lt dow 14-5-15 3 att1Nhants p137 CR France102

MONSELL,Henry Heacock Lt ded 3-12-19 1GarrBn RIrRif p265 CR Lond12

MONSON,Cyril Archibald 2Lt kia 18-5-15 Wilts p153 MR22

MONSON,Edward Charles Sutton.MC.Lt dow 15-6-18 A321RFA p33 CR France10 A331RFA

MONSON,William Herbert.MC.TCapt dow 7-9-16 8DubF p177 CR France66,kia

MONTAGU,Walter Philip Rev 31-10-18 RAChDept att22RGA CR France332

MONTAGUE,Albert Cecil 2Lt kia 16-6-17 117MGC p184 MR29

MONTAGUE,Felix David Lt kia 10/16-3-15 2Lincs p75 CR France525,10-3-15

MONTAGUE,Paul Denys Lt kia 29-10-17 20RB attRFC p19&243 MR37

MONTAGUE,Reginald Marcus Henry Cruise 2Lt kia 8-5-17 3EKent att8SWBord p100 CR Greece6

MONTAGUE,Richard Headley Lt kld 21-9-17 8Hamp p229 MR30,MONTAGU

MONTAGUE,Walter Philip Rev dow 31-10-18 RAChDept att22RGA p199

MONTAGUE-WILLIAMS,Edward Emanuel Lt 10-12-17 RGA 188SB CR Belgium19

MONTAGUE-WILLIAMS,Samuel Roger Thomas Aubon 2Lt dow 25-10-15 EKentYeo p204

MONTEITH,George Michael Capt kia 25-9-15 3 att1GordH p166 MR29

MONTEITH,Henry John Joseph Laurence Maj kia 27-12-15 LanarkYeo p204 CR Gallipoli3

MONTEITH,John Cassels TLtCol kia 1-10-15 2Beds p86 CR France423

MONTEITH,Matthew Rankin 2Lt kia 15-7-16 RE 64FC p47 CR France1890,16-7-16

MONTEITH,Patrick Rankin T2Lt dow 13-11-16 13 att2A&SH p173 CR France40

MONTEITH,Robert John Chap4Cl dow 27-11-17 RAChDept att70ArmyFldArtlyBde p199 CR France711

MONTEITH,William Albert Robertson 2Lt dow 2-9-18 2SfthH p165 CR France14

MONTEITH,William Neve Lt kia 25-9-15 6 att2RB p179 MR32

MONTESOLE,Eric Alfred T2Lt kia 4-3-16 7RSuss p119 MR19

MONTESOLE,Herbert Sarip Roy Lt kia 16/17-5-15 RSuss attBeds p119 CR France279,Sarif 17-5-15 att2Yorks

MONTFORD,Alfred Charles 2Lt kia 3-5-17 208MGC p184 MR20

MONTFORD,Douglas Raymond.MID Capt mbk 30-3-18 IA 98Inf att58Rif p280 MR34

MONTGOMERIE,George Frederick Molyneux Maj kia 22-10-15 GrenGdsResOff att3Bn p50

MONTGOMERIE,Robert 2Lt kia 1-10-18 5RScotsF p222 MR16

MONTGOMERIE,William Graham Capt dow 20-10-14 2Leinst p174 CR France9.

MONTGOMERIE-FLEMING,James Brown TMaj dow 18-8-17 6EYorks p84 CR Belgium16

MONTGOMERY,Albert Barr.MID Capt dow 17-8-17 1/7Worc p225 CR Belgium8

MONTGOMERY,Andrew Graham 2Lt kia 6-9-18 3CamH att1/5SfthH p168 MR16

MONTGOMERY,Arnulf 2Lt kia 22-12-14 3 att2ConnRgrs p172 MR22

MONTGOMERY,Arthur Samuel TLt ded 21-6-16 5RInnisF p105 CR Greece7

MONTGOMERY,Edward Henry 2Lt kia 16-10-16 RFA X9TMB p33 CR France385 &CR France1890

MONTGOMERY,Frederick Alexander T2Lt kia 19-10-16 6KOSB p102 MR21

MONTGOMERY,George T2Lt dow 14-10-17 116MGC p184 CR Belgium132

MONTGOMERY,George Edward Capt kia 22-8-15 5Dors p124 MR4

MONTGOMERY,Hugh Lt kia 13-9-16 1IrGds p53 CR France374

MONTGOMERY,Hugh Bertram Capt kia 9-8-16 10Lpool p216 MR21

MONTGOMERY,Ignatius Diego 2Lt dow 8-11-17 7Lond att4DCLI p247 CR Palestine2

MONTGOMERY,Matthew 2Lt kia 20-7-18 5SfthH p241 CR France1697

MONTGOMERY,Norman Stevenson 2Lt kia 17-6-16 2CldGds p51 CR Belgium73

MONTGOMERY,Ralph Noel Vernon.DSO.Lt ded 1-4-19 D88RFA p33 CR France63,Maj

MONTGOMERY,Raymond Capt kia 25/29-9-15 RAMC p197

MONTGOMERY,Robert Capt 25/29-9-15 RAMC att1Glouc MR19

MONTGOMERY,Robert Taylor 2Lt kia 1-7-16 9RIrF p171 MR21

MONTGOMERY,William Sproat Capt dow 13-3-15 6Lpool p215 CR Belgium59

MONTRESOR,Ernest Henry LtCol kia 14-9-14 RSuss p119 MR15

MONTROSE-EKIN,Leslie.MC.2Lt kia 1-7-16 8Y&L p159

MONYPENNY,Phillips Burnley Sterndale Gybbon.MC.Lt kia 28-6-18 3 att1RWKe p141&258 CR France20

MONYPENY,John Randolph Lt 22-6-20 LNLancs CR Kent61

MOODIE,Douglas Cameron 2Lt dow 15-3-17 1/4YLI p235 CR France345

MOODIE,Harry Morton 2Lt kld 16-9-18 9SfthH &RAF p165 CR France1359

MOODIE,John 2Lt dow 27-8-17 8SfthH p165

MOODIE,John Tully 2Lt dow 27-8-17 8SfthH CR France102

MOODIE,Ralph Wilson Capt kia 17-5-17 6 att1/5GordH p242 MR20

MOODY,Ambrose Capt kia 22-8-15 5Dors p124 MR4

MOODY,Charles Angelo 2Lt kia 21-8-17 GL &1RFC p11 CR Belgium125

MOODY,Henry Fred 2Lt kia 5-4-18 8Lincs p75 CR France798

MOODY,Leonard Leighton T2Lt kia 30-6-16 12RSuss p119 MR19

MOODY,Rowland Harry Mainwaring Capt kia ?-8-14 2LancF p93 MR15

MOODY,Thomas 2Lt kia 1-7-16 1/4Lond p246 MR21

MOODY,Thomas Lewis Vyvian 2Lt kia 21-3-18 1EKent p58 MR20

MOODY-WARD,Richard Guy Torrington Capt kia 9-5-15 2RBerks p139 MR32

MOOLMAN,L.J.H.Capt 21-11-18 EAfrIntelDept CR EAfrica36

MOON,Alfred Edward Capt ded 7-6-18 2RIrRif p171 CR Greece7

MOON,Basil Oliver.MID 2Lt kia 24-5-17 8Lond p247 CR France261

MOON,Clifford Abraham 2Lt kia 22-3-18 YLI att9Bn p143 MR27

MOON,Leonard James TLt ded 23-11-16 10Dev p77 CR Greece6

MOON,Roy Agnew.MC.TLt dow 28-4-18 61MGC p184 CR France145,27-4-18

MOON,Wilfrid James 2Lt kia 17-8-15 3Worc p109 CR Belgium91,Lt 19-8-15

MOON-ORD,Charles Denton 2Lt ded 1-12-16 7DLI p239 CR Durham28,dow 2-12-16

MOONEY,David George T2Lt kia 16-8-17 9DubF p177 CR Belgium45

MOONEY,Francis 2Lt kia 28-2-17 1RDubF p177 MR21

MOONEY,Reginald Herbert T2Lt dow 5-5-17 1Hamps p121 CR France95

MOOR,Christopher 2Lt kia 6-8-15 2Hamps p121 MR4

MOOR,Edward Lewis T2Lt dow 27-1-17 13 att9RWar p65 CR Iraq5

MOOR,George Raymond Dallas.VC.MC&Bar.Lt ded 3-11-18 2Hamps att30DivHQ p121 CR France276
MOOR-RAFORD,Leslie Claude Lt dow 26-10-14 1SStaffs p122 MR29
MOORAT,Francis Ferrers LtACapt dow 23-8-18 6 att4Middx p147 CR France745
MOORCOCK,Frederick Arthur 2Lt kia 3-5-17 YLI att2/5Bn p143 MR20
MOORCROFT,Alfred 2Lt ded 6-11-18 4SStaffs p122 CR Staffs78
MOORCROFT,Richard Lt ded 15-1-21 IA 57Rif p280 MR43 &CR Pakistan50A
MOORE,Alfred Arnold Lt kia 22-10-17 23Manch p155 MR30
MOORE,Albert James T2Lt kld 11-11-17 GL &RFC p11 CR Scot398
MOORE,Albert Reginald 2Lt kia 12-4-17 2/8WYorks p219 CR France568
MOORE,Alexander Holland TLt kia 26-3-18 5SWBord p100 MR20
MOORE,Andrew Douglas T2Lt kia 21-3-18 11Ess p132 MR20
MOORE,Archibald 2Lt kia 26-3-18 13 att22RIrRif p170 MR27
MOORE,Arthur Robert.MC.Capt ded PoW 1-7-16 1/4Lond p246 MR21
MOORE,Athelstan.DSO.MajBtLtCol dow 14-10-18 1DubF p177 CR Belgium84
MOORE,Beaufoi John Warwick Montressor,MC LtTCapt kia 10-6-17 RFC p11 CR Hamps4
MOORE,Brian Ponsonby Fitzgerald Lt dow 9-2-16 IA 62Punjabis p280 MR65,Capt
MOORE,C.2Lt 9-4-17 1/5SfthH CR France15
MOORE,Charles Arthur George 2Lt kia 19-4-18 5N&D p233 CR Belgium102
MOORE,Charles Francis Fitzgerald.MC.Capt 18-2-19 1/123OutramsRif att234Bde HQ CR Egypt2
MOORE,Charles Frederick 2Lt kia 12-3-15 3Worc p109 CR Belgium17
MOORE,Charles Ronald 2Lt 8-3-18 59RFC CR France518
MOORE,Claude Leighton 2Lt kia 26-8-18 7Lond p247 CR France164
MOORE,Clement,Selby Capt kia 19-7-20 IA 1/8 att1/10GurkhaRif p280 CR Iraq6
MOORE,Clifford 2Lt kia 9-4-17 5SfthH p241
MOORE,Clive Goulding Lt kia 15-8-17 GL &43RFC p11 MR20
MOORE,Cuthbert Alex 2Lt ded 25-9-17 14YLI attRFC p11 MR40,Alec
MOORE,Dacre William TLt kia 11-6-16 MGC Inf p184 CR France702
MOORE,Douglas Lewis Lt kia 22-4-18 1SomLI p80 CR France98
MOORE,Douglas Owen Milner Capt ded 23-4-18 RE attRailwayCps p47
MOORE,Edgar Noel.MC.Chap4Cl kld 5-1-18 RAChDept att20Lpool p199 CR Belgium127
MOORE,Edward Hayden.MC.Lt dow 25-4-17 2Y&L p159 CR France80,Capt
MOORE,Edward Kerruish 2Lt dow 25-4-18 8Manch p237 CR France119,Kerruish Lt kia 9Bn
MOORE,Edward Patrick Aylett.MC.2Lt kia 4-11-18 1CldGds p51 CR France1080
MOORE,Ernest Francis Courtney.MC.2Lt kia 24-3-18 5RB p179 MR27
MOORE,Ernest Leonard 2Lt ded 4-7-16 2/4Glouc p225 CR France345
MOORE,Francis Hirst 2Lt kia 7-10-16 7YLI p143 CR France307
MOORE,Francis William.MC.MID TCapt dow 26-4-17 13/10Dev p77 CR Greece1
MOORE,Frederick T2Lt kia 3-7-17 GL &4RFC p11 CR Belgium11
MOORE,Frederick Harry Bedloe 2Lt kia 4-11-18 9Lond p248 CR France939
MOORE,Frederick Henry 2LtTCapt ded 17-5-17 RGA attRAOC p41 CR France46
MOORE,G.B.MC.Capt kld 7-4-18 GL &RAF p191 MR20
MOORE,Geoffrey William Broadbent Lt kia 14-10-18 2Leinst p174 CR Belgium157
MOORE,George Adams 2Lt dow 6-11-17 4Leinst p174 CR France446
MOORE,George Alexander 2Lt kia 2-5-18 14RWar p65 MR32 Ex 28Lond
MOORE,George H.J LtCol 14-3-21 9BhopalInf CR SAfrica26
MOORE,George William 2Lt kia 28-3-18 RGA 288SB p41 CR France729
MOORE,Gerald Alexander Clifford Lt dow 11-7-15 8ScotRif p225 CR Europe1
MOORE,Gerald Francis Hamilton 2Lt ded 12-8-17 3 att9BordR p264 CR Greece6
MOORE,Gillachrist 2Lt kia 7-11-14 2RSuss p119 MR29
MOORE,Harold Thomas Pelham.MC.Lt kia 4-11-18 210RH&FA p33 CR France1081
MOORE,Henry T2Lt kia 15-7-16 3 att2WelshR p127 MR21
MOORE,Henry.DSO.MC.TCaptALtCol dow 30-5-18 RAMC att16FA p197 CR France64
MOORE,Henry Geoffrey Hamilton 2Lt kia 19-5-15 RIrReg p89 MR22,20-10-14
MOORE,Henry Glanville Allen.MID LtCol kia 11-8-15 6EYorks p84 CR Gallipoli5,9-8-15
MOORE,Hugh Stirling 2Lt kia 1-10-17 7N&D p233 MR30
MOORE,Hugh Victor 2Lt kia 22-3-18 4ConnRgrs att48TMB p172 CR France365,21-3-18 Ex BlkW
MOORE,J.A.S.Capt 7-6-18 NyassaFF CR EAfrica90
MOORE,James George.MM.MID Lt 5-7-18 2RB attRAF CR Durham27
MOORE,James Voaden T2Lt kia 2-12-17 6 O&BLI p130 MR17
MOORE,John 2LtACapt kia 26-10-17 3 att2BordR p117 MR30
MOORE,John Aubrey T2Lt kia 7/11-8-15 7SStaff p122 MR4
MOORE,John Clark 2Lt kia 19-4-17 4KOSB p224 MR34
MOORE,John Clifford Dawson 2Lt kia/dow 20-7-18 7WRid p227 CR France1697

MOORE,John Davidson Lt kia 22-3-18 181RFA p208 MR27
MOORE,John Holmes Lyndon Lt kia 9-4-18 37RFA p208 CR Palestine9
MOORE,John O'Hara Capt dow 28-12-14 RE 55FC p46 CR France64,Maj
MOORE,John Ross 2Lt kia 9-9-16 3ConnRgrs att7RInniskF p172 MR21
MOORE,John Rushton.MC.LtAMaj kia 20/23-3-18 3Ches att71MGC p96&184 MR20,21-3-18
MOORE,John William TLt kia 27-8-18 RE 183FC p47 CR France251
MOORE,Keith Hayden Lt kia 26-11-15 1/4LNLancs p234 CR France702
MOORE,Kenneth Hartley T2Lt kia7-7-16 6Dors p124 CR France1890
MOORE,Kenneth William James 2Lt kia 15-9-17 3 att11Ess p132 CR France149
MOORE,Leonard Edwin 2lt kia 6-4-18 4Middx p147 MR27
MOORE,Lionel Watson Lt kia 27-8-16 5Glouc p225 MR21
MOORE,Lionel William Bentinck Lt kia 30-1-18 RFA att34RFC p19&208 CR Italy9
MOORE,Morgan Edward Jellett.MC.Lt dow PoW 27-3-18 2RIrRif p170 CR France1061,kia
MOORE,Percy T2Lt dow 5-5-17 12EYorks p84 CR France95,3-5-17
MOORE,Raymond Cecil Devereux 2Lt kia 9-10-17 HAC Inf p206 MR30
MOORE,Reginald Henry Hamilton Capt kia 11-6-15 1BordR p117 CR Gallipoli6
MOORE,Reginald John T2Lt kld 7-11-17 GL &62RFC p11 CR Kent7
MOORE,Richard 2Lt kia 15-7-16 6WYorks p218 CR France246
MOORE,Richard 2Lt ded 29-10-18 2RIrF p171 CR Greece2
MOORE,Richard Henry 2Lt dow 21-3-18 RFA 6DAC p33 France512
MOORE,Robert T2Lt dow 15-8-17 10RB p179 CR Belgium16
MOORE,Robert Chetwood Capt 16-9-15 S&T Cps MR65
MOORE,Robert Frank.DSO.MC.TLtALtCol kia 30-5-18 1N&D p134 MR18
MOORE,Robert McConnell.MM.2Lt kia 27-3-18 17RIrRif p170 CR France587,1Bn
MOORE,Roger Ludovic Lt dow 20-12-14 SomLI p80 CR Belgium136
MOORE,Ronald T2Lt kia 8-3-18 RFC p16
MOORE,Samuel Johnston 2Lt dow 18-3-17 5RScotF p222 CR France95
MOORE,Samuel Kerr T2Lt dow 25-2-18 2RB p179 CR Belgium22
MOORE,Saxon Weston LtACapt kia 23-8-18 1Herts p252 CR France281
MOORE,Thomas T2Lt kia 15-6-18 1 att1/4 O&BLI p130 CR Italy2
MOORE,Thomas George 2Lt kia 1-7-16 17 att8RIrRif p170 MR21
MOORE,Thomas Harold Lt kia 27-9-15 1/5Glouc p225 CR France742
MOORE,Thomas Sydney Lt dow 30-5-18 3NStaffs p157 MR18
MOORE,Ulick Augustus Lt kia 22-3-18 3 att6ConnRgrs p172 CR France365
MOORE,Victor Cuthbert 2Lt dow 4-9-16 3Leinst att6RIrReg p174 CR France23
MOORE,Waldo Alington Gwennap Capt kia 31-10-14 2WelshR p127 MR29
MOORE,Willfred Englebert Capt dow 11-3-16 1/5SStaffs p229 CR France808,Staffs
MOORE,William T2Lt kia 16-8-17 10RIrF p171 MR30
MOORE,William Addison Hone 2Lt kia 5-5-17 5Ess p232 CR France115
MOORE,William Ernest.MC.2LtACapt kia 14-11-17 86RFA p33 MR30
MOORE,William Henry Lt kia 8-6-16 5Lpool attMGC p215&187 CR France630
MOORE,William Henry Hilme TLt kld 19-10-15 10KRRC p151 CR France706,Helme
MOORE,William Henry Walker T2Lt kia 25-9-15 6Wilts D'Coy p153 CR France260
MOORE,William Joseph 2Lt kia 21-3-18 2RFA p33 MR20
MOORE,William Webb ALt dow 12-6-18 RE Z/SpecCo p47 CR France10
MOORES,Clive Guise Capt dow 30-11-14 RE p47 CR France284
MOORES,Henry Eustace 2Lt kia 7-7-16 3SStaffs att2ELancs p122 CR France267
MOOREY,William Edward 2Lt kia 26-10-17 3Lond p246 MR30
MOORHEAD,Arthur Henry BtCol ded 1-3-16 IA IMS p280
MOORHOUSE,Arthur 2Lt kia 16-11-16 8ELanc p111 MR21
MOORHOUSE,Arthur Edward 2Lt kia 15-11-16 5NumbF p213 CR France385
MOORHOUSE,Arthur John Maj ded 28-11-18 Manch p155 CR Berks42
MOORHOUSE,Harry.DSO.LtCol kia 9-10-17 4YLI p235 MR30
MOORHOUSE,Ronald Wilkinson.MC.Capt kia 9-10-17 4YLI p235 MR30
MOORHOUSE,Rowland Edward 2Lt kia 19-4-18 9Mddx p236 MR30
MOORHOUSE,Samuel LtCol ded 11-12-18 3A&SH p173 CR Hamps218
MOORHOUSE,W.Lt ded 22-8-18 1RWKent &RAF p141
MOORHOUSE,Walter T2Lt kia 22-11-17 1 att2/6WYorks p82 MR17
MOORHOUSE,William Barnard Rhodes.VC.Lt kia 26-4-15 RFC p1
MOORSE,Harold Henry Lt kia 18-3-15 Y&L p159 CR Belgium89
MOORSOM,Alfred Edgar Lt dow 3-8-16 4Suff p217 CR France51
MORAN,Francis TLt kia 22-8-16 9 att2MunstF p175 CR France453,Frank 23-8-16
MORAN,Gerald Charles Lt dow 26-5-15 5 att2DubF p177 CR France145
MORAN,H.J.Lt 24-9-15 8GurkhaRif CR France705
MORAN,John 2Lt kia 7-6-17 8Manch attLond p237 MR29
MORAN,John 2Lt kia 24-3-18 4CamH p243 MR20

MORAN,John 2Lt ded 7-6-18 8Lpool p216 CR France204
MORAN,Samuel Frederick T2Lt dow 1-10-18 9RIrF p171 CR Belgium38
MORAN,William Paul Lt dow 7-7-15 IA 1/10 att2/10GurkhaRif p280 CR Europe4,8-7-15
MORAN,Herbert James Lt dow 25-9-15 IA 1/8 att2/8GurkhaRif p280
MORAND-LEES,James Wright TCapt ded 5-11-18 Manch attBrWI p155
MORANT Gerald Alexander Mackay.MC.TCapt kia 15-4-18 16 att2/5WYorks p82 CR France745
MORANT Norman 2Lt dow PoW 27-3-18 2Yorks p91 CR France1266
MORANT William Hedley T2Lt kia 25-10-16 1 att4NumbF p62 CR France423,12Bn
MORANT William Miles Capt kia 12-4-18 7DLI p239 MR32
MORBEY,Charles Frederick William TCapt kia 9-8-17 7Suff p78 CR France154
MORBEY,J.S.2Lt ded 1-8-18 10Lond attRAF p248&258
MORCOM,Frank Clifford 2Lt kia 8-5-17 5 att18DCLI p227 MR20
MORCOM,Percival John Hosking Lt kia 11-4-18 5DCLI att1MGC Inf p227 MR32
MORDAUNT-SMITH,Lionel St.George 2Lt kia 15/16-5-15 RInnisF p105 MR22
MORDUE,Alfred George T2Lt dow 8-7-17 RE 268Co p46 CR France
MORE,Eric Roy Lt kia 27-10-18 3 att2GordH p166 CR Italy9
MORE,George Lt dow 2-10-17 7WelshR p230 CR France193
MOREHEAD,Robert Evans Capt ded 23-11-19 5RMunstF attGoldCoastR p266&268
MORETON,Ada SNurse ded 7-9-16 QAIMNS p200 MR65
MORETON,Cecil Harry 2Lt kia 17-9-18 RGA 22HB p41 CR France686
MORETON,Edgar.MC.LtAMaj kia 25-8-18 119/27RFA p33 CR France518
MOREY,Alan Wilson.MC.Lt kia 24-1-18 RFC p16 MR20
MORFEY,Kenneth Lt ded 20-5-18 IA 16Rajputs att1/97Inf p280 CR Iraq8
MORGAN,Alan Bertram 2Lt ded 22-4-17 RFC p11 CR France1276
MORGAN,Albert Ernest Capt kld 10-3-15 RFus attRFC p1&69 CR France706,Lt
MORGAN,Albert Sydney 2Lt kia 22-4-17 GL &RFC p261&267 CR France529
MORGAN,Alfred.MC.T2Lt dow 28-4-18 10SWBord p100 CR France41
MORGAN,Alfred Ernest 2Lt kia 29-10-16 Middx att12Bn p147 CR France832
MORGAN,Archibald John Lt ded 29-6-18 6BlkW p271
MORGAN,Arthur T2Lt kld 27-2-18 GL &RFC p16 CR Durham182
MORGAN,Arthur Conway Osborne.MID Lt kia 13-10-15 4/3RFA att5Lincs p208 MR19 &CR France1896,mbk
MORGAN,Arthur Dunbar TCapt ded 14-9-19 RAVC p268 CR Egypt9
MORGAN,Arthur Lewis 2Lt ded 11-9-16 1/5WelshR p271 CR Egypt8
MORGAN,Ashton TLt kld 4-2-18 RFC p16 CR Wilts4
MORGAN,B.Lt kld 16-10-18 6ScotRif &RAF p264
MORGAN,Basil Algernon Cecil 2Lt kia 28-3-18 1Hamps p121 MR20
MORGAN,Brinley Arthur 2Lt kia 4-3-17 RFA &RFC p11&33 CR France285
MORGAN,Cecil Buckley.CMG.DSO.MIDx3 TLtCol dow 29-3-18 22DLI p161 CR France145
MORGAN,Cecil Edward Lt drd 3-7-15 3Hamps p121 MR4
MORGAN,Charles Cecil Lt BombExplode 11-3-16 IARO att6Cav p280 CR France1564
MORGAN,Charles Joseph T2Lt dow 28-4-18 9TankCps p188 CR France145
MORGAN,Charles Sydney Stuart 2Lt ded 2-2-18 RFC p261 CR Lancs7,Sidney kldacc RFA
MORGAN,Clarence William Harding 2Lt kia 23-10-18 5Ess p232 CR France1480
MORGAN,Cyril Edward T2Lt kld 4-12-16 GL &RFC p3&191 CR Egypt9
MORGAN,Daniel Phillips 2Lt kia 26-9-17 1/2Worc p109 MR30
MORGAN,David Lloyd Pophen.MC.Capt kia 9-3-18 PembrokeYeo att2WelchR p205 CR Palestine3,Popkin
MORGAN,Douglas Noel 2Lt mbk 30-6-16 13RSuss p256 MR19
MORGAN,Edward Charles 2Lt kia 18-12-15 1 att5RBerks p139 CR France279
MORGAN,Edward Compton.MC.TCaptAMaj dow 29-9-17 76RFA p33 CR Belgium12
MORGAN,Edward Leslie 2Lt dow 9-11-17 23RFA p33 CR Belgium18
MORGAN,Emlyn Thomas TLt dow 7-2-16 15RWFus p98 CR France345
MORGAN,Ernest Alfred Lt dow 21-8-15 5WelshR p230 MR4
MORGAN,Fothergill Lewis 2Lt dow 3-12-17 1/7Lond p247 CR France398
MORGAN,Frank 2Lt kia 22-8-18 22 att1/24Lond p251 CR France370
MORGAN,Frederick James 2Lt dow 16-5-18 7RFus &18RAF p69 CR France31,Lt
MORGAN,Frederick Ernest.MC.T2Lt kia 23-11-17 12SWBord p100 MR17
MORGAN,Frederick Harold Lewis.MID Capt kia 4-5-15 RFA p33 CR Gallipoli2
MORGAN,Geffrey Evan Lt kia 7-9-17 4A&SH p173
MORGAN,Geoffrey Penney T2Lt kia 14-7-16 1RWFus p98 MR21
MORGAN,George Elton T2Lt dow 19-8-17 15WelshR C'Coy p127 CR Belgium16
MORGAN,George Hamilton.MID TCapt kia 23-11-17 19RWFus p98 MR17
MORGAN,Guy Williams Stuart Capt kia 25-9-15 RWFus p98 MR19

MORGAN,Henry Richard Lt kia 8-11-17 LancsYeo &RFC p204 CR Belgium18,kl
MORGAN,Herbert Glyn Rhys.MID T2Lt dow 31-7-17 17RWFus p98 MR29,1-8-1
MORGAN,Hubert Hoppin Lt kia 30-3-18 17Manch p155 MR27
MORGAN,Idris Anuerin TCapt kia 17-4-18 11 att2SWBord p100 CR France324
MORGAN,James Melvin T2Lt kia 4-3-17 2RE p47 CR France430
MORGAN,James White 2Lt dow 10-8-18 5LancF p221 CR France360,Lt
MORGAN,Jeffery Evan 2Lt 7-9-17 2A&SH CR Belgium15
MORGAN,John 2Lt kia 22-3-18 4GordH p242 MR20
MORGAN,John Cecil Capt kia 7-8-15 6Yorks p91 CR Gallipoli4
MORGAN,John Hywel 2Lt dow 22-11-17 1/4DCLI p227 CR Palestine3
MORGAN,John James 2Lt kia 7-4-17 77RFA p33 CR Belgium21
MORGAN,John Joseph Lee 2Lt dow 16-5-15 2RInnisF p105 CR France80,Leo Lt
MORGAN,John Parkinson 2Lt kia 27-5-18 112RFA p33 MR18
MORGAN,John Towlson Capt kia 29-10-18 1/2RWFus att70RAF p98 CR France263
MORGAN,John Walter Rees 2Lt kia 1-7-16 4 att2DubF p177 CR France643
MORGAN,John William Moore.DSO.LtCol ded 31-3-17 RASC p193 CR France1C
MORGAN,Joseph TLt ded 6-10-18 RE attIWT p47 CR Asia66
MORGAN,Joseph Anthony TLt kia 30-5-17 9KSLI &RFC p11&145 CR Egypt2,2
MORGAN,Leonard(Jack) Lt dow 1-12-17 4EKent p212 CR France439
MORGAN,Lewis Edward 2Lt kia 16-9-18 D275RFA p33 CR France106
MORGAN,L.L.MC.2Lt kia 28-4-18 6WelshR &RAF p230
MORGAN,Matthew Lt ded 8-11-18 4SWBord att4Mon p100
MORGAN,Morgan Hughes Buckley Maj ded 22-11-17 SLancs p264 CR Wales19
MORGAN,Oswald William LtTCapt kld 3-2-18 RFA attRFC p16&33 CR Hamps191
MORGAN,Ralph Lewis 2Lt kia 14-1-17 3 att13WelshR p127 CR Belgium73
MORGAN,Richard Croke.MID Capt ded 18-2-19 LabCps attStaff p266 CR Surrey
MORGAN,Richard Godfrey T2Lt kia 13-11-16 12EYorks p84 CR France156
MORGAN,Ronald Charles Wybrow 2LtTLt dow 27-7-17 3SWBdrs &RFC p3&10 CR Belgium375,28-7-17
MORGAN,R.T.P.2Lt kia 9-7-16 8SLancs p125 MR21
MORGAN,Samuel Valentine Capt kia 10-8-17 2RIrRif p170 MR29
MORGAN,Sidney Herbert T2Lt kia 4-4-17 12ESurr att122TMB p113 CR Belgium
MORGAN,Stephen Beverley 2Lt kia 14-5-15 3 att1Leic p88 CR France276
MORGAN,Thomas Augustus T2Lt kia 8-10-18 13WelshR attMGC p127 CR France234
MORGAN,Thomas Cyril T2Lt kia 12-8-17 11Ches p96 MR29
MORGAN,Vernon Leslie 2Lt kia 21-9-16 4EKent att70RFC p19&212 CR France169
MORGAN,Victor Harold TLt kia 6-9-17 1Lpool GarrBn att1/5LancF p72 MR30
MORGAN,Walter Bassett T2Lt kia 9-8-15 6SLancs p125 MR4
MORGAN,Walter Chapman 2Lt kia 19-7-16 8Norf p74 MR21
MORGAN,Walter Henry T2Lt kia 12-7-16 13 att15Hamps p121 CR Belgium54
MORGAN,Wilfrid T2Lt kia 18-9-18 1 att11RWFus A'Coy p98 CR Greece5
MORGAN,Wilfrid Gilbert T2Lt dow PoW 23-10-17 GL &4RFC p11 CR Belgium381
MORGAN,William T2Lt kia 9-9-16 7RInnisF p105 MR21
MORGAN,William 2Lt dow 23-7-18 62MGC p184 CR France1693
MORGAN,William Lt ded 19-11-18 RH&FA p33
MORGAN,William Alfred T2Lt kia 23-4-17 13RFus p69 MR20
MORGAN,William Anthony Capt ded 22-11-17 LanarkYeo p271 CR Scot803
MORGAN,William Donal T2Lt kia 13-10-15 RE 95FC p47 CR France114
MORGAN,William Hugh 2Lt kia 11-4-18 12SWBord attWelshR p100 MR32
MORGAN,William J.Lt 19-11-18 RFA CR Eire167
MORGAN,William Rich T2Lt kia 2-4-17 9 att1SWBord p100 CR France551
MORGAN,William Vanstone Capt kia 19-4-17 4Norf p216 MR34
MORGAN,W.J.DCM.Lt RFA p259
MORGAN-BROWN,Nigel Martin T2Lt ded 31-10-15 15 att8NumbF p62 CR Egypt3,Lt
MORGAN-GRENVILLE,Hon Richard George Grenville Capt kia 19-12-14 1RB p179CR Belgium71
MORGAN-OWEN,John Guith T2Lt kia 9-4-16 4SWBord p100 CR Iraq5
MORGANS,Thomas T2Lt dow 13-4-18 7KSLI p145 CR France98
MORHAM,Malcolm.MID 2Lt kia 7-3-16 IARO att120Inf p280 MR38
MORIARTY,Denis Joseph 2Lt kia 1-9-18 2RInnisF p105 CR France297
MORIARTY,James Henry.MID Lt kldacc 12-10-15 RGA 18SB p41 CR France80
MORIARTY,Redmond George Sylverius LtCol kia 24-5-15 att2RIrReg p89 MR29
MORICE,Norman Archibald TLt dow 11-3-16 7EYorks p84 CR France102
MORIN,John Archibald Scott Capt ded 4-11-18 RGA 149SB p41 CR France40

MORISON,Alfred James 2LtACapt kia 20-11-17 3 att1EssR p132 CR France1483
MORISON,Douglas Rutherford 2Lt kia 13-3-15 3 att2Wilts p153 CR France706
MORISON,Gerald Patrick John 2Lt kia 13-10-15 3 att1CamH p168 MR19
MORISON,John Sinclair T2Lt kld 13-10-16 GL &RFC p3&191 CR Scot398
MORISON,Robert McKenzie Capt ded 8-5-19 RAMC att31CCS p197 CR Lebanon1
MORITZ,Oscar Frank 2Lt dow 27-7-16 99MGC p184 MR21
MORKEL,Daniel Johannes Cecil 2Lt kia 16-11-16 3 att8ELancs p111 CR France152
MORKILL,Ronald Falshaw Lt kld 23-6-15 1WYorksR attRFC p1&82 CR Yorks462
MORLAND,Charles Bernard LtCol kia 31-11-14 WelshR p127 CR Belgium57,31-10-14
MORLAND,Kenneth Irvine Thomas T2Lt kia 3-9-16 6 O&BLI p130 CR France294
MORLAND,Leonard Mark TLt dow 3-5-16 12WYorks p82 CR France285
MORLAND,William T2Lt kia 2-12-17 17HLI att97L TMB p163 CR Belgium126
MORLEY,Arthur Selwyn.MC.2Lt kia 16-9-16 15DLI p161 MR21
MORLEY,David 2Lt kld 16-6-17 4EYorks p219 CR France644
MORLEY,Frank William T2Lt dow 9-10-18 10EKent p58 CR France80
MORLEY,Frederick Joseph.DSO.MC.CaptAMaj dow 24-4-18 6Dors p124 CR France64
MORLEY,George Thomas.MM.2Lt kia 24-3-18 1Wilts p153 CR France307
MORLEY,Gordon Harper.MID Lt kia 30-12-17 1/4KSLI p235 MR17 Harpur
MORLEY,Harold Lisle.MC.T2LtACapt dow PoW 2-12-17 6EKent p58 CR France660
MORLEY,John Killand Gulson Lt dow 15-5-18 RE E'SpecCo p47 CR France10 Kelland
MORLEY,John Norris Lt kia 25-9-15 7Nhants p137 MR19
MORLEY,Marmaduke Robert Hood TLt kia 1-7-16 8YLI p143 CR France246
MORLEY,William Lt kia 24-3-18 2/1SurrYeo att10RWSurr p205 MR27
MORLEY-BROWN,Alastair James T2Lt kia 29-4-16 9KOSB p102 CR France1182
MORPETH,Stanley Lt ded 22-10-18 PoW 6NumbF p214 CR Europe149
MORPHEY,Henry John Cdr ded PoW 23-12-16 IA IndOrdDept p280 CRIraq8,Lt
MORPHY,Arthur Albert 2LtTLt dow 29-11-17 RASC 42DivTrn p193 CR France98
MORRALL,Edgar Percy Basil TCaptAMaj kia 28-7-17 7BordR p117 CR France604
MORRALL,John Bernard 2Lt dow 23-3-18 10RWar p65 MR20
MORRAR,John Henry Maj kia 18-10-14 RLancs p59 CR Belgium32
MORRELL,Harold Frank TLt kld 19-3-18 3BWIndR &RFC p261 CR Greece3,Francis
MORRELL,Ralph D'Albin Capt kia 8-8-16 4Lancs p213 MR21
MORRICE,Charles Smith 2Lt kia 11-6-17 5SfthH p241 MR29
MORRICE,William Walter LtTCapt kia 30-12-17 3Wilts attabCps p153 CR France398
MORRILL,George Bertie T2Lt kia 23-10-18 KRRC att13Bn p151 CR France1480
MORRIN,William Arthur TCapt ded 1-8-18 RAVC att18RFA p198 CR France145
MORRIS,Albert Evelyn 2Lt kia 27-5-18 NumbF Res att4Bn MR18
MORRIS,Alexander Ramsey 2Lt kia 23/25-4-17 1/7BlkW p231 CR France604
MORRIS,Alfred Arthur Thomas.MC.TLt dow 24-10-18 21Middx p147 CR France661,1Bn
MORRIS,Alfred Ashurst Lt kia 27-9-18 1GrenGds p50 CR France1497
MORRIS,Alfred George 2Lt dow 10-6-16 4GordH p242 CR France95
MORRIS,Allan Duncan TLt kia 30-8-18 13WelshR p127 MR16
MORRIS,Andrew 2Lt dow 26-8-18 4 att12Manch p155 CR France832
MORRIS,Anthony George Attwood Lt kia 13-10-14 1RLancs p59 CR France855
MORRIS,Arthur Capt kia 18-9-18 12Ches p96 MR37
MORRIS,Arthur Cukelyn TLt kia 17-2-18 19RWFus att22RFC p16&98 CR France31,Cuhelyn
MORRIS,Charles 2Lt kia 8-3-16 1Manch p155 MR38
MORRIS,Charles Alan Smith CaptAMaj ded PoW 7-5-17 3Beds p86 CR France452
MORRIS,Charles Geoffrey Noel TLt kia 7-10-16 6 O&BLI p130 MR21
MORRIS,Charles Herbert Lt kia 13-4-17 RWelshFus &RFC p11&98 MR20
MORRIS,Christopher Mowbray Capt&Adjt kia 7/11-8-15 7SStaffs p122 MR4,9-8-15
MORRIS,Clive Wilson 2Lt kia 9-5-15 2KRRC p151 MR22
MORRIS,Colin Dwight T2Lt kia 14-3-16 9RFus p69 CR France423
MORRIS,Duncan Blackett Capt kia 11-9-16 IA 90Punjabis p280 CR Iraq6
MORRIS,E.Lt 24-3-21 RFA MR67
MORRIS,Edward Alan 2Lt dow 1-12-17 3SWBord att25RWFus p100 CR Palestine8,Edwin
MORRIS,Ellis Wayman T2Lt kia 9-11-17 5RFC p11 CR France1361
MORRIS,Ernest John 2Lt dow 17-6-16 1NStaffs A'Coy p157 CR Belgium97
MORRIS,Evan Price 2Lt kia 8-10-18 5NStaffs p238 CR France1345
MORRIS,Eyre Percival T2Lt kia 1-5-17 1EKentR attRFC p11&58 CR France120
MORRIS,Francis 2Lt kld 11-9-16 1/5WSurr p212 CR Iraq6,kia
MORRIS,Francis St.Vincent 2Lt dow 29-4-17 3N&D att3RFC p11&134 CR France145

MORRIS,Frank George Gner.DSO.MajALtCol kia 17-8-17 BordR att16Middx p117 CR Belgium12,Greir 16-8-17
MORRIS,Frederick Lt drd 27-5-18 3ScotHorse p205 MR41
MORRIS,Garfield Hughes T2Lt kia 17-8-17 12RB p179 MR30
MORRIS,George Henry.Hon.LtCol kia 1-9-14 1IrGds p53 CR France1108
MORRIS,George Henry 2LtACapt dow 3-6-17 RGA att2/8HvyTMB p41 CR Belgium11
MORRIS,George Mackelvey T2Lt dow 7-9-16 17Lpool p72 CR Lond4
MORRIS,George Tod Lt kia 11-4-17 RFA att59RFC p19&208 CR France777,RHA
MORRIS,Gilbert Willan TLt kia 1-7-16 8YLI p143 CR France246
MORRIS,Godfrey Maxwell LtCol dow 26-9-15 IA 2/8GurkhaRif p280 CR France705
MORRIS,Harold Henry Lt dow 22-7-17 D150RFA p33 CR Belgium6
MORRIS,Harry Capt kia 26-10-17 2/5LNLancs p234 CR Belgium167A
MORRIS,Henry T2Lt kia 28-9-15 3 att5Middx p148 MR19
MORRIS,Henry Gage Lt kld 23-4-15 DCLI p114 MR29
MORRIS,Hubert Marmaduke T2Lt dow 13-8-18 1/2 att15LancF p93 CR France34,17-8-18
MORRIS,Hugh Lt dow 14-7-15 2ScotRif p103 CR France254
MORRIS,Hugh Anthony Lt ded 18-10-17 RASC 782MT Coy p193 CR Greece4
MORRIS,Hugh Gwilym TCapt kia 14-7-16 RAMC att54FA p197 CR France630
MORRIS,Ian Russell Campbell 2Lt 7-8-15 HertsYeo att1/8LancF p204 MR4
MORRIS,James Lt kia 27-12-17 GlamYeo att24WelshR p203 CR Palestine3
MORRIS,James Hulbert.OBE.Capt ded 1-6-19 RE p262 CR Wales152
MORRIS,John.MC.Maj kia 7-10-18 RAMC p253 CR France375
MORRIS,John Child TLt kia 8-8-15 8WelshR p127 MR4
MORRIS,John Clarke Lt kld 13-1-19 3WRid att19RAF p116 CR France1252
MORRIS,John Glynne 2Lt dow 23-9-17 N&D att16Bn p134 CR Belgium15
MORRIS,John Herbert 2Lt kia 21-9-16 6WelshR p230 CR France453
MORRIS,John Herbert Lt kia 6-3-18 RHA &49RFC p16&33 CR France120
MORRIS,John Torrington 2Lt kia 16-5-15 1RWFus p98 CR France279
MORRIS,John William Gibson Capt kia 1-4-16 12 att6Welsh p127 CR France551
MORRIS,Joseph T2Lt dow 4-11-18 16LancF C'Coy p93 CR France231,Lt
MORRIS,Leslie Tounsend T2Lt kia 1-6-18 Ches att5SWBord p96 MR18,Townsend
MORRIS,Lionel Alfred Harry Blackmore Lt kia 7-7-16 3 att1Wilts p153 CR France293
MORRIS,Lionel Bertram Frank 2Lt dow PoW 17-9-16 3RWSurr &4RFC p3&56 CR France598
MORRIS,Mansell John 2Lt kia 3-5-17 42RFC p11 CR France31
MORRIS,Michael Ambrose TLt kia 6-8-15 2 att13Hamps p121 MR4
MORRIS,Noel Dyke TLt dow 12-5-16 8SLancs p125 CR France40
MORRIS,Oscar David TCapt kia 21-4-17 12SWBord p100 CR France439
MORRIS,Philip Henry T2Lt kia 9-10-17 144MGC Inf p184 CR Belgium126
MORRIS,R.J.Lt ded 8-1-20 1Mon CR Wales85
MORRIS,Reginald Harry 2Lt kia 28-6-18 8RWar p215 CR France21
MORRIS,Reginald Martin 2Lt kia 17-2-17 14 att23Lond p249 MR21
MORRIS,Robert Cochrane MajTLtCol ded 25-3-17 RGA p41 CR France15
MORRIS,Robert Crowe Lt kia 23-9-18 RGA p209 CR Belgium11
MORRIS,Robert Parry.MC.Capt kia 27-10-17 RGA 1/4WelshSB p209 CR Belgium165
MORRIS,Sydney T2Lt kia 7-8-15 6Yorks p91 MR4
MORRIS,Sydney Herbert HonTCapt ded 11-1-18 RAMC p267 CR Surrey70
MORRIS,Thomas Ernest Lt&QM ded 9-1-16 RASC p193 CR Egypt6
MORRIS,Thomas Herbert Picton.MC.MID TLtCol dow 18-9-16 9RB p179 CR France105
MORRIS,Thomas Hodgkinson 2Lt kia 9-8-15 3Y&L p159 MR21
MORRIS,Tom Bernard.MID Lt dow 23-7-17 5RWFus p223 CR Belgium11
MORRIS,Wilfred Cyril 2Lt ded 15-12-18 IA 2/96Inf p280 MR65
MORRIS,William TLt dow 14-4-17 12WYorks p82 CR France40,Capt
MORRIS,William Albert.MC.Capt&QM ded 19-3-17 RInniskF p264 CR Ireland168
MORRIS,William Harold 2Lt ded 23-11-17 3Lincs p75 CR Staffs21
MORRIS,William Henry T2Lt kia 3-2-18 2SWBord p100 CR Belgium22
MORRIS,William James Lt ded 28-3-17 RGA p41 CR Canada742
MORRIS,William Norman 2Lt dow 25-5-16 8Wilts att106MGC p153&184 CR France8
MORRIS,William Oliver Ernest T2Lt kia 17-6-16 16 att12Lpool p72 CR Belgium47
MORRIS,William Percy Lt ded 20-12-18 11KRRC p151 CR France146
MORRIS,William Reginald T2Lt kia 25-9-15 7ELancs p111 CR France727
MORRIS,William Sydney LtTCapt kia 1-6-18 4 att18LancF p93 MR27
MORRIS JONES,O.Lt 31-10-18 14RWFus CR France1478
MORRISH,Donald Bernard T2Lt kia 18-8-16 1YLI att43TMB p143 MR21
MORRISON,Albert Victor 2Lt kia 30-7-16 2RScotF p95 MR21

MORRISON,Alexander Lt dow 25-7-15 RGA p209 MR4
MORRISON,Alexander Capt kia 25-9-15 5CamH p168 MR19
MORRISON,Archibald 2Lt dow 9-4-17 3 att15RScots p54 CR France95
MORRISON,Arnold 2Lt kia 26-10-17 3Lond p271&246 MR30
MORRISON,Arthur Stanley Lt kia 23-8-18 RGA 336SB p41 CR France103
MORRISON,Brian Harford Lt 9-6-19 22Punjabis MR43
MORRISON,Campbell Lt&QM ded 20-1-17 21Lond p251 CR Essex7
MORRISON,Colquhoun Grant.CMG.TBrigGen ded 23-5-16 PresClaimsCommission Staff p1 CR France300 Ex 1Drags
MORRISON,Donald TCapt dow 31-8-15 6RLancs p59 MR4
MORRISON,Douglas St.George Lt ded 3-9-17 RFA attR'A/A Bty p33 CR France518
MORRISON,Duncan Craig 2Lt kia 10-4-17 8A&SH p243 CR France924
MORRISON,Ernest Albert Augustus Lt ded 13-11-18 KRRC attRAF p151 CR Yorks172
MORRISON,Edwin Walter.MC.TLt ded 10-12-18 2DCLI p114 CR Greece2
MORRISON,Frederick Lansdowne.CB.DSO.VD.Col ded 22-12-17 1/5HLI p240 CR Egypt1
MORRISON,George T2Lt dow 25-10-15 12 att10ScotRif p103 CR France88,11 att10Bn
MORRISON,George James.MC.Lt dow 11-4-18 1/6SfthH p241 CR France88,ACapt
MORRISON,Gerard Humphrey Capt kia 31-3-15 5Lond p246 CR Belgium71
MORRISON,Haslett TLt.AMaj kia 23-4-18 61MGC p184 CR France248
MORRISON,J.H.I.Lt 31-3-16 EA Maxims CR EAfrica58
MORRISON,James Lt kia 25/27-9-15 4GordH p241 MR29
MORRISON,James Bough Lt dow 13-10-18 6A&SH &TMB p243 CR Belgium38
MORRISON,James Fyfe TCapt kia 18-11-16 17HLI p163 CR France534
MORRISON,James Ian TLt dow 28-9-16 GL 7RScotF att45TMB p191 CR France40,Iain
MORRISON,James McGregor.MC.TLt ded 15-2-19 GL Mddx att1NigR p201&191 CR WAfrica53
MORRISON,James William Sutton.MC.Lt kia 19-10-18 C'4Huss p21 CR France1237
MORRISON,John Lt kia 28-3-18 HighCycBn p253 CR France531
MORRISON,John TLt kia 24-9-18 1CamH p168 CR France725
MORRISON,John Gray Lt dow 19-8-17 6GordH p242 CR Scot832
MORRISON,John Stewart T2Lt dow 14-5-17 12ScotRif D'Coy p103 CR France145
MORRISON,John Woodley T2Lt dow 30-12-16 16RWar p65 CR France1
MORRISON,Joseph McLaren 2Lt dow 4-12-17 1/19Lond p250 CR France40
MORRISON,Kenneth Rae 2Lt kia 21-9-17 5 att18KRRC p151 MR30
MORRISON,Lechlan Allan 2Lt dow 6-1-16 3 att4SLancs p125 CR Belgium11
MORRISON,Leonard Graeme TLt kia 23-4-17 9BlkW p129 CR France536,Capt
MORRISON,Leslie.MC.Capt kia 25-3-18 1Lpool att1/7LancF p72&258 MR20
MORRISON,Lindsay 2Lt kld 28-7-17 GL &RFC p11 CR Wilts4
MORRISON,Norman Walter T2Lt kia 14-4-17 GL &RFC p11 MR20
MORRISON,Richard Fielding.MC&Bar.MIDx2 CaptAMaj dow 25-4-18 51RH&FA p33 CR Belgium38
MORRISON,Robert T2Lt dow 14-4-18 51MGC Inf p184 CR France924
MORRISON,Robert 2Lt kia 30-8-18 6LancF p221 CR France1484
MORRISON,Robert Cecil 2Lt kia 13-11-16 5Ches p222 CR France293
MORRISON,Robert Cochrane 2Lt ded 13-10-18 3RWar p263 CR Scot253
MORRISON,Robert Stevenson 2Lt kia 7-1-16 2BlkW p129 MR38
MORRISON,Robert Vernon T2Lt kia 13-5-17 Middx att11Bn p148 MR20
MORRISON,Ronald Macdonald 2Lt kia 9-4-17 1EYorks p84 CR France162
MORRISON,Rupert George 2Lt ded 24-8-18 RGA p262 CR Wales681,Lt
MORRISON,Samuel Rev 24-7-20 Chap4Cl CR Lancs34
MORRISON,Samuel Alexander 2Lt kia 3-5-17 7 att2SfthH p165 MR20
MORRISON,Stanley T2Lt kia 9-7-16 19LancF p93 CR France296
MORRISON,Thomas 2Lt kia 21-3-18 30MGC p184 MR27
MORRISON,Vernon MacDonald 2Lt kia 14-11-16 3 att7SLancs p125 CR France384
MORRISON,Walter Scott T2Lt kld 18-3-17 GL &RFC p11 CR Hamps4
MORRISON,William 2Lt kia 20-5-17 9HLI p240 MR20
MORRISON,William.MC.TCapt dow 25-10-17 RAMC att54FA p197 CR Belgium6,23-10-17 14FA
MORRISON,William T2Lt kia 2-12-17 2RB p179 MR30
MORRISON,William Fleming Oliphant Lt kia 2-9-18 9RScots p212 CR France646,8Bn
MORRISON,William Henry Stanley.MID Lt kia 26-5-15 24Lond p252 MR22
MORRISS,John Septimus Lt ded 5-10-17 1RWar p65 MR30
MORRISSEY,Walter George SubCdr mbk 6-5-16 IA IndOrdDept p280
MORRITT,William Graveley.MID Capt kld PoW 27-6-17 1ESurr p113 CR Germany2
MORROGH,Francis Mathew Dominick 2Lt kia 19-5-15 MunstF p175 CR Gallipoli6

MORROGH-BERNARD,Francis Anthony Lt kia 12-12-17 3MunstF p175 CR Palestinr3,11-12-17
MORROW,Hugh Gelston.MC.TLtACapt kia 22-10-18 15RIrRif p170 CR Belgium140
MORSE,Anthony Philip Lt ded 5-6-15 3 att2DCLI p114 CR France134
MORSE,Christopher TLt kia 7-12-17 RE 178TC p47 CR France439
MORSE,Christopher Charles T2Lt kia 14-11-17 GL &RFC p11 CR France1678
MORSE,Edward Hely Templeman 2Lt dow 8-5-17 6Dev p217 CR France512
MORSE,Eric Victor.MC.T2Lt kia 23-10-18 7EKent D'Coy p58 CR France206,Capt
MORSE,Ernest Frederick TLt kia 1-7-16 MGC Inf p184 CR France393
MORSE,Gerald Ernest 2Lt kld 31-10-17 4RWelshF att2RFC p19&223 CR France8
MORSE,Gordon T.H.2Lt kia 12-10-14 4Middx p148 CR France1106
MORSE,Gurth Stephen Lt dow 9-12-14 34RFA p33 CR France284,2Lt
MORSE,Percy Lapper 2Lt dow 20-11-17 1/4Glouc p225 CR France145
MORTEN,Galbraith 2Lt kia 16/19-5-15 Lpool p72
MORTEN,Lewis James 2Lt kia 4-11-18 O&BLI BucksBn p231 CR France1272
MORTENSON,Alfred T2Lt kia 15-4-18 59MGC p184 CR France285
MORTIBOY,William Woolly 2Lt kia 19-8-18 3 att2Manch p155 CR France526
MORTIMER,C.O.2Lt kia 1-4-18 6Dors p124
MORTIMER,Charles Gordon TLt ded 21-10-16 RFA att24A/A p33 CR Europe1
MORTIMER,Cyril Owen 2Lt kia 1-4-18 IARO att6Dors p280 CR France196
MORTIMER,Edmund Lt kia 26-4-15 6NumbF p214 MR29
MORTIMER,Edmund Alfred 2Lt kia 4-7-18 RGA 114HB p41 CR Belgium40
MORTIMER,Ernest George Smith Lt kld 3-4-18 GL &RAF p191 CR France169
MORTIMER,Gerald Henry Walter Capt kia 23-11-14 IA 10Jats att9BhopalInf p280
MORTIMER,Harry Limner LtACapt dow 21-9-17 6ESurr att18KRRCp226 CR France285
MORTIMER,James.CMG.LtCol kia 15-9-16 5Yorks attMGC p187&220 CR France453
MORTIMER,Leonard James TLt dow 24-11-17 9RFus p69 CR France415
MORTIMER,Robert T2Lt ded 27-10-18 10RIrRif p170 CR Ireland33
MORTIMER,W.B Lt 13-6-15 4DLI CR Belgium44
MORTIMER,William Brian Lt kia 13-6-15 4DLI p161
MORTIMER,William George Lt ded 22-3-19 IARO att28LightCav p280 MR66
MORTIMER,William Henry.MID Maj ded 21-2-21 DorsYeo CR Palestine9
MORTIMER,William Lionel Guentz 2Lt dow 10-8-15 6RDubF p177 MR4
MORTIMORE,Owen John Capt kia 22-11-15 3Dev att2Dors p77 MR38
MORTIS,Eric John 2Lt kia 12-4-18 1RGLI C'Coy p201 CR France297
MORTLEMAN,Charles Ibbetson 2Lt kia 9-9-16 1/4Lond p246 MR21
MORTLEMAN,W.R.Lt 29-12-18 HAC
MORTLOCK,Percy George 2Lt kia 20-9-17 26RFus p69 MR30
MORTON,Albert Francis 2Lt kia 8-8-18 8Lond p247 CR France1170
MORTON,Alexander Capt 27-8-18 RAMC att1/7HLI p197 MR16
MORTON,Arthur Darley 2Lt kia 24-8-18 21Lond p251 CR France395
MORTON,Daniel.MID 2Lt kia 10-5-15 4KRRC p151 MR29
MORTON,Eric Lt dow 26-8-18 RE 247FC p210 CR France84
MORTON,Galbraith 2Lt 16-5-15 1Lpool CR France632
MORTON,George Capt kia 13-7-15 5HLI p240 MR4
MORTON,George TLt ded 23-11-18 18NumbF p62 CR Surrey1
MORTON,George Capt 13-7-15 5HLI MR4
MORTON,Gerald Arthur Capt kia 4-5-15 BordR p117 CR Gallipoli3
MORTON,Gordon Reid.MC.T2Lt kia 9-4-17 7CamH p168 CR France1182
MORTON,John Sydney TLt kia 25-4-17 2RScots p54 MR20
MORTON,John William TLt kia 10-4-17 3 att9Leic p88 CR France616
MORTON,Joseph Leonard Milthorpe TLtACapt kia 22-10-17 23Manch p155 MR30,Melthorp
MORTON,Leicester Charles T2Lt dow 19-5-17 1Leic p88 CR France178
MORTON,Norman Donald Rex Lt kia 22-4-17 2/17Lond p250 CR Greece6
MORTON,Percival Clare 2Lt dow PoW 13-4-18 5WRid p227 CR France225
MORTON,Philip Francis TMaj dow 11-8-16 11Suff p78 CR France145
MORTON,Robert Brooke Maj ded 10-2-19 RASC p267 CR Berks117,LtCol
MORTON,Scott Gladstone 2Lt kia 31-7-17 Manch p155 MR29
MORTON,Sidney.MID Maj kia 14-7-15 IA 24Punjabis p280 CR Iraq6
MORTON,Thomas Edward Capt dow 26-3-18 att7RIrReg p24 MR27
MORTON,William Lt kia 5-9-15 5 att2RIrRif p170
MORTON,William 2Lt ded 16-11-18 5SStaffs p229 CR Yorks361
MORTON,William Cattell.MC.Lt dow 22-7-17 C282RFA p208 CR Belgium11
MORTON,William John Edward Lt ?? 5 att2RIrRif MR29
MORTON,William Ronald Capt kia 4-5-17 2/8RWar p214 CR France672
MORTON,William Ross Col ded 21-11-17 RE p47 CR Asia40

222

MORUM,James Pearse 2Lt kia 1-7-16 6 att1RB p179 CR France643
MOSCROP,William Noel Jobson.MC.2LtACapt kia 27-5-18 RFus att5DLI p69&257 CR France1329
MOSELEY,Frederick Arthur Dudley Harris Capt ded 24-5-19 RWKent p265 CR Surrey1,53RSuss
MOSELEY,Henry Gwyn Jeffreys T2Lt kia 10-8-15 RE p47 MR4
MOSELEY,Herbert James Ritchie T2Lt kia 27-6-16 7RB p179 CR France1182
MOSER,Harold Wynn 2Lt ded 22-7-16 3/6ESurr p271 CR Sussex111
MOSES,Frank Samuel TLt dow 31-8-18 1/1WelshRGA p41 CR France1182
MOSES,James T2Lt kia 4-8-16 9LNLancs p136 CR France35
MOSES,Vivian Sylvester 2Lt kia 4-6-17 RFA 11DAC p33 CR Belgium60
MOSGROVE,Robert St.Patrick Capt ded 7-10-17 ArmyPayDept p268 CR Hamps13
MOSLEY,Arthur Roy Lt dow 23-11-17 2/4YLI p235 CR France398
MOSLEY,Geoffrey Kingdon Capt kia 10-4-18 6 att11Suff p217 CR France685,MOSELEY
MOSLEY,George Gordon Maj 7-8-18 IndDefF 37CalcuttaPresBn MR66
MOSLEY,Harold Drewell T2Lt kia 16-8-16 7RBerks p139 CR Greece6
MOSLEY,Nicholas Capt dow 1-8-15 NStaffs p157 CR Mddx26
MOSLEY,Percy 2Lt kia 28-3-18 5WRid p227 MR20
MOSMAN,Hugh 2Lt ded 12-2-16 4Yorks p271 CR Scot239
MOSS,Allan Maj 10-10-16 Worc CR Devon68
MOSS,Charles.MC.Capt kia 6-11-17 1/7Ches p223 CR Palestine1
MOSS,Charles William 2Lt kia 13-6-17 22Lond p251 CR France581
MOSS,Charles William T2Lt kia 8-8-18 RBerks att8Bn p139 CR France247
MOSS,Cyril James 2Lt ded 19-8-16 2Suff p78 CR Kent289
MOSS,Edward Hampton Capt kia 25-9-15 10Glouc p107 MR19
MOSS,Enoch Frank T2Lt dow 17-9-16 9RWFus p98 CR France285
MOSS,Ernest Sumner 2Lt kia 1-7-16 5NStaffs p238 CR France557
MOSS,Frederick Walter T2Lt kia 28-5-18 8Leic attRE 98FC p88 MR18
MOSS,George Percival T2Lt dow 22-12-17 12SWBord p100 CR France214
MOSS,Gerald Alex 2Lt kia 10-8-18 19 att2Manch p155 MR16,Alec
MOSS,Hamilton.MC.TCapt kia 31-5-18 9WRid p116 CR France35
MOSS,Hector Albert Lt kia 7-10-16 7Mddx p235 CR France374
MOSS,Herbert Frank 2Lt kia 30-8-18 RGA 132HB p41 CR France624
MOSS,Herbert Stanley T2Lt ded 4-8-18 2RRofCav attMddxHuss p23 CR Palestine8
MOSS,Howard James Harding 2Lt kia 13-10-15 5Leic A'Coy p220 CR France924
MOSS,John Miles T2Lt ded 6-9-15 RASC 258MechTransCo p193 CR France121
MOSS,John Stephen Noel 2Lt dedacc 24-11-16 RE 57FC p47 CR France169
MOSS,Leonard George 2Lt kia 21-3-18 1 att2/5Lincs p75 MR20
MOSS,M.E.2Lt 29-11-16 6Lpool CR Belgium4
MOSS,Morrice Edgar 2Lt kia 29-11-16 6Lpool p215
MOSS,Percy William T2Lt kia 23-8-18 59MGC Inf p184 CR France924,22-8-18
MOSS,Reginald Barnes Newton T2Lt kia 7-10-16 3 att6EKent p58 MR21
MOSS,Samuel Foden.MM.T2Lt dow 28-3-18 RE J'SpecCo p47 CR France40
MOSS,Sidney Cowan Lt ded 8-3-19 RE p271 CR Lancs1
MOSS,Thomas John.MC.MIDx2 LtAMaj kia 21-3-18 307RFA p33 MR27
MOSS,William Thomas Gregory T2Lt kld 5-7-17 GL &RFC p11 CR Lancs14,dedacc
MOSS-BLUNDELL,Cyril Bertram Lt kia 27-9-15 14DLI p161 MR19
MOSSCROP,Allan.MC.T2Lt dow 11-9-17 9ScotRif p103 CR Belgium19
MOSSE,John TLtCol ded 17-6-16 Leic Commdg Depot p88 CR Leic63
MOSSE,Philip Godfrey T2Lt kia 18-4-16 13RWar att6ELancs p65 MR38
MOSSE,William Oliver Matless Col drd 10-10-18 1GarBnMunstF Ret IA p175
MOSSMAN,Harold Alexander.MC.2Lt kia 25-4-18 3 att2RBerks p139 MR27
MOSSOP,William Nicholson.MC.Capt&Adjt dow 8-5-18 5WYorks p218 CR Belgium353,11-5-18
MOSTYN,Edward Henry Joseph David.VD.LtCol ded 2-8-16 4Suss p271 CR Sussex2,1-8-16
MOTHERSILL,James Neville T2Lt kia 7-6-17 10RWKent p141 CR Belgium29
MOTHERWELL,John Ernest 2LtACapt kia 21-10-16 3 att1RIrRif p170 CR France314,3RIrRif att9LNLancs
MOTHERWELL,William 2Lt dow 5-3-17 2 att7HLI p240 CR France300
MOTION,Sidney Howard.MID TLt dow 1-8-17 7Nhants p137 CR Belgium7
MOTLER,John Frederick 2Lt kia 30-7-16 4 att18Manch p155 MR21 &CR France1890
MOTT,Francis Stanley T2Lt dow 23-7-16 24RFus p69 CR France88
MOTT,Hugh Frederick.MC.Capt kia 1-7-16 16Lond p249 MR21,Fenwick
MOTT,Jacob Ernest T2Lt kia 23-12-17 1RIrFus &21RFC p11&171 MR20
MOTT,John Francis Capt kia 7-8-15 2 att6Y&L p159 CR Gallipoli27
MOTT,Lewes Woodham T2Lt kia 23-4-17 9EssR &RFC p11&132 CR France531
MOTTERAM,Arthur William 2Lt kia 21-5-18 6SStaffs p229 CR France 1/5Bn

MOTTERSHALL,Herbert Stanley 2Lt dow 9-10-17 2/9Manch p155 CR Belgium8
MOTTRAM,Frederick Capt&Adjt dow 9-9-17 RFA 48DAC p207 CR Belgium16
MOTTRAM,John Elliott Lt kia 9-10-17 7LancF p221 MR30
MOTTRAM,Osborne Arthur Capt kia 8-8-16 7Lpool p215 CR France630,9-8-18
MOTTRAM,Piercay John MacQueen Capt kia 6-10-19 IARO att109Inf p208 MR43,Piercey
MOUAT,George Mouat Dundas Capt kia 9/10-5-15 1Lond p245 CR France254,9-5-15
MOUAT-BIGGS,E.2Lt 3-5-16 2Lincs CR France430
MOUATT-BIGGS,John Alborough Lt dow PoW 22-3-18 3 att2RIrReg p89 CR France660,Capt
MOUBRAY,Arthur Russell St John.MC.Maj dow 2-7-18 RGA 200SB p209 CR France29
MOUBRAY,Cyril Lloyd 2Lt kia 10-10-18 RE p210
MOUBRAY,Percy Lionel Capt kia 29-10-14 3 att1BlkW p129 MR29
MOUBRAY,Frank Capt 8-10-18 RFus att4Bn CR France338
MOUCK,Ernest Capt kia 7-8-15 15NumbF p62 CR Gallipoli2
MOUILLOT,Augustus de Thierry Capt dow 15-1-16 IA 51Sikhs p208 CR Iraq5
MOULD,Charles William TCapt kia 25-9-15 5KSLI p145 CR Belgium84
MOULD,David T2Lt kia 13-6-16 1RWar attTMB p65 CR France643
MOULD,Ernest Kingston 2Lt kia 2-9-18 4 att16RWar p65 CR France644
MOULD,James.DSO.MC.ACapt kia 3-9-16 3Worc p109 MR21
MOULDING,Sydney Dormer Lt kia 22-8-15 8Nhants attRInnisF p137 MR4
MOULE,Hugh Elliot Maj mbk 22-5-15 IA 1/4GurkhaRif p280 MR28
MOULSON,Samuel T2Lt kia 4-9-18 18WYorks p82 CR France245
MOULT,Samuel Walker 2Lt kia 15-9-16 2N&D p134 MR21
MOULTON,Charles Eric Lt kia 16-9-15 6Wilts p153 CR France260
MOULTON,William Ralph Osborne T2Lt kia 4-8-16 12Manch p155 CR France400
MOULTSAID,Wesley 2Lt kia 12-11-16 11RIrRif p170
MOUNT,Allan T2Lt kia 18-9-18 EKent p58 CR France369
MOUNT,Edward Alfred T2Lt kia 4-1-16 11RFus p69 CR Belgium28,9Bn
MOUNT,Francis TCapt kia 13-10-15 5RBerks p139 MR19
MOUNTAIN,Allan James 2Lt kia 23-7-16 1/4KLI p235 MR21
MOUNTAIN,Cyril Robert Wightman T2LtACapt kia 5-8-17 13Ches p96 MR29
MOUNTFIELD,Robert Noel Capt dow 5-11-17 8 att2/9Lpool p215 CR Belgium25
MOUNTFORD,Cecil TLt ded 3-3-19 RASC MT p267 CR Ches113,6-3-19
MOUNTFORD,Gordon Capt kia 12-6-17 5NStaffs attRFC p19&237 CR France200
MOUNTFORD,Stanley.MC.Capt kia 24-3-18 9RScots p212 MR 27
MOURITZ,Cecil John Hastings 2Lt kia 5-12-16 5 att2Leinst p174 CR France149
MOURITZEN,Roy Walter T2Lt kld 5-6-17 GL &RFC p11 CR Essex222
MOUSLEY,Alfred Charles 2Lt dow 30-9-17 162RH &FA p33 CR Belgium183
MOWAT,Charles James Carlton Capt kia 28-6-15 8ScotRif p225 MR4
MOWAT,James Maj drd 13-8-15 RAMC p253 MR4
MOWAT,James Dugald Lillie Lt kia 15-6-15 5SfthH p241 MR22
MOWAT,John Farquhar T2Lt dow 15-5-17 7Yorks p91 CR France95
MOWAT,John Graham.MC.Capt kia 27-6-17 1/4WRid p227 CR France258
MOWAT,John Maclellan T2Lt kld 5-1-17 NStaffs &RFC p11&157 CR Scot680
MOWAT,John William 2Lt kia 21-4-17 4 att14A&SH p173 CR France439,21-8-17
MOWAT,Morden Maxwell 2Lt dow PoW 16-5-16 RFC p3 CR France924
MOWAT,Robert James Dugald 2Lt kia 24-9-18 HampsYeo att101MGC p187&204 CR Belgium185
MOWAT,Sinclair Alexander 1917 RFC p257
MOWAT,Sydney Alexander T2Lt kld 2-7-17 GL &RFC p11 CR Scot858
MOWATT,Osmond TLt dow 22-4-17 10Huss p22 CR France113
MOWBRAY,James Seymour Strachan TCapt kia 25-9-15 8BlkW p129 MR19
MOWBRAY,John Leslie.DSO.Maj kia 24-7-16 41RFA p33 CR France630
MOWBRAY,Kenneth John Wharton 2Lt kia 9-4-17 2 att7Suff p78 CR France581
MOWBRAY,Maurice Charles.MC.Lt kia 23-8-17 RE 89FC p47 CR Belgium19
MOWBRAY,William 2Lt dow 14-1-16 IARO att1/9GurkhaRif p208 MR38
MOWES,Alexander Barclay Lt kia 27-3-18 6Ches p222
MOWES,William Bernard 2Lt kia 7-4-17 6RScots p211
MOXLY,John Hewitt Sutton 2Lt kia 13-3-15 Beds p86 CR Belgium59,12-3-15
MOXON,Gerald John Mortimer TCapt kia 27-3-16 4RFus p69 MR29
MOXON,Hugh Cecil 2Lt dow 19-7-17 5 att8Beds p219 CR France80
MOXON,Tom Cyril Lt ded 19-11-18 RFA p271 CR Yorks361
MOYCE,George Herbert Stanley T2Lt dow 19-4-18 2/8Manch p155 CR France145
MOYES,A.B.Lt 27-3-18 6Ches CR France526
MOYES,John Lt dow 14-10-17 2CamH p168 CR Greece3
MOYES,William Lt 7-4-17 6RScots attRFC CR France285
MOYNA,Edward Gerald James TCapt kia 26-9-15 7RScotF p95 MR19

MOYNAN,Harold Otho William 2Lt kia 31-7-17 SWBord BrecknockBn p223 MR29
MOYNIHAM,Michael John Lt dow 3-6-18 8Lpool p215 CR France63
MOYSE,John Jenkins CaptAMaj dow 8-2-17 1Beds p86 CR France80
MOYSEY,Lewis Capt drd 26-2-18 RAMC p254 MR40
MOZLEY,Richard Inger Lt kia 21-3-18 3Y&L att36MGC p159&184 MR27
MUCHALL,George William Stuart 2Lt kia 10-5-17 RLancs p59 MR29
MUDDOCK,Jasper Milton Preston 2Lt kia 30-11-17 ShropYeo att10KSLI p205 CR Palestine3
MUDGE,Ernest Cecil Capt kia 25-9-15 2Wilts p153 CR France423
MUDIE,James Bolingbroke TCapt ded 6-1-16 RASC p193 CR France770,Harold
MUDIE,James T2Lt kia 30-9-16 9RScotF att1RScots p95 CR Greece3,30-9/1-10-16
MUDIE,Robert Allen Capt kia 20-9-17 8LancF p221 MR30,Alan
MUGFORD,Thomas George Lt kia 17-5-19 IA 1/35Sikhs p280 MR43
MUGGERIDGE,William 2Lt kia 14-5-17 RGA 112SB p41 CR France581,MUGGRIDGE
MUIR,A 2Lt 20-9-17 8A&SH CR Belgium83
MUIR,Allan Lt kia 15-5-19 10Lpool p216 MR70 &CR Europe180
MUIR,Alan Steele 2Lt dow 12-11-16 att98RScots p212 CR France41
MUIR,Alexander 2Lt dow 27-7-16 6HLI att4NumbF p240 CR France102
MUIR,Alexander 2Lt kia 20-9-17 8A&SH p243
MUIR,Andrew Lt kia 16-11-15 7ScotRif p224 CR Gallipoli3
MUIR,Andrew Christison Mitchell T2Lt dow 27-10-18 9 att1KOSB p102 CR Gallipoli14,27-10-15
MUIR,Andrew Reid 2Lt dow 7-11-17 B233RFA p33 CR France40
MUIR,Basil 2Lt kia 16-6-15 6 att3Worc p109 MR29
MUIR,Burleigh Leicester TCapt ded 4-11-18 RASC att3Cps HQ p193 CR France1725
MUIR,David Orrock 2Lt kia 20-5-17 9HLI p240 MR20
MUIR,Frederick Bennie Lt kia 15-11-16 3 att2HLI p163 MR21
MUIR,Harry T2Lt kld 18-4-16 11EYorks p84 CR France643
MUIR,Horace Wellesley 2Lt kia 24-4-17 4Beds p86 MR20
MUIR,James Hunter 2Lt kia 7-4-17 RFC p11 MR20
MUIR,James Lester T2Lt ded 11-8-16 10ESurr p264 CR Scot84 Ex 19RFus
MUIR,James Robert Grant Lt dow 17-9-18 1/7HLI p240 CR France686
MUIR,John Hugh TLt kia 26-9-17 1GordH p167 MR30
MUIR,John Huntly Maj dow 11-4-18 17Lancers att1KOSB p23 MR32
MUIR,John Wallace 2Lt kia 12-3-18 46RFC p255 MR20
MUIR,Matthew Andrew TCapt ded 18-7-16 15Huss att1KAR p22&202 CR EAfrica40
MUIR,Philip Denis Grahame 2Lt kia 6-12-16 2LovatScts att10CamH p204 MR37
MUIR,Stanley Keith.MC.T2LtTCapt kld 12-9-17 GL &RFC p11 CR Lincs67
MUIR,William Stewart 2Lt kia 25-9-16 6A&SH p243 MR21
MUIR-MACKENZIE,Robert Cecil.Sir.MC.Lt kia 12-4-18 att95DLI p239 CR France745
MUIRHEAD,Alexander Hugh 2Lt kia 31-7-17 1Camb p245 MR29
MUIRHEAD,George Wilson 2Lt dow 16-12-15 IARO att76Punjabis p280 CR Iraq1
MUIRHEAD,James Love LtTCapt kia 21-11-17 10RScots attTankCps p212&189 CR France1483
MUIRHEAD,John T2Lt kia 16-3-17 GL &59RFC p11 CR France120
MUIRHEAD,John Ritchie 2Lt kia 20-10-18 8ScotRif attTMB RFA p225 CR Belgium140
MUIRHEAD,Langdon 2Lt kia 29-9-18 59RFA p33 MR16
MUIRHEAD,Lennox Lt kia 21-9-18 7RScots p211 CR France1496,5Bn
MUIRHEAD,Phillips Quincy TLt kia 18-7-16 D25RFA p33 CR France453
MUIRHEAD,William 2Lt kia 28-3-18 3CamH att44TMB p168 MR20
MULCAHY-MORGAN,Edward Spread Lt kia 27-10-14 RIrRif p170 MR22
MULCAHY-MORGAN,Francis Campion Lt kia 6-9-16 7RIrRif p170 MR21
MULCUCK,Daniel Henry 2Lt kia 11-10-17 att8Lincs p75 MR30,MULCOCK
MULDOON,John Lt kia 13-9-18 2CamH p168 CR Greece6 2Lt
MULES,William George Horace Mainwaring Lt dow 12-2-16 IA 130Baluchis p280 CR EAfrica56,Capt
MULHALL,Frank Reginald 2Lt dow 15-10-18 RGA 25HB p41 CR France528
MULHOLLAND,Andrew Edward Somerset.Hon.Capt dow 1-11-14 1IrGds p53 CR Belgium57
MULKERN,Hubert Cowell Capt 1-7-16 RAMC att9RInniskF p197 MR21
MULKERN,Lionel Henry T2Lt kia 26-9-17 123MGC Inf p184 MR30
MULLALLY,Brian Desmond TCapt kia 1-7-16 26NumbF p62 CR France393
MULLALY,Charles Mylne Capt kia 9-5-15 IA 2/2GurkhaRif MR28 p280
MULLALY,Dennis Joseph St.Clair.MC.MID Lt kia 17-10-15 RGA 1SB p41 CR France423
MULLALY,Frederick Terence Hastings Capt kia 21-4-17 IA 2/6 att 1/8GurkhaRif MR38 p280
MULLALY,Herbert Maj ded 19-1-20 IA 1/9 att2/4GurkhaRif p280 MR43

MULLANE,Bernard Patrick T2Lt dow 1-4-18 9RFus p69 CR France64
MULLEN,Arnold George Leighton Lt ded 15-2-19 5DLI &104RAF p239 CR France1633,kia 22-8-18
MULLER,Carl Wilhelm Albert 2Lt kia 5-10-16 5Worc p109 CR France423,Charles William 1Bn
MULLER,John Herman Lt kia 31-10-17 9Middx att113RFC p19&236 Cr Palestine
MULLER,Norman Capt kia 28-7-18 6WYorks p218 CR France1689
MULLER-CHATEAU,James Lt ded 29-12-19 RH&FA p261
MULLER-CHATEAU,Leo Lt 27-2-19 RFA CR Norf209 Ex 1AustLtHorse
MULLETT,Walter Stephen 4835 Lt&QM ded 31-1-18 11RScots p54 CR Ireland3
MULLIGAN,Herbert Butler.MC.T2Lt kia 4-7-16 1 att12RScots p54 MR21
MULLIGAN,Sidney Gerald 2Lt kia 23-4-17 3 att4Beds p86 MR20
MULLIN,Archibald T2Lt kld 16-5-17 RAOC p198 CR France57,5-4-17
MULLINS,John Ollis 2Lt kld 30-3-15 Middx &RFC p1&148 CR Mddx29,dedacc
MULLINS,Richard Walter TCapt kia 1-7-16 10Y&L p159 France267
MULLIS,George Edwin LtACapt kia 30-9-16 RGA 14HB p41 CR France251
MULLOCK,Sidney Goss ALtCol kia 12-4-17 2Ess p132 CR France730
MULOCK,Edward Ross 2Lt kia 11-3-15 2GordH p167 CR France279
MULOCK,Henry Collister TLt kia 15-2-17 GL &52RFC p11 CR France105
MULROY,Thomas Bernard T2Lt ded 23-1-16 11Lpool p72 CR Yorks607
MUMBY,Harold Cheffings T2Lt kia 3-10-18 5TankCps p188 CR France375
MUMFORD,Arthur Green 2Lt kia 9-1-17 IARO att105Mahrattas p280 MR38
MUMFORD,Frank Richard Capt kia 8-7-16 2Wilts p153 MR21 CR France390
MUMFORD,John Houston.MC&Bar.Lt kia 13-8-17 B110RFA p208 CR Belgium7
MUMFORD,Louis Richard 2Lt kia 21-10-18 23Lond attRAF p256 CR Mddx17
MUMFREY,B.J.H.LtCol See HUMFREY
MUMMERY,Harry Norman Samuel Capt ded PoW 6-8-18 HLI att14Bn p163
MUNBY,Ernest John Lt kia 31-1-15 RE 1EAngliaFC p210 CR France727
MUNCIE,Daniel McBeth 2Lt kia 3-12-17 2RFA p33 CR France711
MUNDAY,Edwin George Stanislaus 2Lt kia 20-2-17 3 att13Ess p132 CR France39
MUNDAY,Leslie William Crawford 2Lt kld 12-8-18 RGA p209 CR France1170
MUNDEN,John Arnold 2Lt kia 28-8-16 3 att6SomLI p80 MR21 &CR France1890
MUNDEY,Lionel Clement Lt kia 6-6-15 2RFus p69 MR4,5-6-15
MUNDEY,Walter Vivian Lt ded 30-9-19 19RHuss p621 CR Surrey136
MUNDS,Percy T2Lt dow 8-10-18 7RFus p69 MR16,1Bn
MUNDY,James TLt dow 26-11-16 19DLI p161 CR France1182
MUNDY,Jesse Ernest 2Lt dow 24-4-18 PoW Middx att2/2Lond p148 MR27
MUNDY,Lionel Frank Hasting.MID Lt dow 3-9-14 RHA p33 CR France1420
MUNDYE,Arnold T2Lt kld 29-7-16 1RWSurr p56 CR France176
MUNGALL,Robert 2Lt kia 23-4-17 7 att13RScots p211 MR20
MUNGEAM,Ernest George 2Lt dow 25-8-18 17MGC p184 MR6
MUNN,Leslie Vincent T2Lt ded 16-2-17 GL &RFC p11 CR France924 Ex 6Leic
MUNRO,Alexander T2Lt dow 5-11-16 10ScotRif C'Coy p103 CR France145
MUNRO,Alexander Douglas T2Lt kia 2-9-18 11 att1Ches p96 CR France1484
MUNRO,Baillie Chisholm.MC.2Lt kia 10-7-17 12 att2KRRC p151 MR31
MUNRO,Claud Bruce TLt kia 27-9-15 13RScots p54 MR19,26-9-15
MUNRO,Colin Cameron T2Lt dow 23-4-16 A122RFA p33 CR France345
MUNRO,Donald 2Lt kia 28-4-17 15RScots p54 MR20
MUNRO,Donald Rice 2Lt kld 28-7-17 RFC 37TrSqn p11 CR Lincs181,Lt
MUNRO,Duncan Leitch T2Lt dow 13-10-17 8BlkW p129 CR Belgium16
MUNRO,Fergus Fullerton T2Lt kia 20-9-17 att5CamH p168 MR30
MUNRO,Fred Ross 2Lt kia 18-11-16 7 att15HLI p240 MR21
MUNRO,Frederick John 2Lt dow 11-8-17 RGA 4SB p41 CR Belgium20,Lt
MUNRO,George William Lt dow 1-10-18 4 att5CamH p242 CR Belgium173
MUNRO,Guy Horace T2Lt kld 18-8-17 GL 26RFus attRFC p11 CR Mddx80
MUNRO,Hector Charles Seymour.MC.Capt kia 23-10-18 2SfthH p165 CR France1266
MUNRO,Hector William 2Lt kia 23-4-17 7A&SH p243 CR France545
MUNRO,Henry Fraser Capt dow 29-9-15 8SfthH p165 CR France1
MUNRO,Hugh Adam Lt kia 22-9-15 1/8A&SH A'Coy p243 CR France197,Capt
MUNRO,Hugh Donald.MID Lt kia 25-3-18 20DLI p161 MR20
MUNRO,Ian Duncan T2Lt kia 13-9-15 ACycCps att9DCC p181 CR France114,13-9-15
MUNRO,James Donald Sutherland 2Lt kld 17-7-17 RFC p11 CR Surrey150
MUNRO,James John T2Lt kia 31-10-18 1/2 att1/5KOSB p102 CR Belgium140
MUNRO,John.MC.2Lt kia 16-4-18 4SfthH p241 MR32
MUNRO,John Clegg T2Lt ded 10-11-18 3Worc p109 CR France332
MUNRO,John Sutherland Lt ded 16-7-17 RAMC att112FA p197 CR Iraq8
MUNRO,Murdo Simon 2Lt kia 26-4-17 12RB p179 CR France662
MUNRO,Ronald Lt kia 8-8-17 1/5A&SH p243 CR Palestine8

MUNRO,Ronald George.MC.Lt dow 19-9-16 18Lond p250 CR France145
MUNRO,Thomas Mackay 2Lt kia 25-9-15 7SfthH p165 MR19
MUNRO,William 2Lt kia 29-4-18 8Lpool p216 CR Belgium111,Lt
MUNRO,William Dawson Capt kia 16-5-17 8A&SH p243 MR20
MUNRO,William Pearce 2Lt dow 5-9-18 A70RFA p33 CR France421,Lt
MUNSEY,William Frederick 2Lt kia 16-8-17 12KRRC p151 MR30 Ex 28Lond
MUNSON,George Philip 2Lt kia 7-8-15 2Y&L p159 MR29 &CR Belgium453
MUNSTER,John Francis Lt kia 4-2-17 13Huss p22 MR38
MUNT,R.R.2Lt 11-5-16 1/1RFA CR Egypt1
MUNTZ,Joseph Oscar TCapt dow 4-9-18 16Dev B'Coy p77 CR France833
MURCHISON,Donald 2Lt kia 14-4-17 5ScotRif p224 MR20
MURCHISON,Kenneth Bickersteth 2Lt kia 22-8-17 2 att8SfthH p165 MR29
MURCHLAND,Charles TLt kia 26-5-15 RFA p33 CR Belgium101
MURDOCH,Barry Wilkie 2Lt kia 2-2-17 IARO att187MGC Inf p280 CR Iraq5,3-2-17
MURDOCH,James Gordon TLt dow 22-9-15 7SLancs p125 CR France345
MURDOCH,James Hunter George 2Lt kia 4-7-16 95RFA p33 CR France189,3-7-16
MURDOCH,John 2Lt kia 1-7-16 16HLI p163 CR France293
MURDOCH,Louis Farde Campbell 2Lt dow 19-9-16 2ScotGds p52
MURDOCH,Ronald Hamilton William T2Lt kia 28-10-16 21 att4Lpool p72 MR21
MURDOCH,Thomas John Carson TLt kia 6-2-16 24Manch p155 CR France637
MURE,Godfrey Arthur Stanhope Capt kia 3-1-17 ArabRifs CR EAfrica36
MURGATROYD,Ellison.DCM.TCapt kia 26-3-18 16WYorks p82 CR France798
MURGATROYD,Hugh Lester.MC.LtACapt dow 27-9-18 Leic att1/7LancF p88 CR France245
MURIEL,Sidney Herbert Foster Capt kia 30-4-15 BordR p117 CR Gallipoli3
MURLESS,Herbert Reginald.MC.TLt dow 7-2-17 1 att12RFus p69 CR France80
MURLY-GOTTO,James TLt dow 20-8-16 RE 70FC p47 CR France40,2Lt
MURPHY,A.G.Capt&QM ded 14-6-17 GL &RFC p11 CR Hamps1
MURPHY,Albert T2Lt kia 3-10-16 30 att24NumbF p62 CR France922
MURPHY,Alfred Durham.DSO.MC.BtMaALtCol kia 6-11-17 2Leinst p174 CR France528
MURPHY,Allen Ingham 23910 2Lt kld 30-3-17 RFC p11 CR Norf247
MURPHY,Bernard Joseph 2Lt dow 18-8-17 5MunstF attRIrRif p175 CR Belgium8
MURPHY,Christopher Fowler Lt kia 21-10-14 att2 O&BLI p130 MR29
MURPHY,Christopher John 2Lt kia 20-7-16 9MunstF p175 CR France115,1Bn
MURPHY,Christopher Trevor Elias.MID Lt dow 8-5-18 RGA 216SB p41 CR France40
MURPHY,Edward T2Lt kia 2-4-17 19Manch p155 CR France1186
MURPHY,Edward 2Lt kia 21-3-18 8 att1RDubF p177 MR27
MURPHY,Edwin Hale Capt dow 6-5-15 5Leinst p174 CR France141,2Bn
MURPHY,F.Capt 13-3-20 RAMC CR Wilts64
MURPHY,G.F.L.Capt 22-11-18 RAMC CR Ireland24
MURPHY,George TLt kia 6-9-17 13RWar att1/5LancF Res p65 MR30
MURPHY,Harry Eustace Lt kld 22-4-18 1/4RFus &RAF p69 CR Eire78
MURPHY,Hugh Palmer TLt kia 6-8-16 10Lincs p75 CR France432
MURPHY,James 2Lt kia 15-4-18 2/5NStaffs p238 MR32 &CR France298
MURPHY,James Neville Herbert Lt kia 10-5-15 5 att2DubF p177 MR29
MURPHY,John.MID LtTCapt dow 17-8-17 D62RFA p33 CR France113,kia
MURPHY,John Lt kia 25-8-18 6NumbF p214 CR France239
MURPHY,Johnston Lt kia 2-7-16 6 att8RIrRif p170 MR21
MURPHY,Leonard Francis McCarthy2Lt ded 21-7-17 IARO att81Pnrs p280 MR43,121Bn
MURPHY,Lewis William Capt kia 9-4-16 2DCLI att5Wilts p114 MR38,3Bn
MURPHY,Matthew TCapt drd 10-10-18 RAMC p197 CR Eire75
MURPHY,M.J.MID 2Lt kia 12-3-15 3Worc p109 CR Belgium17,11-3-15
MURPHY,Philip Frederick T2Lt kia 2-7-16 RE 201FC p47 MR21
MURPHY,Reginald Graham Capt ded 4-10-18 RDC p256 CR Ches182
MURPHY,Robert T2Lt dow 1-10-18 1RIrRif p170 CR Belgium157
MURPHY,William 2Lt kia 10-3-15 2Leic p88 CR France727,11-3-15
MURPHY,William Joseph.MID TCapt kia 9-9-16 9DubF p177 CR France294
MURRAY,Alastair John Greville 2Lt dow 14-9-14 1CamH p168 CR France1894
MURRAY,Alexander Capt kia 14-8-17 ScotHorse p205 CR Belgium72
MURRAY,Alexander 2Lt kia 29-8-18 4GordH p242 CR France266
MURRAY,Alexander Gordon Wynch.MBE.Capt ded 15-2-19 ULCambUnivOTC p271 CR Kent34
MURRAY,Alexander Roxburgh 2Lt kia 18-11-16 4 att17HLI p163 CR France534
MURRAY,Andrew Lt kia 19-11-16 56MGC p184 MR21
MURRAY,Andrew Buchanan Lt kia 23-4-17 A&SH p173
MURRAY,Andrew Currie Capt kia 20-5-17 9HLI p240 MR20
MURRAY,Anthony Hepburn Poore Lt kia 9-4-17 3 att 1RScotF p95 CR France581

MURRAY,Anthony Stoddart 2Lt mbk 22-3-18 1/8A&SH p257 CR France375,23-3-18
MURRAY,Archibald Capt&QM dow 13-9-14 KOSB p102 CR France870 &CR France1113
MURRAY,Arthur T2Lt kia 8-8-18 7RSuss p119 CR France11770
MURRAY,Cecil James Carruthers Capt kia 15-6-15 6ScotRif p224 CR France260
MURRAY,Charles.MC.2Lt kia 16-10-18 RGA 115SB p41 CR Belgium157,Lt
MURRAY,Charles John Lt kia 25-10-14 1CldGds p51 MR29,26-10-14
MURRAY,Charles Robinson T2Lt kia 18-9-16 9 att7KOSB p102 MR21
MURRAY,Charles Stephenson TCapt dow 1-7-16 12RIrRif p170 CR France44,2-7-16
MURRAY,Charles William 2Lt kia 25-9-15 9KRRC p151 MR29
MURRAY,Cyril 2Lt kia 16-8-17 2Lond p245 MR29
MURRAY,Edward Douglas TLt dow 20-7-16 8BlkW p129 CR France23,2Lt
MURRAY,Eric Dennys 2Lt kia 16-10-14 19Huss p23 CR France263
MURRAY,Ernest Francis Hume.MC.DCM.LtACapt&Adjt kia 9-10-17 2HAC p206 MR30
MURRAY,Fane Wright Stapleton Capt kia 30-11-14 12Lancers p22 MR29
MURRAY,Frederick Stanley Lt dow 19-11-17 3/2KAR &NStaffs p157&202 CR EAfrica11 &CR Tanzania1,NStaffs attKAR
MURRAY,George Capt kia 4-6-16 2Leinst p174 CR Belgium49
MURRAY,George Angus TLt kia 4-10-18 RE att310RFA p47 France910
MURRAY,George Anthony.MC.LtAMaj dow 4-4-18 D47RFA p33 CR France1173
MURRAY,George Ramsay Lt kia 23-12-16 IARO att13Lancers p280 CR Iraq5
MURRAY,Graham Dunmore.MID T2Lt kia 26-1-16 12NumbF p62 CR France922
MURRAY,Harold Gladstone Lt kia 16-12-16 1DivTMB attRFC CR France46
MURRAY,Henry Berkeley TLt kia 18-7-16 10A&SH p173 CR France162 &CR France513
MURRAY,Henry Francis Farquharson MajALtCol kia 23-8-17 9BlkW p129 CR Belgium8
MURRAY,Herbert.MC.Capt kia 25-7-18 1/4GordH p241 CR France622,20-7-18
MURRAY,James Brash Lt kia 21-5-16 8SfthH p165 CR France423
MURRAY,James Eric Capt kia 10-3-15 1A 89Punjabis att1/39GarhwalRif p280 CR France355 &CR France1887,87Bn
MURRAY,James McMillan 2Lt kia 24-6-17 8ScotRif p225 CR France1489
MURRAY,James Thomas Crockatt.DSO.Maj dow 16-2-15 1BlkW p129 CR France202,Crokatt
MURRAY,John 2Lt kia 16-8-17 5 att1KOSB p224 MR30
MURRAY,John Lt ded 30-10-17 1/6A&SH C'Coy p243 CR Belgium11,kia
MURRAY,John Claude 2Lt kia 9-7-16 2SWBord p100 MR21
MURRAY,John Congreve Lt dow 23-9-17 1/8RScots p211 CR Belgium16
MURRAY,John Robertson T2Lt dow 18-9-17 att9SfthH p165 CR Belgium46
MURRAY,Joseph Leonard T2Lt kia 29-5-17 GL &RFC p11 MR20
MURRAY,Kenneth Desmond 2Lt kia 25-9-15 9ESurr p113 MR19
MURRAY,Kenneth Hope 2Lt kia 18-6-16 6SfthH p241 CR France15,dow
MURRAY,Leonard Lt kld 13-3-17 LancHuss attRFC p204 CR Staffs176
MURRAY,Mabel SNurse ded 2-11-18 TFNS 3SGH CR Oxford69
MURRAY,Maurice Austin Lt kia 25-9-15 11Ess p132 MR19,26-9-15
MURRAY,Norman Cairns Capt kia 30-6-16 7War p214 CR France1327
MURRAY,Patrick Austin TCapt kia 1-7-16 25NumbF p62 MR21
MURRAY,Patrick Hallam Capt kia 25-9-15 61/131RFA p33 MR19
MURRAY,Patrick Maxwell Lt kia 20-9-14 2N&D p134 MR15
MURRAY,Percival William Lt dow PoW 2-2-17 6DLI attRFC p19&239 CR France1321
MURRAY,Peter Lt 13-1-20 25 att 152Punjabis MR43
MURRAY,Randolph TLt dow 27-10-17 1CamH p168 CR France545,6Bn
MURRAY,Randolph Noel TLt dow 28-4-16 7RInnisF p105 CR France115,Capt
MURRAY,Raymond Hugh T2Lt kia 12-3-18 155MGC Inf p184 CR Palestine9
MURRAY,Robert Davidson T2Lt dow 2-10-18 11RScots p54 CR Belgium38
MURRAY,Robert Elder Lt kia 11-8-18 5 att5/6RScots p211 MR16
MURRAY,Robert Henry TCapt kia 7-7-16 11Yorks attRMunstF p91 CR France115
MURRAY,Robert Leslie.MID Capt kia 19-4-17 4Nhampt p234 MR34
MURRAY,Robert McDiarmid.MC.TLt dow 25-2-16 RGA 7SB p41 CR France102
MURRAY,Robert William Skinner Capt ded 6-5-19 RAMC att5FlSchl RAF p197 CR Egypt9
MURRAY,Ronald Alexander.MID TCapt dow 19-9-18 8RScotF p95 CR Greece6
MURRAY,Ronald Ernest.DSO&Bar.DCM.LtCol ded 29-6-20 BSAP CR Hamps161
MURRAY,Rupert Auriol Comaut Capt dow 11-3-15 1SfthH p165 CR France201,Conant
MURRAY,Thomas Capt kia 3-7-16 11Ches p96 MR21
MURRAY,Thomas Francis Maj kia 21-12-14 1HLI p163 MR22
MURRAY,Thomas William.MID Capt kia 19-7-20 1A 116Mahrattas p280 CR Iraq6

MURRAY,Victor Bickersteth Lt 28-2-21 2CamH CR Ches22
MURRAY,W.H.E.CB.BrigGen 2-2-15 Staff CR Scot967
MURRAY,William T2Lt kia 24-4-17 1Middx p148 CR France591
MURRAY,William 2Lt kldacc 30-7-18 RFA att17TMB p33 CR Irraq8
MURRAY,William Douglas Gillespie 2Lt kia 3-1-18 RFC p16 CR France285
MURRAY,William Dunmore TLt ded 23-1-16 RAMC p197
MURRAY,William Edward Capt kia 17-9-14 3GordH p167 CR France867,14-9-14 1Bn
MURRAY,William Grant 2Lt kia 16-4-18 7SfthH p165 MR30
MURRAY,William Raymond Croft Capt ded 25-2-17 5GrenGds p50 CR Europe28,26-2-17
MURRAY,William Roland T2Lt kia 11-11-17 GL &RFC p11 CR France44
MURRAY-DIXON,Henry Edward Otto Murray 2Lt dow 10-4-17 1/4SfthH CR France95
MURRAY-MENZIES,Clive William 2Lt kia 25-1-15 1BlkW p129 MR22
MURRAY-MENZIES,Duncan Innes.MC.LtACapt kia 22-8-17 BlkW attC'TankCps p129&188 MR30
MURRAY-SMITH,Arthur George Lt dow 2-11-14 2LifeGds p20 CR France1027
MURRAY-SMITH,Geoffrey Lt kia 29-9-15 6 att3RFus p69 MR19
MURTON,Charles Duncan.TD.Maj 7-9-19 5EKent CR Kent182
MURTON,Charles Evelyn 2Lt kia 30-11-17 35MGC Inf p184 MR17
MUSGRAVE,Cecil David TCapt ded 15-11-18 3RASC 8DivTrn p193 CR France1277
MUSGRAVE,Herbert.DSO.Maj kia 3-6-18 RE Staff 2CpsHQ p47 CR France142,2-6-18
MUSGRAVE,John James Nicholson T2Lt kld 27-2-18 RFC p16 CR C'land&W'land18
MUSGRAVE,Joseph Baxter.MC.Capt dow 16-3-20 4Ches CR Ches28
MUSGRAVE,Kenneth Lt kia 22-3-15 YLI p143 CR Belgium98
MUSGRAVE,Thomas Lt kia 6-2-15 1IrGds SR p53 CR France720
MUSGRAVE,William Martin 2Lt dow 15-4-17 5BordR att16Lond p228 CR France120,MUSGROVE
MUSGROVE,George Henry Stuart TLt kia 1-7-16 8ESurr p113 CR France513
MUSGROVE,John William 2Lt kia 19-7-18 4BlkW p230 CR France324
MUSKER,John Henry 2Lt kia 1-11-17 3 att1Ches p96 MR30
MUSKER,Joseph Walter T2Lt kia 30-7-16 20Lpool p72 MR21
MUSPRATT,Keith Knox.MC.2Lt TCapt kld 19-3-18 2DorsR &56RFC p16&124 CR Hamps15,16-3-18
MUSPRATT,Terence Petty.MC.Capt dow 29-5-18 3Worc p109 CR France1693
MUSSON,Alfred William TLt ded 10-9-18 RAMC p267 CR Lancs226
MUSSON,Graham 2Lt kia 25-3-18 8MGC p184 MR27
MUSSON,Harold Methuen.MC.2Lt dow 26-9-17 D149RFA p33 CR France40
MUSSON,John Henry 2Lt kia 19-7-15 2RWSurr p56 CR France631
MUSSON,Samuel Paynter Maj ded 2-6-17 IA S&TCps p280 CR Leic63
MUSTARD,Robert William 2Lt kia 31-3-18 12/13NumbF p62 MR27
MUTCH,George.DSO.TLt kia 6-7-17 GordH &4RFC p11&167 CR Belgium127
MYBURGH,John Adrian T2Lt dow 10-4-17 GL &55RFC p11 CR France300
MYCOCK,Sam.MM.2Lt kia 21-3-18 7 att2/6N&D p233 MR20
MYDDLETON,Edward Geoffrey 2Lt kia /-9-14 Suff p78 MR15,26-8-14
MYDDLETON-GAVEY,Francis Capt kia 26-9-15 2 att4Worc p109 MR4
MYER,T2Lt kia 14-2-17 GL &RFC p11
MYER,Denzil Grenville Alex T2Lt kia 25-2-17 Worc p109 MR38
MYER,Ernest Alex Maj kld 3-4-15 6Lond p246 CR France279
MYERS,Arthur Francis TLt kia 31-3-18 2RRofCav att4Huss p23 MR27
MYERS,Francis Michael.MC.T2Lt kia 14-2-17 GL 11Suff attRFC 11Wing p11 CR Belgium1
MYERS,Henry John TCapt ded 19-2-19 GL&RASC p255 CR Kent203
MYERS,James Wheatley.MID Capt dow 14-8-17 19Manch p155 CR France102
MYERS,John Coupar Capt kld 4-5-18 ScotHorse p205 MR19,Couper
MYERS,John Flesher TCapt kia 9-10-17 6Yorks p91 MR30
MYERS,John James 2Lt kia 22-10-17 11DLI p161 MR21
MYERS,Lawrence Benjamin 2Lt kia 9-6-16 1ARO att130Baluchis p280 CR EAfrica19,8-6-16
MYERS,Thomas Wrighton T2Lt dow 19-11-17 1Nhants p137 CR Belgium16,Lt Wrightson
MYERS,Wilfrid Herman TCapt ded 10-4-16 12Lpool p72 CR Surrey160
MYLES,Alfred Thomas Charles 2Lt 2-7-18 10Lpool p216MR19,26-9-15
MYLES,Charles William Chester.MC.CaptAMaj ded 19-10-18 RAMC p253 CR Palestine9
MYLES,John Adam Whitson Douglas Capt ded 29-5-18 7HLI attKAR p240&268 CR EAfrica77
MYLES,Philip Henry Lt kia 13-1-16 IA 41Dogras p280 CR Iraq5,Capt
MYLES,R.S.Lt 22-10-19 S&T Cps MR65

MYLES,Thomas Booth.MC.Capt kia 2-8-17 12HLI p163 MR29
MYLES,William Whitson T2Lt dow 20-9-16 10ScotRif &TMB p103 CR France177
MYLIUS,John Kingsford.MID Lt dow 12-10-16 1KSLI p145 CR France105
MYLLES,James Robertson Jack 2Lt kia 30-7-15 3HLI p163 CR Belgium186,Lt 30-12-14
MYLNE,Edward Graham.MID Capt dow 12-6-15 1IrGds p53 CR France145
MYLNE,Euan Louis.MC.Lt dow 15-9-16 1IrGds p53 CR France374,kia
MYLNE,James Graham Lt kia 2-9-18 8RScots p211 CR France646
MYLREA,William Percy Garland TLtCol ded 25-8-15 RFA p271 CR Essex196
MYTTON,Percy Lt kia 2-5-15 8Mddx p236 MR29
MYTTON,Richard Devereux Hugh 2Lt dow 3-10-16 1Lond p245 MR21,1-10-16

N

NADAUD,Henry Louis Frederick Bonnetand.TD.Maj kia 21-3-18 24Lond p252 CR France439,Bonnetaut
NADIN,Trafford Capt ded 8-6-18 2/5N&D p232 CR Lond14
NAGLE,Gilbert.MC.TCapt&Ajt kia 5-7-17 7RSuss p119 CR France1182
NAILER,Edgar Ivan Fitzroy Lt kia 23-8-18 1Beds p86 CR France239
NAINBY,Whinfield Hamilton T2Lt kia 18-8-16 20KRRC p151 CR France513
NAINBY,William 2Lt kia 27-5-18 Lincs att62LTMB p75 MR18
NAIRN,Francis William EngLt ded 9-11-16 RIM p280 CR Iraq6
NAIRN,George 2Lt dow 28-9-16 70RFA 15Div p33 CR France177
NAIRN,Ian Couper.MC&Bar.Capt kia 2-9-18 Fife&ForfarYeo p203 CR France511,Cooper 14BlkW
NAIRNE,Lord Charles George Francis Mercer.MVO.Maj kia 30-10-14 1Drags p21 CR Belgium57
NAIRNE,James 2Lt kia 13-4-18 9HLI p240 MR32
NAIRNE,Ronald.MID 2Lt kia 3-4-18 5RScots B'Coy p211 CR France745,5/6Bn
NAIRNE,William Graham 2Lt dow 11-7-15 3SLancs att2LancF p125 CR Belgium
NAISH,Alfred Herbert TLt kia 13-7-16 20KRRC p151 CR France513
NAISH,Edwin Athelstan T2Lt kia 22/23-7-16 10Glouc p107 MR21
NAISMITH,Noel Lings T2Lt kia 11-1-17 10 att7NStaffs p157 CR Iraq5
NALDER,Frank Shirley Capt kia 21-9-18 8KSLI p145
NANCARROW,John Vivian Capt kia 25-4-15 4Yorks p220 MR29
NANCARROW,William Thomas T2Lt kia 15-4-18 9Norf p74 MR30
NANGLE,Edward Jocelyn TCapt kia 26-9-15 RAMC att1LNLancs p197 CR France219
NANSON,Joseph T2Lt kia 1-7-16 25Manch p155 CR France397
NAPER,Frank Cornewall Capt kia 3-5-17 1RLancs p59 CR France544
NAPIER,Egbert Maj kia 13-11-16 1/5GordH RoO p167 CR France131
NAPIER,Guy Greville Lt dow 25-9-15 IA 35Sikhs att47 p280 CR France924,Capt
NAPIER,Henry Edward.MID TBrigGen dow 27-4-15 88Bde Staff p1 MR4,25-4-15
NAPIER,Henry Lenox Maj kia 17-11-15 11N&D p134 MR40
NAPIER,James 2Lt kld 7-4-18 GL &52RAF p191 MR20
NAPIER,John Chatt Lt kia 29-10-18 4NumbF p213 CR France1034
NAPIER,John Francis SubCdr ded 26-6-21 IA S&TCps 114Coy p280 CR Iraq8
NAPIER,Jonathan 2Lt kia 16-8-17 7YLI p143 MR30
NAPIER,Lennox Robert Murray Capt dow PoW 28-7-16 CamH E'Coy p168 CR France245
NAPIER,Maurice Alexander TMaj kia 27-5-16 Ches att10WelshR p96 CR France707
NAPIER,Rupert George Carrington Lt dow 2-8-17 2GrenGds p50 CR Belgium16,Carrington
NAPIER,William Lennox.Bart.TMaj kia 13-8-15 4SWBord p100 CR Gallipoli17
NAREY,Vincent Gerald TLt dow 15-10-16 11 att8WRid p116 CR France145
NARRACOTT,Ronald William Lt kia 10-8-15 RE p210 MR29
NASBY,Frank Clementine 2Lt kia 1-9-17 4NumbF p213 CR France1461
NASH,Arthur James 2Lt kia 13-6-18 5N&D p233 MR19
NASH,Charles Frederic Wybrow.MC&Bar.Capt kld 27-3-18 7Norf p74 MR27
NASH,Edward Radcliffe Capt kia 21-2-15 16Lancers p23 CR Belgium57
NASH,Fountain O'Key Colbourne CaptTMaj kia 27-4-15 5NumbF p213 CR Belgium113
NASH,Francis Henry.MC.MID TCapt kia 18-7-17 9NStaffs p157 CR Belgium17,7-17
NASH,George 2Lt dow 29-6-15 6 att3Worc p109 CR Hereford166,Lt
NASH,Gordon 2Lt kld 7-5-18 GL &63RAF CR Kent156
NASH,Harold John Lt kia 24-3-18 4 att9RWelshF p223 MR20
NASH,James 2Lt kia 3-4-15 4 att1ESurr p113 CR Belgium17,2-4-15
NASH,James Haran Lt kia 27-3-18 1IrGds 1Coy p53 CR France214
NASH,Llewellyn Charles.MID Lt dow 29-9-15 2KRRC p151 CR France88,Capt 28-9-15

NASH,Manfred Victor Johnstone 2Lt kia 2-11-17 25 att 1/10Lond p252 CR Palestine8
NASH,Phillip Geoffrey T2Lt kia 5-10-17 21Manch p155 CR Belgium308
NASH,William Fleetwood.DSO.TLtCol ded 28-12-15 BordR Maj RoO p117 CR C'land&W'land17
NASH,William Walter 2Lt kia 4-7-18 3 att 2Ess p132 CR France412,2 att 3Bn
NASMITH,Arthur Plater.DSO.TCapt kia 23-4-17 7BordR p117 MR20
NASMYTH,Alfred Wylie 12-10-17 AlbertaR att RFC CR Belgium140
NASON,John William Washington TCapt kia 26-12-16 GL 14Suss att 46RFC p3&p191 CR Belgium4
NASON,Richard Philip 2Lt kia 16-4-18 SNottsHuss p205 MR32
NATHAN,David Lt kia 20-8-17 A155/2RFA p208 CR Belgium10
NATHAN,Leopold Charles T2Lt kia 14-9-16 8WRid p116 MR21
NATHAN,Robert Percy.MC.LtACapt dow 22-3-18 RFA att 36TMB p33 CR France1203
NATHAN,William Sylvester 2Lt kia 14-6-16 RFus att 12Bn p69 MR29,14-6-17
NAUGHTON,H.F.Lt 10-11-17 IARO att 7Lancers MR66
NAYLER,Frederick Augustus 2Lt ded 20-10-18 RASC p193 CR Mddx39
NAYLOR,Cyril Doughty.MC.T2Lt kia 25-8-18 7Lincs p75 CR France392
NAYLOR,Eric Lewin Lt kia 3-12-17 3SStaffs att 2/6RWarR p122 MR17
NAYLOR,Frank 2Lt kia 23-3-18 LNLancs &59RFC p16&136,ded MR20
NAYLOR,Fred Lt kia 12-4-18 4EKent p212 MR32
NAYLOR,G.G.2Lt 8-6-20 GordH CR Yorks417
NAYLOR,Henry Charles 2Lt dow 24-9-17 3 att 11RSuss p119 CR Belgium124
NAYLOR,Herbert William Eastwood Lt&QM kia 17-2-17 1ELancs p111 CR France624
NAYLOR,James Reginald 2Lt kia 26-10-17 1Lond p245 CR Belgium83
NAYLOR,John T2LtACapt kia 11-4-18 9Ches p96 MR30
NAYLOR,Joseph TLt kia 10-4-17 RAMC p197 CR France85
NAYLOR,Rowland Edmund Lt kia 16-5-15 1RWFus p98 CR France279
NAYLOR,Urmston Shaw TMaj ded 3-9-16 13DLI p161 MR21 &MR32
NAYLOR,Walter George 2Lt kia 31-8-18 7Lond p247 CR France218
NAYLOR,William Balme 2Lt kia 16-9-16 1/6WRid p227 CR France246
NAYLOR-LEYLAND,George Vyvyan.MID Lt dow 21-9-14 RHGds p20 CR France1328
NEAL,Harry Beecroft Lt ded 3-11-19 MGC Inf p266 CR Yorks22
NEALE,Algernon Hastings Campbell LtCol ded 7-1-20 8Lpool p271 CR WAfrica17
NEALE,Arthur Hill Lt kia 21-1-16 IA 1Brahmans att 6jats p280 MR38
NEALE,Aubrey Charles T2Lt kia 1-8-17 1/2 att 10Bn ScotRif p104 CR Belgium7
NEALE,Christopher Ernest T2Lt kia 29-9-18 10 att 2Worc p109 CR France665
NEALE,E.A.C.Lt 26-10-20 1/39GarwhalRif MR43
NEALE,George Henry TLtCol.MID kia 28-9-15 3Mddx p148 MR19
NEALE,Guy Dalrymple 2Lt dow 18-5-18 1GrenGds p50 CR France84
NEALE,Herbert Cecil Thubron 2Lt dow 1-1-16 1Nhampt p137 CR France178
NEALE,John Everard Digby Capt kld 22-8-17 4Leic att RFC p19&219 CR Leic63
NEALE,Percy Reginald T2Lt kia 20-12-17 101MGC p184 CR France592 Ex GloucR
NEALE,Robert Edward 2Lt kia 18-3-18 29RFC p16 CR Belgium140
NEALON,Cedric Dunnill 2Lt kia 16-8-17 4RIrReg att RInnisF p89 MR30
NEALON,John Alfred 2Lt kia 4-3-17 10Mddx p236 CR France439
NEAME,Arthur Maj ded 17-3-16 RGA KentHB p209 CR Kent212
NEAME,Geoffrey.MC.TCaptAMaj kia 2-4-18 B190RFA p33 CR France745
NEAME,Gerald Tassell TCapt kia 1-7-16 EKent p58 CR France402
NEATE,Alan Burnaby 2Lt dow 23-4-17 B162RFA p33 CR France113
NEATE,Nelson Rayner.MC.Capt kia 3-5-17 11RFus att HAC p69 MR20
NEATE,William 2Lt kia 24-3-18 24RFus p69 MR20
NEAVE,Alexander Lionel William Capt kia 19-9-18 IA 110Mahrattas att CpsofGuidesInf p280 CR palestine9
NEAVE,Arundell Maj dow 21-2-15 16Lancers p23 CR Belgium57
NEAVE,Gerald Vansittart.MID Capt kia 16-8-17 2/1BucksBn O&BLI p231 MR30
NEAVERSON,Percy Charles 2Lt kia 15-4-18 6NStaffs p238 MR32
NEEDHAM,Arthur Charles TCapt kia 16-11-16 8ELancs p111 MR21
NEEDHAM,Benjamin Llewellyn TCapt kia 1-7-16 2Lincs p75 MR21
NEEDHAM,George Geoffrey.MC.MID Lt dow 22-8-15 LancF p93 CR Gallipoli27
NEEDHAM,Joseph Walter David 2Lt dow 12-11-17 48RFC p11 CR France40,kldacc
NEEDHAM,Pascall 2Lt kia 18-11-16 10RWar p65 MR21
NEEDHAM,Robert Lawrence Laurie Lt kia 21-1-16 5 att 1/4Hamp p228 MR38,Laurence
NEEDS,Charles Richard 2Lt kldacc 27-2-17 RFC p11 CR Gloucl1
NEELY,Clive William T2Lt ded 20-6-16 14RFus p69 CR Iraq5
NEELY,Hugh Bertram 2Lt kia 25-4-15 5Suff p78 CR Belgium4,23-4-15 1Bn
NEEMS,Percy Vincent Nigel T2Lt ded 9-10-15 10Glouc p107 CR Wilts86

NEGRETTI,Norman Charles Achille T2Lt kia 30-1-17 22Mddx p148 CR Belgium28 23Bn
NEGROPONTE,Jack T2Lt dow 29-10-16 8SLancs p125 CR France74
NEGUS,Arthur George 2Lt kia 1-7-16 16Lond p250 MR21
NEGUS,Ralph Albert 2Lt kia 18-4-16 11Glouc p107 CR France149
NEIGHBOUR,Leslie Gulliver 2Lt kld 16-8-15 5Lincs p220 CR Herts
NEIGHBOUR,Walter Bayard T2Lt dow 16-8-16 4RFus p69 MR21
NEIL,John.MC.Lt dow 28-3-18 7A&SH att MGC p187&243 CR Scot752
NEIL,Robert Donald 2Lt kia 26-10-16 1/5RScotF p222 CR France35
NEIL,Stanley Thomas Arthur TCapt kia 1-7-16 15WYorks p82 MR21
NEILAN,Gerald Aloysius TLt kld 24-4-16 10RDubF p177 CR Ireland12,kia
NEILL,David Taylor 2Lt kia 3-5-17 7 att 12RScots p211 MR20
NEILL,Geoffrey William.MC.Lt acckld 8-6-18 6Leinst att RAF p174 CR Egypt8
NEILL,James Dermot TLt kia 1-7-16 108MGC p184 MR21
NEILL,Norman Capt kia 6-11-14 13Huss p22 CR Belgium134
NEILL,Reginald Henry Lt kia 14-7-16 11RIrRif p170 MR21,1-7-16
NEILL,Robert Kirkpatrick T2Lt kia 16-8-17 8NumbF att Res p62 MR30
NEILL,Robert Larmour Lt kia 9-5-15 5 att 1RIrRif p170 MR32
NEILL,Rolfe Mayne 2Lt kia 3-6-17 70RFC p11 CR Belgium410
NEILL,Thom.W.R.T2Lt dow 3-7-16 9RScotF p95 CR France3
NEILL,William Proudfoot Lt ded 24-12-16 6 att 9RScots p211 CR France169,2Lt
NEILSON,Douglas Francis.DSO.MC.LtACapt kia 16-4-18 3Lincs p75 MR30,Donald 15-4-18
NEILSON,John Towers Lt kia 2-11-17 1/8ScotRif p225 CR Palestine8,3-11-17
NEILSON,Malcolm Arthur Lt kia 9-4-17 Worc AMaj 2ndCanInf p109
NEILSON,Richard Clark T2Lt kia 27-8-17 16WelshR p127 MR309
NEILSON,Robert Rowland TLtAMaj kia 13-4-18 3MGC p184 France98
NEILSON,Somerville Montgomerie 2Lt kia 14-4-17 3 att 1Dev p77 MR20
NEILSON,Thomas T2Lt kia 18-11-16 17HLI p163 CR France534
NEILSON,William Capt kia 21-11-17 7ScotRif att 10KRRC p224 MR17
NEILSON,William 2Lt kia 30-5-18 87RFA p33 MR30
NEILY,Frederick Ernest T2Lt kia 22-12-17 GL &16RFC p11 CR France95
NEISH,A.Miss ded 18-10-18 VAD BRCS p200 CR Berks86
NEISH,Alexander Millar.MC.2Lt dow 24-3-18 7A&SH p243 CR France177
NEISH,Herbert Theodore Louis 2Lt kia 31-8-15 3 att 1Nhampt p137 CR France423
NELDER,Gordon Charles Aldridge T2Lt kia 6-8-15 13 att 2Hamp p121 MR4
NELIGAN,Geoffrey Hook Lt kia 8-11-18 1YLI p143 CR France981
NELIGAN,John.MID TLt ded 13-6-17 RAMC 9HospTr p197 CR Egypt7,Capt
NELIGAN,Maurice Alfred Bourke Lt kia 13-10-15 12DLI p161 CR France82
NELIS,James Edward Thornhill TLt kia 15-8-15 5RInnisF p105 MR4
NELL,Basil Frank.MID Maj ded 22-12-18 RE 519FC p209 CR Egypt9
NELLES,Norman Cummings 2Lt kia 29-1-15 1Nhampt p137 MR22
NELSON,Abercromby Anson Craven Maj ded 20-5-16 2/10RScots p271 CR Scot235
NELSON,Alfred Ralph LtCol drd 30-12-15 IA 83Inf p280
NELSON,Craig Capt kia 25-9-15 IA 3Brahmans att 469Punjabis p280 MR28
NELSON,David.VC.LtAMaj dow 8-4-18 D59RFA p33 CR France201
NELSON,Ernest Bertram 2Lt dow 15-3-17 IARO att 1/8GurkhaRif p280 MR38
NELSON,Ethelbert Horatio 2Lt kia 18-11-16 4WSurr p212 CR France535
NELSON,Graham Lt kld 30-8-17 5ScotRif att RFC p11,19,104&224 CR Scot674
NELSON,Harold Griffith 2Lt kld 22-1-18 RFC p16
NELSON,Harry 2Lt kia 15-9-16 20Lond p251 MR21
NELSON,Herbert T2Lt kld 19-3-18 RFC p16 CR War50
NELSON,James Reid 2Lt kia 23-4-17 1/7BlkW p231 CR France604
NELSON,John(Jack) 2Lt kia 1-7-16 8YLI p143 CR France246
NELSON,John Bell.MC.Capt dow 22-9-18 IA 73Inf att 125Rif p280 CR Palestine9
NELSON,Joseph Lawne T2Lt kia 8-3-16 18Manch B'Coy p155 CR France625
NELSON,Richard Owen LtCapt drd 4-5-17 RASC p193 CR Italy14
NELSON,Thomas Arthur Capt kia 9-4-17 Lothian&BordHorseYeo att MGC p187&204 CR France1182
NELSON,Walter 2Lt kia 13-10-15 6SStaffs p229 MR19
NELSON,William Horace Vere TLt dow 8-7-16 10N&D p134 CR France833
NELSON,William Jackson T2Lt kia 27/30-9-18 Lpool att 9Bn p72 MR16
NELSON-COOKES,Henry Capt ded 23-10-18 RGA p41 CR Hamps7
NEPEAN,Evan Cecil Lt kia 4-10-18 3RScotF att 3RFus p95 CR France845
NEPEAN,Francis Molyneux Yorke Capt kia 16-9-15 7SomLI p80 CR France525
NESBIT,Henry George 2Lt kia 23-3-15 1EKent p58 CR France922,Lt
NESBITT,Arnold Stearns Capt kia 7-11-14 3Worc p109 MR29
NESBITT,Frank Wallace Rowland Lt dow PoW 19-4-18 7DLI p239 CR France1027,Rowlands

NESBITT,James Thompson Capt dow 25-3-18 A95RFA p207 CR France40
NESBITT,Terrence Beale 2Lt dow 24-4-16 3Dors p124 MR38
NESBITT,William Charles T2Lt kia 15-8-15 6RDubF p177 MR4,16-8-15
NESER,Frank Charles T2Lt ded 30-9-17 GL &RFC p11 CR Lincs181,François
NESHAM,Charles Frederick Maj ded 24-4-19 HAC p271 CR Surrey160
NESLING,Robert E.2Lt 4-3-18 KRRC &MGC CR Suff83
NESMITH,James Capt kia 12-7-15 5A&SH p243 MR4
NESS,Gordon Stuart Lt kia 10-11-14 3 att 1RScotF p95 MR29
NESS,James Charles Alexander Lt kia 27-6-15 Beds p86 MR22
NESS-WALKER,William Percy.MC.Maj dow 31-12-17 B251RFA p206 CR Belgium11
NESSLING,J.D.Lt ded 30-11-20 RASC CR Sussex23
NETHERCLEFT,Hugh Kirk T2Lt dow 25-12-17 2SWBord p100 CR France145
NETHERSOLE,A.R.LtCol drd 30-12-15 83WallajahbadLI MR41
NETHERSOLE,Timothy Lt kia 22-11-17 IA 87Punjabis att69 p280
NETTLESHIP,Mark T2Lt kia 1-9-18 1 att 1/4KOSB p102 CR France646
NETTLESHIP,Thomas T2Lt kia 22-3-18 att1/5NumbF p6 MR27
NETTLETON,Roy TLt dow 9-10-18 7EKent attTMB p58 CR France146
NEVE,Harold.MID 2Lt kia 27-5-18 1 att7ELancs p111 MR18
NEVE,Rupert Ernest TLt kld 26-1-18 RFC p16 CR Berks71
NEVE,Walter Gregory 2Lt kia 25-8-17 2EKent p58 CR Greece1
NEVEY,Frank 2Lt kld 12-10-18 6WRid p227 CR France718
NEVILE,Bernard Philip TCapt kia 11-2-16 att7Lincs p75 MR29
NEVILE,Guy Lister Capt kia 15-6-15 2Yorks p91 MR22
NEVILE,Hugh George Lt kia 21-8-15 2SWBord p100 MR4
NEVILL,Cuthbert St.John Lt kia 18-4-18 C251RFA p208 CR France98
NEVILL,Edward James Lt 22-12-18 2/4Rajputs MR66
NEVILL,Frederick Pearson 2Lt kia 22-2-17 IARO att92Punjabis p280
NEVILL,Hugh Lewis.DSO.Maj kia 7-8-15 RFA p33 CR Gallipoli26
NEVILL,John Henry Caxthorne 2Lt kia 24-12-14 GrenGds SR p50 CR France727
NEVILL,Robert.MC&Bar..2LtACapt kia 10-4-18 2SLancs p125 MR32
NEVILL,R.W.Capt 3-11-18 RB CR Sussex203
NEVILL,T.Lt 22-11-17 87 att69Punjabis CR Asia62
NEVILL,Wilfred Percy TCapt kia 1-7-16 1EYorks att8ESurr p84 CR France513
NEVILLE,Charles TCapt dow 13-7-16 1N&D C'Coy p134 CR France51
NEVILLE,Frank Septimus TCapt dow 24-11-17 6Nhampt p137 CR Belgium16
NEVILLE,George Henry.MC.MID TCapt kia 2-7-16 1SomLI p80 CR France1890
NEVILLE,Henry George T2Lt dow 10-5-17 GL &20RFC p11 CR Belgium11
NEVILLE,Lionel John Neville Capt dow 17-12-14 RE 5FC p47 CR Norf235
NEVILLE,Philip Percy.MID TLt ded 27-2-19 APayDept p255 CR Italy12
NEVILLE,Robert Patrick.MC.Capt&QM dow 27-10-17 7NumbF p214 CR Belgium25
NEVILLE,Stanley Capt ded 6-11-18 2/8Ess p232 CR Essex146
NEVILLE,Stuart White 2Lt kia 21-9-18 7Lond p247 CR France155
NEVILLE,Thomas Villiers Tuthill Thacker Capt kia 13-5-15 3DragGds p21 CR Belgium167
NEVILLE,William Sim 2Lt kia 25-9-16 RGA p41 CR France374
NEVIN,Alex McDonald Lt ded 24-6-17 RAMC att36GH p197
NEVINSON,Humphrey Kaye Bonney 2Lt dow 5-6-15 10Manch p237 MR4
NEVITT,George Rothwell Capt kia 28-11-17 2/8WYork p219 MR17
NEW,Athelstan William Capt ded 15-5-18 4 att 1Ess p232 CR France84
NEW,Brian Brooke 2Lt kia 16-8-17 7DCLI p114 MR30
NEW,Hedley Bruce Lt kia 31-10-17 4Ess attRFC p19&232 MR20
NEW,Paul Lt kia 19-5-17 3 att1BordR p117 MR20
NEWALL,Leslie 2Lt kia 2-9-15 1Lond p245 CR France347
NEWALL,Nigel Lt kia 12-10-17 1WelshGds p53 MR30,2Lt
NEWALL,William Osborne Lt kia 12-12-17 12WYork p82 MR20
NEWBERRY,William Frederick Capt kld 21-11-20 4RWSurr CR Mddx17
NEWBERY,Gilbert Leonard.VD.T2Lt dow 12-11-17 RASC p193 CR Belgium72
NEWBERY,Richard Fenton Theodore TLt kia 14-7-16 RAMC att6Nhampt p197 CR France630
NEWBIGGIN,John Prentice Lt ded 12-12-18 RGA p41 CR Hamps202
NEWBIGGING,Alexander Tweedie 2Lt kia 3-5-17 3 att 1RScotF p95 MR20
NEWBIGIN,George Nesbitt 2Lt ded 6-4-16 RE 2FC p210 CR Durham15
NEWBOLD,George Harold Lt ded 12-2-17 C241RFA p271 CR Shrop89
NEWBOLD,Philip T2Lt dow 13-7-16 7RWKent p141 MR21
NEWBOROUGH,William Charles.Lord.TLt ded 19-7-16 WelshGds p53 CR Wales714
NEWBOULD,Henry James Frank TCapt kia 2-8-15 6KOSB p102 CR France727
NEWBURY,Fred Peirson 2Lt kia 22-2-17 92Pujabis CR Iraq5
NEWBURY,George Maj kia 11-3-16 IA 130Baluchis p280

NEWBURY,P.F.R.LtCol 25-5-18 Lincs CR Lond4 Ex Cmdg11Bn
NEWBURY,Sydney Eldridge 2Lt dow 30-6-17 7N&D p233 CR France178
NEWCOMB,Charles Stuart Lt dow 5-4-18 6EKent p58 CR France62
NEWCOMB,Harry Reed Lt died 30-6-18 4EKent p271 CR Kent27
NEWCOMBE,Charles Neil TLt kia 27-12-15 7YLI p143 CR France276
NEWCOMBE,Clark Charles Upham 2Lt kia 17-8-17 5 att10Worc p109 CR Belgium106
NEWCOMBE,Cyril T2Lt kia 25/28-9-15 12RFus p69 MR19
NEWCOMBE,Edgar 2LtACapt kia 15-4-18 16Lond p249 MR32
NEWCOMBE,John Carr T2Lt kia 21-3-18 RE 12FC p47 MR20
NEWCOMBE,Richard TLt kia 1-7-16 1ELancs p111 MR21
NEWCOMBE,William TLt kia 3-7-16 1Drags att8SLancs p21 CR France215,Cap
NEWCOME,Basil Rice Maj mbk 8-3-16 IA 1/2GurkhaRif p280
NEWCOME,George Maj kia 11-3-16 130Baluchis CR EAfrica56
NEWDIGATE,Richard Francis Capt kia 4-9-16 3 att1BordR p117 MR29
NEWELL,Arthur Francis ACapt dow 4-4-18 8RB p179 MR27,Frank
NEWELL,Charles TCapt dow 24-3-18 RE 3PontoonPk p47 CR France225,kia
NEWELL,Charles Edward TLt dow 25-5-16 8RInnisF p105 CR France80
NEWELL,Francis Allister 2Lt kia 24-3-18 5Lond p246 CR France245
NEWELL,Matthew Banks T2Lt kia 4/5-4-16 14Ches p96 MR38
NEWELL,Thomas Stanley 2Lt dow 5-7-15 3 att2Ches p96 CR France285
NEWELL,William Joseph LtCol ded 20-12-14 7KSLI p145 CR Mddx48
NEWEY,Reginald Harold Capt 2-11-20 RE MR43
NEWINGTON,Francis Reginald Hayes 2Lt dow 3-12-17 1/20Lond p251 CR France398
NEWINGTON,John Lt kia 22-5-15 3ESurr attChes p113 CR Belgium120,3 att1ESurr
NEWINGTON,Percy Wilmott Lt kia 21-3-18 1EKent p58 MR20
NEWLAND,Arthur Kenyon T2Lt dow 21-11-17 12RE p47 CR France379,Lt
NEWLAND,Cecil Dunbar Capt ded 9-7-20 IA 1GurkhaRif p280 CR Derby39 Ex 3A&SH
NEWLAND,Edward Albert T2Lt kia 23-10-18 24RFus p69 CR France320
NEWLAND,George Michael 2Lt kia 28-3-18 9Lond p248 MR20
NEWLAND,Henry John T2Lt kia 18-2-17 8ESurr p113 CR France314
NEWLAND,Herbert Basil T2Lt dow 18-3-16 1Lincs p75 CR France95,4Bn
NEWLAND,Norman Chester 2Lt dow 31-5-15 PoW 1Mon p244 CR Belgium38
NEWLANDS,Stewart Lindsay Leighton 2Lt kia 27-5-17 7 att1ScotRif p224 MR2
NEWLANDS,Sydney Barron T2Lt kia 1-7-16 16WYork p82 CR France1890
NEWLANDS,Thomas Capt kia 22-3-18 5 att2RScots p211 CR France174
NEWLOVE,John Francis 2Lt kia 25-6-17 9HLI p240 CR France1489
NEWLYN,Walter Tessier T2Lt kia 11-7-16 19WelshR p127 MR21
NEWMAN,Albert T2Lt kia 20-9-17 Suff att 1/9Lpool p78 MR30
NEWMAN,Alfred TLt dow 1-7-16 12SWBord p100 CR France94
NEWMAN,Arthur Cecil T2LtACapt kia 20-9-17 23Mddx p148 MR30
NEWMAN,Cecil Harold T2Lt kia 12-5-17 6RWSurr p56 MR20
NEWMAN,Chafen Cecil.MC.TLtCapt kia 4-9-18 15Hamps attHampYeo p121 C Belgium111
NEWMAN,Cuthbert Alan T2Lt kia 19-4-18 2 att 15N&D p134 CR France232,1 18
NEWMAN,Cyril Arnell T2Lt dow 28-4-17 9NStaffs p157 CR France95
NEWMAN,Cyril Brown 2Lt kia 3-9-16 7WRid p228 CR France293
NEWMAN,Ernest John Lt ded 5-7-19 IARO att27LightCav MR43 &CR Pakistan
NEWMAN,Frederick Arthur TLt kia 31-7-17 GL 13RFus attX37TMB p191 CR Belgium100,Y37TMB
NEWMAN,John Sherwood T2Lt kia 7/11-8-15 6EYorks p84 MR4,9-8-15
NEWMAN,Leslie Cambridge Lt dow PoW 27-12-17 7RWelshF p223 CR France1027
NEWMAN,Neville T2Lt kia 27-6-16 10/11HLI p163 CR France423,28-6-16
NEWMAN,Reginald Bodman 2Lt kia 7-9-16 168MGC p184 MR21
NEWMAN,Reuben McCarthy Lt 23-11-18 IARO att3/2GurkhaRif MR67
NEWMAN,Robert 2Lt kld 27-5-16 RFC p3 CR Lond12
NEWMAN,Vernon William 2LtTCapt kia 25-9-15 4WYork att1NLancs p82 CR France219
NEWMAN HALL,Theodore Lt 15-8-16 1/4 O&BLI CR France145
NEWNHAM,Alfred Geoffrey 2Lt kia 11-11-14 att4RFus p69 MR29
NEWNHAM-DAVIS,Edward LtCol ded 27-2-16 99DeccanInf MR43
NEWNHAM-DAVIS,Nathaniel LtCol ded 28-5-17 RDC p253 CR Hamps120
NEWSAM,Arthur Fowler.MID TLt dow 30-3-18 SL attImpCamelCps p201 MR
NEWSAM,Harry Brightstone T2Lt kia 8-8-18 3TankCps LtBn p188 CR France585
NEWSOME,Clifford William 2Lt kia 14-7-18 20Mddx att26RFus p148 CR Belgium89

NEWSOME,Reginald Horace Arthur.MC.MIDx2 Lt dow 30-8-18 8Lond C'Coy p247 CR France119

NEWSOME,Theodore Edward T2Lt kia 25-9-15 2RWar p65 MR19

NEWSON,Norman Alexander Lt kia 18-2-15 3Ches p96 MR29

NEWSON,Walter Alexander Maj ded 15-4-17 2/3Lond p245 CR France 13

NEWSTEAD,Frederick Lisle Capt kia 7-8-16 3DLI p161 CR France232,6-8-16 2Bn

NEWSTEAD,George Pope LtCol dow 4-3-15 Suff &WAAF p78&201 CR WAfrica28

NEWSTEAD,Rupert Randolph T2Lt kia 7-7-16 17 att13Ches p96 MR21

NEWSUM,Clement Neill Capt kia 26-9-17 5Lincs p220 MR30

NEWTH,Howard Rutherford 2Lt kia 14-4-17 5 att1Ess p232 MR20

NEWTON,Alan Herbert 2Lt dow 7-4-16 2Mddx p148 CR France197

NEWTON,Arthur Douglas.MID Maj kia 27-10-17 265RFA p206 CR Palestine1

NEWTON,Arthur John T2Lt kia 30/31-7-18 2/4SomLI p80 CR France524

NEWTON,Arthur Victor Capt kld 20-10-15 3SomLI att5RFC p1&80,28-10-15 CR Belgium11

NEWTON,Cecil T2Lt kia 15-9-16 6CamH p168 CR France239

NEWTON,Cecil Herbert T2Lt kld 11-3-18 RFC p16

NEWTON,Charles Hercules Augustus Francis TLt kia 13-3-16 10KRRC p151 CR Belgium73 C.H.F.A.

NEWTON,Charles Ronald 2Lt kia 20-9-18 D104RFA p208 CR France1495

NEWTON,Charles Thomas Kemp 2Lt kia 3-6-16 1WYork p82 CR Belgium73

NEWTON,Denzil Onslow Cochrane.MVO.Capt dow 9-1-15 Mddx p265 CR Belgium80 &CR Belgium187,PPCLI

NEWTON,Edwin Brierley Lt kia 10-4-18 RE 182TC p210 MR27

NEWTON,Eric TCapt dow 5-8-17 RAMC att129Baluchis p197 CR EAfrica38,kia CR Tanzania1

NEWTON,Frederick 2Lt kia 15-8-17 4Ches p222 CR Belgium19,1/5Bn

NEWTON,Henry Joseph 2Lt ded 2-8-16 Ches &RFC p3&96 CR France837

NEWTON,Horace Gerard Townsend Capt ded 25-4-17 13Huss p22 CR Iraq6,drd

NEWTON,John 2Lt kia 23-4-17 HAC p206 MR20

NEWTON,Joseph Edmund Lt ded 6-9-19 Ches p263 CR Ireland24

NEWTON,Leslie Abbott T2Lt kia 14-7-16 7Leic p88 MR21

NEWTON,Leslie Cuthbert.OBE.Capt ded 13-1-20 RAOC CR Surrey1

NEWTON,Murray Edell Lt kia 18-6-17 17Lond attRFC p19&250 MR20

NEWTON,Percy TCapt kia 25-9-15 7KOSB p102 MR19

NEWTON,Samuel Thomas Lt dow 13-12-19 1/5SStaffs attMGC CR Hereford186

NEWTON,Thomas.MC.TLtACapt dow 5-8-18 1LancF p93 CR France134

NEWTON,Vivian Frederic 2Lt dow 15-9-16 1RWFus p98 CR France145

NEWTON,Walter Claude Lt kia 4-7-17 4LNLancs p234 CR France525

NEWTON,Walter Kilshaw 2Lt kia 31-3-18 10WYorks p82 MR20

NEWTON,Wilfrid.MID Capt dow 28-9-16 1RWKent p141 CR France40

NEWTON,William Henry T2Lt dow 11-8-18 YLI att2Bn p143 CR France1170

NEWTON,William Howard Capt ded 22-2-19 RAOC p198 CR France1027

NEWTON,William John Maj ded 16-2-15 6Ches p222 CR Ches193

NEWTON,William Leslie 2Lt kia 14-4-17 5DLI p239 CR France162

NEWTON,William Savage Capt kld 6-1-15 HAC Inf p206 CR Belgium17

NEWTON,William Trafford Lt kia 1-7-16 6NStaffs p238 CR France576

NEWTON-DEAKIN,Charles Humphrey Lt kia 11-4-17 3DragGds p21 CR France1182

NEWTON-KING,Alexander Reginald 2Lt dow 12-4-15 2RIrReg p89 MR32,Lt

NEWTON-KING,Pierce Francis Lt kia 25-9-15 2 O&BLI p130 MR19

NIBLETT,Arthur Hilton T2Lt dow 21-9-16 RE p47 CR France833

NICCOL,George McLaughlan Capt ded 30-10-18 RH&FA p33

NICE,Cecil George Lt ded 9-2-20 5RWSurr p271

NICHOL,Anthony Thomas 2Lt dow 16-4-17 1NumbF p62 CR France113

NICHOL,Edward Frank.MC.Capt 24-9-19 3LNLancs &RAF CR Kent27

NICHOL,John Capt kld 5-4-16 1RScotF &RFC p3&95 CR Kent27

NICHOL,Robert C.TLt kia 11-10-17 7SfthH p165 CR Belgium126

NICHOLAS,Francis Mark 2Lt dow 28-9-17 2Manch p155 CR Belgium24

NICHOLAS,J.W.F.Lt drd 2803015 N&D attNigR MR40

NICHOLAS,James Lt&QM ded 5-1-17 RAMC p271 CR Mddx53,6-1-17

NICHOLAS,John Allen Capt ded 28-1-19 266RFA p207 CR France1849

NICHOLAS,Oliffe Richmond Lt kia 17-4-16 3RWKent att1ConnRgrs p141 MR38,18-4-16

NICHOLAS,Thomas Glyn.MID T2Lt kia 18-2-17 18 att14WelshR p127 CR Belgium23,19-2-17

NICHOLAS,Walter Wynne 2Lt kia 29-3-16 7DCLI p114 CR Belgium23

NICHOLAS,William John Worth 2Lt drd 3-4-15 3N&D attNigR p134&201 CR Cornwall20,3-3-15

NICHOLL,Alan Hope Smith 2Lt kia 21-3-18 24RFA p33 MR20

NICHOLL,Alfred Ernest T2t kld 3-2-17 13RIrRif p170 CR France285

NICHOLL,Arnold 2Lt kia 18-7-16 7WRid p228 CR France702

NICHOLL,B.R.Maj 8-3-16 1A 1/2GurkhaRif MR38

NICHOLL,Francis John TLt kia 25-9-15 12HLI p163 MR19,NICOLL

NICHOLL,John William Harford 2Lt kia 29-10-14 2WelshR p127 MR29,29-11-14

NICHOLL-CARNE,Osmond Whitlock T2Lt kia 1-8-17 9WelshR p127 CR Belgium152

NICHOLLS,Alfred John T2Lt dow 12-4-18 Y&L att1/4Bn p159 CR Belgium11

NICHOLLS,Clifford Capt kia 31-7-17 5RWelshF attMGC p187

NICHOLLS,Douglas William Arthur.MC.TCapt kia 10-4-17 7Suff p78 MR20

NICHOLLS,Edward Cecil Henry Robert Lt kia 20-9-18 RWSurr &41RAF p56 CR Essex222

NICHOLLS,Edwin Jesse.MC.T2Lt kia 18-10-18 1Worc p109 CR France196

NICHOLLS,Ernest T2Lt kld 10-3-18 36RFC p16 CR Yorks546

NICHOLLS,Ernest James T2Lt kia 21-5-16 8LNLancs D'Coy p136 CR France68

NICHOLLS,George Arthur 2Lt kia 9-4-17 95RFA &15WarwickRHA p33 CR France418

NICHOLLS,Harold Mayne 2Lt ded 8-11-18 RFA p261CR Cornwall40,NICHOLAS

NICHOLLS,Harry George.DCM.2Lt dow 27-5-18 4 PoW att2RBerks p234 MR18

NICHOLLS,Henry King Capt kia 4-4-18 5 att8ESurr p226 MR27

NICHOLLS,Henry Lewin Faulconer Capt kia 25-2-15 1NumbF p62 CR Belgium166

NICHOLLS,Horace William.MC.2Lt kia 24-8-18 NumbF att1EYorks p62 CR France314

NICHOLLS,John Watson Lt kia 1-7-16 5 att2RFus p69 MR21

NICHOLLS,Leonard Harvey T2Lt kia 26-10-17 21Manch p155 MR30

NICHOLLS,Lionel 2Lt kia 26-8-16 8Lond p247 CR Belgium97

NICHOLLS,R.M.Lt dow 18-7-16 2WelshR p127 CR France833

NICHOLLS,Thomas Rocliffe Capt kia 26-9-17 Res 14Hamps p254 MR30

NICHOLLS,William Howard Capt ded 22-2-16 RAMC attMhowDiv p197 MR66

NICHOLLS,William Montague TLt kia 26-9-15 30/43RFA p33 MR19

NICHOLLS-JONES Thomas Cyril TLt kia 1-8-17 14RWFus p98 CR Belgium86,31-7-17

NICHOLS,Alselan Buchanan Lt kia 23-4-17 3Ess att1Bn 88TMB p132 MR20

NICHOLS,Arthur Robert.MC.Capt kia 23-10-18 4Lpool p72 CR France228

NICHOLS,Charles T2Lt ded 9-11-17 TankCps p188 CR Yorks543 Ex HAC

NICHOLS,Clifford Capt kia 31-7-17 5RWelshF att164MGC p223 MR29

NICHOLS,Cyril Robert Lt kia 23-9-18 3ESurr att5TMB p113 CR France755

NICHOLS,Eustace Alfred Morez T2Lt kia 20-7-16 12 att15N&D p134 CR France374

NICHOLS,Harold 2Lt dow 7-8-18 3 att8ESurr p113 CR France71

NICHOLS,Stanley Lawrence 2Lt kia 12-8-17 GL &19RFC p11 CR Belgium140

NICHOLS,Thomas Leslie T2Lt kia 8/9-5-17 15RWar p65 CR France777

NICHOLS,Walter Henry TMaj ded 15-10-15 8SomLI p80 CR Germany3

NICHOLSON,Alan Grifford Lt kia 10-8-15 4Ches p222 MR4,Gifford

NICHOLSON,Albert T2Lt kia 8-8-18 9RFus p69 CR France141

NICHOLSON,Alfred Francis James Steele 2LtACapt kia 16-8-17 5RIrRif p170

NICHOLSON,Arthur Davidson Maj dow 25-9-15 1CamH p168 CR Germany1,David dedacc

NICHOLSON,Arthur Harry T2Lt dow 9-4-17 19Manch p155 CR France104,10-4-17

NICHOLSON,Arthur Knight 2Lt kia 31-10-14 18Huss B'Sqn p23 CR Belgium118

NICHOLSON,Arthur Stuart Lt kia 4-9-14 1CamH p168 MR15

NICHOLSON,Basil Lee Lt kia 24-7-15 RFA p208 CR Belgium98

NICHOLSON,Bernard George Maurice TLt ded 29-10-18 13NumbF p62 CR Mddx53

NICHOLSON,Bruce Hills 2Lt kia 3-5-17 6 att4RFus p69 MR20

NICHOLSON,Edward Francis Dale Maj dow 12-10-17 1 att7SLancs p125 CR Belgium183

NICHOLSON,Edward Hills.DSO&Bar.MajALtCol kia 4-10-18 3RFus attESurr p69 CR France212

NICHOLSON,Eric N.Capt ded 20-6-17 12Lancers p22 CR Nhampt38

NICHOLSON,Geoffrey Arnold 2Lt kldacc 19-5-17 GL &RFC p11 CR Kent243

NICHOLSON,Geoffrey Alec Shield T2Lt dow 22-8-17 GL &6RFC p11 CR Belgium11

NICHOLSON,Geoffrey Douglas Lothian 2Lt kia 23-4-17 4Worc p109 MR20

NICHOLSON,George Crosfield Norris Capt kld 11-3-16 RFC p3 CR Berks33

NICHOLSON,Gordon Trevor 2Lt kia 28-9-15 IARO att119Inf p280 MR38

NICHOLSON,Harry Reid Lt ?? 24-4-17 1CanPnrs att20RFC MR20

NICHOLSON,Henry William.DCM.Lt kia 3-11-17 RGA 171SB p41 CR Belgium84

NICHOLSON,Harold Willison Capt kia 13-10-15 5Lincs p220 MR19

NICHOLSON,Hugh Hathorn 2Lt kia 24-5-15 2 att3Ches p96 MR29

NICHOLSON,Huntly Warwick Lt kia 17-11-14 1Ches p96 CR Belgium42

NICHOLSON,John Capt ded 16-11-15 RAOC p267

NICHOLSON,John Anthony Lt dow 5-10-18 48/36RFA p33 CR France512
NICHOLSON,John Edward Patrick 2Lt kia 16-9-18 3LNLancs att13KRRC p136 CR France245
NICHOLSON,John Maurice Leonard T2Lt kia 11-7-16 8SfthH p165 CR France423
NICHOLSON,Lancelot T2Lt kia 20-9-17 9Yorks p91 CR Belgium112
NICHOLSON,L.C.DSO.Lt dow 2-11-14 3 att1RBerks p139
NICHOLSON,Leonard Sampson 2Lt kia 2-5-15 12Lond p248 MR29
NICHOLSON,Maurice 2Lt kia 18-8-17 GL ACycCps &11RFC p11&181 MR20
NICHOLSON,Paul Cheesum 2Lt kia 26-4-18 9YLI p143 MR30
NICHOLSON,Randolph Renwick.MC.2Lt kia 18-9-18 4EYorks att2N&D p219 CR France672
NICHOLSON,Richard Le Brun.MC&Bar.TCaptAMaj kia 31-8-18 11 att1/6Ches p96 CR France139
NICHOLSON,T.HonCapt ded 6-11-15 RAOC p198
NICHOLSON,Thomas Edward TLt kia 1-7-16 25NumbF p62 MR21
NICHOLSON,Walter Alan T2Lt dow 27-9-15 2GordH p167 CR France1059
NICHOLSON,Walter Adams see NICOLSON.W.A.
NICHOLSON,William Dukinfield Lt dow 23-2-15 2CamH p168 CR Belgium28
NICHOLSON,William Herbert Hamilton Lt dow 13-4-18 RE p210
NICHOLSON,Winter T2Lt dow 16-3-17 RE 224FC p47 CR France624
NICKALLS,Edward Gilbert T2Lt kia 18-8-16 4Lpool p72 CR France432
NICKALLS,Hugh Quidhampton Lt kia 29-7-17 1DevYeo attRFC p19&202 MR20
NICKALLS,Norman Tom ColTBrigGen kia 26-9-15 BdeStaff 17Lancers p1 MR19
NICKEL,George Gaston T2Lt kia 31-7-17 20Lpool p72 MR29
NICKLIN,Harry John.MC.2Lt kia 16-4-18 2Worc p109 MR32
NICKLIN,William T2Lt dow 24-8-16 RE SpBde C'Coy p47 CR France453
NICKSON,Edmund Reginald T2Lt kia 29-4-18 64LabCps p189 CR Belgium101
NICKSON,Henry Maj kia 30-10-15 4LNLancs p233 CR France251,Harry
NICKSON,John Reginald T2Lt kldacc 2-1-18 35RFC p16 CR Oxford74
NICKSON,William Capt kia 30-7-16 19Lpool p72 MR21 &CR France1890
NICOL,Alexander 2Lt kia 12-7-15 5A&SH p243 MR4
NICOL,Andrew.MID TLt kia 22-5-16 6KOSB p102 CR Belgium136
NICOL,Anthony Thomas 2Lt dow 16-4-17 1NumbF p62
NICOL,C.Sister 6-2-17 QAIMNS CR Surrey160
NICOL,Charles Ashmore Capt kia 8-5-17 10BlkW p129 MR37,C.R.
NICOL,Charles Mill.MID Capt dow 23-10-16 RAMC DADMS 3Div p197 CR France203
NICOL,David TLtACapt dow 26-11-17 14A&SH p173 CR France256,kia 25-11-17
NICOL,Donald Ninian TLt ded 29-12-15 3ScotGds p52 CR Scot4,27-12-15
NICOL,George Moffat TLt kia 25-9-15 9ScotRif p104 CR France114
NICOL,Robert Lt kia 17-4-18 5A&SH attMGC p187&243 MR30
NICOL,Wilfred Edward.DSO.Maj dow 1-10-15 1GrenGds p50 CR France98
NICOLAI,Ronald Claud Lt kia 25-4-15 RWar p65 MR29
NICOLAY,Herbert Cleland Maj mbk 10-3-15 IA 2/2GurkhaRif p281 MR28
NICOLL,Eric Stanhope.MC.Capt kia 19-1-18 2/4RWKent p212&271 CR Palestine3,18-1-18
NICOLL,F.J. see NICHOLL.F.J.
NICOLL,James John McGregor 2Lt ded 9-7-18 RFA p261 CR Scot238,8-7-18
NICOLL,Leonard Orrick 2Lt kia 26-9-17 5BlkW D'Coy p231 MR30,Lt
NICOLLS,John Oliver Lt kia 25-9-15 IA 58Rif p281 MR28
NICOLLS,Richard Jeffreys TCapt kia 1-10-16 9N&D A'Coy p134 CR France151
NICOLSON,Alexander.MSM.T2Lt kia 13-5-18 2N&D p134 CR Belgium3,NICHOLSON Alick
NICOLSON,Donald McDonald 2Lt kia 19-4-17 GL att5KOSB p191 MR34 att3Bn
NICOLSON,Farquhar Murchison 2Lt kia 19-4-17 5HLI p240 CR France1701
NICOLSON,Walter Adams MajTLtCol kia 4-9-17 104RFA p33 CR Belgium183,NICHOLSON
NICOLSON,William T2Lt kia 13-8-16 6RScotF p95 CR France239
NICOLSON,William Alexander Capt ded 20-7-16 10ELancs p111 CR Iraq5
NICOLSON,William Hurst Maj kia 21-1-16 IA 37Dogras p281 CR Iraq5
NIELD,Wilfred Herbert Everard TLt kia 1-7-16 11RFus p69 CR France397
NIELSON,William Christian T2Lt kia 2-9-18 EYork att5YLI p84 CR France1484
NIGHTINGALE,Eric 2Lt kia 25-6-18 GL N&D &RAF p191 CR France526,Lt
NIGHTINGALE,Frank Leslie T2Lt kia 19-12-15 7Lt dow 27-4-17 2SWBord p100 MR20,23-4-17
NILSSON,Geoffrey Burbank T2Lt kia 18-9-18 Yorks att7EYorks p91 CR France415
NIMMO,Adam Prentice.MC.Capt dow 17-11-17 1/4KOSB p223 CR Egypt2
NIMMO,James Ronald 2Lt ded 1-5-17 7ScotRif p271 CR Scot675,kldacc
NIMMO,Stuart Henry TLt kia 19-9-18 8RScotF p95 MR37
NIMMO,William Leslie 2Lt kia 26-7-18 1NumbF p62&539 MR19 &CR France1896
NINIS,Francis Aubrey.MC.LtACapt dow 19-9-18 12Ches p96&257 CR Greece1

NINIS,George Elvey Howard 2Lt ded 29-11-18 RASC p267 CR Lond2
NISBET,Cecil Andrew TCapt dow 21-6-16 12Suff p78 CR France12
NISBET,David Joseph Lt dow 15-1-20 5RWKent p271
NISBET,Douglas Guille Lt kia 10-6-16 3 att5SWBord p100 CR France251
NISBET,Edwin TLt kia 6-9-18 59MGC Divl Inf p184 CR France309
NISBET,Frank Scobell.MID Capt kia 26-8-14 2Manch p155 MR15
NISBET,Frederic William 2Lt kia 14-2-17 YorkDrag att46RFC p19&206 CR Belgium5
NISBET,John 2Lt kia 15-4-15 3RScots p54 CR Belgium17
NISBET,John Andrew T2LtACapt kia 28-9-18 2RScotF p95 CR Belgium112
NISBET,Robert Douglas Morton Lt kia 9-5-15 2Lincs p75 MR32
NISBETT,Frank 2Lt kia 30-11-17 1/5SLancs p230 MR17
NIVEN,Alan Scott T2Lt kia 4-11-17 RLancs att9YLI p59 MR30
NIVEN,Allan Graham TMaj kia 1-7-16 21NumbF p62 MR21
NIVEN,Douglas Scott.DSO.Maj 12-2-19 25Cav MR43
NIVEN,James T2Lt kia 3-5-17 RE 253TC p47 CR France258
NIVEN,John 2Lt kia 13-5-17 RFA p208 CR France266
NIVEN,Kenneth James T2Lt kia 22-8-17 11A&SH p173 MR30
NIVEN,William Adam Mackie 2Lt kia 28-10-18 29RFC p3 CR France158
NIVEN,William Edward Graham Lt kia 21-8-15 BerkYeo p202 CR Gallipoli5
NIVISON,Robert Butler T2Lt kia 15/17-9-16 5 att21KRRC p151 MR21,15-9-16
NIXON,Arthur William Lennox T2Lt kia 1-6-17 GL &16RFC p11 CR France58,L
NIXON,Basil Northcote Capt ded 3-3-19 23Lond p271
NIXON,C.T.Lt 18-10-17 RFC CR Herts115
NIXON,Cyril John Lt ded 8-10-17 5Beds p219
NIXON,David 2Lt dow 29-7-18 5A&SH p243 CR France1225
NIXON,Gerald Ferrers Lt kia 24-10-14 RFA 129Bty p33 CR France706
NIXON,Harold Percival T2Lt kia 26-10-18 6Wilts p153 CR Belgium438,Perceval
NIXON,James Duncan 2Lt kia 11-4-18 4SfthH p241 MR19
NIXON,Lionel Philip T2Lt kia 15-9-16 23Mddx p148 MR21
NIXON,Montagu Alfred Capt ded 26-9-17 5RB p179 CR Hamps202
NIXON,Noel Charles Frederick Capt kia 24-3-18 8 att4Beds p86 MR20
NIXON,Oswald 2Lt kia 17-9-16 Ess &RFC p3&132,ded MR20
NIXON,Philip Henry 2Lt dow 18-12-16 2Glouc p107 CR Greece7
NIXON,Thomas William T2Lt dow 26-10-18 7Y&L p159 CR France214,1/4Bn
NIXON,Walter Henry 2Lt kia 19-9-15 RLancs &RFC p2&59 CR France834,19-7-15
NIXON,William Capt kia 1-7-16 20NumbF p62 MR21
NIXON,William Eric Capt kia 7-5-17 KOSB &40RFC p11&102 CR France1198
NIXON,William Gerald Lt kia 1-7-16 3Hamps att11TMB p121 MR21
NIXON,William Henry 2Lt kld 24-8-17 RGA 298SB p41 CR Belgium4
NIXON-ECKERSALL,Frederick Eckersall Maj kia 10-11-17 RGA 157SB p41 CR Belgium84,Frederic
NOAD,H.C.Maj 28-7-21 RASC CR Iraq1
NOAD,P.H.TCapt ded 3-7-18 RE p47&271 CR Wilts153
NOAKE,Arthur Stratford Maj drd 9-10-18 IARO S&TCps p281 MR40
NOAKES,Frederic Lt kia 25-11-17 1/1StaffsYeo p205 CR Palestine9
NOAKES,Harold Thomas T2Lt kia 23-7-17 GL &32RFC p11 CR Belgium11
NOAKES,James Edward Lt 23-10-20 4/7Mddx CR Surrey8
NOAKES,Stuart Bertram Capt drd 30-12-17 RASC MT p193 MR41
NOAKS,Geoffrey Vaughan 2Lt dow 18-8-16 1Nhampt D'Coy p137 CR France74
NOBLE,Archibald Francis.MID TCapt&Ajt kia 21-5-16 10Ches p96 CR France68
NOBLE,Bertram TLt ded 26-8-16 22 at16LancF att1ArmySch p93 CR France180,23-8-16
NOBLE,Harold Taylor T2Lt kia 28-9-17 GL &20RFC p11 CR France285
NOBLE,Henry Austin 2Lt dow 8-10-18 4Ess p232 CR France379
NOBLE,James Dickson Capt 12-10-14 RAMC 2FA CR Scot259
NOBLE,John Lt kia 28-9-18 5CamH att9MGC p184 CR Belgium58
NOBLE,John Stanley Lt dow 30-3-18 5RBerks p139 CR France62
NOBLE,John Wilson T2Lt kia 25-9-16 10NumbF p62 MR21
NOBLE,Marc Andrew Patrick 2Lt dow 1-7-17 C122RFA p33 CR Belgium1,C121Bde
NOBLE,Norris Heatley 2Lt dow 15-8-16 6 att1KRRC p151 CR France51
NOBLE,Thomas Gilson TMaj kia 1-7-16 20NumbF p62 MR21,Gibson
NOBLE,W.B.Lt 11-12-18 RScots CR Scot639
NOBLE,Walter Frederick T2Lt kia 3-7-16 12 att9Ess p132 CR France393
NOBLE,William Black Lt kia 26-4-15 6NumbF p214 MR29
NOBLE,William McDonald T2Lt dow 31-12-16 EKent attRE DivSig p58 CR France177
NOBLE,William Smyth Jackson T2Lt kia 21-3-18 15RScots p54 MR20
NOBLE-SMITH,John 2Lt kia 9-4-18 165RFA p33 CR France1014

NOCK,Frederick John 2Lt dow 3-6-17 9YLI p143 CR France1184
NOCK,George Goodwin Rudgard T2Lt kia 5-9-18 7Suff att1/1Camb p78 CR France511,6-9-18
NODDER,Frederick May 2Lt kia 14-8-16 48RFA p33 CR France397
NODDER,Ruth Mary Nurse 24-5-18 TFNS MR43 &CR Pakistan50A
NODEN,Frank Hull 2Lt ded 3-12-18 RGA 319SB p41 CR Ches158
NOEL,Alfred 2Lt kia 3-5-17 2Lond p245 CR France537
NOEL,Hon Edward Col ded 9-11-17 SL Staff p268
NOEL,Francis Methuen 2Lt kia 26-10-17 4 att9Dev p77 MR30,Capt
NOEL,Hon,Robert Edmund Thomas More Capt ded 2-2-18 6RFus att1NigR p69&201 CR EAfrica11 &CR Tanzania1
NOEL,Tom Cecil.MC.Lt kld 22-8-18 3KOSB &RAF p102
NOKES,William Herbert 2Lt kia 26-10-17 6 att1SStaffs p229 MR30
NOLAN,Bernard T2Lt kia 21-3-18 2Y&L p159 MR20
NOLAN,Bevan John 2Lt kia 3-9-16 4 att2RIrReg C'Coy p89 CR France402
NOLAN,Howard Stanley T2Lt kld 27-7-17 GL &RFC p11 CR Wilts4
NOLAN,James.MC.DCM.2Lt dow 29-9-18 1RDubF p177 CR Belgium113
NOLAN,Leonard McNeill Lt ded 13-6-20 IA 58Rif p281 MR67
NOLAN,Maurice Edward T2Lt dow 25-9-15 RE p47 CR France554
NOLAN,Maurice Herbert William 2Lt dow 9-12-16 1RIrReg att10RIrRif p89 CR France285
NOLAN,Philip John Noel.DFC.Lt ded 7-4-18 RFA &RAF p33 CR France988
NOLAN,Raymond Philip Drummond Lt kia 3-11-14 3 att1BlkW p129 MR29
NOLAN,Rupert Henry Capt kia 21-10-14 RAMC p197 CR Belgium115
NOLAN,William Henry TLt kia 14-7-16 9Leic p88 MR21
NOLAN-MARTIN,Alfred John Capt dow 22-2-17 3RDubF attMGC Inf p177&184 CR Mddx16
NOON,Alfred Lewis Lt dow 2-4-18 2Dev p77 CR France185
NOON,Gilbert 2Lt kia 29-11-17 6N&D attRFC p19&233 MR20
NOONAN,Joseph Daniel T2Lt kia 24-8-16 6 att2RMunstF p175 MR21
NOOTT,Mervyn 2Lt kia 20-10-14 1EKent p58 MR32
NOPS,Thomas Waldegrave T2Lt kia 21-10-16 GL &RFC 9KiteBallSect p3&191 CR France297
NORBURY,Albert Maj 24-8-21 IndOrdDept CR India97A
NORBURY,Francis Campbell Capt kia 10-1-15 6 att1KRRC p151 CR France727
NORBURY,Philip Giesler TLt kia 1-7-16 7EKent p58 CR France397
NORBURY,Robert Fiddes TLt dow 4-10-17 1 att2SfthH p165 CR Belgium16
NORCOTT,Gerald Alfred Maj died 20-9-18 LNLancs p264
NORCROSS,Arthur Capt kia 9-10-17 4ELancs p226 MR30
NORCROSS,Frank 2Lt kia 30-7-16 23Manch p155 MR21
NORFOLK,Harold Maj kia 23-4-16 WorcYeo attTanks p206 MR34,23-2-16
NORIE,Evelyn William Meadows.ADC.Col ded 29-8-15 Staff AMS WarOff p1 CR Surrey135
NORIE-MILLER,Claud T2Lt drd 4-5-17 RASC p193 CR Italy14
NORKETT,Edward Lt ded 25-3-19 RASC p271 CR Berks29
NORMAN,Albert Edmund.MID Capt dow 11-5-15 3ESurr p113 CR France345
NORMAN,Arthur John T2Lt dow 29-9-16 8Leic p88 CR France145
NORMAN,Basil Chamberlin Qu'Appella Lt dow 30-9-18 4NStaffs p157 CR Belgium10,Qu'Appelle
NORMAN,Charles Capt dedacc 12-2-17 NthIrHorse att5RRofCav p23 CR France74
NORMAN,Edward John T2Lt kia 30-3-18 156RE p47 MR27
NORMAN,Garnet T2Lt dow 2-4-18 26RFus p69 MR27 11Bn
NORMAN,Gilford William T2Lt kia 25-9-16 19N&D att8Leic p134 MR21
NORMAN,Harold Henry Maj kia 10-11-14 Nhampt p137 MR29
NORMAN,Isaac Thomas Victor 2Lt dow 28-3-18 RE 121FC p47 CR France185
NORMAN,James Bertram.MC.T2Lt kia 10-4-18 40MGC Inf p184 MR32
NORMAN,Leonard Frank 2Lt kia 21-9-17 154MGC Inf p184 MR30
NORMAN,Lionel.MC.TCapt kia 15-9-16 1ScotGds p52 MR21
NORMAN,Percy William 2Lt ded 21-5-15 51RGA p41 MR66
NORMAN,Stanley 2Lt dow 16-9-16 7Mddx p235 CR France177,15/16-9-16
NORMAN,Stuart Sheridan Lt kia 23-12-14 Manch p155 MR22
NORMANSELL,John TCapt dow 10-3-17 13Y&L p159 CR France742,kia
NORQUOY,James TCapt kia 3-4-17 Mddx att13Bn p148 CR France570,2-4-17
NORRIS,Alfred James 2Lt kia 28-3-18 7KSLI p145 MR20
NORRIS,Arthur James Lt ded 10-1-17 HAC Inf p206 CR Surrey45
NORRIS,Bertie T2Lt kia 3-5-17 2LancF p93 MR20
NORRIS,Colin Chad Armstrong T2Lt kld 26-12-17 GL &RFC p11 CR Norf256
NORRIS,Cyril Norman T2Lt dow 19-8-17 26RFus p69 CR France855
NORRIS,Edward Fraser LtTCapt kld 15-3-18 RFC p16 CR Oxford74
NORRIS,Ernest Arthur 2Lt kia 22-3-18 21 att17KRRC p151 MR27
NORRIS,Frank Ernest Edwin TLt dow 2-10-18 10RWKent p141 CR Belgium111
NORRIS,Frederick T2LtACapt kia 7-6-17 23Mddx p148 MR29
NORRIS,Frederick George 2Lt kia 4-4-18 4Ches att7RWKent p222 MR27
NORRIS,Gilbert Hume TCapt dow 9-3-18 13KRRC p151 CR Belgium11
NORRIS,Harold Aubrey Blurton T2Lt dow 24-7-17 GL &57RFC 9Wing p11 CR France134
NORRIS,Kenneth Arthur Annesley Lt ded 16-6-16 RWKent p141 CR Iraq6
NORRIS,Leslie Archibald TLt kia 25-3-17 RE att70RFC p11&47 CR France245
NORRIS,Percy Walter T2Lt kia 29-7-18 34MGC Inf p184 CR France524
NORRIS,R.S.Cdr 16-7-15 IOD CR France354
NORRIS,Walter 2Lt kia 7-8-15 8Manch p237 MR4
NORRIS,William Eric 2Lt kldacc 14-1-18 MontgomYeo att17WelchR p204 CR France616
NORRIS,William Forbes Lt kia 25-8-15 5Norf attACycCps p216 MR4
NORRIS,William James George Capt kia 25-9-15 12WYorks p82 MR19
NORRIS,Sydney Frank 2Lt ded 28-4-19 RFA p33 CR Italy65
NORRIS,William John.MID Lt dow 14-10-18 1/10Manch p237 CR France13
NORRISH,Thomas Theodore 2Lt kia 13-9-16 1Dev p77 MR21
NORRISH,William 2LtACapt kia 27-8-17 10Mddx p236
NORSWORTHY,Harold Milford T2Lt kia 18-3-17 1EKent p58 CR France149
NORTH,Arthur Juvell.MC.Capt kia 27-9-18 4NumbF p213 CR France439,Jewell
NORTH,Charles Napier Maj kia 1-11-14 RE 5FC p47 MR29
NORTH,Francis Wilson 2Lt kia 9-9-16 3RIrReg att6ConnRgrs p89 CR France402,Frank
NORTH,Harry Lonsdale Lt kia 27-9-18 3 att2RIrReg p89 CR France1496
NORTH,Hugh Frederic Capt kld 21-1-16 1/4Hamps p228 MR38
NORTH,Julian Capt ded 14-10-16 IA IndTelegraphDept p281 CR EAfrica19
NORTH,Kenneth Croft Lt kia 31-10-14 4Huss p21 CR Belgium118
NORTH,Neville Marriott.MC.Capt kia 27-5-18 5NumbF p213 MR18
NORTH,Robert Dudley TLt kia 3-5-16 2 att13N&D p134 CR Belgium92,2 att14Bn
NORTH,Samuel Frost T2Lt kia 2-11-18 15LancF p93 CR France93
NORTH,Stanley 2Lt kia 16-8-17 19Lond p250 MR29
NORTHAM,John McClure 2Lt kia 15-9-17 15Lond p249 MR29
NORTHAM,Reginald Meek Lt ded 19-2-21 IARO attS&TCps p281 MR43,2Lt
NORTH-COX,Wilfrid Herbert Marshall 2Lt ded 2-3-16 3N&D p134 CR Numb2
NORTHCOTE,Douglas Horace Gilbert.MID Lt kia 12-3-15 3EKent attWilts p58 MR29
NORTHCOTE,Edward Stafford Capt kia 3-9-16 11RSuss p119 MR21
NORTHCOTE,George Barons Capt dow 4-12-15 2Norf p74 CR Iraq5
NORTHCOTE,James Fitz Gaulfield 2lt kia 9-10-17 5WYorks p218 MR30
NORTHCOTE,Hugh Farrar 2Lt kia 28-4-16 IARO att41Dogras p281 MR38
NORTHCOTT,Henry John T2Lt dow 18-10-18 Dors att1/5Glouc p124 CR Devon72
NORTHCROFT,Percival William Cordery Lt kia 31-7-17 6 at3RB p179 MR29
NORTHEY,Alfred.MID Lt kia 12-10-14 3Worc p109 CR France260
NORTHEY,George Evelyn Anson Lt kia 26-8-14 2Ess p132 MR15
NORTHEY,Mervyn Ackland Lt kia 28-10-18 3 att2RWKent p141 CR Iraq8
NORTHEY,William.DSO.Maj dow 22-10-14 2DLI p161 CR France102
NORTHLAND,Thomas Uchter Caulfield Capt kia 2-2-15 2ColdGds p51 CR France720,Ucher Caulfeild 1-2-15
NORTHOVER,Neville Evelyn T2Lt kia 4-9-18 Wilts att15Hants p153 CR Belgium111
NORTHROP,Harold 2Lt kia 9-10-17 8WYorks p219 MR30
NORTON,A.G.2Lt kia 9-5-15 2ELancs p111 CR France566
NORTON,Clement Edgar T2Lt ded 10-10-18 RASC p193 CR Palestine9
NORTON,Eric 2Lt kia 18-8-16 5Suff p217 CR France432,1/4Bn
NORTON,Frank Frederick T2Lt kia 20-9-17 21KRRC p151 MR30
NORTON,Frederick John Lt kia 23-3-18 D187RFA p33 CR France518
NORTON,Frederick William TCapt ded 14-10-16 RE 10LabBn p47 CR France52
NORTON,Hugh TLt kia 24-3-17 GL &8RFC p11 CR France120
NORTON,John Arnold TCapt dow 19-11-15 SL p201&268,ded CR Essex69
NORTON,Leopold Grantley Lt dow 20-10-14 2DLI p161 MR32
NORTON,Richard Conyers Lt kia 23-3-18 E'RHA p33 CR France360
NORTON,Richard Legge 2Lt kia 18-9-18 9Norf p74 CR France1701
NORTON,Tom Edgar Grantley 2Lt kia 20-4-15 4 att1ESurr p113 CR Belgium152
NORTON,William Lt kia 23-3-18 3 att7Leic p88 MR27
NORTON-FAGGE,Frederick Walter Langford Grantly.MIDx2 Lt ded 18-11-16 IARO SpServOff attGHQ p281 CR Iraq6,Frederic Grantley
NORTON-HARPER,Alfred George Montague Capt 16-10-17 SL att4NigR CR EAfrica11 &CR Tanzania1
NORVILL,Frederick Henry 2Lt dow 24-7-17 RGA 81SB p41 CR Belgium16
NORWAY,Frederick Hamilton 2Lt dow 4-7-15 2DCLI p114 CR France64

231

NORWELL,Herbert 2Lt kia 12-4-18 5 att2RFus p69 MR30

NORWOOD,John.VC.Capt kia 8-9-14 5DragGds RoO p21&204,2CountofLondYeo CR France1451

NORWOOD,John Norton 2Lt dow 22-7-16 11RInnisF p105 CR France169,4 att2Bn

NORWOOD,Reginald Harold 2Lt kia 29-9-18 TankCps p188 CR France375

NORWOOD,Robert Cecil Lt kia 18-7-16 BucksBn O&BLI p231 CR France832

NORWOOD,William James 2Lt kia 27-3-18 Mddx att2Nhampt p148 MR27

NOSS,Arthur Rex Hurden.MC.T2Lt dow 15-9-17 GL &48RFC p11 CR France1361

NOSWORTHY,Claude William Michelin Lt dow 6-12-17 RFA att10RFC p11 CR Belgium11

NOSWORTHY,Philip Chorlton 2Lt kia 11-5-15 3 att2Ches p96 MR29

NOTCUTT,Leonard Ernest Lt kia 3-5-17 7RFus att27MGC p69&184 MR20

NOTLEY,Albert Carr 2Lt kia 30-5-18 5RLancs p213 CR France106,31-5-18

NOTMAN,William Graham T2Lt kia 13-8-16 3 att12HLI p163 MR21

NOTT,Charles Lt kia 8-10-15 9Lpool p216 MR19

NOTT,Edward Ross T2Lt dow 13-7-16 9YLI p143 CR France51

NOTT,George Vincent TLt kia 18-8-16 7Nhampt p137 MR21

NOTT,Henry Paton Lt kia 27-4-16 6Glouc p225 CR France1327

NOTT,John Harley Lt ded 25-8-15 RASC 53Welsh DivTr p253 CR Egypt3

NOTT,Louis Cameron.MC.Capt&Adjt kia 18-4-17 1/6Glouc p225 CR France363

NOTT,Louis Phillip Maj ded 4-7-16 RE p271

NOTT,Saumarez Ewen T2Lt kia 9-9-17 13RSuss p119 MR30

NOTT,Thomas Walker.DSO.LtCol kia 18-4-17 1/6Glouc p225 CR France363

NOTT-BOWER,Charles Cecil 2Lt kia 16-5-15 IARO att2/3GurkhaRif p281 CR France631

NOTTIDGE,Edward Capt kia 8-11-16 D79RFA p33 CR France430

NOTTON,Cyril George 2Lt kia 3-12-17 NorfYeo att12Norf p204 CR Palestine3

NOTTON,Frank Gwyer 2Lt kia 27-8-17 5WelshR p230 MR30

NOVERRE,Arthur Kerr Maj ded 18-4-18 RASC 6DivA/C p193 CR Egypt1

NOWELL,Ernest Harold 2Lt kia 1-9-15 1Suff p78 CR Belgium89,Harry

NOWELL,Francis Percival T2Lt dow 2-7-16 18WYorks p82 CR France203

NOWELL,Joseph Kent 2Lt kia 16-8-17 8 att1Lond p247 MR29

NOWELL,Roger Emmett 2Lt kia 22-9-17 RFC p11 MR20

NOWELL,Wilfred James 2Lt kia 9-4-17 RFA 460HB p33 CR France182

NOYES,Claude Robert Barton T2Lt kia 1-7-16 15LancF p93 CR France293

NOYES,Harry Francis Golding TCapt ded 5-9-16 RAMC att17StHosp p197 MR65

NOYES,Ralph Elliot Maj kia 27-9-15 10Yorks p91 MR19

NOYES,Talbot Ronald Arthur Herbert TCapt kia 11-7-16 19NumbF p62 CR France430

NUDDS,Ronald Charles T2Lt dow 30-11-17 RE 219FC p47 CR Belgium3

NUGENT,Charles Capt ded 19-11-18 2RBerks p139 CR France1142

NUGENT,George Colborne.MVO.ColTBrigGen kia 3-5-15 Staff IrGds Cmdg141InfBde p1 CR France80,31-5-15

NUGENT,Gerald William Capt kia 10-8-15 GL Staff HQ29InfBde p191 MR4

NUGENT,Hugh Neville ACapt died 1-7-19 RASC

NUGENT,John Aloysius Joseph 2Lt kia 27-8-17 5Leinst p174 CR Belgium124,2Bn

NUGENT,Raymond Henry 2Lt kia 25-11-17 70RFA p33 CR France415,23-11-17

NUGENT,Richard Francis Robert 2Lt kia 18-12-14 ScotGds p52 MR32

NUGENT,William Andrew.Hon.Capt dow 29-5-15 15Huss p22 CR Lond9

NUNN,Edward Chamberland Lt ded 24-7-17 IARO att2/119Inf p281 CR Iraq8

NUNN,Frederick Arthur William Lt kia 2-4-18 1Lond &65RAF p271 MR20

NUNN,John Henry Maj dow 1-4-17 A149RFA p33 CR France120

NUNN,Mervyn Henry LtCol kia 10-8-15 9Worc Maj RoO p109 CR Gallipoli13

NUNNELEY,George Paterson.MC.CaptAMaj kia 27-3-18 4Beds p86 CR France393

NUNNELEY,Wilford Herbert.MC.2Lt kia 24-4-18 2Ess p132 MR19,Wilfred 23/24-4-18

NUNNELEY,Charles Francis Lt kia 25/27-10-14 3NumbF attYLI p62 MR22

NUNNERLEY,W.P.Lt 24-3-21 SL CR Scot142

NUNNERLEY,Willson Kenwick T2Lt kia 5-12-17 GL &13RFC p11 CR France113

NURSE,Reginald John Cecil 2Lt kia 25-3-18 4 att2/5Glouc p225 MR27,22-3-18

NUTCOMBE,Thomas Arthur 2Lt kldacc 2-8-18 ELancs &101RAF p111 CR France29

NUTHALL,John Constantine T2Lt kia 3-7-17 14MGC p184 CR Belgium24,13-7-17

NUTKINS,Vernon William Lt kld 19-2-18 RScotF att21RAF p16&95 CR Egypt8

NUTTALL,A.2Lt 11-5-16 1/1RFA CR Egypt15

NUTTALL,Albert Armitage Lt dow 15-8-16 1/7WRid p227 CR France2

NUTTALL,Eric John 2Lt kia 21-3-18 12WYorks att59MGC p82&184 MR20

NUTTALL,Harry Norbury T2Lt dow 5-7-17 RASC attMGC HQ HB p193 CR Belgium11

NUTTER,Alan Charles 2Lt dow 15-9-17 40RFC p11 CR France179

NUTTER,Geoffrey Hayward Elliot T2Lt kia 22-3-18 19MGC p184 MR20

NUTTER,Herbert Charles 2LtTLtACapt kia 16-6-17 5Suff p217 CR France421

NUTTING,Ernest Ralph 2Lt kia 18-11-16 3 att10RWar p65 MR21

NUTTLE,James Edward T2Lt ded 6-7-16 RE p47 CR Hamps245

NUTTRALL,Alfred 2Lt ded 11-5-16 RH&FA p209

NYE,Charles TLt kia 17-8-16 8Nhampt p137 CR France700,16-8-16

NYE,Reginald Rayner.MID Capt kia 17-12-15 3RScots p54 CR Belgium70

NYREN,Dudley Richard T2Lt kia 24-3-18 24RFus p69 MR20

O

OAKDEN,Arthur William Lt ded 29-6-18 A124RFA p261 CR France52

OAKDEN,Edward Ralph TCapt dow 22-3-17 10N&D p134 CR Notts84

OAKDEN,Ernest 2Lt kia 22-8-18 RGA 130HB p209 CR France526

OAKE,Douglas.MC.TCapt kld 8-8-18 GL RFA att92TMB p191 CR France19

OAKELEY,William Soulden TMaj ded 11-9-18 RASC MT p193 CR Lond8

OAKENFULL,Herbert Joseph 2Lt kia 7-10-16 10 att1/1Lond p248 MR21 CR France1890

OAKES,George Frederick Thomas.MID Capt dow 15-7-16 RE 130FC p47 CR France833

OAKES,Gerard Edmund Roseingrave Lt dow 19-4-18 1WYorks p82 CR Belgium

OAKES,James Edwards Brooks.MC.Lt kia 10-7-17 RH&FA Z/1TMB p33 MR31

OAKES,Orbell Capt kld 13-3-15 Yorks p91 MR22

OAKES,Robert Claude 2Lt kia 19-7-16 RFA &RFC p2&33,ded CR France366,Lt

OAKES,Samuel T2Lt kia 6-5-17 RE Z'SpCoy p47 CR France560

OAKLEY,Christopher Herbert.MC&Bar.Capt dow 2-9-18 22Lond C'Coy p251 C France630

OAKLEY,Henry Bernard 2Lt kia 3-5-17 8RB p179 MR20

OAKLEY,Reginald T2Lt kia 25-8-16 15 att8Yorks p91 CR Belgium54,Lt

OAKLEY,Reginald William Kennedy TLt kia 1-7-16 8YLI p143 MR21

OAKLEY-BROWN,Valentine Lt kia 9-10-18 3DragGds CR France341

OAKSHOTT,Albert Neville TLt kia 16-8-17 7RIrRif p170 MR30

OATES,Alfred Tennyson Lt dow 1-3-20 IA 10Lancers p281 CR Iraq8,kia

OATES,Herbert Prudent 2Lt kia 20-9-17 5Lpool p215 MR30

OATES,John Stanley TLtACapt dow 11-12-17 9 att6DCLI p114 CR Belgium84

OATES,Walter.MC.T2Lt kia 3-11-18 RE 218FC p47 CR France940

OATTS,Eric Pearce 2Lt kia 3-5-17 4RScotF p222 MR20

O'BEIRNE,Arthur James Lewis 2Lt dow 28-7-17 OxYeo att57RFC p19&205 CR Belgium24

O'BEIRNE,John Ingram Mullanniffe 2Lt kia 3-4-17 RWar att25RFC p11&p65 MR20

O'BRIAN,Walter Vincent 2Lt 20-9-16 1Ches MR21

O'BRIEN,Aubrey Ulick Marshall Capt kia 1-11-14 39RFA p33 MR29

O'BRIEN,Charles Stuart.MC.2Lt dow 27-9-18 1IrGds p53 CR France512

O'BRIEN,Daniel Joseph 2Lt kia 10-11-17 3 att2RMunF p175 MR30

O'BRIEN,Denis Patrick Capt ded 8-8-20 IARO 2EuphratesLevy attPoliticalDept p CR Iraq8

O'BRIEN,Dermot Lt kia 26-9-17 291RFA p208 CR Belgium23

O'BRIEN,Francis Joseph 2LtACapt kia 31-7-17 1Worc p109 MR29

O'BRIEN,Francis Pat T2Lt kia 16-8-16 10 att9ESurr p113 MR21

O'BRIEN,G.P.Capt 3-6-20 IMS MR65

O'BRIEN,Gerard.DSO.MID 2Lt kia 22-3-18 5RMunF att1InnisF p175 MR27

O'BRIEN,Henry Edward TCapt dow 8-9-16 RAMC att99FA No2GH p197 CR France85

O'BRIEN,Hugh Conor Henry Capt kia 21-12-14 2RMunF p175 MR22,22-12-14

O'BRIEN,Hugh Rivers Hamilton(Paddy) TCapt kia 1-6-16 112RFA 19AA Bty p3 CR Belgium127

O'BRIEN,Humphrey Donatus Stafford.MC&Bar.MID Capt kld 14-9-18 1Nhamp &63RAF p137 CR Iraq8

O'BRIEN,James Francis Lt kia 21-12-14 2RMunF p175 MR22

O'BRIEN,James Vincent Capt kia 10-8-16 RAMC att5Bde p197 CR France267

O'BRIEN,Jeremiah James Capt kia 10-3-18 4 att1RIrReg p89 CR Palestine3

O'BRIEN,John.MC.LtTCapt kia 6-10-18 2RMunF p175 CR France845

O'BRIEN,John Dwyer.MC.TLt dow 17-8-17 14RIrRif p170 CR Belgium8

O'BRIEN,Lucius James Francis.MID T2Lt dow 7-4-17 5Wilts p153 CR Iraq8,Frances Ex HAC

O'BRIEN,M.Nurse 21-2-17 QAIMNS CR Hamps1

O'BRIEN,Michael Patrick TLt ded 23-9-17 RAMC p197 CR Hamps1

O'BRIEN,Philip Anderson 2Lt dow 9-3-15 Leinst p174 CR France102

O'BRIEN,Robert Edward 2Lt ded 20-2-19 2 att3A&SH p255 CR Belgium316,2 att18Bn

O'BRIEN,Sidney Joseph Vincent 2Lt kia 7-6-17 5RMunF att2RIrRif p175 MR29

232

O'BRIEN,Terence Donough 2Lt kia 3-3-16 16Lancers att6RFC p2&23 CR Belgium11
O'BRIEN,Timothy John Aloysius Lt kia 7-8-16 27RFA CR France399
O'BRIEN,Thomas Augustine TLt ded 6-10-18 RAVC p199 MR65
O'BRIEN,Thomas Kevin TCapt kia 31-5-16 6ConnRgrs p172 CR France178,30-5-16
O'BRIEN,Walter Hubert Maj kldacc 7-2-17 RE IWT p47 CR France354
O'BRIEN,William Bartholomew Stevenson TLt ded 18-6-18 RE RTO p47 CR France145
O'BRIEN,William Donough TMaj dow 7-6-16 3ConnRgrs att20Manch p172 CR France23
O'BRIEN,William Vincent T2Lt kia 20-9-16 1Ches p96
O'BRIEN-BUTLER,Capel Desmond.MC.Capt kia 7-6-17 4 att6RIrReg p89 CR Belgium17
O'BRIEN-BUTLER,Charles Paget Capt dow 31-10-14 RAMC p197 CR France284
O'BRYEN,Myles Wheeler Lt kld 2-10-16 5RWar p214O'
CALLAGHAN,Duncan Mckay McDonald 2Lt kia 14-3-15 3 att2DCLI p114 CR Belgium28
O'CALLAGHAN,Gerard Arthur Capt dow 24-5-15 RIrReg p89 CR France285
O'CALLAGHAN,James T2Lt kia 21-10-16 13Ches p96 MR21
O'CALLAGHAN,John Charles.MC.TCaptAMaj kia 4-4-18 C190RFA p33 CR France745
O'CALLAGHAN,Thomas Francis 2Lt kia 13-10-15 4Leic p220 MR19
O'CARROLL,Francis Brendon T2Lt kia 10-8-15 6RDubF p177 MR4
OCHS,Ronald Philip 2Lt kia 27-9-15 5 att4Mddx p148 CR Belgium6,26-9-15
O'CONNELL,A.J.Lt ? 4NigR CR WAfrica56
O'CONNELL,C.W.MC.Lt kld 18-6-18 21Lond CR Essex9
O'CONNELL,Donald Charles 2Lt kia 9-9-16 4ConnRgrs att8RInnisF p172 MR21
O'CONNELL,J.M.Dr 7-11-18 SierraLeoneCivilServ CR WAfrica28
O'CONNELL,John Forbes Lt kia 20-9-14 RAMC p197 CR France1329
O'CONNELL,Maurice James Lt ded 30-7-18 222RFA attTMB p33 CR Iraq8
O'CONNOR,Arthur Cathal TCapt kia 27-7-16 1Norf p74 MR21
O'CONNOR,Arthur Patrick.CB.Col 25-1-20 RAMC CR Mddx77
O'CONNOR,Bernard Joseph TLt kia 4-10-18 3RFus p69 CR France234
O'CONNOR,Edward Victor 2Lt dow 12-5-18 RGA 29SB p41 CR Lond9
O'CONNOR,Frederick Henry Pomeroy Maj ded 1-2-16 RAOC p198
O'CONNOR,F.W.Capt&QM 17-10-19 RAMC CR Hamps232
O'CONNOR,Henry.VD.LtCol ded 1-12-15 RGA p209 CR Scot253
O'CONNOR,Hubert Michael.MC.TCapt dow 17-8-17 6KSLI p145 CR Belgium16
O'CONNOR,J.Capt 25-10-16 IA Ord Dept CR Hamps64
O'CONNOR,John McConville 2Lt kia 10-7-18 6ScotRif p224 CR France25,9Bn
O'CONNOR,Joseph Harris Lt kia 10-11-17 5 att2RMunF p175 MR30
O'CONNOR,Richard Dominick Capt kia 25-10-14 RAMC p197 CR France275
O'CONNOR,Roderic Alan Edward 2Lt kia 1-9-16 3Leinst p174 CR France399
O'CONNOR,Roderick Stratford 2Lt kia 28-4-17 4 att2SStaffs p122 MR20
O'CONNOR,William Moyle LtCol ded 21-1-16 RAMC p271 CR Ireland12
O'CONOR,Ronald Ramsay 2Lt ded 30-11-18 ColdGds 51 CR Berks45
O'CONOR,William Owen Rev&TMaj ded 24-1-19 IA IndEcclesEst p281 CR Asia82
O'DALY,Dominic Roe Dathy 2Lt kia 14-11-16 1/7NumbF p214 MR21
ODAM,Cecil Wilfred 2Lt kia 15-9-16 6Lond p247 MR21,Wilfnd
O'DEA,Lawrence Rev ded 4-11-17 RAChDept p199 CR Sussex15,Laurence
O'DEA Mathew Leo Brien Patrick Capt ded 4-6-19 IARO attS&TCps p281 CR Asia82
ODDIE,Francis Arthur Joseph TLt kia 23-10-16 2Mddx att2RBerks p148 MR21
ODDY,Alfred Edward T2Lt kia 27-9-18 8WYorks p82 CR France755,29-9-18
ODDY,James Leslie Capt dow 3-9-16 6WYorks p218 CR France44
ODELL,Oliver Henry Cecil 2Lt kia 10-9-16 3Lond p246 CR France453
ODELL,Philip Ralph Lt 30-4-21 2Beds &Herts MR66
ODELL,Robert Eric TLt dow 20-12-16 8BlkW p129 CR France158,kia
ODELL,William Capt.MC.kia 22-2-17 IA 123Rif att125 p281 CR Iraq5
ODELL,William Ward.MC.TLt kia 4-10-17 9N&D p134 MR30
ODGERS,Robert Blake Lt ded 31-8-17 RASC p271 CR Lond12,Capt
ODHAMS,Valentine Bernand TLt dow 5-10-15 15DLI p161 CR France1
ODLING,Eric Robert Meade Lt kld 25-3-15 RE p47 CR France765
ODLUM,William Henry Maj ded 25-11-20 IA IMS p281
O'DONAHUE,Thomas Henderson T2Lt kia 20-4-17 2/9Manch p155 CR France765
O'DONNELL,Anthony Patrick 2Lt kia 12-6-17 1/4Y&L p238 CR France705
O'DONNELL,Charles Vize Capt ded 12-5-19 SL LpoolRecruitStaff p268 CR Yorks185
O'DONNELL,George Boudrie LtCol ded 20-10-19 RetPay Ex RDC p271 CR Sussex111
O'DONNELL,Hugh Neil T2Lt dow 4-2-17 17WelshR p127 CR France145
O'DONNELL,Percy 2Lt dow 6-5-16 5RFA p33 CR Belgium11

O'DONNELL,Ralph T2Lt ded 25-3-18 61IndLabourCps p189 CR France770,28-3-18
O'DONAGHUE,Algernon Leopold 2Lt ded 22-5-17 RDC p253 CR Somerset25
O'DONOGHUE,Humphrey Patrick 2Lt kia 10-3-15 1Lpool p72 MR22
O'DONOGHUE,John Hamilton 2Lt ded PoW 27-6-16 IARO att110Mahrattas p281 MR38
O'DONOVAN,Miles Henry Capt kia 21-6-16 4 att8RMunF p175 CR France223,20-6-16
O'DOWD,Maurice Vernon 2Lt kia 25-5-15 3 att2NumbF p62 MR29
O'DUFFY,Kevin Emmet TLt kia 15-8-15 7RMunF p175 MR4
O'DWYER,Alfred Stanhope T2Lt kia 29-7-16 14RWar p65 MR21
O'DWYER,John T2Lt dow 11-9-16 GL attTMB p191
O'DWYER,Robert Martin T2Lt dow 18-10-15 D74RFA p33 CR France423
OERTLING,Lewis John Francis Lt dow 8-8-18 5Beds att5RAF p228&271 CR France71
O'FARRELL,Archibald Hugh 2Lt kia 27-9-18 1IrGds p53 CR France1497
O'FARRELL,Haward Patrick Austin TCapt died 6-12-16 SL p268
O'FARRELL,Howard Patrick Curtis LtCol died 6-12-16 14Hamps p121 CR Hamps7,14-12-16
O'FERRALL,Brendon Hynds 2Lt kia 16-8-17 A76RFA p33 CR Belgium12
OFFICER,Arnold Vincent T2Lt ded 10-5-17 12EYorks p84 CR France40
O'FFLAHERTIE,Godwin Joseph Anthony Swifte Lt kld 4-3-18 3KSLI att1Lpool p145
O'FIELD,Alfred T2Lt dow 11-11-17 RE 10CpsSig p47 CR Belgium11
OFIELD,Charles Henry 2lt dow 22-8-18 RGA 139HB p41 CR France119
O'FLAHERTY,Douglas Hill TCapt kia 1-7-16 15RIrRif p170 MR21
O'FLYNN,Dominick Thomas TCapt ded 16-6-18 RAMC att19DAC p197 CR France1415
O'FLYNN,Francis Joseph T2Lt kia 27-4-16 9RMunF p175
O'FLYNN,Michael Joseph TLt dow 24-9-18 RAMC att1Nhampt p197 CR France528
OGDEN,John Herbert 2Lt kia 31-7-17 5LNLancs p234 MR29
OGDEN,Percy 2Lt ded 7-6-17 RFC p261 CR C'land&W'land45
OGDEN,Walter Frederick T2Lt dow 2-12-17 11TankCps p188 CR France446
OGG,Lindsay Ross 2Lt ded 22-9-16 IARO attS&TCps p281 CR Iraq6
OGG,William Kelly Carmichael 2Lt kia 15-7-16 9HLI p240 MR21
OGILVIE,Alexander Walter TLt dow 30-10-18 RASC attRGA 60SB p193 CR Suff3
OGILVIE,Andrew Maxwell 2Lt kia 5-10-17 3 att2GordH p167 MR30
OGILVIE,James Roy 2Lt dow 22-8-18 RE 80FC p210 CR France119
OGILVIE,William Edmond T2Lt kia 27-9-15 9BordR p117 CR France425
OGILVY,Gilchrist Nevill.Bart.Lt 29-10-14 1ScotGds p52 MR29
OGILVY,Patrick Julian Harry Stanley.Hon.MC.ACapt kia 9-10-17 1IrGds p53 CR Belgium83
OGILVY,William Wickham Lt dow 23-3-18 20Huss p23 CR France1063
O'GIOLLAGAIN,John Gabriel T2Lt kld 5-9-17 GL &RFC p11 CR Wilts115
OGLE,Thomas Burton 2Lt kia 23-3-16 3Dors p124 MR38
O'GORMAN,E.M.Sister ded 20-11-14 TFNS CR Glouc6
O'GRADY,Amy Veda Sister 12-8-16 AustArmyNursServ MR65
O'GRADY,de Courcy 2Lt ded 14-2-15 ConnRgrs p266 CR Ireland24
O'GRADY,Standish de Courcy.CMG.DSO.LtCol 23-12-20 RAMC CR Europe1
OGSTON,James T2Lt dow 15-9-16 13RScots p54 CR France188
OGSTON,Kenneth Capt dow 12-4-18 6WRid p227 MR30
O'HALLORAN,John Fernan 2Lt kia 26-7-16 2HLI p163 MR21
O'HALLORAN-GILES,Robert 2Lt dow PoW 26-4-18 KEdwsHorse p24 CR Belgium406
O'HALLORAN,Sylvester North East ACapt kia 9-8-17 2Ess p132 MR20
O'HANLON,Sydney Esmond.MC.TLt kld 3-2-18 RFC p16 CR Lancs30
O'HARA,H.E.2Lt kld 25-5-18 GL &RAF p191
O'HARA,Henry Desmond.DSO.Lt dow 29-8-15 1RDubF p177 CR Europe23
O'HARA,Osborne Capt kia 13-2-15 2RIrF p171 MR29
O'HARA,Patrick Gilbert Warwick 2Lt kia 14-8-16 3ESurr att1/4RBerks p113 MR21
O'HARA,Thomas O.Lt ded 10-3-19 4RScots p211 CR Scot713
OHLMANN,Gerrard Alexander Louis 2Lt kia 29-9-15 3RFus p69 MR19
O'KANE,Paul Lt kia 21-3-18 4 att1RIrRif p170 MR27
OKE,Robert William Leslie LtTCapt kia 25-9-15 3 att2RBerks p139
O'KEARNEY-WHITE Ernest Francis 2Lt kia 9-9-16 9RDubF p177 MR21
O'KEEFE,Joseph Richard T2Lt kia 4-5-16 10LNLancs p136 CR France745
O'KEEFE,William Robert TCapt ded 21-11-18 RAMC 32CCS p197 CR Lebanon1
O'KEEFE,William Henry TLt kia 19-5-17 40RFA p33 CR France1182
O'KEEFFE,Marcus Menus.MC.LtAMaj kia 2-4-18 RFA 48ArmyBde p33 CR France2
O'KELLY,Henry Arundell de Pentheny Capt kia 18-5-15 18Huss CR Belgium4

O'KELLY,Patrick Joseph TLt kia 26-9-16 58RFA p33 CR France393
O'KELLY,Richard Capt ded 18-12-19 RAMC p267 CR Egypt9
OKEY,Leslie Alfred T2Lt kia 15-6-17 214MGC p184 MR20
OKEY,William Ewart T2Lt kia 21-1-16 1ConnRgrs p172 CR Iraq5
O'LAND,Valentine T2Lt kia 1-7-16 15WYorks p82 MR21
OLDEN,Sidney Montague T2Lt kia 4-5-18 1BordR p117 MR32
OLDENDORFF,Friedrich Henrich Maj dow 1-9-16 7Mddx p235 CR France833,Frederick Henry
OLDERSHAW,Leslie Capt dow 2-10-17 RAMC att 1/8Manch p254 CR Belgium24
OLDERSHAW,John Joseph Fritz 2Lt kia 1-7-16 9YLI p143 MR21
OLDERSHAW,Thomas Harold 2Lt kia 14-4-18 3 att2HLI p163 MR20
OLDFIELD,Edmund George William Capt kia 4-6-15 8Manch p237 MR4,5-6-15
OLDFIELD,Fred T2Lt kia 29-6-17 9NStaffs p157 CR Belgium17
OLDFIELD,Guy Christopher Ottley Lt kia 5-9-14 RWSurr attKAR p56&202 MR50
OLDFIELD,John Burleigh Maj&QM ded 9-12-14 7Ess p271 CR Lond14
OLDFIELD,John Burleigh.MC&Bar.T2LtACapt kia 16-8-17 2Nhampt p137 MR30
OLDFIELD,Laurel Cecil Francis TCapt kia 25-9-15 12RB p179 CR France768
OLDFIELD,William Henry 2Lt kia 17-5-15 4 att2HLI p163 MR22
OLDHAM,Joseph Haslope 2Lt kia 18-4-15 3DCLI att2YLI p114 CR Belgium152
OLDHAM,John 2Lt kia 19-4-18 6RWar p214 CR France248
OLDHAM,Leslie William Searles.MID Maj kia 28-7-15 RE 63Coy p47 CR France727
OLDHAM,Llewellyn Haslope T2Lt kia 26-9-15 2Worc p109 MR19
OLDHAM,Wilton Stransham Capt kia 22-11-15 IA 48Pnrs p281 MR38
OLDMAN,Harold Victor T2Lt kld 29-10-17 RFC p11 CR Herts30
OLDMAN,Wilfred Southey Deare TCapt kia 25-9-15 8RBerks p139 CR France552
OLDREY,Gerald Vivian Lt ded 19-2-19 1/1SNottsHuss p205 CR Egypt9,19-1-19
OLDREY,Montague 2Lt kia 26-10-17 3Lond p246 MR30
OLDREY,Robert John Blatchford Capt kia 29-10-14 4DragGds p21 MR22 &CR France1896
OLDREY,Vernon Roy Lt kia 31-8-18 4Lond p246 CR France646
OLDRIDGE,Peter Henry T2Lt kld 26-1-18 RFC p16 CR Hunts83
OLDS,Cyril Austin.DCM.2Lt kia 16-4-16 3Glouc p107 MR20
O'LEARY,Herbert Hornfray Capt kia 14-1-20 IA 2/76Punjabis p281 MR43
O'LEARY,John Maj accrd 9-9-15 IA IMS p281 CR Egypt8
OLIPHANT,Edward Havelock Maj kia 12-7-15 IA 95Inf p281 CR Asia82
OLIPHANT,Marcus Francis 2Lt kia 12-8-15 5Norf p217 MR4
OLIVER,Alfred Donald Capt dow 24-4-17 5/6Manch p236 CR Belgium11,21-4-17
OLIVER,Arthur Harold T2Lt kia 8-11-17 11EYorks p84 CR France184
OLIVER,Charles Gordon 2Lt dow 14-10-15 3Dev attYorks p77 CR France98
OLIVER,Cyril Francis Harrison TCapt kia 14-7-16 12WYorks p82 CR France453
OLIVER,Edgar Alexander T2Lt kia 27-7-16 23RFus p69 MR21
OLIVER,Edward Cole 2Lt kia 22-10-17 1/2 att16Ches p96 MR30
OLIVER,Ernest 2Lt kia 22-9-17 SuffYeo attNigeriaR p205 CR EAfrica22 &CR Tanzania1
OLIVER,Frank Lambton 2Lt kia 13-7-17 SomLI att55RFC p11&80 CR Belgium344
OLIVER,Frederick Richard 2Lt kia 1-7-16 1/6N&D p233 MR21,24-7-16
OLIVER,Frederick Ruddall Lt kia 3-5-17 8Leic p88 MR20
OLIVER,George Baxter T2Lt kia 17-6-16 157RFA p33 CR France631
OLIVER,George Eric 2Lt dow 31-7-17 8ScotRif p225 CR Belgium7
OLIVER,George Frank T2Lt kia 15-7-16 10Ches p96 CR France832
OLIVER,Guy Bertram Maj dow 29-9-16 189RFA p33 CR France400 Ex 116/26RFA
OLIVER,Guy Giffard Capt kia 21-1-16 IA 102Grens p281 CR Iraq5,G.C.
OLIVER,D.Hedley CaptAMaj ded 16-3-19 RE CR Surrey34
OLIVER,Harold Augustus Boyd 2Lt dow 26-5-18 IrGds att4GdsMGR CR France62,served as KING,Norman
OLIVER Harry John T2Lt dow 23-4-18 13MGC p184 CR France31,Henry
OLIVER,Harry Percy Greenwood 2Lt kia 30-6-16 13RSuss p119 MR19
OLIVER,John Milner TLt kia 9-7-16 16Manch p155 MR21
OLIVER,Raymond Edward Creswick 2Lt mbk 28-8-16 2RB C'Coy p256 MR19
OLIVER,Robert.MID Lt mbk 25-9-15 12NumbF p256 MR19
OLIVER,Robert 2Lt kia 20-3-18 6BordR p117 MR19
OLIVER,Roderick Magrath Lt kia 27-8-18 2GrenGds p50 CR France614
OLIVER,Siddartha John 2Lt kia 10-8-17 GL &66RFC p11 MR20
OLIVER,Thomas Alfred Capt kia 14-8-17 GL &RFC p11 MR20
OLIVER,Thomas Frederick 2Lt ded 26-10-18 13N&D p264 CR Sussex183,Lt 12Bn
OLIVER,William Steele T2Lt kia 7/11-8-15 8NumbF p62 MR4
OLIVER-JONES,Alfred Vernon TLt ded 23-7-16 RFA attRFC p2&33 MR20
OLIVER-THOMPSON,John Herbert.MID TLtAMaj kia 21-3-18 40MGC p184 MR20
OLIVIER,Rosaire Henri TLt dow 11-10-17 GL &RFC 6BallCo p11 CR France102

OLIVIER,Jasper George 2Lt kia 16-9-16 3 att7DCLI p114 MR21
OLIVIER,Robert Harold Capt kia 14-9-14 1DCLI C Coy p114 MR15
OLLETT,Alfred Oscar T2Lt kia 27-4-16 13Ess p132 CR France160
OLLETT,Arthur Edmund William Lt ded 20-8-19 RE RlyOpDiv p262 MR66,Capt
OLLETT,Henry Wallace 2Lt dow 28-10-18 17RFA p209 CR France1725
OLLEY,Alfred.DCM.2Lt ded 1-7-19 WRid p264 CR Berks125
OLLIVANT,A.H.CB.CMG.MIDx2 GrigGen 31-8-19 RGA CR Kent217
OLLIVIER,Guy Lancelot CaptAMaj ded 20-1-18 RGA Commdg 65SB p41 CR France85
O'LONE,Robert James.MID 2LtTCapt kia 11-11-15 2RIrRif p170 CR Belgium137
O'LONE,Walter Percy.MID 2Lt kia 25-9-15 2RIrRif p170 MR29
O'LONGAN,Paul Charles Stacpoole 2Lt kia 1-6-17 RIrReg att41RFC p11&89 CR Belgium152
OLPHERT,Frederick John Lt dow 19-5-18 RE 940AreaEmpCoy p47 CR France77
OLPHERT,Hugh Montgomery Archdale 2Lt kia 9-9-16 3MunstF att7Leic p88 MR.
OLSEN,Soren Bendix TCapt ded 20-4-18 RASC p193 CR Durham182
OLVER,John Denis Circuit.MC.2LtALt kia 27-4-17 123/28RFA p33 CR France68
O'MALLEY,Charles Lt kia 25-11-17 17WelshR p127 MR17
O'MALLEY,W.Lt 11-11-19 ConnRgrs CR Ireland12
O'MALLEY,William Joseph 2Lt kia 9-4-17 RFA Y47TMB p209 CR Belgium167
OMAND,Robert Stewart 2Lt dow 25-9-16 4Yorks p220 CR France177
O'MAY,William Shields.MC.LtTCapt dow 3-4-18 5 att15HLI p240 CR France169
O'MEARA,Bulkely Ernest Adolphus.DSO.Capt ded 31-8-16 EAUL CR EAfrica9 &CR Tanzania1
O'MEARA,Leon Alfred 2Lt kia 6-2-17 3 att6ELancs p111 MR38
O'MEEHAN,Isidore James Chap4Cl ded 19-12-19 RAChDept p268 CR Iraq5
OMEROD,James T2Lt ded 27-9-18 Manch att22Bn p155
OMMANNEY,Alfred Erasmus Stuart 2Lt kia 7-10-16 3 att6EKent p58 MR21
OMMANNEY,G.S.Col 21-3-18 58TrnResBn CR Lond4 Ex IA
OMMANNEY,Rupert Capt kia 31-10-14 RE 2DivStaff p47 CR Belgium58
OMMUNDSEN,Arthur Norman Victor Harcourt Lt kia 19-9-15 HAC p206 CR Belgium6
ONCKEN,William Gerrard TLt ded 17-2-19 46MGC Inf p184 CR France341, Gerhard Ex 2/23Lond
O'NEILL,Alfred Edward 2Lt dow 23-9-17 1/7Lpool p215 CR Belgium3
O'NEILL,Arthur Edward Bruce.Hon.Capt kia 6-11-14 2LifeGds p20 MR29
O'NEILL,Douglas Quirke 2Lt kia 26-4-18 10RWar p65CR Belgium185,Quirk
O'NEILL,Frederick 2Lt kia 13-11-16 5RDubF p177 CR France220
O'NEILL,Henry Dubois.MC.CaptAMaj ded 2-6-18 3Beds p86 CR Sussex107
O'NEILL,James Dominick 2Lt kia 24-8-16 5 att2RMunF p175 MR21
O'NEILL,John Teskey TCapt ded 10-10-16 17RIrRif p265 CR Ireland110
O'NEILL,Roderick Lt kia 3-5-17 6WRid p227 MR20
O'NEILL,Samuel Lt kld 12-6-15 6LancF p221 CR Gallipoli1,kia
O'NEILL,Samuel Lt kia 1-7-16 GL RA attTMB p191 MR21
O'NEILL,Thomas 2Lt ded 29-5-19 2RRofCav att 1/1DorsYeo p23 CR Eire451
O'NEILL,Thomas Michael 2Lt kia 8-5-18 9RDubF &43RAF p266 MR20,O'NEIL
ONIONS,Wilfred 2Lt dow 25-4-15 3Mon p244 MR29
ONSLOW,Arthur Denzel.MC.2Lt kia 13-8-16 11RWar p65 MR21,Denzil
ONSLOW,Brian Watton.MID Lt 28-7-15 IA 11Lancers attAust NZ ArmyCps p281 CR Gallipoli30,Walton
ONSLOW,Milo-Richard Beaumont.MID Capt dow 5-11-17 IA 21Cav att33 p281 CR Iraq8
ONSLOW,Tom 2Lt kia 6-1-17 3 att5KSLI p145 CR France420
OPENSHAW,Edward Hyde LtCol ded 23-7-17 4SomLI p218 CR Iraq6
OPENSHAW,Fred T2Lt dow 8-10-18 1/2 att8Lpool p72 CR France256
OPENSHAW,Geoffrey Ormerod TCapt dow PoW 9-8-18 RASC p193 CR Germany3,Omerod
OPENSHAW,Harold Michael Lt dow 28-8-14 Norf p74 CR Belgium205
OPET,Isaac Harold 2Lt dow 22-3-18 PoW 7 att8Lond p247 CR France1893,Isido
OPPE,Henry Sigismund TLt kia 6-11-15 11 att6Yorks p91 CR Gallipoli27
OPPE,Thomas Armin 2Lt kia 20-5-17 4 att1ScotRif p104 MR20
OPPENHEIMER,Lehmann James Lt ded 8-11-16 2/23Lond p252 CR France102
ORBELL,Douglas Lt kia 5-9-18 1Camb p245 CR France511
ORBELL,Ivan Scott 2Lt kia 25-10-17 att4RFus p69 MR22,25-10-14
ORCHARD,Ernest Frank Gordon Lt kia 31-7-17 8Lpool p215 MR29,1-8-17
ORCHARD,Hugh Thomas T2Lt kia 20-8-17 15N&D Y'Coy p134 CR France363
ORCHARDSON,Charles Moxon Quiller.MC.Capt dow 26-4-17 1CotyLondYeo p204 CR Egypt7,MddxHuss
ORCUT,Marcena Hitchcock T2Lt kia 1-3-18 3RFC p16 CR France345
ORD,Ord Ralph TLt kia 18-9-16 10RB p179 MR21
ORD-MACKENZIE,Douglas Allan 2Lt kia 24-9-16 9Lond p248 MR21

ORDE,John Barwick.MC.CaptTMaj dow 12-2-17 B99RFA p33 CR Greece6
ORDE-POWLETT,William Percy 2Lt kia 17-5-15 4Yorks p220 MR29
ORDE-WARD,A.P.Lt 11-11-18 Lincs attMGC CR Sussex144
ORDISH,Henry Thomas.MC.Capt dow PoW 21-3-18 6Lond B'Coy p246 CR France403,25-3-18
O'REILLY,Gerald Joseph T2Lt dow 30-11-16 Lincs p75 CR France297
O'REILLY,H.D.R.Capt 31-5-19 1/4RWSurr att1/5ESurr CR Iraq8
O'REILLY,Herbert Wilson 2Lt dow 20-1-16 4 att2RIrRif p170 CR France285
O'REILLY,Patrick Joseph.MC&Bar.TCapt kia 11-10-18 RAMC att7EYorks p197 CR France658
O'REILLY,Patrick Stanislaus.CMG.LtCol ded 18-11-18 RAMC p197 CR Lond29
O'REILLY,W.T.MC.Capt 19-9-20 Mddx CR Sussex95
ORETT,Claud Cecil Lt 25-9-18 14MGC Inf CR Belgium185
ORFEUR,Howard West Lt kia 23-8-18 8 att10Ess p232 CR France430
ORFORD,Charles Robert Hadfield T2Lt dow 18-7-17 1/2 att16LancF p92 CR Belgium24,19-7-17
ORFORD,Ernest Charles TCapt kia 30-7-16 20Lpool p72 MR21
ORFORD,Ernest Victor Molson 2Lt kia 23-10-16 14 att2Ess p132 MR21
ORFORD,Stephen Mewburn 2Lt kia 25-6-16 11KRRC p151 CR Belgium4
ORFORD,William Kirkpatrick T2Lt kia 1-7-16 GL 17Manch attTMB p191 MR21
ORGAN,Harold Charles 2Lt kia 9-10-17 4Glouc p225 CR Belgium126
ORGAN,Harold Percy TLt&Adj kia 1-7-16 10Y&L p159 MR21
ORGILL,Phillip Ronald T2Lt dow PoW 31-3-18 61MGC Inf p184&257,Philip CR France441
ORKNEY,Robert Lt kia 20-10-15 5A&SH p243 CR Gallipoli2
ORLEBAR,Basil John Capt kia 15-1-15 3 att1Beds p86 CR Belgium98
ORLEBAR,Robert Evelyn Lt kia 9-1-15 2Mddx p148 CR France1157
ORME,Alfred Lyth T2Lt kia 31-7-17 18Lpool p72 MR29,Lytn
ORME,Edward Leslie Lt kia 27-5-17 3 att1RWFus p98 MR20,att2Bn
ORME,Francis Reginald 2Lt kia 7-11-14 1RWFus p98 MR29
ORME,John McCallum.MC.Capt ded 3-4-17 RAMC p197 CR France31
ORME,Owen Felix LtCapt kia 25-9-15 RSuss p119 CR France219
ORME,Peter William Merton 2Lt ded 7-5-17 11RSuss attRFC p261 CR Sussex183
ORMEROD,Andrew T2Lt kia 13-4-17 RH&FA att59RFC p11&33 MR20
ORMEROD,James 2Lt ded 27-9-18 22Manch CR Italy11
ORMESBY,Horatio Nelson Lt kia 4-6-15 12ScotRif attKOSB p104 MR4,ORMSBY
ORMESHER,Herbert TLt kia 4-10-15 7Lincs p75 CR Belgium56
ORMESHER,William TLt dow 7-12-15 16Lpool att2Rfus p72 MR4,3-12-15
ORMISTON,Robert William T2Lt dow 25-3-18 6KSLI p145 CR France987
ORMOND,Alexander T2Lt kia 30-9-16 27 att11Manch p155 MR21
ORMROD,George Lt kia 18-9-18 5RSuss p228 CR France699
ORMROD,Harry TLt kia 1-7-16 8YLI p143 MR21
ORMROD,L.J.2Lt 3-5-15 12Lancers CR Wales664
ORMROD,Lawrence Moreland.MC.Capt ded 25-8-17 1RWFus p98 CR Wales664,dow
ORMROD,Oliver Hugh TCapt kld 12-9-16 RFA attRFC p2&33 CR Wales664
ORMSBY,Francis James T2Lt kia 3-9-16 14 att13RSuss p119 CR France701
ORMSBY,Harold Sydney.MID TLtACapt dow 18-2-17 14RWFus p98 CR Belgium23
ORMSBY,Horatio Nelson Lt 4-6-15 12ScotRif att1KOSB MR4
ORMSBY,Vincent Alexander.CB.BrigGen kia 2-5-17 IA Staff127InfBde p281 CR France363,1-5-17
O'RORKE,Benjamin Garniss.DSO.Rev ded 25-12-18 RAChDept p199 CR Cornwall40
O'RORKE,Denis Clifford.MC.Capt kia 24-3-18 att11KRRC p151 MR27
O'ROURKE,Daniel Lt kia 30-7-18 RGA 170SB p41 CR France343
ORPEN,Walter Selwyn 2Lt kia 6-7-16 2 att10LancF p93 MR21
ORPIN,Ralph Ernest 2Lt dow 6-8-17 A92RFA p33 CR Belgium12
ORR,Alexander Thomas TCapt ded 3-1-19 RE p47 CR Italy11,Thomson
ORR,Arthur James T2Lt kia 23-4-18 24Manch p155 CR Italy11
ORR,Arthur Roxboroughe Capt kia 17-11-15 2ScotGds p52 CR France257,Roxburghe 17-10-15
ORR,Edward Farquharson Burkitt Lt kia 23-3-18 HQ 173RFA p33 CR France1203,24-3-18
ORR,Hugh Brian T2Lt kia 22-3-18 HLI att10/11Bn p163 MR20
ORR,Jack Alexander Anderson Lt kia 12-6-18 3SfthH p165 MR19,2Bn
ORR,James Barbour Capt kia 31-7-17 4RScotF p222 MR29
ORR,James Henry T2LtACapt kia 30-11-17 RGA 210SB p41 MR17
ORR,James Kenneth T2Lt kia 1-7-16 16Mddx p148 MR21
ORR,John 2Lt ded 29-3-19 6DragGds p261 CR Scot525
ORR,John Arthur Capt kia 22-10-14 1CamH p168 MR29
ORR,John Boyd.DSO.Maj dow 24-8-14 1Norf p74 CR Belgium205
ORR,John Compton 2Lt kia 28-4-17 2 att5RBerks p139 CR France1182

ORR,J.L.Maj 10-2-18 IA 20DeccanHorse CR Devan238
ORR,Osborne John.DFC.Lt 23-10-18 204RAF MR20
ORR,Robert Baird Rowley Capt kia 3-7-17 9A&SH att4RFC p243 CR Belgium11
ORR,Robert Clifford Capt kia 19-12-14 3SomLI p80 CR Belgium70
ORR,Robert Duncan Lt kia 10-8-18 9A&SH p244 CR France649
ORR,Robert Watson 2Lt kia 25-9-15 18Lond p250 CR France219
ORR,Walter Leslie 2Lt kia 25-9-15 4 att2RIrRif p170 MR29
ORR,William Gilmour Moore 2Lt dow 12-1-17 3HLI p163 CR Iraq5
ORR-EWING,Ernest Pellew TCapt kia 15-9-16 ScotGds att1Bn p52 CR France374
ORRELL,John Turton 2Lt kia 2-12-17 GL &57RFC p11 CR Belgium140
ORRELL,Keith Faulkener Andrew 2Lt kia 13-1-17 10 att6SLancs p125 MR38
ORRETT,Claud Cecil TLt kia 25-9-18 14MGC p184
ORREY,Frederick William T2Lt dow 16-9-17 5 att3KRRC p151 CR Belgium140,att13Bn
ORRIN,William John T2Lt ded 12-11-18 5RBerks attLabCps p139 CR France85
ORRISS,Walter Gerald Lt dow 29-3-18 3GrenGds p50 CR France62
ORSON,John Tom 2Lt kia 21-3-18 4Leic p220 MR20
ORTON,Cecil Alfred Maj ded 30-9-17 RGA 22SB p41 CR Oxford45
ORTON,Ernest Henry 2Lt kia 9-5-15 2ScotRif p104 MR22
ORTON-SMITH,Geoffrey Ewing Lt ded PoW 1-3-17 6 att1/5RWar p214 MR21
O'RYAN,Francis Joseph T2Lt dow 23-8-18 8RLancs A'Coy p59 CR France103
OSBORN,Alfred Herbert 2Lt kia 23-10-18 8ESurr p113 CR France1478
OSBORN,Arthur Guy Capt kia 6-5-17 12SWBord p100 CR France439
OSBORN,Edward Stanley T2Lt kld 29-11-17 GL &RFC p11
OSBORN,Ernest John.MC.TLtACapt dow 13-4-18 24RFus att5TMB p69 CR France145
OSBORN,George Ashby Chadwick TCapt kia 24-4-17 7Wilts p153 MR37
OSBORN,Gordon Chadwick 2Lt kia 18-4-15 RE p47 CR Belgium165
OSBORN,Walter 2Lt kia 5-11-18 13Lond p249 CR France1142
OSBORNE,Albert John Francis 2Lt kia 10-7-17 3RWSurr p56 CR Belgium15,7Bn
OSBORNE,Alec Ferguson.MC.Capt ded 2-7-21 RASC CR Egypt9
OSBORNE,Archibald Edward Capt kia 21-3-18 5EKent p213 MR20
OSBORNE,Brian Lt kia 11-11-14 15Huss p22 MR29
OSBORNE,Brian Riversdale.MC.T2Lt kia 4-11-18 2GrenGds p50 CR France985
OSBORNE,Derrick Lt kia 21-3-18 3 att2DLI p161 MR20
OSBORNE,Edward Bertram T2Lt dow PoW 1-4-18 2 att2/5ELancs p111 CR France716
OSBORNE,Frank Louis 2Lt dow 21-3-18 2/5Lincs p220 MR20
OSBORNE,Frederick William 2Lt kia 23-4-17 5 att13KRRC p151 CR France1193
OSBORNE,George Edward Bell Maj kia 6-11-17 Fife&ForfarYeo p203 CR Palestine1
OSBORNE,Harold Lt kia 19-7-20 IA 105 att116MahrattaLI p281 CR Iraq6
OSBORNE,Harold John.MID Lt dow 4-8-15 1/4Hamps p228 CR Iraq6
OSBORNE,Harry Edgar Lt kia 10-8-15 5WelshR p230 MR4
OSBORNE,H.C.B.TMaj ded 28-6-16 27RFus p69 CR Kent28
OSBORNE,Henry Douglas 2Lt ded 24-2-19 5EKent p213 CR France34
OSBORNE,Hubert P.Capt kld 7-7-17 104CanadaInf attRFC CR Belgium115
OSBORNE,Hugh Corry T2Lt kia 23-7-16 12WYorks p82 MR21
OSBORNE,John T2Lt kia 2-12-17 17HLI p163 MR30
OSBORNE,John Sydney Lt kia 3-9-16 1/6HLI p240 CR Egypt2
OSBORNE,Leslie Hall TLt kia 7-8-15 9LancF p93 CR Gallipoli27
OSBORNE,Marcus Stuart Lt kia 24-4-18 8Huss att8MGC p22 MR27
OSBORNE,Robert Lionel T2Lt kia 7-10-16 14 att9RFus p69 CR France393
OSBORNE,Trevor Leonard Lt kia 30-9-18 Dev &RAF p77 CR France1483
OSBORNE,Victor Edward 2Lt kld PoW 7-4-18 3 O&BLI attMGC Inf p130&184 CR Germany3,Lt
OSBORNE,William Edward 2Lt dow 11-9-16 1/4Lond p246 CR France23,kia
OSBORNE,William John T2Lt dow 9-8-15 9LancF p93 MR4
OSBORNE-JONES,Noel 2Lt kia 8-5-16 15RWFus p98 MR19
OSBOURNE,Robert Capt kia 2-3-17 9HLI p240 CR France626
OSBURN,Francis Cecil Trousdale 2Lt dow 17-5-17 2 att9Ess p132 CR France113
OSGOOD,Thomas William TLt kia 19-7-16 D23RFA p33 CR France399
O'SHEA,Dermot Patrick Lt kia 11-9-17 IA 69Punjabis p281 CR Asia62
O'SHEA,Dermot Timothy T2Lt kia 10-8-18 14TankCps p188 CR France692
O'SHEA,Harry Arthur TLt kia 14-8-18 SL &92RAF p268 MR20
O'SHEA,Wilfred Bernard 2Lt dow 23-5-16 IA 1/8GurkhaRif p281 MR38
OSLER,Edward Revere 2Lt dow 30-8-17 A59RFA p33 CR Belgium16
OSMAN,Eric Edward 2Lt kia 20-5-17 3 att1InnisF p105 MR20,19-5-17
OSMASTON,Oswald Camplyon Hutchinson.MC.Lt kia 26-8-17 RE 12FC p47 CR France80
OSMASTON,Robert Shirley.MC.2Lt kia 24-9-16 3Suss attRFC p2&119 CR France167

OSMOND,Charles Frederick Squire T2Lt kia 28-11-17 6Yorks p91 CR France551
OSMOND,Cyril Thomas TLt dow 25-8-18 14WelshR p127 CR France84
OSMOND-WILLIAMS,Osmond Traharn Deudraith.DSO.Capt dow 27-9-15 WelshGds p53
OSTLER,Alan.MC.2Lt kld 16-9-18 17RFA &13RAF p33 CR France481
OSTLER,Thomas T2Lt kia 7-6-17 11WYorks att69TMB p82 CR Belgium127
OSTREHAM,Duncan Haldane Lt kia 31-7-17 4LNLancs p234 MR29
O'SULIVAN,John Anthony T2Lt kia 27-5-17 GL &1RFC p11 CR France285,O'SULLIVAN
O'SULLIVAN,Arthur Moore Capt kia 9-5-15 1RIrRif p170 CR France706
O'SULLIVAN,Donald Vincent Chap4Cl kia 5-7-16 RAChDept p199 CR France295,Donal
O'SULLIVAN,Fergus 2Lt kia 23-4-17 6NStaffs attRFC p19&238 CR France366
O'SULLIVAN,Gerald Robert.VC.Capt kia 21-8-15 1InnisF p105 MR4
O'SULLIVAN,Horace Alexander 2Lt kia 22-4-17 RGA 41SB p41 CR France68,Lt 24-4-17
O'SULLIVAN,Hugh Henry 2Lt kia 10-6-15 6NStaffs p238 CR France861
O'SULLIVAN,John Andrew Hamilton Lt kia 28-6-15 13HLI p163 MR4
O'SULLIVAN,Thomas George TLt kia 21-8-18 RE 4LtRlyOpCoy p47 CR France81
OSWALD,William Digby,DSO LtTMaj dow 15-7-16 5DragGds att12WYorks p21 CR France141,LtCol 16-7-16
OSWELL,Percy Vincent T2Lt kia 20-9-18 6RWSurr p56 CR France369
O'TOOLE,Daniel 2Lt kia 23-11-17 1RIrF p171 MR17
OTTER,Robert John Charles Capt dow 15-2-15 Norf p74 CR Belgium98,kia
OTTEY,Raymond Gascoyne 2Lt kia 28-7-17 3Leic att32RFC p11&88 MR20
OTTEY,Thomas William.DCM.Maj ded 3-12-18 RAOC p198 CR Kent175
OTTLEY,Algernon Glendower Capt dow 22-5-15 2EYorks p84 CR France102
OTTLEY,Geoffrey Claude Langdale.DSO.TLt dow 21-12-14 ScotGds p52 CR Scot430
OTTLEY,Glendower George.MID TMaj kia 3-9-16 RFus att9ESurr p69 MR21
OTTLEY,John Lawrence Young 2Lt kia 22-4-17 IA 56Rif p281 MR38
OTTLEY,Kendal Coghill Glendower Lt ded 31-10-16 WIndiaR p192
OTTLEY,Lionel Edward.MID Maj 20-8-21 NumbF CR Sussex200
OTTLEY,Reginald Benade Glendower 2Lt kia 23-12-17 9NStaffs att59RFC p11&157 CR France518
OTTON,Gilbert Charles 2Lt kia 20-9-16 5Y&L p238 MR21
OUCHTERLONY,John Palgrave Heathcote.DSO.Maj kia 7-6-17 RE 102FC p47 MR29
OUDIN,L'Eugene Capt dow 24-8-16 7DCLI p114 CR France141,E.L.
OUGHTON,Reginald 2Lt kia 11-10-18 6WRid p227 CR France612
OUGHTRED,Harold 2Lt kia 23-4-17 4EYorks p219 CR France162
OULTON,Henry Charles 2Lt kia 12-4-17 4Leinst p174 CR France557,Harry
OUTRAM,Edmund T2Lt kia 1-7-16 26Manch p155 MR21
OUTRAM,John 2Lt kia 6-11-17 1DCLI p114 MR30
OVANS,E.H.Capt 23-3-15 125NapiersRif
OVENDEN,Herbert Stephen Lt&QM ded 3-9-16 RASC p193 CR Kent5
OVENS,John Roberts Lt kia 5-11-14 1ConnRgrs p172 CR France1157
OVERMAN,John Gilbert T2Lt kia 9-9-18 9YLI HQ p143 CR France415
OVERTON,Charles 2Lt drd 20-5-17 RE IWT p47 MR38
OVERTON,John 2Lt kia 22-3-18 5 att9RWelshF p223 MR20
OVERTON,Thomas Darwin TLt kia 30-7-15 Lincs p75 CR Gallipoli2
OWEN,Arthur Adrian 2Lt kia 13-3-15 3RWar p65 CR France706
OWEN,Arthur Bankes T2Lt dow 26-10-18 7KSLI p145 CR France380
OWEN,Arthur Edmund Lt ded 18-10-16 1Nhampt att2/4Glouc p137 CR France345
OWEN,Arthur Percy Capt kia 8-3-16 Manch p155 MR38
OWEN,Augustus Charles.MC.TLt kia 6-8-18 8SomLI p80 CR France1014
OWEN,D.G.2Lt ded 23-11-16 3 O&BLI p130 CR Wales212
OWEN,Evan Richard TLtACapt kia 28-4-17 86RH&FA p33 CR France266,Maj
OWEN,Ernest Haddon 2Lt kia 21-12-14 3Lincs att1SWBord p75 MR22
OWEN,Frank LtCol 24-12-18 3/8Lond CR Essex107
OWEN,George Crompton Lt kia 9-4-18 1/4SLancs p230 CR France80
OWEN,George Webster Capt kia 6-6-15 10Manch p237 MR4
OWEN,Godfrey Felix TLt ded 21-10-18 3RIrReg p89 CR Wilts115,30-10-18
OWEN,Griffith Christmas T2Lt kia 31-7-17 11SWBord p100 MR29 &CR Belgium453
OWEN,Henry James T2Lt kia 24-8-18 16RWFus p98 CR France393
OWEN,Herbert Arthur Harold T2Lt dow 23-3-18 2ELancs p111 CR France987
OWEN,Herbert Ernest Malcolm T2Lt kld 18-7-17 GL &RFC p11 CR Wales692
OWEN,Herbert Morris T2Lt dow 25-3-18 9Ches p96 CR France300
OWEN,Horre Solle 2Lt kia 23-11-16 3Manch p155 CR France701
OWEN,Hugh Lt kia 16-5-15 3 att2BordR A'Coy p117 CR France279

OWEN,Humphrey Francis Lt kia 24-3-18 7RWFus p223 MR20,22-3-18
OWEN,Ifor Evan Lt dow 13-4-18 2Mon p244 CR Belgium18,Ivor
OWEN,Iorwerth Roland T2Lt dow 7-5-17 GL &13RFC p11 CR France96,ap Roland
OWEN,James 2Lt dow 20-5-17 5ScotRif p224 MR20
OWEN,John Morris TLtACapt kia 23-4-17 2RWFus p98 CR France593,Capt
OWEN,Leonard Sidney 2Lt kia 20-9-17 19Lond p250 MR29
OWEN,Malcolm de Brissac.MC.LtACapt kia 4-11-18 1Herts p252 CR France206
OWEN,Meredyth T2Lt kia 25-9-15 9WelshR p127 MR19 &CR France260
OWEN,Meurig T2Lt kia 1-8-17 WelshR att9Bn p127 MR29
OWEN,Norman Howell TCapt ded 1-3-19 RASC p267 CR Wales361
OWEN,Norman Moore 2Lt kia 13-9-14 RFA 49Bty p33 MR15
OWEN,Philip Charles T2Lt kia 25-9-15 9 att5KSLI p145 MR29
OWEN,Richard Frank T2Lt kia 30-4-17 102MGC attHamps p184
OWEN,Reginald Frank Leear LtTCapt kia 23-4-17 1Ess att88MGC p132&184 MR20
OWEN,Reginald Mansfield.MID TMaj dow 2-8-16 2 O&BLI p130 CR France141
OWEN,Reuben 2Lt ded 9-11-18 Suff att29Lond p263 CR Essex146
OWEN,Richard Frank T2Lt kia 30-4-17 Hamps att102MGC p121 MR20
OWEN,Rowland Hely Lt kia 18-4-15 3 att2WRid p116 MR29
OWEN,Thomas John 2Lt dow 19-2-17 3 att8RWFus p98 CR Iraq5
OWEN,Thomas John 2Lt kia 8-4-17 29RFC p11 CR France593
OWEN,Thomas Starr T2Lt kia 8-10-18 13RWFus p98 CR France1346
OWEN,Vernon Elias T2Lt dow 29-11-15 9RWFus p98 CR France40
OWEN,Wilfred Edward Salter.MC.Lt kia 4-11-18 5Manch p236 CR France1479
OWEN,William 2Lt dow 27-8-18 16RWFus p98 CR France84
OWEN,William David T2Lt ded 11-10-18 WelshR att15Bn p127 CR France1858
OWEN,William Henry Kenrick.MID TLt dow 1-10-15 9WelshR p127 CR France145
OWEN,William Llewellyn T2Lt dow 12-6-18 KSLI att1/4Bn p145 CR France145
OWEN,William Thomas Lt 14-10-18 213RAF MR20
OWEN,William Vandeleur 2Lt ded 12-11-18 3RScots p54 CR Hamps240
OWEN,Wynne Capt kia 10-3-15 IA 38Dogras att1/39GarhwalRif p281 CR France355 &CR France1887
OWEN-HOLDSWORTH,James Philip.MC.2Lt kld 12-4-18 GL &101RAF p191 C France300
OWEN-JONES,Rhodri Deane Lt bombAcc 5-1-16 IA 36JacobsHorse p281 CR France51,Capt kia
OWENS,Arthur Owen 2Lt kia 22-4-18 15 att16RWFus p98 MR27
OWENS,Charles Arnold TLt dow 10-1-17 13 att10WYorks p82 CR France374
OWENS,Charles Percy.MID ACapt kia 14-4-17 3 att2SWBord p100 CR France162,15-4-17
OWENS,Edward.DCM.2Lt kia 27-6-18 10Ches B'Coy p96 CR France21
OWENS,Frederick Gordon.MID Maj ded 4-10-18 9Lpool p216 CR Egypt2
OWENS,John Philip Edmund 2Lt kia 13-10-15 6NStaffs p238 MR19
OWENS,William 2Lt kia 16-8-17 7RIrRif p170 MR30
OWENS,William Brabazon T2Lt ded 25-6-16 RE 56FC p47 CR Eire168,35FC
OWSTON,William Henry 2Lt dow 23-10-17 4Lincs p217 France32
OXENHAM,Gordon Vincent Lt 27-6-18 1Sqn AustFC MR34
OXLADE,Stanley T2Lt drd 4-5-17 RASC p193 CR Italy14
OXLAND,Nowell TLt kia 10-8-15 6BordR p117 CR Gallipoli5,9-8-15
OXLET,Alan Hayes 2Lt kia 10-12-17 149RFA p33 CR Belgium19
OXLEY,Edith Mary Sister 12-12-18 QAIMNS CR EAfrica101
OXLEY,Fergus Richard ALt kia 20-9-16 GL 10RSuss att1RDubF &TMB p119 CR Belgium4
OXLEY,Harry Alfred Lt kia 21-9-18 4 att10EKent p212 CR France1495
OXLEY,Harry Chamberlain TMaj dow 18-4-18 5SWBord att17NumbF p100
OXLEY,Herman Grant TLt kia 4-11-18 4 att2KRRC p151 CR France190
OXLEY,Malcolm Guy Macdonald 2Lt kia 19-9-17 GL &43RFC p11 CR France92
OXLEY,Richard Stephen T2Lt kia 18-4-18 13RSuss p119 MR30
OXLEY,Robert Duncombe CaptAMaj kia 6-9-16 1 att2GordH p167 MR21
OZANNE,Edward Graeme Capt dow 16-2-15 3RFus p69 CR Belgium59,kia 15-2

P

PACEY,Frederick Carman 2Lt 3-9-18 32 RAF MR20
PACEY,George William 2Lt kia 15-4-18 4Lincs p217 MR30
PACEY,Walter Ernest 2Lt dow 27-6-17 4Yorks p220 CR France518
PACKARD,Henry Norrington.DSO.LtCol kia 12-4-16 RFA p33 CR France1182
PACKARD,Walter Herbert 2Lt kia 15-7-16 4Suff p217 MR21

PACK-BERESFORD,Charles George Maj kia 10-9-14 RWKent p141 MR15,24-8-14
PACKER,Bertram Frith T2Lt kia 19-10-17 9Suff p78 CR France550,23-10-17
PACKER,Gilbert Lt 20-8-19 RE 337 Rd ConstCoy CR Yorks 159
PACKHAM,Eric Frank 2Lt dow 1-11-18 RASC att2Hamp p193 CR Hamps136
PACKMAN,Thomas Alfred Lt kia 10-9-16 RHA att7/8TMB p33 CR France423,9-9-16
PACKWOOD,I.MID Lt 5-1-19 IndianTelDept MR65
PACKWOOD,William Harry 2Lt kia 12-4-18 6RWar p214 MR32
PADDAY,William Hamilton Capt kia 21-12-14 IA 36Sikhs att47 p281 MR28
PADDISAN,Charles Waller Lt&QM kia 29-11-17 1/1LincsYeo p204 CR Palestine9
PADDISON,George Mitford TLt kia 30-7-15 6DCLI D'Coy p114 CR Belgium453
PADDISON,Henry Jepson.MC.2LtACapt kia 16-8-17 4Worc X'Coy p109 CR Belgium106
PADDOCK,Henry Leslie Maj kia 23-3-18 N&D att4ELanc p134 CR France528
PADDOCK,William Francis 2Lt dow 9-4-17 4RFus p69 CR France113
PADGETT,James Philip T2Lt kia 5-5-17 21WYorks p82 CR France97
PADLEY,Percy 2Lt kia 4-11-18 A112RFA p33 CR France231
PAGAN,Gavin Lang Capt kia 28-4-17 15RScots p54 MR20
PAGAN,George Hair Lt kia 30-7-16 1/7BlkW p231 CR France1890
PAGE,Alfred Cecil Dudley T2Lt kia 18-8-16 5 att7Nhampt p138 MR21
PAGE,Arthur Herbert T2Lt kia 19-7-16 8Suff p78 MR21
PAGE,Bernard Robert Lt kia 9-8-16 13Ess p132 MR21
PAGE,Cuthbert Frederick Graham.CMG.DSO.LtCol ded 6-12-19 RGA p262 CR Sussex93
PAGE,Donald Frederick Vincent Lt kia 21-9-18 7Suff &RAF p78 CR France256
PAGE,Dudley Alfred T2Lt dow PoW 14-8-17 Ches &56RFC p11&p96 MR20
PAGE,Francis Trafford 2Lt kia 9-5-15 att2RMunstF p175 MR22
PAGE,Frank.DSO&Bar.LtCol kia 31-7-17 Herts p252 MR29
PAGE,Frank.MC.MM.Capt dow 29-10-17 9Aust LH CR France8
PAGE,Gerald T2Lt dow 9-6-17 33MGC p184 CR France285
PAGE,Henry 2Lt kia 20-7-16 10RWFus p98 CR France744
PAGE,James Horn 2Lt ded 7-10-17 9HLI p240 CR Scot674
PAGE,John Canler 2Lt kia 18-10-16 9Norf p74 CR France307
PAGE,John Kenneth Samuel.MC.Lt dow 21-8-18 9RWar att 1/5LancF p65 CR France643,22-8-18
PAGE,Lionel 2Lt kia 27-5-18 1Worc p109 MR18
PAGE,Lance Stallard March.MIDx2 Lt kia 20-8-18 10EKent &RAF p204&258,Capt CR Iraq8,St.Allard Capt
PAGE,Meaburn Staniland 2Lt kia 21-3-18 4Lincs p217 MR20
PAGE,Raymond Charles 2Lt 24-9-18 8SStaffs CR Staffs57
PAGE,Reginald 2Lt kia 1-7-16 1/6SStaffs p229 MR21
PAGE,Robert Burton Col ded 11-11-14 Staff LancF att7GenBaseDepot p1 CR France85
PAGE,Sydney Durrant Capt kia 19-4-17 1/4Norf p216 CR Palestine8
PAGE,Thomas Spencer T2Lt kia 19-10-16 9Norf att71TMB p74 CR France294
PAGE,Vernon.MC.2Lt dow 23-9-17 D315RFA p33 CR Belgium124,22-9-17
PAGE,Wilfred Frank TCapt dow 28-3-18 Ess att4Bn p132 CR Essex1,Wilfrid
PAGE-GREEN,Reginald Sebastian.MC.T2Lt kia 22-6-17 26RFus p69 CR Belgium154
PAGEN,Wilfred Robert TCapt dow 7-10-16 RAMC att6EKent p197 MR21
PAGET,Albert Edward.MVO.CaptBtLtCol ded 2-8-17 11Huss p22
PAGET,Colin Lt kia 1-9-18 RWar att9Bn p65 MR38
PAGET,Desmond Otho 2Lt kia 21-3-18 KRRC att7Bn p151 CR France1061
PAGET,George Godfrey Brandreth Lt kia 14-9-14 3 att1Nhampt p138 MR15
PAGET,Gerald Lewis Lt kia 13-7-17 RFC p11 MR34
PAGET,John Christopher LtACapt kia 26-4-17 RGA 157SB p41 CR France614
PAGET,Leslie Herbert 2Lt kia 27-9-18 9Manch p237 CR France712
PAGET,Michael Theodore 2Lt kia 17-8-17 3LancF p93 CR Belgium453
PAGET,Samuel James.MID Capt kia 26-3-18 GL attStaff 149InfBde p191 CR France526
PAGET,Wellesley Lyndoch Henr.CB.CMG.MVO.TBrigGen ded 11-6-18 RH&FA p261
PAIBA,Ellis James Alfred TLt kia 20-10-15 15 att2RFus p69 CR Gallipoli4
PAIGE,Jack Brian 2Lt kia 14-6-17 4EKent p212 MR29
PAIN,Edward Davy TCapt kia 18-8-16 6SomLI p80 MR21
PAIN,Wyndham Hackett LtCol 26-9-19 RWSurr CR Surrey134
PAINE,Ernest Louis Evelyn TCapt ded 8-4-17 17Bty MGC Motors p266 CR Palestine2
PAINE,George Gordon.MC.Capt dow 27-3-18 RBerks att6Bn p139 CR France41
PAINE,Harry Arthur 2Lt kia 29-9-18 6N&D p233 CR France375,Auther
PAINE,James Henry.DSO.LtCol kia 25-7-18 Cmdg76RGA p41 CR France209
PAINE,Walter Lionel TCapt&Adjt kia 4-6-15 10RLancs att1LancF p59 CR Gallipoli6

PAINE,William Thomas T2Lt kia 23-8-18 1Beds p86 CR France518
PAINTER,Albert Ernest T2Lt dow 14-4-17 RE 171TC p47 CR France297
PAINTER,Henry Septimus T2Lt kia 29-7-16 16 att12Glouc p107 MR21
PAINTER,John Sigley 2Lt dow 25-4-18 7Worc p226 CR Egypt2,Lt
PAISLEY,George William 2Lt kia 27-12-17 4BlkW p230 CR Palestine3
PAISLEY,Thomas T2Lt kia 25-9-15 10ScotRif p104 MR19
PAKEMAN,Herbert Lt 19-4-17 8Hamps MR34
PAKENHAM,Charles John Wingfield Lt kia 30-4-15 2Hamps p121 MR4
PAKENHAM,Herbert Lt 19-4-17 8Hamps p229
PAKENHAM,John Walter Beaven 2Lt kia 21-9-18 10Lond p248 CR France369
PAKENHAM,Robert Edward Michael Capt dow 17-1-15 2RMunstF p175 CR Lond8
PALARDY,G.2Lt dow 7-5-18 GL &RAF p191
PALETHORPE,Edwin Donald Lt kia 9-10-17 RFA p208 CR Belgium12
PALEY,George Maj kia 31-10-14 RB 1Div Staff p179 CR Belgium58
PALFREE,John William Bateman 2Lt dow 20-9-18 16N&D att8RBerks p134 CR France194
PALFREY,Reginald T2Lt kia 4/5-4-16 9RWar p65 CR Iraq5
PALFREYMAN,A.2Lt dow 9-10-18 RWFus att16Bn p98 CR France906
PALFREYMAN,George Alexander 2Lt kia 26-10-16 3EKent &RFC p3&58 MR20
PALGRAVE-SIMPSON,Evelyn Victor Craig Lt dow 25-11-18 C77RFA CR Lond12
PALIN,Oscar Ernest 2Lt kia 26-10-17 15Lond p249 MR30
PALK,Lawrence Charles Walter.Hon.DSO.TLtCol kia 1-7-16 Cmdg1Hamps p121 CR France643
PALLANT,Herbert Charles Capt ded 21-2-20 IARO attS&TCps p281 CR Asia82
PALLETT,Edward Roy Lt mbk 6-4-18 7RFus p256 CR France252,Capt
PALLING,William Lionel T2Lt kia 15-3-18 8RFus p69 CR France423
PALLISER,John Sylvester.MID Maj kia 9-8-18 5Yorks attMGC Inf p187&220 CR France1170,Silvester
PALMER,Albert Edgar 2Lt kia 27-9-18 8WYorks p82 CR France1483
PALMER,Albert Leslie 2Lt dow 6-3-17 5N&D p233 CR France120
PALMER,Alen Llewellen Maj ded 15-11-16 1WiltsYeo p206 CR France300
PALMER,Ambrose Henry Maj dow 2-5-17 RAMC attStaffsYeo p253 CR Egypt9
PALMER,Arthur Percy.DSO.Capt kia 27-9-15 1WelshGds p53 MR19
PALMER,Bertie William 2Lt dow 25-8-18 8ScotRif p225 CR France1358
PALMER,Cecil Howard.MID MajTLtCol kia 27-7-15 Worc Ex 9RWar p109 MR4,26-7-15
PALMER,Charles TCapt ded 15-1-16 5KSLI p145 CR Eire237
PALMER,Charles Walter 2Lt ded 29-3-16 PoW GL &RFC p3&191 CR France1276
PALMER,David Lt ded 26-2-18 RE IWT p47 MR38
PALMER,David Adams.MC.ACapt dow 25-3-18 3RDubF attTankCps p177&188 CR France177
PALMER,Derek William Onslow TLt kia 4-6-16 10EYork p84 CR France5
PALMER,Edward Anderson 2Lt kia 14-10-18 1Worc p109 CR France1277
PALMER,Edward Charles Maxwell 2Lt kia 23-4-17 13RFus att111TMB p69 MR20
PALMER,Eric George T2Lt kia 4-3-17 3 att2Nhampt p138 CR France439,Lt
PALMER,Francis Reginald T2Lt kia 23-4-17 6Dors p124 CR France531
PALMER,Frederick Edmund Corbett TMaj dow 28-8-15 7Y&L p159 CR Belgium11
PALMER,Geoffrey T2Lt kia 19-11-15 RE 153Coy p47 CR France281
PALMER,Geoffrey Raymond T2Lt kia 30-7-16 10WRid p116 MR21
PALMER,G.H.2Lt 31-10-18 RB CR Somerset186
PALMER,Harry 2Lt kia 27-5-18 8WYorks p219 MR18
PALMER,Henry Edwardes 2Lt dow 5-4-18 5RBerks p139 CR France516
PALMER,Henry John Lt kia 29-3-18 5 att1DCLI p227 MR27
PALMER,Herbert Lt kia 2-10-18 12Lancers p22 CR France375
PALMER,Herbert John TLt dow 21-12-16 RE 121FC p47 CR France285
PALMER,Horace John T2Lt kia 8-8-18 7RSuss p119 CR France247
PALMER,Horace Lewis 2Lt kia 23-10-18 1/4Wilts p236 CR France1477,Harold
PALMER,Hugh Salisbury.MID Capt dow 25-4-18 RAMC FA p254 CR France29
PALMER,John Arthur Stuart 2Lt kia 16-12-17 RGA 343SB p41 CR Belgium20
PALMER,John Stanley Lt dow 18-10-16 2DLI p161 CR France105,2Lt
PALMER,John Walter Edmond 2Lt ded PoW 11-6-18 31MGC Inf p184 CR France1027
PALMER,John William T2Lt dow 25-9-17 12RB p179 CR Belgium16
PALMER,John William Henry TLt kia 20-7-16 20RFus p69 CR France1890
PALMER,Joseph Sidney Herbert 2Lt dow 27-9-16 1LNLancs p136 MR21
PALMER,Leslie Cowper 2Lt kia 26-9-17 4Suff p217 CR Belgium125
PALMER,Leslie Stewart Lt dow 20-9-17 4Dors attMGC Inf p187&229 CR Belgium112
PALMER,Lewis Arthur T2Lt kld 9-11-17 GL &RFC p11 CR Mddx15
PALMER,Percy Eric 2Lt kia 17-7-17 29RFC p11

PALMER,Percy Rogers.MC.2Lt kia 25-5-17 10Leic &55RFC p11&88 CR France421
PALMER,Reginald John Allen.MID Lt dow 22-7-16 1Wilts p153 CR France300
PALMER,Robert Stafford Arthur.Hon.Capt dow PoW 21-1-16 6 att 1/4Hamp p228 MR38
PALMER,Roger Lt dow 13-8-15 2N&D p134 CR France40,2Lt
PALMER,Roland Gaskell Capt kia 25-4-15 2SWBord p100 MR4
PALMER,Ronald William Poulton Lt kia 4-5-15 1/4RBerks p234 CR Belgium53,5-5-15
PALMER,Samuel William Lt kia 27-3-18 10 att 19RDubF p177 MR27
PALMER,Walter Gerard Capt kia 5-3-16 IA 113Inf attRFC p281 MR38
PALMER,Walter Harvey T2Lt kia 23-4-17 17Manch p155 MR20
PALMER,William Henry Eyre Hollingworth Capt ded 26-11-15 20RB p244 MR40
PALMER,William Lucius 2Lt kld 8-5-15 3Mon p244 MR29
PALMER,William Samuel Hudson T2Lt kld 15-9-17 GL &RFC p11 CR Surrey132
PALMES,Guy Nicholas Lt kia 9-5-15 YLI p143 MR29
PALMES,John Philip.MC.Capt kia 1-8-17 3 att 2WYorks p82 MR29
PALMIERI,Alicia Mrs 15-5-17 VAD MR70
PANDFIELD,William Godridge.DCM.2Lt kia 21-8-16 2Worc p109 MR21
PANES,Ernest Philip Morris T2Lt kia 25-9-15 9KRRC p151 MR29
PANK,Adalbert Daniell Lt dow 18-6-15 RE 22FC p47 CR France134,2CavDiv
PANTER-DOWNES,Edward Martin Capt&BtMaj dow 26-8-14 2RIrReg p89 MR15
PANTING,Arnold Clement T2Lt kia 13-1-17 6RMunstF attRFC p175 CR Greece9
PANTON,Arthur William 2Lt kia 3-9-16 RE 234FC p47 CR France339
PANTON,John Gerald.CMG.Col ded 7-12-15 Staff RSuss p1 CR Surrey160
PANZERA,Francis William.CMG.TCol ded 4-6-17 SL p191&268
PAPE,Edmund Rogers 2Lt kia 27-3-18 5Manch p236 MR27
PAPPA,Armaud Francis 2Lt kia 5-5-17 8EYorks p84 MR20
PAPPRILL,Frederick Ernest T2Lt kia 3-6-17 9Leic att 1/4ELanc p88 CR France905,Capt
PAPWORTH,Alfred Wyatt T2Lt kia 2-4-17 RE 129FC p47 CR France480
PARAMORE,Charles Gordon TCapt kia 25-9-15 8RBerks p139 CR France219
PARAMORE,Robert Edward Pynsent Lt kia 23-7-16 1Dev p77 MR21
PARBERRY,Ernest 2Lt kia 27-9-18 13Lpool att 1NumbF p72 CR France,PARBERY
PARBURY,Frederick Nigel Maj kia 9-5-15 20RFA p33 CR France924,10-5-15
PARDOE,George Southey Rev ded 15-10-18 RAChDept p199 CR Palestine3
PARDON,Rolfe Buckland Lt ded 23-11-19 6RRofCav att 13Huss p261 CR Mdd26
PARDY,Thomas Johnston 2Lt dow 7-5-17 4A&SH p173 CR france95
PARDY,William Leslie 2Lt dow 16-9-16 5SLancs p230 CR France,PARDEY
PARE,Charles Percy 2Lt kia 22-3-18 19MGC p185 MR20
PARFITT,Bertram Nowitt 2Lt ded 17-11-18 3Y&L p159 CR Yorks557
PARFITT,Ernest TCapt dow PoW 28-5-17 17Mddx p148 CR Germany3
PARFITT,F.A.2Lt 13-9-18 Y&L CR Yorks557
PARGITER,Henry Cdr ded 26-9-16 IOD p281 CR Iraq6
PARGITER,Reginald Amherst 2Lt kia 10-5-15 3 att 1 Suff p78 MR29,PARGETER 8-5-15
PARGITER,William Herbert TLt kia 12-10-16 24RFA p33 CR France513
PARIS,Harold Graham.MC&Bar.Maj kia 6-10-18 RGA 138HB p41 CR France1461
PARISH,Albert Francis 2Lt kia 18-9-18 3 att 9Ess p132 CR France369
PARISH,Jesse Hugh Lt ded 22-2-19 RGA p255 CR Lond3,28-2-19
PARISH,Robert.DCM.2Lt kia 10-9-16 2NumbF p62 CR Greece3
PARISH,William Harry T2Lt kia 30-11-17 7Norf p74 MR17
PARISOTTI,Luigi Lt kia 2-1-20 IA 4/39GurkhaRif p281 MR43,21-1-20
PARK,Adam St.John Lloyd.MC.Maj kia 21-4-17 A38RFA p33 CR France765,John
PARK,Alexander 2Lt kia 4-11-18 13RB p179 CR France733
PARK,Alexander Crabbe 2Lt dow 29-9-18 46MGC Inf p184 CR France327
PARK,Andrew T2Lt kia 14-7-16 26NumbF p62 MR21 16Bn
PARK,Archibald Kenneth Capt dow 9-5-15 IA 1/10 att 2/2GurkhaRif p281 CR France924
PARK,Frederick Andrew Katchen Lt kia 3-10-18 46MGC Inf p184 CR France1710
PARK,George Alexander T2Lt kia 18-1-18 22RFC p16 CR France31
PARK,Herbert Sidney T2Lt kia 26-10-17 1Bord p117 CR France748
PARK,James Wilfrid Haynes.MID Capt kia 14-1-17 IA 22Cav p281 CR Iraq5
PARK,Victor Herbert Lt ded 4-3-19 2WellingtonR NZEF CR France85
PARK,Walter Williamson Lt kia 2-4-16 1Herts p252 CR France705
PARK,William 2Lt dow 21-3-18 15DLI p161 MR27
PARKE,Allan.MC.Capt kia 27-9-18 9 att 1/8LancF p93 CR France712
PARKE,John Aubrey Lt kia 25-9-15 DLI att 9RB p161 MR29
PARKE,Walter Evelyn Lt kia 13-10-14 DLI p161 CR France193
PARKE,William Henry TCapt kia 15-10-16 6ConnRgrs p172 CR Belgium17
PARKER,Allen Foggett 2Lt kld 31-5-18 1WYorks attRAF p82 CR Yorks294,Lt
PARKER,Alan Capt ded 1-4-17 12RLancs p271 CR C'land&W'land46

PARKER,Alan 2Lt kia 23-9-17 10Lond p248 MR29
PARKER,Albert Alfred.MID Capt kia 25-9-17 A296RFA p207 CR Belgium84
PARKER,Albert Victor 2Lt kia 19-11-16 19Lond p250 MR29
PARKER,Alfred Ernest Capt kia 7-11-14 3BlkW att 2SfthH p129 CR France451
PARKER,Arthur Charles Lt ded 11-9-18 18Huss att 13TankCps p23&188 CR Mddx83
PARKER,Basil Stewart Capt kia 6-8-15 2Hamps p121 CR Gallipoli6
PARKER,Cecil William Hannington Lt kia 27-12-16 WorcR &RFC p3&109 CR France203,Capt
PARKER,Charles Allen.MC.2Lt kld 19-2-18 RFA attRFC p16&33 CR Iraq6
PARKER,Charles Thomas Capt ded 11-7-18 2/4NumbF p213 CR Ches2 Ex 1lincs
PARKER,Colin 2Lt ded 25-10-18 PoW RWFus 3GarBn p98 CR France934
PARKER,Cyril Edmund 2Lt kia 1-1-15 1KRRC p151 MR22
PARKER,Edith Dorothy SpProb ded 7-4-18 QAIMNS p200
PARKER,Edward Thompson T2Lt kia 4-6-15 13WYorks att 1LancF p82 MR15
PARKER,E.K.Matron ded 16-10-16 QAIMNS p200
PARKER,Erasmus Darwin Capt kia 20-3-15 2Manch p155 CR Belgium170
PARKER,Frank Bryan TCapt kld 23-3-19 7 att 6Yorks p91 MR70 &CR Europe180
PARKER,Frederick Neville 2Lt kia 28-4-15 1KRRC p151 CR France80
PARKER,Frederick Richard 2Lt kia 19-7-16 3Wilts p153 MR19
PARKER,Geoffrey 2Lt kia 11-4-17 4 att 10LNLancs p234 MR20
PARKER,George Alec.DSO.MC.Capt kia 27-11-16 Nhampt &RFC p3 MR20
PARKER,George Harvey 2Lt kld 24-3-18 RFC p16 MR20
PARKER,George Hastings Maj kia 19-12-14 1Hamps p121 CR Belgium69
PARKER,George Wilson 2Lt kia 9-10-17 6LancF p221 MR30
PARKER,Gerrard William TLt dow 29-9-15 8Lincs p75 CR France924
PARKER,Gilbert Edmund Anthony Lt kia 10-3-15 3 att 2SStaffs p122 MR22
PARKER,Harold James 2Lt kia 15-4-18 Worc att 2/8 p109 CR France248
PARKER,Harry Prevost England Maj ded 26-2-20 RIrReg Ex 129Baluchis CR Surrey1
PARKER,Henry 2Lt dow 30-4-15 Hamps p121 MR4,Harry Ex 2Worc
PARKER,Herbert John 2Lt kia 27-10-17 RGA 1/1WelshHB p41 CR Belgium115
PARKER,Herbert Proudfoot 2Lt ded 8-10-19 6Lond p271 CR Essex1
PARKER,James TCapt kia 16-6-16 RAMC att 7SomLI p197 CR Belgium4
PARKER,James TLt kia 1-7-16 26NumbF p62 MR21
PARKER,James Stanley Lt kia 9-10-17 7WYorks p218 MR30
PARKER,Jeffery Wimpris TLt kia 7-8-15 RAMC att 11Manch p197 MR4
PARKER,J.H.MajBtLtCol 29-6-18 RMLI CR Surrey37
PARKER,John 2Lt kia 21-7-15 RLancs &RFC p2&59 CR France518
PARKER,John Bradbery LtACapt ded 19-11-18 D84RFA p33 CR Sussex102
PARKER,John Caird T2Lt kia 1-7-17 11Bord p117 CR France293,1-7-16
PARKER,John Ernest Capt kia 8-5-15 12Lond p248 MR29
PARKER,John Norman T2Lt kia 8-9-17 2/6WYorks p82 CR France563
PARKER,John Vincent 2Lt ded 1-9-17 IARO att 112Inf p281 MR65
PARKER,John Womersley.MC.T2Lt dow 13-11-17 3 att 1/5WYorks p82 CR Belgium11
PARKER,Leonard Maj kia 7-1-17 15Huss att 52RFC p11&22 CR France446
PARKER,Leonard George Capt kia 1-9-18 2Ess p132 CR France421,G.L.
PARKER,Leslie Rowland 2Lt kia 29-9-18 1SWBord p100 CR France672
PARKER,Leslie Walter Grosvenor 2Lt dow 20-7-17 6Ess p232 CR France
PARKER,Percy Dolph 2Lt kld 4-1-18 4RRofCav &RFC p16&23 CR Essex210
PARKER,Ralph Windsor Capt dow 28-3-18 3GrenGds p50 CR France225
PARKER,Robert Burton Capt kia 19-9-14 Nhampt p138 MR15
PARKER,Ronald Elphinstone Lt kia 9-9-14 RHA D'Bty p33 CR France1445,8-9-14
PARKER,Rupert Hardy Lt kia 2-12-17 2Lincs p75 MR30
PARKER,Samuel Lt&QM ded 1-11-15 5Norf p216 CR Europe23
PARKER,Sidney T2Lt kia 30-3-17 7ESurr p113 CR France1182
PARKER,Thomas 2Lt ded 11-12-18 2/4RWSurr att 2/22Lond p212 CR Egypt1
PARKER,Thomas Cowper Lt kia 12-10-17 W'land&C'landYeo att 7BordR p206 MR30
PARKER,Thomas Geoffrey Milsome TCapt ded 3-11-18 GL RAMC p191 CR Hamps17
PARKER,Victor Lt ded 5-3-16 1RFA p208 CR Belgium11
PARKER,Walter Henry LtACapt kia 15-6-17 RFus att 2/4Lond p69 CR France148
PARKER,Wilfred Horsley 2Lt kia 9-5-15 2RMunstF p175 MR22
PARKER,Wilfrid Ernest T2Lt kia 8/9-5-17 15RWar p65 MR20
PARKER,William T2Lt dow 31-12-17 10WYorks p82 CR France398
PARKER,William Brabazon Hallowes TLt dow 25-4-16 14 att 8Ches p96 CR Iraq8
PARKER,William George John.DCM.2Lt ded 10-10-18 23Coy H'TankCps p188 CR Lond5

PARKER,William Harold.MC.Lt kia 26-4-18 3Worc p109 MR30
PARKER,William Lefevre Oxley Lt kia 31-10-17 11Huss att13RFC p12&22 MR20
PARKER,William Mackworth Capt&Adj kia 30-7-15 RB att8Bn p179 MR29
PARKER-JERVIS,C.E.LtCol 10-4-18 DLI CR Yorks230
PARKER-SMITH,Wilmot Babington Lt dow 12-9-15 1/3ScotHorse p205 CR Europe1
PARKES,Henry Gordon 2Lt kia 4-6-15 6 att4Worc p109 MR4
PARKES,Horace Frederick.MID 2Lt kia 12-3-15 1RWFus p98 MR22
PARKES,James Arthur Capt 29-3-17 3DLI CR Lancs34
PARKES,James Eric 2Lt kia 20-7-17 RE 69FC p47 CR France581
PARKES,Percy Reginald 2Lt dow PoW 4-4-18 18Lond D'Coy p250 CR France716
PARKES,Robert Lionel T2Lt kia 7-10-16 9RFus p69 MR21,Richard
PARKES,Samuel James 2Lt 13-8-18 205RAF MR20
PARKES,Theodore David TLtACapt kia 5-10-17 1SStaffs p122 MR30
PARKHOUSE,Frank Mayfield T2Lt kia 23-4-17 1Mddx p148 CR France434
PARKHOUSE,Oscar Lt ded 19-11-18 4Dev p220 CR Kent180
PARKHURST,George Henry 2Lt kia 3-6-18 3Manch att2/8Worc p155 CR France1693
PARKIN,Absalom Sydney 2Lt kia 3-5-17 15WYorks p82 MR20
PARKIN,Arthur LtCol kia 25-9-15 7Nhampt p138 MR19,27-9-15
PARKIN,George Frederic T2Lt kia 9-4-17 12WYorks p82 MR20
PARKIN,James Dowell 2Lt dow 27-5-18 DLI p161 MR18
PARKIN,Joseph Henry T2Lt kia 18-6-17 RE 529FC p47 MR20
PARKIN,Thomas Gregory T2Lt kia 9-8-15 6Lincs B'Coy p75 CR Gallipoli5
PARKIN,Thomas Henry LtTCapt dow 4-10-18 Lpool p72 CR France25,Lt 2/21MGC
PARKINSON,Albert 2Lt kia 9-4-18 Lpool att1/5Bn p72 MR19
PARKINSON,Alfred.MC.T2LtACapt kia 12-5-17 21Manch p155 CR France568
PARKINSON,Alfred Louis T2Lt ded 3-6-18 4ResCav att2DGds p23 CR Lancs2
PARKINSON,George Hartley Lt kia 13-4-18 6Norf p217 MR30
PARKINSON,Gilbert Maurice Capt ded 14-11-18 1NumbF att33ItalyDiv p62 CR Italy16
PARKINSON,Horace James Ankers 2Lt dow 1-7-17 4Leic p220 CR War97
PARKINSON,James Herring T2Lt kia 2-7-16 8Lincs p75 MR21
PARKINSON,Joe Anthony Francis Lt kia 13-10-14 Dors p124 MR22
PARKINSON,Leslie Gerard.MC.Maj kia 24-4-17 1/4Glouc p225 CR France365
PARKINSON,Oswald Wright 2Lt kia 1-2-17 3 att6ELancs p111 MR38
PARKINSON,Richard Frank.MC.MID Capt ded 7-11-18 RE 7FldTrp p47 MR38
PARKINSON,Thomas 2Lt kia 12-9-18 6RWFus p223 CR France415
PARKS,George Edwin Harold Lt dow 12-10-18 GL 12Manch p191 CR France1393,kia
PARKS,John Wynard.MC.Capt dow 12-8-19 1ELancs p255 CR Kent102
PARKS,William Francis.MID LtACapt ded 22-12-18 263RFA p33 CR Egypt9
PARKYN,William James 2Lt dow 12-10-18 6WRid p227 CR France214
PARLE,John Audley.MC.2LtACapt kia 30-11-17 12Lpool p72 CR France660
PARMENTER,Gordon William 2Lt kia 26-8-16 6 att12RB p179 CR France513
PARMETER,Francis Robert Bircham LtCol ded 16-10-19 LabCps p266 CR Surrey162,6-10-19
PARNELL,Geoffrey Brooke TMaj kia 15-7-16 1RWSurr p56 CR France4353
PARNELL,John Atherton Parnell TLt kia 8-9-16 1Glouc p107 CR France453,PARNELL PARNELL,J.A.
PARNELL,Leslie Reginald Lt kia 9-10-17 13Lond att2/4ELancsp249 MR30
PARNELL,Mervyn Edmund Capt kia 1-12-17 IA 36Horse p281 CR France417
PARNELL,William Alastair Damer.Hon.MC.Lt kia 25-9-16 att2GrenGds 4Coy SR p50 CR France374
PARR,Bertram Chambré Maj kia 3-9-18 O&BLI att2SStaffs p130 CR France1484
PARR,Denis Fillingham 2Lt kia 7-7-16 10N&D p134 MR21
PARR,Edgar Brian T2Lt dow 21-10-16 11SLancs p125 CR France188
PARR,George Roworth Lt kia 19-12-14 1SomLI p80 CR Belgium70
PARR,Hugh Wharton Myddleton Lt kld 15-5-15 5SStaffs p229 CR Belgium43
PARR,Jackson Webster 2Lt dow 29-3-18 YLI att2/4Bn p143 CR France169
PARR,Wilfred Alexander 2Lt kia 3-5-17 4RFus p69 MR20
PARR,Wilfred Wharton.MC.Capt kia 8-5-17 12Glouc p107 MR20
PARR-DUDLEY,John Huskisson T2Lt kia 1-7-16 11RFus p69 CR France397
PARR-DUDLEY,Walter 2Lt kia 5-4-18 9RFus p69 MR27
PARRIS,Walter Frederick 2Lt kia 15-3-15 3Mddx p148 CR Belgium17,PARRISS
PARRISH,George Lewis 2Lt kld 11-1-18 RFC p16
PARRISH,Harry Thorburn.MC.2Lt dow 23-11-18 Dors att6Bn p124 CR France13
PARROTT,Amy Maud Augusta Sister 24-10-18 VAD CR SAfrica53
PARROTT,Dennis Hele Lt kia 30-4-18 2/17Lond p250 CR Palestine3
PARROTT,Lionel Overton 2Lt kia 7-8-18 19RFA p33 CR France184

PARRY,Claude Frederick Pilkington.DSO.LtCol kia 20-8-18 34RFA p33 CR France745
PARRY,David Thomas 2Lt dow 24-3-17 1/5ELancs att5War p226 CR France145
PARRY,Donald George de Courcy LtAMaj kia 5-4-18 D78RFA p33 CR France41
PARRY,Francis Alexander.MC.Maj kia 27-9-18 16RWar p65 CR France415
PARRY,Frank Marden LtCol ded 2-12-19 RAMC p267 CR Mddx23
PARRY,Frank Meredith T2Lt kia 15-9-16 15Hamps p121 CR France277
PARRY,G.O.Lt 14-4-20 RWFus CR Wales497
PARRY,Harold T2Lt kia 6-5-17 17KRRC p151 CR Belgium4
PARRY,Henry Maysmor Lt dow 11-3-18 2/10Mddx p236 CR Palestine3,Maysmore
PARRY,James Hywell TLt dow 5-9-17 10RWFus p98 CR France512,Hywel
PARRY,John Stanley T2Lt kia 14-7-16 15 att13Lpool p72 MR21
PARRY,Norman Cecil Lt kia 27-7-15 3Y&L p159 CR Belgium96
PARRY,Robert 2Lt dow 26-3-17 1/7RFus CR Palestine8
PARRY,Robert 2Lt dow 23-3-18 7RWFus p223
PARRY,Robert Stephenson T2Lt dow 23-10-17 20LancF p93 CR Belgium106
PARRY,S.2Lt kld 3-5-18 RE &RAF p47
PARRY,Thomas Ellis T2Lt kia 23-10-16 2LancF p93 MR21
PARRY,Wilfred Seaton Bagott T2Lt kia 24-11-15 D53RFA p33 CR Belgium166
PARRY,William Henry Liddon T2Lt dow 29-11-16 24RFus p69 CR France1
PARRY,William Norman Maule 2Lt dow PoW 19-8-17 3Lond p246 CR Belgium140,Lt
PARRY-DAVIES,David Christopher T2Lt dow 10-5-16 9 att2SWBord p100 CR France167,6Bn
PARRY-JONES,Owen Guy.MID Capt dow 29-9-16 RAMC att3Suff p197 CR France74
PARSICK,Charles Edmund Lt sInflictGunshot 28-2-20 IARO att99LabCps p281 MR43
PARSLOE,William Henry.MC.TCapt kia 8-11-18 7Lincs p75 CR France930
PARSLOW,A.J.Lt&QM 7-4-15 RE CR Ireland14
PARSLOW,Albert Jack 2Lt dow 10-10-16 9Lond p248 CR France105
PARSLOW,William Hunt ACapt dow 10-8-18 1Lond p245 CR France69
PARSON,Ernest Edward.MC.TLt dow 1-6-17 124RFA p33 CR France1184
PARSONS,Alfred Cyril Lt kia 29-3-18 3 att1SomLI p80 CR France53,Capt
PARSONS,Alfred Ernest 2Lt kia 3-5-17 4RFus p69 MR20
PARSONS,Alfred Henry Capt kia 8-3-16 IA 2/9GurkhaRif p281 MR38
PARSONS,Algernon George Maj kia 26-4-18 C149RFA p33 CR Belgium11
PARSONS,Arthur Oscar 2Lt dow 26-3-18 5DLI p239 CR France225
PARSONS,Beresford Frank T2Lt kld 23-1-17 GL &RFC p12 CR War10
PARSONS,Desmond Clere LtTCapt kia 15-9-16 2IrGds p53 CR France374
PARSONS,Douglas Montgomery.MID 2Lt kia 10-3-15 RE 5FC p47 MR22
PARSONS,Edgar Vincent Peter 2Lt dow 26-4-18 5 att2Worc p109 MR30
PARSONS,Edward Daniel TLt dow 20-9-15 RAMC p197 CR Surrey57,Daniell
PARSONS,Eric King TCapt kia 15-9-16 9RB p179 MR21
PARSONS,Ernest T2Lt ded 23-7-16 11WRid att1WelshR p116 CR Greece7,24-7-16
PARSONS,Forrest Gale 2Lt kia 26-10-16 RFC p3 MR20
PARSONS,George Jonathan 2Lt dow 31-8-18 4RFus p69 CR France103
PARSONS,Gilbert Newstead 2Lt kia 5-3-17 10Mddx att2RBerks p236 MR21
PARSONS,Hardy Falconer.VC.T2Lt kia 21-8-17 1/2 att14Glouc p107 CR France363
PARSONS,Herbert Lt kia 14-4-17 5 att10WYorks p218 MR20
PARSONS,Herbert T2Lt kia 14-7-16 2RScots p54 MR21
PARSONS,Herbert Mersfield 2Lt kia 13-4-18 50MGC Inf p185 MR32,Hubert Merefield mbk
PARSONS,Kenneth Templeton Jerrard TCapt ded 14-8-17 6RIrRif p170 CR Greece9
PARSONS,Leo Bernard T2Lt kia 12-8-16 EKent p58 CR France164
PARSONS,Maurice Harry Donne TCapt kia 18-7-16 O5RFA p33 CR France1887
PARSONS,P.H.Maj 27-4-20 LondScot CR Surrey9
PARSONS,Samuel Reginald Lt kia 9-4-17 2Wilts p153 CR France214
PARSONS,Septimus Eric Capt kld 14-4-18 8RWar p214 CR France248,kia
PARSONS,Walter Douglas 2Lt kia 13-4-18 7WRid p228 MR30
PARSONS,William Douglas Reynolds 2Lt kia 26-5-18 16RWSurr p56 CR Belgium36,Lt 11Bn See REYNOLDS-PARSONS
PARSONS,William Josiah Capt ded 27-10-18 5RLancs p213 CR Lancs80
PARSONS-SMITH,Eustace Macartney Capt ded 25-5-19 RAMC attEgyptArmy p197 CR EAfrica16,Maj
PARTEUR,William Raymond.MC.LtAMaj kia 10-7-17 102RFA p33 MR29
PARTINGTON,Cyril Walter 2Lt kld 30-8-18 1RWar att22RAF p65 CR France788,Lt
PARTINGTON,Harry 2Lt dow 25-8-18 5LancF att2/4Y&Lp221 CR France226

PARTINGTON,John Bertram Capt kia 3-2-17 4Dev p220 CR Iraq5
PARTINGTON,Leigh Capt kia 28-3-18 1NumbF p62 MR20
PARTON,Roland Thomas T2Lt dow 21-11-17 GL O&BLI att1/10Lond p191 CR Egypt1
PARTRIDGE,Alec John 2Lt kia 3-7-16 9 att5RBerks p139 MR21
PARTRIDGE,Ernest William T2Lt kia 19-11-15 5KSLI p145 CR Belgium84
PARTRIDGE,Geoffrey Dorman Lt kia 3-11-14 2WelshR p127 MR29
PARTRIDGE,Henry Treneman Lt kia 14-7-18 1/4RSuss attRAF p228&258 CR Egypt9,kld
PARTRIDGE,Hugh Roger.MC&Bar.Capt kia 24-7-18 RAMC 1/1WRidFA p254 CR Belgium188
PARTRIDGE,James Henry.MC.2Lt kia 24-3-18 1 att9RIrF p171 MR27
PARTRIDGE,Oswald 2Lt ded 22-10-18 RASC p193 MR41
PARTRIDGE,Richard Crawshay Bailey.MC.Capt kia 28-9-18 ShropYeo p205 CR France756
PARTRIDGE,Robert Charles Capt kia 8-9-14 5DragGds p21 CR France1451
PARTRIDGE,Robert Henry Capt kld 4-9-17 1/5Norf p216 CR Palestine9
PARTRIDGE,Wilfred Issell.MID Lt kia 24-4-17 10Dev p77 MR37
PASCALL,Paul Mervyn.MC.Lt 13-1-18 Mddx att1/2KAR CR EAfrica10 &CR Tanzania1
PASCO,John Crawford Claud 2Lt kia 4-9-18 15Hamps p121 CR Belgium111
PASCOE,Basil Conquest.MC.ACapt&Adj kia 27-5-18 2RB att25InfBdeHQ p179 CR France1753
PASCOE,Eric John 2Lt kia 14-4-17 GL &29RFC p12 CR France783
PASCOE,Frank Guy Buckingham T2Lt kia 2-7-17 9RIrF att53RFC p12&171 MR20
PASCOE,James Sidney.DSO.MIDx2 Maj 28-12-20 RAMC MR65
PASHBY,Frank Edwin 2Lt dow 13-4-18 RBerks att53RAF p139 CR Belgium11
PASHLEY,Eric Clowes.MID 2Lt kia 17-3-17 24RFC p12 CR France699
PASHLEY,Herbert Dudley 2Lt kld 25-12-16 29BallSect RFC p3 CR France397
PASK,Isaac Arthur James.DSO.MC.Capt kia 1-9-16 28RFA p33 CR France397
PASLEY,George Gerald T2Lt kld 19-12-17 RFC p12 CR Eire537
PASLEY,Thomas Edward Sabine 2Lt kia 11-4-18 1KOSB p102 MR32
PASLEY,William Ewart 2Lt kia 17-6-18 4SLancs att1/4LNLancs p230 CR France106
PASLOW,Alfred John Lt&QM ded 7-4-15 RE p262
PASS,Alfred Ernest 2Lt kia 26-8-18 10WRid p116
PASS,Charles Eric 2Lt kia 1-4-17 5BordR p228 CR France672
PASS,Joseph Albert Capt dow 20-5-15 19Lond p250 CR France80
PASSINGHAM,Edward George.MC.Lt 3-5-17 1NumbF p62 MR20
PASSMAN,Kenelm Granby Lt kia 30-8-18 12Suff p78 CR France927
PASSMORE,Arthur William 2Lt kia 4-4-16 9RWSurr p56 MR19
PASSMORE,John Edmund Saunders Capt ded 21-5-16 RAMC p271
PASSY,Cyril Hobart Deare Lt kia 8-3-16 IA 24Punjabis att53Sikhs p281 MR38
PASSY,DeLacy Wolrich Maj dow 12-8-15 IA 25Punjabis att8NumbF p281 CR Gallipoli1,Woolrich kia
PASSY,Logan Deare Capt kia 21-10-15 1DCLI p114 CR France279
PASTEUR,William Raymond.MC.Capt kia 10-7-17 D102RFA CR Belgium15
PASTFIELD,James Thomas Robinson 2Lt kia 21-12-14 5Mddx attNumbF p148 MR22,2-12-14
PASTFIELD,Joseph Victor Robinson Lt kia 9-9-18 5 att13Mddx p148 CR France10
PATCH,Aubrey Melchior William 2Lt kia 16/18-8-16 3 att8RLancs p59 MR21
PATCH,Henry Capt dow PoW 19-10-17 4SLancs attRFC p19&229 CR Belgium140
PATCH,Vernon Lane 2Lt kld 20-11-17 2/4WRid p227 CR France755
PATCHETT,William Ernest TLt kia 25-9-15 1CamH p168 MR19
PATE,George Clarence 2Lt kia 18-9-18 7Lpool p215 CR France530
PATEL,M.B.Lt 20-12-15 IMS att7Rajputs CR Iraq6
PATEMAN,Henry Lewis 2Lt kia 6-2-17 GL &15RFC p12 CR France41
PATER,Hugh 2Lt kld 17-4-17 3WYorks attRFC p12&82 CR Durham28
PATERSON,Alan Foster TLt kia 1-7-16 Mddx att2RFus p148 MR21
PATERSON,Alexander 2Lt kia 13-7-18 5ScotRif p224 MR30
PATERSON,Alistair Finlay 2Lt dow 5-6-15 4CamH D'Coy p243 CR France145
PATERSON,Andrew Melville.CBE.LtCol ded 13-2-19 RAMC p267 CR Lincs1
PATERSON,Arthur Cecil 2Lt kia 22-4-18 1/2 att19DLI p161 CR France296
PATERSON,Arthur Stanley Lt dow 2-10-18 8DCLI p114 CR Greece6
PATERSON,Charles 2Lt kia 28-6-15 4RScots p211 MR4
PATERSON,Charles James.MID Capt dow 1-11-14 1SWBord p100 CR Belgium57
PATERSON,Colin Campbell Lt kia 11-4-17 6CamH p168 MR20
PATERSON,David William Stewart 2Lt ded 20-6-16 RFC p3 CR France518
PATERSON,Douglas William 2Lt dow 31-3-18 1Bord p117 CR Belgium3
PATERSON,Edward Labarte 2Lt dow 23-10-18 10Lpool p216 CR France769
PATERSON,Frank T2Lt kia 1-7-16 9 att1KOSB p102 MR21
PATERSON,Gavin 2Lt ded 21-1-15 9RScotF p95 CR Scot810

PATERSON,Hugh Trevor T2Lt ded 13-5-16 10Suff p78 CR France40
PATERSON,Iain Rose 2Lt kia 12-10-17 3 att6CamH p168 MR30,att5Bn
PATERSON,Isla Scott.MC.Lt kia 1-11-17 4/5BlkW p231 CR Belgium21
PATERSON,J.H.2Lt 24-9-18 3 att1Ess CR France34
PATERSON,James 2Lt dow 20-9-17 8ScotRif p225 CR Belgium18
PATERSON,James.MC.ACapt ded 25-3-19 2ScotGds p262 CR Lond14
PATERSON,Jessie Jane SNurse ded 29-9-16 TFNS p254 CR Greece9
PATERSON,John Herbert Lt 21-6-18 IA 19Lancers &21RAF CR Egypt9
PATERSON,John Jamieson 2Lt kia 21-9-18 18 att10KSLI p145 CR France1495
PATERSON,Lamont Livingstone 2Lt kia 1-9-18 8Lond p247 CR France786
PATERSON,Leslie Arnott 2Lt dow 16-5-15 3Ess attRBerks p132 CR Herts72
PATERSON,Norman Keith TLt kia 29-6-16 A124RFA p33 CR France501
PATERSON,Robert Denzil TLt kia 12-10-16 20Lpool p72 CR France432
PATERSON,Robert Sanderson 2Lt kia 11-3-15 62RFA p33 MR22
PATERSON,Robert Walker.MC.MID 2Lt kia 21/23-3-18 2N&D p134&257 MR20,21-3-18
PATERSON,Stuart T2Lt dow 19-10-16 9KOSB att21MGC Inf p185 CR France389
PATERSON,Thomas Simpson Lt kia 10-11-16 RGA 95SB p209 CR France293
PATERSON,Wallace Campbell T2Lt kia 17-2-16 RE 173TC p47 CR France178
PATERSON,Walter Edward Wadbrook T2Lt ded 26-11-18 RFA p33 CR Kent217
PATERSON,Walter Herbert TLtCol kia 20-4-15 ESurr p113 CR Belgium165
PATERSON,Walter James 2Lt dow 30-10-17 4CamH p243 CR France113
PATERSON,William T2Lt kia 10-8-17 RE 92FC p47 MR29
PATERSON,William 2Lt kia 20-11-17 5 att6Sfth p241 CR France1498
PATERSON,William Brown.MC.2Lt kia 28-4-17 3 att13Ess p132 MR20
PATERSON,William Charles Dawson 2Lt kia 25-9-16 6RScots p211 CR France39
PATERSON,William Paterson TCapt kia 30-7-16 3 att2KOSB p102 MR21
PATERSON,William Wilson 2Lt kia 15-7-16 9HLI p240 MR21
PATERSON-BROWN,Ian Murray 2Lt kia 2-8-16 3A&SH p173 CR Belgium23
PATEY,Edward 2LtACapt kia 2-8-17 5 att3RB p180 MR29
PATEY,Robert Thomas.MC.LtACapt kia 20-5-17 1Lpool p72 CR France434
PATMAN,Harold George 2Lt kia 31-7-17 12RFus p69 MR29
PATON,David Moir Lt kia 24-9-17 GL &66RFC p12 MR20
PATON,Edward Kesson T2Lt dow 3-5-17 54MGC p185 MR20
PATON,George Alexander Lechmere 2LtTCapt kia 7/11-8-15 8NumbF p62 CR Gallipoli5,10-8-15
PATON,George Cyril Olquin TLt kldacc 20-6-16 9RScotF p95 CR Scot119,Olgui
PATON,George Henry Tatham.VC.MC.LtACapt kia 1-12-17 4GrenGds p50 CR France662
PATON,Henry Forsyth T2Lt ded 4-6-17 GL &21RFC p12 MR20
PATON,James Hill T2Lt ded 19-3-19 MGC Inf p266 CR Scot674
PATON,James Ley 2Lt kia 13-10-15 3 att1BlkW p129 MR19
PATON,John Edward.MID 2Lt kld 31-12-14 2Mon p244 CR Belgium33
PATON,John Marvin 2Lt kia 21-3-18 RE DivSigCo p47 CR France1182
PATON,Joseph Train Lt kia 30-5-18 5 att1RScotF p222 CR France33
PATON,Leslie 2Lt kia 21-3-17 11RScots p54 MR20
PATON,Malcolm David Rutter 2Lt dow 12-6-17 22Lond attRFC p19&251 CR France285
PATON,Morton Brown TCapt kia 7-8-15 10SLancs att6LancF p125 MR4
PATON,Norman Macalister 2Lt dow 16-7-17 3 att1GordH p167 CR France512
PATON,Robert 2Lt kia 23-10-18 4RScotF p222 CR France292,24-10-18
PATON,Thomas Howard Moore T2Lt ded 30-6-17 39LabCps p189
PATON,Walter 2Lt kia 26-10-17 LNLancs att2/5Bn p136 CR Belgium126,dow
PATON,Walter Stone T2Lt kia 1-7-16 11Bord p117 CR France293
PATON,William George TCapt kia 14-6-18 10ScotRif p104 CR France423
PATRICK,David Balfour T2Lt kia 18-7-16 11HLI att28MGC p163&185 MR21
PATRICK,Horace.DCM.2Lt kia 13-1-16 Leic p263 MR38
PATRICK,John Bonthrone 2Lt kia 12-7-15 1/4KOSB p224 MR4
PATRICK,Keith 2Lt kia 15-9-16 6HLI att4NumbF p240 2Entries CR France239
PATRICK,T.W.2Lt 25-5-19 EAULGravesRegistn CR EAfrica38 &CR Tanzania1
PATRIDGE,Basil George Nicholas Benedick 2Lt kldacc 27-1-15 IARO att2Rajput p281 CR Egypt7,Benedict
PATRY,Hubert Francis 2Lt kld 13-9-14 NStaffs p157&265,ded CR Camb16
PATTEN,Charles Hill.MID Capt dow 3-10-16 1A&SH p173 CR Greece4
PATTEN,Francis Hope 2Lt kld 15-1-18 RFC p16 CR Scot237
PATTEN,Murray Gladstone.MC.Capt kia 14-4-18 9NumbF p62 MR32
PATTERSON,Alan Capt kia 14-3-16 71RFA p33 CR France554
PATTERSON,Arnott Andrew T2Lt dow 9-11-16 6Bord att34RFC p3&117 CR France882
PATTERSON,Arthur Henry Lt kia 14-10-18 RInnisF att109TMB p105 CR Belgium157

PATTERSON,Aubrey Frederick Albert T2Lt dow PoW 25-9-16 GL &RFC p3&191 CR France598
PATTERSON,Charles Capt ded 20-1-15 3LancF p93 CR Yorks361,19-1-15
PATTERSON,Charles Alfred Capt dow 8-10-16 5NumbF p213 CR France145
PATTERSON,Charles Cox Capt kia 21-10-16 1Ches p96 MR19
PATTERSON,Charles William Ernest Lt ded 12-2-19 RGA 503SB p41 CR France63
PATTERSON,Christian Bingley 2Lt kia 30-12-16 IARO att1/1GurkhaRif p281 CR Iraq5,Lt
PATTERSON,Douglas David John 2Lt kia 16-4-18 7SfthH p165 CR Belgium74
PATTERSON,George Capt kia 13-10-15 RE p210 MR19
PATTERSON,George Beatty 2Lt dow 22-6-18 D168RFA 32Div p34 CR France169,Beattie
PATTERSON,George Gordon 2Lt kia 25-9-16 7Lpool p215 MR21
PATTERSON,Hugh Cecil Lt kia 30-4-17 4Beds att38RFC p12&86 CR France120
PATTERSON,John Agar 2Lt kia 30-11-14 2Beds p86 MR29
PATTERSON,John Hylton TLt kia 1-7-16 23NumbF p62 MR21
PATTERSON,John Keppel Priuli TLt dow 26-12-17 9ESurr p113 CR Sussex57
PATTERSON,Kenneth Scott 2Lt dow PoW 6-12-17 92RFA p34 CR France716,7-12-17
PATTERSON,Philip Leslie T2Lt kia 4-6-16 1NStaffs p157 CR Belgium97
PATTERSON,Robert Arthur 2Lt kia 12-4-17 6RB p180 CR France452
PATTESON,John Dossie 2Lt kia 13-10-14 5DragGds p21 CR France705
PATTINSON,Edwin Potter Lt kia 3-5-17 5YLI p235 MR20
PATTINSON,Ernest 2Lt kia 31-7-17 4 att1N&D p134 MR29
PATTINSON,George Foster 2Lt kia 27-5-18 DLI p161 MR18
PATTINSON,Hugh Lee Capt&Adj kia 4-8-15 3 att9RFus p69 CR France922
PATTINSON,Tom TLt ded 21/22-12-18 GL RE IWT p267 CR Iraq8,22-12-18
PATTINSON,William Graham TLt kia 25-4-17 76MGC p185 CR France531
PATTISON,James 2Lt 27-2-19 10HLI CR Scot812
PATTISON,John Herbert Lt accKld 21-6-18 IARO attRFC p281
PATTISON,John Howell Maj kia 28-4-15 RFA 26Bty 17Bde p34 MR4,PATTISSON
PATTISON,Peterswald Lt ded 22-2-16 RAMC p267 CR Scot253
PATTISON,Robert Capt kia 27-12-17 2/10Lond D'Coy p248 MR30
PATTISON,Robert Macfie 2Lt kia 28-6-15 8ScotRif p225 MR4
PATTON,C.R.Capt 6-11-18 RAMC CR Devon47
PATTON,David 2Lt dow 11-2-18 8 att2ScotRif p225 CR Belgium11
PATTRICK,Arthur Deverus Capt kia 12-8-16 5Norf p216 MR4
PATTRICK,John Harry 2Lt kia 30-11-17 Mddx att8Bn p148 MR17,PATRICK
PATTULLO,Hugh James Lt dow 30-9-18 28RFA p34 CR Belgium126,29-9-18
PATTULLO,Ronald Campbell 2Lt 15-9-18 204RAF MR20
PATULLE,Arthur J.WO ded 20-10-17 RIM p281
PAUL,Alexander Charles T2Lt dow 2-10-17 11RIrRif p170 CR France398
PAUL,Arthur Reginald 2Lt kia 22-1-18 20RAF p16 CR Belgium140
PAUL,Courtenay Talbot Saint.DSO.MID MajALtCol dow 31-7-17 36/45RFA p34 CR Belgium19
PAUL,Edgar.MC.Capt&Adj dow 10-9-18 1SomLI p80 CR France95
PAUL,Edgar Newton TLtACapt kia 28-12-17 6 att12KRRC p151 MR30
PAUL,Ernest Kenneth Montcrieff.MC.2Lt dow 18-4-18 RGA 252SB p41 CR France100
PAUL,Gavin 2Lt kia 30-10-14 2DragGds p21 MR29
PAUL,Herbert James T2Lt kia 20-11-17 12KRRC p151 MR17
PAUL,Jeffery William Ensor 2Lt kia 27-7-16 6 att1KRRC p151 MR21
PAUL,John Andrew Bowring.MC.T2Lt kia 10-10-16 10 att7ESurr p113 MR21
PAUL,Laird Irvine Cassan.MC.CaptAMaj dow 12-8-17 D82RFA p34 CR Belgium7
PAUL,Philip Reid Lt kia 1-10-18 BlkW att8Bn p129 MR30
PAUL,Thomas Bond Lt ded 19-9-15 IA IMS p281 CR Iraq6
PAUL,Thomas Guthrie 2Lt kia 9-4-17 25NumbF p62 CR France265
PAUL,William.DSO.MC.LtACapt dow 1-12-17 1WYorks p82 CR France398
PAUL,William Edgar TCapt kia 31-7-17 8RScotF p95 MR29
PAULET,Cecil Henry 2Lt kia 27-2-16 1/1DorsYeo p203 CR Egypt6,26-2-16
PAULET,Henry Monmouth Basing Lt ded /-/-19 Glouc p264
PAULINE,Victor Reginald 2Lt kia 8-5-18 GL &23RAF p191 CR France134
PAULING,George Francis.MC.Lt kia 25-3-18 3GrenGds p50 CR France924
PAULL,Bryan Dolphin 2Lt kia 30-9-16 RIrRif att8ESurr p170 CR France246,Capt
PAULL,Frederick Major T2Lt kia 27-11-15 14 att9N&D p134 CR Gallipoli4
PAULL,Henry Baynham 2Lt dow 21-8-16 6DCLI C'Coy p114 CR France833
PAULSON,John Sydney 2Lt kia 17-9-14 2LancF p93 CR France874
PAUS,Oscar Lionel T2Lt dow 29-7-17 16WYorks p82 CR France95
PAUSCH,Arthur Walter Lt 16-7-18 GL &RAF CR France792
PAVITT,Charles Frederick.MC.Capt ded 17-8-18 RASC p193&259
PAVITT,Reginald James Lt kia 9-8-15 10EKent p204 CR France247 Ex Suss

PAWLE,Bertram TCapt kia 30-7-15 8RB p180 MR29
PAWLE,Derek Weatherall Capt kia 29-4-15 Bord att2NigR p117 CR WAfrica52
PAWLE,Malcolm Gerald TCapt ded 27-6-17 2BedsGarBn p86 MR67
PAWLEY.R.J.2Lt ded 28-11-18 RGA 92SB p41 CR Sussex200
PAWSEY,Harold Charles 2Lt kia 18-8-16 4Suff p217 CR France432
PAWSON,G.St.V.MC.Lt ded 6-11-18 Wmoreld&CumbYeo &RAF p206
PAXTON,Archibald Francis Campbell 2Lt kia 1-7-16 4Mddx p148 CR France267
PAXTON,Edward Hayton Capt ded 15-2-18 RDC p271 CR Staffs125
PAXTON,Gerald Arthur 2Lt kia 10-8-18 6RSuss att17RAF p228&258 CR Greece1
PAXTON,James William 2Lt kia 21-3-18 15RScot p54 MR20
PAXTON,Robert Michael Mill 2Lt kia 1-1-17 RGA 155SB p41 CR France347
PAXTON,Samuel Turven 2Lt kia 5-11-16 9DLI p239 MR21
PAYN,George Frederick Lt ded 10-8-19 SL p268 CR Essex146
PAYN,Reginald Wallace Capt kia 28-3-18 RE 253TC p47 MR27
PAYNE,Albert 2Lt kld 13-1-18 GL &RFC p16 CR Wales3
PAYNE,Albert James T2Lt ded 27-3-18 RASC p193
PAYNE,Cecil Brandon 2Lt kia 20-8-17 RFA att21RFC p12 CR Belgium36,Brannon
PAYNE,Cecil McKenzie T2Lt kia 22-9-17 GL &16RFC p12 CR France81,21-9-17
PAYNE,Charles Arthur Frank 2Lt ded 15-10-18 RASC 47Div MT Coy p193 CR France769
PAYNE,Charles Geraint Christopher 2Lt kia 12-3-15 HLI p163 MR22
PAYNE,Edward Geoffrey TCapt kia 25-9-15 9RWFus p98 MR19
PAYNE,Frederick Norman TCapt ded 14-11-17 GL attMilGovBaghdad p191 CR Iraq8
PAYNE,George Herbert Lt ded 26-8-14 2Suff p78 CR France716
PAYNE,Harold 2Lt kia 30-11-17 RFA 93ArmyBde p34 CR France755
PAYNE,Hedley Stuart.DCM.2Lt dow 21-2-19 4RWSurr p212 CR Lond1,Lt
PAYNE,Henry Drummond 2Lt kia 20-3-15 EYorks p84 CR Belgium98
PAYNE,Henry James 2Lt drd 4-5-17 6RSuss p228 CR Italy14
PAYNE,Henry Tomkin 2Lt kia 6-8-15 3 att1Ess p131 CR Gallipoli6
PAYNE,Henry William T2Lt kld 12-3-18 RFC p16 CR Surrey153
PAYNE,Horace Abraham 2Lt kia 18-3-18 GL &RFC p16 CR France1269
PAYNE,James Ralph Salisbury Lt kia 8-8-18 1TankCps &SfthH p188 CR France589
PAYNE,James William 2Lt kia 14-4-17 6DLI p239 MR20
PAYNE,John Oswald Lt kia 25-4-17 4 att1RWar p65 CR Belgium96
PAYNE,John Robert 2Lt dow 4-11-17 D82RH&FA p34 CR France145 Ex LCpl WKentYeo
PAYNE,Newman Hayes 2Lt kia 14-9-18 3MGC Divl p185 CR France1890,Inf
PAYNE,Osmond Guy TLt kia 1-7-16 2RBerks p139 MR21,Orsmond
PAYNE,Richard William Lt kia 19-8-15 RGA 6TMB p41 CR France721
PAYNE,Sydney Thomas Lt ded 6-4-18 GL &13RAF p191 MR20
PAYNE,Wilfred Stuart Lane.MC.Lt kia 4-9-17 RGA 13SB att7RFC p12&41 CR Belgium18
PAYNE,William Henry T2Lt kia 17-2-17 22RFus p69 CR France314
PAYNE,William Henry Capt ded 10-12-17 AustEngrs CavDivSigs CR Iraq8
PAYNE-GALLWEY,Maurice Hilton Frankland Lt kia 25-9-16 4GrenGds SR p50 CR France374,Hylton
PAYNE-GALLWEY,Philip Francis Lt kia 30-10-14 21Lancer p23 MR29 CR Belgium168
PAYNE-GALLWEY,William Thomas.MVO.Capt kia 14-9-14 GrenGds p50 MR15
PAYNTER,Francis Pendarvis Maj kia 10-1-16 RFA 4HB p206 CR Belgium127
PAYNTER,John T2Lt kia 8-10-15 RE 174TC p47 CR France637
PAYNTER,Reginald 2Lt kia 26-10-17 2Bord D'Coy p117 MR30
PAYTON,Charles Mervyn.MID Lt kia 18-4-15 3 att1RWKent p141 MR29
PAYTON,John Leslie Lt kia 16-8-18 RFA &84RAF p271 MR20
PAYTON,Ralph Stuart TLt kia 22-7-16 14RWar p65 MR21
PEACE,Hubert Kirkby Lt dow 18-10-14 3Y&L attLincs p159 MR22
PEACH,Bertie Charles TLt kia 9-4-18 12Yorks p91 MR32
PEACH,Crugar Stanley 2Lt kld 24-4-17 1WYorks &16RFC p12&82 CR Surrey160
PEACH,Ernest James 2Lt kia 1-7-16 7N&D att139MGC p187&233 MR21
PEACH,Francis Edward T2Lt dow 23-2-19 N&D p255 CR Staffs135
PEACHE,William Wynter Lt ded 3-12-14 RE p47 CR Europe3
PEACOCK,Alfred Walter T2Lt kia 9-9-17RScots &24RFC p12 &54 CR France251 Ex AustImpForce
PEACOCK,David Ronald 2Lt kia 2-10-16 6DLI p239 MR21
PEACOCK,Frank 2Lt sInflictGunshot 3-12-18 IA TC att2/84Punjabis p281 MR66
PEACOCK,Frederick John ACapt kia 10-10-18 11Manch p155 CR France1301
PEACOCK,John Charles Millard 2Lt kia 27-5-18 5DLI p161 MR30
PEACOCK,John Luddington TLt kia 1-7-16 RE 150FC p47 CR France215
PEACOCK,John Thomas 2Lt kld 16-7-18 3DCLI &49RAF p114 CR France1437,Lt

PEACOCK,Lindsay Capt dow 19-9-18 IA 1/72Punjabis MR34 p281
PEACOCK,Percy Charles 2Lt dow 10-4-16 IARO att125Rif MR38 p281
PEACOCK,Reginald Howard Trees Lt kia 9-4-18 13ESurr p113 CR France924
PEACOCK,Robert Archibald T2Lt kia 27-1-16 12 att10ScotRif p104 CR France423
PEACOCK,Thomas Gordon TLt&Adj kia 25-9-15 8RBerks p139 MR19
PEACOCK,Thomas Harold 2Lt kia 27-6-18 1 att14Worc p109 CR France4
PEACOCK,Walter T2Lt kia 22-12-16 9RIrF p171 CR Belgium49
PEACOCK,William Hubert T2Lt kld 7-4-17 GL &45RFC p12 CR Lincs181
PEACOCK,William James Leonard T2Lt kia 18-8-16 EKent p58 CR France164
PEACOCK,William Webster TLt kia 16-8-16 RE 224FC p47 CR France149,15-8-16
PEACOCKE,Eric Forrester 2Lt kia 20-5-17 15 att16KRRC p151 MR20
PEACOCKE,Evelyn Jeffreys T2Lt kld 4-2-18 RFC p16 CR Wilts115
PEACOCKE,Herbert Parker 2Lt kia 3-7-16 8SLancs p125 MR21
PEACOP,Reginald Trevor 2Lt kia 2-9-17 RFA p208 CR Belgium24
PEADON,Harold Thomas 2Lt dow 27-3-17 1/4WelshR p230 CR Palestine2
PEADON,Percy Hewitt T2Lt dow 7-4-18 8Lincs A'Coy p75 CR France62
PEAK,John Harold Capt kia 16-6-15 4LNLancs p234 MR22
PEAK,Norman T2Lt kia 1-7-16 14Manch p155 CR France397
PEAK-GARLAND,George T2Lt kia 7-6-17 11RInnis p105 CR Belgium60
PEAKE,Arthur Lt kia 24-10-17 3 att11Ches p96 CR France163,2Lt
PEAKE,Cecil Gerald Wyatt.MID LtTCapt kia 10-3-17 2Lincs D'Coy p75 CR France525
PEAKE,Colin Lt kld 13-5-15 LeicYeo p204 CR Belgium152,kia
PEAKE,Henry Arthur Wyatt Capt kia 3-7-16 9Ess p132 MR21
PEAKE,John Lewis 2Lt kia 1-6-17 16Mddx p148 MR20
PEAKE,John Thelwal 2Lt dow 11-12-15 Nhampt p138 CR Kent289,11-5-15
PEAKE,Kenneth John Wyatt Lt kia 9-8-15 61Lincs D'Coy p75 MR4
PEAKE,Malcolm.CMG.TBrigGen kia 27-8-17 RA attStaff p1&34 CR France178
PEAKE,Raymond Lt dow 30-9-16 1ColdGds 1Coy p51 CR France105
PEAKE,William Francis Copson TLt dow 9-7-16 1RWSurr p56 CR France145,7-7-16
PEARCE,Arthur Carlton Lt kia 22-7-18 RASC att1/5N&D p193 CR France109
PEARCE,Charles Denison Fillis T2Lt kia 18-10-16 14Hamps p121 CR France798
PEARCE,Charles Stanley Capt kia 1-7-16 8ESurr p113 CR France513
PEARCE,Cuthbert James T2Lt kia 4-9-16 117MGC Inf p185 CR France220
PEARCE,Dudley George TCapt kia 3-9-16 8EKent p58 CR France1890
PEARCE,Edward Saxelby 2Lt kia 21-3-18 2/7Worc p226 MR20
PEARCE,Edward Sydney Charles Lt 31-3-18 57RFC MR20
PEARCE,Geoffrey Vincent 2Lt dow 18/19-12-14 RWar p65 MR32
PEARCE,George TLt kia 28-1-16 RFA p34 CR France625
PEARCE,Henry.MM.Lt ded 13-10-19 RFA 44ResBty p261 CR Dorset58
PEARCE,Henry Goold.MC.TLtACapt kia 15-7-17 RE 171TC p47 CR Belgium5
PEARCE,Herbert John Lt 24-3-20 RASC CamelTransCoy CR Egypt2
PEARCE,James.DCM.MM.2Lt ded 13-11-18 2WYorks p82 CR France40
PEARCE,James 2Lt ded 4-7-19 Worc 1GarrBn p264 MR67
PEARCE,John Francis Brice Capt kia 29-4-15 3KRRC p151
PEARCE,Maurice Leonard Lt dow 24-9-16 12Hamps attRSuss p121 MR37
PEARCE,Nathaniel Arthur Lt kia 25-11-17 4GrenGds p50 CR France713
PEARCE,Norman T2Lt kia 12-10-17 1RLancs p59 MR30
PEARCE,Richard.MC.Lt kia 27-9-18 23LancF attLabCps p189 CR France297
PEARCE,Robert Swayne 2Lt kia 9-5-15 RB p180 MR32
PEARCE,Sydney Martin Capt ded 7-12-18 4Leic &RAF p219&258 CR Sussex199,Maj 6-12-18
PEARCE,Walter Harry 2Lt dow PoW 24-4-18 RFA attX39TMB p34 CR France716
PEARCE,William Henry 2Lt kia 19-2-18 13Lond p249 CR France184
PEARCE,William James Lt kia 2-12-17 2/5Glouc p225 CR France667
PEARCE-BROWN,Richard 2Lt kia 17-7-16 4DLI p161 CR France832
PEARCE-FLEMING,George Eric Lt ded 1-6-18 IARO att3/39GarhwalRif p281 MR43
PEARCY,Albert 2Lt kia 30-11-17 Dev att7SomLI p77 MR17
PEARKES,Andre Mellard Capt kia 7-8-15 9WYorks p82 MR4
PEARMAN,Humphrey TLt kld 13-8-16 2Leinst attRFC p3&174,ded CR Surrey2
PEARMAN,James O'Hara T2Lt kia 25-1-17 13 att9RWar p65 CR Iraq5
PEARMAN,Thomas Henry 2Lt kia 4-11-18 4Wilts p236 CR France929
PEARS,Charles Martin T2Lt kia 23-11-17 GL &52RFC p12 CR France1361
PEARS,Maurice Loraine.CMG.TLtCol ded 20-10-16 17NumbF p62 CR Sussex112
PEARS,Norman 2Lt kia 24-4-17 4 att1/6Glouc p225 MR21
PEARSALL,Herbert George.MC.Capt ded 19-3-19 1TankCps p266 CR Staffs52
PEARSE,Alister Cullen.MC&Bar.Lt dow 16-9-19 Mddx att45RFus p255 MR70 &CR Europe179
PEARSE,Cecil George Lunnell Lt ded 20-10-18 RFA p208 CR Somerset197,Lunell
PEARSE,Frank Arthur T2Lt kia 2-7-16 1SomLI p80 MR21

PEARSE,Godfrey Maj ded 2-4-20 IA S&TCps p281 MR43
PEARSE,John Francis Brice Capt 29-4-15 3KRRC MR29
PEARSE,Kenneth Herbert T2Lt kia 6-8-15 11ESurr att2Hamps p113 MR4
PEARSE,Phyllis Ada SNurse ded 29-4-15 QAIMNS CR France85
PEARSE,Raymond Stanley T2Lt kia 23-8-16 71RFA p34 CR France239
PEARSE,Samuel LtCol ded 19-11-18 RE p47 CR Lond1
PEARSE,Walter Josiah.MC.2Lt kia 9-4-17 Z5RFA p34 CR France68
PEARSON,Alfred Christopher TCapt kld 4-4-19 9RWar p65 CR Iraq8
PEARSON,Angus John William T2Lt kia 1-7-16 14RFus att1RDubF p69 CR France35,Willans
PEARSON,Arthur James Balfour 2Lt kld 18-8-16 5Ess p232 CR France832
PEARSON,Arthur John.MC.2Lt kia 9-3-17 Nhants att29RFC p12&138 MR20
PEARSON,Athelstan 2Lt kia 13-6-17 5YLI p235 MR19
PEARSON,Bertram Walter Mockley Capt ded 25-10-18 RASC p193 CR France725
PEARSON,Cecil William Lt kia 3-1-18 4NumbF attRFC p19&213 MR20
PEARSON,Charles Hugh 2Lt kia 19-3-16 1/6SStaffs p229 CR France68,18-3-16
PEARSON,Charles Thornhill 2Lt dow 29-8-18 14RWar p65 CR France84
PEARSON,Cyprian Thomas 2Lt dow 6-10-17 A91RFA p34 CR Belgium23
PEARSON,David Easson 2Lt dow 4-9-18 RGA 112SB p41 CR France1484
PEARSON,Edward John 2Lt kia 2-8-17 83RFA p34 CR Belgium19
PEARSON,Ernest William TLt kia 6-8-15 17DLI att6Manch p161 CR Gallipoli1,7-8-15
PEARSON,Evelyn Henry Malcolm Paterson TCapt kld 8-1-16 12Lpool p72 CR France80
PEARSON,Francis Gilbert TLt dow 10-7-17 GL &10RFC p12 CR France98
PEARSON,Frank TCapt ded 5-2-18 GL LNLancs 49TrainingResBn &TMB p136&267 CR C'land&W'land83
PEARSON,Frederick George 2Lt kia 20-10-18 4 att16RWar p65 CR France1396
PEARSON,Frank Shakespeare LtCol ded 5-9-16 RASC p193 CR Dorset94
PEARSON,George Turney TLt kia 12-8-15 9Worc p109 MR4
PEARSON,Gerald T2Lt kia 29-10-17 45RFC p12 CR France200
PEARSON,Harold 2Lt kia 22-5-18 1 att7DCLI p114 CR France924
PEARSON,Harold 2Lt dow 27-9-18 1/7Manch p237 CR France712
PEARSON,Harry 2Lt dow 1-10-18 A/Bty14RFA p34 CR France146
PEARSON,Ignatius Gerald 2Lt kia 30-11-17 LNLancs att1/5SLancs p136 CR France658
PEARSON,James Lt dow 28-3-18 31MGC p185 CR France40
PEARSON,James Alan T2Lt kldacc 9-12-17 RFC p12 CR Norf58
PEARSON,James Bruce 2Lt mbk 25-3-17 IARO att93BurmaInf p281 MR38
PEARSON,John Lt kia 10-10-17 7LancF p221 MR30
PEARSON,John 2Lt dow 11-4-18 10RWar p65 CR Belgium11
PEARSON,John Ashworth TLt kia 4-8-16 8RFus p69 MR21
PEARSON,Joseph Sykes LtACapt ded 7-11-18 RASC MT p193 CR France65
PEARSON,Laumarin Saxe William T2Lt kia 19-7-16 13 att10Ess p132 MR21,Laumann
PEARSON,Maxwell Colquhoun TLt kia 23-11-15 7CamH p168 CR France423
PEARSON,Maurice Murray 2Lt kia 23-4-16 WorcYeo p206 MR34
PEARSON,Neil Mathieson 2Lt kia 17-8-16 5 att1RFus p69 MR21
PEARSON,Oliver Charles 2Lt kia 10-9-17 GL &70RFC p12 MR20
PEARSON,Reginald.MC.Capt kia 9-10-18 7Nhampt p138 CR France916
PEARSON,Reginald 2Lt kia 23-10-18 5WYorks p218 CR France1266,1Bn
PEARSON,Reginald Oswald 2Lt kia 16-6-15 1Lincs p75 MR29
PEARSON,Robert 2Lt dow PoW 7-8-18 1/2Yorks att8WYorks p91 CR France1615
PEARSON,Robert William Capt kld 15-5-15 5DLI p238 CR Belgium84
PEARSON,Stanley Osborne T2Lt kia 30-7-16 12 att10RWar p65 MR21
PEARSON,Stephen Hetley 2Lt kia 1-12-17 2GrenGds p50 CR France364
PEARSON,Sydney James Capt dow 15-8-16 1/8WYorks p219 CR France41
PEARSON,Terence Charles 2Lt kia 26-9-15 2Beds p86 MR19
PEARSON,Thomas Raleigh 2Lt dow 2-7-16 16KRRC p151 MR19
PEARSON,Walter Lt&QM ded 24-5-18 RAMC att41FA p197 CR Iraq8
PEARSON,Wilfred Hearne 2Lt kia 29-9-18 NCycBn ACycCps att57MGC Inf p187&253 CR France256
PEART,Leonard 2Lt dow 12-4-18 18DLI p161 CR France298
PEASE,Charles Capt ded 22-10-19 LNLancs p264 CR Lond28,Maj
PEASE,Christopher York Capt kia 9-5-18 YorkHuss p206 CR France223
PEASE,Cuthbert.MID Lt dow 18-9-16 1IrGds p53 CR France105,Capt
PEASE,Joseph Robinson Maj&HonLtCol ded 17-5-15 F'Res A'RGA Ex Yorks p41 CRYorks45
PEASE,Mark Robinson Lt kia 20-12-14 1EYorks D'Coy p84 CR France1140,20-10-14
PEASE,Ronald Herbert Pike Lt kia 15-9-16 1ColdGds p51 CR France374

PEASTON,Leslie Gordon 2Lt kia 21-3-18 1RFus p69 CR France366

PEATE,John Lt kia 8-9-16 3 att2Glouc p107 MR21 att1Bn

PEATFIELD,Stanley James T2Lt dow 2-7-16 9RBerks att60MGC p139&185 CR Belgium11

PEBERDY,Leonard Montague 2Lt kia 22-12-15 6DLI C'Coy p239 CR Belgium115

PECHELL,George Douglas 2Lt kldacc 21-12-16 IARO att108Inf &66RFC p281 CR Glouc9

PECK,C.W. Lt kia 29-9-15 6RScotF p95 MR19

PECK,Edwin Robert Richmond.MC.T2Lt kia 3-5-17 8Suff p78 CR France1185

PECK,Reginald Geoffrey Lt dow 29-2-16 4ScotRif att10HLI p104 MR32

PECK,Roland Henry.MID TLt kia 5-3-16 Dors &RFC p3 MR38

PECKER,Francis George ACapt dow 18-5-17 7KSLI p145 CR France40

PECKER,Henry Cyril 2Lt kia 20-4-15 3RScots p54 MR29

PECKHAM,Arthur Nyton Lt acckld 14-2-18 IARO att1/112Inf p281 CR Iraq8,Capt

PECKOVER,Reginald Kenneth Capt kia 7-6-17 IA 33Punjabis att7Rajputs p281 CR Asia62,Keith

PECKSTON,Cuthbert Joseph 2Lt kia 22-3-18 25NumbF p62 MR20

PECKSTON,Robert Henry 2Lt ded 22-10-17 7NumbF p214 CR Durham167

PEDDER,Edward Boynton Lt kia 17-1-16 18Huss SR p23 France423

PEDDIE,Alexander William Ponsonby Capt kia 13-9-14 1Lincs B'Coy p75 MR15,14-9-14

PEDEN,George Edward 2Lt kia 25-3-17 3Norf att 133MGC Inf p74&185 MR38

PEDEN,Josef Kormendy Von Ikreny Lt kia 28-3-18 RFA attRFC p19&208 MR20

PEDLEY,Frederick Lewis 2Lt dow 24-8-17 24Lond p252 CR France64,23-8-17

PEDLOW,William.MC.ACapt kia 12-10-18 2RDubF p177 CR France660

PEDRICK,George Richard 2Lt kia 22-3-18 12Suff p78 MR20

PEEBLES,John Adair 2Lt kia 30-4-18 5ScotRif p224 CR Belgium3,9Bn

PEEBLES,John Reid Capt kia 28-6-15 1/7RScots p211 MR4

PEEBLES,Percy Norman Lt kia 9-4-17 12Lond p248 CR France1185

PEEBLES,Peter 2Lt kia 19-7-18 4BlkW p230 CR France324

PEEBLES,William Fleming T2Lt kia 30-4-17 5Wilts att113MGC p153&185 CR Belgium73,MGC attWilts

PEECOCK,Edward Gordon T2Lt kia 7-7-16 9RFus p69 MR21

PEED,Thomas Percy T2Lt dow 10-7-16 11 att8SStaffs p123 CR France833

PEEK,Alfred Taylor 2Lt kia 3-5-17 15WYorks p82 MR20

PEEK,Herbert Thain T2Lt kia 14-7-16 15DLI p161 MR21

PEEK,Roger Grenville Capt 23-3-21 9Lancers CR Devon100

PEEL,Alan Ralph Capt kia 17-11-14 SWBord att5NigR p100 CR WAfrica58

PEEL,Alfred T2Lt kia 5-5-17 6RBerks p139 CR France1185,17-5-17

PEEL,Ambrose Ethelstone 2Lt kia 27-4-18 1Beds p86 CR France346

PEEL,Charles William 2Lt kia 24-4-15 3RDubF p177 MR29

PEEL,Colin Nevill 2Lt kia 3-9-16 3 att14Hamps p121 MR21

PEEL,Geoffrey TLtACapt kia 17-7-17 6Beds p86 CR Belgium100

PEEL,Home.DSO.MC.CaptBdeMaj kia 24-3-18 8Lond p247 CR France374

PEEL,Lawrence Capt kia 24-10-14 Yorks OC 7DivCo p255 MR29,23-10-14

PEEL,Maurice Berkeley.Hon.MC&Bar.Rev kia 14-5-17 RAChDept p199 CR France646

PEEL,Robert Capt ded 7-12-17 Ches 2GarrBn p263 CR Mddx26

PEEL,Robert John De Neuville.MID T2Lt kia 29-3-17 9RWar p65 MR38

PEEL,Robert Lloyd.MC.Lt dow 3-9-17 A58RH&FA p34

PEEL,Thomas Alfred TLt dow 24-8-15 RAMC att5Dors p197 CR Greece10

PEEL,Tom 2Lt dow 21-4-17 2BlkW p129 MR38

PEEL,Walter Sidney.MC.Lt kld 27-9-18 3Lincs att59RAF p75 CR France 1Bn

PEER,Edmund Faithful 2Lt kia 23-4-17 4EYorks p219 MR20

PEERLESS,Cuthbert Henry 2Lt ded 12-5-18 8RSuss p119&257 CR Sussex112

PEERLESS,Charles Stephen T2Lt kia 14-8-16 C166RFA p34 CR France188

PEET,John Edward Grimston 2Lt kld 27-2-15 9RWSurr p56 CR Surrey131

PEFFERS,David Tweedie 2Lt kia 27-2-18 4A&SH p173 CR France162

PEGG,Conrad 2Lt dow 2-6-18 1/2 att6Leic p88 CR France145

PEGG,Hallam William T2Lt dow 3-7-16 8ESurr p113 CR France51

PEGG,Kenneth Hugh Lt kia 20-2-16 3 att2Leic p88 MR38

PEGG,William John T2Lt kld 18-3-18 10RWar p65 CR Norf103,18-3-19

PEGGIE,Alexander Wallace Bruce Lt kia 17-8-17 RGA p209 CR Belgium24

PEGLAR,Harry Sidney 2Lt kia 4-11-18 7RWKent p141 CR France660

PEGRAM,Charles Earnest.MC.TLtACapt ded 9-11-18 RB p180 CR Lond2

PEGUM,Joseph Patrick TCapt kia 26-9-17 RAMC att7KSLI p197 MR30

PEILE,John Selby Chadwick Lt kia 2-6-17 190RFA p34 CR Belgium28

PEIRCE,G.F.2Lt kld 26-5-18 GL &RAF p191

PEIRCE,Sydney Ernest.MC.26-12-15 1/4YLI CR France40

PEIRCE,William Gabriel King Capt kia 30-10-14 3Manch p155 MR22,26-10-14 2Bn

PELHAM,Herbert Lyttelton.Hon.Lt&Adjt kia 14-9-14 2RSuss p119 CR France1329

PELHAM-CLAY,Edward Cecil Granby Lt ded 17-10-19 IARO att3/150Inf p281 CR Egypt7 Ex 2/42Deoli

PELL,Albert Julian Maj ded 28-8-16 4Suff p217 CR Camb91,9Bn

PELL,Beauchamp Tyndall.DSO.LtCol dow 4-11-14 RWSurr p56 CR Belgium116

PELL,Harry Saxon 2Lt kia 6-4-17 40RFC p12 CR France783

PELLETIER,Charles Adolphe Lt 11-5-18 CanadaEngrs &1RAF MR20

PELLEW,James Edward Capt ded 15-12-19 RDC CR Cornwall142

PELLS,Charles Francis Robert Lt kia 11-4-17 6WYorks p218 MR20

PELLS,Cyril Elmore T2Lt kia 27-5-18 Dev p77 MR18

PELLY,Henry Gerald Maj ded 25-7-16 RH&FA p261

PELLY,Herbert Richard Lt kia 9-10-15 1/7Ess p232 CR Gallipoli17,Hubert

PELLY,William Francis Henry TCapt kia 1-7-16 9RInnisF p105 MR21

PELMORE,Bernard Julius TLt kia 18-7-17 RE 247FC p47 CR France184

PELTON,Kenneth Kemble.MC.2Lt kia 1-8-17 5Leinst att7RIrRif p174 MR29

PEMBER,Edward Horace Lt kia 30-9-17 RFA &5RFC p12&34 CR France95

PEMBER,Henry Cecil TCapt kia 3-5-17 HouseholdBn p20 CR France97 Ex 1LifeGds

PEMBERTON,Alan John MacDonald.MC.Capt ded 3-11-16 Leinst &RFC p3&174,Allan CR France614

PEMBERTON,Charles Oliver Paget Lt ded 4-4-16 RDC p253 CR Suff215,4-7-16

PEMBERTON,C.Warren 2Lt kld 25-4-16 RFC p3

PEMBERTON,Francis Percy Campbell Capt kia 19-10-14 2LifeGds p20 CR Belgium157

PEMBERTON,Frederick Despard Capt kia 21-8-17 RFA att50RFC p12&34 CR France660

PEMBERTON,Leigh T2Lt kia 25-9-15 9KRRC att9RB p151 MR29

PEMBERTON,Oswald Capt kia 21-12-14 2MunstF attDubF p175 MR22 1Munst attDubF

PEMBERTON,Percy Leigh 2Lt dow 27-7-16 4Mddx p148

PEMBERTON,Vivian Telfer.MC.Capt kia 7-10-18 RGA 216SB p41 CR France375

PEMBLE,Clarence Arthur Lyon 2Lt kia 1-8-18 RWSurr p56 MR20

PENDER,George.MID Capt dow 24-4-17 1/7RScots p211 CR Egypt2

PENDER,James(Hamish)Granger Gailes 2Lt kia 11-3-15 3 att2GordH p167 CR France525,Geils

PENDER,William Gordon.MC.Capt kia 15-8-17 40RFC p12 MR20

PENDEREL-BRODHURST,Bernard Richard 2Lt kia 1-10-18 RE 82FC p210 CR France631

PENDRIGH,Alexander Conrad Cuthbertson 2Lt dow 17-8-17 6Dev B'Coy p217 CR France145,2Bn

PENFOLD,Bernard Hugh T2Lt kia 20/23-10-17 N&D att15Bn p134 MR30,20-10-17

PENFOLD,Edward Norman Lt kia 29-5-18 2Lincs attLeic p75

PENFOLD,Jeffery Bradley TLt dow 28-1-16 7KOSB p102 CR France178

PENFOLD-WYATT,Hugh Graystone Lt ded 12-11-15 SussYeo p205

PENGELLEY,Rowland Donald.MID T2Lt kia 19-8-17 RE 153FC p47 CR Belgium111

PENGELLY,Edgar Ambrose.MC.Capt dow 31-3-18 RE 213ArmyTpsCo p47&259 CR France145

PENGELLY,William Augustus 2Lt kia 19-5-17 8Mddx p236 MR20

PENHALE,Thomas William T2Lt dow 15-4-17 13KRRC p151 CR France40

PENKETH,Alfred Thomas T2Lt kia 12-5-17 1SStaffs p123 MR20

PENKETH,Robert Charles Capt dow 16-4-17 6NumbF p213 CR France120

PENLINGTON,Arthur Berkeley.MC.2Lt kia 6-10-17 RFA 15ArmyBde p34 MR30

PENMAN,Geoffrey Evans TLt kia 9-5-17 11RWSurr att11MGC p56&185 CR France614

PENMAN,Rowland Arthur T2Lt kia 16-6-17 214MGC p185 MR20 att206Coy

PENN,Eric Frank 2LtTCapt kia 18-10-15 4GrenGds p50 CR France423

PENN,Geoffrey Mark 2Lt kia 11-12-15 6RB attSomLI p180 CR Belgium71

PENN,Thomas 2Lt kia 15-4-18 7Lincs p75 CR France41

PENN-GASKELL,Leslie Da Costa.MID TMaj kld 4-2-16 Norf &RFC p3&74,Lt ded CR Mddx34,SqnCmdr

PENN-GASKELL,William TCapt kia 12-10-16 25Manch p155 MR21

PENNEFATHER,Charles Lewis TCapt kia 14-6-16 2RB p180 CR France251

PENNEFATHER,Somerset Edward Chap2Cl ded 29-8-17 13Lond p271 CR Mddx51

PENNEL,R.H.E.Maj 10-12-15 IAML AcntsDept MR65

PENNEY,Ian Campbell TCapt kia 27-9-15 13RScots p54 MR19,26-9-15

PENNEY,Nicholas Arthur Lt kia 10-4-21 IA 1/25 att28Punjabis p281 MR43

PENNEY,Reginald Harper T2Lt kia 9-11-17 11NumbF p62 CR France1858

PENNEY,Roland Lt kia 2-4-18 B190RFA p208 CR France745

PENNINGTON,Harold Cocking TLt dow 20-6-17 1RFus p69 CR France13

PENNINGTON,Harold Evelyn T2Lt kia 27-9-15 9RSuss p119 MR19

PENNINGTON,John.MID Lt kia 25-9-15 2RWar p65 MR19

PENNINGTON,Thomas T2Lt kia 28-9-15 2EKent p58 MR19,PENINGTON

PENNINGTON,William Henry 2Lt ded 2-3-15 14WYorks p82 CR Cornwall96
PENNINGTON William Herbert Maj kia 9-9-15 IA 12Cav att16 p281 CR Asia82
PENNY,Arthur Hugh Capt dow 1-7-16 1ELancs p111 MR21
PENNY,Arthur Taylor.MVO.Maj ded 28-9-15 2Hamps p264
PENNY,Bernard Willoughby 2Lt dow 18-8-17 2RFus p69 CR Belgium16
PENNY,George 2Lt kia 3-9-16 8WYorks p219 CR France383
PENNY,Stanley T2Lt dow 28-7-16 14RFus p69 CR France141
PENRICE,William Gordon T2Lt kia 7-6-17 20DLI p161 MR29
PENROSE,Algernon Fane Keane Lt kia 10-5-15 RInnisF p105 CR Gallipoli3
PENROSE,Claude Quayle Lewis.MC&Bar.MIDx2 Maj dow 1-8-18 RGA 245SB p41 CR France142
PENROSE,Edward John McNeill.MID Capt kia 25-4-15 1RIrF p171 MR29
PENROSE,Ernest Lt kia 5-4-18 12MGC Inf p185 CR France704
PENROSE,George Alwyn TCapt kia 9-4-17 8RWSurr p56 CR France161
PENROSE,Harold T2Lt dow 27-3-17 12 att8RFus p69 CR France113
PENROSE,Harold Wesley 2Lt kia 26-3-18 4RFus p69 MR20,Henry
PENROSE,Robert John Rowson 2Lt kia 26-4-18 Y&L att1/4Bn p159 MR32
PENROSE-FITZGERALD,Herbert James Cooper Lt kia 12-10-16 3 att1RIrF p171 MR21
PENROSE-FITZGERALD,Maurice J.TLt dow 26-7-16 7RWSurr p56 CR Eire81
PENROSE-WELSTED,Samuel Richard.DFC.Capt kia 17-7-18 5RIrReg &17RAF p89 MR37
PENRUDDOCKE,Charles.MID Lt kia 4-10-18 7Wilts C'Coy p153 CR France1495
PENRUDDOCKE,Cyril Powys Capt kia 3-9-16 11RSuss B'Coy p119 CR France1890
PENRUDDOCKE,Thomas T2Lt kia 25-4-17 8Wilts p153 MR37
PENSON,Thomas Edward 2Lt kia 18-9-18 25RWFus p98 CR France1494
PENTECOST,Charles Gordon 2Lt kia 27-3-18 25RFC p16 MR20
PENTELOW,Arthur Lenton 2Lt dow 28-7-18 62MGC p185 CR France622
PENTLAND,Robert Charles Maj ded 1-3-18 RDubF p266
PENTON,Arthur Herbert 2Lt kia 16-4-18 14Hamps att1/5Manch p121 CR France204
PENTON,E.G.Lt ded 29-5-18 RASC p193
PENWARDEN,William Francis 2Lt kia 31-8-18 4RFus p69 CR France568
PEPLER,Stanley James Lt 6-3-17 51CanadaInf &43RFC MR20
PEPLOE,Keith LtACapt kia 9-11-16 2 O&BLI B'Coy p130 CR France344
PEPPER,Alwyn Tayton Capt ded 6-11-18 RE 100FC 22Div HQ p47 CR Greece9
PEPPER,Cedric William 2Lt ded 21-10-15 3SomLI p80 CR Somerset219
PEPPER,Edith Dorothy SpProb ded 7-4-18 VAD QAIMNS p200&268 CR Egypt9
PEPPER,Enoch.MID 2Lt kia 26-4-18 4SStaffs p123 MR30
PEPPER,Robert Forsythe 2Lt kia 12-10-16 4 att1RIrF p171 MR21
PEPPER,Sydney Whitelock Capt kia 27-8-17 8RWar p214 MR30
PEPPER,William Bramwell Capt dow 4-8-16 RGA 3SB p41 CR France397
PEPYS,Francis.DSO.2Lt kia 12-11-14 2 O&BLI p130 MR29
PEPYS,John 2Lt kia 23-8-14 YLI p143 CR Belgium201
PEPYS,Reginald Whitmore Capt dow 21-9-14 2Worc p109 CR France1329
PERCEVAL-MAXWELL,R.H.Lt 23-7-18 3 att10ScotRif CR France865
PERCEVAL-MAXWELL,Richard Nigel Lt kia 30-3-18 16Lancers p23 CR France988
PERCIVAL,Alfred Jex Blake.DSO.TLtCol kia 31-11-14 NumbR 2DivStaff p62 CR Belgium58,Arthur 31-10-14
PERCIVAL,Anthony.MID TLt dow 15-10-17 95MGC p185 CR France145
PERCIVAL,Cecil Bernard TLtACapt kia 24-11-17 20 att18WelchR p127 MR17
PERCIVAL,Claude Victor Noble Maj kia 14-12-14 2RB p180 CR France1158
PERCIVAL,George Stewart 2Lt kld 13-10-18 4Manch p155 CR France725,Stuart
PERCIVAL,John Lee 2Lt kia 30-9-18 8WYorks p219 CR France755
PERCIVAL,M.Lt att5NigR CR WAfrica58
PERCIVAL,Reginald Frank Lt kia 12-4-18 2Mon p244 MR32
PERCIVAL,Walter Lowe 2Lt dow 24-10-18 YLI att9Bn p143 CR France737
PERCY,George Clark.MC.MID LtACapt kia 31-7-17 3 att2ScotRif p104 MR29
PERCY,Harry Fortescue Lt ded 5-2-17 WiltsYeo p271 CR Surrey150
PERCY,Raymond.MC.LtACapt dow 12-8-18 12 att1Lpool p72&259 CR France84
PERCY,William Francis.MC.Maj ded 12-6-15 Norf p263 CR War143
PERCY-HARDMAN,William Henry Capt dow 1-3-17 4Dev attMGC Inf p187&220 CR Iraq5
PERCY-SMITH,Vernon Maj ded 29-9-20 SL IA 20DeccanHorse attRFC p281&268 MR65
PEREGRINE,John Pryor Puxton Lt kia 1-7-16 1EYorks p84 MR21
PEREIRA,Adrian O'Donnell TCapt kia 20-9-17 10WRid p116 CR Belgium112
PERFECT,Cyril St.Lawrence 2Lt dow 13-10-15 3RLancs att1RWSurr p59 CR France14
PERHAM,Edgar TCapt kia 23-7-16 12WYorks p82 MR21
PERHAM,Ernest Noble T2Lt kia 1-8-17 12 att4Worc p109 CR Belgium7

PERHAM,William Francis George Lt dow 10-3-18 3 att1Beds p86 CR Italy7,2Lt
PERKIN,Albert John T2Lt ded 23-12-17 RE p262 CR Devon73
PERKIN,Philip Kenneth 2Lt kia 1-7-16 12Y&L p159 MR21
PERKINS,Albert T2Lt kia 4-10-17 197MGC p185 CR Belgium20,149MGC
PERKINS,Æneas Charles Maj dow 28-4-15 IA 40Pathans p281 CR France284
PERKINS,Audley St.John Lt kia 2-4-17 9Dev p77 CR France568
PERKINS,Bernard St.George Lt kia 10-8-18 1 att9Ess p132 CR France247
PERKINS,B.T.Capt 14-6-16 N&D CR Somerset196
PERKINS,Cecil Howard Lt kia 22-7-18 2Yorks att21TMB p91 CR France65
PERKINS,Charles Henry Lt ded 14-9-19 11MGC Inf p266 CR Lancs263
PERKINS,Cyril John 2Lt dow 27-6-17 4Yorks p220 CR France518
PERKINS,Frank Arthur Capt dow 8-6-17 21Lond p251 CR Belgium11
PERKINS,Frank Bailey LtACapt kia 19-5-17 23/40RFA p34 CR France1182
PERKINS,George T2Lt kia 1-7-16 2WYorks p82 MR21
PERKINS,John Charles Campbell.DSO.LtCol 28-2-16 IAML AccntsDept MR65
PERKINS,Jukes Ford Rumsey Irving 2Lt kia 8-3-18 27RFC p16 CR France1061
PERKINS,Leonard T2Lt kia 3-11-16 1RWSurr p56 MR21
PERKINS,Reginald Gabriel Beale 2Lt kia 14-9-14 1RBerks p139 MR15
PERKINS,Thorold 2Lt kia 31-5-17 41RFC p12 CR Belgium18
PERKS,Maurice Case T2Lt kia 26-4-17 9LNLanc att74TMB p136 CR Belgium43
PERKS,Robert Clement.DSO.TCapt kia 27-10-18 10WRid p116 CR Italy9
PERKS,Wilfred Lawson 2Lt kia 24-8-16 3Worc p109 MR21
PERKS-MORRIS,Arthur Bois 2Lt dow 14-11-17 2RSuss p119 CR Belgium11
PERN,Montague Lt kia 9-5-15 RAMC att4RFus p197 CR France924
PERNEY,Erland Dauria 2Lt kia 23-11-17 11RFC p12 MR20
PERRAM,George Terrence Clements CaptAMaj kia 3-8-17 RGA att177RFA p41 Belgium10
PERRAM,Henry Charles Capt ded 17-2-19 IA 84Punjabis att66 p281 MR43
PERRATON,Frank Mayvour.MC.2Lt kia 29-4-17 22RFus p69 MR20
PERREAU,Gustavus Arthur LtCol kia 9-3-17 IA 2/4GurkhaRif p281 MR38
PERRET,Gerald Henry Lt kia 9-8-18 5RRofCav att10Huss p23 CR France652,PERRETT 8-8-18
PERRETT,Ernest Henry T2Lt kia 4-10-17 Hamps att1Bn p121 CR Belgium83
PERRETT,Fred Leonard 2Lt dow 1-12-18 17RWelshF p98 CR France34
PERRIER,Hargrave Carroll Lumley 2Lt kia 8-11-18 5RDubF p177 CR France1219,2Bn
PERRIER,William Samuel T2Lt kia 27-3-16 4RFus p69 MR29
PERRIN,Alfred John T2Lt kia 4-10-17 10YLI p143 MR30
PERRIN,Charles Louis Maj kia 23-11-15 IA 76Punjabis p281 MR38
PERRIN,Gilbert Dennis Lt kia 13/15-11-16 2SStaffs p123 CR France742,Capt
PERRIN,Maurice Nasmith Maj ded 28-4-19 RAMC attRAF p267 CR Surrey157
PERRIN,Reginald Percy.MC.Capt kia 27-5-18 GL att7InfBdeHQ p191 MR18
PERRIN,Thomas Frederick TCapt ded 24-7-17 RE IWT p47 CR Iraq6
PERRIN,Thomas Frood.MID Lt 24-5-20 3RIrReg CR Egypt6
PERRIS,Eric Loftus 2Lt kia 27-9-16 4Yorks p220 CR France515
PERRIS,Noel Felix 2Lt kia 20-7-18 2Lond &RAF p245&258
PERROTT,A.H. Lt kia 10-9-14 1RBerks p139 CR France866
PERRY,Alfred Frederick 2Lt 28-11-18 N Flight RAF MR20
PERRY,Arthur Ernest Cecil 2Lt dow 20-6-18 RGA 248SB p41 CR France343
PERRY,Benjamin Lewis Capt kld 26-4-15 1Mon p244 MR29
PERRY,Cecil Robert Lt ded 24-10-19 RASC p267
PERRY,Cecil Victor.MC.2Lt kia 23-4-17 120/27RFA p34 CR France1325
PERRY,Claude William T2Lt kia 1-7-16 7EYorks p84 CR France373,Charles
PERRY,Cullen Hay TLt kld 3-2-18 1/8RFus att23RFC p16&69,ded CR Egypt1
PERRY,Donovan Lt kia 22-3-18 Herts p252 MR27
PERRY,Evelyn Walter Copland 2Lt kldacc 16-8-14 RFC p2 CR France299
PERRY,Francis Ina Lowre Lt kia 2-5-15 1BordR p117 CR Gallipoli3
PERRY,Frank Burgess 2Lt kia 24-4-18 58MGC p185 MR27
PERRY,George Herbert Gresley LtCapt dow 15-3-15 2WYorks p82 CR France
PERRY,George Hugh 2Lt kia 31-3-18 9/41RFA p34 CR France41
PERRY,Henry Bernard.MID Capt kia 6-11-18 13Lond p249 CR France1142
PERRY,John 2Lt kia 23-7-16 3 att2Yorks p91 MR21
PERRY,Kenneth George T2Lt dow 1-11-16 11RSuss p119 CR France74
PERRY,Kenneth William 2Lt dow 8-12-17 1ColdGds p51 CR France40
PERRY,Lawrence Percy 2Lt 2-9-18 48RAF MR20
PERRY,Leslie Harold.MC.2Lt kia 6-10-18 4Glouc att2/6DLI p225 CR France1092,5-8-18
PERRY,Leslie Roy 2Lt kia 15-9-16 6Lond p247 MR21
PERRY,Percy Claude Lt kld 26-4-16 7N&D p233 CR Notts85
PERRY,Robert Proelss 2Lt kia 9-4-17 1/7Mddx p235 CR France420

PERRY,Roy Sinclair 2Lt kia 4-4-16 11 att6LNLancs p136 MR38
PERRY,Stephen Ralph TLt kia 18-9-16 12KRRC p151 MR21
PERRY,Sydney.MC.MM.2LtACapt kia 7-8-18 2RWSurr p56 CR Italy3
PERRY,Thomas 2Lt kia 25-9-15 1CamH p168 CR France553
PERRY,William 2Lt 24-8-20 NumbF CR Numb83
PERRY,William Charles T2Lt kia 30-12-17 GL attRFC p12 CR Egypt1
PERRY,William Claude T2Lt dow 13-7-16 20KRRC p151 CR France141
PERRY,William Everard Hill T2Lt kia 14-4-17 2Dev p77 CR France407
PERRY,William Johnstone 2Lt kld 21-5-16 1/6RWelshF p223 CR Egypt9
PERRY-AYSCOUGH,Henry George Charlie Capt kia 25-9-15 RMunstF p176 MR29,4ConnRgrs attRIrRif
PERRYMAN,Arthur Charles 2Lt kld 7-1-18 Mddx att16RFC p16&148 CR Mddx17
PERSSE,Cecil De Burgh Gordon 2Lt dow 19-7-15 7DragGds attIrGds p21 CR Hamps64
PERSSE,Dudley Eyre Lt dow 1-2-15 4RDubF p177 CR France284
PERSSE,Edward Aubrey Capt kia 14-10-18 A47RFA p34 CR Belgium100
PERSSE,Henry Wilfred.MC&Bar.CaptAMaj dow 28-6-18 2RFus p69 CR France134
PERSSE,Rodolph Algernon 2Lt kia 1-1-15 RB att2KRRC p180 MR22
PERSTON,George Fortescue 2Lt kia 12-2-17 B99RFA p34 CR Greece6
PERY,Cecil de Vere T2Lt kia 25-9-15 1Mddx p148 MR19
PESKETT,Guy Eastcoft Harry 2Lt kia 3-5-17 4WRid p227 MR20
PESKETT,Harry St.Hill Capt dow 13-4-17 10LNLancs C'Coy p136 CR France113
PETER,Alexander Gordon.MC.TCapt dow 5-7-17 RAMC att2/6SfthH p197 CR Belgium12,Alister
PETER,Alfred Edwin 2Lt kia 25-9-16 3NStaffs att9Leic p157 MR21
PETER,Pomeroy John 2Lt kia 19-9-18 10EKent p204 CR France364
PETER,Richard Henry 2Lt kia 30-4-18 16Lond p250 MR34
PETERS,Arthur Stafford 2Lt kia 30-11-17 13 att1/6Lond p249 MR17
PETERS,Albert Wallace 2Lt ded 20-11-18 TankCps p266 CR War23,MGC
PETERS,Ashley 2Lt kia 13-11-16 13EYork p84 MR21
PETERS,Charles Frederick 2Lt kia 18-3-18 6EKent p58 CR France922
PETERS,Charles Walter 2Lt kia 21-3-18 8 att7EKent p58 MR27
PETERS,Cyril Aubrey T2Lt kia 4-7-17 17Lpool p72 CR Belgium115
PETERS,Frank Wesley.MC.2Lt kia 18-7-17 1 att9Ess p132 MR20
PETERS,Gerard 2Lt ded 24-2-17 6Glouc p225 CR France692
PETERS,Henry TLt kia 12-10-16 26Manch p155 CR France744
PETERS,Joseph Henry Gervese Capt kia 10-1-20 IA 51Sikhs att2/152Punjabis p281
PETERS,Lionel Gordon Capt kia 25-3-18 10WYorks p82 MR20
PETERS,Owen Herbert Capt dow 5-8-16 RAMC 36SanitarySect p254 CR France23
PETERS,William John.MC.Lt kia 23-4-17 1Dev p77 MR20
PETERSEN,Aaron 2Lt kia 3-9-18 3EYorks &18RAF p84 MR20
PETERSON,George Benjamin 2Lt kia 31-3-18 4EYorks att6Dors p219 CR France196
PETERSON,J.Lt 20-5-19 14Dev CR Lancs14
PETERSON,William Sinclair 2Lt kia 6-11-14 RHA att2LifeGds p209 CR Belgium134,PETERSEN
PETHERBRIDGE,Henry B.Lt dow 24-7-16 NyasaVolRes att1KAR p268 CR EAfrica40,Victor 2Lt
PETLEY,Hugh Capt kia 16-9-16 1Lond p245 MR21
PETO,Clement Henry Capt kia 17-11-14 10Huss p22 CR Belgium57
PETO,James Archibald Lt kia 23-8-15 4Worc p109 CR Gallipoli4
PETO,Morton.MC.TCapt dow 22-9-16 RAMC p197 CR France177
PETRE,Lionel George Carroll.Lord.LtTCapt dow 30-9-15 4ColdGds p51 CR Essex36
PETRIE,Alex Robertson 2Lt ded 13-2-19 3Manch p265 CR Lancs434
PETRIE,Alfred Hunt 2Lt kia 31-7-17 GL att72TMB p191 MR29
PETRIE,Allan Strachan 2Lt kia 11-9-16 14Lond p249 CR France294
PETRIE,Donald John 2Lt kia 9-9-16 10RScots att2/5LancF p212 MR21
PETRIE,Henry Lawson T2Lt kia 30-7-16 9 att2KOSB p102 MR21
PETRIE,William Wilson LtCol ded 22-2-19 GL RFA p268 CR Norf11,27-2-19
PETT,Joseph 2Lt kia 21-3-18 2/4 O&BLI p231 MR27
PETTER,Harold Rupert 2Lt dow 3-5-17 1RScotF p95 MR20
PETTIGREW,Douglas St.George T2Lt dow 23-10-17 14 att17N&D p134 CR Belgium11
PETTIGREW,Gilbert Thomas Richardson Lt kld 12-9-17 1Hereford attRFC p19&252 CR War151,2Lt 12-8-17
PETTIGREW,John Lt ded 3-11-18 GL attSPersia Rif p191 CR Asia82
PETTIGREW,Robert McCalmont T2Lt dow 10-6-16 8RIrRif C'Coy p170 CR France702
PETTIGREW,Thomas Thomson 2Lt kia 28-7-18 8SfthH p165 CR France865
PETTINGER,Harold Sidney TLt kia 10-10-17 8YLI attHQ70InfBde p143 CR Belgium127
PETTINGER,James Wilson TCapt ded 6-10-17 RAMC p197 CR Somerset139

PETTIT,William Vaughan T2Lt kia 29-6-16 RE 173TC p47 CR France178
PETTITT,William 2Lt kia 19-4-18 1LNLancs p136 CR France1106
PETTS,Cyril Edward Lt ded 14-12-18 IARO att1/8GurkhaRif p281 MR66,C.F.Capt
PETTY,Alfred Hallam 2Lt dow PoW 17-7-16 5N&D p233 CR France1266
PETTY,Charles Henry Capt 2-6-21 6WRid CR Yorks483
PETTY,Eric Bateman Lt kia 23-3-18 5Ches p222 CR France512
PETTY,Nelson Widdup Lt kia 28-6-15 LancF p93 MR4
PETTY,Robert Leach 2Lt kia 31-8-18 WYorks att7NStaffs p82 MR61
PETYT,John Edward 2Lt kia 27-3-18 2/8Manch p237 MR27
PEYTON,Ernest T2Lt kia 1-7-16 4Mddx p148 CR France267
PEYTON,Henry Sydney Charles,MC LtCol dow 24-3-18 3RB Cmdg2Bn p180 CR France692
PEYTON,John Algernon Wynward Lt kia 22-8-18 7Norf p74 CR France196,Wyngard
PEYTON,Montagu Frank T2Lt kia 12-7-17 16NumbF Res p62 CR Belgium173
PHALEN,Ralph Unel 2Lt kia 28-5-17 60RFC p12 MR20
PHARE,Dudley Gershom Lt kia 28-3-18 RASC p193 MR20 RAMC att7KSLI
PHAYRE,Charles Frederick 2Lt kia 27-8-14 2RMunF p176 CR France1751,Lt
PHAYRE,Richard Herbert Lt kia 26-10-14 2Yorks p91 MR29
PHEAR,Henry John Lt dow 17-10-17 RH&FA 14ArmyBde p34 CR Belgium172
PHEAR,Norman Carlyon T2Lt dow 20-11-17 GL &27RFC p12 CR France88
PHELAN,Albert Edward.MC.TLtACapt kia 20-11-17 1NumbF p62 MR20
PHELPS,Duncan 2Lt kia 29-9-18 RSuss attHamps p119 MR30
PHELPS,Leslie James 2Lt ded 3-11-18 1/2 att8Glouc p107 CR Wales149
PHELPS,Wilfred John Lt kia 15-9-16 9Norf p74 MR21,16-9-16
PHETHEAN,Charles Capt kld 30-3-18 5Manch p236 CR France425
PHIBBS,William Griffith Baynes Maj ded 8-11-14 RIrF p171 CR Wales462,5-11-14
PHILBRICK,Edward Hooper Lt ded 6-11-18 RFA 395Bty p34&257 CR Essex81
PHILBY,Denis Duncan Lt kia 12-11-14 RDubF attRMunF p177 CR Belgium96
PHILBY,Harold Payne.DSO.TMaj kia 17-5-16 2Y&L p159 CR Belgium2
PHILCOX,Cecil Ernest.MID TLt ded 24-5-17 1SStaffs p123 CR France518
PHILCOX,Percy Vivian 2Lt kia 1-11-18 RASC attRGA p193 CR France206
PHILIP,Andrew TLt dedacc 30-5-15 RAMC p197 CR Scot127
PHILIP,David Carswell 2Lt kia 29-4-17 23NumbF p62 MR20
PHILIP,Edgar Thomas 2LtTLt kia 18-6-17 RFA att9RFC p12&34 MR20 CR France451
PHILIP,Gerald Huntley 2Lt dow 11-11-16 3 att15Hamps p121 CR Hamps214
PHILIP,John Alexander 2Lt dow 7-5-18 D122RFA p34 CR France100
PHILIP,Kenneth Capt kia 27-3-18 1/4 att11EYorks p219 MR27
PHILIPPS,Ivor John Douglas TCapt ded 8-3-15 16Ches p96 CR Scot237 Ex 3BlkW
PHILIPS,Abraham Zadok TCapt dow 24-10-17 RAMC att56FA p197 CR Belgium18
PHILIS,A.C.2Lt 7-7-16 6KOSB MR21
PHILIS,Arthur Maxwell TCapt kia 11-11-15 11YLI att9WYorks p143 CR Gallipoli27
PHILIPS,Basil Edwin.MID LtCol kia 10-8-15 Cmdg5RWelshF p223 CR Gallipoli5
PHILIPS,Henry Charles T2Lt kia 7-12-17 10RWSurr p56 CR Italy7,PHILLIPS
PHILIPS,Herbert Stanley 2Lt kia 26-3-17 6Ess p232 MR34
PHILIPS,Mark Hibbert 2Lt kia 4-10-17 4 att1SStaffs p123 CR Belgium308
PHILIPS,William Theodore Caldwell 2Lt kia 2-5-18 9RScots p212 CR France33
PHILLIBROWN,Cyril George 2Lt dow 15-11-17 RGA 111SB p209 CR France446
PHILLIMORE,Hugh Bouchier Lt dow 16-6-15 8A&SH p243 MR22
PHILLIMORE,Jasper Prescott TLt kia 13-10-15 6EKent p58 CR France423
PHILLIMORE,Matthew Arden T2Lt kia 25-6-16 9Ess attRE 251TC p132 CR France163,11Bn
PHILLIPPO,Arthur James Cecil Eyre Lt kia 7-6-17 RASC att6RFC p12&193 CR Belgium410,dow
PHILLIPPS,Reginald William 2Lt kia 26-10-15 GrenGds SR att1Bn p50 CR France423
PHILLIPPS,Rowland Erasmus.Hon.MC.TCapt kia 7-7-16 9RFus p69 CR France251,PHILIPPS Roland
PHILLIPS,Arthur 2Lt kia 23-4-17 2RWelshF p98 MR20
PHILLIPS,Arthur Blakeway 2Lt kia 19-6-16 12Lond p248 CR France1327
PHILLIPS,Arthur Cornwallis 2Lt dow 22-5-17 4 att1ScotRif p104 CR France1184
PHILLIPS,Azariah T2Lt kld 12-1-18 RFC p16 CR Wales690
PHILLIPS,Benjamin Wynford Lt kld 14-11-17 RGA &RFC p19&p209 CR Shrop89,PHILIPPS
PHILLIPS,Cecil Ivor 2Lt kia 27-10-17 Glouc att45RFC p12&107 MR20
PHILLIPS,Charles LtCol ded 10-1-19 RGA p262 CR Kent180
PHILLIPS,Charles Ernest.MC.Lt kia 22-10-18 4 att7RIrReg p89 CR Belgium143
PHILLIPS,Christian Gibson Maj kia 10-7-16 RLancs p59 CR France432

245

PHILLIPS,Colwyn Erasmus Arnold.Hon.MID TCapt kia 13-5-15 RHGds p20 MR29 PHILIPPS
PHILLIPS,Cyril Gordon 2Lt kia 10-11-17 3 att 1SWBord p100 MR30
PHILLIPS,David Charles 2Lt kia 16-8-17 4RWelshF p223 CR Belgium106
PHILLIPS,Edward T2Lt dow 27-5-18 NumbF att5Bn p62 MR18
PHILLIPS,Edward George Dunscombe Masters LtACapt kia 13-11-16 2 att6RIrReg p89 CR Belgium17,14-11-16
PHILLIPS,Edward Hawkin.DSO.Maj dow 6-11-14 28RFA p34 CR France80,Hawtin
PHILLIPS,Edward Stone Lt kia 8-5-15 1Mon p244 MR29
PHILLIPS,Edwin Mann Lt dow 29-9-18 2RInnisF p105 CR France34
PHILLIPS,Eric Sutherland TCapt dow 21-2-17 8BordR B'Coy p117 CR France263
PHILLIPS,Ernest Arthur 2Lt kia 2-11-17 4RBerks att1/5Beds p234 CR Palestine8
PHILLIPS,Ernest James T2Lt kia 15-8-17 RE 170TC p47 CR France178
PHILLIPS,Eustace Edward Lovett T2Lt kia 30-10-15 6RBerks p139 CR France515
PHILLIPS,Fenton Ellis Stanley.MC.2Lt kia 13-10-16 3Dev &RFC p3,77&259 MR20
PHILLIPS,Frank Stewart T2Lt kia 23-11-17 13Yorks p91 MR17
PHILLIPS,Frederick Charles 2Lt dow 6-2-16 5NumbF p213 CR Belgium11
PHILLIPS,Frederick George LtACapt kia 25-4-18 5WYorks p218 MR30
PHILLIPS,Gilbert William TLt dow 20-11-17 TankCps p188 CR France415
PHILLIPS,Gwilym 2Lt kia 13-10-18 4Glouc att1/8LancF p225 CR France206
PHILLIPS,Guy Saggerson 2Lt kia 15-9-16 5Yorks p221 CR France239
PHILLIPS,Herbert 2Lt kia 13-10-16 2Yorks p91 MR21
PHILLIPS,Herbert Denis T2Lt kia 24-10-16 57MGC Inf p185 CR France535
PHILLIPS,Hubert Henry Lt dow 4-10-15 2 att3Leic p88 CR France345,7 att3Bn
PHILLIPS,J.Sister drd 20/21-3-17 QAIMNS p200 MR40,21-3-17
PHILLIPS,James Lt kia 1-11-18 RE 203FC p210 CR Belgium167
PHILLIPS,James William TCapt kia 30-5-18 9RWFus p98 MR ?
PHILLIPS,John 2Lt kia 20-7-16 5ScotRif p224 MR21
PHILLIPS,John Harold Montague 2Lt dow 25-1-16 RE 4FC p210 CR France80
PHILLIPS,John Henley Shawe Maj ded 28-9-19 RE p271 CR Mddx77
PHILLIPS,John Noel.MID Capt dow 18-4-15 1Lincs p75 CR France102
PHILLIPS,Joseph Alexander Lt kia 3-5-17 13Lpool p72 MR20
PHILLIPS,Joseph Douglas Lt kia 20-10-14 EKent p58 MR32
PHILLIPS,Joseph Leo T2Lt kld 20-7-17 GL &RFC p12 CR Norf209
PHILLIPS,Leonard Harry Perrins TLt kia 6-11-16 12 att2Worc p109 MR21
PHILLIPS,Leslie Capt kia 25-5-15 1WelshR p127 MR29
PHILLIPS,Maurice Aldcroft Capt kia 21-5-15 RFA 31Bty p34 CR France727
PHILLIPS,Norman Arthur 2Lt kia 25-3-17 54RFC p12 CR France1061
PHILLIPS,Norman Rutherford 2Lt kia 20-9-17 6Lpool p215 MR30
PHILLIPS,Owen Sherwood T2Lt kia 21-8-15 4SWBord p100 CR Gallipoli17
PHILLIPS,Patrick Tewan T2Lt kia 4/5-4-16 10 att6ELancs p111 MR38
PHILLIPS,Percy Montague TLt kia 25-9-16 13Yorks p91 CR France115
PHILLIPS,Philip Roy Capt ded 7-5-18 A55RFA p207 MR38
PHILLIPS,Ralph Aberdeen T2Lt kld 16-8-17 RFC 11TrnSqn p12 CR Lincs61
PHILLIPS,Ralph Noel Capt dow 27-12-14 RWFus p98 CR Berks42
PHILLIPS,Reginald 2Lt kia 23-4-17 2SWBord p100 MR20
PHILLIPS,Reginald Gurwen 2Lt kia 26-1-17 3EKent p58 MR19
PHILLIPS,Richard Glyndwr Lt kia 27-8-17 RGA p209 CR Belgium23
PHILLIPS,Richard Hill T2Lt kia 25-9-16 15RWar p65 CR France374
PHILLIPS,Stanley Cross Lt kia 15-9-16 4Y&L p238 CR France702
PHILLIPS,Sydney Capt kia 25-10-15 12RFus p69 MR19
PHILLIPS,Sydney Vernon T2Lt kia 14-8-16 10 att7Leic B'Coy p88 CR France1182
PHILLIPS,T.Capt 19-8-18 Lancs &RAF CR Lancs76
PHILLIPS,Thomas.MC.DCM.Lt kia 29-8-18 6Lpool p215 CR France106
PHILLIPS,Thomas Frederick 2Lt kia 29-7-16 3HLI p163 CR France397
PHILLIPS,Thomas Glynn Llewellyn Capt kia 26-3-17 5WelshR p230 MR34
PHILLIPS,Thomas McCann.MID Capt dow 4-11-14 RAMC p197 CR Belgium150
PHILLIPS,Tom Vaughan Wynne BtCol ded 29-9-16 RHA p271
PHILLIPS,Walter Ernest.MC.2Lt dow 23-3-18 23Lond p252 CR France177,22-8-18
PHILLIPS,Walter Henry Sherburn 2Lt kia 16-9-16 4EYorks p219 CR France387
PHILLIPS,William Charles Owen Capt kia 24-8-14 RWKent p141 CR Belgium201,23-8-14
PHILLIPS,William David 2Lt dow 28-9-18 15RWar p65 CR France512
PHILLIPS,William Ernest 2Lt dow 29-9-18 RGA 283SB p41 CR France1461
PHILLIPS,William James 2Lt kia 25-7-16 4SfthH p241 MR21
PHILLPOTTS,Brian Surtees.DSO.MajALtCol dow 4-9-17 RE Cmdg38Div p47 CR Belgium16
PHILLPOTTS,Fitzroy Charles TLt dow 9-8-18 7Glouc p107 MR4
PHILLPOTTS,Louis Murray.CMG.DSO.TBrigGen kia 8-9-16 RA Staff56Div p34 CR France394,Murr 24Div HQ

PHILP,Claude Hastings George Capt kia 28-3-18 RAMC att1/7Manch p197 CR France560,26-3-18
PHILP,Edgar Charles 2Lt ded 1-12-18 HAC Res CR Mddx76
PHILP,Richard William Manning Haigh TCapt kia 5-10-16 RFA 91Bde p34 CR France513
PHILPS,Andrew Christie T2Lt kia 17-7-16 6KOSB p102
PHILPOT,Godfrey Capt kia 1-9-16 RGA 25SB p41 CR France329
PHILPOT,John T2Lt kia 25-2-16 RE 253Co p47 CR France423
PHILPOTT,John Reginald.MC.TCapt ded PoW 15-1-18 63RFC p16 CR Iraq8
PHILSON,Samuel Cowell Col ded 4-11-18 RAMC p197 MR66
PHIPPARD,Dudley West T2Lt kia 4-10-17 1Hamps p121 CR Belgium83
PHIPPEN,Henry George Lt dow 9-11-16 4Glouc p225 CR France515
PHIPPEN,Arthur Coryn 2Lt kia 13-4-18 9ACycCps p244 MR32
PHIPPS,Charles Percy Lt kia 19-7-16 O&BLI 2/1BucksBn C'Coy p231 MR19
PHIPPS,Christopher Leckonby Lt kia 14-8-17 RGA 118SB 7BallCo attRFC p12&4 CR Belgium19
PHIPPS,Constantine James.DSO.MC.MIDx3 LtAMaj ded 19-2-19 1Lpool att2DivSigCo RE p72&257 CR Germany1
PHIPPS,Lionel Lush TLt dow 28-9-15 7Nhampt p138 CR France178
PHIPPS,Robert Pickering 2LtACapt kia 13/15-11-16 4 att2SStaffs A'Coy p123 CR France1890
PHORSON,Douglas Stuart 2LtACapt kia 16-12-16 18DLI p161 CR France342
PHRIPP,Arthur Thornton T2Lt kia 19-10-17 WRid p116 CR Dorset67
PIBEL,Leo Maxse T2Lt drd 15-4-17 RASC p193 MR35
PIBWORTH,Frederick James Lt ded 20-12-19 1A TC att2/98Inf p281 MR43
PICK,Alfred James Lt kld 2-12-18 3DLI &RAF p161 CR Numb26
PICKARD,Donald Johnson T2Lt kia 17-7-16 6Leic p88 CR France432
PICKARD,Eugene Cuthbert Llewellyn Capt ded 24-11-18 RE 643FC p256 CR Sussex124
PICKARD,F.F.EngCmdr drd 30-12-15 RIM p281 MR64
PICKARD,Harry Lawson.MC.2Lt kia 20-10-18 1/2 att9RWelshF p98 CR France27
PICKARD,Lawrence Delapons 2Lt kia 10-8-17 5RWSurr p212 MR29
PICKARD,Reginald Gilbert 2Lt dow 2-3-17 1/7WelshF attYLI p230 CR France339
PICKARD,Rubie Mrs 13-4-16 BRCS CR France64
PICKARD-CAMBRIDGE,Herbert Evelyn Winn Lt kia 1-11-17 16Suss p205 CR Palestine1
PICKEN,Ronald Baynton Lt 6-9-18 RAF MR37
PICKER,Herbert Francis.MC.Lt ded 23-5-17 RE SigCo p47&210 CR France102
PICKERING,Albert Edwin.MC.2Lt kia 28-9-18 B165RFA p34 CR France285
PICKERING,Basil Horace 2LtTLt dow 1-12-15 8EKent p58 CR Germany1
PICKERING,Charles Leigh Lt kia 15-4-17 6Ches attRFC p19&222 CR Iraq8
PICKERING,Cyril Aubrey Lt kia 30-8-18 1RB p180 MR16
PICKERING,Edmund Charles 2Lt kia 15-9-16 6Lond p247 MR21
PICKERING,Francis Alexander Umfreville.DSO.MajTLtCol kia 23-12-17 2Drags att9RB p21 CR Belgium101
PICKERING,Frank Wells 2Lt dow 20-9-17 RGA 287SB p41 CR Belgium46
PICKERING,Freeman 2Lt dow 10-10-17 4Manch p155 CR France285,kia
PICKERING,George Anthony Raymond T2Lt kia 2-11-17 2 att1/4Nhampt p138 C Palestine8,3-11-17
PICKERING,Harold Crosby 2Lt kia 7-7-15 NStaffs SR attLancF p157 MR29
PICKERING,Henry Earlam T2Lt ded 9-3-18 SLancs att1/5Bn p125 CR France765
PICKERING,Leonard Lt kia 9-4-18 RE 79FC p210 CR France490
PICKERING,Robert Hackney Lt kia 30-11-17 RFA N'A/ABty p34 CR France379
PICKERING,Thomas T2Lt ded 1-11-15 7Glouc p107 CR Egypt3
PICKERING,William Carrington Lt kia 11-10-18 6 att1RB p180 CR France270
PICKERING,William James 2Lt dow 7-6-17 RFA 113ArmyBde p34 CR France28:
PICKERING-CLARKE,John Norman T2Lt kia 14-7-16 10 att7Leic p88 MR21
PICKERSGILL,John Henry.MC.Lt kia 28-8-18 10 att1/6Ches p96 CR France139,dedacc
PICKERSGILL-CUNLIFFE,John Cunliffe Capt kia 4-6-15 6 att1Worc p109 MR32
PICKERSGILL-CUNLIFFE,John Reynolds 2Lt kia 14-9-14 2GrenGds p50 CR France1112
PICKETT,Frederick Charles 2Lt ded 6-1-15 RScots p54 CR Mddx77
PICKETT,Gerald Molyneux 2Lt kia 9-9-16 3RIrF p171
PICKFORD,Herbert Thomas Reade 2Lt kia 25-4-17 O&BLI p130 MR37
PICKFORD,Howard Arthur T2Lt kia 14-7-16 21Manch p155 MR21
PICKIN,William Thomas TLt kia 25-9-15 2Leic p88 MR19
PICKLES,Clifford Crawshaw Capt 22-12-16 RAMC NumbFA CR Yorks361
PICKLES,Frederick Arthur.MC.Capt dow 5-9-18 12Manch p155
PICKLES,Harry 2Lt kia 14-4-17 4BordR att1/16Lond p228 MR20
PICKLES,Harry Thornton T2Lt kia 26-4-16 11 att9WRid p116 CR France922

PICKOP,James Taylor Greer 2Lt dow 21-6-17 4RFus p69 CR Lond8
PICKOP,William Bannister Augustus Lt dow 24-10-18 4RFus p69 CR France292,1Bn
PICKRELL,Leslie John 2Lt kia 29-3-18 RFA 29Bde MR20
PICKSTONE,Charles 2Lt kia 3-9-17 GL &1RFC p12 MR20
PICKSTONE,Dick T2Lt kia 12-10-16 14 att17Manch p155 MR21
PICKTHALL,Henry Clement Vaughan Capt ded 8-12-18 RGA 320SB p41 CR Greece1
PICKTHALL,William Roy 2Lt kia 16-9-18 A26RFA 26ArmyBde p34 CR France309
PICKUP,Alfred James T2Lt kia 26-9-15 2Yorks p91 MR19
PICKUP,George.MC.ACapt kld 20-8-18 6RLancs p59 CR Iraq1
PICKUP,William 2Lt kia 25-3-18 1ELancs p111 MR20
PICKUP,William Heys T2Lt kld 12-3-18 RFC p17&21 CR Lancs189
PICKWORTH,Arthur William 2Lt kia 28-9-18 16Lond p250 CR Belgium89
PICOT,Philip Simons Capt kia 11-7-15 14N&D p134 CR Gallipoli6
PICSTONE,Charles 2Lt kia 3-9-17 GL &1RFC p12
PICTON,F.J.L.MM.Lt ded 6-2-18 3 att1N&D p134 CR Mddx9
PICTON,James Allanson.MC.TLt kia 23-7-17 9ESurr p113 CR Belgium29
PICTON-WARLOW,Wilfrid Capt kia 20-12-14 WelshR attRFC p2&127,ded MR20
PIDCOCK,Frank Lt ded 17-2-19 RFA 296Bde p34 CR France146
PIDDUCK,Norman Andrews.MID T2Lt kia 1-7-16 102MGC p185 MR21
PIDSLEY,Hayward Gould 2Lt dow 21-5-17 RB ACoy p180
PIERCE,John Basil Lt 2-10-18 53RAF MR20
PIERCE,John Beresford Hudson T2Lt dow 27-4-17 RFA p34 CR France113
PIERCE,Robert Campbell TLtCol kia 1-7-16 1RInnisF p105 CR France339
PIERCE,Ronald Hugh MacGregor T2Lt kia 14-9-16 13 att9WYorks p82 MR21
PIERCE,Sidney Ernest.MC.2Lt dow 26-12-15 1/4YLI p235 CR France40,PEIRCE Sydney see PEIRCE,S.E.
PIERCY,George Bowmaker Lt 28-8-21 4RScots CR Scot561
PIERCY,Wilfred Ashton Lt kld 26-9-15 1/17Lond p250 MR19
PIERREPOINT,James H.TLt drd 4-5-17 RA p34 CR Italy14
PIERSON,Charles Frederick Leonard Capt kia 2-11-14 RGA 114HB p41 CR France260
PIERSON,Christopher Frank Kershaw T2Lt kia 10-10-17 GL &52RFC p12 CR France1361
PIERSON,Leslie Dilworth.MID Lt kia 30-10-16 10EYorks p84 MR21
PIERSON,Roy TLt kia 30-4-15 2Ess p132 CR Belgium20
PIERSON,William Henry Maxwell.MC.LtACapt kia21-11-17 3 att2SWBord p100 CR France911
PIERSSENE,Frederick Andrew Lt dow 6-9-18 4RSuss att26RFus p228 CR France142
PIGE-LESCHALLAS,Gilbert TCapt kia 15-8-15 7RDubF p177 MR4
PIGEON,John Walter Capt kia 3-9-20 IA IMS p281 MR38
PIGG,Bernard William 2Lt kia 3-7-16 6Worc p109 MR21,10Bn
PIGGIN,Frederick Loverseed Lt kia 20-12-16 RhodNatR CR Tanzania1
PIGGIN,Frederick William.MC.Capt drd 27-5-18 NottsYeo p205 MR41
PIGGOT,Arthur Alfred Lt kia 26-9-15 13NumbF C'Coy p255 MR19
PIGGOTT,Deighton Torre.MC.Lt kia 15-10-18 3 att8RWKent p141 CR France270
PIGGOTT,Frederick 2Lt kia 28-9-18 Y&L p159 CR France262
PIGGOTT,Frederick Cecil Holman TCapt ded 26-6-17 RAMC p197 CR Devon239
PIGGOTT,Gerald Wellesley 2Lt dow 14-5-15 127/29RFA p34 CR France284
PIGGOTT,G.F.Lt 23-3-18 5Ches MR27
PIGGOTT,William 2LtACapt kia 24-3-18 2Nhampt p138 MR27
PIGHILLS,John Arthur 2Lt dow PoW 29-5-18 WYorks att11LancF p82 CR France1331
PIGOTT,Christopher Devonshire 2Lt 26-8-16 1Wilts att8LNLancs MR21
PIGOTT,Eric John Keefe Pemberton Lt kia 24-6-15 1RIrReg p89 CR France1140
PIGOT,Ernest Borkman.MC.Lt dow 25-5-20 RGA p262 MR43,PIGOTT
PIGOT-MOODIE,Charles Alfred 2Lt kia 14-1-15 RB p180 CR Belgium17,13-1-15
PIGOTT,Christopher Devonshire T2Lt kia 26-8-16 1Wilts att8LNLancs p153 MR21
PIGOTT,Lancelot Boltry TLt kia 6-8-15 13 att2Hamps p121 MR4,Botry
PIKE,Cecil Francis Browne LtCol 15-3-20 RE CR Cornwall40
PIKE,Geoffrey Davies.MC.TCol acckld 15-8-18 IA 1/9GurkhaRif p281 CR Asia81
PIKE,Henry George 2Lt 30-8-18 65RAF MR20
PIKE,Richard Nicholson Capt kia 8-9-15 PoliticalOff att1NigR p201 CR WAfrica58
PIKE,Robert Maxwell.MID TCapt kia 9-8-15 RFC p2 MR20
PIKE,William.DSO.Capt kia 21-8-15 1RInnisF p105 MR4
PIKE,William Edward T2Lt kia 31-1-17 RE 77FC p47 CR France785
PIKE-STEPHENSON,Daniel Pike 2Lt dow 24-5-15 4NStaffs att1Ches p157 CR France102
PILCHER,Alfred Mark 2Lt dow PoW 6-6-18 15Lond p249 CR France1142
PILCHER,G.Maj 11-11-19 LNLancs CR Surrey160

PILCHER,Gerald Aubrey 2Lt dow 26-10-17 D159RFA p34 CR Belgium16,Lt
PILCHER,Thomas Percy Lt kia 10-3-15 2RB p180 CR France709,12-3-15
PILE,Cyril John 2Lt dow 29-4-17 RFA att12RFC p12&34 CR France531
PILGRIM,Harold Stephen 2Lt 17-2-19 6DCLI CR Leic55
PILGRIM,Henry Bastick 2Lt kia 1-7-16 13Lond p249 CR France1327
PILGRIM,Hugh Thomas.MC.Capt kia 25-8-18 9RFus p69 CR France578
PILGRIM,Stephen Argent Ffennell Lt dow 24-9-18 13TankCps p188 CR France327,2Lt
PILKINGTON,Hugh Brocklehurst.MID Capt kia 4-6-15 6Manch C'Coy p236 MR4
PILKINGTON,John Oscar TLt kia 6-9-17 20RFC p12 CR France285
PILKINGTON,Joseph Bernard Lt kia 20-4-18 1Nhampt p138 CR France260
PILKINGTON,Sam Capt kia 2-7-17 4Leic p219 CR France924
PILLEAU,Arthur Langston Maj dow 10-8-15 10Hamps p121 MR4
PILLEAU,Henry Charles.DSO.LtCol dow 21-9-14 RWSurr p56 CR France462
PILLINER,Rupert Colerick Leybourne 2Lt kia 4-11-14 127/29RFA p34 CR France297
PILLING,Doris Ellen Prob ded 29-3-19 QAIMNS CR Lond7
PILLING,Edgar 2Lt kia 23-4-17 460/15RFA 15Bde p34 CR France581
PILLING,J.E. 2Lt ded 1-7-18 5Lpool &25RAF p215 CR Belgium384
PILLING,Percy Cunliffe Capt dow 6-8-16 1/5LNLancs p234 CR France141
PILLING,Walter T2Lt kld 3-4-17 GL &RFC 5Res p12 CR Lancs211
PILLING,William.MC.2Lt ded 22-10-18 3 att2RWFus p98 CR France146
PILLMAN,Robert Lawrence TCapt dow 9-7-16 10RWKent p141 CR Belgium33
PILLOW,Henry Montgomery Scott T2Lt kia 8-8-17 7RFC p12
PILTER,Charles Lt dow 30-5-15 18Huss p23 CR France285
PIM,Thomas Lt kld 28-8-18 RFA &13RAF p34 MR20
PIMM,Charles William T2Lt kia 18-5-17 12Y&L p159 CR France644
PIMM,Victor Lionel 2Lt kia 10-11-16 2WYorks p82 MR21
PINCH,William 2Lt kia 31-7-17 1/5RLancs p213 CR Belgium10
PINCHES,Edward Harold 2Lt dow 16-11-17 3 att1LNLancs p136 CR Belgium16,Lt
PINCHIN,George Harold Lt dow 27-11-17 1/5Beds p219 CR Egypt1,2Lt
PINCHING,Minden Charles Cardigan.DSO.Maj ded 20-4-17 2DragGds p21 CR Surrey103
PINCKNEY,John William Lt kia 9-4-18 1KEdwHorse p24 CR France644,11-4-18
PINCOMBE,Lionel John T2Lt kia 20-9-17 32RFus p69 MR43
PINDER,Albert Humphrey.MID Lt kia 14-9-16 3 att1Leic p88 CR France374,15-9-16
PINDER,Reginald Maw Capt kia 7-10-17 5WRid p227 MR30
PINDER,S.R.Lt 19-2-18 GL &RFC CR Frnce924
PINE,Albert Arthur Lt kia 16-1-17 4Worc p109 CR Iraq5
PINE,Frank Youatt T2Lt kia 16-8-17 176MGC p185 CR Belgium12,15-8-17
PINE,Leslie William Tattersall 2Lt dow 18-8-17 2Hamps p121 CR Belgium16,Lt
PINE-COFFIN,John Edward.DSO.Maj ded 22-8-19 LNLancs 9264 CR Devon40
PINE-COFFIN,Tntram James Lt mbk 23-9-19 3Dev NR p256 MR70 &CR Europe180
PINFIELD,Guy Vickery TLt kld 24-4-16 8Huss p22 CR Ireland14,2Lt
PINFORD,William Herbert 2Lt ded 9-10-18 IARO attEmbnStaff p281 MR65,PINFOLD
PING,Alan Roy 2Lt kia 21-7-17 3Worc p109 MR29
PINHEY,Hammett Eardley 2Lt kia 19-4-15 3 att2DCLI p114 CR Belgium165
PINHEY,Kenneth Fleetwood Gordon Lt kia 2-8-17 RFA 83Bde p34 CR Belgium19
PINK,Alan Lins Lt kld 30-10-18 1/4RB &41RAF p180 CR Belgium441,Luis
PINK,Harold William 2Lt dow 7-10-16 RE 1/7FC p210 CR Greece4
PINKERTON,Eric Mitchell T2Lt kia 1-7-16 15RScots p54 MR21
PINN,Tyrrell Steventon T2Lt dow 12-10-15 8EYorks p84
PINNEGAR,John Arthur.MC.Capt kia 22-3-18 16RB p180 MR27,23-3-18
PINNEY,John Charles William Adderley.MID Lt kia 1-12-17 1RFus att38Horse C'Sqdn p69 CR France446
PINNIGER,Reginald Charles Lt ded 20-1-20 IARO att26Punjabis CR Devon72
PINNIGER,Wilfred James 2Lt kia 4-10-17 D91RFA 91Bde p34 CR Belgium86
PINNINGTON,Victor 2Lt kia 5-11-16 33 att23NumbF p62 MR32
PINNOCK,Carey T2Lt kld 30-11-17 RFC p12 CR Lincs136
PINSENT,Laurance Alfred.MID TLt dow 15-8-15 7NStaffs p157 CR Gallipoli19
PINSENT,Philip Ryland T2Lt dow 24-9-16 34RFC p3 CR France882
PINSENT,Richard Parker T2Lt kia 9-10-15 10RWar p65 CR France727
PINSON,Ivan Lapworth T2Lt dow 4-5-17 GL &70RFC p12 CR France1031
PIPER,Albert Benjamin Charles Lt ded 4-12-20 IA 120Inf p281 MR43,6-12-20
PIPER,Lawrence T2LtTLt kia 10-6-17 3Worc p109 CR Belgium43
PIPER,Reginald C.MID Capt&Adjt kia 29-4-18 1/6 att1/5SStaffs p229 CR France572
PIPER,Ronald Brandon 2Lt dow PoW 3-4-16 6RWar p214 CR France518

PIPER,Ronald Leslie.MC.MID Lt dow 11-10-17 IA 57Rif att129Baluchis p281 CR EAfrica11 &CR Tanzania1,Capt
PIPPET,John Gilbert.MM.2Lt kia 29-5-18 1Lincs p75 CR France1332
PIRDER,Sidney Rueben 2Lt mbk 19-2-18 80RFC p256
PIRIE,Alexander 2Lt dow 13-12-14 GordH p167 CR France284
PIRIE,Arthur Murray.DSO.ALtCol kia 21-11-17 21Lancers attBerksYeo p23 CR Palestine3
PIRIE,George Lawrence 2Lt ded 16-6-15 NhamptYeo p204 CR Surrey91
PIRIE,George Stephen LtTCapt kia 24-7-17 RAMC att9ESurr p197 CR Belgium29
PIRIE,William Shewan.DCM.Capt kia 19-4-17 5RScotF attMGC p187&222 MR34
PIRRET,James Kay 2Lt kia 4-4-17 11KRRC p151 CR France662
PIRRIE,Robert Bourn Lt kia 9-8-15 3BordR att1KSLI p117 MR29,10-8-15
PITCAIRN,Ellis Gledhill Capt ded 6-10-18 8BlkW p129 CR Belgium38
PITCAIRN,Hugh Francis T2Lt ded 3-6-17 RASC 47Div SplyColmnMechTrans p193 CR France95
PITCHFORD,Arthur Reginald 2Lt kia 17-9-18 att7KSLI p145 MR16
PITE,Horace Victor Walter 2Lt kia 10-4-18 3 att5Hamps p121 CR Palestine9
PITHER,Harold Francis 2Lt kia PoW 6-7-16 9 att5RDubF p177 CR France745,dow
PITHER,Sidney Edward Capt dow 11-6-18 1/2KOSB &RAF p102 CR Egypt15,dedacc
PITMAN,Arthur Frederick Edward Capt kia 3-1-18 5Sfth attRFC p19&241 MR20
PITMAN,Thomas Stuart TLt kia 28-9-17 6Y&L p159 MR30
PITOT,Maurice Leon 2Lt dow 8-10-18 RE &103RAF p47 CR France512,A.L.A.M.
PITT,Bernard T2Lt kia 30-4-16 10BordR attX47TMB p117 MR20
PITT,Bevan William 2Lt kia 10-5-17 55RFC p12 CR Belgium288
PITT,Douglas 2Lt kia 31-7-17 8ScotRif p225 CR Belgium7
PITT,Douglas 2Lt kia 24-3-18 8RWar p215 CR France1203
PITT,Geoffery Stanhope TCapt ded 11-2-19 26RFus p69 CR Lond12
PITT,George Llewllyn T2Lt kld 28-12-15 10Y&L &8RFC p2&159 CR France1205
PITT,James Maxwell Lt kld 13-10-14 1Dors p124 CR France260
PITT,J.H.Capt 16-4-17 SAfrSerCps MR46
PITT,John T2Lt kld 7-2-18 46RFC p17 CR Ches98,Jack
PITT,Robert Frederick Cadet 24-2-19 IndMiscList MR43
PITT,Stanley Lt kia 26-10-17 4RFA p208 MR30
PITT,Stanley Robert.MC.T2Lt kia 23-10-16 RFA 2Bde p34 CR France374
PITT,Vio Douglas Wallace 2Lt dow 24-8-16 8RBerks p139 CR France44
PITT,W.A.Maj 13-6-20 3RFus CR Lond12
PITT,William Neville TMaj dow 20-8-16 2Lincs p75 CR France98
PITT-PITTS,Edward Crewdson Pitt 2Lt kld 17-10-18 4EKent p212 CR France849
PITT-PITTS,Walter John Lt ded 9-8-18 GL &RAF p191
PITTAR,Charles Austin.MC.Lt 28-8-21 CldGds CR Oxford74
PITTIS,Charles Seymour.MC.Capt kia 19-4-17 8Hamps p229 CR Palestine8
PITTMAN,Cecil Frederick Lt kld 20-7-17 14RFC p12 CR Surrey2
PITTMAN,Frederick John 2Lt ded 20-8-18 RGA att14MtnBty p41 CR Iraq8
PITTMAN,Percy SubCdr ded PoW 28-2-17 IA MilWorksServ p281 CR Iraq8
PITTOCK,Herbert Frank Lt ded 27-8-19 MGC p266 CR Sussex107
PITTOCK,Percy Whittle Lt kia 27-9-18 7Lpool p215 CR France686
PITTOM Wenn William Pratt 2Lt ded 10-10-14 4Nhampt p256 CR Nhampt27
PITTS,Francis Burton 2Lt dow 17-5-17 3 att8Leic p88 CR France924,Lt
PITTS-TUCKER,Cecil Mortimer Lt kia 21-12-14 HLI p163 MR22
PITTY,Thomas John 2Lt kia 25-3-18 10Mddx p236 MR20
PIXLEY,John Nicol Fergusson LtACapt kia 12-10-17 4GrenGds p50 CR Belgium106
PIXLEY,Reginald George Hewett.MC.Capt mbk 4-6-17 RFA &54RFC p257 CR France234
PIZA,Daniel ACapt kia 9-4-17 GL att64TMB p191 MR20
PIZEY,Noel Martin Lt dow 27-7-17 NDevYeo att75RFC p19&203 CR Belgium16
PLACE,Frank Clarke.MC.MM.2Lt kia 22-9-18 1/4RLancs p59&258 CR France109
PLACE,Philip Whiteley 2Lt kia 9-8-18 NumbF att12Norf p62 CR France19,19-8-18
PLAISTER,Geoffrey Ratcliffe TCapt kia 11-4-17 RAMC att10Y&L p197 MR20
PLAISTOWE,Alan ACapt kia 24-4-17 8Worc p226 CR France1495
PLAISTOWE,Richard Reeves Lt kia 19-4-17 1/5Norf p216 CR Palestine8
PLANT,Frederic George T2Lt kia 25-9-15 RWSurr p56 MR19
PLANT,George Bede Hornby.MC.Lt kia 18-9-18 NorfYeo p204 CR France369
PLANT,Herbert T2Lt dow 20-12-16 15 att14RWar p65 CR France80
PLANT,Herbert Stanley 2Lt ded 18-2-18 RE 181TC 52InfBde p47 CR France214,Lt
PLANT,Holford Charles Fourdrinier 2Lt kia 3-5-17 3NStaffs att9Leic p157 MR20
PLANT,Hubert Arthur 2Lt kia 24-5-17 6NStaffs p238 MR20
PLANT,John Blayney Llewellyn 2Lt ded 8-8-19 RASC p267 CR Germany1,RDubF att17RFus
PLANT,Percy William 2Lt kia 28-9-15 8RWKent p141 MR19

PLANT,Robert Sydney 2Lt kia 17-10-18 5N&D p233 CR France847
PLANT,Verner Lovelace Lt kia 5-4-18 8SomLI p80 MR20
PLANT,Wilfrid 2Lt kia 28-9-18 5NStaffs p238 CR France375,Wilfred
PLANTE,Arthur Gedge Lt kia 26-3-18 5ESurr att4NStaffs p226 MR27
PLASKITT,Sydney Vernon 2Lt kia 5-11-16 5 att9DLI p239 MR21
PLATER,Richard Henry Lt dow 3-5-17 9RB p180 MR20
PLATNAUER,Leonard Maurice 2Lt dow 3-5-17 16WYorks p82 MR20
PLATT,Charles Henry Morris 2LtLt kia 23-11-17 RWar att52RFC p12&65 CR France1361
PLATT,Claud Lucien Francis 2Lt kia 27-5-18 RH&FA 25DAC p34 MR18
PLATT,Frank Lindsay Capt kia 21-3-18 3 att1KSLI p145 CR France646
PLATT,Henry Evelyn Arthur.MID Capt kia 15-5-16 19Huss att1CldGds p23 CR Belgium6
PLATT,John Rookhurst Lt dow 27-3-16 RFA 3Bde p208 CR Belgium127
PLATT,Lionel Sydney Capt kia 13-4-17 17Lancers att57RFC p12&23 CR France604
PLATTEN,Walter Henry T2Lt kia 10-9-16 14SWBord att19RWFus p100 CR France423
PLATTS,Arthur Leslie Capt kia 20-7-16 2Suff p78 MR21
PLATTS,Edgar Lovell Filmer Lt 28-4-17 RMLI MR20
PLATTS,John Carrick Capt kia 7-3-20 IA 17Cav att10Lancers p281 CR Iraq8
PLATTS,Reginald Hardy Lt ded 31-5-18 RGA p271
PLAYER,Alfred Edward Lt ded 10-7-19 LabCps attChineseLabCps p266 CR France65
PLAYER,Eric Noel TCapt kia 6-8-16 8Yorks p91 CR France515
PLAYER,Gilbert T2Lt dow 30-7-16 21DLI p161 CR France345
PLAYFAIR,A.L.MajGen 10-9-15 BengalStaffCps CR Sussex178
PLAYFAIR,Frank Capt kia 16-7-15 RScots p54
PLAYFAIR,Lambert Lt kia 6-7-15 1RScots att1RFC p2 CR Belgium9
PLAYFAIR,Lyon George Henry Lyon.Hon.Capt kia 20-4-15 RFA 69Bty31Bde p3 MR29
PLAYFAIR,Patrick Lyon Capt dow 11-4-18 7BlkW B Coy p231 MR19
PLAYFORD,Antony Boydell 2Lt kia 28-9-15 1SWBord p100 MR19
PLAYFORD,Patrick Randal Lt kia 1-7-17 A/1RFA p208 CR Belgium10
PLAYNE,Leslie Lt 27-3-18 16RFC MR20
PLEASANCE,Charles Joseph T2Lt kia 31-7-17 24NumbF p62 CR France725
PLEDGER,Earnest Charles 2Lt kia 10-10-17 16LancF p93 MR19
PLENTY,Edward Pellew Lt AMaj ded 21-11-18 1Manch &96RAF p265 CR Berks72,22-11-18
PLESTED,Horace George 2Lt kia 30-7-16 4 att16Manch p155 MR21
PLEWMAN,Charles Edward.MC.Lt kia 9-4-18 7Lpool p215 CR France261
PLEYDELL-BOUVERIE,Jacob Edward Lt ded 1-11-14 2KRRC p151 CR France1
PLEYDELL-BOUVERIE,Samuel Wilfred 2Lt kia 15-9-16 19Lond p250 CR France390
PLIMPTON,Robert Albert.MC&Bar.ACapt kia 27-9-17 A&SH att4BlkW p173 MR30,4/5Bn
PLOWDEN,Francis Charles Lt dow 22-8-18 ShropYeo att10KSLI C'Coy p205 CR France31
PLOWDEN,Godfrey Bruce A.Capt ded 2-2-17 1/7RWelshF p223 CR Egypt2
PLOWDEN,W.F.C.LtCol 28-12-18 CR Mddx77
PLOWES,Errol Sydney 2Lt kia 9-4-18 379/169RFA p209 CR France360,Sidney
PLOWMAN,Charles Hugh Lt kia 24-4-17 7Wilts 153 MR37
PLOWMAN,James.MC.TLtACapt dow 29-4-18 2Leinst p174 CR France24
PLUM,Robert Bagshaw 2Lt dow 2-10-17 RFA p209 CR Belgium183
PLUMB,Edward Stephen TLt dow 8-9-17 3WRid p116 CR France113
PLUMER,William Lt kld 7-2-15 YLI p143 CR Belgium98
PLUMMER,Arthur Henry 2Lt kia 17-5-15 5Lpool p215 MR22
PLUMMER,Charles Benjamin Chap4Cl kia 12-3-17 RAChDept att61InfBde p19 CR France513
PLUMMER,Frederick Charles T2Lt kia 23-9-17 215MGC p185 CR Belgium10
PLUMMER,Frederick Ryle Lt ded 2-11-18 RGA p209 CR France332
PLUMMER,John Humphrey 2Lt ded 10-8-18 3 att2GordH p167 CR Italy11
PLUMMER,John Scott 2Lt kia 18-7-17 Leic att1/5Bn p88 MR19
PLUMMER,Lionel Davey Capt kia 15-9-16 4NumbF p213 CR France239
PLUMMER,Sidney Arthur 2Lt kia 24-4-18 9Lond p248 CR France880
PLUMMER,William Francis 2Lt kia 15-9-16 18Lond p250 CR France390
PLUMPTON,Robert 2Lt ded 25-12-18 6Yorks p91 MR70
PLUMPTRE,Basil Pemberton.MC.Rev kia 16-7-17 RAChDept att1/21Lond p199 Belgium21
PLUNKET,Cedric John Lt kia 5-8-17 RFA 123Bde p34 CR Belgium62,6-8-17
PLUNKETT,Havelock Arthur Terence Lt kia 7-1-16 2BlkW p129 MR38

PLUNKETT,Patrick Lt&QM ded 7-9-16 RAMC p267
PLUNKETT,Reginald Frederick Desmond Lt Accdrd 6-9-18 IA 2/1GurkhaRif att 1/5 p281 MR38
POCHIN,Arthur Campbell T2Lt kia 26-9-16 10Ess p132 MR21
POCKETT,Walter Harold 2Lt kia 24-4-18 410/96RFA 96Bde p34 CR France300
POCKLINGTON-SENHOUSE,Oscar William 2Lt 18-6-15 2CldGds CR France114
POCOCK,Beril Edmund 2Lt kia 13-5-15 5Lond p246 MR29
POCOCK,Charles Arthur T2Lt kia 8-5-17 14RWar p65 CR France777
POCOCK,Charles Clarke T2Lt kld 14-3-16 1ESurr p113 CR France184
POCOCK,Malcolm Robertson.DSO.LtCol ded 5-11-17 IA 28Punjabis p281 MR38
POCOCK,Raglan Lionel Alfred T2Lt kia 25-8-17 8ELancs p111 CR Belgium17
POCOCK,Thomas Guy 2Lt dow 3-4-15 4Lpool p72
PODMORE,Edward Glanville 2Lt kia 25-9-15 9Lpool p216 MR21
PODMORE,Hubert.DSO.MIDx3 TMaj kld 31-12-17 6Nhampt att 12Mddx p138 CR Belgium38,LtCol
POE,Charles Vernon Leslie Capt kia 3-3-15 4KRRC p151 MR29,2-3-15 Charley
POER,Hubert Piers Beresford CaptAMaj kia 24-4-18 RH&FA 91Bde p34
POGOSE,Ivor Reginald 2Lt kia 1-7-16 5Lond p246 CR France203,dow
POGUE,Reginald Thomas.MC.T2Lt dow 28-9-18 4TankCps p188 CR France194
POHL,Frederick Alfred Lt ded 22-10-18 A161RFA p34 CR Essex146,43RFA
POHLMANN,Reginald Peel 2Lt kia 5-2-18 25RFC p17 CR Belgium140
POINTER,Arthur James T2Lt kia 22-3-18 12Mddx att 6Nhampt p148 MR27
POINTER,Henry John Lt ded 13-12-17 RH&FA 130Bde p34
POINTER,Reginald James 2Lt kia 21-3-18 3 att 4ELancs p111 MR27
POLACK,Benjamin James T2Lt kia 9-4-16 9Worc p109 MR38
POLACK,Ernest Emanuel Lt 17-7-16 4Glouc p225 CR France293
POLAND,Guy Bernard 2Lt kia 21-3-18 24Lond p252 CR France439
POLAND,Henry Arthur 2Lt kia 18-4-15 C Coy 3 att 1RWKent p141 MR29
POLE-CAREW,Wymond Nicholas Richard Lt kia 6-11-17 1DCLI p114 MR30
POLEHAMPTON,Frederick William 2Lt kld 26-4-15 8RFC p2 CR France134
POLGE,William Edwin 2Lt kia 16-8-17 7Lond p247 MR29
POLLAK,Harry Leopold TLt kia 23-10-16 17 att 2RB p180 MR21
POLLAK,Otto Dennis Lt kia 8-7-16 17RFus p69 MR19
POLLARD,Alfred Gordon 2Lt kia 16-5-17 9A&SH p244 CR France604
POLLARD,Arthur 2Lt kia 21-3-18 2/6N&D C'Coy p233 MR20
POLLARD,Edward Branch TLt dow 26-7-15 KOSB attRE p102 CR Scot612
POLLARD,Ernest Madel T2Lt dow 16-8-17 KRRC att 12Bn p151 CR Belgium23
POLLARD,Frank T2Lt dow 21/22-3-18 att 2/4ELancs p111 MR27
POLLARD,Geoffrey Blemell.MID Lt kld 24-10-14 RFA 119Btyp34 CR France705
POLLARD,George Edward West 2Lt dow 3-9-18 5YLI p235 CR France103
POLLARD,George Herbert 2Lt dow 7-6-17 PoW 9A&SH attRFC p19&244 CR Belgium140
POLLARD,Gerald Evelyn Gustavus Capt kia 25-4-15 1RMunstF p176 MR4
POLLARD,Harold Ernest T2Lt dow 4-8-16 1KOSB p102 CR Egypt2
POLLARD,Herbert Edward TLt kia 26-6-17 RE 134ArmyTpsCo p47 CR Belgium1
POLLARD,Roger Thompson TLt kia 13-10-15 5RBerks p139 MR19
POLLARD,Stanley Madel 2Lt dow 12-4-18 RHA attAyrBty p34 CR Palestine3
POLLARD,Thomas Regester 2Lt ded 2-7-18 5 att 2Lincs p220 CR France40
POLLARD,Thomas Whittaker TLt kia 16-5-17 10LancF p93 MR20
POLLARD,Wilfrid Downes T2Lt dow 26-4-18 15N&D p134 CR Yorks551
POLLARD,William Marcus Noel 2Lt kia 11-4-17 5NStaffs p238 CR France366
POLLARD-URQUHART,William Edward,MID Lt kia 18-4-15 1RSuss p119 MR43
POLLEY,Frank Clarence Capt ded 16-4-19 SL RE 1WT p255&257 CR Asia81
POLLIN,Robert Kelly 2Lt kia 31-7-17 4RIrRif p170 MR29
POLLOCK,Charles Thomas Anderton Capt kia 31-3-18 Inns of Court OTC att 1/4EYorks p252 CR France988,Anderdon dow
POLLOCK,D.MM.TLtACapt kia 18-9-18 1CamH p168 CR France835
POLLOCK,Daniel TCapt drd 15-4-17 RAVC p199 MR35
POLLOCK,Douglas William Capt kia 6-5-15 4Worc Z'Coy p109 MR4
POLLOCK,Frederick Robert Lt kia 22-10-14 ColdGds p51 CR Belgium63
POLLOCK,George Henry 2Lt dow 18-6-15 4SStaffs att 1RWar p123 CR Belgium9
POLLOCK,John Lt kia 1-7-16 13RIrRif p170 MR21
POLLOCK,John Dunbar Capt kia 28-6-15 4RScots p211 CR Gallipoli6
POLLOCK,Louis T2Lt kia 17-10-18 2DLI p161 CR France849
POLLOCK,Martin Viner Lt kia 9-5-15 3 att 1SWBord p100 CR France924
POLLOCK,Max Kenneth TLtCapt kia 25-9-15 1RScotF A'Coy p95 MR29
POLLOCK,Sidney Geoffrey Lt ded 19-11-18 Glouc p264
POLLOCK-HODSALL,George Bertram Capt kld 9-11-14 3Suff p78 MR29,HODSOLL
POLSON,Geoffrey William 2Lt kia 14/15-9-14 1BlkW D'Coy p129 CR France1341,Lt

POMEROY,Granville George TCapt ded 30-3-17 GL 12Yorks attNigR p202 CR WAfrica54
POMEROY,Norman Ransch 2Lt kia 20-10-16 GL &RFC p3&191
POMFRET,Christopher 2Lt kia 27-3-18 1/4 att 2/5ELancs p226 MR27
POMFRET,John William.MC.T2Lt kia 27-10-18 11NumbF p62 CR Italy9
POMFREY,James Arthur T2Lt dow 4-10-18 9Yorks p91 CR France364
POND,Frederick George 2Lt kia 5-9-18 RGA 144SB p41 CR France568
PONSFORD,Glyn George T2Lt kia 28-8-16 10RB p180 CR France400
PONSONBY,Ashley William Neville Capt kia 8-9-15 2 O&BLI p130 CR France279,M
PONSONBY,Cyril Myles Brabazon.Hon.MVO.Maj kia 27-9-15 3 att 4GrenGds p50 MR19,28-9-15
PONSONBY,Cyril Thomas Lt kia 23-8-16 11KRRC p151 CR France397,24-8-16
PONSONBY,Gerald Maurice.MID Capt dow 31-8-14 2RInnisF p105 CR France1355
PONSONBY,Michael Henry Lt dow 27-8-18 2GrenGds p50 CR France927
PONSONBY,Spencer Lawrence TLt dow 12-1-16 12Mddx p148
PONSONBY,W.R.DSO.Capt 18-1-19 3DragGds CR Hereford129
PONTER,Harry William Francis Lt kia 3-9-18 4RWSurr p212 CR France646
PONTER,William Crossland Lt ded 27-11-18 23RB p244 MR66
PONTIFEX,Dudley Allen Capt kia 31-7-17 2ScotRif p104 MR29
PONTING,Cecil Arthur Lt 26-11-17 10SAfrHorse MR52
PONTING,Edward Frank T2Lt kia 5-10-18 21Manch p155 CR France234
POOL,James Williamson 2Lt kia 20-9-17 6ScotRif p224 MR30
POOL,Samuel.MC.TCapt kia 16-6-17 RAMC att 8Leic p197 CR France1489
POOLE,Arthur George TLt ded 22-11-18 Glouc p264 CR Somerset71,28-11-18
POOLE,Bernard Goldsmith T2Lt kia 22-3-18 53RFC p17
POOLE,Edward Masters Rev ded 31-10-18 YMCA CR France13
POOLE,Eric Skeffington 2Lt dow 10-12-16 11Yorks CR Belgium5
POOLE,Esmond Randolph Lascombe Lt kia 25-5-19 IA 32Lancers p281 CR Iraq8
POOLE,Hugh Edward Algernon.MID 2Lt dow 2-6-15 11Huss p22 CR Berks84
POOLE,John Evered T2Lt dow 22-8-17 RE 33FC p47 CR Belgium11,73FC
POOLE,John Richard T2Lt kia 30-7-16 14RWar p65 MR21
POOLE,L.S.R.Lt ded 3-12-18 GL &RAF p191
POOLE,Richard William.MBE.Capt&QM 21-4-19 6ScotRif CR Scot764
POOLE,Robert Evelyn Sandford Lt kia 4-11-18 6 att 13KRRC p151 CR France1480
POOLE,William Evelyn Stanley Lt kia 19-9-17 5NumbF p213 CR France538
POOLE,William John Rowland Ernest Lt kia 9-10-17 4Y&L p238 MR30
POOLEY,Charles.MC.LtTCapt kia 9-8-18 5DragGds p21 CR France652
POOLEY,Richard Sibthorpe T2Lt kia 23-4-17 8RScotF att 1BordR p95 MR20
POOLEY,Robin Mark 2Lt kia 12-8-16 9Lpool p256 MR21
POORE,Roger TLt kia 19-9-15 A48RFA p34 CR Belgium20
POORE,Roger Alvin.DSO.Maj kia 26-9-17 WiltsYeo p206 CR Belgium126
POPE,Charles Alfred Whiting TCapt drd 4-5-17 RAMC p197 CR Italy14
POPE,Cicely Mary Legh Sister 25-6-21 VAD BRCS CR Europe57
POPE,Cyril Montague Lt dow 24-10-14 5 att 2Worc p109 CR Belgium57 Montagu
POPE,Edward Alexander.DSO.LtCol ded 9-4-19 3WelshR p264 CR Dorset42
POPE,Edwin Albert T2Lt kia 27-2-17 GL &8RFC p12 CR France120
POPE,Ernest William TCapt 18-8-16 7RB p180 MR21
POPE,Harold Edward.MC&Bar.TLtACapt kia 24-8-18 21RGA 118HB Xfer to 1/2LancsHB p41 CR France526
POPE,Henry William Capt kia 24-3-18 7DragGds att 21MGC p21&185 CR France207
POPE,Herbert Arnold Lt kia 16-8-17 9Mddx p236 MR4
POPE,Howard John 2Lt 4-3-19 Glouc CR Glouc9
POPE,J.R.Capt 2-3-22 League of Nations Staff CR Europe150A
POPE,John Herbert 2Lt dow 11-4-17 1RIrF p171 CR France451
POPE,Percy Paris 2Lt kia 1-10-15 WelshR p127 MR19,1/2-10-15
POPE,Philip Gladstone Lt kia 16-10-17 RFA 35BdeHQ p34 CR Belgium19,31Bde
POPE,Reginald Thomas Buckingham Lt kia 16-2-15 1WelshR p127 CR Belgium166
POPE,William Archer TCapt dow 7-10-16 10RWSurr p56 CR France833
POPHAM,Edward Home TCapt kia 6-8-15 13 att 2Hamps p121 MR4
POPHAM,John Francis Watson TCapt dow 3-10-16 8Leic p88
POPPLE,George Marsden T2Lt dow 26-6-16 15 att 16NumbF p62 CR France702
POPPLESTONE,Archibald Harry 2Lt kia 6-12-17 7N&D p233 MR19
POPPLEWELL,Harry Bury Capt kia 22-7-18 3RIrRif att 2/3KAR p170&268 CR EAfrica90
PORKESS,Walter Anderson Lt kia 10-2-17 NottsYeo att 10RFC p19&205 CR France98
PORRITT,Edward Radcliffe T2Lt kia 30-7-16 17Lpool p72 CR France1890
PORRITT,John Ernest T2Lt kia 27-5-18 NumbF att 5Bn p62 MR18

PORRITT,Thomas Handly.MC.2Lt dow 31-7-17 2ColdGds p51 CR Belgium16,Hardley
PORRITT,William Murray 2Lt kia 25-9-15 3SLancs attNLancs p125 MR19
PORT,William Garfield 2Lt kia 4-10-17 1Dev p77 MR30
PORTAL,Oldric Spencer LtTCapt kia 3-5-17 1LifeGds attHousehdBn p20 CR France97
PORTEOUS,Dick MacDonald.DSO.Capt kia 10-5-15 1A&SH p173 MR29
PORTEOUS,Douglas Simpson T2Lt kia 20-10-16 6KOSB A'Coy p102 CR France432
PORTEOUS,Gilbert 2Lt kia 22-11-17 5ScotRif p224 CR Palestine3
PORTEOUS,Harry Morton T2Lt kia 25-9-15 12HLI p163 CR France219
PORTEOUS,James Hunter Capt kia 22-8-17 6A&SH p243 CR Belgium84
PORTEOUS,Thomas Williamson T2Lt kia 23-8-18 12TankCps p188 CR France502
PORTER,Alan Grey.MC.LtACapt dow 29-10-18 1 att6RIrRf p171 CR France34
PORTER,Alex James 2Lt mbk 19-4-17 1Norf p256 MR34,Alec
PORTER,Alwyne Morton Francis Worsley Lt kia 25-4-15 1LancF p93 CR Gallipoli1
PORTER,Aubrey Blackwood Lt kia 3-10-15 4 att2HLI p163 CR France423
PORTER,Edgar George T2Lt kia 20-9-18 10EKent p58 MR16,18-9-18
PORTER,Edgar Wardle 2Lt dow 22-8-16 7Lpool D'Coy p215 CR France66
PORTER,Eric Henry TLt kia 17-2-16 8SStaffs p123 CR Belgium120,14-2-16
PORTER,Ernest James Lt dow 22-9-16 PoW 22Lond p251 CR France598
PORTER,Frederick Ernest Gilchrist TCapt dow 3-11-16 7LNLancs p136 CR France44
PORTER,Gavin Alexander LtTCapt ded 6-12-15 RFA 68Bty att13RFC p2&34 CR France518,5-12-15
PORTER,George Anthony Gordon T2Lt kld 9-3-18 RFC p17 CR Lincs100
PORTER,George Francis Lambert 2LtTCapt kia 8-6-17 11WYorks A'Coy p82 CR Belgium127
PORTER,Graham Hawksworth TLt kia 3-10-16 20RWFus p98 CR Belgium73,2-10-16
PORTER,Harold James TLt dow 15-8-15 5Manch p236 CR Egypt3,2Lt
PORTER,Hugh Gordon 2Lt kia 6-11-16 RGA 155HB p41 MR21
PORTER,John Charlton T2Lt kia 24-7-17 MGC F'HB p185 CR Belgium16
PORTER,John Edward T2Lt kia 23-7-16 7SLancs p125 MR21
PORTER,John Joseph Capt ded 3-8-18 RAMC p271 CR Norf209,kldacc
PORTER,John Thomas T2Lt kia 25-8-18 9 att2/4YLI p143 CR France568
PORTER,John William 2Lt ded 11-7-18 13TankCps p188 CR France300
PORTER,Leslie Capt ded 24-10-16 RFC p3 MR20
PORTER,Reginald Edward Lt kia 26-10-14 RAMC att3RB p197 MR32
PORTER,Robert 2LtACapt kia 25-11-17 1ScotRif p104 CR Belgium125
PORTER,Robert Ernest T2Lt dow 10-8-17 11RFus p69 CR Belgium19
PORTER,Robert Nuttall Lt ded 28-1-19 RAMC p267 CR Wales597,25-1-19
PORTITT,Robert Wilson TLt kia 11-1-18 9 att4/5BlkW p129 MR30,Wilison
PORTER,Roderick Spicer Russell 2Lt kia 9-6-16 IARO att130Baluchis p281 CR EAfrica19
PORTER,Royden Spencer Bayspool 2Lt ded 6-2-17 2HAC Inf p206 CR France40
PORTER,Samuel TLt dow 7-8-15 1Y&L att8Manch p159 CR Gallipoli2,kia
PORTER,Stanley Fitzherbert 2Lt ded 6-6-17 GL &RFC p12 CR Lancs170
PORTER,W.2Lt ded 28-2-19 RH&FA attRAF p34
PORTER,William T2Lt kia 1-7-16 6 att1RInnisF p105 CR France339
PORTER,William Guthrie.DSO.Maj kia 8-6-17 C86RFA p206 CR Belgium15
PORTER,William James Lt dow 3-8-17 2Leinst p174 CR Belgium11
PORTER,Wilson 2Lt kia 24-3-18 RFA att56RFC p17&34 MR20
PORTERFIELD,Leonard Witherow TLt ded 1-11-18 167RFA p34&257 CR Mddx17
PORTLOCK,Alfred Edgar T2Lt kld 6-12-17 RFus &RFC p12&69
PORTWAY,Lionel Felix 2Lt kia 14-4-17 1Ess p132 CR France155
POSENER,Percy Julian T2Lt kia 8-7-16 8 att2Wilts p153 MR21
POSFORD,Benjamin Ashwell 2Lt dow 25-2-15 RASC p193 CR France102
POSNER,Philip Ernest 2Lt dow 27/28-4-17 3SStaffs att8Lincs p123 MR20,27-4-17
POSNETT,William Leonard 2Lt kia 22-6-17 1/13Lond p249 MR20
POSTLES,Charles Ernest 2Lt dow 21-8-18 KSLI att1Ches p145 MR16
POSTLETHWAITE,William T2Lt dow 14-3-18 15WelchR p127 CR France346
POSTLETHWAITE,Christopher Joyce TLt dow 9-1-18 12Suff p78 CR France518
POTTER,Charles Gordon Lt kia 15-9-16 8Hamps p229 MR21
POTTER,Donald Rolls Capt dow 21-12-17 2/4RWSurr p212 CR Palestine3
POTTER,Edward TLt ded 10-11-18 10RWar p65 CR France146
POTTER,Francis George 2Lt kia 24-4-17 7 att1/8Worc p226 MR21
POTTER,Francis John T2Lt kia 1-7-16 GL &RA att94TMB p191 MR21
POTTER,Fred.DCM.2Lt dow 22-9-17 7ELancs p111 CR Belgium183
POTTER,Frederick John 2Lt kia 21-5-16 8Lond p247 MR20
POTTER,Harold 2LtTLt kia 9-4-17 3 att7ESurr p113 CR France1182

POTTER,Henry William Ross Maj mbk 20-12-14 IA 129Baluchis p281 MR28
POTTER,John.DSO.MID T2Lt dow 24-7-16 1SStaffs p123 CR France51
POTTER,John 2Lt kia 24-3-18 1/8 att1Worc p226 MR27
POTTER,Keith Erskine T2Lt dow 13-8-18 Hamps att1Bn p121 CR France10
POTTER,Kenneth Mitchell.DSO.Maj kia 8-7-17 52RFA p34 CR Belgium29
POTTER,Percy Walter 2Lt dow 21-5-17 5 att2Worc p109 CR France214
POTTER,Reginald 2Lt kia 9-5-15 1LNLancs p136 MR22
POTTER,Reginald Funge 2Lt dow 24-7-16 4NStaffs p157 CR France23
POTTER,Robert John T2Lt kia 16-8-17 9RDubF p177 MR30
POTTER,Robert William TLt kia 8-10-18 16RWar att1NumbF CR France338,16-10-18 12Bn
POTTER,Robert.MC.T2Lt kia 14-10-18 BlkW att8Bn p129 CR Belgium88
POTTER,William Rochester T2Lt dow 24-4-17 149MGC Inf p185 CR France120
POTTER,William Robert McCall 2Lt kia 17-9-18 C70RFA p34 CR France179
POTTERTON,Henry 2Lt dow 13-12-17 6WYorks p218 CR France52
POTTERTON,William Hubert TLt kia 24-7-16 RE 23FC p47 CR France430
POTTINGER,Charles Evan Roderick Lt dow 11-5-15 RE p47
POTTINGER,Robert Ormond Brabazon Lt kia 9-5-15 att2RMunstF p176 MR22
POTTS,Arnold Leslie Leopold 2Lt kia 5-11-16 7 att1/9DLI p239 MR21
POTTS,Charles 2Lt dow 11-6-17 4 att11Ches p222 CR France285
POTTS,Ernest Alexander.MC.T2Lt dow 15-10-18 24 att10RFus p69 CR France146
POTTS,Geoffrey Fildes TLt kia 23-4-17 17Manch p155 CR France162
POTTS,Henry T2Lt dow 1-10-16 7Beds att1Ess p86 CR France102
POTTS,Henry Herbert T2Lt dow 31-7-17 RE 254TC p48 CR Belgium11
POTTS,Norman Rhead T2Lt kia 19-7-17 SStaffs att9Bn p123 CR Belgium29
POTTS,Richard Harold Urwin T2Lt dow 2-12-18 1/2WRid att16LancF p116 CR Frnce441
POTTS,Robert William T2Lt dow 24-3-18 25MGC p185 CR France177
POTTS,William Edgar.MM.2Lt kia 13-4-18 5WYorks p218 MR32
POTTS,William Janson.MC.Lt kia 21-9-17 RFA att59RFC p19&208 CR France705
POULLETT,William John Lydston.Earl Capt ded 11-7-18 RHA p256 CR Somerset67,RWar
POULTER,Henry Chapman TCapt dow 29-11-17 8RDubF p177 CR France616
POULTER,Hugh Douglas Michael 2Lt kia 15-7-16 RE 68FC p48 CR France1182
POULTER,John Charles Archibald 2Lt kia 24-2-17 4Hamps p228 MR38
POULTER,Wilfred Forman 2Lt ded 6-3-18 24RFC p17 CR France660
POULTNEY,John Bernard 2Lt kia 18-2-17 3 att8SLancs p125 MR32
POULTON,Frederick James TLt kia 2-11-17 9RWSurr att1/8Hamps p56 CR Palestine8
POULTON,Harry Edward 2Lt dow 26-10-17 3 att1SStaffs p123 MR30
POULTON,Roy Roswell Capt kia 8-8-18 8Lond p247 MR16
POUND,Cecil Davison TLt kia 22-9-18 117MGC Inf p185 CR France836
POUND,John Russell Capt dow 27-4-15 3 att2KSLI p145 MR29
POUND,Murray Stuart 2Lt dow 7-11-14 RWSurr p56 CR Lond14
POUNDALL,William Arthur Lloyd.MC.TLtTCapt kia 31-10-17 SLancs att53RFC p12&125 CR Belgium101
POUNDER,Benjamin William Lt kia 9-10-17 1/5WRid p227 CR Belgium101
POUNTNEY,Percival TLt kia 7-6-17 75MGC p185 MR29
POVAH,Frank Capt kia 16-6-15 RScots p54 MR29 See POYAH
POWELL,Alfred Trevanion 2Lt dow 22-7-16 4CamH p243 CR France15
POWELL,Allan Wentworth.DCM.T2Lt dow 21-8-16 8RWSurr p56 CR France394
POWELL,Brian Baden 2Lt ded 11-1-20 ULIA att1/69Punjabis p281 MR43,Lt
POWELL,Cecil Henry 2Lt kia 15-6-17 O&BLI &RFC p256 MR20
POWELL,Charles.MC.Capt dow 21-3-18 RE 409FC p210 CR Belgium20
POWELL,Charles Swan T2Lt kia 17-7-16 6Leic p88 MR21,14-7-16
POWELL,David Bernard Lt dow 4-9-17 12SWBord p223 CR France398,2Lt
POWELL,David Emrys TLt kia 28-3-18 2DivMGC p185 CR France4,Dafydd Ex 14RWFus
POWELL,Edward Darley.DSO.MC.Maj kia 1-9-18 RE 468FC p48 MR19
POWELL,Edward Ingram Capt kia 22-3-18 6RSuss p228 CR France364
POWELL,Edward Watson 2Lt kia 31-10-17 84RFC p12 MR20
POWELL,Eric Layton T2Lt kia 16-4-17 20RFus p69 MR20
POWELL,Eric Limbery TLt kia 6-4-18 B17H&FA p34 CR France300
POWELL,Ernest Arthur 2Lt dow 15-9-18 7Ches p223 CR France88
POWELL,Eyre Burton Lt ded 4-8-15 3Wilts p153 CR Dorset110
POWELL,Frederick Gill.MC.CaptBtMaj ded 15-4-17 Dors p264 CR Lond8,14-4-17
POWELL,Frederick William 2Lt dedacc 20-1-17 5 att10RDubF p177 CR France74
POWELL,George Alexander Lt kia 28-6-15 15KRRC att1RInnisF p151 MR4
POWELL,George Aubyn 2Lt ded 7-12-16 RFC p261 CR Herts38
POWELL,George Henry T2Lt kia 29-4-17 MGC p185 MR20

POWELL,Gerald Frederick Watson Maj kia 29-7-17 KentCycBn att8RWKent p253 CR Belgium29,28-7-17
POWELL,Harold Osborne 2Lt kia 31-10-14 4DragGds p21 MR29
POWELL,Harry Stranger.MC.Capt dow 5-10-17 1/6RWar C'Coy p214 CR Belgium16,Stanyer
POWELL,Henry Mitchell Capt kia 9-12-14 2SStaffs att1Dors p123 MR29
POWELL,James Henry T2Lt kia 24-11-15 10 att2SStaffs p123 MR19
POWELL,John Allen T2Lt kia 14-1-17 NStaffs att2Y&L p157 CR France423
POWELL,John Harold Slade Maj ded 8-2-15 RH&FA p34
POWELL,John Stewart TCapt kia 2-7-16 11Hamps p121 CR France223,dow 3-7-16
POWELL,Leonard Maurice 2Lt kia 17-6-15 3 att1GordH p167 MR29
POWELL,Lindsay Carlton T2Lt kia 31-5-16 7RSFus &23RFC p3&95 CR France46,Lt
POWELL,Maurice TLt kia 5-7-17 14RFA p34 CR France570
POWELL,Patrick John Gordon Lt kia 2-4-17 RASC attRFC p12&193 MR20
POWELL,Percival 2Lt kia 1-8-15 9 att3RB p180 CR Belgium92
POWELL,Phillip Keith T2Lt kia 7-6-17 8YLI p141 MR29
POWELL,Reginald Walter T2Lt kia 10-7-16 3Worc p109 MR21
POWELL,Rendel T2Lt kia 20-8-18 2YLI p143 CR France526
POWELL,Rhys Campbell Ffolliot 2Lt kia 13-9-14 2HLI p163 CR France1329,14-9-14
POWELL,Richard TLt dow 22-8-17 153RFA p34 CR France13
POWELL,Richard Henry 2Lt kia 9-5-15 5RSuss p228 MR22
POWELL,Richard Oversby TCapt&Ajt kia 16-7-16 36/33RFA p34 CR France1887
POWELL,Robert Keal TLt kia 4-10-17 11NStaffs att2SLancs p157 CR France832
POWELL,Roland Rice 2Lt dow 29-8-18 1SomLI p80 CR France14
POWELL,Scott TCapt dow 4/5-4-16 8RWFus p98 MR38
POWELL,Sidney Lewis TCapt kia 12-7-17 16LancF p93 CR Belgium174,Sydney
POWELL,Thomas.DCM.TCapt ded 1-7-18 8RIrReg p89 CR Ireland14 Ex O&BLI
POWELL,Thomas Clark 2Lt dow 15-7-17 RGA 12HB p41 CR Belgium11
POWELL,Thomas Henry Norman 2Lt kld 24-4-17 RFC p12
POWELL,Thomas William 2Lt kia 25-4-18 4Mddx p148 CR France514
POWELL,Thomas William.MC.TCapt ded 24-11-18 TankCps p188 CR Oxford85
POWELL,Townsend George Capt kia 9-5-15 3 att2Nhampt p138 MR32
POWELL,Victor Edmund TLtACapt kia 26-9-17 3 att7KSLI p145 MR30
POWELL,Wilfred Guy 2Lt kia 26-3-18 7SomLI att61TMB p80 MR27
POWELL,Wilfred Roderick LtACapt kia 9-4-18 4Dors p229 MR34
POWELL,William Arthur 2Lt kia 5-10-18 7 att11N&D p233 CR France234
POWELL,William Edward George Pryce Wynne 2Lt kia 6-11-18 1WelshGds p53 CR France1211,Lt
POWELL,William Uniacke Perry TLt ded 20-10-16 EYorks &RFC p3 CR Hereford/W54
POWELL-AKROYD,Frank Allnutt 2Lt kia 24-8-18 3YLI p143 CR France314,23-8-18
POWELL-JOHNSON,R.B.MC.Lt 19-9-18 RGA 109HB CR Belgium192
POWELL-JONES,Percival Morgan Capt kia 22-4-16 SWBord BrecknockBn p223 MR38
POWER,Charles 2Lt kia 25-9-15 2Leinst att2RWar p174 MR19
POWER,George Henry Fosbrooke Lt dow 9-5-15 6Mddx p148 MR29
POWER,Henry Richard Lt kia 22-8-17 3RIrRif att48RFC p12&170 CR France1361
POWER,Herbert Capt kld 12-3-15 Nhampt p138 MR22
POWER,John James T2Lt kia 19-9-18 7RWSurr p56 CR France1495
POWER,John Wethered Lt kia 10-9-16 WelshGds 4Coy p53 CR France394
POWER,Joseph Leo T2Lt kia 14-2-18 8 att9WRid p116 CR France1483
POWER,Lawrence Henry Capt kia 22-3-18 2TankCps p188 MR27,Laurence
POWER,Pierce Michael Joseph Lt dow 2-3-15 RAMC att1Wilts p197 CR Belgium17
POWER,Raphael Joseph 2Lt kia 19-7-17 IA 46 att33Punjabis p281 CR EAfrica38 &CR Tanzania1
POWER,R.E.Lt kia 17-4-18 SL att4/4KAR p202 CR EAfrica92,Capt
POWER,William Boyle 2Lt kld 17-7-16 RFC p3 CR Hamps1
POWER,William Goodlake Capt kia 16-10-16 RAOC p198 CR France44
POWER-CLUTTERBUCK,James Edward T2Lt kia 25-6-17 RFA att52RFC p12&34 CR France451
POWERS,Bernard Alexander Lt kia 25-9-17 Mddx att19RFC p12&148 MR20
POWERS,Herbert Grendon.MC.Capt&Adjt kia 19-9-18 6Hamps p229&281 IARO att1/1GurkhaRif CR Palestine9
POWLES-CURTIS,Arthur John TCapt dow 11-9-16 17KRRC p151 MR21
POWLESLAND,John Northley Julian 2Lt dow 20-9-16 6Lond p247 MR21
POWLEY,A.D.Lt kia 10-6-16 1KAR p268 CR EAfrica40,2Lt
POWLEY,Joseph T2Lt kia 3-5-17 2Ess p132 MR20
POWLEY,Walter Harry Chap4Cl ded 23-2-19 RAChDept p268 CR Lond10

POWNALL,Allen Claude Morrison 2Lt kia 27-3-18 B104RFA p34 CR France281
POWNALL,Edward T2Lt kia 9-10-17 LancF att8Bn p93 MR30
POWNALL,Hubert Joseph 2Lt kia 23-7-16 4 att10RWar p65 CR France432
POWNALL,John 2Lt kia 30-10-16 6 att2Worc p109 MR21
POWNALL,Lionel Henry Yorke Lt kia 21-3-15 RWKent p141 CR Belgium165
POWNEY,Arthur John T2Lt dow 15-9-17 GL att9RFC p12 CR Belgium16
POWNEY,Joseph Thomas Maj ded 18-12-14 RE p48 CR France85
POWRIE,William T2Lt kia 27-9-18 Y&L att2/4Bn p159 MR16
POWYS,Geoffrey Mappleton TLt kia 19-6-17 1GarBn att8NumbF p62 CR Belgium75,Mapleton
POYAH,Frank Capt kia 16-6-15 RScots p54 MR29 See POVAH
POYNDER,Leopold Eliot Capt bombExplosion 26-6-16 IA 1/6 att2/6GurkhaRif p281 CR Iraq6
POYNDER,Robert Hamilton Lt kia 24-3-18 4 att2SStaffs p123 MR20
POYNTER,Leslie John T2Lt dow 25-10-18 20Manch p155 CR France521
POYNTING,Arthur Lt kia 26-7-16 6RWar att143MGC p187&214 CR France150,27-5-16
POYNTON,Charles Edward Lt kia 30-7-16 26Manch p155 CR France402
POYNTON,John T2Lt kia 4-10-17 RWar attRes 1/6Bn GHQ p65 CR Belgium126
POYNTON,Reginald James Lt ded 29-9-15 RE 2/2SigCoyp210 CR Lond12,kldacc
POYNTZ,H.A.SenAssSurg 5-6-18 IMS MR43
POZZI,Leonard Lambert 2Lt 8-5-15 6AustInf MR4
PRACY,Henry Reginald T2Lt dow 5-9-16 1RWKent p141 CR France23,kia
PRAETORIUS,Alfred 2Lt kia 27-5-18 C155RFA p34 CR France924
PRAGNELL,Archie Ernest 2Lt drd 30-12-17 21Lond p251 CR Egypt1
PRAGNELL,George Frederick TCapt kia 23-7-17 GL 11RWKent Staff 123InfBde p191 CR Belgium15
PRAIN,Theodore.MID Lt kia 21-10-14 1Leic C'Coy p88 MR32
PRALL,Cedric Barkley LtCol 5-4-16 IMS MR65
PRANCE,Arthur Christopher Norman.MC.Lt kia 29-5-18 SWBord p100 MR18
PRANGLEY,Charles Dean 2Lt kia 25-9-16 Lincs p75 CR France374
PRANKHERD,Richard Percy Lt kia 10-11-18 WarYeo attMGC p187&205 CR France937,PRANKERD
PRATKEY,Joseph Edward 2Lt kia 3-5-17 8Leic p88 MR20
PRATT,Alexander Stewart T2Lt kia 24-3-17 12 att10ScotRif p104 MR20
PRATT,Arthur Rev ded 29-6-17 RAChDept att6SStaffs p229&268
PRATT,Arthur 2Lt dow 11-2-18 5Beds p219 CR France1063,7Bn
PRATT,Arthur T2Lt dow 2-7-18 2Beds att6Nhampt p86 CR France516
PRATT,Arthur Victor.MID T2Lt kia 21-3-18 9ESurr p113 MR27
PRATT,Audley Charles.DSO.CaptTLtCol dow 16-8-17 11RInnisF p105 CR Belgium84
PRATT,Aylwin Murray 2Lt kia 21-8-17 186RFA p34 CR Belgium27
PRATT,Christopher T2Lt kia 18-10-16 8CamH p168 MR21
PRATT,Ernest Charles 2Lt kia 14-5-17 2/4RFus p246 MR20
PRATT,Ernest St.George.CB.DSO.BrigGen ded 24-11-18 DLI InspInf Staff p1 CR Lond4
PRATT,Ernest Victor 2Lt kia 25-9-17 C277RFA p34 CR France285
PRATT,Francis Norton Capt kia 18-9-18 2Y&L p159 CR France835
PRATT,Geoffry Cowper Spencer Lt dow 27-11-15 RH&FA 14A/ASect p34 CR France285,Geoffrey
PRATT,George Leslie 2Lt kia 16-5-15 3RWSurr p56 CR France279
PRATT,James Arthur CaptHonMaj ded 25-6-15 SL RecOff p268 CR Eire113
PRATT,John Curdie Lt dow 23-3-18 5 att14HLI p240 MR20
PRATT,John Armstrong.MC.Lt kia 23-8-18 3Lpool p72
PRATT,John Selby.MID TLt kia 11-4-17 10Yorks p91 CR France162
PRATT,Lionel Henry 2Lt kia 25-9-15 18Lond p250 CR France149
PRATT,Mervyn Palles Capt ded 13-4-20 IA 121Pnrs p281 MR43
PRATT,Neville Herbert TCapt dow 8-7-16 10N&D B'Coy p134 CR France207
PRATT,Ralph Lewis Capt kia 18-10-16 2/4Glouc p225 CR France705
PRATT,William George James T2Lt kia 28-9-17 23RFus p69 CR France163
PRATT,William John Armstrong.MC.Capt kia 23-8-18 3 att1Lpool CR France927
PRATTE,Arthur Williams Staples TLt kia 6-8-16 10Lincs p75 CR France390
PREBBLE,Cyril Edgar.MC.T2Lt dow 8-8-18 12Mddx att2/2Lond p148 CR France69
PREBBLE,John 2Lt kia 21-6-17 49/40RFA p209 CR France1182
PREDDY,Edward Fred Spencer LtACapt kia 8-12-17 RGA 36SB p41 CR France379
PREECE,Ellis 2Lt kia 2-10-18 1HLI &RAF p265
PREECE,Henry Raymond Lt kia 8-10-18 6 att4KRRC p151 CR France845
PREECE,P.J.LtCol 29-10-21 8Lond CR Wales497
PREECE,William Henry SubCdr ded 5-11-19 IOD p281
PREEDY,Alban TCapt kia 1-7-16 3Dev p77 MR21,2Bn
PREEDY,John Benjamin Knowlton Lt kia 26-10-17 2Lond p245 MR30

PREEDY,Lawrence Jack 2Lt kia 31-3-18 4 att 1RWar p65 MR20

PREESTON,Philip Southwell 2Lt kia 28-3-18 1RFA p34 CR France582

PRENDERGAST,Charles Randolph Lt kia 21-1-16 IA 84 att28Punjabis p281 MR38,28 att84

PRENDERGAST,James Francis T2Lt kia 27-7-16 6RMunstF p176 CR France115,1Bn

PRENDERGAST,Matthew Vincent Chap4Cl ded 16-9-18 RAChDept p199 CR Egypt9

PRENDIVILLE,Lawrence Anthony 2Lt kia 31-7-17 7Lpool p215 MR29

PRENTER,Dalton T2Lt kia 21-3-18 9RIrF p171 MR27

PRENTICE,Alexander Reid.MC.TCapt kia 9-11-17 12 att 10ScotRif p104 CR France1182

PRENTICE,James T2Lt kld 4-11-17 RFC p12 CR Scot503

PRENTICE,John Ridley 2Lt kia 18-6-15 3Suff p79 MR29

PRENTICE,John Robert 2Lt dow 17-4-18 4A&SH p173 CR France134

PRENTICE,Oliver 2Lt kia 27-3-18 1Lond att2/7LancF p245 MR27

PRENTICE,Thomas Alfred Maj kia 10-8-15 1/4Ches p222 MR4

PRENTICE,Walter Lowry 2Lt dow 3-8-17 4ConnRgs att2Leinst p172 CR Belgium11

PRENTIS,Horace Taylor 2Lt kia 27-4-18 17Manch A'Coy p155 MR30

PRESCOTT,Alec Frank Evelyn TLt kia 8-10-16 124MGC p185 MR21,Alex

PRESCOTT,Ernest Twiss 2Lt dow 26-2-18 34RH&FA p34

PRESCOTT,Lewis William 2Lt 22-4-18 23RAF

PRESCOTT,Reginald Julius 2Lt kia 15-4-17 18LancF p93 MR21

PRESCOTT,Robert Stewart T2Lt kia 1-7-16 10ELancs p111 CR France221

PRESS,George William LtACapt kia 26-10-17 1RWKent p141 MR30

PRESSLY,John Seymour 2Lt kia 15-11-15 1/5YLI p235 CR Belgium23

PREST,William Charles Seagar 2Lt kia 17-8-16 5WYorks p218 CR France702

PRESTIDGE,John Vernon FitzGerald Lt dow 2-5-17 1 att 11Suff p79 CR France95

PRESTON,Arthur John Dillon.MID Capt kia 15-8-15 6RDubF p177 CR Gallipoli4

PRESTON,Alfred James T2Lt dow 21-9-18 8RBerks p139 CR France194

PRESTON,George Allen LtCol Ackld 6-5-19 IA 2/6GurkhaRif p281 CR Asia81

PRESTON,Herbert Stanley T2Lt dow 8-9-16 1BlkW p129 CR France66

PRESTON,Herbert William Lawson Lt ded 19-8-17 RFA M'A/ABty p34 CR France145

PRESTON,James Henry T2Lt ded 11-1-19 LabCps attLpool p266 CR Lancs313

PRESTON,John Abe Stanley Lt dow 6-10-16 11Glouc p107 CR Greece7,Alec

PRESTON,Leslie George.MC&Bar.TCapt dow 10-7-18 8RWKent att6Dors p141 CR France61

PRESTON,Philip Chamberlayne.DCM.TCapt kia 13-10-15 7Norf p74 MR19

PRESTON,Richard Amyas.MC.CaptALtCol dow 7-6-18 RAMC att58FA p197 CR France1415

PRESTON,Rudolph Arthur.MC.Lt kia 15-9-16 RFC p3 CR France1465

PRESTON,Sidney TLt kia 10-4-18 1Ess att98TrResBn p132 CR France745

PRESTON,Stanley CaptAMaj kia 25-9-17 1Mddx p148 MR30,12Bn

PRESTON,Thomas Frederick Lt kia 24-1-17 NorfYeo attRFC p19&204 CR Belgium152

PRESTON,Thomas Harry 2Lt dow 30-9-18 6NStaffs p238 CR Belgium11,4Bn

PRESTON,Thomas Haworth Capt kia 17-11-14 3ELancs p111 CR Belgium68,1Bn

PRESTON,Wilfrid 2Lt dow 4-7-18 7WRid p228 CR France296

PRESTON,William Carter 2Lt kia 10-4-18 8BordR p117 MR32

PRESTWICH,Joseph Lt dow 7-2-16 RASC DivTrn attRFC p19&253 CR Belgium5

PRETOR-PINNEY,Charles Frederick.DSO.TLtCol dow 28-4-17 13RB p180 CR France95

PRETSELL,William Gardiner.MC.T2Lt kia 20-7-18 YLI att5Bn p143 CR France1689

PRETTY,Donald 2LtTLt dow 11-5-15 4Suff p217 CR France80

PRETTY,Harold.MC.CaptAMaj kia 24-3-18 4Suff att10DCLI p217 MR20

PRETTYMAN,Frank Remington Lt kia 4-7-17 2ScotGds p52 CR Belgium12,PRETYMAN

PRETYMAN,Maurice William 2Lt kia 12-8-15 RE 10SigCo p48 MR4,10-8-15

PREVEL,James Alexander Emanuel.MC.TLt kia 29-9-18 2Nhampt p138 CR France212

PRIAULX,George Kendall.DSO.MajTLtCol kia 24-3-18 11KRRC p151 MR27

PRICE,Arthur T2Lt kia 13-11-16 7KSLI p145 CR France742

PRICE,Charles 2Lt dow 18-7-17 1/4SLancs p230 CR Belgium16

PRICE,Charles Lempriere.DSO.Capt kia 16-9-14 2RScots p54 CR France1107

PRICE,Charles Leslie 2Lt dow 15-3-18 1RIrReg p89 CR Egypt2

PRICE,Charles Thomas 2Lt kia 30-11-17 7HLI p240 CR Palestine9,5Bn Ex9HLI

PRICE,David Eleazer 2Lt kia 8-9-16 2WelshR p127 MR21

PRICE,David Leonard T2Lt kia 27-3-18 5 att 3/7KSLI p145 CR France174

PRICE,Eric William Manning 2Lt dow 1-7-16 1Hamps p121 CR France5

PRICE,Ernest Dickenson Lt dow 19-3-16 3RIrReg att2RIrRif p89 CR France924,Dickinson kia

PRICE,F.J.Lt ded 29-11-18 RGA p262 CR C'land&W'land44

PRICE,Francis Maurice 2Lt dow 4-6-17 5Lincs p220 CR France214

PRICE,George Bernard Locking 2Lt dow 23-8-17 3 att8GordH p167 MR30

PRICE,Gordon William Bassett TLt kia 23-11-17 12SWBord p100 MR17

PRICE,Graham T2Lt kia 9-3-16 GL &6RFC p3&191 CR Belgium11

PRICE,Harold.MC.TCapt kia 26-6-16 26NumbF p62 CR France430

PRICE,Harold Strachan T2Lt kia 24-5-15 3RFus p69 MR29

PRICE,Henry Bertram Lt kia 3-5-15 5Lond p246 MR29

PRICE,Henry Wall 2Lt kia 4-7-16 4 att2Manch p155 CR France251

PRICE,Henry Wall Maj ded 19-6-19 4Manch p155 CR Ches53

PRICE,Herbert Allen.MC.T2Lt dow 30-11-17 3SomLI attMGC Cav p80&185 CR Palestine9

PRICE,Hugh 2Lt kia 11-10-18 3WYorks att 1/7WRid p82 CR France270

PRICE,J.F.N.Maj 13-8-18 Beds att2NigR CR WAfrica35

PRICE,James Thirkell.MC.MIDx2 Capt kia 21-4-16 C77RFA p34 CR France423

PRICE,John Esmond T2Lt kia 1-7-16 14Manch p155 MR21

PRICE,John Thomas T2Lt kia 20-7-16 20RFus p69 MR21

PRICE,John Turner 2Lt kia 27-5-18 1/5RLancs p213 MR19

PRICE,Joseph William James 2Lt dow 22-4-17 3 att26NumbF p62 CR France40

PRICE,L.Capt 21-11-20 GL CR Hamps 220

PRICE,Leonard John Joliffe T2Lt dow 15-8-16 2KOSB p102 CR France51,Jolliffe

PRICE,Leonard Charles 2Lt kia 25-4-18 4 att 16LancF p93 MR30,Lawrence Lt 4 att 19Bn

PRICE,Montague Leonard 2Lt kia 26-6-16 1/7Mddx p235 CR France1327

PRICE,Owen Douglas Capt&QM ded 10-12-18 RAMC p267 CR Scot239,12-12-18

PRICE,Paul Adrian Edward 2Lt kia 23-4-17 RGA O'A/A Bty p41 CR France756

PRICE,Reginald 2Lt kia 1-7-16 1/6RWar p214 MR21

PRICE,Robert St.John Locke Capt kia 25-9-15 IA 33Punjabis p281 MR28

PRICE,Samuel Allen Lt ded 11-7-17 GL RE IWT p191 CR Iraq6

PRICE,Sidney James 2Lt kia 15-9-16 9Suff p79 MR21,Sydney

PRICE,Stanley Hastings.MC.T2Lt kia 24-1-18 15N&D p134 CR Belgium83

PRICE,Thomas John Lt 27-5-18 RAF MR34

PRICE,Thomas Joseph.MC.2Lt dow 25-4-18 1/10Lpool p216 CR France88

PRICE,V.M.Capt 15-12-19 3Ess CR Essex123

PRICE,Victor William TLt kld 7-11-17 11Worc attRFC p12&109,1Bn CR Hereford154

PRICE,W.H.Lt&QM 16-10-18 IndDefForce MR 66

PRICE,Walter Edgar Lt ded 31-5-19 3 att9RSuss p119&257 CR Germany1

PRICE,Wilfred T2Lt dow 3-5-17 8EYorks p84 CR France1182

PRICE,William Eric 2Lt kia 2-5-15 5RSuss p228 CR France249

PRICE,William Henry 2Lt kia 23-8-17 42MGC Inf p185 CR Belgium125

PRICE,William Henry TCapt kia 24-3-18 10Mddx p148 MR20 19Bn

PRICE-EDWARDS,Owen Capt kia 22-6-16 18RFus p69 MR21

PRICHARD,Arthur Douglas T2Lt dow 8-10-17 34MGC p185 CR Belgium16

PRICHARD,Edgar Albert CaptHonMaj ded 29-2-16 4Glouc p271 CR Glouc10

PRICHARD,Francis Hesketh Capt ded 1-2-20 RGA p262 CR Asia81

PRICHARD,Frederic Giles Lt dow 9-8-15 2EYorks p84 CR Essex267

PRICHARD,John Walter 2Lt kia 18-9-18 4RWFus p223 CR France365,Lt

PRICHARD,Richard Gerald Mannsell Maj dow 7-6-18 GlamYeo att38CentIndHorse p203 CR Palestine3,Mauncell

PRICHARD,Rowland George Lt kia 24-4-15 1Suff p79 MR29

PRICHARD,Thomas James.MC.TCapt kia 28-3-18 1RLancs p59 CR France452

PRICHARD,Thomas Lewis Capt dow 9-11-14 2RWFus CR France102

PRICKARD,Gerald Thornton 2Lt kia 4-6-15 3SWBord att1RDubF p100 MR4

PRICKETT,Lancelot Capt kld 2-6-16 RGA &RFC p3&41 CR Sussex93 Ex 71HB RGA

PRIDE,A.R.T2Lt kia 3-5-17 8RFus p69 MR20

PRIDE,Harry.MC.Capt kia 23-4-17 10Mddx p236 CR France581

PRIDEAUX,Edwin Ravenhill 2Lt 17-5-18 203RAF MR20

PRIDEAUX,Geoffrey Arthur.MC.TCapt kia 19-1-17 SomLI p80 CR France624

PRIDEAUX-BRUNE,Edmund Nicholas 2Lt kia 22-5-18 3RB p180 CR France81

PRIDHAM,George Frederick TLtCol ded 16-12-16 1 att 1/5WelshR p127 CR Egypt8

PRIDHAM,William Albert Stanley TLt drd 5-1-16 12NumbF p62 CR France102

PRIDMORE,George Harry T2Lt kia 31-8-18 21WYorks att1Ess p82 CR France531

PRIDMORE,Percy Malin.MC.Capt kia 21-9-17 2/6RWar p214 CR Belgium10,2-9-17

PRIDMORE,Reginald George.MC.Maj kia 13-3-18 RH&FA p206

PRIEST,Benjamin.MC.2Lt dow 26-4-18 72/38RFA p34 CR Belgium38

PRIEST,F.T2Lt ded 22-5-18 O&BLI att3Bn p130 p264 CR Berks119

PRIEST,Robert Edgar Priest Lt kld 15-8-17 276RFA p208 CR Belgium41,Paul

PRIEST,Roy Simpson Capt kia 19-4-17 7/103 NZ Bn ImpCamelCps MR34
PRIEST,Walter Samuel Lt&QM ded 25-9-17 RASC p267 CR Hamps8
PRIESTLEY,Archibald Bertram Capt dow 12-9-14 Dors p124 CR France1429
PRIESTLEY,Charles Henry Ryland TLt ded 19-6-18 RGA 120HB p41 CR War23,Harry dow
PRIESTLEY,Charles Homans 2Lt kia 4-9-16 6/12RB p180 CR France294
PRIESTLEY,Charles Lacey 2LtACapt dow 11-11-17 1Glouc p107 CR Belgium22
PRIESTLEY,Douglas Bernard T2Lt kia 31-7-17 2/5LancF p93 MR29
PRIESTLEY,Dyker Stanton 2Lt kia 1-7-16 108MGC p185 MR21
PRIESTLEY,Frederick.MC.Lt kia 27-5-18 1 att5Wilts p153 MR37
PRIESTLEY,Frederick Nicoladies Maj ded 2-9-18 RFA p271 CR Yorks42
PRIESTLEY,Percival Thomas CaptAMaj ded 28-9-18 RAMC att25CCS p197 CR Greece7
PRIESTLEY,Stanley Noel Lt kia 23-7-16 8Glouc p107 MR21
PRIESTLEY-EVANS,Mansfield Capt kia 10-7-20 IARO att231Brahmans attPoliticalDept p281 CR Iraq8
PRIESTLY,Albert Edward 2Lt kia 3-5-17 4WRid p227 MR20
PRIESTLY,Ernest Neville 2Lt 8-5-15 10Jats MR65
PRIESTMAN,Edmund Yerbury T2Lt kia 19-11-15 6Y&L p159 CR Gallipoli27
PRIESTMAN,George Aloysius(Louie) TLt dow 15-5-18 19NumbF p62 CR France84,2Lt
PRIESTMAN,Kenneth Mallone T2Lt kia 31-8-16 RE 105FC p48 CR France246
PRIESTNALL,William Eustace 2Lt kia 27-5-18 NumbF att5Bn p62 CR France1753
PRIME,Arnold 2Lt kia 21-3-18 4 att2/8Manch p155 MR27
PRIMEAU,Cecil Willibrod 2Lt kia 27-10-17 GL &70RFC p12 MR20
PRIMROSE,Neil James Archibald.Hon.MC.Capt kia 15-11-17 1/1BucksYeo p203 CR Palestine9
PRIMROSE,Nigel.MC.TLt ded 25-10-18 64RFA p34 CR France34,Capt
PRIMROSE-WELLS,James Bowen Lt dow PoW 4-4-18 4Beds p86 CR France246
PRINCE,Alfred George Maj 8-2-19 7Lond CR Surrey160
PRINCE,Alick Lancelot Capt kia 8-11-14 1LNLancs p136 MR29
PRINCE,Arthur Alec 2Lt kia 4-10-18 19Lond p250 CR France567
PRINCE,Claude Melnotle T2Lt kia 18-8-16 9RSuss p119 MR21,Melnotte
PRINCE,Frederick George 2Lt kld 18-5-19 2Lond &RAF p245
PRINCE,Frederick Harold T2Lt kia 9-4-17 8EYorks A'Coy p84 CR France581
PRINCE,George Reginald Dudley Lt ded 24-11-18 RE p210 CR Greece9
PRINCE,John Cecil Butter 2Lt kia 27-9-18 9 att16Lond p248 CR France429,Butler
PRINCE,Julius Sefton Lt kia 25-9-15 7Lond p247 MR19
PRINCE,Norman Charlesworth Capt kia 18-4-17 6WRid p227 CR France614
PRINCE,Victor Charles.MC.2Lt kia 1-9-18 4Lond p246 MR16
PRINCE,W.F.J.2Lt ded 30-5-18 9Lond attRAF p248
PRINCE,William T2Lt dow 28-8-17 6Y&L p159 CR Belgium16
PRINCE-SMITH,Donald St.Patrick TLt kia 24-10-17 RDubF att16RFC p12&177 CR France95,2Lt
PRING,Basil Crompton TLt kia 1-7-16 96MGC p185 MR21
PRING,Francis Raleigh Lt kia 25-9-15 9RSuss p119 MR19
PRINGLE,Arthur Stanley TCapt kia 25-9-15 10ScotRif p104 MR19
PRINGLE,Charles Eric T2Lt kia 10-7-16 8 att11LNLancs p136 MR21,11 att8Bn
PRINGLE,James 2Lt ded 8-2-15 14HLI p163 CR Scot253
PRINGLE,Lionel Graham(Leo).MVO.Capt dow 29-12-14 1HLI p163 CR France1027,Leonel
PRINGLE,Matthew 2Lt kia 27-8-17 86RFA p209 CR Belgium19
PRINGLE,Norman Douglas TCapt kia 7/11-8-15 6EYorks p84 MR4,7-8-15
PRINGLE,Norman Robert.Bart Capt ded 18-4-19 GL RE IWT p267 CR Lond4,24-4-19
PRINGLE,Robert Gray 2Lt kia 23-4-17 8HLI p240 CR France1730
PRINGLE,Robert Scott Lt dow 14-9-14 1RWSurr p56 CR France1341
PRINGLE,Robert William Hay TCapt kia 1-7-16 16WYorks p82 MR21 CR France156
PRINGLE,Walter Gerald.MID T2Lt kia 12-10-17 6KOSB p102 CR Belgium126
PRINGLE,William Rennie TLt kia 22-7-16 7SLancs p125 MR21,22/23-7-16
PRINGLE-PATTISON,John Ronald Seth 2Lt kia 5-9-16 2GordH p167 CR France402,6-9-16
PRINTER,Merwanji Dinsha Capt accdrd 2-10-20 IMS CR Egypt2
PRIOLEAU,William Louis St.Julian Maj ded 17-10-19 Norf p263 CR Egypt2
PRIOR,Charles Ronald 2Lt kia 22-8-19 3EKent p58 CR France430,7Bn
PRIOR,Edward Foss TCapt kia 15-9-16 8RB p180 CR France400
PRIOR,Edward Robert Seymour.DSO.MC.TMajALtCol kia 27-5-18 8SLancs att11Ches p125 MR18
PRIOR,Harry Leonard 2Lt ded 3-7-18 1/4RFus att117RAF p69 CR Kent71,kldacc 30Bn
PRIOR,Henry George Redmond TLt kia 7-10-16 11RWKent p141 CR France385,2Lt

PRIOR,Herbert 2Lt dow 27-8-18 5YLI p235 CR France832
PRIOR,John Peter T2Lt kia 9-4-17 24NumbF p62 CR France644
PRIOR,Leslie Montague Sidney T2Lt kia 26-7-16 B156RFA p34 CRFrance453
PRIOR,Leslie Percy Capt dow 7-6-17 10Lond attRFC p19&248 CR France285
PRIOR,Lewis Atkins 2Lt kia 30-6-16 13 att10RSuss p119 MR19
PRIOR,T.A.Lt 10-2-21 5Lond CR Lond14
PRIOR-WANDESFORDE,Christopher Butler 2Lt dow 27-6-17 4Yorks p220 CR France ,Lt
PRISMALL,Arthur Capt kia 14-3-15 13Lond B'Coy p249 CR France710
PRISMALL,Merrick Orville Lt kld 20-12-17 RFA attRFC p12&34 CR Mddx47
PRITCHARD,Andrew Baden Capt ded 26-10-18 StaffsYeo p205 CR Syria2
PRITCHARD,Charles Frederick 2Lt kia 17-9-17 GL &57RFC p12 CR Belgium175,drd
PRITCHARD,Charles Meyrick TCapt dow 14-8-16 12SWBord p100 CR France98
PRITCHARD,David 2Lt kia 19-3-16 1RWFus p98 CR France638
PRITCHARD,Douglas William Lindsay 2Lt kia 27-7-17 2/230RFA p209 CR France161
PRITCHARD,Francis James T2Lt kia 15-11-17 7Lincs p75 CR Belgium23
PRITCHARD,George.MC.Capt kia 3-12-17 2/8Worc p226 MR17
PRITCHARD,Gwynedd William Llewelyn.MC.MID T2Lt kia 23-10-18 20Manch p155 CR France231,Capt
PRITCHARD,Henry T2Lt kia 7-4-18 RWFus attHoodBn p98 MR27
PRITCHARD,H.T.Capt 3-2-20 KOSB CR Devon207
PRITCHARD,Joseph SubCdr ded 12-2-17 IA S&TCps p281 MR61
PRITCHARD,J.F.H Lt 4-9-17 SPersiaRif CR Asia82
PRITCHARD,John 2Lt kia 4-9-17 13RWFus p98 CR Belgium23
PRITCHARD,John Eric Stirling 2Lt dow 27-10-17 RFA 52Bty p34 CR Belgium11
PRITCHARD,John Harold Capt kia 15-5-17 HAC Inf p206 MR20
PRITCHARD,Osborn Brace LtCol ded 27-11-16 WelshR p127
PRITCHARD,Ralph Broomfield.DSO.MC.TCapt dow 26-4-18 14NumbF att2Lincs p62 CR Belgium18
PRITCHARD,Richard T2Lt dow 22-8-16 Dev p77
PRITCHARD,T.L.Capt dow 9-11-14 3 att2RWFus p98
PRITCHARD,Thomas Bradley.MC.T2Lt kld 5-12-17 RFC 39HDSqn p12 CR Mddx29 Ex 52MT RASC
PRITCHARD,Thomas Thompson T2Lt kld 30-8-17 GL &RFC p12 CR Wales440
PRITCHARD,Wilfred Dryden Capt dow 25-9-15 8RFA p3 MR19
PRITCHARD,William TCapt kia 21-6-16 9Y&L p159 CR France430
PRITCHARD,William Alwyn 2Lt kia 26-4-18 DLI att1Wilts p161 CR Belgium126
PRITCHARD,William Bridgett LtCol dow 29-6-15 RAMC attELancsFA p253 MR4
PRITCHARD,William Ernest TLt ded 29-10-18 6YLI p265 CR Suff207,2Lt
PRITCHARD-BARRETT,John Oscar Lt kia 15-6-15 3att2Yorks p91 MR22
PRITCHETT,Edward Guy Lt kia 16-5-18 Hereford att6KSLI p252 MR20
PRITCHETT,George Edgar Kenyon T2Lt dow 3-6-18 18LancF p93 CR France63
PRITCHETT,Walter Penrose Capt dow 26-12-14 1Glouc p107 CR France102
PRITTIE,Francis Reginald Denis.Hon.MIDx2 Capt kia 19-12-14 1RB p180 CR Belgium71,Dennis
PRIVETT,Arthur Bellman T2Lt dow 8-1-16 2Leic p88 MR38
PROBERT,Arthur James T2Lt kia 9-4-17 1 att25NumbF p62 CR France265
PROBERT,Sydney Lt kia 27-5-18 7DLI p239 MR18,ded PoW
PROBYN,John William 2Lt kia 12-4-18 5WRid p227 MR30
PROCKTER,Frederic Lt 2-10-16 7Mddx p235 MR21 CR France390,3-10-16
PROCTER,Alexander Duncan Guthrie T2Lt kia 7-7-17 8RFus p69 MR21
PROCTER,Arthur.MC.Lt kia 1-7-16 1/8RWar p215 MR21
PROCTER,Charles Austin 2Lt dedacc 24-4-18 GL &82RAF CR France52
PROCTER,Charles Edgecumbe TLt kia 2-8-15 1/7Norf p74 CR Belgium71
PROCTER,Harry Mettam 2Lt kia 27-8-17 1 att9WYorks p82 MR30
PROCTER,Herbert T2Lt ded 11-11-17 RE p48 CR France177,kldacc
PROCTER,John Norman William Atkinson.MC.MID Lt dow 2-5-18 1/6WRid p227 CR France142
PROCTOR,Charles Gordon T2Lt kld 20-2-16 10ESurr &RFC p3&113 CR Numb74
PROCTOR,Frank Goodheart 2Lt dow 2-11-17 4Ches p222 CR France40,PROCTER
PROCTOR,Frederick William TMaj ded 13-6-16 SL RWFus p201 CR Berks29,Frederic
PROCTOR,George TLt kia 17-4-18 LancF att19Bn p93 MR30
PROCTOR,George Vincent Lt kia 6-9-17 8LancF p221 MR30
PROCTOR,James Adolphus 2Lt dow 18-9-18 14RFA p34 CR France673,kia 402Bty
PROCTOR,James Claude Beauchamp TCapt kia 1-7-16 10RInnisF p105 CR France383
PROCTOR,John.MID Maj dow 12-8-18 RAMC att9CavFdAmb p197 CR France879

PROCTOR,Leslie Horner Lt kld 17-11-18 RASC &10RAF p193 CR Belgium393
PROCTOR,Maubray T2Lt kia 26-5-17 1Y&L p159 CR Belgium127,Mowbray
PROCTOR,Walter Alan 2Lt dedacc 25-6-19 2ELancs p264 CR Lancs205
PROCTOR,William Fife Capt dow 27-9-15 ScotHorse p205 CR Greece10
PROCTOR,William Harold T2Lt kia 9-4-17 6RWKent A'Coy p141 CR France513
PROCTOR,William Howard.DSO.Capt kia 23-4-17 10LNLancs p136 MR20
PROCTOR-BEAUCHAMP,Horace George.Bart.CB.LtCol kia 12-8-15 5Norf p216 MR4
PROCTOR-BEAUCHAMP,Montague Barclay Granville 2Lt kia 12-8-15 5Norf p216 MR4
PROFEIT,Leopold TCapt kia 25-4-17 8KSLI p145 CR Greece6
PROFFITT,John Thomas Read 2Lt 20-10-18 66Wing 224Sqn RAF MR37
PROFIT,Lodwig Tudor T2Lt dow 20-6-18 Lpool att2/6Bn p72 CR France204
PROPHET,Cecil 2Lt kia 9-10-17 20Lond p251 MR30
PROPHIT,George Craigie Lt ded 10-12-20 IA 1/39GarhwalRif att18Div HQ p281 CR Iraq8
PROSPER LISTON,William Capt 12-4-17 5Leinst CR France557 see also LISTON
PROSSER,Albert Victor TLt kia 26-11-16 Worc attBordR p109 CR France233,9N&D attWorc
PROSSER,Arthur Edward.MID TCapt ded PoW 23-10-18 1Worc C'Coy p109 CR Belgium342
PROSSER,John Lt ded 28-12-17 16Lancers p23 CR Surrey91
PROSSER,John Lt kia 28-9-18 4 att8BlkW p230 CR Belgium101
PROSSER,Walter T2Lt dow 9-10-18 1/6Glouc att38MGC Inf p185 CR France560,Lt
PROTHERO,Francis Isaac TLtACapt ded 13-2-19 LabCps p266 CR Wales135
PROTHERO,James Edward Douglas Capt ded 11-8-18 IA 90Punjabis attPoliticalDept p281 CR Asia82
PROTHERO,Philip Bernard LtTCapt kia 26-7-17 4A&SH &5RFC p12&173 MR20
PROTHERO,Rowland John Lt dow 8-11-18 7Huss p22 CR Iraq8
PROTHEROE,William Bertram TLt kia 12-6-17 GL &53RFC p12 MR20
PROUD,John Dover.MC.LtTCapt dow 1-8-18 RAMC att46FA p197 CR France1225,Maj
PROUD,John Reginald Stanhope TLt dow PoW 6-4-17 GL &RFC p12 CR Belgium406
PROUDFOOT,Colin Andrew Lt dow 7-1-16 IA 53Sikhs p281 MR38
PROUDFOOT,Cyril Dallas 2Lt kia 22-4-18 NottsYeo &RAF p205&258 CR France103
PROUDFOOT,Harold Heafford Capt kia 2-9-16 RAMC att26RFA p197 CR France397
PROUDFOOT,Thomas John Anderson T2Lt kia 23-2-18 54RFC p17 CR France987,kld
PROUGHTEN,Charles Ernest 2Lt kia 23-5-18 SurrYeo att10RWSurr p205 CR Belgium84
PROUT,Douglas William T2Lt kia 3-9-16 8RBerks p139 MR21
PROUT,William Thomas 2Lt kia 28-7-16 3 att1Ches p96 MR21
PROVAN,David Hart.MC.2Lt ded 27-12-18 5LNLancs p234 CR Scot807 see HART.D.P.true name
PROVAND,Dixon 2Lt kia 15-9-16 19Lond p251 CR France390
PROVIS,Ernest Snell 2Lt kia 16-6-16 4 att8RMunstF p176 CR France223
PROWSE,Charles Bertie.DSO.TBrigGen dow 1-7-16 SomLI 11InfBde p80&259 CR France3
PROWSE,Gerald Maurice Warren T2Lt kia 12-4-17 9RSuss B'Coy p119 MR20
PRUDEN,Walter Henry T2Lt ded 27-11-18 34MGC p185 CR Lancs14
PRUDHAM,Thomas Pearson T2Lt kia 28-4-17 25NumbF p62 MR20
PRUNTY,Patrick Gerald Fitzroy 2Lt ded 16-5-16 IARO att33Cav p281 CR Iraq5
PRUST,Henry Royston T2LtACapt kia 20-11-17 7YLI p143 MR17
PRYCE,Alfred Owen Challoner 2Lt kia 14-4-18 8ScotRif p225 MR32
PRYCE,Arthur Meurig Capt ded 21-2-19 RAMC 35GH p197 CR France65,att 129FA 14RWFus
PRYCE,Hugh Beauclerk Mostyn Capt dow 19-3-15 4RB p180 CR France284
PRYCE,Thomas Tannatt.VC.MC&Bar.Capt kia 13-4-18 4GrenGds p50 MR32
PRYCE-JENKIN,Richard Douglas 2Lt kia 31-12-14 1SWBord p100 CR France260
PRYCE-JONES,Reginald T2Lt kia 19-10-17 8Y&L p159 CR Belgium308
PRYDE,James Watson Lt 5-5-18 7BlkW att1KAR p231&268,Capt MR52
PRYKE,Arthur.MC.2Lt kia 11-4-17 2Suff p79 MR20
PRYKE,Edgar King T2Lt kia 30-11-17 GL &3RFC p12 CR France177
PRYN,William Reginald TLt ded 27-6-15 RAMC 9FA p197 CR Belgium11
PRYNN,Norman LtACapt kia 28-3-18 3 att1Hamps p121 MR20
PRYNNE,Edgar George Fellowes TLtACapt kia 16-9-18 4RFus att1/23Lond p69 MR21
PRYNNE,Norman Fellowes Lt kia 24/25-4-17 10Dev p77 MR37
PRYOR,Arthur Henry T2Lt kia 10-4-17 27NumbF p62 MR20
PRYOR,Ferdinand William Lt dow 12-9-16 3RIrRif att6InnisF p170 CR Greece4
PRYOR,Joseph Stoneman 2Lt kia 25-3-18 RE 228FC p210 MR27

PRYOR,Robert Selwyn 2Lt kia 1-5-15 1RLancs p59 MR29
PUCKLE,John.DSO.MID LtCol drd 15-4-17 RASC p193 MR35
PUCKLE,Thomas Norman Capt kia 30-8-14 Leic att2NigR p88 CR WAfrica57,Maj
PUCKRIDGE,Christopher Francis Hewitt ACapt kia 28-3-17 3 att7DCLI p114 CR France907
PUCKRIDGE,Cyril Vincent Noel 2Lt kia 21-7-16 1/5Glouc p225 MR21
PUDDICOMBE,Donald Ramsay T2Lt dow 24-7-16 13EYorks p84 CR France345
PUDDICOMBE,Frank Cecil TLt kia 28-10-18 8Dev p77 CR Italy9
PUGH,Arnold Richard Capt dow 24-6-15 3SLancs p125
PUGH,Cyril Webster Lt kia 21-8-18 RFA att38MGC p34 CR France2
PUGH,David William 2Lt kia 7-10-18 YLI att15Bn p143 CR France1140,Williams
PUGH,Edward Rhodes Capt ded 2-12-18 30NumbF att1KAR p62,267,&202 CR EAfrica86
PUGH,Geoffrey Arthur 2Lt kia 10-10-16 26RFus p69 MR21
PUGH,George Morris 2Lt dow 2-9-18 RGA 91SB p41 CR France785
PUGH,Henry Loyn 2Lt dow 11-9-16 3SWBord p100 CR France833
PUGH,Herbert Elias 2Lt kia 22-7-16 3 att2SLancs p125 MR21
PUGH,Ronald George 2Lt kia 19-8-16 3KSLI att7NStaffs p145 CR France156
PUGSLEY,John Frederick 2Lt kia 30-8-18 1Dev p77 CR France1484
PULFORD,Harvey St.George James.MID Capt ded 28-6-16 IA MilGovNasiriyeh 4Rajputs p281 CR Iraq6,Maj
PULING,R.J.C.Capt 29-2-20 GL &RE IWT CR Iraq6
PULLAM,Frank T2Lt kia 19-6-18 1NStaffs p157 CR France480
PULLAN,Charles Ernest Arbuthnot T2Lt kia 30-12-15 16DLI p161 CR France1140,15Bn
PULLAN,Charles Maxwell 2Lt kld 21-3-17 2WRidRFA p209 CR France614
PULLAN,John Aynsley.MID 2LtTLt kia 28-11-17 DLI att9RFC p12&161 CR Belgium18
PULLAR,Thomas Hume 2Lt kia 24-8-18 8 att 1/7HLI p240 MR16
PULLEIN,Thomas Harold TLt kia 21-3-18 25NumbF p62 MR20
PULLEINE,Robert Percy 2Lt kia 4-9-16 D18RFA p34 CR France515
PULLEN,Alan Collier 2Lt dow 19-8-16 3SomLI p80 CR France833
PULLEN,Charles Tease Lt kia 4-9-17 RGA att25RFC p19&209 MR20,Jesse
PULLEN,Frederick John Edward T2Lt kld 26-3-18 RFC p17 CR Somerset153
PULLEN,Guy Harper 2Lt kia 13-5-15 RHGds p20 MR29
PULLEN,Richard Standeford.MID T2Lt kia 26-10-17 SStaffs att1Bn p123 CR Belgium112
PULLEY,Charles Maj dow 20-7-15 Cmdg68RFA p34 CR Kent287,26-7-15
PULLEYN,Edward Henry 2Lt kia 25-11-17 1/20 att1/2Lond p251 MR17
PULLEYN,James Lewis T2Lt kia 17-10-16 6Dors &RFC p3&124 MR20
PULLIN,Bernard John.MC.Lt dow 21-10-17 D291RFA p208 CR Belgium16
PULLIN,John Henton TLt dow 21-1-16 9LNLancs p136 CR France285
PULLING,O.L.2Lt mbk 25-9-15 RGA att10TMB p256 MR19
PULLINGER,Harold Bessant T2Lt kia 1-9-18 att8ESurr p113 CR France400
PULMAN,Harry Robert Sauve Capt kld 10-3-15 3Lond p245 CR France706
PULVERMAN,Oscar Percy T2Lt dow 1-9-15 1Suff p79 CR Belgium97,Lt
PUMPHREY,Arnold.DSO.MID TCapt dow 21-9-17 20DLI A'Coy p161 MR30
PUMPHREY,Hubert 2Lt kia 26-4-18 10Ches p96 MR30
PUNCHARD,Alfred CaptAMaj kia 29-3-17 2NStaffs p157 MR38
PUNCHARD,Edmund Elgood.MID Lt kia 29-10-14 2Beds p86 MR29,31-10-14
PUNCHARD,James Septimus Lt ded 2-4-19 5RLancs p271 CR C'land&W'land83
PUNCHARD,R Hugh Lt ded 31-10-18 RGA attTankCps p41&188 CR Devon267
PUNTAN,Herbert Forbes 2Lt kia 9-4-17 3 att2GordH p167 MR20
PURCELL,Albert Joseph 2Lt kia 14-7-16 2RWar p65 MR21
PURCELL,Charles Francis Lt kia 15-9-16 2IrGds attMGC p53&185 MR21
PURCELL,Richard Guy.MC.CaptAMaj dow 28-3-18 RGA 31HB p41 CR France182
PURCELL,Stanley Joseph T2Lt dow 26-3-17 RB p180 MR34
PURCHAS,Ernest Charles Lt dow 4-3-15 V'RHA p34 CR France31,3-3-15
PURCHAS,Geoffrey Thomas 2Lt kia 26-9-17 1RWSurr p56 MR30
PURCHASE,Arthur James Lt ded 4-12-19 WYorks attMGC p263 CR Surrey106
PURCHES,Clifford Arthur T2Lt kia 22-3-18 19MGC p185 MR20
PURDEY,M.Sefton TMaj ded 25-5-16 RemountSve 18Huss p24 CR Kent268
PURDIE,David Scott 2Lt dow 30-9-18 9Lpool p216 CR France256
PURDIE,Frank Phillip Maj ded 20-3-19 8Ess p271 CR War151
PURDIE,Peter Robertson 2Lt dow 17-8-17 RGA 14HB p41 CR Belgium24
PURDIE,Thos.Paterson T2Lt kia 10-7-16 13 att20WelshR p127 MR21
PURDON,George Hardress 2Lt kia 23-7-16 2KRRC p151 MR21
PURDON,Harold Reginald 2Lt dow 28-4-18 9Lpool p216 CR France62
PURDON,Robert Gordon 2Lt kia 16-8-16 13Lpool p72 MR21

PURDON,Theodore Oscar TCapt kia 9-9-16 7Leinst A'Coy p174 CR France402
PURDON-STOUTE,Henry T2Lt kia 10-11-17 2RMunstF p176 MR30
PURDY,Archer Kershaw T2Lt dow 20-11-17 1Leic p88 CR France379
PURDY,Harry Wilfred T2Lt kia 23-4-17 19Manch p155 MR20
PURDY,Richard Shaw T2Lt dow 11-9-16 6 att8RInnisF p105 CR France23
PURGOLD,Louis Joseph Lt kld 20-8-17 RFA att RFC p19&208 CR Lancs1
PURKESS,Arthur James T2Lt kia 27-6-18 12Y&L p159 CR France24,13Bn
PURKIS,Harold Arthur T2Lt kia 28-7-17 111MGC Infp185 CR Belgium100
PURKIS,John Nottage T2Lt kia 25-9-15 SomLI att6Bn p80 MR29,Nollidge
PURLL,William Albert George 2Lt kia 3-5-17 11EYorks p84 MR20
PURNELL,Alfred William Howard(Bert) 2Lt dow PoW 20-11-17 RGA CpsHA 120SB p41 CR Belgium140,Albert
PURNELL,Arthur Channing TCapt kia 1-7-16 16Mddx p148 MR21
PURNELL,Stanley George Hardy T2Lt kia 5-6-17 21NumbF p62 MR20
PURSER,Norman Frederick T2Lt kia 28-2-18 GL &12RFC p17 CR France214
PURSER,Philip Addison TLt dow 30-4-16 RASC p193 CR Ireland14
PURSER,Philip Warburton 2Lt ded 11-10-16 3Mddx p148 CR Mddx39
PURSGLOVE,Edwin James Lt kia 6-11-17 5BordR p228 CR Belgium106
PURSLOW,George 2Lt kia 12-10-18 5NStaffs p238 CR France230
PURVER,Bernard Arthur TCapt kia 7-10-16 11RWKent p141 MR21
PURVES,George Gordon de Burgh TCapt dow 8-11-15 2 att6RScotF p95 CR Germany1
PURVES,Harry de Burgh CaptTMaj kia 18-6-16 2A&SH p173 CR France80
PURVES,James Phillip 2Lt kia 11-4-18 6A&SH p243 MR19
PURVES,Thomas Henderson T2Lt kia 22-3-18 2TankCps p188 CR France307
PURVES,Thomas Warren TLt kia 7-6-17 23Mddx p148 CR Belgium111
PURVES,Walter Douglas Laidlaw TLtACapt kia 28-4-17 9ELancs p111 CR Greece6
PURVIS,Eyre Walter Molyneux Maj AccShot 4-3-15 IA 16Cav p281 CR Iraq6
PURVIS,George Bell Capt kia 8-6-17 5Yorks att56MGC Inf p187&220 CR Belgium102
PURVIS,John Ralph TCapt kia 25-9-15 9RB p180 MR29
PURVIS,John William T2Lt kldacc 2-5-17 GL &RFC p12 CR Durham19
PURVIS,Ronald Montague Capt dow 14-3-17 3 att2BlkW p129 MR38
PUSCH,Ernest John 2Lt kia 8-8-16 11RWar p65 CR France453
PUSCH,Frederick Leopold.DSO.Lt kia 27-6-16 IrGds att1Bn SR p53 CR Belgium73
PUTMAN,Edmund 2Lt ded 16-4-18 RGA 383SB p41 CR Egypt1
PUZEY,Arthur Kenneth Capt kia 11-11-14 4RFus p69 MR29
PYATT,Richard Goodwin Lt ded 13-10-15 1/7N&D p233 CR France423
PYBUS,Harold Robert Lt ded 24-7-16 4 att2DLI p161 CR Numb4
PYBUS,Robert 2Lt kia 14-7-16 8DLI p239 CR Belgium97,24-7-16
PYCROFT,Arthur Percival T2Lt kld 16-6-17 GL &RFC p12 CR Notts84,Lt
PYE,Colin T2Lt dow 8-10-18 KSLI att1Bn p145 CR France725
PYE,Francis John Capt kia 15-12-16 5RFus attGoldCoastR p69 CR EAfrica38 &CR Tanzania1
PYE,Walter George 2Lt kia 24-7-17 A277RFA p209 CR Belgium7
PYE,William Wakeley T2Lt kia 14-10-15 6RWKent p141 MR19
PYE-SMITH,Phillip Howson Guy TLt kia 15-5-17 11Lpool p72 CR France581
PYKE,William Edward 2Lt kia 9-9-16 1/4LNLancs p234 MR21
PYM,Claude John Lt ded 27-3-17 2IrGds p53 CR France105,26-3-17
PYM,E.H.Maj ded 11-11-19 RE p262 CR Devon258
PYM,Francis Leslie Melville Lt kia 2-7-16 2IrGds p53 MR29
PYM,John Scarlett T2Lt kia 5-12-16 2RWSurr p56 CR France174,6Bn
PYM,John Walter 2Lt kia 7-7-16 7Lond p247 CR France558
PYMAN,Allan Lt kia 15-6-15 3 att2Yorks p91 MR22
PYMAN,James Capt kld 18-11-14 3BordR attManch p117 MR29
PYMAN,Ronald Lee Lt kia 3-5-17 15 att12Mddx p148 MR20
PYNE,Ernest Sydney 2Lt dow 12-10-17 4 att9WYorks p82 CR Belgium16

Q

QUAIFE,Eric John 2LtACapt kia 30-6-17 RGA 294SB p41 CR Belgium339
QUAIL,Henry Charles T2Lt kia 18-2-18 RE 124FC p48 CR France922
QUAILE,Robert Ernest Browne 2Lt kia 3-10-18 4 att6RInnisF p105 CR France1495
QUALE,Charles Philip 2Lt kia 15-6-17 2/1BucksBn O&BLI p231 CR France706
QUARMBY,Frederick 2Lt kia 18-9-16 7WRid p228 CR France300
QUARMBY,James Scholfield 2Lt kia 2-12-17 7WRid p228 CR France530
QUARRELL,Charles Hubert T2Lt kia 16-6-17 13NumbF p62 MR20
QUARRIER,Edward John 2Lt kia 31-5-18 3 att2Hamps p121 MR32
QUARRY,Herbert TLt kia 2-8-16 RFA F8TMB p34 CR France114
QUARRY,St.John Shandon.MID Maj kia 14-4-18 3RBerks Cmdg14RWar p139 CR France346
QUARTERMAN,Percy Harold Lt kia 9-10-17 23Lond att2/4ELancs p252 CR Belgium125
QUARTLEY,Thomas Warner 2Lt kia 15-1-15 Lancs attSLancs p59 CR Belgium89
QUAYLE,Rupert Charles T2Lt kia 4-10-18 1 att1/4Leic p88 CR France441
QUEEN,John 2Lt kia 7-6-17 12NumbF p62 MR20
QUEKETT,John 2Lt kia 31-7-17 5BlkW p231 CR Belgium96
QUELCH,Arthur Francis T2Lt kld 15-1-18 RFC p17 CR Kent129
QUENINGTON,Michael Hugh.Viscount Lt dow 23-4-16 1/1GloucYeo p203 CR Egypt10,kia
QUEST,Harold.MC.TCapt kia 3-11-16 14Y&L A'Coy p159 CR France1326
QUIBELL,George Edwin 2Lt kia 26-3-17 10Mddx p236 MR34
QUIBELL,Samuel Boyd.MID Maj dow 5-2-16 4EYorks p219 CR Belgium11
QUICKE,Edward Owen St.Ayres Godolphin.MID Capt kia 25-10-14 3Dev p77 MR22,Cyres
QUICKE,Henry Lt kia 23-3-18 4RWFus p223 MR20
QUIGLEY,Christopher T2Lt kia 21-3-18 11 att2RDubF p177 MR27
QUIGLEY,William Grainger 2Lt ded 2-11-18 IA TC attSchoolofInstrn RoO p281 MR65
QUILLER-COUCH,Bevil Brian.DSO.MC.AMaj ded 6-2-19 9/41RFA p34 CR Germany1
QUILLINAN,Lawrence Patrick Capt ded 14-1-20 IA 1/124BaluchistanInf p281 MR67
QUILTER,Frederick Walter 2Lt kia 31-8-15 6Lond p247 CR France149
QUILTER,John Arnold Cuthbert LtCol 6-5-15 GrenGds CR Gallipoli14
QUILTER,Roy Molyneux.MID TCapt kia 19-4-16 8Beds p86 MR29
QUIN,Desmond Hilary Lt kia 18-9-18 5RWSurr p212 CR Greece5
QUIN,Francis John 2Lt dow 2-5-18 50RFA p34 CR France142
QUIN,James Davidson 2Lt kia 19-8-18 2RFus p69 CR France28,18-8-18
QUIN,Leslie William Whitworth.MC.TLtACapt kia 24-4-17 3 att27NumbF p62 MR20
QUIN,Walter Capt 11-7-21 GL CR Iraq6
QUINCEY,Thomas Edmund De Quincey 2Lt kia 9-5-15 6 att2RB p180 MR32
QUINE,Brian Howell TLt kia 27-6-18 2BlkW p129 CR Palestine9
QUINLAN,Charles 2Lt kia 31-7-17 5Leinst p174 MR29
QUINLAN,Harold Daniel Lt kia 26-3-18 4Huss p21 MR27
QUINLAN,James Leonard 2Lt dow 28-12-17 7RWar p214 CR France52
QUINLAN,John Francis Pembroke Boxwell 2Lt kia 3-7-16 RFA attRFC p2&34,ded MR20
QUINLAN,Louis T2Lt kia 27-4-16 8RInnisF p105 CR France219
QUINN,James 2Lt dow 29-7-16 RGA 109SB p41 CR France430
QUINN,James Ewart 2Lt kia 5-10-18 8Lpool p216 CR France256
QUINN,John Henry 2Lt ded 11-8-19 RFA 220Bde AC p261 CR Iraq8,Lt
QUINN,John James Patrick LtCol ded 26-9-15 IA 117Mahrattas p281 MR65,25-9-15
QUINN,John Patrick TLt dow 20-6-17 11RDubF p177 CR France40,2Lt
QUINN,J.P.Lt 6-10-20 2RDubF CR Eire506
QUINN,Thomas Joseph T2Lt dow 18-6-18 9WRid p116 CR France84
QUINN,William Henry Corry 2Lt kia 21-4-18 A70RFA p34 CR France113
QUINT,Henry John T2Lt kia 24-9-18 3Glouc att5Leic p107 CR France699
QUIRKE,Amyas Septimus.MC.T2Lt dow 3-11-18 56MGC p185 CR France40

R

RABAN,Richard Bassett Cockburn LtCol kia 11-5-16 IA 1Lancers att13RScots p281 CR France423
RABONE,Arthur Brian Capt kia 1-7-16 6RWar p214 MR21
RABONE,John Kenneth Capt ded 1-9-15 1/5RWar p214 CR France40,1-12-15
RABONE,Maxwell T2Lt dow 22-8-15 2RMunstF p176 MR4
RABY,William Donald T2Lt kia 8-10-18 1/2RWFus p98 CR France234
RACINE,Ernest Guy 2Lt kia 9-4-17 10Lpool p216 CR France581
RADCLIFF,Herbert Travers Capt kia 15-3-15 5Leinst p174 MR29
RADCLIFF,Robert Sussex Francis Derwentwater 2Lt kia 26-3-18 80RFC p17
RADCLIFFE,Arthur Philip Joseph LtACapt dow 18-8-17 71RFA p34 CR Lond6
RADCLIFFE,David TLt kia 18-3-16 24RFus p69 CR France161
RADCLIFFE,Dering John Jasper Lt kld 31-10-17 5GrenGds p50 CR France112
RADCLIFFE,E.B.Sister ded 10-3-19 QAIMNS p200 CR France65
RADCLIFFE,Ernest Charles Derwentwater T2Lt kia 31-7-17 15RWFus p98 CR Belgium106
RADCLIFFE,Ernest John T2Lt kld 20-2-16 GL &RFC p2&191,ded CR Mddx17

255

RADCLIFFE,Frederick TLt kia 10-4-17 35MGC p185 MR20
RADCLIFFE,George Amyas Lt kia 25-4-17 3A&SH att17RFC p12&173 MR37
RADCLIFFE,George Kan 2Lt kia 1-7-16 14RIrF p171 MR21
RADCLIFFE,James Lt kia 24-2-18 1/7WRid p227 CR Belgium34
RADCLIFFE,Jasper Fitzgerald.DSO.MIDx2 LtCol kia 31-1-16 Dev attEss p77 CR France515
RADCLIFFE,John Douglas Henderson Capt dow 30-7-15 7KRRC p151 MR29
RADCLIFFE,Miles TCapt kia 12-12-14 BordR attRScotF p117 CR Belgium186
RADCLIFFE,Percival Victor Alban Lt dow 25-11-17 5Yorks attMGC Cav p187&220 CR France256
RADCLIFFE,Samuel Roberts.DSO.MID Maj ded 30-4-18 172RFA p34 CR Egypt2
RADCLIFFE,William Thomas 2Lt kia 20-7-18 4A&SH p173 CR France622,7Bn
RADCLIFFE,William Yonge T2Lt dow 19-8-15 5Wilts p153 MR4
RADCLYFFE,Charles Edward.DSO.LtCol kia 25-9-15 11Ess p132 MR19,26-9-15
RADFORD,Amyas Leith Capt kia 12-5-15 9Lpool att8LancF p216 MR4
RADFORD,Basil Hallam TCapt kia 20-8-16 RFC p2 CR France203,dedacc
RADFORD,Charles Oates Lt ded 5-4-18 1KARif p268 CR EAfrica86
RADFORD,Francis Buckley 2Lt kia 25-3-18 3 att13RFus p69MR30
RADFORD,Maurice Clive.DSO.Capt kia 28-9-15 1RBerks p139 CR France423
RADFORD,Oswald Campbel TCapt dow 26-2-16 12KRRC p151 CR Belgium11
RADHILL,P.J.Lt ded 2-6-18 5Ches attRAF p222
RADLOFF,Heinrich Lt kia 14-9-18 1/11Lond &RAF p248&258 CR Palestine3,dedacc
RADMILOVIC,John TLt ded 3-11-18 15 att3WelshR p127 CR Wales17
RAE,Alfred Ian T2Lt kia 24-4-17 13RB p180 MR20
RAE,James TLt drd 13-4-17 RAMC p197 MR35,15-4-17
RAE,James T2Lt kia 4-10-17 SfthH att2Bn p165
RAE,James Albert T2Lt ded 4-9-15 10Beds p86 CR Herts110,kldacc
RAE,James Edmond Pringle TCaptAMaj kia 30-11-17 7DCLI p114 MR17
RAE,John Cairns.MC.LtACapt kia 10-4-17 86RFA p34 CR France266
RAE,Lindsay Leon de'Cram Clement Marsham 2Lt drd 10-10-18 YorkDragYeo p206 MR40
RAE,Reginald Wilson 2Lt kia 30-3-15 3ESurr attSStaffs p113 CR Belgium111,2Bn
RAE,Thomas Keith Hedley T2Lt kia 30-7-15 8RB p180 MR29
RAE,William Alexander 2Lt kia 31-7-17 6BlkW p231 CR Belgium65
RAE,William John Capt 27-3-17 3AustBnImpCamelCps MR34
RAE,William Kenneth T2Lt ded 8-11-18 RASC 1032MT Coy p193 CR Greece2
RAEBURN,Alfred Anthony Douglas 2Lt kia 15-7-16 9HLI p240 MR21
RAEBURN,Gordon Peter T2Lt dow 11-4-17 8ELancs p111 CR France581
RAESIDE,George Forrest.MC.T2Lt kia 9-4-18 1/4Lancs p59 CR France1106
RAFFERTY,John Capt 1-3-21 ConnRgrs CR Wilts115
RAFFIN,Archibald Franklin.MC.TLtACapt ded 30-11-18 9Dev p77 CR France717
RAFTER,James.MC.Capt ded 5-10-19 RAMC p267 CR Lancs169
RAGGETT,Bertram Robert 2Lt kia 5-1-18 RGA att10RFC p17&41 CR Belgium11
RAGHUBIR,Singh LtCol 18-1-15 2KashmirRif MR48
RAHILL,Peter Joseph kld 2-6-18 5Ches attRAF CR Ches28
RAHLES-RAHBULA,Arnold James 2LtTCapt kia 28-4-17 8Lincs p75 MR20
RAIKES,Frank Steward Waddington 2Lt kia 9-5-15 5 att2RB p180 MR32
RAIKES,Frederick Munro 2Lt kia 22-2-17 SWBord BrecknockBn attMGC p187&223,Monro CR Iraq5
RAIKES,John Francis 2Lt kia 11-10-16 3 att9Ess p132 MR21
RAIL,Richard Augwin Lt kia 9-10-17 3CldGds p51 MR30,Angwin
RAILSTON,Spencer Julian Wilfred Lt kia 1-11-14 IA 18Lancers att4DragGds p281
RAILTON,Arthur Temple TLt kld 9-5-15 4SfthH p241 CR France924,kia
RAIMES,Lancelot Capt dow 1-6-16 5DLI p238 CR France285
RAIMES,Leslie Robinson Lt 1-7-16 21NumbF MR21
RAINBOTH,Lawrence John T2Lt kld 24-12-17 GL &RFC p12 CR Canada261
RAINBOW,Albert Edward 2Lt kia 23-7-16 4 att10RWar p65 MR21
RAINBOW,George Lt kia 9-10-18 4SLancs p230 CR France256
RAINBOW,John 2Lt kia 7-8-15 6Manch p237 MR4
RAINBOW,Thomas Welford T2Lt kia 18-11-16 10Worc p109 MR21
RAINE,Charles William 2Lt kia 3-11-18 3WRid att16LancF p116 CR France933
RAINE,Foster Rev ded 7-12-18 RAChDept p268 CR Cornwall61
RAINE,George Kenneth 2Lt dow 2-7-16 16 att18DLI p161 CR France169
RAINE,George Stevenson T2Lt kld 15-3-17 26RFus attRFC p12&69 CR Lond12,56ResRFC attRFus
RAINE,Hubert TLt kia 23-3-18 RE 202FC p48 CR France1203
RAINE,Leonard T2Lt kia 15-8-16 6Y&L p159 CR France420
RAINE,William.MC.Capt&Adjt dow 7-9-18 9Lpool p216 CR France433
RAINES,Leslie Robinson TLt kia 1-7-16 21NumbF p62
RAINEY,Edmund Flower LtCol ded 20-7-16 IA 72Punjabis p281 MR67,30-7-16
RAINEY,Victor Thomas James 2Lt kia 30-9-17 2Dev p77 CR Belgium68
RAINEY,William 2Lt kia 23-11-17 2RIrRif p170 MR17
RAINIE,James Wilson McTurk Lt kia 27-3-16 2RScots p54 CR Belgium15
RAINS,R.H.Capt 23-6-20 RAMC CR Lond14
RAINSFORD-Hannay,Ramsay.MID Capt kia 1-2-17 IA 45Sikhs p281 MR38,Maj
RAISTRICK,F.A.Lt 16-11-18 Leic CR Yorks418
RAISTRICK,John William 2Lt kia 19-5-17 1/8WYorks p219 CR France1887
RAIT-KERR,Sylvester Cecil Capt kia 13-5-15 RFA p34 MR29
RAIT-KERR,William Charles.DSO.Capt kia 10-11-14 RFA 57Bty43Bde p34 MR29
RAITT,Alexander Redmayne Lt kia 8-3-16 IA 2RajputLI p281 MR38,Capt
RALEIGH,George Hebden BtMaj kld 20-1-15 Ess &4RFC p2&132 CR France1359
RALEY,Walter Hugh 2Lt kld 14-5-15 5Y&L p238 CR France276
RALEY,William Henry George Capt kia 15-6-15 3 att2Yorks p91 MR22
RALFS,Francis Arthur Lt dow 16-9-16 5RFus att9LancF p69 CR France74
RALLI,Leonidas,Lucas TCapt ded 24-4-17 RASC p193 CR France1886,20-4-17
RALLI,Lionel Peter Lt dow 14-11-18 20Huss p23 CR France146
RALLISON,Victor Edward 2Lt kia 7-4-17 17Manch p155 CR France1185
RALLS,Frederic Hamilton.MC&Bar.Capt dow 24-8-18 9Lond D'Coy p247 CR France141
RALPH,Henry Bertie 2Lt dow 12-10-18 B255RFA p34 CR France241
RALPH,John Gray 2Lt kia 18-6-16 7Lond p247 CR France558
RALPHS,Arthur T2Lt kia 23-4-17 GL &12RFC p12 CR France531
RALPHS,Walter Joel TLt dow 15-7-16 12RFA p34 CR France399,Capt
RAM,George Edward Capt ded 25-3-16 4NStaffs A'Coy p157 CR Lond4
RAM,Percival John T2Lt kia 1-7-16 26Manch p155 MR21
RAMIER,L.S.Lt 14-9-18 IMS CR Mddx26
RAMNEY,Reginald Van Taerling Lt dow 28-3-18 3GrenGds p50
RAMPLEY,William Temple 2Lt kia 30-9-18 1LovatScts attKOSB p204 CR Belgium157
RAMSAY,Alexander Lt ded 28-4-15 5RFus att1RWar p69 CR Belgium383
RAMSAY,A.G.TCapt ded 6-1-19 KAR p202
RAMSAY,Alan Livingstone LtTCapt kia 24-4-16 3RIrReg p89 CR Ireland24
RAMSAY,Alexander 2Lt kia 28-3-18 4RScotF p222 MR20
RAMSAY,Alexander.MM.2Lt kia 20-10-18 5LancF p221 CR Belgium417
RAMSAY,Alexander Charles Marquis Lt ded 18-12-14 RASC p193 CR Mddx26
RAMSAY,Archibald Hamilton T2Lt kia 13-10-15 9 att2 O&BLI p130 MR19
RAMSAY,David James 2Lt kia 21-3-18 59MGC Inf p185 CR France568,18MGC
RAMSAY,David Winson TLt kia 14-2-16 10N&D p134 MR29,Derrick
RAMSAY,Duncan Gavin.MID 2LtTLt kia 19-12-14 2RSuss att2RWSurr p119 CR France924,18-12-14
RAMSAY,George Strachan Lt 8-8-18 49RAF MR20
RAMSAY,Herbert Cyril Lt dow 22-4-18 1Nhampt p138 CR France260
RAMSAY,John Marmaduke TLt dow 14-4-17 2 att10RB p180 CR France164,13-4-17
RAMSAY,John Richard Maj kia 6-1-17 RFA 160HB p34 CR Iraq5
RAMSAY,Keith Winton TLt kia 3-5-16 7KRRC p151 CR France924
RAMSAY,Louis Nail Griffitt 2Lt kia 21-3-15 3 att2GordH p167 CR France768,Neil
RAMSAY,Norman Lt dow 3-11-14 4DragGds RoO p21 CR Belgium98 Ex RFA
RAMSAY,Norman T2Lt kia 3-9-16 16RB p180 MR21
RAMSAY,Stuart.DSO.TCapt dow 3-6-17 8LNLancs p136 CR Belgium43,2-6-17
RAMSAY,William James Lt kia 27-3-18 RWFus &RFC p17&98 CR France300
RAMSBOTHAM,Geoffrey Bury.MID Lt kia 16-5-15 3RSuss attSStaffs p119 MR22
RAMSBOTTOM,Basil William Lt kia 19-8-18 12Norf p204 CR France19
RAMSBOTTOM,Reginald T2Lt kia 29-7-16 29 att17RFus p69 MR21
RAMSDEN,Edward.MM.T2Lt kia 21-3-18 NStaffs p157 MR27
RAMSDEN,Emsley T2Lt kia 15-9-16 MGC p185 CR France390
RAMSDEN,S.2Lt dow 12-4-18 GL &RAF p191
RAMSDEN,Walter Frederick Stewart T2Lt ded 15-11-18 LabCps att22PoW Co p189 CR France146
RAMSEY,Arthur William Lt kia 12-4-15 3EKent attRInnisF p58 MR29
RAMSEY,Charles Owen 2Lt kia 21-3-18 12/13NumbF Res p62 MR27
RAMSEY,George Bennett 2Lt ded 27-8-15 RE p210 MR4
RAMSEY,Harry Victor Lt ded 5-8-18 RFA p208 CR Beds74
RAMSKILL,William Bliss 2Lt dow 16-9-18 A119RFA p34 CR France34
RANBY,Harvey Lt kia 9-8-17 7Suff p79 MR20
RAND,Charles Herbert Sidney T2Lt kia 18-9-18 21NumbF att2Lincs p62 CR France415
RANDALL,Albert William 2Lt kia 8-8-18 3Lond p246 MR16
RANDALL,Charles Barton TLt kia 31-7-17 A74RFA p34 CR Belgium12
RANDALL,Charles Deschamps TCapt kia 7/11-8-15 9N&D p134 MR4,9-8-15

256

RANDALL,Charles Edwin T2Lt kia 27-5-18 RBerks att2/4Bn p139 CR France248
RANDALL,Edwin Walter Lt kia 23-4-17 7RFus p69 MR20
RANDALL,Frank Horace T2Lt kia 18-7-17 9Norf p74 CR France258
RANDALL,Frederick Percival 2Lt kia 16-9-16 6SomLI p80 MR21
RANDALL,Geoffrey Victor 2Lt kia 30-7-16 ELancs &4RFC p2,261&264 CR France44,20-7-16 Deleted see MR
RANDALL,Guy Philip.MC.LtACapt kia 18-9-18 3KOSB p102 CR France415,2Bn
RANDALL,Herbert Ernest T2Lt dow 20-5-18 7KSLI p145 CR France33
RANDALL,John ACapt ded 17-2-19 RGA p255 CR Wilts156
RANDALL,John Beaufoy TCapt kia 31-10-17 RAMC att82RFA p197 CR Belgium10
RANDALL,Mervyn Gregory.MC.T2Lt kia 6-6-18 8NStaffs p157 CR France622
RANDALL,Reginald Wigmore Sancroft T2Lt kia 9-5-15 att2Nhampt p138 MR32
RANDALL,L.Richard William 2Lt ded 4-2-19 SNottsHuss p271 CR Essex1
RANDALL,Sidney Walter T2Lt ded 31-10-17 GL &11RFC p12 CR France568
RANDALL,Stanley.DCM.MM.MID 2LtTLt ded 31-12-18 EKent attWAFF p58&202 CR WAfrica1
RANDERSON,Robert TCapt kia 7-8-15 6Yorks p91 CR Gallipoli26
RANDLE,Thomas Henry 2Lt dow 11-8-17 3Worc p109 CR Belgium7
RANDLESOME,G.W.Gnr ded 30-11-16 RIM IWT p281
RANDOLPH,Julien TLt kia 27-9-15 1WelshGds p53 MR19
RANEY,Paul Hartley 2Lt kia 21-8-17 66RFC p12 MR20
RANK,Sydney Lt dow 23-10-18 RGA 216SB p209 CR France231
RANKEN,Dudleigh Chalmers TCapt kia 27-7-16 23RFus p69 MR21
RANKEN,Ernest Ford T2Lt dow 25-3-16 7KOSB p102 CR France134
RANKEN,George Lt kia 1-11-18 RGA 19SB p209 CR France521
RANKEN,Harry Sherwood.VC.Capt dow 24-9-14 RAMC p197 CR France1110,25-9-14
RANKIN,Franklin Sharp Lt 23-10-16 CanadaEngrs &18RFC MR20
RANKIN,Frederick Alan 2Lt kia 23-4-17 1/5BordR attD'TankCps p228 CR France162
RANKIN,James 2Lt kia 30-11-17 LNLancs att1/5Bn p136 MR17
RANKIN,James Thomson 2Lt kia 23-12-15 4A&SH att1RScots p173 CR Gallipoli1
RANKIN,John T2Lt kia 23-4-17 7Lincs p75 MR20
RANKIN,John Hall 2Lt ded 2-3-16 RH&FA p34
RANKIN,Robert Herbert T2Lt kia 23-11-17 15RIrRif p170 MT17
RANKIN,William TLt kia 18-2-18 RE HQ VIICps p48 CR France446
RANKIN,William John 2Lt kia 30-6-17 9Y&L p159 CR Belgium127
RANKINE,W.H.Chap2Cl 11-7-21 CR Scot528
RANKING,George Harvey Chap4Cl kia 20-11-17 RAChDept attIV Cps HvyArt p199 CR France529
RANKING,James Gabriel Lancaster Capt kia 12-7-15 IA AssPoliticResident PerianGulf p281 CR Asia82,G.J.L.
RANN,William Alfred.MID SubCdr ded PoW 25-6-16 IA S&TCps p281 MR38
RANNEY,Reginald Van Taerlingh Lt dow 28-3-18 3GrenGds CR France924
RANSDALE,Alfred Charles T2Lt kia 1-9-18 15LNLancs p136 CR Belgium188
RANSFORD,Clement Gascoyen Capt kia 26-10-14 1SStaffs p123 CR Belgium116
RANSOM,Frederick Charles 2Lt kia 9-4-18 5 att9Ess p232 CR France197
RANSOM,Henry Bayly Lt ded 30-10-18 3Wilts p265
RANSOM,Hubert William 2Lt kia 27-3-18 GL &70RFC p12 CR France232
RANSOM,John,MC Capt ded 4-9-19 RBerks attHQ LofC p265 CR France40
RANSOM,Richard Edward Croft TCapt dow 21-7-16 13EYorks p84 CR France345,RANSON
RANSOM,Robert Cyril Starling T2Lt dow 19-10-17 7Beds p86 CR Belgium64
RANSOME,Bertram Colby TLt ded 30-6-18 RASC MT p193 CR France85,Coleby
RANSOME,Cecil Talbot TLt&Adjt kia 1-7-16 16WYorks p82 CR France156
RANSOME,Frederick Ronald 2Lt kia 27-5-18 1RDubF att2WYorks p177 CR France1753,dow
RANSOME,Geoffrey Cyril TLt dow 15-1-18 13Yorks p91 CR France518
RANSOME,Herbert Fullarton TLt ded 14-11-17 RAMC p197 CR Lancs233
RANSOME,John Edwin T2Lt kld 12-12-17 GL &RFC p12 CR Lincs10
RANSON,Charles Sherriff 2Lt kia 16-8-17 13Lond p249 MR29
RANSON,Leslie Edward Lt kia 29-9-18 5 att2Worc p109 CR France665
RAPER,Frank Alexander D'Arbly.MC.T2Lt kia 11-12-17 122MGC p185 CR Italy7
RAPER,Robert George TMaj kia 2-7-16 8SStaffs p123 CR France372
RAPER,Sydney Ernest 2Lt kia 17-8-17 6SfthH attRFC p19&241 CR Belgium132
RAPHAEL,Henry George 2Lt kia 31-7-17 7ELancs p111 MR29
RAPHAEL,John Edward TLt dow 11-6-17 GL 18KRRC p191 CR Belgium11
RAPHAEL,Norman Henry 2Lt dow 8-6-16 2RWar p65 CR France67
RAPLEY,William Godfrey 2Lt kia 25-9-17 Mddx att1Bn p148 CR Belgium63
RAPOPORT,John Lindsay 2Lt kia 27-5-18 6 att12RB p180 MR20
RAPP,Ernest James T2Lt kia 9-4-17 GL attYorks p191 CR France1185

RAPP,Reginald 2Lt kia 18-6-15 7WRid p228 CR France347,Lt
RAPSON,Harold Thomas 2LtACapt dow PoW 23-3-18 3 att7RWKent p141 CR France1717
RASH,Arnold William 2Lt kia 31-7-17 5Suff p217 CR Belgium94
RASH,Ralph Reginald T2Lt kia 12-10-16 7Suff p79 MR21
RASTRICK,Urpeth Lt kia 14-12-14 Nhampt p138 CR France572
RATCLIFF,John Edward Lt kia 20-10-14 2RWar p65 CR Belgium140,19-10-14
RATCLIFF,Sidney Arthur 2Lt kia 31-3-17 C59RFA p34 CR France158
RATCLIFF-GAYLAND, Eric Ronald 2Lt kia 20-7-16 1/5DCLI p227 CR France1887,19-7-16
RATCLIFFE,Alfred Victor TLt kia 1-7-16 10WYorks p82 CR France373
RATCLIFFE,Clifford Stanley 2Lt kia 22-7-18 10RIrF p171 MR32
RATCLIFFE,Frederick Brockwall.MID LtACapt dow 30-3-18 1Drags att6MGC Cav p21&185 CR France145
RATCLIFFE,Frederick Frank T2Lt dow 10-9-17 8RWSurr p56 CR France139
RATCLIFFE,William Henry 2Lt kia 1-7-16 4 att1SStaffs p123 CR France397
RATHBONE,Arnold Richard Capt dow 24-6-15 3 att2SLancs p125 CR France1
RATHBONE,George Benson Lt ded 28-5-19 RGA 1/1HB p41 CR Germany1
RATHBONE,George Henry Lt 29-4-17 AlbertaR &12RFC MR20
RATHBONE,George Powell TLt kia 21-3-18 7Nhampt p138 MR27
RATHBONE,Guy Benson TCapt kia 21-4-16 11 att7Glouc p107 MR38
RATHBONE,John Ernest Vivian Lt 4-6-18 3 att1Dors p124 CR France502,Capt
RATHBONE,Thomas Ford 2Lt kia 26-9-17 5NStaffs p238 CR Belgium125
RATHMELL,E.AssMatron6286 ded 28-7-19 QAIMNS CR Yorks222
RATLIFF,Edward Francis.MC.Capt kia 2-12-17 6 att2RB p180 MR30
RATNAGAR,S.D.Capt 24-4-17 IMS att1/94Inf MR43
RATSEY,Clayton Capt kia 12-8-15 8Hamps C'Coy p229 MR4
RATSEY,Donald White Capt kia 12-8-15 8Hamps D'Coy p229 MR4
RATSEY,Stephen Gilbert Lt kia 19-4-17 8Hamps p229 CR Palestine8
RATTIGAN,Cyril Stanley Capt kia 13-11-16 7RFus p69 MR21
RATTON,Joseph Holroyd Maj kia 2-9-17 RGA 163SB p41 CR Belgium19
RATTON,Wilfrid Holroyd 2Lt ded 9-7-15 22Lond p251 CR EAfrica125
RATTRAY,David 2Lt dow 21-9-18 D23RFA p34 CR France327
RATTRAY,David Lindsay TCapt kia 17-2-17 23RFus p69 MR21
RATTRAY,Haldane Burney.DSO.LtCol kia 1-2-17 IA 45Sikhs p281 MR38
RATTRAY,Malcolm McGregor.DSO.LtCol ded 27-11-19 RAMC 3BritGH p267 CR Iraq6
RATTRAY,James Alec 2Lt kia 23-9-17 RGA 5SB p41 CR Belgium23
RAVEN,Frederick Gifford T2Lt dow 24-3-17 RE p48 CR France85,Frederic
RAVENHILL,Aleck George TCapt kia 25-9-15 8SfthH A'Coy p165 CR France219,Alex
RAVENOR,Geoffrey Paxton T2Lt kia 2-10-16 6RBerks p139 CR France246
RAVENSCROFT,Alan Paddock TLt kia 16-1-17 RFA attRFC p12&34,ded CR Lond29
RAVENSCROFT,Dudley Clement 2Lt kia 1-5-19 18Lond att81MGC CR Greece9
RAVENSCROFT,Guy TCapt kia 18-10-16 18Lpool p72 CR France385
RAVENSCROFT,Richard Birbeck Lt kia 16-8-17 Herts p252 MR30
RAW,Rowland T2Lt kia 7-8-15 9LancF p93 CR Gallipoli27
RAW,Rupert George.DSO.Capt kia 7-8-15 8NumbF p62 MR4
RAWBONE,Charles Robert T2Lt kld 18-12-17 GL &RFC p12
RAWDON-HASTINGS,Edward Hugh Hastings 2Lt ded 25-9-15 2BlkW p129 CR France64,15-9-15
RAWDON-HASTINGS,Paulyn Charles James Reginald Capt kia 13-10-15 5Leic A'Coy p220 MR19
RAWE,Charles Henry 2Lt kia 24-4-18 RFA SR attRGA 309SB p34 CR France210
RAWES,Douglas TLt dow 16-8-15 8KRRC p151 CR Europe28
RAWES,Joscelyn Hugh Russell TLt kia 1-7-19 7Beds p86 CR France513,1-7-16
RAWLE,Charles William Forbes T2Lt kia 5-4-16 9Worc p109 MR38
RAWLE,William Richard Capt dow 8-8-18 1/2Lond p245 CR France95
RAWLING,Cecil Godfrey.CMG.CIE.DSO.TBngGen kia 28-10-17 62SomLI p80 CR Belgium19
RAWLINGS,Charles William Ernest T2Lt dow 28-9-17 1Glouc p107 CR Belgium18
RAWLINGS,George Wilfred Harry Leslie TLt kia 27-1-17 4Hamps p228 MR38
RAWLINGS,Leonard Justly T2Lt kia 7-11-16 2Nhampt p138 CR France744
RAWLINGS,Thomas William T2Lt ded 8-10-18 RWSurr att39RFus p56 CR Palestine8
RAWLINS,Gerald Edmund Adair Capt kia 7-7-16 9RFus p69 CR France393
RAWLINS,Guy Vernon Champion Capt ded 30-1-19 RE att7TankCps p48&188 CR France63
RAWLINS,Hugh Penrose Cardozo 2Lt kia 4-10-17 10YLI p143 MR30
RAWLINS,John Bromley Capt kia 16-8-17 RAMC p254 CR Belgium96

RAWLINSON,Curwen Vaughan 2Lt kia 21-5-15 3 att1Dors p124 CR Belgium82
RAWLINSON,Godfrey Marshall 2Lt dow 16-7-16 1/4 O&BLI p231 CR France203
RAWLINSON,Guy Edward 2Lt dow 23-7-16 1/3Camb p245 CR France924
RAWLINSON,Harry Raymond T2Lt kia 26-9-17 118MGC Inf p185 CR Belgium112
RAWLINSON,Leonard Hugh Lt kia 10-5-15 2Lancs p59 MR29
RAWLINSON,Robert.MID 2Lt kia 25-9-15 3 att2BordR p117 MR19
RAWLINSON,William Gray Lt kia 14-3-15 2DCLI p114 MR29
RAWNSLEY,Gerald 2Lt kia 21-1-17 4WRid p227 CR France503
RAWSON,Arthur.MIDx2 Capt kia 6-10-18 13BlkW p205 CR France1495
RAWSON,Edward Douglas 2Lt kia 23-8-18 4 att2SStaffs p123 CR France214,23/24-8-18
RAWSON,Harry William Capt ded PoW 22-4-18 16RScots p54
RAWSON,Hubert Wyatt Hay Capt kia 15-11-16 3 att2 O&BLI p130 CR France152
RAWSON,Lionel Reginald.MC.LtACapt kia 23-10-16 6 att17KRRC p151 MR21
RAWSON,Philip Colin 2Lt kia 25-9-15 RBerks p139 MR19
RAWSON,Stuart Milner TLt kia 20-7-16 20RFus p69 MR21
RAWSON,Thomas Leonard HonLt ded 28-6-17 RAOC IOD p198 MR43 &CR Pakistan50A
RAWSTHORN,Eric 2Lt kia 15-6-15 4LNLancs p234 MR22
RAWSTORNE,Thomas Geoffrey Maj dow 31-7-17 1/1LancHussYeo p204 CR Belgium23
RAY,Archibald Douglas Hussey Capt kia 30-4-15 Worc p109 CR Gallipoli15
RAY,Frederick Lee 2Lt kia 16-5-18 1Beds p86 CR France21
RAY,Philip Oliphant T2Lt ded 13-4-17 8BlkW &59RFC p12&129 MR20
RAY,Reginald Morison 2Lt kia 27-9-18 7Manch p237 CR France712
RAY,Richard T2Lt dow 26-5-18 RASC MT att40RGA 196SB AC p193 CR France40
RAYMENT,Edward TLt ded 6-4-17 RE IWT p48 CR Scot112
RAYMOND,Arthur Augustus Lt kia 1-8-15 2RIrRif p170 MR29
RAYMOND,Bertram Seymour Maj ded 12-8-17 IA 97DeccanHorse p281 CR Asia82
RAYMOND,Edward Wetherall Hunter Lt dow 29-5-15 RInnisF p105 CR Lond4
RAYMOND,Frederick Charles Motley 2Lt kia 21-8-15 8Hamps p229 MR4
RAYMOND,John Brannan.MC.LtACapt&djt dow 4-10-18 6ESurr att 1/5N&D p226 CR France446
RAYMOND,Wynne Dudley.MID Lt kia 26-10-18 IA 2Lancers attMysoreLancers p281 CR Lebanon1
RAYMOND-BARKER,Cecil Langton T2Lt kia 25-9-15 12RB p180 CR France768
RAYMONT,William Clifton Lt kia 6-5-17 3Mon p244 CR Belgium4,5SWBord
RAYNER,Albert Stanley Lt dow 15-7-18 1/2Nhampt attRAF 21ssSect 2AirSupplyDept p138 CR France792
RAYNER,Arthur Tamplin T2Lt dow 6-7-16 44MGC Inf p185 CR France423,kia
RAYNER,Benjamin Harold Capt kia 14-6-17 1/5NStaffs p157 MR20
RAYNER,Cecil Arthur 2Lt dow 9-11-15 6Ess p232 MR4
RAYNER,Charles Oliver T2Lt kia 1-10-17 GL &25RFC p12 CR France88
RAYNER,Cyril Hood T2Lt kia 24-2-17 18LancF p93 CR France648
RAYNER,Donald Lt kia 8-8-18 1Camb C'Coy p245 CR France196
RAYNER,George Biddulph 2Lt kia 12-5-15 3Ess att2Glouc p132 CR Belgium167
RAYNER,Harold 2Lt kia 4-9-18 4EYorks p219 CR Belgium96
RAYNER,Harold Leslie T2Lt kia 1-7-16 9Dev p77 CR France330
RAYNER,Haydn Eric William 2Lt kia 17-3-17 3 att2 O&BLI p130 CR France786,3 att6Bn
RAYNER,Hubert William TLt dow 5-11-17 GL 10RWFus att76TMB p191 CR France563
RAYNER,James Ernest Robert.MC.2LtTLt dow 10-5-18 C91RFA p34 CR France71
RAYNER,John 2Lt dow 6-7-16 4/10Mddx att1/5EKent p236 CR Iraq5
RAYNER,Leonard Bramhall Capt kia 27-3-17 6Ess p232 MR34
RAYNER,Leslie King T2Lt kia 18-4-17 GL att13RSuss att116TMB p191 CR Belgium4
RAYNER,Noel Roderick Lt kia 27-7-17 WYorks &57RFC p12&82 CR Belgium24
RAYNER,Oliver Crossley Lt kia 18-11-16 3 att2Manch p155 MR21
RAYNER,Percy Thomas.MC&Bar.T2Lt kia 26-8-18 18KRRC p151 CR Belgium11,25-8-18
RAYNER,Roy Balfour Hodgson TLt dow 24-5-16 15WYorks p82 France169
RAYNER,Ryde Guild 2Lt kia 26-10-17 4NumbF p213 MR30
RAYNES,Albert Brainerd 2Lt kia 11-3-15 RSuss att2RBerks p119 MR22,10-3-15
RAYNES,Albert Herbert Lt kia 25-9-15 11Ess p132 MR19,Arthur 26-9-15
RAYNES,Frank Arthur.MC.2Lt kia 27-3-18 3ScotRif att17RScots p104 MR20
RAYNES,Robert T2Lt dow 17-10-15 14DLI p161 CR France1
RAYNHAM,Charles 2Lt dow 19-3-18 1Mddx p148 CR Belgium45
RAYNOR,Harold Arthur Livingston 2Lt dow 7-6-17 6RB D'Coy p180 CR Mddx66
RAYSON,William Humphrey Ronald TLtACapt dow PoW 27-3-18 C47RFA p34 CR France1266
REA,Frank Melton 2Lt kia 27-3-16 1NumbF p62 MR29

REA,Herbert Finlay Lt kia 16-8-17 14RIrRif p170 MR30
REA,Vivian Trevor Tighe Lt kia 25-10-14 4 att2RIrRif p170 CR France279
REACHER,Stanley William TCapt dow 4-7-16 16RB p180 CR France727,kia
READ,Anketell Moutray.VC.Capt kia 25-9-15 Nhampt &RFC p2&138 CR France219
READ,Arthur Beddome 2Lt kia 16-9-14 1SomLI p80 CR France1107
READ,Arthur Herbert TLt dow 28-4-18 1Worc p109 CR France29
READ,Charles TLt kia 5-10-18 1/2 att9Yorks p91 CR France844
READ,Charles Stanley 2Lt kia 6-12-17 GL &52RFC p12 MR20
READ,Clare Moore T2Lt kia 19-7-18 11MGC Inf p185 CR France223
READ,Cyril de Lacy TLt ded 5-3-19 6Lincs p75
READ,Edrick Hurdman Lt kia 26-12-17 16RFC CR France95
READ,Edward Macartney T2Lt kia 2-4-17 9Dev p77 CR France568
READ,Eric Oswald Chap4Cl kia 3-10-18 RAChDept att5Dors p199 CR France273
READ,George Averille Capt kia 8-3-17 3 att7Leinst p175 CR Belgium100,Averil
READ,George Chisholm 2Lt kia 4-1-18 RE attRFC p17&48 CR Belgium18
READ,Harry Esmond Capt kia 10-8-17 LincYeo att24RFC p19&204 CR France660
READ,John Frederick Cullingford T2Lt kia 28-9-15 11Ess p132 MR19,26-9-15
READ,Lawrence William TLt kia 9-12-16 1Ess p132 MR21
READ,Leonard St.Clair T2Lt ded PoW 20-12-16 11Ess p132 CR France924,Lt
READ,Phillips Tower 2Lt kia 23-10-16 2RFA p34 MR21,Towler
READ,Stanley.MC.T2Lt kia 28-4-17 17Mddx p148 MR20
READ,Stephen Tucker TLt ded 11-12-18 GL 15EYorks att1KAR p84,202&267 CR EAfrica77
READ,Terrance Capon T2Lt dow 22-4-17 Norf att1/5Bn p74 CR Palestine8
READ,Walter Felix Lt ded 14-9-15 1/8Hamps p229 CR Egypt6
READ,William Lister.MC.Capt kia 10-3-18 6Ches p222 CR Palestine3
READE,Arnold Baillie T2Lt kia 21-2-18 66RFC p17 CR Italy9
READE,Charlton Leverton Ridout 2Lt kia 9-9-16 2RSuss p119 MR21
READE,John Henry Loftus.MID Lt kia 28-10-14 Manch p155 MR22
READE,Leonard Edwin T2Lt kia 30-8-17 9SLancs p125 CR Greece5
READE,Reginald William TLt kia 4/5-4-16 9RWar p65 CR Iraq5
READER,Bertram Edward T2Lt kia 22-10-17 6SomLI p80 MR30
READER,William Howard 2Lt dow 30-7-16 5SfthH p241 CR France176
READING,Harold Leslie 2Lt kia 5-11-17 108RFA p34 CR Belgium12
READING,John Francis 2Lt kia 29-4-16 7Worc p226 CR France1327
READING,Vernon Jack 2Lt kia 26-3-18 15RFC p17 MR20
READMAN,Wilfred T2LtACapt dow 30-9-18 9 att2/4LNLancs p136 CR France1184
READY,Edward Charles 2Lt dow PoW 2-5-17 3 att1RBerks p139 CR France1276
READY,Nathaniel Henry Alter 2Lt dow 1-8-17 MGC F'HB p185 CR Belgium11
REAH,Kenneth Hudson T2Lt ded 25-11-18 3KRRC p151 CR Greece9
REANEY,Harold Agnew.MC.TLt ded 27-7-18 Beds p263 CR Hunts83
REANEY,Michael Foster Capt kia 2-7-15 IMS att1/5GurkhaRif p281 CR Gallipoli3
REAVELL,Keith Watts TLt kia 9-12-16 12Hamps p121 CR Greece5,10-12-16
REAVIE,Wilfred Laurance 2Lt kia 16-8-17 3RDubF p177 MR30
REAY,Stanley 2Lt kia 28-1-18 11RFC p17 MR20
REAY,Thomas Stanley Lt dow 1-3-18 3 att10DCLI p114 CR France398
REAY,William Roland T2Lt kia 27-5-18 25MGC Inf p185 CR France1332
REBBECK,Edward William Wise T2Lt kld 24-4-16 KRRC &RFC p3&151 CR Hamps15
REBBECK,William Henry.MC.TLt ded 4-11-18 RE 50Div p48 CR France341
RECKENZAUN,Augustus Lt ded 28-1-19 SL EAfrUL p268 CR SAfrica30
REDDEN,George Herbert.MC.2LtTCapt kia 7-6-17 7ELancs p111 CR Belgium102
REDDIE,Francis Graham 2Lt 18-5-18 206RAF MR20
REDDING,Edward Joseph.DCM.2Lt kia 4-10-17 RWKent p141 MR30
REDDING,J.SubCdr 13-2-20 IA ExRFA CR Norf209
REDDING,John Hamilton Montford 2LtTLt ded 2-3-17 RMunstF p176
REDDING,John Wills 2Lt kia 24-4-18 7 att2ELancs p111 CR France304
REDDY,William George Lt ded 4-4-19 1CamH p168 CR France1357,Wilfred kldacc
REDFERN,Frederick Arthur Dudley TLt ded 15-7-17 GL attEmpS PersianRif p191 CR Iraq6
REDFERN,Samuel Lees Capt dow 2-3-17 1/5LNLancs p234 CR Belgium7,2-8-17
REDFERN,Wilfrid ACapt kia 22-3-18 3 att7EYorks p84 CR France560
REDGATE,Bernard Allan 2Lt kia 29-4-18 B15RHA p34 CR Belgium36
REDHEAD,Harold Arthur Lt kia 7-8-18 3 att6Nhampt p138 CR France141
REDMAN,Arthur Sidney 2Lt ded 27-11-19 IA IMS RoO att37Dogras p281 MR67,22-7-18
REDMAN,Wilfred George T2Lt kld 8-11-17 GL &RFC p12 CR Norf259
REDMOND,William Hoey Kearney TMaj dow 7-6-17 6RIrReg p89 CR Belgium183,7-6-16

REDPATH,Harold Edwin 2Lt kia 15-7-16 1NumbF p62 MR21
RADPATH,James Thomas 2Lt kia 25-4-15 KOSB p102 CR Gallipoli3
REDSHAW,Walter Geoffrey T2Lt kia 6-3-16 6EKent p58 MR29
REDWAY,Frank Mercer 2Lt kia 14-2-18 2/21Lond p251 CR Palestine3
REECE,F.B.Capt dow 20-4-18 RE &4RAF p48 CR France134
REECE,Humphrey Stanley TLt dow 2-4-16 1GordH p167 CR Belgium21
REED,Allan Thomas Lt kld 1-11-18 17Lond &RAF p256
REED,Andrew Gordon Capt kia 10-8-15 7RWFus p223 MR4
REED,Bernard TLt kia 12-4-18 10 att15WYork p82 MR32
REED,Bertram Lt kia 12-4-18 15WYorks p82 MR32
REED,Charles Napier TLt kia 24-11-17 12SWBord p100 MR17
REED,Charles Sydney Lt kia 8-5-15 3Mon A'Coy p244 MR29
REED,Charles Sydney T2Lt kia 14-7-16 7Leic p88 MR21
REED,Clifford Hugh.MC.Chap4Cl kia 7-6-17 RAChDept p199 CR Belgium152
REED,Dane Baron TCapt kia 18-8-16 14 att13Mddx p148 MR21
REED,Frederick Capt ded 28-4-15 A&SH p266
REED,Frederick William Carlton 2Lt kia 3-5-17 8RB p180 MR20
REED,George.MC.Lt ded 21-10-17 IARO attS&TCps 5Div p281 CR Iraq8,Capt
REED,Gerald Francis Woolterton.MID TLt kia 21-3-18 8BordR p117 MR20
REED,Gordon Vernon 2Lt kia 22-3-18 7N&D p233 CR France530
REED,Guy Baron Lt dow 23-8-18 8 att2Beds p86 CR France119
REED,Henry T2Lt kia 30-8-18 A57MGC Divl p185 CR France592,Inf
REED,Henry Gerrard Capt kia 29-10-18 IA 114Mahrattas p281 MR38
REED,Henry William Terrent 2Lt kia 2-5-15 2Mon p244 CR Belgium92
REED,Horace Alfred.MC.MID TLt dow 9-4-18 11Suff p79 MR32
REED,James Richard T2Lt kia 24-11-17 8RFus p69 MR17
REED,John Charles.MC.2Lt ded 14-12-18 D280RFA 56Div p34 CR France1142
REED,John Sleeman 2Lt ded 31-3-16 EKent &RFC p3&58,31-1-16 CR Norf131,kld
REED,Leslie Augustus Lt kia 27-8-15 1/4Lincs p217 CR Belgium127
REED,Paul Maurice T2Lt ded 27-12-15 8SomLI att&RFC p80&2,Maurier CR Egypt9
REED,Robert 2Lt kia 24-5-15 1Dev p77 CR Belgium56
REED,Russel Walter 2Lt kia 11-10-18 1RFus p69 CR France270
REED,Sydney George Herbert TLt ded 24-12-18 104MGC Inf p185 CR Belgium393
REED,Talbot.MID Capt kia 12-3-15 IA 67Punjabis att59Rif p281 CR France727
REED,Walter Nelson.MC.TLt kia 27-10-16 RGA 10SB p41 CR France453
REED,William John T2Lt dow PoW 28-10-17 8Dev p77 CR Belgium393
REED,William Percy 2Lt kia 15-9-17 RFA 232ArmyBde p34 CR Belgium34
REED-HARDING,Clarence Henry Lt kld 15-2-18 1/5SomLI attRFC p19&218 CR Egypt1
REEDER,Edward TLt kia 26-9-15 8EYorks p84 MR19
REEDER,Robert Capt kia 6-1-18 10Manch attRFC p19&237 CR France62
REEKS,Frederick Lt ded 7-8-21 IARO attLabCps p281 CR Staffs49
REEP,Alfred Mills T2Lt kia 16-9-16 6DCLI p114 MR21
REES,Albert Lloyd TLt kia 6-11-17 1RWFus p98 CR Palestine1,1/6Bn
REES,Alexander Armstrong TCapt ded 7-2-17 RAMC att7Suss p267 CR France57,4-2-17
REES,Andrew Montgomery Lt kia 18-10-16 9Ess p132 MR21
REES,David John Lt ded 7-7-19 11DLI p265
REES,David Melvyn 2Lt dow 12-4-17 2DLI p161 CR France98
REES,Edris 2Lt dow 27-10-17 3 att 1RWFus p98 MR30
REES,Edward Davies T2Lt 49009 kia 13-6-17 RWFus att16Bn p98 CR Belgium73
REES,Edgar George 2Lt kia 23-11-17 19RWFus p98 MR17
REES,Eric Montague 2Lt kia 8-10-18 6 att13RFus p69 MR16
REES,Ernest Llewellyn T2Lt kia 22-10-18 B113RFA p34 CR Belgium141
REES,Henry Charles TMaj kia 5-8-16 12SWBord p100 CR France550
REES,Henry Hugh Tregarthen T2Lt kia 11-7-16 16RWFus p98 MR21
REES,Ivor Guest TLt dow 5-8-16 9WelchR p127 CR France145,2Lt
REES,John Cyril T2Lt ded 6-11-15 3 att8WelchR p127 CR Egypt6
REES,John Oswald T2Lt dow 8-11-17 SWBord att24WelshR p100 CR Egypt2
REES,John Trevor 2Lt kia 22-1-15 1RWFus p98 CR France684
REES,Kenneth David 2lt dow 29-8-17 4 att5Ches p222 CR France8
REES,Lawrence Sinclair T2Lt kia 10-7-16 13WelshR p127 MR21,Laurence
REES,Leofric Lt dow 4-10-17 4 att1RWar p65 MR30
REES,Morgan James TCapt dow 30-10-16 RAMC 132FA p197 CR France102
REES,Owen George 2Lt dow 20-9-18 10Lond p248 CR Palestine9
REES,Robert Griffith Lt 10-7-16 15RWFus MR21 CR France1890
REES,Roland Gwyn TLt dow 10/11-7-16 15RWFus p98
REES,Rowland.MC.Lt kia 25-3-18 6SfthH p241 MR20

REES,Thomas Stanley TLt ded 18-3-16 46MGC Inf A'Coy p185 CR France658
REES,Tom Lt kia 17-9-16 14RWFus &RFC p3&98 CR France667
REES-MOGG,Louis Leyson Lt kia 11-8-15 RE 68FC p48 MR4
REESE,Arnold.MC.2Lt kia 1-8-17 2WYorks p82 MR29
REESE,David William Capt ded 23-6-21 RAMC CR Devon72
REESE,Richard Tudor Capt kia 23/24-8-18 3Mon att1Lpool p244 CR France214
REESE,William TLt ded 2-2-17 15WelchR p127 CR Wales245
REEVE,Alan Lt 27-3-18 1CentOntarioR &11RFC MR20
REEVE,Charles d'Arcy Edmund Wentworth TCapt kld 18-7-16 Suff attRFC p3&79 CR Suff242,REEVES
REEVE,Charles Frederick T2Lt dow 13-5-17 GL &2RFC p12 CR France80,15-5-17
REEVE,Charles Simms Capt kia 14-2-15 2ESurr p113 MR29
REEVE,Ernest William.MC.Capt kia 3-5-17 11EYorks p84 MR20
REEVE,Garnett Norman Bray Lt kia 1-9-18 9Mach p237 CR France239
REEVE,George.MC.MM.Lt ded 14-10-18 1RIrF attKRRCp265 CR Nhampt ,15-10-18
REEVE,Gilford Montier Capt kia 8-7-16 12Ess p132 MR21
REEVE,Harry 2Lt kia 18-5-16 5Lpool p215 CR France927
REEVE,Herbert 2Lt ded 8-2-17 Ex 10RSuss p264 CR Mddx26
REEVE,Herbert T2Lt kia 30-11-17 9RFus p70 MR17
REEVE,Herbert Joseph 2Lt ded 24-9-15 1Hereford p252 CR Europe1
REEVE,John Stanley Lt kia 29-6-18 2HAC Inf p206 CR Italy8
REEVE,Walter James Lt ded 29-11-18 1/6Dev p217 MR66
REEVE,William Tankerville Monypenny.CMG.LtCol ded 28-9-15 Leinst att1Ess p175 CR Lond4
REEVES,Frank T2Lt dow 30-12-17 247MGC Inf p185 CR France285
REEVES,Geoffrey Browning Capt acckld 28-2- 17 IA 9Horse p281 CR France1564
REEVES,Geoffrey Frederick John 2Lt kia 6-6-15 3Hamps p121 CR Gallipoli2
REEVES,Harry Charles T2Lt kia 24-8-16 21 att2WelshR p127 MR21
REEVES,Harry Gosford TCapt kia 24-1-18 RFC p17CR France285
REEVES,Hugh Charles Maj ded 29-1-15 RGA 4MthBty p41 MR43
REEVES,Laurence 2Lt dow 25-8-18 1Herts p252 CR France84
REEVES,Leslie Leonhardt Capt ded 14-2-19 16/41RFA p34 CR Germany1
REEVES,Stafford Reichel Maj ded 26-3-19 RGA p41 CR India97A
REEVES,Victor Charles Methuen.MID Maj kia 26-2-16 1/1DorsYeo p203 CR Egypt6
REEVES-SMITH,Denys 2Lt ded 2-10-15 RE 87FC p48 MR19
REGAN,Ernest Charles T2Lt kia 21-3-18 9RSuss p119 CR France366
REGAN,James Herbert T2Lt kia 27-9-18 1NumbF p62 MR16
REHM,A.G.MC.Maj 12-4-21 SL &EAPayCps CR EAfrica51
REICHARDT,Paul 2Lt kia 31-7-17 3ELancs p111 MR29
REID,Alex John 2Lt kia 26-4-16 1ESurr p113 CR France1182
REID,Alexander 2Lt kia 15-2-17 1/22Lond p251 CR Belgium127
REID,Alexander.MC.Capt dow 13-10-18 6GordH p242 CR France686
REID,Alexander Daniel.DSO.MajALtCol kia 31-7-17 1RIrRif p170
REID,Alexander William T2Lt kia 4-3-17 6KOSB att43RFC p12&102 CR France924
REID,Annie Campbell SNurse ded 4-3-19 TFNS p254 CR Egypt9,QAIMNS Res
REID,Archibald David 2Lt dow 8-8-17 5 att4Mddx p148 CR France285
REID,Bernard Joseph T2Lt kia 28-6-16 3RDubF p177 CR France423,9Bn
REID,Bruce Simpson 2Lt kia 6-8-18 RGA 192SB p41 CR France247
REID,Charles Douglas 2Lt kia 15-7-16 9HLI p241 CR France296
REID,Charles John Capt 10-8-15 9RWar MR4
REID,David Inglis 2Lt kia 25-8-15 2/5RScot p211 CR Gallipoli4
REID,Donald 2Lt kia 17-8-17 4 att2HLI p163 CR France163
REID,Douglas Leman 2Lt kia 21-9-17 6Ess p232 CR France149
REID,Edward Harrington Capt kia 30-4-15 2Suff p79 MR15,26-8-14
REID,Ellis.Ramsay.CB.DSO.Col 14-10-18 RAPC CR Essex145 Ex Ess
REID,Eric Archdall 2Lt kia 29-3-18 1Hamps A'Coy p121 MR20
REID,Eric Bruce Capt kia 20-10-14 1NStaffs p157 CR France681
REID,Fergus Hamilton Capt kia 16-5-15 RGA 59SB p41 CR France260
REID,G.E.H.Lt kia 9-3-15 SL att4KAR p268 CR EAfrica12 &CR Tanzania1
REID,Geoffrey Percy Nevile Lt kia 14-5-15 EssYeo p203 MR29,13-5-15
REID,George 2Lt kia 9-4-17 1/6GordH p242 CR France184
REID,George Lt kia 12-4-18 8RScots B'Coy p211 MR32
REID,George Lt kia 25-8-18 27HQ RFA p34 CR France239
REID,George Leslie 2Lt kia 1-12-17 7DragGds p21 MR17
REID,George Robert T2Lt kia 15-9-16 1EKent p58 MR21
REID,George Whiteley Capt&Adjt kia 4-5-15 2Hamps p121 CR Gallipoli2,1-5-15
REID,Gerald Mortimer Lt kia 9-5-18 11Lond p248 CR France516

REID,Gordon 2Lt kia 3-5-17 9 att6KOSB p102 MR20
REID,Gordon Alexander T2Lt kia 8-10-18 1Ess p132 CR France611
REID,Guy Patrick Spence.MC.LtTCapt kld 16-10-17 1SfthH attRFC p12&165 CR Lincs181
REID,Hugh 2Lt kia 23-7-18 3 att1/6GordH p167 CR France622
REID,Ian Capt ded 13-6-19 RE CR Canada256
REID,James.MID TCapt kia 25-9-15 10HLI p163 CR France114
REID,James 2Lt kia 23-10-16 4 att2ScotRif p104 MR21
REID,James T2Lt dow 1-2-17 15HLI p163 CR France41
REID,James Lt dow 8-10-18 1LNLancs p136 CR France146
REID,James Archibald John 2Lt dow 16-10-16 1Camb p245 CR France59
REID,James Lestock Ironside Lt kia 2-11-14 IA 1/2 att2/2GurkhaRif p281 MR28
REID,James Robert Lt kia 27-7-16 1RBerks p139 MR21
REID,J.F.W.Lt 25-3-21 2RInnisF CR Dorset57
REID,John T2Lt kia 18-8-16 4Lpool p72 CR France432
REID,John LtACapt kia 4-4-18 15HLI p163 CR France745,Lt
REID,John 2Lt kia 16-9-18 5DLI p239 CR Belgium188,19Bn
REID,John C.M.Lt 12-5-18 213RAF MR20
REID,John Deighton Lewis Lt kia 9-5-18 23Lond p252 CR France516
REID,John Gardner TCapt kia 8-9-16 11Worc p109 CR Greece6
REID,John Lavens 2Lt dow 12-9-16 10Lpool p216 CR France23,13-9-16
REID,John Lawrie T2Lt dow 16-7-16 RFC p3 CR France203
REID,John Lindsay T2LtACapt dow 18-10-17 RE 179TC p48 CR Belgium16
REID,John Shute 2Lt dow 17-8-17 3SWBord att87TMB p100 CR Belgium16,2Bn
REID,Norman Malcolm TCapt ded 12-1-17 GL RASC p191 CR Glouc9
REID,Percy Cargill 2Lt kia 6-5-17 16Lond p250 CR France537
REID,Reginald Harper LtACapt kia 14-9-18 153RFA p34 CR France856
REID,Robert T2Lt kia 22-5-16 9GordH p167 CR France423,21-5-16
REID,Robert T2Lt kia 1-7-16 9 att1KOSB p102 CR France220
REID,Robert TLt kia 1-7-16 15RScots p54 MR21
REID,Robert 2Lt kia 30-7-16 1/7BlkW p231 CR France1890
REID,Robert Neill 2Lt dow 14-5-17 1/2 att4Lpool p72 CR France145
REID,Robert Heslop 2Lt kia 2-12-17 3HLI p163 MR30,Hislop
REID,Robert Logan T2Lt kia 8-8-15 RE 29DivSigs p48 CR Gallipoli1
REID,Robert Robertson 2Lt dow 13-7-16 RE 130Co p48 CR France833
REID,Robert Vernon Lt dow 26-3-18 5LNLancs p234 MR20
REID,Robert Walker TCapt kia 13-8-16 10/11HLI D'Coy p163 CR France151
REID,Robert William 2Lt dow 17-5-16 9BlkW p129 CR France80
REID,Robert William Kerr T2Lt kia 7-7-16 11 att9LNLancs p136 MR21
REID,Stuart Keppel.MC.Capt dow 29-7-18 1/4RSuss p228 CR France864
REID,Thomas Ernest 2Lt dow 18-4-17 3 att9BlkW A'Coy p129 CR France40,Capt
REID,Thomas Mayne,MC 2Lt kia 3-5-17 9 att6KOSB p102 MR20,Capt
REID,William Alexander Lt dow 27-12-17 2/9Lpool p216 CR Belgium13,26-12-17
REID,William Bacon Johnston Capt dow 20-5-15 3SfthH attGordH p165 CR Scot153
REID,William Douglas.MC.TCapt kia 5-10-17 RAMC att21Manch p197 CR Belgium72
REID,William George 2Lt dow 23-2-17 3ScotRif p104 CR France786
REID,William John T2Lt dow 26-11-17 6GordH p167 CR France398
REID,William Leonard Capt dow 17-4-15 Dors p124 CR Iraq6,15-4-15
REID,William Morison T2Lt dow 26-2-16 23Manch p156 CR France345,7Bn
REIDY,Edmund McAyliffe TCapt dow 23-7-16 11Manch p156 CR France46
REIDY,Harold St.John Q.TCapt ded 19-10-18 RASC p193 CR France52
REILLY,Alexander Maxwell T2LtACapt dow 26-11-16 9RInnisF p105 CRFrance285
REILLY,Arthur Frederick Capt kia 30-5-19 IARO attZhobMil p281 MR43
REILLY,Aubrey Spranger Townsend Capt kia 22-2-17 IA 69Punjabis att92 p281 CR Iraq5
REILLY,Henry Duncan Ryan Capt dow 30-5-19 4RWSurr p212
REILLY,James Miller T2Lt kia 20-9-17 12RScots p54 MR30
REILLY,Ralph Alec Lt kia 24-11-14 IA 31Punjabis att58Rif p281 CR France80,23-11-14
REINCKE,Leo Frederick TCapt kia 17-8-17 10WRid att48RFC p12&116 CR France1361
REISS,Stephen Lacy TLt kia 13-10-15 5RBerks p139 MR19
REISS,Willoughby Emil Lt dow 8-8-15 1/6Manch p236 CR Gallipoli1
REITH,Steven Donaldson.DCM.2Lt kia 20-9-18 IARO att2/42Deolali p282 CR Palestine9,21-9-18 Ex 17HLI
REITH,William Robertson T2Lt ded 17-2-19 9TankCps p188 CR France113
RELF,Thomas Joseph Lt kia 4-10-17 7Dev p217 MR30
RELTON,Douglas Edward Lloyd Lt dow 4-6-18 23Bty 40Bde RFA p34 CR France10

RELTON,Gerald Lyons 2lt dow 17-9-14 3ESurr p113
REMINGTON,Felix George 2Lt kia 11-5-17 RGA 3HAG p41 MR20
REMINGTON,Wallace T2Lt kia 23-3-18 24RFus p70 MR20
REMMER,Fred 2Lt kia 12-4-18 5NumbF p62 MR32
REMNANT,Percy Waterland Lt ded 25-12-20 RASC CR Europe149
RENDALL,Francis Holden Shuttleworth.DSO.TLtCol dow 9-7-16 DCLI att5Y&L p114 CR France245
RENDALL,George 2Lt kia 24-3-18 11KRRC p151 MR27
RENDALL,Robert Alexander.MC.TLtACapt kia 18-9-18 8DCLI p114 CR Greece6
RENDEL,Andrew James.MC.CaptAMaj dow 29-6-17 81/5RFA p34 CR France178
RENDEL,Reginald Dacres 2LtTLt kia 16-5-15 2 O&BLI p130 MR22
RENDELL,Leonard Wyndham.MID.2Lt dow 19-10-14 1Beds p86 CR France80
RENDELL-DUNN,Hubert Cecil T2Lt dow 24-11-16 11 att10LNLancs p136 CR France74
RENDLE,Anthony Darley Russell T2Lt kia 10-10-17 9Dev p77
RENDLE,Arthur Edward 2Lt kia 6-11-17 1DCLI p114 MR30
RENDLE,George 2Lt kia 1-10-18 4EYorks p219 MR30
RENNARD,Edward Marmaduke.MID Capt kia 8-8-16 1/4LNLancs p234 MR21
RENNICK,Frank R.LtCol dow 26-4-15 IA 40Pathans p282 CR France200
RENNIE,Cyril Thomas T2Lt kia 25-9-16 9Leic p88 MR21
RENNIE,David Lt 2-6-15 IAUL att25Cav MR43
RENNIE,Donald Williamson 2Lt kia 11-11-14 5RFus p70 CR France451
RENNIE,Edward Clement Lt dow 16-6-18 RGA attRAF p41 CR Greece4
RENNIE,F.Robert T2Lt kia 9-2-16 9ScotRif p104 CR France264
RENNIE,Guy Capt kia 26-10-14 1GrenGds p50 MR29
RENNIE,Hugh Robert 2Lt dow PoW 10-7-18 14Lond attCamH p249 CR Europe149
RENNIE,James Davidson 2Lt kia 9-4-17 1/5GordH p242 CR France184
RENNIE,James Francis.MC.2Lt kia 31-7-17 B70 RFA p34&259 MR29
RENNIE,John Archibald 2Lt dow 25-7-16 3Dev p77 CR Scot212
RENNISON,Harold Leslie Lt kia 12-11-17 IARO att2/3GurkhaRif p282 CR Palestine8
RENNISON,Walter Martyn Lt kia 30-12-16 3 att6RIrReg p89 MR29
RENNY,Gerald Mercer Lt kia 15-4-17 92RFA p34 CR France905
RENNY,James 2Lt kia 26-9-17 5BlkW p231 CR Belgium88
RENNY-TAILOUR,Henry Frederick Thornton 2Lt kia 11-11-14 RE p48 MR29,TAILYOUR
RENSHAW,Alfred Lt dow 7-6-15 5LancF p221 CR Gallipoli1
RENSHAW,Frank T2Lt kia 12-7-16 17N&D p134 CR France727
RENSHAW,Leonard TCapt kia 13-5-16 18Manch p156 CR France625
RENSHAW,Percy Connaught T2Lt dow 24-7-18 Lincs att2/5LancF p75 CR France10
RENTON,Alan John Capt kia 2-12-17 2Ess p132 CR Palestine9
RENTON,Charles T2Lt kia 6-3-17 8 att1Nhampt p138 CR France328
RENTON,Colin Campbell LtCol sInflictedGunshot 2-9-15 IA 98Inf p282 CR EAfrica54,kldacc
RENTON,Cyril William Lt ded 19-7-17 20Lond p251 CR Surrey38
RENTON,Elwyn George TLt ded 29-5-18 RASC attCamelCps p193 MR67
RENTON,Francis Wallace Home TLt kia 30-8-16 8BordR p117 CR France246
RENTON,Harry Noel Leslie TLt kia 30-7-15 9KRRC p151 MR29
RENTON,Stanley.MC.TLtACapt kia 6-5-17 8Dev p77CR France614
RENTON,William Gerald Forrester Capt kia 2-6-15 1 att2DragGds p20 CR Belgium4
RENTOUL,Alexander Lt kia 27-3-18 YorkHuss att25RFC p19&206 CR France514
RENWICK,Donald William Lt dow 14-6-17 3 att1NStaffs p157 CR Belgium127
RENWICK,Gideon Andrew Forrest 2Lt kia 22-8-17 13RScots D'Coy p54 MR30
RENWICK,Hugh Archibald Lt kld 19-8-18 SWBord &RAF p100 CR Hamps145
RENWICK,James Clarence T2Lt ded 21-3-18 10RIrRif p170&257 CR Numb87,Lt
RENWICK,Thomas Buchanan Lt kia 29-4-15 6RB att3Mddx p180 MR29
REPEN,Frederick Capt ded 13-6-19 RFA Lond DAC p34 CR Germany1,Frank
REPTON,C.T.Lt kia 25-4-18 NottsYeo &RAF p205 CR Palestine3
RERRIE,Errol Seymour.MC.Lt kia 12-5-17 3 att7EYorks p84
RESTALL,Kenneth.MID TLt kia 26-9-16 12Mddx p148 MR21
RETALLACH-MALONEY,Henry Richard Capt ded 17-12-18 6Ess p232 CR Essex1
RETTIE,William Philip 2Lt kia 1-7-16 1BordR p117 MR21
REVELL,Robert Arthur Capt dow 13-6-15 1Ess p132 CR Egypt3,Lt 12-6-15
REVELLE,Roy Cyril 2Lt kia 15-9-18 3RWKent &RAF p141 CR Palestine9,16-9-18 8 O&BLI
REVENE,Howard Stephen Lt ded 25-8-17 RGA 72HB p41 CR Iraq6
REVINGTON,John Huleatt 2Lt kia 4-9-16 9Dev p77 MR21
REW,Douglas Jolland 2Lt kia 28-6-17 5Ess p232 CR France115
REW,John Frederick George T2Lt kia 1-7-16 8Dev p77 CR France330

REX,Eustace Charles T2Lt kia 3-9-16 18HLI D'Coy p163 CR France402,2KOSB
REYMES-COLE,William Elmer.DSO.Capt kia 11-11-14 3RMunstF p176 CR Belgium96
REYNARD,Charles Frederick Capt ded 16-6-18 3EYorks p84 CR France772
REYNARD,Henry Corner T2Lt kia 25-9-15 1SStaffs D'Coy p123 MR19
REYNELL,Frederick Henry T2Lt kia 23-4-17 GL &35RFC p12 CR France95
REYNISH,Horace John Cook 2Lt kia 23-3-18 59RFC p17 MR20
REYNOLDS,Albert Stanley 2Lt kia 13-4-18 4DCLI p227 CR France1100,1Bn
REYNOLDS,Alfred Slater 2Lt kia 25-7-17 70/34RFA p34 CR Belgium10
REYNOLDS,Arthur HonCapt ded 2-6-17 RAOC p198 CR France102
REYNOLDS,Benton William Richard.MID Lt ded 20-7-16 IA 103MahrattaLI p282 CR Iraq8,Benbow
REYNOLDS,Charles Edward Lt dow 23-10-18 21Lond &RAF p251&258
REYNOLDS,Douglas.VC.Maj ded 23-2-16 83RFA p34 CR France40
REYNOLDS,Eric Hindle 2Lt ded 26-12-17 10Ches att120PoWCo p96 CR Ches31
REYNOLDS,Francis Daniel.MC.T2Lt ded 9-9-17 8RWSurr p56 CR Kent83,Lt
REYNOLDS,Frank T2Lt kia 13-9-16 2N&D D'Coy att71TMB p134 CR France294
REYNOLDS,Frank Leslie T2Lt kia 20-7-16 11 att15N&D p134 MR21
REYNOLDS,George Hubbard T2Lt kia 9-4-16 10SLancs p125 MR38
REYNOLDS,Guy Beresford Eaton 2Lt kia 18-11-16 3 att2YLI p143 CR France152
REYNOLDS,H.C.Capt kia 20-9-14 3Wilts p153 MR15
REYNOLDS,Harold Henry T2Lt kia 4-10-17 1Beds p86 CR Belgium112 Ex Sgt 4Wilts
REYNOLDS,J.E.2Lt kld 18-5-18 GL &RAF p191
REYNOLDS,John James 2LtTCapt dow 31-12-15 1ScotRif p104 CR France80
REYNOLDS,John William 2Lt kia 7-8-17 4Y&L p238 CR Belgium85
REYNOLDS,Percival 2Lt mbk 19-9-18 10WYorks p256 MR16
REYNOLDS,Percy Basil TCapt ded 4-12-18 RASC p193 CR France34
REYNOLDS,Richard Frederick TLtACapt kia 2-10-18 6RRofCav att15Hamps p24 CR Belgium115
REYNOLDS,Robert Reynold 2Lt kia 31-5-18 41RFA p34 CR France266
REYNOLDS,Sidney Holdsworth Lt dow 16-4-18 1/4Y&L p238 CR Belgium38
REYNOLDS,Thomas James Capt kia 25-10-14 2RIrRif p170 CR France279
REYNOLDS,Thomas Josceline Gordon 2Lt dow 11-10-16 4 att2Beds p86 CR France389
REYNOLDS,Victor Eustace TCapt kia 4-5-16 10WYorks p82 CR France922
REYNOLDS,William Kingsley Lt kia 10-9-15 3 att1Leic p88 CR Belgium126
REYNOLDS-PARSONS,William Douglas Lt 26-5-18 11RWSurr CR Belgium36 see PARSONS
RHEAD,Charles Henry David 2Lt kia 28-3-18 7Manch p237 MR27
RHODES,Arthur Lt kia 25-5-15 7DLI p239 CR Belgium167,24-5-15
RHODES,Charles Frederick Stanley T2Lt kia 7-6-17 11Ches MR29
RHODES,Gerald Rudolph Lt ded 30-10-18 6Ches p256 CR Suff9
RHODES,Henry Capt kia 17-9-17 RFA 33DAC p34 CR Belgium15
RHODES,John Arthur 2Lt kia 24-8-18 6WYorks p218 CR France832
RHODES,John Kenneth T2Lt dow 17-7-16 10 att8BordR p117 CR France44,16-7-16
RHODES,Thomas George Lt 11-6-18 3WRid att57RAF p192 CR France792
RHODES,W.H.Lt 5-5-16 10Lond CR Wilts180
RHODES,William Marvell 2Lt kia 16-9-16 4YLI p235 MR21
RHODES-MOORHOUSE,William Barnard.VC.Lt 27-4-15 RFC CR Dorset6
RHUDE,Foster Weston 2Lt kia 30-11-17 GL &43RFC p12 CR France88
RHYS,Watkin Leoline Tom T2Lt dow 24-4-17 13RB p180 CR France113
RHYS-DAVIDS,Arthur Percival Foley.DSO.MC.2Lt kia 27-10-17 56RFC p12 MR20
RIACH,Gordon Pennington Lt kia 24-9-18 3CamH p168 CR France725,1Bn
RIACH,Walter Hamilton LtTCapt dow PoW 5-5-18 5CamH p168 CR France716
RICARD,Frank 2Lt kia 25-4-15 4 att1RWar p65 MR29
RICE,Arnold Hamilton T2Lt kia 29-11-17 GL &19RFC p12 CR France285
RICE,Arthur Henry TLt kia 20-9-17 17KRRC p151 MR30
RICE,Arthur Hugh Hamilton 2Lt kia 7-2-16 IARO att114Mahrattas p282 MR38
RICE,Bernard Neville TCapt ded 9-7-17 10EYorks p84 CR War83,dow 10-7-17
RICE,Cecil Vincent 2Lt kia 11-5-17 HouseHoldBn p20 CR France546
RICE,Edgar William 2Lt dow 9-8-16 5LNLancs p234 CR France400
RICE,Edward Felix 2Lt dow 18-2-17 5Lond att169TMB p246 CR France345
RICE,Ernest John T2Lt kia 20-11-17 Dev att7SomLI p77 MR17
RICE,Fred T2Lt kia 1-7-16 8 att2SWBord p100 CR France1490
RICE,Frederick Thomas T2Lt kia 12-9-18 13RB p180 CR France530
RICE,Gerard Beechey Howard BrigGen ded 7-5-16 IA Staff 35InfBde p282 CR Iraq5,31Punjabis
RICE,James Alfred.DCM.T2Lt kia 11-10-18 24MGC p185 CR France270
RICE,John Arthur Talbot.MC.Capt dow PoW 14-4-18 5Lancers p22 CR France1061
RICE-Jones,Alfred Theodore TCapt dow 23-3-18 12Lpool p72 CR France1063

RICH,Arthur Capt ded 29-2-16 SL RecOff p201&268 CR Mon67
RICH,Austin Frederick 2Lt kia 27-12-17 2/24Lond p252 CR Palestine3
RICH,Charles Bayard.MID Maj kia 16-8-17 45RFA p34 MR30
RICH,Christopher Stiles Capt kld 22-3-15 RFA attRFC p2&34,ded CR France284,Maj dedacc
RICH,Cyril Shirston 2Lt kia 7-8-16 164RFA p34 CR France80,Lt
RICH,Ernest Evelyn.DSO.Maj dow 1-12-17 U'RHA p34 CR France364
RICH,John Stanser Lt kia 16/19-5-15 3 att1Lpool p72 MR22,17-5-15
RICH,William Suttor Capt dow 9-11-14 Ches p96 CR France1276
RICHARDES,Roderick Alexander William Pryse 2Lt dow PoW 18-9-18 1 att11RWFus p98 MR37
RICHARDS,Arthur 2Lt dow 27-6-17 1Mon p244 CR France550
RICHARDS,Arthur Gough TLt kia 24-4-17 12Worc p109 CR France364
RICHARDS,Arthur Stanley Lt kia 25-6-17 RFA Y8TMB p208 CR Belgium29
RICHARDS,Arthur William Lt kia 28-3-18 A62RFA p34 CR France343
RICHARDS,Bruce Carlton Lt kia 11-7-17 RFA p34 CR Belgium173
RICHARDS,Charles Walter 2Lt kia 27-9-16 1/8Lpool p216 MR21
RICHARDS,Dudley Brookhouse 2Lt dow 20-9-16 6Glouc att15MGC p187&225 CR France105,29-9-16
RICHARDS,Ella Miss ded 14-10-18 VAD BRCS p200 CR Greece9
RICHARDS,Ernest Harry T2Lt kia 2-4-17 21Manch p156 CR France689
RICHARDS,Ewart Wilfred T2Lt dow 10-5-18 10RWar p65 CR France100,11-5-18
RICHARDS,Francis Graham.MIDx2 Maj kia 5-3-15 RAMC 14FA p197 CR Belgium170
RICHARDS,Frank 2Lt kia 14-5-15 2Hamps p121 CR Gallipoli2
RICHARDS,Gwilym Owen T2Lt dow 23-4-18 14RWFus p98 CR France44
RICHARDS,Henry Heaton 2Lt kia 2-4-17 3 att2RWSurr p56 CR France1489
RICHARDS,Henry Scotson T2Lt dow 3-4-17 15N&D att25RFC p12 CR France924
RICHARDS,Henry Stokes 2Lt ded 1-8-18 10Ess &RAF p132 CR Kent180,kld 12Bn
RICHARDS,Hubert Henry Lyster 2Lt kia 7-12-15 5ConnRgs p172 MR37
RICHARDS,Hugh Phelps Maj kia 18-5-16 21Lond p251 CR France924
RICHARDS,James Thomas TLt dow 27-9-16 D180RFA p34 CR France105
RICHARDS,John T2Lt kia 15-3-18 16RWFus p98 CR France275
RICHARDS,John T2Lt dow PoW 30-3-18 1NumbF p62 CR France924
RICHARDS,John Hywell.MC.TLt dow 19-4-18 6SWBord p100 CR France31
RICHARDS,John Leslie Hill TLt dow 15-4-18 1Dev p77 CR France31,2Lt
RICHARDS,John Thomas T2Lt kia 6-11-17 3 att24WelshR p127 CR Palestine1
RICHARDS,Joseph Arthur Capt kia 4-11-18 1/8RWar p215 CR France933
RICHARDS,Leslie John T2Lt kia 1-8-17 9RDubF p177 MR29
RICHARDS,Llewelyn Thomas T2Lt kia 4-9-15 17RWFus p98 CR France217
RICHARDS,Maurice Tom TLt dow 23-9-17 189MGC Infp185 CR France113
RICHARDS,Norman Frederick Kynaston T2Lt kia 24-7-16 12Glouc p107 MR21
RICHARDS,Paul.MC&Bar.TLtAMaj kia 3-10-18 61MGC Inf p185 CR France346
RICHARDS,Percival Morgan T2Lt kia 15-7-16 10RFus p70 MR21
RICHARDS,Peter Austin Willmott T2Lt kia 10-9-16 11Y&L p159 CR France246
RICHARDS,Richard John T2Lt dow PoW 12-5-17 5 O&BLI p130 CR France924
RICHARDS,Robert Ingram 2Lt dow 27-10-17 1Lond p245 MR30
RICHARDS,Roland TLt kia 7-12-15 16RFus att7RMunstF p70 MR37
RICHARDS,Ronald Henry T2Lt kia 2-6-16 11RSuss p119 CR France114
RICHARDS,Stanley Earl 2Lt dow 29-8-16 1Mon p244 CR France120
RICHARDS,W.H.Chap4Cl 19-2-20 CR Wales518
RICHARDS,Walter Edward 2Lt dow 11-12-18 3 att16RSuss p119 CR Sussex226
RICHARDS,William Beresford Lt kia 30-11-17 3 att7DCLI p115 MR17
RICHARDS,William Ernest Cdr ded 14-9-18 IndOrdDept p282
RICHARDS,William Jenkin TCapt kia 27-8-17 16WelshR p127 MR30
RICHARDS,William John TLt dow 12-10-18 15WelshR p127 CR France398
RICHARDS,William Reeves.MID TCapt&Adjt kia 15-8-15 6RDubF p177 CR Gallipoli5
RICHARDSON,Albert Edward Capt ded 24-11-18 RB attMGC Inf p180&185 CR Wales83
RICHARDSON,Alfred Terence Leatham Capt kia 6-11-17 WSomYeo p205 CR Palestine1,12SomLI
RICHARDSON,Allan William TLt kia 11-8-15 6RIrRif p170 MR4
RICHARDSON,Angus MacDonald 2Lt kia 25-9-15 2GordH p167 MR19
RICHARDSON,Archer Stuart 2Lt kia 25-6-17 RGA 13SB p41 CR Belgium29
RICHARDSON,Archie Pelham Lt 19-11-18 IARO CR Egypt2
RICHARDSON,Arthur Archibald Lt kia 26-9-15 11A&SH p173 MR19
RICHARDSON,Arthur Balfour 2Lt kia 21-3-18 8RWKent p141 MR27
RICHARDSON,Arthur Douglas 2Lt ded 12-1-15 10WYorks p82 CR Yorks208
RICHARDSON,Arthur Gordon T2Lt dow 19-9-18 7EKent p58 CR France1468

RICHARDSON,Arthur John Buchannan 2Lt ded 4-1-15 4Yorks CR Yorks126
RICHARDSON,Basil Hutton 2Lt ded PoW 31-5-15 8DLI p239 CR Germany3
RICHARDSON,Basil James 2Lt kia 9-10-17 8WYorks p219 MR30
RICHARDSON,Charles Frederick James TLt kia 23-3-18 RE 80FC p48 CR France1893
RICHARDSON,Daryl Stewart Lt kia 16-5-15 3 att2BordR p118 MR22
RICHARDSON,David Alexander 2Lt kia 21-3-18 7BlkW B'Coy p231 MR20
RICHARDSON,Douglas Birch Capt kia 29-7-16 RE att29RFC p19&210 CR Belgium11
RICHARDSON,Edric Hugh Barnstey Capt kia 15-6-15 3Wilts p153 MR22
RICHARDSON,Edward AssSurg3Cl 2-10-17 IA IMD MR43 &CR Pakistan50A
RICHARDSON,Edward Earle.MM.2Lt kia 9-11-18 1/2ESurr att15RAF p113 CR France1223
RICHARDSON,Ernest Benbow T2Lt ded 28-10-15 RE 67FC p48 MR4
RICHARDSON,Evan John Capt kia 25-9-15 2Yorks p91 MR19
RICHARDSON,Ewart 2Lt kia 27-9-16 4Yorks p220 MR21
RICHARDSON,Francis Aymer.MIDx2 Lt kia 27-5-18 RFA A Bty NumbrianBde p208 MR18
RICHARDSON,Francis James.DSO.Maj ded 11-12-17 4A&SH p173 CR Surrey75
RICHARDSON,Frank Capt. kia 7-6-17 24Lond D'Coy p252 CR Belgium131
RICHARDSON,Frank Arnold 2Lt kld 25-4-18 EYorks att11Bn p84&263,died CR Wilts115
RICHARDSON,Frederick Edward John T2Lt kia 21-11-17 11KRRC p151 MR17
RICHARDSON,Garnet St.John Lt dow 7-12-15 IA 7Rajputs p282 CR Iraq5,Capt
RICHARDSON,Geoffrey Oliver 2Lt kia 26-3-17 1/4Ess p232 CR Palestine8
RICHARDSON,George Alvarez 2Lt kia 27-9-16 6Yorks p91 MR21
RICHARDSON,George Hugh.MC.TCapt kia 29-10-18 22Manch p156 CR Italy9
RICHARDSON,George Sydney TLtACapt kia 20-5-18 RASC MT p193 CR France882
RICHARDSON,Harold Stewart TLt dow 24-4-17 11Leic p88 CRFrance80,2Lt
RICHARDSON,Henry 2Lt dow 21-5-17 RGA 36SB p41 CR France1186
RICHARDSON,Henry Thomas Lt dow 23-8-15 1/5NumbF p213 CR Numb60
RICHARDSON,James Maj ded 24-8-17 7HLI p240 CR Scot683
RICHARDSON,James Freer Capt ded 27-11-19 IA IMS att49IndGH p282 MR43
RICHARDSON,Jasper Myers LtCol dow 30-3-18 RGA p209 CR France40
RICHARDSON,John T2Lt dow 9-9-17 NumbF Res att23Bn p63 CR France1461
RICHARDSON,John Cottier.DCM.Capt kia 4-10-18 2Manch p156 MR16
RICHARDSON,John Ernest Lt kia 7-5-15 2Lond p245 CR France1141
RICHARDSON,John Lowick 2Lt kia 21-8-17 3/4Glouc attRFC p225 CR France1059
RICHARDSON,John Sherbrooke T2Lt kia 9-4-17 26NumbF p63 CR France184
RICHARDSON,John Stanley Capt kia 28-10-14 RE p48 MR22,Maj
RICHARDSON,John Watson Maj kia 3-5-17 4Y&L p238 MR20
RICHARDSON,John William Capt 12-10-17 34Bn AIF MR29
RICHARDSON,Lancelot Lytton.MC.Capt kia 13-4-17 25RFC p12 CR France1321
RICHARDSON,Martin James.MID TLt dow 3-11-14 RAMC 21FA p197 MR29
RICHARDSON,Maurice Lewis George 2Lt kia 28-2-17 3SLancs att2/7RWar p125 CR France526
RICHARDSON,Mervyn Stronge.MID TCapt dow 19-3-16 1RWFus p98 CR France638
RICHARDSON,Percival Blythe L.TCapt ded 3-11-18 MGC 9 att10A/ACoy p185 CR France52
RICHARDSON,Percy William T2Lt ded 12-11-18 RE p262 CR Mddx42,11-11-18
RICHARDSON,Raymond Driver 2Lt dow 26-4-18 4GrenGds p50 CR France180
RICHARDSON,Richard Francis Lt dow 30-9-15 2RWar p65 CR France145
RICHARDSON,Robert 2Lt dow 26-7-18 4RScots p211 CR France134
RICHARDSON,Robert Cecil 2Lt kia 2-12-17 3 att11BordR MR30
RICHARDSON,Robert Harold 2Lt kia 6-11-17 18Lond att6RFC p250 CR Belgium11
RICHARDSON,Robert Scovell.MC.TLt dow 1-9-16 91MGC p185 CR France66
RICHARDSON,Rodney Francis 2Lt dow 31-7-17 3Manch p156 MR29
RICHARDSON,Roger Bryer 2Lt kia 27-5-18 3WYorks p82 MR18
RICHARDSON,Ruskin John Robert kia 25-9-15 3 att2SStaffs p123 MR19
RICHARDSON,Sidney Athelstone T2Lt dow 3-11-17 266RFA p34 CR Palestine1
RICHARDSON,Thomas Capt&QM ded 26-1-19 1/4BordR p271 CR C'land&W'land59
RICHARDSON,Thomas Charles.MC.TMaj dow 4-2-16 RE 185TC p48 CR France430
RICHARDSON,Thomas William.MC.DCM.2Lt kia 28-3-18 32RFA p34 CR France531
RICHARDSON,Thomas William Taylor 2Lt kia 21-3-18 12/13NumbF p63 MR27
RICHARDSON,Victor.MC.Lt dow 9-6-17 4RSuss p228 CR Sussex183
RICHARDSON,Walter Fairfax Capt kia 9-5-15 2ELancs p111 CR France706

RICHARDSON,Wilfrid Frank.MC.TCapt ded 27/28-9-17 7BordR p118 CR France225,Wilfred
RICHARDSON,William Arthur Ingham T2Lt dow 31-8-15 1RWKent p141 CR Kent89
RICHARDSON,William Francis TCapt ded 7-2-20 RE p262 CR Asia81
RICHARDSON,William Harold Lt kia 14-4-17 6DLI p239 CR France162
RICHARDSON,William Quintus Newsom 2Lt kld 6-10-17 RFC p12 CR Essex208
RICHARDSON,William Turner T2Lt kia 1-7-16 12RIrRif att108MGC p185 MR21
RICHARDSON-JONES,Charles Harry 2Lt kia 11-6-16 6RFus p70 CR Belgium28,4Bn
RICHENS,Richard Ivor 2Lt dow 14-4-17 18Lond p250 CR France1185
RICHER,C.E.McG.Lt 3-9-18 14CanadaFA CR France14
RICHER,Frederick Arthur Maj ded 9-2-19 15Huss p261 CR Lancs34
RICHES,George William T2Lt kia 8-10-17 7Suff p79 CR France154,7-10-17
RICHES,Percy William T2Lt ded 6-12-15 10Norf p74 CR Norf110
RICHMAN,Alexander Woolacott 2Lt dow 26-9-17 1/9Lpool p216 CRFrance40,Lt
RICHMOND,Cuthbert Laurence 2Lt kld 24-5-15 5NumbF p213 MR29
RICHMOND,Frederick Robert T2Lt kia 13-3-17 22DLI p161 CR France402
RICHMOND,Harold Christopher Capt kia 25-1-15 Glouc p107 CR France279
RICHMOND,Harold Stedman TCapt kia 24-8-16 9KRRC p151 MR21
RICHMOND,Hugh Bowlin Lt kia 9-12-17 1/21Lond p251 CR France1483,Bowten
RICHMOND,Leslie Lt kia 10-9-14 1GordH p167 CR Belgium242,23-8-14
RICHMOND,Thomas Herbert Capt dow 1-11-14 3YLI p143 CR France102,2Bn
RICKARD,George Henry.MID Maj ded 6-2-19 RGA 79SB p262 CR Sussex4,6-2-18
RICKARD,Victor George Howard TLtCol kia 9-5-15 RMunstF p176 CR France924
RICKARDS,Arthur Traherne.MID LtCapt kia 13-9-17 RGA &43RFC p12&41 CR France88
RICKARDS,David Logan 2Lt kia 19-12-15 1/4YLI p235 CR Belgium23,dow
RICKARDS,Hew Wardrop Brooke Lt kia 28-7-17 RFA &57RFC p12&34 CR Belgium149,51RFC
RICKEARD,William Christopher Lt kia 30-9-15 19Lond p250 CR France219,C.W. 25-9-15
RICKERBY,John Harold Ellerson.MC.Capt kia 22-3-18 5Glouc p225 CR France672
RICKETT,Rupert Alexis TCapt kia 9-7-16 8SLancs p125 MR21
RICKETTS,Clyde Robert TLt ded 11-10-18 RASC p193 CR Mddx9
RICKETTS,Frederick 2Lt kia 18-9-18 3EKent p58 CR France835,1Bn
RICKETTS,Harold Edwin T2Lt dow 14-7-16 RWSurr attMGC p56&185 CR France141
RICKETTS,Henry William Felix Maj kia 10-8-15 IA 93BurmaInf att5Wilts p282 MR4
RICKETTS,James Stuart 2Lt dow 3-10-18 RFA 122A Bty p34 CR France146,5-10-18
RICKETTS,William Falkland Geordie 2Lt kia 1-4-17 4Leinst p175 CR France480,2Bn
RICKMAN,Stuart Hamilton Maj dow 26-8-14 RB p180 CR France1348,27-8-14
RICONO,Martin Capt ded 5-3-17 RAMC attSALabCps CR France40
RIDDELL,David Moore T2Lt ded 23-9-17 16Lpool p72 CR Ireland33,dow
RIDDELL,Frederick James TLt drd 13-8-15 9Beds attEss p86 MR4
RIDDELL,Henry James Maj kia 22-11-15 IA 48Pnrs p282 MR38
RIDDELL,James Riddell 2Lt kia 6-9-15 IARO att2/3GurkhaRif p282 CR France1157
RIDDELL,James Foster BrigGen kia 26-4-15 Staff Cmdg1/1NumbInfBde p1 CR Belgium125
RIDDELL,John Dean 2Lt dow 17-4-17 1/5GordH p242 CR FRance40,RIDDEL
RIDDELL,Richard Cecil Hewat ACapt dow 14-1-20 5SomLI att1A2/76Pujabis p271&282 MR43,RIDDEL
RIDDELL,Robert Anderson 2Lt dow 25-8-16 5ScotRif p224 CR France453
RIDDELL,Robert Mackie T2Lt kldacc 1-7-16 10GordH p167 CR France257,RIDDEL
RIDDELL,Sydney.MC.TLtACapt kia 13-10-17 9Y&L p159&257 CR Belgium112
RIDDELL,Walter.MC.2Lt kia 29-4-18 3 att2RScotF p95 MR30
RIDDELL,William T2Lt kia 1-7-16 11Dev p77 CR FRance330
RIDDETT,Norman Lock 2Lt kia 12-10-17 4 att8ESurr p113 CR Belgium126
RIDDLE,Francis Edmund Langton 2Lt kia 16-5-15 2 O&BLI p130 MR22
RIDDOCK,James Keppie Capt ded 17-10-18 6Hamps p228 CR Iraq8
RIDEAL,Samuel 2Lt kia 27-6-17 1/6Lpool p215 CR Belgium10
RIDEHALGH,Harold Lt kia 23-9-18 1/10Lpool p216 CR France109,2Lt
RIDER,Alonzo Ward 2Lt kia 12-10-17 26MGC Inf p185 MR30
RIDER,Clifford Ernest T2Lt kld 10-10-17 RFC p12 CR Canada1688
RIDGE,Everard Vaughan TLt kia 10-4-17 153MGC p185 MR20,9-4-17
RIDGE,Percy Lt ded 21-2-19 RGA p262 CR Surrey16
RIDGE,Percy Brewster Capt ded 12-3-16 RAMC p254
RIDGEWAY,Edward William Crawfurd Maj kia 23-2-17 IA 1/2GurkhaRif p282 MR38

RIDGWAY,Edward Capt kia 30-11-17 2/6NStaffs p238 MR17
RIDGWAY,Harold Edwin TLt kia 7-6-17 7ELancs p111 CR Belgium102
RIDGWAY,Henry Akroyd Capt kia 13-10-15 5NStaffs p237 CR France550
RIDGWAY,Henry Collinson 2Lt kia 7-10-16 7Lond C'Coy p247 CR France385
RIDGWAY,John Edwin Lt kia 20-11-17 2/5WRid p227 MR17
RIDGWAY,John Herbert.DSO.MajTLtCol kia 23-4-17 1NStaffs att10Y&L p157 CR France924
RIDGWAY,Richard Harry James Willis 2Lt kia 6-12-16 Glouc att1TMB p107 CR France385,H.R.J.W.Lt
RIDGWAY,William 2Lt kia 7-10-16 18KRRC p151 MR21
RIDGWAY,William Thomas 2Lt kia 2-12-17 BordR att11Bn p118 MR30
RIDGWELL,Sydney Causton 2Lt kia 2-11-17 3 att1/7Ess p132 MR34
RIDLEY,Alfred Edwin T2Lt ded 25-7-18 RE IWT p48 CR France65
RIDLEY,Charles Noel Capt dow 7-10-15 NumbYeo p204 CR France134
RIDLEY,Christopher Mellor TCapt kia 31-10-16 10Ess p132 MR21
RIDLEY,Hector 2Lt kia 9-8-15 2N&D p134
RIDLEY,Henry Mills 2Lt dow PoW 23-5-18 9DLI p239 CR Belgium140
RIDLEY,Herbert Leslie.MC.LtACapt kia 15-7-17 RDubF p177 CR Belgium12
RIDLEY,Joseph T2Lt kia 15-6-18 11NumbF p63 CR Italy3
RIDLEY,Lancelot Edwin Lt kia 19-8-16 1/4RBerks p234 MR21
RIDLEY,Pattison Reay.MC.Lt kia 3-5-17 NorthCycBn att5WRid p253 MR20
RIDLEY,Stewart Gordon T2Lt ded 18-6-16 RFC p3
RIDLEY,Thomas 2Lt kia 23-3-18 12/13NumbF p63 MR27
RIDLEY,William Hector Mather Wilson 2Lt 9-8-15 2N&D D'Coy MR29
RIDOUT,Clarence Grosvenor T2Lt dow 22-12-15 9 att1KSLI p145 CR Belgium11
RIDOUT,Gaspard Alweed Evelyn 2Lt kia 21-3-18 331RFA p34 CR France366,Alured
RIDOUTT,William Alexander Lt ded 19-2-19 7DLI p239 CR Hamps9
RIDPATH,Frederick Cecil Lacey Lt kia 27-12-17 2/4WSurr p212 CR Palestine3
RIDPATH,Geoffrey Lionel Chevalier 2LtTLt kia 1-7-16 Mddx p148 CR France267
RIDSDALE,Aubrey Haywood 2Lt kia 22-8-15 CityLondYeo p204 CR Gallipoli5
RIECKE,Arnold Francis Marshall.MID Maj ded 19-6-19 307RFA p34&257 CR Nhampt80,kldacc
RIEKIE,Harry Heatly Lt 4-7-18 9RAF MR20
RIELLY,William Ernest Capt ded 28-11-15 RAMC att3Lond p254 MR4
RIEPLE,Leopold Anthony T2Lt ded 30-10-18 RGA 51SB p41 CR France398
RIGBY,Arthur George.MC.Capt kia 12-10-17 8WYorks p219 MR30
RIGBY,Charles 2Lt kia 4-11-18 6RWar &62RAF MR20,RFus
RIGBY,Douglas Archibald.DCM.2Lt dow 24-4-17 5ScotRif p224 CR France120
RIGBY,Douglas Marshall Lt kia 4-9-18 6Ches p222 CR Belgium89
RIGBY,Edward William TCapt kia 14-7-16 7KSLI p145 MR21
RIGBY,Francis John Capt kia 21-1-16 3 att1SfthH p165 MR38
RIGBY,George.MC.TLt kia 7-6-17 3Y&L p159 CR Belgium127
RIGBY,J.2Lt ded 20-11-18 GL ExtraRegEmployList RAF p267
RIGBY,James Arthur Maj 25-12-16 RAMC CR Lancs111
RIGBY,James Richard Anderton Lt kia 26-9-15 3 att2Yorks p91 MR19
RIGBY,John 2Lt kia 21-3-18 6SStaffs p229 MR20
RIGBY,John H.Capt&QM ded 21-5-18 126MGC Inf p185 CR France1571,20-5-18
RIGBY,Thomas Frank 2Lt kia 27-3-18 3RFC p17 MR20,Franklin
RIGBY,William Geoffrey Morris TLt dow 7-7-16 69MGC Inf p185 CR France
RIGG,George Southerton.DSO.2LtTLt kia 31-7-17 3Y&L att52MGC Inf p159&185 CR Belgium106
RIGG,Samuel AMaj kia 25-3-18 5BordR p256 MR27
RIGG,Stanley 2Lt dow 21-6-18 5BordR p228 CR C'land&W'land74
RIGGENBACH,Frank Arthur Lt kia 19-9-18 1/6Ess p232 CR Palestine9
RIGGOTT,Robert Cyril 2Lt kia 20-9-17 5LancF p221 CR Belgium125
RIGGS,John Stephenson 2Lt dow 19-12-17 RGA 239SB p41 CR France214
RIGGS,Roy Robertson 2Lt kia 22-7-17 19RFC p12 CR France31
RIGHTON,Richard Harry 2Lt kia 27-9-18 6 att7RFus p70 CR France1496
RIHOY,Stanley Alfred 2Lt dow 12-4-18 1RGLI p201 MR32
RILEY,Albert Victor TLt kia 20-8-17 A155RFA p34 CR Belgium10
RILEY,Arthur Cecil Capt kia 25-9-15 19Lond p250 CR France219
RILEY,Ernest 2Lt kia 26-9-18 6SStaffs p229 CR France528
RILEY,George Harold Lt kia 21-8-18 RASC p193 CR France134
RILEY,H.J.Lt 5-4-20 2SLancs CR Lancs150
RILEY,Henry Davison TCapt kia 1-7-16 11ELancs p111 MR21
RILEY,Herbert Angus 2Lt kia 28-6-16 1/9Lpool p216 CR France174
RILEY,James Louis 2Lt kia 29-9-18 1/7Lpool p215 CR France109
RILEY,James Shutt TLt kia 10-8-18 1TankCps p188 CR France649,Capt
RILEY,James Trevor Lt kia 3-9-16 4WRid p227 MR21
RILEY,John Reginald Newton 2Lt kia 3-9-16 5WRid p227 CR France383
RILEY,Leslie T2Lt kld 5-2-18 RFC p17 CR Mddx15
RILEY,Nathaniel Edgar 2Lt kia 21-5-18 3 att2YLI p143 CR France502
RILEY,Paul T2Lt kia 10-10-17 LancF att8Bn p93 MR30
RILEY,Stanley James TCapt kia 12-10-16 1RWar p65 MR21
RILEY,Sydney T2Lt kia 20-9-18 1NumbF p63 CR France530
RILEY,Thomas Capt dow 5-8-16 C158RFA p34 CR France23
RILEY,Thomas Dickinson 2Lt kia 20-9-17 7ScotRif p224 CR Belgium125
RILEY-WATSON,Leslie 2Lt kia 4-7-16 C246RFA CR France215
RIMER,James Cook 2Lt kia 17-3-17 43RFC p12 MR20
RIMER,William Marshall 2Lt kia 1-10-18 4Y&L p238 CR France406
RIMINGTON,Ernest Cameron Waterfield 2Lt kia 2-10-15 3Ches p96 CR France924
RIMMER,Samuel Gerard Lt dow 4-5-16 RFA p208 CR France927
RIMMER,William 2Lt kia 26-10-17 5LNLancs p234 MR30
RIND,Edward Seton.MID Lt kia 22-11-15 1A 24Punjabis p282 MR38
RINDER,Charles Henry 2Lt kia 16-8-17 7Lond p247 MR29
RINES,Edward Thomas 2Lt kia 22-8-17 4SomLI p218 MR30
RING,Charles Augustus Eamonson Capt ded 29-10-18 RAMC p267 CR War88
RING,Leslie Gordon Lt kia 18-9-18 3Lond p245 CR France369
RING,Norman Augustus Manders Lt kia 4-5-17 3 att2RWar p65 MR20
RINTOUL,David Wylie Lt kia 21-10-14 RAMC att3CldGds p197 MR29
RIODAN,Hubert De Burgh Capt kia 10-5-15 ESurr att2nd p113 CR Belgium46
RIORDAN,John Leonard 2Lt kia 8-9-18 5Lond p246 MR16
RIORDAN,Timothy Harold 2Lt dow 6-7-16 4YLI p235 CR France2
RIPLEY,Charles Roger.MID Lt kia 22-10-14 3Y&L p159 MR32,2Bn
RIPLEY,Ens Richard T2Lt kia 31-10-17 GL &53RFC p12 CR Belgium101,Eric
RIPLEY,George Eustace Col dow 16-10-16 6Nhampt p138 CR Nhampt67
RIPMAN,Helmut Armstrong 2Lt dow 16-5-18 RGA 47SB p41 CR France40
RIPPERGER,Harold Alvin Theodore.MC.Lt kia 23-10-18 4Glouc p225 CR France287
RIPPIN,James Harry 2Lt ded 9-3-16 4LNLancs p234 CR Lancs257,Henry 5Bn
RIPPINGILLE,Frank Alexander 2Lt kia 11-11-14 EYorks p84 MR29
RIPPON,Gilbert Harold Earle 2Lt kld 7-6-16 RFC p3 CR Somerset26
RIPPON,Norris 2Lt kia 18-11-15 1/5WRid p227 CR Belgium23
RISELEY,Stanley Maj ded 5-2-15 RAMC p271
RISHWORTH,Henry Holmes 2Lt ded 15-9-15 6WRid p271 CR Yorks439
RISHWORTH,James Lt kld 3-5-15 4EYorks p219 MR29
RISHWORTH,J.R Lt 15-6-15 1A S&TCps CR India164
RISHWORTH,Keith T2Lt kld 6-8-17 GL &RFC p12 CR Yorks3
RISING,Frederick 2Lt kia 15-8-15 5Beds p219 MR4
RISING,Robert Edward.DSO.Maj ded 7-11-14 1Glouc p107 CR Belgium134,dow
RISLEY,Nathan Bright.MC.TCapt dow 20-9-17 16RB p180 CR Belgium15
RISSIK,Bernard 2Lt kia 22-6-15 9RB p180 MR29
RISTEEN,Clifford Fraser 2Lt kia 26-9-17 GL &45RFC p12 MR20
RITCH,William Robertson TCapt kia 23-3-18 1 att9ScotRif p104 MR27
RITCHIE,Alexander 2Lt dow 28-4-17 2ScotRif att23TMB p104 CR France121
RITCHIE,Alexander Stewart.MC.TCapt kia 1-10-18 8BlkW p129 MR30
RITCHIE,Archibald Frederick Lt kia 10-9-14 2YLI p143 MR15.26-8-14
RITCHIE,Arthur Gerald Capt dow 22-11-14 1ScotRif p104 CR France102
RITCHIE,Francis James Dickson 2Lt kia 20-7-16 1ScotRif p104 MR21
RITCHIE,Frank Johnstone T2Lt kia 23-10-16 2Lincs p75 MR21
RITCHIE,Frank Robert 2Lt kia 15-8-15 3RScots att2HLI p54 CR France721
RITCHIE,George Lt ded 15-5-16 6HLI p240 CR Scot674
RITCHIE,Harold.Hon.DSO&Bar.TMajALtCol dow 28-10-18 11ScotRif att1RWSurr p104 CR France332
RITCHIE,Henry Deacon 2Lt dow 27-9-18 1CldGds p51 CR France756
RITCHIE,James Adam T2Lt dow 8-8-18 BlkW att4/5Bn p129 CR France1225
RITCHIE,James Garnck 2Lt ded 3-5-19 CamH p265 CR Scot280
RITCHIE,Jessie SNurse ded 13-8-16 QAIMNS p200 CR Greece7
RITCHIE,John 2Lt kia 25-4-17 6BlkW att66MGC p187&231 CR Greece6
RITCHIE,John Capt ded 28-10-17 6HLI p240 CR Scot674
RITCHIE,John James Austin 2Lt kia 29-9-18 9HLI p241 CR France663
RITCHIE,John Mearns T2Lt kia 15-7-16 12RScots p54 CR France402
RITCHIE,John Nevill 2Lt kia 21-4-16 3SfthH p165 MR38
RITCHIE,John Waugh T2Lt kia 23-4-17 2 att7GordH p167 MR20
RITCHIE,Leonard Albany Lt kia 24-3-18 RE 1/1EdinburghFC p210 CR France1063
RITCHIE,Louis Malcolm Lt kia 5-5-18 4RScots att1KAR p211&268 MR52
RITCHIE,Richard Ayres Lt kia 22-11-15 3 att2Norf p74 MR38
RITCHIE,Richard James Wallace LtACapt kia 20-5-18 4 att18HLI p163 CR France60
RITCHIE,Robin Blackwood LtACapt kia 20-7-16 1ScotRif p104 MR21

RITCHIE,Robert Richard TCapt kia 3-5-17 9ScotRif p104 MR20
RITCHIE,Thomas Arthur 2Lt kia 18-10-16 3 att1ELancs p111 CR France432
RITCHIE,Thomas Pearsall Ayres 2Lt kia 15-3-15 6 att4RB p180 MR29
RITCHIE,William Lancelot 2Lt dow 1-8-17 1Camb D'Coy p245 CR Belgium16
RITCHIE,William Smail 2Lt kia 29-7-18 5A&SH p243 CR France524
RITCHIE-BROWN,John Lt kia 7-11-16 RAMC attHQ 43HAG RGA CR France2
RITCHINGS,Albert Arthur William.MM.2Lt kia 27-9-18 11 att16Lond p248 CR France429,29-9-18
RITSON,Arthur Stuart 2Lt kia 5-11-16 5 att1/6DLI p271 MR21
RITSON,Claude Wilson T2LtACapt kia 28-4-17 13Ess p132 MR20
RITSON,Eustace Blackburne 2Lt kia 8-10-17 204MGC Inf p185 MR30
RITSON,Francis TCapt kia 17-6-17 Dors att5Bn p124 CR Belgium76
RITSON,John Andrew TCapt kia 22-7-16 7SLancs p126 CR France432,23-7-16
RITTER,William Henry TLt kia 2-6-17 GL &15RFC p12 CR France41,dedacc
RITTY,John.MC.TCapt kia 9-9-16 7InnisF p105 MR21
RIVERS,George Claude T2Lt kia 21-8-16 9ESurr p113
RIVERS-SMITH,Edwin Lt 6-11-18 RGA CR Hamps219
RIX,John Cecil TCapt kia 6-7-16 RAMC att9Yorks p197 CR France515
RIX,Leslie Gordon.MID Capt dow 11-2-17 1/4Lond p245 CR France345
RIXON,Theodore Meredith.MC.TMajALtCol kia 19-9-17 6 att8KRRC p151 CR Belgium126
ROACH,Matthew TCapt kia 2-7-16 RE 255TC p48 MR20,225TC
ROADLEY,Thomas Stanley Lt kia 17-8-17 4SStaffs att8RFC p12&123 CR Belgium140
ROADS,Herbert William 2Lt ded 5-5-16 10Lond p271
ROAN,Walter Tait 2Lt kia 29-9-16 8DLI p239 MR21
ROBARTS,Henry Martyn 2Lt dow 26-9-17 4Norf p216 CR France113
ROBATHAN,Douglas Parker Capt kia 10-8-15 5WelshReg p230 MR4
ROBATHAN,Laurence.MID 2Lt kia 28-9-17 2/5Leic p220 CR Belgium16
ROBB,Albert Victor.MM.MID T2Lt dow 12-3-18 5CamH p168 CR France439
ROBB,Alexander Gentle.MC.Lt dow PoW 20-5-18 3ScotRif p104 CR Germany2,1Bn
ROBB,Alexander Kirkland.MID Maj kia 20-9-14 2DLI p161 CR France1329
ROBB,Harold Brindley.MID TLt ded 2-1-17 RASC p193 CR Lond1
ROBB,Henry Alexander Lt kia 10-7-17 3N&D att1LNLancs p134 MR31,Henri
ROBB,J.Lt 13-12-18 RFA CR Kent83
ROBB,John T2Lt kia 21-7-17 16WYorks p82 CR France268
ROBB,Ralph George Campbell TLt kia 25-9-15 10ScotRif p104 MR19
ROBB,Russell Edwin T2Lt ded 5-1-18 65RFC p17 CR Belgium140
ROBB,Thomas Douglas Lt kld 26-9-15 17 att20Lond p250 CR France550
ROBB,Victor Harold TLt dow 3-7-16 14RIrRif p170 CR Ireland33
ROBB,William John Mechan. Lt kia 20-7-18 4 att6BlkW p230 MR18
ROBB-SMITH,Alexander TCapt ded 15-12-17 RAMC attRA &RFA BaseDepot p197&257 CR France85
ROBBINS,Arthur Hodder Capt&Adj kia 21-3-18 7/8RInnisF p105 CR France365
ROBBINS,George Latimer 2Lt dow 10-6-18 6WRid att25MGC Inf p187&227 CR France145,9-6-18
ROBBINS,John Laurence TLt kia 26-3-18 10Ches attStaff 26Div p96 CR France300,Lawrence 25Div
ROBERSON,Frank Hubert Langhorne 2Lt dow 12-8-17 7RWSurr p56 CR Belgium7
ROBERSON,George Lewis T2Lt dow 21-3-18 8RSuss p119 CR France1063
ROBERT,Annie Louise Sister 28-9-16 QAIMNS CR Ches8
ROBERTON,Charles Drinnan 2Lt kia 1-7-16 4LancF p93 CR France156
ROBERTON,David McCulloch SeeROBERTSON.D.M.
ROBERTON,James Leslie SeeROBERTSON.J.L.
ROBERTON,Robert Douglas Finch.MC.Lt dow 12-10-20 1Ess CR Yorks38
ROBERTS,Alan Sheriff T2Lt kia 10-7-16 14RWFus p98 CR France397
ROBERTS,Alfred Frank T2Lt kia 18-11-16 17HLI p163 CR France534
ROBERTS,Anthony Gerald Malpas 2Lt kia 20-10-14 2RInnisF p105 CR France451,Lt
ROBERTS,Archibald Maj dow 22-8-15 6Yorks p91 CR Europe1 Ex IA 95Inf
ROBERTS,Arthur Capt kia 15-9-16 15Lond p249 CR France700
ROBERTS,Arthur Colin.CMG.DSO.BrigGen ded 17-5-17 RFus Cmdg80InfBdeHQ p70 CR Mddx51
ROBERTS,Arthur Doricourt.MC.TLt kld 31-8-17 GL &RFC p12 CR Surrey60
ROBERTS,Arthur Hosbury Starkey Lt dow 4-11-18 3 att15WelchR p127 CR France1478
ROBERTS,Arthur Howell 2Lt dow 20-10-18 5RWelshF p223 CR France1391
ROBERTS,Arthur Wilmot 2Lt ded PoW 16-12-18 DLI p161 CR Germany4,15WYorks
ROBERTS,Benjamin Richard TLt kia 30-7-16 RAMC att98FA p197 CR France23
ROBERTS,Birdsell(Bert) T2Lt kia 9-10-17 WYorks Res att9Bn D'Coy p82 MR30

ROBERTS,Cadwalader Glyn TLt kia 3-7-16 9RWFus p98 CR France393
ROBERTS,Cecil Llewellyn Norton 2LtACapt kia 9-10-17 2RWar p65 MR30
ROBERTS,Cecil Quinlan 2Lt kia 16-5-15 RFA 113Bty p34 CR France727
ROBERTS,Charles Edward.MM.2Lt dow 10-10-16 7Lincs p75 CR France203
ROBERTS,Charles Henry Hill.MC.2Lt kia 15-9-16 21Lond p251 CR France385
ROBERTS,Charles William 2Lt kia 28-12-17 1Dev p77 CR Italy48,Willis
ROBERTS,C.J.Maj 6-11-18 4Hamps CR Hamps13
ROBERTS,Cyril Ainley T2Lt kia 25-4-18 13TankCps p188 MR30
ROBERTS,D'Arcy Granville St.Clair.MC.TCapt kia 26-4-18 4 att1Worc p109 CR France144
ROBERTS,David.MC.TCapt dow 23-4-17 7Lincs p75 CR France1182
ROBERTS,David Charles T2Lt kia 19-7-16 10SWBord p100 CR France643
ROBERTS,David Francis Lt kia 2-11-17 RE 410FC p210 CR Palestine8
ROBERTS.E.SNurse 12-8-17 QAIMNS CR Wales672
ROBERTS,Edgar 2Lt kia 31-8-18 DorsYeo p203 CR Belgium89
ROBERTS,Edmund Percy TLt kia 21-3-18 11Ess p132 MR20
ROBERTS,Edward Elwyn Lloyd 2Lt dow 20-9-18 2/6RWar p214 CR France194
ROBERTS,Edward Owen Lt ded 29-1-17 RDC p253 CR Ches28
ROBERTS,Elwyn T2Lt kia 10-2-17 GL &10RFC p12 MR20
ROBERTS,Eric James 2Lt kia 23-9-16 27RFC p3 MR20
ROBERTS,Ernest Woolley 2Lt kld 6-6-15 7LancF p221 CR Gallipoli2
ROBERTS,F.W.OBE.VD.LtCol 14-7-20 RE CR Norf209
ROBERTS,Francis T2Lt kia 27-10-16 20RFus p70 CR France374
ROBERTS,Francis Bernard TCapt kia 8-2-16 9RB p180 CR Belgium85
ROBERTS,Francis Watson 2Lt kia 14-10-15 14Lond p249 CR France219,ROBARTS 13-10-15
ROBERTS,Francklin Allender 2Lt kia 8-8-18 7Lond p247 CR France141
ROBERTS,Fred TLt kia 23-7-16 11 att6YLI p143 CR France1182
ROBERTS,Frederick John TCapt kia 28-9-15 3Lpool p72 CR France163,25-9-16 1Bn
ROBERTS,Frederick John TMaj dow 17-10-15 6RWSurr p56 CR France98
ROBERTS,Frederick Norman T2Lt dow 19-11-18 3RFus p70 CR Lancs14
ROBERTS,Frederick Roberts 2Lt dow 7-9-16 3GordH p167 CR France833
ROBERTS,Frederick Sheriff 2Lt kia 28-8-18 1 att9RWFus p98 CR France98,29-8-18
ROBERTS,Frederick Sleigh.The Rt Hon.Earl.VC.KG.KP.PC.GCB.OM.GCSI.GCIE.VD:- FieldMarshall ded 14-11-14 ColCommdt RA Col IrGds p1 CR Lond15
ROBERTS,Frederick William.MC.TCapt dow PoW 1-10-17 10RWKent p141 CR Belgium393
ROBERTS,Gavesen Brooke 2Lt kia 26-9-17 GL &19RFC p12 MR20,Gavern
ROBERTS,George Alfred.MM.2Lt kia 21-3-18 1Leic p88 MR20
ROBERTS,George Bradley 2Lt dow 7-5-15 ULIA att1Manch p156&282 CR France102
ROBERTS,George Jewell T2Lt dow 17-6-16 RE 250Co p48 CR France285
ROBERTS,George Peskett TLt dow 26-4-16 134RFA 61HB p35 CR Iraq5
ROBERTS,Gerald Chip-chase TLtCol kia 8-6-16 14Glouc p107 CR France705,Chipchase
ROBERTS,Griffith Evans T2Lt kia 7-6-17 6BordR p118 MR29
ROBERTS,Guy Hepworth LtACapt dow 22-11-17 2/4YLI p235 CR France398
ROBERTS,Harold.MC.TCapt dow 27-10-18 9SStaffs p123 CR Italy7
ROBERTS,Harold Owen Bodvel.MC.Lt dow 18-11-15 7Lond p247
ROBERTS,Harry Cureton Lt kia 27-12-17 MontgomYeo att25RWFus p204 CR Palestine3
ROBERTS,Harry Leslie T2Lt dow 10-9-16 189RFA p35 CR France197
ROBERTS,Henry Norman 2Lt kia 28-4-17 10LNLancs p136 MR20
ROBERTS,Henry Sheriff Capt kia 27-8-17 17RWFus p99 MR30 Ex 5Bn
ROBERTS,Howel Dilwyn T2Lt kia 31-10-18 14RWFus p99 CR France1478
ROBERTS,Idris T2Lt dow 3-9-18 17RWFus p99 CR France41,Lt kia 2-9-18
ROBERTS,Iorworth Cynon 2Lt kia 10-4-18 25MGC Inf p185 MR32
ROBERTS,Ivon L'Esterrre.MID Maj kia 8-6-15 RFA p35 MR4,d'Esterre
ROBERTS,James Roderick Trethowan 2Lt dow 3-3-15 2Suff p79 CR Belgium182,Lt 4-3-15
ROBERTS,James Thursby 2Lt dow 20-7-16 2RWSurr p56 CR Hamps64
ROBERTS,Jane SNurse drd 10-4-17 QAIMNS p200
ROBERTS,John T2Lt kia 14-9-18 1/9Lpool p72 CR France433
ROBERTS,John.MC.Lt ded 11-11-18 S158RFA p35 CR France34,A158
ROBERTS,John Ernest Bate.MID 2Lt dow 23-9-15 IARO att1/5GurkhaRif p282 MR4,WAFF
ROBERTS,John Harry T2Lt dow 11-4-18 EYorks attRes 2Y&L p84 CR Belgium11
ROBERTS,John Henry Charles 2Lt dow 2-5-15 Dors p124 CR France284
ROBERTS,John Herbert Lt kld 24-9-18 RFA &8RAF p35 MR20
ROBERTS,John Lambert.MC.Lt kia 21-3-18 1/2 att6Leic C'Coy p88 CR France212

ROBERTS,John Robert Bowden 2Lt kia 1-2-16 4NumbF p213 CR Belgium127,dow
ROBERTS,John William 2Lt dow 23-3-18 7 att1/4RWelshF p223 MR20
ROBERTS,Laurie Paterson T2Lt kia 23-2-18 20RFC p17 CR France134,Lawrie
ROBERTS,Leslie.MC.T2Lt kia 24-8-18 12ESurr att6RWSurr p113 CR France370
ROBERTS,Lionel John 2Lt kia 3-9-16 16RB p180 MR21
ROBERTS,Llewellyn Hilton 2Lt kia 13-8-16 11RWar p65 MR21
ROBERTS,Matthias Groves 2Lt kia 3-7-17 3 att1RBerks p139 CR France258
ROBERTS,M.C.MC.Capt dow 10-11-18 A Coy CanadaInf CR Belgium202
ROBERTS,M.D.SNurse drd 31-12-17 QAIMNS p200 CR Egypt1
ROBERTS,Noel Humphreys 2Lt kia 23-4-17 1KOSB p102 MR20
ROBERTS,Oscar Howard Salter 2Lt dow 28-9-17 21Lond p251 CR France113
ROBERTS,Philip Hugh Gore 2Lt dow 21-8-15 1/5GordH p242 CR France197
ROBERTS,Ralph Jennings TLt kia 31-10-17 179MGC p185 CR Palestine1
ROBERTS,Reuben TCapt kia 7-7-16 RAOC DADOS 25Div p198 CR France296
ROBERTS,Richard Bowen Lt ded 31-1-18 W'land&C'landYeo p271 CR Wales447,13-1-18
ROBERTS,Richard D'Esterre Capt ded 15-10-18 25DLI p161&266 CR Yorks294
ROBERTS,Robert James T2Lt kia 10-10-16 14 att13Ches p96 CR France280,11-10-16
ROBERTS,Robert Jesse Adams.DSO.TCapt dow 22-9-17 10WelshR att15LudhianaSikhs p127 MR67
ROBERTS,Robert John 2Lt dow PoW 28-10-18 6MGC Inf p185 CR France1211
ROBERTS,Rupert Edward TMaj dow 26-3-18 16Manch p156 CR France145
ROBERTS,S.T.C.Lt 30-7-18 52RAF CR France41
ROBERTS,Samuel HonCapt ded 6-12-14 RE Staff p48 CR France145
ROBERTS,Thomas 2Lt kia 25-5-15 3 att2Ches p96 CR Belgium165,24-5-15
ROBERTS,Thomas TLt dow 11-10-18 6Y&L p159 CR France214
ROBERTS,Thomas Owen 2Lt kia 18-9-18 RWFus att14Bn p99 CR France415
ROBERTS,Thomas William T2Lt kia 30-9-16 7RWKent p141 MR21
ROBERTS,Thomas Wilson T2Lt dow 1-9-16 1Ches p96
ROBERTS,Victor T2Lt kia 19-7-17 9WelshR p127 CR Belgium111
ROBERTS,Victor George 2Lt kia 27-7-17 4WelshReg p230 CR Belgium23
ROBERTS,Walter Rowland Southall Capt kia 16-8-15 RAMC p254 CR Gallipoli27
ROBERTS,William T2Lt dow 8-8-17 218MGC p185 CR Belgium7
ROBERTS,William Lt kia 27-12-17 6RWelshF p223 CR Palestine3
ROBERTS,William 2Lt kia 22-9-18 7SWBord p100 CR Greece5,18-9-18
ROBERTS,William Arthur TLt dedacc 20-8-17 GL RFus 30TrResBn p70&267 CR Kent7
ROBERTS,William John 2Lt kia 21-3-18 1RDubF p177 MR27
ROBERTS,William Lloyd Lt kia 6-11-17 1/7RWelshF p223 CR Palestine1,2Lt
ROBERTS,William Thomas 2Lt kia 28-9-18 3 att1DCLI p115 CR France245
ROBERTSON,Alexander 2Lt dow 17-8-17 RFA &34RFC p12&35 CR France1361
ROBERTSON,Alexander Lt dow 28-1-18 6SfthH att101MGC Inf p187&241 CR France214,kld
ROBERTSON,Alexander Myron Capt kia 4-8-16 1/6GordH p242 CR France1890
ROBERTSON,Alexander Stuart.MC.Lt kia 2-9-18 8RScots p211 CR France1486
ROBERTSON,Alexander Winton.MC.Maj dow 23-4-16 RGA 68SB p209 CR France62
ROBERTSON,Andrew 2Lt kia 13-11-16 7GordH p242 MR21
ROBERTSON,Angus Burns TCapt ded 8-11-18 RAMC p197 CR Scot270
ROBERTSON,Archibald 2Lt kia 9-4-18 20Mddx p148 MR32
ROBERTSON,Archibald Garden 2Lt kia 8-6-17 BlkW att66RFC p12&129 MR20
ROBERTSON,Archibald Watson T2Lt kia 9-6-18 RE 263Coy p48 CR France119,8/9-6-18
ROBERTSON,Athol Lt dow 26-3-16 2A&SH p173 CR France80
ROBERTSON,Barrie Dow T2LtACapt kia 22-8-18 4RFus p70 CR France618
ROBERTSON,Charles.MC.Rev dow 3-10-18 RAChDept p199 CR Greece9
ROBERTSON,Charles Boyd 2Lt kia 16-10-17 A165RFA p35 CR France184
ROBERTSON,Charles Eric 2LtTCapt kia 12-7-17 Cmdg11RFC p12 CR France421
ROBERTSON,Charles Granville T2Lt kia 27-3-18 Ess att2Nhants p132 MR27
ROBERTSON,Charles John 2Lt kia 22-3-17 6BlkW p231 CR France15
ROBERTSON,Charles Thomas Andrews CaptAMaj dow PoW 23-3-18 1/5GordH p167&256 CR France1061
ROBERTSON,Charles William 2Lt dow PoW 22-8-16 3Manch p156 CR France716
ROBERTSON,Clement.VC.TLtACapt kia 4-10-17 3RWSurr attTankCps p56&188
ROBERTSON,David 2Lt kia 31-7-16 6RScots p211 MR29
ROBERTSON,David Hunter Henderson Lt dow 10-3-15 4ScotRif p104 CR France706,2Bn
ROBERTSON,David McCulloch 2Lt kia 13-2-17 1MGC p185 MR21,ROBERTON
ROBERTSON,David Norman 2Lt ded PoW 16-4-17 60RFC p12 MR20
ROBERTSON,David Stephen.OBE.BtLtCol ded 8-12-19 RScotF p263 CR Asia20

ROBERTSON,Douglas Forbes T2Lt dow 28-9-16 15 att8NumbF p63 CR France44,26-9-16
ROBERTSON,Douglas Hill T2Lt kia 14-4-17 1KOSB D Coy p102 MR20
ROBERTSON,Duncan Alexander T2Lt kld 11-11-17 GL &RFC p12 CR Scot677
ROBERTSON,Edmund John Macrory.MID Lt kia 22-5-15 70/34RFA p35 CR France571
ROBERTSON,Edward Craig Maj kia 29-9-15 Y&L p159 MR19
ROBERTSON,Eric Hume 2Lt kia 21-3-18 RDubF att48TMB p177 MR27
ROBERTSON,Ernest Cecil Leonard Lt kia 18-10-15 1/20Lond A'Coy p251 CR France219,Lennox
ROBERTSON,Ernest Guy TCapt ded 28-10-18 GL RAMC p191 MR19 Y&L CR Hamps12
ROBERTSON,Eustace James T2Lt dow 2-3-17 7Glouc p107 CR Iraq5,Capt
ROBERTSON,Fergus 2Lt ded PoW 3-12-18 3 att1/5BordR p118 CR Germany3
ROBERTSON,Frank Capt dow 25-6-15 12Worc p109 CR Egypt6
ROBERTSON,Frank Harding Lt FlyingAcc 22-2-18 IARO attRFC p282 CR Egypt15
ROBERTSON,Frederick Neal Lt kia 11-4-17 7 att1/4GordH p242 MR19
ROBERTSON,Frederick Percival TLt kia 4-3-16 20LancF p93 CR France631,3-3-16
ROBERTSON,George TCapt kia 1-7-16 21NumbF p63 MR21
ROBERTSON,George Arthur Norris TCapt kia 16-8-17 9 att3SWBord p100 CR Belgium106
ROBERTSON,George Cockburn 2Lt kia 21-7-15 6DLI p239 CR France683
ROBERTSON,George Hawthorn Minto TLt ded 10-3-19 GL 13HLI attNigR p202,255&267 CR Scot742,Minot
ROBERTSON,George Seaborn Hyssett 2Lt kia 18-11-16 5 att10Worc p109 MR21
ROBERTSON,Gilbert 2Lt kia 25-9-15 3 att1CamH p168 CR France219
ROBERTSON,Gilbert Swale TCapt kia 27-9-15 13RScots p54 MR19
ROBERTSON,Glagow Archibald William Capt kia 13-11-14 IA 2/39GarhwalRif p282 CR France727,ROBERTSON-GLASGOW
ROBERTSON,Glynn Cuthbert Lt kia 15-3-16 RE 1/2FC p210 CR France68,16-3-16
ROBERTSON,Gordon T2Lt kia 17-11-15 10GordH p167 CR France423
ROBERTSON,Haldane Stanford 2Lt kia 19-4-17 4Nhampt p271 MR34
ROBERTSON,Harold Hay.MC.T2Lt dow 11-9-18 7EYorks p84 CR France307,kia
ROBERTSON,Helenus Macaulay Capt kia 26-1-16 3 att2RWFus p99 CR France114
ROBERTSON,Henry William T2Lt dow 21-4-18 11A&SH p173 CR France95,kia
ROBERTSON,Herbert R.Capt ded 28-7-16 RAMC p271 CR Sussex216,29-7-16
ROBERTSON,Herbert.MC.Maj dow 5-4-18 C86RFA p206 CR France37
ROBERTSON,Herbert Charles Lt kia 1-11-18 135/32RFA p35 CR France1260
ROBERTSON,Herbert Johnston Graeme Lt kia 25-9-15 3 att1BlkW p129 MR19
ROBERTSON,Herbert Neville 2Lt dow 30-4-18 3 att10Ches p96 CR France13
ROBERTSON,Hugh Grant Capt kld 26-4-15 ConnRgrs p172 CR Belgium92
ROBERTSON,Ian Gordon Lt kia 13-11-16 7GordH C'Coy p242 CR France131,2Lt
ROBERTSON,James 2Lt ded 9-7-17 4HLI att19DLI p163 CR France122,dow
ROBERTSON,James LtCol kia 21-3-18 RAMC 2/1FA p253 CR France307
ROBERTSON,James 2Lt kia 21-8-18 4RScotF p222 CR France927
ROBERTSON,James 2Lt dow 5-10-18 19Lond p251 CR France106,7Bn
ROBERTSON,James Duncan.MC.LtTACapt dow 27-8-17 9GordH p167 CR Belgium11
ROBERTSON,James Horan TLt kia 18-7-16 8 att11BlkW p129 MR21,11 att8Bn
ROBERTSON,James Houldsworth Lt 11-3-18 48RFC p258 CR France987
ROBERTSON,James Leslie 2Lt kia 6-9-16 4Yorks attRFC p19&235 MR20,ROBERTON
ROBERTSON,James Whittingham 2Lt kia 23-4-17 1/7BlkW p231 CR France604,Whittingehame
ROBERTSON,John Capt kia 28-6-15 4RScots p211 CR Gallipoli2
ROBERTSON,John Alexander Tower Lt drd 30-12-15 IARO att2/3GurkhaRif p282 MR41
ROBERTSON,John Barclay T2Lt kld 13-11-17 ScotRif att2Bn p104 CR France262
ROBERTSON,John Brewis TCapt dow 17-9-16 9BlkW p129 CR France51
ROBERTSON,John Frederick Maj 12-3-15 11Hamps CR Eire505
ROBERTSON,John Gilfillan 2Lt kia 7-6-17 11RInnisF p105 CR Belgium155
ROBERTSON,John Henry TLt dow 11-3-18 RFC p17
ROBERTSON,John Johnston T2Lt kia 27-9-18 8NumbF p63 CR France272
ROBERTSON,John Keith Grant TLt kia 1-1-17 GL &RFC p12 CR France833
ROBERTSON,John Ross Lt kia 12-5-17 Fife&ForfarYeo attRFC p19&203 CR France272
ROBERTSON,John Stoddart.MID TLt kia 21-5-16 7CamH p168 CR France423
ROBERTSON,John Struan Carmichael 2Lt kia 31-3-18 B46RFA p35 CR France1061,21-3-18
ROBERTSON,Keith Forbes Lt kia 27-8-16 6 att1RB p180 CR Belgium115
ROBERTSON,Laurence Grant T2Lt kia 30-7-16 9 att2KOSB p102 MR21,Lawrance

ROBERTSON,Leonard Dougal.MC.Lt kia 13-11-17 1/4KOSB p223 CR Palestine9
ROBERTSON,Leslie Johnston Walker.MC.Lt kia 3-10-17 3GordH p167 CR Belgium112
ROBERTSON,Lewis Capt dow 7-11-14 1CamH p168 CR Belgium84,3-11-14
ROBERTSON,Magnus Rainer.MC.TCapt dow 22-8-18 2 att11Ess p132 CR France370,Rainier 9Bn
ROBERTSON,Matthew Struan TCapt kia 2-3-16 1GordH p167 CR Belgium21
ROBERTSON,Maxwell Alexander Capt kia 1-7-16 10RInnisF p105 MR21
ROBERTSON,Mowbray Mitcalfe T2Lt kia 31-8-16 9NStaffs p157 CR France397
ROBERTSON,Neil Wallace.MC.Bar.2Lt kia 2-9-18 1RScotF p95 MR16
ROBERTSON,Norman Bethune.DSO.Maj kia 30-11-17 2RFA p35 CR France379
ROBERTSON,Norman Cairns Capt ded PoW 20-6-17 2Hamps p121 CR Germany2
ROBERTSON,Norman McLeod Lt kia 17-10-16 GL RFA att60RFC p3,19,191&208 CR France80
ROBERTSON,Peter Lt ded 16-1-19 3CamH &RAF p168 CR Ches8
ROBERTSON,Ralph 2Lt kld 11-5-17 8Hamps attRFC p19&229 CR Egypt1
ROBERTSON,Robert Arthur Harvey LtCol ded 29-5-20 IA 1/30Punjabis p282
ROBERTSON,Robert Bruce Hope 2Lt kia 28-6-15 8ScotRif p225 MR4
ROBERTSON,Robert Hamilton 2Lt kia 30-11-17 3 att2Hamps p121 MR17
ROBERTSON,Robert Sergius 2Lt dow 20-7-16 1 att3KOSB p102 CR France145,Sergins
ROBERTSON,Robert Ward Shepherd Lt kia 27-5-17 4RWSurr att 19MGC Inf p187&212 CR France593
ROBERTSON,Ronald TCapt ded 13-9-17 10HLI p163 CR Surrey9
ROBERTSON,Sydney T2Lt kia 29-7-18 KOSB att1/5Bn p102 MR18
ROBERTSON,Thomas Arthur TCapt ded 11-7-17 RASC p267 CR Ireland14,drd
ROBERTSON,Walter Raymond T2Lt kia 1-7-16 2BordR p118 CR France394
ROBERTSON,Walter Raymond T2Lt kia 5-3-18 RE p210
ROBERTSON,William 2Lt dow 3-5-17 1RScotF p95 MR20
ROBERTSON,William Adam Lt drd 30-12-15 1ARO att4Cav p282 MR41,att2RRoICav
ROBERTSON,William Bethune Lt kia 25-3-18 RE 404FC p210 MR20
ROBERTSON,William Dickson 2Lt kia 28-7-17 3/5RScots att1/5ancs p212 CR Belgium10
ROBERTSON,William Ford.MIDx2 TCapt&Adjt kia 17-10-17 9NumbF p63 CR Belgium85
ROBERTSON,William George Lt dow 15-12-17 11GordH att156MGC Inf p167&185 CR Egypt9
ROBERTSON,William Haswell 2Lt dow 2-8-18 9RScots p212
ROBERTSON,William John.TD.Maj dow 11-3-15 4SfthH p241 CR France705,10-3-15
ROBERTSON,William Marr 2Lt ded 12-7-19 3NumbF att25Lpool p262 CR Palestine11,Lt
ROBERTSON,William Maxwell Lt ded 28-6-15 2Lincs p75 CR France705
ROBERTSON,William Maxwell 2Lt dow 2-8-18 9RScots CR France1225
ROBERTSON,William Moore.MC.Lt kia 12-11-17 5RScots p211 MR34,1/4Bn
ROBERTSON,William Stewart.DCM.MID 2Lt kia 31-10-14 8BlkW att2GordH p167&264 MR29
ROBERTSON,William Stewart.MC.TLt kia 3-9-16 10 att4/5BlkW p129 CR France701
ROBERTSON-DURHAM,William Hugh TCapt kia 25-9-15 10ScotRif p104 MR19
ROBERTSON-ROSS,Patrick Maitland TCapt kia 26-9-15 8RWKent D'Coy p142 MR19
ROBERTSON-WALKER,Arthur Murdoch Maxwell.MID TCapt kia 7-7-16 8RFus p70 MR21
ROBILLIARD,Francis Humphrey John 2Lt kia 4-10-17 3Lincs p75 MR30
ROBIN,Cecil 2Lt dow 24-5-18 86RFA p35 CR France29
ROBIN,Charles Harold Capt kia 11-5-17 2RJLI att13Y&L p201 CR France1191
ROBIN,John F.TLtAMaj ded 29-11-18 57MGC Inf p185 CR France1030
ROBINETTE,Caroline Amelia SNurse ded 30-3-17 QAIMNS p200 CR Kent38
ROBINS,Charles Frederick TLt dow 2-4-18 5MGC Cav p185 CR France145
ROBINS,George Upton Capt dow 7-5-15 3EYorks p84 CR Belgium127,5-5-15
ROBINSON,Albert Alexander TLt kia 20-7-16 RGA 59SB p41 CR France397
ROBINSON,Alec Maj dow 16-4-18 C177RFA p35 CR France31
ROBINSON,Alexander Joseph 2Lt dow 8-8-17 116/26RFA p35 CR Belgium5
ROBINSON,Alfred Elliot Somers 2Lt kia 16-6-15 2RScotF p95 MR22,Eliott
ROBINSON,Archibald Tyrell.DSO.MajTLtCol dow 11-5-17 ESurr att7 O&BLI p113 CR Greece1
ROBINSON,Arthur Gabriel T2Lt kia 9-3-16 11BordR p118 CR France515
ROBINSON,Arthur Gordon 2Lt kia 9-1-17 RE SpCo p48 CR France115
ROBINSON,Arthur Henry T2Lt kia 11-6-17 25RFus p70 CR EAfrica10 &CR Tanzania1
ROBINSON,Arthur Hine 2Lt kia 26-4-15 1Manch 1Coy p156 MR29
ROBINSON,Arthur Linnell T2Lt dow 25-2-16 8Nhampt attRE 173TC p48 CR France88,Limnell

ROBINSON,Arthur Owen 2Lt kia 21-3-18 N&D att2/8Bn p134 MR20
ROBINSON,Augustine Lt dow 15-3-15 4SStaffs attELancs p123 CR France768
ROBINSON,Benjamin Stanley 2Lt kia 1-7-16 2RBerks p139 CR France393,Lt
ROBINSON,Bernard Oates 2Lt kia 9-10-17 4Y&L p238 MR30
ROBINSON,Bertram Langhorn Capt ded 6-9-17 RASC 4Coy 50DivTrn p253 CRDurham42
ROBINSON,Birketh Waring 2Lt kia 18-9-18 7Lpool p215 CR France530
ROBINSON,Cecil Beaumont TLt kia 14-9-16 13 att9WYorks p82 MR21
ROBINSON,Cecil Rowland 2Lt kia 26-9-17 1Camb p245 CR Belgium116
ROBINSON,Charles TLt.ACapt kia 14-7-16 12WYorks p82 CR Belgium3,15-7-18 1Bn
ROBINSON,Charles Arthur Lt kia 9-4-17 4RInnisF att111MGC p105 MR20
ROBINSON,Charles Edward Lt ded 25-10-18 1/5WYorks p218 CR Yorks123
ROBINSON,Charles Eugene Barnes Maj kia 28-9-15 IA 117Mahrattas p282 MR38,27-9-15
ROBINSON,Charles Lawson.TD.LtCol kld 8-5-15 1Mon p244 MR29
ROBINSON,Charles Surtees.MID TCapt dow 13-9-16 9Norf p74 CR France23
ROBINSON,Claude Gladstone T2Lt kia 20-10-17 7SWBord p100 CR France1472
ROBINSON,Courtney Vyvyan Maj ded 22-1-19 RGA p209
ROBINSON,Cyril Charles Edward Lt kia 28-4-18 59RAF
ROBINSON,De la Pere LtCol 30-10-18 APDept CR Lancs263
ROBINSON,Daniel George Mark 2Lt kia 16-5-15 ULIA att1SStaffs p282 CR France705
ROBINSON,Donald TLt kia 3-5-17 15WYorks p82 MR20
ROBINSON,Douglas Eric 2Lt kia 17-9-16 1/5DLI p239 CR France1890,15-9-16
ROBINSON,Edgar Lt kia 14-9-14 1LNLancs p136 MR15
ROBINSON,Edgar Francis 2Lt kia 20-6-18 6EKent p58 MR27
ROBINSON,Edmond Capt kia 20-3-17 RAMC attSfthH p197 CR France1182
ROBINSON,Edward,Gnr ded 24-5-16 RIM p282
ROBINSON,Edward Lt kld 6-12-17 RFA &RFC p12&261,2entries MR43
ROBINSON,Edward Colston T2Lt kia 26-9-15 8SomLI p80 MR19
ROBINSON,Edwin Winwood Lt kld 25-10-14 5Lancers D'Sqn p22 MR29,erased Voorhezele &CR Belgium454,kia
ROBINSON,Eli Lt kia 1-7-16 1/5NStaffs p238 MR21
ROBINSON,Elizabeth.ARRC.Sister ded 14-7-19 TFNS 3BritGH p271 CR Iraq ,12-7-19
ROBINSON,Eric Arthur TCapt dow 10-9-16 12Glouc p107 CR France23
ROBINSON,Eustace Dixon Sharper 2Lt kia 4-9-17 GL &25RFC p12 MR20
ROBINSON,Francis Bradbury Capt dow 3-7-16 6N&D p233 CR France120
ROBINSON,Francis Edward Lt kia 27-10-14 3 att2SStaffs p123 MR29
ROBINSON,Francis Victor Lt ded 29-7-18 RGA 383SB 59HvyGrp p41 CR Egypt9
ROBINSON,Frank TLt dow 7-7-16 14NumbF p63 CR France23
ROBINSON,Frank Victor TLt kia 3-5-17 18WYorks p82 MR20
ROBINSON,Frank Wright.MC.Lt kia 13-5-17 14 att22Manch p156 MR20
ROBINSON,Fred 2Lt kia 26-1-18 GL att22RFC p17 CR Egypt1
ROBINSON,Frederick 2Lt kia 28-7-18 4GordH p242 CR France622,1/7Bn
ROBINSON,Frederick Andrew.MC.TCaptAMaj kia 4-11-18 10TankCps p188 CR France190
ROBINSON,Frederick Henry.MC.Lt kia 30-9-17 3Lincs att3NigR p75&202 CR EAfrica11 &CR Tanzania1
ROBINSON,Frederick Winwood.DSO.MID MajTLtCol dow 18-4-17 130/40RFA p35&258 CR France52,Maj
ROBINSON,Frederick Wilfred.DSO.MC.Maj dow 29-3-18 8MGC p185 MR27,28-3-18
ROBINSON,Gathorne Clegg 2Lt ded 6-6-18 YLI attRAF p143 CR Yorks570
ROBINSON,Geffrey Wathen TLt kia 25-9-15 10Glouc 4Coy p107 CR France1723
ROBINSON,Geoffrey Francis Capt kia 21-5-15 6KSLI att1/4Ghurkas p145&282,mbk IndVoltrs MR22
ROBINSON,George Whalley Capt kia 15-2-15 3Leinst p175 CR Belgium111
ROBINSON,George Thomas 2Lt kia 3-6-18 2SfthH p165 CR France412
ROBINSON,Gerald Duckworth.MID Capt dow 26-9-16 3 att1ESurr SR p113 CR France329
ROBINSON,Harold Arthur Maj ded 31-5-16 2LNLancs p136 CR SAfrica158
ROBINSON,Harold Fletcher TLt kia 1-7-16 15LancF p93 CR France215
ROBINSON,Harold Godfrey Capt kia 12-6-17 1NStaffs p157 CR Belgium127
ROBINSON,Harold Leefe 2Lt dow 10-4-16 IARO att103MahrattaLI p282 MR38
ROBINSON,Harold Percival 2Lt kia 31-7-17 6Lpool p215 MR29
ROBINSON,Harold Robert 2Lt kia 13-10-18 RGA 10SB p41 CR France716
ROBINSON,Harold William 2LtTLt kia 30-9-17 YLI att3Nigeria p143&202 CR EAfrica11 &CR Tanzania1
ROBINSON,Harry 2Lt kia 15-4-18 2/6NStaffs p238 MR32
ROBINSON,Harry Hesketh Kay 2LtACapt kia 26-3-18 5 att16RB p180 MR27

ROBINSON,Harry Ingham.MID Maj kia 13-10-15 5Lincs p220 MR19
ROBINSON,Harry Stanley Shepley Lt dow 9-6-15 3 att2KOSB p102 CR Belgium28
ROBINSON,Harry William TLt&Maj ded 9-11-18 O&BLI LabCps p266 CR Oxford69
ROBINSON,Henry HonLt&QM ded 3-11-15 RAMC att25GenHospl p197 CR France40
ROBINSON,Henry John T2Lt kia 21-9-17 10RWKent C'Coy p142 MR30
ROBINSON,Henry Awtry T2Lt kld 18-2-18 RFC p17 CR France1844,Harry Awty
ROBINSON,Henry Betham Maj ded 31-7-18 RAMC p253 CR Lond14
ROBINSON,Henry Ellis TCapt kia 25-4-18 RAMC att1/6WYorks p197 MR30
ROBINSON,Henry Harold.DSO.TCapt drd 4-5-17 RAMC p197 CR Italy13
ROBINSON,Herbert Edwin 2Lt kia 10-7-17 189RFA p209 CR Belgium29
ROBINSON,Hercules Edward Joseph.Hon.T2Lt dow 26-9-15 8EKent p58 CR France178
ROBINSON,Hugh Huntley.MC&Bar.Maj kld 3-5-19 RAMC &RAF p253 CR Belgium241
ROBINSON,Horace Victor George 2Lt kia 24-10-17 7Worc p226 MR20
ROBINSON,Hugh Thomas Kay.DSO.LtCol kia 26-4-18 12 att13RSuss p119
ROBINSON,Isaac T2Lt kia 23-10-16 12 att2ELancs p111 MR21
ROBINSON,Isaac Vincent T2Lt kia 14-7-17 RE 67FC p48 CR Belgium36
ROBINSON,James 2Lt kia 20-5-17 9 att4Lpool p216 CR France434
ROBINSON,James Norman T2Lt dow 22-7-18 6LancF att13ELancs p93 CR France28
ROBINSON,James Thompson TLt kia 7-9-18 RWFus att24Bn p99 CR France285,8-9-18
ROBINSON,James Vernon TLt dow 13-8-18 1 att16LancF p93 CR France145
ROBINSON,John 2Lt kia 1-7-16 3 att2SWBord p100 CR France1501
ROBINSON,John Cecil T2Lt kia 5-6-17 YLI att2Bn p143 CR Belgium173
ROBINSON,John Cyril Charles Henry Capt kia 3-6-17 5ELancs p226 CR France905
ROBINSON,John Edward T2Lt kia 3-11-16 Lincs p75 CR France374
ROBINSON,John Henry 2Lt kia 30-11-17 4SomLI att2/6NStaffs p218 MR17
ROBINSON,John Holdsworth 2Lt kia 1-7-16 16WYorks p82 MR21
ROBINSON,John Hunter T2Lt dow 17-9-18 8 att12NumbF p63 CR France145,12/13Bn
ROBINSON,John Langley 2Lt kia 21-1-16 IARO att41Dogras p282 CR Iraq5,Lt
ROBINSON,John Singleton Henry TLt kia 24-9-18 13 att12WelshR p127 CR France673
ROBINSON,John Wilfred Capt kia 15-11-16 4NumbF p213 MR21
ROBINSON,John Yate.MC.TCapt&Adj dow 23-8-16 7NStaffs p157 CR Hereford/W154
ROBINSON,Joseph 2Lt dow 11-10-16 7NumbF p214 CR France145
ROBINSON,Kennett TLt kia 25-9-15 RAMC att12Manch p197 CR Belgium37,Kenneth
ROBINSON,Leonard TCapt kia 22-8-15 9LancF p93 MR4
ROBINSON,Leonard Herbert Frank TLt dow 18-3-16 7ESurr attTMB p113 CR France257,17-3-16
ROBINSON,Leslie Fergus.MC.Lt kia 27-9-18 RFA p208 CR France364,Feargus
ROBINSON,Leslie John Capt kia 12-3-15 Nhampt p138 MR22,1Bn &CR France1896,2Bn
ROBINSON,Louis Francis Woodward TLt kia 25-5-17 RE 153FC p48 MR20
ROBINSON,Max Louis 2Lt kia 22-7-16 2RScots p54 MR21,23-7-16
ROBINSON,Noel Stafford Maj dow 2-8-18 RFA p206 CR France888
ROBINSON,Osmond Cyril.MC.2Lt ded 24-5-18 181RFA p261 CR Yorks173,Lt
ROBINSON,Percy Dickson.MC.Capt kia 31-3-18 RFC MR20 p261
ROBINSON,Percival Bewman Palmer 2Lt kia 1-7-16 8YLI p143 MR21
ROBINSON,Percy Douglas TCapt kia 7-6-16 9NumbF p63 MR21
ROBINSON,Ralf Hubert.MM.T2Lt dow 23-8-17 RB att2Bn p180 CR Belgium11
ROBINSON,Ralph Duncan TCapt kia 7-6-17 9LNLancs p136 CR Belgium43
ROBINSON,Raymond Cecil 2Lt dow 19-10-18 RGA 270SB p41 CR France725
ROBINSON,Reginald Humphries T2Lt kia 4-10-18 1/4RLancs p59 CR France109,Humphreys Lt
ROBINSON,Reginald William TCapt kia 15-8-15 5RInnisF p105 CR Gallipoli4
ROBINSON,Richmond Fothergill T2Lt kia 30/31-7-15 7KRRC p151 MR29,30-7-15
ROBINSON,Robert Ernest T2Lt dow 12-11-18 46MGC p185 CR France123
ROBINSON,Roland Weymouth 2Lt dow 9-9-15 IARO att96Inf p282 CR Asia82
ROBINSON,Sidney Furness 2Lt ded 10-3-15 RH&FA p35 p261
ROBINSON,Stephen Owen.MID Capt kia 5-11-17 13Huss att5DragGds p22 CR Iraq8
ROBINSON,Sydney Francis Lt kia 22-7-17 5SLancs p230 MR29
ROBINSON,Thistle.MC.TLt kia 25-10-18 RFus att26Bn p70 CR Belgium408
ROBINSON,Thomas Botterill 2Lt ded 25-1-20 RFA p271 CR Yorks62,23-1-20
ROBINSON,Thomas Edward Lt kia 18-10-16 11 att2Yorks p91 MR21
ROBINSON,Thomas Naylor T2Lt kia 25-9-16 19 att14DLI p161 MR21
ROBINSON,Walter 2Lt kia 29-9-18 5WYorks attTankCps p189&218 CR France212
ROBINSON,Walter de Horne.MC.LtACapt kia 27-1-17 3 att1BordR p118 MR21
ROBINSON,Wilfred Cane Lt kia 22-3-18 11Hamps p121 CR France365
ROBINSON,William T2Lt kia 1-8-18 1/2 at1/5KOSB p102 CR Frnce524
ROBINSON,William T2Lt kia 22-8-18 8 att12/13NumbF p63 CR France514
ROBINSON,William Alfred Layton 2Lt kia 26-6-17 3RWSurr p56 CR Belgium29,11Bn
ROBINSON,William Charles 2Lt kia 7-1-17 IA 30Punjabis p282 CR EAfrica39
ROBINSON,William Eardley T2Lt kia 26-9-16 11SStaffs attLeic p123 MR32
ROBINSON,William Edwin TCapt kia 18-11-16 16HLI p163 MR21
ROBINSON,William Ewart T2Lt kia 19-8-15 8NumbF p63 MR4
ROBINSON,William Frederick Rokeby Lt 24-9-18 8RAF MR20
ROBINSON,William George T2Lt kia 1-10-17 Leic att8Bn p88 MR30
ROBINSON,William John Lt ded 19-2-19 HAC p271 CR Scot726
ROBINSON,W.Leefe.VC.Capt ded 31-12-18 Worc &RAF p109 CR Mddx23
ROBLIN,Lewis George 2Lt kia 5-5-18 1NumbF p63 MR19
ROBSON,Alfred Styan 2Lt kia 5-11-16 6DLI p239 MR21
ROBSON,Albert Frank TCapt kia 24-3-18 10RWSurr p56 MR20
ROBSON,Alexander 2Lt dow 8-11-17 RIrFus p171
ROBSON,Charles T2Lt dow 2-12-18 18NumbF p63 CR Durham18
ROBSON,Charles Alexander Burleigh.DCM.2Lt dow 8-11-17 2RIrFus CR Palestine1
ROBSON,Charles Henry TCapt kia 1-12-17 RAMC 2/4FA att2/4Glouc p197 MR17
ROBSON,Edgar Capt dow 3-12-14 1SLancs p126 CR France284
ROBSON,Edward Fawcett 2Lt dow 18-5-18 B79RFA p35 CR France84
ROBSON,Edward Moore.MC.Capt kia 11-4-18 5Yorks A'Coy p220 MR32
ROBSON,Frederick William.DSO.LtCol kia 28-3-18 5Yorks p220 MR27
ROBSON,Frederick William.MM.T2Lt dow 22-8-18 5MGC Inf p185&259 CR France281
ROBSON,George Lt kia 20-9-17 4SfthH p241 MR30
ROBSON,George William 2Lt kia 5-11-16 8DLI p239 MR21
ROBSON,Gerald David TLt kia 24-8-17 9KRRC p151 CR Belgium72
ROBSON,Harry Stuart Lt kia 8-8-18 10Lond p248 MR16
ROBSON,Henry Crompton Lt kia 12-3-18 7 att2/10Mddx p235 MR34
ROBSON,John Matley 2Lt ded 17-7-15 9Manch p237 CR Egypt3
ROBSON,Joseph T2Lt kia 20-7-18 2/Y&L p159 CR France1689
ROBSON,Ralph George Griffiths Capt kia 23-12-14 RE 3Coy p48 CR France768
ROBSON,Richard Ivan.MC.Capt dow 6-8-17 15RIrRif p170 CR Belgium11
ROBSON,Stanley 2Lt kia 31-3-18 4EYorks p219 CR France232
ROBSON,Tom Capt kia 22-8-18 19Lond p250 CR France210
ROBSON,William T2Lt ded 30-10-18 17KRRC p151 CR Scot596
ROBSON,William Friend 2Lt kia 3-5-17 296RFA p35 CR France366
ROBSON,William John 2Lt kia 30-11-17 NumbYeo p204 CR France415
ROBSON-SCOTT,Thomas Selby Lt kia 14-12-14 RScots p54 MR29
ROCH,George Powell Capt kia 21-5-18 PembrokeYeo att1KSLI p205 CR Belgium3
ROCH,William Protheroe LtACapt kia 11-3-18 WelshHorse p205 CR Palestine3
ROCH-AUSTIN,Sidney Leslie TLt dow 4-11-18 1/2 att1/4WRid p116 CR France1081
ROCHE,C.MC&Bar.Maj 14-3-21 RAMC CR Scot359
ROCHE,Francis Capt ded 30-6-17 RAVC 10VetHosp p199 CR France40
ROCHE,Francis Cavendish Chap4Cl ded 14-11-15 RAChDept p199 CR Egypt6
ROCHE,Hyacinth Joseph Albert Capt kld 19-1-15 RMunF attRFC p2&176 CR France1360,kia
ROCHE,James Patrick.MC.2LtACapt kia 7-6-17 GL RFA att47TMB p191 CR Belgium17
ROCHE,K.J.2Lt 21-11-18 1/2Madras&SMahrattaRifs MR66
ROCHE,Patrick Joseph.MC.Lt ded 25-8-17 IARO att1Sap&Min p282 CR Iraq8
ROCHE,Richard John Maj&QM ded 6-12-16 RWKent p265
ROCHE,Thomas Maj kia 17-11-14 1Wilts p153 CR Belgium106
ROCHE,Thomas.MC.Capt ded 26-9-19 RMunsF p266 MR40
ROCHE,William Henry T2Lt kia 27-3-18 10RIrFus p171 CR France987
ROCHELL,Alfred LtTCapt dow 14-4-18 1NumbF p63 CR France40
ROCHFORT,Arthur D'Oyly Lt ded 31-10-18 RGA &58RAF p41 CR Egypt15,13-10-18
ROCHFORT-BOYD,Henry Charles.DSO.MajTLtCol dow 4-12-17 16RHA 4CavDiv p35&258 CR France145
ROCHFORT-DAVIES,Wallis Rowland Henry 2Lt 8-3-16 3SomLI CR Somerset197
ROCKE,Charles Owen 2Lt kia 23-8-18 1GrenGds p50 CR France502
ROCKEY,Jim 2Lt kia 2-5-17 1/4Lincs p217 CR France551

ROCKLEY,William Lisle.MC.T2Lt kia 10-10-17 10Y&L p159 MR30,11-10-17
RODAKOWSKI,Raymond Juzio Paul LtACapt kia 9-10-17 1IrGds p53 MR30
RODD,Charles Bouchier 2Lt kia 30-10-16 2Dev p77 MR21
RODD,Frederick Trevor Lt kia 16-7-17 2/3Lond p245 MR20
RODDAM,Robert Collingwood.MC.Capt kia 16-6-15 3 att 1NumbF p63 MR29
RODDAN,Reginald T2Lt kia 1-10-18 9TankCps p188 CR France375
RODDICK,Andrew Maj kia 14-5-15 EssYeo p203 MR29
RODDY,Edwin Louis Maj died 3-7-19 1Ches p263CR Dorset152
RODERICK,Allan Whitlock Nicholl Lt kia 10-8-15 4WelshReg p230 MR4
RODERICK,Francis TLt dow 31-7-17 14WelshR p127 CR Belgium23
RODERICK,Hume Buckley LtACapt kia 1-12-17 1WelshGds 3Coy p53 CR France415,15-12-17
RODERICK,John Victor Tweed Lt kia 27-8-18 1CldGds p51 CR France103,21-8-18
RODERIGUES A.R.G.Maj 18-3-20 IMS MR65
RODGER,Douglas TLt kia 1-7-16 RAMC att90FA p197 CR France44
RODGER,George Swan 2Lt mbk 9-1-17 2Leic p256 MR38
RODGER,James Alexander Valentine 2Lt kia 3-9-16 13 att 14Hamps p121 MR21
RODGER,Lawton Keir Lt ded 15-1-19 RE CR Scot812
RODGER,Matthew Freer Lt kia 23-10-16 1 att2ScotRif p104 MR21,4 att2Bn
RODGER,W.Lt ded 1-11-18 RE 57FC p48 CR Scot86
RODGER,Walter Washington Buchanan 2LtTLt kia 8-7-15 1/5A&SH p243 CR Gallipoli1
RODGERS,Albert Henry Lt ded 7-11-18 4Res RFA p35&257 CR Yorks551,7-10-18
RODGERS,Alan Evison Lt kia 5-6-15 5ELancs p226 MR4
RODGERS,Albert Henry T2Lt dow 17-10-18 50MGC Inf p185 CR France1386
RODGERS,Edward Joseph T2Lt kia 24-4-17 10ScotRif p104 MR20
RODGERS,Henry Frederick T2Lt kia 4-10-17 1/7RWar Res p65 MR30
RODGERS,John.MID LtACapt dow 8-3-17 2YLI p143 CR Belgium12
RODGERS,John.MC.Capt kia 2-9-18 2/4Y&L D'Coy p238 CR France617
RODGERS,John Richard Lt kia 20-11-17 8Hamps attTankCps p189&229 MR17
RODGERS,Joseph Edward 2Lt dow 25-1-15 1CldGds 1Coy p51 CR France202
RODGERS,Robert William Christian Meyer Capt kia 29-7-17 RGA 1HB p209 CR Belgium9
RODHAM,Robert T2Lt kia 17-10-17 27 att9NumbF p63 CR Belgium85
RODNEY,Burnett William T2Lt kia 20-4-17 11RWKent p142 CR Belgium28
RODNEY,Hon William Francis 2Lt kld 9-5-15 RB &3RFC p2&180 CR France98
RODNEY-ANDERSON,Patrick Graham LtCol ded 14-6-16 IA 76Punjabis p282
RODNEY-RICKETTS,Stewart Arthur.MC.T2LtACapt kia 31-10-17 D82RFA p35 CR Belgium10
RODOCANACHI,Paul John T2Lt kia 27-7-17 GL &53RFC p13 CR Belgium76
RODRIQUES,Frank Capt ded 22-1-20 IA IMS p282
RODWELL,Hubert T2Lt dow 10-10-16 9 att 11LNLancs p136 CR France85
RODWELL,Mary SNurse drd 17-11-15 QAIMNS p200 MR40
RODWELL,William Albert.MC.T2Lt kia 9-11-17 RE 171Co p48 CR Belgium3
ROE,Albert John Havilland T2Lt kia 9-8-15 7KRRC p151 MR29
ROE,Arthur Robert Montgomery Capt dow 16-9-14 1Dors p124 CR France1862
ROE,Cyril Charles Lt 28-4-17 RMLI MR20
ROE,Edward Allan.MC&Bar.TLtTCapt kia 2-9-18 ESurr att2/4RWSurr p113 CR Belgium15
ROE,Francis Leslie T2Lt dow 7-1-16 2SLancs p126 CR France40
ROE,Frank Edward Mervyn Capt dow 7-6-16 5 att12RB p180 CR Belgium11
ROE,Harold 2Lt kia 4-9-18 3 att2/5LancF p93 MR19
ROE,Henot Baker T2Lt kia 23-8-18 1ESurr p113 CR France239
ROE,John George 2Lt kia 26-9-17 3 att2/8N&D p134 CR Belgium130
ROE,John Windsor Maj dow 7-8-16 C185RFA RABde IndianEF p35 CR France80
ROE,Samuel George Capt kia 20-10-14 2RInnisF p105 CR France451,21-10-14
ROE,Sidney Charles 2Lt kia 5-5-17 14Lond p249 CR France581
ROE,William Richard T2Lt ded PoW 11-5-17 11RFus attHAC p70 CR France1293
ROEBER,David Arnold 2Lt kia 14-8-16 3 att7Beds p86 CR France82
ROEBUCK,Alfred Eric Eaton TCapt kia 8-9-18 9WRid p116 CR France662
ROFFEY,Harold Bowyer.DSO.MajTLtCol kia 15-4-18 LancF att2/5Lincs p93 CR France285
ROFFEY,J Capt 16-10-16 IA MilWorksServ CR Burma129A
ROFT,Edwin John 2Lt kia 25-7-18 8Lond p247 MR27
ROGER,Edward James Pringle T2Lt kia 19-7-18 RASC 49DivTrn p193 CR Belgium18
ROGERS,Alan Stanley Clark TCapt kia 7-8-15 6EYorks p84 MR4
ROGERS,Albert Edward 2Lt kia 3-5-17 2LancF p93 MR20
ROGERS,Alfred Morris T2Lt kia 18-7-16 15Glouc p107 CR France114
ROGERS,Allen Stanley Clark Lt kia 8-8-15 IA 61Pnrs att6EYorks p282
ROGERS,Arthur 2Lt kia 26-3-17 6RWelshF p223 Palestine8,1/7Bn

ROGERS,Arthur Gerald TLt kia 26-9-16 12Mddx p148 CR France215
ROGERS,Arthur Norman Capt kia 24-11-17 1/7RScots p211 CR Palestine3
ROGERS,Benjamin Richard Corlay 2Lt kia 17-10-18 6 att3RFus p70 CR France190
ROGERS,Cecil Victor De Burgh 2Lt kia 21-4-17 GL &29RFC p13 CR France581
ROGERS,Cecil Walter T2Lt dow 28-12-17 7RWSurr p56 CR Surrey55
ROGERS,Charles Hunter 2Lt dow 9-11-14 RH&FA p35 CR Lond14,Lt
ROGERS,Clarence Elias 2Lt kia 18-6-16 RFC p3 CR France924
ROGERS,Denys Stutely 2Lt kia 21-3-18 189RFA p35 MR20
ROGERS,Edward.MC.CaptAMaj dow 8-12-16 RE 67FC p48 CR France62
ROGERS,Edward Ambrose Gordon Capt ded 9-4-16 RGA 93SB p271 CR Cornwall36
ROGERS,Esmond Hallewell T2Lt kia 3-7-16 10RWar p65 MR21
ROGERS,Francis Caryer Campbell.MVO.Capt kia 15-2-15 2DCLI p115 MR29
ROGERS,Francis Lyttelton Lloyd T2Lt kia 7-1-16 D75RFA p35 CR France705,6-1-16
ROGERS,G.C.MC.Capt 30-10-17 52RFC CR France1361 CR France383
ROGERS,George Murray TLt kia 1-7-16 13RIrRif p170
ROGERS,George Stanley 2Lt kld 10-8-16 RFC p3 CR Canada1602
ROGERS,Gerald 2Lt kia 1-9-18 126AC RFA p35 CR France421
ROGERS,Godfrey Marcus Lt dow 27-4-18 1 att12Glouc p107 CR France31,2Lt 28-4-18
ROGERS,Henry Milward Capt dow 26-5-15 5Manch p236 CR Greece10
ROGERS,Henry Peverell Lt kia 5-7-16 1N&D p134 MR21
ROGERS,Herbert George 2Lt kia 28-12-15 9SomLI p80 MR4,29-6-15
ROGERS,Hermoine Angela Nurse drd 31-12-17 VAD p200 CR Egypt1
ROGERS,James Archibald Lt kia 26-2-18 RE p48 MR38
ROGERS,James Joseph T2Lt kia 28-3-18 11 att2RDubF p177 CR France526,27-3-18
ROGERS,John Lewis Capt ded 15-11-18 1/4DCLI p226 CR Egypt9
ROGERS,Leonard Castel Campbell.MC.MID Lt dow 25-12-14 IA 1/7 att 1/9GurkhaRif p282 CR France727
ROGERS,Leonard Neville TCapt dow 11-4-17 1 att18NumbF Res p63 CR France97
ROGERS,Maurice Croston 2Lt dow 25-2-15 RE 59FC p48 CR Belgium170
ROGERS,N.H.Capt ded 25-4-17 2/4GurkhaRif MR40
ROGERS,Percy Alexander MacKarness Lt kia 9-10-17 7WYorks p218 MR30
ROGERS,Percy Arden T2Lt kia 27-5-18 RE 170TC p48 CR France179
ROGERS,Reginald T2Lt kia 15-9-16 7RB p180 CR France1890
ROGERS,Richard Henry Lyster Lt kia 4-10-17 32RFA p35 CR Belgium86
ROGERS,Robert Carmichael TCapt dow 2-8-18 RAMC att18HAG p197 CR France34
ROGERS,Robert Maxtone T2Lt kia 25-9-16 9 att2KOSB p102 MR21,Maxton
ROGERS,Robert Murray 2Lt kia 2-7-16 8KRRC p151 MR20
ROGERS,Ronald Joseph Capt kia 28-6-15 14RB p180 MR4
ROGERS,Samuel.DCM.2Lt ded 24-11-17 6RWar p214 CR France1778
ROGERS,Sheffield Digby Kissane Lt kia 14-6-15 4RFus attNumbF p70 MR29
ROGERS,Sidney Frederick 2Lt kld 31-12-17 RE p210 CR Hamps8
ROGERS,Sidney Gilbert 2Lt kia 4-10-17 1Dev p77 MR30,3-10-17
ROGERS,Stanley T2Lt kia 4-10-18 Wilts att7Bn p153 MR16
ROGERS,Stanley Arthur Lt kia 21-3-18 2/6N&D p233 MR20
ROGERS,Thomas DepCommy&Capt ded 13-2-15 IA S&TCps p282 CR France356,Lt
ROGERS,Thomas Jerome 2Lt ded 30-10-18 IARO attLabCps p282 CR Pakistan50A,31-10-18
ROGERS,Trevor T2Lt kia 24-11-17 18WelshR p127 MR17
ROGERS,Wilfrid Frank.DSO.MID CaptAMaj kia 19-5-17 45RFA p35 CR France581
ROGERS,William Ewart Lt kia 31-7-17 6Ches p222 MR29
ROGERS,William Frederick 2Lt kld 28-12-15 RFC p2
ROGERSON,Andrew William Maj dow 6-10-17 8A&SH p243 CR Belgium16
ROGERSON,Ernest Sidney TCapt kia 19-8-16 9RSuss p119 MR21
ROGERSON,Harold T2Lt kia 1-8-17 13Mddx p148 MR29
ROGERSON,John Lilly T2Lt kia 5-10-18 9ScotRif att28TMB p104 CR Belgium157
ROGERSON,Noel 2Lt kia 28-2-18 3WYorks att2/4YLI p82 MR20
ROGERSON,William TCapt kia 27-8-18 RAMC att8RBerks p197 CR France515
ROHAN,Patrick Bernard 2Lt kia 16-3-15 2YLI p143 MR29
ROHDE,John Haughton Lt kia 28-10-14 RE att21S&M IA p48 MR22
ROHDE,Harold Turner Capt kia 12-4-16 IA 89Punjabis p282 MR38
ROLASON,Leslie Norton 2Lt kia 26-9-17 9Lond p248 MR30
ROLFE,Ernest Victor T2Lt kia 5-3-17 13Huss p22 CR Iraq8
ROLFE,John Shirley 2Lt ded 4-10-18 IARO att9HodsonsHorse p282 MR65,5-10-18
ROLFE,Philip TCapt kia 24-8-18 RASC att7Norf p193 CR France370

ROLFE,Raymond Harold Lt kia 23-4-18 4GrenGds att1rGds p50 CR France24,22-4-18

ROLFE,Wilfred Edwin 2Lt kia 22-8-17 2/1BucksBn O&BLI p232 MR30

ROLLAND,Frederick James Gordon TLt kia 25-9-15 8 att6KOSB p102 MR19

ROLLASON,Arthur Gilbert Capt ded 30-7-15 1/7Worc p225 CR France3,dow

ROLLASON,Charles Henry 2Lt dow 6-4-18 6N&D p233 CR France145,16Bn

ROLLESTON,Francis Launcelot 2Lt kld 26-4-15 2Lond p245 CR France1141,Lancelot kia

ROLLINS,Harold Victor Lt kia 24-4-18 12Lond p248 MR27 CR France1890

ROLLO,Thomas William T2Lt ded 4-11-18 LabCps p189 CR France34,Capt

ROLPH,Charles Colwyn Capt kia 15-10-15 2Leic p88 CR France765

ROLPH,George William Capt kia 10-8-15 Worc att9th p109 MR4

ROLSTON,Leslie Hicks Lt dow 1-4-18 RGA 182SB p41 CR France37

ROLSTON,William Edward Capt ded 9-8-21 2/5EKent att1D GHQ CR Germany1

ROMANES,Edmund Giles Radcliffe Lt dow 7-6-15 12Worc attRFus p109 MR4

ROME,Hubert Charlton Capt kia 18-12-14 IA 20Inf att129Baluchis p282 CR France571

ROME,James 2Lt kia 18-11-16 5HLI p240 CR France1890

ROMER,Frederick Charles.CB.CMG.HonColTLtCol kia 26-9-15 8EKent Ex LancF p58 MR19

ROMER,Guy Frederick T2Lt dow 3-5-16 13Mddx p148 CR France285

ROMER,Mark Leman Ritchie TCapt dow 20-9-16 7KRRC p151 CR Lond8

ROMILLY,Arthur Hovell Capt kia 21-10-14 DCLI p115 CR France279

ROMILLY,Cosmo George TLt kia 11-8-15 13N&D att1RInnisF p134 CRGallipoli6

ROMILLY,Francis Henry.DSO.Capt kia 25-9-15 2Leic p88 CR France1157

RONALD,James McBain Capt kia 23-4-15 2EKent p58 MR29

RONALDSON,Alexander T2Lt kia 9-6-16 12 att10ScotRif p104 CR France423

RONALDSON,Charles Rashleigh TLt kia 3-9-16 16RB p180 MR21

RONALDSON,James Gray T2Lt kia 20-9-17 10RWSurr attTMB p56 MR30

RONALDSON,John Stein 2Lt kia 9-4-17 3CamH p168 CR France1182

RONAYNE,James Andrew Lt kia 25-9-15 5RMunstF p176 CR France219

RONCA,Edward Henry T2Lt kia 17-10-18 1EKent p58 CR France849

ROOK,Frederick William 2Lt kia 21-7-17 40RFC p13 MR20

ROOK,Reuben Victor Capt kld 30-8-18 20Lond p251 CR France624,kia

ROOKE,Charles Douglas Willoughby.MID Lt kia 19-6-15 1ScotRif p104 CR France83

ROOKE,Claude Eugene 2Lt kld 21-1-18 3KOSB attRFC p17&102 CR Lancs14

ROOKE,Douglas Giles Capt ded 2-11-18 CldGds p51 CR Italy12

ROOKE,Giles Maj kia 9-5-15 IA 2/10GurkhaRif att2/2 p282 MR28

ROOKE,Henry Clive Lt kia 11-4-18 3 att1KOSB C'Coy p102 MR32

ROOKE,Sidney Austin Harold 2Lt dow 20-9-18 RWar att2/7Bn p65 CR France496

ROOKE,Wallace Mortimer.MID Capt ded 8-10-18 RWiltsYeo att2WiltR p206 CR Wilts29

ROOKE,William Albert T2Lt kia 29-7-16 7DCLI p115 CR France344

ROONEY,Bruno Martin Lt kia 25-6-15 9KOSB p102 CR Gallipoli6

ROONEY,Richard James TCapt dow 19-9-17 RE p48 CR France134

ROOPE,Charles Francis T2Lt kia 1-7-16 2RFus p70 CR France1501

ROOPER,Trevor Godolphin Hungerford 2Lt kia 18-1-17 1KSLI p145 CR France423

ROOPER,William Victor Trevor Capt kia 9-10-17 24RWFus attRFC p19&203 CR France285

ROOS,Gustav Oscar Capt kia 1-7-16 14Y&L p159 CR France927

ROOT,Harold Walter Lt dow PoW 22-3-18 36MGC Inf p185 CR France441,102MGC

ROOTH,Richard Alexander LtCol kia 25-4-15 1RDubF p177 CR Gallipoli15

ROOTS,Percy William 2Lt kia 11-6-17 7Lond p247 MR29

ROPE,John Arthur T2Lt kia 24-8-16 9 att1RWSurr p56 MR21

ROPER,Douglas Wingfield 2lt dow 11-11-17 RGA 279SB p41 CR Belgium10

ROPER,Eric Walter TLt&Adj dow 12-9-16 17RFus p70 CR France203

ROPER,Geoffrey Stapylton Rowe.MC.T2Lt kia 12-5-17 3 att7Yorks p91 CR France924

ROPER,George Fitzgerald 2Lt ded 18-5-19 RFA p262 CR Suff83,drd

ROPER,Oliver Stuart LtACapt kia 27-11-17 2/5YLI p235 MR17

ROPER,Reginald Trevor Maj kia 12-10-14 1Dors p124 CR France260

ROPER,William Edward Capt kia 31-7-17 1/5RLancs p213 CR Belgium10

ROPER,William Frank.MC.T2Lt kia 29-9-18 11RFus att54TMB p70 CR France511

ROPER,William Horace Stanley 2Lt dow 11-10-17 3GrenGds p50 CR France16,Lt

RORIE,Thomas Handyside Baxter Capt kia 18-8-16 4BlkW p230 CR France387

RORISON,William Gilbert Don Gurdon Capt kia 9-4-18 3 att10/11HLI p163 MR32

ROSA,Herbert Charles 2Lt kia 31-7-17 RFA 8DAC p35 CR Belgium5

ROSCOE,Arthur.MC.T2Lt dow 5-9-16 8RWKent p142 CR France23

ROSCOE,Ernest 2Lt ded 26-6-15 17WYorks p82 CR Yorks361

ROSCOE,Richard Lang.MC.TCapt dow 4-2-17 22RFus p70 CR France59

ROSE,Alexander Lt kld 6-9-18 7HLI &RAF p271 CR Scot752,2Lt

ROSE,Alexander Daniel.MC.DCM.2Lt kia 31-8-17 17WYorks p82 MR21

ROSE,Algernon Winter.MC.Capt ded 29-10-18 EssYeo &RAF p256&271,2Lt CR Essex256

ROSE,Archibald John Gordon 2Lt kia 26-9-17 12Lond p248 MR30

ROSE,Arthur Hugh Percy Capt kia 23-11-14 3Ess p132 CR Belgium33,2Bn

ROSE,C.V.Lt kia 6-9-18 2KAR p268

ROSE,Eric Dudley Capt kia 30-3-18 22Lond p251 CR Syria2

ROSE,Eric William.MC.T2Lt kia 5-4-18 1/2LancF att1/8Bn p93 MR20

ROSE,Eric Wollaston.MID Capt kia 28-3-18 5Lond Ex SussYeo p246 MR20

ROSE,Frank Stanley D.Bart.Capt kia 26-1-15 10Huss p22 CR Belgium117,26-10-15

ROSE,Frederick Alexander Lt kia 10-8-15 4GordH p241 CR Belgium56,2Lt

ROSE,Geoffrey Craig 2Lt dow 13-2-15 3SfthH att1GordH p165 CR Lond13

ROSE,George 2Lt kia 28-6-18 7 att15RWar p214 CR France20

ROSE,George Douglas 2Lt kia 20-9-17 4GordH C'Coy p242 MR30

ROSE,Harold Emerson Capt dow 7-7-17 RAMC att2CldGds p197 CR Belgium12

ROSE,Herbert John.MID Capt kia 4-6-15 8Manch p237 MR4

ROSE,Hugh Alexander Leslie.DSO.Maj kia 18-4-18 RFA Staff DivHQ p35 CR Belgium11

ROSE,Hugh Price 2Lt kia 11-4-17 2SfthH p165 CR France604

ROSE,John Alexander TCapt kia 9-3-17 17WYorks p82 CR France648

ROSE,John Charles Reginald Lt dow 9-11-14 A&SH p173 CR France284

ROSE,Joseph Harold T2Lt dow 28-12-17 Worc Res att2/8Bn p109 CR Hereford/W110,4-1-18

ROSE,Launcelot St.Vincent.MID Maj kia 27-11-14 RE 55FC p48 CR France525

ROSE,Merton Alfred.MC.2Lt dow 19-9-18 2/5RWar p214 CR France31

ROSE,Osmond Arthur 2Lt ded 12-9-19 5Dors att1/4Wilts p264 CR Egypt2

ROSE,Phillip Vivian TCapt dow 25-4-17 GL 7 O&BLI BdeStaff p191 CR Bucks123

ROSE,Reginald Alfred 2Lt kia 2-8-17 2/7Manch CR Belgium24

ROSE,Reginald Vincent 2Lt kia 1-7-16 1/6RWar B'Coy p214 MR21

ROSE,Ronald Henry Evan TLt kia 28-4-17 6Beds p86 MR20

ROSE,Ronald Hugh Walrond.MID Capt kia 22-10-14 ScotRif p104 MR32

ROSE,Ronald Madoc Tierney.MID CaptTMaj kia 18-9-16 Y&L att2/3KAR p159&202 CR EAfrica39,19-9-16

ROSE,Stewart Alan Lt kia 28-3-18 3NumbF p63 MR20

ROSE,Theodore William Frank 2Lt kia 4-4-18 7RFus p70 MR20,Frederick

ROSE,Thomas Allen.DSO.Capt kia 23-8-14 RScotF p95 CR Belgium206

ROSE,William TLt kia 11-4-17 10HLI p163 MR20

ROSE,William Samuel T2Lt kia 2-12-17 ELancs att2/5Bn p111 MR30,22-12-17

ROSE-CLELAND,Alfred Middleton Blackwood Bingham Lt kia 1-7-16 4RDubF p177 CR France35,1Bn

ROSENBAUM,Laurence Braham Lt dow 17-4-18 3Mon p244 CR Belgium38,1/2Bn

ROSENTHAL,Arthur 2Lt kia 23-11-17 GL &65RFC p13 MR20

ROSEVEAR,Frank Rudolph Capt dow 23-8-18 13Lond p249 CR France103

ROSEVEARE,Francis Bernard Lt dow 9-11-17 IA CpsofGuides Inf att5ScindeInf p282 CR Iraq8

ROSEVEARE,Harold William 2Lt dow 20-9-14 1Wilts p153 MR15

ROSEVEARE,Ronald Chard T2Lt kia 8-8-16 9 att1SomLI p80 CR Belgium73

ROSEVEARE,Ernest William Capt kia 27-4-18 4DCLI p226

ROSEWARNE,Ernest William Capt 27-4-18 4DCLI CR Palestine9

ROSHER,Henry Louis LtCol kia 14-4-15 Cmdg2Dors p124 CR Iraq6

ROSHER,J.R.Capt&QM 19-3-19 23RWFus p13 CR Wales491

ROSIER,James Erle Radcliff Lt dow 20-9-16 A245RFA p208 CR France296,kia

ROSINDALE,Herbert 2Lt kia 11-10-18 1/4EYorks p219 CR France612

ROSKELL,Gertrude Lucinda Nurse ded 31-10-15 VAD att17GH CR Egypt3

ROSKELLY,Wilfred Menadue Lt kia 29-7-17 52RFC p13 MR20

ROSKILLY,Alfred T2Lt kia 3-5-17 7RWSurr p56 MR20

ROSLING,Alan Percy 2Lt kia 4-3-17 1Worc p109 MR21

ROSLING,Charles Holbrook LtACapt dow 22-10-18 3 att7DCLI p115 CR France398

ROSS,A.D.AssSurg 5-6-21 IMS MR66

ROSS,Alaistair 2Lt kldacc 17-1-16 RFC p3 CR Scot280

ROSS,Alexander Aitkin LtCol ded 24-11-15 RAMC 3FA p253 CR Scot244

ROSS,Andrew Beaconsfield TLt kia 6-8-17 RAMC att2RIrRif p197 CR Belgium29

ROSS,Archibald Seymour 2Lt kia 9-5-15 1CamH p168 MR22

ROSS,Arthur Claude 2Lt dow 6-12-17 RScotsF att10RFC p13&95 CR Belgium11

ROSS,Arthur J.Capt kia 16-8-17 5 att1RIrRif p170 MR30

ROSS,Arthur Justin.DSO&Bar.Maj kldacc 2-8-17 RE &RFC p13&48 CR Lond4

ROSS,Cecil Goodall.MC.2Lt kia 23-4-17 3RScots att45TMB p54 MR20

ROSS,Claude Murray 2Lt kia 10-8-17 45RFC p13 MR20
ROSS,Colin 2Lt dow 25-10-18 7 att2A&SH p243 CR France40
ROSS,David.DSO.MC.LtACapt kia 6-11-18 2A&SH p173 CR France521
ROSS,David George 2Lt kia 5-9-15 3Worc p109
ROSS,D.E.2Lt 20-9-18 3Worc CR France632
ROSS,Donald TLt kia 13-11-16 2HLI B'Coy p163 CR France221,13/15-11-16
ROSS,Donald Neil Campbell 2Lt dow 30-11-17 D46RFA p35 CR Belgium18
ROSS,Donald Ord 2Lt kia 11-4-17 6CamH Ex NumbF p168 MR20
ROSS,Douglas Nicol.MM.Lt 17-2-18 BrColumbia &RAF MR20
ROSS,Douglas Stuart Lt kia 1-7-16 Lincs p75 CR France393
ROSS,Douglas William Robertson T2Lt kia 11-1-18 45RFC p17 CR Italy9
ROSS,Edric Crawford Ogilvie Maj AccGunwound 23-4-17 IA 44MerivaraInf p282 CR Iraq6
ROSS,Edward TLt dow 7-10-17 22Manch p156 CR France139
ROSS,Evan Nicholas TLt kia 27-6-18 2BlkW p129 CR Palestine9
ROSS,Findlay McFadyen.MC.Lt kia 1-8-18 1/9RScots p212 CR France524
ROSS,Fleetwood George Campbell Maj kia 2-11-14 IA 2/2GurkhaRif att34SikhPnrs p282 CR France1896
ROSS,Frederic Gordon T2Lt kia 1-7-16 20Manch p156 CR France397,Lt
ROSS,Geoffrey Henry 2Lt ded 18-10-18 Ex 7SomLI p263 CR Lond7,Lt
ROSS,George Augustus Bellair Lt kia 1-6-18 6Lpool attRAF p215&258 CR France1693
ROSS,George Alexander Sinclair Capt kia 28-6-15 4RScots p211 MR4
ROSS,George Duncan 2Lt kia 9-4-17 3GordH att8BlkW p167 CR France729
ROSS,George Harry Thornton 2Lt kia 9-8-16 13Ess p132 CR France402
ROSS,George James T2Lt kld 30-1-18 6/7RScotF p95 CR France57
ROSS,George Munro TLt kia 1-7-16 ACycCps attNumbF p181 MR21
ROSS,George W.2Lt ded 2-3-19 RE p262 CR Canada256
ROSS,Gwilliam Emanuel Henry T2Lt kia 3-7-16 8Glouc p107 MR21
ROSS,Harold 2Lt dow PoW 8-4-18 5LancF p221 CR France716
ROSS,H.E.Clunies Lt ded 27-9-18 2KAR p268 CR Sussex30,Capt See CLUNIES ROSS
ROSS,Hugh Alexander.DSO.MajALtCol dow 27-10-18 2GordH p167 CR Italy9
ROSS,James Andrew Lt kia 26-7-16 4SfthH p241 MR21
ROSS,James Graham T2Lt kia 30-12-17 SfthH att7Bn p165 CR France439
ROSS,James Hamilton 2Lt dow 19-4-17 5RScotF att155MGC p187&222 CR Palestine2
ROSS,James Hector 2Lt kia 23-4-17 8SfthH p165 CR France536
ROSS,James Kenneth T2Lt ded 9-4-17 GL &24RFC p13 CR France403,FltLt
ROSS,James Wilson TLt kld 26-3-18 GL &RFC p17 CR Scot249
ROSS,John Alexander 2Lt kia 26-10-15 17Lond p250 CR France219
ROSS,John Alexander T2Lt kia 13-8-16 RE 178TC p48 CR France453
ROSS,John Alexander T2Lt kia 31-8-18 10HLI p163 CR Belgium115
ROSS,John Edgar(Ian) Capt dow 25-4-16 4Lpool p72 CR France80
ROSS,John McKenzie 2Lt 12-4-17 2SAfrInf MR20
ROSS,Kenneth 2Lt kia 20-6-16 4RIrRif p170 MR29,25-9-15
ROSS,Kenneth Cameron 2Lt kia 11-3-18 7N&D p233 CR France614
ROSS,Kenneth McAlpine TCapt dow 17-9-18 RAMC att1/5HLI p197 CR France686
ROSS,Lawrence George T2Lt dow 30-5-17 7DragGds p21 CR France446
ROSS,Melbourne 2Lt kia 25-9-15 4 att2RIrRif p170 MR29
ROSS,N.M.Maj 5-1-20 18RScots CR Scot1
ROSS,Norman Leslie TCapt dow 15-4-18 8SLancs p126 CR Belgium38,2Bn
ROSS,Peter TCapt kia 1-7-16 16RScots p54 MR21
ROSS,Peter Cunningham T2Lt dow 26-6-17 GL &RFC p13 CR France113
ROSS,Ralph Morison Forbes 2Lt kia 20-2-15 RLancs p59
ROSS,Raymond Glenara Lt kia 4-4-18 RFA p208 MR27
ROSS,Richard(Dickon).MC.2Lt kia 25-9-16 1Dev p77 CR France374
ROSS,Robert.MC.Capt dow 18-4-17 1/7GordH p242 CR France95
ROSS,Robert Simmie T2Lt kia 3-9-16 9 att2KOSB p102 CR France402
ROSS,Robert Stewart T2Lt dow 24-9-17 9ScotRif p104 CR Belgium18
ROSS,Robert Thomas 2Lt kia 29-9-18 5RScotF p222 CR France262
ROSS,Robert Workman SchmasterCl3 11-12-18 Cps of Army Schmasters CR Devon86
ROSS,Ronald Campbell 2Lt kia ?-9-14 2RScots p54 CR France658,26-8-14
ROSS,Ronald Maynard 2Lt kia 4-3-17 1Worc p109 CR France439
ROSS,Simon Fraser Lt kia 23-4-17 4GordH p241 CR France545
ROSS,Thomas Stewart 2Lt dow 13-11-18 3CamH p168 CR France441,1Bn
ROSS,Walter Urquhart TCapt dow 22-2-16 8RWKent p142 CR Belgium11
ROSS,William 2Lt kia 12-4-18 9HLI p241 MR32
ROSS,William Munro Lt kia 11-3-15 2GordH p167 MR22
ROSS,William Samuel Baird 2Lt kia 21-3-18 15RIrRif p170 MR27

ROSS,William Stuart TLt kia 23-7-17 1BordR p118 CR Belgium92,Capt 6Bn
ROSS,Willie LtACapt kia 16-8-17 SWBord p100 CR Belgium106
ROSS-JENKINS,Maurice 2Lt kia 16-6-18 Glouc &RAF p107
ROSS-TAYLOR,Ian Henry Munro T2Lt kia 27-9-16 7Beds p86 MR21
ROSS-THOMPSON,Alexander.MID Lt kia 30-11-14 2RScotF p95 MR29
ROSSE,Martin 2Lt kia 22-2-17 IARO att53Sikhs p282 CR Iraq5
ROSSE,William Edward.Earl.Maj dow 10-6-18 IrGds p53 CR Eire480
ROSSER,Arthur T2Lt kia 10-7-16 14WelshR p127 MR21
ROSSINGTON,Arthur 2Lt kia 13-9-18 6WRid p227 CR France530
ROSSITER,Philip 2Lt kld 19-1-15 RBerks att2RWSurr p140 CR France924
ROSTERN,Joseph Norman Lt kia 26-3-18 2/7Manch p237 CR France511,28-3-18
ROSTRON,George T2Lt kia 21-3-18 59MGC p185 MR20
ROTCHELL,William SubEngr 22-10-18 GoutWatWks &RE MR65
ROTHBAND,Jacob Eustace TCapt kia 19-7-16 23Manch p156 CR France453,Jack
ROTHE,Sidney Ernest Orme 2Lt kia 13-11-16 15 att17Mddx D'Coy p148 MR21
ROTHERAM,Walter Sutton.MID 2Lt kia 29-9-17 A83RFA p35 MR30
ROTHON,Charles Francis T2Lt kia 1-7-16 1Dors p124 MR21
ROTHWELL,Henry.MM.T2Lt kia 2-12-17 14MGC p185 CR Belgium23
ROTHWELL,Reginald Fleetwood 2Lt kia 31-8-18 22 att8Lond p251 CR France624
ROTHWELL,Sidney 2Lt kia 7-1-16 1/5EKent p213 CR Iraq5,Sydney
ROTTMAN,Richard Charles Lt kia 24-4-15 3 att2ESurr p113 CR Belgium167
ROUGHSEDGE,William Lt kia 25-9-17 8Mddx p236 CR Belgium93
ROUGHT,C.G.Lt 31-1-19 RWSurr CR Surrey96
ROUGHTON,Thomas Hende.MC.LtACapt dow 24-3-18 4 att2LancF p93 CR Belgium22,1Bn
ROUILLARD,Charles Louis Amedee Lt kia 18-12-16 IARO att32Lancers p282 MR38
ROUND,Aunol Francis Hay Lt dow 5-9-14 2Ess p132 CR Essex285
ROUND,Edward T2Lt kia 21-4-17 4Worc p109 CR France531
ROUND,Harold Cecil.DSO.MC.TLtACapt kia 24-8-18 6 att9RB p180 MR30
ROUND,James Murray.MC.Capt kia 13-11-16 13Ess p132&259 CR France1890
ROUND,William George.MC.TLt kia 1-5-18 3Worc p109 CR Belgium11
ROUND,William Haldane Capt kia 1-7-16 7N&D p233 CR France281
ROUNSEFELL,Eric de Wolf.MC.2Lt kia 3-9-18 Leinst p175 CR Belgium170
ROUQUETTE,Douglas George 2Lt kia 26-9-17 GL &RFC p13 MR20
ROUQUETTE,John Hector 2Lt kia 17-7-16 1RWSurr p56 MR21,16-7-16
ROUS,Thomas.MID 2Lt dow 22-3-18 D296RFA p35 CR France40
ROUSE,Albert Charles.MID Lt dow 20-3-16 Worc attRE 32Sigs p109 CR France197
ROUSE,Alexander Ritchie Lt dow 31-8-18 C315RFA p208 CR France214,kia
ROUSE-BOUGHTON-KNIGHT,Thomas Andrew Greville 2Lt dow 18-10-16 1RB p180 CR France630,Lt kia
ROUSELL,William Stephen 2Lt kia 8-8-18 3 att7RSuss p119 CR France247,Lt
ROUT,William Owen Nelson TLt kia 25-9-15 10HLI p163 CR France114
ROUTH,John Cyril Capt kia 6-5-15 2Ches p96 MR29
ROUTLEDGE,Arthur Richard.MIDx2 Capt ded 27-6-18 RAVC p199&271 CR Lincs183
ROUTLEDGE,Calvert Capt ded 22-5-16 LNLancs & RDC p271 CR Surrey96
ROUTLEDGE,John T2Lt kia 16-4-17 1KOSB p102 MR20
ROUTLEDGE,John Frederick TLt kia 23-9-17 1NumbF p63 MR30
ROUTLEDGE,Joseph.MM.T2Lt kia 14-9-17 1/2 att15LancF p93 CR Belgium24
ROUTLEDGE,Phillip Charles Lytton LtCol kia 17-5-15 2SStaffs p123 MR22
ROUTLEY,Ernest George.MC.T2Lt kia 7-10-16 6EKent p58 MR21
ROUX,Frank T2Lt ded 26-4-17 RFC p13 CR France924
ROW,Arthur Leslie.MM.2Lt kia 5-6-18 1RBerks p140 CR France120
ROW,Harry Akers 2Lt kia 11-3-15 4Suff p217 CR France705
ROW,John Eric T2Lt kia 29-10-16 8Suff p79 MR21
ROW,Leslie Joseph T2Lt kia 4-6-16 10Norf p74 MR20
ROW,William Burnett T2Lt dow PoW 15-4-18 WYorks att1/5Bn p82 CR France285,14-4-18
ROWAN,John Leck Lt kia 12-7-15 5A&SH p243 MR4
ROWAN,Robert Lt kld 22-8-18 1/2ScotHorse attImpCamelCps p205 CR Palestine9
ROWAN-ROBINSON,William James Maj kia 12-5-15 2KSLI p145 erased from MR29 CR Belgium453
ROWAT,Maurice Alexander TLt kia 12-2-18 66RFC p17 CR Italy48,2Lt
ROWAT,Robert 2Lt kia 16-9-17 GL &8RFC p13 CR France214,Robin
ROWAT,Thomas Finlayson 2Lt 27-11-20 5DragGds CR Scot685
ROWATT,David T2Lt kia 1-7-16 A10RFA p35 CR France630
ROWBOTHAM,Howard Leeson Lt kia 30-11-17 61MGC Inf p185 MR17
ROWBOTHAM,John Edwin.MC.Maj kia 26-3-18 2/7Manch p237 CR France511

ROWBOTTOM,Joseph Arnold 2Lt kia 24-9-17 2/6Manch p237 CR Belgium173
ROWCROFT,E.C.DSO.Maj 27-7-16 IA GS MR65
ROWDEN,Cuthbert Roger.MC.Maj kld 20-4-18 5Worc &78RAF p109 CR Sussex114
ROWDEN,Edmund Percival Lt kia 6-9-17 RE p210 CR France219
ROWDEN,Reginald Colin George TLt kia 30-11-17 RFC p13 CR France446
ROWDON,Alfred William Lt 10-5-18 80RAF MR20
ROWE,Arthur Robert Reginald.DCM.T2Lt kia 7-2-17 17N&D p134 CR Belgium4
ROWE,Benjamin Franklin kia 1-6-17 RFus &RFC p13&70 MR20
ROWE,E.F.Maj 14-4-18 1GarBnSuff CR Lond8
ROWE,Edwin Vivian T2Lt kia 1-9-18 13WelshR p127 MR16
ROWE,Gilbert James Burbery T2Lt dow 17-4-18 5RBerks p140 CR France65
ROWE,Harold Charles 2Lt kia 19-7-17 298RFA p209 CR Belgium131
ROWE,Harvey Wilfrid Warwick.MC.TLtACapt kia 20-8-17 10Ches p96 CR Belgium15
ROWE,Henry Price Capt ded 6-11-18 RE p256 CR Devon47
ROWE,Percy Trevelyan Capt dow 30-11-17 B306RFA p207 CR France1498
ROWE,Philip Henry 2Lt dow 17-9-16 7Mddx p235 MR20 &CR France1890
ROWE,Robert Ronald Lt 3-5-18 73RAF MR20
ROWE,Stafford Gordon Garnet Godfrey Thomas 2Lt kia 10-11-17 3 att6Dors p124 CR Belgium23
ROWE,Thomas 2Lt kia 23-5-16 5Lpool p215 CR France927
ROWED,Charles Henry Lt kia 8-9-16 1/5SLancs p230 MR21,9-9-16
ROWELL,T.MC.2Lt ded 20-5-18 RBerks &RAF p140 CR Nhampt79
ROWELL,William Cecil Capt ded 22-5-19 LNLancs &RAF p136
ROWLAND,Cecil Fred 2Lt kia 21-3-18 RGA 321SB p41 CR France581
ROWLAND,Cyril William.MC.Capt kia 23-8-18 1Lond p245 CR France593,1/4Bn
ROWLAND,John Walter Bruce 2Lt kia 1-11-18 175A D175RFA p35 CR France1257
ROWLAND,Maurice 2Lt kld 4-10-17 YLI att10Bn p143 CR Belgium112
ROWLAND,Rowland Evan Basil 2Lt kia 27-7-16 16RWar p65 MR21
ROWLAND,Stanley Jackson Lt kia 2-11-17 3RWFus att1/8ScotRif p99 CR Palestine8
ROWLAND,Sydney Domville TMaj ded 6-3-17 RAMC att26GenH p197 CR France40
ROWLAND,William Charles Roche TLt kia 4-11-18 9WRid p116 CR France1081
ROWLAND,William Henry 2Lt ded 22-2-19 RWFus att26Bn p99 CR France1359,6Lpool att165TMB
ROWLAND,William Lesingham Lt ded 15-8-19 123ChineseLabCps p266 CR France446
ROWLAND,William Ronald 2Lt kia 1-6-17 17Lond p250 MR29
ROWLANDS,Arthur William TLt kld 15-8-17 RFC p13 CR Lancs2 Ex 10Lpool &RASC
ROWLANDS,Charles William.MSM.T2Lt kia 26-9-17 10RWFus p99 MR30
ROWLANDS,Franklyn Theodore Rowland 2Lt kia 21-11-17 3 att2SWBord p100 CR France911
ROWLANDS,Helena May Nurse ded 10-5-19 TFNS CR Wales568
ROWLANDSON,Thomas Sowerby.MC.Capt kia 15-9-16 4Yorks p220 CR France515
ROWLES,Stanley Walter TLt dow 13-12-17 RASC att10RFC p13&193 CR Belgium18
ROWLETT,George Thomas 2Lt kia 30-7-16 RGA 137HB p41 CR France515
ROWLEY,Albert George T2Lt kia 26-4-18 DLI p161 CR France144
ROWLEY,Charles Edgar T2Lt kld 19-1-18 RE &RFC p17 CR Essex16,Lt
ROWLEY,Charles Pelham Maj kld 29-10-16 RGA p41 CR Hamps60
ROWLEY,Charles Ronald T2Lt kia 10-7-16 9 att1LancF p93 MR21
ROWLEY,Dalbiac Thomas Cotton Capt dow 2-7-16 2 att4Mddx p148 CR France44
ROWLEY,George Cecil.Hon.2Lt kia 17-2-17 5 att1KRRC p151 CR France314
ROWLEY,Gerald.MC&2Bars.Capt dow 15-10-18 6Ches p222 CR France25
ROWLEY,Harold George Lt ded 17-3-16 RE 61FC p48 CR France1182
ROWLEY,Hugh Travers TLt kia 1-7-16 9 att2RBerks p140 MR21,Capt
ROWLEY,John LtTLtCol ded 20-12-16 RFA p271 CR Surrey38
ROWLEY,John 2Lt kia 23-12-17 2Manch p156 CR Belgium126
ROWLEY,John Thomas Lt ded 15-2-21 1ARO attLabCps p282 MR67,16-2-21
ROWLEY,Joseph 2Lt kia 1-7-16 1RLancs p59 MR21
ROWLEY,Joseph Albert T2Lt kia 26-10-18 Ess att10Bn p132 CR France521
ROWLEY,Joshua Robert Capt kia 2-11-17 HLI att1/5Suff p164 CR Palestine8
ROWLEY,Newton T2Lt kia 10-7-16 8Yorks p91 CR France515
ROWLEY,Reginald Frederick Lt kia 21-3-18 A179RFA p35 CR France1061,462Bty
ROWLEY,Walter Austin 2Lt kia 6-7-17 3 att8Leic p88 MR20
ROWLEY-CONWY,Geoffrey Seymour Maj kia 10-8-15 6LNLancs p136 MR4
ROWNTREE,Lawrence Edmund 2Lt kia 25-11-17 A26RFA p35 CR Belgium10

ROWSE,Richard Sidney 2Lt ded 2-9-15 2/5DCLI p227 CR Cornwall109
ROWSELL,Herbert Greaves TCapt kia 3-9-16 14Hamps p121 CR France1890
ROWSON,Stanley 2Lt kia 29-9-16 11LancF p93 MR21
ROWSON,Tom Hollingworth 2Lt kia 15-9-16 19Lond p251 CR France390
ROXBROUGH,William Henry.MC.T2Lt dow 13-4-18 11Suff p79 CR Belgium11,Lt
ROXBURGH,Alan Cameron Lt dow 28-11-17 NottsYeo attRFC p19&205 CR Palestine9
ROXBURGH,George Archibald Capt ded 25-2-20 IA 38CentIndHorse p282 MR67
ROXBURGH,John Capt kia 26-9-15 6RScotF p95 MR19
ROXBURGH,John Hewitt.MC.TMaj kia 2-10-18 MGC RN DivBn p185 CR France530
ROXBURGH,John Wood Lt kia 19-4-17 1/4RScotF p222 CR Palestine8
ROXBURGH,William Fletcher Lt kia 23-3-18 7HLI p240 MR20
ROY,David Charles 2Lt 25-8-18 49RAF MR20
ROY,James Ferrie 2Lt kia 30-7-16 6BlkW p231 MR21
ROY,John James 2Lt kld 13-3-18 7Worc p226 CR France398
ROY,Kenneth James.MID Capt kia 24-8-15 4Mddx p148 CR Belgium242 23-8-14
ROYAL-DAWSON,Oswald Sydney TCapt dow 25-8-17 5 O&BLI p130 CR Belgium11,Sidney
ROYCE,David Costa Lt kia 7-1-16 2Leic p88 MR38
ROYCE,Percival Francis 2Lt kia 10-9-18 2Lond p245 MR16
ROYDEN,Thomas Utting T2Lt kia 14-11-16 19 att1KRRC p151 MR21
ROYDS,John Ilted Lt kia 22-3-18 28Lond p252 MR20
ROYDS,Thomas Alington 2Lt kld 20-4-18 GL &59RAF p191 CR France76
ROYER,Harold Ernest T2Lt kia 27-9-18 4RFus p70 CR France358
ROYLANCE COURT,W.H Capt kia 24-5-15 9Lancers CR Belgium4
ROYLE,Arthur Clegg Fanshawe Lt dow 27-9-14 1NStaffs p157 CR France1110
ROYLE,Dennis Carlton.MC.TCapt kia 21-8-18 4RFus p70 CR France214
ROYLE,Frederick William TCapt dow 8-7-16 19Manch p156 MR21
ROYLE,John Bedward TMaj kia 15-1-17 7SWBord p100 CR Greece6
ROYLE,William 2Lt kia 5-7-16 5YLI p235 MR21
ROYLEY,Harry 2Lt kia 16-9-16 15DLI p161 MR21
ROYLEY,Joseph Holt 2Lt kia 25-4-18 WYorks att1/5Bn p82 MR30
ROYSTON,Basil Drage 2Lt dow 2-10-16 2/1RGA p209 CR France297
ROYSTON-PIGOTT,George Arthur.DSO.TLtCol kia 3-7-16 Nhampt att10Worc p138 CR France393
ROZELAAR,Samuel Louis TLt drd 10-10-18 RBerks att2Bn p140
RUANE,John Patrick T2Lt kia 2-11-17 9RWar att1/5Norf p65 CR Palestine8
RUBY,Joseph Bennett 2Lt kld 4-9-18 RGA attBase Depot Havre p41 CR France1571
RUCK,John Arthur T2Lt kld 25-5-16 GL &RFC p3&191,ded CR Kent232
RUCK,John Egerton TMaj kia 8-8-15 7Glouc p107 MR4
RUCK,Laurence Humphrey Lt kia 14-3-15 1Worc p109 MR22,11-3-15
RUCK-KEENE,Benjamin Corne Chap4Cl kia 26-9-17 RAChDept att8EYorks p199 CR Belgium84
RUCK-KEENE,Ralph Edgar TLt kld 16-1-16 9RWelshF p99 CR France631,kia
RUDALL,Bertram Allen 2Lt kia 17-7-17 4RWKent p234 CR France421
RUDD,Arnold.MID T2Lt kia 27-3-18 RE 63FC p48 MR27
RUDD,Kenneth Sutherland TCapt kia 10-10-18 10WYorks p82 CR France658
RUDD,William Ferris Capt kia 13-11-16 12RWFus p99 CR France742
RUDDIMAN,William 2Lt kia 13-11-16 3RScots p54 CR France742
RUDDLE,Reginald.MC.T2Lt kia 24-7-18 12RB p180 CR France161,Lt 3Bn
RUDDOCK,Edgar Herbert Montague Capt kia 22-6-15 13Worc p109 MR4
RUDDOCK,Joseph John Lt dow 5-6-18 1/4RLancs att55DivHQ p213 CR France10
RUDDOCK,R.B.2Lt 6-4-18 5NumbF att4Beds MR27
RUDDOCK,Richard Fenwick 2Lt kia 18-6-16 6NumbF p214 CR Belgium17
RUDDOCK,Thomas Lt kia 7-8-18 4EKent p212 France116
RUDDY,Thomas Lt ded 1-7-16 1Manch p156 CR Iraq5
RUDDY,William 2Lt kia 26-10-17 4NumbF p213 MR30
RUDELL,Emil Arthur 2Lt dow 27-9-18 3 att16RWar p65 CR France905
RUDGE,Reginald Theodore T2Lt kia 5-11-16 7Yorks p91 MR21
RUDKIN,George Henry.MC.T2Lt ded 28-10-18 21MGC p185&257 CR Lincs34
RUDMAN,Harold Ewart Capt kia 19-7-16 6Glouc D Coy p225 MR19
RUEGG,Kenneth Stanes 2Lt kia 20-9-14 2N&D p134 MR15
RUFF,Samuel 2Lt kia 17-11-16 1/7WRid p228 CR France281
RUFUS,Thomas.MC.TCapt kia 14-4-18 11LancF A'Coy p93 MR32
RULE,John Lindon 2Lt dow 2-11-16 31AustInf CR France432
RUMBALL,George Thomas Sydney.MC.T2Lt kia 13-4-18 RFus att2Bn p70 CR France193
RUMBELOW,Albert 2Lt kia 16-4-18 5SWBord p100 MR30
RUMBOLD,Christian Franklyn Hales Maj kia 22-11-15 4ESurr att2Norf p113 MR38

RUMILLY,Alfred Henry Robinson 2Lt dow 28-6-17 7Worc p226 CR France795,kldacc
RUMSBY,Richard William.MC.Lt dow 9-5-18 9RSuss attRAF p119 CR France792
RUMSEY,Arthur Charles 2Lt kia 24-9-16 9Lond p248 CR France394
RUMSEY,Charles Gordon Lt 25-5-15 3SWBord att 1WelchR MR29
RUNCIMAN,Edmund Inglis 2LtTLt kia 22-10-15 9KRRC p151 CR Belgium44
RUNCIMAN,Keith Stewart T2Lt kia 24-4-17 14A&SH p173 CR France379
RUNDALL,Arthur Montagu Capt kia 20-12-14 IA 1/4GurkhaRif p282 CR France279
RUNDALL,Lionel Bickersteth Lt kia 19-12-14 IA 1/1GurkhaRif p282 MR28
RUNDELL,Leslie Eric.MC&Bar.Capt dow 10-12-17 7Lond p247 CR France755
RUNDELL,Reginald Charles T2LtACapt kia 3-5-17 GL att 10TMB p191 CR France
RUNDLE,Cubitt Noel 2Lt kia 19-5-15 2SWBord p100 CR Gallipoli6,19-6-15
RUNDLE,Horace Liberty 2Lt kia 20-7-16 8Dev p77 CR France432
RUNDLE,James Robson 2Lt kia 20-11-17 4RLancs p213 CR France364
RUNDLE,Raymond Wallis Lt kia 9-5-15 1N&D attRWar p134 CR France525
RUNDLE,Stanley TLt dow PoW 30-4-18 RASC p193 CR B201 ?
RUNGE,Oscar Julius Tolme.MC.Lt kia 15-10-16 Mddx att 18MGC Inf p148&185 MR21
RUNNELS-MOSS,Cyril Gower Vincent 2Lt ded 5-12-17 GL &RFC p13 MR20
RUNNELS-MOSS,Eric Cross Arnold 2Lt ded PoW 9-7-18 2RFA p35 CR Germany3
RUPP,Frederick Albert Lt kia 1-7-16 6 att 11BordR p118 MR21
RUSACK,Louis Amrhein TLt kia 4-7-16 7BordR p118 CR France397
RUSBRIDGE,Robert Thomas Smith TLt ded 11-11-18 RASC 55DivSupplyCol p193 CR Kent83,650MT Coy
RUSE,Edward Wallace Lt kld 31-12-15 RE 128FC p48 CR France275
RUSH,Clement Ward 2Lt kia 3-9-16 5WRid p227 MR21
RUSH,Ernest William 2Lt kia 28-4-17 7Suff p79 CR France312
RUSHBROOK,Sydney Herbert 2Lt kia 6-7-15 Norf attCycCps p74 MR29
RUSHBROOKE,Bartle Davers Capt kia 25-5-15 3 att2Suff p79 MR29
RUSHBROOKE,William Ewart 2Lt kia 26-8-17 7RB p180 CR Belgium125
RUSHBY,Frank Capt ded 26-2-15 RFA p35 CR Berks121
RUSHMORE,Ernest Reginald 2Lt kia 6-9-17 4 att 11LancF p93 MR30
RUSHTON,Arthur 2Lt kia 27-7-18 8RLancs p59 CR France33
RUSHTON,Cecil George Capt kia 16-5-18 GL &RAF p191
RUSHTON,Edward Birley Leigh.MID Capt kia 25-9-16 2Nhampt p138 CR France423,Lever
RUSHTON,Frank Gregson T2Lt kia 1-7-16 GL 2Wilts att53TMB p191 CR France513
RUSHTON,Frederick Hornby Lever.MC.MID Lt kia 15-9-14 2RIrReg p89 MR15
RUSHTON,William Henry LtACapt kia 25-9-16 1Lincs D'Coy p75 CR France374
RUSHWORTH,Frederick Arthur 2Lt kia 29-9-16 6Yorks p91 MR21
RUSHWORTH,Henry T2Lt kia 11-8-18 18KRRC p151 CR Belgium21
RUSHWORTH,Tom.MID Capt kia 16-9-16 7Lond p247 CR France432
RUSS,S.H.Lt 28-10-20 RASC CR Somerset186
RUSSEL,Arthur Richard Lt kia 25-12-15 3Norf p74 CR Iraq1,2Bn
RUSSEL-RENDLE,Anthony Darley 2Lt kia 10-10-17 9Dev CR Belgium112
RUSSELL,A.M.SNurse 4-10-16 QAIMNS CR Berks86
RUSSELL,Alexander Christopher TCapt kia 10-10-15 11N&D p135 CR France680
RUSSELL,Alexander James TLt kia 15-8-15 7RDubF p177 MR4
RUSSELL,Arthur Lt dow 23-7-16 9HLI p240 CR Scot86
RUSSELL,Arthur Charles Lt dow 28-10-18 6RB p180 CR France113
RUSSELL,Arthur Claude Hamilton TCapt ded 27-10-18 RAOC p267 CR Europe51
RUSSELL,Arthur Henry Eric Lt dow 22-3-18 3 att6ConnRgrs p172 CR France987,Capt.
RUSSELL,Bernard.MC.T2Lt kia 25-9-15 RBerks p140&257 MR32 See ABINGER true name
RUSSELL,Charles Lt kia 22-11-17 9EYorks IARO att3/3Gurkhas p84&282 CR Palestine3
RUSSELL,David Leslie Capt dow 23-5-15 8Lond p247 CR France80
RUSSELL,Edward Lt kia 1-7-16 11N&D p135 MR21
RUSSELL,Edward Stanley.MC.Capt kia 6-11-17 1/1Hereford p252 CR Palestine1
RUSSELL,Eleanor AssAdmtr ded 21-2-19 QMAAC p200 CR Leic63
RUSSELL,Ernest 2Lt kia 4-9-18 20DLI p161 MR30
RUSSELL,Francis George T2Lt dow 17-4-18 2EYorks p84 CR Belgium21,1Bn
RUSSELL,Francis Gerald 2Lt kia 28-1-17 RFA &RFC p13&35 CR France744
RUSSELL,Francis Wycliffe.MC.Lt kia 27-8-18 1/16Lond p249 CR France644
RUSSELL,George Launcelot Lighton Capt ded 1-3-18 RE p271 CR Sussex 220,1-3-19
RUSSELL,George Smith T2Lt kia 1-7-16 16RScots p54 MR21
RUSSELL,Glen 2Lt kia 18-3-18 54RFC p17 CR France333
RUSSELL,Guy Campbell Lt ded 21-2-19 16Lancers p261 CR Surrey1,21Bn

RUSSELL,Guy Edward Frank 2Lt kia 14-10-15 4Leic p220 MR19,13-10-15
RUSSELL,Hamish Galbraith 2Lt dow 16-8-15 1/7HLI p240 CR Egypt3,16-7-15
RUSSELL,Harley Raymond Lt kia 13-10-15 att 1Glouc p107 MR19
RUSSELL,Henry TCapt dow 10-6-16 16WYorks p82 CR France5,Harry
RUSSELL,Henry.DCM.2Lt kia 12-7-16 RE 7FC p48 CR Belgium37
RUSSELL,Henry Branfill TLt dow 11-7-16 1Ess p132 CR France169
RUSSELL,Henry Freeman 2Lt kia 6-8-15 4Worc p109 MR4
RUSSELL,Henry Thornbury Fox.MC.Capt kld 18-11-18 6RWFus &RAF p256
RUSSELL,Hubert Leslie 2Lt ded 1-9-19 IA 27LightCav p282 CR Pakistan50A MR43,kldacc
RUSSELL,James.MC.TCapt ded 10-7-17 17HLI p164 CR Scot674
RUSSELL,James Cosmo.DSO.LtCol kia 31-7-17 IA 9HodsonsHorse att6CamH p282 CR Belgium7
RUSSELL,James Forteath Lt kia 2-7-15 IA 2/10GurkhaRif p282 MR4
RUSSELL,James Galloway 2Lt kia 3-5-17 2RScots p54 MR20
RUSSELL,John Maj kia 26-8-15 5RScotsF p222 MR4
RUSSELL,John TLtACapt kia 10-4-17 B76 RFA p35 CR France924,9-4-17
RUSSELL,John 2Lt dow 21-4-17 1/7ScotRif p224 CR Palestine2
RUSSELL,John 2Lt kia 9-8-17 3EKent D'Coy p58 MR29
RUSSELL,John Capt&QM dow 6-10-18 7HLI p240 CR Scot757
RUSSELL,John Fox.VC.MC.Capt kia 6-11-17 RAMC att 1/6RWFus p254 CR Palestine1
RUSSELL,John Guy Harry Stebbing 2Lt dow 29-9-18 RWKent att 10Bn p142 CR Belgium11
RUSSELL,John Hepburn T2Lt kld 12-11-17 GL &40RFC p13 CR Scot674
RUSSELL,John William Binfield TLt kia 7-7-16 9WRid p116 MR21
RUSSELL,Joseph Eric 2Lt kia 23-11-16 7RWSurr p56 CR France646
RUSSELL,Lawrence Dobrée 2Lt dow 2-9-16 7RFC 15Wing p3 CR France833
RUSSELL,Laurence Edward Lt kia 24-8-14 WRid p116 CR Belgium201 Lawrence
RUSSELL,Leonard Maj kia 9-5-15 2ELancs p111 CR France706
RUSSELL,Leonard Cosmo Bolles TCap kia 7-10-16 12RB p180 CR France307
RUSSELL,Leonard William Edward T2Lt ded 14-11-18 8 att2/4Leic p88 CR Germany3
RUSSELL,Lionel William Bowden 2Lt kia 20-9-17 6 att 12ESurr p226 MR30
RUSSELL,Marcus Ralph TLt kia 22-3-18 2RRofCav att8Huss p23 MR27
RUSSELL,Noel John Gilbert 2Lt dow 27-9-18 A26RFA p35 CR France113
RUSSELL,Oswald Bede Plowden.MC.MID Capt kia 3-9-20 IA 10Lancers p282 MR38
RUSSELL,Patrick Alfred 2Lt kia 2-4-17 1LovatScts attRFC p19&204 CR France407
RUSSELL,Peter Currie Stuart Lt dow 19-12-15 5ScotRif attRFC p19&224 CR France285
RUSSELL,Robert Campbell.MID T2Lt dow 31-8-18 7NStaffs p157 CR Asia81
RUSSELL,Robert Ferguson TCapt ded 22-4-17 RAMC 10GH p267 CR France145
RUSSELL,Thomas Capt kia 19-4-16 5ScotRif p224 CR France163
RUSSELL,Thomas T2LtTCapt kia 12-10-16 13A&SH p173 MR21
RUSSELL,Thomas Edward Francis 2Lt kia 3-5-17 2/5Y&L p238 MR20
RUSSELL,Thomas Wallace T2Lt kia 13-11-16 10RDubF p177 CR France220
RUSSELL,Thomas Leopold TLtACapt kia 6-11-17 SL &3/2KAR p202 CR EAfrica33 &CR Tanzania1
RUSSELL,Walter Col ded 4-4-17 RE p48 CR Lond4
RUSSELL,Walter Edward 2LtALt kia 11-5-17 129/42RFA attX29TMB p35 CR Belgium12,13-7-17
RUSSELL,Walter Guthrie 2Lt kia 29-9-16 8DLI p239 MR21,Wallace
RUSSELL,Walter Nicol T2Lt dow 26-8-16 9 att 1RScotF p95 CR France23
RUSSELL,Walter Oswald Lt kia 26-8-18 7NStaffs attDunsterforce p157 MR61,Capt
RUSSELL,Walter Russell Capt kia 21-10-14 Nhampt p138 MR29,23-10-14
RUSSELL,William Capt kia 5-5-15 5RScots p211 MR4
RUSSELL,William Lt kld 3-4-18 RE &RAF p256
RUSSELL,William T2Lt kia 27-9-18 15TankCps p188 CR France530
RUSSELL,William Black Lt kia 19-6-15 14RScots p54 CR Gallipoli6
RUSSELL,William Edward 2LtALt kia 13-7-17 129/42RFA attX29TMB p35 CR France538,12-5-17
RUSSELL,William George Mark Lt ded 8-10-15 4/7Mddx CR Surrey37
RUSSELL-SMITH,Hugh Francis Capt dow 5-7-16 1RB CR France145
RUSTON,Allan Maxwell.MM.2Lt kia 23-4-18 2LancF p93 CR France412
RUSTON,Arthur Cecil Maj kia 2-5-15 8Mddx p235 MR29,26-4-15
RUSTON,Cecil Harold Sowerby 2Lt kia 4-4-18 4 att7EKent p212 MR27,Somerby
RUSTON,Frederick Augustus Lt dow 21-3-18 94RFA p35 CR France987
RUTH,Tom Bertrand T2Lt ded 24-2-17 3BordR p264 CR C'land&W'land17
RUTHERFOORD,David Geoffrey Corry Capt kia 17-4-16 14RFA p35 MR38
RUTHERFOORD,Thomas Corne.MID LtCol ded 18-10-18 IMS att 11CavBde p282 CR Lebanon1

RUTHERFORD,Alfred Fletcher Corrie Capt kia 10-8-15 1 att6BordR p118 MR4,RUTHERFOORD
RUTHERFORD,David Alfred.MC&Bar.Lt kld 1-11-20 7RGA 115SB MR40
RUTHERFORD,George Sparkes 2Lt ded 22-2-19 2BordR p264 CR C'land&W'land17
RUTHERFORD,John Allen TCapt kia 24-8-16 7MGC Inf p185 MR21
RUTHERFORD,Mark T2LtACapt kia 23-7-18 9TankCps p188 CR France987
RUTHERFORD,Norman Edwin T2Lt dow 21-7-16 7RLancs p59 CR France833
RUTHERFORD,R.B.Maj 12-1-21 RAMC CR Scot239
RUTHERFORD,Ralph Baillie TCapt kia 3-7-16 6RWSurr p56 CR France251
RUTHERFORD,Robert Capt kia 15-9-16 9DLI p239 MR21
RUTHERFORD,Robert Witten Glendinning Capt kia 28-6-15 4RScots p211 MR4,Glendenning
RUTHERFORD,Thomas Wood T2Lt kia 22-8-15 6Yorks p91 MR4
RUTHERFORD,William Cecil 2Lt ded 10-3-19 19NumbF p63 CR France134,Lt
RUTHERFORD,William McConnell T2Lt dow 19-4-18 10EYorks p84 CR France64
RUTHVEN,James.MC.Capt kia 9-4-18 4EYorks p256 MR32
RUTHVEN,William Logan Maj kia 3-12-17 1EYorks Cmdg2/6Glouc p84 MR17,2-12-17
RUTLEDGE,John Bedell TCapt kia 1-7-16 7EYorks p84 CR France373
RUTLEDGE,Joseph Ward Lt kia 31-7-17 B103 RFA p35 MR29
RUTLEDGE,Laurence Hugh Nesbitt Capt dedacc 10-1-21 IA 8GurkhaRif attS&T Cps MT p282 MR43
RUTTER,Donald Campbell.MC.Capt kia 7-6-17 RSuss &43RFC p13&119 CR Belgium125
RUTTER,Eustace Frederick.MID Maj kia 13-5-15 1ELancs p111 MR29
RUTTER,Frank Lionel T2Lt kia 14-7-16 2RWSurr p56 MR21
RUTTER,W.R.Capt 27-6-16 UgandaVolRes CR EAfrica123
RUTTLEDGE,John Forrest TCapt kia 1-7-16 2WYorks p82 MR21
RUTTLEDGE,Victor John TCapt ded 3-11-16 RAMC att8MtdBrigFA p197 CR Egypt15
RUTTLEY,Percy Kemp TCapt ded 19-10-18 GL 17WelchR D'Coy p191 CR Wales149
RUXTON,W.H.Lt ded 29-8-18 3RIrReg &RAF p89
RUXTON,William Stewart Mitchell.MC.Lt kia 12-4-18 1BordR p118 MR32
RYALL,Robert William Lt dow 11-10-15 IA 2/8GurkhaRif p282 CR France40
RYAN,Alfred Eric.MC.2LtACapt kia 23-3-18 11RWSurr p56&259 MR20
RYAN,Bliss Wilberforce.MM.Lt kia 20-9-17 CanadaEngrs &RFC CR Belgium18
RYAN,Charles M.J.MC.Lt kia 4-10-18 3RMunstF p176 CR France1495
RYAN,Clement Ignatius Maj kia 8-7-16 Ess att9Bn p132 MR21
RYAN,Donald Whitmore 2Lt kia 9-5-15 Nhampt att2Bn p138 MR32
RYAN,Edward St.John Norwood.MC.TCapt kia 22-10-18 12ESurr p113 CR Belgium140
RYAN,F.D.Lt 18-10-17 SL att3NigR CR EAfrica11 &CR Tanzania1
RYAN,Finley Francis.MC.Capt kia 25-6-17 8Lpool p215 CR France765
RYAN,George Julian.DSO.TLtCol kia 22-1-15 2RMunstF p176 CR France279,23-1-15
RYAN,James T2Lt kld 13-1-18 7Leinst p175 CR France145
RYAN,James Henry Aloysius.MC.LtTCapt kia 25-9-15 1Lpool p72 CR France163
RYAN,John Henry 2Lt dow 2-5-17 57RFC p13 CR France518
RYAN,John Stanley TCapt kia 25-6-16 18KRRC p151 CR Belgium54
RYAN,Martin.MC.TCaptAMaj kia 18-10-17 25RFus p70 CR EAfrica11 &CR Tanzania1
RYAN,Michael Rev ded 1-11-16 RAChDept p199 MR65
RYAN,Patrick Cornelius T2Lt kia 13-10-18 2ELancs p111 CR France777
RYAN,Patrick Joseph 2Lt kia 21-3-18 RWar att6NStaffs p65 MR20
RYAN,Warwick John Norwood 2Lt kia 5-9-16 DorsYeo p202
RYAN-BELL,Hugh Randolph Lt dow 29-8-17 1/8Worc CR Belgium16
RYAN-LEWIS,Wallenstein.MC.Capt dow 25-3-18 RE 284Coy CR France1063
RYCKMAN,Edward Gurney 2Lt kia 4-5-16 7RFC p3 CR France1031
RYCROFT,Henry Frederick Capt kia 7-8-15 3 att2Y&L p159 erased from MR29 CR Belgiu453
RYCROFT,Nelson Wynne T2Lt kia 25-9-15 6Beds p86 MR30
RYCROFT,Robert 2Lt kia 11-10-18 3WRid p116 CR France612
RYDE,John Titcombe 2Lt dow 8-5-17 Beds Res att12Glouc p86 MR20
RYDER,Charles Ernest HonTLt&QM ded 6-11-15 17Lpool p72 CR Wilts115
RYDER,Leonard Charles T2Lt kia 25-4-17 11 att12Worc p109 MR37
RYDER,Reginald Victor T2Lt dow 28-6-17 13Glouc att4RFC p13&107 CR Belgium11
RYDER,Robert Nathaniel Dudley.Hon.Maj kia 30-11-17 8Huss p22 CR France364
RYDER,William Harold Lt dow 6-7-17 YorkHuss attRFC p19&206 CR France44
RYLANDS,Frank 2Lt dow 25-4-17 16Manch p156
RYLANDS,Harold Bertram T2Lt kia 23-11-16 16LancF p93 MR21
RYLANDS,Reginald Victor Capt kia 29-5-15 1/7Manch p237 CR Gallipoli2
RYLE,M.C.Nurse 21-2-15 RussianRedCraoss CR Europe57
RYLEY,Charles Maj ded 4-5-17 RAMC Staff DADMS 40Div p197 CR France446
RYLEY,Donald Arthur George Buchanan Lt kia 11-2-17 NStaffs p157 MR19
RYLEY,Harold Buchanan 2Lt kia 5-9-16 4 att1NStaffs p157 MR21
RYLEY,Harold Buchanan TLt kia 15-12-17 1/5Suff p79 CR Palestine9
RYLEY,Herbert Frank Brownlow Capt kia 2-11-14 att1LNLancs p136 MR29
RYMER,John Henry TCapt kia 7-8-15 11Manch p156 MR4
RYRIE,Arthur TLt kia 10-8-18 6TankCps p188 CR France360

S

SABIME,Gerald TLt kia 22-10-18 N&D att15Hamps p135 CR Belgium408
SABISTON,James Anderson 2Lt kia 22-8-17 4A&SH att7CamH p173 MR30
SACH,Charles Burleigh 2Lt kia 1-7-16 1/13Lond p249 MR21
SACHS,Rudolf Dinges 2Lt kia 20-10-18 1/5ELancs p226 CR France287
SACKVILLE-WEST,Kelvin Frederick.MIDx2 Capt ded 29-6-21 QueensBays CR Kent217
SADD,Philip George TMaj kia 15-9-16 18KRRC p151 MR21 CR France1890
SADLEIR,John Raymond T2Lt ded 26-11-18 MGC p266 CR Lincs61,SADLIER SomLI
SADLER,Charles Edward T2Lt kia 1-7-16 10 att1ELancs p111 MR21
SADLER,Ferrebee 2Lt kia 21-4-17 9DLI attRFC p19&239 MR20
SADLER,Gerald Gloag Capt ded 1-11-14 3DragGds p21 MR29,Gerard
SADLER,Hereward Pattison T2Lt dow 19-7-16 6RBerks p140 CR France513,kia
SADLER,Roland Albert James 2Lt kldacc 23-9-18 RWar &RAF CR Norf24
SADLER,Vyvyan Kendall TCapt kia 17-4-17 RAMC att29RFA p197 CR France97
SADLER,William Douglas 2Lt dow 3-8-17 4ESurr p113 CR Belgium11,9Bn
SADLER,William Edward 2Lt kia 8-5-15 3 att2SLancs p126 CR Belgium132
SADLER,William Harold 2Lt kia 24-8-18 24 att21Lond p252 MR16
SADLIER,Francis Arthur 2Lt kia 14-10-18 2InnskF p105 CR Belgium157
SAFFERY,Leslie Hall 2Lt kia 1-7-16 4RDubF p177 MR21
SAGE,Douglas Michael 2Lt kia 18-12-17 GL &65RFC p13 CR Belgium140
SAGE,Sidney Edward Bush Lt dow 13-9-18 6Glouc p225 CR France686
SAHA,N.N.Lt 7-12-19 IMS CR Lebanon5
SAIDLER,William Tweeddale Lt kia 26-3-18 RGA &RFC p19&209 CR France385
SAILLARD,Phillip 2LtTLt kia 22-8-17 1EYorks attCTankCps p84 CR Belgium16,Philip
SAINES,Charles Edward T2Lt kld 22-10-17 GL &RFC p13 CR Mddx12
SAINSBURY,Charles.MC.TLt dow 7-6-17 1Wilts p153 CR Belgium43
SAINSBURY,Frederick Capt 26-2-19 EAfrLabCps MR46
SAINT,Edward Twelftree.DSO.MID LtCol dow 29-8-18 1Camb p244 CR France119
SAINT,James Harcourt T2Lt kia 4-6-17 RE 428FC p48 CR France905
SAINT,William Bell Lt dow 15-9-16 1/10RScots att70RFC p19&212 CR Frnce446
St.AUBYN,Edward Stuart.Hon.Maj kia 30-12-15 Staff p1 MR41,drd Ex KRRC
St.AUBYN,Francis Joseph TLt kia 10-4-17 7KRRC A'Coy p151 CR France594
St.AUBYN,Morice Julian.MC.TMaj kia 22-3-18 7KRRC p151 MR27
St.AUBYN,Piers Stewart.Hon.2Lt kia 31-10-14 2KRRC p151 MR29
St.CLAIR,Charles Henry Murray.Hon.Capt kia 20-12-14 1SfthH p165 CR France279
St.CLAIR,C.H.D.Maj 31-3-21 RASC DADT CR Asia51
St.GEORGE,Guy Staniforth Wemyss Lt dow 28-4-15 IA 1/1GurkhaRif p282 CR France200
St.GEORGE,Harold Avenel Blight 2Lt kia 15-11-15 1LifeGds p20 CR Belgium134,Howard Bligh 15-11-14
St.GEORGE,Harold Edgar 2Lt kia 13-8-16 6Lpool C'Coy p215 CR France294
St.HILL,Ashton Alexander.DSO.TLtCol kia 27-10-18 1/2WRid att11NumbF p116 CR Italy9
St.HILL,George Herbert.MID LtCol kia 8-7-17 RNDevYeo p203 CR France905
St.JOHN,Esmée Barbara Miss ded 12-10-16 VAD p200 CR France64,B.E.
St.JOHN,Thomas.DCM.2Lt dow 2-7-16 1ELancs att11MGC p185 CR France35
St.JOHN MILDMAY,Bouvene Walter 2Lt kldacc 16-4-18 GL &70RAF CR France169
St.LEGER,Dennis Claude Grant 2Lt mbk 21-3-18 295RFA p256 CR France568,22-3-18
St.LEGER,St.John Richard 2Lt kia 15/17-9-16 2Lond p245 MR21
St.LEGER,William Brett.MC.Lt kia 27-4-18 2ColdGds p51 CR France925
St.QUINTIN,Clifford Jack Lt kia 15-5-17 HAC Inf p206 MR20
St.VINCENT-RYAN,Edmond William LtCol ded 24-8-19 RAMC p256 CR Wales564

SAINTON,Francis Charles.MC.LtACapt kia 18-4-18 2RSuss p119 CR France721
SAKER,Frank Harrison Capt kia 30-10-14 4 att2ConnRgrs p172 MR29
SAKER,Richard Maj kia 25-4-15 4ConnRgrs att5AustralianInfDiv p266
SALAMAN,Euston Abraham 2Lt ded 18-2-16 RFA p209 CR Mddx40
SALAMONSON-SANGSTER,Henry Pryor Saltarn 2Lt mbk 26-9-17 3KOSB att14Hamps p256 MR30
SALATHIEL,Ewart Gladstone T2Lt dow 17-7-16 11SWBord p100 CR Mon83,4Bn
SALBERG,John Beaumont T2Lt ded PoW 30-6-16 12RSuss D'Coy p119 CR France924
SALE,Alexander Gordon Lt 9-3-15 SL att3KAR CR EAfrica12 & CR Tanzania1
SALE,Edward Hanson TCapt kia 25-9-15 10Glouc p107 CR France1723
SALE,Richard Crawford.MID Capt kia 26-3-17 1Hereford p252 MR34
SALE,Richard Lander TLt dow 15-1-18 RHGds p20 CR France446,Lauder
SALES,Norman Lt dow 30-6-18 2YLI &87RAF p143 CR France1525
SALISBURY,Cecil Roland T2Lt kia 7-5-17 14RWar p65 CR France
SALISBURY,Frederick James Lt ded 23-9-19 RE IWT p262 CR Iraq5
SALISBURY,Percy Harold T2Lt kia 27-8-16 10Leic att11Ches p88 CR France246
SALISBURY,Robert Cecil TCapt kia 22-3-18 19Lpool p72 MR27
SALISBURY,Walter Fredk 2Lt dow 30-12-17 28Lond p252 MR21
SALMAN,Clifford T2Lt kia 13-10-15 9 att8RBerks p140 MR19
SALMON,Andrew Frank 2Lt kld 16-8-17 4 O&BLI p231 MR30
SALMON,Bernard Bryant.MC.T2Lt kia 9-7-16 25 att8Manch p156 MR21
SALMON,Cecil Gordon Lt kia 14-6-15 3 att2N&D p135 CR Belgium44
SALMON,Claude Garrett Capt kia 9-5-15 3 att2ScotRif 104 CR France525
SALMON,Gilbert Henry Capt 28-8-20 1/6Dev CR Iraq8
SALMON,J.F.Maj 4-12-19 IA MiscList MilPrison CR Hamps64
SALMON,Reginald Thomas T2Lt kia 12-5-17 7EYorks p84 MR20
SALMON,Stanley Francis T2Lt kia 19-7-17 9WelshR p127 CR Belgium111
SALMON,Wilfred Graham 2Lt kia 7-7-17 RFC p13 CR Kent125,Lt
SALMONS,Harry T2Lt dow PoW 1-4-18 1WYorks p82 CR France1483
SALOMONS,David Reginald Herman Philip Capt drd 28-10-15 RE p210 MR4
SALT,Thomas Frederick Cyril Lt 3-4-15 11SWBord CR France284
SALT,Walter Petit C.TCapt kia 24-10-18 2LancF p93 MR21
SALTER,Albert Leonard 2Lt kia 21-3-18 RWar att2/6NStaffs p65 MR20
SALTER,Donald Sowerby 2Lt dow 22-3-18 RGA 126SB p41 CR France512
SALTER,Francis Henry T2Lt kia 21-10-16 11RSuss p119 CR France383
SALTER,Geoffrey Charles Tayler.MC.2Lt kia 18-3-16 EYorks &RFC p261&263 MR20,Lt 28-5-18 RAF
SALTER,Henry Albert 2Lt kia 7-6-17 7Lond p247 CR Belgium29
SALTER,John Henry Clavell 2Lt kia 9-4-18 att1/5Lancs p59 MR19
SALTER,John Henry Raymond T2Lt kia 13-10-17 GL &54RFC p13 CR Belgium125
SALTER,Reginald Charles Falconer LtTCapt kia 8-6-15 2SLancs p126 erased from MR29 CR Belgium453
SALTER,Robert Capt kia 26-8-16 7WYorks p218 CR France293
SALTER,William TCapt kia 9-8-16 17Mddx p148 MR21
SALTMARSH,John Henry Thomas T2Lt dow 30-12-17 3Ches att2/22Lond p96 CR Palestine3
SALTMARSHE,Oliver Edwin TLt kia 1-7-16 7RWSurr p56 CR France397
SALTREN-WILLETT,Archibald John.MID LtCol kia 11-10-17 RGA p41 CR Belgium10
SALUSBURY,Norman Horace Pemberton T2Lt kia 1-12-15 10BordR att1/7HLI p118 CR Gallipoli3
SALUSBURY-JONES,Ivor Cynric Lt dow 21-9-16 5YLI CR France74
SALVESEN,Edward Maxwell 2Lt kia 25-4-15 4RDubF p177 MR29
SALVESEN,Frederick Malcolm Ross Capt kia 22-12-19 IA 82Punjabis p282 MR43,21-12-19
SALVESON,Cristian Raymond Lt ded 22-5-15 7RScots attRFC p19&211,kld CR Scot249,SALVESEN
SALVESON,Eric Thomas Somervell 2Lt kia 23-4-17 7RScots p211 CR France421,SALVESEN
SAMARSINHA,Leonard Phillip Capt 1-4-20 IA IMS CR India97A
SAMES,Gilbert Fielding T2Lt dow 25-10-18 10TankCps p188 CR France441,24-10-18
SAMES,William Fielding Lt dow 31-5-15 4ELancs p226 MR4
SAMMUT,Herbert Joseph Maj kia 2-5-15 Ess p132 MR4
SAMPSON,Amyas Terrell Lt 8-8-18 3RAF MR20
SAMPSON,Arthur Henry Winn 2Lt kia 1-7-16 4Mddx p148 MR20
SAMPSON,Bertram George T2Lt kia 12-2-17 11RFus p70 CR France251
SAMPSON,Carl Alexander Capt kia 9-8-18 25Lond p252 CR France1170
SAMPSON,Henry Charles DepCommsy&Capt ded 26-12-15 IA S&TCps p282 CR France85
SAMPSON,Horace William 2Lt kia 28-5-18 5Lond p246 CR France41

SAMPSON,Hugh Delaine T2Lt dow 2-9-17 RASC p193 CR Belgium11,Delane
SAMPSON,Richard Harry TLt ded 29-10-18 GL WelchR att114BdeHQ 30Div p191 CR France40
SAMPSON,Ronald Henry 2Lt kia 30-8-18 RGA 122SB p41 CR France593
SAMPSON,T.F.2Lt kia 18-9-18 12Ches p96 MR37
SAMPSON,Tom Burton TLt kia 20-11-17 KSLI p145 CR France379
SAMPSON,Walter Bladen TCapt kia 10-7-16 13RB p180 CR France832
SAMS,Charles T2Lt kia 7-6-17 11RWKent p142 CR Belgium56
SAMSON,Oswald Massey 2LtALt dow 17-9-18 RGA 143SB p41 CR France511
SAMSON,Arthur Legge.MC.Capt kia 25-9-15 2RWFus p99 CR France114
SAMSON,Phillip Edward Lt dow 21-10-18 1/5Lpool p215 CR France163,2Lt
SAMUDA,Cecil Markham Annesley Maj dow 2-7-17 SomLI p80 CR France285
SAMUEL,A.D.T2Lt ded 19-5-18 RASC p193 CR Mddx40
SAMUEL,Cecil Valentine 2Lt dow 6-10-17 4RWar p65 CR Belgium20,Lt 4-10-17 1/8Bn
SAMUEL,Edgar Barnett.MID T2Lt kia 30-1-16 16Mddx p148 CR France924,31-1-16
SAMUEL,George Christopher Capt dow 16-8-18 9/82RFA p207 CR France122
SAMUEL,Gerald George TLt kia 7-6-17 10RWKent p142 MR29
SAMUEL,Gerard Stuart T2Lt dow 14-7-16 8EYorks p84 CR France23,Steuart Lt
SAMUEL,James Frederick T2Lt kia 22-4-18 13RWFus p99 CR France516
SAMUEL,James Roscoe T2Lt kia 25-1-17 7NStaffs p157 CR Iraq5
SAMUEL,Wilfrid Gilbert LtACapt kia 21-9-18 6Suff p218 CR France212
SAMUELS,Arthur Molesworth 2Lt kia 13-10-14 1RIrF p171 CR France324
SAMUELS,Arthur Purfoy Irwin TCapt dow 24-9-16 11RIrRif p170 CR Belgium49,Purefoy
SAMUELS,George Bernard 2Lt kia 22-10-16 21DLI &RFC p3&161,ded MR20
SAMUELS,Lesser Joseph.MC.TLtAMaj kia 29-9-17 A83RFA p35 MR30
SAMUELS,Wilfred Templeton T2Lt dedacc 14-7-17 GL &RFC 47BallSect p13 CR France52
SAMUELSON,Geoffrey Bernard Fitzroy.MC.Lt kia 27-11-17 CldGds p51 MR17
SAMUELSON,Lelia Mathilda.Lady ded 18-6-15 VAD CR Scot80
SAMUELSON,William Denys.MID LtACapt dow 31-12-17 RGA 113SB p41 CR Belgium11
SANBORN,William Reginald T2Lt kld 7-2-18 RFC p17
SANBY,William Worthington T2Lt kia 1-7-16 20NumbF p63 MR21
SANCTUARY,Cecil Reginald 2Lt kia 22-9-18 9Lond p248 CR France665
SANCTUARY,Charles Lloyd.MC.TCapt dow 15-11-16 8Suff p79 CR France102
SANDALL,Horace Cecil Blandford T2Lt kia 9-3-18 12 att10RFus p70 CR Belgium113
SANDALL,James Hosking 2LtACapt dow 23-7-17 RGA 229SB p41 CR Belgium11
SANDALLS,Charles 2Lt kia 18-9-18 1LNLancs p136 MR16
SANDBACH,Frank Stainton 2Lt kia 29-7-17 C93RFA p209 CR Belgium12
SANDBACH,Gilbert Robertson Capt dow 3-7-17 Denbigh Yeo att24RWFus p203 CR Egypt9
SANDBACH,Hugh Handley Capt kia 3-11-14 1Drags Ex DragGds attEAfrForce p21 CR EAfrica28 &CR Tanzania1
SANDBACH,William TMaj kia 10-8-15 6RLancs p59 CR Gallipoli17
SANDBROOK,David Aubrey.MID TCapt kia 31-7-17 14WelshR p127 MR29
SANDELL,Robert Louis T2Lt kia 22-9-16 34MGC Inf p185 CR France832 Ex 13LancF
SANDEMAN,Albert Fitzroy TLtACapt kia 2-12-17 11BordR p118 MR30
SANDEMAN,Charles Vaughan T2Lt kia 4-7-16 RE 184TC p48 CR France1182
SANDEMAN,George Amelius Crawshay Capt kia 26-4-15 3 att1Hamps p121 MR29
SANDEMAN,Kenneth Charles TLt kia 1-9-18 11Hamps att2RInniskF p121 CRBelgium89
SANDEMAN,Sydney Robert Lt kia 22-4-15 RGA p209 MR29
SANDEMAN,William Alastair Fraser Lt ded 19-10-14 1GordH p167 CR France1887
SANDER,A.T.Lt 22-11-20 3GrenGds CR Lond4
SANDERS,Alvin Augustus Maj kia 12-3-15 2ELancs p111 MR22
SANDERS,Archibald Morton 2Lt dow 9-4-17 5KOSB p224 CR France95
SANDERS,Arthur Edward Capt dow 19-5-16 2Y&L p159 CRBelgium5
SANDERS,Arthur Richard Careless.CMG.DSO&Bar.MajTBrigGen kia 20-9-18 RE 50InfBde 17Div p48 CR france906
SANDERS,Charles Phillips T2Lt ded 15-9-18 RE p48 CR Iraq6
SANDERS,Clive ACapt kia 27-5-18 WYorks att2Bn p82 MR18
SANDERS,Frederick Egerton.MC.2Lt kia 10-10-18 5Lpool p215 CR France190,18 Ex19Bn
SANDERS,Frederick John T2Lt dow 6-8-18 23RFus p70 CR France169
SANDERS,George Edward 2Lt kia 19-7-17 2/1NCycBn att1/8Lond p253 CR Belgium118
SANDERS,George Ernest Lt kia 9-10-17 16RWar p65 MR30

SANDERS,Gordon Harry E.2Lt ded 15-5-19 21Lancers p23&257 MR69,14-5-19
SANDERS,Henry Sacheverel Lt kia 21-8-18 6RWar p214 CR France239
SANDERS,James Donald Gerhardt Capt kia 5-1-16 RFA &RFC p3p35 CR France285
SANDERS,John Emerton 2Lt kia 25-8-16 17LancF p93 MR21
SANDERS,John Harry TLt ded 19-1-19 RAOC BaseDepot p198&257 CR Italy15
SANDERS,John Henry T2Lt dow 27-10-17 GL &59RFC p13 CR France446
SANDERS,Joseph Henry T2Lt kia 23-6-17 10ScotRif p104 CR Belgium6
SANDERS,Leslie Yorath T2Lt kia 10-3-17 RGA attRE FldSurvCoy p41 CR France120
SANDERS,Sydney Elphick 2Lt kia 30-11-17 RWKent att6Bn p142 MR17
SANDERS,Vincent Stanton 2Lt kia 4-9-16 1Beds p86 MR21
SANDERS,William Alfred Thomas 2Lt kia 9-9-16 1/13Lond p249 MR21
SANDERSON,Albert Montague Lt 1-10-18 74RAF MR20
SANDERSON,Archibald James Capt dow 2-5-15 att1KOSB p102 MR4
SANDERSON,Arthur Keith 2Lt kia 25-9-15 5Mddx att7Lond p148 MR19
SANDERSON,Arthur Watson Maj kia 28-6-15 7RScots p211 CR Gallipoli6
SANDERSON,Charles Buswell 2Lt kia 25-9-18 27RAF MR20
SANDERSON,Christopher.DSO.T2Lt kia 18-6-17 GordH p167 MR20
SANDERSON,Clement Oliver St.John.MC.TLt kia 27-4-18 RE 58InfBde p48 CR Belgium18
SANDERSON,Eric Harvard 2Lt kia 24-9-18 D149 RFA p35 CR Belgium60
SANDERSON,Francis William TLt kia 2-9-16 RE SpecBde p48 CR France833 Ex28Lond
SANDERSON,Fred Borthwick 2Lt dow 10-8-16 C258RFA p209 CR France145
SANDERSON,Gerald Stanley 2Lt kia 22-7-16 11Lond p248 CR France283
SANDERSON,Geoffrey Evan TLt kia 1-7-16 MGC 107Coy p185 MR21,Euan
SANDERSON,George Edward Lt 30-3-18 1AustBn ImpCamelCps MR34
SANDERSON,Gordon 2Lt dow 13-10-15 IARO att2/2GurkhaRif MGCoy p282 CR France765
SANDERSON,Harold Scott TLt kia 25-9-15 8BlkW p129 MR19
SANDERSON,Harry TCaptAMaj kia 23-4-18 A63RFA p35 CR France1182
SANDERSON,Hugh Capt kia 12-7-15 1/4KOSB p224&271 MR4
SANDERSON,John Topping T2Lt kia 18-12-15 7BordR p118 CR Belgium72,12-12-15
SANDERSON,Philip Noel LtTCapt dow 25-4-15 att1KOSB p102 MR4
SANDERSON,Ronald Harcourt MajALtCol kia 17-4-18 148RFA p35 CR Belgium11
SANDERSON,Roy Broughton 2Lt dow 17-4-18 RGA 6SB p41 CR Belgium38
SANDERSON,Sidney Charles 2Lt kia 11-10-16 2/18Lond p250 CR France68,Sydney
SANDERSON,Thomas Edward.MID Lt kia 13-4-18 1/4Y&L p238 CR Belgium89
SANDERSON,Walter Kerr T2Lt kia 1-7-16 1BordR p118 MR21,Ker
SANDERSON,Wilfrid T2Lt dow 15-4-18 WYorks att1/7Bn p82 CR Belgium38
SANDERSON,William Howard Lt dow 28-9-18 4RIrReg p89 CR France1184
SANDFORD,Charles James Vavasour 2Lt dow 6-5-17 8Mddx p236 CR France113
SANDFORD,Clement Richard Folliot.MC.Capt kia 22-2-17 5YLI p235 CR France163
SANDILANDS,John George T2Lt kia 21-3-17 11RScots p54 MR20
SANDISON,Eric William Wright.MID 2Lt ded 18-11-16 3 att 15RScots p54 CR France64
SANDLAND,William Maj&QM ded 12-11-18 NStaffs p265 CR Staffs125
SANDOE,Charles Frederick.MC.2LtACapt kia 30-8-18 1DCLI p115 CR France518
SANDOE,Montague William Augustus T2Lt kia 8-5-17 9Dev p77 CR France568
SANDOM,William Ernest TLt ded 10-11-18 32MGC p185 CR France146
SANDRY,James Ralph.MC.Capt dow 13-11-17 RGA 329SB p209 CR France40
SANDS,John William.MC.Lt kldacc 20-5-18 RE SigCoy att44RGAp48 CR France106
SANDS,Leslie Kelham TCapt dow 28-4-16 10LancF p93 CR France285
SANDYS,Edwin Thomas Falkiner.DSO.TLtCol ded 14-9-16 2Mddx p148 CR Lond4,13-9-16 dow
SANDYS,Mervyn Keats Capt kia 25-10-14 2Y&L p159 MR32,22/23-10-14
SANDYS,William Edwin TLt kia 5-9-17 GL &32RFC p13 CR Belgium11
SANDYS-THOMAS,Walter Jones 2Lt kia 4-2-17 3 att2SWBord p100 CR France744
SANER,Hubert Evelyn TCapt ded 17-11-18 RASC 372HorseTransCoy p193 CR France34
SANFORD,Walter Henry 2Lt ded 11-2-19 Dev att2/4DCLI p77&257 CR France1849
SANG,Alfred Frederick Joseph 2Lt dow 2-10-14 SL IntelCps p201 CR France16
SANGER,Henry Keith T2Lt kia 13-4-18 10EYorks p84 CR France193
SANGER,Thomas Rudolph 2Lt kia 1-7-16 1/5SStaffs p229 MR21
SANGER-DAVIES,Llewellyn Herbert TCapt kia 1-7-16 15DLI p161 MR21
SANGSTER,Albert Burnett 2Lt 13-8-18 206RAF MR20
SANGSTER,Frederick Charles TLt dow 6-9-16 16RWar p65 CR France23

SANGSTER,William John Campbell 2Lt kia 25-9-15 4GordH p242 MR29
SANIFORD,Noel Pendlebury 2Lt dow 3-4-17 5Ches p222 CR France120,SANDIFORD
SANKEY,C.M.MC.2Lt kld 15-5-18 3EKent &RAF p58 CR Mddx53
SANKEY,Sydney John Capt kld 25-9-15 6SStaffs p229 CR Belgium132,kia
SANKEY,Thomas T2Lt kia 13-12-17 2WYorks p82 CR France134
SANKEY,William Mandeville.MC.Lt dow 23-3-18 2Mon p244 CR Belgium84
SANSOM,Alfred John LtCol kia 5-7-17 5RSuss p228 CR France1182
SANSOM,Edwin Richard 2Lt dow 30-10-18 4EKent p212 CR France380
SANSOM,Roland Charles Lt 16-5-18 GL &55RAF CR Germany3
SANSOM,Walter Edwin Hammond T2Lt kia 16/18-8-16 8Lancs p59 MR21
SANSOME,Howard Victor 2Lt kia 26-10-17 14RWar p65 CR Belgium112
SANT,Edward Medley 2Lt kia 1-9-17 19RFC p13 MR20
SANTLER,William Amos T2Lt kia 13-6-16 8ESurr p113 CR France513
SANTS,Herbert Walter Lt ded 24-12-17 RFA attAOC p35 CR Iraq8
SAPHIN,Alfred Bridge 2Lt ded 15-8-17 3KRRC p265 CR France381,20Bn
SAPHIR,Max.MC.Capt 22-3-18 SAfrInf A'Coy MR27
SAPORTAS,Herbert Arnold Lt kia 17-7-15 2Manch p156 CR Belgium56,16-7-15
SAPTE,Anthony TCapt kia 1-7-16 4Mddx A'Coy p148 CR France267
SARCHET,Hugh le Gallienne.MC.ACapt kia 4-4-18 8RBerks p140 MR27
SARCHET,Leslie Lionel TLt kia 23-10-18 GL att55TMB p191 CR France716,Capt Hamps Xfer to 7EKent
SARDON,Herbert John S.TLt dow 31-10-18 3Dev p77 CR Mddx44
SARGAISON,William Henry T2Lt kia 6-12-15 5RIrF att5ConnRgrs p171 MR37,7RDubF att5CR
SARGEANT,Arthur Percival 2Lt kia 14-7-16 9Leic p88 CR France453
SARGEANT,Bernard Theobald 2Lt kia 11-4-17 8Lond p247 CR France1185
SARGEANT,Harold William 2Lt dow 4-4-18 18Lond p250 CR France37
SARGEANT,Ralph Leslie 2Lt kld 25-3-17 3 att8SomLI p80 CR France1180
SARGEAUNT,Arthur Frederick LtCol kia 31-7-15 RE p48 CR Belgium6
SARGEAUNT,Herbert Gaussen MajALtCol kia 15-6-17 RGA 16HAG p41 CR France285
SARGENT,Alfred George LtCol ded 14-5-18 IMS att25IndGH p282 CR Iraq6
SARGENT,Augustus Montague 2Lt dow 27-4-18 15N&D p135 CR France62
SARGENT,Ernest Vernon Lt kia 27-5-18 5NumbF p213 MR18
SARGENT,Henry Westbury 2Lt dow 6-7-16 1N&D p135 CR France430
SARGENT,Reginald William Fitzgerald T2Lt kia 5-10-17 220MGC Inf p185 CR Belgium308
SARGINT,Edward Eaton.MC.TCapt kia 16-8-17 7RIrF p171 MR30
SARGOOD,Hugh Frank T2Lt kia 10-5-17 16Mddx p148 MR20
SARJEANT,Douglas Leslie Lt kia 21-1-15 1/8RWar p215 CR France281,21-10-15
SARKIES,S.C.LtCol 7-3-17 IMS CR Mddx26
SARSBY,Reginald Ambler T2Lt kia 21-12-15 10Norf p74 CR France279,22-12-15
SARSFIELD,William Stopford Maj dow 20-9-14 2ConnRgrs p172 CR France1107
SARSON,Herbert William Phillips 2Lt dow 20-10-15 1/4YLI p235 CR Belgium11,Phillip
SARTORIS,Charles Frederick Lt kia 24-6-15 10 att7Leic p88 CR Gallipoli6,att2RFus
SARTORIUS,Euston Francis Frederick Capt dow 5-4-15 1GrenGds p50 CR France102
SASSE,Frederick Hugh Capt dow 8-5-15 2EYorks p84 CR Lond4
SASSOON,Hamo T2Lt dow 1-11-15 RE p48 MR4
SATCHWELL,Frank Henry Sandom Capt kia 3-5-17 HAC Inf p206 MR20
SATCHWELL,Henry Lt ded 8-12-18 Res GL p271 CR Numb4
SATCHWELL,Ralph William 2Lt kia 31-1-17 RGA 76SB p41 CR France393
SATTERTHWAITE,G.E.2Lt kld 11-6-18 GL &RAF p191
SATTERTHWAITE,William Herbert Capt kia 7-6-18 2/5RLancs p213 CR France204
SAUERBECK,Charles Theodore William TLt kia 11-9-17 13DLI p161 CR Belgium19
SAUL,Herbert Lepard T2Lt kia 24-10-18 7Suff p79 CR France1259
SAULEZ,Alfred Gordon Capt ded 5-7-21 RASC 83MT CR Iraq8
SAULEZ,Arthur Travers AMaj kia 22-4-17 D64RFA p35 CR France644
SAULL,Harold Truscott T2Lt died 2-10-18 LabCps p266 CR Surrey1,Lpool
SAUMAREZ,Reginald Stafford.MC.Capt kia 23-3-18 22Lond p251 CR France245
SAUNDBY,William Spencer FitzRobert 2Lt kia 17-11-16 Yorks &RFC p3,261&263 MR20
SAUNDER,George Bertram T2Lt kia 15-4-17 1EKent p58 CR France551
SAUNDERS,Albert James 2Lt kia 27-6-17 RGA 58SB p41 CR Belgium1,26-6-17
SAUNDERS,Alfred.MID TCapt dow 16-12-16 6Lancs 1Coy p59 CR Iraq5
SAUNDERS,Alfred George T2Lt kia 29/31-7-16 8NStaffs p157 MR21
SAUNDERS,Alfred Hewgill Lt kia 10-3-15 2RBerks p140 CR France709

SAUNDERS,Arthur Brain TLt dow 4-9-16 17KRRC p151 CR France169,Bryan
SAUNDERS,Arthur Courtenay Capt kia 14-3-15 2DCLI p115 CR Belgium28
SAUNDERS,Arthur Hugh Richard Capt mbk 8-3-16 IA 1/2GurkhaRif p282 MR38
SAUNDERS,Charles T2Lt kia 1-7-16 15WYorks p82 MR21
SAUNDERS,Charles Fabian T2Lt kia 18-8-16 7Nhampt C'Coy p138 CR France402
SAUNDERS,Charles Frederick 2Lt dow 18-4-18 2N&D p135 CR Belgium38
SAUNDERS,Charles Robert Edgar Capt dow 28-4-15 4Lond p246 CR France200
SAUNDERS,Clement 2Lt dow 11-2-17 66/4RFA p35 CR Iraq5
SAUNDERS,Claude Winstanley Capt kia 30-9-19 IA 108Inf att1/7GurkhaRif p282 MR38
SAUNDERS,Clifford William.MC.TLtACapt kia 16-10-17 6Dors p124 MR30
SAUNDERS,Cyril Page Gore ACapt kia 27-9-16 3 att1LNLancs p136 CR France385
SAUNDERS,D M.LtCol ded 2-12-18 RAMC p267 CR Ireland5
SAUNDERS,Edwin Walter Lt kia 5-5-15 1Camb p245 MR29
SAUNDERS,Ernest Manners 2Lt dow 4-12-17 1/4Ess p232 CR Egypt2,Maurice
SAUNDERS,Ferdinand Ward 2Lt kia 25-1-18 WelshR &35RFC p17 CR France446
SAUNDERS,Francis William 2Lt kia 1-8-18 8A&SH p271 CR France866
SAUNDERS,Frank 2Lt dow 17-10-17 1/4Glouc p225 CR Belgium18
SAUNDERS,F.W.Capt ded 29-4-18 12RInniskF p105 CR Shrop93
SAUNDERS,George T2Lt kldacc 30-3-18 51RFC p17 CR Essex13
SAUNDERS,George James Rich LtTCapt kia 26-9-16 SLancs att7Leic p126 MR21
SAUNDERS,George Morley Maj ded 26-2-18 DLI p265
SAUNDERS,Gwilyn Essex T2Lt kia 18-9-18 RWFus att16Bn p99 CR France415
SAUNDERS,Harold Cecil Rich.DSO.CaptAMaj kia 30-5-18 EYorks p84 MR18
SAUNDERS,Harold Macleod T2Lt kia 25-6-18 11ELancs p111 CR France19
SAUNDERS,Horace Victor Bertram T2Lt kia 22-3-18 46MGC p185 CR France258
SAUNDERS,James Renault Lt kia 4-11-18 2CldGds p51 CR France1080
SAUNDERS,Kenneth 2Lt kld 31-12-14 16NumbF p63 CR Numb4
SAUNDERS,Louis Desormeaux T2Lt kia 26-9-15 1SWBord p100 MR19
SAUNDERS,Noel Martyn TCapt kia 20-10-18 7BordR p118 CR France1476
SAUNDERS,Reginald Arthur Lt kia 14-3-16 RFA att1RFC p19&207,TCapt CR Belgium21
SAUNDERS,Robert T2Lt kia 26-10-17 13MGC Inf p185 MR30
SAUNDERS,Robert Stratford Howard Lt dow 12-4-18 D330RFA p35 CR France145
SAUNDERS,Roy Llewellyn T2Lt kia 9-4-16 10 att6ELancs p111 MR38
SAUNDERS,Samuel George Yarrow 2Lt kia 3-11-17 1/4Ess p232 CR Palestine8
SAUNDERS,William Gilbert TCapt&Adjt kia 6-9-16 5Lpool p215 CR France188
SAUNDERS-JONES,Henry St.John Lt dow 3-8-17 IA 20Inf att30Punjabis p282 CR EAfrica10 &CR Tanzania1
SAUNDERSON,Robert de Bedick Lt 18-10-17 GL &NigR CR EAfrica11 &CR Tanzania1
SAUNDERSON,Samuel Treherne Capt kld 22-4-18 NIrHorse &RAF p24
SAVAGE,Alfred 2Lt ded 7-10-17 RFA 4Bde DAC p35 CR Iraq8
SAVAGE,Alfred Charles T2Lt kia 31-7-17 8Suff p79 MR29
SAVAGE,Alphonso Macardle Lt ded 8-3-19 3DragGds p261CR Wilts115,A.N.
SAVAGE,Arthur Raymond Boscawen Maj 18-5-21 RFA CR Ireland14
SAVAGE,Cuthbert Farrar Lt dow 20-6-17 10NumbF p63 CR Belgium11
SAVAGE,Donaldson Lizars 2Lt dow 15-11-16 RE 56FC p48 CR France133,kia
SAVAGE,Edward Hugh Noël Lt kia 29-6-18 RE 1Coy p48 CR France77
SAVAGE,Francis Vandry 2Lt kia 1-5-17 IARO att1/94Inf p282 MR43
SAVAGE,Frederick Quinton T2Lt kia 20-9-17 6Wilts p153 MR30
SAVAGE,George Henry.MM.T2Lt kia 21-10-18 att12ESurr p113 CR B449,C.H.
SAVAGE,Gerald Roderick LtTCapt dow 4-10-17 3 att11Ess p132 MR30
SAVAGE,Harold Wilson Capt kia 10-8-15 10Hamps p121 MR4
SAVAGE,Harry George ACapt kia 20-9-17 4Hamps p228 MR30
SAVAGE,Henry George 2Lt kia 17-10-17 17Lond p250 CR Belgium112,dow
SAVAGE,Henry Osborne Lt kia 26-10-16 RFA X32TMB p35 CR France35
SAVAGE,John Ardkeen Capt kia 18-9-14 1Nhampt p138 MR15,17-9-14
SAVAGE,John Brown 2Lt dow 16-5-15 1RWFus p99 CR France279
SAVAGE,John Geoffrey T2Lt kia 24-7-16 RGA 40 att109SB p41 CR France397
SAVAGE,John Raymond Boscawen 2Lt kia 18-6-16 25RFC p3 CR France161
SAVAGE,Tom Alixander Capt ded 26-6-19 RGA AC att10IndMA Bde p41&257 CR Egypt8, Alexander dow
SAVAGE,Thomas John T2Lt kia 11-10-18 RB att3Bn p180 CR France270 Ex NIrHorse
SAVAGE,Wilfred Clyde Richmond Capt ded 5-5-18 IA 32Lancers p282
SAVAGE,William Beck Lt kia 21-3-18 51MGC p185 MR20
SAVAGE,William Howard T2Lt kia 1-7-16 11RFus p70 CR France397
SAVAGE,William Leslie T2Lt kld 16-6-17 GL &RFC p13 CR Glouc67
SAVAGE-ARMSTRONG,Francis Savage Nesbit.DSO.MID MajTLtCol kia 23-4-17 1SStaffs Cmdg11War p123 CR France452

SAVATARD,Thomas Warner Capt kld 29-5-15 7Manch p237 CR Gallipoli2
SAVEALL,Garrett T2Lt kia 13-7-16 7RWKent p142 MR21
SAVEL,Harold Richard Lt kia 25-5-15 21Lond p251 CR France279
SAVERY,Roger de la Garde Capt kia 7-8-15 10SStaffs p123 MR4
SAVILE,Francis Ewart TLt ded 9-2-16 6RRofCav att9Lancers p24
SAVILE,George Keith 2Lt kia 20-6-15 1/4Glouc p225 CR Belgium48
SAVILE,William Henry Bouchier TCapt kia 14-8-16 70RFA p35 CR France453
SAVILL,F.E.Lt 9-2-16 9Lancers CR Dorset28
SAVILL,John Edward T2Lt kia 24-8-17 RB att9Bn p180 MR30
SAVILL,Ronald John 2Lt kia 30-4-17 3 att9Ess p132 MR20
SAVILL-ONLEY,Frederick Simerville Wroth Capt ded 9-7-20 IA S&TCps p282 MR43,Somerville
SAVILLE,Clifford Allen Capt kia 8-11-17 11EYorks p84 MR20
SAVILLE,Eric T2Lt kia 8-10-18 1RBerks p140 CR France338
SAVILLE,Robert TCapt kld 16-3-18 GL &RFC p17 CR Yorks447
SAVORY,Ernest Harley 2Lt kia 8-7-17 7RWSurr p56 MR29,10-8-17
SAVORY,Francis Richard Egerton Capt dow 5-12-15 2KSLI p145 MR37
SAVORY,Henry Lawrence Scott 2Lt dow 26-4-18 1Suff GarBn att3Worc p79 CR Belgium38
SAVORY,Maurice Jeffery TCapt dow 3-2-17 9WRid p116 CR France105
SAVOURS,Arthur William Lt kia 2-8-18 6 att11RFus p70 CR France209
SAW,Noel Humphrey Wykeham.MC.Capt kia 9-10-17 RAMC att4Worc p197 CR Belgium16
SAWARD,Harry Douglas.MID Capt kia 23-3-15 2RScots p54 CR Belgium104
SAWARD,Ralph 2Lt kia 29-4-17 22RFus p70 MR20
SAWDEN,William Wright Lt dow 5-6-17 RGA att20RFC p209 CR Belgium11
SAWDON,Arthur Tindale T2Lt kia 28-6-17 13EYorks p84 CR France777
SAWER,Edgar 2Lt kia 31-7-17 42/2RFA p209 CR Belgium12
SAWYER,Aleck Makson T2Lt dow 13-12-17 50MGC p185 CR France13,Mayson 12-12-17
SAWYER,Charles Quinton TCapt kia 14-7-16 8EYorks attTMB p84 CRFrance399,C.O.
SAWYER,Frederick William Campion TLt dow 4-4-17 RE 218FC p48 CR France1204
SAWYER,Gordon Stanley 2Lt kia 13-10-17 IARO att113RFC p282 CR Egypt9
SAWYER,Herbert 2Lt kia 12-10-16 7Suff p79 MR21
SAWYER,Maitland Lindsay T2Lt dow 27-4-17 2Y&L p159 France80
SAWYER,Robert Fulwell 2Lt dow 24-8-17 KRRC att17Bn p151 CR Belgium111
SAWYER,William Robert T2Lt dow 8-10-17 6EYorks p84 CR Belgium23
SAXBY,Eric Yardley 2Lt kia 9-9-16 9Mddx att2/5LancF p236 MR21
SAXBY,George Scrase 2Lt dow 22-4-17 9Lond p248 CR France113
SAXELBYE,Frank Norman Lt dow 11-5-15 4EYorks p219 CR France102
SAXON,Ethel Sister ded 3-9-17 TFNS p254 MR43
SAXON,Fredk Thomas 2Lt kia 8-12-17 RGA 143SB p41 CR France415
SAXON,Harry.MID TLt kia 30-11-16 8RLancs p59 CR France133,29-11-16
SAXTON,Arthur Cyril T2Lt kia 30-7-16 1 att2KOSB p102 MR21
SAXTON,Ernest Wilkinson Lt ded 19-12-19 LabCps p266 CR Notts60
SAYCE,George Ben TCapt kia 1-7-16 26Manch p156 CR France397
SAYE,Lancelot Hugo T2Lt dow 11-7-16 6RBerks p140 CR France40
SAYER,Cecil Oversley Lt dow PoW 7-6-15 7DLI p239 CR Belgium393
SAYER,Charles Melville T2Lt kia 17-6-17 GL &4RFC p13 CR Belgium10
SAYER,Harry 2Lt dow 24-10-15 1EKent p58 CR France80
SAYER,Hubert Lionel 2Lt kia 17-8-17 RFA &7RFC p13&35 CR Belgium18
SAYER,James Herbert 2Lt kia 3-4-17 15RFC p13 CR France646
SAYER,Leonard Charles T2Lt dow 4-7-16 17RFus p70 CR France12
SAYER,Robert Bramwell T2Lt dow 19-2-17 11RFus p70 CR France41
SAYER,Thomas Errington TCapt kia 25-9-16 11 att10YLI p143 MR21
SAYER,William Thomas T2Lt kia 5-6-16 RE 180FC p48 MR20
SAYERS,Charlie Ronald T2Lt kia 13-4-17 9Leic p88 CR France616
SAYERS,Horace George David Lt drd 2-6-17 23Lond p252 MR41
SAYERS,Keith Raymond Lt mbk 9-9-17 RWKent &23RFC p256 MR20
SAYERS,Leslie.MC&Bar.TCapt kia 23-8-18 16RWar p65 CR France579
SAYERS,Robert 2Lt kia 21-10-14 2Mddx p148 MR22
SAYES,John T2Lt kia 31-10-18 2Dev p77 CR France1142
SAYLE,George Randall Fysh Lt dow 10-5-15 33/33RFA p35 CR France254,9-5-15
SAYRES,Alexander Ward Fortescue Maj dow 10-10-17 RAMC 2/1FA p253 CR France52,LtCol
SAYRES,Hugh Wingfield Capt kia 1-7-16 1 att2LancF p93 CR France643
SAYWOOD,Charles 2Lt kia 5-7-16 95RFA p35 CR France189
SCAIFE,Joseph 2Lt kia 21-3-18 1WRid att2Y&L p116 MR20

SCAIFE,Thomas Earle Gordon.MC.2Lt kia 26-9-16 6DragGds &RFC p3&21,ded MR20
SCALE,George Devereux T/Capt kia 20-7-16 10RWFus p99 MR21
SCALES,Edwin Herbert Lt dow 11-10-18 RASC att 1EKent p193 CR France446
SCALES,Edward Lionel Capt ded 11-11-18 4Mddx p148&258 CR Lancs472
SCALES,Patrick Joseph T2Lt kia 17-2-17 6Nhampt p138 MR21
SCALES,Walter Alexander.MC.Capt kld 6-1-18 6WYorks p218 CR France62,kia
SCALLAN,Richard Talbot 2Lt kld 31-5-18 RGA attLabCps EscortOffr 90PoWCo p41 CR France1822
SCAMELL,Reginald Frank T/Capt kia 20-4-16 11 att7Glouc p107 MR38,21-4-16
SCAMMELL,Sydney John Alfred 2Lt kia 16-9-16 6SomLI p80 MR21
SCANDRETT,John Jackson T2Lt kia 15-5-16 6/7RScotF p95 CR France423,14-5-16
SCANDRETT,William Frederick T2Lt kia 27-6-16 att2RSuss p120 MR20
SCANLAN,William Jack 2Lt kia 1-9-17 6Lond p247 MR29
SCARBOROUGH,Edward Owen 2Lt ded 25-5-18 6Lpool attRAF p215&258
SCARBOROUGH,Gerald Capt dow 12-9-18 4WRid att15Ess p227CR France31
SCARBOROUGH,Haydn 2Lt kia 17-9-18 3 att 1WYorks p82 CR France835
SCARBROUGH,Michael Claud.MID T/Maj kia 26-9-16 12Mddx p148 MR21
SCARBROUGH,Reginald John Capt dow 2-11-17 3Dev att1/8Hamps p77 CR Palestine2
SCARLETT,Harold Ernest 2Lt kia 17-9-16 3Lond p246 MR21
SCARLETT,Robert Stubbs T2Lt kia 20-12-17 16RScots p54 CR France162
SCARLETT,Thomas Capt ded 31-1-19 SL attHQ Staff RTO p201 CR Belgium265
SCARR,Geoffrey Campbell Lt FlyingAcc 18-11-18 IARO attRAF p282
SCARR,Reginald Graham T2Lt kia 14-7-16 12WYorks p82 CR France432
SCARTH,Alan Edward Capt dow 22-4-17 IARO att53Sikhs p282 MR38
SCARTH,Isaac Hinton Lt kia 23-4-17 4Yorks p220 MR20
SCARTH,James Charles T2Lt kia 14-7-16 10 att7SfthH p165 MR21
SCATCHARD,Thomas Capt kia 8-9-14 RAMC p197 CR France1426
SCATTERGOOD,Tom Victor T2Lt dow 6-6-17 21NumbF p63 CRFrance113
SCAWIN,William Neville Lt kia 15-4-18 5Y&L attMGC Inf p187&238 MR30
SCED,Henry Forbes TLt kia 24-9-17 14NumbF p63 CR Belgium19
SCHAFER,Thomas Sydney Lt kia 26-9-15 13NumbF p63 MR19
SCHALL,Henry Frederick 2Lt dow 24-9-16 RGA 150RotherhamHB p41 CR France833
SCHELL,Frederick Stanley 2Lt kia 22-8-18 RGA 130HB p41 CR France526
SCHENKEL,F.J.Lt dow 19-11-17 EAIntelDept CR EAfrica35 &CR Tanzania1
SCHIFF,Alfred Sydney Borlase 2Lt kia 9-4-17 1RB p180 CR France604
SCHIFF,Martin Noel Lt kia 17-6-16 1ScotsGds p52 MR29
SCHIFF,Mortimer Edward Harold Capt kia 26-9-17 12Suff p79 MR21
SCHILL,Edward Melland TLt dow 25-8-16 21LancsF p93 CR France23,17Bn
SCHINCK,Roger Henry 2Lt ded 31-10-14 3RWSurr p56 CR Belgium57,dow
SCHINDLER,William Barron 2Lt kia 20-7-18 2/5WYorks p218 CR France622
SCHLOSS,Lionel Ernest 2Lt kia 31-7-17 44MGC p185 MR29
SCHLOTEL,Charles Henry Cooper.MC.MIDx2 Capt ded 21-3-19 10DCLI p114 CR Germany1
SCHMIDT,F.P.Acc 4-11-18 IA AccsDept MR61
SCHNEIDER,Alexander Capt kia 29-6-21 IA 2/21Punjabis p282 MR43
SCHNEIDER,Herbert Hugo Lt kia 5-12-14 RE p48 MR40
SCHNEIDER,Stewart Spearing 2Lt kia 1-7-16 2RBerks p140 MR21
SCHOFIELD,Alexander Traies Capt dow 10-11-18 ACycCps &KentCycBn p244&271,HighCycBn CR Iraq6,att2RWKent
SCHOFIELD,Cuthbert TLt kia 25-9-15 14 att12RFus p70 MR19
SCHOFIELD,Henry William Melles Lt ded 2-10-20 IA 123Rif att 104 p282
SCHOFIELD,James Humphrey Clare TLt kia 26-9-16 1 att15DLI p161 MR21
SCHOFIELD,John.VC.T2Lt kia 9-4-18 2/5LancsF p93 CR France1106
SCHOFIELD,John 2Lt dow 24-9-18 5LancsF p221 CR Lancs266
SCHOFIELD,John Douglas Price T2Lt kld 26-5-17 RFC p13
SCHOLEFIELD,Arthur Hoyle 2Lt kia 18-5-17 19Lond att2LondRB p251 MR20
SCHOLEFIELD,Cyril Hamilton Reid CaptAMaj kia 28-3-18 RGA 69SB p41 CR France184
SCHOLEFIELD,Harry 2Lt dow 28-4-17 4YLI p235 CR France40
SCHOLEFIELD,Richard Powell T2Lt dow 25-7-16 16Ches W'Coy p96 CR France66
SCHOLES,Fredk W.2Lt kia 3-5-17 15WYorks p82 MR20
SCHOLES,Wilfred Paul 2Lt kia 13-10-15 4Leic p220 MR19
SCHOLES,William Robert Capt ded 14-7-18 LabCps p189 CR Scot15,12-7-18 HLI
SCHOLEY,Charles Harry Norman T/Capt kia 25-9-15 9RB p180 MR29
SCHOLFIELD,Richard Denham T2Lt dow 10-8-15 6RLancs p59 CR Gallipoli17
SCHONFIELD,Edwin T/Capt kia 20-9-16 2/19Lond p250 CR France68
SCHOOLING Cecil Herbert Rev dow 21-6-17 RAChDept att21InfBde p200 CR Belgium11

SCHOOLING,Eric Charles Capt kia 31-10-14 2RWar p65 MR29
SCHOOLING,Paul Sydney Bedford TLt kia 26-9-16 13 att9LancsF p93 MR21
SCHOOLING,Peter Holt 2Lt dow 30-3-16 9ESurr p113 CR France285
SCHREIBER,Owen Reginald.MC&Bar.CaptAMaj dow 22-10-17 106/22RH&FA p35 CR Belgium11
SCHRODER,Francis Thomas Lt kia 24-3-15 2Suff p79 CR Belgium103,2Lt 15-3-15
SCHRODER,Henry Dudley 2Lt kia 2-12-17 15LancsF p93 MR30,1/5Bn
SCHUH,Rudolf Oscar.MC.Lt ded 8-11-18 1Dev p77 CR France146
SCHULT,Edgar T2Lt dow 28-10-17 2RWSurr p56 CR Belgium11
SCHULTE,D.F.J.MC.Capt 30-7-18 Beds &60RAF CR France1564
SCHULTZ,George Edward T/Capt dow 12-8-17 15Ches p96 CR France363,19-8-17
SCHULTZ,Leonard Elmslie T2Lt kia 27-9-15 2Wilts p153 MR19
SCHULTZE,Hugh Lees T2Lt kia 20-10-18 Dors att6Bn p124 CR France192
SCHUR,Philip Lt kia 15-6-18 9N&D p135 CR France115,Phillip
SCHUSTER,Alfred Felix Lt kia 30-11-14 4Huss SR p21 MR29
SCHUSTER,Christopher John Claude 2Lt kia 10-8-18 5RB 1Coy p180 CR France412,1Bn
SCHUTE,John Hartley TLt kia 15-8-15 6RIrF p171 MR4
SCHWAGE,Sidney Philip T2Lt kia 7-9-18 6RWSurr p56 CR France439,SCHWABE
SCHWALM,Charles Edward Lt kia 22-11-17 6Glouc p225 CR France1327
SCHWARZ,Reginald Oscar.MC.CaptTMaj ded 18-11-18 6KRRC StaffConOfSalv attHQ 1Ech p151 CR France40,19-11-18
SCHWEDER,Archibald Alan.MC.T/Capt kia 26-9-16 9N&D p135 MR21
SCILLEY,James Frederick 2Lt kia 22-1-18 10RIrRif p170 MR21
SCLANDERS,Charles Maclure Lt kia 12-4-18 16Lond p249 MR32
SCOBEY,Richard Campbell 2Lt kia 23-8-17 6DCLI p114 CR Belgium125,5Bn
SCOBIE,C.G.Lt kia 21-5-18 SL &88RAF p268 MR20
SCOBIE,James 2Lt dow 2-8-17 4 att9GordH p242 CR Belgium7,3-8-17
SCOBIE,John Allan Mackay.MC.MID Lt kia 8-3-16 IA 59Rif p282 MR38
SCOBIE,John Angus Nicholson MacEwen Lt kia 29-7-16 RE 225FC p48 CR France727,McEwen
SCOBIE,K.McD.2Lt kld 27-10-18 RGA &RAF p41
SCOGGIN,Harry Cumming 2Lt kia 9-8-16 2Hamps p121 CR Belgium47
SCOLDING,George Henry 2Lt kia 26-3-18 4 att7Norf p216 MR27
SCOLLARD,David Francis.MC.Capt kia 20-4-17 RIrRif att7Bn p170 CR Belgium17
SCOLLICK,Laurence Trevor T2Lt kia 26-6-17 2DLI p161 CR France149
SCOONES,Earl Foster T2Lt kia 23-11-16 13Lpool p72 CR France5
SCOONES,Fitzmaurice Valentine 2Lt ded 18-8-16 3BlkW p129 CR Scot926
SCORE,William Thomas T2Lt kia 27-3-18 6EKent p58 CR France233
SCORER,Herbert Selwyn Capt kia 13-10-15 5Lincs C'Coy p220 MR19
SCORER,Nicholas 2Lt dow 29-3-18 4Yorks p220 CR France64
SCORER,William Harold.MID TLt dow 6-10-18 7Wilts p153 CR France194,Capt
SCOT-SKIRVING,Archibald William Capt dow 9-8-15 5RIrF p171 MR4,Waller
SCOTLAND,David Lothian TLtACapt dow 5-10-18 21MGC p185 CR France13
SCOTT,Alan Dale Wyndham.MC.TLt dow 26-10-16 92RFA p35 CR France,T20RFA
SCOTT,Alexander.TD.CaptHonMaj ded 12-2-15 RGA p209 CR Scot237
SCOTT,Alexander 2Lt kia 24-4-17 10HLI p164 MR20,Capt
SCOTT,Alister Will Henderson Capt dow 16-5-15 6 att2Worc p109 CR France80,kia
SCOTT,Andrew Hamilton Lt kia 3-5-17 4 att6KOSB p223 MR20
SCOTT,Andrew Holmes.MC.Capt kia 31-7-17 RE p48 MR29
SCOTT,Andrew Riddell Lt dow 24-4-17 1/5KOSB p224 CR Egypt2
SCOTT,Archibald T2Lt kia 25-4-17 8/10GordH p167 MR20
SCOTT,Archibald MacDonald T2Lt kia 16-8-17 8NumbF p63 CR Belgium96
SCOTT,Arnold Charles Lt dow 9-6-18 3 att1RScotF p95 CR France10
SCOTT,Arthur Blake 2Lt kia 26-3-17 1/7Ches p223 CR Palestine8
SCOTT,Arthur de Courcy LtCol kia 6-5-15 1Ches p96 CR Belgium134,5-5-15
SCOTT,Arthur Earnshaw 2Lt 24-3-18 A'Coy 4SAfrInf Ex C'Coy 3rd MR27
SCOTT,Arthur Edward T2Lt kia 21-3-18 3RB p180 MR27
SCOTT,Arthur Ernest Mortimer Lt kia 7-11-16 7 att4RFus p70 MR21
SCOTT,Arthur George 2Lt kia 23-12-15 2WRid p116 CR France513,21-12-15
SCOTT,Arthur William Maj ded 23-9-15 RAMC p253 CR Yorks361
SCOTT,Basil John Harrison 2Lt kia 23-10-14 2SStaffs p123 MR29
SCOTT,Bernard Lt kia 21-5-16 15Lond p249 MR20
SCOTT,Campbell Lowe TLt kia 2-9-18 3RScots att81TMB p54 CR Greece6,1Bn
SCOTT,Cecil 2Lt kia 31-7-17 7Ess p232 MR29
SCOTT,Cecil Ewart.MC.TLtACapt dow 9-9-18 8TankCps p188 CR France34
SCOTT,Charles Brough Lt dow 20-11-17 1Drags p21 CR France439
SCOTT,Charles Edward LtCol dow 9-8-16 6WYorks p218 CR France40
SCOTT,Charles Gordon Lt kia 28-10-16 3A&SH p173 CR France744

SCOTT,Charles Lindsay Murray Capt kia 15-2-17 GL 3NStaffs att54RFC p13&157,ded CR France1489
SCOTT,Clarence Trebor 2Lt kia 20-9-17 5Ches p222 MR30
SCOTT,Clifford 2Lt kia 2-8-17 83RFA p35 CR Belgium19
SCOTT,David T2Lt kia 7-4-17 7 att1ScotF p95 CR France57
SCOTT,David Harden.MC.Lt kia 12-11-17 GL &65RFC p13 CR France705
SCOTT,David Lyon 2Lt kia 9-4-17 4GordH p242 CR France531
SCOTT,Desmond 2Lt kia 25-10-16 54/39RFA p35 CR France453
SCOTT,Douglas Brogden Lt kia 9-4-18 6DLI p239 MR32
SCOTT,Douglas Gordon T2Lt kldacc 13-12-17 RFC p13 CR Shrop52
SCOTT,Dudley Holme TLt dow 2-7-16 17Lpool p72 CR France526
SCOTT,Edward Claud 2Lt kia 21-11-14 RGA p41 CR France82
SCOTT,Edward Richard 2Lt kia 19-2-18 1EYorks p85 CR France530,1/7Bn
SCOTT,Elvin Alfred.MC.TL kia 8-4-16 RGA 111HB p41 CR France149
SCOTT,Eric Bertrand Ralph TLt kia 10-7-16 RE 25DivSigCo p48 CR France44
SCOTT,Eric Douglas 2Lt kia 30-10-17 GL &1RFC p13 MR20
SCOTT,Eric Farrow 2Lt kia 30-10-17 D317RFA p209 CR Belgium20
SCOTT,Francis Charles Dudley Lt kia 4-11-18 6DLI &52RAF p271 MR20
SCOTT,Francis Gordon.MM.T2Lt kia 20-10-18 1/5Manch p156 CR France287
SCOTT,Francis Sherwood Lt kia 17-10-18 3 att1YLI A'Coy p143 CR France190
SCOTT,Frank 2Lt dow 8-10-18 5Lpool p215 CR France380
SCOTT,Frank Alexander T2Lt kia 18-9-18 58MGC Inf p185 CR France511
SCOTT,Frank Edward 2Lt dow 4-4-18 RGA 405SB p41 CR France40
SCOTT,Frederick.MC.Capt kia 27-5-18 9Leic p88 MR18,Frederic
SCOTT,George Ernest 2Lt kia 13-4-18 4DCLI p227 CR France18
SCOTT,George Gordon Douglas Lt ded 22-4-18 157RH&FA p262
SCOTT,George Henry Hall TCapt kia 1-7-16 7RWSurr C'Coy p56 CR France397
SCOTT,George Jefferson.MID Capt kia 25-12-15 1/5Yorks p220 CR Belgium5
SCOTT,George Klassen TLt kia 24-2-17 RE 237FC p48 CR Belgium21,Klaassen
SCOTT,George Trotter T2Lt dow 6-5-17 2WYorks p82 CR France1468
SCOTT,George Gordon Douglas Lt ded 22-4-18 157RFA p35 CR Scot280
SCOTT,Gilbert Ernest Josiah Capt kia 25-3-18 12 att19KRRC p151 MR27
SCOTT,Gordon Lt kia 1-7-16 2Mddx p148 MR21
SCOTT,H.G.R.B.Lt 21-3-16 20Punjabis CR EAfrica13
SCOTT,Harold Donald 2Lt kia 16-10-18 3/45RFA p35 CR France1277
SCOTT,Harold George Capt kia 30-7-18 O&BLI &52RAF p264 MR20
SCOTT,Harold Vesey Capt ded 1-9-15 3RB p180 CR France64,Herbert
SCOTT,Henry Arthur 2Lt kia 8-4-17 RE 512FC p210 CR France420
SCOTT,Henry James 2LtTLt dow 29-9-15 4CamH p242 CR Scot581
SCOTT,Herbert Lawson 2Lt ded 6-6-17 2ScotF p95 CR France113
SCOTT,Hugh McLellan Capt kia 6-9-18 3HLI p164 MR30
SCOTT,Ian Archibald Sawers 2Lt kia 1-7-16 1KOSB p102 CR France220,2Bn
SCOTT,J.H.M.Capt 24-3-19 RAMC CR Scot566
SCOTT,James Lt kia 25-9-15 6GordH p242 MR19
SCOTT,James TLt kia 25-9-15 7KOSB p102 CR France219
SCOTT,James 2Lt kia 15-11-16 7A&SH p243 CR France533
SCOTT,James T2Lt drd 26-2-18 RE IWT p48 MR38
SCOTT,James.MC.Lt dow 10-3-18 B302RFA p208 CR Palestine3,9-3-18
SCOTT,James Angus Lt mbk 26-10-17 7NumbF B'Coy p257 MR30
SCOTT,James Francis 2Lt kia 23-4-17 3 att13RScots p54 MR20
SCOTT,James Hall TMaj kia 25-9-15 10ScotRif p104 MR19
SCOTT,James Huggan Lt ded 9-11-18 8RScots att9GordH p211 CR France34
SCOTT,James Robinson T2Lt dow 23-3-18 13KRRC p151 CR France987
SCOTT,James Thompson TLt dow 5-10-17 9Leic p88 CR France40
SCOTT,James Wood 2Lt kia 28-6-15 8ScotRif p225 MR4
SCOTT,James Yuill TLt kia 3-9-16 10RB p180 MR21
SCOTT,John T2Lt dow 27-3-18 22DLI p161 MR27
SCOTT,John Crossfield 2Lt kia 16-10-16 5 att4Worc p109 MR21
SCOTT,John Davie.DSO.CaptALtCol kia 21-3-18 5 att2RIrReg p89 CR France212
SCOTT,John Ellison Lt kia 27-5-18 7DLI 50Div p239 MR18
SCOTT,John George Alec T2Lt dow 15-3-16 16LancsF p93 CR France43
SCOTT,John Gordon 2Lt kia 9-5-15 1BlkW p129 MR32
SCOTT,John Hastings Folliott 2Lt kia 9-4-17 3 att5.O&BLI p130 CR France581
SCOTT,John James.MC.TLtACapt kia 28-6-18 1RWKent p142 MR32
SCOTT,John Kemp T2Lt kia 14-7-16 1ScotF p95 CR France453
SCOTT,John Michael Corse Maj ded 29-3-17 1RScots p54 CR Greece1
SCOTT,John Millar T2Lt kia 18-8-16 11 att1BlkW p129 MR21
SCOTT,John Murray 2Lt kia 2-4-18 295RFA p35 CR France745
SCOTT,John Willoughby.DSO.MIDx3 LtCol kia 23-4-17 OxYeo Cmdg8SomLI p205 CR France924

SCOTT,Jack Voung Lt dow PoW 26-7-18 1RRofCav att10RWSurr p23 CR Germany3,25-7-18
SCOTT,Kenneth Robert.MC.Capt kia 2-11-19 IA 31Punjabis attAdminStaffPostalDept p282 CR Iraq8
SCOTT,Kenneth William Laing 2Lt kia 21-10-16 11Ches p96 CR France383,Lairg
SCOTT,Leonard T2Lt kia 24-3-18 1 att12Suff GarrBn p79 MR20,22-3-18
SCOTT,Leslie TLt kia 12-10-17 HouseholdBn p20 MR30
SCOTT,Lindsay Buchannan TMaj ded 14-11-18 RAOC p198 CR France85,Buchanan
SCOTT,Lionel Keith TLt ded 4-7-16 RE 225FC p48 MR19
SCOTT,Maurice Douglas Guest.MC.LtTCapt kld 17-3-18 3LNLancs &RFC p17&136,ded CR Derby145
SCOTT,Munro Briggs T2Lt kia 12-4-17 12RScots p54 MR20
SCOTT,Nigel Dennistoun 2Lt kld 19-4-16 RWSurr &RFC p3&56 CR Norf255
SCOTT,Noel Edmund.MID Lt dow 21-9-17 RE 422FC p210 CR Belgium18
SCOTT,Norman Sawers 2Lt kia 23-4-15 2KOSB p102 CR Belgium167
SCOTT,Phillip Camm 2Lt kia 8-10-18 7 att1YLI p143 CR France234,Philip
SCOTT,Ralph 2Lt kia 12-4-18 C256RFA p35 CR France1106
SCOTT,Ralph Quintus Lt kia 16-4-17 3ESurr att20RFus p113 CR France434
SCOTT,Reginald Eric Edward Lt dow 13-10-15 7Mddx p235 CR France525
SCOTT,Richard Thomas Folliott Lt kia 16-3-15 1EYorks p85 CR France1140,16-3-18
SCOTT,R.J.2Lt dow 8-5-18 GL &RAF p191
SCOTT,Robert Edward Leslie.MC&Bar.Lt kia 14-9-18 RGA 129HB p41 CR France245,13-9-18
SCOTT,Robert Michael TLt ded 25-12-18 GL attRE Sigs p191 CR Egypt1
SCOTT,Robert Walter Theodore Gordon T2Lt dow 15-8-16 7SfthH p165 CR Scot319
SCOTT,Roger Douglas CaptAMaj kia 13-10-15 2Glouc p107 CR France219
SCOTT,Ronald Burrell Ind 2Lt kia 9-9-16 1Lond p245 CR France402
SCOTT,Ronald Mayne T2Lt dow 20-9-16 13A&SH p173 CR France833
SCOTT,Samuel Geoffrey TCapt ded 6-1-18 RAMC att7DivTrn p197 CR Italy7
SCOTT,Samuel Jervois Capt 27-5-20 RAMC 108FA CR Ireland85
SCOTT,Samuel Lackland T2Lt kia 8-8-18 3Ches att11MGC Inf p96&185 CR France1170,11Ches att58MGC
SCOTT,Sidney Maurice Lt kia 15-9-16 1ColdGds p51 CR France374
SCOTT,Sidney Towers 2Lt dow 12-4-17 5RLancs p213 CR France102,Sydney
SCOTT,Stanley.MC.TLtAMaj kia 6-6-18 19MGC p185 CR France1693
SCOTT,Tampler Henry Capt kia 26-4-15 IA 87Punjabis att47Sikhs p282 CR Belgium167,Templer
SCOTT,Thomas.MC.2Lt dow 21-5-17 4ScotRif p104 CR France214,1Bn
SCOTT,Thomas 2Lt kia 27-5-18 3DLI p255 MR18
SCOTT,Thomas McCreary T2Lt kia 3-9-16 9 att2KOSB p102 CR France402
SCOTT,Thomas Rennie Capt kia 9-5-15 RLancs p59 MR29
SCOTT,Thomas Walter 2Lt kia 13-10-16 1Camb p245 MR21
SCOTT,Victor William.MC.Lt kia 16-3-18 13ESurr attRFC p17&113 CR France924
SCOTT,W.C.Lt 13-3-19 RASC CR Lond14
SCOTT,Walter Lt ded 23-10-15 RFA p208 MR4
SCOTT,Walter Alexander 2Lt kia 22-11-17 10RIrRif p170 MR17
SCOTT,Walter Elvin 2Lt kia 7-5-15 SL 1Wilts p201 CR Belgium111,6-5-15
SCOTT,Walter Falconer Capt kia 25-10-14 IA 59Rif p282 CR France348
SCOTT,William Capt ded 11-11-17 RAVC p268 CR Ireland5
SCOTT,William T2Lt dow 8-10-18 SWBord att13WelshReg p101 CR France375
SCOTT,William David T2Lt kia 3-8-17 26RFus p70 MR29
SCOTT,William Douglas Lt kia 22-8-17 4 O&BLI p231 MR30
SCOTT,William Emiley Oscar Lt kia 29-9-16 9DLI p239 MR21
SCOTT,William Francis T2Lt kia 1-7-16 8SomLI p80 CR France267
SCOTT,William Henry TLt ded 20-11-17 LabCps p189 CR Italy57,RE
SCOTT,William James De Vere 2Lt kia 29-5-15 8Manch p237 MR4
SCOTT,William Leslie Lt kia 17-6-15 5GordH p242 MR22,16-6-15
SCOTT,William McDougall Woodward TLt ded 2-9-18 RASC p193 CR Italy16,2Lt
SCOTT,William Peach Lt dow 9-11-17 1/5HLI p240 CR Palestine8
SCOTT-DEAKIN,Reginald Lt kia 31-7-17 A74RFA p35 CR Belgium12
SCOTT-GATTY,Charles Comyn Scott Maj ded 24-7-16 1Herts p271 CR Herts116
SCOTT-HOGG,James ded 12-8-17 RE p271
SCOTT-HOLMES,B.T2Lt kld 24-10-16 KRRC attMGC p185 CR Somerset185
SCOTT-HOLMES,Henry Favil T2Lt kia 1-7-16 RE 208FC p48 MR21
SCOTT-MacKIRDY,Charles David 22-3-18 11Huss MR27
SCOTT-MILLER,Edward Lt kia 14-5-18 3RLancs p59 CR France106,1/4Bn
SCOTT-MILLER,Walter Dudley 2Lt kld 22-6-17 RFus attRFC p13&70
SCOTT-MONCRIEFF,William BrigGen kia 28-6-15 Staff 1/7ScotRif Commdg156Bde p1 CR Gallipoli6

SCOTT-PILLOW,H.M 2Lt 8-8-17 Mddx att7RFC CR Belgium18
SCOTT-SMITH,Eric Henry 2Lt ded 29-10-15 RE 14FortressCoy p48 CR Greece11
SCOTT-STEVENSON,John Lt dow 9-10-18 RE 90FC Ex 8RScots CR Belgium38
SCOUGAL,Alec Graham.MC.MajALtCol kia 18-9-18 17RScots p54 CR Belgium3
SCOUGAL,Alan Muir T2Lt dow 7-10-15 3Worc p109 CR Belgium11
SCOUGAL,Francis William.MC.TMaj kia 19-9-18 11ScotRif p104 CR Greece5
SCOUGALL,Douglas Muir 2Lt kia 4-5-17 4 att 1/5Lond p246 CR France537
SCOVELL,Reginald Herbert Capt kia 16-8-15 RE 65FC p48 MR4
SCOWEN,Charles Henry T2Lt ded 25-9-17 TankCps p188 p266 CR Hamps13
SCRACE,John T.Lt ded 24-8-18 5EKent att21TrngDepotStn RAF p213&258,kia CR Kent44,kld
SCRACE,Reginald George Lt kia 19-7-16 2/4Glouc p225 MR21
SCRASE-DICKINS,Spencer William.CB.MajGen 23-10-19 Staff CR Sussex13
SCRATTON,Geoffrey Howell.MC.TLt kia 1-8-17 4/5A&SH p173 MR29
SCRIMGEOUR,Michael TLt kia 30-7-15 8RB p180 MR29
SCRIVEN,Arthur Cecil.MC.TLt kia 7-11-16 10Suff att47MGC p185 CR Belgium17,Capt 6-11-16
SCRIVEN,John Barclay LtCol kia 5-9-15 21Lancers p23 MR43
SCRIVENER,Alwyne Twyford.MID Capt ded PoW 5-7-17 5NStaffs p237 MR19
SCRIVENER,Arthur William.MC.Capt kia 2-11-17 1/10Lond p248 CR Palestine8
SCRIVENER,John Sydney 2Lt kia 2-12-17 8LancsF p222 MR30
SCRIVENS,Albert Victor Capt ded 11-1-19 RDC p253 CR Essex81 Ex MddxR
SCROGGIE,Vallentine.MC.T2Lt kia 4-11-18 1 att 1/5Glouc p107 CR France933
SCROGGIE,William Robertson 2Lt kia 2-12-17 LNLancs att 1/5SLancs p136 MR17,30-11-17
SCRUBY,William Samuel T2Lt kia 29-6-16 12Mddx p148 MR21
SCRUTTON,Hugh Urquhart TCapt dow PoW 10-9-16 2NumbF p63 MR37
SCUDAMORE,George Prince Mountford 2Lt kia 8-5-17 2RLancs A'Coy p59 MR29
SCUDAMORE,John 2Lt kia 25-9-15 2KRRC p151 CR France219
SCUDAMORE,John Venables Lt kia 25-4-15 2RFus p70 MR4
SCUDAMORE,Leonard George Lt ded 17-4-17 RAMC p197 p267 CR Wilts167
SCUDAMORE,Robert Capel.MC.TCapt kia 26-2-18 8RFus attRFC p17 CR France1678
SCULTHORPE,William Vaughan 2Lt kia 8-6-17 1/22Lond p251 CR Belgium120
SCURFIELD,Bryan.MC.Lt ded 30-9-18 4 att2ESurr p113 CR Greece9
SEABROOK,Harry Spencer 2Lt kia 12-7-16 16N&D p135 MR19
SEABROOK,James Herbert Lt kia 10-9-14 SL IntelCps 5SigTrp RE att5CavBde p201 CR France1128,2Lt
SEABROOKE,Alexander Stanger TCapt ded 1-7-16 RAMC att2BGH Basra p197 CR Iraq5
SEABURY,Edgar Raymond 2Lt kia 21-9-17 13Lond p249 MR29
SEAFIELD,James.Earl.Capt dow 12-11-15 3 att5CamH p168 CR Belgium11
SEAGER,William Henry T2Lt kia 7-2-16 10SWBord p101 CR France631
SEAGO,George William Edward TLt dow 6-10-18 O&BLI att1/5Glouc p130 CR France194
SEAGRAVE,P.2Lt kia 1-11-18 7Lpool &RAF p215
SEAHOLME,Max Knud T2Lt kia 30-3-18 7RFC p17 CR Belgium18
SEAL,George Hatcher.MC.Lt dow 29-10-18 15Hamps p204 CR Belgium158
SEALE,Theophilus T2Lt kia 22-8-16 7 att2RMunstF p176 CR France453
SEALE,William Henry.MC.2Lt dow 14-3-18 2 O&BLI att5TMB p130&259 CR France398
SEALY,Charles Frederic Noel Prince 2Lt kia 24-5-15 7RFus p70 MR29
SEALY,Edward Molesworth Walpole Capt ded 25-12-15 RE p48 CR Devon39
SEALY-KING,Charles Lt 9-5-15 2RMunstF MR22
SEAMAN,Charles William Frederick T2Lt kia 6-11-18 7Wilts p153 CR France929
SEAMAN,Edwin Charles.CB.CMG.10-5-19 RE CR Lond8
SEAMAN,Leonard James Cameron Lt kia 30-8-18 1RWar p66 CR France421
SEAMANS,Arthur Edward Lt dow 3-12-17 RGA p209 CR Belgium72
SEAR,Eric John Cecil 2Lt kia 8-9-16 2WelshR p127 MR21
SEARGINSON,John Capt kia 10-11-16 4Yorks p220 CR France385
SEARIGHT,G.G.Lt 12-11-20 4RDubFus attRE IWT CR Iraq6
SEARLE,Alec T2Lt kia 23-4-17 RE 202FC p48 MR20
SEARLE,Archibald Henry 2Lt 13-7-17 1AustFC MR34
SEARLE,Arthur Henry Lt ded 18-6-16 9Manch p271 CR Wilts186,11Lond
SEARLE,B.W 2Lt ded 3-10-15 10SStaffs p123
SEARLE,John Arthur T2Lt dow 4-5-17 1N&D p135 CR France122
SEARLE,Percy 2Lt ded 21-2-19 RASC p193 CR France65
SEARLE,Thomas George.MC.MSM.2Lt kia 20-9-17 1/2Beds p86 MR30
SEARLE,Valentine Lang Stuart 2Lt dow 22-6-16 D76RFA p35 CR Belgium11
SEARS,Joseph Patrick T2Lt kia 20-8-18 2 O&BLI p130 CR France214
SEARSON,Harold William 2Lt dow 17-6-17 12Ess att3KRRC p132 CR Greece9

SEATER,George Harold Lt kia 14-9-20 IA 2Rajputs att8 p282 MR38
SEATER,Percival John 2Lt kia 3-5-17 3 att8ESurr p113 MR20
SEATER,Thomas Rendall T2Lt kld 21-1-18 RFC p17 CR Wilts116
SEATH,Douglas Ambrose TLt kia 24-4-17 ScotRif p104 MR20,2 att6BordR
SEATON,Alexander Adam Capt dow 4-9-15 1Camb p244 CR France922
SEATTER,George T2Lt kia 9-9-18 15DLI p161 MR16
SEAVER,Charles TCapt dow 3-10-16 8RInnuskF p105 CR France145
SEAVERNS,Joel Harrison Lt dow 10-5-15 1Lond p245 CR France345
SEBAG-MONTEFIORE,Robert Montefiore Capt dow 19-11-15 EKentYeo CR Egypt5, see SEGBAG-MONTEFIORE below
SEBASTIAN,Skinner Raymond.MC.MIDx2 LtTLtCol dow 27-3-18 3Hamps Cmdg5 O&BLI p121 CR France145
SECKER,Charles William TLt dow 4-11-18 RE 3SpCo p48 CR France658,3-11-18
SECKER,John Devereux 2Lt ded 12-12-16 3/4Ess att1Camb p232 CR Essex146,dow 13-12-16 Ex 5Lond
SECKHAM,Gerald Adair Lt kia 6-1-15 2ELancs p111 CR France924
SECKINGTON,Frank Lt kia 14-7-16 1SStaffs p123 MR21
SECRETAN,Reginald Herbert 2Lt kld 31-7-17 Herts p252 MR29
SECRETT,Albert George 2Lt kia 28-4-17 Mddx att17Bn p148 MR20
SEDDEN,Henry T2Lt kia 8-8-18 6TankCps p188 CR France652,SEDDON
SEDDON,Edward Macmahon.DSO.LtCol kia 24-6-17 RGA 45HAG p41 CR Belgium17
SEDDON,Frank Augustus 2Lt kia 30-11-17 Lpool att1/8Bn p72 MR17,Augustine 20-11-17
SEDDON,Horace 2Lt kia 25-8-18 5 att2/4LancF p221 CR France617
SEDDON,Max Hugo TLt dow 4-11-18 RASC MT p193 CR France206
SEDGLEY,Henry Frederick Lt kia 22-9-18 9Lond p248 CR France665
SEDGLEY,Lionel Edwin 2Lt ded 9-11-18 9Manch p271 CR Surrey156
SEDGWICK,Arthur Edward Lt kia 10-9-16 5Lond p246 CR France66,dow
SEDGWICK,Francis Balfour Capt kld 18-10-18 13Suff &RAF p263
SEDGWICK,Joseph T2Lt kia 9-10-17 2/4ELancs p111 MR30
SEE,Sydney Matthews 2Lt kia 10-10-16 A71 RH&FA p35 CR France453
SEEAR,Christopher Charles Capt ded 30-10-19 SL p268 CR Lond14
SEED,Harper T2Lt kia 20-9-17 17N&D p135 CR Belgium20,Lt
SEED,James Parrott T2Lt kia 17-6-18 2Hamps p121 CR France193
SEEDS,William Albert T2Lt kia 6/7-7-17 10RWSurr p56 CR Belgium111,6/7-6-17
SEEL,Horace Arthur Lt 7-12-15 7Ches p223 MR4
SEELY,Charles Grant Capt kia 19-4-17 8Hamps p229 CR Palestine8
SEELY,Frank Reginald 2Lt dow 13-4-17 1Hamps p121 CR France53
SEERS,Wilfrid.MID TMaj kia 20-9-17 15Hamps p121 MR30
SEFTON,Percy T2Lt kia 22-8-18 13ELancs p111 MR32
SEGAL,Marcus T2Lt kia 19-6-17 13Lpool p72 CR France1182
SEGBAG-MONTEFIORE,Robert-Montefiore Capt dow 19-11-15 REKentYeo p204
SEGGIE,Alexander 2Lt kia 1-7-16 9RIrF B'Coy p171 CR France339
SEGNITZ,Hermann Ferdinand 2Lt kld 25-9-15 19Lond p251 CR France219
SEGRAVE,P.2Lt 1-11-18 7Lpool &RAF CR France937
SEGRAVE,William Henry TLt kld 12-2-17 GL &RFC p13
SEGUIN,Ubalde Hormidas 2Lt kia 6-4-17 16RFC p13 CR France522,Hormisdas
SELBIE,Colin Mackenzie T2Lt kia 14-7-16 11 att9ScotRif p104 MR21
SELBY,Beauchamp Henry Capt kia 20-9-14 1NumbF p63 MR15
SELBY,Gerrard Prideaux Capt kia 26-9-16 RAMC att9LancsF p197 CR France393,Gerard
SELBY,Herbert Richard.MSM.MID Lt 12-4-19 IOD MR65
SELBY,Millin 2Lt dow 29-9-15 3EKent p58 CR France257
SELBY,Millin John TLt kia 7-7-16 2Nhampt p138 MR21
SELBY,William.DSO.LtCol ded 8-9-16 IA IMS p282
SELBY-LOWNDES,Meyrick Edward Lt ded 27-10-18 3 att2SforthH p165 CR Surrey1
SELBY-LOWNDES,Richard Cecil Williams TLt ded 11-7-18 RASC p193 CR Bucks37
SELBY-SMITH,Miles Bury Capt kia 15-3-15 4RB p180 CR Belgium28,SMYTH
SELCH,Frederick William T2Lt kia 4-11-18 9Yorks att7EYorks p91
SELFE,Edgar Donald TCapt kia 7-8-18 9Norf p74 CR Belgium3
SELFE,Hugh Donald TCapt kia 9-7-17 8NStaffs p157 CR Belgium77,Ronald
SELLAR,James Arthur T2Lt kia 3-4-17 6 O&BLI A'Coy p130 CR France568
SELLAR,John Lt kia 9-4-18 6SforthH p241 MR19
SELLAR,John Mill TLt kia 25-9-15 7KOSB p102 MR19
SELLARS,Eric Francis.MC.Capt kia 18-9-18 12Ches p255 MR37
SELLARS,Herbert Whiteley.MC.Lt 15-5-18 11RAF MR20
SELLERS,John Harrison 2Lt kia 24-5-15 3 att2NumbF p63 MR29
SELLERS,Philip 2Lt kld 23-3-17 Worc attRFC p13&109,ded CR Wilts194

SELLERS,Thomas T2Lt kia 22-4-17 RE 173TC p48 CR France178
SELLERS,Vernon Guy Lt ded 27-10-18 RFA X48TMB p208 CR Italy7
SELLMAN,Edgar Nevill Newmark 2Lt kia 4-4-18 3Glouc att5 O&BLI p107 CR France1170,SELMAN Newmarch
SELLON,Bruce Heckford 2Lt dow 16-8-17 11Lond attLondRB p248 Belgium8
SELLON,Marmaduke Heckford 2Lt kia 15-6-18 RGA att1/1War HB p41 CR Italy4
SELLS,Archibald Jenner TLt kia 26-10-16 2 att3RWSurr p56 CR Belgium54
SELLS,C.P.MC.Capt ded 4-7-19 RAMC attRAF p254 CR Dorset93
SELLWOOD,John Dorey 2Lt kia 26-3-18 RE 2FC p48 MR20
SELOUS,Frederick Courteney.DSO.TCapt kia 4-1-17 25RFus p70 CR EAfrica23
SELOUS,Frederick Hatherley Bruce.MC.Capt kia 4-1-18 RWSurr &RFC p17&56 MR20
SELOUS-JONES,Jeffrey Fryer 2Lt dow 26-8-16 RE p48
SELWYN,A.H.2Lt ded 25-1-15 RASC p193 CR Lond4,Lt
SELWYN,Arthur Penrose Lt FlyingAcc 18-5-16 IA 11Lancers attRFC p282 CR Hamps4
SELWYN,Christopher Wakefield 2Lt dow 17-5-15 5Leic p220 CR France284
SELWYN,Colin Redgrave 2Lt kia 22-8-17 6SomLI p80 Cr Belgium112
SELWYN,George Vincent Carus Lt dow 25-10-18 106RFA p35 CR France146
SEMPLE,Henry Spencer.MC.LtAMaj kia 5-9-17 RE 203FC p48 CR France364
SEMPLE,Robert Edward Watson.MC.Capt dow 5-11-18 RFA attGdsDivTMB p35 CR France146
SEMPLE,Robert Woodburn Barnard.MC.T2Lt kia 9-4-17 7CamH p168 CR France1182
SEMPLE,William David 2Lt kia 29-6-16 13KRRC p151 CR France283
SENESCHALL George Rhodely 2Lt ded 16-11-18 5N&D p256 CR Derby120
SENHOUSE,Oscar William Pocklington 2Lt kia 19-6-15 CldGds p51
SENIOR,Albert Morton Capt dow 22-4-16 IA 91Punjabis att92 p282 MR38
SENIOR,Edwin Capt ded 23-6-20 SL &RE IWT CR Iraq6
SENIOR,George Fairburn 2Lt kia 17-11-17 4 att1/7WYorks p82 CR Belgium308
SENIOR,Harold Frank.MC.TCaptAMaj dow 13-4-18 A75RFA p35 CR France40
SENIOR,Herbert Godbert Lt kia 28-5-19 8Manch p237 MR18
SENIOR,Joseph TLt dow 9-5-17 GL &45RFC p13 CR France285 Ex 11WYorks
SENIOR,Robert Mackenzie 2Lt kia 27-3-18 4 att8Norf p216 MR27
SENIOR,Thomas Hugh Sandford TLt kia 11-6-16 2Worc p109 CR France114
SENIOR,Walter Talbot 2Lt kia 3-9-16 6WYorks p218 CR France215
SENSICALL,George Edwin T2Lt kia 9-10-17 6Y&L p159 MR30
SENTER,John Watt TLt dow 9-6-18 RAMC att53FA p197
SEPPINGS-WRIGHT,Frank Thomas 2Lt BombAcc 21-7-15 IARO 113Inf att6Jats p282 CR France345
SERGIADES,John Nicholas Lt kia 30-7-16 19Lpool p72 MR21
SERGINSON,Harold.MC.T2LtACapt kia 27-2-18 16NumbF att96TMB p63 CR Belgium106
SERJEANT,Cyril Lawson TLt dow 21-6-16 1Nhampt p138 CR France149
SERNBERG,Allan TCapt kia 2-7-16 9Ches p96 MR21
SERVANTE,Alfred William T2Lt kia 18-9-18 7RWSurr p56 MR16
SERVICE,Alexander Cumming Lt kia 29-5-18 6A&SH att136MGC Inf p187&243 CR Palestine9
SERVICE,George Brown T2Lt kia 30-3-18 16MGC Inf p185 CR France1170
SESSIONS,F.H.N.Lt 5-6-18 RDubF &RAF CR Ireland24
SESSIONS,John Herford Vivian TLt dow 28-9-18 WelshR att13Bn p127 CR France278
SETCHELL,Alfred Knight 2Lt mbk 21-3-18 9Norf p256 MR20
SETON,Bruce Eglington 2Lt kia 13-1-16 IARO att53Sikhs p282 MR38,15-1-16
SETON-BROWNE,Montague William.MID Lt kia 24-11-14 2Leic p88 CR France727
SETTLE,Mellard Capt ded PoW 23-12-18 1/5NStaffs p237 CR Ches1
SETTLE,Reginald Henry Napier.DSO.MC.MIDx4 TLtCol kia 24-3-18 19Huss att21MGC p23&185 MR27
SETTLE,Reginald William T2Lt kia 23-7-16 GL attRFC p3&191 CR France167
SETTRINGTON,Charles Henry.Lord.Lt dow 24-8-19 IrGds attRFus p255 MR70 &CR Europe179
SEUTER,John Watt Lt 9-6-18 RAMC CR France4
SEVERNE,Henry Francis.MID 2Lt kld 10-5-15 1/6N&D p233 CR Belgium17
SEVERS,Alfred George 2Lt kia 28-3-17 GL &25RFC p13 MR20
SEVIN,Clifford Newton 2Lt dow 25-3-18 15Hamps p121 MR20
SEWARD,Robert Francis T2Lt kia 25-10-16 Bord att2ELancs p118 MR21
SEWARD,Stanley Richard LtACapt kia 30-10-17 7RFus att7RScotF p70 MR30
SEWART,Gerald Evelyn Spuldlam T2Lt kia 8-5-16 10DLI p161 CR France420
SEWELL,Cecil Harold.VC.Lt kia 29-8-18 RWKent att3TankCps p142&188 CR France1484
SEWELL,Douglas Clifford Campbell Lt dow 10-9-14 3RWKent p142 CR Belgium242

SEWELL,Edward John 2Lt dow 10-4-18 RGA 217SB p41 CR France88
SEWELL,Francis Brooke Lt kia 15-5-18 RGA 126HB p41 CR France343
SEWELL,Geoffrey Edward 2Lt dow 2-9-17 1EKent p58 CR France179
SEWELL,Harry Kemp Lt ded 20-8-17 21RFA p35 CR Lond28 Ex WKentYeo
SEWELL,Henry Edward Maj ded 4-6-18 RGA 524SB p262 CR France268
SEWELL,Herbert Victor T2Lt kia 13-11-16 186RFA p35 MR21
SEWELL,Norman Oscar Lt kld 9-5-15 1/13Lond p249 MR32
SEWELL,Sidney Davis Maj kia 18-2-15 RE 3FC p209 CR Belgium58,Davies
SEWELL,William Allan Lt kia 12-11-17 4BordR attRFC p19&228 MR20
SEWELL,William Tait TCapt kia 1-7-16 11RInniskF p105 CR France383,Maj
SEWILL,Arnold Waterlow T2Lt kia 23-7-16 12WYorks p82 CR France630
SEYMOUR,Bertram T2Lt kia 31-7-17 MGC p185 MR29
SEYMOUR,Charles T2Lt kia 13-4-18 61MGC Inf p185 CR France248
SEYMOUR,Charles Benjamin 2Lt 6-9-18 11RAF MR20
SEYMOUR,Constance Emily Mary SpProb ded 12-2-17 QAIMNS CR Hamps1
SEYMOUR,Francis TLt kia 30-7-15 7KRRC p151 MR29
SEYMOUR,Greville Crawford 2Lt kia 15-4-17 3 att1Dors p124 CR France1701
SEYMOUR,Harcourt T2Lt dow 9-11-18 4KRRC p151 CR France658
SEYMOUR,Lewis Thievry Lt kia 13-8-16 2Y&L p159 CR France1012,Thierry
SEYMOUR,William Matthew 2Lt kia 16-8-17 10RIrRfus p171 MR30
SEYMOUR-ISAACS,Maurice T2Lt kia 26-10-17 2Bord p118 MR30
SEYMOUR-JONES,R.Arnold Lt dow 27-3-15 4SLancs CR Belgium28
SEYMOUR-URE,William Bruce T2Lt kia 4/10-10-16 32RFus p70 MR21
SEYS,Roger Cecil.DSO.OBE.Maj 10-4-21 RGA CR Lancs366
SHACKELL,Frank Charles Lt kia 23-5-17 ACycC attRFC p19&244 CR France381
SHACKLE,Frank Guy.MC.LtACapt kia 21-11-17 2Mddx p148 CR Belgium92
SHACKLEFORD,Alfred Edgar John 2Lt kia 9-5-15 1SfthH p165 CR France721
SHACKLES,Kenneth George 2Lt dow 11-5-17 4EYorks p219 CR France214
SHACKLES,Ronald Guy.MC.2Lt kia 19-9-18 KSLI att10Bn p145 MR16
SHACKLETON,Harold.MM.MID TLt kia 26-8-18 1 att9TankCps p188 CR France155
SHACKLETON,James Ernest T2Lt kia 21-3-18 7Leic p88 CR France407
SHACKLETON,James Sutcliffe Lt kia 16-4-17 2/4WRid p227 CR France568
SHACKLETON,Thomas Smith Lt kia 5-5-17 2/6WRid p227 CR France690
SHACKLETON,William Launcelot Collier TLt dow 24-4-17 26NumbF p63 CR France546
SHACKLOCK,George Miller 2Lt kia 12-3-15 1N&D p135 MR22
SHADDICK,Cecil George T2Lt kia 7-8-16 1Dors p124 CR France114
SHAFTO,Arthur Duncombe.DSO.Capt 26-8-14 2RScots D'Coy CR France658
SHAFTO,John Stanley Horsfall T2Lt kia 12-8-16 EKent p58 CR france164
SHAFTO,Thomas Duncombe Capt kia 2-5-15 RFus p70 CR Gallipoli2
SHAIL,William Archibald 2Lt kia 16-8-17 1Lond p245 MR29
SHAIRP,Norman.MC.Capt ded 13-10-18 AyrYeo p203 CR Syria2
SHAKERLEY,Arthur Cecil 2Lt kia 22-4-17 D64RFA p35 CR France644
SHAKERLEY,Eric Piers.MID Capt kia 10-3-15 6 att1KRRC p151 MR22
SHAKERLEY,Geoffrey Charles.DSO.MajTLtCol kia 15-5-15 1KRRC p152 CR France525
SHAKESPEAR,Everard Richard T2Lt kia 23-8-18 2SStaffs p123 CR France927
SHAKESPEAR,George Frederick Cortlandt.DSO.MC.Maj ded 24-2-19 IA 88Inf p282 CR Mddx26
SHAKESPEAR,William Henry Irvine.CIE.Capt kia 24-1-15 17IndCav PolitOff p282 MR53
SHAKLE,Hugh Philip Capt kia 21-11-17 4GordH p241
SHAND,Alexander 2Lt dow 9-5-15 1BlkW p129 MR22
SHAND,Frederick Gordon 2Lt dow 12-10-18 C311RFA p209 CR France113
SHAND,John James Fraser 2Lt kia 6-8-17 RGA 185HB p41 CR Greece6
SHAND,Wilfred 2Lt ded 11-2-19 4Lond p271 CR Kent83,Wilfrid
SHAND,William Gadrow TCapt dow 25-7-16 RAMC att20LancF p197 CR France23,Garrow
SHAND,William Kenwick Willoughby Lt ded 13-10-19 2Norf p263 CR France1571
SHAND-KYDD,William 2Lt kia 16-5-17 51RFA p35 CR France1188
SHANDLEY,Robert Newlyn 2Lt kia 22-8-18 3 att9Ess p132 CR France247
SHANKLAND,Llewelyn Ap Tomas TLt dow 25-11-17 19RWFus p99 CR France398,Aptomos
SHANKS,Daniel Albert 2Lt 21-9-18 108RAF MR20
SHANKS,Edward Ferner T2Lt kia 21-10-16 5ConnRgrs attInniskF p172 MR21
SHANKS,John Arthur Gordon.MC.MID Capt kia 4-10-17 6A&SH attMGC p187&243 CR Belgium165,3-10-17
SHANKSTER,George TLt kia 9-10-16 6Nhampt p138 MR21
SHANKSTER,Stanley 2Lt kia 3-7-16 7Lincs p75 MR21
SHANLEY,Andrew 2Lt kia 25-9-16 MGC 64Coy p185 MR21

SHANN,Alan Webster 2Lt kia 27-11-17 2/8WYorks p219 MR17
SHANN,Albert 2Lt kia 8-5-18 2Yorks p91 MR30
SHANN,John Webster TLt kia 1-7-16 10WYorks p82 CR France373
SHANN,Kenneth 2Lt kia 8-5-15 3 att2NumbF p63 MR29
SHANN,Reginald Arthur Lt kia 21-3-18 3 att4ELancs p111 MR27
SHANNON,Cyril Richmond Capt kia 4-10-15 RE 101FC p48 MR19
SHANNON,George Strangman.MC.MID 2Lt kia 5-5-15 Dors p124 CR Belgium132
SHANNON,Jeremiah 2Lt kia 1-8-18 7/8KOSB p102 CR France864
SHANNON,John James TCapt kia 29-11-17 RAMC att1/1LincsYeo p197 CR Palestine9
SHANNON,John Paterson 2Lt ded 4-3-19 12RB p266 CR Scot596 Ex 5KOSB
SHANNON,Percy Roy TLt dow 3-11-18 RAMC att11FA p197 CR France613
SHANNON,Richard Bernard.Earl of.2Lt kia 13-4-17 4RFus p70 MR20
SHANNON,Robert Mortimer.MC.2Lt dow 29-4-18 50RFA p35 CR Belgium11
SHAPLAND,Adam Francis Terrell TLt kia 20-9-17 6Wilts p153 MR30
SHAPLAND,Herbert George 2Lt dow 2-3-18 36RFA p35 CR France398
SHAPLEY,Alfred Edward TLt kia 1-7-16 23NumbF p63 MR21
SHAPTER,Lewis Henry Capt kia 31-1-15 3Suff attBeds p79 CR France276
SHARER,George Short T2Lt kia 26-9-15 7RScotF p95 MR19
SHARKEY,Thomas 2Lt kia 26-3-18 att1/6DLI p161 MR27
SHARLAND,Frederick James 2Lt kia 24-10-17 23RFC p13 MR20
SHARMAN,Arthur Patrick 2Lt kia 20-9-17 5Lond p246 MR29
SHARP,A.G.TMaj kia 10-8-15 9RWar p66 MR4
SHARP,Albert George 2Lt dow 1-9-18 4BordR p228 CR France805
SHARP,Andrew T2Lt kia 27-9-15 9BlkW p129 MR19,25-9-15
SHARP,Arthur Augustus Charles T2Lt kia 22-3-18 2TankCps p188 MR27
SHARP,Arthur Granville.MC.Lt kia 23-8-18 D72RFA attGdsDivArtly p35 CR France924
SHARP,Beresford 2Lt kia 9-4-18 7Lpool p215 MR19
SHARP,Cecil Jervis Capt kia 9-1-20 IA 13Rajputs att4/39GarhwalRif p282 MR43
SHARP,Charles Gordon 2Lt dow 5-2-16 4NumbF p213 CR Belgium4
SHARP,Christopher Harold 2Lt ded 26-9-18 3Norf att99RAF p74 CR France1667
SHARP,Cyril Robert TCapt kia 14-7-16 3 att12WYorks p82 MR21
SHARP,Eric.MID Lt ded 22-5-17 EKent att2KAR p202&212 CR EAfrica15 &CRTanzania1
SHARP,Fred 2Lt kia 3-8-18 10Mddx p236 CR France522
SHARP,Frederick Arthur Hamilton Lt kia 30-10-18 51/39RFA attStaff p35 CR France1270
SHARP,Frederick Leonard.CMG.LtCol kia 13-8-16 39RFA p35 CR France397
SHARP,George T2Lt ded 29-10-18 GL attIntelCps p191 CR France13
SHARP,George Benjamin 2Lt kia 21-3-18 9ESurr p113 MR27
SHARP,Humphrey TLt kia 5-10-15 11RFus D'Coy p70 CR France637
SHARP,James Calrow 2Lt kia 12-10-16 2LancF p93 MR21
SHARP,John Stanley TMaj kia 17-3-17 5RBerks p140 CR France1182
SHARP,Leon Owen T2Lt kia 1-7-16 2Lincs p75 CR France293
SHARP,Lewis Frederick T2Lt kia 1-7-16 10YLI p143 MR21
SHARP,Matthew.MC.2Lt dow 11-2-18 2/7Lond p247 CR France64
SHARP,Reginald Archibald 2Lt kia 2-9-16 RGA 47SB p209 CR France630
SHARP,Stanley Ernest 2Lt ded 20-10-18 SomLI p80 MR61
SHARP,Stephen Oswald TLt kia 1-7-16 13Y&L A'Coy p159 CR France156
SHARP,William Dalton Colombo 2Lt kia 9-10-17 4Norf p216 MR30
SHARPE,Anthony Herbert LtACapt kia 25-9-17 3 att4Lpool p72 MR21
SHARPE,Arthur Noel Lt kia 3-9-16 5WRid p227 CR France383
SHARPE,Charles Lancelot Arden 2Lt kia 26-4-15 3Mddx p148 CR Belgium151
SHARPE,Douglas Staveley 2Lt kia 7-7-16 3 att1Wilts p153 CR France744
SHARPE,Gerald Norman 2Lt kia 31-7-16 4Y&L p238 CR France246
SHARPE,Henry Norman 2Lt kld 26-1-17 3Leic &RFC p13&88 CR Essex7
SHARPE,John Sutton 2Lt kia 8-8-16 1/8Lpool p216 MR21
SHARPE,Leonard Frederick Robert Lt ded 27-7-18 3Lincs p263 CR Ireland14 &CR Eire77
SHARPE,Maurice 2Lt kia 28-10-16 GL &RFC p3&191 MR20
SHARPE,Robert.MC.T2Lt dow 12-9-18 10 att2Leinst p175&75,Lincs CR France145,Lincs
SHARPE,Stanley Arthur TLtACapt kia 23-11-17 12SWBord p101 MR17
SHARPE,Sydney William T2Lt dow 25-3-18 25RFus p70 CR France103,26Bn
SHARPE,Thomas William.DCM.T2Lt ded 5-7-18 LabCps p189&258 CR Yorks548
SHARPIN,Frank Lloyd T2Lt dow 14-10-16 9 att8Beds p86 CR France105
SHARPLES,Evelyn Horace Guy TCapt kld 19-1-18 RFC p17 CR Yorks138
SHARPLES,George Woods T2LtALt kia 7-6-17 19Lpool p72 CR Belgium127
SHARPLES,Norman.MID TLt kia 20-9-17 7RFC p13 CR Belgium18
SHARPLES,Norman Capt&Adj kia 21-3-18 Manch att16Bn p156 MR27

SHARPLES,Philip Edmund TLt kia 7-6-17 9Y&L p159 CR Belgium127
SHARPLEY,Henry Lt dow 24-3-18 RFA A66TMB p208 CR France770
SHARPS,Herbert Charles Valentine T2Lt kia 22-4-18 RB att1Bn p180 CR France411
SHARPS,Robert T2Lt kia 18-4-18 61MGC p185 CR France202
SHARRATT,Robert Weetman TLt kia 10-3-16 16LancF p93 CR France702
SHATTOCK,Harry Edward TLtACapt dow 7-8-17 7RWKent p142 CR Belgium11
SHATTOCK,Montague Mancha Capt kia 8-1-15 16Lond p249 CR France1140
SHAVE,Leslie Harne T2Lt kia 12-4-17 6Dors p124 CR France531
SHAW,Albert T2Lt kia 12-10-16 9Norf p74 MR21
SHAW,Albert Thomas T2Lt dow 13-6-18 1/7RWar p66 CR Italy11,Lt 18-6-18
SHAW,Alexander Jack 2Lt kia 12-10-16 4 att10A&SH p173 MR21
SHAW,Alexander James Mackintosh TCapt kia 9-7-16 1KOSB p102 CR France339
SHAW,Alexander Morton Capt kia 10-4-18 Yorks p255 MR32
SHAW,Alfred T2Lt kia 1-10-17 Leic att8Bn p88 MR30
SHAW,Alfred 2Lt dow 8-8-19 ACycCps p255 CR Lincs179,Lt
SHAW,Alfred John 2Lt drd 27-5-18 NottsYeo p205 MR41
SHAW,Arthur Gilbey TLt kia 24-12-15 10N&D p135 CR Belgium72
SHAW,Arthur James 2Lt kld 1-2-18 RFC p17 CR Surrey95
SHAW,Bernard Henry Gilbert Lt kia 18-12-14 2WYorks p83 MR22
SHAW,Bernard Hudson T2Lt kia 22-1-17 13Ches p96 CR Belgium54
SHAW,Bernard Lynton Lt kia 23-4-17 4RWFus att2SWBord p223 MR20
SHAW,Charles Athelstan Capt dow 9-1-16 1KEdwardsHorse p24 CR France80
SHAW,Charles Conway.MC.TLt kia 31-8-18 39MGC Inf p185 CR France421
SHAW,Charles Henry 2Lt dow 1-8-17 3Beds p86 MR29
SHAW,Charles Richard 2Lt kia 11-4-18 86WRid p227
SHAW,Charles Salisbury T2Lt dow 30-9-18 1/7Lpool p72 CR France106
SHAW,Clarence Gordon Lt kia 1-7-16 1Lincs p75 MR21
SHAW,Cuthbert Frank 2Lt kia 30-10-14 att2RSuss B'Coy p120 MR29
SHAW,Cyril Trevor Capt kia 23-11-15 IA 122Inf att120 p282 MR38,22-11-15 Rajputs
SHAW,David Perston Maj kia 15/16-6-15 6ScotRif p224 MR22
SHAW,Douglas Sinclair.MIDx2 Lt ded 7-8-17 IARO att61Pnrs p282 CR EAfrica38 &CR Tanzania1
SHAW,Dugald 2Lt dow 27-7-18 1/5SfthH p241 CR France1697
SHAW,Edward Alfred TCapt kia 7-10-16 6 O&BLI p130 MR21
SHAW,Edward Lockhart T2Lt kia 5-8-16 9RWSurr p56 CR France251
SHAW,Edward Wingfield.DSO.Capt dow 7-12-16 1Mddx p148 CR France145
SHAW,Ernest Vernon James 2Lt ded 10-11-18 IARO att2/56Rif p282 MR65
SHAW,Evelyn Fidgeon 24-8-18 FANYC CR France1415
SHAW,Eyre Massey Lt dow 30-7-16 5 att11Mddx p148 CR France44
SHAW,Francis Joseph Marshall 2Lt kia 5-7-16 1N&D p135 MR21
SHAW,Frank Aubrey.MC.Lt kia 16-7-18 6LancF &98RAF p271 MR20
SHAW,George T2Lt kia 12-4-18 2Lincs p75 CR Belgium74
SHAW,George Herbert.VD.LtCol kia 24-4-15 4EYorks p219 MR29,Hubert
SHAW,Gerald Alan Santor T2Lt kia 1-7-17 1/8Lpool p72 CR Belgium10,4-7-17
SHAW,Giles Havergal Lt kia 11-4-17 5Beds p219 MR20
SHAW,Gordon Thompson.MC.TCapt kia 28-8-18 1RMunstF p176 CR France592
SHAW,Guy Trevor TMaj kia 7-7-16 2Nhampt p138 MR21
SHAW,Harold Maj kia 4-6-15 1LancF p93 MR4
SHAW,Harold Lee T2Lt kia 9-6-16 1Lincs p75 CR France281,10-6-16 1/4Bn
SHAW,Harold Joseph T2Lt dow 11-4-18 KRRC att2Bn p152 CR France201
SHAW,Harry 2Lt ded 20-4-19 TankCps p188 CR Ches137
SHAW,Henry Lynn TCapt kia 3-7-16 10RWar p66
SHAW,Herman Lt dow 26-4-17 RE 248FC p48 CR France95
SHAW,Hugh James Capt kld 11-11-14 5 att1RFus p70 CR France348
SHAW,James Capt kia 9-4-16 IA 2Rajputs p282 MR38
SHAW,John T2Lt kia 26-4-18 Manch p156 CR France144
SHAW,John Donald Lt kia 26-7-18 9RScots p212 CR France864,13Bn
SHAW,John Fyffe T2Lt kld 19-2-18 RFC p17 CR Scot386
SHAW,John Herbert 2Lt kia 26-10-17 6NumbF p214 MR30
SHAW,John William T2Lt kia 21-3-18 7KRRC p152 MR27
SHAW,Joshua Harold 2Lt dow 1-5-18 3 att1WYorks p83 CR France142
SHAW,John Thomas Capt ded 8-5-18 20LancF p93&258 CR Lancs2
SHAW,Julius Brinkley 2Lt kia 25-3-18 18Mddx att7Nhampt p148 MR27
SHAW,Leslie Gardner 2Lt kia 13-10-15 5SStaffs p229 MR19
SHAW,Llewellyn William Emile TCapt kia 10-8-18 10A&SH p173 CR France649
SHAW,Marmaduke Marshall.MC.LtACapt kia 21-3-18 3 att2N&D p135 CR France646
SHAW,Maurice TLt dow 30-9-15 12HLI p164 CR France1
SHAW,Max Joseph TLt kia 15-9-16 16 att26RFus p70 MR21

SHAW,Patrick T2Lt kia 30-6-15 1Leinst p175 CR France1140
SHAW,Philip Lt kia 26-10-17 6 att5NumbF p214 MR30
SHAW,Philip Haldane 2Lt kia 25-9-15 8BlkW p129 MR19
SHAW,Ralph.DSO.Lt kia 28-4-17 RWar SR att11Bn p66 MR20
SHAW,Randolph Albert Maj dow 14-11-16 A62RFA p35 CR France188
SHAW,Raymond Pugh Lt Capt kia 28-11-15 5 att2RFus p70 MR4
SHAW,Reginald Thomas Lt kia 9-5-15 RSuss att2Bn p120 MR22
SHAW,Richard Joseph T2Lt dow 26-6-17 11SLancs p126 CR France40
SHAW,Robert Capt kia 20-9-17 7Lpool p215 CR Belgium128
SHAW,Robert Dykes Somerville TCapt kia 23-3-18 7SfthH p165 MR27
SHAW,Robert Edward Fredric.MC.LtCol kia 23-8-18 13Lond p249 CR France924
SHAW,Robert Henderson T2Lt kia 18-9-16 13NumbF p63 CR Belgium83
SHAW,Robert Ramsey Stewart Lt kia 1-7-16 1/6NStaffs p238 CR France576
SHAW,Ronald Percy T2Lt kia 22-3-18 66MGC p185 MR27
SHAW,Rowan T2Lt kia 22-2-16 9Ches p96 CR France705
SHAW,S.TLt ded 13-1-18 GoldCoastR p202 CR EAfrica10 &CR Tanzania1
SHAW,Sydney Thomas T2Lt dow 11-5-16 12 att10WYorks p83 CR France285
SHAW,Thomas 2Lt kia 2-4-18 4SLancs p230
SHAW,Thomas Charles Whitehall 2Lt kia 24-8-18 4Lond p246 CR France395
SHAW,Thomas Gordon 2Lt kia 17-3-18 94RFC p17 MR20
SHAW,Thomas Herbert Lt kia 8-8-17 7RInniskF p105 MR29
SHAW,Victor Charles 2Lt ded 16-10-16 3/1RFA attZ29TMB p209 CR France145
SHAW,Walter Douglas.MC.TLt dow 8-11-18 RFus att1/10Manch p70 CR France1211,7-11-18
SHAW,William 2Lt kia 1-7-16 2SfthH p165 MR21
SHAW,William Lt ded PoW 27-9-16 1Camb p245 CR France598
SHAW,William Bernard TLt kia 12-4-17 9RSuss B'Coy p120 MR20
SHAW,William Cobley T2Lt kia 6-9-17 2Wilts p153 CR Belgium17
SHAW,William Easterby Lt dow 18-5-15 2KSLI p145 CR France102
SHAW,William Henry 2Lt kia 2-11-17 1/5Norf p217 CR Palestine8
SHAW,William Hetherington TLt kia 8-10-18 3MGC Inf p185 CR France358
SHAW,William Lindsay.MC.TLt AMaj kia 16-4-18 RE 228FC p48 CR Belgium20
SHAW,William Maxwell.DSO.Maj kia 29-5-17 102RFA p35 CR Belgium127
SHAW-HELLIER,Arthur Joseph Bradney TLt kia 9-8-15 7SStaffs p123 MR4
SHAW-STEWART,Neil Lt kia 21-8-16 3RB C'Coy p180 CR France402,Niel
SHAW-TWILLEY,J.Lt 9-5-20 RFA CR Yorks38
SHAW-WOOD,Richard T2Lt kld 17-3-18 RFC p17&258,SHAW
SHAWYER,Maurice Arthur Pritchard 2Lt kia 12-10-14 5 att1Mddx p148 MR32,14-10-14
SHEA,Joseph Patrick Lambert.MC.Capt&QM dow 1-12-17 2DLI p161
SHEA,Richard Thomas Lt ded 12-11-18 RGA p41 CR Wales383,2Lt
SHEARBURN,Frank Alan 2Lt kia 14-9-16 4 att10ScotRif p104 CR France703
SHEARBURN,Herbert Henry SubCdr 17-11-15 1AOrdDept CR India164
SHEARD,Arthur William 2Lt dow 17-1-17 5Y&L p238 CR France41,5/6Bn
SHEARD,Fraser Morton.MC.TCapt dow PoW 2-4-18 18Lpool p72 CR France441
SHEARD,Geoffrey Senior 2Lt dedacc 26-6-17 3Ches p96 CR France113
SHEARD,Thomas William Maj ded 29-9-17 RDC p253 CR Ches53
SHEARER,George.MC.TLt ACapt kia 24-8-18 13Y&L p159 CR France324
SHEARER,J.F.Capt 17-7-21 RASC CR Iraq8
SHEARER,William Lt kia 8-6-18 315RFA p208 CR France61
SHEARMAN,Ambrose Augustus Capt dow 20-4-18 2/7Lond C'Coy p247 CR France37,Augustine
SHEARMAN,Eustace Robert Ambrose LtCol kia 13-5-15 10Huss p22 CR Belgium4
SHEARMAN,Herbert Henry Lt dow 5-7-16 1 att2Lincs p75 CR France23
SHEARMAN,Valentine Lt ACapt dow 25-3-18 2RScots p54 CR France103
SHEARS,Arthur Cecil 2Lt kia 3-7-16 7Suff p79 MR21
SHEARS,Edward Hornby Lt kia 4-7-17 IrGds p53
SHEASBY,Edwin William 2Lt kia 15-9-16 1Lond p245 MR21
SHEAY,William 2Lt dow 16-5-15 2Yorks p91 CR France80,Lt
SHECKLETON,Richard Lt kia 8-6-17 8NStaffs p157 MR29
SHEDDEN,Graham Percival Capt dow 31-10-14 RGA 35HB p41 CR Belgium57
SHEDDEN-DOBBIE,Robert T2Lt dow 12-4-17 11A&SH p173
SHEDEL,Rupert Frederick 2Lt kia 12-10-16 3 att1Ess p132 MR21
SHEEHAN,Cornelius T2Lt kld 8-8-17 6MunstF att17RFC p13&176 CR Greece9
SHEEHAN,Desmond Joseph T2Lt ded 10-5-17 66RFC p13 CR France924
SHEEHAN,Gordon Keith Patrick Lt kia 28-8-18 2Nhampt p138 CR France268
SHEEHAN,Martin Joseph 2Lt kld 1-10-18 2RMunstF &RAF p266
SHEEN,Cyril Cross T2Lt dow 3-5-17 11Suff p79 CR France113,2-5-17
SHEEN,George Edward Hayes Capt ded 19-2-15 6RIrRif p170
SHEEPSHANKS,Charles John Harcourt TCapt kia 17-3-16 8Dev p77 CR France188

SHEEPSHANKS,William 2Lt kia 10-7-17 6 att2KRRC p152 MR31
SHEFFIELD,Edward Frederick T2Lt kld 17-5-16 GL &RFC 7KiteBallSect p3&191 CR France68
SHEFFIELD,George Alfred Charles T2Lt kia 26-10-17 1SStaffs p123 MR30
SHEFFIELD,George Nelson Maj ded 1-1-18 3Ess p132 CR Sussex178
SHEFFIELD,Harold Welford Lt kia 23-3-18 1EYorks p85 MR27
SHEFFIELD,Lancelot Hull 2Lt kia 25-3-17 3 att2Dors p124 MR38
SHEFFIELD,Ralph David 2Lt kia 16-6-17 2/3Lond p246 MR20
SHEFFIELD,Surtees TLt kia 6-8-15 13 att2Hamps p121 MR4
SHEGOG,Richard Wellington TCapt dow 1-8-17 RAMC att1/4LNLancs p197 CR Belgium11
SHEIL,Charles 2Lt dow 22-4-18 RMunstF &2RAF p176 CR France179
SHEKURY,Cecil.MC.TLt kia 16-4-18 2Beds p86 CR Belgium12
SHELDON,Archibald Edward 2Lt dow 23-8-15 5Ess p232 CR Gallipoli27
SHELDON,Charles Stanley Lt 27-6-18 70RAF MR20
SHELDON,Reginald Eley 2Lt dow 15-4-18 7N&D p233 CR France102
SHELDON,Robert.MM.Lt ded 3-6-20 1/5SStaffs p264 CR War9 Ex 26War
SHELDRAKE,Archibald Turner Lt kia 28-9-18 7HLI &RAF p271 MR20
SHELLEY,Cecil William Charles TLt kia 17-10-15 2ScotsGds p52 MR19
SHELLEY,Ernest Bowen Lt ACapt kia 12-9-18 1GrenGds p50 CR France1484
SHELLEY,Philip John 2Lt kia 31-7-17 C83RFA p35 CR Belgium115
SHELLINGTON,Percy Gordon T2Lt kld 26-8-17 RFC p13 CR Norf247 Ex CanadaEngrs
SHELTON,Charles Capt kia 21-10-16 8Norf p74 MR21
SHELTON,John Parker 2Lt kia 19-4-17 8Hamps p229 CR Palestine8
SHELTON,Kenneth Lt TCapt dow 14-2-18 3EKent &RFC p17&58 CR France987
SHELTON,Lionel Cartlidge Lt 7-6-20 MGC Inf att RAOC CR Egypt6
SHENKEL,Frank J.HonLt dow 19-11-17 GL p191
SHENNAN,Douglas Francis Fairfax Lt kia 8-5-15 4KRRC D'Coy p152 MR29
SHENTON,Austin Kirk.MC.TLt ACapt ded 26-7-18 RE 12SigCo p48 CR France29
SHEPARD,Bernard Anthony T2Lt dow 26-5-17 RFA attZ24TMB p35 CR Nhampt13
SHEPARD,Cyril Harry T2Lt kia 1-7-16 9Dev p77 CR France330
SHEPARD,Norbert Gerald TLt dow 2-8-16 103RFA D'HB p35 CR France44
SHEPHARD,Ernest Arthur 2Lt kia 11-1-17 5Dors p124 CR France744
SHEPHARD,Ernest Edward.MID 2Lt kia 6-6-18 4Glouc p225 CR France20,12Bn
SHEPHARD,Gordon Strachey.DSO.MC.MID BrigGen kia 19-1-18 RFusstaff Cmdg1RFC p17&70 CR France88
SHEPHARD,Stuart Norman T2Lt kld 17-2-18 GL &RFC p17 CR Essex1
SHEPHEARD,Philip Capt kia 13-6-15 1Ess p132 MR4
SHEPHERD,Alfred Seymour.DSO.MC.2Lt kia 20-7-17 29RFC p13 MR20
SHEPHERD,Arthur Lindesay Moore TLt ded 3-11-16 PoW 6KRRC &RFC p3&152 CR France604
SHEPHERD,C.H.CB.DSO.Col 2-1-20 1Lincs CR India97A
SHEPHERD,Charles Arthur T2Lt kia 12-10-16 7Norf p74 CR France294
SHEPHERD,Edward Alexander Capt kia 3-9-16 4BlkW p230 MR21
SHEPHERD,Edwin Alexander TLt dow 13-4-18 3MGC p185 CR France98,14-4-18
SHEPHERD,Gerald Alexander Gaselee Capt kia 20-12-14 IA 57Rif p282 CR France571
SHEPHERD,Harold Ernest Lt ded 30-12-18 RFA p256 CR Beds75
SHEPHERD,James Duncan.MC.AMaj kia 8-8-19 RE att1S&M p255 MR38
SHEPHERD,James Montague Edward Capt kia 15-2-17 RB &1RFC p13&180 CR Belgium115
SHEPHERD,John Cuthbert Lt kia 25-8-18 4 att10LancF p93 CR France239
SHEPHERD,Norman Robinson Capt kia 4-11-16 7DLI p239 CR France388
SHEPHERD,Richard Malcolm Sisnett 2Lt kia 9-8-16 4RIrReg &RFC p4&89,ded MR20
SHEPHERD,Stanley T2Lt kia 27-9-18 DLI att8Lpool p161 CR France1496
SHEPHERD,Stanley Le Fleming.MC&Bar.Maj kia 10-8-19 Nhampt att45RFus p255 CR Europe179,SHEPPERD
SHEPHERD,Tom Lt kia 17-10-18 4Y&L p238 CR France441,2Bn
SHEPHERD-CROSS,Cecil Herbert.MID Maj dow 15-10-17 DukeofLancYeo att197MGC p187&204 CR Belgium16
SHEPHERD-TURNEHAM,Thomas Percy TCapt kia 28-9-16 6Yorks p91 MR21 Norman
SHEPPARD,A.G.E.Lt kld 12-11-17 1/4KAR p202
SHEPPARD,Asa Frederick T2Lt kld 23-2-17 GL &27RFC p13 CR Lancs474
SHEPPARD,Charles 2Lt kia 27-9-18 16Lond D'Coy p250 CR France429
SHEPPARD,Charles Westcar Lt ded 29-10-18 RE p262
SHEPPARD,Frederick William T2Lt kia 12-6-17 12RSuss p120 CR Belgium126
SHEPPARD,Gordon 2Lt dow 3-11-17 RGA 309SB p41 CR France64,HAC
SHEPPARD,Hubert 2Lt dow 9-12-17 2/17Lond p250 CR Palestine3

SHEPPARD,Illtyd 2Lt ded 3-1-21 IA 1/15Sikhs p282 CR Iraq8
SHEPPARD,Joseph Henry T2Lt kia 24-8-18 7RWSurr p56 CR France116,Lt
SHEPPARD,Lewis Charles Burford 2Lt kia 21-4-17 3SomLI att32RFC p13&80 CR France41
SHEPPARD,Percy Howard.MM.2Lt dow 28-5-18 RGA 119SB p42 CR France1332
SHEPPARD,Reginald Thomas Lt ded 13-5-17 13Lond att2/10Manch p249 CR France163,dow
SHEPPARD,Richard Bellamy.MC.TCapt kia 22-4-18 14WelchR p127 CR France59
SHEPPARD,Samuel Gurney.DSO.LtCol dow 21-8-15 HertsYeo p204 CR Gallipoli5,kia
SHEPPARD,Sidney 2Lt kia 28-4-17 3/10Lond att17RFus p248 MR20
SHEPPERD,S.Le F.MC&Bar.Maj 10-8-19 6Nhampt att45RFus MR70
SHEPPEY-GREENE,Napier Guy Sheppey Lt dow 14-6-18 3 att7RWKent p142 CR France69
SHEPPHARD,W.Lt&QM 29-5-20 RASC CR Surrey115
SHEREK,Paul Lt kld 1-10-18 NStaffs &57RAF p265 CR France658
SHERER,Stephen Frank T2Lt kia 29-9-18 2SWBord p101 CR Belgium116
SHERIDAN,Daniel.MC.DCM.2Lt kia 24-3-18 2HLI p164 MR20
SHERIDAN,Henry Hamilton 2Lt kia 3-5-17 att1RIrFus p171 CR France1896
SHERIDAN,Henry Richards T2Lt kia 3-9-16 6ConnRgrs p172 CR France402
SHERIDAN,John Wilton Lt dedacc 27-9-18 CamH &54RAF CR Essex73
SHERIDAN,Leonard Capt kia 26-3-18 8 att2RDubF p177 MR27
SHERIDAN,Richard Brinsley TLt kld 7-3-16 8RDubF p177 CR France201
SHERIDAN,William Frederick Temple Capt kia 25-9-15 5 att2RB p180 MR32
SHERIDAN,William Nicholas T2Lt kia 1-9-16 17RIrRif p170 CR Belgium49
SHERIFF,Kenneth 2Lt dow 23-6-15 3RWKent att2BordR p142 CR France102
SHERIFF,Leo Frederick David 2Lt kia 13-11-16 4BlkW p230 CR France293,SHERRIFF
SHERIFF,Wilfred T2Lt kia 19-7-17 22DLI p161 CR Belgium29
SHERINGHAM,Hugh Valentine Lt ded 16-10-18 CamelTransCps attRASC p253 CR Egypt9,Capt
SHERLEY,James TCapt kia 27-11-17 RAVC att70RFA p199 CR France415
SHERLOCK,Charles Gregg Capt dow 14-11-17 RAMC DADMS p197 CR Iraq6
SHERLOCK,George Wright Stratford LtCol dow 30-6-21 IA 2/21Punjabis p282 MR43
SHERLOCK,Gerald T2Lt dow 21-4-18 55MGC p185 CR France88
SHERLOCK,Gerrard Loundes Edward Lt kia 25-8-14 3Huss att5NigR p21&202 CR WAfrica58,Capt
SHERLOCK,Ronald Francis Capt kia 23-7-16 2KRRC p152 MR21
SHERMAN,John James Lt kia 20-10-17 15/36RH&FA p35 CR Belgium94
SHERMAN,Palton 2Lt kia 30-4-17 GL &RFC p13 CR France1483
SHERMAN,Reginald TCapt dow 10-10-17 RAMC att4FA p197 CR Belgium12
SHERRARD,Bertram 2Lt kia 22-5-18 D92RFA p35 CR France547
SHERRARD,John Charles TCapt ded 28-3-19 SL p255&268
SHERREN,Arthur Oswald Capt kia 3-8-17 4EKent p212 MR29
SHERREN,Hugh Godwin.MID Maj ded 28-2-20 RAMC p267 CR Asia51
SHERRIFF,Alexander T2Lt kia 22-3-18 1/2 att6/7RScotF p95 MR20
SHERRIFF,Alexander Nimmo 2Lt kia 30-10-14 1Nhampt p138 MR29
SHERRIFF,John George Lt kia 26-4-15 7A&SH p243 MR29
SHERRY,Gerald.MID 2Lt dow 26-7-16 1Beds p86 CR France833
SHERSTON,Somerset Arthur Capt kia 9-5-15 RB p180 MR32
SHERVINGTON,Thomas Robert Munro Capt dow 25-9-15 8EKent p58 MR19
SHERVINGTON,William Hugh Byam T2Lt kia 18-7-16 9 att6Beds p86 MR21
SHERWELL,Ferdinand Nigel TLt kia 13-6-17 7Beds p86 CR France541
SHERWELL,Rex 2Lt kia 3-7-16 3Lincs &25RFC p4&75 CR France88
SHERWOOD,Charles Edward 2Lt kia 22-10-17 3 O&BLI p130 CR Belgium112
SHERWOOD,Clement Walter T2Lt kia 28-11-17 17RFus p70 MR17
SHERWOOD,Hamilton Stanley 2Lt kia 28-8-18 3 att1/4KSLI p145 CR France98,29-8-18
SHERWOOD,Robert T2Lt kia 26-2-18 GL &RFC p17 CR France95
SHERWOOD,William Bernard Lt kia 27-10-17 RFC p13 MR20
SHERYER,Harold John Lt dow 5-8-17 8Hamps p229 CR France139
SHEWAN,Alan Davidson TLt kia 15-9-16 11A&SH p173 CR France453,Capt
SHIEL,John Hubert Trevor 2Lt kia 8-3-18 1Dors p124 CR Belgium12
SHIELD,Clement Ridley.MC.Capt kia 7-10-16 4HLI att51DivHQ p164 CR France3,8-10-16
SHIELD,Frederick Dowson T2Lt kia 6-7-16 8 att5Nhampt p138 CR France251
SHIELD,William James 2Lt kia 2-3-17 6Lpool p215 MR29
SHIELDS,Donald De Vere Lt 10-11-18 42CanadaInf CR Belgium241
SHIELDS,George Hilliard TLt kia 3-2-17 GoldCoastR p202 CR EAfrica38 &CR Tanzania1
SHIELDS,Hugh John Sladen Lt kia 25/26-10-14 RAMC p197 MR29 Haden

SHIELDS,William TLt kia 5-9-17 14Manch &45RFC p13&156 CR Belgium124
SHIELDS,William Francis Waugh TLt kia 25-9-15 9 att5KSLI p145 MR29
SHIFFNER,John Bridger.Bart.2Lt kia 24-9-18 RSuss att2Bn p120 CR France375
SHILCOCK,John Winton Lt kia 22/24-11-15 5RWSurr p212 MR38
SHILLINGFORD,Stanley Charles Lt kia 16-6-18 2RFus &RAF p70 CR France324
SHILLINGTON,Thomas Graham TCapt ded 18-8-17 9RIrFus 108Bde 36Div p171 CR Belgium8
SHIMMIN,Thomas Edward 2Lt kld 22-4-17 NorthDivCyc attRFC p19&253 CR Egypt15
SHINE,Edward.DCM.2Lt kia 20-10-18 15RWar p66 CR France1396
SHINE,Hugh Patrick 2Lt kia 25-5-15 1RIrFus p171 MR29
SHINE,James Rev dow 21-4-18 RAChDept att21Mddx p200 CR France102
SHINE,James Owen Williams.MID Capt kia 16-8-17 2RDubF p177 MR30
SHINE,John Denis 2Lt ded 25-8-14 RIrReg p89 CR Belgium241,Denys
SHINGLER,John Stanley Marsh.MC.Capt dow 4-9-18 4RWFus p223 CR France177
SHINN,Stanley Gilbert Lt ded 13-12-18 20Lond p251 CR France146
SHINNER,William Goodwin Blake Lt dow 2-1-18 28Lond p252 CR France398
SHIPLEY,Arthur Hammond Butler T2Lt kia 27-9-16 6Yorks A'Coy 11Div p91 MR21
SHIPLEY,Harold TLtCol ded 2-10-18 11RLancs att11BrWIndR p59 CR Italy12
SHIPP,Robert Cyril Lt ded 11-1-18 RASC p193 CR Devon1
SHIPPARD,Sanford William Lt kia 10-7-17 1LNLancs p136 MR31
SHIPPEY,Cyril Shaw 2Lt dow 21-12-15 3 att8Beds p86 CR Belgium11
SHIPPEY,James Reginald 2Lt dow 14-10-14 4Beds p86 CR France80
SHIPPOBOTTOM,Frank T2Lt dow 20-11-17 1/4LNLancs p136 CR France446
SHIPSTER,Walter Neville.MC.MID Capt dow 20-9-18 1Manch p156 CR Palestine9
SHIPTON,Cyril Herbert 2Lt kia 25-9-15 2HLI p164 MR19
SHIPWAY,Guy Maxwell Capt kia 23-8-14 1Glouc p107 CR France1752,26-8-14
SHIRLEY,Archibald Vincent 2Lt kia 8-6-17 WelshHorseYeo attRFC p19&205 MR20
SHIRLEY,John George Frederick 2Lt kia 22-4-18 1Hamps p121 CR France411
SHIRLEY,Samuel Myatt 2Lt dow 1-5-17 18Manch p156 CR France214
SHIRREFF,Francis Gordon 2Lt kia 1-7-16 2RBerks p140 MR21
SHIRTCLIFF,Fred T2Lt kia 9-4-18 10DLI p161 MR32,SHIRTLIFF
SHIVES,Robert Kilgour TCapt kld 29-9-16 RFC p4
SHOESMITH,Edward James 2Lt kia 7-6-17 1RFus p70
SHONE,Geoffrey Beville.MC.Lt dow 19-10-17 1SStaffs att56RFC p13,123&259 CR France13
SHONE,Harold Lonsdale T2Lt ded 9-7-18 6RRofCav p24&261 CR Ches,10-7-18
SHONE,Robert Francis 2Lt kia 14-2-15 ESurr p113 MR29
SHOOBERT,Neil TLt kia 31-7-17 23Mddx p148 MR29
SHOOSMITH,Frank Stewart Lt kia 21-8-15 5Beds p219 MR4
SHOOTER,John Harold.MC.2Lt kia 10-4-18 5Y&L &RAF p238 CR France303
SHORE,Florence Nightingale Sister 16-1-20 QAIMNS CR Mddx53
SHORE,Walter Francis LtCol ded 6-12-16 RAVC p199 MR66
SHOREMAN,James.MC.2Lt kia 27-9-18 7Lpool p215 CR France1498
SHORLAND-BALL,Leslie 2Lt kia 6-9-16 3RIrRif p170 SeeSHORTLAND-BALL
SHORROCK,Thomas Dudley Ralph T2Lt kia 20-9-17 26RFus p70 MR30
SHORT,Andrew David Aitkin 2Lt kia 26-3-18 18LancF p93 MR27
SHORT,Cuthbert William.MC.Lt kia 6-3-17 IARO 9HodsonsHorse attRFC p282 CR France833
SHORT,Francis Leslie Capt ded 3-6-16 1RWKent p142 CR Lond7,3Bn
SHORT,James 2Lt ded 8-4-19 LabCps attEgyptLabCps p189 CR Egypt15
SHORT,John TLt ded 28-10-18 11WelshR p127 CR Greec9
SHORT,Oliver James T2Lt dow PoW 3-4-18 10Worc p109 CR Belgium406
SHORT,Vere Dawson TCapt kia 25-9-15 7Nhampt p138
SHORT,Walter TCapt kia 20-7-18 YLI 7 att5Bn p143 CR France 1689
SHORT,William Ambrose.CMG.LtCol kia 21-6-17 286RFA p35&258 CR France922
SHORT,William Innes 2Lt kia 11-8-15 1KOSB p102 MR4
SHORTEN,Henry William 2Lt kia 16-10-18 RGA 19SB p42 CR France1392
SHORTER,Alfred George T2Lt kia 1-7-16 16DLI p161 MR21
SHORTER,Lewis Victor Henry Lt ded 14-11-19 1/4EKent p271 CR Asia60
SHORTER,Vernon Banbury Capt dow 28-9-17 Lincs att10RWSurr p75 CR France139
SHORTER,William John Lt kia 24-3-18 1/8Ess attRFC p19&232 CR France95
SHORTHOUSE,Algernon Geoffrey T2Lt ded 5-6-18 13Yorks p91 CR Camb16
SHORTLAND-BALL,Leslie 2Lt kia 6-9-16 3 att8RIrF p265 MR21 See SHORLAND-BALL
SHORTO,Martin Hubert Lt kia 27-7-17 RE p210 CR Belgium24
SHORTRIDGE,Arthur 2Lt kia 14-3-15 2RIrFus p171 MR29

SHORTT,Vere Dawson Capt 25-9-15 7Nhampt MR19
SHORTT,William Edward Dudley Lt kia 12-10-17 1ScotsGds p52 CR Belgium13
SHOTT,Henry Hammond.DSO.Capt kia 26-8-14 1RBerks p140 CR France944
SHOVEL,Thomas Jasper Rev dow 5-10-18 RAChDept att2/2WessexFA p200 CR France759
SHOWELL,Harold George T2Lt kia 16-7-17 27NumbF p63 CR France366
SHOWERS,H.L.LtCol.CSI.CIE.2-2-16 IA CR Mddx26
SHOWERS,St.George Swaine Lt kia 9-8-15 3 att2Ess p132 MR20
SHRAPNEL,Victor George Fleetwood TLtACapt kia 23-3-18 8ESurr A'Coy p113 MR27
SHREWSBURY,Carl Brannell 2Lt kia 13-10-15 5Lincs p220 MR19
SHRUBSOLE,Arthur Edward T2Lt kia 13-4-17 11Leic p88 CR France223
SHUBRICK,Richard Brian LtTCapt dow 28-4-15 1RInniskF p105 MR4
SHUFF,William Edward Lt&QM ded 20-12-16 SL 4RWSurr p201 CR Mddx66
SHUFFLEBOTHAM,Guy Mynors.MID TLtTCapt kia 3-9-16 7SomLI p80 CR France294
SHUFFLEBOTHAM,John T2Lt kia 25/27-9-15 12NumbF p63 MR19
SHUFFREY,Gilbert Lt kia 9-8-15 6SLancs p126 MR4
SHUMM,Brian Godfrey 2Lt 27-9-18 22RAF MR20
SHUREY,Charles TCapt dow 21-7-16 10RFus p70 CR France833
SHUREY,Edward TLt ded 18-7-18 16WelshR p127 CR Eire322
SHUTE,George Francis 2Lt ded PoW 13-10-17 4 att2/6Glouc p225 MR20
SHUTT,Herbert Cecil Lt kia 13-11-16 3 att1RScotF p95 MR21
SHUTTLEWORTH,Ernest Hebden T2Lt kia 20-7-18 WYorks att8Bn p83 CR France622
SHUTTLEWORTH,Ernest Ronald 2Lt kia 1-7-16 1/8RWar p215 MR21
SHUTTLEWORTH,Henry T2Lt kia 2-10-18 1/2 att16LancF p93 CR France237
SHUTTLEWORTH,Kingsley Christopher Lt kia 19-11-17 1/4Suff p217 CR Belgium125
SHUTTLEWORTH,Robert George Maj kia 10-8-15 IA 110Mahrattas att9RWar p282 MR4
SHUTTLEWORTH,R.W.2Lt ded 15-8-18 9LancF &RAF p93 CR Yorks487,16-8-18
SIBBIT,George Bertrand TLt kia 27-9-18 1NumbF p63 MR16
SIBBIT,Henry T.Maj kia 1-7-16 22NumbF p63 MR21
SIBETH,Charles George Augustine 2Lt kia 9-8-15 RE p48 MR29
SIBLEY,Robert Dymond Gladman Maj 1-10-18 210RAF MR20
SIBOLD,Foster Moverley T2Lt kia 25-9-15 10HLI p164 MR19
SIBOLD,Sidney Sparkling Moverley.MC.LtACapt dow 12-4-18 C165RH&FA p35
SICHEL,Geoffrey Michael John Lt kia 9-2-15 3Mddx p148 MR29
SICHEL,Oliver Walter.MID Capt dow 25-10-18 5 att2/6RWar p214 CR France332
SIDDALL,David Henry 2Lt kia 16-9-18 5YLI p235 CR France97
SIDDALL,Douglas Hamblett T2Lt kia 11-4-18 51MGC p185 MR19
SIDDALL,Joseph Henry Lt 25-7-18 209RAF MR20
SIDDALL,Thomas Arthur 2Lt dow 17-4-17 25Lond p252 CR France120
SIDDLE,Joe 2Lt dow 14-10-17 3 att1/5YLI p144 CR Belgium3
SIDDONS,Henry Thomas Brandon 2Lt dow 24-8-16 5Leinst p175 CR France513
SIDEBOTHAM,Gerald Capt kia 9-3-18 1/4Ches p222 CR Palestine3
SIDEBOTHAM,James Nasmyth Wedgwood TCapt kia 12-10-16 17Manch p156 MR21
SIDEBOTHAM,John Frith TLt kia 12-2-16 6KSLI p145 CR Belgium101
SIDEBOTTOM,Robert Yardley Capt kia 26-8-14 2LancF p93 MR15
SIDEY,William Hepburn 2Lt dow 13-10-17 RGA 62SB p42 CR Belgium16,12-10-17
SIDGWICK,Arthur Hugh 2LtACapt dow 17-9-17 RGA 157SB p42 CR Belgium18
SIDLEY,John Witherington T2Lt dow 2-8-16 16/41RFA p35 CR France23
SIDNEY,Leicester Philip 2Lt kia 2-10-17 17KRRC &29RFC p13&152 CR Belgium140
SIDWELL,Albert Edward.MC.TLt kia 7-7-17 9RFus p70 CR France581,Capt
SIEBER,John Frederick Louis T2Lt dow 4-10-16 6EYorks p85 CR France64
SIEBER,John Lonsdale Lt kia 17-10-17 4A&SH att1/2KAR p173&202 CR Eafrica11 &CR Tanzania1
SIEBERT,Stanley Prentice T2Lt dow 21-9-17 16RB p180 CR France139
SIEDLE,Karl Otto.MC.TCapt.AMaj dow 30-5-18 B174RFA p35 CR France84
SIEVERS,Nowell Johnstone TCapt kia 30-11-17 9Ess p132 MR17
SIFTON,William Alfred T2Lt dow 25-12-15 8SStaffs p123 CR Belgium11
SIKES,Robert Gordon Lt ded 22-2-19 LeicYeo att4Huss p204 CR France146
SILBY,Thomas Stanley.MC.TLt kia 12-9-18 10SWBord p101 CR France415
SILCOCK,Bertram Baker.MID 2Lt kia 10-8-15 7RWFus p223 MR4,Baber
SILCOCK,Percy Bryan T2Lt dow 11-8-17 14 att16Ches p96 CR Belgium7,13Bn
SILCOTT,William Henry Capt ded 9-9-19 RH&FA p262 CR Devon1,H.W.RGA
SILCOX,Baylis.MID T2Lt kia 29-12-17 GL att7RDubF p191 CR Palestine3
SILK,Norman Galbraith Lt kia 9-6-15 2SWBord p101 CR Gallipoli6
SILK,Thomas William Lt kia 26-10-17 9Dev p77 MR30

SILL,John Sutton Capt ded 8-12-18 2EKent p262 CR Hamps7
SILLAR,Tom Cameron TLt kia 30-9-15 9Y&L p159 CR France680
SILLARS,David Robertson TCapt kia 4-5-18 12HLI p164 CR France60,4-6-18
SILLARS,George Alexander 2Lt kia 1-12-17 5HLI p240 CR Palestine9
SILLARS,Harry Frederick Lionel 2Lt kia 1-7-16 4A&SH att2SfthH p174 MR21
SILLARS,Hugh Conn Lt ded 19-2-19 RE IWT p48 CR France85
SILLEM,Arthur Henry Lt kia 24-3-18 4 att8NStaffs p157 CR France380
SILLEM,Augustus Charles Herman T2Lt kia 18-7-16 52RFA p35
SILLEM,Stuart Charles 2Lt kia 12-8-17 GL &RFC p13 MR20
SILLEM,Thomas George TLtACapt kia 14-4-18 16WelchR p127 MR30
SILLENCE,James.MM.Lt dow 24-4-18 1Hamps p121 CR France88,2Lt
SILLERY,Charles Cecil Archibald TLtCol kia 1-7-16 Cmdg20NumbF p63 CR France150
SILLERY,John Jocelyn Doyne.MID Maj kia 7-8-15 11Manch RetIA p156 MR4
SILLS,Charles Caldwell 2Lt kia 26-9-14 1SWBord p101 MR15
SILMON,William Osman de Weld 2Lt kia 28-2-17 8WYorks p219 CR France514
SILVER,Edward 2Lt kia 1-5-18 2/14Lond p249 CR palestine3
SILVER,Humphrey William T2Lt kia 7-6-18 RSuss att2Bn p120 CR France163,W.H.8-6-18
SILVER,John Watt 2Lt kia 26-10-18 4GordH p242 CR France1196
SILVER,Keith T2Lt kia 18-11-16 8Glouc p107 CR France215
SILVER,Sidney Edwin.MC.Capt kia 20-11-17 3 att11Ess p132&259 CR France379,Sydney
SILVER,Thomas Samuel Harper 2Lt kia 16-4-18 RGA 80SB p42 CR Belgium74
SILVER,Walter Barrington Maj ded 4-10-14 RIrFus p171 CR Hamps234,3-10-14
SILVER,Walter Laurence Conningham TLt kia 12-10-16 7Suff C'Coy p79 CR France512
SILVERS,Frank Pitchford.MC.Capt dow 27-5-18 1/6SStaffs p229 CR France10
SILVERTON,Ernest George.MM.2Lt kia 26-7-17 RGA 303SB p42 CR Belgium10
SILVERTOP,Francis Somerled Joseph Lt kia 20-5-17 OxYeo p205 CR France1495
SILVERTOP,William Alexander.MC.Capt kia 27-11-17 20Huss p23 CR France256
SILVERWOOD,Hugh Fletcher Capt kia 27-3-17 6Ess p232 MR34
SILVESTER,Anson Lloyd 2Lt kia 1-1-15 2RSuss p120 CR France720,31-12-14
SILVESTER,Geoffrey Francis TCapt dow 17-7-16 7KSLI p145 CR France66
SILVESTER,Reginald 2Lt kia 7-6-17 20Lond p251 MR29
SILVESTER,William Hugh T2Lt dow 3-11-18 RWar att2/7Bn p66 CR France146
SIM,Alexander Taylor T2Lt kia 12-5-16 13RScots p54 CR France423
SIM,Bueth Vernon Capt dow 7-5-15 Mddx att4Bn p148 CR Belgium35
SIM,Herman Alexander Coysgarne Lt kia 9-5-15 2ScotRif p104 CR France525
SIM,James Robertson Gould 2Lt kia 5-6-17 3RScots p54 CR France1182
SIM,John Moir.MID 2Lt kld 25-3-17 6GordH att70RFC p242&261 CR France518,kia
SIM,Lancelot George Earle 2Lt kia 14-9-16 1GrenGds SR p50 CR France630
SIM,Louis St.George Leslie 2Lt ded 20-12-15 11BlkW p129 CR Lond8
SIM,Norman Young 2Lt kia 9-9-16 9Lond p248 MR21
SIM,William Capt kia 13-11-16 5ScotRif att65SfthH p224 MR21,6Bn
SIM,William George 2Lt kia 14-10-18 5 att8BlkW p231 CR Belgium157
SIMCOCK,Gilbert Alexander 2Lt kia 9-4-14 14Ches p96 MR38
SIMEONS,Edward Emil TCapt dow 17-2-16 8Beds p86
SIMKIN,Horace John TCapt dow 14-7-16 13Lpool C'Coy p72 CR France141,kia
SIMKINS,Walter Francis 2Lt kia 9-10-16 3 att2WRid p116
SIMMANCE,Allan James Spencer TCapt kia 18-8-16 4Lpool p72 MR21
SIMMONDS,Austin Gundry 2Lt drd 2-6-17 5A Res RFA p35 CR Eire506
SIMMONDS,Frederick Daniel T2Lt ded 18-2-19 4Beds p263 CR Lond1
SIMMONDS,Guy Bloxham T2Lt kld 29-12-16 76MGC Inf p185 CR France300,kia 86/5MGC
SIMMONDS,Harold 2Lt kia 31-7-17 18Manch p156 MR29
SIMMONDS,Leslie Bernard 2Lt 16-9-18 57RAF MR20
SIMMONDS,Percy Grabham 2Lt kia 1-7-16 9Lond p248 MR21
SIMMONDS,Richard George T2Lt accdrd 4-7-17 GL 1Worc attRFC X'Depot p13 CR Egypt1
SIMMONDS,Walter Sangster T2Lt kia 7-10-16 10RB p180 MR21
SIMMONS,Arthur George 2Lt kia 7-2-16 IARO att114Mahrattas p282 MR38
SIMMONS,Benjamin Howard TLt kia 29-10-18 14ACycCps p181 CR Italy9
SIMMONS,Eric Warr 2Lt kia 11-8-15 6Y&L p159 MR4,10-8-15
SIMMONS,Frank Wortley Capt kia 22-11-17 2/4Hamps p228 CR Palestine3
SIMMONS,Frederick William T2Lt kia 27-5-18 1 att7Leic p88 MR18,2 att7Bn
SIMMONS,John 2Lt kld 21-8-16 3RB p180 CR Hamps1
SIMMONS,John Marcus Rainsford Lt dow 28-8-20 IA 1/116Mahrattas p282 MR38
SIMMONS,Paul Emery May Capt dow 24-7-15 4Hamps p228 MR38

SIMMONS,Percy Marston 2Lt kia 20-10-18 4Wilts p236 CR France270,2Bn

SIMMONS,Richard Ernest 2Lt kia 5-12-17 RGA 232SB p42 CR Belgium25

SIMMONS,Robert Dendney 2Lt kia 23-9-18 7Lond p247 CR France155,Deudney

SIMMONS,Robert George T2Lt kia 22-3-18 11RFus p70 MR27

SIMMONS,Russell Louis Harry 2Lt kia 25-9-15 RBerks p140 MR32

SIMMONS,Sydney Noël Lt dow 27-10-16 RWiltsYeo p205 CR Surrey157

SIMMONS,Walter John.MC.Lt dow 27-8-18 17Lond p250

SIMMONS,William Aubrey TLt dow 3-11-18 B88 RFA p35 CR France332

SIMMONSl,B.H AssSurg2Cl 8-11-19 IMS MR67

SIMMS,Alexander Capt drd 13-9-18 RE p48 MR40,12-9-18

SIMMS,Alfred George Francis Lt ded 30-12-17 6ConnRgrs p172 MR41,drd

SIMMS,George Norman.MVO.Capt ded 27-8-14 2RMunsF p176 CR France1751

SIMMS,J.B.P.2Lt kld 4-6-18 3NumbF &4RAF p63 MR20

SIMMS,John Sibbald Capt kia 26-10-17 12Lond p248 CR Belgium20

SIMMS,William Capt kia 19-7-16 2/6RWar p214 CR France567

SIMON,Eric Conrad Capt dow 17-8-15 2/5LancF p221 CR France197

SIMON,Henry Hemrick Maj dow 8-9-17 C210RFA p206 CR Belgium11

SIMON,Marcel Andre T2Lt kia 29-4-17 6RBerks att2 O&BLI p140 MR20

SIMON,Norman T2Lt kia 14-7-16 8EYorks p85 MR21

SIMON,Robert M.Sir.LtCol ded /-/-15 RAMC p271

SIMON,Victor Herman.MC.Maj kia 5-6-17 RE 3FSqd p48 CR France363

SIMONDS,Charles Francis.MID TMaj kia 29-6-16 13KRRC p152 CR France501

SIMONDS,Charles Henville.MC.Lt dow 29-4-18 RE 126FC p48 CR Belgium11

SIMONDS,Ernest Hugh T2Lt kia 28-3-18 9RFus p70 MR27

SIMONDS,John De Luze.DSO.CaptAMaj kia 21-4-17 RGA 136SB p42 CR France223,22-4-17

SIMONET,Harold Keith.MC.Capt dow 29-4-18 1/8N&D p233 CR France88

SIMONET,Kenneth William Lee Capt kia 21-1-16 1Yorks p91 MR38

SIMONS,George Henry.DCM.T2Lt kia 26-8-17 10Lincs p75 CR France1462

SIMONS,John Henry Stuart 2Lt kia 10-7-17 3 att1Nhampt p138 MR31

SIMONS,Leon.MC.Capt kia 17-2-17 22RFus p70 MR21

SIMONS,Richard Frederick.MC.Capt ded 9-1-20 12LNLancs attSomalCamCps p271 CR Egypt7

SIMPKIN,Arthur Wilson TCapt kia 30-9-18 13Yorks att8WYorks p91 CR France755

SIMPKIN,Harry Hargreaves TCapt kia 22-3-18 13Yorks p91 MR20

SIMPKIN,Norman Travers Lt 18-8-19 RFA CR USA13

SIMPKIN,Reginald John Henry 2Lt kia 16-7-16 1/5RWar p214 MR21

SIMPSON,Alexander McGregor 2Lt kia 5-9-18 8Lond p247 CR France511

SIMPSON,Allen Ross Fraser T2Lt kia 16-7-16 10YLI p144 MR21

SIMPSON,Anthony Bean Tracey 2Lt kia 6-5-15 2WRid p116 MR29

SIMPSON,Anthony Henry Lt ded 1-2-15 1RWar SR p66 CR France102

SIMPSON,Arthur Ernest 2LtTLt kld 25-1-15 RASC p193

SIMPSON,Arthur Guy 2Lt kia 23-11-17 B'TankCps p188 MR17

SIMPSON,Brian 2LtTLt kia 9-5-15 ScotRif p104 MR22

SIMPSON,Brian George Casson 2Lt dow 29-7-15 RHA p35 CR Belgium11

SIMPSON,Cecil Barclay 2Lt kia 7-10-17 4SfthH p241 CR France536

SIMPSON,Charles Vernon Martin Capt kia 31-7-17 1/5RLancs p213 CR Belgium10

SIMPSON,Christopher Byron TCapt kia 7-10-16 26RFus p70 MR21

SIMPSON,Claude Battwell 2Lt kia 6-11-17 GL &RFC p13 MR20

SIMPSON,Claude Frank Bell Capt dow 3-12-17 9 att14DLI p239 CR France711

SIMPSON,Clifford Sandford TCapt kia 10-7-16 8Yorks p91 CR France515

SIMPSON,Clive Lennox TLt TCapt ded 19-3-17 RE IWT p262 CR Asia45

SIMPSON,Colin.MID 2Lt kia 7-8-16 A79RFA p35 CR France765

SIMPSON,Cyril Woodhouse TLt kia 14-7-16 7Leics p88 MR21

SIMPSON,David.MC.2Lt kia 2-6-17 1WelshR p127 MR37

SIMPSON,David Kilgour 2Lt dow 2-11-16 9HLI p241 MR21

SIMPSON,David Thomson Lt ded 2-12-19 RFA p271 MR40

SIMPSON,Daniel Harrison Lt dedacc 21-12-16 GL Manch p267 CR Lancs30

SIMPSON,Donald.MC.2Lt dow 19-5-17 1/5SfthH p241 CR France95

SIMPSON,Douglas Alexander 2Lt dow 15-10-15 7GordH p242 CR France43

SIMPSON,Douglas Richard T2Lt kia 28-9-18 RE att108RFA p48 CR Frnce511

SIMPSON,Elizabeth Nurse ded 11-5-17 TFNS p254 CR Scot729,10-5-17

SIMPSON,Eric Cograve.MC.TCapt drd 4-5-17 GL p191 CR France1779

SIMPSON,Eric Hadley T2Lt kia 11-4-18 10Ches C'Coy p96 MR32 Ex 4CamH

SIMPSON,Eric Maudsley Capt ded 2-5-16 9Worc p109 CR Iraq5

SIMPSON,Ernest Herbert 2Lt dow 2-10-17 RGA attG'BtyAA AnzacCp p42 CR France134

SIMPSON,Evelyn Victor C.LtRet ded 25-11-18 C172 RH&FA p262

SIMPSON,Frank William Harris Capt kia 16-2-17 RGA att53RFC p13 &42 CR France263

SIMPSON,Frederic TCapt dow 31-3-18 RAMC att2/1LondFdAmb p197 CR Kent127

SIMPSON,Frederick John Rayner 2Lt kia 31-7-17 5 att4Mddx p148 MR29

SIMPSON,Geoffrey Barnsley TCapt dow 12-11-15 7Y&L p159 CR France40

SIMPSON,George TLt kia 4-7-16 18DLI p161 CR France156

SIMPSON,George.MC.T2Lt kia 12-9-18 SWBord att10th p101 CR France415

SIMPSON,George Arnold 2Lt kia 2-7-16 5Leinst att64MGC p175&185,5Leics MR21

SIMPSON,George Duddington 2Lt kia 22-10-17 4RScots p211 MR30

SIMPSON,George Edward TCapt kia 22-10-17 23Manch p156 MR30

SIMPSON,George Fullarton 2Lt kia 29-7-18 5ScotRif p224 CR France864,Fullerton 10Bn

SIMPSON,George Kenneth.MC.TLt dow 7-3-17 RFC 4BallWing 14KiteBallSect p13 CR France164

SIMPSON,George Murdoch T2Lt kia 18-11-16 16HLI p164 MR21

SIMPSON,George Paterson T2LtACapt dow 2-8-18 10ScotRif p104 CR France1225

SIMPSON,George Ricardo Lt dow 30-8-18 3 att1Ches p96 CR France34

SIMPSON,Gerald William Ackroyd Lt died 26-1-19 RAOC p267

SIMPSON,Harry Graham Maj kia 27-5-18 1/4GordH att8MGC Inf p187&241 CR France1753

SIMPSON,Henry Delafosse TLt kia 24-8-17 8KRRC p152 MR30,Hugh

SIMPSON,Henry Gordon.MID 2Lt kia about 16-6-15 9DCLI att1RInniskF p115 MR4,6-6-15

SIMPSON,Henry Lamont 2Lt kia 29-8-18 8LancF p222 MR16

SIMPSON,Henry Leslie TLt ded 26-8-18 TankCps p266

SIMPSON,Henry Richard Deighton TLt kld 20-12-16 6DragGds &RFC p4&22 CR Kent105

SIMPSON,Herbert 2Lt dow 7-7-16 6N&D p233

SIMPSON,Herbert William ACapt kia 23-10-16 2RB p180 MR21

SIMPSON,James 2Lt dow 21-6-15 1/4GordH p242 CR France1

SIMPSON,James Alexander TLt dow 22-10-16 GL &10RFC p4&191 CR France98

SIMPSON,James Ashton 2Lt dow 25-7-16 RGA p42

SIMPSON,James Christian Capt ded 27-6-19 RAMC p271 CR Lond8

SIMPSON,James Francis T2Lt dow 27-10-17 20MGC p185 CR Belgium11

SIMPSON,James Harper Lt dow 12-10-17 8LancF p221 CR France193

SIMPSON,James Hawthorne Lt dow 3-7-16 RE 1/1FC p210 CR France35

SIMPSON,James Jamieson T2Lt kia 28-3-18 1NumbF p63 MR20

SIMPSON,James Kirk.MC.TLt kia 11-4-18 9SfthH p165 CR Belgium111

SIMPSON,James Marsden T2Lt kia 9-5-16 RE 173TC p48 CR France178

SIMPSON,James Cowie T2Lt kia 4-12-16 174RE p48 CR France251

SIMPSON,John Clark 2Lt kia 1-7-16 32RFC 10Wing p4 CR France423,Lt

SIMPSON,John Cornelius T2Lt dow 23-3-18 16RB p180 CR France119,23-8-18

SIMPSON,John Edmund.MID Capt kia 30-10-14 2YLI p144 MR29,31-10-14

SIMPSON,John Eric 2Lt kia 7-7-18 4Lincs att9Norf p217 CR Belgium3

SIMPSON,John Horace 2Lt kia 25-9-15 6 att2KRRC p152

SIMPSON,John Parker Norfolk 2Lt dow 27-5-15 5 att3RFus p70 CR Belgium140

SIMPSON,John Watt T2Lt kldacc 8-12-16 7BordR p118 CR France1568

SIMPSON,John Wyckliffe.MC.2Lt kia 1-8-17 9Lpool p216 MR29

SIMPSON,L.2Lt 5-4-20 3RWSurr CR Herts31

SIMPSON,Odo Mackay Lt kia 13-7-18 4N&D p135 CR Belgium3,2Bn

SIMPSON,Paul James Calvert 2Lt kia 1-10-15 3YLI p144 MR19,4-10-15

SIMPSON,Percy William TLt kia 1-11-16 9WRid p116 MR21

SIMPSON,Reginald Henry 2Lt kia 7-7-15 4 att2LancF p93 MR29

SIMPSON,Robert Arthur Abbs Lt dow 30-10-17 4NumbF p213

SIMPSON,Robert Fraser Lt kia 21-3-18 7 att1/6GordH p242 MR20

SIMPSON,Roger Cordy Capt ded 27-2-19 10WKentYeo p204 CR Surrey41

SIMPSON,Rolf T2Lt kia 26-5-17 18KRRC p152 CR Belgium152

SIMPSON,Rupert Victor Maj kia 28-9-18 1 O&BLI p130 MR38

SIMPSON,Stanley Ashe T2Lt kia 28-9-18 1Dev p77 CR France245

SIMPSON,T.E.2Lt kld 1-6-18 GL &RAF p191

SIMPSON,Thomas TLt kia 1-7-16 27NumbF p63 MR21

SIMPSON,Thomas Henry Capt&QM ded 10-8-19 RASC p267 CR Notts121

SIMPSON,Thomas Liddle.MC.T2Lt dow 30-11-18 DLI att64TMB p161 CR France658,Liddell ded

SIMPSON,Victor James 2Lt kia 24-8-16 5KSLI p145 MR21

SIMPSON,Vivian Samuel.MC.TCapt kia 13-4-18 12Y&L p159

SIMPSON,W.Cdr 14-11-15 IOD MR65

SIMPSON,William Drysdale 2Lt kia 3-10-15 5RScots p211 CR Gallipoli4

SIMPSON,William Herbert Mostyn Lt dow 19-12-14 3ESurr p113 CR France102,1Bn

SIMPSON,William Hugh Maj kia 17-4-16 1A 93BurmaInf p282 MR38

SIMPSON,William Norman TLt kia 31-3-18 YLI att 16EntrenchBn p144 CR France1893
SIMPSON,William Ronald Carde 2Lt kia 16-5-15 2BordR p118 CR France279
SIMS,Charles Henry T2Lt kia 24-4-18 7 att2ELancs p111 MR27
SIMS,Donald Palmer 2Lt kia 23-10-18 2HAC Inf p206 CR Italy9,24-10-18
SIMS,Douglas Henry.MC.T2Lt dow 10-10-18 1Leics p88 CR France725
SIMS,Gordon Lawrence Lt ded 22-2-20 IAUL 1/36Sikhs p282 MR43,2Lt
SIMS,Heber Harold T2Lt dow 1-9-18 4RFus p70 CR France103
SIMS,Thomas Augustus HonCapt&RidgMr ded 19-5-15 RFA p35 CR France85
SIMSON,David Henry Ainsworth Cranstown 2Lt kia 18-9-18 111/24RFA p35 CR France835
SIMSON,Herbert Cyrus Lt ded 12-1-18 RFC p17 MR40
SIMSON,James Robert.DSO.MajTLtCol dow 9-11-17 HLI attKOSB p164 CR Scot237
SIMSON,Noel Charles Spicer Capt dow 26-9-15 RGA 21AA Sec p42 CR France40
SIMSON,Roderick Alexander 2Lt ded 11-11-18 RGA 259SB p42 CR France163
SIMSON,Ronald Francis Lt kia 15-9-14 16/116RFA p35 CR France1341
SIMSON,William Kingsbury T2Lt kia 5-6-17 22NumbF p63 CR France1182
SINCLAIR,Alexander Thomson T2Lt kia 10-9-17 239MGC Inf p185 CR Belgium112
SINCLAIR,Andrew Bremner 2Lt kia 10-12-17 5 att8SfthH p241 MR20
SINCLAIR,A.F.K Capt 19-12-20 RAPC CR SAfrica144
SINCLAIR,Archibald King T2Lt kia 5-12-16 11 att2BlkW p129 MR38
SINCLAIR,Colin Johnston 2Lt ded 30-11-16 27/32 A320RFA p35 CR Lond12,dow
SINCLAIR,Constance Miss ded 22-2-17 VAD p268
SINCLAIR,David Capt kia 20-7-16 7ScotRif p224 CR France432
SINCLAIR,David Williamson Lt dow 22-10-18 RAMC att11RScots p197 CR Belgium140
SINCLAIR,Donald 2Lt dow 18-12-17 7HLI attRFC p19&240 CR France200
SINCLAIR,Donald George Capt dow 15-7-17 RFA 51TMB p207 CR France134,17-7-17
SINCLAIR,Douglas Monteith Farquhar Lt kia 30-3-17 GL &40RFC p13 CR France777
SINCLAIR,Eric Alexander 2Lt kia 23-4-17 5 att2RScotF p222 MR20
SINCLAIR,Eric Russell.MC.Lt kia 13-10-18 7A&SH p243 CR France1196
SINCLAIR,Frank TLt drd 3-10-18 RFus attNigR p70&202 see GRIMSEY,W.J.
SINCLAIR,Gavin Wilson 2Lt dow 7-12-17 19Lond p251
SINCLAIR,George T2Lt kia 9-4-17 11Mddx p148 CR France96
SINCLAIR,George Stanley 2Lt ded 28-5-17 5 att1RIrRif p170 CR France511
SINCLAIR,George Walker 2Lt kia 27-9-18 4RScots p211 CR France484
SINCLAIR,Gerald.MC.2Lt kia 21-3-18 RMunstF att2RIrReg p176 MR27
SINCLAIR,Gerald John LtACapt kia 18-4-18 1BlkW p129 CR France1106
SINCLAIR,Harold Lt kia 17-2-17 4WRid p227 CR France1890
SINCLAIR,Herbert Spencer 2Lt kld 24-12-17 GL &199RFC p13 CR Scot674
SINCLAIR,James Johnston TCapt ded 14-11-18 RAMC p197 CR Scot764
SINCLAIR,John Mitchell T2Lt kia 6-12-15 13ScotRif att5ConnRgrs p104 MR37
SINCLAIR,John Norman.DSO.MajALtCol kia 24-3-18 RFA p35 CR France164
SINCLAIR,Kenneth Lt dow 12-10-18 RE p210 CR France398
SINCLAIR,Lachlan T2Lt kia 28-9-16 12NumbF p63 CR France400
SINCLAIR,Luke Taylor T2Lt kia 2-3-16 11GordH p167 MR29
SINCLAIR,R.B Lt ded 22-3-19 RH&FA attRAF p35
SINCLAIR,Robert 2Lt kia 9-5-15 2BlkW p129 CR France924,Lt
SINCLAIR,W Lt 18-3-16 RIM MR64
SINCLAIR,William T2Lt kia 18-10-16 18Lpool p72 MR21
SINCLAIR,William Everitt T2Lt kld 15-3-18 GL &RFC p17 CR Wilts129,Everett
SINCLAIR-TRAVIS,Norman Brownlie Maj dow 26-3-18 RGA 297SB p209 CR France1182,kia
SINDALL,Richard Edward Capt dow 1-7-15 1/1Camb p244 CR France285
SING,Charles Millington 2Lt dow 7-7-16 7RSuss p120 CR France1890
SINGER,Ernest Henry Percy 2Lt kia 28-3-18 7Ess p232 MR20
SINGLE,Frederick Alexander.MC.Capt dow 30-3-18 2DragGds B'Sqn p21 CR France185
SINGLEHURST,Reginald LtACapt kia 21-3-18 24 att9KRRC p152 MR27
SINGLEHURST,Robert Bruce.MC.T2Lt kia 30-4-16 12NumbF D'Coy p63 CR France1890,Capt
SINGLETON,Frank Chester TCapt kia 3-9-16 17N&D p135 CR France220
SINGLETON,Harold James 2Lt ded 6-4-19 RFA p262 CR Lancs14
SINGLETON,Mark Rodney Lt kia 7-5-15 2YLI p144 MR29
SINGLETON,William James TLt drd 10-10-18 20 att3RWFus p99 CR Ireland14
SINKINSON,Evelyn Henry Le Mesurier Capt kia 14-7-15 IA 24Punjabis p282 CR Iraq6
SINKINSON,Francis Geoffrey 2Lt dow PoW 8-4-18 2TankCps p188 CR Belgium353,Lt

SINNETT-JONES,Gilbert Lloyd TCapt kia 4-4-16 8RWFus p99 MR38,9-4-16
SINNETT-JONES,James Victor 2Lt kia 10/12-7-16 3 att17RWFus p99 MR21
SINTON,Edwin.MC.LtACapt kia 21-8-18 RFA att4LtRlyOpCoy RE p35 CR France81
SINTON,William.MM.T2Lt kia 30-11-17 6BordR C'Coy p118 CR France550
SIORDET,Gerald Caldwell.MC.T2Lt kia 9-2-17 13RB p180 MR38
SISLEY,Arthur Jackson Smith 2Lt kia 10-9-17 GL &RFC p13 MR20
SISLEY,Donovan Laurier 2Lt kia 6-3-18 RFC p17 MR20
SISSON,George Lt dow PoW 20-12-17 RGA 71HB p42 CR France658
SISSONS,Norman Lea TLt kia 9-9-16 11EYorks p85 CR France727
SISSONS,Roland Edward Lt kia 2-6-16 8WYorks p219 CR France251
SISTERTON,Norman Hele 2Lt kia 16-4-18 12/13NumbF att1Lincs p63 MR30,SISTERSON
SITFORD,Leopold John T2Lt kia 2-9-18 1/4Manch p156 CR France308,1/6Bn
SIVEWRIGHT,William George T2Lt kia 26-9-17 RSuss att13Bn p120 MR30
SIVEWRIGHT,William John LtACapt kia 2-11-17 7Manch p237 CR Belgium175
SIZELAND,Charles T2Lt kia 12-10-16 7Norf p74 MR21
SKAIFE,Arthur Frederick Capt kia 1-11-14 1Mddx p148 CR France347,Frederick
SKAKLE,Hugh Philip.MID Capt kia 21-11-17 4GordH CR France256
SKEEN,Oliver St.John.DSO.Maj kia 21-1-16 IA 62Punjabis p282 CR Iraq5
SKEET,John Richard Lt kia 27-4-18 2Lond att7RWSurr p245 MR27
SKEET,William Celington TCapt kia 9-4-17 12WYorks p83 CR France581
SKEFFINGTON,Herbert Neville Southwell 2Lt kia 28-7-17 57RFC p13 CR Belgium149
SKELSEY,Robert Max Lt kld 29-3-18 4WRid att186TMB p227 MR20
SKELTON,Benjamin Dowell T2Lt dow 7-11-18 att10Ess p132 CR France146
SKELTON,Charles George Gordon T2Lt kia 18-11-16 10SLancs att17Bn p126 MR21,7Bn
SKELTON,Francis T2Lt kia 21-10-17 28RFC p13 CR Belgium18
SKELTON,Harry T2Lt dow 12-10-16 8RFus p70 CR France833
SKELTON,Henry T2Lt kia 2-10-18 11 att16LancF p93 CR France237 Ex 28Lond
SKELTON,Sydney Capt ded 20-3-18 1/5EKent p213 CR Iraq8
SKEMP,Arthur Rowland Lt kia 1-11-18 4Glouc p225 CR France190,1Bn
SKENE,Ian.MC.2Lt dow PoW 13-4-18 6LancF p221 CR France1142
SKENE,James Henry 2Lt kia 14-7-16 4RBerks p234 MR19
SKENE,Robin Reginald 2Lt kld 12-8-14 RFC p2 CR Surrey126
SKERRY,James Beadnell TLt kia 1-6-16 17Mddx p148 CR France924
SKETT,Arthur Edwin Pye 2Lt kia 11-11-16 2WYorks p83 CR France744
SKEVINGTON,Arthur Victor T2Lt kia 25-9-16 13 att10YLI p144 MR21
SKEVINGTON,William Percy T2Lt kia 8-9-18 11EYorks B'Coy p85 CR France297
SKEWES,Arthur Courtis T2Lt kia 19-7-16 11Dev att2/6Glouc p77 CR France1887
SKEY,Charles Harland Capt kia 18-8-16 1BlkW p129 MR21
SKIDMORE,John Henry T2LtACapt ded 7-11-18 LabCps att214PoW Coy p189 CR Hereford/W186,8-11-18
SKILL,Harold Jefferson TCapt dow PoW 7-4-18 Mddx att21Bn p148 CR Belgium353
SKILLINGTON,Harry 2Lt kld 18-8-16 4Nhampt p234 CR France832
SKINNER,Alfred Capt kia 31-8-16 4SLancs att27RFC p19&229 CR France662
SKINNER,Charles Edwin TCapt ded 13-1-20 RFA p262 CR Asia81
SKINNER,Douglas Hilton TCapt dow 16-7-16 7RWKent A'Coy p142 CR France119
SKINNER,Edward Dudley T2Lt kia 9-9-17 1/8Manch D'Coy p156 CR Belgium84
SKINNER,Edward Howard 2Lt kia 25-9-16 Dev p77 CR France374
SKINNER,Ernest Archibald 2Lt dow 26-11-17 24MGC p185 CR Belgium3
SKINNER,Ernest Henry 2Lt kia or dow 21/31-3-18 1/1Camb p245 MR27
SKINNER,Frederick Tom TCaptAMaj kia 3-9-16 14Hamps p121 CR France742
SKINNER,Frederick William Fletcher 2Lt dow 13-8-17 2 attD108RFA p209 CR Belgium7
SKINNER,George Arthur TCapt ded 11-10-19 RAMC p267 CR Kent46
SKINNER,Harold Bazalgette Capt kia 8-3-16 IA 2Rajputs p282 MR38
SKINNER,Hilary Francis Cleveland 2Lt kia 25-7-16 1SWBord p101 MR21
SKINNER,James Stuart Capt drd 21-2-17 2KSLI p145,Steuart MR35
SKINNER,Lewis Samuel Corbett Lt ded 31-12-19 IA 39CentIndHorse att38 p282 CR Egypt2
SKINNER,Robert Leonard Grahame 2Lt ded 3-5-18 1/2BlkW &64RAF p129 MR20
SKINNER,Stephen William 2Lt kia 4-10-16 32RFus p70 MR21
SKINNER,Thomas Arnold T2Lt dow 10-8-17 7KOSB p102 CR France145,7/8Bn
SKINNER,Wilfred Henry 2Lt dow PoW 27-5-18 8MGC Inf p185 CR France928
SKINNER,William T2Lt kia 25-9-15 6KOSB p102 CR France114
SKINNER,William Lt ded 21-6-16 RIM p282 CR Iraq6
SKINNER,William.MC.TCapt kia 25-4-18 12RScots D'Coy p54 MR30
SKINNER,William Edward T2Lt kld 4-3-18 RFC p17 CR Lond28

SKIPWITH,Granville Arthur 2Lt kia 16-6-15 RFA 72Bty p35 CR Belgium165,Lt
SKIPWORTH,Bernard William.MC.Lt kia 25-4-18 3RSuss att9MGC Infp120&185 MR30
SKIPWORTH,Frank Peyton Maj kia 25-9-15 7RScotF p95 MR19
SKIPWORTH,Philip John TLt kia 7-8-15 11WRid att5Manch p116 MR4
SKIRROW,Arthur TLt kia 28-3-18 13Y&L p159 CR France745
SKIRROW,Geoffrey LtACapt kia 27-8-18 5WYorks p218 CR France614
SKITT,Harold George T2Lt kia 1-10-18 10 att1RIrFus p171 CR Belgium157
SKOTTOWE,Claude Mannering 2Lt kia 21-10-16 2SLancs p126 CR France384
SKOTTOWE,Gordon T2Lt dow 12-4-18 7RWKent p142 CR France185
SKOULDING,Alfred Cecil T2Lt dow 21-2-17 6 O&BLI p130 CR France105
SKRIMSHIRE,Herbert Eric 2Lt dow 28-3-18 RGA 116SB p42 CR France184
SKRINE,Henry Langton TCapt kia 25-9-15 6SomLI p80 MR29
SKRINE,Sholto Herries.MC.TLt dow 19-9-17 B95RFA p35&259 CR Belgium19
SKUCE,Arthur TLt dow 8-10-17 6 O&BLI p130 CR Oxford74
SKYRNE,Richard Edward Elcho 2Lt kia 6-2-17 3 att1Wilts p153 CR Belgium70
SLACK,A.E.Lt 31-12-20 RASC CR Iraq8
SLACK,John Barnett T2Lt kia 27-5-18 NumbF Res att5Bn p63 CR France1753
SLACKE,Charles Oven TCapt kia 1-7-16 14RIrRif p170 CR France215,Owen
SLACKE,Clulow Orme Capt mbk 12-11-16 12ESurr p256 MR29
SLACKE,Roger Cecil Maj kia 16-5-15 3EKent attRWSurr p58 CR France279,2BordR
SLADE,Charles Godfrey Mitford Maj kia 8-11-14 4WYorks attNLancs p83 MR29
SLADE,Ernest Cowper.DSO.MC.LtCol kia 4-5-18 4 att8Glouc p225 CR Belgium102
SLADE,Robert Blackmore Maj kia 10-7-18 RGA 123SB p209 CR France924
SLADE,Robert Gordon Lt kia 18-4-18 19DAC attA88RFA p35 CR Belgium11
SLADE,Stewart Harold TLt kia 21-8-18 15TankCps p188 CR France214
SLADE,Wilfrid Adolphus 2Lt kia 23-4-17 70RFA p35 CR France1188
SLADE BAKER,Robert Cunynghame.MC.Lt kia 19-8-17 1RBerks CR France572
SLADE-KING,Philip S.TLt ded 13-5-18 2Norf p263 CR Iraq8
SLADE-POWELL,John Harold Maj dow 8-2-15 52RFA CR Suff83
SLADEN,Charles St.Barbe Maj ded 2-9-17 RE p48 CR Hamps11
SLADEN,John Henry 2Lt ded 7-2-19 NumbF p262 CR Numb83
SLADEN,St.Barbe Russell.TD.LtCol kia 12-3-18 5 Cmdg1RWSurr p212 CR Belgium84
SLANEY,Albert Edward T2Lt ded 3-10-17 GL attLabCps p191 CR Yorks547
SLANEY,John Cobley Lt kia 17-2-16 76RFA p35 CR Belgium28
SLATER,Charles Hugh Hope TLt kia 31-7-17 10ScotRif att46InfBde p104 CR Belgium7
SLATER,Gilbert John Leigh Lt&Adjt kia 30-4-16 8Worc p226 CR France1327
SLATER,Harry Lt dow 28-5-18 1/6SStaffs p229 CR France40
SLATER,James 2Lt dow 16-11-16 9DLI p239 CR Yorks45
SLATER,John T2Lt dow 26-3-18 20 att17LancF p93 CR France177
SLATER,John Cyrus 2Lt ded 6-7-17 5Lond p246 CR France40,dow
SLATER,John Elwyn 2Lt kia 3-5-17 5ELancs att2LancF p226 MR20
SLATER,Leonard Capt kia 14-9-14 2RSuss p120 CR France1329
SLATER,R.A.Lt 12-8-19 RAMC CR Scot762
SLATER,Richard Henry.MIDx2 TCapt kia 27-7-16 1KRRC p152 MR21
SLATER,Ronald Mortimer Lt dow 21-11-14 1Worc p109 CR France345
SLATER,Thomas Alexander Fletcher 2Lt kia 16-9-16 3 att5Dors p124 MR21
SLATFORD,Clarence Douglas.MC.Lt ded 31-10-19 2Ess p264 CR Lond14
SLATTER,Roland Percy TCapt kia 15-7-16 1RWSurr p56 MR21
SLATTERY,Duncan Vincent 2Lt kld 3-3-17 Hamps &RFC p13&121 CR Essex43
SLATTERY,Francis James LtACapt ded 9-1-19 RE 8FC p48 CR Eire30
SLATTERY,Francis William 2Lt 17-9-16 3AustLH MGSqn MR34
SLAUGHTER,Arthur Charles T2Lt dow 23-8-16 16Lpool p72 CR France765
SLAUGHTER,Vivian Lt kia 27-9-18 2/20Lond p251 CR France358
SLAUGHTER,William Leonard 2Lt kia 6-9-18 HuntsCycBn attEss p253 CR France511
SLEATOR,Robert John T2Lt ded 8-5-17 9RIrFus C'Coy p171 CR Belgium97
SLEE,John Balhatchet Lt kia 24-3-18 3 att7DCLI p115 MR27
SLEEMAN,William Fraser T2Lt kia 31-5-17 GL &55RFC p13 CR France134
SLEIGH,William Ward TLt kia 25-2-17 18WYorks p83 CR France342
SLICER,Philip Sydney Lt dow 30-9-18 RGA 319SB p42 CR France327
SLICER,Walter Gordon 2Lt kia 13-4-18 8RWar p215 CR France248
SLIDE,G.H.Capt 14-7-18 ScotHorse CR Scot669 Ex 17Lancers
SLIDEL,Sydney Robert T2Lt dow 20-4-18 4Lancs p75 CR Belgium38
SLIGHT,William Hubert 2Lt kia 26-9-17 RE 212FC p48 CR Belgium37,26-9-19
SLINGER,Albert 2Lt 3-5-18 206RAF MR20
SLINGER,George Nicholas 2Lt kia 28-11-16 159RFA p35 CR France452
SLINGER,William TLt kia 23-7-17 12 att1ELancs p111 CR France730

SLINGSBY,Anthony Edward King Lt kia 16-7-15 1/6WRid p227 CR Belgium23
SLINGSBY,Arthur Morris.MC.Capt kia 8-3-16 1A 56Rif p282
SLINGSBY,Charles 2Lt kld 7-8-15 4A&SH p174 CR Yorks250,3Bn
SLINGSBY,Henry Laurence.MC.Capt dow 11-8-17 2YLI att10DCLI p144&259 CR Belgium172
SLOAN,Arthur James 2Lt kia 30-8-18 C315RFA p209 CR France214
SLOAN,Cyril Rennie 2Lt ded 13-5-17 29RFC p13 CR France1483,Cyrie
SLOAN,George Henry Capt dow 16-11-15 2ScotHorse p205 CR Gallipoli26
SLOAN,Harold Alexander 2Lt kia 21-1-17 RGA 198SB p42 CR France786
SLOAN,John Bruce 2Lt kia 23-7-18 5 att7/8KOSB p224 CR France865
SLOAN,Thomas Ian Thompson 2Lt kia 23-4-17 7A&SH p243 CR France545
SLOAN,Thomas William 2Lt kia 20-9-17 8Lond p247 MR29
SLOAN,Wilfred Scott Lt kia 28-4-17 8 att1ScotRif p225 CR France40,Wilfrid dow
SLOANE-STANLEY,Humphrey Henry.MC.LtACapt kia 13-4-18 4GrenGds 1Coy p50 MR32
SLOCOCK,Cyprian Henry Benson LtACapt dow 3-4-18 3 att2 O&BLI p130 CR France102
SLOCOCK,Lancelot Andrew Noel 2Lt kia 9-8-16 1/10Lpool p216 CR France21
SLOCOMBE,Arthur Douglas 2Lt kia 30-7-16 8Glouc p107 CR France432
SLOLEY,Robert Hugh 2Lt kia 1-10-17 RGA att56RFC p13&42
SLOPER,Bruce James.MC.T2Lt kia 31-8-18 3MGC Inf p185 CR France614
SLOPER,Gerard Orby.MC.Capt ded 8-2-19 NumbF att5Bn p63 MR70
SLOPER,Victor Frederick 2Lt drd 10-10-18 4Wilts p236 CR Wilts16
SLOWE,Alfred T2Lt dow 25-8-17 YLI att6Bn p144 CR Belgium11,Abraham
SMAIL,Frank Weddell Lt dow 1-12-15 1/7NumbF D'Coy p214 CR Numb34
SMAILES,Frank Capt&QM ded 21-11-19 GL Yorks p267 CR Yorks159
SMAILES,George T2Lt kia 22-10-16 2WYorks p83 MR21
SMALE,Florence Emily Nurse 13-10-15 VAD 19GH CR Egypt3
SMALL,Alexander Couper.MC.T2Lt kia 23-10-16 2ELancs p111 CR France307
SMALL,Arnold T2Lt dow 12-4-17 8Mddx p148 CR France120
SMALL,Dudley Francis Capt kia 24-3-18 15Ches p255 MR27
SMALL,E.Capt 28-4-21 Beds CR Beds23
SMALL,Frank Gilbert Harrell 2Lt dow PoW 9-6-18 47MGC p185 CR Germany3,Lt
SMALL,Hugh Alexander.MC.T2Lt kia 10-7-16 2OLpool p72 MR21
SMALL,James Bruce Lt kld 2-8-18 1/4RB att101RAF p180 CR France29
SMALL,John TLt kia 29-4-16 9BlkW p129 CR France423
SMALL,John Bertram T2Lt kia 23-3-18 4SStaffs p123 MR20
SMALL,Walter 2Lt mbk 30-7-16 9 att2RScotF p256 MR21
SMALLEY,John Douglas Lt kia 15-3-15 1Camb D'Coy p245 CR Belgium111
SMALLEY,Robert Francis Lt ded 14-5-18 4SStaffs p123 MR32,14-4-18
SMALLEY,Walter Herbert T2Lt dow 28-10-18 2Nhampt p138 CR France113
SMALLEY,William Miles 2Lt kia 9-12-14 N&D p135 CR France924
SMALLMAN,Arthur Frederick Strong 2Lt kia 14-11-16 1HAC Inf p206 CR France339
SMALLMAN,Edward 2Lt ded 19-11-16 RE p210 CR Surrey152
SMALLWOOD,Eric Butter.MC.Capt kia 7-1-17 Herts p252 CR Belgium73,Butler
SMALLWOOD,Frank Graham.CVO.Col ded 30-12-19 RAOC p267 MR65 Ex RA
SMALLWOOD,George Baxter.MM&Bar.2Lt ded 2-11-18 RLancs attMGC p59&185 CR Lancs171
SMALLWOOD,James Fenemore.MC.MID TLt dow 22-5-17 11Mddx p148 CR France40
SMALLWOOD,Reginald 2Lt kia 18-4-17 5Ches p222 MR20
SMALLWOOD,Robert Henry Lt dow 27-5-18 PoW 4NumbF p63 MR18
SMALLWOOD,William Spencer T2Lt kia 25-1-18 GL &22RFC p17 CR France88
SMART,Claude Edward TLt kia 24-7-17 10Worc p109 CR France644,14Bn
SMART,David Lonmer 2lt dow 5-4-17 RE 430FC p210 CR France80
SMART,Edgar Herbert Lt kia 30-11-17 1/6Lond p246 MR17
SMART,Edward Treloar Lt mbk 27-3-18 RGA &2RFC p256 MR20
SMART,Eric Douglas 2Lt kia 18-11-16 10RWar p66 MR21
SMART,Eustace Fowler TLt kia 8-2-16 7Leic p88 CR France745
SMART,George Henry Capt kia 22-12-14 4WYorks attNLancs p83 MR22
SMART,George Orme T2Lt kia 7-4-17 GL &RFC p13 MR20
SMART,Norman Lt kia 16-10-17 1/8LancF attMGC p187&221 CR Belgium88
SMART,Walter TLt kia 3-10-18 6MGC Inf p185 CR France441
SMART,William Ellis 2Lt kia 11-10-18 3Yorks att7WYorks p91 CR France612
SMART,William Leonard T2Lt kia 29-8-18 1/2LancF att8RLancs p93 CR France615
SMARTT,William Francis Capt ded 15-1-16 RAMC p271 CR Norf15
SMEATHMAN,Cecil Lt dow 24-10-14 Leic p88 CR France284
SMEATHMAN,Julian Missenden Lt kia 24-10-14 RE p48 MR29
SMEDDLE,George Robert Graham TLt kld 11-3-18 RFC p17 CR Durham55
SMEE,Arthur Joseph 2Lt ded 28-10-18 3Wilts attRAF p153 CR Surrey15

SMEETH,H.G.2Lt 25-9-18 att2/4RWSurr CR Belgium192
SMEETH,William Sutton T2Lt kld 17-7-17 9RIrRif attRFC p13&170 CR Yorks475
SMELLIE,John Ormond Lt ded 8-8-17 MGC Inf p185 CR Essex86
SMERDON,John Geoffrey T2Lt kia 20-9-17 3SomLI att2/5LancF p80 MR30
SMETHAM,James Eric 2Lt kia 14-11-16 RWar att3MGC p66 MR21
SMETHURST,Frederick James.MC.LtACapt kia 30-11-17 1/5SLancs p230 MR17
SMETHURST,John T2Lt kia 16-9-16 12Lpool p73 CR France374
SMILES,Samuel T2Lt kia 16-8-17 13RIrRif p170 CR Belgium125,1Bn
SMILES,William Alan TCapt kia 9-7-16 2RIrRif p170 MR21
SMILLIE,George Sinclair 2Lt dow 13-8-17 C121RFA p35 CR Belgium16
SMITH,Adam Davidson 2Lt kia 2-10-18 4RScots p211
SMITH,A.H.T2Lt ded 16-8-18 LabCps p189 CR Essex5
SMITH,Alan Douglas Hay 2Lt kia 26-3-17 4Ess p232
SMITH,Alan Francis Broadley Maj kia 16-6-15 5BordR p228 CR Belgium167
SMITH,Alan Joseph 2Lt kia 9-7-18 RGA 49SB p209 CR France19
SMITH,Alan Langdale Capt ded 3-12-19 IA 63Inf att1/80CarnaticInf p282 CR Iraq8
SMITH,Alan Raymond Noel 2Lt ded 10-7-19 IA 130Baluchis p282 MR43 &CR Pakistan50A
SMITH,Alan Wenman Lt kld 18-3-17 6Lpool &RFC p215 p271
SMITH,Albert Edward 2Lt kia 22-3-16 1Lincs p75 MR32
SMITH,Albert Francis 2Lt mbk 9-9-17 9Mddx att13Lond p257 MR21
SMITH,Albert Gower Capt dow 20-5-16 3 att1Manch p156 CR Iraq5
SMITH,Albert Victor T2Lt kia 28-8-18 20Mddx p148 CR Belgium188
SMITH,Alec T2Lt kia 8-7-16 10LancF p93 MR21
SMITH,Alexander Cooper T2Lt kia 23-7-16 2RSuss p120 MR21
SMITH,Alexander Cyril T2Lt kia 23-11-16 10LNLancs p136 MR21,Ayre
SMITH,Alexander Joseph.MM.2Lt kia 31-7-17 11RWSurr p56 MR29
SMITH,Alexander Millar T2Lt dow 26-1-18 16KRRC p152 CR Belgium3
SMITH,Alexander Noel 2Lt dow 26-9-16 7NumbF p214 CR France102
SMITH,Alexander Will.MC.2Lt kia 21-3-18 GordH att1/5Bn p167MR27
SMITH,Alfred Archibald Lt kia 2-4-16 1/5SStaffs p229 CR France68
SMITH,Alfred Percy Capt kia 23-8-15 RAMC att32FA p197 MR4
SMITH,Alfred Victor.VC.2Lt kia 22-12-15 1/5ELancs p226 CR Gallipoli6
SMITH,Alfred William.MM.T2Lt dow 4-10-17 8Leic att8Lincs p88 CR Belgium11
SMITH,Algernon Lindsay Eric.MIDx2 Lt kia 31-11-14 1LifeGds p20 CR Belgium167,31-10-14
SMITH,Allan Bertram.MBE.Lt kia 27-5-18 5 att1/8A&SH p243&258 CR France498
SMITH,Allan Higson.MC.Capt kia 21-8-17 GL &21RFC p13 MR20
SMITH,Allan Wenman Lt kld 18-3-17 6Lpool &1RFC p261 CR Lancs170
SMITH,Allison Gould.MC.Capt kia 18-4-18 7LNLancs p136 MR19
SMITH,Andrew 2Lt kia 14-11-16 6NumbF p214 MR21
SMITH,Archibald MacBrayne 2Lt dow 31-7-17 9A&SH p244 CR Belgium7
SMITH,Arthur T2Lt kia 26-8-18 N&D att10Bn p135 MR16
SMITH,Arthur Lt drdacc 25-10-19 RE CR Lancs43
SMITH,Arthur Borland Lt kia 1-8-18 5ScotRif p224 CR France864,10Bn
SMITH,Arthur Charles Vaughan T2Lt kia 9-10-17 EYorks att8WRid p85 MR30
SMITH,Arthur Gilliat Lt kia 1-11-14 RE p48
SMITH,Arthur Harold T2Lt kia 27-3-18 18 att9Manch p156 MR27
SMITH,Arthur Herbert ACapt kia 6-10-16 2Dev C'Coy p77 MR19
SMITH,Arthur Hodson 2Lt dow 9-6-18 1/5N&D p233 CR France10
SMITH,Arthur Howard T2Lt kia 14-7-16 10Leic p88 MR21
SMITH,Arthur John TLt kia 25-9-15 7Lond p247 CR France550
SMITH,Arthur Jonathan T2Lt kia 28-3-18 36MGC Inf p185 CR France360
SMITH,Arthur Leslie Lt kld 22-8-17 1/4SfthH attRFC p19&241 CR Lond3
SMITH,Arthur Roughton 2Lt dow 22-7-16 1/6Glouc p225 CR France44
SMITH,Arthur William T2Lt kia 7-9-18 23RFus p70 CR France530
SMITH,Aubrey Fairer Lt 24-4-18 RASC MT CR France880
SMITH,Augustus William T2Lt kia 2-2-16 5 O&BLI p130 CR Belgium20
SMITH,Bernard Alfred 2Lt dow 16-4-18 3 att9Norf p74 CR Belgium38
SMITH,Bernard Ridley Winthrope Lt dow 15-11-14 ScotsGds p52
SMITH,Brian Rivers Capt kia 8-8-18 4Lond p246 MR16
SMITH,Burns Crawford 2Lt kia 31-10-17 4NumbF p213 CR Belgium11
SMITH,C.MC.lt 5-6-20 2NumbF CR Iraq8
SMITH,C.SNurse 26-1-21 TFNS CR Yorks361
SMITH,C.F.2Lt kia 9-4-18 12Suff att121TMB p79 MR32
SMITH,Campbell Lindsay TLt dow 10-11-15 11 att8GordH p167
SMITH,Cecil 2Lt kld 12-10-18 ArmyCycCps NorthernCycBn p244&271
SMITH,Cecil 2Lt kia 14-10-18 18WelchR CR France258
SMITH,Cecil Owen 2Lt kia 20-8-17 36/33RFA p35 CR Belgium84

SMITH,Cecil Ramsden T2Lt kia 12-6-17 M'SpecCo RE p48 CR France922
SMITH,Cedric Harry.MC.2LtACapt kia 31-10-17 RGA 229SB p42 CR Belgium19
SMITH,Charles Alfred 2Lt kia 1-10-16 17Lond p250 MR21
SMITH,Charles Arthur.DCM.T2Lt kia 19-9-18 1/2Leic p88 CR France1701
SMITH,Charles Cyril 2Lt kia 25-9-15 5KSLI p145 MR29
SMITH,Charles Edgar Holton TCapt kia 16-9-16 RAMC att10/11HLI p197 CR France239
SMITH,Charles Emanuel Webb T2Lt kld 28-7-17 GL &RFC p13
SMITH,Charles Ernest Lt kia 13-4-18 1/6Lpool p215 CR France88
SMITH,Charles Francis Bateman Lt kia 15-2-15 1Suff p79 MR29
SMITH,Charles Henry T2Lt kia 19-3-16 13WelshR p127 CR France279 Ex 4Ches
SMITH,Charles Henry.MID TMaj kia 27-7-16 8Y&L p159 MR21
SMITH,Charles Hoyle 2Lt kia 23-4-17 9 att13RScots p212 MR20
SMITH,Charles Jervoise Dudley 2Lt kia 16-6-15 1GrenGds p50 MR22,15-6-15
SMITH,Charles John 2Lt mbk 27-5-18 7Worc p257 MR18
SMITH,Charles Jonsing Capt ded 20-12-19 5Mddx p265 CR Surrey84
SMITH,Charles Maxwell 2Lt kia 3-5-17 7Ess p232 MR20
SMITH,Charles Randolph 2Lt kia 22-4-17 RGA 244SB p42 CR France214
SMITH,Charles Sydney.MC.MID TMaj ded 28-11-18 97MGC p185 CR Derby98
SMITH,Charles Theodore 2Lt dow 22-5-15 3DragGds p21 CR France102
SMITH,Clement Roy Blackshaw 2Lt kia 28-4-17 3 att6Beds p86 MR20
SMITH,Clifford Day 2Lt kia 23-10-18 5 att9Norf p217 CR France190,Lt
SMITH,Clifford Thomas 2Lt kia 30-7-17 B122RFA p35 CR Belgium12
SMITH,Colin T2Lt kld 11-3-17 GL &48RFC p13 CR Lincs181
SMITH,David.MC.DCM.2Lt kia 18-10-18 1BlkW p129 CR France1271
SMITH,David Arthur 2Lt kia 26-10-17 4NumbF p213 MR30
SMITH,David Thorne T2Lt kia 3-12-17 14DLI p161 MR17
SMITH,Donald Graham 2Lt kld 10-4-18 1/4Mddx &42RAF Ex RAMC p148 MR20
SMITH,Donald Charnock TCapt kia 1-7-16 16WYorks p83 MR21
SMITH,Donald 2Lt ded 29-1-19 1SfthH p165 CR Egypt2
SMITH,Donald Claud T2Lt dow 13-10-15 7Suff p79 MR19
SMITH,Donovon Richardson McCallum 2Lt dow 27-5-18 4Manch att 1Worc p156 MR18
SMITH,Douglas George.MC.TLt dow 16-8-17 6KSLI p145 CR Belgium16
SMITH,Douglas Robert Capt ded 9-9-18 8Lond att47Div HQ p247 CR France788
SMITH,Douglas Tweedie 2Lt 10-4-16 RFC CR Essex86
SMITH,Douglas Wilberforce TCapt kia 1-7-16 RAMC att20Manch p197 CR France397
SMITH,Dugald T2LtACapt dow 8-10-18 4RFus p70 CR France338
SMITH,Duncan Galloway Capt dow 26-6-16 RE 1FC p210 CR France203
SMITH,Duncan Robertson Moir T2Lt dow 27-8-17 1RScots p55 CR France1461
SMITH,Duncan Vaughan.DSO.LtCol dow 13-4-17 1Lond p145 CR France145
SMITH,E.2Lt kld 29-4-18 GL &RAF p191 CR France184,28-4-18
SMITH,Edgar Ernest.MC.TLt dow 3-12-17 183MGC Inf p185 MR17
SMITH,Edmund Davidson MajGen ded 8-9-16 Staff AQMG p261 CR Lond8
SMITH,Edmund Percival Col kia 2-5-15 17RFA p35 CR Gallipoli2,Perceval
SMITH,Edward Capt 25-3-20 RDC CR Numb4
SMITH,Edward Corrigan Capt kia 30-9-15 2Suff p79 CR Belgium167
SMITH,Edward Frank T2Lt kia 7-7-16 12Manch p156 MR21
SMITH,Edward James TLt kia 28-9-16 8WRid p116 MR21
SMITH,Edward John.MIDx2 TCapt kia 5-10-18 GL &22NumbF p63 CR France163
SMITH,Edward Pelham 2Lt kia 16-8-18 9Lpool att12Norf p216 CR France19
SMITH,Edward Thompson T2Lt kia 19-10-15 8EKent p58 CR Belgium56
SMITH,Edwin Rivers 2Lt ded 6-11-18 RGA p262
SMITH,Eric 2Lt ded 15-10-16 8RWKent p142 CR France32
SMITH,Eric Arthur T2Lt kia 22-7-16 14RWar p66 CR France432
SMITH,Eric Drummond T2Lt kia 4-10-17 9N&D att6Y&L p135 MR30
SMITH,Eric John Garner Lt kia 26-5-15 24Lond p252
SMITH,Eric St.Clare Lt kld 2-7-17 RFA attRFC p13&35 CR Essex1
SMITH,Ernest Lt kia 12-7-15 5KOSB p224 MR4
SMITH,Ernest Edwin Lt ded 26-6-16 RIM p282
SMITH,Ernest Frederick William T2Lt dow 27-12-16 1Leinst attRFC p4&175 CR France833
SMITH,Ernest George Humphrey 2Lt kia 3-11-17 7Ess p232 CR Palestine8,Humphery 1/4Bn
SMITH,Ernest John TMaj dow 28-12-15 7YLI p144 CR France345
SMITH,Ernest Kennedy 2Lt dow 22-12-15 1EKent p58 CR Belgium11
SMITH,Ernest Stuart 2Lt kia 15-5-18 6RWar p214 MR19
SMITH,Ernest Wilson Marshall 2Lt kld 22-3-16 5Leinst attMGC p175&185 CR Lincs61
SMITH,Evelyn Hay Hindley TCapt ded 16-5-18 Ex 5Manch p271

SMITH,Everard Cecil Lt kia 23-8-14 RFus p70 CR Belgium242
SMITH,F.E.S Nurse 1-7-18 QAIMNS CR Lancs32
SMITH,F.de Lisle Lt 30-10-18 RFA CR Ireland14
SMITH,F.J.CB.VD.BrCol 3-6-16 8ScotRif CR Scot756
SMITH,Fereday Fisher Lt kia 28-11-17 4Huss p21 MR17
SMITH,Francis Douglas Matthews 2Lt dow 25-1-16 7Mddx C'Coy p235 CR France525
SMITH,Francis Edwin Lt ded 18-11-18 1Camb p245 CR War151,Capt
SMITH,Francis Geoffrey John LtACapt ded 29-7-18 RASC 3Coy 59Div p253 CR France226,F.J.G.
SMITH,Francis John Lt ded 30-10-18 15Lond p271 CR Oxford24
SMITH,Francis Johnston.MC.2Lt kia 16-5-17 7 att6GordH p242 CR France604
SMITH,Francis Shingleton Capt kia 24-11-15 IA IMS att120RajputsInf p282 MR38
SMITH,Frank Harold T2Lt kia 2-9-18 9TankCps p188 CRFrance426
SMITH,Frank Redfern Lt dow 17-11-17 7Mddx attRE 66DivSigs p235 CR Belgium3
SMITH,Frank William Howard Lt dow 4-12-17 19Lond p250 CR France145
SMITH,Frederick Charles 2Lt kia 10-7-17 4Nhampt att2KRRC p234 MR31
SMITH,Frederick George.MID T2Lt kia 8-10-16 23DLI p161 CR France1182
SMITH,Frederick George T2Lt kld 8-2-18 RFC p17 CR War50
SMITH,Frederick George 2Lt kia 27-8-18 9HLI p240 CR France162
SMITH,Frederick Herbert Corbett Douglas 2Lt kia 10-12-17 RGA 52SB p42 CR France161
SMITH,Frederick John Capt dow 23-8-18 5Beds p219 CR France281
SMITH,Frederick Neville Cowran ALt dow 27-8-16 6Worc att100TMB p109 CR France833
SMITH,Frederick Seaton Chap4Cl ded 15-11-18 RAChDept att13Y&L p200 CR France34
SMITH,Frederick William TCapt kia 25-4-16 1WYorks p83 CR Belgium73
SMITH,Frederick William 2Lt dow 11-4-17 5Lincs p220 CR France113
SMITH,Geoffrey Bache TLt&Adjt dow 3-12-16 19LancF p93 CR France120
SMITH,Geoffrey Cholerton.MC.2LtTLt kia 31-7-17 RASC attRFC p13&193 CR Belgium11
SMITH,Geoffrey H.MC.ACapt mbk 16-10-18 1CldGds p256 CR Belgium242,22-10-18
SMITH,Geoffrey Harold 2Lt dow 10-7-17 1Nhampt D'Coy p138 MR31
SMITH,Geoffrey Herbert T2Lt dow 22-9-16 1EKent p58 CR France145
SMITH,Geoffrey Watkins TCapt kia 10-7-16 13RB p180 CR France832
SMITH,George.MID Capt kia 13-3-15 6GordH p242 MR22
SMITH,George T2Lt kia 15-9-16 10 att9RWKent p142 CR France277
SMITH,George Alan Campbell.MC.TCapt kia 28-9-18 14A&SH p174 CR Belgium185
SMITH,George Alexander.DSO.LtCol kia 28-7-18 4GordH p241 CR France524
SMITH,George Buchanan 2Lt kia 25-9-15 GordH att2Bn p167 MR19
SMITH,George de Ville TCapt kia 1-7-16 13Y&L p159 CR France156
SMITH,George Evanston Lt kia 25-9-15 3A&SH p174 CR France114,2Bn
SMITH,George Lawrence Lotinga T2Lt kia 19-7-17 10NumbF p63 CR Belgium29,Laurence
SMITH,George Maxwell Lt ded 13-9-19 3 att1N&D p264 MR65,10Bn
SMITH,George Morley T2Lt dow 6-10-17 7Leic p88 CR France139
SMITH,George Pringle TLt kia 12-4-17 14RScots p55 CR France604
SMITH,George William 2Lt mbk 28-3-18 8RLancs p257 MR20
SMITH,Gerald Howard.MC.Lt kia 29-3-16 6SStaffs p229 CR France95,dow
SMITH,Gerald Sydney TLt kia 13-11-16 153MGC Inf p185 CR France1502
SMITH,Gilbert Keppal TLt ded 13-3-16 5 att11Mddx p148 CR France423,Keppel dow
SMITH,Gilbert Parker 2Lt kld 5-1-18 2Yorks p91 CR Belgium127
SMITH,Godfrey Garrett 2Lt kia 11-5-17 2RWSurr p56 MR20
SMITH,Godfrey Michael.MC.T2Lt dow 28-10-18 D256RFA p35 CR Yorks438
SMITH,Godfrey Leveson 2Lt kia 29-9-15 1CldGds p51 MR19
SMITH,Gordon Hamilton T2Lt kia 9-5-17 8Dev p77 MR20
SMITH,Gordon Keith.MC.Capt kia 21-8-17 GL &RFC p13 CR France276,Keigh
SMITH,Granville Keith Falconer Lt kia 29-10-14 1CldGds p51 MR29
SMITH,Granville Roland Francis.CVO.CB.Col ded 4-3-17 Ex CldGds p262
SMITH,Harold 2Lt kia 12-10-16 7Norf p74 CR France512
SMITH,Harold.MC.Capt kia 22-11-17 2/6WYorks p218 MR17
SMITH,Harold.MC.TCapt&Adjt dow 28-3-18 15WYorks p83 CR France169
SMITH,Harold Andrew 2Lt kia 21-3-18 N&D att2/6Bn p135 MR20
SMITH,Harold Benjamin 2Lt dow 20-5-17 7Lond p247 CR France568
SMITH,Harold Henderson 2Lt kia 19-9-18 4 att1BlkW p230 MR16
SMITH,Harold Heyworth T2Lt kia 13-2-16 150RFA att1TMB SpBde RE p35 CR France275
SMITH,Harold Robert Lt kia 21-3-18 NStaffs p157 MR20,Rymer

SMITH,Harold Robert.MC.TLt kia 7-11-18 RWKent att8Bn p142 MR16
SMITH,Harold Spencer 2Lt kia 31-7-18 3Lond &53RAF p246&258 CR France20
SMITH,Harry Gordon 2Lt kia 13-3-18 4A&SH p174 CR Greece6
SMITH,Harry Graham TCapt drd 10-4-17 RAMC p197 CR Europe96
SMITH,Harry Leonard Chappell Lt kia 20-10-14 N&D p135 MR32
SMITH,Harry Marsden Lt dow 27-2-17 PoW 1LNLancs p136 CR France1266
SMITH,Harry Norman T2Lt kia 2-3-17 20LancF p93&258 CRBelgium20,23-11-17
SMITH,Headford 2Lt dow 14-9-18 119ArmyBde A119RFA p35 CR France34
SMITH,Henry 2Lt drd 1-1-17 WorcYeo p206 CR Greece16
SMITH,Henry T2Lt kia 19-10-18 13Manch p156 CR France1392,9Bn
SMITH,Henry Crawford 2Lt ded 10-10-16 1OxfHuss p271
SMITH,Henry Dalby Dryden Capt kld 14-12-17 DLI attRFC CR Hamps1
SMITH,Henry James T2Lt kia 4-10-17 8SomLI p80 MR30
SMITH,Henry Leslie 2Lt kia 17-8-18 RFA p209 CR France266
SMITH,Henry Thomas Bayard 2Lt kia 25-3-18 4Huss &9TankCps p21&189 MR27
SMITH,Herbert T2Lt dow 19-7-17 3 att2Manch p156 CR Belgium24
SMITH,Herbert Bennett 2Lt kia 17-7-17 WSomYeo p205 CR Belgium78,12SomLI
SMITH,Herbert Carrington LtCol kia 25-4-15 2Hamps p121 MR4
SMITH,Herbert Dudley T2Lt kia 17-3-18 1/2 att2/7LancF p93 CR France528
SMITH,Herbert Evans 2Lt dow 18-6-17 1/5NStaffs p237 CR France178
SMITH,Herbert Fyfe T2Lt kia 23-4-17 2RScotF A'Coy p95 MR20
SMITH,Herbert George.MC.TCaptAMaj ded 16-2-19 RASC p267 CR Surrey160
SMITH,Herbert James T2Lt dow 29-4-16 10RLancs attRDubF p59 CR France551
SMITH,Herbert James 2Lt kia 9-4-18 7 att13ESurr p113 MR32
SMITH,Herbert Leslie TCapt kia 24-3-18 19Lpool p73 MR27
SMITH,Herbert Norman 2Lt kia 20-11-17 5WYorks p218
SMITH,Herbert Shaw 2Lt dow 12-4-17 9RScots p212 CR France40
SMITH,Herbert Stoney.DSO.LtCol kia 22-10-15 1Leic p88 CR Belgium5
SMITH,Horace 2Lt kia 8-10-16 5Lond p246 MR21
SMITH,Horace Claudian T2Lt kia 11-9-17 52RFC p13 CR Belgium173
SMITH,Horace Richard.MC.2Lt kia 5-11-18 9Lond p248 CR France939,Capt
SMITH,Horace Uchtred T2Lt kia 18-1-18 8SStaffs p123 CR France530
SMITH,Hubert Hector Capt kia 25-9-15 8KOSB p102 MR19
SMITH,Hugh Francis Russell 2Lt dow 5-7-16 1 att6RB p180
SMITH,Hugh Stewart TCapt kia 18-8-16 4 att2A&SH D'Coy p174 CR France432
SMITH,Isham Percy.DSO.CaptAMaj kia 30-11-17 RGA 102SB p42 CR France407
SMITH,Jacob Hardy.DSO.MC.Lt dow 29-8-16 3RB p180 CR France51,Capt
SMITH,James T2Lt kia 9-4-17 10GordH p167 CR France531
SMITH,James Lt ded 1-4-18 6SfthH attLabCps p266 CR Scot874,Capt
SMITH,James Albert 2Lt kia 21-3-18 RFA 30DAC p35 MR27
SMITH,James Bonner 2Lt kia 15-8-17 6BlkW att43RFC p19&231 MR20
SMITH,James Bowman T2Lt kia 28-6-18 7DCLI Ex ScotRif p115 MR20
SMITH,James Clement 2Lt kia 27-3-16 4RFus p70 MR29
SMITH,James Douglas LtACapt kia 27-9-18 ScotRif att1/7Bn p104 CR France484
SMITH,James Montague Lt&Adjt kia 2-5-15 RScots p211 MR4
SMITH,James Norman T2Lt kia 31-7-16 15Lpool att9Ches p73 CR France515
SMITH,James Osbourne Lt kia 2-11-17 1/7ScotRif p224 CR Palestine8
SMITH,James Rockcliffe.MC.TCapt kia 20-5-17 16KRRC p152 MR20
SMITH,James Salsbury Capt kia 17-12-17 LNLancs att1/5Bn p136 MR17,2Lt 30-11-17
SMITH,James Tennant Capt kia 5-6-17 1/4ELancs p226 CR France905
SMITH,James William 2Lt kia 21-3-18 7GordH p242 MR20
SMITH,James William.MID 2Lt dow 30-11-18 RGA 251SB p42 CR Ches28
SMITH,Jeanie Barclay Sister 28-4-16 QAIMNS CR France40
SMITH,John 2Lt kia 14-11-17 6 att4/5BlkW p231 MR30
SMITH,John T2Lt kia 20-7-18 Lpool att5Dev p73 MR18
SMITH,John Lt ded 20-2-19 RGA 200SB p262 CR Scot758,Lt
SMITH,John Adams.MC.T2Lt dow 28-4-17 28 att20NumbF p63 CR France40
SMITH,John Alexander Hay T2Lt kia 14-8-15 11RScots p55 CR France410
SMITH,John Basil T2Lt dow 19-8-17 14RWar A'Coy p66 CR France113
SMITH,John Christie 2Lt kia 21-3-18 6N&D p233
SMITH,John Clarence 2Lt kia 2-12-17 1/20Lond p251 MR17
SMITH,John Dowse Lt ded 3-11-18 DLI CR Lancs43
SMITH,John Fletcher TLt ded 28-7-16 19N&D &RFC p4&135 CR Notts84
SMITH,John Frazer T2Lt kia 11-4-17 7CamH p168 CR France531
SMITH,John Gardiner T2Lt kia 20-9-17 O&BLI att6Bn p130 MR30
SMITH,John Godfrey Bradley TLt drd 15-4-17 RAMC p197 MR35
SMITH,John Grant Lt ded 27-2-19 RE p48 CR France40
SMITH,John Henry 2Lt kia 9-7-18 10Mddx att103RAF p236&258 CR France31

SMITH,John Henry.MM.2Lt kia 28-8-18 Dev att7SomLI p77 MR16
SMITH,John Herbert Michael 2Lt dow 17-9-14 2Manch p156 CR France1113,10-9-14
SMITH,John Hobson 2Lt ded 24-11-18 78RH&FA p35 CR France658
SMITH,John Horne 2Lt kia 23-7-18 6ScotRif p224 CR Belgium3
SMITH,John Lancelot 2Lt kia 9-8-16 1/4SLancs p230 MR21
SMITH,John Macdonald T2Lt kia 12-5-16 12ScotRif p104 MR19
SMITH,John Marshall 2Lt dow 27-9-18 9HLI p241 CR France1184
SMITH,John Rankin Donald 2Lt kia 31-7-17 5RScotsF p222 MR29,2Bn
SMITH,John Richard Gutteridge T2Lt dow 30-12-16 32 att8NumbF p63 CR France40
SMITH,John Samuel 2Lt kia 28-4-17 5SStaffs p229 MR20
SMITH,John Selby Armstrong 2Lt mbk 25-4-17 3 att10WRid p257 MR20,att9Bn
SMITH,John Taylor T2Lt dow 29-3-18 18 att2WYorks p83 CR France650
SMITH,John Veere 2Lt dow 26-7-16 4/8Mddx p236 CR France80
SMITH,John Wilmhurst Grainger ACapt kia31-8-16.1SStaffs p123 MR21,Wilmshurst Granger
SMITH,Joseph 2Lt kia 14-3-17 6SStaffs p229 CR France281,1/5Bn
SMITH,Joseph Basil.MID T2Lt kia 18-9-18 SLancs att9Bn p126 MR37
SMITH,Joseph Cecil Lt kia 28-7-17 RFC p13 MR20
SMITH,Joseph Edward T2Lt kia 15-1-16 12HLI p164 CR France423,18-1-16
SMITH,Joshua Harold Lt kia 12-8-15 6LancF p221 CR Gallipoli2
SMITH,J.S.Lt30-4-20 RFA CR Cornwall140
SMITH,Julian Martin T2Lt ded 10-9-14 SL att9Lancers p201 CR France1441
SMITH,Kenneth Carrington Lt ded 26-3-19 RE p262 CR Staffs41
SMITH,Kenneth Leslie 2Lt kia 20-9-17 LancF p221 MR30
SMITH,Lawrence Brumwell T2Lt kia 14-9-18 10 att1/4LNLancs p136 CR France279,Lt
SMITH,Lawrence Oliver Lt ded 30-6-19 SL attIWT p268 CR Iraq6,GL
SMITH,Leon Walter Lt kia 12-4-18 4DCLI p227 MR32,1/5Bn
SMITH,Leonard George 2Lt kia 1-7-16 2Ess p132 MR21
SMITH,Leonard Hale Lt kld 3-11-17 6Ess attRFC p19&232 CR Essex1,2-11-17
SMITH,Leonard Hearne T2Lt kia 11-8-17 16Mddx p148 MR29
SMITH,Leonard William T2Lt kia 23-10-16 2Mddx p148 MR21
SMITH,Leslie Morgan TMaj ded 20-12-17 1BedsGarrBn p86 CR India48
SMITH,Leslie Phillips 2Lt ded 6-3-15 RGA p42 CR Kent231
SMITH,Leslie Tildero T2Lt kia 16-9-16 7YLI p144 MR21,Tilden
SMITH,Lothrop Lewis de Berniere Lt ded 3-9-16 6RB p180 CR Kent68,kldacc
SMITH,Louis Herbert Collin 2Lt kia 13-10-15 1Mon p244 MR19 CR France1896,Collen
SMITH,Martin Kirke Lt kld 14-12-15 RFA 99TMB p208 CR France637,kia
SMITH,Matthew Frederick.MC.TCapt kia 18-9-18 10WYorks p83 CR France415
SMITH,Neville Field TCapt kia 24-1-16 15DLI p161 CR France922
SMITH,Norman Edward T2Lt kia 20-7-18 1/2LancF att2/4Hamps p93 CR France622
SMITH,Norman Gordon 2Lt kia 19-12-15 HLI &RFC p2&164
SMITH,Norman Havelock 2Lt kia 23-3-18 20Lond att141TMB p251 MR20
SMITH,Norman Herbert 2Lt kia 20-11-17 2/5WYorks CR France1483
SMITH,Norman Louis Lt kia 30-12-17 1/4KSLI p235 MR17
SMITH,Norman McGann Capt dow 12-12-17 RAMC 2FA p254 CR Palestine9
SMITH,Norman McNeill T2Lt kia 1-7-16 21NumbF p63 MR21
SMITH,Norman Spires Lt ded 1-2-19 RASC attRGA 27SB AC p193 CR France63,Spiers
SMITH,Olive Masseuse 24-9-16 ScotWomensHosp attSerbianArmy CR Greece7
SMITH,Patrick Leete TLt dow 27-9-15 10Y&L p159 CR France201
SMITH,Peter TLt kia 28-4-17 RE &12RFC p13&48 CR France46
SMITH,Percival Thomas Lt kia 26-9-15 8RWKent p142 MR19
SMITH,Percy T2Lt dow 13-5-18 1 att2/5LancF p93 CR France10
SMITH,Percy Claude Jacomb 2Lt kia 1-7-16 1EYorks p85 MR21
SMITH,Percy George Cecil T2Lt kia 18-8-18 11RScots D'Coy p55 CR France26
SMITH,Percy Kirk T2Lt kia 12-9-17 RE 212FC p48 CR Belgium37
SMITH,Percy Lloyd T2Lt kia 3-5-17 12WYorks p83 MR20
SMITH,Philip Golding T2Lt kia 5-10-18 13DLI p161 CR France844
SMITH,Quintin Livingstone T2Lt kia 1-7-16 13 att15LancF p93 MR21
SMITH,Ralph 2Lt kia 27-9-15 1WelshGds p53 MR19
SMITH,Ralph Eustace Capt kia 19-4-18 NumbYeo &RAF p204&258 CR France303,18-4-18
SMITH,Ralph Henry T2Lt kia 30-7-16 17Lpool p73 CR France294
SMITH,Ralph John TLt ded 31-7-18 GL RE IWT p48 CR Iraq6
SMITH,Ralph Leslie 2Lt murderedBySowar 16-7-16 1ARO att126Baluchis p282 MR43,124Baluchis
SMITH,Ralph Pritchard T2Lt kia 5-8-17 8NStaffs p158 CR Belgium77

SMITH,Randolph Rae Lt ded 9-8-15 13N&D p264 CR Lond8,2Lt 12Bn
SMITH,Raymond TCapt kia 1-7-16 11BordR p118 MR21
SMITH,Raymond Alexander 2Lt kia 1-7-16 3Lond p246
SMITH,Reginald Lt kia 20-12-16 18RFC p4 CR France518
SMITH,Reginald Frederick 2Lt kia 14-5-17 15Lond p249 MR20
SMITH,Reginald George T2Lt kia 7-10-16 122MGC p185 MR21
SMITH,Reginald Iredale T2Lt kia 18-7-16 10A&SH p174 MR21
SMITH,Reginald John 2512 2Lt dow 1-4-18 D291RFA p35 CR France864
SMITH,Reston Alexander T2Lt kia 25-1-18 73RFC p17 CR France31
SMITH,Reuben Hinton Lt kldacc 10-1-18 4Dev p220 CR Kent38,14Bn Ex 15Bn
SMITH,Rex Johnston TCapt kia 1-7-16 15Y&L p159 CR France246
SMITH,Richard Alfred Capt ded 28-8-18 RAOC p198 CR Mddx77
SMITH,Richard Thomas 2Lt ded 3-5-15 4ELancs p226 CR Lancs193
SMITH,Robert 2Lt kia 1-7-16 2YLI p144 MR21
SMITH,Robert 2Lt dow 9-8-17 BordR att8Bn p118 CR Belgium112
SMITH,Robert 2Lt kia 20-11-17 1/4RLancs p59 CR France844
SMITH,Robert T2Lt kia 15-12-17 2RScotF p95 MR30
SMITH,Robert 2Lt kia 28-3-18 14Lond att7CamH p249 MR20
SMITH,Robert Campbell McIntyre 2Lt kia 20-6-16 8A&SH p243 CR France15
SMITH,Robert Cecil CaptALtCol dow 1-12-17 20DLI att11RWSurr p161 CR Italy76
SMITH,Robert Dunlop Capt kia 12-6-17 IA 33Punjabis p282
SMITH,Robert Fraser 2Lt kia 20-9-17 68MGC Inf p185 MR30
SMITH,Robert Gardner Paget 2Lt kia 15-9-16 9Suff p79 MR21
SMITH,Robert James 2Lt kia 13-11-16 6SfthH p241 CR France131
SMITH,Robert John TCapt kia 6-5-16 15LancF p93 CR France251
SMITH,Robert Paterson.MC.T2Lt dow 2-8-17 8SfthH p165 CR Belgium8
SMITH,Robert Rutherford T2Lt kia 20-9-17 196MGC p185 CR Belgium10
SMITH,Robert Wright 2Lt kia 12-2-17 6HLI p240 CR France35
SMITH,Robert Yearsley Clarke 2Lt kia 21-3-18 2/6N&D p233 MR20
SMITH,Roderick Franklyn.MC&Bar.TCapt kia 28-3-18 6KSLI p145 MR27
SMITH,Roger T2Lt kia 25-1-17 4SWBord p101 MR38
SMITH,Roland 2Lt kia 6-4-17 3YLI Inf &RFC p13&144 MR20
SMITH,Ronald Christian Sundius 2Lt kia 13-3-15 ULIA att2WYorks p282
SMITH,Rowland Siddons Capt ded 21-10-18 3WYorks p263
SMITH,Roy Samuel 2Lt kia 11-4-17 9Lond p248 CR France104
SMITH,Samuel Douard Irvine Lt kia 1-7-16 5 att1RIrRif p170 CR France246
SMITH,Samuel Percy Capt kia 28-2-17 1/5SStaffs p229 CR France502
SMITH,Sergius Holland 2Lt kia 24-11-15 4 att2SStaffs p123 MR19
SMITH,Sidney Lt kia 8-12-15 RGA 113Bty p42 CR France222
SMITH,Sidney Arthur T2Lt kia 10-8-15 10Hamps p121 MR4
SMITH,Sidney Fraser 2Lt dow 3-9-17 D256RFA p209 CR France40
SMITH,Sidney George.VD.TD.LtCol ded 8-10-17 7Hamps p229 CR Iraq8
SMITH,Sidney George 2Lt kia 21-3-18 59MGC p185 MR20
SMITH,Sidney Harold T2Lt kld 23-10-17 GL &RFC p13 CR Shrop52
SMITH,Sidney John Howard 2Lt kia 10-2-17 10Dev p77 MR37
SMITH,Sidney O'Connol 2Lt dow 25-8-16 9RB p180 CR France177,O'Carroll Lt kia
SMITH,Stanley 2Lt kia 18-11-15 1/5YLI p235 CR Belgium23
SMITH,Stanley Fenton Capt kia 9-10-17 5Y&L p238 MR30
SMITH,Stanley Herd T2Lt dow 27-5-18 2TankCps p189 CR France885
SMITH,Susie Marie Colbourn SNurse 12-2-16 QAIMNS CR Staffs78
SMITH,Sydney Capt kia 19-5-18 3 att1ESurr p113 CR France177
SMITH,Sydney Bicheno 2Lt ded 1-12-18 RGA p209 CR Lond3
SMITH,Sydney Ferrar 2Lt kia 7-5-15 1Ches p96 MR29
SMITH,Sydney John T2Lt kia 20-9-17 26RFus p70 CR Belgium22
SMITH,Sydney Newman 2Lt kia 9-8-17 7Suff p79 MR20
SMITH,Sydney Phillip Capt kia 6-4-18 RASC &RAF p271 MR20,Philip
SMITH,T.E.2Lt ded 11-6-18 1/4Worc &RAF p109 CR War60
SMITH,Theodore Thomas 2Lt 29-9-18 11RAF MR20
SMITH,Thomas TMaj kia 23-1-17 6RScotF p95 CR France151,6/7Bn
SMITH,Thomas TLt ded 23-5-17 RAMC p267 CR Mddx26,22-5-17
SMITH,Thomas 2Lt kia 16-5-18 13RScots p55 MR20
SMITH,Thomas Lt kia 28-10-18 NottsYeo p205 MR38
SMITH,Thomas Arthur Lt kia 7-10-16 15Lond p249 MR21
SMITH,Thomas Edmund 2Lt kia 14-7-17 GL &27RFC p13 CR France924
SMITH,Thomas Edward 2Lt kia 5-9-18 8Lond p247 CR France511
SMITH,Thomas Emanuel 2Lt kia 23-4-17 RGA 263SB p42 CR France777,Emmanuel
SMITH,Thomas Lawrie Lt kia 18-9-18 AyrYeo attMGC p187&203 CR France415

SMITH,Thomas Rowland T2Lt dow 30-3-18 N&D attCamelCps p135 MR34
SMITH,Thomas Sidney 2Lt kia 13-10-14 Dors p124 MR22,Sydney
SMITH,Thurston Boyd T2Lt kia 7-6-17 11RWSurr p56 CR Belgium29
SMITH,Valentine Herbert Capt ded 1-6-18 5RWSurr &1KAR p212&268 CR EAfrica77
SMITH,Victor Sidney 2Lt kia 6-10-17 44RFA att113RFC p13&35 CR Palestine2
SMITH,Vivian Norman TCapt kia13-11-16.6Wilts p153 CR France251
SMITH,W.E.2Lt 13-5-17 RFC CR Mddx66
SMITH,Wansey 2Lt kld 2-4-18 11ELancs att 10RAF p111 CR Belgium11,kia
SMITH,Wallace T2Lt kia 23-11-17 RE 129FC p48 CR France528
SMITH,Walter Ernest LtACapt dow 5-7-17 8YLI TrainingRes p144 CR France512
SMITH,Walter Gordon 2Lt ded 5-3-19 RASC 9CpsTroopSplyCo p267 CR Lond12,Lt
SMITH,Walter Sydney T2Lt kia 9-1-18 49RFC p17 CR France238
SMITH,Walter Thomas 2Lt kia 3-3-17 8Beds p86 CR France163
SMITH,Walter Tyrrell 2Lt kia 14-10-16 4BlkW p230 CR France215,Lt
SMITH,Walter Wyville T2Lt kia 18-10-15 9RFus p70 CR France423
SMITH,Wilbraham Fremantle 2Lt dow 28-9-16 5Ches p222 CR France105
SMITH,Wilfred 2Lt dow 9-5-17 4 att6RSuss p228 CR France40
SMITH,Wilfred Robert Abel.CMG.LtCol dow 19-5-15 2GrenGds p50 CRFrance727,Wilfrid
SMITH,Wilfred Vincent 2LtTLt kia 8-8-17 3 att8Glouc p107 CR Belgium17,7-8-17
SMITH,William Lt dow 17-6-15 4LNLancs B'Coy p234 CR France201
SMITH,William 2Lt dow 8-6-17 A275RFA p209 CR Belgium11,Lt
SMITH,William 2Lt kia 1-9-18 20Lond p251 MR16
SMITH,William 2Lt 29-10-18 2/5Lpool CR Lancs193
SMITH,William Alexander TLt dow 3-6-17 RAMC att27RFA p197 CR France95
SMITH,William Alfred.MID TLtCol dow 9-7-16 18Manch p156 CR France23
SMITH,William Arthur Heseltine 2Lt kia 27-5-18 1EYorks p85 MR18
SMITH,William Byron T2Lt dow 25-10-18 YLIatt9Bn p144 CR France332
SMITH,William Cecil 2Lt kia 31-7-18 5Manch p236 CR France5
SMITH,William Charles 2Lt ded 8-2-18 1RFC p17 CR Devon258
SMITH,William Edward.MC.2Lt kia 29-8-18 Mddx att 1/13Lond p148 MR16
SMITH,William George Rae TLt kia 25-1-16 ArmyCycCps p181 CR France922
SMITH,William George Richard 2Lt kia 16-8-17 Mddxatt2Bn p148 MR30
SMITH,William Gerald Furness Lt dow 5-7-15 3 att 1NStaffs p158 CR Belgium44
SMITH,William Gordon.MC.2Lt dow 21-3-18 4 att8Leic p220 CR France716,Lt 22-3-18
SMITH,William Hammond.MID CaptAMaj kia 12-4-17 A52RFA p35 CR France451
SMITH,William Harold Vyvyan 2Lt kia 31-7-17 2ELancs p111 MR29
SMITH,William Henry 2Lt kia 23-4-17 281RH&FA p35 CR France591
SMITH,William Henry T2Lt ded 4-11-18 RBerks Res att2/4Bn p140 CR Essex13
SMITH,William James Capt drd 29-5-17 Dors attEgyptianArmy p124 MR34
SMITH,William James TLt kia 2-10-17 Y&L att8Bn p159 MR30
SMITH,William Joseph 2Lt kia 31-7-17 4Leinst p175 CR Belgium84
SMITH,William Kenneth Ord ded 2-5-17 BRCS 17AmbTrn CR France134
SMITH,William Leslie LtACapt dow 15-4-18 2Worc p109 MR32,kld
SMITH,William Reginald Sturston 2Lt ded 22-10-17 GL &RFC p13 MR20
SMITH,William Robson LtACapt ded 19-11-18 RFA X31TMB 2ndArmy p35 CR France134
SMITH,William Roy TLt kia 24-3-18 RASC att8RWSurr p194 CR France605
SMITH,William Spencer 2Lt kia 23-7-16 2KOSB p102 MR21
SMITH,William Stanley 2Lt kia 25-6-16 RMunstF p176 CR France550
SMITH,William Strain.MC.T2LtACapt dow 23-3-17 1RScotF p95 CR France57
SMITH,William Travers.MID 2Lt kia 20-11-17 RE 174TC p48 CR France689
SMITH,William Watson T2Lt dow 18-10-16 11GordH p167 CR France145
SMITH,Willoughby Willard T2Lt kia 9-7-16 19Manch att21TMB p156 CR France630
SMITH,Wyndham Alexander 2Lt kia 23-4-16 GloucYeo p203 MR34
SMITH-CUMMING,Alexander Mansfield Lt kld 3-10-14 1SfthH p165 CR France1437,Alastair dedacc
SMITH-GRANT,John Gordon Smith Cheetham Capt ded 30-5-18 9RScots att70RAF p212&258 CR France84,kld
SMITH-HOWARD,Kenneth Overend Howard T2Lt kia 16/17-10-16 12RSuss p120 MR21,18-10-16
SMITH-LEE,Jeannie Nurse ded 30-3-17 VAD 30Detachment att9GH p200 CR France145
SMITH-MASTERS,Bruce Swinton.MC.Capt kia 1-7-16 2Ess p132 CR France643
SNITH-MASTERS,George Arthur T2Lt kia 19-8-15 6Beds p86 CR Belgium97
SMITH-MAXWELL,Archibald Findlay TLt kia 1-7-16 17HLI p164 CR France1890
SMITH-REWSE,Henry Bingham Whistler Maj dow 21-11-14 51/36RFA p35 CR Belgium150,22-11-14

SMITH-RYLAND,Henry Dennis Capt dow 7-4-17 1/1WarYeo p205 CR Egypt2
SMITH-SLIGO,Archibald George Roderick Joseph 2Lt kia 14-9-14 1CamH p168 MR15
SMITHER,Charles 2Lt 22-11-18 RFA CR Mddx17
SMITHER,Harold T2Lt kia 6-7-17 GL &48RFC p13 CR France403
SMITHERS,Edward Henry Keith TLt kia 9-7-16 11 att16Manch p156 MR21
SMITHERS,Harold TMaj kia 4-11-16 RGA p42 CR France5
SMITHERS,Reginald Cuthbert Welsford 2LtACapt kia 16-8-17 YLIatt7Bn p144 MR30
SMITHETT,Arthur Cecil Hamilton LtCol dow 24-11-15 IA 76Punjabis p282 MR38
SMITHETT,Graeme Cecil East 2Lt kia 12-10-17 1Nhants &27RFC p13&138 CR Belgium383,Lt
SMITHIES,Ellen Louise SNurse ded 22-2-19 TFNS 3SthGH CR Essex1
SMITHWICK,James Arnold Capt ded 9-11-15 4 att2RIrReg p89 CR Eire350
SMOLLETT-YOUNG,Alexander CaptHonMaj ded 23-5-16 SL 9A&SH p268 CR Scot80
SMOOTHY,Albert Victor 2Lt dow 9-11-18 2Lond p245 CR France1033
SMURTHWAITE,Douglas Stuart Stirling 2Lt kia 26-10-14 1BlkW A'Coy p129 MR29,Donald
SMURTHWAITE,Oscar TLt kia 17-4-18 18NumbF p63 MR32
SMYLIE,Robert Stewart R.TLt kia 14-7-16 7 att1RScotF p95 CR France453
SMUTH,Algernon Beresford Capt kia 15-11-14 2YLI p144 MR29
SMYTH,Arthur Hugo T2Lt kia 13-3-18 RASC 69SB AmmCol p194 CR France15
SMYTH,Donald Seymour 2Lt kia 19-10-14 RIrReg p89 MR22
SMYTH,Edmund Fitzgerald.MC.AMaj kia 3-12-17 11RIrRif p170 CR France379,Fitz-Gerald
SMYTH,Edwin Percy TLt kia 28-6-18 7RWKent p142 CR France21,Percival
SMYTH,George Bostall Jenkinson TLtACapt kia 22-10-18 7RIrRif p170 CR Belgium140,6Bn
SMYTH,Gerald Brice Ferguson.DSO&Bar.MIDx4 LtCol 17-7-20 RE CR Ireland106
SMYTH,Gordon Dill Long T2Lt kia 16-8-17 13RIrRif p170 MR30
SMYTH,Irvine Johnston 2Lt kia 3-9-15 5RInnisKF p105 CR Gallipoli5,6Bn
SMYTH,James Capt kia 9-7-15 3 att2LancF p93 MR29
SMYTH,James 2Lt kia 12-3-17 2RFC p13 CR France924
SMYTH,John T2Lt kia 23-11-17 9RIrRif p170 MR17
SMYTH,John Albert Gordon T2Lt kia 29-6-18 5MGC Inf p185 CR France346
SMYTH,John Fairfax Field 2Lt kia 22-7-17 1ScotsGds p52 CR Belgium12
SMYTH,John Hawkins T2Lt kia 12-4-17 6 att2Leinst p175 CR France557,10-4-17
SMYTH,John Ross 2Lt kia 20-10-14 3 att2RIrReg p89 MR22
SMYTH,Mary Grace AssAdmntr ded 22-2-19 QMAAC p200 CR War74
SMYTH,P.G.4-3-19 VAD CR Egypt9
SMYTH,Philip Joseph T2Lt dow 16-9-16 6ConnRgrs attRFC p4&172 CR France23
SMYTH,Richard Alexander Noel Capt dow 8-11-14 RGA 5SB p42 CR France297,7-11-14
SMYTH,Ross Acheson Maj ded 27-9-17 10RInnisKF p105 CR Ireland201 Ex RIrReg
SMYTH,William Henry TLt kia 17-4-18 2Worc p109 MR32
SMYTH,William Houghton TCapt kia 1-7-16 13RIrRif p170 MR21
SMYTH-OSBORNE,Wilfred Lt kia 29-8-15 1Worc p109 CR France347,Wilfrid
SMYTH-PIGGOTT,Bernard Cecil BvtMaj ded 15-4-16 DLI p161 CR USA23
SMYTHE,Andrew Graham Cowan Maj kia 7-9-17 RGA 140SB p42 CR Belgium83,Conran
SMYTHE,Frederick Fleming 2Lt kia 18-9-14 2Worc p109 CR France1329,Fleming Frednck
SMYTHE,Lee Gordon Fuller Lt ded 26-4-20 IA 2/70BurmaRif p282 MR40
SMYTHE,Patrick Evelyn Lt ded 30-11-18 3 att2BlkW p129 CR Egypt1
SMYTHE,Ralph Conran Maj dow 22-11-15 RGA 2SB p42 CR France1
SMYTHE,Rudolph Meade Capt dow 13-9-15 5Beds p219 MR4,13-10-15
SMYTHIES,Ernest Dudley TCapt ded 16-7-18 RE p48 CR Glouc27
SNAGG,B.C.K.Capt 27-2-19 RM CR Sussex197
SNAITH,Henry T2Lt kia 5-4-15 10KOYLI p144 CR France745,5-4-18 2Bn
SNAITH,William Ernest T2Lt kia 3-5-17 Ex 3Bn 4RFus p70 MR20
SNAPE,Frank William 2Lt kia 7-5-15 2YLI p144 MR29
SNEADE,Charles George.MC.Lt kia 14-10-18 4Worc p109 CR Belgium161
SNEAD-COX,Geoffrey Phillip Joseph 2Lt kia 20-10-14 att1RWFus p99 MR29
SNEAD-COX,Richard Mary 2Lt kia 28-10-14 3RScots p55 MR22
SNEATH,Claude Davis Lt kia 14-10-14 4Mddx p148 CR France1106
SNEATH,Wilfred Archer.MC.TLt dow 11-7-17 RAMC att2FA p197 CR Belgium24,12-7-17
SNEATH,Wilfred Harry Lt 6-4-18 208RAF MR20
SNEDDON,Andrew Beattie 2Lt kia 3-10-17 GL &RFC p13 MR40
SNELGROVE,Frederick Augustus T2Lt kia 24-8-18 6RWKent p142 CR France370

SNELGROVE,Herbert Davys Bernard 2Lt kia 15-8-17 RFC p13 CR France1732
SNELGROVE,Sidney Henry TLt kia 30-7-15 14 att7KRRC p152 MR29
SNELL,Arthur Cyril Everitt 2Lt kia 18-10-16 26MGC p255 MR21,Everett
SNELL,Christopher T2Lt dow 14-7-16 10WRid p116
SNELL,Cyril Herbert Lt mbk 9/10-11-17 DofLancsOwnYeo att12Manch p257 MR30,Hubert 9-11-17 MR34,9-10-17
SNELL,Eric Aylmer Goldney.MID TMaj kia 16-11-17 1Beds att1/4KAR p86&202 CR EAfrica15 &CR Tanzania1
SNELL,Francis Saxon T2Lt kia 11-7-16 8 att9RBerks p140 CR France372
SNELL,Herbert 2Lt kia 7-4-17 24Lond att2/6LancF p252 CR France260
SNELL,Norris TCapt kia 14-7-16 8EYorks p85 MR20
SNELL,Philip Sidney T2Lt kia 9-8-15 6RIrFus p171 MR4
SNELL,Stanley Saxon 2Lt dow 6-5-18 B159RFA p35 CRFrance41
SNELLING,Frederick John T2Lt kia 30-10-17 7RWar p70 MR30,7RFus
SNELSON,Victor Louis T2Lt kia 15-7-17 WelshR att12SWBord p127 CR France439
SNEYD,Dryden George Thompson.MC.Maj ded 7-4-19 RGA p262 CR Lond4
SNEYD,Thomas Humphrey Capt kia 2-11-14 4 att2LancF p93 CR Belgium168
SNITHER,Chas 2Lt ded 22-12-18 RH&FA p262
SNOW,Cecil Longville LtCol kld 11-12-15 IntelDepot CR Egypt19
SNOW,Charles Foote 2Lt kia 30-6-16 RFA p35 CR Belgium136
SNOW,George Wilkie 2Lt kia 20-4-17 8RScots p212 CR France1182
SNOW,Richard Aslin 2Lt kia 4-12-15 1/4Y&L p238 CR Belgium23
SNOW,Tom Cyril Capt ded 10-7-19 LabCps Ex SomLI p266 CR Dorset94
SNOWBALL,John Francis Lt ded 29-9-18 RASC p271 CR Numb43
SNOWBALL,John Hearn 2Lt dow 15-9-16 108RFA p35 CR France294
SNOWDEN,Harcourt John Lt kia 11-1-15 1Herts p252 CR Belgium632
SNOWDEN,Harold Jackson Lt dow 11-8-17 2SLancs attRFC p13&126 CR Lond12
SNOWDEN,Jasper Whitfield Lt kia 25-2-17 9Worc p109 MR38
SNOWDEN,Reginald Wallace TLt kia 10-7-16 8SStaffs p123 MR21
SNOWDEN,Stanley Jackson Capt kia 26-3-17 9Mddx p236 MR34
SNOWDON,Henry Frederick Lt kia 6-10-16 1Lond p245 MR21
SNOWDON,Ralph 2Lt kia 2-10-17 4EYorks p219 CR France162
SNOWDON,Sidney Frank 2Lt kia 15-9-16 1Lond p245 MR21
SNOWIE,George T2Lt kia 15-9-16 8KOSB p102 MR21
SNYDER,Lorne 2Lt kia 23-4-17 Hamps att2Bn p121 MR20
SNYDERS,Emanuel Leon 2Lt kia 17-3-19 RASC p194 MR70 &CR Europe180
SOAME,Everard Nixon Buckworth Herne Capt kia 21-3-18 2/5NStaffs p237 MR20
SOAMES,A.R.Capt 22-7-21 6RWKent CR Lond29
SOAMES,Alfred.DSO.TMaj kia 13-10-15 att6EKent p58 MR19
SOAMES,Arthur Henry Leslie.MC.TLtCapt ded 7-7-15 3Huss attRFC p2&21 CR Wales619
SOAMES,Gilbert Horsman Maj kia 9-6-17 1WYorks p83 CR France114,9-1-17
SOAMES,Harold Martin Lt kia 11-9-14 20Huss p23 CR Belgium201,23-8-14
SOAMES,Maurice Gordon Maj dow 24-9-16 A48RFA p35 CR France833
SOAMES,Oliver Jack T2Lt kia 27-3-18 4Beds p86 CR France516
SOAMES,Robert Eley TLt kia 1-7-16 8ESurr p113 CR France513
SOAMES,William Noel Lt ded 19-5-16 ChesYeo p203
SODDY,James T2Lt kia 23-4-17 Norf p74 MR20
SODEN,Harold Corbet Lt kia 22-5-16 4Lpool p73 CR France163,23-5-16
SOGNO,George Frank T2Lt dow 9-10-17 13RSuss attRFC p13&120 CR Belgium18
SOLLEY,Bernard John 2Lt kia 10-8-18 2Lond p245 CR Belgium79
SOLLY,Arthur Norbury TCapt kia 11-8-17 GL Manch att20RFC p13 CR France134
SOLLY,William Buckle.MC.Lt dow 19-10-18 3LancF att101TMB p93 CR Belgium450
SOLOMAN,Edmund John T2Lt kia 2-8-17 1 att8SLancs p126 CR Belgium34
SOLOMON,Arthur Meyer Capt kia 24-3-18 10 att1/19Lond p248 MR20
SOLOMON,Hubert Philip 2Lt kld 20-10-17 RFC p13&258 CR Lincs136
SOLOMON,Harry M.Lt ded 5-12-18 6Beds &RAF p86
SOLOMON,John Howard 2Lt dow 21-4-17 7Lond att18KRRC p247 CR Belgium11
SOLOMON,Kenneth Maurice Halpen T2Lt dow 18-9-15 11Glouc att11Worc p107 CR Mddx40,Keneth Halgren
SOLOMON,L.B.TLt kia 12-4-18 2RFus attRAF p70 CR France193
SOLOMON,Leonard T2Lt kia 23-4-17 1KOSB p102 MR20
S0MAN,Leon Asher 2LtTLt kia 8-3-17 6LNLancs p136 MR38
SOMERS,Cyril Dermott Fouace 2Lt dow 20-5-17 1RInnisF p105 CR France113
SOMERS-COCKS,Reginald.MC.TCapt kia 24-4-18 GL att7SomLI p191 CR Belgium1, Staff att261InfBde
SOMERS-SMITH,John Robert.MC.Capt kia 1-7-16 5Lond p246 MR21
SOMERS-SMITH,Richard William 2Lt kia 30-6-15 7KRRC p152 CR Belgium165
SOMERSET,Fitz Roy Aubrey.MC.TLt kia 7-7-16 13Ches p96 MR16

SOMERSET,Norman Arthur Henry 2Lt kia 25-10-14 1GrenGds p50 CR Belgium140,23-10-14
SOMERVAIL,William Fulton.DSO.MC.CaptBdeMaj kia 4-10-18 2ScotRif p104 CR France725
SOMERVILLE,Harold Aytoun 2Lt kia 17-6-20 1A 1/129Baluchis p282 MR43
SOMERVILLE,Henry Arthur.MC.2Lt kia 28-3-18 RSuss &82RFC p17&120 CR France1234
SOMERVILLE,Martin Ashwood 2Lt dow 21-9-18 6RB att1/10Lond p180 CR Palestine9,Ashworth
SOMERVILLE,Richard Newman 2LtTLt kia 9-10-15 RE 94FC p48 CR France631
SOMERVILLE,Stafford Dudley 2Lt kia 5-7-16 5YLI p144 CR France702,Lt
SOMERVILLE,Stafford James MajTLtCol dow 16-8-17 1RInnisF att9RIrF p105 CR Belgium8
SOMERVILLE,William 2Lt kia 25-4-18 4RScots p211 CR Belgium168
SOMMERVILL,John 2Lt dow 31-10-18 4RScotF p222 CR Belgium143
SOMMERVILLE,George Little Capt kia 16/18-8-16 3 att8RLancs p59 MR21,16-8-16
SOMMERVILLE,William Henry Lionel.MC.TLt ded 3-12-18 RAOC 550AS p198 CR France34
SONDHEIM,Walter T2Lt kld 4-3-18 RFC p17 CR Wilts28
SONES,Liba 2Lt kia 22-3-18 5 att2LNLancs p234 MR27,Ziba
SONGER,William Arthur T2Lt kia 15-9-16 9RB attTMB p180 MR20
SONGHURST,Charles Edward.MM.T2Lt kia 22-8-18 Ess Res att9Bn p132 MR16
SONNEX,Ernest James Harvey 2Lt kia 24-9-18 4RBerks p234 CR France234,Lt
SOPWITH,Frank Wesley.MC.Lt kia 27-5-18 251RFA att50NumbrianHB p208 CR France1329
SORBY,Charles Malin Clifton 2Lt dow 8-5-15 3Mon p244 CR France284
SORGE,Ivan Percival Campbell T2Lt dow 15-10-16 9 att6BordR Pnrs p118 CR France121
SORLEY,Charles Hamilton TCapt kia 13-10-15 7Suff p79 MR19
SORO,William T2Lt kia 16-4-17 20RFus p70 CR France434
SORRILL,Herbert 2Lt ded 22-5-19 O&BLI p264 CR Staffs52
SORTWELL,Arthur Robert Capt ded 28-3-18 RASC attRFC p267 CR Mddx53,28-2-18
SOTHAM,Ralph Clifford Lt kia 9-1-18 5WSurr attRFC p19,212,271&261,RWKent
SOTHEBY,Lionel Frederick Southwell 2Lt kia 25-9-15 A&SH p174 MR38
SOTHERS,Charles Gordon T2Lt dow 6-12-17 18Mddx p148 CR Belgium45
SOUCHOTTE,C.2Lt kld 23-4-18 GL &RAF p191
SOULE,Francis Lt&QM ded 23-11-19 RAMC p267 CR Hamps62
SOULSBY,Henry Stanley T2Lt kia 6-7-16 9 att6KOSB p102 CR France402
SOULSBY,William Dobson 2Lt kia 31-8-18 6Lond p247 CR France624
SOUNESS,Thomas 2Lt kia 7-9-18 116/26RFA p35 CR France309
SOUPER,Noel Beaumont T2Lt kia 1-7-16 6RBerks p140 MR21
SOUSTER,Albert Edward T2Lt kia 12-4-18 31MGC Inf p185 MR32
SOUTAR,Alexander Henderson.MC.LtAMaj dow 28-5-18 RE 98FC p48 MR18
SOUTAR,Alexander Smith.MIDx2 Capt 15-3-20 RASC CR Egypt9
SOUTAR,Frank Henderson.MID 2Lt kia 21-1-16 3 att2BlkW p129 MR38
SOUTER,George Lt dow 3-9-18 1/7ScotRif p224 CR France103
SOUTER,James Mitchell Lt 11-4-17 59RFC CR France777
SOUTH,Walter Burns Campbell Lt ded 13-10-18 9Mddx p236,189&258 CR Dorset94
SOUTHALL,William Percival Lt 28-5-18 64RAF MR20
SOUTHCOMB,Edward Hamilton 2Lt kia 31-7-17 3 att24Manch p156 MR29
SOUTHERN,Gerald Cameron Lt kia 21-7-15 1A 53Sikhs p282
SOUTHERN,Hugh 2Lt mbk 18-4-16 IARO att47Sikhs p282 MR38
SOUTHERN,Mathew T2Lt kia 12-9-17 10EYorks p85 CR France184
SOUTHERN,Thomas William.MC.2LtACapt kia 29-9-18 11 att4EYorks p219 CR France285
SOUTHEY,Harry Hartley Waite Maj dow 30-3-17 1/5WelshReg p230 CR Egypt2
SOUTHEY,Robert George Melvill Lt kia 23-7-16 1DCLI p115 MR21
SOUTHGATE,Charles Edward T2Lt kia 18-2-17 1RB p180 CR France216,19-2-17 Ex HAC
SOUTHGATE,Henry Albert 2Lt kia 8-4-18 3RWKent attAnsonBn p142 CR France252
SOUTHIN,Charles Alec.MC.2Lt kld 15-2-18 21Lond attRFC p19&251 CR Mddx5
SOUTHON,John Edward.MC.2Lt kia 3-12-17 1/17Lond p250 MR17
SOUTHWELL,Arthur Horace Steadman 2Lt kia 13-11-16 7KSLI p145 CR France1890
SOUTHWELL,Evelyn Herbert Lightfoot TLt kia 15-9-16 13RB p180 MR21
SOUTHWELL,Frederick Edward Granville Lt dow 10-4-17 4EYorks p219 CR France113
SOWELL,Arthur Donald TLt kia 24-8-16 7DCLI B'Coy p115 CR France630
SOWERBY,Frank Douglas 2Lt dow 1-8-16 4Huss SR att18LancF p21 CR France51

SOWERBY,Isaac 2Lt kia 4-9-17 6RWar p214 CR Belgium84,3-9-17
SOWERBY,Maurice Eden.CMG.DSO.Col 28-1-20 CR Egypt9
SOWERBY,Victor Holgate T2Lt dow 31-7-17 2Lincs p75 MR29
SOWINSKI,Joseph Ladislas.MC.Lt kia 28-11-17 RFA &49TMB p208CR Belgium10
SOWLER,F.Capt 8-7-21 RFA
SOWRY,Alfred Allan T2Lt kia 31-8-17 17WYorks p83 MR21
SOWTER,Francis Ingle 2Lt kia 9-8-17 4EKent p212 CR France421
SOWTER,Geoffrey Smart Capt kia 14-10-18 3 att15N&D p135 CR Belgium157,Maj
SOWTER,George Henry Joseph Capt kia 13-10-15 5Lincs p220 MR19
SOWTER,Unwin Henry Etches Lt dow 22-4-17 N&D p135 MR38
SPAFFORD,Alfred Douglas Dale 2LtACapt kia 13-11-16 2RScots p55 CR France742
SPAFFORD,Arthur Langworthy Capt&Adj kia 7-8-15 1 att6LancF p93 CR Gallipoli1
SPALDING,Albert Goodwill T2Lt kia 1-7-16 RInnisF att10th p105 MR21
SPALDING,Robert Gordon 2Lt dow 28-9-15 3 att2SLancs A'Coy p126 CR France40
SPALLE,Ernest James TLt ded 25-2-19 RAOC p268 CR Scot226
SPANKIE,David Noel Lt ded 7-3-19 RASC att 1/5WYorks p253 CR France1142
SPANKIE,Dysart Watt T2Lt kia 5-6-16 104MGC Inf p185 CR France727
SPANKIE,Montague Douglas.MID Lt kia 14-5-15 IA 14Sikhs p282 CR Gallipoli3
SPANNER,Herbert TCapt kia 28-12-16 27RFC p4 CR France620
SPANTON,Cyril Holtby T2Lt ded 23-11-18 RASC MT p194 CR France34
SPANTON,John Woodfield T2Lt dow 13-6-17 13RB p180 CR Sussex178
SPANTON,Thomas Henry.DCM.2Lt kia 1-7-15 3KRRC p152 CR France1141,dow
SPARENBORG,Hans Robert Capt kia 26-8-17 1RLancs p59 MR15
SPARGO,Loris Stiles 2Lt kia 5-8-17 1/5N&D p233 CR France115
SPARGO,Richard Henry Arthur SubCdr dow 14-3-16 IA S&TCps p283 CR Iraq1
SPARK,Archibald Charles T2Lt kia 31-7-17 8GordH p167 CR Belgium101
SPARK,Archibald Graham.MC.TCapt kia 9-4-17 9YLI p144 CR France591
SPARKE,Errol 2Lt kia 22-3-18 20Mddx p148 MR20
SPARKES,Richard Abbot Maj ded 2-11-18 IA 1/54Sikhs p283 MR67
SPARKS,Clive TLt kia 1-7-16 12RSuss p120 CR France924,30-6-16
SPARKS,I.D.Capt 8-3-15 RFus CR Surrey152
SPARKS,James Elliot Lt kia 21-7-16 2RFus p70 MR21
SPARKS,James Frederick TLt kia 9-4-17 8RLancs p59 CR France1182
SPARKS,John Barnes.CBE.29-3-20 RN CR Lond4
SPARKS,Robert Lionel 2Lt kia 22-11-17 2RFus p70 CR France910
SPARKS,Robert William.MC.T2Lt kia 29-4-18 18Lpool 1Coy p73 MR30
SPARLING,Arthur Edward Lt ded 19-2-15 8Ess p271 CR Norf74
SPARLING,Norman Chalmers.MID Maj kia 25-9-15 IA 54Sikhs att6KOSB p283 MR28
SPARLING,Sidney James Belton Maj kia 4-6-15 IA 57Rif attRNDHoweBn p283
SPARROW,Benjamin Charles Capt kia 10-3-15 IA 1/39GarhwalRif p283 CR France355 &CR France1887
SPARROW,Brian Hanbury.MC.Capt kia 26-8-18 3KSLI att7NStaffs p145
SPARROW,Francis 2Lt kia 25-4-15 att2RDubF p177 MR29
SPARROW,Frank Edward TLt dow 13-8-16 RE 129FC p48 CR France141,kia
SPARROW,George Lewis Lt dow 23-12-15 3SWBord attKOSB p101 CR France284,23-12-14
SPARROW,George William Sparrow Capt kia 4-10-18 4KSLI p235 CR France82
SPARROW,Walter Burnaby Lt kia 1-9-18 3 att10Hamps p121 CR Greece6
SPARROW,William Gordon Morgan Capt kia 8-7-17 Nhampt &1KAR p138&268 CR EAfrica40
SPARTALI,Cyril T2Lt kia 13-10-15 8RBerks p140 MR19
SPARTALI,Michael 2lt kia 15-6-15 3 att2SWBord p101 MR4
SPARY,Fred Lt 25-11-20 RE CR Kent46
SPATZ,Walter T2Lt kia 1-7-16 2Mddx p148 MR21
SPAULL,Ernest Mayall Vaughan 2Lt kia 26-3-18 94RFA p35 CR France300
SPEAKMAN,Alan Edwards T2Lt kia 5-9-18 RFusatt2Bn p70 CR France298
SPEAR,A.E.Capt ded 8-3-18 Ex SL p268
SPEAR,Norman Victor T2Lt kld 29-8-17 RFC p13 CR Norf247
SPEAR-MORGAN,Basil Howard Lt ded 16-9-19 1BordR p264 CR Mddx16,Capt dow 16-9-16
SPEARES,Harold Thorne T2Lt kia 16-8-17 10RInnisF p105 MR30
SPEARING,Edward Lt kia 11-9-16 4RLancs p213 MR21
SPEARMAN,John Vanstone T2Lt kia 25-8-15 1KSLI p145 CR Belgium92
SPEARS,Alexander T2Lt kia 18-8-17 12Lpool p73 MR30
SPEARS,Alexander George 2Lt kia 22-8-18 23Lond p252 MR16
SPEARS,G.W.MC.Maj 11-3-21 RAOC CR Germay1
SPEARS,John 2Lt kia 23-4-17 2RScotF p95 CR France539
SPEDDING,Charles Rodney.DSO.Maj kia 19-9-14 2RIrRif p170 MR15
SPEDDING,George 2Lt kia 20-8-17 2/4YLI p235 CR France563

SPEDDING,John Carlisle Decv Maj ded 9-3-19 APD p255 CR Hamps115
SPEECHLY,Thomas Martindale T2Lt kld 8-2-18 RFC p17 CR Wilts129,5RRofCav
SPEED,Arthur Sydney 2Lt kia 4-6-17 1/5SStaffs p229 CR France149
SPEED,David Nelson 9106 T2Lt dow 2-5-17 A&SH att8BlkW p174 CR France113
SPEEDIE,John Gibson 2Lt kia 14-6-17 4RScots p211 CR France644
SPEEDY,Ralph Coggin 2Lt ded 4-12-18 19MGC Cav p185 CR Yorks222
SPEER,Alfred Henry Templeman Loraine Lt kia 9-7-16 RFA attRFC p19&208 CR France1185
SPEIGHT,James Leslie Lt dow 9-10-17 6WYorks p218 MR30,Capt
SPEIRS,George Patrick Maj kia 1-10-18 6HLI p240 CR France602
SPEIRS,Ronald Patrick 2Lt kia 23-4-17 2A&SH p174 MR20
SPEKE,Hugh Tmaj kia 12-8-15 10LancF Ex9SomLI p93 CR Belgium37
SPELMAN,Henry Harington 2Lt dow 22-9-18 YLIatt4Bn p144 MR16,Harrington
SPENCE,Alec William 2Lt kld 25-4-17 GL &51RFC p13 CR Kent197 Ex Mddx
SPENCE,Alexander.MC.Chap4Cl dow PoW 31-3-18 RAChDept attRInniskF p200 CR France987
SPENCE,Bertram T2Lt kia 21-9-18 9RFus p70 CR France369
SPENCE,Charles Bennett.MID Lt kld 9-5-15 RFA att3RFC p2&35 CR France98
SPENCE,David Stuart 2Lt kia 13-12-15 A66RFA p35 MR4
SPENCE,Geoffrey Shalders T2Lt ded 15-4-17 8SWBord p101 CR Beds23
SPENCE,Gilbert Chisholm Drever.MC.Capt kia 1-10-18 2HLI p164 CR France1483
SPENCE,Henry 2Lt kia 13-10-18 7A&SH p243 CR France1196
SPENCE,James Hamilton Lt kia 16-7-18 RGA &54RAF p262 MR20
SPENCE,John Robert Capt kia 9-4-18 RH&FA p207 CR France570,RGA 237SB
SPENCE,Joseph 2Lt dow 8-8-17 RFA p209 CR France285
SPENCE,Lyell Campbell.MC.Lt kia 25-5-18 CanadaFA &RAF CR France10
SPENCE,William Herbert John Shepherd T2Lt ded 23-9-17 GL RE attIWT p191 CR Iraq6
SPENCE,William Kenneth Mackay 2Lt kia 23-4-17 3RScots p55 CR France155,13Bn
SPENCE,William Samuel TLt kia 26-4-17 GL &RFC p13 CR France777
SPENCER,Alfred de Courboisier 2Lt kia 26-9-15 8WelshR att8RBerks p127 CR Gallipoli4
SPENCER,Arthur T2Lt kia 1-7-16 15Y&L p159 CR France246
SPENCER,Arthur Egerton Lt kia 2-7-16 10N&D p135 MR21
SPENCER,Arthur Max 2Lt kia 12-4-17 1RB p180 CR France728
SPENCER,Charles Herbert Slingsby 2Lt kia 5-10-18 C330RFA p35 CR France262
SPENCER,Charles James Capt kia 18-12-14 2Dev p77 CR France567
SPENCER,Edward Lt kia 24-10-14 2Wilts p153 MR29
SPENCER,Eliot Lt dow 18-2-18 5RWar p214 CR Staffs73
SPENCER,Francis 2Lt kia 26-9-17 4 att2/7N&D p135 CR Belgium125,Capt
SPENCER,Francis Leslie.MID Capt kia 2-12-17 2Mon p244 CR France1483
SPENCER,Frederick James Edmund T2Lt ded 9-11-18 PoW Wilts p153 CR Germany3
SPENCER,George Lt dow 5-12-17 20Lond p251 CR France446,4-12-17
SPENCER,George Barton T2Lt kia 25-7-18 13RB p180 CR Frnce614,25-8-18
SPENCER,Gerald Robert Maj ded 13-5-18 RDC p253 CR Sussex128
SPENCER,Gerald William Suckling T2Lt dow 24-2-16 8Norf p74 CR Lond28
SPENCER,Harry John Capt ded 17-11-16 9DLI p239 CR France177
SPENCER,Henry Beresford Capt kia 2-9-18 WSomYeo &TankCps p189&205 CR France646
SPENCER,Herbert 2Lt kia 11-7-16 7Leic p88 MR21
SPENCER,Henry Marston T2Lt kia 12-10-17 7EKent p58&258 CR Belgium126,Hugh Manning
SPENCER,Herbert Cecil Stanhope Lt 26-7-21 RFA CR Sussex183
SPENCER,Hugh Maitland Capt kia 25-4-15 SfthH p165 CR Belgium129
SPENCER,Jack Hamlyn.MC.T2Lt dow 5-6-18 1RBerks p140 CR France63,Capt
SPENCER,James Hilary L.ACapt dow PoW 16-7-18 1LancF p93 CR France1027
SPENCER,James Michael Jeslyn Lt kia 3-11-16 4NumbF attRFC p19&213 CR France927
SPENCER,James Sturtevant 2Lt kia 2-9-16 26RFA p35 CR France397
SPENCER,John Aldersley Craven 2Lt kia 9-8-15 9WYorks p83 MR4
SPENCER,John Clive Capt kia 22-3-18 11Leic p88 MR20,21-3-18
SPENCER,Mowbray Bertram Stovell 2Lt kia 4-8-15 7Worc p226 CR France1327
SPENCER,Richard Isaac Barré T2Lt kia 14-7-16 7 att1RScotF D'Coy p95 CR France453
SPENCER,Richard Martin Lt kia 22-1-16 1RWar p66 CR France643,2Lt
SPENCER,Shirley McTurk Lt kia 10-10-17 290RFA p208 MR30
SPENCER,Stanley 2LtTLt kia 3-5-17 2/5Y&L p238 MR20
SPENCER,Sydney.MC.Lt kia 24-9-18 5Norf p216 CR France369
SPENCER,Sydney Gurton TCapt kia 13-10-15 5RBerks p140 MR19
SPENCER,W.2Lt kia 10-5-18 GL &RAF p191

SPENCER,Walter George Capt dow 26-3-18 23Lond p252 CR France145
SPENCER,Willy Paton Berthold Lt kia 10-3-15 2Wilts p153 MR22
SPENCER-SMITH,Charles Owen Capt dow 3-8-17 16Lond p249 CR France139
SPENCER-SMITH,Gilbert Seymour Worsley Lt kia 9-4-18 5Hamps p228 CR Palestine9
SPENCER-SMITH,Henry.MC.Capt&QM kia 21-3-18 8Leic p88&259 MR27
SPENCER-SMITH,Martin 2Lt kia 10-9-16 16Lond p250 MR21
SPENDLOVE,Gervase Thorpe 2Lt dow 17-11-14 SLancs p126 CR Belgium57
SPENS,Walter Thomas Patrick Lt ded 18-2-17 9RScots p212 CR France95
SPENS,William Lt kld 17-5-15 9HLI p140 CR France413,kia
SPENSLEY,Frank Oswald Capt ded 23-10-18 RAMC attRAF p197&267 CR Dorset110
SPENSLEY,James Richardson TLt dow PoW 10-11-15 RAMC att8EKent p197 CR Germany3
SPERANZA,E.R.2Lt 10-12-18 RMaltaArtly CR Europe4
SPEYER,Cecil Arthur 2Lt kia 16-8-17 4Lond C'Coy p246 MR29
SPEYER,Frederick William Heurick T2Lt kia 14-6-17 att2Suff p79 CR France421,Lt
SPICE,Ernest Robert 2Lt kia 30-4-18 2/20Lond p251 CR Palestine3
SPICER,Cecil Wilfred T2Lt kia 23-11-16 2Lincs p75 MR21
SPICER,Edmund Danniell 2Lt kia 1-2-17 20RFC p13 CR Belgium158
SPICER,Eric Evan Capt kia 28-3-18 1/4Lond p246 MR20
SPICER,Filmer Blake 2Lt dow 6-10-16 3EKent attMGC 111Coy p58&185
SPICER,George Henry T2Lt kia 6-6-18 17RFus p70 CR France745
SPICER,Leonard Baker 2Lt kia 4-10-17 YLIatt9Bn p144 MR30
SPICER,Ronald Murray 2Lt ded 31-5-16 ERidYeo p206 CR Norf210
SPICER,Robert William Capt kia 26-3-17 4RWSurr p212 MR34
SPICER,Stanley Thomas TLt dow 9-8-16 2SStaffs p123 CR France397,kia
SPIEGELHALTER,Leo HonCapt ded 30-4-18 Insp of Army Schls CR Lond3
SPIELMAN,Harold Lionel Isidore Capt kia 13-8-15 10Manch p237 CR Gallipoli3
SPIERS,Archibald Lionel Clive TLt kia 26-9-17 7KSLI p145 MR30
SPIERS,D.2Lt 29-6-18 4RScots CR Scot674
SPIERS,Graham Kinloch 2Lt kia 22-7-18 5ScotRif p224 CR France25,23-7-18 9Bn
SPIERS,William Lt ded 3-8-19 RASC p267 CR Iraq8
SPILLER,Arthur James T2Lt kia 17-9-16 7SomLI p80 MR21
SPILLER,E.SchMstr 15-5-18 Cps of SchMstrs CR Scot288
SPILLING,Charles Nathaniel Jerald T2Lt kia 24-8-17 KRRC att8Bn p152 MR30
SPINDLER,Nellie SNurse kia 21-8-17 QAIMNS att44CCS p200 CR Belgium11
SPINK,Cecil Cooper T2Lt kia 4-6-16 10EYorks p85 CR France5
SPINK,Dennis Boucher 2Lt kia 30-10-17 6Lond p247 MR30
SPINK,Edward Wodehouse Lt kia 23-10-18 1/7LancF p221 CR France287
SPINK,Eric Minor TLtACapt kia 14-9-18 7NStaffs p158 CR Asia81
SPINK,Hubert Octavius Chap4Cl kia 9-8-16 RAChDept att55Div p200 CR France141
SPINKS,W.H.Rev ded 29-5-18 YMCA CR France40
SPINNEY,Frank T2Lt dow 2-10-16 2RScots p55 CR Greece4
SPINNEY,Kenneth Trim TLt kia 3-9-16 17KRRC p152 CR France220
SPINNEY,Robert Eric.MC.TLt dow 1-2-17 GL IntelCps &WRid p191 CR France74
SPINNEY,Ronald Henry Lt dow 2-7-16 2CldGds p51 CR Belgium11
SPITTAL,Robert Haig TCapt kia 4-10-17 RAMC att7LancF p197 MR30,att9Bn
SPITTLE,Thomas Stanley Capt dow 2-10-17 1Mon p244 CR France179
SPILSBURY,Francis James Capt ded 11-10-19 RAMC CR Lincs220
SPOFFORTH,Edward Reginald Lt kia 2-3-16 5Yorks p220 CR Belgium5
SPONG,Frederick William Edward 2Lt dow PoW 2-8-17 2Lond D'Coy p245 CR Belgium140,21-8-17
SPOONER,Charles Norman Capt kia 10-4-18 5Dev p217 CR Palestine9
SPOONER,George Piercy T2Lt kia 20/23-9-17 26RFus p70 MR30
SPOONER,Raymond Wilberforce 2Lt dow 8-6-17 RFC Ex RFA p13 MR20
SPOONER,Ronald Alan TCapt dow 23-9-16 11RWFus p99 CR Greece6
SPOOR,Herbert Mather.MC.TCapt ded 13-12-17 RAMC p198 CR Belgium84
SPOTTISWOODE,John Capt kia 31-10-14 6 att2KRRC p152 MR29
SPRAGG,Charles Edward Wright Capt kia 10-9-18 4EYorks p219 CR France415
SPRAGG,Westley Neal Lt kia 1-1-18 RFC SpSch of AerialGunnery p17 CR Egypt9
SPRAKE,George Harold TLt kia 18-7-16 8 att3BlkW p129 MR21
SPRAKE,Gilbert Edwin Lt kia 4-6-15 5ELancs p226 CR Gallipoli6
SPRANG,Frederick Williamson LtACapt kia 12-4-17 6Dors D'Coy p124 CR France531
SPRATT,David Herbert T2Lt kia 20-9-17 Mddx att6Lpool p148 CR Belgium125
SPRAY,Arthur.MC.TCaptAMaj 5-5-18 5TankCps p189 CR Belgium11
SPREAT,Leicester Hulke.MC.2Lt dow 8-10-16 A91RFA p35 CR France105
SPRECKLEY,Arthur Freer Lt drd 30-12-15 IA 2/9 att1/9GurkhaRif p283 MR41,Capt
SPRECKLEY,Guy Lesingham T2Lt kia 23-4-17 22 att7KRRC p152 MR29

SPRECKLEY,Ralph Lesingham.MC.Lt kia 14-9-14 2ConnRgrs p172 CR France1107,Lessingham
SPRENGER Oliver Howard T2Lt kia 5-6-17 26NumbF p63 MR20
SPRIGG,Henry Aldwin Guildford TCapt kia 9-5-18 14 att2/5Hamps p121 CR Palestine9,9-4-18
SPRING,Harold Albert Arden T2Lt kia 15-9-16 10ScotRif p104 MR21
SPRING-RICE,Gerald TLt kia 26-5-16 11BordR p118 CR France702
SPRINGATE,Arthur Stephen T2Lt kia 25-3-18 2/4Leic p88 MR20
SPRINGFIELD,Arthur Lincoln T2Lt kia 9-4-18 3SomLI p80 CR France532
SPRINGFIELD,George Patrick Osborn Capt kia 12-9-14 2DragGds p21 CR France1110
SPRINGFIELD,Humphrey Osborn.MID 2Lt kia 5-8-16 1/1WarYeo p205 CR Egypt2
SPRINGMAN,Ralph Thomas James 2Lt dow 21-9-18 RGA 169SB p42 CR France1468
SPRINKS,Ralph Cecil 2Lt kia 7-8-17 B83RFA p209 CR Belgium19
SPROAT,Gerald Maitland TLt kia 1-7-16 11 att17Manch p156 MR21
SPROAT,James McCosh.MC.2Lt kia 17-7-16 17Lpool p73 MR21,11-7-16
SPROSON,William Wilson 2Lt kld 7-8-18 17LancF att101RAF p93 CR France29,Lt kia
SPROSTON,Frederick Alvin 2Lt dow 30-7-18 6Ches p222 CR France866
SPROSTON,William Norris.MC.T2Lt kia 4-4-18 8RB p180 MR27
SPROT,Ivan Boyd Lt kia 23-10-14 1CamH p168 CR Belgium115
SPROT,James William Lennox Capt kia 11-11-14 2 att1BlkW p129 MR29
SPROTT,Douglas Anderson Capt ded 4-1-18 4BordR attMGC p187 CR Iraq8
SPROTT,Douglas Andrew Capt ded 4-1-18 4BordR p228
SPROTT,Frederick William 2Lt ded 25-8-16 IARO att92Punjabis p283 CRIraq5,Lt
SPROTT,Maurice William Campbell.MC.TCapt kia 21-3-18 9Norf p74 MR20
SPROXTON,Charles.MC.Capt&Adjt kia 19-7-17 4Yorks p220 CR France592
SPRUNT,Alexander Dalzell 2Lt dow 17-3-15 4Beds SR att2SStaffs p86 CR France201
SPRUNT,Gerald Harper 2Lt ded 15-10-19 2Beds p263 MR40,Lt dow
SPURGE,Henry Wesley LtACapt dow 17-9-17 3 att5 O&BLI p130 CR France40
SPURGEON,Donald Frank Parker Lt kia 10-9-18 20Lond att1/5Beds p251 CR Palestine9
SPURGEON,Percival TCapt dow 18-5-18 RASC att7RWSurr p194 CR Lond1
SPURLING,Francis Eyton TCapt dow 6-12-17 12RB p180 CR Belgium3,7Bn
SPURLING,Henry Stephen T2Lt dow 21-8-16 10 att9ESurr p113 CR France66,Harry
SPURRELL,Frederick John Durnford T2Lt ded 19-2-15 9RSuss p120 CR Norf94
SPURRELL,Herbert George Flaxman TCapt ded 8-11-18 RAMC attRAF p197 CR Egypt1
SPURWAY,Douglas Capt kia 23-3-18 4Yorks p220 MR27
SPURWAY,George Vyvyan.MC.TLt kia 28-3-18 56MGC p185 MR20
SPURWAY,Richard Popham T2Lt drd 13-8-15 2SomLI attHamps p80 MR4
SPURWAY,Sidney Macdonald T2Lt kia 21-9-17 22RFC p13 CR Belgium46
SQUAIR,Robert Hay TLt dow 13-10-17 7SfthH p165 CR Belgium63
SQUIER,Harry Anderton T2Lt kia 19-4-16 10 att8Beds p86 CR Belgium73
SQUIRE,Basil Brett.MID LtACapt kia 23-4-17 15RFA p35 CR France581,450RFA
SQUIRE,D.J.22-10-18 VAD CR Hamps1
SQUIRE,Frederick T2LtACapt kia 31-7-17 11RWKent p142 CR Belgium111
SQUIRE,Leslie Charles Herman 2Lt dow 13-5-15 7Lond p247 CR France80
SQUIRE,Stanley Charles TLt kia 9-8-15 7Glouc p107
SQUIRE,Wallace Henry 2Lt dow 9-4-17 4EKent p212 CR France1182
SQUIRE,Wright Thomas 2Lt kia 30-6-18 RGA 78SB p42 CR France174
SQUIRES,Charles Arthur 2Lt kia 25-4-18 B162RFA p35 CR Belgium3
SQUIRES,Charles Thomas 2Lt dow 30-3-18 4RSuss p228 CR France144
SQUIRES,Edward Constable.MC.TCapt kia 18-8-16 12WYorks p83 CR France453,dow
SQUIRES,Francis Chavasse Capt dow 7-7-15 IA 1/23SikhPnrs p283 CR Asia60
SQUIRES,Francis William 2Lt kia 10-11-16 RGA 95SB p42 CR France294
SQUIRES,John Henry T2Lt kia 12-4-18 SfthH att1/5Bn p165 CR France202
SQUIRES,Reginald Alfred.OBE.Capt ded 25-4-19 16YLI APM 61Div p255&144 CR France52
SQUIRES,Roger Dewar TCapt kia 7-8-15 9N&D p135 MR4,Robert 9-8-15
SQUIRES,Sidney Charles Lt kia 29-10-18 5RWar p214 CR France290,28-10-18
SQUIRL,Montague Ernest Lt dow 15-12-18 2A&SH p174 CR France658,kia
SQUIRL-DAWSON Hugh Dawson Capt ded 31-1-18 1/1RHA p207 CR Palestine2
STABLE,Lascombe Law Capt kia 26-10-14 RWFus p99 CR France705,Loscombe
STABLE,Russell Colin 2Lt kia 9-10-17 2RWar p66 MR30
STABLES,Harold Rolleston Lt 15-11-14 5RFus attChes p70 MR29
STABLES,James Howard Lt mbk 17-2-17 IARO att1/8GurkhaRif p283 MR38

STABLES,Leonard Theodore Drury Lt kia 23-10-18 6Beds att Nhants p86 CR France190

STABLES,Robert Cecil 2Lt kia 13-5-17 IARO att 3Sap&Min p283 MR38

STACEY,Brian John 2Lt dow 26-4-17 B63 RFA p35 CR France40

STACEY,Charles Noble Lt dow 10-5-15 7Mddx A'Coy p235 CR France525

STACEY,Cyril Robert William 2Lt kia 8/9-8-16 3 att 1RInniskF p105 CR Belgium47,9-8-16

STACEY,Dorothy Louise SNurse 5-10-18 QAIMNS CR Dorset87

STACEY,Douglas William T2Lt dow 20-6-17 20RFC p13 France200

STACEY,Gerald Arthur.DSO.Maj kia 9-10-16 2Lond p245 CR France294

STACEY,Harold 2Lt kia 4-8-18 5NStaffs p238 CR France109,1/6Bn

STACEY,Herbert Leonard 2Lt kia 31-7-17 7Lpool p215 CR Belgium125

STACEY,John Brewer T2Lt kia 19-11-16 8ESurr p113 MR21

STACEY,John Charles.MM.2Lt kia 10-4-18 2SfthH p165 MR19

STACEY,John Harold 2Lt kia 4-12-17 5ESurr att RFC p19&226 CR Egypt15

STACK,Edward Hugh Bagot Capt kia 30-10-14 IA 2/8GurkhaRif p283 MR28

STACK,George Hall.DSO.MIDx3 ALtCol ded 16-9-19 RE 3Div p262 CR Palestine9

STACK,James Charles 2Lt kld 30-4-18 LabCps att 4RAF p189 CR France134,Lt

STACK,John Masfen Capt kia 1-7-16 6NStaffs p238 CR France576

STACKE,Oliver George Norman Lt kia 17-5-15 RInniskF p105 MR22,15-5-15

STACKHOUSE,William Thomas Capt kia 12-3-15 1N&D p135 MR22

STACPOOLE,George Eric Guy Lt kia 27-1-15 1RIrReg p89 CR Belgium80

STAFF-BRETT,Henry William T2Lt kia 24-3-18 14Y&L p159 MR32

STAFFORD,Arthur Darrell TLt dow 20-5-18 1RWar att 1/3LancF p66 CR France145

STAFFORD,Charles Edward Trevor T2Lt kia 31-7-17 10/11HLI p164 CR Belgium58

STAFFORD,Claude Charles Lt kia 13-10-14 Beds RoO p86 MR22

STAFFORD,Cyril Francis 2Lt dow 14-4-17 24RFus p70 CR France53

STAFFORD,Frederick John Ewart 2Lt dow 22-4-17 8RFC p13 CR France52

STAFFORD,Henry Herbert Owen T2Lt kia 4-10-16 10WRid p116 MR21

STAFFORD,James Neilson Greenleer Capt kia 16-4-17 6RWar p214 CR France669,Greenlees

STAFFORD,Kenneth James.MC.Lt dow 14-11-18 37/27RH&FA p35 CR France146

STAFFORD,Thomas Colegrave TCapt ded 2-4-16 1Yorks GarrBn p91 MR65,4-4-16

STAFFORD-KING-HARMAN,Edward Charles Capt kia 6-11-14 1IrGds 1Coy p53 MR29

STAGG,Alfred Charles T2Lt kia 19-7-16 11Glouc p107 CR France633

STAGG,Arthur John T2Lt kia 27-5-18 2WYorks p83 MR18

STAGG,Edward Christopher T2Lt kia 18-7-16 14Glouc p107 MR21

STAGG,Harold William 2Lt kia 28-3-18 15MGC p185 MR20

STAGG,John Reginald .DCM.T2Lt kia 17-9-16 27 att 17Mddx p148 CR France156

STAIGHT,Ralph Neville 2Lt kia 24-3-17 3SomLI p80 CR France418 Ex 10Huss

STAINBANK,Arthur Reeve Lt kia 20-7-17 113RFA p35 MR29

STAINBANK,William Denng 2Lt ded 8-4-16 RFA p35 CR Lancs103

STAINER,Claude Hamilton 2Lt kia 15-11-16 6ESurr att 10LNLancs p226 MR21

STAINFIELD,Walter George Lt ded 18-11-18 RGA 115SB p42 CR Kent5

STAINFORTH,George T2Lt kia 14-7-16 13Lpool p73 MR21

STAINFORTH,Herbert Graham.CMG.LtCol ded 11-5-16 IA Cmdg4Cav p283 CR Iraq5

STAINFORTH,Richard Terrick Lt dow 19-10-14 2RWar p66 CR Belgium84

STAINSBY,John Addison TLt drd 26-2-18 RAMC p198 MR40

STAINSBY,Thomas Cecil T2Lt kia 1-10-18 9TankCps p189 CR France375

STAINTON,Ernest Lt dow 25-11-18 7Worc p225 CR Mddx51

STAINTON,Robert Meres T2Lt kia 1-7-16 10Y&L p159 MR21

STAINTON,Walter Adam Lt kia 14-9-16 3GrenGds p50 MR21

STALEY,Edward Vernon Lt kia 18-9-18 D290RFA p35 CR France364

STALEY,Francis Colin Lt kia 8-3-16 5SomLI p218 MR38

STALEY,Frederick Alexander 2Lt kia 25-10-18 3 att 8ESurr p113 CR France1482,23-10-18

STALKER,Daniel TLt dow 12-4-18 169RFA p35 CR France300

STALKER,Francis Brown Douglas T2Lt kia 22-8-15 SL 6BordR p201 MR4

STALKER,James Johnston Harris TLt ACapt kia 28-4-17 11RWar p66 MR20

STALKER,M.B.Sister S1326 18-1-21 1Res QAIMNS CR Scot169

STALKER,Robert Macallan Lt kia 8-9-15 5SfthH att 22RFC p19&241 MR20

STALLARD,Arthur Dudley.VD.Capt 6-2-19 InnsOfCourt ResCps CR Surrey160

STALLWORTHY,Arthur Reynolds 2Lt kia 30-11-17 3EKent att 1/5SLancs p58 MR17

STAMFORD,Gerald Morton 2Lt kia 15-6-15 2Wilts p153 MR22

STAMMAS,Thomas Laurence Capt 6-11-20 RFA CR Lond28

STAMMERS,Joseph Ralph T2Lt kia 9-4-17 5 O&BLI p130 CR France581

STAMP,Douglas Blatspiel Lt dow 10-4-16 EYorks SR p85 CR Belgium1

STAMPE,George Herbert TMaj kia 27-3-18 24MGC p185 MR27

STAMPER,Geoffrey 2Lt kld 25-3-18 4 att 1N&D p135 MR27

STANANOUGHT,Richard Frederick TLt&Adjt dow 5-9-16 12WYorks p83 CR Frnce145

STANBOROUGH,Walter Thomas 2Lt dow 13-5-15 att 2SWBord p101 MR4

STANBRIDGE,Arthur Christian Capt&Adjt kia 18-11-16 8NStaffs p158 MR21 STANDBRIDGE

STANBURY,Lionel Duncan TLt kia 7-7-16 52MGC p185 MR21

STANCER,John William T2Lt dow 17-4-18 23NumbF p63 CR France134

STANDEN,Leslie James Denman Lt kia 18-3-16 5Lincs p220 CR France68,Capt

STANDERWICK,Edwin William 2Lt kia 20-4-18 7Ess p232 CR France250,Lt

STANDRICK,Jones Harold John.MC.Capt dow 21-2-18 2/18Lond p250 CR Palestine3,kia

STANDRING,Benjamin Arthur 2Lt dow 19-12-14 RWar p66 CR France253

STANDRING,Dudley Hethorn Capt dow 30-5-15 8Manch p237 CR Gallipoli2

STANDRING,Frederick John Lt kia 6-9-18 6RScots att 57MGC p187&211 CR France309

STANDRING,William Shuttleworth 2Lt kia 30-7-16 12ELancs p111 CR France298

STANFIELD,Alfred Vivian 2Lt kia 16-8-16 2RWSurr att RFus p56 MR21

STANFIELD,Charles Cecil Capt ded 31-5-17 3EKent att 1NHants p58 CR Hamps1

STANFIELD,Thomas William.MM.T2Lt kia 23-11-17 3Yorks p91 CR France256,13Bn

STANFIELD,William Bowman 2Lt dow 29-9-15 3 att 1Nhampt p138 CR France178,Lt 26-9-15

STANFORD,Donovan Edward 2Lt kia 21-3-18 6RDubF att 2RIrReg p177 MR27

STANFORD,James Vesey TLt kia 25-9-15 8SfthH p165 MR19

STANG,J.S.MC.Capt BlkW p259 See STRANG,J.S.

STANGE,George Nugent.MC.TLt kia 27-10-18 1 att 2LancF p93

STANGER,Nevill Bentley 2Lt dow 5-10-15 4SLancs p230 CR France40,Bentlif

STANGER,Philip James Capt kia 8-11-15 1/20Lond p251 CR France219

STANHOPE,Colin Lundin.OBE.Capt ded 14-10-19 GL p267 CR France457,18-10-19

STANHOPE,Richard Philip.Hon.Capt kia 16-9-16 3GrenGds SR p50 MR21

STANHOPE,Talbot Fitzroy Eden Lt kia 9-5-15 2RB p180 MR32

STANIFORTH,William Moorwood 2Lt kld 23-3-17 YorkDragYeo &RFC p19&206,ded CR War65

STANILAND,Geoffrey 2Lt kia 14-4-15 4Lincs p217 CR Belgium98,13-4-15

STANILAND,Meaborn Capt kld 29-7-15 4Lincs p217 CR Belgium98

STANLEY,Ada SNurse 22-12-15 TFNS CR Yorks639

STANLEY,Arthur Kinnaird Lt kia 15-6-18 6Glouc p225 CR Italy2,1/5Bn

STANLEY,Charles Gordon 2Lt kia 19-9-18 RWar att 34RAF CR Italy11

STANLEY,D.H.Lt 17-8-20 GL CR Iraq8

STANLEY,Edmond Talbot Maj ded 27-2-19 LabCps p266 CR France146,11Dev

STANLEY,George Hopkins 2Lt kia 31-10-14 1ELancs p111 CR Belgium68

STANLEY,Lawrence Aston 2Lt kia 30-11-17 9RFus p70 MR17,Laurence

STANLEY,R.B.Capt ded 17-2-19 RASC &RAF p253

STANLEY,Robert Oliver 2Lt kia 9-4-16 12RWFus p99 MR38

STANLEY,Sidney Edgar T2Lt ded 19-10-17 11RFC p13 CR France1185

STANLEY,James Arthur TCapt kia 27-9-18 RAMC att 15RWar p198 CR France245

STANLEY,John Joseph 2Lt kia 9-12-17 2RIrRif p170 CR France379

STANLEY,John William 2Lt kia 7-6-17 4 att 11LancF p93 MR29

STANLEY,Percy Douglas 2Lt kia 4-10-17 YLI att 9Bn p144 MR30

STANLEY-BAKER,Richard Maj 13-11-18 IARO att 3BurmaMTCoy MR43 &CR Pakistan50A

STANLEY-CREEK,Robert Forbes Stanley.DSO.Capt kia 29-10-14 RWSurr p56 MR29

STANNARD,Alexander Jewell LtAMaj kia 20-8-17 RGA 29SB p42 CR Belgium19

STANNARD,John Arnold.MC.Lt dow 23-4-18 6Hamps p229 CR France88,5Bn

STANNARD,W.L.Capt kia 4-5-15 5SLancs p230 CR Belgium125

STANNUS,Thomas Robert Alexnder.DSO.MajALtCol dow 17-6-17 4Leinst p175 CR France40

STANSELL,Lionel Brough.MM.2Lt ded 26-10-18 3RWKent &RAF p142 CR Kent232,10Bn

STANSFELD,H.A.HonMaj ded 8-12-14 Yorks p91

STANSFELD,Harold Hamer Grey Maj dow 25-9-15 IA 74 Cmdg69Punjabis p283 CR France705

STANSFELD-SMITH,Lyalph 2Lt kld 12-6-15 1Wilts p153 CR Belgium35,Lyulph 13-6-15

STANSFIELD,Frank 2Lt kia 31-5-15 5ELancs p226 CR Gallipoli6

STANSFIELD,Frederick Noel 2Lt kia 2-12-17 17Mddx p148 MR17,STANSFELD Capt 1-12-17

STANSFIELD,John Raymond Evelyn.DSO.MajTLtCol dow 28-9-15 2GordH p167 CR France98,STANSFELD

STANSFIELD,Sydney Pearce 2Lt kia 30-4-17 1/4WRid p227 CR France727
STANTIAL,Frank Evered 2Lt dow 4-5-15 3Suff p79 MR29
STANTON,Claude Wilfred Capt kia 8-5-17 1Mon p244 MR29
STANTON,Clifford.MID TLt kia 31-7-17 10WelshR p127 CR Belgium65
STANTON,Francis Stanislaus 2Lt kia 27-9-18 5RScotF p222 CR France530
STANTON,Gareth Marsh T2Lt dow 20-2-16 8RWKent p142 CR Belgium11
STANTON,George Capt dow 16-8-16 RAMC p198 CR Eire78
STANTON,Oswald Wilfred TCapt ded 6-11-18 15Mddx att10Lond p148&265 CR Lond12
STANTON,Robert 2Lt kia 7-8-15 6RDubF p177 MR4,9-8-15
STANTON,Roydon Ross Lt ded 18-10-18 CldGds p51 CR Berks84
STANTON,Victor George 2Lt ded PoW 29-3-18 RFC p17 CR France511
STANUELL,Charles Martin 2Lt kia 20-9-14 2DLI p161 MR15
STANWAY,Frank T2Lt kia 29-3-17 Glouc att1st p107 CR Iraq8,7Bn
STANWAY,Gerald 2Lt dow 5-10-17 5 att7SStaffs p229 CR Belgium16
STANWELL,William Alexander 2Lt dow 6-7-15 LancF p93 MR29
STANWORTH,Joseph T2Lt dow 11-7-17 2ELancs p111 CR Lancs219
STANYON,Terence George 2Lt dow 23-7-16 WelshR att 1ESurr p127 CR France630
STAPLES,Edmund 2Lt dow 20-8-18 17Lond att44TMB p250 CR France145
STAPLES,Osric Ormsmund T2Lt kia 25-9-15 6RScotF p95 MR19
STAPLETON,Harold Edward Beaumont Capt dow 26-9-17 RGA p209 CR Belgium46
STAPLETON,Harold Frederick Lt kia 15-9-16 1Lond p245 CR France432
STAPLETON,Hubert Capt kia 15-9-16 15Hamps p121 MR21
STAPLETON,Nicholas Capt ded 6-12-18 25Lond p252 CR France146
STAPLETON,William Howell T2Lt kia 26-8-16 2Beds att5RBerks p86 CR France630
STAPLETON-BRETHERTON,Osmund Frederick Lt kia 22-3-18 9Lancers p22 MR27
STAPLETON-BRETHERTON,Wilfred Stanislaus Capt kia 8-11-14 4RFus p70 MR29
STAPLEY,Lawrence D'Arcy 2Lt kia 12-10-16 7Suff p79 MR21,D'Arcy Laurence
STAPYLTON,Granville Joseph Chetwynd Maj kia 25-8-14 RH&FA p36
STARES,Robert Percy Maj kia 30-10-14 Beds p86 CR Belgium115
STARFIELD,Baron T2Lt kia 19-1-18 RFC p17
STARK,James Duncan.MID T2Lt dow 3-9-18 PoW 2 att6KOSB p102 CR Germany1
STARKEY,Francis William T2Lt kia 25-10-17 Manch att21Bn p156 MR30
STARKEY,Joseph Bernard Collins Lt kia 13-11-16 3 att2HLI p164 MR21
STARKEY,Thomas Randle 2Lt ded 13-11-16 RDC p253 CR Notts96,Lt
STARKEY,Vivian George TLt kia 14-10-15 7YLI p144 CR France348
STARKY,James Baynton 2Lt kia 6-7-16 3 att1Wilts p153 MR21
STARLING,Benjamin Alfred 2Lt kia 23-3-18 2Lond p245 CR France184
STARLING,Frederick Leslie 2Lt kia 13-9-16 3Lond p246 MR21
STARR,Alfred 2Lt ded 27-10-18 22Lond p271 CR Lond10
STARR,Arthur James TLt kia 22-3-18 11 att9RInniskF A'Coy p105 MR27
STARR,Dillwyn Parrish Lt kia 14/16-9-16 2CldGds p51&258 CR France374,15-9-16
STARR,Philip Comfort Lt kia 20-2-18 RE 154FC p48 CR Belgium165
START,Lesingham Eden 2Lt ded 23-2-15 13DLI p161 CR Hamps1
STATHAM,Arthur Yates 2Lt kia 3-5-17 5ESurr att9RB p226 MR20
STATHAM,Hugh Kington Llewellyn Lt kia 6-9-17 3Dors p124 CR Belgium24
STATHAM,Noel Horner Lt kia 3-2-17 5ESurr p226 CR Iraq5
STATTON,Percival Graham T2Lt dow 18-4-17 18Lpool p73 CRFrance52
STAUGHTON,A.W.Capt 26-12-16 2RMLI CR France40
STAUNTON,Harvey Chap4Cl ded 14-1-18 RAChDept p200 CR Iraq8
STAVEACRE,James Herbert.MID Maj kia 4-6-15 7Manch p237 MR4 &CR Gallipoli2
STAVELEY,Arthur Godfrey.MID Maj ded 24-3-20 50RFA CR Germany1
STAVELEY,Frederick Simpson Capt kld 15-3-15 EYorks attWRid p85 CR Belgium96,14-3-15
STAVELEY,George Hendley Capt kia 14-4-17 1 att2YLI p144 CR France1890
STAVELEY,Hugh Sheardown TLt kia 3-5-17 11EYorks p85 MR20
STAVELEY,Miles.MC.CaptAMaj dow 29-9-18 340/44RFA p36 CR France194
STAVERT,Robert Elliott Capt kia 25-8-18 4Lond p246 CR France576
STEAD,Aubrey Arthur 2Lt kia 9-4-17 1SomLI attTMB p80 CR France581
STEAD,Brian Desmond Howland Lt kia 21-3-18 1ELancs p111 MR20
STEAD,Charles Brian.MC.Capt dow 28-9-18 8WYorks p219 CR France512
STEAD,Charles Henry 2Lt kia 27-4-15 8Mddx p148 MR29,25-4-15
STEAD,Geoffrey Henry.MC&Bar.TLt dow 22-7-18 Ches att74L'TMB p97 CR France65,Capt
STEAD,Horace Stuart 2Lt kia 26-3-18 1/2 att17LancF p255 MR27
STEAD,John 2Lt ded 15-11-16 5SLancs p230 CR Lancs179

STEAD,John Kenneth Capt dow 4-2-17 4Yorks att20RFC p19&220 CR France285
STEAD,Ralph T2Lt kia 1-7-16 16WYorks p83 CR France742 Ex 19RFus
STEAD,Willie Wouldhave TLt kia 25-8-16 17WYorks p83 CR France630
STEADMAN,William Milton TCapt kld 10-10-17 RE IWT p48 CR France8
STEARN,John Holder.DSO.MID TLt kia 3-12-17 14DLI p161 MR17
STEARNS,Eric Gordon T2Lt dow 7-8-15 4RFus p70 CR Belgium11,6-8-15
STEARNS,Patrick Chillingworth 2Lt kia 4-12-17 5 att7KRRC p152 CR Belgium22
STECKLEY,Ray Clarke 2Lt ded 24-2-19 8Lond p271 CR Hamps2
STEDMAN,Arthur Roy Lt 14-8-18 88RAF MR20
STEDMAN,Philip Bertram Kirk Lt dow 19-8-16 4Lond p246 CR Lond12,Capt
STEDMAN,Raymond Cecil 2Lt dow 20-5-18 4 att1ESurr p113 CR France31
STEDMAN,William Walter Thomas 2Lt kia 13-11-16 18Lond p250 CR Belgium120,10-11-16
STEEDMAN,Arthur Haldane T2LtACapt dow 30-3-17 10ScotRif p104 CR France113
STEEL,Arthur Edward Lt kia 3-5-18 21Mddx &206RAF p148 MR20
STEEL,Alan Ivo Lt kia 8-10-17 2CldGds p51 MR30
STEEL,Angus Murray Russell.MID 2Lt kia 9-6-18 7ScotRif p224 CR Belgium3,5Bn
STEEL,Anthony T2Lt kia 11-9-18 LabCps att8Lpool p189 CR France686
STEEL,Charles Ernest 2Lt ded 28-9-16 7Mddx p271 CR Mddx48,STEELE
STEEL,Douglas Graham.MC.2LtACapt kia 13-11-16 3 att2Suff p79 CR France802
STEEL,Edward Anthony.DSO.LtCol ded 14-10-19 RFA p262 MR70 &CR Europe195
STEEL,Edwin Bedford Maj dow 23-11-14 RAMC p198 CR France284
STEEL,Ernest 2Lt kia 21-3-18 1NStaffs p158 MR27
STEEL,Harold Ponsonby Capt kia 5-8-17 IA 129Baluchis p283 CR EAfrica38 &CR Tanzania1
STEEL,James.MC.Capt kia 2-9-18 RAMC 10FA att1SomLI p198 CR France421
STEEL,James Camplett Lt kld 13-3-15 1A&SH p174 CR Belgium28,Campbell
STEEL,John Gordon.MID 2Lt ded 24-5-17 9DLI p239 CR Numb3
STEEL,Norman 2Lt kia 16-8-17 1/5Glouc A'Coy p225 MR30
STEEL,Robert Archibald 2Lt kia 27-3-18 RB &16RFC p255&257,Lt mbk MR20
STEEL,Stanley Joseph Capt kia 19-6-18 1/4Norf p216 MR34,18-6-18
STEEL,Walter Frank Banfield 2Lt kia 20-10-17 9HLI p241 CR Belgium49
STEEL,Wilfred 2Lt kld 9-5-15 4Y&L p238 CR France276,Wilfrid
STEEL,William Henry Lt&QM kia 28-6-15 5RScots p211 MR4
STEELE,Alfred Charles John 2Lt kia 23-8-18 1RWKent p142 CR France239
STEELE,Alfred Harmer T2Lt dow 5-2-17 GL &16RFC p13 CR France95,4-2-17
STEELE,Allan Robert TCapt dow 6-4-18 9ScotRif p104 CR Scot730
STEELE,Arthur Joseph TLt kia 22-9-15 6EYorks p85 MR4
STEELE,Benjamin Harry 2Lt kia 20-11-17 1Worc p109,258&257,mbk MR30
STEELE,D'Arcy Walter Stewart 2Lt kia 1-10-16 3Dors p124 MR21
STEELE,Ernest Cecil TLt kia 18-9-18 21MGC Inf Divl p185 CR France417
STEELE,Francis Gardner 2Lt kia 18-11-16 4 att2HLI p164 MR21
STEELE,Frederick James 2Lt kia 13-10-15 3Dors att8RBerks p124 MR19
STEELE,Frederick Wilberforce Alexander.MIDx2 Lt dow 25/27-10-14 RFus p70 MR22
STEELE,George Frederick.CMG.LtCol dow 22-5-15 1Drags p21 CR France285
STEELE,Gilbert Bernard Edward Capt kia 5-9-19 3SLancs &IARO att2/3Brahmans p264&283 MR43
STEELE,Norman Leslie 2Lt 20-4-17 1AustFC MR34
STEELE,Oliver Capt kia 25-10-14 1RBerks p140 MR29
STEELE,Robert Balfour Lt dow PoW 22-10-17 IARO att84RFC p283 CR Belgium140,21-10-17
STEELE,Robert Kingsley 2Lt kia 24-5-15 5NumbF p213 CR Belgium96,STEEL Lt
STEELE,William 2Lt dow 27-9-18 LancF att1/7Bn p93 CR France712
STEELE-NICHOLSON,Alfred Francis James Capt 16-8-17 5RIrRif MR30
STEELE-NICHOLSON,William Herbert Lt dow 13-4-18 RE 2/2Div CR Mddx16
STEELE-PERKINS,Cyril Steele Lt kia 31-8/2-9-14 RLancs p59 CR France611,26-8-15
STEEN,Thomas 2Lt kia 1-3-17 5RScotF p222 CR France745
STEENEKAMP,Petrus Andries 2Lt kld 23-5-16 26RFC p4 CR EAfrica56
STEER,Gordon Pemberton Capt dow 26-12-15 3SomLI att2Wilts p80 CR France64
STEGGALL,Hubert Henry TLt kia 18-9-18 N&D att10Bn p135 CR France407
STEHN,Arthur Edward Capt kia 8-11-18 4 att10RWar p66 CR France965
STEIBEL,Charles Lt kia 2-2-17 IMS 1IndGH att62Punjabis p283 CR Iraq5
STEIBEL,Marie Louise AssAdmntr ded 1-12-18 QMAAC p200 CR Lancs34
STEIN,Colin Hunter 2Lt kld 24-5-15 7A&SH p243 MR29
STEIN,John Francis 2Lt kia 28-9-16 3RIrRif p170 CR France293
STEINBERG,George Kenneth.MC.TLt kia 22-3-18 34MGC Divl p185 MR20
STEINMAN,Bernard Puckle Capt ded 26-4-16 1EKent p58 CR France145
STELFOX,George Henry T2Lt kia 9-10-17 1LancF p93 CR Belgium126

STELL,Jack 2Lt ded 19-6-18 13RScots &RAF p55 CR Lancs206
STEMBRIDGE,Jim T2Lt kia 29-9-18 2Yorks p91 CR France273
STENHOUSE,Andrew TLt dow 27-9-15 10ScotRif p104 MR19
STENHOUSE,Herbert Wilson.DSO.Maj kia 26-6-16 RWSurr GSO DivHQ p56 CR France5
STENHOUSE,John Maitland.MC.TCapt dow 25-8-16 RAMC att96RFA p198 CR France145
STENNING,Bernard Clement 2Lt dow 26-7-17 5ESurr attRE 228FC p226 CR France139
STENNING,Leslie Gerald Lt dow 1-9-15 6Ess p232 CR Essex48
STENNING,Sidney Nelson 2Lt kia 21-3-18 189RFA p36 MR20
STENT,Harold Rudolph 2Lt kia 20-7-18 1/2WRid p116 CR France622,2/4Bn
STEPHEN,Adrian Consett.MC.MID LtAMaj kia 14-3-18 D242RFA p36 CR Belgium21
STEPHEN,Alan James 2Lt dow 18-10-18 6 att2KRRC p152 CR France725
STEPHEN,Albert Alexander Leslie.DSO.Capt dow 31-10-14 ScotsGds p52 CR Belgium57
STEPHEN,David James Shirres.MC&Bar.TCapt dow 24-10-17 RAMC att54FA p198 CR Belgium18
STEPHEN,Douglas Clinton Leslie Capt dow 10-9-14 GrenGds p50 CR France1805
STEPHEN,Fred'k Charles Lt kld 25-9-15 6GordH p242 MR19
STEPHEN,George Lt ded 26-10-18 4GordH p256 CR Scot287
STEPHEN,J.Lt kia 14-10-18 3EKent attIA p58 MR38
STEPHEN,James Anderson T2Lt dow 28-10-17 2BordR p118 CR Belgium11
STEPHEN,James Eliot Lt kia 14-10-18 IA 1/19Punjabis p283 MR61 Ex 3EKent
STEPHEN,James Howie Frederic Lt kia 11-1-17 3 att1HLI p164 MR38
STEPHEN,James Pedraza 2Lt kia 23-5-17 46RFC p13 CRFrance354
STEPHEN,John Stephen Lt kia 23-3-18 16Lancers p23 MR27
STEPHEN,Kenneth Travers.MC.LtACapt dow 22-4-18 RFA X2TMB p36 CR France95
STEPHEN,Lionel Henry York TCapt ded 22-5-18 RAMC p198 CR Hamps13,25-5-18
STEPHEN,William Capt kia 13-11-16 5GordH p242 CR France1490
STEPHEN,William Ian 2Lt ded 4-12-17 IA 18Lancers p283 CR Asia60,I.W.
STEPHENS,Alexander Augustus ACapt&Adjt died 25-11-18 RGA p42 CR Hamps11
STEPHENS,Arnold Melvill.MID T2Lt dow 30-12-15 11LancF p93 CR France285
STEPHENS,Cecil Hubert Lt kia 23-10-18 111/24RFA p36 CR France1266
STEPHENS,Dudley Eric 2Lt dow 29-3-18 B70RFA p36 CR France113
STEPHENS,Ernest Stanley T2Lt kia 6-7-17 1Lincs att62TMB p76 CR France593
STEPHENS,Francis John 2Lt kia 30-1-17 22Lond p251 MR37
STEPHENS,Fred Orlando Lt kia 24-4-18 5 att2WYorks p218 MR27
STEPHENS,Frederick Henry Lt 23-11-17 2CentOntanoR &3RFC MR20
STEPHENS,Geoffrey Duncan 2Lt kia 9-7-16 5 att1RFus att17TMB p70 CR Belgium97
STEPHENS,George Harold Lt ded 13-12-20 RGA 219SB CR Lancs1
STEPHENS,Godfrey Gwilym Brychan T2Lt kia 7-7-16 9SWBord att3WelshReg p101 MR21
STEPHENS,Henry French.DSO.MC.TMaj dow 14-10-18 86RFA p36 CR Lond2
STEPHENS,Howell Charles 2Lt kia 31-7-17 1Worc A'Coy p109 MR29
STEPHENS,John Herbert T2Lt kia 3-5-17 16 att12Mddx p148 MR20
STEPHENS,John Lockhart Lt kld 10-3-15 3Lond A'Coy p245 CR France706
STEPHENS,John Parnall Lt 23-7-21 RFA CR Iraq8
STEPHENS,John Stanley 2Lt kia 23-4-17 8SStaffs p123 MR20
STEPHENS,Kyrle Nalder T2Lt ded 31-12-17 RASC p194 CR Dorset22
STEPHENS,Llewellyn T2Lt kld 12-6-17 GL &RFC p13 CR Lond4
STEPHENS,Nasson Barrington 2Lt dow 1-6-16 4EYorks attMGC p187&219 CR France285
STEPHENS,Norman Victor Lt ded 28-1-20 41MGC Inf CR Germany1
STEPHENS,Robert Miller Lt kia 27-9-18 5RWKent p235 CR France415
STEPHENS,Sidney Thompson.MC.2Lt kia 9-10-17 att9Dev p77 MR30
STEPHENS,Thomas Alexander T2Lt dow 22-9-17 RE 250TC p48 CR Belgium165
STEPHENS,William Head T2Lt kia 14-7-16 9Leic p88 MR21
STEPHENS,William Leslie T2Lt ded 19-6-17 RE 143ArmyTroopCo p48 CR Greece4
STEPHENSON,Arthur Frederick Vere Lt kia 23-7-16 4GordH p241 MR21
STEPHENSON,Arthur Thomas Lt kia 28-6-16 7Lpool p215 CR France576,Theodore
STEPHENSON,Charles Lindsay T2Lt kia 28-11-17 9NumbF p63 CR France592
STEPHENSON,Claudius TCapt dow 2-11-16 12Ches p97 CR Greece6
STEPHENSON,Cyril Seymour 2Lt ded 6-12-16 9Lancers p22 CR Sussex204
STEPHENSON,Denys George Lt kia 16-5-15 2ScotsGds p52 CR France279
STEPHENSON,Derek Charles.DSO.MC.Maj kia 23-3-18 CmdgZ5RHA p36 CR France1893
STEPHENSON,Douglas Buchanan.MC.Capt kia 21-3-18 9Manch p237 MR27

STEPHENSON,Erik 2Lt kia 1-7-16 3Y&L p159 CR France246
STEPHENSON,Eric Arthur 2Lt kia 7-2-19 Yorks att17Lpool p255 MR70 &CR Europe180
STEPHENSON,Eric Lionel 2Lt kia 18-3-16 4Lincs p217 CR France68
STEPHENSON,Eric Seymour.DSO.Capt ded 6-5-15 Glouc attEgyptArmy p107 CR Europe3,dow
STEPHENSON,Eric William Rokeby LtCol kia 27-4-15 3Mddx p148 MR29,Ernest 23-4-15
STEPHENSON,Ernest Cooper Apperly 2Lt kia 21-3-18 RFA 18DAC att83Bde p36 MR27
STEPHENSON,Francis Leaman T2Lt ded 6-2-18 att3DLI p161 CR Durham81
STEPHENSON,Gertrude Annie Sister 25-3-18 QAIMNS CR Surrey160
STEPHENSON,Hubert Victor T2Lt kia 8-5-17 1DCLI p115 MR20
STEPHENSON,J.L.Lt 28-12-17 RAMC CR Lancs246
STEPHENSON,John Roberts T2Lt kia 7-8-17 16NumbF p63 MR31
STEPHENSON,Kenneth Langton.MIDx2 T2Lt kia 26-9-15 2Beds p86 MR19
STEPHENSON,L.J.T.Capt 8-6-15 O&BLI CR Surrey2
STEPHENSON,M.Silvia 9-11-15 VAD CR Egypt9
STEPHENSON,Norman Masters 2Lt ded 1-5-16 2RGA p271 CR Kent129
STEPHENSON,Olaf Stephen 2Lt kia 1-7-16 8YLI p144 MR21
STEPHENSON,Rennie TLt kia 16-11-16 10RFus p70 CR France701
STEPHENSON,Robert Brewis.MC.2Lt dow 23-10-17 4 att22NumbF C'Coy p213 CR Belgium16
STEPHENSON,Selwyn Seymour Lt ded 13-3-15 RFA p271 CR Lancs381
STEPHENSON,Urban Arnold Lt kia 23-3-18 1Lincs p76 CR France511
STERLING,George Pomeroy.DSO.MC.TCapt kia 27-10-18 11NumbF p63 CR Italy9
STERLING,John Lockhart 2Lt kia 28-9-15 3 att2RScotF p95 MR19
STERLING,Robert Capt ded 16-10-17 RAMC p198 CR Numb60
STERLING,Robert William Lt kia 24-4-15 3 att1RScotF p95 CR Belgium28,23-4-15
STERLING,William Charles Lt 3-10-18 24RAF MR20
STERN,Leonard Hermann 2Lt kia 9-5-15 13Lond p249 MR32
STERN,Sidney Lt kia 19-7-17 8Mddx att3/3KAR p202&236 CR EAfrica38 &CR Tanzania1,Sydney
STERN,Sydney Lionel T2Lt kld 22-2-18 RFC p17 CR Scot764
STERNBERG,Edgar Adolph Joseph T2Lt kia 16-10-16 11 att2RLancs p59 CR France115
STERNBERG,Rupert Oswald 2Lt dow 1-7-16 83RFA p36 CR France102
STEUART,James William Harvie 2Lt 12-5-20 9RScots CR Scot723
STEUART,Norman Kennedy.MID Capt dow 15-9-16 ConnRgrs att6Bn p172 CR France300
STEUART,Walter Willox T2Lt dow 5-3-17 18HLI &46RFC p13&164 CR Belgium11
STEVEN,Archibald T2Lt kia 25-10-16 10Worc att8Glouc p109 MR21
STEVEN,George Gordon TLt kia 24-10-16 TankCps p189 CR France246 Ex MGC
STEVEN,Harvey Smith Lt kia 7-10-15 1/4BlkW p230 CR France765
STEVEN,Robert T2Lt dow 24-3-18 14HLI p164 MR20
STEVEN,Sidney Herbert Lt kia 25-9-15 4BlkW p230 MR19
STEVEN,William Struan Robertson Capt ded 1-7-19 RAMC p267 CR Devon1
STEVENS,Alexander.DCM.Capt&QM ded 10-4-17 1HLI p164 MR65
STEVENS,Alexander Mackay Lt 28-9-18 202RAF MR20
STEVENS,Alfred James 2Lt kia 21-9-18 1RWar att142RAF p66 CR Palestine9
STEVENS,Albert Charles Capt&QM ded 21-5-17 RE p48 CR Yorks551
STEVENS,Alfred Leslie Lt kia 18-4-17 1Leic p88 MR19
STEVENS,Arthur Eustace.MC.2Lt dow 16-7-15 1Hamps p121 CR France102
STEVENS,Arthur Reginald Ingram TLt kia 4-8-16 9RFus p70 CR France832
STEVENS,Cecil Robert LtCol ded 18-11-19 IA IMS p283
STEVENS,Cyril Stanley Geoffrey ACapt kia 9-10-17 1/2 att3/5LancF p93 MR30,Geoffry
STEVENS,Donald Eustace Lt kia 13-3-18 2/5Manch attRFC p19&236 CR France134
STEVENS,Douglas Alfred Stephen T2Lt kia 9-3-18 GL att76RFC p17 CR France95
STEVENS,Douglas Harcourt 2Lt kia 7-8-18 4EKent p212 CR France247,6-8-18
STEVENS,Edward Alfred Murtagh.MC.2Lt kia 16-6-18 1 att6EKent p58 CR France61,E.H.M.18-6-18
STEVENS,Edward Henry Lt dow 16-6-17 ELancs att25RFC p13&111,16-8-17 CR Belgium406
STEVENS,Ernest 2Lt dow 2-2-15 1SfthH p165 CR France727
STEVENS,Fenwick Charles Lt dow 7-9-18 2/5RLancs attTMB p213 CR France103
STEVENS,Frederick Charles.DCM.TCapt kia 31-7-16 D158RFA p36 CR France329,dow
STEVENS,Frederick George 2Lt dow 21-10-17 RFA p209 CR Belgium25
STEVENS,George Kellner 2Lt kia 4-6-16 3 att1Lincs p76 CR France188
STEVENS,George Percival Lt kia 21-3-18 232RFA attRE p208 MR27

STEVENS,Gorham Ninton 2Lt ded 18-1-18 1/5Lincs p220 CR France98,Vinton Lt
STEVENS,Henry Francis Bingham TLt kia 16-9-15 6RWKent p142 CR Belgium126
STEVENS,James T2Lt kia 9-4-17 5 O&BLI p130 CR France581
STEVENS,John Michael Stanilaus Gregory 2Lt dow 14-7-17 1RFC p13 CR France200
STEVENS,Lottie M.SNurse ded 15-3-16 QAIMNS p200 CR Egypt3
STEVENS,Leonard Frank Lt kia 25-3-18 6ESurr att4NStaffs p226 MR27
STEVENS,Lothian Basil 2Lt kia 9-5-15 SStaffs p123 MR32
STEVENS,Montague Lt kia 7-7-16 5 att1Worc p109 MR21
STEVENS,Norman Walter BtMaj ded 27-7-19 RAMC p267 MR65
STEVENS,Percival Charles 2Lt kia 6-4-17 8RWSurr p56 CR France161
STEVENS,Percy TLt kia 23-9-18 7RWKent p142 CR France364
STEVENS,Reginald Walter Morton.MID Capt dow 29-8-14 RIrRif p170 CR France1395,28-8-14
STEVENS,R.H.B.2Lt kld 30-5-18 GL &RAF p191
STEVENS,Robert LtCol ded 18-11-19 IA IMS CR Devon153
STEVENS,Ronald William.MM.2Lt dow 31-10-17 8Worc Ex 1/4 O&BLI p226 CR France547
STEVENS,Stephen Repton LtCol kia 8-3-16 IA 93BurmaInf p283 MR38
STEVENS,Thomas Tearle TLt kia 26-9-15 9Suff p79 MR19
STEVENS,Walter Sydney John T2Lt kia 7-7-16 11 att9LNLancs p136 MR21
STEVENS,William Philip 2Lt kia 3-8-18 1 att18Lond p245 MR16
STEVENSON,Alan TCapt kia 26-9-16 13 att9N&D p135 CR France296
STEVENSON,Alan McDonald Lt 5-4-18 GL&RAF CR Egypt9
STEVENSON,Alexander 2Lt kia 9-12-16 6GordH p242 CR France393
STEVENSON,Arthur 2Lt kia 27-4-18 RGA 152SB p42 CR Belgium188
STEVENSON,C.A.Lt 21-1-20 ConnRgrs CR Ches51
STEVENSON,Carlos 2Lt kia 2-1-17 20Lond p251 CR Belgium167
STEVENSON,David James 2Lt kia 22-6-16 5ScotRif p224 CR France765
STEVENSON,Douglas Baptiste 2Lt kia 11-3-17 DCLI &45RFC p13&115 CR Belgium11
STEVENSON,Frank Chown Lt kia 22-9-17 4Nhampt &NigR p234 CR EAfrica22 &CR Tanzania1
STEVENSON,Frederick 2Lt kia 29-4-17 22RFus p70 MR20
STEVENSON,George Arthur 2Lt dow 9-5-15 3EYorks p85 CR France102,2Bn
STEVENSON,George Hambly Capt kia 9-1-16 IA 125Rif p283 MR38,6-1-16
STEVENSON,George Herbert Maj kia 25-9-15 2WelshR p127 MR19,26-9-15
STEVENSON,Harold George 2Lt kia 25-6-17 13Y&L p159 CR France777
STEVENSON,Harry Burnett.MID Capt kia 7-8-15 IA 2Rajputs att2/10GurkhaRif p283 MR4,6-8-15
STEVENSON,Henry Fitzroy TLt kia 7-7-16 13Ches p97 MR21
STEVENSON,Hugh 2Lt kia 10-9-16 10 att16Lond p248 MR21 CR France1890
STEVENSON,Hugh Lt kia 9-10-17 6LancF p221 MR30
STEVENSON,Ilston Henry Lt kia 16-2-16 8 att7Nhampt p138 MR29
STEVENSON,J.Lt ded 15-5-18 RE p256
STEVENSON,James T2Lt kld 1-5-17 GL &RFC p13 CR Scot893
STEVENSON,John Lt ded 15-5-18 IARO att1Sap&Min p283 MR66
STEVENSON,John Connell.MID T2Lt kia 23-8-18 6RWSurr p56 CR France370,dow
STEVENSON,John Huntley Wickham 2Lt dow 5-2-17 IA 46 att26Punjabis p283 CR Iraq5
STEVENSON,John Scott Lt dow 9-10-18 RE p210
STEVENSON,Leonard William Hugh.MC.TLt kia 1-7-16 9RInniskF p105 MR21
STEVENSON,Marcus James Lt ded 10-9-15 RAVC attSherwoodRgrs p254 CR Egypt9
STEVENSON,Paul William John 2Lt dow 25-5-15 23Lond C'Coy p252 CR France414
STEVENSON,Philip Noel 2Lt kia 14-1-20 IA 1/109Inf p283 MR43
STEVENSON,Ralph Tapley 2Lt kia 3-8-18 5Lond 1Bn p246 MR16,31-8-18
STEVENSON,Richard John 2Lt dow 10-5-18 3 att1Hamps p121 CR France88
STEVENSON,Robert Capt kia 23-8-17 7 att9BlkW p231 CR Belgium8
STEVENSON,Robert Dennistoun TCapt kia 16-5-16 11A&SH p174 CR France423
STEVENSON,Robert Lyon Capt 9-8-17 EAUL CR EAfrica12 &CR Tanzania1
STEVENSON,Sampson Donald Lt dow 3-10-18 5Hamps p228
STEVENSON,Samuel Bristow 2Lt ded 29-9-16 RGA 138SB p42 CR Greece7
STEVENSON,Talbert.MC&Bar.Capt&Adjt kia 14-11-17 4/5BlkW p230 CR Belgium21
STEVENSON,Thomas Kerr T2LtALt kia 28-1-17 6/7RScotF att45TMB p95 CR France151
STEVENSON,Tom Lt kia 1-8-18 1/9RScots p212 CR France524
STEVENSON,Walter Henry T2Lt kia 5-6-17 29RFC p13 CR France46
STEVENSON,William 2Lt kia 11-6-18 3BordR att10N&D p118 MR27
STEVENSON,William.MC.2Lt kia 18-9-18 RGA 147HB p42 CR France647

STEVENSON,William Alexander Gibb.MID Capt dow PoW 20-12-17 14HLI p164 CR France1142
STEVENSON,William Henry 2Lt kia 21-3-18 11Leic p88 MR20
STEVENSON-HAMILTON,Olmar Charles John Maj ded 12-6-19 IA S&TCps p283 MR43
STEWARD,Arthur Amyot 2Lt kia 6-10-17 RFA &RFC 11BalloonCo p13&36 CR Belgium20,Lt
STEWARD,Charles 2Lt kia 25-5-15 3 att2KSLI p145 MR29
STEWARD,Harold N.Capt FlyingAcc 3-12-16 IA 6Cav &RFC CR Hamps180
STEWARD,John Henry Maj ded 10-5-15 4Norf p74&263 CR Norf139,3Bn
STEWART,Adrian Harry Lt kia 29-8-14 Glouc att3NigeriaR p107&202 CR WAfrica55
STEWART,Alan Dundas T2Lt kld 19-9-15 9RSuss p120 CR France1597
STEWART,Albert Lewis.DSO.TMaj kia 4-10-17 22MGC Inf p185 MR30
STEWART,Alexander Charles Capt kia1 2-4-18 9ACycCps p181 CR France193,12-4-18
STEWART,Alexander Dugald Lorn.MC.Capt dedacc 9-9-19 2GordH p265 CR Scot2
STEWART,Alexander James.MC.LtAMaj dow 30-4-18 2WYorks att59MGC Inf p83&185 CR France100,MGC attWYorks
STEWART,Alexander Leitch Capt kia 21-3-18 9 att1/7A&SH p244 MR20
STEWART,Alexander Vivian 2Lt kia 23-4-17 4GordH p242 MR20
STEWART,Algernon Brigham Anstruther.DSO.LtCol kia 24-5-16 1SfthH p165 CR France157,23-5-16 1/4Bn
STEWART,Alister Douglas TLt kld 13-10-17 GL &RFC p13 CR Wilts116,Alistere
STEWART,Andrew.MC.T2Lt kia 20-9-17 10NumbF p63 CR Belgium132
STEWART,Andrew Christie T2Lt drd 19-4-18 GL RE att1WT p191 MR38
STEWART,Andrew Philip.MC.TLt ded 2-6-18 KOSB p264 CR Scot764
STEWART,Bertrand Capt kia 13-9-14 WKentYeo p204 CR France1110,12-9-14
STEWART,Bryce.MID Lt kia 21-4-16 1SfthH p165 MR38
STEWART,C.G.HonLt&QM ded 26-2-18 Leic p263
STEWART,Charles Edward TLtCol kia 31-8-16 190RFA p36 CR France397
STEWART,Charles Edward 2Lt dow 10-9-16 20Manch p156 CR France51
STEWART,Charles Edward.CMG.TBrigGen kia 14-9-16 BlkW Cmdg154InfBde p129 CR France922
STEWART,Charles Edward.MC.TCapt dow 10-4-17 10DLI p161 CR France120
STEWART,Charles Frederick Somes.MC.TMaj dow 5-4-18 RMunstF att6Nhants p176 CR France587
STEWART,Christopher Codrington Capt kia 24-11-15 IA 20Punjabis attStaff 16Bde p283 MR38
STEWART,David Lt kia 14-6-15 6SfthH p241 CR France705
STEWART,Douglas Alexander T2Lt kia 7-7-16 13Ches p97 MR21
STEWART,Douglas Marshall S.Capt dow 3-1-19 4RScots p271 CR Scot239
STEWART,Duncan Hinshelwood 2Lt kia 20-4-18 9 att11A&SH C'Coy p244 CR France531
STEWART,Duncan John 2Lt kia 23-10-16 6ScotRif p224 CR France374
STEWART,Edward John T2Lt kia 30-11-17 140MGC Inf p185 CR France1496
STEWART,Elizabeth Grace SNurse 15-2-16 QAIMNS CR Hamps1
STEWART,Frederic Arnold TLt kia 16-9-16 10DLI p161 MR21
STEWART,Geoffrey Capt kia 22-12-14 1CldGds p51 MR22
STEWART,George TLtACapt kia 5-6-17 26NumbF p63 MR20
STEWART,George 2Lt kia 11-4-18 1/6WRid p227 CR France297
STEWART,George Lothian.MID 2Lt kia 9-4-17 6 att13RScots C'Coy p211 CR France924
STEWART,Gerald Capt kia 9-4-17 1/6SfthH p241 CR France15
STEWART,Gerald Charles Capt kia 13-5-15 10Huss p22 CR Belgium4
STEWART,George Pemberton.DCM.T2Lt kia 25-9-15 1CamH p168 CR France29
STEWART,George Soutar 2Lt ded 18-6-19 GL &RAF p267 CR USA184
STEWART,Guy Somerville 2Lt kia 28-3-18 49RFC p17 MR20
STEWART,Henry Edward TCapt kia 1-6-17 8RSuss p120 CR France1184
STEWART,Henry Ernest TLt kld 19-11-17 RScotF 55TrgResBn p95 CR Scot119
STEWART,Henry Warburton 2Lt ded 11-2-19 RGA 77SB p42 CR Germany1,Lt
STEWART,Herbert Lt kia 23-4-15 3DLI att2DCLI p161 MR29
STEWART,Herbert TLtACapt kia 9-4-17 9KRRC p152 CR France581
STEWART,Howard William 2Lt kia 27-8-18 GrenGds att4GdsMGReg p50&53 CR France614
STEWART,Hugh TLt kia 25-3-18 12HLI p164 CR France630
STEWART,Hugh.DSO.MC.MajTLtCol kia 12-4-18 RAMC att94FA p198 CR France857
STEWART,Hugh Duncan.MC.Maj kia 12-10-18 RFA p206 CR France612
STEWART,Humphrey.MID TCapt kia 3-7-16 5RBerks p140 MR21
STEWART,James 2Lt kia 28-10-16 22Lpool p73 CR France374
STEWART,James T2Lt dow 25-10-18 CamH Res att5Bn p168 CR Belgium143

298

STEWART,James Alexander Logan Lt kia 13-5-15 1RB p180 CR Belgium126
STEWART,James Aitchison TLt dow 12-10-16 GL &21RFC p4&191 CR France85
STEWART,James Augustus Lt kia 9-5-15 3RMunstF p176 MR22 2Bn
STEWART,James Henry 2Lt kld 21-12-17 413/302RFA p36 CR Palestine3
STEWART,James Robert Chap4Cl kia 2-1-16 RAChDept att2Worc p200 CR France80
STEWART,John Cecil Grahame 2Lt kia 25-9-15 2KRRC p152 CR France219
STEWART,John Charles Miller 2Lt kia 3-7-16 2/7WYorks att25RFC p19&218 CR France88
STEWART,John Ebenezar.MC.TCapt kia 26-4-18 8BordR attSStaffs p118 MR30
STEWART,John Houghton Lt kia 24-5-15 2RInniskF p105 MR22,15/16-5-15
STEWART,John James Erskine Brown 2Lt dow 12-6-17 7 att12RScots p211 CR France40
STEWART,John Kennedy 2Lt dow 2-11-17 4 att 1/7RScots p211 CR Palestine8
STEWART,John Maurice 2Lt kia 1-4-15 IrGds SR p53 CR France279
STEWART,John Morley 2Lt dow 21-8-18 10 att2RScots p212 CR France103
STEWART,John Nelson 2Lt kia 9-4-17 5Lpool p215 CR France595
STEWART,John Robertson 2Lt kia 12-4-18 2/4RWKent p234 CR Palestine3
STEWART,John Stanley T2Lt kia 17-10-16 10 att1RLancs p59 MR21
STEWART,John Stewart 2Lt dow 15-7-15 5A&SH p243 MR4
STEWART,John Walcot.MC.TLt kia 21-3-18 16RScots p55 MR20
STEWART,Joseph 2Lt kia 16-8-17 4RDubF p177 MR30
STEWART,Joseph Charles 2Lt kia 7-2-16 IARO att33Cav p283 CR Iraq6
STEWART,Keith Anthony.Hon.Lt kia 9-5-15 2BlkW p129 CR France924
STEWART,Malcolm Hector Capt dow 15-7-16 2RScots CR France23 served as MALCOLM,R.J.
STEWART,Mungo.MID Lt dow 7-2-17 55RFA HQ Staff p36 CR Iraq5
STEWART,Murdock Sutherland Capt ded 22-9-20 RASC CR EAfrica116
STEWART,Nathaniel William Lt kia 23-1-17 7RScots attRFC p19&211 MR34
STEWART,Norman Sinclair.MID Capt kia 30-9-15 2RScots p55 CR Belgium4
STEWART,Osmer Noel.MC.2Lt kia 31-7-17 B71RFA p36 CR Belgium84
STEWART,Ralph Walker Maj kia 2-9-18 Fife&ForfarYeo p203 CR France511,14BlkW
STEWART,Robert T2Lt kia 1-7-16 1KOSB p102 MR21
STEWART,Robert Arthur Chap4Cl ded 3-11-17 RAChDept att57CCS p200 CR France787
STEWART,Robert Colin TCapt kia 1-7-16 8Y&L p159 CR France246
STEWART,Robert Locke 2Lt ded 18-10-18 IA TC attRGA 1BritMtnArtBde p283 MR66
STEWART,Robert Taylor T2Lt dow 27-9-15 7RScotF p95 CR France98,Lt 28-9-15
STEWART,Ronald TLt drd 15-4-17 RAMC p198 MR35
STEWART,Ronald James.MC.Lt dow 28-1-16 3 att1SfthH p165 CR Iraq5
STEWART,R.S.Maj 13-6-21 Lpool CR Devon50
STEWART,Samuel George.MC&Bar.MID LtAMaj kia 27-10-18 30/39RH&FA p36 CR France1270
STEWART,Sydney Douglas Maj ded 29-11-19 GL &Mddx p267 CR Surrey1
STEWART,Thomas.MC&Bar.Maj kia 12-9-17 8 att5/6RScots p211 CR Belgium24
STEWART,Vernon Forster Lt kia 13-5-17 8DLI att 16RFC p19&239 CR France32
STEWART,Vernon Radcliffe Lt kld 5-12-17 RASC &19RFC p13&194 CR Lancs283,2Lt
STEWART,Walter Robert.DSO.MC.BtMajTLtCol kia 8-4-18 13RB p180 CR France203
STEWART,Walter Ross Taylor 2Lt kia 6-8-16 9A&SH p244 CR France1327
STEWART,Weston Capt dow PoW 27-3-18 1/4 att1/6SfthH p241 CR France560
STEWART,William Maj dow 12-7-15 4RScotFus p222 MR4
STEWART,William Alfred Lindsay.MC.Capt kia 25-9-16 GrenGds att4th p50 CR France374
STEWART,William Beardmore Capt kia 24-5-17 D/HB107RFA p207 CR Belgium15
STEWART,William Debenham McLaren Capt kia 25-9-16 1BlkW p129 MR21,Debnam
STEWART,William Johnston 2Lt kia 1-7-16 10 att9RIrFus p171 MR21
STEWART,William Malcolm.MID TCapt dow 27-10-16 23MGC p185 CR France105
STEWART,William Marshall 2Lt kia 24-3-17 8 att10ScotRif p225 MR20
STEWART,William McEwan Henderson T2Lt kia 16-8-17 11RInniskF p105 MR30
STEWART,William Norman.DSO.LtCol kia 22-3-18 NSomYeo att6Leic p205 MR27
STEWART,William Victor 2Lt kia 8-5-15 1Mon p244 MR29
STEWART,Wilma Bridges SNurse ded 10-7-18 TFNS CR Surrey99
STEWART-CORRY,Eberhardt George Lt kia 26-6-17 5Yorks p220 MR20
STEWART-JONES,Thorold Arthur Capt kia 9-5-15 5RSuss p228 MR22
STEWART-MOORE,Henry TLt kia 10-9-16 6 att7RInniskF p105 CR Greece3
STEWART-MURRAY,Lord George Maj kia 14-9-14 BlkW p129 MR15

STEWART-RICHARDSON,Edward Austin.Bart.Capt dow 28-11-14 3 att1BlkW p129 CR Scot203
STEWART-RICHARDSON,John Lauderdale 2Lt kia 17-5-16 2CldGds p51 CR Belgium44
STEYN,Stephanus Sebastian Lombard TLt kia 8-12-17 B117RFA p36 CR Palestine3
STEYTLER,Edward Dickinson 2Lt kia 25-7-16 SLancs &7RFC p4&126 MR20
STICKLAND,William Alban Lt kia 23-5-16 84/11RFA p36 CR Belgium5
STIDSTON,William Popkiss 2Lt dow 3-8-17 5 att2Leinst p175 CR Belgium7
STIDWELL,Herbert Jenkins 2Lt kia 27-7-16 3 att1RBerks p140 MR21
STIFF,Charles Neville Carleton Capt kia 22-3-18 4Yorks p220 MR27
STIGAND,Chauncey Hugh.OBE.Maj kia 8-12-19 RWKent attEgyptArmy CR EAfrica116
STILEMAN,Cecil Herbert T2Lt kia 29-2-16 RFus &5RFC p4&70 CR Belgium11
STILEMAN,Frederic William Cheere Capt kia 23-7-16 8Glouc p107 MR21
STILES,Arthur James 2Lt kia 3-8-16 8RFus p70 MR21
STILES,Edgar Watson.MID Lt dow 13-4-18 7NumbF p214 CR France88
STILES,Edgcumbe Leopold 2Lt kia 14-4-18 4EKent p212 MR32
STILES,Vincent Harcourt Lt kia 20-9-17 24Lond attMGC p187&252 CR Belgium88
STILL,George 2Lt kia 3-4-18 4CamH &RAF p243 CR Europe20
STILL,Reginald Sidney Hewitt Lt kia 7-10-16 28 att9RFus p70 MR21
STILWELL,Montague James Lt kia 30-6-18 4RWKent p234 CR France516
STIMPSON,John Crockett Lt kia 2-7-16 1/8WYorks p219 MR21
STIMSON,Montague Adolph 2Lt kia 30-9-16 10 att8ESurr p113 MR21
STIRLAND,Joseph Lt kia 24-3-18 22DLI p161 MR27
STIRLING,Colin Robert Hoste.DSO&Bar.MC.CaptALtCol dow 29-5-18 ScotRif att2RBerks p104 CR France145
STIRLING,George Edward 2Lt kia 7-10-16 8Lond p247 MR21
STIRLING,Gordon.MC.Lt kia 15-9-16 ScotsGds attMGC Inf p52 MR21 CR France390
STIRLING,Gordon Sheffield.MC.Capt dow 26-12-16 RoO 1/3KAR attA&SH p202&259 CR EAfrica38 &CR Tanzania1 A&SH attKAR
STIRLING,Harry Francis Dundas.MC.Maj kia 9-1-17 IA 59Rif p283 CR Iraq5,Henry LtCol
STIRLING,James Capt kia 2-1-15 3 att1ScotRif p104 CR France83
STIRLING,John Hunt Lt dow 22-8-17 57/45RFA p208 CR Belgium11
STIRLING,Richard Kellock Lt kia 21-8-15 5 att1RFus p70 MR29 &CR Belgium453
STIRLING,Robert Lt kia 19-2-15 1A&SH p174 CR Belgium28
STIRLING,William Aeneas Capt mbk 14-10-16 2SfthH p257 MR21
STIRLING-COOKSON,Samuel Baillie Capt kia 17-5-15 1RScotF p95 CR Belgium28
STIRLING-STUART,James Lt dow 9-11-14 ScotsGds p52 MR29
STITT,Innes d'Auvergne Stewart 2Lt kia 28-3-18 16Lond p250 MR20
STIVEN,Albert T2Lt kia 24-1-17 2 att6/7RScotF p95 CR France151
STIVEN,Ronald Walter Sutherland Capt dow 15-9-15 RScotF p95 CR Germany3
STOALING,Thomas 2Lt kia 14-5-17 2/4Lond p246 MR20
STOBART,John Geoffrey 2Lt kia 15-3-15 6 att4RB p180 CR Belgium111
STOBART,William TLt kia 24-8-16 10DLI attRFC p4&161 CR Belgium11
STOBBART,Roland Walter T2Lt kld 6-3-18 RFC p17 CR Numb7,Walton
STOBBS,Henry 2Lt kia 26-10-17 4NumbF p213 CR Belgium126
STOCK,Arthur Boy Capt ded 12-12-15 AyrshireYeo p271 CR Surrey160
STOCK,Charles Herbert T2Lt ded 31-5-16 13Hamps att9Worc p121 CR Iraq5
STOCK,Hubert Reginald 2Lt kia 25-10-14 1EKent p58 MR32
STOCK,James Mulock Thompson TLt kia 16-11-16 8ELancs p111 MR21,15-11-16
STOCK,John Launcelot Walmsley 2Lt dow 3-5-17 3Dors att6SomLI p124 CR France581
STOCK,Sydney Albert Cdr ded 31-7-16 IA S&TCps p283 CR Iraq6
STOCKDALE,Arthur William Sinclair 2Lt kia 24-5-15 7DLI p239 MR29
STOCKDALE,Edward Leslie Johnson TLt kia 7-7-16 10LancF p93 MR21
STOCKDALE,Frank TCapt dow 19-9-18 11RWFus p99 CR Greece1
STOCKDALE,Guy Nelson.MC.Maj kia 21-3-18 WYorks att11Ess p83 MR20
STOCKDALE,Norman Henry T2Lt kia 18-9-16 Lincs p76 CR France251
STOCKDALE,Walter Edwin 2Lt kia 10-9-15 NottsYeo p205 CR Gallipoli5,Lt
STOCKDALE,William Lt kia 3-5-17 6WRid p227 MR20
STOCKEN,Kenneth Edgar 2Lt kia 30-8-18 3SomLI att1Dev p80 CR France239
STOCKENSTROM,Andries Lars Lt 22-5-18 70RAF MR20
STOCKER,Arthur Rutterford.MC.ACapt ded 24-1-19 6SfthH attMGC Inf p187&241 CR Belgium316
STOCKER,Edward 2Lt kia 29-5-15 6KOSB p102 MR19,25-9-15
STOCKER,Frederick Luff TLt kia 23-8-18 28 att20RFus p70 CR France927
STOCKER,Harold Victor 2Lt kia 28-3-18 2/6RWar p214 MR27
STOCKER,St.John Crichton TCapt kia 12-3-15 2Nhampt p138 MR22
STOCKER,Thomas Fuller 2Lt kia 19-5-15 RE 171Coy p48 CR Belgium4

STOCKHAM,Thomas Alan Campbell Lt kia 22-3-18 1EYorks p255 MR27
STOCKHOUSEN,Ivan Lancelot 2Lt kia 3-10-17 BritWIndiesR att17RFC p13&192
STOCKINS,William James 2Lt kia 7-6-18 22Lond &RAF MR20,6-6-18
STOCKLEY,Harold Brodie 2Lt kld 22-7-18 2Lond &RAF p271
STOCKLEY,James Pearson Maj kia 7-1-16 IA 102Grens p283 MR38,6-1-16
STOCKLEY,Philip George TCapt ded 12-2-17 EYorks p85 CR Surrey36
STOCKLEY,Philip Lloyd TLtACapt kia 26-4-18 30MGC Inf p185 MR30
STOCKLEY,Walter Edwin TLt kia 9-8-18 14TankCps p189 CR France694
STOCKS,Harris Lawrence.DSO.Maj kia 1-7-16 15RScots p55 CR France296,Laurance
STOCKS,Michael George Lt kia 10-11-14 2GrenGds p50 CR Belgium134
STOCKS,Murdoch MacQueen T2Lt dow 10-4-16 11 att8GordH p167 CR France285
STOCKS,Tom Dixon T2Lt dow 16-4-18 3WRid p116 CR France249,15-4-18 2BN
STOCKTON,James Godfrey Capt kia 22-8-17 4 O&BLI p231 MR30
STOCKWELL,Charles Inglis Maj dow 21-10-14 2SfthH p165 CR France922
STOCKWELL,Eric Craig St.George Maj ded 20-1-19 YLI p265 CRYorks590
STOCKWELL,Frank Roland 2Lt kia 6-8-16 2/13Lond C'Coy p249 MR20
STOCKWELL,George TCapt kia 6-10-17 5Dors p124 MR30
STOCKWOOD,Lawrence Francis T2Lt dow 12-10-17 HouseholdBn p20 CR Belgium83,Finlay
STODDARD,A.A.Lt 27-11-18 IARO att S&M CR Hereford/W56
STODDARD,Ralph Cyril 2Lt ded 3-7-16 SLancs &4RFC p126&4,kia STODDART MR20
STODDART,Frederick William Capt kia 27-10-14 1Wilts p153 MR22
STODDART,George Benjamin Johnstone 89720 2Lt kld 10-4-18 GL 65RAF p191 CR France37,kia
STODDART-MacLELLAND,Chaltair Ruaridh Alwinn Domhnuill CaptHonMaj ded 30-11-14 3Ess p132 CR Scot54,MacLELLAN
STOER,Fred Charles T2Lt kia 17-3-16 6DCLI p115 CR France420
STOKER,Edward Alexander Morris.MC.Lt dow 12-9-16 4 att6RIrReg p89&170 CR France66
STOKER,George.CMG.23-3-20 RAMC CR Devon69
STOKES,Charles Leonard Lt kia 26-9-17 6Hamps att 19MGC Inf p187&229 MR30
STOKES,Claue Harry.DFC.dow 7-11-18 RAF CR Belgium199
STOKES,Clifford 2Lt kia 18-2-17 13Ess p132 CR France314
STOKES,Guy Lennard T2Lt kia 5-7-17 D174 RFA p36 CR Belgium5
STOKES,Haldane Day.MVO.Lt kia 17-2-15 2RLancs p59 CR Belgium133
STOKES,Harold T2Lt kia 20-11-17 E'TankCps p189 MR17
STOKES,Herbert George T2Lt kia 25-3-18 RE 77FC p48 MR20
STOKES,Hugh Adrian Innys Blyth.MC.2Lt dow 28-11-18 3 O&BLI p130 CR Surrey1
STOKES,John Alan T2Lt kia 16-8-17 10RIrFus p171 MR30
STOKES,John Hill.MC.Capt dow 22-3-15 3RWKent att1RBerks p142&259 CR France102
STOKES,John Wilfred LtCol kld 10-2-16 RAMC 3WRidFA p253 CR Lond12
STOKES,Leicester Henry 2Lt kia 31-10-17 18Lond p250 MR30
STOKES,Oliver Chetwode 2Lt kia 5-3-17 2RMunstF p176 CR France1472
STOKES,Philip Durham 2Lt dow 10-4-17 6RB p180 CR France145,11Bn
STOKES,Reginald Alexander 2Lt kia 24-2-17 9YLI p144 CR France163
STOKES,Reginald George Maj kia 28-9-15 2LNLancs p136 CR EAfrica58
STOKES,Robert John 2Lt kia 20-8-16 6 att2KRRC p152 CR France402
STOKES,Terence Fuller Capt dow 7-2-17 IA 82Punjabis p283 CR Iraq5
STOKES,William Allen LtCol 27-8-20 RE attRAF CR Egypt6
STOKES,William Henry 2Lt kia 18-4-18 RGA 101SB p42 CR France200
STOKES-ROBERTS,Edward Rowland Bennett.CB.BrigGen ded 22-11-17 RE HQ Baghdad p48 CR Iraq8
STOKOE,Henry Bertram TCapt kld 12-10-15 6YLI A'Coy p144 CR Belgium105,dedacc
STOKOE,James Clarke T2Lt kia 11-12-15 14Manch att6LNLancs p156 CR Gallipoli5,Lt
STOLLARD,Gordon TMaj kia 3-9-16 17N&D p135 MR21
STOLLERY,John Cecil 2Lt kia 24-5-15 5RFus attRWar p70 MR29
STONE,Alfred Lt ded 17-10-19 3Suff p263 CR France40
STONE,Arnold Capt kia 29-4-17 1/5N&D D'Coy p232 MR19
STONE,Arthur.DSO.TLtCol kia 2-10-18 15LancF p93 CR France836,16Bn
STONE,Arthur Brabazon.MID Maj kia 10-5-15 Ches p97 MR29
STONE,Arthur Cuthbert 2Lt kia 1-2-17 IARO att45Sikhs p283 CR Iraq5
STONE,Arthur Edward Capt kia 24-7-15 A243RFA p207 CR France251
STONE,Charles Douglas Felgate 2Lt kia 9-9-16 4RIrReg att6ConnRgrs p89 MR21
STONE,Docksey 2Lt kia 21-7-16 2/8RWar p215 CR France1887
STONE,Ellis Robert Cunliffe 2Lt kia 26-10-14 2RWFus p99 CR France705,Lt 25-10-14

STONE,Frank Ablett T2Lt kia 20-9-17 Norf att 1/8Lpool p74 MR30
STONE,Frederick James TLtACapt dow 29-12-16 7Glouc p107 CR Iraq5
STONE,George Morrison 2Lt kia 17-8-16 RE 1/1FC p210 MR21,Marrison
STONE,Harold 2Lt kia 7-6-17 23Lond p252 CR Belgium74
STONE,Harold George T2Lt kia 5-4-18 8SomLI p80 MR20
STONE,Henry Brassington Lt kia 18-2-15 RE 3FC p210 CR Belgium120
STONE,Henry Reginald 2Lt dow PoW 17-4-18 13Lond p249 CR France142,Lt
STONE,Herbert John T2Lt dow 15-11-17 19RFC p13 CR France285
STONE,Herbert William Degetan 2Lt kia 26-4-16 2IrRif att4ConnRgrs p172 CR France68,Degetau
STONE,Noel Herbert.MC.LtACapt kia 27-4-18 1Worc p109 CR France144
STONE,Oliver John 2Lt dow 22-9-16 4 att2/41RFA p209 CR France169
STONE,Robert Claude 2LtTLt kia 8-4-17 RLancs att9MGC Inf p59 CR France1701
STONE,Tom Pearce Griffith TLt dow 5-2-17 B66RFA p36 CR Iraq5
STONE,Walter Napleton.VC.ACapt kia 30-11-17 3 att 17RFus p70 MR17
STONE,William.MM.2Lt kia 18-8-18 12NorfR &NorfYeo p204 CR France19
STONE,William Charles 2Lt dow 4-11-18 2RMunstF p176 CR France716
STONE,William Henry.DCM.2Lt kia 26-9-16 6Nhampt p138 CR France1890
STONE-WOOTEN,Frank 2Lt kia 21-9-17 KRRC att 18Bn p152 MR30
STONEHAM,Charles.CMG.Col ded 31-1-16 RAMC p253 CR Mddx26,STONHAM
STONEHAM,Greville Cope 2Lt kia 14-11-16 1RBerks p140 CR France152
STONEHAM,Reginald Percy.DCM.2Lt kia 9-5-15 1N&D p135 CR France566
STONEHOUSE,Charles TLt kia 1-7-16 11ELancs p111 MR21
STONEHOUSE,Ronald Lt kia 1-4-18 RASC &101RAF p253 CR France62
STONEHOUSE,Robert Alfred 2Lt kia 28-4-17 4 att10LNLancs p234 MR20
STONEMAN,William Thomas 2Lt dow 26-7-17 14Lond p249 CR France139,ded
STONES,Francis Dawbarn.MC.Capt dow 28-9-17 2/6N&D p233 CR Belgium18
STONES,George Herbert Lee Lt dow 9-12-17 5 att11N&D p232 CR Italy7
STONES,George Lawden Boys.MC.Capt dow 30-3-17 IA 7Lancers attHQ 6CavBde p283
STONES,Shepherd 2Lt kia 3-11-16 5NumbF p213 CR France387
STONES,Thomas Frederick T2Lt kia 17-9-16 9 att10RWKent p142 CR France401
STONEX,Frank Hugh Tilney 2Lt ded 1-2-18 4RDubF p266 CR Ches182
STONEY,Francis George Duncan TLt dow 25-8-16 RE 204Coy p48 CR France141
STONEY,George Butler.DSO.MajTLtCol kia 15-10-15 KOSB p102 CR Gallipoli3
STONEY,Thomas Ramsay 2Lt dow 10-4-18 6KOSB p102 CR Belgium21,3Bn
STONEY,Thomas Samuel Vesey 2Lt kia 9-10-17 1IrGds p53 MR30
STONIER,William John Lt kia 27-4-17 2Beds att2RFC p13&86 MR20
STONNILL,Frank Roland 2Lt kia 24-3-18 Herts p252 MR27
STONOR,Cuthbert Anthony 2Lt kia 1-7-16 1RInniskF p105 CR France1490
STONOR,Howard Carew.Hon.Lt kia 10-3-15 4Beds att2SStaffs p86 MR22
STOODLEY,Percy Bennett 2Lt ded 9-11-16 7 att2Wilts p153 CR Greece5,Ballard
STOOKS,Herbert Drummond Sumner T2Lt dow 25-4-17 52MGC Inf p185 CR France113
STOPFORD,Frederick Duncan T2Lt kia 15-9-16 15Hamps p121 MR21
STOPFORD,Heneage Frank Maj kia 15-9-16 RFA p36 CR France277
STORAR,Robert Archibald T2Lt kld 16-12-15 18NumbF p63 CR Wilts115,19Bn
STORCH,Herbert.MC.T2Lt dow 24-8-18 13Yorks att1EYorks p91 CR France742
STORE,Albert Cash Lt kia 25-8-16 16 att5KRRC p152 MR21,5 att16Bn
STORE,Leonard 2Lt ded 31-8-15 5Lincs p272 CR Lincs123
STORER,John Young Maj kia 25-9-15 8Lincs p76 MR19
STORER,Patrick George Rawlings 2Lt dow 16-6-18 RH&FA 3DAC p36 CR France33,kia
STOREY,Fawcett 2Lt kia 23-4-17 5BordR p228 CR France1185
STOREY,H.P.2Lt 13-2-21 RASC CR Lancs401
STOREY,Harrison Leetham 2Lt dow 12-9-16 6WYorks C'Coy p218 CR Yorks410
STOREY,Harry Hilton 2Lt kia 13-10-14 DLI p161 MR32
STOREY,Kenneth Cothay Bonnell 2LtTLt kia 9-4-17 3 att5RBerks p140 CR France182
STOREY,Robert William 2Lt kld 9-3-18 1DLI att37MGC p161&185 CR Belgium19
STORIE,John Capt ded 4-10-15 RAVC p272
STORK,William Henry 2Lt dow 11-1-18 3DragGds p21 CR France446
STORKEY,Gordon Coleman T2Lt kia 1-8-17 2Mddx p148 MR29,Colman
STORM,Jack Newton T2Lt kia 23-3-18 5TankCps p189 MR27,28-3-18
STORM,William George.MC.Capt kia 9-10-17 5Y&L p238 CR Belgium125
STORMONT,William Lundie 2Lt kia 31-8-18 5RFA p36 CR France592
STORMOUTH-DARLING,John Collier.DSO.TLtCol kia 1-11-16 1ScotRif att9HLI p104 CR France294,STORMONTH
STORR,Henry.DSO.MajTLtCol ded 15-8-18 18Mddx p148 CR Kent284
STORR,Leycester Benthyn.DSO.Maj mbk 29-3-18 12Lpool att7DCLI p257 MR27,Penrhyn

STORRAR,Andrew Wynne 2Lt kia 16-8-17 2RDubF att48TMB p177 CR Belgium45
STORRIE,Hugh Cochrane Capt kia 12-9-15 RAMC att2RWSurr p198 CR France423
STORRS,James Parker 2Lt dow 8-8-17 6Ches p222 CR Belgium7
STORY,B.C.Agent 22-3-16 EAForce CR EAfrica44
STORY,George Ernest TLt ded 9-9-17 RE 297FC p48 CR Lond1
STORY,Leslie Campbell 2Lt 1-7-18 209RAF MR20
STORY,Tom T2Lt kia 18-11-16 11BordR p118 CR France153
STOTHERD,Sidney Boyle Maj dow 19-10-15 7Suff p79 CR France80
STOTHERT,George Mervyn TLt dow 10-6-17 13WelshR p127 CR Belgium18
STOTON,H.B Capt 3-1-22 SL &IntptrAlliedComm CR Germany1
STOTT,Edward Henry Hussey T2Lt dow 3-9-17 218MGC Inf p185 CR France297
STOTT,Frank Gordon Lt dow 11-7-16 5Ches attMGC p187&222 CR France296,Gorden att14TMB
STOTT,George Whittaker 2Lt dow 8-11-18 6 att9WRid p227 CR France146
STOTT,James Lt kia 19-6-15 10Manch p237 MR4
STOTT,James T2Lt kia 11-10-18 LancF att2/5Bn p93 CR France525,2-10-18
STOTT,Philip Harle 2Lt kia 25-4-18 4 att1/5WYorks p83 MR30
STOTT,Philip Nicholson 2Lt ded 21-3-15 10Manch p237 CR Glouc214
STOTT,Robert Sebastian.MC.2Lt kia 12-10-18 5LancF attL'TMB p221 CR France192
STOTT,Ronald Howorth 2Lt kia 20-9-17 3LNLancs att7RB p136 CR Belgium42
STOTT,Walter Goodwin Lt kia 19-9-18 4Manch att15Ches p156 CR Belgium188,18-9-18
STOTT,William Charles Herbert Ernest T2Lt kia 29-9-18 3YLI p144 CR France357
STOTT,William Ernest 2Lt kia 8-8-18 5LancF p221 CR France156,Lt
STOURTON-LANGDALE,Edward Francis Joseph TLt kia 5-10-16 RE 233FC p48 CR France744
STOUT,George Frederick T2Lt kia 30-9-16 6Yorks p91 MR21
STOUT,George Ronald Yorston.MC.2Lt kia 30-4-17 8A&SH attRFC p19&243 CR France557
STOUT Jnr.Thomas Lt kia 28-6-15 1/8ScotRif p225 MR4
STOVIN,Frederick Cecil Lt 24-4-18 209RAF MR20
STOVIN,George John Lucas Lt ded 2-2-17 IARO att37Dogras p283 CR Iraq5
STOVIN,John Thomas 2Lt kia 28-1-18 6RIrReg p89 CR France212
STOVIN,Lewis John Elliott Lt ded 22-8-17 127RFA p36 CR Kent28,2Lt
STOVOLD,Grosvenor Henry T2Lt kia 10-8-17 11RFus p70 MR29
STOVOLD,Percy Angel Capt kia 1-9-16 2RWSurr p56 CR France402
STOW,Basil T2Lt dow 22-10-18 15RIrRif p170 CR Belgium140
STOW,Montague Bruce TLtCol dow 2-7-16 1EYorks p85 CR France119
STOWE,William Hardwicke T2Lt ded 5-3-18 3Dev p263 CR Yorks447,Lt
STOWELL,Philip Charles Lt ded 12-6-20 IARO attS&TCps p283 MR65,Capt
STOWELL,Robert Cuthbert T2Lt kia 20-11-17 RLancs p59 CR France154
STOWELL,Thomas Brown.MC.2Lt dow 19-11-17 3 att8SLancs p126 CR France80
STOWELL,Wilfrid T2Lt kia 22-3-18 Leinst p175 MR27
STOYLE,A.P.Lt ded 27-2-19 4RFus attRAF p70
STRACEY,Reginald George.MID Capt kia 1-1-15 1ScotsGds p52 CR France644
STRACHAN,Albert 2Lt ded 30-10-18 LabCps attChineseLabCps p189 CR Devon258
STRACHAN,Alexander Macdonald 2Lt kia 20-7-18 4BlkW p256 MR34
STRACHAN,Andrew Robert 2Lt 20-9-18 20RAF MR20
STRACHAN,Aubrey Causton.MC&Bar.Lt kia 28-3-18 C70RFA p36&259 CR France1182
STRACHAN,Benjamin T2Lt kia 18-5-17 GL &12RFC p13 CR France1182
STRACHAN,David Livingston Capt ded 29-12-16 6WYorks p218 CR Yorks361
STRACHAN,Edward Stanley 2Lt kia 14-10-15 8N&D p233 MR19
STRACHAN,George Henry Lt ded 24-11-18 7GordH p242 CR France332
STRACHAN,Henry Lt dow 29-7-18 9DLI p239 CR France145
STRACHAN,James Capt kia 11-4-18 4GordH p241 MR19
STRACHAN,Wellesley Kendle Lt kia 24-8-18 8RScots p211 CR France214,Capt
STRACHAN,William Stead TCapt kia 18-2-18 RE p48 CR France446
STRAFFORD,Percy Belcher Maj kia 24-8-15 WRid p116 CR Belgium201
STRAHAN,Charles Eric Capt kia 28-11-14 2BlkW p129 CR France80
STRAHAN,Geoffrey Bennock 2Lt kia 31-8-15 10Lond p248 CR Gallipoli17
STRAIGHT,Marshall Stuart T2Lt kia 24-12-15 12 att1Ess p132 CR Gallipoli1
STRAIN,John London.MID LtCapt kia 31-7-17 RGA 214SB p42 MR29,Loudon
STRAIN,Thomas TCapt ded 16-9-16 RAMC 6MobLab p198 CR France201
STRAKER,Albert Gray 2Lt kia 3-10-16 7NumbF p214 MR21
STRAKER,Charles Constantine Lionel 2Lt dow 7-7-16 3Mon p244 CR France215
STRAKER,Frank T2Lt dow 16-7-16 RFA attZ39TMB p36 CR France80
STRAKER,Herbert 2Lt dow 9-11-18 6WYorks p218 CR France146

STRAKER,Kenneth Lt kia 23-7-16 3SfthH p165 CR Iraq5
STRANACK,Frederick George Lt kia 27-7-15 3 att1GordH p167 CR Belgium56,28-7-15
STRANG,James Buchanan T2Lt kia 30-7-16 17LancF p93 MR21
STRANG,John S.Capt kia 28-3-18 9BlkW p129&258 SeeStang,J.S.
STRANG,John Traquair 2Lt kia 18-5-18 B79RFA p36 CR France41
STRANG,Robert Capt kia 14-11-16 7A&SH D'Coyp243 CR France131
STRANG,Robert Brown T2Lt dow 12-8-16 6 att7RScotF p95 CR France703
STRANGE,Gilbert John Capt kia 24-9-18 Dors &40RAF p264 MR20
STRANGE,Hector Stanley 2Lt ded 7-10-18 2/4Dors &RAF p124 CR Egypt15
STRANGE,Lionel Cresswell T2Lt dow 22-7-17 9Ess p132 CR France113
STRANGE,Reginald Sydney T2Lt kia 17-10-18 1/2Beds att1Nhampt p86 CR France1270
STRANGE,William Hilbert Charles T2Lt kia 31-10-18 6RIrRif p170 CR Greece3
STRANGE,William Frederick 2Lt kia 1-7-16 2Lond p245 MR21
STRANGER,George 2Lt kia 11-4-18 1RGLI p201 MR32
STRANGER,Harry Easterbrook Knollys.MC.ACapt dow 11-5-18 1RGLI p201 CR France65
STRANGER,John Sercombe Capt kld 3-3-16 6Dev p217 MR38
STRANGER,Richard Henry Lt dow 13-3-15 1N&D p135 CR France102
STRANGWAYS-ROGERS,A.E.F.2Lt 4-11-18 3GrenGds CR France1080
STRANSOM,Norman G.Lt kia 10-5-18 GL &RAF p191
STRATFORD,Ernest Lt dow 21-4-15 RAMC p198 CR Berks112
STRATFORD,Herbert Douglas 2Lt dow 13-4-18 2GrenGds p50 MR32
STRATFORD,Laurence TLt kia 28-3-18 15 att1RB p180 MR20
STRATHAIRN,Hubert William 2Lt dow 16-11-16 6BlkW p231 CR France41
STRATHERN,Tom Dalrymple 2Lt kia 8-7-16 3 att2Yorks p91 MR21
STRATTON,Frederick Arthur 2Lt dow 27-1-17 IARO att82Punjabis p283 CR Iraq5
STRATTON,George Bernard TMaj kia 10/11-8-17 10DCLI p115 CR Belgium173
STRAUGHAN,Thomas Arthur TLt ded 5-1-18 8NumbF p63 CR Numb11,5-2-18
STRAUSS,Bernard Lewis,MC AMaj kia 1-12-17 1EKent p58 CR France439
STRAUSS,Victor Arthur Lt kia 27-11-16 RASC &RFC p4&194 MR20
STRAW,Alexander TLt dow PoW 3-6-18 1N&D p135 CR France1755
STRAW,Frederick Walter Lt kia 7-11-16 3 att14Y&L p159 MR21
STRAWSON,Frank Gordon T2Lt kia 1-10-18 11RWSurr p56 CR Belgium112
STREAM,John Harvey TLt kia 19-2-18 7Lincs att20RFC p17&76 CR Belgium11
STREATER,John Wenban T2Lt dow 22-7-18 15RWar p66 CR France65
STREATFIELD,J.P.S.2Lt ded 3-6-15 6N&D p233&272
STREATFIELD,Thomas Basil Maryon 2Lt dow 7-11-17 3 att1RWKent p142 CR Belgium112
STREATFIELD-JAMES,Ralph.DSO.Capt dow 7-10-16 1ESurr p113 CR France,STREATFEILD
STREATHER,Edward Harry Parsons Lt mbk 11-9-17 70RFC p257 MR20
STREET,Brooks Henry Lt kia 6-8-18 2/7WelshR &34RAF p230&258 CR Italy11
STREET,Cyril TLt kia 26-6-17 GL &1RFC p13 MR20
STREET,Edmund Alger T2Lt kia 2-6-16 22Manch p156 MR21
STREET,Edmund Rochfort.DSO.TMaj dow 15-10-16 2N&D p135 CR France105
STREET,Frank TLt kia 7-7-16 9RFus p70 MR21
STREET,Harold Edward.CMG.MIDx8 LtCol kia 25-8-17 106RFA GenStaff p36 CR Belgium15
STREET,Harry Lt ded 5-10-19 RFA p262 CR Sussex143
STREET,Harvey Ferrington 2Lt mbk 3-5-17 7WRid p257 MR20,Farrington
STREET,Herbert.MM.T2Lt dow 24-11-18 1RBerks p140 CR France40
STREET,Herbert Duke 2Lt ded 26-3-18 4RSuss p272 CR Surrey38
STREET,Hewson.MC&Bar.Capt dow PoW 1-6-18 5Lincs att10Worc p220 CR France622
STREET,Norman Kingsley Capt kia 10-8-15 Worc att39InfBde HQ p109 MR4
STREET,Richard T2Lt kia 24-4-17 WYorks att86MGC p83&185 MR20
STREET,Samuel William Lt ded 9-11-15 IA S&T Cps CR WAfrica61
STREET,Thomas Anderson TLt ded 27-1-18 10Glouc p264 CR Belgium96
STREETEN,Basil Robert Chap4Cl ded 1-11-18 RAChDept att2/5LancF p200 CR France1725
STRETCH,Thomas Noel Heath.MC&Bar.TLt kia 25-3-18 MGC Inf attRASC p185&194 CR France630,2Lt
STRETTELL,William Michael Dashwood Stirling Capt kia 28-11-17 4HLI att1AircraftDepot RFC p13&164 CR France134
STRETTELL-MILLER,Charles Wallace Lt kia 6-10-18 7RScots att4/1MGC p187&211 CR Belgium18
STRETTON,Alexander Lynam De Courcy.MC.Capt kia 16-10-17 SLancs attNigR p126 MR52
STRETTON,John de Courcy.MC.2Lt kia 11-5-18 3 att1RWar p66&259 CR France411

STRETTON,Sidney TLt kia 27-3-17 GL &15RFC p13 CR France62,66Sqn
STRETTON,William Stapleton de Courcy Lt dow 4-9-16 3 att2RWar p66 CR France23,Capt
STRETTON,William Thomas Capt&QM ded 10-4-16 RFA p262 CR Eire49
STREVENS,George William.MC.LtACapt dow 27-9-18 1DCLI p115 CR France146
STRIBLING,Frederick George TLt dow 8-7-16 1N&D p135 CR France44
STRIBLING,Lewis James 2Lt dow 16-11-17 RGA 329SB p42 CR Belgium72,kia 13-11-17
STRICK,Edward Talfourd Capt ded 19-6-15 2/6WelshR p272 CR Wales171
STRICKLAND,Charles John 2Lt kia 5-4-18 1/12 att23Lond p248 CR France232
STRICKLAND,James Edward Trench TLt dow 8-8-16 2SLancs att100MGC p126 CR France40,3ResBn
STRICKLAND,Joseph Chap4Cl ded 15-7-17 RAChDept 12Bde 4Div p200 CR Europe4
STRICKLAND,Reginald 2Lt ded 25-12-15 3 att2 O&BLI p130 CR France80
STRICKLAND,Vincent Norman Lt ded 10-5-17 O&BLI CR Lond8
STRICKLAND-CONSTABLE,Frederick Charles LtCol ded 20-12-17 3EYorks attStaff p85&263 CR Yorks93
STRIEGLER,Henry William 2Lt kia 12-8-16 7ESurr p113 MR21
STRINGER,Albert Edward 2Lt kia 7-6-15 9Manch p237 MR4
STRINGER,Dudley 2Lt kia 3-5-17 10EYorks p85 MR20
STRINGER,Frederick William TLtCol ded 30-6-16 RASC p194
STRINGER,Gerald Moffatt 2Lt kld 15-3-15 13Ches p97 CR Hamps13
STRINGER,Guy Frederick Lt kia 17-6-15 RGA NMidHB p209 CR Belgium9
STRINGER,Henry Francis Godfrey 2Lt dow 3-5-17 RGA 36SB p42 CR France97
STRINGER,John T2Lt kia 7-10-16 26RFus p70 MR21
STRINGER,William Charles 2Lt ded 14-6-17 RFC p13 CR Mddx26
STRITCH,George Seymour Russell TCapt kia 7-2-16 6ConnRgrs p172 CR France178
STROMQUIST,Sydney Goodwin TCapt kia 26-9-15 8Lincs p76 MR19
STRONG,Arthur Penton Lt kia 26-10-17 7NumbF p214 CR Belgium126
STRONG,Cecil Verge.MC.LtAMaj kia 10-3-17 RE 15FC p48 CR Frnce624
STRONG,Edward George 2Lt kia 27-5-18 RE 15FC p48 MR18
STRONG,George Henry 2LtTLt kia 3-1-17 GL att2NigeriaR p202 CR EAfrica36
STRONG,Howard Bertie Lt kia 29-10-14 RWSurr p56 MR29
STRONG,James Mortimer T2Lt dow 26-7-17 23MGC p185 CR Belgium7
STRONG,James William TLt kia 11-6-16 18LancF p93 CR France632
STRONG,Oliver Arthur 2Lt kia 8-5-17 1ESurr p113 MR20
STRONG,Oswald Lucking T2Lt dow 5-8-17 1SomLI att2KSLI attTMB p80 CR Greece9
STRONG,R.Harold 2Lt kia 13-3-15 2ESurr p113 CR Belgium182,Lt 12-3-15
STRONG,Thomas William T2Lt ded 26-5-18 att4SStaffs p123 CR France622
STRONG,William Charles Capt&QM ded 26-7-18 2/4Wilts p236 MR66STRONGE,James Matthew Lt kia 16-8-17 9RIrFus p171 CR Belgium8
STROSS,David 2Lt kld 12-3-17 RFA attRFC attMGC p19,187&209 CR Yorks363
STROTHER,John Marmaduke.MC.2Lt kia 28-4-17 3 att10Y&L p159 MR20
STROUD,Arnold Lt kia 15-9-16 4 att1/7NumbF p213 MR21
STROUD,Eric HubertNoel Lt kia 21-4-18 Leic &53RAF p263 CR Belgium453
STROUD,Henry Clifford Capt kld 7-3-18 RE attRFC p19&210 CR Essex73
STROUD,Reginald Gordon T2Lt kia 1-7-16 9Y&L C'Coy p159 CR France246
STROUD,Stephen George T2Lt dow 13-10-18 Ess Res att9Bn p132 CR France58,Lt
STROUD,Sydney Hill LtACapt kld 20-10-18 78RFA HQ p36 CR France661
STRUBEN,Leicester Frederick 2Lt kia 16-11-16 7DragGds &70RFC p261 2entries CR France307
STRUDWICK,John Meredith Ker 2Lt dow 21-4-18 2 att6RWSurr p56 CR France40
STRUEBIG,Edwin Harold.MM.2Lt kia 8-8-18 10Lond p248 CR France1170
STRUGNELL,Alfred Charles 2Lt kia 1-7-16 2Yorks p91 MR21
STRUGNELL,H.F.H.Maj ded 21-3-19 RM CR Hamps242
STRUGNELL,L.W. 2Lt kld 16-6-18 1/4Mddx &RAF p148
STRUTH,James Scotland T2Lt kia 16-9-17 17RScots p55 France364
STRUTHERS,Andrew Craig T2Lt kia 14-9-16 10ScotRif p104 CR France703
STRUTHERS,James D.Lt ded 8-8-19 87RGA 19SB p262 CR Asia33
STRUTHERS,Kenneth 2Lt kia 7-10-16 14Lond p249 MR21
STRUTT,Anthony Herbert TLt dow 27-4-18 16N&D p135 CR Belgium8
STRUTT,Richard Neville T2Lt kia 25-9-15 12 att2RScots p55 CR Belgium115,dow 15-10-15
STUART,Alexander Rev kia 24-10-17 RAChDept att 12RIrRif p200 CR France755
STUART,Alexander Davidson.MC.TLt kia 12-10-17 7SfthH p165 MR30
STUART,Alexander George LtCol kia 4-6-16 IA 40Pathans attHQ 50Div p283 CR Belgium191 Ex 2RScots
STUART,Andrew John.Viscount TLt kia 25-9-15 6RScotF p95 MR19
STUART,Atholl Archibald Capt kia 12-10-17 10 att11RScots p212 CR Belgium96

STUART,B.DSO.Maj 3-6-2- RFA attPoliticDept CR Iraq8
STUART,C.W.C.E.SubCdr 8-9-20 18DivTrain S&T Cps CR Iraq8
STUART,Cecil Edgar Lt kia 13-9-14 2LancF p93 MR15
STUART,Charles Lt kia 31-7-17 9A&SH p244 CR Belgium96
STUART,Charles Edward Cecil Wilmot SubCdr ded 8-9-20 IA S&TCps p283
STUART,Charles Erskine TCapt dow 15-3-17 2/6Suff p218 CR France41
STUART,David Aymery T2Lt kldacc 29-10-16 7CamH 7RFC p4&168 CR Scot239
STUART,Frank TCapt kia 10-4-18 GL att57TMB p191 MR30
STUART,George Douglas Gordon Lt kia 23-9-17 84/11RFA p36 CR Belgium13
STUART,Herbert Gordon 2Lt dow 7-3-19 3Lond p272 CR Essex86
STUART,James Capt kia 13-4-17 1RInniskF &59RFC p13&105
STUART,James Duff Maj 7-3-17 1CanadaPnrBn &43RFC MR20
STUART,James Maitland Capt 13-4-17 1RInnisF &59RFC MR20
STUART,James Ogilvie Grant.MC.Capt kia 30-3-18 5BlkW p231 MR27
STUART,John T2Lt ded 24-4-18 6RFus p70&258 CR Numb1,kldacc 29-4-18
STUART,John 2Lt kia 28-7-18 3 att9BlkW p129 CR France865,3 att4/5Bn
STUART,John Charles 2Lt dow 23-2-17 5ScotRif p224 CR Scot764
STUART,John Lachlan.MID Capt ded 23-10-18 5RFus p263 CR Camb16
STUART,Joseph Joachim Maxwell Lt kia 2-3-16 3 att9WRid p116
STUART,Karl Edwin Lt kia 25-3-18 2Mddx D Coy p148 MR27
STUART,Kenneth Bruce 2Lt kia 5-11-16 6DLI p239 CR France385
STUART,Maurice Stevenson 2Lt kia 15-6-18 8BlkW p129 CRFrance25
STUART,Morton Hollinshed Crawford 2Lt kia 8-3-16 IARO att2Rajputs MR38,Hollinshead Craufurd
STUART,Robert Alexander T2Lt kia 25-9-15 7CamH p168 MR19
STUART,Robert James Noel 2Lt kia 16-5-15 3 att2RScotF p95 CR France279,17-5-15
STUART,Robert Sheffield.Viscount Lt kia 2-11-14 RScotF p95 MR22
STUART,Vernon Douglas.MC&Bar.Lt kia 29-9-18 RGA 180SB p42 CR France212
STUART,W.A.Lt 30-10-16 RAMC CR Scot764
STUART,W.J.Lt ded 22-8-21 RE CR Canada180
STUART,William Aloysius T2Lt dow 26-5-17 18HLI p164 CR France1468
STUART,William Bruce George.MC.TCapt kia 22-11-17 12RIrRif p170 MR17
STUART,William Esme Montague 2Lt kia 7-10-16 6RWKent p142 MR21
STUART,William Grant Spruell.MC.Capt kia 23-4-17 7CamH p168 CR France1182
STUART-FRENCH,C.H.Maj ded 23-12-16 DAQMG 1MntedDiv p1 CR Herts20,5DragGds
STUART-RUSSELL,Cecil Henry TLt kia 7-9-16 RGA 17HB p42 CR France630
STUART-SMITH,Philip James Lt 8-5-18 CanadaCpsCavR &74RAF MR20
STUART-WORTLEY,John LtCol kia 21-3-18 6SStaffs p229 MR20
STUBBS,Alfred Joseph 2Lt kia 22-10-18 4RWKent p234 CR Belgium408,23-10-18
STUBBS,Cecil Arthur 2Lt dow 2-7-16 2Lond p245 CR France120
STUBBS,Charles Albert TLt ded 9-3-18 RAOC D66Bde p198 CR Greece7
STUBBS,Frank Percival T2Lt dow 25-11-16 15N&D att105TMB p135 CR France46
STUBBS,Frederick William Arthur.MC.2Lt kia 9-5-17 6N&D p233 CR France149,10-5-17
STUBBS,Herbert Edgar T2Lt dow 4-9-17 GL LabCps att65ChineseLabCps p191 CR France134
STUBBS,Lewis Robert.MC.2Lt dow 29-3-18 RGA 123SB p42 CR France40
STUBBS,Reginald Arthur 2Lt kia 8-6-16 4MunstF &RFC p4&176 CR France573
STUBBS,William Norman T2Lt kia 23-10-18 9 att1Ches p97 CR France206
STUCKLEY,Edwin Lane 2Lt kia 25-12-17 17 att4Lond p272 CR France184,STUCKEY
STUCLEY,Humphrey St.Leger Maj kia 30-10-14 GrenGds p50 CR Belgium116,29-10-14
STUDD,Francis Cyril Rupert.DSO.MajTLtCol kia 13-4-18 EKent att22NumbF p58 MR32
STUDD,Lionel Fairfax Capt kia 14-2-15 12Lond p248 CR Belgium58,15-2-15
STUDDY,Melvin Leslie T2Lt dow 22-10-16 1 att8NumbF p63 CR Durham19,15 att8Bn
STUDHOLME,Launcelot Joseph Moore.MID TCapt kia 9-9-16 7Leinst p175 MR21
STUDHOLME,Paul Francis William 2Lt kia 3-10-17 1Dev p77 CR Belgium112,4-10-17
STUDLEY,Charles Carr 2Lt kia 9-10-17 3 att1/8WYorks p83 MR30
STUDLEY,Harry Capt&QM ded 25-2-16 7BlkW p272 CR Scot142,Maj
STUDLEY,Logan 2Lt kia 25-10-14 Yorks p91 CR Belgium57,EYorks
STURDY,Arthur Carlile.MC.Capt ded 1-5-19 RAMC p198 MR65
STURDY,George T2Lt kia 9-10-17 6Y&L p159 MR30
STURGE,Edmund Capt ded 8-2-19 10Mddx attRE Sigs p236 CR Italy6
STURGES,Roland T2Lt kia 21-3-18 1 att2/7Manch p156 MR27
STURGESS,George Minshall 2Lt kld 5-4-18 Ess attRAF p132 CR Egypt8,Lt

STURGESS,Thomas George.MC.T2Lt dow 10-11-18 63MGC Divl p185 CR Belgium236,MM
STURRIDGE,Ernest Arthur Leland TCapt ded 30-12-15 6YLI p144 CR Belgium11
STURROCK,Andrew Lt kia 14-7-16 3 att 1RScotF p95 CR France453
STURROCK,Arthur Hill TLt drd 4-5-17 31MGC Inf p185 CR Italy14
STURROCK,Bernard Silvester Lt kia 26-9-15 4BlkW p230 MR19,Sylvester
STURROCK,George Lt kia 12-7-15 4RScotF p222 MR4
STURROCK,Harry Douglas.MC.Capt ded 1-2-18 ACycCps 1/1HighCycBn p244&272 CR Scot386
STURROCK,Thomas Gibbs Gordon T2Lt dow 16-10-16 17RScots &RFC p4&55 CR France1032
STURT,Douglas Elliott TLt ded 30-10-18 20Mddx p148 CR Mddx66,31-10-18
STURT,Ernest Guy Maclean T2Lt kia 16-8-16 12Mddx att6Nhampt p148 CR France82
STURT,Hon Gerald Philip Montagu Napier Capt dow 11-11-18 CldGds p51 CR Dorset133
STURT,Humphrey Morriston Lt ded 17-1-18 1/8LancF p221 CR France765
STURT,Kate Rosina SNurse 13-12-16 QAIMNS CR Surrey160
STUTTARD,Harold Pierce T2Lt kld 30-10-17 GL &RFC p13 CR Lancs336
STYLES,Alfred Cornwall TLt kia 19-7-16 16Ches p97 CR France630
STYLES,Arthur Horatio TLt dow 26-7-16 17RWFus p99
STYLES,Frederick Ernest Lt kia 27-8-14 2RMunstF p176 CR France1751
STYLES,Harold Thomas T2Lt kia 22-10-17 Manch att23Bn p156 MR30
SUCKLING,Cornelius Vincent Capt kia 16-7-16 1/5RWar p214 MR21
SUDBURY,John Allen TLt kia 29-9-18 2Worc att1GarrBn p109 CR France665
SUDELL,Henry James TCapt dow 28-8-15 RASC 111Coy 10DivTrain p194 MR4
SUDLOW,Horace Stanley T2Lt kia 30-3-18 2 att2/8Worc p110 MR27
SUFFIELD,Ernest 2Lt dow 1-5-18 107RFA p209 CR France145
SUFFOLK &BERKSHIRE,Henry Molyneux Paget.Earl Maj kia 21-4-17 Cmdg1WiltsRFA p206
SUGDEN,Christopher Babington 2Lt kia 25-5-17 4YLI p235 CR France684
SUGDEN,Guy Hatton Lt kia 12-10-16 3 att2WRid p116 CR France374
SUGDEN,Harold Capt dow 20-6-15 9Manch p237 CR Greece10
SUGDEN,John T2Lt kia 29-3-18 1/2 att1/5WRid p116 CR France798,5 att1Bn
SUGDEN,John Edwin,DSO TCapt&Adjt kia 28-9-16 10RIrRif p170 CR Belgium43
SUGDEN,John Paget 2Lt kia 8-8-17 6WRid p227 MR29
SUGG,B.Capt 3-4-21 RE CR Cornwall 40
SULIVAN,Eugene Gilbert Capt ded 8-5-17 4 att1ESurr p113 CR France777,kia
SULIVAN,Philip Hamilton 2Lt kia 27-8-14 2RMunstF B'Coy p176 CR France1751
SULLEY,Alan Hereford T2Lt kia 3-9-16 9 att2KOSB p102 CR France402
SULLINGS,Stephen John Rev ded 21-11-15 RAChDept Chap4Cl attRAMC 54EAngDiv p200 CR War7
SULLIVAN,Arthur John 2Lt kia 15-9-16 2Lond p245 CR France402
SULLIVAN,Cyril Charles Loyola 2Lt ded 16-6-17 3 att1Lincs p263 CR France40
SULLIVAN,Francis Joseph T2Lt kia 28-5-18 2DLI p161 CR Belgium3,27-5-18
SULLIVAN,John Duncan 2Lt dow 26-8-18 24Lond p252 CR France119
SULLIVAN,Timothy 2Lt kia 4-5-15 1RMunstF p176 MR4
SULLIVAN,Walter Ernest.MC.T2Lt dow 19-4-18 13WelshR B'Coy att114Bde HQ38Div p127 CR France62
SULLY,Donovan Ernest T2Lt dow 9-8-16 9SomLI p80 CR Belgium73
SULMAN,Geoffrey 2Lt kld 20-6-17 GL &51RFC p13 CR Lincs181
SULMAN,Paul Loxton.MC.TCapt dow 28-4-18 11Hamps p121 CR Surrey160
SUMMERHAYE,Dudley Leycester 2Lt kia 21-4-15 9Lond D Coy 1Bn p248
SUMMERHAYES,John Alexander T2Lt&ACapt kia 27-8-18 13RInniskF p105 CR France353
SUMMERS,Alfred Spencer Mason Capt ded PoW 15-9-16 19Huss &RFC p4&23 CR France560
SUMMERS,Archibald Young 2Lt kia 22-3-18 12NumbF att11Leics p63 MR20,Archbold
SUMMERS,John Collings 2Lt kia 13-8-18 RGA 120HB p42 CR France1170
SUMMERS,Ranulph Augustus T2Lt kia 28-9-15 9 att1RBerks p140 MR19
SUMMERS,Walter Gordon TCapt kia 28-12-15 7RWKent p142 CR France189
SUMMERS,William Assheton.MC.Capt kia 1-8-16 18Huss &RFC p4,23&259 MR20
SUMMERSCALES,Claude Lt ded 22-7-16 3ConnRgrs p172 CR Iraq6
SUMMERSCALES,Frederick David 2Lt kia 9-3-17 5 att22DLI p239 MR21
SUMMERSON,Herbert Walker T2Lt dow 5-6-18 9LNLancs p136 CR France622
SUMMERTON,Harold TLt kia 29-7-15 7SStaffs p123 CR Gallipoli2
SUMMERVILLE,Joseph.MC.MM.T2Lt kia 29-10-18 8Yorks B'Coy p91 CR Italy9
SUMNER,Charles Maunoir Col ded 30-6-16 SLancs p264 CR Cornwall79
SUMNER,Geoffrey Lt ded 11-5-18 RFA &RAF p272 CR Lancs170
SUMPSTER,Frank Manner Lt kia 21-3-18 8RBerks att53TMB p140 MR27

SUMPTER,George.DSO.MC&Bar.Capt 20-8-20 RFA CR Asia51
SUMPTION,Henry George 2Lt dow 15-10-18 HampsYeo att15HampsR p204 CR Belgium11
SUMSION,Francis Lt kia 4-11-18 3WelshR &RAF p127 CR Belgium218
SUNDERLAND,Alfred Joseph Elton.MIDx3 MajTLtCol kia 31-7-17 2Dev p77 CR Belgium34
SUNDERLAND,Geoffrey TLt&ACapt kia 24-9-18 2RSuss C'Coy p120 CR France1700
SUNDIUS-SMITH,Ronald Christian 2Lt 12-3-15 IARO att2WYorks MR28
SUPPLE,Edward James Collis Lt dow 22-8-15 1/6WRid p227 CR France64
SURGEY,Henry Norris Capt kia 3-1-17 2RWar attArabRifs p66 CR EAfrica36
SURR,Rudolph Vincent 2LtALt kia 31-10-16 5Worc att24TMB p110 MR21
SURRY,Norman Frederick T2Lt kia 12-10-18 16KRRC p152 MR16
SURTEES,Charles Gordon Villiers Lt kia 26-10-14 2BordR p118 MR29
SURTEES,William Beverley TCapt dow 28-9-16 9WYorks p83 CR France59
SUSSEX,Edgar William.MC.LtACapt kia 25-8-17 3ScotRif p104 CR Belgium24
SUSSEX,Reginald Arthur 2Lt dow 20-3-17 4WYorks att1Y&L p83 MR37
SUTCLIFFE,Archibald Alfred Capt died 12-3-15 RAMC p198 CR Germany4,SUTCLIFF
SUTCLIFFE,Fred Malcolm 2Lt kia 29-5-17 8Lond A Coy p247 MR20
SUTCLIFFE,George Mitchele 2Lt kia 21-10-17 RGA 237SB p42 CR Belgium36,Mitchell
SUTCLIFFE,Herbert Richard Charles T2Lt kia 1-7-16 24NumbF att5/24TMB p63 CR France393
SUTCLIFFE,John TLt kia 12-5-16 27Manch p156 CR France370,24Bn
SUTCLIFFE,Kenneth Wilson T2Lt kia 16-9-16 9 YLI p144 MR21
SUTCLIFFE,Oswald 2Lt kia 3-11-16 4YLI p235 CR France1327
SUTCLIFFE,Robert 2Lt dow 5-7-16 16WYorks p83 CR Yorks737,Lt
SUTCLIFFE,Roland Pruett Lt ded 20-10-18 IA 2/53Sikhs Ex 6BnAustInf p282 MR67
SUTCLIFFE,Sydney.MM.2Lt kia 2-10-17 RWelshF &11RFC p13&99 CR France924,Lt
SUTHERLAND,A.N.Chap4Cl 16-1-18 CR Scot764
SUTHERLAND,Alan D'Arcy 2Lt 28-2-17 RAF CR Wilts116
SUTHERLAND,Alister Morphett Lt died 28-8-20 NZ StaffCps MR69
SUTHERLAND,Allan Newton 2Lt kia 22-3-18 7GordH p242 MR20
SUTHERLAND,Anderson.MC.TLtAMaj dow 7-11-18 RHA att51/39RFA p36 CR France441
SUTHERLAND,Andrew Ernest TLt kia 3-10-16 A67RFA p36 CR Greece3
SUTHERLAND,Bessie Gray Sister 26-9-15 ScotWomensHosp CR Europe57
SUTHERLAND,Colin Lt ded 7-11-18 RE p272 CR Scot760
SUTHERLAND,George 2Lt kia 9-4-17 4KOSB p224 CR France924,7/8Bn
SUTHERLAND,George Angus.MC.Capt kia 27-7-18 1/5SfthH p241 CR France1697
SUTHERLAND,George Harry 2Lt kia 21-3-18 2/4 O&BLI att177TMB p231 MR20
SUTHERLAND,George Hay TLt dow 2-11-18 9RInniskF p105 CR France34
SUTHERLAND,George King Lt ded 9-3-19 RE p262 CR Wales13
SUTHERLAND,Goodwin 2Lt kia 9-4-17 4GordH p167
SUTHERLAND,H.W.SubPM 14-5-16 IndP&TDept CR EAfrica56
SUTHERLAND,Hector John.MID TCapt dedacc 2-2-17 6 O&BLI p130 CR France105
SUTHERLAND,Hugh Lt kia 29-10-17 RFA p208 CR France592
SUTHERLAND,J.A.Lt 29-6-17 ELakeBordPolice MR52
SUTHERLAND,James Parker T2Lt kia 9-4-17 2RScots p55 CR France581
SUTHERLAND,James Gilbert T2Lt dow 11-8-15 11HLI p164 CR France727
SUTHERLAND,James Lawrence Cathcart.MC.Lt dow 13-8-18 1RWKent att104RAF p142 CR France1667,19-8-18
SUTHERLAND,James Lindsay T2Lt kia 31-7-17 23Mddx p148 MR29
SUTHERLAND,John 2Lt kld 21-3-18 1/6LancF p221 MR27
SUTHERLAND,John Alexander 2Lt kia 8-12-17 24Lond p252 CR Palestine3
SUTHERLAND,John McIntyre 2Lt kia 23-4-17 9RScots p212 CR France545,Macintyre
SUTHERLAND,Noel Lt kia 21-11-17 4SforthH p241 MR17
SUTHERLAND,Thomas Capt dow 14-6-20 2/6Lpool CR Lancs2
SUTHERLAND,Walter Riddle T2Lt kia 4-10-18 8SfthH p165 CR France106,Riddell
SUTHERLAND,William.MM.T2Lt kia 7-10-18 7RDubF p177 CR France234
SUTHERLAND,William Dunbar.CIE.LtCol ded 27-6-20 IA IMS p283 CR India97A
SUTHERLAND,William Henry.MC.2Lt kia 23-3-18 4GordH p242 MR20
SUTOR,Harry C.N.TCapt ded 23-9-16 GL p191 CR Lond2,SUTER
SUTTHERY,Dorian Melbourne 2LtTLt dow 19-5-17 11A&SH p174 CR Shrop82
SUTTIE,William Campbell 2Lt kia 24-5-15 7A&SH p243 MR29
SUTTON,Arthur Eldred Barker Lt ded 4-7-18 6Lpool &RAF p215&258
SUTTON,Alexander Gordon 2Lt kia 2-1-18 6 att 2RB p180 CR Belgium22

SUTTON,Austin Ivor Spencer 2Lt dow 13-4-18 RFA Y31TMB p209 CR France169
SUTTON,Cyril John T2Lt kia 1-7-16 RFA att5RE p36 MR21
SUTTON,Eric Guy.MC.TLt kia 8-4-16 7RSuss p120 CR France423
SUTTON,Eustace Martin TLt kia 24-3-18 RE 35DivSigCo p48 MR27
SUTTON,Fergus Algernon Lt kia 26-2-15 2SLancs p126 CR Belgium17,27-2-15
SUTTON,Geoffrey Storrs.MC.TCapt kia 23-3-18 19Lpool p73 CR France672
SUTTON,George Nathaniel 2Lt ded 14-10-16 B95RFA p36 CR Lond8,dow
SUTTON,Horace Josiah T2Lt dow 24-11-15 13 att9N&D p135 MR4
SUTTON,Hubert Joselin Lt kia 27-9-15 1WelshGds p53 MR19
SUTTON,John William Wellesley.MC.2Lt kia 29-6-17 RGA att28RFA p42 CR France184
SUTTON,Oliver Joseph.MC.Capt kia 23-3-18 9Manch p256 MR27
SUTTON,Percy Turner Lt kia 24-8-18 RGA 283SB p42 CR France1170
SUTTON,Richard Thomas TLt/ACapt dow 3-10-18 7RInniskF p105 CR France1495
SUTTON,Sir Richard Vincent.Bart.MC.Capt ded 29-11-18 1LifeGds attGdsMGR p20&53 CR France34
SUTTON,Robert William 2LtTCapt kia 16-10-15 2RDubF p177 CR France35
SUTTON,Vivian Charles Woolfe T2Lt dow 14-9-18 RWKent att2/20Lond p142 CR France755
SUTTON,Wilfred Moschary Lt dow 17-9-16 2Y&L p159 CR France23
SUTTON,William Henry TLt kia 23-10-18 2WelchR p127 CR France1268
SUTTON,William Victor Ross 2Lt kia 13-11-17 1/1BerksYeo p203 CR Palestine9
SWABEY,Alan Maurice Eustace 2Lt kia 20-4-15 3SomLI attYLI p80 MR29
SWABY,Sydney Thomas TLt dow 31-8-18 WYorks att2/4YLI p83 CR France103
SWAIN,Basil Fitzroy Lt&QM dow 22-3-18 11RSuss p120 MR27
SWAIN,Charles Douglas Downs Lt kia 29-9-17 RGA 186SB p42 CR Belgium101
SWAIN,Clifford Maxwell 2Lt kld 4-4-18 GL &52RAF p191 CR France37,kia
SWAIN,Ernest George 2Lt ded 4-5-15 RASC p194 CR Hamps64
SWAIN,John George 2LtACapt kia 9-1-17 13N&D att93BurmaInf p135 CR Iraq5
SWAIN,John Henry Lt kia 9-1-17 IA 93BurmaInf p283
SWAIN,L.M SNurse 31-8-15 TFNS CR Egypt3
SWAIN,Robert Ernest T2Lt dow 8-7-16 13RWFus p99 MR21
SWAIN,Thomas T2Lt dow 25-7-16 8Yorks p91 CR Yorks159
SWAIN,William T2Lt kia 22-9-16 14 att8Yorks p91 CR France515
SWAINE,Henry Poyntz 2Lt kia 15-9-14 2RIrRif p170 MR15
SWAINE,S.W.2Lt kld 4-4-18 RH&FA &RAF p36
SWAINSON,Francis Gibbon.MC.Capt kia 1-7-16 16Lond p249 MR21
SWAINSON,John Anthony 2Lt kia 11-1-17 IARO att105MahrattaLI p283 MR38
SWAINSON,Joseph Leonard.DSO.TLtCol dow 9-8-16 6DCLI p115 CR France23
SWALE,Arthur Duncan Lt dow 5-10-18 6 att11N&D p233 CR France194
SWALE,J.V.2Lt 17-2-17 2RMLI CR France41
SWALES,George Middleton LtACapt kia 26-9-17 1RScotF att8/1TMB p95 CR Belgium188
SWALLOW,Arthur Reginald 2Lt kia 24-4-17 8Worc p226 MR21
SWALLOW,Bertie T2Lt kia 31-10-18 1/2 att18LancF p93 MR30
SWALLOW,Ernest Harold 2Lt kia 10-10-17 6 att4Mddx p148 CR Belgium56
SWALLOW,Hervey Lancelot St.George 2Lt mbk 25-9-15 10Y&L p257 MR19
SWALLOW,John Reginald 2Lt kia 8-8-16 1Lpool p73 MR21
SWALLOW,Luther James Lt kia 31-7-17 NStaffs p158 MR29
SWALLOW,William Hugh.OBE.TLtAMaj ded 21-2-19 RAOC DADOS 31Div p268 CR France134
SWAN,Donald Brian 2Lt dow 7-3-17 RHA p209 CR France786
SWAN,George Grieve 2Lt kia 1-7-16 4 att22Manch p156 MR21
SWAN,George Henry T2Lt kia 14-7-16 1RScotF p95 CR France453,Harry
SWAN,George Richard Lt dow 9-8-18 5 att8A&SH p243 CR France145
SWAN,Herbert Thomas 2Lt ded 22-8-18 58MGC p266 CR France116
SWAN,Joseph 2Lt kia 29-9-17 RGA 186SB p42 CR Belgium101
SWAN,Robert John 2Lt kia 29-3-18 A187RFA p209 CR France283,28-3-18
SWAN,William Capt kia 6-10-17 2/5N&D p232 CR France711,6-12-17
SWANN,Cecil Herbert Lt dow 27-8-18 2/6RWar p214 CR France398
SWANN,Gerald Huddart T2Lt kia 18-10-17 GL &41RFC p13 CR France41
SWANN,George William Lt dow 24-3-17 RASC &70RFC p13&194 MR20,SWAN
SWANN,Humphrey Nisbet Capt ded 4-4-17 Lincs Staff15Cps p76 CR France164
SWANN,T.Capt 18-1-17 6N&D CR Derby29
SWANSON,George William Capt drd 10-10-18 4Hamps attRAF p228 MR40
SWANSON,J.W.K.Capt dow 13-4-17 46CanadaInf CR France12
SWANSTON,Charles Oliver.DSO.LtCol kia 2-11-14 IA 34PoonaHorse p283 CR France525
SWANWICK,Russell Kenneth Lt kia 15-9-14 3Glouc p107 CR France1329,14-9-14 1Bn
SWARBRICK,W.Capt 6-9-20 LancF CR Lancs102

SWAYNE,Cecil Walter Harris Lt ded 25-5-17 2SomLI p80 MR43
SWAYNE,Stephen Cormack Lt kia 30-9-15 3EKent p58 MR19
SWEARS,Hugh Miller Lt kia 11-4-17 MGC attD'TankCps p185 MR20
SWEENEY,Gilbert Martin T2Lt kia 5-10-17 1Ches p97 MR30
SWEENEY,Walter Percy 2Lt 20-9-17 3Regt SAfrInf MR29
SWEET,Frederick Gordon Lt kia 26-3-17 3 att1/4Ess p132 CR Palestine8
SWEET,George Charles Walrond Rev ded 7-8-19 RAChDept p268 CR Somerset183
SWEET,Henry George T2Lt kia 25-9-18 RWSurr att2/4Bn p56
SWEET,John Lemon Leslie 2Lt kia 16-6-15 RScotF p95 MR22,Laxon
SWEET,Leonard Herbert TCapt kia 22-6-16 1Hamps att29RFC p4&121 CR Belgium11
SWEET,Roy Thornhill.DSO.Capt ded PoW 17-10-18 IA 2/7GurkhaRif p283 CR Iraq8
SWEET-ESCOTT,Leslie Wingfield TLt kia 25-9-18 5 O&BLI p130 MR29,25-9-15
SWEET-ESCOTT,Murray Robertson Lt kia 20-9-14 3Lpool p73 MR15
SWEET-ESCOTT,William Arthur Lt dow 14-10-18 RFA 50HQBde p36 CR Belgium157,kia
SWEETLAND,Rupert Girard 2Lt dow 26-1-17 3RWFus p99 CR Iraq5 Ex 29CanadaInf
SWEETMAN,Michael James Joseph Maj dow 27-11-15 2Worc att2Dors RoO p110 CR Iraq1
SWEETMAN,John Stephen T2Lt dow 27-4-16 8RIrFus p171 CR France423,SWEETNAM Lt
SWEETNAM,Richard Rodney Stephen TCapt kia 1-7-16 RFA 125Bty p36 CR France643
SWELL,Albert Ernest.DSO.ACapt kia 17-8-16 1Nhampt p138 CR France387
SWETENHAM,Edmund Lt dow 22-10-14 2DLI p161 MR32,27-10-14
SWETENHAM,Foster Maj kia 26-8-14 2Drags p21 CR France1715
SWIFT,Allen Richard 2Lt kia 10-11-17 A246RFA p36 MR30
SWIFT,Harold Heyes T2Lt kia 10-8-17 9LNLancs p136 MR29
SWIFT,Humphrey Morris 2Lt kia 16-11-17 2WelchR p127 MR30
SWIFT,James Herbert 2Lt kia 31-5-18 5Manch p236 CR France1689,Hubert
SWIFT,John T2Lt kia 9-1-17 12Manch p156 CR Iraq5
SWIFT,John 2Lt kia 22-11-17 2/7WYorks p218 MR17
SWIFT,Neville Cropley.DSO.MC&Bar.LtAMaj dow 28-3-18 3 att2ELancs p111 CR France185
SWIFT,Sydney Reginald T2Lt dow 4-12-16 2 att8NumbF p63 CR France59
SWIFT,Wilfred Harold Lt dow 22-4-17 IARO att51Sikhs p283 MR38
SWIFT,William T2Lt kia 1/3-7-16 8Lincs p76 CR France267
SWIFT,William T2Lt kia 11-10-18 WYorks Res att1/7WRid p83 CR France612
SWIFTE-O'FFLAHERTIE,Godwin Joseph Anthony Lt 4-3-18 3KSLI att1Lpool &RFC CR Egypt9
SWINBURNE,Matthew 2Lt dow 5-9-18 PoW 3RLancs p59 CR France1142
SWINBURNE,Thomas Anthony Stewart.DSO.MIDx3 CaptAMaj kia 1-4-18 RE 2FC p48 CR France880
SWINDALL,Arthur Cecil T2Lt kia 11-10-17 7RWSurr p56 MR30
SWINDELLS,Charles Geoffrey Rupert 2Lt kia 9-1-17 2Leics p88 MR38
SWINDELLS,Geoffrey Hillier LtCol kia 1-8-18 1/4Ches p222 CR Frnce524,Hilliers
SWINDELLS,Harold 2Lt kia 15-8-17 1/5SStaffs p229 CR France115
SWINDLE,Jackson 2Lt dow 14-10-16 14DLI p161 CR France52
SWINEY,Ernest Robert Rainier LtCol drd 30-12-15 IA 1/39GarhwalRif p283 MR41
SWINFEN,Percy Courtney 2Lt kld 20-9-17 GL &RFC p13 CR Yorks2
SWINHOE,Edmund Arthur Maj ded 27-10-18 IA S&TCps MR67
SWINLEY,George Dighton Probyn Maj dow 13-5-15 IA 14Sikhs p283 CR Gallipoli3,14-5-15
SWINLEY,Gordon Noël Balfour Lt kia 22-6-15 3 att2KOSB p102 CR Belgium96,dow 23-6-15
SWINNEY,James Herbert Cecil.MC.2Lt kia 16-4-17 7NumbF p214 MR20
SWINNEY,Norman Atkinson T2Lt kia 28-4-16 13NumbF p63 CR France188
SWINTON,A.J.Capt 7-9-20 RE MR65
SWINTON,Ernest.MID 2Lt dow 28-5-15 RFA p36 CR Lancs186
SWINTON,James Gibson 2Lt kia 25-3-18 4BlkW p230 MR27
SWIRE,Alexander Glen 2Lt kld 14-5-15 EssYeo p203 MR29,kia 13-5-15
SWORD,James Hubert 2Lt kia 10-9-14 4Huss p21 CR France1128,Lt
SWORDER,Charles Frederick 2Lt kia 3-7-16 7Suff p79 CR France393
SWORDER,Hubert Pelham Lt kia 2-4-17 RWSurr &57RFC p14&56 CR France924
SWORDER,John Perkins Lt dow 24-7-18 5RWSurr att1/1Hereford p212 CR France864,2/4Bn
SWYNNERTON,Frederick 2Lt ded 18-12-18 IARO attPostalCensorDept p283 MR65
SYDENHAM,Humphrey St.Barbe Lt ded 8-10-16 2/4 att1/4Dev p220 CR Iraq5
SYDES,Edward John Rev AustChap ded 15-11-18 att5FA CR Lond9

SYDNEY,Herbert Lt ded 26-5-17 RE IWT p48 MR38
SYER,Hubert Lionel.MC.Capt dow 18-11-16 1/14Lond p249 CR Lond12
SYERS,Thomas Scott.MC.CaptAMaj ded 14-11-18 D157 RFA p36 CR Sussex183
SYFRET,Edward Tristram Smyth 2Lt dow 17-8-16 3 att1Nhampt p138 CR France833
SYFRET,John Eustace Ridge 2Lt ded 17-1-19 RH&FA p262
SYKES,Arnold Walker TCapt kia 30-9-17 3Y&L A'Coy p159 CR Belgium165,9Bn
SYKES,Claude TLt kia 2-7-16 GL 10Y&L attTMB p191 MR21,Charles
SYKES,Douglas Collett.MC.TLt dow 26-7-17 7BordR p118 CR Belgium24,11Bn
SYKES,Edward Burton T2Lt kia 31-7-17 6/7RScotF p95 MR29
SYKES,Eric Turner Capt kia 3-5-17 2/5WRid p227 CR France644
SYKES,Ernest Edward.MC.Capt kia 4-7-16 4WRid p227 CR France702
SYKES,Frank William Lt kia 14-3-18 RFA p208 CR Belgium21
SYKES,Gerald Wolriche 2Lt kia 25-5-15 7WYorks p218 CR France525
SYKES,Harold Keith Lt dow 29-6-17 GL &42RFC p14 CR France285
SYKES,Harold Widdington TCapt ded 11-11-18 RAMC att14CCS p198 CR EAfrica87,Widdrington Maj
SYKES,Jabez 2Lt dow 25-6-15 4ELancs p226 CR Gallipoli1
SYKES,Jack A.2Lt kld 4-10-18 3GordH &RAF p167
SYKES,James Martyn Strickland 2Lt kia 13-11-16 5GordH p242 CR France1490
SYKES,John Spencer 2Lt kia 3-12-17 Worc att2/7Bn p110 MR17
SYKES,Leslie Gordon 2Lt kldacc 22-3-18 RFA attRFC p17&36 CR Yorks645
SYKES,Leslie Hindle 2Lt kia 3-10-18 6SStaffs p229 CR France375
SYKES,Mark.Bart.Col ded 16-2-19 4EYorks p272 CR Yorks35,5Yorks
SYKES,Oliver John TCapt dow 17-10-16 RGA 23SB p42 CR France296
SYKES,Ronald Arthur Lt dow 28-4-17 7RFus p70 CR France95,Capt
SYKES,Tom T2Lt kia 29-6-17 7Yorks p91 CR France97
SYKES,Walter Ernest Lt kia 20-11-17 5RWKent p235 CR France379
SYKES,William Lt ded 4-4-18 112Bty 6Div RFA p36 CR France102
SYKES,William Ernest MajTLtCol ded 8-1-15 9Worc p110 CR Sussex156
SYKES-BANKS,William Maj 19-2-16 Dors attGenStaff HQ CR France377
SYLVESTER,Charles Percival Haythorn T2Lt kia 3-10-18 SStaffs att 1/6Bn p123 MR16
SYLVESTER,George Harry 2Lt dow 4-11-18 4Lond p246 CR France403
SYM,John Munro.Sir.KCB.3-10-19 IA CR Scot237
SYME,David.MM.2Lt dow 4-7-18 6BlkW p231 CR France95,Lt
SYMES,Charles William Capt ded 10-10-15 1/4 att2Dors p229 CR Iraq5,9-10-15
SYMES,Edward Douglas.MC.Capt kia 13-8-17 9Lond p247 CR Belgium112
SYMES,John Bond Capt kia 3-5-17 2Lond p245 CR France537
SYMES,Henry T2Lt kia 30-9-16 6Y&L p159 MR21
SYMES-THOMPSON,Cholmeley Capt kia 17-11-14 2GrenGds p50 CR Belgium134
SYMINGTON,George Charles 2Lt dow 1-8-17 3 att 12RSuss p120 CR Belgium16
SYMINGTON,Percy George TLt kia 1-7-16 17HLI p164 CR France744
SYMINGTON,William.TD.SurgMaj ded 3-9-16 RAMC att4BordR CR C'land&W'land13
SYMON,John T2Lt kld 5-1-18 2Yorks p91 CR Belgium127
SYMONDS,Arthur 2Lt kia 17-2-17 23RFus p70 MR21
SYMONDS,Bertram Oliver T2Lt kia 21-8-18 34MGC p185 CR Belgium10,Bertan
SYMONDS,Frank James T2Lt kia 1-7-16 16WYorks p83 MR21
SYMONDS,Frederick George.DCM.MM&Bar.MID T2Lt kia 22-10-17 8Norf p74 MR30
SYMONDS,Kenneth Claud Lt 16-10-16 KSLI CR Shrop114
SYMONDS,Spencer Leslie Hatton 2Lt kia 12-11-17 GL &7RFC p14 CR Belgium88
SYMONDS,William Frederick John.DSO.LtCol dow 24-4-18 11Lond p248 CR France37
SYMONDS-TAYLER,Frederick Kingsley Capt dow 17-4-17 3 att 1KSLI p145 CR France98
SYMONDSON,Vernon F.Capt kld 13-11-18 13Huss &RAF p22
SYMONS,Alfred Castell Lt ded 26-2-19 3RScots attTankCps p262
SYMONS,Arthur George.MC&Bar.TCapt&Adjt ded 23-10-18 21Mddx p148 CR Kent180
SYMONS,Charles Fleming Jelinger TLt kia 25-9-15 9RWFus p99 MR19
SYMONS,Charles Handley Lanphier 2Lt kia 20-11-17 5 att8RFus p70 MR17
SYMONS,Charles Leslie 2Lt dow 23-4-18 RE 63FC p48 MR30
SYMONS,Clement Aubrey TLt kia 25-9-15 10Glouc p107 MR19
SYMONS,Douglas 2Lt kia 1-10-16 20Lond p251 MR21
SYMONS,Eric Clarence T2Lt dow 1-9-16 98MGC Inf p185 CR France833
SYMONS,Frank Albert.CMG.DSO.LtColTCol kia 30-4-17 RAMC ADMS 9DivStaff p198 CR France97
SYMONS,Frederick Gordon Lt kia 22-5-16 3 att 12RScotF p95 CR Belgium53
SYMONS,Herbert William.MID Capt kia 20-11-14 1YLI attSomaliCamelCps p144 CR EAfrica60,19-11-14

SYMONS,Hubert Maj dow PoW 22-3-18 D47RFA p36 MR27
SYMONS,Keith William Allardyce Lt 30-7-18 73RAF MR20
SYMONS,James Anthony 2Lt kia 18-7-16 5RSuss p228 CR France296
SYMONS,Rudolph Clifford Lt ded 13-9-15 RASC 3Coy p272 CR Somerset42
SYMONS,T.S.Capt kld 29-9-18 3RSuss &RAF p120 CR France379
SYMONS,Vivian Hood Maj 29-1-17 RAMC CR Wilts115
SYMS,Albert George Ernest.TD.LtCol ded 22-1-18 12Lond p248 CR Lond1
SYNGE,Allen Francis Lt kia 27-11-17 2IrGds p53 MR17
SYNGE,Francis Patrick Hamilton.MC.LtACapt kia 29-7-17 2IrGds SR p53 CR Belgium13
SYNGE,Mark.CIE.DSO.LtCol ded 11-7-21 IA S&TCps p283 CR Sussex200
SYNNOTT,Fitz Herbert Paget 2Lt kia 10-8-15 5RWFus p223 MR4
SYNNOTT,Walter Pierre 2Lt ded 11-10-18 6Drags attMGC p22&185 MR65
SYNYER,Richard Harold 2Lt dow 21-9-18 12Lond p248 MR16
SYRETT,Alfred Montague T2Lt kia 4-5-17 1RWFus p99 MR20
SYSON,Leslie 2Lt kld 17-9-16 RGA &RFC p209 CR War67
SYVRET,Stanley de Beaudenis Lt ded 14-5-18 3RScotF p263 CR Dorset156

T

TABBENER,Thomas Kemp Lt dow 9-12-17 2/19Lond p250 CR Palestine3,kia 8-12-17
TABER,Stacey James Hutley 2Lt kia 20-7-16 2Ess p132 CR France643
TABOR,John Morton T2Lt kia 21-9-17 KRRC att18Bn p152 MR30
TABUTEAU,Rupert Rochefort Moliere Lt kia 28-3-18 3CldGds p51 MR20
TACK,Eldred William.DCM.MM.T2Lt kia 28-9-18 NStaffs Res p158 CR France415
TACKABERRY,John Bailey Capt ded 25-3-17 IMS 83CombStatHosp p283 CR Iraq6
TACKNEY,J.J.Gnr ded 18-8-17 RIM p283
TACON,Ernest John Ballard 2Lt kia 9-10-17 LancHuss p204 MR30
TAFFS,Charles Reginald Lt kia 15-5-15 3 att 1RBerks p140 CR France632
TAFT,Thomas Lt&QM dow 23-12-17 6DLI att4Yorks p239 CR Belgium10
TAGENT,Harold William 2Lt kia 24-3-17 4RIrF &8RFC p14&171 CR France120
TAGG,Charles Hirch 2Lt kia 15-2-15 2ESurr p113 MR29
TAGG,Harold Arthur Lt kia 12-10-14 Mddx p148 CR France1106
TAGGART,Henry Rawson 2Lt kia 24-7-18 3A&SH att 1BlkW p174 CR France258
TAGGART,Herbert Lt kia 8-5-16 11 att15RWFus p99 MR19
TAHOURDIN,Philip Ramsay 2Lt kia 17-4-16 IA 47Sikhs p283 MR38,Lt
TAHOURDIN,Spencer Maxwell Maj dow 8-2-16 IA 12Cav p283 CR Iraq6
TAILFORD,John Wilson.MC.Capt kldacc 22-5-17 BordR &RFC p14&118 CR Kent7
TAIT,David Borthwick 2Lt kia 11-8-18 4 att5/6RScots p211 CR France360
TAIT,Evelyn Euphemia Worker ded 22-10-18 QMAAC CR France85
TAIT,Henry Forsyth T2Lt kia 1-9-16 10 att12ScotRif p104 MR21
TAIT,James Capt kia 16-6-17 7DLI att2/1Lond p239 MR20
TAIT,Kenneth James Capt kia 23-3-18 1/85MC AuklandMtdRif NZEF MR34
TAIT,Robert Andrew T2Lt kia 22-3-18 9LNLancs p136 CR France245
TAIT,Thomas Henderly Lt drd 15-4-17 3A&SH p174 CR Greece14
TAIT,Wilfred Webster Lt dow 19-12-15 10WelchR p127 CR France1106,Wilfrid
TAIT,William Bell T2Lt kia 15-12-17 2RScotF p95 MR30
TAIT-KNIGHT,Alec TCapt dow 27-10-16 22DLI p161 CR France105
TAITE,William Henry Jules 2Lt ded 27-9-18 3Mddx p148 CR Greece9
TALBOT,Ainslie Douglas Capt kia 3-6-15 1LancF p93 CR Gallipoli1,4-6-15
TALBOT,Arthur Aston Lt ded 29-10-18 SWBord BrecknockBn p223 CR EAfrica52
TALBOT,Arthur Charles 2LtTLt dow 17-7-15 2Ess p132 CR France102
TALBOT,Arthur Sydney TLt kld 27-9-17 48RFC p14 CR Essex73
TALBOT,Cecil Melliar 2Lt kia 28-9-15 14 att4Mddx p148 CR Belgium6,27-9-15
TALBOT,Claude Eustace Chetwynd T2Lt kia 25-9-15 6SomLI p80 MR29
TALBOT,Edward Charles.MID Capt dow 29-4-15 IA 47Sikhs p283 CR France200,Maj
TALBOT,Eric Lawrence Lt dow 23-10-14 RHA p36 CR Belgium57
TALBOT,Frank Henry T2Lt ded 15-7-16 RWar att 1BordR p66
TALBOT,Frederick Charles ACapt kia 9-10-17 D'TankCps p189 MR30
TALBOT,Frederic Herbert T2Lt kia 20-7-16 15N&D p135 MR21
TALBOT,Gilbert Walter Lyttelton TLt kia 30-7-15 7RB p180 CR Belgium453,Lyttelton
TALBOT,Humphrey Richard Lt kia 13-11-14 3DragGds p21 CR Belgium57,Humfrey kia
TALBOT,John Lionel Pemberton 2Lt dow 14-10-18 4Worc X'Coy p110 CR Belgium157,kia
TALBOT,Leonard Lane.MC.Capt dow 24-4-17 27RFA p36 CR France95
TALBOT,Norman Hale T2Lt kia 24-8-16 5 O&BLI p130 MR21

TALBOT,Ralph Frederick 2Lt 2-9-18 8RAF MR20
TALBOT,Reginald Fitzroy 2Lt kia 27-8-16 RFC p4 MR20
TALBOT,Rimell Smith 2Lt kia 23-4-18 A121RFA p36 CR Belgium11
TALBOT,Stanley Alfred T2Lt kia 19-10-16 NStaffs att9LNLancs p158 CR France446
TALBOT,Theophilus Edwin 2Lt dow 21-3-18 C160RFA p36 CR France512
TALBOT,William Caithness 2Lt ded 20-7-18 6Leinst &RAF p175
TALBOT-BOWE,Edward TCapt dow 1-11-17 12RBerks att188LabCps p140 CR France145
TALL,John Jeffery 2Lt kia 15-2-18 4Dev p220 MR30
TALLENT,Albert Cecil T2Lt kld 4-11-17 RFC p14 CR Lond10,Charles
TALLENTIRE,Arthur Tom 2Lt kld 20-10-15 28Lond &RFC p19&252 CR Belgium11
TALLON,Moses 2Lt kia 4-8-16 11Suff p79 MR21
TANBURN,Walter Louis 2Lt kia 13-4-17 IARO att1/2GurkhaRif p283 MR38
TANCOCK,Osborne George.MC.Lt kia 17-3-18 RFA att5RFC p17&36 CR France95
TANDY,Archdale Maurice Stratford Lt kia 20-10-14 RIrReg p89 MR22
TANDY,Arthur Jesse 2Lt ded 28-7-19 WYorks p263 CR Scot9
TANFIELD,Arthur Horace 2Lt kia 13-4-17 59RFC p14 MR20
TANKARD,William Joseph 2Lt kia 31-8-18 4 att5LancF p93 CR FRance239
TANNER,Arthur Edward T2Lt dow 10-7-17 16NumbF p63 MR31
TANNER,Charles Cyril Pontin Capt ded 5-10-18 RGA 157HB p42 CR Iraq8
TANNER,Charles Patrick LtACapt kia 30-11-17 59MGC p185 MR17
TANNER,David 2Lt kia 30-8-17 8N&D p233 MR19
TANNER,David Thomas TLt kia 31-8-18 16RWFus p99 CR Belgium73,Capt
TANNER,Edward Joseph Selby T2Lt kia 8-7-16 11Yorks attMGC Inf p91&185 CR France397
TANNER,Gerald Russell.MC.2LtTLt dow 8-4-18 Wilts p153 CR Camb3
TANNER,Harold Herbert TCapt drd 16-8-16 RAMC 13GH p198 CR France102
TANNER,Hubert John T2LtACapt kia 9-4-17 1SomLI p80 MR20
TANNER,John Arthur.CB.CMG.DSO.BrigGen dow 23-7-17 Staff RE 7Cps p1 CR France214
TANNER,John Frederick 2Lt ded 21-2-19 11N&D p264 CR Yorks686
TANNER,John Howard TLt kia 15-9-16 10Hamps p121 CR Greece3
TANNER,Morris Villiers Godwin T2Lt dow 7-4-17 3 att2/8N&D p135 CR France610
TANNER,Percy Valentine Capt kia 27-3-18 79RFC p255 MR20
TANNER,Ralph Eyre Capt dow 23-9-14 1Lpool C'Coy p73 CR France473
TANNER,Raymond Stuart 2Lt kia 31-8-16 3RLancs p59 CR Belgium120
TANNER,Thomas George TLt kia 14-10-17 RFA attRE p36 CR France154
TANNER,Thomas Lanfear Capt kia 18-9-18 4RWKent p234 CR France364
TANNETT-WALKER,Frederick William.VD.Col ded 6-3-17 4RE p48 CR Yorks372
TANQUERAY,Andrew Alexander Truman TCapt kia 30-7-15 9KRRC p152 MR29
TANQUERAY,Frederic Baron 2Lt kia 1-7-16 16Mddx B'Coy p148 CR France221,Lt
TANQUERAY-WILLAUME,F.G.Maj 11-2-19 RHA CR Hamps7
TAPLIN,Albert William 2Lt kia 1-7-16 1/12Lond p248 MR21
TAPP,George Norman T2Lt dow 28-3-16 14Ches p97 CR FRance300,2YLI
TAPP,Harold Donesthorpe Lt dow PoW 25-7-17 RE 3FC att70RFC p19&210 CR Belgium140,Donisthorpe
TAPP,Theodore Arthur.MC&Bar.Capt dow 21-10-17 CldGds att3GdsMGR p51 CR Belgium16
TAPP,William SubCdr ded 16-4-19 IA S&TCps p283
TAPPENDEN,Frank William T2Lt dow 2-7-18 18MGC p185 CR France44,1-7-18
TAPPENDEN,Herbert Frederick 2Lt kia 26-3-17 4RSuss p228 MR34
TAPSELL,William Algernon.DCM&Bar.MM.2Lt dow 18-9-18 1Lincs p76 CR France145
TAPSON-JONES,Herbert.MC.Capt dow 12-11-18 4RFA CR Mon67
TARBET,Arthur Kenneth 2Lt kia 21-8-15 1RInniskF p105 MR4
TARBET,Edmund Alex 2Lt kia 21-8-15 att1RInniskF p105 MR4
TARBET,Victor 2Lt kld 4-10-17 4Dev p220 MR30
TARBET,William Duncan T2Lt kia 9-4-17 7SfthH attC'MGC p165&186 MR230
TARBUTT,Fraser Coventry Lt 16-6-18 56RAF MR20
TARDUGNO,Ray T2Lt kia 7-7-17 17RWFus att57RFC p14&70 CR France134
TARGET,Noel Alexander TLt kia 4-8-16 13DLI p161 MR21
TARGETT,Ernest TLt ded 19-2-19 RASC p255 CR France1076
TARGETT,George Henry Lt kia 18-9-18 1/10Mddx attMGC p187&236 CR France1495
TARR,Francis Nathaniel Lt kia 18-7-15 1/4Leics p219 CR Belgium127
TARR,Henry Charles Hardman 2Lt ded 2-2-19 RASC p194 CR Egypt1
TARR,William Lt 31-10-15 7WYorks CR Belgium73
TARR,William Lt kia 14-7-16 7WYorks p218

TARRAN,Reginald Stuart.MC.2Lt kia 24-3-18 1Lpool p73 MR20
TARRANT,Arthur Ralph 2Lt kia 24-6-18 4RBerks p234 MR19
TARRANT,Henry Geoffrey Nelson.MC.T2Lt kia 31-7-17 6RBerks p140 CR Belgium112
TARRANT,Herbert Sutton Capt kia 27-4-15 HLI p164 CR Belgium101
TARRANT,Percival John TCapt kia 25-6-18 1/2 att11ELancs p111 CR France19
TARRAS,John Rae 2Lt kia 16-10-16 RFA X9TMB p36 CR France385 &CR France1890
TARRATT,Duncan McNeill Fox 2Lt kia 4-10-17 2SfthH p165 CR Belgium83
TART,Cyril James 2Lt kia 1-7-16 RE 219FC p48 MR21 CR France1890
TASKER,Field Pass T2Lt dow 6-10-17 16RWar p66 CR Belgium11
TASKER,Herbert Edwin 2Lt kld 22-8-18 6 att19Lond p247 CR France210
TASKER,Richard Greaves TCapt kia 3-7-16 10Worc p110 CR France393
TASKER,William 2Lt kia 27-5-18 4Leics p220 MR18
TATAM,Leslie Charles 2Lt kia 19-5-16 att8RLancs p59 MR20
TATE,A.C.R.2Lt kld 2-5-18 GL &RAF p191
TATE,Andrew T2Lt kia 20-1-18 NumbF att24/27Bn p63 CR France162
TATE,Charles Bernard Capt kia 1-7-16 15RIrRif p170 MR21
TATE,Frederick Herman.MID Capt kia 11-8-17 10KRRC p152 MR29
TATE,Gerald Charles 2Lt dow 21-3-15 3EYorks p85 CR France284
TATE,Harold Glen TCapt kia 17-2-17 2SStaffs p123 MR21
TATE,Herbert Lloyd T2Lt kia 12-6-16 RFA p36 CR Belgium136
TATE,John Martin TCapt kia 27-5-18 14NumbF p63 MR18
TATE,Johnston T2Lt kia 7-11-17 5RIrFus p171 CR Palestine8
TATE,Lionel Percy T2Lt kia 4-11-18 Res 8NStaffs C'Coy p158 CR France984
TATE,Tom Campbell T2Lt dow 2-9-16 12RSuss p120 CR France203
TATE,William Edward Lt kld 12-8-17 2/5N&D &RFC p232 CR Wilts28
TATE,William Lewis Lt kia 13-3-15 3RFus p70 CR Belgium17 Louis
TATEM,Rolland James.MC.Lt kia 27-9-18 42RFA p36 CR France530
TATHAM,Basil Owen Capt kia 23-4-15 3EYorks p85 MR29
TATHAM,Cautley Lt dow 18-6-15 1HAC D'Coy p206 CR France285,Capt
TATHAM,Geoffrey Bulmer.MC.Capt kia 30-3-18 3RB att116InfBde HQStaff p180 CR France652
TATHAM,George Henry Riley 2Lt dow 11-10-18 5Yorks att1/7WYorks p221 CR France611
TATHAM,Ion Mordaunt T2Lt kld 11-7-17 GL &RFC p14 CR Hamps30
TATHAM,John Savil 2Lt kia 9-2-17 9KRRC att6RLancs p152 MR38,Savill
TATHAM,Lawrence Castell Stanley T2Lt kia 10-1-18 GL &5RFC p17 CR France113
TATHAM,Sherman Trevor.MC.Lt ded 25-5-19 Ex 11Mddx p265 CR Lond14,dow
TATLOCK,Robert Reginald Lt ded 19-6-16 RASC p253 CR Greece7,Rattray 18-6-16
TATLOW,Archibald Henry TCapt kia 4-6-16 15RWar p66 CR France1182
TATTERSALL,Eric T2Lt dow 26-9-17 23Manch p156 CR France446
TATTERSALL,Harold Vaughan TLt ded 22-4-18 PoW 1NStaffs p158 CR Germany4,dow
TATTERSALL,Percival John T2Lt kld 9-1-18 RFC p17 CR Essex11
TATTERSALL,Philip Charles Paul.DSO.Capt accdrd 28-7-17 1/11Lond p248 CR Palestine2
TATTERSFIELD,Neville T2Lt ded 20-11-18 2TankCps p189 CR Dorset94
TATTON-TATTON,C.H.Lt ded 26-11-18 6RB p180 CR Surrey1
TATUM,George Edward 2Lt kia 30-11-17 15Lond p249 MR17
TATUM,Harold Maj kia 4-11-14 IA 101Grens p283 MR47
TAUNTON,Clive Warneford Capt kia 25-11-16 2Mon p244 CR France400
TAUNTON,Cuthbert Andre Patmore T2Lt kia 9-8-15 7SStaffs p123 CR Gallipoli5
TAUNTON,Oscar.MC.Lt dow 14-6-15 RE 1FC attELancs p210 CR Greece10
TAUNTON,Percy Charles James 2Lt kld 7-8-17 RGA 297SB p209 CR Belgium29
TAVERNER,Arthur Frederick 2Lt dow 11-10-16 1KSLI p145 CR France105
TAVERNER,Harold Percy Lt kia 27-3-17 6Ess p232 MR34
TAVERNER,Harold Tait 2Lt dow 12-4-18 B88 RFA p36 CR Belgium11,TAVENER
TAVERNER,Norman Henry Lt ded 4-12-18 GL P267 CR Lond10
TAWNEY,Robert Lionel.MC.2LtALt dow 30-11-17 7SomLI p80 MR17
TAWSE,James Gordon Capt dow 15-4-17 D291RFA p207 CR France518
TAYLER,Eric Hardwick Lt ded 9-2-15 1Y&L p159 CR France200
TAYLER,H.F.TLt ded 8-11-18 RE p48
TAYLER,Jervoise Graham 2Lt kia 15-5-15 3 att2Leic p88 CR France727
TAYLER,St.Cyprian Churchill.MC.Capt mbk 17-3-18 RSuss &80RFC p257 MR20
TAYLER,William Ulric Chevallier Lt kia 10-8-19 7RWKent att45RFus p255 MR70 &CR Europe179,1Bn
TAYLEUR,Charles Edward Lt kia 7-8-15 10NStaffs att8LancF p158 MR4
TAYLEUR,W.OBE.LtCol 8-7-21 ShropYeo Cmdt LabBn CR Shrop81
TAYLOR,A.D.TCapt kld 24-8-18 GL &RAF p191

TAYLOR Adam 2Lt dow 22-3-18 RGA 210SB p42 CR France987
TAYLOR,Adrian Aubrey Charles Capt kia 28-6-15 RDubF attEgyptPolice p177 MR4
TAYLOR,Adrian Connell TLtACapt dow 24-9-17 15HLI p164 CR France1361,Cannell
TAYLOR,Albert Cecil 2Lt kia 20-7-16 Suff p79 CR France402
TAYLOR,Albert Edward.DCM.2Lt kia 9-4-17 2WRid p116 MR20
TAYLOR,Alexander Capt kia 21-4-17 9RScots p212 CR France545
TAYLOR,Alexander John 2Lt dow 8-8-18 16SussYeo p205 CR France31,kia
TAYLOR,Alexander Steven Bain 2Lt kia 23-7-18 1/5SfthH p241 CR France1697
TAYLOR,Alfred Cecil.MM.T2Lt kia 23-10-18 1DCLI p115 CR France1476
TAYLOR,Alfred Francis TLt kia 9-8-16 10 att7Suff p79 MR21
TAYLOR,Alfred Squire LtTCapt kia 31-7-17 RAMC att10/11HLI p198 CR Belgium58
TAYLOR,Alfred Thurston Lt kia 5-10-18 RE 423FC p210 CR France1723
TAYLOR,Andrew Leitch TCapt kia 12-5-17 6SfthH p241 MR20,13-5-17
TAYLOR,Archibald Cameron T2Lt kia 29-4-17 23NumbF p63 MR20
TAYLOR,Archibald McMillan Capt kia 10-8-15 4Ches p222 MR4
TAYLOR,Arnold Bradley T2Lt kia 12-7-16 9Leic p88 MR21
TAYLOR,Arthur Lt kia 10-4-18 4Ches p222 MR32
TAYLOR,Arthur Cuthbert Brooke Lt kia 4-6-15 6Manch p236
TAYLOR,Arthur George 2Lt dow 26-4-18 7RWSurr p56 MR27
TAYLOR,Arthur George Ernest LtACapt dow 26-5-17 7RFus attRN Div p70 CR France95,27-5-17
TAYLOR,Arthur Gilbert Vivian Lt ded PoW 17-10-17 IA 41Dogras attRFC p283 MR20
TAYLOR,Arthur Leonard T2Lt dow 16-11-18 10N&D p135 CR France52
TAYLOR,Arthur Martin T2Lt kia 1-8-17 2Dev p77 MR29
TAYLOR,Arthur McCutheon 2Lt kia 10-11-17 2RMunstF p176 CR Belgium126
TAYLOR,Arthur Montague Lt dow 25-9-15 IA 1Brahmans att2/8GurkhaRif p283 CR France705
TAYLOR,Arthur Rowland T2Lt kld 19-1-18 RFC p17 CR Hamps31
TAYLOR,Aucher Wilbraham 2Lt kia 26-9-16 5RBerks p140
TAYLOR,Bernard Arthur 2Lt kia 30-11-17 166MGC Inf p186 MR17
TAYLOR,Brook Wilbraham.DSO.Maj dow 2-4-16 RFA p36 MR65,8-4-16
TAYLOR,Bruce Mitchell.MC.DSO.Maj kia 6-11-17 1DCLI p115&258 CR Belgium37
TAYLOR,Charles 2Lt ded 9-5-18 C59RFA 11DAC p262 CR France224
TAYLOR,C.de B.Capt dow 24-12-18 RIrRif p265
TAYLOR,Cecil Frederick Lt dow 20-1-18 GlasgowYeo &RFC p203 CR France64
TAYLOR,Cecil Meakin 2Lt kia 7-10-16 4Lond p246 CR France744
TAYLOR,Cecil Salusbury LtCol dow 6-11-16 RGA 28HAG p42 CR France400
TAYLOR,Cedric Charles Okey Lt kia 3-12-16 3EKent attTMB p58 CR France1182
TAYLOR,Charles CaptTMaj kia 5-8-17 3RIrReg p89 MR29
TAYLOR,Charles Christopher Vassell TLt kia 26-12-17 301RH&FA p36 CR Palestine3
TAYLOR,Charles Edward Lt kia 1-11-15 1WYorks p83 MR29 CR Belgium101
TAYLOR,Charles Frederick 2Lt dow 18-2-17 19WelshR p127 CR Belgium18
TAYLOR,Charles Harry Lt drd 17-11-15 10WYorks p83 MR40
TAYLOR,Charles Harry T2Lt kia 25-1-17 9Worc p110 CR Iraq5
TAYLOR,Charles Livingstone LtACapt kia 24-3-18 3 att8ELancs p111 MR27,8 att2Bn
TAYLOR,Charles Manners T2Lt kia 9-4-18 RASC p194 MR32
TAYLOR,Charles Matheson 2Lt dow 20-4-17 121RFA p36 CRFrance68
TAYLOR,Charles Stanley T2Lt kia 3-11-17 1/7Ess p132 CR Palestine8
TAYLOR,Charles Tyerman Lt kia 24-8-14 18Huss p23 CR France206
TAYLOR,Clives Wailes.MC.2Lt dow 25-2-17 17RFus p70 CR France64
TAYLOR,Conrad Paul.MID TCapt kia 28-10-16 8EYorks p85 CR France133
TAYLOR,Coutart-de Butts.MM.Capt dow 24-12-18 RIrRif CR Sussex111 See SgtCOLLINS RFus
TAYLOR,Daniel Martin Lt kia 28-6-15 7ScotRif p224 CR Gallipoli6
TAYLOR,David George 2Lt kia 9-9-16 10Manch attRLancF p237 MR21
TAYLOR,Denis Percival Beauchamp.MC.Lt kia 14-3-16 3Huss att3RFC p4&21,ded CR France782
TAYLOR,Douglas Lt ded 26-7-18 RAMC 41GenHosp p198 CR Greece7
TAYLOR,Douglas John 2Lt kld 29-12-16 21RFC p4 CR Egypt9
TAYLOR,Douglas John Bulpin Capt kia 2-9-18 WSomYeo p205 CR France,12SomLI
TAYLOR,Douglas Merwyn 2Lt kia 4-10-16 3 att7EKent p58 MR21
TAYLOR,E.C.OBE.Maj 26-3-21 RE Staff CR Staffs109
TAYLOR,Edgar Lt 25-8-18 79RAF MR20
TAYLOR,Edmund T2Lt dow 26-9-17 GL &23RFC p14 CR Belgium16
TAYLOR,Edward 2LtTLt kia 13-5-15 18Huss p23 MR29

TAYLOR,Edward Algernon 2Lt kia 11-2-18 1Herts p252 CR France439
TAYLOR,Edward Graham T2Lt kia 25-9-15 7CamH p168 MR19
TAYLOR,Edward Graham 2Lt dow 23-5-17 4HLI p164 CR France40,Lt 2Bn
TAYLOR,Edward Roy.MC.TCapt kia 23-10-18 15WBord p101 CR France1271
TAYLOR,Edward Shillingfleet Sodley 2Lt ded 9-6-18 4NStaffs p265 CR Essex130,Lt
TAYLOR,Edward Staveley 2Lt dow 19-8-16 7Lpool p216 CR France23
TAYLOR,Eric Francis Howard T2Lt kia 27-7-16 23RFus p70 MR21
TAYLOR,Ernest 2Lt dow 16-10-15 1/4WRid p227 CR Belgium9
TAYLOR,Ernest T2Lt dow 7-9-18 7Lincs p76 CR France41
TAYLOR,Ernest Albert Isaac TCapt dow 23-7-18 B98 RFA p36 CR Greece1
TAYLOR,Ernest George 2Lt kia 2-5-15 3 att2RLancs p59 MR29
TAYLOR,Ernest Reginald.MC.Capt kia 11-8-18 7Ess att18KRRC p232 CR Belgium11
TAYLOR,Ernie Rumbold Capt kia 18-4-15 WRid attEYorks p116 CR Belgium152
TAYLOR,Eustace Edmund Marshall TLt kia 1-1-17 169MGC Inf p186 CR France1157
TAYLOR,Ezra Dolphin 2Lt kia 30-4-15 RHA Y'Bty p36 CR Gallipoli14,28-4-15
TAYLOR,Forster T2Lt kia 16-10-18 9ESurr p113 MR16
TAYLOR,Francis Galloway 2Lt kia 23-7-16 12WYorks p83 France432
TAYLOR,Francis Henry 2Lt kia 30-11-17 3Mon B'Coy p244 CR France379,1/2Bn
TAYLOR,Francis Maurice TLt kia 15-7-16 10RFus p70 MR21
TAYLOR,Francis Mortimer.MC.Capt kia 17-3-19 RAMC p198 CR Europe180,Maj
TAYLOR,Frank TMaj kia 13-3-16 10Y&L p159 CR France922
TAYLOR,Frank Wilsher 2Lt kia 1-9-18 5Lond att1/20Lond p246 MR16
TAYLOR,Frederick Cecil LtACapt kia 22-8-18 13KRRC p152 CR France214
TAYLOR,Frederick George T2Lt ded 21-7-17 9NumbF p63 CR Mddx13
TAYLOR,Frederick George Lt kia 14-4-18 4EKent p212 MR32
TAYLOR,Frederick William.TD.LtCol ded 10-7-16 5Ess p272 CR Essex119
TAYLOR,Garth Smithies TLt kia 15-10-16 2N&D p135 MR21
TAYLOR,Geoffrey England 2Lt dow 26-9-18 RFA attY33TMB p36 CR France278
TAYLOR,George TLt drd 30-10-17 RAMC p198 MR38
TAYLOR,George Lt mbk 23-3-18 RE 517FC p257 CR France1472
TAYLOR,George Charles TCapt dow 6-9-18 RAVC att26RFA p199 CR France309,kld
TAYLOR,George Francis Woodland 2Lt kia 4-5-17 2Ess p132 CR France451
TAYLOR,George Gall Lt kia 29-9-18 9HLI p240 CR France663
TAYLOR,George Henry Recknett Capt kia 30-11-17 7Suff p79 MR17
TAYLOR,George Milburn TLt dow 25-5-16 A161RFA p36 CR France43
TAYLOR,George Ossory 2Lt kia 8-10-16 1/5Lond p246 MR21 CR France1890
TAYLOR,George Robert Marmaduke Stanbury Lt dow 30-9-17 295RFA p208 CR Belgium18
TAYLOR,George Stanley 2Lt drd 4-5-17 RASC 905MT Coy p194 CR France1571
TAYLOR,George Thomas T2Lt kia 2-11-17 att1/7Ess p132 CR Palestine8
TAYLOR,George William T2Lt kld 1-10-17 733LabCps p189 CR France285
TAYLOR,George William Lt dow 9-11-17 A150RFA p36 CR Belgium16
TAYLOR,Gerard Bardsley T2Lt kia 24-9-18 11Leic att9DLI p88 CR France835,dow
TAYLOR,Gilbert Elliott Lt ded 13-7-18 4Y&L p272 CR Lancs34
TAYLOR,Gilbert Leslie Frederick Capt dow 26-8-17 3Lond attKRRC p245 CR France64
TAYLOR,Gordon Annesley Capt kia 15-2-15 1Leinst p175 MR29,14-2-15
TAYLOR,Guy Collins Vernon Lt kia 2-10-17 1RWFus p99 MR30
TAYLOR,Guy Hastings Maj mbk 14-11-14 IA 2/39GarhwalRif p283 MR38
TAYLOR,Harold Charles Norman Capt kia 21-5-16 20Lond p251 CR France924
TAYLOR,Harold Harker T2LtACapt drd 11-8-18 LabCps att83ChineseLabCps p189 CR France65
TAYLOR,Harold James 2Lt kia 17-10-18 1EKent p58 MR16
TAYLOR,Harold Richard 2Lt dow 17-3-17 SurrYeo att77MGC p187&205 CR Greece1,Lt
TAYLOR,Harold St.George T2Lt ded 15-4-16 6 att11BordR p118 CR France295
TAYLOR,Harold Victor T2Lt kia 23-8-17 6DCLI p115 MR30
TAYLOR,Harry TLt kia 27-2-16 RE 98FC p48 CR France922
TAYLOR,Harry T2Lt kia 12-10-16 26 att18Manch p156 MR21
TAYLOR,Harry Vivian.MC.Lt kia 22-3-18 17Manch p156 CR France672,Capt
TAYLOR,Helen Batchelor Miss 12-11-15 VAD att4Beds CR Europe1
TAYLOR,Henry TLt dow 9-11-17 12Ess att179MGC p186 CR Palestine1
TAYLOR,Henry Arthur.MC.2LtTCapt kia 27-9-16 RWKent attRFC p4&142 CR France614
TAYLOR,Henry William T2Lt dow 29-5-17 8NumbF p63 CR Belgium102
TAYLOR,Henry Young Cameron Capt ded 25-8-17 RAMC p198 CR Scot241
TAYLOR,Herbert TCapt ded 11-10-15 16KRRC p152 CR Lancs261
TAYLOR,Herbert T2Lt kia 1-4-17 15LancF p93 CR France672

TAYLOR,Herbert Berwick 2Lt kia 31-7-17 4Lond p246 CR Belgium106
TAYLOR,Herbert George Brooks 2Lt kia 16-9-16 1/7Mddx p235 CR France785
TAYLOR,Herbert Hampden TCapt dow 3-4-18 RAMC att4RWFus p198 CR France62
TAYLOR,Herbert Samuel 2Lt kia 28-4-17 O&BLI BucksBn att2/4Bn p232 MR21
TAYLOR,Herbert William Lt ded 12-6-16 2RFA p208 CR Yorks2
TAYLOR,Hugh.MID Capt kia 19-12-14 ScotsGds p52 CR France566,18-12-14
TAYLOR,Hugh Mascie TMaj kia 7-8-15 6RIrFus Ex1Bn p171 MR4,9-8-15
TAYLOR,Ian Cleasby 2Lt kia 4-12-17 7RScots p211
TAYLOR,James T2Lt kia 31-7-17 9BlkW p129 MR29
TAYLOR,James Craik Maj dow 8-6-15 RAMC att4ScotsF p253 CR Gallipoli1
TAYLOR,James Irvine.MC.2Lt kia 28-4-17 3Lincs p76 CR France1194
TAYLOR,James McEwen Thomson.MC&Bar.Lt ded 27-2-19 6CamH p168 CR Scot752
TAYLOR,James Norman.MC.Lt dow 27-7-17 IARO att33Punjabis p283 CR EAfrica38 &CR Tanzania1
TAYLOR,James Wood Colin Lt kia 9-8-15 N&D att2Bn p135 MR29
TAYLOR,John.MC.T2Lt ded 20-9-16 3 att2RScots p262
TAYLOR,John T2Lt dow 13-5-17 RE 233FC p48 CR Belgium11
TAYLOR,John.MC.MM.TLt kia 29-9-18 35MGC Inf p186 MR30
TAYLOR,John Arthur Harold 2Lt kia 24-9-15 1RDubF p177 CR Gallipoli4
TAYLOR,John Birley 2Lt kia 24-12-17 1/4ELancs A'Coy p226 CR France765,25-12-17
TAYLOR,John Cameron.MC.2Lt kldacc 20-9-16 3 att2RScots CR Scot812
TAYLOR,John Edgar 2Lt kld 1-2-17 RE attRFC p210&19,TAYLER CR Staffs156,Lt 6-2-17
TAYLOR,John Edward Middleton T2Lt dow 24-4-17 18Manch p156 CR France214
TAYLOR,John Ogilvie Capt kia 3-5-17 4EKent att1/7Mddx p212 MR20
TAYLOR,John Oswald 2Lt kia 19-4-17 5Beds p219 MR20
TAYLOR,John Tyson 2Lt dow 17-10-18 4SLancs att1/4LNLancs p230 CR France163
TAYLOR,John William Lt kia 12-3-15 1/2Mon p244 CR Belgium33
TAYLOR,John Yates Lt kia 6-7-17 4ELancs attRFC p19&226 CR Belgium112
TAYLOR,Joseph Bertram Lt 28-3-18 GL &RFC MR20
TAYLOR,Joseph Macintyre Lt kia 24-10-18 2A&SH p174 MR16
TAYLOR,Kenneth 2Lt dow 17-6-17 RGA 184SB p42 CR Belgium18
TAYLOR,Leon Eric 2Lt kia 17-2-17 7Beds att54TMB p86 MR21
TAYLOR,Leonard 2Lt kia 27-8-18 3 att2Manch p156 MR16
TAYLOR,Leonard Frank 2Lt kia 14-3-17 1/5SStaffs p229 CR France281
TAYLOR,Leonard William TLtACapt kia 19-2-18 141MGC p186 CR France755
TAYLOR,Leslie Francis.MC.TLt kia 27-5-18 KRRC att8MGC p152&186 MR18
TAYLOR,Leslie Thompson TLt dow 3-6-16 8LNLancs p136 CR France95,Luke
TAYLOR,Matthew Neilson T2Lt kia 27-8-18 MGC Divl Inf p186 CR France1504
TAYLOR,Maurice 2Lt kia 23-3-18 RFus att11Bn p70 MR27
TAYLOR,Maurice Llewellyn 2Lt kia 26-8-16 6 att12RB p180 CR France513
TAYLOR,Maurice William.MC.2Lt kia 12-4-18 4RIrFus p171 MR30,11-4-18
TAYLOR,Merrill Samuel Lt 7-7-18 209RAF MR20
TAYLOR,Nellie Miss ded 27-6-18 VAD BRCS p200 CR France13
TAYLOR,Norman Austin.MC&Bar.Capt dow 26-3-18 1/21Lond p251 CR France40
TAYLOR,Norman Gawan 2Lt kia 24-4-17 3Y&L p159
TAYLOR,Norman Leopold T2Lt dow 18-9-16 19Lpool p73 CR France80
TAYLOR,Norman Robertson.MC.Capt kia 3-5-17 5BlkW p231 MR20
TAYLOR,Percival Harry 2LtTLt kia 13-6-17 2/6LancF p221 CR France765
TAYLOR,Percy Ezra Lt ded 30-3-19 SL RE IWT p201 CR France1571
TAYLOR,Peter 2Lt kia 8-8-16 4 att2ScotRif p104 CR France423,Lt
TAYLOR,Philip Charton Lt kia 15-9-16 2Lond p245 MR21
TAYLOR,Philip Gustave Adolphe T2Lt kia 25-7-17 RE 171Coy p48 CR Belgium5
TAYLOR,Ralph Paton 2Lt kia 10-7-16 3Nhampt att10SWBord p138 CR France397
TAYLOR,Raymond Brewitt.MC.TCapt dow 22-8-18 RAMC att7FA p198&259 see BREWITT-TAYLOR,R.
TAYLOR,Raymond Robert 2Lt ded 19-4-19 2Yorks p263 CR Scot674
TAYLOR,Richard Booksbank Capt kia 30-4-15 BordR p118 CR Gallipoli3,Brooksbank
TAYLOR,Richard Hayward 2Lt kia 20-9-17 8Lond p247 MR29
TAYLOR,Richard Neville T2Lt kia 26-5-16 12EYorks p85 CR France643
TAYLOR,Robert Edward 2Lt kia 17-9-17 41RFC p14 CR France1277,11-9-17
TAYLOR,Robert Edward 2Lt kia 12-10-18 7 att12Manch p237 CR France192
TAYLOR,Robert Fowler 2Lt dow 23-6-18 1/2 att3Glouc Res p107 CR Italy11
TAYLOR,Robert Henry T2Lt dow 13-6-17 RE 102FC p48 CR Lond1
TAYLOR,Robert Leslie 2Lt kia 30-11-17 12Lpool p73 MR17
TAYLOR,Robert Leslie T2Lt dow 11-9-18 Worc 1GarBn att11SLI p110 CR France31,Lester
TAYLOR,Robert Thomson T2Lt kia 22-10-17 6KOSB p102 MR30
TAYLOR,Robert Valentine Capt kia 29-7-18 8RWar att2LNLancs p215 CR France866
TAYLOR,Robert William.MC.Lt dow 24-10-17 8/83RFA p36 CR Belgium16
TAYLOR,Roger Cecil TLt kia 4-10-17 7SStaffs p123 CR Belgium23
TAYLOR,Ronald Francis T2Lt kia 8-8-15 5KSLI p145 MR29
TAYLOR,Ronald Woodhouse T2Lt kia 7-7-16 11NumbF p63 CR France267
TAYLOR,Samuel Alexander T2Lt kia 16-8-17 9RInniskF att109TMB p105 MR30
TAYLOR,Seymour George Frederick Capt kia 20-10-15 2CldGds p51 CR France423
TAYLOR,Sidney Arnold Turner T2Lt dow 17-4-17 12Worc att218MGC p110 CR France145
TAYLOR,Sidney Harold 2Lt kia 4-4-17 3Dors p124 CR France1701,1Bn
TAYLOR,Stanley Gordon 2Lt kia 21-10-16 72/38RFA p36 CR France513
TAYLOR,Stanley Waterman TLt kia 21-3-18 7EKent p58 MR27
TAYLOR,Stuart Campbell.DSO.BrigGen dow 11-10-18 3YLI attStaff 93InfBde p144 CR France25 Ex 15WYorks
TAYLOR,Thomas T2Lt kia 26-3-18 82RFC p17 CR France1242
TAYLOR,Thomas Jesse T2Lt kia 21-3-18 RWKent att52TMB p142 MR20
TAYLOR,Thomas Owen Lt dow 4-11-17 1/5Suff p79 CR Palestine2
TAYLOR,Thomas Ralph Lt kia 7-8-15 6LancF p221 MR4
TAYLOR,Thomas Reekie Morrison 2Lt kia 14-8-18 5RScotF p222 CR France184
TAYLOR,Thomas St Clair Gifford Lt kia 17-3-18 2/10Lond &35RFC p248 CR France446,FltOff
TAYLOR,Vernon TLt kia 15-9-16 7MunstF MGC Inf p186 CR France402
TAYLOR,Vicat Scott 2Lt kld 14-1-17 GL &RFC 10ResSqn p14 CR Lond1
TAYLOR,W.Lt 6-11-18 41MGC Inf CR France934
TAYLOR,Walford Charles Cdr ded 29-7-18 RIM p283 CR Asia82
TAYLOR,Walter 2Lt kia 30-7-16 5GordH p242 MR21
TAYLOR,Walter T2Lt ded 17-7-18 RASC p194 CR Iraq6
TAYLOR,Walter Douglas T2Lt kia 5-7-16 10WRid p116 CR France515
TAYLOR,Whitehead George Edward 2Lt kia 29-9-14 9Lancers p22
TAYLOR,William,Chap3Cl ded 19-10-16 RGA p209 CR Scot398
TAYLOR,William 2Lt kia 18-9-17 4EYorks p272 MR30
TAYLOR,William 2Lt kia 22-9-18 5Glouc p225 CR France1106
TAYLOR,William Alexander TLt kld 10-8-17 GL &RFC p14 CR Scot86
TAYLOR,William Aloysius Capt dow 11-5-15 5SLancs p230 CR France102
TAYLOR,William Anthony TLt kia 31-7-17 166MGC p186 MR29
TAYLOR,William Berrill T2Lt kia 31-7-18 10N&D p135&258 CR France61
TAYLOR,William Bruce T2Lt dow 17-4-17 15 att9Yorks p91 CR France40.2Bn
TAYLOR,William Crookenden TLt dow 5-11-18 13HLI attDivMGC p164&186
TAYLOR,William Currie LtACapt ded 7-11-18 RFA 14DAC p36 CR Scot249
TAYLOR,William Edward 2LtTLt drd 2-6-17 182RASC p194 MR41,482Coy
TAYLOR,William Edward Lt kia 31-7-17 55/33RFA p208 CR Belgium10
TAYLOR,William Ernest Ewart 2Lt kia 27-3-18 3 att13RSuss p120 CR France402
TAYLOR,William Frederick Lt kia 7-6-15 3EKent p58 CR Belgium115
TAYLOR,William Henry SubCdr ded 3-2-15 IA S&TCps p283 CR France145
TAYLOR,William Henry Capt&BtMajTMaj ded 11-2-19 RAVC attStaff p199 CR France134
TAYLOR,William John TCapt ded 1-8-17 8SfthH p165 CR Scot854
TAYLOR,William John Macdonald T2Lt kia 19-12-15 1BordR p118 CR Gallipoli1 Jack
TAYLOR,William Pike 2Lt kia 3-5-17 5Y&L p238 MR20
TAYLOR,William Wadman Capt kia 21-3-18 RASC att2/6N&D p253 MR20
TAYLOR-LOBAN,Gustavus TCapt kld 7-6-17 GL &RFC p14 CR Scot398
TAYLOR WHITEHEAD,George Edward 2Lt kia 29-9-14 9Lancers A'Sqn p22 CR France1337
TAYLOUR,George Ryfield Capt kia 19-10-14 2RWar p66 CR Belgium140
TAYTON,Wilfrid Edward 2Lt kia 10-8-17 Nhampt att6Bn p138 MR29,Wilfred
TEACHER,Norman McDonald.DSO.MajALtCol dow 26-9-17 1/2RScotF p95 CR Belgium84
TEACHER,William George T2Lt kia 14-5-16 15HLI D'Coy p164 CR France702
TEAGUE,Cyril T2Lt kia 4-10-17 SStaffs att1Bn p123 CR Belgium308
TEAGUE,John Gooden Lt kia 3-9-16 RASC att1DCLI p253 MR21 Godden
TEAHAN,John Patrick 2Lt kia 8-10-16 11N&D p135 MR21
TEALBY,Harold Edgar William 2LtACapt kia 5-4-18 6 att7RFus p70 MR20
TEALE,Guy Neville 2LtTCapt kia 20-7-16 20RFC p4 CR France787
TEALE,John Arthur T2Lt dow 27-9-16 11NumbF p63 CR France177
TEAPE,Charles Lewarne T2Lt kia 4-9-16 9Dev p77 CR France402
TEAPE,Cyrud Charles Tulloh Lt ded 26-4-20 IA 21Punjabis p283 MR43,1/26Punjabis
TEARE,John Stewart.MC.TLt kia 3-8-17 108RFA B'Bty p36 MR29

TEASDALE,Eric Henry Janson Lt drd 21-1-17 ASC att1MGC p187&253 CR France102
TEASDALE,Samuel Bird T2Lt kia 31-7-17 10Y&L p159 MR29
TEAZ,Homer Nevin.MC.TLtACapt kia 22-3-18 9YLI p144 CR France511,23-3-18
TEBBITT,I.L.2Lt 4-12-15 19Lond CR Mddx40
TEBBUTT,Arthur Brookes Lt kia 19-4-17 5Norf att163MGC p187&216 CR Palestine8
TEBBUTT,Oswald Nevelle Capt kia 15-3-15 1Camb p244 CR Belgium28,Neville
TEBBUTT,Roger Joseph Capt kia 24-8-18 1Camb p244 CR France430
TEDDER,Oswald Stanley 2Lt kia 27-4-18 8Lincs p76 CR France604,27-4-17
TEDMAN,Basil T2Lt kia 21-3-18 Mddx att13Bn p148 MR27
TEE,Albert Edward 2Lt kia 30-10-17 4Beds C'Coy p86 MR30
TEE,Clifford Vernon 2Lt dow 11-8-18 RGA 153SB p42 CR France34
TEE,Eric William Capt kia 27-3-17 6Ess p232 MR34
TEED,Edmund Maj 25-11-14 5RWSuss CR Sussex178
TEED,Henry Samuel 2Lt kia 24-7-16 1/4RBerks p234 MR21
TEELING,Ambrose Mary Anthony Twibide de Lone Lt kia 24-9-14 3Norf p74 CR France1107
TEELING,Humphrey 2Lt dow 13-10-16 7Norf p74
TEELING,Luke Joseph LtAMaj dow 8-11-18 B87RFA p36 CR France521
TEESDALE,Frank Robinson Maj ded 17-3-16 IA 25Cav attStaff p283 CR Surrey52
TEETON,Percy Randolph.MC.Capt dow 17-10-18 1/6SStaffs p229 CR France146
TEGGART,Francis William Stuart Lt kia 26-10-17 A&SH attGordH p174 CR Belgium115
TEGGART,John Cameron Thomson TCapt kia 21-7-18 RAMC att256RFA p198 CR France1693
TEGGIN,Eugenie Elizabeth SNurse ded 25-12-18 QAIMNS p268 CR Shrop104
TEGLIO,Max T2Lt kia 11-4-17 Dev attWorcs p77 CR Iraq8
TEGNER,Augustus Alfred Becher 2Lt s/iGunshotWound 6-3-18 IARO attS&TCps p283 CR Iraq8
TELFER,Andrew T2Lt ded 15-11-18 Hamps att10Bn p121 CR Greece9
TELFER,Claude William TLt kia 8-11-18 1YLI p144 CR France981
TELFER,Henry Adam TLt kia 1-7-16 YLI att64TMB p144&255 CR France267
TELFER,Leslie Croom T2Lt dow 12-5-16 9 att8Beds p87 CR France102
TELFER,Robert Harold Cecil 2Lt kia 26-9-16 3KOSB attMGC Inf p102 CR France702
TELFER,Somerville Goodman 2Lt kia 8-5-15 12Lond p248 MR29
TELFORD,Carmont Owen 2Lt ded 7-2-19 IA 1/35Sikhs p283 MR43
TELFORD,Hilton Roberts Capt dow 9-9-17 21NumbF p63 CR France446
TELFORD,Robert Bernard Lt ded 21-2-19 RE p262 CR Numb1
TELPER,Richard Greenwell 2Lt kia 7-10-16 4 att12DLI p161,TELFER
TEMPERLEY,Harold Kenyon Lt kia 26-10-17 6 att1/7NumbF p214 MR30
TEMPERLEY,Jesse Hargreaves T2Lt kld 25-10-17 92MGC p186 CR France184
TEMPEST,Basil T2Lt dow 25-4-17 13Manch p156 CR Greece6
TEMPEST,Oswald Aldam Lt kia 28-3-18 RASC att2WYorks p194 MR27,Aidan
TEMPEST,Wilfred Norman TMaj kia 26-9-16 6YLI p144 MR21,2 att9Bn
TEMPEST-HICKS,Charles Edward Henry.MC.Capt dow 9-8-18 16Lancers p23
TEMPLAR,John Franklin Hopwood.MID Capt ded 8-2-19 2RFus p70 CR France34
TEMPLE,Arthur Hilliard William Capt kia 14-12-14 2Suff p79 MR29,Williams
TEMPLE,Edgar 2LtTLt kia 10-9-17 WYorks att12Yorks p83 CR France1461
TEMPLE,Ernest Nelson T2Lt dow 8-4-18 2/7WYorks p83 CR France62
TEMPLE,John Henry 2Lt dow 21-5-18 4EYorks p219 CR France102
TEMPLE,William 2Lt kia 7-6-17 17Lond p250 MR29
TEMPLE,William Arthur Mould Capt dow 23-10-14 1Glouc p107 CR Belgium11,21-10-14
TEMPLEMAN,John Watson 2Lt kia 25-3-18 1LancF p93
TEMPLEMAN,William Henry Lt ded 11-3-19 RAOC p268
TEMPLER,Claude Frank Lethbridge.MID LtACapt kia 4-6-18 1Glouc p107 MR19
TEMPLETON,Archibald Douglas Lt kia 28-6-15 8ScotRif p225 MR4
TEMPLETON,Godfrey Allan 2Lt dow 27-7-18 1/7A&SH p243 CR France1693
TEMPLETON,James Russell 2Lt kia 19-9-18 1 att8RScotF p95 MR37
TEMPLETON,William Fowler Capt kia 1-10-18 4RScotF p222 CR France602
TENCH,Montague Beavan 2Lt kia 10-3-16 9 att5Ess p132 CR France246,10-8-16
TENNANT,Alexander Smith TLt kia 27-9-18 LancF att1/7Bn p93 CR France758
TENNANT,Charles Alan Ramsay(Bunny) 2Lt kia 9-5-15 3Dors att2Dev p124 CR France566
TENNANT,Charles Grant 2Lt kia 9-5-15 4SfthH p241 MR22
TENNANT,Edward Martin Cookes 2Lt dow 16-10-16 4GordH p242 CR France5
TENNANT,Edward Wyndham.Hon.Lt kia 22-9-16 4GrenGds p50 CR France294
TENNANT,George Christian Serocold Lt kia 3-9-17 1WelshGds p53 CR Belgium12
TENNANT,Henry 2Lt kia 27-5-17 2Drags att52RFC p14&21 CR France1486

TENNANT,John Amherst TCapt dow 23-8-15 10Beds att1BordR p86 MR4,22-8-15
TENNANT,John Harold Anthony Lt kld 23-3-21 9Lancers CR Yorks335
TENNANT,Mark Lt kia 16-9-16 ScotsGds attMGC Inf p52 France374,Capt
TENNANT,Philip Eyre 2Lt kia 31-7-17 3ConnRgrs att2Leinst p172 MR29
TENNANT,Robert Edward TCapt kia 28-8-16 6YLI p144 CR France402
TENNENT,Bernard Charles.MC.TLtAMaj kia 22-8-18 RAMC att84FA p198 CR France504,7FA
TENNENT,Oswald Moncreiff 2Lt kia 16-6-15 1WYorks p83 CR Belgium58
TENNYSON,Alfred Aubrey.Hon.Capt kia 21-3-18 4 att9RB p180 MR27,23-3-18
TENNYSON-SMITH,John Alan TLt kia 7-3-17 10RWKent p142 CR Belgium28
TERRAS,James Sutherland T2Lt kia 11-1-17 133MGC Inf p186 MR38
TERRELL,Arthur Clive 2Lt dow 20-4-17 3Mddx p148 CR France40,5 att4Bn
TERRELL,Claud Romako a'Beckett.MC.2LtACapt dow 10-6-17 15RHA p36 CR France113
TERRELL,Frank William Lt kia 3-9-16 8Glouc att3Worc p107 CR France526
TERREY,Harry Leslie LtAMaj dow 22-3-18 RGA 126SB p42 CR France512
TERRIS,William T2Lt dow 3-4-17 2GordH p167 CR France156
TERRY,Charles Edward LtCol ded 11-2-20 Res 5Yorks p272 CR Kent279
TERRY,Harold Millard T2Lt kia 28-6-17 RE 4SpCo p48 MR20 Howard
TERRY,Henry Walter Seymer Lt 22-3-18 2SAfrInf MR27
TERRY,John DepCommsy&Capt ded 9-9-16 IA S&TCps p283 CR Iraq5
TERRY,John Elliott 2Lt ded 16-10-17 RFC p14 CR France145
TERRY,John Norman TCapt dow 20-9-16 6Lond p246 CR France833
TERRY,Leslie Ryder Lt ded 7-8-19 5RWar att 1/5SomLI p256 CR Egypt9
TERRY,Robert Joseph Atkinson.MVO.DSO.Maj kia 3-10-15 2RSuss p120 CR France178,LtCol 1-10-15
TERRY,Sidney Frederic Capt kia 24-3-18 1Wilts p153 MR20
TERRY,Walter John TMaj kia 1-10-15 7Suff p79 MR19
TERRY,William Gregory Capt ded 28-10-16 RGA 36DivArt p42 CR Devon1,Gordon
TERRY,William Gregory Capt dow 27-8-17 2/8LancF p221 CR France1361
TESTI,George T2Lt kia 20-11-17 E'TankCps p189 CR France711
TETLEY,Arthur Calvert T2Lt kia 7-6-17 10WRid p116 CR Belgium127
TETLEY,Clarence Ernest Wand.MID Lt 22-8-15 9LancF MR4
TETLEY,Frederick Noel 2Lt kia 27-9-78 7RWar p214 CR France245
TETLEY,Harold Arthur 2Lt kia 12-4-18 6RWar p214 MR32
TETLEY,John Charlton Lt kia 11-4-18 7DLI D'Coy p239 CR France346
TETLEY,John Christopher Dodsworth Lt kia 9-10-17 3/3GrenGds p50 MR30,Charles
TETLOW,Cyril Lawson Lt kia 22-8-16 RASC attRFC p19&253 CR France727
TETLOW,Joseph TLt kia 25-8-18 KRRC att12Bn p152 CR France578,13Bn
TETLOW,Kenneth Burgess 2Lt kia 21-3-18 7 att2/8Worc p226 MR27
TETLOW,Luke Mallinson Lt kia 29-5-15 1/7WRid B'Coy p227 CR France347,dow 30-5-15
TEUNON,James M.2Lt ded 30-12-18 RFA &RFC p17
TEUNON,M.Lt 4-1-19 RGA attRAF CR Scot378
TEW,Percy T2Lt kld 16-6-17 RFC p14 CR War151
THAANUM,James Conrad T2Lt dow 12-8-15 19RGA 16SB p42 CR France167
THACKER,Herbert Lane 2Lt drd 15-4-17 RASC p194 MR35
THACKER,William Alfred T2Lt kia 12-5-17 7Yorks Ex 5SStaffs p91 MR20
THACKERAY,Frederick Rennel.MC.Lt kia 18-4-15 2WRid p116 MR29
THACKERAY,Frederick Rennell Col ded 15-10-15 RFA 75GdsDiv p36 CR France121
THACKRAY,William Hesling 2Lt dow 26-3-18 5Lancers p22 CR France1063
THAIN,William Skinner T2Lt drd 15-9-18 RWar Res att15Bn p66 CR France13
THARRATT,George Vanes Lt drd 17-11-15 4Lpool p73 MR40
THATCHER,Francis Geoffrey.MC.Capt dow 1-6-18 RAMC DADMS HQ40Div p198 CR France134
THATCHER,George Robin.MC.Lt dow 1-4-18 RGA M'A/ABty p42 CR France103
THAYRE,Frederic James Harry.MC.LtTCapt kld 9-6-17 RFC p14 MR20
THEAK,Horace Leonard 2Lt dow 4-5-17 4Ess p232 CR France8
THEILMAN,Carl Erik Maj kia 24-4-15 4EYorks p219 MR29
THELWALL,Hubert Wallace Maj kia 23-4-16 1WIndiaR att15N&D p192 CR France727
THELWELL,Harry Rowland 2Lt dow 8-7-16 3 att2WRid p116 CR France40
THEOBALD,Arnold.MC.Lt ded 29-6-18 7RScots p211 CR France134
THEOBALD,Frederick George Capt kia 2-9-14 1RLancs p59 MR15,26-8-14
THEOBALD,Reginald.MC.Lt kia 10-4-18 3Suff C'Coy p79 CR France685,11Bn
THEOBALD,Ronald John MacIver Wilson 2Lt kia 21-3-18 5 O&BLI p130 CR France1061
THEODORE-SMITH,Dennis 2Lt kia 30-8-15 RE p48 CR France922

THERON,Lucas Cornelius T2Lt kld 15-7-17 GL &RFC p14 CR Lincs181,dedacc
THESIGER,Frederic Ivor.Hon.2Lt dow 8-5-17 RH&FA 87Bde p36 CR Iraq8,1-5-17
THESIGER,George Handcock.CB.CMG.ADC.MajGen kia 26-9-15 RB Staff Cmdg9ScotDiv p180 MR19
THEW,Frank Atkinson 2Lt kia 12-9-16 2/22Lond p251 CR France157
THEWLIS,Frank.MC.Lt kia 15-9-16 1CldGds p51 MR21
THEWLIS,Harold Darling Lt kia 4-6-15 1/7Manch C'Coy p237 MR4
THEXTON,Percival TCapt ded 20-11-18 RAVC 8MobileVetSec MEF p199 CR France1858
THICKE,Frank Vincent Lt kia 31-10-14 SL att22InfBde p201 MR29
THICKNESSE,Francis William.DSO.CaptAMaj dow 19-10-17 RGA 122HB p42 CR Belgium11
THICKNESSE,John Audley TLtCol kia 1-7-16 Cmdg1SomLI p80 CR France643
THICKNESSE,Raymond Samuel 2Lt kia 10-10-17 4 att2LancF p93 CR Belgium126,9-10-17
THIERRY,Frederick George 2Lt kia 17-9-16 GL &RFC p4&191 CR France439
THIERRY,Leonard Hubert 2Lt kia 10-12-17 GL &15RFC p14,261&267 CR France646
THIERRY,Paul Stanislas.MID Capt 18-2-20 RAVC att317RFA CR Asia9
THILL,John Joseph Lt kia 30-9-15 2Suff p79 MR29
THIMBLEBY,John Egremont 2Lt ded 29-8-15 5Lincs p220 CR Lincs225,Lt kldacc
THIRLBY,Stuart Longston 2Lt kia 22-3-18 6Leics p88 MR27
THIRLWELL,Thomas Albert TLt dow 1-10-17 RE 170TC p48 CR France8,Capt
THIRLWELL,Walter Houlden T2Lt kia 16-8-17 3ESurr att176MGC p186 CR Belgium12,15-8-17
THISTLEWOOD,Percival T2Lt kia 28-8-17 9RB p180 CR Belgium11,dow 25-8-17
THODAY,Albert Eric 2Lt kia 3-5-17 4RFus p70 MR20
THODY,Clarence James Capt kia 30-8-18 8Manch p237 CR France308
THOM,David T2Lt kia 14-9-16 10HLI p164 CR France453
THOM,James Flockhart.MC.Capt dow 27-9-18 Fife&FrfarYeo att17MGC Cav p187&203 CR Syria2
THOM,Laurence Wilson Lt dow 21-4-17 1/8ScotRif p225 CR Egypt2
THOMAS,Albert T2Lt kia 30-5-18 16 att9WelshR p127 MR18
THOMAS,Albert Edward 2Lt kia 17-2-17 3Mon att99MGC p187&244 MR21
THOMAS,Alec Vaughan TCapt kia 6-8-15 11ESurr att2Hamps p113 MR4
THOMAS,Alexander Reginald TCapt kia 3-7-16 10Worc p110 CR France832
THOMAS,Alfred Henry T2Lt kia 21-6-16 15LancF att196TMB p93 CR France702
THOMAS,Alma Cyril Lt dow 8-11-14 RWSurr p56 CR Belgium150,7-11-14
THOMAS,Aneurin Clement Lt ded 13-11-18 RHA p272 CR Wales29,Capt
THOMAS,Arthur Coke T2Lt kia 2-6-16 6 O&BLI D'Coy p130 CR Belgium165
THOMAS,Arthur Crichton AMaj kia 16-11-17 355RGA p42 CR Belgium85
THOMAS,Arthur Hanland,CB.DSO Col ded 8-11-19 RASC p267 CR Hamps146,Havieland
THOMAS,Arthur John Gordon Lt kia 31-5-16 6BlkW p231 CR France15
THOMAS,Arthur Lanham T2Lt kia 11-4-16 9 att7DCLI p115 CR Belgium23
THOMAS,Arthur Laurie Capt dow 30-8-18 20Lond p251 CR France630
THOMAS,Arthur Lewis 2Lt kia 24-4-18 3 att2Nhampt p138 MR27
THOMAS,Arthur Tuder Capt dow 29-9-18 GlamYeo att24RWFus p203 CR France262,Tudor
THOMAS,Arthur William 2Lt kia 8-2-17 IARO att2Sap&Min p283 CR Iraq5
THOMAS,Arthur William Maj ded 9-12-20 IMS p283 CR Iraq6
THOMAS,Aubrey Jocelyn Nugent Capt kia 1-5-15 1LancF p93 CR Gallipoli1,25-4-15
THOMAS,Basil Llewllyn Boyd TLt kia 9-4-17 15RWFus att27MGC p99&186 CR France265
THOMAS,Bryn Atherton Brodie T2Lt kia 16-8-16 13Lpool p73 CR France294
THOMAS,Cecil Rees T2Lt dow PoW 17-8-17 GL &57RFC p14 CR Belgium140
THOMAS,Charles Alexander TCapt kia 23-8-16 16KRRC p152 CR France399
THOMAS,Charles Harold Horatio TLt kia 20-9-17 214MGC Inf p186 CR Belgium310
THOMAS,Charles Herbert.MID Capt dow 5-11-14 2SStaffs p123 CR France102
THOMAS,Charles Humphrey Rittsen Lt dow 16-6-15 3 att2SLancs p126 CR Belgium58,Rittson
THOMAS,Cyril Llewellyn Seymour 2Lt kia 6-9-16 3BordR &RFC p4&118 CR France705,kld
THOMAS,Cyril Raymond T2Lt kia 18-8-18 11 att2SWBord p101 CR France28
THOMAS,Cyril Vaughan 2Lt kia 18-7-17 2RFA p36 CR France115,Lt 21RFA
THOMAS,Daniel Gwyn Lt kia 25-5-15 3RDubF p177 MR29
THOMAS,Daniel Morgan 2Lt 17-11-19 EgyptLabCps CR Europe5
THOMAS,David Arthur T2Lt kia 4-5-17 RWFus p99 MR20
THOMAS,David Cecil Sandby 2Lt kld 16-2-18 3WelshR att57RFC p17&127 CR Egypt8
THOMAS,David Cuthbert 2Lt dow 18-3-16 3RWFus p99 CR France638
THOMAS,David John T2Lt kia 22-4-18 15 att13RWFus p99 CR France339

THOMAS,David Lewis TLt kia 30-3-18 RE 253FC p48 CR France144,2Lt
THOMAS,David Morgan 2Lt ded 15-11-19 LabCps p266
THOMAS,Desmond 2Lt kia 28-6-18 4SLancs &RAF 14N'Wingp272 CR Italy9
THOMAS,Donald James 2Lt kia 21-12-17 2/7Mddx p235 CR Palestine3,Lt
THOMAS,Duncan Collison Willey Capt kia 12-11-14 4A&SH att1GordH p174 MR29
THOMAS,Edward Geoffrey Lt ded 10-10-18 7RWFus p223 CR Shrop93
THOMAS,Edward Palgrave 2Lt kia 9-8-16 7Lpool p215 CR France630,dow
THOMAS,Eric Hand T2Lt ded PoW 18-1-18 2WRid p116 MR20,8-12-17
THOMAS,Eric Lawrence(Dick) TLt kia 18-9-18 13WelshR p127 CR France415
THOMAS,Eric Rowland 2Lt kia 13-6-17 3Mon p244 CR Belgium42
THOMAS,Ernest William Noel T2Lt kia 20-11-17 O&BLI att6Bn p130 MR17
THOMAS,Evan David T2Lt dow 20-4-18 2SWBord p101 CR France180
THOMAS,Evan Llewellyn Lt kia 26-3-17 5RWFus p223 MR34
THOMAS,F.H.Lt 1-8-19 IndMilWksServ MR66
THOMAS,Francis Bernard Vivian Lt kia 22-9-16 4DCLI p227 CR France1887
THOMAS,Francis Stephen Capt kia 16-2-18 16RFC p17 CR France1724
THOMAS,Frank Hender T2Lt kia 1-10-15 RE 175Coy p48 CR Belgium132,Lt
THOMAS,Frank William Henry.MC.Lt dow 5-1-18 1StaffsYeo attRFC p19&205 CR Surrey1
THOMAS,Frederick George Byam Lt kia 6-8-15 1Ess C'Coy p132 CR Gallipoli6
THOMAS,Frederick James 2Lt kia 21-9-17 3 att11WYorks p83 MR30
THOMAS,Frederick Spriggs ACapt dow 21-4-17 1/4WelshR p230 CR Palestine2
THOMAS,Frederick William LtCol dow 26-1-16 IA 9BhopalInf p283
THOMAS,Geoffrey Lynn.MC.Capt kia 6-6-18 95RFA p36 CR France622
THOMAS,Geoffrey Owen 2Lt kia 25-4-18 19LancF p94 MR30
THOMAS,George T2Lt kia 13-11-16 10RWFus p99 MR21
THOMAS,George Oliver Capt kia 26-9-15 2RWFus p99 CR France114
THOMAS,Godfrey Vignolles.Bart.CB.CBE.DSO.MIDx2 BrigGen ded 17-2-19 RFA 24DivArtly p36 CR Essex167
THOMAS,Greville Wynn Lt kia 10-4-18 IA 2/4 att3/3GurkhaRif p283 CR Palestine9
THOMAS,Harold Morris 2Lt kia 10-11-16 4Yorks p220 CR France385
THOMAS,Harry Reid Capt kia 25-12-15 RGA 34SB p42 CR France1106
THOMAS,Heber 2Lt kia 12-10-17 4 att7EKent p212 MR30
THOMAS,Heinrich William Max TCapt kia 1-7-16 1ELancs p111 CR France152
THOMAS,Henry Evan Maj kia 18-4-18 Suff p79 CR Belgium191
THOMAS,Herbert Gordon 2Lt kia 13-11-16 3RWFus p99 CR France156
THOMAS,Honoratus Leigh Murron T2Lt kia 15-9-16 9Beds p87 MR21,8Bn
THOMAS,Horace Wyndham T2Lt kia 3-9-16 14 att16RB p180 MR21
THOMAS,Howard Victor Fraser.MC.Lt kia 22-10-18 3 att11RScots p55 CR Belgium140,Capt
THOMAS,Hugh TLt kia 2-3-17 RFA attY1stTMB p36 CR France692
THOMAS,Hugh Gareth T2Lt kia 30-7-16 8Glouc p107 MR21
THOMAS,Ivan Arthur T2Lt kia 10-5-17 142MGC Infp186 CR Belgium165
THOMAS,James Grant Brandon 2Lt dow 17-11-14 RInniskF p105 CR Lond4
THOMAS,James Leonard Capt kld 28-2-17 3Lond attRFC p19&245 CR Wilts4
THOMAS,James Shepherd T2Lt kia 3-5-17 15WYorks p83 MR20
THOMAS,John Baron Rittson 2Lt kia 18-4-18 4 att2Manch p156 CR France804
THOMAS,John Boaz Lt kia 23-1-18 RFC p17 CR Asia62,Boase
THOMAS,John Clay Lt ded 25-12-19 11WelshR p264CR Asia51
THOMAS,John Dobson T2Lt kld 20-3-18 RFC p17 CR Hamps31
THOMAS,John Mewrig 2Lt kia 22-5-18 3 att2WelshR p127 CR France114,Meung 23-5-18
THOMAS,John Simons T2Lt kia 27-8-17 Lincs p76 CR France1462
THOMAS,John Vick Lt ded 3-12-18 RE p210 MR40
THOMAS,Joseph Henry Lt&QM ded 25-6-19 Ex RWFus p263 CR Sussex93
THOMAS,Kenneth TCapt kia 3-6-16 12KRRC p152 CR Belgium96
THOMAS,Lilian SNurse 14-8-18 QAIMNS CR Lancs14
THOMAS,Lionel George Theophilus 2Lt kia 20-9-17 5WelshR attMGC Inf p187&230 CR Belgium112
THOMAS,Llewellyn 2Lt kia 27-12-17 DenbighYeo att12RWEFus p203 CR Palestine3
THOMAS,Llewellyn Maj&QM ded 29-11-15 6WelshR p230 CR Wales171
THOMAS,Matthew TCapt kia 30-12-15 7LNLancs p136 CR France727
THOMAS,Maurice Wotton Lt kia 5-8-16 RFA &RFC p4&36 MR20
THOMAS,Morgan Lt ded 26-7-19 2SWBord p263 CR Wales95,dow 16-7-19
THOMAS,Noel Lavender 2Lt kia 18-9-18 1 att11RWFus p99 CR Greece5
THOMAS,Oscar Clifford Lt kia 1-12-17 GrenGds att1GdsMGR p50 CR France417
THOMAS,Owen Redrupp 2Lt ded 4-3-19 RE 11DivSig p262 CR Europe51,Lt

310

THOMAS,Owen Richard Capt ded 21-8-17 WelshHorse 54Div p205 CR Palestine2
THOMAS,Philip Edward 2Lt kia 9-4-17 RGA 244SB p42 CR France420
THOMAS,Reginald Ernest 2Lt kia 13-9-18 RGA 193SB p42 CR France729
THOMAS,Reginald Ivor Victor Clifford 2Lt kia 24-11-17 3 att12SWBord p101 MR17
THOMAS,Reginald Percy TLt kia 24-8-18 11 att10SWBord p101 MR16
THOMAS,Reginald Spencer Dudley 2Lt kia 18-9-18 RWFus att25Bn p99 MR16
THOMAS,Rhys Ivor.MC.MID Lt kia 14-9-14 1ConnRgrs p172 CR France1107
THOMAS,Richard Nixon T2Lt dow 23-8-15 9RWFus p99 CR France345
THOMAS,Robert Alfred TMaj ded 3-6-18 15LancF p94 CR France169
THOMAS,Robert Edward Hon2Lt ded 27-11-18 Ex LabCps p266
THOMAS,Robert Newton TCapt kia 23-7-17 GL &RFC p14 MR34
THOMAS,Robert Stanley.MC.T2Lt kia 24-3-18 4Worc p110 CR Belgium22,25-3-18
THOMAS,Rufus Haydon TCapt kia 24-3-18 RAMC att2RScotsF p198 MR20
THOMAS,Rufus William T2Lt kia 9-5-18 16RWFus att113TMB p99 CR France296
THOMAS,Sidney John T2Lt kia 21-9-17 RWKent att10Bn p142
THOMAS,Stanley Meredith 2Lt ded 13-12-18 RFA p209 CR Wales171,Lt
THOMAS,Sydney T2Lt kia 1-7-16 11Suff p79 MR21,Sidney
THOMAS,Sydney Edwin Bailey TLt kia 3-9-16 10 att13RSuss p120 CR France339
THOMAS,T.W.LtCol 26-1-16 9BhopalInf CR Iraq5
THOMAS,Thomas T2Lt kia 10-1-16 16RWFus p99 CR France631
THOMAS,Thomas TLt kia 3-11-16 51MGC Inf p186 CR France374
THOMAS,Thomas TCapt kia 23-8-17 13WelshR p127 CR Belgium23
THOMAS,Thomas Oliver T2Lt kia 10/12-7-16 17RWFus p99 MR21
THOMAS,Trevor Sanby Lt kia 7-4-18 5WelchR p230 CR France804
THOMAS,Tudor T2Lt kia 25-11-17 19RWFus p99 MR17
THOMAS,Walter Edward T2Lt kia 21-9-18 RSuss att16Bn p120 CR France212
THOMAS,Walter Joseph Charles T2Lt dow 22-4-17 11RLancs p59 CR France164
THOMAS,Walter Saunders TCapt ded 15-9-17 NumbF att11GarBn p63 CR Europe1
THOMAS,Wilfred Patrick Otto T2Lt kia 1-7-16 9Y&L p159 CR France246,Wilfrid
THOMAS,William.MM.T2Lt ded 7-11-18 1/2 att1/5ELancs p111 CR France658
THOMAS,William Burton Lt kia 24-10-18 7Worc p225 CR France612
THOMAS,William Edgar.DSO.MC.TMajALtCol kia 20-10-18 7EYorks attBordR p85 CR France1476
THOMAS,William Eric 2Lt kia 31-7-17 118MGC p186 MR29
THOMAS,William Hope 2Lt kia 11-4-18 1Leics attX6TMB p88 MR20,21-3-18
THOMAS,William Humphrey.MC&Bar.MID Capt dow 28-11-17 1/1BerksYeo p203 CR Egypt2
THOMAS,William Norman 2Lt kia 8-4-16 GL KSLI att27RFC p4&191 CR France68,N.W.
THOMAS,William Stanley Lt kia 15-10-16 4 att11Ess p232 MR21
THOMAS-O'DONEL,George O'Donel Frederick.MC.MIDx2 Capt&Adjt kia 16-6-15 4RFus p70 MR29
THOMASIN,Arthur Lt drd 31-12-17 RIM p283 CR Egypt1
THOMASON,Herbert James Bateman T2Lt kia 26-9-17 1/2Leics p88 CR Belgium130
THOMASSET,Gurden Theodore Lt kia 25-9-15 20Lond p251 CR France526
THOMLINSON,John Robert T2Lt kia 8-8-18 4RRofCav att2DragGds p23 CR France526
THOMPSON,A.D.Lt kia 9-3-15 4KAR p268 CR EAfrica12 &CR Tanzania1 Ex DragGds
THOMPSON,Adam Howie 2Lt 7-9-18 4GordH att191RAF CR Hunts90
THOMPSON,Albert Martin T2Lt kia 21-12-15 RFus att1/15Lond p70 MR19
THOMPSON,Alberto Charles.DSO.Maj ded 30-7-19 RDubF p266 CR Lincs69
THOMPSON,Alfred Mussali T2Lt ded PoW 31-7-17 17LancF p94 CR France127,Mussalli dow 3Bn
THOMPSON,Andrew William T2Lt kia 30-5-17 9NStaffs p158 MR20
THOMPSON,Arnold Bosanquet Capt dow 25-12-15 RAMC 1/3ELancsFA p254 CR Gallipoli1
THOMPSON,Arnold Edward Lt 20-9-17 4BrWIndR att26RFus MR29
THOMPSON,Arthur TCapt kia 1-7-16 24NumbF p63 CR France393
THOMPSON,Arthur 2Lt kia 23-10-17 24NumbF attLincs p63 MR30
THOMPSON,Arthur Ernest T2Lt kia 3-9-16 12Lpool p73 MR21
THOMPSON,Arthur George T2Lt kia 2-6-16 14RWFus p99 CR France705
THOMPSON,Arthur Herbert TLtACapt kia 25-9-16 12 att10YLI p144 MR21
THOMPSON,Arthur Herbert 2Lt kia 1-10-16 17Lond D'Coy p250 CR France385
THOMPSON,Aubrey Lloyd Sinclair.MC.LtACapt ded 14-11-17 1Lpool p73
THOMPSON,Brian Wildman-Osborne Capt kia 10-8-15 6LNLancs A'Coy p136 MR4
THOMPSON,C.C.Capt 8-4-19 9Dev CR Staffs84
THOMPSON,Cecil Cuthbert Capt kia 14-7-16 2 att4RInniskF p105 CR France393
THOMPSON,Cecil Victor.MID T2Lt kia 6-2-17 8 att6ELancs p111 MR38

THOMPSON,Cecil William 2Lt dow 6-5-17 3/6LancF att63MGC p187&221 CR France40
THOMPSON,Charles Henry T2Lt kia 3-6-16 2DLI p161 CR Belgium73
THOMPSON,Charles Milburn 2Lt kia 26-8-17 3 att24/27NumbF p63 CR France1461
THOMPSON,Charles John McKinnon Lt dow 27-3-16 1NumbF p63 MR29
THOMPSON,Charles William 2Lt kia 29-6-18 3RWSurr att1EKent p56 CR Belgium3
THOMPSON,Conway Bennett TCapt ded 23-5-16 14Mddx p148 CR Sussex111
THOMPSON,Cyril T2Lt kia 1-6-18 20 att18LancF p94 CR France232
THOMPSON,Cyril James Ockelford Lt dow 25-12-17 18Lond p250 CR Palestine3
THOMPSON,Douglas Blaxland Lt kia 24-10-19 RFA att47RAF p262 CR Asia81
THOMPSON,Edward Homer Boxwell TLt drd 13-8-15 9SomLI attHamps p80 MR4
THOMPSON,Edward James Vibart Collingwood 2Lt dow 10-9-14 3RWFus p99
THOMPSON,Edward Medforth Lt kia 26-2-16 5Yorks p220 CR Belgium5,22-2-16
THOMPSON,Elizabeth Prob kia 1-10-17 TFNS p272
THOMPSON,Ellis T2Lt kia 18-5-17 18DLI D'Coy Ex 4NumbF p161 MR20
THOMPSON,Ernest Edward 2Lt dow 16-10-18 RGA 228SB p42 CR France1392
THOMPSON,Fendall Powney 2Lt kia 1-7-16 1Hamps p121 CR France643
THOMPSON,Francis Clement Lt dow 3-10-17 B59RFA p36 CR Belgium16
THOMPSON,Frank Arthur 2Lt dow 17-8-18 4SfthH p241 CR Surrey76
THOMPSON,Frank Dickinson 2Lt kia 13-1-17 15Lond att17KRRC p249 CR Belgium73
THOMPSON,Frank Samuel Capt kia 23-3-18 17Lond p250 MR20
THOMPSON,Frederic George T2Lt kia 10-4-17 7 att6Beds p87 MR20
THOMPSON,Frederick Charles Maj kia 2-7-16 1/5WYorks p218 MR21
THOMPSON,Frederick Vivian.DSO.MajTLtCol dow 14-10-17 RE att9Ess p48 CR France113
THOMPSON,Geoffrey 2Lt kia 3-9-16 IARO 2S&M attRE 179TC p283 CR France430
THOMPSON,George Lt 16-1-15 RGA 2HB CR Devon2
THOMPSON,George Cyril 2Lt dow 24-10-15 6LancF p221 CR Gallipoli1
THOMPSON,George Eric T2Lt kia 3-9-16 12Lpool p73 MR21
THOMPSON,George Masterman Lt kia 22-8-14 1RScots attGoldCoastR p55&202 CR WAfrica5
THOMPSON,George Samuel Rodie 2Lt kia 14-9-14 2KRRC p152 MR15
THOMPSON,Gerald Pittis Newman Lt kia 4-5-18 1 att8RDubF p177 CR France353
THOMPSON,Gilbert Capt&Adjt kia 24-2-15 ConnRgrs att13Lond p172 CR France707
THOMPSON,Harold 2Lt kia 9-5-15 3 att1Nhampt p138 MR22
THOMPSON,Harold.DSO.TLtCol dow 22-4-17 1 att1/4RScotF p95 CR Egypt2
THOMPSON,Harold T2Lt kia 29-9-18 EKent p58 CR France212
THOMPSON,Harold Blundell Lt kia 2-10-17 RH&FA Staff Lt HQ 29Div Art p36 CR Belgium12
THOMPSON,Harold Eustace 2Lt dow 7-10-16 RFA 23Div X22TMB p36 CR France177
THOMPSON,Harold Francis TCapt kia 12-7-16 9 att12RB p180 CR Belgium5
THOMPSON,Harold Victor 2Lt kia 26-9-17 GL &29RFC p14 MR20
THOMPSON,Hector 2Lt dow PoW 18-9-16 RFC p4 CR France439
THOMPSON,Henry 2Lt 11-6-18 103RAF MR20
THOMPSON,Henry Cedric St.John.DSO.LtACapt dow 30-11-17 2CldGds p51 CR France439,1-12-17
THOMPSON,Henry Herbert Capt 2-1-18 ArmyPayDept Mid CR Hamps1
THOMPSON,Henry Norman 2Lt kia 22-3-18 9 att12RInniskF p105 MR27
THOMPSON,Herbert.MID Capt kia 28-3-18 7DLI p239 CR France700
THOMPSON,Herbert Balfe TCapt kia 18-9-16 Lincs p76 CR France251
THOMPSON,Herbert Henry Capt ded 2-1-18 ArmyPayDept p268
THOMPSON,Herbert Richard TLt ded 3-5-18 Beds 2GarBn p87 MR43,Capt
THOMPSON,Herbert William 2Lt kia 1-7-16 10 att11ELancs p111 MR21
THOMPSON,Horace Brockbank.MC.2Lt kia 24-4-17 7RBerks p140 MR37
THOMPSON,Hubert Roberts 2Lt dow 30-6-18 RGA 99SB p42 CR France31
THOMPSON,Ivan Frank Ross LtCol kia 26-1-17 IA Cmdg26Punjabis p283 CR Iraq5
THOMPSON,J.TLt kia 11-3-17 GL &45RFC p14 CR Belgium11
THOMPSON,J.Capt 20-11-20 Manch CR Ireland33
THOMPSON,James Ambrose 2Lt kia 18-10-16 3 att2Wilts p153 MR21
THOMPSON,James Reginald Walter T2Lt dow 22-3-18 RFC p17 MR20
THOMPSON,James William 2Lt dow 8-8-18 12/13NumbF CR France145
THOMPSON,John.DCM.Lt kia 16-10-16 GL &RFC p4&191 CR France245
THOMPSON,John Cecil Caster 2Lt kia 25-1-15 att1ScotsGds p52 MR22
THOMPSON,John Crawford 2Lt kia 21-3-18 5 att1RIrRif p170 MR27
THOMPSON,John Henry Louis Lt dow 17-9-14 WRid p116 CR Belgium201

THOMPSON,John Oscar 2Lt dow 9-8-16 1/5SLancs p230 MR21

THOMPSON,John Wycliffe 2Lt 5-7-19 7DragGds CR Essex132

THOMPSON,Jonah George 2Lt kld 19-5-17 RFC p14 CR C'land&W'land98

THOMPSON,Joseph.MC.TLtACapt kia 25-10-18 121RFA p36 CR France1391

THOMPSON,J.W.2Lt dow 8-8-18 12/13NumbF p63

THOMPSON,Leslie Northcote 2Lt kia 2-12-17 1/5Lond p246 MR17

THOMPSON,Lloyd Maurice 2Lt kia 25-1-17 7NStaffs p158 CR Iraq9

THOMPSON,M.H.2Lt dow 28-11-14 RWKent p142 CR Hamps173,29-11-14

THOMPSON,Matthew Arnold 2Lt kia 21-3-18 3 att2NumbF p63 MR27

THOMPSON,Morice Bell TLt kia 3-5-17 8MGC p186 MR20

THOMPSON,N.2Lt 5-8-16 17DLI CR France430

THOMPSON,Neville Rudd Lt kia 5-9-15 21Lancers p23 MR43

THOMPSON,Offley Charles Wycliffe Lt kia 20-9-14 1WYorks p83 MR15

THOMPSON,Patrick Stapler.MC.Lt kia 27-4-18 RE 466FC p210 CR France109

THOMPSON,Percy Laughorn T2Lt kia 16-6-17 14DLI p161 CR France115,Langhorn 12-6-17

THOMPSON,Peter Cleasby Lt ded 4-3-19 SL 1NigeriaR p201&202 CR WAfrica41

THOMPSON,Peter Lettice TLt kia 8-8-18 8NStaffs Res p158 CR France33,THOMSON 2Lt

THOMPSON,Philip Capt kia 23-3-18 22RFC p17 CR France245

THOMPSON,Philip Aloysius Xavier Murray 2Lt kia 21-8-15 3 att1RInnisF p105 MR4

THOMPSON,Reginald TLt kia 23-10-16 2ELancs att7Bn p111 MR21

THOMPSON,Reginald Paul 2Lt dow 9-8-16 3SomLI p80 CR Belgium11,1Bn

THOMPSON,Richard Lt dow 20-10-17 2/4ELancs p226 CR France64

THOMPSON,Richard Henry Vaughan.MID TCapt kia 26-9-16 11RFus p70 CR France702 see VAUGHAN THOMPSON,R.H.

THOMPSON,Richard Seward 2Lt kia 16-1-17 18Lond att2/2Lond p250 MR20,16-7-17

THOMPSON,Robert.MC.2Lt kia 26-10-17 7NumbF p214 MR30

THOMPSON,Robert Ellerton 2Lt 1-10-18 80RAF MR20

THOMPSON,Robert Lloyd.MC.LtAMaj kia 1-12-17 C173RFA p36&259 CR France530

THOMPSON,Roger Eykyn Capt kia 12-4-18 15 att2Hamps p203 MR32

THOMPSON,Ronald Fawcett Carrier 2Lt kia 11-9-16 GrenGds SR att4Bn p50 CR France294,TOMPSON Lt

THOMPSON,Ronald William 2Lt kia 11-4-18 1Mon p244 MR20

THOMPSON,Ross Col 5-12-19 RE att2S&M MR66

THOMPSON,Samuel Frederick Henry.MC.DFC.Capt 27-9-18 22RAF MR20

THOMPSON,Stanley TCapt kia 15-9-16 15Hamps p121 CR France188

THOMPSON,Sydney Richmond 2Lt 30-5-20 NumbF CR Durham19

THOMPSON,Thomas John Chichester Conyngham.DSO.Capt kia 24-3-18 4RIrF att2RIrRif p171 MR27

THOMPSON,Walter Capt kia 6-8-15 17DLI att6Manch p161 MR4

THOMPSON,Walter Albert 2Lt ded 8-9-17 10ELancs p111 CR Surrey150

THOMPSON,Walter Lincoln 2Lt kia 9-10-17 3 att2Ess p132 MR30

THOMPSON,Walton Downing Lt dow 2-9-18 3RWFus att1/6HLI p99 CR France145

THOMPSON,Warren Stanley Capt ded 2-9-19 RAVC CR Canada99 p268

THOMPSON,Wilfred Albert 2Lt dow 21-8-17 1/5Lincs p220 CR France80,24-8-17

THOMPSON,Wilfred Bernard T2Lt kia 8-10-18 LNLancs att1/4Bn p136 MR16 att5Bn

THOMPSON,Wilfred John 2Lt kia 31-7-17 7 att10Ess p232 CR Belgium310

THOMPSON,Wilfred Taylor TLt kia 26-9-15 14DLI p161 MR19

THOMPSON,William Frank TLt dow 1-1-16 RAMC 99FA p198 CR France80

THOMPSON,William George Lt kia 14-7-17 5Suff attRFC p19&217 CR France245,Capt

THOMPSON,William John T2Lt kia 26-3-18 6RInniskF p105 CR Palestine3

THOMPSON,W.S.Lt 16-4-20 2GurkhaRif CR Devon33

THOMPSON-HOPPER,James,MC.TLt kia 30-6-16 20DLI p161 CR Belgium137

THOMPSON-McLAUGHLIN,Lee 2Lt kld 19-4-17 4WYorks &RFC p14&83,ded

THOMPSON-SMITH,Kingsley 2Lt kia 23-3-18 11RWKent p142 MR20

THOMSON,Adam 2Lt kia 17-5-18 1/4RLancs p213 CR France106

THOMSON,Alan Graham Lt kia 26-9-17 7RScots p211 MR30

THOMSON,Alexander T2Lt dow 21-4-16 10SfthH p165 CR Iraq5,22-4-16

THOMSON,Alexander Lt kia 22-7-19 IA 3/9BhopalInf attJindInf p283 MR43

THOMSON,Alexander Henry Gouger.DSO.LtCol ded 2-8-18 IA 30Punjabis p283 MR66

THOMSON,Alfred Maurice.MID Capt kia 7-6-16 RAMC att7RSuss p198 MR21

THOMSON,A.L.C.MC.Capt 14-11-17 Lpool CR Hereford/W182

THOMSON,Archibald Walton TLt kia 3-5-17 12RScots p55 MR20,Walter

THOMSON,Arthur Stewart 2Lt dow 15-9-16 7Lond p247 MR21

THOMSON,Arthur Yalden Graham.MC&Bar.Capt kia 30-11-17 CamH attStaff p168 CR France1182

THOMSON,Charles.MC&Bar.Capt kia 2-9-18 7 att2ELancs p111 CR France184,1-9-18

THOMSON,Cyril Ground.MC.Capt kld 22-9-18 WSomYeo att12SomLI p205 CR France1495

THOMSON,David.MC.2Lt mbk 26-11-17 14HLI p257 MR17

THOMSON,David 2Lt ded 1-5-19 9RB p255 CR Notts106

THOMSON,Donald Godrid Campbell Lt kia 31-10-14 2Beds p87 MR29

THOMSON,Douglas Gordon 2Lt kia 30-11-17 10RB p180 MR17

THOMSON,Edmund Peel Maj kia 21-12-14 RMunstF attRIrReg p176 MR22

THOMSON,Edward B.Lt 17-4-20 116/26RFA MR66

THOMSON,Elizabeth Miss kia 30-9-17 VAD BRCS att58GH p200 CR France134

THOMSON,Elizabeth Robertson Sister ded 26-10-18 QAIMNS CR Scot249

THOMSON,Eric James Lt kia 28-6-15 7RScots p211 MR4

THOMSON,Ernest Anderson T2Lt kia 6-11-17 14BlkW p129 CR Palestine1

THOMSON,Francis Wishart 2Lt kia 28-6-15 7RScots C'Coy p211 MR4

THOMSON,Frederick Stanley Capt kia 1-7-16 14Lond att69MGC p187&249 MR21

THOMSON,George 2Lt kia 11-9-16 9A&SH p244 CR France294

THOMSON,George Alastair St.Clair Capt dow 21-7-16 3 att2A&SH p174 CR France23,Sinclair

THOMSON,George Burrell Lt dow 12-7-17 Nhampt p138 MR31

THOMSON,George Ewan Christian 2Lt kia 18-11-17 3 att1BlkW p129 MR30,19-11-17

THOMSON,George Frederick Maynard T2Lt dow 19-5-17 11Lpool p73 CR France214

THOMSON,George Vallance Bruce 2Lt kia 22-3-18 10 att15RScots p212 MR20

THOMSON,Haldane Lt kia 4-6-15 12ScotRif att1KOSB p104 CR Gallipoli2

THOMSON,Henry George Allen Maj dow 28-3-17 RWar Staff 15Div p66 CR France255

THOMSON,Henry Thomas TLt dow 26-9-15 7SStaffs p123 CR Lond4

THOMSON,James TCapt kia 25-9-15 10HLI p164 CR France114

THOMSON,James Capt kia 31-8-17 5BordR p228

THOMSON,James Capt&Adjt 31-10-17 1BordR CR Belgium13

THOMSON,James.MID Maj ded 26-11-17 RGA 130SB p42 CR Greece2

THOMSON,James Thomson HonMaj&QM ded 10-3-18 2NumbF p262 CR Numb7

THOMSON,James.MM.2Lt mbk 21-3-18 6BlkW p257 MR20

THOMSON,James 2Lt kia 22-8-18 4GordH p242 CR France745

THOMSON,James Albert Raymond.DSO.LtCol kia 27-5-18 5Yorks p220 CR France1329

THOMSON,James Pringle TLt dow 15-8-16 6CamH p168 CR France44

THOMSON,James Scott Capt kia 5-5-17 14Lond A'Coy p249 CR France531

THOMSON,James Stein T2Lt kia 22-7-18 1/2WRid att1/7LancF p116 CR France5

THOMSON,James Walter Stewart Lt kia 12-4-18 4GordH att154TMB p241 MR19

THOMSON,J.H.2Lt 9-10-18 5A&SH &107RAF CR Belgium205

THOMSON,John 2Lt kia 18-6-17 5Lpool p215 CR Belgium10,17-6-17

THOMSON,John Lt 27-10-18 CanadaEngrs &N'Flt RAF MR20

THOMSON,John Lt ded 25-2-19 RE &RAF p255 CR Scot115

THOMSON,John Morrison Lt accdrd 26-3-21 1/3KAR CR SAfrica53

THOMSON,John Murray 2Lt kia 21-9-18 4RScots p211 CR France1496

THOMSON,John William Lt ded 4-2-19 RGA att55FdSurvey RE p262 CR Scot274

THOMSON,Kenneth Clarke.MID Lt dow 31-12-14 2RScotF p95 CR France345

THOMSON,Kenneth Douglas T2Lt kia 18-7-16 10A&SH p174 CR France164

THOMSON,Kenneth Sinclair Lt kia 3-3-15 IA 21Cav att16 p283 CR Iraq6

THOMSON,Leslie Charles TLt kia 31-7-17 4Mddx p148 MR29

THOMSON,Minnie Bailey SNurse 18-9-14 TFNS att2GH

THOMSON,Peter McLellan TMaj kia 24-12-15 5HLI p240 CR Gallipoli3

THOMSON,Peter Walls 2Lt kia 24-7-16 RGA 109SB p209 CR France397

THOMSON,Reginald Gresham.MC.MID LtACapt dow 18-9-18 1KSLI A'Coy p145&259 CR France327

THOMSON,Richard Edward John Lt kia 19-5-15 IA 15Sikhs p283 CR France924

THOMSON,Robert Lt dow 20-9-19 10RScots p256 CR Scot247,2Bn

THOMSON,Robert Thoresby 2Lt kia 8-6-17 7Mddx att4Lincs p235 MR20

THOMSON,Ronald T2Lt dow 27-1-17 RE 185TC p48 CR France1

THOMSON,Rowley Stuart Lt ded 1-11-20 IARO att1DForce p283

THOMSON,Samuel Andrew 2Lt 5-9-18 60RAF MR20

THOMSON,Samuel Pestell Donald Lt kld 13-5-15 1/1LeicsYeo p204 MR29 &CR Belgium453

THOMSON,Spencer.MC.TLt kia 24-4-17 14 att2RFus p70 MR20

THOMSON,Stewart Armour Lt dow 24-9-18 SNottsHuss att100MGC Inf p187&205 CR France194

THOMSON,Sydney James Kerr.MID 2Lt dow 12-10-15 3 att1RScotF p95 CR France64

THOMSON,Thomas Lt kia 25-4-17 7A&SH &RFC p19&243 CR France421
THOMSON,Walter Halton 2Lt kia 3-7-16 3HLI p164 CR France293
THOMSON,Wardlaw Ivor T2Lt kld 6-6-17 GL &RFC 27ResSqn p14 CR Lond3
THOMSON,Wilfrid Burrell.MC.Capt mbk 25-3-17 2Dors p257 MR38
THOMSON,William.MC.T2Lt dow 12-4-18 15HLI p164 CR France169
THOMSON,William Lt dow 26-8-18 4 att2KOSB p223 CR France84
THOMSON,William James 2Lt dow 18-11-16 3 att1CamH p168 CR France177
THOMSON,William Robinson Ketchen 2Lt kia 16-10-17 RGA 23HB p42
THONEMANN,Emil Howard 2Lt kia 3-5-17 RFA 13Bty 17Bde p36 MR20
THORBURN,Christopher Cowan 2LtTLt kia 14-6-17 1GordH p167 MR20
THORBURN,Edward Francis Capt kia 23-3-15 12RScots p55 MR27
THORBURN,Edward Francis Lt dow 10-6-15 6Manch p236 MR4
THORBURN,James Capt kia 11-2-17 RGA attRFC p19&209 CR France924
THORBURN,James Walker 2Lt dow 12-3-17 6CamH p168 CR France158
THORBURN,John Morgan TCapt dow 7-8-17 32RFus p70 CR France139
THORBURN,Thomas Orr Lt kia 13-4-18 6ScotRif p224 CR France324
THORBURN,V.TallyClk 16-10-17 S&T Cps CR Iraq6
THORBURN,Walter Ernest.TD.Capt ded 22-1-19 8RScots p256 CR Scot671
THORBURN BROWN,Thomas Elliot Lt dow 20-9-18 3KOSB CR France512
THORBY,Charles Frederick 2Lt kia 30-3-18 11/612NZBn ImpCamelCps MR34
THORLAND,V.S.T2Lt ded 22-7-18 RE 7CpsHQ p262 CR France134,Lt
THORLEY,Gordon Lt dow 7-11-18 1/10Manch p237 CR France929 &CR France955
THORLEY,Horace William 2Lt dow 8-10-18 17Lancers p23 CR France652,8-8-18
THORLEY,William Bowers T2Lt dow 20-4-18 8NStaffs p158 CR France64
THORMAN,Alan Marshall 2Lt kia 1-7-16 1/2Lond p245 MR21
THORMER,Harry T2Lt kld 30-12-17 90MGC p186
THORN,Dudley Oswald Lt kia 7-8-18 5Suff att2/4Berks p217 CR France346
THORN,Harold Lewis 2Lt kia 15-6-17 20Lond p251 CR France581
THORN,Humphrey 2Lt dow 13-10-16 3 att7Norf p74 CR France833
THORN-DRURY,J.G.Lt 12-3-20 1EKent CR Kent37
THORNALLAY,Allatt Barber 2Lt kia 1-7-17 6SStaffs p229 CR France662,THORNALLEY 2/5Bn
THORNBACK,Leonard Thomas Lt ded 2-5-18 29MGC p266 CR France24
THORNDIKE,Francis Herbert Lt dow 17-8-17 LincsYeo att11RFC p19&204 CR France113
THORNE,Charles Everard.MC.T2Lt dow 16-8-17 RE 150FC p48&258 CR Belgium8
THORNE,Cornelius TCapt kia 30-9-16 8ESurr p113 MR21
THORNE,Foster Newton MajTLtCol kia 18-4-17 1RSuss Cmdg6LNLancs p120 MR38
THORNE,Guy Stafford 2LtTCapt ded 18-3-17 13RFC p14 MR20
THORNE,Harold Underhill Hatton ALtCol kia 9-4-17 4Berks att12RScots p234 CR France97
THORNE,Henry Cyril TLt kia 27-6-16 1RBerks p140 CR France161
THORNE,John Parry Lt kia 1-7-16 5SStaffs p229 MR21
THORNE,Marlborough 2Lt kia 28-9-15 8ESurr D'Coy p113 CR France189,27-9-15
THORNE,Norman John 2Lt kia 12-5-17 8Hamps att52MGC CR France97
THORNE,Sigmund Alexander Oscar T2Lt ded 22-12-16 17WYorks CR Sussex111 p263
THORNE,Sydney Charles 2Lt kia 24-4-17 10Dev p77 MR37
THORNE,Thomas Bezly Houghton LtCol kia 21-3-18 2/6NStaffs p238 CR France690,Bezley
THORNE,Thomas Fleetwood Joseph Nicol Capt kia 27-9-15 4GrenGds p50 MR19
THORNE,William Anthony Laroque Capt ded 7-8-18 2RLancs p59 CR Greece4
THORNELY,Maurice T2Lt kld 3-12-16 Nhants &RFC p4&138 CR Yorks178
THORNER,H.A.M 2Lt 30-12-17 90MGC CR Belgium19
THORNHILL,Charles Massy.DSO.MC.Maj ded 19-6-19 IA 24Punjabis attStaff p283 MR67
THORNHILL,Geoffrey Holland Lt ded 10-5-17 3RWar att3LabCps p66 CR Herts84
THORNHILL,George Robert Lt kia 22-10-14 1EKent p58 MR32
THORNHILL,Hubert Burrington LtACapt ded 25-3-19 1Dev &TMB att2RWKent p77 CR Iraq6
THORNHILL,John Evelyn.DSO.BtLtCol ded 2-10-18 SfthH attStaff p165 CR Europe23
THORNHILL,William Ewart T2Lt kia 4-10-17 1/2ELancs p111 MR30
THORNILEY,Percy Arthur Henry.MC.TCapt kia 11-1-17 21Manch p156 CR France221
THORNLEY,Arthur Lincoln TLt ded 12-4-16 RAMC p198 CR Lancs256
THORNLEY,Henry TLt dow 19-12-16 11Manch p156 CR France339
THORNLEY,John Dales.MC.T2Lt kia 24-10-18 8 att6EKent p58 CR France1147,25-10-18
THORNLEY,Reginald Tom Lt kia 1-10-18 1/5LNLancs p234 MR16

THORNS,Francis Joseph T2Lt dow 31-5-16 5RBerks p140 CR France178
THORNSBY,Harold Stansfield T2Lt kia 24-8-18 10WYorks Ex 12Y&L p83 MR16
THORNTON,Claude Arthur Muir 2Lt kia 27-5-18 8WYorks att5DLI p219 CR France1753,Lt 7Bn
THORNTON,Cyril T2Lt kld 5-10-17 GL &RFC p14 CRWar7
THORNTON,Douglas Saville T2Lt kia 1-10-16 11N&D p135 MR21
THORNTON,Francis Arthur TCapt ded 18-11-17 RE 171TC p49 CR Belgium18
THORNTON,Frank T2Lt kia 1-7-16 7EYorks C'Coy p85 CR France373
THORNTON,Frank Cecil T2Lt kld 15-7-16 11Leics p88 CR Belgium1
THORNTON,Frederick Edward Maj kia 25-3-17 IA 105MahrattaLI p283 MR38
THORNTON,George Muir TCapt kia 22-8-17 8SfthH p165 MR30
THORNTON,George Rowland Hart 2Lt kia 9-4-18 RGA 16HB p42 MR19
THORNTON,Godfrey St.Leger.DSO.Maj ded 4-2-18 RFA p36 CR Notts84
THORNTON,Harold James 2Lt ded 25-9-17 RFC p14 MR40,23-9-17
THORNTON,Hedley Thomas 2Lt ded 25-1-16 5RWKent p235 CR Kent82
THORNTON,Herbert Boucher 2Lt kia 9-7-17 9Lond attMGC p187&248 CR Belgium77
THORNTON,James 2Lt kld 9-11-16 RScots &RFC p4&55 CR Scot279
THORNTON,John McLaren TLt kia 20-1-16 RE p49 MR32
THORNTON,John William T2Lt dow 27-3-18 2/4Y&L p159 CR France225
THORNTON,Joseph Henry Banks T2Lt kia 22-9-18 LabCps att23LancF p189 CR France263
THORNTON,Leonard Neville 2Lt kia 22-7-16 11 att10Glouc p107 MR21
THORNTON,Leslie Irvine Lumsden Lt kia 9-9-15 IARO att16Cav p283 CR Asia82
THORNTON,Noel Shipley.DSO.MC.LtTMaj dow 10-4-18 6 att7RB p180 CR France52
THORNTON,Reginald George 2Lt kia 5-9-17 20Lond p251 MR29
THORNTON,Robert West.MID Lt kia 16-6-15 4RFus p70 MR29
THORNTON,Sidney Percy TCapt dow 5-12-16 11Leics A'Coy p88 CR France80
THORNTON,Stanislaw Bonaventure T2Lt kia 29-7-16 2SStaffs p123 MR21,Stanislaus 28-7-16
THORNTON,Victor Hubert TCapt kia 24-10-18 GL 9NumbF p191 CR France739
THORNTON,Wilfred Thomas 2Lt kia 30-7-16 7BlkW p231 MR21
THORNTON-SMITH,Arthur Donald.DSO.MID TLtACapt kia 16-8-17 12KRRC p152 MR30
THORNTON-VARLEY,Charles Richard 2Lt dedacc 25-5-15 RGA p272 CR Yorks2
THORNYCROFT,Edward Gerald Mytton Lt kia 15-9-14 RLancs attKAR p59&202 CR EAfrica43,Capt 12-9-14
THORNYCROFT,John Ralph Mylton Capt kia 21-10-14 3 att1RWSurr p56 MR29
THOROGOOD,Edward Linford Lt dow 3-9-18 8LancF p221 CR France298
THOROWGOOD,Leslie Vernon TCapt kld 22-3-18 RFC p17 CR Wilts3
THOROWGOOD,Rowland William Theodore.MC.TLt kia 7-8-18 11RWar p66&259 CR France412,1Bn
THORP,Austin.CMG.DSO.LtCol kia 30-10-18 RGA att82RFA p42 CR France716
THORP,Edward Henry Courtenay LtACapt kia 21-8-18 1Dev p77 CR France798
THORP,Frederick Horace 2Lt dow 31-3-18 10Manch attRFC p20&237 CR France95,Lt
THORP,Henry Guy Hanwing 2Lt dow 13-3-15 3YLI p144 CR France284,Hanning
THORP,Henry Thomas TLt kia 21-2-18 RFC p17 CR Palestine3
THORP,John Eric 2Lt kia 3-5-17 7WRid &186LtTMB p228 CR France646
THORP,Leslie 2Lt kia 16-11-16 10RFus p70 MR21
THORP,Robert Oakley Vavasour.MC.2Lt kia 22-3-18 3NumbF att64TMB p63 CR France669,1Bn
THORP,Thomas Tudor 2Lt kia 16-8-17 D83RFA p36 CR Belgium125
THORP,Walter Twiss Lt kia 28-3-18 1/7Manch p237 CR France927,T.W.
THORPE,Albert Edward T2Lt ded 6-12-18 Yorks att11EYork p91 CR France134
THORPE,George Robert Capt dow 25-4-17 1HAC p206 CR France113
THORPE,Herbert Gordon.MC.2Lt mbk 24-3-18 1Lpool A'Coy p257 CR France307,Lt kia
THORPE,John Somerled.MC.Maj kia 15-9-16 ScotsGds att2Bn p52 CR France513
THORPE,Norman John 2Lt kia 12-5-17 8Hamps attMGC p187&229
THOULESS,Archibald Cecil T2Lt kia 26-4-16 10Norf &RFC p4&74 MR38,9Bn
THOYTS,Francis Gordon Grant Maj dow 26-8-14 1SomLI p80 MR15
THRELFALL,Herbert Edward 2LtTLt dow 4-11-17 266RFA p36 CR Palestine1
THRELFALL,John Alexander 2Lt dow 10-5-18 9Lpool p216 CR France100,Lt
THRESHER,Oswald Lt dow 2-10-18 RE p210 CR Palestine11
THRIFT,Sydney Henry 2Lt kia 15-7-16 10Ches p97 MR21
THRING,Ashton Edward 2Lt ded 9-2-17 D1RFA p209 CR Beds66
THROCKMORTON,Richard Courtenay Brabazon TLtCol kia 9-4-16 8RWFus Cmdg3Wilts p153 MR38,5Bn
THROSSELL,Horace Claude Sharman 2Lt kia 17-3-17 9Suff p79 CR France423

THRUPP,Maurice Lt kia 31-7-17 1GrenGds p50 CR Belgium106
THRUSTON,Bertie John.DSO.CaptTMaj ded 22-11-18 Lincs attWAfrR p76&202 CR WAfrica30
THUELL,William Johnson T2Lt kia 22-10-16 GL &RFC p4&191 MR20
THUILLIER,George Fleetwood.MC.LtACapt kia 26-3-18 2Dev p77 CR France1472
THUNDER,Michael Hubert Francis 2Lt kia 23-9-16 RFC p4 CR Kent29,24-9-16
THURBURN,Augustus Edward Charlie Sedgwick 2LtACapt kia 28-5-17 9Ess att3KRRC p132 CR Greece9 A.E.S.C.
THURBURN,Eric James Ptolemy 2Lt kia 9-4-17 3ScotRif att16RScots p104 MR20,Erik
THURGAR,Ralph William.MC.Capt kia 19-4-17 1/4Norf p216 CR Palestine8
THURGOOD,Ernest Fuller TCapt kia 31-5-18 16Ches p97 CR France1689
THURLOW,Arthur Geoffrey T2Lt dow 29-8-15 8WRid p116 CR Egypt3,Lt&Adjt
THURLOW,Geoffrey Robert Youngman 2LtTLt kia 23-4-17 13 att10N&D C'Coy p135 MR20
THURLOW,John Kennings 2Lt kia 24-4-18 10Lpool p216 MR19
THURNELL,William Cornelius Gibson 2Lt dow 16-9-16 7Lond p247 CR France177
THURSBY,Arthur Delves TCapt kia 15-2-15 KRRC p152 MR29
THURSTON,Arthur AssCommsy&Lt ded 29-7-16 IndOrdDept p283 CR Iraq6
THURSTON,Hugo Champneys.CB.CMG.Col ded 17-8-19 RAMC p267 CR Glouc190
THWAITES,Guy.DSO.Maj ded 30-5-17 RASC p194 MR34 &CR EAfrica116
THWAITES,Marmaduke LtTCapt kia 30-9-15 Yorks p91 MR19
THWAITES,Robert Capt dow 28-6-17 1/4ELancs p226 CR France755
THWAITES,Robert.MID TCapt kia 24-3-18 22DLI p161 MR27
THWAYTES,John 2Lt kia 18-3-17 BordR att4RFC p14&118 CR France614
THYNNE,Algernon Cateret.DSO.LtCol kia 6-11-17 NDevYeo p203 CR palestine1
THYNNE,Lord Alexander George.DSO.LtCol kia 14-9-18 Cmdg6Wilts p206 CR France80
TIBBS,B.E.Lt ded 9-1-18 SL RE IWT p262 MR38
TIBBS,Robert Dunham Lt drd 30-12-15 IARO att39GarhwalRif p283 MR41
TIBBS,Thomas 2Lt kia 22-3-18 NumbF att1/4Bn p63 MR27
TICE,Ernest William T2Lt dow 1-8-17 17 att11RSuss p120 CR Belgium7,Wilfred
TICEHURST,Gordon Harry Lt kia 20-9-17 5Lond 2Bn p246 MR29
TICHBORNE,John Capt ded 6-4-20 RAMC CR Mddx48
TICHBORNE,Muriel Edith Elizabeth 24-10-18 VAD CR Hamps1
TICKLE,Andrew Brown Lt kia 14-7-17 9Lpool p216 CR Belgium10,1/8Bn
TICKLE,Ernest T2Lt ded 13-7-18 2SLancs p126 CR France806
TICKLE,Frederick Ralph TCapt ded 5-11-18 RAMC att7RB p267 CR Lancs164
TICKLE,Gordon Philip 2Lt dow 30-9-18 6Lond p247 CR France146
TICKNER,Thomas George TLt dow 1-9-16 8SLancs p126 CR France74
TIDD,Ernest George Capt kia 13-6-15 6HLI p240 MR4
TIDDY,Claude Julian 2Lt kia 11-8-18 1Dors p124 MR16
TIDDY,Hector Kingsley Portus T2Lt kia 26-7-17 GL &7RFC p14 CR Belgium18
TIDDY,Reginald John Elliott Lt kia 10-8-16 2/4 O&BLI p231 CR France1887
TIDMARSH,John Moriarty Lt ded 3-9-18 12WRid &RAF p116 CR Eire167,kld
TIDSWELL,Cecil Robert Capt kia 16-10-16 1Drags &RFC p4&21 CR France398
TIDSWELL,William Francis Howard Lt kia 31-10-16 88RFA p36 CR France251
TIDY,Percy Ernest 2Lt kia 24-4-17 12Hamps p121 MR37
TIERNAN,Edwin Lawrence 2Lt dow 29-9-16 C240RFA p36 CR France44
TIERNEY,Herbert Stanislaus 2Lt kia 9-4-18 4Ches p97 MR38
TIFFANY,Harry Waddington.MC.2Lt kia 15-11-16 12RFus p70 MR19
TIFFEN,Harold Vincent 2Lt kia 20-11-17 2/5LancF p221 MR21
TIGAR,Geoffrey Herbert 2Lt kia 13-10-17 6RBerks p140 MR30
TIGAR,Harold Walter Lt kia 9-5-15 3Mddx p148 MR29
TIGHE,James Patrick LtTCapt kia 15-7-16 2RIrReg p89 MR21
TIGHT,Arthur Sidney T2Lt kia 23-3-18 69MGC B'Coy p186 MR27
TILBROOK,Frank Calder Lt dow 10-4-18 7DLI attRE 231FC p239 CR France1094
TILBURY,Arthur TCapt drd 4-5-17 RAMC p198 CR Italy14
TILBURY,Augustus Capt kia 8-6-17 RFA p207 CR France614
TILBURY,Herbert Walter T2Lt kia 5-9-18 Lincs p76 CR France245
TILBURY,Robert William 2Lt ded 18-3-18 95RFC p17 CR Hamps7
TILDESLEY,Harold Vaughan 2Lt kia 14-3-17 1/5SStaffs p229 CR France281
TILEY,George Charles T2Lt kia 21-10-16 9LNLancs p136 CR France384
TILL,Henry T2Lt kia 4-10-17 1Gloucs p107 MR30
TILLARD,Arthur George Capt kia 20-10-14 3 att2Manch p156 MR22
TILLARD,Philip Algernon Capt kia 19-11-16 ShropYeo att8ESurr p205 MR21
TILLARD,Thomas Atkinson Lt kia 6-12-16 NorfYeo attRFC p20&204 CR France285
TILLETT,Albert Edward 2Lt dow 25-3-18 2Mddx p148 MR27

TILLETT,Alexander.DSO.MC.LtALtCol dow 3-12-17 2Dev p77 CR Belgium3
TILLETT,John Edward Lt kia 8-10-18 3 att1Lincs p76 CR France234
TILLETT,Reginald Alfred William 2Lt kia 24-3-17 GloucHuss attRFC p20&203 CR France120
TILLEY,Alan Herbert 2Lt dow 10-4-17 2/4 O&BLI p231 CR France610
TILLEY,Arnold Reid Capt kia 11-5-16 8ScotRif att16RFC p20&225 CR France680,TILLIE Reed
TILLEY,Frank Lewis Cdr 14-2-19 IndMilWksServ MR65
TILLEY,John TCapt kia 28-11-16 7Norf p74 CR France1182
TILLIE,Charles Gordon.MID LtTCapt dow 23-8-15 1RInniskF p105 MR24
TILLIE,John Archibald 2Lt kia 19-7-18 8BlkW p129 CR France324
TILLOTSON,John Lancelot.MID 2Lt kia 23-4-17 4Dors p229 CR France531
TILLY,Charles Wynn TLtCol kia 14-4-18 18DLI att15WYorks p161 MR32
TILLY,John,.MC.TCapt kia 8-6-18 8Yorks p91 CR Italy1
TILLYARD,Sidney Joseph T2Lt kia 2-3-16 35MGC Inf p186 CR France423,Sydney
TILLYER,Richard Bateson Blunt Lt kia 25-4-15 1RWar C'Coy p66 MR29
TILNEY,Leonard Arthur.MC.Maj kia 9-3-18 RHGds att40RFC p17&20 CR France924
TILSTON,John 2Lt kia 18-10-18 RGA 291SB p42 CR France1351,Jack
TILSTON,John Edward T2Lt kia 23-4-17 154MGC p186 MR20
TIMBERLAKE,Roy TLt kia 27-7-17 4Beds p87 CR France644,P
TIMMINS,Frank T2Lt dow 19-12-17 C265RFA p36 CR Palestine9,TIMMANS
TIMMINS,George Oswald T2Lt kia 23-10-18 Beds att1Nhants p86 CR France190
TIMMINS,William Benjamin.MID 2Lt dow 20-5-15 1SStaffs p123 CR France64,Lt
TIMMIS,Richard Sutton 2Lt dow 10-5-15 3KRRC p152 CR France284
TIMONY,Patrick Charles Laurence T2Lt kia 24-8-18 15HLI p164 CR France1170
TIMS,Frederick Maj ded 28-12-15 RAOC p198 CR Lond29
TIMSON,Percy Walter Johnson Lt 26-9-18 57RAF MR20
TINDAL,Archibald Arthur 2Lt kia 8-9-16 177RFA p36 CR France294
TINDAL,David 2Lt dow 18-7-16 11 att8BlkW p129 MR21
TINDALL,Alexander George T2Lt kia 8-10-18 att1/5GordH p167 CR France115
TINDALL,Eric Vickers 2Lt dow 12-9-14 4KRRC p152 CR France1107
TINDALL,Fanny Sister ded 15-1-18 QAIMNS p200 CR Iraq6
TINDALL,Howard Simson TLt kia 31-7-17 6RBerks p140 CR Belgium112
TINDALL,Lawrence.MM.2Lt kia 21-6-18 10WRid p116 CR Italy1,TINDILL
TINDALL,Louis Nicolas Lindsay.MC.Lt kia 27-5-18 2Dev p77 MR18
TINDALL,Richard Frederick 2Lt kia 25-9-15 3Lincs p76 MR32
TINDLE,Kirton 2Lt kia 26-3-18 1/7DLI p239 MR27
TINGLE,John 2Lt dow 16-6-18 23MGC p186 CR Italy11
TINKER,Alan Hirst Capt kia 28-3-18 1/7Manch p237 MR20
TINKLER,George Henry T2Lt kia 25-4-17 7SStaffs p123 MR20
TINKLEY,Horace Arthur 2Lt dow 1-4-18 C2/75RFA p36 CR France169
TINLEY,Gervase Francis Newport.CB.CMG.MIDx2 Col ded 18-2-18 IA BaseCommdtMarseilles p283 CR France1571 Ex 31Lancers
TINLEY,James 2LtACapt kia 20-7-16 1RScotF p95 CR France432
TINLING,George Evelyn.MC.LtACapt kia 4-10-17 1ELancs p111 MR30
TINN,Farquhar Gray Lt ded 6-11-16 5HLI p240 CR Scot508
TINNE,Stuart Christian Capt ded 1-3-18 1RWKent attRFC p261&265 CR Surrey110
TINNISWOOD,Alfred 2Lt kia 1-10-18 RE 412FC p210 CR France484,Lt
TIPLADY,Frank Ewart T2Lt dow 27-9-15 14Mddx att7Lond p148 CR France88,Lt 5Bn
TIPPET,Charles Henry TMaj kia 7-8-15 7RDubF p177 CR Gallipoli5
TIPPETT,Alexander Arnold 2Lt dow 19-8-15 2KSLI p145 CR France275
TIPPING,William 2Lt kia 8-8-16 1/8Lpool p216 MR21
TIPPING,Frank Blamphin Lt kia 19-8-17 RGA &56RFC p20&209 CR France363
TIPTAFT,William Rutherford 2LtTLt kia 21-9-17 62MGC Inf p186 CR Belgium102
TIPTON,Richard James Capt dow 12-3-18 RFA att40RFC p20&207 CR France12
TISDALL,Charles Arthur Maj kia 1-9-14 IrGds p53 CR France1108
TISDALL,Charles Henry T2Lt kia 13-2-16 9RSuss p120 CR Belgium72
TISDALL,Charles Richard.MC.2Lt kia 15-9-16 1IrGds p53 CR France394
TISDALL,John Theodore St.Clair 2Lt kia 8-8-16 1 att1Lpool p73 MR21
TISDALL,Michael Henry Capt kld 23-12-19 NSomYeo &RAF p272
TITCHENER,Leonard Raymond Lt kia 3-12-17 5RLancs att22RFC p20&213 CR France31
TITFORD,Claude Francis 2Lt dow 2-9-18 8 att1/9Lond p247 CR France833
TITJEN,Carsten Francis Henry Lt ded 12-9-16 14Manch p156 CR Sussex178,3Bn
TITLEY,Anthony Graham 2Lt kia 13-4-17 4 att10WYorks p83 CR France311
TITLEY,Richard Guy.MC.Capt dow 13-10-17 1/6Glouc p225 CR Belgium16
TIZZARD,George 2Lt kld 8-3-16 6Dev A'Coy p217 MR38
TOBIAS,Leslie Mark Capt ded 25-2-19 RWFus 2GarBn p99 CR Egypt5

314

TOBIN,Gerald Vere T2Lt ded 15-5-17 11Hamps p121&264 CR Lond9
TOBIN,Richard Patrick TCapt kia 15-8-15 7RDubF p177 MR4
TOBIN-WILLIS,John Galbraith 2Lt kia 17-8-17 RASC att7RFC p14&194 CR Belgium18
TOD,Alexander Revell.MC.Lt dow PoW 18-4-18 5ESurr p226 CR France651
TOD,Frederick Masefield Cockburn T2Lt kia 25-9-15 7KOSB p102 MR19
TOD,William Lennox TCapt dow 29-4-17 15RScots p55 CR France40
TODD,Alexander Findlater Capt dow 21-4-15 3Norf p74 MR29 CR Belgium151,1Bn
TODD,Alfred Guy Eric 2Lt kia 23-4-17 4ESurr att2Hamps p113 MR20
TODD,Alick.MC.Lt dow PoW 16-4-17 4DLI &18RFC p14&161 CR France429
TODD,Charles Bernard 2Lt kia 11-6-17 RGA 184SB p42 CR Belgium4
TODD,Charles Hatt T2Lt kia 12-10-17 att6RBerks p140 MR30
TODD,Charles Leslie Morgan 2Lt dow 4-8-16 4SLancs p230 CR France141
TODD,Chester William Maj ded 9-8-17 A1RFA p206 CR Belgium10
TODD,Frederick George T2Lt kia 12-2-18 2/3Glos attRFC p17&107 CR France1678
TODD,Harold George Winslow TLt kia 12-10-16 7Suff p79 MR21
TODD,Harry T2Lt ded 29-10-18 24MGC p186 CR France40
TODD,Herbert Stanley.MC&Bar.LtACapt kia 18-9-18 4 att8ESurr p113 CR France511
TODD,James Clark T2Lt kia 27-6-17 17HLI p164 CR Belgium173
TODD,James Farquar Capt mbk 30-10-14 IA 39CentIndHorse att2LifeGds p283
TODD,James William T2Lt kld 28-9-17 GL &RFC p14 CR Surrey15
TODD,John 2Lt dow 4-7-18 9HLI p241 CR France268,Lt
TODD,John George TCapt kia 1-7-16 23NumbF p63 CR France150
TODD,Oswald Erick Maj ded 10-7-16 IA 1/5GurkhaRif p283 MR67,Erik
TODD,Richard James Killingworth Lt kia 21-1-16 IA 93BurmaInf p283 CR Iraq5
TODD,Robert Victor.DCM.Lt kia 9-8-18 24 att7Lond p252 MR16
TODD,T.R.Maj 22-9-19 IndOrdDep MR67
TODD,Valentine Otto Capt kia 9-4-17 1RLancs p59 CR France777
TODD,William Capt dow 29-6-15 RGA 1/4MountainBde p209 MR4
TODD,William Drysdale 2Lt kia 15-9-16 6ScotRif att11A&SH p224 CR France453
TODD,William Henry Lt&QM ded 28-8-15 4Ess p232 CR Gallipoli27
TODD-NAYLOR,William Bryan T2Lt kia 24-8-16 8KRRC p152 CR France397
TODD-THORNTON,J.H.B.Maj ded 12-1-18 3NumbF GarBn p63 CR Sussex112
TODMAN,Charles Vincent Lt kia 3-8-18 10Lond att16RAF p248&258CR France95
TODRICK,Thomas.MID Capt kia 14-12-14 8RScots p211 CR France684
TOFTS,Charles Frank Lt kia 7-1-18 5ESurr &1KAR p226&268 CR EAfrica77
TOKELY,Reginald Cyrus 2Lt dow 23-12-16 2Ess p132 CR France105
TOLERTON,Lee TLt kia 15-8-15 6RIrFus p171 MR4
TOLHURST,Alfred Wilfred T2Lt kld 6-10-17 GL &RFC p14 CR Kent130
TOLHURST,Bernard Joseph Lt dow PoW 22-4-17 11WRid &11RFC p14&116 CR France421
TOLLEMACHE,Arthur Henry William 2Lt kia 19-7-16 RE &RFC p4&49,ded MR20
TOLLEMACHE,Bevil Douglas 2Lt kia 22-12-14 1CldGds p51 MR22
TOLLEMACHE,Horace Murray TLt kia 17-7-18 13Hamps p121 CR Belgium11,15Bn
TOLLEMACHE,John Eadred TLt kia 21-8-16 6 att8RWSurr p56 CR France394
TOLLEMACHE,Leo De Orellana Capt kia 1-11-14 1Lincs p76 MR29
TOLLEMACHE-TOLLEMACHE,L.S.D.O.Frandati-Filius Tollemache-Tollemache de Orellana Plantagenet Capt ded 20-2-17
TOLLER,Edward Northcote TCapt kia 20-7-16 20RFus p70 CR France432 [Leic p88 CR France177
TOLLER,George Reginald TLt ded 27-7-17 Lincs 1GarBn p76 CR Iraq8
TOLLER,Richard Arthur Lt ded 24-2-19 2WelchR attRAF p264 CR Lond4,27-2-19
TOLLITT,William Ernest Capt ded 15-5-19 IA 2/48Pnrs p283 MR65,W.G.18-5-19
TOLMIE,George Lester 2Lt dow 19-11-18 6Nhampt p138 CR Yorks11
TOLMIE,Robert 2Lt kia 13-10-18 1/5SfthH p241 CR France271
TOLSON,George Henderson Lt dow 1-12-17 2/18Lond p250 CR Palestine3
TOLSON,Horace 2Lt kia 29-3-18 6RWar Ex RAMC 87FA p214 MR27
TOLSON,James Martin 2Lt dow 20-10-18 A74RFA p36 CR France319
TOLSON,Joseph Capt dow 28-10-17 1/6N&D p233 CR France98
TOLSON,Robert Huntriss 2Lt kia 1-7-16 15WYorks p83 CR France742,Huntriss
TOMBAZIS,James Lyell.DSO.MC.2Lt kia 8-10-18 2N&D p135 CR France849
TOMBLIN,Harold Raymond Lt kia 10-7-16 3 att2Manch p156 MR21
TOMBLIN,James Douglas T2Lt dow 13-11-15 12/12MGC p186 CR Belgium11
TOMBLINGS,Eric Hunter Griffith TLt ded 21-1-16 RE p49&258 CR Yorks504,Honton
TOMBS,James Douglas T2Lt ded 18-2-16 7BordR p118 CR France134
TOMBS,Joseph Simpson McKenzie 2Lt dow 11-9-15 48RFA p36 CR Belgium11
TOMES,Geoffrey Capt kia 10-8-15 IA 53Sikhs att1/6GurkhaRif p283 MR4

TOMEY,Donald Stuart TLt kia 25-3-18 11EYorks p85 MR20
TOMEY,Wilfred T2Lt dow 9-10-18 1RBerks p140 CR France380
TOMKIES,Henry Lea 2Lt kia 25-4-17 RFC p14 MR20
TOMKINS,Albin George 2Lt kia 13-9-16 2IrGds p53 CR France294
TOMKINS,Charles Percy T2Lt dow 29-10-18 Mddx att1Lpool p148 CR Mddx16
TOMKINS,Frank Savell TLt kia 8-8-15 7Glouc p107 MR4 Savill
TOMKINS,Frederick Allen TCapt dow 14-7-16 RFA attTMB p36 CR France141,15-7-16
TOMKINS,Vigor TCapt kia 13-10-15 7ESurr p113 MR19
TOMKINS,William Henry Chap4Cl ded 28-9-18 RAChDept att7SStaffs p200 CR France647
TOMKINSON,C.W.Lt 19-10-18 14Ches CR Ches51
TOMKINSON,Percy Alexander 2Lt kia 4-10-18 6N&D p233 CR France441
TOMLIN,Charles Geoffrey Lt dow 9-7-16 22Lond p251 CR France12
TOMLIN,Harry Francis T2Lt kia 28-9-17 GL &20RFC p14 CR France285
TOMLIN,Reginald Arthur.MC.2Lt kia 1-9-18 1/22Lond p252 CR France785
TOMLINSON,Charles Valentine T2Lt kia 1-7-16 11N&D p135 CR France246
TOMLINSON,Charles William 2Lt kia 3-9-16 1/4WRid p227 MR21
TOMLINSON,Dan T2Lt kia 10-8-15 1Lpool p73 CR France266
TOMLINSON,David Mitchell.MID TMaj dow 13-5-16 13RScots p55 CR France80
TOMLINSON,Ernest 2Lt kia 5-9-18 4Lincs p217 CR France245,7Bn
TOMLINSON,Ferdinand Roger John 2Lt kia 26-10-14 SStaffs p123 MR29
TOMLINSON,Herbert Cecil 2Lt dow 21-3-18 RGA 39SB p42 CR Belgium3
TOMLINSON,Hugh.MC.Lt ded 2-4-17 57RFC p14 CR France924,Capt
TOMLINSON,James Ashworth T2Lt dow 22-11-15 13 att1LancF p94 CR Gallipoli4
TOMLINSON,James Freeman TLt kia 24-3-18 2HLI p164 MR20
TOMLINSON,Robert Henry T2Lt dow 19-7-16 18Lpool p73 CR France145
TOMLINSON,Thomas Harry 2Lt dow 23-7-16 1Dev p77 CR France390 &CR France399
TOMPKINS,Harold Arthur 2Lt dow 1-7-16 10 att1ELancs p111 MR21
TOMPSON,Alan Hawtree 2Lt kia 27-9-15 GrenGds SR att4Bn p50 MR19,Hawtin
TOMS,Arthur Woodland Lt kld 27-11-14 3Dev attScotRif p77 CR France768
TOMS,Horace James Henry T2Lt kia 9-4-17 11N&D p135 CR Belgium127
TOMS,Stanley Muir Lt dow 8-12-17 2/18Lond p250 CR Palestine3
TOMS,William Henry Capt kld 5-12-18 RAOC p198 CR Belgium400
TOMSON,James Wyndham.MID Capt kia 24-9-18 5Leic B'Coy p220 CR France699
TONG,George Lt kia 16-8-18 RE 422FC p210 CR France106,15-8-16
TONGE,Harry TLt ded 25-10-18 2NumbF GarBn p63 MR67
TONGE,John.MID LtCol dow 19-4-17 230RFA p206 CR France98
TONGE,John Richard TLt kia 16-12-17 15LancF p94 CR Belgium20
TONGE,Septimus TLtACapt ded 9-5-18 MGC p266 CR Wales537
TONGE,William Russell T2Lt kia 12-1-16 17Manch p156 MR21
TONGUE,Andrew Leslie 2Lt kia 28-5-18 C175RFA p36 CR France504
TONGUE,Claude Leslie T2Lt ded 26-10-18 Worc 1Res GarBn attLCB Depot p110 CR France34
TONGUE,John William Collis TCapt kia 25-9-15 10Glouc p107 CR France1723
TONGUE,Walter Edward Lt ded 1-5-18 RE p49 CR War10
TONKIN,Edith Mary Miss ded 14-10-18 VolAid BRCS att3GH p200 CR France13,13-10-18
TONKIN,Frederick Cuthbert.DSO.MC.LtTCapt dow 4-11-18 7EYorks p85 CR France1478
TONKING,David Wilson 2Lt dow 29-5-17 3DCLI att10RWar p115 CR France285
TONKS,Leslie Robert James 2Lt kia 11-4-18 4 att9SStaffs p123 MR32,9 att4Bn
TONKS,Samuel William Maj kia 13-10-15 RE p209 MR19
TONSON-RYE,John Reginald Capt ded 25-5-19 RASC MT p255 CR France1571
TOOGOOD,Henry Duncan.MC.T2Lt kia 21-3-18 9KRRC p152 MR27,Harry
TOOGOOD,Percival Frederick 2Lt dow 23-2-17 IARO att2/9GurkhaRif p283 MR38,T.F.24-2-17
TOOHEY,James Thomas T2Lt kia 18-1-17 6RIrReg p89 CR Belgium100
TOOK,Cyril Arthur 2Lt ded 14-8-19 12Suff p263 CR Suff2
TOOKE,Bernard TCapt kia 3-5-17 18WYorks p83 MR20
TOOLEY,Harold Augustus Rupert Lt mbk 20-12-14 RGLI attDCLI p257 MR22,att2Leic
TOOLIS,James Hollingworth Lt kia 1-7-16 2Lincs p76 MR21
TOOMEY,Archibald Roche T2Lt kia 10-8-15 6Leinst p175 CR Gallipoli18
TOON,Harold Phillips T2Lt kia 14-7-16 17 att15DLI p161 MR21
TOOTELL,Bernard 2Lt kia 23-6-17 7N&D att4RFC p20&233 CR Belgium11
TOOTILL,Edward Cecil T2Lt kia 22-8-10 10DLI C'Coy p162 MR30
TOOVEY,Arthur Wilfred TCapt ded 1-12-18 13Beds p87 CR Mddx25,30-11-18
TOOVEY,Kennedy St.Clair Hamilton 2Lt ded PoW 15-10-18 RLancs att166TMB p59 CR Germany3

TOPHAM,Albert Alfred T2Lt ded 7-12-18 GL attSARdCps p191 CR EAfrica36
TOPHAM,Alfred James Tudor 2LtACapt kia 26-9-17 3 att7KSLI p145 MR30
TOPHAM,Charles Henry 2Lt dow 21-10-16 RGA 115HB p42 CRFrance52
TOPHAM,Henry Augrave Cecil 2Lt dow 25-5-15 ULIA att1WelchR p283 CR France285,Angrave
TOPHAM,James Capt&Adjt kia 26-9-15 8Lincs p76 MR19
TOPHAM,Michael 2Lt kia 13-4-17 27RFC Ex 19RFus p14 MR20
TOPP,Richard William 2Lt dow 1-7-16 6 att11RInniskF p105 MR21
TOPPIN,Harry Stanley.MID Capt dow 13-9-14 1NumbF p63 MR15
TOPPIN,Sidney Miles.MC.Maj dow 27-9-17 RGA 151HB p42 CR Belgium11
TOPPING,Eric T2Lt dow 25-4-17 10Y&L p159 CR France113
TOPPING,J.2Lt kia 16-9-18 2BlkW attRAF p129 MR34
TORBIT,James TLt ded 10-9-18 RASC attRGA N'SiegePark p194 CR France34
TORIN,Richard Maynard Lt kia 24-4-15 RE p49 CR France279
TORKILDSEN,W.Cdr 6-11-18 S&T Cps MR43
TORKINGTON,Charles Coke Capt kia 25-5-15 1WelshR p127 MR29
TORKINGTON,John Elmsley Bourchier Capt drd 30-12-15 IA 63PalamcottaLI p283 MR41
TORNEY,Thomas Frederick Hastings Lt kia 3-9-18 3 att13WelshR p127 MR16
TORRANCE,Kenneth T2Lt kia 2-9-18 1RScotsF p95 CR France646
TORRENS,Attwood Alfred Maj kia 8-12-16 RFA p206 CR France832
TORRENS,Gerald Calverley TCapt ded 24-12-16 MGC p186 CR Surrey160
TORRENS,James Claude T2Lt kia 30-5-18 19MGC B'Coy p186 MR18
TORRIE,Louis Eric 2Lt 10-3-21 4KSLI CR Glouc9
TORRIE,Thomas George Jameson TLtCol kia 18-11-16 2LifeGds att7ELancs p20 CR France251
TORRY,Arthur James Dashwood.MC.Lt kia 9-10-17 RGA attRFC p14&42 CR Belgium18
TORRY,John Shirley Archibald T2Lt dow 19-9-15 12RB p180 CR France345
TORTOISHELL,George Henry 2Lt kia 14-3-17 1/5NStaffs p238 MR21
TOSDEVIN,William Cecil 2Lt dow 20-11-17 7Nhampt p138 CR France446
TOSETTI,Douglas.MC.TMaj kia 21-3-18 8RBerks p140 MR27
TOSH,Elmslie Maj kia 25-9-15 4BlkW p230 CR France705
TOSHACK,Thomas 2Lt kia 10-4-17 C'Bn MGC p186 MR20,11-4-17 TankCps Ex 9EYorks
TOSSWILL,Walter Roy Capt dow 12-8-16 1ELancs p111 CR Belgium11
TOTHILL,Geoffrey Ivan Francis 2Lt kia 27-3-16 4RFus p70 MR29
TOTTENHAM,Arthur Henry 2Lt kia 27-6-16 2RInniskF C'Coy p105 CR France296
TOTTENHAM,Charles Gordon Loftus Capt dow 30-3-15 RE att4S&M p49 CR France924
TOTTENHAM,Edward Lowry.MC.2Lt kia 9-4-16 11 att6LNLancs p136 MR38
TOTTIE,Eric Harold 2Lt dow 22-9-14 1NumbF p63 CR France1107,Harald Lt
TOUCHE,Eric Percy Johnstone 2Lt ded 17-5-18 Ess &RAF p132
TOUGH,Arnold Bannatyne TCapt kia 1-7-16 11ELancs p111 CR France802,dow
TOUGH,John James TCapt dow 6-10-18 RAMC att5FA p198 CR France1483
TOUGHILL,C.M.Nurse 14-11-15 ScotWomensHosp CR Europe58
TOULMAN,Philip Musgrave Lt kia 22-6-17 LeicYeo p204 CR France363
TOULMIN,Harold.MC.Lt kia 17-9-18 6LNLancs &46RAF p136 MR2
TOVEY,D.Lt 5-5-18 NRA SchOfMusketry CR Surrey131
TOVEY,Harry Turner LtTMaj dow 22-4-18 A88 RFA p36 CR Belgium18
TOVEY,W.SubCdr 30-5-21 S&T Cps MR65
TOWELL,Gerald Wyman.MC&Bar.LtACapt dow 8-8-18 N'RFA p36 CR France23,kia
TOWER,Bertie Christopher Butler.MC&Bar.MIDx3 CaptAMaj dow 22-8-18 Cmdg4RFus p70 CR France504
TOWER,Christopher Cecil Lt kia 4-10-15 EssYeo p203 CR France178,2-10-15
TOWER,Frank TCapt&Adjt kia 13-4-17 12Manch p156 CR France924
TOWER,Hugh Christopher Capt kia 19-9-16 RFC p4 MR20
TOWER,William Claude Cecil Capt ded 30-11-18 10EKentYeo &RAF p256 CR Sussex144
TOWERS,Grainger Malcolm Lt dow 20-1-16 2Lpool p73 CR France80,1Bn
TOWERS,Wilfrid Goodwin 2Lt kia 2-4-17 4Manch p156 CR France616,Wilfred
TOWERS-CLARKE,John William Lt kia 1-7-16 2RScotsF p95 MR21,CLARK
TOWES,Norman Henry T2Lt kia 4-11-18 7RWSurr p56 CR France737
TOWGOOD,Arthur Cecil Carden T2Lt kia 13-5-17 27 att11Mddx Ex 12Lond p148 MR20
TOWLER,Cyril John 2Lt kld 4-9-18 3RWKent &RAF p142
TOWLER,F.S.2Lt ded 5-10-18 SWBord &RAF p101
TOWLSON,Albert John T2Lt kia 16-10-18 RE 122FC p49 CR Belgium157
TOWLSON,William Holland T2Lt dow 28-9-17 122MGC p186 CR France13
TOWN,Charles Aubrey.MC.TCapt kia 20-9-17 11WYorks p83 MR30
TOWNEND,Cecil Pelham 2Lt dow 24-9-16 1 att2/21Lond p245 CR France95

TOWNEND,Francis William Capt dow 29-3-15 RE 35SigCoy p49 CR France80,Whitchurch 28-3-15
TOWNLEY,Bertram Russell Capt ded 7-11-18 IARO attSPersianRif S&TCps p283 CR Asia82
TOWNLEY,Charles Richard BrigGen ded 15-5-18 Staff Comdg7Dist SuffR p261 CR Hamps13
TOWNLEY,Felix Lionel T2Lt kia 26-10-17 14RWar p66 MR30
TOWNLEY,John Lt ded 1-4-19 7Ches p272 CR Lancs34
TOWNROE,Geoffrey Charles Capt kia 8-9-17 D1/4SLancs p229 CR Belgium10
TOWNSEND,Arthur Eric 2Lt kia 15-2-17 5DLI attRFC p20&239 CR France424
TOWNSEND,Arthur Evans T2Lt kldacc 26-11-15 18Manch p156 CR France300
TOWNSEND,Arthur Gordon TLtACapt kia 5-9-17 2HLI p164 CR Belgium24
TOWNSEND,Charles Victor.MID T2Lt kia 21-3-16 7KSLI p145 CR Belgium28
TOWNSEND,Douglas William Ormond 2Lt kia 16-8-17 GL &7RFC p14 CR Belgium140,TOWNSHEND
TOWNSEND,Eric Lever 2Lt dow 17-9-16 15Lond p249 CR France188
TOWNSEND,Eric Travers Capt kia 8-11-17 1/5HLI p240 CR Palestine8
TOWNSEND,Francis Edward Steavenson Lt dow 30-9-16 5DLI p239 CR France52
TOWNSEND,George John Lt dow 26-11-15 IA 66Punjabis p283 CR Iraq1,Capt
TOWNSEND,Guy Storey Lt kia 23-8-18 5Yorks attMGC Inf p187&220 CR France210,2Lt
TOWNSEND,Harry 2Lt kia 19-7-16 MGC 53InfBde p186 MR21
TOWNSEND,Harry Lt ded PoW 23-2-19 RH&FA p262 CR Yorks361
TOWNSEND,Hugh Vere 2Lt kia 6-5-15 3Mon p244 MR29
TOWNSEND,Ivan Vesey Lt kia 3-2-15 2ELancs p111 CR France924
TOWNSEND,John T2Lt kia 14-7-16 12WYorks p83 MR21
TOWNSEND,John Vernon Lt kia 24-9-18 5Yorks p221 CR France1701
TOWNSEND,Joseph 2Lt kia 21-3-18 5NStaffs p238 MR20
TOWNSEND,Joseph Ernest T2Lt kld 2-1-17 1Worc att66RFC p14&110 CRGlouc9
TOWNSEND,Joseph Leslie T2Lt kia 2-10-17 1/2 att3/5LancF p94 MR30,9-10-17
TOWNSEND,Lionel George Oliver TCapt kia 7/11-8-15 7SStaffs p123 MR4.9-8-15
TOWNSEND,Martha SNurse ded 21-9-18 QAIMNS p200 CR Greece9
TOWNSEND,Richard Stepleton Barry TLt kia 1-7-16 10RIrFus p171 CR France339,9Bn
TOWNSEND,Robert Edward Lawrence TCapt ded 2-3-18 Mddx p265
TOWNSEND,Ronald Travis Robert Lt kia 30-11-17 5HLI attCanadianLocalForce &RFC p261&272 MR20
TOWNSEND,Sidney John 2Lt kia 13-5-15 2LifeGds p20 MR29
TOWNSEND,Thomas T2Lt kia 4-6-16 1EYorks p85 CR France189,Lt
TOWNSEND,Thomas Ainsworth.MC&Bar.Capt kia 24-3-18 RAMC p254 MR20
TOWNSEND,W.H.2Lt dow 23-4-18 GL &RAF p191
TOWNSEND-GREEN,Henry Russell Capt dow 3-3-15 1/16Lond p249 CR France922
TOWNSHEND,Arthur Fitzhenry TLtCol dow 16-9-16 11RWKent p142 CR France833
TOWNSHEND,Dudley Ryder TCapt dow 21-8-15 11LNLancs attLancF p136 MR4
TOWNSLEY,Bryan Hill T2Lt kia 14-9-16 12 att9WYorks p83 MR21
TOWNSON,Herbert Johnston 2Lt kia 21-4-18 15WYorks &RAF p83 CR France52,kldacc
TOWSE,Clifford Henry TCapt kia 8-11-15 6RWKent B'Coy p142 MR19
TOWSE,William Norman Capt kia 15-9-16 4Lond p246 CR France385
TOYE,Hubert Clarence 2Lt dow 15-10-15 2RSuss p120 CR France88
TOYE,Sydney Samuel 2Lt kia 10-10-18 C122RFA p209 CR France190
TOYNBEE,Geoffrey Percy Robert Capt kia 15-11-14 RB p180 MR32
TOZER,Harold Percy 2Lt kld 16-12-16 9DLI attRFC p20&239 CR Wilts128
TOZER,Horace Gordon 2Lt kia 1-10-15 3 att2Yorks p91 MR19
TOZER,John Henry Wallace TLt ded 3-8-17 RASC p194 MR65
TOZER,Sidney Prout TLt kia 8-10-18 Dev p77 CR France844,Sydney
TOZER,William Lt ded 5-5-16 RFA p208 MR38
TRACEY,Geoffrey Eugene TLt kia 25-9-15 9Dev p77 MR19
TRAFFORD,Edmond Thyrkel TLt ded 10-5-16 1Norf GarrBn p74 MR43
TRAFFORD,Geoffrey Thomas Lt kia 23-7-18 1LifeGds att9TankCps GdsMGR p20,53&189 CR France987,Capt
TRAFFORD-RAWSON,John Henry Edmund TCapt kia 18-9-16 1WYorks p83 MR21
TRAHERNE,George Gilbert Capt kia 6-8-16 RGA 15DivArtly p42 CR France44
TRAIL,Robert George Anthony Maj dow 1-12-17 IA CpsofGuidesCav attJodhpurLancers p283 CR France446
TRAILL,Anthony TCapt ded 25-8-17 RAMC att2/4WRid p198 CR France512,att2/4WYorks
TRAILL,Charles Harold.MC.Capt 9-11-20 RFA CR Surrey158
TRAILL,Colin Balfour.MC.TMaj kia 28-6-18 10EYorks p85 CR France19
TRAILL,Henry Rauthwells Capt kia 4-6-19 IA 87Punjabis attSWaziristanMil p283 MR43,Rauthmell 30-5-19

TRAILL,John Murray.MID Maj kia 30-10-14 2Beds p87 MR29,LtCol
TRAILL,Kenneth Robert TLt kia 1-7-16 6RBerks p140 CR France513
TRAILL,Sinclair George Capt kia 24-11-16 1CamH p168 CR France169,Maj kldacc 23-11-16
TRAN,David Rushton T2Lt kia 28-7-18 5SfthH att8Bn p165 CR France865
TRAPP,Andrew Lt kia 23-4-18 41RFA p36 CR France266
TRASK,Charles William Trevor T2Lt kia 18-8-18 3SomLI att24WelshR p80 CR France248
TRASK,John Hedley T2Lt kia 20-11-17 Hamps att14Bn p121 CR Belgium21
TRASK,Sydney Robert T2Lt kia 8-6-16 10 att7Suff p79 MR21,9-8-16
TRATMAN,Harold Wigmore Lt 3-12-17 2/6Glouc p225 MR17,Arnold
TRATMAN,Francis Victor T2Lt kia 25-8-17 14Glouc p107 CR France363
TRATTLES,William Horace T2Lt kia 25-1-17 13Hamps att9Worc p121 CR Iraq5
TRAUNWEISER,G.N.2Lt kld 15-4-18 GL &RAF p191
TRAVERS,Hamilton Henry Lt dow 28-3-15 1SWBord p101 CR France80
TRAVERS,Horace Eden Kennedy T2Lt dow 8-11-16 14N&D att10LNLancs p135 CR France62,kldacc
TRAVERS,Hugh Eaton Frederick Capt mbk 7-8-15 2 att9LancF p257 MR4
TRAVERS,Hugh Mortimer.DSO.Capt kia 8-11-14 5RMunstF p176 MR29
TRAVERS,Hugh Price Maj kia 7-8-15 8WRid p116 CR Gallipoli27
TRAVERS,Spencer Robert Valentine.MID TLt kia 9-8-15 7RMunstF p176 MR4
TRAVERS,Tom Stockholm.MC.MID Capt kia 7-11-17 2/20Lond p251 CR Palestine1,Stockham
TRAVERS-SMITH,Robert Montgomery 2Lt drd 4-10-18 15MGC Inf p186 MR40
TRAVERSE,James Hector T2Lt kia 30-11-17 10RDubF p177 CR France1489
TRAYES,Frederic Kenneth Jackson 2Lt kia 22-3-18 11Ches p97 MR20
TRAYLEN,Norman Algernon.MC.Lt ded 4-11-18 RASC 61SB p253 CR France279
TRAYLOR,John Nelson Capt ded 27-11-15 Res 11Dev p272 CR Somerset71,TRAYLER
TREACY,Eric Henry 2Lt dow 14-12-16 12LNLancs p234 CR France131,kia
TREACY,Michael 2Lt kia 21-3-18 4 att1RMunstF p176 MR27
TREADWAY,Harold Ligomer 2Lt kia 8/9-5-17 15RWar p66 MR20
TREADWELL,George Reuben TCapt kia 5-2-17 6ELancs p111 MR38,Maj
TREADWELL,Robert Naylor.MC.TLt dow 9-9-17 GL 9Ess &22RFC p13 CR France95
TREASE,Reginald Ernest.DSO.MC.Lt ded 5-12-18 28Bde 124Bty RFA p36 CR Notts84
TREASE,Sidney Charles 2Lt mbk 19-9-18 3N&D att11ScotRif p257 MR37
TREASURE,James Herbert.TD.Maj ded 3-12-18 RGA p209 CR Egypt2
TREASURE,William Herbert 2Lt kia 1-7-16 1SomLI p80 MR21
TREBILCOCK,John Archibald.MC.Maj dow 21-5-18 76RFA p36 CR France103
TREBLE,James Noel Capt kia 18-10-15 4 O&BLI p231 CR France1327
TRECHMANN,Kuno Griffith 2Lt kia 2-7-16 12NumbF p63 MR21
TREDENNICK,John Archibald St.Leger Capt kia 23-7-18 2 att1/5SfthH p165 CR France1697
TREDGOLD,John Clarkson.MC.2Lt kia 12-4-17 3RScots p55 MR20
TREE,Charles James Lt dow 20-7-15 9Worc p110 CR Gallipoli 1
TREE,Philip Bevan T2Lt kia 24-3-18 8MGC p186 MR27
TREE,Warren Francis TCapt kld 22-7-16 10Worc p110 MR21
TREFFRY,Dormer Kierulff de Bretton 2Lt kia 15-9-16 4CldGds p51 CR France294
TREFUSIS,Arthur Owen TCapt kia 7-7-16 9LNLancs p136 CR France832
TREFUSIS,Haworth Walter Capt kia 7-11-16 1Nhampt p138 CR France744
TREGARTHEN,Ernest William Lt kld 18-3-18 5RWFus &RFC p223 CR Wales17
TREGASKIS,Arthur 2Lt kia 7-7-16 16WelshR p127 CR France453,Lt
TREGASKIS,Leonard 2Lt kia 7-7-16 16WelshR p127 CR France453,Lt
TREGELLES,Geoffrey Philip.MID TCapt kia 1-7-16 8Dev A'Coy p77 CRFrance330
TREGLOWN,Charles Henry TLt kia 30-3-17 D47RFA p36 CR France1182
TREHEARNE,Leslie Llewellyn T2Lt dow 25-9-15 9WelshR A'Coy p127 CR France98,TREHARNE 24-9-15
TREHERN,Arthur Reginald T2Lt kia 27-7-15 5RBerks p140 CR Belgium71
TREHERNE,Claude William LtTCapt dow 12-8-17 RAMC DADMS 37Div p198 CR France40
TRELAWNY,Henry Wallace Lt kia 23-10-18 1DCLI p115 CR France1476
TRELEAVEN,Noel Houghton Lt kia 23-11-16 5WYorks p218 CR France283
TRELIVING,Arthur Stanley T2Lt kia 29-3-18 23Mddx attTMB p148 CR France745,Lt
TRELIVING,Walter Ricks T2Lt ded 11-10-18 RASC p267&194,Hicks CR Somerset43
TREMBATH,Allen Edward Capt kia 26-5-15 15Lond p249 CR France260
TREMBATH,Arthur Cecil Capt kia 22-12-16 5ESurr p226 CR Belgium127
TREMEARNE,Arthur John Newman TMaj kia 25-9-15 1/22Lond D'Coy att8SfthH p165&251 MR19
TREMEARNE,William Crew 2Lt kia 26-9-15 8SfthH p165 MR19

TREMEER,Sidney Charles T2Lt dow 17-5-17 7Beds p87 CR France13
TREMELLAN,Enner Thorney Capt ded 20-12-17 5WelshR p230
TREMELLEN,Donald Hargreaves 2Lt kia 23-4-17 3 att1DCLI p115 MR20
TREMLETT,Elias.DSO.MC.TLt dow 23-5-17 9Dev att208MGC Inf p77&266 CR France614
TRENBATH,Jack 2Lt kia 8-9-18 4ELancs p226 CR France262
TRENCH,Charles Reginald Chenevix.MID Maj kia 21-3-18 2/5N&D p232 MR20
TRENCH,David 2Lt 23-4-17 4 att2RScotF MR20
TRENCH,David Cunningham 2Lt dow 26-2-16 4RScotsF p222
TRENCH,Derrick Le Poer.DSO.MC.Maj kia 28-8-17 RFA HQ Staff p36 CR France178
TRENCH,Frederick Power Le Poer Lt dow 9-4-16 3Leinst att2RDubF p175 CR France745
TRENCH,Frederick Sydney.Hon.Lt dow 16-11-16 1KRRC p152 CR France131,ded
TRENCH,Nugent Charles Le Poer T2Lt kia 16-1-17 9ESurr p113 CR France115 see LE POER TRENCH
TRENCH,Percy Richard Oliver LtTCapt kia 25-1-17 1RWSurr attRWFus p56 MR38
TRENCHARD,Frederick Alfred Lt kia 24-5-15 RFA p36 CR Belgium92
TRENCHARD,John Wilfrid Hugh Lt dow 3-10-17 RGA 122HB p42 CR Belgium11,Capt
TRENCHMANN,Friedrich Otto T2Lt dow 15-10-16 94RFA p36 CR Durham165,Frederick 14-10-16
TRENERRY,Dudley Goodall 2Lt ded 21-1-18 RFC p261 CR Mddx42,Lt
TRENOW,Geoffrey Foveaux.MC.Lt kia 20-9-17 5Lond 2Bn p246 MR29
TRERISC,Walter Thomas Llewelyn T2Lt kia 15-4-18 1RWar p66
TRERISE,Robert 2Lt dow 13-6-18 RGA 237SB p42 CR France10
TRERISE,Walter Thomas Llewelyn2Lt 15-4-18 1War MR32
TRESIDDER,Charles Tolmie Capt dow 22-4-16 7Glouc p107 MR38
TRESIDDER,Thomas Arthur Capt kia 28-6-15 14RScots p55 CR Gallipoli6
TRESISE,Richard Arthur T2Lt dow 12-10-18 21Manch p156 CR France446
TREVARTHEN,Arthur Francis Vivyan Aubrey TLt kia 28-1-16 2SStaffs p123 CR France279
TREVELYAN,Walter Raleigh TCapt ded 19-4-16 RASC p194
TREVELYAN,Wilfred 2Lt kia 4-5-15 5 att4RB p180 MR29
TREVENEN,Sydney Vyvyan.MC.Capt dow 10-6-18 49/40RFA p36&259 CR France40
TREVES,Wilfred Warwick.OBE.Maj 18-5-20 RAMC CR Mddx26
TREVETHAN,R.SNurse ded 4-9-17 TFNS p254 CR Iraq5
TREVITHICK,Robert Percy 2Lt kia 23-4-17 232RFA p36 CR France536
TREVOR,Ernest Wilberforce Chap4Cl dow 14-11-16 RAChDept att13RB p200 CR France701
TREVOR,Frederick Pelham 2Lt kia 8-5-15 3 att2DCLI p115 MR29
TREVOR,Gruffydd Vaughan TLt ded 5-11-18 RE 256TC p49 CR France34,255TC
TREVOR,Harry Spottiswoode.MID Lt kia 15-8-15 RE att4FC S&M p49 CR France924
TREVOR,Herbert Edward CaptTLtCol kia 11-4-17 Nhampt att9Ess p138 CR France1182
TREVOR-JONES,Evan Edward 2Lt kia 1-7-16 6 att1RB p180 MR21
TREVOR-JONES,John Eric.MC.TCapt kia 22-4-18 6 att1RB p180 CR France411
TREVOR-ROPER,Charles Cadwaladr Capt dow 3-8-17 8Hamps p229 CR Belgium20,14Bn
TREW,John McCammon TCapt ded 28-3-18 RLancs p59 CR Yorks595
TREWARTHA-JAMES,Derric Vernon TLt kia 13-10-15 5RBerks p140 CR France219
TREWBY,Arthur Lt dow 17-5-15 RE 11Coy p49 CR France80
TREWEEKE,Frank Lesley T2Lt ded 7-11-16 RE p49 CR Camb2,Leslie,Lt
TREWHITT,Eric Gerald Lt dow 14-11-16 1HAC p206 CR France44
TREWMAN,Athol Benedict 2Lt dow 22-10-14 1Mddx p148 CR France1887,Lt
TRIBE,A.L.TCapt dow 17-11-17 3/2KAR 2RhodesianR p202 CR Tanzania1,Maj
TRIBE,Charles Walter LtCol kia 13-1-16 IA 41Dogras p283 CR Iraq5
TRICKETT,William Edwin Maj ded 21-11-17 5RWFus p223 CR Wales648
TRIER,Norman Ernest T2Lt dow 6-10-15 2EYorks p85 CR France98
TRIGG,H.F.E.2Lt 8-5-18 GL attRAF CR Hamps15
TRIMBLE,Alan Vincent 2Lt 25-8-18 41RAF MR20
TRIMBLE,Noel Desmond T2Lt dow 29-4-16 12 att8RInniskF p105 CR France115,kia
TRIMBLE,Robert Maxwell.MID Lt kia 21-3-18 5NStaffs p238 MR20
TRIMBY,Henry Thomas Maj&QM ded 19-6-16 RMunstF p266
TRIMBY,T.Maj&QM 19-6-16 RMunstF CR Eire159
TRIMINGHAM,Wentworth Gray T2Lt ded 4-1-18 11LancF att1Lincs p94 CR France512
TRIMMER,Edmund Howard.MID TLt dow 10-8-15 6ELancs p111 MR4
TRIMMER,Frederick George T2Lt kia 12-10-16 26Manch p156 CR France432

TRIMMER,George Ernest Lt ded 16-11-18 2LancF attRE p94
TRIMMER,T.Capt 18-11-18 RE att2FldSurCoy CR France1027
TRIMMER,William Charles 2Lt kia 21-7-16 O&BLI 1BucksBn p232 CR France832
TRIMMER,William Douglas Maclean Lt kia 30-10-14 1Hamps p121 CR Belgium69
TRIMMING,Henry William Noel 2Lt kld 15-5-15 RFA p36 CR Hamps13
TRINDER,Arnold James Lt kia 16-6-15 7NumbF p214 MR29
TRINDER,John Robert.MC.Maj kia 15-9-16 18Lond p250 CR France453
TRINDER,Samuel Louis T2Lt dow 17-8-17 9RIrFus p172 CR Belgium8,Levis
TRINGHAM,Llewellyn Watkins Howell Capt ded 22-11-18 21Lancers attRGA 51BdeHQ p23 CR France146
TRIPE,Alfred King Lt kia 23-11-17 RGA attTankCps p189&209 MR17
TRIPHOOK,Owen Leech.MIDx2 LtACapt ded 6-4-19 RFA attIndMilAccsDept p207 CR Iraq8, Maj
TRIPP,Arthur William Howard BrevCol ded 6-5-17 Lpool p73 CR Devon50
TRIPP,Cyril Claude 2Lt kia 13-11-16 3 att7LNLancs p136 CR France384
TRIPP,Donald Owen Howard.DSO.TCapt kia 18-8-16 1LNLancs p136 MR21
TRIPP,Harold LtACapt kia 16-8-17 3ESurr att1/4Berks p113 MR30
TRISTRAM,Eric Barrington 2LtTLt kia 6-9-17 RFus att1/5LancF p70 MR30
TRISTRAM,John Hutchinson Lt kia 11-3-15 1Worc p110 MR22
TRISTRAM,Lancelot Barrington Crofte Capt kia 31-10-14 2Leic p88 CR France727,Crofts
TRITTON,Alan George Capt kia 26-10-14 3CldGds p51 CR France727
TROLLOP,J.E.2Lt 27-8-18 7Lond CR France164
TROLLOPE,Cyril Harvey 2Lt kld 4-5-17 2/14Lond attRFC p20&249 CR Kent91
TROLLOPE,William Kennedy 2Lt dow 3-5-17 13RFC p13 CR France95
TROMAN,Thomas Joseph Barnsley T2Lt kia 14-7-16 62MGC p186 MR21,13/14-7-16
TRONTON,Frederick Thomas TCapt kia 25-9-15 10ScotRif p104 MR19
TROREY,George Alan 2Lt dow 21-3-18 177RFA p36 MR27
TROTER,Alexander Nigel Lt dow 12-10-14 3RScots p55
TROTMAN,Francis Henry Lionel T2Lt kia 7-11-18 1Dev p77 CR France937
TROTT,Henry George T2Lt dow 16-8-17 10WelshR p127 CR Belgium16
TROTTER,Alexander Nigel Lt dow 12-10-14 3 att2RScots p55 CR France705
TROTTER,Alexander William Lewis TMaj kia 12-7-16 9Leic p88 CR France397
TROTTER,Alick Dunbar.MC.Lt dow 18-9-18 9SLancs p126 MR37
TROTTER,Archibald Lt kia 31-12-14 CldGds p51 CR France727
TROTTER,Arthur Francis Capt ded 27-4-19 11Lpool p263 CR Berks125
TROTTER,Bertram Freeman T2Lt kia 8-5-17 11Leic p88 CR France223,7-5-17
TROTTER,Colin Liddell TLt ded 22-1-18 SL att3/2KAR p202 CR EAfrica10 &CR Tanzania1
TROTTER,Edward Henry.DSO.TLtCol kia 8-7-16 GrenGds att 18Lpool p50 CR France630
TROTTER,Erle,Britt.MC.DCM.Lt ded 28-5-19 3RWKent p142&265 CR Kent46,dow
TROTTER,Henry Baron.MM.2Lt dow 10-9-18 1WelshGds p53 CR France145
TROTTER,James Keith Lt dow 26-8-14 1GordH p167 CR France658
TROTTER,Kenneth Stuart 2Lt kia 26-4-15 6 att1RB p180 MR29
TROTTER,Reginald Baird.MID Capt kia 9-5-15 2 att 1CamH p168 MR22
TROTTER,Ronald Herbert Gillet Lt kia 25-9-15 3 att2RBerks p140 MR32
TROTTER,Warren Francis Col 19-6-16 OC HB RMA CR C'land&W'land100
TROUNCE,Frank 2Lt kia 4-9-18 11Lond p248 CR France439
TROUNCE,Sydney Abel 2Lt kia 5-5-17 5Suff p217 CR France162
TROUP,Frank Monck-Mason TLt dow 10-4-17 13RFus p70 CR France154
TROUP,John Guthrie 2Lt kia 13-5-17 5ScotRif att16RFC p20&224 CR France32
TROUP,Stewart Houghton TLt kia 2-12-17 7 att2RBerks p140 MR30
TROUSDELL,Maurice George TCapt kia 6-8-17 RASC 436GdsDivTrain p194 CR Belgium12
TROUTON,Desmond Gardner ACapt kia 13-10-17 B102 RFA p36 CR Belgium19
TROUTON,Edmund Arthur Lt kia 1-7-16 3 att9RInniskF p105 MR21
TROWER,Alfred Bence 2Lt kia 29-5-18 1ScotsGds p52
TROWLES,Frederick Herbert T2Lt dow 13-9-18 7EKent p58 CR France122
TROWSDALE,Charles Robert 2Lt dow 2-10-18 KRRC att9Bn p152 CR Belgium112
TRUBRIDGE,R.W.Lt dow 6-5-18 GL &RAF p191
TRUBSHAWE,Eric James 2Lt dow 2-2-17 RE 460FC p210 CR France342,kia
TRUBY,George Edward T2Lt kia 31-7-17 2Lincs D'Coy p76 MR29
TRUEMAN,Albert Edward Mackrell 2Lt dow 30-5-18 2RB p180 MR18
TRUEMAN,Arthur Philip Hamilton MajTLtCol ded 26-11-18 EKent p58 CR Notts68
TRUEMAN,Charles Fitzgerald Hamilton Capt kia 26-8-14 2Manch p156 CR France716
TRUEMAN,William Ernest 2Lt ded 30-10-18 IARO att2S&M p283 MR65
TRUMAN,Alfred Holloway 2Lt kia 6-4-16 3 O&BLI p130 MR38

TRUMAN,Donald George Harding Lt kia 1-7-16 2/5RWar p214 CR France1157
TRUMAN,Thomas Archibald T2Lt ded 17-9-18 RASC 56DivTrain p194 CR France113,13-9-18
TRUMBLE,William Acton.DCM.2Lt ded 9-10-18 1/6Ess p232 CR Egypt2
TRUMP,Frederick Joseph.DSO.LtCol kia 2-12-17 1Mon attSStaffs p244 CR France258
TRUSCOTT,Francis George.MC.MIDx2 Lt dow 6-4-17 6Suff attRFC p20&218 CR Belgium406
TRUSLER,George Lt ded 17-7-18 IARO attIOD p283 MR66
TRUSS,George Marquand 2Lt kia 25-9-16 ScotsGds attMGC p52 CR France513
TRUSTRAM,Raymond Prince.MC.Lt dow 28-8-18 121/27RFA p36 CR France84
TRYHORNE,Mark William Lt ded 12-12-20 1/8Gurkhas MR43
TRYON,George Arthur.MC.CaptALtCol kia 7-11-18 6 att4KRRC p152 CR France978
TRYON,Henry TCapt kia 15-9-16 15 att8RB p180 MR21
TRYON,Richard Capt kia 10-1-15 6 att2RB p180 MR22
TUBBS,Seymour Burnell Capt kia 22-8-17 5Glouc p225 MR30
TUCK,Duncan Beresford.MID TCapt dow 30-3-18 16Mddx p148 CR France145
TUCK,Duncan Johnson Capt dow 3-7-16 3 att6 O&BLI p130 CR France46
TUCK,Henry Malpas T2Lt dow 26-10-18 21Mddx att26RFus p148 CR Belgium158
TUCKER,Alan Robert Lloyd 2Lt kia 18/20-12-14 ULIA attRWar p66&283,19-12-14 MR32
TUCKER,Albert Ruthven 2Lt dow 16-5-17 162RFA p36 CR France113
TUCKER,Alfred Capt kld 8-8-15 5YLI p235 CR Belgium85
TUCKER,Arthur Haines Lt kia 16-10-17 4RSuss att9KRRC p228 CR Belgium112
TUCKER,Cecil Hall 2Lt dow 7-9-15 10NStaffs att8LancF p158 CR Gallipoli2,7-8-15
TUCKER,Clifford Francis 2Lt kia 9-4-18 RLancs att1/5Bn p59 MR19
TUCKER,Donald Cecil 2Lt kia 24-3-18 GL &41RFC p13&191 MR20
TUCKER,Edwin George T2Lt kia 13-10-15 10Norf p74 MR19
TUCKER,Frederick Dennis 2Lt kia 25-9-15 1RWSurr p56 MR30
TUCKER,Frederick St.George TMaj kia 3-7-16 10Worc p110 CR France393
TUCKER,H.G.2Lt kld 4-4-18 GL &RAF p191
TUCKER,James Parke LtTCapt kia 23-4-17 3 att10N&D p135 MR20
TUCKER,John Ayre.MID Lt kia 1-11-14 115Bty RFA p36 CR Belgium57
TUCKER,Leslie Archibald 2Lt kia 22-3-18 2TankCps p189 MR27
TUCKER,Lionel Louis Clerici T2Lt kia 1-7-16 20NumbF p63 MR21
TUCKER,Samuel William Joseph Brocklehurst T2Lt dow 13-9-18 Norf att2/5Lancs p74 CR France31,att25Lpool
TUCKER,Sidney.MM.2Lt dow 11-8-18 20Lond p251 CR France69
TUCKER,Stanley Dawson Simm Lt kia 26-10-17 6NumbF p214 MR30
TUCKER,Tudor Henry St.George Maj ded 19-8-17 IA PoiticalDept att21Punjabis p283 MR43
TUCKER,William Henry 2Lt kia 1-7-16 1/12Lond p248 MR21
TUCKEY,Albert William TLt kia 25-9-15 1Nhampt p138 CR France219
TUCKEY,James Caulfield 2Lt kia 31-8-16 13Mddx p148 MR21
TUCKWELL,John Henry Graham 2Lt kia 23-3-18 7A&SH p243 MR20
TUDHOPE,Thomas 2Lt kia 25-9-15 3 att9ScotRif p104 MR19
TUDOR,Alan Roper T2Lt kia 5-6-17 9SfthH p165 CR France97
TUDOR,Percival Bradbury 2Lt ded 1-11-18 RH &FA 26JacobsMtnBty p36 CR Iraq8
TUDOR-JONES,Charles Edward Tudor 2Lt kld 15-12-15 ELancs attRFC p2&111 CR France1144
TUDSBERY,Lancelot 2Lt kia 22-8-17 B70RFA p36 CR Belgium8
TUDWAY,Hervey Robert Charles Lt dow 18-11-14 2GrenGds p50 CR France102
TUFF,Cecil Thomas Capt kia 18-4-15 3 att1RWKent D'Coy p142 MR29
TUFF,Frank Noel 2Lt dow 5-11-15 REKentYeo p204 CR Europe1
TUFFLEY,Victor Evelyn.DSO.MC.MID Lt dow 7-9-18 10Lond p248 CR France511
TUFFREY,Charles 2Lt ded 2-1-17 RDC p272 CR C'land&W'land17
TUFNELL,Carlton Edward Capt kia 15-9-16 3CldGds p51 CR France402
TUFNELL,Carlton Wyndham Lt kia 6-11-14 GrenGds p50 CR Belgium134,Carleton
TUFNELL,Gilbert Jolliffe 2Lt ded 22-2-18 RGA p262 CR Essex128,RFA
TUFNELLA,W.CMG.DSO.Col IA 8Lucknow 17-5-20 CR India97A
TUFT,Gerald Hugh 2Lt kia 27-4-17 6N&D p233 CR France375
TUFTS,George Henry T2Lt kld 26-1-18 KRRC &RFC p17&152 CR Norf285
TUGBY,Leslie Andrew T2Lt kia 18-9-18 13WelshR p127 CR France415
TUGWELL,Claude Buchanan Capt 28-3-17 Dors CR Surrey160
TUGWELL,Frederick William 2Lt ded 2-3-19 RWSurr p262 CR Sussex143
TUGWELL,Geoffrey Arnold.MID Capt kia 23-4-17 4Yorks p220 MR20
TUGWELL,Oswald Norman 2Lt dow 22-4-17 4 att1WYorks p83 CR France80
TUITE,Henry Mark LtCol dow 24-3-18 RMunstF p176 MR20
TUITE,Mark Alan Wallace 2Lt dow 2-12-17 10Lond attTankCps p189&248 CR France398

TUKE,Arthur Harold Seymour 2Lt kia 7-5-15 3 att2NumbF p63&258,Harrington MR29
TUKE,Cyril Stratford TCapt kia 25-9-15 9BlkW attMGC p129&186,27-9-15 MR19
TUKE,Francis Henry Chap4Cl kia 20-7-16 RAChDept att53Bde p200 MR21
TUKE,Ottley TLt kia 17-10-18 7EYorks att 1YLI p85 CR france190
TUKE,Percy George T2Lt dow 21-3-18 20MGC p186 MR27
TULETT,William John HonCapt ded 6-5-17 11N&D p264 CR Yorks561
TULL,Walter David 2Lt kia 25-3-18 5 att23Mddx Ex 17Bn p148 MR20,Daniel
TULLIDGE,Bernard Henry ACapt kia 27-8-17 6 att13Worc p110 MR30
TULLIDGE,Robert Milton 2LtACapt dow 25-1-17 13 att9RWar p66 CR Iraq5
TULLIS,John Drysdale Capt dow 18-11-14 1RScotsF p95 CR France64
TULLIS,Robert Ramsey Capt dow 25-5-15 7A&SH p243 CR France285
TULLIS,William Capt&Adjt 1-7-16 RScotsF att22NumbFp95 MR21
TULLOCH,Edith Sarah SNurse 8-10-18 QAIMNS CR Surrey160
TULLOCH,Ernest St.Clair TLt kia 7-7-16 11NumbF p63 MR21
TULLOCH,William T2Lt kia 20-7-16 53MGC Inf p186 CR France630,TULLOCK
TULLOH,Cecil Falconer Capt kia 13-10-14 Mddx p148 CR France1106
TULLOH,George Swinton LtCol kia 10-5-15 2Glouc p107 CR Belgium167,9-5-15
TULLY,Henry Robson 2Lt dow 27-5-18 8 att4NumbF p63 MR18
TULLY,James Kivas Capt dow 19-9-16 1/7Mddx p235 CR France23
TULLY,Richard Latimer 2Lt ded 22-7-18 4 att12NumbF p213 CR France84
TULLY,Thomas Michael T2Lt ded 9-10-18 GL RE IWT p49 CR Iraq6
TULLY-CHRISTIE,William Kerwin Capt ded 20-2-18 RAVC p199 CR Lond4
TUMILTY,Austin T2Lt ded 10-11-17 11RDubF p177 MR20
TUNBRIDGE,Arthur Thomas Hornby T2Lt kia 12-10-17 RBerks att6Bn p140 MR30
TUNBRIDGE,Gerard Charles 2Lt dow PoW 27-4-18 1Y&L p159 CR Greece3
TUNE,Charles Walter T2Lt kia 23-11-17 13Yorks p91 MR17
TUNKS,Edward Joseph Austin 2Lt kia 3-4-18 4Hamps p228 CR France924,14-4-18
TUNNAH,William T2Lt ded 28-4-18 PoW WYorks att1/6Bn p83 CR Belgium111
TUNNELL,Oliver T2Lt kia 24-10-18 12/13NumbF p63 MR16
TUNSTALL,James Charles Francis T2Lt kia 14-2-17 11KRRC p152 CR France744
TUPMAN,Arthur Lyon Lt kia 22-8-18 3N&D &80RAF p135 CR France329,2Lt 2Bn
TUPPER,Harold 2Lt dow 22-7-18 10RFus p70 CR Kent224,Lt
TURBUTT,Gladwyn Maurice Revell Lt kia 21-10-14 3 O&BLI p130 CR Belgium126
TURK,George Deane 2Lt dow 23-6-17 PoW 7 att1Ess p232 CR Germany1
TURK,Herbert Henry.MC.2Lt kia 3-11-16 11RFC p4 CR France46
TURNBULL,Alexander Miller 2Lt kia 25-4-17 GL &12RFC p13 CR France421
TURNBULL,Arthur Francis X.T2Lt kld 9-2-18 RFC p17 CR Dorset115
TURNBULL,David Stevens Lt kld 15-4-17 6BlkW attRFC p20&231 CR Scot237
TURNBULL,Derwent Christopher Lt dow 14-3-15 RAMC 84FA att1Ches p198 CR Belgium59
TURNBULL,Dudley Ralph.DSO.BrMajALtCol kia 1-10-17 GordH att20Manch p167 CR Belgium308
TURNBULL,Francis Egerton 2Lt kia 27-5-18 DLI att1Wilts p162 MR18
TURNBULL,George T2Lt kia 14-4-18 16RScots p55 MR32
TURNBULL,Gerald Illtyd.MC.TLt dow PoW 9-4-18 18WelshR p127 CR France1027,Gerard 20-4-18
TURNBULL,Henry James 2Lt kia 25-9-16 1/7Lpool p215 MR21
TURNBULL,Hugh McDiarmid Lt kia 5-9-17 4RScots p211 CR Belgium24,Macdiarmid
TURNBULL,Hugh Vincent Corbett Capt kia 13-11-14 2KOSB p102 MR29
TURNBULL,John Oswin Capt kia 8-9-16 3 att2WelshR p127 MR21
TURNBULL,John Seymour Lt 17-6-18 Worc &41RAF MR20
TURNBULL,Laurence 2Lt kia 16-6-15 3 att2Beds p87 MR22
TURNBULL,Maxwell.MC TCapt ded 18-10-18 3 att8BordR p118 CR France40
TURNBULL,Robert.MC.T2Lt kia 25-8-18 13RB p180 CR France518
TURNBULL,Robert Duncan 2Lt kia 5-9-18 RGA 144SB p42 CR France568
TURNBULL,Robert Henry.MC.T2Lt dow 4-6-18 18LancF p94 CR France84,Hendry
TURNBULL,Stephen John.DCM.Lt 19-4-20 RAOC MR43
TURNBULL,Thomas Russell T2Lt kia 11-10-16 11 att9BlkW p129 CR France1059
TURNBULL,William T2Lt kia 12-6-17 53RFC p13 MR20
TURNBULL,William Andrew 2Lt kia 17-7-16 5Yorks p221 CR Belgium60
TURNBULL,William Arthur TLt kia 13-11-16 4Beds p87 CR France220
TURNBULL,William Elliot Lt kia 28-4-15 5RScots p211 MR4
TURNELL,Reginald Leaf T2Lt kia 23-11-17 13 att20Mddx p148 MR17
TURNELL,Robert Douglas.MM.T2Lt kia 27-3-18 52RFC p17 CR France300
TURNER,Alan Fletcher Lt kia 13-5-15 1/1LeicYeo p204 MR29 CR Belgium453
TURNER,Alan Joseph Chamerton 2Lt ded 5-10-18 RASC p267 CR Lancs34,Chamberlain 6-10-18
TURNER,Alan Macfarlane 2LtTLt dow 19-12-15 1/5HLI p240 CR Gallipoli3
TURNER,Alexander Buller.VC.2Lt dow 1-10-15 3 att1RBerks p140 CR France98

TURNER,Alexander Law Lt ded 12-3-16 A1/3RFA p208 CR Egypt3
TURNER,Arthur.TD.LtCol ded 11-8-15 RE p272 CR War
TURNER,Arthur 2Lt kia 26-6-17 4DLI p162 CR France149,2Bn
TURNER,Arthur Charlewood 2Lt kia 16-1-18 6RB p180 CR France154
TURNER,Bernard TLtACapt kia 8-5-17 14RWar p66 CR France777
TURNER,Bingham Alexander.DSO.Capt kia 2-11-14 6RB p180 MR29
TURNER,Charles Hampden.MID TMaj kia 30-9-15 2Suff p79 MR29
TURNER,Charles Rushton 2Lt ded 30-10-15 RH&FA 3C ResBde p36
TURNER,Crosby Russell Swanson 2Lt kia 27-7-16 3Dors attKRRC p124 MR21
TURNER,Cuthbert 2Lt kia 23-4-17 4 att7BordR p228 MR20
TURNER,David Fotheringham T2Lt kia 26-9-15 8EYorks p85 CR France1723
TURNER,David Thompson Capt kia 30-5-18 4NumbF p213 CR France1689
TURNER,Douglas William 2Lt ded 15-2-19 Ess p132 CR Nhampt79,17-2-19
TURNER,Duncan 2Lt ded 16-10-16 IA TC att80CarnaticInf p283
TURNER,Edgar Harold Holmes T2Lt dow 23-10-16 11WelshR p127 CR Greece6
TURNER,Edmund Sanctuary 2Lt kia 21-8-15 RGA 116SB p209 CR France397,21-8-16
TURNER,Edward Percy TLtACapt kia 19-3-17 2RFA p36 CR France115,42RFA
TURNER,Elliott Douglas 2Lt kia 24-8-18 5HLI p240 CR France162,Douglass
TURNER,Eric Walter Carpenter Lt dow 9-8-16 3 att2Hamps CR Belgium165
TURNER,Ernest Arthur Lt kia 3-9-16 1/6WYorks p218 MR21
TURNER,Ernest Augustus Lt ded 10-10-18 UnListEAfr CR SAfrica69
TURNER,Ernest Gilbert.DSO.2LtTCapt kia 12-4-17 11RScots p55 MR20
TURNER,Ernest John 2Lt dow 3-4-18 10 att2/4YLI att20EntrenchBn p144 CR France145
TURNER,Evelyn Victor TLt kia 18-11-16 GL att8NStaffs p191 MR21
TURNER,Frederick Eley 2Lt ded 27-9-18 1/2WYorks &RAF p83 CR France1061
TURNER,Francis Ignatius T2Lt kld 27-9-18 att8WYorks p83 CR France755,8 att1Bn
TURNER,Frederick Harding Lt kia 10-1-15 10Lpool p216 CR Belgium186,2Lt
TURNER,Frederick Harry.MC.TLt kld 10-1-17 GL &RFC p13&191 CR Bucks51
TURNER,Frederick Richard 2Lt kia 15-1-17 A100RFA p36 CR Greece6
TURNER,Frederick Whitecross T2Lt kia 9-4-17 4 att10ScotRif p104 MR20
TURNER,Frederick William Robertson Lt kia 5-8-16 RE 2Coy p210 CR France158
TURNER,George Corrall Capt kia 13-9-17 2/6WYorks p218 CR France563
TURNER,George Henry T2Lt kia 15-10-18 YLI att1/4Bn p144 CR France316,13-10-18
TURNER,George Herbert T2Lt dow 14-6-16 13 att15RWar p66 CR France1
TURNER,George Pernor T2Lt kia 30-6-16 GL 14Hamps att116TMB p191 MR19
TURNER,Gerard Capt kia 4-6-15 IA 1/5GurkhaRif p283 CR Gallipoli3
TURNER,Gilbert Austin 2Lt kia 17-11-16 3RWKent att7LNLancs p142 MR21
TURNER,Harcourt Charles Lt kia 23-8-17 3 att6DCLI p115 MR30
TURNER,Harold Frank Barclay LtACapt dow 1-9-17 Wilts p153 CR Belgium72
TURNER,Harold Lake Compton Maj ded 14-6-18 IA 1/2GurkhaRif p283 MR43,2/9Bn
TURNER,Harold Runciman.MC&Bar.Maj kia 19-5-18 RGA 297SB p209 CR France113
TURNER,Henry Alfred.DCM.T2Lt kia 18-9-18 5 att8KSLI p145 CR Greece5
TURNER,Henry Hamilton Fyres LtCol kia 1-12-17 IA 2Lancers p283 CR France446
TURNER,Henry Scott 2Lt ded 11-3-15 BlkW p129 CR Mddx52
TURNER,Herbert Deacon 2Lt kia 20-8-17 GL &70RFC p13 MR20
TURNER,Herbert Duncan Bruce Lt ded 9-8-17 20/9RFA attRFC p13&36 CR Lancs34
TURNER,Herbert Ellery Capt kia 15-4-18 RGA 169SB p209 CR France881
TURNER,Herbert Guy Capt kia 2/3-3-15 2Ches p97 MR32
TURNER,Herbert Kersey TCapt kia 15-7-16 4Suff p217 CR France453
TURNER,Herbert Norman TLt kia 14-7-16 12WYorks p83 CR France453
TURNER,Herbert Stanley 2Lt kia 24-3-18 15DLI p162 MR27
TURNER,Hubert Samuel Alston 2Lt kia 1-8-17 2Yorks p91 MR29
TURNER,Humphrey Shewell Capt 7-12-15 46Punjabis attRE 31DivSigs MR43 &CR Pakistan50A
TURNER,James Alexander.DSO.MC.LtTLtCol kia 26-7-18 2RScots p55 CR France864
TURNER,James Clifford Lt kia 3-8-16 RFA &RFC p4&36 CR Belgium265
TURNER,John 2Lt kia 29-11-16 7GordH p242 CR France239
TURNER,John AssComsy&Lt ded 11-7-17 IndOrdDept p283 CR Iraq6
TURNER,John 2Lt dow PoW 13-4-18 2TankCps p189 CR Germany3
TURNER,John.MC.ACapt kia 22-10-18 8 att10RWar p215 CR Franxce270
TURNER,John Alvey 2Lt kia 24-2-17 7Mddx p235 MR19
TURNER,John Percival 2Lt kia 26-10-17 3 att14RWar p66 MR30,Capt
TURNER,John Reginald Lt kia 13-10-14 3Dors p124 CR France279

TURNER,Joseph Henry.MC.T2Lt dow 21-9-18 11 att6RWKent p142 CR France194
TURNER,Kenneth Leigh T2Lt kia 2-5-18 5RRofCav attWorcYeo p23 CR Palestine3
TURNER,Maurice Arthur TCapt kia 16-7-16 4Suff p217 MR21
TURNER,Miles Ransome Lt ded 13-1-20 IAUL 25Cav p283 MR43
TURNER,Noel Cuthbert 2Lt ded 29-6-16 IARO p283 CR Surrey34
TURNER,Noel Price James.MID Lt dow 10-5-15 3 att1SWBord p101 CR France80,9-5-15
TURNER,Percival Eric 2Lt dow 5-10-17 143MGC p186 CR Belgium16
TURNER,Percy Herbert 2Lt kia 6-7-15 3 att2SWBord p101 CR Gallipoli6
TURNER,Ralph Pool T2Lt ded 9-3-16 GL &1RFC p4&191 CR Belgium132
TURNER,Reginald T2Lt kia 20-11-17 KSLI att6th p145 CR France379
TURNER,Reginald Allison 2Lt kia 21-3-18 30MGC Inf p186 CR France1701
TURNER,Richard George 2Lt kld 4-5-17 RFC 37ResSqn p13 CR Hamps76
TURNER,Richard Radford 2Lt kia 3-2-17 3RSuss p120 CR Belgium4
TURNER,Robert Henry Lt dow 23-3-18 5Lincs p220 CR France177
TURNER,Roger Bingham Lt kia 9-4-16 3Ches p97 MR38
TURNER,Ronald 2Lt kia 15-8-16 1/5Ess p232 MR4
TURNER,Russell Sandon Capt kia 4-10-17 5RWar p214 MR30
TURNER,Thomas Alfred TLt kia 29-4-17 50RFA p36 CR France96,D5RFA
TURNER,Thomas Edwin Lt kia 9-5-15 13Lond p249 MR32
TURNER,Thomas James 2Lt kia 2-9-18 4RScots p211 CR France646
TURNER,Thomas Norman Leslie 2Lt murderBySepoy 26-3-16 IARO att48Pnrs p283 MR38
TURNER,Walter Gregory 2Lt kia 8-6-17 4Leic p220 MR20
TURNER,Warren Geoffrey Dalton Lt kia 24-5-17 GL &11RFC p13 MR20
TURNER,William Capt ded 6-4-18 RAMC p254 CR Scot501
TURNER,William Ernest 2Lt kia 27-8-17 7Worc p226 MR30
TURNER,William Joseph T2Lt kia 12-10-18 Mddx att4Bn p148 CR France206
TURNER,William Marlow 2Lt ded 28-10-18 IA LabCps att61BurmaLabCo p266 CR Lond8,28-10-16
TURNER,William Rowland.MC.TLt dow 10-11-17 RE 254TC p49 CR Belgium11,Roland MM not MC
TURNER,William Stewart Lt kia 16-6-15 10Lpool p216 MR29
TURNER,William Tom Capt kia 10-8-15 7Ches p223 MR4
TURNEY,Leonard William Maj kia 3-5-17 6 att8RFus p70 MR20
TURNEY,William 2Lt kia 10-7-16 8SStaffs p123 MR21
TURNLEY,John Francis T2Lt kia 16-4-18 9MGC Inf p186 MR30,TURNLY
TURNOR,Christopher Randolph Lt kia 26-10-14 10Huss p22 CR Belgium117
TURNOUR,Arthur William Winterton 2LtTLt kia 25-9-15 2RB p180 MR32
TURPIE,McKenzie Fleming 2Lt dow 23-7-16 7LNLancs p136 MR21
TURPIN,James Knowles Lt kia 14-8-17 A241RFA p208 CR Belgium10
TURPIN,James Stephen T2Lt dow 21-5-16 GL 8SomLI attTMB p191 CR France23
TURRELL,Henry Gifford 2Lt dow 3-11-17 4 O&BLI p231 CR Oxford71
TURTON,Alice Mary SNurse ded 7-5-17 QAIMNS SR att26StatHosp p200 CR Egypt8
TURTON,Cecil William Lt kld 4-2-16 6RSuss p228 CR Sussex112
TURTON,Edmund Spencer Lt kia 1-9-15 YorkHussYeo p206 CR Belgium11,31-8-15
TURTON,Ernest Francis LtACapt kia 27-10-17 RGA 117HB p42 CR Belgium101
TURTON,Richard Dacre TLt kia 24-9-17 9Y&L p159 CR Belgium19
TURTON,Robert Straker Maj ded 15-12-19 RAMC p267 CR CentralAmerica6
TURTON,Thomas Charles T2Lt kia 8-5-17 14Lpool p73 CR Greece6
TURTON,Zouch Austin Lt kia 23-4-15 Norf attEYorks p74 MR29
TUSON,William 2Lt kld 27-3-18 8Manch p237 MR20,26-3-18
TUSON,William.MBE.Capt ded 29-1-20 RAMC CR Hamps1
TUTIN,Guy Lantley Lt ded 27-1-19 3N&D att2/4RBerks p255 CR Notts66
TUTTIETT,Laurence William Capt kia 2-9-16 12RSuss p120 MR21,3-9-16
TUTTON,Francis James.MM.T2Lt dow 26-8-18 RBerks att5Bn p140 CR France630
TUZO,John Atkinson Capt ded 8-4-18 6RSuss attEARlys p228 CR EAfrica36
TWEDDELL,Thomas Lt dow 28-6-18 3 att7Yorks p91 CR France145,att7EYorks
TWEDDLE,William John 2Lt kia 16-4-17 7Ess p232 France423,4Ess att9Suff
TWEEDALE,Eric T2Lt kia 1-7-16 13 att16WYorks p83 MR21
TWEEDALE,Maurice Capt kia 16-5-17 7Lpool p215 CR France279
TWEEDIE,Alexander 2Lt kia 19-4-17 5KOSB p224 CR Palestine8
TWEEDIE,Cunningham Burnside.MC.TCapt dow 17-4-17 6KOSB p102 CR France40
TWEEDIE,David 2Lt dow 5-8-18 5RScotsF p222 CR France27,6-8-18
TWEEDIE,Gilbert TLt ded 21-4-18 RRofCav p261 CR Scot109
TWEEDIE,Leslie Kinloch T2Lt kia 17-1-16 C72RFA p36 CR France423
TWEEDIE-SMITH,Alan Morton.MID T2Lt kia 13-10-15 1RWSurr p57 MR19
TWEEDIE-SMITH,Douglas TLt ded 10-4-16 GL &RFC p4&191
TWEEDY,Cecil Mahon Lt kia 28-2-17 3RDubF p177 CR France215

TWEEDY,Francis Charles Lt kia 9-10-17 5LancF p221 MR30,C.F.
TWEEDY,Gerald Vincent T2Lt kia 13-4-17 BordR att11Bn p118 CR France672
TWEEDY,Maurice Willoughby TLt ded 29-10-17 APCps p268 CR France1180,TWEEDIE
TWEEDY,R.C.Maj 12-7-17 RAMC CR Cornwall163
TWEEDY,Trevor Carlyon Capt kia 15-9-16 6NumbF p213 CR France402
TWEEDY,William Wildman T2Lt kia 27-5-18 RE 3Workshop 3LabBn p49 CR France84
TWEEN,Alfred Stuart.DSO.TMaj kia 23-3-18 10Ess p132 CR France1893
TWELVETREES,Bernard T2Lt kia 4-10-17 RWKent att5Glos p142 CR Belgium128
TWELVETREES,Edward Dudley Lt kia 8-8-18 1Camb p245 CR France196
TWENLOW-ALLEN,William Alfred T2Lt kia 18-10-16 18Lpool p73 CR France385,TWEMLOW
TWENTYMAN,Arthur Capt kia 29-11-14 10Lpool p216 CR France525
TWENTYMAN,Denzil Clive Tate TCapt kia 1-7-16 10Y&L p159 CR France267
TWENTYMAN,Joseph Jefferson.DCM.T2Lt ded 11-2-19 HLI p255&265 CR C'land&W'land9
TWIDALE,Elfric Ashby 2Lt kia 22-4-17 RFA attRFC p13&36 CR France214
TWIGG,Albert Ransom Lt kia 12-4-18 8DLI p239 MR32,Ramsom
TWIGG,Ellis T2Lt kia 18-9-18 4RFus p70 MR16
TWIGG,Francis William LtACapt kia 24-9-18 1Nhampt p138 CR France375
TWIGGE,Francis 2Lt dow 9-4-17 3 att1NumbF p63 CR France418
TWINE,Harold William T2Lt kia 13-5-16 2Y&L p159 CR Belgium73
TWINING,Cecil Francis Harvey Capt kia 3-5-15 3 att1Hamps A'Coy p121 MR29
TWINING,Richard Wake 2Lt kia 1-7-16 1Dev p77 CR France174
TWISS,Arthur Montague Capt kia 17-11-14 RE att3S&M p49 CR Iraq6
TWIST,Francis Cecil Orr 2Lt kia 30-7-16 18Manch p156 MR21
TWITE,Harold Llewellyn Lt kia 1-12-15 RFA attRE 183TC p208 CR France394
TWOMEY,Francis Philip 2Lt kia 22-2-17 IA 54 att51Sikhs p283 CR Iraq5
TWYFORD,Lionel Thomas Campbell.MID ColTBrigGen 24-8-20 NStaffs CR Surrey58
TWYMAN,Percy Gedge T2Lt dow 15-4-17 10RFus p70 CR France40,Lt
TWYNAM,Cyril Francis Frederick Lt kia 15-4-18 3HLI p164 CR France924
TWYNAM,Godfrey 2Lt dow 18-11-16 11BordR p118 CR France153
TYACK,Richard Henry.MID TCapt dow 4-11-18 6DCLI p115 CR France332
TYACKE,Charles Noel Walker Capt kia 23-3-18 5DCLI p227 CR France1203
TYACKE,Edward Humphry TLt kia 29-5-18 25MGC p186 MR18
TYDD,William John Stern 2Lt dow 22-1-17 4ConnRgrs p172 CR France285
TYERMAN,Cyril Laurence Lt kia 9-4-18 6DLI p239 MR32
TYLDEN-PATTENSON,Arthur Dagnall TLt kia 5-1-15 2 O&BLI p130 CR France1106
TYLDESLEY,William Knowles Lt kld 26-4-18 5 att9LNLancs p234 CR Belgium21,kia
TYLEE,Jervis Moore Lt kia 24-8-14 15Huss p22 MR15
TYLER,Albert Lt kia 12-11-14 RE p49 MR29
TYLER,Alfred Herbert Maj kia 11-11-14 RE p49 MR29
TYLER,Cornelius George Capt dow 11-7-16 3 att2Beds p87 MR21
TYLER,E.W.MC.Capt 25-9-20 4RFus CR Iraq8
TYLER,Gilbert Edward.MC.2Lt dow 18-9-16 19Lond p251 CR France177
TYLER,Guy Cromwell TLtACapt kia 22-8-18 1Norf A'Coy p74 CR France281
TYLER,Harold Robert Capt kia 18-8-15 1/4Ess p232 CR Gallipoli4
TYLER,Herbert Henry.MC.Capt kia 17/19-9-18 6N&D p233 MR16
TYLER,John Collett 2Lt kia 18-4-15 RFA p36 MR29
TYLER,Roper Maxwell.DSO.LtCol ded 26-3-19 DLI p162 CR Germany1,26-2-19
TYLER,William Alfred 2Lt kia 27-8-18 7Lond p247 CR France164
TYLER,William Eric T2Lt ded 28-10-18 MGC p186 CR Somerset198
TYNDALE,George Stafford Hilliard Lt dow 13-3-15 WIndiaR att2Mddx p192 CR France102
TYNDALL,Arthur George T2Lt kia 18-11-17 2RB A'Coy p180 MR30
TYNDALL,James 2Lt dow 4-6-17 19Lond p251 CR France518
TYNDALL,Joseph Charles Lt kia 2-3-15 4RDubF attRIrRif p177 CR Belgium17
TYNDALL,William Ernest Marriott.DSO.BtLtCol dow 1-8-16 WRid p116 CR Surrey160
TYNER,Thomas Goodwin T2Lt kia 9-9-16 9RDubF p177 MR21
TYNTE,M.A.TMaj ded 7-12-18 6RMunstF p176 CR Eire532
TYRER,Christopher St.John T2Lt dow 24-7-16 15RWar p66 CR France833
TYRER,John Rawsthorne 2Lt kia 9-10-17 7Manch attRFC p20,8-10-17&p237,Lt CR Belgium23
TYRIE,David T2Lt kia 18-4-18 15DLI p162 MR30
TYRRELL,Arthur James 2Lt kia 7-3-17 10RLancs p59 MR38
TYRRELL,Francis Chichester Lt dow 15-2-15 3CldGds p51 CR France80,2Lt 16-2-15

TYRRELL,Gerald Ernest.DSO.MIDx4 LtCol ded 17-5-17 RGA 64HAG p42 CR Lond28
TYRRELL,John Marcus 2Lt kld 20-6-18 3RIrFus attRAF p172 CR France102,Capt
TYRRELL,John McIntosh T2Lt kia 9-4-17 8EYorks p85 CR France581,Lt
TYRRELL,Joseph Lionel Allanson T2Lt kia 3-3-16 8 att5Nhampt A'Coy p138 MR19,2-3-16
TYRRELL,Launcelot Adrian Hope T2Lt kia 13-11-16 8EYorks p85 CR France742,Lt
TYRRELL,Leonard Collin 2Lt kia 9-10-17 5WYorks p218 MR30
TYRRELL,Oscar 2Lt kia 9-9-16 10Lond p248 MR21
TYRRELL,W.A.Capt kld 9-6-18 GL &RAF p191
TYRRELL,Walter T2Lt dow 4-9-18 1/2 att17RWFus p99 CR France41
TYRRELL-GREEN,Dennis Noel Lt kia 26-3-17 4RSuss p228 MR34
TYRWHITT,Nathaniel Bridges Maj kia 28-12-15 16Lond p249 CR Belgium44,25-12-15
TYRWHITT-DRAKE,D'Urban John 2Lt kia 3-5-17 HouseholdBn p20 MR20
TYRWHITT-DRAKE,Thomas Victor 2Lt kia 29-1-17 1RB p180 CR France439
TYSER,George Beaumont TMaj kia 5-7-16 7ELancs p111 CR France150
TYSER,Henry Erskine T2Lt kia 9-4-17 8BlkW D'Coy p129 CR France729
TYSOE,Leonard T2Lt kia 31-5-17 39LabCps p189 CR France729
TYSON,Alexander Baird LtACapt kia 24-4-17 2A&SH p174 CR France434,23-4-17
TYSON,Claude Richmond 2Lt kia 22-8-17 O&BLI 2/1BucksBn p232 MR30
TYSON,Donald T2Lt kia 8-5-15 7YLI p144 CR France922,7-8-15
TYSON,Eric James.DSO.MC.TMaj dow 11-3-18 5RFC p17 CR France15,12-3-18
TYSON,John Tyson 2Lt mbk 25-9-15 IARO att2/3GurkhaRif p283 MR28
TYSON,Percy Eldin 2Lt kia 8-12-16 3 att2WelshR p127 MR21
TYSON,William Noel Dawson TLt kia 29-9-18 15Ches p97 CR Belgium116
TYTLER,James Hall 2Lt dow 16-9-16 9DLI p239 CR France188
TYTLER,Robert Adam Neilson Maj ded 5-6-19 GordH p255 CR Lond8
TYTLER,William Boyd TLt kia 1-7-16 22NumbF p63 MR21
TYZACK,Eric Delaney 2Lt kia 15-9-17 RE attRFC p20&210 CR France705

———————— U ————————

UDNY,George Richard Murray 2Lt dow 17-5-15 2GordH p167 CR France80
UINT,C.SubCdr 24-9-20 RIM MR65
ULLMAN,Douglas Maurice Jaques T2Lt kia 23-4-17 24RFus p70 CR France777
ULLYOTT,Cecil 2Lt kia 23-8-18 5EYorks p219 CR France215
ULOTH,Arthur Curtis Wilmot.MC.Lt dow 19-9-18 3RSuss p120 CR France194
UMNEY,Basil Charles Lovell 2Lt kia 22-7-16 4RFus p70 MR21,23-7-16
UMNEY,Cecil Francis T2Lt kia 26-9-16 7 att5Dors p124 CR France314
UNCLES,Charles William 2Lt kia 9-10-17 4YLI p235 MR30
UNDERHILL,Charles Bertram TLt kia 27-3-16 12WYorks p83 CR Belgium105
UNDERHILL,Cyril Scott T2Lt dow 21-1-16 9KSLI p145 CR Belgium1
UNDERHILL,Edward Samuel TCapt kia 12-10-16 8LNLancs C'Coy p136 CR France393
UNDERHILL,George TLt kia 6-9-16 9Dev p77 MR21
UNDERHILL,Hugh Caulfield 2Lt mbk 8-8-15 IARO att1/6GurkhaRif p283 MR4
UNDERHILL,Reginald LtACapt kia 18-11-16 11 att4Mddx p148 MR21
UNDERHILL,Thomas William T2Lt kia 19-8-16 EKent p58 CR France164
UNDERHILL,William Annesley Capt kia 21-10-14 Worc p110 MR22
UNDERWOOD,Alexander Russell.DCM.MID AssSurg4Cl drd 13-9-17 IMS att23IndGH CR Iraq5
UNDERWOOD,Cyril Charles 2Lt kia 4-2-17 1/7Worc att 1/8War p226 CR France1472
UNDERWOOD,Cyril Henry ACapt kia 2-5-18 17Lond p272
UNDERWOOD,Edmund Poole T2Lt kia 30-7-16 17 att29RFus p70 MR21,29 att 17Bn
UNDERWOOD,Edward James 2Lt dow 8-6-17 RFA X47TMB p36 CR Belgium11
UNDERWOOD,Francis 2Lt dow 18-4-17 4RWKent attYLI p234 CR France583
UNDERWOOD,George Milne 2Lt kia 6-3-17 GL &16RFC p14 MR20
UNDERWOOD,Harold Henry Capt kia 19-4-17 1/4Nhampt p234 CR Palestine8
UNDERWOOD,Harry.DCM.Lt&QM ded 18-10-17 RAMC att ADMS EgyptHospStaff p198 CR Egypt2
UNDERWOOD,John T2Lt dow 16-4-17 10Leics p88 CR France40,8Bn
UNDERWOOD,John Middleton 2Lt kia 10-11-16 3/45RFA p209 CR France374
UNDERY,John Alfred 2Lt kia 29-10-14 4RFus p70 MR29 26-10-14
UNGER,Michael James 2Lt drd 20-9-15 IARO att 14FerozeporeSikhs p283 MR4
UNIACKE,Henry Percy.CB.LtCol kia 13-3-17 2GordH p167 CR France768
UNIACKE,Robie Fitzgerald MajTLtCol kld 28-5-15 RInnisKF p105 CR France1091
UNSWORTH,Cyril Joseph TLt dow 7-7-16 7SLancs p126 CR France23,2Lt
UNWIN,Ernest Frederick.MID TMaj ded 22-3-16 RASC att10RFC ResSqn p4&194 CR Lond12,dow

UNWIN,Francis John Lt kia 17-9-19 3KSLI &RAF p265
UNWIN,George Ernest T2Lt ded 25-10-18 LabCps p266 CR Yorks547
UNWIN,George Stuart T2Lt kia 30-7-16 15 att11N&D p135 CR France515
UNWIN,Lancelot Urquhart Capt kia 27-4-15 Hamps p121 MR29
UNWIN,Reginald William 2Lt kia 8-10-16 11 att1/5Lond p248 MR21
UNWIN,Wilfrid Peyto T2Lt ded 16-5-16 16RIrRif p170 CR France167
UPFILL,Thomas Henry.MC.Lt kld 18-10-18 RFA att59RAF p36 CR France658
UPHILL,Reginald William James 2Lt kia 22-3-18 1RFus p70 MR27
UPJOHN,William Moon Lt kia 24-8-18 1WelshGds p53 CR France560
UPPERTON,C.B.Capt 31-3-17 SomLI CR Kent27
UPPLEBY,Wyvil Charles Spinola Capt dow 9-2-18 12RSuss p120 CR France1092
UPRICHARD,Henry Albert TMaj kia 1-7-16 13RIrRif p170 CR France383
UPSON,Humphrey Cyril TCapt kia 29-7-16 RGA 109SB p42 CR France397
UPSTONE,Cedric Donovan 2Lt ded 11-7-16 1/4Dev p220 MR65
UPTON,Hon Eric Edward Montagu John.MIDx2 Capt&Adjt kia 9-5-15 2KRRC p152 CR France632
UPTON,John Alberic Everard 2Lt dow 20-8-16 7KSLI D'Coy p145 CR France141,3Bn
UPTON,Ralph Hamon Weeley 2Lt kia 3-5-17 3 att8ESurr p113 CR France162
UPTON,Roger Maitland 2Lt kia 7-6-17 4DLI p162 CR Belgium111
UPTON,Thomas Francis Joseph Capt kia 8-11-18 1YLI p144 CR France981
UPTON,William Edwin Lt&QM ded 5-3-16 19N&D p135 CR Norf209
URBAN,Oscar Arthur T2Lt kia 3-9-16 11 att9ESurr p113 MR21
URCELL,William Lt ded 4-11-18 2Lond p272
URE,Ian.MC.Capt kld 2-2-18 9A&SH A'Coy att 1/6Bn C'Coy p244 CR Italy7
URE,James Mitchell T2Lt dow 16-8-16 8KOSB p102 CR France833
URE,John Andrew Capt kia 21-10-14 3 att2A&SH p174 CR France566
URE,William Alan Lt dow 3-11-17 B262RFA p208 CR Palestine2
UREN,Philip 2Lt kia 18-5-16 1LancF p94 CR France1504
URIDGE,Edgar John Gibbons 2Lt kia 26-7-17 A147RFA p36 CR France149
URINOWSKI,Alexander 2Lt dow 25-8-18 1/2Lpool &RAF p73
URQUHART,Angus Lt kld 26-9-15 4CamH p242 MR19
URQUHART,Alexander 2Lt kia 17-8-17 9HLI attRFC p20&241 MR20
URQUHART,Edward Frederick Maltby Capt kia 23-10-14 1BlkW p129 CR Belgium193
URQUHART,Francis Clement Lt dow 13-4-18 16RScots p55 CR Belgium38
URQUHART,James Lawrance Lt kia 25-9-15 7Nhampt p138 MR19,Lawrence
URQUHART,John TCapt kia 24-4-17 14A&SH p174 CR France662
URQUHART,William TLt kia 7-8-16 11 att1BlkW p129 MR21
URQUHART,William Thomas Bruce T2Lt kia 6-7-17 N&D att1Bn p135 CR Belgium10
URRY,Robert Alexander 2Lt ded 27-4-18 7EYorks p85 CR France62,Lt
URSELL,Victor George T2Lt kia 3-5-17 8 att7KSLI p145 MR20
URSELL,William Lt ded 4-11-18 2Lond CR Mddx53
URWIN,Thomas Alexander T2Lt dow PoW 15-1-18 RFC p17 CR France441
USBORNE,Alfred James TCaptAMaj kia 29-4-17 50RFA p36 CR France96
USHER,Arthur Norman.MC&Bar.2Lt kia 4-11-18 10RFus p70 CR France1480,Lt
USHER,Christopher Lancelot Lt dow PoW 23-4-18 3 att1Wilts p153 CR France987
USHER,Isaac William Lt kia 4-7-16 2RIrReg p89 CR France397
USHER,John Milne T2Lt kia 25-9-15 9GordH p167 MR19
USHER,Robert William Armitage Lt kia 2-5-17 1/7LancF p221 CR France363
USSHER,Beverley Capt kia 19-6-15 Leinst p175 CR Gallipoli6,Beverly
USSHER,Beverley William Reid Maj ded 5-2-16 17DLI p162 CR Mddx48
USSHER,Stephen Capt kia 16-12-14 IA 129Baluchis p283 CR France571
UTTERSON,Henry Kelso.DSO.MIDx3 LtCol kia 10-8-18 Dors att15LancF p124 CR France1022
UZIELLI,Valentine Leslie Douglas 2LtTLt kia 21-7-17 RFA p36 CR Belgium24
UZZELL,Francis Claude 2Lt dow 3-2-18 2/5RWar p214 CR France1203

———————— V ————————

VACHELL,Richard Tanfield.MID Capt dow 1-8-15 5NumbF att3RFC p2&63 CR France98,2-8-15
VACHER,George Herbert 2Lt kia 11-11-14 4 att2RWar p66 MR32
VADE-WALPOLE,Thomas Henry Bourke TLt kia 20-9-15 10GordH p167 CR France554
VAILE,Edward Ernest 2Lt kia 5-10-15 3Worc Ex 1HAC p110 MR29
VAILE,Lawrence Edward Stuart T2Lt kld 29-8-17 GL &RFC p14 CR Norf247
VAILE,Philip Amyas 2Lt dow 14-10-16 2/19Lond p251 CR France85,acckld

VAISEY,Charles Thomas Hilton 2Lt dow 30-6-16 RFC p4 CR France120, 1-7-16
VAISEY,Guy Maddison 2Lt dow 19-4-18 1Glouc p107 CR France10
VAISEY,Roland Maddison Capt kia 7-9-18 36RFA p36 CR France1484
VALE,Andrew Walter T2Lt kia 9-2-17 7EYorks p85 CR France785 Ex 2AustFA
VALENTINE,Guy Capt kia 15-9-16 6Lond p246 CR France277
VALENTINE,James.DSO.CaptTMaj ded 7-8-17 RFC p14 MR70 &CR Europe180
VALENTINE,Moss 2Lt kia 26-10-17 3RWSurr p255 MR30
VALENTINE,Robert Lepper TLt dow 30-4-16 8RDubF p177 CR France178
VALIENT,James Lt dow 28-10-17 7RWFus p223 CR Palestine1,VALIANT
VALINTINE,Rudolf.MC.Capt dow 12-11-17 1WarYeo p205 CR Palestine1
VALLANCE,Harold Leonard 2Lt dow 28-9-18 7HLI p240 CR France52
VALLANCEY,Henry Havelock Delachamps Capt dow 4-5-20 RFA p272 CR Surrey58,VALLENCEY De E
VALLANGE,Lancelot William 2Lt kia 31-10-16 21/2RFA p36 CR France394
VALLANS,Thomas 2Lt ded 28-4-19 RE IWT p49 CR Iraq6
VALLENTIN,John Franks.VC.Capt kia 7-11-14 1SStaffs p123 MR29
VALLINGS,Henry Alan LtCol kia 14-7-15 IA 29Punjabis p283 CR EAfrica56
VAN BUSKIRK L.R.E.Lt 9-12-17 FortGarryHorse &RFC CR Wilts116
VANCE,Charles Richard Griffin 2Lt kia 10-3-15 3Ches p97 CR Belgium59,9-3-15 1Bn
VANCE,Ezekiel TLt dow PoW 15-7-16 11RIrRif p170 CR France657
VANCE,James Lt kia 21-10-14 Ess p132 CR France451
VANDELEUR,Alexander Moore Capt kia 30-10-14 2LifeGds p20 MR29
VANDELEUR,John Beauclerk Lt kia 7-11-14 3Leics attWorc p88 MR29
VANDELEUR,William Mountcharles Crofton Capt kia 26-8-14 2Ess p132 CR France1347
VANDELL,Henry Ivanhoe Lt kia 10-11-14 1Nhampt B'Coy p138 MR29,11-11-14
VANDENBERG,F.A.2Lt kld 20-5-18 GL &RAF p191
VAN den BERGH,James Henry Lt kia 21-5-16 6Lond RFA p208 MR20
VAN den BERGH,Seymour Jacob H.Lt kia 27-10-17 1MddxHuss p204 CR Palestine1,Capt
VAN-den-BOK,Frederick 2Lt kia 1-7-16 2Mddx A'Coy p148 MR21
VAN DER GUCHT,Rupert Lionel LtCol ded 14-8-16 IA S&TCps p283 MR66
VAN der HOFF,Clement Lewis Lt mbk 29-1-18 3RFC p257 MR20
VANDERLINDE,Morris John Thomas 2Lt kia 30-8-18 9Lond p248 CR France624
VANDER-LINDE,Simon T2Lt dow 18-10-17 6Beds p87 CR Belgium11
Van der MERWE,C.S.2Lt 8/9-1-17 EAUL AfrScts CR EAfrica39
VANDERSPAR,Edgar Roland Lt dow 24-6-15 2Manch p156 CR Belgium56
VANDOME,Joseph John 2Lt kia 4-10-17 1ELancs p111 MR30
VAN DUZER,Harry Norman T2Lt ded 25-3-18 RFC p17 CR War97
VANE,Henry Cecil.Hon.Capt ded 9-10-17 298AC RFA p207 CR France145
VAN EEGHEN,Esme Charles 2Lt kia 20-7-17 RGA 324SB p42 CR Belgium23
VANE-TEMPEST,Charles Stewart Lt dow PoW 25-3-17 DSLI att70RFC p20&239 CR France1349
VANGOETHAM,Henry Edward LtTCapt kld 11-7-17 RFC p14 CR Dorset51,VAN GOETHEM
VAN GRUISEN,Nicholas Albert Ray Capt kia 21-8-18 9 att13Lpool p216 CR France745
VAN GRUISEN,Wilfred.MC.Lt dow 1-11-16 1RFus p70 CR Ches8
VANN,Arthur Harrison Allard Capt&Adjt kia 25-9-15 12WYorks p83 MR19
VANN,Bernard William.VC.MC&Bar.LtCol kia 3-10-18 8N&D p233 CR France375,1/6Bn
VAN NECK,Charles Hylton Lt kia 20-10-14 1NumbF p63 CR France924
VAN NECK,Philip Lt kia 26-10-14 1GrenGds p50 CR Belgium116
VANNER,James Charles.DSO.MC&Bar.Capt ded 19-3-19 7Leic p255 CR Dorset49
VAN OPPEN,Pier William Lt dow 16-4-18 4EYorks p219 CR France102,Willem
VAN PRAAGH,Ralp Bertram T2Lt kia 9-4-17 9KRRC p152 CR France581
VANPRAET,Francis Lt kia 1-10-18 RFA p208 CR France375
VANRENEN,Arthur Saunders.MID TLtCol kia 15-8-15 5RInniskF Ex Lincs p105 MR4
VANSITTART,Arthur Bexley 2Lt dow 12-5-15 11Huss p22 CR Belgium6
VAN SOMEREN,Claud Donald 2Lt kia 21-3-18 6MGC p186 MR20
VANSTON,Henry William Frederick Mortimer Capt ded 4-9-17 RIrFus att1/4Ess p172 CR Egypt9
VANSTONE,Charles Douglas Howard 2Lt ded 7-2-17 15RB attTMB p180 CR Devon153
VANSTONE,Stanley Paul TLt dow 29-10-15 10RB p180 CR France345
VARDON,Evelyn Francis Claude 2Lt kia 10-5-16 5RDubF p177 CR France178,8Bn
VARDY,Albert Theodore 2Lt kia 4-7-16 2RWar p66 CR France397
VARDY,Harold Henry 2Lt ded 22-8-18 RE 96LtRlyOpCoy p49 CR Egypt1
VARDY,Marcel Capt kia 27-8-17 A'TankCps p189 CR Belgium72
VARIAN,Walter Osborne 2Lt kia 30-3-16 5RMunstF p176 CR France401

VARLEY,Ernest 2Lt ded 2-3-18 101LabCps p189 CR France512,dow Ex Lpool
VARLEY,John Samuel Lt&QM ded 25-2-19 LabCps p266
VARLEY,Leonard Lt kia 12-11-15 1/6WRid p227 CR Belgium23,11-11-15
VARLEY,William 2Lt kia 24-3-18 RGA 2/1LancHB p42 CR France430
VARNDELL,Charles Henry Essex TLt kia 13-3-16 6RWSurr p57 CR France423,2Lt
VARNDELL,Leslie John T2Lt dow 18-9-16 4Lpool p73 CR France833
VASEY,Sydney.MC.2Lt kia 10-8-19 9 att 16LancF p94 MR16,Capt
VASS,Thomas McKenzie.MM.2Lt kia 4-5-18 8ScotRif p225 MR32
VASS,William Maj&QM ded 23-9-17 6Manch p236 CR Lancs34
VASSALL,Phillip Saumarez Capt kia 7-8-15 7Glouc p107 MR4,Saumerey
VASSIE,Charles Edward T2Lt kia 1-7-16 9YLI p144 CR France267
VASSIE,Richard Lt 13-4-18 Ches CR Scot805
VAUCOUR,Awdry Morris.MC&Bar.DFC.Maj kld 16-7-18 RA &RAF p36 CR Italy11,kia
VAUDREY,Claude Henry Slade Capt ded 2-5-16 3Manch RoO p156 CR Iraq5
VAUDREY,Norman TCapt kia 1-7-16 17Manch p156 CR France397
VAUDREY-BARKER-MILL,William Claude Frederick Capt 15-9-16 8RB CR France402
VAUGHAN,A.E.J.AssSurg 1-9-16 ISM MR66
VAUGHAN,Arthur Owen.DSO.OBE.DCM.LtCol ded 15-10-19 LabCps p266 CR Wales671,YLI
VAUGHAN,Charles.DCM.2Lt kia 6-11-17 1/1Hereford p252 CR Palestine1
VAUGHAN,Charles Alvarez 2Lt kia 25-9-15 7SfthH p165 MR19
VAUGHAN,Charles Davies.DSO.Maj kia 25-4-15 BordR p118 CR Gallipoli3
VAUGHAN,Donald 2Lt kia 30-10-17 3Lpool p73 CR Belgium83,6Bn
VAUGHAN,Edward Wilmot 2Lt kia 15-7-16 12RFA p36 CR France399
VAUGHAN,Evan James Stanley TCapt kia 18-8-16 13Mddx p148 MR21
VAUGHAN,Francis Seymour Lt kld 17-3-18 5RWKent attRFC p20&212 CR Greece3,2/4Bn
VAUGHAN,George Edward.MC.Maj kia 15-9-16 3CldGds p51 CR France402
VAUGHAN,George William T2Lt kia 21-11-17 7SStaffs p123 MR20
VAUGHAN,Guy Carleton TCapt kia 20-7-16 1Dev p77 CR France399
VAUGHAN,Harold TLt&Adjt kia 31-7-17 A74RFA p37 CR Belgium12
VAUGHAN,Harold John 2Lt kia 8-6-16 1Camb p245 MR19
VAUGHAN,Harry Robert 2Lt kia 27-10-14 ConnRgrs attDLI p172 MR32
VAUGHAN,Henry Humphreston Scott.MID Maj kia 24-4-16 83RFA p37 CR Belgium5
VAUGHAN,Horace William Henry Lt kia 4-6-15 10RLancs attRFus p59 MR4
VAUGHAN,James Henry Lionel Maj kia 12-5-18 GL attKAR p202 MR52,5-5-18
VAUGHAN,John T2Lt kia 30-7-16 20Lpool p73 MR21
VAUGHAN,John David.MC.2Lt dow 18-3-17 14WelshR p127 CR Belgium1
VAUGHAN,John Lindhurst.MC.TCapt kia 16-8-16 4 att9ESurr p113 MR21,Lyndhurst
VAUGHAN,John Montgomery 2Lt dow 25-5-15 RFus p70 CR France285
VAUGHAN,John Muir 2Lt dow 18-9-18 3 att2RSuss p120 CR France327
VAUGHAN,Kenelm Cuthbert Maj kia 13-9-16 2IrGds p53 CR France400
VAUGHAN,Leslie Howell 2Lt kld 23-4-17 4SomLI p218 CR France604
VAUGHAN,Percy Cecil 2Lt kia 26-9-17 RGA 294SB p42 CR Belgium19
VAUGHAN,Philip Edmund,DSO Maj ded 4-12-18 6Worc p264 CR Wales201,5-12-18
VAUGHAN,Richard Creswell T2Lt kia 16-4-18 8RWKent C'Coy p142 MR20
VAUGHAN-JONES,Edward Lt kia 11-5-18 3 att11RWFus p99 CR Greece5
VAUGHAN-JONES,Gerald Lt kia 26-2-17 RE att18RFC p20&210 CR France374
VAUGHAN-LEWES,Martyn Tulloch Lt dow 22-7-16 3WelshR &RFC p4&127 CR France285,kld
VAUGHAN-ROBERTS,Richard William TLt kia 30-7-16 19Lpool p73 CR France400
VAUGHAN-SAWYER,George Henry CaptInterpreter kia 29-10-14 IA att34SikhPnrs p284 CR France706,27-10-14 Ex 23Bn
VAUGHAN-SHEEHAN,George M.R.Capt 24-1-19 IARO attLabCps CR Surrey1
VAUGHAN THOMPSON,Richard Henry.mid Capt kia 26-9-16 11RFus CR Frnce702 see THOMPSON,R.H.V.
VAUGHTON,Guy Eglington 2Lt kia 20-11-17 8Ess p232 CR France911
VAULKHARD,John Vincent T2Lt kia 15-9-16 10 att8Beds p87 MR21
VAUSE,John Gilbert TLt kia 1-7-16 15WYorks p83 MR21
VAUSE,Thomas Christopher 2Lt kia 3-9-16 8WYorks p219 CR France383
VAUSE,Wilfrid.MC.Capt kia 23-4-17 5Yorks p220 CR France162
VAVASOUR,Lionel Ormiston Lt ded 24-7-15 2NStaffs p158 MR67
VAVASOUR,Rudolph Dunstan 2LtTLt ded 16-1-17 RFA attRFC p14&37 CR Lond6
VAWDREY,Gilbert Lloyd 2Lt kia 10-11-17 2WelshR p127 CR Belgium20
VAWSER,Thomas Edmund 2Lt kia 21/23-3-18 1Lond p245 CR France1893
VEACOCK,Stanley John TLt dow 17-10-17 1Hamps att20RFC p14&121 CR France200

VEALE,Allan Adolphus T2Lt kia 22-1-18 RFC p17 CR France285
VEASEY,John Sherard Lt kia 12-3-15 1Worc p110 MR22
VEEVERS,Edgar Samuel 2lt kia 10-7-18 1/4RLancs p213 CR France106
VEITCH,Alexander Gordon Lt kia 23-4-17 RFA p208 CR France777
VEITCH,Dawyck Moberly Veitch Capt kia 8-7-16 IA 1Lancers attRFC p284 MR20
VEITCH,James.MC.2Lt dow 19-8-18 5CamH p168 CR France25
VEITCH,John Leonard.MC.MID Maj kia 21-5-18 7 att1Dev p217 CR France20
VEITCH,Michael.MC.2Lt kia 11-8-18 5RScots p211 CR France360
VELLA,Arthur Henry.MID 2Lt kia 28-4-17 1ELancs attRIrFus p111 CR Greece6,att9RLancs
VENABLES,Alfred Ernest 2Lt kld 4-4-17 RFC p14
VENABLES,Aubrey William TCapt kia 2-10-16 RAMC att81FA p198 CR Greece3
VENABLES,Charles Edward T2Lt dow 12-10-16 14Yorks p91 CR France177,9Bn
VENABLES,Charles John.DSO.Maj kia 8-8-15 7Glouc RoO p107 MR4
VENABLES,Gilbert Rowland 2Lt kia 7-3-15 3KSLI p145 CR Belgium111
VENABLES,Vernon Wilson 2Lt dow 18-10-16 3 att2Wilts p153 MR21
VENABLES-LLEWELYN John Lister Dillwyn Capt kia 10-7-17 3/3CldGds CR Belgium12
VENIS,Arthur Raymond 2Lt kia 22-11-15 IARO att48Pnrs p284 MR38
VENMORE,James Frederick.MC.TLt kia 11-7-16 14RWFus p99 CR France397
VENN,Bertram Joseph T2Lt kld 11-7-17 RE &RFC p14&49 CR Glouc9
VENNER,Edgar William 2Lt kia 9-7-16 RWKent att16Manch p142 MR21
VENNER,Ernest Valentine(Nick) 2Lt kia 18-8-16 3RB p180 CR France402
VENNER,George Eric TMaj kia 8-7-16 1 att3N&D p135 CR France397
VENNER,William Frederick Fouracre TLt ded 5-12-16 GL 13Hamps attRE 49MotAir p191 CR EAfrica32
VENNING,Edwin Gerald Capt kia 6-8-15 3Suff B'Coy p79 CR Belgium182,1Bn
VENOUR,Walter Edwin LtCol kia 31-10-14 IA 58Rif p284 CR France80
VENTRIS,Alan Favel 2Lt kia 14-9-15 2SLancs p126 CR Belgium113,Favell
VENUS,Frederick Arthur T2Lt kld 1-7-16 20NumbF p63 CR France393,kia
VERAGUTH,G.F.2Lt ded 18-3-18 19RFA p37 CR Mddx26
VERCOE,Frederick Gordon.MID 2Lt ded 28-4-19 3RWKent p265 MR65,3RWSurr
VEREKER,Robert Humphrey Medlicott 2Lt kia 25-8-14 2GrenGds p50 CR France932,Humphry
VERELST,Harry Wilson.MC.CaptAMaj kia 26-9-16 CldGds p51 CR France374
VERESMITH,Daniel James Christopher Lt dow 14-4-17 1RFA p208 CR France95,Capt
VERESMITH,Evelyn Henry T2Lt dow 9-7-16 14 att9RFus p70 CR France23,Lt
VERGETTE,Samuel.MID 2Lt kia 4-10-17 4 att1Lincs p217 MR30
VERITY,Gilbert 2Lt dow 31-7-17 2/5LancF p221 CR Belgium11
VERLEY,Albert Stuart Leonard TLt kia 16-8-17 9RDubF p177 MR30
VERNALL,Arthur Humphrey.MC.2Lt dow 23-8-18 3 att6Leics p88&259 CR France84,kia
VERNEDE,Robert Ernest 2Lt dow 9-4-17 5 att12RB p180 CR France245
VERNER,Frederick Charles 2Lt kia 25-10-14 1KSLI p145 MR32
VERNER,George de Wet LtCol dow 10-10-15 7KOSB p102 CR France473
VERNER,James Hamilton TCapt kia 5 -12-17 9RInniskF p105 MR17
VERNER,Lancelot Guy T2Lt dow 27-8-16 115MGC p186 CR France145,105MGC
VERNHAM,Noel Mark Hodson T2Lt kia 4-2-17 GL &16RFC p14 CR France95
VERNHAM,Noel Marshall 2Lt kia 28-7-16 4 att1ESurr p113 MR21
VERNIEUX,C.O.Capt 12-3-20 IARO attLabCps MR65
VERNON,Charles Edward Granville TCapt kia 15-8-15 5RInniskF B'Coy p105 CR Gallipoli4
VERNON,Frank Lawson 2Lt kld 8-11-16 12LNLancs p234 CR France62,dedacc
VERNON,Frederick Lewis 2Lt kia 1-7-16 26NumbF p63 CR France393,Capt
VERNON,Frederick Travis 2Lt kia 30-8-15 5Ches p222 CR France625
VERNON,George Francis Augustus Capt 10-11-15 DerbyYeo CR Europe1
VERNON,Grenville Bertie Capt kia 25-4-18 3 att2Nhampt p138 MR27
VERNON,Herbert Douglas Lt kia 15-9-16 GrenGds attMGC p50&186 MR21,attGdsMGR
VERNON,Leonard Patrick.MC.TLt kia 18-6-17 10RWFus p99 CR France531
VERNON,Leslie Godfrey Harcourt 2Lt kia 11-9-16 RWFus &RFC p4,261&263 MR20
VERNON,Lord George Francis Augustus Capt ded 10-11-15 DerbyYeo p203
VERNON,Roger T2Lt kia 14-5-16 8SomLI p80 CR France924
VERNON,Ronald Cecil Lt ded 11-10-18 GenDepot Staff Wynberg CR SAfrica144
VERNON,T.T.LtCol 24-1-19 7Lpool CR Ches32
VERNON,William Harris kia 7-10-16 4Lond p246 MR21
VERNON,William Henry Lovell 2Lt kia 7-10-16 OxfordYeo att6 O&BLI p205 MR21
VERNON,William Walter 2Lt dow 11-10-16 RE 90FC p49 CR France703,Lt
VERNON,William Wood 2Lt kia 7-7-16 4ConnRgrs attRIrF p172 MR21,att2RIrRif
VERNON-INKPEN,Robert Cecil 2Lt kld 21-10-16 12RWar attRFC p4&66 CR Hamps7
VERRALL,Christopher Francis Lt kia 22-12-14 2RSuss p120 MR22
VERRAN,Frank Nicholas Lt kia 18-10-16 2Wilts p153 MR21
VERRILL,William Gibson T2Lt kia 26-10-17 1/5NumbF p63 MR30
VERSCHOYLE,Francis Stuart 2Lt kia 25-4-15 RE R Anglesey 2S'Coy p49 CR Belgium57
VERSCHOYLE,William Arthur Capt kia 11-4-17 1RIrFus p172 MR20
VERSFIELD,Vernon Ferris 2Lt kia 3-4-18 B190RFA p37 CR France745,VERSFELD 2-4-18
VERYARD,Albert Thomas Chap4Cl kia 28-6-17 RAChDept att15TMB p200 CR France184
VESEY,George Walter.MC.Capt dow 26-3-19 9RIrFus p24 CR France1235,Waller
VESEY,James.MC.Lt kia 25-9-15 RBerks p140&259 MR32
VESEY-FITZGERALD,William Herbert Leslie 2Lt kia 14-8-16 2Dev p77 CR France423
VESSEY,Frank Court.MC.MM.Lt ded 25-10-18 RGA 353SB p42 CR France34
VESSEY,John Arthur T2Lt kld 12-6-17 45RFC p14 CR France200
VETTER,H.E.Capt ded 12-1-18 3/4KAR p202 CR EAfrica15 &CR Tanzania1
VEYSEY,Stanley 2Lt dow 21-9-17 RGA 119SB p42 CR Belgium16
VICARS,W.G.Capt 3-10-18 NigR CR Mddx80
VICARY,Gilbert Dake Capt dow 10-11-17 1/5Dev C'Coy p217 CR Palestine2,Doke
VICARY,William Dallin 2Lt kld 8-3-16 6Dev p217 MR38,Lt
VICAT,Frederick Holland 2Lt kia 8-12-17 3 att2WRid p116 CR France155
VICAT,Horatio John Lt kia 18-9-14 RWKent p142 MR15
VICK,Arnold Oughtrad Lt kia 27-9-18 11 att6Yorks p91 CR France611
VICK,Donald Benjamin TLt dow 8-7-16 C162RFA p37 CR France134
VICK,Edward.DCM.T2Lt kia 9-7-17 8Glouc p107 CR Belgium152
VICK,Kenneth Jesson T2Lt kld 5-7-17 GL &RFC p14 CR Yorks12
VICK,Sidney Francis T2Lt kia 20-9-17 att1/7Lpool p73 MR30
VICKERS,Charles Goldthorp Capt kia 22-11-17 2/4Y&L p238 MR17
VICKERS,Eric Leslie.MID T2Lt dow 8-1-17 8RB p180 CR France145
VICKERS,Ernest Charles 2Lt kia 26-1-17 7Ess p232 MR21
VICKERS,Frederick TMaj kia 21-4-17 15N&D p135 CR France674
VICKERS,Godfrey Raymond T2Lt kia 6-1-18 27RFC p17 CR France201
VICKERS,Hugh Gordon Muschamp Lt kia 30-10-18 IARO att13Lancers p284 CR Iraq8
VICKERS,Noel Lt kia 24-3-18 1EYorks p85 MR27
VICKERS,Noel Muschamp TLt kia 3-8-16 13Yorks p91 CR France149
VICKERS,Robert 2Lt dow 10-12-17 C162RFA p209 CR Belgium18
VICKERS,Thomas Bernard Lt kia 16-7-21 IA 2Sap&Min attRE 14FC p284 MR43
VICKERS,Thomas Henry Capt ded 15-11-16 BordR p264
VICKERS,William Burnell T2Lt kia 21-6-17 RGA 184SB p42 CR Belgium10
VIDALL,Lancelot Andrews Lt kia 25-9-15 3 att2 O&BLI p130 MR19
VIDLER,Bertram Hall 2Lt kia 12-4-17 9RSuss p120 CR France480
VIDLER,George Holbrook Eric Lt dow 8-7-16 2Wilts p153 MR21,9-7-16
VIGAR,William Arthur Lt ded 26-10-20 IA TC att120Inf p284
VIGERS,Lancelot Leslie T2Lt kia 1-7-16 RE 30FC p49 CR France513
VIGERS,Robert Stanley Garrard 2Lt dow 5-4-17 6 att10KRRC p152 CRFrance630
VIGOR,William Petter 2Lt kia 13-8-16 4 att11RWar A'Coy p66 MR21
VIGORS,Arthur Cecil T2Lt kia 9-9-16 9RDubF attRMunstF p177 MR21,MunstF attDubF
VIGORS,Charles Henry.MC.Capt kia 18-9-18 12Ches p97 MR37
VIGORS,Philip Wilson.MVO.Capt ded 2-4-17 7Worc p110&272,RoO RIrR CR Hereford/W116
VIGORS,Philip Urban.MVO.Capt ded 2-4-17 7Worc p225
VILE,Herbert Leslie 2Lt kia 3-5-17 2WRid p116 CR France604,VILLE Hubert
VILLAR,Clement John Capt kia 19-9-18 8Hamps p229 CR Palestine9
VILLAR,Robert Peter Capt kia 22-3-18 18Lpool p73 MR27,Maj
VILLIERS,Algernon Hyde Lt kia 23-11-17 Lothian&BordHorseYeo att121MGC p187&204 MR17
VILLIERS,Edgar Fyfe.MID Lt ded 13-11-18 68RFA attSch of Instruct Zeitoun p37 CR Egypt9
VILLIERS,Henry Lister 2Lt kia 4-2-17 6InnisDrags att11RFC p14&22 CR France832,Harry dow
VILLIERS,William Earle LtACapt kia 10-11-17 5 att9KRRC p152 CR Belgium101
VILLIERS-STUART,Charles Herbert Maj kia 17-5-15 IA 56Rif attAust&NZ HQ p284CR Gallipoli30,Punjabis
VINCE,Arthur Neville.DSO.LtCol kia 21-3-18 12Lpool p73&258 MR27
VINCE,William John Douglas 2Lt kld 22-5-17 RFC p14
VINCE,William Lang TLt kia 8-5-17 14RWar p66 CR France777
VINCENT,Alfred Copplestone Waldon TCapt kia 26-9-16 5Dord p124 CR France280

VINCENT,Austin Ears Lt kia 7-11-18 RFA attZ91Bde p37 CR France521,8-11-18
VINCENT,Basil Britton T2Lt kia 23-7-16 8Glouc p107 MR21
VINCENT,Charles 2Lt kia 17-10-18 4EKent p212 CR France849
VINCENT,Charles,RIM EngLtCmdr ded 30-6-21 IA p284
VINCENT,Charles Issam Francis 2Lt kia 16-10-18 1CldGds p51 CR France337,Issard
VINCENT,Frederick Charles 2Lt kia 21-3-18 7KRRC p152 MR27
VINCENT,George Ernest.DCM.2Lt kia 17-2-17 9Mddx p236 CR France314
VINCENT,George Samuel T2Lt kia 4-10-17 13RFus p70 MR30
VINCENT,James Trevor Crawley 2Lt kia 9-5-15 2WelshR p128 CR France631
VINCENT,Leslie Arthur Walter 2Lt dow PoW 31-3-18 4Beds p87 CR France403
VINCENT,Lionel Charles Henry T2Lt kia 3-9-16 12Glouc p107 MR21
VINCENT,Mark Hamilton Capt dow 1-10-15 IA 33Punjabis p284 CR France345
VINCENT,Stanley T2Lt ded 28-3-18 RASC MT p194&258
VINCENT,Vivian 2Lt dow 31-5-18 22DLI p162 MR18
VINCENT,William Capt kia 30-10-14 3DCLI p115 MR29
VINCENT,William Jefferson 2Lt kia 1-10-18 1 att5Dors p124 CR France406
VINCENT,William Morris T2Lt kia 26-3-17 10Suff att 1/4Ess p79 MR34
VINCENT-JACKSON,Montagu John TLt kia 4-2-16 11N&D p135 CR France705
VINE,Christian Courtenay 2Lt dow 25-9-16 19N&D att8Leics p88 MR21
VINE,Christopher Nithsdale Vincent T2Lt kia 18-8-16 6DCLI p115 MR21,C.V.N.
VINE,Robert Saselby 2Lt kia 14-10-16 1Camb p245 MR21,Saxelby
VINE,Wilfred Harold.MC.T2Lt kia 12-10-16 2Y&L p159 MR21
VINER,Alan Bertrand 2Lt kia 7-4-17 8N&D p233 CR France725
VINER,Frank Hillidge.MC.2Lt dow 12-9-18 23NumbF att2/7Lpool p63&259 CR France433
VINER,George Noel(Rex).MID LtACapt kia 12-10-18 4Mddx p148 CR France206
VINER,Rollo Lee T2Lt kia 4-7-16 7SLancs p126 CR France393
VINER-JOHNSON,Percy Joseph Viner Capt kia 12-3-15 3Wilts p153 MR29
VINEY,Cecil Henry 2Lt kia 9-5-15 Nhampt p138 MR32
VINEY,Philip Ernest Capt dow 17-12-14 Leics p88 CR France284
VINEY,Reginald Austin Lt 27-7-18 GL attGoldCoastR MR52 CR WAfrica6
VINICOMBE,Lionel Frank T2Lt kia 29-6-16 8RWKent p142 CR Belgium97
VINNICOMBE,Leslie Lt ded 25-10-18 2Dev attRTE p77 CR Italy12
VINSON,Albert Higgs.MID LtTCapt kld 22-3-18 13RFC p17 CR Kent127
VINT,William Percival ACapt kia 5-8-18 6MGC p186 CR Belgium11
VINTCENT,Charles Aubrey 2Lt kia 13-4-15 5 att4RB p180 MR29
VINTER,B.SNurse 30-5-18 TFNS 2GH CR Lond3
VINTER,Robert Bagster Wilson.MC.2Lt kia 31-10-16 6 att2Worc p110 MR21
VIPOND,Hugh Lt kldacc 28-7-17 1/6Manch p236 CR France518
VIPOND,Sidney James T2Lt dow 20-4-16 8Beds p87 CR Belgium11
VIRGIN,William Job Farnham 2Lt kia 4-11-18 2Wilts p153 CR France521
VIVEAST,William Henry Capt kia 9-8-18 8TankCps p189 CR France526,VIVEASH
VIVERS,John Capt kia 27-10-15 1/5RScotsF p222 CR Gallipoli2
VIVIAN,Charles Augustus LtCol kia 27-4-15 IA 15Sikhs p284
VIVIAN,Gilbert 2Lt dow 22-7-16 4EYorks p219 CR France8
VIVIAN,Robert Trevor.MID Capt mbk 8-3-16 RAMC att1/6Dev p257 MR38,Richard
VIZARD,Harold Talbot.MC.LtACapt kia 1-9-18 ABty 71Bde RH&FA p37 CR France1182
VIZE,Stanley Reed Lt ded 11-10-18 9Hamps p229 CR Egypt1 2/5Bn att4TMB
VOELCKER,Harold Edward T2Lt kia 20-7-16 6SLancs p126 MR21
VOGAN,Lindsay Clarence T2Lt dow 28-4-17 13Mddx p148 CR France12
VOKES,Basil 2Lt kia 15-2-17 O&BLI BucksBn p232 CR France624
VOKINS,Kean Esse T2Lt kia 11-7-16 11RWar p66 MR21
VOLKERS,Frederick Cyril Stowell T2Lt kia 1-7-16 1RB p180 MR21
VOLLER,Herbert William T2Lt kia 6-12-16 10Glouc p107 CR France385
VON POELLNITZ,Herman Walter CaptTMaj kld 11-5-18 2Lincs &72RAF p76 CR Iraq8
VON TREUENFELS,Carl Otto,DSO Maj dow 24-6-17 285RFA p206 CR France8
VON WINCKLER,Myles William Lt 1-8-17 2Mddx p148 MR29
VORES,Geoffrey Bernard 2Lt kia 4-6-15 1LancF p94 MR4
VORLEY,Charles Archibald T2Lt dow PoW 13-9-16 11RSuss p120 CR France657,Lt
VORLEY,W.K.TLt ded 30-11-16 RFA 12A/A Bty p37 CR Lond12
VOSE,Thomas T2Lt kia 13-12-17 2 att12WYorks p83 CR France563,Lt
VOSS,Ernest William Thomas T2Lt kia 24-9-17 11RWar p66 MR30
VOUSLEY,Frederick TMaj ded 5-2-21 1ARO attStaff p284 CR India48
VOWLER,Darrell Francis Stephen TMaj ded 28-2-19 N&D attMGC p135&186 CR Cornwall64
VOWLER,Edward Maxwell 2Lt kia 14-3-15 2DCLI p115 MR29 &CR Belgium453

VOWLER,John Arthur Geoffrey Lt ded 19-7-17 3Leinst attMGC p175 CR Hamps64
VOWLES,Stephen Foster 2Lt kia 28-4-17 3 att13Ess p132 MR20
VOYCE,Henry Eugene T2Lt kia 6-8-15 4Worc Y'Coy p110 CR Gallipoli6
VOYSEY,Alfred Ebenezer 2Lt kia 29-7-17 SR attRGA 21HB p42 CR Belgium9
VYNER,Cuthbert Jack Sigfrid Lt dow 24-7-15 4 O&BLI p231 CR France201
VYVYAN,Beresford Houghton TCapt dow 18-8-17 A121RFA p37 CR Belgium16,Haughton
VYVYAN,Walter Drummond Lt kia 2-3-15 2KSLI p145 MR29
VYVYAN,William Geoffrey Capt dow PoW 24-10-14 RWFus p99 CR Belgium167
VYVYAN-ROBINSON,Courtenay Maj ded 22-1-19 RGA 156SB CR France1030

W

WACE,Henry Edward Capt kia 14-4-18 4KSLI p235 MR30
WACE,Herbert Gordon T2Lt kia 21-8-15 RMunstF p176 MR4
WACE,Percival Beckwith Capt dow 3-7-16 5RBerks p140 MR21
WACHER,John Stewart 2Lt kldacc 5-8-16 1RWKent att7RDubF p142 CR Greece9
WACHER,Walter Ronald TLtACapt kia 12-10-17 2 att6RBerks p140 MR30
WADDAMS,Arthur Richard Lt AccBombExplos 22-11-17 IARO att44MerwaraInf p284 CR Iraq6
WADDAMS,Walter Herbert Leonard.MC.ACapt dow 12-4-17 1/1Lond p245 CR France120
WADDELL,David Adams.MID Lt kia 6-4-17 4GordH p241 CR France266
WADDELL,David Bruce 2Lt kia 21-3-18 2DragGds p21 MR27
WADDELL,James Douglas Capt kia 25-9-15 12RFus p70 MR19
WADDELL,James Hamilton 2Lt kia 5-6-17 11RScots p55 MR20
WADDELL,Thomas Bryson 2Lt kia 8-4-17 5SfthH p241 CR France184
WADDELL-DUDLEY,Robert Rowland Lt kia 15-4-15 3RFus p70 CR Belgium125
WADDINGTON,James Hubert T2Lt dow 6-7-16 16WelshR p128 CR France633
WADDINGTON,Walter Charles 2Lt dow PoW 3-7-18 1/4EYorks p219 CR Germany3
WADDY,John Raymond.MC.MID Lt kia 17-3-15 RAMC attSomLI p198 CR Belgium70
WADE,Albert Luvian TLt kia 28-4-17 17Mddx attTMB p148 MR20
WADE,Arthur Norman T2Lt dow 19-9-15 7YLI p144 CR France705,Lt
WADE,G.A.Maj 17-3-19 RAMC CR Devon239
WADE,George 2Lt drd 1-1-17 7A&SH p243 MR35
WADE,George Edward Ahern 2Lt kia 3-5-17 9RB A'Coy p180 MR20
WADE,Gordon Standley 2Lt dow 13-11-16 5 att17Mddx p148 CR France41
WADE,Graham Hardie Capt kia 26-4-15 1/7A&SH p243 CR Belgium129,25-4-15
WADE,Harold Walter Lt mbk 29-10-14 IA 3Brahmans att9BhopalInf p284
WADE,Herbert.MC.Lt kia 2-11-18 17MGC Inf p186 CR France1475
WADE,Herbert John Clark TLt dow 14-11-17 180MGC Inf p186 CR Egypt7
WADE,Hubert T2Lt kia 9-10-17 YLI att5Bn p144 MR30
WADE,John Mayall 2Lt kia 19-6-15 9Manch p237 MR4
WADE,Lawrence Frank 2Lt kia 28-8-18 9RFus p70 CR France370,Laurence 22-8-18
WADE,Oliver John T2Lt kia 22-10-16 9RWKent &RFC p4&142 MR20
WADE,Richard Curtis 2Lt kia 26-2-18 40RFC p17 CR France924
WADE,Samuel Shorten Arthur 2Lt kia 8-12-14 Lincs p76 MR22
WADE,Sidney T2Lt ded 26-10-18 Lincs p76 CR Notts85
WADE-GERY,Robert Hugh Capt dow 17-7-16 RGA 1SB p42 CR France189
WADESON,Edward Yeadon Lt kia 22-3-18 3 att10LNLancs p136 MR20
WADESON,Frederick William George,CB.MajGen ded 10-12-20 IA Ex KOSB CR Devon71
WADHAM,Vivian Hugh Nicholas.MID Capt kia 17-1-16 1Hamps &RFC p4&121 CR Belgium125
WADLOW,Bernard Victor T2Lt kia 3-4-17 13Mddx p148 CR France570,2-4-17 Ex 5Bn
WADLOW,Harold Maj kia 24-7-16 RGA 109SB p42 CR France397
WADLOW,Harry TCapt kld 1-5-17 GL &RFC p14 CR Glouc38
WADSON,Stanley Parker 2Lt kia 10-8-18 6RWSurr p57 CR France636
WADSWORTH,Ernest Hinchcliffe 2Lt ded 12-3-17 4WRid p227 CR Yorks411
WADSWORTH,Maurice Moxon Lt kia 9-7-15 5YLI p235 CR Belgium85
WADSWORTH,Percy 2Lt kia 22-3-18 1EYorks p85 MR27
WADSWORTH,Wilfred Howard 2Lt dow 22-3-18 RFA X16TMB p37 CR France987
WAGER,Arthur Howell Lt dow 17-7-16 C85RH& p37 CR France630,Capt
WAGER,Willson Stanley 2Lt kia 12-7-17 16NumbF p63 MR31
WAGGOTT,Garibaldi Matthewson 2Lt kia 11-4-18 16 att1/6NumbF p63 MR32,13-4-18

WAGHORN,Herbert Gilmore Capt dow 26-4-17 6NStaffs p238 CR France511

WAGHORN,Leonard Pengelly 2Lt kia 6-11-14 3RWKent att1RBerks p142 MR29

WAGHORN,Percy William 2Lt kia 7-10-16 8RFus p70 CR France512 Ex Sgt 1Drags

WAGHORNE,Harold Frederick 2LtTCapt dow 21-9-16 11YLI p144 CR France833

WAGNER,Ethelbert Godwin Stockwell 2Lt kia 7-1-17 RWar &32RFC p14&66 CR France518

WAGSTAFF,John Carleton T2Lt kia 12-10-17 SStaffs att8Bn p123 CR Belgium126

WAGSTAFF,Robert Arthur 2Lt kia 1-10-18 29MGC p186 CR Belgium84

WAHL,Bruno Wolfgang 2Lt kia 26-9-16 IARO att28Cav p284 MR61,29Cav

WAHL,Matthew Daniel 2LtAMaj kia 21-6-17 RGA 294SB p42 CR Belgium48, Mathew

WAIN,Richard William Leslie.VC.TLtACapt kia 20-11-17 25Manch attA'TankCps p156&189 MR17

WAINE,William Henry Capt kia 6-8-15 14Manch p156 MR4

WAINMAN,Ernest T2Lt kia 2-3-17 20Manch p156 CR France514

WAINMAN,Philip Stafford Gordon CaptBtMaj kia 26-9-15 6 att2Worc p110 CR France423

WAINWRIGHT,Clifford Ernest 2Lt dow 14-10-18 KRRC att11RAF CR France375

WAINWRIGHT,Eric Lawrence Lt ded 15-9-15 IARO att59Rif p284 CR Lond14,2Lt dow 15Sikhs

WAINWRIGHT,Geoffrey Chauner 2Lt dow 22-12-14 3Nhampt p138 CR France727

WAINWRIGHT,Geoffrey Harry Lt dow 8-9-18 3 att2Suff p79 CR France13

WAINWRIGHT,Geoffrey Lennox 2Lt kia 25-9-15 3 att2RSuss p120 CR France219

WAINWRIGHT, Harry Arnold 2Lt kia 16-7-18 15Ches p97 CR Belgium40

WAINWRIGHT,Henry Carrey TLt dow 5-2-16 17Lpool p73 CR France300,Currey

WAINWRIGHT,Samuel Stewart Lt kia 11-3-17 6Norf p217 CR France314,12-3-17

WAISTELL,Walter Edmund T2Lt kia 4-10-17 12/13NumbF p63 MR30

WAIT,Charles Frederick Wells TLt dow 15-7-16 10YLI p144 CR France188

WAIT,Herbert Alfred Vincent 2Lt kia 2-12-17 2RBerks D'Coy p140 MR30,Lt

WAITE,Alfred.DCM.2Lt kia 5-4-18 5RBerks p140 CR France516

WAITE,Arthur Sydney 2Lt dow 25-9-16 1/4NumbF p213 CR France145

WAITE,Charles 2Lt dow 28-3-18 4 att2/8WYorks p83 CR France225

WAITE,Clement William.DSO.TMaj ded 31-1-19 11EYorks p255 CR Yorks22,30-1-19 13Bn

WAITE,Frederick Maxwell 2Lt kia 7-6-15 1/4Leic p220 CR Belgium9

WAITE,Hugh Conyers 2Lt kia 6-4-17 2/8WYorks p219 CR France568 Ex CanadaInf

WAITE,Joseph Thorpe Lt kia 21-1-16 1/5EKent p213 CR Iraq5

WAITES,Charles James 2Lt kia 10-10-18 6ConnRgrs p172 CR France230

WAITT,Reginald Charles 2Lt kia 27-8-17 11Suff p79 MR21

WAKE,Charles Baldwin Drury 2Lt kia 25-9-18 6 att2KRRC p152 CR France375

WAKE,Hugh St.Aubyn.MVC.Maj dow 30-10-14 IA 2/8GurkhaRif p284 MR28

WAKE,Thomas Frederick Henry 2Lt dow 10-4-18 1 att8NStaffs p158 CR Belgium11

WAKEFIELD,Arthur Gibbon Lt kia 29-5-19 IARO att144LabCps p284 MR43,2Lt 28-5-19

WAKEFIELD,Charles John Maj ded 1-7-20 RIrRif att7KAR CR EAfrica36

WAKEFIELD,Frank Mahan Lt ded 2-1-18 DorsYeo attMGC p187&203,2-1-19 CR Hamps64

WAKEFIELD,Jessie Emily Sister ded 7-2-19 TFNS p254 CR France40

WAKEFIELD,Leonard John 2Lt kia 16-6-17 8Lond p247 MR20

WAKEFIELD,Montague Stephen Lt kia 20-11-17 3 att1N&D p135 MR30

WAKEFIELD,Oliver T2Lt kia 12-10-17 HouseholdBn p20 MR30

WAKEFIELD,Roger Owen Birbeck Lt dow 28-8-14 RIrFus p172 CR France657

WAKEFIELD,Sydney Clark 2Lt kia 22-3-18 2TankCps p189 MR27

WAKEFIELD,Thomas Butler T2Lt kia 8-9-17 2/6WYorks p83 CR France563

WAKEFORD,Charles Herbert Stanley Lt kia 7-9-18 GlamYeo p203 CR France446,24WelchR

WAKEFORD,Edward Francis Capt ded 23-2-15 6RSuss p272 CR Sussex58

WAKEFORD,Edward Kingsley TLt kia 14-7-17 7Leic p88 CR France453,16-7-16

WAKEFORD,F.R.S.Lt ded 25-12-18 GlamYeo &RAF p203

WAKEFORD,George Tank 2Lt kia 23-7-16 4RBerks p234 MR21

WAKEFORD,Harold T2Lt kia 4-4-18 10 att6SLancs p126 MR38

WAKEFORD,Owen.MC.Maj dow 21-3-18 RGA 76SB p42 MR20

WAKEFORD,Robert Scott T2Lt ded 22-2-17 RFC p14 CR Berks85

WAKEFORD,Walter Thomas 2Lt kia 7-7-15 2ELancs p111 CR France744

WAKELEY,John Eric Stanley.MID T2Lt dow 9-9-16 1Glouc p107 CR France833

WAKELEY,William Norman 2Lt kia 8-5-17 15Lpool attMGC p73&186 MR37

WAKEMAN,Edward Offley Rouse 2Lt kia 16-5-15 att1GrenGds SR p50 MR22 &CR France1059

WAKEMAN,Frank Trevor Lt kia 30-10-17 5RWar attRFC p20&214 MR20

WAKERLEY,Arthur John Capt kia 8-6-17 1/4Leic D'Coy p219 CR France550

WAKLEY,Bertram Joseph Maj ded 11-2-17 1LNLancs p136 CR lond4

WALBEOFFE-WILSON,William Capt kld 2-8-15 3Mon p244 CR Belgium79

WALBAUM,William Frederick Lt dow 12-9-17 B276RFA p208 CR Belgium16

WALCH,Brian James Brett 2Lt dow 28-10-15 2/4Ess p232 CR Gallipoli18

WALCH,James Bernard Millard T2Lt kia 25-9-15 2RWSurr p57 MR19

WALCOT,Basil.DSO.Maj ded 14-9-18 RE p49 CR Surrey131

WALCOTT,Francis Sharpe TCapt kia 26-9-16 RAMC att8NumbF p198 CR France393

WALCOTT,John Henry Lyons 2Lt kia 2-11-14 IA 2/2GurkhaRif att34SikhPnrs p284 MR28

WALCOTT,Lyons George Edmund Lt kia 2-7-16 5Lincs p220 CR France576

WALDEGRAVE,Edmund John 2Lt kia 10-8-18 D286RFA p37 CR France266

WALDEN,Rand Edwin John T2Lt kia 16-11-17 2LancF p94 CR France154

WALDIE,Charles Percival 2Lt kia 26-9-15 8RWSurr p57 MR19

WALDIE,John Gray TLt kia 31-7-17 11BlkW attt25MGC p129&186 MR29

WALDRON,Benson T2Lt kia 31-7-17 19Manch C'Coy p156 MR29

WALDRON,Cecil Hamersley TLt kia 2-3-17 7Lincs p76 MR29

WALDRON,Fionn Thomas 2Lt kia 23-10-16 2Ess p132 CR France924

WALDRON,Francis Fitzgerald.MIDx2 TMaj ded 3-7-16 19Huss att60RFC p4&23 CR France568,kia

WALDY,Cuthbert Temple 2Lt kia 20-10-14 5Lancs p126 MR22

WALE,Adie Capt dow 30-5-18 186RFA X39TMB p37 CR France84,kld 166RFA

WALE,Alan Ernest T2Lt kld 23-11-17 GL &RFC p14 CR Mddx9,23-7-17

WALE,Alick Arthur ACapt kia 8-11-17 2 att7LNLancs p136 CR Belgium183

WALE,C.C.Augustus Capt 4-4-20 IMS MR65

WALE,Clifford Hardwicke T2Lt kia 19-1-16 RIrRif p170 MR32

WALES,Harold Robert T2Lt kia 14-7-16 9EYorks p85 MR21

WALEY,Aubrey John TLt kia 31-7-17 12RFus p70 MR29

WALFORD,Alexander Ellis TLt kia 16-8-16 2Suff p79 MR21

WALFORD,Alfred Sanderson LtACapt ded 19-1-19 2Ches p97 CR Gallipoli29

WALFORD,Garth Neville.VC.Capt kia 26-4-15 RFA p37 CR Gallipoli15

WALFORD,George Henry Maj kia 19-4-15 Suff p79 CR Belgium59

WALFORD,Hamilton Stewart Lt kia 27-5-18 12Worc att1/4WelshR p110 MR18

WALFORD,Leonard Nithsdale Lt kia 8-5-15 12Lond p248&249 MR29

WALFORD,Oliver Robson 2Lt kia 26-4-15 1Hamps p121 CR Belgium152

WALFORD,Percy Frederic T2Lt kia 11-4-17 7KRRC p152 CR France532

WALFORD,W.G.Capt kia 4-11-18 RE &62RAF p49 CR B218 ?

WALKDEN,Arthur Chamberlain 2Lt kia 28-4-17 4ELancs p226 MR21

WALKER,Adolphus 2Lt dow 15-4-18 1/2 att2/5WRid p116 CR France169

WALKER,Alexander Lamond LtCol ded 27-12-16 RHFA p262 CR Norf11

WALKER,Allan Dixon Lt mbk 16-6-15 2Lincs p257 MR32

WALKER,Alfred English TLt kia 22-8-16 20RFus p70

WALKER,Anthony Thornton T2Lt kia 30-7-15 8RB p180 MR29

WALKER,Archdale Gillam 2Lt kia 17-5-15 4NStaffs att2RScotF p158 MR22

WALKER,Arnold Henry Lt dow 17-9-18 3 att8Ches p97 CR Lancs14

WALKER,Arthur Lt kia 10-8-18 WRid attMGC Inf p116 CR Belgium192

WALKER,Arthur Dight 2Lt kia 18-10-16 7 att19Manch p156 MR21

WALKER,Arthur Dunbar LtCol kia 26-3-18 RE 24DivHQ p49 MR27

WALKER,Arthur John TCapt kia 7-8-15 11Yorks att6Manch p91 CR Gallipoli2

WALKER,Arthur Nimmo LtCol kia 24-9-16 RAMC attRHFA p198&206 CR France703

WALKER,Basil Scarisbrickle 2Lt kld 9-5-15 5Ches p222 CR Belgium35

WALKER,Charles Corbould Capt kia 26-8-14 2A&SH A'Coy p174 CR France716

WALKER,Charles Nigel Gordon TLt kia 7-8-15 10SStaffs att8Manch p123 MR4

WALKER,Clarence Howard T2Lt dow 28-9-16 10 att12Ess p132 CR France74

WALKER,Claud Arthur Leonard Lt kia 10-7-18 2RInniskF p105 CR France296

WALKER,Cornwall Nathaniel Brownlow Lt kia 16-8-17 7RInniskF p105 MR30,Capt

WALKER,Denham 2Lt dow 19-9-16 2/5ELancs att18MGC p187&226 CR France105

WALKER,Denis Henry Capt dow 26-1-16 5Yorks p220 CR Belgium11

WALKER,Edgar Wilmer Capt kia 27-10-14 3EYorks p85 CR France82,29-10-14 1Bn

WALKER,Edmund Basil.MID 2Lt kia 18-4-15 1RWKent p142 CR Belgium152

WALKER,Edward William.DSO.Capt kia 6-11-17 1/7RWFus p223 CR Palestine1

WALKER,Eric Alfred English Lt 22-8-16 20RFus CR France389

WALKER,Eric Arthur T2Lt kia 29-12-15 9 att6KSLI p145 CR France525

WALKER,Ernest James Capt dow 4-10-17 296RFA p207 CR Belgium11

WALKER,F.F.2Lt dow 14-4-18 GL &RAF p191

WALKER,Francis Hercules TLtCol kia 7-1-16 7NStaffs p158

WALKER,Frank Benjamin 2Lt kia 23-7-16 2 att6KRRC p152 MR21,6 att2Bn
WALKER,Frederick Cecil Banes 2Lt kia 9-5-15 Dev p77
WALKER,Frederick Charles T2Lt kia 25-11-15 8Suff p79 CR France430
WALKER,Frederick Clarkson Lt kia 20-9-17 5Lpool p215 MR30
WALKER,Frederick Leslie T2Lt kld 28-12-17 RFC p14 CR Herts30
WALKER,Frederick Ramsay.MC.2Lt ded 6-1-17 2A&SH p174 CR Scot236
WALKER,Frederick Rutley.MBE.Capt ded 26-11-19 31Punjabis attPoliticalDept p284 CR Iraq8
WALKER,Gavin Henry Capt kia 14-3-15 1HLI p164 CR France279
WALKER,George TLt dow 28-11-15 10Beds attNigR p87&202 CR WAfrica58
WALKER,George Bruce TLt ded 1-3-19 17HLI attRFC p265 CR Scot674
WALKER,George Ernest TLt kia 6-6-17 11RScots p55 CR France604
WALKER,George Francis 2Lt kia 7-12-16 5Y&L p238 CR France701
WALKER,George Henderson Lt kia 28-7-17 GL att45RFC p14 MR20
WALKER,George Henry Lt kia 16-6-15 4RLancs p213 MR22
WALKER,George Pybus 2Lt kia 9-8-18 10TankCps p189 MR16
WALKER,George Stafford Lt dow 20-11-17 B79RFA p37 CR France145
WALKER,George Stanley 2Lt kia 23-10-18 20Manch p156 CR France231
WALKER,George William Quarmby Lt kia 7-7-16 7WRid p227 CR France702
WALKER,Gervaise Mapletoft Lt kia 15-4-17 3 att 1Leic p88 MR30,Capt
WALKER,Gideon.MC.TCapt kia 27-11-17 RAMC att3FA p198 CR France755
WALKER,Gordon Henry 2Lt kia 10-11-17 6Nhampt p138 MR30
WALKER,H.Col 26-7-17 WYorks CR Mddx26
WALKER,H.Lt.Col 3-6-19 1WelchR attRAF CR Devon1
WALKER,Harold Saxon.MID Capt dow 12-9-17 2/9Lond p247 CR Belgium16
WALKER,Harry.CMG.LtCol dow 27-9-15 4BlkW p230 CR France705
WALKER,Harry 2Lt kia 28-7-17 RGA 295SB p42 CR France922
WALKER,Harry Brampton LtACapt ded 24-9-17 RFA p37 MR65,Bampton
WALKER,Harry Cullis Steele 2Lt kia 12-3-15 1N&D p135 CR France1059
WALKER,Henry Gerald 2Lt kia 1-7-16 2YLI p144 MR21
WALKER,Henry John Innes Capt kia 25-4-15 att1RWar p66 MR29
WALKER,Herbert John Maj ded 25-9-16 RE Staff p262 CR Greece7,dow
WALKER,Herbert Newton 2LtTLt kia 6-6-17 11SStaffs attMGC p123&186 CR Belgium100,107MGC att11SStaffs
WALKER,Herbert William Capt ded 12-3-19 7N&D p233 CR Notts84
WALKER,Hercules Frank LtCol 7-1-16 7NStaffs MR4
WALKER,Howard Napier.OBE.MC.Lt ded 3-6-19 WelshR &RAF p255
WALKER,Hugh Percy Wonham 2Lt kia 23-4-17 5A&SH p243 CR France1182
WALKER,Ingham 2Lt kia 27-9-18 3MGC p186 CR France756
WALKER,Jack Bertram 2Lt dow 8-3-18 1/5RLancs p59 CR France88
WALKER,James Edward 2Lt kia 3-5-17 1RLancs p59 MR20
WALKER,James Hope 2Lt kld 16-3-17 GL &RFC p14 CR Herts38
WALKER,James Robert.MC.LtAMaj kia 20-3-17 B62RFA p37 CR France1182
WALKER,J.C.2Lt kld 18-10-18 GL &RAF p191
WALKER,Jerome Lennie T2Lt kia 6-5-16 14RIrRif p170 CR France702
WALKER,John T2Lt kia 1-7-16 14NumbF p63 MR21
WALKER,John Prentice 2Lt ded 18-9-16 7A&SH p272 CR Scot64
WALKER,John Alexander 2Lt kia 26-8-18 1RScotF att1/4KOSB p95 MR16
WALKER,John Arthur TCapt kia 19-2-16 10RWFus p99 CR Belgium15
WALKER,John Chinnery 2Lt kia 19/20-12-15 1/5WYorks p218 CR Belgium73
WALKER,John Croxton 2Lt kia 3-9-16 1Camb p245 CR France220
WALKER,John Edward Schlmaster 29-8-14 Cps of Schlmasters CR Kent7
WALKER,John Haslam T2Lt dow 2-11-17 GL att16RSuss p191 CR Egypt9
WALKER,John Henry 2Lt kia 18-9-17 4EYorks p219 MR30
WALKER,John Quintin Frederick 31-3-18 57RFC MR20
WALKER,John West Lt kia 11-4-17 2/5Lincs p220 MR21
WALKER,John Wickham Capt kia 5-7-16 5YLI p235 CR France744
WALKER,Joseph Noel Lt kia 4-7-16 1/5YLI p235 MR21
WALKER,Kenneth MacKenzie 2Lt kia 12-8-18 3Wilts att209RAF p153 MR20
WALKER,Lawrence Hale.MID 2Lt kia 12-10-16 2Beds p87 CR France432,Hall
WALKER,Leslie Bedford Capt dow 1-7-17 5Yorks p220 CR France145
WALKER,Louis Lt ded 22-10-19 IARO att1/10Jats p284 MR43 &CR Pakistan50
WALKER,Lewis Aubrey T2Lt kia 6-8-17 RASC attRGA 118SB p194 CR Belgium11
WALKER,Malcolm Reid 2Lt kia 23-4-17 7A&SH p243 CR France545
WALKER,Maurice John Lea 2Lt kia 3-5-17 6RWKent p142 MR20
WALKER,Miles Lt ded 3-12-18 RASC 29DivTrn p253&272 CR Lond8
WALKER,Norman Crawford Capt kia 25-9-15 4BlkW p230 MR19
WALKER,Norman Reginald Lt kia 23-8-18 RScots att10KOSB p55 CR France19
WALKER,Oscar Lt kia 3-5-17 5WRid p227 MR20
WALKER,Oscar Robert Capt kia 4-6-15 12Worc attRFus p110 MR4

WALKER,Oswald Bethell Capt kia 23-8-14 15Huss p22 MR15
WALKER,Percy Richard Samuel 2Lt kia 5-8-18 RE 103FC p49 CR France161
WALKER,Ralph T2Lt kia 21-4-17 11A&SH p174 MR38
WALKER,Reginald.MID Maj dow 5-9-16 RE 105FC p49 CR France59
WALKER,Reginald Lt kia 25-4-18 1/5WYorks p218 CR Belgium126
WALKER,Reginald Fydell 2Lt dow 21-10-14 2Manch p156 CR France279
WALKER,Reginald Selby.DSO.LtCol kia 30-9-18 RE VI CpsHQ p49 CR France1483
WALKER,Richard 2Lt kia 9-8-16 2/5LancF p221 MR21 Ex 28Lond
WALKER,Robert Coutts 2Lt 12-8-21 2RScots MR66
WALKER,Robert Hugh TLt kia 9-4-17 9SfthH p165 CR France96
WALKER,Robert Jardine.MID Capt kia 25-9-15 GordH SR att1Bn p167 MR29
WALKER,Robert Russell 2Lt kia 23-3-18 7Lond p247 CR France672
WALKER,Robert Sandilands Frowd.CMG.TLtCol ded 16-5-17 SL p201&268
WALKER,Roger Beverley.MC.Capt dow 13-11-18 YorkHuss att9WYorks p206 CR France34
WALKER,Stephen 2Lt ded 14-5-18 Camb &RAF p245 CR Essex246,kld
WALKER,Samuel Hugh T2Lt kia 16-8-17 14RIrRif p170 MR30
WALKER,Samuel Richard Ernest 2Lt dow 11-10-18 1NumbF p63 CR France380
WALKER,Stanley.MC.Capt kia 20-5-18 C246RFA p37 CR Belgium8
WALKER,Stanley Arthur TLt kia 14-10-16 RAMC att1/5Ches p198 CR France293,1/6Bn
WALKER,Sydney 2Lt kia 15-8-17 7DLI p239 CR France1186
WALKER,Sydney Stratton TCapt kia 19-7-16 12EYorks p85 CR France1157,Shatton
WALKER,Thomas Campbell T2Lt kia 14-2-16 10LancF p94 MR29
WALKER,Thomas Cartmel 2Lt kia 5-6-15 1/5Manch p236 CR Gallipoli2,6-6-15
WALKER,Thomas Kynaston Lt kia 24-4-16 1IrGds 1Coy p53 CR Belgium72
WALKER,Thomas Percival Patterson Capt kia 4-7-18 13TankCps p189 CR France1170
WALKER,Turner Russell T2Lt dow 2-7-16 18Lpool p73 CR France630,1-7-16
WALKER,Vernon Lee T2Lt kia 29-5-17 8ELancs p111 MR20
WALKER,Victor 2Lt kia 4-4-18 14Glouc att7RWKent p107 MR27
WALKER,William.DFC.Capt kld 8-10-18 GL &6RAF p191 MR20
WALKER,Walker 2Lt dow 25-8-18 6LancF p221 CR France927,Walter
WALKER,Walter Arthur Beaumont 2Lt dow 30-10-14 Beds p87 CR France80
WALKER,Wilfred Bertram Maj kia 29-10-14 Yorks p91 MR29
WALKER,Wilfred Harold 2Lt kia 3-5-17 Mddx att12Bn p148 MR20
WALKER,William TCapt kia 1-7-16 9YLI p144 CR France189
WALKER,William 2Lt kia 9-1-17 3Manch p156 CR Iraq5
WALKER,William Archibald Smail Maj kia 12-4-15 46Punjabis att130Baluchis p284 CR EAfrica56
WALKER,William Cleland Lt kia 16-4-18 1ScotRif att19TMB p104 MR32
WALKER,William Eaton Guy Capt kia 1-7-16 7N&D p233 CR France281
WALKER,William Francis 2Lt kia 9-4-18 3 att9NumbF p63 MR32
WALKER,William Gray Johnstone.MC&Bar.TLtACapt kia 18-7-17 GL attTMB 8Div p191 CR Belgium5
WALKEY,Francis Ashton 2Lt kia 17-10-18 2RDubF A'Coy p177 CR France190
WALKINGTON,Charles Edward Capt kia 14-10-18 2RIrRif p170 CR Belgium157
WALKINSHAW,James 2Lt kia 26-4-18 att5CamH p168 MR30
WALL,Arthur Geoffrey Nelson T2Lt kld 6-8-17 RFC p14 CR Ches182
WALL,Leonard Comer Lt kia 9-6-17 A275RFA p208 CR Belgium11
WALL,Michael Thomas 2Lt kia 7-6-17 3 att6RIrReg p89 CR Belgium17
WALL,Richard Ralph Baldwin Maj kia 8-6-17 378/169RFA p37 CR France922
WALLACE,Alexander Moultrie Capt kia 12-3-15 3Nhampt p138 MR22
WALLACE,Andrew Capt kia 12-7-15 4KOSB p223 MR4
WALLACE,Arthur Reginald TLt ded 18-1-19 GL RE attIWT p191 CR Iraq8
WALLACE,Charles Arthur Phin 2Lt kia 22-3-18 3 att6KOSB p102 MR27
WALLACE,Cyril John George Lt ded 9-9-18 14NumbF p63 CR France40,24Bn
WALLACE,Cyril Walter 2Lt kia 8-3-16 IARO att47Sikhs p284 MR38
WALLACE,David Stephenson 2Lt kia 19-9-14 2SLancs C'Coy p126 CR France1107
WALLACE,Denis 2Lt dow PoW 18-4-18 4 att9RScots p211 CR France1703,Lt
WALLACE,Dudley Whistler.MC.Lt kia 9-10-17 1/5WYorks p128 MR30,Capt
WALLACE,E.SNurse ded 6-6-16 QAIMNS p200
WALLACE,Geoffrey Robert.MC&Bar.MID Capt kia 27-8-17 7Worc p225 MR30
WALLACE,George Douglas T2Lt kia 26-10-17 21Manch p156 CR Belgium115
WALLACE,George Frederick T2Lt kia 23-5-17 20Mddx p148 CR France439, Capt
WALLACE,Harold Bruce 2Lt kia 26-10-14 3Lpool p73 MR29
WALLACE,Harry Herbert T2Lt dow 21-1-17 27NumbF D'Coy p63 CR France297,Henry
WALLACE,Henry Gilmour 2Lt kia 3-8-17 C86RFA p37 CR Belgium118

WALLACE,Houston Steward Hamilton TCapt kia 22-7-16 10Worc p110 MR21
WALLACE,John 2Lt kia 9-5-15 BlkW p129
WALLACE,John 2Lt kia 1-8-17 TA 4RScots p211 MR34
WALLACE,John Ernest Dudley Lt dow 7-8-17 RE 2FC p210 CR Belgium16
WALLACE,John James Rev dow 8-11-18 RAChDept att8NStaffs p200 CR France332
WALLACE,John Kennedy 2Lt kia 23-4-17 1/7BlkW p231 CR France604
WALLACE,John Robert 2Lt 9-5-15 1BlkW MR22
WALLACE,John Roger 2Lt kia 23-4-15 1RScotF p95 CR Belgium28,22-4-15
WALLACE,Joseph Stephen.MC&Bar. CaptAMaj kia 28-3-18 RAMC p253 CR France266
WALLACE,Kenneth Moss TLt dow 31-5-16 8RIrRif p170 MR19 CR France80
WALLACE,Lillie SNurse 6-6-16 QAIMNS CR Surrey160
WALLACE,Robert Capt ded 6-5-15 2EYorks p85 CR France102
WALLACE,Robert Nelson Capt ded 5-7-18 RAMC att6RScots CR Essex146
WALLACE,Robinson 2Lt dow 2-10-16 8DLI p239 CR France177
WALLACE,Stuart Annesley Lt kia 31-5-17 RGA 156SB p42 CR France1186
WALLACE,Thomas Victor Walter T2Lt dow 2-11-17 1/8Hamps p121 CR Palestine2,kia
WALLACE,Walter Mackenzie T2Lt kia 21-10-15 12Mddx p148 CR France188
WALLACE,William T2Lt kia 29-9-16 54MGC p186 MR21
WALLACE,William Lt kia 16-11-17 3 att1CamH p168 CR Belgium22,17-11-17
WALLACE,William Douglas 2Lt dow 22-8-16 5HLI p240 CR France176
WALLACE,William Edwin T2Lt kia 31-7-17 RE 254TC p49 CR Belgium5
WALLACE,William Ernest Lt kia 17-4-17 8RScots p211 CR France1182
WALLACE,William Middleton Lt kia 22-8-15 5RB attRFC p2&180 CR France924
WALLACE,William Thwaites.MC.TLt kia 12-4-17 B160RFA p37 CR France96,B16RFA
WALLACE-COPLAND,Reginald Capt 16-7-19 3/1GurkhaRif MR43
WALLER,Charles Raymond T2Lt kld 9-6-17 GL &RFC p14 CR Mddx66,9-8-17
WALLER,C.L.LtCol 14-1-15 42DeoliR MR67
WALLER,Francis Ernest.Bart.Capt kia 25-10-14 6 att4RFus p70
WALLER,Hardress Edmund Capt dow 22-11-17 2Y&L p159 CR France398
WALLER,Henry Norman Capt kia 3-7-17 2/4WRid p227 CR France1488
WALLER,Herbert William.MC.TCapt kia 10-4-17 21NumbF p63 CR France96
WALLER,John Raymond T2Lt kld 18-5-17 GL &RFC p14 CR Glouc9,dedacc
WALLER,Richard Alured 2Lt ded 1-11-17 5RFus p70 CR France446
WALLER,Richard Hope Capt kia 3-11-14 IA 38Dogras p284 MR47
WALLER,Thomas Henry Whalley TLt kia 22-10-17 14Glouc p107 MR30
WALLER,Thomas Jenkinson 2Lt dow 28-9-18 2NumbF att4Beds p63 CR France1184,3Bn
WALLEY,Geoffrey Stephen Lt dow 20-8-16 5 att2KRRC p152 CR France177,kia
WALLEY,George John 2Lt dow 25-8-18 7Lincs p76 CR France13
WALLEY,John Clifford 2Lt kia 23-3-18 5 att7Leic p220 MR27
WALLIKER,Lester Charles 2Lt dow 15-5-15 2ESurr p113 CR France102
WALLING,Ernest.MC.MIDx2 CaptAMaj kia 25-4-18 7WYorks p218 MR30
WALLINGTON,Charles Harold T2Lt kia 20-9-17 Dev att 1/6Lpool p77 MR30
WALLINGTON,Frank Courtneay 2Lt dow 6-8-18 SomLI att 1/5SLancs p80 CR France106
WALLINGTON,Geoffrey Stafford 2LtTCapt&Adjt kia 19-9-17 KRRC att10Bn p152 CR Belgium126
WALLINGTON,Nigel Hugh 2Lt kldacc 21-6-17 SomLI p80 CR France729
WALLIS,Alfred Babbington Capt kia 21-3-18 2/6N&D p233 MR20,Bibbington
WALLIS,Alleyne Westaby 2Lt kia 7-6-17 10Lond p248 MR29
WALLIS,Arthur 2Lt dow 2-10-18 1/5LNLancs p234 CR France1184
WALLIS,Arthur Cecil Capt dow 17-9-18 2/5SLancs att4LNLancs p230 CR France13
WALLIS,Arthur Vincent.MID Lt ded 10-7-17 SL EgyptianLabCps p201 CR Iraq1
WALLIS,Harry Bertram T2Lt dow 11-7-16 11RB p180 CR Belgium11
WALLIS,Bertram Henry.MC.Capt kia 18-9-18 RASC att 1/1Camb p194 CR France369
WALLIS,Charles William 2Lt kia 31-7-17 6 att 13Mddx p148 CR Belgium112
WALLIS,Duncan Boyd Lt dow 23-7-15 3ConnRgrs att2RMunstF p172 CR France98,24-7-15
WALLIS,Edward Percy TCapt kia 17-10-16 RLancs att8RSuss p59 CR France150,18-10-16
WALLIS,Francis Herbert Guy Capt dow 17-5-18 11EYorks p85 CR France27
WALLIS,Frederick George TLt kia 30-11-17 EKent p58 MR17
WALLIS,George Arthur Edward.MC.2Lt dow 16-10-18 8RWKent p142 CR France380
WALLIS,George Herbert.DCM.Capt&QM dow 20-9-18 1RWSurr p57&259 CR France278
WALLIS,Harold Legh Lt kld 2-7-16 GL &RFC p4&191,Leigh CR Surrey160
WALLIS,Henry Digby Lt kia 21-10-14 3CldGds p51 MR29

WALLIS,John Buckridge 2Lt drd 10-10-18 4Wilts p236 CR Ireland14,Buckeridge
WALLIS,Nevill Hampton 2Lt dow 25-5-18 C50 RFA p37 CR France102
WALLIS,Noel Veder T2Lt kia 10-4-17 12 Ches p97 CR Belgium102,9Bn
WALLIS,Reginald Robert 2Lt kia 26-3-18 RWar att7Norf p66 MR27
WALLIS,Thomas Francis Capt kia 2-9-18 12SomLI p80 CR France511
WALLIS,Walter Kelburne Lt ded 17-7-18 Lincs attELancs p76 CR Iraq5
WALLIS,William Isaac 2Lt dow 10-10-18 2Hamps p121 CR Belgium38
WALLOND,William John 2Lt kia 22-3-18 13Mddx p148 MR27
WALLWORK,Herbert TLt kia 20-7-16 20RFus p70 MR21
WALMESLEY,Richard Lt kia 23-10-14 3 att2Yorks p91 CR Belgium88,21-10-14
WALMISLEY-DRESSER,Henry Joseph TMajALtCol dow 17-9-16 RWar attESurr p66 CR France833
WALMSLEY,James Blair T2Lt kia 8-8-16 7/8KOSB p102 CR France188
WALMSLEY,Sam Harold Capt kia 5-6-15 5ELancs p226 MR4
WALN,Edward Ashton 2Lt kia 21-10-18 2/6Lpool p215 CR Belgium406
WALNE,Horace George 2Lt kia 11-4-17 2Suff p79 CR France581
WALPOLE,Horatio Spencer Lt kia 9-4-18 1CldGds p51 CR France103
WALPOLE,John Robsart Capt kia 1-7-16 7RWSurr p57 CR France397
WALROND,Francis Hillier T2Lt dow 15-8-16 5 O&BLI p130 CR Sussex111
WALROND,George Basil Stuart TCapt kld 19-3-16 6SomLI p80 CR France420
WALROND,Victor.MIDx2 CaptAMaj kia 26-4-17 15/36RFA p37 CR France265
WALROND,Hon William Lionel Charles TLt ded 2-11-15 RASC p194 CR Devon243
WALSEN,C.W. TLt kia 4-8-17 4KAR p202 CR EAfrica15 &CR Tanzania1,WALSER
WALSH,Albert 2Lt dow 8-8-17 5ELancs att4RFC p20&226 CR Belgium18
WALSH,Archibald Charles Mark 2Lt dow 18-3-15 RHA X'Bty p37 CR Somerset157
WALSH,Arthur.MC.Capt kia 11-4-18 4SLancs p229 MR19
WALSH,Frank 2Lt kia 12-5-17 6 att18Manch p237 MR20
WALSH,Frank 2Lt kia 29-9-18 340/44RFA p37 CR France212
WALSH,Frederick William 2Lt dow 11-7-16 19KRRC att17RWFus p152 CR France833,11Glouc
WALSH,Geoffrey Christian Lansdale 2Lt kia 22-6-17 Ches att 13Bn p97 MR29
WALSH,Geoffrey Pennell Lt kia 9-8-15 N&D att2Bn p135 MR29
WALSH,Gordon James Turnbull.MID Capt 2-7-19 IARO att13Lancers MR66
WALSH,Henry Alfred.CB.Col ded 25-11-18 SomLI Ex Cmdg No8District p263CR Somerset157
WALSH,Herbert T2Lt kia 30-12-17 46RFC p14 CR France49
WALSH,John.MID TMaj dow 19-2-17 22RFus p70 CR France393
WALSH,John Joseph 2Lt kia 8-10-18 5ConnRgrs p172 CR France846
WALSH,Lionel Henry.MC.DCM. ACapt dow 29-8-18 7Lond p247 CR France119
WALSH,Lionel Percy TMaj dow 4-7-16 2RDubF p177 CR France167
WALSH,Martin Oliver.MBE.2Lt kia 3-5-17 2/4YLI p235 MR20
WALSH,Michael Francis 24/1923 2Lt kia 23-12-16 3Bn 3(Rifle)Bde CR France923
WALSH,Patrick Joseph Lt kia 20-9-15 IA IMS p284 CR France354
WALSH,Percival TLt dow 8-7-16 8LNLancs p136 CR France74,2Lt
WALSH,Phillip James T2Lt kia 30-11-17 8RDubF p177 CR France1489,Lt
WALSH,Stephen Barry Lt ded 8-9-15 RAMC att1CavFA p198
WALSH,William TCapt ded 27-2-19 RAVC p268 CR Eire422
WALSH,William Leopold Hampson 2Lt kia 9-8-18 RWKent att8Bn p142 CR France634
WALSHA,Albert Arthur Lt dow 18-9-18 1Norf p74 CR France1701,9Bn
WALSHAM,Harold T2Lt dow 18-9-15 7KRRC p152 CR France40
WALSHAW,Frank Lt kia 20-9-18 IARO att 1/101Grens p284 MR34
WALSHE,Francis Weldon.MC.TCapt kia 25-8-16 3 att1SWBord p101 CR France151
WALSHE,James D.Lt kia 6-4-18 4RWFus p223 CR France232
WALSHE,M.A.SNurse 21-8-15 QAIMNS CR Europe4
WALTER,Alfred Ernest Henry.U.T2Lt dow 13-5-17 2 O&BLI p130 CRLond14
WALTER,Arthur.MM.2Lt kia 21-3-18 1EYorks p85 MR27
WALTER,Bertram.DSO.Maj dow 16-9-16 106/22RFA p37 CR France23
WALTER,Cecil TLtACapt kia 8-10-17 9Dev p77 MR30
WALTER,Harold Ernest CaptTLtCol dow PoW 29-9-15 8Lincs p76 CR France1276
WALTER,Joseph Stanley TCapt kld 21-5-18 RWSurr p57 CR Germany3
WALTER,Raymond T2Lt kia 15-7-16 10Ches p97 MR21
WALTER,Stephen Reginald Parke Lt kia 31-7-17 RWSurr att32RFC p14&57 CR Belgium11
WALTER,Sydney 2Lt kia 25-10-14 1GrenGds p50 MR29
WALTER,William Frederick Maj kia 11-8-15 Staff LancF GSO 53Div p1 MR4
WALTERS,David T2Lt dow 22-5-17 15LancF p94 CR France145
WALTERS,Edward Charles 2Lt kia 22-12-14 3 att1Glouc p107 CR France260

WALTERS,Ernest Beauchamp T.Lt kia 30-7-16 8Glouc p107 MR21
WALTERS,Ernest Henry 2Lt kia 26-9-16 10Manch p237 MR19
WALTERS,Fred 2Lt kia 21-3-18 2/5N&D p233 MR20
WALTERS,Frederick William 2Lt kia 14-10-15 4Leic p220 MR19
WALTERS,Graham Yuille Laundy Lt dow 15-9-16 IrGds attMGC Inf p53 CR France374
WALTERS,Herbert Aidan 2Lt kld 7-4-18 GL &21RAF p191 CR Belgium18
WALTERS,Harold Victor TCapt kia 3-9-16 17N&D A'Coy p135 CR France339
WALTERS,Henry James.MID Lt kia 5-5-15 2Mon p244 MR29
WALTERS,Leslie Hadfield 2Lt dow 17-2-17 5Suff p217 CR France314
WALTERS,Sidney.MC.2Lt dow 4-10-18 SStaffs att1/6Bn p123 CR France446
WALTHER,Kurt Albert 2Lt kia 4-11-18 13KRRC p152 CR France1480
WALTHEW,Ernest John.MC.LtCol kia 22-5-18 RE Cmdg46Div p209 CR France109
WALTHEW,John Syers 2Lt kia 19-9-17 GL &4RFC p14 MR20
WALTON,Albert Bertie.MM.2Lt dow 16-9-18 KRRC att13Bn p152 CR France512
WALTON,Arthur James T2Lt dow 16-10-17 Y&L att9Bn p159 CR France139
WALTON,Charles Hindley T2Lt kia 23-7-16 19Manch p156 MR21 CR France390
WALTON,Eric Alfred 2Lt kia 16-9-16 9DLI p239 MR21
WALTON,Ernest 2Lt kia 27-3-18 18DLI p162 MR27,19Bn
WALTON,Francis John George T2Lt kia 1-7-16 18WYorks p83 CR France742
WALTON,Frank Arthur 2Lt kia 26-9-17 2Lond D'Coy p245 MR30
WALTON,Fred.MM.TCapt kia 15-9-16 18KRRC p152 MR21 &CR France1890
WALTON,Frederick Maxwell 2Lt ded 21-2-19 Worc att1/8Bn p110 CR France1849
WALTON,George Pears Lt kia 22-8-18 4NumbF att2Lincs p213 CR France514,dow
WALTON,Harold Arthur Gordon Lt ded 2-5-17 RFA 33DAC p37 CR France64
WALTON,Harold Foster 2Lt dow 11-4-17 27NumbF p63 CR France95
WALTON,Harold Henry.MC.Capt kia 13-10-15 7N&D A'Coy p233 MR19
WALTON,Harold William Lt dow 24-11-17 13Yorks p91 CR France398
WALTON,Hector Cyril T2Lt kia 9-9-17 Ess att8RWKent p132 CR Belgium19
WALTON,Henry.MC.Capt kia 27-3-18 1/6DLI p239 MR27
WALTON,Herbert Parlby Lt dow 7-12-17 2Yorks p91 CR Belgium165
WALTON,John Leigh Lt ded 22-7-18 21Lond p251 CR Lond14,dow
WALTON,Joseph Cyril Lt kia 29-4-18 4WRid p227 MR30
WALTON,Joseph Frank 2Lt dow 12-11-16 11 att12ESurr p113 MR29
WALTON,Leon Maitland 2Lt kia 17-11-16 1/4LNLancs p234 CR Belgium4,16-11-16
WALTON,Lewin Barlow BrigGen ded 24-5-17 IA Staff p284 MR65
WALTON,Oswald Thomas 2LtTLt kia 12-4-17 3SLancs &18RFC p14&126 CR France568
WALTON,Percy Jackson T2Lt kia 8-3-17 1WYorks p83 CR France115
WALTON,Reginald Frederick William T2Lt kia 26-9-17 12WYorks p83 CR Belgium45
WALTON,Richard Crawhall Lt kia 7-11-14 IA 1/9GurkhaRif p284 CR France705
WALTON,Robert Clare 2Lt kia 10-8-15 5RWFus p223 MR4
WALTON,William Knott 2LtTLt kia 31-7-17 20DLI p162 MR29
WALTON,William Lees Percival 2Lt kia 30-11-17 217MGC p186 MR17
WAND,Wilfred Ernest TLt kia 7-7-16 9NumbF p63
WAND-TETLEY,Charles Ernest Lt kia 22-8-15 9LancF p94
WANE,Hayward T2Lt kia 18-10-16 18Lpool p73 MR21
WANER,Gerald Richard Francis T2Lt dow 2-3-17 RE &25RFC p14&49 CR France88
WANLISS,Alexander.MID Lt kia 9-5-15 1BlkW p129 CR France924
WANKLYN,John Sudell.MC.Lt kia 29-5-18 29RFA p37&259 CR France202,Endell 128RFA
WANKLYN,Kenneth.MID Lt ded 15-11-18 98RFA p37 CR France1858
WANKLYN,William Hibbert T2Lt kia 11-5-17 HouseholdBn p20 CR France452
WANSBROUGH,William Evelyn Capt kia 29-7-16 3 att2SStaffs p123 MR21
WANSTALL,Elton Cyril 2Lt dow 25-9-15 EKent p58 MR19
WARBURTON,Fred Eric 2Lt kia 15-10-17 49RFA 3DivArtAnzacCpsTroops p37 CR Belgium10
WARBURTON,George Augustus Lowe T2Lt kld 1-10-17 GL &RFC p14 CR Norf247
WARBURTON,George Harold Edmondson.MC.LtACapt kia 17-4-18 4Lpool p73 CR Belgium40
WARBURTON,Henry Heap 2Lt dow 9-9-16 7LancF att48MGC p187&221 MR21
WARBURTON,Stanley T2Lt kia 14-9-16 12LancF p94 MR37
WARD,Albert 2Lt kia 28-6-18 15WYorks p83 CR France24
WARD,Albert Joseph 2Lt kia 13-6-18 2Leinst p175 CR France24,18-6-18
WARD,Alec 2Lt kia 28-6-18 15WYorks p83 CR France24
WARD,Alfred Claude Leonard TCapt&Adjt ded 18-11-15 5KSLI p145 CR France64
WARD,Allen Dudley Walter T2Lt ded 23-7-17 7RWSurr p57 CR France145,Allan
WARD,Andrew Rushworth T2Lt kld 21-1-18 RFC p17 CR Lond10

WARD,Arthur 2Lt kia 17-10-14 Lpool p73 CR Belgium126,20-10-14
WARD,Arthur Bowsher 2Lt kia 15-8-18 8 att1EYorks p85 CR France339
WARD,Arthur Claud.DSO.Capt kia 26-8-14 2LancF p94 MR15
WARD,Arthur Edward Martyr Capt&Adjt kia 12-8-15 1/5Norf p74 MR4
WARD,Aubrey Parker Orde Lt ded 11-11-18 4Lincs p217
WARD,Basil Mignot Capt kia 3-5-15 1Ess A'Coy p132 CR Gallipoli1,25-4-15
WARD,Bernard Michael T2Lt kia 20-11-17 11RDubF p177 CR France1489
WARD,Bertram Edmund LtCol ded 22-10-14 1Mddx p148 CR France102
WARD,Charles Albert John Lt ded 15-12-18 IARO attCensorsDept p284 MR34
WARD,Charles Cecil Brooks 2LtTLt dow 11-1-17 7NStaffs p158 CR Iraq5
WARD,Charles Francis Capt kia 15-5-15 RFA p37 MR29
WARD,Charles Sanford TLt kia 7-1-16 10RWar p66 MR19
WARD,Charles Wilson.MC.Capt kia 29-4-18 RHFA attStaff RGA HQ IIICps HAB p37 CR France1025
WARD,Cecil Wellesley 2Lt kia 11-9-17 A/148RFA p37 CR Belgium79
WARD,Cyril Bertram 2Lt dow 1-11-16 21Lond p251 CR France95
WARD,Cyril Richard 2Lt kia 14-7-16 RE 3/1 attChesFC p210 CR France399
WARD,Dacre Stanley 2Lt kia 1-7-16 12Lond p248 MR21
WARD,Dudley Theophilus 2Lt kia 20-9-17 5Lond p246 MR29
WARD,Edward Arthur Hunter Lt kia 11-8-17 6WYorks attRFC p20&218 CR France1314,FltCmdr
WARD,Edward Leslie 2Lt kia 14-7-16 1 att3SStaffs p123 MR21,3 att1Bn
WARD,Edward John.MC.2Lt kia 2-10-17 C50RFA p37&259 CR Belgium10
WARD,Eric 2Lt dow 27-2-18 10RFus p70 CR Belgium11
WARD,Eric Seth Lt kia 10-8-17 O&BLI &32RFC p255 MR20
WARD,Ernest.MC.2Lt ded 19-10-18 A56RFA p37 CR France85
WARD,Ernest Hawksworth Capt kia 30-11-17 1/5LNLancs p234 MR17
WARD,Errol Stephen Remson Lt 8-12-18 9TankCps CR Oxford69
WARD,F.M.2Lt kld 22-4-18 GL &RAF p191
WARD,Francis Welsford Capt kia 9-10-17 4Glouc p225 MR30
WARD,Frank Reginald T2Lt dow PoW 15-10-17 14HLI p164 CR France924,15-12-17
WARD,Frank Saxon Capt kia 31-7-17 8Lpool p215 MR29
WARD,Fred.MC.MID Capt kia 8-12-17 2/19Lond p250 CR Palestine3
WARD,Geoffrey Arthur T2Lt kia 30-9-16 12 att7RWKent p142 CR France383
WARD,George Arthur Ernest 2Lt kia 20-10-18 7Lincs p76 MR16
WARD,George Bernard.MC&Bar.T2LtTMaj kia 21-9-17 GL &10RFC p14 CR France98
WARD,George Cecil 2Lt kia 2-7-16 8WYorks B'Coy p219 CR France215,1-7-16
WARD,George Herbert 2Lt kia 4-6-15 7Manch p237 MR4
WARD,George Duval TCaptAMaj kia 18-5-17 B181RFA p37 CR France439
WARD,George Ernest 2LtTCapt kia 25-9-15 RSuss p120 CR France219
WARD,George Matthews T2Lt kia 24-8-16 7DCLI p115 CR France630,Matthew
WARD,Hon Gerald Ernest Francis.MVO.Capt kia 30-11-14 1LifeGds p20 MR29
WARD,Harold.MIDx2 Maj kia 21-3-18 2/4 att2/5Lincs p217 MR20
WARD,Harold Arthur 2Lt kia 20-4-18 7Worc p226 MR32
WARD,Harold Frederick.MC.TCapt kia 30-11-17 7ESurr p113 MR17
WARD,Henry Ernest Lt ded 13-12-18 RE p49 CR Yorks98
WARD,Hubert Henry T2Lt kia 19-9-18 1/4Ess p132 CR Palestine9
WARD,Jack Bouverie Mallam 2Lt kia 7-11-14 2 O&BLI p130 MR29
WARD,James Eyre Drummond Maj ded 20-6-16 11Mddx attRAOC p148 CR Yorks38
WARD,Jebusa Newton Lt kia 27-8-18 1IrGds p53 CR France214
WARD,J.G.2Lt ded 7-5-18 1/2LancF &RAF p94
WARD,John 2Lt ded 18-12-15 4RLancs p213 CR France22
WARD,John 2Lt kia 30-8-18 3 att2WRid p116 CR France421,31-8-18
WARD,Kenneth Hilary Wodehouse Capt dow 30-8-18 KRRC p152 MR61
WARD,Laurance 2Lt kia 10-4-18 4York p220 MR32
WARD,Maurice Arthur.MC.Capt dow 10-4-18 11LancF p94 CR France1094
WARD,Neville Lascelles 2Lt kia 23-8-14 ESurr p113 CR Belgium201
WARD,Noel Loftus Moore 2Lt kia 15-10-16 3/5Ess p232 MR21
WARD,Norman Hartley T2Lt dow 8-3-17 5Mddx att1LNLancs p148 CR France164
WARD,Norman John T2Lt kia 11-8-16 11RWar p66 MR21
WARD,Otho Charles Capt kia 11-1-17 IA 2/124BaluchisInf p284 CR Iraq5
WARD,Patrick Michael SubCdr ded 28-12-17 IA S&TCps p284
WARD,Paul Francis Seymour 2Lt kia 22-3-18 2/7 att2/8Worc p226 MR27
WARD,Percival Arthur 2Lt dow 16-5-18 50RFA p37 CR France102
WARD,Percy Duncan TCapt dow 11-10-16 11LancF p94 CR France59
WARD,Percy Harry Bavister 2Lt kia 19-5-17 GL &22RFC p14 CR France439,Percival Banister
WARD,Peter Womersley.MC.TCapt&Adjt dow 23-2-17 6SLancs p126 CR Iraq6

WARD,P.F.Lt ded 12-9-15 RAMC p198
WARD,Philip TLt kia 27-12-17 17Manch p156 MR30
WARD,Reginald Ibotson Lt dow 26-5-19 1DragGds p20 MR43
WARD,Reginald Lucian Lt kia 21-4-16 2Y&L p159 CR Belgium73,Lucien
WARD,Robert Oscar Cyril.MIDx2 TMaj kia 20-11-17 EKent attTankCps p58&189 CR France662
WARD,Samuel Leonard.MC.2Lt kia 22-3-18 RWar Res att2/6Bn p66 MR27
WARD,Stephen Remson T2Lt ded 8-12-18 TankCps p189
WARD,Thomas TLt kia 11-6-16 21NumbF p63 CR France515
WARD,Thomas Pillans Lt kia 31-7-17 Nhampt att7Bn p138 MR29
WARD,Thomas Pryce 2Lt dow 10-10-18 1SWBord att1/1Hereford p101 CR Belgium11
WARD,Walter Delay Capt ded 4-9-18 1/9Hamps p229 MR66
WARD,Walter Granby Lt kia 3-9-18 RGA 171SB p42 CR Italy1
WARD,Walter Wallace Capt ded 28-10-18 RASC p194 CR France1512
WARD,William 2Lt kia 4-3-17 5 att1Worc p110 CR France439
WARD,William Alfred Maj ded 30-8-18 RAMC p198 p267 CR Hamps1
WARD,William Arthur Bayford Kirvan.MID TLt dow 2-8-15 RE Sigs p49 MR4,Kirwan
WARD,William Ernest TLt ded 4-11-18 LancF p255 CR Lancs256
WARD,William Leigh 2Lt kia 22-12-17 4SomLI p218 CR Belgium111
WARD-JONES,Frederick Vivian.MC.2Lt kia 17-7-16 1 att9SWBord p101 CR France453,Lt 16-7-16
WARD-PRICE,Leonard Stanley Lt kia 25-3-17 2LifeGds att7ORFC p14&23 CR France846,Capt
WARDE,Basil Charles Conroy 2Lt kia 30-7-16 2 O&BLI p130 CR France402
WARDE,Brian Edmund Douglas Lt kia 16-6-15 6 att4RFus p70 MR29
WARDE,C.A.Maj 14-2-20 15RFus CR Mddx66
WARDELL,Warren Henry Maj mbk 27-11-14 IA 1/39GarhwalRif p284 MR28,24-11-14
WARDELL,William Moss 2Lt kia 23-3-18 1MGC p186 MR27,1TankCps
WARDEN,Edmund Oscar Capt kia 28-6-15 12Ess p133 CR Gallipoli6
WARDEN,Walter George TCapt kia 1-7-16 8SomLI p80 CR France267
WARDILL,Charles Henry T2Lt kia 1-7-16 15 att12Y&L p159 MR21
WARDLAW,A.P.M.Maj 14-5-17 9Suss CR Mddx26
WARDLE,Cyril Ernest 2Lt kia 3-10-18 3 att1N&D p135 CR France441
WARDLE,Frank Lt selfInflictGunshot 2-9-20 IA TC att2/22Punjabis p284 MR65
WARDLE,James Kenneth TLt dow 30-4-16 15WYorks p83 CR France167
WARDLE,John Russell Maj kia 2-1-16 GlasgowYeo p203 CR Gallipoli3
WARDLE,Joseph Frederick TLt ded 14-2-19 RE 334RdConstCo p255 CR Staffs170
WARDLEWORTH,Douglas Lt ded 24-10-14 RAMC p198 CR France85
WARDLEY,Geoffrey Charles Norton TLt dow 24-7-16 RGA 24SB p42 CR France329
WARDLEY,Miles Edward T2Lt kia 29-4-17 22RFus p70 MR20
WARDROP,John T2Lt kia 3-8-16 8RFus p70 MR21
WARDROPER,James Marsh Maj ded 27-3-20 RWSurr CR Hamps241
WARE,Bertram Knight 2Lt kia 19-9-16 15Lond p249 MR21
WARE,Denys C.Capt kld 20-9-18 Lpool &RAF p73
WARE,Eric Wallace 2Lt kia 18-10-16 3 att2Wilts p153 CR France432
WARE,Francis Henry Capt kia 1-7-16 13Lond p249 MR21
WARE,John Wilson 2Lt kia 10-7-16 RE 74FC p49 MR19
WARE,Kenneth Charles Webb 2Lt kia 21-3-18 RGA 77SB p42 CR France1188
WARE,William 2Lt mbk 27-10-18 2RWFus p257 MR16
WAREHAM,Frederick William Lt kia 1-7-16 1/8RWar p215 MR21
WAREHAM,Lawrence John Lt kia 21-7-16 1/7Worc p226 MR21
WAREING,Cecil Hooten Lt dow 1-11-17 4Beds p87 CR Belgium16
WAREING,William Robert Alexander Capt kia 23-3-18 11Lpool p73 CR France1061
WARHAM,Joseph T2Lt dow 7-5-17 8KRRC p152 CR France214
WARING,Edward Robert 2Lt kia 29-10-14 1KRRC p152 MR29
WARING,Frank 2Lt dow 24-8-16 5Y&L p238 CR France40,Lt
WARING,Frederick Royden 2Lt kia 7-7-16 10 att7RSuss p120 MR21
WARING,Holt Maj dow 15-4-18 NIrHorse attRIrRif p24 CR Belgium89
WARING,John.MC.Capt kia 6-10-18 20Manch p156 CR France234
WARINGGILL,Erold Lt 25-7-16 8RFA CR France207
WARK,Hugh Alexander Lt kia 14-3-18 6GordH p242 CR France381
WARLAND,Frederick Leslie 2Lt kia 25-3-18 3 att12ESurr p113 MR20
WARLAND,Maurice George T2Lt dow 20-1-17 8Wilts p153 CR Iraq5
WARLOW,Edmund Jarvis Leith TLt kia 6-11-16 11 att2Worc p110 MR21
WARLOW,Theodore William TLt dow 28-7-16 6YLI p144 CR France102
WARMAN,William Alfred 2Lt 13-10-18 RAF Ex1/4Ess CR Egypt9

WARMINGTON,Alfred Ernest TCapt kia 24-5-16 6RIrReg p89 CR Ireland14,24-4-16
WARMSLEY,Frank Walter 2Lt dow 22-11-17 1/5N&D p233 CR France179
WARN,Wallace Gordon Lt dow 23-9-16 10RSuss &RFC p4&120 CR France245,kia
WARNE,Bertie Joseph 2Lt dow 4-4-18 Mddx att21Bn p148 CR France40
WARNE,William Millar Lt 22-5-15 RGA 7SB p42 CR France260
WARNER,Archibald 2Lt kia 1-7-16 5Lond p246 CR France1327
WARNER,Arnold Ashton Justice 2Lt kia 24-8-18 1GrenGds p50 CR France1489
WARNER,Bernard Oldershaw Lt kia 19-5-17 3 att1Ess p133 CR France311
WARNER,Bertram 2Lt kia 12-4-17 1LondRB p246 MR20
WARNER,Charles Thornton Capt ded 12-9-20 IA 1/22Punjabis p284 MR43,30-9-20
WARNER,Clive Wynyard Lt ded 14-10-18 IA 3Lancers p284 MR43
WARNER,Cornwallis John Lt kia 16-5-15 3 att2 O&BLI p130 MR22
WARNER,Douglas Redston 2Lt kia 1-7-16 4RDubF p177 CR France1500
WARNER,Harry James 2Lt kia 3-6-17 6Nhampt p138 CR France541,Henry
WARNER,Herbert Moline Lt dow 16-11-14 1ELancs p111 CR France284,Capt
WARNER,Robert 2Lt kia 6-3-17 2/5Y&L p238 CR France514
WARNER,Samuel 2Lt kia 1-10-18 12RIrRif p170 CR Belgium157
WARNER,Thomas Lovell.DSO.TMaj ded 27-12-17 8Leic p88 CR France446
WARNER,Thornton Sparr Capt kia 23-7-16 11 att8Glouc p107 MR21
WARNER,William Henry 2Lt kia 21-8-18 5MGC Div p186 CR France281,Inf
WARNER,William James 2Lt kia 3-5-17 18WYorks p83 MR20
WARNES,David Hoggett Lt ded 10-6-17 RFA p208 CR EAfrica38 &CR Tanzania1
WARNINGTON,Charles 2Lt kia 3-5-17 6EKent p58 MR20
WARNOCK,Elizabeth MacMath(Daisy)Nurse ded 5-5-18 VAD 10Detachment BRCS 8GH p200 CR France145
WARNOCK,George Moir.MID Lt dow 29-3-18 6A&SH p243 CR Frnce145,Muir
WARNOCK,Hugh Adolphus Hector Lt dow 16-8-15 4 att1RIrF p172 CR France518,Hector A.Hugh
WARNOCK,Robert.MC.T2Lt kia 12-8-16 6/7RScotF p95 CR France151
WARR,Thomas Edward T2Lt dow 14-10-17 6Dors p124 CR France102
WARR,William Charles Samuel.DCM.2Lt kia 1-7-16 22RFA p37 CR France397
WARRAND,Alastair St.John Munro Capt kld 18-3-15 1BlkW &RFC p2&129,ded CRFrance1027,19-3-15
WARRE,Cecil Alberic Hardy T2Lt kia 24-4-17 88MGC Inf p186 CR France531
WARRE-CORNISH,Gerald Maj kia 16-9-16 6SomLI p80 MR21
WARRELL,Alfred 2Lt kia 9-10-17 5LancF p221 MR30
WARRELL-BOWRING,Walter John 2Lt kia 30-7-16 3 att6RWSurr p57 CR France251,29-7-16
WARREN,Alan John 2Lt dow 10-7-17 12Lond p248 CR France755
WARREN,Alan Rowland 2Lt kia 8-10-16 9Lond p248 MR21
WARREN,Albert T2Lt kia 17-3-18 Leic &35RFC p17&88 CR France446,Lt
WARREN,Archibald Alexander.MIDx2 TLt kia 20-1-16 8BordR p118 CR France924
WARREN,Charles Gordon 2Lt kld 28-8-18 21Lond p251 CR France214
WARREN,Dawson LtCol kia 17-9-14 RWSurr p57 CR France1342
WARREN,Edgar Cecil 2Lt kia 3-5-17 8 att1Lond p247 MR20
WARREN,Francis Purcell 2Lt mbk 14-7-16 2SLancs p257 MR21,3-7-16
WARREN,Fred Langford 2Lt kia 1-7-16 4 att2WYorks p83 MR21
WARREN,Frederick Robert Fulford TLt,AMaj kia 22-10-16 14Hamps p121 CR France384
WARREN,Frederick John Maj ded 14-7-15 9WelshR p128 CR Wilts115
WARREN,Harry 2Lt kia 7-7-17 4Hamps p228 CR Belgium115
WARREN,Ivan John 2Lt dow 8-3-18 3 att1Glouc p107 CR Belgium38
WARREN,James Lionel East Capt kia 2-10-15 att1WelshR p128 MR19
WARREN,John Booker Brough Lt kia 28-10-14 1BordR p118 MR29,James
WARREN,John Crosby.MC.MID Capt kia 21-3-18 7N&D p233 CR France646,Maj
WARREN,Martin 2Lt,ACapt kia 24-3-18 5 att1Worc p110 MR27,25-3-18
WARREN,Peyton Tollemache Capt dow 14-8-15 RAMC 3FA p254 CR Gallipoli27
WARREN,Richard Crawford.MC&Bar.28-6-21 1 O&BLI CR Hamps70
WARREN,Richard Dunn Maj kia 7-4-18 6Leinst p175 CR Belgium72,kld 11Leic
WARREN,Theodore Stewart Wolton T2Lt kia 17-7-16 17DLI p162 MR21
WARREN,William Duncan 2Lt kia 20-9-17 19Lond p251 MR29
WARREN,William Edward AMaj dow 29-3-18 RGA 81SB p42 CR France169
WARREN,William Stanley 2Lt ded 10-10-17 3 att2BordR p118 CR France139,dow
WARREN-SWETTENHAM,Thomas Robert Eaton Wybault Maj kia 6-2-15 2EYorks p85 MR29
WARRINER,Thomas Andrew Latimer 2Lt kia 10-10-16 5Worc p110 CR France631
WARRINGTON,Francis Arnold TLt kia 7-10-16 148RFA p37 CR France374

WARRINGTON,Garfield Lt kia 18-8-17 RASC p253 CR France855
WARRINGTON,Harold Gordon Lt dow 6-12-17 RFA 63A/ASect p208 CR Italy7
WARRINGTON,William Barrett Capt ded 2-2-19 RAMC p256 CRLancs12,Barnett
WARRY,John Lucas Capt dow 27-4-17 8N&D p233 CR France511
WARTER,Henry De Grey Capt kia 20-11-17 4DragGds p21 CR France711
WARTER,Joseph Gordon 2Lt kia 30-9-17 Wilts att66RFC p14&153 MR20
WARTER,William Henry Lt kia 9-5-17 168MGC Inf p186 CR France531
WARTNABY,Charles Richard Arnold Lt kld 11-3-15 NhamptYeo p204 CR France1106
WARWICK,Colin Winder.MC.2Lt kia 22-3-18 5 att8BordR p228 CR France1484
WARWICK,Douglas Charles.MC.LtAMaj ded 20-1-19 NStaffs att11MGC p194&265 CR France1252
WARWICK,John Cedric Geoffrey Lt drd 27-5-18 NottsYeo p205 MR41
WARWICK,John Douglas Barford Maj kia 10-3-17 HuntsCycBn att 1/1BucksBn O&BLI p253 CR France624
WARWICK,J._.2Lt kld 14-6-18 GL &RAF p192
WARWICK,Thomas Harry.MC.2Lt kia 28-4-17 3 att9NStaffs &MGC p186 CR France924,Lt
WARWICK,William Robert St.Clair 2Lt dow 19-12-15 1/4Ches p222 CR Egypt3,WARRICK
WASBOROUGH,Spencer Vere Capt kia 12-4-17 1SomLI p80 CR France728,WASBROUGH
WASBROUGH,William Lewis 2Lt kia 25-9-15 1LNLancs p136 CR France1723
WASEY,Cyril Walter Carleton.MC.Capt kia 28-10-17 2RWar att16RFC p14,66&259 CR France95
WASHBROOK,Harry 2Lt kia 22-8-18 5Lpool p215CR France619
WASHBROOK,Mark Thomas 2Lt dow 21-11-18 5 att11ELancs p226 CR France34,Tomas
WASHINGTON,Frederick.MC.2Lt kia 22-8-18 4 att1RInniskF p105 CR France855
WASHINGTON,Jonathan Noel 2Lt dow 2-10-15 Manch &RFC p2&156 CR France518
WASON,Cyril Ernest T2Lt kia 30-11-17 9RFus p70 MR17
WASTELL,Kenneth 2Lt kld 23-3-18 RFC p17 CR Hunts83
WATERER,M.D.G.2Lt 25-11-19 37Lancers MR65
WATERER,Michael Anthony 2Lt dow 11-10-18 Mon RE &6RAF p49 CR France446
WATERFALL,Vincent 2Lt kld 22-8-14 3EYorks att5RFC p2&85 CR Belgium406
WATERFIELD,Frederick Charles Capt dow 21-5-15 IA 45 att15Sikhs p284 CR France80
WATERHOUSE,Alfred William.MC.MID Capt kia 12-1-16 1Drags p21 CR France423
WATERHOUSE,Arved 2Lt kia 13-10-14 RLancs p59 CR France324
WATERHOUSE,Gilbert 2Lt kia 1-7-16 Ess p133 CR France1890
WATERHOUSE,Gilbert Wilmot T2Lt dow 10-4-17 6RWKent p142 CR France113
WATERHOUSE,Irvin Preston T2Lt kia 8-11-16 10WYorks p83 MR21
WATERHOUSE,Kenneth Capt kia 9-8-16 2/5LancF Z'Coy p221 CR France294
WATERHOUSE,Rennie Capt kia 7-5-15 7LancF p221 MR4
WATERHOUSE,Richard Dalton LtCol kia 7-8-15 8LancF p256 MR4
WATERHOUSE,Robert Bentley Maskill 2Lt ded 26-3-19 5WYorks p272 CR Yorks311
WATERIDGE,Edgar Leake Lt kia 20-11-14 Leic p88 MR22
WATERLOW,Clive Maitland MajTLtCol kld 20-7-17 RE attRNAS p49 CR Lincs86
WATERMAN,Henry Richard Lt kia 28-8-16 3 att1Mddx p148 MR21 CR France1890
WATERS,Bernard Stanley 2Lt kia 3-5-17 4Lond p246 MR20
WATERS,Charles Louis.MC&Bar.CaptAMaj dow 19-10-17 RBerks att1NigR p140&202 CR EAfrica11 &CR Tanzania1
WATERS,Eric Gordon 2Lt kia 24-1-17 HampsYeo attRFC p20&204 CR Belgium11,Lt
WATERS,Eric Joseph Fitzgerald Lt kia 5-3-20 IA 10Lancers p284 MR38
WATERS,George Thorold Capt dow 29-3-18 7Suff p79 CR France64
WATERS,John Patrick T2Lt kia 18-11-17 56RFC p14 CR France177
WATERS,Kenneth Selby 2Lt murdered 30-5-17 IARO att1BritMtnBty p284 MR67
WATERS,Reginald Rigden ACapt dow 24-10-16 4 att1RWar p66 MR21
WATERS,Reginald William 2Lt kia 12-8-18 1LancF D'Coy p94 CR France193,13-8-18
WATERS,William Denne 2Lt kia 12-3-15 3N&D p135 CR France768,Lt dow 1Bn
WATERS,William Nisbet 2Lt kia 28-7-16 1/6A&SH p243 MR21 CR France1890
WATERSON,Frederick Paris T2Lt kia 31-7-17 17N&D p135 MR21
WATERTON,John Edward Mary Claude Pius Augustine 2Lt kia 29-11-17 5Beds p219 CR Palestine9
WATERTON,Joseph Charles Edmund Mary John Reginald ded 18-2-15 5Beds p272 CR Beds48
WATES,Leslie Charles T2Lt kia 9-10-17 GL &29RFC p14 CR Belgium18
WATHERSTON,G.F.Capt 27-11-16 UgandaPoliceBn CR EAfrica127

WATHERSTON,Robert James Henderson Fell 2Lt kia 3-12-17 1/5Leic p220 CR France163
WATHES,Thomas Sidney Capt kia 19-7-16 6RWar p214 MR32
WATKIN,Alfred Charles 2Lt kia 1-7-16 5NStaffs p238 CR France281
WATKIN,Ben Gerald Noel 2Lt dow 25-1-15 40RFA p37 CR France80,27-1-15
WATKIN,Harry Lt ded 21-10-18 1WRid p116 MR67
WATKIN,Henry George Maj kia 21-8-15 4Huss Staff 2MntdBde p21
WATKIN,Frank Ernest Capt kia 3-1-15 1NumbF p63 MR29,1-1-15
WATKINS,Charles Lt ded 30-1-15 GL Res p272 CR Essex1
WATKINS,Eric Leopold Charles Lt ded 2-3-17 2RFA p208 MR65
WATKINS,Eustace Arundel De St.Barbe Sladen Capt dow 31-1-15 3Dev p77 CR France345
WATKINS,Frederick Augustus 2Lt kia 24-3-18 7EYorks p85 MR20
WATKINS,David John George 2Lt kia 21-4-18 1SWBord p101 CR France109,Lt
WATKINS,Horace Holmes 2Lt kia 21-10-14 3 att1SWBord p101 MR29
WATKINS,Howell Cyril.MC.Lt dow PoW 23-10-18 PembrokeYeo p205 CR France716,Howel 24WelshR
WATKINS,Iltyd Edwin Maitland Capt kia 5-5-15 2Mon p244 MR29,7-5-15
WATKINS,Mervyn Holmes Lt kia 18-9-18 C100RFA p208 CR Greece5
WATKINS,Reginald Noel Lt kia 31-3-18 7EYorks p85 MR20
WATKINS,Thomas 2Lt kia 9-5-15 2RBerks p140 MR32 Ex 2GrenGds
WATKINS,Vivian Holmes Capt dow 20-2-15 2Mon p244 CR Mon69
WATKINS,William 2Lt kia 23-7-18 3WelshR att139RAF p128 CR Italy9
WATKINSON,Arthur T2Lt dow 3-8-16 12RScots p55 CR France40,14Bn
WATKINSON,John.MC.Lt&QM ded 10-12-18 18HLI p164 CR France34
WATKYN-THOMAS,Alwyn Capt mbk 13-11-16 2HLI p257 MR21
WATLINGTON,Henry Joseph 2Lt kia 6-7-17 GL &70RFC p14 MR20
WATMOUGH,John Cyril 2Lt kia 10-7-15 att2NumbF p63 CR Belgium37
WATMOUGH,Oscar Oswald 2Lt kia 1-9-18 2WRid p116 CR France421
WATNEY,Valentine Howell TLt dow 3-2-17 152MGC Inf p186 CR Surrey6
WATNEY,William Herbert Lt dow 10-5-15 2RB A'Coy p180 MR32
WATSON,Alastair Fisher T2Lt kia 23-4-17 9BlkW p129 CR France536
WATSON,Albert Edward Lt 6-11-20 20DLI CR Yorks547
WATSON,Alec Philip 2Lt dow 14-4-17 3 att2Hamps p121 CR France113
WATSON,Alexander Bruce 2Lt kia 28-4-17 7HLI p240 MR20
WATSON,Alfred Charles Capt kia 3-9-16 5WYorks p218 CR France293
WATSON,Alfred William T2Lt kia 1-5-17 GL &10RFC p14 CR France98
WATSON,Allan.DSO.Capt 18-1-20 RAMC CR EAfrica116
WATSON,Arthur Paton T2Lt dow 13-10-16 21Lpool p73 CR FRance833
WATSON,Arthur Toward TMaj dow 5-8-17 21KRRC p152 CR Belgium21
WATSON,Arthur Vivian Cradock.MC.Lt ded 21-12-19 7MGC p266 CR Egypt2 see CRADOCK-WATSON
WATSON,Benjamin T2Lt dow 17-6-16 5 att7RInniskF p105 CR France115
WATSON,Benjamin Alexander 2Lt kia 24-10-18 7 ATT12/13NumbF p214 MR16
WATSON,Cedric Gordon Lt kia 9-5-15 RBerks attESurr p140 MR32
WATSON,Charles Chap4Cl ded 22-7-18 RAChDept p200 CR Iraq6
WATSON,Charles Beaumont.MC.Lt dow 12-7-18 21MGC p186 CR France74,kia
WATSON,Charles Challinor.MID Lt dow 1-6-17 A21RFA p208 CR France570
WATSON,Charles Edward Stephen 2Lt kia 1-7-16 1ELancs p111 MR21,Stephens
WATSON,Charles John TLt dow 26-1-17 10Ches A'Coy p97 CR Iraq5
WATSON,Charles Reginald Lt kia 7-4-16 IA 28Punjabis p284 MR38,6-4-16
WATSON,Charles Victor Macgregor 2Lt kia 3-10-17 1Lothian&BordHorseYeo &RFC p204 CR Greece3
WATSON,Clifford Thomas 2Lt dow 3-12-17 7Lond p247 CR France512
WATSON,Cyril Pennefather 2Lt kia 1-7-16 3ELancs p111 MR21
WATSON,David Galloway Lt ded 5-6-15 RAMC att2Beds p198 CR France40
WATSON,Dominic MacAulay Lt dow 3-12-17 WSomYeo p205 CR France446,12SomLI
WATSON,Dorothy Mortimer SNurse ded 13-3-17 TFNS p254 CR Europe1
WATSON,Douglas Christian TCapt ded 16-6-16 RE attSerbianArmy p49 CR Greece21
WATSON,Elizabeth Harvey SNurse ded 5-11-18 QAIMNS p200 CR France658
WATSON,Ernest Guthrie 2Lt kia 19-9-14 2SLancs D'Coy p126 CR France1107
WATSON,Evan Philip 2Lt dow 28-3-18 8RIrRif p170
WATSON,Francis Lt kia 9-5-15 3 att2ESurr p113 MR29
WATSON,Francis George Stuart 2LtACapt kia 23-10-16 2LancF p94 MR21 CR France1890
WATSON,Francis Shuldham.DSO.Maj dow 2-5-18 RGA 276SB p42 CR France63
WATSON,Frank Lt kia 1-7-16 18WYorks att93TMB p83 MR21
WATSON,Frank TCapt kia 2-4-17 Manch att71TrainingRes p156 CR France616,22Bn

WATSON,Frank Fairweather T2Lt kia 4-8-16 14 att 15RScots p55 CR France432
WATSON,Frank McEwan 2Lt kia 3-5-17 55MGC p186 MR20
WATSON,Frederick John 2Lt kia 24-3-18 7DCLI p115 MR27
WATSON,Frederick Johnston Lt 10-6-16 43CanadaInf CR Belgium134
WATSON,Geoffrey Lt kia 21-1-16 IA 28Punjabis p284 MR38
WATSON,Geoffrey Launcelot Capt kia 20-4-15 att 13ESurr A'Coy p113 MR29
WATSON,Geoffrey,William T2Lt kia 1-8-17 11Ches p97 MR29
WATSON,George Carr Capt kld 8-3-16 6Dev p217 MR38
WATSON,George Douglas Lt dow 18-10-18 5ScotRif p224 CR Belgium11,1/8Bn
WATSON,George Edmund Borlase.DSO.MC.Maj kia 29-8-18 O'Bty RHA 5ArmyBde p37 CR France629
WATSON,George Henry Capt dow 18-9-16 RAMC 3FAp254 CR France177
WATSON,George Walker 2Lt kld 29-12-16 1/7RWFus att RFC p223 CR Egypt9
WATSON,George William Annakin T2Lt kia 7-3-18 RFC p17 CR France64,Lt
WATSON,Harry 2Lt kia 12-8-16 1/9Lpool p216 MR21
WATSON,Henry James Arthur Lt kia 23-8-18 5 att 1Beds p219 CR France239
WATSON,Henry Trelss Capt dow 6-3-15 3Lpool attManch p73 CR Belgium165,att2YLI
WATSON,Herbert Sanderson TCapt kia 26-9-15 8GordH p167 MR19
WATSON,Ivan Philip 2Lt dow 28-3-18 12RIrRif CR France145
WATSON,Jack Cecil Lt kia 5-10-17 10Mddx p236 MR30
WATSON,James 2Lt kia 7-7-16 3 att 2RIrRif p170 CR France150,9-7-16
WATSON,James TLt kia 30-7-16 27Manch p156 CR France397
WATSON,James Clarkson Lt dow 31-8-17 3 att6CamH p168 CR France40,2Lt
WATSON,James Frederick 2Lt ded 22-1-16 5BlkW p231 CR Scot398
WATSON,James Laverick T2Lt kia 29-4-17 23NumbF p63 MR20
WATSON,James Norman 2Lt dow 10-8-16 3 att 1RInnıskF p105 CR Belgium11
WATSON,James Roby T2Lt dow 2-12-17 175MGC Inf p186 CR France711
WATSON,James Stennett 2Lt kia 26-11-17 4EYorks att 1/4WRid p219 CR Belgium20
WATSON,John T2Lt kia 7-4-17 16RScots p55 MR20
WATSON,John.Bart.2Lt kia 23-3-18 16Lancers p23 MR27
WATSON,John 2Lt kia 27-4-18 17RScots p55 CR France60
WATSON,John Allan 2Lt kld 31-1-19 RFA attRGA MtnBty p209 MR70 &CR Europe179
WATSON,John Christopher Capt kia 26-9-17 2GordH p167 CR Belgium8,1Bn
WATSON,John Eben T2Lt kia 26-9-15 7RScotF p95 MR19
WATSON,John Edmund Malone.MC.Chap4Cl dow 10-4-18 RAChDept att 21Mddx p200&259 CR France1094
WATSON,John Frederick T2Lt dow 23-10-17 10NumbF p63 CR France102
WATSON,John Irvine 2Lt 14-8-17 B110RFA CR Belgium7
WATSON,John Lawrence Craig Lt kia 9-4-17 5GordH p242 MR20
WATSON,John Mitchell Capt kia 13-11-17 4KOSB p223 CR Palestine9
WATSON,John Mowbray Walter TLt kia 23-8-17 249MGC p186
WATSON,John Peirson 2Lt kia 29-7-17 3EYorks D'Coy p85 MR20
WATSON,Joseph St.John.MC.DCM.Lt&QM dow 30-4-18 2DLI p162 CR France100
WATSON,Joseph Harold 2Lt dow 3-10-18 1/2 att 1/4Leic p88 CR France725
WATSON,Joseph James.DCM.2Lt kia 16-8-18 F99 RFA T'Bty 1TMB p37 CR Greece6
WATSON,Kenneth Charles Forrester.MC.Lt kia 12-4-18 3SLancs att 2/7RWar p126 MR32
WATSON,Kenneth Clennell TLt kia 11-4-17 10LNLancs p136 MR20
WATSON,Laurence Charles 2Lt kia 12-8-15 8Hamps p229 MR4
WATSON,Laurence Stuart Lt kia 29-7-18 8ScotRif p225 CR France524
WATSON,Leslie Riley 2Lt kia 4-7-16 RHFA p209
WATSON,Lord Arthur James 2Lt kia 26-9-18 5Yorks att7EYorks p221 MR16
WATSON,Louis Talbot Capt kia 11-3-15 1Worc p110 CR France525
WATSON,Mark Sanderson 2Lt kia 11-1-17 4HLI p164 MR38
WATSON,Noel Alick Capt kia 22-4-17 IA 55Rif att56 p284 MR38
WATSON,Norman Campion 2Lt kia 24-4-17 6 att 12HLI p240 MR20
WATSON,Norman John 2Lt kia 27-5-18 C246RHFA p37 CR Belgium8
WATSON,Oliver Cyril Spencer.VC.DSO.LtCol kia 28-3-18 1MddxHuss att 2/5YLI p204 MR20
WATSON,Oswald Halley 2Lt kia 9-9-17 2PORif p247 MR29
WATSON,Peter Seton 2Lt kia 9-4-17 5A&SH p243 CR France728
WATSON,Raymond Victor T2Lt kia 16-8-17 8NumbF p63 MR30
WATSON,Reginald 2Lt kia 7-10-16 11RWKent p142 CR France385
WATSON,R.H.17-9-14 1LNLancs MR15
WATSON,Robert Lowson Capt ded 8-2-16 4BlkW p272 CR Scot386
WATSON,Robert Oke Carey Capt kia 26-3-17 2/10Mddx p236 MR34

WATSON,Roger Wentworth TLt kia 30-7-15 8KRRC C'Coy p152 CR Belgium453,20-7-15
WATSON,Samuel Meredith 2Lt kia 1-7-16 64MGC p186 CR France267
WATSON,Stanley John T2Lt dow 28-11-15 8 att2RScotF p95 CR France80,Lt
WATSON,Stanley Lee Capt kia 25-9-15 4BlkW p230 MR19
WATSON,Sydney Fairweather 2Lt kia 6-9-16 2GordH p167 MR21
WATSON,Sydney Towers T2Lt kia 1-7-16 16 att 15DLI p162 MR21
WATSON,Thomas TCapt kia 11-4-17 6RScotF p95 MR20
WATSON,Thomas T2Lt kia 26-3-18 82RFC p17 CR France1242
WATSON,Thomas Colclough.VC.LtCol ded 15-6-17 RE p49 CR mddx26
WATSON,Thomas Hovenden.DSO.MC.ALtCol kia 23-3-18 2/1Worc att 1N&D p110 CR France987
WATSON,Thomas Palmer.MC.TCapt kia 7-3-16 6ELancs p111 CR Iraq8
WATSON,Vesey Clayhills Capt kia 11-4-17 19RFA p37 CR Iraq8
WATSON,Walter 2Lt kia 27-5-18 EYorks att 4Bn p85 MR18
WATSON,Walter John Mowbray Lt kia 22-8-17 249MGC Inf CR Belgium127 Ex NStaffs
WATSON,William.MIDx3 MajTLtCol kia 3-5-17 1SomLI att5YLI p80&235 MR20
WATSON,William Lt kia 21-3-18 4RBerks att 184TMB p234 MR27
WATSON,William Lt&QM ded 18-6-18 SL DLI p201 CR Lancs450
WATSON,William Capt dow 22-8-18 24Manch att 1EYorks p156 CR France131
WATSON,William.CMG.LtCol ded 3-3-19 RAMC p267 CR Mddx26,SomLI attGHQ
WATSON,William Baikie.MC.Lt dow 30-9-18 C95RFA p37 CR France357
WATSON,William Ernest.DSO.Maj kia 31-10-14 6DragGds p21 MR29
WATSON,William Erskine 2Lt kia 24-3-18 17Lpool p73 MR27
WATSON,William George Douglas Capt kia 19-4-17 5KOSB p224 MR34
WATSON,William John 2Lt kld 26-5-17 GL &RFC p14 CR Lond14
WATSON,William Norman.MC.TCapt ded 29-5-19 6KOSB p102 CR France285
WATSON,William Stanley Capt dow 11-8-18 RASC att 15LancF p194 CR France879
WATSON,William Vernon Crowther 2Lt kia 15-10-17 6WYorks p218 CR Belgium126
WATSON,William Wallace T2Lt kia 13-10-16 2Yorks p91 MR21
WATSON-SMYTH,Edward Jeffray Capt kia 27-8-18 2CldGds p51 CR France615,Jeffery
WATSON-TAYLOR,Arthur Simon 2Lt kia 14-9-17 22Lond p252 CR Belgium72
WATSON-THOMAS,Walter Patrick 2LtACapt kia 21-10-16 8BordR p118 MR21
WATT,Alexander Capt dow 20-6-16 4BlkW p230 CR France134
WATT,Alexander 2Lt kia 18-8-18 3 att2RScots p55 CR France26
WATT,Alexander Lyle Capt kld 10-3-15 5BlkW p231 CR France279
WATT,Basil Harry T2Lt kia 25-9-15 7CamH p168 MR19 &CR France1896
WATT,Charles Cecil 2Lt kia 8-5-17 4 att2KOSB p224 CR France777
WATT,Colin Robert Jamieson T2Lt dow 14-8-16 RE 212FC p49 CR France833
WATT,Douglas Gordon.MID 2Lt kia 2-3-16 3 att 1GordH p167 CR Belgium167
WATT,George Macdonald 2Lt kia 17-3-17 16RFC p14 CR France32
WATT,Hugo Burr Craig.MC.Lt kia 24-8-18 8DLI p239 MR16
WATT,J.Capt 22-12-18 SAfrPostalCps MR52
WATT,James 2Lt kld 2-5-17 4RScots attRFC p20&211 CR Greece1
WATT,John 2Lt dow 14-11-16 5GordH p242 CR France131
WATT,John Heigh 2Lt kia 12-4-18 6 att4Worc p110 MR32
WATT,John Grant 2Lt kia 27-8-18 7GordH p242 MR16
WATT,John Vade T2Lt dedacd 30-10-15 14Ches p97 CR Shrop147
WATT,Kenneth Murray 2Lt dow 1-10-17 PoW 3Beds p87 CR Palestine8
WATT,Norman Lindley 2LtTLt dow 27-7-17 KEdwHorse &RFC p14&24,Lindlay CR Belgium76,Lindsey
WATT,Percy Bryden.MID Lt kia 14-4-18 13GordH att 13MGC p167&186,11GordH CR France21,13MGC
WATT,Robert 2Lt kia 10-8-17 11RFus p70 CR Belgium125
WATT,Robert Sherwin 2Lt kia 12-6-17 GL &45RFC p14 CR France200
WATT,Robert Stapleton T2Lt dow 20-11-16 13EYorks B'Coy p85 CR France40
WATT,Thomas Stevenson T2Lt kia 22-9-17 14HLI p164 MR21
WATT,William 2Lt dow 10-4-18 17LancF p94 CR Scot816 Ex 2GordH
WATT,William James 2Lt kia 25-9-15 6GordH p242 CR France219
WATTERS,John Rev ded 7-11-18 RAChDept att 115InfBdeHQ p200 CR France332
WATTERSON,Gerald 2Lt kia 13-3-18 ELancs att 1Bn p111 CR France616
WATTERTON,William Frederick HonLt&QM ded 2-1-17 RAMC p198 CR Hamps1,1-1-17
WATTHEWS,Harold Lt dow 8-6-17 3 att 10WRid p116 MR29
WATTON,Stanley Victor 2Lt dow 27-11-16 3 att3/7SLancs p126 CR France40
WATTS,Albert Edward T2Lt kia 25-9-16 10YLI p144 MR21

WATTS,Albert Edward 2Lt ded 6-3-17 16RFC p14 MR20
WATTS,Albert Edward 2Lt kia 22-4-18 15WelchR p128 CR France59
WATTS,Charles Harold Reynell Capt kia 25-12-14 2Nhampt p138 MR22
WATTS,Cyril George CaptABdeMaj kia 1-10-18 GL 11EYorks Staff93InfBde p192 CR Belgium48
WATTS,Donald William Stuart 2Lt kia 12-10-16 3Y&L p159 CR France307,Stewart
WATTS,Dudley Haldane 2Lt kia 26-9-15 8RWKent p142 MR19
WATTS,F.W.O.Capt 9-5-18 IndDefForce 26Rifs MR66
WATTS,Francis John 2Lt kia 17-7-17 RGA 9SB p42 CR Belgium29
WATTS,Frank Mansell Wall Lt 25-3-20 HLI CR Asia33
WATTS,Frederick Robert 2Lt kia 29-8-18 12Norf p204 MR32
WATTS,George Leonard T2Lt kia 17-10-16 88MGC p186 MR21
WATTS,Graham Harman 2Lt kia 11-7-18 1CamH att2/4KAR p168&202 CR EAfrica52
WATTS,Harland T2Lt dow 22-11-16 7SLancs p126
WATTS,Harold Vaughan Iremonger Capt dow 11-8-17 7 att2Dev p217 CR Belgium18
WATTS,Henry Leonard TCapt kia 20-10-15 9Ess p133 MR19
WATTS,Henry Rowland T2Lt kia 7-6-17 6EYorks p85 CR Belgium21
WATTS,Hubert Lt ded 8-2-19 3NumbF p262 CR Numb4
WATTS,John Howe 2Lt kia 6-11-17 1/1Hereford p252 CR Palestine1
WATTS,Leonard.MM.2Lt kia 9-10-18 3Lond p246 CR France647,Capt
WATTS,Norman Luther TMaj kia 25-9-16 9Lpool p216 CR France397
WATTS,Robin Kenelm 2Lt kia 23-8-18 3 att7RWKent p142 CR France177
WATTS,Ronald William Ailsa.MC.T2Lt dow 12-11-16 13 att2Worc p110 CR France105
WATTS,Samuel TLt ded 28-10-18 2Manch att96TMB p156 CR Ches154,Capt dow
WATTS,Stephen Lt dow 6-9-16 1RMunstF p176 CR France833
WATTS,Talbot Hamilton TCapt kia 1-7-16 16Mddx p148 MR21
WATTS,Thomas William 2Lt kia 25-9-15 9Lpool p216 CR France1723
WATTS,W.Spalding Lt 15-11-20 RE MR40
WATTS,Wilfrid(Val) T2Lt kia 17-1-16 GL &1RFC p4&192 CR Belgium140
WATTS,William John 2Lt kia 12-4-18 49MGC Inf p186 MR30
WATTS,William Kenworthy Capt kia 2-12-17 6Norf att2/6Glouc p217 MR17
WATTSON,Cyril Beaven.MC.2Lt kia 8-10-17 7RFC p14 MR20
WAUCHOPE,James Bourdillon Lt kia 10-3-15 2Mddx p148 MR22,Baurdillon
WAUD,Ernest Henry.MC.LtTCapt kia 16-8-17 22NumbF attRFC p14&63
WAUD,Harold Fenwick T2Lt kia 27-8-17 14DLI p162 CR France551
WAUD,Lionel Douglas Lt kia 8-11-14 ELancs p111 CR Belgium68
WAUD,Wilfred Ernest Lt 7-7-16 9NumbF MR21
WAUGH,Arthur John TCapt kia 17-8-16 RAMC att1NStaffs p198 CR France513
WAUGH,Edward Geoffrey T2Lt kia 4-4-16 10 att6SLancs p126 MR38
WAUGH,George Noel Capt dow 26-5-17 10/86NZ VetCps CR France769
WAUGH,Thomas Hall.MC.TCapt kia 6-6-17 22NumbF p63 CR France1182
WAVELL,Arthur John Byng.MC.Maj kia 9-2-16 1WelshR attArabRifEAfrProtForces p128 CR EAfrica50
WAWN,Frederick Middlemont Capt kia 25-5-15 7DLI p239 MR29
WAY,Frank.MC.Capt&QM ded 25-10-18 RASC p267 CR Hamps1
WAY,Frederick Henry Lt kia 11-9-15 RBerks p140 CR France349
WAY,George Currey TMaj kia 28-1-16 16Mddx p148 CR France114
WAY,Henry Stanley Capt kld 5-5-19 16TankCps p189 CR France788,6-5-19
WAY,Robert Edward Allen T2Lt dow 29-5-17 10LNLancs p137 CR France113
WAY,Roderick Norman 2Lt kia 13-1-16 28RFA p37 MR38
WAYET,Frank Merewether Lt kia 27-9-15 3 att1ScotRif p104
WAYLAND,Richard Bunster 2Lt dow 22-9-16 11ELancs p111 CR France260
WAYLEN,Arthur Francis Capt ded 19-12-19 RFA CR Surrey1
WAYMAN,Fawcitt.MC.TCapt&Adjt kia 31-7-17 20DLI p162 MR29
WAYMAN,William Ambler Lt kia 14-8-16 1/4 O&BLI p231 MR21
WAYMARK,William Ebenezer Capt ded 10-12-19 RAMC p267 CR Asia33,15-12-19
WAYTE,Samuel Wilfred.MC.2Lt dow 7-10-17 103RFA p37 CR France193,Wilfrid
WEAR,Albert Edward T2Lt kia 11-9-17 20RFC p14 CR France134
WEAR,Arthur TLtACapt kia 4-12-17 2Y&L p159 CR France711
WEARE,Albert James Bertram Capt ded 18-4-19 DLI p265
WEARE,Frederick John 2Lt dow 9-10-18 4RFus p70 CR France380
WEARING,Douglas George TCapt ded 11-11-18 SL &RAMC p201&255 CR Eire166,GL
WEARNE,Frank Bernard.VC.2Lt kia 28-6-17 3 att10Ess p133 MR19
WEARNE,Keith Morris Capt kia 21-5-17 3Ess p133 CR France311
WEARNE,Kenneth Martin 2Lt kia 20-9-17 5RWSurr p212 MR30
WEATHERBY,Thomas Capt ded 8-5-15 9WRid p116 CR Sussex138
WEATHERDON,Hugh Eric Capt ded 3-11-20 IA 2/11GurkhaRif p284 CR Iraq8

WEATHERDON,Sidney George T2Lt kia 19-9-17 11Ess D'Coy p130 CR France149
WEATHERHEAD,Andrew 2Lt kia 1-7-16 3 att1RLancs p59 MR21
WEATHERHEAD,George Ernest Capt&Adjt kia 8-5-15 2RLancs p59 CR Belgium58,9-5-15
WEATHERHEAD,Stanley Ernest William 2Lt kia 23-4-17 4Worc p110 MR20
WEATHERILL,Edward Theaker T2Lt kia 15-8-15 7RDubF B'Coy p177 MR4,16-8-15
WEATHERILL,William Brown 2Lt mbk 18-6-18 10 att1/4LNLancs p257 MR19,17-6-18
WEATHERLEY,Lawrence Edwin Martin Lt kia 19-2-18 20Lond p251 CR Palestine3
WEAVER,Augustus Henry 2Lt dow 12-4-18 6WRid attMGC p187&227 CR France185
WEAVER,Cecil Vivian Rupert 2Lt dow 9-8-18 RGA 66SB p42 France924
WEAVER,Humphrey Capt kia 7-2-16 1A 114Mahrattas p284 MR38
WEAVER,John James Capt kldacc 20-4-17 RAMC att2/4ELancs p254 CR Lancs381,later att65LowlandDiv
WEBB,Albert William.DCM.2Lt kia 24-7-16 RGA 109SB p42 CR France397
WEBB,Alfred Henderson 2Lt ded 4-5-16 3Leic p88 CR Iraq6
WEBB,Allan Bonville Hay Capt dow 23-8-15 IA 1/5GurkhaRif p284
WEBB,Arthur Henry 2Lt kia 23-6-17 4EKent p212 MR29,24-6-17
WEBB,Arthur Pelham T2Lt kia 8-4-17 5KSLI D'Coy p145 CR France581,9-4-17
WEBB,Athelstan Sylvester Kenshole Lt kia 21-3-18 7NumbF p214 CR France518
WEBB,Charles Parker.MC.2Lt kia 23-7-17 3 att11RWKent p142 CR Belgium154
WEBB,Cyril Francis Lt kia 25-9-15 2Yorks p91 MR19
WEBB,Dennis Henry TLt kia 10-11-17 2MGC p186 CR Belgium20
WEBB,Denys Stubbs T2Lt kia 21-10-16 13Ches p97 CR France535
WEBB,Duncan Vere.MC.Capt dow 16-10-18 3 att1Leic p88 CR France725
WEBB,Edward Charles Harry 2Lt kia 10-3-15 2Lincs p76 CR France525
WEBB,Edward Melvill Lt dow 1-5-15 4NStaffs attYLI p158 CR France102
WEBB,Ernest T2Lt dow 14-7-16 7Leic p88 MR21
WEBB,Ernest Charles 2Lt kia 17-2-18 8 att4Beds p87 CR France398
WEBB,Evelyn Maxwell Capt kia 23-7-16 2KRRC p152 MR21
WEBB,Frank Ralph 2Lt kia 9-9-16 1/12Lond p248 MR21
WEBB,George 2Lt kia 5-6-18 1/2SStaffs attRAF p123 CR France1235
WEBB,George Henry Duder Capt dow 29-3-18 RAMC p254 CR France62
WEBB,George Tudor T2Lt kia 21-4-16 24RFus p70 CR France559
WEBB,Gerald Vernon Tisdall Capt kia 6-8-15 2Hamps p121 MR4
WEBB,Gilbert Watson Capt ded 1-7-16 3RIrRif &RFC p4&170 CR France518
WEBB,Gordon Arthur TLt kia 20-9-17 10RWSurr p57 MR30
WEBB,Harold Oswald Capt kia 15-9-16 8Lond p247 CR France432
WEBB,Henry 2Lt kia 26-4-18 RGA 9HB p42 CR Belgium20
WEBB,Henry Carlyle Capt kia 19-9-16 5BordR p228 CR France453
WEBB,Henry Rees LtACapt dow PoW 7-5-18 4SStaffs p123 CR Belgiu140
WEBB,Henry Stanley 2Lt kia 21-3-18 4 att9ESurr B'Coy p113 CR France692
WEBB,Herbert Percy 2Lt dow 26-4-17 71RFA p37 CR France1182
WEBB,Horace Maitland Turner Lt kia 10-3-15 3Lpool p73 CR France1106
WEBB,Jack Purnell Capt dow 22-8-18 12Glouc p107 CR France84
WEBB,John Boyer Lt kia 21-4-15 4NStaffs attBeds p158 CR Belgium127
WEBB,John Clifford 2Lt kia 14-9-16 3 att1Leic p88 CR France374
WEBB,John Harold.MC.2Lt kia 9-10-18 21Manch p156 CR France341,dow
WEBB,John Timms 2Lt kia 9-5-15 6Lond p247 CR France260
WEBB,Joseph Gilbert.MC.Lt ded 9-5-18 14RFus p99&259 CR Wales368,dow 14RWFus
WEBB,Louis Victor 2Lt dow 10-1-17 IARO att1/1GurkhaRif p284 CR Iraq5
WEBB,Matthew 2Lt 22-3-18 1SAfrInf MR27
WEBB,Musgrave Maitland Lt kia 18-9-16 16Lond p250 CR France785,Capt
WEBB,Noel William Ward.MC&Bar.Capt kia 16-8-17 70RFC p14 MR20
WEBB,Oswald Brooke TCapt dow 3-7-16 11RIrRif p170 CR France44,4-7-16
WEBB,Philip Edward T2Lt kia 25-9-16 RE 59FC p49 MR21
WEBB,R.B.TMaj ded 26-7-16 25RFus p70 CR EAfrica6 &CR Tanzania1,27-7-16
WEBB,Reginald Brooke Holding 2Lt kia 9-1-17 IARO att53Sikhs p284 MR38
WEBB,Richard Howard 2Lt dow 10-10-16 A237RFA p37 CR France40
WEBB,Richard Joseph 2Lt dow PoW 1-6-18 25MGC Inf p186 CR France1753
WEBB,Samuel Cecil 2LtTCapt kia 3-10-16 6RMunstF p176 CR Greece3
WEBB,Stanley Horace 2Lt dow PoW 26-3-18 3 att7RWKent p142 CR France1707
WEBB,Thomas Frederick Capt kia 7-9-17 6Lond p246 MR29
WEBB,Thomas Henry Basil 2Lt kia 1-12-17 1WelshGds p53 CR France415
WEBB,Thomas Richard Henry T2Lt dow 31-7-17 18KRRC p152 CR Belgium5,1-8-17 14Bn
WEBB,Trevor 2Lt kia 10-5-17 GL &55RFC p14 CR France1266
WEBB-BOWEN,Hugh Ince Capt dow 23-5-15 RWFus p99 CR Gallipoli1

WEBB-WARE,Kenneth Charles 2Lt kia 21-3-18 RGA 77SB p42
WEBBER,Alan Frank Augustus 2Lt kia 24-8-18 5ELancs p226 CR France239
WEBBER,Frederick Henry.MC.2Lt dow 24-10-18 9Norf p74 CR France146
WEBBER,Frederick John T2Lt kia 30-11-17 235MGC p186 MR17
WEBBER,Harold Victor 2Lt kia 5/7-7-15 SomLI B'Coy p80 CR Belgium85
WEBBER,Henry.MID TLt dow 21-7-16 7SLancs p126 CR France188
WEBBER,Leonard Alexander T2Lt dow 9-7-16 9Dev p77 CR France40
WEBBER,Lynden TLt kia 9-8-15 6Lincs p76 CR Gallipoli5,7-8-15
WEBBER,Stanley Albert 2Lt kia 1-7-16 1SStaffs p123 CR France397
WEBBER,William Henry Lt ded 2-6-15 2/4Dev p220 CR Devon72
WEBBERLEY,Reginald Selwyn T2Lt dow 30-9-17 2/6NStaffs p158 CR Belgium16
WEBER,Harry Percy 2Lt kia 15-11-16 3 att7RLancs p59 CR France232,16-11-16
WEBER,Reginald Otho 2Lt dow 4-9-17 3 att8LNLancs p137 CR Belgium11,5-9-17
WEBER,Victor Joseph Lt kld 15-12-18 3BordR &RAF p118
WEBSDALE,Frank Capt 13-7-19 RE CR Ches182
WEBSTER,Alexander 2Lt kia 9-4-17 4GordH p242 CR France184
WEBSTER,Alfred Alexander 2Lt dow 24-8-15 3 att1GordH p167 CR France40
WEBSTER,Arthur Cecil 2Lt kia 3-5-17 4EYorks p219 MR20
WEBSTER,Aubrey Herbert Bower T2Lt kld 25-4-16 6Nhampt p138 CR France164
WEBSTER,Bruce 2Lt kia 5-9-18 RScots att 1/9Bn p55 MR19
WEBSTER,Charles Alexander 2Lt kia 9-4-17 6SfthH p241 CR France15
WEBSTER,Donald Keir 2Lt dow 3-5-17 7ScotRif att 10/11HLI p224 CR France40
WEBSTER,Douglas Gordon.MC.Lt kia 29-9-18 21MGC Inf p186 MR30
WEBSTER,Edward Lt 12-9-20 12Ches CR Asia51
WEBSTER,Edward Mackay 2Lt kia 1-8-16 2RBerks p140 CR France423
WEBSTER,Erwin Wentworth TCapt kia 9-4-17 13KRRC p152 MR20
WEBSTER,Frank Augustus.MC.2Lt kia 1-11-18 1/4Glouc p107 CR Italy4
WEBSTER,George Alan 2Lt kia 18-9-18 4 att1EYorks p219 MR16
WEBSTER,George Alexander Malcolm 2Lt kia 28-2-18 SLancs &RFC p17&126 CR France327
WEBSTER,George Thomas T2Lt dow 7-12-17 203MGC p186 CR France102
WEBSTER,George William.MID 2Lt kia 15-6-15 1RScotF D'Coy p95 CR Belgium126,16-6-15
WEBSTER,Godfrey Vassall George Augustus Lt kia 4-8-17 3GrenGds p50 MR29
WEBSTER,Harold Stanley Lt kia 7-8-17 4EYorks p219 CR France538
WEBSTER,Harold Wolstan Maj dow 12-4-18 RE 497FC p209 CR Belgium11
WEBSTER,Henry Hellyer 2Lt kia 14-4-18 1Lincs p76 MR30
WEBSTER,Hugh Maxwell T2Lt kia 5-7-16 7ELancs p111 CR France150
WEBSTER,John Alexander Croone 2Lt kia 21-4-17 1SfthH p165 CR Iraq8
WEBSTER,John Frederick 2Lt kia 24-8-18 9HLI p241 CR France1170
WEBSTER,John Philip Lt dow 24-10-18 9YLI p144 CR France332,Phillip
WEBSTER,John Ralph Ward 2Lt dow 11-8-16 5Lpool p215 CR France66
WEBSTER,John Richard Capt kia 9-9-16 1/4Lond p246 MR21
WEBSTER,John Ryrie.DSO.MC.LtCol kia 22-3-18 16N&D p135 MR27
WEBSTER,John William Capt dow 29-3-18 2Leinst p175 CR France145
WEBSTER,Joseph Frain.MID 2Lt kia 30-10-14 3BlkW att1/-GordH p129 MR29
WEBSTER,Michael Harold TLt kia 1-7-16 13 att16WYorks p83 MR21
WEBSTER,Robert Bell 2Lt kld 28-4-16 6Dors p124 CR France922
WEBSTER,Sidney Herbert 2Lt kia 30-11-17 3Lpool p73 CR France844,6Bn
WEBSTER,Thomas John 2Lt kia 8-10-16 7Mddx p235 CR France402
WEBSTER,Thomas William 2Lt kia 1-10-16 11 att 1/16Lond p248 MR21
WEBSTER,Walter Henry.DSO.2Lt kia 10-2-17 4Lond p246 CR France525
WEBSTER-JONES,Alfred Owen Webster Lt kia 13-11-16 3 att2 O&BLI p130 MR21
WEDD,Charles Clifford Lt 11-10-17 3MGC AIF MR29
WEDD,Edward Parker Wallman.MC.Capt kia 13-7-18 EssYeo attRAMC p203 CR Belgium12
WEDD,Hermann 2Lt kia 30-4-17 3/1RGA p209 CR France
WEDD,W.S.Lt kia 14-7-15 SL att3KAR p268 CR EAfrica56
WEDDELL,Herbert Lt dow 8-10-16 RFA D4HB p208 CR France177
WEDDERBURN,George Herbert Lt kia 9-8-18 HampsYeo att15Hamps p204 MR30
WEDDERBURN,Robert Hamilton Maclagan 2Lt kia 3-2-15 3ScotRif p104 CR France83,Lt
WEDDERBURN-MAXWELL,James 2Lt kia 30-9-18 3 att6KOSB p102 CR Belgium157,1-10-18
WEDDERSPOON,John Henry Butcher Lt kia 6-4-17 RFA attRFC p20&208 CR Belgium406,Jack
WEDGWOOD,Allen 2Lt kia 19-8-15 8NumbF p63 MR4
WEDGWOOD,Arthur Felix Capt kia 14-3-17 1/5NStaffs p237 CR France800
WEDGWOOD,Cecil.DSO.Maj kia 3-7-16 8NStaffs p158 CR France150
WEDGWOOD,Gilbert Colclough TLt kia 1-7-16 109MGC p186 MR21

WEDGWOOD,Percy Ashworth Lt ded 24-1-18 RAMC att 1/2MddxHuss p198 CR Palestine3
WEDGWOOD,Philip Egerton T2Lt kia 1-7-16 16RIrRif p170 CR France383
WEDGWOOD,William Armstrong 2Lt kia 9-7-16 RE attRFC p20&210 CR France1185
WEEDEN,Charles Harold 2Lt kia 25-3-18 23Lond p252 MR20
WEEDING,John Richard Baggalay.MID 2Lt kia 22-12-14 2WelshR p128 CR France260,Baggally
WEEDING,Thomas Maj kia 26-8-17 1RWSurr p57 CR Belgium24
WEEDON,Dudley Harry T2Lt dow 20-11-17 8NumbF p63 CR Lond14
WEEITCH,James John 2Lt dow 8-10-17 82RFA p37 CR Belgium20
WEEKES,Arthur Nelson Henry.MC.Capt kia 29-7-18 1/4RSuss B'Coy p228 CR France524,Hampton
WEEKES,Cyril Warner.MC.Capt kia 16-9-18 RFA p37 CR France309
WEEKES,Reginald Penkivil Olive T2Lt kia 7-5-17 GL &10RFC p14 CR France98
WEEKES,Sydney Charles Lt ded 28-11-18 IARO att2/72Punjabis p284 MR65,WEEKS
WEEKES,Walter T2Lt kia 23-4-17 Lincs p76 MR20
WEEKS,Francis Mathwin Capt kia 11-4-18 NumbF att8DLI p63 MR32
WEEKS,Henry Russell Capt dow 23-9-18 1WelshR p128 CR Greece5,18-9-18
WEEKS,Herbert Ward Meredith TLt dow 23-11-17 2SWBord p101 CR France446
WEEKS,John T2Lt drd 13-8-15 Dev attHamps p77 CR Greece14
WEEKS,Reginald Skinner 2Lt kia 9-10-16 10Mddx p236 CR France293
WEEKS,Stephen Frederick TLt kia 10-7-16 RE 130FC p49 CR France393
WEGG,Hugh Neville Capt kia 25-3-18 16 att2Mddx p148 MR27
WEGG-PROSSER,Cecil Francis T2Lt kia 3-9-16 15 att16RB p180 MR21
WEIGALL,Richard Edward Cromwell Lt kia 12-3-15 1N&D p135 MR22,11-3-15
WEIGHELL,Frank 2Lt kia 14-4-17 3 att4YLI p144 CR France616
WEIGHTS,James Herbert 2Lt kia 9-8-18 10TankCps p189 CR France1170
WEILL,Abraham T2Lt dow 9-8-16 1RB p180 CR Belgium73
WEINBURG,Philip David Lt kia 9-5-15 3BlkW A'Coy p230 CR France924,2Lt
WEINEL,Edward Eugene 2LtALt kia 7-6-17 RFA attY30TMB p37 CR Belgium127
WEINEL,George Henry 2Lt ded 28-10-18 1/8RWar p215 CR France528
WEIR,Charles Sutherland 2Lt kia 30-5-18 5 att18HLI p240 CR France60
WEIR,Charles William 2Lt kia 28-10-18 261RHFA p37 CR Palestine8
WEIR,Donald Lord.DSO.MC.Capt 21-4-21 2Leic MR43
WEIR,Genge Gordon.MC.Capt drd 9-9-18 7RScots p211 MR40
WEIR,George Lt ded 5-10-18 RFA p208 CR France1858
WEIR,Harold Llewellyn 2Lt kia 31-10-17 4NumbF p213 CR Belgium11
WEIR,Henry Keith Crichton T2Lt dow 3-5-16 10SStaffs att9N&D p123 CR Ireland124
WEIR,Henry Leabody 2Lt ded PoW 28-10-18 12RIrRif p170 CR Germany1,Harry
WEIR,Herbert James Lt dow 9-11-17 AyrYeo p203 CR Palestine1,12RScots
WEIR,John TCapt kia 1-7-16 9RInniskF p105 MR21
WEIR,Peter 2Lt dow 15-8-15 87RFA p37 CR France40
WEIR,Robert Lt kia 16-11-16 1/8RScots p211 CR France221
WEIR,Robert T2Lt kia 9-4-17 15DLI p162 CR France591 Ex 1/7A&SH
WEIR,Thomas Henderson.MC.LtAMaj kia 8-5-18 RE 526FC p209 CR France98
WEIR,William Logan TLt kia 22-10-17 23Manch p156 MR30
WEISS,Edward Stanley T2Lt kia 22-11-17 41RFC p14 CR France62
WEISS,Hubert Foreaux 2Lt dow 3-9-18 8Lond p247 CR France833,Foveaux
WEISS,Thomas Jessop T2Lt dow 27-6-16 151RFA p37 CR France699
WEITZMANN,Cecil Gothet 2Lt dow 25-9-15 4 att1SStaffs p123 CR France109,Goblet
WELBOURN,Ernest Cecil 2Lt kia 21-4-17 5Yorks p221 CR France504,WELBOURNE
WELBURN,Thomas Harold Lt ded 12-6-17 ASC p272
WELBY,Davis 2Lt ded 23-10-18 RGA p42 CR Yorks257
WELBY,Glynne Everard Earle Maj kia 27-9-14 1SWBord D'Coy p101 MR15,26-9-14
WELBY,John Arthur TCapt dow 17-3-17 11Worc p110 CR France41
WELBY,Richard William Gregory Lt kia 16-9-14 2GrenGds p50 CR France1112
WELCH,Arthur Sidney 2Lt kia 29-9-17 RGA 149SB p42 CR Belgium20,Lt
WELCH,Edward Ronald TCapt kia 16-9-16 RAMC att5DLI p198 MR21
WELCH,Eric Arthur T2Lt kia 23-4-17 GL &16RFC p14 CR France269
WELCH,George Frederick Lt planeAcc 11-2-18 IA attRFC p284 MR67,10-2-18
WELCH,Harold Echalaz.DSO.&Bar.LtCol kia 29-3-18 6KSLI p145 CR France360
WELCH,Howard Vyse TMaj ded PoW 4-10-15 9ESurr p113 CR France1724 Ex 4Bn
WELCH,Hugh(Toby) Lt kia 28-3-17 RFA attRFC p20&208 CR France1059
WELCH,James Stanley Lightfoot TLt kia 1-7-16 12YLI p144 CR France802
WELCH,John Eric Haddon 2Lt kia 25-9-15 8Lincs p76 MR19,26-9-15
WELCH,Richard Sydney 2Lt kia 24-3-18 9Ches p97 MR20

WELCH,Stafford Leslie B.2Lt ded 20-7-17 4 att1RWar p66 CR France52
WELCH,Stephen Cocks T2Lt kia 29-4-16 7CamH p168 CR France423
WELCH,Vere Edward Osbaldiston Capt kia 30-8-18 1/5Lond A'Coy p246 CR France568,Osbaldeston
WELCH,Walter George Frederick Lt kia 30-10-14 117RFA p37 CR Belgium59
WELCHMAN,Edward Theodore.DSO.Capt dow 26-10-14 1WYorks p83 CR France102
WELCHMAN,Eric Llewelyn Lt kia 24-8-14 1Lincs p76 CR Belgium202
WELCHMAN,Gerald Harington Capt ded 17-4-19 IARO att1LabCps p284 CR India97A
WELCHMAN,John Charles St.George Lt kia 10-3-15 IA 1/39GarhwalRif p284 CR France355 &CR France1887
WELCHMAN,Patrick Elliot.MC.DFC.Capt dow 28-11-18 1/2KOSB &99RAF p102 CR France1678,Eliot
WELD,Edward Joseph 2Lt dow 27-9-15 72RFA p37 CR Belgium11
WELD,Hugh Edward 2Lt kia 25-1-15 1ScotsGds att28Lond p52 MR22,28Lond att1SGds
WELD,Thomas Joseph Wilfrid.MC.Capt ded 18-11-18 1LovatScts &2/2KAR p204&268 CR Eafrica52
WELD-BLUNDELL,Robert Shirburne 2Lt ded 1-1-16 6Lpool p215&272 CR Lancs168
WELD-FORESTER,Arthur Orlando Wolstan Cecil.Hon.MVO.Maj dow 1-11-14 GrenGds p50 CR Shrop143
WELDON,Anthony Arthur.Bart.CB.DSO.BtCol ded 29-6-17 4Leinst p266 CR Eire313
WELDON,Arthur Steuart Maj kia 25-3-17 2 att7NStaffs p158 MR38,Stewart
WELDON,Geoffrey Capt dow 25-9-15 D48RFA p37 CR France40
WELDON,Henry Walter Cecil T2Lt kia 26-4-16 7RIrRif p172 CR France423,Capt 27-4-16
WELDON,William Joseph 2Lt kia 4-6-17 72/38RFA p37 CR France451
WELDRICK,Wilfred 2Lt kia 12-4-18 25MGC Inf p186 MR32,11-4-18
WELFORD,Alice Sister ded 15-1-18 QAIMNS att65BritGH p200 CR Iraq6,drd
WELFORD,Frederick T2Lt kia 9-10-17 3 att6Yorks p91 MR30
WELHAM,Harry George.MC.TLt kia 4-11-18 3 att9RSuss p120 CR France985
WELINKAR,S.K.C.Lt kia 27-6-18 SL &RAF p201
WELLACOTT,Arthur Cecil Baber 2Lt ded 16-2-19 3RInniskF p264 CR Devon267
WELLBURN,T.A.Lt 12-6-17 RASC CR Yorks98
WELLDON,James Hoste 2Lt kia 30-11-17 6EKent p58 MR17
WELLER,Charles Capt kia 16-8-17 RAMC att1/1Lond p198 CR Belgium72
WELLER,Edward Arthur Walstone.MC.2Lt dow 22-10-18 7RWar attMGC p187&214 CR France146
WELLER,George Herbert LtTCapt kia 12-7-15 7HLI p240 MR4
WELLER,William Richard HonLt&QM kia 18-7-16 10A&SH p174 CR France164
WELLERD,George Godfrey T2Lt dow 15-4-17 1RB p180 CR France102
WELLESLEY,Cyril Gerald Valercan Capt kia 14-3-15 2Lincs p76 CR France525
WELLESLEY,Edmund Ernest Charles TCapt kia 30-4-16 9Norf p74 CR Belgium92
WELLESLEY,Edward Victor Colley William.MC.Capt ded 2-10-16 RE p262 CR Eire531,Maj
WELLESLEY,Eric George 2Lt kia 21-12-15 8Yorks p91 MR32
WELLESLEY,Lord Richard Capt kia 30-10-14 1GrenGds 3Coy p50 CRBelgium112 29-10-14
WELLESLEY-MILLER,John Leslie 2Lt kia 15-9-16 1EKent p58 CR France294
WELLINGS,Charles Henry Clifford T2Lt kia 11-8-17 152LabCps p189 CR Belgium12
WELLINGS,Henry William.DCM.T2Lt dow 20-6-18 KSLI att17MGC p145&186 CR France169
WELLINGS,Thomas Fitch 2Lt dow 16-7-18 RGA 297SB attCRA Bty p209 CR France95
WELLS,Alfred Langton 2Lt kia 9-10-17 1IrGds p53 CR Belgium83
WELLS,Arthur Scott TLt kia 26-9-16 33 att8NumbF p63 MR21
WELLS,Cyril Edward Elliott Lt kia 10-3-15 2ESurr p113 CR Belgium17
WELLS,Douglas Henry.MC.2Lt kia 3-5-17 5Y&L p238 MR20
WELLS,Frank Irving Pascoe Lt kia 9-5-15 2WelshR p128 CR France631
WELLS,Fred 2Lt kia 25-4-18 2/5LancF p221 CR France106
WELLS,Frederick 2Lt ded 1-8-15 2N&D p135 CR France102
WELLS,Frederick Bennett 2Lt dow 10-10-18 23RFus p71 CR France380
WELLS,Frederick Edward TLt&ACapt ded 13-10-18 TankCps p189 CR Surrey41
WELLS,Frederick Neville Lt ded 7-11-18 RASC p194 CR France85
WELLS,Guy Francy Capt dow 15-6-15 RE p49 CR Belgium165,Franey
WELLS,Henry Frederick 2Lt kia 21-9-18 8ScotRif p225 CR France663
WELLS,Henry Maurice Watkins Lt kia 15-9-16 4RBerks attRFC p20&234 CR France382 &CR France1896
WELLS,Herman Theodore T2Lt ded 2-4-16 RASC MT p194 CR France85
WELLS,Hurlestone Vesey Capt kia 12-4-18 2RFus p71 MR32

WELLS,James Ritchie T2Lt kld 17-11-17 1BlkW attRFC p14&129 CR Scot755
WELLS,Leonard Frank.MC.2Lt kia 11-10-18 9WYorks p83 CR France611
WELLS,Leslie Howard Elliott 2Lt ded 4-5-15 3 att2LancF p94 CR B94 ?
WELLS,Louis Conrad 2Lt kia 31-3-18 att2RBerks p140 MR27
WELLS,Maurice Godfrey 2Lt kia 28-3-18 C211RFA p37 CR France745
WELLS,Nigel Grenville Lt ded 9-10-19 WelshGds p262
WELLS,Norman T2Lt dow 25-9-17 1/2 att16LancF p94 CR France1361
WELLS,Norman Albert 2Lt dow 29-12-17 1/1Hereford p252 CR Palestine3
WELLS,Norman Lancaster Lt kia 10-8-15 6LNLancs p137 MR4
WELLS,Norman Septimus LtCol ded 20-4-20 IA IMS p284 CR Mddx26,Maj
WELLS,Reginald William 2Lt dow 3-10-17 1/2 att1ESurr p113 MR30
WELLS,Ronald Graham TLt kia 4-3-16 7RSuss p120 MR19
WELLS,Thomas William Maurice 2Lt kia 1-7-16 2SWBord p101 MR21
WELLS,Walter Neave Capt kia 27-10-14 3EKent att1KRRC p58 MR29
WELLS,William 2Lt kia 13-1-16 2Leic p88 MR38
WELLS,William Leslie T2Lt kia 21-5-16 D235RFA p37 CR France924
WELLS,William Lewis.MC.&Bar.Lt dow 6-5-18 8Mddx att48RAF p20,236,258&237 CR France145,Capt
WELLS-COLE,Neville William.MID Maj dow 6-1-18 28RFA p37 CR Belgium12
WELLS-COLE,William Francis 2Lt kia 31-7-17 1Lincs p76 MR29
WELLSTED,George Wormall TCapt kia 30-6-16 11Hamps A'Coy p121 CR France223
WELLWOOD,Frederick Paton.TD.Capt ded 6-2-17 SL LNLancs p201 CR Scot387,6-3-17
WELLWOOD,Robert Kemp.MC.Lt kia 23-7-18 6SfthH p241 CR France1697,Capt
WELMAN,Noel Yvon Loftus.DSO.Capt kia 25-9-15 1Mddx p148 CR France114,dow
WELSBY,Sydney Walter Humfrey 2LtTLt kia 30-4-17 14Ches p97 MR38
WELSFORD,Geoffrey Joseph Lightbourn 2Lt kia 30-3-16 2Mddx &RFC p4&148 CR France1412,Lightbourne
WELSFORD,George Keith T2Lt kia 20-10-16 11RFC p4 MR20
WELSH,Alexander Torburn 2Lt kia 3-5-17 4RWFus p223 CR France537
WELSH,Anthony Reginald 2LtTLt dow 19-2-16 4Yorks p220 CR France102
WELSH,Cyril Clifton Capt kia 17-7-17 D256RFA p37 CR Belgium5
WELSH,Robert Milne Ballantyne LtACapt kia 23-4-17 7BordR p118 MR20
WELSH,Tom Capt kia 12-7-15 5KOSB p224 CR Gallipoli2
WELSTEAD,Harry Marion TLtCol kia 17-8-15 9LancF p94 CR Gallipoli27
WELTER,Leslie Dingman 2Lt kia 18-6-17 17KRRC p152 CR Belgium10,19-6-17
WEMYSS,Norman Douglas 2Lt kia 27-7-16 1Beds p87 MR21 CR France390
WENBORN,Harold 2Lt dow 24-3-18 47MGC p186 CR France177
WENDEN,Charles Blade 2Lt kia 31-7-17 RGA 104SB p209 CR Belgium34
WENDEN,George TLtTCapt kia 16-3-17 BordR att35RFC p14&118 CR France120
WENDER,Louis.DCM.2Lt kia 16-6-18 Manch p156 MR27
WENDOVER,Albert Edward Charles Robert.Vicount Lt dow 19-5-15 RHGds p20 CR Bucks86
WENHAM,Edward Kimber 2Lt kia 30-10-18 1/7Worc p226 CR Italy4
WENN,William Capt dow 1-4-17 1/5Norf p216 CR Egypt2
WENSLEY,Frederic Martin T2Lt kia 5-8-16 10Lincs p76 MR21
WENSLEY,George Thomas 2Lt ded 31-1-18 1SLancs p126 MR43
WENSLEY,Harold William ded 15-11-18 1Lincs p76 France658
WENTWORTH,Cyril John T2Lt dow 3-2-17 12RSuss p120 CR Belgium11
WENTWORTH,John 2Lt kia 4-7-18 179RFA p37 MR27
WENTZEL,Eric Francis LtACapt kia 23-3-18 3 att8ESurr p113 MR27
WERE,Cyril Narramore Chap4Cl ded 9-1-18 RAChDept p200 CR France193
WERNER,Charles Augustus Capt kia 9-5-15 6 att2RB p180 MR32
WERNET,William Edward ACapt kld 30-7-18 4SWBord attLightTMB p101 CR Iraq8
WERNHER,Alexander Pigott 2Lt kia 10-9-16 WelshGds p53 CR France394
WESCHE,Ernest Brocklesby Capt kia 19-10-14 SLancs attNigR p126 CR WAfrica56
WESLEY,Charles Wallace T2Lt ded 6-2-19 1SStaffs p123 CR France65,Lt
WESSELHOEFT,George Henri T2Lt kia 16-9-16 15DLI p162 CR France744
WEST,Alan Herbert Mainwaring Lt BombExplosAcc 7-1-18 IA 36Sikhs p284 CR Iraq5,dow
WEST,Archibald Stewart.MC.Maj kia 23-3-18 93RFA p37 CR France518
WEST,Arthur Eustace Lockley 2LtACapt dow 28-4-17 RGA 213SB p42 CR France1186,kia
WEST,Arthur Graeme T2LtACapt kia 3-4-17 6 O&BLI p130 CR France568
WEST,Charles Frederick Arthur 2Lt kia 4-10-17 1/2ESurr p113 MR30
WEST,Charles Henry Raymond Lt kia 3-6-15 4 att4Mddx p148 MR29
WEST,Corney.MC.Lt kia 27-5-18 5DLI p239 CR France1753
WEST,Cyril Frederick Ernest 2Lt kia 28-9-18 RSuss p120 CR Belgium115

334

WEST,Edward Lynn TCapt kia 31-7-16 1Norf p74 MR21
WEST,Francis Charles Bartholomew LtCol kia 28-9-16 243RFA p206 CR France251
WEST,George.MM.2Lt kia 22-3-18 9 att6Leic p88&259 MR27
WEST,George Arnold 2Lt dow 8-8-18 1ELancs attMGC p111&186 CR France141
WEST,George Clifford 2Lt kld 12-2-17 3 att7SStaffs p123 CR France818
WEST,George Cyril AssSurg4Cl kia 12-2-16 IMS attRFA 82Bty p284 CR Iraq1
WEST,Gerald William Lt kia 25-9-15 RSuss att2Bn p120 MR19
WEST,Harold 2Lt kia 9-5-15 1BlkW p129 MR22
WEST,Harold Douglas 2Lt dow 25-3-18 1KRRC p152 MR20
WEST,Henry Cave Capt kia 22/24-11-15 RFA att5RHA p37 MR38,22-11-15
WEST,Henry Meldrum Pelham TCapt kia 20-9-17 11NumbF p63 CR Belgium125
WEST,Herbert John.MC.Capt dow 22-8-18 4 att1Beds p87 CR France84
WEST,Herbert St.John Carr Maj dow 27-10-18 12DLI p162
WEST,James Stafford 2Lt dow 20-7-16 RGA 116SB p42 CR France23
WEST,John Preston Sackville 2Lt kia 14-6-17 D189RFA p37 CR Belgium127
WEST,Leslie Gower 2Lt kia 24-10-18 5Lond p246 CR Belgium414
WEST,Lionel Reginald Everard Capt kia 23-4-15 8Lond p247 CR France279
WEST,Mortimer Sackville T2Lt kia 11-11-17 GL &11RFC p14 CR France120,dedacc
WEST,Nevile.MC.Capt kia 16-2-17 1RBerks A'Coy p140 CR France280,17-2-17
WEST,Percy Charles Warren Lt&QM ded 29-7-15 RFC p2 CR Lond8
WEST,Percy Francis 2Lt ded 24-3-18 RFC p17 MR65
WEST,Richard Annsley.VC.DSO&Bar.MC.CaptALtCol kia 2-9-18 NIrHorse attTanks p24,189&259 CR France614,Annesley
WEST,Sidney T2Lt kia 1-4-17 11BordR p118 CR France672
WEST,Stanley James 2Lt ded 20-11-17 2RWSurr p57 CR Lond1
WEST,Sydney Albert T2Lt kia 30-8-17 7MGC p186 CR Belgium72
WEST,Theodore 2Lt kia 24-9-16 RE attRFC p20&210 CR France518
WEST,Walter Montague Lt dow 5-5-15 1Camb p245 CR Belgium102
WEST,Wilfrid Thomas 2Lt kia 25-3-18 9RInnskF p105 MR27
WEST,William T2Lt kia 7-8-15 9N&D A'Coy p135 CR Gallipoli5,9-8-15
WEST,William Anderson.MC.2Lt kia 21-6-18 3 att13RScots p55 CR France113
WEST,William James.MC.MM.2Lt&Capt kia 3-9-18 2Hamps p121 MR32
WEST-THOMPSON,Maurice T2Lt kia 23-11-17 GL &60RFC p14 CR France139
WESTACOTT,Ernest George T2Lt dow 19-5-16 16RB p180 CR France279
WESTALL,Ronald Cameron Lt kia 12-11-14 2RSuss p120 MR29
WESTAWAY,Leslie Thomas T2Lt kia 1-7-16 2RFus p71 CR France1501
WESTBROOK,Edward Worsley 2Lt dow 8-11-15 8Manch p237 CR Gallipoli6
WESTBY,Edmund Henry Herbert Capt&Adjt kia 25-5-15 1WelshR p128 MR29
WESTBY,Edwin John Lt ded 4-1-19 RFA p262 CR Lond4
WESTBY,Percival St.George Charles Capt kia 23-9-17 A296RFA p207 CR Belgium8,Perceval
WESTCOTT,Edgar.MC.Capt dow 4-11-18 9WYorks p83 CR France1084
WESTERBERG,George Herbert 2Lt kia 5-9-16 106RFA p37 CR FRance397
WESTERBY,James Thomas 2Lt dow 5-6-18 7EYorks p85 CR France40
WESTERMAN,Harry 2Lt kia 11-8-18 KRRC att21Bn p152 CR Belgium21
WESTHEAD,John SubCdr accdrd 17-8-20 IA S&TCps p284
WESTHORP,William Hast T2Lt kia 28-4-17 27NumbF p63 CR France604
WESTLAKE,Albert Neave.MC.2Lt kia 1-4-18 4NStaffs att27RAF p17&158 CR France920,Lt
WESTLAKE,Algernon Maj ded 25-5-15 RAMC p253 CR Lincs158
WESTLAKE,Geoffrey Arthur Lt kia 7/8-10-16 1Lond p245 MR21
WESTLAKE,John 2Lt ded 5-12-18 IA S&TCps p284 MR61,T.
WESTLAKE,John Howard T2Lt dow 7-5-17 GL &12RFC p14 CR France113
WESTMACOTT,Frederick Charles 2Lt kia 31-7-17 3 att1RWKent p142 MR29
WESTMACOTT,Spencer Ruscombe Lt kia 8-5-15 2 att1Leinst p175 MR29
WESTMORE,Lawrence Arthur T2Lt kia 1-7-16 1Hamps p121 CR France643
WESTMORELAND,Ernest 2Lt dow 19-2-18 80RFC p17 CR France525
WESTOBY,Frank Durrant 2Lt kia 16-9-16 1/7Mddx attMGC p187&235 CR France785
WESTOBY,Reginald Herbert 2Lt kia 4-10-17 3Lincs p76 MR30
WESTON,Charles Guy TLt kia 1-11-15 7Yorks p91 MR29 CR Belgium35
WESTON,Edmund Culpeper Col ded 7-9-15 Staff Ex Lpool p261 CR Hamps132
WESTON,George Primrose.MC.Capt kia 1-10-16 20Lond p251 MR21
WESTON,John Archibald Lt&Adjt 23-5-20 1RFus CR Hamps1
WESTON,John Cecil 2Lt dow 6-6-17 16Lond p250 CR France518
WESTON,John Douglas 2Lt kia 1-7-16 13 att1Suff p79 MR21
WESTON,John Spencer Theodore,MC LtTCapt kia 20-8-15 3RWar attRBerks p66&259 CR France1106
WESTON,Joseph Capt 17-10-15 14 att9KRRC p149 MR29 Served as CRUIKSHANKS
WESTON,Kingsley Vale 2Lt dow 10-4-18 4WYorks attMGC Inf p83&186 CR Notts84,Lt
WESTON,Maurice Sydney T2Lt kia 27-4-17 N&D att6Bn p135 MR21
WESTON,Ronald John Maj ded 27-10-18 1ARO attRE p284 MR43 &CR Pakistan50A
WESTON,Stanley Valentine.MM.T2Lt ded 18-2-19 MGC Inf p266 CR Kent83
WESTON,Wilfrid James TLt kia 22-8-15 6Y&L p159 MR4
WESTON-WEBB,Henry TLt kia 24-8-16 5 O&BLI p130 MR21
WESTPHAL,Benjamin Augustus 2Lt kia 23-4-17 18Manch p156 MR20
WESTRAY,F.E.2Lt ded 19-12-18 SL UgandaMedServ p255 CR EAfrica40,Lt
WESTRICK,Charles 2Lt kia 31-7-17 3 att1RWKent p142
WESTROPP-DAWSON,Walter Henry 2Lt 24-5-15 2Ches MR29
WESTWATER,Frederick 2Lt kia 28-4-17 3RScots p55 MR20
WESTWELL,Mary AssAdmntr ded 10-10-18 QMAAC p200 CR Ireland14,drd
WESTWOOD,Alexander Cleghorn Lt kia 16-6-15 7BlkW p231 MR22
WESTWOOD,Alfred Herbert Capt kia 21-9-18 10RWar att6Nhants p66 CR France511
WESTWOOD,James 2Lt kia 25-6-17 RGA 321SB p42 CR Belgium10
WESTWOOD,James Henry 2Lt kia 12-7-16 3SStafs att62MGC p123 MR21
WESTWOOD,Stanley Benjamin.MC.2Lt kia 15-4-18 4LNLancs p234 CR France1106
WESTWOOD,Walter Peter 2Lt kia 26-9-17 6Suff p218 MR30
WESTWOOD,Walter Raymond 2Lt dow 26-10-16 3RFA p209 CR France145
WETENHALL,William Thornton TCapt kia 17-7-16 6Leic p88 MR21
WETHERALL,Arthur Hewitt.DCM.2Lt ded 21-1-18 3 att9LancF p263 CR France40
WETHERALL,Eric Francis Cecil TLt ded 27-12-18 LabCps p266 CR France1041,2Lt 12NStaffs
WETHERALL,Francis Gyrth Johnston Lt kia 19-9-18 IA 1/72Punjabis p284 MR34
WEVELL,William Henry Lt kia 14-5-16 3Worc p110 CR France68
WEYMAN,Henry Morton Capt ded 26-8-16 RFA p207 CR Lancs33
WEYMAN,Percy Lt dow 16-10-17 7LancF p221 CR Belgium24
WEYMOUTH,John Alexander.Viscount 2Lt kia 13-2-16 2Drags p21 CR France423
WHALE,William John LtACapt dow 14-6-17 RGA 163SB p42 CR Belgium29
WHALEY,Frank T2Lt kia 31-3-17 2Yorks p91 CR France1186
WHALEY,Oswald Stanley T2Lt kia 10-8-15 10Hamps p121 MR4
WHALL,Anna Marjorie AssAdmntr ded 6-12-18 QMAAC p200 CR France85
WHALL,Edwin Lionel Haversham T2Lt kia 18/21-9-17 1KRRC p152 CR Belgium125,20-9-17 18Bn
WHALL,Walter Edward.MC.Capt kia 6-5-18 7SomLI att11RWFus p80 CR Greece5
WHALLEY,Henry Worthington Capt kia 4-6-15 4ELancs p226 MR4
WHALLEY,Julian Lawson LtACapt dow 3-12-17 3 att9Ess p133 CR France658
WHALLEY,Leonard 2Lt kia 26-3-18 N&D att15Bn p135 MR27
WHALLEY,Reginald Livesey Capt kia 16-9-18 4ELancs &RAF p226&258 CR France403
WHARRAM,Charles Etherington Lt mbk 26-3-18 52RFC p257 MR20
WHARTON,Christopher Willis 2Lt kia 26-10-17 3Lond p246 MR30
WHARTON,Frank Hammond Lt kia 25-9-15 3 att1LNLancs p137 CR France1723
WHARTON,Guy Fitzgerald Lt dow 9-5-15 2DLI att1YLI p162 CR Belgium6
WHARTON,Herbert Lt ded 5-7-17 2/4WRid p227 CR France145
WHARTON,Sidney Alfred T2Lt dow 1-7-16 8Norf attTMB p74 CR France141
WHATELEY,Richard Herschel Lt kia 25-8-16 5 att2RB p180 MR19
WHATELEY,Stephen William Capt dow 25-10-18 1RMunstF p176 CR France528
WHATELY,Percival Vivian Victor TLt kia 27-12-17 179MGC Inf p186 CR Palestine3
WHATFORD,George Lumley Capt 22-11-15 IA 66Punjabis p284 MR38
WHATFORD,Stuart Lumley.CMG.DSO&Bar.TLtCol kld 30-8-19 Yorks att8Y&L p255 CR Italy15,30-9-19
WHATLING,Harold Wilfred T2Lt kia 26-6-16 8Suff p79 MR21
WHATMOOR,Donald Gurney T2Lt kia 17-1-16 7Beds p87 CR France370
WHEADON,James Hansford 2Lt dow 11-3-17 RGA 15SB p42 CR France164
WHEAT,Harold Arthur T2Lt kia 2-12-17 2Y&L p159 MR17
WHEATCROFT,Frederick George 2Lt dow 26-11-17 5 att13ESurr B'Coy p226 CR France256
WHEATCROFT,George Hanson T2Lt kia 13-8-15 RGA 16HB p42 CR France344,11-8-15
WHEATCROFT,Ronald Duncan Lt dow 2-7-16 6N&D p233 CR France120
WHEATCROFT,William Hands T2Lt kia 7-3-17 1NStaffs p158 CR France149
WHEATE,Arthur T2Lt dow 5-4-17 1 att6ELancs p111 MR38
WHEATER,Kenneth Ronald Maclaren T2Lt kia 6-5-17 RE 4SpecBn p49 CR France560
WHEATER,Sydney Capt kia 15-9-16 24Lond p252 MR21
WHEATLEY,Annie Sister ded 1-8-19 TFNS p272 CR Yorks583

WHEATLEY,Arthur.MM.2Lt dow 8-5-18 4RLancs p213 CR France88
WHEATLEY,Arthur Nevin.MID Maj dow 5-7-16 5WRid p227 CR France40
WHEATLEY,Frank Rees T2Lt kia 11-8-16 12Ess p133 CR Belgium44
WHEATLEY,John Charles 2Lt dow 3-10-18 N&D att1/5Bn p135 MR16
WHEATLEY,Joseph Horace Lyncham 2Lt kia 15-6-17 2/4Lond p246 MR20
WHEATLEY,Lionel Frank 2Lt kia 22-11-17 154MGC p186 MR16
WHEATLEY,Ralph Ruthven T2Lt ded 16-2-19 1KRRC p265 CR Scot231
WHEATLEY,Roland 2Lt kia 24-11-16 4 att15N&D p135 CR France182
WHEATLEY,Rutland Villiers 2LtTLt kia 29-11-17 6EYorks p85 CR France184
WHEATLEY,William Clarke 2Lt kia 3-5-17 9RB p180 MR20
WHEATLY,Edward Richard 2Lt dow 10-10-17 156RFA p37 CR France139
WHEELDON,Frank Percy Capt kia 30-10-17 8Lond p247 MR30
WHEELDON,Thomas Victor 2Lt kia 12-7-17 16NumbF C'Coy p63 MR31
WHEELER,Alexander James Paterson 2Lt kld 9-5-18 GL &RAF p192 CR France102
WHEELER,Arthur Leslie Doble Lt kia 10-8-17 3RFA p208 CR Belgium7
WHEELER,Augustus Henry Maj kia 10-8-15 6RWFus p223 MR4
WHEELER,Charles Norman Capt kia 7-1-15 att2SLancs p126 MR29
WHEELER,Charles Palliser Capt kia 25-9-15 RBerks p140 CR France1106
WHEELER,George Godfrey Maj kia 13-4-15 IA 7Lancers p284
WHEELER,Harold Ernest.DCM.2Lt kia 3-9-16 1KOSB p102 CR France402
WHEELER,Harry Lloyd T2Lt dow 26-12-15 9EKent att6RWKent p58 CR France80
WHEELER,Henry Thornton Camden Capt ded 30-10-16 3Lpool CmdgGoldCoastR p73 CR WAfrica2
WHEELER,Howard Sidney 2Lt 5-2-19 3NStaffs CR War10
WHEELER,Hugh Graham 2Lt kia 28-4-17 25NumbF p63 MR20
WHEELER,Jack Douglas 2Lt kia 31-7-17 5Suff B'Coy p217 MR29
WHEELER,John Eric Capt kia 10-11-16 RGA p209 CR France294
WHEELER,John Piggott.MC.LtAMaj kia 30-10-17 D82RFA p37 CR Belgium10
WHEELER,P.F.C.d'Erf Capt 24-7-17 Dors attRFC CR Lond7
WHEELER,Russell Mervyn Lt kia 30-11-16 9 att1/7Mddx p236 CR France705
WHEELER,Wilfrid Henry 2Lt kia 26-4-18 SStaffs att4Bn p123 MR30
WHEELER,William Pierce 2Lt kia 2-7-16 1/6RWar p214 MR21
WHEELER-O'BRYEN,Myles Lt acckld 2-10-16 2/5RWar CR France1887
WHEELHOUSE,George William T2Lt ded 6-7-17 RASC p194 CR Iraq6
WHEELOCK,Charles Herbert T2Lt ded 19-3-18 RFC p17 CR Kent125,Lt
WHEELTON,William 2Lt kia 29-3-18 1 att1/7WYorks p83 CR Belgium72
WHEEN,John Capt kia 15-5-15 Lpool p73 MR22
WHELAN,George.MC.2Lt kia 16-8-17 2WYorks p83 MR30
WHELAN,Harry George,MC Lt ded PoW 11-4-18 2RMunstF p176&259 CR Germany3
WHELAN,John Percy Capt kia 11-12-14 RIrRif att2RIrReg p170 MR29
WHELAN,Joseph Lt 15-7-20 IARO attRGA 35MtnBty MR43
WHELDON-WILLIAMS,Victor TLt kldacc 6-7-16 13Mddx p149 CR France200
WHELTON,Daniel T2Lt dow 29-4-16 8RInniskF p105 CR France423
WHETSTONE,Walter Hugh Lt kia 28-3-18 3CldGds p51 MR20
WHEWAY,Frank Reginald 2Lt dow 14-11-17 RGA 183SB p42 CR Belgium173
WHICKER,Frederick Paul Lt dow PoW 12-4-18 1/22Lond p251 CR France563
WHIDBORNE,George Ferris.MC.Lt dow 24-10-15 2CldGds p51 CR France80
WHIDDETT,Horace 2Lt dow 27-8-18 3Lond p246 CR France119
WHIFFIN,Hartley Allen TLt kia 25-9-15 10Glouc p107 CR France1723
WHIKS,Charles T2Lt kia 10-10-15 9RLancs p59 MR21
WHILE,Frank Richard T2Lt kia 15-7-16 1Mddx p149 CR France432
WHILE,Charles Victor 2Lt kia 26-6-16 8RWar p215 MR19
WHILE,Ivor Austin 2Lt kia 31-8-16 4 att1NStaffs p158 MR21
WHILLIER,Leonard Alfred TLt kia 15-9-16 9Suff p79 MR21
WHILMORE-SEARLE,Bertram T2Lt ded 3-10-15 10 att4SStaffs p123
WHIMSTER,Thomas Forbes 2Lt kia 19-11-16 RE p210 CR France131,Lt
WHINCUP,Frank TLt drd 2-7-17 RAMC p198 CR France85
WHINNEY,Edward Maj kia 26-9-16 7Mddx p235 CR France215
WHINNEY,Frederick Stoddart.MC.Capt ded 17-3-19 Lincs 88InfBdeMaj p76 CR Germany1
WHINNEY,John Arthur Perrot 2Lt kia 22-6-17 OxfYeo p205 CR France212
WHINYATES,Harold Bennet 2Lt dow 14-8-17 3 att8SLancs p126 CR Belgium11,Bennett
WHIPPLE,Herbert Connell Capt dow 24-11-14 Dev p77 CR France284
WHISH,John Kenneth Tulloch Capt dow 8-9-14 1ESurr p113 CR France1445
WHISSON,William Henry 2Lt dow 6-5-17 10Mddx p236 CR France113
WHISTLER,Bertram Charles 2Lt kia 29-9-18 4NStaffs p158 CR Belgium116
WHISTLER,Ralfe Allen Fuller Capt dow 27-4-17 2HLI p164 CR France95,28-4-17
WHISTON,Philip Selwyn Lt kia 21-3-18 5N&D p232 MR19

WHITAKER,Arthur Cecil TCapt kia 1-1-16 11WYorks p83 CR France82
WHITAKER,Charles Frederick Lt kia 5-5-15 3 att2WRid p116 CR Belgium115
WHITAKER,Charles Warburton.MC.Lt dow 18-9-18 8Manch p237 CR France278
WHITAKER,Foster 2Lt dow 3-5-17 5 att2A&SH p243 CR France13
WHITAKER,Frederick TLt ded 28-10-16 RAMC p198 CR Egypt1
WHITAKER,George Capt kia 20-9-17 5Lond p246 MR29
WHITAKER,George Clifford TCapt kia 1-7-16 15WYorks p83 CR France342
WHITAKER,Harold Capt kia 30-11-14 2RB p180 CR France1158
WHITAKER,Harry Garratt.MC.Capt 15-1-20 1/5SLancs CR Lancs160
WHITAKER,Leonard T2Lt kia 16-8-17 YLI att7Bn p144 MR30
WHITAKER,Oscar Frederick TLt ded 10-11-18 5RB p180 CR Mddx83
WHITAKER,Owen.MID T2Lt kia 29-8-15 RGA 65SB p42 CR Belgium85
WHITAKER,Samuel 2Lt ded 26-2-19 10WRid p264
WHITAKER,Sydney George 2Lt kia 22-3-18 40MGC p186 MR20
WHITAKER,Thomas Saville 2Lt kld 7-11-15 1/6WRid p227 CR Belgium23,Savile
WHITAKER,Victor John Lt kia 6-4-17 3Lincs att2RFC p14&76 MR20
WHITAKER,William 2Lt kia 6-12-17 GL &23RFC p14 MR20
WHITBOURN,Walter.MC.2Lt kia 22-8-18 6 at2Beds p87 MR16
WHITBREAD,Basil 2Lt kia 22-7-16 14RWar p66 CR France432
WHITBY,Ernest Victor T2Lt kia 1-7-16 4Mddx p149 CR France267
WHITBY,Eustace Roland.MC.Lt kia 20-11-17 1RMunstF GarBn p176 MR20
WHITBY,Harry Alden TCapt kia 10-7-16 11WYorks p83 CR France832
WHITBY,James Hornby.MID Capt ded 16-3-16 19Lond p250 CR France88
WHITCHER,Charles Edwin 2Lt kia 22-4-17 4Leic p220 MR20
WHITCHURCH,G.Capt 26-5-20 RE 68SigCo CR Suff137
WHITCHURCH,Leslie Sedgwick Capt kia 31-10-14 IA 21Cav attDgnGds p284
WHITCUT,H.M. Lt kld 25-4-18 5SStaffs &RAF p229 CR Wilts115,28-4-18
WHITE,Alexander Maj dow 9-9-15 5RScots p211 CR Scot253
WHITE,Alexander Blair 2Lt kia 23-7-18 5 att8KOSB p224 CR France865
WHITE,Alfred William Lt ded 13-4-19 RASC 1034MTCoy p194 CR Italy15
WHITE,Algernon William 2Lt kia 9-8-18 15Hamps p121 MR30
WHITE,Arthur 2Lt kia 18-1-15 RE 2FC p210 CR France285
WHITE,Arthur Bryan Capt kia 16-8-17 5Lond p246 MR29
WHITE,Arthur Elimen Lt ded 22-7-17 SL IWT p201
WHITE,Arthur Gillmore Lt 15-7-17 RE IWT MR38
WHITE,Arthur Ingram 2Lt dow 23-3-18 KSLI att4th p145 CR France512
WHITE,Arthur Wilfred.MC.Capt kia 7-4-16 IA 117Mahrattas p284 MR38
WHITE,Aubrey Cecil T2Lt kia 1-7-16 8Y&L p159 CR France293
WHITE,Basil Walwyn 2Lt kia 8-4-17 Lpool att35RFC p14&73 CR France481
WHITE,Bernard Charles de Boismaison TLt kia 1-7-16 20NumbF p63 MR21
WHITE,Cecil Augustus 2Lt dow 4-10-17 3 att7SStaffs p123 CR Belgium16
WHITE,Cecil Godfrey.MC.Lt kia 21-4-18 RFA att53RAF p272 CR Belgium453
WHITE,Cecil Hayhoe.MC.T2Lt dow 24-9-17 23NumbF p63 CR France164
WHITE,Cecil William Keane.MC.LtACapt dow 29-7-17 X17RFA p37 CR France178
WHITE,Cecil Wilson Morton T2Lt kia 26-9-15 9Norf p74 MR19
WHITE,Charles Douglas 2Lt ded 10-5-16 12KRRC &RFC p4&152 CR Lond8
WHITE,Charles Kirbell 2Lt kia 1-9-18 8Leic att110TMB p88 CR France560
WHITE,Charles Ramsay.DSO.MIDx3 LtCol 31-3-21 3Yorks CR Yorks569
WHITE,Clement Wiliam.DSO.TMaj ded 31-1-19 11EYorks p255
WHITE,Clifford T2Lt kia 26-9-17 200MGC Inf p186 MR30
WHITE,Cyril Arthur T2Lt kia 28-4-17 17Mddx p149 MR20
WHITE,Cyril William 2Lt kia 4-10-17 1/5RWar p214 CR Belgium125
WHITE,Denis Atholl Pheaneas Terence T2Lt dow 23-11-17 15RWar p66 CR France40
WHITE,Dixon 2Lt kia 29-11-17 StaffsYeo p205 MR34
WHITE,Donald Edward Everard Surg1Cl 2-10-19 IMS att4BritStatHosp MR43
WHITE,Douglas Archibald 2Lt kia 23-3-18 7 att8ESurr p113 MR27
WHITE,Edward Beadon,T2Lt dow 1-7-16 11Yorks attMGC p9&186,kia CR France156
WHITE,Edward Erskine Capt kia 14-9-14 Nhampt p138 MR15
WHITE,Edwin Gordon.MC.LtACapt dow 7-5-18 8Dev p77 CR Italy11
WHITE,Edwin Thexton 2Lt kia 20-9-17 4RLancs p213 MR30
WHITE,Edwin Victor Lt kia 6-9-18 7SStaffs p123 MR16
WHITE,Eric 2Lt kia 6-5-16 RE 2/1WLancsFC p210 CR France504
WHITE,Ernest Lt kia 10-4-18 WSomYeo att55MGC p187&205 CR France279
WHITE,Ernest Norman Lt dow 24-9-17 5 att1Mddx p149 CR Belgium152,25-9-17
WHITE,Ernest William.MC.2Lt ded 20-10-18 RGA 290SB p42 CR France380
WHITE,Esmonde Ricarde Burke 2Lt kia 5-1-16 1/6NumbF p214 CR Belgium127

WHITE,Francis Capt kia 4-9-16 6Ches p222 CR France453,1Bn
WHITE,Francis Herbert.MC.Capt dow 16-4-18 12YLI p144&259 CR France180
WHITE,Francis Reginald 2Lt dow 23-1-17 RE att10RFC p14&49 CR France98
WHITE,Frederick George 2Lt kia 4-9-17 64RHFA p37 CR Belgium8
WHITE,G.C.Lt 17-10-18 1CapeCps CR Palestine8
WHITE,Geoffrey Stewart Augustus Lt kia 10-9-14 2SLancs p126 MR15
WHITE,Geoffrey Wilfred 2Lt dow 1-4-17 6 att10RB p180 CR France164,Capt
WHITE,George TCapt kia 1-7-16 1SStaffs p123 CR France397
WHITE,George Anderson 2Lt dow 30-3-18 3 att1RScotF p95 CRFrance169
WHITE,Gerald John Davis 2Lt kia 6-7-16 2RIrReg p89 MR21,5-7-16
WHITE,Gilbert Clement Whit TLt dow 6-10-15 13Ches p97CR France285
WHITE,Harold Tom 2Lt kld 27-2-17 RE attRFC p20&210
WHITE,Harold Edward TLt dow 21-4-16 3Manch p156 MR38
WHITE,Harold Norton 2Lt kia 6-9-18 57MGC Div p186 CR France309,Inf
WHITE,Henry Thompson Lt kia 8-9-16 3 att1WelshR p128 MR34
WHITE,Herbert Beresford Lt kld 13-4-17 23RFA p37 CR France98
WHITE,Herbert Robert 2Lt kia 1-7-16 3 att2Ess p133 MR21
WHITE,Herbert Thomas T2LtACapt dow 4-10-16 26NumbF att103TMB p63 CR France297
WHITE,Hill Wilson Capt mbk 12-4-18 RAMC p257 MR32,kia
WHITE,Horace Arthur Lt dow 22-11-17 7/8RIrF p172 CR France214
WHITE,H.T.2Lt 27-2-17 RFC CR Surrey157
WHITE,Hugh 2Lt kia 27-8-18 2GrenGds p50 CR France924
WHITE,Hugh Reginald 2Lt kia 27-5-18 5Mddx p149 MR18
WHITE,James Mathew TLt ded 16-3-16 RAVC TC att126RA p199 CR France1016
WHITE,James Pringle 2Lt kia 28-4/26-5-15 10Lpool p216 MR29,16-6-15
WHITE,John Lt kia 4-6-15 2Hamps p121 MR4
WHITE,John 2Lt kia 1-7-16 3 att2GordH p167 CR France331
WHITE,John Finlayson T2Lt dow 7-8-15 6Yorks p91 MR4
WHITE,John Gardner Lt kia 26-8-17 5ScotRif attRFC p20&224 CR France375
WHITE,John Peregrine Robertson Capt ded 7-10-16 RFA p207 CR Scot280
WHITE,John Robert T2Lt kia 23-4-17 7Lincs p76 MR20
WHITE,John Stanley 2Lt kia 18-9-18 2RSuss p120 CR France699
WHITE,John Stephen Grantham TLt dow 31-7-17 12RWFus p99 CR Belgium12,17Bn
WHITE,John Vernon TCapt kia 1-7-16 20Manch p156 CR France397
WHITE,Joseph Wetherall T2Lt kia 26-9-15 8EYorks p85 MR19
WHITE,L.J.H.Lt 2-5-21 2SomLI MR66
WHITE,Leonard Thomas.MC.2Lt kia 21-9-18 RGA 133SB p209 CR France687
WHITE,Leslie Charles Walter 2Lt dow 29-9-18 2RInnskF p106 CR Belgium84
WHITE,Leslie Spencer 2Lt kldacc 15-3-15 1RWKent p142 CR Belgium165,Spender
WHITE,Lewis Scott.MC.TCapt kld 29-9-17 RFC p14 CR Somerset25
WHITE,Lionel TLt kia 19-3-16 10WelshR p128 CR France279
WHITE,Lynton Woolmer Lt dow 10-9-14 1 att2DragGds p20 CR France1420,3-9-14
WHITE,Malcolm Graham Lt kia 1-7-16 6 att1RB p180 MR21
WHITE,Matthew 2Lt dow 13-4-17 5 att1RScotF p222 CR France40
WHITE,Melville Arthur T2Lt kia 23-4-17 3RFC p14 CR France366
WHITE,Nathan T2Lt kia 1-7-16 29 att21NumbF p63 MR21
WHITE,Ralph Ernest 2Lt dow 28-9-17 12ESurr p113 CR Belgium11
WHITE,Richard Finch.DSO.Maj dow 8-12-19 Ess CR EAfrica116
WHITE,Richard Henry.MC.2Lt kia 6-8-17 25Lond p252 MR29
WHITE,Ritchie David T2Lt dow 24-2-18 4RFC p17 CR France98
WHITE,Robert Christian Lt dow 18-9-18 4BordR p228 CR France906,7Bn
WHITE,Robert Edward 2Lt ded 18-3-15 4ScotRif p104 CR Scot235
WHITE,Robert Stewart 2Lt ded 4-11-18 RFA p37 CR Surrey1
WHITE,Roger Wingate Maj kia 18-5-15 364RFA p37 CR Belgium115
WHITE,Ronald Edwin 2Lt dow 5-3-15 RE NumbDiv p210 CR Belgium59
WHITE,Samuel Walton T2Lt kia 16-6-17 13NumbF p63 MR20
WHITE,Sidney Herbert T2Lt dow 9-11-17 1Wilts C'Coy p153 CR France80
WHITE,Spencer John Meadows Capt kia 15-1-17 1/4Norf attRFC p20,216&220,2Lt 4Dev CR Greece7,Lt
WHITE,Stafford Charles Lt kia 31-7-17 1/7Lpool p215 CR Belgium167
WHITE,Stewart Alexander TCapt kia 3-7-16 21NumbF p63 MR21
WHITE,Thomas T2Lt dow 8-7-16 2 att11LNLancs p137 MR21,att8Bn
WHITE,Thomas Herbert.MC.T2Lt ded 24-1-19 7ELancs &RAF p111
WHITE,Thomas James.MC.Lt kia 20-11-17 255RFA p208 CR France662
WHITE,Thomas Leslie.MC.Capt ded 10-7-21 IA S&TCps p284
WHITE,Thomas Pate 2Lt dow 17-10-17 7ScotRif p224 CR France113
WHITE,Wilfred Appleton 2Lt kia 3-10-18 KRRC att4Bn p152 CR France234
WHITE,William 2Lt kia 25-4-15 4RDubF p177 MR29

WHITE,William.MC.Lt kia 12-10-16 2Beds p87 CR France432
WHITE,William Charles 2Lt kia 24-10-18 9TankCps A'Coy p189 CR France1274,Lt 23-10-18
WHITE,William Ewart Cecil 2Lt kia 27-8-18 6Lond p247 CR France329
WHITE,William Gurney Lt dow 23-9-16 281RFA p209 CR France105
WHITE,William Hawtrey.MID Maj kia 15-2-15 1RIrReg p89 CR Belgium80,14-2-15
WHITE,William Kenneth 2Lt kia 31-7-17 4ScotRif p104 MR29
WHITE-BELL,John William Capt kia 9-9-16 5RMunstF p176 CR France294
WHITE-BOWMAN,Alwxander 2Lt 25-9-16 EYorks attMGC Inf CR France785
WHITEFOORD,Charles B.Chap4Cl dow 30-5-18 RAChDept att6Lond p200 CR France84
WHITEFOORD,Lionel Cole Lt kia 15-9-16 IrGds attMGC p53 MR21
WHITEHEAD,Alfred Gordon Lt kia 29-1-18 6WYorks attRFC p20&218
WHITEHEAD,Charles Hugh Tempest Maj kia 25-9-15 IA 56Rif Ex 10HLI p284 MR28
WHITEHEAD,Charles James T2Lt kia 4-10-17 1/2 att1ESurr p113 MR30
WHITEHEAD,Edgar Joseph William Lt ded 17-2-19 RGA 312SB attRE p42 CR France40
WHITEHEAD,Eric Alfred 2Lt kia 13-3-18 GL &24RFC p17 CR France1893
WHITEHEAD,Eric Wilfred T2Lt kld 17-2-18 RFC p17 CR Surrey15,21-2-18
WHITEHEAD,Frank Brenand Lt kia 23-4-17 5Yorks p221 MR20
WHITEHEAD,Geoffrey Nield T2Lt kia 15-10-17 RFC 11BallonCoy p14 CR Belgium20
WHITEHEAD,George Stanley 2Lt kia 2-12-17 D153RFA p37 CR France530
WHITEHEAD,George William Edendale Lt kld 17-10-18 RFA &53RAF p37 CR Belgium140
WHITEHEAD,Henry 2Lt kia 13-6-16 RFA attX4TMB p37 CR France344
WHITEHEAD,Henry Lt ded 4-3-19 RASC p267 CR Yorks469
WHITEHEAD,Henry Montagu Lt kia 14-4-15 4ESurr p113 CR Belgium167
WHITEHEAD,Hugh MacGuire.MID Lt kia 21-3-18 5 att8RSuss p228 MR27
WHITEHEAD,James Edward 2Lt kia 16-9-16 1/7Mddx p235 CR France785,15-9-16
WHITEHEAD,James Hugh Edendale 2Lt ded 13-3-19 9RWKent p265 CR Kent122
WHITEHEAD,John Holberton LtCol dow 12-1-17 IA 93BurmaInf p284 CR Iraq5
WHITEHEAD,John Robert Gobertus T2Lt kld 3-8-16 RFC p4
WHITEHEAD,John Walton Capt kia 1-12-17 246RFA p207 MR30
WHITEHEAD,Lewis Ernest TCapt ded 20-5-19 GL &65RAF p267 MR20,Ewart 20-5-18
WHITEHEAD,Mark 2Lt kia 12-8-16 1/9Lpool p216 MR21
WHITEHEAD,Percy Neil.MC.Capt kia 21-3-18 RE 174TC p49 MR20
WHITEHEAD,Reginald Maurice 2Lt kia 22-11-17 41RFC p14 CR France62
WHITEHEAD,Walter 2Lt kia 6-9-16 3 att8RDubF p177 MR21
WHITEHORN,William Joseph Lt kia 18-9-18 7SWBord p101 MR37
WHITEHORNE-COLE,Arthur George Capt kia 20-9-17 RAMC p198 CR France285
WHITEHOUSE,Alfred Ernest 2Lt kia 8-5-15 12Lond p248 MR29
WHITEHOUSE,Arthur Leslie 2Lt kia 10-9-16 RGA 15SB p42 MR20
WHITEHOUSE,Augustus George Richard.MC.Maj kia 1-8-18 1Hereford p252 CR France524,Augustin
WHITEHOUSE,Charles Thomas 2Lt dow 15-1-15 15RFA p37 CR France80
WHITEHOUSE,Cyril Duncan 2Lt kia 26-5-18 1WelshGds p53 MR20
WHITEHOUSE,Eric 2Lt dow 5-9-18 RGA 144SB p42 CR France568
WHITEHOUSE,Herbert Maj kld 23-3-18 C34RFA p206 CR France245,dedacc
WHITEHOUSE,John Walter Glendenning Lt kia 21-3-18 RE 156FC p49 CR France511
WHITEHOUSE,Percy John 2Lt kia 31-10-14 3RWKent att1Nhants p142 MR29,2-11-14
WHITEHURST,Albert Percival.MID 2Lt kia 25-3-18 1Worc p110 MR27
WHITEHURST,George J.Lt ded 23-12-19 RASC CR Canada180
WHITEHURST,Walter Harry T2Lt kia 22-4-17 NStaffs attY&L p158 MR19
WHITELAM,Lewis 2Lt kia 3-9-16 5WRid p227 MR21,WHITELAN
WHITELAW,Geoffrey Lacy T2Lt ded 14-4-18 HouseholdBn p20 CR Scot886
WHITELAW,James Weir 2Lt kia 11-4-17 6RScotF p95 MR20
WHITELAW,Robert Hilary Lockhart T2Lt dow 28-5-17 HouseholdBn p20 CR France145
WHITELAW,Thomas Capt kia 7-4-18 RAMC att2/7WYorks p254 CR France745
WHITELAW,Thomas Mitchell 2Lt dow 29-5-18 8ScotRif p225 CR Durham26
WHITELAW,William Alexander Lt ded 14-2-19 3A&SH p266 CR Scot240
WHITELEY,Benjamin Eric 2Lt kia 28-8-18 7WYorks p218 CR France268
WHITELEY,Charles Taylor Lt dow 1-7-18 2/8 att1RWar p215 CR France31
WHITELEY,Clifford 2Lt kia 18-9-17 8Y&L p159 CR Belgium96
WHITELEY,Edward Claude Capt kia 14-4-15 RE p49 CR Iraq6
WHITELEY,Hubert 2Lt dow 11-10-16 9DLI p239

WHITELEY,Laurence Lt kia 31-7-17 5BlkW attMGC Inf p187&231 CR Belgium93
WHITEMAN,George Worley 2Lt kia 31-7-17 RHFA 3/4HB p209 CR Belgium21,30-7-17
WHITEMAN,Harold Ernest 2Lt kld 23-10-16 8Hamps attRFC p20&229 CR Sussex107
WHITEMAN,John.MID Maj dow 25-4-17 4Mddx attRND CmdgHawkeBn p149 CR France95,LtCol
WHITEMAN,Ormonde Charles.MID TCapt kia 22-11-17 11RFus p71 CR Belgium13
WHITER,Bertrand Thomas 2Lt kia 27-1-17 10 att20Lond p248 MR21
WHITESIDE,Albert T2Lt kia 6-12-17 17RIrRif p170 MR17
WHITESIDE,Carrol Herbert Marston Lt&Adjt dow 1-11-16 7BordR p118 CR France105,Capt
WHITESIDE,Miles Bruce Dalzell 2Lt ded 13-6-18 1HLI &RAF p164 CR Wales31
WHITESIDE,Robert Borras Capt ded 20-4-15 RASC p194 CR France473
WHITESIDE,Robert Parkinson T2Lt kia 28-4-17 1Lpool p73 MR20
WHITESIDE,William Leslie T2Lt kia 5-7-15 RFA p37 CR Gallipoli6
WHITEWAY,Edward Victor.MC.Capt dow 28-4-18 13ESurr att122BdeHQ p113 CR France40,12Bn
WHITEWRIGHT,Alfred Rutherford 2Lt ded 11-5-16 4N&D p135 CR Glouc9
WHITFIELD,Arthur Henry Lt 14-1-21 TankCps CR Hamps8
WHITFIELD,Arthur Noel Lt kia 14-10-14 2RIrRif p170 CR France1106
WHITFIELD,Edward Hillyard Day 2Lt kia 7-8-15 6Y&L p159 MR4
WHITFIELD,Frederick Ashburnham Hooker 2Lt kia 23-4-15 att3Mddx p149 MR29
WHITFIELD,Gilbert Henry 2Lt mbk 8-8-15 IARO att14Sikhs Ferozepore p284 MR4
WHITFIELD,John T2Lt kia 2-12-17 16HLI p164 CR Belgium123
WHITFIELD,John Burrows Lt dow 20-1-16 RE 104FC p49 CR Belgium11
WHITFIELD,John Lawrence Capt dow 23-6-15 1/4LNLancs p234 CR France102
WHITFIELD,Lewis Hayes T2Lt dow 30-10-17 21RFC p14 CR Belgium16
WHITFIELD,Nigel Bernard Capt ded 7-7-18 RNDevYeo &RAF p203&257
WHITFIELD,Richard Houlbrook TLt kia 12-5-16 RE 104FC p49 CR Belgium138
WHITFORD,Myles T2Lt kia 29-4-16 7RIrRif p170 CR France423,dow 28-4-16
WHITGREAVE,Henry Egerton T2Lt kia 1-7-16 1SomLI p80 CR France1491
WHITHAM,Charles Lt kia 6-10-18 17Lond p250 MR16
WHITHAM,John Edmund 2Lt kia 20-10-16 RGA p209 CR France1327
WHITING,Arthur 2Lt kia 27-3-18 1NStaffs p158 MR27
WHITING,James Oliver Lt kia 22-9-17 60RFC p14 MR20
WHITING,Reginald Cunningham T2Lt dow 31-5-17 Lpool p73 CR Devon72,Cunnynghame
WHITING,Thomas TCapt kia 30-7-16 20Lpool p73 MR21
WHITLARK,Joseph Capt 27-4-16 EAMilLabBureau CR EAfrica44
WHITLEY,A.H.AssSurg 24-2-20 IMS MR66
WHITLEY,Alexander Fauvel Lt kia 23-7-16 RGA 49SB p209 CR France630
WHITLEY,Benjamin Heywood.MID 2Lt kia 17-7-16 3RScots p55 CR France399
WHITLEY,Charles.MC.TCapt kia 11-4-17 7KRRC p152 CR France594
WHITLEY,Harry 2Lt kia 27-3-18 1/2Yorks att2WYorks p91 CR France1472
WHITLEY,Walter Herbert.MID 2Lt kia 21-2-17 4KRRC p152 MR35
WHITLEY,William George T2Lt kia 16-8-16 13Lpool p73 CR France294
WHITLEY-BAKER,Edward.MC.Lt ded 16-12-20 RE attRCpsofS CR Dorset135
WHITLOCK,Frederick Walter 2Lt 25-9-15 6 O&BLI CR France706
WHITLOCK,Tom Oliver T2Lt kia 29-8-16 30 att22NumbF p63 CR France275,24-8-16
WHITMARSH,Alec 2Lt dow 8-9-18 8Lond p247 CR France833
WHITMARSH,Donald Lyle T2Lt kia 22-8-17 12 att2Hamps p121 CR Belgium125
WHITMORE,Harry Cyril 2Lt kld 8-8-18 3Norf att94TMB p74 CR France19,Lt dow 11-8-18
WHITMORE,Roger Searle.MC.Capt dow 20-11-17 1KSLI p145 CR France711
WHITMORE-SEARLE,B.2Lt 3-10-15 SStaffs CR Dorset151
WHITNEY,Thomas Geoffrey 2Lt ded 15-6-16 3RWar p262 CR Hamps240,Geffrey acckld
WHITROD,Roper Henry 2Lt kia 28-5-18 4Lpool p73 CR Belgium36
WHITSIT,John Reginald TLt dow 16-8-15 5RInniskF p106 MR4,WHITSITT
WHITSON,Harold White Lt kia 25-9-15 2HLI p164 MR19
WHITSON,Henry Thomas Capt dow 5-9-18 1/10Lpool p216 CR France10
WHITSON,Wilfred Robert CaptTMaj kia 30-11-17 HLI att9Suff p164 CR France439,Wilfrid
WHITTAKER,Charles Brown.MID Lt kia 22-7-16 12RScots p55 MR21,23-7-16 3 att2Bn
WHITTAKER,Herbert Leonard Charles Lt kia 21-9-18 1RWSurr p57 CR France369
WHITTAKER,James Russell 2Lt kia 29-8-16 9YLI p144 CR France402
WHITTAKER,John Chalton 2Lt kia 28-4-18 6WRid p227 MR30
WHITTAKER,Norman 2Lt kia 12-5-18 3RLancs p59 CR France88

WHITTAKER,Roger D'Arcy Capt&Adjt kia 30-6-16 13RSuss p120 MR19
WHITTAKER,William Gaylard 2Lt kia 22-10-17 3 att23NumbF p63 MR30
WHITTAKER,William Robert Lt 27-3-17 1Hereford p252 MR34
WHITTALL,George William.MC.Lt ded 30-12-19 3DragGds RoO p261 CR Surrey138
WHITTALL,Noel Charles T2Lt kia 13-9-17 7RFus att6RFC p14&71 CR Belgium11,12-9-17
WHITTALL,Roland William T2Lt dow 6-8-15 SL 52DivHQ p201 MR4
WHITTAM,Francis Joseph 2Lt kia 1-7-16 3 att1LancF p94 MR21
WHITTAM,Frederick 2Lt kia 7-8-15 GL att1/5LancF A'Coy p192 MR4
WHITTAM,Matthew John Goldsborough TLt dow 11-8-15 8WRid p116 CR Gallipoli1
WHITTARD,Harold Alfred 2Lt kia 13-8-17 22RFA p37 CR France1489 Ex HAC
WHITTEMORE,Frederick Lt kia 29-3-16 1Beds p87 MR20
WHITTEN,Francis Robert.MC.Maj dow 18-4-18 RE 458FC p209 CR Belgium38
WHITTERON,Claude 2Lt kia 25-4-18 WYorks att1/6Bn p83 MR30
WHITTET,Gilbert T2Lt kia 14-7-16 7RWSurr p57 MR21
WHITTING,Richard Harcourt Cadet 21-9-18 RMilCollCamberley CR Somerset17
WHITTINGHAM,Arthur William.MC.Lt kia 10-10-17 RFA p208 MR30
WHITTINGHAM,Clive Alan Capt kia 9-6-17 RAMC att12RFus p198 CR Belgium15
WHITTINGHAM,Leonard Buxton 2Lt dow 26-4-18 1 att3Worc p110 CR Belgium11,5Bn
WHITTINGHAM,Lewis Stuart 2Lt kia 28-2-17 7RWFus att1InniskF p223 CR France216
WHITTINGHAM,Thomas Lt kia 13-10-15 4Leic p220 MR19
WHITTINGTON,F.Capt 6-11-16 IndMilWksServ MR66
WHITTINGTON,George Edgar 2Lt kia 30-11-17 12Lpool p73 MR17
WHITTINGTON,George William Lt ded 9-6-20 IA 7Lancers p284
WHITTINGTON,William James 2Lt kia 16-5-15 3 att2RInniskF p106 MR22
WHITTINGTON-GREEN,Clifford Capt dow 27-6-15 1RBerks CR France98
WHITTINGTON-INCE,Ralph Piggott.MC.Lt dow 11-11-18 11EYorks p85 CR Belgium143
WHITTLE,Arthur Denton T2Lt kia 16-9-16 10DLI p162 MR21
WHITTLE,Cyril Herbert Spencer Lt kia 24-8-14 15Huss p22 MR15
WHITTLE,Eric Thomas 2Lt kia 23-4-17 7Manch A'Coy p237 MR20
WHITTLE,Walter Victor Patrick Charles 2Lt kia 13-4-15 1Worc p110 CR France684
WITTOCK,Frederick Walter T2Lt kia 25-9-15 6 O&BLI p130
WHITTOME,Arthur George Lt mbk 27-8-20 IA 2/123Rif p284 MR38
WHITTON,Peter Isles Capt kia 28-6-15 7ScotRif D'Coy p224 CR Gallipoli6
WHITTY,John Leo.MC.Capt kia 8-7-16 Leinst &70RFC p4&175 MR20
WHITTY,Michael Joseph LtCol ded 28-3-17 RAMC p198 CR Lancs156
WHITTY,Thomas 2Lt kia 5-10-16 RoO 8Norf p74 CR France215
WHITWAM,Harold Ernest Capt kia 9-10-17 7WRid p227 MR30
WHITWELL,Harry William Maj kia 15-8-20 IA 13Rajputs p284 CR Iraq8
WHITWELL,Patrick Henry 2Lt kld 25-4-18 1/2Yorks &4RAF p91 CR France28,kia
WHITWORTH,Arthur George Richard 2Lt dow 30-3-18 24 att19NumbF p63 CR France62
WHITWORTH,Charles Edward.MID 2Lt dow 22-8-15 6Yorks p91 MR4
WHITWORTH,Ernest Stanley TLt kia 20-12-15 10RWar p66 CR France631
WHITWORTH,Henry Capt kia 27-9-18 8Manch p237 CR France273
WHITWORTH,Henry Parker.MC.Capt dow 29-10-18 RAMC att6KOSB p198 CR Belgium20,Parks
WHITWORTH,Herbert Clifford Lt kia 26-3-18 7SomLI p80 MR27
WHITWORTH,James Frederick Capt kia 21-3-18 RFus Ex WYorks p71 MR20,2Lt 18 att1WYorks
WHITWORTH,James Melville 2Lt kia 6-6-15 9SomLI attEss p80 MR4
WHITWORTH,John Haworth.DSO.MC.MID Maj dow 31-3-18 2/6Manch p236 CR France145
WHITWORTH,Walter Haworth 2Lt dow 14-9-18 7LancF p221 CR France526
WHYATT,Albert Allen 2Lt kia 30-5-18 8Glouc p107 MR18
WHYATT,Percy.MC.TCapt kia 18-10-17 11N&D p135 CR Belgium72
WHYATT,Raymond Selwyn.MC.2Lt kia 13-10-18 10N&D p135 CR France1393
WHYBROW,Harry Thomson TCapt dow 21-3-16 MGC Motors p186 CR EAfrica13
WHUMAN,Richard David Lt&QM ded 10-3-17 5RScots p211 CR France95
WHYMAN,William Arthur 2Lt kia 16-9-16 1/7Mddx p235 CR France785
WHYMARK,William Emerson T2Lt dow 27-11-17 12Suff p79 CR France398
WHYTE,Alan Hill T2Lt kia 9-4-17 11A&SH p174 CR France924
WHYTE,Alexander Cumming TCapt ded 11-4-16 B159RFA p37 CR France254
WHYTE,Alexander Williamson.MC.Lt kia 25-10-18 6ScotRif p224 CR Belgium140,9Bn

WHYTE,Cecil Bertram 2Lt kld 3-5-18 RScots &98RAF p262 MR20
WHYTE,George Henry T2Lt kia 4-12-17 GL &49RFC p14 CR France120
WHYTE,George Herbert.MC.Lt kia 23-12-17 17Lond p250&272,18Bn CR Palestine3,2/18Bn
WHYTE,George Thomas Capt ded 9-6-19 RAMC p267 CR Eire76
WHYTE,John Lt dow 26-4-15 7A&SH p243 CR Belgium151,Capt
WHYTE,John Dudley TCapt kia 13/14-7-16 8RSuss p120 CR France630
WHYTE,John Francis Capt ded 20-10-18 RE IWT p49 CR France65
WHYTE,John Scott.MC.2Lt kia 23-10-18 7 att5ScotRif p224 CR France190,Lt
WHYTE,Mark Gilchrist 2Lt kia 19-8-18 2RFus p71 CR France28
WHYTE,Robert Lt kia 12-4-18 2RScots p55 MR32
WHYTE,Robert Barbour 2Lt kia 25-9-15 3 att1BlkW p129 CR France219
WHYTE,William Lt kia 28-9-18 4/5BlkW p231 CR France699
WHYTE,William Boyd 2Lt kia 21-9-17 9A&SH p244 MR30
WHYTEHEAD,Hugh Holton 2Lt kia 12-7-17 GL &29RFC p14 MR20
WHYTEHEAD,Hugh Richard Augustine Capt kia 12-5-15 IA 1/6GurkhaRif p284 CR Gallipoli6,Augustin 22-5-15
WIBBY,Edward John Lt 2-3-21 IA 73MalabarInf CR Glouc92
WICKETT,Thomas Pemberthy T2Lt dow 20-11-17 5RBerks p140 CR France664
WICKHAM,Anthony Theodore Clephane Lt kia 2-11-14 4 att2ConnRgrs p172 MR29 &CR Belgium453
WICKHAM,Bernard William Theodore.MC.TLt kia 14-4-17 9SStaffs C'Coy p123 CR Belgium127
WICKHAM,Charles Frederick Onslow T2Lt dow 26-6-16 15 att16NumbF p63 CR France702
WICKHAM,Cyril Henry Capt dow 15-1-15 RFus p71 CR France683
WICKHAM,Edmund Theodore Eugene di Christofero de Bourllon TCapt ded 26-6-18 4ConnRgrs att1GBnRWar p266
WICKHAM,John Dobree Durrell Capt dow 22-6-15 1Lincs p76 MR29
WICKHAM,John Seville Deacon T2Lt kia 31-7-17 7RLancs p59 MR29
WICKHAM,Lister Darell TCapt kia 3-7-16 6 att7Lincs p76 MR21
WICKHAM,Montagu Hill Clephane De Cristofero De Bouillon.MID Capt dow 9-5-15 2ConnRgrs B'Coy p172 MR29
WICKHAM,Nigel John Latham TCapt kia 19-4-16 6ConnRgrs p172 CR France178,18-4-16
WICKHAM,Thomas Strange.DSO.Lt kia 25-8-14 Manch att5NigR p156&202 CR WAfrica58,Capt
WICKHAM,William Joseph Capt kia 31-10-14 1ScotsGds p52 MR29
WICKHAM,William Thomas Donald Lt dow 10-10-18 1 att11Manch p156 CR France113
WICKS,G.H.OBE.Maj 21-8-21 GL attRE CR Wilts14
WICKS,Harry Valentine Inwood T2Lt kia 14-4-17 11ESurr att11MGC p113 MR20
WICKS,William Charles.MC.2Lt kia 16-9-17 4 att10N&D p135 CR France604
WICKSON,Edward Arthur Capt kia 16-6-17 51CanadaInf &RFC CR Belgium6
WIDCOMBE,Charles Ingleton 2Lt kia 6-4-16 3 O&BLI p130 MR38
WIDDOP,Arthur Norman Lt kia 30-9-18 4 att7EKent p212 MR16
WIDDOWS,Archibald Lt ded 6-10-18 1/2DCLI att8Ches p113 MR67,7-10-18 11DCLI
WIDDOWSON,A.D.2Lt 18-2-19 RGA CR Notts84
WIDDOWSON,Alfred John Harold Ryder 2Lt kia 25-8-14 2SLancs p126 CR France286
WIDDOWSON,Joseph James TLt dow 23-10-16 1Wilts p153 CR France59
WIDGERY,Philip Henry Lt kia 24-3-18 5 att21Mddx p149 MR20
WIDOWFIELD,George 2Lt dow 14-10-15 1Mon p244 CR France201
WIGAN,William Lewis TLt dow 23-2-16 1 att8RWKent p142 CR Belgium11
WIGFALL,William Edmund Clare.MC.Lt dow 29-8-16 3EYorks p85 CR France102
WIGFIELD,Joshua Biram Crossley Lt dow 21-9-18 RE 74DivSigs p49 CR France194
WIGG,Sydney Harold Capt kia 13-10-18 C255RFA p207 CR France241
WIGGEN,Robert Harrison.MC.T2Lt kia 17-2-17 15 att23RFus p71 MR21,Royal
WIGGETT,Allan James T2Lt dow PoW 15-3-16 13KRRC D'Coy p152 CR France214
WIGGIN,Douglas Holme 2Lt dow 23-12-14 1Glouc p107 CR France202
WIGGIN,George Robert Lt kia 23-4-16 WorcYeo p206 MR34
WIGGIN,Noel Holme TLt kia 11-1-17 RFA 36BdeAmmCol p37 MR38
WIGGINS,Alec Henry 2Lt kia 22-8-18 20Lond p251 MR16
WIGGINS,H.C.2Lt kld 1-4-18 GL &RAF p192
WIGGINS,Thomas 2Lt kia 27-6-18 17LancF att99RAF p94 CR France1667
WIGGINS,Thomas ACapt kia 27-5-18 4 att5Yorks p256 MR18
WIGGINS,William Esmy 2Lt ded 19-8-16 LeicYeo p204 CR Oxford69
WIGGINTON,Arthur T2Lt kia 30-7-16 2EYorks p85 CR France727
WIGHT,Ernest Octavius Col dow 19-12-15 RAMC p198 CR Belgium1
WIGHT,John Guthrie 2Lt kia 1-11-16 6HLI p240 MR21

WIGHT,William Stewart Balmain 2Lt kia 9-4-17 3 att2RScots p55 CR France581
WIGHT-BOYCOTT,Thomas Andrew.DSO.BrigGen ded 30-3-16 WarYeo p205 CR Staffs45
WIGHTMAN,A.B.Capt.MC.2-5-21 2/9Manch CR Lancs471
WIGHTMAN,James.DSO.MC.Maj dow 9-4-18 8ESurr p113 CR France37
WIGHTMAN,John Francis 2Lt kia 4-9-17 GL &11RFC p14 MR20
WIGHTON,George Edwin T2Lt dow 11-3-16 10 att11ELancs p111 CR France631,11-8-16
WIGHTWICK,Sydney 2Lt dow 9-9-17 2/9Lond p248 CR Belgium26
WIGLESWORTH,Godfrey 2Lt kia 8-7-16 24RFC 14Wing p4 CR France46
WIGLEY,Frederick Gwyn Mackay Capt ded 26-3-21 IA 73CarnaticInf p284
WIGLEY,Herbert Henry TLt kia 31-7-17 7RLancs p59 MR29
WIGSTON,Geoffrey Herbert Capt kia 9-9-16 1ESurr at2Suss p113 CR France432
WIILOCK,Neville Gore LtACapt dow 22-11-17 1KOSB p102
WILBERFORCE,W.R.S.2Lt kld 2-6-18 7KRRC &RAF p152 CR Hamps130
WILBRAHAM-TAYLOR,Aucher 2Lt 26-9-16 5RBerks
WILCHER,Harold 2Lt dow 5-7-16 YLI p144 CR France833
WILCHER,Leslie Reginald Victor 2Lt ded 8-5-19 113RFA p37&255 CR Germany1
WILCOCK,Henry Blamires Lt kia 13-11-16 3 att13Ess p133 CR France1890
WILCOCK,Maurice Nettleton Lt kia 18-9-18 13RFus p71 CR France245
WILCOCKS,James Lt&QM ded 20-10-17 RAMC p198 CR Hamps34
WILCOX,Frederick Alexander Cumberland TLt kia 14-7-16 6Nhampt p138 MR21
WILCOX,Frederick Herbert Cumberland Capt kia 14-1-17 4LancF p94 MR38
WILCOX,Harold Ray Capt ded 13-2-19 18LancsF p263 CR Eire534
WILCOX,John Theodore Cumberland Capt kia 12-5-15 IA 2/39GarhwalRif p284 CR France631
WILCOX,Kenneth Dunbar 2Lt kia 8-11-15 9RWSurr p57 CR Belgium82 8Bn
WILCOX,Percy Stracey 2Lt kia 23-3-18 174RFA p37 MR27
WILCOX,Percy William T2Lt kld 31-12-17 RFC p14 CR Sussex111,FltLt
WILCOX,William 2Lt kia 18-5-18 11Manch att34TMB p156 CR France223
WILD,Arthur 2Lt kia 18-9-16 14DLI p162 CR France374
WILD,Basil Warren.MC.Lt kia 1-10-18 9TankCps p189 CR France375
WILD,Henry.MC.Lt kia 21-8-18 14NumbF att1Lincs p63 CR France514
WILD,Jack Douglas Lt ded 21-9-19 EKent att1/4Bn p262 MR67
WILD,Lionel Tudor Capt kia 30-11-17 7SomLI B'Coy p80 MR17
WILDBLOOD,William Arthur TLt kia 16-6-17 RASC 24DivTrain 195Coy p194 CR Belgium15
WILDE,Arthur William 2Lt kia 21-1-16 1Hamps p121 MR21
WILDE,Edwin Joseph Lt kia 1-9-18 3Leic att110TMB p88 CR France307
WILDE,Harold.MM.Lt 3-9-18 11TankCps MR16
WILDE,James Greaves Spencer 2Lt dow 1-11-18 5WYorks p218 CR France1256
WILDER,Arthur James 2Lt dow 23-3-18 32MGC p186 CR Belgium16
WILDER,Frank 2Lt kia 31-3-16 Q'RHA p37 CR France1182
WILDER,Reginald Connor Philip 2Lt kia 18-11-14 3 att2Suff p79 MR29,dow
WILDERS-LEWIS,Henry Charles T2LtACapt kia 31-7-17 10RWSurr A'Coy p57 CR Belgium115,WILLDERS Ex 19RFus
WILDGOOSE,Ernest Henry 2Lt kia 22-3-18 RE 104FC p49 MR27
WILDIG,George.DCM.Lt dow 6-11-18 1KSLI p145&258 CR Wales402
WILDING,Godfrey James 2Lt kia 20-12-16 3RLancs p59 CR France630
WILDING,Horace Holden 2Lt kia 13-9-18 12 att13KRRC p152 CR France245
WILDING,John 2Lt dow 7-12-15 4ELancs p226 CR Gallipoli6
WILDING-JONES,Hugh Wynn Lt dow 22-9-18 3 att11RWFus p99 CR Greece9
WILDMAN,Arthur Henry Lt kia 14-9-15 IA 130Baluchis p284
WILDMAN-LUSHINGTON,Percy John 2Lt kia 3-5-17 3 att6KOSB p102 MR20
WILDON,Edward Harold 2Lt kia 27-4-17 232RFA p209 CR France581,Lt
WILDSMITH,Leonard Charles 2Lt kia 2-3-15 12Lond p248 CR Belgium58
WILDSMITH,Raymond Charles 2Lt kia 7-6-17 25Lond p252 MR29
WILEMAN,Gerald Watkins Brett 2LtACapt kia 8-9-16 2SWBord p101 CR France151
WILES,H Lt 7-8-20 GL RE attArmySigServ CR Egypt2
WILES,John Davenport 2Lt kia 4-10-16 1Suff p79 CR Greece3
WILEY,Donald William 2Lt kia 12-10-18 SussYeo p205 CR France341,Lt
WILEY,Evelyn Otway Scarlett Lt ded 7-11-18 12 att2DLI p162 CR Italy9
WILEY,William.MIDx2 Maj ded 12-2-17 RAMC att42FA p198 CR Mddx48,12FA
WILFORD,Arthur Lucius.DSO.Maj dow 1-7-17 IA 5LtInf p284 CR EAfrica8 &CR Tanzania1,LtCol
WILFORD,Lionel Russell Lt ded 8-11-18 9SStaffs p123 CR France1571
WILFORD,Robert 2Lt kia 23-11-17 5 att13Yorks p221 MR17
WILFORD,William Frederick Shirley.MM.2Lt dow 25-10-18 5Beds p219 CR France441,2Bn

339

WILGERS-LEWIS,Henry Charles T2LtACapt kia 31-7-17 10RWSurr p57
WILKES,Albert Victor 2Lt kia 24-5-18 7N&D p233 MR19
WILKES,Clifford TLtACapt kia 28-4-17 GL 2SStaffs att6TMB p192 MR20
WILKES,George Lionel 2Lt kia 20-4-18 7Lond p247 CR France880
WILKES,Henry James Trevor 2Lt kia 28-2-18 GL &16RFC p17 CR France95
WILKES,James Alwyn 2Lt dow 24-3-18 6MGC Cav p186 MR20 Alwyne
WILKES,Norman Bayley 2Lt kia 29-4-18 1/5SStaffs p229 CR France572
WILKES,Sidney Archer 2Lt kia 24-8-18 4BlkW p230 CR France184
WILKIE,Alexander Buchan 2Lt dow 30-11-17 1RIrRif p170 CR Belgium84
WILKIE,Charles Joseph TLtCol kia 18-10-16 17WelshR p128 CR France149,19-10-16
WILKIE,David.MID Maj kia 24-4-17 5BlkW attRN Div p230 MR20
WILKIE,George Spence Mclean 2Lt dow 4-8-15 5BlkW p231 CR France345,Lt
WILKIE,John Hunter 2Lt dow 9-4-15 1Leinst p175 CR Belgium58
WILKIE,John Stewart TCapt kia 14-4-17 16HLI p164 CR France672,16-4-17
WILKIN,William White 2Lt kia 26-10-17 1/5NumbF p63 MR30
WILKINS,A.R.Lt 10-2-21 RFA CR NZ320
WILKINS,Alfred Henry 2Lt kia 1-7-16 1/7N&D p233 MR21
WILKINS,Archie Raymond Lt kia 8-3-16 3 att1Manch p156 MR38
WILKINS,Bernard Ivan T2Lt dow 6-1-16 9Yorks p91 CR France254
WILKINS,Frank Trevor T2Lt dow 3-7-16 15NumbF att1BordR p63 CR France169
WILKINS,Geoffrey T2Lt dow 4-10-15 2NumbF p63 CR France98
WILKINS,Herbert Jocelyn Ussher Capt kia 10-8-15 1 att6SLancs p126 MR4
WILKINS,John Christopher Martin Lt kia 24-3-18 10DCLI p115 MR20
WILKINS,Laurence Arnold Capt kia 25-8-18 4Y&L p238 CR France614
WILKINS,Mervyn Sydney Lt kia 16-6-18 1/6Glouc p225 CR Italy3
WILKINS,Vernon Spencer Lt ded 11-11-18 4 O&BLI p231 CR France52
WILKINSON,Ambrose Joseph T2Lt kia 26-9-16 6 att12Mddx p149 MR21
WILKINSON,Arthur Benjamin Lt dow 14-11-16 5RSuss p228 CR France515
WILKINSON,Arthur Wilfrid Capt dow 18-4-18 3WYorks p83 CR Belgium8,1Bn
WILKINSON,Arthur William 2Lt kia 12-7-17 5 att13Yorks p221 CR France439
WILKINSON,Bernard.MID 2Lt dow 6-6-17 1/6NStaffs A'Coy p238 CR France149,Lt
WILKINSON,Bernard Jocelyn 2Lt kia 8-7-16 3 att2Yorks p91 MR21
WILKINSON,Bernard Kedington Rodwell TCapt ded 24-1-18 7NStaffs p265 CR Surrey1
WILKINSON,Charles Bliss 2Lt kia 28-3-18 RFA att8RFC p17&37 CR France167
WILKINSON,Charles Harold.MC.2Lt ded 13-10-18 42RHFA p37
WILKINSON,Charles Leslie Lt kia 21-3-18 6 att2/5N&D D'Coy p233 MR20
WILKINSON,Charles Leyburn.DSO.Maj dow 7-4-18 B250/80RFA p206 CR France37
WILKINSON,Clarence Loftus Mason TLtACapt dow 6-11-16 C165RFA p37 CR France74
WILKINSON,Clement Arthur Maj kia 2-5-15 2KSLI p145 MR29 CR Belgium453,12-5-15
WILKINSON,David Stanley TLt ded 26-8-17 GL &56RFC p14 CR Belgium393
WILKINSON,Edmund.DCM.HonLt&QM kia 31-10-14 1LNLancs p137 CR Belgium57
WILKINSON,Edward Wilson T2Lt kia 7-7-16 11 att9WRid p116 MR21
WILKINSON,Eric Fitzwater.MC.MIDx2 Capt kia 9-10-17 8WYorks A'Coy p219 MR30
WILKINSON,Eric Russell.MC.TLt dow 7-10-17 GL &47RFC p14 CR Greece1
WILKINSON,Ernest Alexander 2Lt kia 25-9-15 2Leic p88 MR19
WILKINSON,Eyre Spencer Lt kia 12-1-16 1Lond attRFC p20&245 CR France682,Spenser
WILKINSON,Frank 2Lt kia 27-7-16 3Dors att2/5Glouc p124 CR France1157
WILKINSON,Frank 2Lt dow 13-9-18 2/4YLI p144 CR France1184
WILKINSON,Frank Capt ded 13-11-18 RHFA p272 CR Durham28,3RGA 276SB
WILKINSON,Frederick 2Lt dow 19-6-20 1GarBnYLI Ex 3Huss CR C'land&W'land82
WILKINSON,Frederick James T2Lt kia 9/12-4-17 8RLancs p59 MR20,11-4-17
WILKINSON,Frederick Richardson Lt ded 8-1-20 IA 1/23SikhPnrs p284 CR Asia51
WILKINSON,Geoffrey Ellison T2Lt kia 30-7-16 20Lpool p73 MR21
WILKINSON,Geoffrey Miles 2Lt kia 10-10-17 DCLI &56RFC p14&115 CR France705
WILKINSON,George 2Lt kia 9-4-18 5DLI p239 MR32
WILKINSON,Gordon Frederick Noble T2Lt kia 1-7-16 10YLI p144 MR21
WILKINSON,Harold Reid TLt dow 10-9-17 RFC p14 CR Canada1694
WILKINSON,Horace Capt dow 31-10-18 1/12LNLancs p234 CR France1033
WILKINSON,Hugh Wilmot T2Lt kia 18-7-16 12 att11Ess p133 CR Belgium44
WILKINSON,James Fisher.MC.Maj dow 29-10-18 54/39 RFA p37 CR France1270,Fischer kia

WILKINSON,James Rendell 2Lt ded 20-5-16 PoW 3LancF p94 CR Germany4,Lt
WILKINSON,John 2Lt kia 19-9-18 4 att12A&SH p174 CR Greece5
WILKINSON,John Bright TLt dow 23-6-16 RE 225FC p49 CR France80
WILKINSON,John George T2Lt dow 25-10-17 15DLI p162 CR Belgium11
WILKINSON,John Graham Lt kia 20-7-18 1/4Hamps attDunsterforce p228 MR61
WILKINSON,John Henry Warburton Capt dow 5-5-17 5SStaffs p229 CR France134
WILKINSON,John Laurence T2Lt kia 30-6-16 RE 173TC p49 MR19
WILKINSON,John Rothes Marlow Lt kia 10-9-14 4Mddx p149 CR Belgium242,23-8-14
WILKINSON,John Yeardley 2Lt dow 23-12-17 1/8Manch p237 CR France80,kld
WILKINSON,Marcus Leonard T2Lt dow 8-7-17 10NumbF p63 CR Belgium11
WILKINSON,Maurice Hewson.MC.TLtAMaj kia 31-7-17 RE 177TC p49 CR Belgium5
WILKINSON,Norman Capt kia 21-3-18 9Manch p237 MR27
WILKINSON,Norman Cecil 2Lt dow 24-8-17 RGA 332SB p42 CR Belgium16
WILKINSON,Osborn Cecil Capt dow 5-2-15 5EYorks p85 CR France200
WILKINSON,Percy Lt kia 4-12-17 6LancF att2/7RWar p221 MR17
WILKINSON,Robert Bruce T2Lt dow 12-12-17 LNLancs att1/4Bn p137 CR France446
WILKINSON,Roger Leslie Stuart 2Lt dow 21-11-16 4Beds p87 CR France40
WILKINSON,Robert John LtACapt ded 2-7-18 RIrF p172
WILKINSON,Samuel William 2Lt dow 9-4-18 RGA 237SB p42 CR France201,Lt
WILKINSON,Sidney John.DSO.TLtCol kia 7-7-16 10SWBord p101 MR21
WILKINSON.Thomas Hill Lt 2-2-21 3Lpool CR Lancs149
WILKINSON,Thomas Orde Lawder.VC.TLt kia 5-7-16 7LNLancs p137 MR21
WILKINSON,Thomas William Musgrave Lt kia 20-7-18 8WYorks p219 CR France622,Capt
WILKINSON,Vaudelene Auguste Sydney 2Lt ded 7-6-18 6 att19Mddx p149 CR France1364,Vandeleur
WILKINSON,Walter Lightowler 2Lt kia 9-4-17 1/8A&SH p243 CR France728
WILKINSON,William 2Lt ded 24-2-19 RE p210 CR Germany1
WILKINSON,William Alfred 2Lt kia 2-12-17 256RFA p209 CR France711
WILKINSON,William Andrew 2Lt kia 21-3-18 4InnisF p106 CR France1495
WILKINSON,William Charlton Capt kia 9-4-18 2/5LancF p221 CR France260
WILKINSON,William Donald 2Lt kld 14-11-16 5 att13Ess p232 MR21
WILKINSON,William Jefferson 2Lt kia 25-9-15 Leic p88 MR19
WILKINSON,William Oscar Capt kia 5-8-17 7Ches p223 MR29
WILKINSON,William Thomas TCapt kia 5-7-16 9Yorks p91 CR France515
WILKINSON,W.S.2Lt ded 6-9-15 4WYorks p83 CR Yorks110
WILKS,Harold T2Lt kia 12-10-16 17Manch p156 MR21
WILKS,Harold Douglas Lt ded 18-2-19 4 O&BLI p272 CR Hereford/W58
WILKS,Percy Walter 2Lt drd 10-10-18 RASC p194 CRIreland14
WILKS,Richard Harold 2Lt kia 30-11-17 2/5NStaffs p238 CR France1498
WILKS,Sydney Lt kia 7-10-16 6RWKent p142 MR21
WILKS,Walter Charles.MC.Rev kia 4-10-17 RAChDept att7Staffs SenChapNCofE p200 CR Belgium23
WILL,Alfred William LtAMaj kia 25-5-18 SL attSPersiaRif p201 CR Asia82
WILL,George Kennedy Lt dow PoW 11-9-16 8WYorks p219 CR France245
WILL,John George TLt kia 25-3-17 GL &29RFC p15
WILLANS,Guy Russell 2Lt dow 29-3-18 3 att2LancF p94 CR France40
WILLANS,Robert St.John Lt kia 9-11-14 NumbF p63 MR29
WILLANS,William Alan Jenne ACapt kia 24-3-18 18KRRC p152 MR20,Jeune
WILLARD,Albert Ellis Lt kia 4-7-17 7RSuss D'Coy p120
WILLARD,Alfred George T2Lt dow 7-8-17 9ESurr p113 see MILLARD
WILLARD,Kenneth Hugh 2Lt ded PoW 12-10-17 Y&L att45RFC p159 CR Belgium140
WILLATS,Alton Henry TCapt kia 7-9-17 2/5Y&L p159 CR France563
WILLATS,Harry Ashley 2Lt ded 12-2-17 RFA p37&262 CR Lond10,Lt
WILLATS,Horace Lennan Capt ded 17-12-16 7EYorks p85 CR Lond14
WILLARD,Kenneth Hugh 2Lt ded PoW 12-10-17 Y&L &RFC p15
WILLBOURN,Horace Haynes 2Lt kia 8-5-18 8 att2WRid p116 CR France411
WILLBY,Frank Richard Bagg Lt kld 18-3-19 GL Staff Ex YLI p192 CR Egypt9
WILLCOCK,Frederick Norman T2Lt kia 10-7-16 8SStaffs p123 MR21
WILLCOCKS,Harold Francis CaptAMaj ded 7-5-19 RFA p262 CR Lond28
WILLCOX,Alan George T2Lt kld 14-2-18 GL &RFC p17 CR Egypt15
WILLCOX,Hugh Patterson 2Lt kia 30-11-17 7ESurr p113 MR17
WILLES,Patrick Dalrymple Lt ded 29-9-18 3RLancs &RAF p59
WILLES,William Frances George Capt ded 19-7-16 1Dors Cmdg11Div ACycCps p124 CR France46
WILLETT,John Arnold 2Lt kia 2-7-15 9SomLI att2RFus p80 MR4

WILLETT,Joseph Cyril 2LtTLt kia 15-5-17 19LancF att152MGC p94&186 CR France1194
WILLETT,Nelson Herbert 2Lt kia 11-4-18 2RFus p71 MR32
WILLETT,Richard 2Lt kia 31-7-17 6LancF p221 MR29
WILLEY,Chester Matthew 2Lt ded 9-7-16 RGA CR Lond14
WILLEY,Rupert Harold Duncan Capt kia 14-7-19 SL attRE IWT p201 MR38
WILLEY,Henry Lowes TLt kia 22-10-17 23Manch p156 MR30
WILLEY,John Maj kia 3-4-18 A312RFA p207 CR France745
WILLEY,R.2Lt kld 20-5-18 GL &RAF p192
WILLEY,Thomas Arthur Raymond Robert Ellicott T2Lt kia 1-7-16 15WYorks p83 MR21
WILLIAM,John Rhonwy Capt dow PoW 13-8-16 10Lpool p216
WILLIAM-POWLETT,Oliver Richard Ferdinand 2Lt 30-4-21 7Huss MR65
WILLIAMS,Albert Stanley Gabriel TLt kia 28-10-17 RE 171TC p49 CR Belgium3
WILLIAMS,Alfred Richard T2Lt kia 16-8-17 49MGC Inf p186 MR30
WILLIAMS,Almericus John Falkiner de Courcy 2Lt dow 25-10-14 WIndiaR p192 CR France80,Lt 22-10-14 MddxR
WILLIAMS,Arthur Blount Cuthbert,CB BrigGen 11-7-18 IA MR67
WILLIAMS,Arthur Courtenay T2Lt kld 18-9-17 44RFC p15 CR Canada1694
WILLIAMS,Arthur Ivor Meakin.MID Capt dow 9-10-18 13RWFus p99 CR France906,Ifor 15 att13Bn
WILLIAMS,Arthur Jones T2Lt kia 3-11-17 1/4WelshR p128 CR Palestine1
WILLIAMS,Arthur Llewellyn 2Lt kia 26-3-17 1/6RWFus p223 CR Palestine8
WILLIAMS,Arthur Montague Lt kia 15-6-17 7N&D p233 CR Belgium17
WILLIAMS,Arthur Owen T2Lt kia 16/19-8-16 10RWFus p99 MR21
WILLIAMS,Arthur Trevor T2Lt dow 4-9-17 15RWFus att25RFC p15&99 CR France88
WILLIAMS,Aubrey 2Lt kia 25-4-18 WYorks att1/6Bn p83 MR30
WILLIAMS,Bernard Hallett 2Lt kia 31-7-17 5LNLancs p234 MR29
WILLIAMS,Bleddyn Capt kia 22-1-16 17RWFus p99 MR19
WILLIAMS,Brinley Jenkyn T2Lt kia 20-5-16 19NumbF p63 CR France1106
WILLIAMS,Burton Robert.MID.Bart.Lt kia 3-10-17 3 att1Dev p77 MR30,3/4-10-17
WILLIAMS,Cecil Arthur 2Lt kia 21-3-18 5 att9Norf p217 MR20
WILLIAMS,Charles Aubrey T2Lt kia 3-4-16 8RLancs p59 MR29
WILLIAMS,Charles Beasley TCapt kia 28-8-15 2RIrRif A'Coy p170 MR29A
WILLIAMS,Charles Beresford 2Lt kia 1-9-18 7Lond p247 CR France216
WILLIAMS,Charles Ellicombe.MID LtTCapt dow 27-5-17 7SWBord p101 CR Greece6
WILLIAMS,Charles James TLt dow 19-12-15 8Beds p87 CR Belgium11
WILLIAMS,Charles Montague T2Lt dow 29-7-16 25 att16Manch p156 CR France66
WILLIAMS,Charles Oswald Nicholson TMaj kia 2-12-15 8RLancs p59 CR Belgium15
WILLIAMS,Christopher Manners Capt&Adjt kia 24-3-18 HQ 66RGA p42 CR France1893
WILLIAMS,Claude Cuthbert Lt ded 24-6-21 IARO 2/2GurkhaRif p284 MR65
WILLIAMS,Colin Ernest T2Lt kia 17-10- 17 RASC p194 CR EAfrica38 &CR Tanzania1
WILLIAMS,Collingsby Philip 2Lt kia 26-8-17 GL &RFC p15 MR20,Phillip
WILLIAMS,Cyril Lt kia 30-7-16 HLI &60RFC p4&164 MR20
WILLIAMS,Daniel John 2Lt kia 5-10-17 13MGC Inf p186 MR30
WILLIAMS,Daniel Llewellyn 2Lt kia 15-10-18 1WelshR att1/1Hereford p128 CR Belgium157
WILLIAMS,David Aubrey T2Lt kia 25-7-16 1SWBord p101 MR21
WILLIAMS,David Jenkins 2Lt dow 20-9-17 1Mon att6KSLI p244 CR Belgium83
WILLIAMS,David Marmaduke Lt kia 25-9-15 2SStaffs p123 CR France924
WILLIAMS,David Ransome Vaughan T2Lt ded 20-11-18 1Hamps p121 CR Yorks244,21-11-18
WILLIAMS,Donald Mattieu T2Lt kia 9-4-16 12 att9RWar p66 MR38
WILLIAMS,Douglas T2Lt dow 10-7-16 11 att9YLI p144 CR France145
WILLIAMS,Edgar 2Lt kld 25-1-18 5Y&L p238 CR France184
WILLIAMS,Edward Albert 2Lt ded 31-12-18 GL EgyptLabCps &RAF p189 CR Egypt8
WILLIAMS,Edward Emanuel Montague 2Lt kia 10-12-17 RGA p42
WILLIAMS,Edward Ernest.DSO.TMaj kia 19-8-15 8NumbF p63 CR Gallipoli5
WILLIAMS,Edward Gordon Lt ded 12-8-15 2GrenGds SR p50 CR France495,kldacc
WILLIAMS,Edward Herbert T2Lt kia 31-8-16 2SWBord p101 CR Belgium73
WILLIAMS,Edward Stanley 2Lt kia 3-6-17 3 att8LNLancs p137 CR Belgium43
WILLIAMS,Edward Styant Maj kia 8-5-15 1Mon p244 MR29
WILLIAMS,Edwin Gordon 2Lt dow 13-5-17 10RWFus p99&258 CR France40
WILLIAMS,Einon Lt ded 28-10-18 RE p272
WILLIAMS,Eric Lt kia 27-3-18 18 att2WYorks p83 MR27

WILLIAMS,Ernest Joseph Lt kia 15-10-18 5 att2RIrF p170 CR Belgium157
WILLIAMS,Ernest Thurston Capt kia 3-5-17 6RWKent p142 MR20
WILLIAMS,Evan T2Lt kia 10-4-17 10RWFus p99 CR France531,11-4-17
WILLIAMS,Fawcett Thomas Capt ded 23-2-19 17WelshR attSWBord p264 CR Wales168
WILLIAMS,Felix George 2Lt kia 21-3-18 20Lond p251 MR27
WILLIAMS,Felix Roland T2Lt kia 10-4-17 7KRRC p152 CR France594
WILLIAMS,Francis Christopher Dallas 2Lt kia 19-7-16 3ESurr att2/4RBerks p113 CR France1887,Lt
WILLIAMS,Francis Slaney Lt kia 20-9-17 8N&D p233 MR30
WILLIAMS,Frank Emlyn.MC.Capt kia 7-4-18 1/5WelshR &57RAF p230&258 CR Egypt8
WILLIAMS,Frank Leonard.MC.LtACapt dow 30-5-18 8BordR att25MGC p118,186&259 CR France1693
WILLIAMS,Frederick Lt kia 24-6-18 7RWFus &62RAF p223&258 CR France924
WILLIAMS,Frederick Thesiger TLtCol dow 12-7-16 2Nhampt p138 CR France145
WILLIAMS,G.TLt dow 7-8-17 SL att3/2KAR p202 CR EAfrica10 &CR Tanzania1
WILLIAMS,G.2Lt 22-5-18 4SWBord CR Wales178
WILLIAMS,G.Capt 1-9-20 7WelchR CR Yorks222
WILLIAMS,G.J.2Lt ded 27-4-17 5Y&L p238
WILLIAMS,George Augustus Capt ded 6-2-19 Res p272 CR Lond8
WILLIAMS,George Ernest T2Lt kia 20-11-17 O&BLI att6Bn p130 MR17
WILLIAMS,George Gabriel Lt ded 21-2-19 RE AntiGasSch Etaples p49 CR France40,24-2-19
WILLIAMS,George Henry Spence de Meaker TCapt kia 13-5-16 1/8LancF p94 CR France631
WILLIAMS,George Jackson 2Lt ded 27-4-15 5Y&L p272 CR Wales659,Lt
WILLIAMS,George Stanley Lt kia 20-10-18 WelshR att14Bn p128 CR France230
WILLIAMS,George Stewart Louis Stanislaus Stevens 2Lt kia 8-9-18 6 att25RWFus p223 CR France365,Lt
WILLIAMS,George Trevor TLt ded 19-4-18 RFA 38Bty 9Bde p37 MR43,Capt kldacc &CR Pakistan50A
WILLIAMS,Gerald Leopold.MC.2Lt kia 15-10-18 12RInniskF p106 CR Belgium156
WILLIAMS,Gordon Lt kia 30-10-17 1/28Lond F'Coy p252 MR30
WILLIAMS,Gordon Capt ded 15-11-18 8WelshR p128 MR38
WILLIAMS,Gordon Percy 2Lt kia 16-4-18 1Lpool D'Coy &IntelStaff GHQ p73 CR France924
WILLIAMS,Gwilym T2Lt dow 21-5-16 12 att17RWFus p99 CR France345
WILLIAMS,Guy Grenfell T2Lt kia 6-6-16 9 att7DCLI p115 CR Belgium6
WILLIAMS,H.D.Lt 20-12-20 RE CR Kent95
WILLIAMS,H.I.2Lt kia 18-10-18 4KRRC p152
WILLIAMS,H.W.K.2Lt 11-7-17 RFC CR Gloucl9
WILLIAMS,Harold LtTCapt kia 25-4-17 11Worc p110 MR37
WILLIAMS,Harold Edward 2Lt kia 7/8-10-16 1Lond p245 MR21
WILLIAMS,Harold Garnett 2Lt kia 27-9-18 8RLancs p59 CR France357
WILLIAMS,Harold Justus 2Lt 9-7-16 RFA attGdsTMB CR Belgium73
WILLIAMS,Harold Osborne 2Lt kia 21-1-17 13Mddx p149 MR19
WILLIAMS,Harold Sutton.MID Maj ded 21-3-15 1Dors p124 CR France102
WILLIAMS,Harry Benjamin.MC.2Lt kia 3-5-17 5 att13Lpool p215 MR20
WILLIAMS,Henry Aitken Capt ded 2-11-18 6 att4Mddx attMinofNatServ p265 CR Lond8,Harry
WILLIAMS,Henry Evan Vincent Lt dow 22-5-17 2Lond p245 CR France512
WILLIAMS,Henry Frederick Maj ded 2-5-16 9RMunstF p176 CR Lond28,1-5-16
WILLIAMS,Henry Vincent 2Lt kia 26-5-16 3Worc p110 CR France68
WILLIAMS,Herbert Henry.MID TCapt kia 20-9-17 6Wilts p153 CR Belgium17
WILLIAMS,Herbert Mainwaring.DSO.Maj dow 23-12-17 RAVC 63Div p199&258 CR France398
WILLIAMS,Hilary Evelyn Eccles T2Lt kia 30-9-15 11RB p180 CR France706
WILLIAMS,Horace George Lt kia 17-10-18 2Y&L p159 CR France849
WILLIAMS,Howard Glynne Lt ded 5-1-17 6KRRC p265 CR Wales706
WILLIAMS,Howard Oscar 2Lt kia 11-4-18 23NumbF p63 MR32
WILLIAMS,Howell 2LtTLt ded 21-2-17 RWFus attGoldCoastR p99 CR WAfrica3
WILLIAMS,Howell Morgan 2Lt kia 24-6-17 4WelshR p230 CR Belgium23,19Bn
WILLIAMS,Hubert Cracroft.MC.MID Lt kldacc 18-10-15 2RWSurr p57 CR France114
WILLIAMS,Hugh 2Lt kia 28-7-18 PembrokeYeo att7KSLI p205 CR France33
WILLIAMS,Hugh Osborne Lt dow 12-8-15 5RWFus C'Coy p223WILLIAMS,Hugh Powell TCapt kia 5-6-16 14RWFus p99 CRFrance1730
WILLIAMS,Hywel TCapt kia 10/12-7-16 17RWFus p99 MR21
WILLIAMS,Idris Havard Joseph Capt dow 3-6-15 RFus p71 CR Wales86
WILLIAMS,Idwal 2Lt kia 26-9-17 1/2RWFus p99 MR30
WILLIAMS,Ivor Phillips 2Lt kia 7-1-16 3KSLI att4SWBord p145 MR4

WILLIAMS,J.A.Maj 20-9-19 RGA CR Hamps11
WILLIAMS,J.J.2Lt 6-6-21 RWFus CR Wales725
WILLIAMS,James B.TCapt dow 22-7-16 18LancF p94 CR France66
WILLIAMS,James Alfred 2Lt kia 6-9-16 3RIrF p172 MR21,RIrRif
WILLIAMS,James Ezekiel TCapt ded 27-9-18 GL p267
WILLIAMS,James Griffith Lt kia 27-8-18 RWFus att 17Bn p99 CR France432,29-8-18
WILLIAMS,James Hubert.DSO.Capt ded 30-11-20 IA 1/10GurkhaRif p284
WILLIAMS,James Morgan 2Lt kia 9-5-18 19 att17RWFus p99 CR France296
WILLIAMS,James Trevor 2Lt ded 7-6-18 IARO att 30Punjabis p284
WILLIAMS,Jennie Miss ded 31-1-19 VAD p200 CR France85
WILLIAMS,John TCapt kia 30-6-17 19RWFus p99 CR France439
WILLIAMS,John T2Lt drd 22-10-17 11RDubF att1/5Hamps p177 MR66
WILLIAMS,John Alfred T2Lt kia 18-11-16 11 att2YLI p144 CR France152
WILLIAMS,John Bromfield T2Lt kia 25-9-15 5CamH p168 MR19
WILLIAMS,John Herbert TCapt ded 18-11-17 GL p192 CR Mddx26,6-11-17
WILLIAMS,John Herschell 2Lt kia 17-6-17 C84RFA p37 CR Belgium127
WILLIAMS,John Lewis TCapt dow 12-7-16 16WelshR C'Coy p128 CR France23
WILLIAMS,John Rhonwy(Ronnie) Capt 12-8-16 10Lpool CR France1266
WILLIAMS,John Ronald Watson.MC.Lt kia 12-4-18 RE p210 MR32
WILLIAMS,John Rowland Lt kia 27-9-17 2MonR attMGC p187&244 MR30
WILLIAMS,John Trevor 2Lt ded 7-6-18 IARO att 1/30Punjabis MR43
WILLIAMS,John Tyler 2Lt kia 21-3-18 9 att11Lpool p216 MR27,Tytler
WILLIAMS,John Victor 2Lt kia 26-9-17 4Lpool p73 MR30
WILLIAMS,Joseph Stephenson.MC.LtACapt kia 25-9-17 3 att4Lpool p73 MR30
WILLIAMS,Justus Harold 2Lt kia 9-7-16 RHFA attGdsTMB p37
WILLIAMS,Katherine SNurse ded 6-8-19 QAIMNS p268 CR Wales571,4-8-19
WILLIAMS,Kenneth George TLt dow 21-10-16 74MGC Inf p186 MR21
WILLIAMS,Leigh Roslin Lt kia 27-5-18 B'Bty 251Bde RFA p208 MR18
WILLIAMS,Leonard Lt dow 11-9-15 3 att1SWBord p101 CR France423
WILLIAMS,Leonard Charles 2Lt dow 10-11-17 3Lincs p76 CR Belgium11,1Bn
WILLIAMS,Leonard Vincent TCapt kia 26-5-17 7SWBord p101 CR Greece6
WILLIAMS,Leslie T2Lt kia 1-7-16 23NumbF p63 CR France1890
WILLIAMS,Leslie Caradoc Lt kia 27-8-17 RFA D1/55Div p208 CR Belgium10
WILLIAMS,Lewis T2Lt kia 18-8-16 10RWFus p99 MR21
WILLIAMS,Lionel Murray Capt ded 9-4-17 6Mddx att2Ess p149 MR65
WILLIAMS,Lloyd Capt dow 2-8-17 17RWFus CR Belgium18
WILLIAMS,Lloyd Allison T2Lt kia 20-7-16 1DCLI p115 MR21
WILLIAMS,Martin Floyer TLt kia 11-8-16 A65RFA p37 CR France296
WILLIAMS,Maurice Dingwall 2Lt kia 22/24-10-14 RWSurr p57 CR Belgium83
WILLIAMS,Maxwell Henry 2Lt kia 19-9-17 17Lond p250 CR Belgium10
WILLIAMS,Meredyth Robert Owen T2Lt kia 14-3-17 25NumbF p63 CR France1182
WILLIAMS,Montgomery.MID Capt 23-8-16 RMA CR France296
WILLIAMS,Noel Dyson Lt kia 22-10-18 3 att5SLancs p126 CR Belgium406,dow
WILLIAMS,Norman Lt kia 21-3-18 8RBerks p140 MR27
WILLIAMS,Norman Ernest 2Lt kia 9-11-17 10Lond attRFC p20&248 CRFrance1361
WILLIAMS,Norman Stevens Lt kia 4-11-17 1/4RSuss p228 CR Palestine1,Steevens
WILLIAMS,Osmond Trahairn Deudraeth.DSO.Capt dow 30-9-15 WelshGds CR France88
WILLIAMS,Oswald Michael Maj kia 13-10-15 1Mon p244 MR29 Now known MR19
WILLIAMS,Oswald Morgan 2Lt kia 9-4-16 16WelshR B'Coy p255 MR19
WILLIAMS,Owen Edgar 2Lt kia 19-4-17 Worc att1/4WelshR p110 CR Palestine8
WILLIAMS,Owen Herd Spear LtCol ded 9-1-15 PembrokeYeo p272 CR Wales393,9-12-14
WILLIAMS,Percy John 2Lt dow 17-5-17 6ESurr p226 CR Greece7
WILLIAMS,Peter T2Lt kia 13-11-16 10RWFus p99 MR21
WILLIAMS,Philip Clarence TLt kia 10-8-15 10Hamps p121 MR4
WILLIAMS,Philip Ernest.MC.TCapt dow 24-11-17 19RWFus p99 CR France512
WILLIAMS,Ralph Eustace 2Lt kia 29-6-18 19NumbF attRE p63 CR France84,28-6-18
WILLIAMS,Raymond Burke.MC.TCapt kia 19-9-16 RE 176TC p49 MR20
WILLIAMS,Reginald Joseph T2Lt kia 25-9-15 9RWFus p99 MR19
WILLIAMS,Richard 2Lt dow 2-4-18 17RWFus att41MGC p99&186 CR France169
WILLIAMS,Richard Harte Keatings CaptBtMaj dow 12-12-16 RASC p194
WILLIAMS,Richard Henry T2Lt kia 13-11-16 10RWFus p99 MR21
WILLIAMS,Richard James 2Lt dow 29-4-18 12Lond p249 CR France145
WILLIAMS,Richard Lloyd TCapt dow 2-8-17 17RWFus p99
WILLIAMS,Richard White 2Lt dow 16-8-15 1/10Lond p248 MR4
WILLIAMS,Robert 2Lt kia 8-10-15 GrenGds SR att3Bn p50 CR France423,2Bn
WILLIAMS,Robert John 2Lt kia 31-8-18 3MGC Inf Div p186 CR France614

WILLIAMS,Robert Lukyn Lt kia 27-10-18 IA 23Cav p284 MR38
WILLIAMS,Robin A.W.Lt kia 18-4-15 2YLI p144 MR29
WILLIAMS,Roderick Mathafar Capt kia 12-8-17 2GarBnRWFus &32RFC p15&99 MR20,Rodric Mathafarn
WILLIAMS,Roderick Philip 2Lt ded 8-9-16 IA 72Punjabis p284 MR43.9-9-16
WILLIAMS,Roland Vaughan T2Lt kia 5-6-17 32RFC p15 CR France381
WILLIAMS,Rowland 2Lt kia 23-10-18 9RFus p71 CR France1296 &CR France1080
WILLIAMS,S.R.T.A.M.2Lt dow 25-10-15 REKentYeo CR Gallipoli1
WILLIAMS,Samuel Mervyn 2Lt kia 16-10-16 3 att2N&D p135 MR21
WILLIAMS,Selwyn Coldham TLt kia 18-1-17 B189RFA p37 CR Belgium102,C'Bty
WILLIAMS,Stanley Charles Howard TLt ded 14-10-18 GL att1NigR p192&202 WAfrica53
WILLIAMS,Stanley Norman T2Lt ded 25-10-16 GL &RFC p4&192 CR France514
WILLIAMS,Stuart Duncan 2Lt kia 3-5-17 HouseholdBn p20 MR20
WILLIAMS,Sydney Mansell 2Lt kia 15-6-17 20Lond p251 MR22,15-6-15
WILLIAMS,Theodore Cecil Ormonde.MC.Capt dow 24-3-18 16N&D p135 CR France177,Ormond
WILLIAMS,Theodore Edward 2Lt kia 1-7-15 1SomLI p80 CR Belgium85
WILLIAMS,Thomas Benjamin 2Lt kia 27-5-17 3 att2RWFus p99 MR20
WILLIAMS,Thomas Jones 2Lt kia 28-12-17 1/7LancF p221 CR France765
WILLIAMS,Thomas Langley 2Lt kia 1-9-18 1Lpool p73 CR France646
WILLIAMS,Thomas Rix 2Lt kia 20-7-18 8WYorks p219 CR France622
WILLIAMS,Thomas Wodehouse Lt kia 9-5-15 3Nhampt att1NLancs p138 MR22
WILLIAMS,Timothy Davies 2Lt dow 5-4-18 RGA 248SB p42 CR France41
WILLIAMS,Trevard Lewis T2Lt kia 30-10-17 7RFus p71 MR30
WILLIAMS,Vaughan Floyer 2Lt kia 3-4-17 GL &60RFC p15 CR France518,2-4-17
WILLIAMS,Vivian Pedr 2Lt kia 22-4-18 15RWFus p99 CR France296
WILLIAMS,Walter 2Lt kia 15-5-18 7Lpool p215 CR France106,1/6Bn
WILLIAMS,Walter Frank 2Lt kia 12-9-18 5WBord att10th p101 CR France415
WILLIAMS,Walter Patrick 2Lt kia 17-4-18 3 att4Lpool p73 MR30
WILLIAMS,Wilfred Brynmor T2Lt kia 5-7-16 20 att16WelshR p128 CR France397,dow
WILLIAMS,Wilfred Cyril Lt kia 24-9-16 12Hamps p121 MR37
WILLIAMS,William 2Lt ded 27-2-17 3 att1RWFus p99 CR Lancs4,dow
WILLIAMS,William 2Lt kia 29-8-18 281RFA p37 CR France214,30-8-18
WILLIAMS,William Bernard Lt kia 20-10-18 WelshR att14Bn p128 CR France230
WILLIAMS,William Frederick 2Lt kia 27-9-18 17RFus p71 CR France1497,Lt
WILLIAMS,William George TCapt dow 29-8-17 17RWFus p99 CR Belgium16
WILLIAMS,William George Bransby.MC.Capt kia 12-5-17 19RFC p15 MR20
WILLIAMS,William Harold Lt kia 9-11-18 RGA 326SB p42 CR Belgium214
WILLIAMS,William Harold Trant T2Lt ded PoW 22-8-17 29RFC p15 CR Belgium140,dow
WILLIAMS,William Henry T2Lt kia 6-11-17 9 att1/7RWFus p99 CR Palestine1
WILLIAMS,William Henry 2Lt kia 22-3-18 1/7Lpool p73 CR France765
WILLIAMS,William Henry Capt kia 30-5-18 3Mon att5SWBord p244 CR France622
WILLIAMS,William Humphrey Capt kia 3-5-18 6LancF &RAF p221&258 CR palestine9
WILLIAMS,William Hutton Capt kia 18-5-15 3ESurr att2Beds p113 CR France279
WILLIAMS,William Ifor 2Lt dow 18-3-18 1 att16RWFus p99 CR France275
WILLIAMS,William James.MC.2Lt kia 19-9-17 16RWFus p99 CR France275
WILLIAMS,William James Minister 2Lt kia 7-2-16 3 att2RWFus p99 CR France114
WILLIAMS,William John Lt dow 12-5-15 2Mon p244 CR France102
WILLIAMS,William John TLt kia 25-2-17 14RWFus p99 CR Belgium23
WILLIAMS,William Morley T2Lt kia 7-6-17 14WelshR p128 CR Belgium23
WILLIAMS-BULKELEY,Richard Gerard Wellesley.MC.Maj ded 28-3-18 1WelshGds p53 CR Mddx16,Gerrard
WILLIAMS-FREEMAN,Anthony Peere Capt dow 4/5-4-16 Lincs p76 MR38
WILLIAMS-FREEMAN,Harry Peere LtACapt kia 8-8-18 3 att1/5RWar p66 CR Italy1.9-8-18
WILLIAMS-MEYRICK,Edmund Oswald Griffith TLt ded 7-5-16 RWFus 1GarrBn p99 CR Europe23
WILLIAMS-VAUGHAN,John Christopher Arthur 2Lt kia 18-7-16 SWBord BrecknockBn att 100MGC Inf p187&223 MR21,15-7-16
WILLIAMS-WYNN,Charles Walkin 2Lt kia 29-10-14 1CldGds p51 CR Belgium115
WILLIAMSON,Alan Kennedy 2Lt dow 20-4-17 8A&SH p243 CR France40
WILLIAMSON,Alexander T2Lt kia 31-1-16 9Suff p79 CR Belgium101
WILLIAMSON,Alexander John Neeve 2Lt kia 14-9-14 SfthH p165 CR France867
WILLIAMSON,Andrew Maj kia 21-3-18 RE 12FC p49 MR20
WILLIAMSON,Charles Harry.MC.Capt kia 27-3-17 7Manch attRFC p20&237 CR Egypt2

WILLIAMSON,Charles Percival Lt kia 12-3-17 RE 56FC p49 CR France1182
WILLIAMSON,Cyril George T2Lt kia 2-7-16 10RWar p66 MR21
WILLIAMSON,Edgar Rowe.MC.Lt kia 10-9-16 5Lond att169TMB p246 MR21
WILLIAMSON,Edward Benjamin Bickford 2Lt kia 19-2-17 ConnRgrs att6Bn p172 CR Belgium17
WILLIAMSON,Edward Maurice Lt kia 1-3-15 1N&D p135 CR France706
WILLIAMSON,Frank Lt kia 24-3-18 5Lond p246 MR20
WILLIAMSON,Frank Alfred 2Lt dow 4-6-15 ScotRif att1KOSB p104 MR4
WILLIAMSON,Frederick Lt kia 10-5-17 IARO att 1/4GurkhaRif p284 MR43
WILLIAMSON,George Lt dow 12-11-14 3 att2WRid p116 CR Belgium84
WILLIAMSON,George Hamilton.MC.TCapt dow 12-4-17 7KRRC p152 CR France120
WILLIAMSON,Gerald Coutts 2Lt kia 9-10-17 4Ess p232 CR Belgium115
WILLIAMSON,Gerald Douglas T2Lt dow 1-1-18 7RFC p17 CR Belgium18
WILLIAMSON,Hugh Albert.MID 2Lt kia 2-7-16 3Manch &34RFC p4&156,ded MR20
WILLIAMSON,Harold 2Lt kia 27-5-18 25MGC p186 MR18
WILLIAMSON,Harold Godwin 2Lt kia 1-7-16 6NStaffs p238 MR21
WILLIAMSON,Hugh Henshall Clifford Lt kia 15-9-16 1CldGds p51 MR21,mbk
WILLIAMSON,John 2Lt kia 1-7-16 2SfthH p165 CR France643
WILLIAMSON,John 2Lt kia 24-9-17 246MGC Inf p186 MR30
WILLIAMSON,John Alexander Lt kldacc 10-4-17 10EKent attRFC p20&204 CR Kent34
WILLIAMSON,John Daniel 2Lt kia 15-7-16 1 att4SStaffs p123 MR21,4 at1Bn
WILLIAMSON,John George Joseph 2Lt kia 2-9-18 2 att7RIrReg p89 CR Belgium97
WILLIAMSON,John Maurice 2Lt kia 16-5-15 2GordH p167 CR France279
WILLIAMSON,John McLeod 2Lt kia 12-4-18 4A&SH p174 MR32
WILLIAMSON,John Stanley 2Lt kia 1-5-15 1LancF p94 MR4,25-4-15
WILLIAMSON,Kenneth Harper T2Lt dow 19-4-17 7KRRC B'Coy p152 CR France40
WILLIAMSON,Robert Burdett 2Lt kia 29-10-18 1/2RSuss &RAF p120
WILLIAMSON,Robert Hamilton Lt dow 27-12-14 RGA p42 CR Scot280,2Lt
WILLIAMSON,Stephen de Thierry Lt kia 10-3-15 3ScotRif p104 CR France260,2Bn
WILLIAMSON,Thomas Cockburn 2Lt kia 26-9-15 4BlkW p230 MR19
WILLIAMSON,Wilford Robert.MC.TLt dow 14-8-17 8Norf p74 CR Belgium11,Wilfrid
WILLIAMSON-NAPIER,Alfred Maxwell Lt kia 12-12-18 75RFA p37 CR France1484,12-9-18
WILLINGTON,James Vernon Yates T2Lt kia 6-8-16 6Leinst p175 MR4,10-8-15
WILLINGTON,Reginald Ernest.DCM.Lt dow 31-8-18 2YLI p144 CR France119
WILLINK,George Ouvry William.MC.MID Capt kia 28-3-18 2/4RBerks p234 CR France1170
WILLINK,Herman James Lindale Capt dow 5-11-18 1/6WRid p227 CR France402

WILLIS,Arthur Rhys 2Lt kia 28-7-17 4HLI att20DLI p164 CR Belgium29
WILLIS,Charles Frederick Maj kia 7-3-18 5Y&L p238 CR Belgium307,8-3-18
WILLIS,Cyril Louis 2Lt kia 7-10-16 12Lond p248 MR21
WILLIS,Edgar Reginald TLt kia 13/14-7-16 8RSuss p120 CR France630
WILLIS,Eric Fitzgeorge Lt kia 27-3-18 28Lond p252 MR20
WILLIS,F.A.Sister 15-12-19 TFNS 4LondGH CR Essex5
WILLIS,Frederick LtACapt kia 30-9-18 9 att 1/5Dev p77&258 CR France1483
WILLIS,George Henry Lt dow 10-8-15 6SLancs p126 CR Gallipoli17
WILLIS,Henry George.MID 2Lt dow 22-12-15 2DLI p162 CR France102
WILLIS,Hugh Dudley TCapt dow 12-8-17 RAMC att3Worc p198 CR Belgium7
WILLIS,Justin Charles.MC.Maj dow 7-8-18 RE 18DivSigCo p49 CR France71
WILLIS,Oscar 2Lt kia 20-6-16 5NumbF p213 CR Belgium60
WILLIS,Raymond TLt kia 25-3-18 5RRofCav att18Huss p23 CR France513
WILLIS,Raymond Maurice T2Lt kia 6-11-17 1DCLI p115 MR30
WILLIS,Richard TLt kia 15-5-16 9LNLancs p137 CR France68
WILLIS,Russell 2Lt kia 25-10-14 Y&L att1Lincs p159 CR France705
WILLIS,Samuel Capt kia 1-7-16 14RIrRif p170 MR21
WILLIS,Sherlock Amyas.MID LtTCapt dow 15-5-17 4Mddx p149 CR France40
WILLIS,Thomas Ambrose Lt kia 8-12-17 18Lond p250 CR Palestine,2Bn
WILLIS,William Francis Bucknote T2Lt kia 23-7-16 1DCLI p115 MR21,Frederick Bucknole
WILLIS-FLEMING,Richard Thomas Cyril 2Lt dow 4-8-16 1/5RHA p209 CR Egypt2,kia
WILLISON,John Downie Lt kia 25-7-18 2/9RScots p212 CR France865
WILLMER,Arthur Franklin TCapt dow 20-9-16 9RB p180 CR France145
WILLMER,Walter TCapt kia 13-7-16 19Lpool p73 MR21,30-7-16
WILLMORE,E.G.MC.Lt 31-7-20 RGA CR Herts31
WILLMORE,John 2Lt 5-11-17 2/7Worc MR20

WILLMORE,William Albert 2Lt kia 26-4-18 13 att10Ches p97 MR30
WILLMOT,John Dyott Lt kia 3-7-15 6 att2Worc p110&258 CR France571
WILLMOT,Robert Dyott 2Lt kia 17-2-18 6 att2KRRC p152 CR Belgium63
WILLMOTT,Albert Mckenzie Lt ded 11-2-19 RASC p194 CR Belgium265
WILLMOTT,John Herbert Victor.MC.LtACapt kia 28-3-18 3 att2Ess p133 MR20
WILLNER,John Capt&QM kia 7-4-18 1/6SStaffs p229 CR France480
WILLOCK,Guy Charles Boileau Capt kia 25-9-15 18Lond p250 CR France219
WILLOCK,Neville Gore Capt 22-11-17 KOSB CR France398
WILLOUGHBY,Edwin Charles Capt dow 8-8-15 7Glouc p107 MR4
WILLOUGHBY,Francis George Godfrey TCapt kia 9-8-15 9RB p180 MR29
WILLOUGHBY,James Gerald Capt kia 3-3-15 IA 33Cav p284 CR Iraq6
WILLOUGHBY,John Christopher.Sir.DSO.Maj ded 16-4-18 RASC p267
WILLOUGHBY,Stanley Nelson Lt kia 1-8-17 B70RFA p37 CR Belgium7
WILLOX,George Martin Lt 8-12-18 MilLabCps CR EAfrica36
WILLS,Alban Noel Lt dow 7-3-18 1/5YLI p235 CR Belgium11
WILLS,Alfred James 2Lt kia 18-10-18 RGA 182SB p42 CR France190
WILLS,Alfred Leslie Lt kia 23-4-17 4Worc p110 MR20
WILLS,Arthur George Lt 7-8-15 9N&D p135 MR4,9-8-15
WILLS,Bertram Shera Capt 19-8-19 RAMC CR Leic63
WILLS,John Godfrey 2Lt kia 27-9-18 A93RFA p37 CR France759
WILLS,John Scott Lt kia 4-9-18 20DLI p162 CR Belgium111
WILLS,Mary Elizabeth SNurse 30-3-18 TFNS CR Durham13
WILLS,Oliver Byerley Walters Lt ded 10-11-18 GL &RAF p192
WILLS,Percy 2Lt dow 19-4-15 1DCLI p115 CR Belgium151
WILLS,Robert Bruce Melville.MID Capt kia 15-2-15 RE 2FC p210 MR29,Recommended for VC
WILLS,Robert Dixon.MM.2Lt kia 23-4-17 5BordR p228 CR France162
WILLS,Robert George.MC.MM.2Lt ded 3-12-18 RE 46DivSigs att230RFA p49 CR France717
WILLS,Thomas George Francis 2Lt kia 2-9-18 3SomLI p80 CR France511
WILLSON,Edgar Brian Lt kia 27-5-18 25MGC p186 MR18
WILLSON,Francis George Dudley Lt kia 24-9-18 3 att 1Nhampt D'Coy p138 CR France375
WILLSON,Frederick James Lt dow 10-1-17 IARO att3/1Sap&Min p284 CR Iraq5
WILLSON,Harold Hilton 2Lt dedacc 10-1-17 5Suff D'Coy p217 CR France52,8Bn
WILLSON,Nellie SNurse 16-10-18 QAIMNS CR Lincs76
WILLSON,William Alick Parkinson.MID Lt dow 1-4-18 11RIrRif att22EntrenchBn p170 CR France988,12Bn
WILLSTEAD,Grahame Ernest Lord LtACapt kia 24-3-18 3SomLI p80 CR France1061,7Bn
WILLY,John Howard Cole T2Lt kia 25-11-17 2Dev p77 MR17
WILMER,Harold Gordon Maj kia 4-7-15 IA 14Sikhs Ferozepore p284 MR4,5-7-15
WILMOT,Ben.MC.TLtACapt kia 6-6-17 20NumbF p63 MR20
WILMOT,Edmund Sacheverell 2Lt kia 13/15-11-16 4 att2SStaffs p123 CR France1890,13-11-16
WILMOT,Paul Dominie Lt kia 25-3-18 3 att12RSuss p120 MR27
WILMOT,Ralph Henry Sacheverel.Bart.Capt ded 14-1-18 CldGds p262 CR Lincs60
WILMOT,Robert Coningby TCapt kia 29-10-17 10N&D p135 CR Belgium86,Coningsby
WILMOT,Sachevarel Darwin Capt ded 14-10-18 RGA 159SB p42 MR43,Sacheverel
WILMOT,Thomas Norbury.MC.2Lt dow 25-8-16 2Worc p110 CR France833
WILMOT-SITWELL,Jacinth Sacheverall Lt dow 9-7-16 3CldGds p51 CR Belgium73
WILMSHURST,Cecil Arthur 2Lt kia 5-4-18 4 att5RBerks p234 MR27
WILMSHURST,Edwin Roy TLt dow 1-12-16 29 att20RFus A'Coy p71 CR France145
WILSEY,Edward Henry 2Lt kia 11-1-17 IARO att93BurmaInf p284 CR Iraq5
WILSHAW,Eric James 2Lt ded 23-12-18 A233RHFA p37 Lancs209,dow
WILSHIN,John Howell 2Lt dow 25-4-18 6 att1RFus p71 CR France145,22-4-18
WILSHIRE,Laurence Stanley 2Lt kia 14-4-18 95MGC p186 CR France18
WILSON,Alec Capt kia 26-3-17 1Hereford p252 MR34
WILSON,Alan Hood 2Lt kia 17-3-15 6RB p181 CR Belgium71
WILSON,Alan Mowbray 2Lt kia 19-11-16 3 att8ESurr p113 MR21
WILSON,Alan Sydney Lt kia 23-4-17 2SLancs att51MGC p126&186 MR20
WILSON,Albert Cecil 2Lt dow 8-7-16 14Lond p249 CR France95
WILSON,Albert Knowles Lt kia 14-3-15 1Manch p156 MR22,12-3-15
WILSON,Alexander 2Lt kia 21-3-18 2/7LancF att 1/6Bn p221 MR27
WILSON,Alexander LtCol&QM ded 18-9-19 RAMC p267 CR Kent67
WILSON,Alexander Gordon 2Lt kia 27-8-18 12 att13RInniskF p106 CR France353
WILSON,Alexander Newbigging 2Lt kia 24-11-17 5KOSB p224 MR34
WILSON,Alexander Philip Lt kia 14-4-17 GL &2RFC p15 CR France58

WILSON,Alexander Stewart T2Lt kia 20-4-17 10RDubF p177 MR20
WILSON,Alfred Cairns.MC.2Lt dow 25-9-16 14Lond p249 CR France329
WILSON,Alfred Clarke 2Lt mbk 6-11-18 3 att6Lincs p257 CR Belgium241
WILSON,Allan TLt ded 25-8-15 RE 79FC p49 CR France22
WILSON,Allan Clark 2Lt kia 28-4-17 15RScots p55 MR20
WILSON,Allan Stanley 2Lt dow 12-7-17 5BordR attMGC p187&228,Lt CR France102
WILSON,Andrew 2Lt kia 16-7-18 13RScots p55 CR France139
WILSON,Archibald 2Lt kia 27-3-18 LancF att6Bn p94 MR27
WILSON,Archibald Field TCapt kia 25-9-15 9ScotRif p104 CR France114
WILSON,Arnold 2Lt kia 3-5-17 5WYorks p218 MR20
WILSON,Arthur Alexander 2Lt kia 23-4-17 3A&SH p174 CR France434
WILSON,Arthur Desmond Lloyd TLt kia 1-7-16 9RWKent p142 CR France1490
WILSON,Arthur Dominic 2lt dow 10-9-16 3RMunstF p176 CR France66,1Bn
WILSON,Arthur Edward Lt ded 3-12-18 14RWar p263 CR War3
WILSON,Arthur Henry Capt kia 18-10-14 EYorks p85 MR32
WILSON,Arthur Henry Maitland Capt ded 29-1-18 IA 12Cav p284 CR Iraq8
WILSON,Arthur Holt.DSO.LtCol ded 18-11-19 7ESurr Ex 2Bn p264 CR Suff64
WILSON,Arthur Hone Lt dow 18-11-16 4 att7RFus p71 CR France40
WILSON,Arthur Leslie Lt kia 18-7-18 5CamH p168 CR France285
WILSON,Arthur Stafford T2Lt kia 25-8-16 2RB p181 CR France423
WILSON,Arthur Walker 2Lt dow 22-8-18 251RFA p37 CR France119,Lt
WILSON,Arthur Wesley 2Lt kia 30-7-17 ScotsGds att3MGC p52 CR Belgium20
WILSON,Belford Alexander Wallis.MC.2Lt kia 26-9-17 2 att14Hamps p121 MR30
WILSON,Brodie Wyatt Lt kia 23-9-18 19Lond att20RAF p272 CR France1061
WILSON,Cecil Eustace T2Lt kia 16-4-17 GL &7RFC p15 CR France672
WILSON,Cecil Fred 2Lt dow 27-7-18 4Hamps p228 CR France1693,Lt
WILSON,Cecil Vere TLt dow 31-7-16 1RBerks p140 CR France145,2Lt
WILSON,Charles 2Lt kia 9-5-17 2GordH p167 MR20
WILSON,Charles Edgar Andrew Capt dow 8-4-18 RAMC p198 CR France122
WILSON,Charles Edward Capt&Adjt kia 17-9-14 RWSurr p57 CR France1342
WILSON,Charles Edward T2Lt kia 16-8-16 1Nhampt p138 CR France387
WILSON,Charles George Gordon T2Lt kia 9-4-17 3 att9ScotRif p104 CR France265
WILSON,Charles Henry.MID Lt dow 30-9-18 5YLI p235 CR France512,Capt
WILSON,Charles Lindsay.DCM.2Lt kia 8-8-16 1/5Lpool p215 MR21,9-8-16
WILSON,Charles Oscar Lt kia 26-3-17 1/5Ess p232 CR Palestine8
WILSON,Charles Robert T2Lt kia 24-5-17 88MGC Inf p186 CR France545
WILSON,Charles Wyndham Lt kia 12-3-15 2BordR p118 MR22
WILSON,Christina Murdock A/Sister ded 1-3-16 QAIMNS p200 CR France64,Murdock
WILSON,Clive Harry Adolphus.DSO.Maj 18-1-21 ERidYeo CR Yorks83
WILSON,Conrad Blackadder 2Lt kia 7-2-17 9HLI p241 CR France511
WILSON,Cornelius William 2Lt ded 25-11-18 A76RFA p37 CR France717
WILSON,Cyril Frederick Lt kia 13-5-15 5DragGds p21 MR29
WILSON,Cyril Spencer.MC.Maj ded 27-10-18 RGA p272 CR Somerset35,RE
WILSON,D.H.DSO.LtCol 3-3-20 GL RTO CR Mddx16
WILSON,David.MC.LtCapt kia 30-7-16 24RFC p4 CR France300
WILSON,David 2Lt dow 28-12-16 2A&SH p174 CR France105,29-12-16
WILSON,David 2Lt ded 12-7-18 5SLancs att143RAF p230&258 CR Scot774,21-7-17
WILSON,David Oliver 2Lt dow 8-10-16 1/1Lond p245 CR France105
WILSON,David Rex Lt dow 30-10-14 RWSurr p57 CR Greece4 MR29
WILSON,Denis Erskine TMaj dow 24-9-16 7RDubF p177
WILSON,Denis Grey.MC.LtCol mbk 1-7-16 IA 17Cav att 1/5N&D p284 MR28,D.D.
WILSON,Douglas Jonathan Rogers T2Lt kia 25-9-15 9WelshR p128 MR19
WILSON,Douglas Russell.MC.2Lt kia 25-10-18 6 att16KRRC p152&259 MR16
WILSON,Edward 2Lt kia 26-3-18 7DLI p162 MR27
WILSON,Edward Henry 2Lt kia 8-10-18 14WelchR p128 CR France1345
WILSON,Edwin 2Lt kia 4-11-18 Yorks att9WRid p91 CR France206
WILSON,Edwin Thomas 2Lt kia 23-3-18 10RWar p66 MR20
WILSON,Eric Crawcour Lt kia 28-10-18 2RWKent p142 CR Iraq8
WILSON,Eric Maurice T2Lt kia 1-7-16 17 att10RIrRif p170 MR21
WILSON,Eric Western 2Lt kia 20-9-14 1WYorks p83 MR15
WILSON,Ernest Albert 2Lt kia 6-9-18 3 att 1Lpool p73 CR France518
WILSON,Ernest Edwin 2Lt kia 4-11-18 16 att10N&D p135 CR France735
WILSON,Evan Welldon 2Lt kia 23-4-17 4A&SH p174 MR20
WILSON,Evelyn Seppings TCapt kia 29-9-15 EYorks p85 MR19
WILSON,Ewen Holmes Humphries James Lt kia 8-9-14 1BlkW p129 CR France1451
WILSON,F.A Col 21-3-15 IndStaffCps PoliticDept CR Egypt9

WILSON,Frank 2Lt kia 3-6-16 3 att1Lpool p73 CR France924
WILSON,Fred T2Lt kia 15-9-16 9Suff p79 MR21 &CR France390
WILSON,Fred.MC.DCM.2LtTCapt kia 25-10-17 Manch att22Bn p156 MR30
WILSON,Fred 2Lt ded 13-11-18 10RWar p66 CR France13
WILSON,Fred Brookfields T2Lt dow 7-8-17 12Y&L p159 CR France95,Brookfield
WILSON,Frederick Lawrence 2Lt dow 23-11-16 6WRid p227 CR France120
WILSON,Frederick Thomas Austen 2Lt kia 12-3-18 5 att2RFus p71 MR32
WILSON,Frederick William Lt kia 24-3-18 RInnisksF p106 MR27,25-3-18
WILSON,Gavin Laurie.DSO.MC.LtCol ded 16-2-19 11A&SH p174 CR France40,1/8Bn
WILSON,Geoffrey Lt ded 15-5-15 RASC 19DivTrain &209RAF p194 MR20
WILSON,Geoffrey Hutton Lt ded 23-12-18 RE p49 MR40
WILSON,Geoffrey Mervyn Underhill LtTCapt kia 26-9-15 3 att2Wilts p153 MR19
WILSON,George Andrew 2LtACapt kia 12-7-17 RGA 262SB p42 CR Belgium10
WILSON,George Andrew Glanville ACapt kia 31-7-17 6RSuss p228 MR29
WILSON,George Douglas Lt dow 13-9-16 2RFA p208 France145
WILSON,George Frederick T2Lt kia 1-7-16 21Manch p156 CR France397
WILSON,George Henry.MC.LtAMaj dow 4-11-17 D282RFA p207 CR Belgium36
WILSON,George Reginald Capt kia 10-8-15 4Ches D'Coy p222 MR4
WILSON,Gilbert John 2Lt kia 6-11-17 SussYeo p205 CR Palestine1,16Suss
WILSON,Gordon Chesney.MVO.LtCol kia 6-11-14 RHGds p20 CR Belgium134
WILSON,Gordon Ivor 2Lt kld 12-2-17 YorkDragYeo attRFC p20&205 CR Wilts116
WILSON,Gordon Javot 2Lt kia 12-3-15 NhamptYeo p204 CR France1158,Jacob
WILSON,Guy Denis Capt kia 30-11-17 169RFA p207 MR17
WILSON,Hamish Blacklock Bowes Lt kld 18-7-18 GlasgowYeo &RAF p272
WILSON,Harold 2Lt kia 5-9-18 17Lond p250 CR France511
WILSON,Harold Algar 2LtTCapt kia 6-1-16 1KSLI p145 CR Belgium20,6-1-15
WILSON,Harold Benjamin 2Lt kia 7-4-17 18Lond p250 CR Belgium167
WILSON,Harold John Fossick T2Lt ded 17-2-19 LabCps p266 CR Surrey157,KEdwHorse
WILSON,Harry Stuart TMaj&Adjt kia 9-9-16 1RMunstF p176 MR21
WILSON,Henry T2Lt kia 15-9-16 23Mddx p149 MR21
WILSON,Henry A.MC.2Lt kia 9-5-17 A28RFA p37 CR France28
WILSON,Henry Foss 2Lt kia 21-3-18 16MGC p186 CR France212
WILSON,Henry Ivan De Burgh Capt kia 19-4-17 2/4RWKent p234 CR Palestine8
WILSON,Herbert 2Lt kia 8-11-18 6LancF p221 CR France937
WILSON,Herbert Hayden.DSO.TCapt kia 11-4-17 RHGds p20 CR France1182
WILSON,Herbert Lawson 2Lt ded 2-11-18 Mddx att18Bn p149 CR France332
WILSON,Herbert Raymond Capt dow 9-1-17 IA 114Mahrattas att105MahrattaLI p284 CR Iraq5,kia
WILSON,Herbert Stanley Capt dow 13-5-15 RGA A/ABty p42 CR Belgium102
WILSON,Herbert Villers Lt dow 15-12-19 10Hamps p264
WILSON,Humphrey Hamilton T2Lt kia 19-2-18 RFC p17 CR France369
WILSON,Horace Hayman Maj drd 30-12-15 2RLancs p59 MR41
WILSON,Hugh 2Lt kia 17-10-18 3CamH p168 CR France1268
WILSON,Hugh Russell.MC.Capt kia 11-9-16 5DLI C'Coy p238 CR France515
WILSON,Hugh Stanley 2Lt kia 14-9-15 8Worc p226 CR France1327
WILSON,Hugh Young 2LtTLt kia 14-6-17 2GordH p167 MR20
WILSON,Humphrey Worthington LtTCapt kia 4-10-15 Yorks p91 MR19
WILSON,Ian McLean Lt kia 7-8-15 6Yorks p91 MR4
WILSON,James ACapt kia 15-6-18 3 att 1GordH p167 CR France33
WILSON,James 2Lt ded 12-7-18 CamH att52GordH p168 CR Essex146,Lt
WILSON,James Bannerman Gartly T2Lt dow 30-4-17 15 att12KRRC p152 CR France85
WILSON,James Boyd Lt kia 18-10-18 2NumbF p63 CR France1392
WILSON,James Ernest Studholme.MC.Capt dow 23-8-17 RAMC att2/1 O&BLI p254 CR Belgium11,24-8-17
WILSON,James Gilmour T2Lt dow 15-2-17 2RScotF p95 MR29
WILSON,James Herbert Gray Capt accdrd 7-12-15 IA 103MahrattaLI p284 MR38
WILSON,James Miller 2Lt kia 25-7-17 RGA 333SB p42 CR Belgium10
WILSON,John 2Lt kia 9-5-15 RE p210 MR22
WILSON,John TLt ded 16-10-15 5A&SH p243 CR Egypt3
WILSON,John TLt kia 9-3-16 RAMC att10WRid p198 CR France924
WILSON,John T2Lt kia 1-7-16 2Mddx p149 MR21
WILSON,John T2Lt kia 1-4-17 15LancF p94 CR France672,Lt
WILSON,John 2Lt kia 23-4-17 3 att9BlkW B'Coy p129 CR France536
WILSON,John 2Lt kia 22-3-18 RGA 120HB p42 MR20
WILSON,John Capt ded 30-12-18 RAMC att78GH p198 CR Palestine2
WILSON,John Alexander 2Lt kia 13-11-16 5GordH p242 CR France1502
WILSON,John Andrew Hackett 2Lt dow 19-9-18 9Ess p133 CR France194

344

WILSON,John Barclay 2Lt kia 15-6-15 6ScotRif p224 MR22
WILSON,John Boyd LtCol kia 28-6-15 7ScotRif p224 CR Gallipoli6
WILSON,John Cooper 2Lt kia 17-10-16 4BlkW attRFC p20&230 MR20
WILSON,John Dawson.MC.Lt ded 13-10-18 IA 38CentIndHorse p284 CR Syria2
WILSON,John Dykes Capt ded 16-2-16 IA IMS p284 CR Scot69
WILSON,John Edward Goodwin 2Lt kia 16-8-17 7RWFus p223 MR30
WILSON,John Furnevall TLt kia 29-9-16 RE 9FC p49 CR France246
WILSON,John Graham.MID Capt kia 1-2-17 IA 45Sikhs p284 MR38
WILSON,John Hardy 2Lt kia 7-4-17 8N&D p233 CR France725
WILSON,John Hutton Bowes LtCol kia 7-6-17 WRid att9Y&L p116
WILSON,John James Lt ded 3-1-19 MilLabCps CR EAfrica
WILSON,John Norman Capt dow 4-7-17 1/6BlkW p231 CR Belgium11
WILSON,John Robert.MID Capt kia 20-10-17 RE att9RFC p20&210 CR Belgium140,22-10-17
WILSON,John Soulsby.MID Lt dow 12-10-17 8SStaffs p123 MR30
WILSON,John Thomson T2Lt kia 28-1-17 SfthH att8Bn p165 CR France392
WILSON,John Victor 2Lt kia 27-4-17 5Ches p222 CR Palestine8
WILSON,John Victor 2Lt kia 17-11-17 7RScots p211 CR Belgium20,Lt
WILSON,John William.MM.2Lt kia 21-3-18 7N&D p233 MR20
WILSON,John Wilson T2Lt kia 27-12-17 15RIrRif p170 CR Palestine9
WILSON,Joseph.MC.TCapt kia 30-11-17 6CamH p168 CR France1182
WILSON,Joseph Alec T2Lt kia 14-11-16 149MGC p186 CR France1896
WILSON,Kenneth Felix Capt kia 2-11-17 1/7Ess p232 CR Palestine8
WILSON,Laurence Cecil 2Lt dow 12-8-15 3Norf p74 CR Norf26
WILSON,Laurence Farrer TCapt kia 23-4-17 16Manch p156 MR20
WILSON,Lawrence Trench T2Lt dow 9-8-15 RGA attRE 171TC p42 CR France922
WILSON,Lewis TCapt&Adjt ded 27-11-16 12 att9Ess p133 CR Lond8
WILSON,Lewis McIver T2Lt dow 27-3-16 11HLI p164 CR France285
WILSON,Lloyd 2Lt kia 24-3-18 15DLI p162 MR27
WILSON,Marshall Meredith Lt kld 29-1-18 4BordR attRFC p20&228 CR Greece1,kia
WILSON,Matthew.MC.Capt ded 12-10-18 11A&SH p174 CR Italy6,3Bn
WILSON,Myrtle Elizabeth SNurse ded 23-12-15 QAIMNS p200 CR France64
WILSON,Michael Connal 2Lt kia 20-7-16 8 att5ScotRif C'Coy p225 MR21
WILSON,Neville Inchbold.MC.Lt kia 6-4-18 3 att4RWFus p99 MR27
WILSON,Norman Lt kia 14-7-16 7WYorks p218 CR France702
WILSON,Oswald 2Lt kia 19-3-17 5NStaffs p238 CR France149
WILSON,Philip John Conning Lt kia 9-5-15 CamH att1Bn p168 MR22
WILSON,Philip Stanley 2Lt kia 20-8-16 3 att2RWFus p99 CR France453
WILSON,Ralph Aylmer.MC.2Lt kia 9-4-18 4DLI p162&259 MR32
WILSON,Ralph Edwyn Lt dow 28-9-15 2RScots p55 CR France40
WILSON,Raymond Ernest 2Lt kia 10-3-17 3 att7RWSurr p57 MR29.10-8-17
WILSON,Richard Nelson 2Lt kia 23-8-18 13Lond p249 CR France174,24-8-18
WILSON,Robert 2Lt kia 3-7-16 RBerks p140 MR21
WILSON,Robert.MM.T2Lt kia 30-6-17 9Y&L p159 CR Belgium127 Ex 12Bn
WILSON,Robert Capt ded 12-4-18 GL att6DLI p192&254 MR19 &CR Scot632,RScots
WILSON,Robert Alexander T2Lt kld 2-5-17 19DLI p162 MR21
WILSON,Robert Archibald Scarlyn 2Lt kia 12-10-16 3 att7SfthH p165 MR21
WILSON,Robert Armstrong TCapt kia 18-10-15 D74RFA p37 CR France423
WILSON,Robert Forsyth 2Lt kia 13-11-16 6GordH p142 CR France131
WILSON,Robert Gerald Aldin 2Lt kia 13-3-17 1CldGds p51 CR France786
WILSON,Robert Hamilton Birch Capt kia 1-3-20 IA 2/9GurkhaRif p284 MR43
WILSON,Robert Henry TCapt dow 15-5-17 RAMC att84RFA p198 CR France40
WILSON,Robert Meredith Lt kia 10-8-15 6LNLancs p137 MR4
WILSON,Robert Philip 2Lt kia 7-8-15 6EYorks p85 MR4
WILSON,Robert Sym Capt kia 8-11-14 SfthH p165 MR22
WILSON,Robert Victor Lt dow 13-4-18 1/2 att2/7RWar p66 CR France88,2Lt
WILSON,Ronald Edward 2Lt kia 11-3-16 IA BombayVolRif p284 CR EAfrica56,13-3-16 VolMGC
WILSON,Spence Ross T2Lt dow 13-10-16 13A&SH p174 CR France177
WILSON,Stanley Wright 2Lt kia 18-11-16 11BordR p118 MR21 Ex 8Bn
WILSON,Strawson Lieveslay TLt dow 21-7-16 15N&D D'Coy p135 CR FRance66
WILSON,Sydney Cunningham Maj ded 9-11-18 2RFA p207 CR Scot381
WILSON,Theodore Percival Cameron Lt kia 24-3-18 GL &10N&D p192 MR20,Capt
WILSON,Thomas.MC.TLt kia 29-6-17 RE p49 CR EAfrica38 &CR Tanzania1
WILSON,Thomas 2Lt kia 29-8-18 3 att2/4LNLancs p137 CR France568
WILSON,Thomas Douglas 2Lt kia 23-4-17 7A&SH p243 CR France546
WILSON,Thomas Irving Ward.MC.TCapt kia 28-11-16 21Manch p156 CR France339

WILSON,Thomas James 2Lt kia 21-3-18 295RFA p37 MR20
WILSON,Thomas Lewis 2Lt dow 27-9-18 10Manch B'Coyp156 CR France712
WILSON,Thomas Percy T2Lt kia 28-9-16 7Beds p87 CR France383
WILSON,Thomas Reginald 2Lt kia 20-11-17 E'TankCps p189 CR France711
WILSON,Thomas Wilson Lt kia 5-5-15 6Lpool C'Coy p215 MR29
WILSON,Tom Benholt 2Lt kia 18-7-17 2IrGds p53 CR Belgium12,Bonhote
WILSON,Tristram William Jourdain T2Lt kia 24-11-17 11RWar p66 CR Belgium111,Jordan
WILSON,Victor John Frackleton Lt kia 17-10-18 3 att6RInniskF p106 CR France190,2Lt
WILSON,Walton Ronald TLt dow 12-7-16 RAMC att2SfthH p198 CR France5
WILSON,Wilfred Charles 2Lt kia 9-8-15 1/5SLancs p230 MR21
WILSON,Wilfrid Gordon.MBE.TCapt ded 10-12-18 GL attRE p49&p192 CR EAfrica36
WILSON,William 2Lt dow 12-4-18 18DLI p162 MR32
WILSON,William ACapt ded 4-2-19 1ScotGds p255 CRMddx16
WILSON,William Alderice TLt ded 6-4-19 GL RIrRif att1/7KAR p202 CR EAfrica52
WILSON,William Andrew Rev ded 20-3-18 YMCA CR France85
WILSON,William Arnold T2Lt kia 22-10-17 Manch att23Bn p156 MR30
WILSON,William Charles Davidson Capt kia 18-9-18 RAMC att9SLancs p254 MR37
WILSON,William Clement T2LtTLt kia 25-9-15 1Worc p110 MR32
WILSON,William George 2Lt ded 3-5-18 RASC 17Div MT p194 CR France84,Lt 8-5-18
WILSON,William Graham T2Lt dow 24-8-17 14A&SH p174 CR France398
WILSON,William Harrison 2Lt kia 21-3-18 15DLI p162 CR France439
WILSON,William James 2Lt kia 24-4-17 10Dev p77 MR37
WILSON,William James 2Lt kia 28-3-18 3MGC p186 MR20
WILSON,William John Maj dow 20-6-18 5RFA p207 CR France102
WILSON,William Keates Harrison TCapt ded 12-4-16 Dev 1GarBn p77 CR Egypt9
WILSON,William Scott Banks Capt kia 19-9-18 6ScotRif p224 CR France686,Branks
WILSON-BARKWORTH,Kenneth Arthur.MC.Capt kia 25-10-17 4EYorks p219 MR30
WILSON-BROWNE,Rowland Murray 2Lt ded PoW 21-7-16 RFC p4 CR France543,kldFlying
WILSON ROBERTS,Thomas 2Lt 1-9-16 1Ches Ex 6Lpool CR France329
WILSON-WALKER,Alan Alexander Lt kld 20-3-16 13RFC p4 CR Kent7,2Lt
WILTON,Charles Innes 2Lt kia 21-10-16 3 att2SWBord p101 CR France307
WILTON,Ernest Parkin TLt ded 5-11-18 RFC &RASC p194 CR Yorks643
WILTON,Harold Capt ded 27-11-14 2RFA p272 MR66,28-11-14
WILTON,Richard Birkenhead 2Lt kia 1-10-17 15 att9Yorks p91 MR30,Birkinhead
WILTON,Samuel Brammer.MC.Capt kia 14-3-17 1/5NStaffs C'Coy p237 CR France800
WILTON,Thomas LtCol ded 26-6-16 12Lond Res p272 CR Mddx29
WILTSHIRE,Charles Robert 2Lt dow 13-7-16 BedsYeo p203 CR France176
WILTSHIRE,Healey James Armstrong 2Lt kia 19-4-17 1/7Ess p232 CR Palestine8
WILTSHIRE,Percy Maj dow 25-4-17 1RFA p207 CR France53,kia
WILTSHIRE,William George Earl 2Lt kia 31-3-18 3Wilts p153 CR France1211
WINBUSH,Edward Thomas 2Lt kia 24-9-17 RFA 33DAC p37 CR Belgium15
WINCH,Edmond Arthur 2Lt kia 19-10-15 4 att2WYorks p83 CR France525
WINCH,Edward Hadfield Lt kia 25-3-18 12HLI p164 MR27
WINCH,Edward Maurice 2Lt dow 25-3-15 6RB p181 CR France1,3Bn
WINCH,Edward Nightingale 2Lt dow 9-10-18 8RWKent p142 CR France912
WINCH,Gordon Bluett.DSO.MID Maj dow 10-4-18 A285RFA p207 CR France1094
WINCH,Harry Wilson 2Lt kia 2-4-17 ACycCps 2LondCycCoy att2Manch p244 CR France672
WINCH,Ronald Bluett 2Lt ded 16-4-15 10EKent p272 CR Kent235,18-4-15
WINCH,William Haffenden 2Lt dow 13-1-16 1/5EKent A'Coy p213 CR Iraq6
WINCHESTER,W.H.Capt 2-3-20 RE CR France65
WINCHESTER,William Charles Connor TLtACapt kia 21-10-16 10 att2SLancs p126 CR France384
WINCKLEY,Charles Reginald T2Lt kia 20-7-16 15N&D p135 MR21
WINDELER,Charles Francis Lt kia 10-5-15 4RWar p66 MR29
WINDELER,Herbert Wheelwright Lt kia 28-11-17 4GrenGds p50 MR17,27-11-17
WINDER,Harold 2Lt kia 15-5-17 10ELancs p111 CR France1191
WINDHAM-WRIGHT,John.OBE.Maj ded 14-2-19 5 att11RWSurr p212 CR Germany1
WINDLE,Michael William Maxwell TLt kia 25-9-15 8Dev p77 MR19
WINDRIDGE,E.A.Lt kiaAbout 9-6-18 9NStaffs p158
WINDSOR,Alfred Cooper Lt ded 15-7-15 8Ess attEAngCycCo p272 CR Lond10

WINDSOR,Harold George 2Lt kia 8-10-18 7RWFus p223 CR France1346
WINDSOR,Leslie St.Lawrence T2Lt kia 11-6-15 2Suff p79 MR29,10-6-15
WINDSOR,Mark Gilham 2Lt dow 10-3-15 2Dev p77 CR France1106
WINDSOR-CLIVE,Archer.Hon.Lt kia 25-8-14 3CldGds p51 CR France932
WINDUS,Charles Eric 2Lt kia 9-5-15 1RIrRif p170 MR32
WINES,Walter Wheeler T2Lt kia 24-8-17 8RB p181 MR30
WINFIELD,Frank 2Lt dow PoW 31-5-15 5NumbF p213 CR Belgium383,Lt 31-1-15
WING,Frederick Drummond Vincent.CB.MajGen kia 2-10-15 RA Staff 12Div p1 CR France178
WING,Vincent Sladen 2Lt kia 10-8-17 65/28RFA p37 CR France354
WINGARD,Hume Saunders T2Lt dow 20-9-16 7 att12SWBord p101 CR France178,Sanders Lt 26-9-16
WINGATE,Alexander 2Lt kia 13-10-15 9HLI p241 CR France114
WINGATE,Alfred Douglas Lt kia 16-5-15 ULIA att2RInniskF p264&284,2Lt MR22,15/16-5-15
WINGATE,Malcolm Roy.DSO.MC.CaptBtMaj kia 21-3-18 RE 459FC p49 MR20
WINGATE,Thomas Paterson Capt kia 18-4-15 1KOSB p102 MR29,2Bn
WINGFIELD,Cecil John Talbot Rhys Capt dow 29-4-15 4KRRC p152 CR Glouc138
WINGFIELD,Glanville Harry 2Lt kia 12-7-16 18KRRC p152 CR Belgium54,Granville 5Bn
WINGFIELD,Richard James Trench.MID T2Lt kld 27-4-16 28/9RFA p37 CR Iraq5
WINGROVE,George Frederick 2Lt kia 15-7-16 22Manch p156 MR21,13-7-16
WINGWORTH,Charles Henry Cecil T2Lt kia 25-9-16 10YLI p144 MR21,WINKWORTH
WINK,John Edward T2Lt ded 21-9-16 8SfthH p165 CR France145
WINKLEY,Charles.MC.TCapt kia 30-11-17 235MGC p186 MR17
WINKLEY,Sydney Joseph 2Lt kia 1-7-16 1/6RWar p214 MR21
WINKWORTH,Edwin John 2Lt dow 6-12-17 RGA 219SB p42 CR France518
WINKWORTH,Henry Edward Vernon T2Lt dow 18-2-17 6Nhampt p128 CR France177
WINKWORTH,Kenneth John T2Lt kia 12-8-17 8Suff p79 MR29
WINKWORTH,Walter 2Lt dow 26-8-15 5NumbF p213 CR France285
WINMILL,Thomas George Peyton Capt kia 11-6-18 U16RHA p37 CR France115
WINMILL,Westropp Orbell Peyton Lt kia 22-3-18 1Beds p87 MR27,23-3-18
WINN,Arthur Capt kia 9-9-14 3Suff p79 CR France1113,2Bn
WINN,John 2Lt kia 23-3-18 12Y&L p159 MR20,Yorks att7Y&L
WINNICOTT,Russell.MC.2Lt kia 6-12-17 5Dev att41RFC p20&217 CR France41,Lt
WINNINGTON,Charles 2Lt kia 14-10-18 Ches att1/7Bn p97 MR30
WINNINGTON,John Francis Sartorius.DSO.LtCol dow 22-9-18 1Worc Cmdg 1/4Nhampt p110 CR Palestine9
WINSER,Arthur Cecil.MID TLt dow 22-2-16 8ELancs p111 CR France62
WINSER,Basil Charles TCapt kia 15-2-16 10LancF p94 CR Belgium131
WINSER,Frank Edward 2Lt kia 20-8-17 GL &43RFC p15 MR20
WINSER,Frederick Herbert T2Lt kia 7-10-16 11WYorks D'Coy p83 CR France239
WINSER,Percy Ralph 2Lt kia 23-4-17 149RFA p37 CR France1186
WINSLOW,Benjamin Harmer 2Lt kia 30-11-17 1/6Lond p247 MR17
WINSPEAR,Arthur 2Lt kia 5-11-14 2ConnRgrs p172 MR29
WINSTANCE,William Allsop,DSO.MC LtCol kia 25-4-18 5SStaffs p229 MR30
WINSTANLEY,Bernard Joseph Lt ded 9-9-19 IARO att3S&M p284 MR43,10-9-19
WINSTANLEY,George Clement T2Lt kia 2-7-16 1SomLI p80 MR21
WINSTANLEY,Newnham Leibman Lt kia 13/15-11-16 4 att2SStaffs p123 CR France742
WINSTANLEY,Oswald Coke 2Lt kia 10-8-15 5WelshR p256 MR4
WINTER,James T2Lt kia 28-2-18 70RFC p17 CR Belgium3
WINTER,Laurence Amos Capt ded 15-11-18 RAMC 20GH p198 CR France40
WINTER,R.R.C.2Lt kld 9-8-18 DLI &54RAF p162 CR France526
WINTER,Robert Harold T2Lt dow 17-12-15 10 att7SStaffs p123 MR4
WINTER,Samuel Douglas 2Lt ded 21-11-18 11 att1/4Lond p248 CR France788
WINTER,Thomas Barron 2Lt kia 22-4-18 13RWFus p99 CR France516
WINTER,Wilfred Ormond,DSO CaptAMaj ded 30-11-18 RE p49 CR France1277
WINTERBOTHAM,Cyril William Lt kia 27-8-16 1/5Glouc p225 MR21
WINTERBOTTOM,Charles Percy 2Lt kia 2-8-17 3 att2SLancs C'Coy p126 CR Belgium112
WINTERBOTTOM,Cyril 2Lt kia 14-4-18 8RWar p215 MR32
WINTERBOTTOM,Dudley Dickson Capt kia 7-8-15 5Manch p236 MR4
WINTERBOTTOM,Guy Maj kia 9-8-17 DerbyYeo p203 CR Greece3
WINTERBOURNE,Frank Thomas Capt drd 10-10-18 2Lond p245 CR Ireland14
WINTERSGILL,Gerald Walker.MID Lt ded 26-11-18 RE attATS p49 CR Greece9
WINTERTON,William 2Lt kia 27-9-15 3 att11RScots p55 MR19
WINTHROP-SMITH,Bernard Lt ded 15-11-14 1ScotsGds CR Derby42
WINTLE,Armar Lowry-Corry.MC.Lt dow 22-8-17 9RInniskF p106 CR France64

WINTLE,Ernest de Vaynes LtCol kia 7-2-16 IA 12Cav p284 MR38
WINTLE,Fitzhardinge LtCol 23-3-16 87Punjabis MR65
WINTON,Ernest Walter 2Lt kia 15-12-17 RGA 2SB p42 CR Belgium13
WINTON,Harry George Denys Lt kia 3-5-15 Suff p79 CR Belgium74
WINTON,Harold Barkley 2Lt kld 21-4-18 GL &1RAF p192 CR France134,Lt dedacc
WINTON,John Hubert T2Lt kia 7-7-16 9NumbF p63 CR France393
WINTOUR,Reginald Prince Lt ded 15-12-16 SL RE RTO p201 CR Notts39
WINWOOD,Thomas Ralph Okeden.MC.TLtACapt dow 28-4-17 B199RHFA p37 CR Greece6,B99
WIPF,John Jacob 2Lt kia 8-10-18 3Lincs p76 CR France611,1Bn
WIRKHAM,Nigel John Latham TCapt kia 19-4-16 6ConnRgrs p172
WISE,Arnold Vincent Denys.MC.LtACapt kia 15-5-17 RE 2FC p49 CR France446
WISE,Colin Walter T2Lt kia 31-7-17 74RFA A'Bty p37 CR Belgium12
WISE,Francis Harry Varney TLt kld 13-1-18 RFC p17 CR Mddx77
WISE,Frederick Mortimer T2Lt kia 5-9-16 13Y&L p159 CR France631
WISE,George Edward Foster Lt kia 4-6-16 2/7RWar p214 CR France114
WISE,Henry Lupton Lt drd 30-12-17 6Dev p217 MR41
WISE,Lancelot Charles Lt ded 2-5-17 NIrHorse att3Lancers p24 MR43 &CR Pakistan50A
WISELEY,Francis Joseph TLt dow 14-9-15 RAMC p198 CR Egypt6
WISELY,Alfred Douglas 2Lt kia 12-9-16 4GordH p242 CR France922
WISEMAN,Phillip Henry Franklin Lt dow 27-10-17 2/4LNLancs p234 CR Belgium25
WISEMAN,Stanley 2Lt kia 10-3-17 4Ess p232 CR France624
WISEMAN,Vincent Harvey 2Lt kia 9-4-17 4YLI p235 CR France1186
WISEMAN,Willingham Franklin Gell Capt kia 1-7-16 2Lincs p76 MR21
WISEMAN-CLARKE,Charles Francis Ralph Lt kia 20-2-16 108RGA p42 CR Belgium135
WISHART,Edward George 2Lt dow 21-4-18 1/5GordH p242 CR France31,Lt
WISHART,William Ferguson 2Lt dow 17-6-15 6ScotRif p224 CR France201,Fergusson
WISHART,William Frederick 2Lt kia 15-6-18 4 att1GordH p242 CR France33
WISKAR,Joseph William Capt dow 7-3-17 6Lond p246 CR Lond14,6-3-17
WISSETT,John Noel 2Lt kia 4-6-18 4LNLancs p234 CR France204
WISSMAN,John Rudolph Lt kia 15-9-14 22/34RFA p37 CR France1329
WITCOMBE,Henry James 2Lt kia 23-8-18 Ess att1Bn p133 CR France281
WITHALL,John 2Lt kia 7-10-16 6 att8RFus p71 MR21
WITHEROW,Alexander Hunter T2Lt dow 3-7-16 17RIrRif p170 CR France74
WITHEROW,John Thomas T2Lt dow 5-8-17 9RIrRif p170 CR Belgium7
WITHERS,Charles Garnet T2Lt kia 3-7-16 9 att2SLancs p126 CR France215,10-7-16
WITHERS,Frank Dean T2Lt kia 1-7-16 8SomLI p80 MR21
WITHERS,Victor William T2Lt dow 6-7-16 MGC p186 CR France558
WITHERSPOON,John Clarence Lt kia 11-10-17 13DLI p162 MR30
WITHEY,Charles Elisha Capt kia 20-9-17 4RLancs p213 MR30
WITHEY,Ralph Wallace Lt ded 2-1-18 GordH p167 CR Iraq6
WITHY,Basil TLt dow 2-7-16 18Lpool p73 CR France66
WITT,Cecil Frederick T2Lt kia 28-2-18 KRRC &RFC p17&152 CRFrance327
WITT,Charles 2Lt kia 22-9-18 5N&D attMGC Inf p188&233 CR France836,46MGC att5N&D
WITT,Leonard Stanley 2Lt dow 2-5-17 A104RFA p37 CR Belgium11
WITTER,Harold 2Lt kia 26-4-18 13TankCps p189 MR30
WITTKUGEL,Adolf Frederick Capt dow 15-2-17 SL &SPersiaRif p284,T2Lt CR Asia82
WITTY,James Hannay 2Lt kia 15-4-17 3 att1Dors p124 CR France1701
WIX,Geoffrey Arthur Gibson Lt kia 12-10-17 3ESurr attRBerks p113 MR30
WIXCEY,Herbert Frank 2Lt kia 7-8-18 4RSuss p228 CR France247
WODEHOUSE,Arthur Powys Capt kia 22-11-15 IA PoliticDept att110MahrattaLI p284 MR38
WODEHOUSE,Edward.Hon.MC.2Lt kia 30-3-18 16Lancers p23 MR27
WODEHOUSE,Ernest Charles Forbes.DSO.LtCol ded 10/13-3-15 Worc p110 MR22,12-3-15
WODEHOUSE,Evelyn Charles Bradley T2LtTLt kia 4-10-17 1 att10Beds p87 CR Palestine8
WODEHOUSE,Francis John Ashburnham 2Lt kia 26-8-17 3DCLI att9RFC p15&115 CR Belgium18
WODEHOUSE,Philip.Hon.Lt ded 6-5-19 GL p192 CR Norf118
WOLF,Percy Lt kia 4-6-15 4ELancs p226 MR4
WOLFE,Bernard.MID TLt ded 20-7-18 38RFus p71 CR Palestine3,WOLFFE
WOLFE,Bertram 2Lt dow 12-7-18 5LNLancs p234 CR Ches158
WOLFE,George Capt kia 2-6-15 10RScots p212 MR29
WOLFE,Sidney George TLt kia 22-10-17 18LancF p94 MR30

WOLFE-MURRAY,A.A.CB.LtCol ded 7-12-18 HLI Staff p164 CR Scot668,BrigGen
WOLFENDEN,John Hutton Bowes LtCol kia 7-6-17 WRid att9Y&L p116
WOLFENDEN,Laurence 2Lt kia 24-10-18 2WRid p116CR France1260,Lawrence
WOLFERSTAN,Stanley 2Lt kia 3-4-17 1Dors p124 CR France1701
WOLFF,Gustav Frederick.MID ACapt kia 21-3-18 3RWFus attMGC p99&186 CR France381,Maj
WOLFF,John Alfred LtCol kia 23-10-18 RFA 4HB att14RHA p206 CR France206
WOLLASTON,Frederick Hargreaves Arbuthnot.DSO.MajALtCol kld 8-3-18 4RB Cmdg1/5Suff p181 CR Leic87
WOLLASTON,Keith Roland Lt kia 10-10-18 20Manch CR France611
WOLLEN,Douglas Charles 2Lt kia 13-4-17 GL &25RFC p15 CR France1321
WOLLET-DODD,Frederic Hora 2Lt ded 24-7-19 1YLI p265 CR Asia52,WOLLEY Hova
WOLLEY-DOD,Douglas Kirk TLt kia 25-9-15 12Lpool p73 CR France525
WOLLOCOMBE,Francis T2Lt dow 10-9-16 9Dev p77 CR France66
WOLSELEY,William Bertie TLt dow 5-7-16 160RFA p37 CR France833
WOLSELEY,William Joseph 2Lt kia 11-3-15 2ELancs p111 CR France706,12-3-15
WOLSELEY-JENKINS,Charles Wolseley.MID Capt kia 25-9-15 2RB p181 MR32
WOLSTENCROFT,William Herbert Beau 2Lt kia 12-4-18 1RScotsF p95 MR32,Bean
WOLSTENHOLME,Charles Skaife TCapt kia 17-7-16 12DLI p162 MR21
WOLSTENHOLME,George Mellor.MC.Lt kia 5-10-18 9Yorks p91 CR France341
WOLSTENHOLME,Richard Francis TCapt kia 28-11-16 15Ches p97 CR France1182
WOLTHERSPOON,James 2Lt kia 2-10-18 RScots att5/6Bn p55 CR France375
WOLTON,Owen Biddell 2Lt kia 12-8-15 5Suff p217 MR4
WOMAR,Frederick 2Lt kia 22-10-17 3Glouc p107 MR30
WOMERSLEY,David Norman TLt ded 1-2-17 11MGC p186 CR France13
WOMERSLEY,John William Lt kia 4-6-15 8Manch p237 CR Gallipoli2
WOMERSLEY,Sinclair Patterson 2Lt kia 15-4-18 59MGC Inf p186 MR32,Patteson
WONNACOTT,Thomas Henry 2Lt kia 9-5-17 3Dev p77 MR20
WOOD,Alan Salisbury.MID Lt dow 29-3-18 1/7 att2/9Manch p156 CR France169
WOOD,Alexander Maj dow 12-4-17 3RSuss p120 CR France1182
WOOD,Alfred Godfrey 2Lt kia 11-12-17 1/4Norf p216 CR Palestine9
WOOD,Alfred Lee TCapt kia 1-7-16 15LancF p94
WOOD,Algernon George Newcome.DSO.Maj kia 30-10-15 1Ess p133 CR Gallipoli4
WOOD,Almeric Watkins 2Lt dow 26-9-15 3 att5 O&BLI p130 CR Belgium5
WOOD,Archibald 2Lt kia 29-9-18 att5YLI p144 MR16
WOOD,Basil Vaughan 2Lt kia 3-7-16 6RWKent p142 MR21
WOOD,Brian Robert Philip 2Lt kldacc 2-7-15 7Lond p247 CR France222
WOOD,Bryce 2Lt dow 10-5-18 4 att1GordH p242 CR France10
WOOD,Cecil Gordon TLt dow 20-9-15 6ELancs p111 CR Europe1,Cyril 19-9-15
WOOD,Cecil Strachan Capt dow 3-12-14 3EYorks p85 CR France85,2-12-14
WOOD,Charles Edmund.MID Capt&Adjt kia 11-3-15 1RWFus p99 CR France1158
WOOD,Charles Harold 2Lt dow 25-8-16 8SWBord att8KRRC p101 CR France177,Harald
WOOD,Charles Pascoe 2Lt dow 18-4-18 4EYorks att7N&D p219 CR Belgium38,kia
WOOD,C.K.Lt ded 3-10-18 RASC p267 MR40,drd 3-8-18
WOOD,Claude Ernest TCapt kia 14-9-16 8WRid p116 MR21
WOOD,Clement Percy 2Lt kia 21-11-17 2ELancs p111 MR30
WOOD,Colin Richard Capt kia 18-1-15 5Mddx attGlouc p149 MR22
WOOD,Collingwood Lindsay Capt kia 24-5-15 18Huss A attB'Sqn p23 CR Belgium113
WOOD,Creighton Arthur Bell Lt kia 28-6-15 1Ess p133 MR4
WOOD,David Cardale 2Lt kia 23-7-16 8Glouc p107 MR21
WOOD,Donald TLtCol kia 1-7-16 1RB p181 MR21
WOOD,Donald Theodore.MC&Bar.2Lt dow 25-8-18 77RFA p37 CR France141
WOOD,Edwin Leonard 2Lt kia 26-9-17 1RScotF C'Coy p95 MR30
WOOD,Eric Arthur Walton T2Lt kia 25-2-16 9WRid p116 CR Belgium131
WOOD,Eric Horace 2Lt kia 23-10-16 1Hamps p121 MR21
WOOD,Ernest James Vivian 2Lt dow 9-11-18 36RFA p37 CR France332
WOOD,Ernest Richard Gardner Lt ded 20-7-18 1NStaffs p265 CR France161
WOOD,Frank 2Lt dow 23-10-17 8N&D att86MGC p188&233 CR France134
WOOD,Frank 2Lt kia 30-9-18 1LancF p94 MR30
WOOD,Geoffrey 2Lt kia 6-5-17 GL &2RFC p15 MR20
WOOD,Geoffrey Dayrell TLt kia 13-10-15 7Suff p79 MR19
WOOD,Geoffrey Kershaw Pemberton 2Lt kia 31-10-18 1LancF p94 CR Belgium140,1/2 att 18Bn
WOOD,Harold William Chap4Cl ded 1-11-18 RAChDept attRGA 282SB p200 CR France34

WOOD,Harry Gordon,2LtTLt dow 9-6-17 11WYorks p83 CR Belgium127,7-6-17
WOOD,Harry Douty 2Lt kia 1-7-16 2Mddx p149 MR21
WOOD,Hector Frederick.MC.Capt kia 20-9-17 32RFus p71 MR30
WOOD,Henry T2Lt dow 2-1-16 19RFus p71 CR France80
WOOD,Henry George Capt kia 25-9-15 3 att1LNLancs D'Coyp137 CR France1723
WOOD,Henry George Westmorland.DSO.Capt kia 3-8-18 1/7Worc p225 CR Italy2
WOOD,Henry Percy 2Lt kia 22-3-18 21MGC p186 MR27
WOOD,Henry Stewart.MC.Lt kia 11-8-18 3Dors p125&259 CR France360
WOOD,Herbert Lt kia 1-9-18 20Lond p251 MR16
WOOD,Herbert Bertram TCapt ded 29-1-18 GL &RFA attPoW Coy p267 CR France8,Henry
WOOD,Herbert Frederick Maj ded 11-12-18 9Lancers &RAF p22
WOOD,Horace Lt dow 24-8-18 RASC p253 CR France141,2/10Lond
WOOD,Hubert Kenneth TLt ded 16-5-17 2/2KAR p202 CR EAfrica39
WOOD,James 2Lt kia 5-8-17 1Wilts p153 MR29
WOOD,James 2Lt dow 11-8-18 10Ess p133 CR France119
WOOD,James Capt ded 14-9-18 SL RAMC p201 CR Greece6
WOOD,James Alexander Scott 2Lt kia 12-6-17 1/6WYorks att146TMB p218 CR France1887
WOOD,James Buckley Capt kia 26-3-18 10LancF p94 CR France526
WOOD,James Patrick.MC.2Lt ded 30-3-16 IARO att119Inf p284 CR Iraq1,2/198Inf
WOOD,John T2Lt kia 13-11-16 13EYorks p85 CR France802
WOOD,John 2Lt kia 13-11-16 4KOSB p224 CR Palestine9
WOOD,John George.MC.LtACapt kia 4-10-17 3SfthH p165 MR30
WOOD,John Gervaise 2Lt kia 3-10-16 3Nhampt att149MGC Inf p138 CR France385,Gervase
WOOD,John Goldsmith 2Lt kia 8-12-16 5SLancs p230 MR21
WOOD,John Lockhart.DSO.Capt dow 11-6-15 RoO 18Huss p23
WOOD,John Patrick Hamilton TLtACapt kia 11-1-17 22Manch p156 CR France533
WOOD,John Sendal 2Lt kia 7-2-16 IARO att44MerwaraLI p284 MR38
WOOD,John William Massey.MVO.LtCol ded 9-12-16 Remount Sv SL RecStaff p24&268 CR Lond8 Ex 1DragGds
WOOD,Joseph 2Lt kia 27-9-17 6N&D p233 MR30
WOOD,Joseph Clark T2Lt kld 13-1-18 RFC p17 CR Hamps31
WOOD,Keith Eric.MID Lt dow 27-5-15 23Lond p252 CR France80
WOOD,Leslie John 2Lt kia 4-10-17 14RWar p66 MR30
WOOD,Leslie William 2Lt kia 19-7-16 SLancs att2/7RWar p126 MR19
WOOD,Lewis Ironside.CMG.LtCol kia 16-5-15 Cmdg2BordR p118 CR France727
WOOD,Llewellyn George Capt ded 22-11-18 CityLondYeo att103MGC Inf p188&204 CR France1277
WOOD,Matthew Rodney.MC.TCapt kia 22-10-17 18LancF p94 MR30
WOOD,Maurice Herbert Lt kia 13-4-17 4Lincs attRFC p20&217 MR20
WOOD,Maxmilian,David Francis.DSO.Maj dow 22-8-15 9WYorks p83 MR4,LtCol 21-8-15
WOOD,Noel Ernest 2Lt kia 27-9-15 3EKent p58 MR19
WOOD,Norman Clark.MC.Lt kia 2-9-18 17TankCps p189 CR France46
WOOD,Oswald Ireland Lt kia 3-10-15 1Suff p79 MR19
WOOD,Paul Barnard Lt kia 23-4-17 5 att7RFus p71 MR20
WOOD,Peter Norris T2Lt dow 19-1-17 10RLancs p59 CR Iraq5
WOOD,Philip Capt dow PoW 5-4-16 1A 89Punjabis p284 CR Iraq8
WOOD,Philip John 2Lt kia 25-5-17 4RWSurr attRFC p20&212 CR France62,dedacc
WOOD,Philip Lovel 2Lt kia 4-3-17 43RFC p15 MR20
WOOD,Ralph Lt ded 17-10-18 7WRid &RAF p256
WOOD,Ralph Miles T2Lt dow 9-11-16 9WRid p116 CR France105
WOOD,Reginald Ewart 2Lt dow 3-8-18 EKent p58 CR France209
WOOD,Reginald Harry 2Lt kia 1-4-16 1/5NStaffs p238 CR France68,2-4-16
WOOD,Reginald Nixon T2Lt kia 22-2-16 9RIrF p172 CR France701
WOOD,Richard Poingdestre.MC.CaptALtCol kia 9-10-16 2Y&L p159 MR21
WOOD,Richard Shaw T2Lt kld 17-3-18 RFC p17 CR Hamps31
WOOD,Richard Thomas 2Lt kia 25-4-18 9MGC Inf p186 MR30
WOOD,Robert Basil T2Lt kia 12-10-16 6 att2BordR p118 CR Belgium137
WOOD,Robert Howard TLt ded 27-2-19 RAOC p268 CR B84 ?
WOOD,Robert Smith T2Lt dow 24-11-17 2RScots p55 MR20 &CR France512
WOOD,Ronald Beaumont.MID CaptALtCol kia 21-8-18 12Lancers att6Tanks p22&189 CR France745
WOOD,Rowland Henry T2Lt ded 4-7-17 3Mddx p149 CR Greece7
WOOD,Russell Elliott LtCol ded 8-2-17 RAMC p256 CR Scot253
WOOD,Samuel Herbert 2Lt kia 26-10-17 5RLancs p213 MR30
WOOD,S.G.Lt 3-2-18 1A IMD MR43 &CR Pakistan50A

WOOD,Theodore Herbert Henry 2Lt kia 13-4-15 3Dors p125 CR Belgium59,1Bn
WOOD,Thomas Anthony Capt ded 16-7-18 9KRRC p152
WOOD,Thomas Basil 2Lt kia 13-10-15 4Lincs p217 MR19
WOOD,Thomas Leonard 2Lt dow 26-6-17 16Ches p97 CR France145
WOOD,Thomas Percival Lt kia 25-9-15 IARO att2/3GurkhaRif p284 MR28
WOOD,Thomas Theodore T2Lt dow 14-7-16 9Yorks p91 CR Ches4
WOOD,Thomas Victor T2Lt kia 4-8-16 7RSuss p120 MR21
WOOD,Tom 2Lt ded 17-7-17 RFA attRAOC p37 CR Iraq6,RAVC
WOOD,W.2Lt kia 8-5-15 RB p181
WOOD,Walter Bertram.MC&Bar.Lt kld 11-11-17 2/8Hamps &29 att44RFC p20&229 CR Lincs156
WOOD,Wilfred John TLt kia 1-7-16 6Mddx p149 CR France267
WOOD,Wilfred Thomas 2Lt kia 9-8-17 3 att2WRid p116 MR20
WOOD,William 2Lt 8-5-15 4RB MR29
WOOD,William Allan 2Lt kia 1-10-18 1Dors p125 CR France699
WOOD,William Anthony 2Lt kia 6-11-17 SuffYeo B'Coy p205 CR Palestine1,15Suff
WOOD,William Bertram.MC.2LtACapt kia 25-8-17 2Wilts p153 CR Belgium17
WOOD,William Bryan 2Lt kia 23-7-16 8Glouc p107 MR21
WOOD,William Edmond 2Lt dow 26-4-18 12Lond p248 CR France40
WOOD,William John T2Lt kia 7-11-15 Mddx att16Lond p149 CR Belgium44
WOOD,William Leslie 2LtACapt kia 7-5-17 15RWFus p99 CR Belgium73
WOOD,Williams TCapt kia 31-5-16 8RWKent p142 CR Belgium97
WOOD,Wilfred 2LtTCapt ded 15-3-19 RGA 120SB p262 CR Derby66
WOOD-MARTIN,Francis Winchester Capt kia 17-2-15 1Suff p79 MR29
WOOD-MARTIN,James Isidore Capt kia 12-3-15 2Nhampt p138 MR22
WOODALL,John F.MC.2LtTLt kia 8-11-17 157MGC p186 CR Palestine8
WOODBRIDGE,Austin Hale.MC.Capt ded 28-2-19 8Mddx p236 CR France806
WOODBRIDGE,Stanley George.MC.Capt dow 19-12-18 13NumbF p63 CR Mddx18
WOODBRIDGE,Stephen Antony Ruston T2Lt dow 15-9-16 10RWar p66 CR Mddx48
WOODBURN,Cecil George 2Lt kia 25-9-15 3 att2Leic p88 MR19,Cyril
WOODBURN,Leonard Holt Lt dow 28-8-18 8 att7HLI p240 CR France84
WOODCOCK,Alfred Taylor 2Lt dow PoW 4-6-18 4EYorks p219 CR Germany1
WOODCOCK,Arthur Douglas T2Lt kia 16-8-17 WYorks att10Bn p83 MR30
WOODCOCK,Cecil William Napier 2Lt kia 14-9-18 10RFus p71 CR France245
WOODCOCK,Frank Capt kia 15-9-16 5Yorks p220 CR France453
WOODCOCK,Frederick.MC.Capt kld 31-10-18 RGA &101RAF p42 MR20 &CR France528
WOODCOCK,Geoffrey Herbert 2Lt kia 6-4-18 6 att4RWFus p223&272 CR France232
WOODCOCK,Leonard Albert T2Lt dow 10-4-17 21NumbF p63 CR France95,11-4-17
WOODCOCK,Victor Joseph TLt kia 30-9-17 3RFC p15 CR France398
WOODCROFT,J.SubCdr 23-6-21 S&T Cps MR43
WOODD,Alex.Bethune Peter 2Lt dow 24-8-18 3 att10WYorks p83 CR France805,Alec 25-8-18
WOODERSON,Douglas Henry David TCapt kia 6-8-16 RAMC att6Lpool p198 MR21
WOODFORD,Arthur Francis Lt 29-6-21 2Beds &Herts MR66
WOODFORD,Charles Basil Stanley 2Lt kia 22-8-16 15Glouc p107 MR29
WOODFORD,Harold Vivian T2Lt kia 13-10-15 8RBerks p140 MR19
WOODGATE,Arthur Horace T2LtALt kia 9-4-17 11Suff att101TMB p79 CR France581
WOODGATE,F.J.Lt 12-10-18 3RWFus CR Essex83
WOODGATE,Lionel Streatfield.MID Lt kia 8-9-14 1RLancs p59 CR France1113
WOODHAM,Charles Burnett.DSO.Capt kia 15-6-15 1DCLI p115 CR Belgium121
WOODHAMS,Eric William Lt dow 11-12-17 BedsYeo p203 CR France446
WOODHAMS,Geoffrey TCapt kia 19-3-16 7RSuss p120 CR France423
WOODHEAD,John William Lt ded 27-11-18 6WRid p272 CR Yorks361
WOODHEAD,Percival Lt kia 12-7-15 4KOSB p223 MR4
WOODHEAD,Robert Comber TCapt kia 17-7-16 12DLI p162 MR21
WOODHOUSE,A.F.Lt kia 13-4-18 SL att4/4KAR p202 CR EAfrica92
WOODHOUSE,Alfred James Capt kia 30-10-14 35RFA p37 MR29
WOODHOUSE,Bernard Capt dow 5-9-17 RAMC att10WelshR p198 CR Belgium18
WOODHOUSE,Cecil Herbert Lt kia 6-6-18 12Y&L p159 MR30
WOODHOUSE,Coventry William.MC.Capt 1-11-18 SL attEAfrForce CR EAfrica89
WOODHOUSE,Disney Charles Rev ded 6-10-16 RAChDept att12RSuss p200 CR France102
WOODHOUSE,Earn Faunce 2Lt kia 15-9-17 4ELancs p226 CR Belgium8
WOODHOUSE,Edward John Lt dow 18-12-17 IARO att38CentIndHorse p284 CR France446
WOODHOUSE,Frederick George T2Lt kia 10-7-16 10 att8SLancs p126 MR21
WOODHOUSE,Gordon Stafford T2Lt dow 14-10-15 D64RFA p37 CR France257
WOODHOUSE,Henry 2Lt kia 4-11-18 1/2 att9WRid p116 CR France206
WOODHOUSE,Hugh Egerton Lt ded 1-3-19 5Beds p272
WOODHOUSE,Leslie Douglas TLt kia 3-9-16 17N&D p135 MR21
WOODHOUSE,Lionel Mostyn.MC.DFC.Lt kia 27-9-18 EssYeo &RAF p203&258
WOODHOUSE,Percy Aspden 2Lt ded 11-9-15 9Manch p237 MR4
WOODHOUSE,Percy Wilfred 2Lt kia 28-3-18 5RFC p17 CR France58,Lt
WOODHOUSE,Reginald Courtenay Hulton Lt kia 14-1-16 IA 1/56Rif p284 MR38,13-1-16
WOODHOUSE,Robert Cecil Lt kia 14-8-15 RHA p208 CR Belgium113
WOODIN,Walter Guise T2Lt kia 30-7-16 20Lpool p73 MR21
WOODIWISS,Isaac Newton 2Lt kia 10-5-15 Lincs attRFC p2&76 CR France924
WOODLAND,Clement Arthur Lt ded 1-4-18 4NStaffs att6YLI p158 CR France40
WOODLAND,Herbert Lancelot 2Lt kia 9-8-16 10Lpool p216 MR21
WOODLAND,Leslie Frank 2Lt kia 21-3-18 180RFA p37 MR27
WOODLAND,Richard William Lt kia 9-8-15 1KSLI p145 MR29
WOODLEY,Ada Ann Sister 10-1-18 TFNS CR Essex254
WOODLEY,Charles Albert 2Lt kia 8-10-18 YLI att9Bn p144 CR France234
WOODLEY,Charles Benjamin T2Lt kia 8-10-16 124MGC p186 CR France744
WOODLEY,Stanley William T2Lt kia 22-1-17 GL &10RFC p15 CR France98
WOODLOCK,Francis Joseph T2Lt kia 13-8-17 KRRC att11Bn p152 MR29
WOODMAN,Douglas T2Lt kia 11-3-18 56RFC p17 CR France725
WOODMAN,James Edward Somerville.DSO.Maj kia 25/27-9-15 2LancF att12NumbF p94 MR19
WOODMASS,Kenrick Talbot Capt kia 23-4-15 2EYorks p85 MR29
WOODROFFE,Arthur Henry T2Lt kia 31-7-17 RWKent att10Bn p142 MR29
WOODROFFE,Charles Edward 2Lt kia 27-7-18 N&D att15Bn p135 CR Belgium184
WOODROFFE,Kenneth Herbert Clayton Lt kia 9-5-15 6 att3RB p181 MR22
WOODROFFE,Leslie.MC.TCapt dow 4-6-16 8RB p181 CR France12,14Bn
WOODROFFE,Neville Leslie.MID Lt kia 6-11-14 1IrGds p53 MR29
WOODROFFE,Sydney Clayton.VC.T2Lt kia 30-7-15 8RB p181 MR29
WOODROFFE,Walter Gordon Capt kia 16-9-16 7Mddx p235 CR France329
WOODROW,William Davidson 2Lt kia 23-4-17 5 att13RScots p211 MR20
WOODRUFF,Arthur Hamilton Winthrop Lt kia 28-9-17 4Dors p229 CR Iraq8
WOODRUFF,George Norman Cecil Lt ded 2-12-18 21 att2Lond p272 CR Kent83
WOODS,Alexander Richard Rolleston Lt kia 6-7-15 RE 56FC p49 CR Belgium101
WOODS,Alfred Marcus 2Lt kia 26-2-17 C78RFA p37 CR France785
WOODS,Basil Hamilton 2Lt drd 17-12-14 RE 2FC p210 CR Egypt15
WOODS,Charles Halkett Carson Lt 21-9-17 CanadaArmyServCps &20RFC
WOODS,Edmund.MID Lt kia 12-8-15 4ELancs p226 MR4
WOODS,Edward Hunter Thurtell 2Lt kia 15-7-16 4Suff p217 CR France432
WOODS,Eric Evelyn 2Lt dow 18-5-18 12Lpool p73 CR France145
WOODS,Eric Joseph 2LtTLt kia 9-10-17 9WYorks B'Coy p83 MR30
WOODS,Fletcher Hugh Lionel 2Lt kia 14-11-16 7NumbF p214 CR France385
WOODS,Frank Cecil Lt kia 2-4-17 3RWSurr p57 CR France1489
WOODS,Fred'k William Lt kia 28-8-18 4Dors B'Coy p229 CR France277
WOODS,George Capt kia 9-9-16 9Lond p247 MR21
WOODS,Harold Ernest T2Lt dow 1-5-17 PoW 9NumbF p64 CR France1276
WOODS,Harold Wallace 2Lt kia 23-4-17 4Suff p217 CR France591
WOODS,James Maj kia 9-5-15 IMS p284 CR France631
WOODS,James T2Lt kia 23-10-16 10 att1RLancs p59 MR21
WOODS,James Edwin kia 6-12-17 9RInniskF p106 MR17
WOODS,J.C.TMaj ded 13-5-18 RASC p267 CR Lond28,3-5-18
WOODS,John James Lt ded 17-10-18 5N&D p232 MR65,2Lt
WOODS,John Russell TCapt dow 16-9-16 1ColdGds p51 CR France105
WOODS,John William.MC.T2LtACapt kia 14-4-17 2YLI p144 CR France1701
WOODS,Leslie.MC.Capt ded 25-2-19 RHFA 15DAC p37 CR Belgium316
WOODS,Norman Hill Lt kia 16-8-17 3 att7InniskF p255 MR30
WOODS,Richard Cheetham TLt kia 18-10-17 GL &GoldCstR p202 CR EAfrica11 &CR Tanzania1
WOODS,Richard Hartland 2Lt kia 4-12-17 25Lond att8KRRC p252 CRBelgium125
WOODS,Thomas Cecil Hardwick Lt kia 22-3-18 4 att11Suff p217 MR20
WOODS,William John Peirce T2Lt kia 3-7-16 10Suff p79 CR France393
WOODS,William Thornley Stoker 2Lt dow 27-10-16 62RFA p37 CR France374
WOODS,Walter James TLt dow 24-4-17 1/2KAR p202 CR EAfrica8 &CR Tanzania1,Capt
WOODSIDE,Archibald Mitchell 2Lt dow 23-4-18 9HLI p241 CR France84
WOODSIDE,David Cunningham 2Lt dow 26-2-16 4RScotF p222 CR Scot764,Cunninghame
WOODSIDE,Hugh Marr 2Lt kia 15-7-16 9HLI p241 MR21

WOODSTOCK,Walter Percy TLt kia 1-7-16 8Y&L p160 MR21
WOODTHORPE,Arthur John 2Lt kia 9-10-18 RGA 276SB p42 CR France1355
WOODTHORPE,William Ernest 2Lt kia 13-10-15 3Dors att8RBerks p125 MR19
WOODVILLE-MORGAN,Eric Theodore 2Lt kia 20/23-9-17 6 att26RFus p71 MR30,20-9-17
WOODWARD,Arthur Frederick Albert T2Lt kia 19-11-17 RB att2Bn p181 MR30
WOODWARD,Charles Lt 30-10-14 1RWFus CR France80
WOODWARD,Charles Francis Lt dow 20-5-15 RWFus p99
WOODWARD,Edward Seymer Lt kia 6-1-16 IA 97Inf p284 MR38
WOODWARD,Ernest Harold Hamley T2Lt kia 24-12-16 10RWSurr p57 MR29
WOODWARD,George Ernest 2Lt kia 29-9-18 Worc att2nd p110 CR France665
WOODWARD,Henry Joseph Maj dow 22-8-18 RGA 336SB p42 CR France103
WOODWARD,Leslie.MC.2Lt kia 22-3-18 SLancs att2Bn p126&258 MR27
WOODWARD,Leslie Collins.DSO.Maj dow 3-9-18 63RFA p37 CR France833
WOODWARD,Reginald Rupert T2Lt kia 1-12-17 RLancs att1/5Bn p59 MR17
WOODWARD,Robert Capt kia 9-5-15 3 att1SWBord D'Coy p101 CR France279
WOODWARD,Robert William 2Lt dow 30-8-17 RGA 145SB p42 CR Belgium12
WOODWARD,Sydney Forest.MM.2Lt dow 19-10-18 1 att5Glouc p107 CR France528
WOODWARD,William Thomas 2Lt kia 14-6-17 3 att2Suff p79 MR20
WOODWARK,Ernest Reginald TMaj dow 21-8-15 5Norf p216 MR4
WOODYATT,Nigel Gresley Reginald Capt mbk 8-3-16 IA 1/2GurkhaRif p284 MR38
WOOKEY,Frederick Maurice 2Lt dow 19-3-15 1RIrReg C'Coy p89 CR France284
WOOKEY,Guy Richard Penny Lt dow 10-5-15 EYorks p85 MR29
WOOKEY,William Nehemiah TCapt dow 26-7-17 8Glouc att11TMB p107 CR Belgium60
WOOLASTON,Keith Roland Lt kia 10-10-18 20Manch p156
WOOLDRIDGE,Albert Edward 2Lt kia 19-8-16 6RWar p214 MR30
WOOLDRIDGE,Charles Reginald 2Lt ded 12-10-18 5N&D p233 CRFrance52
WOOLER,Charles Armytage T2Lt dow 20-7-16 12WYorks p83 CR Yorks257,Capt 10Bn
WOOLER,Herbert Sykes.MID T2Lt dow 28-3-16 12WYorks p83 CR Belgium11
WOOLER,Rupert Basil Lt dow 3-5-17 12WYorks p83 MR20
WOOLF,Cecil Nathan Sidney 2Lt dow 30-11-17 SR 20Huss B'Sqdn p23 CR France512,29-11-17
WOOLF,Walter Francis Lt kia 27-3-18 3 att7KSLI p145 CR France174,2Lt
WOOLF,Walter Richard Mortimer 2Lt dow 26-9-15 3 att2BordR p118 CR France98
WOOLF,William Lt kia 21-9-18 24WelshR p128 CR France365
WOOLL,George HonTLt&QM kia 19-8-15 8NumbF p64 MR4
WOOLLACOTT,Cedric Percy 2Lt kia 22-4-17 D64RHA p37 CR France644
WOOLLARD,G.F.Lt ded 3-9-18 6WRid attRAF p227
WOOLLATT,Claud Humpston TCapt kia 21-8-16 8RWSurr p57 MR21
WOOLLATT,Philip Reginald 2Lt kia 14-7-16 7RWSurr p57 MR21
WOOLLCOMBE,Charles Stephenson 2Lt kia 12-10-14 2KOSB p102 CR France260
WOOLLCOMBE,Walter Ley Maj ded 30-8-16 RAMC p272
WOOLLEN,Joseph Alfred 2Lt kia 27-4-18 Manch att17Bn B'Coyp156 MR30
WOOLLERTON,Frank.MC.2Lt kia 3-10-18 14 att2YLI p144 CR France375
WOOLLETT,J.C.Capt 16-11-18 RFC CR Kent230
WOOLLETT,William Charles Capt kia 16-9-16 11 att9YLI p144 CR France744
WOOLLEY,Charles Rupert Lt kia 28-7-16 5DLI p239 CR Belgium60
WOOLLEY,Henry George T2Lt dow 17-4-17 8RWKent p142 CR France80
WOOLLEY,Thomas Hugh Corbett Capt kia 27-4-17 2/8N&D p233 CR France1495
WOOLLEY,Wilfrid Edwin 2Lt kia 11-7-17 1Mddx p236 CR France604,3/10Bn
WOOLLEY,William Lawton 2Lt dow 18-9-18 3 att7SWBord p101 CR Greece5
WOOLLOCOMBE,John Morth Maj kia 3-2-17 1Dev p77 CR Iraq5,WOOLLCOMBE
WOOLLVEN,Gerald Clifton Lt kia 11-9-18 C290RFA p208 CR France369,10-9-18
WOOLLVEN,John Humphrey 2Lt kia 4-9-18 15Hamps p121 CR Belgium111
WOOLMAN,John Gray 2Lt kia 2-11-18 Y&L p160 CR France1196
WOOLMER,Stanley Herbert France T2Lt kia 3-9-16 17KRRC p152 MR21
WOOLNOUGH,Arthur Stanley T2Lt dow PoW 1-12-17 7DCLI C'Coy p115 CR France658
WOOLNOUGH,Charles Walter Fyffe T2Lt kia 22-3-16 10Beds att69MGC Inf p87&186 CR France559,21-3-16
WOOLNOUGH,Frederick Ullathorne Capt dow 22-3-18 3Dors att&6SomLI p125 CR France1203
WOOLNOUGH,George Morton 2Lt kia 7-4-17 159RFA p37 CR France672
WOOSNAM,Richard Bowen Lt kia 4-6-15 6 att4Yorks p91 MR29
WOOSTER,Clarence Daniel Henry.MC.Capt kia 9-8-18 6RWSurr p57 CR France636
WOOSTER,Reginald Joseph TCapt kia 15-9-16 RAMC att9RB p198 MR21

WOOTTEN,William John George 2Lt ded 24-4-19 IARO p284 MR65,WOOTTON
WOOTTON,Donald Herbert ACapt dow 25-8-18 20Lond p251 CR France119
WOOTTON,John Wesley TCapt dow 11-10-17 11Suff p79 CR France134
WORCESTER,Harold Paul TCapt kia 10-9-16 7SStaffs p123 CR France251
WORDINGHAM,Vincent Robert T2Lt kia 16-8-17 GL &Worc p192 CR Belgium106
WORDSWORTH,Alexander Gerald Capt kia 6-12-14 4Mddx p149 MR22
WORDSWORTH,John Lionel Lt kia 6-11-14 5Lancers p22 MR29,4-11-14
WORDSWORTH,Joseph Charles Ditch 2Lt kia 6-4-17 8DLI attRFC p20&239 CR France1321
WORDSWORTH,Osmund Bartle 2LtTLt kia 2-4-17 21MGC p186 MR20
WORKMAN,Edward.MID Lt dow 26-1-16 5 att2RIrRif p170 CR France40
WORKMAN,Charles Service.MC.2LtTLt kia 20-7-17 ScotRif att70RFC p15&104,dow CR Belgium393
WORMALD,Drury Frank Percy Capt ded 4-11-18 RGA p209 CR Shrop125
WORMALD,Frank.CB.LtColTBrigGen kia 3-10-15 12Lancers Cmdg5CavBde p22 CR France1745
WORMALD,Guy TCapt kia 14-9-16 12 att14LancF p94 MR37
WORMALD,Oliver Edward Capt ded 2-2-17 5Suff p217 CR Camb51
WORMULL,Charles Frederic TLt kld 5-10-17 GL &RFC p15
WORNER,Percival Seymour T2Lt kia 4-9-16 9Dev p77 CR France400
WORRALL,Ernest Arthur TCapt kld 20-3-18 51RFC p17 CR Lancs34,Lt
WORRALL,Herbert 2Lt kia 25-4-18 WYorks att1/6Bn p83 MR30
WORSLEY,Charles Sackville Pelham.Lord.Capt kia 30-10-14 RHGds MG Sect p20 CR Belgium58,Lt
WORSLEY,Evelyn Godfrey 2Lt dow 17-9-17 3GrenGds p50 CR France23
WORSLEY,Harold Rapley 2Lt kia 1-9-18 10LancF D'Coy p94 CR France307
WORSLEY,John Fortescue Lt kia 27-11-17 3GrenGds p50 MR17
WORSLEY,Reginald Eric Milne T2Lt kia 8-3-18 AlbertaR GL &RFC p17 CR France214
WORSLEY,Richard Stanley.DSO.MajBtLtCol drd 4-5-17 RASC p194 CR Italy14
WORSLEY,William Reginald 2Lt kia 1-8-17 4SomLI p218 MR29
WORSLEY-WORSWICK,Basil Henry 2Lt 29-4-16 2KEdwsHorse CR Ireland14
WORSNOP,Edgar TLt dow 7-8-15 9WYorks p83 MR4
WORSNOP,John William 2Lt kia 30-6-16 18WYorks p83 MR21
WORSTENHOLM,John 2Lt kia 25-9-17 GL &6RFC p15 CR Belgium11
WORSTER,Alexander Frederick.MC.2LtACapt dow 23-11-17 1EKent p58 CR France398
WORSTER,Frank Copeland,MC LtACapt dow 30-5-18 2Worc p110 CR France1693
WORSWICK,Henry Worsley 2Lt kld 28-4-16 KEdwsHorse p24
WORTH,Bertram Stanley 2Lt ded 8-12-19 LabCps p266 CR Surrey1
WORTH,James William.MC.DCM.2Lt dow 28-11-17 2/6WYorks p218 CR France398
WORTH,Leslie Lt ded 16-8-18 RE p210 CR Egypt2
WORTH,Stanley Seymour T2Lt kia 1-12-17 4RInnskF att14MGC p106 & 186, 2LtTLt CR Belgium23
WORTH,Thomas 2Lt kia 10-8-15 7Ches p223 MR4
WORTHINGTON,Claude Arthur.MID MajTLtCol kia 28-9-15 2EKent p58 MR19
WORTHINGTON,Claude Swanwick.DSO&Bar.TD.LtCol dow 14-10-18 6Manch att5Dors p236 CR France13
WORTHINGTON,Frederick TCapt kia 28-4-17 10Lincs p76 CR France581
WORTHINGTON,Noel Trevor Lt dow 8-8-15 6RLancs p59 CR Gallipoli18
WORTHINGTON,Ralph TMaj kia 17-5-16 16Ches p97 CR France1701
WORTHINGTON,Reginald George Lt kia 16-9-14 2 O&BLI p130 CR France1111
WORTHINGTON,Richard Fitzpatrick Capt dow 4-5-17 2/5Glouc p225 CR Glouc69
WORTHINGTON,Samuel Lt kia 28-11-17 1/1RHA p208 CR Palestine3
WORTHINGTON,Walter Gustavas.MC.Maj dow 27-4-18 12Lond p248 CR France145
WORTHINGTON-EYRE,Lionel George.MID Lt kia 14-7-17 D78RFA p37 CR France418
WORTHINGTON-JONES,George.MC.Maj dow 10-11-17 293RHA CR Belgium18
WORTHINGTON-WILMER,Hugh Ferdinand Mansfield Capt kia 11-5-16 2 att13RScots p55 CR France423,Maj
WORTLEY,John Francis.MC.Capt kia 14-4-18 4Y&L p238 MR30
WORTLEY,Maurice Lester 2Lt kia 3-10-15 3Suff p79 MR19
WORTON,John Paton Lt kia 8-5-15 3Mon p244 MR29
WOTHERSPOON,Andrew Scott Capt kia 16-8-17 4 O&BLI p231 MR30
WOULFE,Gerald Lascelles T2Lt kia 14-7-16 6Nhampt p138 MR21
WRAGG,Frederick William.MID Maj kia 1-7-16 1/5N&D p232 MR21
WRAGG,Norman John Lt dow 18-7-16 3SStaffs att1N&D p123 CR France145

WRAITH,Alfred Osborn.MID TLtAMaj dow 13-6-17 RE 254FC p49 CR Belgium5,kia

WRANGHAM,D'Arcy George Maj 22-7-20 2EYorks MR43

WRAY,Cormac Patrick James T2Lt kia 15-7-16 5 att8InniskF p106 CR France115

WRAY,David Withers Lt died 16-12-19 RIrF 1GarrBn p265 CR Burma129A,Withersow 16-12-18

WRAY,Ernest Warneford Lt kia 23-8-17 RE 517FC p210 CR Belgium8

WRAY,Francis Alan 2Lt kia 31-7-17 8Lpool p216 MR29

WRAY,Harry T2Lt kia 29-12-17 Yorks att 10Bn p91 CR France417

WRAY,John Leonard T2Lt kld 13-2-18 RFC p17 CR USA228 J.C.

WRAY,Kenneth Christopher George Capt kia 9-8-16 1/4SLancs p230 MR21

WRAY,Percy Hugh 2Lt kia 7-6-17 7RIrF p172 CR Belgium111

WRAY,Thomas Ernest T2Lt kia 4-9-17 GL &7RFC p15 CR Belgium18

WREFORD,Bertram William Heyman LtACapt kia 23-4-17 1Dev p77 CR France58

WREFORD,B.F.L.2Lt ded 11-5-18 4Lond &RAF p246

WREFORD,Leslie Warren 2Lt 16-8-17 4Lond p246 MR29

WREFORD-BROWN,Claude Wreford.DSO.Capt kia 25-5-15 2NumbF p64 MR29

WREFORD-BROWN,Oswald Eric TCapt dow 7-7-16 9NumbF p64 CR FRance23

WREN,Christopher Bray 2Lt kia 15-9-16 6Lond p247 MR21

WREN,Thomas Thorpe T2Lt dow 29-7-16 10LNLancs p137 CR Lancs464

WRENFORD,Arthur Leonard.MID CaptALtCol kia 21-3-18 Worc att4ELancs p110 CR France924

WRESSELL,Frank T2Lt kia 2-8-17 1YLI p144 CR Belgium173,1/5Bn

WRIGGLESWORTH,Alfred Gunn 2Lt kia 4-9-16 3Manch p156 MR21

WRIGHT,Aislabie Harcourt Nelson 2Lt kia 2-9-18 1SomLI p80 MR16

WRIGHT,Alan Austin Capt kia 6-9-18 3 att12ESurr p113 MR30,4-9-18

WRIGHT,Albert Harley 2Lt ded 13-1-20 IA 2/2GurkhaRif p284

WRIGHT,Alexander Allen.MC.Capt kia 8-8-16 1/4RLancs p213 MR21

WRIGHT,Alfred Kyrle Terrett 2Lt dow 10-12-17 16Lond p250 CR Egypt1,10-12-16

WRIGHT,Allan O'Halloran.MID Capt kia 13-3-15 1RIrRif p170 MR22

WRIGHT,Arthur T2Lt kia 15-9-16 10War att33MGC p186 CR France251

WRIGHT,Arthur Samuel 2Lt kia 15-8-18 8EYorks p85 CR France352

WRIGHT,Arthur William TCapt ded 13-10-17 GL &RE p192 CR Durham28

WRIGHT,Basil Charles.MC.Lt kia 24-9-18 2RSuss p120 MR16

WRIGHT,Cecil Keith Foyle 2Lt kia 21-8-18 10RFus p71 CR France927

WRIGHT,Cecil Laurence 2Lt kia 7-7-17 RGA 287SB p42 CR Belgium34

WRIGHT,Cecil Medwyn 2Lt kia 6-11-17 22Lond p252 CR Palestine8

WRIGHT,Charles Lt kia 29-11-17 1/1LincsYeo p204 CR Palestine9

WRIGHT,Charles.MC.Lt kia 27-5-18 3 att11Ches p97 MR18

WRIGHT,Charles James T2Lt kia 18-10-16 11SStaffs att26MGC p123&186 MR21

WRIGHT,Charles James Stewart TCapt kia 14-7-16 7Leic p88 CR France1890

WRIGHT,Clarence Haries TLt kia 1-7-16 15LancF p94 MR21,Harris

WRIGHT,Claude Russell Lt kia 21-5-17 5Suff attMGC p188&217 CR France646

WRIGHT,Crossley 2Lt kia 21-11-17 2/6WRid p227 MR17

WRIGHT,Cyril Paul T2Lt kldacc 25-5-16 7RWKent att55/2TMB p142 CR France169,25-6-16

WRIGHT,Donald Samuel T2Lt dow 25-4-17 1 att8Beds p87

WRIGHT,Edmund Capt kia 3-7-16 6RWSurr p57 CR France251

WRIGHT,Edmund Lancelot T2Lt dow 16-7-16 7KSLI p145 CR France66,Capt

WRIGHT,Edward Dearden Lt kia 21-3-18 1/4ELancs p226 MR27

WRIGHT,Edward Frank Macer 2Lt kia 2-4-17 4NumbF p213 CR France1182

WRIGHT,Edward Martin Capt kia 10-4-17 5ELancs p226 MR20

WRIGHT,Edwin Capt kia 17-11-14 3DragGds p21 CR Belgium57

WRIGHT,Edwin George Englesby T2Lt kia 16-6-16 7SomLI p80 CR Belgium4

WRIGHT,Edwin Stanley T2Lt kia 3-7-16 7Suff p79 CR France393

WRIGHT,Egerton Lowndes.MC.CaptBdeMaj kia 11-5-18 O&BLI BucksBn p231 CR France749

WRIGHT,Eric Alfred TLt ded 21-6-15 RAMC p198 CR Egypt3

WRIGHT,Eric Tracey TCapt kia 13-3-16 20RFus p71 CR France114

WRIGHT,Ernest Granville Col ded 27-7-19 IA Staff p284

WRIGHT,Francis Beattie Lt 12-4-18 RFA &10RFC

WRIGHT,Francis John.MID Capt ded 26-9-19 SL attStaff p268 CR France457

WRIGHT,Frederick 2Lt kia 12-4-17 2/5Lincs p220 CR France1494

WRIGHT,Frederick Adams T2Lt kia 19-9-17 DCLI att9RFC p15&115 CR Belgium18

WRIGHT,Frederick Charles 2Lt kia 14-4-18 18Mddx p149 CR France324

WRIGHT,Frederick John T2Lt dow 4-8-17 1/8Lpool p73 CR Belgium7

WRIGHT,Frederick Wilfred TLtCol ded ??? RASC p267

WRIGHT,George 2Lt dow 19-9-16 1/6Lpool p215 CR France40,Georges

WRIGHT,George Bertram 2Lt kia 11-10-18 1RFus p71 CR France270

WRIGHT,George Clinton 2Lt kia 10-3-15 2Dev p77 CR France279

WRIGHT,George Darling Maj ded 26-5-20 IA 2/70BurmaRif p284 CR Hamps64,98Inf

WRIGHT,George Drennan Cron 2Lt kia 23-10-14 2Beds p87 CR Belgium157

WRIGHT,George Edward.MC.2Lt kia 9-10-18 RASC attRGA 276SB p194 CR France1355

WRIGHT,George William 2Lt kia 24-3-18 7Leic p88 MR27

WRIGHT,G.H.Lt ded 15-9-17 Cps of Guides CR Canada740

WRIGHT,Guy Powell 2Lt kia 2-7-18 9 att1Mddx p236 CR France745

WRIGHT,Hannah Elizabeth SNurse ded 22-10-18 QAIMNS p200 CR Italy12

WRIGHT,Harold TCapt dow 14-9-15 6LNLancs p137 CR Leic119

WRIGHT,Harold Ivan Lt kia 8-11-17 4EYorks p219 MR20

WRIGHT,Harold Reginald Lt dow 16-9-18 5WYorks p218 CR France34

WRIGHT,Harry Stevenson.CMG.LtCol ded 1-10-19 RASC p267 CR Hamps 64,30-9-19

WRIGHT,Harry William 2Lt kia 19-12-15 1GordH p167 CR Belgium21

WRIGHT,Henry Gordon Capt kia 6-6-15 8N&D p233 CR Belgium17

WRIGHT,Henry Gordon T2Lt kia 9-4-17 5 att11Mddx p149 CR France96

WRIGHT,Henry Thomas Richard Somerset Capt kld 21-12-16 Manch p156 CR EAfrica116

WRIGHT,Herbert Melville T2Lt kia 2-4-17 2Yorks p91 CR France1186

WRIGHT,Horace William 2Lt kia 3-5-17 7Mddx p235 MR20

WRIGHT,Howard Caldwell.MC.Capt dow 2-9-17 1/17Lond p250 CR Belgium18

WRIGHT,Hugh Stafford Northcote Capt kia 30-10-14 IA 2/8GurkhaRif p284 MR28

WRIGHT,James William Lt kia 10-10-17 5WRid p227 MR30

WRIGHT,John 2Lt kia 4-11-18 18NumbF att8NStaffs p64 CR France940

WRIGHT,John Armer.MC.Lt kia 18-9-18 11 att7RSuss p120 CR France369

WRIGHT,John Crosby Lt kia 10-4-17 RGA p209 MR20

WRIGHT,John George William 2Lt kia 11-5-17 2Lond p245 CR France646,1Bn

WRIGHT,John Major Stanley 2Lt kia 24-2-17 157RFA p37 CR Belgium23,Lt 24-2-18

WRIGHT,John Shilvock 2Lt kia 7-11-18 RGA 219SB p42 CR Belgium143

WRIGHT,Joseph Benjamin 2Lt kia 21-4-16 2DLI p162 MR29

WRIGHT,Joseph Herbert.MC.Capt kia 25-3-18 8Glouc p107 MR20

WRIGHT,Matthew John T2Lt kia 1-7-16 14RIrRif p170 MR21

WRIGHT,Neil James Robert 2Lt kia 15-9-14 15RFA p37 CR France1329

WRIGHT,Noel Tracey LtTCapt dow 1-10-15 3 att2Yorks p91 CR France257

WRIGHT,Norman George T2Lt kia 13-7-16 9RWSurr p57 MR21

WRIGHT,Norman Stanley T2Lt kia 15-9-16 26RFus p71 MR21

WRIGHT,Oscar Capt ded 13-10-17 IARO 31Punjabis attPoliticDept p284 MR66

WRIGHT,Percival Edward 2Lt kia 24-4-18 RFA p209 CR France144

WRIGHT,Percy Andrew T2Lt kld 21-12-16 GL &RFC p4&192,ded CR War7,TLt

WRIGHT,Peter.MC.Maj kia 11-1-18 B186 RHFA p37&258 CR Belgium10

WRIGHT,Reuben.DSO.TCapt dow 17-8-17 7YLI p144 CR Belgium16

WRIGHT,Richard Bertram 2Lt kia 8-7-18 RFus att1/6WYorks p71 CR Belgium188

WRIGHT,Richard Connett 2Lt kia 19-8-18 9 att3RB p181 MR16

WRIGHT,Robert T2Lt kia 7-11-17 18RIrRif attRIrF p170 CR Palestine8

WRIGHT,Robert Maj kia 29-11-17 1/1LincsYeo p204 CR Palestine9

WRIGHT,Robert Kenneth.MC.LtACapt kia 29-9-18 6Beds att2Worc p87 CR France665

WRIGHT,Robert Taylor 2Lt kia 1-11-17 4 att15N&D p135 CR Belgium106

WRIGHT,Samuel Donald 2Lt dow 25-4-17 1 att8Beds CR France8

WRIGHT,Samuel King TLt kia 7/11-8-15 8WRid p116 MR4

WRIGHT,Sidney Harry TLtACapt ded 10-2-19 LabCps att114ChineseLabCo p189 CR France113

WRIGHT,Stamford Walter Seppings Lt kia 9-9-16 1ConnRgrs p172 CR France294

WRIGHT,Stanley.MC.2Lt kia 24-10-17 RE attRFC 21KiteBalloonSect p15&49 MR20

WRIGHT,Sydney John 2Lt kia 23-8-18 Ess p133 CR France281

WRIGHT,T.Maj 19-12-18 attRASC CR Kent7

WRIGHT,Theodore.VC.Capt kia 14-9-14 RE p49 CR France1107

WRIGHT,Thomas 2Lt kia 1-5-15 RBerks att2Bn p140 CR France1158

WRIGHT,Thomas T2Lt kia 13-10-15 1/5Lincs p76&258 MR19

WRIGHT,Victor Albert 2Lt kia 15-4-18 10RWar p66 MR30

WRIGHT,Vivian Arthur Butler T2Lt kia 3-12-15 12Ess att6Lincs p133 CR Gallipoli4,2-12-15

WRIGHT,W.LtCol 13-5-16 RASC CR Kent91

WRIGHT,Walter Horace 2Lt kia 21-3-18 1WYorks p83 MR20

WRIGHT,Walter Tom Crosby Lt kia 8-8-18 2TankCps p189 MR16

WRIGHT,Walter Whitmore 2Lt kia 23-8-17 RGA 276SB p42 CR Belgium19

WRIGHT,Walter Herbert LtCol ded 8-11-15 1/4YLI Res p254&258 CR Yorks361

WRIGHT,Wilfred Eric Capt ded 3-11-18 5SStaffs p272 CR War1

WRIGHT,William TLt kia 7-7-16 6KOSB p102 CR France630

WRIGHT,William 2Lt kia 17-2-17 2SStaffs p123 CR France239
WRIGHT,William 2Lt kia 22-3-18 4GordH p242 MR20
WRIGHT,William 2Lt kia 8-8-18 RFA 175ArmyBde p37 CR France196
WRIGHT,William Clifford TLt kia 10/12-7-16 17RWFus p99 MR21
WRIGHT,William Edward Bellyse TLt kia 22-9-15 7YLI p144 CR France525
WRIGHT,William Gerald 2Lt dow 8-6-17 8Hamps p229 CR Belgium11
WRIGHT,William Joseph T2Lt kia 17-5-16 9Leic p88 CR France745
WRIGHT,William Lake 2Lt kia 20-10-18 17RSuss p120 CR France1054
WRIGHT,William Richardson 2Lt kia 20-4-16 1/4Lincs p217 MR20
WRIGHT,William Sidney 2Lt kia 21-3-18 9Norf p74 MR20
WRIGHT-INGLE,Cecil Hubert T2Lt kia 30-4-16 19RFus att2Leinst p71 CR Belgium49
WRIGLEY,Henry Neville 2Lt ded 30-8-17 RFA 53DAC p209 CR Egypt2,Harry
WRIGLEY,James 2Lt kia 29-9-17 RGA 289SB p42 CR Belgium102
WRIGLEY,Joseph Lt kia 1-7-16 1/5Y&L p238 MR21
WRIGLEY,Leonard Gordon 2Lt kia 9-10-17 2/9Manch p237 CR Belgium125
WRIGLEY,Percy Bernard 2Lt kia 23-3-18 RE 518FC p210 MR20
WRIGLEY,Ralph Mortimer Lt ded 6-11-18 RE 3RlyCoy attRMon Eng p49 CR France52
WRIGLEY,Willoughby Thornton.MC.MID Capt kld 15-8-20 C'Coy 5Wilts CR Iraq8
WRINCH,Harry Durrill TLt dow 20-8-16 BBty 115BdeRFA p37 CR Greece6
WRINCH,Stanley 2Lt kia 8-5-15 3Suff p79 MR29
WRIXON,Arthur Henry TLt kia 2-6-16 13 att11Suff p79 CR France515
WROE,Wilfred Dent TLt kia 13-10-15 10Lincs p76 CR France515,29-6-16
WRONG,Colin Bassett.MC.Lt kia 28-12-17 6RMunstF p176 CR Palestine3
WRONG,Harold Verschoyle Lt kia 1-7-16 15LancF p94 MR21
WROTH,Walter Adams Lt kia 31-5-18 SL &2/4KAR p202 CR EAfrica90
WROUGHTON,Herbert T2Lt kia 8-12-17 12Norf p74 CR Palestine3
WROUGHTON,John Henry Theodore Lt dow 9-5-18 RE 136Co p49 CR France100
WROUGHTON,Musgrave Cazenove.MID 2Lt dow 31-10-14 12Lancers p22 CR Belgium186,30-10-14
WROUGHTON,Philip Musgrave Neeld TMaj kia 19-4-17 1/1BerksYeo p203 CR Palestine8
WYAND,Edward Herbert TCapt kia 30-1-16 16KRRC D'Coy p152 CR France114
WYATT,Alfred John Lt kia 23-10-18 1 att8ScotRif p104 CR France190
WYATT,Arthur Thomas Elford Capt ded 19-2-17 3 att1Lincs p76 CR Lincs142
WYATT,Edwin Wellington 2Lt ded 21-6-19 IA TC attRGA 4MtnBty p284 MR43
WYATT,Esdaile Frederick Burkett.MID TCapt kia 8-1-16 2SLancs &MGC p126&186 CR Belgium28
WYATT,Felix Capt kia 2-7-17 5Suff &RFC p217 CR France439
WYATT,Francis Ogilvy.MVO.LtCol ded 16-12-19 RGA p262 MR43 &CR Pakistan50A
WYATT,Geoffrey Wilfred Penfold 2Lt kia 15-9-16 1EKent p58 MR21 CR France1890
WYATT,Godfrey Louis 2Lt dow 24-5-15 6LancF p221 CR Gallipoli1
WYATT,Henry Edward T2Lt kia 19-1-17 40MGC Inf p186 MR38
WYATT,H.G.P.Lt 12-11-15 1SussYeo CR Egypt3
WYATT,John 2Lt dow 25-10-18 4Glouc p225 CR France292
WYATT,Samuel John Livesley 2Lt kia 23-4-17 18Manch p156 MR20
WYATT,William Herbert 2LtTLt kia 4-5-16 1EYorks p85 CR France188
WYATT,William John T2Lt dow 26-10-17 8Dev p77 CR Belgium11,29-10-17
WYATT-SMITH,John Drummond TLt kia 17-3-18 28RFC p17 CR Italy48
WYBORN,Walter Samuel Lt ded 6-2-19 4RInnisKF p264 CR Sussex185
WYBRANTS,John Holman 2Lt dow 30-7-18 3 att7Lond p246 CR France13
WYKES,Ernest Arthur Inns T2Lt kia 30-11-17 5RBerks p140 MR17
WYKES,Herbert Ivie TCapt dow 30-9-15 6Wilts p153 CR France145
WYLD,Cyril Garnet.MID T2Lt kia 5-7-16 9Yorks p91 MR21
WYLD,George Richard Capt kia 24-12-14 3Wilts attRBerks p153 CR France260,att1RBucksHuss
WYLDE,G.Maj ded 1-1-21 2SStaffs CR War7
WYLDE,Thomas Edgar Lt dow 27-6-17 4Norf attRFC p20&216 CR France113
WYLEY,Francis John Capt dow 23-4-15 1YLI p144 CR Belgium151
WYLEY,William Reginald FitzThomas Lt&Adjt kia 19-9-16 RFA p208 CR France251
WYLIE,Alan Lindsay.MC.T2Lt kia 20-11-17 GL &RFC p15 CR France379
WYLIE,Arrol Edmiston 2Lt kia 18-1-18 56RFC p17 MR20
WYLIE,Arthur William Lt kia 10/16-3-15 2Lincs p76 CR France525,10-3-15
WYLIE,Hamilton MacLaren T2Lt kia 7-1-16 SfthH p165 MR38
WYLIE,J.R.2Lt kld 23-4-18 RDubF &RAF p177
WYLIE,Percival Thomas Lt ded 27-4-19 ArmyPayDept p200 CR Asia81
WYLIE,Robert Downie Capt kia 23-8-17 3 att6CamH p168 CR Belgium7

WYLIE,William Gladstone.MC&Bar.Lt kia 28-3-18 9DLI p239 MR20
WYLIE,William Stanley Lt dow 10-5-15 3Y&L p160 MR29
WYLLIE,Alexander Capt ded 18-4-17 RScotF attEgyptArmy p95 CR EAfrica116
WYLLIE,Andrew Inglis Capt kia 2-9-18 4RScotF attTankCps p189&222 CR France614
WYLLIE,Hugh Alexander 2Lt kia 3-9-16 1/7WYorks p218 CR France252
WYLLIE,Hugh Tweed Walford Capt kia 24-5-15 4DragGds p21 MR29
WYLLIE,Hugh William TLt kia 26-10-16 7ELancs p111 MR21
WYLLIE,William W.Lt ded 6-4-17 LanarkYeo p272 CR Greece6,10-4-17
WYLLIE,William Thomas.MID Capt kia 19-7-16 1DLI p162 CR France397
WYLLY,Edward Vesey TLt ded 17-1-18 SL att2/3KAR p268 CR Tanzania1
WYNDHAM,George Heremon 2Lt kia 24-3-15 3Dev attNumbF p77 CR Belgium98
WYNDHAM,Percy Lyulph Lt kia 14-9-14 CldGds p51 MR15
WYNDHAM,William Reginald.Hon.Lt kia 6-11-14 LincsYeo att1LifeGds p20&272 CR Belgium134
WYNN,Arthur Ernest T2Lt dow 1-11-16 PoW GL &RFC p4&192 MR20
WYNN,Richard Alexander 2Lt kia 14-4-15 Norf p74 CR Iraq6
WYNN,William Alfred Lt ded 28-7-19 8Mddx p256 CR Iraq8
WYNNE,Arnold T2Lt kia 8-4-17 13Lpool B'Coy p73 CR France581,9-4-17
WYNNE,Charles Wyndham T2LtACapt dow 26-6-17 RGA 182SB p42 CR France134,24-6-17
WYNNE,Edward Ernest Capt kia 8-6-17 1/5Leic p220 CR France161
WYNNE,Edward Henry John Lt dow 16-9-16 3GrenGds p50 CR France66
WYNNE,Eric Ralph Lovatt Capt kia 26-10-18 IA 1/10GurkhaRif p284 MR38
WYNNE,Francis George.DSO.Maj kia 10-4-18 9LNLancs att1Wilts p137 MR32,2Bn
WYNNE,Gerald Mansfield Lt ded 22-10-19 RE 455FC p262 CR Germany1,Gerard
WYNNE,Maurice Okeover Mostyn Lt dow 28-8-15 132/1RFA p37 CR France922
WYNNE,Maurice St.Clair Patrick.DCM.MID Lt dow 11-10-18 1/2RInnisKF p106 CR France398
WYNNE,William 2Lt kia 7-2-16 IARO att90Punjabis p284 MR38
WYNNE-JONES,Morys Lt kia 29-10-14 RE 36Co p49 MR29
WYNNE-WILLIAMS,Humphrey Evan T2Lt kia 30-3-16 10RWFus p99 CR Belgium15
WYNSTONE-WATERS,E.Capt 26-8-18 EAMS CR EAfrica52
WYNTER,Cecil Domville Lt dow 5-10-15 IrGds att2Bn p53 CR Leic24
WYNTER,Francis Constantine William Capt kia 22-11-15 O&BLI p130 MR38
WYNTER,Hugh Talbot.MID Maj kia 15-9-14 22/34RFA p37 CR France1329
WYNTER,Philip Cecil Capt dow 20-4-15 1ESurr p113 CR Belgium127
WYNYARD,Damer.MID TCapt&Adjt kia 20-4-15 1ESurr p113 MR29
WYPER,James 2Lt kia 23-7-18 7/8KOSB p102 CR France865
WYPER,James Stewart TLt dow 8-9-16 7/8KOSB p102 CR France145
WYTHES,Claude Aspinall Capt kia 28-4-15 4Worc p110 MR4
WYVILL,Marmaduke Ibbetson TMaj ded 6-3-16 RB p181 CR Yorks138

Y

YALLAND,William Stanley Lt kia 23-10-14 Glouc p107 MR29
YANDLE,Thomas T2Lt kia 10-4-17 13RFus p71 MR20
YANESKE,Walter T2Lt kia 30-7-16 8Glouc p107 MR21
YAPP,William Clarence 2Lt kia 7-8-15 5LancF p221 MR4
YARDE,John Tristram.MC&Bar.MIDx2 Capt dow 21-9-18 1/5Beds p219 CR Palestine9
YARDLEY,Eric Barnes 2Lt dow 20-7-17 5YLI p235 CR Sussex111
YARDLEY,Frederick George T2Lt dow 17-9-15 8NStaffs p158 CR France8,Frederic
YARDLEY,Frank T2Lt kia 7-8-17 246MGC p186 MR29
YARDLEY,William 2Lt dow 30-4-17 9Ess p133 MR20
YARROW,Eric Fernandez.MID 2Lt kia 8-5-15 7A&SH p243 CR Belgium73
YARROW,Henry Edwin Goodwin 2Lt kia 30-7-16 2KOSB p103 MR21
TATE,Charles Allix Lavington.VC.Maj ded PoW 20-9-14 2YLI p144 CR Germany4
YATES,Alec James.DCM.2Lt kia 28-3-18 4MGC DivBn p186 MR20
YATES,Arthur Gerald Vavasour 2Lt kia 1-7-16 16Lond p250 MR21
YATES,Charles Cecil TLt kia 15-5-16 9LNLancs p137 CR France68,16-5-16
YATES,Francis William Capt dow 25-4-15 3 att2YLI p144 CR Shrop111
YATES,Frank Dutton T2Lt kia 15-4-17 13Mddx p149 MR20
YATES,Frederick T2Lt kia 30-11-17 2Hamps p121 CR France910
YATES,George Herbert TLt ded 15-2-19 ArmyPayDept HQ 4Army p200 CR France34
YATES,James Stanley 2Lt kia 8-10-15 3 att6RWKent p142 MR19
YATES,John Carrington Lt kia 21-3-18 160RFA p208 MR20
YATES,John Edwin T2Lt kia 1-11-17 70RFC p15 CR Belgium18

YATES,Richard 2Lt kld 11-2-16 14 RFC p4 CR Egypt3
YATES,Richard 2Lt kia 24-4-18 1EYorks p85 MR30
YATES,Robert Charles Byam Capt mbk 20-10-14 IA 1/4GurkhaRif p284 MR28
YATES,Samuel Benjamin 2Lt kia 22-12-17 10 att8Manch p237 CR France80
YATES,William Grandage.MID 2Lt kia 9-1-17 1Manch p156 CR Iraq5
YATMAN,Dennistoun Hamilton Lt kia 11-4-18 1NumbF p64 MR19 &CR France1896
YAXLEY,Charles William T2Lt dow 23-4-17 8Dev p77 CR France518
YEAMAN,Charles Henry 2Lt ded 15-9-16 7DLI p239 CR Durham8
YEAMAN,Denis John T2Lt kia 5/10-10-16 24KRRC p152 CR France374
YEAMAN,Keith Sanger Capt ded 5-6-18 RFA p207 CR Camb16,Maj
YEARSLEY,Hubert Abram 2Lt kia 9-4-18 RE 79FC p49 CR France490
YEARWOOD,Carleton Douglas T2Lt kia 16-8-17 YLI att7Bn p144 CR Belgium152
YEATES,Stanley Charles Lt kia 14-4-17 16Lond B'Coy p250 MR20
YEATHERD,Motagu Locke Capt kia 11-4-17 12Lancers p22 CR France162
YEATHERD,Raymond Gilbert Hooker.MID Lt kia 15-9-16 2DragGds p21 MR21
YEATMAN,Bernard Joseph Pym Lt kia 23-10-18 9Dev p77 CR France231,2Lt
YEATMAN,Harry Farr Capt kia 21-11-17 DorsYeo p203 CR Palestine3
YEATMAN,Marwood Edwards Capt ded 15-9-14 1SWBord p101 MR15
YELD,Cyril de Clare Lt ded 24-10-18 IARO attS&TCps p284 MR43
YELL,Reuben Harold T2Lt kia 9-3-18 GL &16RFC p17 CR France95
YELLAND,Edward Jonathan 2Lt 15-12-16 4 att2WRid MR21
YELLEN,Cyril Francis T2Lt kia 30-11-17 RFus att 17Bn p71 MR17
YEO,Everard Lisle T2Lt dow 7-10-16 36MGC Inf p186 CR France833
YEO,Frederick George T2Lt kia 26-10-16 8RWKent p142 CR France149,27-10-16 Ex HAC
YEO,Hubert Claud Cater T2Lt kia 24-8-17 6DCLI p115 MR30
YEO,James Frederick Jesse 2Lt kia 1-8-17 11HLI p164 MR29
YEO,Leslie Farquhar Lt dow 10-3-15 2SStaffs p123 CR France80,kia
YEOMAN,Bryan Frank Lawson 2Lt ded 11-5-18 1/4Lond &RAF p246&258,Lt kia CR Oxford97
YEOMANS,Howard William Capt kia 8-10-17 2/1Hereford attMGC p188&252 CR Belgium96,Haywood
YEOMANS,Walter Joseph George T2Lt kia 8-4-17 5KSLI D'Coy p145 CR France581,9-4-17
YEWDALL,Frederick George Lt ded 18-5-18 20DLI p162 CR Durham19
YIRRELL,Percy Tom Wilson 2Lt dow 30-3-17 B240RFA p209 CR France511
YONGE,Geoffrey Bowen 2Lt dow 21-11-18 1/5Dev p77 CR France146
YORATH,Glynne Lougher TLt kia 23-11-17 12SWBord p101 MR17
YORKE,Charles Henry T2Lt kia 7-10-16 11RWKent p142 CR France385
YORKE,David 2LtTLt kia 17-2-15 RLancs p59
YORKE,Frederick Lt kld 13-1-19 6Ches attRAF p256 CR Durham26
YORKE,James Hamilton Langdon.MC.Capt kia 27-12-17 PembrokeYeo p205 CR Palestine3,24WelshR
YORKE-JONES,Kenrick T2Lt kia 26-12-17 17Manch p156 CR Belgium126
YORKE-LODGE,Bryant Wynne.MC.2Lt kia 14-9-16 3 att12LancF p94 MR37
YOUDALE,Alfred Clarence.MC&2Bars.2LtACapt kia 23-12-17 SR 21RFC p15 MR20
YOUDEN,Sidney Edwin Capt kia 27-8-18 1DLI att1/7HLI p162 MR16
YOUENS,Frederick.VC.T2Lt dow 7-7-17 13DLI p162 CR Belgium127
YOULL,John Scott.VC.2Lt kia 27-10-18 11NumbF p64 CR Italy7
YOUNG,Ada Elizabeth Nurse 15-7-18 VAD CR Notts70
YOUNG,Alan Catchpole 2Lt kia 24-3-18 5Lond p246 MR27,Catchpool
YOUNG,Alan Edward Frushard 2Lt kia 25-7-17 RGA p42 CR Belgium24
YOUNG,Alan Emilius 2Lt kia 25-9-15 1/20Lond p251 MR19
YOUNG,Albert Maj dow 14-12-14 IA 2/1GurkhaRif attHQ GarhwalRif p284
YOUNG,Albert Meredyth Lt kia 3-3-16 IARO 16Cav p284 CR Iraq ,3-3-15
YOUNG,Alexander Aytoun 2Lt dow 14-3-17 3 att2BlkW p129 MR38
YOUNG,Alfred Gordon 2Lt ded 31-12-16 3/5RWKent p235 CR France787
YOUNG,Andrew 2Lt kia 27-12-16 3ScotRif att13RScots p104 CR France392
YOUNG,Andrew Gardyne Lt kld 13-10-17 1/6A&SH p243 CR Belgium165
YOUNG,Andrew Yates T2Lt kia 30-9-15 13ScotRif att2RScotF p104 MR19
YOUNG,Archibald Lt kia 28-6-15 4RScots A'Coy p211 MR4
YOUNG,Arthur Maj 14-12-14 1GurkhaRif CR France202
YOUNG,Arthur Cecil TCapt kia 6-7-16 16NumbF p64 MR21,1-7-16
YOUNG,Arthur Conway 2Lt kia 16-8-17 4 att7/8RIrFus p172 CR Belgium125
YOUNG,Arthur Cyril 2Lt kia 2-4-17 8RFC p15 CR France120
YOUNG,Arthur Ernest 2Lt dow 21-5-18 D108RFA p209 CR France196
YOUNG,Arthur John 2Lt dow 10-3-18 1 att7SWBord p101 CR Palestine3,1SWB att7RWFus
YOUNG,Arthur Webster TMaj kia 13-9-15 10N&D p135 CR Belgium6

YOUNG,Benjamin Poyntz TCapt ded 6-11-16 RAMC p198 CR Ireland14
YOUNG,Bertrand John 2Lt kia 5-10-18 5RWar B'Coy p214 CR France375,6Bn
YOUNG,C.Lt ded 20-7-18 GL &RAF p192
YOUNG,Charles Alan 2Lt kia 14-10-18 D256RFA p37 CR France241
YOUNG,Charles Edward Lt ded 17-12-18 MilLabCps CR EAfrica36
YOUNG,Claude Norman T2Lt dow 14-7-16 12RScots p55 MR21
YOUNG,Colin Turner.MID Capt kia 24-4-17 3WRid att17WelshR p116 CR France439
YOUNG,Cyril Rutherford Moffat Maj dow 1-7-17 RGA p209 CR Durham181
YOUNG,David Coley.MID LtCol kia 12-3-15 IA 2/4 att1/4GurkhaRif p284 CR France632
YOUNG,David Goldie TLt kia 25-9-15 10ScotRif p104 MR19
YOUNG,David Lindsay 2Lt kia 26-10-17 4NumbF p213 MR30
YOUNG,David William Laird T2Lt kia 6-1-17 GL 53RFC p15 CR France285
YOUNG,Douglas Campbell Lt ded 18-9-15 RFA p208 CR Egypt3
YOUNG,Edmund Taylor Lt kia 10-6-15 6Manch p236 MR4
YOUNG,Edward Thomas Capt dedacc 14-3-18 LabCps att6ChineseLabCoy p189 CR France134
YOUNG,Eric Templeton Capt kia 28-6-15 6ScotRif p224 MR22
YOUNG,Ernest Joseph 2Lt ded 7-11-18 Mddx att 18Bn p149 CR France398
YOUNG,Fergus Hay TLt drd 23-10-15 RAMC att29DivAmmCol p198
YOUNG,Francis Chisholm.MID 2Lt kia 14-2-17 3RFC p15 MR20
YOUNG,Frank Edward.VC.2Lt kia 18-9-18 1Herts p252 CR France530
YOUNG,Frank Irwin 2Lt kia 24/25-7-16 1NumbF p64 CR France399
YOUNG,Frederick Dobell Lt dow 6-8-17 RGA p209 CR Belgium12
YOUNG,Frederick Henry.MC&Bar.LtACapt dow 25-8-18 3 att1Lincs p76 CR France131
YOUNG,Frederick Sydney Newman.MIDx2 CaptAMaj ded 1-3-18 RASC p194 CR Iraq8
YOUNG,Geoffrey Abbott 2Lt kia 4-3-17 3Nhampt att24TMB p138 CR France439
YOUNG,George Arnold Lt kia 4-10-17 50RFA p37 MR30
YOUNG,George Cooper T2Lt kia 17-3-18 GL &5RFC p17 CR France95
YOUNG,George Edward Savill Maj dow 31-3-17 1IrGds p53 CR France105
YOUNG,George James Taylor 2Lt kia 20-11-17 15RFC p15 CR France379
YOUNG,George Minchin Capt ded 10-3-16 RASC p194 CR France924
YOUNG,George Neville Gardiner.MC.Lt dow 25-7-15 2Leinst p175 CR France64,Patrick
YOUNG,George Walter Capt kia 27-5-18 8EYorks p85 MR18
YOUNG,George William Capt drd 26-2-18 RAMC p198 MR40
YOUNG,George William Lt dow 8-4-18 PoW 4BlkW p230 CR France934
YOUNG,Harold Farquhar 2Lt kia 20-8-17 3 att9N&D att43RFC p15&135 MR20
YOUNG,Harold Victor 2Lt dow 8-12-17 54RFC p15 CR France1359
YOUNG,Harry Capt ded 4-3-19 RGA p209 CR Belgium396
YOUNG,Henry Harman 2Lt kia 24-5-15 3RFus p255 p263 MR29
YOUNG,Herbert Nugent.DSO.MajALtCol kia 25-10-18 7RInniskF att11N&D p106 CR France231
YOUNG,Hugh Hutchinson 2Lt kia 26-5-18 6SfthH p241 CR France324,7Bn
YOUNG,Hugh Roxburgh Maj dow 21-4-17 1/4RScotF p222 CR Egypt2
YOUNG,James Lt kia 5-4-18 RE 258Co p49 CR France144
YOUNG,James 2Lt kia 24-8-18 5DLI p239 CR France314
YOUNG,James Alexander Y.Lt ded 12-8-15 8Hamps p229 MR4
YOUNG,James Cecil 2Lt kia 6-4-18 7RFus p71 CR France252
YOUNG,James Hill 2Lt dow PoW 17-1-18 14Lond attRFC p20&249 CR France441,Lt
YOUNG,James Logie.MC.Lt kia 19-7-18 8BlkW B'Coy p129&259 CR France324
YOUNG,James Vincent T2Lt kia 1-7-16 9 att8SomLI B'Coy p80 CR France267
YOUNG,John Lt kia 9-6-17 13DLI p162 CR Belgium28
YOUNG,John Lt ded 10-1-20 5HLI p272
YOUNG,John Arthur Capt kia 4-10-17 17N&D p135 MR21
YOUNG,John Edward Rostron T2Lt kld 7-7-17 GL attRFC p15 CR Essex84
YOUNG,John Edwards 2Lt 10-1-20 5HLI attIA CR Scot674
YOUNG,John Erskine Capt kia 24-8-14 RScotF p95 CR Belgium206
YOUNG,John Ferrers Harington LtTCapt kia 1-7-16 3 att1RLancs p59 CR France643
YOUNG,John Haddow 2Lt dow 9-6-18 NumbF att5Bn p64 CR France1437
YOUNG,John Stevenson T2Lt kld 3-2-18 RFC p17 CR Scot87
YOUNG,Leonard George Birmingham 2Lt kia 19-5-16 10Ches p97 MR20
YOUNG,Leslie Alexander Capt kia 21-5-16 20Lond p251 CR France924
YOUNG,Leslie Duncan 2Lt kia 7-10-17 2/7Manch p237 MR30
YOUNG,Lucian Albert 2Lt dow 26-10-18 1SomLI p80 CR France646,Lt
YOUNG,Malcolm Henry Lt kia 29-6-16 5LancF p221 CR France1512

YOUNG,Marcus Ernest 2Lt kia 21-3-18 RFA att X58TMB p37 CR France1893,24-3-18

YOUNG,Martin Cortlandt de Budé T2Lt dow 26-9-15 7KOSB p103 CR France178

YOUNG,Mary Ann Eliza ded 13-2-19 VAD att57GH p200 CR France1571

YOUNG,Margaret Cameron Nurse ded 30-7-18 VAD 2GH p200 CR France34

YOUNG,Mervyn Cyril Nicholas Radford 2Lt dow 25-5-15 RDubF p177 CR France200

YOUNG,Nevill Lindsay 2Lt kia 20-8-16 2RSuss p120 CR France402

YOUNG,Norman Mitchell Lt kia 25-4-15 RScots p55 CR Belgium4,23-4-15

YOUNG,Phillip Lt dow 21-8-18 6Mddx att31MGC p149&186 CR Surrey2,MGC attMddx

YOUNG,Philip Mortlock.MID Lt kia 10-3-15 3 att1Lpool p73 MR22

YOUNG,Reginald James.MC.Capt ded 14-2-19 2Mddx p265

YOUNG,Robert Asshelon 2Lt kia 21-12-14 RMunstF p176

YOUNG,Robert Percival.MC.Lt kia 17-12-17 1/4RSuss p228 CR Palestine3

YOUNG,Roger Assheton 2Lt 22-12-14 2RMunstF MR22

YOUNG,Rowdon Morris T2Lt kia 11-8-16 13RFus p71 CR France1890,Rawdon

YOUNG,Samuel Kenneth 2Lt kia 30-11-17 1LondIrRif p250 MR17

YOUNG,Stanley James Lt kld 23-12-17 RFC p15 CR Hamps57

YOUNG,Sydney Vernon 2Lt dow 25-9-15 RE 56FC p49 MR29

YOUNG,Thomas James.MM.2Lt kia 24-9-17 Mddx att1Bn p149 MR30

YOUNG,Wilfred Henry 2Lt dow 30-5-15 1/6Glouc p225 CR Belgium68,Wilfrid

YOUNG,William TLt kia 22-8-17 7CamH p168 MR30

YOUNG,William Alexander.MC.Capt dow 10-6-18 2BlkW p129 CR Palestine9

YOUNG,William Nicholas 2Lt kia 9-9-16 3RScotF p95 CR France727

YOUNG,William Steele Lt kia 2-11-17 RE att412FC p210 CR Palestine8

YOUNG,William Thomas Lt kia 12-7-17 RGA 12HB p209 CR Belgium6

YOUNG-FULLALOVE,George T2Lt kia 13-8-17 55RFC p15

YOUNG-HERRIES,Alexander Dobrée Capt kia 22-7-16 KOSB p103 CR France397,23-7-16

YOUNGE,Frederick George Patrick Lt dow 14-2-15 2Leinst p175 CR France284

YOUNGER,Charles Frierson Lt dow 21-3-17 Loth&BordHorse p204 CR France251,Frearson

YOUNGER,David George T2Lt kia 1-7-16 17HLI p164 CR France293

YOUNGER,John Malcolm Capt ded 31-8-18 CldGds p262 CR Scot608

YOUNGER,John Ramsay T2Lt kia 6-5-16 15LancF p94 CR France251

YOUNGHUSBAND,Harold.DSO.TLtCol kia 20-4-16 Beds Cmdg7Glouc p87 MR38,21-4-16

YOUNGMAN,John Marshall.MC.TLt kia 23-6-16 9ESurr p113 CR Belgium97

YOUNGS,James William Lt dow 12-4-18 3SStaffs att151MGC p123&186 CR France25,John

YULE,Charles Whitehead TCapt kia 11-5-16 13RScots p55 CR France423

YULE,George Udney.DSO.LtCol ded 22-12-18 RE p49 MR65

YULE,John Carmichael.MC.Lt dow 25-12-17 2GordH p167 CR France512

YULE,Louis William.MID 2Lt kia 29-9-15 RFC p2 CR Belgium82,26-9-15

Z

ZACHARIAS,Francis Herbert 2Lt kia 25-9-16 3 att1SWBord p101 MR21

ZACHARIUS-JESSEL,Victor Albert Villiers 2Lt kia 6-4-17 7 att15DLI p239 MR20,Lt

ZEALLEY,Eric Ralph Lt 30-8-18 Lancs attRAF CR France788

ZEDER,Joseph Herbert 2Lt dow PoW 3-7-16 4 O&BLI p231 CR France924,2Bn

ZEEDENBERG Eric 2Lt 20-7-16 20RFus MR21 Served as COVENTRY

ZEIGLER,Philip Harold T2Lt dow 23-9-16 9 att6EKent p58 CR France46,kia

ZELLAND,Edward Jonathan 2Lt kia 15-12-16 4WRid p227

ZIANI de FERRANTI,Basil.MC.TLtAMaj dow 12-7-17 RGA 21SB p42

ZIGOMALA,John Copeland.MBE.Lt kld 25-8-19 IrGds attRE p255 MR70 &CR Europe179

APPENDIX 1

A list of the memorials and cemeteries mentioned in the list of officers.

Memorials

MR4	Helles Memorial, Gallipoli.
MR15	La Ferte-Sous-Jouarre Memorial, France.
MR16	Vis-En-Artois Memorial, France.
MR17	Cambrai Memorial France.
MR18	Soissons Memorial, France.
MR19	Loos Memorial, France.
MR20	Arras Memorial, France.
MR21	Theipval Memorial France.
MR22	Le Touret Memorial, France.
MR27	Pozieres Memorial, France.
MR28	Neuve-Chapelle Indian Memorial, France.
MR29	Ypres (Menin Gate) Memorial, Belgium.
MR30	Tyne Cot Memorial, Belgium.
MR31	Nieuport Memorial, Belgium.
MR32	Ploegsteert Memorial, Belgium.
MR34	Jerusalem Memorial, Israel.
MR35	Mikra Memorial, Salonica, Greece.
MR37	Dorian Memorial, Greece.
MR38	Basra Memorial, Iraq.
MR40	Hollybrook Memorial, Southampton, England.
MR41	Chatby Memorial, Egypt.
MR43	Delhi Memorial, India.
MR46	Mombasa British Memorial, East Africa.
MR47	Tanga British Memorial Cemetery, East Africa.
MR50	Nairobi British and Indian Memorial, East Africa.
MR52	Dar Es Salaam British and Indian Memorial, East Africa.
MR53	Aden Memorial, Arabia.
MR59	Bardera Fort Memorial, Somaliland.
MR61	Tehran Memorial, Iran.
MR64	Bombay (St Thomas) Cathedral Memorial, India.
MR65	Kirkee Memorial, India.
MR66	Madras Memorial, India.
MR67	Karachi Memorial, Pakistan.
MR68	Taukkyan Memorial, Burma.
MR69	Delhi 1914-1918 War Memorial, India.
MR70	Brookwood (Russia) Memorial, England.

Cemeteries

EAST AFRICA
2	Handeni Cemetery.
6	Korogwe Churchyard.
7	Korogwe Military Cemetery.
8	Lindi Cemetery.
9	Mhonda Mission Cemetery.
10	Mingoyo Cemetery.
11	Mtama Cemetery.
12	Mwanza Cemetery.
13	New Moshi British Cemetery.
15	Songea European Cemetery
19	Tanga Main Cemetery.
22	Bweho Chini Military Graves.
23	Chogowali Military Grave
28	Longido Cemetery.
29	Luchomo Military Grave
30	Mahiwa Military Graves
32	Mikese Military Grave.
33	Mkwera Military Graves.
35	Dar Es Salaam (Sea View) Cemetery.
36	Dar Es Salaam (Upanga Street) Cemetery
38	Kilwa Kivinje Cemetery.
39	Morogoro Cemetery.
40	Iringa Cemetery.
42	Kajiado Cemetery
43	Kisii Boma Military Grave
44	Kisumu Cemetery
46	Molo Military Grave.
47	Mombasa Protestant Cemetery.
49	Mumias European Cemetery.
50	Mwele Ndogo Military Grave.
51	Nairobi Forest Cemetery.
52	Nairobi South Cemetery.
53	Naivasha Cemetery.
54	Nakuru Cemetery.
56	Taveta Military Cemetery.
58	Voi Cemetery.
59	Wajir Cemetery.
60	Hargeisa War Cemetery.
61	Mogadishu African War Cemetery.
66	Port Louis Western Cemetery.
77	Mangochi Town Cemetery.
78	Karonga Church of Central Africa Presbyterian Cemetery.
80	Karonga New War Cemetery.
86	Zomba Town Cemetery.
87	Beira Christian Cemetery.
89	Maputo Cemetery
90	Lumbo British Cemetery.
92	Pemba Cemetery.
101	Harare (Pioneer) Cemetery.
116	Khartoum War Cemetery.
124	Entebbe European Cemetery.
125	Jinja Roman Catholic Churchyard.
126	Kabarole Mission Cemetery.
127	Kampala (Jinja Road) European Cemetery.
128	Mbarara (St James) Churchyard.

SOUTH AFRICA
18	Trekkopjes Cemetery
26	Durban (Ordnance Road) Military Cemetery.
30	Durban (Stellawood) Cemetery.
42	Benoni Cemetery.
52	Johannesburg (Braamfontein) Cemetery.
53	Johannesburg (Brixton New) Cemetery.
63	Potchefstroom European Cemetery.
69	Roberts Heights Military Cemetery, Pretoria
72	Tzaneen Estate Cemetery, Selati Valley.
81	Rooidam Military Cemetery, Tempe.
144	Plumstead Cemetery, Cape Town.
158	Simonstown (Dido Valley) Cemetery.
171	Woltemade Cemetery, Cape Town.
172	Wynberg (Church Street) Cemetery, Cape Town.

WEST AFRICA
1	Christiansborg Civil Cemetery.
2	Gambaga European Cemetery.
3	Kumasi European Cemetery
4	Sekondi (Shama Road) European Cemetery now Takoradi European Cemetery, Ghana.
5	Chra Village Cemetery now Whala Cemetery
6	Kumasi Memorial
8	Elisabethville Cemetery
17	Relizane Communal Cemetery.
23	Bathurst Memorial.
28	Freetown Memorial.
30	Freetown (King Tom) Cemetery.
33	Bakundi Military Grave
35	Bauchi European Cemetery.
39	Enugu Military Grave.
40	Ibadan Mission Church Cemetery.
41	Ikoyi New Cemetery, Lagos
42	Kaduna Cemetery
45	Lokoja Town Cemetery.
46	Mamfe European Cemetery

47 Maio Kalei Military Grave
48 Nsanakang Cemetery Enclosure
49 Nsanakang European Cemetery
50 Udi Military Grave
52 Yola Station Cemetery
53 Zaria European Cemetery
54 Zungeru Cemetery
55 Calabar Memorial
56 Ibadan Memorial
57 Lokoja Memorial
58 Zaria Memorial
61 Duala Cemetery.

ASIA
9   Colombo (Kanatte) General Cemetery,Sri Lanka
20   Sai Wan Bay Memorial (UMA & UMB),Hong Kong
33   Hong Kong Cemetery,Hong Kong
40   Yokohama War Cemetery,Japan
45   Kranji War Cemetery,Singapore
51   Haidar Pasha Cemetery,Istanbul
52   Chanak Consular Cemetery,Asiatic side of the Dardanelles
53   Famagusta Military Cemetery,Cyprus
60   Maala Cemetery,Aden
62   Sheikh Othman Cemetery,Aden
64   Horth Point Christian Cemetery,Kamaran Island
66   Muscat Old Cemetery,Oman.
81   Haidar Pasha Memorial
82   Tehran War Cemetery,Iran

AUSTRALIA.
112 Sydney (Waverley) General Cemetery
307 Brighton General Cemetery.

BELGIUM
1   Ferme-Olivier Cemetery,Elverdinghe
2   Hop Store Cemetery,Vlamertinghe
3   Nine Elms British Cemetery,Poperinghe
4   Vlamertinghe Military Cemetery
5   Poperinghe New Military Cemetery
6   Brandhoek Military Cemetery,Vlamertinghe
7   Brandhoek New Military Cemetery,Vlamertinghe
8   Brandhoek New Military Cemetery No 3,Vlamertinghe
9   Hospital Farm Cemetery,Elverdinghe
10   Vlamertinghe New Military Cemetery
11   Lijssenthoek Military Cemetery
12   Canada Farm Cemetery,Elverdinghe
13   Bleuet Farm Cemetery,Elverdinghe
15   Reninghelst New Military Cemetery
16   Dozinghem Military Cemetery,Westvleteren.
17   Kemmel Chateau Military Cemetery
18   Mendinghem Military Cemetery,Proven
19   Huts Cemetery,Dickebusch
20   Duhallow A D S Cemetery,Ypres
21   La Clytte Military Cemetery,Reninghelst
22   Oxford Road Cemetery,Ieper
23   Bard Cottage Cemetery,Boezinge
24   Coxyde Military Cemetery
25   Solferino Farm Cemetery,Brielen
26   Divisional Collecting Post Cemetery,Boesinghe
27   Track "X" Cemetery,St Jean-Les-Ypres
28   Dickebusch New Military Cemetery
29   Dickebusch New Military Cemetery Extension
30   Gunners Farm Cemetery,Ploegsteert
31   Motor Car Corner Cemetery,Ploegsteert
32   Le Touquet Railway Crossing Cemetery,Ploegsteert
33   Calvaire (Essex) Military Cemetery,Ploegsteert
34   Belgian Battery Corner Cemetery,Ypres
35   Divisional Cemetery,Dickebusch Road,Vlamertinghe
36   Gwalia Cemetery,Poperinghe
37   Ridge Wood Military Cemetery,Voormezeele
38   Haringhe (Bandaghem) Military Cemetery
40   Abeele Aerodrome Military Cemetery,Watou
41   Watou Churchyard
42   Kandahar Farm Cemetery,Neuve-Eglise
43   St Quentin Cabaret Military Cemetery,Ploegsteert.
44   Potijze Burial Ground
45   Potijze Chateau Grounds Cemetery
46   Potijze Chateau Lawn Cemetery
47   Potijze Chateau Wood Cemetery
48   La Plus Douve Farm Cemetery,Ploegsteert
49   Ration Farm (La Plus Douve) Annexe,Ploegsteert
50   Underhill Farm Cemetery,Ploegsteert
52   Prowse Point Military Cemetery,Warneton.
53   Hyde Park Corner (Royal Berks) Cemetery,Ploegsteert.
54   Berks Cemetery Extension,Ploegsteert
56   Chester Farm Cemetery,Zillebeke
57   Ypres Town Cemetery,Menin Gate
58   Ypres Town Cemetery Extension,Menin Gate
59   Ramparts Cemetery,Lille Gate,Ypres
60   La Laiterie Military Cemetery,Kemmel
61   Spanbroekmolen British Cemetery,Wytschaete
62   Lone Tree Cemetery,Spanbroekmolen,Wytschaete.
63   St Julien Dressing Station Cemetery,Langemarck
64   Minty Farm Cemetery,St Jan.
65   No Man's Cot Cemetery,Boezinge
66   Welsh Cemetery (Caesar's Nose),Boezinge
67   Colne Valley Cemetery,Boezinge
68   Lancashire Cottage Cemetery,Ploegsteert
69   Ploegsteert Churchyard
70   Ploegsteert Wood Military Cemetery,Warneton
71   Rifle House Cemetery,Warneton
72   Menin Road South Military Cemetery,Ypres.
73   Essex Farm Cemetery,Boesinghe
74   Wytschaete Military Cemetery
75   Derry House Cemetery No 2,Wytschaete
76   Torreken Farm Cemetery No 1,Wytschaete
77   Somer Farm Cemetery,Wytschaete
78   Cabin Hill Cemetery,Wytschaete
79   Lindenhoek Chalet Military Cemetery,Kemmel
80   Dickebusch Old Military Cemetery
81   Reninghelst Churchyard.
82   Reninghelst Churchyard Extension
83   Clement House Cemetery,Langemarck
84   Ypres Reservoir Cemetery
85   Talana Farm Cemetery,Boesinghe
86   Dragoon Camp Cemetery,Boesinghe
87   Ruisseau Farm Cemetery,Langemarck
88   Aeroplane Cemetery,Ypres
89   Wulverghem-Lindenhoek Road Military Cemetery.
90   Westhof Farm Cemetery,Neuve-Eglise
91   La Brique Military Cemetery No 1,St Jean-Les-Ypres
92   La Brique Military Cemetery No 2,St Jean-Les-Ypres
93   Wieltje Farm Cemetery,St Jean-Les-Ypres
94   Buffs Road Cemetery,St Jean-Les-Ypres
96   New Irish Farm Cemetery,St Jean-Les-Ypres
97   Dranoutre Military Cemetery
98   Dranoutre Churchyard
99   Packhorse Farm Shrine Cemetery,Wulverghem
100 Pond Farm Cemetery,Wulverghem
101 White House Cemetery,St Jean-Les-Ypres
102 Klein-Vierstraat British Cemetery,Kemmel
103 Suffolk Cemetery,Vierstraat,Kemmel
104 Godezonne Farm Cemetery,Kemmel
105 Elzenwalle Brasserie Cemetery,Voormezeele
106 Artillery Wood Cemetery,Boesinghe
107 R E Farm Cemetery,Wytschaete
111 Voormezeele Enclosure No 3
112 Hooge Crater Cemetery,Zillebeke
113 Birr Cross Roads Cemetery,Zillebeke
114 R E Grave,Railway Wood,Zillebeke

115	Perth Cemetery (China Wall),Zillebeke.	204	Roisin Communal Cemetery.
116	Zantvoorde British Cemetery.	205	Thulin New Communal Cemetery.
117	Zantvoorde Churchyard.	206	Flenu Communal Cemetery.
118	Oak Dump Cemetery,Voormezeele.	214	Jemappes Communal Cemetery.
120	Woods Cemetery,Zillebeke.	216	Wiheries Communal Cemetery.
121	1/D.C.L.I. Cemetery,The Bluff,Zillebeke.	218	Blaugies Communal Cemetery.
122	Hedge Row Trench Cemetery,Zillebeke.	236	Quevy-Le-Petit Communal Cemetery.
123	Passchendaele New British Cemetery.	241	Mons Communal Cemetery.
124	Voormezeele Enclosures No.1 & No.2.	242	St Symphonen Military Cemetery.
125	Tyne Cot Cemetery,Passchendaele.	243	La Louviere Communal Cemetery.
126	Poelcapelle British Cemetery.	244	Maisieres Communal Cemetery.
127	Railway Dugouts Burial Ground (Transport Farm),Zillebeke.	256	Harveng Churchyard.
128	Dochy Farm New British Cemetery,Langemarck.	261	Nouvelles Communal Cemetery.
129	Seaforth Cemetery,Cheddar Villa,Langemarck.	265	Belgrade Cemetery,Namur.
130	Bridge House Cemetery,Langemarck.	266	Liege (Robermont) Cemetery.
131	Spoilbank Cemetery,Zillebeke.	267	Huy (La Sarte) Communal Cemetery.
132	Larch Wood (Railway Cutting) Cemetery,Zillebeke.	302	Malonne Communal Cemetery.
133	Tuileries British Cemetery,Zillebeke.	307	Polygon Wood Cemetery,Zonnebeke.
134	Zillebeke Churchyard.	308	Buttes New British Cemetery,Polygon Wood,Zonnebeke.
135	Railway Chateau Cemetery,Vlamertinghe.	310	Divisional Collecting Post Cemetery Extension,Boesinghe.
136	London Rifle Brigade Cemetery,Ploegsteert.	316	Halle Communal Cemetery.
137	Tancrez Farm Cemetery,Ploegsteert.	320	Louvain Communal Cemetery.
138	Maple Leaf Cemetery,Romarin,Neuve-Eglise.	321	Nivelles (Nijvel) Communal Cemetery.
140	Harlebeke New British Cemetery.	330	Charleroi Communal Cemetery.
141	Staceghem Communal Cemetery,Harlebeke.	337	Soumoy Communal Cemetery.
143	Vichte Military Cemetery.	339	Berks Cemetery Extension (Rosenberg Chateau Plots),Ploegsteert.
147	Hulste Communal Cemetery.	342	Schoonselhof Cemetery,Antwerp.
149	Wielsbeke Churchyard.	344	Audenarde Communal Cemetery.
150	Poperinghe Communal Cemetery.	349	Bouchaute Churchyard.
151	Poperinghe Old Military Cemetery.	353	Ghent City Cemetery.
152	Oosttaverne Wood Cemetery,Wyschaete.	358	Mooregem Churchyard.
153	Croonaert Chapel Cemetery,Wyschaete.	370	Beveren-Sur-Yser Churchyard.
154	Bus House Cemetery,Voormezeele.	371	Blankenberghe Communal Cemetery.
155	Irish House Cemetery,Kemmel.	375	Hoogstaede Belgian Military Cemetery.
156	Dadizeele Communal Cemetery.	379	Oostcamp Churchyard.
157	Dadizeele New British Cemetery.	380	Oostnieuwkerke Churchyard.
158	Moorseele Military Cemetery.	381	Oostrosbeke Communal Cemetery.
159	Kezelberg Military Cemetery,Moorseele.	383	Roulers Communal Cemetery.
160	Ledeghem Churchyard.	384	Ruddervoorde Communal Cemetery.
161	Ledeghem Military Cemetery.	392	Courtrai (La Madeleine) Cemetery.
162	Moorslede Communal Cemetery.	393	Courtrai (St Jean) Cemetery.
163	Slypskappelle Churchyard,Moorslede.	396	Ath Communal Cemetery.
165	Bedford House Cemetery,Enclosure No.2,Zillebeke.	400	Lessines Communal Cemetery.
166	Bedford House Cemetery Enclosure No.3,Zillebeke.	402	Bisseghem Communal Cemetery.
167	Bedford House Cemetery Enclosure No 4,Zillebeke.	405	Winkel-St Eloi Churchyard.
167a	Bedford House Cemetery Enclosure No.6,Zillebeke.	406	Tournai Communal Cemetery Allied Extension.
168	Messines Ridge British Cemetery.	408	Heestert Military Cemetery.
169	Wulverghem Churchyard.	409	Leuze Communal Cemetery.
170	Neuve-Eglise Churchyard.	410	Menin Communal Cemetery.
171	Adinkerke Churchyard Extension.	414	Bleharies Communal Cemetery.
172	Adinkerke Military Cemetery,Furnes.	417	Esplechin Churchyard.
173	Ramscappelle Road Military Cemetery,St Georges.	420	Froidmont Communal Cemetery.
174	Nieuport Communal Cemetery.	423	La Glanerie Churchyard.
175	Ostende New Communal Cemetery.	428	Orcq Communal Cemetery.
176	Steenkerke Belgian Military Cemetery.	435	Taintegnies Communal Cemetery.
182	Locre Churchyard.	438	Warcoing Churchyard.
183	Locre Hospice Cemetery.	441	Coyghem Churchyard.
184	Locre No.10 Cemetery.	442	Dottignies Communal Cemetery.
185	Grootebeek British Cemetery,Reninghelst.	443	Espierres Churchyard.
186	Kemmel Churchyard.	449	St Genois Churchyard.
187	Dickebusch Churchyard.	450	Wevelghem Communal Cemetery.
188	Hagle Dump Cemetery,Elverdinghe.	451	Strand Military Cemetery,Ploegsteert.
191	Westoutre Churchyard Extension.	453	Sanctuary Wood Cemetery,Zillebeke.
192	Westoutre British Cemetery.	454	Voormezele Churchyard.
193	Boesinghe Churchyard.		
195	Angreau Communal Cemetery.		BURMA.
197	Audregnies Churchyard.	122a	Rangoon War Cemetery.
198	Elouges Communal Cemetery.	129a	Taukkyan War Cemetery.
201	Hautrage Military Cemetery.		
202	Frameries Communal Cemetery.		

CANADA
- 99 Deloraine Cemetery, Souris, Manitoba
- 116 Winnipeg (Elmwood) Cemetery
- 155 Gabriola Island Graveyard, Nanaimo, British Columbia
- 256 Montreal (Mount Royal) Cemetery, Hochelaga, Quebec
- 261 Aylmer (St Paul's) Roman Catholic Cemetery, Hull, Quebec
- 423 Preeceville Cemetery, Mackenzie, Saskatchewan
- 547 Edmonton Cemetery, East Edmonton, Alberta
- 740 Halifax (Camp Hill) Cemetery, Nova Scotia
- 1028 St John (Fernhill) Cemetery, New Brunswick
- 1087 Kincardine Cemetery, Bruce, Ontario
- 1114 Kingsville (Greenhill) Cemetery, Essex, Ontario
- 1143 Chatham (Maple Leaf) Cemetery, Kent, Ontario
- 1245 Ottawa (Beechwood) Cemetery, Carleton, Ontario
- 1380 Peterborough (Little Lake) Cemetery, Peterborough, Ontario
- 1430 Lindsay (Riverside) Cemetery, Victoria, Ontario
- 1464 Brantford (Greenwood) Cemetery, Brant, Ontario
- 1531 St Catharines (Victoria Lawn) Cemetery, Lincoln, Ontario
- 1667 Hamilton Cemetery, Wentworth, Ontario
- 1688 Toronto (Mount Pleasant) Cemetery, York, Ontario
- 1691 Toronto (Prospect) Cemetery, York, Ontario
- 1694 Toronto (St James's) Cemetery, York, Ontario

CENTRAL AMERICA
- 6 Quirigua Hospital Cemetery, Guatemala

EGYPT
- 1 Alexandria (Hadra) War Memorial Cemetery
- 2 Kantara War Memorial Cemetery
- 3 Chatby Military Cemetery
- 6 Chatby War Memorial Cemetery
- 7 Port Said War Memorial Cemetery
- 8 Ismailia War Memorial Cemetery
- 9 Cairo War Memorial Cemetery
- 10 Cairo New British Protestant Cemetery
- 13 Cairo Civil International Cemetery
- 15 Suez War Memorial Cemetery
- 19 Mersa Matruh Military Cemetery

EUROPE
- 1 Pieta Military Cemetery, Malta
- 3 Ta Braxia Cemetery, Malta
- 4 Addolorata Cemetery, Malta
- 5 Rinella Military Cemetery, Malta
- 7 Pembroke Military Cemetery, Malta
- 9 Marsa Jewish Cemetery, Malta
- 17 Plovdiv Central Cemetery, Bulgaria
- 20 Sofia War Cemetery, Bulgaria
- 23 Gibraltar (North Front) Cemetery, Gibraltar
- 28 Lisbon (St George) British Churchyard, Portugal
- 42 Madrid British Cemetery, Spain
- 51 Vevey (St Martin's) Cemetery, Switzerland
- 56 Belgrade New Cemetery, Yugoslavia
- 57 Chela Kula Military Cemetery, Nish, Yugoslavia
- 58 Skoplje (Uskub) British Cemetery, Yugoslavia
- 58a Kuzala Cemetery, Rijeka, Yugoslavia
- 74 Vederso Churchyard, Denmark
- 96 Noordwijk General Cemetery, Holland
- 97 Orthen Protestant Cemetery, Hertogenbosch, Holland
- 149 Poznan Old Garrison Cemetery, Poland
- 150a Malbork Commonwealth War Cemetery, Poland
- 179 Archangel Allied Cemetery, Russia
- 180 Archangel Memorial, Russia
- 193 Churkin Russian Naval Cemetery, Vladivostok, Siberia
- 195 Vladivostok Memorial, Siberia

FRANCE
- 1 Le Treport Military Cemetery
- 2 Forceville Communal Cemetery Extension
- 3 Louvencourt Military Cemetery
- 4 Acheux British Cemetery
- 5 Bertrancourt Military Cemetery
- 8 Calais Southern Cemetery
- 10 Pernes British Cemetery
- 12 Barlin Communal Cemetery Extension
- 13 Mont Huon Military Cemetery, Le Treport
- 14 Ligny-St Flochel British Cemetery, Averdoingt
- 15 Maroeuil British Cemetery
- 16 BoisGuillaume Communal Cemetery
- 18 Morbecque British Cemetery
- 19 Le Grand Hasard Military Cemetery, Morbecque
- 20 Thiennes British Cemetery
- 21 Tannay British Cemetery, Thiennes
- 22 Corbie Communal Cemetery
- 23 Corbie Communal Cemetery Extension
- 24 Cinq Rues British Cemetery, Hazebrouck
- 25 La Kreule Military Cemetery, Hazebrouck
- 26 Le Peuplier Military Cemetery, Caestre
- 27 Caestre Military Cemetery
- 28 Borre British Cemetery
- 29 Crouy British Cemetery, Crouy-Sur-Somme
- 30 Crouy Communal Cemetery, Crouy-Sur-Somme
- 31 Aire Communal Cemetery
- 32 Bruay Communal Cemetery Extension
- 33 Sandpits British Cemetery, Labeuvriere
- 34 Terlincthun British Cemetery, Wimille
- 35 Auchonvillers Military Cemetery
- 37 Picquigny British Cemetery
- 39 Longpre-Les-Corps Saints British Cemetery
- 40 Etaples Military Cemetery
- 41 Varennes Military Cemetery
- 43 Warloy-Baillon Communal Cemetery
- 44 Warloy-Baillon Communal Cemetery Extension
- 46 Avesnes-Le-Comte Communal Cemetery Extension
- 49 Izel-Les-Hameau Communal Cemetery
- 51 Abbeville Communal Cemetery
- 52 Abbeville Communal Cemetery Extension
- 53 Haute-Avesnes British Cemetery
- 54 Dainville British Cemetery
- 55 Dainville Communal Cemetery
- 57 Wanquetin Communal Cemetery Extension
- 58 La Chaudiere Military Cemetery, Vimy
- 59 Contay British Cemetery
- 60 Harponville Communal Cemetery
- 61 Harponville Communal Cemetery Extension
- 62 Doullens Communal Cemetery Extension No.1
- 63 Doullens Communal Cemetery Extension No.2
- 64 Wimereux Communal Cemetery
- 65 Les Baraques Military Cemetery, Sangatte
- 66 La Neuville British Cemetery, Corbie
- 67 La Neuville Communal Cemetery, Corbie
- 68 Ecoivres Military Cemetery, Mont-St Eloy
- 69 Pernois British Cemetery, Halloy-Les-Pernois
- 71 Vignacourt British Cemetery
- 74 Puchevillers British Cemetery
- 76 Toutencourt Communal Cemetery
- 77 Herissart Communal Cemetery
- 79 Molliens-Au-Bois Communal Cemetery
- 80 Bethune Town Cemetery
- 81 Villers Station Cemetery, Villers-Au-Bois
- 82 Ration Farm Military Cemetery, La Chapelle-D'Armentieres
- 83 Brewery Orchard Cemetery, Bois-Grenier
- 84 Bagneux British Cemetery, Gezaincourt
- 85 Ste Marie Cemetery, Le Havre
- 87 Sanvic Communal Cemetery
- 88 Lapugnoy Military Cemetery
- 94 Marles-Les-Mines Communal Cemetery
- 95 Aubigny Communal Cemetery Extension
- 96 Ste Catherine British Cemetery
- 97 St Nicholas British Cemetery

98	Chocques Military Cemetery	202	Lillers Communal Cemetery Extension.
100	Arneke British Cemetery.	203	Couin British Cemetery.
102	Boulogne Eastern Cemetery.	204	Couin New British Cemetery.
103	Bac-Du-Sud British Cemetery, Bailleulval.	206	Romeries Communal Cemetery Extension.
104	Gouy-En-Artois Communal Cemetery Extension.	207	Mericourt-L'Abbe Communal Cemetery Extension.
105	Grove Town Cemetery, Meaulte.	208	Franvillers Communal Cemetery.
106	Houchin British Cemetery.	209	Franvillers Communal Cemetery Extension.
107	Houchin Communal Cemetery.	210	Bonnay Communal Cemetery Extension.
108	Fouquieres Churchyard.	212	Unicorn Cemetery, Vend'Huile.
109	Fouquieres Churchyard Extension.	214	Bucquoy Road Cemetery, Ficheux.
112	Gosnay Communal Cemetery.	215	Connaught Cemetery, Thiepval.
113	Duisans British Cemetery, Etrun.	216	Sailly-Saillisel British Cemetery.
114	Cambrin Churchyard Extension.	217	Morval British Cemetery.
115	Philosophe British Cemetery, Mazingarbe.	218	Rancourt Military Cemetery.
116	Querrieu British Cemetery.	219	Dud Corner Cemetery, Loos.
119	Daours Communal Cemetery Extension.	220	Knightsbridge Cemetery, Mesnil-Martinsart.
120	Warlincourt Halte British Cemetery, Saulty.	221	Beaumont-Hamel British Cemetery.
121	Etretat Churchyard.	222	Mazingarbe Communal Cemetery.
122	Etretat Churchyard Extension.	223	Mazingarbe Communal Cemetery Extension.
123	Tourgeville Military Cemetery.	224	Hersin Communal Cemetery Extension.
131	Mailly Wood Cemetery.	225	St Hilaire Cemetery, Frevent.
133	Courcelles-Au-Bois Communal Cemetery Extension.	226	St Hilaire Cemetery Extension, Frevent.
134	Longuenesse (St Omer) Souvenir Cemetery.	228	Montay Communal Cemetery.
139	Godewaersvelde British Cemetery.	229	Montay British Cemetery.
140	Godewaersvelde Churchyard.	230	Montay-Neuvilly Road Cemetery, Montay.
141	Dive Copse British Cemetery, Sailly-Le-Sec.	231	Pommereuil British Cemetery.
142	Esquelbecq Military Cemetery.	232	Martinsart British Cemetery.
144	Adelaide Cemetery, Villers-Bretonneux.	233	Mesnil Communal Cemetery Extension.
145	St Sever Cemetery, Rouen.	234	Prospect Hill Cemetery, Gouy.
146	St Sever Cemetery Extension, Rouen.	235	Ramicourt British Cemetery.
147	Haynecourt British Cemetery.	236	Joncourt British Cemetery.
149	Maroc British Cemetery, Grenay.	237	Joncourt East British Cemetery.
150	Bapaume Post Military Cemetery, Albert.	238	Joncourt Communal Cemetery.
151	Peake Wood Cemetery, Fricourt.	239	Adanac Military Cemetery, Miraumont and Pys.
152	Munich Trench British Cemetery, Beaumont-Hamel.	241	Ramillies British Cemetery.
153	Waggon Road Cemetery, Beaumont-Hamel.	242	Proville British Cemetery.
154	Monchy British Cemetery, Monchy-Le-Preux.	244	Neuville-St Remy Churchyard
155	Windmill British Cemetery, Monchy-Le_Preux.	245	Lebucquiere Communal Cemetery Extension.
156	Euston Road Cemetery, Colincamps.	246	Blighty Valley Cemetery, Authuile Wood, Authuile and Aveluy.
157	Louez Military Cemetery, Duisans.	247	Beacon Cemetery, Sailly-Laurette.
158	Habarcq Communal Cemetery Extension.	248	St Venant-Robecq Road British Cemetery, Robecq.
160	Bully-Grenay Communal Cemetery French Extension.	249	Gonnehem Churchyard.
161	Bully-Grenay Communal Cemetery British Extension.	250	Gonnehem British Cemetery.
162	Wancourt British Cemetery	251	Aveluy Communal Cemetery Extension.
163	Cambrin Military Cemetery.	252	Aveluy Wood Cemetery (Lancashire Dump), Mesnil-Martinsart.
164	Bray Military Cemetery.	253	Sailly-Sur-La-Lys Churchyard.
166	Bray-Sur-Somme Communal Cemetery.	254	Sailly-Sur-La-Lys Canadian Cemetery.
167	Beauval Communal Cemetery.	255	Anzac Cemetery, Sailly-Sur-La-Lys.
169	Gezaincourt Communal Cemetery Extension.	256	Anneux British Cemetery.
172	Beauquesne Communal Cemetery.	257	Sailly-Labourse Communal Cemetery.
174	Wailly Orchard Cemetery.	258	Sailly-Labourse Communal Cemetery Extension.
175	Fermont Military Cemetery, Riviere	259	Labourse Communal Cemetery
176	Dernancourt Communal Cemetery.	260	Brown's Road Military Cemetery, Festubert.
177	Dernancourt Communal Cemetery Extension.	261	Post Office Rifles Cemetery, Festubert.
178	Noeux-Les-Mines Communal Cemetery.	262	Pont-D'Achelles Military Cemetery, Nieppe.
179	Noeux-Les-Mines Communal Cemetery Extension	263	Pont-De-Nieppe Communal Cemetery.
180	Ebblinghem Military Cemetery.	264	Nieppe Communal Cemetery
184	Roclincourt Military Cemetery	265	Roclincourt Valley Cemetery.
185	Namps-Au-Val British Cemetery	266	Anzin-St Aubin British Cemetery
188	Dartmoor Cemetery, Becordel-Becourt.	267	Gordon Dump Cemetery, Ovillers-La Boisselle
189	Norfolk Cemetery, Becordel-Becourt.	268	La Targette British Cemetery (Aux-Rietz), Neuville-St Vaast
190	Highland Cemetery, Le Cateau	269	Petit-Vimy British Cemetery, Vimy.
192	Neuvilly Communal Cemetery Extension	270	St Aubert British Cemetery
193	Outersteene Communal Cemetery Extension, Bailleul	271	Avesnes-Le-Sec Communal Cemetery Extension
194	Doingt Communal Cemetery Extension	272	Quarry Cemetery, Marquion.
196	Ribemont Communal Cemetery Extension	273	Chapel Corner Cemetery, Sauchy-Lestree
197	Millencourt Communal Cemetery Extension	274	Sains-Les-Marquion British Cemetery.
198	Buire-Sur-L'Ancre Communal Cemetery	275	Erquinghem-Lys Churchyard Extension
200	Hazebrouck Communal Cemetery	276	"Y" Farm Military Cemetery, Bois-Grenier
201	Lillers Communal Cemetery	277	Bulls Road Cemetery, Flers.

278	Thilloy Road Cemetery, Beaulencourt	365	Ste Emilie Valley Cemetery, Villers-Faucon
279	Guards Cemetery, Windy Corner, Cuinchy	366	Jeancourt Communal Cemetery Extension
280	Courcelette British Cemetery	368	Epehy Communal Cemetery
281	Foncquevillers Military Cemetery	369	Epehy Wood Farm Cemetery, Epehy
283	Hannescamps New Military Cemetery	370	Meaulte Military Cemetery
284	Bailleul Communal Cemetery	372	Fricourt British Cemetery (Bray Road)
285	Bailleul Communal Cemetery Extension	373	Fricourt New Military Cemetery
286	Briastre Communal Cemetery	374	Guards' Cemetery, Lesboeufs
287	Belle Vue British Cemetery, Briastre	375	Bellicourt British Cemetery
288	Solesmes Communal Cemetery	376	Uplands Cemetery, Magny-La-Fosse
289	Solesmes British Cemetery	377	Janval Cemetery, Dieppe
290	Crucifix Cemetery, Vendegies-Sur-Ecaillon	379	Fifteen Ravine British Cemetery, Villers-Plouich
292	Vertain Communal Cemetery Extension	380	Delsaux Farm Cemetery, Beugny
293	Lonsdale Cemetery, Aveluy and Authuile	381	Red Cross Corner Cemetery, Beugny
294	Guillemont Road Cemetery, Guillemont	382	Haplincourt Communal Cemetery
295	Bouzincourt Communal Cemetery	383	Mill Road Cemetery, Thiepval
296	Bouzincourt Communal Cemetery Extension	384	Grandcourt Road Cemetery, Grandcourt
297	Trois-Arbres Cemetery, Steenwerck	385	Warlencourt British Cemetery
298	Le Grand Beaumart British Cemetery, Steenwerck	386	Bazentin-Le-Petit Communal Cemetery
299	St Acheul French National Cemetery, Amiens	387	Bazentin-Le-Petit Communal Cemetery Extension
300	St Pierre Cemetery, Amiens	388	Bazentin-Le-Petit Military Cemetery
303	Longueau British Cemetery	389	Thistle Dump Cemetery, High Wood, Longueval
304	Camon Communal Cemetery	390	London Cemetery and Extension, High Wood, Longueval
306	Bancourt Communal Cemetery	392	Martinpuich British Cemetery
307	Bancourt British Cemetery	393	Ovillers Military Cemetery
308	Manchester Cemetery, Riencourt-Les-Bapaume	394	Citadel New Military Cemetery, Fricourt
309	Sun Quarry Cemetery, Cherisy	395	Bray Hill British Cemetery, Bray-Sur-Somme
311	Orange Trench Cemetery, Monchy-Le-Preux	396	Bray Vale British Cemetery, Bray-Sur-Somme
312	Happy Valley British Cemetery, Fampoux	397	Dantzig Alley British Cemetery, Mametz
314	Regina Trench Cemetery, Grandcourt	398	Rocquigny-Equancourt Road British Cemetery, Manancourt
315	Haspres Coppice Cemetery, Haspres	399	Quarry Cemetery, Montauban
316	York Cemetery, Haspres	400	Bernafay Wood British Cemetery, Montauban
319	Quievy Communal Cemetery Extension	401	Longueval Road Cemetery
320	St Hilaire-Les Cambrai British Cemetery	402	Delville Wood Cemetery, Longueval
321	Canonne Farm British Cemetery, Sommaing	403	Cambrai East Military Cemetery
323	Montrecourt Churchyard	404	Drummond Cemetery, Raillencourt
324	Meteren Military Cemetery	406	Sucrerie Cemetery, Epinoy
327	Brie British Cemetery	407	Villers Hill British Cemetery, Villers-Guislain
328	Ennemain Communal Cemetery Extension	410	Hinges Military Cemetery
329	Bronfay Farm Military Cemetery, Bray-Sur-Somme	411	Le Vertannoy British Cemetery, Hinges
330	Devonshire Cemetery, Mametz	412	Mont-Bernenchon British Cemetery, Gonnehem
331	Gordon Cemetery, Mametz	413	Mont-Bernenchon Churchyard
332	Awoingt British Cemetery	414	Annezin Communal Cemetery
333	Awoingt Churchyard	415	Gouzeaucourt New British Cemetery
336	Estourmel Churchyard	417	Heudicourt Communal Cemetery Extension
337	Carnieres Communal Cemetery Extension	418	Beaurains Road Cemetery, Beaurains
338	Forenville Military Cemetery	419	Achicourt Road Cemetery, Achicourt
339	Ancre British Cemetery, Beaumont-Hamel	420	Agny Military Cemetery
340	Busigny Communal Cemetery	421	Vis-En-Artois British Cemetery, Haucourt
341	Busigny Communal Cemetery Extension	423	Vermelles British Cemetery
342	Sailly-Au-Bois Military Cemetery	424	Crucifix Corner Cemetery, Villers-Bretonneux
343	Hedauville Communal Cemetery Extension	425	Hangard Communal Cemetery Extension
344	Mailly-Maillet Communal Cemetery Extension	426	Dury Mill British Cemetery
345	Merville Communal Cemetery	427	Dury Crucifix Cemetery
346	Merville Communal Cemetery Extension	429	Sauchy-Cauchy Communal Cemetery Extension
347	Rue-David Military Cemetery, Fleurbaix	430	Albert Communal Cemetery Extension
348	Rue-Du-Bois Military Cemetery, Fleurbaix	432	Caterpillar Valley Cemetery, Longueval
349	White City Cemetery, Bois-Grenier	433	Ecoust-St Mein British Cemetery
350	Vieux-Berquin Communal Cemetery	434	Heninel-Croisilles Road Cemetery
352	Aval Wood Military Cemetery, Vieux-Berquin	435	Lagnicourt Hedge Cemetery
353	Nieppe-Bois (Rue-Du-Bois) British Cemetery, Vieux-Berquin	437	Morchies Australian Cemetery
354	La Gorgue Communal Cemetery	438	Morchies Military Cemetery
355	Lestrem Communal Cemetery	439	Fins New British Cemetery, Sorel-Le-Grand
356	Calonne-Sur-La-Lys Communal Cemetery	441	Premont British Cemetery
357	Lowrie Cemetery, Havrincourt	443	Montbrehain British Cemetery
358	Grand Ravine British Cemetery, Havrincourt	444	Calvaire Cemetery, Montbrehain
359	Ribecourt Railway Cemetery	445	High Tree Cemetery, Montbrehain
360	Bouchoir New British Cemetery	446	Tincourt New British Cemetery
363	Villers-Faucon Communal Cemetery	448	Aizecourt-Le-Bas Churchyard
364	Villeers-Faucon Communal Cemetery Extension	451	Athies Communal Cemetery Extension

452 Point-Du-Jour Military Cemetery,Athies.
453 Flatiron Copse Cemetery,Mametz.
457 City of Paris Cemetery,Pantin.
461 Levallois-Perret Communal Cemetery.
462 Neuilly-Sur-Seine New Communal Cemetery.
473 Les Gonards Cemetery,Versailles.
477 St Germain-En-Laye Old Communal Cemetery.
480 Aix-Noulette Communal Cemetery Extension.
481 Ontario Cemetery,Sains-Les-Marquion.
482 Triangle Cemetery,Inchy-En-Artois.
484 Moeuvres British Cemetery.
485 Hourges Orchard Cemetery,Domart-Sur-La-Luce.
487 Demuin British Cemetery.
489 Hangard Wood British Cemetery.
490 Gentelles Communal Cemetery.
495 St Venant Communal Cemetery.
496 St Venant Communal Cemetery Extension.
498 Berguette Churchyard.
500 Busnes Communal Cemetery.
501 Berles-Au-Bois Churchyard Extension.
502 Berles New Military Cemetery.
503 Berles Position Military Cemetery.
504 Bellacourt Military Cemetery,Riviere.
505 De Cuisine Ravine British Cemetery,Basseux.
506 Beaumetz-Les-Loges Communal Cemetery.
511 Peronne Communal Cemetery Extension,Ste Radegonde.
512 Grevillers British Cemetery.
513 Carnoy Military Cemetery.
514 Queens Cemetery,Bucquoy.
515 Becourt Military Cemetery,Becordel-Becourt.
516 Bouzincourt Ridge Cemetery,Albert.
518 Achiet-Le-Grand Communal Cemetery Extension.
521 Cross Roads Cemetery,Fontaine-Au-Bois.
522 Thelus Military Cemetery.
523 Nine Elms Military Cemetery,Thelus.
524 Raperie British Cemetery,Villemontoire.
525 Rue-Petillon Military Cemetery.
526 Heath Cemetery,Harbonnieres.
527 Roisel Communal Cemetery.
528 Roisel Communal Cemetery Extension.
529 Hermies British Cemetery.
530 Hermies Hill British Cemetery.
531 Feuchy Chapel British Cemetery,Wancourt.
532 Tigris Lane Cemetery,Wancourt.
533 Frankfurt Trench British Cemetery,Beaumont-Hamel.
534 New Munich Trench British Cemetery,Beaumont-Hamel.
535 Stump Road Cemetery,Grandcourt.
536 Guemappe British Cemetery,Wancourt.
537 Tank Cemetery,Guemappe.
538 Heninel Communal Cemetery Extension.
539 Bootham Cemetery,Heninel.
540 Cherisy Road East Cemetery,Heninel.
541 Rookery British Cemetery,Heninel.
543 Vis-En-Artois Communal Cemetery.
544 Fampoux British Cemetery.
545 Level Crossing Cemetery,Fampoux.
546 Crump Trench British Cemetery,Fampoux.
547 Sucrerie Cemetery,Ablain-St Nazaire.
548 Givenchy-En-Gohelle Canadian Cemetery,Souchez.
549 Zouave Valley Cemetery,Souchez.
550 Loos British Cemetery.
551 St Patrick's Cemetery,Loos
552 Bois-Carre Military Cemetery,Haisnes.
553 Ninth Avenue Cemetery,Haisnes.
554 Fosse 7 Military Cemetery (Quality Street),Mazingarbe.
557 Lievin Communal Cemetery Extension.
558 Bois-De-Noulette British Cemetery,Aix-Noulette.
559 Tranchee De Mecknes Cemetery,Aix-Noulette.
560 Beaulencourt British Cemetery,Ligny-Thilloy.
561 Beugnatre Communal Cemetery.

562 Barastre Communal Cemetery.
563 Favreuil British Cemetery.
564 Bapaume Australian Cemetery.
566 Le Trou Aid Post Cemetery,Fleurbaix.
567 Aubers Ridge British Cemetery,Aubers.
568 H.A.C. Cemetery,Ecoust-St Mein.
570 Fosse No.10 Communal Cemetery Extension,Sains-En-Gohelle.
571 Beuvry Communal Cemetery.
572 Beuvry Communal Cemetery Extension.
573 Quatre-Vents Military Cemetery,Estree-Cauchy.
576 Gommecourt Wood New Cemetery,Foncquevillers.
577 Bucquoy Communal Cemetery.
578 Bucquoy Communal Cemetery Extension.
579 Shrine Cemetery,Bucquoy.
580 Owl Trench Cemetery,Hebuterne.
581 Tilloy British Cemetery,Tilloy-Les-Mofflaines.
582 Cayeux Communal Cemetery.
583 Cayeux Military Cemetery.
585 Le Quesnel Communal Cemetery Extension.
587 Mezieres Communal Cemetery Extension.
588 Beaucourt-En-Santerre Churchyard.
589 Beaucourt British Cemetery.
591 Cojeul British Cemetery,St Martin-Sur-Cojeul.
592 St Martin Calvaire British Cemetery,St Martin-Sur-Cojeul.
593 Boyelles Communal Cemetery Extension.
594 Hibers Trench Cemetery,Wancourt.
595 Neuville-Vitasse Road Cemetery,Neuville-Vitasse.
596 Henin Crucifix Cemetery.
598 Porte-De-Paris Cemetery,Cambrai.
602 Cantaing British Cemetery.
604 Brown's Copse Cemetery,Roeux.
605 Pargny British Cemetery.
609 Voyennes Communal Cemetery.
610 Nesle Communal Cemetery.
611 Naves Communal Cemetery Extension.
612 Wellington Cemetery,Rieux-En-Cambresis.
613 Villers-En-Cauchies Communal Cemetery.
614 Mory Abbey Military Cemetery,Mory.
615 Mory Street Military Cemetery,St Leger.
616 St Leger British Cemetery.
617 Gomiecourt South Cemetery.
618 Railway Cutting Cemetery,Courcelles-Le-Comte.
619 Warry Copse Cemetery,Courcelles-Le-Comte.
620 Ervillers Military Cemetery.
622 Marfaux British Cemetery.
624 Hem Farm Military Cemetery,Hem-Monacu.
625 Suzanne Communal Cemetery Extension.
626 Suzanne Military Cemetery No.3
629 Frise Communal Cemetery.
630 Peronne Road Cemetery,Maricourt.
631 St Vaast Post Military Cemetery,Richebourg-L'Avoue.
632 Rue-Des-Berceaux Military Cemetery,Richebourg-L'Avoue.
633 Morlancourt British Cemetery No.1
634 Morlancourt British Cemetery No.2,Ville-Sur-Ancre.
636 Ville-Sur-Ancre Communal Cemetery Extension.
637 Point 110 Old Military Cemetery,Fricourt.
638 Point 110 New Military Cemetery,Fricourt.
639 Chipilly Communal Cemetery.
643 Sucrerie Military Cemetery,Colincamps.
644 Bailleul Road East Cemetery,St Laurent-Blangy.
645 Bailleul Road West Cemetery,St Laurent-Blangy.
646 Queant Road Cemetery,Buissy.
647 Cagnicourt British Cemetery.
648 Rosieres Communal Cemetery.
649 Rosieres Communal Cemetery Extension.
650 Rosieres British Cemetery,Vauvillers.
651 Caix Communal Cemetery.
652 Caix British Cemetery.
657 Caudry Old Communal Cemetery.
658 Caudry British Cemetery.

660	Honnechy British Cemetery	759	Louverval Military Cemetery,Doignies
661	Inchy Communal Cemetery Extension	760	Iwuy Communal Cemetery
662	Metz-En-Couture Communal Cemetery British Extension	761	Niagara Cemetery,Iwuy
663	Targelle Ravine British Cemetery,Villers-Guislain	765	Gorre British Cemetery,Beuvry
664	Villers-Guislain Communal Cemetery	768	Estaires Communal Cemetery
665	Pigeon Ravine Cemetery,Epehy	769	Estaires Communal Cemetery Extension.
666	Domino British Cemetery,Epehy.	770	Blargies Communal Cemetery Extension.
667	Villers-Plouich Communal Cemetery.	772	Forges-Les-Eaux Communal Cemetery
668	Sunken Road Cemetery,Villers-Plouich	777	Orchard Dump Cemetery,Arleux-En-Gohelle
669	Saulcourt Churchyard Extension,Guyencourt-Saulcourt	779	Lens Communal Cemetery,Sallaumines
672	Savy British Cemetery.	782	Billy-Montigny Communal Cemetery
673	Marteville Communal Cemetery,Attilly.	783	Izel-Les-Equerchin Communal Cemetery
674	Vermand Communal Cemetery	785	Combles Communal Cemetery Extension.
675	Roupy Communal Cemetery	786	Guards' Cemetery,Combles.
680	"X" Farm Cemetery,La Chapelle-D'Armentieres.	787	St Pol Communal Cemetery Extension.
681	Chapelle-D'Armentieres Old Military Cemetery	788	St Pol British Cemetery,St Pol-Sur-Ternoise.
682	Chapelle-D'Armentieres New Military Cemetery	790	Hesdin Communal Cemetery
683	La Chapelle-D'Armentieres Communal Cemetery.	792	Huby-St Leu British Cemetery.
684	Bois-Grenier Communal Cemetery	795	St Georges Churchyard
685	Suffolk Cemetery,La Rolanderie Farm,Erquinghem-Lys	798	Gommecourt British Cemetery No 2,Hebuterne
686	Queant Communal Cemetery British Extension.	800	Rossignol Wood Cemetery,Hebuterne.
687	Dominion Cemetery,Hendecourt-Les-Cagnicourt	801	Luke Copse British Cemetery,Puisieux.
689	Croisilles Railway Cemetery	802	Queens Cemetery,Puisieux.
690	Ecoust Military Cemetery,Ecoust-St Mein.	803	Ten Tree Alley Cemetery,Puisieux.
692	Fouquescourt British Cemetery.	804	Quesnoy Farm Military Cemetery,Bucquoy.
694	Vrely Communal Cemetery Extension	805	Fienvillers British Cemetery
699	Cerisy-Gailly Military Cemetery.	806	Pont-Remy British Cemetery
700	Cerisy-Gailly French National Cemetery	808	St Ouen Communal Cemetery
701	Hamel Military Cemetery,Beaumont-Hamel.	813	Bonneville Communal Cemetery
702	Authuile Military Cemetery	816	Conde-Folie Communal Cemetery
703	Contalmaison Chateau Cemetery.	817	Coulonvillers Communal Cemetery
704	Senlis Communal Cemetery Extension	818	Cramont Communal Cemetery.
705	Pont-Du-Hem Military Cemetery,La Gorgue	832	Pozieres British Cemetery,Ovillers-La Boisselle.
706	Royal Irish Rifles Graveyard,Laventie	833	Heilly Station Cemetery,Mericourt-L'Abbe.
707	Rue-Du-Bacquerot (13th London) Graveyard,Laventie	834	Caulaincourt Communal Cemetery
708	Euston Post Cemetery,Laventie	835	Trefcon British Cemetery,Caulaincourt
709	Neuve-Chapelle British Cemetery	836	Hancourt British Cemetery
710	Neuve-Chapelle Farm Cemetery	837	Beaumetz Communal Cemetery
711	Ribecourt British Cemetery	839	Mons-En-Chaussee Communal Cemetery
712	Ribecourt Road Cemetery,Trescault	840	Tertry Communal Cemetery
713	Trescault Communal Cemetery	841	Vraignes Communal Cemetery
714	Quarry Wood Cemetery,Sains-Les-Marquion.	844	Beaurevoir British Cemetery
716	Le Cateau Military Cemetery	845	Guizancourt Farm Cemetery,Gouy
717	Le Cateau Communal Cemetery	846	Serain Communal Cemetery Extension.
718	Selridge British Cemetery,Montay	847	Fresnoy-Le-Grand Communal Cemetery Extension.
720	Cuinchy Communal Cemetery	848	Brancourt-Le-Grand Communal Cemetery
721	Woburn Abbey Cemetery,Cuinchy	849	Brancourt-Le-Grand Military Cemetery
725	Vadencourt British Cemetery,Maissemy	855	Bertenacre Military Cemetery,Fletre
727	Le Touret Military Cemetery,Richebourg-L'Avoue	856	Mont-Noir Military Cemetery,St Jans-Cappel
728	Highland Cemetery,Roclincourt	857	Borre Churchyard
729	Mindel Trench British Cemetery,St Laurent-Blangy	858	Caestre Communal Cemetery
730	Hervin Farm British Cemetery,St Laurent-Blangy	860	Hondeghem Churchyard
731	Bunyans Cemetery,Tilloy-Les-Mofflaines	861	La Creche Communal Cemetery,Bailleul
733	Ghissignies British Cemetery	864	Vauxbuin French National Cemetery
734	Englefontaine Churchyard	865	Buzancy Military Cemetery
735	Englefontaine British Cemetery	866	Oulchy-Le-Chateau Churchyard Extension
737	Poix-Du-Nord Communal Cemetery Extension	867	Crouy-Vauxrot French National Cemetery,Crouy
738	Preux-Au-Bois Communal Cemetery	870	Chacrise Communal Cemetery
739	Bermerain Communal Cemetery	874	Ste Marguerite Churchyard
742	Serre Road Cemetery No 1,Beaumont-Hamel,Hebuterne and Puisieux	878	Villemontoire Communal Cemetery
743	Serre Road Cemetery No 3,Puisieux	879	Boves East Communal Cemetery
744	A I F Burial Ground,Grass Lane,Flers	880	Boves West Communal Cemetery
745	Bienvillers Military Cemetery	881	Boves West Communal Cemetery Extension
747	Humbercamps Communal Cemetery Extension	882	Allonville Communal Cemetery
748	Bailleulmont Communal Cemetery	885	Frechencourt Communal Cemetery
749	Barly French Military Cemetery	886	Bavelincourt Communal Cemetery
755	Ruyaulcourt Military Cemetery	887	Montigny Communal Cemetery (Somme)
756	Beaumetz Cross Roads Cemetery,Beaumetz-Les-Cambrai	888	Montigny Communal Cemetery Extension (Somme)
757	Beaumetz-Les-Cambrai Military Cemetery No 1	889	Blangy-Tronville Communal Cemetery
758	Bertincourt Chateau British Cemetery	891	Bertangles Communal Cemetery

904 Neuville-Bourjonval Communal Cemetery.
905 Neuville-Bourjonval British Cemetery.
906 Five Points Cemetery, Lechelle.
907 Ytres Communal Cemetery.
908 Manancourt Communal Cemetery.
910 Marcoing Communal Cemetery.
911 Marcoing British Cemetery.
912 Masnieres British Cemetery, Marcoing.
913 Noyelles-Sur-L'Escaut Communal Cemetery.
914 Noyelles-Sur-L'Escaut Communal Cemetery Extension.
915 Rumilly Communal Cemetery Extension.
916 Cagnoncles Communal Cemetery.
920 Niergnies Communal Cemetery.
921 Le Bizet Cemetery, Armentieres.
922 Cite Bonjean Military Cemetery, Armentieres.
924 Cabaret-Rouge British Cemetery, Souchez.
925 Ayette British Cemetery.
927 Douchy-Les-Ayette British Cemetery.
928 Avesnes-Sur-Helpe Communal Cemetery.
929 Fontaine-Au-Bois Communal Cemetery.
930 Dourlers Communal Cemetery Extension.
931 Maubeuge (Sous-Le-Bois) Cemetery.
932 Landrecies Communal Cemetery.
933 Landrecies British Cemetery.
934 Hautmont Communal Cemetery.
935 Berlaimont Communal Cemetery.
936 Berlaimont Communal Cemetery Extension.
937 Pont-Sur-Sambre Communal Cemetery.
938 Sebourg British Cemetery.
939 Sebourg Communal Cemetery.
940 Ors British Cemetery.
941 Aulnoye Communal Cemetery.
943 Grand-Fyat Communal Cemetery.
944 Maroilles Communal Cemetery.
948 Bermeries Communal Cemetery.
949 Brttrechies Communal Cemetery.
952 Ecuelin Churchyard.
953 Eth Communal Cemetery.
955 Gommegnies Communal Cemetery.
957 Hargnies Communal Cemetery.
965 Malplaquet Communal Cemetery, Taisnieres-Sur-Hon.
968 Monceau-St Waast Communal Cemetery.
978 St Remy-Chaussee Communal Cemetery.
979 St Waast-La-Vallee Communal Cemetery.
981 Semousies Churchyard.
982 Taisnieres-En-Thierache Communal Cemetery.
984 Wargnies-Le-Grand Churchyard.
985 Wargnies-Le-Petit Communal Cemetery.
987 Roye New British Cemetery.
988 Moreuil Communal Cemetery Allied Extension.
1003 Hailles Communal Cemetery.
1008 Rouvrel Communal Cemetery.
1012 Englebelmer Communal Cemetery.
1013 Englebelmer Communal Cemetery Extension.
1014 St Amand British Cemetery.
1016 Henu Churchyard.
1017 Mondicourt Communal Cemetery.
1022 Ignaucourt Churchyard.
1027 Lille Southern Cemetery.
1028 St Andre Communal Cemetery.
1029 Tourcoing (Pont-Neuville) Communal Cemetery.
1030 Ascq Communal Cemetery.
1031 Halluin Communal Cemetery.
1032 Linselles Communal Cemetery.
1033 Fretin Communal Cemetery.
1034 Cretinier Cemetery, Wattrelos.
1039 Bousbecques Communal Cemetery.
1041 Croix Communal Cemetery.
1044 hem Communal Cemetery.
1049 Mouvaux New Comunal Cemetery.
1050 Neuville-En-Ferrain Communal Cemetery.
1054 Sailly-Les-Lannoy Churchyard.
1058 Willems Communal Cemetery.
1059 Arras Road Cemetery, Roclincourt.
1061 Grand-Seraucourt British Cemetery.
1063 Noyon New British Cemetery.
1066 Montescourt-Lizerolles Communal Cemetery.
1071 Blerancourt Communal Cemetery.
1074 Jussy Communal Cemetery.
1076 Le Quesnoy Communal Cemetery.
1079 Preseau Communal Cemetery Extension.
1080 Villers-Pol Communal Cemetery Extension.
1081 Ruesnes Communal Cemetery.
1082 Capelle-Beaudignies Road Cemetery, Capelle.
1084 Artres Communal Cemetery.
1087 Maresches Communal Cemetery.
1091 Steenwerck Communal Cemetery.
1092 Croix-Du-Bac British Cemetery, Steenwerck.
1094 Haverskerque British Cemetery.
1095 Laventie Communal Cemetery.
1100 Steenbecque Churchyard.
1106 Vieille-Chapelle New Military Cemetery, Lacouture.
1107 Vailly British Cemetery.
1108 Guards' Grave, Villers-Cotterets Forest.
1110 Braine Communal Cemetery.
1111 Soupir Churchyard.
1112 Soupir Communal Cemetery.
1113 Montreuil-Aux-Lions British Cemetery.
1117 Bezu-Le-Guery Communal Cemetery.
1128 Gandelu Communal Cemetery.
1129 Haramont Communal Cemetery.
1134 Priez Communal Cemetery.
1139 Vieil-Arcy Communal Cemetery.
1140 Houplines Communal Cemetery Extension.
1141 Ferme Buterne Military Cemetery, Houplines.
1142 Valenciennes (St Roch) Communal Cemetery.
1144 Raismes Communal Cemetery.
1147 Bruille-St Amand Churchyard.
1154 Thivencelle Churchyard.
1157 Rue-Du-Bacquerot No.1 Military Cemetery, Laventie.
1158 Fauquissart Military Cemetery, Laventie.
1159 Quesnoy-Sur-Deule Communal Cemetery.
1160 Quesnoy-Sur-Deule Communal Cemetery, German Extension.
1161 Isbergues Communal Cemetery.
1169 St Hilaire-Cottes Churchyard.
1170 Villers-Bretonneux Military Cemetery, Fouilloy.
1172 Fouilloy Communal Cemetery.
1173 Aubigny British Cemetery (Somme).
1180 Neufchatel Churchyard.
1182 Faubourg-D'Amiens Cemetery, Arras.
1183 Boisleux-Au-Mont Communal Cemetery.
1184 Sunken Road Cemetery, Boisleux St Marc.
1185 London Cemetery, Neuville-Vitasse.
1186 Henin Communal Cemetery Extension.
1187 Summit Trench Cemetery, Croisilles.
1188 Feuchy British Cemetery.
1190 Sunken Road Cemetery, Fampoux.
1191 Albuera Cemetery, Bailleul-Sire-Berthoult.
1193 Chili Trench Cemetery, Gavrelle.
1194 Roeux British Cemetery.
1196 Auberchicourt British Cemetery.
1198 Masny Churchyard.
1202 Ham Communal Cemetery.
1203 Ham British Cematery, Muille-Villette.
1204 Foreste Communal Cemetery.
1205 Douilly Communal Cemetery.
1206 Eppeville Churchyard.
1211 Maubeuge-Centre Cemetery.
1216 Sains-Du-Nord Communal Cemetery.
1219 Floursies Churchyard.

1223 Solre-Le-Chateau Communal Cemetery
1225 Senlis French National Cemetery
1227 Compiegne South Communal Cemetery
1228 Royallieu French National Cemetery,Compiegne
1230 Verbene French National Cemetery
1231 Nery Communal Cemetery
1233 Marissel French National Cemetery
1234 Dompierre French National Cemetery
1235 Vignemont French National Cemetery
1236 Annel Communal Cemetery,Longueil-Annel
1242 Hardivillers Communal Cemetery
1252 Denain Communal Cemetery
1254 Famars Communal Cemetery Extension
1256 Maing Communal Cemetery extension
1257 Querenaing Communal Cemetery
1258 Thiant Communal Cemetery
1259 Vendegies Cross Roads British Cemetery,Bermerain
1260 Verchain British Cemetery,Verchain-Maugre
1266 St Souplet British Cemetery
1268 Vaux-Andigny British Cemetery
1269 La Vallee-Mulatre Communal Cemetery
1270 La Vallee-Mulatre Communal Cemetery Extension
1271 Wassigny Communal Cemetery
1272 Le Rejet-De-Beaulieu Communal Cemetery
1274 St Benin Communal Cemetery (Nord)
1276 Douai Communal Cemetery
1277 Douai British Cemetery,Cuincy
1278 Brebieres British Cemetery
1279 Annoeullin Communal Cemetery German Extension
1281 Arleux-Du-Nord Communal Cemetery
1284 Auby Communal Cemetery
1287 Brillon Communal Cemetery
1293 Hem-Lenglet Communal Cemetery
1295 Lallaing Communal Cemetery
1296 Lecelles Churchyard
1301 Paillencourt Churchyard
1308 Somain Communal Cemetery
1310 Beaumont Communal Cemetery
1311 Corbehem Communal Cemetery
1314 Noyelles-Godault Communal Cemetery
1316 Quiery-La-Motte Communal Cemetery
1321 Bois-Carre British Cemetery,Thelus
1325 Vimy Communal Cemetery,Farbus
1326 Hebuterne Communal Cemetery
1327 Hebuterne Military Cemetery
1328 Vendresse Churchyard
1329 Vendresse British Cemetery
1331 hermonville Military Cemetery
1332 Jonchery-Sur-Vesle British Cemetery
1333 Beaurepaire French National Cemetery,Pontavert
1337 Longueval Communal Cemetery
1339 Bourg-Et-Comin Communal Cemetery
1340 Moulins Churchyard
1341 Moulins New Communal Cemetery
1342 Paissy Churchyard
1345 Bois-Des-Angles British Cemetery,Crevecoeur-Sur-L'Escaut
1346 Moulin-De-Pierre British Cemetery,Villeers-Outreau
1347 Esnes Communal Cemetery
1348 Fontaine-Au-Pire Communal Cemetery
1349 Ligny-En-Cambresis Communal Cemetery
1350 Haucourt Communal Cemetery
1351 Becquigny Communal Cemetery
1354 Selvigny Communal Cemetery
1355 Wambaix Communal Cemetery
1357 Bleue-Maison Military Cemetery,Eperlecques
1358 Croix-Rouge Military Cemetery,Quaedypre
1359 Dunkerque Town Cemetery
1360 Malo-Les-Bains Communal Cemetery
1361 Zuydcoote Military Cemetery
1364 Buysscheure Churchyard

1366 Houtkerque Churchyard
1367 Ledeerzeele Churchyard
1369 Steenvorde Communal Cemetery
1372 Wormhoudt Communal Cemetery
1374 Audruicq Churchyard
1386 Quietiste Military Cemetery,Le Cateau
1387 Beauvois-En-Cambresis Communal Cemetery
1388 Bethencourt Communal Cemetery
1391 Bertry Communal Cemetery
1392 Maurois Communal Cemetery
1393 Montigny Communal Cemetery (Nord)
1394 Reumont Churchyard
1395 Troisvilles Communal Cemetery
1396 Viesly Communal Cemetery
1402 Nesles-La-Gilberde Communal Cemetery
1404 Mailly-Le-Camp French Cemetery
1410 Dormans French National Cemetery
1415 Sezanne Communal Cemetery
1416 Soulieres Churchyard
1420 Baron Communal Cemetery
1422 Creil Communal Cemetery
1425 Bassevelle Churchyard
1426 Bellot Communal Cemetery
1429 Coulommieers Communal Cemetery
1432 Fretoy Communal Cemetery
1436 La Haute-Maison,Ferme Des Arceries
1438 Meaux Communal Cemetery
1439 Melun North Cemetery
1440 Montereau Communal Cemetery
1441 Nangis Communal Cemetery
1443 Orly-Sur-Morin Communal Cemetery
1445 Perreuse Chateau French National Cemetery,Signy-Signets
1451 Sablonnieres New Communal Cemetery
1461 Hargicourt British Cemetery
1462 Hargicourt Communal Cemetery Extension
1463 Ronssoy Communal Cemetery
1464 Villeret Churchyard
1465 Hesbecourt Communal Cemetery
1468 La Chapelette British Cemetery,Peronne
1472 Assevillers New British Cemetery
1473 Foucaucourt Communal Cemetery
1475 Vendegies-Au-Bois British Cemetery
1476 Amerval Communal Cemetery Extension,Solesmes
1477 Ovillers New Communal Cemetery,Solesmes
1478 Forest Communal Cemetery (Nord)
1479 Ors Communal Cemetery
1480 Beaurain British Cemetery
1482 Bousies Communal Cemetery
1483 Flesquieres Hill British Cemetery
1484 Vaulx Hill Cemetery,Vaulx-Vraucourt
1485 Vaux Australian Field Ambulance Cemetery,Vaulx-Vraucourt
1486 Vraucourt Copse Cemetery,Vaulx-Vraucourt
1487 L'Homme Mort British Cemetery,Ecoust-St Mein
1488 Noreuil Australian Cemetery
1489 Croisilles British Cemetery
1490 "Y" Ravine Cemetery,Beaumont-Hamel
1491 Redan Ridge Cemetery No 1,Beaumont-Hamel
1492 Redan Ridge Cemetery No 2,Beaumont-Hamel
1494 Templeux-Le-Guerard Communal Cemetery Extension
1495 Templeux-Le-Guerard British Cemetery
1496 Moeuvres Communal Cemetery Extension
1497 Sanders Keep Military Cemetery,Graincourt-Les-Havrincourt
1498 Orival Wood Cemetery,Flesquieres
1499 Demicourt Communal Cemetery,Boursies
1500 Hawthorn Ridge Cemetery No 1,Auchon-Villers
1501 Hawthorn Ridge Cemetery No 2,Auchon-Villers
1502 Hunter's Cemetery,Beaumont-Hamel
1504 Miraumont Communal Cemetery
1512 Fillievres British Cemetery
1525 Wavans British Cemetery

1553 Le Crotoy Communal Cemetery
1564 Quend Communal Cemetery.
1568 Vaux-En-Amienois Communal Cemetery.
1571 Mazargues Cemetery Extension.
1586 Fruges Communal Cemetery.
1597 Rimboval Churchyard.
1615 Rethel French National Cemetery.
1632 Plaine French National Cemetery.
1633 Roppenheim Communal Cemetery.
1643 Neuf-Brisach Communal Cemetery.
1667 Chambieres French National (Mixed) Cemetery, Metz.
1678 Charmes Military Cemetery, Essegny.
1689 Chambrecy British Cemetery.
1690 Courmas British Cemetery.
1693 Epernay French National Cemetery.
1695 La Neuville-Aux-Larris Military Cemetery.
1697 St Imoge Churchyard.
1699 Vandieres Churchyard.
1700 Berthaucourt Communal Cemetery, Pontru.
1701 Chapelle British Cemetery, Holnon.
1703 Guise (La Desolation) French National Cemetery, Flavigny-Le-Petit.
1704 La Baraque British Cemetery, Bellenglise.
1706 Levergies Communal Cemetery.
1707 Ribemont Communal Cemetery.
1710 Sequehart British Cemetery No.1
1712 Brissay-Choigny Churchyard.
1715 Moy-De-L'Aisne Communal Cemetery.
1717 Sery-Les-Mezieres Communal Cemetery.
1723 St Mary's A.D.S. Cemetery, Haisnes.
1724 Carvin Communal Cemetery.
1725 Don Communal Cemetery, Annoeullin.
1726 Phalempin Communal Cemetery.
1730 Wicres Churchyard.
1732 Santes Churchyard.
1744 Monchy-Breton Churchyard.
1745 Nedonchel Churchyard.
1751 Etreux British Cemetery.
1752 Etreux Communal Cemetery.
1753 La Ville-Aux-Bois British Cemetery.
1754 St Erme Communal Cemetery Extension.
1755 Sissonne British Cemetery.
1766 Etroeungt Communal Cemetery.
1775 Nice (Caucade) British Civil Cemetery.
1778 Troyes Town Cemetery.
1779 Gruissan Communal Cemetery.
1788 Dijon (Les Pejoces) Cemetery.
1798 Conches-En-Ouche Communal Cemetery.
1799 Evreux Communal Cemetery.
1805 Maintenon Communal Cemetery.
1822 Talence Communal Cemetery.
1830 Champagnole Communal Cemetery
1839 St Nazaire (Toutes-Aides) Cemetery.
1841 Orleans Main Cemetery.
1844 Vendome Town Cemetery.
1845 Angers West Cemetery.
1848 Tourlaville Communal Cemetery.
1849 Tourlaville Communal Cemetery Extension.
1856 Lyon (La Guillotiere) Old Communal Cemetery.
1858 St Germain-Au-Mont-D'Or Communal Cemetery Extension.
1862 Le Mans West Cemetery.
1866 Asnieres-Sur-Oise Communal Cemetery.
1886 Monaco Principality Cemetery, La Condamine.
1887 Laventie Military Cemetery.
1888 Haubourdin Communal Cemetery.
1890 Serre Road Cemetery No 2, Beaumont-Hamel and Hebuterne.
1891 Thiepval Anglo-French Cemetery, Authuile
1893 Chauny Communal Cemetery British Extension.
1894 Montcornet Military Cemetery
1896 Canadian Cemetery No 2, Neuville-St Vaast.

GALLIPOLI.
1   Lancashire Landing Cemetery, Helles.
2   Redoubt Cemetery, Helles
3   Pink Farm Cemetery, Helles.
4   Azmak Cemetery, Sulva.
5   Green Hill Cemetery, Sulva.
6   Twelve Tree Copse Cemetery, Helles.
13 The Farm Cemetery, Anzac.
14 Skew Bridge Cemetery, Helles.
15 "V" Beach Cemetery, Helles.
17 7th Field Ambulance Cemetery, Anzac.
18 Embarkation Pier Cemetery, Anzac.
19 No.2 Outpost Cemetery, Anzac.
20 New Zealand No.2 Outpost Cemetery, Anzac.
26 Lala Baba Cemetery, Sulva.
27 Hill 10 Cemetery, Sulva.
29 Ari Burnu Cemetery, Anzac.
30 Beach Cemetery, Anzac.
31 Shrapnel Valley Cemetery, Anzac.

GERMANY.
1   Cologne Southern Cemetery.
2   Hamburg Cemetery, Ohlsdorf.
3   Niederzwehren Cemetery, Cassel.
4   Berlin South-Western Cemetery, Stahnsdorf.
9   Coblenz Jewish Cemetery.

GREECE.
1   Sarigol Military Cemetery.
2   Kirechkoi-Hortakoi Military Cemetery.
3   Struma Military Cemetery.
4   Lahana Military Cemetery.
5   Doiran Military Cemetery.
6   Karasouli Military Cemetery.
7   Salonika Anglo-French Military Cemetery, Lembet Road.
8   Salonika Protestant Cemetery.
9   Mikra British Cemetery, Salonika.
10 East Mudros Military Cemetery, Lemnos.
11 Portianos Military Cemetery, West Mudros, Lemnos.
14 Syra New British Cemetery.
16 Suda Bay War Cemetery, Crete.
18 Bralo British Cemetery.
21 Athens New Protestant Cemetery

INDIA.
48 Delhi War Cemetery.
97a Calcutta (Bhowanipore) Cemetery.
164 Madras (St Mary's) Cemetery

IRAQ.
1   Kut War Cemetery.
5   Amara War Cemetery.
6   Basra War Cemetery.
8   Baghdad (North Gate) War Cemetery
9   Baghdad East Jewish Cemetery.

ITALY.
1   Barenthal Military Cemetery.
2   Boscon British Cemetery.
3   Magnaboschi British Cemetery.
4   Granezza British Cemetery.
5   Cavalletto British Cemetery
6   Taranto Town Cemetery Extension.
7   Giavera British Cemetery.
8   Memorial to the Missing, Giavera British Cemetery.
9   Tezze British Cemetery, Vazzola.
10 Dueville Communal Cemetery Extension
11 Montecchio Precalcino Communal Cemetery Extension.
12 Staglieno Cemetery, Genoa
13 Savona Town Cemetery.

14	Savona Memorial
15	Arquata Scrivia Communal Cemetery Extension
16	Bordighera British Cemetery
19	Faenza Communal Cemetery
45	Carmignano Di Brenta Communal Cemetery
48	Padua Main Cemetery
56	Oneglia Town Cemetery
57	San Remo Town Cemetery
59	Testaccio Protestant Cemetery, Rome
65	Turin Town Cemetery
74	Altivole Communal Cemetery
75	Conegliano (San Giuseppe) Communal Cemetery
76	Falze Communal Cemetery, Trevignano

LEBANON

1	Beirut British War Cemetery

NEW ZEALAND

194	Purewa Cemetery
243	Featherston Soldiers' Cemetery
320	Suva Cemetery, Fiji

PAKISTAN

50a	Rawalpindi War Cemetery

PALESTINE or ISRAEL

1	Beersheba War Cemetery
2	Deir El Belah War Cemetery
3	Jerusalem War Cemetery
5	Jerusalem Protestant Cemetery, Mount Zion
8	Gaza War Cemetery
9	Ramleh War Cemetery
11	Haifa War Cemetery
14	Richon-Le-Zion Jewish Cemetery

SYRIA

2	Damascus Commonwealth War Cemetery

TANZANIA

1	Dar Es Salaam War Cemetery, Bagamoyo Road

USA

13	San Francisco (Cypress Lawn) Cemetery, California
77	Avon (St Michael's) Cemetery (Norfolk), Massachusetts
169	New York (Woodlawn) Cemetery, New York
184	Akron (Glendale) Cemetery (Summit), Ohio
187	Chillicothe (Grandview) Cemetery (Ross), Ohio
228	Fort Worth (Greenwood) Cemetery (Tarrant), Texas
234	Arlington National Cemetery (Arlington), Virginia
234a	Newport News (Green Lawn) Cemetery (Warwick), Virginia

WEST INDIES

36	Kingstown (St George) Cathedral Close, St Vincent

ENGLISH, IRISH SCOTTISH and WELSH COUNTIES

BEDFORD & HUNTINGDON

8	Higham Gobion (St Mary) Churchyard, Beds
23	Bedford Cemetery, Beds
34	Pavenham (St Peter) Churchyard, Beds
48	Campton and Shefford Cemetery, Beds
65	Biggleswade Cemetery, Beds
66	Dunstable Cemetery, Beds
70	Eaton Socon Churchyard, Beds
74	Luton Church Burial Ground, Beds
75	Luton General Cemetery, Beds
78	Houghton Regis (All Saints) Churchyard, Beds
83	Huntingdon Cemetery, Hunts
90	Upwood Cemetery, Hunts
102	Ramsey (St Thomas a Becket) Churchyard, Hunts
104	St Ives Public Cemetery, Hunts
113	Wyton (All Saints) Churchyard, Hunts

BERKSHIRE

1	Abingdon Cemetery
2	Abingdon (SS Mary & Edmund) Roman Catholic Churchyard, St Helen Without
19	Bradfield (St Andrew) Churchyard
23	Stratfield Mortimer (St Mary) Churchyard
27	Yattendon (SS Peter & Paul) Churchyard
28	Bisham (All Saints) Churchyard
29	Boyne Hill (All Saints) Chhurchyard, Bray
33	Hurley (St Mary) Churchyard
37	Stubbings (St James the Less) Churchyard, Bisham
39	Ascot (All Saints) Churchyard Extension, Winkfield
42	Cranbourne (St Peter) Churchyard, Winkfield
43	Crowthorne (St John the Baptist) Churchyard
45	Sandhurst Royal Military College Cemetery
47	Warfield (St Michael) Churchyard Extension
56	Hinton Waldrist (St Margaret) Churchyard
71	Maidenhead Cemetery
72	Newbury Old Cemetery
73	Chieveley (St Mary) Churchyard
83	Clewer (St Andrew) Churchyard
84	Windsor Cemetery
85	Reading (Caversham) Cemetery
86	Reading Cemetery
93	Long Wittenham (St Mary) Churchyard
94	Sotwell (St James) Churchyard
112	Wokingham (All Saints) Churchyard
113	Wokingham (St Paul) Churchyard
116	Bearwood (St Catherine) Churchyard, Hurst St Nicholas
117	Earley (St Peter) Churchyard
119	Hurst (St Nicholas) Churchyard Extension
121	Sonning (St Andrew) Churchyard
124	Wargrave (St Mary) Churchyard
125	Wokingham (St Sebastian) Churchyard, Wokingham Without

BUCKINGHAMSHIRE

12	Penn Street (Holy Trinity) Churchyard, Penn
32	Weston Turville (St Mary) Churchyard
36	Beaconsfield Cemetery
37	Bletchley (St Mary) Churchyard
39	Buckingham Cemetery
50	Twyford (The Assumption) Churchyard
51	High Wycombe Cemetery
55	Datchet Cemetery
57	Dorney Burial Ground
69	Wyrardisbury (St Andrew) Churchyard
76	Long Crendon (St Mary) Churchyard
80	Marlow Cemetery
82	Marlow (St Peter) Roman Catholic Churchyard
86	Moulsoe (St Mary) Churchyard
91	Wavendon (St Mary) Churchyard
96	Upton-Cum-Chalvey (St Mary) Churchyard
116	Great Hampden (St Mary Magdalene) Churchyard, Great & Little Hampden
120	Monks Risborough (St Dunstan) Churchyard
123	Tylers Green (St Margaret) Churchyard, Chepping Wycombe Rural

CAMBRIDGESHIRE

1	Cambridge General Cemetery
2	Cambridge (Mill Road) Cemetery
3	Cambridge (SS Gile's & Peter's) Cemetery
16	Cambridge Borough Cemetery, Fen Ditton
19	Cottenham (All Saints) Churchyard
21	Dry Drayton (SS Peter & Paul) Churchyard
31	Horningsea (St Peter) Churchyard
37	Stapleford (St Andrew) Churchyard
39	Trumpington (SS Mary & Michael) New Churchyard
51	Weston Colville (St Mary) Churchyard

84	Chatteris General Cemetery.
91	Wilburton (St Peter) Church.
97	Doddington (St Mary) Churchyard.
103	Wisbech Borough Cemetery.

CHESHIRE.

1	Alsager (Christ Church) Churchyard.
2	Ashton-Upon-Mersey (St Martin) Churchyard.
3	Bebington Cemetery.
4	Bebington (St Andrew) Churchyard.
8	Birkenhead (Flaybrick Hill) Cemetery.
11	Bowdon (St Mary) Churchyard.
18	Northenden (St Wilfrid) Churchyard.
19	Over Peover (St Lawrence) Churchyard,Peover Superior.
22	Rostherne (St Mary) Churchyard.
28	Chester General Cemetery.
30	Christleton (St James) Churchyard.
31	Eccleston (St Mary) Churchyard.
32	Great Saughall (All Saints) Churchyard.
44	Church Lawton (All Saints) Churchyard.
51	Crewe Cemetery.
53	Ashton-Under-Lyne and Dunkinfield Joint Cemetery.
56	Altrincham Cemetery.
62	West Kirby (St Bridget) Churchyard.
72	Macclesfield Cemetery
74	Alderley Edge Cemetery.
84	Prestbury (St Peter) Churchyard.
97	Middlewich Cemetery.
98	Mottram-In-Longdendale Cemetery.
111	Wybunbury (St Chad) Churchyard.
113	Nantwich (All Saints) Church Cemetery.
114	Nantwich General Cemetery.
117	Neston-Cum-Parkgate Cemetery.
123	Lostock Gralam (St John) Churchyard.
127	Northwich Cemetery.
128	Northwich (St Helen) Churchyard.
131	Appleton Thorn (St Cross) Churchyard,Appleton.
137	Halton Cemetery.
143	Stretton (St Matthew) Churchyard.
147	Sale Cemetery.
154	Heaton Mersey Congregational Churchyard.
158	Stockport Borough Cemetery.
160	Stockport (Willow Grove) Cemetery.
175	Waverton (St Peter) Churchyard.
178	Egremont (St John) Churchyard.
181	Woodchurch (Holy Cross) Churchyard.
182	Wallasey (Rake Lane) Cemetery.
183	Lindow (St John) Churchyard.
184	Wilmslow Cemetery.
186	Over (St Chad) Churchyard.
190	Bidston (St Oswald) Churchyard.
192	Eastham (St Mary) Churchyard.
193	Heswall (St Peter) Churchyard.
197	Thurstaton (St Bartholomew) Churchyard.
198	Willaston (Christ Church) Churchyard.

CORNWALL.

1	Bodmin Cemetery.
13	St Mabyn Churchyard.
20	Calstock Cemetery.
36	Mawnan (SS Mawnan and Stephen) Churchyard.
40	Falmouth Cemetery.
56	Ruan Minor (St Ruan) Churchyard.
61	St Martin's Churchyard.
64	Launceston Cemetery.
68	North Hill (St Torney) Churchyard.
79	Morval Church Cemetery.
96	Penzance Cemetery.
106	St Day (Holy Trinity) Churchyard.
109	Redruth Cemetery.
123	St Austell Cemetery.
128	St Columb Major Cemetery.
135	Maker (SS Macra,Mary and Julia) Churchyard.
140	St Stephens-By-Saltash (St Stephen) Churchyard.
142	St Ives Cemetery.
148	Launcells (St Swithin) Churchyard.
163	Kenwyn (St Kenwyn) Churchyard,Kenwyn Rural.
172	Gulval (St Gulval) Churchyard.
177	St Erth (St Ercus) Churchyard,St Erth Rural.

CUMBERLAND AND WESTMORLAND.

6	Aspatria (St Kentigern) Churchyard,Cumberland.
13	Brampton (St Martin) Old Churchyard,Cumberland.
17	Carlisle (Dalston Road) Cemetery,Cumberland.
18	Carlisle (Upperby) Cemetery,Cumberland.
25	Wetheral Cemetery,Cumberland.
40	Cockermouth Cemetery,Cumberland.
44	Silloth (St Paul) Churchyard,Cumberland.
45	Crosthwaite (St Kentigern) Churchyard,Cumberland.
46	Keswick (St John) Churchyard,Cumberland.
54	Great Salkeld (St Cuthbert) Churchyard,Cumberland.
59	Penrith Cemetery,Cumberland.
68	Allonby (Christ Church) Churchyard,Cumberland.
74	Wigton Cemetery,Cumberland.
82	Kendal (Parkside) Cemetery,Westmorland.
83	Kirkby Lonsdale (St Mary) Churchyard,Westmorland.
85	Arnside Cemetery,Westmorland.
86	Barbon (St Bartholomew) Churchyard,Westmorland.
91	Heversham (St Mary) Churchyard,Westmorland.
98	Selside (St Thomas) Churchyard,Whitwell and Selside,Westmorland.
100	Troutbeck (Jesus) Churchyard,Westmorland.
107	Bowness-On-Windermere Cemetery,Westmorland.
108	Windermere (St Mary's) Cemetery,Westmorland.

DERBYSHIRE.

2	Alfreton (Lea Brooks) Cemetery.
3	Alfreton (St Martin) Churchyard.
26	Tideswell (St John the Baptist) Churchyard.
29	Bakewell Cemetery.
30	Baslow (St Anne) Churchyard.
32	Crich (St Mary) Churchyard.
39	Mackworth (All Saints) Churchyard.
42	South Wingfield (Park) Burial Ground.
51	Bolsover (St Mary) Old Churchyard.
58	Fairfield (St Peter) Churchyard.
66	Edale (Holy Trinity) Churchyard.
76	Whittington (St Bartholomew) Churchyard.
97	Derby (Normanton) Cemetery.
98	Derby (Nottingham Road) Cemetery.
99	Derby (Uttoxeter Road) Cemetery.
120	Long Eaton Cemetery.
122	Cromford (St Mary) Churchyard.
127	Dore (Christ Church) Churchyard.
135	Newton Solney (St Mary) Churchyard.
145	Ockbrook (All Saints) Churchyard.
146	Risley (All Saints) Churchyard.

DEVONSHIRE.

1	Plymouth Old Cemetery.
2	Efford Cemetery,Plymouth.
3	Weston Mill Cemetery,Plymouth.
10	Hawkchurch (St John the Baptist) Churchyard.
11	Kilmington (St Giles) Churchyard.
12	Musbury (St Michael) Churchyard.
15	Axminster Cemetery.
29	Horwood Churchyard.
33	Morte Hoe Cemetery.
36	Westleigh (St Peter) Churchyard.
37	Bideford Church Cemetery.
39	Abbotsham Churchyard.

#	Location	#	Location
40	Alwington (St Andrew) Churchyard	151	St Helier (Almorah) Cemetery,Jersey
47	Brixham (St Mary) Churchyard	152	St Helier (Mont-A-L'Abbe) New Cemetery,Jersey
50	Budleigh Salterton Cemetery	156	St Lawrence Churchyard,Jersey
68	Dawlish Cemetery	160	St Peter Churchyard,Jersey
69	Exeter Higher Cemetery	162	St Saviour Churchyard,Jersey
70	Exeter (Exwick) Cemetery		
72	Littleham (SS Margaret and Andrew) Churchyard		**DURHAM**
73	Withycombe Raleigh (St John in the Wilderness) Churchyard	1	Blaydon (St Cuthbert,Stella) Cemetery
74	Great Torrington Cemetery	8	Gateshead East Cemetery
76	Bradworthy (St John the Baptist) Churchyard	13	Jarrow Cemetery
86	Feniton (St Andrew) Churchyard	15	Ryton Cemetery
87	Gittisham (St Michael) Churchyard	18	Harton (St Peter) Churchyard
91	Ilfracombe (Holy Trinity) Churchyard	19	South Shields (Harton) Cemetery
92	Ilfracombe (St Brannock's Road) Cemetery	23	Boldon Cemetery
96	Chivelstone (St Silvester) Churchyard	25	Whitburn (St Mary) Churchyard
100	Loddiswell (St Michael) Churchyard	26	Sunderland (Bishopwearmouth) Cemetery
107	Thurlestone (All Saints) Churchyard	27	Sunderland (Mere Knolls) Cemetery
128	Highweek (All Saints) Churchyard Extension	28	Sunderland (Ryhope Road) Cemetery
132	Northam (St Margaret) Churchyard	39	Annfield Plain (Harelaw) Cemetery
152	Collaton (St Mary) Churchyard	42	Auckland St Andrew Old Churchyard
153	Paignton Cemetery	55	New Shildon (All Saints) Churchyard,Middridge Grange
185	Exminster (St Martin) Churchyard	59	Gainford (St Mary) Churchyard
200	Topsham Cemetery	62	Barnard Castle Roman Catholic Cemetery
206	Seaton (St Gregory) Churchyard	64	Benfieldside Cemetery
207	Sidmouth Cemetery	81	West Pelton (St Paul) Churchyard,Urpeth
230	Marystow (St Mary) Churchyard	88	Darlington West Cemetery
233	Sheepstor Churchyard	97	Durham (St Oswald's) Burial Ground
237	Tavistock New Cemetery	102	Pittington Burial Ground
238	Shaldon (St Nicholas) Churchyard	108	Castle Eden (St James) Churchyard
239	Teignmouth Cemetery	109	Dalton-Le-Dale (Holy Trinity) Churchyard
243	Bradfield (All Saints) Churchyard	124	Hartlepool (Hart Road) New Cemetery
247	Halberton (St Andrew) Churchyard	140	Lanchester (All Saints) Churchyard
248	Huntsham (All Saints) Churchyard	164	Egglescliffe (St Mary) Churchyard
258	Torquay Extramural Cemetery	165	Norton (St Mary) Churchyard
266	Bridgetown and Berry Pomeroy Cemetery	167	Stockton-on-Tees (Durham Road) Cemetery
267	Totnes Cemetery	180	Seaton Carew (Holy Trinity) Churchyard
		181	West Hartlepool North Cemetery
	DORSET AND CHANNEL ISLANDS	182	West Hartlepool (Stranton) Cemetery
6	Parnham Private Cemetery,Beaminster,Dorset		
20	Bridport Cemetery,Dorset		**EIRE or IRELAND**
22	Burton Bradstock Cemetery,Dorset	2	Chapelizod (St Lawrence) Church of Ireland Churchyard,Dublin City
28	Cattistock (SS Peter and Paul) Churchyard,Dorset	3	Clondalkin (St John) Church of Ireland Churchyard
33	Dorchester Cemetery,Dorset	5	Dean's Grange Cemetery,Monkstown
42	Stratton (St Mary) Churchyard,Dorset	12	Glasnevin Cemetery,Dublin City
46	Branksome Park (All Saints) Churchyard,Dorset	14	Grangegorman Military Cemetery,Dublin City
48	Longfleet (St Mary) Churchyard,Dorset	17	Kilgobbin Old Church Cemetery
49	Poole (Branksome) Cemetery,Dorset	24	Mont Jerome Cemetery,Harold's Cross,Dublin City
50	Poole Cemetery,Dorset	27	Royal Hospital Cemetery,Kilmainham,Dublin City
51	Poole (Parkstone) Cemetery,Dorset	30	Ballynacally (Kilchreest) Cemetery,County Clare
52	Broadstone Cemetery,Canford Magna,Dorset	48	Ardnagashel Private Burial Ground,County Cork
53	Kinson (St Andrew) Churchyard,Dorset	49	Ballincollig Military Cemetery,County Cork
57	Portland Royal Naval Cemetery,Dorset	57	Ballynakilla Churchyard,Bere Island,County Cork
58	Portland (St George) Churchyard,Dorset	58	Baltimore (Tullagh) Graveyard,County Cork
67	Gillingham New Cemetery,Dorset	63	Blackrock (St Michael) Church of Ireland Churchyard,County Cork
70	Milton-on-Stour (SS Simon and Jude) Churchyard,Gillingham,Dorset	70	Castlehyde Church of Ireland Churchyard,County Cork
85	Yetminster (St Andrew) Churchyard,Dorset	71	Castlelyons Churchyard,County Cork
87	Sherborne Cemetery,Dorset	75	Cloyne (St Coleman) Cathedral Churchyard,County Cork
93	Swanage Old Cemetery,Dorset	76	Cobh Old Church Cemetery,County Cork
94	Wareham Cemetery,Dorset	77	Cork Military Cemetery,County Cork
95	Affpuddle (St Laurence) Churchyard,Dorset	78	Cork (St Finbarr's) Cemetery,County Cork
102	Kimmeridge Churchyard,Dorset	81	Corkbeg Church of Ireland Churchyard,County Cork
109	Wool (Holy Rood) Churchyard,Dorset	84	Currykippane Jewish Cemetery,County Cork
110	Melcombe Regis Cemetery,Dorset	86	Donoughmore Catholic Churchyard,County Cork
111	Weymouth Cemetery,Dorset	88	Douglas (St Luke) Church of Ireland churchyard,County Cork
115	Owermoigne (St Michael) Churchyard,Dorset	94	Fermoy Military Cemetery,County Cork
133	Witchampton (All Saints) Churchyard,Dorset	95	Fort Carlisle Military Cemetery,County Cork
135	Wimborne Minster Cemetery,Dorset	114	Kinsale (St Multose) Church of Ireland Churchyard,County Cork
139	Fort George Military Cemetery,St Peter Port,Guernsey	122	Millstreet Churchyard,County Cork
141	St Martins New Cemetery,Guernsey	138	Timoleague Church of Ireland Churchyard,County Cork
149	St Brelade Churchyard,Jersey	143	Youghal (St Mary's) Collegiate Churchyard,County Cork

148	Dromod Church fo Ireland Churchyard,Waterville,County Kerry.
159	Tralee New Cemetery,County Kerry.
160	Tralee (Ratass) Cemetery,County Kerry.
161	Ardcanny Churchyard,Mellon,County Limerick.
163	Bruree Church of Ireland Churchyard,County Limerick.
166	Limerick (King's Island) Military Cemetery,County Limerick.
167	Limerick (St Lawrence's) Catholic Cemetery,County Limerick.
168	Limerick (St Mary) Cathedral Churchyard,County Limerick.
185	Clonmel Friends' Burial Ground,County Tipperary.
186	Clonmel (St Patrick's) Cemetery,County Tipperary.
194	Lorrha Old Graveyard,County Tipperary.
205	Terryglass (St Columba) Catholic Churchyard,County Tipperary.
215	Ballynakill House Private Burial Ground,County Waterford.
234	Stradbally Church of Ireland Churchyard,County Waterford.
237	Tramore (Holy Cross) Catholic Churchyard,County Waterford.
238	Waterford Protestant Cemetery,County Waterford.
251	Ballymachugh (St Paul) Church of Ireland Churchyard,County Cavan.
260	Kilmore Church of Ireland Cemetery,County Cavan.
286	Lower Fahan (Christ Church) Churchyard,County Donegal.
301	Galway (Bohermore) New Cemetery,County Galway.
313	Athy (St John's) Old Cemetery,County Kildare.
319	Clane (St Michael) Church of Ireland Churchyard,County Kildare.
322	Curragh Military Cemetery,County Kildare.
336	Nass (Maudlings Or St Magdalen's) Protestant Cemetery,County Kildare.
350	Foulkstown Catholic Churchyard,County Kilkenny.
355	Kilkenny (St Canice) Church of Ireland Cathedral Cemetery,County Kilkenny.
356	Kilkenny (St John) Church of Ireland Churchyard,County Kilkenny.
362	Knocktopher (St David) Church of Ireland Churchyard,County Kilkenny.
381	Durrow Catholic Churchyard,County Leix.
394	Ballymacormick Church of Ireland Churchyard,County Longford.
398	Longford (Ballymacormick) Cemetery,County Longford.
401	Newtown Forbes (St Ann) Church of Ireland Churchyard,County Longford.
406	Drogheda (St Mary) Church of Ireland Churchyard,County Louth.
408	Dromin Old Graveyard,County Louth.
411	Dundalk (St Patrick's) Cemetery,County Louth.
422	Ballina Catholic Cathedral Churchyard,County Mayo.
432	Kilmaine (Holy Trinity) Church of Ireland Churchyard,County Mayo.
437	Ardcath Graveyard,County Meath.
440	Bective (St Mary) Church of Ireland Churchyard,County Meath.
451	Loughcrew Church of Ireland Churchyard,County Meath.
459	Slane (St Patrick) Church of Ireland Churchyard,County Meath.
468	Currin Church of Ireland Churchyard,County Monaghan.
475	Ballyburley Church of Ireland Churchyard,Offaly.
476	Ballycumber (Liss) Churchyard,Offaly.
480	Bir Old Graveyard,Offaly.
487	Killoughy Church of Ireland Churchyard,Offaly.
492	Ardcarn (St Beaidh) Church of Ireland Churchyard,County Roscommon.
499	Killaraght Church of Ireland Churchyard,County Sligo.
505	Ballyglass Cemetery,Mullingar,County Westmeath.
506	Cornamagh Cemetery,Athlone,County Westmeath.
510	Rathconnell Church of Ireland Churchyard,County Westmeath.
512	Toberclare Catholic Churchyard,County Westmeath.
531	Delgany (Christ Church) Church of Ireland Churchyard,County Wicklow.
532	Dunlavin (St Nicholas) Churchyard,County Wicklow.
533	Glenealy Church of Ireland Churchyard,County Wicklow.
534	Greystones (Redford) Cemetery,County Wicklow.
537	Kilcommon Church of Ireland Churchyard,County Wicklow.
539	Killiskey Church of Ireland Churchyard,County Wicklow.
541	Powerscourt (St Patrick) Church Of Ireland Churchyard,County Wicklow.

ESSEX.

1	The City of London Cemetery,Manor Park.
5	Manor Park Cemetery.
7	Woodgrange Park Cemetery.
9	Leytonstone (St Patrick's) Roman Catholic Cemetery.
10	Walthamstow (Queen's Road) Cemetery
11	Walthamstow (St Mary) Churchyard
13	East London Cemetery,Plaistow
14	West Ham Cemetery.
16	Barking (Rippleside) Cemetery
29	Shenfield (St Mary) Churchyard.
36	Thorndon Hall (Our Lady & St Lawrence) Chapel.
40	Chingford Mount Cemetery.
43	Grays New Cemetery.
45	Hornchurch (St Andrew) Churchyard.
48	Ilford Cemetery.
50	Loughton Burial Ground.
56	North Ockenden (St Mary Magdalene) Churchyard.
69	Hockley (St Peter) Churchyard.
73	Rochford (St Andrew) Churchyard.
75	Great Warley (Christchurch) Cemetery.
80	Romford Cemetery.
81	Shoeburyness (St Andrew) Churchyard.
83	Southend on Sea (Leigh on Sea) Cemetery.
84	Southend on Sea (North Road) Cemetery.
86	Southend on Sea (Sutton Road) Cemetery.
88	Wanstead (St Mary) Churchyard.
95	Great Henny (St Mary) Churchyard.
106	Hatfield Peverel (St Andrew) Churchyard.
107	Kelvedon (St Mary) Churchyard Extension.
110	Wethersfield (St Mary Magdalene) Churchyard.
118	Chelmsford (Rectory Lane) Cemetery.
119	Chelmsford (Writtle Road) Cemetery.
120	Springfield (Holy Trinity) Churchyard.
122	Broomfield (St Mary) Churchyard.
123	Danbury (St John the Baptist) Churchyard.
128	Great Waltham (SS Mary and Lawrence) Churchyard.
130	Ingatestone and Fryerning Cemetery.
132	Little Waltham (St Martin) Churchyard.
137	Sandon (St Andrew) Churchyard.
145	Berechurch (St Michael) Churchyard.
146	Colchester Cemetery.
167	Harlow (St Mary) Churchyard.
176	Frinton-on-Sea (St Mary) Churchyard.
185	Dovercourt (All Saints) Churchyard.
196	Great Horkesley (All Saints) Churchyard.
208	Maldon Cemetery.
209	Maldon (St Mary) Churchyard.
210	Bradwell-near-the-Sea (St Thomas the Apostle) Church Cemetery.
211	Goldhanger (St Peter) Churchyard.
212	Great Braxted (All Saints) Churchyard.
222	Stow Maries (SS Mary and Margaret) Churchyard.
231	Woodham Walter (St Michael) Churchyard.
242	Stapleford Abbots (St Mary) Churchyard.
246	Saffron Walden Friends' Burial Ground.
254	Littlebury (Holy Trinity) Churchyard.
255	Newport (St Mary) Churchyard.
256	Quendon Churchyard,Quendon and Rickling.
258	Rickling (All Saints) Churchyard,Quendon and Rickling.
261	Birchanger (St Mary) Churchyard.
267	Alresford (St Peter) Churchyard.
268	Ardleigh Cemetery.
274	Kirby-Le-Soken (St Michael) Churchyard.
275	Little Bentley (St Mary) Churchyard.
285	Witham (All Saints) Churchyard.

GLOUCESTERSHIRE

5	Bristol (Arno's Vale) Cemetery.
6	Bristol (Holy Souls) Roman Catholic Cemetery.
9	Bristol (Canford) Cemetery.
10	Bristol Cathedral Burial Ground.
11	Bristol (Greenbank) Cemetery.
15	Bristol (Shirehampton) Cemetery
19	Westbury-on-Trym (Holy Trinity) Churchyard.
24	Charlton Kings Cemetery.
27	Cheltenham Cemetery,Prestbury
31	Leckhampton (St Peter) Churchyard
32	Prestbury (St Mary) Churchyard,Dowdeswell
38	Frenchay (St John the Baptist) Churchyard,Winterbourne.
40	Little Badminton Churchyard,Hawkesbury.

51	Brimpsfield (St Michael) Churchyard
61	Quenington Cemetery
67	Cirencester Cemetery
69	Lower Cam (St Bartholomew) Churchyard,Cam
72	Slimbridge (St John) Churchyard
86	Gloucester Cemetery
88	Barnwood (St Lawrence) Churchyard.
92	Hempsted (St Swithun) Churchyard.
102	Wotton Congregational Church Cemetery,Wotton St Mary With-Out.
109	Lydney (St Mary) Churchyard.
124	Newnham (St Peter) Churchyard
126	Chedworth (St Andrew) Churchyard.
133	Whittington Cemetery
138	Great Barrington Cemetery.
143	Amberley Church Cemetery,Minchinhampton.
159	Rodborough (St Mary Magdalene) Churchyard.
168	Stroud Cemetery
176	Ashchurch (St Nicholas) Churchyard
182	Berkeley Cemetery.
190	Thornbury Cemetery
203	Eastington (St Michael) Churchyard
214	Stanton (St Michael) Churchyard

HAMPSHIRE.

1	Aldershot Military Cemetery.
4	Gosport (Ann's Hill) Cemetery.
7	Eastney Cemetery,Portsmouth
8	Milton Cemetery,Portsmouth.
9	Portsea Cemetery,Portsmouth.
10	Portsdown (Christ Church) Cemetery,Portsmouth
11	Portsdown (Christ Church) Military Cemetery,Portsmouth
12	Wymering (SS Peter and Paul) Churchyard,Portsmouth
13	Bournemouth East Cemetery
15	Bournemouth (Wimborne Road) Cemetery
17	Christchurch Cemetery.
19	Highcliffe (St Mark) Churchyard.
22	Throop Congregational Churchyard,Holdenhurst
23	Fordingbridge Cemetery
28	Lymington Cemetery
30	Brockenhurst (St Nicholas) Cemetery
31	East Boldre (St Paul) Churchyard
34	Milton (St Mary Magdalene) Churchyard
41	Eling (St Mary) Churchyard Extension
43	Exbury (St Catherine) Church
53	North Stoneham (St Nicholas) Churchyard
56	Southampton (Hollybrook) Cemetery
57	Southampton Old Cemetery
58	Southampton (St Mary Extra) Cemetery
60	Botley (All Saints) Churchyard
62	Hound (St Mary) Churchyard Extension
64	Netley Military Cemetery,Hound
70	Cheriton (St Michael) Churchyard
76	Bentley (St Mary) Churchyard
83	Grayshott (St Luke) Churchyard
85	Headley (All Saints) Churchyard Extension
87	Kingsley (St Nicholas) Old Churchyard
90	Andover Cemetery
98	Penton Mewsey (Holy Trinity) Churchyard
106	Basingstoke (South View) Cemetery
115	Newnham (St Nicholas) Churchyard
119	Sherfield-Upon-Loddon (St Leonard) churchyard
122	Upton Grey (St Mary) Churchyard
130	Shedfield (St John the Baptist) Churchyard
132	Swanmore (St Barnabas) Churchyard
136	Crofton (Holy Rood) Old Churchyard
138	Porchester (St Mary) Churchyard
144	Farnborough Abbey Roman Catholic Churchyard
145	Farnborough Burial Ground
146	Fleet (All Saints) Churchyard

153	Hartley Wintney (St Mary) Old Churchyard
159	Yateley (St Peter) Churchyard
161	North Hayling (St Peter) Churchyard
173	Highclere Cemetery
179	Steep (All Saints) Churchyard
180	Petersfield Cemetery
182	Braishfield (All Saints) Churchyard,Michelmersh.
186	Rownhams (St John) Churchyard
191	Nether Wallop (St Andrew) Churchyard.
192	Stockbridge Cemetery
202	Winchester (West Hill) Old Cemetery
205	Compton (All Saints) Churchyard
214	Ryde Borough Cemetery,Isle of Wight
216	East Cowes Cemetery,Isle of Wight
217	Oakfield (St John's) Cemetery,Isle of Wight.
218	St Helens Churchyard,Isle of Wight
219	Sandown (Christ Church) Churchyard,Isle of Wight
220	Shanklin Cemetery,Isle of Wight
221	Ventnor Cemetery,Isle of Wight.
232	Carisbrooke Cemetery,Isle of Wight
234	Freshwater (All Saints) Churchyard,Isle Of Wight.
240	Parkhurst Military Cemetery,Carisbrooke,Isle of Wight
241	Shalfleet Churchyard,Isle of Wight
242	Shorwell (St Peter) New Churchyard,Isle of Wight
245	Wippingham (St Mildred) Churchyard,Isle of Wight.
246	Whitwell New Burial Ground,Isle of Wight.

HEREFORD AND WORCESTER.

9	Whitbourne (St John the Baptist) Churchyard Extension,Hereford.
18	Hereford Cemetery,Hereford
51	Bosbury (Holy Trinity(Churchyard,Hereford
54	Colwall (St James the Great) Churchyard,Hereford
56	Much Marcle (St Bartholomew) Churchyard,Hereford
59	Ledbury Cemetery,Hereford.
96	Mansell Gamage (St Giles) Churchyard,Hereford
110	Bromsgrove Cemetery,Worcester
116	Martin Hussingtree (St Michael) Churchyard,Worcester
129	Broadway (St Eadburgh) Churchyard,Worcester
144	Kidderminster (St John the Baptist) Churchyard,Worcester
154	Great Malvern Cemetery,Worcester
162	Harpley (St Bartholomew) Churchyard,Lower Sapey,Worcester.
166	Martley (St Peter) Churchyard,Worcester
182	Blockley Church Cemetery,Worcester
186	Stourbridge Cemetery,Worcester
189	Lower Mitton (St Michael) Churchyard,Worcester
191	Tenbury (St Mary) Churchyard,Worcester
201	Kempsey (St Mary) Churchyard,Worcester
208	Worcester (Astwood) Cemetery,Worcester

HERTFORD

10	Shenley (St Botolph) Churchyard
12	Chipping Barnet Church Burial Ground
24	Layston Churchyard
29	Chorley Wood (Christ Church) Churchyard
30	Great Northern London Cemetery
31	Great Birkhamsted (St Peter) Churchyard
37	Harpenden (St Nicholas) Churchyard
38	Bishop's Hatfield (St Etheldreda) Church Cemetery.
60	Tewin (St Peter) Churchyard
72	Knebworth (St Mary) Churchyard
81	Hitchin Cemetery
84	Rickmansworth Cemetery.
87	St Albans Cemetery
91	Redbourn (St Mary) Churchyard
108	Wareside (Holy Trinity) Churchyard,Ware Rural
110	Watford Cemetery
115	Radlett (Christ Church) Churchyard,Aldenham
116	Welwyn Cemetery

KENT.

5	Charlton Cemetery.
7	Dover (St Jame's) Cemetery.
8	Dover (St Mary's) New Cemetery.
15	St Margaret's-at-Cliffe (St Margaret) Churchyard.
24	Birchington (All Saints) Churchyard.
25	Minster Cemetery.
27	Margate Cemetery.
28	Ramsgate Cemetery.
29	Ramsgate (St Augustine) Roman Catholic Churchyard.
30	St Lawrence Cemetery.
34	Walmer (St Mary) Old Churchyard.
37	Hackington (St Stephen) Churchyard.
38	Herne Bay Cemetery,Herne.
44	Luton (Christ Church) Churchyard.
46	Gillingham New Cemetery.
61	Fort Pitt Military Cemetery.
62	Frindsbury (All Saints) Churchyard.
63	Rochester (St Margaret's) Cemetery.
67	Isle of Sheppey General Cemetery,Minster-in-Sheppey.
68	Leysdown (St Clemeny) Churchyard.
71	Sittingbourne Cemetery.
82	Beckenham (St George) Churchyard.
83	Crystal Palace District Cemetery.
85	Bexley Heath Cemetery.
86	East Wickham (St Michael) Churchyard.
89	Bromley Hill Cemetery.
90	Bromley (London Road) Cemetery.
91	Plaistow (St Mary's) Cemetery.
95	Hayes Churchyard.
96	Keston Churchyard.
97	Knockholt (St Katharine) Churchyard.
99	Orpington (All Saints) Churchyard.
100	St Paul's Cray (St Paulinus) Churchyard.
102	Chislehurst Cemetery.
103	Chislehurst (St Nicholas) Churchyard.
105	Crayford (St Paulinus) Churchyard.
109	Darenth (St Margaret) Churchyard.
122	Wilmington (St Michael) Churchyard.
124	Dartford (East Hill) Cemetery.
125	Dartford (Watling Street) Cemetery.
127	Erith (Brook Street) Cemetery.
129	Gravesend Cemetery.
130	Northfleet Cemetery.
141	Fordcombe (St Peter) Churchyard,Penshurst.
147	Riverhead (St Mary) Churchyard.
153	Sevenoaks (Greatness Park) Cemetery.
154	Sevenoaks (St Nicholas) Churchyard.
156	Foots Cray Baptist Chapelyard.
157	Sidcup Cemetery.
160	Ashford Cemetery.
164	Bridge (St Peter) Churchyard.
175	Canterbury Cemetery.
177	Canterbury (St Martin) Churchyard.
179	Cheriton (St Martin) Churchyard.
180	Shorncliffe Military Cemetery.
182	Cranbrook Cemetery.
191	Chilham (St Mary) Churchyard.
197	Wye (SS Gregory and Martin) Churchyard.
203	Saltwood (SS Peter and Paul) Churchyard.
205	Faversham Cemetery.
212	Ospringe (SS Peter and Paul) Churchyard.
217	Folkestone Old Cemetery.
224	Harnetsham (St John the Baptist) Churchyard.
230	Hythe Cemetery.
231	Lydd (All Saints) Churchyard Extension.
232	Maidstone Cemetery.
234	Bearstead (Holy Cross) Churchyard Extension.
235	Boughton Monchelsea (St Peter) Churchyard.
239	Linton (St Nicholas) Churchyard.
243	Staplehurst (All Saints) Churchyard.
252	East Peckham (St Michael) Churchyard.
259	West Malling (St Mary) Churchyard.
261	New Romney (St Nicholas) Churchyard.
267	Rusthall (St Paul) Churchyard.
268	Tunbridge Wells Cemetery.
269	Southborough Cemetery.
279	Brenchley (All Saints) Churchyard.
280	Groombridge (St John) Churchyard,Speldhurst.
281	Hildenborough (St John the Devine) Churchyard.
282	Horsmonden (St Margaret) Churchyard.
284	Matfield (St Luke) Churchyard,Brenchley.
285	Paddock Wood (St Andrew) Churchyard,Brenchley.
287	Speldhurst (St Mary) Churchyard.
289	Tonbridge Cemetery.
298	Westwell Burial Ground.
301	Wrotham (St George) Churchyard Extension.

LANCASHIRE.

1	Allerton Cemetery,Liverpool.
2	Anfield Cemetery,Liverpool.
4	Everton Cemetery,Liverpool.
7	Kirkdale Cemetery,Liverpool.
9	Lingfield Road (Broad Green) Jewish Cemetery,Liverpool.
10	Much Woolton (St Mary's) Roman Catholic Cemetery,Liverpool.
12	St Jame's Cemetery,Liverpool.
14	Toxteth Park Cemetery,Liverpool.
18	Wavertree (Holy Trinity) Churchyard,Liverpool.
19	Birch-in-Rusholme (St James) Churchyard,Manchester.
24	Cheetham Hill Wesleyan Cemetery,Manchester.
30	Manchester Crematorium.
32	Manchester (Gorton) Cemetery.
33	Manchester (Philips Park) Cemetery.
34	Manchester Southern Cemetery.
35	Moston (St Joseph's) Roman Catholic Cemetery,Manchester.
37	Newton Heath (All Saints) Churchyard,Manchester.
40	Barrow-in-Furness Cemetery.
42	Bispham (All Hallows) Churchyard.
43	Blackpool Cemetery.
48	Fleetwood (St Peter) Churchyard Extension.
52	Lund (St John) Churchyard,Clifton-with-Salwick.
71	Grange-Over-Sands Cemetery.
76	Lancaster Cemetery.
77	Lancaster (Scotforth) Cemetery.
80	Bolton-le-Sands (Holy Trinity) Churchyard.
86	Warton (St Oswald) Churchyard,Warton-with-Lundeth.
92	Lytham (St Cuthbert) Churchyard.
95	St Anne's-on-Sea Churchyard.
98	Morecombe (Torrisholme) Cemetery.
102	Preston (New Hall Lane) Cemetery.
103	Broughton (St John the Baptist) Churchyard.
111	Longton (St Andrew) Churchyard.
112	Longton (St Oswald) Roman Catholic Churchyard.
114	Penwortham (St Mary) Churchyard.
149	Great Crosby (St Luke) Churchyard.
150	Great Crosby (SS Peter and Paul) Roman Catholic Churchyard.
152	Huyton (St Agnes) Roman Catholic Churchyard.
156	Liverpool (Yew Tree) Roman Catholic Cemetery.
157	Newton-in-Makerfield Cemetery.
160	Prescot (St Mary) Churchyard.
164	St Helens Cemetery.
168	Ince Blundell Roman Catholic Cemetery.
169	Liverpool (Ford) Roman Catholic Cemetery.
170	Sefton (St Helen) Churchyard.
171	Warrington Cemetery.
176	Hollinfare Cemetery,Rixton-with-Glazebrook.
179	Eccleston (Christ Church) Churchyard.
181	Halewood (St Nicholas) Churchyard.
186	Farnworth (St Luke) Churchyard.
189	Accrington Cemetery.

193	Blackburn Cemetery	117	Sysonby Churchyard
199	Mellor Wesleyan Methodist Chapelyard	119	Quorn (St Bartholomew) Churchyard
205	Burnley Cemetery	120	Shepshed Cemetery
206	Habergham (All Saints) Churchyard		
209	Briercliffe (St James) Churchyard		**LINCOLNSHIRE**
210	Foulridge (St Michael) Churchyard	10	Skirbeck Quarter (St Thomas) Churchyard
211	Haggate Baptist Chapelyard, Briercliffe	14	Fleet (St Mary Magdalene) Churchyard
216	Newchurch-in-Pendle (St Mary) Churchyard, Goldshaw Booth	25	Gosberton Cemetery
219	Wheatley Lane Inghamite Chapelyard, Wheatley Carr Booth	29	Spalding Cemetery
222	Church and Clayton-le-Moors Joint Cemetery	34	Folkingham (St Andrew) Churchyard
226	Clitheroe (St Mary's) Burial Ground	44	Bourne Cemetery
233	Whalley (Queen Mary's Hospital) Military Cemetery	53	Waddington (St Michael) Churchyard
235	Colne Cemetery	60	Stubton (St Martin) Churchyard
246	Padiham Cemetery	61	Grantham Cemetery
255	Bolton (Astley Bridge) Cemetery	67	Harlaxton (SS Mary and Peter) Churchyard
256	Bolton (Heaton) Cemetery	69	Londonthorpe (St John the Baptist) Churchyard
257	Bolton (Tonge) Cemetery	76	Billinghay Cemetery
261	Halliwell (St Peter) Churchyard	86	Leasingham (St Andrew) Churchyard
263	Bury Cemetery	98	Quarrington (St Botolph) Churchyard
266	Bury (St Paul) Churchyard	100	Stamford Cemetery
267	Elton (All Saints) Churchyard	115	Middle Rasen (St Peter) Churchyard
277	Darwen Cemetery	123	Cleethorpes Cemetery
278	Hoddlesden (St Paul) Churchyard	136	Gainsborough General Cemetery
283	Haslingden Holden Hall) Cemetery	142	Broughton Cemetery
284	Haslingden (St James the Great) Churchyard	156	Grimsby (Scartho Road) Cemetery
313	Rawtenstall (Longholme) Wesleyan Chapelyard	158	Scartho (St Giles) Churchyard
321	Tottington (St Anne) Churchyard	162	Stallingborough (SS Peter and Paul) Churchyard
336	Whitworth Cemetery	179	Lincoln (Canwick Road) Cemetery
342	Ashton-in-Makerfield (St Thomas) Churchyard	181	Lincoln (Newport) Cemetery
343	Ashton-in-Makerfield (St Thomas) Churchyard, Heath Lane Extension	183	Louth Cemetery
346	Chorley Cemetery	202	Mablethorpe (St Mary) Churchyard
366	Formby (St Peter) Churchyard	220	Hogsthorpe (St Mary) Churchyard
368	Wigan Cemetery	225	Spilsby Cemetery
380	Southport (Birkdale) Cemetery		
381	Southport (Duke Street) Cemetery		**LONDON**
386	Aughton (Christ Church) Churchyard	1	Wandsworth Cemetery
387	Aughton (St Michael) Churchyard	2	Nunhead (All Saints) Cemetery
401	Douglas Cemetery, Isle of Man	3	Camberwell (Forest Hill Road) Cemetery
403	Kirk Braddan (St Brendan) New Churchyard, Isle of Man	4	Brompton Cemetery, Kensington
405	Kirk Christ Lezayre (Holy Trinity) Churchyard, Isle of Man	5	Fulham Old Cemetery
410	Kirk Malew (St Malew) Churchyard, Isle of Man	6	Fulham (St Thomas of Canterbury) Roman Catholic Cemetery
413	Kirk Maughold (St Machut) Churchyard, Isle of Man	7	Hammersmith Cemetery
416	Ashton-under-Lyne (Hurst) Cemetery	8	Kensal Green (All Souls) Cemetery, Kensington and Hammersmith
421	Audenshaw (St Stephen) Churchyard	9	Kensal Green (St Mary's) Roman Catholic Cemetery, Hammersmith
427	Oldham (Chadderton) Cemetery	10	Abney Park Cemetery, Stoke Newington
434	Eccles (Peel Green) Cemetery	11	City of London and Tower Hamlets Cemetery, Stepney
438	Hindley (All Saints) Churchyard	12	Hampstead Cemetery
441	Hey (St John the Baptist) Churchyard Extension	13	Hampstead (St John) Additional Burial Ground
443	Leigh Cemetery	14	Highgate Cemetery, St Pancras
450	Middleton New Cemetery	15	St Paul's Cathedral
463	Prestwich (St Margaret) Churchyard	28	Charlton Cemetery, Greenwich
464	Prestwich (St Mary) Churchyard	29	Greenwich Cemetery
471	Higher Broughton (St John) Churchyard	32	Eltham (St John the Baptist) Churchyard, Woolwich
472	Kersal (St Paul) Churchyard	33	Plumstead Cemetery, Woolwich
474	Salford (Weaste) Cemetery	35	Woolwich Cemetery
475	Stretford Cemetery		
478	Pendlebury (St Augustine of Canterbury) Churchyard		**MIDDLESEX**
481	Swinton Cemetery	1	Edmonton Cemetery
483	Tyldesley Cemetery	5	Enfield Chase Cemetery
489	Whitefield British Jews' Cemetery	6	Enfield Highway Cemetery
491	Worsley (St Mark) Churchyard	9	Southgate Cemetery
		12	South Mimms (St Giles) Churchyard
	LEICESTERSHIRE	13	Tottenham and Wood Green Cemetery
13	Barrow-upon-Soar Cemetery	15	Islington Cemetery
24	Woodhouse Eaves (St Paul) Churchyard Extension, Woodhouse	16	St Marylebone Cemetery
55	Burbage (St Catherine) Churchyard	17	St Pancras Cemetery
63	Leicester (Welford Road) Cemetery	18	Harrow on the Hill (St Mary) Lower Churchyard
64	Loughborough (Leicester Road) Cemetery	19	Harrow on the Hill Cemetery
87	Shenton (St John) Churchyard	21	Edgware (St Margaret) Churchyard
97	Market Harborough (Northampton Road) Cemetery	23	Harrow Weald (All Saints) Churchyard Extension

25	Pinner Cemetery.
26	Golders Green Crematorium.
27	Golders Green Jewish Cemetery.
28	Hampstead Garden Suburb (St Jude) Church.
29	Hendon Park Cemetery.
30	Hendon (St Mary) Churchyard.
34	Ruislip (St Martin) Churchyard Extension.
37	Wembley Old Burial Ground.
39	Paddington Cemetery.
40	Willesden Jewish Cemetery.
41	Willesden Liberal Jewish Cemetery.
42	Willesden New Cemetery.
43	Willesden Old Cemetery.
44	Acton Cemetery.
46	Chiswick Cemetery.
47	New Brentford (St Lawrence) Churchyard.
48	Ealing and Old Brentford Cemetery.
49	Greenford (Holy Cross) Churchyard.
51	Kensington (Hanwell) Cemetery.
52	Perivale Cemetery.
53	Westminster City Cemetery.
58	Hampton Burial Ground.
62	Harlington (SS Peter and Paul) Churchyard.
66	Heston (St Leonard) Churchyard.
68	New Brentford Cemetery.
70	Ashford Cemetery.
76	Sunbury New Cemetery.
77	Teddington Cemetery.
78	Hounslow Cemetery.
80	Twickenham Parochial Cemetery.
83	Hillingdon Cemetery.

MONMOUTHSHIRE.

4	Abergavenny New Cemetery,Llanfoist.
9	Llanfoist (St Faith) Churchyard.
19	Trevethin (St Cadoc) Churchyard.
34	Caldicot (St Mary) Churchyard.
52	Newport (Christchurch) Cemetery,Christchurch.
67	Newport (St Woollos) Cemetery.
69	Panteg Cemetery.
76	Graig Congregational Chapelyard.
83	Rogerstone (Bethesda) Baptist Chapelyard.
89	Usk (St Mary Magdalene) Churchyard.

NORFOLK.

11	Heydon (SS Peter and Paul) Churchyard.
15	Stratton Strawless (St Margaret) Churchyard.
24	Redenhall (The Assumption) Churchyard,Redwnhall-with-Harleston.
26	Thorpe-Next-Norwich (St Andrew) Church Cemetery.
30	Cromer No.2 Burial Ground.
58	Docking (St Mary) Churchyard.
60	Heacham (St Mary) Churchyard.
61	Hunstanton (St Mary) Churchyard.
73	Marham (Holy Trinity) Churchyard.
74	Runcton Holme (St James) Churchyard,South Runcton.
77	Stradsett (St Mary) Churchyard.
85	Great Yarmouth (Caister) Cemetery,East Caister.
94	Aldborough (St Mary) Churchyard.
101	Mundesley (All Saints) Churchyard.
103	Overstrand (St Martin) Churchyard.
110	West Runton (Holy Trinity) Churchyard,Runton.
111	Weybourne (All Saints) Churchyard
118	Kimberley (St Peter) Churchyard.
128	Little Massingham (St Andrew) Churchyard
132	Great Yarmouth New Cemetery.
137	Colney (St Andrew) Churchyard
138	Cringleford (St Peter) Churchyard.
139	East Carleton (St Mary) Churchyard
151	King's Lynn Cemetery.
162	Hedenham (St Peter) Churchyard.
172	Woodton (All Saints) Churchyard
179	Upwell (St Peter) Churchyard.
184	East Bilney (St Mary) Churchyard,Beetley.
195	Mileham (St John the Baptist) Churchyard.
207	Eaton (St Andrew) New Churchyard,Norwich.
209	Norwich Cemetery.
210	Norwich (The Rosary) Cemetery.
231	Hoveton St John Churchyard,Hoveton.
235	Sloley (St Bartholomew) Churchyard.
247	Narborough (All Saints) Churchyard.
254	Swaffham (SS Peter and Paul) Churchyard.
255	Thetford Cemetery.
256	Blo'Norton (St Andrew) Churchyard.
259	East Harling Cemetery,Harling.
261	Feltwell (St Nicholas) Churchyard.
285	Attleborough Cemetery.
288	Breckles (St Margaret) Churchyard,Stow Bedon.
301	Watton Nonconformist Burial Ground.

NORTHAMPTON.

1	Brackley (St Peter) Churchyard.
13	Church Brampton (St Botolph) Churchyard.
27	Barby (St Mary) Churchyard.
31	Yelvertoft (All Saints) Churchyard.
32	Daventry (Holy Cross) Churchyard.
38	Newnham (St Michael) Churchyard.
55	Castle Ashby (St Mary Magdalene) Churchyard.
60	Northampton (Towcester Road) Cemetery,Hardingstone.
67	Cottingham (St Mary Magdalene) Churchyard.
74	Kettering Cemetery.
76	Middleton Cheney (All Saints) Churchyard.
78	Abington (SS Peter and Paul) Churchyard.
79	Northampton General Cemetery.
80	Dallington Cemetery.
107	Raunds Wesleyan Methodist Chapelyard.
144	Wellingborough (London Road) Cemetery.
151	Peterborough Old Cemetery,Soke of Peterborough.
161	Hambleton (St Andrew) Churchyard,Rutland.
164	Oakham Cemetery,Rutland.

NORTHERN IRELAND.

33	Belfast City Cemetery,County Antrim.
40	Carrickfergus (Victoria) Cemetery,County Antrim.
42	Ballylinney Presbyterian Cemetery,County Antrim.
45	Glenarm New Cemetery,County Antrim.
56	Drumbeg (St Patrick) Church of Ireland Churchyard,County Antrim.
57	Dundrod Presbyterian Churchyard,County Antrim.
68	Kilmore (St Aidnan) Church of Ireland Churchyard,County Armagh.
71	Armagh (St Mark) Church of Ireland Churchyard,County Armagh.
74	Derrytrasna Roman Catholic Churchyard,County Armagh.
79	Seagoe Cemetery,County Armagh.
80	Lurgan (Dougher) Roman Catholic Cemetery,County Armagh.
85	Bessbrook (Christ Church) Church of Ireland Churchyard Extension, County Armagh.
105	Banbridge Roman Catholic Cemetery,County Down.
106	Banbridge Town Cemetery,County Down.
107	Bangor New Cemetery,County Down.
110	Belfast (Dundonald) Cemetery,County Down.
124	Down Cathedral New Cemetery,County Down.
136	Hillsborough (St Malachi) Church of Ireland Churchyard,County Down.
137	Knockbreda Church of Ireland Churchyard,Newtownbreda,County Down.
138	Holywood Cemetery,County Down.
145	Newcastle (St John's) Cemetery,County Down.
146	Colonallan Church of Ireland Churchyard,County Down.
165	kinawley Church of Ireland Churchyard,Derrylin,County Fermanagh.
168	Enniskillen New Cemetery,County Fermanagh.
181	Coleraine Cemetery,County Londonderry.
183	Killowen (St John) Church of Ireland Churchyard,County Londonderry
196	Londonderry City Cemetery,County Londonderry

201 Glendermot Church of Ireland Churchyard, County Londonderry
229 Dungannon Borough Cemetery, County Tyrone
231 Cappagh (St Eugenius) Church of Ireland Churchyard, East Mountjoy, County Tyrone
239 Kilskeery Church of Ireland Churchyard, County Tyrone
248 Strabane Cemetery, County Tyrone

NORTHUMBERLAND

1 Newcastle-upon-Tyne (All Saints) Cemetery
2 Newcastle-upon-Tyne (Byker and Heaton) Cemetery
3 Newcastle-upon-Tyne (Old Jesmond) General Cemetery
4 Newcastle-upon-Tyne (St Andrew's and Jesmond) Cemetery
5 Newcastle-upon-Tyne (St John's, Westgate and Elswick) Cemetery
7 Newcastle-upon-Tyne (St Nicholas) Cemetery
11 Alnwick Cemetery
11a Bolton Churchyard
19 South Charlton (St James) Churchyard
20 Warkworth (St Laurence) Church Burial Ground
26 Bedlington (St Cuthbert) Churchyard
34 Berwick-upon-Tweed Cemetery
36 Blyth Cemetery
39 Horton (St Mary) Churchyard, Blyth
43 North Gosforth Joint Burial Ground
49 Earsdon (St Alban) Churchyard, Seaton Valley
58 Wooler (St Mary) Church Burial Ground
60 Gosforth (St Nicholas) Churchyard
74 Longbenton (Benton) Cemetery
75 Morpeth (SS Mary and James) Churchyard
83 Newburn (Lemington) Cemetery
86 Ancroft (St Anne) Churchyard
87 Norham (St Cuthbert) Churchyard
96 Tynemouth (Preston) Cemetery
99 Whitley Bay (Hartley South) Cemetery

NOTTINGHAMSHIRE

2 Annesley and Felley Cemetery, Annesley
32 Plumtree (St Mary) Churchyard
39 East Retford Cemetery
60 Hucknall Cemetery
66 East Leake (St Mary the Virgin) Churchyard
68 Mansfield (Nottingham Road) Cemetery
70 Forest Town (St Alban) Churchyard
84 Nottingham Church Cemetery
85 Nottingham General Cemetery
96 Halam (St Michael) Churchyard
106 Southwell Minster (St Mary) Churchyard
112 Sutton-in-Ashfield Cemetery
121 Worksop (Retford Road) Cemetery

OXFORDSHIRE

1 Banbury Cemetery
24 Bicester Cemetery
32 Spelsbury (All Saints) Churchyard
36 Dorchester Cemetery
44 Goring (St Thomas of Canterbury) Churchyard
45 Mapledurham (St Margaret) Churchyard
51 Henley-on-Thames Cemetery
69 Oxford (Botley) Cemetery
71 Oxford (Holy Cross) Cemetery
73 Oxford (Rose Hill) Cemetery
74 Oxford (Wolvercote) Cemetery
85 Brize Norton (St Brice) Churchyard Extension
97 Witney Burial Ground

SCOTLAND

1 Applin Old Churchyard, Lismore and Applin, Argyll
2 Applin (St Cross) Episcopalian Churchyard, Lismore and Applin, Argyll
4 Ardmarnoch House Burial Ground, Fillinan, Argyll
9 Campbeltown (Kilkerrean) Cemetery, Argyll
14 Dunoon Cemetery, Dunoon and Kilmun, Argyll
15 Dunoon (Holy Trinity) Episcopalian Churchyard, Dunoon and Kilmun, Argyll
22 Kiells Old Churchyard, Jara, Argyll
26 Kilbride Parish Churchyard, Kilfinan, Argyll
41 Kilmhorn Old Churchyard, Craignish, Argyll
44 Kilmory Castle Burial Ground, Glassary, Argyll
45 Kilmun Cemetery, Dunoon and Kilmun, Argyll
50 Kilvickeon Old Churchyard, Kilfinichen and Kilvickeon, Argyll
52 Lochgoilhead Parish Churchyard, Lochgoilhead and Kilmorich, Argyll
54 Oban (Pennyfuir) Cemetery, Kilmore and Kilbride, Argyll
60 Tarbert Burial Ground, Kilcalmonell, Argyll
64 Alloa (Sunnyside) Cemetery, Clackmannan
69 Tillicoultry Cemetery, Clackmannan
76 Boturich Castle Private Cemetery, Kilmaronock, Dumbarton
77 Cardross Parish Churchyard, Dumbarton
80 Dumbarton Cemetery, Dumbarton
82 Helensburgh Cemetery, Row, Dumbarton
84 Kirkintilloch (Auld Aisle) Cemetery, Dumbarton
86 New Patrick Cemetery, Dumbarton
87 New Kilpatrick Parish Churchyard, Dumbarton
92 Abercrombie Old Chapelyard, Fife
97 Ballingry Cemetery, Fife
105 Cowdenbeath Cemetery, Beath, Fife
109 Cupar New Cemetery, Fife
112 Dunfermline Cemetery, Fife
115 East Wemyss Cemetery, Wemyss, Fife
118 Forgan (Vicarsford) Cemetery, Fife
119 Inverkeithing Cemetery, Fife
122 Kilconquhar Parish Churchyard, Fife
127 Kirkcaldy Cemetery, Kirkcaldy and Dysart, Fife
136 Newburgh Cemetery, Fife
141 St Andrews Eastern Cemetery, Fife
142 St Andrews Western Cemetery, Fife
151 Kinross East Burying Ground, Kinross
153 Orwell Parish Churchyard, Kinross
167 Callander Cemetery, Perth
169 Comrie Cemetery, Perth
171 Crieff Cemetery, Perth
180 Innerwick-in-Glenlyon Parish Churchyard, Fortingall, Perth
187 Kinfauns Parish Churchyard, Perth
199 Perth (Wellshill) Cemetery, Perth
200 Pitlochry New Cemetery, Moulin, Perth
203 St Madoes Parish Churchyard, Perth
204 Scone Cemetery, Perth
208 Trossachs Parish Churchyard, Callander, Perth
211 Denny Cemetery, Stirling
212 Falkirk Cemetery, Stirling
214 Grangemouth Burial Ground, Stirling
226 Stirling (Ballengeich) Cemetery, Stirling
228 Stirling (Mar Place) Cemetery, Stirling
231 Colinton Parish Churchyard, Edinburgh
235 Edinburgh (Comely Bank) Cemetery
236 Edinburgh (Dalry) Cemetery
237 Edinburgh (Dean, Western) Cemetery
238 Edinburgh Eastern Cemetery
239 Edinburgh (Grange) Cemetery
240 Edinburgh (Liberton) Cemetery
241 Edinburgh (Morningside) Cemetery
242 Edinburgh (New Calton) Burial Ground
244 Edinburgh (Newington) Cemetery
245 Edinburgh (North Merchiston) Cemetery
246 Edinburgh (Piershill) Cemetery
247 Edinburgh (Portobello) Cemetery
249 Edinburgh (Rosebank) Cemetery
252 Edinburgh (Seafield) Cemetery
253 Edinburgh (Warriston) Cemetery
259 Cranston Parish Churchyard, Midlothian
262 Dalkeith (Eskbank) Cemetery, Midlothian
263 Dalmahoy (Sr Mary) Episcopalian Churchyard, Ratho, Midlothian
267 Inveresk Parish Churchyard, Midlothian
269 Lasswade Old Churchyard, Midlothian

270	Loanhead Cemetery, Lasswade, Midlothian	627	Dirleton Parish Churchyard, East Lothian
274	Penicuik Cemetery, Midlothian.	632	Haddington Cemetery, East Lothian.
275	Penicuik Parish Churchyard, Midlothian.	639	Prestonkirk Parish Churchyard, East Lothian.
277	Roslin Cemetery, Lasswade, Midlothian.	644	Tynninghame Burial Ground, East Lothian.
279	West Calder Cemetery, Midlothian.	660	Kirkbean Parish Churchyard, Kirkcudbright.
280	Aberdeen (Allenvale) Cemetery.	669	Innerleithen Cemetery, Peebles.
281	Aberdeen (Grove) Cemetery.	671	Peebles Cemetery.
286	Aberdeen (St Peter's) Cemetery.	674	Cathcart Cemetery, Renfrew.
287	Aberdeen (Springbank) Cemetery.	675	Eastwood Cemetery, Renfrew.
288	Aberdeen (Trinity) Cemetery.	677	Greenock Cemetery, Renfrew.
294	Belhelvie Old Cemetery, Aberdeen.	679	Kilbarchan Cemetery, Renfrew.
308	Ellon Cemetery, Aberdeen.	680	Kilmacolm Cemetery, Renfrew.
310	Folla-Rule (St George) Episcopalian Churchyard, Fyvie, Aberdeen.	682	Neilston Cemetery, Renfrew.
313	Fraserburgh (Kirkton) Cemetery, Aberdeen.	683	Paisley Abbey Cemetery, Renfrew.
319	Huntly Cemetery, Aberdeen.	684	Paisley (Hawkhead) Cemetery, Renfrew.
330	Kincardine O'Neil Old Churchyard, Aberdeen.	685	Paisley (Woodside) Cemetery, Renfrew.
333	Kintore Parish Churchyard, Aberdeen.	686	Port Glasgow Cemetery, Renfrew.
341	Lonmay Parish Churchyard, Aberdeen.	696	Kelso Cemetery, Roxburgh.
353	New Pitsligo Parish Churchyard, Tyre, Aberdeen.	711	Ashkirk Parish Church, Selkirk.
357	Old Machar Cathedral Churchyard, Aberdeen.	713	Galashiels (Eastlands) Cemetery, Selkirk.
358	Peterculter Parish Churchyard, Aberdeen.	717	Selkirk Parish Churchyard.
359	Peterculter New Burial Ground, Aberdeen.	721	Bo'ness Cemetery, Bo'ness and Carriden, West Lothian.
378	Turriff Cemetery, Aberdeen.	722	Dalmeny Cemetery, West Lothian.
380	Arbroath Eastern Cemetery, Arbroath and St Vigeans, Angus.	723	Ecclesmachan Cemetery, West Lothian.
381	Arbroath Western Cemetery, Arbroath and St Vigeans, Angus.	725	Kirkliston Burial Ground, West Lothian.
385	Dundee Eastern Necropolis, Angus.	726	Linlithgow Cemetery, West Lothian.
386	Dundee Western Cemetery, Angus.	728	Polkemmet Private Burying Ground, Whitburn, West Lothian.
387	Dundee Western Necropolis, Angus.	729	Uphall Cemetery, West Lothian.
395	Monifieth Cemetery, Angus.	730	Whitburn Cemetery, West Lothian.
396	Montrose (Rosehill) Cemetery, Angus.	742	Portpatrick Cemetery, Wigtown.
398	Montrose (Sleepyhillock) Cemetery, Angus.	746	Stoneykirk Parish Churchyard, Wigtown.
430	Fort William (St Andrew) Episcopalian Churchyard, Kilmallie, Inverness.	752	Glasgow (Craigton) Cemetery.
438	Insh (St Eunan) Churchyard, Kingussie, Inverness.	754	Glasgow Eastern Necropolis.
442	Inverness (Tomnahurich) Cemetery.	755	Glasgow (Lambhill) Cemetery.
447	Kilmallie Old Churchyard, Inverness.	756	Glasgow Necropolis.
455	Kilmuir Old Churchyard, Duirinish, Inverness.	757	Glasgow (Riddrie Park) Cemetery.
458	Kingussie Parish Churchyard, Kingussie and Insh, Inverness.	758	Glasgow (St Kentigern's) Roman Catholic Cemetery.
495	Laurencekirk Cemetery, Kincardine.	760	Glasgow (Sandymount) Cemetery.
500	St Cyrus Upper (Parish) Churchyard, Kincardine.	761	Glasgow (Sighthill) Cemetery.
501	Ardrossan Cemetery, Ayr.	762	Glasgow Southern Necropolis (Central Division).
503	Ayr Cemetery.	764	Glasgow Western Necropolis.
508	Colmonell Parish Churchyard, Ayr.	766	Tollcross (Central) United Free Churchyard, Glasgow.
510	Cumnock New Cemetery, Old Cumnock, Ayr.	774	Cadder Cemetery, Lanark.
514	Darvel Cemetery, Ayr.	775	Cambuslang (Westburn) Cemetery, Lanark.
517	Dundonald (Troon) Cemetery, Ayr.	776	Cambusnethan Cemetery, Lanark.
520	Girvan (Doune) Cemetery, Ayr.	780	Carluke (Wilton) Cemetery, Lanark.
522	Irvine Cemetery, Ayr.	783	Carnwath New Cemetery, Lanark.
523	Irvine Parish Churchyard, Ayr.	789	Culter Parish Churchyard, Lanark.
525	Kilmarnock Cemetery, Ayr.	795	East Kilbride Cemetery, Lanark.
528	Kirkmichael Parish Churchyard, Ayr.	798	Hamilton (Bent) Cemetery, Lanark.
530	Largs Cemetery, Ayr.	799	Hamilton Parish Cemetery, Lanark.
531	Mauchline Cemetery, Ayr.	803	Lanark (St Leonard's) Cemetery.
533	Monkton and Prestwick Cemetery, Ayr.	805	Lanark (St Nicholas) Cemetery.
546	Symington Parish Churchyard, Ayr.	807	Lesmahagow Cemetery, Lanark.
547	Tarbolton Parish Churchyard, Ayr.	808	New Monkland Cemetery, Lanark.
561	Greenlaw Parish Churchyard, Berwick.	810	Old Monkland Cemetery, Lanark.
563	Hutton Parish Churchyard, Berwick.	812	Rutherglen Cemetery, Lanark.
566	Lennel Old Churchyard, Berwick.	816	Strathaven New Cemetery, Avondale, Lanark.
567	Longformacus New Burial Ground, Berwick.	832	Gamrie Old Churchyard, Banff.
569	Mordington Burial Ground, Berwick.	835	Keith (Broomhill) Cemetery, Banff.
581	Annan Cemetery, Dumfries.	838	Macduff Parish Churchyard, Banff.
582	Applegarth Parish Churchyard, Dumfries.	840	Mortlach Parish Churchyard, Banff.
591	Dryfesdale Cemetery, Dumfries.	854	Halkirk Parish Churchyard, Caithness.
596	Dumfries (St Michael's) New Cemetery, Dumfries.	858	Olrig New Cemetery, Caithness.
608	Kirkpatrick-Juxta Parish Churchyard, Dumfries.	862	Thurso Cemetery, Caithness.
612	Moffat Cemetery, Kirkpatrick-Juxta, Dumfries.	871	Duffus Cemetery, Moray.
613	Morton New Cemetery, Dumfries.	874	Elgin New Cemetery, Moray.
617	St Mungo Old Parish Churchyard, Dumfries.	876	Forres (Cluny Hill) Cemetery, Moray.
621	Troqueer New Burial Ground, Dumfries.	877	Grantown-on-Spey New Burial Ground, Cromdale, Moray.
625	Aberlady Parish Churchyard, East Lothian.	886	Nairn Cemetery, Nairn

893 Evie Cemetery,Evie and Rendall,Orkney
900 Lyness Naval Cemetery,Hoy and Graemsay,Orkney
926 Cromarty Parish Cemetery,Ross and Cromarty
935 Fodderty Old Churchyard,Ross and Cromarty
936 Foich Burial Ground,Lochbroom,Ross and Cromarty
963 Rosskeen Parish Churchyard Extension,Ross and Cromarty
966 Suddie Old Churchyard,Knockbain,Ross and Cromarty
967 Tain (St Duthus) Cemetery,Ross and Cromarty
968 Tarbat Parish Churchyard,Ross and Cromarty
975 Brora Cemetery,Clyne,Sutherland
990 Melness Cemetery,Tongue,Sutherland
1014 Lerwick New Cemetery,Zetland

SHROPSHIRE
19 Shrewsbury General Cemetery,Meole Brace
37 Church Stretton (St Lawrence) Churchyard Extension
52 Stoke-upon-Tern (St Peter) Churchyard Extension
60 Little Ness (St Martin) Churchyard
63 Petton Churchyard
67 Ludlow New Cemetery
74 Caynham (St Mary) Churchyard
81 Little Drayton (Christ Church) Churchyard
82 Market Drayton Cemetery
89 Newport Cemetery
93 Oswestry General Cemetery
95 Haughton (St Chad) Churchyard,West Felton
97 Knockin (St Mary) Churchyard
100 Moreton (SS Philip and James) Churchyard,Llanyblodwel
101 Nantmawr Congregational Chapelyard,Oswestry Rural
104 St Martin's Churchyard
111 Donington (St Cuthbert) Churchyard
114 Shifnal (St Andrew) Churchyard
125 Clive (All Saints) Churchyard
130 Shawbury (St Mary) Churchyard
138 Broseley Cemetery
143 Willey (St John the Devine) Churchyard
145 Tilstock (Christ Church) Churchyard,Whitchurch Rural
147 Whitchurch Cemetery

SOMERSET
10 Burrington (Holy Trinity) Churchyard
17 Uphill (St Nicholas) Churchyard
19 Wedmore (St Mary Magdalene) Churchyard
25 Bath (Locksbrook) Cemetery
26 Bath (St James's) Cemetery
30 Bathwick Church Cemetery
31 Bathampton (St Nicholas) Churchyard
33 Bathford (St Swithun) Churchyard
35 Charlcombe (St Mary) Churchyard
37 Lansdown Cemetery,Charlcombe
40 Wellow Cemetery
42 Bridgwater (Wembdon Road) Cemetery (Chapel Portion)
43 Bridgwater (Wembdon Road) Cemetery (Church Portion)
49 Middlezoy (Holy Cross) Churchyard
67 Hinton St George (St George) Churchyard
71 Clevedon (St Andrew) Churchyard
96 Frome (St John the Baptist) Churchyard
101 Corston (All Saints) Church
118 Kingweston (All Saints) Churchyard
126 Easton-in-Gordano (St George) Churchyard
139 Minehead Cemetery
153 Shepton Mallet Burial Ground
157 Taunton (St Mary's) Cemetery
161 Churchstanton (St Paul) Churchyard
172 Staple Fitzpaine (St Peter) Churchyard
173 Staplegrove (St John) Churchyard
183 Sampford Arundel (Holy Cross) Churchyard
185 Wells Cathedral Cemetery
186 Wells Cemetery
196 Wookey (St Matthew) Churchyard Extension
197 Weston-Super-Mare Cemetery
198 Carhampton (St John the Baptist) Churchyard
199 Crowcombe (Holy Ghost) Churchyard
210 Holford (St Mary) Churchyard
219 Redlynch (St Peter) Church,Bruton
222 South Cadbury (St Thomas A Becket) Churchyard

STAFFORDSHIRE
4 Brierley Hill (South Street) Baptist Churchyard
6 Ogley Hay (St James) Churchyard
21 Coseley (Christ Church) Churchyard
41 Codsall (St Nicholas) Churchyard Extensions
45 Pattingham (St Chad) Churchyard
47 Pennfields (St Philip) Churchyard,Trysull and Seisdon
49 Wombourn (St Benedict) churchyard
52 Smethwick (Uplands) Cemetery
57 Tetenhall Regis (St Michael) Churchyard
60 Walsall (Bloxwich) Cemetery
61 Walsall (Ryecroft) Cemetery
67 Rushall (St Michael) Churchyard
73 West Bromwich Cemetery
78 Wolverhampton General Cemetery
84 Burton-upon-Trent Cemetery
85 Horninglow (St John) Churchyard
91 Cheddleton (St Edward the Confessor) Churchyard
93 Kingsley (St Werburgh) Churchyard
105 Norton-in-the-Moors (St Bartholomew) Churchyard
108 Lichfield (St Chad) Churchyard
109 Lichfield (St Michael) Churchyard
114 Cannock Chase Military Burial Ground,Brereton
125 Whittington (St Giles) Churchyard
134 Castle Church (St Mary) Chuhrchyard
135 Stafford Cemetery
140 Great Haywood (St Stephen) Churchyard,Colwick
143 Ingestre (St Mary) Churchyard
152 Normacot (Holy Evangelists) Churchyard
153 Stoke-on-Trent (Burslem) Cemetery
156 Stoke-on-Trent (Hartshill) Cemetery
170 Rangemore (All Saints) Churchyard,Tatenhill
176 Blithfield (St Leonard) Churchyard
177 Denstone (All Saints) Churchyard
180 Newborough (All Saints) Churchyard
183 Uttoxeter Cemetery

SUFFOLK
3 Aldringham (St Andrew) Churchyard
9 Dunwich (St James) Churchyard
45 Bungay Cemetery
54 Felixstowe New Cemetery
55 Felixstowe (SS Peter and Paul) Churchyard
64 Redgrave (St Botolph) Churchyard
69 Badingham (St John the Baptist) Churchyard
83 Ipswich Cemetery
98 Oulton (St Michael) Churchyard
106 Earl Soham Cemetery
121 Brantham (St Michael) Churchyard
126 East Bergholt Cemetery
133 Stutton (St Peter) Churchyard
137 Southwold (St Edmund) Churchyard
138 Stowmarket Cemetery
173 Euston (St Genevieve) Churchyard
176 Bury St Edmunds Cemetery
207 Nayland Cemetery,Nayland-with-Wissington
215 Icklingham (St James) Churchyard
224 Exning Cemetery
225 Sudbury Cemetery
242 Great Livermere (St Peter) Churchyard

SURREY.
1   Brookwood Military Cemetery.
2   Barnes (East Sheen) Cemetery.
3   Barnes Old Cemetery.
4   Mortlake Burial Ground.
6   Bandon Hill Cemetery, Beddington.
8   Carshalton (All Saints) Churchyard.
9   Caterham Burial Ground.
11 Whyteleafe (St Luke) Churchyard.
13 Sanderstead (All Saints) Churchyard.
15 Croydon (Mitcham Road) Cemetery.
16 Croydon (Queen's Road) Cemetery.
18 Shirley (St John) Churchyard.
27 Godstone (St Nicholas) Churchyard.
29 Limpsfield (St Peter) Churchyard.
32 Tandridge (St Peter) Churchyard.
34 Battersea Cemetery, Morden.
36 Morden (St Laurence) Churchyard.
37 Mitcham Burial Ground.
38 Streatham Park Cemetery.
41 Reigate Cemetery.
43 Buckland (St Mary) Churchyard.
45 Chipstead (St Margaret) Churchyard.
47 Kingswood (St Andrew) Churchyard.
52 Walton-on-the-Hill (St Peter) Churchyard.
55 Sutton Cemetery.
57 Wimbledon (Gap Road) Cemetery.
58 Wimbledon (St Mary-on-the-Hill) Churchyard.
60 Byfleet (St Mary) Churchyard.
62 Valley End (St Saviour) Churchyard, Chobham.
64 Addlestone Burial Ground.
70 Holmwood (St Mary Magdalene) Churchyard, Capel.
72 Ockley Cemetery.
75 Dorking Cemetery.
76 East Molesey Cemetery.
78 Egham (St Jude's) Cemetery.
80 Ashtead (St Giles) Churchyard.
83 Cobham Cemetery.
84 Ewell (St Mary) Churchyard.
86 Hatchford (St Matthew) Churchyard, Cobham.
88 Little Bookahm Churchyard.
91 Epsom Cemetery.
93 Claygate (Holy Trinity) Churchyard.
94 Esher (Christ Church) Churchyard.
95 Long Ditton (St Mary) Churchyard.
96 Thames Ditton (St Nicholas) Churchyard.
97 Ash Cemetery, Ash and Normandy.
99 Frensham (St Mary) Churchyard.
102 Shottermill (St Stephen) Churchyard.
103 Tilford (All Saints) Churchyard, Farnham Rural.
104 Wyke (St Mark) Churchyard, Ash and Normandy.
106 Farnham Civil Cemetery.
110 Wrecclesham (St Peter) Churchyard Extension.
112 Frimley (St Peter) Churchyard.
113 York Town (St Michael) Churchyard.
114 Busbridge (St John the Baptist) Churchyard.
115 Godalming New Cemetery.
118 Guildford (Stoke) Cemetery.
126 Send (St Mary) Churchyard, Send and Ripley.
128 Shere (St James) Churchyard.
131 Worplesdon (St Mary) Churchyard.
132 Ham (St Andrew) Churchyard.
134 Bramley Cemetery.
135 Chiddingfold (St Mary) Churchyard.
136 Cranleigh Cemetery.
138 Grayswood (All Saints) Churchyard, Witley.
148 Kingston-on-Thames Cemetery.
150 Fulham New Cemetery, North Sheen.
151 Petersham (St Peter) Churchyard.
152 Richmond Cemetery.
153 Surbiton Cemetery.
154 Malden (St John the Baptist) Churchyard.
156 Walton-on-Thames Cemetery.
157 Weybridge Cemetery.
158 Windlesham Additional Burial Ground.
159 Windlesham (Bagshot) Burial Ground.
160 Brookwood Cemetery (The London Necropolis).
161 Horsell (St Mary) churchyard.
162 Woking Crematorium.

SUSSEX.
2   Arundel Roman Catholic Cemetery.
4   Bognor Regis Cemetery.
5   Chichester Cemetery.
9   Lyminster (St Mary Magdalene) Churchyard.
13 Coolhurst Churchyard, Lower Beeding.
15 Crawley Monastery Burial Ground.
19 Nuthurst (St Andrew) Churchyard.
23 Slinfold (St Peter) Churchyard.
24 Warnham (St Margaret) Churchyard.
27 Horsham (Hills) Cemetery.
30 Easebourne (St Mary) Churchyard.
55 Old Shoreham Cemetery.
57 Southwick (St Michael) Churchyard.
58 Henfield Cemetery.
72 West Dean Cemetery.
88 Westhampnett (St Peter) Churchyard.
93 Heene (St Botolph) Churchyard Extension.
95 Worthing (Broadwater) Cemetery.
102 Sedlescombe (St John the Baptist) Churchyard.
107 Bexhill Cemetery.
110 Brighton and Preston Cemetery.
111 Brighton Borough Cemetery.
112 Brighton Extramural Cemetery.
114 Rottingdean (St Margaret) Churchyard.
124 Glynde Churchyard.
125 Hamsey (St Peter) Churchyard.
128 Ringmer (St Mary) Churchyard.
134 Hurstpierpoint (Holy Trinity) Churchyard.
136 Hurstpierpoint Old Cemetery.
138 Lindfield (Walstead) Cemetery.
139 Newtimber (St John) Churchyard.
143 Cuckfield Cemetery.
144 Eastbourne (Ocklynge) Cemetery.
156 Coleman's Hatch (Holy Trinity) Churchyard, Hartfield.
159 Forest Row Cemetery
165 East Grinstead (Mount Noddy) Cemetery.
176 Fairlight (St Andrew) Churchyard.
177 Guestling (St Lawrence) Churchyard.
178 Hastings Cemetery, Ore.
182 Aldrington (St Leonard) Churchyard.
183 Hove Cemetery.
184 Hove (St Andrew) Churchayrd.
185 Lewes Cemetery.
187 Lewes (St John the Baptist-Subcastro) Churchyard.
189 Southover (St John the Baptist) Churchyard.
190 Kingston-near-Lewes (St Pancras) Churchyard.
197 Rye Cemetery, Rye Foreign.
199 Winchelsea (St Thomas) Churchyard.
200 Seaford Cemetery.
201 Burwash (St Bartholomew) Churchyard.
203 Eridge Green (Holy Trinity) Churchyard, Frant.
204 Frant (St Alban) Churchyard.
216 Framfield (St Thomas Becket) Churchyard.
220 Isfield (St Margaret) Churchyard.
225 Waldron (All Saints) Churchyard.
226 Uckfield Cemetery.

WALES

1	Aberdare Cemetery,Glamorgan
3	Barry (Merthyr Dyfan) Cemetery,Glamorgan
4	Bridgend Cemetery,Glamorgan
7	Nolton (St Mary) Churchyard,Glamorgan
12	Llanfabon (St Mabon) Churchyard,Glamorgan
13	Llanfabon (St Mabon) Churchyard Extension,Glamorgan
16	Ystrad Mynach (Holy Trinity) Churchyard,Glamorgan
17	Cardiff Cemetery,Glamorgan.
19	Cardiff (Llandaff) Cemetery,Glamorgan
20	Llanishen (St Isan) Churchyard,Glamorgan
26	Radyr (St John the Baptist) Old Churchyard,Glamorgan
29	St Fagans (St Fagan) Churchyard,Glamorgan
30	St George-super-Ely (St George) Churchyard,Glamorgan
31	St Nicholas Churchyard,Glamorgan
35	Whitchurch (St Mary) Churchyard,Glamorgan.
37	Llanblethian (St John the Baptist) Churchyard,Glamorgan
54	Reynoldston (St George) Churchyard,Glamorgan
77	Merthyr Tydfil (Ffrwd) Cemetery,Glamorgan
78	Merthyr Tydfil (Pant) Cemetery,Glamorgan
83	Mountain Ash (Maesyrarian) Cemetery,Glamorgan
85	Neath (Ynysmaerdy) Cemetery,Glamorgan
86	Aberpergwm (St Cattwg) Churchyard Private Extension, Neath Higher,Glamorgan
95	Pontrhydyfen (Jerusalem) Calvinistic Methodist Chapelyard, Michaelston Higher,Glamorgan
107	Penarth Cemetery,Glamorgan
118	Pyle (St James) Churchyard,Glamorgan
119	St Bride's Major (St Bridget) churchyard,Glamorgan
135	Pontypridd (Glyntaff) Cemetery,Glamorgan
137	Newton Nottage (St John the Baptist) Churchyard,Glamorgan
149	Rhondda (Treorchy) Cemetery,Glamorgan
152	Cockett (St Peter) Churchyard,Glamorgan
163	Morriston (Horeb) Congregational Chapelyard,Glamorgan
165	Sketty (Bethel) Welsh Congregational Chapelyard,Glamorgan
166	Sketty (St Paul) Churchyard,Glamorgan
167	Swansea (Cwmgelly) Cemetery,Glamorgan
168	Swansea (Danygraig) Cemetery,Glamorgan
171	Swansea (Oystermouth) Cemetery Glamorgan
177	Cwmswyg Congregational Chapelyard,Traianglas,Brecknock
178	Devynnock (St Cynog) Churchyard,Maescar,Brecknock
195	Penderyn (St Cynog) Churchyard,Brecknock
199	Ystradgynlais (St Cynog) Churchyard,Ystradgynlais Lower,Brecknock
201	Llanfihangel Ystrad (St Michael) Churchyard,Cardigan
203	Aberystwyth Cemetery,Cardigan
212	Cardigan Cemetery
214	Llandygwydd (St Tygwydd) Churchyard,Cardigan
231	Llangranog (St David) Churchyard,Cardigan
238	Llangeitho (St Ceitho) Churchyard,Cardigan
245	Carmarthen Cemetery
251	Llanllwch (St Luke) Churchyard,Carmarthen
278	Llanegwad (St Egwad) Churchyard,Carmarthen
289	Llanelly Church Cemetery,Carmarthen
306	Llanfihangel Ar Arth (St Michael) Churchyard,Carmarthen
358	Welshpool (Christ Church) Churchyard,Montgomery
361	Fishguard Church Cemetery,Pembroke
367	Haverfordwest St Mary Church Cemetery,Pembroke
368	Haverfordwest (St Thomas of Canterbury) Churchyard,Pembroke
372	Herbrandston (St Mary) Churchyard,Pembroke
383	Treffgarne (St Michael) Churchyard,Pembroke
389	Milford Haven Cemetery,Pembroke
393	Llawhaden (St Aidan) Churchyard,Pembroke
402	Pembroke Dock (Llanion) Cemetery,Pembroke
416	Stackpole Elidor (SS Elidyr and James) Churchyard,Pembroke
429	Llandrindod Wells Cemetery,Radnor
440	Llanyre (St LLyr) Churchyard,Radnor
447	Llanedwen (St Edwen) Churchyard,Anglesey
460	Holyhead (St Mary) Roman Catholic Churchyard,Anglesey
462	Llangefni Cemetery,Anglesey
491	Bangor (Glanadda) Cemetery,Caernarvon
497	Llanbeblig (St Peblig) Churchayrd,Caernarvon
498	Conway (St Agnes) Churchyard,Caernarvon
518	Clynnog Fawr (St Beuno) Churchyard,Clynnog,Caernarvon
531	Llanwnda (St Gwyndaf) Churchyard,Caernarvon
535	Llandudno (Great Orme's Head) Cemetery,Caernarvon
536	Llandudno (St Tudno) Churchyard,Caernarvon
537	Llanrhos (SS Eleri and Mary) Churchyard,Caernarvon
564	Penmaenmawr (Dwygyfylchi) Cemetery,Caernarvon
568	Abergele Cemetery,Denbigh
571	Colwyn Bay (Bronynant) Cemetery,Denbigh
597	Llanbedr Dyffryn Clwyd (St Peter) Churchyard,Denbigh.
609	St George (St George) Churchyard,Denbigh
613	Wrexham Cemetery,Denbigh
619	Gresford (All Saints) Churchyard,Denbigh.
629	Ruabon Cemetery,Denbigh
637	Hawarden (St Deiniol) Churchyard,Flint
646	Caerfallwch (St Paul) Churchyard,Northop,Flint.
648	Gwernafield (Holy Trinity) Churchyard,Mold Rural,Flint.
658	Pontblyddyn (Christ Church) Churchyard,Mold Rural,Flint
659	Whitford (SS Beuno and Mary) Churchyard,Flint
664	Bangor Monachorum (St Dunawd) Churchyard,Flint
671	Rhyl Church Cemetery,Flint
672	Rhyl Town Cemetery,Flint
673	Bodelwyddan (St Margaret) Churchyard,Flint
677	St Asaph Cathedral Churchyard,Flint
681	Harlech (St Tanwg) Churchyard,Merioneth.
684	Llanfair (St Mary) Churchyard,Marioneth.
690	Trawsfynydd (Penycefn) Cemetery,Merioneth.
692	Brithdir (St Mark) Churchyard,Brithdir and Islaw'roreth,Merioneth
693	Llanaber (St Mary) Churchyard,Merioneth
706	Corwen (SS Mael and Sulien) Churchyard,Merioneth
713	Festiniog (Llan) Cemetery,Merioneth
714	Festiniog (Newborough) Burial Ground,Merioneth
725	Aberdovey Cemetery,Merioneth

WARWICKSHIRE

1	Acock's Green (St Mary) Churchyard
3	Birmingham (Brandwood End) Cemetery
5	Birmingham General Cemetery
6	Birmingham (Handsworth) Cemetery
7	Birmingham (Lodge Hill) Cemetery
9	Birmingham (Witton) Cemetery
10	Birmingham (Yardley) Cemetery
12	Edgbaston (St Bartholomew) Churchyard
14	Erdington (St Barnabas) Churchyard
16	Handsworth (St Mary) Churchyard
19	King's Norton (St Nicholas) Churchyard
22	Northfield (St Laurence) Churchyard Extension
23	Perry Barr (St John) Churchyard
32	Studley (St Mary) Churchyard
37	Atherstone Cemetery
47	Long Compton (SS Peter and Paul) Churchyard
50	Coventry (London Road) Cemetery
57	Farnborough (St Botolph) Churchyard
60	Wyken (St Mary Magdalene) Churchyard
65	Castle Bromwich (SS Mary and Margaret) Churchyard
66	Coleshill Cemetery
67	Curdworth (St Peter) Churchyard
74	Monks Kirby (St Edith) Churchyard
75	Chilvers Coton (All Saints) Churchyard
81	Astley (St Mary) Churchyard
83	Leamington (Milverton) Cemetery
84	Leamington (Whitnash Road) Cemetery
88	Brinklow Cemetery
96	Wolston Cemetery
97	Rugby (Clifton Road) Cemetery
98	Rugby (St Marie) Roman Catholic Churchyard
100	Knowle (SS John the Baptist and Ann) Churchyard
101	Olton Franciscan Cemetery,Solihull
102	Salter Street (St Patrick) Churchyard,Tanworth
115	Southam (St James) Churchyard

- 129 Wellesbourne (St Peter) Churchyard, Wellesbourne Hastings
- 134 Hill (St James the Great) Churchyard.
- 135 Sutton Coldfield Cemetery.
- 143 Budbrooke (St Michael) Churchyard.
- 151 Warwick Cemetery, Budbrooke.

WILTSHIRE
- 1 Amesbury Cemetery.
- 2 Bulford Church Cemetery.
- 3 Durrington Cemetery.
- 4 Figheldean (St Michael) Churchyard.
- 12 Wilsford (St Michael) Churchyard.
- 14 Winterbourne Gunner (St Mary) Churchyard.
- 16 Atworth (St Michael) Churchyard.
- 18 Holt Cemetery.
- 25 East Tytherton Moravian Burial Ground, Bremhill.
- 28 Yatesbury (All Saints) Churchyard.
- 29 Chippenham Cemetery.
- 56 Devizes Cemetery, Roundway.
- 64 Chisledon Cemetery.
- 86 Sopworth (St Mary) Churchyard.
- 100 Melksham Cemetery.
- 115 Tidworth Military Cemetery, North Tidworth.
- 116 Upavon Cemetery.
- 121 Chilton Foliat (St Mary) Churchyard.
- 128 East Harnham (All Saints) Churchyard.
- 129 Salisbury (London Road) Cemetery.
- 142 Swindon (Radnor Street) Cemetery.
- 145 Chicklade (All Saints) Churchyard.
- 153 Swallowcliffe (St Peter) Churchyard.
- 157 Bishopstrow (St Aldhelm) Churchyard.
- 167 Sutton Veny (St John) Churchyard.
- 176 Keevil (St Leonard) Churchyard.
- 179 Wilton Cemetery.
- 180 Barford St Martin Cemetery.
- 186 Burcombe (St John the Baptist) Churchyard, Burcombe Without.
- 194 Salisbury (Devizes Road) Cemetery, Bemerton

YORKSHIRE
- 1 Hull (Hedon Road) Cemetery.
- 2 Hull Western Cemetery.
- 3 Hull Northern Cemetery.
- 5 Hull General Cemetery.
- 11 Beverley (St Martin's) Cemetery.
- 12 Beverley (St Mary's) Cemetery.
- 22 Bridlington Cemetery
- 35 Sledmere (St Mary) Churchyard.
- 38 Fulford Water Burial Ground.
- 42 Filey (St Oswald) Churchyard.
- 45 Hessle Cemetery.
- 46 Hornsea Cemetery.
- 62 Burstwick (All Saints) Churchyard.
- 63 Easington Cemetery
- 81 Barlby (All Saints) Churchyard.
- 83 Kirk Ella Church Cemetery.
- 93 Sigglesthorne (St Laurence) Churchyard
- 97 Withernsea (St Nicholas) Churchyard.
- 98 York Cemetery.
- 100 Aysgarth (St Andrew) Churchyard, Gould.
- 106 Thornton Watlass (St Mary) Churchyard.
- 110 Eryholme (St Mary) Churchyard.
- 123 Huntington (All Saints) Churchyard.
- 126 Guisborough Cemetery.
- 138 Finghall (St Andrew) Churchyard.
- 159 Northallerton Cemetery.
- 171 Thornton Dale (All Saints) Churchyard.
- 172 Coatham (Christ Church) Churchyard
- 176 Richmond Cemetery
- 178 Catterick Cemetery.
- 181 Hipswell (St John) Churchyard
- 185 Scarborough Cemetery.
- 186 Brompton (All Saints) Churchyard.
- 192 Seamer (St Martin) Churchyard.
- 208 Kirk Leavington (St Martin) Churchyard.
- 222 Whitby Cemetery.
- 230 Bishopthorpe (St Andrew) Churchyard.
- 244 Goole Cemetery.
- 245 Acomb (St Stephen) Churchyard
- 249 Little Ouseburn (Holy Trinity) Churchyard.
- 250 Moor Monkton (All Saints) Churchyard.
- 256 Harrowgate (Grove Road) Cemetery.
- 274 Knaresborough Cemetery.
- 292 Rawdon (St Peter) Churchyard
- 294 Ripon Cemetery.
- 303 Selby Cemetery.
- 305 Acaster Selby (St John) Churchyard.
- 308 Healaugh (St John the Baptist) Churchyard
- 311 Kirkby Wharfe (St John the Baptist) Churchyard Extension, Kirkby Wharfe and North Milford.
- 321 Sandal Magna (St Helen) Churchyard.
- 323 Wakefield Cemetery.
- 328 Wath-upon-Dearne Cemetery.
- 335 Spofforth (All Saints) Churchyard, Spofforth-with-Stockeld.
- 344 Calverley (St Wilfred) Churchyard.
- 346 Farsley (St John) Churchyard.
- 361 Lawnswood Cemetery.
- 362 Leeds (Burmantofts) Cemetery.
- 363 Leeds (Gelderd Road) English Hebrew Cemetery.
- 368 Leeds (Hunslet Old) Cemetery.
- 372 Meanwood (Holy Trinity) Churchyard.
- 373 Moor Allerton (St John) Churchyard
- 375 Roundhay (St John) Churchyard.
- 381 Methley (St Oswald) Churchyard.
- 383 Pudsey Cemetery
- 388 Pool (St Wilfrid) Churchyard
- 396 Bingley Cemetery.
- 408 Bradford (Scholemoor) Cemetery.
- 410 Bradford (Undercliffe) Cemetery.
- 411 Buttershaw (St Paul) Churchyard.
- 417 Idle (Holy Trinity) Churchyard
- 418 Idle Upper Chapel (Congregational) Cemetery.
- 425 Wibsey (Holy Trinity) Churchyard.
- 428 Burley-in-Wharfedale Church Cemetery.
- 436 Haworth (St Michael) Churchyard.
- 438 Ilkley Cemetery.
- 439 Keighley (Utley) Cemetery.
- 447 Otley, Newall-with-Clifton and Lindley Cemetery
- 462 Kirkby Malham (St Michael) Churchyard.
- 467 Shelf Wesleyan Chapelyard
- 468 Shipley (Hirst Wood) Church Burial Ground.
- 469 Shipley (Nab Wood) Cemetery.
- 474 Addingham (St Peter) Churchyard.
- 475 Bolton Abbey (SS Mary and Cuthbert) Churchyard.
- 481 Gargrave (St Andrew) Churchyard.
- 482 Kettlewell (St Mary) Churchyard, Kettlewell-with-Starbotton
- 483 Kildwick (St Andrew) Churchyard.
- 485 Rylstone (St Peter) Churchyard
- 487 Thornton-in-Craven (St Oswald) Churchyard, Thornton.
- 500 Doncaster Cemetery.
- 501 Doncaster (Christ Church) Churchyard
- 504 Campsall Old Cemetery.
- 528 Rotherham (Masbrough) Cemetery.
- 543 Ecclesall (All Saints) Churchyard
- 546 Sheffield (Abbey Lane) Cemetery.
- 547 Sheffield (Burngreave) Cemetery.
- 548 Sheffield (City Road) Cemetery
- 551 Sheffield General Cemetery
- 557 Sheffield (St Michael's) Roman Catholic Cemetery
- 561 Wadsley Churchyard
- 569 Tickhill (St Mary) Churchyard.

570 Altofts Cemetery
574 Ardsley (Christ Church) Churchyard
575 Barnsley Cemetery
583 Brighouse Cemetery
588 Dewsbury Cemetery
590 Dewsbury Moor (St John) Churchyard
591 Lower Whitley (SS Mary and Michael) Churchyard
595 Drighlington (St Paul) Churchyard
597 Elland-cum-Greetland Cemetery
606 Halifax (Lister Lane) Cemetery
607 Halifax (Stoney Royd) Cemetery
619 Salterhebble (All Saints) Churchyard
635 Brockholes (St George) Churchyard
639 Armitage Bridge (St Paul) Churchyard
643 Huddersfield (Edgerton) Cemetery
644 Huddersfield (Lockwood) Cemetery
645 Lindley (St Stephen) Churchyard
652 Salendine Nook Baptist Chapelyard
677 Ossett (Holy Trinity) Churchyard
686 Friezland (Christ Church) Churchyard
705 Cleckheaton (St John) Churchyard
719 Outwood Cemetery
730 Shore General Baptist Chapelyard
737 Heptonstall Slack Baptist Cemetery
738 Wadsworth (Wainsgate) Baptist Chapelyard
740 Bradfield (St Nicholas) Churchyard

Appendix 2

This is a list of abreviations used in the list of officers. Some are not mentioned as they are self evident. Others are a combination of the abreviations listed below

ACapt, ALt, etc	Acting Captain, Acting Lieutenant, etc
AA Bty	Anti Aircraft Battery
AC or Amm Col	Ammunition Column
acc	Accidentally
A Cyc Cps	Army Cyclist Corps
Amb	Ambulance
Amm Pk	Ammunition Park
Art	Artillery
A & SH	Argyl & Sutherland Highlanders
Att	Attached
Aux	Auxilliary
Ayr Yeo	Ayrshire Yeomanry
Bde	Brigade
Beds	Bedfordshire Regiment
BlkW	Black Watch
Bn	Battalion
Bord R	Border Regiment
BRCS	British Red Cross Society
Bty	Battery
Bucks	Buckinghamshire Regiment
Cam H	Cameron Highlanders
Can	Canadian
Capt	Captain
Cav	Cavalry
CCS	Casualty Clearing Station
Ches	Cheshire Regiment
Cld Gds	Coldstream Guards
Cmd & Staff	Command and Staff
Cmdg	Commanding
Cmdt	Commandant
Col	Colonel
Co or Coy	Company
Conn Rgrs	Connaught Rangers
Cps	Corps
CR	Cemetery Register
DAC	Divisional Ammunition Column
DCLI	Duke of Cornwall's Light Infantry
Ded	Died
Derby Yeo	Derbyshire Yeomanry
Dev	Devonshire Regiment
Div	Division
DLI	Durham Light Infantry
Dors	Dorset Regiment
Dow	Died of Wounds
Drags	Dragoons
Drags Gds	Dragoon Guards
DubF	Dublin Fusiliers
E Afr or EA	East African
EAUL	East African Unattached List
E Kent	East Kent Regiment
E Lancs	East Lancashire Regiment
E Rid Yeo	East Riding Yeomanry
E Surr	East Surrey Regiment
E Yorks	East Yorkshire Regiment
Emp Coy	Employment Company
Ess	Essex Regiment
Ex	Formerly
FA	Field Artillery (or Field Ambulance if RAMC)
FC	Field Company
Fd Sqd	Field Squadron
Fife & Forfar Yeo	Fife and Forfar Yeomanry
Garr Bn	Garrison Battalion
Gds	Guards
Gds MGC	Guards Machine Gun Regiment
GHQ	General Head Quarters
GL	General List
Glam Yeo	Glamorgan Yeomanry
Glouc	Gloucestershire Regiment
Gord H	Gordon Highlanders
Gren Gds	Grenadier Guards
HAC	Honourable Artillery Company
Hamps	Hampshire Regiment
HB	Heavy Battery
Herts	Hertfordshire Regiment
High Cyc Bn	Highland Cyclists Battalion
HLI	Highland Light Infantry
HQ	Headquarters
HT	Horse Transport
Huss	Hussars
IA	Indian Army
IARO	Indian Army Reserve of Officers
IAUL	Indian Army Unattached List
Imp Cam Cps	Imperial Camel Corps
IMS	Indian Medical Service
Ind	Indian
Inf	Infantry
InniskF	Inniskilling Fusiliers
Intel Cps	Intellegence Corps
Ir Gds	Irish Guards
IWT	Inland Water Transport

KAR	Kings African Rifles	RFA	Royal Field Artillery
KEdw Horse	King Edward Horse	RFC	Royal Flying Corps
KOSB	Kings Own Scottish Borderers	R Fus	Royal Fusiliers
KRRC	Kings Royal Rifle Corps	RGA	Royal Garrison Artillery
KSLI	Kings Shropshire Light Infantry	RHA	Royal Horse Artillery
		RH Gds	Royal Horse Guards
Lab Cps	Labour Corps	RHFA	Royal Horse & Field Artillery
Lanc F	Lancashire Fusiliers	Rif	Rifles
Leic	Leicestershire Regiment	RIM	Royal Indian Marine
Leinst	Leinster Regiment	R Ir Rif	Royal Irish Rifles
Life Gds	Life Guards	R Innisk F	Royal Inniskillin Fusiliers\
Lincs	Lincolnshire Regiment	R Lancs	Royal Lancashire Regiment
LN Lancs	Loyal North Lancashire Regiment	R Munst F	Royal Munster Fusiliers
Lond	London Regiment	RN Dev Yeo	Royal North Devon Yeomanry
Lpool	Liverpool Regiment	RoO	Reserve of Officers
2Lt	Second Lieutenant	RR of Cav	Reserve Regiment of Cavalry
Lt	Lieutenant	R Scots F	Royal Scots Fusiliers
Maj	Major	R Suss	Royal Sussex Regiment
Manch	Manchester Regiment	R War	Royal Warwickshire Regiment
MGC	Machine Gun Corps	R W Kent	Royal West Kent Regiment
MID	Mentioned in Despatches	R W Surr	Royal West Surrey Regiment
Middx	Middlesex Regiment		
Mil Works Serv	Military Works Service	SB	Siege Battery
Min of Muns	Ministry of Munitions	Sfth H	Seaforth Highlanders
Mon	Monmouthshire Regiment	SH	Static Hospital
MR	Memorial Register	SL	Special List
MT	Mechanical Transport	S Lancs	South Lancashire Regiment
Mtd	Mounted	SNurse	Staff Nurse
Mtrs	Moters	Som LI	Somerset Light Infantry
Munst F	Munster Fusiliers	Sp Co	Special Company
		S Staffs	South Staffordshire Regiment
N	North or Northern	S&T	Supply & Transport Corps
N & D	Nottinghamshire & Derbyshire Regiment	St JAB	St John's Ambulance Brigade
N Cyc Bn	Northern Cyclist Battalion	Suff	Suffolk Regiment
Nhampt	Northamptonshire Regiment	Surr Yeo	Surrey Yeomanry
Nig R	Nigerian Regiment	SW Bord	South Wales Borderers
N Ir Horse	North Irish Horse		
N Mid HB	North Midland Heavy Battery	TCapt,TLt,etc	Temporary Captain,Temporary Lieutenant,Etc
Norf	Norfolk Regiment	Tank Cps	Tank Corps
Notts Yeo	Nottinghamshire Yeomanry	TC	Tunnelling Company
N Som Yeo	North Somerset Yeomanry	TFNS	Territorial Force Nursing Service
N Staffs	North Staffordshire Regiment	TMB	Trench Mortar Battery
Numb F	Northumberland Fusiliers	Trn	Train
NZ	New Zealand		
		War Yeo	Warwickshire Yeomanry
O&BLI	Oxfordshire & Buckinghamshire Light Infantry	WGds	Welsh Guards
Obs Grp	Observer Group	Wmoreld&Cumbld Yeo	Westmoreland & Cumberland Yeomanry
OTC	Officer Training Corps	Wilts	Wiltshire Regiment
Oxf Yeo	Oxfordshire Yeomanry	Worc	Worcestershire Regiment
		W Rid	West Riding Regiment
Pnrs	Pioneers	W Som Yeo	West Somerset Yeomanry
Pow	Prisoner of War	W Yorks	West Yorkshire Regiment
QAIMNS	Queen Alexander's Imperial Military Nursing Service	Y & L	Yorkshire & Lancashire Regiment
		Yeo	Yeomanry
RACh Dept	Royal Army Chaplains Department	YLI	Yorkshire Light Infantry
RAF	Royal Air Force	Yorks	Yorkshire Regiment
RAMC	Royal Army Medical Corps		
RAOC	Royal Army Ordance Corps		
RASC	Royal Army Service Corps		
RAVC	Royal Army Vetinary Corps		
RB	Rifle Brigade		
R Berks	Royal Berkshire Regiment		
R Dub F	Royal Dublin Fusiliers		
RE	Royal Engineers		
Res	Reserve